Gotham

Gotham

A History of
New York City
to 1898

Edwin G. Burrows
and Mike Wallace

OXFORD
UNIVERSITY PRESS

OXFORD
UNIVERSITY PRESS

Oxford   New York
Athens   Auckland   Bangkok   Bogotá   Buenos Aires
Calcutta   Cape Town   Chennai   Dar es Salaam   Delhi
Florence   Hong Kong   Istanbul   Karachi   Kuala Lumpur
Madrid   Melbourne   Mexico City   Mumbai
Nairobi   Paris   São Paulo   Shanghai   Singapore
Taipei   Tokyo   Toronto   Warsaw

and associated companies in
Berlin   Ibadan

First published by Oxford University Press, Inc., 1999

198 Madison Avenue, New York, New York 10016

First issued as an Oxford University Press paperback, 2000

Oxford is a registered trademark of Oxford University Press

Library of Congress Cataloging-in-Publication Data
Burrows, Edwin G., 1943–
Gotham / Edwin G. Burrows and Mike Wallace.
p. cm.
Includes bibliographical references (p.   ) and index.
Contents: v. 1. A history of New York City to 1898.
ISBN 0-19-511634-8 (Cloth)
ISBN 0-19-514049-4 (Pbk.)
1. New York (N.Y.)—History. I. Wallace, Mike (Michael L.) II. Title.
F128.3.W35   1998   974.7'1—dc21   97-39308

10 9 8 7 6 5 4 3 2 1

Printed in the United States of America
on acid-free paper

Contents

Introduction

The origin of many a great city lies swaddled in myth and legend.

In Nepal, so the story goes, there was once a mountain valley filled with a turquoise lake, in the middle of which floated a thousand-petaled lotus flower. From it emanated a radiant blue light—a manifestation of the primordial Buddha—and the devout came from near and far to meditate upon the flower. At first they had to live in caves along the shore, but then the sage Manjushri flew down from the north and sliced through the southern valley wall with his flaming sword of wisdom, draining the lake and allowing the city of Kathmandu to rise upon the valley floor.

In Meso-America, according to another urban origin myth, the Aztecs departed their ancestral home and wandered south for centuries, searching for the sign priests had prophesied would reveal their new homeland. Finally, guided by Huitzilopochtli, the Hummingbird God, they reached Lake Texcoco, where, as foretold, an eagle perched on a cactus was devouring a serpent. There the Aztecs built Tenochtitlán, the precursor of Mexico City.

Many European metropoles also traced their beginnings to wandering and divinely guided heroes. Aeneas, Virgil tells us in the *Aeneid*, led a group of Trojan War survivors to the mouth of the Tiber. There he founded Lavinium, parent town of Alba Longa, from whence Romulus and Remus—offspring of the war god Mars—would later go forth to found the city of Rome. Londoners, too, long believed their metropolis had been established by a group of exiled Trojans and called their ur-London Trinovantum (New Troy). Lisbon, according to Portuguese tradition, was begun by Ulysses himself. The citizens of Athens were thus unusual in believing themselves autochthonous—sprung, as Homer claimed in the *Iliad*, from the soil itself. "Other cities, founded on the whim of the dice, are imported from other cities," the playwright Euripides had one of his characters say pridefully, but Athenians "did not immigrate from some other place; we are born of our earth."

"THE THRICE RENOWNED AND DELECTABLE CITY OF GOTHAM"

These origin stories celebrated the founding of urban civilizations as epic acts. Each narrative provided its city with a symbolic bedrock, conferring upon the citizenry a sense of legitimacy, purpose, identity. The cities Europeans built in the New World, however, were of too recent a vintage to allow for legendary beginnings, a fact Washington Irving bemoaned when he sat down to write *A History of New York* (1809). Irving regretted that his town was bereft of the imaginative associations "which live like charms and spells about the cities of the old world, binding the heart of the native inhabitant to his home." Indeed Irving found New Yorkers sadly disconnected from their past; few of his fellow citizens "cared a straw about their ancient Dutch progenitors" or even knew the town had once been called New Amsterdam.

In the very opacity of Manhattan's origin, however, Irving discerned a literary opportunity. Its annals were open, "like the early and obscure days of ancient Rome, to all the embellishments of heroic fiction." Irving decided to portray his native city as "having an antiquity thus extending back into the regions of doubt and fable." He would piece together a saga out of local memories and written records, supplemented with the workings of his lively imagination, and provide New York an epic pedigree, one that ran "from the Beginning of the World to the End of the Dutch Dynasty."

In truth, Irving's *History* is a cheeky mock-epic, a potpourri of fact and fiction that plays knowingly and ironically with myth and history. Its invented narrator, the pedantic and pompous Diedrich Knickerbocker, envies his predecessors "Dan Homer and Dan Virgil" for being able to summon up "waggish deities" to descend to earth and "play their pranks, upon its wondering inhabitants." So Knickerbocker spins a foundation story of his own, a takeoff on a tale Virgil tells in the *Aeneid* of how Queen Dido tricked Libyans out of the land on which she founded Carthage. The Dutch, Knickerbocker says, struck an "adroit bargain" with the local Indians by asking "for just so much land as a man could cover with his nether garments," then producing Mynheer Ten Broeck (Mr. Ten Breeches) as the man whose underwear would be so deployed. The "simple savages," Knickerbocker goes on, "whose ideas of a man's nether garments had never expanded beyond the dimensions of a breech-clout, stared with astonishment and dismay as they beheld this bulbous-bottomed burgher peeled like an onion, and breeches after breeches spread forth over the land until they covered the actual site of this venerable city."

Irving had begun his efforts at coining a lineage for New York in the *Salmagundi* papers (1807), a set of sardonic essays, penned with two equally irreverent and youthful colleagues, in which he affixed the name Gotham to his city. Repeatedly *Salmagundi* referred to Manhattan as the "antient city of Gotham," or "the wonder loving city of Gotham." In the context of the pieces—mocking commentaries on the mores of fashionable New Yorkers—the well-known name of Gotham served to underscore their depiction of Manhattan as a city of self-important and foolish people.

Gotham—which in old Anglo-Saxon means "Goats' Town"—was (and still is) a real village in the English county of Nottinghamshire, not far from Sherwood Forest. But Gotham was also a place of fable, its inhabitants proverbial for their folly. Every era singles out some location as a spawning ground of blockheads—Phrygians were accounted the dimwits of Asia, Thracians the dullards of ancient Greece—and in the

Middle Ages Gotham was the butt of jokes about its simpleminded citizens, perhaps because the goat was considered a foolish animal.

The Gothamite canon, which had circulated orally since the twelfth century, was eventually printed up in jest books, the first being *Merie Tales of the mad men of Gotam* (c. 1565). It included such thigh-slappers as the one about the man who rode to market on horseback carrying two heavy bushels of wheat—upon his own shoulders, in order not to burden his mount. Another tells of the man of Gotham who, late with a rent payment to his landlord, tied his purse to a quick-footed hare, which ran away.

Manhattanites would not likely have taken up a nickname so laden with pejorative connotations—even one bestowed by New York's most famous writer—unless it had redeeming qualities, and indeed some of the tales cast Gothamites in a far more flattering light. In the early 1200s—went the most famous such story—King John traveled regularly throughout England with a retinue of knights and ladies, and wherever the royal foot touched earth became forever after a public highway (i.e., the King's). One day, John was heading to Nottingham by way of Gotham, and he dispatched a herald to

The people of Gotham, according to another of the tales, reasoned that as spring disappears when the cuckoo flies away, capturing the bird would ensure the season's eternal duration. They therefore corralled a cuckoo—in a roofless fence—and when summer came, it flew away. This image is taken from a 1630 edition of the *Merie Tales*. (General Research, The New York Public Library, Astor, Lenox and Tilden Foundations)

THE
MERRY TALES
OF THE Mad-men
OF *GOTTAM*.

Gathered together by *A. B.* of Phyſicke Doctor.

Printed at London by *B. A.* and *T. F.* for *Micha[l] Sparke,* dwelling in *Greene Arbor* at the ſigne of the *Blue-Bible,* 1630.

announce his arrival. The herald reported back that the townspeople had refused the king entry, fearing the loss of their best lands. The enraged monarch sent an armed party to wreak vengeance, but the townsfolk had prepared a scheme to turn aside John's wrath. When the knights arrived, they found the inhabitants engaged in various forms of idiotic behavior: pouring water into a bottomless tub; painting green apples red; trying to drown an eel in a pool of water; dragging carts atop barns to shade the wood from the sun; and fencing in a cuckoo. The chortling knights reported back to the monarch that the townsfolk were clearly mad, and John accordingly spared them.

This rival variant—that Gothamites merely acted silly to gain their ends—was reflected in the old English saying "More fools pass through Gotham than remain in it" (and echoed in Shakespeare's depiction of Edgar in *Lear*: "this fellow's wise enough to play the fool"). It was doubtless this more beguiling—if tricksterish—sense of Gotham that Manhattanites assumed as an acceptable nickname.*

THE $24 QUESTION

Irving's pseudo-classical foundation story never passed into popular lore, but a simpler version did, and it too plays with the notion of New York as a city of tricksters. Encapsulated in a sentence, it asserts: the Dutch bought Manhattan from the Indians for twenty-four dollars. For a century and a half now, this story, like all proper myths, has been transmitted from generation to generation, through all the capillaries of official and popular culture—by schoolteachers and stand-up comics alike—and to this day is well known to New Yorkers young and old, and even to many far from the Hudson's shore.

On its face, the twenty-four-dollar story is not a legend on the order of, or in the same dramatic league as, that of Kathmandu or Rome. Nor is it mythic in the commonplace sense of being readily proved false. Though no deed of sale exists, the event is generally accepted as having taken place. In a 1626 letter, a Dutch merchant reported he had just heard, from ship passengers newly disembarked from New Netherland, that representatives of the West India Company had "purchased the Island Manhattes from the Indians for the value of 60 guilders." In 1846, using then-current exchange rates, a New York historian converted this figure into twenty-four U.S. dollars. In 1877, another historian asserted (on the basis of no apparent evidence) that the sum had been paid over in "beads, buttons, and other trinkets."

What gives the story its legendary quality is the host of meanings attached to the event, starting with the notion—smuggled in via the word "purchased"—that the "Island Manhattes" was a piece of property that could be owned and transferred. This was a European conception, and whatever transpired in 1626 was almost certainly understood by the local side in a profoundly different way.

More to the point, the tale is almost always recounted with glee. What tickles the

---

*The term has gone in and out of popular favor, having great currency in one decade, falling into desuetude the next. It owes its most recent revival to the 1989 movie *Batman* and its sequels, themselves a reincarnation of the late 1930s comic books. When New Yorkers Bob Kane and Bill Finger first created the caped crusader, they were going to call Batman's hometown "Civic City." That seemed a bit dull, however, and Finger "tried Capital City, then Coast City. Then, I flipped through the phone book and spotted the name Gotham Jewelers and said, 'That's it,' Gotham City. We didn't call it New York because we wanted anybody in any city to identify with it. Of course, Gotham is another name for New York." Actually, as a later *Batman* editor perspicaciously noted, Gotham is New York's noirish side—"Manhattan below Fourteenth Street at 3 A.M., November 28 in a cold year"—whereas Superman's Metropolis presents New York's cheerier face, "Manhattan between Fourteenth and One Hundred and Tenth Streets on the brightest, sunniest July day of the year."

tellers is that the Dutch conned the Indians into handing over—in exchange for a handful of worthless trinkets—what became the most valuable piece of real estate in the world. There's racial condescension here, with primitive savages dazzled by baubles of civilization. There's urban conceit as well: New Yorkers love yarns about city slickers scamming rural suckers. The selling of the Brooklyn Bridge to country bumpkins is another staple of local lore. But the twenty-four-dollar hustle stands alone. It is our Primal Deal.

One can also recognize the tale's mythic dimension in its invulnerability to carping critics and deconstructionists. It's possible, for example, to raise an eyebrow at the figure's imperviousness to inflation. If recalculated in current dollars, with the conversion rate pegged to the quantity of gold in the early-seventeenth-century guilder, the sum would come out—so Amsterdam's Nederlandsche Bank tells us—to $669.42. Yet, a variable-rate myth being a contradiction in terms, the purchase price remains forever frozen at twenty-four dollars.

Still, even $669.42 is a bargain basement price by today's standards, and in contemporary Dutch terms, too, sixty guilders was a trifling sum. In 1628, by way of comparison, the capture of a single Spanish treasure fleet netted fifteen million guilders. This fact cannot be gainsaid by indulging in "what if" financial legerdemain, as do those who suggest that if the Indians had invested their twenty-four dollars at 6 percent interest for three and a half centuries they would now have, before adjusting for inflation, somewhere in the vicinity of sixty-two billion dollars, a figure more in line with current Manhattan real estate prices.

A more cogent objection to the "great steal" scenario notes that the values were in fact incommensurable. When the Dutch "bought" Staten Island, we know, they paid for it in axes, hoes, needles, awls, scissors, knives, and kettles. If similar trade goods were involved in the Manhattan arrangement, then the Dutch were engaged in high-end technology transfer, handing over equipment of enormous usefulness in tasks ranging from clearing land to drilling wampum.

More telling still, it appears from a later repurchase agreement that the people who made the original arrangement didn't live in Manhattan and so were in no position to offer up even use-rights or visiting privileges. Perhaps it was the credulous Europeans who got skinned.

But once again mere facts are beside the point. The story, like all good myths, has easily resisted such assaults because it ratifies the popular conviction that deal driving and sharp practice and moneymaking and real estate lie somewhere near the core of New York's genetic material.

The twenty-four-dollar story is also mythically akin to Aztec and Roman fables in bestowing on New York a fundamental legitimacy. It proclaims a city whose acquisition was based not on conquest but on contract. As another local historian put it in 1898: "It was an honest, honorable transaction worthily inaugurating the trade and traffic of America's mercantile and financial capital; satisfying the instincts of justice and equality in the savage breast."

Here, quite apart from the underlying implication that history didn't begin until the Europeans arrived, the myth glosses over uncomfortable realities. It is true and important that in North America the Dutch preferred purchase to pillage. But they were prompted less by ethical niceties than by realistic appraisals of the Indians' superior strength and their indispensability as trade partners. The Dutch, however, were no shrinking tulips: when their power waxed and their need waned, they would engage in ferocious wars of conquest, and Indian heads would roll—quite literally—down Bowling Green.

Finally, however, as is usually the case with myths and legends, the notion that New York is rooted in a commercial transaction gets at a deeper kind of truth.

New York would not become a warrior city, living by raids on its hinterland. Even when centuries later it emerged as an imperial center, it was never a military stronghold. True, the most prominent building in the Dutch town was a fort. But it was never much of one—pigs rooted at its foundations and cows wandered in and out of its crumbling walls—and the Netherlanders never assembled here the kind of military resources they deployed elsewhere in their empire. For all their occasional bellicosity, the Dutch were a trading people, and their town would ever after bear the imprint of its creators.

Nor would New York become an urban theocracy, a citadel of priests. No shrines or temples were erected to which swarms of pilgrims flocked to pay religious tribute or receive inspiration. Despite the formidable number of churches established here, Mammon ruled, not God.

Nor would New York become a great governmental hub, with grand baroque avenues radiating out from imposing seats of state power. There was no regal court to dispense largesse to all comers or lure peasants to bask in its splendors. No monarch founded seats of learning so preeminent as to attract truth-seekers from the ends of the earth. Its civic chieftains would be merchants, bankers, landlords, lawyers; its mightiest buildings, office towers.

As the twenty-four-dollar saga suggests, New York would become a city of dealmakers, a city of commerce, a City of Capital. This book will trace the nature and consequences of that development.

POINTS OF VIEW

We are going to present New York's story as a narrative. Our book will journey along through time, taking each moment on its own terms, respecting its uniqueness. We will adopt the perspective of contemporaries as we relate their experiences, remaining mostly in their "now." Yet, like all histories, *Gotham* is not the simple reflection of an underlying reality, but a construction. The narrative embodies our selections, our silences. It is organized around patterns we discern amid the swirl of events.

So what's our take, our angle, our shtick? Do we concentrate on a particular slice of the city's story? Is this primarily an economic history? Social? Cultural? Intellectual? Political? In truth it's all of the above, or, more precisely, it's about making connections between aspects of municipal life that are usually, of necessity, best studied in isolation. This book is only possible because in recent decades a host of scholars has investigated afresh every imaginable aspect of New York's history: sex and sewer systems, finance and architecture, immigration and politics, poetry and crime. Our intention is to suture these partial stories together and present a picture of urban life as a rounded whole, something that probably only novelists can really do well but that nevertheless seems a goal worth aspiring to.

Do we then have a central argument that has allowed us to reduce New York's mammoth story—especially as defined in such an all-encompassing fashion—to manageable (if hefty) proportions? In fact, no overarching plot line or tidy thesis unfolds incrementally throughout this book; the history of New York is not reducible to a sound bite or bumper sticker. Every page, however, does bear the mark of our central conviction: that it is impossible to understand the history of New York City by looking only at the history of New York City, by focusing, that is, exclusively on events that transpired within the boundaries of what are now its five boroughs. It's hard to understand any place in isolation but utterly hopeless here, because linkages—connections to the wider world—have been key to the city's development.

We do not believe that municipal history was determined from the outside. Rather our claim is that external events provided the context within which the men and women of New York, in conflict and compromise, repeatedly reshaped their city. It seems useful, however, to summarize at the outset those framing forces we think had the greatest impact on local actors. Those inclined to get on with the narrative can turn immediately to chapter 1, which takes up the prehistory of the Primal Deal—recounting Europeans' expansion into the New York area and chronicling their fateful intersection with local peoples. But for those who would prefer to reconnoiter the vast forest that lies ahead before plunging off into its trees, we offer in the remainder of this introduction a sketch of some of our principal arguments.

EDGE TO CENTER

At our highest level of analysis, we chart the ways New York's development has been crucially shaped by its shifting position in an evolving global economy.

From its beginnings as a constellation of Indian communities encamped around the mouth of the Hudson River, the area was pulled into the imperial world system Europeans had begun fashioning in the aftermath of Columbus's voyages. Founded as a trading post on the periphery of a Dutch mercantile empire, New Amsterdam lay at the outermost edge of a nascent web of international relationships. It remained a relatively inconsequential backwater, to which its Dutch masters paid but minimal attention, as they had far greater interest in harvesting the profits available in Asia (spices), Africa (slaves), and South America (sugar).

Once forcibly appended to the rising British Empire, however, New York assumed a more prominent role in the global scheme of things. It became a vital seaport supplying agricultural products to England's star colonial performers—the Caribbean sugar islands—while also serving the English as a strategic base for hemispheric military operations against the French, the latest entrants in the imperial sweepstakes.

After the American Revolution, New York emerged as the fledgling nation's premier linkage point between industrializing Europe and its North American agricultural hinterland. The city adroitly positioned itself with respect to three of the most dynamic regions of the nineteenth century global economy—England's manufacturing midlands, the cotton-producing slave South, and the agricultural Midwest—and it prospered by shipping cotton and wheat east while funneling labor, capital, manufactured and cultural goods west.

After the Civil War, the metropolis became the principal facilitator of America's own industrialization and imperial (westward) expansion. Capital flowed through and from its great banking houses and stock exchanges to western rails, mines, land, and factories; it became the preeminent portal for immigrant laborers; and it exported the country's industrial commodities as well as its traditional agricultural ones.

By century's end, New York had gained the ability to direct, not just channel, America's industrialization. Financiers like J. P. Morgan established nationwide corporations and housed them in the city, making Manhattan the country's corporate headquarters. When World War I ended European hegemony, and the United States became a creditor nation, New York began to vie with London as fulcrum of the global economy.

It finally captured that position after World War II when the United States emerged as a superpower. In subsequent decades, when American corporations and banks expanded overseas, New York became headquarters for the new multinational economy; and the arrival of the United Nations made New York a global political capital as well as a financial one. When European and Japanese competitors revived in the latter decades of the twentieth century, the emergence of a more decentered transnational capitalism challenged New York's former preeminence, but it remained most prominent among the handful of world cities directing the workings of the global capitalist order.

Since its inception, therefore, New York has been a nodal point on the global grid of an international economy, a vital conduit for flows of people, money, commodities, cultures, and information. Its citizens were always well aware of this, and in the intermittent jubilees we call Festivals of Connection, they hailed each development—ratification of the Constitution, opening of the Erie Canal, laying of the Atlantic Cable, Lindbergh's solo flight to Paris—that wove the city tighter into the networks of trade and communication on which its livelihood depended.

More than simply a point of confluence, however, New York was a place of ever-increasing potency in global affairs, and as the United States evolved from colony to empire, the city migrated from the edge to the center of the world.

CITY AND COUNTRY

In its relations with the country, New York traveled a more bell-shaped trajectory.

When still a Dutch town, tiny New Amsterdam was as peripheral to the continent as it was to the planet, and it affected relatively few people beyond the Indians with whom it traded or warred. When integrated into England's empire, its impact grew as it drew an expanding hinterland into widening networks of regional and international commerce. New York became the political capital of the new nation after the Revolution but soon lost that status, in part because southern gentry were leery of leaving affairs of state in the ambit of northern merchants. Departure of the Federal City meant that New York would never become the urban colossus of the United States, the way London was for England, or Paris was for France.

Though no longer de jure capital, New York emerged as de facto capital over the course of the nineteenth century, its centrality reflected in the accepted custom of identifying points in its landscape with nationwide functions. Wall Street supplied the country with capital. Ellis Island channeled its labor. Fifth Avenue set its social trends. Madison Avenue advertised its products. Broadway (along with Times Square and Coney Island) entertained it. Its City Hall, as befit an unofficial capitol, welcomed heroes and heroines with keys and parades and naval flotillas, and paid farewell respects to national leaders by organizing processions along Manhattan's black-draped streets. New York, moreover, was the nation's premier source for news and opinion; like a magnet, it attracted those seeking cosmopolitan freedom; and as the biggest city of the biggest state it exercised extraordinary influence in national politics.

Hegemony generated ambivalence. The country envied and emulated the city, but feared and resented it too. Farmers, planters, and industrialists needed its capital but disliked their indebted and dependent status. New York's connections to Europe gave it a glamorous sheen but made it seem the agent of imperial powers and host to an "alien" population that spawned political machines, organized crime, labor unions, anarchists, socialists, Communists, and birth controllers. In the 1920s, relations between New York and its national hinterland came to a rancorous boil, and Governor Al Smith's defeat in 1928 stemmed in part from widespread repudiation of his metropolis.

With Franklin Roosevelt's accession to the presidency, however, New York's national influence expanded again. Under his aegis, unionists, settlement workers, professors, and politicians flocked to Washington, winning a tremendous expansion of federal power to deal with the Depression (along lines pioneered in the city). Ironically, the New Dealers' success undermined their city's position. Strengthening Washington saved New York from catastrophe but also directed a huge and transforming flow of resources to the West and South, converting former dependencies into regional rivals— a process accelerated by the Second World War.

The power of the federal state was enhanced yet again during the Cold War, in part at the behest of a New York-based foreign policy elite. In terms of U.S. relations with the world, Washington and New York emerged as partners: the city on the Hudson the multinational empire's commercial center, the city on the Potomac its military core. In domestic matters, however, no such parity existed. Washington commanded the heightened federal taxing power; New York was just another hard-pressed metropolis. Cold War Washington, moreover, speeded the transfer of wealth from Northeast to Sunbelt, from cities to suburbs. The arms economy bypassed the demilitarized city, industrial jobs fled to other states, and other harbors undercut the aging port. Population shifts diminished New York State's power in federal councils. The consequences for the city became evident in the urban crises of the 1960s, the so-called fiscal crisis of the 1970s ("Ford to City: Drop Dead"), and the 1980s ascendancy to national power of suburban and Sunbelt/Gunbelt constituencies.

MUNICIPAL REMAKINGS

As the city shifted position and function in global and national arenas, the ways in which its citizens went about earning their livings and generating wealth for collective endeavors underwent repeated rearrangement.

Indian peoples lived off the bounty of the harbor, fields, and hills—fishing, farming, and hunting. The Dutch supported themselves and developed a rudimentary infrastructure chiefly by trading with the Indians for beavers (a rodent duly honored in the city's seal). The English-era merchants who oversaw New York's transformation into a significant seaport accumulated their profits from the West Indian trade—as supplemented by privateering, slaving, fencing pirate loot, and provisioning British forays against the French. These enterprises in turn spawned a subsidiary artisanal sector, which manufactured the tools of trade (ships, barrels) and processed raw materials (sugar, hides).

From the Revolution to the Civil War, New York remained preeminently a seaport, as did the adjacent city of Brooklyn, but a host of associated enterprises sprang up to accommodate and enhance the city's mercantile outreach. New Yorkers built canals and railroads; established banks, insurance companies, and a stock market; developed means of communication (newspapers, telegraph); fostered new forms of wholesale and retail merchandising (auction houses, department stores); and augmented their capacity for hosting and entertaining (hotels, restaurants, theaters). Manufacturing capacity surged as entrepreneurs and workers churned out consumer goods for the new markets tapped and created by an expanding commercial network, and New York became the nation's largest manufacturing center. An ever-widening stream of immigrants provided the labor power for all these activities and, in swelling the internal market, further increased demand for clothing, food, housing, and popular amusements.

Between the 1870s and the 1940s, New York's mercantile sector underwent relative decline. The financial sector, meanwhile, expanded to underwrite continental industrialization and western expansion. A business services sector emerged to manage the new corporate economy and merchandise its products. The industrial sector burgeoned, fueled by new immigrants. And the entertainment industry emerged as an independent powerhouse, with New Yorkers hawking plays, vaudeville acts, books, magazines, newspapers, sheet music, records, movies, and radio shows to the nation.

V-E Day ushered in a brief Augustan age when New York was simultaneously major port, largest manufactory, financial center, headquarters of a corporate sector rapidly expanding to multinational dimensions, and vortex of cultural production. But World War II's convoys proved the seaport's last hurrah, and though its loss was partially counterbalanced by expanded air traffic, the growth of alternative hubs— notably West Coast ports attuned to Pacific Rim trade—undermined its gateway status. Manufacturing, which had begun to slip away into the national hinterland, now scattered across the globe, its departure offset only in part by the expansion of local government services. The culture industry remained potent, though regional competitors (and federal funding) continued to undermine its former predominance. Pieces of the corporate command post were dismantled and reassembled in outer suburbs, leaving finance, once an inconsequential component of the city's economy, as its central and precarious prop.

OSCILLATIN' RHYTHMS

These large-scale municipal remakings provide our book its macrostructure, its division into parts. There are five such parts in this volume, the first two of which—"Lenape Country and New Amsterdam to 1664" and "British New York (1664–1783)"—hinge on the establishment or loss of imperial power. The remaining parts encompass eras marked by relatively coherent and stable macroeconomies, with transitions between them marked, provoked, or accelerated by war, economic crisis, and/or internal conflict. These eras include "Mercantile Town (1783–1843)," "Emporium and Manufacturing City (1844–1879)," and "Industrial Center and Corporate Command Post (1880–1898)." The last of these closes out this volume with an account of the consolidation of once separate cities and townships into Greater New York, whose hundredth anniversary we marked in 1998.

When blocking out the city's centuries-long story as a whole, it is these grand epochs of municipal development that command our attention. But when telling New York's story on a year-by-year basis, a more sinuous rhythm demands consideration: the alternation of peaks of prosperity with troughs of hard times that dominated the experience of everyday life.

When the city was still subordinate to the interests of either Holland or Great Britain, the pattern of ups and downs was shaped primarily by imperial decisions. Irv-

ing's brief Dutch "dynasty" had time for only one such cycle. In the twenty years preceding the mid-1640s, while the Dutch empire prospered, New Netherland's fortunes
ebbed; in the twenty subsequent years, when the empire declined, the town's situation
improved. Under the subsequent century of English rule, imperial dynamics of war
and trade sustained an undulating cadence of abundance and adversity.

It was in the nineteenth and twentieth centuries, however, when imbricated in the
U.S. nation-state and the world capitalist economy, that New York commenced its characteristic roller-coaster ride in earnest, now surging to heights of affluence, now plunging into sloughs of depression. The city first rose to national preeminence in the
wartime trade boom of the Napoleonic nineties; then its ascent was punctured by
embargo and peace. The canal era boom of the 1820s and 1830s raced to culmination
and crisis in 1837, then tumbled into a seven-year depression. The rail-spurred prosperity of 1844–57 was interrupted by the Panic of 1857, reignited by the Civil War, then
snuffed out by the Panic of 1873, which inaugurated a lengthy period of hard times.

Industrialization-based resurgence in the 1880s gave way to depression in the
1890s. Corporate consolidation and war with Spain ushered in prosperity in the 1900s,
which subsided after the Panic of 1907. World War I and a consumer goods revolution
led to the 1920s boom, which collapsed into the 1930s depression. Lifted again by the
Second World War, the city flourished during the long postwar boom, until laid low by
the mid-1970s recession. A 1980s quasi-boom buckled in 1987, making way for the stagnant early 1990s and the brisker but still problematic fin de siècle.

These cycles created characteristic and remarkably similar cultures of boom and
bust. The jaunty and expansive 1830s, 1850s, 1900s, 1920s, 1950s, and 1980s (times of
comparably frenetic construction and high living in the city) gave way to the depressed
1840s, 1870s, 1890s, 1930s, and 1970s (periods marked by unemployment, homelessness, and contentious protest movements).

This pattern inscribed itself in the city's skyline and streetscape. In boom times,
speculative capital cascaded into real estate, generating frenzied building sprees. When
the fever broke, office and housing construction halted abruptly. By the time the economy regathered its energies, a new generation of promoters and architects had come
along, new cultural fashions were in vogue, new technologies and construction practices
had materialized, and the latest spurt of building bore little resemblance to its predecessor. This spasmodic evolution of New York's spatial geography allows us to "read" the
cityscape, rather as archaeologists decipher stacked layers of earth, each of which holds
artifacts of successive eras. Here, remnants of built environment offer clues to New
York's periodization.

Working from the bottom up, we find traces of New Amsterdam's prosperous
upswing in the archaeological remains of the gabled Stadt Huys (the Dutch City Hall)
uncovered beneath Pearl Street, visible now through a Plexiglassed hole in the ground.
Nearby Fraunces Tavern, a conjectural reconstruction of the De Lancey family's urban
town house, recalls a heyday of England's mid-eighteenth-century empire. Federal
mansions betoken 1790s affluence. The upsurge of the 1830s is immortalized in Wall
Street Greek temples like the Merchants' Exchange and Federal Hall, and that of the
1850s lives on in Italianate mansions like the Salmagundi Club and Litchfield Villa.
Turn-of-the-century flush times are traceable in neo-Roman artifacts like the New York
Stock Exchange, and remains of the 1920s boom include exuberant art deco skyscrapers
like the Chrysler Building. The post–Second World War surge is invoked in modernist

glass boxes, from modest Miesian beginnings to berserk apotheosis at the World Trade Center, built just before the crash of the mid-1970s. And the totems bequeathed by the economic upsurge of the 1980s are postmodernist structures ranging from the World Financial Center to AT&T's (now Sony's) jocular pink Chippendale tower.

PAST AS PROLOGUE

It is indeed remarkable that so many tangible traces of earlier eras remain, given that few structures in New York were ever hallowed by mere age. As the city's economy shifted from commercial to industrial to corporate, older buildings were exuberantly torn down to make way for newer ones—higher, more fashionable, more convenient, more profitable—and these ruthless remakings gave the cityscape a chameleon-like, quicksilver quality that matched the mutability of its economy, its populace, and its position on the planet.

The city's well-merited reputation as a perpetual work-in-progress helps explain why from Washington Irving's day New Yorkers were famous for being uninterested in their own past. "New York is notoriously the largest and least loved of any of our great cities," wrote *Harper's Monthly* in 1856. "Why should it be loved as a city? It is never the same city for a dozen years together. A man born in New York forty years ago finds nothing, absolutely nothing, of the New York he knew."

One of our ongoing avenues of inquiry follows New Yorkers as they slowly developed the conviction that their past was worth knowing, even worth preserving. Indeed we believe there is a greater degree of interest in Gotham's history today than was ever the case before. We hope to nourish this ripening historical sensibility by telling the city's story in a spirited way—a relatively easy task given that it's intrinsically dazzling, a claim we think transcends both the fond boasting of all historians for their subject and the legendary conceitedness of New Yorkers (we notorious braggarts).

More difficult, perhaps, because it goes against the American ahistorical grain, we also hope to show that temporal analysis can be as useful as it is entertaining, that it can be helpful for New Yorkers (and Americans) to better situate themselves in time. This does not mean adopting the narrow presentism that runs through some of the narratives advanced by present-day commentators—sagas of rise and dirges of decline aimed at providing a pedigree for their purveyors' optimistic or pessimistic takes on the state of the contemporary city.

Optimists portray New York as a magnificent and never-better metropolis. They point to the inrush of new immigrants, no longer streaming past the Statue in the harbor but airlifting their way into Kennedy, as evidence that much of the world sees New York as a place of opportunity, a mecca for the talented and ambitious. The newcomers' belief that they can survive and prosper (say the optimists) rests on solid foundations. Wall Street's enormous corporate and financial sector churns out professional and business services jobs. New York hosts the nation's publishing, advertising, fashion, design, and network television industries. Its museums, concert halls, playhouses, nightclubs, and festivals draw vast numbers of tourists, who in turn help sustain an enormous array of restaurants and hotels. Some see a high-tech, Silicon Alley, bio-medical future lying just around the corner.

New housing blooms amid the outer borough ruins, these boosters note, and new capital improvements head toward completion. Refurbished subways are cleaner and swifter. Crime is down dramatically. The City University of New York, though under attack, provides opportunities for the newly arrived and the less advantaged, while the city's tradition of social caring sustains a network of public support services, albeit one in parlous condition. Despite cultural antagonisms, moreover, the city remains a model of rough-hewn cosmopolitanism and multicultural tolerance, with an astonishing mix of peoples living side by side in reasonable harmony. Indeed the incessant interplay among its heterogeneous citizens makes New York a font of creative human energy, an unsurpassed site for personal development, a stupendous collective human accomplishment, and the glorious, glamorous, greatest city in the world.

Pessimists reject this cheery portrait and fashion from the shards of morning headlines and nightly newscasts a grim mosaic of urban decay. They point to the homeless who line up at soup kitchens, camp out in parks or under bridges until driven off by police, or burrow into subterranean warrens: subway tunnels, abandoned railway shafts, the roots of skyscrapers. A vast army of the unemployed poor subsists on welfare, living in squalid ex-hotels, rat-ridden tenements, bleak housing projects. Infant mortality rates in parts of the city match, even surpass, those of "underdeveloped" countries. And its vaunted opportunities are, as they long have been, largely limited to those with the means to seize them. "You can live as many lives in New York as you have money to pay for," ran a contemporary judgment in *The Destruction of Gotham*, an apocalyptic novel of 1886, which also recorded the maxim that the "very first of the Ten Commandments of New York [is]: 'THOU SHALT NOT BE POOR!'"

Perched one precarious step above these nether ranks are millions more working poor—the sporadically or marginally employed who cobble together a living from minimum-wage jobs that might vanish in an instant—for jobs, the city's lifeblood, have been draining away for decades. Hundreds of thousands of manufacturing slots, many of them unionized and decently paid, have vanished since the 1960s (though it is true that a new sweatshop sector is busy being reborn, with immigrants once again serving as entrepreneurs and exploited workforce, a dubious achievement). Many corporate headquarters have departed, downsized, or dispatched their back offices elsewhere, and the financial sector remains all too vulnerable to the next downturn. Giant department stores have gone bankrupt, and while malled superstores replenish some retail positions they (together with soaring commercial rents) knock out mom-and-pop shops. The seaport is long gone to Jersey—only rotted wharves and tombstone pilings recall the once flourishing waterfront—and rusted railyards have been converted to high-priced condos, with airport and truck traffic picking up only some of the slack.

Despite recent improvements, pessimists note, a once magnificent infrastructure continues to crumble. Ancient water tunnels explode, flooding brownstones, drowning avenues, shorting out decrepit subway lines. Tired bridges and eroded highways close repeatedly for repairs. Pitted streets clog with traffic. JFK has been voted the world's worst airport. Garbage has piled to mountainous heights in Staten Island. More oil lies beneath the streets of Brooklyn than was spilled by the *Exxon Valdez*. For all the brave new housing efforts, block after Bronx block remains lined with shuttered factories and abandoned apartment houses, while the tendrils of a long-stymied nature creep through the rubble of burned-out buildings.

Those who present such stark readings of New York's present and future often supply matching versions of the past. Those convinced of New York's decline recall its glory days, the better to indulge in rueful nostalgia or stoke a bitter anger at what has come to pass. They see the past as a reverse *Guinness Book of Records*—a catalog of fabulous accomplishments now, alas, never to be surpassed. Those more sanguine about New York's future assemble an indictment of the bad old days. They seize on catastrophes past: the British invasion and torching of the town; the great fever and cholera plagues, when coffin carts rattled through the streets and rats swam across the East River to gnaw the corpses piled high on Blackwell's Island; the horrific draft riots when African-American New Yorkers were lynched from lamp poles and armies bivouacked in Gramercy Park; the tenement squalor and sweatshop misery; the horrors of the Great Depression and myriad littler ones. Such a legacy, they argue, renders contemporary misfortunes modest by comparison.

We strongly endorse the idea of New Yorkers' turning to the past for perspective on their present—comparing different eras can bring balance to contemporary judgments—but *Gotham* is not about ransacking the past for evidence of Spenglerian decline or Panglossian progress. Straight-line scenarios, whether optimistic or pessimistic, usually pose false questions and offer false alternatives. Our hope, rather, is that a history that respects the complexity and contingency of human affairs can offer well-grounded insights into our current situation.

We believe that the world we've inherited has an immense momentum; that actions taken in the past have bequeathed us the mix of constraints and possibilities within which we act today; that the stage onto which each generation walks has already been set, key characters introduced, major plots set in motion, and that while the next act has not been written, it's likely to follow on, in undetermined ways, from the previous action. This is *not* to say that history repeats itself. Time is not a carousel on which we might, next time round, snatch the brass ring by being better prepared. Rather we see the past as flowing powerfully through the present and think that charting historical currents can enhance our ability to navigate them.

We are historians, not mythmakers, but like Washington Irving we appreciate the power of the past and its centrality to the life of a place, and our choice of title represents a tip of the hat to his endeavor. Our Gotham is not Irving's, but like Diedrich Knickerbocker we think that the more we know about the city's past the more we will care about its future. We therefore dedicate this book to the citizens of New York City and to the many historians who have labored to tell its story.

Now, on with the show.

PART ONE

LENAPE COUNTRY AND NEW AMSTERDAM TO 1664

The Castello Plan of New Amsterdam, c. 1660. (I. N. Phelps Stokes Collection. Miriam and Ira D. Wallach Division of Art, Prints and Photographs. The New York Public Library. Astor, Lenox and Tilden Foundations)

I

First Impressions

O this is Eden!" exulted the Dutch poet Jacob Steendam. A "terrestrial *Canaan*," echoed the English essayist Daniel Denton, "where the Land floweth with milk and honey."

That was the usual reaction of the Europeans who began to settle the lower Hudson Valley and the islands of New York's harbor, three and a half centuries ago. Nowhere else in North America would the beauty and abundance of the physical environment evoke such consistently extravagant praise.

Initially it was what Denton called the "sweetness of the Air" that bewitched explorers and travelers. "Dry, sweet, and healthy," Adriaen van der Donck wrote. "Sweet and fresh," the missionary Jaspar Danckaerts noted in his journal as his ship came up past Sandy Hook. "Much like that of the best parts of France," declared the Rev. John Miller. What could produce such air, or where it came from, was the subject of extensive speculation. Miller traced it to the surrounding "hilly, woody Country, full of Lakes and great Vallies, which receptacles are the Nurseries, Forges and Bellows of the Air, which they first suck in and contract, then discharge and ventilate with a fiercer dilation." Denton, too, emphasized the region's sweeping woods and fields, "curiously bedecked with Roses, and an innumerable multitude of delightful Flowers" whose fragrance could be detected far out at sea. The effect was magical, and there was speculation that it might cure colds, consumption, and other respiratory ailments.

But it was the miraculous size and quantity and variety of things—the sheer prodigality of life—that left the most lasting impression. Travelers spoke of vast meadows of grass "as high as a mans middle" and forests with towering stands of walnut, cedar, chestnut, maple, and oak. Orchards bore apples of incomparable sweetness and "pears larger than a fist." Every spring the hills and fields were dyed red with ripening strawberries, and so many birds filled the woods "that men can scarcely go through them for the whistling, the noise, and the chattering." Boats crossing the bay were escorted by schools of playful whales, seals, and porpoises. Twelve-inch oysters and six-foot lobsters crowded offshore waters, and so many fish thrived in streams and ponds that they could be taken by hand. Woods and tidal marshlands teemed with bears, wolves, foxes, raccoons, otters, beavers, quail, partridge, forty-pound wild turkeys, doves "so numerous that the light can hardly be discerned where they fly," and countless deer "feeding, or gamboling or resting in the shades in full view." Wild swans were so plentiful "that the bays and shores where they resort appear as if they were dressed in white drapery." Blackbirds roosted together in such numbers that one hunter killed 170 with a single shot; another bagged eleven sixteen-pound gray geese in the same way. "There are some persons who imagine that the animals of the country will be destroyed in time," mused Van der Donck, "but this is an unnecessary anxiety."

IMMIGRANT ICE

The formation of this lush ecosystem had begun seventy-five thousand years earlier, when packs of glaciers crept down from Labrador into the almost featureless plain that then stretched east of the Allegheny Mountains to the Atlantic, and halted in the middle of modern New York City. Approximately fifty thousand years ago, a sheet of ice a thousand feet thick lay across the area. Its immense weight, and the continual flow of ice from the north, crushed and flayed the land beneath, depressing riverbeds, scooping out deep valleys, and dragging along boulders, gravel, sand, and clay like a huge conveyor belt. In parts of Manhattan and the Bronx, it peeled away everything above the bedrock—layers of gneiss, marble, and schist, five hundred million years old, that now lie naked to the passing eye, scarred and battered by their ordeal. So much of the earth's water was captured in this and other ice sheets that the sea level fell three hundred feet or more and the shoreline bulged out a hundred miles. Arctic gusts blew off its face across a desolate tundra, inhabited only by mosses and lichens, that reached as far south as Philadelphia.

About seventeen thousand years ago, the climate of the northern hemisphere began to warm. As the ice sheet melted back, the line of its furthest advance was marked by a terminal moraine—the still-visible ridge of glacial debris that arcs down from northern Queens through places named Jamaica Hills, Highland Park, Crown Heights, and Bay Ridge (which in turn overlook such neighborhoods as Flatbush and Flatlands, settled on the ice sheet's sandy outwash plain). Extending across to the south side of Staten Island, the moraine reaches its maximum elevation of 410 feet at Todt Hill (the highest natural point on the Atlantic seaboard south of Maine), then turns north across New Jersey and Pennsylvania.

Trapped behind the moraine, runoff from the retreating ice pooled into icy lakes that drowned the region for several thousand years before their waters broke through a mile-wide gap, now called the Narrows, and drained off toward the ocean. Scrubby pines and birches took root in the thawing tundra, then gave way, perhaps twelve thousand years ago, to stands of spruce and fir, interspersed with open meadows. Woolly mammoths, mastodons, bison, musk oxen, bears, sloths, giant beavers, caribou, saber-toothed tigers, and other large animals moved in. Trailing behind them came small bands of nomadic hunters—the region's first human occupants—who stalked game for a couple of thousand years, leaving behind only flint spear points and heaps of bones as evidence of their presence.

The hunters left nine thousand years ago, when the effects of continued climatic warming drove away the big beasts on which they depended. Hardwood forests of oak, chestnut, and hickory took over from the pines and spruce. Fed by the melting ice packs, the ocean rose again, inundating coastal lowlands and pouring back through the Narrows, creating the commodious Upper Bay that would serve as the harbor of New York. In the glacially scoured terrain north of the terminal moraine, it sculpted a fantastic topography of new islands, fjords, inlets, tidal marshes, and peninsulas. The Hudson River gorge was transformed into a broad estuary, while drowned valleys became Long Island Sound, the Harlem River, the East River, and Arthur Kill. Below the Narrows, protecting the Upper Bay from the Atlantic Ocean, sprawled the great Lower Bay—a hundred-square-mile watery expanse whose entrance was guarded by Rockaway Peninsula, a barrier beach on the Queens shore of Long Island, and by Sandy Hook, a long sandspit that jutted up from New Jersey. A broad underwater sandbar running between Sandy Hook and Coney Island, pierced here and there by navigable channels, presented arriving mariners with the only natural obstacle to the 770 miles of waterfront that lay beyond.

WHERE THE LENAPES DWELL

About sixty-five hundred years ago, this altered environment attracted a second generation of human residents. The newcomers were small-game hunters and foragers who subsisted on a diet of deer, wild turkey, fish, shellfish, nuts, and berries. Although they possessed a limited repertoire of tools, their campsites may have been occupied by as many as two hundred people at a time. Roughly twenty-five hundred years ago, they discovered the use of the bow and arrow, learned to make pottery, and started to cultivate squash, sunflowers, and possibly tobacco. Later, about a thousand years ago, they may also have begun to plant beans and maize. These changes supported larger populations. By the time Europeans appeared on the scene, a mere five hundred years ago, what is now New York City had as many as fifteen thousand inhabitants—estimates vary widely—with perhaps another thirty to fifty thousand in the adjacent parts of New Jersey, Connecticut, Westchester County, and Long Island. Most spoke Munsee, a dialect of the Delaware language in which their name for themselves was Lenape—"Men" or "People." Their land was Lenapehoking—"where the Lenapes dwell."

The Lenapes comprised a dozen-odd groups living between eastern Connecticut and central New Jersey. To the west were the Raritans (of Staten Island and Raritan Bay), the Hackensacks (of New Jersey's Hackensack and Raritan river valleys), the Tappans (northern New Jersey), and the Rechgawawanches (Orange County). Their counterparts (and sometime enemies) to the east included the Wiechquaesgecks (northern Manhattan, the Bronx, and Westchester) and the Siwanoys (along the northern banks of the East River and Long Island Sound as far as the Connecticut line), as well as the Matinecocks, Massapequas, Rockaways, Merricks, and others of Long Island.

These weren't the well-defined, organized "tribes" or "nations" that populated the imaginations of European colonizers. Except under very unusual circumstances, the Lenapes identified themselves primarily with autonomous subgroups or bands consisting of anywhere from a few dozen to several hundred people. Nor did they reside in "villages" as that word was understood by Europeans, but rather in a succession of seasonal campsites. In the spring or early summer, a band could be found near the shore, fishing and clamming; as autumn approached, it moved inland to harvest crops and hunt deer; when winter set in, it might move again to be nearer reliable sources of fire-wood and sources of smaller game. As the Rev. Charles Wolley put it, the Lenapes lived "very rudely and rovingly, shifting from place to place, accordingly to their exigencies, and gains of fishing and fowling and hunting, never confining their rambling humors to any settled Mansions."

Within the five boroughs of modern New York alone, archaeologists have identified about eighty Lenape habitation sites, more than two dozen planting fields, and the intricate network of paths and trails that laced them all together. On Manhattan, the primary trail ran along the island's hilly spine from what is now Battery Park in the south to Inwood in the north. Just north of City Hall Park it passed by an encampment near a sixty-foot-deep pond, fed by an underground spring, which together with adjacent meadow and marsh lands almost bisected the island. Farther north, where the trail passed Greenwich Village, a secondary path led west to Sapokanikan, a site of fishing and planting on the Hudson River near the foot of Gansevoort Street. At about 98th Street and Park Avenue the trail ran by a campsite known as Konaande Kongh and, on the broad flats of Harlem just to the north, still more fishing camps and planting fields. (From an East River landing at about 119th Street, fishermen paddled out in tree-trunk

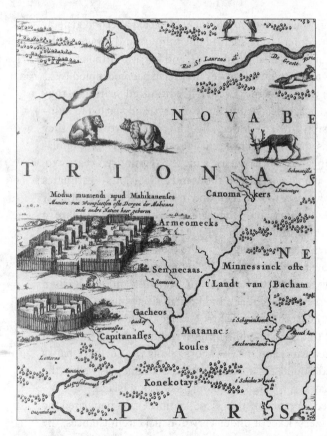

The largest Lenape habitation sites were occupied by several hundred or more people and probably resembled these villages depicted in western New Netherland, but without the enclosing palisade. Detail from a map by Nicolaes Visscher, 1656. (I. N. Phelps Stokes Collection. Miriam and Ira D. Wallach Division of Art, Prints and Photographs. The New York Public Library. Astor, Lenox and Tilden Foundations)

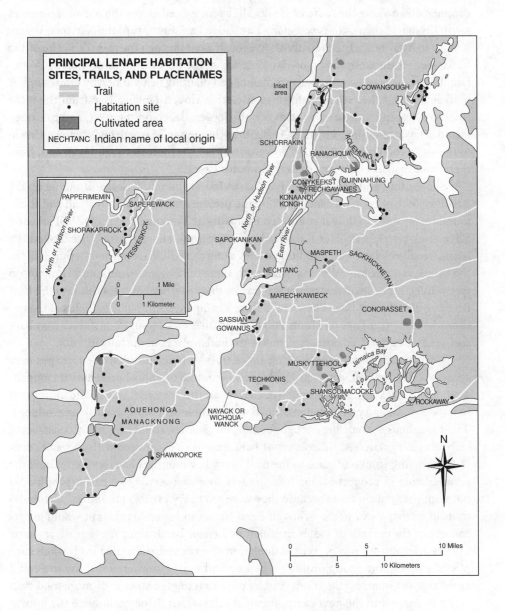

PRINCIPAL LENAPE HABITATION
SITES, TRAILS, AND PLACENAMES

Trail

• Habitation site

Cultivated area

NECHTANC Indian name of local origin

COWANGOUGH

Inset
area

SCHORRAKIN

AQUEHUNG

RANACHQUA

CONYKEEKST QUINNAHUNG
RECHGAWANES

KONAANDI
KONGH

PAPPERIMEMIN

SAPEREWACK

SHORAKAPROCK

KESKESKICK

North or Hudson River

SAPOKANIKAN

MASPETH

SACKHICKNETAN

NECHTANC

0   1 Mile

0   1 Kilometer

MARECHKAWIECK

CONORASSET

SASSIAN
GOWANUS

MUSKYTTEHOOL

Jamaica Bay

TECHKONIS

AQUEHONGA
MANACKNONG

NAYACK OR
WICHQUA-
WANCK

SHANSCOMACOCKE

S/ROCKAWAY

SHAWKOPOKE

N

North or Hudson River

East River

0   5   10 Miles

0   5
10 Kilometers

canoes to net or spear striped bass.) Its northern terminus was a cluster of three camps along the Harlem River, two of which now actually lie on the mainland, severed from Manhattan by the Harlem Ship Canal.

Across the East River, in Brooklyn and Queens, another major artery ran just below the terminal moraine, following the present course of Jamaica Avenue west from the Nassau County line. At Evergreen Cemetery, on the Brooklyn-Queens border, it dropped down along the route of Kings Highway, looped across the outwash plains of south Brooklyn, then swung west along Bay Ridge Parkway toward the Narrows. Where Kings Highway now crosses Flatbush Avenue, it went through the main campsite of the Canarsees. At the western end of Bay Parkway, in the Fort Hamilton section of Brooklyn, it passed a camp whose residents maintained planting fields at nearby Gravesend. A half-dozen branches reached down to sites that ringed Jamaica Bay from the main Rockaway camp on the east to what is now Bergen Beach on the west, and to Coney Island, a favorite summering place. Other branches ran to Maspeth on Newtown Creek, to the shores of Wallabout Bay, to downtown Brooklyn (near Borough Hall), and, from there, over to maize lands lying along Gowanus Creek.

Similar trail grids can be traced on Staten Island and in the Bronx. Running up the Atlantic shore of Staten Island, marking the present course of Amboy Road and Richmond Road, was a path that connected campsites at Tottenville, Great Kills Park, and Silver Lake Park. At Silver Lake Park, it intersected shorter paths that circled the island's central hills to reach additional sites along the Kill Van Kull and Arthur Kill. In the Bronx, most major trails ran north-south along the Harlem, Bronx, and Hutchinson rivers and sundry smaller streams and creeks that together empty south into the East River or Eastchester Bay. These trails linked campsites and planting fields along the shore—among them one on Hunts Point and another on Clasons Point, which may have sheltered three hundred or more people—to similar places in the hilly interior.

Their seasonal movement along these trail systems afforded the Lenapes easy access to fish, shellfish, game birds, and deer—sources of animal protein that compensated for the lack of domesticated livestock—but this transient way of life meant that tools, weapons, and cooking utensils had to be simple and light, or easily reproduced. Their longhouses, some big enough for a dozen families, could be quickly constructed of bent saplings covered with sheets of bark, the crevices plugged with clay and cornstalks. Moving from one place to the next every few months likewise discouraged the accumulation of property. (Dutch fur traders soon discovered that native peoples did not want iron pots in trade because they were too heavy.) It also minimized accumulations of garbage and waste—though Pearl Street in lower Manhattan would get its name from the mounds of oyster shells left by Lenape bands along the East River shore. Constant relocation also prevented depletion of firewood and arable land: when supplies dwindled, the group simply packed up and went elsewhere until the site could again support human habitation. And by discouraging the storage of more food than could be carried to the next camp, seasonal relocations helped minimize the human impact on local plant and animal populations, giving them a chance to rebound before the Lenapes returned the next year.

Lenape bands prepared and maintained their woodland planting fields by the slash-and-burn method, clearing out all but the largest trees and bushes, then burning off the rubbish and undergrowth every spring. This brought fallow land into cultivation quickly and returned essential nutrients to the soil, extending its productive life well beyond the two or three years possible with the European system of crop rotation. Sowing a variety of crops together in the same field—maize, sunflowers, beans, squash, melons, cucumbers, and tobacco—maintained high concentrations of nitrogen; it also required less work, because cornstalks, for example, could support the beans as well as man-made poles. What was more, the simple stone and wood implements of the Lenapes turned the soil easily without the damage caused by European plows and draft animals.

No less than the colonists who came after them, in other words, the Lenapes had "settled" the land by manipulating it to their purposes. Consciously or not, they used it in ways that extended the diversity of plant and animal life on which their survival depended. The heavy use of firewood around their principal habitation sites, combined with the annual spring burnoff of active planting fields, left vast, open, parklike forests where deer, rabbit, birds, and other game flourished. Their abandoned planting fields became the meadows and prairies that were home to a tangle of flowers and edible berries. And because Lenape spiritual beliefs emphasized the interdependence of all life, hunting was an enterprise loaded with such supernatural significance that excessive killing was avoided. The abundance that so amazed early European visitors was thus no mere accident of nature, for "nature" was an artifact of culture as well as geology.

LAZY AND BARBAROUS PEOPLE

Nothing made it harder for Europeans to see the link between the Lenapes and their environment than the fact that kinship—not class—was the basis of their society. Private ownership of land and the hierarchical relations of domination and exploitation familiar in Europe were unknown in Lenapehoking. By custom and negotiation with its neighbors, each Lenape band had a "right" to hunt, fish, and plant within certain territorial limits. It might, in exchange for gifts, allow other groups or individuals to share these territories, but this did not imply the "sale" or permanent alienation known to European law. In the absence of states, moreover, warfare among the Lenapes was much less systematic and brutal than among Europeans. As Daniel Denton said disdainfully: "It is a great fight where seven or eight is slain."

More perplexing still, kinship in Lenape society was traced matrilineally. Families at each location were grouped into clans that traced their descent from a single female ancestor; phratries, or combinations of two or more clans, were identified by animal signs, usually "wolf," "turtle," and "turkey." Children belonged by definition to their mother's phratry: if she was a turtle, they were turtles. Land was assigned to clans, and the family units that comprised them, for their use only: they did not "own" it as Europeans understood the word and had no authority to dispose of it by sale, gift, or bequest. If the land "belonged" to anyone, it belonged to the inhabitants collectively.

On one point European and Lenape societies seemed similar: the division of labor by gender. Lenape women, along with cooking and childrearing, did the bulk of agricultural work—planting, weeding, harvesting, drying, packing, sorting—which made them responsible for as much as 90 percent of the food supply. During seasonal changes of settlement, it was also their job to strike and rebuild dwellings as well as to carry the communal goods.

Lenape men, by contrast, thought agriculture unmanly and devoted their energies to hunting and fishing. European observers were often appalled to find them relaxing after their return while their women toiled away in the fields, though this reaction had less to do with sympathy for the women than with ideas about "laziness." Europeans

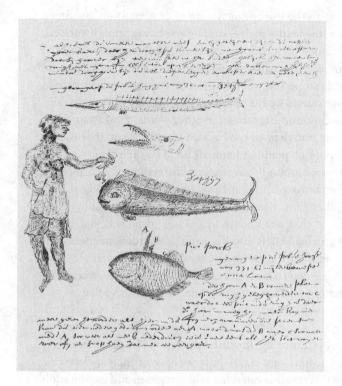

Pen and ink sketch of a Native American woman and local fish
by Jaspar Danckaerts, c. 1679/1680. (United States History,
Local History & Genealogy Division. The New York Public
Library. Astor, Lenox and Tilden Foundations)

believed that agriculture was a respectable occupation for men, while hunting and fishing were chiefly recreational: one was work, the other mere sport. ("They labour not
much, but in absolute necessity," Charles Lodwick reported to the Royal Society, and
"mostly employ themselves in hunting and fishing.") Indeed, the apparent reluctance of
their men to work only reinforced the impression that the Lenapes had done little to
subdue and develop the land.

The sexual division of labor and the matrilineal organization of clans and phratries
accorded women considerable importance in communal affairs. Each sachem was chosen from among the sons—sometimes even daughters—of a sister of the old sachem,
and the actual choice might well have been made by the older women of his phratry.
There is also evidence that after divorce, which was a simple matter for Lenape women
(as well as for men), they retained possession of all household effects and that their children invariably remained with them because they were of the same lineage.

Seasonal habitation sites, few tools and personal possessions, the lack of domesticated animals, disorderly planting fields, a classless and stateless social system, matrilineal kinship, indifference to commerce—what all of this added up to, for many Europeans, was a deeply inferior way of life, mired in primitive poverty. It seemed the very
antithesis of civilized existence, a devilish inversion of the proper order of things. To
the Dutch, all Indians were *wilden*—savages—while the English likened them to the
despised "wild Irish," whose seasonal migrations with their sheep and cattle appeared
utterly incompatible with civilization.

True, they didn't appear to be suffering. "It is somewhat strange," Nicholaes van Wassenaer admitted, "that among these most barbarous people, there are few or none cross-eyed, blind, crippled, lame, hunch-backed or limping men; all are well-fashioned people, strong and sound of body, well fed, without blemish." "Some have lived 100 years," Charles Lodwick marveled. "Also," Jasper Danckaerts added, "there are among them no simpletons, lunatics or madmen as among us."

Indeed, that the Lenapes lived so contentedly in what looked to Europeans like a setting of wonderful "natural" abundance made them all the more contemptible. How could people living in such a place fail so utterly to take advantage of the opportunities that lay all around them? They ought to have been civilized and rich, but they weren't. It was only a short step to the conclusion that they didn't deserve to be there at all.

THE FUR TRADE

A map of the New World drawn by Juan de la Cosa in the first decade of the sixteenth century hints that Europeans—probably anonymous fishermen looking for cod—may have visited Lenapehoking when Christopher Columbus was still exploring the Caribbean. The first solid evidence of such a visit, however, comes with the arrival of a French vessel, *La Dauphine*, piloted by the Florentine navigator Giovanni da Verrazzano. King Francis I of France and a syndicate of Lyons silk merchants had commissioned Verrazzano to find a northern route to China and Japan—the same "Indies" that Columbus dreamed of finding. In March 1524, after a fifty-day crossing from Madeira, *La Dauphine* began crawling up the coast from Cape Fear. By mid-April she passed Sandy Hook and anchored in the Narrows between Staten Island and Brooklyn.

As they had already done many times before, the crew of *La Dauphine* lowered the ship's longboat and rowed out to see what they could see. They soon found themselves, Verrazzano said, in "a very beautiful lake"—the Upper Bay—where they were surrounded by several dozen small boats whose occupants, "clad with feathers of fowls of diverse colors," greeted them "very cheerfully, making great shouts of admiration." This happy encounter ended almost as soon as it began, however. A sudden squall forced *La Dauphine* to stand out to sea again, so Verrazzano decided to resume his search further to the north—"greatly to our regret," he added, for this was a "hospitable and attractive" country, "and, we think, not without things of value." He dubbed the "lake" Santa Margarita, in honor of the king's sister, and the surrounding land Angoulême, the name of the king's principal estate. (When the Verrazano Narrows Bridge opened in 1964, the Triborough Bridge and Tunnel Authority, in its wisdom, spelled the explorer's name with one *z* rather than two.)

One year after Verrazzano's brief visit, Esteban Gomez, a black Portuguese pilot who had sailed with Magellan, ventured a fair distance up the Hudson (which he named Deer River) before concluding it didn't lead to China. Various French and English pilots are thought to have scouted the region as well in the years that followed. An Englishman supposedly crossed the Hudson in 1568 during an epic overland trek from the Gulf of Mexico to Canada. Marooned sailors and fishermen are rumored to have wintered along the Delaware or lower Hudson rivers in the late 1590s and early 1600s. On occasion, English and Spanish skippers raided the area to take slaves, an enterprise inspired by Gomez, who had seized fifty-seven New England Indians for sale on the Lisbon slave market.

But the most numerous and persistent successors of Verrazzano and Gomez were fur traders. Furs had always figured importantly in the European luxury trades; beaver in particular was highly prized for both its soft, deep pelt and its alleged medicinal properties. As Adriaen van der Donck would explain midway through the seventeenth century, beaver oil cured rheumatism, toothaches, stomachaches, poor vision, and dizziness; beaver testicles, rubbed on the forehead or dried and dissolved in water, made an effective antidote to drowsiness and idiocy.

Traditionally, most of the furs marketed in Europe came from Russia. Trapped in Siberia or along the shores of the Baltic, they were dressed and marketed in the ancient city of Kiev. But when French explorers and traders opened the St. Lawrence River valley in the 1580s, the influx of Canadian skins created a wider market in Europe and prompted rival traders to seek additional sources of supply elsewhere in North America. By 1600 exchanging beaver and other pelts for European wares had become routine for at least some Indian peoples along the Atlantic coast, the Lenapes undoubtedly among them. European trade goods from the 1570s have turned up in habitation sites well into the interior of New York State, and Dutch traders claimed to have "frequented" the lower Hudson Valley as early as 1598, "but without making any fixed settlements, only as a shelter in winter."

Not all the Lenapes were anxious to do business with Europeans. Some must have heard stories of captives carried off into slavery. Others seemed unwilling to get into the spirit of a market economy. "They take many beavers," Johannes de Laet remarked in 1615, "but it is necessary for them to get into the habit of trade, otherwise they are too indolent to hunt the beaver." Even a half century later, Daniel Denton would note that many Long Island Lenapes still showed a marked indifference to material possessions. "They are extraordinarily charitable to one another," he wrote, "one having nothing to spare, but he freely imparts it to his friends, and whatsoever they get by gaming or any other way, they share to one another, leaving to themselves commonly the least share."

What the Europeans offered the Lenapes—blankets, brass kettles, iron drills, hoes, knives, combs—were nonetheless obvious improvements on familiar things and could readily be incorporated into prevailing patterns of production and exchange. Slowly at first, then more rapidly after the addition of guns and alcohol as trade goods, even reluctant curiosity would give way to habit, and habit to dependency. By the early seventeenth century, the demand for items of European origin among the Lenapes had begun to undermine their way of life.

Even as the first colonists arrived on the scene, Lenape men were devoting more and more of their time to gathering furs for exchange with Europeans rather than for the use of their families and clans. They were away from home longer and returned with less food, which every spring left a few more communities a little closer to real famine when their stores from the previous harvest finally gave out (and in time virtually exterminated fur-bearing animals throughout the lower Hudson region). Then, too, as the work of men shifted from stalking to setting and checking traps, territorial boundaries became a matter of escalating controversy. The reciprocity that sustained complex kin networks weakened. Bands dissolved, re-formed, and dissolved again in a search for stability. Old intergroup alliances broke up. War became increasingly likely and, with the spread of firearms, increasingly deadly.

As European commodities supplanted their Lenape equivalents, a widening array of traditional skills, duties, and knowledge became less and less important. Lenape women assumed ever greater responsibility for supplying the camp with food and managing its internal affairs. Lenape sachems gained new prestige as the managers of trade with Europeans, though every year it would be more and more difficult to manage their often conflicted communities, let alone mobilize them for resistance. Alcohol hastened the disruption of earlier ways. As early as 1624 Nicolaes van Wassenaer could report that excessive drinking had destroyed the authority of at least one sachem, who "comes forward to beg a draught of brandy with the rest."

Another danger for the Lenapes had meanwhile appeared to the north in the form of the Iroquois League. According to legend, the idea of the league originated around the middle of the sixteenth century with a Huron prophet and philosopher named Deganawidah, who wandered among the Iroquois-speaking peoples of upper New York State preaching a gospel of unity, brotherhood, and equality. Around 1570, assisted by a certain Ha-yo-went'-ha (Longfellow's Hiawatha), Deganawidah brought the Mohawk, Oneida, Onondaga, Cayuga, and Seneca "nations" together in a single federation known as the League of the Great Peace. The league stretched from the Hudson to Niagara, encompassing perhaps a dozen semipermanent, stockaded villages whose combined population approached fifteen thousand.

Once Deganawidah and Ha-yo-went'-ha had gone—not died, it was said, merely moved on to spread their message among less fortunate peoples elsewhere—the league entered a new, aggressively expansionist phase. Its armies, sometimes numbering more than a thousand warriors, ranged west to the banks of the Mississippi, south to Virginia and the Carolinas, east into New England, and north, across the St. Lawrence, deep into Canada. Not unlike the crusading chivalry of medieval Christendom, they ventured out among the infidel with news of the Great Peace of Deganawidah and Ha-yo-went'-ha, a scourge to all who opposed them. Like the crusading chivalry, too, they had practical motives as well.

Their initial encounters with European commodities and weapons, which must have occurred around the same time that Deganawidah and Ha-yo-went'-ha were finishing their work, impressed upon the Iroquois the importance not only of direct access to the traders but also of controlling the supply of furs. In the 1580s, a decade or so after the league had been formed, the Iroquois attempted to establish a foothold on the St. Lawrence but were turned back by a combined force of Hurons and Algonkians, armed with French weapons. The erection of a French trading post at Quebec in 1609 completed the Iroquois defeat and enabled the Hurons and their allies to organize a vast, complex trading empire in which they used European goods to obtain food from agricultural peoples living above Lake Erie, exchanged the food for skins brought in by hunting groups in the far north, then brought the skins to Quebec and exchanged them for more trade goods.

In desperation, the Iroquois turned south toward the Susquehanna, Delaware, and Hudson valleys. Before 1600 they had subjected or driven off many of their original inhabitants. The Algonkian-speaking Mahicans who lived on the west side of the Hudson, near modern Albany, were the next in line. If they too succumbed—when they succumbed—all the peoples of the lower Hudson would be endangered in turn. With Europeans at their front door and Iroquois at their back, the Lenapes were doomed.

2

The Men Who Bought Manhattan

On the second day of September 1609, a three-masted Dutch carrack, the *Halve Maen* (Half Moon) dropped anchor off Sandy Hook. Her skipper, an English seaman named Henry Hudson, had started out six months earlier to find an Arctic shortcut to the Indies. Blocked by ice in the waters off Novaya Zemlya, and with his half-frozen crew threatening mutiny, Hudson then turned west and ran five thousand miles across the Atlantic to Nova Scotia. Since July, the *Halve Maen* had been scouting the coast between Cape Cod and Chesapeake Bay in search of the same northwest passage that Verrazzano failed to find eighty years before.

For more than a week Hudson and his men explored the Lower Bay, marveling at its wild beauty and fertility. Robert Juet, one of Hudson's officers, said the surrounding hills were "as pleasant with Grasse and Flowers, and goodly Trees, as ever they had seene, and very sweet smells came from them." The inhabitants seemed "very glad of our comming, and brought greene Tabacco, and gave us of it for Knives and Beads," Juet added. "They appear to be a friendly people," Hudson himself reported, "but are much inclined to steal, and are adroit in carrying away whatever they take a fancy to." That may explain why the situation suddenly turned ugly. A fight broke out, a crewman named Coleman was killed with an arrow through the neck, and Hudson decided to move on.

On September 12 Hudson guided the *Halve Maen* through the Narrows between Staten Island and Long Island. Crossing the Upper Bay, he warily purchased "Oysters and Beanes" from some "people of the Country" who paddled out to his ship in canoes, then entered the river that now bears his name—"as fine a river as can be found," in the words of another contemporary report, "wide and deep, with good anchoring ground on both sides." One week later and ninety miles upstream, near the present site of Albany, Hudson realized that he wasn't going to reach the Pacific. He turned back, dis-

appointed yet deeply impressed by what he had seen. "The land is the finest for cultivation that I ever in my life set foot upon," he asserted, "and it also abounds in trees of
every description. The natives are a very good people; for, when they saw that I would
not remain, they supposed that I was afraid of their bows, and taking the arrows, they
broke them in pieces, and threw them in the fire."

Nor did he leave empty-handed. The "loving people," in Juet's words, "came flocking aboord, and brought us Grapes and Pompions, which wee bought for trifles. And
many brought us Bevers skinnes, and Otters skinnes, which wee bought for Beades,
Knives, and Hatchets." That they made better hosts than the inhabitants of the
seaboard was confirmed as the *Halve Maen* sailed down "that side of the River that is
called *Manna-hata*" and dodged a hail of arrows fired by "savages" on the shore. (The
meaning of "Manna-hata" has been debated ever since; the preferred translation nowa-
days is "hilly island.")[1]

MIGHTY AMSTERDAM

Though Hudson's reconnaissance was no more successful than that of Verrazzano or
Gomez, it proved the more important because the political climate of Europe had
changed markedly by the early 1600s. At issue was the condition of Hapsburg Spain, still
the most powerful European state but surrounded now by adversaries. Over the course of
the sixteenth century, under Charles V and his son Philip II, the Spanish had absorbed
Portugal, taken possession of the Holy Roman Empire, overrun the principal islands of
the Caribbean, subdued Mexico and Peru, and invaded the Philippines. At the same
time, they became involved in a series of costly military adventures aimed at rolling back
the Protestant Reformation. Eventually, despite the riches extracted from its far-flung
possessions, the crown ran out of money and embarked on a disastrous program of
forced loans and debt repudiations that sent shock waves through European political and
financial systems. France and England, would-be entrants on the global imperial stage,
preyed mercilessly on Spanish shipping and launched their own colonizing projects in
those parts of the western hemisphere where Spanish power seemed weakest.

Nowhere were Spain's afflictions more apparent than in the Low Countries, or
Netherlands. Inherited by Charles V and subsequently granted by him to Philip II, they
had flourished under Spanish rule. Their leading cities—Antwerp, Bruges, Brussels—
grew rich as the marketplaces where Spain obtained, with gold and silver from the New
World, the food, clothing, manufactures, naval stores, and luxuries that it could not produce for itself. But when Protestantism spread across the Netherlands in the 1560s, a
revolt broke out against Spain. The seven Dutch-speaking provinces of the northern
Netherlands formed the United Provinces or Dutch Republic (foreigners called it Holland after the largest and wealthiest of the seven). Its governing body was the States-
General, in which each province had a single vote.

---

1. More than 150 years later, the Lenapes gave a Pennsylvania missionary their version of what happened when
the first white men landed on Manhattan: they sighted a "large canoe or house" moving across the water and
decided that it belonged to the Supreme Being, "the great Manitto," who then appeared before them dressed
entirely in red. After a preliminary exchange of courtesies, he offered them a toast and they all got happily
drunk—whence the site came to be known as Mannahattanink, "the island or place of general intoxication." If
authentic, this almost certainly alludes to events that occurred before Hudson arrived. Hudson and his mate, who
kept a fairly full record of their activities, made no mention of landing on Manhattan. It doesn't appear, either,
that the Lenapes he encountered were especially surprised to see him.

The United Provinces occupied a mere corner of Europe, not much bigger than the states of Connecticut, Massachusetts, and Rhode Island combined, and inhabited by fewer than two million people. Its struggle for independence would nonetheless become a central event of the early modern era. Year after year, Spanish armies ravaged the Netherlands. Year after year, the rebels fought back, fired by Calvinist zeal and led by the brilliant Prince William of Orange. Along the way they assembled the greatest fleet in Christendom, owning, Sir Walter Raleigh once estimated, more ships than eleven other nations combined.

Even before Dutch fireships helped England fend off the Spanish Armada in 1588, the war in the waters had spread far beyond the confines of Europe. Dutch squadrons, flying their orange, white, and blue banners, plundered Spanish ports throughout the Americas, Asia, and Africa. *Oranje boven!* was their war cry—"Orange above!" They hounded Spanish shipping in the Caribbean and swept Spain's Portuguese allies from the Indian Ocean. Dutch troops fought in Puerto Rico, Africa, South America, India, China, Japan, and Malaysia. Holland was already one of the world's great maritime powers when, in 1609, weary, frustrated, and bankrupt, the Spanish at last agreed to a twelve-year truce that gave their former subjects de facto independence.

Although true independence did not come for another forty-odd years, Holland's Golden Age had begun. Dutch traders, never far behind the fleets and armies, cornered the international markets in African slaves, Brazilian sugar, Russian caviar, Italian marble, Hungarian copper, fish from the North Sea, and furs from the Baltic. "The factors and Brokers of Europe," Daniel Defoe called them. "They *buy* to *sell* again, *take* in to *send* out, and the greatest Part of their vast Commerce consists in being supply'd from All parts of the World, that they may supply All the World again."

The fates of faraway kingdoms were decided in the countinghouses of Dutch bankers. Dutch investors bought Russian grain fields and German vineyards. Dutch engineers taught foreign princes the most advanced methods of building forts and draining swamps. Rich merchants and aristocrats across Europe collected the works of Dutch painters, filled their homes with the fine china and glass produced by Dutch artisans, and shipped their sons off to Dutch universities to study at the feet of scholars and philosophers who were changing the face of Western law and science.

Integral to Holland's success was the city of Amsterdam. Protected by a forbidding network of estuaries, Amsterdam rose to international prominence as the home base, nerve center, and symbol of the Dutch revolt. It expanded rapidly as the struggle wore on, nourished by the spoils of war and the capital of merchants fleeing the devastated cities of the south. With them came religious outcasts of every denomination—Walloons (French-speaking Protestants from what is now Belgium), Huguenots (French Protestants, many of whom joined Walloon churches), Baptists, Quakers, Sephardic Jews, and a party of English Calvinists (known to their day as Separatists and to ours as the Pilgrims)—all drawn by the city's tolerance for diversity and dissent. Together they made Amsterdam one of Europe's liveliest and most cosmopolitan urban centers. In 1585, the year that a Spanish army laid waste to Antwerp, Amsterdam's population numbered a mere thirty thousand. When Spain and Holland called their truce in 1609 it had risen to nearly sixty thousand. By mid-century it would exceed 150,000.

Amsterdam's burghers, moreover, were open to newer ways of doing business. Profitmaking and capital accumulation, still the objects of medieval scorn in much of Europe, were civic virtues in Amsterdam. Before the seventeenth century was more than a decade old, the city could already boast of the world's most up-to-date credit and banking facilities. It had Europe's most important stock exchange, specialized commodity exchanges, and a legal system swept clean of medieval obstructions to the free circulation of money and goods. Out of its well-equipped shipyards came swarms of privateers and fleets of a cheap but efficient new cargo ship—the *vlieboot* or flyboat—with which Dutch traders prowled the seas in search of gain. When they returned, holds bulging with the merchandise of distant lands, it was to an ingenious new system of canals that linked the waterfront with blocks of new warehouses and municipal markets, sharply reducing the time needed to find buyers, make up an outward-bound cargo, and set off again.

In time, half Europe's foreign trade would be in Dutch hands, and half its ships would have been built in their yards. Andrew Marvell, the English poet, linked the city's preoccupation with moneymaking to what he thought was its appalling indifference toward dissenters. "Staple of sects and mint of schism," he called Amsterdam—a "bank of conscience, where not one so strange/Opinion but finds credit and exchange."

THE WEST INDIA COMPANY

Amsterdam was also the headquarters for a pair of giant trading companies whose fortunes would determine the course of Dutch exploration and settlement around the world. Their purpose was to reduce destructive competition among smaller firms while simultaneously prosecuting the war with Spain. To that end, each had its own private army and navy, almost unlimited powers of peace and war, and control over vast human and material resources.

Senior of the two was the Vereenigde Oost-Indische Compagnie—the United East India Company—created in 1602 by the States-General to manage all Dutch trade east of the Cape of Good Hope. Capitalized at over six million guilders, an enormous sum at the time, the giant company quickly established Holland as a global power. East India Company merchants, backed by the company's own armed forces, set up trading posts, or "factories" (not to be confused with modern industrial enterprises), at Bandar-Abbas (Gombroon) near the mouth of the Persian Gulf, at Batavia on the vital Sunda Strait in the Spice Islands, at Chinsura in Bengal, and at Canton in China. They negotiated exclusive trading privileges in Nagasaki, the only Japanese port open to Europeans. Company troops expelled the English from Bantam, close by Batavia, and they seized a whole network of strategic bases from the Portuguese, including Malacca, Colombo, Cochin, Negapatam, and Macassar.

By the second half of the seventeenth century, this aggressive expansion had brought the East India Company undisputed commercial hegemony in the Malay archipelago and a fat share of the carrying trade throughout Asia. Its shareholders made fortunes, often receiving annual returns on their investments in excess of 30 percent—occasionally as much as 200 or 300 percent. The company itself became one of Amsterdam's largest employers and a bulwark of the city's prosperity. Manning, outfitting, provisioning, and servicing its lines of great East Indiamen required the labor of thousands—seamen, artisans, stevedores, laborers, and clerks—in addition to the thousands more employed in sugar refining, cloth finishing, tobacco cutting, silk throwing, glassmaking, distilling, brewing, and other industries related, directly or indirectly, to the company's operations.

In 1609, encouraged by the prospect of a long truce with Spain, the East India

Company commissioned Henry Hudson to find a northeast route to the Orient. When he failed, it turned its attention to other matters, not least of all the 329 percent dividend it had just declared for 1610. For merchants outside the company, though, Hudson's report that he and the crew of the *Halve Maen* had carried on a brisk trade in furs with obliging natives was tantalizing news. Despite the recent settlement of a French trading post at Montreal, the European market for furs remained so strong that smaller traders could still expect high returns with only a modest initial investment and little risk.

In 1610 a company of Amsterdam *particuliere kooplieden* (private merchant-traders) sent a single ship to the river "called Manhattes from the savage nation that dwells at its mouth" (soon renamed the Mauritius and, eventually, the North River). Rivals were close behind, and in the vigorous competition that followed, flinty Dutch captains like Hendrick Christiaensen, Cornelis May (after whom Cape May is named), and Adriaen Block won fame if not fortune.

Block's voyage of 1613–14, his fourth to the Hudson, must have been the talk of the Amsterdam waterfront. When fire destroyed his first ship, the *Tyger*, he and his men wintered on Manhattan and, with Indian help, built a new ship, the *Onrust* (Restless), with which they explored the East River and Long Island Sound in the spring of 1614.

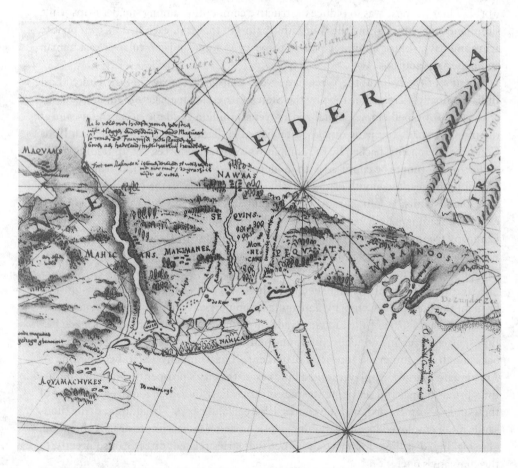

New Netherland, 1613/1614. Detail of the chart drawn by Adriaen Block. (© Collection of The New-York Historical Society)

(A mulatto from San Domingo named Jan Rodrigues remained on Manhattan with a stock of goods to organize trade pending Block's return.) The "Figurative Map" that Block brought back to Amsterdam later that year was the first to apply the name "Man-hates" to Manhattan, first to show Long Island as an island, first to show the Connecticut River and Narragansett Bay, and first to use the name "New Netherland" for the lands between English Virginia and French Canada. (Block's monument is the small island off the eastern end of Long Island that bears his name.)[2]

In 1614, knowing that competition was better for discovery than for profits, a group of Amsterdam's principal merchants persuaded the States-General to set up a single firm, the United New Netherland Company, with exclusive rights to traffic in American pelts (much as had been done earlier in the East Indian trade). The company sent out at least four expeditions and established a fortified year-round factory, or trading post, on Castle Island in the North River, just below modern Albany. It was called Fort van Nassouwen (Nassau), a name already applied to two other Dutch factories elsewhere in the world, one on the Amazon River in Brazil and the other at Mouree, in West Africa. A contemporary report described the fort as "a redoubt, surrounded by a moat eighteen feet wide" and garrisoned by ten or twelve men with a dozen-odd cannon. Under its protection, company traders began to tap the river's "great traffick in the skins of beavers, otters, foxes, bears, minks, wild cats, and the like." A smaller "redoubt or little fort," apparently not intended for year-round occupation, was erected the following year "about the Island Manhattans."

Expiration of the New Netherland Company's charter at the end of 1617 touched off another competitive free-for-all. The end of the Twelve Year Truce with Spain was approaching, moreover, and a controversy raged about what would come next. One party, known as the Remonstrants because of their opposition to dogmatic Calvinism, advocated peace; the other, whose less tolerant interpretation of Calvinist doctrine gave them the name Counter-Remonstrants, urged the resumption of all-out war. The war party scored its first major victory in 1619 at the Synod of Dordrecht (Dort in English), which gave the Dutch Reformed Church a strictly orthodox foundation and identified it irrevocably with a new, more aggressive Dutch nationalism.

A second Counter-Remonstrant victory came in 1621, when the States-General handed New Netherland and the fur trade over to a new and far larger enterprise, the Geoctroyerde West-Indische Compagnie, or West India Company. Capitalized at 7.5 million guilders, the West India Company received a monopoly over all Dutch trade with west Africa and the Americas. Like the East India Company, it had two purposes: to make money by trade and to make money by making war on Spain.[3]

---

2. The *Tyger* burned and sank on the Hudson shore of Manhattan near what would now be (thanks to subsequent landfill) the intersection of Greenwich and Dey streets, due east of the World Trade Center's North Tower. In 1916 workmen excavating the site for the IRT subway uncovered the ship's prow and keel. Portions were sawed off and are now preserved by the Museum of the City of New York; the rest is still there, twenty feet below street level.
3. The charter divided the company into five provincial chambers, one of which was in Amsterdam proper (and cost a hefty six thousand guilders to join). A nineteen-member central committee, consisting of delegates from the provincial chambers and the States-General, supervised the company's business, but day-to-day matters were delegated to particular provincial chambers. The administration of New Netherland and Curaçao, for example, always belonged to the Amsterdam Chamber. Similarly, the colony's spiritual affairs were entrusted to the Classis of Amsterdam, an association of churches that had the exclusive right to examine and license dominies, or ministers.

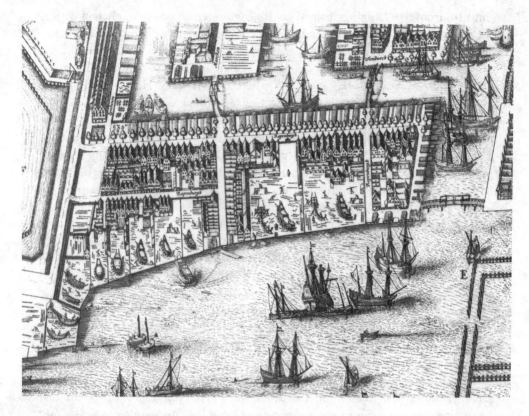

Amsterdam's waterfront. The West India Company's compound can be seen at the foot of the bridge on the right. Detail of a map by Balthasar van Berckenrode, 1625. (Municipal Archives, Amsterdam)

Shares in the West India Company sold briskly, and the company geared up for business. In 1623 it launched a campaign to seize the Portuguese sugar plantations in Brazil. In 1624 it sent out some seventy ships to prey on Spanish commerce. In 1625 it attacked and sacked San Juan, Puerto Rico. Over the next dozen years it would dispatch some seven hundred additional ships manned by sixty-seven thousand men. They took over five hundred prizes worth almost forty million guilders. Counting damages as well as booty, they are said to have cost Spain alone nearly 120 million guilders. *Oranje boven!*

NEW NETHERLAND

Nor did the company neglect its interests in North America. As early as 1622, according to a contemporary English account, its agents had appeared along "the river Manahata and made plantation there, fortifying themselves in two several places" where "they did persist to plant and trade." One of the company's ships spent the winter of 1623–24 trading in the Hudson and Long Island Sound. She was still anchored in the East River in the early summer of 1624 when Captain Cornelis May brought in the *Nieu Nederlandt* with thirty families, mostly Walloons from Leyden who had previously tried without success to get permission to settle in Virginia. May immediately sent eighteen families north to establish a base along the west bank of the Hudson, not far from the site of Fort Nassau (now fallen into disrepair), which they called Fort Orange. Some sixty years later a female survivor recalled that "as soon as they had built themselves some hutts of Bark," the people there were doing a good business in furs with the local Mahicans, who were "all as quiet as Lambs."

The remaining families of colonists were sent to establish outposts along the Delaware and Connecticut rivers—the western and eastern boundaries, respectively, of New Netherland. (Perhaps because no one could think of a better name, the Delaware site, like its North River counterpart, was also called Fort Nassau.) A small party also occupied Noten (now Governors) Island and were soon at work clearing and planting at least one farm on nearby Manhattan.

By December of that same year, the company's ships had returned to Amsterdam with pelts worth fifty thousand guilders and the cheerful news that New Netherland had begun "to advance bravely and to live in friendship with the natives." And such was the region's astounding abundance and fertility, according to one report, that the colonists lacked almost nothing. "Had we cows, hogs, and other cattle fit for food (which we daily expect in the first ships) we would not wish to return to Holland, for whatever we desire in the paradise of Holland, is here to be found."

Several more company ships arrived in the spring of 1625. Led by Willem Verhulst, who replaced May as director of New Netherland, this second expedition deposited over a hundred additional colonists (again, mostly Walloons) plus a wide variety of livestock (103 head in all) and a mountain of supplies—wagons, plows, tools, clothing, food, seeds, plant shoots, firearms, and cheap goods for the fur trade. The cattle were put to pasture on Manhattan ("a convenient place abounding with grass"), and Verhulst ordered more land there to be cleared for planting wheat, rye, and buckwheat.

Verhulst and Cryn Fredericks, an engineer, also chose Manhattan's southern tip as the best location for a massive fortification whose masonry walls, bristling with cannon, would anchor West India Company operations throughout New Netherland (in light of the fact, it was said, that "the Spaniard, who claims all the country, will never allow any one to gain a possession there"). They called it Fort Amsterdam, and Fredericks had the site staked out before the end of the year.

Nobody liked Verhulst. He bullied the colonists, doctored the books, and managed to lose track of vast quantities of trade goods. In the spring of 1626 he was replaced as director by forty-year-old Peter Minuit, a Walloon whose family had lived in Wesel, Germany, until driven out by a Spanish army a couple of years earlier.

FARMS OR FACTORIES?

Verhulst was really the least of New Netherland's problems, however. Far graver was a sharp division of opinion within the West India Company itself about its long-range expectations for the colony.

The original idea for the company had come from Willem Usselinx, a wealthy Flemish refugee who believed that its primary objective should be settlement, not the establishment of trading posts. To his way of thinking, Holland in particular and the Protestant cause in general would never throw off Spanish rule until Spain's grip on the New World and its resources had been broken. The surest way to do that, he reasoned, was to establish extensive colonies where free European farmers and converted Indians could produce agricultural commodities for the markets of Europe. The company's preoccupation with conventional trade and warfare left Usselinx bitterly disappointed, and he refused its repeated offers of employment. At least a few of its directors nonetheless thought he had been on the right track. Led by Kiliaen van Rensselaer, an

Amsterdam diamond merchant, these dissidents fought for years to make something more out of the company's American holdings than a collection of thinly populated trading posts.

From the very beginning, consequently, New Netherland's status was anomalous. In 1624, just before the Walloons set out with Captain May on the *Nieu Nederlandt*, the West India Company promulgated a set of regulations for the colony known as the Provisional Orders. The Orders implied that it would be run as a collection of thoroughly typical factories in which the company's interests came first, the company made the rules, and the company decided what was best. Prospective colonists were explicitly warned "to obey and to carry out without any contradiction the orders of the Company then or still to be given, as well as all regulations received from the said Company in regard to matters of administration and justice." The company would tell them where to live. The company would tell them what to plant on their land. They would work on the construction of fortifications and public buildings at the direction of the company. Their able-bodied men would perform military service for the company as needed.

Yet the Provisional Orders also hinted that other intentions besides those of the company were to be served as well. Perhaps because the Walloons had driven a hard bargain, colonists bound for New Netherland were promised things that matter only to people seeking to put down roots: cheap livestock, easy credit for the purchase of supplies, freedom of conscience in private worship, and, after six years' service to the company, free land on which to settle. The company likewise instructed the director to appoint some of them to a council that would advise him on matters of general concern. It was this council that in 1626 brought in Minuit to replace the unpopular Verhulst.

WAR AND WAMPUM

Complicating the company's confusion about its purposes in New Netherland were momentous changes in the organization of the fur trade. Intensive trapping had severely depleted the Lenape peltries of the lower Hudson Valley by the mid-1620s, with the result that more and more of the furs exported from New Netherland were now coming from Mahicans who lived on the west bank of the Hudson around Fort Orange. The Dutch were not alone in appreciating the significance of this development. Iroquois-speaking Mohawks, recently repulsed from the St. Lawrence by the French and Hurons, saw a chance to recoup their losses by wresting control of the fur trade away from the Algonkian-speaking Mahicans. War between the Mohawks and Mahicans broke out in 1624 and escalated rapidly.

Concurrently, both Dutch and English discovered the value of "sewan" or "wampum." True wampum consisted of long strings of tiny purple and white beads sewn together into belts; a large belt, six feet or so in length, would have contained six or seven thousand beads ("loose" or unstrung wampum was never considered the genuine article). The beads themselves were made from certain clam and whelk shells that could be found only along the shores of Narragansett Bay and Long Island Sound—Sewanhacky was in fact the Lenape name for Long Island—and the peoples native to those regions had long been accustomed to collecting, drilling, and stringing the shells for trade with groups far into the interior of the continent. With the introduction of European metal awls or drills, perhaps as early as the final quarter of the sixteenth century, it became possible for them to manufacture wampum in significantly greater quantity.

In 1609 Hudson's men received "stropes of Beades" from some upriver Indians, but it was a crafty Dutch fur trader named Jacob Eelkes (or Eelckens) who became the first European to grasp the significance of wampum. In 1622 Eelkes seized a Pequot sachem on Long Island and threatened to cut off his head unless he received "a heavy ransom." The sachem gave him over 140 fathoms of wampum, which Eelkes then discovered would fetch more furs than conventional European trade goods. Before long West India Company agents were buying up all the wampum they could get from the coastal Algonkians and trekking it north to Fort Orange to buy furs from the Mahicans—which made the Mahicans all the more inviting a target for the Iroquois, who relied heavily on wampum for ceremonial and diplomatic purposes. Isaack de Rasieres, a Walloon serving as the company's chief commercial agent and the colony's official secretary, took the news of wampum up to Governor William Bradford of Plymouth, a settlement of English Separatists founded in 1620. Bradford spread the word, and almost overnight, as he put it, "a great alteration" was wrought in the affairs of the entire region.[4]

Suddenly the fur trade was no longer a simple matter of direct barter between assorted Europeans and assorted native American peoples. Henceforth it would also involve a pair of transactions in which wampum functioned rather like money. In the first, European traders and coastal Algonkians exchanged manufactured goods for wampum; in the second, European traders used wampum (as well as manufactured goods) to obtain furs at Fort Orange. Not too many years later, wampum would become legal tender throughout both New England and New Netherland.

NEW AMSTERDAM

As the Mohawk-Mahican war intensified, the West India Company weighed the idea of an alliance with the Mahicans. But after Mohawk warriors killed three soldiers from the Fort Orange garrison and "well roasted" a fourth, the company's managers lost confidence in the Mahicans and cast their lot with the Iroquois. Realizing that New Netherland's far-flung trading posts couldn't be defended if they were caught up in the fighting, the company also resolved to abandon those on the Connecticut and Delaware rivers and move the women and children from Fort Orange to an encampment on the southern tip of Manhattan. This was an attractive site because company agents stationed there could still supervise the flow of commerce out of the Hudson Valley and Long Island Sound. It was big enough for the company to maintain its own farms and herds for provisioning the camp. Apparently, too, many of the island's original inhabitants had recently succumbed to epidemic disease or been driven away by rival groups. (De Rasieres, writing c. 1628, noted that only about two or three hundred of "the old Manhatans" still lived on the island. Along the East River, he added, "is a little good land, where formerly many people have dwelt, but who for the most part have died or have been driven away by the Wappenos [Wappingers].")

In May or June of 1626, shortly after taking over from Verhulst, Director Minuit began to implement the new policy by "purchasing" Manhattan from the Lenapes for sixty guilders' worth of trade goods. It's impossible to say which Lenapes, or what kind

---

4. Jasper Danckaerts later remarked that native American peoples knew nothing of theft or greed prior to the European invasion "because *zeewant*, which they all treasure and now serves as their money, didn't exist previously but was only their decoration as beads are for children." According to the Hiawatha legend, wampum was invented by the Iroquois.

New Amsterdam, c. 1626. Perhaps drawn by Cryn Fredericks, the company's engineer, this view greatly exaggerates the size of the fort but accurately depicts the mill and cabins that huddled outside its walls. Engraved and published by Joost Hartgers in 1651. (© Museum of the City of New York)

of trade goods, because no deed or bill of sale has survived—if indeed there ever was one. However, when he and five other colonists also "bought" Staten Island on August 10, 1626, they paid the local sachems "Some Diffies [duffle cloth], Kittles [kettles], Axes, Hoes, Wampum, Drilling Awls, Jew's Harps, and diverse other other wares"— probably the same kind of trade goods with which they had obtained Manhattan. (Probably, too, those "drilling awls" were the very kind used by coastal Algonkians to manufacture wampum.)

Engineer Fredericks and his workers meanwhile scaled back their plans for a real fortress and threw up a simple blockhouse surrounded by a palisade of wood and sod. Other workmen hurriedly erected a sawmill on Noten (Governors) Island, then heavily wooded, and used the lumber to build thirty cabins. These were followed by a stone countinghouse "thatched with reed" and "a horse-mill, over which shall be constructed a spacious room sufficient to accommodate a larger congregation." The mill was to have a tower where bells captured the year before at the sack of San Juan would be hung. The new settlement was dubbed New Amsterdam. It had about 270 inhabitants, including a handful of newborn infants.

Was it a settlement, though? Many of those 270 inhabitants, undoubtedly the Walloons and perhaps Minuit as well, wouldn't have objected to the term. They saw themselves as settlers and thought—not without reason, considering the terms of the Provisional Orders—that the West India Company did too.

A majority of the company's shareholders saw things differently. Continuing to favor trade over colonization, they viewed New Amsterdam as a commercial "factory" or trading post indistinguishable from dozens of other such installations scattered along the coasts of Africa, India, Malaysia, and China. It wasn't a beachhead of imperial conquest or a citadel to overawe a subject population. It wasn't a seedbed for transplanting Dutch culture in the New World. It wasn't a workshop or plantation for the production

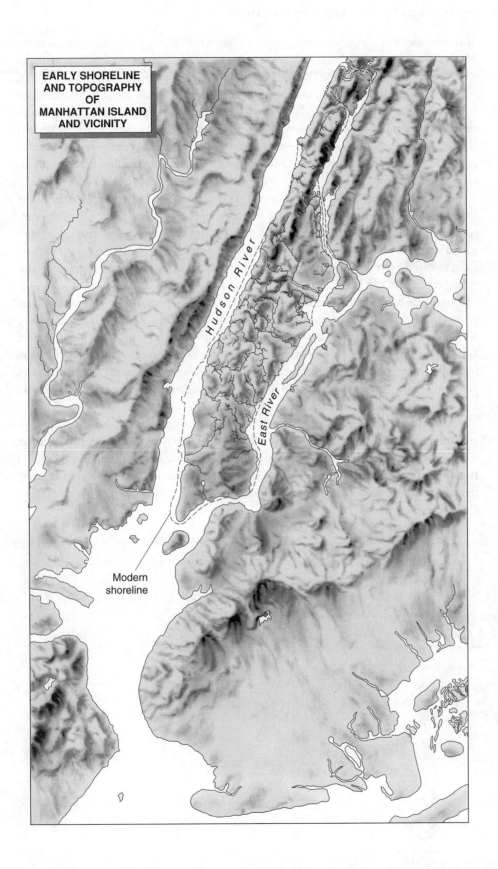

EARLY SHORELINE
AND TOPOGRAPHY
OF
MANHATTAN ISLAND
AND VICINITY

Hudson River

East River

Modern
shoreline

of commodities. It was, purely and simply, a place where cheap European manufactured goods (knives, axes, blankets, iron pots, nails) would be exchanged for those items of local origin (dressed and cured pelts) that would fetch a good price back home.

From this perspective, the company would actually do itself more harm than good by promoting a proper colony in New Amsterdam. Settlers would require constant support and protection—both of which cost money—and the more there were, the trickier it would be for the Company to maintain its authority. Besides, settlers would inevitably squabble with the Indians over land and livestock, jeopardizing the flow of furs into the company's storehouses.

As a factory, New Amsterdam seemed a far sounder proposition. Because the labor-intensive drudgery of preparing furs for market could be done by the native inhabitants, the colony would be able to get along very nicely with a skeleton staff of salaried officials plus a small number of hired artisans, soldiers, and laborers. A few husbandmen and farmers could keep it supplied with fresh food (just as, for example, the company maintained cattle herds on Bonaire to feed Curaçao). Employees wouldn't expect the company to provide much in the way of amenities, either. They would sleep in company barracks, work with company tools and equipment, and eat in the company mess. Nor would the company have to be particular about who they were: they needn't be Dutch, and they surely didn't need to be respectable. It wasn't even essential for the company to have all of them on the payroll: anyone, strictly speaking, could go to New Amsterdam and deal in furs—as long as they sold them to the company, at the company's price, and bought their trade goods at the company's stores.

Thus the little community that gathered on Manhattan in 1626 was a hybrid—something more than what a majority of West India Company directors intended yet something less than what many of its inhabitants must have hoped, a confused mix of private and public aspirations, of commerce and colonization, of employees and settlers. It wasn't the most solid of foundations.

Company Town

According to Nicolaes van Wassenaer, the Dutch physician-journalist who published a semiannual compilation of intelligence from America, New Amsterdam's first year had gone remarkably well. "Men work there as in Holland," he rejoiced. "One trades, upwards, southwards and northwards; another builds houses, the third farms. Each farmer has his farmstead on the land purchased by the Company, which also owns the cows; but the milk remains to the profit of the farmer; he sells it to those of the people who received their wages for work every week. The houses of the Hollanders now stand outside the fort, but when that is completed, they will all repair within, so as to garrison it and be secure from sudden attack."

People with firsthand knowledge of conditions on Manhattan were less sanguine. Isaack de Rasieres worried that few colonists had come prepared to establish anything more than a grubby little trading post. Some, not having contracted to perform manual labor, expected the company to provide them with food and shelter while they got rich in the fur trade. The rest, de Rasieres wrote in a letter home, were a "rough lot who have to be kept at work by force." "I cannot sufficiently wonder at the lazy unconcern of many persons, both farmers and others, who are willing enough to draw their rations and pay in return for doing almost nothing," he added.

De Rasieres's criticism paled alongside the fulminations of Dominie Johannes Michaelius, New Amsterdam's first regular minister of the gospel. Fresh provisions were scarce and overpriced, Michaelius wrote angrily to friends back in the Netherlands; it was impossible to get a horse or a cow, rations distributed by the company were disgusting—"hard stale food, such as men are used to on board ship"—and there were no decent houses, only "hovels and holes" where the colonists "huddled rather than dwelt." Nobody seemed really interested in improving things, either. Some of the Walloons had already given up and gone home. A few years later, the dominie himself followed.

Criticism of New Amsterdam flared at company headquarters as well. Expenses were running well ahead of initial projections, and income from the fur trade hadn't lived up to expectations. After two or three profitless years, investors as well as directors were clamoring for the company to cut its losses, abandon Manhattan, and concentrate on operations in the West Indies and Brazil.

PATROONS AND PURITANS

New Amsterdam's future brightened temporarily when Admiral Piet Heyn, commanding a flotilla of thirty-one company vessels and three thousand men, captured the Spanish treasure fleet outside Havana in 1628. Heyn returned to Amsterdam with two hundred thousand pounds of silver, 135 pounds of gold, and a mountain of sugar, pearls, spices, hides, and other merchandise—worth, all told, a whopping fifteen million guilders. This triumph of organized banditry enabled the company to pay a fat 50 percent dividend and made Heyn a national hero. Over the next half-dozen years, largely financed by Heyn's coup, company forces would drive the Portuguese from their lucrative sugar plantations in Brazil and seize Curaçao, which commanded the vast salt pans on nearby Aruba and Bonaire.

In the general euphoria that followed Heyn's coup, the prosettlement faction led by Kiliaen van Rensselaer persuaded the West India Company to give New Netherland a second chance. In the Freedoms and Exemptions of 1629 (also known as the Charter of Liberties) the company agreed to give large chunks of New Netherland to "patroons" who would promise to buy the land from the Indians and import fifty or more settlers at their own expense. It also agreed to supply the colonists with slaves and to build a better fort on Manhattan. The reward for these concessions would be continued control of New Netherland's trade: all goods coming into and out of the colony, furs included, would have to travel in company vessels at company rates and pay specified duties to company agents at New Amsterdam.

Van Rensselaer promptly applied to the company for a "patroonship" called Rensselaerswyck, a seven-hundred-thousand-acre domain surrounding Fort Orange. A half-dozen other directors associated with Van Rensselaer followed with applications for their own patroonships. Michael Pauw set his sights on Pavonia, which included Staten Island and the west bank of the Hudson across from Manhattan. Most of the projects existed only on paper, however, quietly forgotten when the would-be patroons came to their senses or failed to overcome the skepticism of potential investors. Pauw did build a house on the site of present-day Jersey City but lost too much money, quarreled with the local Indians, and ultimately sold his rights to Pavonia to the company in 1637. Rensselaerswyck alone survived, a thorn in the company's side for years.

The patroonship fiasco was compounded by the vigorous expansion of settlement in neighboring New England. In 1630 Puritan immigrants founded the town of Boston in a colony they called Massachusetts Bay; thousands more followed over the next decade. They were a doctrinaire and disputatious people, and dissidents soon began streaming out of Boston to plant a crop of new settlements elsewhere in Massachusetts as well as in New Hampshire, Rhode Island, Connecticut, and eastern Long Island.

From the West India Company's point of view, the Puritans couldn't have showed up at a less opportune moment. As trappers and traders from Massachusetts joined those from Plymouth and fanned out across the dwindling peltries of northern New England, the company's chances of turning a profit in the fur trade grew steadily slimmer. What was more, the arrival of actual settlers—besides undermining Dutch claims to the Connecticut River Valley and Long Island—threatened the wampum-manufacturing Lenapes who lived along Long Island Sound. Their displacement or conquest by the English would strike directly at the company's ability to obtain furs from the Mohawks at Fort Orange.

An all-out buildup of Dutch settlement along the New England frontier might still save the situation. The question was whether the West India Company, distracted by big-budget campaigns in the West Indies and Brazil, cared enough to work out an acceptable alternative to patroonships.

THE CASE FOR COLONIZATION

Back in New Amsterdam, it seemed that everyone had fixed the blame for the colony's lack of progress on Peter Minuit ("a slippery man," fumed Dominie Michaelius, "who under the treacherous mask of honesty is a compound of all iniquity and wickedness.") The company decided to replace Minuit with Wouter van Twiller, a twenty-seven-year-old former clerk in its Amsterdam headquarters and, not unimportantly, the nephew of Kiliaen van Rensselaer.

Van Twiller arrived in 1633 with a hundred-odd soldiers, the first regular troops to be stationed in the colony. He made a show of sealing the border between New Netherland and New England by erecting a fortified trading post called the House of Good Hope (now Hartford) on the Connecticut River, but to no avail. The English coolly ignored the House of Good Hope, and the callow Van Twiller, unwilling to make a fight of it, abandoned the company's jurisdiction over the Connecticut River Valley.

Van Twiller's administration of New Amsterdam was no more successful. He attempted to rehabilitate the fort and did manage to build a new bakehouse, a "small house" for the midwife, a goathouse, and a proper church. He drank too much, on the other hand—once, in an alcoholic rage, he even chased Dominie Everardus Bogardus, Michaelius's replacement, around town "with a drawn knife"—and spent too much time scheming to acquire land for himself and his cronies under the company's patroonship plan. At one time or another Van Twiller owned what are now Governors, Wards, and Roosevelt islands, as well as tobacco plantations in what are now Greenwich Village and the Red Hook section of Brooklyn. (Easily grown on fields already cleared by the Lenapes, tobacco was a profitable and popular crop.)

Ironically, although the West India Company hadn't yet decided to try again to promote settlements outside New Amsterdam, Van Twiller's landgrabbing helped establish the first Dutch colonists across the East River on Long Island. Between 1636 and 1638 he registered the "purchase" from various Lenape sachems of better than fifteen thousand acres of land at three locations in what is now Brooklyn. One site, in Gowanus, belonged to William Adriaense Bennett and Jacques Bentyn. Another, on Wallabout Bay, belonged to Joris Jansen de Rapalje, a Walloon. The third site, by far the best and largest, lay on the broad, treeless plains just to the north and west of Jamaica Bay where the Canarsees had maintained planting fields. Part of it was reserved by Van Twiller for his own use, part belonged to Jacob van Corlear, and part was held by two partners, Andries Hudde and Wolphert Gerritsen (for whom Gerritsen Beach is named).

Only Hudde and Gerritsen attempted to occupy their portion—known variously as

Achtervelt (i.e., after or beyond the plains or flats of south-central Brooklyn), New Amersfort (Gerritsen's hometown in Holland), or simply Flatlands. The two partners broke ground in 1636 near where the Flatlands Dutch Reformed Church now stands at the intersection of Flatbush Avenue and Kings Highway. An inventory made two years later reveals that they had put up a house, barn, and hayrick. The house was twenty-six feet long, twenty-two feet wide, and forty feet high, "covered above and all around with boards" and "surrounded by long, round palisades"—evidently a precaution against Indian attack. The partners had thirty-two acres of land sown with summer and winter grain as well as a garden planted with fruit trees. Their livestock included a half-dozen cows, several oxen, and five horses. This brave little beginning didn't inspire others to follow in their footsteps, however: a full decade would pass before the West India Company could point to more than a sprinkling of settlers anywhere on Long Island.

While New Amsterdam struggled along, Holland was seized by the Tulip Mania, a bizarre speculative frenzy that boosted the price of tulip bulbs to unheard-of levels before it collapsed in February 1637, wiping out innumerable unwary investors and generating widespread unemployment. The States-General began to talk of exporting the indigent to New Netherland—at which point it became more obvious than ever that the West India Company had done little over the previous decade to populate the colony or protect it from being overrun by the English. Under pressure to remedy the situation or surrender New Netherland to the nation, the company's directors decided to act.

Their first move was to fire Van Twiller and annul his various land purchases. The second, which took two years to complete, was a revision of the Freedoms and Exemptions that made the first deliberate provision for settlements outside New Amsterdam. Prospective emigrants to New Netherland were now promised cheap transportation, up to two hundred acres of land, and a schoolmaster for the education of their children. Except for minor regulatory taxes on imports and exports, the company also consented to permit free trade in the colony, abandoning the commercial monopoly it had so jealously guarded for twenty years.

The fate of the new policy hinged on the company's third move, its appointment of Willem Kieft as director of New Netherland. Kieft was a merchant with excellent family connections and a reputation for learning. He was also rumored to be something of a crook. According to one story, he had recently left France "in a hurry." According to another, he had once absconded with money raised to ransom Christians imprisoned by the Turks. Considering the havoc Kieft would wreak on New Netherland over the coming eight or nine years, the company's directors would have done well to inquire into such talk a bit more closely.

PERSONNEL AND CHATTEL

When Kieft stepped ashore in 1638, New Amsterdam was a collection of eighty or ninety structures occupied by four hundred or so people—not much bigger, in other words, than it had been a dozen years earlier in the days of Peter Minuit. (Boston, four years younger, already boasted a thousand inhabitants.) Most of the town lay along crooked footpaths to the east and south of the ramparts of Fort Amsterdam. A string of buildings followed the East River shore along what is now Pearl Street as far as a sluggish creek known as Blommaert's Vly (Broad Street). No more than a handful stood on the far side of Smit's Vly (the foot of Maiden Lane).

Everything in sight belonged to the West India Company, and the company had never been diligent about maintenance, let alone appearances. Everywhere Kieft looked he saw chaos, squalor, and dilapidation. Fort Amsterdam, he informed the West India Company, was "totally and wholly in a ruinous condition, so that people could go in and out of said fort on all sides." The director's house needed "considerable repairs," as did the company's five stone workshops, the wooden church built by Van Twiller, and the smith's house. The thirty cabins built a decade earlier were still standing, though many were now occupied by sheep and pigs. Of the four windmills belonging to the company, only one gristmill and one sawmill remained in operation. Owing to a recent fire, "the place where the Public store stood can with difficulty be discovered." North of town, along the axis still called the Bowery, the company's five farms lay "vacant and fallen into decay; there was not a living animal on hand belonging to the Company on said Bouweries." (In New Netherland, a "bouwerie" was a fully developed farm with live-stock, in contrast to a "plantation," which produced tobacco and other crops.)

As for the inhabitants of New Amsterdam, they had a good claim to being the motliest assortment of souls in Christendom. Probably only a narrow majority of the heavily male European population was Dutch, for Manhattan ran a distant fourth to Asia, Brazil, and the West Indies as a magnet for fortune seekers from the Netherlands. The rest were Walloons, English, French, Irish, Swedish, Danish, and German, among others—not to mention various Frisians sometimes confused with the Dutch, one Cicero Alberto (known around town as "the Italian"), and Anthony Jansen van Salee (a Muslim mulatto of mixed Dutch and Moroccan ancestry whom everyone called "the Turk"). Between them, Kieft told Father Isaac Jogues, a visiting Jesuit missionary, they spoke no fewer than "eighteen different languages."

About the only thing they had in common was that nearly everyone was an employ-ee of the West India Company. First among them—making up what might be called New Amsterdam's official establishment—were the director, the provincial secretary, and the *schout-fiscall* (a combination sheriff and prosecutor). The director made rules and regulations for the colony by outright fiat; the director and his appointed council sat as a court to hear both civil and criminal cases brought by the *schout*. Others were a mar-shal or constable who acted as court messenger, a few commissaries and their assistants who ran the "public store" and kept track of company property, and a labor foreman. Dominie Everardus Bogardus was on the company payroll too, as were Catarina or "Tryn" Jonas, the official midwife, and New Amsterdam's first schoolmaster, Adam Roelantsen.

Also in the company's employ were fifty or sixty soldiers and officers stationed in the fort, various sailors who manned harbor lighters and North River sloops, and at least one mason, blacksmith, armorer, cooper, house carpenter, ship carpenter, shoemaker, hatter, brewer, baker, surgeon, wheelwright, tailor, locksmith, sailmaker, and miller. Often these artisans pursued more than one line of work to supplement their meager wages. Schoolmaster Roelantsen took in washing. Other employees worked company land as tenants, producing small crops of maize, beans, barley, and tobacco. They occu-pied the lowest level of New Amsterdam's corporate hierarchy—except, that is, for the company's slaves.

Slavery had most likely existed in New Amsterdam from the outset, although the details are sparse and ambiguous. In 1625 or 1626 the company imported eleven bondsmen, among them Paulo d'Angola, Simon Congo, Anthony Portuguese, and John Francisco. It acquired three female slaves from Angola in 1628. Handfuls of others followed, women as well as men, and in 1635 Jacob Stoffelsen was hired as "overseer over the negroes belonging to the Company." Stoffelsen used the men on a variety of official projects, from repairing the fort and cutting wood to "splitting palisades, clearing land, burning lime, and helping to bring in the grain in harvest time." In 1641 he had them remove dead hogs from the streets of New Amsterdam, "to prevent the stench, which proceeds therefrom." The women appear to have been employed as domestic labor, although an irate Dominie Michaelius said that as maidservants "the Angola slaves are thievish, lazy and useless trash." By 1639 slave quarters were reportedly established on the East River shore across from Hog (now Roosevelt) Island, well outside of town.

None of this meant that the West India Company was ready to invest heavily in slave labor for New Netherland. Dutch opinion remained divided about the morality of owning and selling human beings, and the company (which consulted theologians on the matter) had shied away from the slave trade before 1637, when it captured the Portuguese station at Elmina on the west coast of Africa and began to take over the key sources of supply. Not indeed until 1640, when Portugal broke away from Spain and lost the *asiento*, the license to supply slaves to Spanish colonies, did the company become systematically involved in the trade. And despite occasional promises to import slaves for use on the bouweries and plantations of New Netherland, it did so only twice before the mid-1650s. As a result, there were never more than a few dozen or so slaves at a time throughout the colony, most of them contraband seized from the Spanish or Portuguese or purchased from the occasional visiting privateer (Virginia settlers bought their first slaves in 1619 from a West India Company warship). Not all were Africans, either: some may have been Indians or even captured Spanish or Portuguese sailors. Few if any were privately owned.

Nor was slavery in New Netherland the system of absolute racial subjugation it would later become. The West India Company never tried to formalize the status of slaves in the colony, and local custom accorded them a measure of respect and autonomy. Slaves were subject to the same laws and judicial procedures as whites. They could own property and testify in court. They could bear arms in time of emergency. They were encouraged to attend services and to observe religious holidays. They could marry and have their matrimonial bonds registered in the Dutch Reformed Church, the first such surviving record being a double wedding in 1641 that united Anthony van Angola with Catalina van Angola, and Lucie d'Angola with Laurens van Angola.

Blacks were hardly considered equals, to be sure. Adulterous intercourse with "heathens, blacks, or other persons" was banned by a 1638 ordinance. Whites convicted of serious crimes were made to work in chains next to the blacks, while company policy excluded slaves from employment in skilled trades, avoiding possible conflict with white labor. Similarly, punishments meted out to blacks were calculated less to maintain racial supremacy than to ensure a tractable labor force. In 1641 eight slaves confessed "without torture or shackles" to murdering a ninth. Plainly reluctant to hang all eight, the court decided to hang one, chosen by lot. The choice fell on Manuel of Gerrit de Reus, but when the executioner pushed him off the ladder with "two good ropes" around his neck, both ropes broke and the bystanders "very earnestly" called for mercy. The court thereupon pardoned him and the other slaves "on promise of good behavior and willing service"—which was doubtless what they were most concerned about anyway.

All nine of the slaves involved in the 1641 incident—including Big Manuel, Little Manuel, Simon Congo, Paulo d'Angola, and Anthony Portuguese—were among those who received something called "half-freedom" in 1644. They had petitioned the company for emancipation, and Kieft thought it was a good idea, observing that they "are burthened with many children so that it is impossible for them to support their wives and children, as they have been accustomed to do, if they must continue in the Company's service." He therefore granted the men "and their wives" their liberty and gave or leased them land on which to support themselves. They weren't completely free, however. Kieft required them to pay an annual tribute of "thirty skepels of Maize or Wheat, Pease or Beans, and one Fat hog" or forfeit their freedom; they had to work for the company, for wages, whenever it called on them; and their children remained in bondage.[1]

Half-freedom for slaves offered the company manifold practical advantages. It lifted the burden of providing for those who were older and less productive—some of the 1644 petitioners had already served for eighteen or nineteen years—while allowing the company to employ their labor as needed. Allowing manumitted slaves to take up land was also expedient, for "the Negroes' Farms," as they became known, were situated on the outskirts of town where their presence would help alert New Amsterdam to the danger of an Indian attack. Some lay just north of the present site of City Hall, near a former Lenape encampment on the pond that the Dutch called Kalch-hook (meaning "lime-shell point," from the shell-covered promontory above it). Others lay above what is now Houston Street, between Lafayette Street and the Bowery. A third group was concentrated in what is now Greenwich Village. Domingo Anthony's plot occupied the southwest corner of today's Washington Square Park; most ran along the marshy banks of Minetta Creek, with Paulo d'Angola's lying between Minetta Lane and Thompson Street.

Not on this roster of New Amsterdam's personnel and chattel were the "free inhabitants" who lived outside the company's authority. Some Walloons still raised cattle and wheat on the outskirts of New Amsterdam, staying to themselves except when they came in to trade at the company store. There were also various independent merchants and their families, a few widows, and a handful of former (or part-time) company servants who, like Hudde and Gerritsen, had begun to set up as farmers on Long Island.

WILD WEST ON THE HUDSON

The diversity of New Amsterdam's inhabitants when Kieft arrived was matched only by their turbulence. Fully one-quarter of the town's buildings were "grog-shops or houses where nothing is to be got but tobacco and beer," he reported, and immoderate drinking caused daily "mischief and perversity." This probably came as no surprise to company officials back in the Netherlands, as their profits from liquor sales ran second to those from the fur trade. For years the company had operated a brewhouse, which gave Brouwer Straet its name. It also sold imported wines and brandies at the company store and wholesaled liquor to the inhabitants, who were urged to retail it from their homes. Kieft himself proceeded to establish, on Staten Island, the first distillery in New Netherland.

---

1. In 1649 white residents criticized the company for enslaving the offspring of free Christian mothers. Taken aback, the company moderated its claim to occasional labor and noted defensively that only three children were then in service.

During his first year in office alone, the new director heard over forty criminal cases involving slander, theft, assault, adultery, rape, and murder, with much of the trouble stemming from a skewed sex ratio as well as excessive drinking. Because the company had shown so little interest in promoting permanent settlement, there were many more men in town than women—and too many of those men were footloose bachelors, down-and-out adventurers, fugitive husbands, runaway servants, and waterfront riffraff who had decided to spend a few years toiling for the company while on their way from wherever to God-only-knows.

Particularly troublesome were the men of the Fort Amsterdam garrison, one or another of whom was always up on charges for drunkenness, fighting, destruction of civilian property, larceny, sleeping on duty, refusing to work, desertion, or insubordination. In June 1638 Kieft and the council hired Nicolaes Coorn as the company sergeant, explaining that "it is necessary to have some one to drill the soldiers in the proper use of arms" (a striking admission in its own right). Within months, however, Coorn's unmilitary conduct had the barracks in an uproar. He stole from the troops and looked the other way when the troops in turn stole "turnips, chickens and tobacco pipes" from the company. He traded company property to the Indians for furs, then hid the contraband in his bunk. "Likewise," according to the *schout*, he "has at divers times had Indian women and Negresses sleep entire nights with him in his bed, in the presence of all the soldiers." The council eventually broke Coorn to the rank of private and condemned two fellow soldiers "to ride two hours on the wooden horse"—a military version of the pillory in which the culprit was made to straddle a high sawhorse, with weights up to fifty pounds attached to each leg. But nothing changed. The very next year a soldier named Gregoris Pietersen was executed by firing squad for urging the troops to mutiny.

Not only were there too few women in New Amsterdam, but too few women disposed to Calvinist order and decorum. In Europe, unmarried Dutch women struck foreigners, especially the French, as shockingly improper, given to public kissing, lewd talk, and a general lack of regard for chastity, though married housewives were as a rule accounted pillars of sobriety and virtue. On the colonial frontier, mores grew even more relaxed. Over and over again the magistrates came up against bawds and doxies like Nanne Beeche, who went to a party at the house of wheelwright Claes Cornelissen and, "notwithstanding her husband's presence, fumbled at the front of the breeches of most all of those who were present," setting off a near riot. Grietjen Reyniers, wife of Anthony "the Turk" Jansen, was said to have "pulled the shirts of some sailors out of their breeches and in her house measured the male members of three sailors on a broomstick"—which perhaps explained why when the crew of a departing ship caught sight of her on the shore they began chanting, "Whore, Whore, Two pound butter's whore!" When she and her husband were finally expelled in 1639, they took up farming on Long Island in the vicinity of what is now New Utrecht. Their place was known for years as Turk's Plantation.

A further complication here was the proximity of native women who seemed entirely lacking in sexual restraint—"utterly unchaste and shamefully promiscuous," in the words of Adriaen van der Donck. They "are exceedingly addicted to whoring," agreed Dominie Johannes Megapolensis, who arrived in 1642 to serve as the minister to Rensselaerswyck. "They will lie with a man for the value of one, two or three schillings, and our Dutchmen run after them very much." The dominie's point was clear: not until this sexual carnival had been brought under control (by way of law as well as the immigration of respectable women from Europe) could New Amsterdam be considered a properly settled colony, much less a stable community.

DEVELOPMENT

It seemed for a while that Kieft might succeed in taming New Amsterdam. He forbade the sale of liquor except at the company store. He promulgated ordinances to prevent "adulterous intercourse with heathens, blacks, or other persons; mutiny, theft, false testimony, slanderous language and other irregularities." He prohibited householders from harboring "fugitive servants" from other colonies (a frequent source of trouble) and forbade sailors from vessels in the harbor from staying ashore overnight. He told company craftsmen and laborers to go to work punctually "when the bell rings" and to keep working "until the bell rings again to break off." He ordered the construction of a two-story stone inn on the East River called the Stadts Herbergh, or City Tavern, later designated as the site for public auctions and the posting of official notices. Inside Fort Amsterdam, Kieft saw to the erection of "a pretty large stone church" as well as a new residence for himself "quite neatly built of brick" (and decreed "that no one shall make water within the Fort"). Although the church was built by contractors from the English colony of New Haven, and the Stadts Herbergh provided food and lodging for many visiting New England traders, Kieft served notice on the English that the West India Company would defend New Netherland's borders. He also vigorously protested when former director Minuit planted a colony of Swedes on the lower Delaware in 1638 and began diverting the local fur trade away from the Dutch.

That same year, moving to implement the company's decision to promote large-scale settlement, Kieft began to buy extensive tracts of land from the Lenapes in what are now Kings, Queens, and Bronx counties, as well as Jersey City on the western side of the Hudson. He obtained the area between Wallabout and Newtown Creek, as far inland as "the Swamps of Mespaetches"—later known as Bushwick—for "eight fathoms of duffels [cloth], eight fathoms of wampum, twelve kettels, eight chip-axes [adzes] and eight hatchets and some knives, beads, and awls." At the same time, in a major step toward the institution of private property in New Netherland, Kieft also authorized the first "ground-briefs" or deeds for "free people" who took up land in the colony.

Thus the same Andries Hudde who began farming Achtervelt in 1636 received, in 1638, a patent giving him the right "peaceably to possess, inhabit, cultivate, occupy and use, and also therewith and thereof to do, bargain and dispose" of a tract of land lying north of New Amsterdam in what is now Harlem. In return, Hudde agreed that after ten years he would pay the company "the just tenth of the products with which God may bless the soil, and from this time forth annually for the House and Lot, deliver a pair of capons to the Director for the Holidays." That stipulation resembles what would have been called a quitrent in English law, not rent in the ordinary sense. Hudde now "owned" the land and could do with it as he pleased, but he (as well as his heirs or anyone who bought the land from him) would be required to acknowledge the sovereignty of the West India Company with a yearly payment that "quit" or absolved him of any other obligations to the company.

Soon enough the inhabitants of New Amsterdam were buying, selling, and leasing land among themselves, just like the inhabitants of settled European communities— land that only a few years earlier, when occupied by the Lenapes, had supported a fundamentally different network of social and productive relations. Not all land in the

Manhattan Lying on the North River, c. 1639, also known as the Manatus Map. Possibly drawn by Andries Hudde, a surveyor as well as farmer, it depicts the recent settlement of twenty-two bouweries and plantations in upper Manhattan, Brooklyn, Staten Island, the Bronx, and New Jersey. The presence of Lenape longhouses in Brooklyn was a pointed reminder that Europeans were still heavily outnumbered throughout the region. The house said to have been provided for company slaves can be seen on the Manhattan shore across from what is now Roosevelt Island. (© Collection of The New-York Historical Society)

colony was turned over to private owners, to be sure, and the company continued to rent its remaining property to tenants as well as to hire farmers and laborers (and buy slaves) to work its bouweries.

Over the succeeding four or five years, free settlers did trickle into New Netherland, and the colony began to flesh out a bit. On western Long Island men named Ryker, Wyckoff, Stoothoff, Teunessen, and Francisco the Negro settled at places they called, informally, Amersfoort, Boswijk, Breuckelen, and Midwout (Vlachte Bos)—not the compact, open-field villages of New England, but isolated, fortified cabins and farmsteads. An initial motive for this dispersion was to trade with the Indians without paying required duties to nosy agents of the West India Company. But when a ferry began operating across the East River in the early 1640s, settlers began to furnish New Amsterdam with tobacco, corn, wheat, and cattle (Kieft opened New Amsterdam's first annual cattle fair in 1641 on the Marktveldt, just outside the walls of the fort). Similar settlements sprang up on Staten Island under the leadership of David de Vries, a ship captain who had been involved in the ill-fated Swanendael patroonship, and Cornelis Melyn, an Antwerp merchant and sometime director of the West India Company.

Outside the half-dozen Dutch settlements of Long Island, however, many of these colonists, perhaps as many as half of them, represented the same broad mixture of nationalities as New Amsterdam itself. Among them were Swedes, Germans, French, Belgians, Africans, and Danes (such as a certain Jonas Bronck who owned a five-hundred-acre farm on the mainland near what is now Morrisania, and who left his name on the Broncks or Bronx River—whence the modern borough of that same name). Their presence didn't, in the long run, augur well for the company's ability to preserve New Netherland as a Dutch colony.

Most serious were the mounting numbers of English dissidents seeking refuge in New Netherland from the Puritan regime of Massachusetts. In 1639 Kieft ordered all Englishmen in the colony to swear an oath of allegiance to the States-General. The next year a small group from Lynn, Massachusetts—eight men, one woman, and one child—tried to take up land at Schout's Bay (now Manhasset) on the north shore of Long Island, but Kieft drove them away with troops.

For reasons that aren't clear, and over the objections of powerful men like Kiliaen van Rensselaer, Kieft dealt more leniently with subsequent arrivals. In 1642 he allowed the Rev. Francis Doughty and his followers, fugitives from Plymouth, to settle a thirteen-thousand-acre tract at Mespat (Newtown). That same year he also permitted the Rev. John Throgmorton and thirty-five families, mostly Quakers, to take up land on Throg's Neck, only twenty-five miles from New Amsterdam on the shore of Long Island Sound; shortly thereafter, Anne Hutchinson, perhaps Puritan New England's most famous nonconformist, settled nearby on what is now Pelham Neck.

DISASTER

Despite the colony's development, Kieft failed to win the hearts and minds of its inhabitants. Prominent colonists complained of his arrogance and his contempt for the council, which he reduced to a single member on the grounds that no one else was qualified to advise him (he did, after all, write his letters in Latin and was a talented watercolorist). His law-and-order campaign lost momentum, and Dominie Bogardus, for one, was furious that Kieft "permitted the officers and soldiers to perform all kinds of noisy plays during the sermon, near and around the church, rolling ninepins, bowling, dancing, singing, leaping, and other profane exercises." (Kieft, in turn, accused Bogardus of frequently delivering his Sunday sermon in a drunken stupor.) Everybody quickly found out, too, that Kieft was a grafter whose cunning and greed made Van Twiller look like a saint. His morals were compared to those of ravens, "who rob whatever falls in their way." In the end, though, it was Kieft's Indian policy that brought the opposition to a head and nearly finished off the colony.

New Amsterdam's first dozen years hadn't been happy ones for its Lenape neighbors. With the influx of colonists came the unfamiliar diseases—smallpox, typhus, measles, diphtheria—that would in time cut the Lenape population to a mere 10 percent of what it had been at the beginning of the century. Their conflicts with settlers, magnified by the increasing availability of guns and alcohol, grew more frequent as well as more violent. European cows and swine trampled their planting fields, while heavy cutting for firewood and building materials wiped out the forests where they hunted game. The Lenapes retaliated by killing the livestock (and occasionally their owners), but this shrinking resource base left them increasingly dependent on the production of maize and wampum to obtain trade goods.

As suppliers of wampum, the Lenapes became increasingly tempting prey for rival fur-trading interests. After the fighting between them ended in 1628, both the Mohawks and Mahicans sent raiding parties to collect tribute from Lenape groups in the lower Hudson region. In the bloody Pequot War of 1637, the New England colonies won control of wampum production on the shores of Long Island Sound. The Dutch were slower to act, and cancellation of the West India Company's monopoly touched off a furious competition for pelts by independent traders called *bosch loopers* (runners of woods), many of whom were former company functionaries, tradesmen, and farmers. By the time Kieft arrived on the scene, protecting their sources of wampum—now legal tender in New Amsterdam—had become a matter of real urgency.

In 1639, on the preposterous theory that the West India Company was protecting them from their enemies, Kieft demanded "contributions" in wampum, maize, and pelts from Lenape bands living near New Amsterdam. They were perplexed and irritated by the idea: Kieft "must be a very mean fellow," the Tappans grumbled, "to come to live in this country without being invited by them, and now wish to compel them to give him their corn for nothing." The following spring angry Raritans drove a Dutch trading party off Staten Island in a shower of arrows.

In the summer of 1641, when the Raritans again refused to pay and allegedly killed some swine from David de Vries's new plantation on Staten Island, Kieft dispatched Provincial Secretary Cornelius van Tienhoven with eighty-odd soldiers to teach them a lesson. After the soldiers slew three or four Indians and tortured the sachem's brother "in his private parts with a piece of split wood," the infuriated Raritans fell upon De Vries's plantation, killed four of his people, and burned all the buildings. To the nervous inhabitants of New Amsterdam this Pig War, as it came to be known, was entirely Kieft's fault (De Vries himself charged that company soldiers, not Indians, had killed his pigs). In a bid to placate the critics, Kieft invited the heads of families in New Amsterdam to choose twelve men to help him decide what to do next.

And what, Kieft asked the Twelve, should be done about the recent killing of an elderly Dutch wheelwright, Claes Smits, by Wiechquaesgecks? If they refused to hand over the culprit—and the sachem allegedly said "he was sorry that twenty Christians had not been murdered"—"shouldn't his whole village be ruined?" Of course, replied the Twelve, Smits must be avenged. But that wasn't the only issue, they added, and handed Kieft a list of demands for the creation of a responsible municipal government. Furious, Kieft threw out the list and in January 1642 ordered the Twelve to disband.

He didn't, however, abandon the idea of punishing and extracting tribute from the Lenapes. Over the summer of 1642 another Dutch colonist was killed by a Hackensack near Pavonia, just across the Hudson River. Kieft told the Hackensacks to give him the murderer, but they refused. Some months later, at the very beginning of 1643, a large and well-armed raiding party of Mahicans attacked Tappan and Wiechquaesgeck settlements above Manhattan, killing seventy and driving over a thousand survivors to seek protection of the Dutch at New Amsterdam. The Wiechquaesgecks still hadn't turned over the murderer of Claus Smits, and when they chose to make camp at Pavonia with the Hackensacks, who also continued to harbor the murderer of a Dutchman, Kieft saw the opportunity to strike.

On the night of February 25, vowing to "wipe the mouths of the savages," he launched a surprise attack on the Pavonia encampment. Company troops massacred scores of men, women, and children, Wiechquaesgecks as well as Hackensacks. At daybreak, wrote David De Vries, the exulting soldiers returned to Manhattan with stories of how infants were "torn from their mother's breasts, and hacked to pieces in the presence of the parents, and the pieces thrown into the fire and in the water, and other sucklings, being bound to small boards, were cut, stuck, and pierced, and miserably massacred in a manner to move a heart of stone." Some of the victims, De Vries added, "came to our people in the country with their hands, some with their legs cut off, and some holding their entrails in their arms." Volunteers attacked a smaller Wiechquaesgeck camp at Corlear's Hook, the bulge on the East River side of Manhattan, with similar results. The heads of more than eighty victims were brought back to New Amsterdam for display, and Kieft made a little speech congratulating his forces on their valor.

The carnage at Pavonia and Corlear's Hook touched off full-scale war. Within weeks eleven major Lenape groups representing virtually the entire native population of the lower Hudson Valley had banded together to fight the Dutch. According to one contemporary account, the enraged Indians "killed all the men on the farm lands whom they could surprise" and "burned all the houses, farms, barns, stacks of grain, and destroyed every thing that they could come at." Among the casualties that year were the New England exile Anne Hutchinson and fourteen of her followers, slain on the banks of the river that now bears her name.

As the panic-stricken survivors streamed into New Amsterdam for safety, Kieft's authority crumbled. Two attempts were made on his life in March. In September, with an angry crowd gathered outside his house, he agreed to the formation of a Council of Eight to advise him in the crisis. The Eight at once dispatched a memorial to the company directors, detailing the colony's desperate circumstances. Virtually every other settlement had been abandoned, and their former inhabitants now "skulk, with wives and little ones that still survive, in poverty together, in and around the Fort at the Manahatas where we are not safe for an hour." There were only a few score poorly equipped company soldiers in the fort and two hundred men able to bear arms—hardly enough to hold off an estimated fifteen hundred Lenape warriors. The fort itself looked more like "a molehill than a fort against an enemy."

Salvation arrived in the person of John Underhill, a hard-drinking, short-tempered Indian fighter renowned for his brutality in the Pequot War of 1637 as well as for a pamphlet extolling the charms of New Netherland. Underhill and a small contingent of New England troops rallied the Dutch over the winter of 1643–44, attacking Indian villages in Connecticut, on Staten Island, and on Long Island, killing hundreds and taking many prisoners. Some of the captives were brought back to the fort, and an eyewitness reported that Kieft "laughed right heartily, rubbing his right arm and laughing out loud" as they were tortured and butchered by his soldiers. The soldiers seized one, "threw him down, and stuck his private parts, which they had cut off, into his mouth while he was still alive, and after that placed him on a mill-stone and beat his head off." Secretary Van Tienhoven's mother-in-law allegedly amused herself all the while by kicking the heads of other victims about like footballs. In a later raid on an Indian camp near Pound Ridge in Westcheser, Underhill and the Anglo-Dutch force were said to have slaughtered somewhere between five hundred and seven hundred more with a loss of only fifteen wounded.

Before the war finally ended in the summer of 1645, some sixteen hundred Indians and scores of colonists had died. Dozens of settlements throughout Long Island, Staten Island, present-day Westchester County, and southern Connecticut had been abandoned or destroyed. As one observer summed up the situation, Kieft's misguided attempts to wring tribute from the Indians had "in a short time nearly brought this country to nought." With the States-General again fretting that New Netherland would be lost to the English, the directors of the West India Company decided that Kieft would have to go. Orders for his recall were on their way to New Amsterdam before the year was out.

LOSING GROUND

During a lull in the fighting in the summer of 1643, it occurred to Kieft that New Amsterdam would be safer if more people lived in its immediate vicinity. Stepping up the pace of private land grants, he distributed nearly two dozen patents to prospective settlers whose farmsteads, mostly on Long Island, would create a buffer around Manhattan and serve as tripwires in the event of further attacks. (The following summer, to the same end, he would begin to settled manumitted slaves north of New Amsterdam.)

First to accept Kieft's terms were Lady Deborah Moody and a phalanx of Anabaptists—ardent opponents of infant baptism and forerunners of Quakerism. Expelled from Massachusetts in the summer of 1643, they came down to New Netherland looking for a place to settle. They found it at a place they called Gravesend, on the sandy south shore of Long Island, just north of Coney Island. Kieft gave them a patent, but Canarsee raiders—possibly the same band that had just killed Anne Hutchinson—drove them away. The return of peace in 1645 brought them back, armed with a second patent from Kieft, and they soon had their town laid out for a second time.

Testifying to the links between Anabaptism and social egalitarianism, the Gravesend town plan was an unusual variation on the compact, open-field communities typical of New England. The village center—its ghost still visible 350 years later in the street pattern of modern Brooklyn—consisted of four squares or commons, each about four acres in extent and surrounded by ten house lots. Every male householder was assigned one of these house lots—twenty-three of the forty were distributed within the first year or two—as well as a hundred-acre farm or planter's lot in the fields outside the village.

Other English settlers established Hempstead in 1644, and the following year eighteen English families founded Flushing. The irony of an English town named Flushing in New Netherland would have been lost on no one. Its namesake, Vlissingen, was one of the first towns in Holland to revolt against Spain. When the States-General appealed to Queen Elizabeth for military and financial assistance, Flushing-Vlissingen was one of two "cautionary" towns they allowed the English to occupy as a pledge of good faith. English forces held both for years, much as English settlers were now occupying towns in New Netherland.

Everywhere the West India Company's directors looked, they seemed to be losing ground. A new round of fighting with Spain had gone badly, and the Portuguese were on the way to retrieving Brazil, despite the company's tremendous and expensive efforts to fend them off. By mid-decade the directors confronted a million-guilder debt, half of it traceable to losses in New Netherland alone. The Board of Accounts, summarizing "the confusion and ruin" into which that unfortunate colony had fallen, wondered again if they shouldn't give up and bring everyone home.

4

Stuyvesant

But the West India Company didn't abandon New Netherland. Instead, reasoning that it could be used to provision Brazil—and if Brazil were lost, that it might be the only Dutch possession of consequence in the New World—the company's directors resolved to make another attempt to get the colony on its feet. Their first step was to find a man tough enough to ride herd on its turbulent inhabitants, and the obvious choice was a company veteran named Petrus Stuyvesant.

Stuyvesant came from Friesland, in the northern Netherlands, where his father, a Reformed clergyman, preached the stern, bellicose Calvinism of the Counter-Remonstrant party and the Synod of Dort. He enrolled in the University of Franeker at the age of twenty but was expelled two or three years later for seducing his landlord's daughter. His father then sent him to Amsterdam, where he wangled a job with the West India Company and began to make something of himself (as "Petrus" rather than "Pieter" because the Latin form of his name showed that he had university training). In 1630 the company appointed young Stuyvesant its commercial agent on Fernando de Noronha, a tiny island off the coast of Brazil used for operations against the mainland. He was transferred to Pernambuco in 1635, and in 1638 the company moved him to Curaçao, now its American headquarters and principal naval base in the Caribbean. In 1642, barely thirty years old, he became acting governor of Curaçao, Aruba, and Bonaire.

Stuyvesant's principal assignment on Curaçao was to organize an expedition against the island of St. Martin. The Spanish had pried St. Martin away from the company some years earlier, and the Dutch sorely missed its valuable salt pans as well as its proximity to Puerto Rico, which had almost fallen to company forces in 1625 and remained an inviting target. In the early spring of 1644 Stuyvesant fell upon St. Martin with twelve ships and over a thousand men. When the Spaniards refused to surrender, he laid siege. He failed to prevent supplies getting through from Puerto Rico, however, and an enemy cannonball crushed his right leg. Surgeons amputated it just below the knee. Four weeks later, in excruciating pain, he called off the assault. Later that year he went home to the Netherlands to recuperate and get fitted for a wooden leg. It was, he always said, a sign that God had spared him for great things. The West India Company, for its part, hailed Stuyvesant's peg-leg as a symbol of "Roman" sacrifice and named him director-general of New Netherland at the salary of three thousand guilders per year—fifty times the purchase price of Manhattan and twenty times the annual wages of a company sailor or seaman.

While waiting for the States-General to confirm his appointment, Stuyvesant married Judith Bayard, the daughter of a Huguenot clergyman from Breda. He and his bride left Amsterdam in December 1646. After a quick stop on Curaçao, they reached New Amsterdam in August 1647.

The place was a wreck. Kieft's "land-destroying and people-expelling wars with the cruel barbarians," Stuyvesant later reported, had stripped the country of inhabitants, obliterated all but a handful of villages, and driven many settlers to head for home. Barely "250, or at farthest 300 men capable of bearing arms" remained in the entire colony. Around seven hundred people, still fearful of reoccupying their farms, cowered in makeshift huts around Fort Amsterdam, which "I found resembling more a mole-hill than a fortress, without gates, the walls and bastions trodden underfoot by men and cattle." Kieft himself was holed up in his quarters counting all the money he

Petrus Stuyvesant, painted in New Amsterdam by Hendrick Couturier, c.1660. (© Collection of The New-York Historical Society)

had made—reportedly more than four hundred thousand guilders—and drinking him-self into oblivion. The rest of New Amsterdam's besotted inhabitants, Stuyvesant said, were "grown very wild and loose in their morals."

Certain that this was the work for which the Lord had spared his life on St. Martin, the new director waded in with the same combination of ruthlessness and piety with which the English Puritans were just then consolidating their power under Oliver Cromwell. "I shall govern you as a father his children," he informed the townsfolk.

TOWN BUILDING

Uppermost in Stuyvesant's mind was the need to turn New Amsterdam into the kind of community that would appeal to the Dutch taste for well-regulated urban life. For the Netherlands (unlike, say, England) was a nation of town dwellers, known for their civic consciousness and for the love of public tidiness that had led them to adopt the broom as a symbol of national identity and purpose. No sooner had he arrived, therefore, than Stuyvesant began to sweep New Amsterdam into shape with a succession of edicts, decrees, and orders. They would continue to stream from his pen for the next seventeen years—joined, after 1653, by a torrent of ordinances from the burgomasters he appoint-ed to New Amsterdam's first municipal government.

One of his earliest targets was the town's confounding jumble of lanes and foot-paths. Stuyvesant named three surveyors to establish reliable property lines and lay out regular streets, some of which even received names. He ordered the removal of building materials and other obstructions from the streets and imposed a speed limit on wagons and carts. In 1658 the residents of Brouwer (Brewer) Street received permission to pave their lane with cobblestones, creating New Amsterdam's first properly surfaced road-way, now Stone Street.

In 1648 Stuyvesant declared war on New Amsterdam's pigs, cows, goats, and hors-es. Residents had been accustomed to letting their animals forage freely through the town; while this helped remove accumulations of garbage it also damaged gardens and orchards, and rooting swine had pretty well ruined the fort's sodded ramparts. Hence-forth, Stuyvesant announced, the *schout* would seize wayward animals and drag them to a public pound, and soldiers were authorized to shoot on sight any hog grunting its way toward the fort. What was more, residents were forbidden to throw "rubbish, filth, ashes, oyster-shells, dead animal or anything like it" into the streets. Householders were required to clean the road in front of their dwellings. Any privy that released excrement at ground level was banned, for it "not only creates a great stench and therefore great inconvenience to the passers-by, but also makes the streets foul and unfit for use." Butchers were warned not to discard offal in the streets. In 1657 an ordinance estab-lished five official sites for the dumping of garbage.

To guard against the danger of fire—"most of the houses here in New Amsterdam are built of wood and roofed with reeds," Stuyvesant explained, and "in some houses the chimneys are of wood, which is very dangerous"—he prohibited further construc-tion of wooden chimneys; later, thatched roofs and haystacks were banned as well. Four fire wardens were appointed to see that all chimneys in town were regularly swept. The wardens banned the use of fireplaces on dangerously windy days. After 1647 a fire cur-few required that each evening all fires must be put out or covered up. A decade later the burgomasters began to assemble a municipal firefighting apparatus. Two cordwainers (shoemakers) were hired to produce 150 leather fire buckets, copied from a Dutch sam-

New Amsterdam, c. 1650–53, copied so often that it has become known as the "Prototype View." On the far left, just east of what is now Bowling Green, stands the company gristmill, while to its right the twin gables of the Reformed church rise above the walls of the fort. At Schreyers Hook in the foreground—just below what is now the intersection of Whitehall and Pearl streets—are the company's wooden wharf, crane, and a beam for weighing merchandise (which may also have served the burgeoning community as a gallows). At the extreme right, the City Tavern faces the East River shore on present-day Pearl Street, near the head of Coenties Slip. (© Museum of the City of New York)

ple, and after being painted with the city seal by glazier Evert Duyckinck—the town's first artist—they were placed at various street corners. The following year the town got ladders and fire hooks. As conditions improved and a sense of permanence began to take hold, Dutch brick "alla moderna"—some imported as ship's ballast, some turned out in local kilns—began to replace wood as a building material.

From the outset, the company had supplied New Amsterdam with a succession of midwives and *zieckentroosters* (comforters of the sick)—lay pastors who assisted ordained clergymen by reading Scripture and prayers to the ill. A year before the arrival of Governor Kieft, it sent over the first formally trained physician, Dr. Johannes La Montagne, a Huguenot refugee and graduate of the University of Leyden. The company balked at the expense of a proper hospital, however, until Stuyvesant decided that unsanitary conditions impeded the recovery of sick slaves and soldiers billeted in private homes. In 1658, as a result, New Amsterdam got its first hospital under the direction of matron Hilletje Wilbruch (in the Netherlands such charitable institutions were often run by women).

In 1649 and again in 1653, on the other hand, Stuyvesant refused requests to build an orphan asylum and appoint orphanmasters, claiming that the idea was inconsistent with "the weak state of this just beginning city." Let the deacons of the church "keep their eyes open," he said, and look after any destitute children they saw. Matters changed only after 1654, when company officials arranged with the burgomasters of

Amsterdam to send children from that city's orphan asylum to New Amsterdam, there to be bound out as apprentices and servants. Now Stuyvesant not only rented a house to lodge the first group—the town's first public home for orphans—but, in 1656, established an Orphan Masters' Court.

The company likewise resisted appeals to provide for the relief of the poor—a responsibility, it said with some justice, that properly lay with religious institutions. In 1653, accordingly, New Amsterdam's Reformed Church opened an almshouse or "deacons' house" for the aged poor on what is now Beaver Street. For funding, the deacons relied on contributions collected in church and at weddings, where guests dropped offerings in a poor box. In time, the system acquired a public character as the deacons began to assist the needy in general and were assigned revenues raised from municipal fines. In 1655 the first lottery took place in New Amsterdam as a fund-raising device for the almshouse.

Company involvement expanded in 1661, after the deacons complained that needy people from outlying villages had begun drifting into town for help, diminishing their ability to care for New Amsterdam's own poor. Stuyvesant and his council enacted the colony's first poor law, "to the end that the Lazy and Vagabond may as much as possible be rebuked, and the really Poor the more assisted and cared for." The law required every village to take up weekly collections for its own poor. It also specifically relieved the New Amsterdam Church from caring for nonresidents who could not present a certificate of character and poverty from the deacon at their place of residence.

So, too, the company responded grudgingly when New Amsterdam's residents asked for schools comparable to those in the Netherlands, where publicly funded education was widely available, even to the poor. The company had launched a common school in 1638, but it refused to build a schoolhouse, forcing teacher and pupils to find temporary quarters. Residents complained repeatedly—in 1649 they appealed again for construction of a "public school, with at least two good teachers"—but the company still declined to spend the money.

Townspeople petitioned as well for a Latin school that would provide more advanced instruction to the many children who could now read and write. The nearest grammar school, they pointed out, was in Boston, 250 miles away, and without an establishment of its own, New Amsterdam was not likely to become a "place of great splendor." In 1659 the company belatedly agreed to help defray the expense of a teacher's salary (but not erection of a school building), and a certain Dominie Curtius, "late professor in Lithuania," soon commenced classes with seventeen pupils. By 1664, with the additional assistance of private teachers—the only schooling available to non-Dutch-speaking children—probably a majority of New Amsterdam's white population could read and write. As in Holland, a larger number of women had received an education than was common in other European countries or their colonies.

The company also resisted establishing a police force until 1658, when, partly inspired by fears of Indian trouble, the magistrates organized a rattle watch. A captain and eight men received twenty-four stivers a night (plus an allowance for firewood) to walk around town and "call out how late it is, at all corners of the streets from nine O'Clock in the evening untill the *reveille* beat in the morning." Given the absence of streetlights, keeping a lookout for crime or fire wasn't the easiest of tasks. If the watchmen discovered anything amiss, they were to use their rattles to rouse the populace.

Stuyvesant was, however, prepared to spend "a considerable amount of money" for "very proper and highly necessary public works"—by which he usually meant projects that enhanced the town's security, commerce, or moral order. He had masons patch up the fort and oversaw renovations to the church. He established a post office and authorized a municipal pier on the East River, at the foot of what is now Moore Street. Drawing on Dutch skill in mastering marshy terrains, he had a sullen creek on the site of modern Broad Street deepened and widened into what became known as "the Ditch"— and then had its sides planked up to make a little canal, rather grandly called the Heere Gracht. The canal in the heart of town was both useful and, like the windmills, a comforting reminder of life in the Netherlands. To pay for all this the director-general placed "a reasonable excise and impost on wines, brandy and liquors which are imported from abroad."

Within a decade of his arrival, and despite bouts of official penny-pinching, Stuyvesant's campaign to tidy up New Amsterdam helped spur its evolution from a seedy, beleaguered trading post into a well-run Dutch town. His success was hardly total, and a conspicuous gap remained between prescription and practice: foraging swine, wooden chimneys, overflowing privies, smelly accumulations of garbage, and tavern brawls continued to frustrate municipal authorities for years. Nor indeed would he have been able to accomplish so much had he not also been able to resuscitate New Amsterdam's economy.

A WELL-REGULATED ECONOMY

One of Stuyvesant's most pressing concerns was to create more orderly markets in the city. To combat widespread fraud in the sale and transfer of real estate—the transition to private ownership in New Netherland had given rise to a rather chaotic land market—he announced that all conveyances of real estate would be invalid without his approval and until properly recorded by the provincial secretary. To regulate the sale of local produce and ensure an adequate supply of food—the indispensable precondition for municipal growth—Stuyvesant directed that a municipal market be held every Monday along the East River shore for "meat, bacon, butter, cheese, turnips, roots, straw, and other products of the farm." Eight years later, in 1656, Saturday officially became the day when "country people" might offer their goods and wares to townsfolk "on the Beach or Strand, near the end of the Heere Gracht," and farmers from Brooklyn, Gowanus, and Bergen sold produce from their boats parked in the canal, their dickering with householders reminiscent of similar scenes in the Netherlands. Stuyvesant also established a ten-day free market, to be held every St. Bartholomew's Day (August 24). "Corresponding to the legal Amsterdam Fair," it would be a time when ordinary municipal regulations were suspended, prices would be subject only to the law of supply and demand, and no stranger could be arrested. In 1659, moreover, the burgomasters made the space in front of the fort available for a forty-day-long "market for fat and lean cattle" each autumn; soon the market would be housed in a new building with tiled roof, later called the Broadway Shambles. Proclamations for these events were issued in English as well as Dutch and attracted farmers and their herds from as far away as Southampton.

Stuyvesant kept close watch on retail markets too. He required all persons who kept a "private shop" in cellar or garret, or who carried "on any Trade by the small weight and measure," to use "genuine Amsterdam ells, measures and weights" that had been inspected at the fort. He was not, on the other hand, prepared to establish price controls. When townsmen petitioned him in 1657 about the high cost of "Necessary commodities and household supplies"—charging that not only "Merchants, but also, consequently, Shop-keepers, Tradesmen, Brewers, Bakers, Tapsters and Grocers, make a difference of 30, 40 & 50 percent when they sell their wares"—he took no action. Instead, he banned "Scotch traders"—itinerant merchants from Holland or elsewhere who began visiting the colony soon after the West India Company abandoned its monopoly on trade in 1639. By selling their wares at steep discounts and paying outrageous sums for beaver pelts, these "destroyers of trade," as Stuyvesant called them, could beggar the town's permanent residents. He therefore prohibited anyone from doing business in New Amsterdam who had not built a "decent citizen dwelling" and lived in it for three consecutive years. The directors of the West India Company were avid supporters of free trade, however, and they overruled his ban on "Scotch traders."

Stuyvesant was prepared to impose stricter controls on artisans than on merchants, especially in such vital local enterprises as brewing, slaughtering, and baking. In the face of repeated complaints about the supply and quality of "black" bread—a mainstay of the local diet—he established the assize of bread customary in the Netherlands, ordering bakers to produce only eight-, four-, or two-pound loaves, at fixed prices, using unadulterated wheat or rye flour "as it came from the mill." At the same time, to stimulate domestic production, Stuyvesant handed out monopolies for the manufacture of tile, bricks, potash, salt, and other products (it isn't clear how many such enterprises were actually launched, or how long they survived). Here again West India Company officials rejected policies they thought might discourage prospective settlers. Interference with the law of supply and demand, they explained, reduced "the expectation of gain" that "is the greatest spur to induce people to go thither." Similarly, Stuyvesant's monopolies seemed "very pernicious and impracticable especially in a new country, which begins only to develop, and must be peopled and made prosperous by general benefits and liberties to be granted to everybody."

Soon, however, the burgomasters were issuing ordinances to the same effect. "All bakers, brewers, shopkeepers and merchants" should "sell their goods at reasonable prices to the people," they announced in 1658. Porters, cartmen, tradesmen, and laborers were told what they could charge for their services; outsiders or "strangers" were forbidden to offer their wares for sale except at stated times and places.

Now it was the bakers who protested, openly defying the ordinance requiring them to sell coarse bread at fixed prices. Squeezed by the rising cost of grain, they routinely sifted their flour with bran, short-weighted loaves, and surreptitiously produced more of the higher-priced white bread and cakes than the law allowed. In 1661 the most frustrated bakers, led by Joost Teunissen, suspended work altogether on the grounds they could no longer earn a living. The magistrates were sympathetic but unrelenting: they warned the bakers to resume production or face the loss of their licenses, raised the fines for substandard loaves, and appointed inspectors to check the weight and quality of all bread sold within New Amsterdam. As the court told Reynier Willemsen, the public interest always came first: to practice your trade in New Amsterdam, you must agree to "bake good and fit bread for the best possible accommodation of the community."

Stuyvesant did address one of the greatest concerns of the bakers, and of everyone else in the colony: the steady inflation of wampum, New Netherland's principal currency. Too much of it, Stuyvesant observed, wasn't the genuine article—"unpierced and only half-finished, made of stone, bone, glas, shells, horn, nay even of wood, and broken." As always, bad money drove out the good, and people were complaining that "they cannot go to market and buy any commodities, not even a little white bread or a mug of beer, from the traders, bakers and tapsters." At the same time, the quantity of wampum in circulation was rising sharply. The New England colonies had recently demonetized wampum, started to coin their own money, and begun to dump huge quantities of wampum, good and bad, on their Dutch neighbors. Wages and prices in New Amsterdam soared, and it was getting hard for anyone to make a living in the fur trade.

Stuyvesant responded by ordering that all wampum used as money must henceforth be strung ("upon a wire, as hitherto it has usually been done") and that its value would be fixed at the rate of six white or three black beads per stiver for high-quality "merchantable" or "trade" wampum and eight white or four black beads per stiver for inferior wampum. Shopkeepers and tradesmen who refused to accept the poorer grade, if properly strung, faced stiff fines. Stuyvesant also pleaded with the company to ship over enough hard coinage to serve the colony's needs or let it mint coins of its own, as the English had done. Neither he nor the company considered demonetizing wampum, however, and it remained legal tender.

But Stuyvesant's most far-reaching suggestion for New Amsterdam's economic revitalization came in response to events unfolding on the international scene. In 1648 the Dutch finally won their long struggle for independence—a boon for the nation's private merchants but a disaster for the West India Company, which had always depended on war with Spain to justify its existence and generate income. Soon after Stuyvesant arrived in New Amsterdam, the company's prospects looked grimmer than ever. By 1649 it couldn't afford to launch a single ship for the defense of Brazil, and the price of its shares on the Amsterdam Exchange had sunk to an all-time low.

As Brazil slipped from its grasp, the company instigated a momentous revolution in the Atlantic slave trade. During the 1630s and 1640s it had imported nearly thirty thousand slaves from Africa to work the Brazilian sugar plantations. The increasing precariousness of those markets prompted the company to direct its attention elsewhere—above all to the British and French West Indies, where white indentured servants had been producing tobacco on myriad small holdings. On one island after another, company agents as well as independent Dutch merchants not only convinced the planters to adopt slave labor but loaned them money and equipment to make the switch to sugar, several times more profitable than tobacco. By the early 1650s sugar was well on its way to becoming the principal crop of the Caribbean, large plantations were emerging as the basic unit of production, and the company was funneling tens of thousands of African slaves every year into the region. (On Barbados, richest of the new sugar colonies, the black population soared from a few thousand to better than thirty-two thousand by the 1670s.) Dutch slavers had even started probing Virginia and Maryland, and there was good reason to believe that Chesapeake planters would soon follow their West Indian counterparts in adopting slavery.

It was in this context that it occurred to Stuyvesant and company strategists that New Amsterdam would make a convenient entrepôt for the slave trade in North America and a source of vital supplies for the plantation economies developing to the south. It might also be profitable to establish a local market for slaves, perhaps even bring them directly from Angola, thus bolstering New Amsterdam's labor force, hastening the reoccupation of its hinterlands, and securing the entire colony against encroachment from

Nieu Amsterdam, mid-seventeenth century. The figures in this Dutch print—two colonists, a woman holding a basket of fruit and a man with tobacco leaves, as well as the bare-chested slaves behind them—are identical to those in a contemporary depiction of Barbados, except they are seen here with New Amsterdam in the background. Which came first is unknown, but this version nicely conveys the West India Company's growing involvement with slavery and the slave trade in New Netherland. (I. N. Phelps Stokes Collection. Miriam and Ira D. Wallach Division of Art, Prints and Photographs. The New York Public Library. Astor, Lenox and Tilden Foundations)

New England. Stuyvesant was one of the new policy's most ardent supporters. His tour of duty on Curaçao coincided with the construction there of vast pens capable of holding thousands of slaves at a time, and it was he who suggested the administrative unification of Curaçao with New Netherland.

The last Dutch stronghold in Brazil fell to the Portuguese in 1654, and implementation of the new policy got underway the very next year. A company ship, the *Witte Paert* (White Horse), anchored in the East River with nearly three hundred Guinea slaves—the first specifically intended for local buyers—stowed below decks in conditions so cramped and filthy that residents must have been able to smell the ship from the far side of town. Additional shipments arrived before the end of the decade, though the real surge of imports did not come until after 1660, when some four hundred slaves were sold at public auction in the space of three or four years. By the mid-1660s New Netherland had about seven hundred slaves all told, three hundred of whom were held in New Amsterdam, far outnumbering its seventy-five or so free blacks and constituting over 20 percent of the town's total population.

That population had meanwhile grown rapidly, for at the same time it began importing slaves, the West India Company had mounted its most ambitious campaign yet to attract free colonists. It issued a more liberal set of Freedoms and Exemptions and published a barrage of promotional pamphlets praising New Netherland's abundance of rich, easily cultivated land.

Although immigration figures are incomplete and inexact, it appears that the company's efforts—in tandem with Stuyvesant's reform program—succeeded admirably. By the mid-1650s New Netherland's population had climbed to perhaps thirty-five hundred men, women, and children; a decade later, to nine thousand. Of that number, some fifteen hundred lived in New Amsterdam alone, roughly three times as many as Stuyvesant found fifteen years earlier. Only one-fourth of the town's three hundred adult white males could claim to have lived there longer than he had. The newcomers were as diverse as ever, too: half of them hailed from Germany, England, France, and the Scandinavian countries. By the mid-1660s, indeed, only 40 percent of New Netherland's population was actually Dutch, while 19 percent was German and 15 percent English. But these weren't the same kind of people who had been drawn to the colony during its first twenty or thirty years. Seventy percent came over in family groups, many of them couples in their early twenties with small children. Only one in four was a single male, and for the first time a small but significant proportion, about 6 percent, were single women. Better than half were farmers or skilled craftsmen (a few fishermen showed up as well). Only one in eight was a laborer or servant. The rest were soldiers.

"PERSONS OF QUALITY"

Travelers disembarking at the new East River pier in these years would have found themselves near the heart of a bustling, cosmopolitan little seaport. Directly in front of them, facing the river, lay the Strand, a two-block stretch of Paerle Straet (Pearl Street) crowded with taverns, workshops, warehouses, cottages, and brick residences built in the Dutch manner, one or two stories tall, gable-ends out. Just upriver, one block to the right, was the entrance to the Heere Gracht, now lined with houses almost up to what is now Exchange Place. A block to the left stood Stuyvesant's new Great House, a "costly and handsome" two-story residence of whitewashed stone—later known as the White Hall (whence the present Whitehall Street)—which boasted extensive gardens and a private dock for the director-general's barge of state. From there it was a short walk across the Marktvelt, past Brugh (Bridge), Brouwers (Brewers, now Stone), and Marktvelt (Marketfield) streets—all densely built up—to the parade-ground (now the site of Bowling Green) at the front gate of Fort Amsterdam. The Heere Wegh (Broadway), which led north from the parade-ground, past the company's garden, was only beginning to attract construction, though. Indeed most of the area beyond the upper end of the Heere Gracht was still occupied by orchards, gardens, and grazing cows.

Although the physical transformation of New Amsterdam was remarkable enough, the really striking change, less apparent to the casual observer, was the appearance of an embryonic class system where once there had been only employees of the West India Company. At the top of this new social order stood a few dozen wealthy, socially established, and politically well-connected private merchants from Holland. They were a new phenomenon in town, so much so that in 1656 an embarrassed *schout* had to ask where he should jail "persons of quality, or of good name and character," who broke the law. (He was told they could be held in a tavern, if they had the money to pay for their lodgings.)

Some of these "persons of quality" were representatives of the handful of Dutch commercial syndicates that dominated the colony's trade after the West India Company abandoned its monopoly in 1639. Their business consisted for the most part of exchanging a few basic items of local origin (furs, skins, tobacco, timber) for imported essential trade goods (duffel cloth, liquor, gunpowder). Johannes Pietersen Verbrugge and his cousin Johannes Gillissen Verbrugge came over for the firm of Gillis Verbrugge and Company; Allard Anthony, a prosperous Amsterdam merchant, served as New Amsterdam agent for the firm of Pieter Gabry and Sons. Other important newcomers—Abel de Wolff, Cornelis Steenwyck, Jan Baptiste van Rensselaer, and William Beekman—enjoyed close family and professional ties with leading West India Company stockholders, private merchants, government officials, and military men. Cornelis van Werckhoven had served as governor of the Amsterdam poorhouse and was an officer in that city's burgher guard. Arent van Hattem was a nobleman and former alderman of the city of Culemborg.

Women like Annetje Jans played a major part in the accumulation of wealth by this nascent upper class. Jans was one of two daughters of Tryn Jonas, the West India Company's midwife. Around 1630 Annetje married Roeloff Jansen, an Indian trader and agricultural foreman up at Fort Orange. Thanks largely to her business acumen, the couple prospered, and later they moved down to Manhattan, where they occupied a sixty-acre farm along the North River shore near the foot of what is now Jay Street. Roeloff's sudden death in 1636 left Annetje with several children to raise on her own but with an attractive estate. Two years later, after getting him to sign a prenuptial agreement that protected the interests of her children by Jansen, she married Dominie Bogardus, moved into his new house near the fort, and leased out her North River farm. Over the next ten years, while bearing several more children, she parlayed the farm's income into a modest real estate empire. After the dominie's death in 1647 she did not remarry but continued to manage her various properties and the marriages of her numerous children. By the time of her own death in 1663 she had become the titular head of a large and powerful clan that included affluent merchants and entrepreneurs (women as well as men), influential magistrates, and the colony's only physician.

Annetje's younger sister, Marritje, was equally gifted at making her way in the world. Her first husband was the West India Company's chief shipwright on Manhattan, her second a carpenter turned farmer. When she married for the third and last time it was to Govert Loockermans, a fur trader and landowner who was probably New Amsterdam's richest man at the time of their marriage in 1649. As it happened, Govert's sister, Anneken, had married Oloff Stevensen van Cortlandt, one of the soldiers who came over with Van Twiller. Although Oloff, like Govert, had a talent for making money and knew the right people (Kieft helped him along with the job of company commissary), it was Anneken who guided the family fortunes for thirty-odd years. She invested heavily in real estate around New Amsterdam (acquiring along the way a big farm in what is now Greenwich Village), and she is said to have talked Oloff into opening a lucrative brewery by the fort. Like her sisters-in-law Annetje and Marritje Jans, she also passed her business and social talents on to her children. One daughter, Maria, having run the family brewery while still in her teens, married Jeremias van Rensselaer and ran Rensselaerswyck by herself for fifteen years after his death. Two other daughters found husbands in the Philipse and Schuyler families, while a son, Stephanus, would become one of the colony's greatest landowners.

None of this would have seemed odd or unusual back in the Netherlands, where strong and assertive Dutch wives were commonplace. In Dutch law, a unique mixture of Roman and Germanic antecedents, women enjoyed far greater autonomy than they did in the patriarchal English-speaking world. A Dutch woman had recourse to legal process and could file claims against a man. She could own property and retain control of it after marriage. With her husband's permission, she could borrow money, conduct business, and make contracts in her own name. Prenuptial agreements spelling out these rights were mandatory, and the law allowed husbands and wives to prepare mutual wills stipulating that the death of one would not deprive the other of their common property. A Dutch wife wasn't her husband's peer: the law gave him extensive authority to control her actions and allowed him, among other things, to sell or bequeath their common property without her consent. Even so, culturally as well as legally, his power was qualified by the conviction that a submissive wife was incompatible with a strong household.[1]

In other ways as well—and in sharp contrast to the bulk of New Amsterdam's inhabitants—the members of this emerging municipal elite were unmistakably Dutch in taste, manner, and outlook. They commissioned comfortable brick and stone townhouses whose steeply pitched gables, high stoops, double doors, and manicured gardens of roses, tulips, and lilies wouldn't have looked out of place in one of Amsterdam's better neighborhoods. Those who could afford to followed Stuyvesant's example in furnishing their houses, as did wealthy inhabitants of Amsterdam, with furniture of rare woods, paintings, fine china, and heavy silver. Wives of wealthy merchants dressed in the fashionable styles of Amsterdam and Paris, with dresses sent over from Europe or made locally by seamstresses. Their husbands' tastes ran to silk or velvet breeches and to coats flowered with silver lace. Emulating the merchant nabobs of the Dutch empire in the East Indies, they surrounded themselves with servants and slaves. Many imported spinets and virginals to satisfy their love of music. A few amassed modest libraries. Jonas Bronck, for one, owned twenty printed books, eighteen pamphlets, and seventeen manuscript books. Some even wrote themselves: Jacob Steendam, a man of substance with interests in the slave trade and local real estate, found time to compose poetry. His "Complaint of New Amsterdam to her Mother"—the city's first poem—presented the town-as-narrator describing ill treatment at maternal hands ("I, of Amsterdam, was born,/Early of her breasts forlorn," etc.).

They were highly sociable, too. The director, the council, the burgomasters, and the orphanmasters frequently held meetings in taverns. Many commercial bargains were struck in the taprooms where merchants gathered to exchange and discuss news. Jollier still were the drinking clubs whose members gathered at favorite taverns to eat and drink. Arguably the best-known establishment was the Stadts Herbergh or City Tavern on the East River. Its ground-floor taproom was always thronged with merchants, sea captains, and Indian traders, and it was one of three places in town designated for the posting of official notices. Metje Wessels's tavern over on Pearl Street was noted for its terrapin feasts. On the Sabbath, after the sermon, many families dined at an inn, and some publicans provided bowling greens, where customers could play ninepins at all times except during divine service. The more vigorous enjoyed ice-skating, boat racing, and angling parties, especially up at an island in the middle of the Kalch-hook pond where the Lenapes once fished.

---

1. Note too that Dutch names were patronymic but not patrilineal, meaning that the family lineages typical of England and English colonies didn't exist in New Netherland. Thus, if Roeloff Jans had a daughter named Volckje, she would be known as Volckje Roeloffse (or Roeloffsen). If she married Jan van Hoesen, she could keep the name Roeloffsen or take the name Jansen (also spelled Jansz or Janse); it wouldn't be unusual to find her listed both ways in the records.

COMMON FOLK

Below the mercantile elite of New Amsterdam's new social hierarchy were the white working people of modest means, not exclusively Dutch, who provided the growing community with its basic goods and services. The backbone of this middling class consisted of a hundred or so skilled craftsmen and their families, plus a few dozen innkeepers, boardinghouse owners, surgeons, and notaries.

Only a few artisans still worked for the West India Company. Back in 1644, surveying the havoc wrought by Kieft's War, the company's Board of Accounts had recommended slashing the number of its salaried "officers and servants" throughout New Netherland. "Carpenters, masons, smiths and such like ought to be discharged," the board added, "and left to work for whomsoever will pay them." The directors evidently concurred, for over the next ten or twenty years company employees became a distinct and shrinking minority of the colony's population. In New Amsterdam, counting everyone from Stuyvesant down to the poorest laborer, only seventy-five of the town's adult white males, roughly one in four, remained in the company's service after 1660.

Many former employees stayed on and put down roots in New Amsterdam. Abraham Willemsen, for example, had been a seaman in the company's service who married a local girl in 1647, petitioned the court to release him from his obligations to the company, and settled in town as a carpenter. (It's more than likely that he'd been moonlighting as a carpenter for some time already. As Stuyvesant explained to his superiors in 1659, a common soldier employed by the company, "except on extraordinary expeditions, has only to go on guard duty in his garrison every third day" and the rest of the time endeavored "to earn elsewhere something to supplement his small pay and board-money"—no better, in most cases, than thirty guilders per month.)

By the early 1660s old-timers like Willemsen had been joined by a new generation of immigrant artisans representing a wide variety of trades. Coopers made the barrels, hogsheads, pipes, and kegs in which merchants exported flour, salted meats, fish, and beer. The town's bakers (ten of them now) made bread, special cakes for festivals and weddings, and the hard biscuits that formed a large part of the diet of sailors at sea. Evert Duyckinck, the glazier and fire-bucket artist, installed leaded glass, painted with family coats of arms, in the windows of the church at two and a half beaver skins a pane. There were brewers like Isaac and Joannes Verveelen, who ran the famous Red Lion Brewery, carpenters like Frederik Flipsen and Thomas Lambertsen, shoemakers like Coenraet ten Eyck, and tailors like Hendrick Kip, along with twelve butchers, several tanners, three silversmiths, and assorted hatters and masons.

These middling people of New Amsterdam tended to live in houses like the one built for schoolmaster Roelantsen. Made entirely of wood, it was thirty feet long, eighteen feet wide, and eight feet high, with a small garret above the beams. The single chamber served as a combination dining room, living room, and bedroom, with a built-in corner bedstead for the husband and wife (children slept on straw pallets in the garret). It was illuminated by transom windows by day, homemade candles at night. In the rear was the fireplace, where Mevrouw Roelantsen kept her iron pots and pans, and a door to the back garden, where she grew Indian corn. In quarters like these, furniture was crude, books few, and paintings absent. With the arrival of housewives skilled in domestic arts, however, came an increase in the apparatus of domestic production—vessels and implements for making butter, cheese, candles and soap, for spinning and dyeing yarn, and for cutting and stitching imported duffle cloth into articles of clothing. These shirts and shifts, along with household linen, were washed and dried by the housewife or her young daughter, down by the grassy banks of a pebbly brook that ran from Nassau Street to the East River, along what is today Maiden Lane.

The remainder of New Amsterdam's free white inhabitants comprised a diverse, shifting lower class of laborers, cartmen, transient sailors, apprentices, soldiers, minor West India Company functionaries, farmhands, and indentured servants (too many of the latter, Stuyvesant complained, were runaways)—the same kind of people who until recently had made up the bulk of the colony's population.

Popular culture in New Amsterdam centered on the town's always numerous taverns, grogshops, and pothouses, where noisy, pipe-smoking crowds of men and women drank, gambled, and played games like backgammon, handball, and bowling. (Women were particularly fond of a pipe, Nicasius de Sille observed in 1654. "Young and old, they all smoke.") The Wooden Horse, a particular favorite of sailors and soldiers, was located in a thatched cottage on the corner of Whitehall and Stone streets. In its small single room, boasting only one window and reeking of smoke and stale beer, men sat at long wooden tables, dimly lit by flickering candles, drinking West Indian rum, French brandy, and local brews. The owner was a Frenchman named Philip Gerard, who had once been sentenced to ride the wooden horse in his days as a soldier for the West India Company.

Places like the Wooden Horse tended to treat the nine o'clock closing law casually, and their patrons often disturbed the peace with drunken brawls, sometimes involving knives, cutlasses, and pikes. Jan Peeck, a cantankerous old Indian trader, lost his license for entertaining "disorderly people" in his taproom near Smits Vly on the East River shore. (His equally troublesome wife would be banished from New Amsterdam ten years later for selling liquor to the Indians.)

The upsurge of immigration to New Netherland during the mid-1650s and early 1660s was accompanied by an exuberant revival of holidays long associated with popular culture in Europe. For centuries, peasants and craftsmen, soldiers and sailors had periodically thrown restraint to the winds and indulged themselves with feasts, games, mock courts, races, processions, and wild merrymaking that inverted the everyday order of society. A King of Misrule presided over Twelfth Night festivities, maidens chased young men about the streets on St. Valentine's Day, servants frolicked in the market on Pinkster (Whitsunday or Pentecost to the English), and whole villages cavorted about maypoles on May Day. In the Netherlands, the Shrove Tuesday festivities, marking the end of Carnival and the beginning of Lent, involved Rabelaisian consumption of meat and drink (hence Mardi Gras, "Fat Tuesday").

By the end of Stuyvesant's first decade in office, the people of New Amsterdam were celebrating these and other *volksvermaken* or "folk pleasures" with gusto. Just as in the Netherlands, they greeted Pinkster with singing and dancing while a "Queen of the Feast" or "flower bride," dressed in white and holding a May-branch in her hand, led a procession of maidens through the streets of the town. In 1663 the tranquility of Harlem was shattered by young men "shouting, blowing horns, etc." around a maypole. Shrove Tuesday, too, was now routinely commemorated by the traditional bacchanal of eating and drinking while, as in Europe, young men dressed up like women and paraded about the streets. Another traditional bit of Shrove Tuesday fun, likewise resurrected in New Netherland, was Pulling the Goose. In this rough country sport, a live bird, its neck smeared with oil or soap, was tied by a rope between two poles: contestants on horseback then rode at full gallop toward the tethered goose and tried to yank off its head.

THE NEGROES' LOT

The bottom rungs of New Amsterdam society were occupied by Africans, though their lives and working conditions varied widely. Most still belonged to the West India Company and worked on important agricultural, public, and military projects. In 1660 Stuyvesant requested additional slaves be sent up from Curaçao for company use: "They ought to be stout and strong fellows," he explained, "fit for immediate employment on this fortress and other works; also, if required, in war against the wild barbarians, either to pursue them when retreating, or else to carry some of the soldiers' baggage." Four years later he reported that he had utilized a recent shipment of slaves to harvest food, chop wood, and repair oxcarts.

In time, because of the company's chronic unwillingness to spend money, its slaves were also trained for more highly skilled tasks. In 1657 Stuyvesant appealed to the directors in Amsterdam to send him some ship's carpenters, only to be told that Dutch workmen were far too expensive and that carpentry, bricklaying, and other trades "ought to be taught to the Negroes as it was formerly done in Brazil." He appears to have followed orders, inasmuch as contemporary deeds begin referring to Negro caulkers, blacksmiths, and carpenters.

Other of New Amsterdam's slaves worked in private households, either as domestic servants or agricultural laborers. Stuyvesant himself acquired forty slaves, far more than anyone else in the colony; some were domestics, the rest labored in the fields and orchards of his private bouwerie, a country estate lying between what are now 5th and 20th streets, east of Fourth Avenue all the way to the East River—a "place of relaxation

The Peasant Dance, by Pieter Brueghel the Elder. After 1650, such scenes of fun and frolic were becoming more common in New Amsterdam and neighboring villages. (Art Resource, Inc./ Kunsthistorisches Museum, Vienna)

and pleasure" (as one admiring visitor described it) that Stuyvesant acquired by taking over, either by purchase or fiat, several of the "Negro Lots" or "Negroes' Farms" the West India Company had previously set aside for former slaves. (Nicholas Bayard, his son-in-law, combined six others into a two-hundred-acre farm nearby.) Most privately owned slaves in the colony, however, belonged to farm families in outlying villages like Flatbush, where they and their masters often slept in the same houses, ate the same food, and worked side by side in the fields. Overall, they were predominantly male— roughly 130 men for every hundred women.

Some Africans were free because the company continued with its half-freedom policy of conditional manumissions. In 1662 three slave women were liberated, on condition that one of them do housework for the director-general each week. The next year Mayken, an old and sickly black woman, was granted outright freedom by the West India Company, "she having served as a slave since the year 1628." Mayken was almost certainly one of the original three females imported from Angola thirty-five years earlier, whom Dominie Michaelius had accounted "lazy and useless trash."

Disparities in condition and location made it difficult for Africans in New Amsterdam to establish communities of culture, yet not impossible. Men and women formed families against great odds—there were twenty-six black marriages recorded in the Dutch Reformed Church between 1641 and 1664—although the dominies were increasingly reluctant to baptize either slaves or their children. In 1664 Dominie Henricus Selyns informed the Classis of Amsterdam that he and his colleagues had halted the latter practice altogether—"due to their lack of knowledge and faith, and because of their worldly aims. The parents wanted nothing else than to deliver their children from bodily slavery, without striving for Christian virtues." In some instances couples adopted orphans, gathering them into kin units at great cost. In 1661 free blacks Emanuel Pietersen and his wife, Dorothy Angola, sought freedom "for a lad named Anthony Angola, whom they adopted when an infant and have since reared and educated." Their petition was granted, after they paid the West India Company three hundred guilders (five times the original purchase price of Manhattan).

5

A City Lost,
a City Gained

Although New Netherland appeared to be recovering nicely, Stuyvesant grew increasingly fearful that its very progress had undermined the authority of the West India Company. The arrival of thousands of settlers—too many, he said, lured by "an imaginary liberty in a new and, as some pretend, a free country"—seemed only to have raised the level of irreligion, immorality, and lawlessness in the colony. This was the worry as well of New Amsterdam's Reformed dominies: Johannes Megapolensis, formerly the pastor at Rensselaerswyck, whom Stuyvesant had persuaded in 1649 to lead the "feeble lukewarm and faint hearted congregation" that still worshiped in the church in the fort; and Samuel Drisius, who came over in 1652 to assist Megapolensis. Staunch Calvinists, the two dominies would join with Stuyvesant (himself the son of one clergyman and son-in-law of another) in an attempt to establish order and righteousness in the colony before it was too late.

Stuyvesant and the dominies were especially troubled by the resurgence of popular holidays, feasts, and carnivals in the colony. For well over a century, European churches, militant Protestant and reforming Catholic alike, had been waging a campaign to stamp out or regulate all such folk pleasures, both because they had popish (or pagan) roots and because they often spilled over into riot or rebellion. Like its Puritan counterparts in England, the Dutch Reformed Church had been very vigorous in this regard. Since the 1580s—and inseparably linked to the struggle for national independence—synods of the Reformed Church had repeatedly attacked popular music, maypoles, plays, dances, and even such apparently innocent amusements as filling children's shoes, on the feast of St. Nicholas, with sweets and toys. Ecclesiastical suppression of these traditional practices was also strongly endorsed by the Dutch upper classes, who though once willing to join in the general merriment were now cultivating distinctively genteel patterns of recreation, entertainment, speech, and conduct.

In the Netherlands, the outcome of this great conflict over the form and content of public culture was as yet far from certain, for the ever pragmatic Dutch had struck a series of compromises between religious and secular imperatives, between Calvinism and humanism, between sobriety and festivity. In New Netherland, however, Stuyvesant and the dominies had no intention of compromising. When told about a man who "last Shrove Tuesday walked along the street in woman's clothes," Stuyvesant announced that while such behavior "may be tolerated and looked at through the fingers in some places in the Fatherland," he wouldn't permit it on this side of the Atlantic.

In 1654, accordingly, Stuyvesant banned all Shrove Tuesday festivities, calling it "altogether unprofitable, unnecessary and censurable for subjects and neighbors to celebrate such pagan and popish feasts and to practice such evil customs in this Country." Two or three farmers' servants defied the ban and were caught at a game of Pulling the Goose. Hauled before Stuyvesant to account for themselves, the culprits behaved "in an insolent and contumacious manner, threatening, cursing, deriding and laughing at the chief magistracy." Stuyvesant, in a sulfurous rage, threw them into prison and reiterated his determination to combat the "sins, scandals, debaucheries and crimes" to which the "rabble" of the colony were prone.

In an effort to reform popular manners and morals, Stuyvesant likewise ordered all "brewers, tapsters, and innkeepers" to close their doors at nine P.M. and directed them to apply to him for proper licenses. He warned the people against "quarreling, fighting and hitting each other" and imposed harsh new penalties (up to a year and a half at hard labor on a diet of bread and water) for those convicted of fighting with knives or swords. He outlawed sexual intercourse with Indians and (because "we see and observe daily drunken Indians run along the Manhatans") forbade the sale of liquor to them under any circumstances. Unlike officials in Amsterdam, he favored the building of a proper schoolhouse, not only (or even primarily) for the sake of learning but "to keep the youth off the street, and bring them under discipline." He and the magistrates decreed that "no male and female shall be allowed to keep house together like man and wife, before they have legally been married," and he summarily deported women "of bad reputation."

Mindful that the residents of New Amsterdam were indifferent churchgoers, Stuyvesant scheduled Sunday services for the afternoon as well as the morning and charged "all officials, subjects and vassals" of the West India Company to attend both. He enjoined everyone from "going on pleasure parties in a boat, cart, or wagon" on the Sabbath and banned "all tapping, fishing, hunting and other usual occupations, handicrafts and business, be it in houses, cellars, shops, ships, yachts or on the streets and market places." In the same spirit, he set aside the first Wednesday of every month for fasting and obligatory prayer. The travails of "our sister state of Brazil," Stuyvesant said, should serve as a premonition of the wrath that would rain down "from a sky laden with vengeance" if the people of New Amsterdam failed to mend their ways. Observed one townsman, "Stuyvesant is starting a whole reformation here."

The rabble continued nonetheless to have their fun, which may help to explain why Stuyvesant and the magistrates resorted to more and more draconian punishments. In 1658 a man found guilty of deserting his bride-to-be after the publication of their marriage banns was sentenced to have his head shaved and his ears bored, then to be flogged and put to work for two years with the company slaves. In 1660 a soldier convicted of a "crime condemned by God as an abomination" was ordered "to be taken to the place of execution and there stripped of his arms, his sword to be broken at his feet and he then to be tied in a sack and cast into the river and drowned till dead." (Sodomy had been fiercely punished once before, in 1646, when a black man named Jan Creoli was sentenced "to be conveyed to the place of public execution, and there choked to death, and then burnt to ashes"; Manuel Congo, "a lad ten years old, on whom the above abominable crime was committed," was tied to a stake and flogged.) In 1662 a runaway servant was hanged for resisting arrest and his head set on a stake as an example to others. In 1664 Lysbet Antoniosent—one of the three children of half-freed slaves whom the company had kept in bondage—set her master's Nieuw Utrecht house on fire. The court ordered her chained to a stake, strangled, and burned, though it commuted the sentence on the day appointed for her execution.

SERVANTS OF BAAL

Vexing Stuyvesant as much as the intransigence of traditional popular culture were challenges to the supremacy of the Reformed Church. The revised Freedoms and Exemptions of 1640 and 1650 had stipulated that "no other religion shall be publicly admitted in New Netherland except the Reformed," as defined by the Synod of Dort. That was the rule in the Netherlands as well, where it had been interpreted over the years to mean that other Protestants, Roman Catholics, and Jews wouldn't be molested by the authorities so long as they worshiped in private. The West India Company expected that similar allowances would be made for immigrants to New Netherland who didn't belong to the Reformed communion: they could worship as they pleased, providing they did so out of the public eye. But the company underestimated Stuyvesant's fanatical loyalty to the national church. On several important occasions during the 1650s it would be embarrassed to discover that he, Megapolensis, and Drisius seemed bent on imposing a degree of religious conformity on the colony that was unthinkable as well as impracticable in the Netherlands.

First to feel the heat of Stuyvesant's displeasure was New Amsterdam's growing Lutheran population—mostly Swedes, Germans, and Finns. At issue was their opposition to the Reformed rule that at baptism both parents be present and acknowledge the authority of the Synod of Dort. In 1653 the Lutherans asked Stuyvesant to let them organize their own church. He refused, and New Amsterdam's two dominies urged the Classis of Amsterdam to advise the directors of the West India Company to support Stuyvesant's decision. If they didn't, the two said, other sects would want similar privileges and "our place would become a receptacle for all sorts of heretics and fanatics." The directors did as asked.

The Lutherans didn't go away, though, and in 1656 Stuyvesant learned they were holding conventicles—unauthorized services—in Newtown and perhaps elsewhere on Long Island. He issued a strongly worded ordinance banning all such gatherings and threw a few offenders in jail. Unluckily for him, the directors of the West India Company (three of whom were Lutherans) now began to worry that too much zeal would discourage settlement. They told Stuyvesant to let the Lutherans enjoy "free religious exercises in their houses." He did so, but it was all he did, and the controversy continued to simmer for years. (Megapolensis and Drisius were pointedly warned that if they failed to accept the compromise the company would replace them with younger ministers who weren't "infected with scruples about unnecessary forms, which cause more division, than edification.")

As with the Lutherans, so with the Jews. New Amsterdam's first known Jewish residents, two traders from Holland named Solomon Pietersen and Jacob Barsimson, arrived in the summer of 1654. A little while later, around the beginning of September, they were joined by twenty-three exhausted refugees from Brazil. Mostly Sephardim, the newcomers—four couples, two widows, and thirteen children—had been trying to get to Holland since Recife fell to the Portuguese the previous January. After their first ship was captured by Spanish pirates, they were rescued by a French privateer, which then took them to New Amsterdam.

Their ordeal was far from over, however. When they couldn't raise the money to pay for their passage, the magistrates authorized the French captain to auction off whatever property they had brought with them and held a few in jail as hostages until the entire sum had been paid. Stuyvesant let it be known that he wanted no Jews in New Amsterdam. "Their usual usury and deceitful business towards the Christians" made them undesirable colonists, he explained to his superiors in the company.

More Jews arrived from Holland in 1655—five wealthy merchants and their families, to whom the company gave passports, partly in the hope they would "take care of their own poor." Rumors flew around New Amsterdam that many others were on their way and that construction would soon begin on the town's first synagogue. To Stuyvesant, Drisius, and Megapolensis, this sounded even more ominous than conventicles of Lutherans. "For as we have here Papists, Mennonites and Lutherans among the Dutch; also many Puritans or Independents, and many atheists and various other servants of Baal among the English," Megapolensis told the Classis of Amsterdam, "it would create a still greater confusion, if the obstinate and immovable Jews came to settle here." After all, he grumbled, "These people have no other God than the Mammon of unrighteousness, and no other aim than to get possession of Christian property."

The company's managers didn't see it that way. Under pressure from Amsterdam's Jewish leaders, they rebuked Stuyvesant for his intolerance and pointed out to him that it would be "unreasonable and unfair" to expel the Jews from New Amsterdam, because they had done so much for the defense of Brazil and also—no small point—"because of the large amount of capital, which they have invested in this Company." They ought to have the same civil and political rights in America as in Holland, the directors concluded, "without giving the said Jews a claim to the privileges of exercising their religion in a synagogue." Stuyvesant obediently withdrew an order expelling the Jews from New Amsterdam "forthwith," but his persistent harassment of them forced the directors of the company to rebuke him again in 1656. The next year he reluctantly admitted the Jews to full citizenship in New Netherland. Although neither he nor the company was ready to let them build their synagogue, they were allowed to worship in a private house on the corner of the Heere Gracht (Broad Street) and Slyck Steegh (Mill Lane). Asser Levy, one of the Recife refugees, pressured Stuyvesant for even more extensive civil rights. He eventually won the right to serve in the militia, to engage in retail trade, to be licensed as a butcher, and to own a house—the first Jew to do so in New Amsterdam or anywhere in North America.

Stuyvesant had no better luck with the various radical sectarians, mostly English, who arrived in New Amsterdam during the later 1650s. Unlike the Presbyterians, Congregationalists, and other mainstream Calvinists whose views broadly conformed to the Reformed creed, these newcomers appeared to reject all existing forms of religious and political authority. In 1656 one William Wickendam—"a troublesome fellow, a cobbler from Rhode Island," said Megapolensis—began to preach at Flushing, claiming "he had a commission from Christ." When he started baptizing people in the East River as well, it became obvious that Wickendam was some kind of Baptist or Mennonite. Stuyvesant promptly threw him out of the colony.

One year later, in 1657, a boatload of English Quakers showed up and astounded everyone with their behavior. Their ship flew no flag and fired no salute; their leader, one Robert Fowler, spoke with Stuyvesant but (Megapolensis said) "rendered him no respect, but stood still with his hat firm on his head, as if a goat." Fowler departed on the next tide, leaving behind two young women who immediately "began to quake and go into a frenzy and cry out loudly in the middle of the street, that men should repent, for the day of judgment was at hand." Megapolensis added dryly, "Our people, not knowing what was the matter, ran to and fro, while one cried 'Fire,' and another something else." The *schout* marched them both off to prison "by the head," and they too were soon on their way out of the colony.

Only a few months later, another Quaker, one Robert Hodgson, began preaching to enthusiastic crowds in the English towns of Long Island. Stuyvesant, informed of Hodgson's arrest at Hempstead, had him bound to a cart and dragged back to Manhattan, there to be thrown in a dungeon, tried and convicted without an opportunity to defend himself, and sentenced "to work at the wheelbarrow two years with the negroes." When he refused, Stuyvesant had him hung in chains and whipped until near death. After a number of appeals for clemency from the shocked inhabitants of New Amsterdam, Stuyvesant deported the unfortunate Hodgson to Rhode Island—"a place of errors and enthusiasts," Megapolensis explained.

Stuyvesant now issued a proclamation that any ship bringing a Quaker into New Netherland would be confiscated and anyone caught harboring a Quaker would pay a stiff fine. In December 1657 thirty-one residents of Flushing signed an eloquent defense of religious toleration—known ever after as the Flushing Remonstrance—declaring that they couldn't in good conscience abide by such regulations. Remember, they said, that in the Netherlands, the "law of love, peace and libertie" extended even to "Jews, Turks and Egyptians." Dismissing the Remonstrance as a "seditious, mutinous and detestable letter of defiance," Stuyvesant ordered the arrest of the town's officials.

The Quakers, who thrived on persecution, continued to gain adherents on Long Island, prompting Stuyvesant in January 1659 to order a day of fasting and prayer throughout the colony against their "unheard of abominable Heresy." The effect, if any, was short-lived. By the summer of 1662 the magistrates of Jamaica advised him that a majority of the town's inhabitants attended Quaker conventicles at the Flushing home of John Bowne. Stuyvesant had Bowne returned to New Amsterdam for trial and, following the now predictable conviction, banished him to Holland. Soldiers were quartered in Jamaica while the town's officials attempted to administer an anti-Quaker oath to its inhabitants. When Bowne shrewdly took his case to the West India Company, however, the company's directors decided that, once again, Stuyvesant had gone too far. Quakers might well be disagreeable, they rebuked him in early 1663, but trying to "force people's consciences" would almost certainly discourage immigration.

"OUR GREAT MUSCOVY DUKE"

In matters of government, too, Stuyvesant was forced to accept limitations on his authority. The company's instructions to him (as to his predecessors) had vested the "supreme government" of New Netherland in a council composed of the director, a vice- or deputy director, and the *schout*. Stuyvesant made it clear from the outset that this system left no room for discussion, much less dissent. "We derive our authority from God and the West India Company," he thundered, "not from the pleasure of a few ignorant subjects." When Cornelis Melyn asked for a retrospective investigation of Kieft's administration, Stuyvesant warned him that private citizens had no business questioning the conduct of lawful authorities, even a scoundrel like Kieft. When Melyn suggested that only company employees need obey the council, Stuyvesant had Melyn clapped in irons for sedition and banished. Ironically, Melyn sailed for home on the same ship that carried Kieft and Dominie Bogardus. Kieft and Bogardus were drowned when the ship foundered off the English coast, but Melyn survived. To Stuyvesant's dismay, the States-General suspended Melyn's sentence and allowed him to return to New Amsterdam, where he continued to stir up opposition.

Stuyvesant's expectation of obedience from the residents of New Amsterdam quickly ran up against their own expectation, derived from conventional Dutch practice, of a proper municipal government. The Netherlands had no landed aristocracy to speak of, urban capital dominated its agricultural production, and a decentralized political system ensured the power of merchant oligarchies over its cities. So the more Stuyvesant insisted on his authority, the more he was resented—above all among the colony's burgeoning merchant elite. "Our great Muscovy Duke," they called him (behind his back). He set up an advisory council of prominent colonists—the Board of Nine, it was called—but only made matters worse by treating them too with contempt. He often "burst into a violent rage," they complained, "if we in our advice didn't fall in with his humor." Some thought he was mad. His "head is troubled," one said; he "has a screw loose."

After a year or so of intolerable abuse, the Board of Nine became the nucleus of a loose alliance of men who called themselves the "commonality" of New Amsterdam and agitated tirelessly to have Stuyvesant recalled. They derided him for issuing proclamations that nobody paid any attention to. They accused him of paying too much attention to the company's balance sheets and too little to the well-being of the colony. They blamed him for arbitrary taxation, political favoritism, and corruption.

Stuyvesant responded by arresting their ringleader, the suave young Adriaen van der Donck, and throwing him too out of the colony. Van der Donck and ten current or former members of the board then sent off a blistering "Remonstrance" to the States-General that depicted Stuyvesant as a "vulture [who] is destroying the prosperity of New Netherland." "All the permanent inhabitants, the merchant, the burgher and peasant, the planter, the laboring man, and also the man in service," despised him, declared Van der Donck and his allies (who included Melyn as well as former director Wouter van Twiller). The only solution was for the West India Company to surrender the colony and let the States-General provide it with a regular government of "godly, honorable and intelligent" men. Besides, now that the conflict with Spain had ended, what good was the debt-ridden West India Company anyway?[1]

"Frivolous talk!" Secretary Van Tienhoven scoffed in reply. "Gross ingratitude."

---

1. Van der Donck later retired to his estate overlooking Spuyten Duyvil, where he set himself up as a *jonkheer*, or squire—whence the present town of Yonkers. His death in 1655 coincided with the publication of his famously lyrical *Description of the New Netherlands*.

Yet for a time it seemed that the States-General might indeed revoke the company's charter and assume direct control of New Netherland. Plainly nervous, Stuyvesant's superiors warned him to be more circumspect. "Govern the people with the utmost caution and leniency," they wrote, "for you have now learned by experience, how too much vehemence may draw upon you the hatred of the people."

What saved Stuyvesant, in the end, was the threat of war between England and the Netherlands. The Puritans had now executed Charles I, and Parliament was aflame with plans to protect the nation's trade—primarily from the Dutch, who were driving the English out of one market after another in Europe and the Caribbean. In 1650 Parliament authorized privateers to begin seizing Dutch vessels; the following year it adopted the first of numerous Navigation Acts that restricted trade with England and English colonies to English merchants. For the Dutch, whose prosperity hinged on freedom of the seas, this belligerence on the part of their sometime ally was alarming indeed. By the spring of 1652, reluctant to tamper with things in New Netherland at so critical a juncture, the States-General had decided against revocation of the West India Company's charter. The company in turn decided to keep Stuyvesant as director-general. To placate his critics, however, he was told to equip New Amsterdam with a proper municipal government—"a Burgher Government," the company emphasized, with a *schout-fiscall*, two burgomasters (co-mayors), and five *schepens* (aldermen).

Naval warfare between the Netherlands and England erupted three months later. Close to home, the fighting went badly for the Dutch, who lost twelve hundred ships and thousands of seamen in clashes off the coast of Britain. Elsewhere, however—in the Baltic, the Mediterranean, the Caribbean, and Asian waters—English losses ran so high that within a year Parliament had declared its willingness to make peace.

THE STRUGGLE FOR POWER

Early in February 1653, as he had been instructed to do, Stuyvesant launched New Amsterdam's first municipal government in a large second-floor room of the Stadt's Herbergh (soon renamed the Stadhuis, or City Hall). Clad in their long cloaks and huge bell-crowned hats, the burgomasters and *schepens* appointed by Stuyvesant solemnly took their oath of office and bowed their heads for a benediction. "We thank Thee that . . . it has pleased Thee to make us the rulers of the people in this place," they prayed. "Incline also the hearts of the subjects to dutiful obedience," they added somewhat apprehensively. They would have done better to pray for Stuyvesant's cooperation.

For as the magistrates settled into their seats it still wasn't evident who in fact governed New Netherland. Were they really "the rulers of the people in this place"? Or did ultimate authority in the colony still reside with the authoritarian director-general and his advisory council?

There wasn't time to get an answer from the company, even if the company had an answer, for the spring and early summer of 1653 brought warnings that the New England colonies were preparing to attack Manhattan. Captain Underhill, moreover, had called for the English inhabitants of Hempstead and Flushing, where he was now the *schout*, to throw off "the iniquitous government of Peter Stuyvesant." Ordered out of New Netherland, Underhill went to Rhode Island to raise troops for an invasion of the Dutch colony.

At an emergency meeting between Stuyvesant, his council, and the magistrates, it was agreed that repairs should begin immediately on Fort Amsterdam. It was also decided to build a "high stockade and a small breastwork" across the town's northern frontier (the site of present-day Wall Street). Stuyvesant contributed the labor of "the Company's Negroes," and the magistrates collected five thousand guilders from New Amsterdam's forty-three wealthiest citizens, who loaned the funds at 10 percent interest, creating the town's first municipal debt. Ironically, the stockade's fifteen-foot planks and oaken posts were supplied by an Englishman, Thomas Baxter. (In the early 1660s the wall would be strengthened by the addition of six bastions with brass cannon and two gates—the Water Poort at the East River road, today the corner of Wall and Pearl, and the Landt Poort, at what is now the intersection of Wall and Broadway.) No sooner was the wall finished, though, than Stuyvesant demanded more money to complete work on the fort and pay for weapons distributed to the public from the company armory.

Coolly, the magistrates informed Stuyvesant that they had run out of funds and wouldn't think of soliciting more until he turned the wine and beer excise over to the municipal treasury. An independent revenue, they knew, would allow the municipal government to be something more than a rubber stamp for the director-general. Impossible, Stuyvesant said: without the excise he couldn't pay the soldiers in the fort, and the city would be left defenseless. When this argument failed to impress, he announced that he was calling in all the West India Company's "outstanding debts [and] the tithes and other royalties that are due" from the town's inhabitants. The magistrates stood their ground.

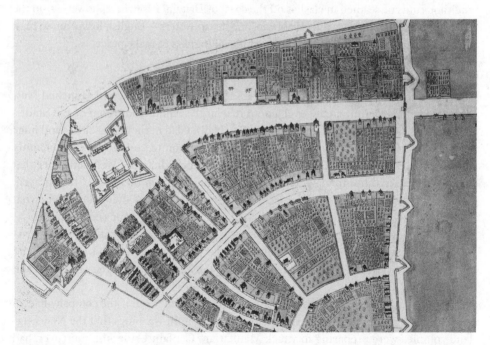

In 1660 surveyor Jacques Cortelyou drew up a map of the town that served as the basis for this bird's-eye view (sometimes called the Castello Plan because it was discovered in a villa of that name near Florence). There were now over three hundred houses in New Amsterdam, but when the directors of the West India Company saw this plan of the city, they complained that the place still didn't seem built up enough. Much of the property below the "Cingle," the area adjoining the new city wall, was in fact being used for gardens or orchards while the owners waited for property values to rise. (I.N. Phelps Stokes Collection. Miriam and Ira D. Wallach Division of Art, Prints and Photographs. The New York Public Library. Astor, Lenox and Tilden Foundations)

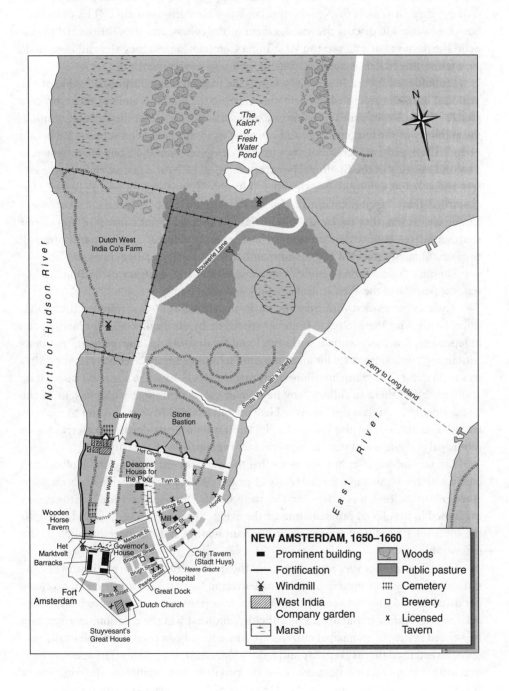

"The Kalch" or Fresh Water Pond

North or Hudson River

Dutch West India Co's Farm

Bouwerie Lane

Smits Vly (Smith's Valley)

Ferry to Long Island

East River

N

Gateway

Stone Bastion

Het Cingle

Deacons' House for the Poor

Tuyn St.

Prince St.

Hoogh Street

Wooden Horse Tavern

Heere Wegh Street

Mill

Marktvelt St.

Governor's House

Brouwer Street

Snyck St.

City Tavern (Stadt Huys)
Heere Gracht

Het Marktvelt Barracks

Brugh Street

Pearle Street

Hospital

Great Dock

Fort Amsterdam

Pearle Street

Dutch Church

Stuyvesant's Great House

NEW AMSTERDAM, 1650–1660

- ▬ Prominent building
- — Fortification
- ✕ Windmill
- ▨ West India Company garden
- ⌇ Marsh
- ▨ Woods
- ▨ Public pasture
- ▥ Cemetery
- ▫ Brewery
- x Licensed Tavern

A showdown of sorts occurred in the autumn of 1653, when Stuyvesant convened a "General Assembly" of delegates from New Amsterdam and the Long Island towns, English as well as Dutch. He wanted them to deal with the Englishman Thomas Baxter, who, having sold the town the lumber for its wall, had promptly turned pirate and was now preying on vessels of New Netherland and New England alike. The delegates, however, wanted to discuss the management of the colony, and they threatened to suspend the payment of taxes to the West India Company unless they were allowed to do so; a few muttered darkly about setting up their own government.

Emboldened by the Assembly's stand, the magistrates summoned "some of the principal burghers and inhabitants of this City" to the Stadhuis and got them to sign a pledge—New Amsterdam's Mayflower Compact, as it were—that they would submit to the authority of the burgomasters and *schepens* "in all things as good subjects are bound to do." Then, early in December, they invited delegates from the Long Island towns to a second meeting in the Stadhuis. Nineteen men, all of New Amsterdam's burgomasters and *schepens* among them, signed a "Humble Remonstrance and Petition" that described their "apprehension of the establishment of an Arbitrary Government among us." It was, they declared, "one of our privileges that our consent or that of our representatives is necessarily required in the enactment of . . . laws and orders." Stuyvesant curtly rejected the petition and ordered the "so-called delegates" to disperse at once "under pain of our extreme displeasure and arbitrary correction." They sent the petition to the West India Company and went home.

The company sided with Stuyvesant. In the spring of 1654 it rebuked the magistrates for allowing themselves to become "stirred up by the disaffected," for holding "an independent Assembly without authority," and for drawing up "inexpedient" petitions containing "forged pretexts for an imminent factious sedition." Yet Stuyvesant didn't win everything. The company allowed the magistrates to have the wine and beer excise and authorized them to collect "any new small excise or impost with consent of the Commonality . . . unless the Director General and Council have any reason to the contrary." The magistrates also received a city seal for registering deeds and mortgages on municipal real estate and were given permanent occupation of the City Hall.

The summer of 1654 brought news that the war between England and Holland had ended with the signing of a formal treaty of peace. Although neither side had won, New Amsterdam at least was safe—for the time being. "Praise the Lord!" Stuyvesant exclaimed in his official proclamation of the event. "Praise the Lord!" In mid-August the town celebrated its deliverance with a giant bonfire and free beer supplied by the magistrates.

Over the next decade, Stuyvesant and the magistrates jointly ran the town, constantly bickering over precedence and maneuvering for petty advantages with no clear-cut division of duties between them. On one important measure, however, they managed to cooperate without apparent difficulty, and that was the creation, in 1657, of a two-tiered system of municipal citizenship. Any native-born resident of the town, anyone who had lived there ("kept fire and light") for at least one year and six weeks, or anyone willing to spend twenty guilders for the privilege was eligible for the common or small burgher-right. This provided full freedom of New Amsterdam and the all-important right to practice a trade or carry on business. For fifty guilders, city residents, ministers of the gospel, and military officers could purchase the great burgher-right, qualifying them to fill all "offices and dignities within this City, and consequently be nominated thereto." Both the great and small burgher-rights were open to women.

Stuyvesant and nineteen others immediately had themselves enrolled as great burghers. Their ranks included one woman, Ragel (Rachel) van Tienhoven, wife of Cornelius. An additional 238 persons subsequently received the small burgher-right, among them ten carpenters, six shoemakers, five tailors, four coopers, two masons, two smiths, two sawyers, one pot baker, one chimney sweep, and one carter.

IMPERILED PERIPHERY

In 1650 Stuyvesant journeyed up to Hartford to resolve the long-standing boundary dispute between New Netherland and the New England colonies. The resulting Treaty of Hartford recognized English control over all of Connecticut east of Greenwich and over Long Island east of Oyster Bay. It wasn't a bad deal, since the English had previously claimed sovereignty over the whole of New Netherland, but New Amsterdam's resurgence underscored the need for settlements on western Long Island and upper Manhattan—both to provision its growing population and to create a buffer against the English and Indians. For obvious reasons, Stuyvesant hoped that their inhabitants would be Dutch and that they would see the need to live together in compact villages, like the people of New England. Yet here too his authority came under attack, and things didn't turn out as he wanted.

New Amersfoort (Flatlands), the oldest Dutch village on the periphery of New Amsterdam, came closest to fulfilling Stuyvesant's expectations. Its few dozen residents—Schencks and Strykers, Van Sigelens and Van Kouwenhovens—lived close by one another in palisaded farmhouses near the intersection of Flatbush Avenue and Kings Highway, not far from where Andries Hudde and Wolphert Gerritsen first broke ground in the mid-1630s. Breuckelen, chartered by Kieft in 1646, was somewhat larger and less well defended. Dominie Henricus Selyns, who arrived there in 1660 to preach the gospel, counted 134 people in thirty-one households, predominately Dutch, scattered along what is now Fulton Street, not far from the ferry landing—"an ugly little village with the church in the middle of the road," he said.

In 1651 Stuyvesant set out to organize a new settlement in the thickly wooded land between Breuckelen and New Amersfoort. He christened it Middlewout, or Midwout; to its residents and neighbors it was also known as Vlachte Bos (Flatbush). Land was distributed to settlers, and in 1654 they received a formal charter permitting them to choose their own magistrates, to raise taxes, to build a church and school, and to provide for their common defense.

Despite Stuyvesant's repeated demands and warnings, the residents of Midwout stubbornly refused to live near one another, as did the English or their New Amersfoort neighbors. After much argument, he ordered them to lay out forty-odd plots of about fifty acres each along an Indian trail (now Flatbush Avenue) that ran down from Breuckelen to Jamaica Bay. Where Church Avenue now crosses Flatbush Avenue, he had them build a stockade and blockhouse as well as a small house of worship for the village's first dominie, the Rev. Johannes Polhemus, who arrived in 1654 from Brazil.

In 1652, the year after creating Midwout, Stuyvesant permitted fifty-odd English Independents and Presbyterians to settle west of Flushing Creek near Mespat Kill. He called the place Middelburgh after the capital of Zeeland; they called it Newtown. The West India Company didn't want them there under any name, however, for with war looming between Parliament and the States-General, the English settlements in New

Netherland looked too much like "serpents in our bosom, who finally might devour our hearts." Stuyvesant realized his mistake when Middleburgh joined Gravesend, Hempstead, and Flushing in the clamor against him. In retaliation, he reneged on his promise to give Middleburgh a charter and slammed the door on further English settlements in the colony.

Stuyvesant's settlement-building program very nearly came to grief when he turned his attention to New Sweden, a colony of four-hundred-odd fur traders and tobacco planters on the western flank of New Netherland. For a dozen years the West India Company had done little or nothing to dislodge the Swedes, but after 1650 they became more troublesome, building new trading posts along the Delaware and Schuylkill rivers and harassing Dutch merchants. Stuyvesant vowed to erase New Sweden from the map, and in the autumn of 1655 he descended on the Delaware community with four heavily armed ships and several hundred soldiers. The Swedes gave up without firing a shot.

There was no time to celebrate, however, for bad news had arrived from New Amsterdam. In Stuyvesant's absence, nearly two thousand Hackensacks, Mahicans, Wappingers, and assorted other "river Indians" came down the Hudson to raid Canarsee camps on Long Island. While gathering food and water on Manhattan, one of their women was killed by a Dutchman for taking peaches from his orchard. That night, enraged Indians poured into town, hammering on doors, ransacking houses, and terrifying the residents. Though no one was seriously injured, the panicky burgomasters, urged on by Secretary Van Tienhoven, organized a militia and drove them away with the loss of several lives on both sides. The Indians then turned their wrath against settlers in upper Manhattan and on Staten Island. Colonists on Long Island feared they would be next.

Before the so-called Peach War sputtered out a month or so later, several dozen of the invaders and fifty whites lay dead. More than a hundred whites, mostly women and children, had been taken captive. Twenty-eight bouweries were destroyed, along with six hundred head of cattle and twelve thousand bushels of grain. Stuyvesant, who hurried back from the Delaware to marshal the colony's defenses, was shocked at the extent of the destruction. New Netherland has "gone backward so much," he wrote pessimistically to the States-General, "that it will not be in the same flourishing state for several years." The burgomasters complained to the company that Stuyvesant and Secretary Van Tienhoven had failed to protect New Amsterdam and again demanded their immediate recall. Stuyvesant survived, but the company sacked Van Tienhoven. (He later vanished, and his hat and cane were found floating in the river. Suicide? Murder? No one knew.)

Despite Stuyvesant's initially dismal assessment of its impact, the Peach War marked the end of Lenape resistance to European expansion on western Long Island. Not long after the fighting ended, a Massapequa sachem named Tackapousha pleaded with Stuyvesant not to exact revenge on his people. They had done no harm to the Dutch, he said, "even to the value of a dog." In 1656, on behalf of a half-dozen Lenape groups, including the Canarsees and Rockaways, Tackapousha signed a treaty with Stuyvesant accepting the governor of New Netherland as their "protector" and vowing to live in peace with settlers.

After Tackapousha's treaty, the pace of Dutch settlement on the island picked up noticeably. Stuyvesant approved the "purchases" of at least a half-dozen large tracts of land from Lenape groups during the later 1650s and early 1660s. As colonists moved in, many of the Lenapes drifted away, often merging with Algonkian-speaking peoples in New Jersey, Pennsylvania, and further west; those who remained fell prey to one or more epidemics of smallpox. By the mid-1660s, less than fifty years after Minuit's purchase of Manhattan, virtually all of modern Kings and Queens counties lay in European hands.

The pacification of Tackapousha's followers didn't necessarily strengthen Stuyvesant's authority in the villages around New Amsterdam, however, least of all in Nieuw Utrecht. Situated on the headlands of western Long Island overlooking the Narrows—including also what are now the Bay Ridge and Fort Hamilton sections of Brooklyn—Nieuw Utrecht originally belonged to the inhabitants of a Lenape campsite called Nayack. In 1652 Cornelis van Werckhoven, a sometime magistrate of Utrecht and major shareholder in the West India Company, persuaded two Nayack chiefs to sell him the entire area, a thousand or more acres in all, for "six shirts, two pairs of shoes, six pairs of socks, six axes, six hatchets, six knives, two scissors, [and] two combs." (When the Nayack realized that Van Werckhoven expected them to leave, they asked for, and got, a second payment of "six coats, six kettles, six axes, six hatchets, six small looking glasses, twelve knives and twelve combs" before decamping to Staten Island.) Van Werckhoven himself died shortly thereafter, but the project went ahead under the leadership of Jacques Cortelyou, Nicasius de Sille, and others, who received an official charter from Stuyvesant in 1657.[2]

By the terms of the charter, twenty initial settlers would each receive fifty acres, divided between small house lots in a central village and elongated out-lots behind it. Despite repeated warnings, though, many grantees failed to build on or enclose their land, and three years later Nieuw Utrecht consisted of only eleven houses and one barn. Its inhabitants were bitterly divided by allegations of fence stealing and by disputes over use of the common meadows, the organization of a watch, and the construction of a palisade.

Stuyvesant came out for a personal inspection of the troubled town. Its residents raised the Dutch flag and gave him "a dinner or public entertainment in as good a stile as the place could afford." In return, he obligingly let them borrow some slaves to finish the palisade and sent "a half dozen shackles with an iron rod and a good lock" to help maintain law and order. But Nieuw Utrecht wasn't going to be built in a day. A year later Stuyvesant learned that it was still torn by "controversies, misdeeds, and difficulties" and that new measures were needed "to stimulate the people to build dwelling houses, a block house and public pound, and to dig wells for the benefit of the community."

In Nieuw Haarlem, by comparison, things proceeded rather more smoothly. Several attempts had been made between the later 1630s and the early 1650s to plant settlements on the rich flats that bordered the Manhattan side of the Harlem River, several miles to the north of New Amsterdam. None had survived Kieft's War and subsequent Indian troubles, but the land was too valuable to ignore, and settlers there would form

---

2. When the missionaries Jaspar Danckaerts and Peter Sluyter visited New Utrecht in 1679, they found that seven or eight of the original Nayack families, fewer than two dozen people in all, had returned to their former lands to scratch out a "poor, miserable" existence. Cortelyou rented them "a small corner" of what was now his property for "twenty bushels of maize yearly"—an illustration of how quickly the balance had swung against native peoples.

an important line of defense for New Amsterdam. (Dutch residents of the colony wouldn't have forgotten how Nieuw Haarlem's namesake in the Netherlands put up a legendary seven-month resistance to the Spanish army before capitulating.)

In 1658 Stuyvesant tried again. Grants of between forty and fifty acres of arable land were offered to prospective colonists, along with promises of a court, a minister, and regular troops in time of danger. Two parallel streets, cutting the modern block pattern diagonally, were laid out to meet the Harlem River between the present 125th and 126th streets. The first twenty-odd house lots were sandwiched between them in two ranges, with garden plots and planting fields assigned to each on the surrounding flats. To emphasize his support for the fledgling settlement, Stuyvesant set company slaves to work on a wagon road linking it with New Amsterdam.

Within a few years Nieuw Haarlem had thirty male residents. Most were heads of families and landowners; some were probably tenants of well-to-do investors in New Amsterdam who had begun to speculate in real estate. They nonetheless made up a strikingly diverse group, including eleven Frenchmen, four Walloons, four Danes, three Swedes, three Germans, and seven Dutchmen. One, Jean La Montaigne, was a veteran colonist, an experienced Indian fighter, and a perennial member of Stuyvesant's council. The majority of La Montaigne's fellow settlers, by contrast, were recently arrived tradesmen who had little or no experience with farming. One was a butcher, one a carpenter, another a mason. Others had previously occupied themselves with making barrels, shoes, pots, soap, or beer. Their diversity and inexperience seem not to have been sources of conflict, however, and they appear to have escaped the troubles that beset their counterparts elsewhere in New Netherland.

Despite the differences among these and a half-dozen other such towns and villages, they were the raw material out of which a distinctive rural society was taking shape on the outskirts of New Amsterdam. These Dutch towns and villages were quite different from the closed, self-sufficient, egalitarian, organic communities of New England. Their inhabitants were essentially strangers, often of widely mixed national backgrounds—imagine the confusion of tongues in Nieuw Haarlem—and they had been brought together by nothing more elevated or complex than the West India Company's promises of land and protection. None had the history of communal sacrifice and struggle, much less radical dissent, that solidified early New England towns, although Flatbush residents strove to maintain a rough equality in the ownership of land and to emphasize cooperative rather than competitive behavior (each household, for example, owned a share of the village's public brewery).

Nor did the Dutch towns encourage the broad popular participation characteristic of their English counterparts. As a rule, each was governed by a court—made up of three *schepens* and a *schout*—who were appointed by the director in New Amsterdam. Although many of the English towns of New Netherland had contrived to obtain charters with more liberal provisions for self-government, they never felt at ease with the West India Company's unwillingness to relax its grip on New Amsterdam's hinterland.

JAMES STUART, DUKE OF YORK

The challenges to Stuyvesant's authority in and around New Amsterdam might not have mattered so much as they did, or mattered so quickly, were it not for events unfolding abroad. Although the first Anglo-Dutch War had ended without a clear-cut victor, England now had the Netherlands on the defensive. In 1655, just a year after the loss of

Brazil, parliamentary forces seized Jamaica from Spain and turned that strategically located island into a base for the further expansion of English influence in the Caribbean. By the end of 1655, as word of New Netherland's recent Indian troubles deepened the gloom on the Amsterdam exchange, West India Company stock had sunk to 10 percent of par, an all-time low. It soon fell to 5 percent, then 3.

Then, in 1660, after a decade of Puritan rule, Parliament restored the Stuarts to the throne. Charles II, the new king, was a cordial and witty man, conciliatory by temperament and conviction. Trailed by mistresses and illegitimate children—his court nicknamed him "Old Rowley" after one of the stallions in the royal stud—he would give his country twenty-five years of jolly sexual intrigue, extravagant private entertainments, and baroque scandals. When Parliament refused him enough money to pay for it all, he accepted secret bribes from Louis XIV of France.

The Restoration didn't derail England's pursuit of the Dutch, however, for even royalists now believed that the proper business of the state was business. Within months of Charles II's accession, Parliament adopted a second Navigation Act reiterating Britain's intention to drive the Dutch out of the American colonial trade. The new measure stipulated that the most valuable colonial products—sugar, tobacco, and indigo—could be shipped only to England in English ships, while all goods imported into British colonies from elsewhere were required to pass first through English ports. Concurrently, Charles II created a new body, the Lords of Trade, to supervise relations between the colonies and the mother country. The first imperial customs collectors weren't far behind.

The King's younger brother, James—duke of York, lord high admiral, master of vast estates in England and Ireland, and a far more conscientious man—played a key role in charting the course of British commercial policy. During the early 1660s, not quite thirty years old, he joined a circle of peers, navy officers, and great merchants whose envy of the Dutch was exceeded only by their visions of the rewards to be reaped in the field of colonial enterprise. Their diverse activities included the organization of several firms to spearhead the British assault on Dutch commercial supremacy. One, the Royal Fishery Company, undertook to break Dutch control over the lucrative Baltic fishing industry. Two others, the Morocco Company and the Company of Royal Adventurers Trading to Africa (later reorganized as the Royal African Company), both led by the duke, aimed to smash the Dutch West India Company's domination of the slave trade and to monopolize the importation of slave labor into the British colonies of the Caribbean and North America. The first expedition of the Royal Adventurers, sent out in 1663 in vessels borrowed from the Royal Navy, quickly captured almost every West India Company factory on the African coast, a blow that doomed the company's hope of making New Amsterdam a base for the slave trade.

The duke's circle also collected detailed accounts of rising Anglo-Dutch tensions along the borders of New Netherland. Only a few years earlier, Gravesend's troublesome magistrates had raised Parliament's colors over the town and declared that it would henceforth be subject only to the "laws of our nation and [the] Republic of England." Stuyvesant threw them into jail. Despite the Hartford Treaty of 1650, however, and despite his efforts to reestablish Dutch communities in their path, Stuyvesant was powerless to stem the flood of English settlers into his colony. By the early 1660s thirteen English towns had been planted on Long Island as against only five Dutch. In 1663, then again in 1664, Stuyvesant tried to bolster the authority of the West India

Company by inviting all the towns to send delegates to provincial meetings, but it didn't work.

Connecticut governor John Winthrop Jr. meanwhile opened a campaign to bring the English towns on Long Island and Westchester under the authority of his government. Connecticut agents stirred up support for the idea; in Gravesend, where they caused "a greate Hubbub and furie," it was rumored that armed parties were planning to put both "English & Dutch to fyre & to Sword." With the entire island in an uproar, the English towns rejected Winthrop's meddling and banded together in a combination with an adventurer named John Scott as their president. Scott tried to force the Dutch towns into the combination as well, assisted by none other than Captain John Underhill, lately returned to Flushing. Justifiably alarmed, the West India Company ordered Stuyvesant to hold the line. But in February of 1664, with the situation completely out of hand, Stuyvesant arranged a one-year truce with Scott. The alternative, he explained, was "an inevitable surprise and capture of all the Dutch villages on Long Island."

As New Netherland disintegrated, York and his friends closed in. Ousting the Dutch from North America, they reasoned, would make Britain master of the whole eastern seaboard from Maine to Cape Fear, linking settlements of the Chesapeake and New England and clearing the way for more effective enforcement of the Navigation Acts. By virtue of New Amsterdam's position at the southern end of the Hudson-Champlain corridor to Montreal, its conquest would also give Britain an invaluable base of operations against the French in Canada and their Indian allies. This would mean not only enhanced security for the frontier of New England but a stronger grip on the fur trade as well.

Furthermore, as the West India Company too had known, the plantation economies of the West Indies needed an entrepôt on the mainland from which they could obtain slaves and food in exchange for raw sugar and molasses. Because it was the only city of any size between Boston and Havana, New Amsterdam was the obvious choice: to wrest it from the Dutch West India Company would be an act of mercantile acumen, not to mention the highest patriotism.

The acquisition of New Netherland promised to improve the duke's own finances too. According to his personal Commission of Revenue, possession of the colony could bring him between ten and thirty thousand pounds a year in rents and customs duties. (On the Amsterdam exchange in 1664, Stuyvesant's annual salary of three thousand guilders was the equivalent of just three hundred pounds.) Finally, as many people suspected but few knew for certain, the duke was about to abandon Anglicanism for Roman Catholicism. An American province the size of New Netherland would make an attractive refuge for his sorely oppressed coreligionists, and perhaps for himself as well.

NEW YORK, NEW YORK

In March 1664 York persuaded the king to make him the proprietor of all the territory between the Delaware and Connecticut rivers, plus part of Maine and various islands off the coast—the entirety, that is, of New Netherland. In return for this vast domain, he was to acknowledge the sovereignty of the king with a token gift of forty beaver skins a year. At his own expense, York immediately dispatched Colonel Richard Nicolls with four frigates and nearly two thousand fighting men to secure the "entyre submission and obedience" of his new estate. Nicolls anchored in Gravesend Bay on August 26 and began disembarking his troops. An advance party of 450 soldiers and sailors marched up from Gravesend to seize the ferry at Breuckelen, just across the East River from Manhattan. A smaller force occupied Staten Island.

Loyal to the end, Stuyvesant prepared to make a fight of it. He had little to work with, however. Fort Amsterdam was (as usual) in no condition to withstand an assault, and its 150 or so soldiers were short on guns and ammunition. The town itself had no more than 250-odd men capable of bearing arms, and owing to the recent arrival of nearly three hundred slaves, its reserves of food were insufficient for a siege. After years of acrimonious strife with Stuyvesant, moreover, few of its residents were willing to risk themselves and their property for him or the West India Company.

So when Nicolls sent him a letter guaranteeing "every man in his Estate, life, and liberty" if New Amsterdam capitulated peacefully, Stuyvesant showed it to no one, certain that the revelation of its contents would only increase "popular murmurs and disaffections" in the town. Three days later he tore up a "friendly" letter from Governor Winthrop of Connecticut repeating Nicolls's offer and begging him to "avoid effusion of blood." But word of both letters had leaked out. A crowd of irate workmen and magistrates gathered at the Stadhuis, where they made Stuyvesant reassemble Winthrop's letter and read it aloud. That same afternoon he suffered a second humiliation when Nicolls moved his frigates up through the Narrows and trained their guns on the town. Stuyvesant climbed the bastion of the fort and made ready to open fire, but Dominie Megapolensis took him firmly by the arm and led him down again.

Early the next day, ninety-three of New Amsterdam's most prominent men, including virtually every present or former municipal officeholder as well as his own seventeen-year-old son, sent Stuyvesant a petition reiterating the folly of resistance against "so generous a foe." Finally accepting the hopelessness of his position, Stuyvesant informed Nicolls that he would give up. Negotiators from both sides met at his bouwerie and drafted formal Articles of Capitulation.

On September 8, 1664, the West India Company's colors were struck, and the soldiers of the garrison marched down to the East River shore, drums beating and flags flying, to board a ship for the long trip home. Scarcely had it raised anchor than Nicolls announced that in honor of his master Fort Amsterdam would henceforth be called Fort James, while Fort Orange would become Albany. Both New Amsterdam and New Netherland would be known as New York.

When he received news of New Netherland's capitulation, the Dutch ambassador in London hurried to the court to demand that Charles II return the colony at once. Not only did the king refuse—the Dutch had no right to be there in the first place, he said—but the duke of York added an angry warning that the crown was as determined to put the States-General in its place as Cromwell had been. The idea of another fight with Holland was in fact becoming more and more popular by the day. Parliament appropriated the money for it in February 1665; in March Charles II declared war.

The West India Company had meanwhile ordered Stuyvesant home to explain what had happened. He gathered his papers—including a testimonial from the magistrates that he had always been "an honest proprietor and patriot of the province and a supporter of the reformed religion"—and left for Amsterdam in the spring of 1665. The company, he discovered on his arrival, wanted a scapegoat. It publicly accused him of lying, incompetence, and cowardice, adding that New Amsterdam's merchants and clergy hadn't exactly distinguished themselves, either. Stuyvesant angrily rebutted the charges in a remonstrance to the States-General. If anything, he wrote, it was the company's own penny-pinching stupidity that had lost the colony, not his eighteen years of "trouble, care, solicitude and continued zeal."

The States-General had other things to think about, though. Its war with England was going better than expected, and in June 1667 a Dutch fleet sailed boldly up the Thames, burned three British men-of-war, and towed off the *Royal Charles*, pride of His Majesty's navy. This blow, falling less than a year after the Great Fire that destroyed much of London, prompted Charles II to sue for peace. In the negotiations that ensued, the States-General agreed to let the English keep New Netherland in exchange for Surinam (Dutch Guiana), whose slaves and sugar plantations were more highly valued by the West India Company. Aware that his quarrel with the company was now moot, Stuyvesant returned to Manhattan in the spring of 1668. He, Judith, their children, and their slaves lived quietly on his beloved bouwerie until his death in February 1672.

PART TWO

BRITISH NEW YORK
(1664–1783)

Plan of the City of New York, 1767–1774. (I. N. Phelps Stokes Collection. Miriam and Ira D. Wallach Division of Art, Prints and Photographs. The New York Public Library. Astor, Lenox and Tilden Foundations)

6

Empire and Oligarchy

The surrender of New Amsterdam didn't, strictly speaking, mean a shift from Dutch to English rule but from that of the Dutch West India Company to that of James Stuart, the duke of York. As its proprietor, the duke of York wielded greater power in his new province than his brother the king did over England. His charter gave him personal title to all its "lands, islands, soils, rivers, harbors, mines, minerals, quarries, woods, marshes, waters, lakes, fishings, hawking, hunting and fowling." He had "full and absolute power and authority to correct, punish, pardon, govern, and rule" its inhabitants—with no duty to establish a representative assembly and subject only to the requirement that his "statutes, ordinances, and proceedings" conform as nearly as possible to those of England. Landholders in the colony would be his tenants, obliged to pay him an annual quitrent in lieu of personal service. He decided who could trade with his colony, and he could impose duties on its imports and exports. Nowhere else in British America were the rights and privileges of colonists so limited, or those of government so vast.

The harshness of these provisions was mitigated, however, by the Articles of Capitulation, which were the essence of moderation, conciliation, and even compassion. There would be no punitive expulsion of Dutch settlers, no expropriation of Dutch property (including slaves), no assaults on Dutch culture. Dutch settlers could stay or freely leave, with all of their possessions, as they pleased. Those who stayed, providing they took an oath to the king, wouldn't be deprived of their ships, goods, houses, or land, nor would they be compelled to take up arms against the United Provinces in the future. They wouldn't have to change their religion, language, or inheritance customs. Contracts between them would continue to be enforced "according to the manner of the Dutch," and the Reformed Church could still collect taxes, run schools, and hold services in Dutch.

In negotiating the Articles with Stuyvesant, Nicolls had been generous because both he and the duke knew that no useful purpose would be served by acting "rigorous and scrutinous." With few English merchants as yet residing in New York, and with taxes and customs duties expected to supply the bulk of ducal revenues, the oppression of the colony's Dutch inhabitants and the disruption of established commercial interests could well ruin the proprietary and leave the duke with little or nothing to show for his efforts. It would certainly damage the fur trade, which depended on satisfying the Indian demand for cheap Dutch duffel (a coarse woolen cloth). Religious toleration, too, made sense if someday the duke wanted to make New York a haven for English Catholics.

The Dutch seemed prepared to cooperate. Not only did few of them leave, but the town's former Dutch magistrates thanked the duke for sending "so gentle, wise, and intelligent a gentlemen" as Nicolls to be their governor and expressed the hope that he would make New York "bloom and grow like the Cedars on Lebanon." Johannes van Brugh, an affluent merchant and son-in-law of Annetje Jans, hosted a dinner where Nicolls and his entourage could meet the town's leading citizens. Nicolls came away more convinced than ever that without "ill usage" the Dutch would make tractable and productive subjects. New York City itself, he told the duke, was "the best of all his Majesty's towns in America."

COLLABORATORS

It was the kind of people who asked him to dinner that Nicolls got along with best, and over the next several years he cultivated their good will with numerous courtesies and concessions—above all, allowing them to continue direct trade with the Netherlands. Toward the end of the second Anglo-Dutch war, Nicolls pleaded with the crown to exempt New York completely from the Navigation Acts. He also confiscated what remained of the West India Company's property, a cause for celebration among the burghers who had for years chafed under company rule. He reaffirmed the law, first embodied in the Burgher Right of 1657, that only freemen of the city could conduct business there. He let the powerful Van Rensselaers keep their patroonship and became fast friends with ex-director Stuyvesant, whiling away many pleasant evenings at his bouwerie outside of town. Nicolls even introduced the burghers to the gentlemanly sport of horse racing, laying out the first racetrack in North America on Long Island's Hempstead Plain.

In June 1665 Nicolls formally confirmed the right of the residents of New York City to govern themselves "according to the custom of England in other [of] his Majesty's corporations," changing the offices of burgomaster, *schout*, and *schepen* to mayor, alderman, and sheriff, respectively. Nicolls also filled the new municipal administration with men who wouldn't be offensive to the Dutch. A majority of the aldermen was Dutch, and the first mayor, Thomas Willett, was an English merchant who had lived in New Netherland for years and become friendly with former director Stuyvesant. The first sheriff, Allard Anthony, had also lived among the Dutch for years and served Stuyvesant as *schout*. A few years later, New York even got a Dutch mayor, Cornelis Steenwyck. Nicholas Bayard, Stuyvesant's nephew and Steenwyck's sometime business partner, held a number of lucrative municipal posts too.

Well-to-do Dutch New Yorkers, pragmatic men and women, began to admit that New Netherland might be gone for good. As Jeremias Van Rensselaer said, "it has pleased the Lord that we must learn English." In the years that followed, more and more people of his class and connections likewise began to "anglicize"—speaking English, reading English books, observing English holidays, and allowing their sons and daughters to marry into English families.

When the duke called Nicolls back to England in 1668, New York's most prominent citizens gave him a sumptuous farewell dinner, then escorted him to his ship with a grand procession that included two brand-new militia companies, the first reorganization of the city's burgher guard since the conquest. If Stuyvesant attended the festivities, he must have marveled at how positively amiable the burghers had become since forcing him to hand over the city four years earlier.

Colonel Francis Lovelace, Nicolls's successor, proved equally solicitous. To stimulate trade, he slashed import duties by 30 percent and named as customs collector a Dutchman who immediately threw out most port regulations. By fiat, Lovelace gave city merchants a monopoly of the Hudson River carrying trade and ordered Long Island farmers, even those for whom New England markets were more convenient, to ship all their surplus produce through Manhattan. He fixed grain prices to benefit exporters and required that hogs must be brought to the city for slaughter, a boon to local butchers and coopers.

To improve the flow of news, Lovelace arranged monthly mail deliveries between the city and Boston, the first regular postal service in any of the colonies. Near the present intersection of Pearl, Broad, and Bridge streets, where a small bridge crossed the town's canal and merchants liked to gather for business, he established the city's first mercantile exchange, complete with a bell and a drop-box for transatlantic mail. Communication with England remained maddeningly unpredictable, even so; Lovelace complained that it could be counted on to occur, like the reproduction of elephants, no more than once every two years.

Besides continuing the horse races on Hempstead Plain, Lovelace strengthened the proprietary's ties with influential Dutch New Yorkers by organizing one of the town's earliest social clubs. Once or twice a week its sixteen members—ten Dutch, six English—gathered at one another's houses to discuss matters of common concern and drink punch from silver tankards. "I find some of these people have the breeding of courts," Lovelace later told the king. He didn't mention that he'd become involved in extensive private dealings with a number of the very same people, including Cornelis Steenwyck. Nor did he reveal that, at his own expense, he'd built a tavern right next to the old Stadhuis, now called City Hall, and equipped it with a connecting door that opened directly into the chambers of the municipal court, a convenience for which it may be supposed the magistrates were often grateful.

By the early 1670s, thanks in no small measure to the attentions of Nicolls and Lovelace, New York's economy was showing signs of life again, and people with names like Van Rensselaer, Schuyler, Van Cortlandt, and Beekman were both richer and more securely in control of the town than ever. Former mayor Steenwyck, reportedly Manhattan's wealthiest resident, had just built an opulent house on the corner of Bridge and Whitehall streets that would become famous for its Russia-leather chairs, French cabinets, oils by old Antwerp masters, statuary, and other luxuries.

The rewards of collaboration with the English shone even more brilliantly, perhaps, in the career of Margaret Hardenbroeck. She had first come to New York in 1659 as the agent for an Amsterdam merchant and soon after her arrival married a local trader named Rudolphus de Vries. De Vries dealt in such diverse commodities as lumber, bricks, sugar, furniture, tobacco, and wine. He also owned quite a bit of land and was one of a group of investors who in 1660 established the village of Bergen, just across the Hudson from New Amsterdam. After his death in 1661, Hardenbroeck inherited his various interests and went into business for herself, becoming one of New Amsterdam's richest citizens, known throughout the province for her "miserable covetousness" and "terrible parsimony."

In 1662 Hardenbroeck married a former West India Company carpenter, now turned trader, named Frederick Vlypse (also spelled Flipsen or Flypsen), with whom she formed a highly profitable partnership. They were among the merchants who pressured Stuyvesant not to oppose the English invasion, and in its aftermath they became intimates of Nicolls and Lovelace, a connection that earned them valuable privileges and exemptions from English trade regulations. In time they owned all or part of fifteen vessels that ranged from Albany to Europe to Virginia to the West Indies with cargoes of furs, lumber, tobacco, hides, and wine. One of Hardenbroeck's ships was the *King Charles*, and another, partly owned by Governor Lovelace and Cornelis Steenwyck, was the *Duke of York*—a choice of names that suggests the lengths she would go to flatter authority.

Ten years after the conquest, Hardenbroeck and Vlypse had amassed an empire that included, besides ships and goods, extensive real estate holdings throughout the lower Hudson Valley and a plantation in Barbados; Vlypse himself was a moneylender, wampum manufacturer, land speculator, and mill owner as well. It was around this time, too, that he changed his name to the more English-sounding Philipse.

DISSIDENTS

Steenwyck, Philipse, Hardenbroeck, and others of their ilk thought the transition from Dutch to English government was going well. Others didn't, the duke of York among them. He worried that trade with England failed to develop as rapidly as his bookkeepers would have liked. No more than a few English merchantmen were ever in the harbor at once, and in the entire decade following the conquest, only five are known to have made a direct voyage from England to Manhattan.

Some of this was the duke's own fault. He never actually set foot in New York and, like the West India Company, didn't always put a high priority on its interests. In 1665, for example, he impulsively gave all of the colony between the Hudson and Delaware rivers to two old Civil War cronies, John Lord Berkeley and Sir George Carteret. They called it New Jersey and began handing out land to prospective settlers. No one informed Nicolls, however, and he had been doling out the same land on his authority as governor of New York. The ensuing legal confusion crippled the development of New Jersey for years. What was more, by removing the west bank of the Hudson from New York's jurisdiction, the duke foolishly divided an economic whole into political parts.

Communities to the north and east of Manhattan had other reasons to be dissatisfied with the transition from Dutch to English rule. One of Nicolls's first decisions after the conquest had been to incorporate Long Island, Staten Island, and Westchester into an English-style county named (inevitably) Yorkshire. Its inhabitants assumed that he intended to set up the self-contained, nearly autonomous, English-style local governments for which they had been clamoring over the previous two decades. But at a special meeting in Hempstead in 1665—attended by delegates from thirteen English and four Dutch towns as well as from Westchester—Nicolls promulgated a code of laws for Yorkshire that granted nothing of the kind.

The Duke's Laws, as they came to be known, made no provision for freemanship (i.e., the right to a voice in town affairs) or for representative government on the provincial level. The code obliged townsfolk to submit to new land surveys and registration fees, to pay taxes they didn't consent to, and to practice religious toleration. Obviously, Nicolls admitted, this was "not contrived so Democratically" as the codes of other colonies: his goal had been to "revive the Memory of old England amongst us" and establish the "foundation of Kingly Government in these parts, so farre as is possible, which truely is grievous to some Republicans." The disappointed Long Island towns were indeed crawling with Stuart-hating commonwealthmen, and their staunch opposition to the Duke's Laws, sometimes spilling over into violence against justices of the peace and tax collectors, caused the proprietary government no end of trouble. As the representative of one of the greatest landowners in the realm in an age of rural insurrection, Nicolls found it all too familiar. "The Late Rebellion in England, with all ye ill consequences thereof, began with the selfe same steps and pr'tences," he grumbled.

The largest group of malcontents were New York's five or six thousand Dutch inhabitants, who together constituted almost 70 percent of the population of the colony and as much as 75 or 80 percent of the population of the city. One of their continuing grievances was the conduct of what Stuyvesant called the "dissolute English Soldiery."

Maria Abeel Duyckinck (1666-1738), portrait by her husband, Gerrit Duyckinck, c. 1700. Mrs. Duyckinck, who inherited large tracts of real estate around Albany as well as on Manhattan, was one of the many second- and third-generation Dutch residents of New York who did not eagerly accommodate themselves to English rule. (© Collection of The New-York Historical Society)

Nicolls had had to quarter many soldiers in Dutch households, and their lack of regard for persons or property was a source of frequent conflict. Wherever there were garrisons or posts—in New York City, in Albany, in Kingston—hard words, fisticuffs, and rioting between troops and citizens were endemic.

The major targets of Dutch resentment, however, were the men and women of their own nation who had collaborated with the English. Merchants like Steenwyck and Hardenbroeck were particularly despised for their prosperity and arrogance. Within the Reformed church, anti-English factions regarded Megapolensis and the other dominies as little better than English flunkies because of their friendship with Nicolls and Lovelace. When some congregations attempted to withhold the dominies' salaries as punishment, their English patrons had them paid out of public tax monies instead— which only made the dominies more odious still in the eyes of their parishioners.

NEW ORANGE

Stung by his failure to defeat the Netherlands in the second Anglo–Dutch War, Charles II had begun preparations for a third. In 1670 he signed a secret accord with Louis XIV of France that committed both nations to combine forces against the Dutch. All he lacked was a plausible excuse to open hostilities, and that came in the spring of 1672, when English and Dutch naval forces clashed in the Channel. Within days, both England and France had declared war. Rallied by the young Prince William of Orange, the Dutch fought back (one of their first victims was Colonel Richard Nicolls, felled by a Dutch cannonball as he stood next to the duke of York on the deck of an English warship). Before the year was out, they had dispatched a heavily armed squadron to raid English and French possessions in America.

In the spring of 1673, led by Admiral Cornelis Evertsen—whose derring-do on the high seas had earned him the nickname of "Kees the Devil"—the Dutch squadron attacked British possessions in the Caribbean, seizing a fortune in sugar and slaves. Evertsen then headed for Virginia and Maryland. In midsummer he entered the Chesapeake, capturing or destroying numerous English ships and making off with thousands of hogsheads of tobacco. His next target was New York.

At the end of July 1673 the Dutch squadron dropped anchor off Sandy Hook just below the Narrows. Some Dutch farmers from New Utrecht made their way out to Evertsen's flagship to complain "about the hard rule of the English." They also said that Governor Lovelace was away on business in Connecticut, that Fort James was in no condition to repel an invasion, and that the town would welcome the Dutch. Evertsen decided to attack.

On the twentieth, while Dutch saboteurs spiked the guns on the East River shore near City Hall, Evertsen brought his frigates within range of the fort and ordered its temporary commander, Captain John Manning, to surrender. "We have come to bring the country back under obedience to their High Mightinesses the Lords States General," he announced. When Manning stalled, Evertsen bombarded the fort and landed Captain Anthony Colve with six hundred marines on the Hudson shore near the present site of Trinity Church. Cheered on by "demonstrations of joy" among the Dutch populace, Colve and his marines advanced down Broadway and took possession of the fort without firing a shot. With "enemy in our Bowells," Manning glumly explained, resistance was impossible. Evertsen promptly renamed the city New Orange in honor of

New Amsterdam formerly called New York, 1673, issued shortly after the Dutch reoccupation. Note the soldiers marching along the waterfront. (I. N. Phelps Stokes Collection. Miriam and Ira D. Wallach Division of Art, Prints and Photographs. The New York Public Library. Astor, Lenox and Tilden Foundations)

Prince William. He also declared that the entire colony would again be known as New Netherland and designated Captain Colve its governor-general.

Evertsen sailed off in September to attack Newfoundland, leaving Colve to continue the work of restoring Dutch control—with the assistance of prominent men like Cornelis Steenwyck and Nicholas Bayard, whose patriotism seems to have overcome their close ties to the English. He restored the old Dutch forms of government, administered oaths of loyalty, collected taxes, strengthened the city's defenses against an expected counterattack, and faced down the English villages of Long Island. For good measure, he confiscated the property of leading English officials and merchants; when Lovelace foolishly returned to town, Colve clapped him in jail on the complaint of some Dutch merchants who said he owed them money, then shipped him back to England. There the duke cashiered him for incompetence and Charles II threw him into the Tower.

But New Orange was a chimera. The Dutch were growing weary of the war—their forces had done well at sea, but French troops occupied four of their seven provinces—and defending New Netherland was certain to require more money and resources than they could afford. (New Orange authorities had in fact warned the States-General that the colony couldn't survive without prompt and substantial help.) The States-General asked for peace and offered to return all conquered territories, including New Netherland. Charles II, himself nearly bankrupt and under intense pressure from Parliament to recover the colony, agreed. A formal treaty of peace was signed in February 1674.

When rumors of the sellout reached Manhattan several months later, the Dutch were incredulous. Some, in "a distracted rage and passion," hurled "curses and execrations" at the States-General, demanded a chance to fight, and vowed to "slay the English Doggs"; others vowed "to fyre the Town, Pluck downe the ffortifications [and] teare out the Governours throats, who had compelled them to slave soe contrary to their priveledges." A small number packed their belongings and struck out for Dutch Surinam, while a few went back to the Netherlands with Colve, who officially surrendered the city in October. Jeremias Van Rensselaer, always the pragmatist, resolved to make the best of it. "Well, if it has to be," he shrugged, "we commend the matter to God, who knows what is best for us." He added, almost as an aside: "We didn't count on such a blow, God knows."

ANDROS

Although angered by their enthusiasm for New Orange, the duke of York rejected suggestions that his Dutch subjects be relocated to the Albany area or expelled altogether. He did, however, obtain a new charter that enlarged his already considerable powers as proprietor. He also dispatched a new governor in the person of Major Edmund Andros, a thirty-eight-year-old royalist soldier and aristocrat, highly regarded by the king and recommended by extensive experience in the West Indies and the Netherlands (where he had learned to speak fluent Dutch).

Andros was instructed to be firm but forgiving toward the Dutch and to reestablish the proprietary's ties with the principal Dutch merchants, landowners, and clergymen. Accordingly, Andros promised Colve that the Dutch needn't fear for their property, that they could continue to enjoy perfect freedom of religion, and that they would never be asked to fight against the States-General—basically the same guarantees written ten years earlier into the Articles of Capitulation.

Andros soon came to terms with the same group of collaborators that had surrounded Nicolls and Lovelace (except Cornelis Steenwyck, with whom he never got along). Frederick Philipse, Steven Van Cortlandt, William Beekman, Nicholas Bayard, Johannes de Peyster—they and a handful of other men, many already linked together by business and marriage, willingly served Andros as councillors, mayors, aldermen, and other officials. He in turn spent much of the next six years transforming New York into a more efficient and more profitable commercial emporium.

Conscious that New York's economy depended more and more on the export of foodstuffs to Barbados and other plantation colonies of the West Indies—the fur trade had by now dwindled to one-fifth of its peak in the mid-1650s—Andros took steps to protect city merchants from competition. Ignoring cries of outrage from Albany and elsewhere, he ordered that all goods imported into the colony pass through New York

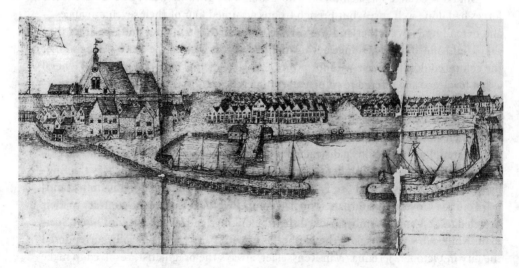

New York from Brooklyn Heights, 1679. Drawn by the Labadist missionary Jaspar Danckaerts, its most conspicuous features are the recently completed Great Dock or mole and the new stone pier. (I. N. Phelps Stokes Collection. Miriam and Ira D. Wallach Division of Art, Prints and Photographs. The New York Public Library. Astor, Lenox and Tilden Foundations)

City. He then designated it the only place in the colony where cargoes could be loaded for export. He decreed that no one outside the city could bolt (sift) flour or pack wheat, beef, or pork for export, and he appointed a small force of inspectors to see that the city's reputation in foreign markets wouldn't be injured by inferior goods. After 1680 its merchants enjoyed a virtual stranglehold on the trade of the entire colony. Of course what was good for them tended to be good, in turn, for millers, bakers, coopers, rope-makers, sailmakers, carpenters, and smiths.

Andros gave particular attention to improving the waterfront. In 1675 residents along the Heere Gracht were ordered to fill in the old Dutch canal level with the street and "then to pave & pitch the Same before there dores with stones." The foul inlet, reincarnated as what is now Broad Street, was destined to be the city's principal commercial street well into the next century. Near where the bridge had crossed the canal, Andros erected a new mercantile exchange and covered market, the city's first. At the foot of Broad Street he built a new stone pier into the East River. On either side of the pier he constructed a massive stone and timber mole, or breakwater, that arced out in two great semicircles from the foot of Whitehall Street and City Hall. Known as the Great Dock, it provided secure anchorage for cargo ships plying the West Indian trade.

And Andros didn't stop with the waterfront. Because the supply of water for fighting fires had been reduced by filling in the canal, he ordered the digging of six new wells (the brackish water brought up by buckets proved unfit for drinking, however). He moved malodorous tanneries and slaughterhouses to locations outside the city gates. He fixed up Fort James, ransacked by departing Dutch troops, and designated "the Plaine afore the Forte"—now Bowling Green—as the site of an annual fair for the display and sale of "all graine, Cattle, or other produce of the Country." He made much-needed repairs to the city wall and ensured that its gates were closed every night by nine o'clock. When the city's twenty-three coopers banded together to fix a uniform rate for casks and barrels, Andros had them prosecuted and fined for violating the law against illegal combinations. Those employed by the city were fired.

When Long Island farmers and stockmen raised the familiar complaint that they had been enslaved to the mercantile interests of the city, Andros likewise told them to pay up or leave the province. He also advised York that it might be a good idea to set up some kind of representative assembly so they could tax themselves. And when New England governments responded sympathetically to appeals for help from the English towns on the eastern end of Long Island, as they had done so often before, Andros warned them off so convincingly that New York's jurisdiction over the entire island would never again be called into question.

It was under Andros, too, that municipal authorities forged stronger ties with local cartmen, whose one-horse wagons were the principal means of transporting commodities into and around town. In 1667 the cartmen had formed a "fellowship" or guild and contracted with the city to work at fixed rates. In return for this privilege, the magistrates required them to perform "public work as desired"—picking up rubbish from the streets, fighting fires, maintaining roads, repairing the fort, and transporting felons to the gallows. Slaves and free blacks were later prohibited from operating carts in town—a measure that gave the cartmen relief from a troublesome source of competition but also further reduced their independence and hastened their transformation into semi-official municipal employees.

THE COVENANT CHAIN

Andros had been in New York less than a year when the Algonkian-speaking peoples of English America rose up in a last, desperate attempt to stem the advance of white settlement. Perhaps the greatest Indian war in American history, it produced political and social revolution in the Chesapeake colonies and such devastation in New England (where it was known as Metacom's or King Philip's War) that complete recovery, economic and demographic, would take a generation.

While his New England and Chesapeake counterparts dithered, Andros acted decisively. He disarmed Long Island Indians, cut off their communication with insurgents on the New England side of the Sound, drilled town militias, and saw to the construction of fortifications. He ordered Westchester Indians to move closer to the city, where they could be kept under constant observation. He summoned sachems of the Hackensacks and other New Jersey Indians to Fort James, making them swear allegiance to the crown and requiring hostages from each to guarantee their compliance.

Andros's shrewdest stroke was to open talks with the Five Nations of the Iroquois, ancient enemies of the Algonkian peoples who were embarked on a course of imperial expansion not unlike that of the English. Armed with Dutch weapons, they had previously attacked and all but annihilated their Huron rivals to the north; by the early 1660s their power stretched from the Carolinas to Hudson's Bay.

Between 1675 and 1677 Andros and the Iroquois forged the so-called Covenant Chain, an alliance of English and Iroquois ambitions that would decisively influence the future of New York City. Its terms were simple. Andros agreed to support Iroquois domination of the coastal Algonkians, while the Iroquois agreed to attack Algonkian insurgents in New England; both agreed to make common cause against the French in Canada, and both agreed to respect what would later be called spheres of influence, English to the east, Iroquois to the west.

Early in 1676 Mohawk war parties crossed over from New York to Connecticut and destroyed a major Algonkian encampment. By that summer the uprising had collapsed. The negotiations that followed, adroitly managed by Andros, brought peace to the colonies and ensured the safety of settlements all the way to the Appalachians. The duke's province came through unharmed. What was more, New York City had become one pole of an Anglo-Iroquoian axis around which the affairs of North America south of Canada and east of the Mississippi would turn for another century. A grateful Charles II rewarded Andros with a knighthood.

For the Lenapes of the lower Hudson Valley, by contrast, the Covenant Chain was a confirmation of their impotence and irrelevance. Jaspar Danckaerts, a Labadist missionary who visited New York several years later, was one of the last Europeans to study its original inhabitants in anything like their original setting, and the observations he recorded in his diary—by turns embarrassed, angry, and despondent—depict a people thoroughly ruined by contact with Europeans. So few were left, Danckaerts wrote, that they would soon "melt away and disappear" from the face of the earth. "I have heard tell by the oldest New Netherlanders," he noted, "that there is now not 1/10th part of the Indians there once were, indeed, not 1/20th or 1/30th; and that now the Europeans are 20 and 30 times as many." Legend has it that the last of the Lenapes—known as Jim de Wilt or Jim the Wild Man—died in Canarsie in 1803.

NEW YORK IN 1680

To a casual observer, it might have appeared that Andros had made little headway against the Dutchness of New York. By 1680 the bulk of its four-hundred-odd buildings, even the fine new residences of anglicized families like the Steenwycks, Van Cortlandts, and Philipses, were still built in the Dutch style: high stoops, stepped-gable end to the street, roofs sheathed with the same red and black tiles that graced houses in Holland. The twin peaks of the Reformed church still poked above the ramparts of the fort, Stuyvesant's former Great House (now White Hall) still commanded the East River shore, the great stone warehouse built by the West India Company still stood on Pearl Street, and the old Stadhuis still served as City Hall. Dutch was still the language of the streets and markets, and Dutch culture was still everywhere in evidence. During the winter of 1678, his first on Manhattan, the Rev. Charles Wolley marveled at the quintessentially Dutch spectacle of "Men and Women as it were flying upon their Skates from place to place, with Markets upon their Heads and Backs."

But New York was hardly the same place it had been in 1664, or even 1674. It had many more people—around three thousand of them, give or take a few hundred (another sixty-six hundred or so were scattered across Long Island and up the Hudson). The ethnic balance was shifting as well. Immigration from the Netherlands had fallen off sharply, and by 1680 about half of the Dutch inhabitants who witnessed Stuyvesant's surrender had either died or moved away. During the later 1660s and early 1670s, meanwhile, affluent English merchants had come to Manhattan in pursuit of economic opportunities. Some, like John Darvall, arrived via Boston or other North American seaports. John Lawrence moved in from Long Island, and Robert Livingston came over from Scotland. Still others came up from the West Indies, most notably a rich Barbadian planter named Lewis Morris. By 1670 or so Morris and his brother Richard had established themselves in New York as importers of sugar and flour. They began buying property in and around the city, including a town house on Bridge Street next door to their friend and sometimes business associate, former mayor Cornelis Steenwyck. Another of the colonel's purchases was the five-hundred-acre Westchester estate once owned by Jonas Bronck; he promptly renamed it Morrisania. The influx of English merchants quickened after 1674, as London mercantile houses began for the first time to take an active interest in the New York market. By 1680, although the English still accounted for under 20 percent of New York's overall population, they represented nearly 40 percent of the town's *taxable* population. Of the forty-eight merchants with estates worth over five hundred pounds, twenty-two were English.

Thanks to these newcomers, New York's trade improved markedly. After six years in office, Andros reported that the volume of New York's shipping was "at least ten times" higher than when he arrived. Ten to fifteen vessels now came across the Atlantic every year with cargoes worth in excess of fifty thousand pounds, and by 1684 some eighty ships and boats were owned in the port itself, including three barks, three brigs, and twenty-six sloops. It exported sixty thousand bushels of wheat annually, along with furs, meats, peas, horses, lumber, and fish—more and more of it to the plantation economies of the West Indies.

This expansion meant not only that New York now had "plenty of money," as Andros put it, but that the city's merchants were getting a bigger share of its wealth. In

1664 the merchants who comprised the richest 10 percent of New York taxpayers had accounted for 26 percent of its assessed wealth. A dozen or so years later, the richest 10 percent of the city's 313 taxpayers—some thirty merchants—held 51 percent of its assessed wealth; the richest 15 percent—fewer than fifty merchants—owned fully 65 percent, the richest five individuals alone accounting for some 40 percent. At a time when a merchant worth a thousand to fifteen hundred pounds was "a good substantial merchant," according to Andros, the wealthiest of them all, Frederick Philipse (who possessed "whole hogsheads of Indian money or wampum" according to Wolley) was assessed at thirteen thousand pounds, about 14 percent of the city's total. Cornelis Steenwyck, now the second-richest man in New York, was assessed at four thousand pounds.

Between 1664 and 1676, by contrast, the assessed wealth of New York's hundred-odd poorest taxpayers declined from 6.6 to 5.9 percent of the total. The assessments of the hundred or so just above them plunged from 23.1 percent to 10.4 percent. Many other inhabitants of the city—casual laborers, apprentices, small craftsmen—were simply too poor to be assessed at all. Still worse off were the city's four or five hundred slaves, perhaps half again as many as had been present at the time of the English conquest, crowded into garrets, cellars, and outbuildings.

Pockets of poverty now dotted the urban landscape, throwing the prosperity and comfortable residences of the possessing classes into sharper relief. The city's predominately Dutch carters, who ranked among its poorest taxpayers, lived in shabby dwellings along a back alley called Smith's Street Lane, not far from the Dutch Reformed church. Shoemakers congregated along Broad Street until Andros banished their tanning pits to the outskirts of town, but a handful of streets crossing Broad—Beaver, Marketfield, Mill—continued to have a disproportionately large share of poor taxpayers. So did places like Smith's Valley (or Vly), which lay on the East River between Wall and Maiden Lane, and along the roads and trails that led to villages still further to the north. In 1679, when Jaspar Danckaerts visited Stuyvesant's bouwerie, he passed "many habitations of negroes, mulattoes and whites" who had simply "settled themselves down where they have thought proper" and cultivated "ground enough to live on with their families." In the following decade, however, a number of free black families would sell or abandon their Manhattan holdings and move to more secluded corners of New Jersey and Pennsylvania.

A comparable gap was opening up between the wealth of the city and that of the fishing and farming towns of the Long Island hinterland. Southampton, the most prosperous, was assessed at a total of thirteen thousand pounds—barely more than Frederick Philipse alone. The combined assessments of Brooklyn, Bushwyck, Flatbush, Flatlands, and New Utrecht—the five Dutch towns on the western end of the island—were calculated to be only half that much. Not surprisingly, the towns believed they were oppressed and exploited by the merchants on Manhattan, where the law required them to market their produce. What was more, as population growth and the practice of partible inheritance combined to reduce the size of individual farms, many of their residents were beginning to move elsewhere in search of arable land.

STANDING MORE ON NATURE THAN NAMES

These transformations sharpened the discontent of those Dutch craftsmen, farmers, and small traders who had declined to embrace English ways or ingratiate themselves with their English rulers. After the collapse of New Orange in 1674, they grew more determined than ever to maintain their distinctiveness as a nation, for in an age of conflict and upheaval, who could say they would never again be delivered from captivity?

One index of Dutch intransigence was their low rate of intermarriage with other national groups. In New York City, only one Dutch woman in six married a man who wasn't Dutch. Dutch men almost never married non-Dutch women; those in Flatbush, for example, were known to range as far as the Dutch villages of New Jersey and the upper Hudson Valley in search of wives. With the passage of time, this pattern of behavior ensured that Dutch families and communities everywhere in New York would be closely linked by kinship networks. These guaranteed that the essentials of communal life—the preservation of order, the settlement of disputes, the care of widows and orphans and the needy—could be handled quietly and smoothly without recourse to external (that is, English) authority.

The intensity of Dutch resistance to assimilation was also demonstrated by their loyalty to Holland's Roman-Dutch legal tradition. With the resumption of proprietary authority in 1674, the use of Dutch was no longer permitted in New York courts. But Dutch New Yorkers showed little inclination to accept the English notion of a common law or to yield to the unfamiliar procedures of English courts (Dutch courts relied on arbitrators and referees rather than juries). Instead they effectively boycotted the English judicial system for the resolution of commercial as well as private disagreements, often appealing instead to the consistory of the Reformed Church. Dutch residents of New York City rarely sued one another after 1674.

Even more telling was their aversion to the patriarchalism that dominated English attitudes toward property, inheritance, and gender. English practice stressed the descent of both realty (land, buildings) as well as personalty (clothing, household goods, livestock, cash) through the male line. Only in the absence of male heirs did females inherit real property, and their rights to personalty were sharply limited. When she married, a woman became *feme covert*—legally "covered" by her husband, who thereafter represented her interests. She took his name; he took control of the real and/or personal property she possessed, subject only to the restriction that he couldn't sell or bequeath her realty. If he died before her, she was entitled as a rule to a "dower right"— the use of or rent from one-third of the real property belonging to his estate (including what she had brought to the marriage). The balance of his estate would be divided between their children and his kin, with real property going to males whenever possible. If she died before him, on the other hand, he kept everything until his death, at which time it passed to their children.

In defiance of the conqueror's laws, Dutch women continued to use their own surnames rather than their husbands'; some went on doing business in their own names. Dutch husbands and wives still employed the Roman-Dutch mutual or joint wills that kept their common property intact if either one died. Dutch children, daughters as well as sons, still inherited equal portions of the family estate, but only after both parents had died. It "was the manner amongst them," the Rev. Charles Wolley wrote in his journal, that they preferred "standing more on Nature than Names; that as the root communicates itself to all its branches, so should the Parent to all his offspring which are the Olive branches about his Table." This proved increasingly difficult in the country villages outside New York City, where farms couldn't be subdivided indefinitely, and some rural Dutch families did attempt to keep the land in the hands of one son—on condition that he provided his brothers with property elsewhere, and his sisters with tools, animals, furniture, kitchen equipment, and the like. Often, though, it was the youngest who kept the farm, because his older brothers had already moved away. Flatbush and other Long Island towns routinely dispatched expeditions to find land for young men who needed it. In 1677, for example, several dozen residents of Flatbush obtained a patent to settle the eastern part of the town, called the New Lots; another group moved en masse to new settlements on the Raritan and Milstone rivers in New Jersey.

Not every Dutch New Yorker clung to the old ways. One who didn't was Frederick Philipse, Margaret Hardenbroeck's husband and by far the richest man in the colony. In his will he would convey his vast holdings in Westchester and New York City to his sons and their male heirs, all of whom he expressly prohibited from breaking up or selling the property. His daughters would inherit no land at all unless both of their brothers died without male issue. No olive branches about the table for Philipse, then: his was an English landlord's dream of the future—great estates handed down from first-born son to first-born son, unbroken, generation after generation.

It wasn't the Dutch who put an end to Andros's career in New York, however, but rather the town's new crop of English merchants. They criticized his partiality toward prominent Dutch traders and accused him of one crime after another—violating the Navigation Acts, taking bribes, extortion, obstructing trade, and pocketing the colony's taxes. He in turn excluded them from public office, harassed them with legal proceedings, and threw one or two into jail without trial. In the summer of 1680, bowing to pressure from the merchants' connections in London—a clear signal of where the fulcrum of New York's destinies now stood—the duke summoned Andros home pending an investigation of the charges against him. Captain Anthony Brockholls of the Albany garrison tried to maintain order pending the arrival of a new governor, but the victorious merchants, now joined by the English towns of Long Island, declared a tax strike that made a shambles of the colony's affairs for the next year or two. Frustrated and running out of money, the duke talked of selling the place to anyone who would make him a reasonable offer. His friend William Penn, whose own colony was just getting underway on the banks of the Schuylkill, urged him to hang on a while longer.

7

Jacob Leisler's Rebellion

Andros was acquitted of the charges that prompted his recall, but he lost his job anyway. In 1683 the duke replaced him with Colonel Thomas Dongan, the fourth royalist veteran of the Civil Wars to be sent to govern New York. Dongan was also an Irish Catholic landlord, the younger brother of Irish peer Baron Dongan (soon to be earl of Limerick), and an experienced imperial functionary who had previously served as the military governor of Tangier. Manhattan's Anglo-Dutch oligarchs liked him at once. They admired his "knowledge, refinement, and modesty," as Dominie Selyns put it. They were also grateful that although he gave a majority of the seats on his council to prominent English residents, he had the tact and good sense to seek the advice of leading Dutch merchants like Philipse, Van Cortlandt, and Steenwyck (the latter of whom Dongan appointed as mayor). Above all, they appreciated his readiness to give them the freedom to manage local affairs more or less as they saw fit.

THE REORGANIZATION OF GOVERNMENT

Dongan launched his administration by calling for elections to the first representative assembly in the colony's sixty-year history. The Assembly's eighteen delegates met at Fort James for three weeks in October 1683. Their main accomplishment was to draft a "Charter of Libertyes and Privileges."

The charter defined the form of government for the colony (governor, governor's council, assembly), recognized basic political and personal rights (trial by jury, no taxation without representation), and affirmed religious liberty (for Christians). It divided the colony into twelve "shires" or counties: New York (all of Manhattan), Kings (now Brooklyn, including the Dutch towns of western Long Island), Queens (the English towns of western Long Island), Richmond (Staten Island), Suffolk (the eastern remainder of Long Island), and seven others. As in England, these were to be the fundamental units of local government. Each had its justices of the peace, collectively known as the County Court, plus a county clerk, high sheriff, and militia officers—all appointed by the governor. Each was also an election district whose freeholders were empowered to elect representatives to the Assembly (although the definition of a "freeholder" was left rather vague).

The Assembly wound up its work by awarding Dongan a "free and voluntary" cash gift for his good will. Obligingly, he proclaimed the Charter of Libertyes aloud at City Hall—the townspeople "having notice by sound of Trumpet"—and passed it along to York for final approval.

At the behest of Mayor Steenwyck and the aldermen, the ever cooperative Dongan then issued a new charter for the government of New York City. "Dongan's Charter," as it came to be known, made New York City a self-governing corporation, one of only a dozen-odd communities ever incorporated in English America. It divided the city into five inner wards (South, Dock, East, West, and North) plus an Out Ward comprising the remainder of Manhattan. Every year each ward's "inhabitants" were to elect assessors, a constable, an alderman, and an assistant, the latter two of whom served as delegates to the Common Council. The mayor, who presided over the council, would continue to be selected by the governor, as would the recorder, sheriff, coroner, and clerk.

With Dongan wielding his appointive powers on their behalf, the Anglo-Dutch oligarchy easily gained control over both provincial and municipal governments. They lost no time deploying their new powers for a wide range of purposes—straightening out public finances, establishing courts of justice, repairing municipal facilities, fixing the qualifications of physicians and surgeons, providing relief for the poor, standardizing marriage procedures, and, not the least, regulating city land sales in their favor.

THE GATHERING STORM

Dongan's amiable relations with the Anglo-Dutch oligarchy were clouded, however, by the baronial land grants with which he favored a select group of insiders. Seven of these grants were formally styled "manors," over which their "lords" received quasi-feudal legal and governmental powers subject only to the authority of the governor. The biggest, Rensselaerswyck Manor (an anglicized version of the old Dutch patroonship), encompassed 850,000 acres or better than eleven hundred square miles—fifty times the area of Manhattan. The Van Rensselaers' Lower Manor at Claverack added another 250,000 acres. Robert Livingston, the ambitious young Scot who had worked for the Van Rensselaers and linked himself by marriage to the Schuylers and Van Cortlandts, obtained Livingston Manor, some 160,000 acres in extent. Smaller grants went to James Lloyd (Lloyd's Neck Manor), John Palmer (Cassilton Manor), Christopher Billop (Bentley Manor), and Thomas Pell (Pelham Manor). Dongan also distributed a number of substantial nonmanorial patents, among them three separate patents for Frederick Philipse (fifty thousand acres in all) and one for Stephanus Van Cortlandt of several thousand acres.

The ostensible purpose of this largesse was to improve the colony's revenue while strengthening its defenses against the French and their Huron allies. Anglo-French competition in the Mississippi Valley had heated up during the 1670s and 1680s—La Salle, Marquette, Joliet, and other French explorers were scouting the interior of North America from Wisconsin to Louisiana in these years—and the danger of an invasion from Canada couldn't be ignored. (All the more so, Dongan thought, because the Albany Dutch couldn't be trusted to support the English in the event of war.)

None of this assuaged the wounded ambitions of men the governor overlooked while making free with the proprietor's real estate. Land, not money, was still the key to power and status in the English-speaking world: a rich man without estates was a man of limited influence—which explains why rich men on both sides of the Atlantic dreamed of acquiring land and moving into the ranks of the country gentry (or better yet, the titled nobility). It was galling indeed that Dongan gave so much to so few. And galling, too, that he didn't fail to help himself along the way. On Manhattan, he used dummy partners to lop off hefty slices of real estate along both sides of the city wall and drove a new road (now Park Row) diagonally through the town common from Broadway to the Bowery, appropriating a two-acre plot for his own use (and leaving a wedge-shaped remnant now occupied by City Hall Park). On Staten Island he acquired a twenty-five-thousand-acre tract that he named Castleton Manor after his estate in Ireland (its approximate location is marked by the modern Dongan Hills).

Resentment against the Charter of Libertyes was also brewing outside the oligarchy, among the colony's Dutch population. Only eight of the first Assembly's eighteen members had been Dutch, and the charter contained a string of provisions offensive to Dutch traditions and sensibilities—allowing a widow to remain in her house for only forty days after the death of her spouse and building primogeniture into the colony's law of intestate succession, among others. In 1684, the new Assembly adopted "An Act for Quieting of mens estates" that further affronted Dutch custom by denying a married woman the right to purchase land or conduct business in her own name. As for access to public office, most of the Dutchmen who found their way by election or appointment into the new city government were the same anglicized merchants who had collaborated with provincial officials for years; what was the likelihood that ordinary Dutchmen would be appointed to the new county offices in proportion to their numbers in the colony?

Working people, regardless of ethnic origin, didn't have much to gain from the new charter, either. Among the first acts of the new colonial and municipal governments were regulations for the stricter disciplining of unruly laborers, apprentices, servants, and slaves. The cartmen, still a virtually all-Dutch trade, received special attention. Early in 1684, when numerous merchants signed a petition complaining that city cartmen were "engrossing" firewood—going out of town to buy in quantity from suppliers, then returning to sell at inflated prices—the city council prohibited the cartmen from selling firewood themselves, then made them pay for inspectors to check the length and quality of all firewood sold in the city. Another measure forced the cartmen to drop whatever other work they were doing and make themselves available at the waterfront whenever shipments of perishable foodstuffs arrived. Dongan ordered each to make 104 deliveries to the fort every year, an average of two per week, without compensation. Outraged, the cartmen began the first transport strike in the city's history. The council declared them "Suspended and Discharged," then announced that "persons within this Citty have hereby free Lyberty and Lycence to Serve for Hyre or Wages as Carmen." After a week the strikers pleaded to return, but the council refused to rehire any until they had paid a fine and taken an oath to accept the new order of things.

Two additional circumstances sharpened dissatisfactions. One was the colony's faltering trade, mainly the result of competition from Philadelphia. Founded in 1682, only a year before Dongan arrived, William Penn's City of Brotherly Love had grown with alarming speed—by 1690 its population reached four thousand, already equal to or exceeding that of Manhattan—and its merchants were cutting deeply into New York's business with Chesapeake tobacco planters, New Jersey farmers, and the Iroquois of the upper Susquehanna. Nobody had a remedy as yet, least of all Dongan, but everyone, merchants and tradesmen and farmers alike, was worried.

Dongan's Catholicism rankled too. He'd come to New York in the company of several Jesuit priests and immediately celebrated Mass in Fort James, the first such occasion in the city's history. He also named Roman Catholics to strategic positions in his administration and authorized the Jesuits to open a Roman Catholic school. New York was a comparatively tolerant place and its residents didn't complain at first, not openly anyway. As Captain William Byrd of Virginia discovered while touring the city a couple of years later, the sheer diversity of its creeds had made the residents so forbearing that they "seem not concerned what religion their neighbor is of, or whether hee hath any or none." According to Dongan's own tally, there were "not many of the Church of England; few Roman Catholics; abundance of Quakers . . . Singing Quakers; Ranting Quakers; Sabbatarians; Anti-Sabbatarians, some Anabaptists, some Independents, some Jews; in short, of all sorts of opinions there are some, and the most part of none at all."

The problem was that the duke of York too now belonged to the Roman Catholic Church—and because his brother the king had failed as yet to sire a legitimate male heir, he stood next in line to the throne. Sending Dongan to New York had been only the latest of many signals that, in the event of his accession, the duke fully intended to restore Catholics to positions of power and influence from which they had been excluded by 150 years of Protestant supremacy. Horrified by this prospect, a parliamentary faction known as the Whigs was maneuvering to exclude the duke from the succession, put a Protestant on the throne, and curb the power of the monarchy. Anti-Catholic hysteria swept the country, aided and abetted by intriguers like Titus Oates, who in 1678 claimed to have uncovered a "Popish Plot" to assassinate Charles II and hasten the duke's accession. In the spring of 1683, just as Governor Dongan left for New York, Protestant fanatics were foiled in an attempt to murder both the king and the duke.

The failure of the so-called Rye House Plot gave the crown and its allies in Parliament, known as Tories, an excuse to crack down on the Whigs. Two of their leaders, Lord Russell and Algernon Sidney, were executed for complicity in the scheme; a third, the earl of Shaftsbury, friend and patron of John Locke, was driven into exile in the Netherlands. At the same time, crown lawyers attacked the chartered corporations and colonies that served as bases of Whig power outside Parliament. When the duke's advisers laid the Charter of Libertyes before him at the end of that same year, he had second thoughts.

Then, in February 1685, Charles II died and the duke of York became King James II. New York was now a royal colony, meaning that the governor, the council, and all other appointive officials would henceforth be named by the crown. Other changes were on the way as well. Shortly after his ascension, James II and the Lords of Trade created the Dominion of New England, a super-colony incorporating all of New England plus New York, New Jersey, and Pennsylvania. New York's Charter of Libertyes was disallowed, and with it the provincial legislature. Although the city's new charter survived royal scrutiny, Manhattan's affairs and fortunes were now inextricably married to those of King James.

The king's subjects in New York were struggling to make sense of these events when they learned, only months later, that Louis XIV had revoked the Edict of Nantes and unleashed a hurricane of official brutality against French Protestants. Thousands of Huguenots, as they were known, fled the country to England, Switzerland, the Netherlands, and America. A small number of them arrived in New York as early as 1686. By 1688 there were two hundred Huguenot families in the city, and they had erected a house of worship, the Eglise du Saint Esprit (originally the Eglise des Réfugiés Français à la Nouvelle York), on Petticoat Lane (Marketfield Street). Its congregation included Jays, De Lanceys, Boudinots, and other well-to-do merchants and shipbuilders known for their extensive business connections throughout Europe and their visceral hatred of Roman Catholicism. Not surprisingly, on hearing that the new English king had congratulated Louis for his diligence in persecuting them, New York's Huguenots—along with the great majority of the city's other Protestants—began to see the outlines of a deep-laid conspiracy, international in scope, against everything they held dear. After 1687, when James II suspended by royal decree all anti-Catholic legislation in England, they were sure of it.

A GLORIOUS REVOLUTION

In August 1688 Sir Edmund Andros returned to New York. He was now governor of the new Dominion of New England, and for the past year or so he had been up in Boston, its capital, bringing one colony after another under its authority. Now it was New York's turn to submit. Andros removed Dongan from office, broke the provincial seal, hoisted the flag of New England over the fort, and seized all the provincial records. He then returned to Boston, taking the records with him and leaving Colonel Francis Nicholson behind as lieutenant governor. Nicholson, though not a Roman Catholic like Dongan, was no less ardently devoted to the Stuart cause. He was also a passionate admirer of French culture and French political institutions.

The succession crisis in England was meanwhile coming to a head. What had held the Whigs in check thus far was the fact that James II, having no male heir, would in time be succeeded by one or the other of his two daughters, both of whom had remained Protestants. The elder of the two, Mary, was the wife of none other than Prince William of Orange—awkward, to be sure, but preferable, the Whigs figured, to having a Roman Catholic on the throne.

But in the summer of 1688, even as Andros was preparing for his journey down to New York, the queen gave birth to a son. Now faced with the certainty of a Roman Catholic succession, the Whigs reached out to William and Mary for assistance. A Dutch army landed on the coast of England in November 1688 and marched toward London. James chose not to make a fight of it and fled to France. Early the following year William and Mary accepted the crown from a grateful—not to say relieved—Parliament.

This bloodless coup, hailed by Whig apologists as the Glorious Revolution, proved to be a turning point in Anglo-American history. It secured the Protestant succession. It laid to rest the theory of royal absolutism in England. It established the supremacy of Parliament. In time, too, as Whig propagandists like John Locke labored to justify what had taken place, it would alter, fundamentally, the structure and vocabulary of Anglo-American political discourse. Natural rights, popular sovereignty, constitutionalism, the inherent tendency of power to encroach upon liberty—these and other Whig commonplaces would become the conventional wisdom on both sides of the Atlantic, so broadly accepted as to seem self-evident and timeless, a national creed rather than sectarian dogma.

"THIS CONFUSED BUSINESSE"

Secret dispatches at the beginning of March 1689 brought the first sketchy reports of "a total Revolution att home" to Lieutenant Governor Nicholson in New York. Uncertain of his own authority and unwilling to act without further information, Nicholson sat on the story for the next six weeks. His anxiety increased toward the end of April when word came down from Boston that Governor Andros and other dominion officials were under arrest. The dominion had been extremely unpopular in New England, where attempts by Andros to reorganize local government aroused exactly the same kind of discontent that he and his predecessors in New York had stirred up on Long Island. When word of James II's abdication reached Boston, an angry mob clapped Sir Edmund and other dominion officials in jail. They were later shipped back to England in chains.

By mid-April (if not earlier) everybody in New York as well knew of the Glorious Revolution—that an English king after whom the city was named had been replaced by a Dutch prince after whom the city had previously been named (during its brief incarnation as New Orange), that Andros was finished, that the Dominion of New England had collapsed. Then came news that England had joined the League of Augsburg against Louis XIV and that a declaration of war against France could be expected momentarily. Rumors may also have reached the city around this time that Louis XIV had ordered the governor of Quebec to attack New York in the autumn of 1689 and drive out all the Protestants.

Nicholson and his council (Stephanus Van Cortlandt, Frederick Philipse, and Nicholas Bayard), together with the captains of the city's six militia companies (among them Abraham De Peyster, Nicholas Stuyvesant, and one Jacob Leisler), took steps to fortify the city and strengthen the garrison in the fort. The governor said nothing, however, to indicate that he would accept the accession of William and Mary, and more rumors now began to fly around town—that Nicholson, Irish Roman Catholics (including former governor Dongan), renegade Jacobites (supporters of the deposed king), the French, and Iroquois befriended by Andros were planning to seize the city for James II.

The English towns of Long Island responded to the alleged Catholic-Jacobite-French threat by electing new magistrates and calling out their militias to march against New York City. As the militias advanced slowly westward, Nicholson reported, they were assisted by "some ill affected and restless spiritts amongst us" who "used all imaginable meanes to stirr up the Inhabitants of this Citty to sedition and rebellion." Nicholson, his council, and the the city's militia captains reiterated their determination to defend New York against foreign enemies and to suppress "mutinous persons nigh us." The Long Island militiamen went no further than Jamaica and dispersed, but apprehensive merchants, Captain Leisler among them, began withholding payment of customs duties until the legitimacy of the government had been clarified and the customs collector, a Roman Catholic, was removed from office.

Nicholson still hesitated to acknowledge the abdication of James II. When he gave refuge to some soldiers from the Boston garrison, then threatened to "pistol" a Dutch militia officer and "sett the town in fyre" rather than tolerate insubordination, his authority disintegrated. Excited city militiamen poured into the streets, beating drums and calling on Captain Leisler to lead them in preventing a papist rising. On the last day of May, led by Ensign Joost Stol of Leisler's company, the militia swarmed into Fort James and disarmed the little garrison of regular troops. Joined by a mass of civilians, they declared all laws made under the authority of King James to be null and void and formed an "association" to hold the city for William and Mary. To all intents and purposes, the colony's government had ceased to exist. Nicholson took the first boat back to England to get help (and in the bargain got himself appointed governor of Virginia, where he founded the College of William and Mary and laid out Williamsburg).

Toward the end of June what Nicholson called "this confused businesse" took another turn when orders at last arrived from England for all public officials to proclaim William and Mary. When Mayor Van Cortlandt and Nicholson's council continued to stall, their authority too collapsed. Angry crowds drove them out of office, shut the courts, and closed down the customhouse. Van Cortlandt went into hiding. Bayard, having narrowly escaped an armed assault, decided to get out of town.

The insurgents immediately set up a ten-member Committee of Safety (four of whom were Huguenots) to govern both city and province. Over the summer of 1689 the committee reopened courts, resumed the collection of duties and taxes, allocated money for the city's defenses, and dispatched an emissary to England to tell William and Mary that all was well. The committee also chose Jacob Leisler to command the fort; by mid-August, the committee had become so impressed by Leisler's zeal and popularity that they made him commander-in-chief of the entire province. When William and Mary finally sent a commission for Nicholson or "such as for the time being take care for Preserving the Peace and administering the Lawes in our said Province of New York in America," Leisler decided—not unreasonably, in light of Nicholson's hasty departure—that he should assume the office of lieutenant governor. He began to organize a government, handing out commissions to scores of militia officers, justices of the peace, tax collectors, sheriffs, and notaries throughout the colony. As the year drew to a close his control of New York seemed complete.

LEISLER AND THE LEISLERIANS

Leisler was not unprepared for the work that lay ahead. Born forty-nine years earlier in Frankfurt-am-Main, he came from an illustrious family whose members included well-known Reformed clergymen, wealthy merchants and bankers, and highly placed government officials throughout Germany and Switzerland. After graduating from a Calvinist military academy in Nuremberg, he moved to Amsterdam and got a job as a translator for Cornelis Melyn. In 1660, probably with Melyn's help, he was commissioned an officer in the forces of the West India Company and led a contingent of troops over to New Amsterdam. He stayed on after the English conquest, set himself up in the fur and tobacco trade, and by the mid-1670s had become one of the half-dozen richest men in New York, owning a large town house, a farm on the present site of City Hall Park, and numerous other properties in and around the city. He became even wealthier in 1683, when the courts finally awarded him control over the vast estate of Govert Loockermans, whose stepdaughter, Altye (Elsie) Tymans, he had married some years before. Active as well as prosperous, Leisler was a deacon of the Reformed Church, captain of the militia, justice of the peace, and—thanks to close family and personal connections with the international Huguenot community—a respected figure among New York's French Protestants. It was largely through Leisler's efforts, in fact, that a settlement of Huguenots had been started in 1687 at New Rochelle (named after La Rochelle, the epicenter of French Protestantism).

Leisler never quite made it into the innermost circle of the Anglo-Dutch oligarchy, however. One reason was a nasty, protracted dispute with the Bayards and Van Cortlandts over the estate of his wife (who was related to both families). Another was his ardent Calvinism and passionate devotion to the House of Orange, which linked him to anti-English elements in the Reformed Church. During the brief Dutch reconquest of 1673–74, moreover, Leisler had been closely identified with Governor Colve and was thereafter never entirely trusted by the English.

Leisler's goal in the summer of 1689 was to hold New York for his new sovereigns against the "Popish Doggs & Divells," foreign and domestic, who threatened it. The identity and motives of his followers cannot be summed up so neatly. Many were second-generation Dutch, born in the city around the time of the 1664 conquest. A few, like Johannes De Bruyn, Abraham Gouverneur, and Nicholas Stuyvesant, were successful merchants; others, such as Cornelius Pluvier, baker, and Johannes Van Couwenhaven, brewer, were well-to-do artisans. Gerardus Beekman, a physician, supported Leisler. So did Samuel Staats, also a physician, who had returned to the Netherlands after the English conquest "rather than endeavor to make himself an Englishman," then came back again to join Leisler. But this wasn't simply a Dutch uprising against English oppression. Some prominent Dutch merchants opposed Leisler, as did Dominie Selyns of New York and Dominie Varick of Long Island, while Leisler's most trusted lieutenants included a number of Englishmen, among them Jacob Milborne and Samuel Edsall, a New Jersey hatmaker and Indian trader. Among Leisler's followers, moreover, were the shopkeepers, craftsmen, sailors, cartmen, and laborers of every nationality who formed the bulk of the city's population. Somewhat more than half the militiamen who initially took over Fort James came from England, Scotland, Wales, Denmark, France, Germany, or other parts of North America; outside the city itself, the Stuart-hating villagers of English Long Island would prove to be among Leisler's staunchest supporters.

What united these disparate insurgents was a rhetoric of loyalty to the Protestant cause that encompassed a broad range of social and political discontents. As Leislerian pamphleteers and spokesmen told the story, they had lived for years in "great dread" that the late King James planned "to Damn the English Nation to Popery and Slavery." His minions in New York—"our grandees," Leisler called them—had already made great strides in that direction, aided by Reformed clergymen who collaborated with the English. Then "the Hand of Heaven sent the glorious King William" to save the colony. When the governor and council delayed in declaring for the new government, the people rose up to defend both "the Holy Protestant Religion, and the Rights and Liberties of English men."

Nowhere was this layering of social and religious resentment more apparent than in the case of Jacob Milborne. Eight years younger than Leisler, Milborne was the son of a tailor who had been deeply influenced by the radical Protestantism that flourished among English working people during the Civil War. Jacob's brother William was one of the Fifth Monarchy Men who believed that Christ's kingdom was at hand and in 1661 attempted an armed uprising to prevent the restoration of the Stuarts. He eventually settled in Boston as a Baptist preacher. Jacob, in the meantime, went to America as the apprentice of a Hartford merchant. In 1668 he came down to New York, found work as a clerk for Thomas Delavall, and then went into business for himself.

During the 1670s and early 1680s, Milborne often traveled to Europe as a factor for Delavall and other city merchants, building a modest fortune as well as contacts with powerful English Whigs like Shaftsbury. On both sides of the Atlantic, his loathing for the Stuarts and his egalitarian contempt for puffed-up authority got him into trouble on more than one occasion. He helped spread the tale of the Popish Plot and served as a spy for Samuel Pepys. He also joined Leisler in opposition to the anglicized dominies who led the Reformed Church in New York. The Glorious Revolution found him in the Netherlands on business, but rumors of a Catholic plot to deliver the colony to the French brought him hurrying back in the summer of 1689.

Like his brother, who took part in the Boston uprising that toppled Andros and the Dominion of New England, Milborne threw himself into the struggle to defend his new sovereigns against their enemies. His pronouncements on social equality and the popular basis of political authority—far more extreme than anything ever heard from Leisler himself—soon made him one of the city's most conspicuous and controversial figures.

As for Leisler's "grandees," whose version of events is more fully recorded, they knew, without a shadow of doubt, what they were up against. "Hardly one person of sens & Estate . . . do countenance any of these ill and rash proceedings," Nicholson had said after giving up the fort, striking a note that would be played over and over again by Leisler's opponents and victims in the months and years to follow. Thirty-six merchants, including a half-dozen deacons of the Reformed Church, sent an address to William and Mary depicting the Leislerians as "a Rable . . . who formerly were scarce thought fit to bear the meanest offices among us." Still other "men of quality" and "Persons of Note" scoffed at Leisler's "ignorant Mobile," his "most abject Comon people," his "drunken crue," his "Olleverians" (a reference to Oliver Cromwell's supporters). Van Cortlandt spoke grimly about the approach of "people's Revolucions."

To Nicholas Bayard, perhaps his most vitriolic critic, Leisler was a man of Cromwellian insolence, driven by "unsatiable Ambition," unable to accept "the station nature had fitted him for, and placed him in, but his soaring, aspiring mind aiming at that which neither his birth nor education had ever qualified him for." Jacob Milborne was a "dark politician" who had an "affected ambiguous way of expressing himself [which] renders him unfit for the conversation of any but the vulgar, who in this age are so apt and ready to admire and applaud that they understood not." The rest of the insurgents, Bayard continued, were "poor ignorant innocent and senseless people who suffer them to be ruled and hectored by about twenty or thirty ill drunken sots." (Bayard also alleged that the insurgents were egged on by a woman, Trijn Jans, and women appear to have been among Leisler's most active and vocal supporters.)

"KILL HIM! KILL HIM!"

Something very like a "people's Revolucion" did indeed appear to be approaching New York between the autumn of 1689 and the spring of 1691. When the Committee of Safety called for a general election of local officers in September 1689, it decided (perhaps at Milborne's urging) to broaden the range of elective positions: justices of the peace and militia captains were to be chosen directly by voters for the first time, triggering a dramatic shift in the distribution of political power in the city. Bakers, bricklayers, carpenters, innkeepers—workingmen heretofore thought unfit for public responsibility—captured a majority of seats on the board of aldermen. Johannes Johnson, carpenter, became sheriff, and William Churcher, bricklayer, became marshal. Peter Delanoy, a Huguenot and one of Leisler's inner circle, was elected mayor of the city. Joost Stol, the militia ensign who had led the initial takeover of the fort, accepted the crucial task of presenting the Leislerians' case in London.

Scenes of open class conflict now became commonplace in the city. Bands of Leislerian rebels waylaid grandees who ventured out of doors, ransacked their homes and stores, intercepted their mail, and hauled them off for questioning. Bayard was arrested, marched in irons around the parapets of the fort, then thrown into jail for almost a year. Arrest warrants went out for such other prominent anti-Leislerians as Van Cortlandt, Robert Livingston, and former governor Dongan—so many, in fact, that a little colony of fugitives and refugees sprang up across the Hudson in New Jersey.

In retaliation, anti-Leislerian saboteurs reportedly tried to blow up the fort, and one day in June 1690 thirty-odd anti-Leislerian merchants set upon Leisler himself, shouting "Kill him, kill him!" "I will not suffer this to happen," cried sixty-year-old John Langstraet, a prominent carter, who jumped into the fray, giving Leisler time to draw his sword and escape. While his outraged followers flooded into town to protect him against further attempts, thirteen of the plotters were arrested, including Major Thomas Willett. Inexplicably, they were all soon released. Willett returned to his home in Queens, where he raised a small body of troops and marched back toward New York. Milborne rallied the city militia and drove the Long Islanders off after a brief skirmish near Newtown. Willett escaped to New England, and Milborne's militiamen contented themselves with looting his house. Seven of his captains were subsequently convicted of treason and rebellion at a court-martial in Flatbush.

In the spring of 1690 Leisler ordered elections for a new Assembly, which proceeded to raise taxes and strike down the monopolies and trade regulations with which every governor since Nicolls had favored New York City and its merchants. At a second session in the fall of the same year, the Assembly demanded the return of all disaffected persons who had fled the colony and provided heavy fines for those refusing civil or military employment in Leisler's government.

The striking thing, under the circumstances, was what the Assembly didn't do— how utterly it failed to address the piled-up political and social grievances that had plunged New York into near-chaos. Leisler himself bore a large share of responsibility for what happened. He never really wanted to deal with a legislature, it seems, and when talk at the first session turned to things like fundamental rights and liberties, he angrily sent the delegates home. If Leisler's rebellion was to become a revolution, he wasn't the man to lead it.

Besides which, Leisler had his hands full. To suppress the grandees' strong and active opposition, he relied more and more heavily on arbitrary arrests, oppressive taxation, and confiscations, with the result that some of his most trusted collaborators lost their nerve and began to drift away. Then, too, there loomed the problem of French Canada. In February 1690, six months after the outbreak of the War of the League of Augsburg (known as King William's War in the colonies), a mixed force of French and

Indians burned Schenectady and slew some sixty of its citizens and their slaves. Leisler promptly began to organize a retaliatory strike against Montreal, but after months of time-consuming, often acrimonious preparations the attack failed to materialize. Had he not been confronted with so serious an external threat to the entire colony so early in his regime—or had he not chosen to respond with such single-mindedness—it is arguable that his fate might have been different.

"FOR THEY HAVE DEVOURED JACOB"

New York's grandees had better connections at court than did Ensign Stol, the Leisler-ian emissary. Over the summer of 1690 they convinced King William to disavow Leisler. Colonel Henry Sloughter was commissioned governor and given a council consisting of Philipse, Van Cortlandt, Bayard, Willett, and other oligarchs. Proclaiming his intention to rid New York of Leisler and the "rabble," Sloughter set sail for New York toward the end of 1690.

The first contingent of English troops, commanded by Richard Ingoldsby, reached the city in March 1691. With several hundred well-armed followers, Leisler and Milborne barricaded themselves in the fort and refused to surrender until shown Sloughter's commission. A tense six weeks passed, punctuated by exchanges of gunfire, as both sides waited for Sloughter himself to arrive. When Sloughter finally turned up, commission in hand, Leisler and Milborne had no choice but to lay down their arms. A hastily appointed court (including Ingoldsby) convicted them and six others of treason, then directed that they be "hanged by the Neck and being Alive their bodys be Cutt Downe to the Earth that their Bowells be taken out and they being Alive burnt before their faces that their heads shall be struck off and their Bodys Cutt in four parts and which shall be Desposed of as their Majesties shall Assigne."

While he waited for this grisly sentence to be approved back in London, Sloughter ordered elections for a new Common Council and provincial assembly. Both bodies began at once to apply pressure on the city's working people and its large Dutch population, the two overlapping groups that had formed the mass base of the insurgency. The council imposed a licensing requirement on cartmen, made it more difficult to obtain the privileges of freemanship, and drew up the first municipal ordinances specifically regulating apprenticeship. The Assembly facilitated the suppression of future dissent with legislation providing that anyone who disturbed "the peace good and quiet of this their Majestyes Government" would be guilty of high treason. It also allocated public funds to compensate individuals for losses sustained during Leisler's regime and encouraged punitively large private damage suits against dozens of leading Leislerians.

The Assembly's most important thrust against the Leislerians, however, came in the form of the Judiciary Act of 1691. Designed to anglicize New York's legal system once and for all, the Judiciary Act set up a centralized Supreme Court of Judicature, erased the remaining traces of Roman-Dutch law in the colony, and instituted a new, uniform legal system based on the English common law. (That this was the Assembly's work underscores its vindictiveness: English courts traditionally derived their authority from the crown, not legislatures.) The act also empowered county sheriffs and justices of the peace to prosecute "moral" as well as civil and criminal offenses—a de facto license to homogenize local custom and culture. Under English law "moral offenses" were a matter for church courts. No such courts existed in New York, and by shifting their responsibilities to county justices and sheriffs, the Assembly made those officials more powerful than their English counterparts.

In response to public appeals for clemency and to a Huguenot riot on Staten Island, Sloughter paroled all the condemned rebels except Leisler and Milborne (who was now Leisler's son-in-law, having married his daughter Mary just before their arrest). Bayard talked Sloughter into signing their death warrants; it was later alleged that he took advantage of the governor when he was drunk. The Assembly concurred, and on a rainy May 16, 1691, the two were taken "on a sledge" to the gallows on the eastern edge of what is now City Hall Park.

Leisler spoke briefly, begging forgiveness for the errors and excesses of his regime and insisting on the purity of his motives. "This confused City & Province," he said, needed "more wise & Cunning powerful Pilotts than either of us ever was." Milborne, always the more defiant, swore that he would have his day of reckoning with his enemies "before gods tribunal." No carpenter would provide a ladder for the scaffold, so Dominie Selyns fetched one himself, and the executions proceeded while the crowd sang the Seventy-ninth Psalm: "Pour out thy wrath upon the heathen that have not known thee, and upon the kingdoms that have not called upon thy name. For they have devoured Jacob, and laid waste his dwelling place."

One eyewitness later recalled that "Milborne was not dead when the executioner took him down from the gallows, and lifted up his arm as if to parry the blow of the axe that was to cut his head off." Another remembered that "the shrieks of the people were dreadful—especially the women—some fainted, some were taken in labor; the crowd cut off pieces of his [Leisler's] garments as precious relics; also his hair was divided out of great veneration as for a martyr." (It was also reported that the executioner cut out Leisler's heart and gave it to a lady, possibly Bayard's wife, who held it aloft, screaming, "Here is the heart of a traitor!")

Leisler and Milborne, heads sewed back on, were buried side by side on property Leisler owned not far from the place of their execution, in the area now bounded by Park Row, Spruce Street, and Frankfort Street. Legend says the latter was named after the place of Leisler's birth. If so, it is the city's only surviving monument to his memory.[1]

---

1. A Jacob Street, also said to have been named for Leisler, no longer exists. Gouverneur Street, Gouverneur Lane, and Gouverneur Slip were all named after Abraham Gouverneur, a leading Leislerian who later married Milborne's widow, Mary Leisler. Hester Street was named after another Leisler daughter, while Nicholas Bayard is remembered in Bayard Street. After World War I a bronze tablet commemorating Leisler was placed on a boulder in City Hall Park, only to be banished a decade or so later by Parks Commissioner Robert Moses.

8

Heats and Animosityes

Leisler's death split New York like an ax. Colonel Benjamin Fletcher, who succeeded Henry Sloughter as governor in the autumn of 1692, found the hostility between Leislerians and anti-Leislerians running at such a pitch that neither faction "will be satisfied with less than the necks of Theire adversaries." An Irishman, Fletcher understood how bad these "heats and animosityes" could get, but he had no intention of remaining neutral. His job was to carry on the work of anglicizing the colony, and he needed the cooperation of the anti-Leislerian dominies and merchants who had, for the better part of thirty years now, cast their lot with the English.

CHURCH AND STATE

At the top of Fletcher's agenda for New York was the creation of a secure Protestant establishment—"a settled Ministry"—the one guarantee, he said, "that neither heresy, sedition, schism nor rebellion be preached amongst you, nor vice and profanity encouraged." Vice and profanity in particular were rife, observed the Rev. John Miller, newly arrived Episcopal chaplain to the fort's two companies of grenadiers. New York had become a sink of "irreligion, drunkenness, cursing and swearing, fornication and adultery, thieving, and other evils," he reported to the bishop of London. If the locals go to church at all, it is but "to find out faults in him that preacheth rather than to hear their own." Too many residents believed the "sweet and unconfined pleasures of the wandering libertines" an acceptable alternative to holy matrimony, while "ante-nuptial fornication" had become so widespread that New Yorkers often didn't marry until "a great belly" obliged them to.

In 1693 Fletcher more or less forced the Assembly to pass the Ministry Act, which provided for the public election of vestrymen and churchwardens in New York, Westchester, Queens, and Richmond counties. These county vestries (secular bodies, not to be confused with those governing individual churches) were empowered to tax all residents to pay the salaries of "good and sufficient Protestant ministers." In England, this meant only Anglicans. Fletcher, a staunch adherent of the national church, said it meant only Anglicans in New York as well.

Anglicans were a distinct minority in New York, however. The colony's only Anglican clergyman was the chaplain attached to the garrison on Manhattan, and his congregation comprised fewer than ninety families, at best 10 percent of the city's twenty-one hundred white adults. Except for a comparative handful of Roman Catholics and Jews, the vast majority of New Yorkers were nonconformists or "dissenters"—Protestants not affiliated with the Church of England. The Act of Toleration, adopted by Parliament in 1689, guaranteed their right to public worship, as did legislation by the New York Assembly in 1691, which extended the same right to all orderly Christians other than Catholics. Even Fletcher's official instructions required him to allow "a liberty of Conscience to all persons (except Papists)." Not surprisingly, then, dissenters saw the governor's interpretation of the Ministry Act as a subterfuge for evading the law and establishing the Church of England: what good is the right of public worship, they asked, if they must pay the salaries of Anglican clergy and, worse yet, allow Anglican clergy to occupy their pulpits?

The dominies who had opposed Leisler were especially indignant, and to them the governor offered a compromise. In return for their acquiescence, the Dutch Reformed Church, representing some 650 adults in the city alone, could have a charter exempting it from any obligation to support the Church of England and granting it complete autonomy in the appointment of clergy. The dominies accepted. In 1696 they got their charter, presented the governor with a silver plate as a token of gratitude, and set aside richly appointed pews for him and his entourage in the new Dutch church on Garden Street (Exchange Place).

In 1697 Fletcher granted New York Anglicans a corporate charter of their own. A vestry of wealthy laymen began at once to organize construction of Trinity Church, the city's first Episcopal house of worship, on the west side of Broadway at Wall Street, overlooking the Hudson River. By 1698 the building was ready for services, with the Rev. William Vesey serving as first rector. Satisfied that the Church of England now had a foundation for future expansion in New York, the vestry happily declared that the days were over when "for want of a Temple for the public Worship according to the English Church, this seemed rather like a conquered Foreign Province held by the terrour of a Garrison, than an English Colony, possessed and settled by people of our own Nation."

Ties between the Anglican and Reformed communions remained strong, nevertheless. During Trinity's construction, Dutch carters were paid handsomely for transporting building materials, while Dominie Henricus Selyns made the Garden Street church available for Anglican services and assisted Fletcher at Vesey's induction on Christmas Day of 1697. For the first three months, moreover, Vesey and Selyns preached alternately at Trinity, the former officiating in English, the latter in Dutch.

Yet this unique arrangement—really a dual establishment—failed to have the calming effect that Fletcher promised. Dissenters refused to concede the Church of England's right to public maintenance and initiated a decades-long conflict with militant Anglicans. Provincial authorities responded by leaving Trinity to fend for itself, thus ensuring the colony's reputation for heterodoxy and toleration. Only Roman Catholics remained officially unwelcome. In 1700, when there were still fewer than a dozen Catholics in the city, the Assembly required all priests ordained by the pope to leave before the end of the year; anyone hiding a priest was subject to a fine of two hundred pounds.

Nor did the privileged status of the Reformed Church quiet the wrath that swept New York's Dutch population following Leisler's execution. County sheriffs and judges, linchpins of local English government outside Manhattan, reported case after case of Dutch opposition to their authority, often to the point of open violence. On one occasion, in 1696, a party of Dutchmen armed with "swords guns and Pistoles" attacked the Kings County courthouse, and Myndert Courten, a prominent Leislerian, announced that "he didn't value the Courts order a fart for their power will not stand long."

More odious still for truckling to the English were the Reformed dominies them-selves—Selyns of Manhattan, Varick of Long Island, and Dellius of Albany. Angry congregations tried to starve them out of office by withholding their salaries; those in Harlem, Staten Island, and New Jersey announced that they could "live well enough without ministers or sacraments" and refused to have anything to do with the three. Once the sanctuary of the Garden Street church was "attacked by violence and open force." Thousands of men and women throughout the colony simply abandoned the Reformed communion altogether. By the mid-nineties, according to Dr. Benjamin Bul-livant, a visitor from Boston, the Dutch residents of Manhattan generally ignored the Sabbath, "some shelling peas at theyr doors children playing at theyr usuall games in the streets & ye taverns filled." As the decade came to a close, Reformed churches everywhere in the colony complained of 80 or 90 percent declines in membership, fre-quently because of wholesale exoduses—"ten, twenty or more families" at a time—to the wilds of Ulster County, northern New Jersey, or Pennsylvania.

THE PIRATES OF NEW YORK

While attempting to erect an Anglo-Dutch religious establishment in New York, Fletcher also secured the fealty of the colony's anti-Leislerian oligarchs by serving them gluttonous helpings of real estate. The most fortunate received manors over which they exercised quasi-feudal authority. Stephanus Van Cortlandt became lord of eighty-six-thousand-acre Cortlandt Manor in Westchester County and of Sagtikos Manor on Long Island's south shore. Chief Justice William "Tangier" Smith was made lord of St. George Manor, which ran for fifty miles along the north shore of Long Island. Lewis Morris (nephew and heir of Colonel Lewis Morris of Barbados) became lord of Morrisania Manor, now encompassing some three thousand acres near the mouth of the Harlem River. Frederick Philipse became lord of ninety-two-thousand-acre Philipsburgh Manor in Westchester, while the municipal government awarded him the exclusive right to operate a toll bridge across Spuyten Duyvill Creek at the northern tip of Manhattan. (King's Bridge, as Philipse called it, opened for business in 1693.) A host of other anti-Leislerians—Peter Schuyler, Henry Beekman, Dominie Dellius, and a rising young merchant named Caleb Heathcote—accepted hundreds of thousands of acres without the trappings of lordship.

In addition to rewarding his friends with the crown's territory, Fletcher gave them free rein in the piracy business. As King William's War dragged on—it didn't end until 1697—both Britain and France bolstered their regular navies by relying on privateers,

privately owned warships empowered by "letters of marque" to despoil enemy shipping. The law required that captured ships and cargoes—known as "prizes"—be legally condemned in a proper court of law before they were disposed of. Privateering
proved so lucrative that many captains and owners dispensed with the formalities and
turned to out-and-out piracy, attacking the vessels of any country, including their own.
There were only two details to worry about. One was being caught and hanged. The
other was disposing of loot.

Fletcher rolled out the red carpet for pirates, allowing them and their crews to enter
New York without fear of arrest, dispose of their treasure, and refit for another voyage—all for a mere one hundred Spanish dollars each. Over the next four or five years
he hosted a remarkable collection of villains and cutthroats. When pirate captain
Thomas Tew put into port in 1694, the governor invited him to dinner, escorted him
around town, and presented him with a gold watch as an inducement to return. Taken
aback, the Lords of Trade in London asked for an explanation. Tew was "what they call
a very pleasant man," Fletcher answered serenely. "When the labours of my day were
over it was some divertisement as well as information to me, to heare him talke. I wish'd
in my mind to make him a sober man, and in particular to reclaime him from a vile habit
of swearing."

With Fletcher's blessings, some of New York's best-known captains hoisted the
black flag and sailed off to ply the waters between Africa and India, trailing mayhem and
murder in their wake. Richard Glover, captain of the *Resolution*, seized two East India
Company ships off the coast of Aden, burned their crews alive, and then blockaded the
port of Calicut for ransom. Edward Coates came home with stolen goods valued at sixteen thousand pounds (including twenty-eight hundred pieces of eight) and gave
Fletcher his ship, the *Jacob*, as a present. William Mason, captain of the *Charming
Mary*, returned with booty worth thirty thousand pounds. Mason's quartermaster,
Samuel Burgess, subsequently went into the business on his own account and became
one of the most feared pirates along the east coast of Africa.

Frederick Philipse, Nicholas Bayard, William Nicoll, Stephanus Van Cortlandt,
Peter Schuyler, Thomas Willett, Tangier Smith, and other anti-Leislerian merchants
financed these pirate cruises, provisioned pirate ships, and smuggled pirate contraband
back into the city. They invested heavily in the illegal trade between New York and
Madagascar, a notorious haven for marauders where goods of both colonial and European origin—clothing, shoes, tobacco, rum, sugar, firearms—fetched fantastic prices. A
cask of wine worth nineteen pounds in New York was said to sell for three hundred
pounds on Madagascar, and local merchants sometimes made profits of ten thousand
pounds on a single voyage. A few maintained their own agents on St. Mary's Island, just
off the Madagascar coast, where a former New York mariner named Adam Baldridge
had set up a kind of trading post for merchants and pirates.

All told, according to one report, this boodling was worth a hundred thousand
pounds a year to the city. Tavern keepers, whores, retailers, and others flourished as
buccaneers swaggered through the streets with purses full of hard money—Arabian
dinars, Hindustani mohurs, Greek byzants, French louis d'or, Spanish doubloons. Merchants reaped huge profits (as great as "200, 300, yea sometimes 400" percent, according to the Rev. John Miller) on silk carpets, muslins, ivory fans, ebony and teakwood
chairs, East India cabinets, looking-glasses, vases of hammered silver and brass, and
other exotic merchandise whose provenance didn't always bear close scrutiny. The most

successful built fine new residences, prompting Dr. Bullivant to remark on the "multitudes of greate & Costly buildings" that went up in New York during Fletcher's administration.

Few New Yorkers did better than Fletcher himself, however. In addition to the protection money he collected from pirates, he extorted bribes from licensed Indian
traders, bilked the customs service, padded military payrolls, and embezzled funds
raised to pay the provincial debt. "He takes a particular delight in having presents made
to him," wrote Peter Delanoy, the former Leislerian mayor, a trait that "has found
employment for our silversmiths and furnish'd his Excellency with more plate (besides
variety of other things) than all our former Governours ever received." Altogether, his
profiteering reportedly netted him thirty thousand pounds. His luxuriously appointed
residence in the fort, staffed by nineteen servants, was the talk of the town.

THE ANGLICIZATION OF CITY LIFE

While working to attach the anti-Leislerian dominies and oligarchs ever more firmly to
his government, Fletcher accelerated the process of anglicization begun by the Judiciary and Ministry acts. In 1693 he informed New Yorkers that Long Island would henceforth be called the Island of Nassau so that the memory of William III "may live forever
amongst you" (prior to the Glorious Revolution the new king's title had been Prince
William of Nassau; it survives in Long Island's Nassau County). That same year
Fletcher tightened New York's connections with other English colonies by reviving regular mail service to New England. Except in the dead of winter, a post rider left New
York once every week, following the Post Road through New Haven to Saybrook, where
he exchanged mailbags with the Boston rider, who had come down via Providence,
Stonington, and New London. Service to Philadelphia was added shortly thereafter.

On November 4, 1694, likewise at Fletcher's behest, the city celebrated the King's
Birthday with a bonfire—the first instance of what soon evolved into an elaborate annual civic ritual "essential," in the words of a later royal governor, "to preserve and keep
up in the minds of the People that respect which is due to His Majesty." One day later,
another bonfire was lit to commemorate the discovery of Guy Fawkes's Gunpowder
Plot of 1605, a Catholic scheme to blow up Parliament. Also called Guy Fawkes Day (or
Pope Day in New England), the fifth of November was a popular English holiday
marked by fireworks, anti-Catholic effigy processions, and general rowdyism. As a spur
to political loyalty and patriotism its value in post-Leislerian New York was self-evident, and it too would become a key element of an ever more anglicized municipal culture. At some point early in the eighteenth century, it also became customary for the
governor to host a fancy-dress ball for well-to-do New Yorkers of English descent on
St. George's Day (April 23). St. George, of course, was the patron saint of England, and
in time, private national societies sprang up to celebrate the feast days of St. Andrew
(Scotland), St. David (Wales), St. Patrick (Ireland), and even St. Nicholas (the Netherlands) as well.

Fletcher pressed his anglicization program still further by persuading the Assembly to hire thirty-year-old William Bradford of Philadelphia as public printer. Over the
summer of 1693 Bradford opened a printshop at the Sign of the Bible in Dock Street
(now Pearl) and promptly ran off a glowing testimonial to Fletcher's martial exploits by
Nicholas Bayard and Charles Lodwick. It may have been the first book ever printed in
New York.

Because of its close association with dissent, and of the thin line that seemed to separate dissent from sedition and revolution, printing had always been closely controlled in England (as elsewhere); the duke of York, not long before ascending to the throne as James II, warned Governor Thomas Dongan to let no one operate a printing press in his province since "great inconveniences may arise by the liberty of printing." After the Glorious Revolution, though, Parliament virtually eliminated restrictions on the press and the expression of opinion. Well before the end of the century, as a result, the English-speaking world was awash in books, pamphlets, journals, magazines, and newspapers.

Bradford's shop connected New York to this burgeoning print world, attuning its residents to every nuance of British social and political discourse (although his audience was narrow by modern standards: in 1700 no more than one out of five residents of the city could read, and by 1750 no more than two out of five). Over the next thirty or forty years, he served up a steady diet of English-language almanacs, religious tracts, courtesy books, and excerpts from English newspapers (most often the *London Gazette*). His editions of Richard Lingard's *Letter of Advice to a Young Gentleman Leaving the University Concerning His Behavior and Conversation in the World* (1696) and Francis Daniel Pastorius's *A New Primmer, or Methodical Directions to Attain the True Spelling, Reading & Writing of English* (1698), as well as his own *Secretary's Guide, or, Young Man's Companion* (1698), were obvious attempts to promulgate British standards of correct behavior. So, too, the first American edition of the Anglican Book of Common Prayer would come off Bradford's press in 1710. In 1725 he would launch New York's first newspaper, the weekly *Gazette*.

As the government's mouthpiece, Bradford issued a stream of official edicts, statutes, ordinances, petitions, and notices that imparted legitimacy as well as substance to the imperial order. His annual edition of the Assembly's journals was the first publication of its kind anywhere in the colonies, for nowhere else did government have a more urgent need to inform and instruct the literate classes. Similarly, in 1698, Bradford would issue the first locally printed account of Leisler's Rebellion, an anonymous anti-Leislerian diatribe entitled *A Letter from a Gentleman of the City of New York to Another, Concerning the Troubles Which Happen'd in the Time of the Late Happy Revolution.* (True freedom of the press was an idea whose time hadn't yet come, though: the Leislerian response—another anonymous polemic, entitled *Loyalty Vindicated*—had to be printed in Boston.)

In this increasingly anglicized climate the city acquired its first coffeehouse. Created by Puritans in the mid-seventeenth century, coffeehouses were now quite fashionable in London as alternatives to the taverns and gin mills frequented by the lower classes. They offered men of affairs a comfortable place to talk business, discuss current events, and peruse the latest books and newspapers. Lieutenant John Hutchins, an officer who had come over with Sloughter, decided that New York was ready for a coffeehouse of its own. In 1696 he opened for business at the sign of the King's Arms.

Standing on the west side of Broadway between Crown (Liberty) and Little Prince (Cedar), just north of Trinity Church, the King's Arms quickly became the unofficial headquarters of English New York. Municipal and provincial officials, merchants, and officers from the fort thronged the barroom, some milling about on foot, others occupying small curtained booths to sip coffee or dine in comfort and privacy. Committees of both the provincial assembly and Common Council routinely convened in its spacious

THE
LAWS & ACTS
OF THE
General Assembly
FOR
Their Majesties Province
OF
NEW-YORK,
As they were Enacted in divers Sessions, the first of
which began *April*, the 9th, *Annoq; Domini*,
1691.

At *New-York*,
Printed and Sold by *William Bradford*, Printer to their Majesties, King
William & Queen *Mary*, 1694.

(The New York Society Library)

upstairs meeting-rooms, whose windows and balconies afforded sweeping views of the river and harbor below. As early as 1699, Hutchins may have allowed his establishment to be used for theatrical performances, now considered very chic in London.[1]

In these same years, the Common Council decided to replace the Dutch Stadhuis, half a century old now, with a proper City Hall at the intersection of Wall and Broad streets. (The parcel was donated by Abraham De Peyster, who had bought up many of the Dongan lots on Wall Street.) Completed in 1700 at a cost of some three thousand pounds, the new building was as much a symbol of the anglicization of New York as Trinity Church, Bradford's printshop, or the King's Arms. Facing down Broad, still the city's premier commercial thoroughfare, it held rooms for the Common Council, the Assembly, the Mayor's Court (also known as the Court of Common Pleas), the new Supreme Court of Judicature, and, in the basement, the municipal jail. After 1716 "a publick Clock" of local manufacture embellished the tower.

Yet another vestige of New Amsterdam was erased when colonial authorities demolished the old city wall, erected almost half a century earlier to keep out the English. In 1694 the Common Council had asked to have the wall removed, citing the

---

1. The only rival of the King's Arms was the Two-Mile or Bowery Village Tavern operated by John Clapp, sometime clerk of the Assembly. Situated two miles north of town on the Bowery Road, roughly on the present site of Astor Place, the Two-Mile Tavern was billed as a place where "Gentlemen travellers . . . may have very good Entertainment for themselves and Horses." It also became the resort of choice for refreshments during a genteel outing into the country. Dr. Bullivant, who was driven out to Clapp's by Governor Fletcher himself, testified that it offered "good Cyder & mead."

"Incroachment of Buildings" on those parts of the palisade "Along the Wall Street" that hadn't already been turned into firewood. The last of it finally came down in 1699, just in time for the stones from its bastions to be incorporated into the foundation of the new City Hall—a symbolic touch that would have been lost on no one.

The wall's removal didn't cause an immediate surge of building north of Wall Street, however, for the Dongan Charter had given all vacant land on Manhattan to the municipal corporation, which proved quite unwilling to part with any of its endowment. The resulting shortage of building plots, along with the attractions of living and working next to the Town Dock, would keep New Yorkers tethered to lower Manhattan for many years to come. In 1695 the built-up part of town covered no more than an eighth of a square mile, and most new construction took place below what is now Fulton Street. In 1704, when there were around 750 houses for the city's five-thousand-odd inhabitants, Sarah Kemble Knight, a visitor from Boston, pronounced it "well compacted." And crowded: as one harried colonial official complained to the Board of Trade only a few years earlier, he had been unable to find a place to live. "I have eight in family and know not yet where to fix them, houses are so scarce and dear, and lodgings worst in this place."

Scarce and dear, but increasingly solid: most houses in New York were now built of stone or brick—the latter, Knight reported, "are of divers Coulers and laid in Checkers, being glazed [they] look very agreeable." Aesthetics aside, the new building materials greatly reduced the menace of fire. So did the municipality's relentless attention to fire prevention. In 1691 Direck Vandenburg, the mason who would direct Trinity's construction, headed a committee that regularly examined chimneys and fireplaces; in 1697 the Common Council shifted that responsibility to inspectors in each ward who checked every house weekly. The city's sixteen wells were put also put under ward supervision, and as many as fifteen more would be drilled in the middle of Manhattan streets by 1720, with residents covering the expense. In addition, new Common Council regulations required residents to keep fire buckets handy—compliance to be monitored by two city inspectors, assisted by constables.

The condition of the streets was another story. Dr. Bullivant agreed (in 1697) that "most of theyr new buildings are magnificient enough, ye fronts of red and yellow (or Flanders) brick looking very prettily." But, he added caustically, "theyre streets are Nasty and unregarded, ye which they excuse at this time, saying the Multitudes of buildings now going forth are ye Occasion." Improvements were nonetheless underway. In 1691 the Assembly resolved that, for the "Encouragement of Trade and Commerce," streets, lanes, and alleys should "be conveniently regulated" and empowered the municipal corporation to lay out new ones. It did so in 1691, 1694, and again in 1700—mostly in the area below Wall Street, with the addition of some roads in the Out Ward after 1707.

The most important new street was built on landfill adjacent to the Town Dock. In 1686, intending to raise cash for the payment of its debts, the Common Council began the process of selling "water lots" along the East River shore to merchants who agreed to fill them in. In 1691, when the town again needed funds for a new market house and ferry house, and later in the decade, when it built the new City Hall, additional lots were sold along the waterfront between the old Stadhuis and Fulton Street. But this time the Common Council attached strings. Purchasers were required to fill in their lots and erect on each a stone- or brick-fronted building at least two stories high—after which the entire stretch of new-made land was to be designated Dock Street. By 1692 purchasers were hard at work, filling in their lots with dirt obtained by digging and leveling as much of "the hill by Mr. Beekmans" as belonged to the city. Increasingly, the city gave preference in the sale or lease of water lots to inhabitants (usually wealthy) who owned property fronting the new lots.

Dock Street's residents, like those along other roadways, were also required to pave the section of street in front of their house, at their own cost, with "good & sufficient peeble Stones," and to pull up any "poysonous and Stinkcking Weeds" (Broadway residents had to plant trees as well). By 1707 most of the city's major thoroughfares were covered with cobblestones, except in the middle, where a gutter or channel was left to funnel off rainwater. Residents of Broad Street had petitioned the city for a "Common Sewer" in 1696, but when the parsimonious Common Council discovered that a proper sewer would cost £865, they promptly dropped the matter. As a result, the channels on Broad and elsewhere were constantly clogged with dirt and refuse, much of the latter dumped there by householders themselves, in lieu of paying cartmen the prescribed fee for taking it away. Official scavengers were employed from time to time to tackle the problem, but without notable success.

The streets presented other perils—being run down by galloping horses, for example, or bowled over by the ever ubiquitous pigs (whenever they weren't rooting about in the city graveyard). At night, footpads were so common that pedestrians were obliged to travel in pairs. Finally, in 1697, the magistrates—remarking on "the great Inconveniency that Attends this Citty, being A trading place for want of Lights"—ordered that every house have a light "hung out on a Pole" from an upper window "in the Darke time of the Moon." When homeowners objected to the expense, the magistrates retreated to a requirement that only every seventh house need present "A Lanthorn & Candle," and only in winter, the cost to be shared by the owners of the other six.

In 1684, moreover, the Common Council instructed the constables in each of the five wards south of the Fresh Water Pond to hire eight citizens as watchmen. This "Constables Wattch" was a more substantial force than in other colonial (or most English) towns. Besides patrolling the streets at night, staffs in hand, the watchmen were to ensure that no violations of the drinking laws occured during Sunday worship. In 1685 the Assembly increased the fines for public drunkenness, describing that "Louthsome and Odious sin" as "the root and foundation of many other Enormous Sinnes as bloodshed, stabbing, murther, swearing, fornication, Adultry, and such like." That same year the Common Council outlawed "Pockett Pistols" and other concealed weapons. It was becoming somewhat more difficult, too, to open a "public house" or tavern for the sale of liquor. Municipal authorities now requested applicants for a license to present a certificate attesting they were "of good life & Conversation and fitt to keep such a house."

"TRUMPET AND DRUMMS"

The anglicization of New York also meant the closer synchronization of provincial "heats and animosityes" with the rhythms of party politics in England. Within a year of Leisler's execution, his son, Jacob Leisler Jr., and his old friend Abraham Gouverneur were in London, lobbying members of Parliament, cabinet officers, and other highly placed government officials to clear his name. The complexion of affairs in London was changing rapidly, and powerful Whigs agreed to help.

By 1694 King William had become impatient with the Tories who remained in his cabinet after the Glorious Revolution. They criticized the war with France as excessively expensive and complained when the Whigs set up the Bank of England to stabilize government finances. Before the year was done, the king had forced them all out of office, leaving the Whigs in complete control of the machinery of state. Moving swiftly to strengthen the government's hand abroad, the Whigs established a new Board of Trade, adopted the first comprehensive Navigation Act, announced a full-scale crackdown on piracy and illegal trade, and poured money into the Royal Navy.

For New York's Leislerians, the Whig ascendancy was a new beginning; for Governor Fletcher, it spelled disaster. In 1695 Parliament declared that both Leisler and Milborne had been unjustly convicted. Robert Livingston, one of Fletcher's keenest enemies, rushed to London bearing lurid testimonials, largely accurate, to Fletcher's corruption. As the protégé of certain Tories no longer in the king's favor, Fletcher was helpless. In 1697, after a lengthy investigation that focused on his relations with pirates, the Board of Trade ordered him home.

Fletcher's successor was Richard Coote, the earl of Bellomont, a gouty Irish peer with impeccable Whig credentials. Bellomont reached New York in the spring of 1698 and found that "there are parties here as in England." The local Tories included Bayard, Philipse, and other anti-Leislerians—disgraceful "vermin," Bellomont called them, who with former governor Fletcher's backing had turned New York into "a sink of corruption." He promptly brought the leading anti-Leislerians up on charges of smuggling, graft, landgrabbing, election fraud, and piracy. He started legal action to recover the millions of acres of prime land they had obtained from Fletcher, including the property occupied by Trinity Church. He gave the job of mayor back to Peter Delanoy and ordered customs officers to enforce the new Navigation Act with utmost vigor.

With Bellomont's help, the Leislerians soon regained control of the Assembly and began to settle old scores—granting pardons to Leisler's followers, canceling punitive lawsuits, restoring illegally seized property, voiding Fletcher's most excessive land grants, and writing new legislation to protect the livelihood of city artisans. They broadened the suffrage for Assembly elections (Catholics excepted, of course). But nothing gave the Leislerians greater satisfaction than the day in October 1698 when the bodies of Leisler and Milborne were exhumed and reburied in the Dutch church on Garden Street amid the "sound of trumpet and drumms." Despite a "rank storm," an estimated fifteen hundred people took part, many coming in from Long Island, New Jersey, and Pennsylvania for the occasion. Excited spectators reported seeing "Leisler's apparition in a Coach" near the church.

The anti-Leislerians were meanwhile actively scheming against Bellomont. Already, he warned the Board of Trade, they had sent a delegation to London to bring charges against him and were "cock sure of carrying the point and getting me turned out of this government." It proved to be Captain Kidd, however, who would wound Bellomont most deeply.

THE STRANGE CAREER OF CAPTAIN KIDD

A Scot by birth, William Kidd went off to sea as a young man and at length found his way to the Caribbean. There, along with thousands of other restless, ambitious seamen, he drifted from port to port looking for work, a background that later prompted Leisler to call him, with considerable justice, a "blasphemous privateer."

When war broke out between England and France in 1688, Kidd got a privateering commission from the governor of Nevis, an English colony in the West Indies. He attacked French ships and colonies until his crew, who preferred piracy to honest plunder, absconded with his ship. Kidd set out after them in another vessel, and over the winter of 1690–91 the chase brought him to New York, where he astutely chose to help Ingoldsby and Sloughter recapture the town from Leisler. The Assembly voted Kidd a reward of one hundred fifty pounds, and he became fast friends with Nicholas Bayard, Stephanus Van Cortlandt, Frederick Philipse, and other anti-Leislerian worthies implicated in piracy and illegal trade. On the very day of Leisler's execution, he obtained a license to marry Sarah Bradley Cox Oort, widow of a prosperous merchant whose property included a flour warehouse, the fine home on River Road (Pearl Street) once owned by Govert Loockermans and Annetje Jans, and a capital of nineteen hundred pounds. After a few more years, Kidd had acquired fine silverware, a large plot of land north of Wall Street, and an excellent wine cellar; his wife was the proud owner of the first "Turkey worked" carpet seen in New York. When construction began on the new Trinity Church, he provided the block and tackle for hoisting the stones.

In 1695, while marshaling his case against Governor Fletcher, Robert Livingston met Kidd in London and arranged for him to take a heavily armed frigate, the *Adventure Galley*, into the Indian Ocean to hunt pirates. A syndicate of rich Whigs, organized by Bellomont and Livingston on the eve of Bellomont's departure for New York, agreed to finance Kidd's expedition in return for a share of the proceeds.

Kidd returned to New York and filled out his 150-man crew with the kind of restless spirits who usually signed up for risky ventures at sea—mostly young, overwhelmingly poor, and, except for a handful of experienced mariners, thoroughly weary of trying to make a living on land as farmers, laborers, carpenters, shoemakers, bakers, and the like. Two out of three were English, and one out of six was Dutch. There was one African and one Jew—Benjamin Franks, a jeweler from Jamaica who was trying to get to India, then the world's leading supplier of precious gems.

The *Adventure Galley* set sail for Madagascar in the early autumn of 1696. Somewhere along the way Kidd decided to turn pirate and spent the next couple of years preying on trade in the Indian Ocean. When he headed back for New York in the spring of 1699, he was rumored to be carrying a treasure worth half a million pounds. His backers, though, were deserting him. He had thumbed his nose at the government, embarrassed important people, defied the navy, outraged the budding imperial bureaucracy, and done harm to the mighty East India Company. The Tory opposition was clamoring for his head, and by early 1699, even as Kidd reentered American waters, the Whigs knew they might lose control of Parliament if they didn't wash their hands of him at once.

Kidd's relationship with Governor Bellomont was a particularly sensitive issue for the Whigs. When Kidd showed up in Boston in July, Bellomont had no choice but to order his arrest—a decision probably made easier by the discovery that Kidd's loot was worth a paltry forty thousand pounds or so, far too meager to make it worth anyone's while to protect him (though rumors persist that just before his arrest he stashed a huge treasure somewhere on the forks of eastern Long Island). In May 1701, after six months

THE
Arraignment, Tryal, and Condemnation
OF
Captain William Kidd,
FOR
MURTHER
AND
PIRACY,
Upon Six feveral Indictments,

At the Admiralty-Seffions, held by His Majefty's Com-
miffion at the *Old-Baily*, on *Thurfday* the 8th. and *Friday* the 9th.
of *May*, 1701, who, upon full Evidence, was found Guilty,
receiv'd Sentence; and was accordingly executed at Execution-
Dock, *May* the 23d.

AS ALSO,

The TRYALS of *Nicholas Churchill*, *James Howe*, *Robert*
Lamley, *William Jenkins*, *Gabriel Loff*, *Hugh Parrot*, *Richard Barlicorn*,
Abel Owens, and *Darby Mullins*, at the fame Time and Place
for PIRACY.

Perufed by the Judges and Council.

To which are added,
Captain *KIDD*'s Two Commiffions:
One under the Great Seal of *ENGLAND*, and the Other under
the Great Seal of the Court of *Admiralty*.

Kidd's fate, like Leisler's, had been played out on the Anglo-American political stage, before an audience that was increasingly eager for printed news and information. This account appeared on the market very soon after the execution. (© National Maritime Museum, Greenwich, London)

of solitary confinement in Boston, followed by a year in London's infamous Newgate prison, Kidd was hanged for murder and piracy while his erstwhile Whig patrons looked on in stony silence. (Hanged twice, actually, because the first rope broke and he had to be dropped a second time, after which his body was tarred, bound in an iron cage, and left swinging alongside the Thames as a warning to sailors contemplating a pirate life.) Exactly ten years had passed since Leisler's execution, and it couldn't have been clearer that the political trail between New York and London was now shorter, and more treacherous, than ever.

"A VERY WELL HUMOURD AFFABLE GENT."

Just weeks before Kidd's execution, Lord Bellomont died suddenly in New York. By the time his replacement was chosen in 1702, the Tories were back in power in Parliament and Queen Anne had taken the throne. The new royal governor was the queen's Tory cousin Edward Hyde, Viscount Cornbury. Former governor Fletcher's private secretary welcomed him as "a very well humourd Affable Gent.," and so he no doubt appeared to his political supporters—all the more so after Cornbury removed Bellomont's Leisler-ian appointees and resumed the practice of handing out land to backers; the largest ran to two million acres, better than half the size of Connecticut. The large number of New Yorkers belonging to Reformed and dissenting congregations, on the other hand, saw nothing affable about Cornbury or his campaign to impose the Church of England on the colony.

A zealous Anglican like Fletcher, Cornbury favored Trinity Church with a gener-ous portion of Manhattan real estate known as the King's (or Queen's) Farm, which stretched up the island's west side as far as modern Christopher Street. He increased the salary of Trinity's rector, the Rev. William Vesey, and persuaded the Assembly to raise taxes to pay for it. He welcomed missionaries dispatched by the Church of Eng-land's new Society for the Propagation of the Gospel (SPG), chartered by King William in 1701 to invigorate the colonial church. It was, he said, his intention to pro-mote the SPG's "good and pious designs, to the utmost of my power."

In 1707 Cornbury ordered the arrest of the Rev. Francis Makemie, one of the founders of American Presbyterianism, for preaching in the city without a license. After languishing in jail for three months, Makemie successfully defended himself under the English Toleration Act (which Cornbury said didn't apply in New York). In Jamaica, where the Presbyterians had just built a new church, Cornbury evicted the minister, William Hubbard, and replaced him with an Anglican. When the congrega-tion rioted and retook the building, Cornbury barred Hubbard from ever preaching there again.

Cornbury bore down heavily as well on the Reformed Church, despite decades of collusion by its dominies. Claiming the authority to do so under the Ministry Act, he began to fill vacant Reformed pulpits with Anglicans—a tactic, he said, that in conjunc-tion with English-language schooling was the best way to "make this Colony an English Colony, which I am afraid will not easily be done without it." Under his aegis, Anglicans also took over Dutch Reform missions to the Indians, and when they began to distribute Dutch-language editions of the Anglican Book of Common Prayer—suggesting that Netherlanders were also fit objects for proselytizing—the dominies abandoned their collaborationist policy and went over into opposition.

Only a few years after he arrived in New York, Cornbury was tangled in sheets of trouble. Stories began circulating on both sides of the Atlantic about his eccentric, out-landish personal behavior. On one memorable occasion he allegedly scattered the patrons of the King's Arms by riding his horse through the front door and up to the bar. It was charged, too, that he made a habit of addressing the Assembly and strolling the fort's parapets in female attire. "His dressing himself in womens Cloths Commonly [every] morning is so unaccountable that if hundred[s] of Spectators didn't dayly see him, it would be incredible," said Robert Livingston (who in fact never actually wit-nessed such a scene himself and was only spreading rumors). Cornbury was a casual chiseler, on top of everything else, and soon had city merchants clamoring for him to pay off better than ten thousand pounds' worth of bills and promissory notes. Lady Cornbury was accused of swiping clothes and jewels from the town's best-dressed women; the sound of her carriage at the door, people said, was a warning to hide any-thing of value.

In 1708, when the Whigs won a crushing majority in Parliament, Cornbury's ene-mies, rallied by Lewis Morris, persuaded the government to remove him from office. Stephen De Lancey and assorted other creditors immediately had him thrown into debtor's prison. "A Porter in the streets of London is a happier man than a Governor in America," Cornbury wailed. He got out only when the timely death of his father made him the third earl of Clarendon, rendering him immune from prosecution. No one shed a tear when he left New York later that same year, except perhaps those unlucky towns-folk who were still trying to collect the money he owed them.

POLITICAL INTERESTS

Cornbury hadn't yet taken up his post in New York when, in 1702, Parliament renewed the war with France, this time to prevent the grandson of Louis XIV from inheriting the Spanish empire. The War of the Spanish Succession—"Queen Anne's War" in America—soon blossomed into a kind of national crusade for the great Whig traders and financiers of London, who fattened their purses on military contracts, loans, and colonial commerce.

In New York, on the other hand, city merchants suddenly found themselves up against a Spanish embargo on their exports to the West Indies and mounting losses to enemy privateers. In the first two years of the war alone the French captured nearly thirty New York vessels, about one-fourth of those that worked out of the port. The economy nosedived. "Their Trade is in effect quite gon," said a contemporary report; "the produce of the Country is of little or noe value, nor is there any markett for it any where." Local shipyards eventually did some business replacing vessels taken by the enemy; some merchants traded illegally with the French West Indies; and privateering helped cushion the losses. Between 1703 and 1712, New York privateers returned with more than fifty prizes worth as much as sixty thousand pounds, but this was a trifling sum compared to the wages of piracy a decade earlier, and it cost the lives of nearly three hundred seamen, almost half the colony's total.

The end of Queen Anne's War was in sight after 1710, when the wheel of political fortune turned again and the Tories won a majority in Parliament. Viscount Boling-broke, a Jacobite who had become the party's chief tactician, set out at once to make peace with France and restore the Stuarts to the line of succession. He achieved the former in 1713, but his plans for the latter were foiled by Queen Anne's death in 1714 and the accession of the Hanoverian George I. In desperation, Bolingbroke cast his lot with a Jacobite rising in Scotland in 1715. (For reasons of commerce as well as defense, the Whigs had engineered the unification of Scotland and England in 1707.) "The '15" ended in defeat, however, and from that point forward the Whigs had a firm grip on the government.

As the likelihood of counterrevolution receded and Parliament settled in for a long period of one-party rule, the "heats and animosityes" between Leislerians and anti-Leislerians slowly dissipated. Robert Hunter, governor between 1710 and 1719, has-tened the process by administering timely doses of both intimidation and compromise to suppress dissent. By 1717 he could inform his superiors back home that New York seemed at peace for the first time in a generation, "a perfect harmony reigning among all parties." Among the old parties, that is, for new lines of conflict were already being drawn as Britain's escalating rivalry with France spawned two competing cliques or "interests" within New York's propertied classes.

The "mercantile interest," headed by the De Lancey, Philipse, and Schuyler fami-lies, spoke for those residents who regarded the Anglo-French conflict as bad for busi-ness. The deep-water merchants among them were fearful of the toll an all-out war would take on international commerce; others traded regularly with French Canada. The De Lanceys, in particular, had relations with both sides. Stephen, who had helped establish New York's French Church, had prospered as a merchant (in 1719 he built the handsome mansion on Broad and Queen that would later become Fraunces Tavern). His success was due in part to adroit anglicizing, notably by marriage into the wealthy

Van Cortlandt family. His son James had studied in England, where the archbishop of Canterbury had been his college tutor, and the family had impressive connections with influential men in Parliament, the cabinet, and the Anglican Church.

The rival "landed interest," dominated by the Livingstons, Beekmans, Van Rensselaers, and Morrises, was an alliance between Hudson Valley manor lords and the assorted speculators, lawyers, and city retailers whose fortunes were tied to theirs (and leaned, as they did, toward Presbyterianism or other dissenting sects). They wanted no expense spared for the defense of the frontier, they welcomed war as a source of profit, and they dreamed of conquering Canada, not trading with it.

The landed interest was dominant in the early 1720s owing to the support of Governor William Burnet, Hunter's hand-picked successor. Bookish and courtly, Burnet liked nothing more than to sit on the porch of White Hall, Stuyvesant's old residence, gazing out over the harbor while taking his afternoon tea. On three occasions after 1720, at the instigation of Livingston, Morris, and their friends, the Assembly halted sales of "Indian goods" to the French, hoping thereby to keep the Iroquois tied to Britain while ruining Montreal. With the arrival of Governor John Montgomerie, who replaced Burnet in 1728, the mercantile interest got its turn to luxuriate in the warm embrace of official preferment, while the landed interest became increasingly identified with opposition to the colony's royal governors.

The full meaning of these factional twists and turns was not yet apparent, however, for by 1720 New York was on the upward slope of an economic boom that would completely change the contours of public life in the city.

9

In the Kingdom
of Sugar

Sometime over the spring or early summer of 1717, an obscure artist-engraver named William Burgis finished a six-foot-wide panoramic drawing entitled *A South Prospect of the Flourishing City of New York in the Province of New York in America*. Better known as the "Burgis View," it depicts the East River waterfront of Manhattan from the Battery to the foot of Catherine Street (slightly north of where the Brooklyn Bridge now stands). That Burgis meant to emphasize the Britishness of the city is readily apparent. At the very center of his panorama he placed Trinity Church, topped by a steeple disproportionately taller than nearby buildings. Besides drawing attention to the privileged status of Anglicanism, this device defines a visual axis of power that runs down Wall Street, passes through the Royal Navy's Station Ship, and terminates in the coat of arms of the royal governor, Colonel Robert Hunter. A bevy of oversized Union Jacks and Red Ensigns reiterates that the city is a British possession, while the absence of other national flags serves as a reminder that the Navigation Acts excluded vessels of foreign nations from every British port.

Equally apparent in the Burgis View is New York's prosperity. The economy of the town had perked up since the end of Queen Anne's War a couple of years before. Imports as well as exports were advancing vigorously, and over the next decade it was the rare year that didn't see at least two hundred vessels clear the port. Burgis's perspective evokes and celebrates this latest round of expansion by exaggerating the density of the built environment and depicting every structure that could be taken as evidence of municipal progress—churches, markets, substantial private residences, wharves, shipyards—each carefully rendered and identified by number. Lilliputian merchants walking to the Exchange, shipwrights at work on the hull of a new vessel, a man driving a steer along the waterfront, and other figures not only make the scene more lifelike but suggest the scope and variety of enterprise in the city as well. So does the impressive

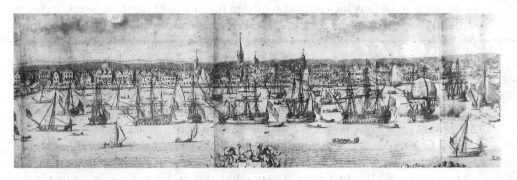

The Burgis View, 1717. Visible in the lower right-hand corner is the Brooklyn ferry landing, where cattle and produce from Long Island were brought across to the growing city. Almost directly above the ferry house, on the Manhattan shore, are the shipyards that built vessels for the West Indian trade. (© Collection of The New-York Historical Society)

throng of merchantmen, sloops, warships, yachts, and ships' boats on the river, perhaps celebrating a royal birthday or other special occasion (two vessels can be seen firing salutes).

WHITE GOLD, BLACK SLAVES

New York was flourishing when William Burgis saw it thanks mainly to a prodigious rise in the English market for sugar. In 1660, when it was a luxury associated with social privilege, England consumed a thousand hogsheads of sugar. That figure had since increased a hundredfold while the per capita annual consumption of sugar doubled, driven up by a combination of improved purchasing power and falling prices. By 1730 sugar would be as embedded in English culture as Whig principles were in English politics. A cup of heavily sweetened chocolate or coffee—accompanied by candies, cakes, or bread slathered with molasses—was integral to the daily rituals of middle-class life and a practical way to supplement the caloric intake of poorly nourished workers.

Changes in production and exchange moved in tandem with the rise in consumption. Until 1710 or so, half of England's sugar came from the tiny (166 square miles) island of Barbados. Between 1710 and 1720, however, notwithstanding the fact that its annual output continued to rise, Barbados was eclipsed by the development of numerous new plantations on Jamaica and four of the Leeward Islands: Antigua, Nevis, St. Kitts, and Montserrat. By the 1730s their combined production accounted for fully 85 percent of the sugar exported from the British West Indies, and sugar from all sources had emerged as the single most valuable article of British overseas trade. "White gold," they called it.

By then, too, wealthy West Indian planters—far wealthier, as a group, than their tobacco- and rice-cultivating counterparts on the North American mainland—were leaving their affairs in the hands of agents and returning home to England, where they set themselves up on sprawling estates and elbowed their way into social prominence alongside the old landed aristocracy and commercial bourgeoisie. The most ambitious went to Parliament, where they fought tenaciously to promote what came to be known as the West Indian "interest." Among their most notable achievements were the rum ration ordered by the Royal Navy in 1731 (half a pint per man per day) and the Molasses Act of 1733, which gave the planters a virtual monopoly of the North American market by laying prohibitively high duties on foreign (i.e., French) sugar, molasses, and rum imported into the mainland colonies. Not surprisingly, protecting the West Indies from foreign rivals, especially the French, became a central imperative of British foreign policy, a fact acknowledged by the placement of permanent British naval stations on Jamaica and Antigua.

Sugar also brought wealth to British refiners, shippers, bankers, insurers, and investors, not to mention the royal treasury, which came to depend on the taxes and duties sugar and sugar products could be made to bear. Thousands of workers were employed in the refineries and distilleries of London, Glasgow, Edinburgh, and other British ports. Their need for food and clothing and shelter created jobs, in turn, for additional thousands of laboring people and was an important reason for that great upsurge of manufacturing around the middle of eighteenth century—the industrial revolution.

No less momentous was the parallel Africanization of the West Indian populations. Between 1678 and 1745 the number of whites living on the Leeward Islands declined from 10,400 to 9,500 while the number of African slaves rose from 8,500 to 59,500. In the half century from 1651 to 1700 some 78,000 slaves had been brought to Jamaica; between 1701 and 1750 imports ballooned to 339,000. All told, between 1700 and 1775 the West Indies absorbed 1.2 *million* slaves.

After 1713, when Britain was awarded the *asiento*—the coveted exclusive right to supply Spanish America with slaves—the business was almost entirely in British hands. When Parliament broke the Royal African Company's monopoly two years later, independent slavers raced in to open new markets as well as new sources of supply. A report of 1753 said that British captains purchased 34,250 slaves every year from Africa; a second report, fifteen years later, put the figure at 53,100.

THE WEST INDIAN CONNECTION

It became so profitable to raise sugar that West Indian planters, preferring to cover their land in cane rather than waste it growing food or raising stock, turned to New England and the Middle Colonies for essential supplies. New York merchants had traded in the islands for a long time, of course; some, like Colonel Lewis Morris, maintained extensive business and family connections there. But in the opening years of the eighteenth century the West Indian market became a cornerstone of the city's economy. By 1720 or so half the ships entering or leaving the port were on their way to or from the Caribbean; another one-quarter to one-third were on their way to or from other North American colonies, moving goods often as not destined for reexport to the Caribbean.

Outward bound, New Yorkers hauled the flour, corn, pork, beef, and naval stores (tar, pitch, turpentine, lumber, and the like) without which the West Indian plantations couldn't survive (New York flour, in particular, was regarded as the finest available). They returned with bills of exchange, bills of credit, warehouse certificates, and (infrequently) specie—plus sugar, rum, molasses, cotton, indigo, lime juice, salt, cocoa, pimento, ginger, and other tropical commodities for which there were markets in the city itself, elsewhere on the North American mainland, or in London.

It wasn't specialized work. Most merchants were jacks-of-all-trades who dealt in whatever goods came their way and almost always functioned as both wholesalers and retailers. The typical vessel was a modest, all-purpose sloop or brig with a single deck, a few hands, and multiple owners (who often as not held "eights," or one-eighth shares). Its cargo represented the combined "ventures" of several traders, including members of the crew, who trusted the ability of the master or captain (who not only ran the ship but also served as the business agent of its owners) to find the best market for their goods and return with something of value. Prevailing winds and currents dictated a standard route that looped down to Barbados, swung up into the Leewards, crossed over to Jamaica, then pointed for home through either the Gulf Passage (between Florida and Cuba) or the Windward Passage (between Cuba and Santo Domingo). In practice, such a voyage would ordinarily be broken by frequent return visits to this port or that as the captain hunted among the islands to find the most favorable prices for his wares or to assemble a cargo for the homeward voyage.

Success was never a foregone conclusion. Pirates ceased to plague the Caribbean after a British expedition ran down Edward Teach ("Blackbeard") in 1718. Even so, untimely gluts or shortages, bad weather, poor judgment by a master or supercargo, an unexpected outbreak of war—any one of them could doom a voyage and bring its sponsors to ruin. To minimize such dangers, the merchants of New York and other colonial ports developed networks of correspondents upon whom they could depend for credit, for the disposal of a cargo, for the collection of debts, and for reliable news about distant crops, weather, prices, and public affairs.

As they matured, these networks facilitated intricate multilateral exchanges in both commodities and commercial paper that involved other New York merchants, indirectly but no less deeply, in the West Indian trade. Around the middle of the century, for example, Gerard G. Beekman (grandson of the Leislerian Gerardus Beekman) ran a store on Beekman Street from which he presided over a remarkable variety of projects that depended in one way or another on Caribbean products and markets. He sold limes and indigo on commission for a Philadelphia merchant, bought ginger from another Philadelphia merchant and paid for it with a shipment of logwood, bought more ginger at New London, Connecticut, that a commission agent sold for him at Boston and Newport, sold rum on commission for a Rhode Island merchant, shipped bread and flour to Rhode Island for reexport to the West Indies and used the proceeds to buy molasses that he sold on his own account in New York, and invested in a large order of cocoa that he meant to sell either there or in Philadelphia, depending on the market. Beekman's quick thinking must have saved the day more than once for his correspondents, as it did for the Rhode Islander whose shipment of cheese "Spoiling with maggets" seemed lost until Beekman hired a cartman to peddle it on the streets of New York. It was a safe bet that he would one day take advantage of a similar favor in return.

Knowing that the difference between profit and loss might well be a matter of whether or not they complied with the Navigation Acts, Beekman and his correspondents didn't scruple at evasive measures—bribing customs collectors, doctoring ships' manifests, circulating fraudulent bond certificates, and outright smuggling. After Parliament passed the Molasses Act in 1733, such conduct became almost a way of life. Planters on Guadeloupe, Martinique, and other islands of the French West Indies responded to the law by offering premium prices for North American provisions and asking less for sugar and molasses than did their British counterparts. When it became evident that customs officials were making only halfhearted attempts at enforcement, the profitability of illicit trade for North American merchants was assured. (It may have accounted for one-third of all northern commerce.) Beekman himself became so accustomed to smuggling that he would complain bitterly if circumstances compelled him to pay full duty on the rum and molasses he imported by way of Rhode Island.

What Beekman and men like him almost never did was invest their profits in plantations. Trade, not production, was the New Yorkers' forte, and they tended to think of the West Indian plutocracy as wildly dissolute and irresponsible. Nor did more than a handful of them engage in direct trade with England. Local products alone couldn't fetch high enough prices in the mother country to pay for imported manufactures. Also, because the prevailing winds blew out of the west, getting back to New York from, say, Bristol or Liverpool was a hazardous and time-consuming proposition. Ships outward bound from British ports usually took tropical routes to the New World, dropping down to Madeira to catch the Canaries Current, then winging across to the West Indies and working up the North American coast. Over time, improvements in ship rigging and design—the appearance of the gaff-rigged "schooner," the development of jib and headsails, and the adoption of the helm wheel—gradually made it easier to sail in the teeth of the westerlies. Even then, however, the majority of New York merchants continued to concentrate on the West Indies and other North American colonies.

The net result was the economic triangulation of three strikingly different systems of production: the small-farm hinterlands of northern seaports, the slave-labor plantations of the Caribbean, and the wage-labor workshops of early industrial England. New York now lived by feeding the slaves who made the sugar that fed the workers who made the clothes and other finished wares that New Yorkers didn't make for themselves. Along the way, they closed in on their old objective of breaking Boston's grip on the economies of southern New England. Lying a week closer to Barbados and ten days closer to Jamaica, the city enjoyed a natural advantage over Boston in competition for the lucrative West Indian markets. Inexorably, pressed by Philadelphia's domination of the mid-Atlantic region, New York merchants took control of the New England coasting trade. Commercially becalmed, Boston sank into a depression from which it wouldn't recover for years. After 1750 New York ranked second only to Philadelphia in wealth and population.

THE TOWN THAT TRADE BUILT

By 1720, if not earlier, the economy of New York advanced and receded throughout the year in a seasonal rhythm that was unmistakably West Indian in origin. Between November and January, the East River waterfront buzzed with activity as merchants and captains rushed to get down to the islands in time to take delivery of the new sugar crop, usually ready soon after the first of the year. The pace slackened in the early spring, then picked up again between April and June as the ships raced back to escape hot-weather diseases and hurricanes. Another brief lull was followed, in the high summer, by the arrival of additional vessels from other mainland ports (usually Boston) and, in the fall, from Britain.

The effects of the West Indian connection were visible as well in the expansion of commercial agriculture around the city. On innumerable small and medium-size plots, ranging from a few dozen to a few score acres in extent, the rural populations of Long Island, Staten Island, New Jersey, and Westchester—many relying heavily on slave labor—produced an ever-growing volume of foodstuffs for the Caribbean market. Bigger and richer landowners like Lewis Morris, nephew and heir of Colonel Lewis Mor-

ris, built productive complexes that combined elements of slave plantations and industrial villages. From Morrisania, his nineteen-hundred-acre estate in what is now the
southwest corner of the Bronx, he and his workforce—which in 1691 included one of
the area's largest concentrations of slaves (twenty-two men, eleven women, six boys,
two girls)—sent corn, wheat, barley, oats, lumber, and a variety of livestock to Manhattan for export to the West Indies. (The Morris property ran west from the Harlem River
to Intervale Avenue, with the manor house near the junction of 132nd Street and
Cypress Avenue, overlooking Long Island Sound.) Morris ground the grain in his own
gristmill and cut the lumber in his own sawmill. He kept his own sloop, and even operated an ironworks at Tintern, New Jersey. His products—as was the case with all lumber, grain, flour, meat, and leather exported to the West Indies—were carefully scrutinized by government inspectors as to size, weight, and quality and labeled accordingly.
All exported butter, for example, was packed in firkins branded "N.Y."

Shipbuilding grew rapidly to meet the demand for the single-masted sloops and
two-masted brigs needed for Caribbean and coastal commerce. In 1728, having made a
fortune in the West Indies, "Boss" William Walton founded a shipyard on the East
River at the foot of Catherine Street (just north of the Brooklyn Bridge, about where
the Alfred E. Smith Houses now stand), and another five were soon in operation nearby.
Sail lofts and ropewalks (the enlongated workshops that made rigging and lines for
ships) likewise enjoyed unprecedented prosperity—as did millers, cartmen, chandlers,
and other trades heavily dependent on oceangoing commerce. Coopers worked hard to
keep up with mounting demand for wooden firkins, casks, tubs, and vats, their livelihoods protected by duties on the importation of empty containers from other colonies.

Other New Yorkers flourished by processing imports from the West Indies, above
all sugar. In 1730 Nicholas Bayard announced in the *Gazette* that he had erected, virtually next door to City Hall, a "Refining House for Refining all sorts of Sugar and Sugar-
Candy, and has procured from Europe an experienced artist in that Mystery." In time,
Livingstons, Roosevelts, Van Cortlandts, and Rhinelanders would follow him into the
business of turning brown sugar into clean white loaves of table sugar, suitable for
export to Europe or the West Indies. By the early 1720s, moreover, sixteen distillers
were turning molasses into rum (much of the raw material having been smuggled in
from Martinique). In addition, after 1715, New Yorkers began importing tobacco for
conversion into snuff, a process that involved the grinding and flavoring of dried tobacco leaf.

The movement of these exports and imports would have been impossible without
the labor of "Jack Tar," the seafaring man who loaded, sailed, and unloaded the city's
growing merchant fleet. Mariners had been a familiar presence on Manhattan ever since
the West India Company first set up shop, but never in such quantities: by the second or
third decade of the eighteenth century, not counting the masses of transients who drifted from port to port in search of work on the docks or merchant vessels, perhaps one
out of every four or five adult male residents of New York earned his livelihood as a
mariner. It was a notoriously hard existence—periodic bouts of unemployment punctuated by long, isolating voyages on ships where the dangers, atrocious conditions, harsh
discipline, strict division of labor, and exploitative wages prefigured the industrial factories of a later era. Since most men quit (or died) after fewer than ten years at sea, the
average age of crews tended to fall somewhere between twenty-five and thirty. No other
trade or occupation in the city developed a stronger sense of collective identity and

interest, however. More than once, crowds of "Brother Tars" in their distinctive attire—baggy breeches (tarred to keep out water), checked shirts, "fearnought" jackets, Monmouth caps—swarmed out of waterfront gin mills and rookeries to confront a tyrannical captain, dishonest "crimps" (the recruiting agents who filled out crews for merchants), or a press gang from one of His Majesty's warships. Their fine disdain for thrift, sobriety, polite speech, and organized religion constituted a standing challenge to the values of respectable society. "A merry life and a short one": that was the sailor's motto.

Because the perils of the sea threatened the owners as well as crews of ships, access to reliable marine insurance was a matter of increased importance in the city. Rather than rely solely on underwriters in London or Amsterdam, a few prominent New York merchants began to insure voyages on their own, forming consortiums of wealthy residents willing to share the risks at an attractive rate of interest. Similarly, the need for access to capital promoted the expansion of private banking. One lawyer went so far as to advertise his services as an intermediary, inasmuch as "many Persons in this Province have often Occasion to borrow Money at Interest, and others have sums of Money lying by them which they want to put out." All transactions, he added, would be managed with the "greatest Secrecy and Integrity."

Indeed the legal profession too was changing significantly in these years. Until quite recently, all but a few of New York's two dozen or so lawyers had been self-taught "attorneys" rather than formally trained "barristers." Their knowledge of the law was often rudimentary, most of their work consisted of collecting debts or making out conveyances, and even the busiest of them doubled as tavern keepers, ferry operators, and tradesmen. Now, however, the demands of an increasingly complex international economy, together with the new, anglicized legal system, gave the edge to professionals with expensive university educations. Their desire to set higher standards had already led to the formation of the city's first bar association in 1709.

With the expansion of trade, too, came more taverns and coffeeshops. Between 1694 and 1720 fifty-four tavern keepers, victuallers, and vintners were granted the "freedom" of the city. New inns and ordinaries like the Black Horse Tavern joined the old King's Arms in providing residents and travelers alike with food, lodging, and a convivial setting for business. The Exchange Coffee House, which opened in 1729 at Broad and Water, became the principal scene of real estate transactions, while the Merchants' Coffee House (originally named the Jamaica Pilot Boat) catered to merchants active in auctions and shipping.

Taverns, and the dozens of dramshops that catered to seamen and the laboring classes, were often run by widows who received free licenses from the Common Council, an inexpensive form of relief. Women were also prominent in the retail shops that boomed after the late 1720s. The Widow Lebrosses carried Canary wine and olive oil in her store at Hanover Square, the city's shopping center, while the Widow Vanderspiegel and her son sold imported window glass. Mrs. Edwards started a cosmetics business in 1736, offering "An admirable Beautifying Wash, for Hands Face and Neck, it makes the Skin soft, smooth and plump, it likewise takes away Redness, Fredkles, Sun-Burnings, or Pimples." The continuing role of women in trade, English as well as Dutch, promoted a certain feistiness among their ranks that ran contrary to prescriptions for proper female behavior. In 1733 the Widow Lebrosses and other "She Merchants" complained bitterly to the press that while they were "full as Entertaining" as men, and certainly as brave, the governor never invited them to dinner "at Court." As taxpayers who "in some measure contribute to the support of the government, they reasoned, "we ought to be entitled to some of the sweets of it."

The typical retail shop carried a wide range of goods. In 1733 George Talbot displayed beds, chairs, tables, chests of drawers, and andirons. In 1736 the "New Store in Hanover Square" offered haberdashery, dry goods, laces, pictures, pipes, snuff, cutlery, hardware, and glassware. Visitors to William Bradford's printing office could buy coffee, Bohea tea, and "Very good oatmeal" in addition to books. Thomas Adams, a stationer, had also begun selling reading matter, and by 1719 there were perhaps four booksellers in town.

The diversity of imported goods in New York was matched by their costliness. Governor Hunter asserted that a 100 percent advance over London prices was "reckoned cheap" on Manhattan, where profits from the West Indian trade, swollen by indirect earnings from insurance and interest on loans, were contributing to a relentless rise in the concentration of wealth. As early as 1716 John Fontaine, a visitor from Virginia, met "many rich people" in New York; ten years later the richest 10 percent of the population—mostly merchants, with a sprinkling of lawyers and landed gentlemen who had taken up residence in town—controlled half the city's wealth. Judging by estate inventories of upper-class households, these rich New Yorkers proceeded to accumulate luxuries—silver, fine furniture, carpets—at a significantly greater rate than their seventeenth-century forebears.

The demand for luxury goods and services in turn spurred the formation of a pool of skilled local artisans and tradespeople. By the 1720s fine work was being turned out by New York goldsmiths, silversmiths, watchmakers, potters, and jewelers. Families of means seeking self-portraits patronized a small group of local artists (known more colloquially as "phiz mongers"), including old Evert Duycinck. "Crooked women" seeking to "appear strate" could get help at the stay shop run by James Munden and Thomas Butwell. Nichols Bailey, coachmaker, sold chaises and chairs for ladies. Barbers and periwig makers arrived to cater to their husbands.

For food and other provisions, New Yorkers shopped at the municipal markets, of which (by 1728) there were five along the East River waterfront—one at the end of each major street (Broad, Coenties Slip, Wall Street, Old Slip, and Maiden Lane). But much of what city households needed was grown and made by its women. Housewives, aided by daughters and perhaps female slaves, produced soap and candles, smoked meats, put up garden fruits and vegetables, spun flax, dyed yarn, wove cloth, and sewed clothes. Governor Cornbury observed in 1705 that New Yorkers made "very good linen" for domestic use as well as "very good serges [and] linsey-woolseys." Several years later, the Board of Trade was advised to make them stop, because if they began to produce cloth for the market it would be "very much to the prejudice of our manufactures at home."

Finally, New York's developing connection to the West Indies brought a sharply higher frequency of epidemic disease. A ship from the islands was blamed for a major outbreak of smallpox in 1690, and after the turn of the century malaria, yellow fever, and other tropical scourges became an all too familiar part of life in the city. In 1702 a visitor informed William Penn that "at York they are visited with a mortal distemper . . . which sweeps off great numbers; tis such a visitation as that place, they say, never knew before, carrying off eight, ten, or twelve in one day." Over a three-month period, smallpox and "malignant fever" claimed 570 lives—better than 10 percent of the population. Because well-to-do residents "left their usual habitations and Retired into the Country"—Lord Cornbury retreated as far as Albany—the poorer classes suffered a disproportionate share of the fatalities and the immiseration that often followed.

New York had plenty of doctors, among them Cadwallader Colden, who graduated from the University of Edinburgh and studied medicine in London before migrating to Philadelphia. When he moved up to New York in 1718, Colden discovered to his dismay that twenty "Chirurgeons" and two "Barber-Chirurgions" had been admitted into free-manship over the previous two decades. "The practice of Physick being undervalued," Colden found it necessary to supplement his income by wholesaling imported drugs (and stockings) to local shopkeepers and apothecaries (Mrs. Colden occasionally moved some of his merchandise at retail). Of course it wasn't only the oversupply of doctors that caused New Yorkers to undervalue "the practice of Physick," for the current state of medical knowledge still put great stock in such useless practices as purging and bleeding. Colden's own contribution to the problem was to take an active part in oppos-ing the introduction of inoculation in 1722, although his colleagues eventually accepted the idea in time to minimize fatalities in the epidemic that struck the city in 1731.

CITY OF SLAVES

Nowhere was the impact of the West Indian trade on New York more obvious than in its burgeoning population of African slaves. Stuyvesant, York, Bellomont, and others had dreamed in years past of making the city an entrepôt in the slave trade or exploiting slave labor for the production of commodities. Yet despite the best efforts of the Dutch West India Company and York's Royal African Company, slavery remained a marginal feature of the municipal economy. Decade after decade, New York merchants took only a fitful interest in slaving, and the number of slaves on and around Manhattan rose more slowly than the rest of the population. When Stuyvesant surrendered in 1664, New Amsterdam counted about fifteen hundred whites, three hundred slaves (half the colony-wide total of six hundred), and seventy-five freedmen. Forty years later, the 1703 census found forty-four hundred whites and somewhere between six and seven hundred blacks in New York City alone—more than twice as many, but down from 20 percent to around 12 or 13 percent of the total (enslaved Indians, never common, were exceedingly rare after 1700).

Everything changed during the second and third decades of the eighteenth century, as the city became more closely tied to the plantation colonies of the West Indies. Their insatiable demand for servile labor and foodstuffs drew growing numbers of city mer-chants into the slave trade. By 1730 it had become big business in the countinghouses of Pearl Street and Hanover Square, never representing more than a minor share of the total tonnage involved in overseas commerce yet sufficiently lucrative that few mer-chants weren't involved at one time or another.

In the city itself, where cheap labor was always in short supply, the economic advan-tages of slaveowning became harder to overlook as greater availability brought down costs. By the early eighteenth century, the price of a prime slave was roughly equivalent to the annual wages of a skilled craftsman, and direct imports began to soar. In the first quarter of the eighteenth century, twenty-four hundred slaves would be legally import-ed into New York, with another five thousand to follow over the next fifty years (maybe six hundred or so of whom would be smuggled in): seventy-four hundred in all, greater than the entire population of the city in 1700. More blacks came involuntarily to

New York in the eighteenth century, in other words, than whites came voluntarily in the seventeenth.

The proportion and distribution of slaves in the city's population increased accordingly. In 1712 nearly a thousand of New York's sixty-four hundred inhabitants—somewhat over 15 percent—were black, and better than 40 percent of its households owned a slave. By 1746 African Americans comprised about 21 percent of the city's residents—more than 2,440 in a total population of nearly 11,720. This was the highest concentration of slaves north of Virginia. At least half the city's households now contained one or more slaves.

Merchants bought slaves to fill out their crews and toil on their docks. Shipbuilders put them to work in the bustling East River yards. Coopers, butchers, carpenters, blacksmiths, tinners, and other artisans prospered by training them up in the mysteries of their crafts. In 1715 Governor Hunter remarked on the manumission of a butcher's slave, "who by his faithful and diligent service, had helpt to gain most part of his masters Wealth." Tradesmen unable to afford slaves found themselves at a competitive disadvantage, and in 1737 the provincial assembly received a report of widespread opposition to the "pernicious custom of breeding slaves to trades," which "reduced [whites] to poverty for want of employ."

Wealthy New Yorkers began to utilize slaves as domestic servants. ("Please to buy mee two negro men about eighteen years of age," Cadwallader Colden instructed his commercial agent in 1721. "I design them for Labour & would have them strong & well made. Please likewise to buy mee a negro Girl of about thirteen years old my wife has told you that she designes her Cheifly to keep the children & to sow.") And if ever there wasn't enough work to do, owners could hire their slaves out at half the going rate of free labor—enough, as a rule, to bring an annual return of between 10 and 30 percent on

TO be Sold, a Young Negro Woman, about 20 Year old, she dos all sortr of House work; she can Brew, Bake, boyle soaft Soap, Wash, Iron & Starch; and is a good darey Women she can Card and Spin at the great Wheel, Cotten, Lennen and Wollen, she has another good Property she neither drinks Rum nor smoaks Tobacco, and she is a strong hale healthy Wench, she can Cook pretty well for Rost and Boyld; she can speak no other Language but English; she had the small Pox in *Barbados* when a Child. Enquire of the Printer here of and know the Purchase.

N.B. She is well Clothed.

From *New York Weekly Journal*, April 15, 1734. (© Collection of The New-York Historical Society)

the initial investment. This business was already so brisk by 1711 that the Common Council designated the Meal Market at the foot of Wall Street as the authorized site for the purchase, sale, and hire of slaves. From time to time the council itself appropriated funds to hire slaves for construction and cleanup projects around town.

Across the East River, in Kings and Queens counties, slaves did almost everything. They worked for merchants, grocers, physicians, attorneys, tallow chandlers, coach-makers, ropemakers. Samuel Hallet's slave piloted ships on the river. But the bulk of rural slave labor was employed in agriculture. Bondsmen and bondswomen cut, hauled, and split firewood; carted dung, mended fences, thatched roofs, and repaired farm buildings; raised vegetables, fruits, animals; plowed fields, mowed meadow grasses, har-vested potatoes, cut and husked corn; butchered hogs and salted and barreled the meat; cooked, kept house, sewed, spun, knit, repaired clothing, attended table—and in their off-moments were hired or leased to others.

The 1738 census turned up twenty-three hundred people in Kings County, of whom one in four was a slave. Brooklyn, whose 705 inhabitants made it the largest vil-lage, had 158 slaves (22 percent). Flatbush, second largest with 539 inhabitants, con-tained 129 slaves (24 percent). In Bushwick, population 327, there were another 78 slaves (24 percent). The 185 whites of tiny New Utrecht owned 84 slaves (an astonish-ing 31 percent). By contrast, the overall proportion of slaves stood at 14 percent in Queens and Suffolk counties, 18 percent in Richmond, and 13 percent in Westchester.

The highest concentrations of slaves occurred on the great Westchester and Hud-son Valley estates, where slavery settled in alongside indentured servitude and tenantry. Caleb Heathcote, created lord of Scarsdale Manor in 1702, depended on dozens of slaves, indentured servants, and tenants to produce lumber, grain, cloth, and leather goods for export. By mid-century, Frederick Philipse's son Adolph had some eleven hundred tenants and two dozen slaves on Philipsburg Manor, an agricultural-industrial complex that not only produced a variety of grains for the New York market but ground and bolted (sifted) them in its own mills, packed them in its own barrels, and shipped them downriver in its own sloops.

But these high concentrations of slaves were extremely unusual, for most New York masters owned no more than two or three slaves. Their need for slaves, their ability to purchase slaves, and their capacity to house and feed slaves were on an utterly different scale from the masters of cash-crop plantations in the southern colonies. Even so, the life of a slave in a small household could be as harsh, in its own way, as in the rice and tobacco fields of Carolina or Virginia. When an SPG catechist named Elias Neau began to baptize slaves in New York, masters resisted on the grounds that conversion imposed constraints on their property rights—even after a 1706 law, supported by Neau, affirmed that it did not. It was almost impossible, moreover, for slaves to form enduring family units because masters routinely opposed slave weddings, broke up husbands and wives to raise cash, sold off infants as well as superannuated adults, and wrote wills dividing up their chattel among their heirs. In 1717 Cadwallader Colden sold a slave woman to a purchaser on Barbados precisely because he wanted to remove her from her children. "I could have sold her here to good advantage," he admitted, "but I have sev-eral other of her Children which I value and I know if she should stay in this country she would spoil them."

New York slaves were divided on cultural lines as well: those imported from the West Indies and thus already "seasoned" (perhaps speaking Spanish), or those—two out of every five in these years—who arrived directly from Africa. Typically, the latter had roots in the Akan-Asante society of the continent's west coast, a fact reflected in the large numbers named, according to Akan-Asante practice, after the days on which they were born—e.g., Quashee (Sunday), Cudjo (Monday), Quaco (Wednesday), Cuffee or Cuff (Friday), and so on.

Notwithstanding such obstacles, many slaves found common ground in practicing and perpetuating African customs, both sacred and secular. Burials were a focal point of the wider slave community, a chance to engage in traditional funerary rites. The interment ground lay north of the city, in a low-lying area that ran east from Broadway toward a deep ravine that continued to the Fresh Water Pond. It may have been used by the Africans since before the English conquest, because it lay near many of the plots granted half-freed slaves. It was certainly well established by 1713, a year after blacks were denied interment in Trinity's graveyard. "They are buried in the Common," wrote the Rev. John Sharpe in 1713, "by those of their country and complexion without the office, on the contrary the Heathenish rites are performed at the grave by their countrymen." Bodies were wrapped in shrouds fastened with brass pins and placed in wooden coffins; some had coins placed over their eyes, while others were adorned with seashells, glass beads, or buttons of bone and pewter. They were laid to rest with their heads facing west, as was done in Africa.[1]

These nighttime ceremonies were disturbingly outside white jurisdiction, although whites themselves habitually foreclosed other options. In 1722, for example, the Common Council passed a law requiring that "all negroes and Indian slaves dying within this corporation on the South side of the fresh water be buried by daylight at or before sunset," while three years later a Bushwick town meeting resolved that "no negro at all shall be buried in this aforesaid churchyard." Similarly, whites attempted, with at best mixed success, to prevent slaves from coming together in great and occasionally raucous gatherings, especially on the Sabbath. "On Sundays while we are at our Devotions," Elias Neau remarked in 1703, "the streets are full of Negroes, who dance and divert themselves." In 1710 they were said to "feast and Revell in the Night time."

"BONNY COUNTRY"

The same demand for labor that led New Yorkers to purchase slaves in record numbers stimulated an upsurge of immigration from Europe in the early decades of the eighteenth century. First to arrive were the Palatine Germans. Mostly Lutherans and Calvinists, they had barely recovered from the terrible devastation of the Thirty Years War when they were overrun, again and again, by the armies of Louis XIV during Queen Anne's War. In the wake of the catastrophic epidemics and famines that followed the French invasion of the Rhineland in 1707, they appealed to the British government for help. Queen Anne, eager to rescue Protestants from the clutches of a Catholic despot, said the Palatines could take up land in British North America; Parliament,

---

1. The African Burial Ground was part of land deeded by Governor Colve in 1673, during the brief Dutch reconquest of the city, to Cornelius van Borsum, in recognition of the services of his wife, Sara Roeloff. A daughter of Annekje Jans, Roeloff had acted as an interpreter in negotiations between Dutch officials and the Esopus Indians. Subsequent disputes over the title, lasting well into the eighteenth century, probably delayed the development that would eventually cause the burial ground to be filled in. The site was rediscovered in 1991, during excavations in the block bordered by Broadway, Duane, Elk, and Reade streets. The remains of four hundred men, women, and children were removed to Howard University for further study.

eager to populate the colonies, passed a law naturalizing foreign Protestants.

No one was prepared for the response. By the end of 1709 at least thirteen thousand German refugees had already crowded into London, and thousands more were said to be on the way. All manner of schemes were developed for putting the Palatines to work in Ireland, Wales, or one of Britain's overseas possessions. Most promising was a proposal to settle them in communities along the Hudson River in New York, "where they might be useful to this kingdom, particularly in the production of naval stores, and as a frontier against the French and their Indians." A small advance party reached New York in 1708 and began a settlement at Newburgh, fifty-five miles north of the city.

The main body of Palatines, some twenty-five hundred in all, arrived in the summer of 1710 with Governor Hunter. Flabbergasted at the sheer magnitude of this invasion, which amounted to roughly 40 percent of the city's population, and frightened by an outbreak of typhus among the exhausted and malnourished newcomers, the Common Council quarantined the Palatines on Nutten (Governors) Island. There they languished while Hunter tried to find them land and city merchants cashed in on their desperate need for food, clothing, and shelter. Several hundred Palatines died in the course of the summer and were buried in unmarked graves. Of those who survived, about eighteen hundred were subsequently transported up to several tracts of land lying along the Hudson, where they founded half a dozen small communities. The rest, around 350 individuals, settled in New York City. Forty or so were apprenticed out to local residents, including John Peter Zenger, who went to work in William Bradford's printshop. The others were probably widows and children.

Things got worse. The Palatines soon learned that they weren't to be independent proprietors but indentured servants of the crown, obliged to work at the pleasure of the governor until the costs of transporting and relocating them had been paid off. Hunter's agents herded them into labor gangs to do the noisome, unfamiliar work of extracting turpentine, tar, and pitch from pitch pines; children orphaned by the typhus epidemic were apprenticed off in Albany and other towns. Enraged, the Palatines mutinied, and Hunter sent troops to restore order. It then became clear that the land chosen for them was poorly suited for cultivating pitch pines—whereupon Hunter turned them loose to fend for themselves. Some found their way to the Mohawk Valley. Others scattered into New Jersey and Pennsylvania. Still others returned to the city. No one could have been happy with the outcome except perhaps the merchants who, like Lewis Morris and Robert Livingston, realized tidy profits selling them spoiled food and second-rate supplies at inflated prices. Livingston also wound up with sizable numbers of Palatines as his tenants.

Close behind the Palatines came the Irish, though on their own rather than with official backing. Roughly two out of three were the so-called Ulster Scots or Scots-Irish, the descendants of hundreds of thousands of Scottish Presbyterians driven by chronic poverty and religious persecution to settle Ireland's northern counties during the seventeenth century. After 1715 a succession of blows—parliamentary suppression of the Irish woolens industry, crop failures and famine, rack-renting by absentee English landlords—forced them to move again, first to Irish coastal ports, then to America. Between 1720 and 1730 the mainland colonies as a whole absorbed more than fifteen thousand Ulster Scots.

With them came between sixty and eighty thousand Roman Catholics (many of them possibly Gaelic-speaking) from Ireland's southern counties, driven out by legal proscription, Protestant prejudice, and the erosion of traditional communities. While cheap land on the frontier was their primary goal, a substantial though undetermined number made their way to New York City. Many arrived as indentured servants who contracted to serve an employer for a stated period of time, in exchange for passage and keep ("sufficient Meate drinke and App[arel] during his said time," as one indenture phrased it). Sometimes this was arranged in Europe, as in 1729, when tailor William Presland agreed, in the presence of the lord mayor of Dublin, to serve New York merchant John Colgan for four years. Others were advertised for sale in the *New-York Gazette* on their arrival. ("Redemptioners" were those who agreed to pay for their passage within a stated period after arriving in America; if they failed to "redeem" this debt, the captain who brought them could sell their services to the highest bidder as indentured servants.)

When the ship *Thomas* arrived from London in October 1728, its owners invited the public to purchase the indentures of "several Men, Women and Boys, Servants, amongst whom there are several Tradesmen, as Bakers, Weavers, Bricklayers, Carpenters, Shoemakers, Glassiers, Coopers, &c." Not infrequently, entire families were on the market. "To Be Sold," read one advertisement at the middle of the century: "A German Servant Man, with his Wife and Son, of about Six Years old, who are to serve five Years, he is as compleat a Gardner as any in America; understands a Flower and Kitchen Gardens to Perfection." (Only a tiny fraction of these were the convicted felons routinely sent out from the mother country as indentured servants: most such "transported" convicts wound up in the plantation colonies of the Chesapeake or the West Indies.)

What drew artisans to New York was the good pay they could expect after they had served their terms. In "York city," James Murray wrote home in 1737, "a Wabster gets 12 Pence a Yeard, a Labourer gets 4 Shillings and 5 Pence a Day, a Lass gets 4 Shillings and 6 Pence a Week for spinning on the Wee Wheel, a Carpenter gets 6 Shillings a Day, and a Tailor gets 20 Shillings for making a Suit of Cleaths, a Wheel-wright gets 16 Shillings for making Lint Wheels a Piece."

Despite Murray's assurances to those left behind that his new homeland was a "bonny Country," a servant's life could be a harsh one, as attested by the mounting number of advertisements for runaways published in the *Gazette* during the 1730s. One Hugh Agen, his master advised, "wears a light coloured blew Coat" and "is an Irish man" though he "pretends to be a Doctor and to let Blood." Nevertheless, well before

(The New York Society Library)

the middle of the eighteenth century the Irish, Protestant and Catholic, had become the most numerous and rapidly expanding element of the city's working population. New York's reputation as a market for Irish servants was indeed so well established by then that Dublin could boast two inns, both named the New York and Philadelphia Arms, where shipping agencies processed prospective immigrants for the voyage over.

Not to be confused with the Scots-Irish were immigrants from Scotland proper. Like Robert Livingston, handfuls of native Scots had found their way to New York in search of fame and fortune during the final decades of the seventeenth century. But after 1707, when the Act of Union with England opened a period of sweeping economic and social upheaval, immigration from Scotland accelerated. As in Ireland, enclosures and rack-renting displaced tens of thousands of cotters from their traditional holdings; the failure of the Jacobite rising of 1715, and of a second rising in 1745, drove away thousands more, at least some of whom were banished prisoners of war. All told, more than twenty-five thousand Scots—perhaps as many as fifty thousand—found their way to America before the end of the colonial period. Most settled in the Carolinas, New Jersey, or Pennsylvania, but there was always a regular trickle to New York, where "Presbyterians," Scots as well as Scots-Irish, had become a force in the life of the city by the third decade of the century. In 1716, "att the desire of a few especially Scots people," visiting minister James Anderson began preaching and was soon called to serve as pastor of the First Presbyterian Church, conducted in the manner of the Church of Scotland. The erection of its first building, on the north side of Wall Street between Broadway and Nassau streets, offered clear evidence of how much the climate had changed since Cornbury's persecution of the Rev. Francis Makemie, an Ulster Scot.

Though at first, as Anderson reported in 1717, his church's supporters were "yet but few & none of the richest," the expanding commercial ties between New York and Scotland (which after the Union of 1707 was allowed to trade directly with the American colonies) drew a number of well-to-do merchants and professionals. So did the appointment of a string of Scotsmen—Hunter, Burnet, and Montgomerie—to serve as governor of the colony. Indeed Hunter, a Scot well known in the coffeehouses of London and boon companion of such literary luminaries as Joseph Addison, Richard Steele, and Jonathan Swift, prompted a miniature Scottish Enlightenment in the city. Described by one admiring colonist as "a gentleman of as refined a taste as any we have known or perhaps heard of in America," Hunter gathered unto himself a small group of intellectuals united in the belief that fortune had set them down in a cultural wasteland. Together they discussed books, conducted experiments with pendulums and telescopes, and collaborated on an Italian translation of Addison's play *Cato*. Hunter himself composed Latin odes and achieved a certain literary renown in 1714 with the publication of *Androboros: A Biographical Farce in Three Acts*, the first play written and printed in America.

Conspicuous in Hunter's circle were the attorney James Alexander, the physician Cadwallader Colden, and the proprietor of Morrisania, Lewis Morris. Alexander, one of the Jacobites transported to America after the 1715 rising, had an aptitude for mathematics and engineering that immediately brought him to the governor's attention; under Hunter's aegis, he embarked on a long and illustrious public career (along the way training an entire generation of New York lawyers in his office). Colden, whom Hunter appointed surveyor-general of the province, possessed one of the most original minds in the colonies. His copious writings on physics, botany, history, and ethnography (especially his *History of the Five Indian Nations*, first published by William Bradford in 1727) would earn him an international reputation—New York's answer, as it were, to Benjamin Franklin. Boasting a library of three thousand books, not much smaller than that of Harvard College, Colden was a devoted student of Cicero, Virgil, Tacitus, Shakespeare, Milton, and Addison. He composed poetry, dabbled in the natural sciences, and taught the Linnaean system of plant categorization to his daughter Jane, whose subsequent research made her something of a celebrity among botanists on both sides of the Atlantic.

The same need for mercantile and professional expertise that helped break down resistance to dissenting Protestants helped revitalize New York's Jewish community. The first generation of immigrants had moved elsewhere by the early 1660s—Asser Levy was for many years the only one remaining in town—but the 1680s brought a steady trickle of Portuguese-speaking Sephardim from the West Indies, Surinam, France, and England. Religious services had resumed in 1682, and although its appeals for formal recognition of the right to public worship were consistently rejected, the congregation wasn't molested. By the mid-eighties it had acquired a private burying ground (a corner of which still survives on St. James Place opposite Chatham Square); by the mid-nineties, if not earlier, it was openly using a house on Beaver Street as a synagogue.

Yet New York Jews faced legal hurdles to earning a livelihood in the city. The great majority weren't English citizens, and the Navigation Acts explicitly prohibited them from doing business in England or in any English colony (even the right of native-born Jews to engage in trade or own property remained less than secure). Legal naturalization didn't provide an attractive solution to the problem, since Parliament required prospective subjects to swear an Anglican oath of allegiance. The alternative was to obtain a patent of denization from the crown, allowing the recipient to settle and trade in specified parts of the realm. But this required money and political connections, and only a dozen or so Jewish residents of New York ever managed to become endenizened in England. In addition, the provincial assembly, in 1683, had decreed that anyone wishing to be naturalized in New York would have to be a professing Christian.

Almost immediately, however, the potentially adverse effects of such a restriction on the city's commercial interests compelled local authorities to be more accommodating (just as they had once compelled the West India Company to make Stuyvesant accept the presence of Jews in New Amsterdam). Governor Fletcher began the practice, continued by his successors, of granting letters of endenization to Jews and other aliens, for a fee, few or no questions asked. After 1718, moreover, the Assembly routinely naturalized Jews on its own authority and permitted them to omit the phrase "on the true faith of a Christian" from the necessary oaths. The municipal corporation meanwhile quietly ignored instructions from England that the privileges and duties of freemanship be restricted to native-born, naturalized, or endenizened subjects. Even before the turn of the century, as a result, Jews were serving on juries, in the militia, and on the Common Council; many would hold the office of constable (one of whose duties was to collect taxes for the Anglican Church). Similarly, although the English Test Act of 1673 barred Jews (and Catholics) from sitting in the Assembly or holding appointive office, local custom allowed Jews to vote freely in provincial as well as municipal elections. (When this was called into question in 1737, the Assembly voted to deprive Jews of the franchise. The decision wasn't strictly enforced, though, and within a few years Jews were again going to the polls without interference.) Of equal importance, Jews inherited the economic right—for which Asser Levy had fought decades earlier in New Amsterdam—to trade in local commerce like other burghers. This right to make a living as they pleased, without constraint, wouldn't be available to them in England for another half century.

In this climate, New York Jews flourished. Nathan Simson made his mark in the West Indian trade and retired at the end of the 1720s with an estate valued at sixty thousand pounds. His son Joseph was one of several Jewish merchants who did so well marketing kosher beef in the islands and elsewhere that by the 1740s the stamp *K.Sh.I.*, *kasher* (Congregation Shearith Israel, kosher) was recognized throughout the colonies. The marriage of Jacob Franks to Bilah Abigail Levy in 1712 not only ensured Franks's success in trade but was also the beginning of a mercantile dynasty that would be renowned in London and Philadelphia as well as in New York. Luis Moses Gomez shipped New York wheat to Lisbon, used the profits to import wine from Madeira, then expanded his operations to include furs, slaves, rum, and English manufactured wares. In addition to such families, who ranked among the city's wealthiest residents, Jews occupied positions as peddlers, candlemakers, butchers, watchmakers, goldsmiths, and shopkeepers.

The community was not without its internal divisions. The immigration of more and more German speakers in the early eighteenth century—by 1730 a majority of the 225 Jews in New York were Ashkenazim—stirred resentment among the Sephardim. Proud, socially conscious families like the Gomezes resisted intermarriage with "Tudescos" (i.e., Germans), even wealthy ones like the Franks, and tensions between the two groups were reflected in their tendency to live in different parts of town: Sephardim in the East Ward, Ashkenazim in the Dock Ward. When the congregation decided to erect

Bilah Abigail Franks. "Still it Gives me a Secret pleasure to Observe the faire Chareeter Our Family has in [this] place by Jews and Christians," she once wrote. (American Jewish Historical Society)

a new synagogue on Mill Street (South William) in 1728, the Sephardim made no secret of their apprehension that it would adopt Ashkenazic liturgical practices. By the mid-thirties, however, Ashkenazim and Sephardim came up with an arrangement that enabled them to present a more unified front to their sometimes hostile neighbors: henceforth the president of the congregation would normally be an Ashkenazi, while services continued to follow Spanish-Portuguese ritual under the leadership of a Sephardic *hazzan*. The use of Portuguese in congregational records and on tombstones nonetheless slowly but surely yielded to English; before the middle of the century it had disappeared altogether.

Despite New York's reputation for allowing "perfect freedom of conscience for all, except Papists" (as one Dutch dominie put it in 1741), the attainment by some Jews of social and economic standing stirred resentment. On one occasion, in 1743, a mob attacked a Jewish funeral cortege, seized the corpse, and subjected it to a mock conversion. A less clear-cut case of anti-Semitic violence would occur half a dozen years later, when Oliver De Lancey organized a mob to attack the home of a recently arrived Jewish merchant. They smashed all the windows, broke down the door, wrecked the interior, and threatened to rape the man's wife—on the grounds, De Lancey allegedly said, that she looked like the wife of Governor George Clinton, "and if he could not have her, he would have her likeness." Oddly, De Lancey's own wife was Phila Franks, daughter of Jacob and Bilah.

AN EPITAPH FOR DUTCH NEW YORK

As New York grew ever more integrated into the English empire, and trade with Holland ever more attenuated, the position of the city's Dutch declined accordingly, more so than met the eye. Well into the second decade of the eighteenth century, travelers continued to marvel at the tenacity of Dutch speech, Dutch dress, and Dutch architectural conventions in New York. Sarah Kemble Knight, in 1704, was astonished at how *different* its Dutch women looked. "The English go very fashionable in their dress," Mrs. Knight wrote. "But the Dutch, especially the middling sort, differ from our women, in their habitt go loose, were [wear] French muches wch are like a Capp and a head band in one, leaving their ears bare, which are sett out wth Jewells of a large size and many in number. And their fingers hoop't with Rings, some with large stones in them of many Coullers as were their pendants in their ears, which You should see very old women wear as well as Young." A dozen years later John Fontaine remarked that most houses still went up "after the Dutch manner, with the gable-ends toward the street," and in the Burgis View of 1717 it is indeed possible to make out, huddling along the waterfront below Wall Street, the stepped gables and sharply pitched roofs that bore silent witness to the days when New York was New Amsterdam.

Yet between 1700 and 1720 the Dutch component of the city's white population fell below 50 percent for the first time, and its marginalization, underway for a generation, passed the point of no return. A select company of Dutch traders with good connections in London or the West Indies—Rip van Dam, Abraham De Peyster, Jacobus Van Cortlandt—prospered in the boom that followed Queen Anne's War. As a group, however, Dutch merchants now formed a distinct minority of the city's wealthiest inhabitants, and proportionally fewer Dutch New Yorkers owned slaves than either the English or the French. What was more, fully 80 percent of the families in the city's poorer neighborhoods were Dutch. The Dutch had managed to carve ethnic niches in the labor force—they were disproportionately represented among the ranks of coopers, smiths, masons, cordwainers, cartmen, and other laboring people—but these niches were at the lower end of the city's economy. The Dutch were losing ground politically too. Prior to Leisler's Rebellion, most mayors of New York had been Dutch; after Leisler, not only were most mayors English or French, but as a rule the Dutch held a third or fewer of the seats on the Common Council.

After 1720 Dutch was almost exclusively reserved for private communication or worship. Subsequent attempts to provide Dutch-language schooling for the young invariably failed, and by the early 1740s even bilingualism was a thing of the past. "The Dutch tongue Declines fast among Us Especially with the Young people," wrote a saddened Cornelius van Horne, grandson of a New Amsterdam settler. "All Affairs are transacted in English and that Language prevails Generally Amongst Us."

Affirmatively Dutch communities did survive along the Hudson River, over in New Jersey, on Staten Island, or out on Long Island. Dutchess, Orange, and Ulster counties remained predominately Dutch for years; Albany was almost exclusively Dutch, and would long remain so. Overall, nevertheless, the Dutch now constituted a clearly dwindling minority of the colony's population, and Dutch settlements outside the city were becoming more clannishly isolated from the rest of the world.

Dwindling population and waning prosperity were accompanied by a pietist movement that tunneled through the Reformed Church during Queen Anne's War. The pietists' message—part denunciation of orthodox clerical authority, part attack on liturgical formalism, part summons to individual spiritual renewal—reaped bountiful harvests of souls along the rural frontiers of New York and New Jersey, home to large numbers of Leislerians who hadn't forgotten the Church's complicity in their leader's defeat and execution. When an evangelical dominie named Theodore Frelinghuysen began preaching among the villages of New Jersey's Raritan Valley in 1720, the movement erupted into an open revolt.

These afflictions, combined with the chronic shortage of Dutch-speaking dominies, the missionary efforts of the Society for the Propagation of the Gospel, and the growing social status commanded by the Church of England, helped expand Anglican congregations. Every year prominent Dutch families went over to the Church of England—Beekmans, Roosevelts, Schuylers, Stuyvesants, Van Cortlandts, Verplancks, Van Dycks. Huguenots too embraced Anglicanism, most notably Elias Neau, who had been an influential elder in the Huguenot Church before enlisting with the SPG. By the 1730s the French Church had all but vanished.

Other institutions that had shielded the Dutch way of life in the first generation or two after the English conquest were in comparable disarray. No longer recognized in provincial courts since the Judiciary Act, the mutual will—last line of defense against British patriarchalism—virtually disappeared from use in the early eighteenth century. As among the English, married women used their husbands' names; a husband enjoyed full control of his wife's personal property (clothing, housewares, money) and had the right to administer (though not dispose of) her real estate until his death, even if she should die before him. Though some Dutch women continued to run businesses, they were now almost always widows, far outnumbered by men. (And perhaps because they had more to lose from Anglicization, Dutch women were slower than their husbands to abandon the Reformed communion. After 1700 women comprised two-thirds of the new members of the Dutch Church.)

De Lanceys, Livingstons, Schuylers, Van Rensselaers, Beekmans, Morrises, Philipses: New Yorkers now tended to speak of them in the plural not merely because these families spread so luxuriantly as time went on, but because in an anglicized environment it was the family name that determined social standing and political influence. Outsiders could and often did acquire money and reputation, but the price was going up all the time and more and more rich men were starting out as the sons (or sons-in-law) of other rich men.

Rich women, by the same token, were being held to new standards of purity and obedience with the expectation that they would devote themselves to childrearing, household management, and the mastery of such parlor rituals as the serving of "high tea" (now de rigueur among the English upper classes). "Let your Dress your Conversation & the whole Business of your life be to please your Husband & to make him happy & you need not fail of being so your self," Cadwallader Colden wrote his daughter Elizabeth De Lancey in 1737. It was advice that might well serve as the epitaph of Dutch New York.

10

One Body Corporate and Politic?

On the morning of February 11, 1731, Mayor Robert Lurting and two dozen other municipal officials gathered at City Hall to prepare for a ritual that none had ever taken part in before. At precisely ten o'clock, no doubt after some last-minute fussing with wigs and robes, they proceeded "in their formalities" down to Fort George and were escorted into the presence of Governor John Montgomerie. Montgomerie greeted them with a little speech, then handed Lurting "his Majestys Royal and most Gracious Charter to the Mayor Aldermen and Commonality of this City." The New Yorkers, who had already paid Montgomerie an £840 cash bribe to get them the charter, praised the governor for his "Just Good and wise Administration." After a round of drinks and toasts, they returned to City Hall.

Twice before, from Governor Nicolls in 1665 and from Governor Dongan in 1686, New York City had received municipal charters. Neither grant bore the royal seal, though, and doubts had arisen over the years as to their validity. In 1729, after repeated appeals to have its status clarified, the Common Council petitioned the crown for a new charter ratifying the city's "ancient Rights and Priviledges." The delivery of the "Montgomerie Charter" a year later was a happy occasion—all the more so because in the charter His Majesty praised New York for having "become a considerable seaport and exceedingly necessary and useful to our kingdom of Great Britain in supplying our governments in the West Indies with bread, flour, and other provisions."

"A FREE CITY OF ITSELF"

The Montgomerie Charter established, or confirmed the existence of, a corporation— "one body corporate and politic"—bearing the name of "the Mayor, Alderman, and Commonality of the City of New York." The charter also gave the corporation an "estate" consisting of the City Hall as well as all municipal market buildings, docks,

The Lyne-Bradford Plan of 1730/1731, drawn by surveyor James Lyne and printed by William Bradford. The first map of New York to be printed in the city itself, and probably intended to accompany the Montgomerie Charter, it shows that the built-up area of town now extended almost up to what is now Fulton Street. Wall Street remains the municipal axis, running east from the "English Church" (Trinity), past the new City Hall and the Meal Market, to the Coffee House on the corner of Water Street. The East Ward, lying east of William Street between Hanover Square and John Street, has begun to replace the Dock Ward as the city's commercial center of gravity. (© Collection of The New-York Historical Society)

wharves, cranes, and bridges; the "waste and common land" of Manhattan; the land surrounding Manhattan out to the low-water mark, plus an additional four hundred feet around the southern end of the island; the waterfront of "Nassaw Island" (Long Island) "from the east side of the place called Wallabout to the west side of Red Hook"; and the exclusive right to operate ferries between Manhattan and Long Island. Like other individual property owners, the corporation could increase, improve, sell, lease, or otherwise dispose of this estate as it saw fit. It could sue and be sued.

Like other property owners, too, the corporation was accorded powers of self-determination commensurate with the size and nature of its estate. In the words of the charter, it was a "free city of itself." It could lay streets, regulate markets, license trades, and charge fees. It could make laws and promulgate ordinances not only for "the good rule and government of the body corporate" but for the "common profit, trade, and better government" of all the city's inhabitants. To enforce such laws and ordinances it could set up courts, erect jails, collect fines, confiscate goods and chattels, and administer punishments "not extending to the loss of life or limb."

The "free city of itself" was not perfectly autonomous. It had to abide by English and provincial law. It could not tax its inhabitants (that was a power reserved for the provincial legislature and perhaps, depending on one's point of view, Parliament). What was more, the corporation's top officials—the mayor, sheriff, coroner, and recorder—continued to be appointed by the colonial governor. When petitioning for a new charter the Common Council had pleaded for an elective mayor; the crown's refusal was a clear signal that the corporation must answer to interests over and above those of its members.

Likewise the charter's distinction between "freemen" and "freeholders." "Freemen" were residents enrolled as voting members of the corporation after swearing an oath of loyalty and paying a modest fee—initially £3 12s. for a "Merchant, Trader or Shopkeeper," £1 4s. for a "Handy-craft Tradesman," and mere pennies for native-born residents of the city or those who had completed an apprenticeship there (the exact amounts varied over time). Counting white women and slaves of both sexes over the age of twenty-one, about one-third of the city's adult population qualified for the freemanship. "Freeholders" (a term not used in either the Nicolls or Dongan grant) were defined by existing provincial statute as persons owning real property worth forty pounds in the ward where they voted. They needn't be residents of the ward, or even residents of the city, and were permitted to vote in *every* ward where they met the property qualification. Here too the charter gave outsiders a voice in the corporation's governance; to wealthy outsiders it offered the prospect of more than one.

Freemanship conferred genuine benefits. As under the old burgher-right, only freemen could practice an "art, trade, mystery, or occupation" or sell "any manner of goods, wares, merchandises, or commodities by retail . . . within the said city." Every Michaelmas (September 29), they assembled ward by ward to elect their aldermen, assessors, collectors, and constables for the year to follow. Though bona fide headcounts are very rare, throughout the first half of the eighteenth century, probably three or four of every five adult white males in the city had the right, as freemen of the corporation, to determine by whom they would be governed. This made the freemen of New York one of the most inclusive political communities in British America.

Some freemen were affluent merchants, lawyers, landowners, and "gentlemen." The majority consisted of carpenters, bakers, bricklayers, butchers, cordwainers, cartmen, mariners, tavern keepers, weavers, tanners, laborers, and other working people of moderate means, or less. (Between 1700 and 1745 better than two thousand individuals representing ninety-one trades would be admitted to freemanship; after mid-century half the new admissions were laborers.) Rich or poor, all freemen were created equal under the charter, and the charter held them all equally responsible for the management of the corporation's business. "Ye Shall be Contributing to all Manner of Charges within this City," ran the oath to which they were required to swear, "as summons, Watches, Contributions, Taxes, Tallages, Lot and Scot, and all other Charges, bearing your Part as a Freeman Ought to do."

Freemen did not, however, enjoy access to the corporation's real estate. In many villages of England and New England, the "commons" were available to all members of the community for hunting, cutting hay and firewood, pasturing livestock, and the like. Not so in New York, where the Montgomerie Charter gave the corporation absolute ownership of its estate, unencumbered by old-fashioned "use-rights." The Common Council would in fact spend considerable time prosecuting trespassers, encroachers, poachers, and others who allegedly threatened the value of its holdings.

Suffusing the charter was the idea of a collective civic good that transcended the private interests of individual freemen. The most direct and tangible expression of this belief was a welter of regulations (some dating back to the Dutch era) that protected all freemen from the destructive effects of economic competition, dishonest practices, and shoddy workmanship. Periodic "assizes" fixed the weight, quality, composition, and price of every essential commodity offered for public sale in the city. Other regulations prevented "forestalling," the practice by which sellers bought up and withheld goods from the market in the hope of boosting prices. Wages too were typically set by statute, and there was close supervision of trades deemed vital to the public interest—carters, butchers, bakers, tavern keepers, gravediggers, porters, chimney sweeps, river pilots, midwives, and assorted municipal functionaries (gaugers, packers, watchmen, weigh-masters, and so on).

Yet the welfare of the corporation as a whole was an ideal that could mean different things to different people. Building and repairing docks, for instance, were improve-ments to the municipal infrastructure that arguably benefited everybody. But how should the work be done? Municipal authorities favored a policy of selling the "water lots" that lay between high- and low-water marks along the East River. Purchasers were required to fill in the lots and construct buildings, wharves, bulkheads, and streets—which looked like a reasonable way to raise revenue while developing the port. It was also, however, a device for moving some prime urban real estate into the hands of wealthy speculators and developers. So, too, when municipal authorities refused to let the cartmen raise their rates, it was hard to avoid the conclusion that the livelihoods of working people were secondary to the interests of merchants.

DEFERENCE OR INDIFFERENCE?

Merchants and the propertied classes usually got their way, moreover, for freemen of modest means—the "middling" classes who comprised perhaps 60 percent of the city's white population—generally failed to sustain an organized presence in either municipal or provincial politics. From time to time, small merchants, shopkeepers, and master craftsmen occupied as many as half the seats on the Common Council, while others served regularly as constables, assessors, market inspectors, and the like. Yet for several decades, elections grew duller by the year, polling was generally slow, and incumbents were almost always returned to office without opposition.

For rich and influential New Yorkers, the kind who dominated the Assembly and Common Council, this was exactly as it should be. To their way of thinking, a political-ly engaged "commonality" meant instability and upheaval because men of little or no property, even freemen of the corporation, lacked the judgment and self-discipline needed for participation in public affairs. And because they depended on others for trade, patronage, and employment, such men (like women and children) could never be trusted to think or act independently: when they entered the political arena it was cer-tain to be as mere tools of someone else. A stable, effective system of government was thus one in which the mass of citizens deferred to the leadership of their social superi-ors—just as they now appeared to be doing in New York.

But there were other reasons for the torpor of public life in the city. For one, except for the annual Common Council elections, the freemen had few venues for sustained political activity. All the important citywide offices were appointive, besides which Assembly elections occurred only at the discretion of the governor or on the death of the monarch (not until 1743 was legislation adopted that mandated elections at least once every seven years). All told, in the eighty-four years between 1691 and 1775 New Yorkers voted for assemblyman on only thirty-one occasions.

For another, the law required viva voce or "voice" voting in both charter and provincial elections, meaning that every voter declared his preference, openly, before election officials, candidates, and neighbors. While the chilling effect of this procedure cannot be discounted, freemen were not altogether vulnerable to the blandishments of powerful men. Master craftsmen owned their own shops and tools, determined for themselves how often and how hard they would work, and took a fierce pride in the "mysteries" and traditions of their trades; journeymen weren't employees but prospective equals sharing similar assumptions and expectations.

New York's political quiescence in the early eighteenth century thus had less to do with deference, as such, than with a combination of institutional constraints and popular indifference to the issues that tended to dominate public affairs. Governors fought with the Assembly for control over the public purse. Landed and mercantile interests jockeyed for advantage. But what did any of that matter to ordinary freemen of the municipal corporation? When they needed to sit up and take notice, they would—and did.

THE MASTER'S VOICE

And what of all those residents, roughly two out of every three adults, excluded from the corporate community by reason of gender, race, or poverty? How did the freemen expect to secure *their* compliance with municipal rules and regulations?

The maintenance of law and order depended—by day—on the constables of each ward (one of whom seems to have been designated high constable). From nine o'clock at night to daybreak the following morning the night watch took over—"four good And honest Inhabitants householders," as the Common Council described them in 1698, who were paid to "go round the Citty Each Hour in the Night with a Bell and there to proclaime the season of the weather and the Hour of the Night and if they Meet in their Rounds Any people disturbing the peace or lurking about Any persons house or committing any theft they take the most prudent way they Can to Secure the said persons." Attempts were made from time to time to improve on the system, now by adding more men, now by paying the men for their efforts. The thinness of municipal police power was unmistakable, however, and it was never regarded as the city's main line of defense against the multitudes who lived beyond the pale of membership in the corporation. (The county sheriff and city marshal, as agents of the county and mayor's courts respectively, had no responsibility for routine police work in the city.)

It was no accident that the Common Council wanted "Inhabitants householders" for the night watch. The typical workplace in eighteenth-century New York was part of a private house, or something in close proximity to a private house. Merchants, lawyers, and physicians saw clients and patients in their parlors. Importers and exporters kept their "stores" in attics and back cellars. Retailers displayed their wares, and tavern keepers served their customers, in small ground-floor front rooms. Master craftsmen set up workshops in their own homes—on the first floor, in the basement, in backhouses, or in yards—while their apprentices, slaves, and indentured servants, if any, slept in garrets or nearby outbuildings. Even sugar refineries, shipyards, ropewalks, and tanneries— trades that required heavy, bulky equipment as well as ample space—were located as close as possible to the residences of their owners.

In this domestic mode of production, the heads of households were managers of labor as well as parents. More exactly, their "families" included one or more dependents to whom they weren't biologically related but over whom they exercised, by law as well as custom, paternal authority ("paternal" more than "parental" because after 1700 only one New York household in six was headed by a woman, typically a widow).

Other than the small handful of constables and the night watch, the freeman-pater-familias, master of his household, was the primary bulwark of public order, because throughout the eighteenth century the freemen's apprentices ranked among the most troublesome elements of the city's population. Mostly they were young men between the ages of ten and twenty-one (though William Reade was apprenticed to a tailor in 1701 at the age of five) or girls bound out to learn housewifery, cooking, and sewing. Most were British in origin (because the Dutch rarely made use of formal apprentice-ship agreements). Their rights and responsibilities derived from the Elizabethan Statute of Artificers (1562), which was the explicit basis of regulations relating to apprenticeship in New York after 1695. Apprentices swore to serve their masters well and faithfully for a specified period of time (a 1711 ordinance required a minimum of seven years). In return, their masters promised to teach them a trade, to give them adequate room and board, and, at the end of their terms, to release them with whatever clothing, tools, or "freedom money" was required by their written deed, or indenture. Nearly all indentures, moreover, offered to provide some education. In 1693 Frances Champion was apprenticed as a house servant to Elizabeth Farmer, who agreed to "Instruct the said Frances to Reade and to teach and Instruct her in Spining, Sewing, Knitting or any other manner of housewifery." Night schools for apprentices became popular after 1700, and indentures often included arrangements for them to attend after work.

As surrogate parents, masters also had full authority to discipline their apprentices by any means not causing death or permanent physical injury. In theory, the good behavior of apprentices was ensured by the promise of admission to a trade and automatic membership in the corporation when their terms were over. But apprentices were frequently too young, too homesick, too restless, or (as a printer's apprentice named Benjamin Franklin said of himself) "too saucy and provoking" to heed their masters. Often they refused to work or worked indifferently. Some returned to their parents or signed up with other masters, actions that could embroil everyone in long and acrimo-nious litigation. So many simply took to their heels, never to be seen or heard from again, that the runaway apprentice would become a stock figure of the eighteenth-century urban scene. Nor did masters invariably live up to their part of the bargain. Abusive or negligent masters weren't hard to find, and ill-clad, ill-fed, and ill-treated apprentices were an all too common sight on city streets.

Repeatedly, the Common Council tried to bolster the authority of masters with ordinances that prohibited apprentices from loitering, gambling, bartering or selling goods, fighting, swearing, drinking in taverns after eight or nine o'clock at night, and other offenses against the peace of the city (especially on the traditional popular holi-days: in 1719 the Court of General Sessions complained of the "Disorders and Other Mischiefs that Commonly happen within this City on Shrove Tuesday by Great Numbers of Youths Apprentices and Slaves that Assemble together in throwing at Cocks"). Apprentices who broke the law could be fined, whipped by the public whipper, or sentenced to longer terms of service, at the discretion of the magistrates.

Masters who failed to abide by their contractual obligations, especially those guilty of cruelty, were increasingly likely to be fined or to have their apprentices released. James Jamison's indenture to Henry Brughman was voided in 1718 when the magistrates learned that Brughman had so disfigured Jamison's face that he stood "in Danger of loosing his Eyes." In 1728 eleven-year-old Margaret Anderson won a discharge from her apprenticeship to Benjamin Blake, a cordwainer, who was found guilty of "very often Immoderately Correcting her & not allowing her reasonable time to rest several times in the Night."

Indentured servants presented the corporation with a somewhat different kind of dilemma. Although servants too were subject to the *in loco parentis* authority of masters, they were probably older than apprentices, on the whole, and doubtless included a higher percentage of women. Some already knew a trade, having gone into service for the sole purpose of obtaining passage to the colonies. They also appear to have been rather less tractable than apprentices. Masters griped constantly about disobedient servants, larcenous servants, and idle servants. Ann Sewall savagely beat Ann Parsons and kept her "in Chains and Irons for several Weeks upon bread and water only," explaining "she didn't know itt was the breach of any Law her said Servant having highly offended her." Small wonder that hardly a day seemed to go by when the sheriff and constables didn't have to contend with servants who, like apprentices and slaves, struck back or ran off. (In 1734 maidservants formed an organization and declared that "we think it reasonable we should not be beat by our Mistrisses Husband[s], they being too strong, and perhaps may do tender women Mischief.")

Maintaining order was complicated by the town's so-called bawdy or disorderly houses—unlicensed groggeries and gin mills catering to boisterous crowds of apprentices, servants, free women, and even slaves. The better part of them also sheltered a brisk underground traffic in stolen goods as well as aiding and abetting prostitution; many were located in the homes of widows or unmarried women unable to support themselves by other means. In 1710 Elizabeth Green spent a week in jail because she regularly permitted "sundry Negro slaves to assemble and meet together to feast and Revell in the Night time" at her house. Such an establishment, besides endangering public safety, was an ominous inversion of the social order—a world turned upside down, an underworld beyond the authority of masters, where the conventional boundaries between races and sexes were flagrantly ignored.

THE CITY AND THE POOR

Further complicating the management of servants and apprentices was the sharply unequal distribution of wealth in the city. According to the 1730 census, New York's population stood at 8,622: 7,045 whites and 1,577 blacks. That same year, a comprehensive property assessment revealed that the richest 10 percent of the city's taxable population, some 140 merchants and landowners, held almost half its taxable wealth. By contrast, 49 percent of white taxables held property worth ten pounds or less—a pathetically meager sum, indicating that around one-third of all whites were more or less destitute. On the assumption that virtually all blacks were no better off, nearly three-fifths of the city's inhabitants thus lived at or near the subsistence level. (Poverty wasn't just an urban problem. In rural Newtown, just across the East River, the pressure of population on the community's supply of land had begun as early as the 1720s to diminish the size of holdings and multiply the numbers of those without any land at all.)

In New Amsterdam, the care of the indigent had been left to the city's religious bodies. In New York, this approach seemed less and less satisfactory as the seventeenth century drew to a close. Not only were the numbers of poor people rising, but on both sides of the Atlantic poverty as such was increasingly regarded as an aspect of the general problem of labor discipline. In the comprehensive Settlement Act of 1662, Parliament prohibited the indigent from seeking relief outside their native parishes and drew up precise classifications of poverty to prevent the able-bodied from evading work. The New York Assembly followed Parliament's lead in 1683 with the first colony-wide measure "for Maintaining the Poor and Preventing Vagabonds." The law combined relief for needy residents of every community with provisions for the prompt eviction of newcomers who lacked visible means of support (to which end it also required ship captains to give the magistrates a list of all their passengers). Because each town and county had to maintain its own poor, governor Dongan remarked, "no vagrants, beggars, nor idle person" would be allowed in the colony.

The poor didn't go away, though. In 1685, at Dongan's urging, the Common Council ordered the aldermen of each ward to identify their "deserving poor"—established residents who had fallen on hard times through no fault of their own—and for the first time accepted the responsibility to provide "for their Reliefe out of the publique Treasury." This decision was affirmed in the Ministry Act of 1693, which created a special tax known as the "poor rate" and made the proceeds available to five "overseers of the poor" or "churchwardens" (secular officials, despite the name). So-called outdoor relief, or outrelief, the most common form of aid, involved grants of fuel, clothing, food, and even cash. Persons unable to care for themselves could be boarded with families. In New York City, the very sick and infirm were placed in an almshouse on Broad Street, the first of a succession of private residences that the corporation rented for this purpose after 1700. Denied assistance of any kind were nonresidents and all able-bodied persons judged fit to work for a living. In 1707, moreover, the Common Council told the churchwardens to "put a Badge upon the Clths of such persons as are clothed by this city with the Mark N:Y in blew or Red Cloathh." (Only ten years earlier Parliament had passed a similar law requiring pensioned paupers to wear the letter *P*.)

During Queen Anne's War, warnings about the inadequacy of the poor rate became a standard feature of the annual churchwardens' report. In 1713 the wardens said their resources had been exhausted by the many people in the city "who are in great want and a miserable condition and must inevitably perish unless some speedy method be taken for their support." Next year the tax was raised to £438, three times the amount collected in 1697.

Relatively few New Yorkers received municipal assistance (one reason being that local congregations continued to give food, clothing, shelter, pensions, and medical care to their "own" poor, who therefore weren't counted as public charges). Between 1721 and 1725 the names of only two-hundred-odd residents appear on the relief rolls—ninety-nine women, fifty-five men, fifty children—170 of them on outrelief, twenty in the almshouse, and fourteen as boarders. Nearly all the boarders and residents of the almshouse were men too old or sick to work; the bulk of those on outrelief, by contrast, were indigent widows with children.

Vagrants and beggars—the undeserving poor, men and women deemed unwilling to work by the authorities—got no pity. In 1699 Governor Bellomont proposed the construction of a workhouse to "employ the poor and also vagabonds," but the Assembly rejected the idea. "They smiled at it because indeed there is no such thing as a beggar in this town or country," Bellomont wrote. Just one year later, the Common Council nevertheless adopted legislation for removing the "Vagabonds & Idle Persons that are a Nuisance & Common Grievance of the Inhabitants." (Perhaps two dozen individuals and their families were actually expelled from Manhattan in the first half of the century.) For those worthy of sterner treatment, "a Cage, Whipping post, pillory and Stocks" were erected in front of the new City Hall on Broad Street. Subsequent legislation authorized thirty-five lashes for anyone returning to town after deportation and required all citizens to report the presence of strangers to the authorities.

"A TERROR TO OTHERS"

When the Montgomerie Charter went into effect, some sixteen hundred of the city's residents, roughly 18 percent of the total population, were black slaves. Prominent officials were beginning to wonder if the presence of so many slaves didn't discourage white immigration, and working people had already complained on numerous occasions that the increasing employment of blacks in the trades was costing them jobs. None doubted, though, that preserving order among this large servile labor force had become one of the corporation's most pressing challenges.

Legally, there was no longer any doubt as to the subordinate and dependent status of blacks. By the beginning of the eighteenth century, the comparatively broad rights enjoyed by slaves under Dutch rule—to hold property, to carry a weapon, to serve in the militia, to sue in court, to obtain half-freedom—had all been whittled down or stripped away. New York's first comprehensive slave code, adopted in 1702, underscored the association of slavery with black skin by banning the enslavement of Indians and defining indentured servitude as a condition for whites only. It granted masters nearly unlimited powers of correction, set up special tribunals to try slaves accused of crimes, and authorized a Common Whipper for the city. Subsequent enactments by either the legislature or Common Council confirmed that slavery was heritable through the female line, prohibited more than three slaves gathering together at a time (twelve for funerals), restricted the movement of slaves after nightfall, banned slaves from selling food or other goods in the streets (a practice known as "huckstering"), and eliminated conversion to Christianity as grounds for manumission. Innkeepers couldn't sell liquor to slaves, and severe penalties were decreed for whites who helped slaves break the law or failed to take appropriate action when they did. In 1738 Elizabeth Martin was "Reputed a Common Whore as with Negro Slaves as to others and a great Disturber of the Peace." Declared a "very Low Notorious Wicked Woman," she was ordered out of city. When she refused to go, she received thirty-one lashes and was chased out.

It proved next to impossible to enforce such laws. Slaves moved about the city almost at will in the course of their work and were often unsupervised by their masters for extended periods of time, even at night. Despite the profusion of statutes, therefore, municipal authorities were inundated year after year with demands to stop slaves from illegally congregating, brawling, breaking curfew, playing in the streets on Sundays, and drinking at "bawdy houses" whose white proprietors were suspected of keeping prostitutes and fencing stolen goods. Their brazen defiance of whites was notorious. In 1696 Mayor William Merritt ordered a group of noisy slaves to disperse and got punched in the face; half a dozen years later Governor Cornbury expressed alarm at the "great

RUN AWAY

THE 18th Inftant at Night from the Subfcriber, in the City of New-York, four Negro Men, Viz. LESTER, about 40 Years of Age, had on a white Flannel Jacket and Drawers, Duck Trowfers and Home-fpun Shirt. CÆSAR, about 18 Years of Age, cloth-ed in the fame Manner. ISAAC, aged 17 Years cloathed in the fame Manner, except that his Breeches were Leather; and MINGO, 15 Years of Age, with the the fame Clothing as the 2 firft, all of them of a middling Size, Whoever delivers either of the faid Negroes to the Subfcriber, fhall receive TWENTY SHILLINGS Reward for each befide all reafon-able Charges. If any perfon can give Intelligence of their being harbour'd, a reward of TEN POUNDS will be paid upon conviction of the Offender. All Mafters of Veffels and others are forewarn'd not to Tranfport them from the City, as I am refolved to profecute as far as the Law will allow. WILLIAM BULL.
N. B. If the Negroes return, they fhall be pardon'd. - 88

New-York Gazette; or, *the Weekly Post-Boy*, October 27, 1763. Notices such as this, common in colonial newspapers, typically provided as much detail as possible about the fugitives and their destinations. (© Collection of The New-York Historical Society)

insolency" of slaves in the city. Everybody complained about runaways, especially as it became known that fugitives could find refuge with the Seneca, Onondaga, and other Indian tribes to the north, or the Montauks, Shinnecocks, Massapequas, and others of eastern Long Island.

A mere hint of restiveness among black New Yorkers could throw whites into a near panic. And not without justification. New York slaveowners knew full well that the price of slavery in the West Indies had been a long ordeal of racial violence and bloodshed. Between the 1670s and the 1730s half a dozen major slave insurrections and numerous small revolts took place on Barbados and Antigua alone; on Jamaica, armed bands of escaped slaves known as Maroons kept the authorities at bay for decades. New Yorkers knew, too, that slaves convicted of serious crimes in the West Indies—even arson and murder—were frequently sold to unsuspecting buyers on the mainland. Beginning in 1702 the Assembly tried to deter nonresident merchants from dumping these "refuse Negroes" on the colony by permitting local merchants to pay much lower tariffs on slaves imported directly from Africa. How many veteran insurrectionaries had ended up in New York? No one knew for sure. Everyone feared, however, that a mere handful could do terrible damage to the city and neighboring communities.

Could it happen in New York? A gang of runaway slaves allegedly robbed and ter-rorized Dutch farmers in Harlem in 1690. In 1706 Governor Cornbury learned that "several N's in Kings County (Brooklyn) have assembled themselves in a riotous man-ner, which if not prevented may prove of ill consequence." To make certain the turmoil didn't spread, he ordered the arrest of "all such Negroes as shall be found to be assembled—& if any of them refuse to submit, then fire upon them, kill or destroy them, if they cannot otherwise be taken."

Two years later, Queens County was thrown into an uproar by the slaying of William Hallett Jr., a prominent landowner and self-styled "gentleman" whose plantation bordered Hallett's Cove in present-day Astoria. Hallett, it seems, had tried to stop his slaves "from going abroad on the Sabbath days." In retaliation, an Indian slave named Sam and his African wife murdered Hallett, Hallett's wife, and their five children. The culprits were quickly seized, convicted, and executed on the plains east of Jamaica. Sam was impaled and hung in chains. His wife was burned alive. Two other black men were executed as accessories. A witness reported the four "were put to all the torment possible for a terror to others."

The city got its first taste of servile rebellion in 1712—less than a year after the municipal slave market opened for business. One night in early April, two dozen slaves who, Governor Hunter reported, "had resolved to revenge themselves, for some hard usage, they apprehended to have received from their masters," gathered in an orchard of Mr. Crook, "in the middle of the town." According to John Sharpe, the Anglican chaplain, the majority were unchristianized Kormantines and Pawpaws from the Akan-Asante society of the Gold Coast—probably imported within the previous year or two (so much for the assumption that newcomers from Africa were more docile). They had pledged themselves to secrecy "by Sucking ye blood of each Others hands" and attempted to make themselves invulnerable by rubbing their clothes with a powder supplied by one Peter the Doctor, "a free negroe who pretends Sorcery." Arming themselves from a secret cache of stolen muskets, swords, knives, and hatchets, the conspirators set fire to a nearby building and ambushed residents who rushed to put out the flames. Nine whites were shot or slashed to death before Governor Hunter raised the garrison and marched against them, but the rebels "made their retreat into the woods, by the favour of the night." The next day, Hunter sealed off "the most proper places on the Island to prevent their escape," then dispatched militia to "drive the island." Hunted down, six of the conspirators cut their own throats (one man killing his wife and himself) rather than be captured. Seventy others were arrested and brought back for trial before a special court convened by the governor. Twenty-three were convicted of murder, two others of attempted murder. Twenty were hanged outright. Three were burned to death—among them Tom, a bondsman of Nicholas Roosevelt, who was condemned to roast over a slow fire "in Torment for Eight or ten hours & Continue burning in the said fire untill he be dead and Consumed to Ashes." Another, named Robin, was sentenced "to be hung up in chains alive and so to continue without any sustainance untill he be dead." Still another, named Clause, was "broke alive upon a wheel." Spread-eagled and fastened face upward on a wheel, he was laid flat on the ground in front of City Hall. A Dutch sailor (who said he'd seen the thing done in Rotterdam and knew how to go about it) then took a crowbar and over a period of many hours smashed the bones in Clause's body, one by one, stopping now and again for refreshment at Jan Peterson's Broad Street tavern. Clause finally expired at two o'clock the next morning, having suffered, as had the others, what Hunter assured the Lords of Trade were "the most exemplary punishments that could be possibly thought of."

In the wake of the trials the Common Council ordered that no slave could travel about the city after dark without a lantern. (Elias Neau, the SPG catechist, was widely blamed for sowing discontent among the city's slaves; the new lantern law was in part an attempt to cut attendance at his school, which held classes only at night.) The Assembly drafted a tough new slave code. Among other things, the law made manumission almost prohibitively expensive for masters and stipulated that no freed slave could henceforth own a house or land in the colony. But this merely codified the status quo. By the early eighteenth century very few free blacks remained on Manhattan; most of them lived on the fringes of the city on land granted them or their forebears by the Dutch West India Company.

The real legacy of the 1712 uprising was a new era of routinized brutality and official cynicism toward slaves. Crowds of townsfolk often gathered now to watch slaves hanged or burned to death for one offense or another. A slave girl named Rose was arrested "foar Damning the White Peoples Throats and Yours too (Speaking to a White Woman) and divers other Vile Expressions against the White People"; the magistrates gave her nine lashes at the whipping post, had her tied to a cart and dragged around town, gave her thirty-nine more lashes for good measure "on the Naked Back," and then transported her to another colony. And when John van Zandt horsewhipped his slave to death in 1735 for being on the streets at night, an all-white coroner's jury found that the "Correction given by the Master was not the Cause of his Death, but that it was by the Visitation of God."

II

Recession, Revival, and Rebellion

y 1730, even as municipal officials prepared to receive the new city charter, New York was sliding into a deep recession. Part of the problem was that cheap flour from Pennsylvania had cut into New York's share of the West Indian trade. Merchants and farmers, now heavily reliant on wheat production, responded by cutting prices—then expanded output in order to maintain their profits, glutting the market and driving prices still lower. At the same time, climaxing years of overproduction on West Indian plantations, the price of brown sugar at the London Custom House fell off sharply. Pressed by their creditors, numerous planters failed, and those who didn't fail retrenched. Trade between the islands and the mainland colonies slumped for the first time in nearly two decades, then sagged further still when the Molasses Act of 1733 took effect. Being part of an international commercial network, it was clear, could bring severe dislocations as well as create opportunities. An alarmed Lieutenant Governor George Clarke advised New Yorkers to consider manufactures as the solution to their dilemma. "The markets for your flour, the present staple of the Province, are already so much overdone by the great importations that are made of them from this and the other northern colonies," he warned, that unless New York could begin to produce goods "that are wanted in Great Britain" (and didn't interfere with British manufactures), then soon "there will be no way to employ the people to any advantage."

In New York, the ramifications of the recession were multiplying quickly by the mid-1730s and continued for the remainder of the decade. The city offered "nothing but the melancholy Scene of little Business, and less Money," it was reported in 1732. Shipyards languished; by 1734 only one or two vessels were under construction, and the governor was seeking ways to "give life to the expiring hopes of ship carpenters." Indeed everyone whose livelihood depended on overseas trade was in trouble. "The Baker, the Brewer, the Smith, the Carpenter, the Ship-Wright, the Boat-Man, the

Farmer, and the Shopkeeper"—all were suffering, "John Scheme" wrote to the *New-York Weekly Journal* in 1734. Many residents had been forced "to seek Other Habitations so that in these three Years there has been above 300 Persons who have left New-York." Sailors were hit hard as the town's merchant fleet, 124 ships strong in 1700, shrank to fifty in 1734. Residents wondered how the prosperity of the previous decade could have ended so quickly. As one poetically inclined writer asked in the pages of the *New-York Gazette* in 1733: "Pray tell me the cause of trade so dead, / Why shops are shut up, goods and owners fled, / And industrious families cannot get bread?"

Disease made matters worse. Epidemics of measles and smallpox claimed 549 victims, some 6 percent of the population, before running their course at the end of 1732. "Many Children dye . . . and the Country People are afraid to come to Town which makes Markets thin, Provisions dear, and deadens all Trade, and it goes very hard with the Poor." Between 1731 and 1735, almost four hundred people required public assistance—twice as many as a decade earlier—while the poor rate soared to £649 (although the churchwardens and vestrymen were unwilling to raise taxes to support able-bodied artisans out of work). Prosecutions for larceny, fencing stolen goods, and prostitution rose swiftly, accompanied by a skittish clamor for a new jail and a better watch. Courts imposed increasingly severe exemplary punishments, and the municipal gallows were moved up to the Common to accommodate larger crowds.

Hard times increased racial animosities. In 1737 Lieutenant Governor Clarke received petitions from skilled craftsmen who "complain with too much reason of the pernicious custom of breeding slaves to trades. The honest and industrious tradesmen are reduced to poverty for want of employ" and must "seek their living in other countries." For this too Clarke had a solution. New York, he said, needed to be "replenished with white people" and made an all-white city. But white outmigration continued, the flow of white immigrants fell off, and the city—its economy and society now hooked on slavery—continued to import African slaves. By 1741 nearly one in five New Yorkers would be black.

THE PARTY OF THE PEOPLE

In the summer of 1731 Governor John Montgomerie died unexpectedly. His replacement was William Cosby, formerly governor of Minorca, who regarded his appointment as an invitation to gorge at the public table. No sooner had he reached New York in 1732 than he forced the Assembly to give him a "present" of a thousand pounds and sued Rip Van Dam, president of the council, for half the salary that Van Dam had collected as acting governor in the months since Montgomerie's death. Van Dam's lawyers, William Smith and James Alexander, persuaded Chief Justice Lewis Morris to throw out the governor's suit, over the objections of Associate Justices James De Lancey and Frederick Philipse. Cosby, in a rage, kicked Morris off the bench and named De Lancey to be chief justice instead.

This was no routine dispute over political spoils. Nor was it the usual dispute over who should pay the bulk of the tax burden—the gentlemen of New York's mercantile interest (who advocated a tax on land and were now in favor) or those of the landed interest (who championed a tax on imports and were now out). Cosby was a protégé of the duke of Newcastle, a great Whig nobleman, secretary of state, and staunch ally of Robert Walpole—the canniest and most controversial politician of the era.

During the 1720s, as lord of the treasury and chancellor of the exchequer, Walpole had acquired such influence over both cabinet and Parliament that he became known as the "prime" minister, Britain's first. He also earned the implacable hatred of "country party" Tories and old-fashioned True Whig "commonwealthmen." Despite their differences, they were unanimous in the belief that Walpole's lavish use of patronage had corrupted Parliament, the last bastion of English liberty, and infected the nation with avarice, speculation, luxury, and sloth.

By 1730 attacks on Walpole permeated British literature and public discourse. John Trenchard and Thomas Gordon, two radical libertarians, won renown for their savaging of Walpole in *The Independent Whig* (1720) and *Cato's Letters*, a series of essays that first appeared in the *London Journal* (1720–22) and were widely reprinted in the colonies. At the other extreme of the political spectrum stood the *Craftsman* (1726–76), in which Bolingbroke, William Pulteney, and other Tories flayed Walpole as the "man of craft" who had driven the country to the brink of moral and political ruin. When Walpole proposed a new excise on wine and tobacco in 1733, angry crowds thronged the streets of London chanting "No slavery, no excise!" and—*The Craftsman*'s motto—"King George, Liberty, and Law!"

The gentlemen of the landed interest in New York, who knew all about the ties between Walpole, Newcastle, and Cosby, decided that Cosby's venality possessed a deeper, more sinister meaning than first met the eye—that its real purpose was to accelerate the subversion of English liberty by exporting ministerial corruption to America. Their response was to reach out for public support, drawing upon the full range of anti-Walpole "opposition" rhetoric. By the spring of 1733, against a background of epidemic disease and the most serious economic depression in the town's history, the stage was set for New York's first broad-based political confrontation in decades.

The struggle began in Westchester County, where Morris mounted a campaign against the Philipses for possession of a vacant Assembly seat. When the polls opened in the village of Eastchester on the appointed day in October, hundreds of Morris's supporters, many on horseback, converged on the village green behind "two Trumpeters and 3 Violines" and a banner emblazoned with the motto of the *Craftsman*: KING GEORGE on one side, LIBERTY & LAW on the other. After circling the green three times, they retired for refreshments supplied by Morris and his friends. Morris's rival, a schoolmaster appointed by the Society for the Propagation of the Gospel, then made his appearance, escorted by Frederick Philipse, James De Lancey, and nearly two hundred horsemen. They paraded twice around the green and likewise trooped off for refreshment. The high sheriff, "finely mounted" in the scarlet and silver regalia of his office, then summoned the electors back to the green and began to record their votes.

Morris won handily and returned to New York City, where his supporters had just arranged for William Bradford's former apprentice, John Peter Zenger, to launch a new newspaper in opposition to Bradford's semiofficial *Gazette*. The Morrisites hoped to crack the government's virtual monopoly on the dissemination of information and to create a means for mobilizing the city's artisans, shopkeepers, and laborers.

Zenger's *Weekly Journal* proceeded to belabor Governor Cosby and his circle for "tyrannically flouting the laws of England and New York and . . . setting up personal henchmen with unlawful powers to control the judicial system of New York." Over the next year the Morrisites, billing themselves as "the party of the people," widened their popular appeal by calling for the adoption of electoral procedures already in place in Boston and Philadelphia: annual or triennial Assembly elections, the reapportionment of that body to reflect population growth, and adoption of the secret ballot (which would allow ordinary people to vote "for the Man they Love, and not for the haughty Tyrant they fear, and consequently hate"). They further proposed that mayors, sheriffs, and other officials be popularly elected and that judges be appointed during good behavior, protecting them from gubernatorial whim. They promised the city's artisans to build a permanent almshouse (a project that would promote employment). They also pledged to issue paper money for the construction of fortifications (yet another public works project that would have the additional benefit of easing credit, bringing down interest rates, and affording relief to debtors).

The Morrisites swept the hotly contested municipal elections of September 1734, capturing control of the Common Council. Laboring New Yorkers voted for the upper-class candidates who most convincingly claimed to be favorable to their interest. But they elected men of their own kind as well. Among the popular party's councilmen that year were a painter, three bakers, a bricklayer, and a bolter—"the meanest labourers, tradesmen and Artificers" in town, Cosby sniffed. At no time since the suppression of the Leislerians a generation earlier had working people been so actively engaged in city politics, or so successful.

THE CASE OF THE POOR PRINTER

Nor had political rhetoric been more strident. Week after week, Zenger's *Weekly Journal* lashed Cosby for incompetence, influence peddling, corruption, collusion with the French, election fraud, and tyranny. His confederates were sycophantic politicians, rich merchants, "people in Exalted Stations," and haughty "courtiers" who regarded their opponents as "*Canaille* or Dregs of the People." By contrast, the "industrious poor" who backed Morris were truly "the support of any country." Writers named "Timothy Wheelwright" and "John Chisel" urged honest working men—men like "Shuttle" the weaver, "Plane" the joiner, "Drive" the carter, "Mortar" the mason, and "Tar" the mariner—to defend their "rights and liberties" from "Gripe" the merchant, "Squeeze" the shopkeeper, and "Spintext and Quible" the lawyers. To be sure that his readers would see all this in its wider, British frame of reference, Zenger also reprinted essays from the *Craftsman* as well as lengthy excerpts from *Cato's Letters*. Stylistically, too, the *Journal* imitated the *Craftsman* by treating its readers to the same outrageous lampoons, brutal caricatures, mocking ballads, and double-entendre advertisements that had delighted the denizens of London's coffeehouses year after year.

The *Gazette* labored to respond in kind. It attributed the *Weekly Journal* to "a parcel of griping lawyers" who had failed to receive the patronage they hoped for from the governor. It reprinted selections from the standard English defenses of the established order and itemized the *Journal*'s not infrequent errors of omission and commission. Others in the gubernatorial party issued pamphlets denouncing Morrisite appeals to "unthinking" people who were "of no Credit or Reputation, rak'd out of Bawdy-Houses and Kennels."

Soon, however, Cosby and De Lancey tired of bandying words and resolved to silence the *Journal* by force. De Lancey asked a grand jury to indict Zenger for two "scandalous" songs published after the "popular" party's victory in the 1734 elections. The jurors balked, claiming they couldn't confirm the printer's identity. Cosby then ordered the sheriff to arrest Zenger for "seditious libel" and burn four especially offensive issues of his paper. Both the Assembly and Common Council objected, to no avail.

Zenger went to jail in mid-November 1734. De Lancey set his bail at a preposterously high four hundred pounds, which not only ensured that the printer would remain behind bars until the end of his trial, eight months later, but also enabled the Morrisites to portray him as a martyr to the cause of liberty. James Alexander and William Smith (both of whom bore some responsibility for getting Zenger into trouble in the first place) began to prepare his defense.

In April 1735, Smith and Alexander made their first move on Zenger's behalf by challenging the legality of Cosby's commissions to De Lancey and Philipse. De Lancey found them in contempt, ordered them disbarred, and assigned John Chambers, a skilled attorney but one of Cosby's men, to represent Zenger instead. Shrewdly, Alexander then enlisted the help of Andrew Hamilton of Philadelphia—the best trial attorney in the colonies. Hamilton's decision to participate in Zenger's defense changed everything.

Zenger's trial began in August 1735. Hamilton's strategy, from a strictly legal point of view, was extremely risky. As the English common law then stood, "seditious libel" meant simply the publication of any material undermining the authority of government. The truth or falsity of such material was irrelevant; juries were to determine only whether, as charged, it had been made public and referred to the persons or institutions in question. Hamilton conceded that Zenger's articles were malicious, seditious, and

The New-York Weekly Journal, December 17, 1733. Ten months after it appeared, this issue was burned by order of Cosby and the provincial council. (© Collection of The New-York Historical Society)

scandalous—which should have ended the matter then and there. But in a dazzling appeal to "reason" and "natural rights," Hamilton argued that truth must be accepted as a defense against the charge of libel. What was at stake, he told the jury, was nothing less than the right of a free people to criticize their rulers. "It is not the cause of a poor printer, nor of New York alone, which you are now trying. No! It may in its consequences affect every freeman that lives under a British government on the main of America. It is the best cause. It is the cause of liberty."

Hamilton's oratory carried the day. Despite De Lancey's insistence that they stick to the law, the jurors took only minutes to acquit Zenger of all the charges against him. The crowded courtroom burst into cheers, and the jubilant Morrisites marched the Philadelphia lawyer off to the Black Horse Tavern (at what is now the corner of William Street and Exchange Place) for a feast. Shortly thereafter, the Common Council hailed Hamilton for "his learned and generous defense of the rights of mankind, and the liberty of the press" and made him a freeman of the corporation. Additional plaudits followed as word of the verdict percolated throughout the Anglo-American world, moved along by James Alexander's *Brief Narrative of the Case and Trial of John Peter Zenger*, which came off Zenger's press in 1736. Often reprinted on both sides of the Atlantic, it was probably the most famous book yet published in America.

No one imagined that Zenger's acquittal set a legal precedent for the elimination of restrictions on the press—it was an instance of jury nullification, not a judicial opinion—and indeed decades would pass before printers in either America or Great Britain were safe from official scrutiny. What made the case so significant to contemporaries, rather, was that it sent a clear warning to judges and prosecutors that the law of libel was out of step with popular sentiment and that they could no longer rely on juries to shield government from public censure. In doing so, moreover, the Zenger verdict endorsed assumptions about relations between "the people" and their rulers long familiar to readers of *Cato's Letters* or the *Craftsman*—that executive power tends to expand at the expense of liberty, and that to protect themselves, freemen must be able to speak their minds without fear of official retribution.

"SUCH A STRUGLE I NEVER SAW"

Although the Morrisites had won an important skirmish, the war still raged. Governor Cosby died of tuberculosis in 1736, and George Clarke, one of the richest men in New York, was installed as acting lieutenant governor. Clarke dissolved the Assembly, issuing writs for new elections in 1737, and the Morrisites embarked on what Cadwallader Colden remembered as one of the city's wildest campaigns on record. On election day, "the sick, the lame, and the blind were all carried to vote," Colden said. "Such a strugle I never saw and such a hurraing that above one half of the men in town are so hoarse that they cannot speak." Morris and the popular party won handily. Lewis Morris Jr., who with his father swept to victory in Westchester, was chosen speaker of the new Assembly. John Peter Zenger got the nod as official printer.

Clarke now discovered, however, that if the Morrisites couldn't be beaten, their leaders could be bought off. He won over Smith and Alexander by having them reinstated to the bar, he endorsed a few Morrisite reforms (including a one-year revenue bill and a triennial election act), and he appointed key Morrisites to public offices in Westchester and other counties. Morris himself accepted an offer from Newcastle to become the royal governor of New Jersey and promptly turned into an advocate of executive authority—which only proved, as Walpole liked to say, that every man has his price. Abandoned by its founders, the "popular party" fell into disarray, and when prosperity returned, it disappeared altogether.

The Morrisites had nonetheless opened the door to a new and potentially more turbulent political environment in the city. The freemen had returned to politics, books and newspapers were full of talk about threats to "liberty," and gentlemen—as one assemblyman put it—increasingly had to think of public office as "a fine laced Livery coat of which the vain Lacquey may be stript at the pleasure of his proud Master [i.e., the electorate] & may be kikt out of Doors naked."

What was more, the Morrisites had actually delivered on some campaign promises, establishing yet another precedent. To alleviate the shortage of specie and attendant high interest rates, they issued twelve thousand pounds of paper money in 1734 and added another £48,350 three years later, to repair "the Decay of Trade & other Difficulties which this Colony has the Misfortune to have Laboured Under." In 1737 the first Assembly elected in the colony in a decade remodeled the militia, agreed to hold triennial elections, and reduced the legal interest rate.

The Morrisites also made good on their promise to construct New York's first permanent almshouse. Completed in 1736, the two-story stone and brick building stood on the Common at the very outskirts of town (the northern end of what is now City Hall Park). Although a boon to its contractors, it was greeted with considerably less joy by those for whom it was intended. Really three institutions under one roof—a Poorhouse, a Workhouse, and a House of Correction—its inmates were a cross-section of the city's lower classes, ranging from "Poor Needy Persons and Idle Wandering Vagabonds" to "Sturdy Beggars," petty criminals, rogues, and "parents of Bastard Children." All inhabitants of the city had "free Liberty and Lycence to send to the said House all unruly and ungovernable Servants and Slaves there to be kept at hard labour." Despite rudimentary attempts to separate them—one basement room was reserved for the inmates at forced labor, another for those considered "unruly"—the vestrymen were soon expressing concern at mixing the elderly sick with incorrigible rogues.

Whatever the reasons for their confinement, all inmates were held, insofar as possible, to a strict daily regimen calculated to teach them self-discipline, industry, and deference. Inmates were supplied clothing "marked with the first letters of their names," deprived of meals if they refused to attend prayer sessions, and set to work carding wool, shredding old rope for reuse, or raising garden crops. The idea, according to the Common Council, was that "such Poor as are able to work, may not Eat the Bread of Sloth & Idleness, and be a Burthen to the Publick." Inmates who learned "decorum" and exhibited a "bashful, modest, humble, and patient temper" would be "encouraged and comforted"; "troublesome and discontented" inmates would get a "moderate whipping."

The rigid order imposed on inmates of the almshouse was quite different from what the poor experienced when they were lodged in rented private dwellings. This might explain why the new institution drew only nineteen people its first year (twelve adults and seven children) and why some inmates, though prohibited from leaving without permission, fled at the return of clement weather—only to come back "almost naked," as the Common Council complained in 1738, when winter again approached.

Once the almshouse was in operation, moreover, the city drastically slashed outdoor relief—the traditional system of granting aid to the poor in their own homes. By 1747 it had been all but eliminated, and the gulf between those who enjoyed the privileges of membership in the municipal corporation and those who didn't was wider than ever.

"GETHSEMANE! GETHSEMANE!"

The transformation of public life in New York received further impetus during the depression from that outpouring of piety known as the Great Awakening. Linkages between politics and evangelical religion were nothing new. Nearly two decades had now passed since Theodore Frelinghuysen began drawing on the pools of Leislerian resentment that still lay under the Dutch churches in the Raritan Valley. In the mid-1720s William Smith (Zenger's sometime attorney) and Gilbert Livingston led a faction within the New York Presbyterian Church that struggled against clerical orthodoxy and managed the installation of the Rev. Ebenezer Pemberton as pastor.

After 1710, moreover, Baptists began gaining ground among the city's laboring population when the Rev. Valentine Wightman came down from Groton, Connecticut, to preach. Wightman kept a low profile, speaking only at private homes and performing baptisms by night, until several converts, disdaining further subterfuge, demanded daylight baptism. Governor Hunter offered his protection and even went to the waterfront to watch, accompanied by other gentlemen. By 1715 Baptists in the city were meeting at the Broad Street home of a brewer named Nicholas Eyres. In 1724 the Baptist Church was formally organized and moved into a new building atop Golden Hill, along what is now Cliff Street (near John).

Enter now George Whitefield, a young preacher from Oxford University who had been closely associated with Charles and John Wesley in the budding Methodist movement. Whitefield was an unusually talented orator and within a few years after his graduation in 1736 became renowned in England for his attacks on clerical laxity as well as for his ability to awaken the slumbering religious fervor of popular audiences. So large were the crowds that flocked to hear him—and so hostile were the established clergy to his speaking in their churches—that Whitefield took to preaching outdoors, a practice that soon became his trademark.

In the summer of 1739, aware that many of his printed sermons had already aroused great interest in America, Whitefield crossed the Atlantic for a tour of the colonies. His first stop was Philadelphia, where he spoke to excited multitudes of as many as six thousand people. In mid-November he went up to New York, staying at the home of William Smith, the prominent Presbyterian layman. Seeking a pulpit from which to speak, Whitefield approached the Rev. William Vesey, now in his forty-fifth year as rector of Trinity and more doggedly conservative than ever. Vesey refused the use of his church, charging Whitefield with various violations of canon law (to which Whitefield replied that the aging cleric spent too much time in the taverns). Faithful to the arrangement struck years before with the Anglicans, Dominie Henricus Boel likewise refused to let Whitefield speak in the Dutch Reformed church. Whitefield had his sympathizers, however, and when the Rev. Ebenezer Pemberton granted him permission to use the Presbyterian church, everything was in place for a dramatic confrontation between the Awakeners and their critics.

On the afternoon of November 15, Whitefield launched his New York tour with an open-air prayer meeting in the Common. His theme was the need for a "New Birth"—a reawakening of the faith without which there can be no salvation. According to a newspaper account probably written by Pemberton, "many Hundreds of People" turned out to hear him. Most were "very serious and attentive," but a fair number of hecklers also gathered on the fringes of the crowd, "Giggling, Scoffing, Talking and Laughing." Whitefield faced them down, delivered a blistering attack on "the boldness and Zeal with which the Devil's Vassals serve him," and left the entire crowd "hush'd and still," their faces glowing with "solemn Awe and Reverence."

Pemberton was hard-pressed for words to describe what had taken place. "A mighty Energy attended the Word," he said. "I heard and felt something astonishing and surprizing." So, evidently, had many others. Over two thousand people jammed into the Presbyterian church that evening, during which an awed Pemberton reported, "The Peoples Eyes and Ears hung on his Lips. They greedily devour'd every Word. I came Home astonished!"

Whitefield continued for four days, speaking at least twice a day, afternoons in the Common and evenings in the Presbyterian church. Despite chilly weather, the crowds grew ever larger and more emotional. People who couldn't find a seat or get close enough to hear him wept openly with disappointment. One member of the audience, finding himself seated next to a lady who sobbed loudly through the entire service, later asked "which part of the sermon had most particularly affected her." "Oh! Sir," she told him, "it was when he said *Gethsemane! Gethsemane!*" Whitefield himself wrote in his journal that "the people seemed exceedingly attentive, and I have not felt greater freedom in preaching, and more power in prayer, since I came to America, than I have had here in New York. I find that little of the work of God has been seen in it for many years."

It was the same story when he returned the following year, once in the spring and again in the autumn. Five, six, and seven thousand people at a time allegedly thronged the Common to hear him speak, now from a specially constructed scaffold. New York—polyglot, urbane, skeptical New York—appeared to be in the throes of a full-scale religious revival.

Whitefield was probably tapping the same vein of popular restiveness mined by the Morrisites just a few years earlier. His chief targets—complacent and even corrupt leaders, a loss of old-time zeal, indifference to basic principles, the advent of a heartless, legalistic formalism—echoed almost exactly, albeit with a religious rather than political vocabulary, the opposition to Cosby. If there was a difference it lay in the breadth of Whitefield's audience. The crowds that flocked to hear him in 1739–40 included numerous representatives of the city's lower classes—apprentices and laborers, the poor and the enslaved—whose exclusion from the municipal corporation rendered them invisible to the Morrisites. During his 1740 tour, indeed, Whitefield had called openly for the humane treatment of slaves and for instructing them in the Christian religion, issues that had never troubled Morris (one of the city's leading slaveowners) or his followers.

Leaders of New York's Anglican-Reformed establishment were horrified. As one conservative Dutch dominie declared in 1741, Whitefield's attacks on the sincerity of the orthodox clergy struck at the authority of all organized religion. A "spirit of confusion is ever blazing up more and more," he wrote. Many went further and insisted that the revivalists had called into question the authority of all institutions—a not unreasonable fear, it turned out, for only months after Whitefield's last visit, it appeared that scores of slaves and poor whites had banded together in a frightful plot to burn the city.

"G — D D —— N ALL THE WHITE PEOPLE"

On March 18, 1741, the soldiers of Fort George—Irish and non-Irish alike—were recuperating in the barracks from their hearty celebration of the Feast of St. Patrick the day before. The garrison was undermanned as well as under the weather, for the Empire was at war again. In the autumn of 1739, after years of heavy losses to Spanish privateers, West Indian planters demanded action from London. Walpole wanted to avoid costly foreign conflicts, but Pulteney roused Parliament to a declaration of war by waving around the pickled ear of one Captain Robert Jenkins—cut off, it was said, by an arrogant Spaniard who told him to give it to King George as a warning. The so-called War of Jenkins' Ear reached New York during the summer of 1740, when an expedition of six hundred troops left the city for an assault on Cuba. Now, six months later, only a relative handful remained on Manhattan.

Shortly after noon on the eighteenth, smoke and flames poured from the governor's house; soon the adjoining chapel was ablaze as well. A bucket brigade and the town's recently purchased hand-pump fire engines failed to control the wind-whipped flames, and by late afternoon the Fort's buildings were in cinders. Precisely a week later, on March 25, another fire broke out, at the home of Captain Peter Warren, brother-in-law of Chief Justice De Lancey, but this one was successfully contained. Another week passed, and then another fire incinerated Winant van Zant's warehouse near the East River docks on April 1; astonishingly, given its contents of hay, fir, and pine, this conflagration too was kept from spreading farther. Three days later fire flared again, this time at a Maiden Lane cow stable filled with dried fodder. On the following day a passerby sniffed smoke and discovered coals burning at the base of a haystack in attorney Joseph Murray's stables on lower Broadway, just in time to prevent the wealthy neighborhood from going up in flames.

Fires were common in the mid-eighteenth century, so the first catastrophe had aroused few suspicions. But as the number of incidents mounted, so did the conviction that they were the product not of accident but of arson. Perhaps (one council member hypothesized) "a combination of villains" was creating diversions, under cover of which they could make "a prey of their neighbor's goods." Most white residents suspected the slaves, however. All New York had heard about the massive uprising that had rocked Stono, South Carolina, in September 1739 and of the ongoing disturbances in that colony that culminated, in November 1740, in an apparent attempt to destroy Charleston by fire.

Then *another* round of fires broke out on April 6—four in one day. A black man was spotted near one of them, running. A white tried to catch him, yelling, "A negro, a negro." The cry, swiftly taken up, soon turned into terrified screams of "The negroes are rising"! The man seen running—Adolph Philipse's slave Cuffee—was quickly captured and incarcerated. This did nothing to quiet the hysteria. Crowds of white vigilantes rounded up more blacks and threw them in jail with Cuffee.

Although the City Council launched an intensive investigation, two weeks of examining the blacks in custody and searching for evidence of arson yielded nothing except increased anxiety among the white townspeople. The council now turned the inquiry over to Daniel Horsmanden. Horsmanden was the city's recorder as well as a justice on the supreme court of the province (a position he had gained through loyalty to the late Governor Cosby). Horsmanden, who had long believed that New York was far too lax in its handling of slaves, set out to track down the conspirators he was sure were behind the fires.

A special grand jury was convened and directed to investigate whites who sold liquor to blacks—men like tavern keeper John Hughson. A poor and illiterate cobbler from Yonkers, Hughson had come down to New York in the mid-1730s with his wife, Sarah, his daughter, and his mother-in-law. Unable to find employment, he opened a tavern on the East River waterfront that "very much offended his neighbors" by catering to a disreputable clientele. This was at the height of the Morris-Cosby struggle, and according to a number of witnesses, Hughson soon became convinced that "the country was not good," that there were "too many gentlemen" in the city, that they "made negroes work hard." Some even said he had urged slaves to burn the town and kill their masters.

In 1738 Hughson opened a new tavern on the Hudson River waterfront, not far from the Trinity churchyard. This establishment, like its predecessor, acquired immediate notoriety as a rendezvous for slaves, free blacks, poor whites, soldiers from the nearby fort, and even (as rumor had it) the occasional "young gentleman" inclined to after-hours carousing and gaming. (In the winter of 1740–41, after constables raided his tavern, Hughson had been convicted of illegally "entertaining Negro slaves" but let off as a first offender.) Hughson's also became the residence of one "Margaret Sorubiero, alias Salingburgh, alias Kerry, commonly called Peggy, or the Newfoundland Irish beauty," said to be a prostitute "of the worst sort, a prostitute to negroes." Her room and board was paid by a slave of baker John Vaarck, named Caesar, by whom Peggy had recently had a child.

Hughson also fenced stolen property. He got to be so well known in this line of work that city slaves laughingly referred to his place as "Oswego," after the Indian trading post on Lake Ontario. Although the constables had their eye on him, they had as yet failed to catch him red-handed. Nor had they caught John Romme, a publican-shoemaker and friend of Hughson's whose tavern stood on the Battery near Fort George. Like Hughson, Romme trafficked in stolen goods—protected, perhaps, by his kinship with a member of the Common Council and connections in the right places. Yet he too had been heard to speak bitterly of "how well the rich people at this place lived" and likewise advised slaves to "burn the houses of them that have the most money, and kill them all, as the negroes would have done their masters and mistresses formerly"—an obvious allusion to the abortive 1712 uprising.

Two weeks before the fire in the fort, Hughson had been arrested for receiving goods stolen by Caesar and Prince (slave of merchant John Auboyneau) from Rebecca Hogg's general store on Broad Street. The crime came unraveled when on March 3 the Hughsons' sixteen-year-old indentured servant, Mary Burton, had been enticed to give evidence against John, Sarah, and Peggy by a promise to free her from her indenture.

Caesar and Prince were arrested—and not for the first time. The two, along with Cuffee, had been caught stealing barrels of Geneva (Dutch gin) back in 1736 and denounced as "the ringleaders of a confederacy of negroes who robbed, pilfered and stole whenever they had opportunity." Caesar and Prince had faced the death penalty then—burglary committed by slaves was a capital crime—but had been let off with a public whipping. They had carried on, however, boldly assuming the name "Geneva Club." (According to one observer they had even had the "impudence to assume the style and title of Free Masons, in imitation of a society here: which was looked upon to be a gross affront to the provincial grand master and gentlemen of the fraternity . . . and was very ill accepted.") Caesar languished in jail; the Hughsons and Prince were freed on bail; and all were awaiting trial on burglary-related charges when the fires started.

Horsmanden's grand jury now called Mary Burton to testify. She confirmed her earlier account of the Hogg burglary but refused to talk about the fires. When ordered jailed for contempt, however, she quickly agreed to cooperate and proceeded to describe what she said was a conspiracy between slaves and poor whites to burn the city. To Horsmanden's delight, Burton declared that the three Geneva Club members had met frequently at Hughson's, that they had often talked of burning the fort and town, and that the Hughsons had agreed to help. Though Burton's testimony didn't prove that a crime had actually been committed, it did constitute evidence of criminal conspiracy. Seeking additional corroboration, the Common Council posted rewards for anyone coming forward with information about the fires—one hundred pounds to whites (an amount equal to at least five years' wages for anyone lucky enough to be working steadily during the hard times), forty-five pounds to a free black or Indian, and, for a slave, twenty pounds plus freedom.

On May 1 the court found Caesar and Prince guilty of burglary and condemned them to death. The next day, just across the river in Hackensack, New Jersey, seven barns were set ablaze; two blacks were caught and immediately burned at the stake. On May 6 the Hughsons and Peggy were found guilty of receiving stolen goods, and Peggy, in fear of her life, decided to talk. So did some of the blacks crammed in the dungeons below City Hall. Two who didn't confess to anything were Caesar and Prince: on May 11 they were hanged for burglary. Caesar's corpse was then dangled from a platform near the city's powder house, on the little island between the two arms of the Fresh Water Pond.

Now, "witnesses" in hand and with the backing of the mayor, governor, and Common Council, Horsmanden proceeded to trial against Cuffee and Quack, a slave belonging to butcher John Roosevelt. He summoned all the town's lawyers and got each of them, including William Smith and James Alexander, to agree to assist Attorney General Richard Bradley with the prosecution. Eleven witnesses were called for the prosecution. They reported on conversations they'd overheard, such as the time Cuffee declared "that a great many people had too much, and others too little, that his old master"—Adolph Philipse, wealthy merchant, speaker of the Assembly, and prominent supporter of Governor Cosby—"had a great deal of money, but that, in a short time, he should have less." The defendants, who had no legal counsel, called witnesses, including their owners, who offered at best limited support to avoid rousing the wrath of their neighbors. The jury returned a guilty verdict in minutes, and Horsmanden instantly pronounced sentence—death by fire the following day. Chained to the stake, faggots piled at their feet, Cuffee and Quack both confessed to burning the fort. They also began naming names, eventually accusing some fifty others of complicity. Horsmanden, thrilled, considered saving them as future witnesses. But the crowd was howling, and the sheriff said it would be unwise to stop. So, as Horsmanden later recounted, "the executions proceeded." The two screaming men, having bought but a few extra hours of life, were soon engulfed in flames.

Trials followed quickly now. The Hughsons and Peggy were sentenced to hang, with John Hughson's body to be suspended in chains next to Caesar's rotting corpse. More verdicts, more burnings, more confessions, more verdicts. At the height of the hysteria, nearly half the city's male slaves over sixteen years of age were in jail.

From Horsmanden's point of view, however, something was still lacking: a white mastermind who could be held accountable for the whole diabolical conspiracy (given that Africans, in his view, clearly lacked the intelligence for such a scheme, and the illiterate Hughson didn't quite fit the bill). As candidate for head conspirator, Horsmanden nominated John Ury. Only recently arrived in town, Ury had been working as a private tutor and schoolmaster. Because his expertise in Latin made him conspicuous around town, he now found himself under arrest on the suspicion of being a Roman Catholic priest and a secret agent of the Spanish. Arrested with Ury were several soldiers from the garrison—among them Peter Connolly, Edward Kelly, Edward Murphy, and Andrew Ryan—who were also suspected of being Catholics and conspirators. The ever-obliging Mary Burton now remembered that Ury, too, had been among the plotters at Hughson's; William Kane, another of the soldiers, offered a corroborative confession.

Ury's grand scheme, the prosecution now proposed, had been to have Hughson purchase arms and organize all participating slaves into two companies, the Long Bridge Boys and the Smith's Fly Boys, who would set fire to the fort, slay their masters, and burn their homes. Led by Hughson and Caesar—the former as king, the latter as governor—they would hold the city until the arrival of Ury's Catholic masters, the Spanish or French. After that, the conspirators would divide up their booty and make their way to freedom.

During the unfortunate Ury's trial, a hysterical warning arrived from Governor Oglethorpe of Georgia, saying that Spanish agents were "preparing to burn all the magazines and considerable towns in the English North America" and that some were priests "who pretended to be physicians, dancing masters, and other such kinds of occupations." That sealed Ury's fate, and he too was dispatched to the gallows at the end of August.

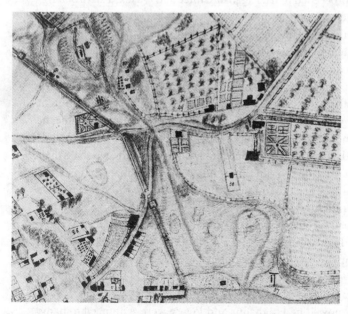

Gallows of the 1741 conspirators. Note also the stake with flames on it. Detail of a map drawn from memory by David Grim in 1813. (© Collection of The New-York Historical Society)

By then, all told, some 160 blacks and twenty-one whites had been arrested. Four whites—John Hughson, Sarah Hughson, Peggy Kerry, and John Ury—were hanged, as were seventeen blacks; one white, sentenced to be hanged, escaped. Thirteen Africans were burned at the stake. Seventy-two were subsequently banished from the colony, twenty-seven to the Portuguese island of Madeira, and most of the rest to colonies in the West Indies.

But had there in fact been a conspiracy? Certainly the autumn and winter of 1740–41, the time when Hughson, Romme, and the Geneva Club allegedly began planning a rebellion, had been a miserable period in the city. To the effects of years of depression were added dwindling supplies of fuel and food, the result of record snowfalls and the lowest temperatures in memory. By February 1741 the Hudson was a solid mass of ice all the way up to Poughkeepsie, and huge drifts blanketed the smaller houses and shacks that were home to New York's poorest inhabitants. Funds for the relief of the needy had already run out, and many were in imminent danger of freezing or starving to death. City bakers had gone on strike to protest what they considered the unfairly low price of bread set by the city. Zenger's *Weekly Journal* reported that their refusal to bake caused "some Disturbance, and reduced some, notwithstanding their Riches, to a sudden want of Bread." (Similar shortages had also led to rioting in Wales and England, the paper reported.)

Certainly the slaves were angry enough, particularly those forced to live apart from their spouses. Quack resented Lieutenant Governor Clarke for prohibiting him from visiting his wife, the governor's cook, and he had had several fights with the fort's sentry during repeated attempts to visit her. Quack might well have fired the governor's house, as he confessed to doing. And the sailors and soldiers in town, particularly the Irish, had grievances of their own. Private Edward Murphy reportedly said, "Damn me if I won't lend a hand to the fires as soon as anybody." Moreover, this milling, interracial discontent might well have been brought into sharp focus by the recent outbreak of war. By 1741 so few troops remained in Fort George, one slave reportedly said, that only "an hundred and fifty men might take this city." If the Spanish or French did come to their aid, they stood a reasonable chance of getting away with it.

The actual evidence, however, is less than convincing. John Hughson, Hughson's wife, John Romme, and more than a few of the most important blacks denied to the very end that a conspiracy existed. Key witnesses against them—Mary Burton, Peggy Kerry, Hughson's daughter, Sarah, an indentured servant named Arthur Price, the soldier William Kane—gave confused, frequently contradictory, and invariably self-serving testimony. Equally suspect were the sixty-odd "confessions" wrung out of terrorized slaves. Much of the trial testimony vital to the official conspiracy theory is likewise tainted. The presiding judges—Horsmanden, De Lancey, and Frederick Philipse—took pains to follow accepted rules of evidence and procedure. Yet none of the accused, slave or free, had legal representation. As a result, key witnesses weren't cross-examined, obvious exculpatory evidence was ignored, and no alternative explanation of events was ever presented to the juries. Only Ury, the suspected Catholic priest, mounted anything like an informed and organized defense, explaining that he was just a dissenter from the Church of England and had no knowledge whatever of any conspiracy. Bradley and his assistants got a conviction by haranguing the jury on the dangers of Catholicism—a "hocus pocus, bloody religion," cried Bradley—but Ury's calm eloquence, first in the courtroom and then on the gallows, threw a shadow of doubt across the entire business.

So, in the end, did Mary Burton herself, by hinting that the conspiracy had involved "some people *in ruffles* (a phrase as was understood to mean persons of better fashion than ordinary)." Incredulous, the court demanded names, whereupon "she named several persons which she said she had seen at Hughson's amongst the conspirators, talking of the conspiracy, who were engaged in it; amongst whom she mentioned several of known credit, fortunes and reputations, and of religious principles superior to a suspicion of being concerned in such detestable practices." Knowing that the veracity of its star witness would crumble if Burton kept talking, the prosecution began to wrap up the proceedings soon after Ury's execution. One who escaped the hangman as a result was Hughson's friend John Romme. "The devil couldn't hurt me," he had boasted, "for I've a great many friends in town, and the best in the place'll stand by me." Although he was arrested in New Jersey after fleeing to escape prosecution, the New York authorities made no attempt to bring him back.

If the official conspiracy theory cannot be taken at face value, that doesn't rule out the possibility of some less widespread or well-organized coup—by slaves against their masters, by the poor against the rich, or a combination of both. It's quite likely that Hughson and a number of slaves often speculated casually about their chances of getting away with some such project. Alternatively, Hughson and perhaps another half-dozen or so whites and blacks may have planned the rash of fires in February and March to cover up multiple burglaries.

Whether or not they had really planned an uprising, the mass of casual, incidental evidence—corroborative detail supplied in page after page of depositions, confessions, and trial testimony—makes it apparent that by 1741 New York's two-thousand-odd slaves had the organizational ingenuity and the political sophistication to do so. Over and over again, witnesses testified to the inability or unwillingness of their masters to keep them under close supervision. They regularly held clandestine meetings, passed long hours drinking, gaming, and dancing together away from the prying eyes of whites, easily got away with petty larceny and the small-scale destruction of property, and even managed to own weapons.

Conspiracy or no, moreover, the Geneva Club and its mock-Masonic rituals had been real enough. The existence of two paramilitary companies said to have been formed by the conspirators—the Long Bridge Boys and the Smith's Fly Boys—undoubtedly made perfect sense to prosecutors because they corresponded to groups or affiliations or divisions within slave society. Judging by reactions to the departure of the expedition to Cuba and the hopes of a Spanish or French attack, at least some slaves knew a good deal about international events and their ramifications for the city. Many clearly remembered or knew of the 1712 revolt, how it had been organized, and what came of it. A few had participated in revolts elsewhere; one was a veteran of risings on both St. John's and Antigua. No doubt some of them were ready for a revolt in New York too, despite the tremendous odds against success. "G—d d——n all the white people," one was said to have cried, "if he had it in his power, he would set them all on fire."

Prosecution of the alleged conspirators also disclosed the numerous points of contact and mutuality between the city's slaves and its burgeoning population of poor whites. Witness after witness reported blacks and whites as partners in crime, partners in drink, partners in bed, partners in survival, partners in their contempt of the rich and well-born few who dressed in ruffles and ran the town—a vast, restless, interracial underworld.

One response by municipal authorities to these discoveries was to demand increased vigilance on the part of slaveowners. Another was to insist on closing down the sleazy disorderly houses whose owners, like Hughson, observed the "most wicked and pernicious practice . . . of entertaining negroes, and the scum and dregs of white people in conjunction." Yet another was to accuse "Suspicious, Vagrant, Stroling Preachers" of stirring up the lower classes, especially "Youths and Negroes." George Whitefield's tumultuous revivals in 1739 and 1740 drew particular criticism in this regard. As one SPG missionary put it, Whitefield's "impudence and indiscretion" in advocating the conversion of blacks to Christianity—still a very unpopular idea among slaveowners—gave "great countenance" to the plot. Even Ury was said to have blamed "all the disturbances" on "the great encouragement the negroes had received from Mr. Whitefield."

But the ultimate response, one on which prosecutors often fell back in their final summations, was to drown out the noise of class conflict by beating the drums of racial hatred. Bradley berated city slaves as "silly unthinking creatures." Horsmanden called them "cannibals." Not only did they dare to think of killing white men, Smith ranted, but they intended to make white women the victims of their "rapacious lust" as well. "The monstrous ingratitude of this black tribe is what exceedingly aggravates their guilt," he added. As for Hughson, he "could not be content to live by the gains of honest industry, but must be rich at the expense of the blood and ruin of his fellow citizens! miserable wretch!" His crimes "have made him blacker than a negro."

It was indeed mysterious, Horsmanden reported, that the rotting cadavers of Hughson and Caesar, after hanging on the gibbet in the summer sun for several weeks, had changed color—the former becoming "a deep shining black, rather blacker than the negro placed by him, who was one of the darkest hue of his kind," while the latter "somewhat bleached or turned whitish." Crowds gathered to ponder the meaning of these "wonderous phenomenons," and "many of the spectators were ready to resolve them into miracles."

Mindful that many slaves implicated in the "conspiracy" had come by way of the West Indies, white New Yorkers concluded they would be safer with chattel imported directly from Africa, a decision that in time would significantly alter the composition of the city's servile population. The mass deportation of male slaves also helped transform the city's gender balance. During the depression the outmigration of unemployed artisans and seamen had changed the sex ratio from 117 white men for every 100 white women in 1731 to 91:100 in 1731, then to 89:100 in 1741—producing a substantial excess of white women. At the same time, male-heavy slave imports had continued. While in 1731 there had been 99 black men for every 100 black women, by 1737 the ratio was 111:100, and by 1741 it was 119:100—a substantial excess of black men. Demographics like these, together with well-known sexual alliances between black men and white women, like that of Caesar and Peggy, had given rise during the hysteria to lurid fantasies of bondsmen seizing white mistresses. The post-hysteria shift in slaveholders' preferences from males to females, together with the opposition of white male artisans to the use of skilled black labor, had by 1746 diminished black males to under 47 percent of the African population.

New York didn't soon forget the "Great Negro Plot" of 1741. A printed version of Ury's last words from the gallows was a standing reminder of the panic that had gripped the city, and it was rumored for years that Hughson's ghost haunted his place of execution. When renewed political squabbling began to dissolve the united front forged by racial and religious fear, critics of the governor's party hinted that Horsmanden had imagined the whole conspiracy and committed judicial murder. Stung by such rumors, he defended himself by writing a book. It appeared in 1744 bearing the unwieldy if accurate title of *A Journal of the Proceedings in the Detection of the Conspiracy Formed by Some White People, in Conjunction with Negro and other Slaves, for Burning the City of New-York in America, and Murdering the Inhabitants.*

12

War and Wealth

While New York recovered from the "Great Negro Plot," the Anglo-Spanish war that began in 1739 grew wider. By 1743 both Prussia and France were fighting alongside Spain, and virtually all Europe and America had plunged into a conflict, at once dynastic and imperial, known to His Majesty's American subjects as King George's War. Peace returned in 1748, without a clear-cut victory for either side, and hostilities soon resumed.

In 1754 a detachment of Virginia troops under young Colonel George Washington surrendered to French forces on the frontier near what is now Pittsburgh. When General Edward Braddock's attempt to repulse the French ended in a humiliating disaster, Britain declared war—this time with the intention of driving France out of North America once and for all. The war went badly, however, until George II brought in William Pitt, arguably the most brilliant wartime leader in British history. Between 1757 and 1761 the French were expelled from India and Canada, a French invasion fleet was smashed in the English Channel, and choice sugar islands in the French West Indies passed into British hands. Pitt might have achieved even more, but George II died in 1760. His twenty-two-year-old grandson, George III, was eager for peace and forced Pitt's resignation in 1761. Two years later, the fighting was ended by the Treaty of Paris. To Europeans, it would be remembered as the Seven Years War. Americans called it the French and Indian War.

Throughout these twenty-odd years of conflict, New York's strategic proximity to Canada—Montreal lay only three hundred miles to the north along the Hudson-Champlain corridor—kept the city in a state of almost constant alert. French raiding parties struck as far south as Saratoga and Albany during King George's War, and during the French and Indian War heavy fighting erupted around Lakes George and Champlain as well as on the shores of Lake Ontario. Often (as in 1741) New Yorkers believed themselves in imminent danger of attack. Militia companies camped on the Common, drilling incessantly, and in 1745 municipal authorities took the precaution of erecting a palisade along the northern perimeter of the town (raising the necessary funds by a public lottery). Made of fourteen-foot-long cedar logs set in a three-foot-deep trench, the barrier zigzagged from Cherry Street and James Slip on the East River to present-day Chambers Street on the Hudson, broken by only four gates and guarded by six blockhouses. This second city wall, like the first a century earlier, was a grim reminder that New York's fortunes often hinged on events unfolding oceans away from Manhattan.

SPOILS OF WAR

Even gentlemen of the mercantile "interest," always leery of getting entangled in imperial conflicts to the detriment of trade, conceded that both King George's War and the French and Indian War were good for business. ("War is declared in England—Universal joy among the merchants," William Smith wrote in his diary in 1756.) Legislative bodies in New York and other colonies spent unprecedented amounts of money on military operations, while the British government poured troops into the colonies in numbers that staggered contemporary imaginations. The first contingent arrived in 1756, when a thousand soldiers set up winter camp in the city after losing to the French at Oswego. When the barracks in the fort proved inadequate, the earl of Loudon, commander-in-chief of His Majesty's armed forces in America, billeted soldiers in private homes. This practice brought so many complaints from residents that the Common Council authorized construction of additional barracks up on the Common. And none too soon, for by 1758 some twenty-five thousand soldiers and a vast fleet manned by fourteen thousand mariners would be stationed in America—most of them in either New York or Boston.

Provisioning His Majesty's forces required gargantuan quantities of food, clothing, shoes, alcohol, horses, wagons, and other materiel, and in 1755 New York was made the "general Magazine of Arms and Military Stores" as well as a station for military and naval forces. (That same year, the British government inaugurated monthly fast-sailing packets from Falmouth to Manhattan, underscoring its selection of New York as its link with the colonies.) Contracts to deliver any of those items to royal or provincial commissaries made fortunes for well-connected New York merchants like Hayman Levy, Peter Van Brugh Livingston, James Alexander, William Bayard, Gerard G. Beekman, Oliver De Lancey, and John Watts. None did better than the firm of De Lancey and Watts, which by virtue of Oliver De Lancey's marriage to Phila Franks enjoyed close ties to her brother Moses, chief purveyor to His Majesty's troops in America after 1760. Yet there was plenty of room for newcomers as well. Young Uriah Hendricks, representing one of London's best-known Jewish firms, settled in the city in 1755 and was soon doing a substantial business supplying the sutlers, mostly Jews, who set up store wherever the military made camp. By 1756 an envious Benjamin Franklin observed "that New York is growing immensely rich, by Money brought into it from all Quarters for the Pay and Subsistence of the Troops."

Provisioning His Majesty's enemies was another lucrative wartime preoccupation. "Scarce a Week passes without an illicit Trader's going out or coming into this Port," one New Yorker remarked in 1748, "who are continually supplying and supporting our most avowed Enemies [the French]." In the French and Indian War, Manhattan merchants who traded with the French islands offloaded their cargoes beyond Sandy Hook and proceeded to port while their illicit goods were smuggled in by wagon. When increased fighting in the Caribbean made such expeditions too risky, one annoyed merchant crankily informed a correspondent that "I am now about trying a Voyage to our own Islands, since Trading with the Enemy has turn'd out so very ill."

Still another way to get rich in wartime, especially for merchants without friends in high places, was that old standby, privateering. During King George's War, about three dozen New York privateers prowled the Caribbean, taking several hundred French and Spanish prizes, worth some £618,000 to their investors. One ship, the *Royal Hester*, seized forty prizes, generating £63,800 for a dozen backers, among them men with such names as Aspinwall, Beekman, Cuyler, and Livingston. Seven other privateers cleared over forty thousand pounds for their investors, and Captain Peter Warren sailed into port in the summer of 1744 with a single French merchantman carrying nine thousand pounds' worth of sugar and indigo. Such exploits won "the general acclamation of the Public," and when Captain John Burgess's *Royal Catherine* took *Le Mars,* after only three broadsides off Sandy Hook, the corporation presented him with a gold box and freedom of the city.

In the next war, seventy-odd privateers operated out of New York—now the greatest such fleet by far in the colonies, and fabulously successful to boot, capturing more than six hundred prizes worth at least 1.4 million pounds to 150-odd investors. Between September 1756 and May 1757 alone, according to an official report, prizes worth two hundred thousand pounds arrived in the city. Their cargoes included coffee, cotton, sugar, wine, dry goods, pottery, indigo, ironware, lumber, bricks, and "live wares" (slaves), not to mention strongboxes of specie—gold doubloons, louis d'or, pieces of eight. Again the champion privateer proved to be the *Royal Hester*, which brought its fourteen owners a total of twenty-five prizes worth £115,000. "Such a Spirit of Privateering prevails here," trumpeted the *Post-Boy* in December 1756, "that by the most Judicious account, no Colony has exceeded it since the Discovery of North America."

All told, between 1739 and 1763 legalized plunder poured something like two million pounds into the pockets of two hundred or so investors—an immense accession of wealth at a time when, as Gerard G. Beekman observed, an income of three hundred pounds a year was sufficient to live "Like a Gentleman" in New York. Not all of this was profit, of course. As a rule, the crew of a privateer signed on for 60 percent of the value of prizes taken. An experienced captain received an extra two to three hundred pounds for a voyage of nine or twelve months. There were also multitudes of contractors, suppliers, and lawyers to be paid, not to mention the costs to be absorbed when a ship returned empty-handed, or didn't return at all. Inevitably, some shareholders in privateers lost everything, while still others barely covered expenses.

As a group, however, they did well enough that the average investor could expect to double or even triple his money in less than a year. Christopher Bancker refitted one of his merchantmen as a privateer in 1744 at a cost of twelve hundred pounds. He then sold shares to seven other merchants and captains, probably at a small profit to himself. Three cruises resulted in the capture of prizes worth £42,400. After the crew received its share, and after all other expenses were paid, each investor realized a profit of eighteen hundred pounds—a return of around 140 percent on the initial investment, perhaps more for shares that had changed hands at a discount.

More than a few found ways to multiply their winnings. They speculated in shares in privateering expeditions, creating a rudimentary futures market. They invested in city real estate, as land appreciated steadily in response to the pressures of population and economic growth, provided a hedge against recession, and could be mortgaged to obtain credit. They also loaned out their funds to friends and business associates at 6 or 7 percent interest, creating a system of private credit that partially compensated for the absence of banks.

INDUSTRY AND EMPIRE

A second source of New York's prosperity during the 1740s and 1750s was that great transformation of the British economy known as the industrial revolution. Its essential components were many and varied: the application of water and steam power to textile production, a burst of road- and canal-building, a new flowering of banks and insurance companies, improved agricultural output, accelerated demographic expansion, and urbanization. The population of London, largest city in the Western world, climbed from 676,000 to 900,000 between 1750 and 1800.

For British America, these changes spelled enhanced importance both as a market for cheap manufactured goods and as a source of raw materials and foodstuffs. By mid-century roughly half of all British shipping was engaged in trade with the American colonies, and the colonies were buying nine hundred thousand pounds' worth of British products annually—around 25 percent of all Britain's exports and 50 percent of all manufactures other than woolens. By the early 1760s that figure had soared to over two million pounds. (Because the Navigation Acts prohibited direct imports from other European countries, 80 percent of the finished wares shipped to New York from British ports were of British origin.)

Colonial exports rose almost as rapidly, from seven hundred thousand pounds at mid-century to some £1.5 million in the early 1760s. For New York and other northern ports, the mainspring of this business remained the British craving for sugar, which in the 1740s and 1750s triggered a new round of expansion in the West Indies. The demand for North American lumber and foodstuffs drove the prices of those commodities to new heights. By the early 1760s New York merchants were shipping over four hundred thousand pounds' worth of bread, flour, wheat, and livestock to the islands every year. Their ships returned with valuable cargoes of mahogany, slaves, raw sugar, rum, molasses, and, perhaps most important, bills of exchange that helped finance imports of manufactured goods from Great Britain. Direct sales to the mother country remained relatively rare: between 1751 and 1765 the *total* value of New York exports to Great Britain came to a mere £559,000.

Because the prices of imported British manufactures rose more slowly than the value of agricultural exports, the purchasing power of colonial Americans climbed throughout the later 1740s and 1750s, pushing their overall standard of living higher and higher. British exporters encouraged the trend by allowing colonial merchants, vendue houses, and even individuals to buy on credit. Merchants, in turn, extended credit to shopkeepers, who passed it on to artisans and farmers, drawing them as well into the international web of money and commerce. By 1760 or so the mainland colonies had run up some two million pounds in debts to English creditors; in another dozen years they would owe more than four million pounds. The residents of New York, meanwhile, became the leading American consumers of British wares.

Along with easy credit came restrictions aimed at protecting British merchants and manufacturers from colonial competition. In 1732 Parliament outlawed the exportation of American-made hats, and the Molasses Act of 1733 effectively prevented colonial merchants from trading with the French West Indies. In 1750 Parliament likewise prohibited the manufacture of iron products and certain classes of textiles in the colonies. Enforcement of these laws was lax, however, and many otherwise law-abiding colonial businessmen simply ignored them, even—perhaps especially—in time of war.

By 1750 New York was thriving again. The stores and countinghouses of Hanover Square, still the retail center, were stuffed with imported hardware, glassware, furniture, books, and clothing. Along Queen, Dock, Smith (William), Wall, Broad, Duke (Stone), and other nearby streets the houses of leading mercantile families—De Peysters, Beekmans, Livingstons, Philipses, Verplancks, Roosevelts, Crugers—presided over a lively hodgepodge of shops, taverns, and public markets. The Customs House showed 157 vessels registered out of the port, with a combined burden of sixty-four hundred tons; something on the order of twenty-five thousand tons of shipping entered and cleared it every year. A dozen years later, in 1762, the fleet consisted of 477 vessels with a combined burden of 19,500 tons, a threefold increase. Some 33,700 tons of shipping were by then passing through the port, providing employment for some

The Rhinelander Sugar House, constructed 1763, photographed c. 1890. This massive stone building on the corner of Rose and Duane streets was one of the largest structures in the pre-Revolutionary city and a tangible symbol of its prosperity after 1750. Like other New York "sugar houses," it was used to refine the sugar produced by West Indian slave labor into the loaves and other products that were in high demand throughout the colonies as well as England. (© Collection of The New-York Historical Society)

thirty-six hundred seamen, nearly five times the number only fifteen years earlier.

Overall, the city's population had now swelled to nearly eighteen thousand—almost twice what it had been in the 1740s. Philadelphia remained the largest North American city, with a population of 23,750. Boston, which actually lost population between 1740 and 1760, had slipped from second to third place with a population of 15,600.

REFINEMENT

When Dr. Alexander Hamilton of Philadelphia came up to New York in 1744, he often dined with the members of the Hungarian Club at Robert Todd's tavern on Broad Street. It wasn't, he reported, an easy thing to do. His companions seemed to think that "a man could not have a more sociable quality or enduement than to be able to pour down seas of liquor and remain unconquered while others sank under the table. . . . To drink stoutly with the Hungarian Club, who are all bumper men, is the readiest way for a stranger to recommend himself." Crude puns and dirty jokes were their idea of wit. Their arguments were "incoherent," their table manners execrable.

The good doctor's revulsion honored a code of taste and conduct known as "refinement." Detailed in countless British magazines, novels, and "courtesy books" over the previous half century, "refinement" was what distinguished people of quality from the vulgar masses—not just money, that is, but an inner discipline of body and spirit, a natural smoothness, for which money was a necessary though far from sufficient precondition.

"Refined" men and women had a poised yet complaisant manner. They avoided coarse speech, gross or lewd behavior, uncouth gestures, and sharp displays of emotion. They could make their way through a roomful of strangers without embarrassment, and at table they didn't give offense by using improper utensils or chewing with their mouths open. They conversed easily on history, literature, music, science, and other basic subjects. They read a little Greek and Latin and spoke at least one modern language besides English—hopefully French. For recreation, gentlemen rode and hunted while their ladies did needlework; both danced gracefully and played cards competently. Both, too, paid close attention to appearances: they kept their bodies clean, they wore fresh and fashionable clothing, they lived in commodious and agreeably furnished houses.

Notwithstanding Dr. Hamilton's verdict on the Hungarian Club, there had always been handfuls of ladies and gentlemen in New York who qualified as "refined." Earlier in the century they gathered round Governor Hunter, sipping Madeira, discussing Shakespeare, and peering through telescopes. In the early 1730s they patronized what may have been the city's first regular playhouse: the New Theater, located in the loft of a Nassau Street warehouse owned by Rip van Dam. When it closed after a season or two, genteel audiences contented themselves with puppet shows, pantomimes, and assemblies in the "long Room" of dancing master Henry Holt. Only after 1750, however, did refinement become de rigueur among the Manhattan gentry. By then, wartime affluence and buy-now-pay-later offers from British exporters finally afforded them access to the full range of goods and services that signaled a refined way of life.

Evident almost at once was a new opulence and complexity in upper-class attire. Guided by the life-size fashion dolls with which Britain's garment manufacturers advertised in distant markets, wealthy New York women began to accumulate closetfuls of "smart" clothes and accessories—girdles, hooped petticoats, gowns, cloaks, hoods, bonnets, pocketbooks, muffs—preferably constructed out of such exotic materials as India damask, China "taffety," Irish and Venetian poplin, Turkey Tabby, German serge, or Genoa velvet. They teased their hair into "towers," slathered their faces with fancy creams and pastes and powders, and splashed their bodies with costly oils and scented waters. Upper-class men developed comparable collections of "gallant" wigs, toupees, hats, shirts, waistcoats, cloaks, cravats, breeches, shoes, stockings, buttons, pocket watches, silk handkerchiefs, ribbons, snuff boxes, swords, walking sticks, and toothpick cases.

For Gerard B. Beekman, as for other wealthy New Yorkers, the wish to appear refined required a conscious adaptation to higher standards. Beekman resolved to wear stockings of the "best Silk" instead of plain linen. He sent to London for "a good fashionable Shass [sash]" of the sort favored by officers, plus "a fashionable Silver Mounted Sword . . . with a sword knot." He also vowed to take up the "Glorious sport" of hunting and sent away, again to London, for a "Genteel fowling Piece." One morning on Long Island, seated in his carriage, he experienced the sublime pleasure of shooting fifteen brace of plovers. The fact that he had a carriage to sit in wasn't unimportant either. Before 1740 only a handful of New Yorkers owned carriages, and the town had no resident coachmaker. Over the next twenty-odd years, though, carriages became securely linked to gentility and thirteen coachmakers set up shop to meet the demand.

Jane Beekman (1760-1841), by John Durand, c. 1768.
Miss Beekman's genteel upbringing is apparent not
only from her fashionable clothing but the book
she holds, open to a page in Latin from Erasmus.
(© Collection of The New-York Historical Society)

By the mid-1770s there were eighty-five coaches, chaises, and phaetons in New York, and the sixty-nine families to whom they belonged ranked among the city's richest and most powerful.

But stylish clothes and carriages alone weren't enough. Refinement also demanded superior diction, posture, and gesture—knowing which, the gentry flocked to elocutionists, music teachers, singing masters, dancing masters, and dentists. Gentlemen practiced the lazy nasal drawl and elaborate slang of London bluebloods. "Split me, Madam," they declared. "By Gad." "Dam me." Ladies learned to blush at such talk and studied the techniques of genteel correspondence.

Ultimately, the only way to assess one's own progress toward refinement was by comparison with other aspirants in a suitable setting. New York's biggest social event— the occasion when pretensions to refinement came under the keenest scrutiny—was still the Governor's Ball, which took place every year at the fort following public celebrations of the King's Birthday. During the 1750s and 1760s formal dancing assemblies, a fixture of polite society in Britain, became very influential in New York as well. Like the Governor's Ball, they were selective. Admission was by invitation only, and the "managers" of an affair bore the solemn responsibility of ensuring that only the right kind of people got in.

"Turtle-feasts" were much in vogue too. "There are several houses, pleasantly situated on the East River, where it is common to have turtle-feasts," one visitor reported. "These happen once or twice in a week. Thirty or forty gentlemen and ladies meet and dine together, drink tea in the afternoon, fish and amuse themselves till evening, and then return home in Italian chaises . . . a gentleman and a lady in each chaise."

Intimate card parties became quite fashionable, whist and backgammon being all the rage at court. Private eating and drinking clubs remained a fixture of city taverns, though literary and scientific "societies," which multiplied rapidly after mid-century, were considered more respectable. The New York Harmonic Society sponsored musical recitals and benefit concerts featuring the works of Handel, Bach, Corelli, Haydn, and other fashionable composers. Even the besotted members of the Hungarian Club were capable of a "great deal of talk about attraction, condensation, gravitation, rarification [and] the mathematical and astronomical problems of the illustrious Newton," Dr. Hamilton admitted. "I was tired of nothing here but their excessive drinking, for in this place you may have the best of company and conversation as well as att Philadelphia."

Chaperoned "routs" and "frolics" not only allowed young men and women of genteel families to socialize among their own kind but helped inculcate appropriate rules of courtship and marriage. Refined young bachelors learned to expect sexual favors only from serving girls or prostitutes (though that too was frowned on in some quarters). Without a chaste reputation, conversely, young women of quality couldn't hope to find acceptable husbands.

Even at their funerals, refined New Yorkers knew, they would be on trial. Lest they appear stingy or unsociable, they took care to set aside enough money to provide mourners with an abundance of food, drink, and tobacco. In time, gifts of gold rings, silk scarves, silver spoons, and gloves for pallbearers and other important guests became practically mandatory; private family vaults created an especially favorable impression. As a result, funerals costing a hundred pounds or more weren't unusual after the middle of the century—an amount equal to or exceeding the annual wages of a skilled craftsman and sufficient to support three or four laborers and their families for an entire year.

Probably the most challenging environment for the observation and exercise of gentility was the theater. Beginning in the early 1750s a succession of theatrical companies occupied the New Theater on Nassau Street, abandoned fifteen years earlier, where they indulged enthusiastic audiences with performances of *The Recruiting Officer*, *Richard III*, *The Beggar's Opera*, *Beau in the Suds*, *The Intriguing Chambermaid*, and other favorites of the contemporary London stage. The renowned Lewis Hallam, a Covent Garden veteran, brought his London Company of Comedians to Manhattan in 1753 and erected a new New Theater on the same site as the first, only bigger, and with more attractive accommodations for the gentry. The gentry turned out in force—"a player is a new thing under the sun in our good province," explained the young Philip Schuyler—even though they didn't have the players to themselves. Occupants of the cheaper gallery seats frequently interrupted performances by talking, singing, fighting, and hurling eggs at the well-dressed boxholders below. The experience wasn't lost on David Douglass, Hallam's successor as manager of the London Company: when he put up a new playhouse on the corner of Nassau and Chapel (now Beekman) streets in 1761, he wisely added partitions to the boxes for the protection of "select Companies."

GENTEEL RESORTS

To partisans of refinement everywhere in the Anglo-American world, the noise, squalor, and capricious intimacy of city life—the unpredictable, unintended encounters with people beneath one's station—were sources of constant irritation. Country estates afforded occasional relief, above all in the summer, but year-round rural isolation had obvious disadvantages. A more practical solution was to define places within cities where polite people could promenade, ride carriages, converse, and socialize among themselves without having to take notice of their inferiors. Prototypes of such "resorts" already existed. The Mall in London's St. James Park and the Tuilleries in Paris, for example, were restricted to the refined classes. London also had its "pleasure gardens" like Vauxhall and Ranelagh, ornate sanctuaries where properly dressed and well-behaved visitors could stroll, take refreshments, attend musical concerts, and the like.

In 1732 the Common Council of New York leased a portion of the large open space fronting the fort to three prominent citizens—John Chambers, Peter Bayard, and Peter Jay—who agreed to lay out and maintain a "Bowling-Green" on the site, with "Walks therein." The little park was intended for "the delight of the inhabitants of this city," the council said, besides which it would enhance the "Beauty & Ornament" of lower Broadway. Abigail Franks, wife of the wealthy Jewish merchant Lewis Franks, affirmed a couple of years later that Bowling Green's "handsome Walk of trees" and neatly painted fence did indeed make a "very Pretty" retreat from the hustle and bustle of the waterfront.

By the 1760s some of the city's most fashionable residences could be found in the immediate vicinity of Bowling Green, including those of the Van Cortlandts, Livingstons, De Lanceys, Morrises, Bayards, and De Peysters. Since the governor's mansion stood there as well, some residents referred to this as the "court" end of town. Yet Bowling Green was neither large enough nor exclusive enough to function as a truly genteel resort.

Because few private residences had rooms of sufficient size for entertaining on a grand scale, committees of leading citizens in towns all over England and America organized the construction of special assembly rooms. As early as 1751 "several gentlemen" of New York hit upon a plan to replace the tottering eighty-year-old market house on Broad Street with a structure that could serve both commerce and genteel society. They had no trouble raising the necessary funds—the Common Council alone contributed twelve hundred pounds—and work proceeded so swiftly that the new building was ready the following year. Known as the Royal Exchange, it had an arcaded ground floor suitable for an open-air marketplace. Upstairs was a large hall with twenty-foot ceilings, ideal for balls, dinners, and concerts. Several smaller adjacent rooms provided space for more intimate gatherings or meetings. One would sometimes be used by the Common Council; another would be leased for use as the Exchange Coffee House, which was for many years the best place in town to get news of distant ports and the preferred location for privateers to auction off prizes.

Taverns often had plenty of space, but their association with drunkenness, cursing, fighting, and other plebeian vices disqualified them as milieux for polite recreations. Alert tavern keepers responded with inducements calculated to attract a wealthier, more decorous clientele. They cleaned up, laid on decent food, improved service, and even relocated in better neighborhoods; more and more of them advertised "long rooms" decorated like genteel parlors, only spacious enough for an assembly or recital of music. Samuel Fraunces, a West Indian of mixed French and African descent, had opened his first New York tavern, the Mason's Arms, on upper Broadway near the almshouse—not a name or a location with which an ambitious man could rest content. In 1763 Fraunces moved down to the old De Lancey mansion on the corner of Broad and Pearl, still one of the handsomest buildings in town and the perfect location for a tavern where ladies and gentlemen would feel at ease. Its very name was a step up: the Queen's Head, presumably in honor of Charlotte, wife of King George III. For two decades the Queen's Head would be recognized as the premier establishment of its kind in the city.

The enterprising Fraunces also had a hand in bringing "pleasure gardens" to New York. Several had opened during the 1740s and 1750s, though only two remained: Spring Garden, situated at the northeast corner of Broadway and Ann Street, and Catiemuts Garden, located on the brow of a small hill of the same name about where the Boston Post Road (Park Row) now crosses Chambers Street—the same hill, some residents remembered, where the "Negroes were Burnt." In 1765 Fraunces opened Vauxhall Garden on a prominence overlooking the Hudson near the present junction of Greenwich and Warren streets. Its attractions included a wax museum, Italian fireworks, and afternoon teas. That same year, a rival opened Ranelagh near the corner of Church and Thomas streets, advertising band concerts on Tuesdays and Thursdays.

No public space in New York attracted higher concentrations of the refined, however, than Trinity Church. Of all the city's religious bodies, Judge Thomas Jones later recalled, Trinity enjoyed "the most influence, and greatest opulence. To this Church, the Governor, the Lieutenant-Governor, most of his Majesty's Council, many members of the General Assembly, all the officers of Government, with a numerous train of rich and affluent merchants, [and] landholders, belonged." During the 1740s and 1750s its parishioners began renovations to Trinity's now cramped and aging building (including the purchase of its first organ) that were aimed at creating an environment more hospitable to their genteel brand of Christianity. What they had in mind reflected the legacy of the renowned Christopher Wren and his students, who had utilized principles and themes of classical Roman architecture—strict symmetry, geometric proportions, temple-front porticos—to create buildings perfectly attuned to the ambitions and self-confidence of the propertied classes in Georgian Britain (whence the term "Georgian" architecture). Trinity paid homage to the link between this neoclassicism and gentility as early as 1752, when it erected St. George's Chapel on Chapel (Beekman) Street for the convenience of members living on the east side of town. St. George's columned portico, balustrades, gracefully arched windows, and hexagonal steeple wouldn't have been out of place in a fancy London suburb.

St. George's was soon eclipsed by Trinity's second chapel, St. Paul's, erected between 1764 and 1766 on the corner of Broadway and Fulton streets. Its builder, Thomas McBean, studied under the London architect James Gibbs, arguably Wren's most eminent disciple. St. Paul's closely resembles Gibbs's elegant St. Martin's-in-the-Fields Church in London. Its dominant features—temple-front portico, giant Ionic columns, massive pediment, and elaborately decorated tower—gave visible expression to the desire for order, balance, and harmony that denoted the genteel way of life. (A second Wren-Gibbs-style building, the North Dutch Church on William Street, went up in 1769 to accommodate members of the Reformed faith who wanted English-language services.)

St. Paul's domestic counterparts were the fashionable residences built by well-to-do New Yorkers in imitation of the Georgian-style mansions already ubiquitous in Britain. The most famous of the city's "Spacious Genteel Houses" (as one visitor called them) was erected in 1752 by William Walton, son of the "Boss," on the east side of Queen (today Pearl) Street between Peck Slip and Dover Street—not far from the Walton shipyards on the East River. Three stories high, fifty feet wide, and built of costly, yellow-hued "Holland" brick, Walton's house was a manifesto of Georgian refinement. The details of its facade—including a majestic front door framed with fluted classical columns and topped by a broken pediment with the Walton coat of arms—conveyed not only wealth but good taste, social confidence, and family dignity. The same effect was achieved inside by oak-paneled halls, marble floors, gilt mirrors, silk damask curtains, and drawing rooms wainscoted in black walnut and hung with crystal chandeliers. An ornately carved mahogany staircase led to the second floor, one corner of which was devoted to a ballroom. Outside, to the rear of the house, lay carefully groomed grounds that sloped down past flower gardens and grape arbors to the grassy banks of the East River, where the family had a summer cottage and boathouse.

Nothing like it had ever been seen in New York, and for decades it was considered one of the finest private residences in North America. When Walton threw a victory party for British officers after their conquest of Canada in 1759, the splendor of his home made such an impression that it would be offered to Parliament as proof of the colonies' ability to pay their fair share of imperial expenses (and of the need to boost the compensation of royal governors and other imperial functionaries, who were finding it more and more difficult to keep up).

As the interior of the Walton house demonstrated, refined standards of sociability necessitated newer, more complex approaches to the organization and furnishing of domestic space. Well-to-do New York families had long since replaced the clunky Dutch-style furniture of the William and Mary period: first with the more graceful walnut pieces in the newer Queen Anne style; then with the self-consciously classical style popularized by the London cabinetmaker Thomas Chippendale after 1750; and then again, in the 1760s, with the more ornate classicism advocated by Scottish designer Robert Adam. Out, as well, went the plain, old-fashioned, often home-made canvas floor-cloths once favored by the rich as well as middling classes; in came expensive, imported "Turkey fashion" carpets, no two exactly alike.

Each room now served a specific public or private function, identified by specialized furniture, distinctive imported wallpaper, and suitable pictures. Nothing graced a drawing room or parlor more than a family portrait by Benjamin West or John Singleton Copley, whose blunt materialism appealed to the gentry's pride in its power and possessions. The hallmarks of a genteel dining room, by contrast, were a sideboard stuffed with Wedgwood china and an abundance of specialized silver, pewter, and crystal implements, many of them associated with the serving and consumption of tea. Afternoon tea had now become a vital upper-class ritual on both sides of the Atlantic, presided over by ladies equipped with a fantastic technology of kettles, lamps, stands, urns, strainers, trays, and canisters of fine imported teas.

New rural "seats" and country houses enabled the gentry to pursue refinement outside the city as well as in. The trendsetter here was Peter Warren, whose fame as commander of the fleet that took Louisbourg in 1745 had won him a promotion to vice-admiral, a knighthood, and a seat in Parliament. Sir Peter acquired several hundred acres of land at Greenwich, a mile or so above the city, and built a comfortable Georgian country house to which he and his family could flee during the hot, pestilential months of summer.

The Warrens soon had company. In 1750 Captain Thomas Clarke acquired a tract between what are now Eighth and Tenth Avenues, running north from 14th Street to roughly 29th Street. He called it Chelsea, after the London borough, and just below the present intersection of Ninth Avenue and 23rd Street he too built a fine Georgian home. In 1760 Abraham Mortier, commissary to His Majesty's forces, leased an estate from Trinity Church called Richmond Hill—a promontory between the present King, Varick, Charlton, and MacDougal streets—where he wined and dined a host of dignitaries, including Lord Jeffrey Amherst, who until 1763 served as supreme British commander in America. Other gentlemen, too, developed a taste for refined country life—William Bayard, James Jauncy, and John Morin Scott among them—enough that by the mid-1760s there was an almost unbroken line of great estates up the west side of Manhattan.

Much the same thing occurred on the east side. South of the present Seward Park, just below the intersection of Division and Rutgers streets, lay the hundred-acre estate of the wealthy Rutgers family, whose money came from trade and brewing. Chief Justice and later Lieutenant Governor James De Lancey occupied 340 acres on what is today 120 blocks of the Lower East Side, running from the Bowery to the East River, and north from Division Street (so named because it separated his property from that of the Rutgers family), across Delancey, to Stanton. (Orchard Street was cut through the governor's fine stand of fruit trees.) The Stuyvesants still held Director Pieter's original estate, encompassing most of the land west of Fourth Avenue from 5th to roughly 20th streets. Gerardus Stuyvesant (the Director's grandson) still lived in the old family house, while his two sons, Petrus and Nicholas, occupied more up-to-date mansions nearby; Petrus dubbed his Petersfield, and Nicholas's was known as the Bowery.

Above the Stuyvesants lay John Watts's Rose Hill (now 29th Street and Park Avenue) and, still further north, Inclenberg, the estate of John Murray, whose mansion stood on what is now Park Avenue between 36th and 37th streets (an area known today as Murray Hill). In the early 1760s James Beekman (cousin of Gerard G. Beekman and son of William) built Mount Pleasant, an elegant villa overlooking Turtle Bay on the East River, near the foot of what is now 50th Street. Further upriver lay the mansions of Schermerhorns, Rhinelanders, Lawrences, and others. On Harlem Heights, Colonel Roger Morris and his wife, Mary Philipse, were building Mount Morris, a beautiful Georgian showplace commanding a view down the length of Manhattan. Some gentlemen preferred the comparative isolation of Westchester or Long Island. Frederick Van Cortlandt built a substantial mansion in the Bronx in 1748. Cadwallader Colden located his country seat in Flushing. Philip Livingston erected his in Brooklyn Heights, while William Axtell went all the way out to Flatbush to build his Melrose Hall.

Although some of these estates grew crops for profit, their primary purpose— besides providing refuge from epidemics—was to serve as theaters of refinement. Many New York gentlemen, inspired by the rage for gardening and landscaping among English estate owners, surrounded their country homes with vast lawns and flowerbeds, orchards, greenhouses, conservatories, fish ponds, and fanciful grottos. The great demand for flowers, shrubs, and trees prompted William Prince to found a nursery in Flushing, later called the Linnean Botanic Gardens, famous throughout the colonies.

Such embellishments conveyed an appreciation of order and harmony, paid lip service to scientific agriculture and horticulture, and provided a setting for such recreations as golf, tennis, cricket, hunting, and horse racing. Some estates boasted deerparks and game preserves—Governor Cosby may have set the local precedent when he designated Governors Island as his private game preserve—and the De Lancey estate even had its own race course just off the Bowery Road, between the present 1st and 2nd streets.

POLITICS AMONG GENTLEMEN

One thing the spread of refinement didn't do was improve the tone of New York politics. During King George's War, the Morris-Livingston "landed interest" and the De Lancey-led "mercantile interest" waged increasingly rancorous public battles around the problem of Canada. With the help of Governor George Clinton, who replaced George Clarke in 1743, the landed interest clamored for wider military operations against the French. The mercantile interest resisted the idea, fearing a disruption of the Albany trade and new taxes that would jeopardize New York's reviving commerce. When the two factions turned to voters for support, they hurled pamphlets, broadsides, and newspapers at one another with furious abandon—without, however, eliciting much of a response among the freemen of the city, who remained content to leave politics to gentlemen. The merchant interest was thus able to get a firm grip on the provincial assembly, and when Clinton's successor, Sir Danvers Osborne, committed suicide shortly after his arrival in 1753, it was James De Lancey who took control of the government as lieutenant governor.

By then, too, religion had again become an ingredient in the colony's factional strife. The gentlemen of the landed interest had always leaned toward Presbyterianism or one of the other dissenting sects, while those of the mercantile interest mostly identified with the Anglican establishment. At mid-century this line was drawn more sharply by a trio of young men connected with the landed interest: William Livingston, John Morin Scott, and William Smith Jr., often referred to as the "Triumvirate." Each was a recent Yale graduate. Each had read law in the office of Smith's father, William

Smith Sr., who had defended Zenger and helped prosecute the 1741 "conspirators." And each was (or would be) a member of the Presbyterian Church (the elder Smith had been a leading Presbyterian layman).

In 1752 Livingston and his friends launched the *Independent Reflector*, a political journal that combined the oppositional intensity of Trenchard and Gordon's *Independent Whig* with the didacticism of the *Reflector*, a contemporary British literary magazine in the style of Addison and Steele. One of their primary concerns was the adverse impact of prosperity on the manners and morals in New York. Dedicated to "correcting the taste and improving the Minds of our fellow Citizens," the *Independent Reflector* ridiculed the grasping, pretentious people "who call themselves the Polite and Well-bred." "Our extraordinary success during the late War has given Rise to a method of living unknown to our frugal Ancestors," Livingston wrote scoldingly. The journal ceased publication at the end of 1753—done in, Livingston wrote, by "the fears of my enemies and the spite of malignants." But like Zenger's *Weekly Journal*, with which it shared a common intellectual ancestry, the *Independent Reflector*'s influence would resonate long after it had disappeared. When William Smith Jr. published the first volume of his *History of the Province of New York* (1757), sharply critical of the De Lanceys, he too mocked the sudden concern for refinement among well-to-do residents of the city. "Our affluence during the late war introduced a degree of luxury in tables, dress, and furniture, with which we were before unacquainted," Smith wrote.

Yet nothing gave the Triumvirate greater cause for concern than De Lancey's effort to make New York's first publicly supported college an Anglican institution. Back in 1746 the Assembly had approved a lottery to raise money for a college, and when a board of trustees was finally appointed in 1751, seven of its ten members were Anglicans. They decided to build on a thirty-acre portion of the King's (formerly Queen's) Farm on the west side of Manhattan, donated by Trinity Church on condition that the school's presidents belong to the Church of England and that it use the Anglican liturgy in religious services. The board then invited Samuel Johnson, the Anglican rector at Stamford, Connecticut, to lead the new institution.

William Livingston, one of the three non-Anglicans on the board, was apoplectic. He revered higher learning as a beacon of enlightenment in a crassly materialistic age and believed that a college would do much to improve New York's reputation (there were, after all, only four other such institutions in all of British North America: Harvard, William and Mary, Yale, and the College of New Jersey, now Princeton). "Our Neighbours have told us in an insulting Tone, that the Art of getting Money, is the highest Improvement we can pretend to," he had written in the *Independent Reflector*. In the spring of 1753, accordingly, Livingston, Smith, Scott, and Alexander launched an all-out attack on the Anglican plan.

Their contention, in Livingston's words, was that the Anglican scheme would make the college "a contracted Receptacle of Bigotry" and was part of an SPG conspiracy— "so perilous, so detestable a plot"—to impose religious conformity on the colony. The stakes were thus political as well as religious. Inasmuch as the Ministry Act of 1693 hadn't actually established the Anglican Church, use of the Anglican liturgy in college services constituted an invasion of hard-won legislative prerogatives. Natural rights, constitutional liberty, rational toleration, freedom of thought, diversity of opinion, separation of church and state—those were the real issues, Livingston declared. "The

Absurdity of a Religion, supported and inforced by the Terrors of the Law, is too apparent to need much farther Display."

These Whiggish accusations made the proposed New York college a transatlantic cause célèbre by tying it, like the Zenger affair fifteen years earlier, to issues and ideas deeply imbedded in Anglo-American political experience. Thomas Bradbury Chandler, Samuel Seabury Sr., Samuel Auchmuty (rector of Trinity), and other Anglican spokesmen fought back in a succession of pamphlets and newspaper essays. (Belfast-born Hugh Gaine's *New-York Mercury*, published at the sign of the Bible and Crown on Hanover Square, was their favorite outlet; the Livingston forces labeled it a "priestly Newspaper.") Inequality, hierarchy, monarchy, patriarchy, obedience to authority, and an established church—these were the true principles of social organization, the Anglicans declared. Religious toleration was one thing, the anarchy of complete religious freedom quite another. The Church of England symbolized and served the British people as a whole; its clergy acted as custodians of British values, tradition, and culture; its preeminence was as vital in the colonies as in the mother country. Opposition to the proposed college wasn't merely ignorant: it smacked of treason and rebellion as well.

In 1754, to no one's surprise, Governor De Lancey granted a charter for King's College. By July of that year the new institution had opened in the vestry room of Trinity Church with Samuel Johnson as president. Later that year Livingston and his friends founded the New York Society Library. Their intent was not only to serve the city's inhabitants generally but to maintain some influence over the new college by establishing a collection of books for the use of its students.

Wrangling continued over whether the Assembly would allow public money to be spent for the college. The arrival of Osborne's replacement, Sir Charles Hardy, cleared the way for a compromise in 1756. The Assembly agreed to give half the lottery money to the college and the other half to the city for a new municipal jail and pesthouse (a quarantine hospital for the victims of contagious diseases). Construction of a proper academic building began at once on the plot now bounded by Murray, Barclay, West Broadway, and Church streets; Bedloe's Island in the Upper Bay—which the city purchased in 1758—was chosen as the site for the pesthouse, completed by 1760. Compromise or no, Livingston and company continued for years to view King's College with deep suspicion.

WAGES OF WAR

Throughout the King's College controversy, the Livingstons, unlike their predecessors in the "popular party" of the 1730s, made no real attempt to mobilize a broad following. Freemen continued to pay little attention to local elections, and the numbers of small shopkeepers and artisans on the Common Council fell to levels not seen in forty years. Nor was there much popular interest in official ceremonies, as the traveler Peter Kalm discovered. "The King of England's Birthday was celebrated in town to-day," Kalm wrote in November 1749, "but the people didn't make a great fuss over it. A cannon was fired at noon and the warships were decorated with many flags. In the evening there were candles in some windows and a ball at the governor's. Some drank until they became intoxicated, and that was all."

When the occasion seemed to warrant it, however, the common people didn't hesitate to defend their interests—in the streets rather than at the polls. Over the winter of

1753–54, for example, a self-appointed committee of merchants agreed that by devaluing copper pennies in relation to the shilling they could improve the colony's balance of payments with the mother country. Outraged that devaluation would also raise the price of bread and depress wages, laboring people "armed with Clubs and Staves" took to the streets to protest, though without success.

Trouble could erupt, too, over the tendency of soldiers stationed in town to supplement their meager pay by moonlighting as tradesmen or laborers. As their numbers increased, their competition with native working people became the subject of more than a few dockside rows and tavern brawls. What really riled townspeople, however, was raids by naval press gangs. One spring morning in 1756 marines armed with clubs and pistols came ashore at Murray's Wharf, hurried through the Fly Market, and, ignoring orders to seize "only such as had the appearance of seafaring or labouring men," entered houses and grabbed people indiscriminately. One man was chased down Wall Street, beaten unconscious, and dragged off. The following spring, when Lord Loudoun's expeditionary fleet was delayed from sailing against Louisbourg by a scarcity of hands, he had three thousand men cordon off the city at two o'clock in the morning, then sent press gangs to search "the Taverns and other houses, where sailors usually resorted." By dawn, they had hauled in eight hundred people, including "All kinds of Tradesmen and Negroes"—a number equal to more than a quarter of New York's adult male population. Even after half had been released, the four hundred or so "retained in the service" were more than enough to meet Loudon's needs. In 1760, when the fifty-gun HMS *Winchester* fired a shot over the bow of the privateer *Sampson* and dispatched a party to board it, the *Sampson*'s crew locked the captain in the cabin, then blasted the press gang with a volley of musketry, killing or wounding several. The mariners then took refuge in the town, where sympathetic citizens helped them escape the clutches of the sheriff.

Despite such incidents, seamen were doing well in the war years; indeed the navy's resort to impressment was a consequence of the mariners' prosperity. New York seamen had been swept by "almost a kind of madness to go a-privateering," Lieutenant Governor De Lancey noted in 1758. They had been quickly joined by farmers, laborers—and deserters from the Royal Navy. In 1759 alone, forty-eight ships were commissioned out of New York as privateers manned by 5,670 seamen.

Reality rarely lived up to expectations. The crew of a privateer that returned to port with thirty-five thousand pounds or more in prizes would have £12,600 to divide among themselves (subtracting court costs and the shares for the owners, captain, and mates). On a typical ship of around seventy-five or so hands, that could mean £168 per man—a lot of money at a time when common laborers earned thirty pounds a year. Most privateers came home empty-handed, however, and in nearly two decades of war the average tar probably received no more than eleven pounds for his troubles. Assuming he came home at all, that is: one out of every two or three was killed, captured by the enemy, or injured.

So many common seamen continued nonetheless to sign up with privateers that New York shipowners were obliged to offer five shillings per day for regular voyages (over three times the peacetime rate), while the government had to offer five pounds a month to recruit sailors for service on troop transports (a master's rate in peacetime). That was good news for the three thousand or so seamen working on New York vessels by 1762.

The town's artisans flourished as well. The East River shipyards, stretching up the waterfront toward Corlear's Hook, did a booming business refitting merchantmen with the cannon and extra sail required for a Caribbean expedition and repairing those that returned to port with damages. Ropemakers, sailmakers, coopers, chandlers—all had steady employment now for the first time in recent memory. Cordwainers struggled to keep up with huge military orders for boots and shoes, a boon also for the city's tanners, whose operations had been moved from Beekman's Swamp to the Fresh Water Pond, where they were allowed to dig their tanning pits and draw water. British troops needed hats too, so officials winked at violations of the 1732 parliamentary law that limited colonial hatmaking. In 1755 New York's bakers, on hearing that the army would need fifty thousand pounds of bread, jacked up their prices a hefty 14 percent. His Majesty's forces likewise paid good money to cartmen for hauling supplies and gunpowder. Merchants, too, needed cartmen more than ever, and Mayor John Cruger, himself a powerful merchant, began to expand their ranks in 1756. Over his nine-year term Cruger licensed 386 new carters, a nearly tenfold increase. (Cartmen remained tightly regulated, though. The Common Council set standard rates on over a hundred commodities and listed them in chapbooks distributed throughout the city. Violators could be tracked down easily as each cartman had to put his number, using red paint, on his wagon.)

The presence of hundreds of military and naval officers, together with surging civilian demand, caused a burst of new construction that raised the number of houses in New York from 1,991 in 1753 to nearly twenty-six hundred by 1760. Housewrights, bricklayers, stonemasons, glaziers, plasterers, painters, and carvers commanded wages about 25 percent higher than prewar levels, and the demand for building materials led the city to allow manufacturers to set up brick kilns on the Common or on leased land farther north. Similarly, the influx of officers created a rich new market for the luxury goods produced by local carvers and gilders, watchmakers, furniture makers, painters, pewterers and potters, silversmiths, perfumers, glovers, seamstresses, hoopmakers, and mantua makers. During the war years, forty-one wigmakers and hairdressers found employment in New York, providing men with perukes and ladies with fashionable towers. Shoemakers offered goods "equal if not superior to any made in London," and as word of the provincial demand for finery crossed the Atlantic, milliners and staymakers began arriving from London and Bath with the latest fashions.

Specialty shops around Hanover Square thrived on the demand for wines, tobacco, china, glassware, stationery, and teas. Much of this retailing continued to be done by women—widows as well as the wives of merchants and sea captains—who tended to specialize in dry goods and millinery. Some did so well as the city's economy charged forward that they crossed the line separating shopkeepers from she-merchants. Martha Carrick ran an ordinary "shop" until 1761, when she moved into the "store" (short for "storehouse") of a former merchant and began selling only at wholesale. Frances Willett in Wall Street sold sugar and rum by the hogshead, which she fetched from St. Kitts on her own two ships, a schooner and a snow.

The most successful wartime retailers were the tavern owners who sold food and drink to the thousands of seamen and soldiers passing through town every year. New York, in fact, could boast of more licensed public houses than any other colonial city—334 by 1752, up from 166 only eight years earlier. Local merchants who had once imported rum now began making their own: of the ten rum distilleries in 1753, the leading

"works" were those of Livingston and Lefferts, erected "at great expence" just behind
Trinity Church. After 1760 Pierre Lorillard did his best to keep the city's nicotine output
on par with its alcohol production. Having served an apprenticeship as a snuffmaker,
Lorillard opened his own "manufactory" in a small rented house on Chatham Street.
Here he packed snuff into animal bladders, which had first been dried and tanned, then
sold it to wholesalers, thereby launching Manhattan's tobacco industry.

The pursuit of refinement by war contractors and others provided work for a small
army of gardeners, coachmen, butlers, footmen, and maids, although many domestic
servants remained unpaid slaves. In 1756 New York counted 695 female slaves over the
age of sixteen and another 443 under it, constituting a pool of over a thousand black
women to serve a population of almost 10,800 whites. Black men continued to do much
of the town's heavy labor, as well as to be used by their owners as fishermen, coopers,
barbers, or boatmen. At the same time, the institution of slavery was gradually coming
under more severe criticism throughout the English-speaking world, and white New
Yorkers were exposed to a growing number of books, pamphlets, and newspapers that
argued for abolition on economic as well as religious grounds. One essayist, after a careful statistical analysis, pronounced "the labor of freemen to be much more productive
than of slaves" and concluded "that slavery is impolitic as well as unjust."

MUNICIPAL IMPROVEMENTS

Although years of war boosted the city's income from licensing fees, rents, fines, and
other charges, both the mayor and the Common Council proved reluctant to spend
money on municipal improvements. They made little effort, for example, to upgrade
harbor facilities in response to the upsurge in waterfront traffic and made only occasional repairs to the municipally owned Great Dock, now used mainly for fishing boats,
market boats, and other small craft. Rather, the magistrates continued the old practice
of granting water lots, often to one another, for the building of quays (wharves that paralleled the shore) rather than substantial piers. Similarly, despite the expansion of overland traffic between Westchester and Manhattan, the city built no new bridges over the
Harlem River. King's Bridge, erected by Frederick Philipse in 1693, was still the only
crossing, and still charged exorbitant tolls. Its monopoly was finally broken by private
entrepreneurs in 1759, when Benjamin Palmer and Jacob Dyckman—blacksmith, tavern keeper, and the owner of a riverfront farm—constructed their Freebridge.

The Common Council was diligent, to be sure, about keeping streets and roads in
good repair, inasmuch as they were vital to the local economy. Maintaining the up-
island Kingsbridge and Bloomingdale roads cost little or nothing because the law
required all inhabitants to do roadwork two days a year, using their own spades and
pickaxes, or pay a large fine (wealthy residents routinely paid). Not until 1764 would the
council create the first rudimentary highway department, hiring laborers and surveyors
whose wages were paid out of a general tax levy. Around the same time, recognizing the
need for better roads within the city itself, the council ordered boatloads of cobblestones from Westchester to pave streets near public buildings—the fort, Bowling
Green, City Hall, and the Old Slip Market. It also enforced street-cleaning laws rigor-
ously, though packs of feral swine and dogs continued to roam about with impunity.

The council proved much less attentive to the sanitation problems created by
steady population growth and overcrowding. After ten P.M., householders and servants
were allowed to empty ordure tubs of human waste into the rivers, where it coated the

wharves and quays with a fecal slime. A storm sewer under Broad Street, reinforced with stone in 1747, was designed to drain into the East River, but even with the addition of trunk lines in Wall Street and elsewhere, it never functioned properly, and pools of rank, debris-filled water were a frequent challenge to pedestrians. Although residents complained loudly about the appalling stench and clouds of flies that blanketed the city as a result—a hot day in summer could be almost unbearable—the Common Council seemed unwilling or unable to act.

Nor did it cope effectively with the increase of crime that accompanied the city's new prosperity after 1750. Prostitution, for example, had been relatively unobtrusive in New York as late as 1744, when Dr. Hamilton learned that an after-dusk stroll on the Battery "was a good way for a stranger to fit himself with a courtezan; for that place was the generall rendezvous of the fair sex of that profession after sunset." The mass arrival of troops and privateers prompted more aggressive and organized approaches to commercial sex—bolder women venturing out to board ships at anchor in the harbor, others setting up "Houses of Ill Repute" in town. Raids on these establishments in July 1753 netted twenty-two "ladies of Pleasure," five of whom received fifteen lashes before "a vast Number of Spectators" and were then banished. These measures were utterly ineffectual, though, and prostitution became a more and more conspicuous element of the city scene in the years that followed.

So did assault, mugging, robbery, and other crimes against persons and property, which residents blamed on the influx of disreputable outsiders like the "Gang of Fellows of no good Aspect" who arrived one day on the stage from Philadelphia. As early as 1749 one local paper reported that it had "become dangerous for the good People of this City, to be out late at Nights, without being sufficiently strong or well armed," and half a dozen years later the printer Hugh Gaine estimated that at least one house in New York was burgled every night. The unpaid citizen watch, consisting chiefly of residents who couldn't afford to buy their way out of obligatory service, was useless—a "Parcel of idle, drunken, vigilant Snorers, who never quelled any nocturnal Tumult in their lives," the *Gazette* scoffed in 1757, "but would, perhaps, be as ready to join in a Burglary as any Thief in Christendom." Equally ineffective as a deterrent were the public floggings and other forms of corporal punishment ordered by the courts. Mary Anderson, "a loose and profligate Wretch," was given thirty-nine lashes for theft in 1754, and "she afforded some Diversion while at the Post to the Mob, as she was very obstinate and resisting."

In 1759 the Common Council responded to the rising clamor for action by erecting a new city jail in the Common (at the northeast corner of today's City Hall Park). The New Gaol was quickly filled with French and Indian prisoners of war, however, and the council had to begin making plans for a second structure. Three years later the council took the further step of creating a paid watch to patrol the streets at night. It decided, too, to begin installing whale-oil lamps around town and hired municipal lamplighters to keep them lit.

Besides crime, the council had to contend with the ever-present danger of fire, magnified now by the great stockpiles of pitch, tar, resin, turpentine, and gunpowder that His Majesty's armed forces had located in and around town. New regulations were adopted for the storage of flammable materials, and official inspectors were appointed to secure compliance. Because the new density of buildings in lower Manhattan heightened the risk of a major conflagration, the provincial assembly ordered, in 1761, that all

One of the city's first fire engines, detail from a notice of the Hand-in-Hand Fire Company. (I. N. Phelps Stokes Collection. Miriam and Ira D. Wallach Division of Art, Prints and Photographs. The New York Public Library. Astor, Lenox and Tilden Foundations)

new buildings erected after 1766 south of the Fresh Water Pond be roofed with slate or tile rather than the highly combustible white fir or cedar shingles (then delayed implementation of the law for an additional ten years after residents objected to the expense).

Back in 1731 the council had ordered two firepumps of the very latest design from London. Because they required teams of men to operate—some for the bucket brigades that kept the reservoirs supplied with water, others to work the levers that forced water out through a hose—the council appointed thirty "Strong able Discreet honest and Sober Men" to run "the said ffire Engines" (in lieu of wages they were exempted from serving as constables, highway laborers, or jurymen). When this force proved deficient in dealing with the blazes of 1741, the city immediately bought a hundred new buckets (marked "City of N.Y."), purchased two more London engines, and expanded the force to forty-four men. Additional engines arrived in 1758, at which time the magistrates ordered construction of sheds to house them—at least one in each ward, with the largest at Hanover Square.

If its interest in civic improvements thus seemed haphazard—driven as much by a concern to protect the estate of the municipal corporation as by a sense of duty to an abstract public interest—the Common Council must have taken considerable satisfaction from the stream of visitors who praised the city's busy, well-regulated appearance. As one of His Majesty's naval officers admitted in 1756, it caught Europeans off guard. "The nobleness of the town surprised me more than the fertile appearance of the country," he remarked. "I had no idea of finding a place in America, consisting of near 2,000 houses, elegantly built of brick, raised on an eminence and the streets paved and spacious, furnished with commodious keys and warehouses, and employing some hundreds of vessels in its foreign trade and fisheries—but such is this city that very few in England can rival it in its show."

ARTISANAL WARDS

City authorities also spruced up the municipal almshouse in the 1740s and 1750s, for despite the general prosperity of the war years, poverty remained a problem. Some inmates were casualties of combat, others of inflated currency, others of the death of a provider. One widow told a local newspaper in 1752 that her husband's death had left her "in the greatest poverty," with only her eldest boy, twelve years old, able to support the family selling oysters. Oysters, in fact, were the mainstay of the poor. As Peter Kalm observed, many "lived all year long upon nothing but oysters and a little bread."

Other working people had better luck. A few butchers, innkeepers, and sugar boilers got rich during the war years; blacksmith Matthew Buys, cordwainer John Sickles, and baker John Orchard did well enough to purchase estates of over 150 acres.

The bulk of New York's laboring population happily settled for reaping the rewards of constant employment at high wages. Many saved enough to buy a piece of property on which to set up a house and shop—though not in the dock area, where competition between merchants, retailers, and real estate investors had driven the price of land near Hanover Square and Bowling Green beyond the reach of any but the most prosperous craftsmen. A standard lot there, measuring twenty-five by a hundred feet, could rent for as much as twenty pounds a year for the land alone (the "ground rent"), exclusive of improvements. A house in the Dock Ward or East Ward might rent for as much as two hundred pounds a year. It wasn't any easier finding cheap land outside of town, where thousands of acres had long since been engrossed by the country estates of Stuyvesants, Bayards, Warrens, Rutgers, and other prominent families.

Virtually the only place open to residents of modest means was the hundred-acre tract owned by Trinity Church on Manhattan's west side. Known familiarly as the Church Farm, it lay in the West and Out wards between what are now Cortlandt and Christopher streets. In 1762, hoping to generate additional income, Trinity's vestry had the property surveyed and mapped into rectilinear blocks. It then offered to lease two hundred lots, most of them measuring twenty by a hundred feet, for periods of twenty-one, forty-two, or sixty-three years and for attractively low ground rents—two pounds per year for the first seven years, three pounds per year for the next seven, and four pounds per year for the remainder of the lease—on the assumption that land values would double over time. Artisans and laborers realized that for the same money it would cost to rent near the wharves they could erect their own wooden houses on the Church Farm (improvements remained their own property).

The largest single group of working people to settle this part of town were the cartmen, whose numbers and incomes had swollen during the war. They built homes and stables and declared their presence by planting cart-and-horse signs in front of their houses. (Because Trinity permitted subletting, some leased two or three lots for purposes of speculation.) Second in numbers to the carters were bricklayers, masons, house carpenters, stonecutters, and other representatives of the flourishing construction trades. Like cartmen, many of them worked not in their own homes but at job sites around town. Some artisans (cabinetmakers, for example) and retailers moved west to set up combined work-and-living households, from which they could practice their trades. There were virtually no merchants or professionals (or blacks, who had been legally barred from owning property since 1712).

This proto-working-class neighborhood was set off by more than distance from the wealthier East River wards. The discrepancy between the Georgian grandeur of upper-class brick residences and the rough-and-ready wooden housing of artisans was readily apparent—inside as well as out. One knowledgeable observer calculated that while New York's finest private homes averaged seven hundred pounds' worth of "Plate and furniture," and those of the "Middling" class some two hundred pounds, the contents of "lower Class" houses averaged a mere forty pounds, and many fell below twenty pounds. Then, too, the cobblestoned solidity of Hanover and Broad streets stood in marked contrast to the west side's raw, unpaved roads, which frequently became quagmires of mud, garbage, and manure.

It was a comfortable quarter nonetheless, not too far from the city's commercial district and anchored by institutions like Abraham Montayne's tavern on Broadway, just across from the Common. Montayne's became an informal neighborhood headquarters, a place to read a newspaper and talk over the latest news, a rendezvous for personal or public celebrations, a magnet for canny politicians who appeared on election day to buy a round for the voters. Its clientele could play at dice and cards (ignoring the provincial law that promised to fine innkeepers who let youths, apprentices, journeymen, servants, or common sailors gamble). They might also take a chance, between beers, on one of the "private Lotteries" that were springing up (also illegal because they encouraged "Labouring People to Assemble together at Taverns where Such Lotteries are usually Set on Foort & Drawn"). From time to time, as well, they could take in the display of a live leopard, a waxworks show, a bullbaiting, and other entertainments hosted by the proprietor.

Montayne's was far from the only such establishment in New York. Dozens of waterfront dives like the Pine Apple, the Dish of Fry'd Oysters, or the Dog's Head in the Porridge served similar functions for seamen and shipyard workers. Out-of-town drovers and city butchers congregated in the smoky, low-ceilinged rooms of the Bull's Head Tavern, which stood just below modern Canal Street amid a jumble of stables, cattle pens, and slaughterhouses. Increasingly, moreover, the sweaty, wood-and-pewter camaraderie of these workingmen's hangouts was shunned by persons of fastidious sensibility, who preferred the more genteel ambience of the King's Arms or the Queen's Head.

And if gentlemen still rubbed elbows with workingmen at cockfights, horse races, and the theater, the widening cultural distance between them was readily apparent now in the contrast between the fancy wig-and-powder fashions of the upper classes and the practical costumes of ordinary craftsmen or the hand-me-down garb of the poor. Nowhere, indeed, did the splendor of a refined gentleman in full regalia shine more brilliantly than in the light of advertisements for runaway servants during the 1750s. These often noted in detail what New York's poorest inhabitants wore from one day to the next: "a coarse Linnen Jacket"—"a Half worn blue Broadcloth Coat"—"half worn Shoes, with plain Brass Buckles in them"—"homespun Cloth Colour'd Jacket"—"blue Plush Breeches pieced behind with Buck-Skin, an old Felt Hat, blue Stockings, old ribbed leggings over them"—"old Leather Breeches patched before, a half worn Wool Hat, coarse light coloured ribbed Stockings, old Shoes"—"blue homespun coat and jacket, greasy leather breeches, old grey stockings."

Plebeians as well as patricians remarked on the new, increasingly visible distances between the classes. Some working people began to use terms like "silk-stocking" or "big-wig" as an epithet. In 1761 a certain "Sally Tippet" wrote sarcastically that many women still adhered to "home-bred fashions and complements," adding that "I believe

Silver beaker, engraved by Joseph Leddel of New York in 1750 with scenes of the devil leading the Pope and Pretender into the mouth of Hell. The full inscription reads: "Three mortal enemies Remember. The Devil Pope and the Pretender./ Most wicked damnable and evil. The Pope Pretender and the Devil. / I wish they were all hang'd in a rope. The Pretender Devil and the Pope." These figures were no doubt very similar to the effigies carried in the city's annual Pope Day celebrations. (© Museum of the City of New York)

the one-half have neither milliners, dolls, dressing-maids, dancing-masters, nor indeed pier-glasses."

This same trend can be traced in the emergence of Pope Day as a distinctively popular festival. The fifth of November, nominally a patriotic holiday commemorating the failed plot of Guy Fawkes to blow up Parliament, had had a kind of semiofficial standing in New York since the British conquest. It was an opportunity for the governor to make a speech, for gentlemen to toast the health of the monarch, for the artillerymen of the garrison to fire their cannon, for right-thinking inhabitants to illuminate their houses with candles in every window. Beginning in the later 1740s, however, the city's working people appropriated the day's festivities for their own purposes. Speeches by persons in authority gave way to raucous, torch-lit parades by tradesmen, sailors, apprentices, laborers, boys, and slaves that culminated with the marchers throwing effigies of the pope, the Pretender, and the devil into a roaring bonfire.

13

Crises

In September 1760 His Majesty's troops captured Montreal, completing the conquest of French Canada. The focus of the war now shifted from the North American mainland to the Caribbean, where British forces were preparing to assault France's island possessions. When the Spanish government appeared ready to assist France, Britain declared war on Spain as well. For New York, this turn of events proved disastrous.

Once-lucrative war contracts evaporated almost immediately, and in May 1761 the East River shipyards fitted the last fleet for an expedition against French Martinique and Dominica—both of which fell to Britain the next year, followed shortly thereafter by the capitulation of Havana. Privateering, vital to the well-being of every American port since the early 1740s, fell off sharply as the Royal Navy harried French and Spanish forces out of the Caribbean. The navy also shut down the clandestine traffic in molasses and sugar from the French West Indies on which many colonial merchants had depended, while an invigorated British customs service cracked down on American smugglers. The departure of British troops from Manhattan meanwhile constricted the flow of coins into the tills of local retailers and tavern keepers. As the merchant John Watts observed sadly: "The Tipling Soldiery that use to help us out at a dead lift, are gone to drink it in a warmer Region, the place of its production."

The 1763 Treaty of Paris confirmed Britain's triumph. France ceded the whole of Canada, abandoned its claims to land east of the Mississippi (except New Orleans), and withdrew from India. Spain had suffered losses in the Americas from which it would never recover, British merchants stood poised to take over the lucrative European trade with Africa and Asia, and London was positioned to become the financial axis of the world market. New York, though, sank into a depression worse than that of the 1730s.

British mercantile houses, reacting as well to a recession at home, cut back on credit and pressed merchants in New York and other colonial ports to settle outstanding accounts. Some firms abandoned long-established relationships to deal with newer, smaller importers and exporters in the colonies—aggressive upstarts ready to trade on the narrowest of margins—or with public auctioneers, known as vendue masters, who could dispose quickly of great quantities of goods at sharply reduced prices. Others sent out their own agents to bargain directly with local shopkeepers and suppliers. "The weak must go to the wall," warned one New York merchant, and for craftsmen engaged in the production of finished goods for the local market—ironware, furniture, shoes, hats, and the like—the influx of cheap imports from Britain's overstocked mills and factories looked similarly ominous.

Hard-pressed merchants called in debts from shopkeepers and tradesmen—who then bore down on artisans, farmers, and country storekeepers. Hard money, of which there was never enough, virtually disappeared. The exchange rate soared, in effect siphoning the profits of recent years back to the mother country as importers scrambled to stay solvent. Domestic consumption fell off, markets languished, inventories of unsold goods mounted. Overextended merchants went bankrupt. Stores and shops stood empty. Journeymen, apprentices, and laborers found themselves out of work for the first time in years. "Our business of all kinds is stopped," declared the *Post Boy* in December 1765. "Great numbers of our poor people and seamen without employment and without support . . . many families which used to live in comfortable plenty daily falling to decay for want of business." In effect, one merchant declared, "Trade in this part of the world is come to so wretched a pass that you would imagine the plague had been here." Before 1760 there had never been more than sixteen actions against debtors in any given year; by 1763 there were forty-six; by 1766, eighty. So many debtors were locked up in the recently completed New Gaol (conveniently located in the Common next to the almshouse) that it was already being called the debtors' prison.

The crisis was exacerbated by relentless increases in the cost of living, which had already doubled during the war and now continued to rise as Britain's burgeoning demand for colonial grain helped push prices higher still. Small houses renting for ten or fifteen pounds were in such short supply that families of modest means were beginning to double up. Food was more expensive than ever, and during the winter of 1760–61, with unemployment spreading, the cost of firewood rose drastically. Taxes, chiefly regressive imposts and excises, mounted sharply. Even steadily employed craftsmen and established shopkeepers found themselves badly squeezed. As one artisan wrote in 1762 to the *New-York Gazette*, "the Expence of living in the most frugal Way has increased so exorbitantly, that I find it beyond my ability to support my Family with my utmost Industry—I am growing every Day more and more behind hand, tho' my Family can scarcely appear with Decency, or have necessaries to subsist." This, he insisted, "is really the Case with many of the Inhabitants of this City." Things remained equally grim five years later according to a "tradesman" writing in the *New York Journal*: "What a dismal Prospect is before us! A long Winter, and no Work; many unprovided with Fire-wood, or Money to buy it; House-rent and taxes high; our Neighbors daily breaking; their Furniture at Vendue at every Corner."

The times were even harder for widows, transients, former indentured servants, British deserters, ex-privateers, recent immigrants—people with the smallest savings, who spent most of their scarce resources on the hard-to-trim items like food, rent, clothing, and fuel. Worst off were the aged or infirm slaves whose owners set them free to save money, a practice so widespread by 1773 that in order to keep down the cost of relief, the legislature imposed a fine of twenty pounds on the last owner of any freedman found begging in the city.

To make matters worse, working people faced competition for jobs, food, and firewood from the numerous military personnel who remained in the city. By law, off-duty sailors and soldiers could take odd jobs or even practice trades to supplement their normally low wages. It was notorious that they would work for next to nothing. The anger this generated was intensified by the Royal Navy's ongoing attempts to fill out crews by impressing seamen from town. When four fisherman were taken from their boat and carried to a nearby man-of-war in July 1764, an infuriated crowd dragged the ship's barge to the front of City Hall, burned it, then forced municipal officials to negotiate for the release of the captives.

Spiraling municipal expenditures for relief bear witness to the spread of poverty. Between 1740 and 1760 the city's average annual expenditure for poor relief was £667 (some £39 per 1,000 population), but between 1761 and 1770 the annual average soared to £1,667 (£92 per 1,000). In 1765 the churchwardens informed the Common Council that money raised for the relief of the indigent "had been "Long Since Expended," yet the "distresses of the Poor" had become "so Extremely Great" that many "must unavoidably perish" without additional assistance for food and firewood.

Private charity, churches, and national groups like the St. George's Society and the St. Andrew's Society shouldered much of the burden, as always. In 1767 some Irish officers in the British army formed the Ancient and Most Benevolent Order of the Friendly Brothers of St. Patrick in the Sixteenth Regiment of Foot; by 1769 its sixty members included civilians as well, and in 1771 they relieved some of their countrymen languishing in the debtors' prison. Such efforts weren't nearly enough, and the Common Council discussed various schemes for simply removing the poor from the city, often to places like Staten Island.

Not everyone suffered. Wealthy merchants, lawyers, crown officials, and naval officers lived no less comfortably than they had at the peak of wartime prosperity. The annual cycle of musical recitals, masquerades, balls, and routs went on as before. Performances continued at the Chapel Street Theater. Better shops continued to stock a full range of imported luxuries, and, as one New Yorker informed a London newspaper, "notwithstanding the great complaints of the distressing times, we have here no less than four coaches which were brought hither from London in the last ship." By 1770, according to one count, a mere sixty-two people owned all the city's eighty-five fashionable "equipages"—twenty-six coaches, thirty-three chariots, and twenty-six phaetons.

In 1764 a party of rich young aristocrats organized a "macaroni table" at London's fashionable Almack Club. Their foppish, devil-may-care manner of dressing—short waistcoats, huge wigs, small cocked hats, tasseled walking sticks—represented the height of Italianate fashion. Hard times or no, the so-called macaroni style was at once picked up in New York, which boasted a Macaroni Club of its own at least by the autumn of 1764. That same year the club proclaimed its indifference to the city's straitened circumstances by offering purses of £100 and £150 for the fastest horses at the Hempstead races.

These excesses attracted a good deal of unfavorable attention around town, and local newspapers soon began to carry letters from indignant residents that had a distinctly radical edge. "Some Individuals," one writer told the *New-York Gazette* in 1765, "by the Smiles of Providence or some other Means, are enabled to roll in their four wheel'd Carriages, and can support the expense of good Houses, rich Furniture, and Luxurious Living. But is it equitable that 99, rather 999, should suffer for the Extravagance or Grandeur of one? Especially when it is considered that Men frequently owe their Wealth to the impoverishment of their Neighbors?"

NEWCOMERS

Faltering trade, unemployment, inflation, poverty—to this litany of trouble was added another: a sudden rise in the city's population. In 1760 New York had roughly eighteen thousand inhabitants. Over the next ten years or so, the city's population jumped by four thousand—a 20 percent increase. By 1775 it stood between twenty-two and twenty-five thousand. Only Philadelphia, with forty thousand inhabitants, was larger; Boston now trailed far behind, having barely reached sixteen thousand.

Behind this demographic expansion lay an unprecedented surge in transatlantic migration. Between 1760 and 1775 better than 137,000 Europeans poured into the thirteen colonies—roughly fifteen thousand people every year, three times the average rate before 1760. The great bulk of them—125,000 or so—came from the British Isles, some fifty-five thousand from Ireland (predominately but not exclusively Protestant), another forty thousand from Scotland, and the remaining thirty thousand from London and Yorkshire. Of those whose occupations are known, most were trained artisans and craftsmen, directly or closely tied to the beleaguered textile industry, which was going through a period of massive unemployment. About two-thirds of the Irish and English emigrants, generally young men and women on their own, came as indentured servants. Fewer than one-fifth of the Scots did so, presumably because they were somewhat older, included a higher proportion of laborers, and traveled as families, sometimes entire communities.

Land was the goal of the overwhelming majority of these immigrants, and they headed as quickly as possible for the rapidly expanding colonial frontier. No one kept count of how many went to the province of New York, but estimates place the figure at roughly twenty-five thousand. Most were recruited by local merchants to settle and develop property they had purchased far to the north and west, so only a small minority of these new arrivals, probably fewer than one out of every six or seven, actually took up residence in town. (That was enough, however, to make a noticeable difference in its racial balance, for while the absolute number of slaves in New York rose from 2,278 in 1756 to 3,137 in 1771—a growth of 38 percent—the proportion of Africans in the population fell from 18 percent to 14 percent because the number of whites grew even more rapidly.)

For the permanent residents of New York as well as for transients, the hubbub on waterfront wharves and piers—the confusion of accents, the clattering, milling congestion of it all—was something to behold. Between 1773 and 1775 alone, forty-odd vessels disgorged as many as thirty-three hundred men, women, and children in the city, equivalent to 15 percent of its population.

The newcomers brought additional competition for scarce jobs and resources. They also brought new voices of protest, for they included some of Britain's most militantly disaffected urban craftsmen and rural laborers—unemployed journeyman weavers from the Spitalfields district of London who tried to storm Parliament in 1765 and followed George III about with black flags; shipwrights recently discharged from the royal naval yards after striking for higher wages; and some of the bands of White-boys, Oakboys, and Steelboys who were now throwing down fences and mobbing land-lords in Ireland. Their anger against the British government, and the experience they had gained while fighting it, ensured that the postwar political climate of New York would become increasingly volatile.

POLICY

Even before the war with France was over, young George III began fiddling with the political system in England. It now appeared that his break with Pitt was only the begin-ning of a campaign to reassert the power of the monarchy by arranging a permanent majority for it in Parliament. Year after year, more and more impatient with long-estab-lished alliances, the king shuffled ministers, shifted policies, and shoveled out patronage on a scale that would have made Walpole himself cringe.

Also on the royal agenda was a new get-tough attitude toward the colonies. Like a good many people, the king no longer believed that America could be controlled, as in the past, by the easygoing, solicitous policy that Edmund Burke famously defined as "salutary neglect." Uncooperative colonial courts and legislatures had repeatedly obstructed the recent war effort, or so it was said; now, without the threat of French Canada hanging over their heads, there was every reason to expect the colonies would become more rather than less difficult to manage in the future. Besides, customs fraud, smuggling, and illicit manufacturing had flourished so extravagantly during the war that respect for imperial regulations seemed to have sunk to an all-time low, even among the richest and most respectable elements of colonial society.

The crux of the matter was money. Given that customs duties accounted for well over a third of the crown's income, how was the government to finance the defense of Britain's vast new conquests, much less pay off the nation's sky-high war debt, if the colonies continued to flout the law? Increased domestic taxation was next to impossible: the landowning classes refused to accept a higher land tax, while stiffer excises looked very risky in light of widespread industrial and agrarian unrest. Considering how much the mother country had already done for the colonies, let alone the precarious state of her finances, surely the time had come for them to bear their fair share of imperial expenses. What were colonies for, after all?

In that frame of mind the king and his ministers began to tighten the administra-tive screws of the Empire. As early as 1761 customs officials were authorized to use writs of assistance, a kind of search warrant, to ensure compliance with the Navigation Acts. In 1763, in addition to banning further settlement across the Appalachians, the government announced it would station ten thousand British regulars in America to make certain that His Majesty's subjects did as they were told.

The following year, Chancellor of the Exchequer George Grenville won parliamen-tary approval for a sweeping American Revenue Act. Popularly called the Sugar Act, it raised duties on a variety of items imported into the colonies, provided more efficient collection of duties on sugar and molasses imported from the foreign West Indies, required all duties to be paid in silver, and lengthened the list of colonial products that could be shipped only to Britain. A companion bill gave the customs service broad new powers to catch and prosecute merchants who violated trade regulations. Still another measure, the Currency Act, prohibited colonial governments from issuing paper money to meet the need for specie. If necessary, Grenville said, he would also ask Parliament to raise a revenue in the colonies by means of a stamp tax.

In New York, Grenville's program looked all the more threatening thanks to the dour, petty, self-righteous, and dogmatic Cadwallader Colden. For nearly half a century now, ever since Governor Burnet put him on the council, Colden had complained to anyone who would listen that the crown's interests were being thwarted by the venality of New York's great landlords and merchant princes—to say nothing of the lawyers who trailed behind them (Colden's contempt for lawyers knew no bounds). They in turn cordially despised him. Even the Livingstons, perhaps more sympathetic than any other of the colony's great families, felt uneasy about the man.

When Lieutenant Governor De Lancey died unexpectedly at the end of July 1760, Colden, senior member of the council at the age of seventy-two, became acting governor. True to form, Colden promptly threw himself into a series of amazingly ill timed and provocative reforms that made him a target for the wrath of both the Livingston and De Lancey factions. He infuriated New York's powerful legal community by undermining the finality of jury verdicts and insisting that judges in the colony served at the pleasure of the crown (one of his few backers on the bench was Chief Justice Daniel Horsmanden, recently restored to official favor). He angered merchants and artisans alike by making a special effort to prevent any revival of illegal trade with the French West Indies. He enraged the great landholders by trying to annul some of the largest land patents in the colony. The furor died down when Robert Monckton arrived to take over as imperial governor—then resumed with even greater ferocity when Monckton returned home in the summer of 1763, having spent only eighteen months on the job, and Colden was once again in charge of the colony.

RESISTANCE

Alarmed by the altered tenor of affairs at home and abroad, New York's merchants spent much of 1764 drawing up petitions—to the Assembly, to the House of Commons, to the House of Lords, to the king himself. The basic message was always the same: don't try to squeeze more revenue out of the colonies, don't saddle the West Indian trade with additional duties, don't prohibit paper money, don't meddle with the system of trial by jury, don't tax the inhabitants of America without their consent. Over the winter of 1764–65 the Common Council took the additional step of declining to provide firewood for regular troops quartered in the New Barracks above the Common. It had always done so in the past. But this year, Mayor John Cruger informed Major General Thomas Gage, the new commander-in-chief of British forces in America, the city simply didn't have the money.

One group of wealthy New Yorkers applied pressure from a different direction. In the autumn of 1764 they set up the Society for the Encouragement of Arts, Agriculture, and Economy to promote the domestic production of manufactured goods hitherto imported from Britain, above all linen cloth. The loss of American markets would send an important message to Parliament, the society's backers theorized. What was more, domestic manufacturing would slow the drain of specie to the mother country and create work for the city's growing numbers of jobless poor. By teaching frugality and self-reliance, it would counteract the enervating effects of "the vast Luxury introduced during the late war." It looked like a good investment too.

Within months, prompted by the society's offer of cash bounties for the purchase of equipment, a linen factory with fourteen looms opened on Mulberry Street, near the Fresh Water Pond. Several spinning schools for the children of paupers were set up as well, and a new municipal market was designated for the sale of flax and yarn. Before failing a year or so later, the enterprise would employ some three hundred people, mostly poor women. It also accorded a certain legitimacy to an upsurge of popular resentment against the ostentatiousness that had so greatly altered the city over the previous two decades. "All pride in Dress seems to be laid aside," Robert R. Livingston observed, "and he that does not appear in a Homespun or at least a Turned Coat is looked on with an Evil Eye." Well-to-do women resolved that they would "let a horrid homespun covering (which can become none but a country wench) take the place of the rich brocade and graceful satin." Even Governor Colden and members of his council were seen in homespun coats.

Parliament took no notice and in the spring of 1765 made good its threat to pass a Stamp Act. The measure taxed a broad range of paper and paper products sold in the colonies, and the revenues raised were to be paid into the royal treasury for the maintenance of British troops stationed in America—meaning, of course, a proportionate reduction in the flow of military appropriations from Britain that had boosted the colonial standard of living in the 1740s and 1750s.

The drive to reduce American dependence on British imports prompted Peter Curtenius and Company to build this iron foundry on the Hudson River in 1767. It produced kettles, pots, plows, and other items for the local market. In 1775 Curtenius contracted to make bayonets and muskets for local patriots. (© Collection of The New-York Historical Society)

More important, the Stamp Act put at risk the power and authority of every colonial political establishment by violating the old assumption that the inhabitants of America could be taxed only by representatives of their own choosing. Partly in response to Gage's prompting, Parliament also adopted a Quartering Act that required civil authorities in the colonies to provide shelter and supplies for British troops. Never before had Parliament attempted to tax the colonies directly; never before had it ordered them to help pay imperial bills. To many colonists this was tantamount to slavery. Britain "will make Negroes of us all," cried Robert R. Livingston.

By the summer of 1765 urban America was in an uproar. In New York, the Assembly agreed to host an emergency Stamp Act Congress in October for the purpose of coordinating colonial opposition. There was talk of refusing compliance with the Quartering Act on the grounds that it, like the Stamp Act, violated the ancient principle of no taxation without representation. What, after all, was the difference between a tax levied directly by Parliament and a parliamentary order that a colonial legislature spend money for one purpose or another?

RIOTOUS PROCEEDINGS

Mid-August brought word from Boston of a violent disturbance that forced the stamp distributor there to resign in fear of his life. James McEvers, a rich merchant who had accepted appointment as New York's distributor, announced that he too would resign to avoid "the like treatment." "My House would have been Pillag'd, my Person Abused and His Majestys Revenue Impair'd," he advised Governor Colden. McEvers's announcement was followed by reports of more trouble in Boston and the spread of rioting to Newport, Rhode Island. The stamp distributor from Maryland appeared at the gates of Fort George to tell how he had fled from a mob in that colony with just the clothes on his back.

Colden, now grasping what he and Parliament had wrought, began to prepare for the worst. He informed Gage that Fort George couldn't be defended "in its present state, from a Mob, or from the Negroes"—an allusion, perhaps, to the events of 1741— and Gage obligingly sent down reinforcements from Crown Point. Major Thomas James, commander of the Fort George artillery, wheeled up new guns and positioned them on the walls to enfilade Broadway. Colden had the cannon on the Battery spiked to prevent their being turned against the fort, strengthened its gates, and had two frigates moved up to provide additional firepower if necessary. The more the truculent old governor prepared for trouble, however, the more it was said around town that he wanted trouble—and would get it if he tried to enforce the Stamp Act.

On October 7, 1765, twenty-seven delegates from nine colonies assembled at the City Hall for the long-awaited meeting of the Stamp Act Congress. Over the next eighteen days the Congress adopted declarations and petitions that denied Parliament's authority to tax the colonies and cautioned that its attempts to do so "have a manifest Tendency to subvert the Rights and Liberties of the Colonists."

On the evening of October 23, just as the Congress finished its work, the booming of cannon from a man-of-war in the harbor signaled the arrival of the stamps. The following day, as an angry crowd of two thousand gathered on the Battery, the *Edward*, escorted by two warships, dropped anchor under Fort George's ninety-two guns and awaited orders concerning the disposition of more than two tons of stamped paper, parchment, and vellum in its hold. Handbills circulated in the streets threatening violence against anyone assisting in their distribution ("the first Man that either distributes or makes use of Stampt Paper let him take Care of his House, Person, and Effects"). Ships in the harbor flew their flags at half-staff "to signify Mourning, Lamentation, and Woe." Colden had marines bring the stamps into the fort under cover of darkness, temporarily averting a confrontation.

One week later, two hundred of New York's "principal merchants" gathered at the City Arms Tavern on Broadway to sign a nonimportation agreement. It was the first pact of its kind anywhere in the colonies.

No British goods would be bought or sold in the city, vowed the merchants, until Parliament repealed the Stamp Act and removed the objectionable parts of the Revenue and Currency acts. They assumed that British exporters would pressure Parliament to act quickly, and in the meantime nonimportation would give local importers a chance to dispose of swollen inventories. It would stimulate the local production needed to pay for imports in the future. It would also toughen a people overly fond of foreign luxuries. Although this all went well beyond what the Assembly had been prepared to do, a crowd of artisans, mariners, and laborers had gathered outside the Coffee House in the expectation of still stronger measures. Disappointed, they staged a mock funeral for "liberty," then roamed the streets "in a mobbish manner," breaking lamps and windows and threatening to pull down houses.

On November 1, 1765, the day the Stamp Act took effect, business in the city came to a halt. An eerie calm descended over the usually busy waterfront. Little or no traffic moved in the streets. Toward sundown, a crowd began to assemble in the Common, eventually some two thousand strong. Witnesses reported that it consisted of numerous sailors, youths, artisans, laborers, and blacks, along with many "country people" who had flocked to town from nearby farms and villages. With the upcoming Pope Day celebrations clearly in mind as a model, the crowd hoisted a scaffold from which hung an elaborate effigy of Governor Colden. One hand held stamped paper and a boot (symbol for the unpopular earl of Bute, the king's current minister). The effigy's other hand held a drum (recalling Colden's service as a drummer boy in the Jacobite rising of 1715). Beside him sat the devil, whispering instructions in his ear.

A second column of demonstrators appeared, dragging Colden's private coach and another effigy of the unpopular governor. "With the grossest ribaldry," according to one witness, the two groups marched with gallows, coach, and effigy down Broadway to the fort, their way lit by candles and torches. They hurled bricks and stones at the walls and challenged the garrison to open fire; according to the chief engineer of His Majesty's forces, "300 Carpenters belonging to the mob were collected & prepared to cut down the Fort Gate on the first Shot fired from thence." Although Colden wouldn't give the order to fire, a letter was nailed on the gate warning him that if he used force to uphold the Stamp Act, "you'll die a Martyr to your own Villainy, and be Hang'd like Porteis, upon a Signpost, as a Momento to all wicked Governors, and that every Man, that assists you, Shall be, surely, put to Death." The crowd then dragged his private coach over to Bowling Green and burned it along with the effigies.

From Bowling Green some "Volunteers" proceeded back uptown to Vauxhall, where they sacked the home of Major James, the fort's artillery commander, who had incautiously sworn to "cram the Stamps down their Throats with the End of my Sword." "Looking Glasses Mehogany Tables Silk Curtains A Libiry of Books all the China and furniture"—anything, in short, that bore witness to the refinement of its owner—was thrown into the street and smashed. The major's private papers and personal effects were destroyed; his wine cellar was broken open and its contents consumed or destroyed; his garden was torn up. (The Assembly later awarded the major £1,745 to cover the damage, a generous sum. Colden put his losses at around £195. The Assembly gave him nothing.)

Men of property and reputation in the city, even those who had been outspoken in opposition to the Stamp Act, floundered in disbelief at what was happening. The governor's council believed New York to be in a state of "perfect anarchy." Robert R. Livingston, proprietor of Clermont and a Dutchess County assemblyman, found the mayor and his advisers "extremely dejected" and paralyzed with "despondency and irresolution." Crowds, including armed newcomers from Connecticut and New Jersey, milled about the streets waiting for something to happen. Rumors flew of an impending attack on the Fort on November 5 (Pope or Guy Fawkes Day), of attempts on the lives of officials, and, worse, of "an open Rebellion" by a "secret party, who called themselves *Vox Populi*." Colden, who believed that "a great part of the Mob consists of Men who have been Privateers and disbanded Soldiers whose view is to plunder the Town," fled with his family to the warship *Coventry* for protection. An apprehensive group of merchants associated with the Livingston faction met at the Merchants' Coffee House to discuss ways of preventing "all riotous proceedings," but broke up in confusion.

Tensions eased when Colden, fearing "the Effusion of blood and the Calamities of a Civil Warr," turned the stamps over to municipal officials, who carried them off for safekeeping in City Hall. A huge throng of five thousand lined the streets to watch. Everyone breathed a little easier, too, when a new royal governor, Sir Henry Moore, arrived on November 13 to relieve Colden. Moore's appointment was his reward for brutally crushing a Jamaican slave revolt, but he had no intention of using force to make New York accept the stamps. Instead, on the theory that a few months of economic stagnation would bring the colonists to their senses, the governor simply refused to permit any business to be conducted that would require the use of stamped paper. "All their commerce must inevitably be ruined if they persevere in their obstinacy," he explained smugly.

SONS OF LIBERTY

New York's obstinacy, as Governor Moore called it, reflected the rising influence in municipal affairs of persons and groups that spoke for the city's middling and laboring classes. One, as Livingston reported, went by the name of Vox Populi. Another was known as the Sons of Neptune, yet another as the Free Sons of New York. Most famous was the Sons of Liberty, which seems to have been formed in late October or early November 1765, just prior to Governor Moore's arrival.

The Sons of Liberty was the creation of Alexander McDougall, Isaac Sears, John Lamb, Hugh Hughes, Marinus Willett, and others—plain-spoken, self-taught, self-made men, the kind who had carried little weight in municipal affairs since at least the end of the last century, if ever. McDougall's family had emigrated from Scotland when he was a boy, and his father operated a profitable dairy farm on the outskirts of town. At the age of fourteen, McDougall left the farm and went to sea. Diligent and reliable, he worked his way up to become a highly successful captain of privateers during the Seven Years War. With the end of the war, still in his early thirties, he came back to New York and set himself up in the West Indian trade. He prospered, bought a lot of land up in

Albany County, and scandalized the refined classes with his flamboyant manner and flashy taste in clothes. Through the Presbyterian Church he also became a disciple of the Whig Triumvirate—William Livingston, John Morin Scott, and William Smith Jr.—under whose influence he read everything from *Cato's Letters* to nonconformist religious tracts.

Like McDougall, Isaac Sears was an immigrant to New York—from Norwalk, Connecticut, where his family had lived modestly for many years, and from where he also had gone off to sea. Like McDougall, he made his way up through the ranks and by his early twenties was a captain in the West Indian trade regularly employed by prominent New York merchants. Like McDougall, too, Sears turned privateer during the Seven Years War, won a reputation for heroism under fire, and made himself a small fortune, some of it in clandestine trade with the French. After the war, Sears established himself as a West Indian merchant in New York, where by his mid-thirties he was living like a gentleman—though everyone could tell by his quarterdeck manners that he wasn't one.

John Lamb's father had been convicted of burglary in his native England and transported to New York, where he found work making optical instruments. His son made mathematical instruments. Marinus Willett, whose early history is almost as vague as Lamb's, was a successful master cabinetmaker still in his mid-twenties when the Stamp Act crisis erupted. The dominant influence on his life seems to have been the evangelical Protestantism that periodically swept through the city beginning in the early 1740s. He moved restlessly through a succession of sects, unable to find one that quite suited his temperament, and played a leading part in the city's annual Pope Day celebrations.

What made the likes of McDougall, Sears, Lamb, and Willett so formidable was the fierce loyalty they inspired among New York's artisans, apprentices, seamen, and laborers. They were easy men to respect and good men to follow. They had come up in the world, but without the advantages of inherited wealth, fancy educations, or powerful connections—and without forgetting where they came from. They were still, unmistakably, workingmen themselves. They talked like workingmen—McDougall's Scottish burr and Sears's Yankee twang were nothing like the flat, nasal English of the upper classes—and they could still make the rounds of crowded workingmen's taverns and coffeehouses, pumping hands and slapping backs, with a straightforward, natural confidence. Willett's father, in fact, operated the Province Arms, while Sears's father-in-law owned Drake's alehouse on Water Street near Beekman's Slip, very popular among the Sons; at one time McDougall may even have owned a sailor's "slop shop." It was precisely this common touch that enabled them to link popular social and political grievances to the formal constitutional issues raised by British policy.

"OUR PORT IS SHUT UP"

Toward the end of November 1765 the Sons of Liberty posted notices around New York headed LIBERTY, PROPERTY, AND NO STAMPS and calling for a meeting at Burns's Coffee House. Enfranchised freemen or not, all residents were invited to take part. On the agenda were radical proposals that the provincial assembly "repeal" the Stamp Act and that merchants resume trade in defiance of Governor Moore's prohibition. Alarmed by this bold attempt to take charge of New York's resistance movement—let alone the extremism of the Sons' proposed remedies—the Livingston and De Lancey factions first tried to prevent the meeting, then, when that failed, determined to prevent it from getting out of hand. They succeeded, barely. A slate of moderate resolutions was adopted and forwarded to the Assembly, which used them as the basis for yet another petition to Parliament.

From the early winter of 1765 through the spring of 1766, the Livingstons and De Lanceys, jointly or at cross-purposes with one another, continued their efforts to tame the Sons of Liberty. Governor Colden, General Gage, and other officials always took it for granted that the Sons couldn't be acting independently of either one or the other faction—mostly on the grounds that common people couldn't act in concert unless led by gentlemen. "The Plan of the People of Property has been to raise the lower Class to prevent the Execution of the Law," Gage wrote. "The whole Body of Merchants in general, Assembly Men, Magistrates, &c. have been united in this Plan of Riots, and without the Influence and Instigation of these the inferior People would have been quiet."

In truth, the New York Sons of Liberty followed no one's direction but their own. Just a few days before Christmas they formed a Committee of Correspondence and charged it with the task of seeking a military alliance or union with their comrades elsewhere in the colonies; their idea, which owed nothing to either the Livingston or De Lancey faction, was to be ready to go "to the extremity with lives and fortunes" to prevent enforcement of the Stamp Act. The committee's efforts were successful. By the following spring the New York plan for a "Union of the Colonies" had been greeted with enthusiasm from Massachusetts to South Carolina—except, of course, by crown officials and handfuls of ministerial sympathizers who understandably viewed it as out-and-out treason. Even when word began to get around that Parliament would soon repeal the Stamp Act, the New York Sons continued to emphasize that the liberties of America couldn't be preserved without vigilance and organization.

On their own authority, too, the Sons took to the streets of New York so often over the winter and spring of 1766 that, as Governor Moore told Lord Dartmouth in January, the magistrates were terrified of displeasing them. They had "Children nightly trampouze the Streets with lanthorns upon Poles & hallowing." They led noisy crowds around town with effigies of Colden, Grenville, and other unpopular officials; once they depicted Colden "mounted on a Cannon drilling the vent"—a ribald commentary on his orders to spike the fort's cannon. Tongues in cheek, they warned that all persons caught selling or eating lamb in New York would have their houses pulled down.

Early in May, a party of Sons interrupted the opening performance of the Chapel Street Theater. It was "highly improper that such Entertainments should be exhibited at this Time of public distress, when great numbers of poor people can scarce find subsistence," they announced. Shouting, "Liberty, Liberty," they then drove the audience out in a shower of "Brick Bats, sticks and Bottles and Glasses," stripping many along the way of "their Caps, Hats, Wigs, Cardinals, and Cloak Tails"—all symbols of wealth and disdain for a virtuous frugality. The crowd then reduced the building to kindling and carted it off to a giant bonfire in the Common.

In the meantime Sears and troops of Liberty Boys brought pressure to bear on merchants who broke the nonimportation agreement, routinely inspecting papers, confiscating goods, and forcing offenders to recant in public. So effective were these measures that when spring arrived the Sons virtually controlled business in the city. "The people of this province seem to have such an aversion to taking the stamp papers, that they will sooner die than take them," declared one resident. "Our port is shut up, no vessel cleared out, no law, and no money circulating."

The radicalism of New York's Liberty Boys had its limits, though, as events in the countryside soon demonstrated. Early in 1766 word began to reach the city that tenant farmers in the Hudson Valley had risen against their landlords. First in Dutchess, then in Westchester and Albany counties—on the vast estates of the Philipses, Van Rensselaers, Livingstons, Beekmans, Van Cortlandts, and other great proprietary families—disciplined bands of rebels, some said to number in the thousands, were shutting down courts, throwing open jails, and fighting pitched battles with hastily organized posses. Most sought only more secure leases and lower rents; others wanted to buy their land outright and pay no rent at all. A few at least professed to be "levelers" and looked to the day when the land would be divided equally among those who worked it. All were keenly aware that among their landlords were men who had lately been talking a great deal about liberty and freedom.

In April 1766 as many as two thousand insurgents massed at King's Bridge, which linked northern Manhattan and Westchester. Calling themselves true "Sons of Liberty," they made ready to march into New York City, join forces with "the poor people there," and pull down the town houses of big landowners. If anyone got in the way, they warned, they would "kick their Arses as long as we think fit." Even the king would get such treatment, declared William Prendergast, one of their leaders, "for Kings had been bro't to by Mobs before now."

But the city's poor didn't respond as hoped. Nor did the Sons of Liberty, who, after some initial stirrings of sympathy, recoiled from the farmers' more radical egalitarianism. Governor Moore called out the militia and drove them away without bloodshed.

REPEAL

Grenville had meanwhile quarreled with the king, who replaced him with the marquis of Rockingham. Rockingham, eager to disentangle his new government from Grenville's controversial policies, promptly abandoned the Stamp Act. Parliament passed a repeal bill in March 1766, and George III signed it into law a month later.

When word of the repeal reached New York on May 20, the town went berserk with joy. Crowds of merrymakers surged through the streets, roaring out their approval against a background of clanging church bells, exploding firecrackers, and sporadic musket fire. The Common Council added its voice to the festivities by appropriating funds to erect a statue of George III in Bowling Green.

Grander festivities followed on June 4, the king's official birthday. A throng of thousands gathered in the Common to devour, at public expense, two barbecued oxen, twenty-five barrels of "strong Beer," and a hogshead of rum. While a band played "God Save the King," a flagstaff was erected with the standard of George III and a banner with the word LIBERTY in large letters. Near the flagstaff went up a liberty pole—ancient symbol of popular defiance to tyranny—with a dozen tar and pitch barrels suspended from the top. A "Grand illumination throughout the city" followed in the evening, after which the day "ended in Drunkeness, throwing of Squibbs, Crackers, firing of muskets and pistols, breaking some windows and forcing off the Knockers off the Doors."

Royal Navy transports arrived in June with two regiments—three or four thousand men in all—to reinforce the British garrison, and General Gage promptly dispatched one of the two to mop up what remained of the tenant insurgency. His redcoats arrested scores of rebels, dispersed them at gunpoint, and caused considerable property damage in the process. A special court—consisting of Chief Justice Daniel Horsmanden and seven associate justices, including Oliver De Lancey, assisted by lawyers John Morin Scott and William Smith Jr.—met in July 1766 to hear the cases of some seventy men charged with riotous assault. Most received stiff fines and jail terms. William Prender-gast, denied counsel, was found guilty of high treason and sentenced to death. The king pardoned him six months later, but the court's harshness wasn't forgotten. Scott's role in it remained a sore point with the insurgents for years.

After much discussion about forming a permanent political club, the Sons of Liberty decided to suspend operations until such time as the rights of America were again in danger. That time was nearer than most realized. For even as it repealed the Stamp Act, Parliament had also passed a little-noticed Declaratory Act, reaffirming its right to tax the colonies "in all cases whatsoever."

Nothing, in short, had been settled.

14

The Demon
of Discord

During the summer of 1766 New York's prospects grew more dismal. Parliament passed a new Revenue Act that not only failed to lift the burdens of the 1764 Sugar Act but actually made them heavier. Thousands of redcoats were now pouring into town too, and because the Assembly refused on principle to requisition salt, vinegar, and beer for them as required by the Quartering Act—no taxation without representation, it said—His Majesty's forces were spoiling for trouble. One day in August 1766 fed-up soldiers from the barracks poured into the Common and chopped down the liberty pole erected there in May. When Isaac Sears and a party of Liberty Boys tried to put it up again, they were driven off. Sears and his men returned in strength to raise an even grander pole, after which they pressured local retailers, tradesmen, tavern keepers, and householders to shun all military personnel. Again the redcoats destroyed the liberty pole—now obviously a vital symbol for both sides—and again Sears and company replaced it.

Toward the end of November 1766, summoned by the reactivated Sons, 240 merchants signed a lengthy petition to Parliament explaining (again) why the West Indian trade was vital to the city's long-term prosperity and should not be sacrificed for the short-term purposes of raising revenue. Arriving at the same time as news that the New York Assembly still refused to comply with the Quartering Act, the petition was ill received in London. "Highly improper," harrumphed Prime Minister Chatham, "most absurd . . . most excessive . . . most grossly fallacious and offensive. What demon of discord blows the coals in that devoted province I know not."

Charles Townshend, the new chancellor of the exchequer, asked Parliament to suspend the New York Assembly. Because the Lords and Commons had recently slashed the land tax, throwing the government further into the red, Townshend also urged Par-

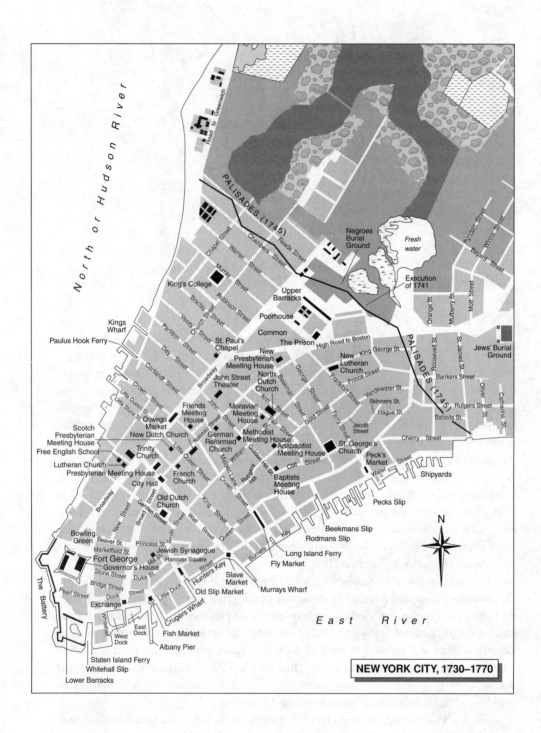

North or Hudson River

Road to Greenwich

PALISADES (1745)

Negroes Burial Ground

Fresh water

Chambers Street

Reade Street

Chapel Street

Warren Street

Murray Street

King's College

Robinson Street

Bradley Street

Upper Barracks

Execution of 1741

Church Street

Vesey Street

Poorhouse

Common

Partition Street

Kings Wharf

Paulus Hook Ferry

St. Paul's Chapel

The Prison

High Road to Boston

New Presbyterian Meeting House

North Dutch Church

New Lutheran Church

King George St.

Jews' Burial Ground

Orange St.

Mulberry St.

Mott Street

Dey Street

Broadway

John Street Theater

Beekman Street

George Street

Prince Street

Frankfort Street

Roosevelt St.

St. James Street

Oliver St.

Cortlandt Street

Crown Street

Little Queen Street

Little Stone St.

Oswego Market

Friends Meeting House

Moravian Meeting House

Ann Street

Fair Street

Gold Street

Vandewater St.

Skinners St.

Hague St.

Bankers Street

Rutgers Street

Batavia St.

Catharine St.

Scotch Presbyterian Meeting House

New Dutch Church

Free English School

German Reformed Church

Methodist Meeting House

Jacob Street

Trinity Church

Lutheran Church

Presbyterian Meeting House

French Church

City Hall

Nassau Street

Little Queen Street

William Street

Maiden Lane

Golden Hill St.

Anabaptist Meeting House

Baptists Meeting House

Ferry Street

St. George's Church

Cherry Street

Peck's Market

Shipyards

Old Dutch Church

Broadway

New Street

Broad Street

Garden Street

Smith Street

Wall Street

King Street

Crown Street

Rutgers Hill

Cliff Street

Queen Street

Water Street

Pecks Slip

Bowling Green

Beaver St.

Princess St.

Marketfield St.

Mill St.

Jewish Synagogue

Hanover Square

Burnets Key

Beekmans Slip

Rodmans Slip

N

Fort George

Governor's House

Stone Street

Duke St.

Hunters Key

Slave Market

Long Island Ferry

Fly Market

Bridge Street

Pearl Street

Dock Street

Old Slip Market

Murrays Wharf

The Battery

Exchange

Whitehall

West Dock

East Dock

Little Dock

Crugers Wharf

Fish Market

East River

Staten Island Ferry

Whitehall Slip

Lower Barracks

Albany Pier

NEW YORK CITY, 1730–1770

liament to create a new Board of Customs Commissioners to stiffen enforcement of the Navigation Acts and improve the collection of revenues from the colonies. Finally, he proposed the imposition of new taxes on paper, lead, glass, ink, paints, and tea imported into the colonies. By June 1767 his program had become law.

THE TRANSFORMATION OF POLITICS

Boston, roused over the late summer and early autumn by the oratory and organizational skills of James Otis and Samuel Adams, led the opposition to Townshend. Its merchants drew up the first in a new series of colonial nonimportation agreements, and early in 1768 the Massachusetts House of Representatives adopted a Circular Letter, inviting coordinated American protest against the Townshend program. Unwilling to back down a second time, Parliament and ministry responded with a show of force. The Massachusetts legislature was summarily dissolved—the second such body in as many years to fall before imperial wrath—and troops were dispatched to Boston as well to quell what was being referred to in London as a virtual insurrection.

For New York, the events of 1767 and 1768, though less dramatic than what took place in Boston, were no less tumultuous. In December 1767, at one of many protest meetings, residents chose a committee to devise yet another plan for promoting local manufactures, employing the poor, and encouraging frugality. The following April, the city's merchants organized its first Chamber of Commerce and agreed to join the nonimportation movement providing their counterparts in Philadelphia did likewise. In late August 1768 "Nearly all the Merchants and Traders in town" signed an agreement to begin nonimportation on November 1. Artisans and tradesmen, rallied by the Sons of Liberty, pledged to support the agreement and to use "every lawful Means in our Power" to see that everyone else did too. By the end of the year business in the city had once again come to a halt.

Two back-to-back elections for the provincial assembly had meanwhile strained long-established political practices and institutions to the breaking point. Although it escaped dissolution by Parliament on a technicality, Governor Moore dissolved the provincial assembly for objecting to the Townshend Duties, which led to an election in March 1768. Then he dissolved it again, for endorsing the Massachusetts Circular Letter and issuing a bold "Declaration of Rights," and another election followed, in March 1769. Sears and the Liberty Boys, who thought the Livingston-dominated Assembly hadn't done enough, threw their support to the De Lanceys, who won back much of the ground they had lost over the previous decade. Never before had the outcome of a faction fight between gentlemen been so influenced by men who weren't gentlemen.

Neither had gentlemen ever before faced such insistent popular demands for changes in the political process: open sessions of the Assembly, secret ballots, and strict adherence to the principle that legislators should do what they were instructed to do by their constituents rather than what they thought best for them. In response, the Assembly opened its doors to the public for the first time in early 1769. In municipal elections, too, more and more working people were involving themselves in the political process. Local elections brought steady increases in the numbers of artisans winning seats on the Common Council, and three out of five constables, collectors, and assessors were artisans.

The 1769 election even brought a hint of organized ethnic involvement in politics, when it was alleged that in the previous year's contest lawyer Thomas Smith, of the

Livingston faction, had said "that the Irish were poor beggars, and had come over here upon a bunch of straw." The whole body of Irishmen, it was observed, "immediately joined and appeared with straws in their hats." Fearful that Irish voters would desert en masse to the De Lancey side, the Livingstons hastened to publish a broadside utterly denying that Smith had been involved in "abusing or reflecting upon the *Irish* People" and asserting that indeed he had "expressed his Disapprobation of such Conduct."

A CITY "ALIVE TO GOD"

Dissatisfaction with established hierarchies was heightened by a new eruption of evangelical Protestantism in the city. George Whitefield, who had an instinct for showing up at key moments in the Anglo-American crisis, swung through town in 1763–65 and again in 1769–70 to remind his vast audiences of the difference between an authentic "religion of the heart" and the sterile "legal Christianity" of an unregenerate clergy. The thousands of working-class immigrants descending on New York from England, Scotland, and Ireland also proved fertile ground for the exertions of Methodists like Philip Embury, a Palatine German carpenter who had been preaching Methodism in Ireland and came to New York in 1760. At the instigation of his cousin Barbara Heck, who had been upset to find her brother playing cards in a hayloft in John Street, Embury began preaching to a small group in his home in 1766. A Methodist organization was formed, led by Embury and Captain Thomas Webb, a British army officer who had been conducting interracial services in Brooklyn. The fledgling Manhattan congregation met in a sail loft on William Street until Wesley Chapel was completed in 1768, fittingly enough on John Street.

New York's tiny Baptist congregation flourished as well. While its old church on Golden Hill hadn't survived the 1730s, the denomination had been revitalized in the 1740s by shipbuilder Jeremiah Dodge, who held prayer meetings at his house. Now, in the early 1760s, the First Baptist Church moved into a stone meetinghouse on Gold Street, just south of Fulton, and by 1763 had forty members.

Against this background, the city's principal dissenting sects set out to incorporate themselves as had Trinity many years earlier (incorporation permitted them to receive bequests, acquire and convey property, and the like). In March 1766, with the Stamp Act controversy raging around them, John Morin Scott, Peter R. Livingston, and other trustees of the First Presbyterian Church had petitioned the crown for a charter of incorporation. They were turned down on the grounds that the king had a duty to uphold the exclusive rights of the Church of England. The bishop of London and other imperial officials had also strongly advised against such a charter, fearing that it would encourage discord and undermine the dignity of His Majesty's government. It was a severe but revealing disappointment. When petitions from the Lutherans, Huguenots, and Reformed churches likewise failed, the established order, especially the Anglican Church, gathered a harvest of bitterness.

In May 1766 more than eighty Presbyterian and Reformed clergymen and deacons from around the colonies assembled in New York to voice their opposition to the appointment of an Anglican bishop for America. Arguments for such an appointment, though not new, had recently been revived by Samuel Johnson, president of King's College, and the Rev. Thomas Bradbury Chandler; they would be heard again the following year, with still greater force, when John Ewer, the bishop of Landaff, denounced the colonists as "infidels and barbarians" in an address to the Society for the Preservation of the Gospel, and the society began an all-out push for the creation of an Anglican episcopate in America. Read in light of Townshend's simultaneous attempt to tax the colonies, news of the SPG offensive was received by dissenters as well as secular radicals with indignation and apprehension. Their objection, as John Adams later explained, wasn't just to the office of bishop as such "but to the authority of parliament, on which it must be founded."

In New York, William Livingston, probably with the help of William Smith and John Morin Scott, entered the fray with a series of essays entitled "The American Whig." Running in the *New-York Gazette* from March 1768 to July 1769—thus overlapping the spirited Assembly campaigns of those years, the failure of dissenting congregations to secure charters of incorporation, and the new upsurge of evangelical fervor—Livingston's "American Whig" assailed the proposal for an American episcopate with arguments and a fervor reminiscent of the Triumvirate's attacks on King's College a decade earlier.

Evidence of Livingston's effectiveness came early in 1769, when New York's leading Baptists and Presbyterians—Alexander McDougall, William Livingston, John Morin Scott, David Van Horne, and several members of the Livingston clan, among others—formed the Society of Dissenters to fight episcopacy. One of the society's first recommendations was to urge the public to support dissenters rather than Anglicans in that year's Assembly elections. It subsequently advocated legislation relieving dissenters of the duty to pay taxes for the upkeep of Anglican clergy in the colony and, in 1770, got a bill through the Assembly repealing the Ministry Act of 1693. The bill died in the heavily Anglican council, however, and several years later Governor William Tryon would rule that the Anglican Church in New York was in fact legally established and immune from legislative interference. The whole experience confirmed that the line between religion and politics in New York had grown exceedingly fine indeed.

By the end of the decade, as one Methodist preacher reported to John Wesley in May 1770, the "religion of Jesus" had become a "favorite topic in New York." Even the city's "gay and polite" inhabitants were now "alive to God." "A person who could not speak about the grace of God and the new birth was esteemed unfit for genteel company," testified another observer. Thirteen of eighteen Protestant congregations in Manhattan had already gone over to pietism, while Trinity, that citadel of Anglicanism in New York, harbored a budding minority of evangelicals. (There was also a burst of church building and renovation. Between 1750 and 1776 half of the city's twenty-two religious houses were built or substantially refurbished.)

Religious orthodoxy and denominationalism had always been vital to the order of things in British New York. Their precipitous retreat during the 1760s not only made the rehabilitation of imperial power next to impossible but threw into question the authority of all social and political institutions as well. What was more, the corresponding advance of pluralism, individualism, and antiauthoritarianism—habits of mind whose meanings are as much religious as secular—increased the willingness of evangelicals to associate and cooperate with one another regardless of the doctrinal formalities that nominally divided them. Out of their concerted assaults on the religious establishment would come an organizational sophistication that mirrored—perhaps indeed helped lay the foundations for—the emergence of new secular political associations.

THE WILKES OF AMERICA

Opposition to the Townshend program was now at the end of its second year. In March 1769 New York merchants assembled at Bolton and Sigel's tavern near the Exchange (formerly the Queen's Head) to set up a Committee of Inspection for enforcing their nonimportation agreement. Headed by the indefatigable Sears, and widely believed to be an arm of the Sons of Liberty, the committee patrolled the waterfront, checked papers, and searched warehouses in search of violators. The best measure of its success was that imports from Britain fell to a mere seventy-six thousand pounds by the end of 1769, an 85 percent decline from the £491,000 reported just the year before, steeper than in any other colony.

In September 1769 Governor Henry Moore died, setting in motion an extraordinary train of events. Taking over again as acting governor was none other than Cadwallader Colden, now eighty-one (he "fairly lives himself into office," grumbled the merchant John Watts). Colden, who saw this as his last chance to score points with the ministry and snare an appointment as governor in his own right, negotiated an alliance of convenience with the De Lancey forces. Early in December, as part of their deal, the De Lancey-led Assembly—though it had just endorsed the Virginia Resolves of May denying Parliament's right to tax the colonies—abruptly chose to comply with the Quartering Act by appropriating two thousand pounds to provision His Majesty's troops stationed in New York. It was a spectacular blunder.

On December 16 an anonymous broadside entitled *To the Betrayed Inhabitants of the City and Colony of New York* appeared on the streets. Signed only by "A Son of Liberty," it attacked Colden and the Assembly as corrupt minions of British tyranny. It also recommended that the friends of liberty in New York, and indeed throughout America, "Imitate the noble example of the friends of Liberty in England; who, rather than be enslaved, contend for their right with k——g, lords, and commons."

This was an unmistakable reference to the controversy then boiling around John Wilkes, a radical member of Parliament who had been imprisoned in 1763 for his part in the publication of an allegedly libelous political pamphlet, *The North Briton, no. 45*. In 1768, a hard year for England's laboring classes, Wilkes won reelection to Parliament from Middlesex County and got himself thrown into jail again on the old charge of seditious libel. Crying, "Wilkes and Liberty!"—"Wilkes and No King!"—his indignant supporters, primarily small property owners and working people, paralyzed London with strikes, rallies, marches, and riots. On May 10, the day Parliament opened, as many as forty thousand demonstrators in St. George's Fields (a crowd exceeding the population of New York City) was fired on by troops, with considerable loss of life.

Amid spreading disorder, Parliament refused to let Wilkes take his seat. Three times more the Middlesex electors sent him back; three times more Parliament turned Wilkes away. By mid-1769 the government had more or less lost control of London to an array of spontaneously organized radical clubs and popular associations—among them the famous Society of Supporters of the Bill of Rights—for whom Wilkes's ordeal now symbolized the need for massive reform, even revolution. To suggest, as had the author of *To the Betrayed Inhabitants*, that New York needed a dose of the same thing was a provocation of the first rank.

While the De Lancey-led Assembly labored to uncover the identity of "A Son of Liberty," ill will between soldiers and civilians escalated sharply. The liberty pole in the

Common was the scene of frequent mass meetings at which John Lamb and other popular orators assailed the Assembly's decision to provision the troops both because it violated the sacred rights of Englishmen and because it imposed new hardships on the city's working people as well. On the night of January 13, 1770, a Saturday, soldiers of the Sixteenth Regiment swarmed out of the barracks and again attempted to blow up the liberty pole with a charge of gunpowder. When the pole didn't fall, the soldiers trashed Montayne's Tavern, the westside cartmen's hangout that had become the headquarters of the Liberty Boys. Monday night the soldiers tried a second time to topple the pole, and a second time they failed. Tuesday night they finally succeeded, leaving sawed-up pieces of the pole in a pile by Montayne's front door.

The denouement came on Friday, January 19. Led by Isaac Sears, a crowd of angry seamen and workingmen armed with cutlasses and clubs brawled with bayonet-wielding soldiers on Golden Hill, a former wheatfield at the crest of John Street (near William). That the Sixteenth had just completed a tour of duty in Ireland must have been an inspiration to those of Sears's followers who had so recently escaped that island. The ensuing Battle of Golden Hill—perhaps the first head-on clash between colonists and redcoats of the American Revolution—resulted in numerous injuries and one fatality, a seaman who was run through by a bayonet. It ended when officers ordered the soldiers back to their barracks, but scattered confrontations between civilians and troops took place the following day as well. The biggest took place in Nassau Street, when a large party of seamen, fed up with the loss of jobs to moonlighting military personnel and vowing to revenge the death of a fellow Jack Tar the day before, came to blows with some soldiers. Timely intervention by the mayor and members of the City Council quelled the disturbance before anyone had been seriously injured. Word of the clashes in New York roused the ire of British troops in Boston, however, and six weeks later the colonies would be horrified by news of the Boston Massacre.

Well before then, a committee chaired by Sears and McDougall had arranged for the erection of a new liberty pole. On February 6, escorted by flag-bearers and a marching band, a team of six horses drew a huge eighty-foot pine mast up from the East River shipyards to a site just across from the Common on private land. Several thousand onlookers cheered as the mast was then sunk in a hole twelve feet deep, girded with iron bars and hoops, crossed by a twenty-two-foot topmast—the influence of sailors on its design and construction couldn't have been plainer—and capped off with a gilt weather vane inscribed with the word LIBERTY. There it stood for the next half-dozen years, virtually impregnable. Weary of seeing his establishment used as a battleground, publican Montayne refused to host the Sons' annual celebration of the repeal of the Stamp Act. Sears, Scott, McDougall, and eight others quickly put up the money to purchase a nearby tavern for the Sons, which they promptly christened Hampden Hall in memory of John Hampden, who had given his life to the struggle against arbitrary taxation a century earlier.

One day after the new pole went up, McDougall was identified as the author of *To the Betrayed Inhabitants* and arrested for seditious libel. Chief Justice Daniel Horsmanden, now seventy-six years old, set bail at two thousand pounds—a prohibitive figure—and McDougall was hustled off to prison to await formal indictment. New York's Sons of Liberty promptly hailed him as the "American Wilkes." The allusion was astute. By linking McDougall to Wilkes, the Sons made McDougall's arrest and imprisonment common knowledge everywhere in America. Prominent visitors from other colonies came for interviews and returned home with reports of McDougall's selfless struggle against corruption and tyranny. In the city itself, crowds gathered outside his cell window to hear him speak while his friends ingeniously employed the Wilkseite number "45" to emphasize the political nature of his arrest. On the fourteenth of February, the forty-fifth day of the year, forty-five gentlemen dined with McDougall in his cell, consuming forty-five pounds of steak from a steer forty-five months old. Forty-five "virgins of this city went in procession to pay their respects," ending their visit with a rendition of the Forty-fifth Psalm. Dinners held in McDougall's honor were concluded with forty-five toasts to him and other heroes of English freedom.

At the end of April, after nearly three months of this, the grand jury finally met to hear the case against McDougall. His lawyer, John Morin Scott, argued that the acquittal of John Peter Zenger in 1735 had established truth as a sufficient defense against the charge of seditious libel. But Horsmanden would have none of it, besides which the sheriff had carefully packed the jury with friends, relatives, and business associates of both De Lancey and Colden. McDougall was indicted for publishing a "wicked, false, seditious, scandalous, malicious, and infamous libel." After posting a reduced bail, he was released to await trial. Unlike Zenger, though, he never got his day in court. The case against him collapsed after the death of the government's key witness, the printer.

NONIMPORTATION DEFEATED

In April 1770 Parliament at long last succumbed to the pressure of nonimportation. All the Townshend Duties were withdrawn except the one on tea—a reminder, said the new prime minister, Lord Frederick North, that Parliament still claimed the right to tax the colonies at its pleasure. The Sons of Liberty, more than two hundred of them, drafted a petition urging that nonimportation continue until the tea tax as well had been removed (many could sign only with a mark).

But after two years of little or no business, finishing off a decade-long economic slump, the pressures for a resumption of trade were formidable. Although a few "rich merchants" were holding their own, observed General Thomas Gage, "traders in general are greatly hurt. Many testify to their dissatisfaction, and the country people begin to complain of the dearness of the commodities they stand in need of." Also complaining were a sizable number of the craftsmen and seamen and laborers who depended on the merchants for work. In 1768 and 1769 journeyman tailors, waterfront stevedores, and workers in the building trades struck for higher wages. A newly organized Friendly Society of Tradesmen House Carpenters had begun dispensing sick benefits and funeral expenses for its members, obligations previously assumed by the municipal government or religious bodies.

Through the spring and early summer of 1770, the Sons of Liberty tried to keep nonimportation alive, but house-to-house polls in New York suggested that a three-to-one majority of the inhabitants also favored the resumption of trade. By mid-July New York's nonimportation movement had collapsed. The following month, entertained by brass bands, roaring cannon, and a military parade, a festive crowd converged on Bowling Green for the unveiling of the new equestrian statue of George III, commissioned four years earlier after repeal of the Stamp Act. A statue of William Pitt was subsequently erected in Wall Street, also at public expense.

Yet all the king's horses and all the king's men couldn't repair the damage done to the traditional order of things in New York. The Assembly had capitulated to the ministry and betrayed the cause of American liberty. Merchants, slow to endorse nonimportation and quick to abandon it, had punctured any illusion that men of wealth could be trusted to subordinate their private interests to the good of the whole community. Working people, drawing on the antiauthoritarianism of evangelical Protestantism as well as on a long tradition of robust plebeian communalism, had rallied behind leaders of their own making and in pursuit of their own interests, outside existing institutions. The De Lancey and Livingston factions, latest (and last) representatives of the old political order, responded accordingly, the former heading off in the direction of Colden and the ministry, the latter moving carefully toward the Sons of Liberty headquartered in Hampden Hall. As William Smith later wrote, for "both the Assembly and People without Doors . . . the old Despotism was broke."

The Empire, however, was not. In October 1770 London dispatched to New York a new royal governor in the person of John Murray, the earl of Dunmore, an alcoholic and corrupt Scottish nobleman whom the ministry soon sent away to take over as governor of Virginia. He took the news badly, wandering drunkenly through the streets roaring: "Damn Virginia . . . I ask'd for New York—New York I took, and they have robbed me of it without my consent." Dunmore's successor, William Tryon, arrived in July 1771. Tryon was another military man, well connected at court, and famous for his recent suppression of the Regulators in North Carolina, whose residents remembered him as "the Butcher."

"A NEW FLAME KINDLING IN AMERICA"

Fleetingly, for a year or two after the end of nonimportation, New York's economy seemed to be on the mend. But in June 1772 the British credit system collapsed, dashing hopes of an early recovery. More merchants in the city went under, more tradesmen closed their shops, more mechanics sought work. And more Scots, Irish, and English immigrants arrived, full of bitterness toward the landlords, employers, and politicians who had driven them out of their homelands.

During and after the winter of 1772–73 (so cold the East River froze over and people walked to Brooklyn), the condition of the city's poor again became desperate. Over four hundred men, women, and children jammed the old municipal poorhouse while the Common Council made more and more frequent appropriations for apprehending and transporting vagrants beyond the city limits. The council's yearly appropriations for outdoor relief climbed swiftly toward the twenty-eight-hundred-pound mark—better than four times what the city spent in 1760 and almost eight times what it spent in the 1730s. By 1773 the spread of sickness and disease had so severely strained the old municipal hospital that the council was obliged to order the construction of a new hospital near Broadway and Duane streets, on the outskirts of town. General Gage, serenely oblivious, praised New York's "domestic tranquility."

Crime too was on the rise again, a problem the council addressed by spending more money than ever for street lamps and the watch. By 1773 it had sixteen paid watchmen on duty every night and was placing "Centinal Boxes" at strategic locations around town (not enough, however, to protect James De Lancey Jr., son of the former governor and New York's best-known politician, who was mugged by a pair of footpads the very next year). So many convicted felons were being packed into the New Gaol, erected only a dozen-odd years before, that the council decided, also in 1773, to confine them in a proper "Bridewell" (named after London's notorious Bridewell House of Correction, which ever since the seventeenth century had been used to confine runaway appren-tices, vagrants, prostitutes, and debtors). Completed two years later near the New Bar-racks at the north end of the Common, the Bridewell's two stories and gray stone walls made it New York's most impressive public building.

Given that hard times always bore down hardest on widows and unmarried women, it wasn't surprising that more women turned to crime—as did Mary Daily and Mar-garet Siggins, who were hanged as pickpockets in 1771—and prostitution. Just west of the Bridewell, a red-light district had recently sprung up on land belonging to St. Paul's. Residents called it the "Holy Ground." Patrick McRobert, a Scot who visited New York in the summer of 1774, reported that "above 500 ladies of pleasure" kept lodgings in the "Holy Ground." They included "many fine well dressed women, and it is remarkable that they live in much greater cordiality one with another than any nests of that kind do in Britain or Ireland. . . . One circumstance I think is a little unlucky," McRobert added primly, "is that the entrance to [King's College] is thro' one of the streets where the most noted prostitutes live." The *New-York Gazette* went farther still, urging municipal authorities to wipe out these "nests of villainy" that catered to sol-diers of the king.

Relations between the colonies and the mother country went from bad to worse after passage of the Tea Act of May 1773. Ostensibly, Parliament wanted nothing more than to revive the fortunes of the ailing British East India Company, bulwark of British influence in India, by allowing it to sell tea directly in America. It was bad enough that this would cut out colonial middlemen, but Americans also suspected that Parliament really wanted the company to grab control of the colonial tea market in order to collect the duty on tea held over from the Townshend program—a devious ploy to make the colonists swallow the principle of parliamentary taxation.

By September 1773 half a million pounds of East India Company tea were on their way to selected consignees in the major American ports. For the next two months, as everyone awaited the arrival of the tea, another wave of defiance rolled through the colonies. Perhaps the first public demonstration of opposition anywhere occurred in New York, where, in mid-October, Sears and McDougall formed a Committee of Vigilance to plan a course of action and congratulate ship captains refusing to handle cargoes of duties tea. McDougall launched a series of inflammatory essays called *The Alarm*. "A New Flame is apparently kindling in America," William Smith wrote in his diary.

Summoned by the Committee of Vigilance, a huge crowd assembled on November 5 (Guy Fawkes Day) outside the Coffee House. After denouncing Parliament and East India Company agents, they hanged in effigy one local merchant who had advised the company to ship to New York. Later that same month the Sons of Liberty formed an association to defeat the Tea Act. Anyone who stood against them, they declared, would be treated as "an enemy to the liberties of America." Governor Tryon ruefully admitted that this resolution was "universally approved by all the better sort of the Inhabitants."

No doubt remembering the fate of stamp distributors eight years earlier, the East India Company's agents hastily resigned. Sears and McDougall began to talk of shut-ting down the port altogether to prevent the landing of tea. McDougall went even fur-ther: "What if we prevent the Landing," he asked a horrified William Smith, "and kill [the] Gov[ernor] and all the Council?" On December 17, 1773, as many as three thou-sand of the city's inhabitants gathered at City Hall to protest the Tea Act. They pledged to use force, if necessary, to resist the unloading of East India tea and elected a Committee of Correspondence, consisting of Sears, Lamb, McDougall, and several other Liberty Boys, to reopen communications with patriots in other colonies. Not until Paul Revere brought the news to town four days later did anyone know that on December 16 patriots disguised as Mohawk Indians had dumped several hundred chests of East India tea into Boston harbor. Word soon arrived that Philadelphia too had turned back a tea ship. Two ships were reported on their way to New York.

Sears and McDougall had ample time to prepare. Hampered by bad weather, New York's tea ships didn't arrive until mid-April 1774. The captain of one, told by "sundry gentlemen" on a Committee of Inspection that "the sense of the citizens" wouldn't permit him to land his cargo, quietly turned around and sailed for home. He was seen off by the greatest crowd "ever known in this city" and a "band of music" playing "God Save the King." The captain of the other (already notorious for having brought the hated tax stamps to New York in 1765) failed to bluff his way past the inspection committee and was forced to apologize before a public meeting at Fraunces Tavern. A party of "Mohawks" dumped his cargo into the harbor, "and it was not without some risk of his life that he escaped." Lieutenant Governor Colden—now eighty-seven and once again in charge of the colony because Tryon had gone back to England for a year-long leave of absence—didn't intervene, on the grounds that no one had asked him to.

Outraged by the Boston Tea Party, the government in London had meanwhile resolved to make an example of Massachusetts. From its point of view, it could do no less. Ten years of American defiance had upset a trading empire worth thirty million pounds a year in combined imports and exports. Besides, when perhaps only one in thirty Englishmen could vote, and at a time of ballooning internal disorder, American theories of representation struck at the very heart of Britain's political and social order. As George III himself declared: "The colonists must be reduced to absolute obedience, if need be, by the ruthless use of force." (Otherwise, he would later say, India, Ireland, and the rest of England's possessions would go their own way as well, and "this Island, reduced to itself, would be a poor Island indeed.") The upshot, in April 1774, was a series of so-called Coercive Acts—soon referred to throughout America as the "Intolerable Acts"—by which Parliament shut the port of Boston, reorganized the colony's courts to facilitate the prosecution of political troublemakers, and sharply restricted the power of the colony's legislature and town meetings. Commander-in-Chief Thomas Gage was named governor and sent up from New York with additional troops to help him enforce the law.

THE "NEW ARCADIA" OF LIBERTY

Initial reports of the Intolerable Acts began to arrive in New York in mid-May. "This intelligence was received with Great abhorence & indignation," McDougall noted in his diary. The Sons of Liberty and the Livingston faction immediately moved to organize "an impartial spirited Committee of Correspondence" for the purpose of drawing up new nonexportation as well as nonimportation agreements and reviving the idea of a continental congress. They were only partially successful. At a turbulent mass meeting at the Exchange on May 16, moderate merchants rallied by the De Lancey faction voted to postpone a decision on nonimportation and nominated a fifty-member committee with only a dozen-odd seats reserved for the Sons.

The very next day, however, Paul Revere returned to town with the Boston Circular

Letter, which advocated an immediate embargo on trade with Britain until Parliament repealed the Intolerable Acts. Heartened by this evidence of patriotic zeal elsewhere, and ready now to act independently of the merchants, a group of the city's mechanics nominated a Committee of Correspondence having only twenty-five members, mostly Sons of Liberty and Livingston adherents. Revere was sent off with letters for the patriots in Philadelphia and Boston, explaining the confusion in New York and stressing the need for a general congress.

The showdown occurred at a tumultuous public meeting in the Coffee House on May 19. At issue was the size and composition of the Committee of Correspondence: fifty, as the moderates wanted, or twenty-five, as the new Mechanics Committee had proposed. Equally difficult was the question of who in the city had a right to vote on the matter: "none but the Freeholders & Freemen," as one of the moderates argued, or "every man whose Liberties were concerned," as Sears maintained. On both points the moderates again carried the day. All fifty moderate nominees won election, with the addition, as a conciliatory gesture, of one radical. A compromise plan for a house-to-house canvass of the city broke down when the details couldn't be worked out. The following day Sears and McDougall reluctantly persuaded the Mechanics Committee to accept what was now the Committee of Fifty-one on the understanding they would be removed "if they misbehaved."

Although the moderates gained the upper hand, the appearance of the Mechanics Committee was a milestone in the political history of New York City. A plebeian counterpart to the merchants' Chamber of Commerce, it confirmed the growing political sophistication of the city's working people and their ability and willingness to act without the prompting even of men like Sears, Lamb, and McDougall. Its leaders over the next few years—Jonathan Blake, Daniel Dunscomb (a cooper), Nathan Tylee, Christopher Duyckinck (a sailmaker), Lewis Thibou, and Malcolm McEwen—had hitherto been on the fringes of municipal affairs. Now they were at the very center.

Joining them there were the many women who played an increasingly visible role in mobilizing resistance to British policy, above all by vesting ordinary domestic decisions with political significance. As shoppers, retailers, and housewives, they refused to buy or sell British goods, made clothes of homespun, and served coffee instead of tea. Some called themselves Daughters of Liberty, and their patriotic fervor suffused the letters that a New York teenager named Charity Clark sent to a cousin in England. She and other young women of the city had begun to knit "stockens," she wrote, dreaming of the day when "a fighting army of amazones . . . armed with spinning wheels" would free America from its dependence on British imports and thus put it beyond the reach of "arbitrary power." Do not underestimate us, she warned her distant correspondent: "Though this body is not clad with silken garments, these limbs are armed with strength, the Soul is fortified by Virtue, and the Love of Liberty is cherished within this bosom."

THE CONTINENTAL ASSOCIATION

For the next six weeks, according to one observer, New York was "as full of uproar as if it was beseiged by a Foreign force." City papers reported a succession of raucous meetings, rallies, demonstrations, and fistfights. Isaac Sears received a "drubbing" on one occasion from a British officer stationed in the city.

Despite pressure from its more radical members, the Committee of Fifty-one managed to sidestep a commitment to nonimportation by insisting that it should be proposed first by a "Congress of Deputies from all the Colonies in general"—although the committee's moderate majority didn't much like the idea of such a meeting, either, given its radical origins.

By early July it had become certain that a congress would convene in Philadelphia in September. The Fifty-one grudgingly nominated five delegates to attend for New York City: Isaac Low, John Jay, Philip Livingston, John Alsop, and James Duane. Dismayed that no one to their liking had been included, and conscious that events had begun to turn in their favor, the Mechanics Committee met at Bardin's Tavern (the former Hampden Hall) to draw up its own slate of candidates: Low, Livingston, Jay, Leonard Lispenard, and Alexander McDougall. Called by the Sons of Liberty, a public meeting in the Fields on July 6 approved the mechanics' slate, along with resolutions instructing the five, if elected, to support a nonimportation agreement. It took three weeks of tense, byzantine maneuvering to work out a compromise: the Mechanics Committee agreed to support the original nominees of the Fifty-one, while the Fifty-one in turn assured the mechanics it would wholeheartedly support a nonimportation agreement if one were adopted by the upcoming congress.

Several weeks later John Adams and other New England delegates passed through New York en route to Philadelphia. With McDougall as their semiofficial host, they toured the city and spent hours in deep conversation with patriots. The starchy Adams was less than impressed. "At their entertainments there is no conversation that is agreeable," he noted in his diary. "They talk very loud, very fast, and altogether." (They did know how to eat, however: invited to John Morin Scott's "elegant Seat" overlooking the Hudson, Adams was taken aback by the profusion of silverware and abundant food.)

Adams tore himself away, and New York's delegates embarked for Philadelphia on

To the PUBLICK.

NEW-YORK, OCTOBER 5, 1774.

BY Mr. Rivere, who left Boſton on Friday laſt, and arrived here laſt night, in his way to the General Congreſs, we have certain intelligence that the Carpenters and Maſons who had inadvertently undertaken to erect barracks for the ſoldiers in that town, upon being informed that it was contrary to the ſentiments of their countrymen, unanimouſly broke up, and returned to their reſpective homes, on the 26th of laſt month; which, it is hoped, will convince the Mechanicks of this city, how diſagreeable it will be to the inhabitants of that place, for them to afford any manner of aſſiſtance to thoſe, who are made ſubſervient to the deſtruction of our American brethren.

Printed by JOHN HOLT, near the COFFEE HOUSE.

Paul Revere was an important conduit of information between radical artisans in New York and Boston. This broadside announces one of his several appearances in the city. (© Collection of The New-York Historical Society)

September 1, "with Colours flying, Music playing, and loud Huzzas at the End of each Street." Four days later the Continental Congress, attended by fifty-six delegates from twelve colonies, got down to business. To the delight of radical patriots everywhere, it advised the people of Massachusetts to form a new government and take up arms. It rejected a conciliatory Plan of Union with Great Britain and adopted resolutions attacking the entire course of British policy toward the colonies since 1763. In mid-October it created the Continental Association, a "nonimportation, nonconsumption, and nonexportation agreement" to be enforced by Committees of Inspection in every county, town, and city in America—a clear usurpation of the authority of legal governments throughout the colonies.

In New York, one immediate casualty of the Association was David Douglass's theatrical troupe. Douglass had returned to the city in 1767 and enjoyed a string of profitable seasons in a spacious new playhouse on John Street. But he had also drawn heavy abuse—from radical Whigs, who saw theatergoing as a manifestation of genteel self-indulgence (it was said that the price of a season's subscription had risen to an amazing fifty pounds), as well as from evangelicals, who believed that theaters promoted idleness, debauchery, and blasphemy. Douglass now learned that the Association agreement had committed all patriotic Americans to "discountentance and discourage every species of extravagance and dissipation, especially all horse-racing, and all kinds of gaming, cock-fighting, exhibition of shews, plays, and other expensive diversions and entertainments." Fearing the worst—he could hardly have forgotten the violent destruction of his old playhouse on Chapel Street a decade earlier—Douglass promptly closed his doors and took his actors to Jamaica, expecting no trouble from "the Ladies and Gentlemen of that polite and opulent island."

The moderate Committee of Fifty-one tried to preserve its control over the course of events by proposing that it supervise enforcement of the Association through teams of inspectors chosen by the electors in each ward. But the Mechanics Committee demanded instead dissolution of the Fifty-one and enforcement of the Association by a new sixty-member Committee of Observation on which popular leaders would have

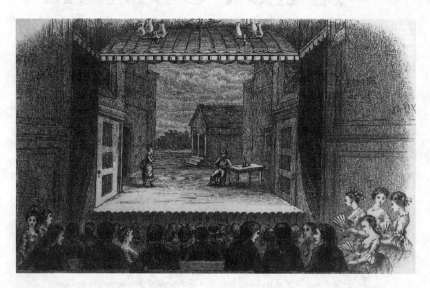

Interior of the John Street Theatre, from *The New York Argus*, March 13, 1797.
(© Museum of the City of New York)

half the seats. Bolstered by the success of radical patriots in other colonies, the mechanics had little trouble getting the Fifty-one to cooperate. Nominations for the new committee were published in the papers and confirmed without incident at a public rally on November 22.

WHIGS OF THE OLD STAMP

From the very beginning of the struggle with Great Britain, New York had been regarded on both sides of the Atlantic as a nursery of loyalty to the mother country. Nowhere else in the colonies, after all, did the ground lie quite so thick with royal functionaries, generals, admirals, Anglican churchmen, big landowners, and merchant princes. They were rich men, on the whole, well born, well educated, well married, and well connected—precisely the kind of men on whom the Empire had relied, for more than a century, to govern its American provinces. Few approved the idea of taxing the colonies, but they were obstinate in their devotion to British institutions and knew what they stood to lose if the Empire failed to keep a firm grip on America. By 1773 or 1774 many had already cast their lot with king and Parliament, and the potential scope of their influence troubled patriots everywhere.

Not until Congress set up the Association, though, would a concerted, broadly based loyalism begin to emerge in New York (or indeed anywhere else). For as the Committee of Sixty and other such extralegal bodies plunged into their work over the winter and spring of 1774–75—chasing down rumors of violations, examining backsliders and the contrary-minded, confiscating property, prescribing what good patriots should buy and sell and wear, often indeed administering oaths of support for the Association—substantial numbers of New Yorkers finally decided that matters had got out of hand. Hundreds of shopkeepers, tradesmen, and farmers joined loyalist associations to affirm their loyalty to the crown and the old order; many talked of forming loyalist militia companies. Jacob Walton, a careful man, built a secret escape tunnel from his country house at Hell Gate to the East River shore (workmen uncovered portions of it in Carl Schurz Park in 1913).

Hardcore loyalists were a distinct minority in the province, never amounting to more than 15 percent of the colony's 168,000-odd inhabitants. (Some 60 percent of the population, by contrast, supported the patriots; the rest were fence-straddlers and switch-hitters.) Queens, Kings, and Richmond counties—the agrarian periphery of New York City—proved notably cool to the patriot cause. Staunch patriots comprised only 12 percent of the nearly eleven thousand residents of Queens County (which then included what is now Nassau County). With loyalists often outnumbering patriots by better than two to one, a succession of Queens communities—Jamaica, Newtown, Oyster Bay, Flushing, Hempstead—openly defied Congress and issued protests condemning the Association. Indecisiveness seemed epidemic among the thirty-six hundred inhabitants of Kings County. A mere 6 percent have been counted as hardcore patriots, but they outnumbered hardcore loyalists, and the half-dozen towns of Kings County silently ignored the Association. The Flatbush Reformed Church hedged its bets by having services conducted by two ministers, one patriot, the other loyalist.

The strength of loyalism in these counties reflected a long-standing dependence on the export markets of New York City and, through them, on the entire system of international exchange protected by British imperial power. In parts of Kings and Queens counties, if not Richmond, loyalism drew as well on local traditions of hostility to New

England-style radicalism dating back to the mid-seventeenth century (neighboring Suffolk County, still closely tied to New England, was overwhelmingly patriot). Also to be reckoned with was the role of religious, cultural, and ethnic heterodoxy: the *least* "English" areas of Long Island were most heavily loyalist, presumably because they had flourished under British rule and would have the most to lose in a new, majoritarian social and political order.

Nowhere, however, was loyalism rooted in formal ideological differences with the patriots. A shower of Tory placards, handbills, broadsides, pamphlets, and newspaper essays fell on New York in 1774 and 1775—many appearing courtesy of James Rivington's printshop, source of the *New-York Gazetteer*, the single most important loyalist journal in the colonies. The bulk of this literature appealed to essentially the same Whiggish fears about tyranny, corruption, and conspiracy that shaped patriot thought. Many Tories, in fact, waited until the very last moment to decide which side they were on, for they saw Congress, not Parliament, as the immediate danger. Parliament may well have acted unwisely or unjustly, loyalist writers conceded. But Congress was an illegal and unconstitutional body, controlled by unscrupulous men whose secret objective was to gain wealth and power for themselves. They would stop at nothing until they had destroyed every remnant of British authority—and with it the prosperity, stability, and security the colonies had enjoyed for generations.

Still, there was something fundamentally elitist, even aristocratic, about loyalism. New York's leading Tories—John Watts, Isaac Low, Cruger, Thomas Jones, William Smith, Peter Van Schaack, William Johnson, James and Oliver De Lancey, Frederick Philipse, William Bayard—were all men of wealth and power, long identified with British high culture. A large majority of the hundred members of the Chamber of Commerce sided with the crown, as did, overall, half of the city's merchants, who as a group tended to be wealthier than their patriot counterparts. Religion too set New York Tories apart. Anglican clergy and their congregations by and large opposed independence, while dissenters favored it. Only one of the city's Presbyterian ministers became a loyalist, and many rebel leaders, like John Lamb and Isaac Sears, had evangelical connections. Thirty-seven of forty-four Dutch Reformed ministers in the colony backed independence; the four exceptions were conservatives with a record of opposition to the church's evangelical wing.

The most energetic and compelling loyalist propaganda in the middle colonies emanated from a circle of learned, profoundly conservative Anglican clerics: the Rev. Thomas Bradbury Chandler of New Jersey; the Rev. Charles Inglis, assistant rector of Trinity Church; the Rev. Myles Cooper, president of King's College; the Rev. John Vardill, a sometime professor at King's College moonlighting as a British spy; and the Rev. Samuel Seabury of Westchester County. To their way of thinking, constitutional liberty could be maintained only by the better sort of people—people of rank and distinction in society—because they alone possessed the capacity for reason and disinterested virtue. Common folk, ruled by base passions, always looked first to their own self-interest and could not therefore be trusted with power. No wonder, then, that law and order had broken down: all those congresses, committees, and conventions now oppressing the colonies were the handiwork of vulgar upstarts, men ill equipped to govern themselves, much less others. A sad spectacle indeed, declared Cooper: "I feel indignation and shame mingling in my Bosom, when I reflect that a few men (whom only the political storm could cast up from the bottom into notice) have presumed to act in the character of *representatives and substitutes of the Province.*" That one Tory pamphlet after another would be consigned to the flames on the day of their publication by cheering crowds merely underscored the oppressive nature of mob rule. And it made perfect sense to Anglican loyalists that men who resorted to such desperate, illiberal measures frequently proved to be religious dissenters.

"THE MOB BEGIN TO THINK AND REASON"

Often only the finest of lines divided Tories from moderate or conservative patriots. For young Gouverneur Morris, a Whig like his grandfather Lewis but no admirer of the lower classes, these were gloomy and troubling days. "The mob begin to think and reason," he declared after watching the mass meeting of May 19, 1774, in the Coffee House. "Poor reptiles! It is with them a vernal morning; they are struggling to cast off their winter's slough, they bask in the sunshine, and ere noon they will bite, depend upon it. The gentry begin to fear this." If this quarrel with Britain continues, Morris added dramatically, "we shall be under the worst of all possible dominions; we shall be under the domination of a riotous mob." Yet Morris's fears didn't, in the end, fix his course. For whatever reason—the stirrings of national pride, a revival of confidence that the upper classes could maintain control, a sense of obligation to the Whiggism of his ancestors—he cast his lot with the patriots and supported independence.

So did James Duane, the city-born son of a well-to-do Irish immigrant merchant and landowner. After studying law in the offices of James Alexander, Duane built a practice of his own that by the early 1770s, just as he turned forty, was earning a handsome fourteen hundred pounds a year. Marriages to Maria Livingston and, after her death, to Gertrude Schuyler cemented Duane's position in society. He became a vestryman of Trinity and a trustee of King's College. He maintained a fashionable town house, a country seat, and a thirty-six-thousand-acre estate west of Schenectady where he managed 235 tenants and engaged in potash-making and milling.

It would hardly have been surprising if Duane, like so many other men of his class and connections, had drifted into loyalism by 1774 or 1775. He didn't think highly of the intelligence or intentions of ordinary people and helped prosecute Alexander McDougall. He worried about the advent of mob rule and warned Robert Livingston, his father-in-law, about the dangers of "a great and respectible Family becoming obnoxious to Government" by even appearing to associate with the Sons of Liberty. Though deploring Parliament's attempts to tax the colonies, he revered the British constitution, regretted the absence of an American peerage, and abhorred republicanism. "God forbid that we should ever be so miserable as to sink into a Republick!" he exclaimed.

Yet Duane remained a patriot. In the First Continental Congress, he fought for a cautious statement of American rights, conceding almost everything but the right of the colonies to tax themselves. He returned home and plunged into the work of enforcing the Association and preparing the colony for armed conflict. While men no more conservative than he were turning their backs on colonial resistance, he attended the provincial convention and was named a delegate to the Second Continental Congress. In 1775 he moved that each inhabitant of the city take up arms and prepare for war.

John Jay was another unlikely rebel. Grandson of the Huguenot refugee Augustus Jay, he was reputed one of the most promising young attorneys in New York by the early 1770s. Besides a quick mind and natural eloquence, he possessed impeccable social credentials and was related to the Bayards, Stuyvesants, Van Cortlandts, and De Lanceys.

Robert Livingston Jr. was for a time his law partner, and in 1774, not yet thirty years old, Jay married William Livingston's daughter Sally. There was talk that year of getting him a royal judgeship.

As conservative as Gouverneur Morris and James Duane—"those who own the country ought to govern it," he liked to say—Jay too found himself drawn step by step into revolution. His election to the Committee of Fifty-one marked his entrance into the struggle. Sent down to the Congress in Philadelphia, he signed the Association and drafted an *Address to the People of Great Britain* that was widely applauded for its ringing defense of American rights ("we will never submit to be hewers of wood or drawers of water for any ministry or nation in the world"). By the time he returned to New York, even radicals like Sears and McDougall were hailing Jay's accomplishments.

Some of his friends worried that "to please the Populace he must have thrown aside his *old Principles*," but events proved them wrong. The more prominent Jay became, the more certain he was that men of property ought never yield to force from above or pressure from below. He became a revolutionary, in the end, because he couldn't see an honorable way out of a predicament created by obstinate, venal politicians in London. "It has always been and still is my opinion and belief," he said many years later, "that our country was prompted and impelled to independence by necessity and not by choice."

15

Revolution

In February 1775, when the Assembly refused to choose delegates for a Second Continental Congress, the authority of New York's legal government collapsed. The Committee of Sixty, assuming quasi-governmental power, called for a public meeting at the Exchange in early March to devise a plan for choosing a congressional delegation. To ensure a strong patriot turnout, the Sons of Liberty rallied at the liberty pole on the appointed day, then marched downtown in force, "round all the docks and wharves, with trumpets blowing, fifes playing, drums beating, and colours flying." The excited crowd that followed them to the Exchange endorsed the Sixty's proposal that the selection of delegates be entrusted to a special provincial convention of representatives from every county in the colony, to convene at the Exchange six weeks later. Governor Colden talked about preventing the meeting by proclamation, but neither he nor the Assembly had the nerve to do so—which made the royal government look even more ineffectual. New York's Provincial Convention met on April 20 and put together a congressional delegation. The old Assembly adjourned, never to meet again.

Three days later the city learned that Gage's redcoats had been bested by mere militia at Lexington and Concord. Isaac Sears, John Lamb, and Marinus Willett quickly gathered a crowd and headed for the East River docks, where they emptied two ships of provisions intended for the British forces. Willett then led a second raid on the City Hall arsenal, removing nearly six hundred muskets, bayonets, and cartridge boxes for distribution among the patriots. Next day, April 24, a crowd of some eight thousand people—roughly a third of New York's population—assembled in front of City Hall to hear from the Committee of Sixty. Crossing the line between resistance and revolution, the Sixty proposed that all New York patriots subscribe to a General Association, that a Provincial Congress assume control of the colony, that government of the city be turned over to a new Committee of One Hundred, and that immediate steps be taken to defend the city from a British attack—a distinct possibility, given that Gage's position in Boston was clearly untenable. "People here are perfectly fearless," Robert R. Livingston told his wife, Mary.

Nominations and elections for the Committee of One Hundred took place within a few days. Though dominated by moderates, its members included such radicals as Daniel Dunscomb, chairman of the Mechanics Committee, whose presence helped push the committee to widen its authority. At a mass meeting of city residents on April 29, the One Hundred promulgated Articles of Association drafted by James Duane and John Jay. Those who signed pledged "never to become Slaves" and to obey the measures of the Continental Congress, the Provincial Congress, and their local committees.

Three hundred and sixty armed men, led by Isaac Sears, meanwhile seized the keys of customs collector Andrew Elliot. Sears declared the port of New York closed until further notice. For another week or two, Sears's house on Queen Street seemed to be the effective seat of government and headquarters for the company of militia that nightly patrolled the city. William Smith Jr. could hardly believe what was happening. "It is impossible," he wrote on April 29, "fully to describe the agitated State of the Town since last Sunday, when the News first arrived of the Skirmish between Concord and Boston. At all corners People inquisitive for News. Tales of all kinds invented believed, denied, discredited. . . . The Taverns filled with Publicans at Night. Little Business done in the Day. . . . The Merchants are amazed and yet so humbled as only to sigh or complain in whispers. They now dread Sears's Train of armed Men."

This was revolution—"total revolution," in the words of one Tory. Even if Great Britain and the colonies did manage to compose their differences—the Continental Congress continued to insist that the colonies weren't seeking independence—the legitimacy of colonial political institutions had boiled away. Governmental power was passing to a network of committees that responded to, and included representatives of, what another Tory called "the lower class of people." The city is now ruled, said yet another, "by Isaac Sears & a parcel of the meanest people, Children & Negroes."

Isaac Low, Abraham Walton, and a handful of other prominent Tories, still clinging to the hope of a peaceful solution, remained in New York to take part in the Provincial Congress. Most took flight. James De Lancey, merchant John Watts, and Colonel Roger Morris scrambled to get on the May 4 packet to England. Printer James Rivington fled to the protection of a British warship in the harbor. Governor Colden retreated to his Flushing estate, writing to Lord Dartmouth that "Congresses and committees are now established in this Province and are acting with all the confidence and authority of a legal Government."

President Myles Cooper of King's College left town as well, chased from his bed one night in May by "a murderous band." A student named Alexander Hamilton is said to have helped Cooper escape by delaying his pursuers with a lengthy "harangue" on Cooper's front porch. Hamilton, who had come up to New York from the West Indian island of Nevis only two years earlier, was already the author of two highly regarded pamphlets supporting the Continental Congress; like other conservative patriots, however, he detested mobs.

"GOOD AND WELL-ORDERED GOVERNMENTS"

The New York Provincial Congress took over the vacant Assembly chamber in City

Hall on May 23 and moved quickly to consolidate its authority. It called for the creation, where they didn't already exist, of "county committees, and also sub-committees . . . to carry into execution the resolutions of the Continental and this Provincial Congress." It instructed Queens and Richmond counties to send delegates at once. It warned everyone who hadn't yet subscribed to the General Association to do so by July 15 or suffer the consequences. It also stepped up the pace of military preparations by creating a Military Association—in effect, a revolutionary militia—and launching a campaign to recruit five regiments. Alexander McDougall, the Wilkes of America, personally took charge of raising a regiment from the city; the First New York, as it would be known, consisted largely of workingmen.

Association militia were soon drilling in the Fields and patrolling the streets while gangs of laborers erected barricades, dug trenches, and threw up breastworks. The Committee of One Hundred, assuming the duties of municipal government, meanwhile began to grapple with such familiar problems as regulating wages and prices and providing relief for the poor.

The speed with which both the One Hundred and the Provincial Congress got to work reflected not only the quickening pace of events but also the continued concern among more cautious patriots that popular enthusiasm not be allowed to get out of control. "Good and well-ordered governments in all the colonies," explained John Jay, would "exclude that anarchy which already too much prevails." James Duane, who admitted that "licentiousness is the natural effect of a civil discord," felt "it can only be guarded against by placing the command of the troops in the hands of men of property and rank." Easier said than done, Gouverneur Morris reflected, inasmuch as "the soldiers from this Town [are] not the Cream of the Earth but the Scum" and are "officered by the vulgar." Even Alexander McDougall felt apprehensive. "I fear liberty is in danger from the licentiousness of the people," he confessed.

For many moderates, these fears were underscored on June 6, when the last of the Fort George garrison, a hundred or so soldiers from the Royal Irish Regiment, were withdrawn from the city to the sixty-four-gun warship *Asia* (in part, according to one source, because too many of them had deserted to the patriots). Led by Marinus Willett, some Liberty Boys intercepted the column as it marched down Broad Street, commandeering its muskets, ammunition, and baggage. Escorts provided by the Provincial Congress and Committee of One Hundred endeavored to stop the outrage, without success. Shortly thereafter, a party of Liberty Boys raided a royal storehouse at Turtle Bay, likewise over the objections of representatives from the Provincial Congress. Knowing that a failure to respond might well explode its authority, the Congress ordered Willett to return everything he and his men had made off with. Independent "attempts to raise tumults, riots, or mobs" couldn't be tolerated, it said sternly.

Willett backed down, but no one expected that to end the matter. When a crowd burned a supply barge from the *Asia* in July, the embarrassed Congress built a replacement; when that too was destroyed, Congress again condemned unauthorized attacks on persons and property and ordered the construction of another replacement, this time dispatching militia to guard it.

The rapidly escalating crisis between Britain and the colonies made it all the more difficult for the Provincial Congress to stay on top of the situation in New York. On June 25, 1775, General George Washington passed through town on his way to take command of the troops besieging Gage in Boston. Cheering crowds lined the streets and church bells pealed as a battalion of militia and members of the Provincial Congress escorted him down Broadway to Hull's Tavern, where he would spend the night.

Later that same day, Governor Tryon returned to resume his duties after a fourteen-month absence. A smaller and much more restrained crowd greeted the governor at the foot of Broad Street and walked with him over to Hugh Wallace's town house on Bowling Green, where he had lodgings for the night. It was the first of many hard lessons, he said, in the "impotence of His Matys Officers and Ministers of Justice in this Province," and it now seemed "very probable I may be taken Prisoner, as a state Hostage, or obliged to retire on board one of His Majestys Ships of War to avoid the insolence of an inflamed Mob."

It came to that more quickly than the governor might have imagined. Only a week before he and Washington reached New York, a second clash between colonial forces and Gage's redcoats took place at Bunker Hill. Then, over the summer of 1775, Congress rejected a conciliatory plan proposed by Lord North. It offered instead the so-called Olive Branch Petition, pleading with the king to cease hostilities. It also drew up a "Declaration of the Causes and Necessity of Taking Up Arms," explaining that the colonists had acted only in self-defense and were "with one mind resolved to die freemen, rather than to live slaves." In August Congress launched an invasion of Canada to prevent its use as a base of operations against the colonies. "The Americans from Politicians are now becoming Soldiers," Tryon reported to the home government.

YANKEE DOODLE COMES TO TOWN

On the night of August 23 John Lamb's artillery company undertook to remove two dozen cannon from the Grand Battery at the southern tip of Manhattan. While they were at it, they exchanged fire with a boatload of soldiers from the *Asia*, lying in the East River just off the foot of Wall Street. In retaliation, the commander of the *Asia* ordered a full thirty-two-gun broadside of solid shot into the sleeping town. Apart from a hole in the roof of Fraunces Tavern, no great damage was done. But for the thousands of half-dressed, panic-stricken residents who tumbled out of their beds into the streets, it was an effective reminder of the city's vulnerability to naval bombardment. Many made plans to leave.

Isaac Sears soon left town too, albeit for reasons of another kind. In October 1775 the Continental Congress recommended the arrest of all royal officials remaining in the colonies; not only did the New York Provincial Congress seem reluctant to take so decisive a step, but when soldiers pilfered a royal store, the Congress ordered everything returned rather than risk another bombardment from the *Asia*. Incensed by this timidity, Sears sold his house, moved to Connecticut, and proceeded to organize an armed troop made of sterner stuff. "There are many Enemies to the cause of Freedom" in New York, he declared. Governor Tryon, suspecting that Sears had set his sights on him in particular, slipped off to William Axtell's Flatbush estate; from there he made his way to a merchant ship, the *Duchess of Gordon*, anchored safely under the guns of the fleet in the harbor.

The winter of 1775–76 brought a steady stream of news confirming that Tryon would never again set foot in the city without a fight. Parliament rejected the Olive Branch Petition. The king formally proclaimed the colonies to be in a state of rebellion and closed them to all trade. General Gage had been replaced by General Sir William Howe, and a punitive expedition force under General Henry Clinton, General Charles

Cornwallis, and Admiral Peter Parker was expected to descend on North Carolina sometime in January.

Throughout the colonies, the reaction to these developments was an eruption of popular resentment against the monarchy that killed the chances of a reconciliation with the mother country. Americans now began to talk openly of independence; the case for it was clinched in January 1776 by Tom Paine's *Common Sense*, which denounced "the Royal Brute of Great-Britain" and catalogued all the reasons why the colonies would be better off on their own.

Tryon's departure left New York's Tories both demoralized and defenseless. During the late summer of 1775 the pressure on them became intolerable. A series of resolves by the Provincial Congress provided that anyone aiding the enemies of America, or even denying the authority of congresses and committees, could be disarmed, fined, imprisoned, and banished. To Isaac Sears, this was the long-overdue summons to action. He galloped down from Connecticut with one hundred men and smashed up James Rivington's printshop. After announcing that they acted independently of all congresses and committees, Sears and his band galloped away again singing "Yankee Doodle." (Who, it will be recalled, stuck a feather in his cap and called it "macaroni"— a deft little dig at the flamboyant style of the same name associated with the upper classes on both sides of the Atlantic.)

Printer Samuel Loudon came in for similar treatment the following March when he printed *The Deceiver Unmasked*, an attack on Paine from the pen of the Rev. Charles Inglis. Led by Sears, Lamb, and McDougall, a band of Liberty Boys raided Loudon's shop, destroyed his press, and burned every one of Inglis's pamphlets.

Lukewarm patriots as well as Tories fled New York in droves. By the end of 1775 more than ten thousand of the city's twenty-five thousand inhabitants had gone; thousands more would go in the months that followed. By July 1776 only five thousand or so remained. "To see the vast number of houses shut up, one would think the city almost evacuated," wrote one departing Tory. "Women and children are scarcely to be seen in the streets. Troops are daily coming in; they break open and quarter themselves in the houses they find shut up. Necessity knows no law."

Outside the city, however, the Tory problem proved harder to resolve. Opposition to the Association ran so high in Kings County that in August 1775 the Provincial Congress dispatched a committee to rally the fainthearted and disarm enemies to the cause. General Nathaniel Woodhull was likewise ordered to secure Queens County, but the task there was so difficult that the Provincial Congress finally appealed to the Continental Congress for help. Congress answered by sending Colonel Nathaniel Heard of New Jersey. Heard marched through Queens in January 1776 with twelve hundred militia and a list of "inimicals" who had refused to sign the Association. Nearly a thousand Tories or suspected Tories were rounded up and disarmed; nineteen were taken away to Philadelphia for questioning. Heard made a similar sweep of Staten Island a month later.

No sooner had Colonel Heard departed than General Charles Lee arrived in New York with two regiments of New England militia. A strange and moody man who surrounded himself with dogs, Lee was already something of a sensation among the patriots. His soldiers adored him, Washington depended on him, and the Continental Congress seemed to think he could do no wrong. For one thing, Lee was a retired British officer with more impressive military experience than anyone else on the American side, experience that had proved vital during the siege of Boston in the summer and fall of 1775. He was also an out-and-out radical who detested monarchy, spoke admiringly of democracy, and advocated immediate independence for the colonies.

To Lee's way of thinking, the struggle against Great Britain was an authentic popular uprising, which required the kind of grass-roots mobilization that French revolutionaries would later call a *levée en masse*. If the war continued, he argued, it could be won only by citizen-soldiers who made up the rules as they went along, not by professional troops employing the aristocratic "Hyde Park" tactics of conventional European armies. True to his principles, he made his headquarters at Montayne's tavern on Broadway, just across from the Fields and once the principal meeting place for radical patriots. It isn't hard to see why the New England troops and the city's mechanics loved him—or why he made the Provincial Congress extremely nervous. Paine thought him a marvel well before they met.

Congress wanted Lee in New York partly to keep up the pressure on local Tories (Lee relished that kind of assignment) but mostly because a British attack on the city was becoming more likely every day. The American invasion of Canada had just ended in disaster: General Montgomery was dead, and the First New York had suffered heavy casualties (one of McDougall's sons had been killed, the other taken prisoner). General Howe was meanwhile preparing to leave Boston, most likely for New York.

Until General Gage had left to occupy Boston in 1768, after all, New York had served as the headquarters for British forces in North America. It was familiar territory, socially and politically as well as militarily. Its central location and unsurpassed harbor and port facilities made it the logical staging area for further operations against the rebels, while control of the Hudson-Lake Champlain axis would isolate rebellious New England from the rest of the colonies. The many Tories in and around the city would surely give His Majesty's forces a warmer welcome than they had received in Boston; their presence would, of course, eliminate an important center of political and social radicalism and boost the morale of Tories throughout the colonies. Taking New York would be an easy matter, in any case: as Peter Stuyvesant had learned a century before, New York couldn't be defended without a navy, and Congress had no navy to speak of. "I feel for you and my other New York friends," said an Englishman sympathetic to the American cause, "for I expect your city will be laid in ashes."

Lee knew full well that New York couldn't be held against an all-out assault by an enemy army and fleet; he also knew that handing it over without a fight would give the enemy a dangerous military and psychological advantage. The only course, he reasoned, was to put up a stout resistance and extract as high a price for the city as possible.

As the spring of 1776 approached, Lee threw himself into the business of preparing New York for invasion. To prevent hostile warships from entering the East River, he ordered construction of thirteen forts and batteries on Manhattan and Long Island. To forestall an attack by land, he barricaded the city's major streets and placed an additional half-dozen forts and batteries at strategic points between the city and King's Bridge at the northern end of Manhattan; one, near what is now the intersection of Grand and Center streets, was nicknamed "Bunker Hill." To keep an enemy from taking Brooklyn Heights, the high ground that commanded the city from across the East River, Lee strung a chain of forts, redoubts, breastworks, and trenches between Gowanus Creek and Wallabout Bay (built, for the most part, by levies of Kings County slaves.) He sent Isaac Sears with an armed party over to Long Island to keep the Tories there in line. He also issued manifestos to inspire the citizenry and hosted a dinner party for Tom Paine, who came up from Philadelphia.

After little more than a month of this feverish activity, Lee moved on to organize the defenses of Charleston, leaving General William Alexander in command of the city. He'd done his work well: New York wasn't safe, but it was getting ready.

"PEOPLE TREADING ON THEIR LEADERS' HEELS"

In mid-March, as expected, Howe finally pulled out of Boston and headed for Halifax, there to prepare for the move against New York. At once Washington began shifting Continental troops down to the city, then came down himself in mid-April to oversee military preparations. Every able-bodied man in the city, including servants and slaves, was pressed into work on fortifications.

New batteries were built on Red Hook, Governors Island, Paulus Hook, and elsewhere, bringing the total to fourteen, with 120-odd cannon. To prevent enemy ships from entering the Hudson, construction began on a pair of forts that straddled the river between upper Manhattan and New Jersey—one dubbed Fort Washington, the other Fort Lee.

By the beginning of the summer of 1776, the arrival of better than ten thousand troops had transformed the city into an armed camp, and (Washington hoped) more were on the way. Military authorities established two huge bivouacs, one just north of town near present-day Canal Street, the other across the East River on the slopes above the Brooklyn ferry landing, and many other pieces of open ground were crammed with tents, huts, shacks, wagons, and piles of supplies. To build barricades and meet the demand for firewood, work parties ripped up fences and cut down the many trees for which the city had been famous. Warehouses and loft buildings, especially those belonging to departed Tories, were commandeered for military purposes, as were the new city hospital and the classrooms of King's College.

Town houses and country retreats belonging to the Apthorp, Bayard, Watts, Stuyvesant, Walton, and Morris families—every one a talisman of the old order in the city—were turned over to soldiers who draped their feet on the furniture, tore up the parquet floors for fuel, threw garbage out the windows, and corralled their horses in the gardens. Washington himself settled the army's general headquarters on Richmond Hill, the country estate of Abraham Mortier. Protests were pointless; indeed protesting seemed only to make matters worse. Oliver De Lancey, brother of the late governor and uncle of Captain James De Lancey, ordered army woodcutters off his estate on the west side of Manhattan at 23rd Street. Once they might have retreated before the wrath of so great a personage; now, fired with a new egalitarian zeal, they brushed him aside and set upon his prized orchards with a vengeance. By June, De Lancey too had fled to the *Duchess of Gordon.*

Everybody complained about price-gouging by shopkeepers, tradesmen, and ferryboat operators. Nobody knew what to do about waste disposal and sanitation, which—along with the inadequate supply of potable water, always a problem—constituted an open invitation to epidemic disease. The provost marshal imposed a curfew on the troops and struggled to control the sale of alcohol, but drunkenness and rowdyism were a source of constant concern. So was the "Holy Ground" district west of Broadway, where (as one American officer wrote his wife) "bitchfoxy jades, jills, hags, strums, [and] prostitutes" flourished as never before. At Washington's request, the authorities removed the four hundred indigent residents of the almshouse and ordered that the "women, children, and infirm persons in the City of New York be immediately removed from the said City" to nearby rural counties.

Despite the best efforts of military and civilian officials, the city and its environs were still crawling with Tory spies and sympathizers, many in positions of considerable importance. Throughout the spring and early summer, rumors flew that Tories in New York and New Jersey were recruiting soldiers, stockpiling weapons, and sabotaging military equipment and installations on the assumption that the redcoats would show up any day. Tensions ran especially high on Long Island, where patriot troops didn't get along with rural villagers and Tory "skulkers" hid out in the Rockaway marshes.

The New York Provincial Congress hadn't been much help. Since the previous summer—specifically, some said, after the *Asia* cannonaded the city in August—that body seemed to have come down with a bad case of the jitters. It agonized about prohibiting local merchants and farmers from selling supplies to British warships still in the harbor. It agonized about raising money. It agonized about spending money. It agonized about the havoc wrought by ten or twenty thousand young men under arms (especially Lee's New Englanders, some of whom were allegedly talking about burning the city if all else failed). After agonizing, too, about the Tories, it created a special Committee for the Detection of Conspiracies to chase them down, but without much success. Washington thought the Provincial Congress was a pack of dithering nincompoops and quarreled with it about almost everything. Patriots elsewhere spoke of New York as the weakest link in the chain.

In New York City, as opposed to the colony as a whole, the revolutionary movement actually gained momentum after mid-1775. The final disintegration of royal authority, the flight of thousands of Tories, the impending attack by His Majesty's forces, and the presence of a revolutionary army had completed the shift to radical rule. There, in the words of Hugh Hughes, "the people are constantly treading on their leaders' heels, and, in a hundred cases, have taken the lead of them." Suspected Tories were forced to recant in public, then tarred and feathered, ridden through town on rails, or forced to parade the streets holding candles.

The well-organized and militant Mechanics Committee (soon referring to itself as the Mechanics Union) had now become the dominant voice in municipal affairs. It carefully watched—and criticized, when necessary—every move of the Committee of One Hundred. When a local printer advertised a pamphlet attacking *Common Sense*, the mechanics urged him not to sell it; when he refused, they confiscated and burned all the copies. When it seemed the Conspiracy Committee wasn't moving fast enough, the mechanics ran suspected Tories out of town. When elections were held for a new Provincial Congress in April, the mechanics refused to endorse McDougall because he had stayed in town when his regiment marched off to Canada; McDougall lost. All spring, while the Provincial Congress hemmed and hawed about a final break from Great Britain, the mechanics stressed the essential connection between revolution and independence: revolution needn't have led to independence, nor independence to revolution, but neither could get very far without the other.

"I THOUGHT ALL LONDON WAS AFLOAT"

At the end of May, prodded by the Continental Congress in Philadelphia, the Provincial Congress recommended new elections so that New Yorkers could vote on the issue of forming a new state government. The result was an exhilarating, free-wheeling debate over fundamental political principles, in which the city's mechanics advocated ideas that not too many years earlier would have landed them in jail: republicanism, constitutionalism, unicameral legislatures, limited executive power, annual elections, the secret ballot, universal manhood suffrage, rotation of office, equal apportionment, the popular election of all local officials, religious toleration, and even the abolition of slavery. The Mechanics Union also declared that no frame of government should be adopted for the state without having first been ratified by the people.

When the new Provincial Congress assembled in mid-June, a number of the most conservative delegates had been unseated by men whose views were decidedly more radical—among them Daniel Dunscomb, a former chairman of the Mechanics Committee—and there now appeared to be a slim majority in favor of national independence.

Under the leadership of John Jay, moreover, the Conspiracy Committee finally began to show some initiative in dealing with the Tory problem. Its biggest discovery was that one of Washington's own bodyguards, a certain Thomas Hickey, had conspired with several others, probably including Mayor David Mathews, to kidnap or assassinate the American general. Hickey was court-martialed and hanged near the Fields in the presence of a huge throng of soldiers and civilians. Matthews was seized at his Flatbush residence and taken to prison in Connecticut.

On June 29, the day after Hickey's execution, lookouts saw the long-awaited fleet from Halifax streaming past Sandy Hook toward the Narrows between Staten Island and Long Island—better than a hundred vessels in all, bearing thousands of regular troops. To one amazed American rifleman, the harbor resembled "a wood of pine trees." "I could not believe my eyes," he recalled. "I declare that I thought all London was afloat." Within a day or so nine thousand redcoats had been landed on Staten Island and set to work building fortifications.

Washington meanwhile exhorted his soldiers to be ready to fight to the last, convinced that the city was defensible. He wasn't alone. Colonel Henry Knox, a self-taught

The British fleet anchored off Staten Island, 1776. Sketch by Archibald Robertson. (Spenser Collection. The New York Public Library. Astor, Lenox and Tilden Foundations)

artilleryman from Massachusetts, assured Washington that the cannon emplacements now ringing the city would deter a British attack. The Provincial Congress, more cautious, thought it best to move up to White Plains.

On July 2, 1776, Congress voted in favor of independence; two days later it adopted Jefferson's Declaration. New York's Provincial Congress gave its assent on July 9. At six P.M. that same day, the Declaration was read to Washington's troops mustered in the Common. A rowdy crowd of soldiers and civilians ("no decent people" were present, one witness said later) then marched down Broadway to Bowling Green, where they toppled the statue of George III erected in 1770. The head was put on a spike at the Blue Bell Tavern near Fort Washington at present-day Broadway and 181st Street; the rest of the statue, some four thousand pounds of lead, was hauled off to Connecticut. There it will "be run up into musket balls for the use of the Yankees," declared one soldier. "It is hoped that the emanations from the leaden George will make . . . deep impressions in the bodies of some of his red-coated and Tory subjects."

Within a week the King's Arms on City Hall had likewise come down, along with other trappings of monarchy adorning Trinity and St. Paul's. "Every Vistage of Royalty, as far as been in the power of the Rebels, [is] done away," said Tryon glumly. Reported another observer: "The Episcopal Churches in New York are all shut up, the prayer books burned, and the Ministers scattered abroad. . . . It is now the Puritan's high holiday season and they enjoy it with rapture."

SUCH UNSOLDIERLY CONDUCT

His Majesty's army was ready for a fight too, convinced it would make short work of the rebels defending New York. Despite the recent unpleasantness in Boston, its officers still believed that Washington's so-called army was a mere republican rabble, without

Symbolic regicide in New York, a nineteenth-century interpretation, painted by John C. McRae, of New York patriots pulling down the statue of George III. Legend has it that the head was later rescued by a British officer and shipped back to England. (© Museum of the City of New York)

the training or leadership necessary to hold off seasoned veterans. This unshakable class contempt was reinforced by the knowledge that large numbers of recent immigrants had thrown in with the patriots. "The chief strength of the Rebel Army at present consists of Natives of Europe, particularly Irishmen," observed Captain Frederick Mackenzie of the Royal Welsh Fusiliers.

General Howe, though, didn't want an all-out fight for New York. It wasn't a question of winning but of how much it would cost to win. He couldn't forget the carnage at Bunker Hill, where a frontal assault against entrenched American positions had cost him 40 percent of the men under his command in a single afternoon, and it was clear that Washington expected him to try the same thing again. Howe knew, too, that if Washington fought well the city could easily be left unfit as a base for further military operations.

As always, there were also political considerations. Sympathy for the American cause had widened steadily among the British middle and laboring classes, who linked it to demands for domestic political reform. London voters chose two Americans as sheriffs in 1773. John Wilkes, installed as mayor of London in 1775, was pressuring the crown to remove ministers hostile to American rights. A new generation of radical Whig pamphleteers—Catharine Macaulay, Major John Cartwright, Granville Sharp, James Burgh, Richard Price, Joseph Priestly—were all the while bombarding the reading public with warnings that liberty was in mortal peril on both sides of the Atlantic. New York readers paid careful attention. Local papers reprinted long extracts from parliamentary debates, British journals, and private correspondence. Local bookstores stocked a full range of controversial books and pamphlets, including Price's famous *Observations on the Nature of Civil Liberty, and the Justice and Policy of the War with America* (1776).

Aware that further conflict with America would require expenditures of blood and money that the government could ill afford—resistance to domestic recruiting had already obliged it to hire soldiers from the Landgrave of Hesse in Germany—even moderate Whigs like Edmund Burke were urging Lord North to go easy. General Howe's brother, Admiral Lord Richard "Black Dick" Howe, was in fact already on his way to the colonies at the head of a commission authorized by the king, reluctantly, to negotiate with Congress.

Both the Howe brothers felt personally well disposed toward the colonies. Both remembered with gratitude that the Massachusetts legislature had erected a monument in Westminster Abbey to the memory of an older brother killed at Ticonderoga during the Seven Years War. Both believed, vaguely, that the Americans had some cause for complaint. Both continued to believe in the possibility of a peaceful reconciliation. Both sensed that the annihilation of Washington's army in New York would make reconciliation impossible and doom Britain to resolve the American crisis by force of arms alone—an unhappy prospect even for men who made a profession of war.

The course that both preferred, all things considered, was to make the colonies realize the danger they faced without closing the door to negotiations. Confronted with the combined might of His Majesty's army and navy, Washington and the Congress (so the theory went) would come to their senses and return to the fold. A case could be made, in fact, that General Howe's arrival off Staten Island was already having the desired effect. Virtually the entire Staten Island militia had joined the British army, and every day, from New Jersey, from Long Island, and even from Manhattan, scores of Tories were slipping through rebel lines to join the fleet. At a moment's notice, they said, thousands more were ready to rise against the tyranny of Congress; Washington's army, they said, was disintegrating.

Howe's first move, accordingly, was a modest but revealing probe of the American defenses. On July 12 a pair of British warships, the gunship *Phoenix* (forty-four guns) and the frigate *Rose* (twenty-eight guns), detached themselves from the fleet anchored off Staten Island and crossed the upper bay toward the mouth of the Hudson. American cannon blazed away from Red Hook, Governors Island, Paulus Hook (New Jersey), and Manhattan, but to no effect. While the captain of the *Rose* and his officers sipped claret on the quarterdeck, the two sailed serenely into the Hudson, past the city, and all the way up river to Tarrytown, some thirty miles to the north.

Washington was appalled. His artillery did more harm to themselves than to the enemy—the only casualties of the day occurred when an ill-trained gun crew on the Battery blew themselves up—while many of his men and officers abandoned their positions to gawk at the spectacle. "Such unsoldierly conduct," he explained to the Provincial Congress, would "give the enemy a *mean* opinion of the army."

Just as unfortunate, casual return fire from the British warships, though doing no great damage, caused pandemonium among the civilian population. A few of Washington's staff were convinced by what had happened that this was the wrong place and the wrong time for a head-on battle with the British. Washington, however, remained obstinate in his determination to fight for the city. Admiral Lord Howe and his fellow commissioners, who had by coincidence arrived on the evening of the twelfth (along with 150 ships and fifteen thousand more troops), got nowhere with the American commander in the days that followed. He firmly refused to see them; negotiation was a matter for Congress, he explained, besides which Howe had made the mistake of writing to "Mr. George Washington" rather than "General George Washington."

Two weeks passed. Generals Henry Clinton and Lord Charles Cornwallis, having failed to capture Charleston, came up through the Narrows on August 1 with eight regiments of veterans and several men-of-war. (For Clinton this was a homecoming of sorts: the son of Admiral George Clinton, royal governor of New York from 1743 to 1753, he had spent much of his boyhood in the city.) Several days behind Clinton and Cornwallis came a convoy of twenty-two ships with additional regiments from England and Scotland. On August 12 a fleet of over a hundred vessels crossed the bar at Sandy Hook, bringing in nearly nine thousand Hessian mercenaries under General Philip von Heister. To Ambrose Serle, Lord Howe's secretary, it was a scene never to be forgotten. "So large a fleet made a fine appearance upon entering the harbor, with the sails crowded, colors flying, guns saluting and the soldiers . . . continually shouting." In New York, "the tops of the houses were covered with gazers," the wharves were "lined with spectators," and apprehension mounted as "ship after ship came floating up" to drop anchor off Staten Island in the distance. Hundreds more residents gathered their belongings and fled. Within days, as Pastor Schaukirk of the Moravian Church described the scene, the city looked "in some streets as if the Plague had been in it, so many houses being shut up."

General Howe now had at his disposal two men-of-war and two dozen frigates mounting a combined twelve hundred cannon, plus four hundred transports, some thirty-two thousand disciplined and well-equipped troops in twenty-seven regiments, and thirteen thousand seamen. It was the largest force ever assembled in the colonies and the largest British expeditionary force in history thus far, marshaling better than 40 percent of all men and ships on active duty in the Royal Navy. Already the cost exceeded £850,000—a breathtaking sum for the time. Washington, by contrast, had no ships to speak of and probably fewer than twenty-three thousand men under his command, mostly raw militia without adequate equipment, training, or experience. About half of them weren't fit for duty thanks to an epidemic of camp fever (dysentery) that had broken out in the overcrowded town across the bay.

But still Washington didn't waver, not even when the fever laid up Nathanael Greene, his best general and the commander of the all-important Brooklyn Heights defenses. Instead, to replace Greene, Washington turned to John Sullivan of New Hampshire. Sullivan not only lacked Greene's ability, he knew nothing about the terrain on which he was supposed to fight.

By this time six weeks had passed since General Howe's arrival on Staten Island, and it was clear that he was going to have to do something fairly soon. On August 17 Washington ordered warnings posted throughout the city that an attack was near and urged all civilians to get out immediately. Next day the *Phoenix* and the *Rose* dropped back down the Hudson from Tarrytown. Again the American batteries thundered away at them, again with no effect.

THE BATTLE OF BROOKLYN

On August 22 the British finally made their move. Under the cover of six warships, scores of flatboats, longboats, and bateaux ferried fifteen thousand redcoats across the Narrows to what is now Dyker Park on the Gravesend shore of Long Island. Set against "the Green Hills and Meadows after the Rain and the calm surface of the water," Ambrose Serle observed, the landing made "one of the most picturesque Scenes that the Imagination can fancy or the Eye behold." Similarly impressed, a light guard of two hundred Pennsylvania riflemen stationed near the beachhead withdrew without offering any opposition. More redcoats and five thousand Hessians followed on the twenty-third and twenty-fourth, bringing the total enemy force to around twenty-one thousand.

As the British settled in, their positions stretched in a four-mile arc from the village of New Utrecht on the west (site of Howe's temporary headquarters) through Gravesend to Flatbush (where the Hessians were billeted) and Flatlands (the main British camp, at the intersection of what is now Flatbush Avenue and Kings Highway). Governor Tryon appeared on the scene and called out the local militia, some six hundred men in all, to aid the regulars. Joined by two Tory regiments raised among refugees from New York, they imparted to this invasion the tensions of civil war. Eight hundred slaves had fled to the British as well and were being organized into a labor regiment.

Howe and his officers professed to be delighted by their reception on Long Island. "The Inhabitants receiv'd our people with the Utmost Joy, having been long oppress'd for their Attachment to Government," said one. "They sell their things to the Soldiers at the most Reasonable Terms & they kept up their stock in spite of the Rebels." In Flatbush and other Kings County hamlets, however, fear and confusion reigned. Many years later, the elderly mother of Gertrude Lefferts Vanderbilt still remembered when a "rumor reached us that the soldiers were rapidly approaching. The whole village was in commotion. . . .Women and children were running hither and thither. Men on horseback were riding about in all directions."

On the twenty-third Washington sent reinforcements to Sullivan and went over from New York to study the situation personally. On the twenty-fourth he dispatched more reinforcements under General Alexander, bringing the American total to around seven thousand. He also ordered General Israel Putnam of Connecticut to go over and see what he could do. "Old Put" was a capable veteran of the French and Indian War who had faced Howe at Bunker Hill. "Don't fire until you see the whites of their eyes," he is supposed to have said. "Then, fire low."

Putnam took charge of the Brooklyn Heights defenses, leaving Sullivan with around twenty-eight hundred men to cover the outer line along the Heights of Guan, the rocky, heavily wooded ridge of the glacial moraine that ran down the middle of Long Island. Only four roads traversed this barrier—at Gowanus, Flatbush, Bedford, and Jamaica—and even a relatively small force should have been able to defend it against an army advancing north toward Brooklyn Heights.[1]

Someone, however, had neglected to place troops at the Jamaica Pass, on the far left of the American line. A civilian spy (probably one of many Kings County Tories who attached themselves to the British army) soon brought word to General Clinton of the gap, and Clinton persuaded Howe to attack it in strength. Just after sundown on the twenty-sixth, a Monday, Howe, Clinton, and Cornwallis led better than ten thousand regulars in a two-mile-long column out of Flatlands toward New Lots in the east; with them went two companies of Long Island Tories under Oliver De Lancey. To deceive any watching Americans, they moved quietly and left their campfires burning. At New Lots they turned north to Jamaica; at about three A.M. on the twenty-seventh, they marched through the Jamaica Pass without opposition. They then turned west along the Jamaica Road toward the village of Bedford—today the intersection of Nostrand Avenue and Fulton Street in Bedford-Stuyvesant—where they arrived around 8:30 A.M. and fired two signal guns to alert the rest of the army.

Two smaller enemy forces now swung into action. At the Flatbush Pass in the center of the American line, five thousand Hessians attacked eight hundred Americans under General Sullivan. Realizing from the signal gun that Howe had somehow worked his way around him, Sullivan tried to fall back but couldn't. Trapped between Howe's light infantry coming down from Bedford and bayonet-wielding Hessians pouring up from Flatbush, his men broke and were slaughtered. "The greater part of the riflemen," reported one German officer, "were pierced with the bayonet to trees." A jubilant British officer gloated: "It was a fine sight to see with what alacrity they dispatched the Rebels with their bayonets after we had surrounded them so they could not resist." Hundreds of Americans threw down their weapons and raced to reach safety behind the lines in Brooklyn Heights. Sullivan himself was captured in a cornfield near what is now Battle Pass in Prospect Park. It was over before noon. Although most of the American dead were buried on the grounds of the Flatbush Reformed Dutch Church, area farmers were still turning up bones in their fields well into the next century.

At Gowanus, on the far right of the American line, General James Grant had meanwhile thrown seven thousand redcoats and two thousand Royal Marines, supported by two companies of Long Island Tories, against two thousand troops from Maryland,

---

1. The Heights of Guan are visible today in the high ground that begins in Bay Ridge and runs west to east through Green-Wood Cemetery, Prospect Park, Eastern Parkway, Evergreen Cemetery, and Forest Park in Queens. The Gowanus Pass is now 37th Street between Green-Wood and Sunset Park, while the Flatbush Pass is the East Drive of Prospect Park. Bedford Pass was where Bedford Avenue now meets Eastern Parkway. Jamaica Pass lies at the junction of Jamaica Avenue and Evergreen Cemetery.

Pennsylvania, and Delaware commanded by General Alexander. Alexander's men fought gamely to keep control of the high ground—now called Battle Hill in Green-Wood Cemetery—until the collapse of the American center at Flatbush made their position hopeless. Redcoats from Bedford were closing in behind them, while Hessians were crashing through the woods on their left. To give the rest of his force time to escape across the tidal flats along Gowanus Creek, Alexander counterattacked with barely four hundred Maryland troops.

Washington, who watched Alexander advance from a vantage point where Court Street now crosses Atlantic Avenue, reportedly wrung his hands and cried out: "Good God! What brave fellows I must this day lose!" Survivors remembered the "confusion and horror" as the fleeing Americans tried desperately to cross eighty yards of muddy flats under a hail of British canister, grape, and chain. "Some of them were mired and crying to their fellows for God's sake to help them out; but every man was intent on his own safety and no assistance was rendered." After savage fighting on the Gowanus Road near the Cortelyou House (now known as the Old Stone House, at Fifth Avenue and 3rd Street), Alexander was captured. By two P.M. all but nine of the Marylanders had been killed or taken prisoner. Thanks to their valor, however, hundreds of other Americans managed to wade or swim to solid ground on the other side of the creek, and hence to safety in Brooklyn Heights.

Had Howe kept up the chase, it is likely that the demoralized remnants of Washington's army would have been driven into the East River. In only a few hours of fighting roughly twelve hundred Americans had died, and another fifteen hundred were wounded, captured, or missing—among them three generals and ninety-odd junior officers. The British, by contrast, reported only sixty dead and three hundred wounded or missing.

The American retreat across Gowanus Creek, by Alonzo Chappel. (© Collection of The New-York Historical Society)

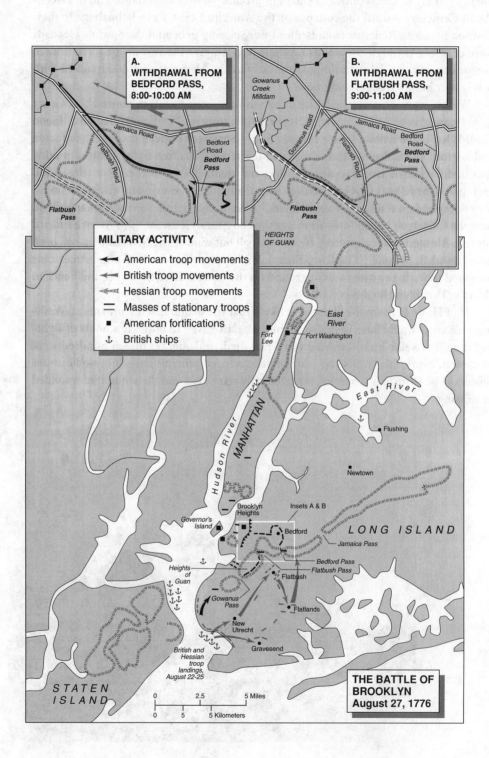

A. WITHDRAWAL FROM BEDFORD PASS, 8:00-10:00 AM

Jamaica Road

Flatbush Road

Bedford Road

Bedford Pass

Flatbush Pass

B. WITHDRAWAL FROM FLATBUSH PASS, 9:00-11:00 AM

Gowanus Creek Milldam

Gowanus Road

Jamaica Road

Flatbush Road

Bedford Road

Bedford Pass

Flatbush Pass

HEIGHTS OF GUAN

MILITARY ACTIVITY

- American troop movements
- British troop movements
- Hessian troop movements
- Masses of stationary troops
- American fortifications
- British ships

East River

Fort Lee

Fort Washington

East River

Flushing

MANHATTAN

Hudson River

Newtown

Brooklyn Heights

Governor's Island

Insets A & B

Bedford

LONG ISLAND

Jamaica Pass

Heights of Guan

Bedford Pass

Flatbush Pass

Flatbush

Gowanus Pass

Flatlands

New Utrecht

British and Hessian troop landings, August 22-25

Gravesend

STATEN ISLAND

0   2.5   5 Miles

0   5   5 Kilometers

THE BATTLE OF BROOKLYN August 27, 1776

Despite pleas by Clinton, Cornwallis, and others to finish what they had begun, Howe halted and began preparations for a formal siege—either because he didn't have the heart for another Bunker Hill–like frontal assault or because he hoped that the rebels would give up without a struggle. Tuesday evening and all day Wednesday his forces dug trenches and probed the American defenses in a cold, soaking rain that made it impossible for men on either side to build campfires or keep their powder dry. Although the storm ended by noon on Thursday the twenty-ninth, two days after the battle, Howe continued to bide his time—and gave Washington the opening for one of the boldest strokes of the war.

That evening, as night fell, Washington ordered all units to form up and move down from the Heights to the ferry landing on the East River shore. "We were strictly enjoined not to speak, or even cough," one private recalled. "All orders were given from officer to officer, and communicated to the men in whispers." At water's edge, a regiment of fishermen from Salem and Marblehead with commandeered rowboats, barges, sloops, skiffs, and canoes waited to ferry the army across to New York. Working silently, hour after hour, they rowed back and forth, under the cover of a thick fog that concealed the maneuver from enemy sentries. The last of ninety-five hundred men—Washington's entire force—reached Manhattan just as dawn broke on Friday. Not until 8:30 would a chagrined Howe learn that the Americans had slipped his grasp.

Even though everyone knew that Washington's audacity had saved the Revolution, there was no celebrating in New York. Pastor Schaukirk, roused out of bed to watch the soldiers straggle into town, saw only shock and exhaustion on their faces. "The merry tones on drums and fifes had ceased," he reported. "It seemed a general damp had spread, and the sight of the scattered people up and down the streets was indeed moving. Many looked sickly, emaciated, cast down, etc.; the wet clothes, tents—as many as they had brought away—and other things were lying about before the houses and in the streets to dry."

Washington's escape from Brooklyn Heights, by J. C. Armytage. (© Collection of The New-York Historical Society)

THE FALL OF NEW YORK

On September 11 Lord Howe met with a congressional delegation consisting of Benjamin Franklin, John Adams, and Edmund Rutledge at the stone manor house Captain Christopher Billopp had built around 1680 in Tottenville, Staten Island. If Congress would revoke the Declaration of Independence, Howe repeated, the British would pardon all who had taken up arms against the king (essentially the same offer they had made to Washington a month before). Independence isn't negotiable, replied the American delegates—with which the so-called conference came to an end.

Now even Washington could see that his days in New York were numbered. His dispirited army was falling apart—in one week six thousand of eight thousand Connecticut militia simply picked up and went home—and the longer he stayed in the city, the greater the danger he would be encircled and destroyed. At a war council on September 12, Washington accepted the advice of his officers to abandon all of Manhattan to the enemy except for Fort Washington at the northern end of the island. Greene (supported by John Jay, among others) argued strongly that New York should be burned as well as abandoned. ("That cursed town from first to last has been ruinous to the common cause," exclaimed one officer.) Congress firmly rejected the idea. Two days later, leaving Putnam and five thousand men behind to cover his rear, Washington shifted his headquarters ten miles out of town to the home of Roger Morris on Harlem Heights (now the Morris-Jumel Mansion on 162nd Street).

On October fifteenth, the Howe brothers finally roused themselves for another move against Washington. That morning, Connecticut militiamen crouched in trenches a few miles above the city at Kip's Bay (34th Street) observed so many flatboats of redcoats massing just across the East River at the mouth of Newtown Creek that it looked "like a large clover field in full bloom." As they pushed off, five warships anchored nearby poured barrage after barrage into the American positions—"so terrible and so incessant a Roar of Guns few even in the Army & Navy had ever heard before," declared Lord Howe's secretary, Ambrose Serle. Awestruck spectators on the shore at Bushwick watched as four thousand British troops swarmed toward Manhattan to "the strains of exciting music, and the peals of thundering guns, the tall ships vomiting flames and murderous shot" under "rolling volleys of smoke." The militia ran off in fear, and the British waded ashore without opposition. "The rogues have not learnt manners yet," scoffed one of His Majesty's officers; "they cannot look gentlemen in the face." By early afternoon the British had taken possession of the Robert Murray farm—atop what is now Murray Hill—and were prepared to descend on the city below.

Washington, racing down from Harlem Heights, found his troops in complete disarray, "flying in every direction and in the greatest confusion." He tried to rally them in a cornfield north of what is now 42nd Street, near where the Public Library now stands, but the sight of advancing redcoats sent them running again up the Bloomingdale Road (Broadway). At this, witnesses recall, Washington went berserk with rage. "The General was so exasperated," a Virginia officer reported, "that he struck several officers in their flight, three times dashed his hat on the ground, and at last exclaimed, 'Good God! Have I got such troops as those?'" Aides led him away, fearful he would be captured. The disgraceful rout became a more orderly retreat only after his panic-stricken soldiers reached McGowan's Pass at the south end of Harlem Plains.

In the meantime, Howe arrived at the Murray farm and stopped to wait for reinforcements—or perhaps, according to legend, to have some cake and wine with Mrs. Murray, who saw a chance to distract him from the business at hand. Howe's dallying gave Putnam and the rest of the army, guided by Lieutenant Aaron Burr, time to slip out of New York along the Greenwich Road and reach Harlem Heights before the red-coats crossed Manhattan to cut them off. They left behind about half of the army's heavy guns and what Greene called "a prodigious deal of baggage and stores."

The city itself was in a state of utter chaos as thousands of civilians, including the last remaining members of the Mechanics Committee, scrambled to get out as well. Only a few thousand remained when some officers from the fleet rowed ashore that evening to announce that New York was again in British hands. A small but delirious crowd of Tories paraded them "upon their shoulders about the streets and behaved in all respects, women as well as men, like overjoyed Bedlamites," Ambrose Serle report-ed. "One thing is worth remarking," he added: "A woman pulled down the rebel stan-dard upon the fort, and a woman hoisted up in its stead His Majesty's flag after tram-pling the other under foot with the most contemptuous indignation."

The next day, September 16, a reconnaissance party of Connecticut rangers tan-gled with an advance column of several hundred redcoats on a farm near present-day 106th Street and West End Avenue. As the rangers pulled back toward the Hollow Way, a ravine where West 125th Street now meets the Hudson River, enemy buglers taunted them with the same call that traditionally ended a successful fox-hunt. "I never felt such a sensation before," wrote Washington's adjutant, Joseph Reed, who witnessed the retreat. "It seemed to crown our disgrace." Perhaps even more sharply stung—no one appreciated better than Virginians the upper-class associations of fox-hunting—Wash-ington ordered up reinforcements and counterattacked, driving the redcoats back through a buckwheat field in the vicinity of 120th Street and Broadway before breaking off the engagement two hours later. About thirty Americans and fourteen British had been killed. This "brisk little skirmish," as Washington called it, was the first time sol-diers under his command had bested the British in a stand-up fight; it did much to lift their flagging spirits.

HEAVEN IN FLAMES

Patriot morale got another boost from the conflagration that engulfed the now-occupied city soon after midnight on the twenty-first. It began, apparently, in a tavern called the Fighting Cocks that stood on a wharf near Whitehall Slip. From there, driven by a brisk wind from the southwest, the flames raced uptown across Bridge, Stone, Marketfield, and Beaver streets, sweeping through whole blocks of houses and shops at a time. According to one newspaper account, the confused shouting of men and the terrified shrieks of women and children, "joined to the roaring of the flames, the crash of falling houses and the widespread ruin . . . formed a scene of horror great beyond description." Clutching what few possessions they had managed to gather up, hundreds of people plunged through the heat and choking smoke toward the relative safety of the Com-mon, "where in despair they fell cowering on the grass." Far to the north, on Harlem Heights, Alexander Graydon watched the blaze grow until "the heavens appeared in flames."

At two A.M. the wind shifted to the southeast, driving the flames across Broadway, then up toward Trinity Church, which was consumed in minutes. A contingent of rebels watching from Paulus Hook, across the river in New Jersey, cheered as its steeple collapsed in "a lofty pyramid of fire." St. Paul's, half a dozen blocks to the north, escaped a similar fate thanks to the efforts of a hastily organized bucket brigade. British soldiers and seamen were rushed in at daybreak to provide assistance, but not until the blaze reached the empty lots north and west of St. Paul's, around midmorning, did it finally burn out. Smoldering in the mile-long swath of destruction were the ruins of better than five hundred dwellings, one-fourth of the city's total.

Many jumped to the conclusion that the fire was the work of rebel arsonists. Furious mobs killed several suspicious characters during the night—one or two for carrying "matches and combustibles under their clothes," another for "cutting the handles of fire buckets," a couple of others for being "in houses with fire-brands in their hands." Various eyewitnesses remembered other things as well: missing fire-alarm bells, broken fire engines and pumps, empty cisterns, and wagonloads of combustible materials concealed in cellars and basements.

Military authorities rounded up about two hundred men and women for questioning, among them a young captain in the American forces named Nathan Hale. Hale confessed that he had come to New York to spy on the British, and because he was out of uniform, General Howe had no choice under the rules of war but to have him hanged the next morning. Hale's final words from the gallows (most likely located in an artillery park at today's Third Avenue and 66th Street)—"I only regret that I have but one life to lose for my country," paraphrased from Addison's play, *Cato*—made him famous but didn't settle the question of whether he, or anyone else, had attempted to burn the city. Although no credible evidence of deliberate arson ever came to light, it was Washington who delivered the final verdict while studying the red glow on the horizon from the balcony of the Roger Morris house on Harlem Heights: "Providence, or some good honest fellow, has done more for us than we were disposed to do for ourselves."

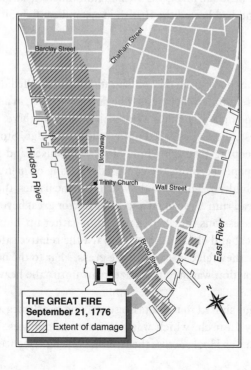

THE GREAT FIRE
September 21, 1776
Extent of damage

FINALE

The clash on Harlem Heights convinced the ever cautious Howe to encircle the American army rather than attack head-on. On October 12, three weeks after the fire, he took four thousand redcoats up the East River to Long Island Sound and landed on a peninsula called Throg's Neck (Fort Schuyler Park in the Bronx). Their task was to seize King's Bridge, a few miles to the west and Washington's only means of escape across the Harlem River to the mainland. A small party of riflemen gave the redcoats some trouble at Westchester Creek, however, and Howe decided to wait for reinforcements. He waited for six days, then put everybody back on the boats and shifted the attack three miles north to Pell's Point (Pelham Bay Park), where a much smaller force of Americans held him up again on the road to the little hamlet of Eastchester. Washington, meanwhile, moved his army off Manhattan up to White Plains, leaving only a twelve-hundred-man garrison at Fort Washington.

Howe finally worked his way up through Eastchester and New Rochelle to White Plains, which he attacked and drove Washington out of on the twenty-seventh. Again he didn't pursue the Americans, this time because he needed to return to Manhattan and deal with Fort Washington, which continued to threaten his communications with New York. On November fifteenth, following a heavy bombardment from British batteries on the east side of the Harlem River and a frigate anchored in the Hudson, about twenty thousand Hessians and redcoats converged on Washington Heights. After a brief struggle, the fort's bedraggled and vastly outnumbered defenders surrendered. "A great many of them were lads under fifteen and old men, and few had the appearance of soldiers," observed one British officer. "Their odd figures frequently excited the laughter of our soldiers." Washington, who had meanwhile divided his army and taken part of it across the Hudson to New Jersey, watched in horror from Fort Lee as the last American forces on Manhattan were marched off into captivity. He wouldn't set foot on Manhattan again for seven years.

The fall of New York didn't doom the Revolution, as many on both sides had initially expected, but it did change matters profoundly. All told, the American army had taken a terrible beating trying to hold the city. Some thirty-six hundred men lay dead or wounded, and another four thousand, along with three hundred officers, were prisoners of the enemy. Thousands of others had simply gone home in disgust or despair. Mountains of ammunition and equipment had been lost.

This dismal accounting persuaded many army officers and members of Congress to think twice about the best way to carry on the struggle. Lee's notion of relying on militia and home-grown amateur officers seemed discredited; Washington, among others, now believed the Revolution wouldn't survive unless Congress created a standing army of regular, professional troops who obeyed their officers, held their ground under fire, and didn't head for home whenever they wanted (to which Henry Knox added pleas for a military academy to provide the army with proper officers).

Similarly, the loss of Long Island in August and of Fort Washington in November appeared to demonstrate that the British couldn't be beaten in a Bunker Hill-style confrontation. Instead, Washington decided, he would endeavor to keep the army intact, avoiding the big battle that could lose everything and concentrating instead on striking the smaller, sharper blows that would wear away the enemy's resolve. Thus when Howe finally retired to New York City for the winter, Washington lashed back with surprise raids on the small British garrisons at Trenton and Princeton in late December and early January, two modest but morale-building victories.

Howe would receive the Order of Bath for capturing New York, but his foot-dragging was the subject of recurring controversy. In 1778, after the loss of Saratoga, he was recalled in favor of Clinton and Cornwallis, both of whom promised to be more aggressive generals. Fortunes also changed for the English radicals who between 1764 and 1776 had spoken out so vigorously on behalf of the colonies. With a few prominent exceptions, they were thrown off balance by the American demand for independence, for while they accepted it as a legitimate expression of the popular will, colonial self-determination would blast all hopes that reformers on both sides of the Atlantic could work together toward the same objective.

Republicanism, too, was a problem. By rejecting monarchy and aristocracy, by insisting on the primacy of reason over tradition and traditional authority, and indeed by at least asserting the principle of full political equality, the Americans had moved far beyond all but their most radical counterparts in Britain.

The outbreak of fighting, finally, dampened public enthusiasm for America. British merchants, fearful of the loss of trade, rallied behind the ministry and sent addresses of loyalty to the crown; British crowds turned increasingly patriotic, snapping the connection between radicalism and working-class discontent. Pottery manufacturer Josiah Wedgwood, a longtime supporter of colonial protest, observed ruefully that the town of Newcastle "went wild with joy" when word arrived that His Majesty's army had captured New York. Even in London, once a stronghold of pro-American sentiment, there was a noticeable decline of enthusiasm for the rebel cause. Not for another generation, by which time the world had greatly changed, would British and American radicals again come within hailing distance of one another.

16

The Gibraltar of North America

For the thousands of Tories who fled New York between 1774 and 1776, its capture by the British was the signal for a jubilant homecoming. Sporting red badges in their hats as tokens of loyalty, they streamed into town behind Howe's troops; the general's personal chaplain, inspired by this devotion to the royal cause, reopened St. Paul's Chapel with a sermon on Jeremiah 12:15: "And it shall come to pass, after I have plucked them out, I will return again and have compassion on them, each man to his heritage, and every man to his land." Hundreds of people thronged City Hall in October to sign a memorial congratulating General Howe and his brother on their victory. Another crowd turned out in November to sign a "declaration of dependence," reaffirming their "loyalty to our Sovereign, against the strong tide of oppression and tyranny, which had almost overwhelmed this Land."

By early 1777 the Tory flood tide had lifted New York's population to some twelve thousand; two years later, swollen by successive waves of Tory refugees from elsewhere in the colonies, the city had a record thirty-three thousand inhabitants. Conspicuous among the returnees was James Rivington, who won an appointment as "Printer to His Majesty the King" and resumed publication of his *New-York Gazetteer* (later the *Royal Gazette*). The *Gazetteer*'s reappearance, along with Hugh Gaine's *Weekly Mercury* and James Robertson's *Royal American Gazette*, would make New York the headquarters of Tory opinion for the remainder of the war. Also back in town, having been run out of Virginia by the rebels, was former governor Dunmore; joining him, at one point, were four other colonial governors and swarms of lesser imperial functionaries with similar stories to tell. All told, an estimated fifty thousand Tories had gathered behind British lines in and around New York City by 1782.

Those were the civilians. As the war waxed and waned in distant theaters, tens of thousands of troops also shifted in and out of the city—Waldeckers in their gaudy yellow-trimmed cocked hats, huge mustachioed Hessians, kilted and tartaned Highlanders, black-capped Anspach grenadiers—all trailed by numerous dependents and camp followers. Between November 1777 and July 1778 their numbers leaped from five thousand to nearly twenty thousand. By December 1779 they had fallen to four thousand, only to rise again to ten thousand by August 1781 and seventeen thousand by December 1782.

Organized rebel activity on Long Island and in much of Westchester County came to an abrupt end. Soon after Washington's retreat from Brooklyn Heights, perhaps as many as five thousand patriots from Kings, Queens, and Suffolk counties fled across the Sound to Connecticut. In their absence one town after another disbanded its committees, repudiated the authority of Congress, and drafted congratulatory addresses to General Howe and Governor Tryon. Tryon toured the island in October 1776, handing out thousands of certificates of loyalty and administering an oath of allegiance to the militia in his capacity as head of the provincial forces. In Kings County, 593 out of the 630 militiamen took the oath; in Queens, roughly twelve hundred of a possible fifteen hundred did likewise, while some thirteen hundred "freeholders and inhabitants" put their names on a declaration denouncing the "infatuated conduct of the Congress" and describing how they had "steadfastly maintained their royal principles." The army obligingly sent eight hundred stands of arms to Queens, where they were received "with demonstrations of joy."

Military recruiters had an easy time of it for the next few years. Long Island men flocked to Tory militia regiments under the command of Oliver De Lancey, brother of the late governor. In Westchester County, Oliver's nephew James De Lancey (not to be confused with James De Lancey Jr., the late governor's son) raised a troop of some five hundred light horse to hunt for deserters and patrol the regular army's supply routes through the Neutral Ground—a thirty-mile-wide no-man's-land that ran north of Morrisania to the mouth of the Croton River, marking the unofficial boundary between British- and American-held territory.

Thousands of other New Yorkers joined a parade of colorfully named Tory units— the King's American Regiment, the King's Orange Rangers, the Loyal American Regiment, the British Legion, and the Volunteers of Ireland, among others—some of which would see action as far away as Georgia, Canada, and Jamaica. In all, around sixteen thousand New York men bore arms for the king as against thirty-six thousand for Congress. Over the winter of 1779–80, when Washington was rumored to be preparing an attack on New York, it took only five days to raise two thousand volunteers for the city's defense.

Female Tories served the British as spies and couriers. Lorenda Holmes had carried messages to Howe's forces in 1776. Captured by rebel committeemen, she was stripped naked and exposed to a patriot crowd but, she wrote, "received no wounds or bruises from them only shame and horror of the mind." Holmes carried on, helping to slip loyalists through rebel lines into occupied New York City. When the rebels apprehended her a second time, they held her right foot on hot coals until it was badly burned.

It was men and women such as these, said one British commander, that made New York the principal bulwark of royal power and influence in the colonies. The "Gibraltar of North America" he called it—a proud allusion to the royal fortress that was, even as he spoke, standing fast against the combined forces of France and Spain.

"TOUJOURS DE LA GAIETÉ"

Superficially, at least, the British occupation restored some of the prosperity that New York had enjoyed in the 1750s. The city's rebounding civilian population opened lucrative new markets for area farmers and, after years of nonimportation, for British manufacturers eager to reduce inventories of clothing, hardware, and other finished goods. Provisioning the huge military machine—five hundred ships jammed the harbor within a month after the city's fall—generated windfall profits for the Waltons, Bayards, Lows, and other Tory merchants. When Parliament authorized a fleet of 120-odd privateers to be fitted out in New York to prey on rebel shipping, it created work for thousands of seamen and attracted immense quantities of goods and money into the local economy. (In one six-month period, between September 1778 and March 1779, privateers came in with 165 prizes worth over six hundred thousand pounds.) Shopkeepers, cloakmakers, milliners, dressmakers, wigmakers, and coachmakers were busy again trying to meet the demand of His Majesty's officers and their wives for all the comforts of home. There was money to be made, too, in illicit trade between the city and rebel-held areas of Westchester, New Jersey, and Connecticut, despite efforts of authorities on both sides to stamp it out. Alexander Hamilton calculated in 1782 that upstate patriots were buying thirty thousand pounds' worth of luxuries from New York merchants every year, plus an additional eighty thousand from sources in New Jersey, Pennsylvania, and New England. Cartloads of specie were said to arrive in the city every week.

Thanks to this sudden wealth, plus General Howe's own weakness for extravagant living—"Toujours de la gaieté!" he cried as the occupation got underway—New York's fashionable classes were soon caught up in a social whirl that would have been unthinkable only a year or two before. Fox-hunting and golf made a fast comeback, dispelling the gloom of republican austerity. Billiards were all the rage at the King's Head Tavern. Horse racing returned to Hempstead Plains, and its popularity prompted the opening of a new course, Ascot Heath, on the Flatland Plains, five miles east of the Brooklyn ferry. Two rival cricket clubs, the Brooklyn and Greenwich, squared off on Bowling Green or near Cannon's Tavern on Corlear's Hook. Ladies and gentlemen of quality entertained themselves with saltwater bathing parties and concerts, and every two weeks at the City Tavern on Broadway there was a "Garrison Assembly" where local girls danced with dashing officers like the young Captain Horatio Nelson—"genuine, smooth-faced, fresh-coloured" Englishmen "of family and consideration" (as the American prisoner of war Alexander Graydon described them). The John Street Theater, renamed the Theatre Royal, reopened in January 1777 with a production of *Tom Thumb*. Some 150 performances followed over the next half-dozen years, including works by Shakespeare, Garrick, and Sheridan. The actors, mostly officers, were fondly known as "Clinton's Thespians." Audiences usually numbered around 750.

Especially lavish festivities accompanied the Queen's Birthday celebration of 1780, when "a transparent painting of their majesties at full length, in their royal robes" was suspended over the gate of the fort and "illuminated with a beautiful variety of different colored lamps." The presentation of this tribute was followed by an elegant ball and formal supper. "It is said that the ball cost above 2000 Guineas, and they had over 300 dishes," the Rev. Schaukirk noted sourly in his diary. When Prince William Henry (later King William IV) visited New York in September 1781, the social whirl became positively frantic. The prince especially liked the informal skating parties on the Fresh

Water Pond, during which an attendant pushed him around in a chair mounted with runners.

Eating and drinking societies like the Old Church and King Club again crowded into the private rooms of Hull's Tavern or the King's Head, roaring out their loyalty to the crown in song and endless toasts. The St. Andrew's Society, the St. George Society, and other fraternal organizations resumed their annual rites with gusto and aggressively loyalist overtones. In March 1779 the Volunteers of Ireland, a British regiment organized in Ireland that had arrived in New York the previous June, sought to win Irish recruits to the British cause by staging one of the first St. Patrick's Day parades in the city's history. According to the *Weekly Mercury*, "the Volunteers of Ireland, preceded by their band of music," marched out to the Bowery, where a dinner was provided for five hundred people.

"EVERY NEGRO WHO SHALL DESERT THE REBELL STANDDARD"

If anyone had reason to rejoice at the British occupation, it was New York's suddenly flourishing population of runaway slaves and freedmen. Many rebel slaveowners in the city had manumitted their slaves after 1775—partly in response to increasing immigration (which according to one traveler had already produced a surplus of cheap free labor in the city), partly in recognition that human bondage violated their professed attachment to liberty and natural rights, and partly because, fleeing the British invasion, they didn't want the continued trouble and expense of extra dependents.

Besides, in December 1775 Lord Dunmore, governor of Virginia, issued a proclamation freeing all of that colony's indentured servants and slaves who were willing to support the crown. As word of Dunmore's proclamation spread north in 1776, nervous masters everywhere noted the rising numbers of runaways and fretted about the growing likelihood of a black insurgency. Within months, hundreds of slaves from the New York–New Jersey area ran off to seek refuge within the British lines. Some reportedly joined regular British units in preparation for the August invasion of Long Island. General Nathanael Greene warned Washington that eight hundred blacks were drilling on Staten Island, and the Provincial Congress provided a detachment of militia to "guard against the insurrection of slaves." Once His Majesty's forces moved in, moreover, they found area slaves ready and willing to help them plunder the property of their masters. As one patriot recalled many years later, "The negroes of [Long] Island were all Tories, and pointed out to the enemy the places where goods and plate had been concealed."

During the next half-dozen years, additional thousands of slaves from Long Island, Staten Island, New Jersey, and Westchester County ran off—a revolution-within-a-revolution that dwarfed the events of 1712 and 1741. (Fully two-thirds of the slaves in Westchester, nearly twenty-two hundred people in all, were said to have fled their masters in the course of the war.) At one point, the volume of fugitives from New Jersey became so great that city officials ordered Hudson River ferryboat operators to stop transporting blacks until further notice. New Jersey's rebel government underscored the magnitude of the problem by advising masters to transport their slaves into the interior of the state, from where it would be more difficult to reach British lines.

The movement of runaways and freedmen into the city quickened after June 1779 when General Clinton, following Dunmore's lead, issued a proclamation of his own promising "every Negro who shall desert the Rebell Standdard full security to follow within these lines any Occupation which he shall think Proper." Many chose to take up arms against their former masters and enlisted in one or another of several army units composed of blacks from all over the colonies, among them the Black Pioneers and Guides, the Royal African Regiment, the Ethiopian Regiment, and the Black Brigade. Led by the dashing Captain Tye, an escaped slave from New Jersey, the Black Brigade won notoriety for its lightning raids on patriot farms and villages in nearby Monmouth County. As early as 1777 a unit of Virginia freedmen occupied a redoubt guarding the strategically important Boston Post Road (now Van Cortlandt Avenue East in the Bronx); area residents called it the "Negro Fort."

Numerous other fugitives served with regular British units as pilots, guides, and couriers or worked as laborers for the Quartermaster General's Department, the Wagonmaster, or the Forage and Provision departments of His Majesty's army. Still others found employment as cartmen, carpenters, and the like, trades from which they had hitherto been excluded. More than a few married, established families, and sent their children to the school for blacks opened in 1778 by the Anglican Church. Many found shelter in or around various "Negro Barracks" located on Broadway, Church Street, and elsewhere. When they died, they were interred in the Negro Burial Ground above Chambers Street—as happened to "great numbers" of Virginia runaways, whose camp in an open field on the west side of Broadway was swept by a smallpox epidemic. The burgeoning numbers, autonomy, and self-confidence of New York's freedmen were unmistakable and got a good deal of attention throughout the colonies. "Ethiopian Balls," where African Americans and British officers mingled freely, drew particular criticism in the rebel press.

"HERRINGS IN A BARREL"

Rich men, officers, and runaway slaves excepted, most inhabitants of occupied New York had little to cheer about. Their hopes for the prompt restoration of civilian government proved embarrassingly naive. General Howe imposed martial law on the city and environs and resisted every appeal to relent, as did his successors, Generals Henry Clinton (1778–82) and Sir Guy Carleton (1782–83). Year after discouraging year, the provincial assembly, city council, and courts remained officially dormant. Governor William Tryon and Mayor David Mathews, though restored to their offices, exercised little or no real power. Nor did William Smith, former stalwart of the Whig Triumvirate, who showed up in New York in 1778 and accepted appointment as chief justice of the colony.

Under martial law, a commandant, appointed by the commander-in-chief, exercised more or less dictatorial power over the day-to-day administration of municipal affairs. Answerable to the commandant was a small coterie of other officials and bureaucrats. A police department enforced military regulations, maintained a night watch, and regulated ferries (by the end of 1780 a two-judge police court had been set up to try cases involving civilians). Andrew Elliot, head of the department for many years, also supervised the collection of customs as superintendent of exports and imports. A Barracks Board arranged housing for soldiers. The Chamber of Commerce, which resumed its meetings in 1779, informally advised the commander-in-chief and commandant on economic matters. Two volunteer companies, the Military Club and the Fire Club, equipped themselves with buckets and pumps to protect the town from the kind of disaster that befell it in 1776.

General Clinton and other officers talked of the need "to gain the hearts & subdue the minds of America," but the military regime produced exactly the opposite effect. Merchants lost patience with the maddeningly arbitrary system of restrictions, passes, and permits; it didn't help that the wharves and warehouses of loyal traders were often summarily commandeered for military use, or that the Royal Navy routinely harassed privateers on the grounds that they lured away too many of His Majesty's sailors. Merchants and seamen alike railed against the press gangs that periodically scoured the city to fill out crews. One "very hot press" in 1781 carried off several hundred able-bodied men, whose affections for the crown must have been sorely tried as a result. White New Yorkers of all classes disapproved of the city's increasingly conspicuous population of free blacks and runaway slaves. Oliver De Lancey bowed to the prevailing opinion by discharging "all Negroes Mullattoes and other Improper Persons" from his corps in 1777.

Conflicts with poorly paid, poorly provisioned, often poorly disciplined troops sharpened civilian discontent. The first redcoats to enter town in September 1776 went on a rampage, looting private houses and vandalizing City Hall, where they smashed equipment belonging to King's College, mutilated paintings, and destroyed books. On New Year's Eve 1777, after performing in a play entitled *The Devil to Pay in the West Indies*, a party of drunken officers—one dressed up like Old Nick himself, complete with horns and tail—disrupted services at the John Street Methodist Church. Nor was that the worst of it. "I could narrate many and very frightful occurrences of theft, fraud, robbery, and murder by the English soldiers which their love of drink excited," said one dismayed German officer.

Elliot's police proved next to useless in dealing with the problem, and the police court was thought unreliable because it functioned without the juries that had always been considered a bulwark of English liberty. Civilian complaints against military personnel rarely got anywhere. Courts-martial tended to sympathize with the men in His Majesty's services and were notoriously lenient on officers accused of wrongdoing; everyone indeed knew of cases in which officers charged with robbing, assaulting, raping, and even murdering civilians had gone free.

Military officials appeared equally unwilling or unable to remedy the city's desperate shortage of adequate shelter. One-quarter to one-third of its housing stock had been destroyed by the great fire of September 1776 (which drove three hundred persons to seek admission to the almshouse) and by a second conflagration in August 1778. Agents of the Barracks Board marked rebel-owned buildings with the initials *G. R.* (for George Rex) and confiscated them for the use of refugees and troops. The Baptist Church, the Brick Presbyterian Church, the First Presbyterian Church, the South Dutch Church, the Middle Dutch Church, the North Dutch Church, the French Church, the Scotch Presbyterian Church, and the Quaker Meeting House—tangible symbols of the dissenting principles to which many loyalists traced the Revolution—were commandeered for barracks, stables, prisons, or storehouses. (Presbyterian churches everywhere on Long Island were also routinely vandalized after 1776.) The two chapels of Trinity Church, St. Paul's and St. George's, escaped such ill treatment, although King's College was used as a military hospital. The Mill Street synagogue, occupied by a loyalist remnant of the Shearith Israel congregation, suffered no appreciable damage either.

Sporadic efforts were made to ease the crisis by regulating the influx of refugees and shifting troops to camps outside the city; at the end of 1777 Commandant General James Robertson also authorized the city vestry to employ rents from Whig-owned property for the relief of the poor and municipal improvements. No steps were taken, however, to rebuild or enlarge the city's supply of housing. With blocks of scorched and crumbling ruins at their backs, civilians and military personnel waged prolonged, sometimes violent struggles for the possession of anything with four walls and a roof. Rents rose 400 percent in the first year of the occupation alone. Few households got through the war without a redcoat or two quartered in a spare room or seated at the dinner table, many with wives and children in tow.

Hundreds, perhaps thousands, of destitute refugees had nowhere to go but "Canvas Town," a pestiferous camp of makeshift tents that sprawled west from the foot of Broad Street through the ruins left by the 1776 fire. The results of so many people jammed together "like herrings in a barrel, most of them very dirty," as the Englishman Nicholas Cresswell observed, were the foul odors that often left city residents gasping for air. "If any author had an inclination to write a treatise upon stinks," Cresswell sniffed, "he never could meet with more subject matter than in New York."

Food and fuel were as hard to come by as fresh air. Within one year of the British takeover, driven by the combination of military and civilian demand, the cost of food in the city jumped 800 percent. Higher prices didn't, however, generate increased supplies. International law at the time allowed armies a right to the "contribution" of food and other essential material—at a fair rate of compensation—from populations under their protection. For farmers in the hinterland of occupied New York, this meant surrendering crops, animals, and equipment, on demand, to army foragers, who paid them with certificates drawn on the Office of Forage in New York City. Inasmuch as the army never matched the going rate for what it took—and from time to time actually froze prices at absurdly low levels—growers and stockmen quickly learned to divert what they produced into the city's flourishing black market or else to restrict production to the bare minimum.

Hard-pressed quartermasters took to importing food, at great expense, from elsewhere in the Empire. Between 1776 and 1778 victualing fleets arrived from Ireland and England with twenty-eight hundred tons of beef, ten thousand tons of pork, twenty thousand tons of bread and flour, a thousand tons of butter, and twenty-four hundred tons of oatmeal and rice. There was never enough to go around, however. Prices continued to go up, not down, and poorer New Yorkers found themselves trying to keep body and soul together on a diet of rice or baked beans. When a French fleet briefly blockaded the city in the summer of 1778, food supplies dwindled so quickly that officials talked of evacuating everyone to avert massive famine. It was the same story in 1779, when mountains of Iroquois corn destined for the army were seized by patriot forces. Periodic epidemics of yellow fever, cholera, and smallpox only underscored the appalling circumstances to which many residents of the city had been reduced.

"BLOOD-SUCKING HARPIES"

The ultimate insult to the patience and principles of loyal New Yorkers wasn't red tape, crime, overcrowding, or chronic shortages—all of which might have been bearable, somehow—but the miasma of decadence and corruption that gradually enveloped the city. Pastor Schaukirk never quite comprehended how the city's most privileged and powerful residents could live so extravagantly at a time of widespread privation. One day he noticed that "the walk by the ruins of Trinity Church and its grave-yard has been railed in and painted green; benches placed there and many lamps fixed in the trees, for gentlemen and ladies to walk and sit there in the evening. A band plays while the commander is present, and a sentry is placed there, that none of the common people may intrude." As if this weren't bad enough, Schaukirk continued, "a house opposite is adapted to accommodate the ladies or officer's women, while many honest people . . . cannot get a house or lodging to live in or get their living."

Respectable New Yorkers, according to Judge Jones, took particular exception to the vices of sixty-year-old Commandant Robertson. These included openly keeping a mistress, "smelling after every giddy girl" who caught his eye, and "waddling about town with a couple of young tits about twelve years of age under each arm." Visitors gaped at the numbers and brazenness of the city's prostitutes. Said one after attending services at St. Paul's Chapel: "This is a very neat church and some of the handsomest and best-dressed ladies I have ever seen in America. I believe most of them are whores." Patriots up and down the continent were scandalized by stories about the city's commissary of prisoners, a Boston Tory named Joshua Loring, who allegedly promoted an affair between his wife and General William Howe in exchange for a free hand with the shady wheeling and dealing that would make him rich before the war was over. "Profaneness and Wickedness prevaileth," cried Pastor Schaukirk. "Lord have Mercy!"

Not since the days of Governor Fletcher had official cynicism and venality bedded down so amiably together. One royal investigator reported "peculation in every profitable branch of the service." According to Jones, army quartermasters, barrack-masters, and commissaries—"blood-sucking harpies" to a man—made away with no less than five million pounds by the end of the war. Even the royal chimney sweep saw his opportunities and took them. "He keeps a half-dozen negroes," said an irate German officer, "each of whom can sweep at least twenty chimneys a day, and often must clean more; and for each chimney his master, who sits quietly at home, is paid two shillings. . . . The negroes get nothing out of it save coarse food and rags." General Howe pocketed money intended for farmers whose cattle had been taken by the army. Admiral Arbuthnot sold blank warrants allowing merchants to conduct illegal trade. Proving that civilians could feed at the same trough, Mayor Mathews embezzled money, stole provisions intended for the poor, charged excessive fees, and ran protection rackets.

"KENNEL, YE SONS OF BITCHES!"

The most chilling stories to come out of occupied New York, however, concerned the thousands of American prisoners of war held in and around the city. Captured officers were permitted to find private accommodations in boardinghouses and taverns, but not common soldiers. As many as eight hundred at a time were jammed into the New Gaol, now called the Provost's Guard or Prison, on the northeast corner of City Hall Park. Hundreds of others languished in Livingstons' Liberty Street "sugar house"—a cavernous building formerly used for refining and storing sugar. Sugar houses owned by the Van Cortlandts (near the northwest corner of Trinity churchyard) and by the Rhinelanders (at the corner of Rose and Duane) were also used to hold prisoners, as were the Middle Dutch Church on Nassau Street and the North Dutch Church on William.

Conditions in the sugar houses and the Provost's Guard dismayed even the most unyielding Tories. Hungry, half-naked prisoners huddled together in appalling squalor, racked by waves of smallpox, yellow fever, and cholera. Many starved or froze to death after scratching out final messages on the walls with their fingernails, and every morning the "dead cart" rumbled up to remove the bodies of those who had succumbed the night before. Abraham Leggett, confined in a room of the Provost's with a dozen other rebels, remembered being thrown some raw salt beef and spoiled bread. "As soon as the bread fell on the floor it Took legs and Ran in all Directions," he wrote.

Two men bore special responsibility for these horrors: Commissary Joshua Loring, who made a fortune selling off provisions meant for the prisoners, and the sadistic Provost Marshal William Cunningham, who had once been roughed up by the Sons of Liberty and now took his revenge in merciless brutality. Every evening, Alexander Graydon recalled, "he would traverse his domain with a whip in his hand, sending his prisoners to bed, with the ruffian like *Tattoo* of *Kennel ye sons of bitches! Kennel, G—d damn ye!*" Some years after the war, on his way to the gallows for forgery, Cunningham confessed to murdering as many as two thousand American prisoners by starvation, hanging, or poisoning their flour rations with arsenic. Typically, he said, inmates were hustled out at midnight, bound and gagged, to be hanged from a hastily erected gallows on Barrack (now Chambers) Street. Area residents were under strict orders to shutter their windows and say nothing.

The suffering inflicted on the inmates of the sugar houses and Provost's Guard paled, even so, by comparison with the agonies of rebel prisoners confined to prison ships anchored across the East River in Wallabout Bay. All told, the British employed at least twenty of these ships in the course of the war, using them first for captives taken during the Battle of Long Island and then exclusively for seamen taken on the high seas. The conditions on board were atrocious—hundreds of men packed together in squalid, reeking holds without adequate food or water and brutalized by their guards. Alexander Coffin remembered that his eleven hundred fellow captives on the *Jersey*, most infamous of the prison ships, were "mere walking skeletons . . . overrun with lice from head to foot." Dysentery was rampant, said Christopher Hawkins, and because only two prisoners at a time were allowed to relieve themselves on the upper deck, he and the others below spent many nights smeared with "bloody and loathsome filth." Every morning

The prison ship *Jersey*, by James Ryder van Brunt, 1876. (General Research. The New York Public Library. Astor, Lenox and Tilden Foundations)

the ships awakened to the call "Prisoners, turn out your dead!" Before the war ended 11,500 men had perished, their bodies simply cast overboard or buried in mass graves on the shore. Bones littered the beach for years.

"ONE GENERAL SCENE OF RAVAGE AND DESOLATION"

Military oppression and corruption also weighed heavily on the areas immediately adjacent to the city. Hessians and redcoats ran amok after the American retreat from Long Island, assaulting civilians and pillaging at will. The Tory Philip Van Cortlandt heard "many frightful accounts" of "cruel unnatural & inhuman" acts committed by His Majesty's troops on friend and foe alike. Soldiers murdered several persons "in cold blood, plunging bayonets in their bodys & then trampling them under their horses feet, women without distinction taken into the lascivious embraces of Officers & then turned over to the Soldiery, torn from the arms of husbands & parents by Brutal force." Colonel Stephen Kemble reported that rampaging redcoats had destroyed "all the fruits of the Earth without regard to Loyalists or Rebels, the property of both being equaly a prey to them."

Little of this havoc was accidental. From the very beginning of the war it was taken for granted, especially among the subordinate officers responsible for day-to-day discipline, that the Americans were a cowardly, contemptible rabble—either descended (like the third- and fourth-generation Dutch of Long Island) from Europe's most benighted and boorish classes or (as in the case of New York's burgeoning Irish population) the genuine article, fresh off the boat. Rebel and Tory alike would benefit from a dose of Britannic wrath, wrote Lord Francis Rawdon, Sir Henry Clinton's aide-de-camp, in September 1776. Only by giving "free liberty to the soldiers to ravage at will" could "these infatuated wretches" be made to realize "what a calamity war is." "At heart they are all rebels," agreed a high-ranking Hessian.

The yearning to bayonet and torch reached new heights in 1780 when William Franklin, Benjamin's Tory son and former royal governor of New Jersey, organized the Board of Associated Loyalists in New York. Franklin's plan was to unite supporters of the crown for self-preservation and revenge, and until Generals Clinton and Carleton put them on a short leash, the four hundred armed Associators compiled a record of atrocities unrivaled on either side. They plundered the country around New York, Jones wrote tersely, "without distinction of Whigs or Tories, Loyalists or rebels."

Besides Associators, residents of Westchester County had to contend with a vicious little civil war between De Lancey's "Refugees" and irregular "Cowboys," who pillaged indiscriminately while pursuing rebel "Skinners" through the Neutral Ground. On Staten Island, said Lord Rawdon, "a girl cannot step into the bushes to pluck a rose without running the most imminent risk of being ravished" by soldiers "as riotous as Satyrs." On Long Island, hundreds, often thousands, of regulars were stationed at Bedford, Flushing, Brooklyn, Newtown, Jamaica, Oyster Bay, Hempstead, and other villages after 1776. Clashes with civilians were common and all the more bitter when the troops belonged to one or another of the crown's special black regiments. Officers and public officials with the authority to protect the local population did little or nothing. The Nassau Blues, a regiment of provincial troops commanded by Colonel William Axtell of Flatbush, entered local lore as the "Nasty Blues" thanks to their thuggish abuse of the town's residents. Axtell himself allegedly tortured rebel prisoners in the secret chambers of his country house, Melrose Hall.

Always a sore point with loyal civilians was the obligation to quarter troops and prisoners, and the system of "contribution," pitting military foragers against local farmers and householders, ensured that His Majesty's forces would never be really welcome, even among their most patient friends. A more and more frequent source of friction, as time went on, was competition for rapidly dwindling stocks of firewood. After making fast work of city fences and shade trees, scavengers and foraging parties turned their attention to the orchards, woodlots, and forests of upper Manhattan and western Long Island. Not even loyalist estates escaped the ax: a Tory regiment stripped Morrisania of livestock and leveled 450 acres of timberland.

The heaviest cutting occurred during the terrible winter of 1779–80, when snow fell almost every day from early November to March and the East River, Hudson River, Long Island Sound, and the Upper Bay became a solid mass of ice. Military authorities couldn't, or wouldn't, distribute firewood to civilians, and it became so expensive that some of the city's poorest inhabitants quietly froze to death. A year or so later, while studying the enemy's positions on Manhattan from the New Jersey palisades, Washington was astonished to see that "the island is totally stripped of trees; low bushes . . . appear in places which were covered with wood in the year 1776."

"CURSES UPON THEIR KING"

Only a few years after deliriously celebrating General Howe's seizure of the city, New York's Tories were thus a good deal sadder and wiser. Pastor Schaukirk began to hear it said around town that corruption among "great men" had needlessly prolonged the war, perhaps lost it altogether. Recruiters for Tory units found their work increasingly difficult and started to look elsewhere for men. As General Robertson explained to Lord Jeffrey Amherst: "Those who formerly wishd our approach, and would with Joy have seen Us triumph Over the rebels, will now Arm to defend their All from Undistinguished Plunder." By 1780 or so De Lancey's battalions depended heavily on Connecticut refugees, while the Queen's Rangers, initially made up of New York Tories, consisted chiefly of newly arrived Irish and Scots volunteers.

A few New Yorkers even began working covertly for the Americans. James Rivington, printer of the *Gazette*, became one of Washington's most valuable spies (among other things, he helped obtain the code signals of the British fleet). The well-organized Culper Ring sent female spies into the occupied city, under the pretext of taking baskets of fruit and food to relatives; they relayed information on the disposition of British patrols by hanging a black petticoat and an agreed-upon number of white handkerchiefs from a clothesline behind Mary Underhill's boardinghouse on Queen Street. One of the ring's agents, a woman known only by the code number 355, was captured in 1779 and later perished on board the prison ship *Jersey*. That same year, Elizabeth Burgin eluded arrest after helping over two hundred American prisoners of war escape from the city. "The British offered a bounty of two hundred pounds for taking me," she reported to General Washington. Smuggled down to Philadelphia by friends, she later returned to New York under a flag of truce to retrieve her children.

Toward the end of October 1781, New York Tories received the almost unbelievable news of Cornwallis's capitulation to the combined American and French forces at

Yorktown. A few die-hards insisted that the war could still be won. But the winds of opinion in Britain now began to shift decisively toward peace, and a new government formed by the marquess of Rockingham in mid-1782 announced its willingness to begin negotiations with the rebels.

Sir Guy Carleton, who replaced General Clinton as commander-in-chief in May of that year, won praise in the city for a long-overdue anticorruption drive, but his diligence couldn't dispel the pall of gloom that enveloped New York as the loss of the war became more and more obvious. In August the London government accepted the principle of American independence. William Smith, his hand shaking, wrote that the news "shocks me as much as the Loss of all I had in the World & my Family with it." "God d——n them," ranted William Bayard, booking passage on the first ship back to England. "What is to become of me, sir? I am totally ruined, sir. I have not a guinea, sir." Perhaps as many as eleven hundred other Tories would also leave town before the year was out. Local shops advertised china, glassware, and "Genteel furniture" at fire-sale prices.

Preliminary Articles of Peace were agreed to at the end of November 1782. A royal proclamation in February 1783 officially suspended hostilities; Congress quickly followed suit, clearing the way for the completion of a definitive peace treaty in Paris five months later. New York Tories were dumfounded. When an apprehensive throng gathered in early April to hear the royal proclamation read aloud from the steps of City Hall, they responded with "groans and hisses," showering "bitter reproaches and curses upon their king, for having deserted them in the midst of their calamities." Soldiers walked away from their units. Panicky civilians put their houses up for sale, gathered their belongings, and prepared to flee at a moment's notice; a few, utterly overwhelmed, took their own lives.

THE STATE OF NEW YORK

The hopelessness and fear that engulfed the Tories in occupied New York arose not only from the trauma of defeat but also from the recognition that, while they were waiting for the victory that never came, their enemies had revolutionized the world around them. In 1777 the fourth Provincial Congress adopted a written constitution for the "State" of New York that signaled a break with the past more radical than most Tories would have believed possible only a year or two earlier. It required annual elections for the state assembly. It guaranteed trial by jury, due process of law, and freedom of religious worship. It disestablished the Anglican Church and drew a firm line between church and state by prohibiting any form of religious establishment. It opened all public offices to freeholders of the state and halved the old forty-pound colonial property qualification: henceforth residents of the state owning twenty-pound freeholds, paying two pounds (forty shillings) a year in rent, or admitted as freemen of New York City or Albany could vote in elections for the Assembly. It eliminated representatives from corporations, manors, boroughs, and townships and doubled the number of seats in the Assembly—creating thereby a legislature more responsive to popular opinion. Finally, striking a blow against the old system of viva voce voting, the constitution also required the secret ballot in gubernatorial elections and gave the legislature discretion to experiment with ballots in the elections of its members.

Certain features of the new constitution were more conservative, to be sure. It vested executive authority in a governor elected every three years by male residents of the state owning freeholds worth at least a hundred pounds—a sum big enough to ensure that only men of property and standing would occupy the office. At the same time, the power of the Assembly was checked by creation of a Senate, a Council of Revision (empowered to review and veto all legislative action), and a Council of Appointment (which filled appointive offices above the local level). There was no bill of rights as such, and the constitution was declared to be in effect immediately, without popular ratification. What was more, the preamble of the constitution pointedly warned that popular committees had become the source of "many and great inconveniences" and were no substitute for properly founded governments and the rule of law.

Vis-à-vis New York City, the constitution expressly affirmed the municipal charter granted by Governor Montgomerie in 1730, with one technical adjustment: instead of being appointed by the royal governor and council, the city's principal officials—mayor, recorder, clerk, and sheriff, among others—would henceforth be chosen by the Council of Appointment. New York would thus remain the "free City of itself"—an autonomous private corporation with absolute title to its own personal "estate." Its day-to-day affairs would continue to rest in the hands of a private body legally protected from the will of the now sovereign people. Only freemen and freeholders—the "commonality" of the corporation—elected aldermen, assistants, collectors, and constables (and these "charter" elections remained viva voce for another two decades, in defiance of the trend toward secret ballots).

Just months after the constitution was ratified, George Clinton of Ulster County edged out General Philip Schuyler, John Jay, and John Morin Scott to win the state's first gubernatorial election. Born to a Scotch-Irish Presbyterian family of modest circumstances, Clinton was a country lawyer who got into politics in the mid-1760s as an anti-De Lancey Whig. When the war began he wangled an appointment as a brigadier general in the militia. His ardent republicanism and plainspoken manner made him a hero to the small farmers and tenants who were the backbone of the Revolutionary movement in the Hudson Valley outside New York City. But to the great landowning families he remained an outsider, a "new man" thrust into public life by the press of events, and they regarded his elevation to the state's highest office as a scandal. His "family and connections do not entitle him to so distinguished a predominance," Schuyler protested. "A humiliation to the ruling classes," declared Gouverneur Morris. It humiliated them further that over the next half-dozen years Clinton built a devoted following among other "new men" who found their way into the state legislature—radical Whig farmers, shopkeepers, schoolmasters, and exiled workingmen from the city like Daniel Dunscomb (the cooper and former chairman of the Mechanics Committee), Abraham Brasher (silversmith), Abraham P. Lott (a baker active in the Sons of Liberty), and Robert Boyd (blacksmith). Although "unimproved by education and unrefined by honor," in Robert R. Livingston's phrase, the Clintonians were ambitious, upwardly mobile men who saw in independence the promise of both republicanism and opportunity. Several, including Clinton himself, would go on to amass significant fortunes.

Their immediate objective, however, was the suppression of Toryism in the state, and in 1778 the Clintonian-dominated legislature established a permanent Commission for Detecting and Defeating Conspiracies. Dozens of subsequent laws gave the new commission virtually unlimited authority to ferret out "inimicals" and subjected them to increasingly harsh penalties. The Act to Regulate Elections (1778) deprived disloyal persons of the right to vote or hold office. The Banishing Act (also 1778) provided that even "Persons of equivocal and suspected Character" could be summarily expelled from the state. In 1777, moreover, the legislature created commissioners of sequestration for each of the counties not under British control, empowering them to seize but not sell livestock, tools, furniture, and other personal effects belonging to active Tories. The Forfeitures Act of 1779 confiscated all such property, adding houses, land, and slaves to the list. That same year an Act of Attainder declared fifty-nine leading Tories guilty of treason, seized their property, and ordered their immediate execution upon capture. In 1780 the legislature authorized the sale of confiscated Tory property. All told, the estates of some fifteen hundred Tories, including those belonging to the Philipses, Johnsons, and other great landowning families, were forfeited; hundreds of individuals were convicted of treason and banished. No other state, in the end, did more than New York to suppress and punish enemies of the cause, real or suspected.

After 1781, with American independence and the liberation of New York City now a virtual certainty, the Clintonian legislature adopted a pair of measures designed to make life difficult, if not impossible, for Tories who chose to remain in the city once the war ended. The Citation Act of 1782 protected patriots from suits by Tory creditors, while the Trespass Act of 1783 permitted patriots to sue loyalists for damages to property in occupied areas of the state, even when ordered by British authorities.

Over the winter of 1782–83, encouraged by this legislation, patriots began heading for New York to recover houses, land, and other possessions left behind six or seven years earlier. By mid-April, one report said, upwards of two thousand former residents had already returned to the city. Their insistence on the immediate restoration of abandoned property, often coupled with demands for the payment of damages and back rent, produced frayed tempers and tense confrontations. When the merchant John Broome came down from Connecticut to inspect his house on Hanover Square, he found it occupied by British officers. "I am the owner and I should like to make some arrangements respecting the rent," he announced. The officers laughed in his face.

A joint Board of Claims, consisting of officers of both the British and American armies, struggled to resolve such disputes peacefully. Brawls and even organized attacks on Tories nonetheless became common during the summer and fall of 1783. Some of these "violent and interested associations," General Carleton said, were actually planning the outright seizure and redistribution of Tory property once His Majesty's forces withdrew from the city (one group openly described themselves as "levellers"). Pamphlets and newspaper letters warned of more severe measures to come, and mass meetings around the state clamored for immediate action.

Little wonder, under the circumstances, that many Tories decided to get out of New York as quickly as possible. By the end of June 1783 an estimated ten thousand of them had already accepted the government's offer of free passage with the fleet and left town. Another eight thousand departed in September, followed by eleven thousand more in December.

Of the forty thousand or so Tories who thus abandoned New York between 1782 and 1783—the bulk of whom originally came from Connecticut, New Jersey, Pennsylvania, and other colonies—few returned to their homes or found refuge elsewhere in the United States. Most, perhaps three out of four, made their way to Canada. Many settled in New Brunswick (St. John was incorporated in 1785 with a constitution modeled after the charter of New York City; Hempstead, in Queens County, was founded by former residents of Long Island). Others joined the eight-thousand-odd Tories who established a settlement called Shelburne on the coast of Nova Scotia below Halifax; the Rev. Charles Inglis, rector of Trinity Church since 1777, won appointment as the bishop of Nova Scotia. Adherents to the crown wound up in Ontario, Cape Breton Island, the Bahamas, and elsewhere. Former mayor David Mathews became president of the Cape Breton council. William Smith accepted Carleton's offer to become chief justice of Quebec.

And what of the thousands of slaves and free blacks who had gravitated to New York during the British occupation? All summer long, slaveowners from other colonies turned up in the city looking for their property; Boston King of South Carolina remembered how he and other runaways were filled "with inexpressible anguish and terror . . . when we saw our old masters coming from Virginia, North Carolina, and other parts, and seizing upon their slaves in the streets of New-York, or even dragging them from their beds." Washington (ever the slavemaster, no matter his exertions on behalf of American liberty) told Carleton that he wanted the British to return all runaways to their rightful owners. Carleton honorably refused on the grounds that those with the British on or before the signing of the provisional peace treaty in November 1782 had been liberated by Clinton's proclamation of 1779. Perhaps four thousand blacks from all over America thus managed to escape the city while it was still in British hands, most of them, too, destined for Canada or Nova Scotia.

The subsequent history of these black refugees wasn't a happy one. Most settled at Shelburne, Nova Scotia, or St. John, New Brunswick, where trouble with white veterans erupted into race riots in 1784, forcing many to run for their lives yet again. Former members of the Black Pioneers and Guides regiment who founded Birchtown, Nova Scotia (named after the British commander who signed their passports to freedom), stuck it out for a few years longer, but in 1790 over one thousand of them decamped for Sierra Leone. Some individuals made out comparatively well. Bill Richmond, who escaped his Staten Island master in 1776, sailed to England with General Percy and became a celebrated pugilist.

EVACUATION DAY

Protesting "the violence in the Americans which broke out soon after the cessation of hostilities," General Carleton held on to New York until every Tory who wanted to get out had left. On November 21, 1783, satisfied that he had done his duty, Carleton ordered all British forces to begin withdrawing from Long Island and upper Manhattan. Governor Clinton and General Washington met at Tarrytown and rode down through Yonkers to Harlem, where they waited at a tavern (near the present intersection of Frederick Douglass Boulevard and 126th Street) for word of the final British departure.

Three days later, on the morning of November 25—long celebrated in the city as Evacuation Day—the last redcoats in New York paraded glumly down the Bowery to the East River wharves, from where they were rowed out to the fleet in the harbor. When a certain Mrs. Day prematurely ran up the American flag over her boardinghouse on Murray Street, Provost Marshal Cunningham, resplendent in his scarlet coat and wig, ordered her to take it down. She bloodied his nose with her broom, however, and drove him off. Delirious patriots now thronged the streets, many sporting a special "Badge of Distinction" that consisted of "a Union Cockade, of black and white Ribband, worn on the left Breast, and a Laurel in the Hat." High-spirited seamen pulled down the signs of taverns that had welcomed the trade of Tories and British soldiers.

A contingent of Continental officers, including General Alexander McDougall, Colonel John Lamb, and numerous other old Sons of Liberty meanwhile assembled at the Bull's Head Tavern on the Bowery to escort Washington and Clinton into town. Joining them there were some eight hundred Continental troops from Massachusetts and New York and a party of mounted townsfolk. Careful to keep a discreet distance behind the British, the Americans marched in formation down the Bowery to Pearl Street, turned west along Wall Street, then stopped opposite Cape's Tavern on Broadway. "The troops just leaving us were as if equipped for show," one eyewitness recalled, "and with their scarlet uniforms and burnished arms, made a brilliant display. The troops that marched in, on the contrary, were ill-clad and weather-beaten, and made a forlorn appearance. But then they were *our* troops, and as I looked at them, and thought upon all they had done for us, my heart and my eyes were full, and I admired and gloried in them the more because they were weather-beaten and forlorn."

At Cape's, a group of patriot citizens formally welcomed Washington. "In this place, and at this moment of exultation and triumph," they declared, "while the Ensigns of Slavery still linger in our sight, we look up to you, our deliverer, with unusual transports of Gratitude and Joy." An infantry and artillery detail meanwhile discovered that the enemy, in a parting insult, had nailed the royal ensign to the flagstaff of Fort George and greased the pole to prevent its removal. John Van Arsdale, a sailor wearing cleats, climbed up and replaced it with the Stars and Stripes while a throng of spectators cheered their approval. Except for Cunningham's bloody nose, there had been no violence. Said one witness: "One day the British patrolled the streets, next day the American soldiers."

Washington's Triumphal Entry, 1783. Washington and his retinue on Broadway, passing St. Paul's Church.
(© Museum of the City of New York)

That same evening, Governor Clinton hosted a grand public banquet at Fraunces Tavern for Washington and his officers. Thirteen toasts were drunk, concluding with "May the Remembrance of this DAY be a Lesson to Princes." More banquets followed over the next week, all marked by "good humour, hilarity and mirth." Clinton's dinner for the French ambassador at Cape's Tavern drew 120 guests who consumed 135 bottles of madeira, thirty-six bottles of port, sixty bottles of English beer, and thirty bowls of punch; they also broke sixty wine glasses and eight cut-glass decanters. Bowling Green was the site of a huge display of fireworks on December 2. Spectators saw a "Balloon of Serpents," a "Yew Tree of brilliant fire," and an "Illuminated Pyramid, with Archemedian Screws, a Globe and vertical Sun," climaxed by "Fame, descending" and the launching of a hundred rockets. Printer James Rivington, who had just stripped the British arms from the masthead of his *Gazette*, said the show that night "exceeded every former Exhibition in the United States."

On the morning of December 4, Washington bade farewell to his officers in another gathering at Fraunces Tavern. After a brief toast, marked by "extreme sensibility on both sides," he embraced each of those present in turn. "In every eye was the tear of dignified sensibility and not a word was articulated to interrupt the eloquent silence and the tenderness of the scene." Escorted by a column of infantry, the Father of His Country walked silently to the foot of Whitehall Street, where a barge waited to take him across to Paulus Hook on the New Jersey shore.

PART THREE

MERCANTILE TOWN
(1783–1843)

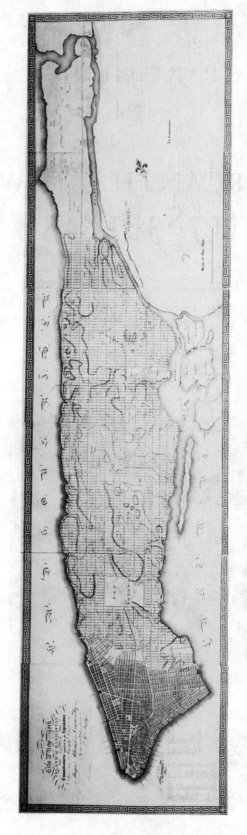

The Commissioners' Plan of 1811. (I. N. Phelps Stokes Collection. Miriam and Ira D. Wallach Division of Art, Prints and Photographs. The New York Public Library. Astor, Lenox and Tilden Foundations)

17

Phoenix

As Washington made his way back to Mount Vernon, New Yorkers got down to the business of rebuilding a city that seven years of enemy occupation and two calamitous fires had reduced to a shambles. In the burned-over district east of Broadway, the spectral shell of Trinity Church loomed menacingly over block after rubble-choked block where, as William Alexander Duer recalled, the skeletal walls of gutted buildings "cast their grim shadows upon the pavement, imparting an unearthly aspect to the street." Many private residences were unfit for human use. James Duane returned on Evacuation Day and found two of his houses looking "as if they had been inhabited by savages or wild beasts." Churches and public buildings, commandeered for service as stables or hospitals or barracks, stood in desperate need of repair. Many streets, stripped bare of trees, were obstructed by trenches, redoubts, and other fortifications. Garbage and refuse lay everywhere. Wharves and warehouses had crumbled from years of neglect. The merchant fleet had all but vanished.

Vanished too were the Caribbean markets on which New York's prosperity had hinged for the better part of a century. British orders in council of July and December 1783 opened the British Isles to American trade but banned American meat, fish, and dairy products from the British West Indies and restricted trade in all other goods to British ships—a tremendous blow to the livelihood of every merchant and artisan in town, not to mention commercial farmers and stockmen in the city's hinterland. According to some observers, this was only the beginning. John Adams, the American ambassador in London, believed that His Majesty's government actually had *"disigns of ruining, if they can our carrying Trade, and annihilating all our Navigation, and Seamen."* It didn't improve matters that Spain and France, having opened their West Indian possessions to American trade during the war, promptly closed them again with the return of peace.

The ruins of Trinity Church, 1776. (© Collection of The New-York Historical Society)

Perhaps the only really good news was that the Continental Congress had decided to meet in New York pending the selection of a permanent seat for the national government. Congress arrived in the spring of 1785 and took up quarters in City Hall at the head of Broad Street. It was a tight fit: the building already housed the Common Council, the state legislature, and a school. Desperate for space, a rare commodity in the war-damaged city, Congress eventually occupied parts of various other public buildings as well and leased rooms in Fraunces Tavern.

RADICAL RESURGENCE

For the first year or two after Evacuation Day, it appeared that New York's future in these parlous times, if indeed it were to have a future, would be determined by the same radical Whigs who had been driven out by the British in 1776. Their return to power began when the Council for the Southern District, a provisional government set up by the state legislature for the formerly occupied counties, scheduled Common Council elections for mid-December 1783. Revived by rumors that Tories would attempt to cast ballots—thousands still remained in town, and even conservative Whigs like Robert R. Livingston worried about their intentions—the Sons of Liberty mobilized working people to ensure a substantial margin of victory for radical Whig candidates. Concurrently, a "Committee of Mechanicks" put forward a slate of nominees for the Assembly and Senate elections to be held later that same month. Again there were warnings that Tories might try to participate.

Polling began at City Hall on December 29 and closed a week later, with the Mechanics Committee candidates—including Marinus Willett, John Lamb, and Isaac

Sears (who had just moved back from Boston)—winning by a four-to-one margin. Instructions for the new assemblymen soon followed from a committee of "late exiled Mechanics, Grocers, Retailers and Innholders." The committee, whose members included a tallow chandler, a saddler, and a pewterer, demanded that Tories be explicitly disfranchised and excluded from all "advantages of trade and commerce."

Early in 1784 the Council of Appointment tapped the rich and conservative James Duane for the job of mayor. At first glance this looked like a setback for the radicals, but they raised no complaint. Duane was a proven patriot, after all, and following his inauguration in February, he demonstrated that he was public-spirited as well by donating money earmarked for the customary entertainment, some twenty guineas, to the poor. A Committee of Mechanics, Grocers, Retailers, and Innholders made a special point of complimenting the new mayor on his good judgment.

Duane's ability to influence the course of events was limited, in any case. Under the terms of the Montgomerie Charter (reaffirmed by the 1777 state constitution) he presided over the Common Council, the Mayor's Court or Court of Common Pleas (for civil cases), and the Court of General Sessions (for criminal cases). He was clerk of the markets, he appointed subordinate officials such as the high constable and marshals, and he licensed all butchers, tavern keepers, scavengers, cartmen, and porters. The powers of the Common Council, however, were at least as extensive. It regulated all markets and trades in town. It set the terms under which the mayor granted licenses and made appointments. It also had a fair number of lesser municipal offices at its disposal, and it could change the mayor's compensation by raising or lowering the various market and license fees out of which his salary was paid. With the subsequent appointments of Marinus Willett as sheriff and John Lamb as collector of the port, those posts too belonged to the radicals. So long as Governor Clinton ran the state, they had little to fear from Mayor Duane.

Clinton had in fact already given city radicals their cue to step up the pace of their anti-Tory campaign. Toward the end of January 1784 he opened the new session of the legislature—the first to be held in New York City since independence—with a lament on "the ruins of this once flourishing city" and an impassioned attack on the Tories for the "cruelty and rapine" with which they had opposed the cause of American freedom. Stirred by Clinton's rhetoric, the Sons of Liberty—along with shadowy ad hoc radical groups like the Whig Society—organized a series of mass meetings, culminating in a huge demonstration in the Common at the end of March, to demand not only stricter penalties for former adherents to the crown but also their immediate expulsion from the city by the first of May. Particularly unpopular Tories were tarred and feathered or hamstrung. A party of visiting British officers was set upon and beaten.

With equal zeal, the legislature's radical majority began to spin off anti-Tory legislation. One law barred Tories from holding public office. Another, enacted over the veto of the Council of Revision, authorized election officials to disfranchise any Tory on the testimony of a single witness. A subsequent law ordered the immediate sale of all confiscated property, though doing so plainly violated the Treaty of Paris. Still another imposed a punitive tax of one hundred thousand pounds on those residents of the five lower counties who had chosen to remain under the British occupation and thus hadn't yet paid their fair share for "the blessing derived from freedom and independence."

The state commissioners of forfeitures meanwhile proceeded to auction off confiscated property. James De Lancey's huge Manhattan estate went on the block, the purchasers including some fifty butchers, gardeners, cartmen, grocers, carpenters, farmers, and assorted other working people—at least some of whom had been De Lancey's tenants before independence. For fifty-eight pounds, a ropemaker named William Arnold bought a half interest in seven lots of De Lancey's West Farm; John Buchanan, mariner, obtained four lots for £271; James Galloway, rigger, spent eighty pounds for a half interest in eight lots.

The radicalized Common Council now moved to enlarge the powers and responsibilities of the municipal corporation. For seven years now the assorted rents and fees that were the corporation's sole sources of revenue had gone uncollected, leaving it no money with which to repair the ravages of war or pay its outstanding debts. Taxation was the obvious solution. But the mayor and council only had the authority to govern the estate of the municipal corporation: they couldn't levy taxes on residents of the city generally.

At the corporation's request, therefore, the legislature passed a law granting its officers the power to levy a tax on all inhabitants of the city. Although this was a one-time measure—if and when the corporation wanted to impose additional taxes, it would again need to seek legislative approval—it was nonetheless a momentous extension of the corporation's power to govern. Ratifying the popular impulse to local self-determination expressed in the Revolutionary committee system, it began a gradual but inexorable metamorphosis of the corporation from a "private" into a "public" entity that governed as a surrogate of the legislature. Necessarily, too, it cast new doubt on the restrictiveness of the municipal suffrage. Who should now constitute the "commonality" of the corporation: merely those property-owning (male) residents formally admitted to the freemanship, or a broader cross-section of the city's population?

Conservative Whigs protested the delegation of legislative power to the municipal corporation, all too aware that both corporation and legislature were dominated by radicals. The Council of Revision vetoed the tax bill, in part because it permitted assessments "according to the estates *and other circumstances and abilities to pay taxes*" (thereby pitting rich against poor), and in part because it could elevate the city into an "independent republic," a rogue state-within-a-state, immune from higher authority. But the legislature easily overrode the veto, and the law stood.

Equally disturbing to conservatives was the radical assault on two other powerful corporations—King's College and Trinity Church. A group of prominent Whigs led by Mayor Duane had petitioned the legislature to give King's College a new charter embodying "that Liberality and that civil and religious Freedom" secured by the Revolution. What they got instead from the radical majority was an act creating the University of the State of New York. King's College, renamed Columbia, would henceforth be only one among many prospective institutions of higher learning belonging to and controlled by the university. Furthermore, the university was to be governed by a giant board of regents, most of whose members came from rural parts of the state and could be counted upon to harbor no particular sympathy for an elitist, Anglican institution in the city. This was borne out when the board proposed three highly controversial candidates for president of the university: Joseph Priestly and Richard Price, radical dissenters who had actively supported the American cause, and John Jebb, a reformist Anglican cleric.

Trinity Church presented an even more complicated and potentially explosive case. Only weeks before Evacuation Day, the Tory vestry of Trinity had picked a staunch supporter of the crown, the Rev. Benjamin Moore, to take over as rector (the Rev. Charles Inglis having lately realized that his future looked brighter in Nova Scotia). Even moderate and conservative Whigs were dismayed by Moore's elevation—he "preached and prayed against us during the war," Robert R. Livingston recalled—and the Council for the Southern District decided to place the church under the control of nine trustees, all Whigs, including James Duane, Francis Lewis, Isaac Sears, and William Duer. For rector the trustees chose the Rev. Samuel Provoost, whose forebears had years before drifted with so many other well-to-do Dutch families into the Anglican fold.

Moore refused to step aside. Accordingly, in April 1784, the legislature issued a new charter for Trinity, empowering the trustees to call and induct a rector. Simultaneously, in conformity with the principles of religious liberty embodied in the 1777 constitution, the legislature repealed the Ministry Act of 1693, disestablished the Anglican Church, and adopted a law for the incorporation of non-Anglican religious bodies in the state. Later that same year New York Anglicans hosted a convention that organized the American Episcopal Church in strict accordance with the practices of the Church of England.

What really caught the imagination of the legislature's radical majority, though, was Trinity's valuable Manhattan real estate. Its centerpiece was the sprawling tract known as the King's Farm, bestowed upon the church almost a century earlier. Soon after Evacuation Day, heirs of Annetje Jans, the original owner, petitioned the legislature for recovery of the property, whereupon the Assembly decided the land properly belonged to the state. In February 1785 it ordered the attorney general to sue the church for possession. The judicial expropriation of Trinity's holdings, if successful, would be a milestone in the transformation of society and an invitation to push that transformation still further.

How much further wasn't clear, although there were plenty of hints. Since Evacuation Day, the Sons of Liberty, the Mechanics Committee, and other radical groups had expressed an interest in such matters as the popular election of mayors, free public schooling, easier naturalization laws, and the abolition of primogeniture and entail. During the war, many had urged the state to combat inflation with policies not unlike those exercised by the municipal corporation—wage and price controls, prohibitions against monopolizers and hoarders, stiff penalties for profiteering, and heavy taxation of unimproved land as well as personal property. John Holt, editor of the *New-York Journal*, had been especially outspoken against the notion that merchants should be free to charge what the market would bear.

At least some radicals seem to have had a penchant, too, for the moral legislation that always lurked just beneath the surface of Anglo-American Whiggism. In March 1784, as a case in point, the Common Council enacted the city's strictest Sabbath law to date, strictly prohibiting labor, public gatherings (except of course at church), sports, games, and even children making noise or playing in the streets on Sunday. Petitions were said to be circulating for "the annihilation of taverns, coffee-houses, billiard tables, ale-houses and theaters." Next year, when Lewis Hallam's Old American Company returned from exile and applied for license to reopen the John Street Theater, the Common Council turned them down with the stern rebuke that this was no time for frivolity. What was more—putting a new spin on an old complaint—the theater's notorious tendency to corrupt manners and morals was a danger to the republic. "Attendance on public Stages intoxicates a populace and diverts their minds from what ought to be the grand object of their study, the public good," asserted one newspaper writer.

NEW NEW YORKERS

Thousands of people had meanwhile continued to pour into New York, boosting its population from twelve thousand at the end of 1783 to twenty-four thousand two years later. Most were refugees hoping to pick up the pieces of their former lives in the city. Scattered among them, however, were wealthy and cosmopolitan newcomers from elsewhere in the state, from other parts of the United States, and even from abroad.

Preeminent among these newcomers—and soon to take the lead in organizing an opposition to the radical resurgence—was twenty-seven-year-old Alexander Hamilton. Although he had lived briefly in the city while a student at King's College, Hamilton spent the first four years of the war traveling the country as Washington's confidential aide and secretary, then settled in Albany after marrying General Philip Schuyler's daughter, Elizabeth. In the company of men like Washington and Schuyler, moreover, Hamilton had become convinced of the need for a strong national government to combat what he considered to be state parochialism and fiscal irresponsibility. His *Continentalist* essays of 1781 called for a constitutional convention to replace the Articles of Confederation (adopted back in 1777) and lavished praise on his friend Robert Morris, a wealthy Philadelphia merchant who served as superintendent of finance for Congress and was largely responsible for the creation of the Bank of North America. The following year, Hamilton appeared before a joint committee of the state legislature to urge "a solid arrangement of finance" for the state and drafted a plan for overhauling state taxes. New York's "radically vicious" system of taxation, he confided to Morris, was a symptom of "the general disease which infects all our constitutions—an excess of popularity. The inquiry constantly is what will *please*, not what will *benefit* the people."

Needing an occupation, Hamilton took a crash course in the law and was admitted to the New York bar in the summer of 1782. A year later he moved his family down to the city, opened a law office on Wall Street, and began to build a practice by representing Tories ensnared by the Trespass Act. "Legislative folly has afforded so plentiful a harvest to us lawyers that we have scarcely a moment to spare from the substantial business of reaping," he gloated to Gouverneur Morris. Publicly, Hamilton professed to have no political ambitions and fended off attempts to nominate him for office. Privately, though, he made no secret of his alarm at the radical clamor for retribution against the Tories. This "epidemic phrenzy," he said, could only be the work of "levellers."

Like Hamilton, William Duer was a newcomer who needed no introduction to New York. Born in England and educated at Eton, Duer had served briefly as an aide to Lord Clive in India before making his way to the West Indies, where his family owned plantations on Antigua and Dominica. In 1768 he came up to New York to buy lumber and was introduced to General Schuyler, a prominent Hudson Valley landowner as well as Hamilton's father-in-law. On Schuyler's advice, Duer purchased a tract on the east side of the Hudson near Saratoga, took up permanent residence there, and over the next half-dozen years did a handsome business supplying masts to the Royal Navy and speculating in land. By 1776, now a prominent Whig, Duer had become the main supplier of the Continental forces in New York, raking in profits of a thousand dollars per month. He married Kitty Alexander, daughter of General William Alexander, and with his father-in-law outfoxed their mutual creditors by paying off prewar debts with depreciated Continental paper. Unfazed by the occupation of New York, he arranged to sell flour, cattle, and other provisions to His Majesty's army under flags of truce and bragged of regularly making 500 percent profits on his investment. When Congress balked at the price General Alexander asked for iron shot manufactured at his New Jersey ironworks, Duer coolly sold it to the British army instead. In another scheme, he took money appropriated to buy food for Continental troops, funneled it into his private account, then bought 6 percent Loan Office certificates—i.e., loaning the money back to the government at a tidy, risk-free profit to himself.

Long before the war ended, radical patriots everywhere had come to regard Duer as the kingpin of corruption among military suppliers and a perfect illustration of the self-seeking that, if unchecked, would sooner or later destroy the republic. In New York, Duer's wheeling and dealing made him a ready target for radical critics and fed widespread resentment against "mushroom gentlemen" who prospered while their fellow citizens did without. Contemptuous of public opinion, like so many of his associates, Duer brushed off such criticism as the carping of "Paine lovers." During the spring or early summer of 1783, now very rich and heavily engaged in the business of supplying provisions to the army, he shifted his residence down to the city.

New Jersey-born Richard Varick, another of Washington's wartime aides, had been admitted to the New York bar on the very eve of independence, but he too didn't settle permanently in the city until after Evacuation Day. Neither did Varick's better-known compatriot, Aaron Burr. Born in Newark, New Jersey, Burr, like Hamilton, had made a name for himself as a gallant young officer in the first years of the war, rising to the rank of major at the age of twenty and joining Washington's military entourage. Unlike Hamilton, Burr soon broke with Washington, resentful of the commander-in-chief's dependence on Hamilton and alleged opposition to his, Burr's, further advancement. Transferred to the staff of General Israel Putnam, Burr subsequently won a promotion to lieutenant colonel and, for a few months, commanded the West Point defenses and the American forces patrolling Westchester County's Neutral Zone. The Zone's much-abused civilians praised his diligence and honesty; his men respected him as a fair yet quick-tempered disciplinarian (he once allegedly lopped off the arm of a mutinous soldier with a single stroke of his saber). By 1779, however, in ill health and believing his prospects still clouded by the rift with Washington, Burr resigned his commission to study the law. He was admitted to the bar in Albany in 1782 and moved down to New York the next year, launching his practice from a house on Wall Street near Hamilton's residence and only two doors from City Hall. In no time at all he was making ten thousand dollars a year and setting his sights on a political career.

Melancton Smith arrived in New York only months behind Duer, Hamilton, Varick, and Burr. A native of Jamaica, Long Island, Smith had moved to Poughkeepsie in his teens and set himself up as a merchant. Well-to-do if not wealthy when the Revolution began, he joined the local Sons of Liberty and, like so many other "new men," saw his public career accelerate. Dutchess voters sent him to the Provincial Congress, where he sat on the Committee for Detecting Conspiracies and developed a reputation as one of the most articulate radical Whigs in the state as well as a close adviser to Governor George Clinton. He also served as a contractor and purchasing agent for the new state government (in which capacity he struck a number of profitable deals with William Duer). In 1784, though, Smith abandoned Poughkeepsie and shifted his business to New York City. One year later, city voters sent him to Congress.

Another Dutchess transplant was Edward Livingston, younger brother of the chancellor, who forsook life among the upstate landed gentry to open a law office in the city. William Constable, born in Dublin but raised in Schenectady, moved up from Philadelphia (where, among other things, his name had been linked with Duer's in a smuggling scheme) to take over the New York business of an English firm, Phyn and Ellice. John Pintard, a fourth-generation Huguenot born in New York but raised on Long Island and educated at Princeton, got to know the city while serving as the American deputy commissary for prisoners of war. Well before the last British troops had pulled out, Pintard had set himself up in trade. By the end of the decade he presided over one of the city's leading mercantile houses.

A procession of merchants came down from New England, among them Daniel Parker, a native of Watertown, Massachusetts, who had prospered during the war selling flour and forage to the Continental Army, most of the time in partnership with Duer; early in 1783, spurred by news of the impending peace, Parker moved to New York and lobbied Sir Guy Carleton for a contract to supply the British army.

This migration also figured in the founding of Olympia, a speculative development just across the East River from Manhattan. Its story began with two Long Island brothers of New England extraction, Comfort and Joshua Sands, who had clerked with city merchants before the Revolution, taken part in the resistance to British policy, and left when New York fell in 1776. During the war they made a fortune in military provisioning (Washington, among others, considered them crooks), and when they returned to New York in 1783 they founded the highly successful firm of Comfort and Joshua Sands. They also bought the former Rapelje farm, a 160-acre tract lying northeast of the road (now Fulton Street) that ran down to the Brooklyn Ferry.

There the brothers laid out the "City of Olympia," dividing the property into lots and selling them off to a group of interrelated Connecticut families. Many came from the New London area, where they had been employed in the maritime trades, and they seem to have envisioned Olympia as a shipbuilding center; the Sands themselves erected wharves, warehouses, and a huge ropewalk for the production of rigging and cables. A New England-style Independent church followed within a year or two, and by the end of the decade the little community appeared to be thriving.

In addition to this migration from New England there was an influx of well-to-do, ambitious businessmen from the British Isles. Some had settled in town during the war and collaborated with the British yet chose to stay after Evacuation Day, often to carry on the business of or manage property belonging to departed Tories. Others came over as soon as the outcome of the war was certain.

John Delafield, a thirty-five-year-old English merchant, arrived in the spring of 1783, traveling on the same ship that brought the provisional treaty of peace between Great Britain and the United States. Dominick Lynch, the son of a rich Galway merchant with extensive connections on the Continent, had been in Bruges when he learned that the war was over. Early in 1783, not yet thirty years old, he formed a partnership with Thomas Stoughton to do business in New York. Stoughton sailed immediately and had the firm of Lynch and Stoughton up and running on Greenwich Street well before Evacuation Day. Lynch followed in mid-1785, carrying, it was said, more cash than had been brought to America by any other single individual in living memory.

With "Don" Stoughton—so named because of his subsequent appointment as Spanish consul—Lynch also assumed a leading role in the city's small yet burgeoning

Roman Catholic community. Probably fewer than a thousand Catholics lived in New York at the end of the Revolution. Ferdinand Steenmayer, a Jesuit, had slipped into the city during the war to celebrate Mass secretly in a house on Wall Street. With the elimination of restrictions on Catholic worship, Steenmayer gathered his flock in a loft over a Barclay Street carpenter's shop. The postwar surge of immigration, virtually doubling the Catholic population overnight, prompted Lynch, Stoughton, and other lay leaders, led by Hector St. Jean de Crèvecoeur, the French consul in New York, to arrange for the construction of St. Peter's Church, the city's first Roman Catholic house of worship. Lots were purchased on Barclay Street, and the cornerstone was laid in October 1785.

Only months behind Delafield and Lynch was Archibald Gracie. A Scot by birth, Gracie had gone to Liverpool and worked his way up to the position of chief clerk in the branch office of a London shipping house. When the war ended he decided to go into business for himself, setting off for New York with a cargo of textiles, tin ware, watches, cheese, and "fine London Porter and Liverpool Beer." By the spring of 1784, not yet thirty years old, Gracie had a house and shop on Queen (now Pearl) Street and was taking an interest in the tobacco trade. He moved to Petersburg, Virginia, in 1785 but often came up to New York with cargoes of tobacco destined for transshipment to European markets. In 1793 he would move back to the city for good.

Cornelius Heeney left Ireland for New York in 1784 and found work as a bookkeeper with a furrier named William Backhouse. Backhouse taught him the business, and Heeney was soon dealing in skins and furs on his own account out of a store on Little Dock (now Water) Street. Both Backhouse and Heeney (another benefactor of New York's Catholic church) were sometime associates of another young immigrant, a short, stout, square-faced German named John Jacob Astor.

The third son of a butcher in Walldorf, a small village near Heidelberg, Astor had left home at the age of seventeen to seek his fortune in London, where an older brother was established in a musical-instrument house founded by their uncle. When word arrived several years later of the signing of the Treaty of Paris, Astor quit London for New York, where another brother, Henry, had gone to provision Hessian troops and was now flourishing as a cattle trader and butcher (he would soon own the Bull's Head Tavern on the Bowery). Jacob arrived in March 1784, not quite twenty-one years old, with a modest financial stake in hand. His marriage to Sarah Todd the following year brought him a connection to the Brevoort family and a small dowry. In 1786 he went into business selling imported flutes, pianofortes, and violins in a building on Queen Street owned by his mother-in-law, but his future lay in the fur trade.

PHOCION SPEAKS

Over the winter of 1783–84, moderate and conservative Whigs became increasingly fearful that radical assaults on the city's Tories would impede economic recovery, perhaps even precipitate some kind of social cataclysm. There were also international repercussions. "Violences and associations against the Tories pay an ill compliment to Government and impeach our good Faith," John Jay wrote from France. Unfortunately, said Robert R. Livingston, "violent Whigs" had gained the upper hand. Reasonable men—men of property and social position—still hoped "to suppress all violences, to soften the rigor of the laws against the loyalists, and not to banish them from . . . social intercourse." But never, Livingston intimated, had things looked so grim for them.

In January 1784 Hamilton published a little pamphlet entitled *A Letter from Phocion to the Considerate Citizens of New-York.* (Phocion was the Athenian general who helped defeat the Macedonians in 339 B.C. and then, over the objections of Demosthenes, advocated conciliation with his former enemies. When the democrats came to power, they forced Phocion to drink hemlock.) Hamilton's *Letter*, the first sustained appeal for forbearance toward the Tories, "excited a general sensation" by saying openly what the propertied classes had been saying privately for months: that radical Whig attacks on the rights and property of men and women who had ended up on the wrong side of the Revolution were ruining the city's chances of recovery from years of war and military occupation.

Besides putting at risk the rights and liberties for which the Revolution had been fought, Hamilton argued, such attacks violated the Treaty of Paris. This made the United States look irresponsible in the eyes of other nations and destroyed the climate of confidence essential to international trade. It infringed, too, upon the power of Congress to determine how, and upon what conditions, the war would end—diminishing in turn the ability of that body to lead the nation in time of peace. Finally, persecution of the Tories drove away the very men whose wealth and abilities were essential to the prosperity of a commercial society.

That last point was vital, and key passages in *Phocion* warned the city's radical mechanics to take heed. Driving away Tory merchants and craftsmen, Hamilton wrote, will not raise your wages: the former are essential to the city's economic health; the latter do you no harm. Wages in town have risen "sufficiently high" as it is, and "those classes of the community who are to employ you" will not in any case go on paying "exorbitant prices" for labor even if its supply dwindles. Besides, if you disturb "the economy of the political machine" by trying to elevate any of the "departments of industry" above its "natural height," then "society at large suffers." Indeed, "the only object of concern with an industrious artisan, as such, ought to be, that there may be plenty of money in the community, and a brisk commerce to give it circulation and activity."

The Revolution is over, Hamilton continued. Direct popular intervention may have freed the nation from tyranny, but the liberty of the people—meaning "their *right* to a *share* in the government"—is now secure. The citizens of New York should return to their shops and countinghouses, leaving public affairs in the hands of those persons most fit to rule.

Just as dangerous as popular interference in government was the corporatist ethos that had in the past gone virtually hand in hand with radical Whig demands for economic and social justice. The truth was, Hamilton wrote, "that all monopolies, exclusions and discriminations in matters of traffick, are pernicious and absurd." This applied not only to repeated attempts by local and state authorities to regulate wages and prices during the war but also to their continuing vendetta against the Tories. It didn't necessarily apply to the central government. Unlike his mentor Robert Morris, Hamilton always saw a role for vigorous government intervention at the national level, now to promote trade, now to mitigate the competitive "jealousy" between states that could shatter the republic. Municipal laissez-faire and federal activism, in other words, were opposite sides of the same coin. New York's future prosperity depended on both. And both, Hamilton repeated, had been gravely impaired by local and state abuse of the Tories.

Phocion, together with a *Second Letter from Phocion* that appeared in April 1784, underscored what many people in New York already suspected: Colonel Hamilton, as he was generally known, was the only moderate or conservative Whig gifted with a coherent vision of the city's political economy. Resolutely opposed to arbitrary government and anchored in the principle of equality before the law, that vision was undeniably republican—the kind of republicanism that scorned popular opinion and trusted only governments led by the rich and well-born few.

THE EMPRESS OF CHINA

Perhaps, though, New York's future was brighter than Hamilton imagined. One morning in late February 1784, only a month or so after the appearance of his first *Letter from Phocion*, crowds of spectators lined the East River waterfront to mark the long-awaited resumption of overseas trade. For months ice had jammed the Narrows and East River, bringing business in the city to a standstill while acute shortages of food, shelter, and firewood, exacerbated by heavy snowfalls, wore at everyone's nerves. Now, as winter began to relax its grip on the city, ship after ship slid away from the East River wharves, shook out its sails, and filled away down toward the harbor.

As the fleet passed the Battery, said a report in the *New York Packet*, "A large party of gentlemen" could be seen, "congratulating each other on the pleasing prospect of so many large ships being under sail in the bay." One ship in particular commanded their attention: the copper-bottomed, black-hulled *Empress of China*, bound for the Orient. She was, boasted the *Independent Gazette*, "the first ship from this new nation, to that rich and distant part of the world." New York owed a special debt of gratitude to "the gentlemen, whose ambition to discover new resources of wealth, by forming new channels for the extensions of our commerce" had thus prompted them to "risque their property" in the voyage.

Such an undertaking would have been unthinkable before the Revolution, when trade with the Chinese was an exclusive privilege of the British East India Company. Independence removed that obstacle, and as the end of the war drew near China had beckoned to entrepreneurs in every American port. First off the mark was John Ledyard, a Connecticut adventurer who had served as a corporal of marines on the third and final voyage of Captain James Cook. Ledyard turned up in New York City in the summer of 1783, touting a scheme to trade for furs along the Pacific Northwest coast and peddle them in Canton. Unable to find backers, he went to Philadelphia and got the attention of the financier Robert Morris. Intrigued, Morris agreed to raise some $120,000 for the purchase of ships and trading goods, eventually putting up half the money himself. The other half came from the New York firm of Daniel Parker and Company, one of whose partners was William Duer.

Over the autumn of 1783, amid all the commotion of the British evacuation, Parker and Company found a ship on the ways in New England, hired a crew, and began to assemble a cargo. Three thousand pelts were purchased, but when the idea of a second voyage to the Pacific Northwest fell through, causing Ledyard to go off in a huff, Morris and Parker shifted their focus to another commodity: ginseng root. Ginseng was prized in China as a cure for everything from indigestion and high blood pressure to impotence; one Chinese emperor was said to have paid ten thousand dollars for an especially rare sample. Happily, ginseng also grew wild in the Ohio and Mississippi valleys, where native peoples had been harvesting it for trade since the 1750s. Agents of Morris and Parker scoured the backwoods of Pennsylvania and Virginia for all they could get their hands on, and eventually they had some thirty tons of it stashed in the holds of the *Empress of China* when she passed the Narrows on her way to the Far East.

Six months later, having been escorted part of the way by friendly French warships, she dropped anchor in the Pearl River below Canton. Another four months of bartering ensued, during which her pelts and ginseng were exchanged for several hundred tons of tea and fifty tons of "export" chinaware (so called because it was manufactured specifically for the Western market). Trading on their own accounts, agents of the investors and members of the crew also packed in a wide variety of other commodities, including silk and satin clothing, wallpaper, lacquered fans, umbrellas, exotic plants, and even delectable Shanghai roosters.

A five-month return voyage brought the *Empress of China* back to New York on May 11, 1785, fifteen months after her departure. Her return caused a sensation. Local papers hailed it as a promise that the city would soon be out of the economic doldrums. New Yorkers could now look forward, said one, to "a future happy period in our being able to dispense with that burdensome and unnecessary traffick, which hitherto we have carried on with Europe—to the great prejudice of our rising empire. . . . Providence is countenancing our navigation to this new world." Constable, Rucker, and Company of New York, whose partners included Robert Morris and Gouverneur Morris, easily sold the *Empress of China*'s cargo, returning profits of between thirty and forty thousand dollars to her investors.

This was a 30 percent return on their original investment, but given the time and risks involved, it was disappointing. So was the venality of Daniel Parker. Scarcely had the *Empress of China* cleared New York than Parker's creditors began to hear rumors of certain irregularities in his accounts. He finally admitted to embezzling huge sums of money, then skipped to Europe, leaving Duer and other investors to sort things out. Angry, embarrassed, and teetering on the edge of disaster themselves, they were looking for ways to cut their losses even before the *Empress of China* returned to New York. Years of recrimination and litigation would follow.

Five ships left New York for China in 1786. There was excited talk around city taverns and coffeehouses about opening new routes to Russia too, and at least one New York vessel, *Betsy*, had already ventured out to Madras. In the decade or so to come, trade with China and the East Indies would make rich men of such merchants as John Pintard, John Broome, and Robert Lenox.

Isaac Sears wasn't so lucky. After moving to Boston in 1777, Sears made a fortune during the war and was almost certainly the "Captain Sears of Boston" to whom Duer and his associates offered shares in the *Empress of China* in 1783. He too returned to New York late in 1783, moved into a mansion at Number 1 Broadway, opposite Bowling Green, and took an active part in the revitalization of the Sons of Liberty. By 1785, however, Sears was in trouble. Besieged by creditors, he pleaded immunity from arrest as a member of the Assembly and sailed for China. He died and was buried in Canton in October 1786.

The fate of the *Empress of China*—let alone what became of Isaac Sears—made it clear that no new trade route, even at a 30 percent rate of return, was in and of itself sufficient to ensure New York's future prosperity. Two or three years after Evacuation Day, the fitful condition of business had become a subject of debate in local newspapers, taverns, and coffeehouses. It would also make Alexander Hamilton the man of the hour.

18

The Revolution Settlement

In February 1784, finally free from imperial constraints, a group of merchants assembled at the Coffee House to organize New York's first bank. Banks were considered essential for commercial expansion, and proposals for one kind or another had been circulating around the city since before Evacuation Day. Hamilton had been trying to arrange something with Robert Morris's Bank of North America at Philadelphia, but when the Coffee House meeting came out with an attractive proposal for a Bank of New York, he changed his mind and resolved to "fall in" with the project. He also helped turn the new bank into an instrument for reconciling former enemies and deflecting radical attacks on the Tories. Alexander McDougall became the bank's first president; William Seton, a Tory, took the job of cashier. Its board of directors included Thomas Stoughton, lately arrived from England, and such prominent Tories as Joshua Waddington and Nicholas Low. Patriots like Melancton Smith, Marinus Willett, Isaac Sears, and John Lamb signed its petition to the legislature for a charter. As early as June 1784 the bank was doing business out of the old Walton Mansion on Pearl Street.

Prominent merchants also revived the Chamber of Commerce, the bulk of whose pre-Revolutionary members had sided with the British. Like the bank, the chamber heeded Hamilton's plea for reconciliation. Many Tories gained admission at its first meeting in April, and one of them, John Alsop, was elected president. More Tories joined up over the next few years, along with Whigs of every description, including William Duer, John Lamb, Alexander McDougall, and Isaac Sears, who became the chamber's vice-president. This was a signal that the town's principal men of business were welcome regardless of their opinions (allegiance to money being the only really reliable test of character) and that at least some radical Whigs too were eager to advance the city's trade and commerce.

Hamilton's program for rehabilitating Tories moved into the courts in the summer of 1784 with the case of *Rutgers v. Waddington*. Widow Elizabeth Rutgers had fled New York in 1776, leaving behind the family's brewery on Maiden Lane. Joshua Waddington, a very rich and highly unpopular Tory merchant, became the agent for two British brewers who took over the Rutgers brewery and operated it under license of the British commissary-general and, later, the commander-in-chief. When Rutgers pressed Waddington for eight thousand pounds in damages and back rent under the 1783 Trespass Act, Waddington refused to pay. Rutgers sued, and the case went before the Mayor's Court in June. To represent her, Rutgers hired a team of distinguished attorneys that included John Laurence, Robert Troup, and Attorney General Egbert Benson. Hamilton appeared for Waddington.

Hamilton took the position, as he had in his *Phocion* letters, that the Trespass Act was null and void. It violated a maxim of international law that citizens could not be held liable for actions, otherwise illegal, committed at the order of military forces. It also specifically violated the Treaty of Paris. Congress had negotiated and approved the treaty in the name of the Confederation, Hamilton reminded the court: it was the law of the land and couldn't be repealed at the whim of one or another state. Benson and Troup responded that the Trespass Act was a proper exercise of legislative power and couldn't be set aside or repealed except by the legislature.

Duane's ruling, handed down in August, was a split decision. Rutgers could recover for the period when Waddington held the property under license from the commissary-general; she couldn't recover for the time Waddington held it by authority of the British commander-in-chief, who was acting in accordance with the law of nations. As for the validity of the Trespass Act itself, Duane found no legislative intent to overrule international law. He did allow, on the other hand, that when a legislature failed to anticipate all the consequences of a statute, courts were obliged to interpret or even disregard it altogether.

Radical Whigs were appalled. The Assembly hauled in Duane to explain himself, censured his decision as a violation of legislative autonomy and a threat to law and order, then reaffirmed the Trespass Act. Hamilton was savaged in the papers for giving aid and comfort to "the most abandoned and flagitious scoundrels in the Universe," and there were rumors of a plot to have him killed. Waddington, worried that the case might be lost on appeal (if not that his attorney would go down in a blaze of pistol fire), negotiated a compromise settlement with Mrs. Rutgers.

As the first anniversary of Evacuation Day approached, New York's Tories, reassured by Hamilton's exertions on their behalf, had begun to make their peace with independence and republicanism. This in turn facilitated the growth of an alliance with conservative Whigs that would, in Hamilton's words, confront the radicals with "all the mercantile and monied influence" of the city—old Anglo-Dutch merchant families, newly arrived exporters and importers, resident agents of British trading firms, key members of the bar and other professions, and leading public creditors. For Robert Troup, one of Hamilton's most dedicated lieutenants, this was perhaps the most decisive event of the city's postwar history. "Soon after we regained possession of New York," Troup later recalled, "we permitted the Tories to enlist under our banners; and they have since manfully fought by our side in every important battle we have had with the democracy."

Over the fall and winter of 1784–85, Hamilton broadened the scope of his alliance by wooing the great Hudson Valley landowning families—Livingstons, Schuylers, Van Cortlandts, and their ilk. Their incessant jockeying for precedence had always made it difficult for them to work together, but Hamilton's message was brutally frank: cooperate or go under. As he told one of the redoubtable Livingstons, this was no time for men "concerned *for the security of property* or the prosperity of government" to quibble among themselves.

RAPPROCHEMENT

Hamilton's bid for the support of New York City's laboring population also began to get results. When elections were held for the state assembly in June 1784, defecting mechanic voters scuttled the radical ticket. Even Isaac Sears went down to defeat, running behind conservatives like Comfort Sands. (Among the new assemblymen that year was Aaron Burr, making his political debut with no principles to speak of—a development almost as noteworthy as the election of former Tories.) Several months later, the Tory merchant Nicholas Bayard drew enough votes in the balloting for City Council to defeat the incumbent Out Ward alderman Thomas Ivers. Stunned, Ivers protested that Bayard was ineligible because of his previous collaboration with the enemy. The council seated Bayard anyway, which must have struck even Hamilton as something of a miracle.

The movement of artisans and tradesmen into Hamilton's camp gathered momentum over the next several years as Governor Clinton and his supporters appeared to lose interest in restoring the city's trade and grew increasingly disdainful of Congress. Toward the end of 1784 the legislature's radical majority slapped a 2.5 percent duty on goods imported into the state and a punitive 5 percent duty on British goods entering from the West Indies. Outside the city, Clinton's impost was wildly popular, not least of all because the hundreds of thousands of dollars it soon funneled into the state treasury kept land taxes low.

Inside the city, however, the impost threatened disaster. New Jersey and Connecticut, over half of whose imports came through the port, objected vociferously to the New York impost and threatened an all-out trade war that could devastate the municipal economy. Britain not only kept its West Indian islands off limits to American shipping but began dumping its own products in the New York market. By 1786 almost twice as much tonnage had entered the port from the former mother country than from all other foreign nations combined. Local artisans and mechanics, confronted with an avalanche of cheap British manufactured goods—thirty thousand hats and ninety-seven thousand pairs of shoes between 1784 and 1786 alone—charged that Clinton had played into Britain's hands with a policy "which tends in some degree to defeat the purposes of our late revolution."

Nor were they happy with Clinton's go-it-alone strategy for the state. In 1786, buoyed by revenues from the impost, the legislature enacted a financial program that was tantamount to a declaration of independence from the Confederation. The law provided for an issue of two hundred thousand pounds in paper money. It also set aside revenues sufficient to "fund" (i.e., pay off) the entire state debt as well as that portion of the federal debt represented by Continental Loan Office certificates and notes issued for supplies furnished to the Continental Army. Holders of Continental securities (worth around $2.3 million in all) could exchange them for state securities of equal value, at the same rate of interest. Some fifty thousand pounds of the new paper money would go to pay part of the back interest that the United States had thus far failed to pay on these securities.

Clinton's program dismayed Hamilton and his circle. For years moderate and conservative Whigs had urged *federal* assumption of all Revolutionary War debts on the theory that the surest way to strengthen the Confederation government was to get the resources and influence of the public creditors behind it. Now, at least in George Clinton's New York, public creditors would be harnessed to the state government instead, and the idea of a stronger Confederation seemed suddenly more remote than ever. The city's working people had their own reasons for repudiating the governor's policy. His veiled threats of secession from the rest of the country were an affront to people who had for twenty years advocated both republicanism *and* national union.

In the 1785 Assembly elections, accordingly, conservative and moderate Whigs ran well ahead of the field, capturing the votes not only of former Tories but of many working people as well. Isaac Sears received the fewest votes of any winner, and only two mechanics were elected, shoemaker William Goforth and smith Robert Boyd, neither strongly identified with the radicals. Only James Duane's defeat by Thomas Tredwell in a race for the state senate could have been construed as a radical victory. The Mechanics Committee, recently reorganized as the General Society of Mechanics and Tradesmen, played a key role in swinging public opinion against radical candidates. It endorsed three conservative merchants known for their close ties to Hamilton: Robert Troup, William Duer, and Evert Bancker.

During the summer and fall of 1785, city newspapers were full of talk that merchants and artisans had begun to realize that each had an interest in the prosperity of the other. Popular hostility to Clinton mushroomed the following year, when the city stumbled into a mini-recession that was widely blamed on the governor's paper-money and funding bills. Caught short by a sudden rise in the price of depreciated public securities, a number of prominent investors went under, dragging their creditors down too. Others dumped huge quantities of imported goods on the market to raise cash, driving down prices and, briefly, causing a spasm of unemployment in the city's laboring population. Although timely loans from the Bank of New York saved a few of the better-connected casualties, among them the Sands brothers, petitions for bankruptcy inundated the legislature.

The almshouse, built to hold no more than four hundred people, became so overcrowded during the summer and fall of 1786 that the city government ran out of funds for public assistance and had to borrow nine hundred pounds from the bank. New commissioners of poor relief appointed by the City Council (which had only the year before scrapped the old system of elected vestrymen) struggled to rid the town of nonresident paupers. So many debtors were languishing in jail by the beginning of 1787 that a Society for the Relief of Distressed Debtors was organized to provide them with bread, wood, clothing, and other essentials.

Against this background, Hamilton's conservative alliance swept into power. Richard Varick, Nicholas Bayard, and Hamilton himself won seats in the Assembly in 1786 (this was the only elective office Hamilton would ever hold). Nicholas Bayard, Richard Harison, Comfort Sands, and Richard Varick followed suit in 1787 along with two former Tories, Gulian Verplanck and Nicholas Low. That year's local elections confirmed that Clinton and the radicals had lost their grip on the city and its environs.

Former Tories were voting openly throughout the region, and in Queens nearly one-fourth of the successful candidates had supported the crown during the Revolution.

THE RADICAL RETREAT

Though Governor Clinton won reelection in 1786—no conservative was even willing to run against him—the radicals were already too weak to prevent the reversal of nearly the entire body of anti-Tory laws for which they had been responsible over the previous decade. In 1784 and 1785 the legislature removed the acts of attainder against thirty-odd loyalists. By 1785 numerous rank-and-file Tories began to make their way back to New York from Canada and other places of refuge, hopeful that the worst was at last over.

Tories not banished by name were restored to full citizenship in 1786, and the act disqualifying them from the practice of law was repealed. In 1787, led by Hamilton and Varick (now speaker), Assembly conservatives easily beat back an attempt to deny seats to a number of former Tories. They then removed all election laws denying Tories the vote and methodically revoked the Trespass Act, the Citation Act, and, early in 1788, all other statutes inconsistent with the Treaty of Paris. In 1792 the legislature would decide to allow even banished Tories to return, providing only that they recognized the state's title to confiscated property, including slaves.

Radical threats against Trinity Church and Columbia College were repelled as well. One of Hamilton's law clerks dug up a long-lost deed that rescued Trinity's Manhattan real estate from confiscation, and shortly thereafter the relieved vestry began construction on a new church building. The college was saved when Duane, Jay, and Hamilton convinced the legislature to let Columbia elect its own board of governors, leaving it within the state university yet well insulated from meddlesome radicals. The new board promptly offered the job of president to William Samuel Johnson, the Tory son of William Johnson, first president of King's College.[1]

ESTATE SALES

Perhaps the most telling sign of the ebbing of anti-Tory radicalism came in 1788, when the state commissioners of forfeiture closed their books on the formerly occupied counties. Over the previous five years they had confiscated, broken up, and sold off the estates of more than two dozen prominent Tories in the New York area, including James De Lancey, Oliver De Lancey, William Bayard, Roger Morris, John Watts, Frederick Philipse, and Isaac Low. Their combined losses exceeded $1.2 million (claims for compensation they filed with the British government put the total closer to $10 million).

Yet given contemporary assertions that Tories owned two-thirds of the property in the city, this was a far cry from the leveling frenzy initially feared by moderate and conservative Whigs. Statewide, some 70 percent of all confiscations had occurred in Albany

---

1. Local place names continue to reflect the outcome of the struggle over Trinity's holdings. When the first streets were cut through the King's Farm in February 1790, four were named after conservative Anglicans who helped beat back the radical offensive: Duane, Jay, Harison, Provoost. Two streets honored former Tory clergymen: North Moore Street (for the Rev. Benjamin Moore) and Beach Street (for the Rev. Abraham Beach, who with Moore was appointed an assistant minister of Trinity after Provoost became rector in 1784).

and Tryon counties. New York, Kings, and Queens counties together represented a mere 2 percent of the total, and the estates of some very conspicuous Tories survived more or less intact.

Nor had there been a serious shift in the class composition of landownership in the city. While some tradesmen and shopkeepers had purchased parts of confiscated estates, a substantial majority of buyers were well-to-do Whig lawyers, merchants, and established landowners. Nearly two hundred individuals acquired pieces of James De Lancey's holdings on the east side of Manhattan. Yet fully half of the total sales can be attributed to no more than fifteen or so buyers, including William and James Beekman, four members of the Livingston clan, merchants John Delafield, Dominick Lynch, and John Delameter, and sugar refiner Isaac Roosevelt. Many of De Lancey's former tenants, unable to compete against these high bidders, promptly found themselves thrown off land they had occupied for years, with no compensation for the often extensive improvements they had made at their own expense.[2]

It was much the same story in neighboring counties. In Kings, Colonel Aquila Giles, Esq., snared all of William Axtell's Flatbush estate. The bulk of John Rapalje's estate, the largest in Brooklyn, went to ex-Tories Comfort and Joshua Sands. In Queens, property belonging to the Ludlow and Colden families went to no more than a dozen purchasers. The Manor of Bentley, Christopher Billopp's Staten Island estate, went to a single purchaser. North of the city there was a more democratic redistribution of confiscated Tory property, and many tenants of Frederick Philipse's ninety-two-thousand-acre Westchester estate purchased their holdings.

Big buyers, in fact, had an edge. State law gave preference in the purchase of confiscated estates to holders of soldiers' pay certificates and allowed purchasers to pay for land with state securities. Speculators had been purchasing both kinds of government obligations at fire-sale prices from the original holders—who either needed cash or didn't believe that the government would ever make good on its promise to pay off, or both. The gamble was that if the government did redeem the certificates and securities at or near par (face value), the current holders would pocket a very considerable profit. This so-called stockjobbing—buying and selling government notes to make money— had a very unsavory reputation. Nonetheless, by the mid-1780s millions of dollars' worth of depreciated securities had already been engrossed by a handful of New York's leading merchants and financiers.

Confiscated-estate sales gave the speculators a splendid opportunity to convert still-doubtful paper into solid land, overwhelming smaller buyers as they did so. Many then subdivided their new tracts for profitable resale, thus sustaining secondary speculation in forfeited Tory property well into the next decade. The legislature did little to deter any of this, since a number of radical as well as conservative Whigs were deeply implicated in the game. Indeed, Sears made such a poor showing in the 1784 Assembly elections partly because of revelations that he, Marinus Willett, John Lamb, John Morin Scott, and other sometime Sons of Liberty were using depreciated veterans'

2. The final indignity may well have been the survival of so many street names originally chosen by De Lancey when he staked out the area for development prior to the Revolution. These include, besides Delancey Street itself, Rivington Street (named for the sometime Tory printer), James and Oliver streets (named for the onetime governor's sons, both ardent Tories), Stanton Street (named after George Stanton, the De Lanceys' agent), and Grand Street (which was to have run through a Great Square).

pay certificates to speculate in confiscated Tory estates. In his two *Phocion* letters, Hamilton had warned the city's mechanics that their heros had feet of clay. Who could deny it now?

ORDER OUT OF CONFUSION

Four or five years after Evacuation Day, radical and conservative Whigs had come to agreement on a number of fundamental political and social questions. This "Revolution Settlement," to borrow a term from British history a century earlier, was unplanned, informal, tacit, unenforceable, and extremely fragile. It was nonetheless real, and its effect, as James Hardie would later recall in his *Description of New York* (1827), was that "the British had scarcely left our city, when order seemed to arise out of confusion."

Key elements of New York's Revolution Settlement read like an obituary for the radical resurgence of 1783–84. By 1786 or 1787 it was accepted on all sides that the rule of self-appointed committees should give way to the rule of law, that there were to be no further confiscatory assaults on private property, that former Tories should be admitted to the full privileges of citizenship, and that vital institutions—the municipal corporation itself, Columbia College, Trinity Church—would remain in the hands of the propertied classes.

Conservative Whigs knew, however, that the radical insurgency had been blunted, not defeated, and that the base lines of public discourse in the city would have to change. To avoid the taint of royalism, they could no longer dispute such principles as natural rights, government by consent of the governed, and popular sovereignty. Never again could they advocate religious establishments as essential for the preservation of order and property, and they raised no objection when the state legislature adopted a succession of laws between 1782 and 1787 that repealed primogeniture and entail, provided for the commutation of quitrents, and abolished all feudal obligations and tenures in the state—gutting, that is, the legal infrastructure set up in the wake of the 1664 conquest and Leisler's Rebellion. They squirmed but didn't resist when the legislature divided every county into townships, further weakening the power of the great upriver manor lords. They likewise accepted the fact that the legislature would henceforth determine the powers and privileges of banks, colleges, benevolent societies, and other chartered corporations. Even former Tories understood that from now on the issue wouldn't be *whether* to have a republic but *what kind* of republic to have.

What was more, following Hamilton's lead, conservative Whigs and former Tories had begun to acknowledge that the route to public office now ran through a mobilized, demanding electorate. Gone forever were the days when men of wealth and social position could presume the deference or indifference of voters: political power henceforth required organization, a readiness to curry support among ordinary people, and a willingness to abide by what happened at the polls. That Hamilton and company had virtually driven the Clintonians out of town by 1787 or 1788 only clinched the point. Public life in New York would never be the same.

Some things, on the other hand, did not change, and the outer limits of the Revolution Settlement were defined by its failure to address issues of gender and race.

DAUGHTERS OF LIBERTY

For New York women, as women, the Revolution was an ambiguous experience. On the one hand, they had helped mobilize resistance to Britain and made often crucial contri-

butions to the war effort—spying on the enemy, collecting money and clothing and provisions for the army, making bandages and ammunition, tending the wounded, carrying
water and powder during battle, on occasion fighting alongside regular troops (women
were active on the Tory side too, but much less so). The state legislature acknowledged
the extent of their involvement when it allowed that women could be convicted of treason—an unprecedented admission that they had the capacity to choose their own political allegiances, independently of their husbands and fathers. None of this, on the other
hand, led to fundamental changes in the gender system itself—the different roles and
rights assigned to men and women—which survived the conflict with Britain
unchanged, even strengthened.

Most important, republicanism put new emphasis on defining the right to participate in politics and government as an attribute of property. It was axiomatic among male
revolutionaries that republics were vulnerable to persons with the wealth, power, and
influence to make others do their bidding. This meant, among other things, that voters
as well as officeholders must possess sufficient property to be politically independent—
free, that is, to discern and serve the public good without fear for their livelihoods.

By the same token, people having little or no property should be disqualified from
taking part in public affairs because they were too easily led, swayed, and dominated.
Inasmuch as New York law continued to follow the doctrine of "coverture," which
didn't allow women to hold property in their own names, it seemed more obvious than
ever (to men) that women, like children and slaves, had no right to vote, much less hold
office. Thus, while colonial authorities sometimes permitted well-to-do widows to cast
ballots in municipal and provincial elections, that practice would not survive the Revolution. In fact, New York became the first state to officially disfranchise women when
the constitution of 1777 specifically defined the electorate as *male*. No matter the extent
of their contributions to the struggle against Britain: republican women were destined
by republican men to be passive, second-class citizens.

Then, too, what conventional male wisdom considered to be the inherent foibles of
women—their impulsiveness, their love of luxury and self-indulgence, their limited
powers of reason—only made it more apparent that they deserved no role in republican
politics and government. Not surprisingly, the new republic's ideal citizen was unfailingly identified by male attributes and duties: *his* preparedness to take up arms in
defense of the state, *his* authority as the head of a household of dependents, *his* pride as
an autonomous producer of wealth, *his* responsibility to sit on juries and pay taxes. If
anything, "woman" and "citizen" were considered irreconcilable opposites, states of
being forever at war with one another.

Among the propertied classes, this resurgent patriarchalism gave rise to a notion
that the chief duty of women was to bear and raise sons for service to the republic. But
while it seemed to endow their work with new public significance, what came to be
called Republican Motherhood essentially compelled women to return to the "sphere"
of family and household. For women of the white laboring classes, republican patriarchalism could have still more calamitous consequences. War heroine Elizabeth Burgin,
finding herself penniless, wrote General Washington directly: "I am now Sir very Desolate without Money without Close or friends to go to," she explained, as "helping our
poor preseners Brought Me to Want Whitch I dont Repent." Her plea brought results,
but it was an isolated success: few women who worked for the army, or widows of enlisted men, ever received equitable assistance. Poor women, moreover, could hardly afford

to devote their lives to childrearing and found the new standard of republican mother-hood virtually impossible to meet—which to men and women of property became prima facie evidence of irresponsibility and moral depravity. Although propertylessness brought poor men too under increased suspicion, they at least could derive some small measure of comfort from knowing that the republic belonged to men.

EMANCIPATION

Within a year of the Treaty of Paris, Massachusetts, New Hampshire, Vermont, Pennsylvania, Rhode Island, and Connecticut—all of the northern states, that is, except New York and New Jersey—had either abolished slavery outright or adopted programs for its gradual abolition. When Gouverneur Morris and John Jay tried to insert a clause into the 1777 state constitution "recommending" the eventual abolition of slavery, they ran into a wall of resistance; Morris himself admitted that "it would at present be productive of great dangers to liberate the slaves within this state." In 1781 the legislature did agree to manumit slaves who had taken up arms against the British, but this was a grudging response at best to General Clinton's offer of freedom to slaves who remained loyal to the crown. When the Society of Friends took steps to free all slaves owned by the state's Quakers, their example inspired little or no imitation. (The appropriateness of indentured servitude was another matter. In 1784 a group of citizens purchased the freedom of a parcel of servants, observing that "the traffick of White People" was contrary "to the idea of liberty.")

Slaves in and around the city grew increasingly restless after the war, stirred by the ideals of the Revolution as well as by local traditions of resistance and rebellion. For Jupiter Hammon, a slave who had published occasional religious verses and essays while serving three generations of the Lloyd family in Queens, this new mood was profoundly troubling. In *An Address to the Negroes of the State of New-York* (1787), the seventy-year-old Hammon urged his fellow bondsmen not to dwell upon the idea of freedom and not to forget their duty to obey their masters. Many slaves had nonetheless already rejected that advice. Some pressured their masters for improved treatment, occasionally even extracting written promises of freedom. Large numbers of others simply disappeared—so large, in fact, that runaway notices filled local papers and gangs of white "blackbirders" were able to make a living as free-lance slavecatchers.

In January and February 1785, frustrated by the state's foot-dragging on abolition and alarmed by a recent attempt to seize free blacks for sale as slaves, thirty-two prominent citizens of widely divergent political views—radical Whigs, conservative Whigs, even the odd Tory or two—met at the Coffee House to organize the New York Manumission Society. Among those present were Governor George Clinton, Alexander Hamilton, Egbert Benson, Mayor James Duane, Melancton Smith, and a strong contingent of Quakers (including Robert Bowne and John Murray). John Jay was elected president of the society, notwithstanding the fact that he owned five slaves—no disqualification, to be sure, considering that at least half the society's founders were slaveowners; Governor Clinton alone owned eight.

That same year, antislavery members of the legislature—urged along by the New York Society of Friends and the Manumission Society—brought in a bill for the gradual abolition of slavery. After a ferocious fight with assemblymen from Kings, Richmond, and Ulster counties, whose predominately Dutch constituents still relied heavily on slave labor to work their farms, the bill passed. The Council of Revision promptly vetoed the measure because it denied free blacks the right to vote or hold public office.

Some weeks later, however, the council did approve a voluntary emancipation law that allowed masters to manumit slaves between twenty-one and fifty years of age without any obligation for their subsequent upkeep (a break with colonial precedents)—on condition that local overseers of the poor first certified, in writing, that the slaves would be able to provide for themselves. (Manumission of a slave over fifty still required owners to post a bond of two hundred pounds to ensure that he or she wouldn't become a public burden.) Getting the "poor certificate" now became central to the process for obtaining liberty. In Quamio Buccau's case, as he later recalled, his master, William Griffith, having decided to free him and his wife, Sarah, summoned the overseers of the poor to the house. The couple was called into Griffith's office "and there we stood as if we were just married. Squire Adams asked me how I felt—and I told him 'I feel very well. I tank you, Sir: I feel very well in my limbs.'"

Though the Manumission Society prodded other masters to free their slaves, few New Yorkers followed Griffith's example during the next fifteen years. The society, lowering its sights, concentrated instead on publicizing cases of abuse and set up a registry to protect freedmen against reenslavement. In 1786 it won adoption of a law freeing all slaves who still remained state property as the result of the confiscation of Tory estates. (How many is unknown, though a dozen or so men and women formerly belonging to the Philipse, Axtell, Bayard, and other Tory families were being supported at public expense as late as the 1820s.)

That same year, too, the society founded an African Free School in a one-room building on Cliff Street. There, besides learning to read and write, boys could acquire the values and discipline that would keep them from "running into practices of Immorality or Sinking into Habits of Idleness." Girls were admitted after 1792. To be accepted, however, free blacks had to stay sober, not associate with slaves, and live clean lives—by which the society meant, among other things, that they would tolerate no "Fiddling, Dancing or any noisy Entertainments in their houses."

In 1788, having discovered that numbers of New Yorkers were selling a "very considerable" number of slaves to agents of southern planters in anticipation of further restrictions, the society persuaded the legislature to stop the sale of slaves for removal to another state and to prohibit the importation of slaves into the state. It did not, on the other hand, oppose the adoption of New York's first comprehensive slave code since 1730—a severe setback to the antislavery cause inasmuch as it ensured that the institution would have a solid legal foundation for the foreseeable future. Nor did it press to have the port closed to ships involved in the slave trade, as other northern states had done.

By 1790 slavery had been solidly reestablished in New York. True, the percentage of blacks in Manhattan's population had fallen to 10 percent, and roughly one-third of the 3,096 African Americans in the city were now free. Yet the absolute number of slaves was growing, and, taking the southern six counties of New York as a whole, nearly three of every four blacks were still slaves. Moreover, those 9,447 men, women, and children represented an investment of nearly one and a half million dollars, a sizable obstacle to emancipation.

The use of slave labor remained as widespread as ever. One in five white households in the city, scattered broadly through every ward and representing all but the very poorest classes, owned at least one slave. Two-thirds of the merchants kept slaves, mostly for use as domestic servants—cooks, butlers, gardeners, stable hands, and the like. (Females still significantly outnumbered males, constituting 57 percent of the total black population in 1786.) One of every eight artisans held slaves too; numerically, artisans remained the city's largest group of slaveholders and continued to depend on slave labor for production in workshops, breweries, ropewalks, sail lofts, and shipyards. In the immediate hinterlands of Manhattan, the pervasiveness of slave labor was even more striking. Forty percent of the white households within a ten-mile radius of the city owned slaves—a higher proportion than in the whole of any southern state. In Kings County, still strongly Dutch and still heavily dependent on its servile work force to produce goods for the urban market, blacks comprised one-third of the forty-five hundred residents; in some parts of the county, two of every three white households owned slaves. Only in Westchester, two-thirds of whose slaves disappeared between 1776 and 1783, did it appear that the Revolution had inflicted any lasting damage on the institution of slavery.

19

The Grand
Federal Procession

In May 1787 delegates from a narrow majority of the thirteen states met in Philadelphia to identify "defects" in the Articles of Confederation and propose such remedies "as shall appear to them necessary to render the constitution of the Federal Government adequate to the exigencies of the Union." To represent New York, the state legislature had chosen Alexander Hamilton and two veteran Clintonians, Robert Yates and John Lansing, declaring that the three would attend "for the sole and express purpose of revising the Articles of Confederation." But when the Philadelphia Convention got down to work at the end of the month, it became apparent at once that the delegates were ready to draw up a brand-new frame of government for the United States.

Hamilton treated the convention to a remarkable five-hour lecture in which he confessed his admiration for the British system and proposed his own plan for a "completely sovereign" national government, all but eliminating the states and stipulating the election of a president and senate for life. But he realized that such notions "went beyond the ideas of most members," and at the end of June, bored and irritated, he returned to New York. Yates and Lansing followed in short order, protesting that their instructions didn't "embrace an idea of such magnitude as to assent to a general constitution." In their absence, the convention proceeded to draft a federal constitution. Congress (still sitting in New York) officially transmitted the resulting document to the states, ratification by nine of the thirteen being required for it to take effect.

In New York, the proposed government faced an uphill fight. Advocates of ratification, now called Federalists, looked very strong among the wealthiest classes throughout the state and among all segments of the population in the city—thanks in no small part to Hamilton, who finally signed the Constitution as better than "anarchy and

Convulsion." In the rural upriver counties, however, home to the bulk of the state's population and the heartland of Clintonianism, it was the "Antifederalists" who seemed unassailable.

"WHAT ARE YOU, BOY, FEDERAL OR ANTI-FEDERAL?"

Both sides rehearsed their arguments in a heated newspaper and pamphlet war that began in the summer of 1787 and raged for the better part of a year. Hundreds of essays and pamphlets and broadsides, for as well as against ratification, would be published in the city, and no one, it seemed, could talk of anything else. Apologizing to readers who wanted "NEWS, as well as POLITICS," Thomas Greenleaf of the *New-York Journal* explained that "the RAGE of the season is, Hallow, damme, Jack, what are you, boy, FEDERAL or ANTI-FEDERAL?" (There were now half a dozen papers published in the city. Francis Childs's *Daily Advertiser*, founded in 1785, appeared daily, only the third paper in the country to do so. The *New York Morning Post*, founded in 1783, became a daily in 1786. John Holt's *New-York Journal*, taken over by Greenleaf early in 1787, briefly became a daily in 1787–88 because Greenleaf said he would otherwise be unable to print half of the essays he received supporting or opposing the Constitution.)

Antifederalist opinion drew heavily on the radical Whig conviction that concentrated power was a menace to liberty. Under the Constitution, Antifederalists charged, the federal government's broad prerogatives—to tax, to raise armies, to regulate commerce, to administer justice—would sooner or later overwhelm the states, pulverize individual rights, and sink the republic under a mass of corruption. Then, too, large republics had always succumbed to tyrants or dissolved in civil war. The great diversity of the American people, to say nothing of the distances separating them, offered no reason to hope that the United States could escape a similar fate.

Under the Constitution, Antifederalists also stressed, Congress would be too small and too remote from the people to represent them effectively. The widely circulated *Letters from the Federal Farmer*, a pamphlet that first appeared in November 1787 (probably written by Melancton Smith), stressed the inadequacy of representation under the Constitution. "Natural aristocrats" and demagogues, it argued, would have a better chance of winning election to Congress than men drawn from "the substantial and respectable part of the democracy." No wonder, other Antifederalists said knowingly, that the Constitution was supported by the rich and well-born few.

Federalists, defending the Constitution, asserted that under the Articles of Confederation the country was falling apart. While Congress looked on helplessly, violent factionalism and insurrection had afflicted one state after another—most recently Massachusetts, where insurgent farmers led by Daniel Shays had closed courts in the western part of the state and in January 1787 mounted an abortive attack on the federal arsenal at Springfield. Trade and commerce meanwhile continued to languish, public credit had evaporated, and Congress, powerless to defend its own interests against foreign nations, had become an international laughingstock. The Constitution would end this misery by establishing a stronger, more energetic national government—which of course, Federalists said, explains why it had met with such opposition from popular demagogues and state politicians fearful of losing influence.

Toward the end of October 1787, the *Independent Journal* ran the first of eighty-five essays by "Publius." Published together the following May as *The Federalist*, they were the fruit of a brilliant collaboration between Hamilton, Jay, and Congressman James Madison of Viriginia. Their exhaustive, clause-by-clause defense of the Constitution remains the most famous contribution to the debate on either side and a landmark of American discourse on government. Two crucial arguments of *The Federalist*, both related to the issue of representation, would have seemed especially compelling to readers in New York.

First, under the Articles of Confederation too many decisions of national importance depended on state governments that had been taken over by the wrong sort of men: men unprepared by wealth or education to conduct public business, "men of factious tempers, of local prejudices, or of sinister designs . . . [who] practice with success the vicious arts by which elections are too often carried"—exactly the kind of "democratical" leaders, in other words, who had followed George Clinton into office in New York after 1776. But the Constitution would set things right by causing an "ENLARGEMENT of the ORBIT" of government sufficient to exclude from power all but the "proper guardians of the public weal." Congress, having powers commensurate with its responsibilities, would draw more "fit characters" into public life, and large electoral districts would ensure the election of those "who possess the most attractive merit and the most diffusive and established characters"—which was, of course, the very thing that worried the Antifederalists.

Second, it was wrong to think that these "diffusive and established characters"—in New York City, this meant the merchant elite—would be unable to comprehend "the interests and feelings of the different classes of citizens." They had to stand for election, after all, and would always want to pay close attention to the "dispositions and inclinations" of the voters. Also, by virtue of their ties to all segments of the laboring population, merchants had a very clear picture of what was good for the mass of their fellow citizens. Indeed, honest tradesmen knew that "the merchant is their natural patron and friend; and they are aware, that however great the confidence they may justly feel in their own good sense, their interests can be more effectually promoted by the merchant than by themselves. They are sensible that their habits in life have not been such as to give them those acquired endowments, without which, in a deliberative assembly, the great natural abilities are for the most part useless."

But for many New Yorkers it was a third contention of *The Federalist* that must have clinched the case: ratification of the Constitution was indispensable to their future prosperity. By giving Congress the exclusive power to regulate foreign commerce, "Publius" declared, the Constitution would permit the United States to extract "commercial privileges of the most valuable and extensive kind" from Great Britain—above all to reopen the lucrative West Indian markets that had anchored the city's economy before independence. Similarly, allowing Congress to create a navy "would enable us to bargain with great advantage for commercial privileges" in the event of war between European nations; it would also provide employment for seamen as well as for the many artisans engaged in building and outfitting ships. A string of other powers bestowed on Congress—to borrow and coin money, to establish post offices, to fix the standard of weights and measures, to make uniform laws of bankruptcy—would meanwhile remove annoying obstacles to the expansion of domestic markets. The only alternative to ratification, in fact, was national ruin. "Poverty and disgrace would overspread a country which, with wisdom, might make herself the admiration and envy of the world."

VOX POPULI

By January 1788, when the regular session of the legislature got underway, five states—Delaware, New Jersey, Pennsylvania, Georgia, and Connecticut—had ratified the Constitution, and conventions were deliberating in several others. After stalling for several weeks, the Clintonian legislature called for a ratification convention to meet in Poughkeepsie in mid-June. The election of delegates would take place at the end of April. Each county would send as many delegates as it had assemblymen. And—in an unusual but noncontroversial move—existing property requirements would be waived so that all free male citizens aged twenty-one and over would be entitled to vote.

During February and March upstate Antifederalists organized a network of county committees that distributed literature, nominated candidates, and aroused voters in anticipation of the election. In New York City, though, they moved hesitantly at best. Public opinion there was running strongly in favor of the Constitution, and news that Massachusetts had ratified in early February was greeted with spontaneous demonstrations and a parade. John Lamb, Melancton Smith, Marinus Willett, and other city Antifederalists finally set up a committee in April, but it stuck to dispatching essays and pamphlets to Antifederalist committees throughout the northeast and didn't even bother to get up a proper municipal ticket for the Poughkeepsie convention. Most of the key Manhattan leaders put their names up in Ulster, Dutchess, and Queens counties, where they were almost certain of victory. By contrast, the New York City "Federal Committee" pulsed with activity. It got up an impressive slate of candidates, including John Jay, James Duane, and Alexander Hamilton, and had its slate endorsed by special meetings of the "German inhabitants," the "Master Carpenters," a group of "Mechanics and Tradesmen," and the St. Andrew's Society, among others.

When the votes were tallied at the end of April, Antifederalists came out well ahead statewide. Queens went Antifederalist by a five-to-four margin. Kings, Richmond, and Westchester came in solidly Federalist. Manhattan produced a Federalist landslide: all told, 2,836 men went to the polls there—the highest turnout thus far in the city's history—and John Jay paced the Federalists with 2,735 votes, an impressive 96 percent of the total. Nicholas Low, who trailed the ticket, got 2,651. Governor Clinton received a paltry 134 votes, and Marinus Willett and William Denning garnered just 108 and 102 votes, respectively. Willett, chastened, was said to be coming round to the view that the Constitution "might be right—since it appears to be the sense of a vast majority."

The convention thus promised a face-off between rural and urban forces, and between delegates whose backgrounds differed in other ways as well. Federalists were predominantly merchants, lawyers, former officers in the Continental Army, Anglicans, socially prominent, well-off, and college educated; most had had experience in high public office. Antifederalists were mostly older than their counterparts and had entered politics later in life. They were the "new men" associated with Governor George Clinton: farmers, rising entrepreneurs, sometime militia officers, Presbyterians, self-educated, self-made, radical Whig in outlook, and utterly lacking the social connections and graces that had been essential to political advancement before the Revolution.

On Saturday, June 14, 1788, while crowds cheered and cannon boomed, New York's delegates to the ratifying convention boarded Hudson River sloops for the village of Poughkeepsie, seventy-five miles upriver. Governor Clinton and his party left later the same day, almost unnoticed. When the convention got underway in the village courthouse the following Tuesday, however, Clinton had a happier time of it. The Antifederalist majority, obviously in control, settled him in the chair and had two staunch opponents of the Constitution appointed secretaries.

The outnumbered Federalists weren't without resources, even so. Alexander Hamilton, Robert R. Livingston, and John Jay were three of the foremost orators in the nation. Of them one observer remarked: "Hn's harangues combine the poignancy of vinegar with the smoothness of oil: his manner wins attention; his matter proselytes the judgment. . . . L pours a stream of eloquence deep as the Ganges. . . . Mr. Jy's reasoning is weighty as gold, polished as silver, and strong as steel." Melancton Smith readily admitted that the Federalists had all the "advantages of Abilities and habit of public speaking."

Time was now on the Federalists' side too. Eight states had already ratified the Constitution, and conventions in two more, New Hampshire and Virginia, were in session. Ratification by either one would be sufficient to dissolve the old Confederation and launch the new federal union. All the Federalists in New York had to do was keep the opposition from bringing the issue to an early vote. They thus scored an important tactical victory of their own on the opening day when the convention agreed to discuss the Constitution clause by clause before deciding whether to ratify.

Six days later, on June 25, express riders reached New York City and Poughkeepsie with word that New Hampshire had ratified. In Poughkeepsie the Antifederalists insisted that the news didn't upset their calculations—without Virginia, they reminded everyone, federal union remained highly problematic—but Virginia, it soon turned out, had ratified that very day. The news got to New York City at three o'clock in the morning of July 2. Bells began to peal and continued until dawn, when ten twenty-four-pounders fired a loud salute to the new government. William Livingston, who had set out immediately for Poughkeepsie, galloped up to the courthouse around noon the same day and burst in upon the convention with the story. Federalist delegates cheered, and spectators paraded around the building with fife and drum. With only New York and Rhode Island now out of the Union, it seemed certain that the Antifederalists would accept the inevitable and vote for the Constitution.

They didn't. Rallied by Smith, the Antifederalists put forward a plan for limited or conditional ratification: they would agree to the Constitution providing that, within a specified period of time, a "bill of rights" was added to safeguard freedom of the press, freedom of conscience, and other individual liberties. If the desired amendments failed to materialize, the state would withdraw its ratification. Hamilton and the Federalists denounced the idea, contending that it would cause more trouble and confusion than outright rejection of the Constitution. The Antifederalists were adamant, however, and for another several weeks it remained unclear what the convention would do.

THE FEDERAL SHIP *HAMILTON*

Down in New York City, the Antifederalists' demand for a bill of rights raised a hurricane of indignation, not least of all because Congress had already started talking about where to go if the Poughkeepsie convention failed to ratify the Constitution. "You have no idea of the rage of the Inhabitants of this City," Samuel Blachley Webb wrote a friend, adding that if ratification did not happen soon, "I do not believe the life of the Governor & his party would be safe in this place."

Many people suggested that the city should secede from the state and ratify the Constitution separately. Newspapers in Pennsylvania and Connecticut as well as New York carried reports that Richmond, Kings, Queens, Suffolk, and Westchester counties were also prepared to cast their lot with a new state if the convention failed to ratify. There was speculation about the likelihood of civil war, and when John Lamb led a party of Antifederalists down to the Battery to burn a copy of the Constitution, they had to fight their way out of the angry crowd that surrounded them.

Federalist spokesmen in Poughkeepsie reminded the opposition that Congress was important to the city and that the city was indispensable to the state. Jay told the convention that Congress pumped a hundred thousand pounds a year into the municipal economy. In fact, he said, "All the Hard Money in the City of New York arises from the Sitting of Congress there." Chancellor Livingston worried that the state's isolation from the Union would be economically ruinous and raised the possibility that "the Southern part of the State may separate."

Hamilton went further: a separation was inevitable, he warned, if New York rejected the Constitution. Although Governor Clinton reprimanded Hamilton from the chair for this "highly indiscreet and improper" threat, Antifederalists were now clearly worried about the mood of the city.

It was in this setting that city Federalists mounted a "Grand Federal Procession" to celebrate the Constitution. Similar events had been staged in Boston, Philadelphia, Charleston, and other cities, and during June, if not earlier, arrangements were underway for something equivalent in New York. Originally scheduled to coincide with the city's Fourth of July festivities, the New York procession was repeatedly postponed because its organizers kept waiting for word of ratification from Poughkeepsie. Finally, their patience at an end, they called for participants to assemble in the Common at eight o'clock on the morning of July 23.

Five thousand men and boys representing sixty-odd trades and professions showed up despite a light drizzle, all in costume and accompanied by colorful floats and banners proclaiming the happiness and prosperity that would follow from stronger national union. The Bakers, positioned near the front of the column by white-coated assistants with speaking trumpets, held aloft a ten-foot "federal loaf" and "a flag, representing the declension of trade under the old Confederation." After them came the other trades with banners proclaiming the certain return of prosperity under the new government. "May we succeed in our trade and the union protect us!" declared that of the Peruke Makers and Hair Dressers; further down the line of march were the Black Smiths, hammering away on an anchor and chanting: "Forge me strong, finish me neat, I soon shall moor a Federal fleet."

Towering over every other display was the "Federal Ship *Hamilton*" in the Seventh Division. A scaled-down thirty-two-gun frigate, twenty-seven feet in length, it rumbled along behind a team of ten horses "with flowing sheets, and full sails . . . the canvass waves dashing against her sides, the wheels of the carriage concealed." A "federal ship" had figured in similar processions elsewhere, but none honored a specific individual. Its preeminent role in the New York proceedings was dramatic testimony to Hamilton's effectiveness in linking adoption of the Constitution to the city's economic well-being. As the nearby banner of the Ship Joiners proclaimed: "This Federal Ship Will Our Commerce Revive / And Merchants and Shipwrights and Joiners Will Thrive." There was even talk that day of renaming the city "Hamiltoniana" in his honor.

The marchers headed down Broadway to Great Dock Street, where the *Hamilton* exchanged salutes with a Spanish packet, then swung over to Hanover Square and moved through Queen, Chatham, and Arundel streets to Bayard's Tavern on Bullock Street. The Committee of Arrangements, members of Congress, and "the Gentlemen on Horseback" reviewed the marchers outside the tavern, and the *Hamilton* changed pilots to guide it from the "Old Constitution" to the new. More cannon were fired. Everyone then sat down to a banquet at tables set up around a canvas pavilion designed

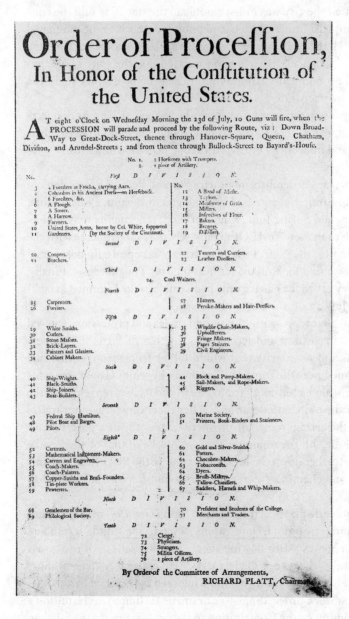

Artisans dominated the first eight "divisions" in the line of march, followed by lawyers, merchants, and clergy—testimony not only to the depth of support for the Constitution among working people, but also to the importance of the organized trades in the public life of the city after Independence. (© Collection of The New-York Historical Society)

by a French architect, Major Charles Pierre L'Enfant. After a feast of roast ham, bullock, and mutton, the day-long festivities concluded with a toast to "the Convention of the State of New York; may they soon add an eleventh pillar to the Federal Edifice."

Antifederalists scoffed and sneered, but the Grand Federal Procession was an event of almost transcendent significance in New York's post-Revolutionary history. Nominally, it dramatized the breadth of local support for the Constitution and, by implication, the city's determination not to be left out of the new federal union. No less important, arguably even more so, the massed presence of the trades also gave tangible expression to the organized artisanal presence that was already altering the course of municipal affairs. After two decades of upheaval and war, New York's numerous mechanics had come to see themselves as equal citizens, actively engaged in the life of the community. Their best qualities—their respect for labor, their selfless interdependence, their usefulness to society, their unflinching patriotism—were the very essence of republican virtue.

Up in Poughkeepsie, the Antifederalists had already decided to surrender. That morning, even as the marchers were moving out of the Fields, Samuel Jones, the Queens Antifederalist, made a motion to ratify the Constitution "in full confidence" that a bill of rights would be forthcoming. Melancton Smith supported the motion, explaining that he feared the consequences if New York spurned the Union—"Convulsions in the Southern part, factions and discord in the rest." Jones's motion passed. The Federalists, in turn, accepted thirty-two "recommendatory" and twenty-three "explanatory" amendments to the Constitution and agreed to urge a second convention to consider them. A final vote next day produced a margin of thirty to twenty-seven for ratification—the narrowest in any state.

Silk banner carried by the Society of Pewterers in the Federal Procession. (© Collection of The New-York Historical Society)

An express rider carried the news down to New York City on the evening of the twenty-sixth. Jubilant crowds again surged through the streets. One group ransacked the office of Greenleaf's Antifederalist *Journal* and made off with his type. Another paraded over to Governor Clinton's residence, gave three hisses, and beat the rogue's march; there was talk of going after John Lamb as well, but nothing came of it. More commotion followed a few days later when the Federalist delegation returned from Poughkeepsie. Cheering crowds greeted them at the waterfront, and eleven-gun salutes were fired before each of their houses.

INAUGURATION DAY

At the end of the summer of 1788, the Confederation Congress designated New York City as the temporary seat of the new federal government. Both it and the City Council then vacated City Hall so the building could be converted into a suitable capitol by L'Enfant. He gave it a complete facelift and turned its interior into a showcase of plush, some said extravagant, neoclassicism. In November, as elections for the new government got underway, the old Congress adjourned for good, leaving the country with no central government for the next five months.

L'Enfant's work was substantially complete by March 4, 1789, when the new Congress convened in what was now Federal Hall—over which, in honor of the occasion, flew the flag of the "Federal Ship *Hamilton*." After waiting anxiously for a month to get quorums, the Senate and House were at last able to count the ballots cast by presidential electors. To no one's surprise, George Washington was the unanimous choice. Genuinely dismayed by the news, Washington left Mount Vernon for New York in mid-April, hoping to have "a quiet entry to the city devoid of ceremony." He felt, he said, like "a culprit who is going to the place of his execution."

His week-long journey to Manhattan proved anything but quiet. Every town, village, and hamlet marked the president-elect's passage with ecstatic crowds, honor guards, booming artillery, ringing church bells, banquets, speeches, triumphal arches, and rose-strewn streets. New York churned with anticipation. "All the world here are busy in collecting flowers and sweets of every kind to amuse and delight the President in his approach and on his arrival," one man wrote. Washington portraits went up everywhere. The initials *G. W.* appeared on front doors, buttons, and tobacco boxes. Local taverns and boardinghouses were besieged by excited visitors, many of whom had to settle for lodgings in nearby villages and campgrounds.

On April 23, Washington entered Elizabethtown, New Jersey, where an official welcoming committee from New York (Robert R. Livingston, Richard Varick, Egbert Benson) was waiting in a red-canopied barge to escort him across the Hudson River. As the barge pulled away from the New Jersey shore, rowed by thirteen harbor pilots in sparkling white uniforms, it was surrounded by a dense mass of vessels, one of which bore musicians and a chorus whose voices were barely audible above the roar of cannon from shore batteries and a Spanish warship in the harbor. One witness, who watched the barge pass the Battery, commented that the "successive motion of the hats" of cheering bystanders "was like the rolling motion of the sea, or a field of grain." Governor Clinton and Mayor Duane greeted Washington at Murray's Wharf at the foot of Wall Street on the East River. Clinton said a few words, which almost nobody could hear over the din, and then, preceded by a military guard and two marching bands, escorted Washington up Wall Street through throngs of well-wishers. Turning into Pearl Street, the procession moved slowly along to Cherry Street and the Presidential Residence, a private mansion that had been handsomely refurbished at a cost of twenty thousand pounds (all of it raised by private contributions).

Thursday, April 30, was Inauguration Day, and the city awakened at dawn to a salute from the guns on the Battery. At nine o'clock, hour-long services got under way in all churches. Congress assembled at noon and dispatched a party of dignitaries to fetch the president-elect from his Cherry Street residence. After some inevitable confusion over the formalities—there were no precedents to rely upon, after all, and nobody remembered to bring a Bible—Washington stepped out on the second-floor balcony of Federal Hall, dressed for the occasion in a plain suit of "superfine American Broad Cloth" from a mill in Hartford, Connecticut. He hoped, he had said, that it would soon "be unfashionable for a gentleman to appear in any other dress" than one of American manufacture.

"The scene was solemn and awful beyond description," wrote one spectator. Chancellor Livingston administered the oath of office, then, overcome by emotion, bellowed, "Long Live George Washington, President of the United States!" The densely packed crowd below responded with "loud and repeated shouts" of approval, and Washington went back inside to deliver his inaugural address. Afterward, he and the members of Congress walked up to St. Paul's on Broadway for a worship service.

That evening, visitors and residents jammed the streets to gawk at "illuminations"—huge backlit transparent paintings of patriotic subjects erected here and there around the city. One, at the lower end of Broadway, showed Washington with the figure of Fortitude, flanked by the Senate and House and surmounted by the forms of Justice and Wisdom. Another, displayed at the John Street Theater, showed Fame descending

Inauguration of General George Washington as President, 1789. Engraving by Montbaron & Gautschi.
(© Collection of The New-York Historical Society)

from heaven like an angel to bestow immortality on the new President. Even the residence of the Spanish minister was bedecked with moving transparencies that depicted the past, present, and future glories of America. Bands played, houses and ships in the harbor blazed with candles, and the skies above crackled with a two-hour-long display of fireworks. Washington, who watched the show from Chancellor Livingston's house, had to get home on foot because the streets were too full of people for his carriage to pass.

20

Capital City

New York had been the de facto capital of the nation since 1785, but the transition from Confederation to Constitution gave new snap and sophistication to life in the city. Trailing behind President Washington came a multitude of Revolutionary heroes and near-heroes—"the most celebrated persons from the various parts of the United States," as the French reformer Brissot de Warville wrote in his *New Travels in the United States* (the first American edition of which appeared in New York in 1792). A brief stroll through the streets of lower Manhattan could bring residents face to face with Vice-President John Adams, Secretary of War Henry Knox, Attorney General Edmund Randolph, Congressman James Madison, or Senator John Hancock; Thomas Jefferson, currently American ambassador to France, would arrive in another six months or so to take up his duties as secretary of state. So many of the republic's most famous men converged on New York over the spring and summer of 1789 that the painter John Trumbull moved to the city in December to finish the portraits on his monumental canvas *The Declaration of Independence*.

Washington drew numerous prominent New Yorkers into the new federal orbit. John Jay became the first chief justice of the Supreme Court. Alexander Hamilton was named secretary of the treasury on the recommendation of Senator Robert Morris (Hamilton was "damned sharp," Morris told Washington, who surely knew it already); Hamilton in turn chose William Duer for assistant secretary of the treasury. Gouverneur Morris took the post of ambassador to France, General John Lamb became collector of the port, and Richard Harison got the office of U.S. attorney. Chancellor Livingston thought he deserved a cabinet-level appointment but came up empty-handed—the only notable New Yorker to be snubbed by the administration. Although James Duane wanted to join General Philip Schuyler in the Senate, Governor Clinton arranged for the selection of Rufus King, a well-connected Massachusetts politician who had just moved down to the city. Instead, Duane got the job of first judge of the federal district court of New York. Richard Varick took over as mayor.

Municipal and state officials did their best to accommodate the federal government's need for space and quiet deliberation. Congress complained that the ringing of bells at funerals disturbed its deliberations; local authorities obligingly banned the practice. The chief executive's hemorrhoids flared up, and his doctors insisted that he stay in bed for six weeks; a chain was stretched across the street outside his residence to reduce the clatter of traffic. Additional renovations were required on Federal Hall; officials organized a lottery to raise seventy-five hundred pounds.[1]

There was even talk about turning lower Manhattan into the federal district envisioned in the Constitution, complete with government offices, residences, parks, and gardens; one plan designated Governors Island, just across the harbor, as the site for a presidential mansion. Eager to cooperate, the city demolished the old Anglo-Dutch fort on the Battery over the summer of 1789, uncovering, among other things, the coffin of Lord Bellomont and the cornerstone of the church erected during Willem Kieft's regime a century and a half earlier. Once the fort was down, workmen began construction of a three-story brick building with ample quarters for all three branches of the government. When finished two years later, Government House, as it was called, commanded spectacular harbor views and an elegant waterfront promenade.

Provisions were dear and housing hard to come by, as ever, but New York's cosmopolitan attractions made up for a good deal of discomfort. As wide-eyed St. George Tucker of Virginia recorded in his diary, the "hurly burly and bustle of a large town" held a unique fascination of its own. "You may stand in one place in this City and see as great a variety of faces, figures, and Characters as Hogarth or Le Sage (author of Gil Blas) ever drew."

There were plenty of other things to do, however. Opposition to playhouses had receded again, and Lewis Hallam the younger had reopened the John Street Theater with a performance of Royall Tyler's *The Contrast*, a sentimental comedy set in postwar New York. A new racetrack, the Maidenhead, was now operating just behind the old De Lancey mansion, and two new pleasure gardens had appeared: Brannon's, near the southwest corner of present Spring and Hudson streets, and the United States, an establishment on Broadway once run by the widow Montayne. Much frequented by students from Columbia College, Brannon's was renowned for its "curious shrubs and plants" and excellent ice cream; the United States pitched its advertisements to the "Fair Sex" and noted that "select companies or parties, can always have an apartment to themselves, if required."

A "VORTEX OF FOLLY AND DISSIPATION"

But would the federal government stay? The selection of a permanent site for the national capital remained a topic of passionate controversy around the country, New York being a far from popular choice. Its raw juxtapositions of wealth and poverty, its

---

1. In 1785 and again in 1792 Congress established the decimal "dollar" as the basic monetary unit of the United States. New York State officially switched to the dollar in 1797, and the Common Council of New York City seems to have followed suit shortly thereafter. Merchants and shopkeepers, however, continued to use pounds, shillings, and pence alongside "federal money" well into the nineteenth century, at an exchange rate of eight shillings per dollar (thus city shoppers were accustomed to seeing the price of a book, for example, expressed as either 3/ or 37$^{1}/_{2}$ cents.) Foreign coins remained legal tender in the United States until 1857.

preoccupation with commercial profit, its tolerance (even laxity) in matters of religion and morality, its raucous crowds—none of these recommended the city to the nation's overwhelmingly rural and agricultural population. Leading the opposition were hard-shell republicans who feared that New York's "British" and "aristocratic" tendencies, to say nothing of its fleshpots, would sooner or later fatally corrupt the leaders of a free people. Everything they heard or saw over the next couple of years convinced them the end was already in sight.

Much would be made of Brissot's observation that "if there is one city on the American continent which above all others displays English luxury, it is New York, where you can find all the English fashions." One evening at dinner he encountered two ladies in "dresses which exposed much of their bosoms. I was scandalized by such inde-cency in republican women." And was it really true, as a horrified Senator William Maclay of Pennsylvania reported, that many New Yorkers still observed the King's Birthday "with great festivity"? Or what about Mrs. John Jay, the former Sarah Van Brugh Livingston, handsome and high-spirited daughter of William Livingston (long-ago editor of the *Independent Reflector* and later revolutionary governor of New Jersey)? She had married Jay in 1774, accompanied him on his diplomatic missions to Spain and France (becoming a favorite of Parisian society), and had now made their house on lower Broadway the center of New York's smart society. Had she actually thrown her doors open to Lady Kitty Duer, Lady Mary Watts, Lady Christiana Griffin, and other American matrons not yet reconciled to republican forms of address? And what manner of idolatry prompted the Common Council to hire John Trumbull to paint a portrait of Washington for City Hall? ("Flattery to the living rulers is always dangerous," scolded "Vox Res Publica.") If Thomas Jefferson is to be believed, when he arrived to take up his duties as secretary of state in the spring of 1790 he was the only republican in town.

Very worrisome indeed, notwithstanding the suit of plain brown broadcloth in which Washington took the oath of office, was the courtly style of entertaining adopted by the chief executive and his wife. His Tuesday afternoon levees and her Friday evening receptions were, as one observer wrote, "numerously attended by all that was fashionable, elegant, and refined in society; but there was no places for the intrusion of the rabble in crowds, or for the more coarse and boisterous partisan—the vulgar elec-tioneer—or the impudent place-hunter—with boots and frock-coats, or round abouts, or with patched knees, and holes at both elbows. . . . Full dress was required of all." When the president appeared in public, it was noted, bands sometimes struck up "God Save the King." His lady, it was noted, always returned visits on the third day, preceded by a footman.

Not overlooked, either, was the president's cream-colored coach, drawn by a team of six horses—reputedly the finest equipage in the city—or the "bountiful and elegant" dinners served up by Samuel Fraunces, now the president's head steward, who also supervised a household staff of twenty servants, maids, housekeepers, cooks, and coach-men. It didn't help that in 1790 Washington moved his official residence from Cherry Street to the mansion built by Alexander Macomb at Number 39 Broadway, an even grander house at a better address. The rent was a breathtaking twenty-five hundred dol-lars per year. To the *Boston Gazette,* New York was a "vortex of folly and dissipation" into which republican virtue and simplicity had long since vanished.

New York's champions, numerous and articulate, pooh-poohed all the commotion. Oliver Wolcott (related to the Livingstons, after all) made the city sound like a bastion of propriety: "There appears to be great regularity here," he testified; "honesty is as much in fashion as in Connecticut; and I am persuaded that there is a much greater attention to good morals than has been supposed. So far as an attention to the Sabbath is a criterion of religion, a comparison between this city and many places in Connecticut would be in favor of New York." Other advocates of the city emphasized its beauty and temperate climate (notwithstanding an influenza epidemic and heat wave in 1789 that resulted in numerous fatalities). According to one newspaper, only a single member of Congress fell ill while in New York—a point that became the subject of an extended commentary by Dr. John Bard, a local physician and president of the Medical Society, who pronounced New York "one of the healthiest cities of the continent." The proof of this assertion, he said, was readily visible "in the complexion, health and vigor of its inhabitants."

MONEYED MEN

What couldn't be shrugged off so easily was New York's growing notoriety as a cauldron of financial speculation. Over the previous half-dozen years, "moneyed men" through-out the United States, often as not in league with European financiers, had come to think of heavily depreciated state and Continental securities as good investments. (As early as 1786, William Duer owned sixty-seven thousand dollars' worth of Continental paper outright, and another two hundred thousand in partnership with half a dozen other New York investors.) If the American experiment in self-government succeeded, they reasoned, the value of their holdings would be multiplied many times over. The tempo of speculation quickened in the months before Washington's inauguration, as investors became more and more certain that the new federal government would take immediate steps to put the nation's finances in order.

New York afforded speculators two advantages. Rapid population growth—and above all a stream of immigrants with cash, credit, and connections—favored the city with an abundance of capital. "More money is to be had in Your City" than anywhere else in the country, a Philadelphia merchant complained to Andrew Craigie in 1789. As the national capital, furthermore, New York churned with valuable rumors, tips, and inside information that took days, even weeks, to reach buyers and sellers elsewhere. There was no substitute for rubbing elbows with important people in the government on a day-to-day basis, Craigie said. "I know of no way of making safe speculations but by being associated with people who from their Official situation know all the present & can aid future arrangements either for or against the funds."

The early summer of 1789 brought word that southern state securities were both cheap and plentiful, some selling for as little as ten cents on the dollar. Over the next six months, seventy-odd New Yorkers scooped up $2.7 million worth of South Carolina, North Carolina, and Virginia obligations—roughly a third, all told, of their outstanding debts. Leading the pack was the firm of Herman LeRoy and William Bayard, with a combined investment of over $580,000. Andrew Craigie and four others were each in for a hundred thousand dollars or more. William Constable, another participant, told an English investor that *"those in the secret"* expected to come away with huge profits in the very near future. "My opinion is founded on the best information," he wrote. "I cannot commit to paper my reasons, nor explain from whence I have my information, but I would not deceive you."

Constable's "secret" was that Treasury Secretary Hamilton ("our Pitt," Constable called him reverently) would soon go before Congress with a financial plan calculated to boost the value of state and federal securities. How did Constable know? No evidence exists that Hamilton breached the confidentiality of his office. Assistant Treasury Secretary Duer, on the other hand, talked freely to Constable and their other New York friends and was himself deeply involved in speculation. Hamilton surely knew of Duer's activities and did nothing—which encouraged the widespread suspicion that he was masterminding a corrupt conspiracy against the republic.

The denouement came in mid-January 1790, when Congress received from Hamilton a fifty-page *Report Relative to Public Credit*. According to Hamilton's figures, the unpaid foreign and domestic debts of the United States amounted to some fifty-four million dollars. Outstanding state debts came to another twenty-five million. The total—nearly eighty million dollars—was the country's "price of liberty," Hamilton said. Yet, he added, neither the old Confederation nor many of the states had fulfilled their duty to pay off this sacred debt as promised. The annual revenues of the new federal government weren't even enough to cover the interest on the debt (currently around $4 million a year), let alone retire the principal, and numerous public creditors had been waiting for their money for years. This intolerable negligence had brought the nation to a "critical juncture" in its history. Not only was "the individual and aggregate prosperity of the citizens of the United States" in jeopardy, but their very "character as a People" and "the cause of good government" hung in the balance as well.

No one in Congress opposed paying the national debt. At issue was who owed how much to whom, and where the money would come from. Hamilton's recommendation followed what he, Robert Morris, and other conservative nationalists had been advocating for a decade or more. First, Congress should consolidate the various foreign and domestic debts incurred by both the confederation and federal governments since 1776 and "assume" (i.e., take responsibility for) unpaid state Revolutionary debts, with accumulated interest. Second, it should "fund" the whole amount "at par" (i.e., face value), meaning that it would provide sufficient revenue to pay the interest and part of the principal every year. As to the mechanics of the process, Hamilton gave Congress a choice of six different plans. The one eventually chosen called for state and federal creditors to exchange their old notes for new 6 percent federal "stock." Accumulated interest, if any, would be paid in 3 percent stock.

Without funding and assumption, Hamilton reasoned, the United States could never achieve the stability, prosperity, and strength it needed to survive. As in Britain a century earlier, the creation of a funded national debt would restore the government's credit among those persons, at home and abroad, who possessed "active wealth, or in other words . . . monied capital." The assumption of *state* debts, Hamilton continued, would bind every public creditor to the new federal system by powerful "ligaments of interest." If it succeeded, they would profit; if it failed, they would lose. Politically, in other words, funding and assumption together would cement the union by enhancing the authority and reputation of the central government vis-à-vis the states. Economically, too, funding and assumption would do wonders for the country. Public confidence in government stock would enable it to function like money, thereby increasing the money supply, driving down interest rates, and stimulating the development of agriculture, commerce, and industry.

No sooner had Hamilton's report become public knowledge, Chancellor Livingston reported sourly, than a mania for speculation in public securities immediately "invaded all ranks of people." New York went wild. Even prominent Antifederalists like George Clinton and Melancton Smith took the plunge. Big investors became celebrities. Stories circulated of their high-stakes derring-do, richly embroidered with talk of secret couriers and chests full of cash.

Prince of the New York speculators was none other than William Duer. After less than six months on the job, Duer abruptly resigned from the treasury—"I have left to do better," he explained—and promptly threw himself into daring and complex schemes. Through his wide network of connections in the United States and Europe, he arranged for or encouraged the influx of millions of dollars from investors in Boston, Philadelphia, Amsterdam, Paris, London, and elsewhere. Suddenly one of the richest men in the country, he lived like an Eastern potentate in the former Philipse mansion, attended by a regiment of servants and fawned over by important visitors. Jefferson called him "the king of the alley." The Rev. Manasseh Cutler, who attended one of the chic dinner parties given by Duer and his wife, the former Kitty Alexander, had never seen anything like it. "I presume he had not less than fifteen different sorts of wine at dinner, and after the cloth was removed, besides most excellent bottled cider, porter, and several other kinds of strong beer."

THE COMPROMISE OF 1790

Outside New York, and to no small degree because of the financial delirium there, Hamilton's proposals roused fiery resentment. Funding at par, by allowing creditors to swap depreciated obligations for new interest-bearing paper at face value, was legalized fraud, critics said. Speculators with money and inside information—for surely Hamilton was in cahoots with Duer and other New York speculators—were raking in immense unearned profits at the expense of patriotic republicans who had been tricked out of their property. Assumption especially angered the South. Northern states owed a disproportionate share of the debts Hamilton proposed to take over, meaning they stood to gain a financial windfall at the expense of southern taxpayers. Besides, northern speculators had by now bought up so much of the outstanding southern state debt that they would pocket the real profits of assumption—again at southern expense.

In Congress, James Madison of Virginia rallied opponents of Hamilton's proposals with two of his own: no assumption of state debts at all, and no funding of the national debt without making a distinction between the original and subsequent holders of government paper. The debate over Madison's alternatives went on, inside Congress and out, for weeks. Toward the end of February, the House defeated his discrimination idea. Assumption failed a preliminary vote in mid-April. By early June, while more or less certain his funding scheme would get through, Hamilton was increasingly fearful that assumption wouldn't survive a second and decisive ballot.

It was at this juncture, Jefferson later recalled, that Hamilton offered a compromise. The two men chanced to meet one day in the street, just outside the president's house, Hamilton appearing "sombre, haggard, & dejected beyond despair, even his dress uncouth & neglected." Hamilton begged Jefferson to reassure southern congressmen that assumption was vital to the well-being of the republic; in return, he would round up enough northern votes to move the national capital to a site on the Potomac River.

Anxious to get the government out of the clutches of New York "moneyed men,"

Jefferson suggested that Hamilton and Madison join him for dinner the next evening at his house on Maiden Lane. There the bargain was sealed.[2]

At the Poughkeepsie convention, New York Federalists had more or less promised that the federal government would remain in New York if the Constitution were ratified. Now, shocked and embarrassed by this latest turn of events, they geared up for a fight to keep the federal government in the city as long as possible (or, failing that, to locate the federal district along, say, the Susquehanna, or even in Baltimore). Hamilton was adamant, however. His financial program, he told Senator Rufus King, was "the primary object; all subordinate points which oppose it must be sacrificed." King and the others did as they were told. Early in July, Congress voted to build a permanent capital in a ten-mile-square federal district on the Potomac; for the remainder of the decade, pending completion of the necessary construction, the government would return to Philadelphia. In due course, both houses approved assumption as well as funding, completing Hamilton's victory.

On August 12, 1790, Congress met for the last time in Federal Hall. Two weeks later, on August 30, Washington stepped into a barge moored at Macomb's Wharf on the Hudson and left Manhattan, never to return. Abigail Adams vowed to make the best of Philadelphia but knew that "when all is done, it will not be Broadway."

" Cong_ss Embark'd on board the Ship Constitution," a New Yorker's satirical view of the decision to move the federal capital to the Potomac. It is the Devil who lures the ship of state onto the rocks, but his words — "This way, Bobby" — echo the widespread belief that Robert Morris and other Pennsylvanians were behind the move. (Library of Congress)

---

2. Or maybe not. There are no eyewitness accounts of this famous incident other than Jefferson's—two versions of which came to light many years after the fact. Hamilton and Madison left no mention of any such deal, and the linkage of assumption and residence is at least open to question: for many members of Congress, as indeed for Hamilton himself, the really tough issue was whether to fund at 6 percent or 4 percent, not where the capital would be. Everybody, on the other hand, knew that some kind of understanding had resolved the crisis—if not the one described by Jefferson—and that getting the capital out of New York was somehow a part of it.

New Yorkers watched the federal departure with both regret and irritation. "No more Levee days and nights, no more dancing parties out of town thro' the summer, no more assemblies in town thro' the winter," lamented one resident. Everyone blamed the Pennsylvanians—to which Senator William Maclay, who had never liked New York anyway, testily replied that its residents "resemble bad school-boys who are unfortunate at play: they revenge themselves by telling notorious thumpers." Even Washington came in for a share of abuse when he signed the Potomac bill into law. Hamilton, whose role in the deal wouldn't come to light for years, emerged unscathed.

Yet by the end of the summer, the loss of the capital had been forgotten. Passage of the funding and assumption bills restored between forty and sixty million dollars in hitherto virtually worthless certificates of indebtedness to face value—a sudden accession of wealth that bathed the city (or at least its successful speculators) in prosperity. Even the state government had invested a couple of million dollars in securities that, redeemed at par, brought a tidy sum into the treasury. Eager investors were meanwhile bidding up the price of the new 6 percent and 3 percent federal securities, dreaming of fortunes to come.

To a visiting British diplomat, the city's future seemed utterly secure, capital or no capital. New York, he said, "is certainly favored to be the first city in North America, and this superiority it will most assuredly retain whatever other spot be made the seat of government."

It was an arresting thought: henceforth the United States would have two centers, one governmental, the other economic. This separation of powers, as emphatic as anything in the Constitution, had no parallel in the Western world. London, Paris, Amsterdam, Berlin, Vienna, Rome, Madrid, Lisbon—these were capitals in the fullest sense of the word, hubs of national politics, business, and culture (only the rivalry between Moscow and St. Petersburg even vaguely resembled the American case). That New York already promised to become the first city of the United States, independent of the apparatus of state power, was an augury of its uniqueness. Nowhere else in the republic would the marketplace come to reign with such authority, or painters and politicians alike bow so low before the gods of business and finance. No longer the capital city, its destiny was to be the city of capital.

THE PROBLEM OF MANUFACTURES

Some New Yorkers wanted the city to become a center of industrial manufacturing too—filled with English-style factories, not just the small artisanal workshops with which it had long been well supplied. In January 1789, over "wine, cakes, etc." at Rawson's Tavern on Water Street, a committee of prominent businessmen formed the Society for the Encouragement of American Manufactures, commonly known as the New York Manufacturing Society. The promotion of industry was nothing new: the nonconsumption and nonimportation movements twenty-five years before had inspired similar projects, none of which met with much success. Yet the inception of a new federal government, President Washington's words of encouragement for the country's infant textile industry, and the strength of the city's capital market suggested that large-scale manufacturing was an idea whose time had come. Even Governor Clinton, idol of the state's rural republicans, had been heard to say that "the promotion of manufactures is at all times highly worthy of the attention of government." No one was surprised when nearly two hundred investors bought up all Manufacturing Society stock at twenty-five dollars per share.

Before the year was out, the Manufacturing Society had opened a textile factory on Crown (later Liberty) Street. It had a carding machine and two hand-operated spinning jennies, and it employed fourteen weavers and 130 spinners, an impressive labor force by contemporary standards; it was also said to have cost $57,500—almost as much as the city had spent to renovate Federal Hall. A young Derbyshire immigrant named Samuel Slater offered to build and install, from memory, the spinning jennies whose design the British government guarded as carefully as the crown jewels. The factory's managers turned him away, however, and within a year or two were forced to close their doors. Slater moved on to Pawtucket, Rhode Island, where he built the first successful cotton mill in the United States for the firm of Almy and Brown.

Advocates of manufacturing didn't quit. The New York Society for the Promotion of Agriculture, Arts, and Manufactures, founded in 1791 by Robert R. Livingston and others, remained for years one of the country's leading exponents of direct government support for American industrial development. Local organizations of manufacturers and workingmen likewise bombarded Congress with demands to protect infant industries from foreign, especially British, competition. Individual entrepreneurs, including many British immigrants and New Englanders, went on experimenting with cotton mills, iron foundries, pottery works, breweries, and thread mills. One visitor saw a cotton mill at Hell Gate on the East River in 1794.

The demise of the Manufacturing Society was nonetheless a signal that large-scale industrial manufacturing faced immense obstacles in New York. Manhattan lacked the water power necessary for mills and factories. City real estate was already very expensive, almost prohibitively so for high-risk ventures that might take years to show a profit. Inexperienced management, the lack of up-to-date technology, and competition from low-cost British imports compounded the problem. Besides, investors could almost always do better, with less danger, in shipping, insurance, and other mercantile enterprises, to say nothing of land or stock speculation. Over time, more and more of New York's merchants and financiers came to think of manufacturing as a nuisance. It threatened to open competitive outlets for capital, they charged, while the protectionist trade policies advocated by its proponents posed a danger to the free movement of goods, money, and credit across national boundaries.

SCRIPTOMANIA

Fighting over the direction of the nation's political and economic future resumed in Philadelphia in mid-December 1790 when Hamilton dispatched a second report on public credit to Congress. Among other things, the report recommended creation of a Bank of the United States. British experience proved, Hamilton said, that a bank was vital to national stability and prosperity. It would facilitate the financial operations of the treasury. Bank stock, a portion of which could be bought with the new public stock, would forge yet another link between public creditors and the federal government. Because its notes would serve as a circulating medium, and because its capital could be loaned out to private entrepreneurs, a national bank would further stimulate the nation's trade and commerce. Jefferson and Madison protested that the Constitution gave the federal government no authority to charter such a bank, but the necessary legislation sailed through Congress and was signed into law by the president at the end of February 1791.

The new Bank of the United States got off to a shaky start. Against Hamilton's wishes, the BUS board of directors decided to open a branch in New York, where the Bank of New York had just lost another attempt to get a charter from the state. The BONY's capital resources were larger than ever, but the number of shareholders had dwindled to twenty-five or so, mostly wealthy merchants like Rufus King, Isaac Roosevelt, and Nicholas Low—exactly the men to whom the BUS branch could be expected to appeal for support. Was there room for two banks in New York? Would the potential danger to the BONY cause a local backlash against the new federal institution? Certainly Governor Clinton and his friends thought a state bank might offset the power of the BUS, and they decided to give the BONY a charter after all, reserving the right for the state to buy a hundred shares of stock for fifty thousand dollars.

None of this had been sorted out when, on July 4, 1791, BUS stock went on sale in Philadelphia at twenty-five dollars a share. Within two hours, frenzied buyers—led, as Madison and Jefferson had feared, by northern and European "moneyed men"—snapped up the entire offering. In no time at all, bank stock as well as federal loan certificates were on the auction blocks in New York as well, and as Madison reported to Jefferson, the Coffee House was in "an eternal buzz with the gamblers." City newspapers began printing the latest quotations, and special express couriers rode in with current prices on the Boston and Philadelphia markets. "O that I had but cash" was the general cry, reported the *New-York Journal*, "how soon would I have a finger in the pie!"

The value of BUS "subscription shares" or "scrip" climbed steadily—from $25 to $45 to $60 almost overnight, from $60 to $100 in two days, from $100 to $150 in a single day. Toward the end of October shares in the bank were selling for $170. It was clear by this time that a number of Hamiltonians had acquired big stakes in the BUS as well as seats on its board; some indeed had seats on the BONY board as well, giving the two banks something close to interlocking directorates. (The state of New York hedged its bets by investing sixty thousand dollars in BUS stocks.) In the meantime, according to one of Andrew Craigie's associates, ordinary mechanics and shopkeepers had begun to dream of making easy money in the market—a danger because "ideas of this kind being disseminated amongst the various Classes of people become subversive of private industry, happiness, & economy."

Hamilton too worried about the "scriptomania" raging in New York, but his attention was momentarily diverted by another of his projects, the Society for Establishing Useful Manufactures. The purpose of the SUM was to promote the industrialization of the United States, diversifying the country's economy and reducing its dependence on imported, chiefly British, manufactures. SUM shares, valued at a hundred dollars each, could be purchased with either federal securities or BUS stock as well as specie—an ingenious arrangement that not only enabled the project to draw upon the increasing sums of foreign as well as domestic capital sluicing into the New York financial market but would also, in the process, help brake excessive speculation by stabilizing the demand for government bonds.

Although its operations would be located at Paterson, New Jersey, the SUM's New York connection was repeatedly underscored—by the fact that a majority of its directors were big New York speculators, by the board's decision to make William Duer its first governor or president, by the speed with which its stock was taken up by New York investors, and by its selection of L'Enfant to lay out a company town (his sense of grandeur proved too expensive, however, and he was let go). As of November 1791 over $625,000 had been raised toward an initial capitalization of one million dollars—the bulk of it from the city, where SUM stock was selling at or above par. A month later Hamilton gave Congress a *Report on Manufactures* that urged federal support for all such undertakings (because, among other things, idle "women and Children are rendered more useful" by employment in manufacturing).

PANIC

At the end of December 1791, former assistant secretary of the treasury William Duer mobilized a small group of New York speculators—among them Alexander Macomb, John Pintard, William Livingston, and Royal Flint—for a daring attempt to manipulate the city's stock market. The plan called for "the Company" or "the Six Per Cent Club," as it was known, to make massive secret purchases of government paper and bank stocks (Duer himself had bought over half a million dollars' worth in the previous nine months alone). To keep the market percolating, the club would also announce the formation of a new bank with an initial capitalization of a million dollars, then hint that this so-called Million Bank would merge with both the Bank of New York and the Bank of the United States. Stocks of all three institutions were certain to rise in value. When they had gone up far enough, the club would unload its holdings at tremendous profits—and perhaps (though Duer's exact intentions remain hazy) seize control of the Bank of New York as well.

Shares in the Million Bank went on sale in January 1792. Excited investors bought the entire offering within a matter of hours, and the ensuing cry for bank stocks of every description threw the city into what startled participants referred to as a "bancomania." By the end of the month, competing groups of speculators had entered the fray with two more banks having a combined capitalization of $1.2 million. As the financial market surged higher and higher, New Yorkers feverishly bought and sold stocks in all five banks. "The merchant, the lawyer, the physician and the mechanic, appear to be equally striving to accumulate large fortunes" through speculation, marveled one witness to the hysteria. Duer and company plunged deeper and deeper into debt to finance their purchases, Macomb even kicking in fifty thousand dollars from the SUM treasury—practically its entire cash surplus.

Early in March, while promoters of the three new banks maneuvered for money and legislative approval, stock prices leveled off, then declined. Coincidentally, the government notified Duer of a $250,000 discrepancy in his accounts as assistant treasury secretary. Cornered, and no longer able to raise cash, Duer began to sell. On March 10, as panic engulfed New York, he stopped payment on all his debts; two weeks later his creditors had him arrested and thrown in debtor's prison. Macomb and Walter Livingston soon went to jail as well; John Pintard escaped his creditors by fleeing across the Hudson to Newark.

New York appeared to have been struck by a disaster of staggering proportions. Duer alone owed more than $750,000. Judge Thomas Jones said that estimates of all losses ran as high as three million dollars—a huge sum, representing the savings of "almost every person in the city, from the richest merchants to even the poorest women and the little shopkeepers."

"Everything is afloat and confidence is destroyed," one man grieved. "The town

here has rec'd a shock which it will not get over in many years." No one escaped—
"shopkeepers, widows, orphans, butchers, carmen, Gardeners, market women & even
the noted bawd, Mrs. McCarty," lost their life savings. "Such a revolution of property
perhaps never before happened." All told, two dozen leading merchants were ruined;
the Million Bank and its competitors never opened their doors. Business languished,
and ships lay at the wharves with no one to buy their cargoes. Artisans, mechanics, and
cartmen couldn't find employment. Farmers couldn't sell their produce. Over in Paterson, the directors of the SUM (absent Duer and Macomb) forged ahead with plans for
the construction of factories and housing for workers, but the wounds were fatal, and
within a few years the project foundered.

Hamilton, watching the nation's first financial crisis unfold, was appalled. The
whole point of his financial program was to transform the nation's public creditors into
a class of proto-capitalists able to lend the government stability and facilitate the production of tangible wealth—not reel off on speculative binges that paralyzed the economy. "There should be a line of separation between honest men and knaves," he fumed,
"between respectable stockholders and mere unprincipled gamblers." In March and
again in April he ordered the treasury into the market in an effort to restore confidence
and give "a new face to things." It helped, but not much. Where, and how, to draw the
line between "respectable stockholders" and "gamblers" would remain a central dilemma of American capitalism for the next two centuries. The demise of the SUM had
meanwhile soured Hamilton's interest in such projects, and when Congress refused to
act on his *Report on Manufactures*, he quickly lost interest in the subject.

Duer was lucky to be behind bars. Everyone blamed him for the panic, and threats
against his life were commonplace. "I expect to hear daily that they have broken open
the jail and taken out Duer and Walter Livingston, and hanged them," wrote one resident. On the night of April 18 a stone-throwing crowd of between three and five hundred persons, working people as well as merchants, converged on the jail shouting, *"We
will have Mr. Duer, he has gotten our money."* Nothing much happened, but the scene was
repeated for the next several evenings and the mayor prudently increased the guard at
the jail. Duer appealed to his old ally Hamilton for assistance. Hamilton advised him,
stiffly, to make a clean breast of his affairs and settle with his creditors. "Adieu, my
unfortunate friend," wrote Hamilton. "Be honorable, calm, and firm."

UNDER THE BUTTONWOOD TREE

Like Hamilton, New York's "moneyed men" came out of the Panic of 1792 eager to
draw the line between honest investment and knavish speculation. When trading in
public stocks began two or three years earlier, the market was dominated by auctioneers
who knocked down consignments of government paper to the highest bidder like any
other commodity (and often, indeed, side by side with other commodities). Two of the
most active, Leonard Bleecker and John Pintard, formed a partnership in July 1791 and
held auctions in the Long Room of the Merchants' Coffee House, three times a week at
one P.M. and three times a week at seven P.M. Although these events were open to the
general public, the great majority of stock purchases appear to have been made either by
wealthy "dealers," also known as "jobbers," who bought and sold on their own accounts
(often, like Duer, using borrowed money), or by "brokers," who acted on behalf of
specific customers. Between auctions, dealers and brokers would meet outside to trade

stock among themselves. During the summer of 1791 they gathered under a button-wood (sycamore) tree on Wall Street.

That September, as the volume of sales increased and bank stocks joined public stocks on the market, the city's auctioneers, dealers, and brokers drew up the first set of rules governing the sale of securities. Five months later, in February 1792, the auctioneers opened a Stock Exchange Office in "a large convenient room for the accommodation of the dealers in stock" at 22 Wall Street. Then, in March, Duer failed and the market collapsed.

In the ensuing panic, the auction system came under heavy criticism for having been too easily manipulated by unscrupulous auctioneers and dealers who rigged prices and circulated false rumors. At the end of March, hoping to restore confidence in the market, a number of dealers and brokers met at Corre's Hotel and signed a promise to boycott future auctions and find "a proper room" in which to do business; several weeks later, the legislature flatly outlawed the auctioning of federal or state securities.

On May 17, 1792, twenty-four brokers and dealers drew up the so-called Button-wood Agreement, which laid the foundations for a structured securities market without the now discredited auctions. The signers agreed to a fixed minimum commission rate, and they promised "that we will give a preference to each other in our Negotiations." Early in 1793 the brokers and dealers moved into an upstairs room of the elegant new Tontine Coffee House, situated on the northwest corner of Wall and Water streets. Wags dubbed it "Scrip Castle." (The Wall Street "curb market" didn't disappear, how-

The Tontine Coffee House, by Francis Guy, c. 1820. The Coffee House was the large building on the left, occupying the northwest corner of Wall and Water streets. Note the merchants and traders gathered on its balcony, as well as the presence of women in the street below—a reminder that private residences were still common in this part of town. (© Collection of The New-York Historical Society)

ever: in warm weather, stock traders continued for many years to assemble on the pavement outside.)

Construction of the Tontine Coffee House symbolized the fear of disorderly capital markets that became a recurring feature of the city's economic life. It was also an early indication that the Panic of 1792 wouldn't, as some had feared, cause prolonged harm to the city's economy. By the following June a local paper could declare that rumors of New York's problems "have been very exaggerated and falsified. . . . Credit is again revived—and prosperity once more approaches in sight. . . . Trade of every kind begins to be carried on with spirit and success." Events unfolding in France would accelerate the recovery and thrust New York further ahead of its rivals than anyone could have imagined.

21

Revolutions Foreign and Domestic

The summer and fall of 1789 found New York agog with the news of revolution in France. Parisian rioters sack the Bastille! The National Assembly issues a Declaration of Rights! The nobility surrenders feudal privileges! For many residents, this was the death knell of despotism and the dawn of the republican millennium. Manhattan crowds hailed "the Friends of revolution throughout the world," and French liberty caps enjoyed a sudden vogue. The new Uranian Society, founded by thirty recent Columbia graduates to debate current events, resolved that the French Revolution was a blessing to mankind. Even Alexander Hamilton was caught up in the excitement. "As a friend to mankind and to liberty I rejoice in the efforts which you are making," he confided to Lafayette.

By the autumn of 1792 the situation had grown more complicated. Prussian and Austrian forces had invaded France; fighting had broken out in the streets of Paris; Louis XVI had been arrested; a new National Convention had abolished the monarchy and proclaimed France a republic. The winter of 1792–93 brought still more astonishing intelligence: the Prussians and Austrians had been repulsed; Louis had been guillotined for treason; France had declared war on Great Britain, Spain, and Holland. In the summer of 1793 word came that Maximilian Robespierre's radical Jacobins were preparing a campaign of terror against all enemies of the Revolution.

These distant events were made startlingly immediate by the arrival in New York of a stream of political refugees or *émigrés*—Bourbon absolutists, constitutional monarchists, and republicans, among them such literary and political luminaries as Charles-Maurice de Talleyrand, the duc de La Rochefoucauld-Liancourt, Victor-Marie du Pont de Nemours, Chateaubriand, Volney, and Prince Louis Philippe, the future monarch. "The City is so full of French," observed the English traveler William Strickland in 1794, "that they appear to constitute a considerable part of the population." A *French and American Gazette* was founded in 1795 as a bilingual paper; the following year it became the purely French *Gazette Française*.

The ferment of revolution was at work nearer home too, in the French colony of Saint-Domingue (modern Haiti). Inspired by appeals for liberty, equality, and fraternity and by the April 1792 decree abolishing slavery, Saint-Domingue's 450,000 blacks rose against their masters. Troops sent from France to restore order were routed by insurgents under the command of Toussaint Louverture. By the end of 1793, 90 percent of the colony's forty thousand whites, royalists as well as republicans, had fled to the United States. All told, four or five thousand people, creole planters and black servants alike, debarked in New York City.

Like the French, the exotic Domingans were a conspicuous addition to the population. John F. Watson, an early nineteenth-century antiquarian, remembered well how their appearance caused frissons of excitement among townsfolk who thought they had seen everything: "Mestizo ladies, with complexions of the palest marble, jet black hair, and eyes of the gazelle, with persons of exquisite symmetry, were to be seen escorted along the pavements by white French gentlemen, both dressed in the richest materials of West India cut and fashion; also coal black negresses in flowing white dresses, and turbans of 'muchoir do madras,' exhibiting their ivory dominos, in social walk with white, or mixed creoles." Altogether, Watson recalled, they formed "a lively contrast with our native Americans, and the emigrés from old France, most of whom still kept to the stately old Bourbon style of dress and manner; wearing the head full powdered à la Louis, golden headed cane, silver-set buckles, and cocked hat."

Maintaining such appearances wasn't easy, even for the most eminent *émigrés*. Many found work as dancing masters, fencing masters, milliners, musicians, gunsmiths, jewelers, weavers, furniture makers, watchmakers, booksellers, printers, and the like. Antheleme Brillat-Savarin, the future gastronome, played in theater orchestras, taught French, and, at Little's Tavern, gave the proprietor instruction in how to prepare partridges *en papillote* and other delicacies. Other *émigrés* earned their livelihoods as laborers, dockworkers, hod carriers, or draymen. The widow and children of John Bérard du Pithon, once a wealthy Domingan planter, were supported by their slave, Pierre Toussaint, a successful hairdresser—so successful that he eventually became the city's most celebrated coiffeur and a trusted confidant of powerful society matrons.

WARS AND RUMORS OF WARS

President Washington's cabinet was sharply divided on the issue of how the United States should act toward the belligerents in Europe. Jefferson favored recognition of the French republic, strict compliance with the 1778 Franco-American treaty, and prompt accreditation of the new French ambassador, Edmond Genêt. Hamilton, now concerned that the revolution in France had gone too far, advised withholding diplomatic recognition, suspending the treaty, and ignoring Genêt. A second war with Great Britain, he argued, would ruin his program for national growth and development. President Washington tried to steer a middle course. At the end of April 1793 he issued a Neutrality Proclamation, declaring that while the United States government would abide by the treaty and receive Genêt, it wouldn't take sides in the conflict. American citizens were advised to act in a "friendly and impartial" manner toward all the warring powers. Three months later Jefferson submitted his resignation.

New York's merchants applauded neutrality. The city had only just rebounded from the 1792 panic, and the local economy remained dependent on Great Britain. Not only did virtually all foreign manufactured goods come from the British Isles, but many New York importers continued to function on British capital and credit as well. Furthermore, although the export business was gradually diversifying as city traders sought new markets in China and elsewhere, there was still hope on the docks of fully restoring trade with the British West Indies. If war with France, a sister republic, was almost unthinkable, war with Great Britain might well sink the city's economy.

European war might nevertheless do wonders for business—assuming the United States could remain neutral and trade with all the warring parties. As early as May 1793 the highly regarded mercantile firm Lynch and Stoughton noted that demand on the Continent for American produce was growing fast and should realize handsome profits. The future looked even better after France opened its West Indian colonies to American commerce. Staple exports to the Caribbean soared during the summer of 1793, along with the earnings of more than a few city merchants.

But neither Britain nor France accepted American neutrality for long. Britain said it sustained French colonial trade; France claimed that it reneged on the 1778 alliance and perforce aided the British. Each proceeded by turns to punish the United States for its impartiality, and for the better part of the next decade, New Yorkers contended with a succession of diplomatic crises, international incidents, and threats of war.

First to strike were the British. In the summer of 1793 His Majesty's government began a massive deployment of naval power to enforce a blockade of France and French colonial possessions. Neutral commerce with the French West Indies was banned under the so-called Rule of 1756, according to which trade with enemy colonies prohibited in time of peace couldn't be legalized in time of war. This was a direct blow at the United States, whose vessels dominated the carrying trade throughout the Caribbean. Hundreds of American ships, dozens of them from New York, were seized and confiscated by the British over the winter and spring of 1793–94. Numerous American seamen, among them many New Yorkers, were impressed into the Royal Navy or imprisoned in West Indian jails. Lurid stories circulated that the British, who continued to occupy five forts on New York territory in violation of the 1783 peace treaty, were urging the Iroquois to attack frontier settlements.

It was an uprising by some home-grown Manhattan "Indians," however, that almost put an end to Washington's neutrality policy.

REPUBLICAN SPIRITS

On October 12, 1792, several hundred New Yorkers in war paint, bucktails, and feathers had gathered solemnly around a fourteen-foot obelisk dedicated to the memory of Christopher Columbus. "Transparent devices" on each face of the obelisk depicted key events in the career of that "nautical hero and astonishing navigator"—Columbus receiving a compass from Science, Columbus wading ashore in America, Columbus at the end of his life, neglected by all but the "Genius of Liberty." Many of those present would have recalled the figure of Columbus that led the Grand Federal Procession of 1788, but this ceremony— marking the three hundredth anniversary of his initial landfall—was the new nation's first proper Columbus Day celebration. It was also one of the first public events staged by a new organization in town, the St. Tammany Society, or Columbian Order.

Twenty years earlier, back in the tumultuous 1770s, Philadelphia patriots had celebrated a St. Tammany Day in honor of the mythical chief Tamamend, whom the Delawares credited with carving out Niagara Falls and other heroic feats. After Independence, Tammany Societies arose in many parts of the country as vehicles for the expression of popular patriotism and republicanism; often they represented hostility to the Society of the Cincinnati, an elitist organization of former Continental Army officers. A Tammany Society had appeared in New York in 1786 or 1787 but languished until 1789, when the merchant John Pintard and a onetime Tory upholsterer named William Mooney took it over, charging it with a new sense of purpose.

One of his principal goals, Pintard told Thomas Jefferson, was to "collect and preserve whatever relates to our country in art or nature, as well as every material which may serve to perpetuate the Memorial of national events and history." Two years later, in 1791, the society's American Museum opened in an upper room of City Hall; when those quarters proved inadequate, the museum moved to the Merchants' Exchange on Broad Street. Contrary to Pintard's expectations, though, its holdings consisted mostly of stuffed animals and doleful curiosities like the "perfect Horn, between 5 and 6 inches in length, which grew out of a woman's head in this city." In 1795 the society washed its hands of the whole thing.

More fruitful was Pintard's wish to put the society on a "strong republican basis" and to endow it with "democratic principles" that would help check the resurgence of New York's "aristocracy" (a curious ambition given Pintard's association with William "King of the Alley" Duer). Any citizen able to pay a small initiation fee and modest dues could join, and by the mid-nineties some five hundred residents of the city had done so. Some Tammany members were youthful lawyers and merchants, but most were "artisans" or "mechanics" (masters and journeymen in the skilled trades, as distinct from apprentices, cartmen, sailors, and laborers).

At first Tammany stuck to displaying its republican zeal via comic-opera appropriations of Native American nomenclature and ritual. Rank-and-file members, called "braves," were assigned to "tribes." They elected a board of directors or "sachems," who in turn picked the society's "grand sachem" (a position Mooney held for many years), and once a month they all congregated in their headquarters or "Wigwam" for an evening of eating, drinking, singing, storytelling, and debates on issues of current interest. The braves' choicest moments were a handful of holidays—Washington's Birthday, Independence Day, Columbus Day, Evacuation Day, and the society's own Anniversary Day (May 12)—when they paraded through town in full Indian regalia, cheered patriotic orations, then sat down for mammoth open-air banquets along the East River. By the mid-1790s their Anniversary Day spree was widely considered the premier public event in the city.

Under the spur of revolutionary events abroad, however, Tammany became increasingly involved in local politics. New York's laboring population was showing signs of restlessness with Hamilton and the Federalists. The General Society of Mechanics and Tradesmen, irate because it had failed to pry a charter of incorporation out of the legislature, had run its own ticket in the 1791 elections, four of its nominees capturing seats in the Assembly. Artisans grew even more disaffected—and drew closer to the rival Clintonians—during the national furor over the Federalist financial program. Though Hamilton's handiwork remained more popular in New York than elsewhere in the country, its less savory consequences—rampant speculation in public stocks, followed by the unnerving Panic of 1792—raised troubling questions about

The Tammany Society celebrating the Fourth of July, 1812, by William Chappel. Line of march up Park Row, with the Brick Presbyterian church in the rear and Tammany headquarters on the left. This was one of the last occasions on which the braves and sachems appeared in their original Indian costumes. (© Collection of The New-York Historical Society)

privilege, greed, corruption, and other antirepublican tendencies in Washington's administration. The General Society, increasingly vocal on this point, warned city residents against an "overgrown monied importance" and "the baneful growth of aristocratic weeds among us." Philip Freneau, poet-editor of the antiadministration *Daily Advertiser*, complained in verse that "some have grown prodigious fat / And some prodigious lean!"

Governor George Clinton, joined by the disaffected Livingston clan, had meanwhile opened lines of communication with Madison and Jefferson. The two Virginians came up for a tour of the state in 1791, saying they intended only to "botanize." Yet there was enough political talk thrown in along the way to justify the later belief that their trip founded the Virginia–New York axis of a new national opposition party.

The 1792 gubernatorial elections confirmed that the Federalist chokehold on New York was weakening. Clinton survived a tough contest with John Jay to capture his sixth three-year term, drawing 603 votes in the city to Jay's 739—a substantial broadening of support for the governor, who had received only a hundred or so votes in the city as an Antifederalist candidate for the Poughkeepsie convention.

The spirit of opposition ripened during 1793 as the tempo of the French Revolution quickened. Mechanics, laborers, and some smaller merchants began to believe that international republicanism was in mortal danger—here from the machinations of Tory-loving "moneyed-men" like Hamilton and Duer, there from the armies of reactionary despots, and on both sides of the Atlantic from the malevolent influence of British agents, British arms, and British gold. Did not American neutrality at such a moment smack of political heresy and betrayal?

New York Federalists, on the other hand, shocked by the execution of Louis XVI and the rise of the radical Jacobins, concluded that the revolution had gone off the rails. The upheaval in France was being "conducted with so much barbarity & ignorance," said Rufus King, that sensible people could no longer countenance it. American neutrality was more imperative than ever, Federalists argued, and the Chamber of Commerce, a Federalist stronghold garrisoned by the city's principal merchants, reiterated that American involvement in the war would mean economic disaster.

While remaining officially nonpartisan, the Tammany Society began to mobilize popular support for the French Republic. Tammany braves and their friends greeted every scrap of good news from France with noisy parades and raucous banquets. After its Anniversary Day festivities in May 1793, four hundred participants trained through the streets in red liberty caps. When the French warship *L'Embuscade* (Ambush) docked in New York in June, Tammany men led a tumultuous throng down to Peck Slip, where they showered the arriving officers and crew with tricolor cockades and chorus after chorus of "La Marseillaise," the Revolutionary anthem. In July, Tammany turned the "Glorious Fourth" into a celebration of international revolution, a day-long carnival of parades, fireworks, bell ringing, singing, guzzling, stuffing, sermonizing, and speechifying.

Later that same month, a British frigate, the *Boston*, hove into port. Her crew fell to brawling with the crew of *L'Embuscade* and the pro-French regulars of waterfront grogshops. At one point, a large party of French sailors and sympathetic residents marched down to Bowling Green, where they dug up and demolished fragments of the statue of George III torn down some seventeen years earlier. The captain of the *Boston* then challenged his French counterpart to a naval duel. On August 1 both ships dropped down to positions off Sandy Hook, trailed by nine boatloads of excited spectators from the city. To their immense satisfaction, *L'Embuscade* claimed the victory after a fierce two-hour exchange of cannon fire and was escorted back to Manhattan by the French fleet, fifteen ships of the line that miraculously sailed into view just as the smoke was clearing. Thousands of cheering residents converged on the Battery to greet the French. Women collected old linen to make bandages for injured French sailors, and in an emotional ceremony, *L'Embuscade*'s colors were presented to the Tammany Society as a token of republican fraternalism.

Republican fraternalism had its limits, though. Only days later, Edmond Genêt, the French ambassador, arrived on the scene, cockily predicting that New York would give him a hero's welcome. "The whole city will fall before me!" he crowed. The problem was that "Citizen" Genêt had repeatedly thumbed his nose at Washington's Proclamation of Neutrality by commissioning American privateers to prey on British and Spanish commerce in the West Indies. This undiplomatic behavior caused a furor around the country, and the cabinet had just voted to ask the French government to bring him home; even Secretary of State Jefferson admitted that Genêt had become a political liability. His reception in the city was thus chillier than he had bargained on. White Matlack of the General Society of Mechanics and Tradesmen escorted him to a banquet at the Tontine Coffee House, and over the next few months he dined with various opposition leaders—mostly, it was said, because he had tens of thousands of dollars to spend

The French warship *L'Embuscade* off the Battery in 1793, drawn by John Drayton.
Washington Irving said the flagstaff on the right looked like a giant butter churn, and the
"churn" was a local landmark for years. (I. N. Phelps Stokes Collection. Miriam and Ira D.
Wallach Division of Art, Prints and Photographs. The New York Public Library. Astor,
Lenox and Tilden Foundations)

on refitting the French fleet. (Recalled by the Jacobin regime in early 1794, Genêt
applied for asylum, took an oath of allegiance to the United States, and retired to a farm
near Jamaica on Long Island. He later married Governor Clinton's daughter, Cornelia,
and settled down to dabble unsuccessfully in business and tinker with steam-propelled
balloons and other mechanical gadgets.)

THE DEMOCRATIC-REPUBLICANS

Genêt notwithstanding, the French Revolution still commanded a broad following in
New York. In mid-January 1794 boisterous celebrations erupted again over reports
(subsequently proved false) that the French had captured the Duke of York. The "lower
class of citizens," Peter Livingston noted with satisfaction, still loved the French so
much that they were "almost to a Man . . . Frenchmen."

Consistent with Livingston's judgment was the success of a new organization, the
Democratic Society. One of forty similarly named groups around the United States—at
least some of which seem to have been founded with Genêt's assistance—the New York
Democratic Society made its debut in early February 1794, vowing "to support and
perpetuate the EQUAL RIGHTS OF MAN." Its leaders were a cross-section of "old Whigs"
and Clintonian "new men" like Commodore James Nicholson (the president), David
Gelston, Henry Rutgers, Melancton Smith, and two young lawyers of whom much
would be heard in the very near future, Tunis Wortman and William Keteltas. Rank-
and-file members, somewhere between one and two hundred strong, included master
craftsmen, apprentices, and laborers, among them many recent Scottish and Irish
immigrants (Donald Fraser, president of the Caledonian Society, was another of the
Democratic Society's founders).

Resolutely pro-French, the Democratic Society clamored for war with Britain. Throughout the spring and summer of 1794 New York churned with rallies, demonstrations, and marches. When French forces recaptured Toulon, the Democratic Society organized eight hundred working people to parade through town in liberty caps, arm-in-arm with French officers, as thousands of cheering onlookers lined the sidewalks. At Corre's Tavern the celebrants downed toasts to the armies and fleets of France (nine cheers) and to the destruction of Britain's "venal and corrupt" government (nine cheers). That evening, republicans and Frenchmen gathered at the Tontine Coffee House to sing the "Marseillaise" and dance the carmagnole. The Tammany Museum exhibited a guillotine, complete "with a wax figure perfectly representing a man beheaded!"

New York's Federalists were horrified, all the more so when residents of the city, anticipating a British attack, decided to build fortifications on Governors Island. Every morning for nearly a month, drums beating and banners flying, shipwrights, cordwainers, journeymen, tallow chandlers, sailmakers, and Columbia College students trooped down to the Battery, where boats waited to carry them over to the island. "To-day," wrote an amazed English visitor, "the whole trade of carpenters and joiners; yesterday, the body of masons; before this, the grocers, school-masters, coopers, and barbers." Never, however, was the demise of the merchant-mechanic alliance more apparent than at the city polling places, where a fledgling "Democratic-Republican party"—a confederation of Clintonians, Livingstons, and popular societies—whittled down big Federalist majorities with organization, discipline, and conscious appeals to the interests and sentiments of workingmen.

New York's Democratic-Republicans didn't invent their electioneering practices out of whole cloth. The genealogy of such tactics reached back through the ratification struggle of 1787–88 to the pre-Revolutionary committees, perhaps as far back as the Morrisite "party of the people" in the 1730s or even the Leislerian movement in the 1690s. Nor had political parties or "factions" suddenly acquired legitimacy: their presence continued to be widely regarded as prima facie evidence of corruption and conspiracy. But in the furious press of events, actions ran far ahead of ideas. Federalist foreign and domestic policies had united disparate opposition forces and prompted them to seek power, in concert, by means not yet considered entirely right or proper. Unlike any of their predecessors, moreover, the Democratic-Republicans of New York had already begun to establish close working relations with similar parties emerging in Virginia, Pennsylvania, and elsewhere around the country—not yet a national party in the modern sense, but close.

In the spring 1794 legislative elections, thanks in great part to exertions by the Democratic Society, the Democratic-Republican ticket ran extremely well among small masters, tradesmen, mechanics, and apprentices, especially in the city's poorer wards. It wasn't enough to win, but it set the stage for the December congressional elections, in which Edward "Beau Ned" Livingston challenged the Federalist incumbent John Watts for the privilege of representing New York City. This was a race, said one excited Democratic-Republican, between "friends and enemies to the French or the swinish multitude and the better sort" (on the theory that Beau Ned, despite his wealth and connections, was really a man of the people).

Livingston defeated Watts by a margin of eighteen hundred to sixteen hundred— an upset that not only gave local Democratic-Republicans a voice in Congress but demonstrated the party's increasing strength among the city's middling and lower classes. Beau Ned did exceptionally well, it was noted, in the uptown wards that were home to the same working people who had so recently trooped out to work on the Governors Island fortifications. Once again, it was the Democratic Society that got them to the polls.

BROKEN HEADS

In an effort to avoid another conflict with the former mother country, President Washington dispatched Chief Justice John Jay to Britain to negotiate. It wasn't a popular mission in Jay's hometown. When he left for England in May 1794, only a couple of hundred well-wishers came to see him off. The militia, many of whose members belonged to the Democratic society, flatly refused to parade. As Jay's ship weighed anchor, Governor Clinton, Chancellor Livingston, and the French consul stood together on the deck of a nearby French man-of-war, loudly singing French revolutionary anthems.

Democratic-Republicans worried because Jay, like other New York Federalists of his class, was an acknowledged Anglophile. Indeed, when Jay arrived in England and found his counterparts in a conciliatory mood, he quickly came to terms. By November 1794 Britain had agreed to evacuate the frontier forts, open British ports in the West Indies to American vessels, and submit disputed pre-Revolutionary debts to joint commissions.

But the United States paid a stiff price for these concessions. Jay tacitly abandoned the principle of freedom of the seas. He consented to give Britain most-favored-nation status in its trade with the United States. He promised that foreign (i.e., French) privateers would not be allowed to operate out of United States ports. He accepted a commercial accord in which American ships not exceeding seventy tons burden would be allowed to enter the British West Indies—providing the United States renounced the international carrying trade in cotton, sugar, and molasses. On the impressment of American seamen and compensation for slaves carried off during the war—two issues that had poisoned Anglo-American relations for years—Jay's treaty said nothing.

In the uproar that followed, Jay and his party were very nearly destroyed. While still in England, and before his treaty's terms were made known, Jay had been elected governor after George Clinton declined to stand for a seventh term. Soon after Jay returned at the end of May 1795, the U.S. Senate, after weeks of intense secret debate, narrowly ratified the treaty, except for the article limiting American trade with the West Indies. By July 1, when Jay was sworn in as governor, critics had begun a furious campaign in New York and elsewhere to dissuade President Washington from signing the pact. This opposition was bolstered by a new British crackdown on neutral vessels carrying provisions to France. Twenty-seven ships owned by New Yorkers were seized in the course of the summer, more even than in the 1793–94 crisis.

It was in this context that, in mid-July 1795, New York's Democratic-Republicans scheduled a Saturday noon "Town Meeting" to express their "detestation" of the Jay Treaty. "Our demagogues always fix their meetings at the hour of twelve," scowled one Federalist, "in order to take in all the Mechanics & Labourers—over whom they alone have influence and who in public meetings have a great advantage as they are not afraid of a black eye or broken head."

It was by all reports the greatest such assemblage in twenty years and reminded everyone of the tumultuous popular rallies of the 1770s—except, that is, for the French tricolor flying alongside the American flag on the balcony of City Hall and the presence of numerous radical *émigrés* and political fugitives from Ireland and Scotland, overwhelmingly sympathetic to the Democratic-Republicans. Grant Thorburn, an immigrant Scottish artisan whose earlier radical sympathies had by this time cooled, recalled what to him were the most frightening and disreputable elements of the crowd: "The Irish (patriot) laborer, his face powdered with lime, shirt sleeves torn or rolled up to his shoulders, came rattling up with his iron shod brogues; and the clam-men were there; and the boat-men were there; and the oyster-men were there; and the ash-men were there; and the cart-men were there."

Alexander Hamilton was there too, surrounded by a small contingent of Federalists, who "looked on the multitude like affectionate parents beholding with sorrow the frantic tricks of their erring children." Hamilton began to speak, Thorburn said, and although "his clear, full voice sounded like music over the heads of the rabble," he was shouted down and pelted with stones. A large body of demonstrators, led by Peter R. Livingston, newly elected grand sachem of the Tammany Society, then marched off to Bowling Green, where they burned a copy of the treaty.

Later that day a group of Revolutionary War veterans paraded with French and American flags and burned a picture of Jay "holding a balance containing American independence and British gold, the latter predominating." Hamilton, still full of fight, quarreled on the street with Commodore James Nicholson, head of the Democratic Society and honorary captain of the Federal Ship *Hamilton* in 1788. Nicholson accused his former ally of being "an abetter of Tories" and used "other harsh expressions." Hamilton promptly challenged Nicholson to a duel, and Nicholson accepted. Moments later Hamilton had a second confrontation with prominent opponents of the treaty, shouting that he would "fight the whole party one by one . . . the whole detestable faction." The former secretary of the treasury had become a mere "street Bully," sneered Beau Ned Livingston.

The following Monday saw another and bigger crowd, perhaps as many as seven thousand people, return to City Hall and adopt a package of resolutions denouncing the Jay Treaty. As for Hamilton and Nicholson, their seconds worked out a face-saving settlement. Hamilton had nonetheless become so worried about the safety of his friends and himself in New York that he asked the federal government to station troops on Governors Island—a striking reversal of fortune for the man who eight years earlier had been the hero of New York's working people.

Washington assented to the treaty in August, but despite his tremendous prestige, it continued to create controversy. In the city's volatile, superheated atmosphere it became more and more difficult for organizations like the Tammany Society to maintain even an official political neutrality. Over the winter of 1794–95 Tammany Federalists pressed the membership to endorse President Washington's criticism of "self-created" societies in the United States—above all the Democratic Societies, which Washington held responsible for the recent Whiskey Insurrection in Pennsylvania. When Tammany Democratic-Republicans, many of whom belonged to the New York Democratic Society, refused, the Federalists pulled out en masse. By spring Tammany allied itself openly with the new Democratic-Republican party, which now began to use "Tammanial Hall"—the Long Room of Abraham (Bram) Martling's Tavern on Chatham Street (now Park Row)—as a kind of campaign headquarters on election day.

"Gallomania" also gripped the Democratic-Republican wing of fashionable society. Ladies and gentlemen with advanced principles as well as advanced means acquired a taste for French expressions, French food, French waltzes, French opera, French books, and French mattresses. Fancy boardinghouses became *pensions françaises*; upscale taverns became "restaurants" and began serving dinner at three in the afternoon, in the French manner, instead of noon. Well-to-do Democratic-Republican wives adopted low-cut gowns and gauzed coifs *à la française*, spurning the buckram and brocades still favored by Federalist matrons. Similarly, their husbands rejected powdered wigs, knee britches, and shoe buckles as insignia of the *ancien régime*. Instead, they wore their hair in the radical "Brutus Crop"—brushed forward from the crown—and affected the bloused shirts, linen cravats, and baggy pantaloons that were the uniform of continental revolutionaries.

But this was 1795 not 1775; New York, not Paris. Despite the liberty caps, choruses of "La Marseillaise," and take-no-prisoners rhetoric, neither the Democratic-Republican party nor the popular societies allied with it were in a revolutionary frame of mind. They were rising enterprisers, successful craftsmen, aspiring journeymen, and respectable mechanics, not a mass of propertyless proletarian levelers. They demanded equality of opportunity and participation, not equality of condition. Their class-consciousness (if that is the word for it) admitted distinctions only between the productive and nonproductive classes of society—between those who came by their money through hard and honest labor, and those, like parasitic bankers, speculators, stockjobbers, and idle landlords, who relied on privilege and politics, money and monopoly to gain their position.

For all its limits, on the other hand, this artisanal republicanism was infused with egalitarian, democratic aspirations scarcely imagined a decade or two earlier. Over the next decade, indeed, it would bring about fundamental changes in the political system of the city.

"AS GOOD AS ANY BUGGERS"

One day in mid-November 1795 Gabriel Furman, a well-to-do merchant and prominent alderman, set out to return from Brooklyn to Manhattan via the ferry that docked at the foot of Fulton Street. Furman ordered the ferrymen, Thomas Burk and Timothy Crady, both recent arrivals from Ireland, to leave ahead of schedule. They refused. An argument ensued, Furman yelling that he would have "the rascals" thrown in jail, Crady yelling back that he and Burk "were as good as any buggers" and would use their boat hooks on anyone who tried to arrest them. As soon as the ferry got across to Manhattan, Furman summoned a constable and had the two marched off to the Bridewell while he thrashed them with his cane.

After twelve days behind bars, Burk and Crady came up for trial before the Court of General Sessions on charges of insulting an alderman and threatening the life of the constable. Neither man was allowed legal counsel; there was no jury; Furman was the only witness; and the presiding judge, Mayor Richard Varick, was clearly out to make an example of them. "We'll learn you to insult men in office!" he shouted. The court found Burk and Crady guilty on both counts and sentenced them to two months at hard labor. For extra measure, Crady also received twenty-five lashes on his bare back.

The case took a new turn some weeks later when Burk and Crady broke out of jail and escaped to Pennsylvania. Writing as "One of the People," lawyer William Keteltas (a youthful newcomer from Poughkeepsie) wrote an account of their ordeals for

Thomas Greenleaf's *Journal*. Keteltas denounced the court for its "tyranny and partiality." Burk and Crady had been punished, he said, merely to "gratify the pride, the ambition and insolence of men in office." The accusation stung, coming at a time when the mayor and aldermen were under fire for turning nine prisoners from the Bridewell over to a British man-of-war as alleged deserters.

The case of the long-gone Irish ferrymen suddenly blossomed into a republican cause célèbre in which upper-class arrogance menaced the dignity of ordinary citizens. "Do we live in a city," asked one angry newspaper writer, "where the Mayor or an Alderman or two have a right to strip us naked and give us as many lashes as they please at a whipping post for what they may deem an insult to a magistrate?" Keteltas stoked the fires by petitioning the Assembly to impeach Varick and the magistrates for their "illegal and unconstitutional" conduct. In January 1796 the Assembly rejected the petition. Keteltas wrote another article for the *Journal* berating the Assembly for "the most flagrant abuse of [the people's] rights" since independence. The Assembly in turn censured Keteltas for his "unfounded and slanderous" remarks. Keteltas repeated his attack on the Assembly.

Early in March, in an uncanny reenactment of Alexander McDougall's experience twenty-five years before, the Assembly summoned Keteltas to explain himself. He showed up with two thousand supporters, admitted authorship of the offending newspaper articles, and refused to apologize (amid loud "clappings and shoutings"). When the Assembly then sentenced him to jail for "a breach of the privileges" of the house, the crowd hoisted him into a "handsome arm chair" and carried him off to the Bridewell, chanting, "THE SPIRIT OF SEVENTY-SIX! THE SPIRIT OF SEVENTY-SIX!" After Keteltas got out a month later on a writ of habeas corpus, another crowd pulled him through the streets in a phaeton decked out with French and American flags, a liberty cap, and a large picture of a man being whipped, above which was the inscription *"What, you rascal, insult your superiors?"*

The Keteltas affair helped siphon away more of the Federalists' popular constituency. A record four thousand residents of the city went to the polls in the spring 1796 legislative elections, and while the Democratic-Republicans failed to capture any of New York's twelve Assembly seats, they pulled five hundred votes more than the year before. More important, two-thirds of the Democratic-Republican voters were men of little or no property, many of them the immigrants whose numbers had grown markedly in recent years. Six months later, in the September Common Council elections, two Democratic-Republican candidates, including a leader of the Democratic Society, won by substantial majorities.

New York's Federalists fumbled the 1796 congressional and presidential elections too. Beau Ned Livingston easily beat back a Federalist attempt to capture New York City's congressional seat, not only solidifying Democratic-Republican control of the wards "chiefly inhabited by the middling and poorer classes of the people" but mobilizing hundreds of new voters as well.

Washington's decision not to seek a third term set off a scramble in both parties for acceptable candidates. Democratic-Republicans united around Thomas Jefferson but had trouble agreeing on a vice-presidential nominee. Aaron Burr was the front-runner. Many Democratic-Republicans didn't trust him, however: too young, too pushy, too devious, they said. Some knew that Burr's notorious love of fine clothes, luxurious household furnishings, expensive wines, fancy carriages, and big houses was driving him further and further into debt. Characteristically, when he acquired the lease for Richmond Hill, the estate in Greenwich built years before by Abraham Mortier, he borrowed huge sums—from friends, from family, from law clients—to refurbish it in the opulent style with which he wished to be identified; General John Lamb alone signed more than twenty thousand dollars' worth of Burr's notes, a gesture he came to regret many times over. Burr even dammed Minetta Creek to create a grand ornamental pool by the main gate (approximately the present junction of Spring Street, MacDougal Street, and Sixth Avenue).

The Federalists' problem was their standard-bearer, John Adams. Because Adams had never quite approved of Hamilton's financial program—he once described banking as "downright corruption"—Hamilton and a corps of New York Federalists labored behind the scenes to have a narrow majority of electoral ballots cast for Thomas Pinckney, a former U.S. envoy to the Court of St. James. Adams won anyway, leaving a residue of bitterness that would in time help destroy the party. Worse yet (owing to the fact that electors didn't yet distinguish between presidential and vice-presidential candidates) Jefferson trailed Adams by only three votes and was therefore elected vice-president. Nationwide, the Democratic-Republicans' organizational sophistication, their mastery of electoral politics, and the mass appeal of their democratic credo had never been more obvious. Locally, their strength was underlined in the 1797 elections, when for the first time Democratic-Republicans won every seat on the city's delegation in the state assembly.

BLACK COCKADES

In 1798 trouble with France abruptly derailed the Democratic-Republican express. A new right-wing government, the Directory, ousted the radical Jacobins and took immediate steps to upset the Anglo-American rapprochement. It embargoed American vessels in French ports, refused to honor bills for goods received from American merchants, and looked the other way while colonial authorities illegally plundered and confiscated American property. Squadrons of French "picaroons," or privateers, descended on the West Indies over the winter and spring of 1795–96, taking several hundred American prizes and abusing American seamen. In December of 1796 the Directory broke diplomatic relations with the United States. The following March it announced that all neutral ships carrying enemy goods would be liable to seizure and that Americans impressed by the British navy, willingly or not, would be hanged if captured.

John Adams, just inaugurated as Washington's successor, offered to negotiate, but the attempt fell apart when Talleyrand, the Directory's minister of foreign relations, demanded a bribe from the American delegation. (Talleyrand's contempt for Americans owed much to his experiences as a refugee in New York, where he had been reviled as a libertine and intriguer.) In the wake of this so-called XYZ Affair, Congress enlarged the army and navy, strengthened coastal fortifications, slapped an embargo on American trade with France and French colonies, closed American ports to French vessels, raised taxes, and authorized the arming of privateers.

By 1798 a furious quasi-war raged on the high seas. American losses to Caribbean picaroons rose steadily, and French corsairs ranged as far north as Long Island Sound to prey on American commerce, making it unsafe to sail from New York to Philadelphia without a convoy. Maritime insurance rates in New York ballooned, sometimes reaching as much as 40 percent of the value of a ship and its cargo—too high for many merchants, whose inability to carry on business sent ripples of unemployment through the city's working population. American trade with Great Britain seemed to be in some danger too. The Bank of England had suspended cash payments, two ominous mutinies had shaken the Royal Navy, a rebellion had broken out in Ireland, and the Directory's brilliant young general, Napoleon Bonaparte, was massing an army in preparation for an invasion of England itself.

As national opinion swung heavily against France, the Federalist Chamber of Commerce and the Federalist Common Council appropriated sixty thousand dollars for another frenzy of fortification building in New York. Congressional Federalists, sensing an opportunity to crush the Democratic-Republican opposition, meanwhile rammed through a series of bills, collectively known as the Alien and Sedition Acts, that set new standards for nativist paranoia and political repression. One, the Naturalization Act, aimed to stanch the flow of immigrants into the Democratic-Republican party by changing the residence requirement for full citizenship from five to fourteen years. The Alien Act authorized deportation of aliens suspected of "treasonable or secret" inclinations. Another measure authorized the jailing, for up to two years, of anyone convicted of publishing "false, scandalous and malicious writing" that might bring the U.S. government into disrepute. President Adams signed all this legislation into law and made it known that he was prepared to ask Congress for an open declaration of hostilities against France at any moment.

New York's Democratic-Republicans were all but swept aside. Four thousand city residents signed a memorial to President Adams, praising his patriotism and firmness. Federalist crowds tore down a liberty cap from the Tontine Coffee House and gathered at night outside the residence of Representative Livingston, cursing Beau Ned as a Jacobin and singing "God Save the King." Companies of eager young men began drilling on the Battery every evening between five and eight o'clock. The black cockade, once a Tory insignia, became fashionable again as a symbol of scorn for the French tricolor. Governor Jay, who had taken a leading role in the building of fortifications, won reelection easily, beating Chancellor Livingston, the Democratic-Republican candidate, by the greatest majority to date in a gubernatorial election.

Galvanized by this sea-change in the public mood, Hamilton dashed off a series of newspaper essays called "The Stand," urging Congress to step up preparations for war, and more or less accusing the Democratic-Republican opposition of cowardice and treason. He soon got a chance to take up sword as well as pen. Washington came out of retirement to head a new fifty-thousand-man Provisional Army and tapped Hamilton for his second in command. Hamilton immediately began preparing a list of "Jacobins" for the army to round up once the shooting started.

Over the next year or so, the demoralized Democratic-Republicans assembled bravely now and then to sing the "Marseillaise." A liberty pole or two went up in westside neighborhoods that remained strongholds of Democratic-Republicanism and "Gallomania." From time to time, too, Democratic-Republicans held their own in street brawls with Federalists (during one melee on the Battery somebody even beat up the president's personal secretary). Every election nonetheless showed the party losing ground at an alarming rate.

Democratic-Republican gloom was lifted somewhat by a spunky young Irish immigrant named John Daly Burk. Expelled from the University of Dublin as a deist and republican, Burk fled to America. He arrived in New York in 1797 and made a modest name for himself with the production of two patriotic, passionately anti-British plays: *Bunker Hill* and *Female Patriotism, or the Death of Joan d'Arc*. In June of the following year, probably with the help of Aaron Burr, Burk became part owner and editor of a small weekly paper called the *Time Piece* and quickly turned it into one of the hottest, most widely read antiadministration papers in the country. Federalists up and down the continent soon demanded something be done to shut him up. The *Time Piece*, declared Abigail Adams, was a "daring outrage which called for the Arm of Government," and quotations from Burk's inflammatory essays helped speed passage of the Sedition Act through Congress.

Burk vigorously defended freedom of the press, winning the admiration of Democratic-Republicans in every state. They admired him all the more when, as head of the New York lodge of the United Irishmen, he repeatedly expressed his hopes for the success of an Irish rebellion against England and for a French invasion of the British Isles. But Burk's career as a New York journalist proved short-lived. In July 1798, following the appearance of two provocative articles in the *Time Piece*—one intimating that President Adams had falsified a diplomatic communiqué, the other that Secretary of State Timothy Pickering was a murderer—Burk was arrested on charges of sedition and libel. Federal district judge Robert Troup, Hamilton's right-hand man in the city, applauded the arrest as an opportunity to find out "whether we have strength enough to cause the constituted authorities to be respected."

Prominent New York Democratic-Republicans, led by Aaron Burr and Tammany sachem Peter R. Livingston, stood bail for Burk. He promptly went back to hammering the administration and denouncing the charges against him as an attempt to muzzle the press. Disputes among the owners of the *Time Piece* caused them to suspend publication in September 1798, however, and, suspecting that the legal odds were stacked against him, Burk now offered to settle out of court. He would voluntarily leave the country, he said, if the government dismissed the case against him. Adams and Pickering agreed. When Burk boarded a ship for France six months later, British secret agents tried to grab him—or so he charged afterward—at which point "some of the best men in America" persuaded him to go instead to Virginia. He lived there under an assumed name until the expiration of the Alien and Sedition Acts several years later.

New York Federalists had no time to savor their victory over the *Time Piece*. Party moderates, believing there was still room for negotiations with France, made clear to President Adams that he couldn't get a formal declaration of war through Congress. Adams, for his part, was annoyed that most of his cabinet took their cues from Hamilton, and he came to see the New Yorker's hubristic visions of military and imperial glory as positively dangerous. "That man," he told Abigail, "would in my mind become a second Buonaparty [*sic*] if he was possessed of equal power." Though prowar Federalists fought him bitterly, Adams prevailed, and soon American negotiators were on their way to Paris, where the Directory had developed sober second thoughts about war with the United States. The Irish rebellion fizzled. Admiral Horatio Nelson smashed the French fleet in the Battle of the Nile. In the maritime quasi-war, the scales shifted in favor of the United States as a thousand-odd privateers and three new frigates—the *United States*, the *Constellation*, and the *Constitution*—cleared American coastal waters of enemy vessels. By the end of 1799, if not before, they controlled the Caribbean as well. In November of that year Napoleon overthrew the Directory and communicated his readiness to settle quickly. French and American negotiators came to terms in 1800.

FEDERALISTS IN RETREAT

Having reaped major political benefits from the quasi-war with republican France, New York Federalists contemplated the prospect of peace with something akin to panic. With the spring 1800 elections at hand, Hamilton appealed to the mechanic vote by arranging a legislative ticket that included a ship chandler, a baker, a potter, a mason, a shoemaker, and two grocers. However, deprived of war with France, none of the Federalists did well at the polls. Dr. Samuel Latham Mitchill, a Democratic-Republican Columbia professor, won the city's congressional seat, taking over from Edward Livingston. All thirteen of the city's Assembly seats went to Democratic-Republicans, giving the party a narrow majority in the state legislature. As that body chose the state's federal electors, the sweep guaranteed that New York would back Jefferson's second run for the presidency against Adams later that year.

No one deserved more credit for the victory than Aaron Burr. As head of the General Republican Committee, Burr prepared a roster of all voters in the city and had party workers visit every known Democratic-Republican to round up support and contributions. His house was crowded with messengers and committeemen and poll watchers who ate while they mapped strategy and napped on the floors rather than go home to sleep. Burr also introduced "fagot voting" into the party's political repertoire during this campaign, enfranchising scores of working people who failed to meet the property requirement for voters by making them joint owners of a single piece of property. "Fagot" or "bundle" voters made all the difference in several close contests.

Suddenly, everyone in the country knew about Aaron Burr. Democratic-Republicans hailed the New Yorker as a master of the electioneering arts—a political genius who had found the fulcrum upon which the mighty Federalists could be levered from power. Even Federalists were impressed. One asked Burr how the Democrats had won the election. He replied: "We have beat you by superior *Management*." When the congressional Democratic-Republican caucus nominated Jefferson for the presidency, it selected Burr as his vice-presidential running mate.

Among the Federalists, all was confusion and recrimination. In an extraordinary letter to Governor Jay, Hamilton proposed a maneuver to prevent the state legislature from choosing Democratic-Republican electors. Call a special session of the outgoing legislature, he advised Jay, and have it alter the procedure so as to ensure victory for the Federalists. No matter that everyone would see this as a brazen attempt to thwart the popular will. "In times like these in which we live," Hamilton wrote, "it will not do to be overscrupulous." Jay, whose sense of rectitude wasn't so easily laid aside, refused.

President Adams blamed the loss of New York on Hamilton. That "bastard" New Yorker, he said, had organized a "damned faction" of "British partisans" who would destroy the Federalist party unless checked by moderates such as himself. Hamilton struck back with a pamphlet accusing Adams of "disgusting egotism," "ungovernable indiscretion," and "distempered jealousy." As election day drew near, all semblance of unity among the Federalists vanished in a riot of charges and countercharges. "Wonderful," declared Jefferson from the sidelines.

By mid-December 1800 all America knew that the Democratic-Republicans had captured the presidency by an electoral college margin of seventy-three to sixty-five, that the outcome in New York had been decisive, and that that outcome rested on the Democratic-Republicans' ability to mobilize the artisans and laborers of New York City. What was not clear was who the president *was*. As Jefferson and Burr had each received seventy-three votes, the final decision was up to the outgoing House of Representatives, where Federalists would have the decisive role.

Jefferson or Burr? Most congressional Federalists favored Burr, but New York Federalists—notably Hamilton—warned party leaders around the country that Burr was a self-serving, unprincipled rogue and demagogue—"the most unfit and dangerous man of the community." True, Hamilton said, Jefferson was "a contemptible hypocrite." The Virginian was nonetheless basically decent, and manifestly the lesser of two evils. The House deadlocked for six days and thirty-five ballots, with talk of civil war growing on all sides, until the lone congressman from Delaware, a Federalist, changed his vote to Jefferson and the thing was done.

On March 4, 1801, rejoicing New York Democratic-Republicans celebrated the inaugurations of President Jefferson and Vice-President Burr. A month later George Clinton dragged himself out of retirement to lead the party in that year's gubernatorial election. He defeated the aristocratic Stephen Van Rensselaer to win a seventh term; for the first time in his long career, he won a majority among city voters as well.

The Democratic-Republican takeover of the state legislature in 1800 vaulted yet another Clinton to a position of power in New York: the governor's nephew and political heir apparent, De Witt Clinton. Born in 1769, De Witt was the third son of Mary De Witt and General James Clinton, an Irish-Presbyterian veteran of the Revolutionary War. He graduated from Columbia College in 1786, studied law in the office of Samuel Jones, then served a five-year political apprenticeship as his uncle's private secretary, during which he was an active Antifederalist and became involved in upstate canal projects and real estate speculation.

In 1796 De Witt married the beautiful Maria Franklin of New York City. She was the daughter of wealthy Quaker merchant Walter Franklin, a founder of the New York City Chamber of Commerce and former owner of the Cherry Street mansion briefly occupied by President Washington. Franklin had died during the Revolution, leaving his daughter a sizable inheritance, including a country estate in Newtown, Queens.

A year after his marriage, Clinton entered politics. His commanding appearance—handsome, heavily framed, and over six feet tall, he would come to be known as the Magnus Apollo—helped him win a seat in the state assembly along with his rival-to-be Aaron Burr. In 1798 Clinton moved up to the state senate. After the Republican sweep of 1800, he was elected one of the four members of the all-powerful Council of Appointment (and its informal leader). Using his command of state patronage, he had former congressman Edward Livingston installed as mayor and rewarded a small army of party regulars with municipal and county jobs.

"POLITICAL EQUALITY AND THE CORPORATION"

Behind Clinton and Burr, the Democratic-Republicans were now ready to attack the last bastion of Federalist power in New York, the Common Council. Federalists had controlled the council more or less continually since the mid-1780s, thanks in large part to ancient constraints on political participation. Under the city charter, voting in elections for the Common Council was restricted to freeholders owning property worth at least twenty pounds (fifty dollars) and to residents of the city admitted as freemen. In 1790, out of sixty-seven hundred adult white males in New York, only eighteen hundred (28 percent) were qualified to vote in municipal elections. Federalists likewise benefited from the old practice of viva voce voting. Voters in charter elections declared their preferences aloud in the presence of election inspectors; the Federalist-controlled council naturally took pains to see that at least two of the three inspectors in each ward favored that party. The candidates were there too, making careful note of who voted for whom. Journeymen, small shopkeepers, carters—men whose livelihoods might well depend on the patronage of big merchants or successful master craftsmen—needed more than a little courage to stand up for what they believed when doing so could cost them their jobs.

The formal case for changing all this was laid out by James Cheetham, an admirer of Tom Paine who fled England in 1798 and become a political journalist. His landmark *Dissertation Concerning Political Equality and the Corporation of New York*, published in 1800, argued with clarity as well as conviction that the city charter violated the Spirit of Seventy-six and broke every precept of republican government. The time had come, Cheetham announced, for the popular election of mayors, for secret balloting, and for the extension of the suffrage in municipal elections to every resident who could vote in assembly and congressional elections—by 1801, an estimated 62 percent of adult city males compared to the 23 percent currently eligible.

The political stakes were evident. The excluded body of voters embraced small shopkeepers, mechanics, and journeymen who were by this time overwhelmingly Democratic-Republican; if they took part in charter elections, nothing would save the Federalists from defeat. Predictably, the Federalist council refused all appeals to democratize the charter. When Democratic-Republicans turned to the state legislature for help, Federalists objected strenuously to legislative interference with the ancient "rights and privileges of the Freeholders." One newspaper writer warned less high-mindedly that liberalizing suffrage requirements would hand the municipality over to "*Irish freemen.*" A reform bill passed the Assembly in March 1803, only to be tabled in the Senate.

Then, in the summer of 1803, an audit of the federal attorney's office in New York revealed the disappearance of some forty-four thousand dollars. The head of that office was Mayor Edward Livingston. Although his own integrity was not in question, Livingston resigned both posts and moved to New Orleans. In his place the Council of Appointment named De Witt Clinton, who only the year before had been sent to the United States Senate by the state legislature. As Clinton told his uncle George, being mayor was the better job because its influence in presidential elections made it "among the most important positions in the United States" (besides, it was worth as much as fifteen thousand dollars a year).

Clinton's return to New York helped break the deadlock over democratizing the municipal charter. In April 1804 a compromise reform bill passed both houses of the legislature. While rejecting suffrage for all taxpayers, the bill enfranchised twenty-five-dollar renters and introduced the secret ballot into municipal elections. It also defined "freemen" as all freeholders and rentpayers eligible to vote—to all intents and purposes abolishing freemanship as a privilege distinct from the ownership of property. Cheetham hailed the new law as a "Second Declaration of Independence to the Citizens of New York." And in that year's more democratized municipal elections, the Democratic-Republicans added the Common Council to their list of conquests.

Whipped by Jefferson and now evicted from City Hall, many party elders—John Jay, Rufus King, Gouverneur Morris, Richard Varick, Philip Schuyler, Comfort Sands, and others—decided to quit public life altogether until the voters came to their senses. After twenty-five years of struggling to contain the democratic impulses unleashed by the Revolution, they had had enough.

Other, typically younger, Federalists drew the opposite conclusion from defeat. As Hamilton advised the King, do not lose hope that "the people, convinced by experience of their error, will repose a *permanent* confidence in good men." Elections clearly had their drawbacks, but good men had to go along or they would be doomed to political extinction (a point Hamilton had been making since the early eighties). If they lost this time around, there was no alternative other than to try again the next. Even in New York, after all, Federalists continued to enjoy a strong following in certain trades, and they hadn't yet fully tapped nativist hostility to the foreign-born, especially Irish, immigrants crowding into the city.

In 1801, accordingly, Hamilton helped establish the *New York Evening Post* as a party organ, with William Coleman as editor. The following year he unveiled his plan for a new, nationwide Federalist organization to be called the Christian Constitutional Society. As he envisioned it, the society would finance the publication of newspapers and pamphlets in every part of the country. It would "promote the election of *fit* men." It would also encourage—especially in "the populous cities"—the formation of clubs, charities, and schools to uphold the true principles of Christianity and the United States Constitution. Initial reactions to the idea were cool. There is no telling where it might have led, however, for two years later Hamilton was dead.

INTERVIEW IN WEEHAWKEN

Early in 1804 George Clinton, governor of New York for twenty-one of the last twenty-seven years, announced his intention not to seek an eighth term (rumor had it that he would replace Burr as Jefferson's vice-presidential running mate later in the year). The state's Democratic-Republicans, now divided by mushrooming hostility between pro- and anti-Burr factions, couldn't agree on a replacement. The Clinton-Livingston wing put up Chief Justice Morgan Lewis; Burrites raised their leader's standard. Jefferson denounced Burr's candidacy. So did Hamilton, who, reiterating his belief that Burr was a scoundrel, threw his support to Lewis. Burr narrowly carried New York City, but Lewis won by a huge margin statewide.

His political career in shambles, Burr lashed out at the man who had thwarted him ever since their days as young officers on Washington's staff. Soon after the election he wrote to Hamilton demanding an explanation for a certain newspaper report that he, Hamilton, "looked upon Mr. Burr to be a dangerous man, and one who ought not to be trusted with the reins of government." Hamilton let it be known, through an intermediary, that his remarks "turned wholly on political topics, and did not attribute to Col. Burr any instance of dishonorable conduct, nor relate to his private character." Burr nevertheless demanded an "interview" on the field of honor. Hamilton's views on dueling had shifted after his eldest son was killed in a political duel only three years before. To run from Aaron Burr, however, was unthinkable. He accepted the challenge.

Early on the morning of July 11, 1804, Hamilton and Burr, accompanied by their seconds, crossed over to Weehawken, New Jersey, on the west bank of the Hudson opposite the present foot of 42nd Street. Their seconds cleared a proper site near the shore, loaded the pistols, and positioned the two men a mere ten paces apart. At the signal, Burr slowly raised his weapon, aimed, and fired. Hamilton, who had previously declared his intention to let Burr get off the first shot, fell mortally wounded. Burr fled the scene at once. Hamilton's seconds brought him back across the river in a small boat, docking at the foot of what is now Horatio Street in Greenwich Village. He was carried to the nearby home of William Bayard, where he died the next day after what his doctor termed "almost intolerable" suffering.

Hamilton's funeral two days later was a poignant reminder of the political consensus he had once inspired in New York—and had subsequently done so much to destroy. The Democratic-Republican Common Council instructed "all classes of inhabitants" to suspend their usual business and ordered muffled bells to toll from dawn to dusk. At noon a long, somber funeral cortege wound its way through the streets toward Trinity Church. Every social group and civic organization—military officers, students of Columbia College, merchants, attorneys, the Society of Cincinnati, the General Society of Mechanics and Tradesmen, even the Tammany Society—was represented in the procession, trailed by a mass of "citizens in general." Warships in the harbor fired their minute guns. Merchant vessels flew their colors at half-mast. Gouverneur Morris delivered a moving funeral oration at Trinity.

While tributes to Hamilton poured in from all over the country, Burr kept out of sight. Two weeks after the duel, facing a murder indictment and fearing his house would be attacked by a mob, he slipped out of town into obloquy everlasting.

22

Queen of Commerce, Jack of All Trades

American neutrality during the Napoleonic Wars paid off handsomely for New York. Despite persistent losses to belligerent navies and privateers, fifteen or so years of supplying distant combatants transformed the city into the nation's premier port and marketplace.

In war-ravaged Europe, the demand for American products became almost insatiable. As early as 1795 Noah Webster reported that French purchases of meat, flour, leather, and cloth were opening a new era of affluence for the United States. Between 1795 and 1800, as a result of the Jay Treaty, the value of American exports to Great Britain trebled, while the United States emerged as the single most lucrative overseas market for British exports. The West Indies plantation economies, isolated from Europe, also grew more dependent on supplies of grain, meat, and timber from the mainland. West Indian officials coolly ignored attempts by their home governments to restrict neutral commerce and allowed American ships to come and go without interference.

Thanks to the turmoil in Europe, moreover, the United States captured much of the international carrying trade. Sugar from the West Indies, wine from Madeira, cotton and spices from India, manufactures from Europe—all of them and more crisscrossed the oceans in American bottoms by the turn of the century. From 1795 to 1800 American shipments of Caribbean sugar to Europe doubled—over six hundred U.S. ships engaged in trade with Saint-Domingue alone—while American reexports of European goods to Latin America grew by a factor of seven.

The consequences for New York were astounding. Between the early 1790s and 1807, the value of imports through the city rose from $1.4 million to $7.6 million. By the later 1790s New York had pulled decisively ahead of Philadelphia as the leading port of entry in the United States. In 1806 alone, the value of New York's imports was almost twice that of Philadelphia's. More striking still was the jump in exports through New York, which went from around $2.5 million in 1790 to $26 million in 1806, a tenfold increase. By 1799 the port handled nearly one-third the nation's overseas trade; almost one-fourth its coasting trade also moved through the East River waterfront.

Little or none of this would have happened had Europe been at peace, or had the United States been dragged into war on one side or the other. But neutrality doesn't explain why New York proved so much more successful than, say, Philadelphia or Boston in responding to heightened foreign demand for American products. How did the city become the principal link between the United States and world markets?

CONNECTIONS

Geography was part of the answer. That New York possessed one of the best harbors in the world—deep, directly accessible to the open sea, and rarely blocked by ice, even in the depths of winter—was an old story. But those assets counted for relatively little until the final decade of the eighteenth century, when merchants began to employ big, deep-draft vessels—brigs, barks, and ships—that could make Philadelphia, one hundred miles from the mouth of Delaware Bay, only on a flood tide. The bottom-line case for New York was simple: larger cargoes could move in and out more rapidly and surely than elsewhere.

This efficiency helped New York reestablish its old commercial partnership with Great Britain. By the early 1790s more ships were leaving Liverpool for New York than for any other American port, and New York had regained its former role as the American terminus of the transatlantic postal "packet" service from Falmouth, providing city merchants with vital mercantile information days, even weeks, ahead of competitors in other seaports. Ratification of the Jay Treaty, followed by the appointment of Rufus King (another pro-British New Yorker) as American ambassador to the Court of St. James, all but sanctified this special neocolonial relationship.

Equally critical was the expansion of New York's continental hinterlands. In the mid-1790s, following Anthony Wayne's victory over the Indians at Fallen Timbers and ratification of the Jay Treaty, tens of thousands of settlers began occupying western territories wrested from the Six Nations of the Iroquois after the Revolution. Most were land-hungry New England Yankees, squeezed off their rocky farmsteads by overpopulation and declining yields. Up the Mohawk Valley and over the Adirondacks they raced, aiming for the rich country below Lake Ontario, a few even setting their sights as far west as Ohio.

This migration dwarfed anything of its kind in the previous history of the New World. During the winter of 1794–95 alone, some twenty thousand migrants flooded through Albany, and that was only a hint of what lay ahead. All told, between 1790 and 1800 the population of New York State rose from 340,000 to 589,000—the great majority of the increase attributable to the rapid occupation of the frontier. By 1810 the state had 959,000 inhabitants, nearly three times as many as when Washington was first inaugurated.

From this vast region's burgeoning towns and villages—Buffalo, Rochester, Syracuse, Elmira, Ithaca—an ever-widening stream of farm produce cascaded down toward the Atlantic seaboard, where New York merchants hustled it out along well-traveled sea routes to markets in the West Indies and Europe. So relentless was the pressure for improved transportation between the coast and the interior that in the first two decades of the nineteenth century, the legislature granted charters of incorporation to hundreds of bridge and turnpike companies; as early as 1808 New Yorkers had already invested more money in road company stock than had the residents of any other state. The legislature also handed out exclusive franchises for stagecoach service that markedly improved the city's connections with Albany, Boston, and Philadelphia. In 1792, moreover, the state subsidized two private canal companies, one to link the Hudson with Lake Champlain, the other to connect the Hudson with Lake Ontario. Both did much to facilitate trade and communication, further helping the city establish dominion over an agricultural hinterland that stretched, at its fullest extent, from the upper Connecticut River Valley to the shores of Lake Erie, encompassing sizable portions of northern and western Pennsylvania as well.

For wealthy and well-connected residents of New York City, the rapid settlement of the state's northern and western territories brought additional rewards from land speculation and development. In 1791 state commissioners, chaired by Governor Clinton, auctioned off 5.5 million acres of Iroquois land for better than a million dollars. Syndicates of city investors grabbed most of it, some purchases dwarfing the grants made by Fletcher and Cornbury a century earlier. Alexander Macomb got his hands on a princely 3.6 million acres; Melancton Smith, Marinus Willett, James Clinton, Jonathan Lawrence, James Kent, and many others came away with thousands of acres apiece.

At almost the same time, New York merchants were gaining control of another agricultural hinterland, this one in the American South. Here the story hinged on cotton rather than foodstuffs. The world's chief markets for raw cotton were Manchester and other great British textile manufacturing centers, where the production of muslin and broadcloth continued to drive the industrial revolution. Prior to 1790 North America had supplied relatively little of Britain's voracious demand for cotton, in part because the time-consuming work of removing seeds from the lint made it commercially less attractive than other cash crops. Only scattered shipments passed through New York in the 1780s and early 1790s, city merchants shunning it as a "dull article."

Then, in 1792 or 1793, a Connecticut inventor named Eli Whitney devised a hand-cranked mechanism—afterwards called the cotton engine, or "gin"—that did the job quickly and cleanly. Virtually overnight, the production of cotton below the Mason-Dixon line doubled, then doubled again. In 1796 over six million pounds were exported from the United States, the bulk of it to Great Britain. By 1804 cotton exports had climbed to thirty-five million pounds, and British manufacturers were buying more cotton from the United States than from Britain's own colonial possessions. Cotton suddenly became a major component of American trade with the former mother country, and it was on the way to becoming the nation's single most valuable export.

New Orleans shipped out more cotton than any other American city because it was cheaper and easier to raft bales down the Mississippi River than to send them overland to eastern ports. However, New York possessed several distinct advantages of its own that enabled its merchants to divert a significant part of that traffic through the East River waterfront of Manhattan.

For one, New York commanded a much stronger regional market. Slave societies couldn't generate the same level of consumer demand for foreign manufactures as did seaboard cities and midwestern towns, so British buyers coming to New Orleans for cotton found themselves unable to sell their own exports as quickly or profitably as they could along Pearl Street or in Hanover Square. New York's attractiveness was enhanced by a superior commercial infrastructure and abundant human resources—ships, wharves, storehouses, auction rooms, sailors, cartmen, dockworkers—which made it possible to move mammoth quantities of cotton directly to European mills more efficiently and reliably.

Above all, New York enjoyed financial resources second to none in the country. By the turn of the century Manhattan had more banks and a greater volume of financial transactions than any other American city. New York's primacy in trade with the British Isles had also made it the nation's principal market for the bills of exchange that were the lifeblood of international commerce. As cotton production mounted, southern planters relied more heavily on the New York financial market to turn the receipts they received from exporters into cash. Shrewd merchants like Isaac Hicks soon took to advancing money to southerners (at customary rates of interest) and, in the absence of southern banks, to handling transactions between them and northern creditors (for a percentage). From time to time Hicks also acted as an agent for southerners wanting to use the proceeds from cotton sales to speculate in other commodities on the New York market. Using "factors" (resident agents) and correspondents, other city merchants bought cotton outright from planters for shipment back to New York or, more often, directly to Liverpool or Le Havre.

New York also had an unrivaled concentration of insurance firms. During the war-torn nineties, the mounting cost of private insurance for ships and cargoes had prompted a number of wealthy New York merchants to organize marine insurance companies. Three appeared in 1796 alone: Archibald Gracie's New York Insurance Company, Nicholas Low's United Insurance Company, and Comfort Sands's Associated Underwriters—all of which soon expanded their operations to include coverage of houses and lives as well as vessels. Within the first half-dozen years of the next century, five additional insurance firms would be established in the city.

As a hub of speculation too, New York was now far ahead of its rivals. While the pace of activity on the Tontine exchange was glacial by modern standards, rarely exceeding a hundred shares a day, and few businesses as yet relied on issues of stock to raise money, New York brokers nonetheless offered more than stocks to wager on—elections, sporting events, international affairs, even the weather—and siphoned cash from all over the country. As one envious Philadelphia merchant said in the mid-nineties, the "immense capital" pouring into the city lubricated every aspect of trade and commerce and explained why New York "now far exceeds us in her exports and imports."

The upshot was the renowned "Cotton Triangle," in which New York brokered the exchange of southern cotton—and, more important, the money from sales of southern cotton—for British manufactures. New York ships ran cotton from Charleston or Mobile or Savannah to Europe, returned to New York with manufactured goods (and immigrants), then worked down the coast again to exchange their goods for more cotton—ringing up, at every turn, substantial profits in sales, freight charges, and commissions. By 1798 cotton already accounted for half of the city's domestic exports; a decade later one-fourth of the cotton reaching Liverpool from the United States came through the East River waterfront. Eventually, New York superintended so great a share of the South's output that forty cents of every dollar paid for southern cotton allegedly wound up in the pockets of city merchants.

Once again, New York had hitched its economic well-being to the institution of slavery.

RIDING THE WAVE

The quickened tempo of local commerce drew throngs of aspiring businessmen to Manhattan, and their lean and hungry willingness to take entrepreneurial risks further accelerated the velocity of trade. In 1790 the city directory listed 248 merchants; by 1800 there were over eleven hundred—a fourfold increase.

A large body of newcomers came down from New England, bringing new expertise, capital, and connections—the urban wing, as it were, of the great exodus populating upstate New York and the Ohio country. The brothers Nathaniel and George Griswold arrived from Old Lyme in 1794 and established the firm of N. L. and G. Griswold, whose blue-and-white checkered house flag was known in the West Indies, South America, and China. (Local wags liked to say that a cargo stamped "N.L. & G.G." meant "No Loss and Great Gain.") They were joined by Lows from Salem, Grinnells from New Bedford, Goodhues from Salem, and a host of other Connecticut Yankees, including Anson G. Phelps, Elisha Peck, and William E. Dodge—more than enough, all in all, to warrant formation in 1805 of the New England Society in the City of New York. At their annual dinner, the members drank toasts to "the Universal Yankee nation!"

With the New Englanders came additional numbers of Scots, English, Irish, and French immigrants eager to make their fortunes in the city's surging economy—none more successfully, as it happened, than young John Jacob Astor. Since his arrival in New York shortly after Evacuation Day, Astor had developed a keen interest in the fur trade. He began buying furs in Manhattan and shipping them back to London, soon accumulating enough capital to open his own warehouse in Montreal (still the center of the North American fur trade) as well as to purchase a lot and building on Little Dock Street, in the heart of the business district, for an office and residence. By 1793 he had become the most important fur merchant in the United States. When Britain agreed to abandon its western posts in the Jay Treaty of 1794, Astor moved aggressively into the Great Lakes and began to pull trade away from the St. Lawrence toward the Hudson. Over the next decade his agents ranged as far west as St. Louis, sending thousands of pelts every year back to New York City.

In the mid-1790s, recognizing the limits of European and American demand for furs, Astor also began to participate in the China trade. At first he bought space on Canton-bound ships owned by other merchants, shipping otter, beaver, and fox skins (along with ginseng) and bringing back tea, silk, and porcelain. He consigned these goods to local auction houses, to local retailers, or to Manhattan wholesalers for reshipment to Bordeaux or Hamburg. In the early 1800s Astor began building his own ships and had become the executive manager of a far-flung mercantile empire, with employees and agents in several countries and headquarters in New York. By 1808, when the state legislature chartered his American Fur Company, he had become the city's first and only millionaire.

Early on, convinced that Manhattan—and Manhattan real estate—had a golden future, Astor began to invest his profits in land. He bought two lots and four half-lots from his brother Henry in 1789. Two years later, he acquired the first of what would become sizable holdings along the waterfront. After the turn of the century, flush with China trade profits, his interest in real estate grew more systematic, more ambitious, and more calculating. Weekends often found him on his horse, scouring the countryside north of the city for parcels—as in 1803, when he bought a seventy-acre farm that ran west of Broadway to the Hudson River between 42nd and 46th streets. That same year, he also gained control of Richmond Hill when the high-living Burr, hard pressed for cash, sold Astor the leasehold on 241 lots for $62,500; the following year, with Hamilton in his grave, Burr sold off still more land to Astor before heading into exile. Over the next decade, Astor continued to buy or lease additional parcels just north of the developed city—then sat back to await further developments.

CONCOMITANTS OF COMMERCE

The success of Astor and his fellow businessmen had innumerable ramifications for New York, perhaps the most obvious being the transformation of its waterfront. Ships from all over the world jammed the East River docks during the wartime boom—more ships "than I ever before saw, except on the Thames below London Bridge," wrote the English traveler William Strickland. "Bales of cotton, wool, and merchandize; barrels of potash, rice, flour, and salt provisions; hogsheads of sugar, chests of tea, puncheons of rum, and pipes of wine; boxes, cases, packs and packages of all sizes and denominations, were strewed upon the wharfs and landing-places, or upon the decks of the shipping," observed another English visitor, John Lambert.

Presiding over this waterfront whirl were the merchants, great and small, who according to the English actor John Bernard worked harder and lived faster than any he had seen in America:

> They breakfasted at eight or half past, and by nine were in their counting-houses, laying out the business of the day; at ten they were on their wharves, with aprons around their waists, rolling hogsheads of rum and molasses; at twelve, at market, flying about as dirty and as diligent as porters; at two, back again to the rolling, heaving, hallooing, and scribbling. At four they went home to dress for dinner; at seven, to the play; at eleven, to supper, with a crew of lusty Bacchanals who would smoke cigars, gulp down brandy, and sing, roar, and shout in the thickening clouds they created, like so many merry devils, till three in the morning. At eight, up again, to scribble, run, and roll hogsheads.

No less dramatic was the increased size and scale of enterprise in the city. As shipping boomed in the 1790s and early 1800s, importers and commission merchants began consolidating capital into partnerships, expanding their operations, and erecting grand new brick warehouses. These massive structures—importer William Lupton's four-story building covered two town lots and ran back sixty feet—changed the ambience of the waterfront by crowding out artisanal workshops. A mere eight merchants amassed 75 percent of the property along Front Street between Wall Street and Old Slip, and Pearl Street was well on its way to becoming a solid block of wholesale establishments.

The mounting demand for access to the waterfront prompted the merchants who ran the municipal corporation to extend the shore around Manhattan's southern tip. In 1798 the city began the filling, grading, and paving of South Street, a new seventy-foot-wide border, and by 1801 new wharves, slips, and piers were under construction from Whitehall to the Fly Market. Spiked wooden poles were drop-hammered into the river bottom to form sea walls, then the water lot they enclosed was filled in with rubbish, earth, and cinder. In some places the traditional sheet piling was supplemented by crib-works—wood-frame, boxlike receptacles filled with loose stone and sunk to the river bottom as a base for larger and sturdier docks.

As in the past, the city enjoined proprietors of adjoining land to carry out these projects, under the direction of municipal surveyors. On completion, the developers received clear title to the filled water lots along with the right to collect the fees from pier users. The Common Council did, however, require that dockside fronting slips be reserved as "publick property," to ensure that private wharf owners would not be able to jack up food prices by charging monopoly rents to market boats. In 1806, moreover, the city began to develop public basins at its own expense, retaining the right to wharfage.

The increase in traffic coming down the Hudson from the interior prompted commercial development along the west side of Manhattan as well. By 1810 West Street had been created on landfill, its new facilities for docking providing a grand counterpart to South Street across town. By 1807 the Hudson side had fifteen wharves, nearly half the thirty-plus on the East River. By then, too, ships that through the 1790s had still been forced to anchor offshore and transfer their cargoes to smaller boats—lighters—for loading and unloading were now able to pull directly into shore, their bowsprits arcing out over South Street. The result was a circumferential forest of spars, and the "tall masts mingled with the buildings," John Lambert wrote in 1807, "together with the spires and cupolas of the churches, gave the city an appearance of magnificence."

Streets adjacent to the eastside docks were equally alive with commercial activity. Bankers and brokers elbowed their way into the blocks nearest the Tontine Coffee House at Wall and Water, epicenter of mercantile transactions (and the site, not coincidentally, of New York's first hackney station). Insurance companies, accountants, and law firms rented space in subdivided old town houses—one ad placed in 1803 announced the availability of an "Office and Cellar in Pearl Street near the Coffee Houses"—their presence announced by shiny brass plates.

Merchants' operations also grew more specialized in the 1790s and 1800s. Emerging alongside the all-purpose general traders were new commission merchants, brokers, jobbers, factors, importers, and auctioneers. Many devoted themselves to handling just one or two lines of goods (textiles, drugs, provisions, hardware) or one kind of trade (retail or wholesale, import or export). Businessmen advertised on a much larger scale too, and papers began to carry ever greater quantities of the commercial information merchants needed to operate in an ever larger and more impersonal market. From 1796 a weekly newspaper, the *New-York Price-Current*, devoted itself entirely to covering these complex affairs.

Business took on a newly organized quality as well. In the twenty-odd years after Evacuation Day, for example, the number of booksellers in the city jumped from five to thirty, and the importance of the New York print market was in turn recognized, in 1802, by formation of a national trade organization, the American Company of Booksellers. In June of that year it held the "first Literary Fair ever in the United States." Dealers from every part of the country converged on the Long Room of the Coffee House, snapping up half a million books in five days. The New-York Association of Booksellers, a local organization, appeared shortly thereafter.

Book buyers weren't the only out-of-town merchants to descend on the city. Some came to attend fairs and auctions, others to shop (along with locals) in the expanding retail district above the wharves or in the fine specialty shops that lined lower Broadway, William Street, and Maiden Lane. (There was, however, as yet "no appearance of shop windows as in London," one English observer noted, "only stores which make no shew till you enter the houses.")

So many transients arrived, for business as well as pleasure, that taverns and board- inghouses proved unable to accommodate the influx. This dilemma led to the construc- tion of New York's first hotel in the modern sense—the five-story, 137-room City Hotel, which opened in 1794 on the west side of Broadway just north of Trinity Church. Besides room and board, it offered the facilities for public dining and dancing hitherto provided by taverns. Its gracious accommodations and excellent wine cellars were specifically designed to attract a wealthy clientele, and its "very handsome" street- level shops, elegant barroom, and coffeehouse fronting Broadway became important mercantile gathering spots. So did Pearl Street House (which opened around 1810). Aimed specifically at commercial travelers from around the nation, especially western New York and Ohio, it advertised explicitly that it was not intended "for the accommo- dation of families or ladies."

By the first decade of the new century, Manhattan's downtown district, like its docks, was a pandemonium. Bankers, brokers, and insurance men darted in and out of offices, contending for elbow room in the old Dutch streets with craftsmen, hucksters, slaves, women hurrying to market, and a noisy cavalcade of wagons, carts, and carriages. "Everything in the city is in motion!" exclaimed a French traveler, adding that New York's opulence reminded him of "ancient Tyre, which contemporary authors called the queen of commerce and the sovereign of the seas."

DOWN TO THE SEA IN SHIPS

Shipbuilding in New York languished during the British occupation, and by Evacuation Day the old East River yards at Dover and Roosevelt streets were no longer in use. Dur- ing the 1790s, however, new shipwrights arrived to meet the rising domestic demand for the big, deep-draft vessels needed to link the city with the Far East, Latin America, and Europe. One of the first was London-born Charles Brownne (who managed to evade parliamentary restrictions on the emigration of skilled craftsmen to the United States, perhaps in part by adding *ne* to his given name of Brown). Another was Forman Cheeseman, who started a yard near the foot of present-day Rutgers Street in the 1790s, then joined with Brownne in 1800 to open a larger yard on a parcel bounded by what are now Montgomery, Clinton, Cherry, and Monroe streets. Scotsman Henry Eckford, who learned his trade in Quebec, moved to the United States in 1796, built one vessel in Brooklyn near the ferry in 1801, then joined with Edward Beebe in making boats near the bottom of Jefferson Street. One of Eckford and Beebe's most famous commissions was the *Beaver*, commissioned by John Jacob Astor for the China trade and specifically designed for larger cargoes. When the *Beaver* came down the ways in 1805, it was the equal of anything the great British East India Company had afloat.

As the expanding city engulfed adjacent farmland, the shipyards pushed up to and around Corlear's Hook, whose fine-sanded beach had long been used for bathing and Baptist immersions. Christian Bergh opened a yard there, and in 1804 Brownne too moved up to a spot near the foot of Stanton Street known as "Manhattan Island"—an oasis of solid ground near the shore but almost isolated from Manhattan proper by salt meadows or marshes. When Brownne moved on again in 1810, Eckford, together with Adam and Noah Brown, would take over the famous "island."

The revival of shipbuilding was accelerated by government contracts for naval vessels. Forman Cheeseman got one in 1800 to build the frigate *President*. Shrewd merchants encouraged this federal connection by bankrolling construction of another frigate at the yards of Peck and Carpenter, then handing the ship over to the navy for use against the Barbary pirates. But the biggest beneficiary of government orders lay across the East River in Brooklyn. Back in 1781 John Jackson and his brothers had purchased a crescent-shaped, half-mile-long parcel of land on muddy Wallabout Bay, part of the old Rapalje estate. They eventually built a shipyard on the site and, in 1798, contracted with the navy to build the *John Adams*, one of the biggest ships afloat. Three years later, when the Jacksons put their forty-two-acre yard up for sale, the navy bought it for a hefty forty thousand dollars. The Common Council encouraged the sale by granting the U.S. government New York's rights to the Brooklyn shoreline between the high and low water marks.

Although Brooklyn's Navy Yard built no new ships during the remainder of the Napoleonic Wars, it did outfit many privateers and helped establish the East River as the site of the nation's best and most active shipyards. With both sides of the river providing ample work for brass founders, caulkers, joiners, riggers, and sailmakers, the city became a mecca for skilled maritime tradesmen. In 1792 there had been no more than thirty shipwrights and ship carpenters in town; in 1805 there were 117.

The city's most notable achievement in nautical construction, however, involved not sail but steam. Many people had thought of applying steam power to ships—among them a Connecticut Yankee named John Fitch, who had built a steamboat that successfully paddled up and down the Delaware River in 1787. Fitch won a monopoly from New York state to build and run boats propelled "by the force of fire or steam." Lacking money for development and promotion, however, he got nowhere. (The legend that he tested another prototype on the Fresh Water Pond in 1797 is almost certainly not true.)

Chancellor Robert R. Livingston, on the other hand, had both cash and connections. An ardent amateur inventor, he had long sought a way to speed travel between the city and Clermont, his Hudson River estate, 110 miles to the north. In 1798 Livingston, aided by his political ally De Witt Clinton, got the legislature to assign him the monopoly over future steamboat travel, on the condition that he produce, within a year, a vessel capable of running upriver from New York to Albany at an average speed of four miles per hour. Livingston tinkered away but, no engineer and too pigheaded to take advice, botched one prototype after another. In 1801, disheartened, he left for France, charged by President Jefferson with securing permission for U.S. ships to sail past New Orleans up the Mississippi. In Paris, Livingston *bought* the Mississippi, along with the rest of the Louisiana Territory, and also met the man who would bring his steamboat quest to fruition.

Robert Fulton, a Pennsylvania-born Irish American, had gone to London in 1786 to study painting, then switched to civil engineering. Fulton moved to Paris in 1797, drawn by the promise of government subsidies for technological development. He was working on a torpedo to blow up the English fleet when he met Livingston there in 1802. Livingston was attracted by Fulton's theoretical knowledge, practical experience, and access to prominent French scientists (he also dressed well and had the manners of a gentleman). Fulton, attracted by Livingston's money and influence, embraced the New Yorker's project and in 1803 tried out an experimental steamboat on the Seine, with great success. On the strength of this, an excited Livingston got his monopoly rights extended.

In 1806 Fulton moved to New York City and set out to construct a full scale steamboat. In doing so, he sought out and took the advice of talented local craftsmen. He contracted with shipwright Charles Browne's Manhattan Island establishment to build a 146-foot-long, twelve-foot-wide, flat-bottomed, straight-sided vessel. He engaged Scotch millwright Robert McQueen to construct the ironwork paddle mechanism and a local coppersmith to produce the boiler (with metal supplied by importer Harmon Hendricks). From England, Fulton obtained a Boulton and Watt twenty-four-horse-power engine with piston, rods, and air pumps made to his own specifications.

By August 17, 1807, Fulton was ready for his initial voyage. A crowd of New Yorkers trekked two miles up to the Christopher Street dock to watch. The venture seemed comically crackpot, even (given the danger of exploding boilers) excitingly suicidal. But Fulton's boat departed without mishap, hissing and churning its way northward, steadily overtaking assorted sloops and schooners. By midmorning next day it arrived at Clermont, having averaged a speed of four and a half miles per hour. Livingston came on board, and the partners pressed on to Albany. Arriving the following morning, Fulton immediately hung a placard over the side advertising places for the return trip at seven dollars—more than twice what sloops charged. Only two Frenchmen dared clamber aboard a vehicle that resembled, as one spectator put it, a sawmill mounted on a raft and set afire. Still, on the way back, the riverbanks were filled with kerchief-waving, cheering people and huzzahing West Point cadets.

Robert Fulton's sketch of his steamboat on the Hudson River accompanied his application for a patent in 1809. The vessel was not called the *Clermont* until after the inventor's death in 1815. (American Society of Mechanical Engineers)

In September Fulton began scheduled service from a dock at the foot of Cortlandt Street. He officially enrolled the vessel as the *North River Boat*—only later was it renamed the *Clermont*—but most people simply called it "the steamboat": there was, at that time, no other in the world.

Well aware that he needed the social sanction of New York gentry as much as their capital, Fulton made steamboating socially acceptable, even fashionable. He revamped his boat, concealing its ugly boiler and furnace. He added a deck awning, sleeping accommodations for fifty-four, and a bar. He fitted up cabins for men and ladies with elegant mahogany furnishings and posted regulations dictating proper comportment. Wealthy passengers flocked aboard.

Fulton meanwhile settled into New York City. In 1808 he married Harriet Livingston, the chancellor's second cousin, a move rendered socially acceptable, despite Fulton's plebeian background, by his technological and commercial success. Fulton bought a fine mansion on the corner of Marketfield and State, obtained servants (one a young slave woman), and joined the General Society of Mechanics and Tradesmen.

By the end of 1812 Fulton had six steamboats in operation, most of them built at Charles Brownne's yard. (His 1808 contract for *Car of Neptune* called for having "all the joiners' work done in the best New York style, and of seasoned stuff.") He and his partner had also dispatched boat builder Nicholas Roosevelt and a team of New York workmen to Pittsburgh in 1811, having won an exclusive franchise to service the New Orleans Territory. Following plans supplied by Fulton, Roosevelt built the *New Orleans*, which made its way down the Ohio and Mississippi to the Gulf, outracing a Chickasaw war party. The partners' dream of monopolizing steam traffic on the Mississippi was soon blocked by local opposition, but by providing planters and farmers in the South and West with the capability of sending their goods up the great inland waterways—reversing the hitherto natural flow of commerce down to New Orleans—they had done New York City an inestimable service.

CAPITALIZING CRAFTS

Alongside these impressive maritime developments came subtler but arguably more profound changes in Manhattan manufacturing. The revitalization and expansion of trading networks, and the city's emergence as the nation's premier entrepôt, spurred some master craftsmen to revise traditional processes of production. The presence of out-of-town buyers, the ready availability of raw materials, and the general increase in population and wealth all suggested to would-be artisan-entrepreneurs that by expanding production for distant consumers they could reap far greater profits than by catering only to a walk-in, custom-made trade.

When Scotland-born Duncan Phyfe came down to New York in 1792, all of twenty-four years old and just out of his apprenticeship to an Albany cabinetmaker, he faced an uncertain future. The city's economy was rebounding from the shock of that year's financial panic, and with the outbreak of war between Britain and France shortly thereafter, local taverns and countinghouses rang with talk of the windfall profits that lay just ahead in neutral commerce. Cabinetmaking was a fiercely competitive line of work, however. There were already scores of cabinetmakers in town, plus scores of chairmakers, carvers, gilders, turners, upholsterers, and practitioners of other closely related crafts. More were on the way too, carried toward the city on gusts of revolution from

France, the British Isles, and the West Indies. For young journeymen like Phyfe, merely surviving, let alone getting ahead, didn't promise to be easy.

One thing in Phyfe's favor was the latest of those abrupt shifts in taste that periodically shook the Anglo-American markets in art, architecture, and interior design. On the very eve of American independence, British builders and designers had made their own break from the increasingly intricate Greco-Roman motifs characteristic of Georgian country houses and Chippendale furniture. Recent archaeological excavations at Pompeii, Herculaneum, and Paestum had thrown new light on the classical world and inspired more nuanced interpretations of antiquity.

The best of these interpretations came from architect-decorator Robert Adam and a pair of talented cabinetmakers, George Hepplewhite and Thomas Sheraton. Soon after the war, their work—lighter, thinner, more decorative than Chippendale's—began to attract attention among the propertied classes of the United States as well as England. Its appeal on this side of the Atlantic derived partly from the traditional linkage of classical learning to social status (New York's Columbia College, for example, still required applicants to prove their competence in ancient Latin and Greek by translating long passages from Cicero and the Gospels). At the same time, however, the purity and restraint of the new classicism seemed tailor-made for a republican political culture, and during the Federalist administrations of George Washington and John Adams its influence became so pervasive in America that it has since been called the Federal style.

Phyfe, who had a nose for opportunity, built up an affluent clientele with adept interpretations of Adam, Hepplewhite, and Sheraton designs (later incorporating French Directoire motifs as well). He was no mere copyist: his workmanship equaled or excelled the best that London or Paris had to offer, and his finely carved lyres, eagles, acanthus leaves, wheat ears, reedings, and moldings were matchless. He wasn't cheap either. A single cane-bottom mahogany side chair could run as high as twenty dollars— close to a month's wages for an ordinary workingman. Card tables fetched sixty-five, and a carved rail sofa $122.

A chance encounter in 1798 with John Jacob Astor's daughter, who touted his work among her friends, sent demand for Phyfe's work soaring. Orders began pouring in from other parts of the country too, and by the end of the first decade of the nineteenth century well-to-do residents of every state regarded a Duncan Phyfe settee, sofa, or sideboard as the ne plus ultra of refinement; Henri Christophe, the black emperor of Haiti, wanted a Phyfe bed for the royal bedroom. Phyfe had meanwhile become a rich man and was investing heavily in Manhattan and Brooklyn real estate.

One key to Phyfe's increased output was his reduction of the complexities of cabinetmaking to a sequence of elementary steps, making it possible to replace expensive journeymen with semiskilled workers from abroad. (At his peak he employed as many as a hundred journeymen at a time in his large workshop on Partition Street.) Phyfe maintained high standards, nevertheless, but many of his contemporaries, by simplifying designs and standardizing parts, began to mass-produce cheap "stick furniture," knowing that New York's wholesale merchants stood ready to purchase entire inventories for shipment to out-of-city markets. In 1795 one master cabinetmaker was able to dispatch five thousand Windsor chairs to the West Indian market.

Duncan Phyfe wasn't the only New York artisan to break with traditional practices and make a fortune in the buoyant 1790s and early 1800s. Stephen Allen, an enterprising sailmaker, claimed to have amassed thirty-two thousand dollars between 1796 and

Cowperthwaite's Chair Manufactory in the 1820s. Although his establishment was less famous than Duncan Phyfe's, Cowperthwaite's advertisement conveys both the scale and fierce competitiveness of manufacturing in the city. (© Collection of The New-York Historical Society)

1802 alone. Allen's breakthrough—a by-product of the wartime shipbuilding boom— came when he began buying his materials (sail duck and bolt-rope, marlin and twine) directly from wholesalers and auctioneers, cutting out the ship chandlers who tradition- ally supplied the city's sailmakers.

The Lorillard brothers took a different path. During the Revolution, old Pierre Lorillard, the Huguenot immigrant who had launched New York's first tobacco "manu- factory" back in 1760, sided with the patriots, fled town, and was killed by Hessian sol- diers. His widow held the family and business together until her sons George and Peter were able, in 1792, to move their production operations to the banks of the Bronx River, where they harnessed its water power to turn the wheels of a wooden snuff mill. (In about 1800 they replaced it with one of native field stone, which sits today in the New York Botanical Garden in Bronx Park.) They added a warehouse and homes for workers, and soon they were operating the largest tobacco-producing unit in the United States. Innovative at marketing, they would later print up broadsides advertising their snuffs, cigars, and cut tobacco and send them to every postmaster in the United States (many of whom also ran general stores). The third brother, Jacob, borrowed three thousand dollars from George and Peter and went into the tanning trade. He too opted for increasing production while lowering costs, investing in newly invented leather-rolling machinery and erecting his own bark mill for making tannic acid. Jacob prospered so rapidly that by the early nineteenth century he owned three houses, two leather stores, and forty acres of Manhattan real estate and was ready to move into banking and politics.

On a less spectacular scale, myriad entrepreneurially inclined master tailors and shoemakers cut costs and raised output by reorganizing the labor process of their trades. They purchased leather or cloth on a wholesale basis—either on their own or with the backing of merchant-investors—and distributed it to immigrant journeymen or poor women to turn into low-quality ("slop") shoes or shirts, paying them a fraction of the piece rates customarily earned by skilled journeymen. (This, of course, required workers to put in longer hours to stay in the same place, forcing shoemakers, for instance, to peg and stitch from five in the morning till eight at night.) By relying on wage-workers who labored either in the large workplaces of master craftsmen or in their own home or basement shops, artisan entrepreneurs were able to churn out an ever-growing volume of clothing and shoes for the slave populations of the American South and the Caribbean, for farmers in the western hinterlands, and for the laboring poor of New York and other seaboard cities. The new entrepreneurs marketed these products as well, either taking to the road themselves or turning the goods over to established merchants to retail.

Once artisan-entrepreneurs entered this world of volatile markets, brutal competition, and a growing influx of cheap British manufactures, their ability to make a profit depended on their ability to hold down labor costs. One of the easiest ways to do this was by circumventing their customary responsibility to train up apprentices in the "mysteries" of their crafts. Taking on many more youths than they could care for, masters paid them low wages and offered cash payments in lieu of room, board, and education. The arrival every year of thousands of immigrants further corroded relations between masters and journeymen by steadily enlarging the pool of "free" labor—men and women who could be hired and fired at will, who required no initial capital investment or long-term care and feeding, and whose desperate need to earn a livelihood allowed employers to pay them subsistence wages.

Women Working in a Millinery Shop, n.d. by Alexander Anderson. Although it discloses nothing about the organization of the shop, Anderson's engraving is a reminder that female waged labor figured importantly in the municipal economy. (Print Collection. Miriam and Ira D. Wallach Division of Art, Prints and Photographs. The New York Public Library. Astor, Lenox and Tilden Foundations)

THE END OF SLAVERY

When the English traveler William Strickland visited New York in 1794, he discovered himself in a place that looked like most provincial British cities, except for the thousands of blacks "who may be seen of all shades till the stain is entirely worne out." "Most of the inferior labor of the town is performed by Blacks," he added, and on the surface it might well have seemed that slavery had become even more entrenched in the city since 1790. Between 1790 and 1800, as New York's economy took off and its population leapt toward the sixty-thousand mark, the absolute number of slaves jumped by nearly 25 percent to twenty-five hundred—one of the sharpest such increases on record. After 1790, moreover, the number of white households relying upon some form of black labor more than tripled, and many of them had purchased their human property quite recently. By 1800 three-fourths of New York's slaveholders had not owned slaves ten years before.

Yet support for the institution of slavery in New York was thinner and more fragile than ever. New slaveowners were by and large the big winners in the economic sweepstakes of the nineties—merchants, lawyers, bankers, brokers, artisan-entrepreneurs, speculators—and their primary interest was domestic service, chiefly by women. Artisans had continued their decades-long retreat from the use of black male labor, preferring to draw as needed on the plentiful numbers of cheap wage-workers who didn't have to be housed, clothed, or fed. Some masters in more traditional trades like baking and butchering still found slaveowning an attractive proposition, but by 1800 only about one artisan in every seventeen owned slaves, proportionally just half as many as a decade before. The Manumission Society had meanwhile continued to promote its African Free School as evidence that blacks were as capable as whites as becoming "safe and useful members" of society, while its Standing Committee frequently attempted to win freedom for slaves whose masters violated the law against purchasing or selling slaves out of state.

What was more, the proportion of slaves in the black population had declined sharply because the number of free blacks rose from eleven hundred to thirty-five hundred between 1790 and 1800—a threefold increase, the result of a high birthrate, migration from elsewhere in the United States, and the arrival of the "French Negroes" swept up in the West Indian exodus. Once it was a safe assumption that virtually any African American in New York was enslaved. By 1800 well over half the city's black residents were free, and the impact of this shift on the city's racial dynamics was profound.

Free blacks harbored and aided runaways, and the number of escapees escalated sharply in the 1790s. Some fled to nearby free states, but many vanished into the city itself. Thus, in 1795, eighteen-year-old Calypso was "seen running with a bundle of cloaths and her shoes in her hand through Pearl and Cherry Streets, then turning into Oliver, then into Rutgers, and finally into Roosevelt Street on the left hand; here were lost her tracts [sic]." Even African-born slaves who could barely speak the local language found refuge there: one fifty-year-old man who "talks bad English" had run away from Flatbush and was, his master complained in the press, rumored to be living in the city, where he "pretends to be free."

On occasion free blacks actively resisted white dominion. In 1798 Sally Gale stole some items from a store and was chased by Finch, a white man, to a cellar in Hague Street. Here, however, a "Mulatto Man Stood at the Door with some kind of weapon in his hand and Declared he would knock the said Finch's Brains out if Offered to Come in." Militant West Indian blacks, in particular, brought their own long experience of concerted resistance to the institution. In 1796 some "French Negroes" started several fires by throwing burning coals wrapped in oiled paper into open cellars. Soon frightening rumors were commonplace about plots to burn the city. Lewis Morris wrote that gentlemen had taken to serving on the watch every night and had succeeded in securing some suspicious blacks, while others had been "shot down owing to their not answering quick." Even the most obdurate masters must have wondered whether owning one's cook or butler might not be getting too difficult—too *dangerous*—to be worthwhile.

Politics also played a role in eroding support for slavery. When the French Revolution broke out, popular enthusiasm for liberty, equality, and fraternity more than once spilled over into demands for emancipation of the slaves—as it did in 1789, when the crowd at the John Street Theater gave a thunderous ovation to an epilogue that linked the liberation of "Afric's sable Sons" to the cause of international republicanism:

> Shall Freedom's Sons on others put the chain!
> Detested thought! soon may we hope to see,
> Columbia, Europe, Asia, Afric, FREE,
> One Genius reigns through all—ETERNAL LIBERTY.

In the years that followed, the General Society of Mechanics and Tradesmen, the Sailmakers Society, and other organizations representing or allied with the city's mechanics openly endorsed abolition. The Democratic-Republican party, despite its alliance with southern slaveowners in national politics, absorbed these sentiments—along with radical refugees from Britain who strongly favored emancipation—and party papers like the *Argus* published antislavery articles by authors who signed themselves "A Consistent Democrat" and "An Invariable Friend to the Equal Rights of Man." Condemning slavery became all the easier as city artisans retreated from slaveholding and the proportion of slaves in the overall population shrank, calming old anxieties about competition from new-made freemen (by 1800 slaves comprised a scant 4.5 percent of the city's inhabitants).

Federalists as well found the dynamics of party rivalry propelling them to a more activist position on the slavery question. As anglophiles, they were well aware of the rise of abolitionism in Britain and the moral opprobrium with which transatlantic opinion increasingly regarded slaveholders. After passage of the Alien and Sedition Acts, when Federalists needed to prove that they remained genuine friends of liberty, antislavery seemed an attractive and responsible reform. Given that Federalists like John Jay had been conspicuous in the Manumission Society and as advocates of gradual emancipation, it also seemed likely that freed slaves would support them at the polls. (The black vote indeed later provided a margin of victory for Federalists on at least one occasion, and it would be Democratic-Republicans who protested; in 1811, 1814, and 1815 they voted to limit black access to the ballot.)

While the critics of slavery grew stronger, its defenders grew weaker. Resistance to emancipation still ran highest among the Dutch inhabitants of Kings, Queens, and other rural counties where the system remained economically vital. In 1800 nearly 60 percent of the white households in Kings County owned at least one slave, more than had done so in 1700. In towns outside of Brooklyn, between 70 and 80 percent of house-holds held slaves (three out of every four in New Utrecht, for instance). The political influence of Dutch farmers had nonetheless declined because the bulk of farm com-modities sent to Manhattan—certainly those destined for export—now came from upstate communities settled by New Englanders, old opponents of slavery, and a reap-portionment of the legislature in 1796 gave them greater political clout.

Encouraged by John Jay's election as governor at the end of 1795, the Manumission Society had in the meantime decided to make another attempt to get a gradual emanci-pation act through the legislature. A bill to that effect was introduced early in 1796, and after three years of intense public debate and parliamentary maneuvering, the legisla-ture adopted a gradual emancipation plan in January 1799 (approval by the Council of Revision followed in March). In both the Assembly and Senate, delegates from New York City joined forces with their upstate counterparts to overcome opposition by Dutch legislators from Long Island and elsewhere. As Senator Erastus Root recalled, the Dutchmen "raved and swore by *dunder* and *blixen* that we were robbing them of their property. We told them that they had none and could hold none in human flesh . . . and we passed the law."

But this was *gradual* emancipation, carefully designed to minimize the cost to slaveowners. Not one slave was freed by the new law: all who were currently slaves would remain so for life, and while any of their children born after July 4 of that year would be technically free, they were required to remain in service to their mother's mas-ter until reaching the age of twenty-five (if female) or twenty-eight (if male). Further-more, masters had five years to turn over ill or elderly slaves to the local overseers of poor without incurring the usual financial obligations for their support. They were like-wise allowed to jettison without penalty all slave children over the age of one, a provi-sion that proved popular in the lower six counties of the state, where hundreds of infants were abandoned.

Assured now of slavery's eventual demise, owners hastened to cut their losses. Many put their slaves on the market at once, and in spite of the ban on out-of-state sales it was soon being reported that the exportation of slaves to the West Indies had increased "to an alarming magnitude," often under "circumstances of great barbarity." Other masters allowed slaves to negotiate self-purchase arrangements or promised them early emancipation in exchange for a commitment to trouble-free service for a fixed number of years.

After the passage of the gradual emancipation act, therefore, slavery disintegrated with unexpected speed. Between 1800 and 1810 the number of officially recorded man-umissions in the city jumped to 260 while the total number of slaves shrank by 43 per-cent to just under fifteen hundred. The free black population meanwhile climbed to some seventy-five hundred. By the end of the first decade of the nineteenth century, 84 percent of nearly nine thousand New York blacks were free, as against 33 percent in 1790.

PROGRESS AND POVERTY

Freedom had decided drawbacks. African Americans found themselves pitched into the new wage-labor market, but on unequal terms that ensured they would occupy the bot-tom of the city's occupational hierarchy. Some black women, perhaps one out of twenty, were able to secure positions as shopkeepers, fruiterers, bakers, boardinghouse keepers, or hawkers selling buttermilk or hot corn in the city's streets and markets. Some took in washing as independent entrepreneurs. But the vast majority continued to perform the same heavy domestic work, albeit for wages, that they had done as slaves—and in much the same circumstances too, living in the garrets, cellars, or outbuildings of white households.

Two-thirds of the free black community, however, resided in independent black households, headed by men who for the most part earned their livelihoods as laborers. Perhaps one in four retained artisanal skills from slavery days, and while black men were increasingly excluded from many crafts, some managed to earn a living in shoemaking, baking, butchering, tanning, and carpentry. A few black New Yorkers established themselves as tavern or dance hall keepers, shopowners, peddlers, and service providers. A majority of the city's two dozen oystermen (and later its oyster shops) and probably all of its two-hundred-odd chimney sweeps, for example, were free blacks, and several freedmen became well-known tobacconists, barbers, and caterers.

Given their limited options, perhaps 40 percent of adult freedmen took to the sea, and there were some appealing aspects to life as a black Jack Tar. During the war years, seafaring jobs were plentiful, and seamen's wages on risky but profitable "neutral" voyages were three times what they had been previously. Captains offered new sign-ups a portion of their wages in advance—especially important for recently freed slaves. And not only did African Americans receive equal pay for equal work, but maritime custom and the rough egalitarianism of deep-sea tars helped insulate skilled black seamen from white antagonism and broke down racial barriers. Black and white sailors not only lived, worked, and ate together, they often looked alike, wearing their hair in queues secured with eelskin and tattooing themselves with a similar array of anchors, mermaids, and crucifixes.

But if racism weakened at sea, it hardly disappeared—as John Jea, an ex-slave from New York, found out in 1806 when he took a job as ship's cook (a position, like that of steward, often reserved for blacks). Initially Jea "was very much pleased in going on board the vessel, but the case was soon altered" as brutal white sailors "used to flog, beat, and kick me about, the same as if I had been a dog."

During their stints on land, many black sailors supplemented their pay by working as day laborers—toting and hauling in warehouses, rigging ships, and unloading cargoes along the docks. While they were at sea, their wives bore the burden of keeping the household together by taking in washing and ironing. If their husbands abandoned them or were lost at sea, they might have to resort to prostitution. Black men too might turn to crime as an available option, and African-American New Yorkers were active in the establishment of a thriving underground market in stolen clothing.

Most freed blacks in New York thus lived a precarious existence in which sudden unemployment, illness, or old age could easily push them into pauperism. In some years, as many as 70 percent of black families in the city received outdoor relief, and the number of those in municipal institutions rose steadily, from nine in 1790 to 72 in 1810: ten in debtor's prison, seventeen in the public hospital, and forty-five in the almshouse.

They weren't alone. As the commissioners of the almshouse reported in 1795, the ranks of the truly impoverished included a growing percentage of white immigrants—some 44 percent, in fact, of the 620-odd paupers under their care. Two years later the commissioners observed that the Irish alone accounted for 148 out of the 770 paupers in the almshouse. The problem became steadily worse after the turn of the century. In 1801 the *New-York Gazette* reported that nine hundred immigrants had entered the port in a four-week period, many "without money, and without health and strength to enable them to earn even the most scanty subsistence." Camped out in outerward hovels, some were actually *"expiring from the want of sustenance."*

Then, too, notwithstanding the general prosperity of the 1790s and early 1800s, more city residents than ever were becoming vulnerable to the seasonal fluctuations of trade that always brought misery to small tradesmen, common laborers, journeymen, seamstresses, and their families. Their "incessant application to labor," as the Society for the Relief of Distressed Debtors put it as early as 1788, "will not enable them to subsist themselves, and their families, and at the same time, secure a small provision for their support during a temporary failure of supplies." A writer in the *Daily Advertiser* in 1791 observed, "Many of our small tradesmen, cartmen, day labourers and others dwell upon the borders of poverty and live from hand to mouth." In January 1797 "Six Hundred Journeymen Mechanics and Tradesmen now out of Employ" petitioned the city that they were, "in consequence of the season, without work; and many of them, by reason of large families, in want of sufficient FIRE and FOOD."

The revolution in the organization of work that lay at the bottom of this phenomenon didn't occur overnight, and the city's vibrant economy served—up to a point—to cushion its impact. Yet every year the gulf between rich and poor grew wider. At the beginning of Washington's first term, in 1789, already more wealth was concentrated in fewer hands than at any time prior to independence. The richest 2 percent of the population—a mere eighty-eight individuals—owned almost 25 percent of the city's total assessed wealth. The richest 20 percent owned nearly 75 percent; the poorest 50 percent owned under 7 percent. By 1800 the richest 20 percent owned almost 80 percent of the city's wealth. The bottom half owned under 5 percent.

In that bottom half, moreover, were numerous small masters, journeymen, and apprentices for whom the advent of capitalist production had meant not prosperity and respectability but traumatic decline. Instead of the decent independence they could have expected a generation earlier, they now found themselves slipping into the ranks of casual wage-laborers, domestic servants, food hawkers, tea-water men, chimney sweeps, seamen, dockhands, and the other propertyless poor who lived on the margins of society. They had to compete with immigrants and freed blacks for jobs. When too old or too sick for work of any kind, they had to apply to the city for outdoor relief or—perhaps the cruelest blow of all to a respectable mechanic's aspirations of independence—beg for shelter in the almshouse. Given that the number of city households headed by women grew by 30 percent during the 1790s—from one in twelve to one in nine—it appears that quite a few workingmen simply disappeared, perhaps to look for work elsewhere in the country but leaving their wives and children behind. As in the past, women—sick, abandoned, or widowed—outnumbered all other residents of the almshouse.

Worse was yet to come. After 1800 wage rates in New York leveled off, then fell, sinking to eighty cents a day by 1805. The cost of food, fuel, and shelter continued nonetheless to climb, stripping innumerable laboring people of the last hope that they could maintain a decent standard of living. A string of extremely hard winters around the turn of the century deepened the distress caused by a string of yellow fever epidemics. Scarcely a winter now passed in which city officials didn't have to find food, fuel, and medical care for thousands of destitute residents.

It was becoming more and more apparent, in short, that the expansion of opportunity for some New Yorkers meant its constriction for others.

23

The Road to City Hall

The revolution did little to change either the structure or orientation of municipal government. Aldermen continued to be elected by freeholders and freemen of the corporation (until the right of representation was expanded in 1804), and the Common Council was still composed overwhelmingly of merchants and lawyers, with a sprinkling of substantial master craftsmen. Its standing committees—like Lamps, Streets and Roads, Public Buildings, Auditing of Accounts—carried on as they had before the Revolution, supplemented, as necessary, by special committees for, e.g., repair of the Brooklyn ferry house, improvements at the Battery, or building a new watch house. The mayor and council continued to function as the Court of Common Pleas (for civil cases) and the Court of General Sessions (for criminal cases).

Beneath this apparent stability, however, lay an ongoing metamorphosis in the city's relationship to the state. In colonial days, all council actions had to be approved by the governor, who could veto them at will. Now there was much more give and take. The city often asked the state legislature—the acknowledged font of sovereign authority—for explicit grants of power to undertake actions not authorized under the Montgomerie Charter. Almost always the legislators approved these ad hoc requests for specific delegations of authority to raise money or undertake particular public projects. At other times, however, the legislature intervened in municipal affairs on its own initiative, overriding the city on matters that were clearly within its competence under the charter. The state was particularly active where patronage was concerned, and the first decades after independence witnessed a considerable transfer of appointing power from the mayor and Common Council to the statewide Council of Appointment (which appointed the mayor).

By increments, without anyone expressly intending it to happen, the corporation gradually came to be recognized as primarily an agent of the state, with its "private" personality, so jealously guarded by earlier generations, remembered, if at all, as a relic of the rapidly receding colonial past. New York City did not, however, become a puppet of New York State: politically, the municipality remained active in shaping its own destiny, with the state acting in tandem rather than in opposition to its initiatives.

As the city-state association grew ever closer, the two governing bodies drew physically farther apart. Before 1796 the state Legislature and Common Council often cohabited in the Broad Street Exchange. In January 1797 however the state government moved north to Albany. A variety of reasons were advanced for the change of venue: epidemics, threats of war, the high cost of living, and proximity to the state's developing hinterland. Also a factor was the already well advanced rivalry between upstate and downstate interests. Perhaps not coincidentally, the decision to relocate came shortly after John Jay became the first Manhattanite in state history to win the governorship.

Whether together or at opposite ends of the Hudson River, however, the two jurisdictions agreed in continuing many colonial-era mercantilist policies in the new republican world. While the state relinquished control of customs-related matters to the national government—after 1789 the Port of New York's collector, gaugers, weighmasters, land and tide waiters, surveyors, and searchers became federal officers—it was the Council of Appointment that chose the seaport's harbormasters, wardens, and pilots.

The state also took control of monitoring exports, even though its charter specifically authorized the corporation to do so. The state gave the Council of Appointment the right to name the surveyors and packers of bread, flour, beef, and other inspectors of commodities being shipped out from the port, and a series of laws between 1785 and 1799 laid down elaborate specifications regarding the quality and packing of flour and meal and the dressing, grading, branding, casking, and storing of beef and pork. Staves, lumber, flaxseed, pot and pearl ashes, butter and lard—all were examined and certified by state inspectors.

When it came to examining products brought to the city for local consumption, an army of municipal measurers, weighmasters, gaugers, and inspectors took over. Stationed at markets, slips, and wharves, they measured, weighed, gauged, and inspected timber, planks, grain, salt, hay, lime, charcoal, coal, hemp, flax, hides, anchors, and cables—for a fee, half paid by the buyer, half by the seller. By 1800 there were at least sixty-four public measurers, five weighmasters, four weighers of hay, twenty-two inspectors of hay, two gaugers of liquor, and thirteen inspectors of firewood.

The city-run system of public markets was flourishing at century's end. Although two of the five leading pre-Revolutionary markets had been abandoned, three new ones had been added (including Catherine Market near Catherine Slip). The old ones had been improved, including the oldest—the Fly Market, at the foot of Maiden Lane— which now consisted of three market houses, for meat, country produce, and fish. Under the aegis of the mayor, who served as clerk of the market, and the council, which regulated the deputy clerks, markers and sealers of weights and measures, inspectors, porters, packers, and cullers, the city prohibited forestalling, engrossing, and regrating and paid close attention to sanitary conditions (oysters could not be sold between June 1 and September 30). As a result, the quality of food sold in New York City was generally good.

At the same time the city was maintaining close oversight of distribution, however, it was dismantling pre-Revolutionary restrictions on production. In this they were supported by entrepreneurial masters, who believed that the explosive commercial and

The Fly Market, 1816. Women are conspicuous in this scene both as venders of produce and, in the covered meat market (background), as consumers. (© Collection of The New-York Historical Society)

demographic expansion of the nineties would pay off only for those having the freedom as well as the character to act. What was the point of the Revolution, they asked, if not to free individuals from arbitrary, artificial, and oppressive restraints?

During the later 1780s and 1790s the old requirement that none but freemen be permitted to engage in "any art, trade, mystery, or occupation, within the city, saving in time of fairs" was permitted to lapse. On the books, violators remained subject to five-pound fines, but as one observer noted in 1807, "no prosecutions are brought against those who carry on business without taking out their freedom."

For a time, the city insisted that all butchers have their cattle slaughtered at the municipal abattoir, but vigorous protests won a ruling that licensed butchers could kill their own livestock on their own premises. The city would continue to crack down on fraudulent practices—for example, falsely designating meat as having been slaughtered according to Hebrew law—but tended to overlook sharp practices such as forestalling (meeting drovers up-island, cornering whole herds, and charging other butchers what the market would bear), in this case a latitude butchers deplored, as they were the ones who got skinned.

A similar ambivalence marked the bakers' response to the assize—the regulation of bread prices by a committee of the Common Council. Although officials kept close track of the price of flour and adjusted bakers' charges to bakers' costs, the breadmen grew increasingly restive. Finally, in 1800, the Common Council acceded to demands by master bakers that the price of bread, like that of other commodities, be determined in the marketplace. Competition, they argued, "would create an Emulation among the Bakers and would of course produce good Bread . . . at a reasonable price." A year later, however, when the cost of flour fell sharply, the bakers refused all appeals to lower their prices accordingly. The council then reinstated the assize, at which point the bakers went on strike, refusing to bake until allowed the price they wanted for their bread. Although the council got them back to work with a substantial increase, a group of "wealthy citizens" formed the New York Bread Company to manufacture bread in such quantities that residents would never again have to pay more than the market would bear. This wasn't at all what the bakers had intended in denouncing the assize: free markets were one thing, industrial enterprises operated by semiskilled labor another. Besides driving them out of business, cried the bakers, the Bread Company was the opening wedge of a capitalist labor system that would in time annihilate the crafts, reduce mechanics to mere wage-slaves, and destroy the republic. The threat receded after a spectacular fire—apparently accidental—destroyed the Bread Company's main building in May 1803, but wrangling over the pros and cons of unfettered market economies went on in earnest. Not until 1821 would the City Council finally abandon the assize once and for all.

Cartmen continued to be strictly supervised. The mayor issued licenses, the council set prices they could charge to haul loads, and city officials disciplined violators of ordinances. To avoid monopolization and price-gouging, the city insisted that all cartmen remain independent one-horse entrepreneurs; fleets of company-owned carts driven by wage-workers were strictly forbidden. The city did, however, organize the men into companies of forty-nine (each under supervision of a foreman), and by 1800 there were twenty such, comprising a thousand truckmen. In an effort to rein in street chaos, moreover, a 1799 state law required that carts, carriages, wagons, and sleighs keep to the left when passing other vehicles; the city adopted a like ordinance in 1800.

Like bakers and butchers, cartmen were ambivalent about municipal regulation, though in general they found paternalism in their interest. The freemanship requirement, dropped for others, continued in effect for carters, protecting them against competition from farm-based laborers, Irish immigrants, and black slaves. On the other hand, cartmen complained that by issuing so many licenses, the city created excessive competition and lowered their incomes, keeping many on the edge of subsistence.

SHAKING HANDS WITH DEATH

In 1793 an epidemic of yellow fever battered Philadelphia, and compassionate New Yorkers raised five thousand dollars for the suffering city. There was, however, no agreement on what caused the yellow fever (in fact, the agent was a virus transmitted by the *Aedes aegypti* mosquito), and in a politicized era the dispute quickly took on political overtones. Federalists tended to depict it as a foreign contagion—the biological counterpart, so to speak, of French Jacobinism. Republicans answered that it was the product of "nauseous stenches" rising up every summer from the city's "abominably filthy" waterfront and other unsanitary conditions for which only the negligence and incompetence of Federalist magistrates were to blame. Yet etiological positions were not rigid. Many merchants, generally Federalist in their politics, preferred to fault the local environment rather than imported contagions, which could lead to trade-disrupting quarantines. Indeed, virtually every city body that addressed the problem chose to sidestep the controversy by advocating *both* quarantine and sanitation.

In 1793 the predominately Federalist municipal government established a semiautonomous Health Committee, composed of aldermen and citizen volunteers, which cut off communications with Philadelphia, presumed source of the pestilence. Committee inspectors patrolled the waterfront with full power to turn away or quarantine persons as well as goods arriving from that city. In close conjunction with these efforts, the committee also set out to track down "Nuisances in this City," such as the "dead horses, dogs, cats, and other dead animals lying about in such abundance, as if the inhabitants accounted the stench arising from putrid carcasses a delicious perfume," as one letter to an editor put it sardonically.

The fever passed by in 1793, and the following year Governor George Clinton officially reinsitituted the Health Committee. The group in turn got the Common Council to lease Bellevue, a rustic estate owned by Quaker merchant Lindley Murray that overlooked the East River north of the settled city, for the use of fever victims.

In 1795 yellow fever was reported to be widespread in the West Indies. Early summer, while hot and humid, passed uneventfully, though Dr. Valentine Seaman noticed (without understanding the significance of his observation) that "musquetoes were never before known, by the oldest inhabitants, to have been so numerous as at this season, especially in the *south-eastern* part of the City." In mid-July, the health officer was summoned to attend three sick seamen aboard a vessel in the East River. He caught the disease and died eight days later. More cases surfaced on the waterfront. The Health Committee denied any occasion for alarm, but many wealthy men sent their families out of town in August. Then the number of cases shot upward, touching off a mass September exodus. Well-to-do residents shuttered their businesses and decamped for Greenwich, Harlem, and other nearby country villages, leaving thousands of unemployed mechanics and laborers to fend for themselves. Health Committee members made daily rounds, giving medical treatment, distributing relief, and sending victims up to Bellevue. The fever burned on through October until cool weather brought a sharp reduction in mortality, but by then the epidemic had claimed a record 732 victims—and had proved, according to Mayor Richard Varick, "most fatal among the poor emigrants, who lived and died in filth and dirt."

Milder outbreaks followed in the summers of 1796 and 1797, during which the Health Committee removed the sick to a new "pesthouse" on Bedloe's Island, while at the same time moving to purchase Bellevue outright, as well as the adjoining property of merchant Samuel Kipp, for an isolation hospital. The legislature, meanwhile, created a permanent Health Office, staffed by commissioners selected by the Council of Appointment, and gave it the right to make and enforce ordinances for cleaning the city.

In 1798, amid frantic preparations for war with France, the fever slammed into New York with greater fury than ever. The first cases came to light at the end of July, again in the dock areas by the East River. Within weeks every resident able to do so had fled, crowding into "every vehicle, from the humble dungcart to the gilded carriage" to escape, as Grant Thorburn described the scene, "fear quickening their pace, and the destroying angel at their heels." Left behind were the poor and dependent, many made destitute by the death or incapacity of the household wage-earner. The doctors of New York remained on the job—twenty of them falling victim to the fever—while the new state health commissioners, aided by zealous watchmen, carted the sick up to Bellevue and established three "cook houses" where the poor were given soup, boiled meat, and bread. At the peak of the epidemic in September and October, sixteen hundred to two thousand were fed each day, and another eight hundred at the almshouse, the cost covered by Common Council appropriations and donations from wealthy merchants and other towns. Thorburn too stayed on, making nails for a Warren Street carpenter who was trying to keep up with the demand for coffins; two little boys hawked the pine boxes around town on a handwagon, stopping at intersections to sing out, "Coffins! Coffins of all sizes!" "Death and we shook hands so often in those times," Thorburn recalled, "that his bony fingers appeared as soft as a lady's glove."

When the crisis finally passed, the disease had claimed 2,086 lives—close to 5 percent of the population. While a number of prominent citizens lay dead, Melancton Smith and printer Thomas Greenleaf among them, the great majority of victims, as in previous epidemics, were poor. Many were buried in the new potter's field, just opened in 1797, to the north of town on the site of today's Washington Square.

Shaken by this catastrophe, the Common Council established a committee to investigate its causes. Their report, made public in 1799, came down hard on unsanitary conditions, attributing the disease to "filthy sunken yards" filled with offal, putrefying matter in pools of stagnant water, damp cellars, foul slips, decayed docks, open sewers, and overflowing privies. The report called for sweeping reforms, which it admitted would inconvenience and abridge the property rights of citizens. But the public welfare came before individual rights, the committee concluded, and the Common Council should have "great and strong power, to clean up the city."

The Common Council drafted a bill for the legislature embodying virtually all the recommendations. The legislature enacted it promptly, and in the next few years municipal authorities would embark on a series of unprecedented interventions in hitherto private affairs. (The state also passed a new quarantine act in 1799 and built a quarantine station on Staten Island, at Tompkinsville. By 1800 the first buildings of the new Marine Hospital were ready to receive fever victims and to accommodate sick passengers removed from incoming vessels.)

While these initiatives were underway, fever flare-ups remained mild until the summer of 1803, when again, one physician wrote, "the wealthy early abandoned the city, and the poor are daily falling victims to its ravages." The state-appointed Health Commission did excellent work, but in the wake of this latest epidemic the Common Council decided to establish its own Board of Health, to be headed by Mayor De Witt Clinton. The legislature agreed and ceded all powers to the new body, including the authority to order any vessel into quarantine. The city supplemented the new Board of Health with an even more novel office, that of city inspector. Its mission would be to gather information about public nuisances and propose ordinances to "remove or correct" them, in order to ensure "the future health of the City." The task was soon assigned to John Pintard, who had on his own been collecting mortality statistics for the city since 1802. At his urging, the Common Council soon expanded the city inspector's tasks to include maintaining a Register of Births and Marriages and keeping a record of admissions and deaths at Bellevue.

The first Board of Health was constituted just as the epidemic of 1805 broke—during which time, Pintard reported, twenty-seven thousand of the city's estimated seventy-five thousand residents fled town, most to Greenwich Village, taking along the Customs Office, the post office, and the offices of many newspapers and businesses. The Board of Health didn't hesitate to use its powers, and the Common Council backed it up with a virtually unlimited expense account. The board evacuated all contaminated streets near the East River and set up tents and barracks at Greenwich and Bellevue for anyone who couldn't afford to rent temporary quarters. This proved effective, though the Board didn't know why (evacuation left no one for the infected mosquitoes to bite).

After 1805 yellow fever disappeared from New York for fourteen years. While this probably had more to do with a parallel decline of the disease in the West Indies, it was due in part to the burst of municipal action triggered by the disaster of 1798, above all a drainage campaign that might have reduced, albeit inadvertently, breeding places for mosquitoes.

EXCREMENT AND FROG-SPAWN

When city authorities cast about for possible sources of pollution, they didn't have to look much farther than the no-longer Fresh Water Pond. The seventy-acre-wide, sixty-foot-deep spring-fed basin where the Lenapes had once caught fish and killed ducks was, by 1800, what one contributor to the *Daily Advertiser* termed "a shocking hole . . . foul with excrement, frog-spawn and reptiles." Nearby residents had made the pond a "very sink and common sewer. It's like a fair every day with whites, and blacks, washing their clothes, blankets, and things . . . sudds and filth are emptied into this pond, besides dead dogs, cats," and the like. Worse yet were the potteries, breweries, tanneries, rope-walks, and furnaces that lined the pond's southern and eastern banks. Landed and mercantile interests meanwhile complained that runoffs from the pond fed a stretch of marshes and swamps between modern Chambers and Canal that nearly cut the island in two, blocking the northward flow of population. One outlet, a sluggish stream, ran along modern Canal Street before losing itself in the swampy wooded salt marshes known as Lispenard's Meadows, where for decades gentlemen had taken guns and dogs to shoot woodcock and snipe. To the southeast, a second outlet ran through a smaller tidal marsh, still known as "the Swamp," and along the course of Roosevelt Street, a foul muddy alley, to the East River.

The city had been eyeing these obstacles for some time, and in 1791 it purchased all claims to the pond from the heirs of Anthony Rutgers. It could not, however, decide on what to do next. Some advocated a Venetian strategy: making the pond into an inland harbor by cutting broad canals to both rivers. Others wanted to embark on a giant real estate development. But in the aftermath of the 1798 epidemic, the health commissioners pressed for and got a Common Council decision to drain the swamps, then in 1803 ordered the Fresh Water itself filled in. A drain was cut through the marsh along the line of present-day Canal Street to carry off water from the underground springs that fed the pond and meadows. Then Bunker Hill, east of Broadway on what is now Grand Street, was leveled and its earth and stone dumped in the pond. By 1807 the pond was "rapidly turning to dry land"; by 1813 (some say 1815) it had disappeared.

But not completely. Although the springs remained (as they do to this day), the landfill process, having ignored the old watercourses, upset the area's natural drainage. The result was a boggy tract that oozed and sank unevenly. The principal street across it—first called Collect, later Centre—had to be laid with planks to be passable, and the cellars of the buildings that soon covered it were constantly full of water.

To correct the situation, the Common Council had an eight-foot ditch dug down the middle of Canal Street to convey storm water from the Collect Street area to the Hudson. Because the canal didn't flow swiftly enough, however, it became a stinking open sewer. When the city covered it over in 1819, the engineers failed to install air traps, and it became a stinking closed sewer.

Canal Street was not the only pathway along which New Yorkers were forced to hold their noses despite dramatic new cleanup efforts by fever-fearing municipal authorities. The 1798 post-epidemic report had urged the city to assume direct responsibility for cleaning the streets, rather than leaving the job to individual householders, and in 1798 it created a Street Commission. The commission hired carts and laborers to clear the streets of dirt, manure, and offal twice a week. In 1802 a separate Superintendent of scavengers was appointed to oversee the collection of garbage. The sweepers and scavengers were never particularly effective, however, and the city continued to rely heavily on its ever-present hogs to clean up.

Human excrement compounded the problem. Backyard privies routinely overflowed, sending their effluvia to mix with street debris and storm water in polluted puddles. In 1800 the city required that all privy pits on the east side be cleaned out, a labor largely undertaken by poor blacks attracted by the wages, but even then problems remained. Night soil was still dumped in the river, and the haphazard construction of docks and slips had so obstructed the natural movement of water that the noxious mass piled up along the waterfront, generating nauseous stenches in warm weather. Under the 1799 legislation, the Common Council had the power to require renovation of piers and wharves, with alterations to be assessed against the property owner; this brought some relief, but it was not a real solution. Only sewers that went beyond conveying excess storm water to carrying human wastes might do the job. And although an 1803 report on the London sewer system sent back by Rufus King, ambassador to England, was well received, nothing came of it, because only indoor water closets could supplant privies, and they in turn were dependent on a nonexistent supply of water.

WATER

New Yorkers were keenly aware that the city had a water problem. The 1798 postepidemic report had blamed many of the city's health problems on the lack of plentiful fresh water. Some citizens began agitating to revive a municipal waterworks project that had been launched just before the Revolution.

In 1774 Irish-born civil engineer Christopher Colles had begun construction of a thirteen-mile conduit system of bored pine logs, connected to a well and pump just west of the (still) Fresh Water Pond. War intervened and the project lapsed. By the 1780s contamination of Manhattan's underground streams had fouled nearly every source of drinking water, except Colles's waterworks and the privately owned Tea Water Pump on Chatham Street, and they too were worsening rapidly.

When citizens called on the Common Council to revive Colles's project, however, the authorities demurred, pointing to the expense involved. The populace pressed on, and many inhabitants signed a petition in 1788 requesting the city to begin laying pipes; again the corporation pled financial inability. Then came the epidemics, the 1798 report that called for a fresh water supply, and the launching of a public effort by Philadelphia. Responding to proposals for an aqueduct from the Bronx River, the Common Council now approved a municipal waterworks and drafted a bill for the legislature's approval, explicitly disavowing a for-profit solution on the grounds that such an enterprise would "not be undertaken by a Company unless upon the Prospect of considerable Gain; and that such Gain must be acquired at the Expense of the City." Aaron Burr, John Murray (president of the Chamber of Commerce), and Peter H. Wendover (president of the Mechanics Society), argued that the aldermen should abandon their plan in favor of a privately operated water company, a position Alexander Hamilton hammered home to the Council in a separate concurring opinion. Within weeks the Federalist-controlled legislature had approved a charter of incorporation drafted by Burr, for the Manhattan Company. The charter empowered the company to build dams, dig wells, divert streams, lay pipes, and do whatever else might be necessary to supply the city with fresh water (which, it was generally assumed, would be tapped from the Bronx River, as per the city's original plan). A crucial, vaguely worded clause also permitted the company to use its surplus capital for any "monied transactions or operations" consistent with the law—including trade, insurance, and, Burr's real object, a bank.

Burr and his wealthy backers had long been interested in launching a third bank in the city. The Bank of New York and the local branch of the Bank of the United States (known to all simply as "the Branch Bank") had done very well since the outbreak of war in Europe, both moving into larger quarters before the end of the decade. Yet their clubby, interlocking directorates and their habit of loaning money only to shareholders had given rise to much discontent in countinghouses around town. There was ample capital for a third bank too, but Burr and his associates, worried that the two existing banks would fight if the legislature tried to create a third, devised the idea of using the water company as a front. No one was really fooled, in any event, and by September 1799 the bank of the Manhattan Company (forerunner of the Chase Manhattan Bank) was up and running. It soon proved extremely profitable.

The waterworks were another story. The Manhattan Company had no intention of tying up its capital in an expensive Bronx River Aqueduct and instead revived the Colles project, sinking new wells at Reade and Centre, right near the anything-but Fresh Water Pond. Although engineers urged iron pipes, the company, keeping the interests of its stockholders uppermost, opted for cheap hollow logs. And despite estimates that New York needed three million gallons a day—for which the city plan had envisioned a reservoir of a million gallons—the company erected on the north side of Chambers Street one that would hold only 132,600 gallons, then, perhaps in compensation for its fundamental inadequacy, grandly decorated its facade with four Doric columns and a statue of Oceanus standing guard. Instead of buying a steam engine, it made do with a horse-powered pump. By mid-1800 it had laid but six miles of pipe, which supplied only four hundred homes with water.

Complaints mounted rapidly—of inadequate delivery, of the company's refusal to provide water to flush gutters, of its unwillingness to pipe water into the markets, of its habit of not filling in streets it dug up. Burr was removed from the board of directors, but his replacement and soon-to-be company president De Witt Clinton, himself one of the leading investors in the enterprise, proved to be no more public-minded. Indeed, after he became mayor in 1803, Clinton routed a bill through the Common Council stipulating that all city funds be held by the bank of the Manhattan Company, and despite now vociferous outcries at negligent management and insufficient facilities, a Democratic-Republican state legislature renewed the charter in 1808.

Thanks to Burr and his cohorts, who had hijacked a civic movement in order to launch a profit-making venture, New York would remain without a decent water supply for another four decades, the city would grow steadily dirtier as it grew steadily bigger, and in the not too distant future it would again be visited by yellow fever and even deadlier plagues.

FIRE

The Manhattan Company didn't do much to help the city's efforts at expanding its firefighting capacity either. While in the beginning it refrained from charging the corporation for the use of its water in putting out blazes, its system was so limited that it reached only a small portion of the city. Also, it had no hydrants, only hard-to-find and harder-to-open fire plugs, forcing firemen to drill holes in the wooden mains to gain access.

The city nevertheless pressed ahead, energetically expanding its activities, though not to the extent of establishing a professional fire department. (The Fire Department of the City of New York, established in 1791 and incorporated in 1798, was not a municipal agency but rather an organization for the relief of disabled and indigent firemen and their families, to which the city contributed money from fees and chimney fines.)

What the city did do, in 1791, was pass an ordinance appointing fire wardens in each ward, who entered houses to check fireplaces and stoves and to make sure that each had its requisite number of leather fire buckets. Apart from the three hundred men named from among the freeholders and freemen to man the seventeen engine companies and two hook-and-ladder brigades, every citizen was required to turn out, buckets in hand, and assemble into bucket lines under the supervision of the wardens. The mayor, recorder, and aldermen were also expected to show, and they were supplied with special white wands, five feet long and topped by a gilded flame, to help direct the action.

In December 1796, however, a big fire swept through the commercial district and destroyed a million dollars' worth of stores and merchandise, prompting city officials to adopt more effective approaches. In 1799 New York imported from Hamburg "two fire Engines with long Hoses, to convey Water from the River into the interior of the City," and created Supply Engine Company No. 25 to man the new machines. Hoses, connected from one engine to another, soon proved more efficient than bucket lines, and after another great fire, in 1804, the Common Council redoubled its efforts to add engine companies. In 1806 it obtained authority from the legislature to pull down or blow up buildings to stop the progress of a fire. By 1807 City Inspector Pintard reported that the city's firefighting force, under direction of a chief engineer, now included seven engineers, forty-eight fire wardens, thirty-six hook-and-ladder men, and 778 men to work the fire engines. It also invested in new equipment, soon acquiring 13,087 feet of hose. By 1811 bucket lines, and with them the colonial-era reliance on mass mobilization of the citizenry, were a thing of the past.

The municipality's growing involvement in firefighting was echoed by its increased commitment to regulating construction. A statute requiring that new buildings be made of brick or stone and topped with slate roofs had been passed back in 1761, but its implementation had been postponed repeatedly. State laws of 1791 and 1796 resurrected the rules, and in 1801 the city got the legislature to grant it even more sweeping regulatory authority. Henceforth it could appoint surveyors to see that all new buildings (as well as streets, wharves, and slips) were constructed in a manner laid down by the Com-

Scene at a fire, c. 1800, from *Ye Olde Fire Laddies*, by Herbert Asberry. Rapid improvements in the city's firefighting equipment would put an end to these citizen bucket brigades by 1820. (© Museum of the City of New York)

mon Council: builders had to obtain certificates before starting work and adhere to city codes governing the quality of building materials.

The city also received authority to make property owners correct or improve existing structures. An act of 1800 allowed the Common Council, within certain designated areas, to buy, at fair valuation, any houses or lots below city standards and dispose of them in such manner as "will best conduce to the health and welfare of the said city." Municipal authorities even won the right to tear down houses and oversee the erection of "proper & wholesome Buildings thereon"—apparently the city's first warrant to engage in slum clearance—though in the next decades such powers were usually exercised only in the case of abandoned buildings. The Board of Health, for its part, was given the right to enforce hygienic standards that went beyond issues of simple cleanliness to matters of population density. An 1804 Common Council ordinance regulating lodging houses was the first piece of legislation to specify maximum densities in housing.

Municipal powers were likewise expanded to include oversight of existing and future roads. In 1793 systematic house numbering and street signs ("direction boards") were introduced, helping to rationalize the city's built environment. The next year, one of intensely anti-British excitement, brought some overdue change in street names too. King, Little Queen, Prince, Princess, and Duke became Liberty, Pine, Cedar, Rose, Beaver, and Stone, respectively. Eventually, several dozen city streets would be named or renamed after Revolutionary heroes and other patriot worthies: Broome, Clinton, Duane, Franklin, Gansevoort, Greene, Horatio (Gates), King, Lafayette, Madison, Mercer, MacDougal (Street and Alley), Magaw, Montgomery, Sullivan, Thompson, Varick, Washington (Fort, Mews, Place, and Square), Willet, and Wooster, among others. A considerable number of Tory street names remained unchanged, however, including Beech, Cornelia, Desbrosses, Delancey, Abingdon, Fort Charles Place, Great Jones, Hanover, Nassau, Oliver (De Lancey), Pell, Pitt, Prince, Rivington, and Warren.

Strategic improvements were effected on key routes. In 1796 the city horse market was removed from Wall Street. In 1802 the Common Council pushed to have the main roads leading in and out of town "turnpiked" (paved). Broadway was extended north and regulated up to Canal—which involved leveling a fifty-foot-high hill at Duane Street—and then on till it intersected the Bowery at 14th Street. The Bowery, meanwhile, was turnpiked from Bullock (Broome) Street on up to the forks of Kingsbridge and Bloomingdale roads, at modern-day 233rd Street, and another two new bridges were thrown across the Harlem River. Finally, and most grandly, in 1804 the corporation decided to regulate the city's future expansion and ordered the commissioner of streets to prepare a plan for "new streets hereafter to be laid out and opened."

POVERTY

Via the commissioners of the almshouse, the municipality continued to provide outdoor relief—usually food, clothing, and firewood—to residents pitched into temporary dependency. In February 1796 the commissioners visited and subsidized forty families, "either by giving them money, where they supposed they might be trusted with it, or by leaving orders on neighboring grocers." In addition, they supported, as of 1795, 622 paupers inside the almshouse, including the aged, lunatic, and blind. Some residents had been there for decades, like blind Susana Wilson, who had entered in 1761.

Between the mid-eighties and the mid-nineties, the almshouse budget soared from $12,500 to over $29,000, far exceeding all other municipal expenditures. A report to the mayor and aldermen by the commissioners of the almshouse in 1796 said: "We cannot help being alarmed at the enormous and still growing expense of this department, arising not so much from the increase of our own poor, as from the prodigious influx of indigent foreigners in the city," especially the Irish, who often wound up in the almshouse. The almshouse, however, was falling apart. By 1796 there were 770 dependents in a sixty-year-old building capable of handling half that number. It was agreed that the structure was in such "Ruinous Condition" that repairs were useless. The state legislature authorized a municipal lottery, and in 1797 the new three-story, $130,000 almshouse (on the site of today's Tweed Courthouse) was ready for occupants. Yet it was soon as outrageously overcrowded as its predecessor—by January of the following year it housed a record nine hundred paupers—and the Common Council began debating the possibility of erecting an enormous new edifice up at Bellevue.

Governor Jay proposed more immediate relief. Reacting to pleas from municipal officials, Jay urged the state legislature to assume some financial responsibility for alien dependents, suggesting they be treated as "the poor of the state." The 1798 legislature agreed and authorized a 1 percent tax on auction sales in New York City to support the "foreign poor" there. The law also supported Manhattan's first efforts at professionalizing the administration of relief, by allowing the Common Council to appoint and pay commissioners. After 1800 these commissioners in turn delegated direction of outdoor relief to an almshouse superintendent and his hired aides. By 1802 the city was spending thirty-five thousand dollars on outdoor relief alone, better than twice as much as a decade earlier.

Beyond this, authorities wouldn't go. In the winter of 1804 City Inspector John

Pintard told the council that winter fuel shortages were becoming endemic and that it was the "duty" of municipal government to relieve the situation. He urged the council to buy five hundred cords of firewood before winter then resell it according to ability to pay, using robust paupers from the almshouse to saw, stack, and deliver. The aldermen rejected the proposal, only to find that very winter an ice-clogged harbor forcing suspension of fuel deliveries from Westchester and New Jersey. In the ensuing crisis, committees of volunteers in each ward distributed fuel and food to the needy (fifty-four hundred persons were aided in just one week in January). But in June of that year, when warm weather had returned, Mayor Clinton authorized the chief marshal and his forty-plus deputies to round up "all idle Strollers, Vagabonds and disorderly persons whom you shall suppose would become chargeable to the City." The magistrates would give them sixty days in the Bridewell or transportation out of the city.

UP THE RIVER

Throughout these decades, as the city expanded its involvement in fire prevention, market regulation, sanitation, and poor relief, it also enhanced its police powers. Beside the marshals, it could call on an expanded constabulary, under the direction of High Constable Jacob Hays. Appointed by Mayor Livingston in 1802 to the position he would hold for nearly fifty years, Hays, of Jewish parentage though reared in the Presbyterian faith, would convert the job from its eighteenth-century role as a server of court writs into that of de facto police commissioner. Under his command were sixteen elected constables and seventy-two members of the watch.

Hays's men increasingly absorbed the responsibility of the magistrates to maintain public order. The mayor and aldermen were still expected to appear at major disturbances to assert municipal authority, and while they still possessed considerable political and economic influence, the city was getting too big for such measures. In addition, upstanding citizens could no longer be counted on to rally on behalf of authority, any more than they could be counted on to show up with buckets at fires. Hays relied more on physical coercion than social deference to break up disturbances, plunging into crowds with his staff to seize individuals in a viselike grip and haul them off to jail.

The mayor and aldermen also drew back slowly but surely from the exercise of their judicial functions, giving rise to a de facto separation of powers. Under De Witt Clinton, the jurisdictional reach and number of meetings of the Mayor's Court increased steadily, forcing him to turn its proceedings over to the recorder. He maintained his involvement in the Court of General Sessions, but there too specialization took hold, and the adjudication of petty criminal cases was spun off to new special justices of the peace. Since 1798, moreover, a new Police Office had been established, in which police justices sat to examine all those detained overnight by the watchmen; this new layer of judicial officials heard complaints, examined witnesses, imposed small fines or penalties, and passed only the serious cases on to the higher courts.

For those placed in detention while awaiting trial for violation of municipal ordinances or state laws, or those few found guilty and sentenced to prison—only eighty-three during the ten years between 1784 and 1794—the destination was the old New Gaol (1759) on the northeast corner of the Common. Here too were incarcerated debtors, who were expected to pay for their own food, clothing, and fuel. At the northwest corner—separated from the New Gaol by the almshouse—sat the Bridewell, built on the eve of the Revolution, with space for 400 vagrants, disorderly persons, and prostitutes. This creaky, colonial-era institution was about to undergo a transformation, however.

In 1764, an Italian nobleman named Cesare Beccaria had published his landmark *Essay on Crimes and Punishments*, denouncing inhumane punishment as both the major cause of crime and an instrument of despotism. During the seventies and eighties Beccaria became a pillar of enlightened opinion on both sides of the Atlantic. His ideas influenced John Howard, an English penologist who fought the death penalty and advocated imprisonment at hard labor in place of corporal punishment. Howard and Beccaria in turn fired the imagination of Thomas Eddy. Born in Philadelphia in 1758 to a prominent family of Tory sympathizers, Eddy had settled in New York after the Revolution and become a successful insurance broker, a Federalist, a Quaker philanthropist who promoted a variety of humanitarian causes (including antislavery), and a commissioner of the almshouse. In the mid-1790s, Eddy marshaled politically influential acquaintances—Philip Schuyler and George Clinton, among others—to reform the state's antiquated criminal code. It was, he said, a relic of "barbarous usages" and "monarchical principles" ill suited to "a new country, simple manners, and a popular form of government."

The idea was to replace a system of harsh laws, mitigated by frequent grants of clemency, with milder statutes and fewer pardons. There were good practical as well as ideological reasons for modernizing the criminal code. It had, for one, patently failed to stop criminal behavior. The list of offenses punishable by death in New York had grown longer and longer during the eighteenth century and by Eddy's day had come to include housebreaking and malicious mischief as well as murder; lesser infractions were punished by lashing, branding, flogging, and the pillory (though a 1785 city ordinance had given magistrates limited authority to substitute confinement at hard labor in the Bridewell for corporal punishment). Even so, the incidence of crime in every category had seemed to rise at least as rapidly as the city's population, and its law enforcement officials had real trouble keeping up. In certain neighborhoods their authority had virtually evaporated. One resident later recalled that this was a time when "no man would venture beyond Broadway towards the North River by night without carrying pistols, and the watchmen marched on their beats in couples; one to take care of the other."

Eddy now proposed to use imprisonment as an alternative to corporal punishment. In New York, as elsewhere, prisons had always been thought of only as places to detain idle and suspicious persons, vagrants, and debtors. Soon after the Revolution, however, this notion had begun to give way before the arguments of Beccaria and Howard—not merely that prisons could also be employed to punish, correct, and deter lawbreakers but that they were the most humane, effective, and politically appropriate means of doing so. After all, what more fitting penalty could a republican people impose on those who violated its laws than the loss of their personal liberty?

Eddy's reform campaign bore fruit in 1796 when the state legislature abolished corporal punishment and trimmed the number of capital offenses from sixteen to three (treason, murder, theft from a church). Persons convicted of lesser crimes like burglary and arson were to be sentenced to hard labor in Newgate Prison, the state's first penitentiary, which stood on the Hudson River shore at the foot of Amos (now 10th) Street in Greenwich Village. Named warden when it opened in November 1797, Eddy saw Newgate as a historic opportunity to prove that a rational legal system, affording certain

Newgate Prison from Greenwich Street. "Unseen from the world," according to a contemporary account, evildoers here "expatiate their transgressions in contrition and repentence." (© Collection of The New-York Historical Society)

yet humane retribution for infractions of the law, would actually reduce crime and promote public virtue. To that end, he arranged religious and moral instruction for all inmates while subjecting them to strict discipline. Those who responded positively won special privileges; those who didn't wound up in solitary confinement, which Eddy considered a progressive way to make prisoners "perceive the wickedness and folly" of their conduct, experience "the bitter pangs of remorse," and prepare themselves for "future amendment."

In reality, Newgate was a fiasco. Designed to house 432 inmates in fifty-four eight-person cells, it soon became overcrowded, dirty, pestiferous, and violent. Its inmates resisted prison regulations and failed to work together productively. (Eddy himself described them as "wicked and depraved, capable of every atrocity, and ever plotting some means of violence and escape.") Many were West Indian blacks—the "French Negroes"—who had a history of opposition to white authority. About 20 percent of the prison's population, moreover, were women. They had separate quarters and exercise facilities, but their presence made for trouble. "The utmost vulgarity, obscenity, and wantonness characterizes their language, their habits and their manners," said one scandalized ex-con. "Their beastly salacity, in their visual amours, is agonizing to every fibre of delicacy and virtue."

Frequent riots—no fewer than four in its first seven years of operation alone—caused severe damage to prison buildings and at least several fatalities among the inmates. Breakouts grew so common that the city formed a special squad of armed watchmen to surround the prison at night; after an especially serious riot in 1804, the public outcry forced Eddy to resign.

DEPARTMENTS AND DEBTS

Despite the failure or limitations of some of its parts, the municipal-state administrative apparatus as a whole had been transformed by the time Eddy departed office. Where power had been almost completely centralized in a handful of magistrates at the time of Washington's inauguration, responsibility for various aspects of city government had now been parceled out to administrators with sharply defined duties. A superintendent of scavengers looked after the cleaning of streets, while their repair was the province of the Street Department. A Board of Health oversaw disease-related issues. A superintendent of wells and pumps concerned himself with water supply. A superintendent of public buildings and grounds (1800) had oversight of the Battery, the Common, and the potter's field (with his own force of special constables and marshals to prevent injury to trees or grass). The chief engineer looked after firefighting, the high constable ran the police force, the almshouse commissioners tended to poor relief, the city jailer dealt with correctional facilities, and the city inspector had a wide range of responsibilities, including the collection of municipal statistics. In 1801, the legal responsibilities of the recorder were transferred to a new official, the corporation attorney. That same year, some duties of the city treasurer were transferred to a new office of the comptroller, whose particular duty was to audit municipal accounts.

This growing division of labor among financial officers was accompanied by a profound shift in the way the city met its expenses. The rising cost of poor relief, police, jails, street cleaning and repair, fire equipment, lamps, wells, and the compensation of public officials had quadrupled the city's budget between 1790 and 1800 alone, driving per capita expenditures up from $1.87 to $4.29. To pay for it all, the city drew on two funds. The first, its revenue account, consisted primarily of receipts from corporate properties, franchises, and fines—including income generated by slips, docks, markets, the rental of corporation lands, and, particularly lucrative, the monopoly income gained from leases to ferry operators plying the East River between Peck Slip, Fly Market, and Catherine Slip and various points on the Brooklyn and Queens shorelines. The second fund, its tax account, consisted mainly of income from state-authorized taxes and from a liquor excise levy.

At first, the city drew most of its income from revenues, but as its initiatives and expenses mounted, it began calling on the state ever more routinely for authorization to tax. In 1787 the mayor, recorder, and aldermen were constituted as a Board of Supervisors to set tax rates when special levies were allowed; the board in turn appointed city tax assessors. Soon the bulk of the city's income was coming not from the corporation's private "estate" but from taxes. In 1800 they amounted to $112,000.

Still the city's income couldn't keep pace with its spending. To cover the shortfall the corporation began to borrow—mainly from the Bank of New York—to cover specific contingencies, such as the costs of dealing with yellow fever, building a new almshouse, or acquiring Bellevue and the lots for a new potter's field. Sometimes the city borrowed in anticipation of forthcoming tax returns. Finally, in 1812, the city was allowed to set up a permanent bonded debt of nine hundred million dollars at 6 percent interest, known as New York City Stock.

CITY HALL

All of this activity—constructing wharves, fighting fevers, draining swamps, charting the future development of the city—had silently revolutionized municipal government, giving it, in practice if not yet in law, an increasingly "public" identity and legitimacy. Now the Common council decided that it needed a proper home. Nothing much was wrong with the old building down on Wall Street, elegantly renovated only a decade before. Nor was there a pressing need for additional office space. Government House, having served as the official residence of the governor, was currently being leased for a hotel and could easily have been pressed into service. What the council sought, rather, was the kind of public "ornament" that New Yorkers had never really given much thought to. The city's present wealth and future prospects now exceeded those of any other in the country, the council complained, but it lacked even a single public structure of suitable size and opulence.

The Common Council chose the Common or Park—recently fenced and lavishly stocked with a variety of shade trees—as the site for a new city hall, then held a competition for the building's design. Twenty-six architects and builders, including the renowned Benjamin Henry Latrobe, submitted plans. The winning entry, awarded a prize of $350, came from the firm of Joseph François Mangin and John McComb Jr.

Mangin was an *émigré* architect who had worked on the place de la Concorde in Paris and (allegedly) made his way to New York via Saint-Domingue in the mid-nineties. On Washington's recommendation, he was commissioned to design fortifications for the city. Appointed city surveyor soon thereafter, Mangin, along with a German engineer named Casimer Goerck, prepared an official map of the town and projected new streets into the rolling meadows of northern Manhattan. By the end of the decade his credits also included Rickett's Equestrian Circus on Greenwich Street, the Park Theater, and Newgate Prison in Greenwich. The exterior he and McComb proposed for the new City Hall clearly reflected his sense of scale and proportion.

Mangin's role in the project soon faded, however. Nervous about expenses, the council insisted upon alterations—reducing the depth of the building, shortening its wings, and substituting Newark brownstone for marble on its rear (which was obscured by the nearby almshouse anyway). Maybe Mangin quit in a huff, maybe the council fired him for fighting the changes: one way or the other, he was out of the picture when construction got underway in the summer of 1803. McComb, his erstwhile partner, was now the supervising architect (at a salary of six dollars per day), and it was McComb who in the end got the credit for seeing the building through to completion eight years later (at a cost of half a million dollars—twice the initial estimate).

McComb, a home-grown "mason and master builder," was to architecture in New York what Duncan Phyfe was to furniture—an enterprising artisan who would win fame and fortune purveying the new Federal style to the city's propertied classes. In the facade of Government House, completed in 1791 when he was just thirty, McComb had combined a Georgian portico with four slender Ionic columns of the kind favored by the English architect Robert Adam. On the pediment above the roofline, along the cornices, and at the sides of the building, his judicious deployment of pilasters, dentils, and other classical motifs created an effect that was up-to-date and elegant without being pretentious.

As the work on City Hall progressed, McComb achieved the same effect with even more convincing artistry. He deftly blended the principal elements of Mangin's French Renaissance facade—its palace-like horizontal massing, central pavilion, and swagged window panels—with Federal-style detailing derived from the design book of Robert Adam. Inside, inspired by plans of an English Palladian mansion, McComb created a magnificent rotunda that rises the full height of the building to a skylight at the center of the coffered dome. From the ground level of the rotunda, a pair of flying marble staircases sweep up to a second-story circular gallery ringed by Corinthian columns. In the wings that extend off the rotunda on both floors, McComb placed offices for the mayor and governor, the City Council chambers, and assorted other hearing rooms, committee rooms, and courtrooms, all finished with the moldings, swags, and pilasters that were by now his trademark.

When it was finally done, Benjamin Henry Latrobe sourly dismissed the new City Hall as a "vile heterogeneous composition . . . the invention of a New York bricklayer and a St. Domingo Frenchman." Prevailing opinion, however, held that McComb had produced a masterpiece. As an emblem of the municipal corporation's enlarged sense of responsibility for the city's affairs—for its legitimacy as a "public" entity in a republican society—the building could hardly have been more apt.

24

Philosophes and Philanthropists

A year or so after Evacuation Day, Robert R. Livingston bought a house on Bowling Green—only to discover that the municipal corporation meant to sell off a dozen nearby lots fronting the Hudson River for commercial development. This was a terrible mistake, Livingston warned Mayor James Duane. The corporation should stop construction along the Hudson River waterfront, not encourage it. Ban new streets and wharves. Let the "opulent persons" living in this part of town close off Greenwich Street and extend their gardens all the way to the river. Thus, "instead of the noxious odor of warves & dram shops they will in the midst of a town enjoy the pure air of the country—Few among them are so tasteless or so interested [i.e., selfish] as to permit the sight of wretched houses smokey chimneys & dirty streets to shut off their prospect of one of [the] finest rivers in the world."

Livingston's attempt to find a home insulated from the seamier aspects of urban life was as yet far from typical among well-to-do New Yorkers. Like master craftsmen, they were accustomed to living and working in the same building, and the boundaries between "family" and "business" life, between "private" and "public" spaces, were highly porous. Every day their families rubbed elbows with customers and clients, clerks and apprentices, servants and slaves. Indeed the households of prominent merchants ranked among the largest work establishments of the eighteenth century. Typically the first floor contained a store or counting room, with patrons, employees, and family members alike moving freely through adjacent hallways and rooms. Not even the second-floor drawing rooms and bedrooms were ever completely sequestered from this traffic, and the third would be filled with children, clerks, and servants engaged in domestic as well as business-related chores. It was the same story out of doors, for commercial neighborhoods, like commercial households, were spaces shared by all classes.

In 1790 merchants constituted only a third of the residents of the dockside area. The majority of their neighbors were artisans, shopkeepers, and the laboring poor.

After 1790, however, Livingston's peers began to follow his example. The frequency of pestilential diseases, the increasing tempo of business, the construction of ever bigger warehouses, the conversion of older residences into boardinghouses, the proliferation of artisanal workshops, and the profusion of shanties and cellars filled with impoverished Irish immigrants—all of these transformed the waterfront streets that wealthy New Yorkers had called home for a century or more. So, too, the impact of republicanism on class relations meant that gentlemen and their wives could no longer command an easy deference from the mechanics, sailors, and laborers living nearby. Thus, like Livingston, they decided to look for houses in less congested and troublesome parts of town.

More precisely, they decided to live and work in different places. Merchants transferred their countinghouses to their warehouses near the East River wharves, using the ground floors to sell and display goods while keeping the upper floors for storage. They then moved their families across town, into new residences whose richly ornamented interiors, generous yards, and many amenities—carriage houses, smokehouses, icehouses, liquor vaults, private pumps—were clearly designed for domestic isolation rather than trade. Once underway, the movement to separate home and work advanced rapidly. In 1800 one in ten merchants or professionals listed separate houses and workplaces in city directories. By 1810 better than half did so.

The west side of Manhattan meanwhile became New York's most exclusive quarter. Not only did this part of town lie within convenient walking distance of coffeehouses, storehouses, and offices, but thanks to recent municipal improvements it was acquiring certain unique charms as well. After razing Fort George, the city had extended Broadway through the site, erected a bulkhead from Battery Place to Whitehall Street, and installed a spacious walk along the water's edge shaded by elm trees. As early as 1793 civic boosters were hailing the emerging little park as "one of the most delightful walks, perhaps in the world," much frequented by the city's "genteel folk." Another local attraction was nearby Bowling Green, recently refurbished with brick or fieldstone sidewalks and planted with stately Lombardy poplars to replace trees lost during the war.

As early as 1786 a notice in one of the local papers called lower Broadway "the center of residence in the fashionable world," and over the next decade it would be lined with four-story Federal-style mansions occupied by Jays, Gracies, Delafields, Macombs, Lawrences, and Varicks. (Hamiltons, Morrises, and Hoffmans lived close by on Whitehall, Beaver, and lower Greenwich streets.) "There is not in any city in the world a finer street than Broadway," La Rochefoucauld proclaimed in the mid-nineties. "From its elevated situation, its position on the river, and the elegance of the buildings, it is naturally the place of residence of the most opulent inhabitants."

The "opulent inhabitants" hadn't entirely escaped their less affluent fellow citizens, for members of other classes lived on adjacent streets, virtually next door. Greenwich Street, for instance, was home to numerous artisans and shopkeepers as well as a small population of free blacks. Petty crime was a recurring problem, and by the turn of the century weekend crowds of working people converged on the Battery. There, as Washington Irving observed condescendingly, "the gay apprentice sported his Sunday coat, and the laborious mechanic, relieved from the dirt and drudgery of the week, poured

In the early nineteenth century, Bowling Green was a center of fashionable society in the city. The fence encircling the little park still stands. (© Museum of the City of New York)

his weekly tale of love into the half-averted ear of the sentimental chambermaid." Newspapers deplored the parties of naked boys and young men who could always be seen swimming off the Battery in hot weather—an offense against refined sensibilities that the Common Council struggled for years to eradicate. Far more disturbing was the neighborhood's vulnerability to disease. In 1799 Elizabeth Bleecker, who lived on lower Broadway, was shocked when a black man dying of yellow fever "came up our alley and laid himself down on the ground."

These plebeian intrusions didn't precipitate another patrician exodus, but some merchants, professionals, and prosperous master artisans did begin to drift a bit farther north, searching for houses that (as one builder advertised in 1803) were "in so healthy and airy a situation as to render retirement to the country unnecessary during the summer." Streets running west to the river were popular—Vesey, Barclay, Park Place, and Murray—especially where they fronted open spaces like the campus of Columbia College. Broadway north from Cortlandt Street attracted the likes of John Jacob Astor, who settled on Broadway in 1803, along with assorted Kings, Rutherfords, and Roosevelts. After 1806, when Trinity began requiring its tenants to build with brick rather than wood, genteel housing reached as far as Chambers Street, on the north side of the Park where City Hall was under construction. Indeed it was widely assumed, as the Common Council asserted, that "the Elegance and situation of this Building" would so increase the value of nearby real estate that it was destined to be "the center of the wealth and population of this City."

When the Englishman John Lambert passed through New York in 1807, the mile-long stretch of Broadway from Bowling Green to the Park was firmly established as the axis of respectable society. At the lower end of the street, rich merchants and lawyers and brokers lived side by side in rows of "lofty and well built" town houses. Above them ranged block after block of "large commodious shops of every description . . . book stores, print-shops, music-shops, jewelers, and silversmiths; hatters, linen-drapers, milliners, pastry-cooks, coachmakers, hotels, and coffee-houses." From eleven to three every day, Lambert remarked approvingly, the whole of Broadway from Bowling Green to the Park was the "genteel lounge" of New York, "as much crowded as the Bond-street of London" with strolling ladies and gentlemen turned out in the latest European fashions.

Few wealthy residents as yet were prepared to venture farther north, however—as Trinity Church found to its cost. Inspired by the soaring real estate market, the ever alert vestrymen decided to develop part of the old church farm near the Hudson River into an elite residential square of the kind that graced London's West End. In 1807 the church obtained Common Council permission to enclose a grassy pasture bounded by Varick, Beach, Hudson, and Laight (near what is now the entrance to the Holland Tunnel). To lure the right kind of people so far from the center of town, the vestry hired John McComb to put up a suitably refined chapel in honor of St. John, facing the proposed square from the east side of Varick Street. McComb directed the building of St. John's between 1803 and 1807 while continuing to supervise construction of City Hall, and it proved to be a gem of patrician neoclassicism. Its pedimented portico, supported by four Corinthian columns and topped by a 214-foot clock tower and steeple, made it the most imposing church in the city; its bells could be heard as far south as the Battery and as far north as Greenwich.

Delighted, the vestrymen of Trinity began laying out, grading, and planting their development on the opposite side of Varick. But Hudson Square, also known as St. John's Park, failed to attract settlers. The vestry's terms—ninety-nine-year leaseholds on lots surrounding the park—didn't appeal to the city's property-savvy upper classes, and except for a handful of stonecutters and other artisans who settled nearby, McComb's church was left virtually alone in its pasture for another twenty years.

Genteel families would nonetheless venture farther north for summer homes. Some well-to-do city merchants even built or rented country estates for their families on Brooklyn Heights, from which Washington had so narrowly escaped a scant twenty years before. There they had everything—cool ocean breezes, stunning views of the harbor, and ready access to their places of business. "The men go to New York in the morning," it was said, "and return . . . after the Stock Exchange closes." Vacationers also flocked to places like Governors Island, Harlem, and even New Jersey; in 1797 President John Adams came up to Eastchester in the Bronx to escape the yellow fever in Philadelphia.

PARLOR SOCIETY

When James Watson, a wealthy merchant, decided to enlarge his Federal style residence on State Street, he hired John McComb, who embellished it in 1806 with a distinctive curved porch and graceful Ionic columns, purportedly carved from ships' masts. (Watson's house still stands, sole survivor of an entire block of elegant town houses that once faced the Battery.) The basic elements of the Federal style—brick facade, high stoop, recessed front door, discreet trim—were nonetheless inherently simple, and from the street it wasn't usually so easy to gauge who occupied a residence or how it was being used. Indeed, the unpretentiousness of its dwellings was a matter of some pride to an elite that took republicanism seriously and eschewed much of the "reserve and *haut ton* so prevalent in the old country," as visiting British astronomer Francis Baily put it.

A Federal-style townhouse, therefore, could easily be sheltering people in relatively modest circumstances. Between 1790 and 1820 master builders erected hundreds, probably thousands, of such residences for the prosperous master craftsmen, smaller merchants, and up-and-coming professionals who constituted the city's middling classes. Other, almost identical domestic structures accommodated commercial or professional operations or had been recycled into boardinghouses. This very uniformity obscured significant and growing differences in wealth and power among residents of the city, and veiled as well important changes taking place within the buildings themselves.

One such change was the expanded use of genteel homes for socializing. In the seventeenth and eighteenth centuries, well-to-do New Yorkers were accustomed to "entertaining" one another in taverns and coffeehouses (with results often verging on the riotous). They continued to do so in the early nineteenth century, taking advantage of the more commodious public rooms in new city hotels to host gatherings of the St. Andrew's, St. George's, St. David's, Friendly Sons of St. Patrick, the German, St. Stephen's, and New England societies. In 1792 a number of New York gentlemen founded what was perhaps the nation's first country club, the exclusive Belvedere House, at what is now Cherry and Montgomery streets. It boasted an octagonal ballroom, two private dining parlors, two card rooms, a barroom, and overnight accommodations for members. Dancing-assemblies continued to play a crucial role in determining social status—an invitation from the City Assembly was more highly prized than one from the rival Juvenile Assembly. Subscription concerts were another draw, and at least seven fashionable musical companies—the New York Musical Society, the St. Cecilia Society, the Columbian Anacreontic Society, the Harmonical Society, the Polyhymnian Society, the Philharmonic Society, and the Euterpean Society—flourished at one time or another during the eighties and nineties. Equally prestigious was the fancy new (1798) two-thousand-seat playhouse on Chatham Street (now Park Row) facing the Common. Designed by *émigré* engineer Mark Isambard Brunel, the Park Theater, as it came to be known, cost a princely $130,000 and was specifically calculated for the comfort and convenience of the city's respectable classes.

At the same time, however, the disappearance of clerks, clients, and customers from the genteel household facilitated the redeployment of its interior spaces for less public forms of socializing. Formal parlors, drawing rooms, and dining rooms acquired new prominence as the setting for gentlemen to entertain business associates as well as for those events—suppers, teas, receptions—with which their families solidified ties to others of similar wealth and status. With this shift, too, came a heightened emphasis on the role of upper-class women as domestic managers. On New Year's Day, when city gentlemen threaded their way through the streets to call at one another's homes, it was their wives and daughters who remained behind to serve food and drink to visitors—assisted by a growing domestic labor force. The ensuing demand for household help was largely responsible for the brief revival of slavery during the 1790s, after which it fostered the growth of "intelligence offices," recruiting agencies for waged servants. By the early 1800s, upper-class women in New York were expected to hire, train, and supervise swarms of household workers, overwhelmingly female, who cooked, served, cleaned, washed, drew water, hauled wood, mended clothes, minded children, and emptied the slops. It wasn't easy, either, as newlywed Eliza Southgate Bown discovered in 1803. "Mercy on me," she cried, overwhelmed by the myriad details of setting up a proper home, "what work this housekeeping makes! I am half crazed with sempstresses, waiters, chambermaids, and everything else—calling to be hired, enquiring characters, such a fuss."

LEARNED MEN AND CULTIVATED WOMEN

When the federal capital departed for Philadelphia, Manhattan's intellectual life suffered a grievous setback. Losing Thomas Jefferson would, alone, have been a blow to any cultured community. But New York had lost the entire federal establishment, something it could ill afford for, as one French traveler remarked, "this city does not abound in men of learning."

During the 1790s, however, would-be New York philosophes—primarily youthful merchants and professionals who aspired to be men of letters as well as men of affairs—began to create associations to incubate a worthy municipal culture. In the parlors of their new town houses, and in Manhattan's taverns and coffeehouses, earnest young men gathered to debate and discuss literary, political, and scientific ideas in their Uranian, Horanian, Calliopean, Law, and Philological societies, or their Sub Rosa, Turtle, Black Friars, and Belles Lettres clubs.

The most fruitful of these group efforts at civic and self-improvement was the Friendly Club, creation of Elihu Hubbard Smith, a twenty-two-year-old, Yale-educated physician who came down to New York from Connecticut in 1793 to join the staff of the New York Hospital. Smith soon became acquainted with a handful of other ambitious men just embarking on what would prove to be distinguished careers. Among them were William Woolsey, future financier and corporate president; James Kent, soon to be one of America's leading legal scholars and chancellor of New York State; and William Dunlap, who as playwright, theater manager, and drama critic would help establish the professional stage in the city.

In addition, Dr. Smith linked up with Dr. Samuel Latham Mitchill, Manhattan's closest approximation to a native renaissance man. In 1797 Smith and Mitchill collaborated on launching the *Medical Repository*—the country's first professional journal of medicine, and a source of original scientific essays, book reviews, and reports on scholarly work in Europe. The versatile, Hempstead-born Mitchill had attended King's College, received his medical degree from Edinburgh in 1786, then served as surgeon general of the state militia. After the Revolution he became "Professor of Natural History, Chemistry, Agriculture, and other Arts Depending Thereon" at Columbia; cofounded, with his good friend Robert R. Livingston, the New York Society for Promoting Agriculture, Arts, and Manufactures (1791); carried out the first geological survey of the Hudson River Valley; promoted sanitary reforms in the city; helped found the College of Physicians and Surgeons in 1807; and served, as an ardent Jeffersonian Republican, three terms in the state assembly and thirteen years as U.S. congressman and senator.

Sometime near the end of 1793, Smith's formidable coterie formed themselves into the Friendly Club and embarked on a program of intellectual improvement. Once a week for the next five years, members assembled in one another's private lodgings or in taverns to discuss literature, science, philosophy, and politics. As inhabitants of what Smith liked to call the "republic of intellect," they avidly explored the most progressive ideas of the age. They pored excitedly over William Godwin's *Inquiry Concerning Political Justice* (1793), an electrifying attack on monarchy and property. They rejected the "vulgar superstitions" of Christianity, according to James Kent, and cast their lot with deists.

One of the most popular subjects to occupy the all-male membership of the Friendly Club was the rights of women. The works of European feminists were readily available in the United States by the mid-nineties. Many Manhattanites thrilled to Mary Wollstonecraft's *Vindication of the Rights of Women* (1792), her generation's most articulate statement of what women deserved and what they might become with equality. Only a year or two after its initial publication, pamphlets for and against Wollstonecraft were standard fare in New York bookshops. Newspaper and magazine editors openly competed for readers of "the fair sex" by reprinting excerpts from the *Vindication* and running lengthy exchanges between its critics and defenders. Articulate and well-informed women sent in essays to local newspapers and magazines, disputing offensive characterizations of female intelligence, attacking the sexual double standard, challenging legal and political discrimination, and questioning the institution of marriage. In 1796 Wollstonecraft's partisans got their own periodical, the *Lady and Gentleman's Pocket Magazine of Literature and Polite Amusement*, which promoted women's rights with zeal, though not profitably enough to keep it from going out of business after a few issues.

In 1798 the Friendly Club persuaded Charles Brockden Brown to move up from Philadelphia. Described sometimes as the first American to make a profession of literature, Brown was a catch—an authentic man of letters, widely read as well as sociable, whose views owed much to both Wollstonecraft and Godwin. During his three-year residence in the city, besides publishing two novels with female protagonists, *Wieland* and *Ormond*, Brown produced an influential women's rights tract entitled *Alcuin: A Dialogue*.

Against this background, well-to-do New York families began to place a higher priority on the education of young women. How, it was asked, could respectable wives and mothers contend with their new social and managerial responsibilities without some degree of formal schooling? How could they inculcate republican virtue in their children without some knowledge of history, natural science, and philosophy? Aaron Burr, who had pronounced Wollstonecraft's *Vindication* "a work of genius" and vowed to read it aloud to his wife, had their daughter, Theodosia, tutored in Latin and Greek; at the age of nine she was reading two hundred lines of Homer and half a dozen pages of Lucian every day. The Jays, Kents, Duanes, and other prominent families shipped their daughters off to one or another of the many new female boarding schools that had sprung up around the country since independence (the three most favored by New Yorkers being the Moravian Young Ladies Seminary in Bethlehem, Pennsylvania, the Philadelphia Young Ladies Academy, and Miss Pierce's School in Litchfield, Connecticut). Still other well-to-do New York families came to depend upon the academy for women founded in 1789 by Mrs. Isabella Graham, a widow recently arrived from Scotland. The earliest institution of its kind in the city's history, "Grandmother" Graham's school was quartered in an old Georgian mansion on lower Broadway, a reputable address for what was still considered daring work.

CULTIVATING CITIZENS

"The history of the City of New York," Elihu Hubbard Smith once wrote with some asperity, "is the history of the eager cultivation & rapid increase of the arts of gain"; its residents think of nothing but "Commerce, News, & Pleasure." From the outset, accordingly, he and other members of the Friendly Club made a special point of disseminating a wide range of literary and scientific "information" to the reading public. By 1793 or 1794 they were providing all the original articles for the *New York Magazine*, a publication launched in 1790 by Thomas and James Swords and edited initially by Noah Webster. The journal featured a mélange of materials ranging from sentimental romances to essays on the rights of man and woman by Godwin and Wollstonecraft. It wound down in 1797, about the time that the members of the Friendly Club disbanded. A number of former members founded the *Monthly Magazine and American Review* in 1799, the editorial philosophy of which closely followed that of the *New York Magazine*; it too sputtered out within a year. In 1801 Hocquet Caritat, the *émigré* proprietor of the most influential bookstore in town, established a "Literary Assembly" in a reading room of the old city hall. Caritat hoped it would become a place where writers, lawyers, scientists, doctors, and clergymen would come to discuss books and ideas, but like the efforts of the Friendly Club, it made little headway against the city's preoccupation with money making—even after Caritat took the radical step in 1803 of inviting women to attend.

The struggle against municipal materialism finally began to bear fruit when it engaged the formidable energies of city inspector John Pintard. For years, inspired by the example of the Massachusetts Historical Society (1791), Pintard had advocated the creation of a similar institution in New York to improve its intellectual and cultural tone. In 1804 he assembled a group of Friendly Club alumni, merchants, attorneys, and clergymen to found the New-York Historical Society. Its mission was "to collect and preserve whatever may relate to the natural, civil or ecclesiastical History of the United States in general and of this State in particular."

Historical preservation—especially of relics and records—held special meaning for men who had seen the city's only two substantial libraries destroyed during the Revolution—that of Columbia College, and the New York Society Library, of which Pintard had been a trustee. The latter had made a comeback, and by the time it moved into its new quarters on Nassau Street in 1795 it owned over five thousand books, but it remained a general reading library for well-to-do shareholders. Pintard hoped the Historical Society would in time "become like the extensive Libraries of the Old World inestimably valuable to the erudite Scholar."

The Historical Society swiftly attracted prestigious supporters, including Dr. Samuel Latham Mitchill, Dr. David Hosack (physician, botanist, and founder in 1801 of the Elgin Botanical Gardens), members of old New York families (like Peter Gerard Stuyvesant, the director's great-great-grandson), judicial luminaries (like state attorney general Egbert Benson, the society's first president), and political leaders (like Governor Daniel D. Tompkins and Mayor De Witt Clinton, who provided the group with rent-free quarters in Federal Hall on Wall Street). Though its finances were precarious, the Historical Society quickly published an *Address to the Public* (1805) calling for donations of materials and for answers to queries concerning points of local and national history. In 1809—the year the society was incorporated and in which it purchased Pintard's own library—members gathered to commemorate the bicentennial of Henry Hudson's voyage by listening to the Rev. Dr. Samuel Miller's *Discourse on the Discovery of New York*, followed by a banquet at the City Hotel. Two years later, the Historical Society issued the first volume of its *Collections*, which featured documents on city life under the Dutch and the never-before-printed Duke's Laws of 1665.

As it happened, Pintard's labors on behalf of the Historical Society coincided with a mounting interest among wealthy New Yorkers in painting and the fine arts. Some of the country's foremosts artists—Ralph Earl, James Sharples, Charles Willson Peale, Gilbert Stuart, John Trumbull, John Wesley Jarvis—all set up shop in the city at one time or another in the eighties and nineties. Prosperous burghers, as the poet William Cullen Bryant later recalled, "began to affect a taste for pictures, and the rooms of Michael Pfaff, the famous German picture dealer in Broadway, were a favorite lounge for such connoisseurs as we then had, who amused themselves with making him talk of Michael Angelo." What was more, reformers and civic improvers like Pintard began to sense that art—the right kind of art, under the right kind of circumstances—could also help lift the sights of New Yorkers and teach them virtues vital to a republican society.

In 1802 Chancellor Robert R. Livingston and his brother Edward, the newly appointed mayor, raised several thousand dollars to establish the New York Academy of the Fine Arts (later the American Academy of Fine Arts), with none other than John Pintard as its first secretary. The academy was not an association of artists but of wealthy patrons. Its purpose, Mayor Livingston explained, was to expose New Yorkers to the best European sculpture and painting, thereby affirming "the intimate connection of Freedom with the Arts—of Science with Civil Liberty." It would also be "useful and ornamental to our city." That proved overly optimistic. The academy's first exhibition, which opened in the summer of 1803 at the Greenwich Street Pantheon (formerly Rickett's Equestrian Circus), was a disappointment. Consisting mostly of plaster casts of "the great remains of Antiquity" owned by the Louvre, it failed to attract popular interest and was cut short by that year's epidemic of yellow fever. John Vanderlyn, a young artist introduced to New York art patrons by Aaron Burr, was dispatched to Europe to make more casts and paint copies of Raphael, Caravaggio, Titian, Rubens, and other Old Masters. The academy's shareholders, businessmen ill-prepared to promote art appreciation among the general public, began to bicker among themselves, however, and the academy soon languished.

Its prospects brightened again in 1804, when John Trumbull returned to New York to take over as director. Trumbull was immediately swamped with commissions, private as well as public. Between 1805 and 1808 he produced a series of portraits for City Hall that included such local luminaries as De Witt Clinton, James Duane, Alexander Hamilton, John Jay, Peter Stuyvesant, Richard Varick, and Marinus Willett (all of which would hang alongside his *George Washington in New York*, painted back in 1790). Yet Trumbull paid more attention to his own work than to the academy's affairs, and after his departure in 1808, the organization again went into decline. Its officers ceased to meet, and by 1815 its collections were put in storage.

The academy's demise did not mean, on the other hand, that the new Historical Society would have to carry on by itself. Business-minded New York wasn't ready for art, but neither were men like John Pintard ready to abandon the campaign for municipal uplift and enlightenment.

"ACTIVE EXERTIONS & USEFUL IMPROVEMENTS"

It wasn't accidental that Pintard, Clinton, Mitchill, Dunlap, and many of their friends were also active in Freemasonry, an international movement devoted to personal betterment, fraternal loyalty, and the diffusion of knowledge to dispel (as Mitchill put it) "the gloom of ignorance and barbarism." Under the leadership of Robert R. Livingston, grand master from 1784 to 1801, the Masons founded ten lodges in the city. Arguably the most influential was the Holland Lodge, whose masters included both Clinton and Pintard, and whose members included such eminent and powerful residents as John Jacob Astor, Cadwallader D. Colden (grandson of the colonial governor), and Charles King (president of Columbia College).

De Witt Clinton, in particular, was an ardent Mason. From master of the Holland Lodge (1794) he rose to become grand high priest of the Grand Chapter, grand master of the Grand Encampment of New York, and grand master of the Knights Templar of the United States, the highest office of the Cerneau Scottish Rite body. What attracted him, apart from the opportunity lodge work gave him to establish links with powerful men throughout the city, state, and nation, was the fraternity's lineage of descent from "scientific and ingenious men" and its commitment to having each member "devote to the purposes of mental improvement those hours which remain to him after pursuing the ordinary concerns of life."

Even when his public life was at its busiest, Clinton found time for an impressive range of intellectual interests. He belonged to, and often led, the most prestigious literary and learned organizations of his day. He studied botany, zoology, geology, ornithology, ichthyology, and chemistry, and his published papers, which earned the praise of scientific societies throughout the United States and Europe, covered such disparate subjects as the fish of New York State, Iroquois language and customs, archaeology, and the cockroach. Justifiably proud of his achievements, Clinton could describe himself with aplomb—others called it insufferable vanity—as "distinguished for a marked devotion to science; few men have read more, and few men can claim more various and extensive knowledge."

Clinton was never content with private scholarly pursuits, however, and he was among the first New Yorkers to say that people of his class had a duty to improve the lives of others. As early as 1794, in an address to the Black Friars Club, he summoned patrician New Yorkers to reject "selfishness" and enlist in the cause of "disinterested benevolence." They should rise "from the couch of affluence and ease," he said, not only to encourage the "polite arts and useful sciences" but to build schools and hospitals, care for the poor, and modernize the penal system. This was an idea practically unknown in New York before independence, and it drew heavily on Clinton's identification with the Masonic movement ("the most *antient benevolent institution in the world*," he called it), on his frank admiration for contemporary British reformers, and on his personal connections with such prominent Quaker philanthropists as Thomas Eddy and John Murray Jr. (both of whom he met through his wife, also a member of the Society of Friends). What Clinton added was an emphasis on the urgency of benevolence— not simply to rectify social ills but also to overcome the privatism of the propertied classes and reaffirm their legitimacy.

During the 1790s and 1800s, Clinton and other well-to-do New Yorkers would create a battery of humanitarian and educational associations to improve the lot of their fellow citizens. In time, their membership rolls comprised a who's who of the city's most successful and influential citizens—merchants, lawyers, bankers, brokers, physicians, clergymen, Columbia College faculty—many of whose names turn up over and over again in an astonishing variety of causes.

As a rule, these associations were solidly Protestant and determinedly bipartisan. (The Society for the Promotion of Agriculture, Arts, and Manufactures, for example, was founded in the early nineties by George Clinton, John Jay, Philip Van Cortlandt, Edward Livingston, and James Duane, among others, a judicious balancing of political tendencies and temperaments that would be duplicated often in years to come.) Nominally private, they often received generous support from both municipal and state governments—as well they might considering the roster of governors, mayors, legislators, assemblymen, and other public officials who were their founders and managers. They were guided by an awakening sense of civic pride, by compassion, and by an absolute certainty that the best people ought to toil, directly and personally, for the public good—as they defined it. "What a field our large city presents for active exertions & useful improvements!" exulted John Pintard.

No one was more active than Pintard himself. After leaving the office of city inspector in 1809, he became secretary of the Mutual Insurance Company, his sole source of income for the next twenty years (during most of which time he and his family lived frugally in rooms above the company's Wall Street office). It was abundantly clear by then, however, that his real work lay in benevolence and philanthropy. In all, over the course of thirty-odd years, he would be the prime mover in dozens of similar organizations.

Never far from Pintard's mind was the knowledge that men such as himself were all too scarce in New York. The city's wealthiest residents were on the whole unable or unwilling "to attend to the multiplied demands on humanity & benevolence," he once told his daughter. "Here, these duties fall oppressively heavy on a few public spirited citizens." But in the end virtue was its own reward. "The further I go down the hall of life," he added modestly on another occasion, "the more I rejoice in the retrospect of being a coadjutor in some of our great benevolent and charitable institutions and that when I depart—it will cheer me that I am leaving the world better than I found it."

When genteel reformers like Pintard talked about leaving the world a better place, they meant, above all, ameliorating the misery of their city's lower classes. Pintard himself admitted that this mass of humanity—immigrants, working poor, the aged and infirm, blacks, widows, orphans—seemed hardly worth the trouble. They were, he said censoriously, "improvident, careless, and filthy." Yet if Pintard and his colleagues believed anything, they believed in what De Witt Clinton had called "the progressive improvement of human affairs." Shown the way, they thought, even the meanest people (the bulk of them, anyway) could become decent, productive citizens. This wasn't simply altruism. A permanent class of paupers, unincorporated into legitimate political and social institutions, posed a threat to the republic.

In this spirit, the Society for the Relief of Distressed Debtors set out in 1787 to provide short-term assistance to some of the city's neediest residents. Its managers— almost exclusively business and professional men—would include, at one time or another, such luminaries as Clinton, Pintard, Eddy, Dr. Hosack, and Divie Bethune, a wealthy Scottish merchant. At first, the society's aim was to provide occupants of the debtors' prison with food, blankets, clothing, fresh water, and firewood. This was no small task. Over five hundred debtors were arrested in New York County every year. By posting a bond with the sheriff, those with means could be released to live within prescribed "gaol limits." Those without means, rarely fewer than a hundred at a time, were locked up and required by law to supply their own necessaries. Conditions in the prison verged on the nightmarish.

In the later 1790s the society distributed food to indigent victims of the yellow fever, and after 1800 its charitable horizons widened steadily. In 1802 the society opened a permanent "soup house," near the jail on Frankfort Street, that dispensed soup to the urban poor at four cents a quart—or free, during epidemics and depressions. New Yorkers took to calling it the Humane Society (a change of name that became official in 1803). During the hard winter of 1804–5, their Frankfort Street operation, and a second "soup house" they opened on Division Street, distributed eighty-four hundred gallons of soup to residents of the city's poorest wards. The group also dispensed soup tickets for handing out to street beggars in place of money and provisions, lest the poor convert such offerings into liquor.

The city's doctors had meanwhile taken steps to provide impoverished residents with medical care. In 1791, inspired by similar projects in Europe and Philadelphia, the Medical Society opened the New York Dispensary on Beekman and Nassau streets. Supported by private donations, it treated over two thousand patients in its first five years. In 1791, too, the state provided money to reopen New York Hospital, originally founded in the 1770s but soon forced to suspend operations because of a devastating fire and the turmoil of war. Now designated "the public hospital," it provided free treatment to the "sick poor" from immigrant ships and the city's emerging slums. It housed the first nursing school in the United States, established in 1798 by the Quaker physician Valentine Seaman, and soon after the turn of the century it absorbed another charitable institution, the Lying-In Hospital, which had been founded in 1799 to provide care for impoverished pregnant women. In time, and at federal expense, the hospital also began to take in indigent seamen from the navy and merchant marine.

Genteel ladies too immersed themselves in philanthropic work among the poor and laboring classes. In 1797, by which time she was earning a comfortable income from her school, Isabella Graham joined forces with others, notably Elizabeth Ann Seton, wife of a successful merchant, to organize the Society for the Relief of Poor Widows with Small Children. Applicants for assistance were to receive only "necessaries," never money, and only after "particular enquiry" had determined their moral fitness; no assistance would be given, either, unless younger children were sent to school and older ones placed into trades or into service with "sober virtuous families." Efficient and resourceful, the society expanded quickly. Within two years it was supplying firewood, food, shoes, clothing, and meal tickets to 150-odd widows and some 420 children.

Mrs. Graham followed up this project with a workhouse for needy women. After a protracted campaign for municipal support, she and her followers, organized as the Society for the Promotion of Industry, founded the House of Industry and won an annual appropriation of five hundred dollars from the legislature. At one time or another over the next decade (it failed in 1820), the House of Industry employed more than five hundred women as tailors, weavers, spinners, and seamstresses.

These and other female charities enabled women (well-to-do women, at any rate) to break the male monopoly on the city's public life and assert for the first time a separate and distinct role in municipal affairs. Although respectable to a fault and indifferent to women's rights as such, these initiatives worried even reform-minded men. Women calling meetings, women running organizations, women raising money, women contending with local officials about budgets and leases and regulations—where would it end? Many men nodded approvingly when Bishop John Hobart of New York publicly denounced the whole idea "of *females* laying aside the delicacy and decorum, which can never be violated without the most *corrupting* effects on themselves and public morals" to become agents of social change.

"THE SLOW PROCESS OF EDUCATION & RELIGIOUS INSTRUCTION"

Although committed to charitable works, New York's philanthropic pioneers did not trust charity alone to bring lasting improvements in the lives of the urban poor. Their assumption—increasingly common among the mercantile and professional classes, successful artisan-entrepreneurs, and well-off mechanics alike—was that poverty stemmed from moral turpitude, not merely, or even mainly, from misfortune. With the breakdown of traditional relations of production, households and workshops could no longer be relied upon to teach the habits of self-discipline and self-reliance necessary for survival in a wage-labor economy. Prudence, decency, sobriety, thrift, punctuality—these and similar virtues would now, more than ever, have to be instilled through what Pintard described as "the slow process of education & religious instruction."

Ample precedents already existed, in fact, for using schools to provide poor children with the kind of guidance once supplied by households and workshops. By the mid-1790s there were half a dozen so-called "charity schools" in town, plus a dozen-odd "pay schools" run by free-lance masters. Together, they enrolled better than half the children in the city between the ages of five and fifteen—girls as well as boys, blacks as well as whites, representing a broad cross-section of social classes. Additional charity schools sprang up around the turn of the century, including one organized by Isabella Graham's Society for the Relief of Poor Widows. The Female Association, founded in 1798, opened a school to teach poor girls the "principles of piety and virtue."

In 1806 Mrs. Graham and her daughter, Joanna Bethune (wife of wealthy reformer Divie Bethune), conceived the idea of founding an orphanage where working-class children could be brought up to lead productive lives. Orphanages were unknown in the United States—New Amsterdam's short-lived orphan asylum was now a dim memory at best—but they had been strongly endorsed by European reformers. When Graham and Bethune unveiled their idea before a meeting of prominent ladies at the City Hotel (one of those in attendance was Elizabeth Hamilton, Alexander's widow), it won enthusiastic approval and led at once to the formation of the Orphan Asylum Society. In 1807 the cornerstone of its first home was laid at the corner of Barrow and Asylum (now 4th) streets in Greenwich. (Nearby Bethune Street commemorates Joanna Bethune's long career as a philanthropist and educator.)

It seemed doubtful, though, that these scattered, uncoordinated initiatives could bring about major improvements in the manners and morals of the poor. Thomas Eddy, the wealthy Quaker who served as almshouse commissioner and warden of Newgate, raised this problem in his correspondence with Patrick Colquhoun, a London police magistrate active in the famed British Society for Bettering the Condition of the Poor. In 1803 Colquhoun warned Eddy that if American schools weren't soon put on more solid foundations, the country's rapidly expanding population would cause a crisis "manifested by extreme ignorance and immoral conduct, as it respects a considerable proportion of the lower classes of society."

That was enough for Eddy. With the help of Pintard, Colden, Mitchill, Clinton, and other influential friends— and with financial assistance from the Masons—he set about organizing the New York Free School Society (1805). Its purpose, in Pintard's phrase, was to eradicate crime and pauperism in the city by inculcating "habits of cleanliness, subordination, and order" in the children of the lower classes.

To that end, its first school, which opened the following year in rented quarters in the Fourth Ward, adopted the Lancasterian system of instruction. Devised by the English Quaker Joseph Lancaster, this involved the selection of older and better pupils as "monitors," or assistant teachers, who were trained to drill information and biblical precepts into their younger charges. The system was cheap and efficient. To speed the morning roll call, pupils were each assigned a number that was posted on the wall against which they lined up, allowing monitors to see at once who was absent. Learning meant rote memorization, imagination was actively discouraged, and while Lancaster prohibited corporal punishment, pupils in need of additional motivation could be shackled to their desks or made to carry six-pound logs on their shoulders.

Pintard had said that the eradication of poverty required religious instruction as well as education, and here too he and other Manhattan reformers took their cues from abroad. William Wilberforce's *Practical View of the Prevailing Religious System of Professed Christians* (1797), widely reprinted in the United States, urged the responsible classes to spread Christian virtue among their social inferiors via bipartisan, nonsectarian organizations like his own Society for the Suppression of Vice. During the later 1790s and early 1800s, in accordance with this and similar recommendations, New York clergymen and lay leaders assembled an arsenal of specialized associations for moral uplift and humanitarian reform.

In 1794 John Stanford, an English Baptist who had migrated to the city in 1789, helped establish the New York Society for Promoting Christian Knowledge and Piety Among the Poor. Stanford had no regular pulpit in Manhattan, but he conducted a private school, instructed theological students, wrote and distributed religious tracts, and preached frequently around the city. Now his New York Society took up the task of distributing Bibles and religious pamphlets to the poor.

In 1796 the Dutch Reformed and Baptist churches jointly established the New York Missionary Society, which initially targeted Long Island Indians and published the *Theological Magazine* (1796–99). There was no mistaking the aims of the Society for Aiding and Assisting the Magistrates in the Suppression of Vice and Immorality on the Lord's Day (1795), of the Society for the Suppression of Vice (1802), of the Society for the Suppression of Vice and Immorality (1810), or of such periodicals as the short-lived *New-York Missionary Magazine and Repository* (1800–1801), which ran articles demonstrating the divinity of Jesus, the coherence of the Bible, and the like. Hamilton's Christian Constitutional Society (1802)—an attempt to tap this impulse on behalf of the Federalist party—went nowhere, as direct political intervention breached the separation of church and state, already a sacrosanct element of American republican thought.

Another British import, the Sunday school, reached New York in 1792, when Isabella Graham founded an evening Sunday school for adults, black as well as white, on Mulberry Street. The following year a former slave named Catherine Ferguson opened a Sunday school for both children and adults: Katy Ferguson's School for the Poor in New York City. After 1800 the Sunday school movement in New York accelerated dramatically. In 1803 Graham, her daughter Joanna Bethune, and her son-in-law Divie Bethune—the Bethunes too were in regular contact with British reformers and followed closely the work of the London Sunday School Society—started a new Sunday school on Mott Street. Using the Bible as a textbook, the school offered reading and writing classes along with religious instruction. A decade later there were fifty Sunday schools in New York with a combined enrollment of six thousand.

As the campaign for popular religious instruction gained momentum, evangelical Protestant clergymen began to preach among the poor (more and more of them immigrant Catholics) confined in municipal institutions. The Rev. John Stanford became the semiofficial chaplain to the almshouse in 1807. He was soon preaching to the inmates of the hospital, debtors' prison, insane asylum, and penitentiary as well, and in 1810 was joined by Ezra Stiles Ely, a young Presbyterian minister. Stanford and Ely published such shocking details about the physical and moral condition of their charges that Divie Bethune and other prominent reformers resolved to support their work with yet another organization, the interdominational Society for Supporting the Gospel Among the Poor of the City of New-York (1812). Both Stanford and Ely were named New York's first municipal missionaries. For a score more years, Stanford in particular would maintain a herculean schedule of ministerial rounds, reporting annually on his sermons and the number of deathbed conversions among the paupers.

THE PICTURE OF NEW YORK

Never before in the city's history had its upper classes gone to such lengths to rescue the souls and bodies of working and impoverished folk, or to educate their children. To Senator-Doctor-Professor Samuel Latham Mitchill—Friendly Club alumnus, Freemason in good standing, cofounder of the New-York Historical Society, the New-York Society for the Promotion of Agriculture, Arts, and Manufactures, and the New-York Free School Society—the time had therefore come to spread the good news that New York was no longer solely a center of commerce but one of culture and benevolence too. In 1807, accordingly, he published a pocket-sized volume entitled *The Picture of New-York; or The Traveller's Guide, Through the Commercial Metropolis of the United States, By a Gentleman Residing in this City*.

Basically the city's first guidebook, Mitchill's *Picture of New-York* assailed the dearth of knowledge about this "great and growing capital" (even among its own residents) and denounced writers like Jedediah Morse, whose often-reprinted *American Geography* (1784) had ridiculed New York for its artistic, literary, and scientific backwardness. To set the record straight, Mitchill diligently compiled evidence of the city's breathtaking growth over the previous twenty-odd years: the multiplication of banks and insurance companies, the upsurge in overseas and domestic commerce, the expansion of municipal services. What made him proudest, however, were the signs of New York's cultural maturity. Its numerous newspapers, booksellers, reading rooms, theaters, parks, medical and scientific organizations, literary societies, and the new apparatus of reform and benevolence—all of these now put the city far ahead of erstwhile rivals like Boston or Philadelphia. For the men and women of his class who envisioned New York as something more than an island of benighted shopkeepers, this was praise indeed.

25

From Crowd to Class

In 1788, New York's African-American community petitioned the City Council to stop medical students from stealing corpses out of the Negro Burial Ground. The petitioners understood "the Necessity of Physicians and Surgeons consulting dead subjects for the benefit of mankind," but they were dismayed that the students, under cover of night, would carry away the bodies of their relatives and friends "without respect to age or sex, mangle their flesh out of a wanton curiosity and then expose it to beasts and birds." Nothing was done, however—not, that is, until the body snatchers or "resurrectionists" began raiding Trinity's whites-only graveyard as well. Digging up blacks was one thing, whites quite another, and indignation ricocheted around town.

On Sunday, April 13, a boy peered in a window at New York Hospital and observed a cadaver being dissected. The medical student at work waved a severed arm at the boy and told him it belonged to his mother, who had in fact recently died. The boy ran off to tell his father, a mason at work on a nearby building. The man gathered some friends, went to the graveyard, and found his wife's coffin empty. Soon an enraged crowd charged into the hospital, wrecking dissection equipment and gathering up bits and pieces of human bodies for respectable reburial. They also captured and abused several medical students, but surrendered them to magistrates when promised that legal action would be taken.

The next day another crowd, perhaps as many as five thousand strong, demanded to reexamine the hospital. Finding no more stolen bodies, they searched the buildings of Columbia College and the residences of city doctors (including that of Sir John Temple, the British consul, mistakenly identified as "Surgeon" Temple). At sunset, their wrath still unappeased, the rioters regrouped and headed for the jail, where a number of doctors and medical students had taken refuge. Governor George Clinton, Chancellor

Robert Livingston, John Jay, Baron Friedrich von Steuben, and Mayor James Duane all pleaded for restraint, only to be answered with a hail of bricks and stones. Jay, struck in the head, was carried home unconscious. Duane summoned a troop of militia to disperse the crowd and was met with another shower of missiles. Baron von Steuben, also struck in the head and bleeding profusely, shouted, "Fire, Duane! Fire!" Duane, or perhaps Clinton, gave the order. The first volley killed three rioters outright and wounded many others. Before a second could be fired, the crowd had scattered.

Spontaneous, short-lived, and aimed at redressing a specific offense against communal sensibilities, the so-called Doctors Riot closely resembled pre-Revolutionary popular disorders in the city. That resemblance was strengthened by the willingness of public authorities to address the rioters' grievances. Within a year the state legislature passed an act banning "the Odious Practice of Digging up and Removing, for the Purpose of Dissection, Dead Bodies Interred in Cemeteries or Burial Places." (The law also allowed the bodies of executed criminals to be assigned to the doctors.)

But in certain crucial respects the Doctors Riot was unprecedented. No colonial mayor or governor had ever ordered soldiers to open fire on a crowd. Never before had gentlemen ever proved so ineffectual in controlling the actions of a crowd or (with the possible exception of Leisler's Rebellion a century earlier) actually come under attack themselves. In retrospect, indeed, that violent clash in front of the jailhouse was an early manifestation of what would become increasingly antagonistic relations between patrician and plebeian residents of the city. For over the next ten or twenty years, even as the rich grew more clannish and disdainful of laboring people, laboring people grew more conscious of themselves as a class with markedly different interests, values, and social practices.

WORKING NEIGHBORHOODS

In the 1790s the streets of the East Ward, hard by the East River waterfront, were home to watchmakers, printers, bookbinders, tailors, hatters, and other skilled craftsmen who catered to an affluent clientele. Typically, they lived and worked under one roof—as did silversmith Daniel van Voorhis, who resided above his workshop and retail store on Hanover Square, along with his wife, Catherine Richards, their children, and some of his journeymen and apprentices. But Van Voorhis and his kind were a vanishing breed. Artisans in the capitalizing and competitive trades, caught between rising rents and declining incomes, found themselves obliged to adopt new living arrangements. One downtown shoemaker bundled both his family and his workshop into the household's first floor, then rented out the upstairs to a Scotch journeyman carpenter and his family. The carpenter's wife, in turn, took in boarders to meet the rent, and two immigrant nailmakers moved into the attic along with three of the carpenter's sons.

Even with this additional income, the shoemaker found himself squeezed out of the wharf district and pushed uptown. With other priced-out artisans, he trekked to the northern wards, especially the Fifth, Sixth, Seventh, and Tenth, which together formed a broad band across Manhattan. Anchored on the west by Trinity's Church Farm along the Hudson, this plebeian belt ran through the mid-island area dominated by the slowly disappearing Fresh Water Pond and its swampy tributaries, and on into the now parceled-out Rutgers and De Lancey estates, before terminating in Corlear's Hook on the East River. By the turn of the century, migrants had pressed this perimeter of settlement as far north as modern Houston Street.

Sledding at the corner of Greenwich and Warren streets, 1809, by the Baroness Hyde de Neuville. In the one- and two-story frame buildings of this plebeian quarter it was still possible for artisans to maintain their traditional single family house-and-shop living arrangements. (© Museum of the City of New York)

One of the artisan communities within this zone lay just west of City Hall Park in the blocks bounded by Greenwich, Hudson, Warren, Murray, and Chambers streets. Chambers Street, for one, had been unpaved and largely uninhabited at the end of the Revolution. By 1800 the now cobbled thoroughfare was a neighborhood of independent proprietors, the kind of community no longer sustainable near the docks. Its seventy-six row houses, built on land leased from Trinity, were occupied by the representatives of twenty-five different trades: carpenters, joiners, coachmakers, carters, grocers, stone-cutters, and others. These houses employed the neoclassical motifs of Federal architecture, like the residences of wealthy downtown merchants, but were smaller (often only eighteen feet wide) and more cheaply made (some entirely of wood). Signboards on or above their front doors made it clear, too, that their interiors were organized to suit the needs of domestic production. The family lived on the second floor. The first floor (in front) was given over to workbenches, tools, and storage space, along with (in the rear) a kitchen, spinning wheels, bins, and tubs. In the back yard, protected from ambulatory hogs by high fences, were the vegetable garden, fruit trees, privy, woodpile, cistern, smokehouse, and open fires over which the housewife boiled the wash.

The Chambers Street community proved short-lived, however. Merchants and professionals edging their way northward, away from downtown disease and disorder, bid up land prices. After 1806 Trinity demanded that its leaseholders put up only substantial brick houses, driving out small builders. By 1812 most of the artisanal home-and-workshops were gone, along with their occupants. Chambers Street had been gentrified.

Some dislocated building tradesmen, grocers, and cartmen headed farther up-island to Greenwich. The opening of Newgate Prison in 1797 and repeated infusions of fever refugees had transformed the rural hamlet into a booming village in need of their services. "The demand for houses at Greenwich," noted a Boston paper in 1805, "is scarcely greater than the rapidity with which they are raised." A Greenwich Market opened in 1808, just below Christopher Street, and quickly filled with wagons and carts. The Greenwich Hotel (1809), established on the prison's doorstep, became the terminus for the stagecoach that rumbled back and forth from Federal Hall at least five times a day.

Other artisans headed across town to Bowery Village, the community that had grown up around Petrus Stuyvesant's country house and chapel. Throughout the eighteenth century it had remained sparsely settled—a few houses plus blacksmith, wagon shop, general store, and tavern—partly from fear of highwaymen lurking in the Bayard woods. But now the developmentally minded Petrus Stuyvesant III laid out a street system on his ancestral property, squared with the points of the compass, and he donated land and construction funds for an Episcopal parish church. By 1807 St. Mark's in the Bowery (completed in 1799 at what is now East 10th Street and Second Avenue) attracted as many as seventy worshipers in winter and two hundred in summer, reflecting the village's new popularity as a fever refuge for city folk (the Manhattan Company erected a branch office there for banking during epidemics).

Because Bowery Village lay just outside the city limits, farmers could sell there without paying a market tax. Wagon stands soon flourished along 6th and 7th streets, along with a weigh scale for Westchester hay merchants. Comfortable residences went up along the upper Bowery, still a country road edged with blackberry bushes, drawn perhaps by the continuing presence at Petersfield of Mrs. Stuyvesant, the former Margaret Beekman, who stayed on after Petrus died in 1805. Artisan house-and-shops arrived too; so did groceries, a brothel, and a post office (in truth an oyster house where the postrider left mail for the village). From 1804 the community even had its own (short-lived) newspaper, the *Bowery Republican*.

Farther down the Bowery Road, just above Chatham Square, the city's meat-processing industry expanded outward from the Bull's Head Tavern, abattoir, and stockyards, owned since 1785 by Henry Astor. In the early 1800s, as additional butchers herded into the area, slaughterhouses multiplied along Chrystie and Elizabeth streets. With them came a profusion of new taverns—the Gotham Inn, the Duck and Frying Pan, the Pig and Whistle, the Crown and Thistle—and in 1801 the New Circus in the Bowery, whose bill included bullbaiting and bearbaiting. Chatham Square itself featured a horse market, a livery stable (headquarters for the Boston stagecoaches), Hendrick Doyer's distillery (at the present Doyers Street), a watch house, and blocks of stores and workshops.

Chatham Square, in turn, bordered the former Rutgers estate, now the Seventh Ward. Colonel Henry Rutgers, grandson of Harmanus the Second, who remained in residence at the family mansion on the East River, cut up and leased out much of his land on a long-term basis. Strict building covenants required each leaseholder to erect a "workmanlike brick building." This drew merchants and professionals to the high ground along East Broadway, Rutgers, and Monroe streets. But Rutgers's terms were reasonable enough, and the area close enough to the Corlear's Hook shipyards, that his property attracted shipwrights, coopers, chandlers, joiners, sailmakers, and ropemakers as well.

From the shipyards, it was but a short ferry ride to two other outposts of the old artisanal world. In Brooklyn Village, at the foot of the Old Ferry Road (now Fulton

Street), lay a clustering of houses, taverns, stables, and shanties, through which the country road straggled on and out through Bedford Corners toward Jamaica. Just to Brooklyn Village's right—from an arriving horse-ferry passenger's perspective—rose the bluff generally known as Clover Hill, studded still with farms, orchards, gardens, and pastures.

To its left, a little way up the East River shore, lay the "City of Olympia," founded by Comfort and Joshua Sands back in the mid-eighties. Since 1795 it had been accessible directly, via the "New" or Catherine Street Ferry that docked at Main Street. This artery, which wandered toward an inland connection with the Old Ferry Road, was lined with wood-frame buildings that housed ex-Manhattanites and settlers from Connecticut (a big contingent of whom had come down after yellow fever devastated New London in the late nineties). Slightly further upriver, between Olympia and Wallabout Bay, shipbuilder-turned-developer John Jackson had laid out yet a third village. Having sold most of his holdings to the government, the savvy promoter now began advertising his remaining lots, on the Navy Yard's western border, as Vinegar Hill. His intention was to attract fugitives from the ill-fated Irish rebellion, the climactic battle of which had occurred at a place of the same name in 1798.

Between 1790 and 1810 the population of Brooklyn township nearly tripled, rising from sixteen hundred to just over forty-four hundred—a rate of growth only slightly below that of New York City proper—and the influx of Yankees, Irish, Manhattanites, and freed slaves from Kings and Queens counties engulfed the area's old Dutch inhabitants. The bulk of the town's residents lived within Brooklyn Village, a thriving artisanal community whose growth was marked by the purchase of its first Town Bell in 1796 (it hung in a cupola on top of Buckbee's Hay Scales on Fulton Street), by the

"Winter Scene in Brooklyn," by Francis Guy, c. 1817-20. Imitating Pieter Brueghel's paintings of peasant life in the Netherlands, Guy meticulously documented the life of what was still a close-knit village from a second-floor window of his house on Front Street. This view along Front, ranging from Fulton Street (the old Ferry Road) on the far right to Main Street on the far left, records a mix of small shops, stores, and private residences (the dark building in the center was a slaughterhouse and butcher shop). Each of the figures is a portrait of one of Guy's neighbors. Much of the area now lies under the approaches to the Brooklyn Bridge. (Eno Collection. Miriam and Ira D. Wallach Division of Art, Prints and Photographs. The New York Public Library. Astor, Lenox and Tilden Foundations)

advent of its first newspaper, the *Long Island Courier*, in 1799 (also the first in Kings County), and by the construction, in 1802, of its first "cage, or watch-house." Besides numerous shops of coachmakers, pumpmakers, tailors, and cordwainers, the village boasted gristmills that used the East River tides to grind wheat for export as well as for local consumption and manufactories that produced chairs, tobacco, and floorcloth. Throngs of local carpenters, riggers, caulkers, coopers, and other craftsmen were employed in the maritime trades spreading along the waterfront, and the village's many butchers maintained stalls in the old wooden market near the ferry slip, where they sold the meat wheelbarrowed over from nearby slaughterhouses (by black employees) or shipped it across the river to Manhattan's Fly Market.

The more remote farming hamlets that dotted Kings and Queens counties—Bushwick, Flatlands, New Utrecht, Gravesend, Newtown, Flushing, Jamaica—likewise experienced a modest rush of prosperity by supplying the New York market with food for consumption and export. The tiny village of Flat Bush (still often spelled as two words) got itself a new private academy, Erasmus Hall (two hundred students), and a lovely new Reformed church—both of which still stand at the corner of Church and Flatbush avenues.

FIVE POINTS

Back in Manhattan, the negative consequences of economic restructuring were coming to malign fruition in the neighborhood known as Five Points. Ever since the Revolution, artisan proprietors had been colonizing the area east and south of the Fresh Water Pond, raising modest house-and-shops near its breweries, potteries, tanneries, and tobacco manufactories. The neighborhood had always been squalid, situated amid the swampy runoff from the ever more polluted pond. By the early nineteenth century, many of the streets here—Mulberry, Orange, Roosevelt, Bancker (now Madison), James, Oliver, Catherine, and Rutgers—were little better than foul, muddy lanes blocked by refuse-choked pools of slime and silt that washed down from hills around the pond. Some houses were half buried by erosion; when it rained, their cellars and kitchens filled with water, and many back yards were perpetually covered with green, stinking muck.

Sanitationists hoped that filling in the pond would revitalize the area, which many considered a breeding ground for yellow fever. It did, though not in the manner intended. Absentee landlords began to buy up houses once occupied by artisans, subdividing them or replacing them with new wood-frame structures: the dapper Edward Livingston, New York's first Jeffersonian mayor, owned eight on Orange Street alone. Landlords then packed the buildings with tenants, transforming them into de facto boardinghouses for the wage-laborers now settling the area.

Some of these renters were artisans pushed out of gentrifying neighborhoods and no longer able to establish independent households. Others were the recent Irish immigrants who began settling near the docks in the 1790s, then spread inland after the turn of the century. Still others were African Americans whose ancestors had been in the area since receiving half-freedom plots from the Dutch West India Company. Most of their forebears had long since sold off their little grants to white proprietors; still legally barred (until 1809) from inheriting or bequeathing property, they had rented or squatted near the pond. Now, together with recently freed relatives and friends coming in from the countryside, they settled in the sodden basements of buildings whose upper stories were filled with whites. Certain lanes, however, notably Bancker Street between Pearl and Catherine, became known for their concentration of all-black tenant houses, some of which packed in five men to a room.

As the Fresh Water was filled in, streets and housing crept out across the boggy terrain, followed by grocers, tavern keepers, glue factories, slaughterhouses, and turpentine distilleries. As early as 1798 it was remarked that the area was "generally full of poor and dirty people." By 1810, though the area was but a scant few blocks from the nearly completed City Hall, it had become a slum known as the Five Points, named for the intersection of five streets: Mulberry, Anthony (now Worth), Cross (now Park), Orange (now Baxter), and Little Water (now gone). The Five Points housed the city's poorest residents, including the greatest percentage of those receiving public assistance in the form of outdoor relief. For years the neighborhood remained a notorious breeding ground for disease and a source of hefty profits for local landlords.

The emergence of the Five Points slum was only the most tangible sign of the rise of a class of permanent tenants in New York City. Around the city, master artisan householders were rejecting the paternalistic practice of providing year-round room and board to apprentices and journeymen. Instead, just as they hired and fired wage-workers according to seasonal demand, they now rented out household space (along with the domestic services provided by their wives) to boarders on a cash basis.

In an increasingly competitive economy such rental income could well provide the margin that smaller masters needed to preserve their own independence. For the more entrepreneurially inclined, profiting from real estate could become an end in itself. Some masters subdivided their houses into apartments, rented them out to lodgers, and then moved their own families to separate domestic quarters.

Some members of the new tenant class found liberty in mobility. They were free to move when and where they wished, just as they had an unfettered right to sell their skills to the highest bidder. But with housing a commodity rather than a customary right, purchasers could get only what they could pay for. For the majority—the 60 percent who worked in capitalizing trades and faced declining wages—this meant a steady erosion of living standards. Some journeymen formed their own "trade" houses, pooling the incomes of four or five skilled workers and crowding into a single residence. But most had to settle for one- or two-room apartments, wooden rear houses, or, in the case of ill-paid laborers and mariners, boardinghouses that squeezed four to six men in a room.

Mobility did increase, but less out of choice than coercion. In a tight, impersonal, and utterly unregulated housing market, where landlords pressed to maximize returns, tenants outbid by competitive renters were compelled to move. The resulting dislocations—voluntary and involuntary—were apparent every year on the first of May, the date on which, by Dutch tradition, all New York City leases expired simultaneously. Of no great consequence in more settled times, Moving Day now became an ever more frenetic affair. Especially in neighborhoods composed primarily of propertyless renters, thousands packed their belongings, hired a cartman (if they could find one), and moved to new quarters. As one commentator noted in 1799, the people "of this city are seized, on the first of May, by a sort of madness, that will not let them rest till they have changed their dwelling."

TURMOIL IN THE TRADES

For New York journeymen, the degradation of housing in the city was only one element

May Day, from H. P. Finn, *Comic-Annual of 1831* (Boston, 1831). New York's tumultuous "Moving Day" was now nationally famous. (Print Collection. Miriam and Ira D. Wallach Division of Art, Prints and Photographs. The New York Public Library. Astor, Lenox and Tilden Foundations)

of the crisis they faced after the turn of the century. As capitalist relations of production penetrated one trade after another, fewer and fewer journeymen could look forward to becoming independent masters. Instead, they had to contemplate a future as permanent "hirelings"—mere wage-workers, thrown into the same proletarian pot as ex-slaves, former indentured servants, half-trained apprentices, and casual laborers. They knew who to blame, too: entrepreneurial masters whose hot pursuit of personal profit had caused them to betray time-honored principles of craft solidarity and mutual responsibility.

In many trades, journeymen attempted to mitigate the loss of personal independence by forming associations for the relief of members in distress. Pooling weekly or monthly dues, they built up common treasuries from which the sick or infirm could draw, thus forging the kind of mutual aid institutions that seemed ever more necessary in a postpaternalistic society. Some of these associations also fought against the growing use of poorly trained labor in the trades. In 1785 "a considerable number of Principal Journeymen Carpenters" criticized the master carpenters for hiring workers "so very ignorant of their business, that some of them have been at a loss to know the right end of their tools." Similar concerns led journeyman printers to form the New York Typographical Society in 1794. The Journeyman Shipwright's Society required members to refuse to labor alongside any other than "fully skilled and trained journeymen."

The most aggressive journeymen went even further. As early as 1785 journeyman cordwainers banded together and refused to work until paid higher wages—arguably the first authentic "strike" or "turn-out" in the city's history. (The latter term alluded to soldiers "turning out" for combat, the former to sailors "striking" or lowering a ship's sails.) In 1802 white sailors and black seamen joined forces to demand that merchants and shipowners raise the basic wage from ten to fourteen dollars per month. For several days the two allied "combinations," one white and one black, paraded the docks "with drums beating and colors flying," but the strike collapsed when municipal authorities jailed its leaders.

In 1802 journeymen broadened their repertoire of tactics to include formation of worker-run businesses. When master cabinetmakers announced a 15 percent reduction in wages, eighty journeymen walked off the job and opened their own warehouse on John Street to sell furniture directly to the public. Sales proved disappointing, however, and after a six-month fight the strikers capitulated.

Masters answered the militant journeymen with combinations of their own— none more influential than the General Society of Mechanics and Tradesmen, which while open to all resident artisans had become an organ of the city's entrepreneurial masters. Its members (488 as of 1798) stoutly defended their right to lock out trouble-makers, to import out-of-town labor to break strikes, and to hire ill-trained workmen. Such tactics, they said, were necessary to preserve the very things for which the Revolution had been fought: equality of opportunity, unfettered markets, and the sanctity of private property.

In effect, a kind of ideological mitosis was under way. Artisanal republicanism, reasonably coherent during the 1770s and 1780s, had begun to divide along its main social axis—one version for masters, another for journeymen and apprentices. The effect of this development on political alignments in the city was wrenching. Most artisans had switched from the Federalists to the Democratic-Republicans during the 1790s, believing that society should be governed by those who engaged in "real" labor—yeoman farmers in the countryside and independent craftsmen in the cities—as opposed to speculators, bankers, and lawyers. But the divisions within the trades gave Federalists no end of opportunities to drive a wedge between the masters of the Democratic-Republican leadership and the journeymen who made up the party's rank and file. Federalists pounced on one Democratic-Republican candidate for advising master tanners not to sell leather to any journeyman shoemaker in the city who attempted to get his wages raised. They likewise denounced the opposition for urging master cordwainers to hire only journeymen who had obtained a regular discharge from their last employer— a "rascally proposal" which put the journeymen on "the same footing with a hired negro wench, that must have a recommendation before she can get a place."

Democratic-Republican masters parried such thrusts by stirring popular resentment against the poor as well as against the rich. Like riches, poverty implied a whole range of dangers to republican values and institutions—dependency, sloth, ignorance, immorality—and was thus a condition to be feared and despised by free people. The economic dislocations of the 1790s and 1800s, robbing even the most industrious workingman of the certainty that his labors would keep him and his family out of the almshouse, made it all the more urgent to hold the line. By 1800 no one in New York condemned poverty more insistently than those who seemed at greatest risk of winding up poor themselves.

In 1803 Mayor Edward Livingston proposed the creation of municipally owned and operated workshops where immigrants, ex-convicts, widows, and the indigent could learn such crafts as shoemaking or hatmaking. Reducing unemployment, Livingston reasoned, would reduce crime and vagrancy. Outraged mechanics protested that competition from Livingston's workshops would drive hard-pressed masters as well as journeymen out of business, rewarding "idle and dissolute" elements of society at the expense of the most industrious. After a huge uproar, the state legislature quietly tabled Livingston's proposal.

The impact of the turmoil in the trades was magnified by the movement of masters and journeymen alike into a wider world of political and social discourse. An upswing in literacy rates during the 1780s and 1790s opened new, assertively artisanal markets for the printed word, and a string of local papers—the *New York Journal* (1787–1800), the *Argus* (1795–1800), and others—geared their contents toward a politically conscious mechanic readership. Record numbers of artisans were also buying books and magazines, and they accounted for half the initial subscriptions to the *New-York Magazine* (1790–97), among whose contributors were such eminent radicals as Joseph Priestly, William Godwin, Mary Wollstonecraft, and Thomas Erskine.

Equally important was the parade of radical *émigrés* that passed through the city in the 1790s, along with numerous representatives of popular societies—United Irishmen, United Englishmen, Friends of the People, Levellers—that blossomed all over the British Isles in the early 1790s, only to be crushed in spasms of official repression and mob violence. Republican France was their inspiration, Thomas Paine their idol, the Rights of Man their creed, and when they reached New York they were still full of fight. Grant Thorburn remembered how he and a party of other young men, members of the Scottish Friends of the People, were rounded up and put on a boat to New York in 1794. "We had some hot characters among us," Thorburn wrote, "which all the waters of the Atlantic could not cool."

Like John Daly Burk, editor of the *Time Piece*, and James Cheetham, editor of the *American Citizen*, these firebrands gave a powerful impetus to the militancy of New York artisans by identifying their concerns with an international struggle for political and social justice. Foreign and home-grown radicals likewise rubbed elbows, compared notes, and cemented friendships at Hocquet Caritat's famous bookstore on Broadway. The energy and excitement they generated there inspired Caritat to found a circulating library from which the principles of the Enlightenment and the ideals of the French Revolution could be disseminated at modest charges to working people throughout the country.

INFIDELS AND EVANGELICALS

By the mid-nineties Jacobin assaults on the French church and Thomas Paine's attack on the authority of Holy Scripture in *The Age of Reason* (1794) were finding a receptive audience among New York's book- and newspaper-reading mechanics. Some gravitated toward Elihu Palmer, a blind Baptist preacher devoted to spreading deism among the working classes. Palmer's association with New York began in 1788 when he was called to the pulpit of the Presbyterian church of Newtown, Long Island. En route from his native Connecticut, he preached a Thanksgiving Day sermon that proved him "ill adapted for a Presbyterian pulpit," in the words of his friend John Fellows (Paine's American publisher and Hocquet Caritat's sometime business partner). "Instead of expatiating upon the horrid and awful condition of mankind in consequence of the lapse of Adam and his wife, he exhorted his hearers to spend the day joyfully in innocent festivity, and to render themselves as happy as possible." After six months at Newtown, Palmer moved on to Philadelphia, joined the Baptists, and set up a Universal Society. He lost his sight during the 1793 yellow fever epidemic and was run out of town the following year by "an immense mob" for attacking the divinity of Jesus Christ.

Returning to New York in 1794, Palmer treated the new Democratic Society to a raise-the-roof oration against clerical interference with the revolution in France. The society's warm response convinced him to remain in the city, and later that same year, in a pamphlet defending Paine's just-published *Age of Reason*, Palmer denounced Christianity itself as a system of "ignorance and credulity" designed to hold the lower classes in thrall and prop up monarchy. His alternative, the subject of frequent essays and addresses over the next decade, was a "natural morality" or "religion of nature" that acknowledged a divine Creator without violating the dictates of reason or subjecting its adherents to ecclesiastical tyranny.

A tireless organizer as well as publicist, Palmer founded a Deistical Society in the mid-nineties that actively recruited members from the city's laboring population. He established two newspapers, the *Temple of Reason* (1800–1803) and the *Prospect, or View of the Moral World* (1803–5), that became the foremost vehicles of deistic thought in the country. In 1804 Palmer launched a "Theistic Church" and announced plans to build a Temple of Nature in Manhattan. This buzz of activity attracted other prominent deists to the city, including John Foster, the radical universalist and friend of Paine, and Dennis Driscol, a defrocked Irish priest who served as editor of the *Temple of Reason*.

Yet Palmer failed to ignite the mass movement he hoped for. Despite the crowds that initially turned out for his public lectures, membership in the New York Deistical Society dwindled to a mere handful of working people too poor even to pay their modest dues on a regular basis. Respectable mechanics and even hardened skeptics were shocked at his virulent disdain for Christianity. (He once scolded Christians that their "pretended Saviour is nothing more than an illegitimate Jew, and their hopes of salvation through him rest on no better foundation than that of fornication or adultery.") Not surprisingly, Palmer's allure soon paled alongside that of more temperate personalities like the Unitarian John Butler, who came to town in 1794, rented a hall on Cortlandt Street, and lectured before "truly alarming" crowds while the mainstream clergy railed against him from their pulpits. So, too, when Dr. Joseph Priestly, renowned both as a chemist and as a Unitarian advocate, visited New York that same year, he got a warm reception from the Tammany, Democratic, and other popular societies.

Neither Unitarians nor deists, however, were able to keep up with the itinerant evangelists who began trolling for souls among New York's laborers, sailors, apprentices, and journeymen during the later 1790s and early 1800s. Prominent among these were Dominic van Velsor, known as the stove-fence preacher; Amos Broad, an upholsterer often at odds with the law; Johny Edwards, a Welsh scale-beam maker who harangued sinners from the back of his wagon and once stood in Wall Street, shouting through a three-foot tin trumpet for the moneylenders to repent; John Leland, the Baptist abolitionist, who came to town with a twelve-hundred-pound "Mammoth Cheese" inscribed "Rebellion to Tyrants is Obedience to God"; and the Methodist circuit-rider Lorenzo Dow, who looked and talked like an Old Testament prophet.

Their open identification with the poor, their scorn for fancy educations and fine clothes and high-toned manners, their biblical literalism, millennialism, and mysticism—all of these qualities located the evangelicals in a tradition of charismatic "mechanick preachers" going back to the days of Cromwell. Dow in particular employed a "colloquial vulgarity" to which Palmer, much less Priestly, never stooped even though it purportedly attracted "large multitudes" of the city's laboring poor whenever he preached. Dow "understood common life," admitted a contemporary, "and especially vulgar life—its tastes, prejudices and weaknesses; and he possessed a cunning knack of adapting his discourses to such audiences." At the same time, their frequent appeals to reason, science, natural justice, and the Rights of Man—Dow often began his sermons with quotations from Paine—linked the evangelicals to the radical republicanism let loose by the revolutions in America and France. Unlike George Whitefield a half century earlier, Dow and his fellow revivalists made it a point to steer newborn Christians away from the suffocating metaphysics and imposed authority of the established denominations. Theirs was to be a democratized Christianity—a religion of, for, and by the people in which the individual conscience blazed its own, independent trail toward salvation, free at last of sectarian organization, inherited theological systems, and clerical oppression.

Respectable people, inevitably, stressed the connection between this disdain for conventional forms of piety and the tenets of mechanic republicanism. In 1785 the Synod of the Dutch Reformed Church in New York and New Jersey pointed to the burgeoning interest of working people in universalism, rationalism, freethinking, deism, and other newfangled theologies closely identified with the international republican movement—a "mighty flood of errors," in their words, that threatened the very foundations of the faith.

Nothing, however, concentrated attention on republican religion in the city quite so effectively as Tom Paine, who had returned to the United States from France in 1802. His first destination was Washington, D.C., where the resumption of his old friendship with President Jefferson caused such an uproar in the Federalist press that he decided to settle on the farm in New Rochelle that the State of New York had given him in recognition of his services to the nation. When he reached Manhattan in March 1803, his supporters, including many radical immigrants from England, Scotland, and Ireland, hailed him with a dinner at the City Hotel. Over the next year or two Paine often came down from New Rochelle to visit with freethinkers and republicans, stroll the streets, and attend parties (one evening he dined and jousted good-humoredly with John Pintard). In 1804 Elihu Palmer, who had proclaimed Paine "probably the most useful man that ever existed on the face of the earth," drafted him to write articles on religion for the *Prospect*. Paine obliged with a series of forceful essays that reiterated his belief in God but emphasized that a narrow-minded, dogmatic, bigoted Christianity was inconsistent with a pluralistic and democratic republic.

Paine's enemies retaliated with scurrilous personal attacks, he ran out of money, and his erstwhile admirers began to desert him, embarrassed now by his aspersions on Christianity, his increasingly unkempt appearance, and his unpaid bills. Mrs. Elihu Palmer, the young portraitist John Wesley Jarvis, Thomas Addis Emmet, and a few other steadfast friends struggled to keep Paine clean and well fed, and though he rallied briefly after taking up permanent residence in the city, his health deteriorated rapidly. For a while he lived with a baker's family on Broome Street, then found quarters above a squalid tavern on Partition (now Fulton) Street, then moved again to lodgings in Greenwich Village on Herring Street (at what is now 293 Bleecker), where he was cared for by his old friend Madame Marguerite Bonneville. In 1809 she moved the ailing revolutionary into the back room of a small frame dwelling on the site of what is now 59 Grove Street.

There, in the last month of life, Paine was harried by devout visitors, determined to save his soul with an eleventh-hour conversion. Once two Presbyterian ministers pushed their way in, only to be rebuffed. "Let me have none of your popish stuff," the invalid declared. "Get away with you, good morning, good morning." He would be badgered one last time, in his final waking moments on June 8, 1809, when the attending doctor asked: "Do you wish to believe that Jesus Christ is the son of God?" "I have no wish to believe on that subject," he replied, and died peacefully in his unfaith. Paine's theological and political adversaries did not give up, however, and spread rumors that he had undergone a deathbed conversion. When New York's street commissioners, shortly after Paine's death, named an adjacent lane Reason Street in his honor, Trinity Church managed to get it renamed Barrow Street, honoring a minor watercolorist who had done a drawing of their new building.

OUT FROM THE BACK OF THE CHURCH

Although the rapid pace of European immigration after 1800 made New York whiter than at any time since the mid-seventeenth century, the continued growth of its black population made African Americans an important element of the city's new wage-earning class—and made the city in turn the largest center of African-American life and culture in the United States. Black impatience with slavery and racism became an increasingly visible part of the city's public life, as in 1807, when a "numerous and respectable meeting of the Africans" was held at the African Free School on Cliff Street to celebrate the new federal ban on slave imports. Similarly, emancipated men and women quickly abandoned the surnames of their former Dutch or English masters, choosing replacements that affirmed their release from bondage (Freeman) or advertised their artisanal skills (Cooper, Mason, Carpenter). For their children, they rejected the derisive and comical given names bestowed by slaveowners (Pompey, Caesar, Cato), often preferring those of biblical origin—not surprisingly, for black churches were anchors of the emerging African-American community.

Most New York denominations had long routinely segregated their black worshipers, confining them (as visiting Englishman William Strickland reported) to so-called Negro Pews—"usually the back rows in the Galleries"—whose occupants "are not permitted or never presume to mix among the whites." Methodists were different. From 1787 the Methodist Episcopal Church condemned slavery and welcomed blacks as full participants.

The number of black congregants at the Wesley Chapel on John Street increased rapidly in the mid-1790s, and in 1800 the denomination provided for the ordination of deacons among its "African brethren." This initial enthusiasm for integration soon peaked, however. Whites grew uneasy with integrated worship, fearful that blacks might yet exercise leadership authority, and worried that antislavery sentiments were dividing northern Methodists from their southern coreligionists. Blacks, pushed to the fringe where other white churches consigned them, asserted their autonomy and pushed to form an independent church.

The mainstay of this movement was sexton Peter Williams. Born of slave parents in a cowshed adjacent to their masters' Beekman Street town house, Williams had been purchased as a young man by tobacco merchant James Aymar and become an expert cigar maker. He also became a Methodist. In 1778 the Wesley Chapel purchased Williams, for forty pounds, and made him its sexton. He left the city during the British occupation, returned in 1780, bought his freedom out of his earnings, and became a successful tobacconist while retaining his position with the church.

In 1796 Williams joined with James Varick and other Methodists of color to establish the Zion Chapel in a cabinetmaker's shop on Cross Street between Orange (Baxter) and Mulberry. The Zionites didn't intend to withdraw from the John Street congrega-

Methodist Church on John Street, c. 1817. The figure in the doorway may be Peter Williams, the sexton. (I. N. Phelps Stokes Collection. Miriam and Ira D. Wallach Division of Art, Prints and Photographs. The New York Public Library. Astor, Lenox and Tilden Foundations)

Peter Williams, sexton of the John Street Methodist Church. (Schomberg Center for Research in Black Culture. The New York Public Library. Astor, Lenox and Tilden Foundations)

tion, merely to worship together in an atmosphere free of racial animosity, but by 1799 they had concluded that they would be better off on their own. Encouraged by the example of Richard Allen, who had just founded the African Methodist Episcopal Church in Philadelphia, they obtained permission from Bishop Francis Asbury to form a new congregation.

In 1801 the dissidents incorporated as the African Methodist Episcopal Zion Church and raised a house of worship on the corner of Leonard and Church streets. In remembrance of the little Cross Street chapel, it would be known as "Mother Zion." Williams didn't join Zion; though he supported and shepherded the separatist project, he stayed at John Street out of gratitude. By decade's end, Zion had attracted many blacks to settle nearby, and it had become the nucleus of a mini-community within the larger Five Points neighborhood.

Brooklyn blacks traveled a similar road. In 1794 a small integrated congregation built the Sands Street Church on the same location where in 1766 Captain Thomas Webb had first conducted outdoor services. Blacks, who constituted a third to half of the communicants, were relegated to an "end gallery." As friction with whites increased, they broke away to form the Bridge Street African Methodist Episcopal Wesleyan Church (1818), the oldest black church in Brooklyn. In 1809, meanwhile, nineteen African-American men and women, unwilling to accept racially segregated seating, had withdrawn from Manhattan's First Baptist Church on Gold Street and established the Abyssinian Baptist Church in a building on Anthony, between Church and Chapel streets.

At Trinity too African Americans moved toward greater autonomy. Black Episcopalians had been worshiping apart from whites since the revolution, and they had been buried apart since 1696. Now Trinity acceded to their request for a separate chapel, the germ of what would later emerge as St. Philip's Church. In 1794, moreover, a group of blacks, possibly these same Episcopalians, noted that the Negro Burial Ground was slated for development and petitioned the Common Council for a new cemetery. The city granted the request, set aside four lots on Chrystie Street, and contributed funds (as did Trinity) toward establishing a graveyard there.

Blacks organized themselves in secular society as well, in response to gradual emancipation and the rise of systematic prejudice. Most whites simply couldn't imagine blacks as full members of a republican society, and there were plenty of veterans in town who remembered, as one man told a local paper, that area slaves "fought against us by whole regiments" during the Revolution and therefore didn't deserve freedom. Free blacks responded by forming associations for (in the words of a contemporary report) their "mutual support, benefit, and improvement." In 1808, for example, Peter Williams joined with other blacks to form the New York African Society for Mutual Relief. In doing so they followed a now common practice among the city's artisans; indeed, the society's first president was a house carpenter, and six of its founders were bootmakers. In 1810, with the aid of Mayor De Witt Clinton, the society received a charter from the state legislature. That same year the legislature chartered an African Marine Fund and the Brooklyn African Woolman Benevolent Society, named for the eighteenth-century Quaker abolitionist John Woolman.

No black antislavery organization per se emerged, though the community occasionally engaged in direct action. When Madame Jeanne Mathusine Droibillan Volunbrun, an *émigré* slaveholder, tried to ship twenty slaves south in 1801 in violation of state law, hundreds of city blacks, led by "French Negroes," threatened to "burn the said Volun-brun's house, murder all the white people in it and take away a number of Black Slaves." The crowd was dispersed by fifty watchmen, two dozen blacks went to jail, and Madame Volunbrun's slaves went south as planned.

"IRISHTOWN"

In much the same way that racism prompted the black community to circle its wagons, nativism prompted Irish immigrants to coalesce around the Roman Catholic Church. Probably fewer than a thousand Catholics lived in New York at the end of the Revolution. Ferdinand Steenmayer, a Jesuit, had slipped into the city during the war to celebrate the Mass secretly in a house on Wall Street. With the elimination of restrictions on Catholic worship, Steenmayer gathered his flock in a loft over a Barclay Street carpenter's shop. The postwar surge of immigration, virtually doubling the Catholic population overnight, prompted Dominick Lynch, Thomas Stoughton, and other lay leaders, led by Hector St. Jean de Crèvecoeur, the French consul in New York, to arrange for the construction of St. Peter's Church, the city's first Roman Catholic house of worship. Lots were purchased on Barclay Street, and the cornerstone was laid in October 1785. Although the founders of St. Peter's had envisioned a multiethnic congregation, the massive influx of Irish immigrants after the 1798 rebellion, boosting the number of Catholics in the city to some 10,000 by 1806, soon gave the new church a distinctly Hibernian orientation.

That was a matter of no small importance, because ethnic hostilities had mounted in tandem with the growing crisis in the trades. The Catholic Irish, abjectly poor, desperate for work, and alarmingly numerous, made a perfect scapegoat for the economic and social pressures rending mechanic republicanism—better even than the city's relatively smaller and more marginal black population. Virulent anti-Irish sentiment spread rapidly among the city's white Protestant laboring population during the 1790s and was further encouraged by the Federalist Alien and Sedition Acts. During the final years of the century, journeymen and apprentices revived the pre-Revolutionary Pope's Day festivities and repeatedly marched about town bearing straw-stuffed effigies designed to mock St. Patrick. These "Paddy processions" met with militant resistance, often terminating in wild brawls and arrests. In 1799, only a year after the French-backed rebellion in Ireland had been crushed, marchers invaded the Irish neighborhood along lower Harman Street (East Broadway), touching off a melee that resulted in one fatality and many serious injuries. Three years later, after another explosion, the Common Council passed an ordinance outlawing the flaunting of Paddies or other insulting effigies.

In the new century, a set of gifted revolutionary leaders arrived from Ireland, among them lawyers Thomas Addis Emmet and William Sampson, physician William MacNeven, and printer John Chambers. Though all were Anglicans except for MacNeven, they helped make the Irish Catholic community a political force in New York. Emmet, perhaps the United Irishmen's most gifted orator, had been arrested for his part in the abortive uprising of 1798. The British proposed deporting him to America, but Ambassador Rufus King persuaded the Adams administration to exclude Emmet and the other Irish "Jacobins." As a result, Emmet spent nearly four years in prison (during which time his brother Robert was hanged and beheaded for conspiring against the British). Finally, with Jefferson in power, Emmet and the other United Irish leaders, like Paine, made their way to New York City.

Taken up by George and De Witt Clinton, themselves of Irish extraction, Emmet gained admission to the bar, over the protests of Federalist attorneys, and soon emerged as one of the city's most popular and successful lawyers as well as a potent force in Democratic-Republican party. Rufus King had bragged of winning the "cordial and distinguished Hatred" of United Irishmen like Emmet. He was right, and in election after election, Emmet's blistering denunciations of King as a British collaborator helped Clintonians win the burgeoning Irish vote.

One thing the Irish vote could not do, however, was elect Catholics to public office. A naturalization clause in the 1777 state constitution had required all new citizens of the state to "abjure and renounce all allegiance and subjection to all and every foreign King, prince, potentate, and state, in all matters ecclesiastical as well as civil." Although this requirement was superseded by the U.S. Constitution ten years later, it had mean-while been incorporated into a test oath required of all state officeholders—meaning that Catholics could become citizens but were effectively barred from serving in the leg-islature. They protested in vain until 1806, when Francis Cooper became the first of his faith to be elected to the Assembly. The congregation of St. Peter's rounded up thirteen hundred signatures for a petition protesting the oath, De Witt Clinton won passage of a bill to abolish it, and Cooper took his seat.

Political victories, in turn, exacerbated tensions on the street. On Christmas Eve of 1806, less than a year after Cooper's victory, fifty members of the Highbinders (or Hide-Binders)—a nativist gang of apprentices and propertyless journeyman butchers—gathered outside St. Peter's to taunt worshipers leaving midnight Mass. The watch pre-vented a serious disorder, but on Christmas Day, Irishmen fearing a Highbinder attack armed themselves with cudgels, stones, and brickbats. When the watch attempted to disperse a crowd on Augustus Street (now the site of the Municipal Building), a bloody skirmish broke out, and one watchman was killed. The Highbinders and a nativist crowd now invaded "Irishtown," wreaking havoc until the magistrates managed to restore order.

Tensions on the street encouraged the Irish to greater political exertions. In 1807, when the anti-immigrant Rufus King stood for election to the Assembly, Emmet denounced him as a "royalist" and a "political dupe" of the British. King haughtily announced he would "enter into no explanations, leaving the Public to decide between me and these foreigners." The voters decided emphatically against him and torpedoed his subsequent bid in 1808 for the governorship as well.

"HONEST FOLKS IN THE PIT"

One of those who took part in the 1806 Christmas riot against Irish Catholics was William Otter, a young plasterer's apprentice from England, but he was there for plea-sure, not principle. Otter was a rowdy, one of a growing number of young men who scorned journeymen's associations, radical bookshops, and Methodist chapels. They preferred instead to go out on "sprees"—nighttime forays into the city's brothels, rum holes, and oyster shops that often ended in drunken brawls. As Otter recalled in the careful notes he kept of these adventures, he and his mates once went to Mr. Green's "for the express purpose of raising a row and were gratified to our heart's content." On another, they descended on Mr. Drake's, where they "broke every glass in the whole house, and cleared it of men, women, and children," then "scampered off to a grog-shop."

Among their favorite targets were the city's now-numerous dancehalls. "The dancing fever began to rage in Harman street," Otter remembered, and he and his gang
began dropping in at places like Mrs. Cunningham's or the "Negro dancing cellars"
on Bancker Street. Horace Lane, a white sailor, also recollected his 1804 visit to one
such establishment: a "small room, well filled with human beings of both sexes," with
"a big darkie in one corner sweating, and sawing away on a violin." Lane continued, "To
increase vigour, and elate the spirit of fun, there stood by his side a tall swarthy female
who was rattling and flourishing a tambourine with uncommon skill and dexerity"
while in midfloor dancers were "jumping about, twisting and screwing their joints and
ankles as if to scour the floor with their feet."

Interracial camaraderie had shocked Daniel Horsmanden back in 1741, and despite
all that had transpired in the intervening sixty years poor whites and poor blacks continued to mingle in gin mills, dance halls, and brothels that catered to both races. Such
fraternizing took place, on occasion, in more public spaces, especially on Sundays and
holidays like Pinkster. Although the old Dutch celebration of Whitsuntide had disappeared from anglicized New York City during the eighteenth century, it survived
among the Dutch villages of Long Island and the Hudson Valley, where it was appropriated as a holiday by slaves, who then brought it back to the city in the 1790s and
1800s. As one resident remembered: "All made it an idle day; boys and negroes might be
seen all day standing in the market laughing and joking and cracking eggs. In the afternoon the grown up apprentices and servant girls used to dance on the green in Bayard's
farm [west of Broadway]."

"Negro dancing" was a familiar feature of Pinkster time. Slaves or country free
blacks trooped in to the marketplace at Brooklyn Village from Long Island or New Jersey (the former with their hair tied up in a queue with dried eelskin, the latter favoring
plaited forelocks fastened with tea leaves). Sometimes as many as two hundred would
perform exhibition dances, toot on fish horns, play games, and drink. Others crossed
over to Catherine Market or the fish market in front of Burnel Brown's Ship Chandlery.
There they sold roots, berries, herbs, and birds to raise money for the holiday. Some
were hired by resident butchers to engage in a jig or "break-down." This pastime, performed at home on a barn floor, became a competitive display of skill, performed on a
springy board, with percussive accompaniment made by beating hands on sides of legs,
followed by the taking up of a collection from bystanders.

When white rowdies attended interracial gatherings, however, they were likely as
not to indulge in violence: victimizing blacks (like attacking Irish) seemed part of the
natural order of things. "A parcel of us lads," Otter reminisced, went to John M'Dermot's oyster shop in George's Street, played "patent billiards" for drink and oysters, got
loud and obstreperous, and stomped M'Dermot when he tried to stop them; "some of
the spare hands fell upon the negroes who were employed by him to shuck oysters, and
drove them into the cooking room, and beat them, poor d——ls, into a jelly."

Traditional "blood sports" like cockfighting and bearbaiting remained another
popular pastime, and as promoters vied to stage more and more bizarre contests they
drew larger and more turbulent crowds. One impresario threw up a two-thousand-seat
amphitheater for such spectacles; box seats sold for seventy-five cents, while admission
to the pit could be had for as little as a quarter. By the mid-nineties several circus
troupes were also competing for public attention. The most successful was led by John
Bill Ricketts, whose inventive deployment of clowns, tightrope walkers, tumblers, acro-

batic riders, mounted Indians, and fireworks lured sellout crowds to his New Amphitheater on Greenwich Street.

Rowdies turned up as well among theatergoers, the bulk of whom still consisted of working people because only the poorest apprentices and journeymen were unable to scrape together the price of admission. In 1789 ticket prices at Lewis Hallam's John Street Theater ranged from fifty cents for the gallery to seventy-five cents for the pit and a dollar for the boxes. The fancy new Park Theater on Chatham Street, for all its appeal to the Broadway-area gentility, was even cheaper, at twenty-five cents for the gallery and fifty cents for the pit. While some impresarios dreamed of performing only for cultivated audiences, this simply wasn't possible. John Howard Payne, who made his debut on the New York stage in 1809, ruefully observed that the "judicious few" were "always to be found in a Theater, like flowers in a desert, but they are nowhere sufficiently numerous to fill one."

Like the city itself, New York's playhouses were in fact increasingly divided into distinct social zones, their boundaries defined as much by deportment as dress. At John Street, occupants of the pit and gallery—"Blacksmith's apprentices and Canvastown girls," in the words of Grant Thorburn—smoked and drank incessantly, talked loudly, traded punches, besieged the orchestra with calls for their favorite tunes, harangued the players, clambered onto the stage, and consorted with the numerous prostitutes who worked the halls. Box seats offered no immunity from the commotion: a series of incidents in 1795 prompted Hallam to place an announcement in local papers reassuring boxholders that bolts would be placed inside the door of each box "to prevent any interruption" and that "no persons of notorious ill fame will be suffered to occupy any seat in a box where places are already taken."

It was the same at the Park. Not long after opening night, the management offered a fifty-dollar reward for information leading to the arrest and conviction of "certain ill-disposed persons [who] have made a practice of throwing at the performers in the Orchestra and on the Stage." It did no good. Several years later, in his *Letters of Jonathan Oldstyle, Gent.* (1802), the youthful Washington Irving described how the "honest folks in the pit" milled about near the Park's stage, noisily commenting on the play before them, while rowdy "gallery gods," including platoons of prostitutes, added to the general din by "stamping, hissing, roaring, whistling," "groaning in cadence," and flinging "apples, nuts & ginger-bread" at those below. Even some boxholders carried on as if they were in "a coffee house, or fashionable lounge, where [they can] indulge in loud conversation, without any regard for the pain it inflicts on their more attentive neighbors."

Their more attentive neighbors knew better than to object, too. The theater rules and idioms accorded audiences extensive powers of self-regulation as well as a voice in the content, length, and pacing of performances. Irving's gallery gods and honest folks in the pit considered themselves, and were considered by others, an integral part of the production, with a right, even a duty, to make their views known.

Managers, accordingly, arranged programs and assembled troupes calculated to appeal to plebeian sensibilities. For the 1789 season at the John Street Theater, Hallam advertised thirty-one comedies, twenty-six farces, nine comic operas, six tragedies, and two pantomimes. Thirty-five different authors were represented, the most frequently produced of whom included David Garrick (*Clandestine Marriage*), Richard Sheridan (*School for Scandal*), and William Shakespeare (*The Tempest, The Merry Wives of Wind-*

sor, Richard III)—a repertoire that seems remarkable only because (thanks partly to critics like Irving) the behavior of audiences has become confused with the extent of their sophistication. Shakespeare was a perennial favorite at both the John Street and Park theaters (a full-length statue of the bard stood in the Park's lobby). By day, journeymen recited passages from Shakespeare to their shop mates; by night, they cheered, booed, argued, and whistled in possessive familiarity with the drama unfolding on both sides of the footlights.

Increasingly popular were plays that linked patriotism and republicanism. In 1787 John Street patrons hailed *The Contrast*, a sentimental comedy set in contemporary New York, which demonstrated the superiority of republican honesty and simplicity over European sophistication (at one emotion-charged point in the production, the entire house rose to sing "Yankee Doodle"). When the popular actor John Hodgkinson appeared in the red coat of a British officer, hecklers wouldn't allow him to continue until he had explained, at length, that he was merely playing the part of an unworthy character.

Between 1798 and 1805 the young playwright (and Friendly Club habitué) William Dunlap, manager and part owner of the Park Theater, staged elaborate reenactments of the battles of Bunker Hill and Yorktown Heights. And his own efforts (like *The Glory of Columbia—Her Yeomanry!*) practically invented the "stage-Yankee," a two-fisted patriot who became as recognizable to New York mechanic audiences as any Shakespearean character. Like him, they took pride in being plain people who produced objects of genuine usefulness with their own hands. Like him, they sensed that they had been ennobled by the Revolution—a despised and powerless rabble transformed into free citizen-craftsmen. Their best qualities, like his, now seemed the very essence of republicanism: bluntness, self-reliance, unaffected decency, instinctive egalitarianism. They pursued an honest living, not wealth. They scorned privilege, ridiculed ostentation, despised avarice, and stood by their fellows.

As in matters of work, residence, religion, and politics, leisure-time pursuits became a bone of contention between the city's working classes and its elites. In some respects this was nothing new; since the days of Peter Minuit, civic and religious authorities had been trying to impose decorum on the heterogeneous, turbulent inhabitants of Manhattan and to curb the popular predilection for swearing, blasphemy, Sabbath-breaking, alcohol, and blood sports. What gave these concerns a new edge was the desire of entrepreneurial masters to create a more disciplined workforce.

Masters especially were dismayed by the continuing interpenetration of leisure and work. City artisans still observed the practice of "jeffing"—periodic trips to nearby taverns and "groceries" for beer or gin—and they continued to take the frequent breaks for doughnuts, candy, and cakes that were a time-honored prerogative of journeymen and apprentices. They often observed "Saint Monday," as well, taking the day off for horse races, boxing and shooting matches, drinking bouts, billiards, gambling, semiorganized brawling, and other long-established popular pastimes.

Many masters began challenging such traditions in their shops, promulgating strict work codes, and constructing in the process a new bourgeois standard of order and personal decorum. The General Society of Mechanics and Tradesmen—that bastion of master craftsmen—bore down especially hard on the customary drinking rights of journeymen and apprentices, blaming them for drunkenness, gambling, swearing, and other antisocial evils. Duncan Phyfe, a pillar of the General Society known for his Scotch

Calvinist rigor, was said to require that even the members of his own family be in bed by nine o'clock. At least a few mechanics, too, contended that the traditional values and attitudes of working people led only to poverty and misery. As one wrote with heavy sarcasm: "Pursue the gay and jocular companion through his weekly round of plea-sures—On Monday evening at the play, Tuesday at Piken's public dance, Wednesday at Rickett's Circus, Thursday to see Gibonne and Coco, Friday Seely's long room, and Saturday's theater closes the week of mirth—*Sunday*, that long, that tedious heavy day hangs heavy on their heads."

Some masters and merchants appealed to the authorities for help, at least in keeping the Sabbath holy (as they understood the term). After independence, church atten-dance failed to keep pace with population growth, and reports of Sabbath violations became standard fare for New York newspapers. As an indignant "Friend to Order" told the *Weekly Museum* in 1792, he had seen "near two hundred Negroes, Boys and *Gentle-men* (I mean those who have the appearance of Gentlemen)" skating on a recent Sunday. State as well as municipal authorities responded by renewing the old colonial prohibi-tions against profaning the Lord's Day with work or sport; at one point the Common Council even appointed a special peace officer to go after offenders. It made little or no difference, for as one "Journeyman Mechanic" with an ear for rhyme declared, the working classes had the right to do as they pleased on Sundays:

> Of rich and poor the difference what?—
> In working or in working not
> Why then on Sunday we're as great
> As those who own some vast estate.

"THE LIFE OF A CITIZEN IN THE HANDS OF A WOMAN"

Although white working-class women in New York led widely divergent lives—hot-corn girls and the wives of Episcopalian master craftsmen had very little in common—the changes sweeping the city during the 1790s and early 1800s left them collectively worse off than ever. Lowered property requirements for the suffrage, for example, boosted the political visibility of working-class men, but they also magnified the power-lessness and dependency of their still-voteless wives. The erosion of household produc-tion and the growth of wage-work likewise tended to privilege the labor that brought home the bacon over the unpaid labor that cooked it—along with raising the children, mending clothes, cleaning, and nursing the sick.

As jobs for men in the trades became less secure and wages declined, many work-ing-class women found themselves obliged to shoulder additional responsibilities to supplement the incomes of their husbands: taking in piecework as milliners or seam-stresses (black women took in laundry), hiring out as domestic servants in middle- and upper-class households, or renting rooms to boarders. A lucky few may have been able to earn an independent living—by 1800, eighty-eight of the 150 boardinghouses listed in the city directory were run by women—but the income generated by this kind of work was as a rule far too meager for that. For women whose husbands had died or run off, and who proved unable (or unwilling) to support themselves as domestic drudges, prostitution was frequently the only alternative to public assistance.

Indeed, the heightened vulnerability of working-class women to sexual exploita-tion—above all by upper-class men—became a familiar and explosive topic during the

1790s. Seduction dramas in which unscrupulous aristocratic cads took advantage of simple but pure working girls were hugely popular on the New York stage. Arguably the most widely read book of the era was Susannah Haswell Rowson's novel *Charlotte Temple*, first published in London in 1791. Set in Revolutionary New York, her tale concerned an innocent fifteen-year-old schoolgirl seduced by a dashing British naval officer named Montraville, who then abandons her to take up with a wealthy local belle. Charlotte dies giving birth to his child, scorned by all except the laboring people, who haven't lost sight of her innate decency and virtue.[1]

In 1793 life provided an ugly imitation of art, when a seventeen-year-old girl named Lanah Sawyer alleged that a certain Henry Bedlow had lured her into Mother Carey's bawdy house on Ann Street, where he then raped her. Rape in eighteenth- and early nineteenth-century New York was a crime of the poor: well-to-do women rarely if ever brought formal accusations of rape before the courts, and the men charged with rape were almost invariably mechanics and laborers. Sawyer, a sewing girl whose father was a little-known sea captain, fit the pattern perfectly. "Harry" Bedlow didn't. His family was wealthy, and he had a reputation around town as a rake and libertine.

Bedlow's trial before an all-male jury raised questions of power, privilege, gender, and class in a republican society. To the prosecution, Sawyer was a "poor and unknown" girl victimized by an arrogant rogue "of rich family and connections." Bedlow's attorneys, Richard Harison, Robert Troup, and Brockholst Livingston, admitted that a seduction had occurred. But they denied the charge of rape, arguing that Sawyer's plebeian standards of "discretion and prudence"—why had she been out in the streets without an escort? why had she failed to reject Bedlow's advances at the very outset?—were obviously looser than those observed in respectable society. And because a casual accusation of rape could put "the life of a citizen in the hands of a woman, to be disposed of almost at her will and pleasure," its disposition was thus a matter of grave consequence for the (male) political community.

Bedlow was a "fellow citizen" regardless of his private shortcomings or station in life: to convict him just because Sawyer alleged he raped her was to violate an essential distinction between those who were active, useful members of the republic and those who stood outside it. All the more so in this case, the lawyers said, because Sawyer came from the most vicious and depraved class of society. Respectable women learned to tame their wanton passions; laboring women, exposed to the coarsest aspects of life, could not. No matter that Sawyer's neighbors described her as modest and polite, Brockholst Livingston told the jury. They seemed "an obscure set of people, perhaps of no character themselves," while she was just another working-class slattern who "had the art to carry a fair outside, while all was foul within."

---

1. Rowson's plot allegedly draws upon the affair between a certain Charlotte Stanley and John Montresor, the author's cousin and a Royal Engineer stationed in New York during the Revolution (he is still remembered for an exquisitely detailed 1775 map of the city). During the rebuilding of Trinity Church in the mid-1840s, Charlotte Stanley's tombstone was somehow reinscribed "Charlotte Temple." As such, it became a shrine for the novel's many readers and one of New York's premier tourist attractions. Year after year weeping pilgrims strewed the site with flowers and other testimonials to their devotion. They were still doing so, according to one report, as late as 1905. Local historians, meanwhile, battled furiously over the exact site of Charlotte's death, though everyone agreed it must have been in the vicinity of Chatham Square, perhaps on the lower Bowery. The crumbling Walton House, supposedly where Rowson's pregnant heroine made a dramatic final appeal for help, gained a similar renown. When it burned in 1853, hundreds of distraught townsfolk gathered at the scene to mourn the loss.

When the jury acquitted Bedlow after fifteen minutes' deliberation, workingmen went on a rampage. The disorders centered around Greenwich, Warren, and Murray streets on the west side of town, home both to mechanics, shopkeepers, cartmen, and laborers and to "the Holy Ground," the red-light district whose prostitutes and brothels were well known to young men of genteel backgrounds, not least of all those enrolled at nearby Columbia College.

For three days crowds of "Boys, Apprentices, Negroes, and Sailors" roamed through the Holy Ground and its immediate vicinity until chased off by mounted horsemen. The rioters—hundreds strong—focused their attention on Mother Carey's bawdy house as well as two others operated by Mother Giles and Mother Gibbons. (Bawdy houses, like so many of the city's boardinghouses, tended to be run by women, often widows.) All three establishments were looted of their luxurious appointments— "petty-coats, smocks, and silks, together with downy couches, or feather beds"—and then, after their roofs were unshingled, the houses were utterly dismantled. There were doubtless other possible targets in the area, but they escaped unscathed, and for good reason. Mother Carey and her girls had testified on Bedlow's behalf. They were accessories to a system of upper-class sexual exploitation of young working-class women that might yet claim more of the rioters' sisters and daughters. As anchors of that system in the city's poorer communities, their house (and those of Mother Giles and Mother Gibbons) had to come down.

What was finally at issue here was not so much the insult to Lanah Sawyer's honor, or the existence of bawdy houses per se, but whether working-class men or upper-class men would control the bodies of working-class women. The anonymous "Justicia" made this point forcefully, protesting to a local newspaper that the bawdy houses in question had been patronized over the years by the very magistrates who sprang to Bedlow's defense and scrambled to quell the riots.

Street battles over gender rights thus joined strikes, ethnic tangles, racial tensions, and popular revivals as indications of growing strains in New York society. But the same prosperity that had helped generate these conflicts helped mute their consequences as well. Only a significant downturn in the economy would truly test the depth and degree of civic disaffections, and that was just what onrushing global events were about to provide.

26

War and Peace

One evening toward the end of April 1806, two miles off Sandy Hook, the sixty-gun British frigate *Leander* spied the American schooner *Richard* making her way up the coast to New York from Brandywine Creek in Pennsylvania. *Leander* was searching for deserters from the Royal Navy and fired a shot across *Richard*'s bow as an order to heave to and prepare for boarding. The American promptly complied, but a second shot followed, and then a third—possibly meant for another vessel nearby—which smashed into Richard's stern, decapitating the helmsman, John Pierce.

Pierce's death was a grisly reminder that since the resumption of the Napoleonic Wars in 1803, both Britain and France had redoubled their efforts to curb the lucrative carrying trade of neutral nations, the United States above all. For Britain's Royal Navy, that task had been made immeasurably easier by Admiral Nelson's 1805 destruction of the French fleet at Trafalgar. But the Royal Navy was experiencing severe shortages of manpower. Able seamen were deserting by the thousands—more often than not for the rapidly growing American merchant marine, where conditions and pay were vastly better and captains wouldn't look too closely at a man's documents. So new instructions had gone out for British warships to search neutral vessels with particular vigor and "press" deserters back into service. Since Britain didn't recognize U.S. naturalization laws—and since her captains were also given to a certain carelessness about paperwork—as many as a thousand men every year, the innocent along with the guilty, American as well as British, found themselves serving time before the mast in the Royal Navy.

As the hub of American neutral commerce, New York was an obvious place for His Majesty's forces to ferret out both contraband and deserters (virtually every British vessel that put into the port after the turn of the century was said to leave shorthanded). Since as early as 1804, the Royal Navy had been patrolling nearby waters so relentlessly that the British consul in the port admitted it was as good as under blockade. The *Leander*, one of three frigates on station outside New York in the spring of 1806, routinely detained a score or more ships at a time. Any seaman suspected of being a British subject was impressed on the spot.

As word of *Leander's* attack on *Richard* raced through the city, angry crowds converged on the waterfront. One party of volunteers set out in a pilot boat to recover a pair of merchantmen taken by the *Leander* and about to be sent up to the prize courts in Halifax, Nova Scotia. Other parties seized five of the *Leander*'s supply boats, and a "prodigious mob—huzzaing" hauled their contents off to the almshouse for distribution to the poor.

When John Pierce's headless corpse went on display at the Tontine Coffee House a day or so later, the mood in New York turned so ugly that the British consul predicted his house would be burned by a mob and he himself would be taken hostage. Mayor Clinton and the Common Council had Pierce buried at public expense and directed all ships in the harbor to fly their flags at half-mast. President Jefferson barred *Leander* from American ports and issued an unenforceable order for the arrest of her captain (who, to no one's surprise, was afterward exonerated by a Royal Navy court-martial). Newspapers in Philadelphia and Richmond talked of war.

O GRAB ME

But there was to be no war—not yet.

A week before the *Leander* incident, already incensed by British violations of neutral commerce and the impressment of American seamen, Congress had passed a Non-Importation Act. Reminiscent of American resistance to parliamentary taxation in the 1760s and 1770s, the measure promised to end the sale of numerous British manufactures in the United States, effective the following November—unless, that is, His Majesty's government mended its ways before then. Secretary of State James Monroe sailed at once for London to open negotiations.

The threat of American economic retaliation could not overcome the momentum of events. In mid-May, with the American public still in a furor over the *Leander*, the British blockaded the European coast from Hamburg to Brest. Napoleon's answer came in the Berlin Decree of December 1806, which demanded that all neutral nations discontinue further trade with Great Britain. More concerned with bringing pressure to bear on France than avoiding trouble with the United States, His Majesty's government scuttled a treaty just negotiated by Monroe and Ambassador William Pinkney. Nonimportation had failed.

The year 1807 opened with a volley of British orders in council further curtailing neutral trade between France and France's allies. American hostility to the former mother country mounted in June when HMS *Leopard* fired on the USS *Chesapeake* off Norfolk Roads, Virginia, killing three sailors. Jefferson, in a fury, directed all British warships to leave American waters. His Majesty's government replied that it intended to pursue deserters with even greater zeal—and its resolve was stiffened by outrages like the one that occurred in New York the following September, when a crowd of dock-workers and sailors prevented six escaping British seamen from being returned to their ship. In a General Blockade Order of November 1807, the British then prohibited all neutral trade through ports closed to English shipping: if France barred British trade, in other words, France would have *no* trade. Napoleon retaliated in December 1807 by asserting that any vessel that submitted to British inspection, willingly or unwillingly, was subject to seizure. If the Americans didn't make Britain respect their rights as neutrals, the emperor would treat them as Britain's de facto allies.

As the probability of American involvement in the Anglo-French struggle increased month by month, "fortification fever" swept New York. The invasions of 1664, 1673, and 1776 left no doubt as to Manhattan's vulnerability to attack by sea, but only Fort Jay on the northern end of Governors Island—thrown up during the war scare of 1794 and rebuilt as Fort Columbus in 1806—afforded the city any protection from enemy warships. Over the spring and summer of 1807, therefore, teams of military engineers got to work on a system of forts and batteries for the Upper Bay that would take four years to complete.

President Jefferson was now coming round to the view that a second war with Great Britain was both inevitable and necessary. In mid-December 1807 the president asked Congress to place a total embargo on vessels leaving American ports—not to bring economic pressure on the belligerents, he explained, but to get American ships and seamen "out of harm's way" and give the nation time to prepare for war. An Embargo Act quickly passed both houses and was signed into law three days before Christmas.

It was a colossal blunder. Besides causing no appreciable harm to the British economy, the embargo gave Napoleon the opportunity to grab ten million dollars' worth of legitimate American shipping on the grounds that it must perforce be illicit. In a single stroke, moreover, the embargo brought a decade of unprecedented American prosperity to a dead stop. Exports tumbled 80 percent in 1808. Imports fell 60 percent. What this amounted to, one critic charged, was a deranged act of self-mutilation—an attempt "to cure the corns by cutting off the toes."

In New York the whole leg seemed to have been amputated. John Lambert, who returned to the city in April 1808, was overwhelmed by its "gloomy and forlorn" appearance. "The coffee-house slip, the wharfs and quays along South-street, presented no longer the bustle and activity that had prevailed there five months before," Lambert wrote. "Not a box, bale, cask, barrel, or package, was to be seen upon the wharfs. Many of the counting-houses were shut up, or advertised to be let; and the few solitary merchants, clerks, porters, and labourers, that were to be seen, were walking about with their hands in their pockets. Instead of sixty or a hundred carts that used to stand in the street for hire, scarcely a dozen appeared, and they were unemployed."

A few quick-witted merchants managed to stay afloat in the crisis, here slipping through loopholes in the law, there falling back on old-fashioned smuggling. John Jacob Astor got permission from President Jefferson to let an "esteemed citizen" of China named Punqua Wingchong return home on the *Beaver*. No sooner had the *Beaver* cleared port than Punqua Wingchong was rumored to be "a common Chinese dock-loafer" conscripted by Astor to hoodwink the government (in fact Wingchong appears to have been a Hong merchant sent to collect some outstanding American debts). When the *Beaver* eventually returned to New York, its cargo netted Astor a profit of two hundred thousand dollars.

Few New Yorkers were so nimble. By the spring of 1808, some 120 firms had already gone out of business, the sheriff held a record twelve hundred debtors in custody (five hundred owing sums less than ten dollars), and a pandemic of unemployment was savaging the city's laboring population. Over the winter of 1807–8 the tally of destitute persons was said to have grown tenfold. Residents grimly spoke of the crisis as "O Grab Me"—"embargo" spelled backward.

"BREAD OR WORK"

No one suffered more than sailors. There were, Lambert reported, "above 500 vessels in the harbor, which were lying up useless and rotting for want of employment" while thousands of seamen were "destitute of bread." Unable to find shore jobs, many braved the icy winds to fish for food off the Battery. Early in January 1808 a committee of the Common Council declared that the municipal government should do something "to alleviate the evils which must result from a suspension of the ordinary vocations of the laborious part of the community"—perhaps by hiring "industrious persons" to improve Broadway.

Shortly thereafter, on Saturday, January 9, unemployed Jack Tars rallied in the Park, then paraded through the streets with placards that demanded "bread or work." They dispersed peacefully after presenting a petition to the mayor that was respectful but laced with hints of menace. If municipal authorities failed "to provide some means for our subsistence during the winter," they said, "we shall be necessitated to go on board foreign vessels." What was more, many of them could no longer pay their boardinghouse bills. "By what means shall we discharge these debts? Should we plunder, thieve or rob, the State prison will be our certain doom."

A special session of the Common Council promptly organized relief operations. By Thursday a soup kitchen had been built; by Friday the almshouse was supplying food to over a thousand of the unemployed, five times more than the week before. By early February nearly six thousand were lining up for rations at the almshouse three times a week—receiving a quart of soup, a pound of bread, and three-quarters of a pound of beef. The program was terminated in the spring, then started up again the following fall. All told, between 1807 and 1809 municipal expenditures for relief climbed from forty-six to seventy-eight thousand dollars—a 70 percent increase.

The city also initiated the nation's first work-relief project for persons "who are capable of labouring and who are destitute of occupation." The street commissioner hired workers to help fill the Fresh Water Pond, raise streets and lots near Corlear's Hook, lower Murray Hill, and dig the foundation for City Hall. The Common Council also devised a plan for the Navy Yard to hire unemployed seamen, at city expense, paying them not with money but "victuals, drink, fuel, candles, and accommodation for lodging." Many tars, however, feared being "trepanned"—kidnapped—by the navy, and only fifty-three accepted the offer. They did, on the other hand, flock to a War Department program, initiated at the urging of city authorities, which hired men to work on forts around the city.

Private relief organizations like the Humane Society contributed to the relief effort as well. To coordinate their work, forty civic leaders formed the General Committee of the Benevolent Associates for the Relief of the Poor. In December 1808 it organized a new, broadly based Assistance Society, which promised "to combine moral improvement by the recommendation of religion, with temporal relief distributed in the most economical and cautious manner." In the last week of February 1809, the society provided food, clothing, and fuel to over eight hundred indigent families (after first dispatching visitors to investigate the applicants).

It was beginning to look, however, as if no amount of governmental ingenuity or private charity could save New York from Jefferson's embargo. Not perhaps since the terrible depression of the early 1760s had the city experienced privation and despair on such a scale. Its streets swarmed with beggars, and "thousands of mariners, mechanics, and laborers" remained "destitute of cloathing, food and a lodging." Obviously, wrote the Democratic-Republican newspaper editor James Cheetham, New York faced a crisis of such magnitude that it could only be solved at the federal level. "The NATION," Cheetham insisted, "should provide for the distress which the nation inflicts."

UNLAWFUL COMBINATIONS AND RIOTOUS ASSEMBLIES

While protests against the embargo poured into Washington from every corner of the country, Jefferson defiantly bore down, tightening enforcement of the law until he exercised near-dictatorial powers. By the beginning of 1809, however, Congress was in open revolt. On March 1 it killed the fifteen-month-old embargo, adopting in its place a Non-Intercourse Act that permitted trade with all nations *except* Britain and France. It also provided for the resumption of trade with whichever of those two agreed to respect neutral rights. Jefferson, in one of his last official acts as president, resignedly signed the measure. New York greeted the news with ringing bells, fireworks, and cannonades.

Business picked up a bit in the months to come, but not enough to neutralize anxiety and contentiousness in the city. One symptom of the mood was the increased appeal of the "mechanic preachers" who had been active in New York since the turn of the century. Seasoned evangelists like Jesse Lee and Johny Edwards drew record crowds after 1808—Lee said he "never knew so great a revival of religion in the city before"—while the messianic Amos Broad preached to exuberant throngs of worshipers (mostly apprentices and mechanics) in his new hall on Rose Street. Alarmed municipal authorities tried to crack down on these meetings, so inconsistent with established religious practices, and when Edwards and the female evangelist Dorothy Ripley sponsored an open-air revival in May 1810, a squad of city marshals dragged Ripley off the pulpit while she cried out, over and over, "Lord have mercy upon them; Lord have mercy upon them for Christ's sake!"

Violent outbreaks against African Americans became common. In 1807, and virtually every year thereafter, the trustees of the AME Zion Church pleaded with the City Council to do something about the gangs of white working-class youths that routinely harassed worshipers on Sundays; the Common Council wondered whether a watch box should be built outside the church. The Abyssinian Baptists faced similar problems.

Paralleling this new eruption of racial hatred were sharply rising tensions between masters and journeymen. As unemployment caromed through the trades after 1807, the bricklayers, printers, carpenters, cordwainers, masons, tailors, and cabinetmakers were plunged into a succession of acrimonious confrontations and strikes. Journeyman printers established a New York Typographical Society, whose 120 members protested that they were "sinking in the estimation of the community" and denounced master printers for employing half-trained apprentices and "full-grown men (foreigners)." Journeyman house carpenters issued an 1809 manifesto asserting that "every class of society ought to be entitled to benefit in proportion to its usefulness."

The most significant clash took place among the city's shoemakers. In 1808 the Journeyman Cordwainers' Society expelled one of their members for nonpayment of dues and "raising a rumpus" during a meeting. The society's by-laws required the offender's employer, the firm of James Corwin and Charles Aimes, to discharge him at once or lose the services of all other members. Corwin and Aimes obliged, which might have ended matters, except they refused to fire the man's apprentice as well. When the journeymen in their shop awoke to the fact that this apprentice was now doing a journeyman's work for less than a journeyman's wages, they walked out. Then, discovering that the city's master cordwainers had banded together to help Corwin and Aimes by filling the firm's orders, the journeymen struck them all.

To this the master cordwainers responded by swearing out a complaint charging two dozen leaders of the journeymen's society with illegal conspiracy. Early in 1809 the journeymen were duly indicted for "perniciously and deceitfully forming an unlawful club and combination"—the first time New Yorkers had been prosecuted for uniting to raise their wages. To represent them at the subsequent trial, they hired William Sampson, the exiled Irish revolutionary and well-known Jeffersonian. The masters, shrewdly, retained Thomas Addis Emmet, whose reputation eclipsed even Sampson's.

Emmet's argument before the Mayor's Court in 1809 played upon the still-widespread belief that extragovernmental associations had no place in a republic. In banding together to advance their private interests, Emmet contended, the journeymen had breached their sacred duty as citizens to uphold the common good. By the same token, their so-called right to strike violated the right of masters in every trade to dispose of their property as they saw fit. But Sampson too appealed to republican principles. The real problem here, he said, was "the rapacity of the masters." They, not the journeymen, had put private gain ahead of the public interest, forming their own "sordid combination" to sustain excessive profits while "crowding their shops with more apprentices than they could instruct." Besides, when merchants could meet to fix prices, politicians to nominate candidates, and sportsmen to wager on horses, why should poor men be indicted for "combining against starvation?"

Judicial hostility, if not Emmet's oratory, carried the day. Mayor Jacob Radcliff instructed the jury that the accused journeymen had indeed employed "arbitrary and unlawful means," whereupon the jury found in favor of the masters. Not all was lost: the journeymen received comparatively mild fines of one dollar apiece, and the court acknowledged their right to "meet and regulate their concerns, and to ask for wages, and to work or refuse" as they saw fit—so long as they didn't do it together.

Strife continued nevertheless, and in 1810 the city's "architects and surveyors" issued an unusual appeal for calm, condemning the "increasing evils and the distressing tendency of the disputes between the Master and Journeymen Mechanics." It did no good. Six months later, several hundred striking journeyman house carpenters converged on Mechanic Hall, headquarters of the General Society, smashing all the windows in what may well have been New York's first labor dispute involving serious violence.

"MUCH EXULTATION AMONG THE FEDERALISTS"

Political strife also grew as Jefferson's foreign policy handed New York Federalists one issue after another. They vilified the president for his cautious response to British and French attacks on American shipping. They criticized nonimportation as ineffectual and cited it as further proof of the government's indifference to the welfare of saltwater ports like New York. When Treasury Secretary Albert Gallatin balanced the budget by cutting back on naval expenditures, they accused the administration of disregarding the safety of American ships and seamen. When work on the new harbor fortifications seemed not to move along briskly enough, they scolded Governor Tompkins and Mayor Clinton.

Nothing, though, gave the Federalists more cause for hope than the outcry against the embargo. During the winter of 1807–8, as the city's economy croaked to a halt, public opinion swung heavily against the administration. Federalist writers and pamphleteers made a great show of concern for the miseries Jefferson had inflicted on working people and urged them to put their trust, again, in the party of Washington and Hamilton. In the spring 1808 elections, although Democratic-Republicans held on to both the city and state, the Federalists doubled the number of seats they occupied in the legislature. Some began to discern a chance of victory in the upcoming presidential election as well.

Over the spring and summer of 1808, a new Federalist organization, the formidable Washington Benevolent Society, took the field to rally the faithful. What the Tammany Society did for the Republicans, the Washington Benevolents now set out to do for the suddenly rejuvenated Federalists: mobilize disaffected voters and lead them away from the party in power on election day. Its Tammany-like tactics—secret rituals, colorful parades, public banquets, low dues, inexpensive loans to members—succeeded brilliantly. Before the year was out, thousands of New Yorkers had joined the Washington Benevolents, and chapters of the society were sprouting up all over New England and the mid-Atlantic states.

Toward the end of August 1808, Federalists from eight states gathered secretly in New York to hold what has been called the first national political convention in the country's history. The delegates chose Charles Cotesworth Pinckney of South Carolina for president and Rufus King of New York for vice-president (the same ticket Jefferson and Governor George Clinton had clobbered four years earlier). A caucus of congressional Republicans then nominated Jefferson's Virginia neighbor, James Madison.

Madison won the election handily, a blow to the Federalists that was partly offset by the continuing good news from New York. In the 1809 elections, notwithstanding repeal of the embargo, the Federalists captured the Common Council, the state legislature, and the Council of Appointment and broke the Democratic-Republican hammerlock on the city's congressional delegation. Their revival as a party was celebrated on July fourth of that year when the Washington Benevolents marched through town, two thousand strong in thirteen divisions, to the corner of Broadway and Reade Street, where the cornerstone was laid for the society's new headquarters, Washington Hall.

DIEDRICH KNICKERBOCKER

Since the Revolution, writers and editors from all over the country had been trickling into New York City, drawn by its energy, its wealth, its clubs and theaters, its expanding book and newspaper markets, its contentious public life. Noah Webster arrived in the late eighties, Philip Freneau in the early nineties, Charles Brockden Brown later in the decade. Following them, soon after the turn of the century, came James Kirke Paulding, Samuel Woodworth, Fitz-Greene Halleck, and John Howard Payne, among others—including one southern newspaperman who explained in 1806 that he moved to New York in order to work "at the confluence of the greatest number of the streams of knowledge."

None of these out-of-towners, however, held the promise of an easygoing, blue-eyed, twenty-year-old native named Washington Irving. The fifth son of an English-woman and a Scots hardware merchant who had settled in the city before the Revolution, Washington was born the year the British evacuated New York and was named by his mother in honor of the general. The prosperous William Street household was Federalist and strictly Calvinist, and young Washington began a legal apprenticeship in 1802 with Josiah Hoffman, a prominent Federalist judge. Hoffman introduced him to the cream of city society and affectionately indulged his obvious passions for convivial company, for the theater, and for literature. Irving was still with Hoffman when he wrote the *Letters of Jonathan Oldstyle, Gent.* (1802), a series of high-spirited if callow forays into dramatic criticism that initially appeared in the *Morning Chronicle*, edited by his older brother Peter. In 1804 his brothers William and Ebenezer, worried about Washington's health, sent him off on a lengthy grand tour of Europe.

On his return to New York in 1806, Irving resumed his man-about-town life and emerged as ringleader of the Lads of Kilkenny, a loosely knit pack of literary-minded young blades out for a good time. They haunted the Park Theater, Dyde's London Hotel (which stood next to the theater and advertised hospitality "in the true Old English Style"), and Thomas Hodgkinson's Shakespeare Tavern, which opened in 1808 at the corner of Nassau and Fulton streets and was for the next thirty years the rendezvous of New York literati. None of the Lads lived by pen alone. Like the members of the old Friendly Club, they were men of affairs—lawyers, merchants, physicians—except, that is, for Irving himself, whose adoring brothers actually gave him a share of the family business so he could continue his literary pursuits without having to depend on what he wrote (or indeed the law) for his livelihood.

And write he did, along with his brother William and William's brother-in-law, the sensitive, bookish James Kirke Paulding. Over the course of 1807 the trio collaborated on *Salmagundi*, a running collection of droll essays on current events in "the thrice renowned and delectable city of GOTHAM" (thereby affixing a nickname to New York). Their irreverent commentaries—named after a spicy appetizer of chopped meat, pickled herring, and onions—were intended "to present a striking picture of the town; and as every body is anxious to see his own phiz on canvas, however stupid or ugly it may be, we have no doubt but that the whole town will flock to our exhibition."

Few Salmagundian sallies were intended to do serious injury—apart, perhaps, from those ridiculing the American "mobocracy" or mocking Jefferson as "a huge bladder of wind." Irving and his circle were, after all, gentlemen (or aspiring gentlemen). They knew their way around respectable society, and they knew that no true gentleman would wish to shock, offend, or inflict original ideas upon his readers: light, facile essays, in the knowing and self-ironic tone of the *Spectator* or the *Gentleman's Magazine* were the objective. As Richard Henry Dana later said, *Salmagundi* made "exceedingly pleasant morning or after-dinner reading, never taking up too much of a gentleman's time from his business and pleasures, nor so exalted and spiritualized as to seem mystical to his far reaching vision. It was an excellent thing in the rests between cotillions, and pauses between games at cards."

Salmagundi's strict adherence to the cultivated standards of eighteenth-century English letters didn't bother Irving any more than it did Duncan Phyfe or John McComb: "We are," he would write, "a young people, necessarily an imitative one, and must take our examples and models, in a great degree, from the existing nations of Europe. There is no country more worthy of our study than England." (The original

"Gotham," immortalized in proverb and nursery rhyme, was of course that old English village whose inhabitants turned aside King John's wrath by pretending to be fools.)

Yet the denizens of Shakespeare Tavern were poised to transcend the merely provincial. Imbued with a sense of patrician stewardship, they would take on the task of originating a genuinely American tradition of thought and expression—a "National Literature," in Paulding's phrase—reflecting the country's growing cultural as well as political autonomy and bolstering the republican character of its institutions. Paulding, a more ardent nationalist and republican than Irving, was soon building a career out of twisting John Bull's tail. The passionately anti-British, pro-American essays, poems, and satires that followed *Salmagundi* would make him a major figure in the "paper war" waged between British and American writers over the next several decades.

Irving himself, for all his aesthetic and political conservatism, had taken a step in that direction as "Jonathan Oldstyle"—"Jonathan" being the current shorthand for an uncouth American—and his contributions to *Salmagundi* rivaled Paulding's in lampooning British snobbery. But he was soon to go considerably farther and become the first American writer to exploit the full literary potential of local speech, characters, scenery, folkways, and history.

On October 26, 1809, the *Evening Post* carried the following notice: "Left his lodgings some time since, and has not since been heard of, a small elderly gentleman, dressed in an old black coat and cocked hat, by the name of KNICKERBOCKER. As there are some reasons for believing he is not entirely in his right mind and as great anxiety is entertained about him, any information concerning him left either at the Columbian Hotel, Mulberry-street, or at the Office of this paper will be thankfully received." Two weeks later, a letter writer to the *Post* reported that he had spotted the man, just above Kingsbridge, trudging wearily northward. The proprietor of the Columbian Hotel then announced that he had discovered "a very curious kind of a written book" in Knickerbocker's room—and that if the vanished lodger didn't soon pay his bill, the manuscript would be sold off. Finally, on November 28, New York's cleverest prepublication publicity campaign to date culminated with an announcement of the availability of *A History of New York from the Beginning of the World to the End of the Dutch Dynasty . . . by Diedrich Knickerbocker*.

Irving later explained that the idea for *Knickerbocker's History* came to him after reading Samuel Latham Mitchill's *Picture of New-York*. Irving found it shallow and self-important—the Lads had already mocked it in *Salmagundi*—and it seemed a perfect target for a spoof "written in a serio-comic vein, and treating local errors, follies, and abuses with good-humored satire." Accordingly, with the assistance of his brother Peter, Irving concocted a "crude mass of mock erudition," brimming with mordant sarcasm, goofy wordplay, and spurious footnotes, jumbling hilarious make-believe events together with bona fida history.

Casting himself as a serious scholar—though admitting that his name probably came from *knicker*, "to nod," and *boeken*, "books," hence a great nodder or dozer over books—Knickerbocker/Irving recounted the story of New York's origins, doing for it what Virgil had done for Rome but with tongue in cheek. When Hudson first sights Manhattan, for example, he is given the memorably vacuous line: "See! There!"

It helped that in Irving's day knowledge about the city's Dutch roots was very skimpy. The New-York Historical Society had only recently issued a plaintive request for information: "Is there any thing known concerning *Wouter Van Twiller*, or *William*

Kieft, who preceded Governor *Stuyvesant* in the Chief Magistracy of the *New-Nether-lands?* How long did each remain in office? What stations or offices did they fill prior to their appointment here? Were they removed by death or resignation, or for ill behaviour?" William Smith's *History of the Province of New York* (1757) didn't have the answers: it gave only nine pages to the entire half century of Dutch rule. Small wonder, then, that readers often couldn't tell when Irving was pulling their leg, and in later editions he had to warn that the *History* was a "whimsical and satirical work, in which the peculiarities and follies of the present day are humorously depicted in the persons, and arrayed . . . in the grotesque costume of the ancient Dutch colonist."

Knickerbocker's History was certainly in part a sendup of contemporary politics, particularly Jefferson's foreign policy. It portrays Kieft ("William the Testy," Knickerbocker calls him) as an intellectual who lacks the ability or patience to run a government and whose notions of defense against foreign aggression are limited to empty proclamations and self-defeating limitations on trade—an unmistakable allusion to the recently retired president. Stuyvesant, by contrast, was an ur-Federalist who believed that "to render a country respected abroad, it was necessary to make it formidable at home."

Irving/Knickerbocker also took a jaundiced view of contemporary cobblers, blacksmiths, and tailors—the "swinish multitude," the "enlightened mob"—who, believing themselves competent in "matters above their comprehensions," attempted to "attend to the measures of government." He ridiculed modern "hoydens" who, unlike the domestic *goede vrouws* of yore, were "very fond of meddling with matters that did not appertain to their sex." He bemoaned the "pride of family and ostentation of wealth, that has since grown to such a height in this city," and heaped scorn on the "satisfied struttings of wealthy gentlemen with their brains in their pockets" and on "smart young gentlemen, with no brains at all." Indeed Irving's *History* can be read as one long screed, tempered somewhat by self-irony, that denegrates the "degenerate days" in which he lived, by comparing them to a fictive Dutch Golden Age "when every thing was better than it has ever been since."

The *History* was also an exercise in literary nationalism. For all its obeisance to Sterne and Swift, Knickerbocker's earthy irreverence, extravagant bombast, and blustery tall tales would soon be considered hallmarks of American humor. Walter Scott claimed that reading it made his sides "absolutely sore with laughter," Dickens wore out his copy with repeated reading, and Coleridge, who picked up a copy at an English inn (a remarkable fact in itself), couldn't put it down until he'd finished. Irving's was the first American book so favorably received abroad. It put the United States—and New York City—on Europe's cultural map.

And Irving really had provided Manhattan with a past, of sorts. "Cities *of themselves*," Knickerbocker told his readers, tongue only partly in cheek, "are nothing without an historian," and Irving believed that creating his book had been an act of the highest civic patriotism. Although his version of colonial New Amsterdam was a burlesque, and deeply resented by New Yorkers of Dutch descent (Gulian Verplanck excoriated it as "coarse caricature"), Irving had done some real research, rummaging in documents and collecting family legends and lore from those same Dutch New Yorkers—who like it or not were soon known as Knickerbockers. Through Diedrich Knickerbocker, Irving wrote, "I hailed my native city, as fortunate above all other American cities, in having an antiquity . . . extending back into the regions of doubt and fable." And he credited

Knickerbocker's flights of fancy with provoking serious research into that antiquity: "It is only since this work appeared that the forgotten archives of the province have been rummaged, and the facts and personages of the olden time been rescued from the dust of oblivion."

Irving would recall, in the preface to a much later edition, that he had set out to give the Manhattan cityscape historical depth and texture—"to clothe home scenes and places with imaginative and whimsical associations, which live like charms about the cities of the old world." He believed that he'd succeeded, too, claiming that the "popular traditions of our city" now formed a "convivial currency" and "link[ed] our whole community together in good-humor and good fellowship."

Too good, perhaps, for Irving's "community" was devoid of slavery, Indian wars, poverty, and other unpleasantness—and too many New Yorkers would for too long accept his affectionate mythmaking as authentic history. He had accomplished something remarkable, nevertheless. In inventing a past for his city, he chose not to revel in "gunpowder and carnage" but rather to detail the amiable everyday life of a contented and pleasure-loving people. Virgil he wasn't, but New York could have done worse.

INTERNAL IMPROVEMENTS

While Irving was imagining a past for New York, some of his fellow citizens were busily imagining its future. Their vision, however, would be inscribed on the landscape itself.

In the spring of 1810 De Witt Clinton threw his influence behind the efforts of Gouverneur Morris, Thomas Eddy, Philip Schuyler, and Jonas Platt—Federalist land developers and empire builders—to drive a canal between the Hudson River and the Great Lakes, a distance of some 360 miles. That summer, named by the legislature to a new Board of Canal Commissioners, Clinton accompanied a team of engineers and surveyors up the Mohawk, through the Finger Lakes, and on to a rude little frontier village called Buffalo. Their report, issued in March 1811, proposed construction of a single continuous waterway from Albany to Lake Erie at a cost of five million dollars.

It was an idea—a dream—of pharaonic proportions. This great "national work," the commissioners proclaimed, was the "key to the commerce of our western world," a conduit through which thousands of tons of lumber, furs, flour, and other products of the Great Lakes would pour down to New York every year, enriching the city as well as hastening the conquest of the frontier. Generations to come would stand in awe of it.

Clinton and Morris went down to Washington to lobby for the plan, but Madison refused: federal aid for "internal improvements," the president said, was probably unconstitutional. Clinton didn't lose heart, however, and over the next fifteen years he crusaded so zealously for the canal's completion that it would come to be known as "Clinton's ditch."

Other momentous changes, more local in scope, lay closer to realization. In the spring of 1811, as workmen were finishing the facade of City Hall, New Yorkers got their first glimpse of a remarkable new plan—intricately engraved on an eight-foot-long map—for the city's future expansion up the island of Manhattan. Some four years in preparation, the plan was the work of a state-appointed Streets Commission made up of Gouverneur Morris, Simeon De Witt (the state surveyor), and John Rutherford (a respected city businessman and former New Jersey senator). After a decade of yellow fever epidemics, the Assembly had charged the commissioners with laying out "streets, roads, and public squares" in such a manner "as to unite regularity and order with the Public convenience and benefit, and in particular to promote the health of the city," by allowing for the "free and abundant circulation of air."

The commissioners had hired John Randel Jr., a young man in his early twenties, for the herculean task of surveying all 11,400 acres of Manhattan Island. He began in the spring of 1808, hiking each day from his residence in lower Manhattan to field head-quarters at the corner of Christopher and Herring streets (passing Tom Paine's house, where "frequently in fair weather [I] saw him sitting at the south window"). From there Randel and his men tramped on to distant parts of the island, often so thickly wooded as to be "impassable without the aid of an ax." Additional obstacles included hostile prop-erty owners and squatters, who unleashed dogs on any who approached with measuring instruments, or barraged them with cabbages and artichokes.

Randel had worked (he later said) "with a view to ascertain the most eligible grounds for the intended streets and avenues, with reference to sites least obstructed by rocks, precipices, steep grades, and other obstacles." But by the time he'd finished, in the fall of 1810, the commissioners had settled on an overlay pattern that brooked no such obstacles. Inasmuch as Morris (like Clinton) was also an active member of the Erie Canal Commission, it comes as no surprise that their vision of the streets of Manhattan had much in common with their vision of a great canal plowing across the state.

Several years before, the Salmagundians had playfully credited the right-angled, logical temperament of Philadelphians to the right-angled, logical pattern of their streets. "Whereas the people of New York—God help them—tossed about over hills and dales, through lanes and alleys, crooked streets—continually mounting and descending, turning and twisting—whisking off at tangents, and left-angle-triangles, just like their own queer, odd, topsyturvy rantipole city, are the most irregular, crazy-headed, quicksilver, eccentric, whim-whamsical set of mortals that ever were jumbled together in this uneven, villainous revolving globe, and are the very antipodeans to the Philadelphians."

Now all that was about to end. In the Commissioners' Plan, twelve avenues, each a hundred feet in width, would slice north, canal-like, from the edge of town (then rough-ly Houston Street), paralleling Manhattan's central axis. Every two hundred feet, cross-ing these avenues at right angles, were fifty- or sixty-foot-wide streets (one of which, every half mile or so, widened to one hundred feet). The resulting grid appealed to the same republican predilection for control and balance, the same distrust of sinuous nature, that shaped the neoclassical architecture of John McComb and the furniture of Duncan Phyfe. It combined "beauty, order, and convenience," the commissioners boasted.

There was nothing new about grids. City planners had relied on them for thou-sands of years, and they were deployed throughout the American colonies, from small New England towns to larger urban centers like Philadelphia, Savannah, Charleston, and New Orleans. When Lady Deborah Moody founded Gravesend in the mid-seventeenth century, she laid out a grid adapted from the town plan of New Haven. What was new about the Manhattan grid was its ruthless utilitarianism.

In 1803 Joseph François Mangin and Casimir Goerck had come up with a plan for the future of Manhattan that served varying needs (health, recreation, commerce, com-munity) with variable means: small blocks with streets close together in commercial

The Commissioners' Plan of 1811. (I. N. Phelps Stokes Collection. Miriam and Ira D. Wallach Division of Art, Prints and Photographs. The New York Public Library. Astor, Lenox and Tilden Foundations)

areas, spacious and more separated blocks in residential districts, and plenty of parks. But the Commissioners' Plan of 1811 would have none of this. Like the proposed Erie Canal, it was an "internal improvement" that gloried in the supremacy of technique over topography. Manhattan's ancient hills, dales, swamps, springs, streams, ponds, forests, and meadows—none would be permitted to interrupt its fearful symmetry. The commissioners admitted that it "may be a matter of surprise that so few vacant spaces have been left, and those so small, for the benefit of fresh air and consequent preservation of health." Certainly, if New York had been situated alongside a small stream, "such as the Seine or Thames," it might have needed more ample public places. "But those large arms of the sea which embrace Manhattan Island render its situation, in regard to health and pleasure, as well as to the convenience of commerce, peculiarly felicitous."

The commissioners hastened to add that they had indeed incorporated *some* open spaces into the grid. A huge 240-acre tract bounded by Third Avenue, Seventh Avenue, 23rd Street, and 34th Street was set aside for a "Grand Parade"—big enough, they said, "for Military Exercise, as also to assemble, in case of need, the force destined to defend the City." Above the Grand Parade, four smaller squares—Harlem, Hamilton, Bloomingdale, and Manhattan—afforded further relief from the grid's rectilinear monotony. Two final squares were set aside, one for a reservoir on an elevated bluff, another for a fifty-four-acre wholesale "Market Place" between 7th and 10th Streets from First Avenue to the East River.

Of "circles, ovals, and stars" there were to be none, however. Such "supposed improvements," the commissioners argued—sniping at features incorporated by L'Enfant in his plan for Washington—not only obstructed traffic but violated "the principles of economy." Cities are "composed principally of the habitations of men," and it is self-evident that "strait-sided and right-angled houses are the most cheap to build, and the most convenient to live in." Carving Manhattan up to 155th Street into roughly two thousand long, narrow blocks, each further subdivided into standardized lots (usually twenty-five by one hundred feet), each of which was easily located in reference to numbered streets and avenues, would also make land easier to market: Randel later pointed with pride to the way his handiwork heightened opportunities for "buying, selling, and improving real estate."

The grid enshrined republican as well as realtor values, in its refusal to privilege particular places or parcels. All plots were equal under the commissioners' regime, and the network of parallels and perpendiculars provided a democratic alternative to the royalist avenues of Baroque European cities. The shift from naming streets to numbering them, beyond promoting efficiency, also embodied a lexicographical leveling; no longer would families of rank or fortune memorialize themselves in the cityscape. Indeed William Duer complained that the commissioners had swung "the scythe of equality" across the island, replacing the country estates of the privileged classes with block after democratic block, no one necessarily better than any other, each equally exposed to the ebb and flow of the market.

In a remarkable assertion of public authority over large estate owners, moreover, the city decided to shut up any previously laid-out streets that were not retroactively accepted by the Common Council. Petrus Stuyvesant's Bowery Village grid, devised twenty-odd years before, ran afoul of the Commissioners' Plan, as it had been laid out on a true north-to-south and east-to-west basis, rather than adopting Manhattan's skewed axis. When the city began opening streets and avenues in the area—Third Avenue was cut through Stuyvesant property as early as 1812—the old roads were closed and the houses on them demolished or moved. After much bitter fighting with city officials, the powerful family was able to salvage several residences on Stuyvesant Street; it still survives, cutting diagonally between Second and Third avenues, a ghost of defunct ambitions.

Yet it was really the commissioners who were most ambitious of all. Their system of streets, which started at 1st and swept grandly and numerically up-island, was an implicitly imperial blueprint with no logical stopping point. Indeed the commissioners felt compelled to apologize for having halted at 155th Street. The reason "the whole island has not been laid out as a city," they explained, was not from any lack of expansionary will; they had, after all, already provided space enough "for a greater population than is collected at any spot on this side of China." Going farther would simply have been pointless for the time being, both because "it is improbable that (for centuries to come) the grounds north of Harlem Flat will be covered with houses," and because extending the grid higher "might have furnished materials for the pernicious spirit of speculation." For—like the Erie Canal in yet another sense—their grid was intended to hasten the real development of the city's hinterlands, not to encourage unproductive shenanigans. And no sooner were map and plan approved than Randel and his crew were set to work on staking out the actual landscape. Over the next decade they would place 1,549 yard-high white-marble markers at imagined intersections, each engraved with the number of its street-to-be, and wherever rocks barred the way, half-foot iron bolts, ninety-eight in all, were driven in to mark the spot.

New York's dominant commercial classes thus engraved their vision on the city, reshaping it to meet their evolving needs, unhindered by the presence of powerful national or state officials who, following a different urbanist calculus, might have imposed corridors of power and display. In Manhattan—a city of capital, not a capital city—considerations of efficiency and economy came first.[1]

---

1. Yet even in these terms, New York's new spatial arrangements were hardly flawless. Though longitudinal traffic would perforce be heavy on a long and narrow island, the grid provided two and a half times more latitudinal streets than it did north-south avenues. The absence of major diagonals—apart from Broadway, which the commissioners had originally intended to eliminate—forced cartmen and coaches to zig and zag around squared-off blocks, colliding at intersections that invited gridlock. Nor, as was customary, had the commissioners provided service alleys through the center of blocks: this maximized salable land but impeded access to it.

THE MAYOR WHO WOULD BE PRESIDENT

In the spring of 1811, while the streets commissioners staked out the Manhattan grid, President Madison's fumbling attempts to protect the rights of neutral carriers moved the United States and Great Britain ever closer to open conflict. The idea of a second war of independence with the former mother country had become popular in many parts of the country, but not in New York, still reeling from the havoc wrought by the embargo. With a notable lack of enthusiasm, the city prepared for the worst by completing the construction of four forts designed to protect it from naval attack.

The circular West Battery, built on a rocky outcropping about two hundred feet off the tip of Manhattan, had been designed by John J. McComb. Its eight-foot-thick walls were pierced with embrasures for twenty-eight cannon to sweep the Upper Bay and the mouth of the Hudson River. Only a few hundred yards away, on the shore of Governors Island, stood Castle Williams, designed by the Army's chief engineer, Lieutenant Colonel Jonathan Williams (later the first superintendent of West Point and namesake of Williamsburgh). Three stories high, Castle Williams bristled with a hundred heavy guns that could lay down a deadly crossfire with both the West Battery and Fort Columbus (formerly Fort Jay), which commanded the north shore of Governors Island, facing the East River.

The West Battery was also designed to crossfire with the North Battery, which stood on the Hudson shore at the foot of Hubert Street (and whose walls of red Newark sandstone caused it to be nicknamed the Red Fort.) The North Battery, in turn, could crossfire with Fort Gansevoort, located further upriver near the foot of Gansevoort Street (and dubbed the White Fort because of its whitewashed brownstone walls).

All told, these installations, plus numerous mortar batteries and smaller forts sprinkled around on Bedloe's, Ellis, and Staten islands, could train more than three hundred guns on enemy ships daring to enter the Upper Bay through the Narrows.

The day was fast approaching when they might be called upon to do so. In February 1812 Madison restored nonimportation against Great Britain. Two months later, on his recommendation, Congress adopted a ninety-day embargo that everyone knew to be the last step prior to an actual declaration of war. Everyone, that is, except the British government, which was just then preoccupied with rampant inflation, massive unemployment, labor unrest, and, early in May, the assassination of Prime Minister Spencer Perceval.

On June 16 Perceval's successor, Lord Castlereagh, finally got around to repealing all restrictions on neutral trade offensive to the United States. But Madison had already asked Congress for a formal declaration of war. On June 18, unaware of Castlereagh's action, Congress obliged him. Southern and western members tended as a rule to vote aye; northerners generally voted nay.

Well-to-do New York received the news sullenly. The state's congressional delegation had overwhelmingly opposed the declaration of war, and as one woman wrote, it came "like an Electric shock upon the great part of the people who have been too sanguine, in regard to peace Measures." Some feared that the city's defenses remained inadequate. In Broadway dining rooms and at the bar of the City Hotel, the greater concern was that a second conflict with Britain would inflict irreparable damage on the city's wounded economy. As Gouverneur Morris would remind the New-York Historical Society, "war with the greatest naval power is no happy condition for a commercial people." Four days before the declaration was finalized, the *Evening Post* published a memorial of protest signed by fifty-six of the city's principal merchants.

The man who took the helm of national opposition to Madison's war policy was the mayor of New York, De Witt Clinton. Clinton had been thinking for some time about a run for the presidency in 1812. Knowing he couldn't expect much encouragement from Republicans, the bulk of whom would surely remain loyal to Madison, Clinton had been making himself attractive to the Federalists, and they in turn had expanded their popular base by presenting themselves as the party of order, prosperity, and peace. In the spring of 1812 the Federalists put his name into nomination against Madison. Anti-administration Democratic-Republicans in the state followed suit. When war broke out only weeks later, Clinton was positioned as the candidate of bipartisan moderation and prosperity—willing to defend the nation's honor yet unwilling to put its commerce at risk in an ill-advised struggle with the former mother country.

New York City Democrats (as the urban Democratic-Republicans had begun calling themselves) rallied patriotically around President Madison. Indeed Tammany Hall—the party headquarters maintained by the Society of St. Tammany—and the Long Room of Bram Martling's Tavern on Chatham Street (Park Row) became bastions of the "Martling Men" or "Bucktails" (terms soon synonymous with "Tammanyite"), whose efforts to wrest the party away from Clinton would torment him for years to come.

Tammany belligerency reflected sentiment in the city's plebeian quarters. Down by the East River docks, in taverns and seamen's boardinghouses, or along the alleys that converged on the filled-in Fresh Water Pond, the prospect of war with Britain elicited significant enthusiasm. Many hundreds of workingmen signed on with regiments hastily formed for the defense of the city. One, the aptly named Old Butcher Troop, paraded through town behind banners proclaiming "Free Trade and Butcher's Rights / From Brooklyn's Fields to Harlem's Heights," and "Skin me well and Dress me neat / And Send me on board the Federal Fleet." Another unit, the Irish Greens, was a reminder that in 1812 as in 1775, New York harbored numerous and vengeful victims of His Majesty's attempts to pacify the Emerald Isle.

At the end of June, gangs of sailors roamed the waterfront attacking crewmen from Spanish and Portuguese vessels, on the theory that because their nations were allies of Britain, they were now enemies of the United States. Mayor Clinton moved swiftly to crush the disorders, however. Warning that "anarchy and tyranny" went hand in hand, he put the city's constables, firemen, and militia on alert; at the next sign of trouble, he announced, they would be called out by signal rockets launched from the cupola of City Hall. The sailors grumbled and cursed—whose side was the mayor on, anyway?—but Clinton remained presidentially firm.

Although senior New York Federalists like Rufus King and John Jay still weren't quite sure about Clinton, they proved to be in the minority. John Pintard and Gouverneur Morris, Clinton's de facto managers, summoned Federalists throughout the Northeast to support the mayor as the party's best hope of political resurrection and the only chance for maritime states to escape a ruinous war. In mid-August, at a meeting of the Friends of Liberty, Peace, and Commerce in Washington Hall, Morris went so far as to advocate secession of the northern states from the Union if Madison could not be stopped. A month later, when the Federalists gathered for a three-day national convention at Kent's Tavern on Broad Street, Morris played a key role in persuading the delegates to endorse Clinton.

When election day came, however, even with the Federalists on his side, Clinton could muster only eighty-nine electoral votes to Madison's 131. Besides New York, which he held thanks to the labors of a thirty-year-old upstate legislator named Martin Van Buren, Clinton carried New Jersey, all of New England except Vermont, and Maryland. Although the race was tighter than the final tally suggests—had he carried Pennsylvania, the mayor would have become president—the outcome was a clear warning to Clinton and his friends that if respectable New York didn't approve of the war, much of the rest of the United States did.

THE WAR OF 1812

The war effort required two things above all else from New York City, money and skilled manpower; it got the first reluctantly, the second with enthusiasm.

For Secretary of the Treasury Albert Gallatin, financing the war proved to be a hellish task. As military expenditures ballooned, a British naval blockade cut deeply into tariff revenues that remained the federal government's main source of income. In the past, Washington might have borrowed from the Bank of the United States, but in 1811 the Democratic-Republican Congress refused to renew its twenty-year charter. Opponents charged that much BUS stock was held in England and that the national bank had been hobbling boom-era venture capitalists by restricting the availability of credit. Proponents of development urged that federal deposits be transferred to the growing number of state banks, to use as a basis for expanding loans. In New York State, the legislature incorporated ten new banks between 1810 and 1812, including the chiefly Federalist Bank of America, the primarily Democratic-Republican City Bank of New York, and the Mechanics' Bank, dedicated to supplying artisan entrepreneurs with capital.

After the demise of the BUS, the federal government was forced to borrow from private lenders. In 1813 Congress authorized a loan of sixteen million dollars, but selling the bonds proved hard going with so many New York merchants opposed to the war. Secretary Gallatin therefore turned to a small syndicate organized by the country's two wealthiest capitalists, John Jacob Astor (an old friend of Gallatin's) and Stephen Girard of Philadelphia. They invented the practice of American loan contracting by purchasing the bonds wholesale (at enormous discounts), then selling them retail to friends in the States and associates in Europe. In 1814 the syndicate agreed to grant the government an additional eight to ten million dollars—if it gave them generous discounts, and if it created a second national bank. They wanted a new bank on the theory that it would stabilize the economy by curbing reckless speculation; they also expected to make tidy profits for themselves by purchasing bank stock with depreciated federal bonds, at full face value. In the final desperate months of the war, with the treasury bare, congressional resistance crumpled. Presented with an ultimatum from a "deliberate concert among the Capitalists," the government agreed to charter a new bank in exchange for emergency loans, chiefly from New Yorkers and Philadelphians.

Manhattan shipbuilders were less grudging in their contributions to the war effort. Henry Eckford, Christian Bergh, and Noah Brown led teams of ship's carpenters from Corlear's Hook to the shores of Lakes Erie and Ontario. There, over the winter of 1812–13, the New York artisans helped build the brigs and gunboats with which Captains Isaac Chauncey and Oliver Hazard Perry would defend the Niagara frontier with Canada. When Perry smashed a British squadron in the Battle of Lake Erie in September 1813, the city celebrated with abandon. It subsequently accorded Perry a hero's welcome, gave him the keys to the city, and named a street in his honor.

Eckford, Bergh, Brown, and other New York shipbuilders had plenty to do in Manhattan as well. In 1814 Adam and Noah Brown built for the U.S. Navy the world's first steam-driven vessel of war—*Fulton the First*, or *Demologos*. The New York yards also constructed, outfitted, and repaired privateers. Enemy warships blocked the Narrows, but Long Island Sound remained open, and hastily armed merchant vessels of every description were soon streaming out to prey on British commerce. In the first year or so of the war, some 125 privateers operated out of New York alone, employing nearly six thousand men and returning with seven hundred prizes.

As in past wars, however, the profits of privateering were elusive. The typical privateer was fitted out and owned on shares, and if she returned with a prize, there were court costs, fees, and duties to be paid even before her shareholders, officers, and crew took their cuts. So few investors came out ahead, much less struck it rich, that New York merchants petitioned Congress to make the business more lucrative. Offer a twenty-five-dollar bounty for every enemy national captured or killed, they asked; give pensions to disabled privateersmen and their widows. Congress agreed, but it made no difference. By the end of 1813 the Royal Navy had extended its blockade along the entire New England coast, including the entrance to Long Island Sound. For the remainder of the war nothing under sail could get in or out of the port.

Importers of finished wares coped with the blockade by moving cargoes up the Delaware River to South Trenton, overland to the Raritan River, and thence across the Hudson to the city. The volume of traffic was considerable—in November 1813 some fifteen hundred wagon teams reportedly worked the South Trenton-Raritan leg of the journey—but it was no substitute for direct access to the port's wharves and warehouses. Nor did it appeal to exporters of bulky agricultural products, increasing numbers of whom found it easier (and a lot more profitable) to sell their goods to the British forces poised just across the Canadian border. New York's business with the enemy would in fact grow so rapidly in the course of 1813 that President Madison was compelled, at the very end of the year, to slap another embargo on all American exports.

As the second winter of war approached, New York was once again like a city under siege. As during the embargo crisis of 1807–9, hundreds of vessels lay idle along the waterfront. Shuttered shops and stores lined every street, and on Broadway the cacophonous traffic of carts and wagons and carriages subsided to a mere rumble. Because profiteers had diverted so much of the city's essential supplies to the British in Canada, food and fuel were almost prohibitively expensive. Unemployed working people deluged municipal authorities with appeals for relief, and in December a committee of gentlemen, including Thomas Eddy and John Pintard, organized the Fuel Association to provide the "meritorious" poor with firewood; over the next several months the association distributed wood to three thousand addresses in the city. "The times are very hard," said one resident. "Money almost an impossibility. The necessaries of life are very high. . . . We are obliged to use beans steeped in hot molasses. Many are living on black butter-pears, apples and quinces stewed together—the poverty in the city is very great."

Militarily, moreover, the first eighteen months of war had gone badly. Except for Captain Perry and a young frontier general named William Henry Harrison, American field commanders committed one blunder after another, allowing the enemy to capture Detroit, repulse two assaults on Montreal, and burn Buffalo. When Napoleon abdicated in April 1814, further humiliations seemed certain. His Majesty's government, able at last to concentrate on the American theater, immediately shifted fourteen thousand veterans across the Atlantic and began massing naval forces off Sandy Hook and Gardiner's Bay. As the summer began, New York braced for another British invasion.

Mayor Clinton and his Federalist allies extracted every ounce of political capital they could from the situation. They assailed Madison for getting the country into the war, and they assailed him for failing to wage it with vigor and dispatch. Time and again, they reminded the city's mechanics of the years just after independence, when "industrious laborers had work, and having work they had money; and having money their wives and children were well clothed and well fed and well warmed. These were Federal times."

Maybe so. But as in the mid-1770s and the mid-1790s, that sort of argument could not overcome the combination of nationalist pride and hatred of Great Britain that was integral to popular culture in New York. With every British victory, every new hardship, Clinton and the Federalists lost rather than gained credibility. In the charter elections at the end of 1813, branded by Republicans as the "*Peace Faction*—or to use a more correct term—the enemy," their majority on the Common Council evaporated. The following spring, they lost control of the state legislature as well. Many a mechanic, it was observed, had come to the conclusion that "his children can freeze, but he must not let the Tories in."

Over the summer of 1814, with the war's opponents now effectively silenced, New Yorkers made ready for the expected British invasion. By the beginning of August, if not before, it was known that the enemy intended to strike down through Lake Champlain while diversionary forces harassed the Atlantic ports—meaning that the fortifications erected in the city between 1807 and 1812 were not likely to be of much use. On August 11, with the blessings of the City Council, thousands of residents turned out for a meeting to consider what ought to be done. After an impassioned speech by an aged Marinus Willett recalling popular resistance to British tyranny forty years earlier, it was agreed to form a Committee of Defense consisting of representatives from every ward. Like its Revolutionary predecessors, the committee was empowered by direct popular consent to form new military companies through the "voluntary enrollments" of ablebodied citizens, to organize citizens for "voluntary labor" on additional defense works, and to apprehend "all persons who shall be concerned in any illicit commerce or improper intercourse with the enemy."

New York boiled with activity. Marshaled by the Committee of Defense, its residents rallied to construct additional forts, breastworks, and blockhouses on Brooklyn Heights, upper Manhattan, and other newly defined danger points. City artisans, organized by trade, contributed over a hundred thousand days' worth of free labor. Patriotic ladies, lawyers, cartmen, merchants, and shopkeepers felled trees, dug trenches, and hauled artillery. The "free people of color" offered their collective services to the Committee of Defense and assisted in the erection of fortifications on Brooklyn Heights. In response to a congressional appeal for volunteers to defend New York, some 23,000 militiamen meanwhile flocked in from the surrounding countryside. From dawn to dusk they drilled and paraded, and the City Council appropriated money to pay them until they could be officially mustered into the regular service.

At the end of August, an enemy column burned Washington. The tension in New York became excruciating. "Your capital is taken!" cried one newspaper. "In six days the same enemy may be at the Hook. . . . Arise from your slumbers! . . .This is no time to talk!" Even Federalists professed their willingness to bear arms. "The enemy is at our doors," Rufus King announced, "and it is now useless to enquire how he came there." Gouverneur Morris, though, testily informed King that "anything like a Pledge by Federalists to carry on this wicked War, strikes me like a Dagger to my Heart." When Morris learned that antiwar Federalists in New England planned a secret convention in Hartford at the end of the year, he rejoiced at the possibility of a New York–New England confederation. The Hartford Convention, he declared, was "a star in the East . . . the dayspring of freedom and glory. The traitors and madmen assembled at Hartford will, I believe, if not too tame and timid, be hailed hereafter as the patriots and sages of their day and generation." (This wasn't the first time Morris flirted with sedition, but it was the last: he died less than a year later, having attempted to relieve a urinary obstruction by forcing a whalebone through his penis.)

Inside of two weeks, however, the sense of crisis in New York subsided. The British were turned back at the gates of Baltimore. Captain Thomas Macdonough's victory in the Battle of Lake Champlain removed the threat of an attack from Canada. Militiamen who had come to fight for the city soon started for home, and the Committee of Defense began to plan its final report to the Common Council.

PEACE! PEACE! PEACE!

One frigid evening in mid-February 1815, in the middle of a concert at the City Hotel (a witness recalled), "the door of the concert-room was thrown open and in rushed a man breathless with excitement. He mounted on a table and, swinging a white handkerchief aloft, cried out 'Peace! Peace! Peace!' The music ceased, the hall was speedily vacated, I rushed into the street, and oh, what a scene! In a few minutes thousands and tens of thousands of people were marching about with candles, lamps, torches, making the jubilant street appear like a gay and gorgeous procession." Over the next several days, in the wake of word that American and British commissioners had agreed to a treaty of peace, the still-rejoicing residents were treated to a spectacular display of fireworks from Governors Island and the erection of elaborate transparencies on public buildings and private houses depicting the long-awaited return of prosperity.

No one worried about the actual terms of the treaty: it was enough that the war had ended and that life could begin to return to normal. But what did "normal" mean—and how, exactly, was the city going to prosper now that the strife in Europe, the foundation of its expansion following independence, had ended as well?

27

The Canal Era

New York's postwar recovery proved to be quick and convincing, though not quite problem-free. Annoyingly enough, Britain and France once again closed down the West Indies to American trade, and British exporters began using the Pearl Street auction houses to dump a huge backlog of cheap manufactures on the American market. But if local importers and retailers suffered for a time, deep-water merchants and shipbuilders adjusted without serious difficulty—partly because the success of anticolonial revolutions in Latin America cracked open markets once monopolized by the Spanish and Portuguese, but mainly because industrializing and urbanizing Europeans remained willing to pay high prices for American cotton and wheat.

Whether or not New York would continue to dominate the trade in those lucrative commodities was an open question, however. Thousands of settlers were flooding into the Ohio and Mississippi valleys every year, shifting the heartland of American agricultural production ever westward, ever farther from Manhattan. Every year, too, increased the likelihood that the output of these myriad farms and plantations would be siphoned off by rival ports—New Orleans, for example, or Philadelphia (now linked to Pittsburgh by turnpike), or Baltimore (eastern terminus of the new National Road, which ran to Wheeling on its way toward Columbus and Indianapolis).

It was the heightened urgency of maintaining New York's connections to the West that enabled De Witt Clinton to bring his campaign for the Erie Canal to fruition. At the end of December 1815, he assured a conclave of businessmen at the City Hotel that the canal would make New York "the greatest commercial emporium in the world" and easily persuaded them to sign a memorial to the legislature calling for construction to begin as quickly as possible. Although his Tammany opponents denounced the "big ditch" as a costly folly and depicted it—not incorrectly—as a vehicle for Clinton's political ambitions, the legislature established a Canal Commission to consider costs and routes. When the Madison administration refused federal aid, an action some saw as a Virginia-based effort to forestall New York's ascendancy, Clinton persuaded the state to proceed on its own. In April 1817 Albany formally authorized the project. Two months later Clinton was elected governor. On July 4, three days after he assumed office, construction commenced on the state-owned, state-financed, state-run enterprise.

THE WEDDING OF THE WATERS

Work on the canal advanced swiftly, despite the carping of skeptics, daunting natural obstacles, and a financial crisis that shook the country in 1819, when—in part reflecting a severe postwar depression in England—the price of American cotton in Europe fell off sharply, dragging down western land values and triggering an avalanche of bank failures and foreclosures. Eight years after the first spade went into the ground and an amazing two years ahead of schedule, the great project was finally done—a marvel of human ingenuity and sacrifice by its engineers, who learned their trade on the job, and its laborers, many of them Irish and Welsh. Three hundred sixty-three miles long, forty feet wide, and four feet deep, the canal rose and descended a distance of 660 feet through eighty-three massive stone locks and passed over eighteen stately aqueducts.

On October 26, 1825, in Buffalo, Governor Clinton and assorted dignitaries boarded a flat-bottomed canal boat, the *Seneca Chief*, to begin a triumphal "aquatic procession" east to Albany and down the Hudson to New York harbor. Their arrival ten days later touched off one of the most spectacular celebrations in the city's history—a grand Festival of Connection. On November 4—one of those brilliant autumn days for which the city is famous—the *Seneca Chief* drew near the Battery and was hailed by city officials on an elegantly appointed steamboat: "Whence come you and where are you bound?" "From Lake Erie," came the reply, "bound for Sandy Hook!" Crossing the Upper Bay, the procession wound its way through an "Aquatic Display" of gaily decorated vessels while bands played, the Battery's guns fired salutes, and dense masses of cheering spectators packed the wharves and rooftops of Manhattan and Brooklyn. When it reached the Narrows, the *Seneca Chief* was met by the U.S. schooner *Porpoise*— a "Deputation from Neptune"—and Governor Clinton solemnized the "wedding of the waters" by pouring two casks of Erie water into the sea.

Everyone then returned to the Battery for a "Grand Procession" through the streets of Manhattan. As in the Federal Procession of 1788, the seven thousand marchers lined up in ranks, each "bearing their respective standards and the implements of their arts"—lawyers, physicians, militia officers, firemen, and artisans of every description—tangible affirmation that all elements of the social order endorsed the canal and understood its significance for the city's future. (Only the presence of some journeymen's societies, marching apart from the master craftsmen, hinted at the ongoing conflict in the shops.) Up Greenwich Street they marched, six abreast, to Canal and over to Broadway, up to Broome and across to the Bowery, and down Pearl to the Battery again, whence they rolled up Broadway to City Hall. As they marched they passed through a throng estimated at over one hundred thousand people—nearly two-thirds of the city's entire population. It was the largest such gathering ever witnessed in North America.

As night fell, New York came ablaze. Private houses and public buildings, theaters and hotels, coffeehouses and museums, all were brilliantly illuminated. Most impressive

Grand Canal Celebration, drawn by Archibald Robertson and lithographed by Anthony Imbert, 1826. The building in the background, called Castle Clinton when built as a harbor fortification in 1808, was now a theater known as Castle Garden. (I. N. Phelps Stokes Collection. Miriam and Ira D. Wallach Division of Art, Prints and Photographs. The New York Public Library. Astor, Lenox and Tilden Foundations)

was City Hall, lit up with 1,542 wax candles and 764 oil lamps and covered with glowing transparencies depicting the canal. At ten P.M. ten thousand people elbowed into the Park for a dazzling display of fireworks.

Cadwallader Colden (grandson of the colonial governor and one of the Erie Canal's most energetic promoters) boasted that "this extensive channel" would make New York "one of the greatest commercial cities in the world" before the end of the century. But even he underestimated the speed and scope of the canal's impact. Within the year, Erie boatmen were steering forty-two barges a day through Utica, bearing a thousand passengers, 221,000 barrels of flour, 435,000 gallons of whiskey, and 562,000 bushels of wheat. Shipping costs from Lake Erie to Manhattan plummeted from a hundred dollars a ton to under nine dollars. A few more years of this brought the annual value of freight transported along the canal up to fifteen million dollars, double that reaching New Orleans via the Mississippi; by mid-century the figure would approach two hundred million. Enough money would be collected in tolls—nearly half a million dollars the first year alone—to repay the cost of construction and help subsidize an additional six hundred miles of canals in the state over the next fifteen years.

At first, most of the goods cascading down the Erie Canal toward New York came from farms and villages along the canal's route. Its success inspired a frenzy of digging elsewhere in the country, however, and a burgeoning network of canals between western waterways and the Great Lakes soon drew more distant agricultural regions into the city's orbit: Ohio by 1830, Indiana by 1835, Michigan by 1836. Produce and timber that once rafted southward along the Ohio River now reversed course and headed east toward Manhattan. One collateral consequence was the transformation of agriculture on Long Island: when local wheat, barley, corn, and rye proved unable to compete with cereal grains from the West, Queens farmers switched to market gardening, raising potatoes, cabbage, peas, beans, asparagus, and tomatoes for booming Manhattan and Brooklyn.

The growing power of the New York market to pull commodities out of distant regions was confirmed by a trio of "anthracite canals" that funneled coal from the mines of northeastern Pennsylvania to Manhattan: the Delaware and Hudson Canal (1828), which linked the Lackawanna Valley to Kingston; the Morris Canal (1832), which connected the Lehigh Valley to Newark and Jersey City; and the Delaware and Raritan Canal (1834), which ran from Bordentown to New Brunswick.

UNDER STEAM AND SAIL

When Robert Fulton died in 1815, his fame as inventor of the steamboat earned him a hero's funeral in Trinity Church and the rare distinction of having his name attached to the streets that ran down to the Brooklyn Ferry terminals on both sides of the East River. Not everyone mourned his passing, however. A charter from the state legislature had given him and his partner, Robert Livingston, a monopoly of the steamboat business in New York. With the help of eminent lawyers like Thomas Addis Emmet and Cadwallader Colden, the duo had ruthlessly suppressed one competitor after another. Even Livingston's brother-in-law, Colonel John L. Stevens, couldn't get permission to operate a steamboat of his own design across the Hudson to develop his property near Hoboken. After both partners died, their company continued to swat down rivals, forcing them to settle for the use of horse ferries—a much slower form of transport that employed eight draft animals to drive a central water wheel. By 1820 many New Yorkers considered the Fulton-Livingston monopoly as annoying an obstacle to the city's growth as the swamps and escarpments that confronted engineers on the Erie Canal. But in this case it would be the United States Supreme Court, not pick and shovel, that would solve the problem.

Aaron Ogden, onetime governor of New Jersey, had purchased a franchise from the monopoly to operate a steamboat between Manhattan and Elizabethport, New Jersey. From there, passengers could continue to New Brunswick on a steamboat run by Thomas Gibbons, a tough and irascible lawyer from Savannah. Gibbons didn't need a New York franchise, because his route lay entirely within New Jersey. But in 1818 Gibbons and Ogden had a falling out. The Georgian decided to steam all the way to New York, in direct competition with Ogden and in open defiance of the monopoly. To pilot his vessel into these lawyer-infested waters, Gibbons turned to a lanky, quick-fisted young Staten Islander named Cornelius Vanderbilt.

Vanderbilt's family traced its New York origins to Jan Aertsen van der Bilt, who had arrived in Flatbush from Holland somewhere around 1650. In 1715 Jan's grandson established a farm near New Dorp, Staten Island, from where he and his descendants carried their produce to Manhattan markets in their own small boats. Cornelius, born in 1794 at Port Richmond on Kill van Kull, loathed farming, however. He escaped it by hauling freight and passengers in a flat-bottomed, two-masted periauger that the brawny six-footer poled through the marshes rimming the island. During the War of 1812 the sandy-haired young Dutchman made great profits delivering beef and firewood to blockaded Manhattan and also won a lucrative military contract to ferry supplies to the harbor's six forts. He gained a reputation for reliability, pugnacity, thriftiness (some said meanness), and world-class profanity. After the war, it was obvious to Vanderbilt that "b'ilers"—steamboats—were the wave of the future, and when Gibbons offered him command of his *Mouse of the Mountain*, he leapt at the chance. He dodged writs brandished by the monopoly's lawyers with such skill that Gibbons gave him the helm of a much larger boat, the 142-ton *Bellona*. Again, Vanderbilt successfully evaded sheriffs and process servers, darting into different Manhattan landings to offload passengers and hiding in secret onboard compartments to avoid the law.

When the enraged Ogden won an injunction against Gibbons and Vanderbilt from the New York courts, Gibbons hired Daniel Webster and appealed the case to the Supreme Court. A powerful current then running through American jurisprudence favored eliminating legal constraints on capitalist enterprise, and Chief Justice John Marshall was also eager to assert greater national authority over the states. Accordingly, in *Gibbons v. Ogden* (1824), the court ruled the monopoly unconstitutional on the grounds that only Congress could impose constraints on interstate commerce.

New York greeted the decision with enthusiasm, and within a year the number of steamboats serving the city jumped from six to forty-three. Steamer traffic on the East River, the Hudson River, and Long Island Sound grew so rapidly that competition between rival operators often degenerated into brawling and boat-ramming. It was a game Cornelius Vanderbilt soon proved he could play better than anyone else. By the end of the 1830s he had reestablished a degree of order in the business and was worth half a million dollars, making him one of the richest men in New York. People called him "the Commodore."

Steamboats, like the Erie Canal, ensured that the sprawling interior of the United States would remain within the economic orbit of New York. But no steam-powered vessel was yet capable of crossing the open sea, which meant that corresponding improvements in the city's ties to foreign markets—its ability to find buyers for huge quantities of Ohio wheat or Mississippi cotton while keeping up with the domestic demand for imports—would have to come by less conventional means.

One snowy day in January 1818, a small crowd gathered at the East River docks. Notices in local newspapers had promised that at an appointed date every month the new Black Ball Line would dispatch one of its four ships to Liverpool. "The regularity of their times of sailing, and the excellent condition in which they deliver their cargoes," it was said, "will make them very desirable opportunities for the conveyance of goods."

This innovation, the brainchild of Jeremiah Thompson, a transplanted English merchant, met with considerable skepticism. Traditionally, ships sailed only when their holds were full, and only in reasonably fair weather, so people turned out on the appointed day to see if the firm would make good. Despite the snow squall and a light cargo of passengers, mail, and fine freight, the square-rigged James Monroe weighed anchor precisely as St. Paul's clock struck ten. It reached Liverpool twenty-five days later. Battling in the opposite direction through westerly winter gales, its sister ship took forty-nine days to make New York.

The Black Ball's punctuality impressed Manchester magnates, who, with their capital tied up in plants and labor, could ill afford cotton shortages. It also attracted competitors. An eccentric Connecticut whaling captain named Preserved Fish and his cousin-partner Joseph Grinnell shifted from hawking New Bedford whale oil to running the Swallowtail line. Others followed, and within two decades fifty-two packets would be traveling regularly from New York to Liverpool and Le Havre, an average of three sailings weekly, with an average transit time of thirty-nine days.

The packets also carried human cargoes. At first, the lines sought only wealthy passengers; those with more limited means had to find a captain willing to take them in "steerage"—between decks, near the rudder. In 1815, however, Belfast merchants started-ed a full-time passenger trade, and after 1820 merchants in Liverpool began buying space on New York-bound packets, into which they stuffed the maximum number of immigrants (an art they had perfected in the slave trade). The result was that as more and more people left for the United States, more and more of them followed existing trade routes to New York. Between 1820 and 1832 the number of immigrants entering the port rose from thirty-eight hundred to some thirty thousand; in 1837 it swelled to nearly sixty thousand—almost 75 percent of the national total. Fed by this stream of humanity as well as internal migration, Manhattan's population climbed from 124,000 in 1820 to 166,000 in 1825 and 197,000 in 1830. By 1835 it exceeded 270,000. No other place in the country was growing so fast.

Joining the packets on the Atlantic run were ships flying the distinctive pennants of the city's principal commercial houses. Some of these, like LeRoy, Bayard, and Company, were venerable Knickerbocker establishments. But in the 1820s mercantile supremacy passed to New England Yankees: the Grinnells, Griswolds, Howlands, and Goodhues who had come down in the Napoleonic boom and a swarm of newcomers that now followed them.

The newcomers tended to specialize in particular commodities. Anson G. Phelps and Elisha Peck, originally from Hartford, opened a metal import firm in 1818. Phelps, in New York, shipped southern cotton to England. Peck, in Liverpool, used the proceeds from cotton sales to purchase tin plate, sheet copper, and brass wire, which he sent over to New York. Phelps then shipped the metal goods south by packet or, via the Erie Canal, upstate and out west to thousands of country stores. When Peck retired in 1832, Phelps partnered with another Connecticut Yankee, his son-in-law William Earl Dodge. Like Phelps, Dodge, and Company, the Tappan Brothers carved out a specialty niche in the European trade. Arthur Tappan moved from Boston to New York City in 1815. By 1827, when his brother Lewis came down to join him, he had built up the nation's largest silk-importing house, drawing on suppliers in England and Italy.

Other New York firms broke into new Latin American markets. Spain and Portugal's South American colonies had long been off limits to American traders, but now the creole revolutions were in full swing. John Jacob Astor ran guns and flour past Spanish blockades to revolutionary governments, a profitable if dangerous enterprise. With *independista* victories, a steadier and more sedate trade emerged: between 1816 and 1822 the number of ships returning to Manhattan from Central and South America rose from nine to fifty-two; by 1825 it had climbed to 111. In their holds were Brazilian coffee, hides from Argentina (a specialty of the De Forests), and Mexican silver (a speciality of Edward K. Collins). In exchange, the New Yorkers sent flour, domestic textiles, furniture, carriages, horses, and machinery for sugar mills. In manufactures, however, they were at a disadvantage because the British could better tailor their products to local markets. Despite President Monroe's insistence that Europeans should clear out of the hemisphere, British finance, British industry, British diplomacy, and the British navy remained paramount in the region.

In the Caribbean, however, British policy backfired. By stubbornly blocking American trade to Jamaica, as it had done since the Revolution, Britain succeeded only in destroying the island's economy while New York merchants moved on to new opportunities in Cuba and Puerto Rico. Though the islands were still Spanish possessions, the mother country had opened them up to free trade, lest they join South America in revolt. Proximity gave New Yorkers an advantage over their British rivals, and the city finally reestablished its old Caribbean lifeline. South Street commission merchants took up residence in Havana, Cuban planters fell into chronic debt, and Spain's former ward became an economic dependency of the United States in general, and of New York in particular.

In the 1820s the city also assumed the lead in trade between China and the United States. The Chinese preferred to be paid in silver or gold for their wares—those teas, silks, furniture, fabrics, and blue porcelain tureens, platters, and punch bowls so beloved by well-to-do New Yorkers. With no American mines to supply precious metals in quantity, merchants had to rely on expensive silver imports from Mexico, and they were always on the lookout for cheaper alternatives. Fur was one—which was why John Jacob Astor dominated the China trade in the postwar years. His American Fur Company shipped skins from Mackinac and St. Louis to company warehouses in New York, where clerks repacked them for shipment to Canton.

Another alternative to specie was opium, and in 1816 Astor became America's first large-scale drug dealer, smuggling five thousand pounds of Turkish opium from Smyrna to Canton. In the 1820s Astor shifted into other ventures and was replaced by Thomas H. Smith, a speculator who in 1826 brought in so much tea that he glutted the market and went bankrupt. By the early 1830s great firms like Griswold, Goodhue, Grinnell-Minturn, and Howland and Aspinwall were preeminent in the Pacific. These in turn gave way to the House of Low, launched in 1829 when Seth Low moved his business from Salem to New York. It would be brought to fruition by Abiel Abbot Low, the eldest of Seth's twelve children, who went out to Canton in 1833, spent seven years learning the business, and returned with enough contacts and market knowledge to dominate the industry. Yet here too the British remained the primary power, not least because the Empire controlled access to the opium of Bengal, while Astor and his successors were relegated to supplying an inferior Levantine product.

EMPORIUM

The web of canals, steamboats, and packets that New York flung out across the world in the 1820s and 1830s captured a wider and wider share of the nation's import business—from 38 percent in 1821 to 62 percent in 1836. It also brought an unprecedented multitude of ships into the harbor. One day in 1824 there were 324 at anchor off Manhattan, a huge number by comparison with prior years, but nothing in light of those to come. On a single day in 1836, 921 vessels lined the East River bulkhead, their bowsprits and carved figureheads looming over South Street, while another 320 bobbed along the Hudson (still known to sailors as the North River).

With this increased traffic came important changes in the scale, organization, and tempo of the city's commercial life. Dozens of new wharves, hastily constructed of hewn log frames filled with loose stone and earth, sprouted out from the shores of both the East River and the Hudson River, all tidily numbered (a practice that began in 1815, when the municipality began to rationalize the waterfront as it had the streets).[1] The

---

1. Cheap docks kept wharfage rates down, enhancing the port's competitiveness. They wore out quickly, however, and their narrow little basins, clogged with filth, became breeding grounds for disease. They were thus a far cry from the great enclosed stone piers of London—the West India Docks (1800–1806), London Docks (1800–5), East India Docks (1803–6), and the sumptuous new St. Katharine's Dock (1823) beside the Tower of London, which allowed direct unloading from ship to warehouse—all of which were linked directly with England's inland waterways via the new Regent's Canal (1812–20). But such enterprises were fantastically expensive—the London Dock Company alone spent 1.2 million pounds—and technically unnecessary in New York. The tides of the Thames

South Street from Maiden Lane, by William J. Bennett, c. 1828. Only a few years after the opening of the Erie Canal, activity along the East River waterfront had increased dramatically. That well-dressed family in the center appears ready to board the *Leeds*, one of the Swallowtail packets. (The Metropolitan Museum of Art, Bequest of Edward W.C. Arnold, 1954. The Edward W.C. Arnold Collection of New York Prints, Maps and Pictures)

auction system created a new breed of businessman, the wholesale merchant or "jobber," who bought, say, cheap imported British manufactured goods at auction and shipped them, on commission, to far-off country storekeepers via coastal packets and the Erie Canal. The low cost and abundance of these goods further spurred rural demand, inducing farmers to concentrate more and more heavily on the production of food and fuel for the Manhattan market—which in turn drew still more city merchants into the business. By 1840, in addition to the 417 commercial houses active in foreign trade, New York had 918 commission firms that consigned goods to domestic markets in every region of the country.

Every spring and fall, moreover, thousands of the most prosperous and adventuresome storekeepers converged on the city in person, prowling its countinghouses and auction rooms in search of bargains. The clamor for space in boardinghouses, inns, and the city's few hotels (only eight in 1818) attracted the attention of builders and investors, who flung up a score of new hotels during the 1820s and 1830s. Grandest of the lot was the six-story, three-hundred-room Park Hotel that John Jacob Astor opened on Broadway, directly west of City Hall Park, in 1836. Eventually renamed Astor House, it remained the nation's most prestigious hostelry for decades.

In 1827 two brothers from Switzerland named Giovanni and Pietro Del-Monico—

(and Liverpool's Mersey) rose and fell twenty feet. The vast dock enclosures were designed to accept vessels at high water and then, by closing their locks, keep them afloat when the tide receded. New York's rivers and estuaries fluctuated only four or five feet. This allowed the city to make do with less costly, less sightly, and less healthy versions.

the one a wine importer, the other a pastry chef—opened a shop on William Street with a half-dozen pine tables where customers could sample fine French pastries, coffee, chocolate, wine, and liquor. Three years later, the Delmonicos (as John and Peter now called themselves) opened a "Restaurant Français" next door that was among the first in town to let diners order from a menu of choices, at any time they pleased, and sit at their own cloth-covered tables. This was a sharp break from the fixed fare and simultaneous seatings at common hotel tables—so crowded (one guidebook warned) that your elbows were "pinned down to your sides like the wings of a trussed fowl." New Yorkers were a bit unsure about fancy foreign customs at first, and the earliest patrons tended to be resident European agents of export houses, who felt themselves marooned among a people with barbarous eating habits. The idea soon caught on, however; more restaurants appeared, and harried businessmen abandoned the ancient practice of going home for lunch.

Visitors and native New Yorkers alike shopped in retail outlets, another new and specialized institution. Previously, importers had sold off their ships, and artisans from their workshops. As importers withdrew from retail and artisans concentrated on production, the gap was filled by independent stores clustered on streets behind the waterfront and along fashionable Broadway, which sold sugar, coffee, hardware, and other commodities harvested by the city's merchants. After 1827 well-to-do consumers could stroll though the New York Arcade, a skylight-covered corridor shared by forty stores, which ran parallel to Broadway between Maiden Lane and John Street. Display methods too grew more sophisticated. Where an 1817 Broadway clothier simply hung samples of his ready-mades outside the door, leaving "the coat-tails and pantaloons" (one visitor warned) to "flap around the face of the pedestrian, like the low branches in a woodpath," by the 1830s, as another traveler observed, "plates of the newest London Fashions" were "displayed in the shop windows of every tailor in New York."

But it was a clutch of dry-goods stores that made the most lasting impression on the city's commercial history. In 1818 Connecticut-born Henry Sands Brooks founded a men's clothing store on Cherry Street, a waterfront location that he described as convenient to "the Gentry and Seafaring Men alike." (His sons, who inherited the concern on his death in 1833, would later adopt the name Brooks Brothers.) In 1825 Englishman Aaron Arnold opened a small Pine Street establishment dealing in "silks, woolens, laces, shawls, and novelties from Europe and the Orient." By the 1830s, when he took on James Mansell Constable as a partner, his thriving firm had relocated to Canal Street near Mercer. In 1826 another English immigrant, Samuel Lord, went partners with George Washington Taylor, his wife's cousin, to sell "plaid silks for misses' wear," hosiery, and "elegant Cashmere long shawls" at their Catherine Street store.

The proliferation of mercantile firms multiplied the number of clerks, bookkeepers, copiers, and errand boys: the Tappans alone had a clerical staff of more than twenty. Virtually all were males, many were sons of the merchant's kin or associates, and most were, in effect, merchants-in-training. Some labored over manifests and correspondence, seated on high stools and supervised by a chief clerk ensconced on a raised platform in the rear, rather like a ship's quarterdeck. Others were deployed as salesmen or dispatched to lodging houses to "drum up" sales from visiting storekeepers.

Manual as well as mental labor was required of these early white-collar workers. Before William Earl Dodge joined Anson Phelps as a partner, his clerical duties had included fetching water from the pump at Peck and Pearl with which to sweep the sidewalk, putting out refuse to be collected by the city's "dirt-carts," taking letters to the post office, delivering goods, stocking shelves, and distributing handbills in the streets. Still heavier labor could be demanded. When longshoremen hauled barrels, bales, crates, or sacks out of ships' holds, they lugged them across the wharves to South Street. There cartmen set them on horse-drawn wagons and rumbled them through crowded cobbled streets to the warehouses, where the clerks winched them up and in, using a thick hemp cable strung over a hoisting wheel.

The mercantile firms that housed all this activity bulked ever larger on the cityscape, growing in size as well as complexity. By the 1820s three- to five-story office buildings and warehouses cost as much as a brig. By the late 1830s some cost as much as a full-rigged ship. Their style changed too, from Georgian brick to granite-faced Greek Revival (the earliest example of which, designed by Ithiel Town for Arthur and Lewis Tappan, went up on Pearl Street at Hanover Square in 1829). In 1832 Phelps and Peck built a new store and warehouse that towered six stories over the corner of Cliff and Fulton. It was one of the wonders of the city—until it collapsed under the weight of cotton bales within, killing seven clerks.

Similarly, because the mounting volume and complexity of commercial transactions made it inefficient to conduct business in coffeehouses, city merchants responded eagerly when William Backhouse Astor (John Jacob's son) and Stephen Whitney pro-

Bowne & Co.'s stationery shop on Pearl Street, c. 1830.
As in other retail establishments, its clerks not only
dealt with customers but hoisted wares for storage on
the building's upper floors. (Bowne & Co. Stationers,
South Street Seaport Museum)

posed construction of a building where they might "transact in a few minutes, the business, which, if each were to seek the other at his counting-house, would require as many hours to accomplish." By 1827 the two had raised a hundred thousand dollars for a new Merchants' Exchange on Wall Street. Faced in Westchester marble, the neoclassical building boasted a fifteen-foot-high statue of Alexander Hamilton in its grand rotunda and a cavernous Exchange Room, as well as rooms for auction sales of real estate and stocks, a post office, and the Chamber of Commerce.

New York's attractiveness as a marketplace was further enhanced by the adoption of gas lighting in the mid-twenties. Nobody liked the smoky oil lamps—few in number and not much brighter than lightning bugs—that had provided unreliable illumination on Manhattan thoroughfares since the 1760s. When Baltimore became the first American city to install gas lights, following the example of London, the Common Council decided to try an experiment. In 1816 a crude gasworks was set up near City Hall and tin pipes run down to several street lamps and store windows on Broadway. Merchants loved the new system, but opposition from tallow interests and a dispute over the merits of public versus private development delayed further action. Finally, in 1823, the city awarded a franchise to the New York Gas-Light Company, a private firm organized by banker Samuel Leggett and others. By early 1825 the company had a gasworks up and running at Hester and Rhynder—one of the largest edifices in the city—and over the next couple of years it ran cast-iron lines into the principal commercial streets. First to be lit was Broadway from the Battery up to Grand Street, soon followed by Wall, Pearl, Broad, William, Nassau, and Maiden Lane. The city paid for installing the street lamps, for "fitting" them up to the mains, and for gas consumed. Office buildings, fine stores, and plush hotels arranged their own connections, and printed warnings—"Don't Blow Out the Gas!"—began appearing on the bedroom walls of up-to-date hostelries.

By the early 1830s, as Frances Trollope noted, many of the city's retail shops, now brilliantly illuminated, stayed open as late as those of London and Paris, giving New York a lively nighttime appearance in marked contrast to Philadelphia's. The contrast with other parts of New York City was equally striking. The gas company did lay mains under residential streets, but only fashionable (hence profitable) ones, leaving most neighborhoods, especially the working-class wards on the east side, blanketed in a darkness punctured only feebly by oil lamps.

THE WORD FROM MANHATTAN

In 1815 New York newspapers still closely resembled their colonial predecessors in form and function. Aimed primarily at merchants, their pages featured lists of ship arrivals and departures, current wholesale prices, money conversion rates, stock and bond quotations, real estate transactions, and—in long columns of minute type—"advertisements" placed by wholesalers, retailers, patent medicine vendors, and transport companies. Many, though not all, contained accounts of events in Albany or Washington or Europe (often clipped from papers elsewhere and typically well out of date), extracts from congressional speeches, and political editorials. None could claim to have many readers. In 1820 the two largest papers in New York were the *Commercial Advertiser*, edited by Colonel William Leete Stone, and the *Evening Post*, Alexander Hamilton's old sheet, still edited by William Coleman. Neither sold more than two thousand copies daily.

Over the next decade, however, publishers awoke to the fact that no other city in the country was receiving better information about distant markets and conditions, or getting it faster—or making more money from it. In 1824 the price of cotton in Liverpool shot up unexpectedly. When the news reached New York a few weeks later via the Black Ball Line, its owner, Jeremiah Thompson, dispatched agents by fast pilot boat to New Orleans, where they turned a quick profit buying cotton at the old price from unsuspecting suppliers. Stories like this, repeated over and over as canals and steamboats quickened the flow of intelligence toward Manhattan, whetted the entrepreneurial imaginations of a new generation of publishers. By 1830 New York had forty-seven newspapers, eleven of them dailies, each determined to bring the news to its readers ahead of the others.

Semaphore or "telegraph" poles on Staten Island, visible by telescope from the Battery, already signaled the arrival of packets from Europe off Sandy Hook, and another semaphore, atop the Exchange, was adjusted accordingly, relaying the information to all interested parties. Impatient and aggressive editors now dispatched swift news boats to dart out and retrieve the latest overseas intelligence in time for an extra edition; some even ordered construction of schooners that could range a hundred miles into the open sea to intercept incoming vessels. For domestic news, they arranged teams of relay riders and steamboats that could make the trip up from Washington, Baltimore, and Philadelphia in a couple of days or less.

Most influential of the new papers was the *Courier and Enquirer* (1829), the offspring of a strange political marriage between James Watson Webb, editor of the *Morning Courier*, and Mordecai M. Noah, editor of the *Enquirer*. Bellicose and supercilious, Webb, a West Point graduate, had fought in the War of 1812, fought Indians in the Northwest, and fought duels with fellow officers. He also loathed blacks, Irish immigrants, and Jews—especially, among the latter category, Mordecai Noah. Noah had moved to New York after a brief diplomatic career and established himself as a journalist, playwright, and Tammany influential. Appointed interim high sheriff of New York in 1821, he failed to win relection the following year when opponents raised a rumpus about having a Jew supervise the hanging of Christians. ("Pretty Christians to need hanging at all" was Noah's tart retort.) In 1825 Noah proposed to found a refuge for Jews of the world on an island in the Niagara River and proclaimed himself "high sheriff of the Jews." When that project failed, he turned to editing the *Enquirer*, with the aid of a squint-eyed Scotsman named James Gordon Bennett. After Noah supported Andrew Jackson for president in 1828, the victorious Jackson appointed him "surveyor and inspector of the New York Port," a sinecure that allowed him to continue editing the *Enquirer*. But Webb too had backed Jackson, and in 1829 party pressure forced the two editors to combine their papers.

The new *Courier and Enquirer* became the largest and most powerful paper in the United States, famous for the lengths to which Webb would go to scoop his rivals. In 1830 he contrived to get his hands on the text of President Jackson's annual message to Congress in twenty-seven and a half hours. But this coup failed to discourage Arthur Tappan's *Journal of Commerce* (1827), which retaliated with an express system of twenty-four horses that covered the distance from Washington to New York in twenty hours flat. The *Journal's* readers were often privy to the proceedings of Congress and news from the South as much as two days ahead of everyone else.

New York's hegemony as a clearinghouse for foreign and domestic news pulled in subscribers from every part of the country and compelled editors elsewhere to cannibalize Manhattan papers for stories. By 1828 160,000 newspapers were shipped out monthly through the New York post office; by 1833 nearly a million. In 1838 some two tons of mail left each day for the South alone, three-fourths of it printed matter.

Not surprisingly, and for many similar reasons, it was during these same years that Manhattan became the center of book publishing in the United States. New York's leading authors—Irving, Paulding, Halleck, and two newcomers in the 1820s, James Fenimore Cooper and William Cullen Bryant—now commanded national audiences, and the printers who brought out their books were handsomely rewarded; one, Charles Wiley, did so well that he became a full-time publisher. The big money, however, came from pirated editions of English authors (who didn't have to be paid royalties because the United States government refused as yet to recognize foreign copyrights). Printers and book dealers in New York and Philadelphia competed furiously to bring out the first American editions of new English novels. Some sent agents to England with orders to grab volumes from bookstalls, or sheets from printshops, and ship them west by fast packet. Copy was then rushed from the dock to the composing room, presses run night and day, and books hurried to the stores or hawked in the streets like hot corn.

No one was better at this than the Harper brothers of New York. Their firm began as a printshop in 1817 and evolved over the next decade into a full-time publishing house that kept popular titles in circulation (birthing the backlist). On one celebrated occasion, borrowing techniques from the newspaper trade, the Harpers retrieved the third volume of Walter Scott's *Peveril of the Peak* from a packet before it docked. Working nonstop, they got the finished product to the bookstalls twenty-one hours later, well in advance of the edition issued in Philadelphia by Mathew Carey. It was the Harpers, too, who became the first American commercial publishers to make effective use of stereotyping, a printing process brought to the United States from England in 1811 that was ideal for books frequently reprinted in large editions.

What really assured New York of an unassailable lead in the book trade was cheap and easy access to western readers via the Erie Canal. Every fall, just before the onset of winter, and then again in the spring—a seasonal pattern that still rules the industry—city publishers dispatched crate after crate of books via the canal to retailers scattered across upstate New York, around the Great Lakes, and along the Ohio and Mississippi rivers. Like small-town newspaper editors, local book printers were hard-pressed to compete with the low prices and big-name authors offered by their Manhattan counterparts. The canal helped make it clear, indeed, that selling books wasn't so very different from peddling hats or chamber pots, and the business soon attracted men who knew nothing about printing but had a talent for marketing. Daniel Appleton, for one, was a Massachusetts storekeeper who moved to New York in 1825 and began to sell books along with groceries. He prospered and by 1831 had decided to become a publisher.

INDUSTRIAL REVOLUTIONS

After 1815, if not earlier, the greatest concentration of shipbuilding facilities in the United States lay along the shores of the East River, two or three miles above the Battery. On the Manhattan side, circling around Corlear's Hook, were the yards of Foreman Cheeseman, Charles Brownne, Henry Eckford, Christian Bergh, Adam and Noah Brown, and other principal builders—piled high with stacks of fresh-cut white oak, live oak, locust, and cedar (some now brought down the canal), the air fragrant with the smells of pitch, tar, and burning coke in the blacksmiths' forges. Directly across the river, at the mouth of Wallabout Creek, sprawled the rapidly growing Brooklyn Navy Yard, which in 1815 launched the *Fulton* (the inventor's war frigate) and in 1820 the *Ohio*, the country's first ship of the line and its largest vessel yet. All told, they would send a prodigious number and variety of vessels down the ways over the next couple of decades—sturdy packets for the Black Ball Line, sharp brigs and schooners for the China trade, swift slavers that could outrun naval patrols, warships for the navies of several different nations, and steamboats by the score.

At first glance, the basic processes of shipbuilding hadn't changed much over the previous century or more. Vessels of every description were still constructed by teams of leather-aproned axmen, carpenters, riggers, caulkers, and other craftsmen, employing tools and materials and techniques known to their trades for generations. To control costs and keep pace with demand, however, leading builders had already taken the first steps toward a more factory-like organization of their yards. Where smaller firms made hulls and subcontracted out the final stages of construction—making and raising masts, painting hulls, finishing cabins—to the city's host of independent specialists, the bigger yards hired the necessary workmen directly, in some cases boosting the number of their employees to several hundred or more. They added specialized buildings, covered the ways with sheds, and embraced the use of steam power to drive saws, derricks, and pumps. The Browns even built a boardinghouse for two hundred apprentices. In 1824 several of the biggest builders banded together to form the New York Dry Dock Company, which was incorporated, given banking privileges, and capitalized at seven hundred thousand dollars the following year. By 1826 trials had begun on a three-hundred-foot-long inclined marine railway, installed at the foot of East 10th Street, capable of pulling vessels out of the water for repairs and application of copper sheathing to their hulls.

The transformation of shipbuilding on the East River owed much to the vision and diligence of James Allaire, a gifted mechanic who had worked on Fulton's first steamboat. Allaire proved so adept at assembling engines shipped from England that he began to build them himself. When Fulton died, Allaire purchased the Fulton-Livingston engine shop in Jersey City and moved it to his ironworks on Cherry Street, close to the Corlear's Hook shipyards. The yards awarded him contract after contract (in 1818 he turned out the *Bellona* for Gibbons and Vanderbilt), his designs became larger and more elaborate, and by 1829, with hundreds of employees, Allaire had become the premier manufacturer of engines and boilers in the country.

Nor was shipbuilding the only industry in New York to be transformed by the introduction of steam power or the reorganization of production into larger and larger units. Ropewalks and sugar refineries experienced comparable changes, as did the leather-making business, aided by an influx of hides from Argentina (Gideon Lee's New York Tannery Company was capitalized at sixty thousand dollars). Printing too was transformed: in 1823 Jonas Booth printed an *Abridgment of Murray's English Grammar*, the first American book manufactured by steam power; in 1830 Robert Hoe imported the country's first Napier cylinder press, then improved it, and soon Harpers was using the new machine in a four-story plant on Cliff Street. By 1824 a sixteen-acre site on the north shore of Staten Island was occupied by a textile dye and printing works that employed 150 hands and had become the center of a growing community named Factoryville (later West New Brighton). Visiting dignitaries hailed it with a toast to "the

Ladies and Gentlemen of New York and its vicinity—may they all resolve to dye on Staten Island."

But the industrial revolution in New York wasn't primarily about big machinery and factories. The great bulk of manufacturing after 1815 took place in small frame or brick houses near the waterfront, without steam power or other elaborate equipment, and typically involved the production of light consumer goods—shoes, furniture, and clothing—for wholesalers or auction houses. After 1815 Brooklyn was a beehive of small shops that churned out playing cards, pocketbooks, combs, tinware, patent leather, iron chests, marble mantles, mustard, writing ink, pencil cases, white lead, paint, glass, and more. It was exactly in places such as these, moreover, that the decay of artisanal skills and traditions advanced most quickly as masters-turned-employers— among them Duncan Phyfe, now a wealthy furniture manufacturer—struggled to get ahead at the expense of their employees. Ambitious shoemakers, for example, coped with competition from New England factory towns by packing their workrooms with low-paid apprentices, distributing cheap leather to journeyman outworkers, and hiring women and girls as binders.

The process was particularly quick and brutal in the men's clothing trade. Before 1820 the bulk of the male population wore clothes made at home by their wives, mothers, and daughters or made to order by custom tailors. Only poor seamen, laborers, apprentices, and hapless bachelors wore the cheap ready-made clothing known as "slops." Between 1825 and 1835, however, New York wholesalers, auctioneers, and jobbers presided over the creation of a huge new national market in men's ready-mades. Local retailers and country storekeepers received generous credit to stock up on "negro cottons" for slaves and dungarees for farmers and miners, as well as slops for the urban working classes. Manufacturers, who were likewise given easy terms for the purchase of raw materials, stepped up production by expanding the number of women employed. As they worked in their own households, "outwork" saved on overhead (no small consideration at a time when real estate was becoming more and more expensive), and it avoided the managerial and disciplinary problems presented by a large, concentrated workforce. Female outwork was particularly attractive because it saved on wages—the wages of women were less than half those of men—while reinforcing the conventional wisdom that a woman's place was in the home. By the 1830s some New York shops had five hundred women on the payroll, and men's garment making had become one of the city's (and the nation's) most important industries.

WALL STREET

Western farmers and southern planters, notoriously cash-poor, usually bought goods from country storekeepers on credit—who in turn acquired their stock from wholesale jobbers in New York, also on credit. Although this chain of indebtedness was good for business, it also left New York creditors waiting for payment, usually until harvest time. Commercial banks solved the problem by turning accounts payable into cash. A Pearl Street jobber, for example, might send a thousand dollars' worth of goods to an Ohio storekeeper. He would include a bill requesting payment in ninety days, which the Ohioan would sign and return to New York. The jobber could now wait three months and (hopefully) collect his full thousand. Or he could take the storekeeper's promissory note to a bank and get, say, $950 immediately—his thousand less the percentage (or "discount") charged by the bank—thereby gaining immediate access to most of his capital. When necessary, the jobber could also borrow from the bank to replenish his stock, or even purchase goods with a bank draft or "check" drawn against his account (a service that was becoming quite common in the early decades of the nineteenth century).

In 1815 there were only five banks in the city—among them Hamilton's Bank of New York and Burr's Bank of the Manhattan Company—and their boards were top-heavy with old-stock Knickerbocker merchants who preferred loaning money only among themselves. The relentless expansion of domestic and international trade created a demand for new banks, however, and within the next two decades eighteen more would extract charters from the legislature (including one created in 1824 by the directors of a Hudson River chemical plant, who dubbed it the Chemical Bank).

In theory, these institutions kept their credit under tight control, following the conservative precepts of a banker and banking philosopher named Isaac Bronson. Bronson had come down from Connecticut after the Revolution, made a fortune speculating in securities, and become one of New York's ten wealthiest men. To his way of thinking, banks should provide only short-term credit (no longer than ninety days) and accept only the best collateral (actual goods in transit). Nor should banks give their money to farmers, manufacturers, and other high-risk borrowers: that was a job for independent investors.

Because their counterparts elsewhere tended to be less cautious with their assets, New York bankers wanted Congress to create a new national bank that could rein in irresponsible lenders and stabilize the country's financial system. John Jacob Astor, having invested heavily in federal securities during the War of 1812, helped secure the legislation that established the second Bank of the United States in 1816.

Headquartered in Philadelphia, the BUS was to be the fiscal agent of the federal government—holding its revenues, paying its bills, and ensuring a uniform currency. As a central bank, it would restrain state banks' lending by refusing to accept their notes if not adequately backed with specie and by demanding payment as soon as it did accept them. It also had the authority to open offices in other parts of the country. Astor, a director of the parent body, became the first president of the Manhattan branch.

Disaster struck the national bank almost immediately. In the get-rich-quick climate of 1817–18, Astor and his friend Stephen Girard of Philadelphia, the two most conservative members of its board, lost control to incompetent and corrupt plungers who issued loans far in excess of reserves. When swooning cotton prices on the European market brought sudden ruin to thousands of unwary land and commodity speculators, the BUS called in its loans to overextended state banks—which then demanded payment from their customers. A financial panic swept the nation in 1819, followed by two or three years of deflation and stagnation that caused great suffering in the South and West. Although the BUS survived, it was widely blamed for the crisis; some casualties, among them a planter named Andrew Jackson, vowed revenge.

In the meantime, a new kind of bank was making its New York debut, summoned into existence to help finance the Erie Canal. The legislature had resolved to pay for the project by selling bonds, but commercial banks as well as wealthy individual investors hung back, unconvinced they would get their money back if the canal failed (all the more so once the panic started). To solve this problem, William Bayard, John Pintard, Thomas Eddy, and other canal men proposed creation of a savings bank. Its capital would consist entirely of deposits made by working people, and it would be allowed to invest only in government securities—thus encouraging thrift among the improvident classes and having them bear risks that the rich considered unacceptable. In 1819, impressed by the ingenuity of this scheme, the legislature chartered the Bank for Savings in the City of New York; within five years it boasted thirty thousand depositors and assets of $1.5 million and was the single largest holder of Erie bonds. More savings banks weren't far behind—the Seamen's Bank for Savings (1829), Greenwich Savings Bank (1833), and Bowery Savings Bank (1834), among others.

Concurrent with the appearance of savings banks was the advent of a second new institution, the investment bank. Its story centers on the stout, short figure of Nathaniel Prime. A onetime coachman to a Boston merchant, Prime had arrived in New York in 1795. He made money buying and selling bank stocks; married Cornelia Sands, daughter of a wealthy merchant; and became a private banker, holding customers' funds on deposit and loaning them money. As the business grew, he took in partners—first Samuel Ward, scion of an aristocratic New England family, then the commission merchant James Gore King. In the early twenties the firm moved into loan contracting, a field that Astor's syndicate had pioneered during the war when it bought government bonds wholesale and sold them retail (a radical departure from the previous practice of selling new issues of stocks or bonds directly to purchasers). Prime, Ward, and King applied the same technique to Erie Canal bonds, buying up large quantities for resale to their clients.

Among their best clients was the highly respected Baring Brothers firm of London. Britain's leading "American house," the Barings had sold the bonds of the young republic since its foundation, helped it finance the purchase of Louisiana, and acted on its behalf even during the War of 1812. In 1823 the Barings bought their first Erie Canal bonds from Prime, Ward, and King. Eager British investors snapped them up, and the Barings began to buy more. Other financial houses jumped in, and by 1829 a majority of Erie Canal debt was owned overseas.

Prime, Ward, and King moved on to underwrite internal improvements in the American West. The firm purchased bond issues offered by Ohio, Louisiana, and Mississippi and retailed them to London banking houses. The Bank for Savings too looked west, financing a canal that connected Cleveland, on Lake Erie, with Portsmouth, on the Ohio River. These initiatives were not only fabulously profitable in themselves, but they also ensured the diversion of more and more commerce toward the Erie Canal.

New York's prominence in national and international banking was enhanced by yet another canal-related phenomenon: the quickening tempo of trade on the floor of the Tontine Coffee House stock exchange. In 1817, no longer content with the old "Buttonwood Agreement" of 1792, the city's several dozen brokers had formed the New York Stock and Exchange Board, tapping Nathaniel Prime to serve as its first president. The ability of the reorganized market to attract capital was confirmed by the millions of dollars that soon poured through the doors of the Coffee House in pursuit of canal stocks—not only those of the Erie but of private ventures like the Delaware and Hudson (whose promoters set up a grate in the Coffee House to demonstrate the value of anthracite coal as a fuel). The profitable and regular trading in canal securities gave new vitality to Manhattan's capital markets, but the Exchange also proved a source of instability. In 1825 unscrupulous dealers whipsawed the stocks of the Morris Canal and Banking Company, driving the price up and down until the entire market broke under the strain and required several years to recover fully.

Rampant speculation could be good for the banks, however. Speculators borrowed heavily from bankers, who were happy to make "call" loans—payable whenever the bank "called" or demanded repayment—because the stocks that served as collateral could be sold without difficulty. It was a wonderfully profitable business, and it enabled New York banks to pay higher rates of interest than those in other cities. This in turn induced out-of-town "correspondent" banks to leave their excess funds in Manhattan, swelling the amount available for loans to speculators.

By 1830—less than two decades after construction began on the Erie Canal—New York had overtaken Philadelphia as the nation's premier money market. Its banks controlled significantly more capital (and were safer too, because the state had just established an insurance fund to guarantee notes issued by member banks). The New York Stock and Exchange Board handled a greater volume of stocks, and its prices, quoted in newspapers throughout the country, were now the norm everywhere. So, too, the collective assets of the city's insurance companies exceeded those of Philadelphia, Boston, and Baltimore combined.

New York's ascendancy in finance inspired a burst of architectural assertiveness along Wall Street, which like Pearl Street got a facelift during the 1820s. No longer satisfied with quarters in renovated private residences, some dating from before the Revolution, prosperous bankers and brokers now demanded proper offices of suitable scale and grandeur. In 1825 Martin Euclin Thompson, a carpenter turned architect-builder, finished a monumental Federal-style building for the Branch of the Bank of the United States (its sixty-foot facade now stands in the American Wing of the Metropolitan Museum of Art). Two years later, in 1827, the Stock and Exchange Board moved into Thompson's new Merchants' Exchange, and he completed a new home for the Phoenix Bank that was the city's first taste of the new Greek Revival style in architecture, rivaling the BUS headquarters on Chestnut Street in Philadelphia.

It was the latter institution, in fact, that presented the only obstacle to New York's complete domination of the nation's finances. Although conservative New York bankers applauded BUS commitment to a stable currency, they chafed at regulations constraining their own freedom of action and squirmed when the giant bank undercut their interest rates, putting downward pressure on profits. Most galling of all was the knowledge that the BUS continued to serve as the depository for the revenues of the federal government, although the great bulk of these came from customs receipts collected at the Port of New York. Like Andrew Jackson, the New Yorkers watched and waited for a chance to strike back.

LAND LORDS

Speculation in western lands was an old game for Manhattan merchants with extra money in their pockets, and the very thought of the Erie Canal, lancing toward the Great Lakes through mile after mile of prime real estate, had them quivering with temptation. Every year the canal advanced, tens of thousands of acres along its route were feverishly bought, sold, and sold again by many of the same men who at first shunned canal stock as too risky an investment. The mercantile house of LeRoy and Bayard acquired over three hundred thousand acres; De Witt Clinton himself bought up choice parcels he expected to rise in value with the completion of his big ditch.

None did more than banker Isaac Bronson to make an exact science of the business. Going beyond mere speculation, Bronson employed local businessmen, judges, and politicians to steer him toward the best land. He then resold it to farmers, granting five-year mortgages at 6 percent to those whose financial standing his agents had scrutinized and certified. By the early 1820s Bronson owned or held mortgages on property in over half the counties of the state. His enterprise was so solid that conservative bankers like Prime, Ward, and King invested substantial sums with him.

For the adventurous speculator, though, there was still no place like home. Manhattan land values had risen 750 percent between the Revolution and the War of 1812, and with the Erie Canal in place the future looked even more promising. Plenty of land awaited development in the rolling countryside north of 14th Street. But much of it was tightly held—either by assorted Stuyvesants and Brevoorts and Dyckmans, descendants of seventeenth- and eighteenth-century landowners, or by merchants and artisans who had acquired their estates in the Revolutionary era and fiercely clung to them as talismans of gentility. Although a few speculators got their hands on parcels here and there during the 1820s, new purchasers often hung on to their lands for rural retreats. Scottish merchant Robert Lenox, for one, bought thirty uptown acres between 68th and 74th streets, put up a country house, and refused to sell or develop his new estate.

Downtown was a different story. Astor, who before the war had amassed substantial holdings just above the settled city, now prepared for new arrivals. In 1820 he had Aaron Burr's old Richmond Hill mansion rolled downhill on logs to a site on the corner of Charlton and Varick streets. In 1822, to lend tone to the neighborhood, he reopened it as a "public house, with a Music Room, Reading Room, newspapers, gardens, wines, liquores, etc." He then leveled the hill, opened streets Burr had previously charted, and sold or leased lots to carpenters and masons, who erected row after row of houses on speculation. By the mid-twenties this once remote neighborhood was full of people, and Astor had multiplied his initial investment many times over.

Astor's prescience seemed about to be rewarded again in the village of Greenwich, where he had been amassing real estate ever since 1805, until planned development touched off a vigorous backlash, led by a most unlikely agitator. Clement Clarke Moore was a conservative Knickerbocker whose father had been Episcopal bishop of the Diocese of New York for thirty-five years. Clement too was deeply involved in church affairs, and a classical scholar as well. He was also proprietor of Chelsea, the largest estate in the area, which consisted mainly of open countryside. When the city, obedient to the commissioners' 1811 grid plan, thrust Ninth Avenue through the middle of his property in 1818, Moore penned an indignant pamphlet. Addressing his fellow "Proprietors of Real Estate," he decried urban development as a destructive conspiracy by patronage-hungry and politically well connected "cartmen, carpenters, masons, pavers and all their host of attendant laborers." More galling still, the city was taxing Moore to pay for this and other street openings, in effect compelling him "to become a capitalist for the public"—a tyranny "no monarch in Europe would dare to exercise."

The Common Council backed down in 1818, agreeing not to extend the grid into the area west of Sixth Avenue from Houston Street up to 14th—a corner of Manhattan still famed for the eccentric and baffling pattern of its streets. Two years later the victorious Moore helped Trinity organize a parish church on Hudson Street. Its name—St. Luke's in the Fields—evoked the pastoral nature of the area and, by association with the physician-apostle, Greenwich's role as haven for the multitudes fleeing disease in the city. It proved all too apt a name.

In 1822 yellow fever again broke out in New York, this time on the stylish streets west of Broadway and near the Battery, supposedly the healthiest part of town. The municipal government declared everything below City Hall an "infected district" and established a picket-fence barricade along Chambers Street. Thousands of residents fled north. "From daybreak till night one line of carts, containing boxes, merchandise, and effects, were seen moving towards Greenwich Village," one paper reported. The city pitched tents for refugees, and carpenters hastily erected hundreds of wooden houses.

Although many refugees went home when the fever broke, enough stayed on that local builders had their hands full trying to keep up with the demand for housing. St. Luke's trustees had carpenter James Wells flank the church with brick row houses, which it maintained as rental property, while Hudson Street filled with residences equipped with such middle-class conveniences as brass grates for burning the new anthracite coal, brick cisterns with pumps, and servants' apartments. Smaller houses went up on other streets to accommodate a burgeoning number of artisans, especially the carpenters, masons, painters, and stonecutters employed in the booming construction trades. Christopher Street was paved and its sidewalks flagged by 1825, and the blocks around Newgate Prison became so residential that no one complained when the state shut it down in 1829 (having just opened a new facility, Sing Sing, up the river at Ossining).

North of 14th Street, meanwhile, even Clement Clark Moore had begun to play the landlord, carving out lots along Ninth Avenue and promoting them to genteel purchasers. To provide a community anchor, Moore gave the Episcopal diocese an apple orchard lying west of Ninth between 20th and 21st streets, where construction of the General Theological Seminary got under way in 1827; a second Moore-donated parcel, along 20th Street east of Ninth, became the site of the elegant St. Peter's Episcopal Church a decade later.

Astor's successes at Richmond Hill and Greenwich would be duplicated a mile or so to the east, where in 1804 he had purchased a large garden farm near what is now Astor Place. A Frenchman named Delacroix then leased the site from Astor to build Vauxhall Gardens, a resort for fashionable New Yorkers that offered leafy walks, pavilions serving juleps and ice cream, bands, theatrical entertainments, and fireworks. By 1809 the city had extended and paved Broadway all the way up to Vauxhall, and by 1820 streets just to the south—Bleecker, Bond, and Great Jones—were rapidly filling up with genteel residents. In 1825, when the Vauxhall lease expired, Astor cut a broad street through the gardens that he named Lafayette Place, in honor of the Revolutionary War hero (who had just paid a return visit to the city.) Lots along both sides of Lafayette Place sold briskly, earning Astor many times what he had paid for the property twenty-one years before.

By 1830, now in his late sixties, Astor had become the richest man in the United States—almost as rich, according to certain estimates, as European magnates like the duke of Bedford, Sir Francis Baring, and Nathan Rothschild. He had also created something akin to a perpetual moneymaking machine. Between 1800 and 1820 he invested $715,000 in Manhattan real estate, roughly two-thirds of which had come out of the profits of his fur and tea businesses. Between 1820 and 1835 he purchased another $445,000 worth of land on the island, but most of this sum derived from the sale, lease, or rental of property he already owned. By 1830 he had pulled out of the China trade entirely, sold his interest in the American Fur Company, and was running a real estate operation that employed a sizable staff of rental agents, contractors, accountants, book-keepers, and lawyers—all overseen by his son, the colorless but meticulous William Backhouse Astor, who could recite the family's rent rolls by heart. Between 1835 and his death in 1848, Astor and his son would put another $832,000 into New York real estate, a sum generated entirely from rents on existing properties. Small wonder that he is supposed to have said, just before he died: "Could I begin life again, knowing what I now know, and had money to invest, I would buy every foot of land on the Island of Manhattan."

ON THE HEIGHTS OF BROOKLYN

Across the East River, another speculative drama was unfolding on Brooklyn Heights. Hezekiah Beers Pierrepont, grandson of a minister-founder of Yale, had come south from New England, made good money speculating in the national debt, founded a mercantile firm in 1793 that exported provisions to Paris, and in 1802 married Anna Marie Constable, whose father, William Constable, one of the largest landowners in the state, gave the couple half a million acres as a wedding present. Abandoning commerce for manufacturing, Pierrepont bought Philip Livingston's gin distillery at the foot of modern Joralemon Street and added a large wharf, a windmill, and storehouses. His Anchor Gin proved successful, but in 1819, after competitors diluted his profits, he abandoned the business. By then he had discovered his true calling, land development.

Pierrepont began purchasing property on Clover Hill, the bluff overlooking Brooklyn Village, eventually amassing sixty acres, including an eight-hundred-foot stretch overlooking the harbor. His plan was to subdivide the property into large plots on which wealthy merchants and professionals could build substantial houses. But Pierrepont knew that (unlike Astor) he couldn't expect the right kinds of buyer to appear unless they were pulled in from across the river. His realtor rivals John and Jacob Hicks, descendants of a Dutch artisanal family, faced no such problem. They too had been acquiring property on Brooklyn Heights, to the north of Pierrepont's holdings, but their intention was to create numerous small lots, cheap enough for the tradesmen and artisans who already lived down by the ferry landing.

Pierrepont's vision of the future began to look more promising in 1814, when his good friend Robert Fulton formed the New York and Brooklyn Steam Ferry Boat Company. Pierrepont eagerly contributed money and influence, knowing that improved transportation to New York would do wonders for Brooklyn real estate values, and after Fulton's death he became a part owner and director of the operation. Soon the *Nassau*—the East River's first steam ferry—was shuttling people, carriages, and wagons back and forth to Brooklyn forty times a day, each trip lasting a mere four to eight minutes.

In 1816 Pierrepont and a committee of prominent Brooklyn residents successfully petitioned the state legislature for a village charter, which authorized a new board of trustees to open streets, build sidewalks, install water pumps, and establish a watch—much-needed improvements that would enhance Brooklyn's image among affluent New Yorkers. When the trustees received a street plan that favored the Hickses' vision of development, Pierrepont hired his own surveyor, worked up an alternative proposal, and got it adopted for the area south of Clark Street, leaving the Hickses predominant above that line. Pierrepont likewise blocked the powerful Schermerhorns from establishing a ropewalk in his part of the Heights, forcing them (and their workers) over to what is now Schermerhorn Street.

Pierrepont's readiness to combine the roles of land speculator, local politician, and community booster—so unlike Astor, who preferred to work behind the scenes—began to pay off during the yellow fever epidemic that struck New York in 1822. Like Greenwich, Brooklyn received an influx of well-to-do refugees (the steam ferry *Nassau* skipped downtown Manhattan and plied back and forth between the two locations), and Pierrepont began at once to advertise his lots on the Heights. They were "elevated and perfectly healthy at all seasons," he wrote—ideal for "Families who may desire to associate in forming *a select neighborhood and circle of society*," and especially convenient for "Gentlemen whose business or profession requires daily attendance into the city." These and similar claims by Hoyts, Boerums, and other landowners stimulated a construction boom that raised nine hundred new buildings on and around the Heights over the next half-dozen years. By 1830 Brooklyn had become the country's first commuter suburb, and Hezekiah Pierrepont a very rich man.

"THE LONDON OF THE NEW WORLD"

As the Erie Canal neared completion, the *Times* of London predicted it would make New York "the London of the New World." The city's meteoric growth over the next ten or fifteen years largely bore out that prediction. Though the Hudson River town could hardly be compared with the colossus of the Thames, it had established itself as America's preeminent seaport, emporium, and financial center. After an 1831 visit, even the hard-to-please Mrs. Trollope found herself gushing about New York that, "situated on an island, which I think it will one day cover, it rises, like Venice, from the sea, and like that fairest of cities in the days of her glory, receives into its lap tribute of all the riches of the earth."

New York's success owed much to the entrepreneurial daring of its businessmen, who had proven themselves more willing than counterparts in other cities to take risks in pursuit of profit. Immigrant Yankee and European capitalists, having demonstrated their feistiness in the very act of relocating, seemed more flexible, less bound by tradition. They didn't always succeed—New York firms failed more often than did the dynastic enterprises of Boston—but their collective ambition stoked the city's economic furnace.

Yet if New Yorkers were willing to hustle in the marketplace, it was a marketplace both cosseted and regulated by the state. Public enterprise was as much a part of New York's civic culture as private ambition, and a raft of governmental initiatives helped the city embrace and enhance its natural advantages.

Above all, it was the state-run Erie Canal that secured New York City's position as the nation's entrepôt, galvanizing its commerce, its banking, its stock market, and its manufacturing sectors: in 1825, the year the Erie commenced operation, five hundred new mercantile operations opened their doors in the city. Government aided entrepreneurs in many other ways as well. Fulton and Livingston perfected their steamboat under the aegis of a state monopoly without which they would not likely have spent the time, money, and energy it took to bring the project to completion. A similar monopoly encouraged the New York Gas-Light Company to illuminate the streets—by warding off competitors, subsidizing construction, and guaranteeing an initial market. State law also undergirded the monopolistic auction system, which generated some of the largest fortunes of the era, and its Safety Fund assured local bankers of the most stable operating environment in the nation. Finally—the ultimate boon—the New York legislature dispensed, in ever-increasing numbers, the privileges of incorporation, a grant of limited liability originally intended to achieve public purposes, which now became a device to undergird private profitability.

Federal initiatives, too, provided an extensive support system for Manhattan's risk-takers. Washington dispensed shipbuilding contracts, dispatched the navy to protect city merchants in hostile waters, maintained forts to safeguard the harbor, banned foreign vessels from the American coastal trade, and, by charging the same postage for long- as for short- haul mailings, helped New York publishers undersell their regional competitors.

Municipal government continued to serve as custodian of the economic order by exercising a broad regulatory authority. In 1828 the Common Council licensed or appointed nearly seven thousand people—including the cartmen, porters, longshoremen, dray carriers, and hackney-coach drivers who moved commodities and people around the port—and municipal regulations had an impact on 255 occupations. Manhattan also maintained an expanding public market system. Though the old Fly Market closed in 1821, the Franklin Market opened that same year at Old Slip, the Fulton Market arrived in 1822, and in 1828 Washington Market was expanded by filling in adjacent wetlands, becoming by the end of the 1830s the leading revenue producer of the city's twelve venues.

The city corporation, moreover, while continuing to run its own "estate" (with some ancient franchises, notably the ferries, now more lucrative than ever), focused more attention on providing a planned and predictable public environment within which market actors could operate and invest. Waterfront improvements and mandated low wharfage rates kept the docks competitive. The grid underwrote real estate development by making clear where property-enhancing roads would run. The new administrative agencies created back at the turn of the century worked to abate public nuisances and speed the flow of commerce. And tax policies favored capital accumulation: real and personal property were flagrantly underassessed, while bank stocks, bonds, and mortgages were not taxed at all until 1823.

Laissez-faire rumblings did emerge from several quarters. The Rev. John McVickar, professor of moral philosophy at Columbia and scion of a leading mercantile family, was a disciple of David Ricardo and a stout opponent of government intervention in the economy. "I cannot but reverence the claims of free commerce as something holy," he declared. Yet even McVickar, in his *Outlines of Political Economy* (1825), admitted there was a role for government in executing expensive infrastructure projects, and he specifically praised the Erie Canal.

It was easier for most Manhattan businessmen to hew to mercantilist convictions inasmuch as, given their continuing hold on political power, public projects were in effect overseen by the merchants themselves. Beyond that, the commercial elite's belief that they were entitled to direct the workings of the municipal economy was rooted in a still deeper sense of stewardship—a conviction, bolstered by their ongoing preeminence in a wide array of civic arenas, that New York City remained a little republic, over which it was their right, indeed their duty, to exercise a collective oversight.

28

The Medici of
the Republic

When Frances Trollope wrote about New York in her *Domestic Manners of the Americans* (1832), she praised the city's upper class as a "small patrician band"—"the Medici of the Republic"—whose refined manners and genteel way of life met the highest European standards. The Medici were flattered, not least of all because Mrs. Trollope had endorsed their belief that they were better than everyone else, yet had remained true to the nation's republican heritage. What she didn't relay to her readers were the conflicting denominational sensibilities and ethnic allegiances that divided the snug little patriciate into at times competing factions.

One camp consisted of the recent arrivals from New England, who were inclined toward evangelical reform and found the Presbyterian Church an acceptable substitute for the Congregationalism of their native region. The other comprised old-stock Anglo-Dutch and Huguenot bluebloods—dubbed Knickerbockers after the character in Irving's history—who tended to think of religious zeal as fanaticism and felt most comfortable in the Episcopal fold. As one of them would tartly put it: "Our graceless Knickerbockers danced around the May-Pole in the Bowery, while the Puritan Anglo-Saxons burned witches at Salem."

A characteristic point of conflict between Yankees and Knickerbockers was their attitude to the theater. Knickerbockers loved the stage, and a performance at the Park Theater—which Mrs. Trollope identified as the only house in town "licensed by fashion"—was certain to bring out an abundance of Beekmans, De Lanceys, Kents, LeRoys, Bayards, Livingstons, and Van Renssalaers. More than eighty can be identified in the painting that John Searle made of the Park's audience one night in 1822. Pious Yankees, however, are conspicuously absent from Searle's canvas, having no doubt heeded the admonition of the Rev. Gardiner Spring, pastor of the Brick Presbyterian Church (just up the street from the Park), that playgoing encouraged licentious habits,

Interior of the new Park Theatre, 1822, watercolor by John
Searle. Fire destroyed the original Park Theatre in 1820, but its
replacement, which opened the following year, was no less
fashionable. Searle's portraits of the audience comprise a
visual directory of the Knickerbocker elite. William Bayard, the
wealthy merchant who commissioned the work, is standing in
the first tier, behind the lady who has draped her shawl over
the rail. (© Collection of The New-York Historical Society)

especially among the young. Spring's views were shared by Arthur Tappan, a successful
silk merchant and evangelical who felt about vice (according to his younger brother,
Lewis) as he would about a toad in his pocket. Although his annual income reached as
high as thirty thousand dollars during the 1820s, Tappan pointedly poured his money
into charity rather than preening display or self-indulgence. His usual lunch consisted
of a cracker and a tumbler of cold water. He held his clerks to equally strict standards,
insisting that they attend divine service regularly (twice on Sundays), get home by ten
each night, and never, ever, visit a theater or consort with actresses.

Yankees likewise vilified horse racing, another Knickerbocker enthusiasm that
enjoyed wide popular support. Although the state banned the sport in 1802 as a vestige
of aristocratic dissipation, Long Island gentry got the ban reversed, though only for
Queens County, on the ground that it impeded the improvement of breeds. The Union
Course, out on the plains of Jamaica, soon became one of the premier tracks in the
country, famous for its huge purses and the multitudes who came out from the city to

watch, gamble, and carouse. In May 1823 the track tapped sectional rivalries by hosting a match race between the fastest mount in the North, Eclipse, and a southern challenger, Henry. Some twenty thousand spectators showed up, a million dollars in wagers allegedly changed hands, and the *Evening Post* brought out a special edition to announce that Eclipse had carried the day. The victory did nothing to dispel Yankee convictions that racing was wicked, and when the Union Course was later bought and refurbished by Cadwallader Colden, the eminent Knickerbocker, they knew who to blame for encouraging it.

Waltzing too was in disfavor. Exclusive, meticulously arranged dancing "assemblies" were no less a feature of upper-class socializing than they had been before the Revolution, but the younger and more adventuresome set now regarded the cotillion or quadrille (ancestor of the modern square dance) as unbearably old-fashioned. They preferred the "valse," which came to New York via Paris in the 1820s and was thought quite daring because dancers whirled around the ballroom in couples. Yankees and Presbyterian ministers denounced it as the devil's work. Knickerbockers and Episcopalians seemed less concerned, even tolerant.

Nothing raised Yankee hackles like Sabbath-breaking, however. True, the bustle and frivolity of Sundays in New York had been a sore subject among devout residents for nearly two hundred years now. But newcomers from Connecticut and Massachusetts had still-warm memories of communities where families observed the Sabbath by abstaining from all forms of recreation, dining on cold collations of Saturday-baked meats, and attending multiple church services. They could see, too, that the city's recent growth had spawned alluring new opportunities for diversion on Sunday—pleasure gardens serving punch and wine, even to unescorted single women, and steam-powered pleasure boats providing musical excursions around Manhattan ("a refinement, a luxury of pleasure unknown to the old world," their proponents preened)—all apparently aided and abetted, and some owned as well, by easygoing Knickerbockers.

In 1821 the Rev. Spring and the Sabbatarians launched a boycott of newspapers that advertised Sunday excursions and won the support of Mayor Stephen Allen. Then they got up a petition asking the city to enforce biblical injunctions to keep the Sabbath holy by closing down pleasure gardens, markets, livery stables, newspapers, and the post office. In time, they meant to sweep the Hudson free of sloops and steamboats "filled with profaners of the Lord's day."

The reaction was swift and overwhelmingly negative. Most newspapers defended steamboat excursions as innocent amusement. The *Evening Post* justified keeping markets open on Sunday as necessary for the poor, who went unpaid until late Saturday and couldn't afford iceboxes to keep fish, meat, and milk fresh during hot weather. Thousands of residents signed a rival petition denouncing clerical interference in public affairs as "highly improper," while handbills and placards went up around town attacking Spring and his ministerial allies as bigots. When Spring's forces announced a public rally at City Hall, the *Mercantile Advertiser* urged anti-Sabbatarians to show up en masse. They did so, seized control of the meeting, and adopted a resolution stating that the citizens of New York wanted the clergy to mind their own business. ("The excited multitude looked daggers at us," Spring recalled.) The Sabbatarians retreated, and the Knickerbockers congratulated themselves on their stand for tolerance and bonhomie.

What the Knickerbockers lacked was an organization comparable to the New England Society, whose annual dinner to commemorate the landing of the Pilgrims generated endless bragging about Yankee virtues and Yankee achievements. More than a few Knickerbockers took up Freemasonry, which combined fraternalism with a commitment to religious toleration and rationalism. By 1827 there were forty-five Masonic Lodges in New York, each of which met twice monthly, either at old St. John's Hall or at the imposing new Gothic-style Masonic Hall on the east side of Broadway, between Duane and Pearl, nearly opposite the New York Hospital.

Eventually, in 1835—after two years of prodding by Washington Irving—the Knickerbocracy gave birth to a club all its own, the St. Nicholas Society. One of its declared purposes was to gather information on the history of the city, a subject that seemed to particularly interest old-guard New Yorkers. What mattered to the wealthy merchant and former mayor Philip Hone, though, was the promise "to promote social intercourse among native citizens"—meaning men of "respectable standing in society" whose families had resided in New York for at least fifty years. A "regular Knickerbocker Society," Hone noted in his diary, would serve "as a sort of setoff against St. Patrick's, St. George's, and more particularly the New England [societies]." Peter Gerard Stuyvesant, great-great-grandson of Petrus, was elected first president, and three hundred men with names conspicuous in the city's history—De Peysters and Duers, LeRoys and Roosevelts, Lows and Fishes—signed up at once. A second St. Nicholas Society soon sprang up across the East River, rallying Sandses, Leffertses, Bergens, Suydams, Strykers, and Boerums to the defense of Brooklyn against insolent and upstart Yankees.

E PLURIBUS UNUM

But not every question that roiled upper-class New York followed this pattern: partisan political alignments cut across the Yankee-Knickerbocker boundary, as did controversies over such economic issues as the tariff. More important still, none of these clashes of style, principle, or interest provoked permanent rifts in New York's upper registers. Numerous circumstances allowed old-timers to fashion a detente with newcomers and construct a common class identity, rather as the wealthy Dutch and English had worked out a rapprochement a century earlier.

The city's galloping prosperity, for one thing, enabled Yankees and Knickerbockers alike to make so much money so fast that their differences paled alongside their combined riches. In the buoyant economy, profits rose to the top like cream: by 1828 the top 4 percent of taxpayers possessed roughly half the city's assessed wealth—more than the top 10 percent had owned a half century earlier. Then, too, although New Englanders now ruled the wholesale and retail mercantile trade—LeRoy and Bayard, the last great Knickerbocker firm, folded in 1826—their rivals hadn't died out. Rather, they moved nimbly into banking, lawyering, transportation, shipbuilding, insurance, the stock market, and, above all, real estate. As ever, money begat money, and if the son of a rich man didn't stay in the family business, the family could get him off to a fast start in some other line of work. In fact, nine out of ten affluent New Yorkers in the 1820s and 1830s were wealthy before they embarked on their careers.

Besides money there was style, and nowhere were the commonalities among well-to-do gentlemen and ladies in New York more plainly visible than in their evolving sense of fashion. Beginning in the 1790s the peacock regalia of eighteenth-century males—cocked hats, greatcoats with turned-up cuffs and gilt buttons, embroidered waistcoats, snowy cravats, lace ruffles, buckskin knee breeches, silk stockings, and shoes with silver buckles—had fallen rapidly out of favor. Well-dressed men now favored trousers or close-fitting pantaloons ("pants"), along with double-breasted frock coats, preferably in a circumspect black (a color once reserved for mourners and the clergy). They wore their own hair, unpowdered, closed their shirts at the collar with the simple white neckcloths known as "stocks," and covered their heads with high-crowned top hats. Dandies affected tighter pants, flashy vests, bright green gloves, and an eyeglass for inspecting curiosities—and were scorned by etiquette advisers as effeminate. The trend was unmistakable. Aristocratic plumage had succumbed to republican simplicity and bourgeois restraint: a gentleman conveyed social superiority through consummate tailoring and impeccable grooming, not color and ornamentation.

Female fashion followed a similar trajectory. Heavy brocaded skirts with whale-boned bodices and hooped petticoats, all the rage in the mid-eighteenth century, yielded during the first two decades of the nineteenth to lighter, neoclassical designs inspired by the French empire and then the Greek struggle for independence. Their objective was a free and natural silhouette: high-waisted dresses of sheer white muslin, featuring low rounded necklines and a bandeau (precursor of the bra) that emphasized the bosom, typically worn with a shawl and with the hair piled up in reckless masses of curls. After 1830, however, the prevailing taste retreated to more constrained, less revealing styles. Waistlines became lower and narrower, necklines rose, and the natural contours of the body were concealed with boned corsets, voluminous skirts, layers of petticoats, padded bustles, and enormous leg-of-mutton sleeves. Modesty now required that hair be pulled back, drawn into a demure knot, and covered with a frilly bonnet.

Shared tastes in costume were accompanied by a similar determination to settle in neighborhoods where the better sort of people, Yankees and Knickerbockers alike, could insulate themselves from the seamier elements of urban life. In 1820 the choicest addresses in town still lay on the lower west side of Manhattan, along Broadway (from Bowling Green up to Chambers), Greenwich Street (which paralleled the Hudson), and the quiet, tree-shaded blocks in between. From here gentlemen could easily walk to their places of business on Wall Street or Hanover Square, and their families could walk to one of the many houses of worship nearby—the great Episcopal bastions of Trinity and St. Paul's on Broadway, say, or perhaps the First Presbyterian Church on Wall, Brick Presbyterian on Beekman Street, St. Peter's Roman Catholic Church on Barclay Street, John Street Methodist, the Dutch Reform triplets (Old South on Exchange Place, Middle on Liberty Street, and Old North on William Street), South Baptist on Nassau Street, or Shearith Israel on Mill Street, still the only synagogue for New York's four hundred Jews. Also within easy walking distance was the Battery. Spruced up in the early 1820s with lawns, shade trees, and an ornamental iron railing, it remained the city's premier park and promenade. Its appeal was further enhanced in 1824, when the city acquired Castle Clinton from the federal government and leased it out as a "place of resort," tethered to the Battery by a wooden bridge ninety paces long and illuminated by gas lamps. Two years later, refurbished as a theater, it became Castle Garden. The high price of tickets to the Garden's varied performances guaranteed respectable audiences.

Throughout the 1820s some of New York's most prominent Yankees and Knicker-bockers nestled around the Battery and its adjacent blocks, so many that Bowling Green was irreverently dubbed Nobs' Row. Other affluent families settled along Broadway itself. In 1828 over one hundred of the city's five hundred richest men lived there.

Broadway between Park Place and Barclay Street, 1831 (now the site of the Woolworth Building), directly opposite City Hall. The private house on the right was occupied by Philip Hone, who had settled there a decade earlier, when Broadway was still lined with fashionable private residences. Only a half-dozen years later, surging commercial growth—marked by the expansion of the adjacent American Hotel and construction of Astor House one block to the south—would transform the neighborhood. (© Museum of the City of New York)

Among them was Philip Hone, who had retired in 1821 at the age of forty from the auctioneer business with money enough to purchase a house directly across from City Hall (making for an effortless commute during his 1825 term as mayor). Even the censorious Mrs. Trollope loved Broadway, that "noble street." Though lacking "the gorgeous fronted palaces of Regent-street," it was nevertheless "magnificent in its extent." Its "neat awnings, excellent *trottoir* [sidewalk], and well-dressed pedestrians" were so appealing that she might have moved there herself, she confessed, "were it not so very far from all the old-world things which cling about the heart of an European." Roosevelts, Astors, Grinnells, and Aspinwalls were nonetheless quite content to occupy the elegant three-story row houses that fronted blocks running west from the strip of Broadway adjacent to City Hall Park down to the Hudson shore.

Yet for all its charms, lower Broadway was losing its exclusivity in these years. Clerks, shopkeepers, and laborers trod its excellent *trottoir* on their way to and from work. Pigs wandered over from all-too-near poor neighborhoods. Commerce and the business district expanded rapidly northward. Old private homes were converted to boardinghouses for young merchants, clerks, and out-of-towners. The growing number of shops, hotels, restaurants, and theaters produced, said the *Mirror*, a "confused assemblage," mixing people of high and low degree.

More and more wealthy residents thus began a long, reluctant march uptown in search of more hospitable enclaves. One destination was Hudson Square, also known as St. John's Park, which had been opened by Trinity twenty years earlier but had failed to attract residents. In 1827, however, the vestry decided to sell rather than lease lots and deeded the square itself to purchasers. They poured in by the score, threw up a tall iron fence around the square, and landscaped it with catalpas, cottonwoods, horse chestnuts,

Battery Park, 1830. A field of fashionable bonnets and top hats, well-behaved children, carefully maintained grounds—everything in this scene of the Battery conveys its continuing prominence as a hub of respectable New York. (© Collection of The New-York Historical Society)

silver birches, flowerbeds, and gravel paths. The neighborhood for blocks around soon bristled with Hamiltons, Schuylers, Delafields, Tappans, and other prominent families whose elegant brick town houses afforded refuge from the sweaty commotion of the city below. Nothing else in New York so closely approximated the beauty and exclusiveness of the great squares of London's West End. It was, according to one contemporary report, "the fairest interior portion of this city."

A second destination for rich urban refugees lay even further uptown, where Broadway sliced through Bleecker, Bond, Great Jones, and East 4th streets, just below John Jacob Astor's Vauxhall Gardens. Building sites on this northern frontier of the city were ample enough for patrician-sized dwellings with commodious yards, gardens, and stables; one guidebook announced that they "may vie, for beauty and taste, with European palaces." Arguably the most desirable addresses lay along Bond Street, where Jonas Minturn built the first house in 1820. Its white marble facade set the pattern for the expensive three-and four-story residences that stretched the length of the street, from Broadway to the Bowery, by the mid-thirties.

Bond Street's principal rival was the wide nine-block sweep of Bleecker Street from the Bowery to Sixth Avenue, and in 1828 the portion of Bleecker between Mercer and Greene streets became the site of New York's first experiment with terraces— grand residential blockfronts of the kind seen in the most fashionable London neighborhoods. Christened LeRoy Place in honor of the Knickerbocker merchant Jacob LeRoy, its Federal-style row houses sold for a hefty twelve thousand dollars. But LeRoy Place was promptly eclipsed by the resplendent La Grange Terrace, completed in 1833

St. John's Chapel and Hudson Square, from the New York *Mirror*, April 11, 1829. This genteel bastion—bounded by Hudson, Varick, Ericsson, and Laight streets— fell abruptly out of fashion after 1850 and was sold to Commodore Vanderbilt, who built a four-acre freight depot on the site in 1866. It is now overrun by automobiles exiting the Holland Tunnel, and the memory of McComb's chapel is recalled only by St. John's Lane, a block east. (© Museum of the City of New York)

on the west side of Lafayette Place (itself opened by the canny Astor only half a dozen years earlier). Also known as Colonnade Row, for its magisterial procession of two-story Corinthian columns, La Grange Terrace consisted of nine residences that sold for as much as thirty thousand dollars apiece. They were reportedly "the most imposing and magnificent in the city."

The exodus of well-to-do New Yorkers out of lower Manhattan took a toll on many downtown churches—even Gardiner Spring moved up to Bond Street—and their denominations, Yankee and Knickerbocker alike, moved quickly to establish new congregations uptown. A Dutch Reformed church opened on the corner of Houston and Greene streets in 1825; the Bleecker Street Presbyterian Church, just east of Broadway, in 1826. The Episcopalians consecrated the stately, Gothic-style St. Thomas's at Houston and Broadway in 1826, followed ten years later by the sumptuous St. Bartholomew's, at Lafayette and Great Jones.

Even these houses of worship were inaccessible to affluent New Yorkers who fled still farther away from the city, all the way up Third Avenue until it dwindled to a country lane in the higher latitudes of northern Manhattan. In May 1831 their mansions caught the eye of Alexis de Tocqueville and Gustave Beaumont, two Frenchmen who had come to explore America's jails and America's democracy. As their steamboat from Providence cruised past the East River shore, the two marveled at the "unbelievable multitude of country houses, big as boxes of candy," whose grassy lawns and orchards sloped down to the water. More and more of these bucolic summer retreats had become full-time residences, from the Stuyvesant estate just below 14th Street (where boys still filched pears from trees planted by old Petrus), and the thirty-acre Phelps estate at Kip's Bay between 29th and 31st streets, all the way up to Archibald Gracie's lovely Federal-style mansion between 86th and 90th streets. By the 1820s these regions had so many permanent inhabitants that St. James's Church—a wooden Trinity outpost at 69th and Lexington—began year-round worship.

The isolation that wealthy New Yorkers sought in their uptown encampments made travel into the city something of an ordeal. Bond Street merchants and bankers occasionally walked the two miles down to Wall or Pearl. Yet daily commuting required swifter, less tiresome transportation, and absent the use of a private carriage or cabriolet (a two-wheeled vehicle drawn by a single horse), the alternatives proved sadly limited. One option was to suffer through an uncomfortable ride atop one of the stagecoaches that ran downtown from the corner of Broadway and Houston Street. Another was to hail one of the licensed hackney carriages that congregated at stands by the Park, Bowling Green, Trinity Church, and Hanover Square. Hacks weren't plentiful, though (only 180 served the entire city in 1828); they weren't cheap; and as Mrs. Trollope discovered, "it is necessary to be on the *qui vive* in making your bargain with the driver; if you do not, he has the power of charging immoderately." At the least, a Bond Street gentleman might spend two hundred dollars a year getting to and from work.

The demand for better transportation between the downtown business district and elite uptown neighborhoods inspired New York coachmakers to introduce the omnibus, an innovation that had recently appeared in London and Paris. Seating a dozen or more passengers, and drawn by huffing teams of two or four horses, the first of these boatlike vehicles began rumbling along Broadway from Bowling Green to Bond Street in 1829. The idea caught on quickly. Within a decade there were over a hundred omnibuses in operation along the city's principal thoroughfares, gaily painted and sporting heroic names like the *General Washington*, the *Benjamin Franklin*, and the *Thomas Jefferson*. Philip Hone, who himself had moved uptown to the corner of Broadway and Great Jones Street, reveled in the ease with which they allowed him to get downtown. "I can always get an omnibus in a minute or two by going out of the door and holding up my finger," he said.

Although *omnibus* means "for all" in Latin, this was class, not mass, transit. It cost twelve and a half cents for a one-way trip down to Wall Street, which was cheaper than the hacks but well beyond the reach of common laborers earning a dollar a day. Even well-to-do passengers found things to complain about, to be sure: grime, unpadded benches, poor ventilation in the summer, no heat in the winter, an often maddeningly slow pace through downtown traffic, and frequent overcrowding. For people living on their estates north of town, omnibuses were no use at all.

SPHERES OF INFLUENCE

Nor were the omnibuses generally able to get gentlemen back uptown in time for dinner. Until 1830 or so, dinner had been the main meal of the day for upper-class New Yorkers, served *en famille* at two or three in the afternoon, followed by a light and informal supper in the early evening. As the distance between home and office increased, however, men of affairs found it more convenient to make a quick midday snack of oysters or clams bought from street vendors ("Here's your fine clams, as white as snow, on Rockaway these clams do grow") or to have "lunch" together at business-district restaurants like Dyde's on Park Row or the Porter House on John Street. Back home, meanwhile, wives and small children made do on cold meat, soup, bread, cheese, and other breakfast leftovers. "Dinner" now waited until Father returned in the early evening, while supper was pushed back to nine or ten o'clock or abandoned altogether.

The rescheduling of dinner was accompanied by changes in the consumption and presentation of food that would make the meal as much an emblem of gentility as restraint in fashion or a choice address. Guests no longer arrived to find the table already laden with dishes, which the genial host would dispense, amid much communal passing of plates. Instead, servants (who no longer ate with the family) distributed dishes in a carefully specified order: first soup and fish, then meat and vegetables, finally pies and puddings, which Americans had begun to call "dessert." The new manners did encounter some opposition—"This French influence must be resisted," Philip Hone declared—but the more ceremonial and "refined" mode eventually prevailed.

Food preparation too changed in upper-class households. Breads, hoecakes, and johnny cakes, once made in an open hearth, were baked in new cast-iron cookstoves, using the new "refined" white flour that came down the Erie Canal from the new Rochester mills. Meat wasn't boiled in a pot or spitted over a fire, as in the past, but oven-roasted and served with fancy sauces. The mistress crafted ornate pastries and compotes from recipes gleaned out of increasingly complex domestic manuals like Lydia Maria Child's *Frugal Housewife* (1829). Costly imported porcelain and silverware, once reserved for guests or special occasions, were now considered de rigueur for everyday use.

Changes in the dinner ritual were further evidence that for upper-class New York households "work" and "home" increasingly occupied distinct social spaces, one ruled by men, the other by women. By the 1820s the downtown commercial district was well on its way to becoming a separate male preserve—virtually empty of respectable families, and scrupulously avoided by respectable women except for shopping expeditions to lower Broadway or visits to the Ladies' Dining Room of the City Hotel. John Pintard, then living over the offices of the Mutual Insurance Company on Wall Street, realized that his wife and daughter were "nearly prisoners during the hours of business in Wall Street." In 1832 a popular guide to the city advised "distant readers" that no women appeared in its pictures of the area because women rarely went there. So, too, the *Mirror* reported a few years later that "the sight of a female in that isolated quarter is so extraordinary, that, the moment a petticoat appears, the groups of brokers, intent on calculating the value of stocks, break suddenly off, and gaze at the phenomenon."

This was as it should be. Decent women didn't belong in the heartless, bare-knuckled free-for-all that raged downtown, for according to the conventional wisdom, proclaimed over and over again in the pulpit and in the press, nature designed the female of the species to be pacific, nurturing, and cooperative. Her proper sphere was the Home, and her duty— essentially a refinement of the ideal of republican motherhood—was to make the Home a haven for her weary husband and a nest where she imbued her children with Christian love and humility. A genteel household was thus the very antithesis of the marketplace yet indispensable to it, a place where men returned at the end of the day to be refreshed for battle the next and where the young acquired the moral armor they would need as adults.

THE DOMESTICATION OF CHRISTMAS

Wealthy New Yorkers didn't invent this new cult of domesticity, which was a characteristic of emerging bourgeois culture throughout the Atlantic world. They did, however, give it Christmas—a holiday that became synonymous with genteel family life and a quintessential expression of its central values.

For 150-odd years, probably since the English conquest, the favorite winter holiday of the city's propertied classes was New Year's Day (as distinct from the night before, which was an occasion for revelry and mischief among common folk). Families exchanged small gifts, and gentlemen went around the town to call on friends and relations, nibbling cookies and drinking raspberry brandy served by the women of the house. Sadly, according to John Pintard, the city's physical expansion after 1800 rendered this "joyous older fashion" so impractical that it was rapidly dying out.

As an alternative Pintard proposed St. Nicholas Day, December 6, as a family-oriented winter holiday for polite society. In *Knickerbocker's History*, Pintard's good friend Washington Irving had identified Nicholas as the patron saint of New Amsterdam, describing him as a jolly old Dutchman, nicknamed Sancte Claus, who parked his wagon on rooftops and slid down chimneys with gifts for sleeping children on his feast day. It was *Salmagundi*-style fun, of course: although seventeenth-century Netherlanders had celebrated St. Nicholas Day, the earliest evidence of anyone doing so on Manhattan dates from 1773, when a group of "descendents of the ancient Dutch families" celebrated the sixth of December "with great joy and festivity." Certainly nothing remotely like the Sancte Claus portrayed by Irving had ever been known on either side of the Atlantic.

Mere details were no obstacle to Pintard. On December 6, 1810—one year to the day after the publication of Irving's *History*—he launched his revival of St. Nicholas Day with a grand banquet at City Hall for members of the New-York Historical Society. Their first toast was to "Sancte Claus, goed heylig man!" and Pintard distributed a specially engraved picture that showed Nicholas with two children (one good, one bad) and two stockings hung by a hearth (one full, one empty)—the point being that December 6 was a kind of Judgment Day for the young, with the saint distributing rewards and punishments as required. St. Nicholas Day never quite won the support Pintard wanted, and he eventually ran out of enthusiasm for the project. Sancte Claus, on the other hand, took off like a rocket. Only a few years later, in a book for juveniles entitled *False Stories Corrected*, he was already under attack as "Old Santaclaw, of whom so often little children hear such foolish stories."

Other New Yorkers of Pintard's ilk were meanwhile taking a second look at Christmas as a substitute for New Year's Day. Since the Reformation, Protestants had dismissed Christmas as another artifact of Catholic ignorance and deception: not only was the New Testament silent on the date of Christ's birth, they noted, but the Church had picked December 25 to coincide with the beginning of the winter solstice, an event traditionally associated with wild plebeian bacchanals and challenges to authority. Well-bred New Yorkers in the early nineteenth century weren't so vehemently opposed to Christmas as Petrus Stuyvesant had been, and often marked the day with private family devotions, dinners, and "Christmas logs." Patricians with New England roots knew that churches there had recently begun a movement for public worship on December 25 to counteract the spread of popular rowdyism. Then came Washington Irving's *Sketch*

Book (1819), a collection of short stories that not only gave to American literature the characters of Ichabod Crane and Rip Van Winkle but sparked widespread interest in Christmas as a cozy domestic ritual.

It remained only to get Sancte Claus into the picture, and that was the achievement of another of Pintard's friends, Clement Clarke Moore (still fuming over the intrusion of Ninth Avenue into his beloved country estate, Chelsea). During the winter of 1822, Moore wrote a poem for his children entitled "A Visit from St. Nicholas," arguably the best-known verses ever written by an American. Moore's saint was an obvious derivative of Irving's—"a right jolly old elf" who sneaks down the chimney of a gentleman's house in the dead of night, not to rob him but to put toys in the stockings hung up by his children. Moore had him arrive on December 24, however, a small revision that deftly shifted the focus away from Christmas Day with its still-problematic religious associations.

A friend sent "Visit" to an upstate newspaper for publication, other papers picked it up, and within a decade it was known throughout the country (though Moore didn't acknowledge writing it until some years later). In the meantime, genteel New Yorkers embraced Moore's homey, child-centered version of Christmas as if it they had been doing it all their lives. "A festival sacred to domestic enjoyments," the papers called it; a time when men "make glad upon one day, the domestic hearth, the virtuous wife, the innocent, smiling merry-hearted children, and the blessed mother." In 1831, his earlier promotion of December 6 long since forgotten, Pintard asserted that the new rituals of Christmas were of "ancient usage" and that "St. Claas is too firmly riveted in this city ever to be forgotten." (Christmas trees reached New York in the mid-thirties, courtesy of German Brooklynites; they were popularized by Catharine Maria Sedgwick, the novelist, who wrote the first American fiction including a Christmas tree in 1835.)

PARLOR BUSINESS

Despite its prominence in the consciousness of upper-class New Yorkers, the ideal of a genteel household—quarantined from the rough-and-tumble of commerce by distance, nurturing mothers, and yuletide cheer—often collided with the day-to-day realities of household affairs. Only the very wealthiest women, for example, had enough servants to relieve them entirely of cooking, cleaning, laundering, and other menial chores. John Pintard employed an all-purpose maid, but his wife and younger daughter were responsible for sewing, tailoring, preserving food, baking, liming the basement, whitewashing fences, clearing the yard, and basic carpentry. Increasingly, moreover, even rich families were replacing lifetime African-American retainers with part-time or seasonal help, typically Irish, and the mistress of the house needed to be as adept as her husband in recruiting and managing a wage-labor force. Everyone had stories of servants who stalked out in a dispute over their duties or pay or were lured away by promises of better accommodations. When John Pintard's "unfaithful, ungrateful" maid left without notice, he found it "vexatious in the extreme" and (as was his wont) formed an organization in 1825 to deal with the entire "problem"—the Society for the Encouragement of Faithful Domestic Servants.

Business and public affairs were no more absent from the genteel home than labor. If the back parlor remained a family sanctum, the dining room and front parlor, where children were allowed only on Sunday mornings, hosted a good deal of work-related socializing. New York gentlemen often entertained one another at home and although

Mr. and Mrs. Ernest Fiedler and family at their home on Bond Street, painting by
F. Heinrich, 1850. "The houses of the higher classes," Frances Trollope wrote, were
"extremely handsome, and very richly furnished" with the chandeliers, mirrors,
carpets, and upholstered furniture that here attest to the Fiedlers' respectability. Note
also the pianoforte and—partially concealed by the Greek Revival ionic columns in the
background—a Christmas tree. Not depicted, almost inevitably, are the servants whose
labor was essential to maintaining these cozy domestic sanctuaries. (Photograph
courtesy of Mr. Nicholas L. Bruen)

Mrs. Trollope deplored the exclusion of women from these male affairs as "a great defect
in the society" that "certainly does not conduce to refinement," they were nonetheless
a vital forum for the private exchange of views about economics and politics.

Women too utilized the parlor, for Bible readings, charity meetings, after-church
teas, and the formal "morning calls" that maintained class boundaries by defining the
people to whom one was, or was not, "at home." For both sexes, moreover, every room
accessible to outsiders was a stage for displaying the family's wealth and sophistication.
The most refined houses boasted pianofortes, which cost as much as six hundred dollars
(more than a year's wages for a carpenter or cabinetmaker) and were the basis for fashionable "at home" musical performances. Technologically advanced households also
had coal-burning stoves, iceboxes, and gas lights, whose installation and upkeep exceeded the annual rent bill of many poor families.

The genteel parlor was likewise an important adjunct to the upper-class marriage
market. Well-bred young men and women took note of one another during the annual
cycle of assemblies, balls, and concerts, but a proper courtship didn't begin until a
"beau" gained the privilege of an "at home" visit. Such occasions were closely chaperoned and, as James Fenimore Cooper observed, governed by taboos so strict that a
young woman would assume "a chilling gravity at the slightest trespass." And not
without reason, for much hung in the balance: a careless match could plunge an entire
family into dishonor and ruin; a good one would bring money and connections sufficient for generations of preeminence. Here, too, Yankees and Knickerbockers saw eye to

eye, and many a Yankee entrepreneur won his future in the parlor of a genteel Knickerbocker girl.

The permeability of the membrane separating the spheres of family and business
was no less apparent at Christmas, the holiday dedicated to domesticity. By 1830, if not
earlier, the week before Santa arrived had become a time for heavy shopping at toy
shops, confectionery stores, jewelers, and booksellers. Shopkeepers flogged luxury
goods few people purchased at other times of the year, and indeed the season helped
legitimate indulgence for a culture that was still consumption-shy. In this context as
well, genteel households managed both to lock out commerce and simultaneously contribute to its relentless advance.

TRUE REPUBLICANS

August 16, 1824, a fine summer day: thousands of New Yorkers jammed the Battery to
greet the flotilla of steamboats escorting the marquis de Lafayette to Manhattan for the
start of a year-long tour of the United States. Stepping ashore at two P.M., the aging
Revolutionary hero was swept in magnificent procession out the Battery's Greenwich
Street gate, through Bowling Green, and up Broadway toward City Hall, preceded by
mounted buglers. The route was thick with tens of thousands of cheering men and
ladies waving handkerchiefs, while a rain of flowers fell from the upper windows of
nearby buildings. After a reception at City Hall, Lafayette was settled at the City Hotel
and feted at a state banquet that concluded with a balloon ascension.

Any resemblance to an ancient Roman triumph was completely intentional. Conscious of the hoary canard that republics were ungrateful to their benefactors, the Corporation of the City of New York had set out to arrange a reception that, while avoiding
unrepublican "pomp" and "ostentatious ceremonies," would nevertheless pay magnificent homage to one who had labored selflessly for the common weal. A committee
chaired by the civic patriarch William Bayard (assisted, inevitably, by John Pintard)
devised a schedule that honored Lafayette and showed off the city to best advantage.
Before setting out on his U.S. tour, he took in a gala performance of *Twelfth Night*,
endured another state dinner at the City Hotel, and attended a reception at the Rutgers
mansion. He visited the Navy Yard. He met with clergymen, officers of the militia, and
delegates from the French Society and the New-York Historical Society.

Lafayette swung through New York again the following July on his way south.
Speaking at the city's Independence Day celebrations, he assured his listeners that of all
the wondrous improvements he had seen on his journey thus far, "Nowhere can they be
more conspicuous than in the state of New York, in the prodigious progress of this
city." Another busy week ensued, including a trip to Brooklyn, where he picked up and
kissed six-year-old Walter Whitman (or so the poet insisted in later life). Lafayette
returned to New York a third and final time in early September for another round of
sightseeing (Columbia College, the Academy of Arts, the hospital, the almshouse) and a
spectacular sendoff that was soon to become the talk of the country: a grand fete at Castle Garden on the evening of September 14, at which six thousand guests danced until
two in the morning.

For upper-class New Yorkers, Lafayette's three visits, each carefully staged-
managed, constituted a running advertisement for the legitimacy of the municipal
social system. They demonstrated that huge crowds of citizens could assemble peacefully to honor a national hero—or, as Cadwallader Colden forthrightly put it, that an

"exhibition of bayonets is not essential to the preservation of order in New York." They affirmed, too, that even the city's wealthiest residents hadn't forgotten their Revolutionary antecedents and remained fully committed to the cause of constitutional republicanism around the world.

Not coincidentally, rich New Yorkers were already deeply involved in marshaling popular support for the Greek War of Independence from the Ottoman empire. Since raising the standard of revolt in 1821, the Greeks had won support from radicals and reformers throughout Europe by presenting themselves both as heirs of Athenian democracy and as Christian crusaders against the heathen Turks. In 1823 a meeting of sympathetic New Yorkers set up a Greek Committee, chaired by William Bayard, to raise money for the rebels, while another group, headed by Chancellor James Kent, appealed to Congress to recognize Greece as an independent nation. They were soon joined by a long line of wealthy Yankees and Knickerbockers.

By the mid-twenties, even as Lafayette made his triumphant rounds of the city, New York was in the grip of a Greek mania. The Greek Ladies of Brooklyn and New York erected a twenty-foot Grecian Cross on Brooklyn Heights. Churches and schools took up collections, theaters gave benefit performances, and tickets were sold for a military ball ("as exclusive an affair as was practicable"). Politicians made speeches, and poets churned out verses on Greek themes; Mordecai Noah wrote a play, *The Grecian Captive or the Fall of Athens*, in support of "the present struggle for liberty in Greece."

There was money to be made as well as raised. In 1824 Greek agents in London asked LeRoy, Bayard, and Company to arrange manufacture of two fifty-gun frigates in New York. The firm placed the order with Eckford and with Smith and Dimon, two local yards, and once again a fund-raising frenzy swept the city. In October 1825, with the ships ready to sail, the Greeks discovered the final bill was twice as high as the price they'd been quoted, having been inflated by fat commissions and brokerage fees, and the builders refused to release the vessels until the sum was paid. The rebels were forced to sell one of the frigates to the U.S. Navy in order to redeem the other. Both purchasers soon discovered that the vessels had been constructed using cheap green timber rather than the expensive live oak stipulated in the contract. The ensuing scandal embarrassed old Bayard, head of the Greek Committee, though his sons appear to have been the ones at fault. When the old man died in 1826, the business failed almost immediately.

None of this dampened the enthusiasm of the propertied classes for international republicanism. In 1830, when the July Revolution in France toppled the regime of Charles X, a committee chaired by Philip Hone chose Evacuation Day, November 25, for a massive show of solidarity. Thousands of merchants, manufacturers, and tradesmen, many accompanied by elaborately decorated floats, turned out to march from the Battery up to a rally at the Washington parade-ground. Several old Revolutionary soldiers were present as well, among them John Van Arsdale, who had pulled down the last British flag in 1783 and now carried the banner he had hoisted in its place.

The clamor for Greek independence (nudged along by a recent British fad for Greek antiquities) had meanwhile sparked a demand among wealthy New Yorkers for buildings designed to look as if they belonged on the Acropolis in ancient Athens. Greek Revival architecture, as it came to be known, seemed particularly well suited to the United States. Its basic elements—massive fluted columns, triangular pediments, heavy cornices—created a highly satisfying sense of kinship with the Athenian city-state famed as the birthplace of Western democracy. The first full-blown example of

Greek Revival architecture in America was the headquarters of the Bank of the United States in Philadelphia, a Parthenon-like edifice completed in 1824. Only a few years later, New York's booming financial district got its first taste of the new style in Martin Euclin Thompson's Phoenix Bank.

The spread of Greek Revival architecture in the city quickened with the arrival of a Yankee engineer-architect named Ithiel Town. Town moved down from New Haven in the mid-twenties, certain that New York was about to become the pivot of the republic—and that its rich patricians would pay generously for the new style. His first commission, a Greek Doric design for the New York [later renamed Bowery] Theater, came in 1826. The following year he went into partnership with Thompson to form the city's first professional architectural firm, Town and Thompson, which quickly produced the Church of the Ascension on Canal Street (1827–29), among other notable structures, as well as renovations to St. Mark's in the Bouwerie (1828).

Thompson left Town in 1829 and went on to fame as the architect of the gracefully proportioned row houses on Washington Square North (1829–33) and, with another newcomer named Minard Lefever, of Sailors' Snug Harbor on Staten Island (1831–33)—both still among the best surviving examples of Greek Revival building in the country. Town had meanwhile teamed up with Alexander Jackson Davis, a native New Yorker nineteen years his junior. Davis was a skilled architectural draftsman who had thrived by furnishing plans and elevations to the burgeoning ranks of speculative builders. After Davis won a commission to remodel the old almshouse—New York's first civic building in the new style—Town took him on as a partner and opened an office in the Merchants' Exchange. The two soon made Greek Revival architecture as prevalent a symbol of genteel New York as Santa Claus. Their temple-fronted churches and columned town houses sprang up throughout Greenwich Village, Chelsea, and other fashionable new neighborhoods. The Greek Revival facade that Town designed for Arthur Tappan's store at Pearl and Hanover streets in 1829 was the first to make use of post-and-lintel construction, so obvious an improvement for displaying as well as storing wares that it quickly became the norm for downtown commercial buildings.

CIVIC PATRONS

Ever since the 1790s, De Witt Clinton and a small handful of like-minded gentlemen had been urging more systematic support for the arts and sciences—equally to encourage republican virtue among the people and to counter the city's reputation for benighted money-grubbing. Culture was as much an "internal improvement" as the Erie Canal, they argued, and equally the responsibility of government. In 1816 the Common Council agreed. New York had "too long been stigmatized as phlegmatic, money making & plodding," the aldermen admitted, and they determined to "speedily retrieve the reputation of our City," by providing "municipal aid" to cultural institutions as Edinburgh, London, Paris, and Amsterdam, and other European capitals did. Moving inmates of the Chambers Street almshouse up to a new facility near Bellevue, they gave McComb's three-story 1797 building a new name: the New York Institution of Learned and Scientific Establishments. The idea, as Pintard put it, was that "by concentrating all our resources we may give a greater impulse and elevation to our intellectual character."

Seven prominent "establishments" agreed to take up quarters in the Institution: the recently reorganized American Academy of Fine Arts, the New-York Historical Society, the new Literary and Philosophical Society, the New York Society Library,

John Scudder's Museum (successor to the old Tammany Museum), the U.S. Military and Philosophical Society, and John Griscom's Chemistry Laboratory. (Not all of them actually moved in. The Society Library, for one, kept its formidable collection of twenty thousand volumes down on Nassau Street.)

The leadership of the institution's member organizations was drawn from a small, frequently overlapping group of affluent merchants and lawyers. As they understood matters, elevating the city's intellectual character required them not simply to patronize creativity but to ordain and enforce standards for it as well. So in 1816, when John Vanderlyn asked the academy for space to exhibit a reclining nude entitled *Ariadne Asleep on the Island of Naxos*, the horrified members turned him down on the grounds that the painting offended public decency. Their notions of good art ran to the inspiring historical canvases of John Trumbull, whose full-length portraits of Washington, Hamilton, Jay, and other worthies already graced City Hall—and who, as it happened, had just been elected president of the academy. In 1819, when Trumbull finally completed his *Declaration of Independence*, destined for the Capitol in Washington, the academicians proudly let the public in for a preview (at twenty-five cents a head).

Vanderlyn, in the meantime, had taken his revenge by soliciting money from Astor and a hundred other gentlemen to build his own gallery on Chambers Street, directly east of the institution. This was the Rotunda, a Pantheon-like building, fifty-six feet in diameter and capped by a thirty-foot dome. Its main attraction, which went on display in the summer of 1819, was Vanderlyn's own *Panoramic View of the Palace and Gardens of Versailles*, twelve feet high and 165 feet long. The public wasn't impressed, and critics advised him to depict American rather than European scenes in the future.

In 1824 the effort to improve the intellectual climate of New York took a new turn when Pintard and a number of its "wealthiest and most learned" citizens met at the City Hotel for the purpose of creating an athenaeum. Modeled on similar organizations in Liverpool (1798), Boston (1807), and Philadelphia (1814), the New York Athenaeum was to be a "genteel place of resort" for the perusal of books, magazines, and newspapers. It would also sponsor lectures, which would be open to women as well as men, by prominent artists, writers, and scientists. The lecture series started up almost immediately in the chapel of Columbia College: Gulian Verplanck speaking on political economy, Professor John McVickar on the philosophy of mind, Professor James Renwick on applied mechanics, and the Rev. Jonathan Wainright on oratory, among others, drawing audiences "distinguished for fashion, beauty, and accomplishments." As intended, the athenaeum subsequently opened a public reading room at the corner of Broadway and Pine that became quite popular (Tocqueville and Beaumont dropped by almost every day during their visit to the city).

The machinery of genteel cultural legislation and patronage made its most enduring contribution to the city, however, by launching the artistic careers of newcomers like Samuel Finley Breese Morse and Thomas Cole. Morse, an itinerant painter from New England, moved down to the city in 1823 because he believed that the "influx of wealth from the Western canal" would soon make it a good place to look for commissions (and because he hoped to succeed the aging Trumbull as president of the academy). It was slow going at first. "This city seems given wholly to commerce," Morse grumbled. "Every man is driving at one object, the *making of money*, not the spending of it." But in 1825, thanks to Philip Hone, Morse was tapped to paint a portrait of Lafayette for City Hall. His dynamic rendering catapulted him to fame, and commissions poured in. Dr.

David Hosack of the academy asked Morse to do anatomical paintings for his medical classes. The athenaeum made him its secretary and invited him to lecture on the arts. By 1831 Morse had come round to the view that "New York is the capital of our country and here artists should have their rallying point."

Cole's was a similar story. Born in 1801 in Lancashire, England, where his father was a failed woolens manufacturer, Cole came to the United States in 1818 and became an itinerant painter of landscapes and portraits. In 1824 he came to roost in a Greenwich Street garret and began to exhibit scenes of upstate New York in local shops. Three of his works, displayed in the window of William Colman's bookstore, caught the eye of Trumbull, who reported his discovery to engraver Asher B. Durand and the playwright-painter William Dunlap. Each bought one, and they exhibited their acquisitions at an academy show in the New York Institution, where they caused considerable excitement. Philip Hone, William Gracie, Gulian Verplanck, and David Hosack ordered paintings from Cole for themselves, and Cole headed back upstate to produce more. He returned with a new batch, sold them at the academy, and left again for the mountains—a cycle that would be repeated over the next four or five years.

Like Morse and Cole, writers William Cullen Bryant and James Fenimore Cooper found the support of New York patricians crucial at the beginning of their literary careers. Bryant, originally from the Berkshire town of Cummington, Massachusetts, had been practicing law unhappily in Great Barrington before he came to Manhattan in 1825 to promote a book of poems and start life over as a journalist. The athenaeum hired him to edit its *New-York Review and Athenaeum Magazine*; the venture didn't flourish, and Bryant (echoing Vanderlyn and Morse) began to complain that "nobody cares anything for literature" in New York, where the only man considered a genius was "the man who has made himself rich." Then William Coleman, editor of the *Evening Post*, took Bryant on as his assistant. In 1829 Coleman died, and the thirty-four-year-old succeeded him as editor, giving "America's First Poet" a secure base of employment.

Cooper had grown up on his family's extensive Cooperstown estate, got himself kicked out of Yale, and drifted into the navy. When his father died he inherited an ample fortune and seemed destined for the life of an Episcopal squire in Westchester. But in 1821, now thirty-one, Cooper walked into the New York office of publisher Charles Wiley, carrying the manuscript of a novel about the Revolution entitled *The Spy*. Its publication made him famous and prompted him to move to the city to be near his publisher. Over the next six years he churned out *The Pioneers* (1823), *The Pilot* (1823), *The Last of the Mohicans* (1826), and *The Prairie* (1827). Meanwhile, in 1822, he began a series of midday get-togethers for writers, artists, and interested gentlemen in the back room of Wiley's New Street bookstore. First known as Cooper's Lunch, the conclave soon became the Bread and Cheese Club, named after the formalized balloting system for electing new members (a bit of bread signified acceptance, a piece of cheese rejection).

In one sense, Bread and Cheese was only the latest in a long line of fraternities organized in the city by dabbling amateurs and self-taught connoisseurs among the elite—most recently, the Knickerbocker wits who had held court at the Shakespeare Tavern and preserved their repartee in print, as much for their own amusement as for the public's. Yet it also contained the germ of something quite new. Among its members were artists and writers who regarded their crafts as full-time vocations, not hobbies to be pursued in moments snatched from law or commerce, and the club helped them forge a new kind of professional identity. Morse, Cole, Bryant, Durand, John Wesley Jarvis, and Dunlap cemented friendships there, as did Fitz-Greene Halleck, versifier and man about town; Gulian Verplanck, writer on law and theology, editor of Shakespeare, and spokesman of the New York Dutch; and James Kirke Paulding, still grinding out material for *Salmagundi*, his old venture with Washington Irving (who, now abroad, was a Bread and Cheese man in absentia).

Although the club failed to survive Cooper's departure for a long European sojourn in 1826, the growing sense of solidarity it bred among professional artists had already laid the foundation for a confrontation with Trumbull's Academy of Fine Arts. When some young painters sought access to the academy's collections to practice their drawing, Trumbull, full of patrician hauteur, barred the way and advised them to "remember that beggars are not to be choosers." Late in 1825 the painters struck back by founding their own organization, the New York Drawing Association, with Morse as president and Cole and Ithiel Town among the founding members. The following year it became the National Academy of Design, which unlike the Fine Arts Academy was to be run strictly by and for artists—"on the commonsense principle," Morse wrote, "that every profession in a society knows what measures are necessary for its own improvement." Artists all over the country came to think of the National Academy's annual exhibition as the most desirable place to show their latest work. In a similar spirit, Morse, Bryant, Cole, Durand, and Verplanck, with other professional writers and artists, came together in 1829 to form the Sketch Club.

All this was a frontal assault on the notion—an article of faith for men like Pintard and Clinton—that the propertied classes were competent to steer artistic and literary production for the greater municipal good, and it marked the beginning of a decline in genteel cultural authority. Artists had effectively shifted relations with the Hones and Hosacks, Gracies and Griswolds to a less paternalistic, more market-mediated footing, which in turn summoned professional "critics" into being. Before 1825 literary magazines hadn't covered the negligible fine arts world; now the weekly *New-York Mirror* began reviewing the annual exhibitions at the National Academy and reproducing some of the artwork via engravings and woodcuts.

The older model of patrician patronage, having helped foster a cultural community, now began to fade away. As early as 1828 the athenaeum abandoned its lecture program because too many well-to-do families were moving too far uptown (the reading room was eventually absorbed by the Society Library). The New-York Institution collapsed when the Common Council, on the recommendation of councilman James Roosevelt in 1830, refused to renew its lease on the almshouse and took the building over for municipal offices (after renovations by Alexander Jackson Davis). The Literary and Philosophical Society dissolved shortly thereafter, followed by the Academy of Fine Arts itself.

NATURE AND NOSTALGIA

For all their differences, patricians and artists had in common a lack of interest in New York City as a literary and artistic subject. Instead, they echoed the pastoral romanticism currently in vogue among European intellectuals (neither Wordsworth, Coleridge, Byron, Shelley, nor Keats located most of a major poem in contemporary London). Addressing the Academy of Fine Arts in 1816, Governor Clinton suggested that exposure to the "wild, romantic, and awful scenery" of the American wilderness had the power "to elevate all the faculties of the mind, and to exalt all the feelings of the heart" (both of which, by implication, suffered in the nation's cities). Within a decade, thanks less to Clinton's oratory than to canny steamboat operators and the appearance of fashionable rustic "resorts" far removed from Manhattan, hundreds of affluent New Yorkers left town every summer to experience the restorative powers of uncontaminated Nature. Their favorite destination was the Catskill Mountain House (1824), the first successful hilltop hotel in the United States and a must-see stop for Europeans on the American Grand Tour. Ladies and gentlemen disposed to visit the seashore went to Coney Island House (1824), a retreat famed for its first-class accommodations, well-prepared meals, and up-to-date bathing facilities.

New York writers fostered the new sensibility with a widening stream of novels and poems that depicted the American wilderness as an antidote to alienated urban life (rather as the refined home was held up as a sanctuary from city hurly-burly). Cooper's frontier romances were an extended paean to the nobility of the Catskills, while Irving, who had never been closer to the forest primeval than the deck of a river sloop, wrote lovingly of the supernal beauty of the Hudson highlands and their quaint inhabitants, who, like Rip Van Winkle, belonged to an earlier, less complicated time. Bryant, having fled the countryside for the big city, built an entire career on poetry that taught respectable merchants and bankers to yearn for woods, pastures, and streams.

Cole and his many disciples would convey the same message with even greater force in landscapes where all evidence of human presence was dwarfed by scenery so majestic and inspiring as to seem almost other-worldly—a point of view that garnered princely commissions from the very land speculators, canal boosters, and manufacturers who were doing their best to tame that scenery in the name of trade and commerce. What was more, some of Cole's earliest and best-known paintings—*Falls of Kaaterskill* (1826); *The Clove, Catskills* (1827); *Scene from "The Last of the Mohicans"* (1827)—were of subjects already immortalized, or soon to be, by Irving, Cooper, and Bryant. Though Cole's representations carefully deleted all signs of the new tourism, Catskill resort operators drew on his panegyrics, and those of Irving and Cooper, for use in advertisements. James Kirke Paulding, in his *The New Mirror for Travellers; and Guide to the Springs* (1828), urged "the picturesque tourist" not only to stay at the Mountain House but also to buy paintings from Cole and other landscape artists.

One of the few ways in which New York's artists were willing to appreciate the city was by turning to its past—or a sentimentalized nostalgic version thereof. Like Home and Nature, History seemed a sanctuary from the hurried present. In 1827 the *New-York Mirror* began a series called "Antiquities of New York" that combined wistful, Irvingesque stories of New Amsterdam with engravings of old Dutch buildings by Alexander Jackson Davis.

Bryant often escaped from downtown to explore groves along the Hudson or ramble past old Dutch farms in Brooklyn, looking for traces of history. In 1829–30, he and Gulian Verplanck wrote "The Reminiscences of New York," published in two successive issues of their annual, *The Talisman*. The fictive narrator of the piece fretted about the lack of "chivalric" associations common in Virginia or South Carolina: "I do not know whether any romance actually remains in New-York at the present moment," because "the progress of continual alteration is so rapid" that a few years can "sweep away both the memory and the external vestiges of the generation that precedes us." European cities changed little from decade to decade, but the narrator, having returned to Manhattan after an absence of just two years, found "every thing was strange, new and perplexing, and I lost my way in streets which had been laid out since I left the city."

Worse still was the prevailing antihistoric sensibility, evidenced by even so distinguished a citizen as Cadwallader Colden. In 1825, when hailing the opening of the Erie Canal, Colden had remarked: "We delight in the promised sunshine of the future, and leave to those who are conscious that they have passed their grand climacteric to console themselves with the splendors of the past." Bryant and Verplanck suspected that "New-Yorkers seem to take a pleasure in defacing the monuments of the good old times, and of depriving themselves of all venerable and patriotic associations." All the more imperative, therefore, to preserve any remaining "fragments of tradition and biography," and the authors accordingly chronicled the little church where Whitefield used to preach, the site of Washington's inauguration, Jefferson's home on Cedar Street.

Cooper too cherished the few Dutch dwellings that remained—"angular, sidelong edifices, that resemble broken fragments of prismatic ice"—regretting a growth rate that forced old buildings "out of existence before they have had time to decay." Asher Durand would try to conjure them back into existence by painting picturesque tableaux of New Amsterdam's past—as interpreted by Washington Irving—in works such as *The Wrath of Peter Stuyvesant*.

In the end, however, the ties that bound many Knickerbocker artists to the city would prove tenuous indeed. When Cooper returned from Europe, he withdrew to the old family manor at Otsego Lake. Irving would establish himself as a country squire at an old Dutch farmhouse near Tarrytown. And Cole retreated to a country home just north of Catskill. Nevertheless, New York's merchants, financiers, and lawyers were delighted with their artists' achievements. Given "the growing Fame" acquired by Irving and Cooper, Philip Hone believed, in time the city would "become as celebrated for taste and refinement, as it already is for Enterprise and public spirit."

Indeed, the Manhattan Medici had every reason to feel proud about the direction the civic ship was taking under their collective captaincy. They felt secure in their position as patrons of the arts and sciences, directors of economic enterprise, chief celebrants at municipal pageants, leaders in the political arena, and owners of most of the city's terrain. True, there were intramural debates between Knickerbockers and Evangelicals, but none had proved sufficiently divisive to override their common republican conviction that they could and should assume responsibility for the common good. But this serene self-confidence in their ability to speak for the city as a whole, without rebuke from below, was at the same time being called into question in a series of confrontations with obstreperous lower orders, who, day by day, were developing opinions and judgments considerably at variance with their own.

29

Working Quarters

On New Year's Eve, as the city bade farewell to 1827, several thousand workingmen—laborers, apprentices, butcher boys, chimney sweeps—set out from the Bowery on a raucous march through the darkened downtown streets, drinking, beating drums and tin kettles, shaking rattles, blowing horns. The crowd headed down Pearl Street into the heart of the city's commercial district, smashing crates and barrels and making what one account described as "the most hideous noises." From there the marchers wheeled across town to the Battery, where they knocked out the windows of genteel residences and attempted to tear down the iron railing around the park. At two in the morning they tromped up Broadway, just in time to harass revelers leaving a fancy-dress ball at the City Hotel. A contingent of watchmen appeared but, after a tense confrontation, gave way, and "the multitude passed noisily and triumphantly up Broadway."

During the seventeenth and eighteenth centuries, New York's propertied classes had more or less tolerated such instances of plebeian revelry because they were relatively harmless and (as Petrus Stuyvesant found out) difficult to uproot. Even after the Revolution, "Callithumpian bands"—echoing ancient European traditions—had continued to parade about, beating on pans, shouting and groaning, mocking the powerful and overly dignified. Respectable opinion had grown steadily less tolerant of self-organized plebeian frolics, however, partly because they affronted genteel notions of correct behavior, and partly because every year they became more truculent, more defiant of authority. It was one thing for great throngs of working people to rejoice noisily at Lafayette's visit or the opening of the Erie Canal, civic ceremonies orchestrated by gentlemen; it was quite another for rowdies to take over the streets, wantonly destroying property and terrorizing law-abiding citizens.

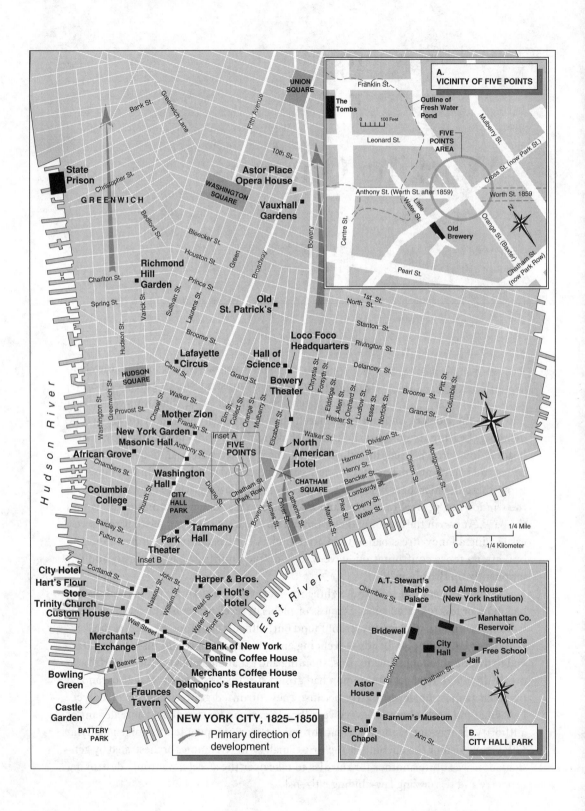

A. VICINITY OF FIVE POINTS

Franklin St.

The Tombs

0   100 Feet

Leonard St.

Mulberry St.

FIVE POINTS AREA

Cross St. (now Park St.)

Anthony St. (Worth St. after 1859)

Outline of Fresh Water Pond

Centre St.

Little Water St.

Worth St. 1859

Old Brewery

Orange St. (Baxter)

Chatham St. (now Park Row)

Pearl St.

N

UNION SQUARE

Bank St.

Greenwich Lane

Fifth Avenue

10th St.

State Prison

Christopher St.

WASHINGTON SQUARE

Astor Place Opera House

GREENWICH

Bedford St.

Bleecker St.

Vauxhall Gardens

Charlton St.

Richmond Hill Garden

Houston St.

Green

Broadway

Bowery

1st. St.

Spring St.

Varick St.

Sullivan St.

Prince St.

Laurens St.

Old St. Patrick's

North St.

Broome St.

Hudson St.

Lafayette Circus

Canal St.

Loco Foco Headquarters

Stanton St.

Rivington St.

HUDSON SQUARE

Walker St.

Grand St.

Hall of Science

Bowery Theater

Chrystie St.

Forsyth St.

Eldridge St.

Allen St.

Orchard St.

Ludlow St.

Essex St.

Norfolk St.

Delancey St.

Broome St.

Pitt St.

Columbia St.

Grand St.

Hudson River

Washington St.

Greenwich St.

Provost St.

Chapel St.

Elm St.

Collect St.

Orange St.

Mulberry St.

Hester St.

Mother Zion

Franklin St.

New York Garden

Masonic Hall

Anthony St.

Elizabeth St.

Walker St.

North American Hotel

Division St.

African Grove

Chambers St.

Inset A FIVE POINTS

Harmon St.

Henry St.

Bancker St.

Montgomery St.

Clinton St.

Columbia College

Washington Hall

Church St.

Duane St.

Chatham St. (Park Row)

CHATHAM SQUARE

Lombardy St.

Pike St.

Cherry St.

Water St.

Barclay St.

CITY HALL PARK

Bowery

James St.

Oliver St.

Catherine St.

Market St.

Fulton St.

Park Theater

Tammany Hall

Inset B

East River

City Hotel

Cortland St.

John St.

Harper & Bros.

Hart's Flour Store

Nassau St.

William St.

Holt's Hotel

Trinity Church

Custom House

Wall Street

Pearl St.

Water St.

Front St.

Merchants' Exchange

Beaver St.

Bank of New York

Tontine Coffee House

Merchants Coffee House

Bowling Green

Delmonico's Restaurant

Fraunces Tavern

Castle Garden

BATTERY PARK

NEW YORK CITY, 1825–1850

→ Primary direction of development

0   1/4 Mile

0   1/4 Kilometer

A.T. Stewart's Marble Palace

Chambers St.

Old Alms House (New York Institution)

Manhattan Co. Reservoir

Bridewell

City Hall

Rotunda

Free School

Jail

Broadway

Chatham St.

Astor House

Barnum's Museum

St. Paul's Chapel

Ann St.

N

B. CITY HALL PARK

The very next year, accordingly, Mayor Walter Bowne ordered the watch to disperse all crowds on New Year's Eve, and there was no Callithumpian procession. But such street confrontations would not fade away, in part because they were rooted in widening divisions between working-class wards and gentry precincts over the proper canons of public and private behavior.

WORKING QUARTERS

One point of divergence concerned the seemliness of living where one worked. While some prosperous entrepreneurial artisans had joined the gentility in commuting to their place of business from uptown bedroom communities, few master craftsmen, journeymen, or unskilled laborers could afford the expensive new omnibuses. They stayed, accordingly, in craft-based communities, within which they could walk to work.

Greenwich Village remained one such house-and-shop stronghold. Especially after the Christopher Street pier (1828) became the main point of entry for building materials used in transforming the uptown cityscape, the area grew dense with carpenters, masons, painters, turners, stonecutters, dock builders, and street pavers. Brooklyn Village too continued as a working community based on agricultural processing and transport, its streets lined with household-shops of coachmakers and coopers, saddlers and blacksmiths. Butchers remained prominent: one was elected first village president. By the mid-1820s the booming hamlet had more than tripled its prewar population, creating additional jobs for resident carpenters and masons.

Corlear's Hook still hosted the shipwrights, sailmakers, coopers, and chandlers whose livelihoods depended on the nearby shipyards—along with sailors, including a group of Chinese tars on Market Street who constituted the first significant Asian presence in New York. The Five Points also housed a great array of trades: breweries, potteries, and tobacco manufactories; tailoring, shoemaking, and printing establishments.

Bowery Village remained notorious for the stomach-turning stench of its slaughterhouses and tanyards. As late as 1825, upstate drovers like Daniel Drew were herding an estimated two hundred thousand head of cattle across King's Bridge each year and making their way, accompanied by hordes of pigs, horses, and bleating spring lambs, down Manhattan to Henry Astor's Bull's Head Tavern and adjacent abattoirs. A butcher who acquired an exceptionally fine cow would then parade it through the streets, preceded by a band and followed by fellow butchers in aprons and shirtsleeves, stopping before homes of wealthy customers, who were expected to step out and order part of the animal.

Some of those customers, bolstered by gentry families filtering in from the lower wards, wanted to transform the Bowery into a more genteel neighborhood. Taking aim at the stink, the endless whinnying, lowing, and grunting, and the occasional steer running amok and goring passers-by, they set about driving the Bull's Head from the area. In the mid-1820s, an association of socially prominent businessmen bought out Henry Astor and dismantled his enterprise. (A new Bull's Head opened in semirural surroundings at Third Avenue and 24th Street and soon attracted cattle yards, slaughterhouses, pig and sheep pens, and a weekly market; the area became known as Bull's Head Village, the city's northern frontier.) Meanwhile, in place of the old tavern, the consortium set about erecting Ithiel Town's splendid Greek Revival playhouse—the New York (soon to be Bowery) Theater. Mayor Philip Hone hailed the transformation as marking "the rapid progress of improvement in our City." But neither theater nor street was destined for gentility, and the Bowery would soon evolve into an entertainment strip for surrounding communities.

Within such working-class neighborhoods, the families of small masters, journeymen, and laborers lived in housing far different from the spacious abodes rising along Bond Street. Some speculative builders did raise modest but decent worker residences along streets carved out of the old De Lancey estate—many of them, including Eldridge, Ludlow, Forsyth, and Chrystie, named for military and naval heroes of the late war—or along 1st to 6th streets, the newly opened first fruits of the grid, which ran down to the East River.

However, with low incomes and expensive transportation tethering working people downtown, it proved equally profitable to exploit the captive market by cramming renters into preexisting spaces. In these aging structures, conditions varied from decent to squalid, but even at their best, the coal stoves, gas lights, iceboxes, and other improvements on display in the residences of the uptown gentry were unheard of. People made do with candles and oil lamps or scavenged winter wood along upper Manhattan's roadsides. Few households had a sufficient number of privies. Many laborers relied on cheap ceramic chamber pots from England, except for the very poor, who, in the phrase of the day, were "without a pot to piss in." Better-off families might have bedsteads or display clocks and prints on the wall. The poorest lived together in a single room, furnished with little more than a straw mattress, a few cast-off chairs, and a sawed-off barrel top for a table.

The plebeian quarters grew steadily more crowded, and the Sixth Ward's Five Points became the most densely packed neighborhood in the city. Its two- and three-story buildings, designed originally as one-family houses, housed an average of thirteen people as early as 1819, and by some estimates, building density doubled by the early 1830s. On Mulberry Street, homes with thirty-five occupants were not unknown; 122 Anthony housed eighty-three residents; 10 Hester Street contained 103; later in the decade, a brewery erected back in 1797 on the shores of the Fresh Water was transformed into a boardinghouse (known to all as the Old Brewery) that housed several hundred people. The mushrooming number of tenants in the area became overwhelmingly evident each Moving Day—by 1820 a scene of utter pandemonium, with thousands of people relocating at once, clogging the streets with wagons full of household possessions. It looked, Mrs. Trollope observed, as if the population were "flying from the plague."

WOMEN AT WORK

Within working-class neighborhoods, in further contrast to the more "refined" parts of town, women's labor was deemed indispensable. Given the declining fortunes of proletarianized males, and employer calculations of a "living wage" that implicitly included the value of women's unpaid domestic labor, many families were unable to make ends meet without the contributions of wives and children. A skilled wife whittled down the family's cash expenditures. She hauled in water and firewood, lugged out waste and garbage, washed, mended, and made clothes, tended the sick, and raised the children, passing on values of hard work, honesty, loyalty to family, and neighborliness.

Laboring women did not dress up and pay each other formal parlor visits—they had no parlors—but they socialized through open windows and dropped in at one another's kitchens, children in tow, to exchange gossip and information. Neighbors intervened in quarrels, sat up with sick infants, swapped news of market bargains, and helped out in crises (removing goods and furniture in case of fire, or rallying to block evictions). They also bickered and brawled in public, often engaging in extravagant donnybrooks that attracted crowds of cheering female onlookers.

Poorer women spent much of their time on the streets. Rather than retreat to domestic sanctuaries, they pawned and redeemed possessions, bargained with shop-keepers and peddlers for goods and credit, and scavenged for such discarded items as wood to burn, scraps of old clothing, and bits of food: one could scoop a week's worth of flour from a broken barrel on the docks. Children were dispatched to forage for manu-facturing wastes—nails and screws, old rope, broken glass, shreds of cotton plucked from wharves where southern packets docked. These could be sold to waterfront junk dealers, who in turn recycled them to iron founders, shipwrights, glassmakers, or mak-ers of shoddy (the cheap cloth used in producing "slop" apparel for the poor).

Women worked hard to supplement a diet that consisted largely of bread and potatoes, corn and peas, beans and cabbage, and milk from cows fed on "swill"—by-products of the city's distilleries. In good times, they might add salt meat and cheese, a little butter, some sugar, coffee, and tea. But meat and poultry, though widely available in city markets, were expensive, even when purchased for a reduced price at the end of the market day. Many working-class wives therefore kept their own animals, notably pigs; lacking the space to board them, they let the hogs run free to scavenge for them-selves. New York had long been infamous for its thousands of porcine prowlers, and when city fathers once again tried to sweep them from the streets, they touched off a raucous confrontation with poor mothers.

In 1818 Mayor Cadwallader Colden regretted that "our wives and daughters cannot walk abroad through the streets of the city without encountering the most disgusting spectacles of these animals indulging the propensities of nature." Copulating and defe-cating porkers were a decidedly ungenteel sight, and their "grunting ferocity" could be dangerous to children. Colden empaneled a grand jury, which indicted a butcher, Chris-tian Harriet, as a public nuisance for keeping hogs on the streets. He hired a lawyer, who contended that customary social practices, especially those "of immemorial duration," could not be declared a public nuisance unless they violated standards held in common by the entire population. Pigs might offend ladies and dandies, "who are too delicate to endure the sight, or even the idea of so odious a creature." But "many poor families might experience far different sensations, and be driven to beggary or the Alms House," if deprived of this source of sustenance. Mayor Colden, in charging the jury, ruled the food factor irrelevant, and Harriet was convicted, establishing the absence of a legal right to keep pigs in the street. In 1821 the Common Council ordered a roundup of the swinish multitudes, but when pig-owning Irish and African-American women discov-ered city officials seizing their property, they mobilized, hundreds strong, and forcibly liberated the animals. Further hog riots broke out in 1825, 1826, 1830, and 1832, invari-ably ending with the women saving their bacon.

Women also earned hard cash for their households. They took in laundry, catered for boarders, or sewed pantaloons and vests as outworkers. Some worked as neighbor-hood midwives; others assisted their artisanal or shopkeeping husbands (butchers' wives cut meat for market, junk-shop owners' spouses took care of customers). Still others roamed the city streets as hucksters, hawking roots and herbs they had dug up, clams collected from beaches, muffins purchased cheap at the end of the previous day's market, or berries and apples bought from country women at the edge of town. African-American hot-corn girls were famed for their street cry: "Hot corn, hot corn, here's your lily white hot corn / Hot corn all hot, just come out of the boiling pot."

If a huckster could afford the fee, she rented a stall at a city market; if not, she circulated among the market's customers. Those whose husbands could afford a backyard garden vended their own fruit and vegetables alongside the farmers' wives selling pot cheese, curds, and buttermilk. Others opened small shops and sold cookies, pies, and sweetmeats of their own manufacture or retailed sundries, needles, and pins. The most destitute became ragpickers, perambulating the streets with hooks and baskets, poking into gutters.

The most common way for a woman to earn money, however, was to work as a domestic servant. The expanding number of upper-class dwellings and artisanal boardinghouses generated a huge demand for household help. Most white American women considered the job degrading. Apart from the harsh conditions, heavy work load, low pay, and often antagonistic relations with employers, the position was tainted by its associations with slavery and aristocracy. As a European visitor noted in 1819, "if you call them servants they leave you without notice." When one domestic was asked to tell "your mistress" something, she exploded: "My *mistress*, Sir! I tell you I have no mistress, nor master either. . . . In this country there is no mistresses nor masters; I guess, I am a woman citizen." Poor immigrant women, of necessity, were more willing to put up with the job; by 1826 a survey found that 60 percent of New York's servants were Irish.

On the whole, however, while a woman's wages might well be instrumental in keeping her household afloat, she could seldom earn enough to support herself on her own. This was particularly evident from the condition of wage-earning widows, who often lived closeted in tiny garrets or huddled in cellars or half-finished buildings, at the edge of destitution.

"THE VILEST RABBLE, BLACK & WHITE, MIXT TOGETHER"

Working wards were different from genteel quarters, too, in their social composition. The Five Points in particular, as the *Evening Post* observed, was "inhabited by a race of beings of all colours, ages, sexes, and nations."

Immigration boosted and diversified the population throughout the city, of course. The number of people living in what are today the five boroughs rose from 119,734 in 1810 to 152,056 in 1820 (an increase of 27 percent), and by 1830 it had jumped to 242,278 (up another 59 percent). The immigrant percentage of this growing populace rose steadily (6.3 percent in 1806 to 9.8 percent in 1819) until by 1825 over a fifth of the city's residents were foreign-born.

Affluent arrivals might settle in the westside or uptown gentry wards, but relatively few were in a position to do so. Irish immigrants were getting steadily poorer. Ireland's cotton and linen industries had collapsed with the end of wartime demand, generating widespread unemployment and destitution. Agriculture too sagged badly, once Britain's wartime dependence on Irish foodstuffs slumped, cutting grain prices in half. Landlords responded by squeezing tenants, upping evictions, and consolidating lands, exacerbating a universal depression that led many to consider emigration to America "a Joyful deliverance."

In 1818 alone, some twenty thousand Irish crossed to America. Most, as in colonial days, were Presbyterian and Anglican Scotch-Irish migrants from Ulster, many lured by jobs on roads and canals (especially the Erie). The Panic of 1819 slowed the rate of arrival, and emigration remained modest through the early 1820s. When packet ships between Liverpool and New York began providing cheaper passage, poorer Catholics from Ireland's southern provinces began coming in growing numbers. Responding to intractable hard times at home and employment opportunities abroad, artisans, laborers, and single young women struck out on their own: passenger lists of vessels landing in New York in 1826 reveal that 62 percent of the Irish on board were traveling solo, and two-thirds of them were male. Many of those disembarking had exhausted their slender resources and were drawn—by its cheap rents and available jobs—to the Five Points' soggy terrain, moving, as it were, from bog to bog.

The Points was home as well to many newly freed blacks. As the emancipation clock ticked toward its scheduled rendezvous with freedom on July 4, 1827, New York's slave system collapsed. With immigration augmenting the supply of cheap free labor, manumissions mounted. The slave population of 2,369 in 1790 dwindled to 518 by 1820. African Americans declined as a percentage of New York's total population (from 8.8 percent to 6.9 percent over the 1820s), reflecting the quickening pace of European immigration. But the absolute number of blacks in the city grew substantially, from 3,262 in 1790 to 13,976 by 1830, as freedpeople flocked in from surrounding rural regions.

Slavery's grip had lasted longest in outlying farm country; as late as 1820 slaves constituted one-sixth the population of the agricultural communities of Kings County. When liberated, blacks relocated to nearby towns, flowing into Brooklyn Village, Jamaica, and Flushing's Crow Hill. They were also drawn to Manhattan, by the availability of jobs as domestics, barbers, caterers, launderers, hucksters, wood sawyers, whitewashers, swill gatherers, ragpickers, chimney sweeps, and day laborers.

The Five Points, 1827 (from *Valentine's Manual*, 1855). A cartoonish rendering of Paradise Square, heart of the Points—now the southwest corner of Columbus Park. Anthony Street (now Worth) heads diagonally off to the left while Orange Street (now Baxter) angles off to the right; Cross Street (later Park) runs left to right. The emphasis is on liquor, brawling, and pigs—all of which no doubt scandalized the dandyish outsider in the foreground. (© Collection of The New-York Historical Society)

In Manhattan, some blacks settled in the northern countryside: in 1825 members of the African Methodist Episcopal Zion church purchased parcels of farmland between 83rd and 88th streets and Seventh and Eighth avenues and erected several one-story unpainted cabins, forming the core of what would emerge as Seneca Village. A larger number moved to Greenwich Village, especially near Minetta Creek, where blacks had lived since Dutch days. Coachmen settled along a stable alleyway (it would evolve into Gay Street), but most took rooms in cramped and segregated boardinghouses. A bit farther south, still more blacks were drawn to the sunken Fifth Ward lots of the filled-in Lispenard Meadows, just behind New York Hospital. Others situated themselves along the strip of land spearing east along Chambers and Anthony (atop the Negro Burial Ground) or in the Five Points itself, where they occupied houses perched on insecurely reclaimed swampland, often in cellars, a scant few feet above water level, which flooded routinely.

Many of New York's African Americans thus lived in close proximity to the newly arrived Irish and longer-established Anglo-Dutch working people—creating a mélange one genteel observer characterized as "the vilest rabble, black & white, mixt together." There was no black ghetto, though some blocks were more single-hued than others. Bancker Street was notably black, overcrowded, and susceptible to disease. Of the 296 people killed by fever in the latter half of 1820, 138 were African Americans, and half of these died in the vicinity of Bancker Street. So bad was its reputation that the Bancker family (Rutgers relatives) demanded their name be struck off, and in 1826 Bancker was renamed Madison.

THEY GATHERED AT THE RIVER

The broad-spectrum quality of the working-class quarters extended to their religious institutions. Though the plebeian wards were theologically underserved in comparison to the thickly steepled gentry precincts, new houses of worship did arise, usually Catholic, Jewish, or evangelical Protestant, rather than Episcopal, Presbyterian, or Dutch Reformed (the dominant patrician denominations).

Even before the war, Father Kohlmann, Jesuit rector of St. Peter's on Barclay Street, believed that many of his sixteen thousand parishioners were "so neglected in all respects that it goes beyond conception." A second building was needed, especially for the growing number of Catholics "outside the city." As New York had been made a see in 1808, Kohlmann decided to provide the forthcoming new bishop with a cathedral. A site was selected on the corner of Prince and Mott streets, north of the settled town, in an area of country villas and scattered farm dwellings. Joseph Mangin (coarchitect of City Hall) provided a design; wealthy laymen, among them Dominick Lynch and Cornelius Heeney, helped raise the funds; and in 1815, the same year in which Irish Dominican John Connolly arrived to serve as bishop of New York, St. Patrick's Cathedral was dedicated. What is now referred to as Old St. Pat's was, moreover, the largest church in the city.

Bishop Connolly also presided over the Church's expansion into Brooklyn. In 1823 St. James Church, at the corner of Jay and Chapel streets, became the first Roman Catholic edifice in a community exclusively Protestant for two centuries. In that same year, Connolly invited Félix Varela y Morales to New York to begin a pastoral ministry among the Irish. They liked the Havana-born priest, an advocate of self-government and the abolition of slavery in Cuba, who published a bristling political magazine, *El Haberno*, and smuggled it down to Havana. Varela visited the sick and poor at all hours and purchased an old Episcopal church at Ann Street near the Five Points as a base of operations. By the time Connolly died in 1825, New York had thirty-five thousand Catholics, the great bulk of them poor Irish immigrants, and Gaelic working people dominated St. Patrick's. The Irish had begun to be possessive of the ethnically mixed St. Peter's too. When the Rev. John Dubois was installed as New York's new bishop, Irish parishioners angrily opposed the move, stirring irate French Catholics to describe their Irish confreres as "an ignorant and savage lot."

The House of Israel in New York City also fissured along ethnic, theological, class, and spatial lines. As of 1817 most of the city's four hundred Jews still lived by the Battery, and Shearith Israel on Mill Street was the only synagogue in town. There was talk of relocating farther north: the edifice was showing its age; some wealthy members, including copper manufacturer Harmon Hendricks, had moved uptown, a long Sabbath walk away; and commercial development was making the area less desirable. Nevertheless, in 1818 the community rebuilt and enlarged the synagogue on its original site.

During the 1820s, however, Jews definitively migrated uptown, sorting themselves out geographically on class lines. The richer families generally stayed west of Broadway, the modestly well off settled between Broadway and the Bowery, and the poorest repaired to Centre, White, and Pearl streets, in or near the Five Points. When German immigration picked up—7,729 Germans arrived in the United States in the 1820s, and 152,454 in the 1830s—it included (beginning in the late 1820s) a substantial number of Jews. As most of these were working class or poor, they too headed for the laboring quarters.

The Germans, along with Jewish migrants of Polish, Dutch, and English descent, were accustomed to Ashkenazic rites, but the established city Jews who ran Shearith Israel insisted on Sephardic ritual, alienating newcomers. The Mill Street temple was also far away, overcrowded, and required a payment of two shillings (for charity) before one could read from the Torah. In 1825, after protesting the latter practice (at the same time poorer Protestants and Catholics were attacking pew rents), the Ashkenazim split away from the parent body. Forming a new congregation, B'nai Jeshurun, they purchased a church on Elm Street, close to where less affluent Jews had settled, and adopted Ashkenazic ritual. In 1828 another split produced Anshe Chesed; more secessions followed as national groups sought their own synagogues. Finally, in 1833, the old Mill Street synagogue was sold off, and Shearith Israel erected an imposing gas-lit edifice on Crosby Street; its consecration in 1834 was attended by the mayor, several Christian clergymen, and many "of the most distinguished gentlemen of the city."

In working-class Protestant ranks, the Methodist and Baptist "mechanick preachers" of the turn of the century were followed by revivalists energized by the Second Great Awakening, then rolling into Manhattan from the frontier. Making use of successful camp-meeting techniques, they got urban congregants clapping, jumping, and screaming in holy ecstasy. Those seeking salvation were coaxed from their pews and "called to the altar," where they were prayed over until the spirit struck. Baptists gathered outdoors at the shoreline point of Corlear's Hook and performed rites of immersion in the East River. Between 1816 and 1826, at least ten Baptist churches were enlarged, rebuilt, or constructed in working-class wards, and shopfront chapels became

Baptising Scene, lithograph by Endicott and Swett, 1834. Immersions were a common sight along the Hudson as well as the East River. This one took place near the foot of modern Horatio Street in Greenwich Village, just below the White Fort erected during the War of 1812. (I. N. Phelps Stokes Collection. Miriam and Ira D. Wallach Division of Art, Prints and Photographs. The New York Public Library. Astor, Lenox and Tilden Foundations)

a common sight along the Bowery. Though popular evangelicalism would remain predominantly a western and rural phenomenon, by 1825 New York City had nevertheless become one of its three leading centers.

Methodists won working-class male and female converts by offering "free churches" that did not charge pew rents, allowing prayer in mixed-gender assemblies, and teaching that possession of earthly riches did not signify grace and might even suggest sin. On July 4, 1826, at potter's field, a gardener and lay preacher named David Whitehead invoked divine wrath against the "pretty set" who lived in luxury. Also in the mid-1820s, a group including Sarah Stanford, Baptist and daughter of almshouse chaplain John Stanford, began denouncing elite Presbyterians for their luxurious diets, clothing, and home furnishings.

Not all evangelicals were pleased with this turn of events. Nathan Bangs, "preacher in charge" of the Methodist Circuit of New York City since 1810, believed that the revivals had "degenerated into extravagant excitements." A severe, self-educated son of a Connecticut blacksmith, Bangs denounced the "impatience of scriptural restraint and moderation, clapping of the hands, screaming, and even jumping, which marred and disgraced the work of God." Bangs also demolished the old John Street chapel in 1817 and replaced it the following year with a much grander edifice. Gradually he marginalized the more enthusiastic preachers, curtailed the singing of spirituals, and imposed order, efficiency, and method. Bangs's emphasis on disciplined self-repression appealed to some Methodists, especially second-generation members who sought to combine spiritual salvation with dignified respectability. But others were distressed at Bangs's restrictions and the imposing new John Street Church. They broke away in 1820, formed their own "Methodist Society," and erected three more modest structures in the uptown wards.

African Methodists too were roused to new assertiveness. In 1821 Mother Zion broke from its parent body and, with two other black churches, formed its own denomination, the African Methodist Episcopal Church (later the African Methodist Episcopal Zion Church). African Zion became the largest black congregation in the city; its recruits included Isabella Van Wagenen, a newly arrived (1828), recently freed, Hudson Valley slave who would later rename herself Sojourner Truth.

Black Episcopalians also established a presence in the Five Points area. Peter Williams Jr., son of the sexton at John Street Methodist, studied for the Episcopal priesthood and in 1818 supervised the emergence of Saint Philip's Episcopal Church. With encouragement and financial aid from the parent denomination, members of St. Philip's, some of them skilled mechanics, constructed their own wooden church on Collect Street between Anthony and Leonard, right in the middle of the Fresh Water Pond landfill. In 1820 Williams was ordained a deacon; in 1826, elevated to the priesthood, he became rector.

ON THE TOWN

The spread of piety proved no barrier to a simultaneous expansion of prostitution throughout the city, but especially in working-class districts. Before the war, fee-for-service sex had been largely restricted to the old Holy Ground (just behind St. Paul's Chapel) and to a few blocks near the East River docks. Here streetwalkers and brothel strumpets made carnal connection with visitors, sailors, shipyard workers, and (according to various complainants) "idle Negroes," "dissolute persons," and "droves of youth." Outside these clearly defined waterfront districts, commercial sex in the early republican city—certainly by European standards—had a decidedly low profile.

In the 1820s, however, the sex trade boomed. Heightened demand came from the surging influx of single young male immigrants, sailors on shore leave, out-of-town businessmen, and the growing numbers of proletarianized journeymen who, facing an uncertain future, postponed marriage until their late twenties.

Heightened supply came from a pool of female migrants, deserted and widowed wives, and the expanding ranks of the working poor. When "respectable" employment garnered women one or two dollars a week and even low-end whoring fetched twenty to thirty dollars, some turned to part-time prostitution to supplement abysmal wages. Others abandoned miserable jobs as servants or seamstresses only when lashed by hard times—"going on the town" temporarily until conditions improved. (Some estimates suggest that perhaps 5 to 10 percent of all women between the ages of fifteen and thirty prostituted themselves at some point, with the figure rising above 10 percent during depressions.) Still others actively embraced the trade on a full-time basis. It paid well, allowed (indeed required) the purchase of fancy clothes, and offered entree into fashionable worlds from which their poverty-scarred mothers were forever barred. All-female brothels, moreover, offered a heady freedom from surveillance by male employers and from subjection to parental authority (or abuse).

The number of brothels in the city rose rapidly in the 1820s. By decade's end there were probably more than two hundred. Though the docks remained a haven for the coarsest bawdy houses, the riverfronts lost their monopoly on the business. Brothels thrived almost everywhere, their form varying with the local clientele. Elegant and expensive "parlor houses"—so called for their genteel furnishings and fashionably dressed residents—could be found just west of Broadway, a short walk from imposing elite homes, the big hotels, and the theatrical district by City Hall Park. Here native- or New England-born women held sway, many of them well spoken and well educated, some of them accomplished musicians. Parlor house girls could fetch fifty to a hundred dollars a week, working only afternoons and early evenings.

At Corlear's Hook, adjacent to the shipyards, coal dumps, and ironworks, droves of streetwalkers brazenly solicited industrial workers, sailors, and Brooklyn ferry commuters. So notorious was the Hook's reputation as a site for prostitution that (according to one theory) the local sex workers were nicknamed "Hookers," generating a new moniker for the entire trade.

It was the Five Points, however, that emerged as the summit of public sexuality. Prostitutes walked the streets day and night and worked out of saloons and "houses of bad fame" strewn along Anthony Street and the Bowery. Whoring here was famous for its interracial character. African-American New Yorkers, barred from all but service trades, assumed a significant role in the illicit economy. Some of their establishments catered exclusively to other blacks, but numerous Points saloons and brothels accommodated a mixed clientele with a mixed staff. Some haunts featured miscegenational sex; Cow Bay Alley's black-and-tan cabarets attracted venturesome young gentlemen from the proper west side to what municipal authorities in 1830 called the "hovels of negroes."

Some madams did extremely well. Maria Williamson, who by 1820 was already running what one contemporary called "one of the greatest Hoar Houses in America," reinvested her profits in additional brothels and soon owned over half a dozen. But the people who did best in the business were slum landlords. Rentiers delighted in housing madams, who paid hefty rents, and paid them right on time, unlike most tenants in poor neighborhoods, who paid late or not at all.

One of the most enterprising de facto whoremasters was John R. Livingston, brother of Chancellor (and steamboat financier) Robert Livingston. By 1828 he controlled at least five brothels near Paradise Square and a score more elsewhere in the city, with a tenant roster that included some of the best-known madams in New York. His involvement was well known, and when irate neighbors complained, he simply reshuffled the offending women to another of his buildings. Tobacco entrepreneur George Lorillard and Matthew Davis, a founder of Tammany Hall, were also among the ranks of patrician sex profiteers.

Theater owners, including John Jacob Astor (who had purchased the Park back in 1806), encouraged erotic third tiers as drawing cards, providing special entrances from which the *femmes du pavé* could reach the upper house. There assignations were struck and rendezvous arranged at nearby brothels (in the 1820s there were bordellos within easy walking distance of every major theater). Nor were hoteliers (Astor again chief among them) overly chagrined when whorehouses set up shop near their lobbies. The tourist-boosting potential of brothels was one of many reasons they were seldom bothered by the police, nor their landlords punished. Besides, prostitutes who did not solicit openly on the streets violated no law, and few men in positions of power were in any hurry to criminalize their activities. Police did occasionally raid low-life brothels, notorious for robbing patrons, but the arrested women were usually booked on charges of vagrancy or disorderly conduct.

If the sex trades flourished with the not-so-covert acquiescence of the town's male elite, genteel women upheld strict social sanctions against its female participants, no matter how much money they accumulated. Eliza Bowen Jumel, daughter of a Providence, Rhode Island, prostitute and herself a professional of some standing in her youth, had married French-born wine merchant Stephen Jumel, who in 1810 gave her the old Roger Morris mansion above Harlem. For all her wealth, she was barred from Knickerbocker society. Even after 1826, when she returned from a decade in France, where she'd won social acceptance, she was unable to crack the wall of disapproval and lived in splendid manorial isolation at 160th Street. (She did, however, manage a short-lived marriage in 1833 with the equally notorious Aaron Burr, who had returned to New York eight years after the duel with Hamilton and resumed the practice of law.)

"LET'S LIQUOR"

The eruption of commercial sex was accompanied by a surge in commercial drink— again, a phenomenon that suffused New York society but flourished particularly in the laboring quarters. Drinking was a long-established component of male working-class life. On the job, frequent drams fortified tiring workers: shipyard bosses would pass a pail of brandy, then suggest raising another timber. In hot weather, iced beer helped make steamy workshops bearable. Swigging was a preindustrial work habit, to which laborers clung all the more stubbornly in the face of drives for efficiency and punctuality launched by employers. Alcohol also lubricated rites of civic and communal solidarity—from militia musters to elections—and bouts of social drinking fueled unofficial holidays, such as boisterous wakes. The first words two just-met strangers might likely utter were "Let's liquor."

What changed in this era was the nature and availability of that liquor. After the Revolution, declining West Indian sugar imports, along with duties on rum and molasses, forced importers and distillers to hike prices. Western whiskey filled the breach, as farmers, using improved still technology, sent ever greater quantities of more potent liquor coursing eastward. Rampant overproduction hammered the price down to twenty-five cents a gallon, less per drink than tea or coffee. Urban outlets competed briskly to dispense the cheaper and higher-proof spirits. In 1819 thirteen hundred groceries and 160 taverns were licensed to sell "strong drink," with the Sixth Ward home to 238 of them. By 1827 there were more than three thousand approved outlets, and on some Five Points blocks over half the houses accommodated a grogshop or grocery. Brooklyn did its best to keep up: in 1821, of the village's 867 buildings, ninety-six were groceries or taverns.

Taverns were particularly popular with the vast numbers of young men stacked in dreary boardinghouses. Saloons became workingmen's parlors—places to eat, play, and affirm one's generosity by treating comrades. Saloons and groceries also served as informal labor exchanges; out-of-state employers set up temporary hiring halls there. In addition, publicans and grocers offered loans and lines of credit, posted bail bond, and provided workers a cushion in difficult times—while further encouraging consumption of booze.

Like commercial sex, commercial drink had powerful patrician supporters, including the city fathers, as a group of outraged petitioners discovered in 1829. Some twen-ty-four hundred memorialists from outside the Five Points urged the Common Council to tear down a triangle of the section filled with tenants, taverns, and "horrors too awful to mention" and build a new jail on the site. The Street Committee backed the propos-al, noting that the buildings in question were "in ruinous Condition" and occupied only by the "most degraded and abandoned of the human species." Others in government responded that the area produced great income for the Corporation "on account of its being a good location for small retailers of liquor who have located themselves in the vicinity. What may be considered a nuisance," they concluded, "has in reality increased the value of the property."

ON THE BOWERY

Men played as hard as they drank in the working-class wards. Though official opposi-tion had almost eliminated the baiting of bulls and bears by 1820, cockfighting contin-ued to thrive, as did ratbaiting, a blood sport even more suitably scaled for urban life. Patsy Hearn's Five Points grogshop, across from the Old Brewery, had a "Men's Sport-ing Parlor" famous for its ratfights. Seated on pine planks around a railed-in sunken pit, fifteen feet square, two hundred men at a time watched while an escaped slave named Dusty Dustmoor released packs of rats collected by neighborhood youths. While the rodents engaged in losing combat with trained terriers, spectators wagered furiously on the number of rats the dogs would kill.

Trotting flourished too, as plebeian drivers ran informal matches along Third Avenue from after work to dusk or on Sunday afternoons, after which they repaired with their panting steeds to one of the taverns dotting the high road. Eventually a track for harness racing was built in Harlem, and, in the winter of 1824–5, the New York Trotting Club was formed, dominated by prosperous butchers.

New circus theaters arrived as well. The Lafayette (on Laurens near Canal), the Broadway (in a large wooden building between Canal and Grand), and the Mount Pitt (on Grand Street nearer to Corlear's Hook) featured dancing girls, equestrian displays and races, and shows by traveling musicians and acrobats.

The most novel development in popular amusements was the transformation of the Bowery itself into a full-blown working-class entertainment strip. On Saturday night, after weekly wages were paid, pleasure seekers headed for its lamp-lit sidewalks. Bowery taverns, brothels, porter houses, oyster houses, dance halls, and gambling dens filled up with sailors, young butchers, day laborers, small employers, journeymen and appren-tices from nearby furniture shops and shipyards, and smartly dressed young women as well.

The street's premier institution was the Bowery Theater. For a few years after it replaced the Bull's Head Tavern, Ithiel Town's faux-marble Greek temple had, as planned, attracted genteel patrons. They liked its sumptuous crimson curtains, its gas-illuminated globes (the nation's first), its boxes painted gold in front and apple blossom in back—a color, the *Mirror* noted, that showed off the occupants "to best advantage." And the Bowery charmed the fashionable with fare similar to that offered by its Park and Chatham rivals: Shakespeare, sentimental dramas, farces, French dances, English operas, and Italian singers.

But the Bowery was far bigger than its competitors. It could hold a thousand more spectators than the Park. Usually it didn't, as patrician fare didn't lure plebeian audiences. So the management adjusted the entertainment mix to include more spectacular offerings. It ran equestrian events. (One paper noted that though the Bull's Head had been evicted only recently, "now horses are again prancing where they were formerly.") Tubes transported water to center stage for aquatic displays. Novelty acts abounded, including one in 1828 during which sixteen Indian warriors did the Pipe Dance on stage. The narrator-chief was shockingly nude from the waist up, but one newspaper assured New Yorkers that the "difference in color removes all the idea of indelicacy, which a similar exposure of white men would occasion."

Charles Gilfert, the Bowery's manager, also found that tragedies seldom drew audiences sizable enough to cover the large salaries required to win top actors—already known as "stars"—away from rival theaters. So he turned to melodramas, a recent British import that provided blood-and-thunder action, spectacular mechanical enhancements, and starkly moralistic plots. Melodramatic heroes and villains—their characters written all over their faces—battled to an invariably happy ending, in which the forces of evil were overcome.

The Bowery nurtured America's first master of the form, the Manhattan-born Shakespearean actor Edwin Forrest. Though he made his debut at the Park in 1826, Gilfert won him away to the Bowery for the next several years. Forrest's bombastic, muscular style matched the demands of melodrama and the proclivities of the working-class portion of the Bowery's audience. Their roars of approval lofted him to heights of fame unmatched by any contemporary American actor.

Gilfert tried to keep his elite attendees happy too, with English dramas and English stars, who worked in the British style featured at the Park, but the balancing act proved difficult to sustain. Gilfert died suddenly in 1829 and was succeeded in 1830 by Thomas Hamblin, who wholeheartedly cast his lot with the Anglo- and Irish-American artisans and laborers who peopled the surrounding neighborhoods. The Bowery ostentatiously promoted "native talent," and its hyperpatriotism, lower prices, stage pyrotechnics, and shrewd choice of plays (Hamblin immediately doubled the number of melodramas) garnered an intensely loyal and vociferous audience of shopkeepers, small masters, wage-earners, and prostitutes. The elite decamped. By the time Mrs. Trollope arrived, it was evident that although the Bowery was "as pretty a theater as I ever entered," it was decidedly "not the fashion."

JUMP JIM CROW

New York's theaters and working-class communities nurtured into vigorous life a peculiarly American cultural product: the minstrel show, a racially charged entertainment form that would eventually sweep the nation and much of Europe. Minstrelsy had many seedbeds, but one of the most important lay in black Manhattan.

In the summer of 1821 William Henry Brown opened a pleasure garden in his back yard. Brown, a West Indian black, had served as a steward on Liverpool packets before giving up the sea and buying a house at 38 Thomas (between Chapel and Hudson), a street well known for its brothels. Now he dispensed brandy and gin toddies, porter and ale, ice cream and cakes to black patrons, who were barred from the other private gardens in town. The African Grove, as Brown called it, was a smashing success. As the *National Advocate* noted, "black dandies and dandizettes" gathered in their finest (the

men particularly resplendent in their fashionably cut blue coats, cravats, white pantaloons, and shining boots) to saunter and flirt, listen to music from a "big drum and
clarionet," and, occasionally, hear songs sung by James Hewlett, a waiter at the City
Hotel.

In the fall of 1821 Brown moved his entertainments inside, a shift hastened by complaints from white neighbors about the noise, and launched his African Theater. Brown
offered mostly Shakespeare—Hewlett, who proved a gifted thespian, opened as Richard
III—and modern plays as well. As in white theaters, hornpipes were danced and comic
songs sung between acts. The African Theater was a great success with black men and
women. More remarkable, white patrons began showing up in substantial numbers,
allowing Brown to move to a thrice weekly schedule, and he replaced "African" with
"American" in the company's name.

The entrepreneurial Brown decided to expand still further. He rented a house way
uptown, on the southeast corner of Mercer and Bleecker, and again whites turned out,
especially "laughter loving young clerks," though some were more interested in heck-
ling than listening. The *National Advocate* noted in October 1821 (with conventional
condescension) that the troupe had "graciously made a partition at the back of their
house, for the accommodation of the whites" who, the group's handbill said, "do not
know how to conduct themselves at entertainments for ladies and gentlemen of color."

Giddy with success, Brown now overreached. He audaciously rented space in a
hotel right next door to the Park Theater and put on three performances a week during
January 1822. The Park's manager hated the competition and hired ruffians who
cracked jokes, threw crackers onto the stage, and started a riot. The watch responded
but, rather than ejecting the provocateurs, arrested the cast, with Hewlett wittily tossing
off Shakespearean lines as he was hauled away.

Brown set up shop again at his former quarters, and his patrons, now predominantly white, followed him. For a brief time, audiences could watch the earliest work of one
of the era's great actors, Ira Aldridge, until the teenager's father, a deacon at Mother
Zion, made him quit to pursue a ministerial career. (To no avail: Aldridge, aware he had
no chance to develop his talents in race-bound New York, fled to London, where he
would play Othello at the Royal Theatre, and become the rage of Europe for a quarter
century.)

Brown's troupe carried on through the summer of 1823, surviving a nasty assault in
August 1822, when fifteen members of a nearby circus, camped above Canal Street,
attacked the theater, beat Brown severely, stripped the actors and actresses, and demolished the furniture and scenery. Whether the company fell victim to further white violence, a yellow fever epidemic, or limited financial resources is unknown, but Brown
closed on a militant note, offering a drama of his own creation, *The Drama of King
Shotaway, Founded on facts taken from the Insurrection of the Caribs in the Island of
St. Vincent*.

Apart from a final attempt to establish a black theater later in the 1820s, African
Americans would not again stride the boards in New York City for many decades. What
replaced genuine black performance was "blackface minstrelsy," in which white men,
painted up as black men, mimicked what they alleged to be Negro culture.

Blackface "masking" had been familiar to colonial Americans, in the form of rioters
blacking up to hide their identity and in onstage portrayals of Negroes by Caucasians.

But probably the first white person to deliberately appropriate elements of black culture for the purpose of performance was Charles Mathews, an English actor who toured the United States in 1822–23. Mathews, known for his benignly humorous renderings of Scots, Yorkshiremen, and other regional British "types," quickly added a "Yankee" characterization for local audiences. He also began assembling scraps of song and dialect from black preachers, stagecoach drivers, and the actors at William Brown's African Theater. From this body of transcribed lore, speeches, and sermons, Mathews built up a "black" characterization, which became a staple of his new act, *A Trip to America*. Mathews later claimed he'd seen the audience at the African Theater demand that Aldridge, playing Hamlet, stop his soliloquy and sing the popular freedom song "Possum up a Gum Tree." Aldridge denied Mathews's story, though claiming not to mind, as Mathews was a fictional humorist. But Mathews's use of the song appears to be the first certain example of a white borrowing black material for a blackface act.

Others followed Mathews—in 1823 Edwin Forrest took the boards as a plantation black, and in 1828 George Washington Dixon sang "negro melodies" such as "The Coal-Black Rose"—but the man who created blackface minstrelsy was a New Yorker named Thomas Dartmouth "Daddy" Rice.

Rice, born in the Seventh Ward in 1808, apprenticed as a woodworker but abandoned the artisanal life for a theatrical one (he was not alone in segueing from a collapsing craft into the flourishing world of commercial culture). Drifting west, Rice worked as a stagehand and bit player throughout the Mississippi Valley. In 1828, according to one version of the story, he came across a crippled old slave named Jim Crow who did an odd shuffling dance. Rice borrowed the man's style, his persona, even his clothes, and fashioned a song-and-dance routine that became an instant sensation. Dressed in a dilapidated, ill-fitting costume, with patched breeches, a broad-brimmed hat, and holes in his shoes, Rice would roll his body lazily from one side to the other while singing his waggish signature ditty in exaggerated dialect. Audiences used to the high-stepping tapping of Irish jigs thrilled to the black-derived shuffle (ancestor of the soft shoe), in which the feet remained close to the ground and upper-body movements carried the action.

By the late 1820s Rice was serving up his alleged Negro songs and dances as brief burlesques and bits of comic relief in circuses, theaters, museums, and pleasure gardens throughout the West. In November 1832 he brought his routine back home. Spectacularly successful, Rice regularly "jumped Jim Crow" at the Bowery Theater, sandwiched between plays as an entr'acte. In January 1833 he staged a full "Ethiopian Opera"— *Long Island Juba, or, Love by the Bushel*—featuring a group of "blacks." And in May 1834 he put his character to topical use as a participant in a play called *Life in New York, or, the Major's Come*, in which Rice tunefully discussed a ride in an omnibus, a trip to Harlem, and life in the Five Points.

Guised in blackface, the artist could also safely mock elites, snobs, and condescending moralists. But if Rice's Ethiopian operas skewered upper-class manners and pretensions, they mainly lampooned blacks. Jim Crow, the slow-witted, irrepressibly comic "plantation darky," was soon joined by Zip Coon, the second essential stereotype of the nascent minstrel tradition. Where Jim Crow evoked the rural South, Zip Coon, a fancied creature of the urban North, was a foolish, foppish, self-satisfied dandy. An ultramodish dresser, he was given to skintight pantaloons, a lacy jabot, a silk hat, a lorgnon

T.D. Rice as Jim Crow, 1833. During Rice's performances at the Bowery Theater, enthusiastic audiences routinely clambered onto the stage, leaving him little room to perform. (© Collection of The New-York Historical Society)

held with effeminate affectation, and his beloved "Long Tail Blue," an indigo coat with padded shoulders and long swishing tails.

Rice and other minstrels assembled the Zip Coon image from fact and fiction. There were blacks who thrived on imitating (or parodying) white dandies—who enjoyed wearing flamboyant, brightly colored, occasionally mismatched articles of clothing, purchased cheaply in urban markets. White minstrels gained familiarity with black manners, games, and dances in the racially integrated streets, taverns, and brothels of the Five Points or waterfront.

Crow and Coon were paradoxical creations. Their primary import was racist ridicule. Slavery was presented as right and natural; slaves as contented, lazy, and stupid; northern blacks as larcenous, immoral, and ludicrous. At the same time, Rice's act (like those of his colleagues) was laced with envy. At a time when employers, ministers, and civic authorities were demanding productivity, frugality, and self-discipline, Crow and Coon shamelessly indulged in sensual pleasures. Minstrelsy projected unbuttoned modes of behavior onto "blacks," allowing spectators to simultaneously condemn and relish them.

Minstrelsy was an exercise in creative cultural amalgamation, something for which New York would become famous. It blended black lore with white humor, black banjo with Irish fiddle, African-based dance with British reels. Rice's act embraced the promiscuous racial reality of America—nowhere more dramatically evident than in the Five Points—yet it was received with greatest enthusiasm by white Boweryites, who were increasingly concerned to demarcate their culture from that of blacks. By constructing a spurious image of "blackness," it helped develop a category of "whiteness." At the Bowery Theater, Anglo- and Irish-Americans, in laughing together at "niggers," forged a common class identity built on a sense of white supremacy.

RUNNING WITH THE MACHINE

Whiteness, however, was far too broad a social category to be serviceable as an everyday identity marker, especially given the diminishing percentage of African Americans in the city. Working-class communities spawned numerous social organizations, keyed to work or neighborhood, within which working-class males gained a sense of participation and belonging.

With bucket brigades obsolete—the department formally abandoned them in 1820—firefighting became ever less a civic enterprise, ever more the private prerogative of the (as of 1825) fifty volunteer fire companies. These groups were changing, getting younger, and drawing in far more journeymen and laborers than masters and merchants. They were evolving into a species of workingmen's fraternal order, replete with mottoes, ornate insignias, and names that honored heroes and heroines of the republic, the theater, or the turf. After work, mechanics would rendezvous at their engine house, socializing while they polished their elaborately painted machines, or they would repair to the particular bar or oyster house their company had adopted as a haunt. The volunteers developed tremendous esprit de corps and marched together, with their gleaming machines and colorful banners, in every municipal celebration.

Rivalry between these fiercely proud and intensely macho companies led to regular scuffles, ranging from prankish raids on rival firehouses to capture their regalia right on up to battles over who had the rights to a particular fire. At first alarm, some companies would send out an advance guard to put a barrel over the nearest hydrant, sit atop it, and defend it until his comrades arrived. This precipitated fierce fights for possession of the water supply, rather than conjoint concentration on wetting down the flames.

Such combat drew in others. Most fire companies attracted a set of hangers-on, usually boys (over half the school-age population was not in school). The youths were drawn by the excitement and physicality of firefighting: nothing else in urban life could match it. There were also large numbers of men—temporarily or seasonally or permanently unemployed—who enlisted as informal volunteers, helping to drag the engines. In 1824 the Common Council, complaining of the number of boys, idlers, and vagabonds hanging about the firehouses, ordered the companies to dispense with their services, but soon they were back again.

Clusters of young workingmen also formed themselves into gangs. These groups swaggered about the city after work and on Sundays, staking out territories, picking fights, defending the honor of their street or their trade. Butcher's-boy gangs like the Highbinders were particularly obstreperous, hardened as they were by the bloody work of dispatching cattle, but watermen brawled as well, taking on bookbinders and printers.

Religion too became a rallying ground and point of contention. On July 12, 1824, the anniversary of the Battle of the Boyne, Irish Presbyterian laborers took up fife, drum, and Orange flag and commenced a celebratory parade through Greenwich Village. Awaiting them were a grim assembly of Irish Catholics, mostly weavers, who demanded the Orangemen lower their colors. Someone threw a punch, out came clubs and brickbats, and a furious donnybrook got underway. After countless rioters had fallen, the watch arrived and arrested thirty-three participants, all Catholics.

At the ensuing trial, Emmet and Sampson got their compatriots off by recounting to the judge, Recorder Richard Riker, the long history of Irish mistreatment. Riker responded evenhandedly, chastising the Orangemen for introducing to the United

States the "dangerous and unbecoming practices, which had caused so much disorder and misery in their own [country]," and blaming the Catholics for letting themselves be provoked. He then lauded all the combatants as valuable accessions to the nation and urged them to set aside ancient quarrels and forge amicable relationships in their adopted homeland.

Like the Callithumpian bands, bumptious volunteers and fractious gangs, as emblems of disorder, would draw increasing attention from civic authorities concerned over what appeared to be growing numbers of masterless men.

30

Reforms and Revivals

In the spring of 1817 a New York charitable agency announced, with mingled pride and dismay, that during the previous winter "fifteen thousand, men, women, and children, equal to one-seventh of the whole population of our city, have been supported by public or private bounty and munificence!" Already the alarming size of this dependent population had prompted New Yorkers active in benevolent work to begin reemphasizing the centuries-old distinction between the "deserving" and "undeserving" poor—or, as such leading British political economists as Thomas Malthus, David Ricardo, and Jeremy Bentham were now putting it, between poverty and pauperism.

These were held to be very different conditions, meriting very different responses. Poverty was providential. The sick and crippled, the old and orphaned, the widowed and deserted, the victims of epidemics and casualties of war were poor through no fault of their own, and their plight warranted at least a minimalist benevolence. Pauperism, however, stemmed from laziness, fraud, and assorted moral degeneracies, and it called for chastisement and correction, not charity.

Thomas Eddy, one of New York's most influential reformers and sometime warden of Newgate Prison, agreed. As he explained to De Witt Clinton, he had grown "tired assisting them in their distress, and it appears to me more wise, to fix on every profitable plan to *prevent* their poverty and misery." His decades-long correspondence with Patrick Colquhoun had kept him well informed about the work of the London Society for Bettering the Condition of the Poor, and he had decided that the time was ripe for a similar body in New York. In December 1817, together with master organizer John Pintard and the Quaker chemist John Griscom, Eddy called a meeting out of which emerged the Society for the Prevention of Pauperism (SPP).

The SPP membership was top-heavy with prominent merchants, lawyers, and clergy, representing a cross-section of political and denominational loyalties, Yankees as well as Knickerbockers. These were essentially the same men who for the past two or three decades had led the Humane Society, the Free School Society, New York Hospital, the New-York Historical Society, the Literary and Philosophical Society, and other cultural and benevolent organizations in the city. Many were also deeply involved in promoting the Erie Canal.

They now threw their collective weight behind the view that pauperism stemmed from ignorance, idleness, intemperance, extravagance, imprudent marriages, and deficient childrearing practices—what Griscom called the lack of "correct moral principle." Willy-nilly benevolence only made it worse. Giving alms to the undeserving poor not only undermined their independence but also drove up taxes and sapped the prosperity of the entire community. For their good as well as everyone else's, therefore, the SPP recommended that all paupers in the city be cut off from all public assistance forthwith.

Not all the elite subscribed to the new sink-or-swim wisdom. Mayor Cadwallader Colden, for one, expressed doubts that the multiplication of New York's poor was "justly to be imputed to either her public or private charities." He blamed it, instead, on a wave of unemployment triggered after 1815 by Britain's "reduction of great naval and military establishments, the abridgment of her commerce, the curtailment of her manufactures, and the astonishing operations of her labor-saving machines." Almshouse chaplain Stanford was another holdout, arguing that since the poor had helped "multiply the treasures of the rich" through their labor, the rich were "morally obligated to relieve a necessitous person." These dissenters made no headway against the massed prestige of the SPP, and both municipal and state governments began to implement its recommendations. The Common Council halted contributions to all charitable enterprises except for the Humane Society and the City Dispensary. Governor De Witt Clinton proclaimed his intention to wipe out pauperism "by rendering it a greater evil to live by charity than by industry." In 1823 the legislature charged Secretary of State John Van Ness Yates to report on the condition of the poor and the administration of relief throughout the state. Echoing the SPP, Yates's committee attributed pauperism to "vice of all kind"—especially in New York City, which attracted the "idle and dissolute of every description." Subsequent legislation ended outdoor relief throughout New York State, except (to the SPP's annoyance) in New York City, where the dramatic fluctuations of the economy made it as yet impracticable and impolitic to do so.

Private benevolence slacked off as well. The ad hoc ward committees that had helped the victims of hard times during the embargo and war years now vanished, nowhere more abruptly than in Brooklyn. In the terrible winter of 1817, when the thermometer plummeted to twenty-six below zero and Buttermilk Channel iced over so thickly that horse-drawn sleighs crossed to Governors Island, the Brooklyn Humane Society had set up a soup house for the distressed poor. But as the new maxims of British political economy made their way across the East River, the society announced that its benevolence had been misguided. Alms-giving, it now realized, had "a direct tendency to beget, among a large portion of their fellow citizens, habits of imprudence, indolence, dissipation and consequent pauperism." Accordingly, the Humane Society announced that no food or firewood would be forthcoming the following winter, and to hammer the point home, the group disbanded.

The efficacy of charity likewise fell under suspicion among the genteel women who led the Society for the Relief of Poor Widows with Small Children. As recently as 1815 the ladies had rejected the lazy-poor line and indeed reported that "an attentive observation has thoroughly convinced us that it is an impossibility for a widow, with the labor of her own hands, to support her infant family . . . even if work abound." Then, however, the men of the SPP denounced the Relief Society's work on the grounds that giving charity to widows with children incited those without to become pregnant, "which is highly immoral, and ought not be tolerated in a christian land." Despite the best of intentions, in other words, the women had been "encouraging population among the poor, and increasing the number of paupers," a line of reasoning that won converts.

So how did the SPP propose to prevent pauperism in New York, beyond shutting down the flow of ill-advised charity? The answer was to inculcate the undeserving poor with the values that would make them useful and productive members of society: sobriety, cleanliness, industriousness, frugality, punctuality, good manners, and the like. European precedents suggested a host of tactics, among them savings banks, workhouses, Sunday schools, and a ban on street begging, all of which the SPP advocated. Another possibility, currently underway in Glasgow and Hamburg, was the "moral superintendence of neighborhoods." The idea was to divide the city into districts, each of which would be assigned to two or three well-bred visitors who could advise the poor on such matters as domestic management, childrearing, and proper conduct. For several years SPP "visitors" fanned out through the city, diligently compiling information on the background and character of every resident. By 1821, though, the project had foundered. Only one district had a visitation system fully in place, and that was a fashionable neighborhood where 90 percent of the householders were found to be of "good" character and there wasn't a pauper in sight.

URBAN MISSIONARIES

Evangelicals in the city had meanwhile discerned a connection between pauperism and religious absenteeism. It was no secret that many poor New Yorkers were still unchurched—according to the SPP itself, some fifteen thousand of the city's twenty-five thousand families rarely if ever took part in worship services—at least in part because poor neighborhoods had too few churches and their residents weren't often welcomed by congregations in well-to-do parts of town. Until it became linked with the genteel revolt against charity, however, urban irreligion had aroused only fitful interest among mainstream Christian denominations. The New-York Missionary Society, founded back in 1796, targeted Indians and settlers on the frontier. The Society for Supporting the Gospel Among the Poor of the City of New-York had been formed back in 1812, but its primary concern remained the underwriting of John Stanford's preaching to hospital, prison, and almshouse inmates.

All this changed after 1815, when a new generation of evangelicals began work "among the destitute of our own city." In 1818 the Female Missionary Society for the Poor of the City of New-York established a free church in African-American Bancker Street—the very "seat of Satan." The following year they planted another chapel on Allen Street, near Corlear's Hook. The ladies retained ministers to garrison these outposts but also took the field themselves, visiting the poor, praying with them in their homes, and coaxing destitute mothers to church. Clerics found such female initiatives alarming, and in 1821 the Rev. William Gray told the women that because they "had engaged in an enterprise beyond your appropriate sphere," active management had

"been wholly transferred from the hands of the Ladies into those of the Gentlemen."
Ministers applauded when the Presbyterian Young Men's Missionary Society of New-
York built a church near Corlear's Hook and staffed it with eager young preachers, and
when the Presbyterian New-York Evangelical Missionary Society of Young Men set up
mission stations in the Hook and on Bancker Street, where they conducted services,
visited families, and held prayer meetings.

Like the SPP, evangelicals believed in "moral superintendence." The Rev. Ward
Stafford, Female Missionary Society preacher-at-large, argued in his *New Missionary
Field* (1817) that "the very sight of the moral and pious is a check to the wicked."
Because New York wasn't a "well-regulated village," where the "character, and circumstances of every family are almost necessarily known," it was imperative for godly men
and women to make their presence felt, dispensing not charity but their own righteousness. Stafford also accepted the reigning orthodoxy: "If people believe, that they shall
be relieved when in distress," he asserted, "they will not generally make exertions, will
not labour when they are able and have the opportunity." But "let it be known that death
or extreme suffering will be the consequence of idleness, or profligacy, and the number
of the idle and the profligate will soon be diminished."

The urban mission movement expanded steadily in the next few years, with the
waterfront and its "vastly wicked" sailors drawing particular attention. Stafford helped
organize both the New-York Marine Missionary Society (1817) and the Port of New-
York Society for Promoting the Gospel Among Seamen (1818). Together they erected
the interdenominational Mariner's Church (1819) on Cherry Street near the East River
docks. In 1821, even more aggressively, the New-York Bethel Union began holding
nightly prayer meetings aboard wharfed ships and in sailors' boardinghouses and
offering comfort to families whose breadwinners had been lost at sea. In 1822 many of
the new missions came together in the United Domestic Missionary Society, which
four years later took the lead in founding the nationwide American Home Missionary
Society.

SPREADING THE GOOD NEWS

In 1816 a group of prominent reformers—Henry Rutgers, David Low Dodge, Divie
Bethune, Gardiner Spring, Richard Varick, and Governor De Witt Clinton, among others—founded the American Bible Society (ABS) for the purpose of printing and distributing Bibles throughout the United States. New York was deemed the appropriate
headquarters city for such an organization—indeed, the ABS constitution required that
twenty-four of its thirty-six managers reside in Manhattan or vicinity—because of the
advanced state of its printing industry. In particular, New York printers had been the
first in the country to adopt a revolutionary new British technique called stereotyping.

Formerly, a printer set a page by locking movable type into a form that would be
disassembled once the required number of impressions for a given press run had been
taken. In stereotyping, however, the printer made a mold of the page before disassem-
bling the form, then cast a metal plate that could be inserted in the press over and over
again, whenever a new printing was wanted, so the page would never have to be reset.
(The plate was the stereotype itself, from the Greek *stereo*, or solid; thus "stereotype"
would come to mean any often-repeated concept or image.) It was an expensive process
but made good economic sense with books destined for massive and repeated print runs.
Not surprisingly, one of the first objectives of the ABS was to acquire a full set of "well-

executed stereotype plates" of the Bible, and within a few years the presses in its sumptuous Nassau Street headquarters, nicknamed Bible House, were producing tens of
thousands of Bibles every year. Completion of the Erie Canal in 1825 ensured that the
reach of Bible House would extend into every corner of the developing West.

Nor did the ABS neglect the widening war on irreligion in the city itself. It too
believed that pauperism could be defeated by the Word, and it helped organize an
expanding network of local groups—including the New-York Female Auxiliary Bible
Society (1816), the Female Juvenile Auxiliary Bible Society (1816), the New-York
Union Bible Society (1816), the New-York African Bible Society (1817), and the New-
York Marine Bible Society (1817)—whose members distributed Bibles in slums, brothels, grogshops, gambling dens, hospitals, and jails. Sometimes they ran into trouble. "A
respectable man, not long since, who was distributing Bibles," the Rev. Stafford reported in 1817, "was attacked, knocked down, and had his clothes literally torn off, and was
so beaten as to lose considerable blood." Sometimes they were laughed at by sailors
brandishing books by "Hume, Gibbon, Paine," and other infidels. Nor did Jews appreciate being the target of conversion drives: printer Solomon H. Jackson's *The Jew*
(1823–25), the first Jewish periodical published in the United States, consisted mainly
of monthly diatribes against Christian missionaries.

Their biggest problem, however, often proved to be the Bible itself—too big, too
long, too complex to be a convenient instrument of urban evangelism. Not so the pamphlets and booklets distributed by the New York Religious Tract Society, founded back
in 1807 by many of the same men who subsequently created the American Bible Society. Initially, the Tract Society had been content with British imports—such inspirational tales as "The Duties and Encouragements of the Poor," "Destructive Consequences of Dissipation and Luxury," "Happy Poverty," and the like—which it
forwarded in bulk to frontier missionaries. After 1815, however, it joined the evangelical
crusade against urban pauperism and gave rise to a pair of auxiliaries that dispensed
tracts among the city's poor: the Young Men's Tract Society (1821) and a special Female
Branch (1822) organized by Mrs. Divie Bethune (the former Joanna Graham), which
enlisted the support of several hundred prominent women.

In 1825 the New York Tract Society combined forces with the New England Tract
Society to form the American Tract Society (ATS). Like their counterparts in the ABS,
the directors of the new group readily agreed to set up headquarters in New York,
knowing that the Erie Canal would ensure them easy access to western settlements—
and because the city was home to wealthy benefactors like textile importer Arthur Tappan, banker Moses Allen, and merchants David Low Dodge, Anson Phelps, and
Thomas Stokes. Tappan and Allen paid for the construction of Tract House on Nassau
Street, which, like the ABS's nearby Bible House, held the organization's offices,
foundry, bindery, and stereotype-finishing functions. (The availability of stereotyping
in Manhattan, the directors said, had been "a powerful argument in favor of union.") It
was likewise Arthur Tappan's gift of five thousand dollars that led, in 1826, to the
installation of New York's first steam-powered press on the fourth floor of Tract House.
By 1829, four years before Harper Brothers became the first commercial publisher to
install one, the Tract Society had sixteen of the machines, all built by Robert Hoe, soon
the country's leading manufacturer of printing presses.

The offspring of this marriage of technology and evangelism was an unprecedented outpouring of printed matter—six million tracts (61 million pages in all) in 1829

alone, plus better than three hundred thousand Bibles. No less impressive was the invention of marketing and distribution techniques, later the norm in American business, by which the evangelicals moved their wares from New York to the rest of the country. Corps of agents in every state, organized into hundreds of local branches, handed out Bibles and tracts door to door, founded circulating libraries, advertised in newspapers, and even made special deliveries to sailors and boatmen aboard whalers, packets, ferries, canal barges, and steamboats. There was even a Tract of the Month program that offered "book dividends" to subscribers.

In New York itself, the American Tract Society considered the systematic distribution of its publications to be "the lever which shall move the foundation of Satan's empire in this city" (and in Brooklyn too, which got its own auxiliary Tract Society). In 1829 the ATS launched a "General Supply" campaign whose goal was to place in the hands of every resident a copy of a different tract every month. Each ward had a committee and a chairman and was divided into districts encompassing sixty families each. Each district (over five hundred in all) was assigned a team of distributors who received printed instruction cards, forms for reporting back to the central committee, and a supply of the tract of the month. By March 1829 the ATS had visited all 28,771 families in the city. Only 388 declined to take a tract. Evidently, as the secretary of the ATS put it, "The concentration of tract work in New York was what God designed."

OFF TO SCHOOL

Complementing the labors of missionaries and tractarians came a new burst of interest in the use of schools to combat pauperism and licentiousness: children who acquired good moral training at an early age (it was said) would become productive, law-abiding, self-supporting adults. The difficulty—as Eddy, Pintard, Clinton, and other reformers began to appreciate soon after the turn of the century—was that New York still had no system of public education that could be mobilized to provide such training to the people who needed it the most. Affluent residents sent their sons and daughters to private day schools or boarding schools; artisans and journeymen, if they could afford it, relied on a small number of "pay schools" that taught the rudiments of reading, writing, and arithmetic.

Some merchants and entrepreneurs had begun to experiment with educational institutions targeted at specific elements of the laboring population. In 1820, for example, the Chamber of Commerce established the Mercantile Library Association to impart commercial skills and sober habits to the city's growing number of clerks—too many of whom, surrounded by "excitements to pleasure," had "become the votaries of vice and depravity." The association's hope was that its mammoth book collection (eventually comprising thirty-seven thousand volumes, second largest in town), supplemented with regular lectures by leading business, professional, and public men, would help the clerks resist "these moral foes." That same year, prompted by John Pintard and the Society for the Prevention of Pauperism, the General Society of Mechanics and Tradesmen—dominated by wealthy former mechanics like bankers Jacob Lorillard and Stephen Allen—established an Apprentices Library, a lecture series, and a school for the sons of poorer or deceased members. Their goal too was to teach good habits and skills. In 1826 the General Society opened a school for girls as well.

For the vast majority of children, however, so-called charity schools remained the only chance for an education. By 1825 city churches sponsored fourteen such schools,

First Infant School in Green Street New York, by Archibald Robertson, c.1827. Located in the basement of the Presbyterian Church on the corner of Canal and Green streets, the school was run by the newly founded Infant School Society. Like many "charity schools," it used the monitorial system devised by the English reformer Joseph Lancaster. (The Metropolitan Museum of Art, Bequest of Edward W.C. Arnold, 1954. The Edward W.C. Arnold Collection of New York Prints, Maps and Pictures)

with a combined enrollment of nearly thirty-four hundred pupils, virtually all from poor families. The African Free School, founded by the Manumission Society in 1786, drew nearly nine hundred pupils in 1823—more than half the African-American youths of school age in the city. Another eleven charity schools were operated by the nondenominational Free School Society (FSS), which Eddy, Clinton, and other gentlemen had founded back in 1805 to educate poor children "who do not belong to or are not provided for by any religious society." After 1815, against the background of mounting concern over pauperism and lawlessness, the FSS strenuously promoted its Lancasterian approach to education—a combination of Bible study, rote memorization, and rigorous discipline—as "the main instrument by which extreme poverty & grovelling vice, & high-handed crime are to be banished from society." In 1825 John Griscom boasted that over the years some twenty thousand children, "taken from the most indigent classes," had passed through FSS schools.

More successful still were the scores of Sunday schools that sprang up in the city during the twenties. The Sunday school movement, launched just after the turn of the century, really took off in 1816, when merchants Divie Bethune and Eleazer Lord founded the New York Sunday School Union. The purpose of Sunday schools, said the union, was "to arrest the progress of vice and to promote the moral and religious instruction of the depraved and uneducated part of the community." Thousands of students were quickly recruited by handbills offering an "education free of expense" and promising that those who attended regularly, read their Bibles, and behaved well would be recommended for admission to an FSS school. The two hundred-odd volunteers who signed up as teachers (many, like Melissa Phelps, from genteel families) were pointedly charged to help their pupils become honest and useful citizens: "While you instill in their young minds the duty of contentment in the stations allotted to them by Providence, you will of course embrace the occasion to point out to them the self-degradation which attend idleness and vice; and the certain rewards which await industry and a virtuous life."

By 1823 better than seven thousand male and female students were attending seventy-four Sunday schools in New York. Roughly a quarter of the pupils were African-Americans—half of them adults, women as well as men. The Episcopal Church refused to join the Sunday School Union but started its own program, which over the next decade grew to some two dozen schools with a combined enrollment of six thousand. The movement spread quickly to communities on the Long Island side of the East River, and in 1829 the Kings County Sabbath School Society was formed to coordinate Sunday school work in Flatbush, Flatlands, Gravesend, New Lots, Brooklyn, and Bushwick. Memorization remained the technique of choice, and its results were toted up meticulously. (Some students were paid for each verse memorized—with coupons redeemable in Bibles).

All of this convinced evangelicals that they were at last beginning to make some inroads on pauperism and related social evils. Even "Bancker-Street Sabbath-breakers of the vilest class [i.e., blacks]," exulted Eleazer Lord, had become "decent in their dress, orderly in their behavior, industrious in their calling, *and punctual at school and church!*" In 1829, to celebrate the "mighty machinery of Sunday schools," twelve thousand scholars were paraded down Broadway in orderly rows to Battery Park, where they sang songs and heard congratulatory speeches.

But the apparent success of the Sunday School Union was clouded by an acrimonious fight over public support among the city's charity schools. Since 1812 the state government had provided financial assistance to the charity schools (funneled through the Common Council after 1824) in proportion to their enrollments. As the number and size of church-run schools increased, however, the Free School Society's share of the pie dwindled alarmingly, and it began to attack all aid to "sectarian" schools as a violation of the separation of church and state. In 1825 the FSS called for the creation of a single public school system, under its management, that would be open to all city children, "not as a charity, but as a matter of common right." New York, it declared, needed classrooms where "the rich and the poor may meet together; where the wall of partition, which now seems to be raised between them, may be removed; where kindlier feelings between the children of these respective classes may be begotten; where the indigent may be excited to emulate the cleanliness, decorum and mental improvement of those in better circumstances." The Common Council agreed and, despite bitter opposition, cut off aid to denominational schools. In 1826 the Free School Society renamed itself the Public School Society, though it remained in fact a privately run institution.

Over the next several years, although the society's schools did manage to attract somewhat more students from what it called "the middle walks of life," the effectiveness of free common education as a cure for pauperism and immorality remained largely hypothetical. New public schools were opened only in neighborhoods of "a quiet and orderly cast"—there were none in the Five Points throughout the 1820s—and they tended to expel pupils who didn't readily conform to their values. By 1829, of the roughly forty-three thousand children in New York between the ages of five and fifteen, as many as twenty thousand—overwhelmingly from the city's most indigent house-holds—still attended no school whatever. Of the remainder, about fourteen thousand went to private schools, as against the five thousand in public schools and the four thou-sand or so served by church-run charity schools (which coped with the loss of public support by scaling back enrollments). Many working-class youths withdrew once they were old enough to help support their families; few stayed past fourteen, the traditional age for beginning an apprenticeship. What was more, the manifestly genteel and Protes-tant leadership of the new system proved unattractive to Roman Catholics, who now began to construct their own network of parochial schools.

Sunday schools reacted to the new climate by cutting back on the three R's and giv-ing more emphasis to formal religious instruction, the effect of which was to discourage enrollment outside their own congregations—most notably by African-American adults. Although the Manumission Society expanded the number of African Free Schools from two to seven, the Public School Society absorbed them all in 1834. Renamed Colored Free Schools, they experienced a precipitous decline in quality that soon drove away many students.

JUVENILE DELINQUENTS

With only half of the city's children in school and the old apprenticeship system in dis-array, it was almost inevitable that thousands of ragamuffins would become a fixture of the city scene—lolling along the wharves, begging on the streets, thronging the ship-yards, hanging about Brooklyn ropewalks on the Sabbath, playing cards and spouting profanity. Some edged into criminality. Groups of girls stole sugar, coffee, or tea from the docks and sold them to market women. Boys pilfered brass rods, rope, or sheets of copper and sold them to junk dealers. Marauding bands robbed grocery stores and van-dalized houses. Boys became accomplished pickpockets. Girls as young as twelve drift-ed in and out of prostitution.

The conventional response to errant or merely "vagrant" children was to put them in jail, but chaplain John Stanford began to argue as early as 1815 that incarcerating youthful offenders with adult criminals merely trained a new generation of professional outlaws. Stanford thought that these children should be placed in an "Asylum for Vagrant Youth" where they could be instructed in moral and religious principles and apprenticed to a trade. Stanford's idea languished until the Society for the Prevention of Pauperism fastened on the notion that wayward youths formed the true "core of pau-perism." In the fall of 1819, just back from one of his visits with British reformers, John Griscom spoke to a packed City Hotel meeting about the work with delinquent children currently underway in London. Over the next several years the SPP became so enthusi-astic about the youth-oriented solution to poverty that in 1823 it reconstituted itself as the Society for the Reformation of Juvenile Delinquents. Convinced that they could smother pauperism in its cradle, the society's spokesmen lobbied city and state officials to incorporate and fund the country's first juvenile reformatory.

The New York House of Refuge opened on January 1, 1825, in an abandoned fed-eral arsenal on the Bloomingdale Road between 22nd and 23rd streets, amid farms and orchards on the outskirts of town. The Refuge's charges were children under sixteen, committed by the courts for indefinite terms (not to exceed the age of twenty-one for boys or eighteen for girls). Their "indolent and worthless" parents, in the Rev. Stanford's phrase, had allowed them to roam the streets, frequenting theaters and taverns until ensnared by alcohol, immorality, and crime. Stanford didn't believe that they were beyond redemption, on the other hand, for as the directors of the Refuge put it, it was necessary only to put them through "a vigorous course of moral and corporal discipline" to make them "able and obedient."

Upon entering the Refuge, accordingly, the children were stripped and washed and given uniforms, their hair was cut to a standard length, and they were placed in windowless five-by-eight-foot cells. Day after day they followed the same lockstep routine, parsed by bells. Bells rang at sunrise and fifteen minutes later, when guards unlocked their cells. Bells herded them to the washroom, to the chapel, to school, and to breakfast by 7:00 A.M. They worked from 7:30 till noon (boys making brass nails or cane seats; girls washing, cooking, or mending clothes), when bells called them again to the dining room for dinner. Back-to-work bells sounded at 1:00 P.M., wash-and-eat bells at 5:00, work bells again at 5:30, school bells at 8:00. Bells summoned everyone to evening prayers, then for the march back to the cells, where absolute silence was enforced all night.

But Joseph Curtis, the Refuge's first manager—chosen for his experience in superintending workers at James Allaire's ironworks—soon discovered that the young reprobates had minds of their own. They used "improper language," talked during silent periods, played during work sessions, and ran away. When reprimands proved useless, Curtis resolved to be "as harsh as any other father." The infractions and punishments recorded in his daily journal for 1825–26 included:

E. D. paddled, with his feet tied to one side of a barrel, his hands to the other.

J. M. . . . neglects her work for play in the yard, leg iron and confined to House.

Joseph R.: Disregarded order to stop speaking, given a bit of the cat [i.e., the whip].

John B.: A few strokes of the cat to help him remember that he must not speak when confined to a prison cell.

Ann M.: Refractory, does not bend to punishment, put in solitary.

William C.: Questioned guard's authority, whipped.

Amid some uneasiness at his methods on the part of the overseers, Curtis was replaced by a new manager, Nathaniel C. Hart. Hart proved an even more thoroughgoing disciplinarian, and he ringed the Refuge with a two-foot-thick wall to prevent escapes. Nevertheless, the institution was pronounced a great success. In its first ten years 1,120 boys and girls were admitted, and those "reformed" to the satisfaction of the authorities were released to parents, friends, or masters for apprenticeship; the more refractory were bound over to captains of whaling ships or sent into service as domestics.

THE BELLEVUE INSTITUTION

Almost due east of the House of Refuge, on a twenty-six-acre site overlooking the East River, stood a complex of buildings, likewise enclosed by a wall, known as the Bellevue Institution. Dedicated in 1816, by the mid-twenties Bellevue comprised—in addition to the pesthouse opened during the yellow fever epidemic of 1794—the city's new almshouse, Bellevue Hospital, and a penitentiary, plus a school, a morgue, a bakehouse, a washhouse, a soap factory, a greenhouse, an icehouse, and a shop for carpenters and blacksmiths. It was here that New York reformers faced, even more directly than at the House of Refuge, the task of holding the line they had drawn between the deserving and undeserving poor.

The three-story, blue stone almshouse paralleled the water; 325 feet long, with wings at either end, it was the largest structure in the city. Nevertheless, within a decade of its opening, it was overflowing with people too old, too young, or too sick to heed the summons to greater self-reliance. During the year ending September 30, 1825, when the annual cost of running the almshouse had climbed to $81,500—better than 10 percent of the total city budget of $780,400—the number of its inmates fluctuated from a high of 1,867 to a low of 1,437 (with deaths totaling 495). Ninety-five percent of the inmates were white and were more or less equally divided between men and women (with genders, like races, segregated in their own quarters). The number of those whom guidebook writer James Hardie referred to as "wretched emigrants from Europe" had multiplied, but they were still outnumbered, three to two, by "needy adventurers from most parts of our own country."

Jews were conspicuously absent from the almshouse rolls as, ever since New Amsterdam had made Jewish settlement contingent on their poor not becoming a burden to the Dutch West India Company, the tiny community had been taking care of its own. Suddenly faced with large numbers of poor immigrants in the 1820s, but determined that no Jew would beg on the streets, Shearith Israel (spurred by its president Harmon Hendricks) dispensed aid to the needy. In 1822 Ashkenazic members formed the Hebrew Benevolent Society, which affiliated with B'nai Jeshurun after it seceded.

Catholics too formed their own institutions. In 1817 the Roman Catholic Orphan Asylum was founded by the Sisters of Charity, an out-of-town order organized by ex-New Yorker Elizabeth Ann Seton (who in 1797 had cofounded the Society for the Relief of Poor Widows). In 1805, two years after her husband died, Seton had converted to Catholicism and been baptized at St. Peter's. Ostracized by her Episcopalian family and friends, she had moved with her five children to Baltimore in 1808, taken vows before the bishop, and formed the American Sisters of Charity in 1809 in Emmitsburg, Maryland; it was the first Catholic religious order in the United States. Seton never returned to New York, but four years before she died in 1821, she dispatched three sisters to open the city's first Catholic orphanage, a small wooden structure on Prince Street near the new cathedral. The ranks of its charges grew steadily, swollen by the hard lives and piety of immigrants like Bridget McGlone, who in 1820 left her infant daughter on the steps of Bishop Connolly's house, with a note saying she hadn't taken it to the almshouse as she didn't want it exposed to Protestant teachings. In 1826 the diocese erected a three-story brick building for the sisters' now 150 orphans; a second followed in 1830 for half orphans (children with one surviving parent).

Like the almshouse, the new Bellevue Hospital was soon overcrowded, thanks both to the epidemics that swept the city in the early 1820s and to an influx of patients turned away from the New York Hospital downtown. That old charitable establishment, though it still served the respectable poor, had begun to exclude dangerous or morally reprehensible cases. It now sent the contagiously ill up to Bellevue's pesthouse, the chronically ill to Bellevue's hospitals and infirmaries, and the wicked ill—sailors with syphilis—to Bellevue's almshouse, where they could be "made to work." This policy at once lowered the downtown institution's patient load and diminished its mortality rate by whisking away terminally ill patients before they could blemish the hospital's good name.

The pressure on Bellevue Hospital and the almshouse was somewhat alleviated by the appearance of specialized institutions for indigent New Yorkers of good character, among them the New York Eye Infirmary (1820), the New York Infirmary for the Treatment of Diseases of the Lungs (1823), a Deaf and Dumb Asylum (1817), and the New-York Asylum for Lying-in Women (1823). Similarly, in 1821 "maniacs" and "lunatics" were shifted from city hospitals to the new Bloomingdale Insane Asylum, located on a rustic seventy-seven-acre plot several miles north of town (now occupied by Columbia University). Besides removing a source of constant disruption in the hospitals, its construction was a victory for Eddy, who had been urging for years that New York adopt Europe's humane new system of "moral management" for mental illness, which all but eliminated chains and straitjackets.

That both the almshouse and Bellevue Hospital ran out of room so quickly suggests the extent to which genteel reformers had underestimated the population of deserving poor in the city. It was in the penitentiary, moreover, where the consequences of their drawing such a thin line between pauperism and criminality became increasingly apparent. The penitentiary, a three-story stone structure situated just to the rear of the new almshouse, housed criminals and poor alike. It took those convicted at the Court of Sessions of relatively minor offenses—petty larceny (theft of goods valued under twenty-five dollars), fraud, misdemeanors, disorderly conduct, assault—and set them to hard labor for terms up to three years. It also received those convicted of vagrancy—the offense of being unemployed, poor, and on the streets during one of the occasional sweeps by city marshals. These roundups came at the behest of merchants and shopkeepers determined to improve New York's business climate by scouring away peddlers, scavengers, beggars, and potential criminals. In 1826 the 210 vagrants (fifty-nine white men, ninety-three white women, sixteen black men, forty-two black women) substantially outnumbered the eighty-four criminals (fifty-two white men, two white women, twenty-seven black men, three black women), in part because prostitutes were charged as vagrants.

Vagrants too were set to hard labor, for up to six months, which took various forms. Some prisoners worked alongside almshouse inmates, making shoes or mending clothes, further blurring the line between poverty and criminality. Others were set to opening and improving city streets. Still others were assigned to the treadmill, or "stepping wheel," another English import beloved by reformers, which was installed at Bellevue in 1822 at the urging of Mayor Stephen Allen. Housed in a two-story stone building erected for the purpose, the wheel was a cylinder, twenty feet long and six feet in diameter, attached to a grain-grinding millstone. Sixteen prisoners would mount the wheel and start it turning, trudge for eight minutes, then give way to another set of sixteen, their alternations paced by the inevitable bell. Mayor Allen—who preferred the term "discipline mill"—applauded it as a device for terrorizing "sturdy beggars," those outside the walls as well as in.

New York City's more serious offenders—those convicted of highway robbery, burglary, forgery, counterfeiting, or rape—were subject to terms ranging from three to twenty-one years (arson and murder were capital crimes). Such miscreants, overwhelm-

The Stepping Mill, 1823. (© Collection of The New-York Historical Society)

ingly male, were sent not to Bellevue but to the state-run Newgate Prison, hulking on the Hudson's edge at Greenwich. By the 1820s, however, Newgate's viability was in serious question. Even dedicated supporters like Eddy conceded that the old prison had been an almost total failure. The place was appallingly overcrowded, stuffed to twice its capacity. After prisoners rioted in 1818, nearly destroying the jail, the legislature responded in 1819 by legalizing flogging—up to thirty-nine lashes per occasion—as well as reviving stocks and irons. In prereform days, a thief would have been whipped and then set free; now he could be held for years and flogged repeatedly if he didn't conform to prison discipline.

Lengthy internments were the exception, however, as the state issued pardons to alleviate the crush. At the end of 1821 Newgate held 817 inmates, but it would have held over two thousand had it not been for repeated mass releases, sometimes of fifty convicts a day, which petrified the now burgeoning community of Greenwich Village. By 1826 the inmate population was down to 448—more than half of whom, sniffed James Hardie in his *Description of the City of New York* (1827), were miscreants from foreign countries or other states, many of them no doubt "attracted by the hopes of getting more abundant plunder in this metropolis than they could expect in any other place."

Critics also condemned Newgate's design because it allowed convicts almost unlimited interaction, letting them pool their experiences. As one Society for the Prevention of Pauperism lawyer pointed out, the place operated "with alarming efficacy to increase, diffuse, and extend the love of vice, and a knowledge of the arts and practices of criminality." Some thought it might be worth trying to immure prisoners in silent isolation, as did Philadelphia's celebrated Eastern State Penitentiary. Others thought that as stretches in solitary had been shown to drive many to madness and suicide, the system used upstate at Auburn might be preferable: isolating prisoners at night but setting them to (profitable) gang labor by day, under the rule of absolute silence, enforced by summary flogging. In the end, however, Newgate was deemed hopelessly beyond repair, and the legislature authorized a brand-new prison, on the Auburn model, at Ossining, near the large marble deposits discovered in Westchester County.

In 1828 the state closed Newgate and transferred its prisoners to Sing Sing, which almost instantly won an awesome reputation, potent enough to draw Tocqueville and Beaumont across the Atlantic to investigate its workings three years later. They were astonished to find nine hundred completely unfettered prisoners, overseen by only thirty guards (who meted out merciless floggings with cat-o'-nine-tails for the tiniest infractions), laboring assiduously in open-air quarries, digging up marble to grace the Greek Revival homes, banks, and churches of New York City.

In 1835 the Bellevue Institution took on one last function, that of serving as Manhattan's execution ground. This represented a major change for New York's criminal justice system, which had relied for centuries on highly public hangings, staged, in recent years, at sites around the city. In 1816 Ishmael Frazer, a colored man, and Diana Silleck, a white woman, were hanged at Bleecker and Mercer, for arson and murder respectively. In 1820 Rose Butler, a black servant convicted of arson, was dispatched in the potter's field at what would become Washington Square.

Until the 1820s these public executions had remained sober communal rituals, in which the condemned, the crowd, and the civic authorities all played their respective roles: the first contrite, the second awed, the third magisterial. One of the last executions to follow the traditional script came in 1825, with the hanging of James Reynolds, a twenty-two-year-old seaman convicted of murdering his ship's captain with an ax. A vast crowd had already assembled at the old prison near City Hall when, at ten A.M., the high constable and the sheriff, the marshals and ministers, and a battalion of infantry and company of dragoons took their places. At 10:30 the prisoner, wearing white trousers, a white frock, and a white cap trimmed with black, was led out from his cell and seated on a small stage. The Rev. John Stanford (as the *Commercial Advertiser* recounted) gave a "very solemn and affecting" sermon, which "caused the tear to flow from many an eye."

Then the procession rumbled off, led by the sheriff on horseback, with Reynolds in an open carriage preceded by a wagon carrying his coffin, the entire convoy surrounded by the military and trailed by the crowd. At the scaffold, two miles out of town, the sheriff read the death warrant, and Reynolds addressed the assembled. He had led a moral life, he explained, until corrupted by drink and the brothels of Corlear's Hook, and he exhorted youthful onlookers "to take warning by the awful spectacle, and shun the paths of vice." Finally Reynolds sang a psalm with the minister, the cap was drawn over his eyes, and he was hanged at 12:45 while "earnestly praying to God for pardon."

Prompted in part by a new delicacy of feeling, however, elites were beginning to turn against such spectacles. Essayists, editors, ministers, and legislators began to denounce them as "disgusting exhibitions," finding them revolting rather than uplifting. It was not executions that troubled them—few of the critics sought an end to capital punishment—but rather their public character. Hangings summoned up mammoth crowds at a time when crowds (like the Callithumpians) were falling out of favor with the gentry. At a minimum, they clogged public space, wasted time, and were bad for business. Worse, these affairs—increasingly festivals of disorder plagued by drunks and pickpockets—seemed to excite base and brutal passions among the populace, to blunt rather than cultivate moral sensibilities. Formerly awe-inspiring drama was turning into counterproductive farce, more blood sport than solemn ceremony.

Lingering republican convictions that private executions smacked of star-chamber despotism led authorities to seek a compromise by keeping them public but limiting popular access. For the 1829 double execution of convicted murderers Richard Johnson (white) and Catharine Cashier (black), the authorities selected Blackwell's Island as venue. At eight A.M. the two were whisked from the Bridewell, in separate carriages, "with such rapidity [said the *Post*] as to prevent the rabble from keeping pace with the cavalcade." But when the entourage reached Penitentiary Wharf, where a steamboat waited, it was accompanied by several thousand men, women, and boys "eager to witness the dying struggles of two of their fellow beings." Worse, when the boat carrying the condemned left the dock, the assembled thousands piled into hundreds of small vessels, which tagged along, then ringed Blackwell's shore. In addition, four or five steamboats cruised back and forth, crammed with passengers "animated by the strange, savage, and fierce desire to see the disgusting spectacle." In the aquatic jostling, one boat was upset, and several spectators drowned.

Finally a New York legislative committee recommended that public executions, being "of a positively injurious and demoralizing tendency," should henceforth be conducted in private, where they could not excite "animal feelings." The legislature concurred in May 1835 and, to forestall objections to "private assassinations," required that executions be witnessed by at least "twelve reputable citizens." In 1835 the first such execution was held behind the walls of Bellevue: the hanging of Manuel Fernandez, a Portuguese seaman, went off with satisfying solemnity.

ON TO BLACKWELL'S ISLAND

The New York gentry were proud of the array of institutions they had created. On the day before Tocqueville and Beaumont sailed back to France, the mayor and aldermen, some thirty notables in all, conducted them, as Tocqueville recalled, "with great ceremony to all the prisons or houses of charity of the city." A cortege of five carriages departed City Hall at ten A.M., headed up to the House of Refuge, where they inspected the premises (at the northwest corner of today's Madison Square), carried on to the Bloomingdale Asylum for the Insane (on today's Columbia University campus); swung over to the Deaf and Dumb Asylum on Fifth Avenue, and then, after an aquatic excursion to Blackwell's Island, they repaired to Bellevue's almshouse for a banquet. Tocqueville was appalled by the dinner, which "represented the infancy of art: the vegetables and fish before the meat, the oysters for dessert. In a word," he sniffed, "complete barbarism." But on the whole he found the postprandial toasts, given with great solemnity by speakers enveloped in clouds of cigar smoke, accurate enough in their self-congratulatory assessments.

The present, moreover, was clearly mere prologue. So pleased were the city fathers with their various walled compounds that they had decided to expand their initiative. Three years earlier, in July 1828, the Common Council had purchased from James Blackwell the island around which the visiting Frenchmen had just "made two or three charming promenades." Here the magistrates planned to erect a city of asylums. Many of the recently constructed institutions, for all their worthiness, were already crammed full; Manhattan was surging north toward once bucolic Bellevue; and the success of colossal projects like Sing Sing had led Manhattan officialdom into thinking big. Surveyors had already selected a southerly site for a new penitentiary, to be modeled on Ossining's pride. Plans were afoot to shift the almshouse to bigger quarters on the island, perhaps in company with a workhouse. A new smallpox hospital was in the offing. And a mammoth lunatic asylum, an intricately designed complex of centers, octagons, and wings, was being discussed. The city's disordered and disorderly of tomorrow would be transported to Blackwell's and be aided if worthy, punished if found wanting.

Captivated by this vision of the unruly, ruled, the city's elite were ill prepared for the emergence of some sharply different diagnoses of New York's social ills—and some startlingly different proposals for how to cure them.

31

The Press of Democracy

On January 3, 1829, Frances (Fanny) Wright began a series of lectures at Masonic Hall before a capacity crowd of more than fifteen hundred. In her hour-and-a-half-long speech, the rousing orator, garbed in a white muslin tunic, denounced evangelical clergymen for raising tremendous sums for tracts and missions while opposing reasonable efforts to improve people's living conditions. Such ministers, she said, were intent on reconciling Americans to an unjust status quo, especially by working on "the minds of weak and deluded women" who had been "humbugged from their cradles." Virtue was not something to be dictated by the clergy; it would follow naturally when people were happy and secure and free.

Using the class-conscious European feminism of Mary Wollstonecraft, with which the gentry had flirted in the 1790s, to denounce the cult of domesticity the bourgeoisie had more recently adopted, Wright shockingly demanded sexual equality for women. Sexual passion was among "the noblest of the human passions," yet "ignorant laws, ignorant prejudices, ignorant codes of morals," Wright argued, "condemn one portion of the female sex to vicious excess, another to as vicious restraint, and all to defenseless helplessness and slavery, and generally the whole of the male sex to debasing licentiousness, if not to loathsome brutality." A marriage, she said, should last only as long as a couple's emotional attachment. Addressing herself to plebeian males as well as gentlemen, she cried: "Fathers and husbands! Do you not see how, in the mental bondage of your wives and fair companions, ye yourselves are bound?"

Wright also weighed in on the debate over the educational system. As did the Public School Society (PSS), she favored inculcating republican virtue in pupils. She also agreed that schools had to counteract the time children spent on the streets "learning rudeness, impertinent language, vulgar manners, and vicious habits." But Wright wanted schooling to produce egalitarian-minded citizens who would struggle against economic and social injustice. Such education was impossible in New York so long as the wealthy sent their children to private schools while the rest attended charity institutions run by the PSS.

The PSS gentry, Wright charged, condescendingly called working-class parents who kept their children at home ignorant, intemperate, and improvident. They refused to recognize that poor families could not dispense with their children's earnings, especially with artisans' wages being pummeled downward, nor could they even afford to clothe the youngsters decently enough to send to school. America had to live up to the promise of its revolution by providing full and equal education to all—including the poor, and slaves, and women. This required more than free day schools. Rather the state should provide free boarding schools to which all citizens would go and be treated equally, wearing the same plain clothing, eating the same food, receiving the same instruction. In the "State Guardianship Plan of Education" formulated by her comrade Robert Dale Owen, the state would assume educational responsibility for children starting at age two.

As Wright laid out these ideas, the crowds and the applause grew. At each lecture working-class freethinkers crushed into Masonic Hall to hear and hail the "female Tom Paine." Paine's ideas had undergone quite a revival since his death in Greenwich Village back in 1809 and its disturbing aftermath, when Paine's body had been carried back to New Rochelle and no Christian graveyard would bury him. He had finally been laid to rest on his farm under a walnut tree, where he had remained until 1819, when William Cobbett got permission to dig him up and take his remains to a place where they would be more honored.

Cobbett, a radical English journalist, had fled to New York City in 1817 when the British government, responding to riots in depressed industrial and agricultural regions, suspended habeas corpus and drastically curbed the press. Facing incarceration, Cobbett chose exile, and for the next two years issued his paper from a basement in Wall Street. When he sailed back home, he took Paine's bones with him, hoping to get English democrats to build a mausoleum for them. The project never came to pass, and Paine's remains eventually went missing. His ideas, however, helped fuel a renaissance of deism and anticlericalism in 1820s England. Radical urban artisans argued that religion bolstered authoritarian regimes, crippled freedom of thought, and undermined the independent rationality essential to citizens of the republican society they longed to create. English radicals took to celebrating Paine's birthday each year, and when many of them fled depression and repression in the late 1820s, they transplanted the custom to New York City. Joining forces with local freethinkers, they gathered at Harmony Hall on each anniversary and raised their glasses in toasts such as "Christianity and the Banks, on their last legs." In 1827 a weekly lecture series on deism was regularly drawing three hundred people, and George Henry Evans, a journeyman printer of English parentage, had begun bringing out fresh editions of Paine, Elihu Palmer, and other freethought advocates.

Radicals hoped thus to inoculate New York's workers against the tractarians who, they believed, threatened the separation of church and state, and thus reason and republicanism itself. When Sabbatarians tried in 1828 to prohibit mail deliveries on Sunday, radicals denounced them as a would-be Christian party in politics, intent on compelling the citizenry to their standards. Proving themselves as disciplined as the evangelicals, the freethinkers, aided by a still-widespread anticlericalism, helped beat back the Sabbatarian offensive. Not surprisingly, when Fanny Wright arrived, they hailed her as a spectacular champion of their cause.

At first, however, distinguished elites, men like Cadwallader Colden and Philip Hone, also came to hear Wright speak, in part because for all her radicalism Fanny had impeccable social credentials and was no stranger to Manhattan's upper class. Wright's father was a linen merchant who admired Tom Paine, and her mother a child of the British aristocracy. Born in Scotland in 1795, she had first visited New York in 1818, aged twenty-three, with her sister Camilla, to meet liberal thinkers and political exiles. Back in Europe in 1820, she published her *Views of Society and Manners in America*, an enthusiastic, prorepublican book that won her the attention and affection of Lafayette. With characteristic boldness, Wright suggested he either marry or adopt her.

In 1824 she followed Lafayette to the United States, and in New York her special relationship to the hero won her special attention. She returned yet again in 1828, to undertake a speaking tour of U.S. cities, and quickly became the most notorious orator of her age. In January 1829 Wright decided to "pitch [her] tent" in New York City. "All things considered," she wrote, New York "is the most central spot both with respect to Europe and this country," and whatever worked on the Hudson would soon "spread far and wide."

Wright's support from the likes of Colden evaporated even before her six-lecture series ended. Not only were the gentry unsettled that a woman was speaking to large sexually mixed audiences, they were appalled by what she was saying. William Leete Stone, editor of the *Commercial Advertiser*, championed many of the same causes Fanny stood for—he admired Lafayette and supported Greek independence—but Wright's attacks on clergymen and Christianity drove him to near-pathological rage. Declaring that she had "unsexed herself," he denounced "her pestilent doctrines" and labeled her a "bold blasphemer, and a voluptuous preacher of licentiousness." Newspapers attacked her boarding-school idea as an infringement of parental rights and an assault on the family and refused to print letters written on her behalf. Old friends denounced her. Society refused to receive her. "Fanny Wrightism" became an epithet in gentry circles and would remain one for decades.

By the time Wright's fifth lecture got underway, opponents had moved from words to deeds, setting a barrel full of oil of turpentine afire at the entrance door. Suffocating smoke billowed up the staircase into the hall above, touching off a panic-stricken race to escape. None of this daunted her followers, including a young Brooklyn carpenter and follower of the radical Quaker Elias Hicks, Walter Whitman. Heartened by this support, Wright dug in. She began publication of the *Free Enquirer*, printed by George Henry Evans, aimed at the city's working class (Whitman became a subscriber). The *Free Enquirer* declared war on "priestcraft," fought the Sabbatarians, attacked legal disabilities of women, and wrote respectfully of birth control.

In April 1829, for seven thousand dollars, Wright bought the old Ebenezer Baptist Church on Broome Street near the Bowery, in the heart of an artisanal neighborhood. She remodeled it to include a Greek-columned facade and rechristened it the Hall of Science; its front window, which faced a Bible repository across the street, was cheekily festooned with pictures of radical heroes (Paine, Shelley, Godwin). On April 26 Wright gave an opening address dedicating the hall to promulgating "universal knowledge" and to helping working people apply rational standards to the problems of the age.

The Hall of Science, a radical counterpart of the gentry's athenaeum and the evangelicals' missions, offered a day school and a deist Sunday school where working-class youngsters could learn reading, writing, and arithmetic using texts shorn of biblical reference. Its main focus, however, was adult education. The Hall of Science had a bookstore and a circulating library, well stocked with editions of Wright's pamphlets. It offered speeches and debates every Sunday—admission ten cents—and the twelve-hundred-seat hall was regularly filled. Free lectures were offered as well on mathematics, anatomy, geometry, chemistry, natural history, and debating, all aimed at preparing workingmen to think, speak, and legislate for themselves.

ARISTOCRATS AND DEMOCRATS

Political activism was the more attractive to crowds at the Hall of Science because in the late 1820s remaining constraints on popular participation had just been dismantled. Even after the 1804 law had lowered suffrage requirements for city dwellers, large numbers of tenants, clerks, journeymen, and laborers had still lacked sufficient property to vote. Indeed the growth of propertylessness worsened the situation. As of 1821 three-quarters of New York City's male population could not vote for governor or state senator (women couldn't vote at all), and even the less rigorous requirements for casting a ballot for assemblyman or congressman still barred roughly a third of the electorate. Popular participation was further circumscribed by the fact that power to select most state, county, and municipal officials—nearly fifteen thousand in all as of 1821, including the mayor of New York City—was still vested in the Council of Appointment consisting of the governor and four senators. The Council of Revision, yet another undemocratic body, retained the right to veto any act of the legislature.

The 1819 recession had quickened demands for political reform. Debtors petitioned the state legislature for assistance but were refused. Many believed this disregard for their interests was a function of the property qualifications that disfranchised them. A clamor went up for ending electoral restrictions, now characterized as undemocratic holdovers from the colonial era.

What finally battered down the old constraints was the thrust and parry of electoral politics. The Federalists' opposition to the War of 1812 had been their undoing, and they did not long survive the truce. Their Democratic-Republican antagonists, however, soon divided into two factions: those who backed De Witt Clinton, and those who followed Tammany Hall and the upstate Bucktails led by Martin Van Buren, a successful country lawyer who had defended tenants and small landowners against the Hudson River manor lords.

Tammanyites and Bucktails denounced Clinton as an aristocrat. With his autocratic style and ruthless wielding of the Council of Appointment's patronage power, Clinton, his enemies charged, was bent on perpetuating the eighteenth-century patrician system of family and personal factions. The Democrats, on the other hand, proclaimed themselves a modern political party whose very structure, which relied on open-to-all caucuses to select candidates and policies by majority vote, was responsive to the popular will.

Clintonians and Tammanyites competed for popular support. The governor focused on wooing the Irish, with the aid of his good friend Thomas Addis Emmet. Clinton had successfully sponsored the bill abolishing the Test Oath (something Catholics in Ireland would struggle for another two decades to achieve) and had let it be known, through the Shamrock Friendly Association, that jobs in canal construction awaited Irish immigrants.

Tammanyites' initial response to the Clinton-Irish alliance was a knee-jerk nativism. Not only did they refuse to court the Irishmen crowding into the Sixth Ward, but in 1817 the Wigwam's General Committee flatly refused to nominate Emmet for an Assembly position. On the night of April 24, two hundred Irishmen expressed their displeasure by breaking into Tammany Hall, destroying most of the furniture in the Long Room, and sending several Tammanyites to the hospital before the arrival of the mayor and police ended the brawl. Forcibly alerted to their self-destructive chauvinism, Tammany now began to woo the Protestant Irish. Eldad Holmes, prominent banker and sachem, gave a toast at the St. Patrick's Day dinner of the Hibernian Provident Society, hitherto a Clintonian hotbed, and slowly the party began to make some inroads.

When the surge of popular sentiment for electoral reform came along, moreover, Tammanyites and Bucktails rushed to head it. They initiated and won a referendum—over Clinton's ill-advised resistance—that decreed the holding of a constitutional convention in 1821. The convention laid an ax to the hated Council of Revision. It also abolished the Council of Appointment and transferred the choice of most local officials to local voters—though reserving selection of the mayor of New York to that city's Common Council. These decisions were relatively easy. The suffrage issue proved more contentious.

The most radically democratic delegates demanded an immediate end to all constraints on white male suffrage. In response, the upstate landed gentry, led by Chancellor James Kent, mobilized forthrightly against the "evil genius of democracy." In particular they pointed to "the growth of the city of New York," which in itself should have been sufficient, Kent declared, to "startle and awaken those who are pursuing the *ignis fatuus* of universal suffrage." New York, after all, was home both to "men of no property" and to "the crowds of dependents connected with great manufacturing and commercial establishments." If the poor were enfranchised, they would seek to plunder the rich, debtors would try "to relax or avoid the obligation of contracts," and factory workers would become the electoral adjutants of industrialists.

Many New York City delegates had their own reservations about total enfranchisement, given the rising numbers of impoverished residents against whom the Society for the Prevention of Pauperism was then inveighing. In the end, moderate forces led by Van Buren conferred the suffrage on all twenty-one-year-old white males who had lived in their district for six months and had either paid taxes, served in the militia, or worked on the roads.

The proposed constitution was impressively endorsed at the polls. In 1822 De Witt Clinton, facing clear defeat, retired from the governorship rather than run again. His good friend John Pintard reflected sourly that power had passed to those with "no stake in society" and that New York City would "hereafter be governed by a rank democracy." In fact, Clinton would have one last hurrah. His triumphant opponents, unable to resist kicking him when down, removed him from the Canal Board, a patent injustice that won him instant martyrship and, in 1824, reelection as governor. By 1826, nevertheless, calls for total eradication of the remaining restrictions on voting had become irresistible, and a constitutional amendment completed the democratization of New York's political system.

For white men. Suffrage for women was not on the agenda, and the same convention that emancipated poor whites disfranchised most blacks. Indeed ardent Democrats took the lead in drawing the color line, because African-American voters had long supported the Federalists. This was hardly surprising, given that the 1799 abolition law had been enacted by a Federalist legislature and signed by a Federalist governor, but Democrats chose to assume that Federalists (or their Clintonian successors) would continue to command black votes because the freedmen were dependent, illiterate, and easily manipulated by their former masters. "If we may judge of the future by the past," one Democratic militant cautioned the 1821 convention, "I should suppose that there was some cause for alarm, when a few hundred Negroes of the city of New York, following the train of those who ride in their coaches, and whose shoes and boots they had so often blacked shall go to the polls of the election and change the political condition of the whole state." Northern Democrats, moreover, had been moving toward an alliance with slaveholding southerners, a strategy that only enhanced their desire to bar blacks from the polls.

In the end, Peter A. Jay, an abolitionist like his father, John Jay, prevailed on the convention's majority not to exclude all black men but only those who didn't pay taxes on $250 worth of property. This proved acceptable, as Democrats were quite confident that the provision would effectively exclude African Americans. They were right. In 1826, of a total black population of 12,499 in New York County, only sixty were taxed at all, and of these only sixteen qualified to vote. New York was to remain a republic—or a democracy, as it was now increasingly called—of white males.

TAMMANY DEMOCRACY

The Democratic Party, which now unequivocally defined all European immigrants as "white," vigorously cultivated newcomers. It established a "naturalization bureau" to hurry new voters into being; held special meetings for Irish, French, and German immigrants; placed influential Irishmen on local tickets, and dispensed patronage to ethnic supporters. Within a few years, an estimated one-third of Democratic voters would be of foreign birth, and Philip Hone would be complaining that Irishmen "decide the elections in the city of New York."

In 1828 Tammany solidified its position by helping make Andrew Jackson president. Jackson had received the largest number of electoral votes for the presidency in 1824. However, failing of a majority, he had been defeated in the House of Representatives, which elected John Quincy Adams in what Democrats charged was a "corrupt bargain." Tammanyites itched to support the popular war hero in the 1828 rematch but were at first dissuaded by the fact that his biggest supporter in New York was De Witt Clinton. Eventually Martin Van Buren, his eyes on national prizes, made peace with Clinton and swung the Democrats behind Jackson. Clinton's unexpected death that year removed any remaining reservations.

During the campaign, Tammanyites sponsored elaborate dinners to commemorate the Battle of New Orleans—packing sixteen hundred into the Long Room and holding smaller affairs in all the wards. They established Hickory Clubs throughout the city, which ceremonially planted hickory trees (Jackson was known as Old Hickory) and then retired to local taverns to toast the general's health. They reminded Irish audiences that Jackson was their compatriot and had humiliated their British oppressors. New York (city and state) went for Jackson and also sent Martin Van Buren to the governor's mansion, a position he soon resigned to become Jackson's secretary of state.

Though Tammany trumpeted Jackson's election as the triumph of democracy, some of the demos thought otherwise, pointing to the fact that the commanding heights of the Democratic Party were occupied by the mercantile elite itself. In truth, the Tammany Society, the party's inner sanctum, embraced many well-connected attorneys, merchants, bankers, and entrepreneurial craftsmen. Such men often effectively dominated as well the ward committees and caucuses that chose candidates for the Common Council, as only they, or career politicians, could afford to undertake such time-consuming, unpaid political activity. Rich men remained vigorously involved in the electoral arena because they were determined to keep a firm hand on the public tiller. In 1829, when a convention to draw up a new city charter was proposed, Philip Hone and a large number of civic notables ran for delegate, lest others, as Hone put it, adopt "indiscreet measures"; 60 percent of those elected were wealthy men, many of them from prominent families.

As a result, in 1826 two-thirds of the Common Council were well-off or extremely wealthy men. (Across the river, 75 percent of Brooklyn's identifiable trustees and aldermen hailed from rich families through most of the 1830s.) The mayors, when the council appointed—among them Cadwallader Colden, Walter Bowne, Philip Hone, and Gideon Lee—tended to be affluent as well.

The strong presence of elite gentlemen in the party's leadership was one reason that, for all the Democrats' rhetorical populism, when a nascent labor movement emerged in New York during the late 1820s, it insisted quite forcefully that Tammany did not speak for or address the issues about which its membership was concerned. Within a year of the Jacksonian Democrats' victory, therefore, the city's workingmen launched an independent political party that advanced a very different vision of New York's future.

WORKERS AND "BOSSES"

During the 1820s the transformation of the trades had accelerated. Craft work had grown more subdivided, less respected. In printing, entrepreneurs bought presses and hired "halfway journeymen" who had not completed full apprenticeship. In marine construction, nearly all shipwrights now worked as wage-earners for boatyard owners. In the building trades, speculative developers let out competitive bids to contractor-entrepreneurs who agreed to erect structures for a package price; they in turn subcontracted the actual work to builders, who subdivided the labor among crews of semi-skilled carpenters and masons, thus circumventing experienced journeymen, whose status and pay eroded further.

Journeymen, recognizing that their employers were more often antagonists than craft-partners, began to draw sharper lines of demarcation within the trades. In 1816 journeyman printers banned employers from their meetings. Masons followed suit in 1819. Cabinetmakers, chairmakers, ship carpenters, caulkers, cordwainers, coopers, house carpenters, and tailors—all established journeymen's societies. Like the groups formed at the turn of the century, these remained primarily fraternal associations, which provided benefits to sick and elderly members, arranged recreational outings, and marched together in civic parades. Increasingly, however, they also operated as labor unions and began appealing to the public for support against capitalizing masters, whom they branded as self-seekers whose "only object is to accumulate money."

Before 1825 journeymen's associations rarely engaged in strikes. One reason for such caution was that the press uniformly and vehemently condemned such actions as unrepublican and cast participants as criminals consorting against the public interest, rather than as aggrieved members of the larger community. In addition, the state refused to grant such organizations charters unless they explicitly included provisions disavowing any intention of regulating work or wages.

Nor was it always clear who the enemy was. Many small masters were as badly squeezed as their journeymen. Many upheld the leather-aproned camaraderie of the Trades, refused to sweat more out of their workers, balked at hiring cheaper unskilled labor, and marched with their employees on civic occasions. But they faced sharp competition and grim choices. Either they struggled on as principled but ever poorer independents; or they became subcontractors to merchants and/or large manufacturers and thus accomplices in the degradation of their trade; or they themselves tumbled into permanent wage work. With the distinction between small master and journeyman fast disintegrating, New York's working people began, as early as 1817, to employ a new term to describe their entrepreneur-employers: "boss," derived from *baas*, the Dutch word for master.

In the 1820s laborers were more aggressive than skilled artisans, in part because wage differentials between unskilled and skilled workers kept rising sharply, in part because working conditions were particularly hard. The riggers and stevedores who fitted ships for sea and loaded or unloaded goods, for instance, faced long hours, low pay, and intermittent employment (winters were slack time, and the waterfront instantly registered any curtailment of trade).

In March 1825, accordingly, these waterfront workers (both white and black) marched along the wharves nearly a thousand strong, chanting, "Leave off work, leave off work." Forcing all dockworkers to join them, they effectively shut down the port. Police arrested the leaders and dispersed the strikers. But 1828 brought additional protests; shipowners reduced wages during a trade slump, and hundreds of strikers rolled along the East River wharves, knocking down and beating up nonstriking workers, then crossed to the Hudson River docks, where they showered a Le Havre packet with ballast stones. The merchant community was not about to put up with anything that threatened its port's new reputation for regularity and efficiency, and in short order the mayor, several magistrates, a posse of constables, and a troop of cavalry put the strikers down.

Labor violence also broke out that year in Greenwich Village, where handloom weavers, most of them British and Irish immigrants, struck for higher wages. In late June, employing a tactic used hundreds of times in England during that period, one anonymous weaver threw a note through the window of Alexander Knox, the city's leading textile employer. Addressed to "Boss Nox," the crudely lettered warning from "the Black Cat" advised him to "either Quit the Business Or else pay the price you ought to for if you don't you will be fixed." When several weavers continued to work for Knox at a lower wage, scores of angry journeymen stormed the shop and cut webs off looms.

Such outbursts received no support from skilled workers. Nor did the country's first all-female strike, in 1825, when tailoresses turned out. Indeed male tailors refused to allow women in their organization and sought to drive them out of the trade altogether. Seamstresses had been garnering much of the slop work on which many tailors depended, and already in 1819 one journeyman had expostulated in print: "Is it reasonable that the best of workmen should be unemployed half of the year" because "mercenary" employers knew that "women work cheaper than men?" Ignoring women's own survival needs, the men demanded a "family wage" for themselves—the "natural" breadwinners—which would enable them to keep their women at home, thus restricting labor competition while reaping the benefits of a wife's housework. Faced with lack of male support, and possibly inspired by Fanny Wright's Jacobin feminism, an independent Tailoresses Society emerged in 1831, asserting in a startling departure from conventional wisdom about female dependency: "Long have the poor tailoresses of this city borne their oppression in silence," but "*patience* is no longer a virtue." The women embarked on a months-long strike—"If we do not come forth in our own defence," unionist Sarah Monroe asked, "what will become of us?"—but, cut off from male support, their effort withered and their group disbanded. Master and merchant tailors continued to hire ever larger numbers, for ever lower wages, until by the 1830s some employers had as many as five hundred women outworkers sewing coarse "Negro cottons" for export to the slave South.

The quiescence of New York's skilled craftsmen was misleading, however, for their growing resentments were about to explode, but in the world of politics, not production. They would be galvanized, in part, by analyses advanced by two self-taught mechanic-intellectuals, which set workplace developments in the context of a larger and more menacing threat to the city, and to the republic itself.

In 1826 Langton Byllesby, a thirty-seven-year-old printer of English ancestry who had failed as an independent master, was doing wage-work as a proofreader at Harper Brothers, New York's largest shop. In that same year he brought out *Observations on the Sources and Effects of Unequal Wealth*, a book in which he predicted that New York City would soon match London's levels of crime, pauperism, and spending on prisons and welfare. Where Byllesby's analysis differed from the equally gloomy reports of the gentry-run Society for the Prevention of Pauperism was in refusing to put the blame on working-class slatterns and slackards.

Instead Byllesby faulted the rich. It was they, he said, who were plunging the producing majority into "resourceless distress, and intense misery." Merchant capitalists fostered rampant speculation. Auctioneers like Philip Hone got rich by drowning local industry in a flood of cheap British imports. The wealthy deployed new labor-saving machinery but harvested its benefits for themselves. Bankers monopolized credit and manipulated money for private gain. Landlords, having seized far more than their fair share of the soil in the old days, were now able to wax fat on levied rent-tribute.

Hard work, thrift, and the other practices recommended in the gentry's book of virtues would never offset such class advantages, Byllesby said. Instead, city tradesmen should supplant the competitive production system with a cooperative one, by pooling their shops and tools, then offering equal pay for equal labor. Producers, moreover, should use their newly expanded political power to tackle the privileged position of parasitic merchants, bankers, lawyers, and bureaucrats. In particular, speculative uses of land should be forbidden, and land ownership restricted by need and use.

Thomas Skidmore had an even more incendiary analysis. The Connecticut-born Skidmore had been a peripatetic teacher up and down the eastern seaboard, then a tinkerer-inventor seeking ways to improve the manufacture of gunpowder and paper. When he moved to New York City in 1819, he labored as a machinist, worked on an improved telescope, and read widely in radical political philosophy and political economy, including Byllesby and Robert Owen.

In 1829 Skidmore issued *The Rights of Man to Property!* This tract not only lengthened Paine's title but also deepened his argument. Skidmore attacked existing property relations as the ill-gotten fruits of a corrupt, colonial-era disposition of vast grants to a few landed proprietors and the ensuing failure to recycle this property over time to the wider community. As long as property remained "so enormously unequal" in its distribution, Skidmore argued, "those who possess it *will* live on the labor of others." In addition to private property, Skidmore said, private banks, privately owned factories, and private educational institutions also worked to replenish the wealthy while depleting the workers. The solution was not education, *pace* Wright and Owen. Maldistribution of wealth was not the effect of knowledge inequality but its cause. Instead, journeymen and small masters—the backbone of the producing class—should use their political power to force an equal division of property, achieving redistribution by changing inheritance practices. Banks and manufactories should be publicly run. Land, the basis of republican independence, should no longer be treated as a commodity. "Why not sell the winds of heaven," Skidmore asked, "that man might not breathe without price?"

Skidmore's goal was a patriarchal utopia of free and independent producers in which there would be "no lenders, no borrowers; no landlords, no tenants; no masters, no journeymen; no Wealth, no Want." To achieve this, men of modest fortunes had to combine with the propertyless poor and take electoral control of the government.

Both Skidmore and Byllesby believed something had gone terribly wrong in city and country, that social inequality and privilege were on the rise, that the republic was being undermined from within, that the new industrial system was immoral in its promotion of a lust for quick riches, individualism over community, and speculation, gambling, and usury. Such propositions had deep roots in the republican tradition. So did the argument that nonproducing parasites were able to appropriate the wealth labor created because government had granted them monopolistic rights. This diagnosis came bundled with its own prescription: the producing classes should elect men who would abolish the monopolies that bred aristocrats.

WORKINGMEN'S ADVOCATES

In April 1829 a crowd of more than five thousand mechanics turned out for a meeting in the Bowery to protest a rumored scheme by employers to lengthen the ten-hour day. After resolving to fight any such move, the gathering appointed a Committee of Fifty and instructed it to prepare a report on "the causes of the present condition of the poor." In setting up this counterpart of the Society for the Prevention of Pauperism "great care was taken to have no 'Boss' on the committee," recalled George Henry Evans, one of the workingmen's leaders and the party's first historian. The committee labored over summer and fall, under the influence of member Thomas Skidmore.

On October 19 another mass meeting of "Mechanics and other Working Men" assembled, heard the Fifty's report, and invited "all those of our fellow-citizens who live on their own labor, AND NONE OTHER," to join them in supporting an independent slate of candidates in the upcoming November elections for the state assembly.

The meeting also adopted a platform for what soon would be called the Workingmen's Party (Brooklyn would form its own such organization). They unanimously endorsed the essence of Skidmore's program, calling for "equal property to all adults." They also backed Fanny Wright and Robert Dale Owen's demand for equal educational opportunity and elected Owen himself secretary. Signaling their anticlerical bent, they called for an end to tax exemptions on ministers and church properties. They also briskly denounced government-created "chartered monopolies," urging the wider community to "destroy banks altogether." Banks flooded society with "rag money"—depreciated banknotes—that were often bought at steep discount by employers and used at face value to pay employees' wages. The Workingmen advocated a purely metallic currency—so-called hard money—employing the sophisticated argument that bank-created inflation led to a rise in prices, a rise in imports, a fall in exports, an outflow of specie, and then an inevitable contraction and depression.

The Workingmen also advocated a mechanic's lien law, a plank that appealed greatly to the carpenters, masons, and stonecutters who were major supporters of the new party. In the 1820s boom, contractors bid low to get a job, then gave workmen only part of their pay (perhaps 25 percent), promising the balance later. Later never came. Instead, the contractor pocketed the remainder and declared insolvency, making it impossible to collect monies due. The Workingmen proposed a law giving a lien on the building to all those who had been employed in erecting it. The propertied fought this vigorously, saying it would discourage investment.

Proclaiming that "we have nothing to hope from the aristocratic orders of society" and that "our only course to pursue is, to send men of our own description, if we can, to the Legislature at Albany," the Workingmen, using an elaborately democratic procedure, nominated eleven candidates: two carpenters, two machinists, a painter, a whitesmith, a brassfounder, a printer, a cooper, a grocer, and a physician.

The new party decided it needed a newspaper. George Henry Evans, who had brought out Wright and Owens's *Free Enquirer*, now launched the *Workingman's Advocate* from his office on Thames Street, where he served as editor, compiler, and printer. The first issue, on October 31, 1829, carried the slogan "All children are entitled to equal education; all adults to equal property; and all mankind, to equal privileges." Only the second labor paper in the United States (the first having been started in Philadelphia the year before), the *Workingman's Advocate* would be the voice of New York's artisanal radicalism for the next fifteen years.

A brief but frenzied campaign followed. Bosses and the established mercantile press branded the Workies a "Fanny Wright ticket," with editor Stone in the *Commercial Advertiser* calling them "poor and deluded followers of a crazy atheistical woman." Tammany's General Society disavowed any connection with the ticket, belittled its program, and called on "all sober, respectable mechanics of New York" to shun it.

The Workingmen lost, but they lost well. In an impressive debut they elected one candidate to the Assembly, placed a narrow second in six other races (including Skidmore's), and won nearly one-third the total vote. The Democrats prevailed, but there was consternation in the Tammany camp.

As the Workingmen's Party girded for the following year's contest, however, it experienced tremendous internal upheavals. New recruits poured in, including many whose politics were quite different from those of the progenitors. One was Noah Cook. A commission agent for an Erie Canal boat line, Cook sold items ranging from cordwood to country real estate. He had also been an active Adams supporter in 1828 and was an editor of the *Evening Journal*. Cook's faction, which included employers, evangelicals, large-scale manufacturers, and residents of the "aristocratic" First Ward, hoped to transform the Workingmen into an anti-Jackson vehicle. Cook allied with Owen and Evans to drive Skidmore out of the party he had started, then turned on the Owen faction and ejected it too, denouncing its education plan as a plot to break up families and undermine religion. Some journeymen, too, including the New York Typographical Society, attacked the state guardianship plan as dangerously visionary, though the Workingmen still demanded education for all and wondered aloud "if many of the monopolists and aristocrats in our city would not consider it disgraceful to their noble children to have them placed in our public schools by the side of poor yet industrious mechanics."

Even as the party quarreled and split, one demand remained constant: more democracy in New York City. In particular, the Workingmen pressed for direct election of the mayor. They also asked that aldermen and assistants be paid, because "poor men cannot afford to spend their time without receiving an equivalent for their labor," and under the current system "none but large property holders can be elected." Workies wanted an end to compulsory militia service, an obnoxious obligation for men who couldn't afford to take time off from work, or to pay for substitutes as merchants did. They wanted smaller electoral districts, which would allow "*all interests* to be represented" and thus offset "the misrule of the dominant party in this state, and especially in this city"—a reference to Tammany, which they believed was under the corrupt control of "idlers, office holders, and office seekers."

The Workies were of mixed mind as to what to do with city government should they get hold of it. Some advocated an activist policy of mechanic's liens, aid to internal improvements, government funding of education, and an ongoing regulation of the municipal economy in the public interest. But a greater number denounced government intervention in the economy—both the grant of special corporate privileges and the maintenance of municipal regulations—as an unwarranted colonial holdover, a violation of democracy on a par with the now eliminated suffrage restrictions.

In 1828 the Common Council still appointed or licensed nearly seven thousand people, including butchers, grocers, tavern keepers, cartmen, hackney coachmen, pawnbrokers, and market clerks, together with platoons of inspectors, weighers, measurers, and gaugers of lumber, lime, coal, and flour. From the Workingmen's perspective, licenses sheltered their privileged holders from competition that could lower prices. Regulations and fees indirectly taxed food and drink, as vendors passed on the costs they accrued in obtaining licenses, buying market stalls, paying fines, and bribing corrupt city inspectors. (Grocers, in particular, complained that inspectors had "a long Pocket for themselves.") The whole system was kept in place, Workies suspected, less for the public's convenience than to provide the government with revenue, which it could then share out with cronies and patronage recipients.

In an 1830 petition to the City Council, the Workingmen demanded an end to privileged monopolies in the local economy. They called for abolition of market laws and chartered licenses, the sale of all city-owned property in markets, an enhanced reliance on property taxes for revenue, the granting of permission to butchers and hucksters to sell anywhere in the city, the establishment of tax-free country markets (with adjacent taverns) that would entice farmers to the city, and the exemption of market produce from ferry or bridge tolls.

The closely watched trades—some of them well represented in the new party— were ambivalent about deregulation. Butchers, grocers, and tavern keepers were enticed by free enterprise but nervous about it. Some butchers came out for economic freedom: in 1829 one rebel, refusing to rent a market stall, opened New York City's first private meat shop. But city protection had served butchers well, and most demanded more of it, not less, asking the city to clamp down on unlicensed (and overhead-free) hucksters. Grocers complained of being pestered by inspectors, yet griped that the city didn't protect them from black, Irish, and female peddlers. Tavern keepers sought the freedom to sell alcohol on Sunday but also wanted authorities to crack down on unlicensed Irish groggeries. Bakers, after wobbling on the issue earlier in the century, had come out definitively against regulation in 1821. Calling themselves the "slave of corporation dictation," they demanded that buyers and sellers be allowed to bargain freely and that bakers be freed from special responsibility for feeding the poor. The Common Council repealed the assize in 1821, abdicating its authority over prices, but continued to require that bread be sold in standard-weight loaves, to lessen the possibility of fraud.

Cartmen, on the other hand, definitely favored regulation. American-born carters complained to the city fathers that Irish immigrants, who had been licensed during the war while Anglo-Dutchmen were off soldiering, were undercutting established rates and stealing customers. Mayor Colden limited future alien licensing to dirt carting, a field the Irish quickly dominated. When they continued to challenge the Anglo-Americans in other areas, the Society of Cartmen petitioned the Common Council to reaffirm their "ancient privileges." The municipal government agreed, rejecting calls for the decontrol of carting, as the business and trade of the city depended on it, and in 1826 the council banned aliens from carting, pawnbroking, and hackney-coach driving; soon all licensed trades were closed to them.

One deregulatory demand that nearly all Workingmen supported was abolition of imprisonment for debt. Attacks on the practice, which the Humane Society had begun making in the 1790s, had accelerated in New York just after the war, winning passage of an 1817 law ending incarceration for debtors owing less than twenty-five dollars. In 1828, nevertheless, more than a thousand defaulters served time in city jail, without bed, fuel, or food, other than a quart of soup every twenty-four hours. Most debtors, to be sure, spent only brief periods in actual custody, as "gaol limits" had been extended to the lower wards of the city. The Workingmen's first demand was only that these prison boundaries be extended to the whole city, because most of those affected by the law lived and worked in the upper wards. By 1830, however, they (along with businessmen) were petitioning Albany for a complete abandonment of the practice.

Workingmen pressed their positions through a new paper, the *Daily Sentinel*, launched in February 1830 by Workie printer Benjamin Day and five other directors. But by the time of the fall elections, the party's internal conflicts had torn it apart. Drubbed at the polls, finished as an electoral force, by 1831 the Workingmen's Party had disintegrated.

The Workies' collapse had many causes, including factional division, political ineptness, simple inexperience, a lack of funds, infiltration by the opposition, press hostility, the pull of regular party loyalty, and the arrival (with the 1830s) of a fevered prosperity that turned attention from politics to trade unionism. Perhaps superb leadership could have offset these handicaps, and if Frances Wright had in fact been at the party's helm she might have made a difference. But in June 1830 Wright had announced her return to Europe to a packed (and half-female) Bowery Theater crowd, and she departed on July 1, to Philip Hone's great delight, and that of his opposite political number, Tammanyite Mordecai Noah. Further sighs of relief attended Robert Dale Owen's closure in 1831 of the Hall of Science and its sale to a Methodist congregation.

If the independent workingmen's voice was stilled for the moment, their words had entered irreversibly into civic discourse. Fanny Wright's "doctrines and opinions and philosophy," Noah noted, "appear to have made much greater progress in the city, than we ever dreamt of." And labor's political awakening would have both immediate and long-term consequences for New York City. The short-term impact was registered in the Democrats' decision to woo disaffected Workies by assuming their language and their issues. Rhetorically, they denounced banks and condemned monopolies. Symbolically, they took the lead in organizing the 1830 parade celebrating the overthrow of the French monarchy. Practically, they helped enact such Workingmen planks as were compatible with entrepreneurial agendas. In 1830 legislators passed a mechanic's lien law. In 1831 the state abolished imprisonment for debt in all cases except where fraud was alleged. The same year brought support for direct mayoral elections, a reform effected two years later with an amendment to the city charter. Such concessions brought many artisans back to the Tammany fold, and the following year Workie wards voted Democratic.

THE SUN SHINES FOR ALL

A more long-term—and more indirect—legacy of the Workingmen's Party was the creation of a popularly oriented commercial journalism. In the *Free Enquirer, Workingmen's Advocate,* and *Daily Sentinel*, Workies and freethinkers had passionately protested the gentry's monopolization of knowledge, insisting that equal access to education, culture, and information was vital to a democracy. Most of their fire had been directed at New York's stratified school system, but they also blasted the city's press as being of, by, and for the mercantile and political elite.

Only the affluent could afford the dailies, which sold for six cents each (annual subscriptions cost a hefty ten dollars), and only the affluent cared to read them. The papers featured ship arrivals and departures, market and financial conditions, importers' offerings, legal notices, verbatim congressional speeches, and vitriolic editorials denouncing freethinkers and trade unions or proclaiming the current party line. Editors, paid to merchandise wares and politicians, paid attention to little else, certainly not to the daily life of most New Yorkers. The lack of interest was reciprocated, and as a result the average circulation of all seven daily papers in 1835 was a mere seventeen hundred, with Colonel Webb's *Courier and Enquirer*, the largest, boasting only four thousand.

Working-class New Yorkers were not lacking in literacy or interest. For all the schools' limitations, they had helped nurture a plebeian reading audience, which publishers readily reached with religious papers, tracts, Bibles, broadsides, pamphlets, ballads, gallows confessions, and adventure tales. Well aware of this, the youthful labor journalists of the 1820s had attempted to bypass the established press and to break its monopoly of information and perspective.

One of these media rebels was Benjamin Day, the twenty-year-old journeyman printer who had helped launch the *Daily Sentinel* in 1830, when he was twenty. Son of a Massachusetts hatter, Day had apprenticed on a Springfield paper. Drawn to New York City, he worked for the *New York Evening Post*, then opened his own job shop; like many young activist printers, he became part of the workingmen's movement. During Day's tenure, however, the *Daily Sentinel* did not adopt innovations in content, style, or pricing. It relied on politics to win readers and did not long survive the death of the Workingmen's Party.

Day soon decided to start another mass circulation daily (in part to advertise his printing plant). He was encouraged in this by the example of London's *Penny Magazine*. Published from 1832 by the Society for the Diffusion of Useful Knowledge, ostensibly to educate and improve the poor, the *Penny Magazine* was cheap and hugely successful. By 1833 its circulation was twenty thousand, and many copies were being sold in the United States.

On September 3, 1833, Day launched the *New York Sun*. Unlike the sixpenny papers, which were printed on mammoth-sized paper (some were known as "blanket" sheets), the *Sun* was a tiny affair of four tricolumned pages on $8^{1}/_{2}$-by-11-inch paper. With job printing his only source of income—"Capital! Bless you, I hadn't any capital," he recalled later—Day started by imprinting two hundred copies an hour on a hand-cranked flatbed press. He experimented boldly, however, with pricing, distribution, format, and content. The *Sun* cost a penny, well within artisanal reach, and Day did not require prepayment of subscriptions. Instead, using a London plan, he sold bundles of a hundred *Sun*s for sixty-seven cents, cash in advance, to newsboys drawn from the city's pool of orphans and unemployed. If a newsboy sold all his papers, he pocketed thirty-three cents. Some plied regular routes, collecting six cents per customer each Saturday. Others hawked *Sun*s on the street, adding their cries to the cacophony of oyster sellers and hot-corn girls.

The *Sun*'s slogan—"It Shines for All"—proclaimed Day's intention of reaching a wide spectrum of New Yorkers. So did his assertions that the paper would be "vended at a price which the poorest laborer can afford," while being "of a character (we hope) deserving the encouragement of all classes of society." But if the popular classes were not the exclusive target, as had been the case with the *Sentinel*, the paper's demotic thrust was obvious from what it did and did not cover.

Conspicuous by their absence were ponderous articles on national and world affairs. (Even had he wanted to, Day couldn't compete with the *Journal of Commerce* and its twenty-four-horse express relays from Washington.) There were no announcements about pending arrivals of cargoes of bombazine; artisans didn't care, and merchants could find out elsewhere. There was no partisan politics as traditionally understood—no vituperative harangues, no lengthy discussions of public affairs; though the *Sun* tended to support Democratic candidates, it was out of conviction, not patronage.

Missing also was the radical language, the incendiary tone, of the workingmen's press; Day well remembered the *Sentinel*'s failure. Instead he proclaimed his mission in language acceptable to an elite eager to educate the disorderly classes so as to improve their behavior and productivity. In an early issue, Day stressed (echoing his London predecessors) that the *Sun* was "effecting the march of intelligence" by "diffusing useful knowledge among the operative classes of society." Yet Day would firmly back unions, strikes, and the ten-hour day. The *Sun*, said its founder, helped produce a "decided change in the condition of the laboring classes" by enabling them to "understand their own interest, and feel that they have numbers and strength to pursue it."

What the *Sun* did have was local news that would interest an audience of artisans. Breezy, brightly written pieces sketched the daily life of ordinary New Yorkers. Snappy, even sensational stories covered unusual events—"fires, theatrical performances, elephants escaping from circus, women trampled by hogs."

Crime news was made to order for Day. There wasn't any competition—the blanket sheets found such stories embarrassing and bad for business—and it was cheap and easy to gather. For four dollars a week, Day dispatched unemployed printer George Wisner to record the vivid dramas of police court. With coarse humor and flippant style, the *Sun* offered accounts of domestic tribulation and drunkenness (husband beats and chokes wife to death in drunken rage), scandals (reverend arrested for rape), tales of thieves, whores, and arsonists. Chronicles of crime were not new, but crime news was.

"Police Reports" became the *Sun*'s most popular section for many reasons. Sex and violence were titillating. The narratives were familiar to readers accustomed to sensational street literature. They comfortably incorporated everyday speech, the kind of dialect, colloquialisms, and slang never found in elite papers. They provided New Yorkers with useful and important information about the way their city worked. They often contained a sharp-edged, critical component—reminiscent of the radical papers—in holding up instances of gentry pretension, hypocrisy, favoritism, violations of equal justice, abuse of state power, corruption. In one instance—the provision of gruesomely detailed accounts of executions, which had been recently privatized—crime news served to reassure a populace that remained highly suspicious of such closed-door dealings.

Crime stories were paralleled in popularity by the occasional hoaxes the paper concocted. In August 1835 Day began publishing a series of articles recounting life on the moon—spherical amphibians rolling about—as supposedly revealed by a powerful new telescope. These good-humored impostures, together with reports of curiosities and monstrosities, resembled crime reports in offering readers a chance to play detective and decide their truth or falsity. Both were forms of voyeurism at a distance, dependent for their impact on the fact that some parts of the city were now as little known as the surface of the moon.

The *Sun* was a runaway success. Within four months its circulation of four thousand brought it abreast of Webb's *Courier and Enquirer*. By 1834 Day had made enough money to install a machine press with a capacity of a thousand copies per hour, equal to the demands of his paper's now ten thousand purchasers. A year later, with readership at fifteen thousand, he switched to a steam press with an hourly capacity of fifty-five hundred. During the moon hoax, daily circulation hit twenty thousand: four times that of the most successful sixpenny, more than the Methodists' weekly *Christian Advocate and Journal*, and more than the *London Times*. The *Sun* had become, for the moment, the biggest-selling paper in the world.

Day had promised that the *Sun* would be an "advantageous medium for advertising," and circulation figures like these brought advertisers flocking. Ads were not new, of course. The mercantile and political sheets had long filled six or eight columns of a page with tiny ten-line squares of text that, in minuscule typeface, called the attention of a select audience to goods and services. Day sold space on a cash, not an annual, basis and included "Help Wanted" notices for cooks, maids, coachmen, bricklayers, and men to open oysters in restaurant kitchens. These increased the paper's popularity with readers looking for jobs—or for servants—and though many of the elite denounced the *Sun* for pandering to the vulgar mob, businessmen were not about to pass up the opportunity to purvey their wares to the enormous local market it had revealed.

Success bred competition. In 1834 two former colleagues of Day's started the *New York Transcript*, placing it under the editorial control of Asa Greene. A native of western Massachusetts, Greene, a printer, had come to New York in 1829 at the relatively advanced age of forty and edited a comic weekly for several years. The *Transcript* offered his lighthearted commentaries, in the form of a letter written by a recent arrival to his country friend back home, which sensitively detailed urban manners and customs.

Like the *Sun*, the *Transcript* was a working-class-friendly paper. Not only did it support workers' right to organize unions, but one of the owners was himself a printer's delegate to a trade union body. Greene reported on local boardinghouse price increases, theater and sporting events, and the Mechanic's Fair, along with meetings of the Common Council and sessions of the police court, which were humorously recounted and spiced with dialogue between magistrate and accused. Soon the paper was selling nearly as well as its penny rival within Manhattan, and even better in nearby cities and towns. Dozens of penny dailies now entered the field—some lasting but a few weeks—and flourishing imitations were started in Boston, Philadelphia, and Baltimore (several by veterans of Day's shop).

EXHILARATING THE BREAKFAST TABLE

One of the newcomers—the *New York Herald*—soon surpassed all others, including the *Sun*. Its proprietor, a gaunt Scotsman named James Gordon Bennett, was born in a Highlands hamlet in 1795 to a Catholic family. After study in a seminary in Aberdeen, Bennett broke with the Church and adopted the laissez-faire classics as his new sacred texts. In 1819 inspired by Ben Franklin's *Autobiography*, he sailed for the United States, becoming part of a resurgent Scottish migration. Bennett spent three years in Boston clerking for a bookseller and proofreading; then he worked for ten months in South Carolina on the *Charleston Courier*, one of the best papers in America, honing his writing skills and absorbing white supremacist views.

In 1823 Bennett settled down in New York City, where he did free-lance writing for party papers, specializing in economic analysis. His 1825–26 exposure of stock speculations drew considerable attention, and in 1826 Mordecai Noah hired him to report on Washington politics and society for the *New York Enquirer*. Bennett's informed, irreverent reportage, written in a flamboyant but authoritative style, won him considerable standing in the trade. When party pressure forced the merger of Noah's *Enquirer* and James Watson Webb's *Courier* in 1829, Bennett became associate editor of the new *Courier and Enquirer*. His steady rise through the world of party newspapers was halted in 1832: when the *Courier and Enquirer*, encouraged by money from Biddle's Bank, switched its allegiance to Jackson's opponents and muzzled the pro-Jackson Bennett, he quit. Bennett started his own Democratic paper in 1833, but the party, considering him too unpredictable, gave him skimpy support, and he finally abandoned the partisan press altogether.

Bennett applied, unsuccessfully, for jobs at the *Sun* and *Transcript*, then decided to start his own penny paper. Never having set type or operated a press, Bennett needed a partner. He turned to a twenty-two-year-old printer named Horace Greeley.

Greeley, born to struggling New Hampshire farm folk, had arrived in New York in

1831, with ten dollars and a small sack of belongings, fresh from an apprenticeship in a small-town printshop. An earnest, downy-haired beanpole of a man, Greeley first found work setting type on projects ranging from an annotated Bible to William T. Porter's *Spirit of the Times*, a new weekly devoted particularly to racing news. Then he set up a printshop, purchased type on credit, and looked about for business. In 1832, approached by a physician with a yen to publish, Greeley agreed to collaborate on a twopenny paper, the *New York Morning Post*. The first issue appeared January 1, 1833, eight months before the *Sun* saw the light of day, but the doctor was a ponderous writer, and the paper went belly up within three weeks. When Bennett showed up, asking if he'd like to launch a penny paper, Greeley declined.

In May 1835, therefore, Bennett went ahead on his own. He rented a basement apartment on Wall Street, stretched some pine boards between a set of flour barrels for a desk, and began singlehandedly to produce the *Herald*. Like his penny predecessors, Bennett set out to reach a mass audience, but not because he had a message to convey. He had no prior association with the Workingmen's Party, no ties to New York City's laboring class, no particular interest in its welfare. He just wanted to make a lot of money, and Day's success had made clear that the road to riches ran through a mass market.

The *Herald*'s proprietor also wanted to reach the city's elites for whom he was accustomed to writing. Besides, combining gentry with plebeian audiences would boost revenues. Bennett accordingly set out to combine the zest and local identification of the *Sun* and *Transcript* with the broader news coverage of the *Courier and Enquirer* and *Journal of Commerce*.

In the *Herald*'s first issue, on May 6, 1835, Bennett announced his intention to transcend existing boundaries of class. His new four-page sheet was "equally intended for the great masses of the community—the merchant, mechanic, working people—the private family as well as the public hotel—the journeyman and his employer—the clerk and his principal." Aware that a penny paper would be automatically suspected of working-class proclivities, Bennett ingratiated himself with the mercantile elite by denouncing Day as a "Fanny Wright infidel." The *Herald* offered not radicalism but relief from the "dull business air" of the large morning papers. It would "exhilarate the breakfast table."

As promised, Bennett delivered "brevity, variety, point, piquancy, and cheapness." His prose was fresh, pointed, and zestful. And he offered far more for a penny than did the *Sun*. Bennett entered the national news race. In short order, his express relays were outpacing those of the *Courier* and the *Journal* by three hours, and by 1837 his news boats rivaled those of the mercantile press. Bennett also went after New York news, even more assiduously than Day. The *Herald* covered City Hall and the police, court trials and executions, sports and theater, docks and coffeehouses, and sermons and church meetings to boot.

Bennett investigated Wall Street with unprecedented accuracy and acumen. Many sixpenny editors had entered into secret and lucrative collaborations with brokers, hyping or disparaging stocks to their mutual advantage. Bennett savaged them for "catering to speculators, hypocrites, stock-jobbers, bankers, brokers, and political and moral rascals of all kinds." He, Bennett, would deal "justly, honestly and fearlessly with every institution in Wall Street—every broker—every bank—every capitalist." Again, he delivered. His first "Money Markets" column demonstrated that a recent "uncommon rise in the stock market [was] not produced by accident," and he repeatedly blasted stock speculations as a "secret conspiracy of our large capitalists."

Bennett's stance won artisanal applause. His exposés of chicaneries shrouded from the general public echoed the old labor press's attack on privileged monopolies. Yet the bulls and bears themselves pored over his daily column, so accurate were his analyses, and so poorly did the plungers understand the market. The result was precisely the one Bennett sought: where the *Sun* and *Transcript* didn't penetrate the downtown financial world, and the *Courier and Enquirer* and *Journal of Commerce* were "never seen in the crowd," the *Herald* reached all parts of town.

The same breadth of appeal marked the pioneering coverage of society he would develop over next few years. Converting gossip into news, and private lives into public commodities, Bennett reported on the doings at Broadway mansions and the social season at Saratoga Springs, often with a whiff of mockery. Ordinary New Yorkers delighted at this peek behind the curtains. With classes segueing off to different parts of town, elite lives had become less accessible to the curious, the critical, and the covetous alike.

Patricians loathed Bennett's violations of their newly prized privacy. But they too bought the penny press, as fascinated as the plebeians with its revelations about personalities. "Everybody wonders how people can buy these receptacles of scandal, the penny papers," Philip Hone wrote in 1837, "and yet everybody does encourage them; and the very man who blames his neighbors for setting so bad an example, occasionally puts one in his pocket to carry home to his family for their and his own edification."

Even the *Herald*'s advertisements were bright, shocking, useful, and broadly appealing. Where the blanket press might run the same ad for a year, Bennett demanded fresh copy every two weeks, eventually every day. He also opened his pages promiscuously to anyone who would pay. He started a "Personals" column that included communiques from women looking for husbands, mothers searching for lost children, prostitutes soliciting clients, abortionists seeking customers.

Caveat emptor was Bennett's guiding principle; complaints about advertisers were briskly dismissed. When one correspondent denounced Dr. Brandreth's Pills as a quack nostrum, Bennett replied: "Send us more advertisements than Dr. Brandreth does—give us higher prices—we'll cut Dr. Brandreth dead—or at least curtail his space. Business is business—money is money. . . . We permit no blockhead to interfere with our business."

And business was phenomenal. Within fifteen months, the *Herald* claimed a circulation of twenty thousand. Bennett plowed profits back into a new steam press (from Hoe and Company), a new building at the corner of Nassau and Beekman, a bureau in Washington, and a network of European correspondents, making the *Herald* the first American paper to offer systematic foreign coverage. Within four years of its founding, it surpassed the *Sun*—and the *Times* of London, assuming first place in the global circulation sweepstakes.

A GLANCE AT NEW YORK

In 1836 a Philadelphia journalist exploring New York and Brooklyn found people reading penny papers in virtually every street, lane, and alley. "Almost every porter and drayman, while not engaged in his occupation, may be seen with a paper in his hands." The penny press offered New Yorkers a broadly encompassing look at the range of groups that had clambered into visibility during the previous democratizing decades. It did not speak to or for any one of them in particular. It did not reflect, and help shape, a single constituency, as did the era's many religious, ethnic, racial, and radical papers. It was not limited by eighteenth-century print culture's pinched definition of urbanity and restrictive repertoire of urban types and settings. Instead, it addressed something that had never quite existed before except in republican theory: a "public" at large, a civic demos. In doing so, it offered New York's citizenry the technical and textual means to grasp their city's growing miscellaneity.

In 1837 this new way of seeing the city was transferred to urban guidebooks, when Asa Greene, editor of the *Transcript*, authored *A Glance at New York*. Greene's style was far livelier than his predecessors'. He included anecdotes, dialogue, and personal musings, described people and places with flair, and presented arguments illustrated with everyday events and characters.

Glance was the first critical guide to New York City. Greene felt no need to present the urban milieu in an unambivalently positive light, as his forebears had. Indeed he gently mocked New Yorkers for their insatiable need to proclaim their city biggest and best. Noting the negatives in sharp but jovial language, Greene cited corrupt municipal politics, inadequate public services (poor water and sparse parks), rampant hucksterism, superficial values, and, particularly, class stratification. Greene conveyed a sympathy for the city's working classes that had never appeared in any previous guide. *Glance* had a political edge: it attacked the greed and opportunism of those in power while twitting fatuous nouveau riches.

Not content to rattle off a list of worthy civic institutions—hotels, theaters, churches, jails—Greene set out to capture the panorama of city life, embracing such novel subjects as rogues, mobs, monopolies, and hoaxes. This comprehensive way of seeing turned powerful floodlights on all corners of the civic stage. Its arrival, during the tumultuous decade of the 1830s, meant that these years of fevered prosperity and riotous contention would be the first in the city's history to receive instant amplification in a mass medium. From that day to this, New York, communications capital, would be the most closely watched city in the world.

32

The Destroying
Demon of
Debauchery

In the summer of 1829, an upstate Presbyterian evangelist named Charles Grandison Finney descended on New York City to establish the Kingdom of God in Manhattan. The revivalist's energetic and colloquial style—"We must have exciting, powerful preaching," Finney thundered, "or the devil will have the people, except what the Methodists can save"—had recently ignited a spiritual firestorm in sin-soaked towns along the Erie Canal. Unlike most millenarians, who believed Christ's Second Coming would inaugurate the thousand years of holiness promised in Revelations 20, Finney argued that Jesus' arrival would culminate—indeed be predicated upon—a ten-century reign of peace and justice. Finney's millennium would be attained by human action, not divine fiat: pious men and women who had saved themselves had now to save society.

Finney's upstate activities had brought him to the attention of the Manhattan-based Association of Gentlemen. This informal junta of transplanted Yankee merchants and bankers—among them Anson Phelps, Arthur Tappan, and David Low Dodge—had abandoned their parents' gloomy belief in predestination. Self-made men, they believed that sinners could be saved by applying the kind of disciplined effort that garnered success in the business world. They begged Finney to bring his crusade to (as Phelps put it) "our Stupid, Poluted, and Perishing City," promising him to put up the money for a "free" church that would allow the poor to attend without paying the pew-rents still required by every denomination except the Methodists. Finney accepted, and by the fall of 1829 he had been installed as the temporary pastor of the First Free Presbyterian Church on Thames Street.

Finney's arrival under the auspices of the Association of Gentlemen was a signal that the cause of social reform in New York had entered a new and more aggressively evangelical phase. Those genteel Knickerbockers who had dominated the work of charity and benevolence from 1790 to 1820 were passing away—Divie Bethune in 1824, Thomas Eddy in 1827, De Witt Clinton in 1828—and even the venerable John Pintard, now approaching seventy, was beginning to slow down. The wealthy Yankees who took over from them made no secret of their intention to do things differently. Nominally Presbyterians, they had lost patience with divines like Gardiner Spring of the Brick Presbyterian Church and Samuel Cox of the Laight Street Presbyterian Church, who opposed Finney-style revivals as theologically unsound as well as undignified. From the Yankee point of view, too, the older generation of reformers had been insufficiently concerned with a swarm of new threats to social stability and tranquility: trade unions, Tammany politicians, the Catholic Church, and the freethinkers flocking to Fanny Wright's Hall of Science.

Over the next half-dozen years, accordingly, the Association of Gentlemen stepped up their support of Finney by providing him with bigger and better church buildings. In 1832 they converted the former Chatham Street Theater into the Chatham Street Chapel, also known as the Second Free Presbyterian Church. The huge barn of a place, hard by the burgeoning Five Points, had been deserted by fashionable patrons, while working-class customers opted for its competitor, the Bowery Theater. Finney worried about the neighborhood—"Is not the location too filthy for decent people to go there?" he queried Tappan—but it could seat twenty-five hundred worshipers, and he moved in anyway. Several years later, in 1835, the association established him in the massive new Broadway Tabernacle (at what is now Worth Street) directly across from New York Hospital and near the new Masonic Hall and Columbia College. The tabernacle's great rotunda, with tiers of pews rising steeply from the central pulpit, served to focus all eyes on the preacher and carried his voice clearly to the throngs that came to hear him.

By the end of the decade, Finney's crusades in New York had spawned eleven "free" churches with several thousand members, all bundled into a Third Presbytery created by the Synod of New York (the alternative being schism). He saved disappointingly few working-class men, however: three-fourths of his followers consisted of working-class women, many of them recent rural migrants employed as domestics and seamstresses. (Frances Trollope wrote that evangelical congregations often consisted of "long rows of French bonnets and pretty faces," resembling "beds of tulips, so gay, so bright, so beautiful.") Most of the men Finney did manage to win over were affluent merchants, manufacturers, retailers, and professionals who, like the Associated Gentlemen, believed that an awakened Christian asceticism was the answer to urban poverty and vice. Many more were drawn from the city's embryonic middle class—shopkeepers, small master craftsmen, clerks, salesmen, bookkeepers, and bank tellers—who embraced evangelicalism as a way to dissociate themselves from both the dissolute poor and the idle rich.

ONWARD, CHRISTIAN SOLDIERS

The real measure of Finney's impact on the city wasn't the number of souls he saved but rather the boost his preaching gave to a wide range of evangelical efforts during the 1830s. Reform projects that had once absorbed a relative handful now enlisted the energies and emotions of much greater numbers of middle- and upper-class New Yorkers.

Evangelical fervor revitalized the old American Tract Society, which by 1835 had over a thousand men and women distributing its publications in the city's stores, taverns, countinghouses, markets, asylums, and hospitals. The reinvigorated American

Bible Society embarked on a "general supply" campaign to deliver a Bible to every family in the United States by the end of 1831 and actually managed to distribute 481,000 copies—well short of its goal but an impressive display of renewed organizational resolve and sophistication. Thanks largely to Finney, moreover, these groups, along with Sunday schools, home missions, and a steadily growing number of other such organizations, found it easier to raise money and develop a national outreach. Each May, generals and foot soldiers from moral uplift organizations throughout the country descended in great numbers on New York for conclaves at the Chatham Street Chapel or the Broadway Tabernacle, underscoring the city's position as headquarters of the Benevolent Empire. By 1830 the thirteen leading societies had already received contributions of $2.8 million, compared to the $3.6 million Congress had spent on internal improvements since the founding of the republic. Soon their annual receipts would surpass the annual federal budget.

Mainstream Christian denominations struggled to keep up with the evangelical juggernaut. Anglicans, under the leadership of Benjamin Onderdonk (consecrated as bishop of New York in 1830), established a Protestant Episcopal City Missionary Society to open free churches in poor neighborhoods. That initiative was followed by the Bible and Common Prayer Book Society, the Protestant Episcopal Tract Society, and the New York Protestant Episcopal Sunday School Union, which by 1833 embraced twenty-four schools with some sixty-two hundred pupils. Finney-style exhortations had no part in the Anglican program, however. "The transformation of character we propose to effect," said the Episcopalian New York Mission Council in 1832, would be achieved "by the simple agency of plain instruction and cheering counsel."

In 1835, several years after the formation of the evangelical Third Presbytery, Finney's adherents in the Presbyterian Church resolved to build a seminary to train a new generation of clergymen. Meeting at the home of Knowles Taylor—a prominent merchant, elder of the Bleecker Street Presbyterian Church, and treasurer of the American Home Missionary Society—they set in motion plans for the New York Theological Seminary. In 1839, a year after moving into its first building on University Place, it was renamed the Union Theological Seminary in the City of New York.

Evangelical Presbyterians also figured prominently in forging an alternative to the Episcopalian stronghold of Columbia College. Despite its central location, Columbia in the 1820s drowsed on the margins of New York's intellectual life, expounding the classics to upper-class boys destined for careers in the clergy. But its critics were growing more numerous and vocal. Mercantile and professional families wanted their sons trained for commerce, not the cloister. Workingmen and democrats sought equal educational opportunity for all residents. Old Jeffersonians like Albert Gallatin argued that no proper college could function under clerical control. Powerful evangelicals like Eleazar Lord and the Rev. Samuel H. Cox pressed for a Presbyterian version of Columbia.

In the autumn of 1830 a three-day "literary and scientific convention" convened in City Hall to discuss proposals for a municipal institution of higher learning comparable to the new University of London (1826). After some sharp debate, the hundred-odd delegates agreed on a plan for a University of the City of New York (now New York University). When both the state and city governments refused to provide financial support, the university's trustees raised a hundred thousand dollars from private donors, hired faculty, and tapped Gallatin to serve as its first president. Less than a year later, however, Gallatin resigned in disgust. Evangelical Presbyterian and Reformed ministers had succeeded in drawing up a curriculum for the university that neglected the "rational and practical" learning he considered essential. By 1832, as classes got underway in rented quarters in Clinton Hall (at Nassau and Beekman streets), it was no surprise that twice as many Presbyterian students registered as those of any other denomination. Three years later, the university moved into its first permanent home, a white marble Gothic Revival building on Washington Square designed by A. J. Davis.

SPIRIT VERSUS SPIRITS

By the mid-1820s the massive growth of western grain production, combined with improved technologies of distillation and ever more efficient means of transportation, left New York awash in cheap liquor. It also triggered a new eruption of concern over the scope and consequences of excessive drinking. John Pintard remarked as early as 1821 that "grovelling drunkenness increases among the lower vulgar owing to the reduced prices of ardent spirits." Growing numbers of well-to-do residents—already in revolt against the swilling customary on New Year's and other holidays—were alarmed that alcohol was taking a heavy toll among their own kind as well, eroding ambition, dissipating wealth, and spawning domestic violence. So, too, manufacturers challenged the customary drinking rights of their employees as a threat to higher profits, while journeyman unionists and freethinkers denounced drunkenness as an obstacle to effective organization in the trades.

It was evangelical merchants and industrialists, however, who would inspire and lead the city's first temperance movement. Hat manufacturer Joseph Brewster, for one, was an idealistic and determined Finneyite who also calculated that banning alcohol from the workplace could boost profits by up to 25 percent. He moved his family from a 4th Street mansion (today's Old Merchant's House museum) to a shabby Bowery dwelling on Rivington Street, joined one of the free Presbyterian churches, and began to hand out abstinence tracts (he slipped one inside each hat he sold) and to lead raiding parties on nearby saloons. Lewis Tappan likewise organized a network of Christian spies to infiltrate taverns and report infractions of long-ignored ordinances to municipal authorities.

When grocers, publicans, distillers, and the landlords who rented them space started to fight back, evangelicals assembled at the Masonic Hall in 1829 to organize the New-York City Temperance Society. The society's first president was banker Samuel Ward (of Prime, Ward, and King); its leadership included Tappan, engine maker J. P. Allaire, Eleazar Lord (president of the Manhattan Insurance Company), and other prominent businessmen and professionals. Over the next several years, the society launched its own newspaper, the *Genius of Temperance*, and began an aggressive recruitment campaign. By 1835 it had chapters in each ward, forty-five additional subsidiaries attached to individual churches, and societies for sailors, stonecutters, and silversmiths—better than fifty thousand members in all. (A parallel Brooklyn Temperance Society, headed by Adrian van Sinderen, first president of the Brooklyn Savings Bank, made equally rapid headway, as did the black-run Society for Temperance, which recruited through African-American churches.)

Members did more than pledge personal abstinence. They distributed tracts, addressed civic groups, launched boycotts, and pushed for legal restrictions. One measure of their effectiveness was a sharp drop in alcohol consumption (which fell, nationwide, from four gallons per capita in 1830 to less than two gallons a decade later); there was also a modest reduction in the number of liquor licenses, especially in working-class wards. The Brooklyn temperance movement won passage of an ordinance curbing the sale of liquor by the glass, after which the number of taverns fell from 178 to fifty, even as Brooklyn's population rose from over twelve thousand to nearly thirty thousand.

"THE DESTROYING DEMON OF DEBAUCHERY"

In 1831 and 1832, at the invitation of New York's temperance leadership, Philadelphia activist Sylvester Graham delivered lectures on the relationship between diet and disease. New Yorkers, Graham argued, had been fatally weakened in their ability to resist epidemics by the improper eating habits spawned by big-city life. Graham opposed the use of stimulants—not only liquor, wine, and cider but tea, coffee, and tobacco too. He advocated vegetarianism. He denounced urban bakers who used "refined" flour—stripped of husks and dark oleaginous germ and whitened with "chemical agents"—because it baked more quickly than traditional bread, even though the result was an almost crustless loaf without granular texture or nutritional value. He railed, too, against marketplace milk, much of which came from cows fed on leftover distillery mash (swill), with the anemic, liquor-inflected product made presentable by the addition of chalk, plaster of Paris, and molasses.

Graham's proposed antidotes for such urban ills were—like most evangelical suggestions—personal, not social. Rather than calling for regulations on production, he advised New Yorkers to alter their consumption patterns. Ideally they should bake their own bread; he gave them directions for selecting, preserving, and grinding wheat, then fermenting it to produce the old-fashioned, whole-wheat bread that later bore his name. They should also consume more fresh fruits and leafy vegetables—perishables still in short supply in urban markets and considered unhealthy if not cooked.

In 1833 some of his followers opened a Graham Boardinghouse, a kind of temperance hotel where men (no women were allowed) could follow a Grahamite regimen. No alcohol, tea, or coffee was allowed, as the sign in front advised. Bells rang at five o'clock summoning residents to cold baths, followed by a breakfast of fruit, wheat pudding, tepid gruel, and cold water or milk, after which the lodgers—Arthur Tappan, Horace Greeley, and, when he was in town, William Lloyd Garrison were among the noted guests—went off to work in Pearl or Wall Street. They came back for a midday vegetarian meal accompanied by wheat-meal bread and cold filtered rainwater, then returned again in the evening for exercise and a cold-water wash before lights were doused, and clients locked in, at "precisely" ten o'clock.

Avoiding spirits and highly seasoned "flesh-meat" was an aid to sexual abstinence as well, as Graham told an enthusiastic audience at New York's American Lyceum (in a talk later published as a *Lecture to Young Men* [1834]). Male orgasms, he warned, were inherently destructive; the loss of vital semen lowered men's life force, making them easy prey to diabetes, jaundice, consumption, and premature death. Sex was as bad for business as it was for health. Reckless "spending" of sperm could lead to financial as well as moral and physiological bankruptcy. Properly subdued, however, sexuality, like nature, could be made useful—its energies harnessed, accumulated, put to productive purposes.

Unfortunately a saturnalia of carnality was underway in the city. The locus of the problem was the all-male boardinghouses where growing numbers of country boys and immigrant youths were lodged, unsupervised by family, church, or community. These single young men, freed from constraints, drank in saloons, visited brothels, and practiced self-abuse (a "loathsome and beastly habit" that produced debility, weakness, dyspepsia, impotency, and "masturbatory insanity"). Such practices, moreover, were being picked up by children of the higher classes, transmitted via the debasing influence of servants or through the schools, where youths learned filthy habits from their peers.

Continence was the only answer. Sex was to be avoided before one got married—in one's late twenties or thirties; interim masturbatory relief was strictly enjoined. Even with the conjugal state safely attained, sexuality was best proscribed.

The pursuit of sexual self-discipline became the subject of a flood of self-help books, tracts, manuals, and magazine articles addressed to males (passionlessness was presumed to come naturally to women). Abstinence, like temperance, was presented as a prescription for personal, social, and financial well-being. Alas, the theory availed its progenitor little: for all his careful rationing of intake and outflow, Sylvester Graham suffered a nervous breakdown in 1837 and spent the rest of his life a semi-invalid.

Grahamites evoked ridicule, some hostile but most affable: vegetarianism and cold-water cures, after all, were voluntary affairs. But reformers did not settle for reining in their own bodies, and when they set out to discipline the sex lives of other New Yorkers, they provoked an uproar.

As Charles Finney was winding down his first New York City revival in the spring of 1830, John Robert McDowall arrived in town. A twenty-nine-year-old Amherst graduate and Princeton divinity student, McDowall spent the summer as an American Tract Society missionary, with Arthur Tappan covering his expenses. Dispatched to the Five Points, he visited slum cellars, distributed Scripture, taught Sunday school classes, and gave temperance lectures. McDowall also began visiting brothels, where he led prayer meetings and remonstrated with the women and their customers.

McDowall also started a Sunday school and Bible class in New York's almshouse and prisons, with access arranged by Finneyite supporter Anson Phelps. Pious genteel women, many recently converted by Finney, taught in these classes, led prayer meetings, and, like McDowall, developed a particular interest in the problems of female convicts, most of whom were prostitutes.

In 1831 McDowall and his female adherents launched the New-York Magdalen Society with funding provided by Arthur Tappan and his male evangelical associates. The society opened a house of refuge for penitent prostitutes in the Five Points, modeled on the famous Magdalen Asylum in London, with McDowall as curate and on-site superintendent to "the daughters of guilt and sorrow."

The Magdalens quickly ran into trouble. In the summer of 1831 McDowall issued a shocking pamphlet declaring that New York City had been overrun with harlots—ten thousand of them. Nor was their clientele limited to sailors and laborers, he charged; it included gentlemen from the most prominent and respectable families. Lewdness and impurity were tainting all sectors of civic society, and unless something was done, "multitudes will probably be immolated on the altar of the destroying demon of debauchery."

McDowall's statistics were wildly off, but he was responding to a real phenomenon. Commercial sex had become ever more ubiquitous. By the 1830s the Five Points was notorious, with twenty-seven of the forty-three blocks surrounding Paradise Square hosting brothels in whose windows girls in varying stages of undress paraded to lure street trade. In more genteel zones, the expensive carriages of judges, merchants, lawyers, and statesmen could routinely be seen lined up in front of their owners' favorite parlor houses, and some clients went so far as to pay traditional New Year's calls on madams. These gentlemen, some of them in flight from the new domesticity, could indulge their lustful pastimes reasonably sure that no one would trumpet their misdeeds.

This tacit approval of officially illicit sex extended to the vast numbers of visiting businessmen for whom parlor-house patronage was fast becoming a customary part of commercial transactions. During 1835 New York's leading hotels housed nearly sixty thousand guests, many of them country merchants come to arrange credit and place orders. More than a few banks and businesses dispatched "drummers" to show them a good time. As one critic described the process in 1836, drummers invited potential clients "to champagne parties, to the theatre, and to houses of infamy, with the offer to bear all the expense."

Into this civic conspiracy of masculine silence stepped John Robert McDowall, loudly blowing the whistle. Not surprisingly, his *Magdalen Report* was greeted with an avalanche of criticism, which the *Evening Post* summed up by saying: "The report should never have been printed, and being printed should be as speedily as possible suppressed." Gentlemen of standing argued that McDowall's lurid picture of urban vice was itself prurient and pornographic—"a disgraceful document," said Philip Hone. Even more shocking, as William Cullen Bryant observed, its statistics of whoredom had been read out at a public meeting "composed three-fourths of respectable females." City boosters protested its slandering of New York's fair name and pronounced it bad for business. Workingmen and freethinkers denounced it as yet another theocratic initiative by church and state busybodies. Some suggested that McDowall's zealotry stemmed from a morbid fascination with vice. This accusation was not entirely off base; as Lewis Tappan remarked of his brother, Arthur—McDowall's patron and one who also liked to boldly "explore [the] recesses of Satan"—he "gloried in all the soiling that attaches to one in such efforts."

Knickerbockers who resented the rising social influence of New Englanders in the city were much in evidence at an August 1831 meeting in Tammany Hall that called for and swiftly obtained a grand jury investigation of McDowall's charges. This body could locate a mere 1,438 working girls—a deflated claim the press found risible—but it nevertheless flayed Tappan and the Magdalen trustees. Members of the society, even female ones, were verbally abused and threatened with ostracism. In short order, the campaign for public reticence triumphed. Tappan, taken aback by the rage and respectability of his opponents, quit the Magdalen Society, McDowall resigned his chaplaincy in September, and by November the group had suspended its activities and disposed of its asylum.

Utterly isolated, McDowall was about to give up and leave the city when two groups of genteel Presbyterian women—most of them wives of businessmen or of ministers—joined his purity crusade, thereby transforming the debate over sexuality in the city.

In December 1832 the New York Female Benevolent Society (FBS) was formed to help fallen females who "manifest[ed] a desire to return to the paths of virtue from which they have swerved." By May 1835 the FBS had opened the House of Reception, a refuge for prostitutes in Yorkville, four miles north of City Hall. Its bell-driven daily routine included scripture readings and sewing classes to train the magdalens for future

Prostitution Exposed, by "A Butt Ender." A droll parody of the anti-prostitution campaign organized by McDowall and other reformers, the book conveniently supplies the names and addresses for more than a hundred local courtesans and brothels. (General Research Division. The New York Public Library. Astor, Lenox and Tilden Foundations)

jobs with Christian families. The FBS severely limited the appeal of their refuge, however, by refusing to accept any but "worthy" candidates, which required turning away "bigoted Papists" and impious Protestants. After two years they had gathered in only 145 penitents, and of these only four seemed "serious and industrious." Worse, in the summer of 1836 inmates seized control of the institution, and the bitterly discouraged managers dismissed their charges, closed the building, and turned to dispensing tracts about the Seventh Commandment.

In May 1834, however, some of the FBS's more militant members had split off to form a new citywide group, the New York Female Moral Reform Society (FMRS). This body quickly won powerful evangelical backing, with Lydia Andrews Finney, the revivalist's wife, becoming its first directress and Arthur Tappan stepping in as its financial backer. The FMRS now appointed McDowall as missionary-general to New York's prostitutes, and he began leading teams of men and women on "active visits" to brothels. Arriving early on Sunday morning, just as the ladies of the night and their customers were waking up, the reformers stationed themselves across the street, knelt in prayer, and began reading Bible passages and singing hymns. When they tried this at some of the rougher venues in the Points and the Hook, the crusaders were often met with curses and threats. At the westside parlor houses, however, they seemed to have something of a deterrent effect: closed coaches would circle for an hour or so, then clatter off. Encouraged, McDowall and company upped the ante by noting down names of the more determined patrons and printing them in *McDowall's Journal*, alongside editorials excoriating brothels as "stagnant pools of moral filth" whose owners "ought to be executed."

McDowall also lit into New York's pornography trade. Charging that "obscene prints and licentious figures and paintings" were sold widely in the city, he collected a variety of "obscene books, prints, music-boxes, [and] snuff-boxes," which he displayed at a meeting of three hundred clergymen in May 1834. Out of probity or prurience, *McDowall's Journal* did well. Circulation that year topped fourteen thousand a month, with half the issues handed out around town, the other half dispatched to rural subscribers.

Another grand jury, impaneled in 1834 to investigate *McDowall's Journal*, declared it patently "offensive to taste, injurious to morals, and degrading to the character of [the] city." Even the Third Presbytery, the body that licensed McDowall to preach and supported his campaign, advised him to discontinue the journal. Accordingly he offered his press to the FMRS, which purchased it, renamed it the *Advocate of Moral Reform*, and staffed it exclusively with women—editors, typesetters, even financial managers. The *Advocate* gathered 16,500 subscribers within three years, becoming one of the nation's most widely read evangelical papers.

Under the women's direction, the *Advocate* went beyond unmasking men who visited brothels to asking prostitutes who had "ruined" them—it being an article of faith with the ladies that many women "on the town" had been victimized by licentious males—and publishing the names of men whom its investigations showed to be guilty. It sued seducers for civil damages on occasion and launched a petition campaign to lobby public officials in Albany to make seduction a criminal offense.

The newspaper seethed with visceral antagonism to salacious males, and in its pages FMRS members raged against predators who "basely and treacherously" seduced and ruined trusting women. Behind the outrage at particular individuals lay a much deeper resentment of the "despotism" of "lordly man" in general. These pious wives and middle-class mothers insisted that men be held to the same requirement of sexual purity that women were. The double standard, said the *Advocate* in 1835, permitted a "state of licentiousness, systematized as it is in our cities," that constituted "a regular crusade against the sex."

Within a year of its formation, the New York Female Moral Reform Society had hired ministers, missionaries, and agents and had organized five auxiliaries in New York and another twenty-eight outside the city. By 1838 there were 361 auxiliaries and an estimated twenty thousand members, principally in New York State and greater New England. In 1839 the city group reorganized as a national operation, the American Female Moral Reform Society, and within two years it boasted 555 auxiliaries and a combined membership of approximately fifty thousand.

Male clergymen attacked this female initiative, as they had the work of the Female Missionary Society nearly two decades earlier, as being beyond women's proper sphere. But the Female Moral Reform Society strenuously resisted clerical injunctions. As an early issue of the *Advocate* asserted, "This work must be begun with ladies. They are the injured, and they must rise and assert their rights." Rather than meekly returning to the home, militant women elbowed male philanthropists aside and made a place for themselves in the quest for the Millennium.

"IS IT NOT MORE LIKELY THE WORK OF A WOMAN?"

At three A.M. on Sunday, April 10, 1836, brothel keeper Rosina Townsend was awakened by smoke billowing out of Helen Jewett's room. She screamed for the watchmen, who discovered Jewett's body—hacked up ("the bone was cleft to the extent of three inches") and partly consumed by flames. The rear door was ajar. Just outside lay a hatchet and a blue cloth cloak belonging to one Richard P. Robinson. Townsend explained that Robinson had arrived the previous evening to spend the night with Jewett and had been there at eleven P.M., when she had served the couple champagne. The watch hastened to Robinson's lodging house. There they found pantaloons smeared with what appeared to be lime from the whitewashed fence behind the brothel. Charged with murder, Robinson was imprisoned at Bellevue.

The slaying of Helen Jewett became an instant sensation. "For the last ten days," James Gordon Bennett wrote in his *Herald* on April 20, "this tragedy and the accused have occupied every tongue—been the leading topic of every conversation—is discussed in every drawing room and gin shop throughout the extent of New York. . . . No point of interest—no event—no contingency ever took place in New York, which has so completely divided public opinion, and created a general debate."

Premeditated murders were rare—only seven had been reported in all of 1835—but the uproar over the Robinson-Jewett affair stemmed from more than shock. The protagonists were perceived, correctly, as emblematic players on the city's gender stage, whose relationship afforded the citizenry yet another opportunity to debate New York's rapidly changing sexual and class dynamics.

Helen Jewett, daughter of a poor Maine shoemaker, was keenly intelligent, extremely beautiful, and the possessor of social graces acquired in service to a prominent Augusta family. Since 1830, then aged seventeen, she had been a girl "on the town," first in Portland, then in Boston, finally in New York City. From 1833 on she lived in a series of elegant brothels in the lower Fifth Ward, ending up at 41 Thomas Street in 1835.

Rosina Townsend ran an elegant establishment. Her girls met potential clients in fashionable venues like the third tier at the Park Theater or were screened and deemed acceptable by Madame Townsend herself. Many of the visitors paid a kind of court to the courtesans, in earnest emulation of bourgeois mating rituals. Helen, glamorous and erudite (she read Byron), received from three to eight love letters a day, which she picked up at the post office or had delivered by public porters.

Robinson, a handsome, ruddy youth of nineteen who dressed in the height of fashion, was one of Jewett's most ardent suitors. Scion of a fine old Connecticut family, Robinson worked for Joseph Hoxie, a Yankee cloth merchant. Hoxie was a charter member of the New-York City Temperance Society, and he supported a lecture series promoting industrious habits and moral deportment among young clerks. So far as his employer knew, Robinson was an unblemished exemplar of proper behavior.

In fact, Robinson was a habitué of whorehouses. Since meeting Jewett in June 1835, Robinson had been visiting her several times a week. He sent her romantic epistles, books, literary periodicals. He went with her to the Park and Bowery theaters. He boasted of his relations with her to his friends, many of whom also shared her favors.

Like their plebeian male counterparts, Robinson and his confraternity of "sporting men"—clerks, cashiers, and fledgling merchants—adopted promiscuous bachelorhood as a way of life, defying the culture of chastity demanded by the evangelicals, and even the conventional proprieties adhered to by Knickerbocker businessmen. Many of these macho clerks lived on their own, as did the single male laborers in working-class boardinghouses, and were equally beyond the moral surveillance of employer, family, or church. Robinsonian dandies, in satisfying their sexual needs through the marketplace, benefited as well from the differential standard of sexual propriety for men and women.

In 1831 McDowall and his Magdalen Society had forced issues of sexuality into the public forum; they had been ruthlessly suppressed and civic silence restored. In 1834 the New York Female Moral Reform Society had redeclared war against male promiscuity, but its crusade remained a marginal and minority preoccupation.

The Jewett murder injected the issue of class into the debate about sex in the city at just the moment when the penny press had arrived, with the result that the conversation was catapulted into the mainstream of popular discourse. Traditional sixpenny editors had preferred not to talk about such sordid issues. Bryant pronounced the case a "disagreeable subject." But the *Herald, Sun,* and *Transcript* lavished oceans of lurid prose on the murder, making it the most intensely covered story of the decade. And, as they took violently opposing positions on the guilt or innocence of the parties, their pugnacious exchanges generated additional excitement, further boosting the circulation of all three.

Bennett led off with a melodramatic recounting of his visit to the scene of the crime. His alluring description of Jewett's body—"the perfect figure, the exquisite limbs, the fine face, the full arms, the beautiful bust, all surpassed in every respect the Venus de Medici"—was a bit odd, to be sure, given that the corpse had been hacked and roasted. His report of an exchange with Madam Townsend, replete with verbatim dialogue and generally considered the first formal interview ever recorded in an American newspaper, was rendered similarly suspect by Townsend's denial, related in the *Sun*, that she had ever talked with him.

But Bennett was after more than mere facts—or what he called "dull police reports." He had a thesis to promote: that Robinson, despite appearances, was a "young, amiable, and innocent youth." In the role of murderer, Bennett cast a series of candidates. First he said one of the other prostitutes had killed Jewett out of jealousy. After all, he asked, given the brutality, "is it not more likely the work of a woman?" Then he blamed Townsend, an "old miserable hag, who has spent her whole life in seducing and inveigling the young and old to their destruction." He even implied that Jewett herself bore moral responsibility for her own death: in becoming one of the "licentious inmates of a fashionable brothel," she had violated the canons of true womanhood and put herself beyond the protective pale of respectability.

Like McDowall, Bennett expressed indignation at vice while closely portraying its lineaments for the delectation of respectable readers. Yet Bennett avoided McDowall's fate, partly by vigorously upholding the established class and gender order, which McDowall had challenged, and partly by fashioning a new journalistic persona. Bennett became the intrepid reporter, the public's representative, duty bound to expose even the most sordid aspects of New York's underworld. This proved a winning and lucrative formula: in one week, the *Herald*'s circulation shot up to fifteen thousand per day.

Benjamin Day's *Sun* and the *Transcript* took the opposite tack. Robinson was no innocent boy but a villainous man about town. Jewett hadn't seduced him; he had seduced Jewett, yet another instance of an upper-class dandy sexually exploiting a working-class woman. He had murdered poor Helen and now would now try to cheat the gallows with help from highly placed friends. This egalitarian analysis, worthy of the penny papers' Workie roots, accorded with assumptions many working-class readers brought to the issue.

After more than a month of discussion in the court of public opinion, the courtroom trial commenced at City Hall on June 2, 1836. Each of its five days was a circus. Even on the second morning, when it rained fiercely, five to six thousand would-be spectators thronged the area. Crowds of clerks—a Robinsonian claque—jammed the courtroom almost daily. They were permitted to whoop and cheer testimony favorable to the prisoner and hiss and boo prosecution witnesses.

To defend Robinson, his employer hired three of New York's most celebrated lawyers: William Price, Hugh Maxwell, and Ogden Hoffman. The evidence against their client was circumstantial but plentiful. Robinson's roommate swore he had been out late the night of the murder. Townsend and a bevy of the prostitutes placed him at the crime scene. Townsend testified about motive as well, noting that Robinson, recently engaged to a young woman of good family, was anxious to retrieve letters he had sent Jewett, two score of which were found in her room.

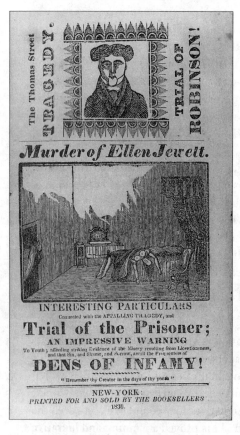

Intense coverage of the Jewett murder in the penny press created a market for cheap pamphlets that provided graphic embellishments while drawing moral lessons from the event. (© Collection of The New-York Historical Society)

In rebuttal, Robinson's lawyers produced a witness—a respectable grocer named Furlong—who insisted the youth had been reading papers in his shop a mile and a half from Thomas Street that evening. Well aware that many believed Furlong's testimony had been purchased with Hoxie's cash, the lawyers also attacked the credibility of the prosecution's witnesses—on *moral* grounds. Women like Townsend, who had led an "infamous and abandoned" life, could not be trusted to tell the truth.

Here the lawyers were bucking convention. Legally, madams had been treated like small businesspersons and protected against threats to their person or property—threats that had increased dramatically in the 1830s. Brothel riots, expressions of community disapprobation of sin, were an old story, but recently small groups of working-class toughs had been bursting into fancy brothels, physically assaulting and sometimes raping the women, breaking furniture and windows. Some of these incidents were drunken sprees. Some were fueled by misogyny: brothel bullies found the prosperous independence of prostitutes intolerable at a time when working-class males' income and prerogatives were being undermined. Some were driven by class animosity: attackers were furious that upscale brothels barred their access to women who were readily available to clerks and merchants.

When ruffians went on rampages, prostitutes did not hesitate to initiate legal proceedings against them. In 1833, after three men had barged into Mrs. Townsend's Thomas Street house shouting indecent language, she had them charged with assault and battery. The municipality was prepared to defend prostitutes from attacks by lower-class antagonists; would they do so when the accused, by birth and association, was one of the city's elite?

The issue was decided by the presiding judge, Ogden Edwards. Judge Edwards was a distinguished member of the patriciate, a grandson of Jonathan Edwards and cousin of Aaron Burr. Originally a conservative Tammany man—at the constitutional convention of 1821 he had opposed universal suffrage—Edwards was active in the New-York City Temperance Society. He now decreed that the testimony of prostitutes was likely to be as corrupt as their way of life. The judge instructed the jury not to credit their testimony unless it was otherwise corroborated. Robinson was acquitted in less than ten minutes.

The *Sun* denounced the verdict as a miscarriage of justice and an affirmation of class privilege. It noted that "an opinion is prevalent and openly expressed that any man may commit murder, who has $1500 to give to Messers Hoffman, Price and Maxwell." The Female Moral Reform Society's *Advocate of Moral Reform* also bristled at the ruling, outraged that prostitutes' testimony—and lives—were not deemed the moral equal of their clients'. Some elite males were outraged too—Philip Hone called the verdict the "foulest blot on the jurisprudence of our country"—but Robinson's acquittal pleased privileged gentlemen determined to suppress challenges to their masculine prerogatives.

In the trial's aftermath, antifeminists grew bolder. When Fanny Wright returned later in 1836 and attempted to renew her speaking campaign, she was met not simply with verbal brickbats—the *Courier and Enquirer* attacked her "disgusting exhibition of female impudence"—but with outright suppression. On September 23, maddened males at Masonic Hall drove Wright from the stage with hisses, pounding of canes, stink bombs, and a "volley of expressions of the most vulgar and indecent kind." She soon found the doors of every major public hall in New York City shut against her.

33

White, Green, and Black

J ust as debauchery, drunkenness, and Sabbath desecration were impediments to fashioning a heavenly city, so too was Catholicism, in evangelical eyes. Popery was idolatrous, theocratic, and despotic, and any further spread of its pernicious doctrines would hinder the Second Coming of Christ. Given the growing presence and power of Catholics in New York City, such a stance resonated widely within Protestant communities. Not only did the evangelicals' nativist denunciations of immigrant Irish win them plaudits from citizens who in other respects were put off by the pious crusaders, but they touched off violent sectarian confrontations in the streets.

At the same time the evangelicals were stirring up anti-Catholic bigots, they were denouncing slavery as an evil, one America had to purge if it were ever to attain a state of grace. Abolitionism, like nativism, would rouse rage in the city. Those who believed that tampering with the South's peculiar institution menaced Manhattan took to the streets, hell bent on suppressing antislavery.

THE COMING OF THE GREEN

When Thomas Addis Emmet died in 1828, he was perhaps the foremost lawyer in New York, ranked by many with Massachusetts's Daniel Webster, and his funeral, by some accounts, was the largest ever seen in the city. Emmet's death, though deeply mourned within the Irish community, coincided with the waning of support for his ideas and values. Together with the other distinguished middle-class emigrés who had arrived in the aftermath of the failed 1798 United Irishmen uprising, Emmet had staunchly opposed religious sectarianism. He, his fellow Protestant attorney William Sampson, and Catholic physician William James MacNeven had organized the Association of the Friends of Ireland in New-York. The group had raised funds and rallied support for Daniel O'Connell's civil rights movement in Ireland and helped win emancipation for British Catholics in 1829. The Friends of Ireland, however, like the allied Society for Civil and Religious Liberties, was vigorously ecumenical. So was the *Shamrock, or Hibernian Chronicle*, New York's first Irish-American paper (1810–17), which reflected the exiles' values. The Shamrock Friendly Association of New York (1816), too, sought to create a united Protestant and Catholic Irish-American community imbued with American and republican values. By forging alliances with highly placed Manhattan sympathizers of varying religious persuasions, the United Irishmen served as links between New York's growing numbers of laboring Catholics and the city's Protestant elite.

Over the 1820s, however, the nonsectarian integrationist vision of the '98ers came to seem less compelling to the Irish working class packing into the Five Points. Feeling engulfed and unwanted, they were drawn instead to a defensive ethnic separatism. They preferred the pages of the newly founded and distinctly pro-Catholic weekly, the *Truth Teller* (1825), which routinely excoriated Protestants who viewed the urban newcomers "with the most determined hostility, hatred and contempt." They liked the paper's bold attacks on the American Bible Society, which distributed only Protestant versions of the Scriptures, even though Catholics indignantly refused them. Immigrants purchased their Bibles instead, patronizing newly established Catholic publishing firms like John Doyle's on Broadway, which put out the popular edition of 1833 known as the Doyle Octavo.

Foreswearing the Shamrock Friendly Association, they turned to groups like the Hibernian Universal Benevolent Society (HUBS), organized by small businessmen and artisans of radical republican bent. Each July fourth, Hibernian painters, coopers, tailors, and cordwainers paraded proudly, displaying their ethnic insignias. Until 1830 the HUBS celebrated St. Patrick's Day with a procession that wended its through the city's Irish neighborhood from Harmony Hall to old St. Patrick's Cathedral. After that its destination was Father Varela's church on Ann Street (though a Cuban, Varela was hailed as a fellow nationalist and appointed as chaplain of the HUBS). After the parade and church services, celebrants moved on to the plebeian McDermott's Sixth Ward Hotel for open house festivities (covered in the *Truth Teller*) that were in sharp contrast to the more exclusive dinners of the Friendly Sons of St. Patrick at Bank's Coffee House or Niblo's Garden.

In the late 1820s and early 1830s, the marchers' ranks were rapidly reinforced. In 1827, when Britain repealed all restrictions on emigration, over twenty thousand Irish had flocked to the new world. By 1835 over thirty thousand Irish were arriving in New York each year, the majority of them poor, unskilled, male, young, and—for the first time in New York City's long history of Gaelic immigration—Catholic. Fed by this influx, the Church expanded at an unprecedented pace. "The Catholics have a considerable establishment in New-York," Tocqueville noted. It included such new additions as St. Mary (1826) on Grand Street, for the shipyard workers, and St. Joseph (1829) on Sixth Avenue, which served Greenwich Village contractors and builders. By 1833 Felix Varela's mission church to the Irish had evolved into two parishes, St. James and Transfiguration—the latter centered from 1836 in a former Presbyterian church on Chambers Street. (St. Paul's Catholic Church in Cobble Hill, Brooklyn, was completed the same year.) The diocese also established a "national" parish, a multiethnic response to a multinational city. In 1833 Bishop John Dubois approved construction of the tiny but quasi-autonomous St. Nicholas Church on East 2nd Street for the three thousand resident Catholic Germans who had up till then had worshiped, unhappily, with the Irish and French.

Newly fortified, the Catholic community displayed a new feistiness in its relations with the Protestant majority. In 1834, for instance, Bishop Dubois suggested to the Public School Society that at least in PSS No. 5 (on Mott Street near St. Pat's) it remove defamatory language from schoolbooks and allow after-hours use of the building for religious instruction, in order to "ensure the confidence of Catholic parents." Dubois promised the trustees he had no sectarian motives, no desire to proselytize, but the PSS insisted that its pan-Protestantism was truly "nonsectarian" and refused any accommodation. Balked, the hierarchy continued its piecemeal construction of an alternative parochial school system.

"POPERY OUGHT ALWAYS TO BE LOATHED AND EXECRATED"

As New York's Catholic Church changed during the 1820s—became more working class, more militant, more Irish, less middle class, less French and Spanish, less respectable—anxieties and resentments rose in various Protestant quarters. These concerns were heightened at decade's end by a particular confluence of events. Catholic emancipation in England (1829) generated a flood of antipopery books and tracts decrying the new license; many of these were exported to New York, where they agitated local activists. The advent of Finney's revivals exacerbated tensions by generating millennial enthusiasm and heightening denominational aggressiveness. The sudden spurt of Irish Catholic immigration seemed menacing too, in the light of Vatican support for various reactionary European governments. Some believed it signaled an attempt by monarchists and despots to establish a beachhead in New York City, as a step toward infiltrating and overthrowing the republic.

In January 1830, accordingly, a small group of clerical and lay militants established the *Protestant*, an avowedly anti-Catholic weekly. In its initial number of January 2, 1830, the Rev. George Bourne declared that the paper's goal would be to expose the papacy's "present enterprising efforts to recover and extend its unholy dominion, especially on the western continent." This initiative was followed, in January 1831, by formation of the New York Protestant Association under the leadership of the Rev W. C. Brownlee, a Dutch Reformed pastor. The group began disseminating anti-Catholic literature and, in 1832, sponsoring public meetings to discuss the history and character of popery. Attendance at these biweekly gatherings soon swelled from three hundred to fifteen hundred (not counting the spinoffs in Brooklyn), in part because Catholics began showing up as well, to cheer on their spokesmen. Brownlee, somewhat incautiously, had dared Catholic priests to come debate the issues, only to find that Felix Varela and other apologists proved formidable opponents.

These battles spilled over into the sectarian press, with the *Truth Teller* leading the Catholic camp, and the Protestant side upheld in Brownlee's new biweekly, the *American Protestant Vindicator and Defender of Civil and Religious Liberty Against the Inroads of Popery* (1834). The *Vindicator*'s prospectus (endorsed by twelve clergymen) announced that as "Popery ought always to be loathed and execrated," Brownlee would lay bare its "detestable impieties, corruptions and mischiefs." Agents fanned out across the country, offering lectures, selling *Vindicator* subscriptions, and inspiring local imitations of the New York Protestant Association.

Also in 1834, Samuel F. B. Morse, just back from Europe, published a series of letters in the *New York Observer*, an evangelical paper, concerning a "Foreign Conspiracy against the Liberties of the United States." The artist announced that in Vienna he had discovered the existence of a plot by European monarchs leagued in the Holy Alliance to flood the United States with Catholics. In another Morse series, issued as a pamphlet in 1835, the newly appointed NYU professor warned of "foreign turbulence imported by ship-loads" at the behest of "priest-controlled machines" and rhetorically demanded: "Can one throw mud into pure water and not disturb its clearness?" The answer was clear: Morse called on all New York patriots to stand tall against the growing power of the Catholic hierarchy and the onrushing influx of Irish.

"DAMNED IRISH!"

By March 1835 the Irish were in a fury. When the New York Protestant Association sponsored a meeting at Broadway Hall to discuss the question "Is Popery Compatible with Civil Liberty?" a crowd of Catholics forced their way in, broke up furniture, and destroyed the fixtures while the speakers escaped through the back passageway.

Catholic clergymen disavowed the Broadway Hall riot, but nativists seized on it as justification of their concerns. In June, with James Watson Webb, pugnacious editor of the *Courier and Enquirer*, serving as a prime mover, the Native American Democratic Association was organized—the first explicitly nativist political party in the United States. It established ward committees, set up its own newspaper (the *Spirit of '76*), and warned Anglo-American voters, chiefly small masters and journeymen, of the "swarms of foreign artisans who are more destructive to native American industry than the locusts and lice were to the Egyptian fields."

Violence erupted again in 1835 when a Bowery saloon keeper announced plans to form an Irish militia company, to be called the O'Connell Guards in honor of the Irish patriot. The nativist press shrieked about a "foreign armed force stationed among us," and on June 21, 1835, the American Guards, a Bowery gang proclaiming native ancestry, clashed with Irishmen in Chatham Square. The battle, fought with clubs and brickbats, took the life of a passerby—a physician, struck by a brick, fell to the sidewalk and was trampled by struggling combatants. Rioting spread throughout the Five Points and elsewhere in the city, until subdued by Mayor Lawrence and two hundred policemen.

That fall, the Native American Democratic Association ran its first ticket, on a platform demanding that only native-born Americans be permitted to hold office, but the new party, snarled in internal divisions, had little impact. Philip Hone wrote gloomily in his diary that December that "low Irishmen"—"the most ignorant, and consequently the most obstinate white men in the world"—were now able to "decide the elections in the city of New York." In time, he feared, "the same brogue which they have instructed to shout 'Hurrah for Jackson!' shall be used to impart additional horror to the cry of 'Down with the natives!'"

Nativists emerged in Brooklyn too; its populace, friendly to the Irish in the 1820s, had grown alarmed by the 1830s, their fears played on by politicians and editors (like Alden Spooner, who raised a hue and cry against "foreigners"). Here, too, Native American candidates did poorly and moderates remained in command: the Rev. Evan Johnson, rector of St. John's Episcopal, used his 1835 Thanksgiving Day sermon to preach against nativism.

Seeking a more combustible issue, nativists spiced their theology with sex. In January 1836 Harper Brothers published *Awful Disclosures of the Hotel Dieu Nunnery of*

Montreal, by one Maria Monk. (The Harpers, though nativists themselves, were concerned enough about their firm's reputation to set up a dummy company to bring *Awful*
out.) In the book, which Benjamin Day excerpted in the *Sun*, Monk told of her Protestant upbringing, her embrace of Catholicism, and her arrival at the Canadian convent,
where she discovered that nuns were forced to have intercourse with lustful priests
(those who refused were executed). Children born of these criminal unions were baptized, then strangled and thrown into a large hole in the basement. Monk, impregnated
by one Father Phelan, escaped to New York City, tried to commit suicide, was taken to a
charity hospital, and confessed all to a kindly Protestant clergyman.

The anti-Catholic press gave *Awful Disclosures* complete credence. Indeed the Rev.
George Bourne of the Protestant Association capitalized on the furor to launch a new
organization, the Protestant Reformation Society, and more ministers joined the
antipopery crusade. Catholic clerics, led by Father Varela, charged that the "revelations" were a manufactured smear, and so they proved to be. Maria's mother came forward to say her daughter's tale was the product of a brain injured in infancy when the
child had run a slate pencil into her head. Growing up wild, Maria had been confined in
a Catholic Magdalen asylum. She had escaped, with the aid of a former lover, and come
to New York, where leading nativist ministers—including the Rev. Bourne—had written up her "disclosures."

Many nativists doggedly refused to doubt Monk's story until Colonel William
Leete Stone, the mildly antipapist editor of the *Commercial Advertiser*, examined the
convent in the fall of 1836 and pronounced the priests and nuns completely innocent.
Monk's star now faded quickly, but not before it had helped spark another outburst in
the streets.

In 1836, with excitement still running high, a nativist crowd resolved to attack St.
Patrick's Cathedral. Forewarned, the faithful rallied. The church's cemetery had just
been enclosed by a high brick wall, in which loopholes were now cut for muskets. More
armed men lined Prince Street, the expected avenue of attack. Others tore up cobblestones and hoisted baskets full of them to the upper stories along the route. As the anti-
Catholic army roiled up the Bowery, its advance scouts reported back on the fearsome-
ness of the Gaels' military preparations and the fortress-like impregnability of their
walled cathedral. Disheartened, the nativists retreated, and their movement, for the
moment, subsided.

LIFE ALONG THE COLOR LINE

On July 4, 1827—Emancipation Day—all the city's black churches held services of
prayer and thanksgiving. The largest celebration was in African Zion Church (at
Church and Leonard). In his oration, church trustee William Hamilton placed the day
in historical context, recalling the bloody events of 1741, the complex relation of blacks
to the Revolution of '76, and the years of postwar degradation. Then he joyously proclaimed that "this day we stand redeemed from a bitter thralldom." "No more," he
rolled on, "shall the accursed name of slave be attached to us—no more shall *negro* and
slave be synonymous [*sic*]."

Then the celebrants quietly dispersed, refraining from a more public jubilation lest
they be assaulted by whites hard at their Independence Day revels. Instead they gathered the next day, four thousand strong, near St. John's Park. Then they paraded

through the principal streets to Zion Church and on to City Hall, where the grand marshal, with drawn sword, saluted the mayor as the crowd roared cheers.

The city's blacks called for making July fifth their annual day of commemoration and reserving the fourth for bitter reflection on the continuing disparity between America's rhetoric and its reality. For as the Rev. Peter Williams Jr. said: "Alas! the freedom to which we have attained is defective." It remained the case, he sadly observed, that in New York City "the rights of men are decided by the colour of their skin." Even the briefest of strolls around segregated Manhattan would have quickly confirmed the accuracy of Williams's assessment.

All the new forms of transport drew the color line. Blacks were banned from cabins on Hudson River steamers and restricted to the exposed deck, on spring day and stormy night alike. The Rev. Williams himself had been refused passage on an American packet bound for Europe and been forced to sail on an English vessel. Blacks were not allowed on street stages, and when a black man hailed one of the new omnibuses going up Broadway, the driver warded him off with a whip, convulsing white bystanders with laughter.

Many commercial facilities were also off limits to African-American New Yorkers. Vauxhall Gardens flatly denied them admission; the Park Theater sequestered them in a roped-off section. An English visitor in 1819, questioning a black barber as to why he had rejected a prospective black customer, was told that if he hadn't the shop would have lost all its white patrons. A black minister was refused a cup of tea by a "foreigner in a cellar cookroom" as the "customers would not put up with it"—customers who included agents of the American Bible Society.

Blacks were barred from the Free School Society's institutions, as well as the charity schools of most denominations. A light-skinned African-American Presbyterian minister found his children rejected from Presbyterian schools "on account of their complexion, they being mixed blood, a few shades below the pure white." The Quaker-run African Free School was exclusively for blacks and provided a good education, but as one graduate noted, the diploma wasn't much help. "What are my prospects?" he asked. "To what shall I turn my head? Shall I be a mechanic? No one will employ me; white boys won't work with me. Shall I be a merchant? No one will have me in his office; white clerks won't associate with me. Drudgery and servitude, then, are my prospective portion."

Even servitude couldn't be taken for granted. Irish women were rapidly displacing black women in domestic service jobs, driving some to the streets to hawk fruits or vegetables, or themselves. Most black men found work as waiters, coachmen, servants, or unskilled laborers, though their political powerlessness barred them from most licensed trades (notably jobs as cartmen) and public offices (such as weighers and measurers). Hackney drivers and chimney sweeps were an exception, as their ranks had been opened to blacks by grateful Federalists.

Many black men still took to the sea, as sailors, stewards, or cooks, so many that in the late 1820s the African Free School added navigation to its curriculum. Though wages and working conditions were miserable as ever, foredeck gangs were substantially integrated, forecastles (the cramped bunkrooms below decks in a ship's forward end) maintained a rough equality, freedmen could get wages equal to those of whites, a ship's job came complete with room and board, and often one's compatriots constituted the majority. In 1835 nearly 25 percent of the black men sailing out of New York City were members of predominantly black crews.

Although blacks formed mutual aid societies—like the African Clarkson Association (1829)—to provide sick benefits, burial allowances, and widows' allotments, with economic options so pinched, many nevertheless wound up in public institutions. Here too they received "special" treatment. The almshouse was segregated. Until 1833 the House of Refuge refused to accept black juvenile delinquents. And blacks landed in jail more readily than whites, in part because authorities arrested them for minor infractions ignored when committed by Caucasians.

Things were no better in most churches. Trinity had actively encouraged formation of St. Philip's as a separate (though closely watched) institution, but the General Theological Seminary continued to reject black applicants, and when the New York Diocese did vote to admit a black man to candidacy in holy orders, it stipulated that neither he nor any congregation he might head would be entitled to a seat in the diocesan convention. White churches that received blacks at all sent them aloft to "Nigger Heaven" or shunted them to a "Nigger Pew" (with seats marked *B.M.* for Black Members). Whites who deeded pews to their children generally covenanted that blacks never be permitted to purchase them, lest this depreciate the value of adjacent pews.

Finally, of course, there was the all but total exclusion from the polls.

Some whites, unsatisfied with this segregated status quo, wanted blacks out of the city altogether. The American Colonization Society (ACS, 1817), whose New York branch was run by the cream of Manhattan society, advocated shipping blacks to Liberia in Africa, or elsewhere out of the country. David Hale, editor of the *Journal of Commerce*, declared that New York City would be much better off without its black population, and Tammany spokesman Mordecai Noah agreed. After all, he asked in 1826, "what do our colored citizens do but fill our almshouses and prisons and congest our streets as beggars?"

As late as the latter 1820s, leading evangelicals like Arthur Tappan and Anson Phelps backed the American Colonization Society's efforts, with Phelps actually serving as president of the organization's New York branch. In Brooklyn, Adrian Van Sinderen, president of the Long Island Bible Society and the Brooklyn Temperance Society, also headed the Brooklyn branch of the ACS (founded in 1830). It was only when Arthur Tappan realized how deeply the New York African-American community detested the back-to-Africa project that he swung the evangelical battalions in a radically different direction, and that realization, in turn, came through his affiliation with the city's black Presbyterian community.

During the 1820s prosperous evangelicals, dismayed by what they saw as the ignorance and viciousness of poor African Americans, helped found and finance a black congregation. In the process, they cultivated some outstanding African leaders, most notably Samuel Cornish. Born free in Delaware in 1795, Cornish had moved to Pennsylvania in 1815, where he was tutored for the ministry by members of the Philadelphia Presbytery. Licensed to preach, he was recruited by New York evangelicals to missionize poor blacks in the Bancker Street area. In 1821 Cornish set up a rough-hewn church, held two or three services there on Sunday, conducted a Sunday school, gave Bible lectures, held prayer meetings, and visited families in their homes. The next year he drew together the twenty-four initial members of the First Colored Presbyterian Church. In 1824, with loans from the presbytery and financial aid from Jacob Lorillard, tobacco merchant and real estate investor, the group built and settled into a brick home on Elm Street near Canal, with Cornish formally installed as pastor. (It would later relocate to Duane and Hudson, then to Frankfort and William, where it would remain for the next twenty years.)

Samuel Cornish soon tested the limits of denominational support by refusing to draw sharp lines between the black community's theological and political concerns. He began by speaking out against the American Colonization Society and then, in 1827, took an even more decisive step. For almost ten years, the city's white press had cooperated with the ACS by refusing to print the anticolonization resolutions passed by black gatherings in New York and across the country. Cornish now met with a small group that included the Jamaican-born John Russwurm, recently graduated from Bowdoin College (only the second black college graduate in the United States), and church leaders William Hamilton of AME Zion and Peter Williams Jr. of St. Philip's. In March 1827 they launched *Freedom's Journal*, the first black newspaper in the United States. By the summer it had well over twelve hundred subscribers, with perhaps several thousand reading at least parts of each weekly issue.

Freedom's Journal, as edited by Cornish and Russwurm, covered activities in the African-American community, both the extraordinary (like Emancipation Day) and the everyday (marriages; funerals; the doings of mutual relief, literary, temperance, and fraternal societies), together with advertisements from local black businessmen. Its pages presented a portrait of the community strikingly at variance with the negative picture promulgated by the ACS. Not that the paper denied the existence of a rougher element. But Cornish noted that whites constituted, proportionately, a substantially larger percentage of almshouse residents than blacks. And while he conceded that the per capita number of blacks in prison was higher than whites, he argued that "the coloured man's offence, three times out of four, grows out of the circumstances of his condition, while the white man's, most generally, is premeditated and vicious." Cornish did deplore coarse conduct by unrefined and uneducated blacks—which he attributed to slavery, not emancipation—but believed they should be uplifted, not exiled. *Freedom's Journal* exhorted its readers to eschew "loose and depraved habits" and cultivate sobriety, industry, honesty, and self-discipline; like Fanny Wright, the editors hailed education as the way to overcome economic deprivation. They also ran inspirational biographies, published articles on the black revolution in Haiti, of which they were intensely proud, and proclaimed that "every thing that relates to Africa, shall find a ready admission into our columns."

Freedom's Journal did not hesitate to lash whites and denounce racism. The paper called for the abolition of property requirements for black voters, denounced the colonization project, and condemned fellow Presbyterians for excluding blacks from church-connected academies. Most critically, *Freedom's Journal* demanded the immediate abolition of slavery. While Cornish and Russwurm did not advocate a slave rebellion in the South—though their Boston agent, David Walker, would do so in 1829—their call for the immediate confiscation of property in slaves was an extremely advanced position, one that not even William Lloyd Garrison would adopt until 1830.

Influential white Presbyterian clergymen were upset by Cornish's denunciations of the American Colonization Society and by what they deemed his insufficient appreciation for their altruism. This created an awkward situation at a time when Cornish was visiting white churches to solicit funds for First Colored Presbyterian. In September

John Russwurm, left, and the Rev. Samuel Cornish with the masthead
of *Freedom's Journal*—the first African-American newspaper in the
United States, famous for its pioneering, no-holds-barred attacks on
both slavery and racism. (Schomberg Center for Research in Black
Culture. The New York Public Library. Astor, Lenox and Tilden
Foundations)

1827, therefore, having completed his agreed-upon six months, Cornish resigned as
editor and accepted instead a position as agent of the African Free Schools. (Working
with black women who formed the African Dorcas Association in 1828, he managed to
double pupil enrollment in a few years by opening four new schools nearer the black
community and by mending and providing clothes for children to go to class in.)

In 1828 Cornish also withdrew as pastor of First Colored Presbyterian and was succeeded by Theodore Wright. Born in 1797 in New Jersey—his father was from Madagascar—Wright had attended the African Free School and in 1825 been admitted to
Princeton Theological Seminary, where he served as one of *Freedom's Journal*'s fifteen
agents, getting many students and faculty to subscribe. On graduating in 1828—the
first Afro-American alumnus of a theological seminary—Wright was engaged by the
Presbytery of New York. He rapidly expanded First Colored Presbyterian's membership, was installed in 1830 as its pastor, and would go on to transform a small struggling
institution into the second largest black church in the city, one heavily involved in educational, reform, and protest efforts.

Freedom's Journal, meanwhile, had fared poorly under Russwurm's sole control.
The young man had been won over to the support of the American Colonization Society, and he began printing articles (usually by whites) in favor of colonization, though
still including articles (usually by blacks) opposing it. Finally, on March 28, 1829, repu-

diated by his community, Russwurm resigned; the ACS sent him to Liberia as superintendent of public schools, and the paper ceased publication. Cornish started a new one to replace it, but the *Rights of All* lasted only a few months, and for much of the next decade, the black community's newfound voice fell silent.

"CRUSH THIS HYDRA IN THE BUD"

Before doing so, however, it had won some powerful converts. Editor Samuel Cornish's anticolonization broadsides had unsettled Arthur Tappan. So had the staunch opposition of Peter Williams Jr., rector of St. Philip's, who in an Independence Day speech in 1830 pointedly evoked anti-immigrant sympathies by noting: "We are natives of this country, we ask only to be treated as well as *foreigners*."

White evangelicals could hear the black antislavery ministers in part because they felt quite comfortable with them. They shared religious values, after all, as well as a belief in temperance and self-improvement. In 1833, for example, the Revs. Cornish and Wright founded the Phoenix Society of New York, declaring that the condition of "people of colour" could "only be meliorated by their being improved in *morals, literature,* and the *mechanic arts.*" Such acceptance of the need to refine, educate, and employ New York's African Americans appealed to Tappan, who signed on as treasurer and donated the funds to hire Cornish as general agent.

This extremely unusual degree of association—in some cases outright friendship—between middle-class blacks and whites in New York City helped galvanize an antislavery movement. Tappan reversed course on colonization, as did Garrison up in Boston, where he started the *Liberator,* an antislavery paper, in 1831. Soon Garrison came out with a sharp attack on the American Colonization Society, a polemic that received wide circulation with the help of financial assistance from Arthur Tappan.

Before long the silk merchant essayed bolder interventions, urged on by Charles Finney, who declared slavery one of the evils America had to shed if it were to attain the millennium. Tappan set out to form an integrated antislavery organization. He secured the collaboration of black ministers Williams, Wright, and Cornish, and he also recruited youthful white evangelicals from the Third Presbytery, seat of Yankeedom in New York. William Goodell, editor of the *Genius of Temperance,* signed on. Joshua Leavitt, editor of the *New York Evangelist* (and, like Garrison and Tappan, a sometime resident at the Grahamite Boardinghouse), also saw the abolitionist light. So did the Rev. George Bourne, editor of the anti-Catholic *Protestant Vindicator,* and Presbyterian minister Samuel H. Cox, a close friend of Cornish and Wright and, like Bourne, a religious bigot, though he focused his ire on Quakerism ("infidelity in drab").

In the spring of 1833 Tappan launched the *Emancipator,* a newspaper devoted solely to abolition, and underwrote its distribution to clergymen across the North. Next, he and his associates set about organizing a New York Anti-Slavery Society. They decided they would formally inaugurate it whenever English abolitionists succeeded in their campaign to end slavery in the British West Indies. Such a transatlantic linkage would underscore the fact that the abolitionists' views, rather than those of slaveholders and their apologists, were becoming the norm of the "civilized" world. When news reached New York in September 1833 that Parliament had voted for emancipation, Tappan announced an organizational meeting for 7:30 Wednesday evening, October 2, at Clinton Hall.

On October 1 a worried group of colonizationists met in the office of James Watson

Webb, editor of the *Courier and Enquirer*. The American Colonization Society was in deep financial trouble. Its Liberian colony was faring poorly. It was smarting from rebukes (by Arthur Tappan and other temperancites) about its importation of liquor. And now abolitionist rivals were poised to take the field.

For Webb, the abolitionists presented a clear and present danger not just to the ACS but to New York City itself. Though he proudly traced his lineage to Puritan Massachusetts, Webb was an ardent Episcopalian and a member (by marriage) of New York's wealthy mercantile class. A staunch traditionalist, he had appointed himself the journalistic defender of the city's patriciate. Webb was particularly concerned to guard against any dilution of old American bloodlines by inferior breeds—above all, blacks— and to his way of thinking, Tappan's newest venture threatened just such miscegenation. If slaves were emancipated but not exiled, they would have to be assimilated. Given that many freed slaves would move north, the abolitionist enterprise might mulattoize New York society.

On the morning of Tappan's planned meeting, Webb's *Courier and Enquirer* fulminated: "Are we tamely to look on, and see this most dangerous species of fanaticism extending itself through society? . . . Or shall we, by promptly and fearlessly crushing this many-headed hydra in the bud, expose the weakness as well as the folly, madness, and mischief of these bold and dangerous men?" He urged "patriots" to assemble at Clinton Hall a half hour before meeting time to take remedial action. During the day placards went up around town, addressed (ostensibly) TO ALL PERSONS FROM THE SOUTH (and signed "Many Southerners"), summoning people to Clinton Hall to show their displeasure. Tempers flared yet higher when it was learned that William Lloyd Garrison planned to attend.

That evening at least fifteen hundred New Yorkers arrived at Clinton Hall, yelling for the blood of Tappan and Garrison, only to find the building locked. The trustees of Clinton Hall, having learned of the proposed onslaught, had withdrawn permission to use it, and Tappan's troops had surreptitiously shifted uptown to Finney's Chatham Street Chapel. By the time the crowd of "highly respectable citizens" (in the words of a later newspaper report) learned of the new venue and arrived to storm the building, the New York Anti-Slavery Society had whipped through its organizational meeting, elected Arthur Tappan president, and slipped out the back door. The abolitionists were in business.

Indeed New Yorkers now seized the mantle of national antislavery leadership from the Garrisonians in Boston. On December 4, 1833, sixty black and white delegates founded the American Anti-Slavery Society (AASS), establishing its national headquarters at 143 Nassau Street and requiring all members of the Executive Committee to be residents of New York City. Arthur Tappan was named president. His brother, Lewis, joined the Executive Committee, along with some white merchants and the black ministerial trio of Cornish, Wright and Williams.

The worst fears of negrophobes had been realized. New York had become a center of antislavery agitation—at who knew what cost to the city's business links with the South. Worse, the integrated organization had put blacks in positions of responsibility and signaled an assault on local segregation by inviting blacks into white evangelical churches (though continuing to seat them separately). Tappan and team—having told New York it had problems with drink and sex—now informed the city it had a racial problem, which it would not be allowed to ignore.

WHITE SLAVES AND "SMOKED IRISH"

Abolitionists hoped to win support from New York's white working class. Most radical leaders were disciples of Tom Paine and Robert Owen, both of whom were ardent enemies of servitude. Fanny Wright was antislavery. So was George Henry Evans, editor of the *Workingman's Advocate*. Evans, indeed, specifically opposed colonization, defended free speech for abolitionists, and urged workers to support their project, insisting that "EQUAL RIGHTS can never be enjoyed, even by those who are free, in a nation which contains slaveites enough to hold in bondage two millions of human beings."

Many white workers agreed with Evans that slavery was unjust: republican artisans considered chattel slavery the antipode of liberty. Many artisans and shopkeepers were among the three thousand who signed an abolitionist petition submitted to Congress in 1830, calling for an end to slavery in the District of Columbia. The plebeian-oriented *Sun* occasionally printed antislavery material, and the *Transcript* defended abolitionists' right to speak.

Nevertheless, most New York laborers hated the men in command of the abolitionist apparatus and refused to separate the message from the messengers. Abolitionism was inextricably linked to other evangelical initiatives that many workers found objectionable. Evans, a freethinker, rejected Tappan's revivalism and Sabbatarianism and wondered if the abolitionists weren't "actuated by a species of theological fanaticism" in hoping "to free the slaves more for the purpose of adding them to their religious sect, than for love of liberty and justice."

Worse, many of the wealthy merchants who championed black slaves were in the front ranks of those condemning workers who rallied to defend their rights (the Tappan-initiated *Journal of Commerce* had led the assault on Workie-ism). Tappan and his colleagues drew a sharp line between slavery and capitalism. Under slavery, the misery and poverty of working people was clearly attributable to the slaveocrats who owned them. Under capitalism—given the evangelical premise that ascribed success or failure wholly to individual character—a working person's poverty could not be laid at his employer's door.

The absolute clarity of this evangelical distinction between free and unfree labor seemed a good deal muddier to those whose lives had been abraded by capitalist development. To such men, setting the plight of distant slaves above that of local workers seemed hypocritical. Some labor radicals, including George Henry Evans, were drawn for a time to the metaphor of "wage slavery" (or "white slavery") as a linguistic device for emphasizing the analogies between their own sinking condition and that of already submerged bondsmen.

True, New York laborers had their political independence, no trifling matter. But the Revolution had been fought for economic independence as well, and by that criterion, the growth of wage-work, the declining respect for manual labor, the rise of rent-tenantry, the transformation of proud craftsmen into "hirelings"—all these together constituted a disturbing trajectory, whose end point might yet be dependency, even bondage, for whites as well as blacks.

For most New York artisans and laborers, however, the metaphorical equation of Northern wage-work and Southern slavery was not simply overdrawn but psychologically intolerable. Such men opted for a different linguistic strategy, one that sharply differentiated their condition from that of slaves by referring to capitalist employers as "bosses" rather than "masters" (reserving the older term for the small workshops where an owner was master of his craft, not his men).

There was another, uglier vocabulary that could be used to underscore the gulf between free and unfree labor: the language of racism, which insisted on the difference between "white men" and "niggers." The problem was, the emancipation of New York City slaves made it more difficult to sustain such a sharp symbolic separation between whites and blacks. Emancipation had erased any grounds for assuming that the black person one passed on the street was of inferior legal status. True, white supremacy had been written back into the state constitution, denying nearly all black men the right to vote, at just the time all white males were being awarded the franchise. Unfortunately the argument used to justify that denial was not per se racist but rather the assertion that African Americans were dependent, powerless, and therefore easy pawns of the rich and powerful. But this was uncomfortably close to Chancellor Kent's grounds for seeking to deny the suffrage to economically dependent white wage-workers. Once the provision was in place, however, it was but a short step to arguing that it rested on blacks' inherent incapacity for self-government, just as some southerners were busily justifying slavery itself as the result of an innate black "slavishness" rather than of any forcible imposition of unfreedom.

White workers who rejected the evangelical gentry's insistence that the poor were responsible for their own poverty accepted the premise when applied to blacks. If slavishness and slavery were attributes of blackness, and citizenship a function of whiteness, then whites were at least guaranteed that declining economic status would never lead to political disfranchisement. Such a position further undercut the appeal of "wage slave" imagery: one could not easily boast of being a citizen while claiming to be a slave.

Whites relied on more than language to distance themselves from unfreedom: they insisted that worksites be segregated on race lines. Few white artisans faced a direct challenge from African Americans: skilled black craftsmen were increasingly rare, a situation guaranteed by white refusal to accept black apprentices. Laborers, unskilled workmen, and servants were in more direct competition, though in most categories whites clearly held the upper hand. Still, it was increasingly felt that the mere presence of blacks degraded a job category (the expression "to work like a nigger" entered American English at this time). Only their complete expulsion from a trade could truly preserve its dignity, one reason New York's blacks were being steadily driven from all but the most "servile" occupations.

Segregation in living arrangements served the same differentiating function: whites received psychic reassurance from not having to share schools, churches, playhouses, or pleasure grounds with blacks. There was, however, a yawning loophole in New York's system of urban apartheid: neighborhoods were not segregated. Low-waged, or intermittently employed, or widowed, or orphaned, or unskilled whites, could and did easily find themselves domiciled in the same slum quarters as blacks. Living next door to African Americans (occasionally even in the same household) effectively stripped away all the hard-earned badges of racial difference. This was humiliatingly underscored when the gentry—including abolitionists like Arthur Tappan—moved to lily-white enclaves where it was all but certain that any black faces in evidence belonged to domestic servants, not residents. Even this was less and less the case, as Irish domestics replaced African Americans in gentry households and as black women in domestic service opted for living with their own families.

Nothing undermined the separation of colors as rapidly as sexual fraternization, raising as it did the dreaded specter of what the era called "amalgamation." The growing hysteria over amalgamation was exacerbated by the attenuated patriarchal power of laboring males. Not only were they seldom in a position to govern an independent household, but their generic gender authority had been put in question. Nothing rubbed this in more painfully than seeing "their" women have sexual relations with black men—or worse, bear black men's children, thus mulattoizing "their" posterity.

Nowhere did these fears flame more fiercely than in the densely integrated Five Points, where interracial sex was a common fact of life. Four working-class wards contained over half the black population and had the highest black-to-white ratios in the city. Interracial liaisons came easily, moreover, in an area where, unlike in gentry enclaves, women like men were constantly out-of-doors. Especially galling was the fact that numerous Five Points saloons and brothels housed both black and white prostitutes, accommodated a mixed clientele, and in some cases specifically featured miscegenational sex; many blacks with leading roles in the city's vice economy had white wives or mistresses. As had been true since Dutch days, it was in the urban underworld that New York's races mixed with greatest abandon.

One solution to this blurring of racial borders was to violently reinscribe them. The same Callithumpian bands that roistered through upper-class neighborhoods on New Year's also paid their disrespects to blacks. They singled out for attack the sites where blacks and whites indulged in common sensual pleasures: brothels, taverns, the homes of interracial couples. They also policed places where African Americans had managed to create community institutions that signaled their aspirations to dignity and demonstrated their moral equality. In 1828 a Callithumpian procession paused at the African Church in Elizabeth Street, where the congregation was holding a "Watch Night." They smashed the windows, demolished the doors, tried (unsuccessfully) to pull down the building, solaced themselves by beating churchgoers with sticks, then resumed their march. Such assaults weren't limited to holidays: rowdies routinely disrupted services at St. Philip's, knowing that unsympathetic magistrates wouldn't intervene, and butcher boys from the Centre Street Market delighted in setting dogs on students at the nearby African Free School.

Racial anxieties ran particularly high in the city's Irish-American community. More than any other white group, they lived side by side with Africans. They took on the same jobs—"nigger work"—laboring as degraded apprentices, domestic servants, prostitutes, seamen, and casual laborers. When they submitted (of necessity) to oppressive and despotic treatment, they were derided for "slaving like a nigger."

The advent of abolitionism, moreover, created particular problems—and possibilities—for Irish Americans. The Irish at home had never been particularly race-conscious, and some of their greatest champions, like Daniel O'Connell, would strongly support the abolitionist cause. But evangelicals and employers condemned the Irish for drinking, brawling, and irregular work habits in much the same way they condemned black behavior, labeling both groups alike lazy, improvident, and irresponsible. Some New York gentry placed ads in the *Herald* for cooks, washers, and ironers that specified "any color or country except Irish." Anti-Tammany nativists challenged the immigrants' right to citizenship, which, given the new-forged connections between race and nationality, was tantamount to questioning their whiteness. And just as the English had long characterized their neighboring islanders more harshly than they had Africans, plenty of Anglo New Yorkers routinely used adjectives like *low-browed, savage, bestial, wild*, and *simian* to describe the Catholic Irish "race." More disturbingly, the Irish were sometimes referred to as "niggers turned inside out," as, conversely, blacks were occasionally termed "smoked Irish."

One way to avoid the taint of blackness was to loudly assert whiteness, and the Irish quickly learned that in New York City blacks could be despised with impunity. Another route to permanent certification as members of an Anglo-Celtic racial majority was through affiliation with Tammany Hall. Northern Democrats had bonded with southern planters in a common negrophobia; now racism would do similar duty on the home front, smoothing divisions between New York's Angles and Celts, allowing the party to swell its ranks from both sides. The theater, too, allowed white working people of all backgrounds to come together as an audience to laugh at derogatory representations of black "others." Not surprisingly, minstrel songs singled out abolitionists—particularly Arthur Tappan—for merciless ridicule. Indeed abolitionism and blackface ascended the political stage arm in arm.

"HE CALLED MY SAVIOUR A NIGGER!"

In May and June of 1834, Arthur and Lewis Tappan stepped up their abolitionist drive. Among other initiatives, they underwrote formation of a Female Anti-Slavery Society. The participation of white ladies in a mixed-race movement jangled the nerves of New York racists—which were soon further tautened by pronouncements from the Rev. Samuel Cox, the antislavery (and anti-Catholic) cleric.

Arthur Tappan was a pewholder in Cox's Laight Street Church. One Sunday morning on his way to church, Tappan encountered Samuel Cornish on the street. As Cox's institution was nearby—two miles closer to Cornish's home than where the black clergyman usually worshiped—Tappan invited him in, and the two sat together in Tappan's pew. This led to a tremendous row, with some church members threatening to resign and the elders insisting that Tappan not repeat the offense. (Arthur would never again be seen in public with any of his African-American associates, even one as light-skinned as Cornish.) Cox, however, chided his congregation for its intolerance. Arguing that as Christ was probably of a dark Syrian hue, he might well have been ejected along with Cornish, Cox denounced "nigger pews" and called for church integration. He was instantly subjected to citywide attack. As one merchant spluttered, "And would you believe it? he called my Saviour a nigger! God damn him!"

By June lurid rumors were flying around town (recycled by colonizationalist champion James Watson Webb in his *Courier and Enquirer*). The abolitionists—so the stories went—had told their daughters to marry blacks. Arthur Tappan had divorced his wife and married a Negress. Presbyterian minister Henry Ludlow was conducting interracial marriages. Abolitionists were encouraging black dandies to parade up and down Broadway on horseback to seek white wives. William Leete Stone, secretary of the New York Colonization Society and editor of the *Commercial Advertiser*, joined in stoking popular fury, assuring his readers that amalgamation appealed only to those of "morbid or vicious tastes." A startled English traveler reported that even the "nicest people" talked about "sexual passion, with a vehemence of manner, and in a tone of earnestness, utterly abhorrent from the generally received notions of propriety."

By July racial tensions were at full boil. On the fourth, an integrated group met at Chatham Street Chapel to celebrate New York's emancipation of its slaves seven years earlier. Angry spectators complained the meeting looked like "the keys of a piano forte," and rioters proceeded to break up the assembly with hoots, stamps, and shouts of "Treason."

The celebration was rescheduled for July 7. The chapel's sexton gave the mostly black group permission to use the building's large hall. Normally it was used on Monday evenings by the New York Sacred Music Society, but the society's president had agreed to use a smaller room. The sexton, however, had not explained to the chorister the racial composition of the supplanting group. When the musicians arrived they were enraged to find a black choir seated in *their* stalls. Hotly ordering the intruders out, they also tried to drag the speaker from the stage. This triggered a full-scale brawl, which the outnumbered whites lost; indeed, they were pitched out of doors and windows.

The police came and arrested six African Americans. A large white crowd forced the remaining blacks to flee. Excited rumors flamed through the city, fanned by the colonizationist press. Webb described the incident as a Negro riot, in which innocent whites had been beaten, and blamed it all on "Arthur Tappan's mad impertinence." Stone's *Commercial Advertiser* reported that gangs of blacks were threatening to burn the city. "If this state of things is to be suffered to continue," Stone shrilly declared, "neither white men nor women can much longer leave their doors in safety."

On Wednesday evening, July 9, one of the hottest nights of the year, three interconnected riots broke out. Early on, two or three thousand whites gathered at Finney's Chatham Street Chapel to break up a planned antislavery meeting. When the abolitionists, forewarned, failed to show, the crowd broke in and passed resolutions calling for black deportation. One young white man preached in a "mock negro style" (so the newspaper *Man* reported), and his fellows "struck up a Jim Crow chorus" in the style of Daddy Rice's popular Bowery act.

At about the same time, another crowd, composed chiefly of butcher boys and day laborers, converged on Lewis Tappan's Rose Street home (he and his family had fled to Harlem). Spurred on by well-dressed merchants, the rioters smashed windows and doors, demolished the interior, dragged Tappan's artwork and furniture to the street, piled it high, and set it ablaze. A Gilbert Stuart portrait of Tappan's father-in-law was being carted to the bonfire when one rioter shouted, "It's Washington! For God's sake don't burn Washington!"—and the republican hero (as they supposed) was borne safely off. Mayor Lawrence arrived with the watch but was shouted down, three cheers were raised for Webb, and the police were driven off with brickbats.

Some of the anti-Tappan group, joined by rioters from Chatham Street, now descended on the Bowery Theater, where a benefit performance was underway for George Farren, the playhouse's English stage manager. The Britisher had allegedly cussed out Yankees and called them jackasses. In addition, the English were associated with the antislavery cause. Four thousand people stormed the theater. Perhaps a quarter of them broke in and drove Edwin Forrest and the cast from the stage. The riot was quelled only when Thomas Hamblin, the Bowery's manager, came out waving two American flags, apologized for the Farren benefit, then summoned a performer to sing "Yankee Doodle" and "Zip Coon," popular anthems of country and color.

Violence escalated over the next two days. Crowds moved methodically through the city assaulting precise targets. Messengers darted to and fro, keeping rioters apprized of the whereabouts of the forces of order. Battle plans were advertised in handbills or spread verbally in marketplaces. At some points the belligerents formed up into squares, putting smaller men armed with stones on the inside, and sturdier clubwielding ones on the outside to ward off the military, which they believed had been forbidden to fire at them.

The crowds went after the homes, businesses, and churches of white "amalgamators." Throngs stoned Arthur Tappan's Pearl Street store until his employees, armed with muskets, drove them away with the help of a troop of one hundred watchmen. At the Laight Street Church, on the corner of Varick, rioters began smashing windows as one shouted, "Dr. Cox says our Savior is a nigger, and [damn] me if I don't think his church should be torn down!" Another contingent broke into Cox's home on Charlton Street. When the police and two squadrons of cavalry showed up, rioters ripped down fences for clubs and hurled paving stones but were driven off. Later in the evening, several thousand headed to Spring Street, where they attacked Henry Ludlow's church, demolishing its organ and pews and tearing down its galleries. To ward off a cavalry charge, they carried out the wreckage and built a barricade, which they bolstered by chaining carts together. The Twenty-seventh National Guard Regiment hacked its way through with axes and dispersed the crowd—which then reassembled on Thompson Street to trash Ludlow's home.

A second set of targets consisted of churches and institutions associated with black abolitionists. The African Baptist Church on Anthony Street was among those pelted with rocks, the African schoolhouse on Orange Street was heavily damaged, and a huge crowd totally demolished Peter Williams's St. Philip's African Episcopal Church (and his home as well).

The greatest ferocity was reserved for the black community in the Five Points area—though isolating it from the white community with which it was so intermixed proved challenging. Taking a cue from Exodus, rioters spread the word that white families should keep lit candles in their windows and stand before them, so their homes might be passed over. Households with dark windows or dark faces were sacked, torn down, or burned. All night long, individual blacks were caught and beaten. Roughly five hundred fled their homes, many to the watch house in the Park. No one was killed, however, and guns were kept under wraps (though a black barber on Orange Street did fire off his pistol as whites stormed in).

On Friday, Mayor Lawrence, himself an active colonizationist, weakly urged citizens to refrain from further violence, while agreeing that the abolitionists' program was "repugnant." By that evening, however, Lewis Tappan sensed that "the 'respectable' portion of the community, that had, thus far, looked on with indifference, or a willingness to see the hated band of abolitionists punished to a certain extent by popular violence, began to be alarmed for the safety of their own property."

And indeed the Twenty-seventh, which had handled the nativist outbreaks easily enough, was having serious trouble dealing with these upheavals. It didn't even try to intervene in the Five Points, where the rioting was heaviest. Saturday promised worse. Mayor Lawrence, deluged with desperate communications from citizens, estimated that sixty-two sites had been slated for destruction, including businesses, churches, schools, newspapers, the prison, and the state arsenal. With violence threatening to spread, the press demanded bringing it to an immediate end—by firing on the crowd if necessary.

Lawrence now issued a second, stronger proclamation and swore in one thousand volunteers as special constables. Irish laborers, who had been noticeably absent from the affray, now volunteered in the hundreds to aid in suppressing rioters perceived to be nativists. The New York First Division was ordered out and its officers authorized to hand out ammunition. Troops paraded through the streets and took up stations at such key sites as St. John's Park and the arsenal. Cavalry squadrons patrolled all through the night. The upheaval tapered down. By Tuesday evening it was over.

When it came time to apportion blame, some denounced scaremongers Webb and Stone for whipping up the crowds. Some denounced the rioters and declared civil disorder intolerable, no matter what its cause. But the bulk of respectable and popular opinion alike argued that the abolitionists had brought it on themselves.

In this repressive atmosphere, abolitionists made some tactical retreats. The American Anti-Slavery Society (AASS) plastered handbills around the city, denying it encouraged intermarriage. It sent an official disavowal of amalgamationist proclivities to the mayor. Lewis Tappan, who left his house on Rose Street unrepaired as "a silent Anti-Slavery preacher," was criticized by fellow abolitionists for allowing black and white choirs to sing in the same church, even though seated separately. And when Tappan later requested that a black minister address an antislavery gathering, nervous colleagues insisted that "the time has not come to mix with people of color in public."

Abolitionists also suffered some defections. Under strong pressure from Bishop Onderdonk, Peter Williams Jr., pastor of the ruined St. Philip's, resigned from the AASS—though he refused to recant his principles and declared the abolitionists "good men, and good Christians, and true lovers of their country, and of all mankind." Charles Grandison Finney, shocked at New York Christian businessmen's approval of racist outrages, resigned the country's leading pulpit and retired to Oberlin College, a Tappan-backed institution in northern Ohio.

After a year of lying low, however, the abolitionists aggressively expanded their operations—albeit outside the city itself. In May 1835, employing the skills and resources they had used in fashioning the benevolent empire, the Tappans set out to inundate the entire United States—South as well as North—with antislavery propaganda. In 1834 the AASS had distributed 122,000 pieces of literature. In 1835 its high-speed presses pumped out over a million tracts—graphically illustrated exposés of slavery's horrors. The AASS also circulated newspapers, plaster statuettes of slaves in chains, handkerchiefs, medals, emblems, and blue chocolate wrappers. Mixing business and politics, Lewis also advertised the sale of silk prints depicting "The Poor Slave."

This amazing mass communication machine provoked anxiety throughout the North and outrage throughout the South. Mainstream northern opinion had not been overly worried about the impact on the Union of ravings by a few fiery Bostonians. But now the abolitionist movement was being directed from New York City by masters of the new media, possessed of awesome organizational skills. Within four years the AASS would boast 1,350 auxiliaries and a million members nationwide. Conservative regional elites in Illinois or Ohio could handle local radicals: gentry-directed riots to suppress home-grown abolitionists multiplied throughout the North. But competing with New Yorkers presented a more formidable challenge. Indeed Manhattanites' newfound ability to disseminate a political gospel, coupled with their command over capital and credit, was positively alarming.

White Southerners were infuriated. Inflamed by the torrent of tracts that began reaching their ports, by mid-August of 1835 they were hysterical. Vigilantes stopped, boarded, and searched ships and stages, hunting for subversive literature; they patrolled slave quarters to make sure none had gotten through. They denounced the New Yorkers in blazing speeches at torchlit parades. A band of men broke into the Charleston post office, carried off mailbags newly arrived from the Hudson, and used the intercepted abolitionist tracts and magazines to kindle a huge bonfire. In it they burned effigies of Arthur Tappan and Samuel Cox, as thousands cheered.

Some southerners were not satisfied with symbolic gestures. East Feliciana, Louisiana, posted a fifty-thousand-dollar reward for the delivery of Arthur Tappan, dead or alive. Some demanded the Tappans be extradited. This, however, got New Yorkers' backs up, angering even those opposed to antislavery agitation. "I do not choose," said Philip Hone, "to surrender the power of executing justice into the hands of the slaveowners." Governor Marcy flatly refused to consider such requests.

Balked, southerners organized an economic campaign against Tappan's firm—one of the first attempts to bankrupt a national business. Some called for a boycott of all New York City goods. Alarmed delegations from the Chamber of Commerce pleaded with Arthur to call off his campaign. "You demand that I shall cease my anti-slavery labors," he responded fiercely, *"I will be hung first!"* Webb in the *Courier and Enquirer* seemed quite prepared to oblige him, demanding that "modern haberdashers of murderous negro tracts" be crushed like "reptilian eggs."

By mid-August, excitement was so intense that the AASS barricaded its doors with inch-thick planks. The mayor of Brooklyn instituted sundown-to-sunup patrols in Arthur Tappan's new neighborhood (he had moved across the East River after the riot of 1834). "I have not ventured into the city," wrote abolitionist Lydia Maria Child. "'Tis like the times of the French Revolution, when no man dare to trust his neighbors."

The abolitionists were spared another dose of violence, for two reasons: city authorities wanted no repetition of the previous year's lawlessness, and federal authorities intervened to quash the AASS outreach effort. Charleston's postmaster had asked New York City's postmaster, Samuel Gouveneur, to extract antislavery tracts from his southbound mail. Gouveneur agreed and informed the postmaster general that he planned to deny postal access to Tappan and his colleagues. The issue went up to Andrew Jackson, who informally authorized Gouveneur's embargo on "offensive papers" and explicitly denounced the AASS in his Annual Message. For the moment, the abolitionists were stymied.

THE RAILROAD THAT RAN UNDERGROUND

The mercantile elite were not prepared to turn Arthur Tappan over to planter justice, no matter how much they despised his politics. But they did not yet contest the right of southern slaveocrats to reach into New York City itself when their intended targets had black skins.

Since emancipation, New York had become a haven for fugitive slaves—and slavehunters. Under the provisions of the federal Fugitive Slave Act of 1793, anyone claiming that a person residing in the North was a runaway from the South had only to appear before a local magistrate, personally or represented by counsel, and submit "proof" of ownership; an affidavit would do.

"Blackbirders"—stalkers who were not above seizing free blacks and shipping them into slavery—began prowling the city on a regular basis. Their only opposition consisted of sporadic and spontaneous riots by local African Americans. In 1819 forty blacks on Barclay Street tried and failed to rescue a man being taken by a slavecatcher and a city marshal to a Hudson River steamboat dock. In 1826 blacks bombarded a slavecatcher giving evidence at City Hall with bricks, sticks, and stones but were suppressed by the police and given severe sentences.

By the 1830s bounty hunting had become big business. One lawyer, F. H. Pettis, offered to search for and return runaway slaves for $250 a head. Blackbirders Elias Boudinot and Daniel D. Nash ran an operation known as the New York Kidnapping Club, notorious for snapping up victims. Straight-out kidnapping was illegal, but if blackbirders brought a captive before City Recorder Riker and produced (paid) witnesses to swear he or she was a recent runaway, Riker usually authorized deportation.

With young girls being snatched on trips to the water pump, black parents began keeping their children off the streets after dark. Then, with white abolitionists on the defensive or concentrated on their national campaign, the city's African Americans formally organized for their own protection. On November 20, 1835, David Ruggles led in setting up a New York Committee of Vigilance. Ruggles, a migrant from Norwich, Connecticut, had opened a bookshop and circulating library at 67 Lispenard Street, specializing in antislavery publications. Now he became the eyes and ears of the black community.

Ruggles identified slavecatchers by name in the *Emancipator*. He pointed them out to blacks on the street. He publicized descriptions of missing Afro-Americans. He went door to door in fashionable neighborhoods inquiring as to the status of black domestics, implementing a New York law that freed any imported slave after a residence of nine months. At hearings of accused runaways before Recorder Riker, Ruggles presented counterwitnesses, though, as they were usually black, their testimony seldom helped. He also boarded incoming ships, to see if slaves were being smuggled in, and on one occasion won an indictment against a Frenchman from Guadeloupe. (Such actions were denounced by the *New York Express*, a militant Whig organ, as an embarrassment to trade.) Ruggles had to change lodgings repeatedly to foil efforts at kidnapping *him*.

The Vigilance Committee also aided those they called "persons arriving from the South." They explained to fugitives their rights, protected them from blackbirders, and established them in new locations. In his first annual report, presented at Theodore Wright's church in 1837, Ruggles announced that the group had protected 335 persons from slavery. The following year he sheltered the young Frederick Douglass for two weeks, before sending the penniless fugitive on to New Bedford, Massachusetts.[1] The bulk of funds for the Committee of Vigilance's work—efforts Lewis Tappan later praised as crucial to the developing Underground Railroad—was (Ruggles acknowledged) "obtained by the efforts of the Ladies, who collect from their friends one penny a week." In Brooklyn, Bridge Street African Methodist Episcopal Wesleyan became a major underground station, eventually providing refuge, food, and clothing for hundreds of escaped slaves. Some whites too took serious risks: Quaker Isaac T. Hopper's home, at 110 Second Avenue, became a noted way station, and in 1835 Hopper was accused of harboring a fugitive slave in his store on Pearl Street.

The Vigilance Committee was not always successful. On July 23, 1836, George

---

1. Not everyone in the black community got behind this effort. Douglass later recalled being told by another escapee that "New York was full of slaves returning from the watering places of the North, that the colored people were not to be trusted; that there were hired men of my own color who would betray me for a few dollars; that there were hired men on the lookout for fugitives; that I ought not to think of going upon the wharves or into any colored boarding house, for all such places were closely watched." Ruggles hid Douglass in his home.

Jones, a "respectable" free black man, was arrested at his workplace, an attorney's office at 21 Broadway, supposedly for assault and battery. At first he refused to go along with his captors, but his employers advised him to submit, promising they would help. However, once in custody, Jones was whisked before Recorder Riker, where several notorious blackbirders declared him a runaway, a proposition to which Riker assented. Less than three hours after his arrest, Jones, bound in chains, was dragged through the streets of New York "like a beast to the shambles" and carried south. Ruggles described the kidnapping in the *Sun*. The piece, widely reprinted, helped Ruggles win public support for granting accused "fugitives" a trial by jury—a right secured five years later.

34

Rail Boom

New York's rival coastal cities, badly undercut by the Erie Canal and facing commercial catastrophe, retaliated by building their own canals, but frenzied ditch digging availed them little. Boston was just too far from the western wheat fields, and its capitalists shifted their funds into manufacturing. Philadelphia's businessmen, lacking New York's break in the Appalachians, redirected their investments into mining. Baltimore was closest to the fertile West, but constructing a canal proved prohibitively costly. With the daring of desperation, at a town meeting in 1826, its citizens decided to build a railroad. In 1827 the Maryland legislature chartered the Baltimore and Ohio, and on July 4, 1828, Charles Carroll, last surviving signer of the Declaration of Independence, broke ground for the B&O amid fireworks, floats, and speeches.

The B&O planned to use horses for motive power. Locomotive engines had been around since England's Richard Trevithick had built the first one back in 1804, but as of the mid-1820s they were still cumbrous affairs, suitable only for hauling coal cars. Then, at trials on the Liverpool and Manchester Railway in the fall of 1829, George Stephenson's *Rocket* proved astonishingly successful, confirming that the future belonged to steam. The B&O, realizing it had to switch from horses in midstream, turned for help, oddly enough, to a New Yorker.

Peter Cooper, of mixed Dutch, English, and Huguenot ancestry, was the son of a Methodist hatmaker who had moved his family down to the city from Newburgh in 1808. After trying his hand at hatting, brewing, coachmaking and cabinetmaking, young Peter made a go of selling a cloth-shearing machine he'd developed. In 1816, however, Britain's postwar dumping spree drove his customers out of business, and the twenty-five-year-old Cooper opened a grocery store in Bowery Village. He also continued tinkering with mechanical devices; among his inventions was an endless chain for drawing Erie Canal boats, which won De Witt Clinton's applause but was never used.

In 1821 Cooper bought a glue factory at Sunfish Pond, amid clover fields and buttonwood trees near the village of Kip's Bay. When the new Bull's Head market opened nearby, providing a plentiful supply of cows' and calves' feet, Cooper devised new methods for using them to produce glue, gelatin, household cement, isinglass, and neat's-foot oil. He thus became the premier supplier of such items to the city's tanners, paint manufacturers, and dry-goods merchants. He also became a pioneer polluter: his factory so fouled the pond's waters that it had to be drained and filled in 1839.

Cooper invested his profits in land purchases around town. In 1828, convinced the proposed new B&O would send Maryland's land values skyrocketing, he purchased three thousand acres near Baltimore and began large-scale development there. While leveling hills and draining swamps, he discovered iron ore. Immediately he set up furnaces and forges, positioning himself to sell rails to the B&O.

When the company on which his future depended ran into technical trouble, Cooper promised to invent them an engine. "I got up a little locomotive," he later explained, cobbling it together from old wheels, musket barrels, and a small brass steam engine he'd built in New York City. In August 1830, with Cooper at the controls, *Tom Thumb* hauled a carload of B&O officials at the breathtaking speed of eighteen miles per hour. Investors now snapped up B&O bonds, and the B&O used the proceeds to buy Cooper's iron rails, making him his first fortune.

Now it was New York that faced a threat to its canal-based preeminence, and powerful Manhattanites quickly jumped into railroading. By 1831 the Mohawk and Hudson Railroad Company—with Stephen Van Rensselaer as titular head, John Jacob Astor an active director and major stockholder, and officers and promoters with such august names as Jay, Fish, Stuyvesant, Schuyler, and King—had completed a link between the Hudson and Mohawk rivers, connecting Albany and Schenectady.

Its success sparked a rail boom. Entrepreneurs and communities deluged the legislature with requests for corporate charters. Funds flowed into lines linking other Erie Canal towns, and within a decade through service was available from Albany to Buffalo. In 1832 New York City promoters won a charter for a New York and Erie line that would cut out Albany and slice diagonally across the state to Dunkirk, on Lake Erie, from Piermont, on the Hudson. The Erie's backers—including leading merchants (Eleazar Lord), bankers (James Gore King), and land developers (Samuel B. Ruggles)—also had the clout to win three million dollars in state credits toward construction.

While these distant enterprises were getting under way, closer to home another set of investors had set out to connect the two ends of Manhattan Island. Banker John Mason and two large landholders interested in promoting their uptown real estate won a charter in 1831 for a New York and Harlem Rail Road, and its initial stock offering of $350,000 was immediately oversubscribed. The Common Council granted the NY&H the right to operate cars over a double track from City Hall to the Harlem River along Fourth Avenue—and did so with great good cheer, as most of the incorporators were associated with Tammany, and many of the aldermen received blocks of stock as thank-you presents. Workingmen's spokesman George Henry Evans protested this cozy symbiosis, arguing that while the road was a good idea, it wasn't necessary to "give a regiment of rich aristocrats the exclusive privilege of increasing their wealth by the profits of it. We have already too many laws to favor *capitalists*." In 1831, however, the Court of Chancery upheld the legislature's right to delegate the power of eminent domain (an attribute of sovereignty) to a railroad (a private corporation), even if that company would permit only its own cars to use its tracks.

Construction of the Harlem began in February 1832. The rails were bolted not to wooden ties but to foot-square granite blocks, which, as they rose several inches above street level, made crosstown traffic a teeth-jolting ordeal. In the meantime, John Stephenson, a local omnibus operator, built the *John Mason*, which closely resembled a traditional stage, driver perched above in front. In November 1832 horses pulled the *John Mason* along the Bowery from Prince Street (near old St. Patrick's Cathedral) up to 14th Street, speeding its thirty passengers along smoothly at a seven to twelve miles per hour clip. Soon the New York and Harlem's tracks reached Fourth Avenue and 27th Street, where the line built a depot complex that included company offices, a produce terminal, and stables for the horses.

In the fall of 1833 the tracks reached their first formidable obstacle, Murray Hill; driving a tunnel (still in use) through solid Manhattan schist from 32nd Street to 42nd Street would take until 1837 to complete. In the meantime, tracks were laid on wooden ties through mid-island rural terrain and the village of Yorkville, near 86th Street. Between 92nd and 94th streets, another tunnel was cut (in 1836) through the domelike rise of Mount Pleasant, where the line opened the Prospect Hall hotel, in hopes of enticing passengers to visit the fields and woodlands bordering the East River. Finally the engineers and laborers forded Harlem Creek and adjacent marshlands with a 658-foot timber viaduct, and from there reached the Harlem River terminus by 1837.

By 1838, therefore, it was possible to travel from City Hall to Harlem for twenty-five cents, but south of 27th Street the cars were pulled by horses. The NY&H had intended to use engines all the way, but a clamor against noise, smoke, sparks, and danger—one blew up in 1834—led to a city ordinance requiring the line to use horses in its lower regions. At 27th Street, just before diving under Murray Hill, the horses were unhitched and a little steam locomotive hooked up (to the chagrin of Peter Cooper, whose house at Fourth Avenue and 28th Street, once amid open country, now lay a block from the station and the railroad's cattle pens). Downtown the Harlem's cars—the first street vehicles to be operated on iron rails in the United States—became known as "horsecars," and, along with the other lines that soon followed, they became a regular part of the downtown transport system.

In time the horsecar would challenge the omnibus for control of the city's streets. It was more stable, easier to pull, more maneuverable, and lower to the ground, and it could negotiate cobblestoned, potholed thoroughfares far more smoothly. In the thirties, however, omnibuses still ruled the roads. There were eighty in service by 1833, 108 by 1837. Indeed the *New York Gazette and General Advertiser* suggested in 1834 that New York might well be termed "the City of Omnibuses," as they generated much of downtown's "noise and bustle." Asa Greene, in his guidebook, *A Glance at New York* (1837), reported that it was "almost as much as your life is worth" to cross Broadway south of City Hall Park. "To perform the feat with any degree of safety," Greene counseled, "you must button your coat tight about you, see that your shoes are secure at the heels, settle your hat firmly on your head, look up street and down street, at the self-same moment, to see what carts and carriages are upon you, and then run for your life."

Negotiating Brooklyn's streets was nowhere near as hazardous, but there too the transportation revolution had arrived. In 1832 the state legislature chartered the Brook-

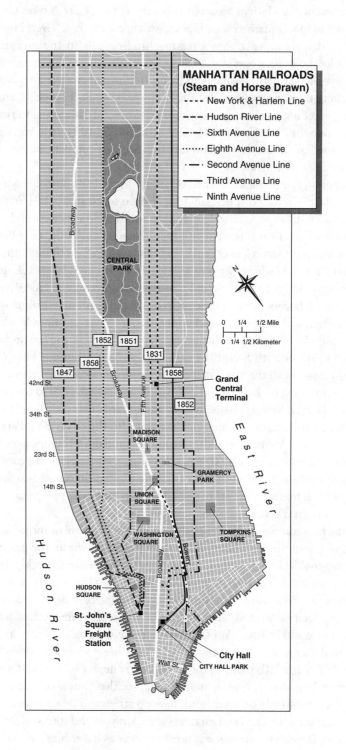

MANHATTAN RAILROADS
(Steam and Horse Drawn)
- - - - New York & Harlem Line
- - - Hudson River Line
-·-·- Sixth Avenue Line
········ Eighth Avenue Line
·-·-·- Second Avenue Line
——— Third Avenue Line
——— Ninth Avenue Line

CENTRAL PARK

Broadway

Broadway

Fifth Avenue

Bowery

Broadway

Wall St.

Hudson River

East River

42nd St.
34th St.
23rd St.
14th St.

1852
1851
1858
1847
1831
1858
1852

Grand Central Terminal

MADISON SQUARE

GRAMERCY PARK

UNION SQUARE

WASHINGTON SQUARE

TOMPKINS SQUARE

HUDSON SQUARE

St. John's Square Freight Station

City Hall
CITY HALL PARK

0   1/4   1/2 Mile
0   1/4   1/2 Kilometer

lyn and Jamaica Rail Road, with the aim of linking the two oldest communities on the western end of Long Island. In 1834 (the same year omnibuses were introduced to Brooklyn) the line received permission to lay track down Atlantic Street. But it had barely started running its first locomotives (in 1836) when it was subsumed by the far more ambitious Long Island Rail Road (LIRR). The LIRR, chartered in 1834, was intended in part to foster the economic vitality of Kings, Queens, and Suffolk counties—whose farms were being outpaced by the fertile enterprises of Genesee and Cayuga counties now accessible via the Erie Canal—by enhancing the exchange of market garden produce for urban manure. Primarily, however, the LIRR was intended to speed travelers between New York and Boston, through the center of the island, by connecting Jamaica with the harbor at Greenport. Most local traffic in Brooklyn and Queens would continue to be handled by stagecoaches traveling along turnpikes (privately owned toll roads), though a glimpse of the far future arrived in June 1833 when Charles Durant lifted off from the Battery in a balloon and sailed eastward to a safe landing in Jamaica.

SMOKESTACKS AND SPECULATORS

Peter Cooper wasn't the only one who realized that railroads needed tracks, engines, and boilers. New York's iron foundries and machine shops, already flourishing in tandem with the city's shipyards, expanded to meet the new needs. Happily, the local iron furnaces could now count on expanded and regular deliveries of coal, as the completion in 1832 of the Morris Canal across New Jersey had linked New York's harbor to the Lehigh River. In 1830, moreover, a German-American ironmaster had smelted iron ore with anthracite coal at a laboratory furnace in the city, a process he patented in 1833, thus helping launch a new era in the commercial manufacture of iron.

Demand generated additional supply. The Allaire Works, hitherto the city's biggest, faced new competition from the Novelty Iron Works (1830), Browning and Dunham's North River Iron Foundry and Locomotive Engine shop (1837), and the Morgan Works (1838). Harmon Hendricks's Soho Copper Works boomed as well with the demand for boilers, flues, and boxes. Hendricks, joined by his sons, Uriah and Henry, had moved their operations to Belleville, New Jersey. Eventually, most rail-spawned metal and machine work would follow them across the Hudson—Paterson, in particular, would lead the country in producing locomotive engines—but for the moment New York City remained a major site of industrial production and innovation.

The coming of the railroad also revitalized the city's capital markets. Transactions had been relatively sedate on the New York Stock & Exchange Board (NYS & EB) in 1830, when shares of the Mohawk and Hudson Railroad first traded there. By 1831, however, with investors scrambling after the NY&H offering, a frenzied boom in stocks of the new technology got underway. By 1835, at the height of the mania, rail trades had outstripped those in all the NYS&EB's hundred-plus listed stocks and bonds. Total volume reached six thousand shares a day, with orders pouring in from across the country.

Much of the investment business was handled by private bankers and loan contractors who bought up trustworthy securities and sold them to investors seeking safe and steady dividend income. The city's most substantial investment banker, the so-called king of Wall Street, was Nathaniel Prime. Reputedly the third wealthiest man in New York in 1830, Prime avoided speculative operations, and his conservatism appealed to continental capitalists who, frightened by the Revolution of 1830, were seeking a secure

Browning and Dunham's foundry stood on the Hudson River shore at the foot of North Moore Street. Water color, 1837. (The Metropolitan Museum of Art, Bequest of Edward W. C. Arnold, 1954. The Edward W. C. Arnold Collection of New York Prints, Maps and Pictures)

haven for their funds. Europeans who had soured on Latin American loans and been excited by the Erie's success now joined English investors in pouring cash and credit into the U.S. market. Much of this new money was channeled by the House of Baring into state (especially New York) and federal bonds. Even during the runaway market of 1832–34, when the Barings curtailed their involvement in anticipation of a crash, the house continued to deal with substantial firms in New York City, primarily Prime, Ward and King.

The Barings were right to be cautious, for the rail boom had provided an opening for traders far less circumspect than Nathaniel Prime. Younger men, despised by their seniors as gamblers, seized on the opportunity for speculative scheming. Playing the stock market, after all, was much easier than dealing in real estate. Securities could be bought and sold quickly, and the invention of "margin trading" (a form of securities purchase on credit that was indigenous to the United States) allowed one to play at the table without anteing up huge sums: five dollars to a broker could buy fifty dollars' worth of stocks.

Railroad issues were risky, glamorous, and potentially highly profitable—perfect for the adventurously inclined investor. But speculative traders didn't often bother with assessing a company's real-world chances. Instead they manipulated the virtual reality of the market itself. By the early thirties warring cliques of bulls and bears were driving prices up and down, using underhanded maneuvers that were not only legal but were widely admired for their daring.

Jacob Little, the New York stock market's first full-time "operator," was one of the most famous and successful of the manipulators. Little, a tall, tense, preoccupied-looking man, started out on Wall Street clerking for a private banker. He opened his own office as a money broker in 1822, joined the NYS&EB in 1825, and by the 1830s was known as "the Napoleon of Wall Street." In his heyday, 1832–35, Little speculated in cotton, securities, canals, and above all railroads, with spectacular success.

Little was credited with inventing—and was certainly a master of—the "manipulated short sale." He would promise to sell someone shares of stock, shares he didn't yet own, for delivery in, say, sixty days. Then he would launch a campaign to drive the price of the stock down, perhaps by planting false rumors about the company's impending insolvency. If all went well, just before the sixty-day limit expired, he had forced the shares well below the price he had promised to sell them for. He could then buy the shares, make his delivery, and pocket the difference between what he had paid for them and the price the buyer had obligated himself to pay. The spread could be enormous.

Politicians who could influence a railroad's destiny were quick to follow Little's lead. State Senator Kemble made a speech opposing any enlargement of the NY&H's capital. When the news of impending scarcity hit Wall Street, the price of Harlem stock rose. At the top of the market, Kemble's broker sold short. Kemble then pushed a bill through the legislature enlarging Harlem's capital, and the price plummeted. As these were early days, and such behavior was still considered inappropriate, Kemble was expelled from the Senate.

Bulls countered such bearish tactics by trying to "corner the market" in a contested stock. If they could round up most available shares, they could block bears from buying the amount of stock necessary to fulfil their contracts. Better still, if they secured a complete monopoly, they could hoist the price as high as they chose, forcing bears to buy at the inflated price, then sell at the lower, promised one—likely driving them into bankruptcy. Profits of 200 percent were routine for successful corners. In the 1830s boom, corners were common.

Little was a master of this tactic too. In 1834 he drove Morris Canal and Banking stock from ten dollars a share to $185, the price at which shorts were forced to buy from him. The following July he cornered NY&H—with the road itself still only in construction—and realized a profit of over 60 percent. These unearned windfalls enraged many, and in 1836 it was proposed to outlaw such practices. But the NYS&EB argued that regulation would only drive business to Philadelphia, and the legislation was not passed.

Speculation raised moral hackles, but it also helped the city's economy by generating a volume of trade that, together with respectable investment transactions, kept New York's financial markets extremely "liquid." Both buyers and sellers knew that the NYS&EB could execute trades at short notice. New York thus became ever more a pacemaker of the nation's financial activities. Its market quotes were reproduced in Philadelphia, Boston, Baltimore. Its brokers became the country's largest traders in state, federal, bank, canal, and insurance company offerings and the primary promoters of new issues. More than any other economic factor, railroad financing helped solidify New York City's role in the national credit system.

PIONEERS OF CAPITAL

Those seeking less volatile outlets for accumulated pools of capital turned to western land. In the Black Hawk War of 1832, the Sac and Fox Indians were defeated in their attempt to reoccupy former homelands, paving the way for a burst of settlement into Illinois and the Wisconsin Territory. Along with the Conestoga wagons came New York money men—pioneers of capital—eager to speculate in western acres.

In 1833, with the embers of war still warm, Charles Butler and Arthur Bronson traveled by steamboat, horse, and canoe, loaded with cash and connections to local notables like General Winfield Scott, military commander in the area, who pointed out choice sites. Butler and Bronson (son of Isaac Bronson) bought town lots in as-yet-little-known places like Chicago (population five hundred), picked up great swatches of rich agricultural land in Indiana, Illinois, and the Michigan Territory, and constructed a network of agents—leading citizens, Indian agents, and military personnel—to handle their buying in the future.

John Jacob Astor garnered western holdings too. At first Astor had been hurt by the wars, which by driving the Indians west cost his American Fur Company its cheap labor supply. But when many of the locals who had been dependent on the now defunct fur trade went bankrupt, they paid their debts to Astor with land claims, leaving him in possession of prime real estate just as immigrants began to swarm in.

Settlers and speculators ignited a land-buying frenzy. In 1830 the U.S. government had sold a respectable two million acres of public land. In 1833 it moved nearly four million acres, in 1835 over twelve million went, and in 1836 twenty million followed. For the easterners who had gotten there first, average net proceeds (after deducting agent's share, lawyers' fees, travel, and other administrative costs) hovered close to 20 percent, though windfall profits of 100 to 500 percent were not uncommon, especially on city property.

Much of the New York capital flowing into western lands traveled via the medium of trust companies, financial institutions established to manage old Knickerbocker and recent Yankee fortunes. These outfits were always on the lookout for prudent long-term investments—they happily settled for modest dividends of 6 to 9 percent in exchange for stability of income—and western real estate seemed like just the thing.

The New York Life Insurance and Trust Company, one of the earliest such institutions, was established in 1830. The company was dominated by conservative bankers, merchants, and land investors, many from the city's highest social and economic echelons. Individual investors like Astor, Bronson, Kent, Lorillard, Prime, and Stuyvesant anted up a million dollars for the capital pot. Banks and foreigners added an additional five million (England's House of Baring, with fifteen hundred shares in 1834, was by far the largest single holder of its stock). New York Life and Trust then invested judiciously in farm mortgages. Its agents examined the value of the land each borrower proposed to buy, checked the borrower's status and character, and refused loans to pioneer settlers, subsistence farmers, or "men who are irresponsible, improvident and intemperate," in Charles Butler's words.

Twenty-five more such trusts were set up in the 1830s. Some of them competed to boom the value of their respective properties. In 1835–36 a Bronson-led firm built up Cassville, Wisconsin, laid out streets named after its New York investors (Prime, Ward, Arthur), and tried to make it the territorial capital, but a rival consortium, led by John Jacob Astor, succeeding in getting the governmental seat awarded to Green Bay (then called Astor).

New York land speculators were hard at work in the South too, especially after gold was discovered on Indian lands and President Jackson picked up the pace of forced dispossession. The Indian Removal Act of 1830 secured the evacuation of remaining Choctaw and Chickasaw by 1833, and the Cherokee were gone by 1835. In the latter year, the coast now clear, Butler formed the American Land Company. Pooling a million dollars from wealthy men and politicians in New York City, Albany, and Boston, it soon owned about 350,000 acres in eight states, 70 percent in cotton lands. A similar entity, the Colorado and Red River Land Company, had amassed half a million acres by 1835.

Texas proved particularly attractive. Samuel Swartwout, collector of the Port of New York and a close friend of Sam Houston, created the New Washington Association in 1834 to purchase and develop Texas land. Swartwout and his Manhattan associates strongly supported the "Texian" revolt against Mexico, and after Houston's victory at San Jacinto in 1836, a Swartwout-convened meeting of four to five thousand people in Masonic Hall backed recognition of Texas.

New York's growing financial, landed, and political involvement in the South and West provoked mixed responses there. Many local merchants, bankers, and agricultural entrepreneurs relied on eastern capital for new infrastructure, long-term mortgages, and credit for land and slaves. They considered the charges for procuring capital and marketing their commodities to be reasonable, or at least unavoidable, costs of doing business.

Others feared the political consequences of financial dependency. Southern planters remembered their subordinate position in the British Empire and worried about falling into a neocolonial relationship with northeastern capital. Some westerners feared they were in one already, pointing to the Ohio Life Insurance and Trust Company as evidence. Ohio Life was the West's largest financial institution, but 70 percent of its stock was controlled by easterners, primarily New Yorkers. Bronson and Butler had written its charter, selected its officers and stockholders, raised its capital, and won an amazingly nonrestrictive charter from Ohio (in part by liberally dispensing stock to influential Cincinnatians). As the state had bound itself not to repeal or even amend this charter until 1870, one opponent worried that by that time "it will have so wormed itself into the vitals of the land, that nothing short of revolution can put it down." Outcries appeared regularly in Ohio newspapers against the "Wall St. Gentry of New York," noting that in 1836, with other easterners, they owned over 70 percent of all bank stock in the state. Such protests were met with blunt rejoinders from New Yorkers, reminding westerners of the stark facts of economic life. Ohio, having rejected public financing of internal improvements, was "an interior state new and without surplus capital [and] could do nothing without the aid of capitalists of the City of New York."

BANK WAR

For all the grumbling about Wall Street, the country's most vigorous protests were still directed against "Chestnut Street," for it was in Philadelphia that the country's most powerful financial institution—the Second Bank of the United States—made its Greek Revival home. The BUS was the only bank in the nation with a federal charter, the only one allowed to have branches in more than two states, the only institution in which the U.S. Treasury deposited its funds. It was, as its name implied, the government's fiscal agent, and it had the de facto authority of a central bank.

Since his accession to power in 1823, Nicholas Biddle, the bank's brilliant and well-born president, had skillfully forged a reliable national currency, sustained an ample but controlled growth of credit, and provided some security against economic fluctuations by acting as lender of last resort. These accomplishments—and the prosperity associated with them—had won him many supporters.

They had also won him enemies. Westerners and southerners seeking rapid development disliked his tight control over credit, and President Andrew Jackson saw in Biddle's bank a Money Power that menaced the republic. In 1829, though the bank's federal charter still had seven years to run, Jackson announced his preference for having a publicly owned and treasury-operated institution at the helm of the country's finances. New York City's leading Tammany politicians quickly concurred, as did upstate Democrats led by Martin Van Buren.

Many Wall Street financiers were also vexed by the Philadelphia institution. They bristled at what James Hamilton (Alexander's son) called its ability "to exercise a dangerous power over the monied and mercantile operations of the great city of New York." Wall Streeters also resented competition from the BUS, which had a branch in Manhattan itself. It galled them, too, that as the federal government's official depository, its coffers and profits were swelled by customs revenues extracted from New York merchants. A lot of money was at stake. In 1828 New York custom duties paid all federal expenses apart from interest on the debt, and receipts were rapidly increasing. The Custom House staff was growing rapidly, and in 1834 the U.S. government would break ground for a grand Greek Revival headquarters, designed by Town and Davis at Nassau and Wall (today's Federal Hall). Leading bankers, it was reported to Jackson, were unhappy at "the wrong done to New York in depriving her of her natural advantages by the legislation of Congress, which undertook to make Philadelphia the financial centre of the Union."

Nevertheless, the Bank of the United States had powerful supporters in New York City—bankers, politicians, and conservative businessmen who had developed ties to Biddle's operation because it was an inescapable fact of financial life, and who applauded Biddle's demonstrated wizardry at stabilizing national money markets. Some key journalists backed Biddle too, in part because he lucratively backed them. After receiving a "loan" from Biddle, James Watson Webb of the Jacksonian flagship *Courier and Enquirer* took his paper into the camp of those supporting the bank. Tammany Hall denounced Webb as a traitor, and William Leggett, an assistant editor of the Democratic *Evening Post*, approached him on Wall Street, saying, "Colonel Webb, you are a coward and a scoundrel, and I spit upon you." They exchanged blows until a crowd pulled them apart, but not before Leggett scored with another gob. Political editors were a truculent breed. Leggett's boss, William Cullen Bryant, took a cowskin whip to William Leete Stone of the *Commercial Advertiser* in 1831, who riposted with a sword cane, a thrust Bryant parried with his whip until onlookers broke them apart. In 1836 James Watson Webb would assault James Gordon Bennet in the middle of Wall Street.

By 1831 Jackson's various opponents had coalesced into a new political party, the National Republicans, which nominated Henry Clay to run against the president in 1832. Clay got Biddle to apply for an early recharter, which Congress granted, only to have the president veto it. In New York, Tammany firmly supported the veto and held an enormous antibank rally on Jackson's behalf. George Henry Evans and former members of the Workingmen's Party supported the president too, believing that many of the artisanate's problems stemmed from the control of finance by a privileged class. Many Workies advocated eliminating all banks, not just Biddle's, and relying on "hard money"—a purely metallic currency.

The alliance of Jacksonians and Workingmen alarmed conservative Democrats like John Jacob Astor. Many broke ranks and condemned Jackson's veto, thus splitting the Democratic Party. Jackson triumphed nevertheless in his 1832 reelection bid, winning

59 percent of the vote in New York City, and promptly declared full-scale war on Biddle's "Monster." He announced he would soon remove all U.S. funds from the BUS and transfer the money to selected state bank depositories.

During May and June of 1833 Jackson toured the Northeast to test his policy's popularity. Huge and affectionate crowds turned out—nowhere more so than in New York City. When the president landed at Castle Garden, a hundred thousand people jammed the Battery and its adjoining wharves and housetops to watch Jackson mount a horse and lead a procession of cabinet members, governors, congressmen, and mayors across the wooden causeway connecting the old fort to Manhattan. Unfortunately for his followers, the moment Jackson reached dry land, the bridge collapsed behind him, tumbling the assorted notables into the shallow waters. No one was seriously hurt, and the grand parade of dripping-wet dignitaries proceeded up Broadway to City Hall Park, led by the president on horseback, with the crowds huzzahing lustily for Old Hickory. And when seven state banks were chosen to receive the federal deposits, three of the "pet banks" (as his enemies dubbed them) were in New York City.

Biddle struck back. Convinced that only a massive economic crisis would galvanize the citizenry into demanding that Congress overrule Jackson, he jammed on the fiscal brakes by engineering a credit contraction. Withholding loans and calling in debts, Biddle singlehandedly deflated the national economy, producing widespread financial prostration, especially in New York. By Christmas, stocks on the NYS&EB were plummeting. "Panic prevails," wrote Hone, who himself lost thirty thousand dollars in two months. With many dealers and merchants verging on bankruptcy, disaster rippled through the city; laborers were discharged by the hundreds.

Biddle remained remorseless. "All the other Banks and all the merchants may break," he said, "but the Bank of the United States shall not break." As he hoped, delegations of businessmen now descended on Congress with pleas to restore the deposits. The president declared that the distress was only affecting "brokers and stock speculators and all who were doing business on borrowed capital" and that "all such people ought to break." When New York financiers went to plead with him in person, an angry Jackson thundered, "Go to Nicholas Biddle," as he was the one with the millions.

Jackson's opponents—National Republicans and Conservative Democrats—denounced the autocratic "King Andrew" and coalesced into a new "Whig" Party. The name, first suggested by Colonel Webb in the *Courier and Enquirer*, invoked Revolutionary-era resistance to King George III and gained rapid acceptance. In April 1834 the fledgling Whigs entered the political lists in New York City.

BANK RIOT

On the morning of April 8, voters slogged their way to the polls through rain-muddied streets. Over the next three days, for the first time in the city's history, they would be casting ballots in a mayoral election; the city charter had been amended in 1833 to finally give New Yorkers the right to elect their own chief magistrate. With the Bank War at its height, the city's election was widely viewed as a referendum on the president's policies. Daniel Webster declared that Whig hopes for winning national power "rely mainly upon the success of the great struggle which is to take place in New York."

The election would also measure the ability of Whig amateurs to compete with Tammany professionals. The new party's inner circle was comprised chiefly of merchants, bankers, and rentiers—powerful paladins like Philip Hone, Arthur Tappan,

Samuel Ruggles, and Cornelius Vanderbilt—but they were not seasoned political operatives. The Whigs chose the ruddy-faced Dutchman and former Democratic congressman Gulian C. Verplanck as their mayoral standard-bearer.

Democratic orators branded Whiggery a tool of the city's elite and portrayed the coming contest as "one of the rich against the poor" (William Cullen Bryant) or the "bank aristocracy against the people" (George Henry Evans). Whigs retorted that Democratic ranks too were laced with men of wealth and position—starting with the Democrats' mayoral candidate, banker Cornelius Lawrence—though they did not deny their party's affiliation with the rich and influential, and indeed denounced Lawrence as a traitor to his class.

Whigs were well aware, however, that winning the mayoralty would require popular support. Some Whig employers bluntly relied on economic muscle, threatening to dismiss employees who voted Democratic. Others solicited support on the basis of converging class interests—the old Alexander Hamilton strategy. At a Masonic Hall rally Whigs appealed to the traditional interdependence of merchants and "all trades connected with commerce"—winning some converts among cartmen, draymen, porters, sailors, ship carpenters, coopers, stevedores, riggers, and longshoremen. Whigs also appealed to American-born workers' growing resentment of the Catholic Irish. Tammany, they said, was using the new immigrants to consolidate municipal power, and in fact Irishmen had flocked to the party that had courted them.

With the stage thus set for confrontation, James Watson Webb, the combative *Courier and Enquirer* editor and former soldier, took command of Whig troops. On Tuesday, April 8, pro-Whig sailors fitted out a float-size frigate. They named it the *Constitution*, mounted it on wheels, attached Whig pennants to its rigging, and hauled it through the streets with two bands and five hundred seamen following along behind. The parade marched through Broadway and Greenwich Street, picking up a thousand more supporters from among the vast pool of idled employees (Whig employers had decreed afternoon business shutdowns for the duration). After being vigorously cheered at the Merchants' Exchange on Wall Street, the crowd headed into the heavily Democratic Sixth Ward. At the polls there, Whigs insulted the locals, with one invader shouting, "We should get along well enough if it were not for the low Irish." Words led to blows, and the Whigs were driven from the area. Webb proclaimed the repulsion a "REIGN OF TERROR" in his *Courier and Enquirer*, and at a Masonic Hall conclave that evening, Whigs resolved to march en masse into Democratic terrain the next day.

On Wednesday hundreds of Whigs proceeded "in military order" into the heart of the Sixth Ward, bellowing epithets such as "damned Irish." Gaelic Democrats retaliated by attacking Whig headquarters on Broadway. In the ensuing battle, shots were exchanged and many were injured. The Tammanyite crowd then headed to Wall Street, determined to destroy the *Courier and Enquirer*'s office. Webb, forewarned, erected a barricade of bundled papers and retired to the roof with thirty young merchants, seventy muskets, one hundred pistols, and six loads of paving stones. When rioters filled the street below, Webb threatened to shoot the first man who moved toward his property, and eventually the crowd dispersed.

On the third and final day of the election, fifteen hundred Whig freemen again did battle with Jacksonians armed with clubs and brickbats, and when the mayor tried to intervene he was knocked to the pavement and struck on the head with a stick. Hun-

dreds of youthful Whigs now cleaned out the gun shops on Broadway and marched to
the state arsenal at Elm and Franklin streets, led by such prominent merchants as Simeon Draper. They broke in and began passing out arms. Irishmen raced to the site. Soon
an estimated twenty thousand merchants, mechanics, cartmen, and laborers filled the
area. "We were indeed in the midst of a revolution," said the *Sun*. With Armageddon in
the offing, the mayor called out the troops—twelve hundred infantry and cavalrymen—
and order was restored.

The election proceeded with military guards stationed at the arsenal, City Hall,
Merchants' Exchange, and the local branch of the Bank of the United States. Huge
crowds milled around Masonic and Tammany halls while the votes were counted.
Finally it was announced that Mayor Lawrence, the antibank Democrat, had defeated
Verplanck, the Whig, by the whisker-thin margin of 180 votes out of thirty-five thou-
sand cast, but the fledgling Whig Party captured a majority of the Common Council.

"THE CITY IS REDEEMED," crowed the *Commercial Advertiser*. To celebrate what
Hone called a "signal triumph," the Whigs threw a Castle Garden banquet on April 15.
Tables were set for ten thousand, but the multitudes jamming the Battery were great
enough to require several shifts. Hundreds of boiled hams and rounds of beef, along
with three pipes of wine and forty barrels of beer, disappeared down the collective gul-
let. Afterward, thousands marched up Greenwich Street to where the visiting Daniel
Webster was quartered; he gave a fiery speech of congratulations. The later inauguration of Mayor Lawrence was the occasion for a turbulent gathering of his Democratic
supporters, but Tammany had been badly shaken.

Happily for the Democrats, the Bank War now moved to a victorious conclusion.
Biddle had overplayed his hand, his colossal arrogance alienating even his supporters.
When elder statesmen like Albert Gallatin and Isaac Bronson demanded Biddle relax
the pressure, the Philadelphian refused, and New Yorkers mobilized to fend off his
attack. The Safety Fund made available a multimillion-dollar line of credit to member
banks, enabling them to defy Biddle and stabilize the markets, and another state agency,
the Canal Commission, permitted the banks maximum use of its massive revenues, further helping undercut Biddle's strategy.

With New York holding the line and angry denunciations of Biddle's abuse of
power sweeping the country, House Democrats mustered a majority for a resolution
upholding removal and opposing recharter. Even Whig politicians felt compelled to
abandon the BUS. By summer Biddle had given up, his bank was on the road to extinction, and New York City had emerged from the crisis as the undisputed financial capital
of the country.

Business revived quickly, and in New York City support for Whigs eroded just as
rapidly. Aided by a burgeoning labor movement, Tammany swept the fall 1834 elections. Discouraged by their swift rise but even swifter fall, downcast Whigs didn't even
contest Mayor Lawrence's reelection bid in April 1835.

CITY BUILDERS

The Bank War interrupted the 1830s boom but failed to stop it. With the dramatic
imbroglio over, stock speculators, railroad promoters, and real estate investors resumed
their fevered dealings. Land developers, in particular, set a torrid pace, especially
in New York City itself, and speculative building emerged as one of Manhattan's

(and Brooklyn's) largest enterprises. Annual investment in new construction exceeded three million dollars, rivaling the stakes in shipbuilding, shoemaking, and clothing manufacture.

Ground zero for the building boom was the commercial area at the island's lower tip, as a rapidly expanding mercantile and financial community tried to elbow itself into the seventeenth-century streetscape. Lot owners petitioned for wider roads, and the city responded with a massive program of prying open narrow and gloomy lanes. Between 1831 and 1834 Pine, William, Ann, Cedar, Hanover, and Exchange Place were among the many streets that had their residential houses relocated or, more often, torn down and replaced by purely commercial structures. The successful conclusion of the Bank War galvanized the process, with the victors determined to build a central business district worthy of the city's new status. The year 1835 brought a surge of street widenings—Mill, Stone, and John streets were among the stretched thoroughfares—and a new surge in the erection of Doric banks.

Uptown, a residential-based boom was underway, spurred by developers seeking to profit from housing the exploding population. Manhattan had contained roughly 124,000 residents in 1820, 167,000 in 1825, and 200,000 in 1830. Fed by a tripling in the rate of immigration, by 1835 the population topped 270,000, and with the annual overseas influx doubling again, Manhattan was headed toward an 1840 total of 313,000. During the 1830s New York was the fastest-growing city in the United States, and at some point during the decade it surpassed Mexico City in population, becoming the largest city in the New World.

Between 1821 and 1835 the population of every ward tripled or quadrupled, generating crowding, congestion, and soaring real estate prices. The value of land in Manhattan went from $64.8 million in 1826 to $87.6 million in 1830 to over $143 million in 1835—then shot to $233 million within the next twelve months, for a total rise of 280 percent over the previous decade. These numbers reflected both speculative expectations and actual improvements. Developers built commercial structures and private dwellings at a fantastic pace. In 1834, 877 commercials and 654 residentials went up; in 1835, 1259 and 865 of each were added; and in 1836, 1826 and 868. Buildings grew taller, too. In 1824 three-fourths of all new buildings had been two stories high, and none was over three; in 1834, a third of the structures surpassed three stories, and over two-thirds of the city's new stores (15 percent of all new construction) had three or more floors.

The money for all this flowed in from private investors, many of them old landed families. Stuyvesants, Livingstons, Roosevelts, Goelets, Cuttings, Rhinelanders, Lenoxes, Lispenards, Brevoorts, and Bayards plunged into the real estate market, as, of course, did John Jacob Astor. Financial institutions also invested, after New York State removed restrictions on banks' ability to make loans on urban land. Merchants, professionals, and shopkeepers, too, combined their savings with mortgage-backed loans to build speculative housing on an ever larger scale. A survey in 1831 showed that over six and a half million dollars had been loaned out on mortgages, two-thirds of it from individuals residing in the city, another third from "incorporated companies."

Most actual construction continued to be undertaken by small, independent contractor-entrepreneurs, who put up perhaps one to three houses a year and operated on the thinnest of margins. But a handful of developers emerged on the order of London's Thomas Cubitt, a carpenter who had risen to preside over much the biggest construction firm England's capital had ever seen. Cubitt supervised the raising not of single buildings or even rows of them, but whole ensembles of houses, arranged in squares, crescents, and terraces—the grand estate developments like Bloomsbury, Belgravia, and Pimlico that blossomed in the 1820s and 1830s.

The New Yorker who most closely approximated Cubitt's accomplishment was Samuel Bulkley Ruggles, though his social status was quite different from the Londoner's. Ruggles, born in 1800 in New Milford, Connecticut, grew up in Poughkeepsie, where his father was a prominent lawyer. After graduating from Yale in 1814, he studied law, moved to New York in 1821, set up his own practice, and married Mary Rosalie Rathbone, daughter of a rich merchant. Her financial and social patrimony helped him establish close ties with the old Knickerbockracy, many of whom found payment of taxes and street assessments on their inherited estates to be a growing burden. Ruggles suggested he could turn their assets into profitable sources of income. Noting that canal development had helped push the value of Manhattan's taxable real estate from fifty-two million dollars in 1825 to ninety-five million in 1831, he predicted that the impact of railroad construction would be even greater. "Within five years after the railroad from Albany shall reach Lake Erie," Ruggles declared, "the real estate upon this little rocky island will be taxed at 250 millions of dollars." It made sense, therefore, to buy and build. Ruggles had used his wife's inheritance to purchase farmland from the Stuyvesants and other families, often drawing them into jointly financing his speculative ventures. In 1831 he gave up law altogether and plunged into real estate full time. By 1833 Ruggles had purchased over five hundred building lots, many of them in contiguous bunches, most of them heavily mortgaged.

One such pieced-together block of land covered roughly the area between 19th and 22nd streets and Third and Fourth avenues, with the former Gramercy Farm as its twenty-two acre core. The terrain—swampy in spots, hilly in others—was traversed by the spring-fed Crommessie Vly, which over the years had gouged out a gully almost forty feet deep on its way to the East River at 18th Street. In the early 1830s Ruggles undertook a mammoth landscaping job that eventually required moving approximately a million horsecart loads of earth, at a cost of $180,000.

At the center of his rearranged domain, Ruggles laid out Gramercy Square. Inspired by the example of Trinity's St. John's Park, he deeded the square collectively to the owners of the sixty surrounding plots he had platted out. Ruggles sought tax-exempt status for the private park, and the Board of Aldermen agreed (in 1832), expecting that it would soon be surrounded by valuable (and taxable) properties. They were right. By 1833, when the square was fenced in, most of the lots had been sold, despite their distance from town. Actual housing construction, however, would be delayed until the 1840s.

To enhance access to Gramercy Square, Ruggles prevailed on the state legislature to insert a new north-south artery between Third and Fourth avenues. He named the northern extension Lexington Avenue, for the famous battle, and the southern strip Irving Place, honoring Washington Irving, though the writer never lived there. Irving Place served another function for Ruggles, as it led to his second mammoth enterprise, Union Square.

Union Place, as it was known until Ruggles got it changed to Union Square, was situated, as the name implied, at a junction of many roads. Left open by decree of the grid commissioners, it remained in the early 1830s a collection of vacant lots—apart from some shacks and a potter's field. In 1832 Ruggles obtained a fifty-year lease on most of the area between 15th and 19th streets, then got the city to approve opening Fourth Avenue north of 17th Street. In 1834 he convinced the Board of Aldermen to enclose, regulate, and grade the square (with much of the cost assessed to the Ruggles-owned land between there and Gramercy Park). Finally, Ruggles built curbs and sidewalks along the new streets. Then he sold most of his leases and, in 1839, built a four-story house for himself on the square's east side, into which he moved from his Bond Street quarters. In time Ruggles would be surrounded by affluent neighbors, but, as at Gramercy Square, actual construction would await the next decade.

Due west of Gramercy Park, on Manhattan's Hudson River side, another grand project was afoot on the domain of Father Christmas, Clement Clarke Moore. Once his resistance to lower Manhattan's northward sprawl proved futile, Moore had decided to make the best of things and systematically developed Chelsea as a fashionable quarter, anchored by the green grounds of the General Theological Seminary. Working with James N. Wells, the Hudson Street carpenter who had developed Trinity's St. Luke's property, Moore laid out streets. Again, smoothing out Manhattan's cragginess took heroic efforts: Eighth Avenue had to be beveled down by six to twelve feet to reach the required grade. By 1832, his friend John Pintard noted, Chelsea was laid out with streets "where, but a few years ago, all was open country." Soon Moore was leasing lots, with restrictive covenants to guarantee the proper tone.

Laborers excavating Union Square, engraving by James Smillie, c. 1831. The leveling of Manhattan's original terrain for real estate developers like Samuel Ruggles was done by pick and shovel. This view looks south from what is now 18th Street, with Broadway on the right and Fourth Avenue on the left. (I. N. Phelps Stokes Collection. Miriam and Ira D. Wallach Division of Art, Prints and Photographs. The New York Public Library. Astor, Lenox and Tilden Foundations)

Way across town, where the high, dry land west of Second Avenue tumbled down into marshes that ran on to the East River, the Stuyvesant family took the lead, albeit reluctantly, in developing Tompkins Square. For quite some time, they and other swamplords (including Pells, Fishes, and Astors) had refused to underwrite the mammoth job of draining and filling their boggy empire. At one point they threatened to dump the property back on the city as not worth improving. Thus prodded, and having taken note of the "depressed state of property in this part of the city," the municipal authorities allocated sixty-two thousand dollars of taxpayers' money to compensate the landowners (in particular, the Stuyvesant family) and set aside another twenty-two thousand to transform the muddy flat into a park. Opened in 1834, Tompkins Square was surrounded the following year with an ornamental cast-iron fence, then studded with shade trees. This upgrade immediately lofted the value of all the swamplords' nearby holdings, and boosters predicted a brilliant and genteel future for the neighborhood.

The city supported the Stuyvesant and Ruggles developments so handsomely largely because it was running out of money. As expenses for infrastructure and poor relief soared, traditional revenues had failed to keep up. For over a century the municipal corporation's treasury had relied mainly on rental income from its own property (water lots, wharves, common lands) and on license and franchise fees. By the 1820s, with these sources no longer generating sufficient revenues to cover expanding costs, city officials relied more on property taxes.

Previously, property (especially "farmland") had been taxed lightly or not at all, one reason eighteenth-century merchants had regarded it as such a good investment. But as land values catapulted, the city began to demand a portion of the profits, and total assessments leapt from just over two hundred thousand dollars in 1830 to over $1.1 million in 1837. With their fiscal fate now tied to the value of private holdings, aldermen adopted a policy of aggressively enhancing the value of private property, in the name of promoting the public good.

Street openings were central to this strategy. The municipality's Street Committee steadily expanded its building program, and in 1835, responding to numerous complaints about limited access north of 14th Street, it decided to open all grid-plotted thoroughfares up to 42nd Street. Ignoring the grid designers' egalitarian inclinations, however, it began subsidizing creation of elite neighborhoods. Partly this was simply a matter of sanctioning exceptions in street design, like the creation of residential squares—elements that enhanced a location's status and raised its values. Occasionally this entailed actively constructing new spaces with public money, as at Washington Square, which now completed a thirty-year transformation from ugly duckling to civic swan.

Originally sodden marshlands, the area had been drained in the 1790s and become a graveyard for paupers and fever victims, receiving more than twenty-two thousand bodies over the next two decades. It also served occasionally as execution ground, with prisoners carted up Christopher Street from Newgate Prison and hanged from an elm before jeering crowds (the resident gravedigger doubling as hangman). After the yellow fever epidemic of 1823, with Greenwich booming just to the west and Bond Street burgeoning just to the east, the city barred further burials and routed new corpses north to what is today Bryant Park. In 1826 the city purchased additional land here (paying a hefty seventy-eight thousand dollars) and created the Washington Parade-Ground, a setting for militia exercises. It opened to the public that July 4—the Declaration's jubilee anniversary—with an old-fashioned fete in which two roasted oxen, two hundred hams, and a plentiful supply of ale were disbursed to the crowd of ten thousand.

Though heavy guns sometimes caved in the parade-ground's surface, exposing the yellow-shrouded corpses of fever victims, it quickly became a plebeian gathering spot, attracting visitors from nearby Greenwich. Almost immediately, however, developers began raising handsome new town houses along the square's southern border. Then, from 1828, northside farmers and estate owners began subdividing their property and erecting aristocratic rowhouses. In 1831 Sailors' Snug Harbor leased a northside stretch from Fifth Avenue to University Place to developers, imposing restrictions to guarantee homogeneity. By 1833 another Greek Revival terrace had emerged, spanning 1 to 13 Washington Square North, known collectively and colloquially as "the Row."

Washington Square, like its Hudson Square prototype, drew posh residents. Many decamped uptown together from homes near the Battery. Bankers and merchants predominated, including former mayor Allen, who arrived in 1835. Most families came from New England or Scottish backgrounds and worshiped at the Presbyterian Church on Christopher Street.

Rising out of Washington Square like a thermometer from its bulb, Fifth Avenue was not yet an address to boast about, having only recently graduated from open stream to muddy rutted road. In 1824 Fifth was opened to 13th Street, covering over the Minetta Waters that continued (as they do today) to course beneath its surface. The road reached 21st Street by 1830, and 42nd by 1837, but remained sparsely populated, certainly by gentry. The first sign of its future eminence was the construction in 1834, by Henry J. Brevoort Jr., of a Greek-ornamented mansion (perhaps designed by Town and Davis). It lay at the northwest corner of Fifth and Ninth Street, in the midst of what remained of the farm that Henrick Van Brevoort had bought back in 1714, and it represented the profits the family had accrued by selling off portions over the years and investing the proceeds in the stock market.

SECOND CITY

New York's gains, at first, seemed Brooklyn's loss. Manhattan's expansion had created a powerful up-island real estate lobby of landowners, speculators, developers, and politicians, and this phalanx was determined to thwart any move by New York's increasingly feisty neighbor to lure potential customers across the East River.

One mechanism for stanching any such outflow lay in New York's continuing control of the river and its ferries. Under its colonial charter, the municipal corporation's boundaries lapped to the shores of Long Island. It also had exclusive authority to license ferries across the East River. It used this to ensure that its lessees remained untroubled by competitors, thus allowing them to keep both their fares and payments to the city high.

Brooklyn villagers pleaded with New York's Common Council to award leases to men who would run the ferry as a public utility instead of charging whatever the monopolized traffic would bear. They petitioned as well for boats to go to new locations, like Atlantic Street. Manhattan dismissed such requests. As one alderman baldly admitted in 1834, he legislated for New York, not Brooklyn, "and if I shall think that the establishment of this ferry will abstract from the southern extremity of New York and centre of its commerce of population which would otherwise reside upon this island, I am bound to vote against it."

In 1834 Brooklyn abandoned direct appeals and turned to the state for support. Fashioning novel legal weaponry, the villagers attacked New York at a vulnerable spot, the independent authority of its venerable municipal corporation. Chancellor Kent had justified its right to control water traffic as being in the interest of the public, by which he meant residents of the city. But Brooklynites argued that the "public" encompassed the entire state and that the ferry's paramount function was to serve that public's convenience, not generate revenues for the corporation by exacting tribute from its smaller neighbor. New York should be made to treat its franchise as an administrative responsibility delegated by the state—of which, they pointedly reminded Albany, it was but a creature—or to transfer its ferry-licensing power to a state commission. If the courts accepted this reasoning, one of the last perquisites of the "private" corporation would vanish.

In March 1835 stockholders of Fulton Ferry decided to compromise. They agreed to permit New York City to grant a license to a different group of investors. The Common Council agreed, though it designated the new ferry's terminus as Whitehall, Manhattan's most remote and inconvenient point. Tensions eased. New York had bought itself a ten-year truce in the ferry wars. (Concessions were made on the Hudson side too: in 1833, New York and New Jersey settled their boundary dispute by fixing Manhattan's boundary in midriver, not at water's edge as long claimed.)

New York proved unable, however, to stave off Brooklyn's emergence as a full-fledged city. Since its formation, the town around the ferry landing had been growing at a rate exceeding Manhattan's. The Village Council wanted enhanced authority, both to press disputes with its bullying big neighbor and to promote local development by installing street lights, clearing pigs from the streets, and cleaning up grogshops. The council also sought more substantial headquarters, cramped as it was in the upper floor of the Apprentices' Library, which, since a fire in 1832 had destroyed the new Flatbush courthouse, it had been forced to share with the county government as well.

In 1833 a bill to incorporate Brooklyn as a city passed the Assembly. New York's opposition killed it in the Senate. In 1834 Brooklyn tried again. New York officials countered with a remonstrance requesting that all of Kings and Richmond counties be made part of New York City. Brooklyn won, aided by upstaters. An act passed April 8, 1834, invested their community with the privileges of a city. But Brooklyn's charter was quite different from New York's. This city was to be an administrative agency, not a private and propertied corporation. It had specific responsibilities, as well as things it was forbidden to do—like regulating the prices of any commodity except bread, or infringing the chartered rights of the Corporation of the City of New York. The new city promptly set up wards, elected aldermen, and chose its first mayor, George Hall—son of a Flatbush Irish farm family, an Erasmus Hall graduate, and a leading temperance advocate.

In July 1834 a town meeting began to talk of building a City Hall that would outdo New York's. This suited Hezekiah Pierrepont perfectly. In 1833 Hezekiah had sent his son Henry Evelyn Pierrepont to Europe to study cities. Like Ithiel Town, he came back enamored of crescents and squares. The Pierreponts decided to map out the old Livingston lands behind Brooklyn Heights in the same grand manner. The terrain was still open country, however, and nearly a mile from the waterfront. To lure commercial and professional interests it needed an anchor. A grand City Hall would do nicely. In May 1835, accordingly, the Pierreponts and Remsens sold Brooklyn a triangular site at the intersections of Fulton, Joralemon, and Court streets. In 1836 a cornerstone was laid for a Greek Revival structure. It would be by far the most conspicuous building in Brooklyn, rivaling anything in fashionable Manhattan.

The formation of the City of Brooklyn stimulated the cupidity of many local landowners and touched off an extravagant binge of speculation in town lots. This fever soon spread way beyond Brooklyn proper. For miles in all direction, farms were surveyed, subdivided, laid out into streets, and sold off at auction sales—at the manic pace of the land booms in Manhattan and out west.

To the north, on the other side of Wallabout Bay with its Navy Yard, flourished Williamsburgh. Incorporated as a village in 1827, Williamsburgh extended its borders in 1835, set up a board of trustees to manage itself, built large wharves along its stretch of the East River, and started a new ferry to Peck Slip (over the strenuous opposition of New York). In 1836 a company of gentlemen purchased a farm and estate traversed by the present Grand Street. There they erected fourteen first-class model homes for a planned model city, which they trumpeted in lithographic property maps as a great investment opportunity. The population jumped. Merchants established residences along the shore. And just to Williamsburgh's north, the village of Green Point experienced a similar heightening of expectations. In 1832–34, Neziah Bliss, a Connecticut Yankee ironworker who married into one of the original Dutch families, bought up farmland, had the area surveyed, and laid out streets and lots.

Activity was equally frenzied below the City of Brooklyn's southern border of Joralemon's Lane. Two and a half miles from the ferry lay Hoyt's (or Prospect) Hill, where Charles Hoyt had planted streets back in 1826. By 1833, amid a marketing blitz of lithographic maps and auction sales, Hoyt was harvesting his speculative profits. At the same time, the hills, marsh meadows, and mill ponds of Red Hook were fetching astonishing prices: one ten-acre patch went for forty-seven thousand in 1833. In 1834 the old Van Dyke lands were transmuted into the Red Hook Building Company, which issued stock on Wall Street. In 1835 poplars, cedars, locusts, and sassafras were hatcheted down. Hills were tossed into marshes, and old mill ponds, like that on which Nicholas Luquer had raised oysters and ground grain for Pierrepont's distillery, passed into history. The Red Hook Building Company's ambitions outpaced its abilities, however, and in 1835 it was taken hold of by Messrs. Voorhees and Stranahan, who organized the Atlantic Dock Company, which in the next decade would construct an engineering masterpiece.

Still farther south, across Gowanus Bay, the land rose again toward the wooded Heights of Gowanus. It was here, in 1832, that Henry E. Pierrepont proposed to build a city of the dead. Pierrepont had been inspired by a visit to Mount Auburn Cemetery, the country's first rural, parklike necropolis, which had opened in 1831 in Cambridge, Massachusetts. He was also inspired by a vision of the fortune he could make importing corpses from Manhattan.

New York had banned burials south of Canal Street, and by 1830 several enterprising businessmen had opened New York Marble Cemetery as a profit-making venture. The city's first nonsectarian cemetery—its 156 underground vaults were open to the wealthy of any faith—was situated on a half-acre plot just west of Second Avenue between Second and Third streets. An inscription blazoned on its east wall read PLACE

OF BURIAL FOR GENTLEMEN. It was so successful they opened a second one, a block east, in 1832. Further annexes were ruled out the following year by the real estate boom, which drove the value of downtown lots to such heights that the City Council extended the ban on new interments north to 14th Street. Pierrepont saw an opportunity here and, once Brooklyn had become a city, proposed creation of Green-Wood Cemetery, a plan that would come to fruition in the next decade.

Below the Heights of Gowanus, Brooklyn rolled south to the sea. Here the landscape of scattered farms and villages was largely untouched by the 1830s boom, with one exception. At its southwestern rump, across the Narrows from Staten Island's easternmost extension, federal defense spending catalyzed new development. On June 11, 1825, the cornerstone was laid for Fort Hamilton, commencing a seven-year, half-million-dollar construction project. Wharves rose along the shore for landing supplies. Fort Hamilton village, also known as Irishtown, grew up on the bastion's northwestern side. Its shacks housed construction workers, many of them recent immigrants, and the Irish women who did laundry and opened small stores. By the mid-1830s stage service connected the fort with New Utrecht, two and a half miles away, and from there, via Gravesend and Flatbush, with the City of Brooklyn.

In November 1831 Fort Hamilton received its first garrison, the fifty-two men and two officers of Battery F of the Fourth U.S. Artillery Regiment. During the peaceful 1830s the citadel remained undermanned, but the village continued to grow. There was only one church, however—Dutch Reformed—so many soldiers had to travel to Brooklyn or New York to worship. In 1834, accordingly, soldiers and locals joined in building St. John's Episcopal Church just outside the fort (its cornerstone was laid in 1835). In 1836, seeking to supplement its grandly named dirt roads, the city engaged a company to build a railroad from Brooklyn to the fort, then on along Gravesend Bay to New Utrecht, Bath, and Coney Island.

Grand schemes were conceived far to the east of Brooklyn too. For a century and a half the conservative farmers of New Lots had gone about their traditional business. In 1835 things changed abruptly. John R. Pitkin, a wealthy Connecticut merchant, began buying up large portions of land (above today's New Lots Avenue) from local villagers. He intended to found a great city—East New York—that would rival Manhattan. The new metropolis would have access to cheap food from local farmers, low rents that would allow manufacturers to undercut competitors, and a vast transportation center all its own along the shores of Jamaica Bay. By 1836 Pitkin had assembled a vast tract, laid out streets and lots, and prepared a prospectus that spoke glowingly of future buildings, markets, factories, parks, and schools.

In 1835 Pitkin had jumped border boundaries to Queens, where he launched another model village, Woodside (later Woodhaven). But the county in general remained unaffected by the boom. Flushing's population remained stable at about two thousand and was only incorporated as a village in 1837, while Jamaica's railroad-spurred growth remained in the future. Staten Island too remained largely isolated from the speculative fever. One group of speculators formed an association to develop the island's northeastern sector as a resort center, to be named New Brighton. They borrowed $470,000 from bankers and erected a large hotel and some houses, but the enterprise didn't get much farther. The area did attract "Commodore" Vanderbilt, however; in 1835, now among the city's richest men, he built a porticoed and Corinthian-columned house on the family farm, between Stapleton and Tompkinsville.

GOOD TIMES

Philip Hone, an active player in the real estate game, was a very happy man in 1835. Land values, he noted elatedly, had soared "beyond all the calculations of the most sanguine spectators," with the consequence that "immense fortunes have been made and realized within the last three months." Abounding in newfound wealth, Hone set out to enjoy himself.

New York's boom-era Knickercrats spent their off-work hours differently than did their evangelical class counterparts. While Arthur Tappan and his colleagues were stamping out sins, Philip Hone and his comrades were merrily indulging them. Hedonism was not universal, to be sure: reaction to good fortune varied with the individual. Old Nathaniel Prime had speculated heavily in stocks, bonds, and real estate and had won big. He retired in 1832, vastly wealthy, his sons well launched, his daughters well married. But Prime became seized by a strange fantasy. He grew convinced he was becoming poor and would die in the almshouse. Unable to shake this monomania, he cut his throat with a razor and died instantly.

Something akin to Prime's anxiety infected even Hone's optimism, for the noted bon vivant's pursuit of the good life mixed celebration of pleasure with a search for security. He and his peers fashioned one enclave after another dedicated to gregarious fun—men's clubs, opera houses, pleasure gardens; each was as much a sanctum as a playpen. They were places, as were the elite's exclusive neighborhoods, where a newly flush bourgeoisie could experiment with an aristocratic lifestyle, safely segregated from the hoi polloi of an increasingly democratic city.

In June 1836 a little group met at the athenaeum and formed the Union Club, choosing as first president Samuel Jones, chief justice of the Superior Court of New York City. As Hone explained to his diary, the intention was to create an establishment of four hundred "of our most distinguished citizens." It would "be similar in its plan and regulations to the great clubs of London, which give a tone and character to the society of the London metropolis." The Union Club was an instant success. Merchants and lawyers from the city's established families flocked to it. Even James Gordon Bennett was asked to join, though he declined, publicly and noisily, in the pages of his *Herald*, on the grounds it refused to admit females ("Society without woman is a farce," he declared). Undeterred, the Union Club leased the Le Roy house at Broadway and Leonard, where local businessmen, out-of-town visitors, and bachelor men-about-town could entertain in exclusive and comfortable surroundings, which included the services of a chef from Paris and a cellar stocked with excellent wines.

Not all Knickerbocker nightlife was so relentlessly male. Soirees were all the rage in the boom era, as gentry couples gathered at the homes of their friends for late supper, music, and games. Hone regularly invited sixty or so to evenings featuring tableaux vivants. Costumed ladies and gentlemen arrayed themselves before elaborate backdrops as "Madonna" or "Lady Jane Grey" or "Highland Chief" or formed groups to depict a "Scene from Waverly" or "Cato's Death." Women also attended the round of elaborate parlor parties customarily triggered by society weddings, such as the 1834 union of Charles Augustus Heckscher with the daughter of John G. Coster, which dismayed even Hone with its costliness.

In 1833 the Knickerbockracy flirted with grand opera. Lorenzo Da Ponte, librettist of Mozart's *Don Giovanni*, had introduced the masterpiece to New York in the mid-

1820s, arranging a staging of it thirty-nine years after its world premiere. (Da Ponte translated his libretto into English and sold copies in the lobby.) Opera had not proved a social success, however, which the dogged Da Ponte put down to the absence of a proper theater. He therefore convinced a group of patricians to subscribe $150,000 and construct the Italian Opera House, the first building in the United States designed exclusively for that purpose. But its multicolumned, Greek-white exterior and sumptuous, gas-lit interior drew but a few hundred regular attendees. The first season ran a deficit; the second was a terminal disaster. New York simply lacked the social and cultural structures—state subsidies, aristocratic patronage—that underlay Europe's operatic system. Its burghers were prepared to consume culture as aristocrats did, but not to underwrite it as aristocrats were expected to do. Besides, the whole business still seemed a bit culturally rich for Knickerbocker blood. No matter how much they envied European elites their prestigious cultural emblems, Knickerbockers were not yet prepared to emulate them. The New York Opera Company was liquidated, its palace sold off.

Pleasure gardens were more the local style, and here too exclusiveness was key to success. After 1830 the upper classes deserted the déclassé Vauxhall and turned to William Niblo's new concern, established in 1828 at the northeast corner of Broadway and Prince. Niblo's Garden surpassed all others in elegance and respectability, its status sustained by high entrance fees, expensive food, and urbane entertainments. Its only competitor for posh patronage was Contoit's New York Garden, across from the Park, a cozy and quiet resort for wealthy and well-bred ladies and unchaperoned genteel couples. Waiters in white jackets and aprons dispensed lemonade, pound cake, and vanilla,

Broadway, etching by Thomas Horner, 1836. This view, looking north from Canal Street, captures the fast pace of Manhattan's principal artery during the 1830s boom. Niblo's Garden can be glimpsed in the distance, on the corner of Broadway and Prince Street. (Eno Collection. Miriam and Ira D. Wallach Division of Art, Prints and Photographs. The New York Public Library. Astor, Lenox and Tilden Foundations)

lemon, or strawberry ice cream of a Sunday afternoon, and from sundown to midnight it was illuminated by colored whale-oil lamps on stanchions and branches of trees.

From the pleasure gardens to the blooming new gentry preserves, from Vanderbilt's mansion to the rising village of Harlem, from one side of the harbor to the other, the sound of hammers and saws was everywhere as the rail and realty boom shifted into hyperdrive. But the feverish "good times," hailed so exuberantly by those who under-wrote the construction and investment boom, were experienced quite differently by many other New Yorkers.

35

Filth, Fever, Water, Fire

The 1830s boom improved living conditions for many working people, notably the two-fifths of the city's artisans who worked in the building trades, erecting the thousand-plus structures going up each year. The street contractors, stonecutters, and yard owners who paved, curbed, and guttered the city's roadways, as well as many of the cartmen who hauled commodities over them, could aspire to the comfortable housing going up above Houston and below 14th Street. Some entrepreneurial contractors, especially those who invested in land, rocketed to the ranks of the wealthy.

But the majority of the working class saw their living standards deteriorate, partly because of boom-fostered inflation—especially the rapidly rising rents exacted by those the City Inspector (in 1835) called "mercenary landlords"—but primarily because constructing housing for poor people wasn't profitable. Some speculative developers did erect three-story brick structures, partition each floor into four rooms, and rent out each of six two-room "apartments" to one or more families. In 1833 industrialist James Allaire raised Manhattan's first "tenement" house on Water Street near his foundry: a four-story, sixty-foot-deep, barracks-style building for his workforce.

On the whole, however, speculative builders—especially those operating on thin credit margins—had little incentive to house the poor. Nor did established landlords have reason to replace their rundown, two-story, brick-fronted wooden houses with better structures. Given the tremendous housing shortage and most workers' continued need to live within walking distance of their jobsites, landlords harvested tremendous rents just by packing people into preexisting buildings. Indeed, the more they reduced maintenance and let their properties deteriorate, the more the city reduced their tax assessments, thus boosting their profits.

As ever more people crammed into ever more dilapidated quarters, the consequences of crowding became blatantly apparent—to both eye and nose. New York, it
was widely agreed, was the filthiest urban center in the United States; Boston and
Philadelphia gleamed by comparison. This dubious distinction, ultimately rooted in the
perverse dynamics of the housing market's response to immigration, was exacerbated
by the city government's hands-off approach to the increasing production of garbage.

Since the turn of the century the Common Council had had ample authority from
the state to oversee sanitary conditions, but the aldermen had made infrequent or
incompetent use of their power. Municipal collecting remained lackadaisical at best.
Great heaps of mud, garbage, and animal excrement piled up in the streets, forming a
stinking mash labeled "Corporation Pudding" by a disgusted citizenry. To this base
were added the noxious by-products of slaughterhouses, tanneries, dyers, distilleries,
glue works, bone boilers, and stables, which had once been banished to the periphery
but had now been overtaken by rapid expansion and were back in town. Roving herds of
scavenging pigs made some inroads on the resulting accumulation, but what goes in
must come out, and the porkers added their own contributions to the vile stew.

So did humans, albeit more indirectly. Excrement was still stored in privy-vaults—
temporary holding bins placed beneath backyard outhouses. An 1823 city ordinance had
required they be made of stone, be sunk at least five feet deep, and pass city inspection.
In practice, brick or wood remained common, many were shallowly positioned, and
exemptions were liberally granted. But no matter how well or ill they were made, the
city's privies were not prepared for the torrent of shit that now descended on them,
courtesy of a proliferating population. One (admittedly notorious) building between
Christopher and Grove housed forty-one families, all of whom shared one indescrib-
ably disgusting privy, but the routine state of affairs was bad enough. When porous
vaults were situated higher than adjoining basements, their contents oozed downward
into the living quarters of invariably poorer neighbors. And when backed-up privies
overflowed, which was often, or when storms produced local flooding, human effluvia
was swept into the streets, where it mingled with the rest of the awful offal.

Privies were emptied periodically by "necessary tubmen"—one of the few jobs
reserved exclusively for blacks. Hired by the city, they were mandated to carry their
loads in closed carts, in dead of night or early morn, though this hardly mitigated their
impact. In stifling summer months New Yorkers slept with their windows open, and the
stench from passing "night carts" was powerful enough to wake the most somnolent.
Also, to brace themselves for their revolting labors, some tubmen fortified themselves
with strong liquor, and their consequently raucous behavior generated additional complaints, particularly in working-class neighborhoods.

Their routes run, the tubmen either laid their burdens down in landfill areas,
dumped them directly into the rivers (where they quickly coated the docks with slime),
or delivered them to fertilizer dealers who mixed them with sawdust and spent charcoal,
producing a light manure they sold to farmers. The one thing tubmen were *not* allowed
to do with human waste was put it in the sewers.

Sewers were for water, not garbage of any description, and had been since drains
were first built in Manhattan in 1676. The first sewers had been open trenches for carrying off storm water from low-lying areas and preventing hazardous accumulations. By
1800 such trenches were common; made of stone, brick, cement, or planks, they ran
down the center or along the sides of streets. They were built wide enough to permit

access for cleaning, but the breadth made them slow running, stagnant, and foul; to avoid decomposition by the sun, some were dug six feet deep, or below low-water mark. The covered-over sewer under Canal Street, in the absence of air traps, continued to reek on warm days, and the resulting decline in property values was long remembered.

In 1819 the Common Council had explicitly prohibited the use of sewers to carry off fecal matter. It further required installation of grates at the junction of common sewers with household drains, which allowed flood water in and kept solid wastes out. Dr. Hosack argued against this, proposing instead adoption of water closets connected to sewers that would then convey "every species of filth" to the rivers. He admitted, however, that the requisite flushing process would depend on New York's obtaining a far more abundant source of water than currently available.

The city's water was not only scarce, but brackish, and it was fast becoming deadly. In 1829 researchers from the Lyceum of Natural History estimated that in every twenty-four hours New Yorkers deposited over one hundred tons of excrement into the alluvium, from whence, accompanied by other soluble waste, it percolated down to the water table. In the 1830s, due to the increase in privies and to seepage from old graveyards, downtown wells were bringing up a tainted brew.

With pure water now a scarce commodity, it became allocated according to marketplace rules, by ability to pay. The poor continued to use city wells, including the ancient "tea water pump." Artisans bought water, at a penny a gallon, from enterprising carters who carried hogsheads of "pure" country springwater around the city; it too was often polluted. Even the well-to-do had problems, if they relied on Aaron Burr's old gambit, the Manhattan Company. The firm expanded its skimpy service at a sludge-like pace, just enough to keep its banking privileges from being revoked. As the city moved north, the Manhattan's waterworks grew more remote from more people (the company didn't operate above Grand Street). By the end of the War of 1812, its scant twenty-three miles of wooden pipes delivered perfunctory service to its select (and increasingly furious) clientele. Municipal authorities, albeit reluctant to take on one of the city's leading bondholders, came around slowly to the notion that water was a public good, which should be publicly produced.

In 1821 Mayor Allen again proposed diverting the Bronx River into a municipal reservoir. In 1825 the state chartered a private company to bring water down from Westchester, but nothing much was done until 1829, when the city built its own reservoir. A huge cast-iron tank—forty-three feet in diameter, twenty feet high, with a capacity of 305,422 gallons—was set atop an octagonal stone tower twenty-seven feet high, at the corner of the Bowery and 13th Street. Water was carried from here south to the city by iron pipes, one running down Broadway to Canal, the other down the Bowery to Catherine.

Farther than this the city would not go. For the affluent and powerful, the absence of abundant fresh water remained an annoyance, not a crisis. But in the slums, the consequences of pollution, squalor, and crowding were about to become lethal.

CHOLERA

In 1832 the cholera roared into town. New Yorkers had seen it coming. They had read in their papers of its devastating march across Asia and the trade routes to Europe, reaching Poland, then France, then England. City authorities knew the plague might well ride the sea lanes to the Hudson, but did next to nothing with this foreknowledge.

New York's old Board of Health certainly had authority to act. Yet it had been lulled into quiescence in the ten years since the yellow fever epidemic of 1822. Its approach to disease prevention, moreover, now concentrated almost exclusively on quarantining ships from dangerous southern waters. Even there, it was under constant pressure not to render too hasty a diagnosis that would cut off the flow of trade and profit. The board, one critic noted caustically, was "more afraid of the merchants than of lying."

As spring turned to summer, the corporation's inactivity spurred men of medicine to demand action. The Medical Society, which represented two-thirds of the city's licensed physicians, urged immediate cleaning of streets, yards, and vacant lots, disinfection of privies and cesspools with quicklime, and establishment of a network of emergency hospitals. The city administration responded with an apathy partly rooted in the conviction—widely shared, but advanced most ardently by evangelical clergymen—that the plague, should it come, would pass over the virtuous parts of town and descend, like God's wrath, on its sin-infested quarters. Ministers told the pious that the path of righteousness was the road to health. Temperance activists plastered Manhattan's walls with notices like QUIT DRAM DRINKING IF YOU WOULD NOT HAVE THE CHOLERA. (There was nothing like the possibility of suffering and death for bringing sinners to their knees, wrote Lewis Tappan, with something approaching glee.)

Physicians' belief in "predisposing causes" also suggested the likeliest victims would be those who, through indulgence in vice, intemperance, and filthy living habits, had weakened and predisposed themselves to the disease. Science and religion thus sailed on parallel courses, with their essential interconnections drawn out most clearly by Sylvester Graham, who lectured that liquor, impure foods, and sexual dissipation undermined the body's ability to resist the cholera. Bon vivants ridiculed the Grahamites and advised citizens to fortify themselves with a hearty diet of meat, spices, and brandy.

On June 15 the Albany steamboat brought word that the cholera had forded the Atlantic, wreaking havoc in Quebec and Montreal. By June 18 it was reported at Ogdensburg. Mayor Walter Bowne proclaimed a severe quarantine. No ship was to approach closer than three hundred yards to the city, no land-based vehicle to come within a mile and a half. The *Courier and Enquirer* printed a cholera extra of ten thousand copies. Apothecaries posted handbills advertising opium, camphor, and laudanum. On June 20 a large group of clergy and prominent laymen met at the American Bible Society and called for a day of fasting and prayer. They were seconded by the Common Council, but workingmen's advocate and freethinking editor George Henry Evans urged his readers to ignore the recommendation as an "insidious and dangerous encroachment" on the separation of church and state.

Late Monday night, June 26, an Irish immigrant named Fitzgerald came home violently ill; he recovered, only to have two of his children die after being struck by the identical agonizing stomach cramps. The city fathers pressured the Board of Health into declaring them the victims of nothing worse than diarrhea, a common summer complaint. But many physicians had seen and diagnosed Asiatic cholera, and beneath the blanket of official silence, word spread fast.

Methodists began prayer meetings each morning. June 29, the day of fasting and humiliation, was observed in scores of churches. The Medical Society, fed up with the dilatory Board of Health, stated publicly on July 2 that cholera had struck nine people and that only one had survived. John Pintard attacked this "impertinent interference" with the constituted authorities and asked if the doctors knew the disaster their announcement would wreak on the city's business.

On July 3 Leggett reported in the *Evening Post* that a great exodus had begun. For all the certainty about their moral and physiological invulnerability, the city's comfortable classes weren't about to stake their lives on it. The roads, Leggett noted, were lined with "well-filled stage coaches, livery coaches, private vehicles and equestrians, all panic struck, fleeing from the city, as we may suppose the inhabitants of Pompeii or Reggio fled from those devoted places, when the red lava showered down upon their houses." Oceans of pedestrians trudged outward with packs on backs. Steamboats bore refugees up the Hudson, among them Sam Ruggles and his family—he would correspond with his Gramercy Park contractor from Newburgh—generating substantial profits for Commodore Vanderbilt. Every farmhouse and country home within a thirty-mile radius was soon filled with lodgers. By the end of the first week in July, almost all who could afford to flee had fled; by the *Post*'s estimate of August 6, that figure eventually reached 100,000, roughly half the population.

Of the other half, 3,513 died, most of them horribly, the lucky ones swiftly. The young editor Henry Dana Ward wrote his parents that some "are taken like lightning from the midst of their families and daily work." One paper reported smugly that a prostitute who had been adorning herself before her glass at one was in a hearse by half past three.

Cartloads of coffins rumbled through the streets but couldn't keep up with demand. One day Finney noticed five hearses drawn up at five different houses, all at the same time, all within sight of his door. In other neighborhoods, dead bodies lay unburied in the gutters. At the potters' field, putrefying corpses lay in shallow pits, the prey of rats.

As the city reeled, some sought to calm hysteria among the better-off still in town or camped nearby, by noting that, as predicted, the plague was mainly scything the poor. John Pintard, observing that the plague was "almost exclusively confined to the lower classes of intemperate dissolute & filthy people huddled together like swine in their polluted habitations," drew the terrible conclusion that the sooner this "scum of the city" was dispatched, the sooner the fever, deprived of fodder, would pass. Most New Yorkers who stayed in town, however, sprang into action in an effort to succor or rescue plague victims, sinners or no. The Board of Health assumed governmental functions. Streets, lots, cellars, and docks were cleaned of a decade's accumulation of filth and strewn with lime. The clothes and bedding of the sick were taken out and burned, the fumes filling the air.

With thousands of wage-earners thrown out of work by the abrupt cessation of the city's business, private citizens and churches established a Committee of the Benevolent. A July 16 meeting at the Merchants' Exchange collected about seventeen hundred dollars for poor relief; thousands more dollars flowed from prominent merchants. The committee divided into fifteen subcommittees, one for each ward. These groups paid local residents for "cleansing and purifying their own dwellings," established soup kitchens, and distributed food and clothing. This was hands-on charity. Gentlemen searched out "the abode of poverty, filth, and disease" and administered "personally to the wants of the wretched inmates" while "not omitting to warn the wicked of their evil ways, and point them to the Great Physician of the Soul."

1	47 Greenwich		1	do corner Greenwich,	dead
1	13 Leonard		1	115 Orange,	dead
1	38 1-2 Thomas		1	do	dead
1	46 do		1	do	con
1	———	dead	1	95 Sherriff,	dead
1	Laurens		1	do	
1	417 Greenwich		1	———,	
1	13 Leonard	dead	1	156 Leonard,	
1	39 1-2 Thomas		1	81 Mulberry,	dead
	46 do		1	do	
1	———	dead	1	86 do	
1	Laurens, between Broome and Spring,	dead	1	85 do	
1	Hudson and Perry		1	170 Hester, convalescent	
1	22 James	dead	1	79 Mulberry, collapse	
1	17 Bank	dead	1	93 Orange, collapse	
1	8th Avenue & 20th st.	dead	1	58 do convalescent	
1	123 Delancey	dead	1	White & Elm	dead
1	318 Washington	dead	1	68 Orange	
1	Foot of Christopher	dead	1	95 Firrst	
1	Spring	dead	1	79 Mulberry	
1	53 Leonard	collapse	1	215 Orange	
1	do	Convalescent	1	76 Mulberry	
1	do	will not recover	1	156 Leonard	
1	———	dead	1	46 Elm	dead
1	147 Christie	convalescent	1	80 Duane	Convalescent
1	17 Eldridge		1	27 Cross	Recovered
1	87 Norfolk,		1	19 do	
1	217 Wooster,	dead	1	39 Orange,	
1	8 Republican Alley,	dead	1	61 do	
1	51 Broome,		1	7 do	
1	——— Chatham,		1	56 do	dead
1	119 Mulberry,		1	11 Little Water,	
1	112 do		1	21 Orange,	
1	29 Burton,	con,	1	27 Mulberry	
1	53 Grove,	con.	1	83 Duane	
1	115 Charles,	con.	1	21 Augustus	dead
			2	21 Augustus	

As reported in this daily tally of its victims, the cholera epidemic raged through the streets of the Five Points and other crowded downtown districts with particular severity. (© Museum of the City of New York)

For some, the poor swam into focus for the first time. At the height of the epidemic Mrs. P. Roosevelt noted that while ordinarily "no one notices the poor" who are "frequently are to be found lying in the streets," now they were being "picked up and taken to the hospitals." "Only on occasions such as this," she reflected, "is the true extent of the misery of the City known."

Despite earnest solicitations by the Board of Health, the trustees of the privately run New York Hospital (who included Philip Hone and James DePeyster) flatly refused to accept cholera patients. The brunt of the onslaught therefore fell on Bellevue, the public institution. By July 7 it had already admitted 555, of whom 334 would die by August 8. Soon the place was swamped with the quick and dead alike. Patients lay on the floors crying for water. There were often forty bodies at once in the deadhouse, as the morgue was known. Before it was over, Bellevue would admit two thousand people, over a sixth of all victims, and tally six hundred deaths.

To supplement its work, the Board of Health established five cholera hospitals around the city—in the Hall of Records, a school, an old bank, an abandoned workshed, and a workshop at Corlear's Hook (the arrival of the latter precipitating a mass exodus of workers from adjoining shipyards). Most poor people forcibly blocked efforts to remove their sick to these hospitals, regarding them as charnel houses run by incompetents. Doctors and city officials who insisted were attacked and brutally beaten.

Following precedents from earlier battles against yellow fever, the authorities set out to disperse the deadly concentrations in the slums. A Committee to Provide Suitable Accommodations for the Destitute Poor evacuated tenants, over the protests of anguished landlords. It moved them to buildings and shanties around town (including one at 10th Street and Avenue C for "colored people in health"), which they leased from other landlords, often at extortionate rents. It then arranged with the commissioners of the almshouse to supply food, medicines, and clothing. The Court of General Sessions discharged all prisoners convicted of misdemeanors and removed felons from the penitentiary and Bridewell to temporary shelter at Blackwell's Island.

Many churches closed down, especially the wealthier ones whose flocks had fled (St. George's shut for almost a month), but many clergy and religious stayed and did heroic work. The Catholic Church won highest praise, with the Sisters of Charity and Father Varela singled out. (It was said that Varela "lived in the hospitals.") The Episcopal Mission Society expanded its outdoor relief efforts. Evangelist Finney stayed at his post and caught the disease; he survived but was incapacitated for months.

By the third week in July, with the epidemic at its height, great swathes of the city were deathly silent, their streets deserted. Then it ended. Moving on almost as rapidly as it had blown in, the cholera continued its journey along the trade routes, through the Erie Canal towns of western New York, down the Ohio Canal to the Ohio and Mississippi rivers, tracing the pathways of the market economy with a finger of death.

In August the number of new cases began a steady decline. By the second half of the month, refugees began to trickle back. On August 29 medical authorities pronounced the city safe. Pintard was thrilled at the commercial resurrection. All was "life & bustle," he rejoiced, with stores all open, sidewalks lined with bales and boxes, streets crowded with carts, and "clerks busy in making out Bills." Beneath his notice, hundreds of beggars, vast numbers of them newly orphaned children, plied the streets. Benevolent ladies started up a Brooklyn Orphan Asylum to deal with the youthful survivors.

Stocktaking in the aftermath generally followed the lines of prior opinion. The Rev. Gardiner Spring saw in the pestilence "the hand of God," with His sanitary and salutary purpose apparently having been "to drain off the filth and scum which contaminate and defile human society." Sabbatarians declared the disease "owing to vices which a proper regard to the Sabbath would check more effectually than anything else." Others blamed drink and slovenliness, including the governor of New York, who opined that "an infinitely wise and just God has seen fit to employ pestilence as one means of scourging the human race for their sins, and it seems to be an appropriate one for the sins of uncleanliness and intemperance."

The immigrant poor, who had fared worst, came in for the greatest opprobrium. The Board of Health reported that "the low Irish suffered the most, being exceedingly dirty in their habits, much addicted to intemperance and crowded together into the worst portions of the city." They were poor—due, of course, to their own idleness and fondness for drink—and poverty was the "natural parent of disease." Philip Hone brought a more succinctly brutal indictment: "They have brought the cholera this year, and they will always bring wretchedness and want."

Radicals insisted cholera was the result not of divine intervention but of human injustice. "It may be heretical," said George Henry Evans, "but we firmly believe that the cholera so far from being a scourge of the Almighty is a scourge which mankind have brought upon themselves by their own bad arrangements which produce poverty among many, while abundance is in existence for all." Certainly there was a correlation between poverty and mortality. But poverty was not a moral failing, Evans wrote that August in the *Workingman's Advocate*, it was "occasioned by unjust remuneration of labor." He urged New Yorkers to impose a graduated income tax that would secure funds from the wealthy to make recurrence of the disease impossible. Other radicals called on the city to create a park at Corlear's Hook for working people, akin to facilities it was helping develop at Washington, Gramercy, and Union Squares; this was vetoed as too costly and unlikely to generate significant new tax revenues.

WATER

On one thing, there was general agreement: New York City needed fresh, clean water. Even those who saw divine intervention at work didn't contest physicians and sanitarians like William MacNeven and John Griscom who pointed to the polluted drinking supply and the poisonous vapors rising from the streets as major contributors to the plague.

In October 1832 the Common Council appropriated a thousand dollars for an inquiry into how to fetch water to New York. A December report concluded that the Croton River in upper Westchester County was the best source for an "inexhaustible" supply. In 1833, at the Common Council's behest, the legislature authorized creation of the New York State Water Commission, headed by former mayor Stephen Allen, to supervise the city's ongoing investigations. Surveyors declared the Croton feasible, but the cost of building an aqueduct was pegged at five million dollars, an alarming estimate that abruptly halted proceedings.

Opposition to the enormous expense might have postponed or even precluded the project, but for the existence of *another* proaqueduct lobby. This coalition of landowners, speculative developers, banks and insurance companies feared a different urban scourge—fire. Fire threatened to undermine the real estate boom of which they were primary beneficiaries. Fires had been decimating rich areas, not just poor ones, and with increasing frequency in the thirties. The year 1834 had been a terrible one for property owners in the dry-goods district, the worst to date, and fire insurance companies had been hit with claims approaching a million dollars. Afflicted businessmen joined the campaign for new municipal initiatives, arguing that public costs were justified by private savings.

New York's fire prevention efforts to date had concentrated on extending the "fire limits," the part of the city where special building codes regulated the material and design of private and commercial structures. In 1812 the fire limits covered Manhattan south of Chambers Street. In 1815 they were extended to a line crossing the island just above Washington Square. In 1833 they jumped north to Second Street, and the following year, to 14th Street.

The city also abandoned reliance on church sextons to sound the alarm in case of fire, shifting to purpose-built bell towers, with the number of clangs indicating in which of five fire districts a blaze had been reported. Because these wooden stanchions too often fell prey to flames themselves, in April 1835 officials placed a twenty-four hour sentinel in the cupola of City Hall to clang a large, newly installed fire bell and hang a light in the direction of any perceived blaze.

To enhance the water-for-fire supply the Common Council had built a stopgap network of some forty cisterns, usually beside a church, to catch rainwater (at times convicts were set to filling them). In the event of a conflagration, fire engines were dragged to the nearest cistern, or if it was dry (as was often the case, given low levels of rainfall), firemen would link their machines in a chain to the nearest river. Neither method, however, could generate enough pressure to reach the upper levels of newer, taller buildings. The 13th Street Reservoir, once connected to hydrants, proved capable of lofting water to the roofs of most three-story houses, even without engines. The number of hydrants grew rapidly, accompanied by street boxes containing coiled hemp hoses, and some predicted that eventually there would be a hydrant on every block, making engines obsolete. However, one big tank could not handle simultaneous blazes nor drive water to the tops of the four-to-five-story warehouses going up downtown.

Sam Ruggles was deeply concerned—doubly so because he, like many large property owners, including Mayor Cornelius Lawrence, held substantial shares in fire insurance companies. Insurance company directors, moreover, were heavily represented on the Common Council and on the New York State Water Commission, and together with the landed interests they formed a formidable lobby. Additional support came from the manufacturing and service sectors. Industrialists needed water. The New-York Gas-Light Company's well was drying up. Chemical works, sugar houses, brewhouses, distilleries, tanners, dyers, and soap makers: all faced dwindling liquid resources. Many businesses also relied on steam engines—there were sixty of them around town in 1834—and taverns, hotels, livery stables, and cake shops were all increasingly parched.

The water lobby was spurred on by another outbreak of cholera in 1834, which drove the number of reported deaths up 50 percent over that of 1833, in sharp and sorry contrast to Philadelphia's success in curtailing the disease, widely credited to a vigorous street-washing campaign. The *Sun* pronounced acquisition of an aqueduct to be a matter of "our city's honor and our city's pride." The penny presses' blanket rivals, including the *New York Commercial Advertiser*, joined them in calling for Croton water.

The conjoint pressure burst through remaining opposition, now chiefly from the Manhattan Company and from uptown property owners who feared weakened demand for their real estate if water came to the lower wards. In February 1835 the Common Council, citing both health and safety crises, finally wrested the water supply from Burr's progeny. The aldermen authorized a reinvestigation of the Croton project and its submission to a popular referendum. In preparation for the April 1835 vote, Ruggles and his colleagues paid the cost of printing pro-Croton tickets and of hiring poll watchers. When the results were in, 17,330 backed the idea, 5,963 opposed it. Support was highest in the elite First Ward, resistance strongest in the poorer districts, where many believed they would be priced out of access. By July 1835 preconstruction surveys were underway.

New York had taken decisive steps toward revolutionizing its water supply. But action came too late to prevent or contain the greatest fire in the city's entire history, one of the most destructive anywhere since London had been ravaged 169 years earlier.

FIRE

On the frigid evening of December 16, 1835, high winds pummeled downtown Manhattan. The temperature kept plunging; before the night was over, it would bottom out at seventeen degrees below zero. Just before nine P.M., as Watchman Hayes passed the corner of Exchange and Pearl streets, he smelled smoke and summoned other watchmen. They quickly discovered the source in a five-story warehouse. (Subsequent investigation "incontrovertibly established" that stove coals had ignited gas escaping from a broken line.) Forcing open the door, they found the interior all aflame. They watched helplessly as the inferno blew through the roof and jumped across the narrow and crooked streets, whipped by the wind. Within fifteen minutes, fully fifty of the area's tightly packed buildings were ablaze.

The watchmen spread the alarm. The new City Hall sentinel clanged his bell. The jail next door took up the pealing. Church belfries chimed in.

The firemen who now crawled out of their beds, exhausted from fighting two bad fires the night before, were members of a shorthanded and demoralized department. The cholera epidemics had taken a heavy toll on their ranks, which in any event had not kept pace with the growth of population. The city had more than doubled in size since 1823, but the number of volunteers in 1835 stood at fifteen hundred, up only 285 over the same period. Chief Engineer James Gulick, the six-foot-two idol of the department, had cut down on slugfests between companies for control of hydrants, but feuds still festered. Some of the firemen's troubles were of their own making. The manly volunteers stubbornly insisted on dragging their hand-operated engines to the scene, rather than permitting horses to be used, and had no tolerance whatever for the new steam fire engines London had deployed since 1829.

Even had they been in peak condition, the firemen faced an impossible task. By midnight the freezing winds had lashed the fire to an awesome and unmanageable ferocity; many thought the last days of Pompeii the only fitting comparison. The sky was lit so brightly the glow could be seen in Poughkeepsie, New Haven, and Philadelphia, where firemen turned out thinking their suburbs were aflame. Help came from near and far. Brooklyn sent company after company by ferry. A locomotive was rushed from Jersey City to Newark and returned with a train of flatcars loaded with fire engines. One company came all the way from Philadelphia.

As the flames roared down to Water Street—jumping "like flashes of lightning," Philip Hone recalled later—arriving volunteers discovered that all the wells, cisterns, and hydrants were frozen solid. Gulick sent a dozen engines to the East River. It was frozen too. Hook-and-ladder men took their axes, ran to the ends of the piers, chopped holes in the ice, dragged an engine over, rigged up a series of machines along Coenties Slip and up Water Street—only to discover that water froze in the hose. By jumping up and down on the lines to break the ice clots and pouring alcohol into the engine pumps, they worked up some feeble streams, only to have the wind hammer the water back in their faces. Some, reduced to "the apathy of despair," stood about helplessly, pouring brandy into their boots to keep their feet from freezing. Others turned to salvage operations, dragging tons of silks, satins, laces, and shawls out of warehouses. One phalanx piled a thirty-foot-high mountain of goods in the center of Hanover Square, only to watch it vanish in flames that vaulted out from the warehouse of Peter Remsen and Company. Later, there were bitter complaints about the predatory behavior of cartmen

View of the Great Fire in New York, December 16 & 17, 1835, aquatint by Nicolino Calyo, 1836. All that remained of the Merchant's Exchange was the burned-out shell on the left. (© Collection of The New-York Historical Society)

who charged exorbitant rates for moving possessions away from flames and refused to serve any but the wealthy.

The fire headed north, seizing the marble and supposedly fireproof Merchants' Exchange. Heroic rescuers saved the trading records charting the speculative movements underway at the New York Stock & Exchange Board. But efforts to salvage the statue of Alexander Hamilton failed, and the would-be recovery men just escaped being buried in the collapse of the great sixty-foot cupola.

Around four A.M. the Tontine Coffee House went up. Foreman Mills, of Eagle Engine No. 13, realized that if the flames crossed Wall Street the upper half of the city would go. Two buildings were blown up to block the fire's passage by depriving it of fuel. The gambit worked and, with Mayor Lawrence's permission, was deployed more vigorously. Lawrence dispatched Charles King, editor of the *New York American,* to the Navy Yard for officers and sailors to do the demolitions and for the necessary gunpowder, but these supplies proved inadequate. While Mayor Lawrence and Colonel Hamilton raced from grocery to grocery scraping together portions of powder, and others ransacked the arsenal tearing open cartridges, King and a boatload of marines fought their way through the ice-obstructed river to the Red Hook Point powder house and ferried back enough twenty-five pound kegs to prevent the inferno from crossing Coenties Slip.

By morning the fire, though balked, raged uncontrollably. Its domain—from Maiden Lane to Coenties Slip, from William Street to the East River—was a thirteen-acre ocean of burning waves. As if alive and determined to break out, it forayed out into the river, from which boats had been hastily removed: gallons of blazing turpentine cascaded down the shore and rolled across the ice, setting a few vessels on fire. The conflagration took another night and day to burn itself out. Even then, thick black clouds spewed into the winter sky. It would not be completely quenched for two weeks.

Troops were brought in the first night to control looting. Sentinels stood guard for days amid ruins littered with charred merchandise: scorched silks, laces, prints, a "mountain of coffee" at the corner of Old Slip and South Street. The night of the fire, over ninety people were seized in the act of carrying away property; the next day, two hundred more were arrested. Hone ranted to his diary about "the miserable wretches who prowled about the ruins, and became beastly drunk on the champagne and other wines and liquors with which the streets and wharves were lined." Worse, they "seemed to exult in the misfortune, and such expressions were heard as 'This will make the aristocracy haul in their horns!'"

In the aftermath, voracious demands for information spurred the new penny press to innovative heights. The *Sun* published a morning edition of twenty-three thousand and an "extra" of thirty thousand, for a record-shattering one-day circulation of fifty-three thousand. The *Herald*, in its December 21 issue, used illustrations for the first time: one two-column woodcut showed the remains of the Merchant's Exchange; another mapped the area of destruction. Nathaniel Currier, a twenty-two-year-old lithographer from Massachusetts who had set up shop on Nassau Street the previous year, leapt to prominence with his prints of the fire; one of them inspired a scene in Harrington's New Grand Moving Diorama, which opened at the American Museum in 1836.

In succeeding days, the press and others counted costs. Eighty buildings had burned on Front Street alone, 674 in all. Almost every structure south of Wall and east of Broad was to some degree a casualty. Estimates of losses in buildings and merchandise ranged from eighteen to twenty-six million dollars, more than three times the cost of the Erie Canal. Twenty-three of the city's twenty-six fire insurance companies went bankrupt. Four thousand clerks were temporarily thrown out of work, along with thousands of cartmen and porters.

The most telling statistics, however, were these: only two people died in the fire—a function of the commercial district's almost complete lack of residential housing. And within a year, five hundred new buildings had been built, the area entirely restored, indeed dramatically improved—testimony to the underlying strength of the mercantile economy and the tremendous momentum of the real estate boom.

PHOENIX

On December 19, less than two weeks after the fire, city officials, bankers, brokers, manufacturers, and merchants met to map the course of recovery. A committee of 125 citizens—"all the best and most influential men in the city," said Hone—turned to the tasks of thanking neighbors (Philadelphia, Brooklyn, Newark), providing emergency relief, investigating the fire, and applying for aid from the federal, state, and city governments.

Former treasury secretary Albert Gallatin and Mayor Lawrence went to Washington, where Lawrence argued that the national government should consider itself as "a large capitalist, with an overflowing treasury . . . whose duty it is to promote the welfare and prosperity of the people." Congress kept its treasure to itself, though it did authorize the Treasury to remit duties already paid on imports newly destroyed and to extend the time importers had to pay duties on goods that survived.

Philip Hone's delegation fared better in Albany. In January 1835 the state authorized the city to float a loan of up to six million dollars, a new precedent for disaster relief. Municipal authorities borrowed a million, then provided loans at 5 percent, increasing the credit available in the city. The Canal Commission doubled this line of credit by shifting another million of its funds to the city's banks, thus allowing them to accommodate strapped customers and forestall mercantile failures.

In the meantime, business went on virtually uninterrupted. The stock exchange resumed trading after four days. Over six hundred dislodged firms set up operations in temporary accommodations nearby, driving rental prices in lower Manhattan up by 100 to 150 percent almost overnight. That instant boomlet triggered a far bigger one. The area's businesses had long been trying to insert their nineteenth-century institutions into seventeenth-century streets by widening them one at a time, at great expense. The calamity, by demolishing the old structures, opened the way to transform crooked alleys into straight, broad, gas-lit thoroughfares. City officials announced plans to render "the entire surface of that section much cleaner, drier and more eligible for the transaction of business than it has heretofore been."

This promise, coupled with the bid-up of prices by dislocated firms, sent land values soaring. Within a month, Hone noted, lots in the "burnt district" were selling "at most enormous prices, greater than they would have brought before the fire, when covered with valuable buildings." One parcel of lots purchased earlier in the century for ninety-three thousand dollars now yielded $765,000 at auction.

Postfire reconstruction started almost instantly, with Arthur Tappan first off the mark. At dawn the day after, he told his clerks: "We must rebuild immediately." One went to fetch an architect; the rest fitted up temporary quarters. At noon the *Journal of Commerce* carried a notice announcing the store was open for business as usual, "by the blessings of God," and by midafternoon workmen began clearing the still warm rubble.

In short order, the new-style high-rise, Greek Revival granite warehouses were going up everywhere, with iron shutters and independent foot-thick brick walls as fire protection. Even buildings still standing were transformed; masons knocked out the old brick and brownstone ground floors and hoisted stylish granite piers into place. Block after block took on a dignified new look. The Delmonicos, whose establishment had been wiped out, bought a triangular plot at the junction of Beaver, William, and South William (formerly Mill) streets. Work started in August 1836 on a three-and-a-half-story brick-and-brownstone structure with marble trim; in a nicely defiant touch, the marble porch pillars were brought from Pompeii. By December the carpets and gas fixtures were being fitted into the luxurious first- and second-story saloons—of an "appearance far surpassing anything of the kind in the city"—and the third floor had facilities for private dining, evoking Parisian splendor, as did the immense wine vaults for sixteen thousand bottles.

Grandest of all was the new Merchants' Exchange. Within a week of the fire, the Merchants' Exchange Company solicited plans, choosing an aggressive Greek Revival design by Isaiah Rogers, with a twelve-columned Corinthian colonnade. A million dollars in subscriptions was raised by February 1836. By April construction was underway on the site of its predecessor, expanded to cover an entire block. Built of Massachusetts granite—not a sliver of wood was used in constructing the floor—it featured an enormous central hall surmounted by a vast saucer dome eighty feet in diameter. When it opened for business five years later, it would include offices for insurance companies, bankers, brokers, the Chamber of Commerce, and, later, the New York Stock and Exchange Board, as well as a reading room stocked with papers from every state in the union and countries overseas, together with a foreign letter office. It was frequently compared to the Paris Bourse.

All along Wall Street, banks and insurance companies began demolishing their former residences—those red brick facades, fanlight doorways, and dormer windows that now seemed so old fashioned—and erecting stone-front porticoed Doric temples. Within a few years, the street boasted perhaps the greatest concentration of classical columns built since the fall of Rome. By the anniversary of the catastrophe, Hone observed, "fine and commodious stores, much improved in their appearance and construction" nearly covered the "burnt district."

Ramifications rippled outward. The fire expelled much of the dry-goods trade from Pearl Street, making it more strictly a financial center, and many firms shifted west toward the fashionable quarter around lower Broadway. Retail shops—jewelers, watchmakers, bookstores, merchant tailors, hatters, confectioners, carpet and fancy dry-goods stores—spread northward up the thoroughfare. Broadway became a business district up to and beyond the City Hall Park area, where numerous publishers, law firms, and newspapers now clustered.

This development touched off a pell-mell flight of the wealthy. Private dwellings were turned into boardinghouses, converted into offices, or torn down to make way for warehouses and shops. A writer in the *New-York Mirror* in April 1836 reported: "It is said that in one year, there will be scarcely a private residence or boarding house below Wall Street." He added, "Ladies will, hereafter, scarcely extend their promenades further down than the Park; and what will become of the Battery, heaven only knows." Some suggested the corporation sell it off to private owners for storehouses and dockyards, though this touched off a preservationist uproar that saved the park for the present.

Hone himself was swept away in March 1836 when he sold his house at 235 Broadway, across from City Hall, to the owner of the adjacent American Hotel, who wanted an annex. Hone received sixty thousand dollars for a building he had purchased fifteen years earlier for twenty-five thousand dollars. "I have turned myself out of doors," he wrote wryly, "but $60,000 is a great deal of money."

If the new Merchants' Exchange was the symbol of the Wall Street financial district, then Astor House, a block from Hone's former residence and just across from the Park Theater, became the emblem of the expanding commercial sector. Astor had long been attuned to the fortune awaiting those who cultivated the city's entertainment and hostelry industries. In his prior ventures as landlord-impresario, including the Park Theater, Vauxhall Gardens, and the City Hotel, Astor had let others take the lead, then moved in to absorb a going concern. Now he decided to be an innovator. Even before the great fire accelerated downtown development, Astor had grasped that the area around City Hall, having been on the town's periphery for two hundred years, was emerging as New York's new civic and commercial center, with its park and churches, theaters and newspapers. By the mid-1830s, moreover, there was an enormous flow of tourists and visiting businessmen—over seventy thousand annually (nearly half the city's population of two hundred thousand). Astor would capitalize on this traffic with a mammoth luxury hotel to rival Boston's Tremont House.

When it opened in 1836 many thought the Greek Revival structure the "grandest mass" in town—not beautiful, but impressive. Five stories of Quincy granite were arranged around a central courtyard. Its 309 rooms at times housed up to eight hundred guests. Each floor offered bathing and toilet facilities—a real novelty, something even the finest mansions and elegant boardinghouses usually lacked. Astor House also featured gas lighting provided by its own plant, as well as a table d'hote eatery at which guests and city merchants could choose from among oyster pie, round of beef, roast wild duck—in all, thirty meat and fish dishes each day. Soon its main hallway was bustling with guests, the street in front was piled with luggage, and a New York institution had launched its long career.

FEVERED FINANCE

The city's economy did more than simply rebound from the triple blows of cholera, Bank War, and fire; it shifted into overdrive. Peter Cooper had hoped the great blaze—which in his opinion had been a "flagrant providential warning"—would curb the frenzied speculation on Wall Street, but in 1836 the volume of trading on the NYS&EB soared upward. Land transactions in the city set astonishing records. The value of Manhattan real estate, registered at $143 million in 1835, mounted to $233 million within twelve months. Most of this also represented speculation, Governor Marcy warned in 1836, with plots and buildings being purchased "not for the purpose of being occupied by the buyers, but to be again put in the market, and sold at still higher prices."

The surge was stoked by a tremendous expansion in the availability of credit. Money was cheap and plentiful, inspiring diligent entrepreneurs and speculative manipulators alike to expand their operations with borrowed funds. State banks, freed from Biddle's fierce scrutiny, pyramided their modest specie bases into mountains of paper credit, and across the country legislatures chartered over two hundred new banks in three years, pushing the total to over six hundred. In New York State the Bank Commission fought to slow the increase, and the legislature refused all new charter proposals in 1835. But 1836 brought a torrent of new banks, many of which quickly issued notes far beyond any reasonable ratio to their holdings of specie. The nation's specie supply was itself rising, in the form of a fortuitous glut of silver, occasioned by a rising Mexican output of the precious metal and a declining demand for it in Britain and China. Banks bulging with bullion multiplied their treasure by pumping out more paper banknotes. In addition, by 1836 the tariff and land sale revenues pouring in to the federal government had extinguished the national debt. The treasury, awash in a two-million-dollar surplus, was obliged under the new rules to turn it over to the pet banks, some of which, engorged with cash, went on a reckless lending spree. All told, the country's money supply, which had jumped from $144 million in 1831 to $172 million in 1834, climbed to $276 million in 1836.

This touched off an inflationary firestorm. The cost of living rose rapidly through 1834 and 1835, then shot up 66 percent in the first two months of 1836. Philip Hone noted in his diary: "Living in New York is exorbitantly dear, and it falls pretty hard upon persons like me, who live upon their income, and harder still upon that large and respectable class consisting of the officers and clerks of public institutions, whose support is derived from fixed salaries." Beneath the range of his troubled gaze lay the great mass of the population, upon whom the great upward leap in the cost of living wreaked far greater havoc than it did on any of the victims he'd mentioned.

Indeed the disparate ways New Yorkers experienced the inflationary spiral was characteristic of their differential experience of the boom years as a whole. For some it meant fabulous profits and pursuit of pleasure; for others, degraded work, higher prices and rents, poorer living conditions, a rigidifying class structure, and a new determination to organize in defense of a crumpling way of life.

36

The Panic
of 1837

On Sunday, June 5, 1836, handbills went up around the town. Headlined THE RICH AGAINST THE POOR! they denounced Judge Ogden Edwards, who had just acquitted Richard Robinson of the murder of Helen Jewitt, as "the tool of the Aristocracy, against the People!" A week later, a gigantic evening rally drew nearly thirty thousand workingmen—roughly one-fifth of New York's adult male population—to City Hall Park, where they berated the judge again, hanging and burning his effigy for good measure. This time, however, the huge throng was not protesting Edwards's role in acquitting Helen's killer but rather his sentencing of twenty journeyman tailors who had been found guilty of going on strike.

The tailors' trial capped an employers' effort to crush New York's fledgling labor union movement, which had been launched three years earlier by workingmen caught in the boom era's downdraft. In 1833 inflation had sent the cost of food, fuel, and rent climbing. To restore their real wages and reverse their declining control over the workplace, skilled journeymen set out to make Manhattan a union town.

In the spring of 1833 the Journeymen House Carpenters struck for higher wages. Other sweated carpenters joined them, multiplying the union's ranks fivefold. The Typographical Association of journeyman printers rallied behind the carpenters' walkout. Journeyman tailors offered support. So did stonecutters and painters.

With fraternal backing, the carpenters won. Almost immediately the allies formalized their ad hoc mutual assistance compact. Representatives of nine crafts formed the General Trades Union of the City of New York (GTU), an organization, the carpenters declared, that would stand as "one great phalanx against the common enemy of workingmen, which is *overgrown capital* supported by AVARICE."

The GTU made clear, in the preamble to its constitution, that an irreparable breach had opened up between masters and journeymen—former partners in the

Trades—to the latter's detriment. "We the JOURNEYMAN ARTISANS and MECHANICS of the City of New York," the document proclaimed, believe that "as the line of distinction between the employer and employed is widened, the condition of the latter inevitably verges toward a state of vassalage while that of the former as certainly approximates towards supremacy."

Unionists denied their labor was a mere commodity, something to be regulated by the marketplace. Wage-work could be squared with a just society only if journeymen were paid the full value of their labor, that value to be determined by the workers themselves. Unionists were not mindlessly opposed to mechanization, chairmaker John Commerford stressed, but they wanted assurances that any worker facing replacement by a new machine would be secured "from want, until he could obtain a situation at least as good as that from which he was about to be driven."

The General Trades Union swiftly established a vivid presence in the city. On Evacuation Day (November 25) of 1833—the "anniversary of our entire liberation from *foreign* thralldom"—the GTU's now twenty-one member organizations underscored their separation from former craft masters by parading, four-thousand strong, along the Bowery and Broadway. For the first time in New York City's history, organized labor was independently on the march.

The new movement sprouted a panoply of union songs, banners, and insignias. It launched a newspaper—the *Union*—to complement George Henry Evans's popular *Working Man's Advocate*, his new prolabor organ the *Man* (1834), and the editorial support offered by the *Sun* and *Transcript* penny papers. In 1834, moreover, New York workers formed (and dominated) the National Trades Union (NTU), a clearinghouse for reports on the state of labor around the country. It too started up its own paper, the *National Laborer*.

Though dominated by native-born journeymen, the GTU reached out to newly naturalized immigrants in the city. To discourage ethnic division in its ranks, the organization prohibited discussion of religion and eschewed organized politics.

Not everyone was welcome in New York's house of labor, however. Blacks and women were left outside; indeed the GTU and NTU opposed female labor altogether. Having seen employers use women operatives as wedges to transform the textile, shoemaking, and tailoring trades, the men insisted that women's place was in the home, supported by adequately waged fathers or husbands. The tailoresses once again made bold to disagree, with one seamstress demanding: "If it is unfashionable for the men to bear the oppression in silence, why should it not also become unfashionable with the women?" The sewing women attempted once more to organize on their own, but faced with male unionists' stubborn patriarchy, their efforts proved evanescent.

GTU-backed strikes mounted steadily between 1833 and 1835. Many skilled journeymen, day laborers, sailors, and canal workers won higher wages and better conditions. New York workers also pushed successfully for a ten-hour day. Skilled shipwrights, their labor irreplaceable in the booming riverfront yards, won the right to hang their own "mechanics bell" at the corner of Stanton and Goerck streets, on a twenty-five-foot-high tower next to Isaac Webb's yard. Signaling the end of each ten-hour day, the bell overrode the customary "dark to dark" schedule, and President Jackson ordered the Navy Yard to adopt the new standard.

One of the GTU's most vehement demands was the abolition of prison labor, which undercut wage levels and forced laborers to compete with "felons and scum."

Stonecutters and masons were incensed that New York building contractors could purchase marble cut and hewn at Sing Sing. The Manufacturers of Marble Mantels and 325 journeyman marblecutters joined in petitioning the state legislature to outlaw the practice. The GTU also condemned the "State Prison Monopoly." All to no avail.

When the newly established New York University contracted in January 1833 to purchase prisoner marble for their University Building going up on the east side of Washington Square, workers resorted to direct action. On the evening of October 24, 1833, roughly 150 men marched to the Broadway and 4th Street marble works of Elisha Bloomer, a contractor notorious for his use of prison products. Hurling rocks and brickbats, the crowd smashed Bloomer's doors and windows and broke some marble mantels. The mayor called out the Twenty-seventh Regiment, which dispersed the protestors, then camped out on Washington Square for four days and nights to forestall further outbursts. Continued union pressure did wring a weak ban on prison labor from the state legislature, but the law had little effect, and NYU continued to use Sing Sing stone.

In 1836 unions expanded their organizing drive in a desperate attempt to keep up with rocketing inflation. "The *nominal* value of every article of necessity has been greatly increased," union leader Seth Luther told a Brooklyn labor audience, and working people were being "compelled to pay enormous rents or to be turned out of doors." Yet despite climbing costs, Luther noted, the "price of labor has not received a proportionate advance." Tailors, stonecutters, shoemakers, and cabinetmakers launched industrial actions—ten major turnouts in the skilled trades alone. Coal heavers and other unskilled laborers walked out as well. Even manure carters struck for an increase in pay from the Common Council.

As usual, the most convulsive strikes came on the waterfront. In February stevedores and riggers marched from ship to ship, pulling hundreds off the job, effectively shutting the port. Police efforts to disperse the strikers landed one watchman in the hospital with a fractured skull. The strike spread. One body of stevedores hived off from the docks and marched through the streets of the commercial district. Hundreds of laborers cleaning up postfire debris downed tools and joined them. High Constable Hays coaxed the fire workers back to their job, but the ongoing disruption of commerce led the mayor to call out the Twenty-seventh Regiment yet again. The troops paraded at City Hall Park in a show of force daunting enough to drive the stevedores back to work. For the first time, New York City had used the military to break a strike.

Despite this success, employers were thoroughly alarmed. In 1833 there had been virtually no labor movement. Now, in 1836, two-thirds of New York's workingmen were enrolled in fifty-two confederated unions. Businessmen counterattacked by organizing pugnacious employer-only trade associations, like the Society of Master Tailors, which attacked unions for subverting the civic weal. Labor, the businessmen declared, *was* just like any other commodity, and its value should be set by the free market. Labor unions might in the short term interfere with the market's "natural" workings and extort higher wages from businessmen, but this would only drive up prices, thus hurting consumers while making New York products uncompetitive. In the end strikers would only bankrupt their employers and liquidate their own jobs.

Workers, employers argued further, should pursue individual not collective improvement. An industrious and virtuous workman, especially if he stayed sober, would surely rise in society. Workingmen should quit unions, practice self-discipline, and join groups like the New-York City Temperance Society, which under evangelical merchant Robert Hartley's leadership explicitly opposed trade unions.

Employers' groups adopted tougher tactics too. Early in 1836 the Society of Master Tailors' member-bosses cut wages and announced they would not employ union men. Journeyman tailors responded by launching a GTU-supported strike and by establishing cooperative workshops as an alternative to the wage system. February's use of troops to end the dockworkers' strike only redoubled the tailors' militancy. Battles broke out among strikers, strikebreakers, and policemen. Other unions "turned out" too, so many that Bennett's anti-union *Herald* perceived "a general movement over the city."

The master tailors now turned to the courts, encouraged by a recent upstate ruling from Chief Justice Savage of the state supreme court. Declaring trade unions "monopolies of the most odious kind and injurious to trade," Savage found that "a man has the right to work as he pleases" and that existing law forbade strikes. In late March the boss tailors, citing this precedent, won a conspiracy indictment against twenty strikers. In response, the unions took to the streets. Several thousand workers marched up Broadway with bands and banners, proclaiming their right to regulate their own wages and denouncing banks, politicians, and corporations. "Are we not on the eve of another revolution," the *Herald* wondered, such "as we witnessed among the mechanics in 1829?"

The tailors' trial began in May, Judge Ogden Edwards presiding. Edwards, a Whig and soon-to-be-nativist, had no love for labor unions. His charge to the jury followed Savage closely in stigmatizing them as illegal combinations. This enraged the *Union*. In a June 1 tirade, the labor paper warned that "if an American judge will tell an American jury that the barriers which the poor have thrown up to protect the growing avarice of the rich are unlawful, then are the mechanics justified the same as our own fore Father's [*sic*] were in the days of the revolution, in ARMING FOR SELF-DEFENSE!!" Handbills were plastered throughout the city declaiming that *the Freemen of the North are now on a level with the slaves of the South!*, with no other privileges than laboring that drones may fatten on your life-blood!" Blazoned with a coffin, it summoned freemen to City Hall, where "the Liberty of the Workingmen" was to be interred by Judge Edwards.

On June 6 Edwards delivered the tailors' sentence, levied heavy fines totaling fourteen hundred dollars, and lectured the courtroom that "in this favoured land of law and liberty, the road to advancement is open to all, and the journeymen may by their skill and industry, and moral worth, soon become flourishing master mechanics." Labor unions, Edwards added, were a foreign idea, "mainly upheld by foreigners."

"DOWN WITH MONOPOLIES!"

Over the next week, union men collected money in taverns and shops to pay the men's fines, while arranging for the giant rally at City Hall Park on June 13. Though the assembled multitude cheered the incineration of Edwards's effigy, they opted in the end for a less incendiary strategy, agreeing with orators that the outlawing of strikes called for a counteroffensive at the ballot box. Since the two major parties, speakers argued, were as one in their efforts to "crush the laboring men," the gathering resolved to form a "separate and distinct party, around which the laboring classes and their friends can rally with confidence."

The word "friends" was crucial. The laboring men were not prepared to act on their own—as the Workingmen had in 1829—but they were willing to work with the

Friends of Equal Rights, a party recently founded by veteran Workies and dissident Democrats. The new group's leadership, after all, included such labor activists as Alexander Ming Jr. and Levi Slamm. Ming, a printer, had been prominent in freethought circles, a close associate of Thomas Skidmore, and a candidate of the Workingmen's Party back in 1829. Locksmith Slamm was a delegate to the General Trades Union. The new party, moreover, backed repealing restraints on organizing unions, instituting a mechanic's lien law, expanding the public schools, adopting a metallic currency, and curtailing banks.

Yet the Equal Righters were not a strictly labor party. They believed rather in a united front of all "producing classes"—including sweated journeymen, small manufacturers, shopkeepers, and professionals—against parasitic bankers, aristocrats, monopolists, corporations, and undeserving paupers. Most Equal Righters were grocers, tradesmen, editors, lawyers, small masters, or Tammany politicians disgruntled at the preeminence of bankers in their party. While open to unionist concerns, their core convictions were a hatred of "monopolies" and an insistence that New York City's economic life be democratized.

The man who had inspired the Equal Rights movement was William Leggett, assistant editor at the *Evening Post*. Leggett, a native New Yorker, was a dashing and tempestuous firebrand, as passionate in his hatred of despotism and oppression as were his favorite poets, Byron and Shelley. In 1823, when a midshipman in the navy, Leggett's railings against a tyrannical captain got him court-martialed and cashiered. Back in New York in 1825, he published verse, tried and failed to become an actor like his friend Edwin Forrest, got a job (in 1827) writing theater criticism for the *New-York Mirror*, then branched into writing about literature and established his own magazine, the *Critic*. In 1829, his journal having proved an intellectual success but a financial disaster, Leggett took the *Post* position as William Cullen Bryant's second-in-command.

Leggett's fiery editorials against banks and monopolists won him enthusiastic supporters. So did his reputation as a duelist and his street-trouncing in 1833 of editor James Watson Webb. In the summer of 1834 Bryant departed for a lengthy European sojourn, and Leggett, left in charge, escalated his war on "monopoly."

Leggett argued that growing municipal inequality and declining working-class fortunes were alike the result of special privileges that the rich and well-connected extracted from government through cronyism and corruption. These privileges gave their holders an edge over smaller competitors, while injuring consumers by boosting prices artificially. To bring down this state-supported "order of American Barons," Leggett demanded government cease all regulation of the economy and replace case-by-case chartering of companies with a general incorporation law. This would allow "the humblest citizens" to combine their small savings into "a vast aggregate of capital," which could compete "with the capitals of the purse-proud men who now almost monopolize certain branches of business."

For all his blistering denunciations of "monopolists," Leggett was no anticapitalist. His principles were, in fact, widely accepted by many "purse-proud" businessmen: Whig organs like the *Journal of Commerce* cheered when the *Post* attacked usury laws (restraining interest rates banks could charge) as "arbitrary and unjust." Yet Leggett pushed his antimonopolism with such ruthless consistency that it transmuted into an almost revolutionary challenge to New York's traditional political economy, which had long fostered mutually profitable links between magistrates and merchants.

Leggett attacked the monopoly on ferry service to Brooklyn as a prime example of "exclusive privileges." City authorities, by refusing to license new ferry operators, enabled existing ones to jack up the price of crossing the East River, generating fat profits, which they then shared with the city. Not surprisingly, affluent ferry operators and their supporters on the Common Council were as one in branding Leggett a dangerous radical. But his rationale was essentially the same as that which the Supreme Court used to dismantle the Fulton-Livingston combine, and the limits of Leggett's radicalism quickly became apparent when the *Sun* advocated public ownership of, and free access to, all ferries. Leggett indignantly denounced the idea. "Why not free omnibuses, markets, and houses?" he sputtered. The city, he insisted, should simply allow "unrestricted competition with no other restraint but the laws of supply and demand and we will have enough boats."

Leggett and his followers tackled such powerful corporations as the New York and Harlem Rail Road, the New York Gas-Light Company, and the New York Life Insurance and Trust Company. They went after the fire insurance industry and denounced the auction system that had made Philip Hone's fortune. They lit into banks, particularly those that secured their charters by bribing politicians. And to forestall further corruption of legislators by would-be monopolists, they demanded incorporation be thrown open to all.

Equal Righters also tore into the ancient network of municipal regulations, dismissing the notion that government had any moral obligation to intervene in the economy on the public's behalf. Society was "too much governed," they thought, and they demanded root-and-branch deregulation. They sought to abolish inspectorships and end Common Council interference with trade. They wanted to scrap the licensing system, which fattened the purses of butchers and grocers and cartmen by protecting them from competitors, while filling the city's coffers with fees from the protected. Licensing constituted an indirect tax on consumers. "We cannot pass the bounds of the city," said the new party in 1836, "without paying tribute to monopoly; our bread, our meat, our vegetables, our fuel, all, all pay tribute to monopolists."

Leggett and friends also chopped away at municipal backing for literary and cultural institutions, which privileged the established vis-à-vis newcomers. They criticized government aid to asylums for the insane poor, preferring care by kin. They decried regulation of the medical profession as a ploy by conventional doctors to drive homeopathic, botanicalist, and patent medicine rivals out of business.

In 1835, after a year at the editorial helm during which he'd managed to alienate most of the city's elite, Leggett proceeded to outrage the leaders of his own Democratic party. He denounced President Jackson for banning abolitionist literature from the mail: the editor disapproved of the antislavery group's tactics, but he detested government censorship. Tammany in return cut off the paid announcements that the *Evening Post* received as a party organ, and the post office—which Leggett had urged be stripped of its monopoly and turned over to private enterprise—likewise canceled its advertising.

In early October the Hall read Leggett out of the party altogether, which galvanized Leggett's antimonopoly supporters into action. They had been meeting as an informal faction at the Military and Civic Hotel (on Bowery and Broome). Now they decided to wrest the Democratic party from the faction led by bankers Gideon Lee and Preserved Fish, by taking control of the general meeting. On the appointed evening,

however, canny Tammany men arrived early, entered by the back door, quickly organized the meeting, nominated a bank president as chair, and were about to ram their
ticket through when the antimonopoly forces burst in and forced the Tammanyites out.
As they left, departing Tammany men turned off the gas lights, plunging the hall into
darkness. But this was an old trick—it had been used against Fanny Wright years
before—and the antimonopolists had come prepared. Whipping out their "loco focos,"
the new friction matches, they lit candles and completed their business, winning the
nickname of "Loco Focos" in the process. In February 1836 they formally established
the Friends of Equal Rights Party and started their own paper, the *Democrat*.

In the April 1836 mayoral elections—which the new organization considered a test
of "whether the rich or the labouring classes, the few or the many, are to rule this wide
Confederation," the Equal Rights Party ran Alexander Ming for the mayoralty. He was
opposed by the "Bank Democrats," who chose the incumbent, Cornelius Lawrence,
and the "Bank Whigs," who selected Seth Geer. Both, in Loco Foco eyes, were agents of
the "souless [*sic*], cadaverous, unmanly aristocracy of Wall Street." A fourth entrant,
Samuel F. B. Morse, entered on behalf of the Native American Party.

Democrats worked hard to recapture Loco Foco supporters by incorporating their
issues and personnel. Tammany came out for government control of the banking system. It supported the GTU's former president Ely Moore for congressman. Democrats
also appealed to party (and local) loyalty, noting that favorite son Martin Van Buren was
running for the presidency. In addition, the pressure for independent action by journeymen slackened when another upstate conspiracy trial reversed direction, acquitted
some accused unionists, and ushered in a more prolabor climate.

The election, quiet and orderly, proved a triumph for the Democrats. Lawrence
won easily, with 60.2 percent of the vote. The Whig, Geer, got 23.5 percent. Ming and
Morse pulled down a mere 10.4 and 5.9 percent respectively. Whigs and Democrats
split the Common Council equally, eight and eight. The Equal Rights movement had
failed to establish itself as a serious rival of the major parties, but it had succeeded in
pressuring the Democrats into adopting some of its positions. For the next half century,
Tammany Hall would represent itself as the de facto party of New York's working
classes, even while providing a haven for bankers and merchants with quite different
interests and sensibilities.

Certainly the newly reelected Mayor Lawrence was not prepared for the enthusiasm of his followers when, on New Year's Day 1837, he opened his house to the public
in the traditional manner. To the delight of Philip Hone, who recorded the proceedings
in his diary, the Democratic masses treated Lawrence's house like a Five Points tavern.
"Every scamp who has bawled out 'Huzza for Lawrence' and 'Down with the Whigs'
considered himself authorized to use him and his house and furniture at his pleasure; to
wear his hat in his presence, to smoke and spit upon his carpet, to devour his beef and
turkey, and wipe his greasy fingers upon the curtains." Served Lawrence right, Hone
thought. Having pandered to the lower orders, he'd have to put up with them, lest they
throw him out of City Hall in favor of one of their own class, who would be even "less
troubled than him with aristocratical notions of decency, order, and sobriety."

"TO HART'S FLOUR STORE!"

Over the next several months, as the speculative binge continued at a frenzied pace, inflation ravaged the populace. By February 1837 the price of flour had shot up to nearly

$12.00 a bushel—from $4.87 back in December 1834—and pork went from $13.00 to $24.50 per barrel over the same period.

Rumors circulated that the city's flour merchants—firms like Eli Hart and Company and S. B. Herrick and Son—were hoarding great quantities of flour and grain, hoping to drive prices even higher. New York's commission merchants had traditionally bought farmers' crops, stored the grain in huge warehouses, and waited for the most profitable moment to sell. Such behavior, perfectly in tune with the new market universe, was utterly at variance with the old but not forgotten moral economy, and it touched off a spate of angry editorials. "An atrocious and wicked conspiracy by rich speculators" was underway, the *Herald* claimed, and the *New Era*, a new penny press, castigated "monopolists" as "veritable vermin who prey upon the community."

More than food was surging in cost. Coal prices were going up, and the *New Era* suggested forming cooperatives for the purchase and sale of fuel. Rents too were climbing rapidly, and the same paper called on the city to build small one-family dwellings, a pioneering proposal for what would come to be called public housing. Bennett counseled (in the *Herald* on February 3) that tenants who could not meet the exorbitant demands of the "real estate monopoly" should refuse to leave their apartments after leases expired May 1, thus forcing landlords into court. He proposed a mass meeting in the Park to consider such propositions.

A week later, with the city enveloped in snow and icy winds, placards went up around town, over the signature of several Loco Foco leaders, calling for a four P.M. rally at City Hall on Monday, February 13, to air grievances. "BREAD, MEAT, RENT, FUEL! THEIR PRICES MUST COME DOWN!" it blared. "The People will meet in the PARK," it explained, to "inquire into the Cause of the present unexampled Distress, and to devise a suitable Remedy. All Friends of Humanity, determined to resist Monopolists and Extortioners, are invited to attend." The *Post* and *Herald* urged participation.

Monday the thirteenth was winter's bitterest day to date, with wind whipping through the Park, but roughly five thousand people showed up. Loco Foco speakers, among them Alexander Ming, argued the connections between the flood of paper currency and the inflationary spiral. They read off and won assent to resolutions demanding hard money and an end to ferry and market monopolies and to municipal interference in trade. But what really got the crowd's blood up were those speakers who bluntly blamed landlords and flour merchants for the outrageous price of shelter and provisions.

The last speaker, a man whose identity was never ascertained, tore into Hart and Company, ending with the peroration: "Fellow-citizens, Mr. Eli Hart has now 53,000 barrels of flour in his store; let us go and offer him eight dollars a barrel for it, and if he will not take—" at which point someone touched his shoulder, and he concluded: "We shall depart in peace."

A voice in the crowd bellowed, "To Hart's flour store!" Over the protests of Loco Foco leaders, the crowd headed to Hart's, on Washington Street between Dey and Cortlandt, where they found the large brick building barricaded in anticipation of their arrival. Mayor Lawrence arrived to remonstrate with the rapidly swelling multitude. He was shouted down, barraged with stones and barrel staves, and "compelled to retreat for his life," according to the *Post*.

A furious assault now carried the building. After entering the counting room, where they smashed desks and scattered papers, rioters hurled hundreds of barrels of flour and sacks of wheat to the street below. There—although a "tall athletic fellow in a carman's frock" shouted, "No plunder, no plunder; destroy as much as you please"—women (in the words of one hostile account) "like the crones who strip the dead in battle fill[ed] the boxes and baskets with which they were provided, and their aprons, with flour, and ma[de] off with it."

At dusk, a detachment of rioters marched to the South Street store of E. and J. Herrick, but spared it when a company representative persuaded them the firm had sold off its flour at low prices. The crowd carried on to S. H. Herrick and Son, at Coenties Slip, where it broke in and began a similar process of destruction but agreed to desist when an agent promised to give every barrel in the store to the poor. Meanwhile, the mayor had called out the militia, the marshals and watchmen having proved ineffective. The troops took several hours to assemble, but by nine P.M. they had cleared remaining rioters from the vicinity of Hart's, and the affair was over.

The flour riot was a throwback to the colonial (and beyond that the English) tradition of crowds enforcing the moral economy by punishing those who profited from economic hardship. It constituted a violent petition to the city's elites, a demand they act responsibly for the common good. But the appeal fell on ears more attuned than ever before to the ethics and logic of the marketplace. Conservatives, not surprisingly, denounced those who had deluded the "pillaging canaille, the colored people, thieves and Irish" into stupidly trying to lower the price of flour by making it scarcer. But the radical William Leggett concurred with their analysis. With perfect consistency, he denounced unionists who would combine to raise wages "yet attack Capital for raising flour prices." The crisis was due to a deficient crop and inflated paper money. Violent interference with the laws of trade was useless and indefensible.

The riot did not, therefore, produce a restoration of the assize on bread. What it did do was galvanize those who had been pushing for a strengthened police force. Within twenty-four hours of the riot a hitherto becalmed plan for adding 192 more watchmen sailed into law.

It was clear to at least some of the gentry, however, that repression would not be a sufficient response to the crisis. Philip Hone, foreman of a grand jury investigating the flour riot, agreed it had been an outrageous event. But Hone couldn't help sympathizing with the "poor devils," at least in the privacy of his diary. "What is to become of the labouring classes?" he asked himself on February 18. "It is very cold now, if it continues so for a month, then will be great and real suffering in all classes." Presciently, Hone added the thought that "the present unnatural state of things cannot continue."

"THE VOLCANO HAS BURST AND OVERWHELMED NEW YORK"

On the ides of March 1837, the granite office building of J. L. and S. I. Joseph and Company caved in with a crash that shook every building on Wall Street. Two days later the firm itself collapsed, frightening the financial district far more than had the tumbling stonework, for the fall of the House of Joseph presaged general disaster.

The firm failed because New Orleans merchants, caught short by a drop in the price of cotton, had defaulted on vast sums they owed their Manhattan creditor. Soon hundreds of other New York City brokers, commission houses, and dry-goods jobbers also found their bills to southerners coming back unpaid. Many of these companies were far weaker than the defunct Josephs, who had been agents of the mighty Roth-schilds. One after another, dragged down by the foundering cotton economy, they sank into default.

Mayor Lawrence's firm—Hicks, Lawrence, and Company—suspended payment on its debts and closed its Wall Street office. Brown and Hone defaulted too. It was "a dark and melancholy day," former mayor Philip Hone informed his diary. "My eldest son has lost the capital I gave him, and I am implicated as endorser for them to a fearful amount."

Failure after failure jolted Wall and Pearl streets. By April 8, the *Journal of Commerce* reported, ninety-three firms had gone under. Three days later the total reached 128. "The merchants are going to the devil *en masse*," wrote George Templeton Strong, a student at Columbia College who had begun keeping a diary as meticulous and opinionated as Hone's.

Demands from overseas creditors escalated the pressure. "The accounts from England are very alarming," Hone noted; "the panic prevails there as bad as here." At April's end a businessmen's committee informed newly inaugurated President Van Buren that there had been "more than 250 failures of houses engaged in extensive business" and that the merchandise in New York's warehouses had lost a third of its value. As their fortunes melted away, some desperate merchants set fire to their own stores, seeking insurance payouts worth double and treble the value of their stock.

The disaster rolled on. On May 1 Arthur Tappan went belly up. The Liverpool packet had brought heavy demands from British creditors, demands his once flourishing silk firm could not meet. Weakened by the great fire, the boycott by irate southern antiabolitionists, and now the default of country and city retailers, Tappan's debts had mounted past the million-dollar mark, a sum few merchants grossed in a year. The devout merchant's evangelical brethren were bewildered to find God scourging saints as well as sinners. Local antiabolitionist enemies were gleeful. "Arthur Tappan has failed!" gloated George Templeton Strong. "Help him all ye niggers!" But most men on Wall Street shuddered, for if Arthur Tappan could break, a complete collapse of wholesale merchants seemed inevitable.

Other sectors of the city economy reeled and staggered. The overheated real estate boom of the 1830s abruptly iced over. The price of lots plunged. Landowners near Bloomingdale Village had been getting $480 an acre in September 1836; by April 1837, Hone noted, they were lucky to clear fifty dollars. Stunned merchants calculated that the value of their real estate had "depreciated more than $40,000,000" in a scant six months. Hundreds of Manhattan landowners and builders defaulted on mortgages and lost their property through foreclosure.

Grand development schemes—like Samuel Ruggles's Gramercy Park and Union Square—were put on hold. Brooklyn suspended construction of its City Hall, leaving an unfinished basement in a weed patch. Greater Williamsburg winked out. So did John Pitkin's would-be metropolis of East New York. On Staten Island, New Brighton's developers crumpled; their hotel and houses went to the block.

Far more damaging for the city's future was the virtual cessation of wholesale speculative building. New York's supply of housing fell behind the growth of population. Crowding in working-class districts worsened rapidly, setting the stage for future social disaster.

The stock market fell apart too. The value of locally held shares declined twenty million dollars. The average number of shares traded daily dropped from 7,393 in January to 1,534 in June. Hot new rail stocks nosedived as their companies collapsed. On April 5 work was halted on the Long Island Rail Road with only fifteen track miles laid between Jamaica and Greenport; it would remain stalled for years. Other projected lines—including one intended to connect Brooklyn with Fort Hamilton—died and were not resurrected. The Erie Rail Road survived, thanks only to a three-million-dollar loan extracted from the state legislature by influential directors.

The crisis of the railroads sped the disintegration of city manufacturing. Cutbacks in orders for iron and engines crippled foundries and machine shops, wounding even the giant Allaire works. Failed locomotive builders defaulted in turn on notes due metal dealers like Hendricks and Brothers. The economic storm flattened less industrialized operations as well: virtually all of New York's major clothing firms foundered in 1837.

The ruin of merchants and manufacturers alike had been hastened by, and in turn exacerbated, a crisis of the financial system. To protect their reserves of specie—gold and silver coin—banks virtually ceased lending, turning away even the most respectable merchants. Leading brokerage houses were equally tightfisted. When the well-connected sugar merchant Moses Taylor applied to Brown Brothers, he was told they would not accommodate even "the U.S. Bank with J. J. Astor to back it as security." Interest rates skyrocketed to 24 percent. "Money is exorbitantly dear," wrote Hone in March. "The bloodsuckers are beginning to be alarmed, and keep their unholy treasures locked up."

Worse, banks began calling in outstanding loans, pushing more merchants over the edge into default. In turn, businessmen, who feared the banks might not survive, rushed to convert their deposits and bank notes into precious metal.

So did the citizenry. The Loco Focos, who all along had been denouncing banks and paper money, called a mass meeting in City Hall Park on March 6. Over thirty thousand people turned out, more than had attended the February rally preceding the flour riot. The assemblage urged noteholders to cash in their banknotes, "and thus make these soulless corporate extortioners pay their debts to the people as promptly as they compel payment from the people." In April, with the panic spreading, angry crowds of the "poor and laboring classes" (Hone noted) gathered at the banks, demanding the return of their deposits "in a most alarming manner."

On May 3 milling crowds besieged the Dry Dock Savings Bank. Mayor Lawrence managed to convince them that their money was safe. But the next day, the president of the Merchants' Bank was found dead—"Some say prussic acid," Strong reported—and the bank runs began again. Captain Frederick Marryat, a noted English writer, arrived to find that "suspicion, fear, and misfortune have taken possession of the city" and that "the militia are under arms, as riots are expected."

Early next morning, the Dry Dock stopped payment. A score more merchants promptly failed. Throughout the city, people began jamming toward bank tellers shouting "Pay! Pay!" By May 9 $652,000 in coin had been drained from Manhattan vaults. Then, on May 10, all twenty-three of Manhattan's banks announced they would henceforth refuse to exchange specie for paper. An infuriated crowd boiled into Wall Street. But the city had summoned up the Twenty-seventh Regiment—"the monopoly aristocracy of New-York garrisoned their fortresses with arms and men," as one Loco Foco put it—and the day passed with much tumult but no bloodshed.

"The volcano has burst and overwhelmed New York," Hone told his diary, and the repercussions spread swiftly throughout the country. Within twenty-four hours, most

banks in the Northeast had stopped gold and silver payments. More distant states followed suit as soon as the news from Wall Street reached them. In most places—and certainly New York—suspending specie payments was blatantly illegal, but metropolitan
bankers prevailed on the Albany legislature to suspend the law. This saved them from
bankruptcy and enabled them to continue doing business. Indeed, now freed from having to redeem their notes in specie, banks issued them in abundance. James Gordon
Bennett, noting that the banks still had millions in coin, denounced this as "legalized
and chartered swindling, without a parallel in the annals of crime and imposture."

Merchants in debt were delighted: though legally obligated to pay their debts in
specie, it was now impossible to do so, and this saved them from collapse. Some businesses carried on using notes and checks. Others resorted to barter and promises.
Stores, hotels, and oyster cellars issued their own scrip, called shinplasters. "Go to the
theater and places of public amusement," wrote Captain Marryat, "and, instead of
change, you receive an I.O.U."

But the city's overall economy, tied as it was to international markets, could not so
easily finesse the crisis. At the end of May, Hone wrote, "a deadly calm pervades this
lately flourishing city. No goods are selling, no business stirring, no boxes encumber the
sidewalks of Pearl Street." Barges and boats lay idle at the docks. "Many of the counting houses were shut up, or advertised to be let," wrote a British traveler. "The coffee
houses were almost empty, the streets near the water side were almost deserted; the
grass had begun to grow upon the wharves."

Panic had given way to depression.

CAUSES AND REMEDIES

What had happened? This was the prime topic of conversation throughout the city.
Explanations came in many sizes and shapes, but three predominated: some people
blamed the government, some the banks, others the English.

Whig businessmen indicted Andrew Jackson. He had destroyed the Bank of the
United States, the financial system's only regulator, and then, in July 1836, decreed the
government would accept only gold or silver as payment for public lands. In requiring
hard coin, Jackson had hoped to halt the runaway inflation, and also the monopolization
of land by northeastern speculators who had been using borrowed paper money to gobble up millions of midwestern acres. The real consequence, Whigs argued, had been to
deepen the monetary crisis, and the *Journal of Commerce* savaged Jackson for "permitting government to investigate and direct the affairs of private business."

From Jackson's perspective, the panic was a necessary corrective—and deserved
retribution—for the inflationary expansion generated by bankers and their paper
money system. It would pass once all the "speculators and gamblers are broke." Jacksonian politician A. Z. Flagg agreed that New York City bankers had blown up "land
bubbles and stock bubbles" and now were "reaping the bitter fruits"—an animus
strengthened when investigators found that bank officers had filched perhaps $1.5 mil-
lion from various Manhattan institutions. Jacksonian Senator Silas Wright gave this
analysis an anti-Semitic spin when he wrote that the failure of the Joseph brothers—
"Jew brokers of New York"—was cause for rejoicing.

Jacksonians and Whigs agreed, however, that the crisis also had international roots.
"The barometer of the American money market hangs up at the stock exchange in Lon-

615

don," one Democratic congressman said, and Philip Hone believed that the Bank of England was "arbiter of the fate of the American merchant."

They were right. Both boom and bust had originated in Europe. British and Continental investors had poured capital into U.S. canals, railroads, and lands, first cautiously, then at a frenzied pace. In addition, Old World creditors let New World merchants import goods on credit. New York City had been America's link to these money markets. Anglo-American merchant bankers like the Barings and Rothschilds had funneled capital and credit to Hudson River firms like Prime, Ward, and King, and Alexander Brown and Sons, who relayed them to the Continent, stoking the boom. New York wholesalers, and through them country storekeepers, ran up an enormous tab. State governments accumulated huge debts, then borrowed more to pay the interest. Gold and silver imports enabled banks to issue more paper money, facilitating speculation and generating inflation.

In the summer of 1836, what the English had given, the English decided to take away. The Bank of England raised its discount rate and reined in British bankers it thought too accommodating of Americans. The transatlantic flow of capital was suddenly and severely restricted. Eurocreditors demanded U.S. merchants remit their balances due, just as cutbacks in cotton purchases were driving down the price of America's staple. This forced U.S. businessmen to pay in gold. Specie sailed back to Europe. New York City, which had facilitated the boom, now helped terminate it. Its hard-pressed banks and merchants called in *their* debts. When New Orleans cotton factors and country retailers couldn't pay, Pearl Street failed, Wall Street suspended, and a vicious contraction radiated out along the same trade routes upon which credit and capital had earlier traveled.

Proposed remedies varied dramatically with ideology and interest. Whigs called for reversing Jackson's policies and bringing back a national bank. President Van Buren and the Loco Foco Democrats wanted to *extend* Jackson's policies by severing all connections between the banking system and the government.

Debtors, for their part, wanted to suspend or scale back what they owed. They favored inflating the currency so they could repay their debts with dollars cheaper than those they had borrowed. Above all, farmers, producers, and thousands of businessmen across the country—including many Pearl Street merchants, leagued in the New York Board of Trade—wanted to postpone resumption of specie payments, which they feared would force them into bankruptcy.

Creditors wanted to put the country through the wringer of deflation and depression. They favored restoring the gold standard, which would force debtors to repay them with dollars more valuable than those they had borrowed. A phalanx of New York City financiers, led by the venerable Albert Gallatin and the firm of Prime, Ward, and King, called for resuming specie payments as soon as the banks were strong enough to withstand runs. Restoring paper money's interconvertibility with gold would regain the good graces of overseas bankers—something deemed crucial for a country dependent on imported capital—while also deflating the economy.

Gallatin and the New York bankers succeeded, with some crucial governmental assists from the Erie Canal Fund (which lent beleaguered banks over two million dollars) and the Bank of England (which chipped in one million pounds sterling). Their vaults now stuffed with metal, New York banks resumed specie payments in May 1838.

The country, including Philadelphia, reluctantly followed Manhattan's lead. Wall Street, once a lionized lender, now became a hated creditor. The hard-nosed policies of New York's banks were complemented by the tough tactics of its land speculators. Arthur Bronson, acting for himself and for eastern and English interests, lobbied vigorously and successfully against all western and southern moratoria and debt reduction schemes.

For a short time, it seemed that resumption had indeed resurrected the economy. Credit and capital flowed again from east to west. Businesses revived. States and corporations sold their bonds on the London market and launched new projects. The price of cotton rose. But when a bad harvest in 1839 forced England to export gold in order to import wheat, the Bank of England clamped down again, and the story repeated itself.

The depression deepened through the early 1840s. Imports fell. Real estate values sagged. Railroad construction fell by two-thirds between 1838 and 1843; canal construction plummeted 90 percent. Deflation replaced inflation: prices declined 46 percent between February 1839 and February 1843. Recompense for craftsmen and unskilled workers—for those lucky enough to find work at all—dropped about one-third between 1836 and 1842, often falling faster than prices and rents, thus driving real wages down.

FROM BOOM TO BUST

The panic wrought startling reversals of condition at all levels of city society, noted the Common Council, making many "who but two years since considered themselves rich, poor." General Winfield Scott had been invited by a group of leading New Yorkers to a public dinner in his honor, but after the crash he tactfully withdrew his acceptance, deeming celebration unseemly when so many of his hosts had gone broke.

The New York elite had long been more volatile than that of other American cities, as its members' fortunes were more closely tied to mercurial mercantilism and speculative enterprise. But the novelty and thoroughness of changes in fortune wrought by the Panic of 1837 fascinated observers, generating a novel lore and literature of bankruptcy.

One visitor, Francis Grund, noticed that the commercial insolvency of New Yorkers "changes at once their friends, their associates, and often their nearest relations, into strangers. How many ties are thus broken by a single failure in business!" Some, Grund reported, positively relished news of others' misfortune. One lady, on hearing of the return from London of "the wife of that vulgar auctioneer that wanted to outdo everybody," remarked with satisfaction: "Well, she will find a sad change; her husband has failed since she was gone, and is said not to pay ten cents in a dollar."

New York writer Charles Francis Briggs, who in 1839 penned perhaps the first depression novel—*The Adventures of Harry Franco, a Tale of the Panic of 1837*—followed it up, in 1843, with *The Haunted Merchant*, a study of ruination. Briggs compared the sudden collapse of a businessman to the shutting of a wild bird in a cage while its fellows soared above. The real horror, Briggs suggested, was less the loss of luxuries than the way former associates shifted their tone from familiarity to suspicion, from deference to insolence.

Such observations caught the brittleness of social ties within New York's upper class but missed a deeper change in attitude toward failure ushered in by the panic. New York businessmen—and American capitalists in general—began shuffling off the stigma and shame once attached to insolvency. In the summer of 1839 city merchants started a

campaign to allow them to discharge their debts through bankruptcy proceedings, freeing themselves to start up business again with a clean financial and moral slate. Reformers passage of the Federal Bankruptcy Act of 1841, which, though repealed in
1842, lasted long enough for twenty-eight thousand debtors to shed $450 million dollars
of debt.

Focusing on examples of the high-brought-low also overstated the collective vulnerability of the New York rich. Their ranks were far from decimated. Some had the
wherewithal to survive even such a substantial setback. In 1838 Philip Hone declared
that he, like half his friends, was deeply in debt, with no prospect of ever getting out. A
year later, Hone was free and clear—albeit shorn of two-thirds his fortune—and had
taken up his accustomed lifestyle again.

Hone did have the grace to wonder "how the poor man manages to get a dinner for
his family," as well he might have. Mass bankruptcies had produced massive layoffs. By
April 1837 collapse of the real estate industry had already devastated the construction
trades; one paper reported that "six thousand masons and carpenters and other workmen connected with building had been discharged." A citywide survey that month estimated that one-third of all New York workers had lost their jobs and that in addition to
these fifty thousand unemployed, another two hundred thousand were without adequate means of support. In May Captain Marryat observed that "mechanics thrown out
of employment, are pacing up and down with the air of famished wolves." Newcomers
were particularly hard hit: "The Irish emigrant leans against his shanty, with his spade
idle in his hand, and starves."

The Times, a cartoon depicting the Panic of 1837 and its consequences. Lithograph by Edward W. Clay.
Unemployed mechanics look for work on the right, a mother and child plead for assistance from a fat banker
on the left, and a run on the Mechanics Bank unfolds in the background. (© Museum of the City of New York)

Men posted notices in City Hall offering to do work of any kind for three dollars a week. In August, when a job for twenty laborers was advertised at four dollars a month plus board, five hundred applied. Asa L. Shipman, in his early twenties when the calamity struck, lost his job, looked bootlessly for work, lived for a time on credit from a local grocer, then began subsisting on one meal a day. Shipman was lucky, however. A regular at church, he attracted the attention of a gentleman who decided he was worthy of assistance and lent him money weekly until the worst was over.

Most men were not so fortunate. Some camped out in Chatham Square, hungrily eyeing the corn that African-American girls were selling at a prohibitive three cents an ear, waiting until ten P.M.—clearance sale time—when the chants switched to "Hot corn! Two cents!" Others camped out at the grogshop, downing homemade liquor at three cents a glass. By the end of 1837 many were panhandling outside oyster-cellar doors. Others had joined the throngs of women—many of them mothers with children—who begged in the streets or went door to door seeking alms.

For a time, the working-class movement of the 1820s and 1830s retained some collective energy. Laborers packed into a series of Loco Foco-orchestrated demonstrations. To cries of "Our families are famishing around us," they backed calls for hard money, economy in city government, jobs on public works, and removal of destitute immigrants to the country. One protest meeting in Greenwich Village threatened to march on the banks unless given work. Respectable observers shivered, with one witness reminded of the "Jacobins, and the Guillotine." No heads or tumbrels rolled, however, and the agitation came to little. Loco Foco Democrats soon effected a rapprochement with their Tammany Hall counterparts, winning concessions on the monetary issues that most agitated them. Their departure left workers leaderless, because by then their unions had been destroyed.

In May 1837 the *Journal of Commerce* had bugled an antilabor offensive. "Now is the time to deliver mechanics and their families from the cruel oppression of the unions," the paper urged. "The rules of the unions as to hours, pay, and everything else ought to be thoroughly broken up." Employers should lengthen the working day. "The ten-hour system is one of the worst deformities of their deformed code," the *Journal* ranted.

Given the availability of thousands of desperate unemployed, the employers' offensive to increase hours, reduce wages, and rid themselves of union troublemakers proved highly successful. By the end of June, as one journeymen's association noted, bosses had effectively leagued together "to take advantage of the present depressed state of our trade and business in general, in order to reduce our present prices, and to render us, if possible, obedient vassals to the nod of the oppressor." By midsummer the union movement in New York City was dead, the National Trades Union interred alongside it.

37

Hard Times

As the city's shattered labor force headed into its first depression winter, Horace Greeley—publisher and editor of the *New-Yorker*, a weekly paper— warned that at least ten thousand of the jobless were "in utter and hopeless distress" and not likely to survive the frigid season. Greeley had urged the poor to "fly, scatter through the country, go to the Great West, anything rather than remain here," but few had heeded him. Now he believed that only massive charity stood between the poor and utter calamity.

Many New Yorkers agreed. As in prior downturns, civic relief groups sprang up in each ward. In December 1837 a Central Committee for the Relief of the Suffering Poor was organized to coordinate these volunteer efforts, the mayor serving as chair. The committee raised money by sponsoring lectures and concerts, solicited donations in kind or cash, and established depots for receiving and dispensing aid. Greeley himself was active in the Sixth Ward's Citizens Relief Committee, and it was there that he discovered both the terrible suffering of the poor and the hopeless inadequacy of eighteenth-century measures for dealing with nineteenth-century problems.

The relief committees were quickly overwhelmed by the numbers of the needy. Twenty-five hundred requested and received aid in the Seventh Ward (roughly one in every ten residents). In the Fifth, six thousand were assisted, approximately a third of the ward's population. Soon hundreds were being turned away each day. Provisions dwindled at local soup kitchens. In mid-February, the Fifth Ward's money gave out. Almsgiving stopped. People starved, froze, or contracted fatal diseases through exposure and privation. The ad hoc, civic-minded approach was discredited. In the subsequent hard winters of 1839–42, ward committees were not revived.

Some of the relief burden was picked up by the churches, especially evangelical

Presbyterians. Even during good times, American Tract Society visitors, horrified by slum conditions, had begun to offer "temporal goods" along with tracts and prayers. Acting as individuals, they had paid the rent for families about to be evicted, brought clothing and food to the hungry and ill clad, and sought jobs for those without work. When hard times struck, tractarians continued and expanded these efforts. But the dimensions of the crisis engendered a growing sense of helplessness and a hardening of old convictions that most of the poor had only themselves to blame for their misery.

In February 1838 the evangelical ladies of the New York Female Moral Reform Society, having discovered the great and growing destitution among the laboring classes, began distributing charity to those deemed virtuous and receptive to the word of God. But most of the poor proved neither, in their judgment, being either intemperate or Catholic. As one visitor to Ann Street put it that year: "Alas! few were found deserving of relief, [as] nearly all were reduced to their present suffering by a course of vice." Their mid-1830s optimism about the perfectibility of man gave way to renewed pessimism about the intractability of poverty, a gloom deepened further by the bankruptcy of many of their staunchest supporters. The Protestant Episcopal City Mission Society also found donations hard to come by. Saddled with debt for churches built and clerics hired in the halcyon thirties, it soldiered on through the depression years—growing more and more convinced that the poor were an alien and inferior class, mostly incapable of salvation—and by 1843 it was facing bankruptcy.

In July of that year the New York City Tract Society, also buckling under its charitable burdens, decided to spin off almsgiving to a separate organization. After investigating contemporary European approaches to poverty, it established, at the end of 1844, an Association for Improving the Condition of the Poor (AICP). The new organization proposed a centralized and scientific approach to managing the city's now seemingly permanent underclass of indigents. (A Brooklyn AICP was established the same year, with Seth Low as president and a plan of operation identical to Manhattan's.)

The directors, who included some of the richest bankers, merchants, and industrialists in New York, were only too aware of the devastation wrought by the depression. They insisted nevertheless that poverty was caused not by failures of the economic system over which they presided but by deficiencies of the poor themselves, in essence reviving the analysis and strategy adopted nearly three decades earlier by the Society for the Prevention of Poverty (a continuity underscored by the prominence in the AICP of Dr. John H. Griscom, son of SPP founder John Griscom).

To direct the new association's work the managers chose Robert Milham Hartley as executive secretary. The English-born Hartley, a devout Presbyterian, had served from 1833 to 1842 as secretary of the New-York City Temperance Society; like most of the directors, he believed poverty bespoke depravity. As "pauperism" was the problem, Hartley wrote, and "the chief cause of its increase among us is the injudicious dispensation of relief," the AICP's "primary" goal would be "to discountenance indiscriminate almsgiving."

What Hartley advocated instead was "scientific philanthropy," by which he meant not only rationalizing the distribution of relief citywide but also using it as an incentive to better behavior. The AICP would visit the poor in their homes to "inspire them with self-reliance and self-respect; to inculcate habits of economy, industry and temperance; and whenever it shall be absolutely necessary, to provide such relief as shall be suited to their wants." Under Hartley's leadership, the AICP divided Manhattan into several hundred sections with approximately sixty poor families apiece. Each section was assigned a visitor who would regularly canvass his charges and assess their condition and character. To discourage the poor from shopping around for handouts, Hartley had AICP visitors file their reports with a central registry; he also warned residents not to give money to panhandlers, advising them instead to disburse tickets bearing the address of the nearest AICP visitor.

The point of establishing this moral credit-rating agency was to sort out the poor, deciding who was truly needy and who was idle or depraved; it would act, Hartley said, as "a vast sieve" to separate "the precious and the vile." If the visited were victims of temporary illness or adversity, the visitor would get them medical help and dispense relief, judiciously, until health and employment returned; if they suffered from drink or other vices, the visitor could hold out the promise of assistance as an incentive to reform. Persons deemed unable to support themselves because of age, chronic illness, or physical handicap would be dispatched to the appropriate municipal institutions. Ever wary of creating temptations to fraud, Hartley warned that people confined inside such places should never live better than the laboring poor outside; inmates who gained weight, he said, should have their daily rations cut back. "Paupers" and "vagrants"— the idle and dissolute poor—should be put to hard labor in a workhouse until ready to become productive members of society. For the hopelessly "debased" and "depraved," there was no choice except a sentence to the penitentiary, where they must suffer "exemplary punishments as a warning to the community."

THE POLITICS OF LAISSEZ-FAIRE

The decline of civic volunteerism and the curtailment by evangelicals of "indiscriminate almsgiving" left the primary burden of aiding depression casualties to the city itself. New York would indeed succor many of the poor, but with ill grace and limited funds, its reluctance a function of penury, ideology, and a transformed political system.

Hard times reshaped the electoral landscape. Since the 1820s New York had been a Democratic town. The Whig Party, born during the Bank War, had lapsed into somnolence at its conclusion. After the crisis of 1837, Whiggery was born again, and over the next few years its candidates rode the depression first into City Hall, then into the governor's mansion, and finally into the White House itself.

The parties had different core constituencies and policies. The Democrats, who cast their Whig opponents as aristocrats, drew upon new immigrants, antibank radicals, merchants trading with the South, workers tied to the port economy, and, thanks to Tammany's long command of municipal patronage, a small army of grateful contractors, thankful work crews, and appreciative officeholders. Democrats opposed high tariffs, a smart strategy in a city with five times as much capital invested in trade as in manufactures; they also aimed to divorce government from banking, curb speculation, and reduce government expenses.

Whigs could usually count on evangelical and Episcopalian merchants, bankers, and businessmen, master craftsmen and the middling classes, and working-class voters hard hit by the depression. Whig planks backed governmental underwriting of internal improvements and stronger oversight of banking while defending the credit system. The party promoted itself as a bastion of "order, morals and religion" and portrayed Democrats as agrarians, Fanny Wrighters, and people associated with "infidelity, anarchy, the riot, butchery, and blood of the French revolution."

In 1837 Aaron Clark, the Whigs' mayoral candidate, won office in part because Loco Foco radicals ran an independent candidate and siphoned off votes from Tammany's man. When President Van Buren adopted the Locos' approach to currency questions, the disaffected Democrats trooped back to Tammany Hall, only to see the Conservative Democrats, many of them bankers or bank stockholders, decamp en masse, make common cause with Whigs, and get Clark reelected in 1838. A brief economic upturn helped Democrat Isaac Varian squeak into City Hall in 1839 and 1840, and Democrat Robert H. Morris proved able to hold the mayoralty for three successive terms (1841–43), though again by slender majorities. Meanwhile the Common Council teetered back and forth, Whigs winning control in 1837–38, Democrats in 1839–41, Whigs in 1842, Democrats in 1843. At the state level, the governorship passed in 1838 from Democrat William Marcy to Whig William Seward, who was reelected in 1840 (though he lost in the city); then Democrats recaptured Albany in 1842 with William C. Bouck.

Whigs scored heavily among those who blamed the governing party for the depression, but they also did well because they finally turned to a new breed of professionals: Whig politicians who had mastered the art of Tammany-style electioneering. Thurlow Weed, an Albany newsman turned full-time politico, was a robust and florid fellow, a man who liked his oysters and wine. He was also shrewd, manipulative, and determined to whip the hitherto disparate elements of Whiggery into a cohesive party. Weed tapped New York City's community of rich Whig and Conservative Democrat merchants for campaign contributions and amassed a sixty thousand dollar war chest his first year out. Spending cash as effectively as he raised it, he made use of promotional techniques invented by the penny press. In 1838 Weed rescued Horace Greeley, whose *New-Yorker* was foundering in choppy depression seas, and hired him to edit a party sheet, the *Jeffersonian*, which contributed substantially to Seward's victory.

Weed could play political hardball too. In the 1838 campaign Whig agents were dispatched to Philadelphia, where they hired two hundred lowlifes at thirty dollars a head. These "floaters," conveyed to New York City, were trooped from poll to poll, casting fraudulent ballots. Once Whigs gained power they happily deployed Tammany tactics to keep it, giving prison inmates one-day passes contingent on their voting the anti-Tammany ticket, and marching almshouse paupers to the polls en masse, their gray uniforms temporarily exchanged for new clothing. Whigs also embraced the spoils system with delight and, when they captured the municipal government in 1837, handed out jobs and contracts to party members only. To block Tammany's penchant for mass naturalizations, Whigs passed a state law—applicable to New York City only—that required voter registration. They also cut the length of elections from three days to one.

In the 1840 presidential race, Weed again drew upon Greeley's skill as political publicist. New York Whig magnates opened their purses as never before, allowing Weed and Greeley to spend fabulous sums transforming patrician William Henry Harrison into a Man of the People. When Democrats incautiously charged that General Harrison had, since retirement, been guzzling hard cider in a log cabin in Ohio, Weed and Greeley transformed both wooden house and apple drink into badges of honor. New York imagemakers contrasted Harrison-as-backwoodsy-pioneer to a putatively aristocratic Van Buren. Greeley's new subsidized sheet, the *Log Cabin*, was also chock-a-block with woodcuts, cartoons, large-type slogans ("Tippecanoe and Tyler, too"), and the words and music for campaign songs. A smash success, its circulation soon topped eighty thousand.

Weed and Greeley took their presidential campaign to the New York streets as well, advancing an urban politics of spectacle. A totemic log cabin, capable of holding four to five hundred, was erected on MacDougal Street across from Washington Square; another went up near Prince Street. Tippecanoe Clubs paraded up and down the town with portable log cabins, ploughs, and barrels of hard cider, shouting, "Van, Van is a used-up man." Despite the hoopla—diverting fare for a depressed populace— Van Buren held the city, in part because Tammany could still deploy superior force at the polls.

Amid the clash and uproar of electoral combat, it was easy to miss the fact that while these realigned and oscillating parties in general presented New York voters with real alternatives on the issue of governmental responsibilities, when it came to depression-era relief they had worked their way, from opposite directions, toward a convergent position.

In 1838, when a group of citizens petitioned the Whig Common Council to restore the assize on bread—to put the city back in the business of regulating its price and quality—the supposed governmental activists refused. Indeed they continued to chip away at any regulations that hampered freedom of action in the marketplace.

Democrats, having long equated government intervention with special privilege, also adopted laissez-faire policies when they were in power. Democratic administrations cut expenses, sold off city-owned lands (at bargain prices) to reduce the debt, and in 1841 and 1843 repealed centuries-old privileges of cartmen and butchers, declaring that such market laws "no longer are observed and do not serve the people's interests." Some zealots proposed shuttering the city's markets altogether and selling off the municipal docks, but neither side was prepared to go to such extremes.

A similar convergence marked their attitude toward aiding the unemployed. On the surface, the municipality's response seemed munificent. The number receiving relief in New York City leapt from under thirty thousand in 1837 to over eighty thousand in 1838. Most of this aid took the form of outdoor relief: provision of food, fuel, and money to the impoverished in their own homes. In addition, the population of the almshouse jumped by a third, to over twenty-five hundred, with immigrants outnumbering native-born for the first time. The amount of money appropriated, however, as distinct from the numbers of people assisted, increased only marginally—though enough to hit a record level of $281,000 by 1839. Conditions in public institutions worsened accordingly; almshouse commissioners found "neglect, and filth and putrefaction, and vermin." The Bridewell, city hospital, and penitentiary were also crammed way beyond their physical capacities.

Mayor Clark nevertheless claimed in 1838 that Manhattan was being too generous. Clark worried that New York would get a reputation for liberality that would attract desperate out-of-towners. Even at present aid levels, he fretted, "New York is likely to become the general rendez-voux of beggars, paupers, vagrants and mischievous persons." Tammany men pointedly busied themselves in private relief efforts, dispensing baskets of cakes, pies, and meat to the needy, but when they assumed power, their position was much the same.

Both parties, to be sure, confronted declining municipal revenues, a function of the falling assessed real estate values, and when the rate of taxation was compensatorily increased by 38 percent in 1842, bellows of protest arose from propertied Whigs and Democrats alike. Indeed large landowners demanded municipal retrenchment and threatened to move to Brooklyn, which publicized itself as a refuge from onerous impositions.

City fathers of both parties justified limits on relief by insisting, in tandem with the directors of the Association for Improving the Condition of the Poor, that healthy and able-bodied men and women seeking public assistance were not depression victims. The 1838 Whig Common Council committee harrumphed that charity would only "increase pauperism" and "promote a lamentable dependency." In 1840 Democrat William Cullen Bryant's *Evening Post* said the managers of public charity "were so grossly lavish and so careless of the consequences, that to them we must attribute a great deal of the demoralization, improvidence and misery that exists."

In 1841 Mayor Morris called for isolating able-bodied paupers in a separate workhouse on Blackwell's Island and assigning them to productive labor. The 1843 City Council agreed that this might well discourage "our dissolute and idle population" from seeking public aid in the first place.

Zealots urged more ruthless measures. One 1843 letter writer to the *Tribune* called for the complete elimination of *any* public aid that would keep paupers alive, fulminating in fine Malthusian fashion that "they who will marry and beget children in dirty cellars are a curse to the world." Such sentiments remained beyond the pale of decent opinion, but so did Horace Greeley's assertion that it was the depression that had made it impossible for many who wanted work to find jobs. During his relief stint in the Sixth Ward, Greeley had heard "stout, resolute, single young men and young women" pleading, "Help us to work, we want no other help; why is it we can have nothing to do?" What New York needed, Greeley declared, was not a workhouse but a "House of Industry" that could provide temporary employment in hard times. The elite consensus, however, followed Mayor Morris and his counterparts at the AICP, and before the decade was out, a workhouse would be up and running on Blackwell's Island.

Dominant opinion was equally opposed to government's providing public works jobs for the unemployed, as had been done in the embargo crisis. When petitions were submitted in 1837 "in behalf of the unemployed operatives, for relief," a Common Council committee conceded that the petitioners were "not paupers" and "merely ask for employment to enable them to procure food for their wives and little ones"; nevertheless, it declared its general opposition to work relief. The council did authorize a few street and sewer projects (in part to take advantage of low wages) but established such stringent conditions for contractors that no bids were submitted, and no work provided.

At the statewide level Whigs did support internal improvements. Whig Assemblyman (and Gramercy Park developer) Samuel B. Ruggles proposed an ambitious program of state-backed canals and railroads. Governor Seward, who had written an admiring biography of his hero De Witt Clinton, supported one such project after another, running up an unprecedented state deficit of eighteen million dollars.

Democrats denounced Whigs for increasing the state's debt and endangering New York's standing with its creditors. The principal bankers of New York City, including many Whig paladins, agreed that further borrowing would be "highly inexpedient and improper" (especially as their institutions held nearly $750,000 of shaky state obligations). Democrats demanded that all public construction be halted. Seward, Greeley, and Ruggles argued this was short-sighted and inhumane and would flood the state with perhaps four thousand new unemployed. But Democrats took power in 1842, and New York's grand program of public works came to a complete halt.[1]

"WATER! WATER!"

With one magnificent exception. The Croton Aqueduct had been authorized before the panic struck, and powerful backers would sustain the gigantic state undertaking throughout the depression. Its construction would serve as New York's de facto jobs program.

By early 1837 the Corporation had wrested control of the municipal water supply from Aaron Burr's Manhattan Company, purchasing its works, pipes, and water rights. Lawsuits by Westchester County dwellers protesting land confiscations by big-city interests were overcome, as was opposition from northern Manhattan landowners. Albany authorized issuance of $2.5 million in stock, and despite the panic, so sterling was the state's Erie Canal track record that the Rothschilds and others were able to round up investors. Eventually an unprecedented twelve million dollars was raised.

Government-appointed commissioners took charge of the project and selected John B. Jervis as chief engineer. Jervis had learned his craft on the Erie Canal—working his way up over eight years from axman to surveyor to Resident Engineer—and honed his skills further on the Delaware and Hudson Canal and the Mohawk and Hudson Railroad. Now Jervis managed construction of the forty-one-mile aqueduct, parceling out the work to private contractors in half-mile sections. Fierce competition kept bids low. To clear a profit, builders had to keep wages down, which they easily accomplished by recruiting their labor force from the port's vast reservoir of unemployed workers. Eventually three to four thousand were employed, including many mechanics from the devastated construction trades and large numbers of recently arrived Irish immigrants.

Laborers who resented the rock-bottom wages and strict work rules periodically launched violent strikes. In April 1840, when men working in upper Manhattan demanded higher pay, the city called out the reliable Twenty-seventh Regiment. The troops traveled to 42nd Street by railroad, dispersed the strikers, and returned to the city by late evening. There were further labor protests, which halted progress until slight raises were extended, as well as riots between immigrants from different Irish counties, each determined to channel precious jobs to their own community.

Despite this, progress was rapid. By the spring of 1840, work crews had run the masonry conduit, over eight feet high and seven feet wide, down to the city's edge, while others were laying pipes and constructing reservoirs in Manhattan itself and launching the spectacular 1,450-foot granite High Bridge that would span the Harlem River.

On June 23, 1842, water was successfully conveyed—along with a four-person boat, the *Croton Maid*—from the dammed-up Croton River to the giant receiving reservoir bounded by 79th and 86th streets and Sixth and Seventh avenues—a basin capable of holding 180 million gallons. Fifteen to twenty thousand New Yorkers traveled by

---

1. Whigs also passed a law in 1838 that threw open the right of incorporation—including all its privileges and immunities—to anyone who could meet minimal requirements. In this Whig magnates had the support of Loco Foco radicals, who were convinced that they were ending the monopolization of banking and attendant legislative corruption by special interests. In fact, they had opened the door to concentrations of capital and accumulations of corporate power far beyond anything they were capable of imagining.

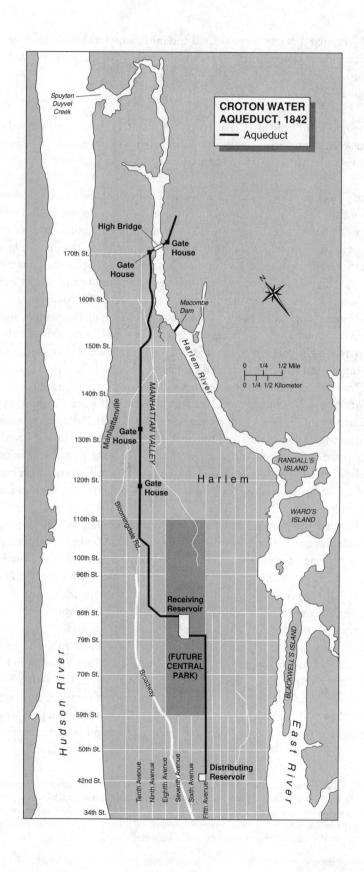

CROTON WATER AQUEDUCT, 1842

━━ Aqueduct

Spuyten Duyvel Creek

High Bridge

Gate House

Gate House

170th St.

160th St.

Macombe Dam

150th St.

Harlem River

140th St.

MANHATTAN VALLEY

Manhattanville

Gate House

130th St.

Harlem

120th St.

Gate House

RANDALL'S ISLAND

Bloomingdale Rd.

110th St.

WARD'S ISLAND

100th St.

96th St.

Receiving Reservoir

86th St.

79th St.

BLACKWELL'S ISLAND

(FUTURE CENTRAL PARK)

70th St.

Broadway

59th St.

East River

50th St.

Hudson River

Distributing Reservoir

42nd St.

Tenth Avenue
Ninth Avenue
Eighth Avenue
Seventh Avenue
Sixth Avenue
Fifth Avenue

34th St.

0   1/4   1/2 Mile
0   1/4   1/2 Kilometer

N

Croton Water Celebration, October 14, 1842. As the huge procession came down Broadway and swung into Park Row, it passed the new fountain in City Hall Park. The prominence of fire engines in the line of march reflected the importance of the new water system for fire protection as well as health and sanitation. (© Museum of the City of New York)

foot, horse, carriages, or trains to Yorkville for a preliminary celebration, as the *Croton Maid* came sailing out of the great aqueduct to cheers, cannon salutes, and toasts of the "sweet, soft, clear water." On July 4 water flowed through three-foot-diameter pipes down Fifth Avenue to the distributing reservoir at Murray Hill. Located at Fifth Avenue and 42nd Street, this fortress-like container, whose embankments rose thirty-eight feet above street level, was topped by a railed promenade, reachable by a stone staircase. It held twenty-four million gallons and fed water down to the 13th Street tank, and thence into the network of underground piping that supplied the heart of the city.

On October 14 New York gave itself over to one of its most extravagant Festivals of Connection, on the order of those celebrating the Federal Union and the Erie Canal. In what the *Commercial Advertiser* called "the largest procession ever known in the city," a parade five miles long marched through town with noisy jubilation, every bell pealed, and a hundred-gun salute honored the eruption of a fifty-foot plume of water from a fountain in City Hall Park. "Nothing is talked of or thought of in New York but Croton water," Philip Hone recorded. "Fountains, aqueducts, hydrants, and hose attract our attention and impede our progress through the streets. . . . Water! water! is the universal note which is sounded through every part of the city, and infuses joy and exultation into the masses."

Charles King, president of Columbia College, hailed the new system as "the crowning glory and surpassing achievement of the latter part of the half century," and the Croton Aqueduct was indeed one of the era's great engineering achievements. But it proved to be the last gasp of New York's governmental activism. By 1842 the great enthusiasm for state-supported internal improvements had run dry. Governmental underwriting no longer seemed so necessary, nor state control so appropriate. City merchants and bankers would not hesitate to demand government aid for themselves whenever it suited their purposes, even while ritually denouncing government meddling in the economy. But for now, Croton would be the culmination—and conclusion—of a grand tradition of municipal enterprise.

RUM, REVIVALS, . . .

The depression galvanized an outpouring of the holy spirit as well as of water in New York City. Upper- and middle-class worshipers flocked to Episcopalian and Presbyterian churches to hear ministers declare the panic to be God's punishment for the sin of greed and the evil of reckless speculation. Plebeian Protestants, too, filled churches as workshops emptied. In the mid-1830s most artisans had resisted evangelical blandishments and devoted themselves to labor organizing. Now, their unions in ruins, artisans packed into Methodist and Baptist tabernacles and feasted on fiery sermons.

Brand-new sects appeared. William Miller, a modern-day prophet, predicted the end of the world would arrive on April 23, 1843, and be followed promptly by the Second Advent of Christ. Miller's New York disciples met in a large hall on Chrystie Street. Led by Joshua Himes, a brilliant publicist dispatched to the country's communications capital to spread the good news, Manhattan's Millerites helped blanket the nation with four million prophetic charts and pamphlets. In the city itself, believers put out a weekly, the *Midnight Cry*, and roamed the sidewalks auguring doom. As the final day neared, some gave away their possessions. Many garbed themselves appropriately for their impending transformation into angels by purchasing the "White Muslin for Ascension Robes" advertised in Bowery dry-goods stores. When the end failed to arrive, Miller announced an error in calculations; a revised forecast postponed Judgment Day until October 23, 1844. After a second disappointment, the leadership recanted and the movement dispersed.[2]

Born-again workers seeking strength and solace also created a working-class temperance movement. In the flush years of the 1830s, most artisans and laborers had spurned the evangelicals' calls to give up drink, and hard times had driven many more to hard liquor. Yet within a year of the panic, journeymen and day laborers had formed the Temperance Beneficial Association, which set up street-corner pulpits from which reformed drunkards testified that alcohol made bad times worse, not better.

In 1841 journeymen and small masters launched the New York Washington Temperance Society, opening a mission on Chatham Street. Many in the panic-strengthened sects took the temperance pledge hoping Washingtonianism would bring order and self-respect to depression-buffeted lives. With elites insisting that poverty was a sign of dissoluteness, sobriety was a way of attesting respectability. The Washingtonian movement spread swiftly. In six months, it claimed twenty thousand male members in fifty chapters. Thousands of working-class women joined the Martha Washingtonians:

2. One of those who left town after the first disappointment was a freed slave named Isabella Van Wagenen, who over the previous decade had been a housekeeper and cobeliever of James Latourette, a Manhattan fur merchant who had broken with the Methodist Church to lead a New York group of Wesleyan perfectionists. After that, she became a member of the Kingdom of the Prophet Matthias, an anti-Finneyite cult. In June 1843, having renamed herself Sojourner Truth, she commenced an itinerant ministry, traveling first to the City of Brooklyn, then out into Long Island, where Millerite camp meetings proved receptive to female preaching, and then up to New England, where she began her abolitionist career.

wives who watched their husbands squander precious wages or savings on drink had their own reasons for being drawn to the movement.

Washingtonian temperance became the largest popular movement in New York City's history. While merchants, professionals, and masters held some leading positions, the movement sustained an egalitarian tone, rejected pious coercion, and refused to insist on conversion in Christ. Aware of drinking's key role in male working-class sociability, Washingtonians sought alternatives to the saloon. They sponsored weekly experience meetings—confessional self-help groups—and offered alcohol-free amusements like steamboat excursions, picnics, dances, bazaars, and concerts. The evangelical American Temperance Union criticized these vulgar innovations; at *their* meetings, also burgeoning, people listened decorously to clergymen and doctors expound on the evils of liquor. But it was precisely the Washingtonians' ability to foster individual survival skills within a congenially communal context that made them popular.

Communalism had its downside, however. Temperance helped respectable Anglo-Protestant artisans distinguish themselves from the (putatively dissolute) Catholic poor, a source of psychic comfort at a time when the line dividing the two communities had become thinner than ever. But the depression had also galvanized New York's Irish Catholics. They too pursued consolation in consolidation and asserted an ever greater cultural and political presence in the city. In a context of frightening economic insecurity, heightened communal sensibilities could and did easily degenerate into urban tribalism. Soon the mid-thirties dream of working-class solidarity would be drowned in a sea of ethnic and religious bitterness.

. . . AND ROMANISM

The depression had badly battered the Catholic Church. Father Varela's Transfiguration was in particularly grim shape. Back in prosperous 1836 he and the lay trustees had borrowed tens of thousands of dollars, in small sums, from the poor people of the parish to buy a vacated Presbyterian church on Chambers Street. Now desperate parishioners, many of them out of work for months and "in the utmost distress," implored him to return their money lest landlords seize their few pieces of furniture as payment for rent. Transfiguration itself was on the verge of being auctioned off, however, and only managed to stave off creditors by mortgaging its organ.

Bishop John DuBois was not prepared to deal with a crisis of this magnitude. Now seventy-four, he had been a priest for nearly fifty years and head of the diocese since 1826. Even before the panic, the aging Frenchman, long resented by the Irish community and hierarchy, had signaled his readiness to pass power to the immigrant-strengthened Gaels. The American bishops, accordingly, now dispatched John Hughes, a priest in Philadelphia, to aid DuBois and his flock.

Hughes was himself an Irish immigrant. The son of poor farmers, he had arrived in the United States back in 1817, aged twenty, and supported himself as a gardener while studying for the priesthood. More than ethnicity distinguished him from DuBois. Where the bishop had shied away from controversy, fearing to raise the profile of an outnumbered community, Hughes thrived on conflict and had long urged Catholics to fight for political and civil rights. With his stern mouth, muscular body, and intimidating presence, Hughes *looked* like a fighter. His nickname of "Dagger John" rested on more than his penchant for inscribing a stiletto-like cross next to his signature.

Two weeks after Hughes arrived in 1838, DuBois suffered a paralytic stroke, and the newcomer took effective control of the diocese. In 1842, on DuBois's death, Hughes would become bishop, the first prelate to be consecrated in St. Patrick's, and his elevation would mark the ascendancy of the Irish in the New York church. The dethroned French, perhaps by way of consolation, were awarded their own parish of St. Vincent de Paul in 1841.

In the fall of 1839 Hughes sailed to Europe seeking aid from wealthy Catholics. He did receive funds from the Austrian Leopoldine Society, but these were earmarked for a college and seminary—the future Fordham—and for recruiting priests and teachers for Catholic schools. The troubled New York church would have to make it on its own.

With Catholics still a small minority—the diocese had only eight of the city's 150 churches—Hughes was convinced the community had to rally round its faith, as various Protestant sects had been doing. In 1840 Father Varela founded the New York Catholic Temperance Association; hundreds took the pledge at Transfiguration gatherings, and within a year the group had five thousand members. Hughes, however, decided to focus on the schools.

Missionary protestantism still permeated Public School Society classrooms. The King James Bible—which Catholics would not accept even when the American Bible Society gave them away free—remained required reading. Schoolbooks slurred Catholicism. Teachers derogated Irish culture. And the PSS refused to open branches for Five Points immigrants, as "it is not thought proper to associate them with the respectable and orderly children who attend the Public Schools." The Church had expanded its own schools, but with public funding having ceased in 1825, they were overcrowded and understaffed. Thousands of Catholic children received no education at all.

Hughes wanted to restore public funding for church schools. This would relieve depression-aggravated poverty and end Catholics' second-class status in the city. The bishop soon discovered an ally in Governor Seward. An ardent advocate of Irish freedom and Irish immigration, Seward believed education was crucial for assimilating and elevating the arriving poor. Less high-mindedly, the governor knew that if Whigs were to sustain their depression-era victories, they would have to break Tammany's grip on the city's Catholic Irish.

In January 1840 Seward recommended funding for schools in which children "may be instructed by teachers speaking the same language with themselves and professing the same faith." Catholic leaders promptly applied to the Common Council, which controlled distribution of school monies. They promised, if funded, to limit religious instruction to after-school hours and to require parental approval. A Hebrew congregation and a Scotch Presbyterian church joined the appeal.

Cautious aldermen arranged a debate. A battery of Protestant lawyers and divines supported the current arrangements as a satisfactory separation of church and state. Hughes, standing alone, gave a three-and-a-half-hour speech arguing that Catholics' religious liberties could be upheld only in Catholic institutions. Appealing to Loco Foco antimonopoly sentiments, Hughes also cast the PSS as unacceptably authoritarian, paternalistic, and undemocratic—a "complex monopoly, of mind, and money, and influence, in the city of New York." Nevertheless, a nervous Democratic council turned him down.

Hughes appealed to Albany, where the Whig legislature and governor backed a school decentralization plan giving each ward authority to decide what kind of schools it wanted. The PSS countered that—given the city's shifting population—New York needed more, not less, uniformity in its schools. Besides, the Catholic claim was unconstitutional. Also it was unrepublican, one Protestant paper said, to train up children "to worship a ghostly monarchy of vicars, bishops, archbishops, cardinals, and Popes!" Renascent nativists formed (in May 1841) the American Protestant Union (led by S. F. B. Morse) to back candidates in the upcoming November elections who were deemed safe on the school issue.

With Tammany waffling and city Whigs backing away from Seward, Hughes decided to enter politics directly. Days before the election, he called a meeting in Carroll Hall, which endorsed ten of the thirteen Democratic nominees for the Assembly but ran independent Catholic candidates for the three remaining slots. All ten joint selectees won, but the Carroll Hall ticket drew sufficient Democratic votes away from the contested trio to let three Whigs win. Hughes had demonstrated two things conclusively to the Democrats (who had regained both houses of the legislature): given the roughly equal strength of Whigs and Democrats, Catholics held the balance of political power in New York City, and they would not hesitate to wield that power against Tammany.

Democrats, accordingly, passed the Maclay bill on April 9, 1842. It authorized each ward to elect commissioners who would supervise local schools and, acting together, constitute a citywide Board of Education. It also barred the teaching of any sectarian doctrine. Seward signed the bill. For the first time in its history, New York City had an education system financed entirely from the public treasury and directly controlled by the people.

Some of the people were less than pleased, however. On the night Seward signed, crowds stoned Hughes's home, forcing authorities to call out the militia. The editor of a new twopennny paper, the *Aurora*, applauded the attack. Already known for his diatribes against "villainous priests" and "Irish rabble," Walter Whitman now declared that if the missiles had been directed against "the reverend hypocrite's head, instead of his windows, we would hardly find it in our soul to be sorrowful."

Protestant die-hards quickly won control of the new Board of Education and ruled that classroom readings from the King James Bible were not precluded by the ban on sectarianism. Catholics also lost the battle for funding of their church schools. So Hughes returned to the task of building up a parochial school system, staffed primarily by nuns, that would parallel the city's network. At Hughes's request Mother Madeleine Sophie Barat founded the Convent of the Sacred Heart in 1841 and opened an academy on Houston and Mulberry, near the cathedral.

THE RETURN OF THE NATIVES

Bishop Hughes's brief foray into politics, combined with the pressures of hard times, had reawakened New York's slumbering nativist movement, which now dramatically asserted its power.

At first, the panic had actually soothed anti-immigrant anxieties by diminishing the influx of Irish. "Times is hard and wages low," an Ulster-American warned his relatives back home, and the word got around. In 1837 forty-eight thousand crossed over; in 1838 only eleven thousand did. Still, the stream of new arrivals helped swell relief rolls, increase taxes, and heighten competition for scarce jobs and housing. Hughes's Carroll Hall gambit of 1841 raised fears of Catholic political ambitions, and in spring 1842 newly reelected Mayor Morris rewarded Irishmen for their support by giving them jobs and licenses in the public markets.

Enraged Anglo-Protestant butchers, suddenly facing Irish competitors, spearheaded an anti-immigrant offensive. By August an American Republican Party was up and running, and in November its candidates received an astounding 22.9 percent of the vote for local offices. Spurred by this showing, a wide variety of New Yorkers clambered aboard the new party. Merchants, professionals, editors, and shopkeepers—furious at high taxes, financial profligacy, patronage abuses, outright corruption, and the yielding of Democrats and Whigs to Catholic pressure—hailed the American Republicans as a party of municipal reform. Small masters and journeymen in as yet unindustrialized trades like building, butchering, blacksmithing, and shipmaking signed on as well, in hopes that halting the immigrant flow might forestall the capitalist reorganization of work that had devastated the tailors, printers, and shoemakers. The new party also exalted the artisanal republican values of manly independence, Christian brotherhood, and craft solidarity and promised to restore the Trades to prominence.

What tied these disparate groups together was a shared Protestant culture, a nostalgic belief that New York City had been a far better place just after the Revolution, and a conviction that the evils now afflicting it—rising rates of crime, pauperism, and immorality—were foreign imports. The party's platform reflected these premises. The American Republicans wanted to extend the naturalization period to twenty-one years, effectively eliminating foreigners from politics and reserving government offices and market licenses to citizens. The nativists aimed to repeal the 1842 school law to guarantee preservation of Bible reading and "nonsectarian" religion in the schools. The party also promised budget cuts, tax reductions, law and order, sobriety, bipartisan appointments, and an end to corruption.

In 1844 the American Republicans ran publisher James Harper for mayor. An ideal candidate, Harper was native born and a devout Methodist, head trustee of the John Street Church. He was staunchly anti-Catholic: his firm had brought out Maria Monk's *Awful Disclosures*. He was a temperance man, a Washingtonian. Harper cast himself as "a mechanic"—he was a member of the General Society of Mechanics and Tradesmen—and evoked the old artisanal town. He was also the city's largest employer, in command of its most technologically sophisticated plant, and thus appealed to propertied taxpayers and the men forging an industrial metropolis.

Many city Whigs deserted their party to support Harper's candidacy—some openly, most tacitly, given Governor Seward's opposition. With their support, American Republicans swept the spring 1844 elections, placed James Harper in City Hall, and won control of the Common Council.

Harper set out to forge a new civic order. On the Fourth of July, the Mayor banned the sale of alcohol, offering up instead a large basin of iced Croton water in City Hall Park. He enforced tavern laws prohibiting Sunday liquor sales (though he exempted the downtown hotels patronized by more elite clienteles). Foreigners disappeared from the city's payroll. Apple women and other vendors were driven from the streets. Some salaries were cut, though taxes and expenditures continued to increase. Plans were launched for reforming the almshouse. In the end, however, Harper's crusade went nowhere: partly because under the charter the mayor lacked real power; partly because his moral fervor was transparently class-partial; partly because he was inept at governance; but primarily because a sequence of shocking events discredited his nativist movement.

In May 1844 word arrived that Philadelphia, which had also been riven by debates about schools and Bibles, had exploded in violence, with frenzied nativists hunting down Irishmen by the light of burning homes and churches. Excitement spread through New York. Some local nativists were eager for combat; an hours-long battle with Irishmen had broken out in Brooklyn a few days before Philadelphia erupted. Now they called for a giant rally on May 9, to greet a delegation of Philadelphia nativists.

Bishop Hughes stationed a thousand armed Irishmen around each Catholic church and told his community to keep the peace but defend their property at all costs. Hughes met with the mayor, who asked if the bishop was afraid for his churches. "No, sir," he replied, "but I am afraid that some of *yours* will be burned." Hughes went on to make it utterly clear to the nativist administration that "if a single Catholic church were burned in New York, the city would become a Moscow." The authorities, fearing a bloodbath, pressed their Protestant allies to abandon their mass meeting, a request to which they reluctantly acceded a scant few hours before it was to take place.

The riots in Philadelphia and New York's near brush with Armageddon deeply shocked many citizens. Nativists, now associated with riot and lawlessness, lost sympathy. In the 1845 mayoral election, the Seward wing recaptured control of city Whiggery and refused to back Harper's bid for reelection. Deserted by their allies, the American Republicans managed to win only a single ward constableship. The Democrats elected respected sugar merchant William Havemeyer Mayor on a reform ticket. Within two years the American Republican Party was dead, and with it, for the moment, nativism as a political force.

ROACH GUARDS AND DEAD RABBITS

Before receding, nativism contributed to an increase in street gangs, many of them ethnically based. "The city is infested by gangs of hardened wretches," Philip Hone told his diary in 1839. They "patrol the streets making the night hideous and insulting all who are not strong enough to defend themselves."

Gangs were no novelty in New York City. Citizens had complained of them since the early eighteenth century, and evanescent constellations of rowdy young men had been common enough after 1800. The Chichesters, perhaps the first gang with staying power, had commanded attention during the 1830s boom years, particularly for its assaults on brothels. But during the depression scores of gangs crystallized, each distinctively named and garbed.

The grocery-groggeries in the heart of the Five Points became headquarters for turf-based Irish gangs like the Forty Thieves, Kerryonians, Shirt Tails (from their shirts-out sartorial style), and Plug Uglies (from their enormous plug hats, which they stuffed with wool and leather and drew down about their ears like helmets when entering battle). The Roach Guards were conspicuous in their blue-striped pantaloons, and the Dead Rabbits, snappy in red stripes, adopted a name that meant "seriously *bad* dudes" in Points argot.

The Bowery was another gang locus. Here resided the Bowery Boys, O'Connell Guards, Atlantic Guards, American Guards (of nativist bent), and True Blue Americans (Irishmen, whose costume consisted of long black frock coat and stovepipe hat—a send-up, perhaps, of the outfits favored by dandified young merchants and clerks). African Americans coalesced as well, a phenomenon one of Frances Grund's local informants blamed on Arthur Tappan and his colleagues: "Our black servants are getting worse and worse every day ever since that bigoted scoundrel T*** has commenced preaching abolition," he fulminated. "Those black devils have always been a nuisance; but now 'a respectable white man' can hardly walk up and down Broadway of a Sunday afternoon without being jostled off the sidewalk by one of their desperate gangs."

Some gangs were pacific and merely took in the theater or circus together, but many were fiercely territorial. They guarded (as the names of many groups implied) particular pieces of city turf or invaded those of nearby bands. Neighborhood frontiers crackled with border wars. Combatants fought with bludgeons and brickbats, clubs and hobnail stomping boots, and occasionally, though still rarely, knives and pistols. At times, local rivals would league together into a giant horde and sally forth to challenge a gang-combine from some other part of town. Such combat was a customary entertainment in Ireland and England but increasingly frowned upon by the authorities over there. Over here, immigrants found, they could indulge in donnybrooks with virtual impunity; indeed spectators massed on rooftops or gathered at windows to cheer the scrappers on.

Gang members also latched onto volunteer fire companies and transmuted their traditional tussles into increasingly nasty confrontations. In 1839 over a thousand men and boys battled with sticks and brickbats. More and more often, such fire fights ended with stabbings or broken skulls. In January 1840 the mayor and Common Council found that "a great excitement prevails in this community, in consequence of frequent breaches of the peace, alleged to have been committed by a large number of dissolute and profligate young men."

Tribalism provided camaraderie, protection, identity, and also a sense of being in charge, something increasingly hard to come by in the workplace. Many gang members were technically "apprentices" or "journeymen," but few harbored any hope of becoming a "master." Jobs seldom gave a worker status or a chance to display skill. And if being a waged employee diminished one's sense of autonomy and control, being fired devastated it. The panic had made painfully clear that the new economic order could pitch a worker into desperate poverty, virtually overnight.

Security and self-esteem were best pursued elsewhere. After work a butcher, tailor, or cartman could doff his smock, apron, or overalls, don colorful gang regalia, rendezvous with his comrades, and regain at least the illusion of being in control of his life, of being a man among men. Rude lads esteemed precisely those qualities the emerging bourgeoisie devalued: muscular prowess, masculine honor, swaggering bravado, and colorful display. Uptown precincts exalted domesticity and sanctified femininity, but the lower wards were dominated demographically by single young men, most of whom, given their limited prospects, married late or not at all, and there, rowdy masculinity ruled. Women might assist in battle by bringing stones to frontline fighters but were seldom full-scale participants. There were, however, some spectacular exceptions, like the Dead Rabbits' Hell-Cat Maggie, whose teeth, filed to points, and fingers, embellished with brass nails, made her a welcome companion on forays against the Bowery Boys.

Gang warfare reflected and exacerbated conflicts between old-timers and newcomers. Some groups took ethnic chauvinism or blustering nativism as a raison d'être. Others avoided straight-out trials of strength with evenly matched opponents, preferring to prowl the streets singling out victims to bash (as in an 1840 assault on German immigrants).

The emergence of a vigorous two-party system drew the gangs into politics as well. Democrats, especially, sought the services of well-organized and well-muscled groups. Many Tammany ward and district leaders were on familiar terms with gang members, being proprietors of the Bowery saloons where they congregated. It was easy enough, therefore, especially in straitened times, to hire men to strong-arm party opponents and to guard, steal, or stuff ballot boxes.

Some of these outfits had political ambitions of their own. Mike Walsh, brought over from Ireland as a child, was a lithographer and journalist by trade. A militant defender of the city's workers, Walsh was hugely popular for his vitriolic and hilarious speeches excoriating assorted elites as "curs," "grub-worms," and "vultures." An effective fighter as well as eloquent speaker, Walsh formed the Spartan Band, one of the city's most effective gangs, in 1840. In elections that year, he and his men, forty or fifty strong and armed with clubs, invaded Whig headquarters, assaulting all present. In the November 1841 election, Walsh's Spartan Band, with three hundred members, became something of a loose cannon when he and his shoulder-hitters strong-armed their way into *Tammany*'s precincts and forced the Democratic General-Committee to put Walsh's name on their ticket.

Captain Isaiah Rynders, for whom politics was strictly a business, was more typical of the new breed of gang leaders who tied up with Tammany. The Captain had earned his title commanding a Hudson River sloop, then headed west, where he became a celebrated gambler and knife fighter, working the Mississippi River steamboats. Back in New York by the late 1830s, he opened half a dozen groceries and Bowery saloons. In 1843 Rynders organized the Empire Club, a group of bruisers who operated out of the Arena saloon at 28 Park Row—recruiting immigrants, breaking up Whig meetings, doing whatever Tammany called for.

At the same time some gang leaders were forging fateful partnerships with New York politicians, others were dedicating their energies to criminal enterprise. Complaints of robberies and muggings increased rapidly during the depression years. "The property of the citizen is pilfered, almost before his eyes," declared a special committee of the Common Council in 1842. "Dwellings and warehouses are entered with an ease and apparent coolness and carelessness of detection which shows that none are safe."

"A CIVIC ARMY"

New York's patriciate had long tolerated crowds rather than maintain a "standing army" of professional police. As late as the rowdy Callithumpian processions of the 1820s, some gentlemen had still considered the occasional civil disorder to be compatible with civic order. No longer. Crowds had gotten too big, too unruly, too organized, too Irish, and (Hone feared) "will ere long be difficult to quell."

They were *already* difficult to quell. In the riots of the 1830s, mayors attempting to overawe crowds with the majesty of their office had been unceremoniously trampled on. Nor, given existing instrumentalities for maintaining law and order, did reliance on physical force work much better than relying on social deference.

The police force was not inconsequential, to be sure. Jacob Hays, appointed high constable back in 1802, was a seasoned enforcer of the law. During the 1830s disturbances he had plunged gamely into the thick of a crowd, armed only with his staff of office, and seized rioters with a viselike grip. Hays, moreover, was backed by an expanded cadre of peace officers. By day these consisted of two dozen elected constables (two per ward) and scores of mayorally appointed marshals. By night hundreds of watchmen roamed the streets; though primarily on the lookout for fires, they were empowered to arrest any criminals they caught in the act. By 1834, indeed, New York's constabulary was among the largest and most efficient in the United States.

But not efficient enough. Old Hays, as he was known, was in his sixties. The daytime men were unsalaried and often corrupt political appointees, more interested in earning fees than preventing crime. The "leatherheads" (as watchmen were jeeringly known, after their leather helmets) were poorly paid moonlighters, scantily trained and ill respected. In the big upheavals of the 1830s civil authorities had been repeatedly forced to resort to the militia—usually the elite Twenty-seventh—but frenzied last-minute responses to street turbulence no longer seemed acceptable.

After the shipworkers' strike of February 1836—an affair that underscored the vulnerability of the city's commercial core—an elite consensus had emerged in favor of strengthening the forces of law and order. The Twenty-seventh was issued standing orders to be ready to deal with street violence, and the state legislature (in March 1836) specifically authorized the mayor to order out the militia to "quell riots, suppress insurrection, to protect the property, or preserve the tranquillity of the city." Yet widespread sentiment still held reliance on the military to be inappropriate for a republican government. In 1836, accordingly, Mayor Lawrence had asked Police Justice Oliver M. Lownds to consider ways of reorganizing the police department.

Lownds proposed that New York establish a twenty-four-hour professional police force, modeled on the one created in London by Robert Peel back in 1829. Lownds's "System of Police" envisioned the creation of multiple stationhouses, each armed with alarm bells. It won the approval of Mayor Lawrence, but opponents killed it by rousing old fears of a standing army and playing on new antigovernment sentiments, distrust of professionals, and fears that political parties might control the police. Besides, the Twenty-seventh Regiment had done such a sterling job suppressing riots. "Six hundred strong," one paper noted, and "composed entirely of the respectable young men of the city," they "may be considered the most efficient police we have, and we believe the Mayor and Common Council look upon them as such." So, apparently, did the federal government, which in 1839 allowed the Twenty-seventh to drill at Fort Hamilton (making it the first National Guard training camp in the nation); in 1840 granted the fort twenty thousand dollars for additional armaments; and in 1841 dispatched Captain Robert E. Lee for a five-year stint as post engineer, charged with improving the fort's defenses along with those of other military installations in the area.

The council did agree that New York needed a new jail. The old Bridewell was a nuisance, and the Bellevue Penitentiary was too distant from the downtown courts. In 1835, accordingly, construction commenced on a Hall of Detention and Justice. Situated on the grounds of the old Fresh Water Pond, along Centre Street between White and Leonard, the structure had a highly distinctive appearance. John L. Stevens of Hoboken had returned from the Holy Land with illustrations of an Egyptian tomb that caught the fancy of the Common Council. Completed in 1838, the new and imposing city prison became popularly (if mordantly) known as the Tombs.

In the depression, the propolice movement revived. The Twenty-seventh no longer seemed quite so potent a weapon since the panic had bankrupted many of its officers and men, and each passing year had underscored the inadequacy, inefficiency, and outright corruption of the existing force. The daytime marshals and constables, unsalaried, were compensated by fees, supplemented by privately offered rewards. The officers, not surprisingly, concentrated on crimes that seemed most likely to generate emoluments, such as thefts from a rich merchant's warehouse. With New York in effect having evolved a system of privatized justice, some enterprising detectives went a step farther. They actively colluded with thieves by "recovering" stolen property, then splitting the reward with the perpetrator. Hearings in 1840—the first of many and many to come—produced shocking accounts of organized police corruption.

The night watchmen—"postmen" at fixed stands and "roundsmen" patroling the streets—were equally problematic. As their numbers expanded from 512 in 1830 to 1096 in 1845, their reputation declined. Many leatherheads were elderly retirees or working a second job: "While the city sleeps," New Yorkers quipped, "the watchmen do too."

In 1839 Mayor Clark pushed for a municipal "military arm," on the grounds that having "the character of a riotous city fastened upon us would be truly calamitous." Editors called for a force that would *prevent* crime, not just catch criminals after the fact. Yet reluctance to expand police powers stalled further action until the sensational death of Mary Cecilia Rogers generated a demand strong enough to overbear all objections.

Mary Rogers, known as "the Beautiful Cigar Girl," had come to New York from Connecticut in the panic year of 1837. In 1838 she took a job selling cigars and tobacco at John Anderson's popular Broadway haunt for journalists and politicians. (This too was a depression-era phenomenon: as an 1838 story in the Sunday *Morning Atlas* noted, "times are so hard" that out-of-work young women were taking jobs in cigar stores despite the potential threat to their virtue from rakish young customers.) Early one Sunday morning in the summer of 1841, Mary Rogers left the boardinghouse her mother ran at 126 Nassau Street and went missing. Three days later, her bruised and waterlogged body was found floating in the Hudson River near Hoboken.

The penny press turned Rogers's death—like that of Helen Jewett—into a sensational event. Initial reports had it that Rogers had been gagged, tied, beaten, and raped by several men, then strangled and dumped in the water. Many assumed, with Philip Hone, that Rogers had "no doubt fallen victim to the brutal lust of some of the gang of banditti that walk unscathed and violate the laws with impunity in this moral and religious city." James Gordon Bennett blamed a gang of "fire rowdies, butcher boys, soaplocks, and all sorts of riotous miscreants," or perhaps a "gang of negroes."

When police made no headway in solving the crime, the press, led by Bennett, escalated Mary's death into a metaphor of New York's social and moral disintegration. In a scathing editorial on August 12, 1841, Bennett denounced "the apathy of the great criminal judges, sitting on their own fat for a cushion bench—and the utter inefficiency of their police." Such incompetence was "leading fast to reduce this large city to a savage state of society—without law—without order—and without security of any kind."

Hysterical rhetoric about the proliferation of crime was seriously overdrawn, as an 1842 district attorney's report demonstrated, but sentiment proved more compelling than statistics. Governor Seward, citing the Rogers case, called for improving the police in his 1842 Annual Message. Local influentials now swung round and reached a consensus, as one advocate put it, about "the necessity (as in London) of a civic ARMY, a numerous Municipal Police."

In 1843 the state legislature passed a New York Municipal Police Act, which the governor signed on May 7, 1844. The new law abolished the Watch Department and the offices of marshals, street inspectors, health wardens, fire wardens, dock masters, lamp lighters, bell ringers, and inspectors of pawnbrokers and junk shops. All these responsibilities and more were turned over to a semimilitary "Day and Night Police," not to exceed eight hundred men.

New York's force was closely modeled on London's, with one crucial difference. London's Metropolitan Police was an arm of the national government, divorced from local control. New York's was totally decentralized. Each ward became a patrol district, with its own stationhouse. And each ward nominated its own candidates for police officers; if accepted by the mayor, they were required to live and serve in that ward. New York's police, beholden to politicians, would be inextricably enmeshed in local politics.

The new policemen were salaried—all fees were abolished—and each was expected to make policing his only and full-time job. Preventing crime became as important as apprehending criminals. Officers assigned to surveillance were required to report "all suspicious persons, all bawdy houses, receiving shops, pawn brokers' shops, junk shops, second-hand dealers, gaming houses, and all places where idlers, tiplers, gamblers and other disorderly suspicious persons may congregate."

The 1844 state law, however, was merely permissive legislation. It was up to the city to accept it. Mayor Harper's nativist administration, which took power after Albany acted, refused to ratify it. Instead, leaving the old system intact, the American Republicans added a body of two hundred men—native born and strictly temperance. Officially called the Municipal Police, they were known informally as "Harper's Police," as the mayor, not the wards, selected each man.

Harper also chose their wardrobe. The state law had explicitly rejected uniforms as a sign of despotic government, requiring only a star-shaped copper badge (hence "copper" or "cop"). Mayor Harper demanded a blue frock coat with covered buttons, a dark vest, blue pantaloons, and a standing coat-collar with the letters *M.P.* and a number in woolen embroidery. The men bitterly opposed the uniform, which they felt made them look like butlers. The public booed them in the streets, denouncing them as "liveried lackeys" of the nativists.

In 1845, when Democrats retook the city, they scrapped Harper's Police and adopted the state law. Mayor Havemeyer, striving to establish a bipartisan department, appointed a political opponent, George W. Matsell, to be the first chief of police. Tammany men on the Common Council, having no such high-minded compunctions, promptly parceled out the eight hundred new positions to Democratic activists (some of them members of the new strong-arm gangs).

BOTTOMFEEDERS

Hard times had a golden lining for more than newly minted policemen. Indeed, the depression laid or strengthened the foundation for several of Manhattan's foremost fortunes.

On May 14, 1837, August Belmont, aged twenty-three, arrived in New York City. His intention was to take the next boat to Havana, where he was to check on the Cuban interests of his employer, the House of Rothschild. Belmont immediately noticed the idle docks, the subdued streets, the general air of a city suffering from plague. He walked over to Wall Street to enquire of the Rothschilds' American agents what was happening, only to discover that the House of Joseph and Company had folded its tent. An ambitious young man—he had worked his way up with the Rothschilds from errand boy to confidential clerk to private secretary—Belmont decided on the spot to set up as the Josephs' replacement. Canceling his Havana trip, he rented a small room at 78 Wall Street and established August Belmont and Company, gambling on his employers' approval. When the Rothschilds' blessing arrived—along with a salary of ten thousand dollars a year, a fortune in shattered New York—he used Rothschild credit to buy up banknotes, securities, commodities, and property at severely depressed prices. With building lots going for a tenth of their former value, he could hardly help but flourish.

Unto those who already had, even more was given. Jacob Little, the notorious short seller, positively thrived during the crisis, reaping vast returns as the market plunged. John Jacob Astor, profiteer of calamity, snapped up land and houses at fire sale prices, spending over $224,000 in 1838 alone. At the same time, Astor ruthlessly foreclosed on hundreds of property owners who fell behind in their mortgage payments. Cornelius Van Shaack Roosevelt also accumulated land all over Manhattan during the panic years, betting it would rebound in value. Henry E. Pierrepont, whose proposed cemetery had been stymied by high land prices, now found old Dutch farmers willing to sell out for far less. Green-Wood was incorporated in 1838; the first lots went on sale in 1839. At the opposite end of the opportunity spectrum, James Weeks, an African-American stevedore, purchased land in 1838 from the Lefferts family estate, site of the future Bedford-Stuyvesant's Weeksville.

Bottomfeeding was not the only route to success. Alexander Turney Stewart, born in 1803 near Belfast (where he was educated for the ministry), emigrated to New York in 1818 and found work as a schoolteacher. In September 1823 he opened a tiny dry-goods store on lower Broadway just north of City Hall Park, offering Irish linens, French cambrics, damask, and similar items "on reasonable terms." The business flourished, and over the next twenty years Stewart moved from one location to another, each one a little bigger and fancier than the last. By 1837 his five-story, double-width emporium at 257 Broadway was one of the city's largest. In the panic, Stewart bought up great amounts of distressed merchandise from bankrupt wholesalers and resold it at low-price high-volume, emerging as one of the city's first millionaires.

Lewis Tappan fashioned a new industry out of hard times. At first, he and his brother, Arthur, had concentrated on simply staying afloat. Prevailing on their creditors to let them to stay in business, they cut expenses to the bone—Arthur moved into a boardinghouse and slashed his aid to abolitionists—and in eighteen months repaid all outstanding obligations, an amazing accomplishment. Still, the silk business remained a day-to-day struggle, and in 1840 Lewis departed to launch the Mercantile Agency, the country's first credit rating firm (and ancestor of Dun and Bradstreet). Even in good times, New York wholesalers had lacked information about the solvency and reliability of the far-flung country storekeepers to whom they annually entrusted goods worth millions of dollars. The depression had underscored the problem, as unscrupulous (or merely desperate) retailers used evasion or fraud to escape their liabilities. Tappan's solution was to establish a network of trustworthy informants—recruited from abolitionists, evangelical clerics, and solid young lawyers like Abraham Lincoln of Springfield, Illinois—who forwarded to New York confidential reports on the merits of local storekeepers. These communiques assessed net worth, liquidity, and "character." They flagged storekeepers who had intemperate habits, led a sporting life, or were "mixed up with a bad woman" (marriage was deemed essential to good credit, though having too many children was thought to cut into capital). From these raw files Tappan fashioned reports he sent to subscribers twice each year, just in time for the fall and spring seasons, when inland storekeepers descended on the city. He thus secured his own fortune and strengthened New York's position as a commercial center and haven for creditors.

"LAUGH AND GROW FAT"

Clearly, New Yorkers' responses to the drawn-out depression varied widely. Some failed, others made fortunes; some gave charity, others accepted it; some plunged into politics, others into religion, others still into crime. But one reaction was well-nigh universal: a search for diversion, something to drive one's cares away. For all but the rich, this dictated a search for inexpensive pleasures. At first, the panic had sandbagged the city's entertainment trades, but it quickly became apparent to a new breed of entrepreneurs that substantial profits could be made in hard times by providing cheap amusements to mass markets.

In 1837 popular papers had suffered along with their working-class readers. The panic killed off most of the penny dailies, including the *Transcript*. Even pioneer Benjamin Day lost heart. Facing declining circulation and advertising revenues, Day sold the *Sun* to his brother-in-law, Moses Yale Beach, another Connecticut Yankee. Soon, however, it became clear that working people considered penny papers an excusable indulgence in difficult days. Beach infused the *Sun* with capital, jettisoned what remained of its insurrectionary character (though retaining its democratic air), and filled its pages with romantic fiction, racy crime, theatrical and sporting news, and such "Help Wanted" notices as came along, making it popular with the unemployed. By 1843 the *Sun* was shining brightly, with a claimed daily circulation of thirty-eight thousand, and twelve thousand for the weekly edition.

Bennett's *Herald*, aimed at a more middling market niche, flourished too. Readers enjoyed his misanthropic maunderings, scathing editorials, accounts of scandals, and attacks on deceitful politicians and venal financiers. On March 2, 1840, Bennett broke new ground yet again, when he devoted his front page to the "Grand Fancy Dress Ball, at Brevoort Hall." The story, mixing fawning society reportage with exposé, recounted a tale of outrageous extravagance amid widespread suffering. Nearly six hundred costumed gentry had partied from eight in the evening until five the next morning at the Brevoort mansion on Fifth Avenue and 9th Street. (The article included a layout plan of the first two floors.)

Philip Hone—who attended as Cardinal Wolsey, garbed in scarlet merino robe and ermine cape—was delighted with the event. "Never before," he told his diary, "has New York witnessed a fancy ball so splendidly gotten up, in better taste, or more successfully carried through." But the racy reportage—which aroused both fascination and fury among the city's middle and working classes—led the old mercantile elite to declare total war on James Gordon Bennett.

"This kind of surveillance is getting to be intolerable," Hone fumed, "and nothing but the force of public opinion will correct the insolence." He, along with leading merchants, bankers, and civic notables, worked to have "respectable people withdraw their support from the vile sheet." Genteel readers and advertisers boycotted the *Herald*, rooted it out of homes, clubs, hotels, and coffeehouses, and ostracized Bennett. To no avail. The so-called moral war cost Bennett a quarter of his readership and a chunk of his ad revenue, but he soon bounced back, and voyeuristic society columns, offering mass audiences a window into elite sanctums, became a permanent feature of New York journalism.

The "moral war" was, however, a great opportunity for any publisher willing to step in as a champion of respectable values, and Horace Greeley seized the moment. On April 10, 1841, backed by the Whig magnates who had underwritten his log cabin journalism, Greeley founded the *New York Tribune*. His entrant in the penny press sweepstakes, Greeley declared, was intended for the "cultivated and influential families of the city," those a notch above the *Herald*'s and two notches above the *Sun*'s. To penetrate "the parlors or sitting rooms of the uptown residents," the *Tribune* would eschew the "immoral and degrading Police Reports, Advertisements and other matter which have been allowed to disgrace the columns of many of our leading Penny Papers." Greeley's efforts to win "the hearty approval of the virtuous and refined" soon garnered him a circulation of ten thousand a day.

Like the penny papers, city book publishers fared poorly at first. Prices and profits plummeted; so did the number of titles the houses issued. Even the largest were imperilled. Unable to transact business or secure credit in London, Harpers considered bankruptcy in 1837, before opting for retrenchment. The industry recovered, however, and even flourished, when eager newcomers, deploying penny press techniques, revolutionized the book trade.

Park Benjamin had been literary editor of Horace Greeley's *New-Yorker* until, as Greeley wrote later, "the Commercial Revulsion of 1837 swept over the land, whelming it and me in the general ruin." Benjamin then tried publishing the *American Monthly Magazine*; it collapsed in 1838. Finally, in 1839, he devised a publication suited to an era of cutthroat competition. *Brother Jonathan*, a weekly magazine, combined news with serialized novels pirated from England. It was printed cheaply, on a single giant sheet of paper, then folded but not bound; because of a postal regulation loophole, it could be mailed at cheap newspaper rates. Given the excess capacity of New York's depression-idled presses, *Brother Jonathan* could be priced at six cents, an attractive bargain.

With *Brother Jonathan* launched, Benjamin departed to start up a rival, the *New World*. Each now vied to include the most material. The sheets grew larger and larger, winning the name "mammoths." The *New World*, eventually six-feet-seven by four-feet-four, comprised forty-eight columns of small type and was best read on the floor. The mammoths also issued "extras" or "supplements," which crammed entire books into this format. They offered melodramas and high romances, English novels and French fiction in translation, as well as books by local authors, such as *Franklin Evans*, a temperance novel by the journalist Walter Whitman. Newsboys hawked them on the streets and delivered them to subscribers' doors, offering premiums (Bibles) for quick renewals. Profit margins were slim, but volume was enormous. Circulation soared past that of all other magazines, even that of most penny papers, forcing book prices ever lower.

Suffering publishers loudly protested the ruinous competition. In 1842, Harpers decided to do battle. Slashing prices on its own English knockoffs, it overcame the attendant deficits with steady profits from schoolbook sales. Then, in 1843, postal authorities ruled that the mammoths' "supplements" had to be mailed at the more expensive book rate. The newcomers—undercapitalized and overextended—collapsed, succumbing at last to the depression they had up till then ridden so masterfully. What remained was a meaner, leaner New York book trade, geared more than ever before to low-cost, high-volume production.

A similar trajectory characterized the development of New York's theatrical life in these years. The panic devastated city playhouses. Ticket prices plunged, without attracting patrons. Some smaller theaters closed their doors; larger ones cut wages sharply. At the Bowery Theater, manager Hamblin hoped spectacular effects might improve attendance. In an 1840 drama, *The Pirates' Signal*, he replaced the stage with a tank of water, upon which a full-rigged ship sailed from rear to footlights, actors declaiming on deck. Equestrian spectacles followed, among them *The Battle of Waterloo*, which boasted fifty horses, two hundred supernumeraries, and cannons. Neither fared well; both were too expensive.

Elsewhere along the Bowery and Chatham Street new approaches were percolating. Taverns and small hotels provided free entertainment to draw in drinkers. These venues—known as "free and easies" or "varieties" or "vaudevilles"—offered an ever-changing if incoherent assortment of music, dance, magic, ventriloquism, comedy, skits, and tall tales, frequently provided by the audience itself. Hamblin discovered that his Bowery Theater, too, did best when it ran circus shows, comic routines, and low-budget acts appropriated from the streets and marketplaces. William Mitchell followed suit, halving his Olympic Theater's admission prices and focusing almost exclusively on what he called "tragico-comico-illegitimate" productions: travesties of local events, topical commentaries, and Shakespearean burlesque (*Julius Sneezer* and *Dars-de-Money*).

Shipbuilders and cartmen, butchers and firemen, tradesmen and laborers, domestics and launderers—the vast numbers of single men (and growing numbers of single women) who lived in nearby boardinghouses—began packing their way into such shows. New theaters (the Franklin, the Chatham) went up to house the overflow. The plebeian fare fit comfortably into the expanding spectrum of Bowery entertainments, which included scores of cheap dance halls, dime museums, brothels, billiard rooms, bowling alleys, saloons, oysterhouses, and amphitheaters offering bare-knuckle prizefights or cockfights. At the district's northern end, the shabby but genial Vauxhall Gardens, one-eighth its former size, still offered substantial food at reasonable prices, and its promenades, deserted by toffs, were thronged with toughs.

The Bowery came into its own during the depression as a plebeian recreation zone, one that rivaled, even outshone, the constellation of patrician venues around City Hall. Working people gravitated there after hours, attracted by the life and color, the array of services (including pawnshops, stage offices, butcher and grocery shops, and livery stables), and above all the vitality of crowds of people determined to have a good time.

The neighborhood was not all-inviting, however; the audiences at most festivities were white-only. The New York Zoological Institute, at 37 Bowery, had a sign reading: "The proprietors wish it to be understood, that PEOPLE OF COLOR are *not permitted to enter*, EXCEPT WHEN IN ATTENDANCE ON CHILDREN AND FAMILIES." When one African American challenged the edict by driving up with his own family in a hired carriage, he was barred, punched, and ejected. The *Emancipator*, an abolitionist paper, seethed at "these savage proprietors and managers," these "sordid knaves," and wondered if they would "allow *animals* of color in their institute!"

Blackness, barred from the audience, remained near the heart of the Bowery's art. "Negro delineations"—brief bits of burlesque, comic relief, and entr'acte songs and dances—grew ever more popular. At the Bowery Theatre, Hone noted, Jim Crow "is made to repeat nightly, almost *ad infinitum*, his balderdash song, which has now acquired the stamp of London approbation to increase its *éclat*." In February 1843 these solo performances evolved into the depression era's most remarkable innovation.

Four unemployed musicians, living in a Catherine Street boardinghouse, decided to pool their talents and work up a marketable routine. All had performed as blackface entertainers with circuses. Hoping to ride the coattails of a successful touring company, the Tyrolese Minstrel Family, the quartet called themselves the Virginia Minstrels. Their act featured presumed southern slave culture ("Virginia Jungle Dance") and employed a heavy "nigger" dialect. Their eccentric movements, wild hollers, infectious music, captivating dancing, rollicking humor, and earthy jokes set Bowery audiences to whistling, shouting, and stomping their feet. From the second they strutted onstage at the Branch Hotel, the Virginia Minstrels were a sensation. They soon departed for an English tour, leaving behind a swarm of imitators. New York City had birthed the minstrel show—a baby that would soon reshape American popular culture.

Race was central as well to the career launch of the titan of the New York entertainment world, the era's (and arguably the century's) most important impresario, the master of humbug himself, the one, the only, Phineas Taylor Barnum. Barnum was yet another Connecticut Yankee who, loathing life on the family farm, had cast about for alternatives. He clerked for a time in a country store, learning the local arts of hard bargaining and sharp practices. He opened his own fruit and confectionery store. He became a lottery manager. In 1834 he moved to New York City, where he ran a boardinghouse, then a grocery on South Street. Finally, in 1835, Barnum discovered his true calling.

Barnum learned that in Philadelphia a Yankee showman was exhibiting a gnarled black woman who claimed she was 161 years old and had been George Washington's slave nurse (with a 1727 bill of sale for herself to prove it). Joice Heth, toothless and totally blind, offered affecting stories about "dear little George," but only meager audiences came. Barnum, convinced he could repackage Heth into a paying proposition, sold his grocery store, borrowed more money, and bought the rights to her for a thousand dollars.

Barnum quickly displayed a genius for promotion. He got up a promotional pamphlet, festooned New York with posters, and persuaded the papers to discuss Heth. Most intriguing, he invited doubt about the truth of her story, even hinted she was a fraud, sure that audiences would be as interested in testing their ability to discover the truth as in the real facts of the matter. He was right. After exhibiting Heth at a coffeehouse on the corner of the Bowery and Division Street, he moved her up to Niblo's Garden, eventually clearing fifteen hundred dollars a week.

Joice Heth died within a year, and Benjamin Day reported in the *Sun* that an autopsy showed her age to be half what Barnum claimed. By then the showman was on the road. For much of the next four years he traveled the country with a blackface dancer and a juggler, ran an entertainment steamboat on Mississippi, and sold Bibles. Then he abandoned itinerancy, returned to New York, and launched his career as impresario.

In May 1840 Barnum leased Vauxhall Gardens. Rather than assemble the usual (and costly) summer stock company, he brought in performers by the night. His "variety shows," like those up and down the Bowery, drew on popular plebeian entertainments ("grand Trials of Skill at Negro Dancing"). They featured familiar city types ("the Fireman," "the Fulton Market Roarer"). They redeployed street activities (like amateur slack-rope walking). In effect the self-styled Director of Amusement's variety show had appropriated the natural (and low-budget) theatricality of the street and market and made it pay.

The format proved popular. Its zestful novelty and continual change suited an audience quickly and easily jaded, and its miscellaneity mirrored metropolitan diversity. An ad in the *Herald* noted the performances "are exceedingly various, and full of life and merriment. This is what we want. The public have enough to groan and sigh about at home these times, they go out to such places as Vauxhall to 'laugh and grow fat,' and Barnum is determined they shall not go in vain."

"Blackness" remained central to Barnum's formula, though the tricky conventions of popular racism could present problems for a fledgling cultural entrepreneur. In 1841 his star performer, a white blackface dancer who specialized in "negro break-downs," struck out for greener pastures. Barnum (as editor Thomas Low Nichols of the *New York Aurora* later remembered) scouted the dance houses of the Five Points. He soon found a lad who could do the dance even better, "but he was a genuine negro; and there was not an audience in America that would not have resented, in a very energetic fashion, the insult of being asked to look at the dancing of a real negro." Barnum rose to the occasion. "He greased the little 'nigger's' face," Nichols recalled, "and rubbed it over with a new blacking of burnt cork, painted his thick lips with vermillion, put on a wooly wig over his tight curled locks, and brought him out as the 'champion nigger-dancer of the world.' Had it been suspected that the seeming counterfeit was the genuine article," Nichols chuckled, "the New York Vauxhall would have blazed with indignation."

By 1841, when Barnum was ready for a grander venue, he learned that the old Scudder's Museum was up for sale. Scudder's had a great location, on Broadway at Ann Street, near to both plebeian quarters and patrician precincts (the Astor House Hotel and City Hall were just across the way). Barnum took over the building and its collections, renamed it the American Museum, and made it the nucleus of New York popular entertainment.

Barnum stocked his American Museum, as he had Vauxhall, with jugglers and ventriloquists, curiosities and freaks, automata and living statuary, gypsies and giants, dwarfs and dioramas, Punch and Judy shows, models of Niagara Falls, and real live American Indians. (Barnum advertised the latter as brutal savages, fresh from slaughtering whites out west, though privately he groused that the "D——m Indians" were lazy and shiftless—"though they will *draw*." Animal acts had their problems too: when his orangutan got sick in 1843, Barnum pinned his hopes on a goat but soon realized that "he *shits* so I can do nothing with him.)" After 1842 attendees could also see a two-foot, one-inch midget named Charles Stratton, better known as General Tom Thumb, whom crowds adored (especially after Barnum took him to Europe in 1844, where he performed for royalty). And, of course, he featured blackface dancers, Ethiopian melodists, and the new minstrel shows.

One key to Barnum's success was his mastery of the art of imposture. Hoaxes had been a staple of the penny press since 1835, when Benjamin Day's *Sun* had run its series reporting life on the moon. The failure of so many oversold speculations during the panic and the subsequent exposure of deceptions by swindling businessmen had lessened the public's appreciation for plausible rogues, to be sure. But Barnum's brand of humbug was neither malicious nor costly. In offering up such forgeries as the Fejee

Mermaid he sold his audiences the sheer fun of debating truth or falsity, of outmaneuvering the hoaxer, of discovering how the deception was done. "The public," as Barnum observed, "appears disposed to be amused even when they are conscious of being deceived."

Barnum was also a brilliant promoter. "It was my monomania to make the Museum the town wonder and town talk," he wrote in his autobiography, and he developed merchandising into a daring new art form. Barnum deployed all the familiar tactics—extensive ads in the papers, lithographs, pamphlet biographies, posters, flags, bright banners—and a slew of new ones. He installed the first "Drummond lights" in New York City, which illuminated Broadway with limelight "from the Battery to Niblo's." He stationed a band on his balcony. He covered the entire building with five-foot-high transparencies depicting over a hundred species of animals. He hired street performers and sent "bulletin wagons" with their sides plastered with ads rolling through the metropolis. Barnum imposed his institution on New York City with much the same flair and fanfare Thurlow Weed had used to hawk William Henry Harrison. And with even greater success, for by the mid-1840s, Harrison was in his grave, but P. T. Barnum's Museum had become the boast of city guidebooks, a shrine for visiting tourists. More than anyone else, Barnum had realized and seized upon the essential compatibility of hard times and high times. His triumph would stand as an inspiration to countless successors in New York's world of entrepreneurial entertainment.

PART FOUR

EMPORIUM AND MANUFACTURING CITY (1844–1879)

Currier and Ives lithograph, city of New York, 1876. (© Collection of The New-York Historical Society)

38

Full Steam Ahead

J ust before noon on April 23, 1838, the *Sirius*, a small paddlewheel steam packet nineteen days out of Cork, limped across the Upper Bay, its coal supply all but exhausted, and made landfall to the cheers of a great crowd gathered at the Battery. A scant four hours later, a second steamer, twice as big and half again as fast, hove into view, belching black smoke. This was the *Great Western*, fourteen days out of Bristol. She had been chasing *Sirius* across the Atlantic, and the sight of her churning toward the city touched off even more exuberant rejoicing, as it was now doubly clear that New York had established a maritime steam link to Europe.

Over the next twenty years, a growing fleet of transatlantic steamers would nourish the city's economic revival, but the newcomers would be *English* ships, which boded ill for the future of the port's merchant marine. More disturbing, when Samuel Cunard began twice-monthly steamer service out of Liverpool in 1840, he chose Boston as his line's terminus. Cunard was heavily subsidized by the British government, and New York editors and lobbyists bombarded Washington with appeals for equivalent support. In 1845 Congress grudgingly agreed to provide subsidies for steamships that carried the mail (and could be used by the navy in time of war). Still, no New York competitor materialized, and though Cunard did extend service to the Hudson, he built his piers in Jersey City.

Finally, in 1848, a city champion emerged. Edward Knight Collins, a well-connected New York packet operator, promised to build the biggest and fastest steamships afloat. Collins won a mail contract from the government, raised over a million dollars from New York merchant bankers, and organized the United States Mail Steamship Company. Commencing a prow-to-prow competition with Cunard, Collins's captains tore across the Atlantic. Where the *Great Western* had taken fourteen and a half days on

The Arrival of the Great Western Steam Ship off New York on Monday 23rd April 1838, artist unknown. Once again, the opening of new connections between the city and the world beyond became an occasion for delirious celebrating. (I. N. Phelps Stokes Collection. Miriam and Ira D. Wallach Division of Art, Prints and Photographs. The New York Public Library. Astor, Lenox and Tilden Foundations)

her maiden run in 1838, Collins's *Pacific* made Liverpool in a record nine days, twenty hours in 1851. A grateful Congress raised the line's annual subsidy from $385,000 to $853,000.

But Collins never made money. His costs were higher than Cunard's, in part because English wages were lower, and he was hammered by disasters. In 1854 his *Arctic* collided with a French steamer off Cape Race and sank with a loss of 318 passengers and crew, including Collins's own wife and children. In 1858 Congress scuttled the mail subsidy program, largely at the behest of Jefferson Davis and other southerners at odds with New York. Once the federal government left the private enterprise to sink or swim on its own, it promptly sank. The last Collins sailing, in February 1858, marked the end of New York's bid to establish itself in transatlantic steam shipping. The field—and the future—were left to Cunard and newer British or German entrants. For the present, however, the decision of foreign steamers to make Manhattan their primary port of call, along with a spectacular efflorescence of New York's sailing fleet, sustained the city's commanding position as the nation's premier port.

New York's trim, square-rigged packets—products of the East River's thirty-odd yards—had been steadily growing in speed, agility, and size. By 1850 New York ship-builders routinely constructed packets three times larger than the pioneer Black Ballers. Whenever one of these leviathans slid down the ways, thousands of spectators converged on the scene to watch and applaud. They were the city's pride and glory, bulwarks of its wealth, instruments of its power. But now they were superseded by still more awesome vessels: the breathtaking "clippers" for which the East River yards gained fame in these years.

The first true clippers were promoted by the city's traders in China tea, a fragile commodity that fetched exorbitant prices only if brought to market quickly after harvest. In 1844, hoping to shorten the voyage from Canton, which normally took more than a hundred days via the Cape of Good Hope, the firm of A. A. Low and Brothers invested forty-five thousand dollars in a packet-like vessel designed specifically for speed. Named the *Houqua* after a highly regarded Chinese merchant, she was slender and heavily sparred and canvassed, with a bow that cut rather than butted the waves. Inspired by her example, the South Street firm of Howland and Aspinwall ordered the *Rainbow* and the black-hulled *Sea Witch* from the yard of Smith and Dimon. In 1849 *Sea Witch* completed the run from Canton, a distance of fourteen thousand miles, in an astonishing seventy-four days, fourteen hours.

The production of clippers increased steadily over the next decade, and the enormous expense of constructing them led to further consolidation of the trade in a handful of wealthy firms. By the late fifties, with some fifty ships returning to port from China every year, half a dozen New York companies dominated the business completely. After the repeal of the British Navigation Acts, New York clippers managed as well to capture a large share of the carrying trade between China and London. In 1850 one of the Low clippers, *Oriental*, brought a cargo of tea from Hong Kong to the Thames in a record-breaking ninety-seven days; the proceeds nearly covered her original cost of construction.

The discovery of gold in California in 1848 gave the clippers their most lucrative mission. Inflamed by stories of egg-size nuggets lying about for the taking, men from all over the country headed west. "Nothing else is talked about but the quick fortunes to be made in California," one New York paper reported that autumn. In 1849, with the Gold Rush in full swing, eighty thousand people converged on eastern ports to book passage on anything that would float for the long and dangerous passage around Cape Horn to San Francisco. Between 1849 and 1852 California's population ballooned from twenty thousand to 223,000.

The price of milk, coffee, work shirts, boots, and other necessities rose accordingly—a barrel of flour worth six dollars back in Manhattan would fetch two hundred in the goldfields—and merchants in the China trade soon saw that routing their outbound clippers west, around South America with a stop in California, rather than east, around Africa, was the way to maximize returns. Among the earliest China clippers out of New York to Frisco were the *Samuel Russell* and *Sea Witch*, each of which returned profits beyond the wildest expectations of its owners. Low and Brothers netted eighty-four thousand dollars on the initial voyage of the *Samuel Russell*, more than it cost the firm to build her. A load of flour, nails, and steam engine parts sent out on the *Sea Witch* made $190,000 for Howland and Aspinwall.

Other firms jumped into the business. When news of the strikes reached the William Street store of Joseph Seligman and his brothers, they plunged all they had into small merchandise, sent it posthaste to San Francisco, and made a fast fortune. The Strauss brothers, a family of Bavarian emigrés in the dry-goods trade, sent young Levi to San Francisco in 1853 to peddle wares that Jonas and Louis sent him round the Horn.

New York shipbuilders designed scores of clippers for merchants working the California market. Some of the best of the new crop were the work of William Henry Webb, whose yards stretched from 5th to 7th streets along the East River—notably the two-thousand-ton *Challenge*, which flew the checkered flag of N. L. and G. Griswold and was able to make San Francisco in 110 days or less. Webb's father had taught the art of shipbuilding to Donald McKay of Boston, who now built the *Flying Cloud*—loveliest of all clippers on the California run—for Grinnell, Minturn, and Company of New York. On her maiden voyage, in 1851, she dropped anchor in San Francisco Bay eighty-nine days and twenty-one hours after leaving the foot of Maiden Lane, a week under the previous record.

The demand for speedy service to the West Coast tempted some merchants into imperial adventures. Back in 1847 William Aspinwall and a tough river steamboat operator named George "Hell Fire" Law had won federal subsidies to move mail and freight across the Isthmus of Panama. Law's firm ran steamers from New York, by way of Havana and New Orleans, down to the east coast of Panama. From there their cargoes were conveyed overland by canoe and mule train to Panama City, and thence up to San Francisco on the ships of Aspinwall's Pacific Mail Company. The entire trip took five weeks, and once the Gold Rush got underway it became fabulously profitable despite the unpleasant trek through the snake-infested, mosquito-plagued Panamanian jungle. Aspinwall's Panama Railroad, completed in 1855, improved transport considerably, and Panama City became an economic satellite of New York.

Law and Aspinwall's success whetted the cupidity of Commodore Vanderbilt, who calculated that a route across Nicaragua would be five to seven days faster than the one across Panama. Vanderbilt's initial plan called digging for a canal, at a cost of thirty-one million dollars, through the twelve miles of jungle and mountains that separated Lake Nicaragua from the Pacific Ocean. When that idea ran afoul of British interests in the region, Vanderbilt set up the Accessory Transit Company and wangled a franchise from the Nicaraguan government to run a macadamized road that, combined with bay and river steamers, connected San Juan del Sur on the Pacific and San Juan del Norte on the Atlantic. The new line's first passengers and a shipment of gold reached New York from San Francisco in August of 1851; within a few years it was earning Vanderbilt a million dollars a year, despite complaints about his penny-pinching disregard for public health and safety.

In 1855 an American filibuster named William Walker seized control of Nicaragua, installed himself as president, and revoked Vanderbilt's charter, transferring it to competitors who promised to pay more. This audacity made Walker a hero in New York— some Boweryites went down to join him—but it earned him the enmity of the ruthless and powerful Commodore. Without setting foot outside New York, Vanderbilt underwrote an invasion of Nicaragua by four other Central American republics, and Walker's hated American Phalanx was overthrown in 1857.

Most New York businessmen worried that such tactics could lead to war with Spain or Great Britain, but armed diplomacy became an acquired taste among some big merchants and railroad financiers, including August Belmont, Prosper M. Wetmore, Royal Phelps, and John A. Dix. Cheered on by such prominent editors as James Gordon Bennett and John Louis O'Sullivan (of the *Democratic Review*), these "Young Americans" clamored for further expansion, especially in Central America and the Caribbean. It was the Manifest Destiny of the United States, they said, to spread republicanism, Christianity, and progress around the world—by trade if possible, by force if necessary.

In Asia, force seemed particularly appropriate, England having demonstrated its efficacy by ramming unwanted drugs into China during the Opium War. (The Lows and other China traders had also been smuggling in Turkish opium in exchange for tea, using fast little schooners turned out by the East River yards, and after Britain's success they too expanded their operations.) All New York celebrated when Commodore Matthew C. Perry took the navy's East India Squadron to Japan in 1853 and bullied the shogun into opening his country to American trade. Perry was almost a native son, having spent a decade at the Brooklyn Navy Yard pioneering the application of steam power to warships. Besides, he was Belmont's father-in-law. New Yorkers could be forgiven for thinking that Tokyo too was now an economic satellite of Manhattan.

From around the world, commerce poured into New York City. In 1849 over three thousand ships sailed or steamed into the harbor from more than 150 foreign ports—three times the number that had arrived in 1835—and they carried with them half the nation's imports and departed with nearly one-third its exports. In the Gold Rush decade (1849–59), ship tonnage through the port jumped another 60 percent.

As trade grew, so did the size and tempo of the waterfront. By 1850 a collar of piers, wharves, docks, and slips circled Manhattan below 14th Street—sixty on the East River, another fifty or more on the Hudson. Those along the East River were favored by sleek Liverpool packets and great square-rigged clippers, those on the west by deeper-draw coastal and transatlantic steamships (the Collins Line pier, for example, lay at the foot of Canal Street). East side or west, however, there was never enough room to accommodate the thousands of vessels now moving in and out of the port every year. At its busiest, the harbor looked (to landlubbers anyway) dangerously anarchic: pilots and crews jockeying for berths while schools of sloops and lighters darted in and out among canal boats, schooners, yachts, barges, ferries, and two-thousand-ton steamers that plowed along at speeds approaching twenty miles per hour.

It wasn't any calmer on shore, either. In 1857, 598 licensed hacks, forty-five hundred carts, and 190 express wagons competed to tote cotton bales from southern packets to steamers heading to Liverpool; lug finished bolts just in from Manchester to storage warehouses, Pearl Street wholesalers, or Broadway retailers; carry ice, coal, or wood to consumers; haul brick, stone, and earth to construction projects; and fetch passengers from ferries and steamer berths. The number of omnibuses shot up from 255 in 1846 to 683 in 1853 (when they carried over a hundred thousand passengers a day). After 1840, cabs too began clattering about town. The din was terrific, what with hundreds of iron horseshoes striking cobblestone pavements, boxes rattling, drivers cursing and fighting. The racket was not much alleviated when, in 1853, the city began to substitute Belgian blocks—bread-loaf-size cut-granite chunks that were better able to withstand iron-rimmed wagon wheels than circular cobblestones and provided firmer footing for horses.

This profusion of conveyances soon swamped the downtown streets. On an average weekday in the mid-fifties, fifteen thousand vehicles rumbled by St. Paul's at the corner of Broadway and Fulton. "The throng and rush of traffic in the business part of New York is astonishing even for London," noted a visiting correspondent for the *London Times*. "There is a perpetual jam and lock of vehicles for nearly two miles along the chief thoroughfare." Along the riverfronts, West Street and South Street were lined by block after block (as *Gleason's Pictorial Magazine* put it in 1857) of bustling "sail-lofts, shipping offices, warehouses of every description, cheap eating-houses, markets, and those indescribable stores, where old cables, junk, anchors, and all sorts of cast-off worldly things, that none but a seaman has a name for, find a refuge." Like Broadway, these dockside streets were clogged with horsedrawn wagons, carts, and carriages, which by the 1850s often choked off movement altogether.

Decay and disrepair was as pervasive as congestion along both rivers. Pilings wobbled and shook. Wharves vanished under the waves at high tide, some never to reappear. Rotting piers suddenly gave way, tumbling people and cargoes alike into the water. Pools of effluvia from open sewers and drains, trapped by masses of floating debris, lapped at crumbling bulkheads; except in the dead of winter, the stench and flies could be over-powering. By 1855, almost in defiance of the port's burgeoning traffic, New York's waterfront had deteriorated so badly that state investigators found no more than a dozen-odd piers in fair to good repair on either side of Manhattan. The one positive consequence was that wharfage rates remained low, maintaining New York's strong competitive advantage over ports having better but more expensive facilities. In 1852, for example, it cost one packet $4.88 to unload seventeen hundred bales of cotton at a Hudson River pier over a two-day period; in Boston or Baltimore it would have cost sixty-eight dollars.

If there was short-term method in the madness, the city would pay a long-term price, as the deplorable condition of the Manhattan waterfront prompted new con-struction on the opposite side of the East River. From Green Point in the north to Red Hook in South Brooklyn, gangs of workmen filled in tidal marshes, built breakwaters, and threw up blocks of docks and warehouses. One of the largest projects was merchant and landowner Daniel Richards's plan to transform forty acres of Red Hook marsh-lands into the Atlantic Basin. Surveying began in 1839; the first dock blocks were sunk in 1841; the initial warehouse rose in 1844 under the direction of contractor James S. T. Stranahan; the port's first steam grain elevator was installed in 1846; and by the end of the decade, its forty acres of basin were capable of sheltering a hundred ships at a time. The docks in turn were covered with twenty acres of four-story brick and stone ware-houses, erected by developers like Samuel Ruggles, and enough grain elevators to make it the main terminus for Erie canal boats. In the Brooklyn Navy Yard, meanwhile, the federal government spent two million dollars over a ten-year period on the construction of a massive masonry drydock.

Just as these sea-oriented projects were coming to fruition, new railroads began pumping even vaster quantities of cargo and passengers into the New York maelstrom.

Built in reponse to overcrowding and deterioration along the Manhattan waterfront, the huge Atlantic Basin in Brooklyn became an important destination for grain and other bulky cargoes entering the port from the Erie Canal. From Henry Stiles, *History of the City of Brooklyn*. (United States History, Local History and Genealogy Division. The New York Public Library. Astor, Lenox, and Tilden Foundations)

RAIL

In May 1851, with great fanfare, President Fillmore and a party of civic notables boarded a steamer at the foot of Duane Street and chugged twenty miles upriver to the west-bank port of Piermont. There the party transferred to a New York and Erie Rail Road car and proceeded to travel 447 miles to Dunkirk, a hamlet on the shores of Lake Erie.

An ecstatic Common Council hailed completion of the long-delayed line as "emphatically the work of the age," and for good reason. Incorporated in 1832, the New York and Erie had not only survived the bankruptcy of most of its original backers during the Panic of 1837, but its engineers and immigrant laborers had contrived to run a double track of six-foot gauge over a major mountain system. The economic significance of this linkage was manifest to all. As director and ironmonger William E. Dodge jubilantly exclaimed: "The Empire City and the great West, the Atlantic Ocean and inland seas, are by this ligature of iron made one!"

Also in 1851, a second force of engineers and laborers was driving the Hudson River Rail Road within sight of Albany, having laid 144 miles of track along the bank of the Hudson. Like the Erie, the Hudson Line had overcome more than natural obstacles—including the opposition of powerful Hudson River steamboat operators who had been pouring money into the development of mammoth floating palaces to attract customers, with great success. Roused by the threat of a rival road out of Boston, however, the legislature assented to a charter for the Hudson Line. By the end of 1851 it was scooting passengers from New York to Albany in less than four hours as against seven and a half hours by steamboat. By 1853 its passengers could transfer to a set of interconnecting roads that stretched all the way to Buffalo. Unlike the Erie, moreover, the Hudson Line ran directly into Manhattan. Its cars rolled south down Eleventh Avenue to a massive depot covering the area between 30th and 32nd streets. There, since municipal regulations prohibited steam engines below that point (the danger of explosion still being very real), passengers and freight were transferred to horse cars, which clopped downtown along Tenth, West, and Hudson, stopping at 23rd, 14th, and Christopher, skirting the west side of Hudson Square, and finally terminating at a shed on Chambers Street.

The arrival of the railroad on the city's West Side, coupled with the increasing preference of steamships for the Hudson River docks, pulled vast numbers of dry-goods merchants across town from their Pearl Street quarters. By 1855, speeded by a city-engineered program of street widenings that cleared vast tracts for real estate speculators, some two hundred warehouses had been erected, many handsomely designed in the latest Italianate mode with white marble or brownstone facades. Rents and prices doubled in three months, quickly driving out groggeries and boardinghouses. "From the old worm of Decay," exulted the *Tribune*, "flutters forth the gorgeous butterfly of Wealth and Beauty."

Together, then, the Erie and Hudson lines sustained New York's overwhelming advantage in the movement of western produce to the East Coast. By the late fifties, the city was handling half again as much rail tonnage as Philadelphia and Baltimore combined. In 1860, counting the still-heavy volume of traffic on the Erie Canal, it received $161 million worth of goods from the West, just about the value of that year's cotton crop.

A third line, the old New York and Harlem, was meanwhile acquiring a new look. It still ran cars every ten minutes from Union Square up to Harlem village, but in 1840 it bridged the Harlem River at 135th Street and began to push north. Two years later, construction crews had crossed the Bronx River and were driving into Westchester County. By the mid-fifties the Harlem Line had opened a feeder from its Melrose station in the Bronx (at 162nd Street) to Port Morris on the East River near Riker's Island, and at Woodlawn it had linked up with the New York and New Haven coming down from Connecticut. This vigorous expansion shortened the commute to Manhattan from the Bronx, Connecticut, and Westchester suburbs like White Plains. Harlem Line locomotives ran down the East Side, along Fourth Avenue and through the Murray Hill tunnel. At 32nd Street, passengers switched to horsecars for the short ride to Madison Square Depot, a grand, multitowered station in the newly popular Italianate manner the line had erected in 1845 in the block bounded by Madison and Fourth avenues and 26th and 27th streets. From that point passengers could catch a horsecar directly to Astor House while freight continued on south to a terminal occupying the blocks between Center, Franklin, Elm, and White streets. Built in 1853, it was thought to be the largest structure in the city at the time.

By 1852 the Hudson, Harlem, and New Haven lines were channeling 2.5 million passengers a year into the city. At the same time, carriers like the New Jersey Railroad funneled traffic from Philadelphia and elsewhere into Jersey City. There, at a new terminal built in 1858, people and vehicles transferred to the 850-ton ferries that carried two thousand passengers plus horses, wagons, and carriages back and forth across the Hudson every ten minutes all day, every fifteen minutes all night. To the east, travelers could ferry across the East River and hook up with the Long Island Rail Road for a rail-sea voyage to Boston—until 1848, when the New York and New Haven established a direct and far more expeditious overland service.

DOLLARS AND DRY GOODS

Building railroads, clippers, and steamships took money—and money was something New York had plenty of. Between 1851 and 1854 alone, $175 million in gold reached the city from California. A good part of it was brought in by the new American Express Company, organized in 1850, or by Henry Wells and William G. Fargo, who left American Express in 1852 and set up their own company "to forward Gold Dust, Bullion, Specie, Packages, Parcels & Freight of all kinds, to and from New York and San Francisco."

This western bounty induced an upsurge in the banking business, which the state had opened to all comers back in 1838. New banks flowered even more profusely than railroads: twelve in 1851, another thirty by 1853, sixty in all before the middle of the decade. These institutions, in turn, served as depositories for six hundred of the nation's seven hundred commercial banks, which maintained permanent balances in New York to expedite domestic and foreign transactions.

The efficiency of the banking system improved as well. For years now, it had been the practice of the city's banks to close their accounts every day by settling up with one another directly—squadrons of clerks and porters rushing to and fro in an atmosphere of comic-opera frenzy, here with checks or notes for payment, there with hand trucks piled high with satchels of specie. But as the number of banks mounted, the financial system, like the streets, approached gridlock, and the need for a more rational approach became apparent. In 1853, accordingly, local bankers created the New York Clearing House, which enabled clerks to do in minutes what had previously taken hours.

More capital, more banks, and more efficient banking enabled New York to pull far ahead of its nearest competitor, Boston, in the moneylending business. By August 1857 local banks carried better than forty million dollars in outstanding loans on their books, a deep reservoir of credit that lubricated the expansion of trade, transportation, and manufacturing throughout the United States. Banking evolved from being an adjunct institution, created and controlled by merchants to facilitate their trading operations, into a distinct business enterprise, with a profit motive all its own.

Growing numbers of merchants—men like Moses Taylor—segued from commerce to finance. Taylor, like many of his contemporaries who amassed fortunes in business, had been born (in 1806) into relative affluence. His father, Jacob Taylor Moses, was a cabinetmaker who had invested successfully in Manhattan land and become John Jacob Astor's "general agent." Young Moses apprenticed as a clerk with G. G. and S. S. Howland, by 1830 the leading house in the Latin American trade. After he proved himself with diligent wharf and countinghouse service, the Howlands allowed him to trade on his own account. In 1832, with his accumulated profits, a loan from his father, and sterling references from Astor and the Howlands, Taylor set up on South Street as a commission merchant specializing in trade with Cuba.

In addition to arranging the transport of sugar from Havana to New York, Taylor advised Cuban planters on how to invest their excess funds and advanced them credit for land and slaves. In the 1840s Taylor turned much of his mercantile work over to Percy Rivington Pyne—successively Taylor's clerk, partner, and son-in-law—and concentrated on investing.

Taylor first favored cautious, capital-preserving vehicles like bonds, mortgages, real estate (especially wharves and stores near Manhattan's shore), and trust companies (like the well-established New York Life Insurance and Trust Company). Taylor branched out into gas and telegraph companies, and in the 1850s he became one of a small group of venturesome merchant-financiers who supplied capital to, and gradually assumed control over, many of the coal mines and blast furnaces in Pennsylvania. Taylor, Belmont, and other New Yorkers also became the nation's premier railroad financiers, with Taylor concentrating on lines in and out of the eastern coal fields. In 1851 one group established the Illinois Central Rail Road, with blueblood Robert Schuyler, Hamilton's nephew and the country's leading railroad tycoon, as its first president.

Taylor also moved directly into banking. In 1837 he had become a director of the City Bank of New York, acting as J. J. Astor's representative. He and the other directors invested in one another's ventures, and Taylor brought his own associates into the bank's management. In 1856 Taylor assumed the bank's presidency.

Entrepreneurs also turned to New York's capital markets to raise money, jolting the stock market out of the torpor that had gripped it during the recent depression. By the late fifties, hundreds of new brokerage houses had appeared in the city. These firms helped attract leery European capital—badly burned by American defaults during the panic years—back into U.S. businesses. The Barings had refused to participate the boom as late as 1850, but the discovery of gold fired the imagination (and avarice) of investors, just as the Revolutions of 1848 frightened Euroelites into seeking safely distant havens for their money. By 1853 26 percent of all U.S. rail bonds were in the hands of overseas investors, notably English and German. During a typical week in the 1850s, hundreds of thousands of shares in railroads, banks, canals, and coal mines were traded, making New York one of the largest and most sophisticated capital markets in the world.

Speculators and stock manipulators also zoomed in on the glamorous new railroad issues. Jacob Little, the stockbroker who had already won the nickname "Ursa Major," the "Great Bear," now dazzled the city with ever more brazen feats of financial legerdemain. Little rigged prices with fake tips, false rumors, phony accounts, and fictitious sales. He outfoxed short sellers by organizing clandestine pools to corner the market, and he fleeced friends as well as enemies by working through other brokers to screen his movements. Not since the days of William Duer, if ever, had Wall Street witnessed such single-minded predation.

Little's methods inspired a new generation of wheeler-dealers, most notably a country boy named Daniel Drew. Drew got his start in business as a drover, buying cattle from upstate farmers and herding them down to Manhattan to satisfy the growing city's demand for beef. In 1830, at the age of thirty-three, he became manager of the new Bull's Head Tavern on Third Avenue at 24th Street. Thrifty and clever with money, Drew became a trusted private banker for the drovers and butchers who met at the Bull's Head, cashing their notes and extending them credit for a modest 1 percent interest. In 1838 he retired from the cattle business, moved down to Bleecker Street, and set up a banking and brokerage house in the basement of the City Bank building at 40 Wall, directly across from the Merchants' Exchange.

Over the next twenty years, playing the market with the nerve of a riverboat gambler, Drew accumulated a personal fortune estimated in the millions. He took particular interest in the high-risk "fancies"—wildly fluctuating stocks of troubled companies, typically railroads that had underestimated costs and overestimated traffic. Drew learned to minimize his risks and maximize his profits by purchasing enough stock to get himself named an officer or director of the issuing company. Insider trading violated no laws in this feverish, cynical era, and Drew's privileged position helped him decide when to buy or sell the company's stock, as well as to manipulate its market value to his own advantage—something he did on numerous occasions as treasurer of the New York and Erie Railroad. Legend has it that while still a drover, Drew bamboozled Henry Astor by selling him cattle fattened on water just prior to sale; it didn't happen, but it served as a convenient origin myth for the term "stock watering," which came into currency to describe the practice of artificially inflating the value of securities.

While Drew himself never succumbed to the temptation, it wasn't uncommon to see a company straightforwardly looted by its own management. In 1854 directors of the New Haven line discovered that Robert Schuyler, their powerful and distinguished president, had privately printed up twenty thousand shares of bogus New Haven stock, sold them for two million dollars, and pocketed the proceeds. In the ensuing uproar, Schuyler slipped across the Canadian border; neither fugitive financier nor funds were ever recovered.

The results of all this commercial and financial activity, licit and illicit, were soon palpable on Wall Street. Many new banks set up shop in built-to-order Renaissance palazzos—monumental structures made of New Jersey brownstone and cast-iron columns and designed by stylish architects like Richard Upjohn and James Renwick. The new buildings, in addition to keeping up with the latest London fashion in commercial architecture, were more flexible than the now passé Grecian temples. Banks could rent the front rooms to other institutions (private bankers, insurance companies) and still have room in back for the small army of clerks, copyists, and accountants needed to handle their growing paperwork.

Still, the demand for office space kept burgeoning. The members of the Stock and Exchange Board burst out of their quarters in the Merchants' Exchange and sought new shelters. So did the legions of ever more specialized wholesalers—dealers in cotton, provisions, dry goods, hardware, drugs—and the formal organizations like the New York Produce Exchange (1851), which they established to standardize the grading, inspection, and marketing of their particular commodities. On top of this came the space requirements of brokers, agents, commission merchants, auctioneers, jobbers, and credit reporting firms. Tappan retired from his Mercantile Agency, but the company expanded under his successors Benjamin Douglass and Robert Graham Dun, and indeed attracted rivals, like the Bradstreet Agency.

Insurance companies added to the crush. By 1860 ninety-five insurance outfits protected against losses from fire; seventy-one of them had been founded in the 1850s. A dozen firms covered maritime risks, with fully a third of the city's business being transacted by the Atlantic Mutual Insurance Company (dominated by the Jones family, which had invested its rentier inheritance in the firm).

The life insurance industry finally took root, as businessmen, scarred by the depression, responded to new hard-sell campaigns. Agents warned that "experience demonstrates that the possession of property is almost equally unstable with that of life," presented statistics demonstrating that "the merest fraction" of those in mercantile pursuits "leave any property to their surviving relations," and printed up chilling lists of men who had died shortly after taking out a policy. Using the new domesticity to counteract religious objections that insurance interfered with the workings of Divine Providence, agents pleaded with merchants and professionals not to let their "beloved wife or children" be left "often worse than penniless, to the cold charities of the world." Eleven life insurance companies soon were thriving in the city, paced by the Mutual Life Insurance Company (1843), which by 1860 had over twelve thousand contracts on its books.

IRON AGE

During the 1850s, fattened on trade and gold, New York became the nation's leading manufacturing center—indeed one of the fastest-growing industrial areas in the world. Testifying to this transformation were the ironworks that hunkered down along the East River and Hudson River waterfronts, attended like economic royalty by flotillas of barges full of New Jersey pig iron and Pennsylvania coal. (In 1854 alone over one million tons of the latter came down the Delaware and Hudson Canal.)

Some of the biggest—the Globe Iron Works, the Morgan Iron Works, and the Delameter Iron Works, each acres in extent and employing hundreds of workers—were creatures of the boom in railroads and steamships, producing entire trestles, thirty-ton marine engines, and the enormous bed-plates on which a ship's machinery rested. Largest of the lot, an acknowledged wonder of the age, was the sprawling Novelty Iron Works on the East River shore at the foot of 12th Street. Founded in the 1830s by Thomas B. Stillman and Horatio Allen, Novelty was a five-acre maze of buildings that employed as many as twelve hundred workers by the early 1850s. Highly systematized,

Novelty was sectioned into eighteen departments, each directed by a foreman who in turn answered to the "front office"—one of the city's first—staffed by a superintendent and eleven clerks.

Another set of foundries turned out cast iron for warehouses and stores. In the mid-forties James Bogardus, a New York watchmaker and inventor, developed and patented a method for mass-producing prefabricated building elements. Columns, panels, and arches—in any architectural style—were cast from molds, laid on the foundry floor, primed, and assembled into small numbered units. Then, packed in straw, they were loaded on a horse-drawn dray, taken to construction sites, and raised and bolted into place, ready for painting (usually a light earthen color) and the installation of plate-glass windows. At first Bogardus's modular facades were simply fastened to the front of existing brick buildings, converting downtown structures from domestic to commercial use. In 1849, he designed a complete cast-iron facade, for a Broadway drugstore, and in 1850 he patented an all-cast-iron building.[1]

Bogardus broke the logjam in commercial construction, and his structures—inexpensive to make, easy to erect and maintain, supposedly fireproof—were soon in great demand. Foundries were created or converted to supply them. Daniel D. Badger had moved to New York in 1846 to make iron shutters. Now he relocated his Architectural Iron Works to East 14th Street and Avenue C, where he churned out Corinthian columns, roof cornices, and (from 1852 on) complete cast-iron storefronts. Though Badger dominated the field, competitors flourished as well—notably the Jackson, Cornell, and Etna ironworks—most also located near the rivers for ease of access to coal and pig iron.

There were, however, serious drawbacks to erecting giant industrial plants in Manhattan. Apart from the overcrowded streets and jammed docks, the rapid rise in the price of land (and of taxes tied to assessed valuation) meant that, as of 1855, two-thirds of all fixed capital invested in iron foundries was tied up in real estate, and only one-third in machinery. It still made economic sense for the big foundries to keep close to customers like the shipyards lining the East River from Grand to 12th streets, just as this great maritime complex, which launched one out of every seven steam-powered vessels built in the United States between 1850 and 1860, preferred proximity to its suppliers. But for many growing enterprises, cheaper land and more fluid transportation were the key desiderata. Some big operations like Steinway and Sons' piano-manufacturing plant (1853) found a satisfactory perch on the northern edge of the built-up city. But for many, it was Brooklyn that proved most enticing.

Sugar refineries were among the first to migrate. Back in the early nineteenth century, when the Havemeyer family operation required but five employees, a little building on Vandam Street had been perfectly adequate. But as Moses Taylor and other merchants funneled vast amounts of Caribbean sugar to the city, and as refinery technology underwent explosive development, the Havemeyers engineered a drastic change in scale and location. In 1858 Frederick C. Havemeyer bought a sizable waterfront tract in Williamsburgh and erected a million-dollar plant complete with its own docks and

---

1. In 1845 Thaddeus Hyatt patented a unique lighting system that neatly complemented Bogardus's creation. Thick glass discs set within iron grilles were placed in the sidewalk in front of a warehouse, letting natural light into the basement and avoiding the need for gas lighting and its attendant fumes.

warehouses. By 1860, the Havemeyers and their thirteen competitors were producing half the nation's supply, and Brooklyn had become the greatest sugar-refining center in the world.

Other industries followed suit. By the 1850s Brooklyn's factory district stretched along the shoreline from Greenpoint and Williamsburgh in the north, down past the Navy Yard at Wallabout Bay, and on to South Brooklyn, where the building of the Atlantic Basin and the decision to construct a canal from Gowanus Bay to Douglass Street to drain the surrounding marshland spurred development.

Iron foundries flourished. So did drug companies: Pfizer started up its Williamsburgh plant in 1849, and Squibb opened on Furman Street in 1858. The Brooklyn Flint Glass Works and the Cartlidge porcelain factory paced two newly substantial industries. The city's distilleries produced over five million gallons of whiskey annually, its steam-powered ropeworks thrived, and its white-lead manufacturers turned out more product than anyplace else in the United States.

Queens too proved attractive, especially as new transport increased its accessibility. In 1849 Peter Cooper transplanted his glue factory to a ten-acre site along the Maspeth Avenue Plank Road. And in 1854, Conrad Poppenhusen set up a factory in College Point to produce household goods made of the hard rubber patented in 1839 by Charles Goodyear. Around his Enterprise Rubber Works, Poppenhusen constructed a company town—by draining marshes, bringing in water, streets, and gas, building a road to Flushing, and erecting houses he rented or sold to workmen and their families, whose ranks grew to two thousand by 1860.

To the north, the bucolic Bronx remained heavily forested, divided into sizable estates, with here and there some small farms, and a few minuscule villages and townships along the New York–Boston post road. The advent in 1841 of Jordan L. Mott, inventor of a coal-burning stove, and the arrival in 1842 of the Harlem Railroad opened up a small industrial beachhead. Mott purchased from Gouverneur Morris II a site on the Harlem River bounded by Third Ave and 134th Street. (After the sale he asked if he might name his new settlement Mott Haven. "I don't care what he calls it," Morris grumped. "While he is about it, he might as well change the name of the Harlem and call it the Jordan.") Here Mott erected a sprawling ironworks, with a tall brick smokestack, where his workforce produced stoves, sinks, and ornamental ironwork. He also laid out the Mott Haven Canal to facilitate access to the foundry and purchased additional acres from the Morris family on which to found a community for craftsmen, near what is now Washington Avenue and 160th Street (this time he tactfully chose the name Morrisania). Other, grander operations soon followed, including the Janes and Kirtland Iron Works (on Westchester Avenue between Brook and St. Ann's avenues); a mammoth plant, it turned out mammoth products, most spectacularly the 8,909,200-pound Capitol dome, which was transported to Washington section by section and set in place by 1863. Still farther north, large New York-owned firms operated out of Yonkers, Bridgeport, and Danbury—manufacturing bricks, stoves, and locomotives—while the output of the Catskills' leather tanneries, when finished in Manhattan, allowed New York to dominate regional and national markets in yet another industry.

To the south, the agricultural and sea-based economy of Staten Island also began to draw large manufacturing operations to its wide open spaces. By 1860 the pioneer New-York Dyeing and Printing Establishment was employing 160 men, forty women, and eight steam engines to process nearly five million yards of cotton muslin annually, and rival firms had emerged—like Crabtree and Wilkinson, whose 183 workers turned out 1,520,000 silk handkerchiefs annually. New manufactories made wallpaper, furniture, carriages, and Charles Goodyear's India rubber cloth. The village of Factoryville boomed. Nearby Tompkinsville benefited from the arrival of the Dejonge brothers' paper plant, which produced gift, art, commercial, and (a U.S. first) white-coated lithograph paper. Three Staten Island manufacturers devoted themselves to producing and bottling artificially carbonated or "soda" water for dispensation at "soda fountains."[2] On the southwest shore, along the Arthur Kill, discovery of clay and kaolin deposits led to the emergence of a major brick-manufacturing industry. The earliest, largest, and most influential company was founded near Rossville in 1854 by Balthazar Kreischer; by 1860 his sixty employees, housed in the company village of Kreischerville, were producing a million firebricks annually.

Even Staten Island's most traditional occupation, oyster gathering, changed scale and structure. Most of the natural shellfish beds in Kill van Kull, Arthur Kill, and Prince's and Raritan bays had been exhausted as early as the 1810s. To preserve their livelihood and meet increasing demand, watermen imported and transplanted small "seed" or tiny, larval "set" oysters from fertile Virginia beds. By the 1840s oystering had become an extensive business. By the 1850s it was one of the region's foremost industries, dominated by large commercial firms that, collectively, employed perhaps a thousand men raking and tonging the sea bottom with long wooden-handled iron tools, then culling, hauling, shucking, preparing, and cleaning the planting grounds.

Manufacturing also blossomed to the west, across the Hudson River, in a string of New Jersey towns easily accessible to the emerging national rail grid: Elizabeth, Jersey City, Newark, Orange, Passaic, and Paterson. Many manufactories had been transplanted from Manhattan and were still owned and operated by New Yorkers. The Colgate Soap Company moved to Jersey City in 1847. The Hendricks copper factory at Belleville had become one of the largest of its kind. Even so ardent a New York booster as Peter Cooper moved his ironworks to the banks of the Delaware at Trenton, where it would be closer to Pennsylvania anthracite, Jersey ore, and his biggest buyer, the Camden and Amboy Railroad. Cooper's son, Edward, and Abram Hewitt then expanded the business by combining the whole process of iron manufacture from ore to finished product in one enormous complex, employing over two thousand workers, in the hills of northern New Jersey.

By the mid-fifties, then, considerable numbers of larger companies had situated or resituated themselves in an industrial belt girdling Manhattan, a regional economy that included such powerhouse cities as Brooklyn (fifth in manufacturing) and Newark (ranked sixth). Yet New York City remained number one—with one of every fifteen people employed in U.S. manufactures working on the island of Manhattan— because king-size iron works, factories, and refineries were not the be-all and end-all of industrialization.

---

2. Artificially carbonated soda water, made by Noyes Darling and first served at the Tontine Coffee House in 1809, became a serious industry in the thirties, with the arrival of Englishman John Matthews, whose factory at First Avenue and 26th Street became the nation's leading plant for production of soda water, bottles, glasses, and designs for soda fountains. Natural effervescent mineral water, discovered in upstate New York in the 1780s, was also popular; it was known as seltzer, after Selters, a village in Prussia associated with the drink.

METROPOLITAN MANUFACTURING

As of 1855 roughly two-thirds of the city's industrial workforce was employed in firms with fewer than a hundred hands, half of them in firms with under twenty-five—big by the standards of 1840, but nonetheless lilliputian alongside a behemoth like Novelty. Even in the iron industry, small- to medium-size firms were the rule. By 1860 New York had 539 iron works with 10,600 employees—an average of twenty per shop—producing gas meters, plumbing fixtures, printing presses, cutlery, iron beds, springs, nails, bolts, and the like. In woodworking, giant companies turning out pianos were far outnumbered by small furniture shops where handfuls of workers turned out cheap tables, cane chairs, sofas, beds, and chests. Shipmaking required huge yards but depended also on the sixty-odd firms that produced sails, blocks, and other marine equipment. All in all, in 1860 Manhattan housed 4,375 manufacturing establishments, which employed 90,204 workers. Most of these were small operations, crammed into the upper stories of buildings used otherwise for trade and commerce (44 percent were in the downtown warehouse district bounded by the Second Ward). Why did New York attract such a bevy of manufacturers?

Partly it was a matter of finance. Banks were still unwilling to lend to small manufacturers. Hence enterprising artisans either paid their own start-up and overhead costs, which limited them to the cheap rental spaces available in the warehouse district, or they relied on loans (and orders) from downtown merchants, who preferred their partners (and investments) close to hand.

Partly it was a matter of markets. For manufactures destined for export, it made sense to locate production facilities near the port, the place where it was easiest to get information about, and ship to, distant markets. When items were destined for Manhattan—and the city consumed most of what it made—it was proximity to local purchasers that dictated the choice.

Partly it was a matter of access to other manufacturers. New York was a warren of interlocking suppliers. Iron foundries produced steam boilers for shipyards, gas tanks for gas companies, architectural ornaments for contractors; and they relied in turn on a network of repairmen, machine shops, and importers of raw materials. Cabinetmakers prized nearness to sawmills, dealers, and auction houses. Papermakers, rag collectors, publishers, printers, and even pencil factories (the country's biggest was on the East River) developed synergistic relationships. P. J. Lorillard cut and cured tobacco at his plant in the Bronx and packed it downtown on Broome and West Broadway. While there were areas of topographical specialization, most manufacturing areas were a jumble of businesses. In the 1850s, when the blocks south of Houston and west of Broadway began to change from residential to industrial, they filled with foundries, copper and brass shops, locksmiths, China and glass manufactories, cabinetmakers and furniture makers, and the lumber yards that supplied them.

Partly—principally—Manhattan's was a labor-intensive economy. Most New York workshops relied on skill and muscle, not steam. Powered firms were roughly three times as expensive to establish as unpowered ones, so by 1860 only 18 percent of New York's shops were engine driven. This was up considerably from the 4 percent using steam a decade earlier, but it still left three-quarters of Manhattan's workers in firms where people-power was the only source of energy. Not surprisingly, most firms planted themselves close to the low-wage, walk-to-work proletarians who were stacked into the island's lower wards.

The most characteristic form of metropolitan manufacturing was the transformed textile trade. After 1840 the ailing artisanal system of production, unable to withstand the pressure of low-paid immigrant labor and a new national demand for ready-to-wear men's clothing, had succumbed to capitalist relations of production. Ready-mades had once been a synonym for slop clothes—cheap flannel shirts and dungarees fit only for sailors, slaves, and backwoodsmen. The tremendous expansion of southern slavery increased demand for such inexpensive products, and the Gold Rush touched off a clothing rush in flannel drawers, overalls, and calico shirts. Falling labor costs also made it possible to manufacture high-quality reproductions of European fashions at half the cost of imports. As the national market for New York ready-mades ballooned, the wholesale value of clothing sold in the city between 1841 and 1853 leapt upward, rising from two and a half to twenty million dollars. By 1855 the garment industry was far and away the city's largest, embracing 35 percent of all manufacturing employees. In 1860 New York produced roughly 40 percent of the country's clothes.

Crucial to this rapid expansion was a reorganization of the trade into three distinct but interdependent levels: a small elite of wholesale firms at the top, a large corps of subcontractors who supervised final production in the middle, and, at the bottom, an army of outworkers. Wholesale firms like P. L. Rogers, D. and J. Devlin, and Lewis and Hanford (the nation's biggest) brought cloth straight from the mills to their own in-house tailors, who cut it to the desired pattern. These "cutters," aristocrats of the trade, were among the city's best-paid workers. The constituent parts of garments were then turned over to outworkers, men and women who worked in their own homes or shops sewing the pieces together into a final product. As one cutter could keep many outworkers busy, the ratio of employees was wildly skewed toward the latter. In 1854 Hanford's had seventy-five insiders and four thousand outsiders; Brooks Brothers (the former custom tailors turned wholesalers) had seventy-eight inside, fifteen hundred outside.

In time, as the volume of business grew, more and more wholesalers subcontracted their finishing work to smaller manufacturers. Many were immigrant artisans who had made the transition from wage-worker to proprietor. It didn't require much capital. A tailor might get a contract from a wholesaler or a larger shop, do his own cutting at home, and parcel out the sewing to outworkers, thus passing on the costs of space, light, fuel, and even needles and thread. Competition among subcontractors was fierce—vicious—and success depended on holding the wages of outworkers to an absolute minimum. ("If they were compelled to pay living wages for their work," Horace Greeley observed, "they must stop it altogether.") Even then, profit margins were slim, and the whole enterprise could easily collapse, tumbling a boss back down into the ranks of his workers.

Everything, in the end, came down to the workers, tens of thousands of them—male tailors and their families as well as unmarried seamstresses. Many of the men had fled Europe aiming to reestablish themselves as traditional artisans, only to discover that too many had come too late for that to be possible. Apprenticeship disappeared. Wages plummeted. The best and luckiest became contractors or cutters; most found themselves irredeemably proletarianized. By the 1850s piece rates in New York were so low that journeyman tailors couldn't earn enough to stay alive unless they had families and became, in effect, foremen of their own family shops. They negotiated with employers, did the heaviest or most skilled work, and supervised the labor of their wives and children. Working sixteen hours a day, seven days a week, they and their families together might take in ten dollars a week (compared to the twenty dollars an inside male cutter could earn).

Life was even more precarious for single women working as seamstresses, dressmakers, milliners, shirtmakers and collarmakers, embroiderers, tasselmakers, and artificial-flower makers. A woman's wages reflected the assumption that she didn't need to support herself but was merely supplementing the income of her husband. Single women and widows, frequently with children to support, made between fifty cents and two dollars a week (unskilled male laborers in other fields got seven dollars a week)— when they could find work at all in this highly seasonal and competitive business. This relegated them to the cheapest rooms in the upper floors of the worst housing, where they often worked without heat or light because firewood and candles were too expensive; they and their children routinely suffered from eyestrain, fatigue, malnutrition, pneumonia, and consumption. Sometimes groups of women banded together, sharing quarters in boardinghouses and turning them into all-female cooperative workshops. Some made ends meet by part-time prostitution. Even Bennett's *Herald*, no friend of labor, said in 1853, "We know of no class of workwomen who are more poorly paid for their work or who suffer more privation and hardship."

The plight of New York garment workers worsened after Isaac Merritt Singer came to the city in the early fifties to build and sell the first practical sewing machine. Raised in upstate New York, where his father was a village millwright, Singer apprenticed at a machinist's shop, worked briefly in New York in the mid-1830s at Hoe's press works, then knocked about the country as an actor till discovering his true metier was inventing. In 1850, having produced rock-drilling and type-carving machines, he was solicited by a Boston machine shop owner to help improve the sewing machine, which Elias Howe had invented and patented in 1846. Singer came up with a working model incorporating a foot treadle.

In 1850 Singer moved to New York City, center of the garment industry, to market and manufacture his product. After settling a patent dispute with Howe by pooling their rights, he began production in a twenty-five-by-fifty-foot room over the New Haven Railroad Depot in Centre Street. At first, skilled craftsmen produced almost all the parts by hand, a process that was slow and costly and made each machine unique, thus hard to fix. Then the recently invented milling machine allowed Singer to make precision-measured interchangeable parts and introduce mass-production techniques heretofore employed only in armories. In 1857 I. M. Singer and Company opened a new factory, more advanced than any in Britain, in a six-story building on Mott Street, between Broome and Spring, complete with an up-to-date Badger and Company cast-iron front. Production soared from 2,564 machines in 1856 to thirteen thousand by 1860.

Demand for Singer's heavy industrial models grew brisk as wholesale clothing manufacturers insisted their subcontractors use them to standardize stitching and increase output: a gentleman's frock coat took sixteen and a half hours to make by hand, two and a half hours by machine. Contractors in turn demanded that outworkers buy machines. When few seamstresses proved able to afford them, Singer offered another innovation, installment buying, but the women soon discovered that if they fell behind on monthly payments, even if the machine was all but paid for, it was repossessed, and their money was not returned. Most women, and many men, were therefore forced to pay tailors who had managed to acquire machines to do the requisite stitching, shaving their incomes yet farther.[3]

Some garment manufacturers responded to Singer's invention by recentralizing production. Detail work (cuffs, buttonholes, sleeves) was put out to homeworkers to sew, and the garments were then assembled by machine operatives in inside shops under tight supervision. Fashion had a hand in this reconcentration, as the new "hoop skirts" required that cloth be sewn onto iron frames made in Connecticut and brought to New York factories for assembly. By 1858 one hoopskirt factory alone employed 350, mainly women, to turn out three thousand skirts a day.

These factories or "sweatshops" tended to hire single girls between the ages of sixteen and twenty-five who lived either with their families or in boardinghouses. Their wages were higher than those of outworkers, and the work was steadier (owners being reluctant to leave costly machines idle); some even had a little money left over to spend on clothes and recreation. The setting had its drawbacks, especially given the power wielded by male foremen, but the factory girls, partly by virtue of their massed numbers, were seldom pliant and docile. Indeed a high-spiritedness characterized the shops at first, with much socializing and bantering, to the point where some bosses complained that "men are considered more reliable and more easily managed." Employers soon began to impose stricter discipline—Brooks Brothers, for example, forbade all conversation—and as conditions worsened, turnover soared.

Factory production, in turn, increased pressure on small employers, who responded by lowering piece rates, forcing seamstresses to work ever faster and ever longer; fifteen-to-eighteen-hour workdays for seamstresses became common in the 1850s. And machine work proved just as taxing as hand sewing; it simply shifted the strain from arms to hips, while the jarring mechanisms generated altogether new nervous disorders. The Shirt Sewers and Seamstresses Union spoke out against the Singers, but they had come to stay.

PALACES OF CONSUMPTION

As production of commodities soared, local retailers began to adopt radically new marketing techniques to increase the volume and velocity of sales. The vanguard of this revolution was the department store, and the man who introduced it to New York was dry-goods merchant Alexander T. Stewart.

This slight, taciturn man with sandy-gray hair and whiskers, who had done so well during the Panic of 1837, came to realize that retail merchandizing was not keeping pace with the boom-era surge in industrial productivity. Even in larger shops like Brooks Brothers or Lord and Taylor, stock turnover could be glacially slow. According to time-honored custom, each prospective customer who came through the door was engaged by a clerk, and prices, rather than being fixed, depended on the outcome of

---

3. Singer introduced a family machine in 1856. Home sales were sluggish at first, until Singer offered them at half price to ministers' wives and to sewing societies connected with churches, after which sales to "respectable" women picked up. Singer also sold abroad, arguably becoming the first multinational corporation in the process. Sales agencies were installed in Paris in 1855 and Rio in 1858, and remittances from abroad helped tide the company over during domestic recessions. By 1861 Singer was doing more business in Europe than in the United States.

leisurely dickering. It was Stewart's genius to see that if he wanted to sell more goods, and to sell them more rapidly, he would have to sell them differently.

As early as 1832 Stewart, like Arthur Tappan, had advertised "regular and uniform prices"—an inspired tactic, as E. L. Godkin remembered half a century later, which made Stewart popular among female shoppers by "delivering them from distrust of their own power as hagglers or bargain-makers." Over the next dozen-odd years he perfected his appeal to women with periodic price reductions, special sales, auctions, and canny advertising that depicted his establishment as "the most desirable place to which ladies can resort." It was reported in the newspapers that he even sent salesmen outside to deliver "eulogies on silks, laces, and french muslin" to preferred customers while they sat outside in their carriages, "which must have won their hearts."

Stewart's most famous innovation, however, dates from 1846, when he opened a cavernous new store on the east side of Broadway between Chambers and Reade streets. The former site of Washington Hall, headquarters of the Federalist Party, this was now a prime retail location—close to wholesale clothing manufacturers, rail and ferry terminals, fashionable hotels, sumptuous private residences—and Stewart built accordingly.

Stewart's Marble Palace on Broadway and Chambers Street, 1851, the pioneer department store in the United States. Fifteen years after it opened, Stewart moved to larger quarters uptown and turned the building into a wholesale outlet and warehouse. It still stands, having served (among other things) as the headquarters of the *Sun* in the early twentieth century. Engraving by J. A. Bogert. (© Collection of The New-York Historical Society)

Instead of adhering to the Greek Revival style, he erected a magnificent Italian Renaissance palazzo, five stories tall and sheathed in dazzling white Tuckahoe marble. Its street-level facade, supported by great cast-iron Corinthian pilasters, boasted fifteen huge plate-glass windows. The interior, airy as well as opulent, was organized around a large circular court covered by a domed skylight. Nothing remotely like it had ever been seen in New York before; well-traveled residents knew it had no equal in London or Paris, either. People began to call it the "Marble Palace."

Consistent with his previous experiments in retailing, Stewart encouraged customers to stroll at leisure around the selling floors, inspecting wares laid out on polished mahogany counters and marble shelves, everything clearly tagged with a set price and organized into separate "departments." He instructed his sales staff, as always, to be helpful but unobtrusive and never to bargain. Above all, he continued to look for ways to make shopping agreeable to women of the propertied classes: by hiring handsome young men as clerks, by advertising aggressively in ladies' magazines, by staging the first American fashion shows, and by locating a "Ladies' Parlor" on the second floor featuring full-length Parisian mirrors.

Stewart's store was a sensational success. Outside, private carriages jammed Broadway; inside, two hundred clerks allegedly took in ten thousand dollars a day, an unheard-of sum (a decade later, in 1859, sales topped nine million, almost twenty thousand dollars per day). Admiring newspapers paid homage to the owner as "Stewart the Great" or "King Stewart." So did his competitors. During the 1850s one after another of them moved to Broadway—albeit a little to the north, to the five-block-long strip intersected by Canal, Grand, Broome, Spring, Prince, and Houston. Arnold, Constable opened a new "Marble House" facing Canal Street; its brass-buttoned, blue-uniformed porters opened carriage doors and held umbrellas over crinolined customers. Lord and Taylor opted for a palace of cast iron, an elegant emporium that opened a block farther north in 1859. There were other broad-gauged arrivals, such as Brooks Brothers and the Hearn Brothers, but specialized stores flocked to the strip as well. Badger's ironworks cast a Venetian-style palazzo for E. V. Haughwout, an importer of silver and glass, who also manufactured fine chandeliers and handpainted china. Tiffany and Company, too, chose a Badger iron-and-glass front to show off its "diamond jewelry, watches, clocks, silverware and bronzes," and assured would-be customers "that they may examine our collections, without incurring the least obligation to make purchases." Cheny silks, Gunther furs, and W. and J. Sloane carpets were soon displayed in their own retail outlets.

By the mid-fifties throngs of "window-shoppers" were promenading up and down Broadway delighting (as Henry James later remembered) in the goods "heaped up for our fond consumption." The street became an extension of the stores, a stage for the fashion conscious. Hundreds of people "spend their lives in sauntering through Broadway during fashionable hours seeing and being seen," the *Tribune* observed. Most were smartly dressed women, all ribbons and silks and Parisian fashions, who formed "one sheet of bright, quivering colors," though men were also in evidence, conservatively dressed businessmen as well as dandies with hornlike mustaches, kid gloves, thin trouser legs, and patent leather shoes. At night the effect was almost magical as gas lamps and illuminated store windows captured the streams of pedestrians in their glow and the colored lamps on carriages and omnibuses transformed Broadway into a river of light.

A PALACE OF CRYSTAL

After 1853 omnibus riders could continue north past Houston, past Madison Square, and out beyond the settled fringes of the city, toward the only structure in town that put Stewart's emporium to shame. Journalist George Foster described the journey: "For some blocks we have been aware, by the accumulation of coffee houses, grog shops, 'saloons', peep-shows of living alligators, model-artists and three-headed calves, that we were approaching the newly discovered, Sedgwickean centre of the metropolis. 'Fortieth street, Crystal Palace'—says the conductor, stopping the cars handily on the crossing."

Two years earlier, in 1851, the Great Exhibition of the Works of Industry of All Nations had opened in London's fabled Crystal Palace, a soaring, glittering wonder of cast iron and glass. Later that same year, a group of influential New Yorkers— Theodore Sedgwick, August Belmont, Edward Collins, and William Cullen Bryant, plus assorted Schuylers and Livingstons and Hamiltons—resolved to build a rival Crystal Palace on Manhattan, as big as or bigger than the original. The site they chose lay far uptown, in a four-acre site along Sixth Avenue between 40th and 42nd streets (now Bryant Park)—the same field across which, seventy-five years earlier, Washington's troops had been chased by jeering redcoats.

Construction advanced quickly, and New Yorkers soon had a Crystal Palace to boast about: eighteen hundred tons of iron supporting fifteen thousand panes of translucent enameled glass that peaked in a 123-foot dome, the highest ever built in

The Crystal Palace, 1853, by Nathaniel Currier. The Latting Observatory rises to the left, on the north side of 42nd Street. "In remote districts of this great and growing country," declared *Scientific American*, "young men, and old, too, have begun to lay by a few shillings weekly or monthly that they make be enabled to come from the far prairie and backwoods to see the Crystal Palace in New York." (© Museum of the City of New York)

America. When the Exhibition of the Industry of All Nations officially opened on July 14, 1853, tens of thousands of residents and visitors turned out for the occasion. President Franklin Pierce and Charles Lyell, the great English geologist, made speeches hailing the event as the birth of a new era, in which war would be replaced by the heroic advances of science and technology. There was art, too, "to educate and refine the masses" (said the catalog), including a colossal equestrian statue of Washington and thirteen gigantic sculptures of Christ and His Apostles.

For the next five years, crowds roamed the building's halls past shimmering fountains and glaring clusters of gas lights, marveling at the miracles of the age, great and small: scales, meters, guns, lamps, safes, clocks, carriages, scientific instruments, agricultural implements, a Fresnel lighthouse lens, telegraphy and photography equipment, fire engines, ships, and plans for an elevated railroad above Broadway. And machinery, everywhere machinery—machinery to pump water, sew, print, finish wood, refine sugar, set type, make ice cream, and wash gold.

The machine that would have the most dramatic impact on New York's cityscape— the elevator—was on display in a sideshow area across 42nd Street, in two different versions. One lifted passengers to the first- and second-floor landings of the Latting Observatory, a 350-foot-high viewing structure of iron-braced timber. The second elevator, less spectacular but more momentous, hoisted a mountable platform just high enough to clear the heads of onlookers. The man who mounted it was Elisha Graves Otis, a master mechanic turned inventor. Some years earlier, Otis had produced a machine that made bedsteads, and when the Yonkers bedstead plant where he worked needed an elevator, Otis was asked to install one. He did, and he also added an automatic device to prevent it from falling. Otis was just about to seek his fortune in the California goldfields when an unsolicited order for two "safety" elevators arrived from a Hudson Street manufacturer and Otis realized his fortune lay in New York City. Canceling his trip, he borrowed funds, set up a small shop to make the devices, and then introduced one, with theatrical flair, on 42nd Street. When the elevating platform reached its highest level, an assistant presented the inventor with a dagger on a velvet cushion. Otis cut the cable holding them aloft and, voilá, nothing happened, thanks to the invisible safety catches. Three years later E. V. Haughwout and Company installed a passenger version in its new five-story Broadway store, and Manhattan took a decisive step upward.

The Crystal Palace pulled people to New York from across the country. Seventeen-year-old Sam Clemens came all the way from Missouri. Entranced by the "perfect fairy palace—beautiful beyond description," he reported that it drew an average of six thousand visitors each day, "double the population of Hannibal." On October 5, 1858, however, a fire broke out in one of the Palace's storage rooms. Although its cast-iron beams were believed to render the building fireproof, the flames spread quickly through some 750,000 board feet of wood flooring. In the intense heat, the roof and walls literally melted away, and within minutes the entire structure had collapsed in a spectacular shower of sparks and smoke. All of the two thousand visitors inside that day escaped with their lives, but the contents were lost. Scavengers later picked through the rubble looking for souvenirs, and a certain Mrs. Richardson went into business selling "vitrified masses of glass, metals, &c." They were, she said, relics "of the finest building ever erected in America."

PALACES FOR TRAVELERS

Before its blazing demise, the Crystal Palace, by boosting New York's tourist trade, had nourished an ongoing spate of hotel construction. Until mid-century, the premier hostelry had continued to be the elegant Astor House, on Broadway opposite City Hall, just down the street from Stewart's Marble Palace. But as Manhattan's commercial center of gravity shifted northwards in the fifties, Astor House came to seem too "downtown." Spurred by vast ranks of Crystal Palace gazers and burgeoning numbers of commercial travelers, dozens of hotels sprang up. Nineteen deluxe establishments appeared on Broadway alone between 1850 and 1854.

Grandest of these newcomers was the six-story, six-hundred-room St. Nicholas Hotel (1853), whose white marble facade dominated the west side of Broadway between Broome and Spring streets, fourteen blocks above the Astor House. Its guests, upward of eight hundred at a time, were pampered by a million dollars' worth of walnut wainscotting, frescoed ceilings, and such technological wonders as gas-light chandeliers (supplied by Haughwout's across the street), hot running water, central heating, annunciators, a telegraph in the lobby, and steam-powered washing machines in the basement. There were opulent parlors for gentlemen and ladies, a richly ornamented reading room, and a stately main dining room where a regiment of liveried servants (mostly Irish) escorted guests to their seats. Downstairs, right next to the hotel's main entrance, was Phalon's Hair-Dressing Establishment, the most fashionable place in town for gentlemen to be shaved, barbered, and groomed with grease, scent, and pale rum. It was, said one English visitor in 1853, "like an introduction to the palace of some Eastern prince."

The St. Nicholas Hotel on Broadway, flagship of the new fleet of hotels built to accommodate the city's burgeoning tourist trade in the 1850s. Lithograph by F. Heppenheimer. (© Museum of the City of New York)

Other hotels nestled within a few blocks of the St. Nicholas, interspersed among Broadway's emporiums and theaters—like the Metropolitan (on the corner of Prince, next to Niblo's Garden), famous for its "sky parlors" that allowed lady guests to observe the well-dressed throngs below. Additional grand establishments situated themselves along Broadway, marking fashion's uptown progress. James Renwick's St. Denis held down the corner of 11th Street across from the new and very stylish Grace Church; the Clarendon Hotel, famous for its huge bathtubs, overlooked Union Square; and the wave crested at the corner of Fifth Avenue and 23rd Street, three blocks below the New York and Harlem's Madison Square Depot, where in 1859 Amos Eno opened his Fifth Avenue Hotel. Costing two million dollars and employing four hundred servants, the Fifth Avenue was hailed as the most spectacular building of its kind yet erected in the city: "a larger and handsomer building than Buckingham Palace," raved a correspondent for the *London Times* who came to New York the following year with the prince of Wales (later King Edward VII). Among other wonders, the Fifth Avenue offered private bathrooms, an unprecedented extravagance, as well as the city's second passenger elevator (equipped with Otis's safety device), described variously as a "perpendicular railway intersecting each story" or "a little parlour going up by machinery."

Visitors of means clearly had no problem finding accommodations in New York City. What they needed—as did less affluent arrivals and even long time residents—was orientation. The cozy republican town had metamorphosed into a bewildering metropolis, and citizens and strangers alike sought ways to grasp its scale and meaning.

THE PIGEON PERSPECTIVE

In 1845–46, under the direction of E. Porter Belden, 150 artists, craftsmen, sculptors and mechanics collaborated on building a scale model of New York City. It represented Manhattan from 32nd Street down to the Battery and threw in part of Brooklyn for good measure. The model, twenty feet long by twenty-four feet wide, included two hundred thousand miniature buildings, two and a half million windows and doors, and 150,000 teensy chimneys. It was surmounted by a fifteen-foot-high Gothic canopy festooned with a hundred oil paintings depicting the "leading business establishments and places of note in the city." This wonder, exhibited at the Minerva Room (406 Broadway, between Walker and Canal), became a principal sight for visitors and residents.

Belden went on to publish *New York: Past, Present, and Future* (1849), one of a large number of prideful, self-congratulatory guidebooks that appeared during the boom years. New York was delighted by its emerging metropolitan status and not shy about trumpeting its virtues. Addressing a national, indeed an international, audience, the volumes—many of which were underwritten by the new monster hotels or prepared for visitors to the Crystal Palace—proclaimed the city's civic grandeur, its commercial entrepôts, its palaces of pleasure, its charitable and educational institutions. In Bunyunesque prose they boasted of the sheer scale of it all: their city had the greatest concentration of wealth and energy and people in America, it was the largest market in America, it had "become so enriched that she may call Ohio her kitchen-garden, Michigan her pastures, and Indiana, Illinois and Iowa her harvest fields."

In addition to encomiums, the guidebooks offered solid information: where to stay and eat; how to get around the city (with rail and omnibus timetables appended). Beyond providing pathways through the city's labyrinthine corridors, the books helped readers grasp the city in its entirety by including "panoramic" representations of it as seen (or imagined) from elevated vantage points. C. S. Francis, the publisher who brought out Audubon's *Birds*, offered in his *New Guide to the Cities of New-York and Brooklyn* (1853) a view from atop the recently completed Trinity Church.

Such representations broke with traditional ways of seeing the city. Manhattan had customarily been presented as it appeared from the opposite bank of an adjacent river. In colonial days, the waterways—New York's commercial lifelines—featured as prominently as the land; in the early nineteenth century, the ensemble was often framed with a pastoral foreground scene in the manner of Thomas Cole. The new panoramic views, however, planted themselves squarely inside the city, generally atop one of its many steeples, presenting a pigeon's-eye view of the bustling streets below.

In the 1850s the pigeons took wing. Inspired, perhaps, by experiences at the Latting Observatory, where visitors could use telescopes to inspect the island and its surrounds, artists began imagining the city from ever higher perspectives. An 1853 electrotyped woodcut, *Bird's Eye View of the City of New York* from *Frank Leslie's Illustrated News*, encompassed the town as a whole. And in John Bachmann's spectacular fish-eye view, *New York & Environs* (1859), the Empire City seemed to stretch to the ends of the earth.

39

Manhattan, Ink

From a pigeon's point of view, the most obvious sign of New York's metropolitan transformation was the bulky physicality of its railroads, steamboats, factories, warehouses, and department stores. However, the city's metamorphosis could be measured as well by its production and distribution of something less tangible than clipper ships or steam boilers. In the 1840s and 1850s Manhattan became the nation's information center, a fountain from which news and novels, stock quotes and lithographs flowed in ceaseless profusion. A mountain of printed matter, generated by a growing army of publishers and printshops, was delivered by rail. But data was also dispatched, almost magically, through an expanding latticework of wires, itself the progeny of New York's scientific and commercial cultures.

WIRING UP

After painter Samuel F. B. Morse returned from Europe in 1832, the renaissance New Yorker devoted himself, more or less simultaneously, to art, politics, and science. He served as professor of the literature of the arts of design at the University of the City of New York. He joined the crusade against popery and ran for mayor on the Native American ticket. And he set out to design a device that would "transmit intelligence by electricity."

Morse was no theorist, though he had picked up the rudiments of electromagnetism at New York Athenaeum lectures. But in 1837, after years of dogged experimentation, he and his colleagues succeeded in transmitting signals through the hundreds of feet of wire Morse had looped around his university rooms overlooking Washington Square. Patenting their "telegraph," the inventors developed a dot-dash code system and set out to convince a skeptical public the machine was practicable.

In October 1842 Morse insulated two miles of copper wire with tar, pitch, hemp, and India rubber, put it on board a rowboat, and paid it out, one moonlit night, while a boatman paddled him over to Governors Island. In the morning the *New York Herald* announced that at noon Morse would transmit a message back to Castle Garden. The receiver worked for a bit, then died when the wire snagged on a departing ship's anchor and was hauled up and sliced apart by puzzled sailors. The crowd, believing itself hoaxed, dispersed with jeers.

Morse had better luck in 1844 when, having convinced Congress to underwrite a telegraph line between Baltimore and Washington, he inaugurated the hookup with an exultant "What hath God wrought!" Morse, a good republican, offered to sell his invention to the government for development as a public network, but Congress in its laissez-faire wisdom declined to accept. Some businessmen shied away too, thinking Morse's device too risky an investment. Jacob Little, worried that vandals would make short work of poles and wires, preferred carrier pigeons. But scores of other entrepreneurs plunged with gusto into developing a new industry.

Morse himself rounded up enough backers, including the owner of a Nassau Street beanery, to establish the Magnetic Telegraph Company and begin service between New York and Philadelphia (actually, the line ended at Jersey City and messengers rowed telegrams across to Manhattan). In 1846, when speculators used stock and commodity news relayed from New York to manipulate prices on the Philadelphia exchange, even Jacob Little became a believer.

By 1846, also, independently owned telegraph lines were converging on New York from Washington, Boston, and Albany. Less than a decade later, better than fifty companies had sprung up around the country, and thousands of miles of wire coupled New York to such far-away places as Pittsburgh and Cincinnati.

The city's commanding position in the new communications web was bolstered by establishment of a telegraphic link with Europe—the project of Cyrus West Field. A Massachusetts migrant, Field had worked as an errand boy at A. T. Stewart's store, then gone into paper manufacturing. Given the explosion of the penny press, the market for bank notes and bonds, and a surge in long-distance letter writing, Field's firm flourished, making him one of the city's richest men. At thirty-four he retired, bought a house in Gramercy Park, and turned to telegraphy.

In 1854, encouraged by the recent discovery of a shallow submarine plateau between Ireland and Newfoundland, Field teamed up with industrialist Peter Cooper (his Gramercy Park neighbor), ironmaster Abram Hewitt, banker Moses Taylor, and Morse. After securing a charter and a fifty-year monopoly, the New Yorkers subscribed $1.5 million, hired battalions of laborers to hack an eight-foot-wide path through four hundred miles of rugged Canadian wilderness, and succeeded in linking St. John's, Newfoundland, with Nova Scotia, then the terminus of lines from the United States.

In 1855, anticipating the European connection, Field, Taylor, Cooper, and Hewitt formed the American Telegraph Company to expand their control over the U.S. network. The New York-based firm quickly swallowed up smaller lines, Morse's among them. By the end of the decade its consolidated system stretched from Maine to the Gulf of Mexico, making it the largest telegraph company in the eastern states; its only rival was Western Union, a Rochester-based firm that had acquired lines in the Midwest.

In 1857, having raised additional capital in England, two sidewheel steamships provided by the U.S. and British governments began spooling out 1,950 miles of cable.

The Eighth Wonder of the World: The Atlantic Cable. When the cable was finally hooked up again in 1866, this print hailed the event—an iconographic echo of earlier Festivals of Connection in the city's streets. (Library of Congress)

After several setbacks, the mighty work was completed in 1858. On August 16 Queen Victoria sent President Buchanan a congratulatory message in "Morse" code officially opening the line; it was shortly followed by the first transatlantic news dispatch: "Settlement of Chinese Question; Chinese Empire open to trade; Christian religion allowed; Mutiny being quelled, all India becoming tranquil."

In a keystroke, what the *Times* hailed as the most "wondrous event of a wondrous age" had solidified New York's position as principal link between New World and Old. In a jubilant Festival of Connection, cannons boomed, church bells pealed, and public buildings were illuminated. The fireworks at City Hall were so tumultuous they touched off a conflagration that destroyed the cupola before it was brought under control. On September 1 a parade with Field and the mayor in the lead carriage marched from the Battery to the Crystal Palace, past stores, hotels, and businesses festooned with banners, placards, and transparencies; the celebration was capped that evening by a torch-lit procession. The ecstasy proved a mite premature, however, as the cable fell silent at the beginning of September, spurring accusations of humbuggery, and would not be reconnected until 1866.

"EXTRA, EXTRA, READ ALL ABOUT IT!"

The telegraph, nurtured to fruitful life in New York City, in turn helped reshape the metropolis. By the 1850s the city's railroads had adopted the device to route and dispatch trains, all police stations were telegraphically interconnected, and the New York Stock Exchange was setting securities prices for the entire nation. Nowhere, however, did the new technology have greater repercussions than in journalism. New York's newspapers, driven by their mania for speed, became the telegraph's most crucial supporters. In doing so, they won for themselves and their metropolis an insurmountable advantage in the collection and dissemination of information.

The rise of the penny press in the 1830s had put a premium on ever swifter access to news. Newsboy-hawked "extras" that scooped rivals by even an hour could harvest a bonanza in street sales. By the mid-1840s, New Yorkers were being bombarded by fast-breaking stories—garnered by pony express, chartered locomotives, express steamships, or carrier pigeons—and the race for news had itself become good copy.

Telegraphy accelerated the frenzy. Morse himself, after marveling at what God had wrought, had promptly tapped out a second message: "Have you any news?" Soon James Gordon Bennett of the *Herald* was paying a five-hundred-dollar bonus to news entrepreneur Daniel Craig for every hour his dispatches preceded those received by other papers, and when the Mexican War broke out in 1846, Bennett bankrolled an extension of telegraph lines to get up-to-the minute intelligence from the front.

No one was more adept at speeding news to press than Moses Yale Beach, proprietor of the *Sun*. But it was obvious to Beach that telegraphy required rewriting the rules of the news-gathering game. Wire companies swamped with usage demands had restricted each paper to a scant fifteen minutes of transmission time before passing the wire to competitors, effectively eliminating electric scoops. As the construction of private lines was beyond the capacity of even the biggest metropolitan dailies, cooperation, not costly competition, was now in the interest of the New York papers—especially as they faced a collective threat from Boston, where Cunard's vessels still made first landfall in the States, bearing the latest news from Europe.

In June 1846, accordingly, Beach brokered an arrangement among six leading papers (the *Sun, Tribune, Herald, Journal of Commerce, Courier and Enquirer*, and *Express*). They agreed to collaborate in procuring Mexican War updates and, as well, to share the cost of transmitting political and congressional news from Washington. The associated papers also deftly bypassed Boston in 1849 by spurring Britain's Maritime Provinces to link New York to Halifax, the Cunarders' first hemispheric port of call. The group also formally established a Harbor News Association and jointly chartered a steamer—the *Newsboy*—to intercept incoming vessels off Sandy Hook. New Yorkers had locked in their control over the collection of information from Europe.

In the 1850s, the combination—soon to be known as the Associated Press (AP)—moved to dominate news distribution as well. AP agents, placed in major cities, gathered stories produced by local papers, then flashed them to headquarters in New York. There they were consolidated and wired back out to a client base that soon included the great majority of America's newspapers. Opponents cried monopoly, and they were right. The AP, in conjunction with New York City's cable and telegraph companies, had cornered the information market. Subscribing newspapers were forbidden from any independent use of telegraphy, barred even from receiving dispatches written by their own reporters.

Manhattan's papers thrived. By 1853 the circulation of Bennett's *Herald* had jumped to fifty-two thousand, making it the country's most profitable daily. Horace Greeley's *Tribune* was running a close second, and its weekly edition was probably the most widely circulated journal in America. Within the city itself, combined daily circulation shot from one paper per every 16 residents in 1830 to one for every 4.5 in 1850 (and 1 per 2.2 on Sundays).

The rise was due in no small part to the penny papers' explicitly addressing themselves to both sexes as readers, unlike the older, strictly male-oriented commercial press. The newspapers proved hospitable to women writers as well. In 1841 the Boston abolitionist Lydia Maria Child was a rarity when she moved to New York to edit the *National Anti-Slavery Standard*, and as the first woman to edit a journal of public policy, she was kept at arm's length by the male New York press. But after Child dramatically increased the *Standard*'s circulation and published her urban reportage as *Letters from New York* (1843, 1845), professionals like Bryant accepted her claim to a literary vocation.

Margaret Fuller, another pioneer, had been a highly respected editor of the *Dial*, the literary magazine founded by Emerson up in Concord. In 1844, at Horace Greeley's urging, she moved to New York and joined the *Tribune*'s staff. Mostly she wrote on acceptably female subjects like literature and music, but Fuller also did pieces on slums, prisons, and almshouses—becoming the *Tribune*'s woman-about-town. In 1846 Greeley even dispatched Fuller, an avid supporter of Garibaldi and Mazzini, to cover the fight for an Italian republic. (In 1850 the ship bringing her back to New York sank off Fire Island in a storm; a search party including Walter Whitman combed the beach, but her body was never found.)

Along with new readers and new writers, new technology made the expansion possible. What the telegraph was to getting a story, the rotary press was to getting it out. Patented in 1846 by New York City's Richard Hoe, it could produce over twenty thousand copies per hour, permitting a paper to be printed far more quickly, with far fresher news. In the 1850s, moreover, papermaking machines emerged to provide Hoe's "Lightning" presses with newsprint made from wood pulp rather than scarce cotton and linen rags, breaking another bottleneck.

The housing of mammoth presses, the steam engines to power them, and growing numbers of correspondents, bookkeepers, typesetters, and press operators required ever larger accommodations. By the 1850s the *Tribune* employed fifty people (not counting the hundred employees it shared with the Associated Press) and filled a five-story Park Row building. Bennett had moved the *Herald* to larger quarters on Fulton and Nassau in 1842, but after 1848, when he switched to Lightning presses and his workforce topped two hundred, he was forced to expand into three adjoining buildings.

Large premises, costly presses, sizable staffs, and telegraphic services—all drove expenses skyward. To offset rising costs, owners boosted advertising rates, justifying hikes by pointing to increased circulation. As Greeley noted in 1841, "We lose money on our circulation by itself considered, but with 20,000 subscribers we can command such Advertising and such prices for it as will render our enterprise a remunerating one." In the late 1840s, while a firm might still pay sixty dollars a year for ads in the old-fashioned *Journal of Commerce*, a similar amount of copy in the *Herald* could cost over a thousand.

The increase in business precipitated the first advertising agencies. Enterprising young brokers tramped lower Manhattan's publishing district, buying space from newspapers, then hawking it to patent medicine manufactures and dry-goods emporiums. No one touted the new profession's benefits more ardently than Volney B. Palmer, self-styled "Morse of commercial intercourse." By the end of the 1840s Palmer had established offices in Philadelphia, New York, Boston, and Baltimore and was proclaiming that "the day will come when a man will as readily think of walking without feet . . . as of success without advertising."

Even with enhanced ad revenues, it now required substantial capital to establish a newspaper. It was still possible—at least in Brooklyn—for artisan printers to enter the business, especially when backed by politicians. The *Brooklyn Eagle and Kings County Democrat*, established in 1841 to promote the party's fortunes, would remain more or less a one-man operation for years. But in Manhattan, only one entrant in the mass circulation sweepstakes succeeded during the mid-century boom: Henry Jarvis Raymond's *New-York Daily Times*.

Unlike the founding generation of penny press entrepreneurs, Henry Raymond had no links to the Trades. He came to work for Horace Greeley straight from college, then moved to James Watson Webb's *Courier and Enquirer*, where he rose to become managing editor. Here Raymond established solid conservative credentials by attacking socialism (a "stupendous humbug") in a six-month print duel with his former employer. In 1849 he was elected as a Whig to the Assembly. In 1851, as a leader of what Bennett called the "Wall Street clique," the thirty-year-old Raymond was chosen as speaker.

That summer a group of Whig bankers surveyed the penny press field with disaffected eyes. Bennett's *Herald* seemed too flamboyant, the *Sun* too plebeian, and Horace Greeley, though a stalwart Whig, had dedicated the *Tribune* to promoting social justice "causes." The dailies' collective prosperity, however, suggested there might be room for another penny press—more agreeably conservative in style and politics. The Whig magnates, accordingly, chose the reliably orthodox Raymond to found the *Times* (the eighth to bear that name). They raised $110,000, making the *Times* the most amply funded newcomer in American journalism.

Raymond acquired a Lightning press, hired a large staff, and joined the Associated Press. He also set out to establish a clear identity for the *Times*, one professing objectivity, detachment, and bourgeois respectability. The paper's first issue, in September 1851, declared, with unmistakable reference to Greeley's tubthumping, that "we shall *make it a point to get into a passion as rarely as possible*." Raymond's mix of prudent politics, good manners, and sober design found a readership at once—ten thousand in ten days—drawn, he claimed, from "business men at their stores" and "the most respectable families in town." Advertisers flocked in, circulation doubled, and the *Times* replaced the *Tribune* as the favored organ of New York Whiggery.

Raymond and his backers had entered an extremely influential circle. By 1860 the five leading New York dailies, with a combined per diem circulation of 250,000, wielded immense power. Printing House Square had become the hub of American journalism, and city editors and publishers would become national celebrities—better known than manufacturers, department store moguls, or clipper ship captains.

A PAGEANT OF TEXT

Newspaper publishing, the city's fourth largest manufacturing sector by the late 1850s, proved crucial to making the printing trade New York's fastest growing industry. But a vast array of quite different kinds of material also rolled from the city's presses, helping make Manhattan an ink-drenched town.

Ads were everywhere. Aleksandr Lakier, a Russian visitor in the 1850s, was struck by the steady flow of "notices and announcements [that] are thrust in your hands" along

Broadway. Trade cards—four-by-six-inch handbills promoting everything from patent medicines to prostitutes—blossomed with the spread of lithography. "Bill-stickers" with paste buckets mades their rounds late at night, plastering their posters over those of their rivals, creating a patchwork of odd and quintessentially urban juxtapositions.

"New York is distinguished for its display in the way of signs," noted chronicler John F. Watson in 1846; "every device and expense is resorted to, to make them attractive." Not only were stores festooned with ever more and ever bigger placards and announcements, but so were warehouses, carriages, buses, fences, lampposts, trees—and people: men walked the streets with sandwich boards on their shoulders. One commentator noted with mock surprise that umbrellas had as yet been left blank, "their ample and conspicuous surface bearing no announcement of any new pill, new adhesive gum, bankrupt's sale, or What is it?"

Civic text added to the visual pageant—banners draped over buildings for celebration, broadsides for political campaigns, and "Direction Boards" erected at the Board of Aldermen's insistence "for the accommodation of the whole public, and especially strangers." Often these street signs appeared only on gas-light stanchions, making it difficult, complained visiting novelist Anthony Trollope, to know when to get off the horsecar. There were, however, remarkably few injunctions in the cityscape—little by way of traffic regulations or health warnings telling people what they should or should not do—though omnibuses did post warnings to BEWARE OF PICKPOCKETS.

Some of the cleverest trade bills on the street were designed to resemble paper

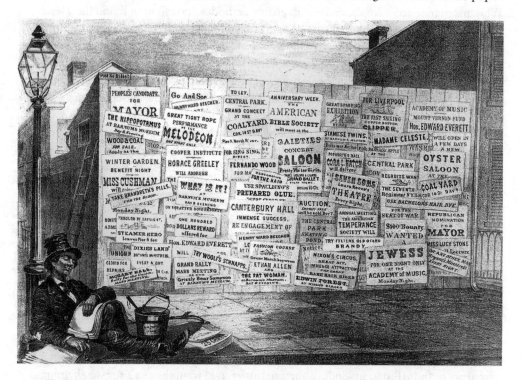

"The Bill-Poster's Dream," an 1862 cartoon spoofing the proliferation of signs in the city. When read down, beginning in the upper left, the juxtaposition of messages makes an amusing commentary on local persons and events: "People's Candidate for Mayor . . . The Hippopotamus," "Miss Cushman will . . . take Brandreth's Pills," "The American Bible Society will meet at the . . . Gaieties Concert Saloon," "$100 Bounty Wanted . . . A Jewess for One Night Only," etc. (Eno Collection. Miriam and Ira D. Wallach Division of Art, Prints and Photographs. The New York Public Library. Astor, Lenox and Tilden Foundations)

money—no surprise, given the city's role in producing the real thing. Manhattan was headquarters for the nation's three largest banknote manufacturers, whose clients included many of the over ten thousand institutions empowered to issue currency. It was also home to those who produced bogus bills. "We have never known counterfeiting carried on to a more alarming extent than at present," wrote the *Sun* in 1840. "We were shown yesterday a one dollar bill on the Atlantic Bank of Brooklyn, altered to a ten in so ingenious a manner as to have deceived all but the most wary." This in turn gave rise to an impressive array of daily, weekly, and monthly journals—like *Day's New-York Bank Note List and Counterfeit Detector*—produced by more than a dozen different publishers to help store clerks and bank tellers identify failed banks and fraudulent currency. By the late 1850s, as well, ninety-four engraving establishments and twenty-three lithographic works were churning out such other print-tools of the commercial and financial trades as checks, bills of lading, and bills of exchange.

BOOK MART

The widespread assumption, by all these print publicists, of near-universal literacy was largely accurate. During the 1840s and 1850s—thanks to the country's growing number of schools and colleges, a general conviction that literacy was essential to republican citizenship, the tremendous evangelical commitment to teaching sacred texts, and the emergence of a cheap popular press—the literacy rate among white adults climbed past 90 percent in the city and throughout the nation.

With the national market for reading matter growing briskly, and with the economy rising, postal rates dropping, and railroads affording inexpensive access to the interior, New York publishers flourished as never before. By 1860 seventeen book-printing firms were manufacturing over three million dollars' worth of volumes for the national marketplace. New York City, with 2 percent of the country's population, produced over 37 percent of its total publishing revenue.

Harper and Brothers retained its preeminence. By 1853, when its workforce of five hundred issued more than four and a half million volumes, it had become the largest employer in New York City. After its Cliff Street plant burned down that year, the firm immediately set James Bogardus to building two splendid five-story cast-iron structures, which between them covered half an acre on Franklin Square. One combined all of Harpers' editorial, management, inventory, and wholesaling operations. The other, the factory, devoted a separate floor to each stage of the production process. This powerhouse secured Harpers' position as the largest publisher in the world.

The company distributed its tremendous output with smooth efficiency. Advertising extensively—it placed notices in 844 local papers during 1856 alone—Harpers circulated its wares through a network of over a thousand booksellers and a phalanx of colporteurs (peddlers of religious material). Harpers, indeed, had great success with religious works, especially *Harper's Illuminated and New Pictorial Bible* (1846) a gilt-edged, gold-embossed, morocco-bound edition that set new (and rococo) standards for taste and elegance. The firm did well, too, with inexpensive book sets: the 150 volumes of the *Harper's Family Library* could be had for sixty-five dollars. And state legislative appropriations underwrote widespread and profitable purchase of the two-hundred-plus titles in its *Harper's School District Library* series.

The firm continued to pirate European authors: Dickens, Thackeray, the Brontë sisters, and above all Thomas Babbington Macaulay, whose confident assertions in the

History of England from the Accession of James II (1848) about the benefits of industrial progress helped it to sales of four hundred thousand copies. It also extended growing attention to a wide array of American texts embracing Prescott's *Conquest of Mexico* (1843), a miscellaneity of geographies and travel accounts, including *Harper's New York and Erie Rail-road Guide Book* (1851), and the domestic advice books of Catharine Beecher.

Harpers' success spurred competitors. The House of Appleton retained its number two status by producing Spanish-language books for the Latin American trade, commencing the *New American Cyclopedia* (the greatest literary enterprise yet attempted in the United States), and securing rights to *Webster's Elementary Spelling Book* (which became the number two seller in the world, right behind the Bible). Behind the Appletons lay a pack of up-and-coming rivals including A. S. Barnes, Charles Scribner, David Van Nostrand, E. P. Dutton, and, scrappiest of all, the youthful George Palmer Putnam.

Putnam teamed with John Wiley in 1840 and quickly established an agency in England to forage for European books with which to rival Harpers. He also propelled Wiley and Putnam into building a strong domestic list, a focus he continued after setting up on his own in 1848.

Again, women writers and readers proved crucial to the expansion of the publishing world, particularly after 1850, when Putnam published Susan Warner's *The Wide, Wide World*. Warner had grown up in the fashionable town house of an affluent and genteel New York family, received an excellent education, and thrived on the city's cultural offerings. In the Panic of 1837, however, her father lost his fortune and took the family into impoverished upstate exile. Warner took to writing in hopes of making money and submitted a pious and sentimental novel to Harpers, which rebuffed it with the single word "Fudge." Brought out by Putnam, however, *Wide, Wide World* became a publishing phenomenon. It went through fourteen editions in two years, becoming the most successful novel yet written in the United States, and touched off a flood of domestic parlor books by and for women. Despite the strictures against women speaking in public, which if anything had sharpened since Fanny Wright had been howled from her platform, writing for the public became an acceptable extension of woman's sphere. Male publishers were simply not prepared to turn down the kind of revenue ladies generated, and "scribbling women," with the help of their consuming sisters, carved out a niche in the flourishing industry.

By 1857 there were at least 112 publishers in New York City. While most were "respectable" houses, emphasizing genteel, religious, and domestic literature, others catered to a rougher readership. These outfits churned out blood-and-thunder adventures, sadomasochistic romances laced with sex and horror, and lurid accounts of patrician villainy or plebeian roguery. Nearly 60 percent of all fiction published in the United States between 1830 and 1860 was of this ilk.

In 1846, four years after the federal government banned importation of erotic material, an indigenous pornographic publishing industry arose when William Haynes, an Irish surgeon who immigrated to New York, reinvested the money he'd made publishing *Fanny Hill* in the United States in the production of cheap erotic novels like *Confessions of a Lady's Waiting Maid* (1848). Most such paperbacks—usually octavo-sized pamphlets with yellow or pink wrappers, priced at twenty-five cents—were aimed at a youthful male audience and written by men, some of whom achieved heroic levels of productivity. In the 1850s New York sensationalist George Thompson whipped off nearly one hundred steamy potboilers—with titles like *City Crimes* (1849), *New-York Life* (1849), and *The Gay Girls of New-York* (1853)—portraying group sex, nymphomania, miscegenation, and incest in the Five Points. This plethora of pornographic confections, often replete with lustful woodcuts, led one New York reformer to wonder: "Will not the steam-presses create licentiousness faster than police regulations can drain it off?"

In the 1850s New York's competing book publishers discovered, as had their counterparts in journalism, that cooperation could be in the interest of all. The market's growth in size and scale had made it ever more difficult for companies to inform back-country stores about new titles. Nor was it easy for distant booksellers to get to New York for the fall and spring trade sales. Some of these problems were alleviated by the establishment of a trade paper in 1851, *Norton's Literary Advertiser*, which included book news, ads, and reviews, and in 1855 the city's bookmen decided to establish the New York Publishers Association. It was inaugurated with a banquet for six hundred at the Crystal Palace, the biggest-ever gathering of literary personalities in American history. This self-congratulatory conclave of authors and editors marked publishing's arrival as a full-fledged metropolitan industry.

Book selling flourished too. Stores along Broadway between Pine and Houston concentrated on new titles. Secondhand volumes were found at shops on Nassau Street and Pearl or farther uptown along Canal, Mulberry, and the Bowery. When the Astor Library opened, Fourth Avenue between Astor Place and 14th Street became the city's used-book center; and it remained so for a century. In addition streetcorner bookstalls served as outlets, especially for the fledgling pornography trade: in 1843 one paper claimed that nearly every stand sold "libidinous books with the most revolting and disgusting contents."

"THE CENTRE OF LITERARY POWER"

The efflorescence of book publishing boosted magazine production as well. Political, literary, domestic, and religious journals had long flourished in New York. Now commercial periodicals began to circulate at a hitherto unmatched pace. As Henry Wadsworth Longfellow noted as early as 1839, in "the Great Metropolis . . . new literary projects in the shape of Magazines and Weekly papers are constantly started, showing great activity, and zeal, and enterprise."

Two of the grandest were offshoots of great publishing houses. In June 1850 Fletcher Harper set up *Harper's New Monthly Magazine*, in handsome format, with sumptuous engravings. The raw material was filched from the best English authors, supplemented occasionally by local talent. The magazine also featured columns of light commentary—including "The Editor's Easy Chair," a seat filled in the late 1850s by George William Curtis—and offered travel sketches by genteel tourists just back from perambulating Italian art galleries and classical ruins. The formula worked to perfection in a culture that still set its course by European stars. Harpers printed seventy-five hundred of the first number; in six months circulation hit fifty thousand; by 1860 it reached two hundred thousand.

With figures like these it wasn't hard for Charles F. Briggs, the New York editor (and author of *Harry Franco*), to convince Harpers' rival George Palmer Putnam to found another monthly. *Putnam's Magazine*, with Briggs at the helm, sought out American authors, compensated them well, and attracted sophisticated contributions on art, literature, and society.

Robert Bonner's unaffiliated *New York Ledger* outpaced both *Harper's* and *Putnam's*. An Irish immigrant printer turned entrepreneur, Bonner purchased the *Ledger* in 1851 when it hung on the brink of collapse. Over the next several years he aggressively improved its circulation by lowering the price to three cents a copy and offering a class and gender-straddling mix of adventure stories, domestic romances, and first-rank writing.

Bonner, an advertising genius, spent twenty-five thousand dollars a week on promotions. A pioneer in the use of "white space," he took out full pages in the *Herald*, *Tribune*, and *Times*, only to leave the entire space blank but for a single line in the center or a corner: "Read Mrs. Southworth's new story in *The Ledger*." In this manner, Bonner promoted a star system that featured the writer as much as the written word. He paid unprecedented sums—thirty thousand dollars for a novel by Henry Ward Beecher, three thousand for a poem by Longfellow—then advertised his expenses. In 1855 Bonner signed Fanny Fern to write for the *Ledger*. Born Sara Payson Willis, Fern had won national acclaim in Boston for a volume of essays, *Fern Leaves from Fanny's Portfolio* (1853), that sold over a hundred thousand copies. Now she moved to New York, where Bonner paid her one hundred dollars a column, making her the most highly paid newspaper writer in the country. By 1860, with circulation topping three hundred thousand, the *Ledger* was the most widely read magazine in the nation.

Below these Everests lay ranges of more specialized weeklies and monthlies. New York published fifty-two religious periodicals at mid-century. There were magazines devoted to ethnic affairs, banking, sports, ladies' fashions, politics, culture, science, humor, trade and industrial technology. Even the *American Agriculturalist* made its home in Manhattan, noting that "more Farmers and Planters resort here than to any other city in the Union."

The magazine spectrum too had its spicier bandwidth, represented most notoriously by the *National Police Gazette*. In 1845 journalist George Wilkes, the New York-born son of an artisan cabinetmaker, was convicted of criminal libel while coediting the *Subterranean* with the pugnacious Mike Walsh. After serving four weeks in jail, Wilkes penned a pamphlet (*Mysteries of the Tombs*) exposing corruption in the city's criminal justice system, then founded the *Gazette* to continue and extend his investigations. Imitating London's *Police Gazette*, Wilkes gave his readers lurid capsule reports of crimes in the city and around the nation (in columns titled "Seductions," "Rapes," and "Murders"), interspersed with criminal biographies ("The Lives of the Felons"), trial coverage of crimes involving sex and violence, and a glossary of criminal slang (the "Rogue's Lexicon"). Lively, at times quasi-pornographic graphics helped boost *Police Gazette* sales to over forty thousand by 1850.

The *Gazette* and its hundreds of periodical rivals made New York's literary marketplace intensely competitive. With journals being founded and folded almost daily, Manhattan was perilous for entrepreneurs but a magnet for would-be professional authors, whose arrival further altered the process of literary production. Writing had long been an amateur affair. Gentlemen authors wrote for their friends and peers; they lived *for* literature, not *off* it. Now, as one disgruntled Boston literatus put it in 1843, "literature begins to assume the aspect and undergo the mutations of trade," with authors hoping to sell their literary goods to impersonal and far-flung audiences, addressed by advertisement.

Writers found *themselves* advertised as well; they were packaged as commodities, their portraits and biographies promoted. Horace Greeley, acting as Henry David Thoreau's informal literary agent (an emerging profession), told him: "You may write with an angel's pen, yet your writings have no mercantile, money value till you are known and talked of as an author." Marketing, in turn, increased the importance of reviewing—another budding profession. When Margaret Fuller moved to the city to work on Greeley's *Tribune*, she became the first full time book reviewer on an American paper. Laudatory excerpts were cited in ads or the book itself, and while most were honestly come by, others were bought and paid for.

Writers were ambivalent about publishing's transformation into a capitalist enterprise. Formerly authors had financed their own books, kept the profits, and paid publishers a percentage for printing and distributing the work. Now the flow of funds had reversed itself, with publishers fronting costs and paying only "royalties" to authors. Yet the new system, along with the creation of a national market, clearly increased potential sales. Authors might therefore be simultaneously dismayed at being encouraged to tailor their output to the marketplace and exhilarated at the chance to become self-supporting.

As writers poured into the city, supply outstripped even the surging demand and further tilted the balance of power from authors to publishers. By 1851 editor Nathaniel Parker Willis warned that New York City was the "most overstocked market in the country," noting, "I have tried to find employment for dozens of starving writers, in vain." Horace Greeley cautioned one upstate hopeful: "You do not realize how little the mere talent of writing well has to do with success or usefulness. There are a thousand at least in this city who can write very good prose or verse," he added, "while there are not fifty who can earn their bread by it." Few heeded such advice, for it was clear, as a writer in the *Literary World* noted in 1847, that "the seat of commerce" was fast becoming "the centre of literary power."

YOUNG AMERICA

One thing this "centre" lacked was a center. New York's literary world was fissured into warring factions, each with its own complement of writers, critics, and magazines. The two leading circles—Knickerbockers and Young Americans—disagreed on almost everything. The former were Whigs, Episcopalians, anglophiles, and hostile to all political and literary radicalisms. The latter were Jacksonians seeking a democratic literature and politics and an end to America's cultural subservience to Europe.

Knickerbockers and Young Americans also related differently to the marketplace. Knickerbockers were prosperous gentleman amateurs—businessmen and professionals who dined well, told good stories at table, and wrote lightly ironical essays in the style of Charles Lamb. At the center of their circle was man-about-town Lewis Gaylord Clark, who since 1834 had piloted the *Knickerbocker* magazine, a literary monthly. Clark's chatty "Editor's Table" kept the nation apprised of the Rabelaisian wit of his glamorous circle, which included Henry Brevoort and Charles Astor Bristed (J. J. Astor's grandson).

Clark didn't pay his well-heeled writers; he considered publication its own reward. But the *Knickerbocker* wasn't utterly divorced from the marketplace. Clark often "puffed" books for favored authors or publishers, tossing off glowing reviews of volumes he hadn't necessarily bothered to read. Whig newspapers then circulated his opinions to the nation, which meant a *Knickerbocker* puff could sell out a book in several weeks or, conversely, kill it. By 1840, much to the annoyance of Young Americans, the conservative *Knickerbocker* was the most influential literary organ in America.

Clark's nemesis, Evert Augustus Duyckinck, represented the young professionals. He himself had been bred to the business—his father was a Water Street bookseller and publisher—and unlike Clark, an upstate New Yorker, Duyckinck was an authentic Knickerbocker (his name in Dutch meant "diving duck"). An ample inheritance allowed him to attend Columbia, study law, and do the Grand Tour of Europe, after which, in 1840, he settled down in a Clinton Place town house, surrounded by a ducal library of seventeen thousand books.

Around Duyckinck gathered the first generation of New York intellectuals for whom literature was a vocation. These youthful writers shared a generational distaste for the clique of conservative critics, publishers, and magazine editors whose mutual backscratching made it difficult for newcomers to penetrate the market. But Duyckinck's circle focused on more than moneymaking. At rollicking Saturday night suppers they debated the future of U.S. culture. They adopted the name Young America, emulating and expressing solidarity with Mazzini's Young Italy and Daniel O'Connell's Young Ireland. Most *were* young, in their late twenties or early thirties. Like Duyckinck's fellow Columbia alumnus Cornelius Mathews, an ardent (verging on shrill) literary nationalist, they considered New York "the seat and stronghold of this young power." From their metropolitan base they set out to foster an American literature.

In 1840 Duyckinck and Mathews established *Arcturus*, a monthly literary magazine that quickly rivaled Clark's *Knickerbocker*. Two years later they organized an American Copyright Club, hoping that if Harpers and other pirates were forced to pay their European sources, they might turn more often to American authors. In 1845 Duyckinck urged city writers to develop the kind of labor solidarity common in other New York trades, for only a "union among authors, bringing together the force of their aggregate works, would create a sentiment, a feeling in their behalf, a voice to which booksellers would be compelled to listen."

In 1845 Duyckinck became literary editor of the *Democratic Review*, a broad-circulation political magazine edited by John Louis O'Sullivan, a fiery and charming Irishman. O'Sullivan was a vigorous supporter of western expansion and European revolution. In both cases, he said, it was America's "manifest destiny" to extend the domain of democracy (though as a staunch Democrat, O'Sullivan exempted black slaves from this destiny). The swashbuckling O'Sullivan reached out to the scholarly Duyckinck because the latter's literary vision dovetailed perfectly with the former's political project. Both believed New York to be the ideal seedbed for a new American culture because it was home to writers from the West, South, and North, thus a more representative American city than provincial Boston. And New York, Duyckinck pointed out, was the country's "true publishing center," the only place technologically and financially capable of underwriting a people's art.

George Palmer Putnam, the aggressively entrepreneurial publisher, was Young America's perfect ally. Putnam was eager to promote America's cultural independence, especially if it could help him contest Harpers' domination of the literary marketplace, and he was prepared to pay authors fair dividends while distributing inexpensive editions of their books to ordinary American audiences. Duyckinck became general editor of Wiley and Putnam's watershed project, the Library of American Books, and enlisted some of the city's (and country's) outstanding younger writers in forming a new literary canon. In 1847, moreover, Wiley and Putnam joined Appleton and Company in launching the *Literary World*, with Duyckinck at the editorial helm. The new magazine would survey and publicize the nation's burgeoning literary output. It would assess, as well, the accomplishments of America's visual artists, who, like the writers, had been profoundly affected by technological and social developments in New York City.

ART IN THE AGE OF MECHANICAL REPRODUCTION

The Panic of 1837 had disrupted Manhattan's patronage system. Cole, Sully, and Asher Durand found that merchants laughed wanly at the notion of buying paintings with their businesses facing bankruptcy. Spurred by hard times, artists fashioned new and more collective ways of supporting their work.

In 1838 portraitist and engraver James Herring established the Apollo Gallery, where painters could exhibit and share in the proceeds of a twenty-five-cent admission fee. When this foundered, Herring decided to reach out to a far broader audience. In 1839, drawing on a model developed in several European cities, he created the Apollo Association, a noncommercial joint stock company. Subscribers contributed five dollars each to a fund, which then purchased works from artists. These were exhibited to the public free of charge and, at year's end, distributed by lottery to subscribers. Association members also received engraved reproductions of some of the artworks, as well as the group's *Bulletin*, the first magazine devoted exclusively to American art. In 1844 the enterprise, now going strong, was renamed the American Art-Union (AAU).

The AAU was run by managers whom Herring drew at first from the pool of gentleman art enthusiasts—among them Philip Hone, rentier James W. Beekman, and editors Henry Raymond and William Cullen Bryant. Some were attracted by old republican ideals of stewardship and civic patronage; others hoped art might exert what the Rev. Henry Bellows called "exalting, purifying, calming influences" on the increasingly agitated masses. Young America rallied to the AAU, seeing in it a democratizing project akin to their own. Duyckinck, Mathews, Putnam, and O'Sullivan, delighted to make art available to the many, also hoped that artists freed from dependence on Eurofixated patrons might create an American art.

By the late 1840s the American Art-Union was the nation's primary market for U.S. paintings other than portraits. Each year roughly nineteen thousand subscribers purchased an average of four hundred artworks, benefiting painters, sculptors, and the engravers and die casters who prepared prints for reproduction. The AAU's gallery, one paper reported, had "grown to be a kind of municipal Institution, visited by the whole people." The managers had established a luxurious setting on bustling Broadway, replete with ottomans and gas lights, that stayed open at night when working people could come. The gallery drew from "every section of the social system," the press noted, "from the millionaire of 5th Avenue, to the B'hoy of 3d." Half a million people visited in 1848, the organization claimed, a number roughly equal to the city's entire population.

The AAU collected enemies too: envious and profit-seeking private art galleries; disgruntled rejected artists; connoisseurs who sniffed at the sometimes mediocre work submitted by sign painters, itinerant portraitists, lithographers, and banner painters;

and the National Academy of Design, which, though many of its members participated in AAU affairs, worried about dwindling attendance at its own exhibitions. What finally brought the AAU down, however, was an assault by powerful antigambling forces (backed by Bennett's *Herald*) who managed in 1852 to have its lottery ruled illegal.

The private art market now flourished. The National Academy's annual spring exhibit blossomed into a major event. Galleries catered to wealthy collectors like department store owner A. T. Stewart, and Broadway showrooms attracted a steady patronage—occasionally a spectacular one: when Edwin Church's *Niagara* was first exhibited in May of 1857 thousands crowded into the gallery each day. The Art-Union had left its mark, however, in a heightened public interest in art, in the precedent it had set for a municipal museum, and in boosting the growing popularity of reproductions and strengthening the city's role in their supply.

Engraver and printer Nathaniel Currier, who had long been producing and marketing images from his Nassau Street shop in the heart of the newspaper district, was joined after 1852 by James Merritt Ives, a self-trained artist, who became his partner in 1857. Currier and Ives used the latest in steam-driven press technology to churn out lithographs from sketches drawn by staff artists. They also hired hundreds of women to hand-color the prints. Their inexpensive "Colored Engravings for the People" provided uplifting images of family life for moderate-income households.

They also portrayed New York City. Currier and Ives views of Broadway, the burning of the Crystal Palace, P. T. Barnum's galleries, and the clipper ships all sold briskly. The firm's success spurred competitors into providing urban imagery. Specialized producers turned out lithographed advertisements for ironworks, inexpensive wall prints of tourist spots, engravings of local scenes for guidebooks, and—for banks, shops, hotels, real estate promoters, and tourist operators—the bird's-eye views that presented a coherent and comprehensible metropolis, laid out for delectation and consumption.

The great national monthlies like *Harper's* and *Putnam's* joined in the preening. In 1853 *Putnam's* offered an illustrated series called "New-York Daguerreotyped" that depicted the emblematic edifices—the Crystal Palace, the department stores, the newspaper headquarters, the monster hotels—deemed "worthy of her pretensions as the metropolis of the Union." In 1854 another running commentary appeared in *Putnam's*—"The World of New York"—which hailed the city's energy, wealth, and culture. City sights and scenes also saturated the popular press, with *Harper's, Putnam's*, and journals like *Frank Leslie's Illustrated Newspaper* (1855) and the *New York Illustrated News* (1859) helping make New York the most represented city in the country.

The process of urban imaging was further accelerated by the debut of photography. When news of Louis Daguerre's success in fixing images on silver-coated copper plates arrived in New York City in 1839, the omni-capable Samuel F. B. Morse, together with scientific instrument maker George W. Prosch, devised a rudimentary camera. From the doorway of Prosch's workshop, Morse captured an image showing City Hall, the Park, and a "coachman sleeping on his box." Then he established a glass-walled rooftop studio on a Nassau Street building. From here he produced some of the first urban cityscapes, including one, a visitor reported, with "very clear, distinct views of Brooklyn in the distance."

The novelty of daguerreotypy, along with its low start-up costs, attracted many to commercial photography during the depression. In 1843 the New York correspondent of a Washington newspaper wrote whimsically that "in these Jeremiad times" only two classes were making money in Manhattan: "the *beggars* and the *takers of likenesses by daguerreotype*." Indeed, he added, ever since a Frenchman had set up shop selling apparatuses, "any pedlar can take up the trade."

Mathew Brady was no peddler, though he did clerk for A. T. Stewart after moving to Manhattan from upstate New York in 1839. Then the young Irishman met Morse and discovered his life's profession. In 1844, aged twenty-two, Brady opened the Daguerrean Miniature Gallery at Broadway and Fulton, on the top floor of a building directly across from Barnum's.

Brady was an instant success, thanks to his talent and a Barnumesque flair for self-promotion. Taking up residence at Astor House, he pursued and captured visiting celebrities so successfully that it was soon considered a mark of social standing and public distinction to be daguerreotyped by "Brady of Broadway." He and his peers also made photography a public art form by opening their galleries to passersby. Strollers headed for Brady's (or Gurney's, Edward's, or Anthony's—all on Broadway near City Hall Park) to socialize and gaze at likenesses of the famous and notorious.

Brady had little interest in depicting ordinary working people (though in 1846 he did photograph inmates of the Blackwell's Island penitentiary for a book on "reading" criminal heads). But others soon jumped into the business of providing "occupationals"—pictures of artisans in daily dress holding the tools of their trade. By 1850 there were seventy-one daguerreotype studios (employing 127 "operators") ready to take one's picture, and at least one that advertised a willingness to make house calls in order "to take Likenesses of sick or deceased persons." By 1853 there were more such studios in Manhattan than in England, more on Broadway than in all London. By then, one magazine writer remarked, it was hard "to find the man who has not gone through the 'operator's' hands from once to half-a-dozen times, or who has not the shadowy faces of his wife and children done up in purple morocco and velvet, together or singly, among his household treasures."

As mechanized "daguerreotype factories" sprang up, driving down prices and speeding up delivery, photographers who sought an upscale clientele proclaimed themselves artists, not mechanics. Brady, to underscore his superior status and keep up with his migrating market, repeatedly moved uptown into ever finer surroundings. By 1853 his gallery on upper Broadway boasted satin walls, gilded chandeliers, and a mirrored parlor for the ladies.

The streets themselves continued to draw droves of daguerreotypists, especially in the latter 1850s, when new technologies made collection and dissemination of outdoor images easier. Such photographs could now be turned into lithographs, for reprinting in newspapers, and in the 1850s photographs became the basis of urban scenes published in *Harper's* and *Leslie's*.

Seizing on the latest technical improvements, Edward Anthony snapped freeze-frame images of Broadway street life (including pedestrians caught in midstride) and mounted two such shots, taken from slightly different angles, on a double print card called a stereograph. Viewers could insert these into an inexpensive and widely available stereoscope, a double magnifier that produced the illusion of three-dimensionality. Oliver Wendell Holmes raved at Anthony's ability to "snatch at the central life of a mighty city, as it rushed by in all its multitudinous complexity of movement!" By 1859 Anthony had over two hundred stereographs on the mass market and was hard at work on factories capable of producing thousands of such cards a day. Within five years there would be stereoscopes in parlors across the country, further enhancing New York's position as the most visually represented city in the country.

Photographs of street life and urban residents were also touted as enabling a new, more veracious knowledge of reality. Soon, inspired by the new way of seeing, journalists and novelists were busy turning out what they claimed were "daguerreotypes" of city life.

40

Seeing New York

In the 1820s city watching became a highly developed art form in Europe. Gentleman spectators sauntered the streets observing and recording impressions, then published amiable commentaries for coffeehouse and parlor readers that made bewildering, stressful cityscapes seem knowable and negotiable. One of the most popular of the genre was *Life in London, or The Day and Night Scenes of Jerry Hawthorn Esq and his elegant friend Corinthian Tom, in their Rambles and Sprees through the Metropolis* (1821). Written by Pierce Egan, an Irish-born London printer and journalist, and illustrated by the brothers Cruikshank, *Life in London* recounted the fictional peregrinations of two men-about-town. Tom and Jerry, though well-born, were equally at home in the West End or at gin parlors and cockfights—places respectable people didn't go in person.

Over the next fifteen years, London's slums attracted ever-increasing interest, penny papers commenced their Bow Street Police Court reporting, and Charles Dickens started evoking London's lowlife. *Sketches by Boz* began appearing in December 1833, and soon, in *Pickwick Papers* (1836–37) and *Oliver Twist* (1839), Dickens had provided thousands of armchair Londoners with a guide to their city's hidden terrains.

New Yorkers loved these European flaneurs. They bought American reprints of Egan's *Life in London*, perused city sketches in the *London Quarterly* and *Edinburgh Review*, and devoured Dickens. Their own city, alas, was not deemed flaneurable. Lacking the spectacular variety of European metropoles, it didn't seem worth perambulating for publication. Would-be urban spectators went abroad instead. They sent back dispatches on London's immensity, on Paris's complexity, on the power of great cities to induce disorientation—even insanity!—in unwary tourists. Washington Irving was an early American master of the form, and Nathaniel Parker Willis carried on the tradition. In 1835, after he joined George Pope Morris as coeditor of the *New-York Mirror*, the dandyish Willis went abroad and sent back somewhat precious urban sketches done in a pun-filled style. But flaneurism made Willis New York's first successful profession-al "magazinist." ("My rubbish, such as it is, brings me a very high price.")

In the 1830s the *Sun* and its penny press competitors began defining everyday life in New York as something worthy of coverage. Benjamin Day published a vivid account of a visit to the Five Points in 1834 ("they endure literally, a hell of horrors"), launched police court reporting, and paid episodic attention to everyday life. But it was in the 1840s that New York became fully flaneurable. As Manhattanites turned their attention homeward—newly enchanted (or appalled) by their city's growing size and diversity, the kinetic flow of its crowds, and its flowering as a cultural center—street narratives by middle-class walkers became omnipresent.

Willis turned his practiced eye on Manhattan in "Daguerrotypes of the Present," a series of urban essays for the *New-York Mirror*, and bundled up another batch of sketches as *Hurry-Graphs*. Lewis Gaylord Clark and the *Knickerbocker* crowd filled their magazine with sketches like " 'Loaferina' in New York," which celebrated the immensi-ty and diversity of the "London of America," and their Young American rivals at *Arc-turus* provided equally urbane commentary on New York's passing show. For Duyck-inck's circle, moreover, the shift of sensibility suggested a new frontier for American literature. Cornelius Mathews argued this thesis vigorously in an 1840 manifesto, declaring that writers should embrace "the crowded life of cities, the customs, habi-tudes, and actions of men dwelling in contact." In 1842 Mathews took his own advice. His *Career of Puffer Hopkins* was the first fictional attempt to capture the color of New York, as its flaneurial hero wandered about from fancy shops to dingy alleys, exploring the city's various worlds.

CROWDS AND CIVILIZATION

Much of this city scrutinizing zeroed in on particular features of urban life, and among the closely watched phenomena none seemed more fascinating than the "crowd." "Crowd" had long been disturbingly interchangeable with "mob," but now it evoked something benign: a vibrant street life, an exciting tempo, a flood of sensation. Charles Loring Brace, a young seminarian arriving to study at Union Theological Seminary after graduating Yale in 1846, was astonished by Broadway. "Faces and coats of all pat-terns, bright eyes, whiskers, spectacles, hats, bonnets, caps, all hurrying along in the most apparently inextricable confusion. One would think it a grand gala-day. And it's rather overpowering to think of that rush and whirl being their regular every-day life." Guidebooks trumpeted the sensuous excitement as a prime reason for visiting, with William Bobo's *Glimpses of New York* (1852) typical in hailing "the throng upon the sidewalks" as "one grand kaleidoscope in perpetual motion."

Natives might grumble at the rush and whirl's impracticality—trying to cross Broadway was considered a risky business—but they too were taken with its poetry. One set of local enthusiasts—admittedly a committee of Broadway merchants—celebrated their chief thoroughfare's bustle and color, its collisions and complexity. "The din, this driving, this omnibus-thunder, this squeezing, this jamming, crowding, and at times smashing, is the exhilerating [*sic*] music which charms the multitude and draws its thousands within the whirl. This is Broadway—this *makes* Broadway. Take from it those elements, the charm is gone."

"Living in crowds," the *Times* suggested in 1852, "gives to the business, the daily life, the whole character of great cities, such wonderful energy and vigor. Men in cities live and work constantly *under high pressure*. It is almost impossible to go on a walk on Broadway or Wall Street in business or pleasure; one naturally and unthinkingly quickens his pace to a run." Living in crowds (the *Times* continued) gave a distinctively modern shape to the way people experienced life, in "gusts of passion and excitement." Any "startling incident—the arrival of a steamer, the perpetration of a crime, the advent of a celebrity—anything at all calculated to stimulate curiosity or startle attention—comes upon half a million of people at once," courtesy of the morning papers, and then "every man sees it in his neighbor's face and hears it from his lips the moment he meets him."[1]

Crowds offered more than mere sensation, it was believed; they fostered interactivity, hence progress. *Tribune* reporter George Foster argued in 1849 that "a great city is the highest result of human civilization," the place where people's energies could be developed "to their utmost power and excited to their highest state of activity by constant contact with countless other souls."

Going hand in hand with this new metropolitan self-confidence was a brash disdain for rural life and people. The author of an 1859 treatise called *Civilization in New York* suggested that living in the country "stupefies rather than deepens character." A "human being dwelling alone, or in sparsely settled districts, without any communication with cities, remains unacquainted with his own capabilities," he explained, and thus "deteriorates in prejudice and ignorance." New York banking authority J. S. Gibbons reported that "any one who has travelled among our country villages, out of the immediate influence of cities," was struck by "the lack of energy, the rudeness of life and character, and the almost savage features of the common people"—but once urban institutions arrived "a less brutal and more intelligent spirit beams from their eyes."

Ruralites responded with defensive counterassaults. An upstate doctor, Joel H. Ross, addressing his *What I Saw in New York* (1851) to the young men and women fleeing farms and villages, warned that city life consisted of "trials, losses, frowns, failures, pestilence, poverty, and hypocrisy." Places like New York, he said, were "to dwellers in the country, very like what white lights at night are to flies—brilliant and attractive, but certain ruin." But the destiny of America, metrophiles rebutted, lay less in taming the continental wilderness and creating independent homesteads and small towns than in establishing large cosmopolitan cities that harbored the greatest diversity of human types. By these lights, New York was in the vanguard of American development. As George Francis Train boasted in 1857, it was "the locomotive of these United States," pulling the rest of the nation faster and faster into the future: "twenty miles an hour—thirty—forty"![2]

---

1. Observers often presented "crowds" as socially undifferentiated organisms, seldom providing a breakdown of their class composition. One exception was a journalist who in 1845 noted that the Broadway "crowd" changed markedly with the time of day. In the early morning clerks, mechanics, and laborers went by. Then masses of merchants and children made their way to work and school. Forenoon brought out people of leisure, many of them ladies or strangers, to promenade the shops. At noon mechanics paraded by on their way to dinner, as did the merchants at three, and so forth. The streets were never crowded in the same way.

2. Such vigorous assertions unsettled even Nature's chief apostle, Ralph Waldo Emerson. When in 1842 Emerson made a lecture swing down to the city, he inveighed against "this world of material & ephemeral interest" but confessed that maybe it was only his own "poorness of spirit" that kept him from the city. Perhaps in his next "transmigration," Emerson speculated, he would "choose New York."

LONELY CROWDS, CONFIDENCE MEN

Amid the din of celebratory oratory, some city-based critics could be heard suggesting that the crowded life had some distinct minuses, among them anonymity. Boosters, to be sure, relished it for facilitating the pursuit of private pleasures. New York City "is the most free and easy place conceivable," wrote Thomas R. Gunn, author of a treatise on the city's boardinghouses. "The right to do as you d——n please," Gunn exulted, "is nowhere so universally recognized or less curbed by authority." Others, however, observed that one woman's liberation was another's loneliness.

Lydia Maria Child had her rhapsodic moments as she rambled Manhattan compiling the "Letters from New York" she dispatched to the *Boston Courier*, and she regularly praised the city's "many agreeable sights and sounds." Overall, however, she had a most un-flaneur-like perspective on street life. "It is sad walking in the city," Child reported. "For eight weary months, I have met in the crowded streets but two faces I have ever seen before." She discovered that in the city, "the loneliness of the soul is deeper, and far more restless, than in the solitude of the mighty forest." Confluence didn't guarantee connection, and indeed could underscore its absence. Child encountered much human suffering on her walks, "hungry eyes, that look as if they had pleaded long for sympathy, and at last gone mute in still despair," but "the busy throng, passing and repassing . . . offer no sympathy."

Crowding brought vulnerability too, especially in an era of humbug and flimflam. City people had to size up a stranger's character from externals, which, like paper money, were all too easy to counterfeit. In 1849 William Thompson, a man of "genteel appearance," struck up conversation on Broadway with a well-dressed stranger, greeting him as an old acquaintance. After a short time Thompson asked affably: "Have you confidence in me to trust me with your watch until to-morrow?" The victim, embarrassed at having forgotten such an agreeable fellow, and reluctant to deny such a forthright request, handed over his timepiece, and Thompson faded away into the crowd. The city wasn't yet vast enough to swallow him up forever, though, and when the mark happened upon Thompson a second time, he got him arrested, convicted, and sent to the Tombs.

A local journalist called Thompson a "confidence-man," and the coinage achieved instant currency. New Yorkers' reactions to Thompson were mixed. Some admired, even hailed his enterprise. But the phenomenon of the Confidence Man proved deeply worrying to many—it earned the longest entry in the *National Police Gazette's Rogue's Lexicon*—as it underscored the increasing difficulty city folk had in distinguishing benign stranger from malign trickster. Fortunately these were skills that could be improved with time. Those most vulnerable to being conned were newcomers, hayseeds, "greenhorns"—and innumerable guidebooks, pamphlets, and newspaper articles were published to alert such novices to the scams and scammers awaiting them in the big city. The really polished New Yorker, as editor Walter Whitman noted in an 1856 "Advice to Strangers" piece, was one who could coolly respond to a con man's pitch by looking him in the eye and saying: "You've waked up the wrong passenger."

UNQUIET BONES

Another worrisome feature of New York life was the very "fluctuation, and never-ceasing change" so beloved by boosters. "Overturn, overturn, overturn! is the maxim of New York," declared former mayor Hone in 1845. "The very bones of our ancestors are not permitted to lie quiet a quarter of a century, and one generation of men seem studious to remove all relics of those who precede them." *Putnam's* 1853 series "New York Daguerreotyped" fretted that the businesses spreading "with such astounding rapidity over the whole lower part of the city" were "prostrating and utterly obliterating every thing that is old and venerable, and leaving not a single land-mark, in token of the former position of the dwelling-places of our ancestors." Manhattan was a "modern city of ruins," agreed the *New-York Mirror*, where "no sooner is a fine building put up than it is torn down."

The result, said *Harper's Monthly* in 1856, was that "New York is notoriously the largest and least loved of any of our great cities. Why should it be loved as a city? It is never the same city for a dozen years together. A man born in New York forty years ago finds nothing, absolutely nothing, of the New York he knew." The city's relentless focus on the future was ravaging its past, undermining the sense that New York was a home, not just a grid of opportunities.[3]

The razing and rebuilding generated nostalgia for an older, quieter, more comprehensible city and fostered efforts at commemoration. James Miller's guidebook, *New York as It Is*, lamented that the city had sacrificed "to the shrine of Mammon almost every relic of the oldentime" and offered as counterweight a walking tour of such historic sites as remained. A more thoroughgoing intervention got underway when David Thomas Valentine, clerk of the Common Council, began issuing *Manuals of the Corporation of the City of New York*, an annual compilation published and widely distributed by the city between 1841 and 1866. Though mainly an assemblage of official data, the *Manuals* included woodcut and lithographic reproductions of old paintings, prints, drawings, maps, and documents that Valentine had rescued "from oblivion, to which they were hastening down the stream of time." Nevertheless, Valentine worried in 1856, "the present rapid progress of the City" threatened "soon to obliterate all the natural landmarks of the island," and he urged still greater efforts to preserve "for future generations" images of what remained.

Painters began tackling historical subjects: William Walcutt recalled *Pulling Down the Statue of George III at Bowling Green* (1857). Plays like *Charlotte Temple* and *Jacob Leisler, or New York in 1690* became popular fare at the Bowery Theater. Autobiographies appeared lamenting the passing of the Knickerbocker era, such as Grant Thorborn's *Fifty Years Reminiscences of New York* (1845). Evacuation Day was celebrated with fife-and-drum parades by ancient veterans in cocked hats and buff breeches and with full-scale reenactments of the British departure. And the New-York Historical Society took on nearly a thousand new members in the 1840s and 1850s, growing prosperous enough to erect a neo-classical headquarters at Second Avenue and 11th Street, in genteel proximity to St. Mark's Church.

This wave of looking backward also spurred historical scholarship. When E. Porter Belden researched his model of New York in the late 1840s, he reported in astonish-

---

3. This hyperinstability was compounded, Joel Ross noted, by the hypermobility so dramatically evident each May Day. "It is so customary to *'move'* on this day, that it would seem that many change their residences just to be in the *fashion*," but whatever their motives, the result was that New Yorkers "are more like travellers who stop on their journey for the night, and start on the next morning, with little attachment to their lodging-place, and well nigh forget it by the next sun."

ment that "no history of the city had ever been published, and that no accurate descriptive work had been issued in the last twenty years." He wasn't far wrong, as remarkably little had been published since William Smith's *History of the Province of New-York* back in 1757.

There was, however, much newly available raw material for would-be scholars, thanks to the state legislature. In 1839, following up a suggestion by the New-York Historical Society, Albany had authorized and paid for a "historical agent"—John Romeyn Brodhead—to spend several years in Dutch, French, and English archives, laboriously copying documents relating to New York's colonial history. Brodhead's eighty manuscript volumes were eventually brought out in eleven printed tomes edited by Edmund Bailey O'Callaghan, beginning in 1855, again with state support.

O'Callaghan, an expatriate Irish physician and activist in the Catholic emancipation movement, was chosen to compile Brodhead's documents in part because he himself had published a pioneering *History of New Netherland; or New York under the Dutch* (D. Appleton, 1846–48). His two-volume study, which ended with the English conquest of 1664, drew on original documents and interviews with old Dutch families in Flatbush and Gravesend, and it came as a revelation to those who had incautiously assumed Irving's satirical "history" was the real thing.

James Fenimore Cooper set out to follow O'Callaghan's treatment with a more comprehensive study—oddly enough, given that Cooper's 1820s enthusiasm for New York City had given way in the 1830s to caustic derogation. Perhaps it was because he believed that Manhattanites, in their infatuation with wealth, displayed an "intensity of selfishness which smothers all recollection of the past" that he began researching *Towns of Manhattan*, for publication by Putnam. In July 1851, however, with only eight chapters completed, doctors ordered the ailing Cooper to stop writing. He died that September, and the manuscript was later lost in a fire at Putnam's.

John Romeyn Brodhead stepped into the breach, and Harpers brought out the first of his planned series of volumes in 1853. Brodhead too got only as far as 1664. He'd hoped to get down to 1702, he recalled, but had been tempted by the mass of original documents he'd unearthed, and the volume "in spite of laborious condensation" had "grown unfashionably large." Daniel Curry's *New-York: A Historical Sketch of the Rise and Progress of the Metropolitan City of America* (1853) told more of the tale, but only because his book (he admitted) made "no pretensions to originality, nor yet to deep and thorough research," as doing so would "have swelled the work to ten times its present volume." Curry's study was nevertheless notable for being among the first to advance the Manhattan-as-melting-pot theme. "From whatever point the denizen of that city may have come, a residence in New-York surely and speedily makes him a NEW-YORKER," Curry asserted, as "New-York energy acts as a solvent to fuse the motley masses that Europe is pouring upon our shores into a consistent body of valuable and happy freemen."

It was left to Mary Louise Booth to produce the first comprehensive study written in the nineteenth century, *A History of the City of New York* (1859). Formerly a Williamsburg schoolteacher like her father, Booth had been drawn, at age eighteen, to a literary career, and she moved to Manhattan to be nearer its newspapers and libraries. For several years Booth worked by day as a vestmaker while studying at night and writing without pay for educational and literary journals. Finally she was engaged by the *New York Times* as a piece-rate reporter on educational and women's topics.

Booth was commissioned by a group of merchants to write a city history that would combat New Englanders' denigration of New Yorkers as crassly commercial, while contesting their arrogation of the nation's historical narrative. She produced an eight-hundred-plus-page study; even so, it left out many "curious and interesting events of the past" (she apologized), as their inclusion would have swollen the volumes "to so formidable a size that they would terrify the public."

Booth argued that pluralistic New York, not provincial New England, best embodied the nation's history. She hailed Manhattan's "cosmopolitan character," so evident "in its freedom from exclusiveness, in its religious tolerance, and in its extended views of men and things," and she traced these admirable traits to the "genial hospitable nature ingrafted on the city by its early settlers" and the subsequent arrival of "all the races of the earth." In New England, one stock of settlers predominated, but Manhattan's populace "is blended with all the races of the earth; and if it be true, as one of our most eminent philosophers asserts, that a mixture of many materials makes the best mortar, there is no reason to regret it."

MYSTERIES OF THE CITY

None of the misgivings about the isolation or the chicanery or the rootlessness or the ahistoricism of New York life did much to cloud the prevailing sunny optimism. But a much harsher take on the city was emerging in these years, promoted by a host of popular journalists and urban fiction writers. This genre dismissed the showier aspects of New York's street life as inconsequential froth and proposed a troubling thesis. The *real* essence of metropolitan life was a stark, indeed shocking, contrast between two new social classes: a monied aristocracy of debauched nouveaux riches and a threatening mass of degenerate immigrants. These critics offered a darker way for New Yorkers to see, and evaluate, the new urban scene, a perspective summarized with brutal succinctness by *Harper's* in 1857: "What was then [1827] a decent and orderly town of moderate size, has been converted into a huge semi-barbarous metropolis—one half as luxurious and artistic as Paris, the other half as savage as Cairo or Constantinople—not well-governed nor ill-governed, but simply not governed at all."

This perceptual framework, like flaneurism an import, was first formulated by writers in Paris and London. In 1842–43, Eugene Sue serialized his *Mysteries of Paris* in the popular French press, a work that exposed two shadowy and corrupt worlds, one of the criminal underground, the other of a decadent elite. Sue's *Mysteries* was widely pirated and reprinted in England and on the Continent—it appealed greatly to artisans and became the sensational reading of Chartists and the revolutionaries of 1848—and in New York Mike Walsh brought out excerpts in his *Subterranean.*

A still more influential lesson in how to read the contemporary city was delivered to Manhattan, in person, by Charles Dickens. His books had depicted a London where the center no longer held, where a well-ordered and harmonious world had split into realms of squalor and splendor, of civilization and barbarism. The depraved paupers and grasping nouveaux riches responsible for these appalling changes merited and received condemnation in his pages, but they were also fascinating in their very repulsiveness. Part of Dickens's phenomenal popularity was the opportunity he afforded readers of feeling simultaneously superior to, and enthralled by, villains of the upper and lower registers.

New Yorkers were thrilled when Dickens arrived in the city in January 1842, partly for sightseeing, partly in a fruitless attempt to promote an international copyright law that would require Americans to pay for the pleasure of reading him. New York's elite threw a Boz Ball in the Park Theater for twenty-five hundred people—"the greatest affair of modern times," said Philip Hone—and in an encore, Washington Irving presided over a feast for 230 diners at the City Hotel.

Later that year New Yorkers had the additional pleasure of being able to pick up *American Notes* (in a pirated twelve-and-a-half-cent edition Harpers brought out in November 1842) and find out how Dickens applied his way of seeing to their very own city. On the whole, his account of "the beautiful metropolis of America"—in a book whose revenues Dickens counted on to cover his travel costs—was quite flattering. Dickens had nice words for Broadway, the city's pride, apart from some catty remarks about its pigs—"two portly sows are trotting up behind this carriage, and a select party of half a dozen gentlemen hogs have just now turned the corner"—which called embarrassing attention to Broadway denizens routinely excised from boosterish lithographs. More delightfully, New Yorkers discovered, through Dickens's account of an expedition to the Bowery, that *Oliver Twist* was alive and well in their very own city.

On leaving Broadway, "the lively whirl of carriages is exchanged for the deep rumble of carts and wagons," Dickens noted. "The stores are poorer here, the passengers less gay. Clothes ready made, and meat ready cooked." Then, with two police escorts, he plunged into the dark heart of the Five Points, along "narrow ways, diverting to the right and left, and reeking everywhere with dirt and filth," passing "coarse and bloated faces." Now, deeper still, through "lanes and alleys, paved with mud knee-deep," past "hideous tenements which take their name from robbery and murder"; groping down pitch-dark rickety stairs, past rooms where "some figure crawls half awakened, as if the judgment hour were near at hand, and every obscene grave were giving up its dead," past rooms from which "vapors issue forth that blind and suffocate," culminating at "underground chambers" at the bottom of "the world of vice and misery" where blacks and whites "dance and game" together. A final judgment: "All that is loathsome, drooping, and decayed is here."[4]

From this rich storehouse of ready-to-wear metaphors, some popular New York authors drew heavily—and heavy-handedly, being far less talented than Dickens or Sue. In 1848 E. Z. C. Judson, better known by his nom de plume of Ned Buntline, penned the mammoth *Mysteries and Miseries of New York*. In it, he promised, he would provide "a perfect daguerreotype of this great city" from "above Bleecker" to the "horrors of the Five Points." Advertising himself as a "Friend of the Working Man," Buntline dwelt in lascivious detail on the plutocratic lifestyle of the city's rich, and his hero also visited an underground nightclub—remarkably similar to the one described by Dickens—where, again, all is dirt and chaos and where blacks frolic with whites. In the manner of the *Police Gazette*, Buntline offered statistics on urban crime and provided a four-page glossary of underworld argot. *Mysteries and Miseries* proved enormously successful. First serialized in popular journals, it was reprinted in the Harpers Family

4. The interracial heart of darkness was Almack's, "the assembly-room of the Five-point fashionables," wittily named after an exclusive London club. Despite Dickens's mordant rhetoric, the smartly dressed and cordial African-American proprietor, Pete Williams, arranged a "regular break-down" for Dickens's delectation, featuring the brilliant dancing of Master Juba. Not one to miss an opportunity, after *American Notes* came out, Williams renamed his now notorious venue "Dickens' Place."

Library series, and the firm promoted it heavily in small-town and rural America as a testament to urban wickedness. It sold perhaps a hundred thousand volumes in all and helped mold perceptions of the metropolis.

With the public devouring Buntline's *Mystery*, George Foster, who covered the city beat for Greeley's *Tribune*, decided to collect his columns in book form. Foster, one of the first professional flaneurs, had long walked about the city, "eating with his eyes" and boasting of the "varieties of human nature" he encountered in New York: "Every face you meet is a character, every scene affords a piquant contrast. Talk of your Eastern bazaars and Parisian arcades!" Yet his articles also drew heavily on the conventions of urban sensationalism. Foster promised to get beneath the tall spires, commercial palaces, and princely mansions "where life flows so brightly and so gaily" to explore the profoundest recesses of the "deep, dark, sullen ocean of poverty, crime and despair" and "bring to light of day the horrid monsters that live and gender in its oozy depths."

Foster's city was as polarized as Buntline's. Above, the deceitful parvenus— "pompous without dignity, gaudy without magnificence, lavish without taste, and aristocratic without good manners." Below, a degraded underclass of drunken Irishmen, grasping Jews, and black men who danced (in the same old underground dance halls reached via the same old labyrinthine passageways) with "sluttishly-dressed women, in whose faces drunkenness and debauchery have destroyed every vestige of all we expect in the countenance of women, and even almost every trace of human expression."

Foster's *New York in Slices* (1849) did well. A second series, published in 1850 as *New York by Gas Light*, surpassed his own record (and Buntline's too), eventually selling about two hundred thousand copies. He followed this up with *Fifteen Minutes Around New York* (a guide book for Crystal Palace visitors) and a last effort, *New York Naked* in 1854.

Foster and Buntline believed that the metropolitan transformation of the 1840s and 1850s had destroyed the old republican town. New York was now a segmented city of poor and rich, each with their own territorial strongholds from which they issued forth to prey upon the other. Those in the middle ground—the assumed audience for this literature—were addressed but not described, and the result was a chiaroscuro portrait of pools of light and darkness, resembling the way radiance from gas-lit street lamps was swallowed up by surrounding blackness.

This noir-ish city was a far cry from the clearly legible one sketched by the flaneur, praised by the guidebooks, and portrayed in the bird's-eye views. Those official New Yorks were civic spirited, filled with noble vistas. This New York was jumbled and anarchic, an incoherent labyrinth, a polarized city ruled by rapacity. It was not a site of civilizing encounters: it was a battleground, fractured along lines of class and sex.

The mysteries' New York was peopled with dangerous and endangered women. Harlots lured victims to their dens, notably in the Five Points, where "squalid females," or so William Bobo claimed in *Glimpses of New York* (1852), perched "about the windows, stoops and cellar doors, like buzzards on dead trees." Conversely, beautiful innocent females routinely fell into the clutches of sinister monied men against whom their virtue was no defense. Tales of sex and murder based on real-life incidents were particularly popular. George Wilkes of the *Police Gazette* vividly recounted *The Lives of Helen Jewett and Richard P. Robinson*, and the prolific Joseph Holt Ingraham was but one of many who recycled the Mary Rogers murder in his *La Bonita Cigarera, or The Beautiful Cigar Vender*.

Thus was born the sunshine-and-shadow tradition, a way of seeing New York that became the era's central cliché about the city. Countless writers were forced to grope for new and fresh ways to describe stark juxtapositions, usually without success. "It is but a step from the mansion where wealth gathers its luxuries," declared an anonymous clergyman in *Life in New York* (1847), "to the cellar or garret where hunger gnaws and cold pinches." Joel Ross spoke of "success and defeat, health and disease, wealth and poverty, comforts and misery, plenty and beggary." George Lippard, in *New York: Its Upper Ten and Lower Million* (1853), went with "empire of palaces and hovels, garlands and chains, churches and jails." Lydia Maria Child commented drily on the rage for "vituperative alliterations such as magnificence and mud, finery and filth, diamonds and dirt, bullion and brass-tape, &c. &c."

Much of this language was clearly formulaic, rhetorical, overblown. The writers, journalists, clergymen, and public officials who wielded it exaggerated the declension from the old order. But the melodramatic prose was a response to new realities: the transformation of public space and the transmutation of class and gender cultures and relationships. Sunshine-and-shadow hyperbole was reductive, but not ridiculous. When a trio of great writers turned their attention to metropolitan life, they incorporated these metaphors of popular culture in their poetry and prose, even while transcending them.

MAN OF THE CROWD

In April 1844 Edgar Allan Poe arrived in New York—dead broke but still optimistic that even at age thirty-five he could reestablish his career as a "magazinist." Poe had done well in Philadelphia editing *Graham's Magazine* but, sick of "fashion-plates" and "love-tales," he'd resigned, hoping to launch a serious literary journal. Having failed to raise the capital—due, he was sure, to the machinations of a Philadelphia clique—Poe headed for Manhattan, accompanied by his tubercular wife, Virginia, and a reputation for drunken irresponsible conduct.

Poe found New York hard to afford and hard to take. He perched briefly in a Greenwich Street boardinghouse but was soon complaining about "insufferably dirty" streets and the din of clam-and-catfish vendors—"intolerably a nuisance." Seeking more salubrious surroundings, the Poes moved to Patrick and Mary Brennan's two-hundred-acre working farm, five miles outside town, just off the Bloomingdale Road near 84th Street. Here they would board until early 1845.

Poe was no fan of cities. They connoted heartless commercialism, poverty, pollution, and crime. He loved upper Manhattan and often rambled its woods and streams but believed the area "doomed." Soon it would be withered by the "acrid breath" of "the spirit of Improvement," its waterfronts lined with "nothing more romantic than shipping, warehouses, and wharves."

Disdainful but needy, Poe plunged into New York's expanding publishing world. Soon after arriving, he sold Moses Beach's *Sun* a hoax he'd concocted about an Atlantic balloon crossing. Then he landed a spot at the *Evening Mirror* run by Willis and Morris. Hiking each day from the farm to Nassau Street, he scribbled anonymous filler for fifteen dollars a week, helping turn out a magazine he thought "frivolous and fashionable." He did hackwork for other presses too, including a "Doings of Gotham" series for a small-town Pennsylvania paper.

In his tales, however, Poe was forging new ways to read the city. "The Man of the

Crowd," published in *Graham's Magazine* in 1840, recounted the story of a balked flaneur. The narrator lounges in a London coffeehouse, observing the street scene, sorting passersby into familiar categories. Suddenly he sees an old man whom he can't place, whose behavior challenges his ability to read and interpret the crowd. Leaping up, he follows his quarry through the metropolis, without stopping, for over twenty-four hours. He discovers that the old man drives himself ceaselessly through the streets out of terror that if he stopped he would have to confront his own emptiness. The flaneur's confidence in civic legibility, Poe suggests, is shallow and misplaced. Crowds and cities are indecipherable.

A subsequent trio of tales, published in Philadelphia magazines between 1841 and 1843, extended and deepened this approach. "The Murders in the Rue Morgue," "The Mystery of Marie Rogêt," and "The Purloined Letter" all presented cities teeming with activity and possibility (as did the flaneurs) yet shot through with crime and random violence (as did the mysteries). "Marie Rogêt," putatively set in a Paris described as "odious" and a "sink of pollution," was in fact based on the death of Mary Rogers in New York City. Rogers's fate symbolized for Poe the vulnerability of city folk, how easily one could go missing and turn up a brutalized corpse. Yet Poe *solved* Marie's "mystery" by introducing an analytical investigator, C. Auguste Dupin, who acknowledged what flaneurs denied: that the city was hard to read, dangerous, even terrifying. Dupin is no amateur idler but a credentialed specialist, a master of the skills of decoding a cityscape. Poe had invented a genre—the detective story—that played upon but in the end relieved his readers' urban anxieties. Social order was possible after all, Poe implied, if authorities adopted scientific methods of investigation and control. The detective, embodiment of this reassuring message, became a fixture on the urban literary scene.

So did Poe. Hoping to improve his chances of starting a magazine, he tried to get Harpers to publish his tales, but it turned him down. Then, in "the bleak December" of 1844, he wrote "The Raven," a shivery poem ideal for reading aloud, which Willis published in January 1845 to uproarious acclaim. Buoyed by overnight fame, Poe renewed his efforts to launch a journal. He moved back to the city in early 1845 and perched, variously, on Greenwich Street, East Broadway, and Amity Street near Washington Square during the coming year.

Poe wrote a piece, which Willis published, called "WHY HAVE THE NEW YORKERS NO REVIEW?" In it, he proposed establishing a "proper indigenous vehicle" for rallying Manhattan's literati against derisive Boston intellectuals. Charles Briggs did just that by launching the *Broadway Journal*, a literary review with a strong focus on the cultural life of New York City. Citing Poe's celebrity—everybody was "raven-mad about his last poem"—Briggs took him on as junior partner.

In 1845, at the behest of Duyckinck (whose *Arcturus* Poe had praised lavishly), Wiley and Putnam published editions of Poe's tales and poems in the Library of American Books. Social success followed commercial success. Poe was welcomed to literary salons sponsored by wealthy New York women determined to repudiate the city's money-grubbing reputation. He was often found at Anne Charlotte Lynch's Saturday evening "conversaziones," which attracted the likes of Irving, Bryant, Emerson, and Fuller to Lynch's Waverly Place drawing room.

Poe worked fourteen-hour days at the *Broadway Journal*, but in the brutally competitive magazine world it failed to make money. A disenchanted Briggs turned it over to Poe's exclusive management. Poe finally had his own magazine, but not the resources to promote it. He borrowed. He ran every aspect of the journal himself and wrote for it as well. Circulation kept falling, and in January 1846 it collapsed, leaving Poe destitute.

To bring in funds and to revenge himself on real and fancied enemies, he began writing "The Literati of New York City," a series of thirty-eight sketches published between May and October of 1846 in a Philadelphia magazine, *Godey's Lady's Book*. The pieces mixed brilliant if vitriolic criticism with venomous vignettes about local authors, gossip he'd picked up at salons. For all its pettiness, the series had an underlying ambition: to rid New York—which he considered "the focus of American letters"—of the curse of amateur writers. Poe, like Duyckinck and the Young Americans, had long railed against Lewis Gaylord Clark and his *Knickerbocker* puffery. He denounced the ability of "coteries in New York" to "manufacture, as required from time to time, a pseudo-public opinion by wholesale." Puffery impeded America's literary development by subordinating independent professionals to established cliques of privileged gentlemen.

These sallies precipitated full-scale war. Clark accused Poe of duplicity and drunkenness, impotence and cowardice. Poe sued for libel and won but was nevertheless banished from literary circles. Increasingly depressed and erratic, he raged at his foes from a cottage in Fordham, thirteen miles out of town amid hills and heavy foliage, where he had moved in hopes that country air would aid his failing wife. It did not: she died in January 1847, their first winter there.

Poe hung on a while longer. He took long walks atop the Croton Aqueduct, visited Jesuit faculty friends at St. John's College, and did some writing (with mixed success), including "Mellonta Tauta," a tale that imagined the future destruction of New York City by earthquake. By 1849, having concluded that the entire northern literary establishment was conspiring to thwart him, Poe decided to move south. Two weeks after Mathew Brady took his photograph, he set off to explore Richmond. On his way back, he stopped off in Baltimore, where in 1849, drunk and delirious, he died, aged forty, in a public house.

"DOLLARS DAMN ME"

Herman Melville had a bleaker yet more complex view of New York City than did Poe. Melville appreciated his hometown's energy and diversity, but he could never forget that Manhattan's marketplace had destroyed his father and stripped his family of its social position. Herman's mother, Maria Gansevoort, traced her family to Hudson Valley Dutch aristocrats, and his father, Allan Melvill [*sic*], a descendant of Scottish nobility, had been educated as a gentleman. Allan, a successful Boston merchant, became convinced that New York was "destined to become the Commercial Emporium of our Country" and relocated there in 1818. Setting up as an importer of French luxury goods, he quartered his family in an elegant house on Pearl Street near the Battery.

Maria Melvill craved social distinction—she was thrilled when the mayor's wife paid a welcome call—and soon after Herman was born in 1819 the family began a rapid ascent. Within two years they were ensconced in finer accommodations on Courtlandt Street, along with a housekeeper, cook, nurse, and waiter. In 1824 they climbed farther up-island to 33 Bleecker, whose proximity to "our Stylish Neighbours in Bond Street" delighted Maria. In 1828 the Melvills reached the pinnacle, a spacious house on Broadway, between Great Jones and Bond Street itself. Along the way, Maria gave her children the skills and graces appropriate to their would-be station. She taught them etiquette herself and sent Herman and his elder brother, Gansevoort, to the New-York Male High School, Mrs. Whieldon's dancing school, and the prestigious Columbia Grammar School, attended by pupils from the finest families.

Then catastrophe struck. Hard-pressed to compete with New York's auctioneers, and dangerously overextended, Allan entered secretly into a speculative scheme that went sour. Maria's wealthy brother reluctantly bailed him out, but Melvill was soon on the skids again, sliding toward an 1830 bankruptcy. The family fled to Albany, where they lived, humiliatingly, on the charity of relatives and where Allan, broken, died in 1832. Maria, hoping to give her children a fresh start, added an aristocratic *e* to their name, and for a time it seemed Gansevoort would make a go of his fur-and-cap business. But the Panic of 1837 wiped him out, plunging the Melvilles into indigence.

With the depression dragging on, Herman shipped out in 1839 as cabin boy on a square-rigger to Liverpool. In 1841 he signed up for a four-year cruise on a "blubber-hunter" but jumped ship in the Marquesas, drifted about the South Pacific for a year, then returned and wrote up his recent adventures in a narrative that he submitted to Harpers. The firm turned him down, believing the tale untrue, but after his brother Gansevoort sold the work to an English company, Wiley and Putnam brought it out in New York, published, under the direction of Evert Duyckinck, as *Typee: A Peep at Polynesian Life* (1846).

Melville's "peep" proved popular. His account of swimming nude with savage damsels was titillating yet not vulgar. His favorable comparison of Polynesian women's free and uncomplicated sexuality to the "stiffness, formality and affectation" of Victorian ladies back home struck a chord. So did his sympathy for the South Sea natives, whom arrogant American missionaries had "evangelised into beasts of burden." Irate religious papers assailed the sailor-author, but Margaret Fuller reviewed *Typee* favorably for the *Tribune*, and Harpers grabbed his next book—*Omoo: A Narrative of Adventures in the South Seas*—which came out in 1847 to good reviews and further fierce attacks.

Now a celebrated author, Melville moved to New York City with his new bride, Elizabeth Shaw. Pooling resources with his lawyer-brother, Allan, they bought a brownstone on Fourth Avenue, just behind Grace Church, a short walk to Barnum's Museum and Astor House and a few blocks away from Duyckinck. The critic championed Melville against the religious press (an Episcopalian, Duyckinck had little sympathy for Methodist evangelists) and became his patron and mentor, inducting him into the ranks of Young America and guiding him into literary society.

Melville thrived in New York. Salon hostesses sought him out much as they had Poe. He read voraciously, borrowing from the New York Society Library and burrowing happily in Duyckinck's massive book collection. He loved Duyckinck's Saturday night suppers, where the Young America set debated literature, democracy, philosophy, and art over brandy and cigars. Embracing their cultural program, he rejected the *Knickerbocker* gentry (as had Poe) and luxuriated in metropolitan sensations (as he was sure the Bard would have: "I would to God Shakspeare [*sic*] had lived later," he wrote Duyckinck in 1849, "& promenaded in Broadway").

He wasn't making much money, however, a situation that worsened after his next book, *Mardi*, departed from his established format and turned off reviewers and readers alike. Melville now reluctantly tailored his output to the marketplace, turning out two adventure stories, *Redburn* (1849) and *White-Jacket* (1850). "They are two *jobs*," he complained, "which I have done for money—being forced to it, as other men are to saw-ing wood."

Melville broke free again with *Moby-Dick*, not only from literary conventions but from New York City, the "insular city of the Manhattoes" whose citizens he character-ized as "tied to counters, nailed to benches, clinched to desks." In 1850 Melville moved to a 160-acre farm near Pittsfield, Massachusetts. He continued to make trips to Man-hattan to visit friends and publishers, but his disenchantment with the city and its liter-ary marketplace grew stronger. "Dollars damn me," he wrote Hawthorne in 1851. "What I feel most moved to write, that is banned,—it will not pay."

After *Moby-Dick* came out to cursory reviews and limited sales, Melville began to see readers as adversaries. Most enraging of all, his Young America allies at the *Demo-cratic Review* published a devastating critique, and his mentor Duyckinck, discomfited by the book (and perhaps by the fact that Harpers had published it), gave it a tepid review in the *Literary World*.

In *Pierre* (1852) Melville purged his anger with lacerating indictments of, among other things, New York City and its literati. The book's doomed hero, Pierre Glendin-ning, cast out of his pastoral upstate world, comes to Manhattan, intending to support his Isabel by writing. In the end, however, both sink into urban depths as black as any in the city mystery genre. From their first arrival by coach at night, jounced along on cob-blestones as hard as "the buried hearts of some dead citizens," Melville depicts a men-acing city, where money rules and the poor can expect no pity. He now disdains Broad-way's "proud-rustling promenaders" as "drooping trains of rival peacocks"—peacocks, moreover, who little realized how close pavement was to gutter in a city where (and here Melville spoke from experience) families "rise and burst like bubbles in a vat." As for denizens of the gutter itself—"diseased-looking men and women of all colors"—they seemed to have been "poured out upon earth through the vile vomitory of some unmen-tionable cellar." In the end Pierre falls into the city's very bowels, the Tombs, where he commits suicide.

Pierre was a monumental failure—condemned (as the *American Whig Review* put it) for morals "repulsive to a well constituted mind"—with the critical establishment's fury no doubt exacerbated by Melville's having singled them out in the book as mon-sters. Now a literary outlaw, Melville was in desperate financial straits when Charles Briggs, Poe's former partner at the *Broadway Journal* and now editor of *Putnam's Mag-azine*, courageously solicited his work. *Harper's New Monthly Magazine* followed suit, and the author soon gained greater success as a magazine writer than he ever had as a novelist.

Melville continued to blast away at the city as the apotheosis of America's money-mad society, a place of deceit and despair. In 1853 *Putnam's* brought out "Bartleby, the Scrivener: A Story of Wall-Street," about a clerk in the office of an elderly Episcopalian lawyer who does a "snug business among rich men's bonds, and mortgages, and title-deeds." Bartleby—"pallidly neat, pitiably respectable, incurably forlorn"—copies legal documents "by sun-light and by candle-light," working "silently, palely, mechanically" in his cubbyhole, until the day he politely but firmly responds to the lawyer's assign-ments with "I would prefer not to," eventually declining all duties. Fired, he refuses to leave, and indeed moves in. His baffled employer, by turns concerned and furious, aban-dons the office to a new landlord, who has Bartleby thrown into the Tombs. There the inscrutable scrivener—more unknowable even than Poe's Man of the Crowd—starves himself to death, declining life itself.

Melville also explored the sunshine-and-shadow mode. *Harper's* published his "Poor Man's Pudding and Rich Man's Crumbs," which excoriated the hypocritical wealthy, particularly "the criticisms made on the habits of the poor by the well-housed, well-warmed, and well-fed." "The Two Temples," which decried the snobbish atmosphere at a fictionalized Grace Church, proved too hot to print; even Briggs feared it "would sway against us the whole power of the pulpit."

The Confidence-Man: His Masquerade, Melville's ferocious judgment on marketplace civilization, was brought out in 1857 by a small New York house that folded shortly thereafter. The title borrowed the label affixed to swindler William Thompson, and many of its characters were modeled on New Yorkers. More to the point, *The Confidence-Man* was set on a symbolic Mississippi riverboat, which represented a commodity culture, peopled by highly mobile strangers, of which Manhattan was the epitome (in "Bartleby" Melville referred to "the Mississippi of Broadway"). One trickster after another peddles bogus products—stocks, patent medicines, plots in a real estate development called "the New Jerusalem"—in a sardonic satire on the prevailing chicanery and manipulation of urban encounters. More darkly still, Melville indicts a civilization where all human exchange, including language itself, has become deeply corrupted.

Moody, depressed, and increasingly dependent on drink, Melville took a trip abroad. On his return he tried lecturing to make money. He first proposed a sarcastic talk on the "daily progress of man towards a state of intellectual & moral perfection, as evidenced in the history of 5th Avenue & 5 Points," but in the end opted for safer subjects like the South Sea islands. Abandoning prose altogether, Melville tried poetry, only to have Charles Scribner decline to publish his poems on the grounds they wouldn't pay. As the 1850s wound down, the frustrated professional writer, largely dependent on Elizabeth's family, began casting about for a job in the New York Custom House. His long slow slide into obscurity had begun.

"MY CITY!"

Both Walt Whitman and Herman Melville spent many hours standing in the Battery, gazing at the bay, but apparently they never met. Nor did the two men, though exact contemporaries, see their city the same way. Melville, a patrician on the way down, regarded it with an embittered eye, while Whitman, an artisan on the way up, became its exuberant celebrant.

Walter Whitman was born in 1819, two months before Herman Melville, in West Hills, Long Island. The Whitmans, English Quakers, had long been substantial farmers and landholders. So were the Dutch Van Velsors, and as a boy Walter often accompanied his maternal grandfather delivering produce to Brooklyn, a forty-mile wagon ride over tortuous roads. Walter's father, apprenticed as a carpenter, raised houses as well as crops, and in 1823 he took his pregnant wife, Louisa, and their three children to seek his fortune in booming Brooklyn. He fared poorly. An old-fashioned artisan, he was shunted aside by contractors who hired unskilled and poorly paid laborers to throw up prefabricated dwellings. Over the next decade, the hard-pressed family shuttled repeatedly around the Brooklyn waterfront in search of affordable housing.

Young Walter was occasionally sent to Saint Ann's Sunday school, but mainly for its free lunch, the elder Whitman having been a friend of Tom Paine and a follower of Fanny Wright. From 1825 to 1830 Walter attended Brooklyn's only public school, on Adams and Concord, until family finances forced him, at age eleven, to seek employment. He worked for a time as an office boy at a Fulton Street law firm, then was apprenticed as a printer to the editor of the *Long Island Patriot*. In 1833 his family, defeated by the city, moved back to farm country. Walter stayed on, learning his trade, exploring Brooklyn, ferrying across to New York's theaters.

In 1835, now a journeyman printer, Whitman moved to Manhattan. After a year spent in setting type, he too retreated to Long Island in the difficult aftermath of the Great Fire. Between 1836 and 1841 he started up and sold off a penny paper, set type for a Jamaica weekly, participated in politics as a Loco Foco Democrat, and taught school. In 1841 Walter plunged back into the world of Manhattan journalism, where, despite the ongoing depression, the mammoth weeklies and penny dailies offered opportunities for would-be writers and editors. Whitman worked awhile as a printer for Park Benjamin's *New World*. He also wrote poems and stories and published some in the *New World*, its rival *Brother Jonathan*, and John O'Sullivan's *Democratic Review*. In the spring of 1842, just shy of his twenty-third birthday, Whitman was hired to edit a recently established twopennny paper, the *New York Aurora*, completing his transformation from artisan printer to Grub Street professional.

Assuming a flaneuresque persona, the *Aurora*'s editor promised his readers a regular reckoning with "this great, dirty, blustering, glorious, ill-lighted, aristocratic, squalid, rich, wicked, and magnificent metropolis." Duding himself up—his daguerreotypes depict a sophisticated dandy in frock coat and fashionable hat—he strolled around town, sporting a polished cane, absorbing scenes and characters. Whitman particularly explored the plebeian world of popular culture, visiting fire companies, gambling dens, whorehouses, and theaters, and he wrote up richly detailed sketches of newsboys, pawnbrokers, stage drivers, salesclerks, and butchers. He also captured the excitement of being on Broadway, reporting from atop a mobbed Yellow Bird omnibus or from a pavement crammed with enough people "to make one continued, ceaseless, devilish provoking, delicious, glorious jam!"

As a New York booster, Whitman was hard to top. Manhattan, he wrote, was "the great place of the Western Continent, the heart, the brain, the focus, the main spring, the pinnacle, the extremity, the no more beyond of the new world." Yet he was not blind to its negatives. Whitman worried particularly about the city's obliteration of its past, its "rabid, feverish, itching for change." At one point he recounted the efforts of a large crowd of women to block workmen from digging up a Baptist cemetery at Crystie and Delancey, noting that in the end the speculators—"a set of miserable wretches" who wanted the land for house lots—succeeded in "desecrating the *very grave* in order to add something to their ill won heaps of gold."

Dismissed from the *Aurora*, Whitman leapt nimbly from job to job. He worked as a penny-a-liner for the *Daily Plebeian*, run by Loco Foco Levi Slamm. He knocked out a popular temperance novel, *Franklin Evans the Inebriate*, admixing praise for the Washingtonian temperancites with sensational descriptions of miscegenation and murder ("damned rot," he'd later say). He covered the courts and prison for Beach's *Sun* (he would write a piece on jailhouse lawyers called "Tomb Shysters of Gotham"), contributed to Willis and Morris's *New-York Mirror*, edited the *Democrat* (a party paper), and wrote for the *Broadway Journal*, where he met Poe when picking up his pay and found him "very kindly and human" if "perhaps a little jaded." Clearly Whitman had mastered the art—better than had Poe—of staying afloat in a quicksilver literary marketplace.

Whitman's housing arrangements were equally peripatetic. He moved repeatedly between boardinghouses on Spring, John, Vesey, and Duane streets until 1845. Then, after four years in Manhattan's fast lane, dismayed to be still earning less than five dollars a week in an ever more viciously competitive industry, he returned to slower-paced Brooklyn, where his parents and five siblings had come to take another stab at house-building and where he would stay for the next seventeen years.

In March 1846 Whitman became editor of the *Brooklyn Daily Eagle*. In the morning he penned editorials in his Fulton Street office, which commanded a good view of the ferry landing, then set out in search of stories. He might take a stagecoach to Fort Greene or Green-Wood Cemetery, attend a Sunday school picnic in Jamaica, drop in on sermons by Brooklyn preachers, or head south to Coney Island for a swim in its "beautiful, pure, sparkling, sea-water!"

Whitman was now a Brooklyn booster—he began referring to New York as "the Gomorrah across the river"—but didn't shy from pointing out its downsides. He ran stories about crime and violence. He complained about filthy, ill-paved, and unlit streets. He criticized real estate developers for their "pull-down-and-build-over-again spirit" and sought to strengthen Brooklynites' historical sensibilities by campaigning to commemorate the Prison Ship Martyrs. He even chided the crowds heedlessly rushing on and off the Brooklyn ferry and sighed: "How it deadens one's sympathies, this living in a city!"

The *Eagle* was a Democratic paper, and Whitman was a vigorous party supporter. He also considered himself a foot soldier in Young America's ranks, though he didn't move in their social circles, and applauded projects O'Sullivan advanced in the *Democratic Review*, seconded Duyckinck's efforts to foster a national literature, and hailed Melville's *Typee*. But in 1848, with the Democrats split into radical and conservative wings, the radical Whitman found himself at odds with the *Eagle*'s conservative owners and, once again, out of a job.

In the 1850s Whitman drifted away from journalism. He joined his brothers in speculative building ventures—purchasing lots, then erecting and selling frame houses. He abandoned his foppish dandy's outfit for a workingman's slouch hat, checked shirt, and baggy pants. But he never stopped his urban peregrinations. Whitman explored the two cities from end to end. Tuning his ear to the "superb music" of the streets and worksites, he jotted down slang expressions (among them "cave in," "dry up," "bully for you," "that's rough," and "the New York Bowery boy—'Sa-a-a-y! What-a-t?'"). He loved the voices of "workmen and apprentices in the spar-yards, on piers, caulkers on the ship-scaffolds, workmen in iron, mechanics to or from their shops, drivers calling to their horses." He dropped in often at Brady's daguerreotype gallery (and called an essay series in the *New York Leader* "City Photographs"). Entranced by the Crystal Palace, he returned so often that officials assigned detectives to shadow the tall and roughly garbed man.

In 1854 a recession halted Brooklyn's building boom. Unemployed, Walter returned to professional writing. On completing a dozen poems, he took them to a friend's printshop (setting some himself), had himself daguerreotyped wearing an open-collared shirt, rumpled pants, and tilted round hat, adopted a new name ("Walt"),

In 1854, Whitman posed as a New York rough for the
Brooklyn daguerreotypist Gabriel Harrison, who
specialized in the images of workingmen that were
known as "occupationals." The daguerreotype was
then copied onto a lithographic plate and used as the
frontispiece for *Leaves of Grass* (1855). (© Collection of
The New-York Historical Society)

and by Independence Day of 1855 had eight hundred copies of *Leaves of Grass* ready
for sale.

An ode to New York, *Leaves* was perhaps the first great urban epic. English poets
had flinched from London. Poe and Melville found only alienation in the New York
milieu. But Walt Whitman was gloriously at home in the city. Indeed, Whitman *was* the
city. No aloof, flaneurial observer, he incorporated into himself the masses crossing
Brooklyn's ferry or thronging New York's streets. "When million-footed Manhattan
unpent descends to her pavements," he wrote, "I too arising, answering, descend to the
pavements, merge with the crowd, and gaze with them."

Yet Whitman maintained his individuality. Immersed in "Manhattan crowds, with
their turbulent musical chorus!" he experienced not dissolution or isolation but sensuous delight. "Give me interminable eyes—give me women—give me comrades and
lovers by the thousand!" he cried. "The life of the theatre, bar-room, huge hotel, for
me!" he exulted. "Give me the streets of Manhattan!"

The crowd's "million hued and ever changing panorama" inspired him to new
metaphors with which to capture its sounds—"the blab of the pave, tires of carts, sluff

of boot-soles, talk of the promenaders"—and its range of movement. Grace Church became a "ghostly light-house looming up over the porpoise-backs of the omnibuses, as they lift and toss in that unquiet sea."

Whitman's omnivorous curiosity embraced far more than crowds and streets. "This is the city and I am one of the citizens," he declared. "Whatever interests the rest interests me, politics, wars, markets, newspapers, schools, / The mayor and councils, banks, tariffs, steamships, factories, stocks, stores, real estate and personal estate." He hailed its industry: "On the neighboring shore, the fires from the foundry chimneys burning high and glaringly into the night, / Casting their flicker of black, contrasted with wild red and yellow light, and down into the clefts of streets." He cherished its multiplicity: "city of the world! For all races are here; all the lands of the earth make contributions here." He revered its superb shoreline—"hemm'd thick all around with sailships and steamships"—and its "high growth of iron, slender, strong, light, splendidly uprising toward clear skies." "City of hurried and sparkling waters! city of spires and masts!" he exclaimed. "City nested in bays! my city!"

Yet in all this the poet was protesting a bit too much. The dazzling perfection of his "Manahatta" seems strangely distant from Manhattan, the city of grime and crime that journalist Whitman knew. "Manahatta" was Manhattan without a dark side, Manhattan with its contradictions resolved, dissolved. Broadway had become a metaphor—the highway of equal souls—and New York City the symbol of egalitarian and democratic community.

Whitman's poetry finessed social and class tensions of which he was only too aware, which he himself embodied. It was, to be sure, saturated with a workingman's sensibility. He was "Walt Whitman, an American, one of the roughs," "one who does not associate with literary people—a man never called upon to make speeches at public dinners . . . rather down in the bay with pilots in their pilot-boat . . . or riding on a Broadway omnibus, side by side with the driver." And he could be severe with the "upper ten," referring in "Song of Myself" to the "many sweating" and the "few idly owning" (in his notebooks he denounced the "vast ganglions of bankers and merchant princes"). He disliked posh Grace Church even more than Melville did, and on one occasion, when an overzealous usher removed Whitman's hat, he grabbed it back, beat the man over the head with it, and swept out in a fury.

Yet Whitman didn't grapple with the transformations these classes were undergoing. He rhapsodized the city's growth and progress as if it came without cost, as if skilled artisans like his father were not plummeting in status and income. Nowhere were such changes more pronounced and more obvious than in the world of printing and publishing, where Harpers and the penny press were crowding out small artisanal publishers and one-man newspapers. Whitman himself had abandoned the compositor's trade and sustained his artisanal journalism and artisanal authorship by moving to Brooklyn, where older ways remained viable. But if Whitman the journalist expressed dismay over aspects of modern publishing, Whitman the poet elided such concerns with a rapid-fire cataloging of the undoubted marvels that world had wrought: the "story papers, various, full of strong-flavored romances, widely circulated . . . the one-cent and two-cent journals—the political ones, no matter what side—the weeklies in the country—the sporting and pictorial papers—the monthly magazines, with plentiful imported feed—the sentimental novels, numberless copies of them—the low-priced flaring tales, adventures, biographies—all are prophetic; all waft rapidly on . . . swell wide . . . What a progress popular reading and writing has made in fifty years! What a progress fifty years hence!"

There was little sense in *Leaves* that the artisanal and republican city was passing and ushering in the metropolis of slums and mansions to which the urban mysteries were calling relentless attention. Whitman didn't see the imperiled city Melville did, perhaps because he had been relatively successful at negotiating his way in the new order. Or perhaps he hoped to suspend those changes, to freeze the present moment with the power of his poetry, thus holding in suspended animation the baleful metamorphosis against which Melville and Poe ineffectually railed.

Whatever its evasions, his masterpiece was an astonishing—and ironic—development. Here was the powerful urban voice Young America had long been calling for, yet the survivors of that movement never noticed its coming. They had not expected their literary messiah to be a half-educated carpenter's son, a political journalist who consorted with b'hoys and coachmen. They'd been expecting the Great American Poem to issue from the parlor. Instead it bubbled up from the streets.

Whitman's language threw them too. Young America sought a literary democracy but shied away from the country's ruder idioms. Cornelius Mathews insisted it be American in the "purest, highest, broadest sense. Not such as is declaimed in taverns, ranted off in Congress." In *Pierre*, a disillusioned Melville had warned Young Americans they would never produce a native literature because "vulgarity and vigor—two inseparable adjuncts" were denied them. What, then, were they to make of a poet whose work drew sustenance from minstrel shows, blood-and-thunder romances, and the penny press, who boasted that "copulation is no more rank to me than death is" and proclaimed "the scent of these arm-pits is aroma finer than prayer"?

Much of polite New York shuddered at *Leaves of Grass*, reviling Whitman as a disgusting barbarian, but not all the reviews were bad. Whitman the journalist had many friends in the press—Charles A. Dana said nice things in the *Tribune*, Fanny Fern applauded him in Bonner's *Ledger*—and besides, Whitman had taken the precaution of publishing three glowing reviews himself. New Englanders, curiously, were the most supportive, perhaps because, with Charles Eliot Norton, they saw Whitman as fusing "yankee transcendentalism and New York rowdyism." Emerson sent a splendid salutation and came to pay respects (Whitman took him to a rowdy Mercer Street firehouse for a glass of beer). Bronson Alcott made a pilgrimage to Whitman's home on Classon Avenue, then came again with Thoreau in tow. Not all Yankee intellectuals were taken with *Leaves of Grass*, however: James Russell Lowell threw his copy in the fire and warned off a foreign visitor by declaiming, "Whitman is a rowdy, a New York tough, a loafer, a frequenter of low places, a friend of cab drivers!" But cab drivers didn't buy the book either. Despite the workingman-poet's strenuous efforts to reach a wider audience, he sold only several hundred copies.

Like Melville, Whitman had failed to get the hearing he wanted. Unlike Melville, Whitman didn't fade away. Instead he went underground, joining the bohemians, New York's first self-declared counterculture.

"Bohemians" was the French term for gypsies, based on the erroneous assumption that Bohemia was their original homeland. In the 1840s the name was affixed to the poor artists of Paris's Latin Quarter—first in derision, then in fascination. Henry Murger's romantic tales about the left bank's denizens, serialized between 1845 and

1846, then published as *Scenes de la vie de bohème* in 1851, presented them as principled people who repudiated middle-class morality, held money in contempt, and adopted alternative work habits and domestic arrangements. The French bourgeoisie, initially scornful, became intrigued by their lifestyle, and some of the affluent adopted or affected their ways.

The apostle who brought the boho gospel to New York City was a Nantucket-born journalist and theatrical critic named Henry Clapp Jr. After several years' residence in Paris, Clapp moved to Manhattan in the mid-fifties and gathered a like-minded group around him. Its members included Fitz-Hugh Ludlow, who would write *The Hashish Eater* about his drug experiences, and Ada Clare, the Charleston-born and independently wealthy writer who scandalized respectable New York by publishing torrid love poems and flaunting her illegitimate son. Bohemia also attracted writers, actors, artists, and students from the now sizable class of professional cultural workers, many of whom felt insufficiently remunerated or attended to.

Clapp's circle found a home in 1855 when Charles Pfaff, a rotund German Swiss, opened a basement beer hall on Broadway, just north of Bleecker Street. Modeled on the rathskellers and underground grottos becoming popular in Europe, Pfaff's offered the best coffee in town along with rich German beers, fine wines, and cheeses. At the cellar's far end, extending beneath the sidewalk upon which Broadway's endless crowds promenaded, was a vaulted "cave." Here Pfaff reserved a long table for Clapp's crew, who would filter in by late afternoon and again after an evening at the theater, to eat, drink, and inveigh against dull, respectable Manhattanites.

The bohemians adopted the departed Poe as their patron saint, attracted by his morbid writings, but they made Walt Whitman their reigning luminary. Even if he was not the most loquacious of the regulars ("my own greatest pleasure at Pfaff's," Whitman recalled, "was to look on—to see, talk little, absorb") he nevertheless spread the tavern's fame by writing of "The vault at Pfaff's where the drinkers and laughers / meet to eat and drink and carouse / While on the walk immediately overhead pass the myriad / feet of Broadway." By decades end, Pfaff's vied with Castle Garden, Tammany Hall, and Barnum's Museum as a New York City landmark.

The bohemians, in turn, promoted Walt's reputation. In 1858 Clapp founded the *New York Saturday Press*, an irreverent weekly with radical perspectives on art and politics that showcased new American writing, especially Whitman's. In distant Ohio, the youthful William Dean Howells was so impressed by the journal—it "really embodied the new literary life of the city"—that he made a pilgrimage to Pfaff's in 1860 to visit its resident poet.

None of this paid Whitman's bills. Having failed to support himself as a free-lance writer, he had returned to full-time journalism in 1857, becoming editor of the *Brooklyn Daily Times*. His poetry had dried up too (though shortly to reflower), perhaps because he had exhausted the material he'd been ingesting for years. *Leaves of Grass*, he would later say, "arose out of my life in Brooklyn and New York from 1838 to 1853, absorbing a million people, for fifteen years, with an intimacy, an eagerness, an abandon, probably never equalled."

41

Life Above Bleecker

In 1845, with the great mid-century boom just getting underway, only two men—John Jacob Astor and Peter G. Stuyvesant—possessed estates whose value topped the million-dollar mark. So many and so great were the fortunes accumulated over the next decade, however, that by the mid-fifties New York was home to dozens of so-called millionaires—a new word for a new social reality.

"Wealth," mused George Templeton Strong, "is rushing in upon us like a freshet," and it was clear who had navigated the current most successfully. In 1856 9,122 individuals were assessed for tax purposes as having a net worth of at least ten thousand dollars. Of this group, which collectively possessed the overwhelming bulk of the city's wealth, close to half engaged in mercantile pursuits, with merchants, auctioneers, brokers, and agents being far and away the richest New Yorkers in this, their Golden Age. Rentiers and others who profited from soaring land values did well too, making up about a fifth of the top taxpayers. Roughly another fifth owned goods-producing firms, a category that embraced ironmasters like Peter Cooper and contractors like Alexander Masterson, the Scots stoneyard owner who erected the Customs House. A tenth of the rich were professionals, though many owed their ranking more to capital than credentials, having parlayed substantial fortunes and family connections into lucrative careers in law, doing probate and trust work, or in medicine, attending to fellow patricians.

New York's economic elite had ballooned in size and complexity as well as wealth. The city teemed with bankers, brokers, importers, exporters, manufacturers, insurance tycoons, blueblood professionals, real estate moguls, department-store lords, railroad barons, and publishing magnates. So diverse a constellation was sometimes hard to recognize as a discrete social entity, riven as it was by divergent interests and styles.

Industrialists, for example, tended to be dependent upon but antagonistic to merchants. The latter demanded high prices for raw materials, paid low prices for the manufacturers' products, offered credit on harsh terms, and promoted free trade. Culturally, moreover, genteel wholesalers had little in common with manufacturers, many of whom came from artisanal backgrounds and worked on a daily basis with grubby proletarians.

Respectable old clans like the Beekmans, Livingstons, Stuyvesants, DePeysters, and Schermerhorns, for their part, claimed that recently acquired wealth didn't count for as much as riches that were properly patinaed, and that nouveaux like the Vanderbilts, Laws, and Stewarts did not belong in their category, much less their company. To help keep them out, hostesses like Mrs. James D. Roosevelt, Mrs. Hamilton Fish, Mrs. Henry Brevoort, and Mrs. William Schermerhorn—whose invitations still signified social acceptance—relied on Isaac Brown, the sexton of Grace Church who doubled as society's majordomo. Brown screened their guest lists, using his formidable grasp of Knickerbocker bloodlines to sort social aspirants into "old family, good stock" or "new men."

"Old stock" families wishing to wall themselves off from vulgar "new men" had other gatekeeping institutions besides Sexton Brown. The Society of St. Nicholas and the Union Club were joined by the New York Yacht Club (1844), whose cachet was assured in 1851 when John Cox Stevens took the yacht *America* to England and beat Britain's best while Queen Victoria and Prince Albert looked on. Another newcomer, the Century Association (1847), was in theory open to talent and accomplishment in every field—"Artists, Literary Men, Scientists, Physicians, Officers of the Army and Navy, members of the Bench and Bar, Engineers, Clergymen, Representatives of the Press, Merchants and men of leisure." In practice, by the mid-fifties, the bulk of the Century's members were merchants, bankers, railroad executives, insurance officials, and leading lawyers and physicians. Some Centurions fancied their club the American equivalent of the august French Academy, but while gentleman authors like Lewis Gaylord Clark of the *Knickerbocker* set were indeed on board, on the whole the Century's clubhouse tended more toward hearty masculinity than intellectual discourse.

Some of the rich even tried on the trappings of aristocracy, riffling through the pages of Gwilt Mapleson's *American Hand Book of Heraldry* in search of noble forebears. There was a certain appropriateness in making lineage a prerequisite for status, as kinfolk had supplied the capital for many of the elite's enterprises. Roughly seven of every ten New Yorkers whose wealth was assessed at over a hundred thousand dollars— men like Moses H. Grinnell, Robert B. Minturn, Samuel Shaw Howland, and Abiel Abbot Low—had inherited substantial fortunes and thus stood on the shoulders of their forebears.

On the other hand, most of those forebears weren't New Yorkers. Forty-three percent of the top taxpayers in 1856 had been born in other parts of the United States (especially New England and upstate New York). And fully 25 percent had come from foreign countries (especially England, Ireland, and Germany), making the overseas contingent nearly as big as the fewer than one-third born in the metropolis. Manhattan had an old guard, but it had been swamped by outsiders. Requiring a civic ancestry might make sense for provincial Boston's upper class, but in cosmopolitan New York it would exclude two-thirds of the rich, and the miffed might decide to form alternative, competing power centers.

Most old residents, therefore, accepted the newcomers in time. The Union Club blackballed A. T. Stewart—an Irishman, it was pointed out, and a mere shopkeeper-writ-large to boot—then invited him in, a few years later, when his wealth and prominence could no longer be denied. The Yacht Club snubbed Cornelius Vanderbilt, notorious for his swearing, womanizing, and general disdain for bourgeois domesticity. Vanderbilt's revenge was to build the first American-owned, oceangoing steam yacht, the *North Star*, furnished with a plush saloon in the style of Louis XV. After a decent interval, the club relented.

The old monied even accepted August Belmont. Favored by an unrivaled knowledge of high finance and access to Rothshild credit, the German-Jewish Belmont had amassed a major fortune since his arrival in 1837. One of the leading private bankers in the country, he had also become one of the most colorful figures on the New York social scene. He was multilingual, handsome, and suave, a connoisseur of food and wine and art and horses and dogs. He hosted fancy soirees and led a pack of young uptown bachelors in late-night adventures around town. He limped romantically, the result of a duel over the attentions of a certain Mrs. Coles. His position improved even further in 1849 when he married nineteen-year-old Caroline Perry, daughter of Commodore Matthew Perry. Jewishness was not yet a bar to genteel status—the Hendrickses were honored members of the Union and St. Nicholas—but polite society took comfort from the fact that the wedding occurred in an Episcopal church (not to mention that he gave the bride an entire city block as a wedding present).

Other such alliances—such as the 1853 nuptials of William Backhouse Astor and Caroline Webster Schermerhorn—further blurred the distinction between arrivistes and aristocrats. Sniping at social climbers would continue, to be sure, as when Episcopal Bishop William Kip tartly observed that "wealth came in and created social distinctions which took the place of family, and thus society became vulgarized." But New York's pragmatic patricians accommodated newcomers and thereby made themselves a more durable and coherent elite.

But what to call themselves? Some were quite happy to be known as "aristocrats," though this was still a fighting word in republican America. Others preferred more neutral, though still hierarchical, language: "best society," "higher classes," and (given the craze for things French) "*bon ton*." "Bourgeoisie" had some appeal, though it had disparaging connotations: one local informant told Francis Grund, Viennese-born author of *Aristocracy in America*, that the "aristocracy here is itself nothing but a wealthy overgrown *bourgeoisie*, composed of a few families who have been more successful in trade than the rest." The most New York City-specific solution was a numerological one. The phrase "upper ten thousand" (often awkwardly abbreviated as "uppertendom") was originated by social arbiter Nathaniel Parker Willis and ratified by Charles Astor Bristed, Cambridge-educated grandson of John Jacob Astor, who used *The Upper Ten Thousand* as the title for his 1852 sketch of elite life in New York City.

Membership in uppertendom required but two things: having a lot of money and spending it in approved ways. Willis's checklist of appropriate consumption patterns awarded upperten status to those "who keep carriages, live above Bleecker, are subscribers to the opera, go to Grace Church, have a town house and country house, give balls and parties." There were rival definitions, but all focused on measurable behavior: one had only to observe how—and especially where—an aspirant for elitehood lived.

"FLED BY DIGNIFIED DEGREES UP BROADWAY"

"Startled and disgusted with the near approach of plebeian trade," one observer noted in 1853, New York's wealthiest "fled by dignified degrees up Broadway." By the mid-fifties private residences had virtually disappeared from once fashionable blocks around lower Broadway, Greenwich Street, and Park Place. Amos Eno, the hotel builder, stuck it out on Greenwich (his daughter recalled) "until we were surrounded by immigrant boarding houses, and then went uptown to live." Yachtsman John Cox Stevens had incautiously erected an extravagant Greek Revival mansion on a corner of the Columbia College campus in 1846, only to see the the area became a black and Irish slum. In 1856 Cox tore down his "palace" and built warehouses on the site; that same year Columbia College itself headed north to 49th Street.

Neighborhoods thought immune from urban squalor as recently as the 1820s and 1830s became undesirable in the 1840s and 1850s. St. John's Park denizens fled in droves, especially after Vanderbilt's Hudson River Railroad ran tracks down its west side in 1851. A few blocks to the east, so many beer halls and tobacco shops had spilled off Broadway onto Bleecker and Bond streets that those addresses, as one paper put it in 1853, could no longer be considered "the *ultima thule* of aristocracy." Even in the Astor Place district, Charles Astor Bristed wrote sadly, "the dwellings are interspersed with shops; elegant mansions are beginning to be elbowed by dentists and boarding houses, and to assume an appearance of *having been* in the aristocratic precincts."

Willis had warned wealthy New Yorkers that they must settle "above Bleecker" to be socially acceptable. But how far above Bleecker? One answer was the brand-new neighborhood around Union Square Park, the three-and-a-half-acre elliptical oasis laid out in the 1830s on the northern frontier of the city at the instigation of developer Sam Ruggles. Building, halted by the panic, began anew with recovery. The park itself was fitted up with a fountain, gas lights, birdhouses named for prominent municipal buildings, and a bronze equestrian statue of Washington on the exact spot where he'd been received by citizens on Evacuation Day in 1783. In 1848 the *Herald* announced that 14th Street, the square's southern boundary, was "now nearly the center of the fashionable *faubourgs*."

Gramercy Park, another panic-stalled Ruggles project, took off as well. By the mid-fifties the discreet little square was snugly enveloped by expensive residences. Among the wealthy new arrivals were Peter Cooper, Cyrus Field, James Harper (who relocated his mayor's lamps to the front of Number 4), and George Templeton Strong, who had married Ellen Ruggles, the developer's daughter.

But it was Fifth Avenue, a block west of Union Square, that drew the very wealthiest New Yorkers. When Henry Brevoort had built his mansion on 9th Street in 1834, the "avenue" was a near-deserted country lane running up from Washington Square to the municipal parade-ground on 23rd Street. In 1847 the city replaced the parade-ground with Madison Square, a seven-acre park that by the early fifties was being touted in the press as a sure bet to become "the most fashionable part of our rapidly increasing city." A parade of commodious row houses and ornate mansions advanced quickly up Fifth, lodging the likes of August Belmont, Moses Grinnell, and William Lenox. By the end of the fifties, when Caroline Schermerhorn Astor convinced her husband, William Backhouse Astor Jr., to erect a mansion (with a capacious ballroom) between 33rd and

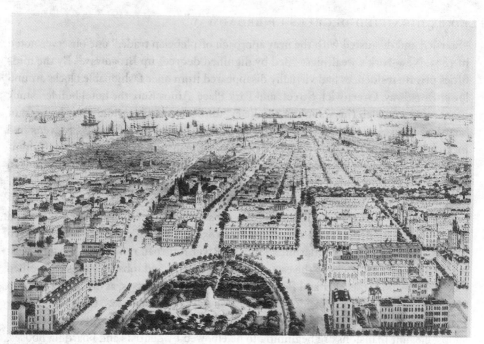

Union Square, 1849, looking south across 14th Street. Lithograph by Sarony & Major. On the square's east side, between 15th and 16th streets, is the row of fancy bow-fronted residences erected by Samuel B. Ruggles. (© Museum of the City of New York)

34th streets, next door to that of his brother, John Jacob Astor III, it qualified as the richest thoroughfare in America.

Upperten housing was as distinctive for its architecture as its location. Economic depression had put paid to the reigning Greek Revival style, and returning prosperity brought to the fore designers captivated by the Italian Renaissance. A. T. Stewart's Marble Palace had been the first New York structure inspired by fifteenth-century palazzos, a style with which Londoners and Parisians had been experimenting for a decade. Now Herman Thorne, who had lived stylishly in France, engaged Stewart's architects, Trench and Snook, to design him an Italianate residence. Completed in 1848, the freestanding mansion, sited on 16th Street just off fashionable Fifth, was an instant hit. Magazines and guidebooks raved about its courtyard, carriage drive, and Tuscan portico, and with startling speed other detached mansions boasting rusticated basements and winter gardens went up within a few blocks of Thorne's.

Equally startling, most of the new structures were made of a triassic sandstone, which, thanks to the presence of hematite iron ore, turned from pink to chocolate as it weathered. Brownstone, as it was called, was a familiar building material in New York City—St. Paul's (1766) had used it along with Manhattan schist—but until now it had mainly been a substitute for marble or limestone, reserved for basements, stoops, and details. Suddenly it became a luxury item, deemed more dignified than brick or wood and more in tune with the current romantic aesthetic favoring "natural" darks over "artificial" whites.

The soft brown stone also allowed for richly carved facades and lavish ornamentation, to the delight of the wealthy, who were sick of simplicity and republican restraint.

Federal houses now seemed dowdy, while brownstones (as one magazine observed) allowed their owners to "make a gratifying display of knowledge and taste." This wondrous material, moreover, was relatively inexpensive, thanks to new steam-cutting technology, and readily available from nearby Paterson, New Jersey, and Portland, Connecticut. Soon nearly every architect and builder in the city was putting up Italianate brownstone mansions for rich clients, and four- or five-story brownstone row houses for the merely affluent. Marching up Fifth and its adjacent avenues, these buildings created block after chocolate block of monumental streetscapes, and by the 1850s it was agreed that, as one magazine put it, "the prevailing tint of New York is fixed."

As uppertens clambered uptown, they drew their institutions up with them. The Union Club relocated to a Florentine mansion on the corner of Fifth Avenue and 21st Street, while the Century settled into a clubhouse on East 15th Street, just off Union Square. But churches remained the anchors of choice.

In 1839 the wardens of Trinity Church, fearing their building was about to collapse, had pulled it down and begun work on what would be the third Episcopal house of worship to occupy that site since 1699. Designed by Richard Upjohn, an up-and-coming young architect, and completed in 1846, the new structure of reddish-brown sandstone was a paragon of the "pointed" or spiritualized Gothic style newly popular among "high church" adherents. Its "very ornaments," one writer enthused, "remind one of the joys of a life beyond the grave."

But the flight of the propertied classes out of lower Manhattan meant that Trinity could no longer claim to be the *ne plus ultra* of city churches. That distinction now belonged to Grace Episcopal, housed on Broadway at 10th Street in a Gothic masterpiece designed by James Renwick. Situated only a few blocks below the refined precincts of Union Square, Grace served a congregation notable for long pedigrees and deep pockets. Pews sold for as much as sixteen hundred dollars, and it became the preferred setting for baptisms, weddings, and funerals among well-to-do New Yorkers. (The cachet of the nearby Church of the Ascension got a huge boost when August Belmont married Commodore Perry's daughter in its sanctuary.)

As in the past, the Presbyterian wing of respectable society came closest to matching Episcopalians in wealth and influence, and several Presbyterian congregations, almost as exclusive as Grace, also struck out for uptown. In 1845 a high-powered group that included James Brown and Henry Raymond called a meeting, subscribed the money, purchased a site, hired Richard Upjohn, and put up a church on University Place at 10th Street. Pew for pew, the congregation was probably the wealthiest in New York. The very next year, led by the redoubtably rich James Lenox, First Presbyterian abandoned Wall Street for an imposing Gothic edifice and tree-shaded grounds on Fifth Avenue between 11th and 12th streets. A decade later, in 1857, the venerable Brick Presbyterian auctioned off its valuable lot across from City Hall Park, shifted all unclaimed bodies from its vaults to Cypress Hills Cemetery in Brooklyn, and resettled on the brow of Murray Hill, at Fifth Avenue and 37th Street. Brick's old building was razed and replaced by the headquarters of the *New York Times*.

Other wealthy New Yorkers attended the Unitarian Church of All Souls on the corner of Fourth Avenue and 20th Street, close to Gramercy Park. Erected in 1855 at a cost of over a hundred thousand dollars, All Souls was vaguely Romanesque in appearance, with alternating bands of black and white stone and a 106-foot dome that towered over the neighborhood—the irreverent called it the Church of the Holy Zebra—and prominent pewholders were attracted by its dynamic minister, Henry Bellows.

SUBURBS AND SUMMER SPOTS

The rich were prepared to abandon downtown Manhattan, but not the city itself. Though surrounded by vast open spaces, newly accessible by speedier transport, most of the wealthy preferred to cluster together, living literally side by side, cooped up in narrow row houses on relatively tiny lots. The urbane inclinations bequeathed by the Dutch remained vibrant as ever.

A minority, however, did defect to the countryside, seduced by the siren song of Andrew Jackson Downing. A Newburgh-based landscape gardener for the Hudson Valley gentry, Downing wrote a series of books in the forties advocating villa living as an antidote to "the too great bustle and excitement of our commercial cities." Villas—asymmetrical, natural-hued country mansions—really belonged on properties of several hundred acres, Downing admitted. But he allowed that one might opt for a smaller villa (with as few as three servants) if grouped with others around a common park, in the manner of English "romantic suburbs." When Downing died in 1852, his close friend Alexander Jackson Davis took up the campaign for rural residency. Hitherto a Greek Revival man, Davis nimbly embraced the Gothic and received several commissions for baronial homes in quasi-rustic settings.

In Brooklyn, Edwin Clark Litchfield, a lawyer who made a fortune in midwestern railroad development, had Davis erect Grace Hall, a grand Italianate villa, on the crest of Prospect Heights from where he could survey his square mile of virtually vacant land. Costly villas and sloping lawns also began to dot the Bronx (Richard March Hoe's Brightside in Hunt's Point), Riverdale (actor Edwin Forrest's Font Hill), Queens's East River shore (a cluster at Ravenswood), and far-off hillsides in Staten Island.

In New Jersey one venturesome contingent of affluent New Yorkers experimented with Downingesque suburban living. In the mid-1850s, aided by Davis, Llewellyn Haskell, a wealthy drug merchant, built Llewellyn Park, a collection of villas set along curving roads ranged around a fifty-acre park called the Ramble. Situated in the Jersey foothills of the Orange Mountains, the elaborately landscaped suburb succeeded, but there would be no more planned communities in this era. Those willing to leave Manhattan preferred to settle in nearby, already established villages made newly accessible by rail, and depot towns such as Mott Haven, Morrisania, Tremont, and Fordham experienced substantial growth during the 1850s. Deeper Westchester was deemed inconvenient; it took ninety minutes to do the nineteen miles to Bronxville.

Outlying villages in Queens were even less enticing to uppertens, though real estate speculators hoping to boom Maspeth, Newtown, and Flushing tried hard to woo them. Even when bumpy stagecoach rides over plank roads gave way to rail connections direct from the Hunter's Point ferry landing, these county towns remained too far out. As one commuter complained in 1854: "The inability to get to a meeting or a lecture—to a place of amusement, or to do a little shopping are tolerable; but to be half a day in getting to and from business is a bore."

The only suburb that really enticed elite New Yorkers lay a scant ten minutes away, in Brooklyn Heights, and Pierrepont's genteel bastion on the cliffs overlooking the East River was no romantic confection, but rather a Manhattan clone. Its gridded, tree-lined streets were reassuringly covered with brick and brownstone row houses, in up-to-date styles with modern conveniences, and punctuated by churches designed by Renwick, Upjohn, and Minard Lafever.

Brooklyn was also a tax haven: its promoters publicized it as an offshore financial refuge from Manhattan. This in turn generated some proposals for annexation, the solution Philadelphia authorities embraced in 1854 to recapture runaway taxpayers. (One New York state senator proposed physically uniting the two islands by filling up the East River with gravel and covering the cost of the enterprise by selling the new-made land at high prices.) But it was Brooklyn, not New York, that resorted to annexation. Absorbing neighboring Williamsburgh and Bushwick in 1855, it became the nation's third most populous city. Brooklyn not only bolstered its status as an independent municipality but emerged as a credible competitor to Manhattan itself, complete with its own imposing City Hall; construction, halted by the panic, had recommenced in 1845 and been completed by 1849.

Though most of Brooklyn's newly rich merchants and financiers joined old established families on the Heights, more venturesome types pioneered other exclusive locations. Just to the south lay the Heights' fashionable offshoot of Cobble Hill, where in short order the assessed value of houses almost matched those of its progenitor. To the east lay "the Hill," where General Greene's Fort Putnam—renamed Fort Greene in the War of 1812—had been replaced by Washington Park, thanks largely to a campaign waged by *Eagle* editor Walter Whitman.

Those who found the Hill too close to the Navy Yard could opt for Bedford Corners. A sleepy Dutch village as late as 1850, it first became accessible via the Long Island Rail Road along Atlantic Avenue. Then, after 1854, the Brooklyn City Railroad Company began running forty-passenger horsecars along the recently opened Fulton Avenue (now Street) and Myrtle Avenue. Large rural landowners like the Lefferts and the Lotts began to sell off property to speculators, who subdivided it for individuals or small developers. Ads in the *New York Times* soon proclaimed the availability of "villa plots" and residences complete with stables, gardens, and "all modern improvements," just thirty minutes from downtown Brooklyn.

Farther than this uppertens seldom went. Developers in the 1850s tried promoting Fort Hamilton, Bushwick, and East New York as suburban retreats—promising trees, parks, nuisance clauses, minimum plot sizes, an escape from city taxes and dirt, and a good investment to boot. But these were too far away, scattered amid small farming communities like Flatbush, Flatlands, New Lots, New Utrecht, and Gravesend. Cannier developers, like Park Slope's Edwin Litchfield, patiently accumulated property and bided their time.

Brooklyn did have one Downing-type suburb, which griddish New Yorkers liked. The spectacular if belated success of Green-Wood Cemetery proved that while they didn't want to spend their lives in such locations, they had no objection to spending eternity there. With its landscaped terrain, pastoral winding paths, weeping statues, and plots enclosed by iron railings, Green-Wood was a romantic suburb for the deceased. Indeed early suggestions that it be called the Necropolis had been rejected precisely because the word would have conveyed "an idea of *city* form and show." The quick as well as the dead flocked to Green-Wood. On pleasant days hundreds of carriages headed for the Hills of Gowanus, taking the Hamilton Avenue ferry that Henry E. Pierrepont had started up in 1846, then crossed Gowanus Creek over the Hamilton Avenue toll bridge. By the early 1850s Green-Wood had become, in effect, the preeminent park for both Brooklyn and Manhattan.

In the summertime, uppertens pursuing relief from city heat would press on farther still. Their carriages headed south—often on Sundays, to the dismay of Gravesend's religious element—toward the exclusive hotels and beaches of Coney Island. There they spent the Lord's day watching the waves from porch chairs, eating clam chowder, or hunting snipe and duck near the marshes. But Coney Island couldn't solve the more difficult dilemma confronting society's upper echelons: how to maintain class cohesion when once compact precincts had been scattered into far-flung enclaves.

Traditional customs like New Year's Day visits were becoming increasingly unwieldy. "The extent of the visiting circle in New York has become too great for the operations of one day," Philip Hone lamented as early as 1840. The grand promenade hour along Broadway served as a partial substitute. In the late afternoon, reporter George Foster observed in 1849, the street became "a perfect Mississippi, with a double current up and down" of bourgeois ladies and gentlemen acknowledging—or not acknowledging—one another in prescribed ways. This ritual did help define and police social boundaries. But it remained awkwardly open to disruption—performed as it was on a very public stage—by any rowdies who declined to accept their assigned roles as awed spectators.

Uppertens began to rely more heavily on the summer season and the summer resort, and as a result, Saratoga Springs blossomed in the boom. Far from the hoi polloi—and Coney Island, even the Catskills, were no longer far away enough—the city's elite constructed a town-away-from-town, a place to mix and mingle among themselves. At first the notion of spending an entire summer lolling in leisure grated on still-sensitive republican nerves, so Saratoga's properties as a restorative health spa were emphasized (the "Bath of America," Willis called it). In the 1850s such scruples dropped away, and visitors to the elegant United States Hotel devoted themselves to matchmaking, horse racing, gambling, and gamboling in what was universally agreed to be the nation's most brilliantly fashionable resort. So popular did it become that by decade's end, New York's crème de la crème—the Fish, Rhinelander, Lenox, Schermerhorn, Taylor, and Belmont families—began moving on to Newport, Rhode Island, settling into a growing number of "country houses" there.

Uppertens routinely traveled to Europe, too. The entire family might go, or just the wives and children, or bourgeois scions would decamp by themselves on extensive grand tours. Foreign travel provided the extra bonus of allowing the New York rich to keep abreast of the forms of display currently fashionable among Europe's titled aristocracy and haute bourgeoisie—forms they set about duplicating the minute they got home.

"I NEVER SAW SUCH LUXURY AND EXTRAVAGANCE"

The elite's retreat from downtown Manhattan was also a farewell to older standards of reticence and restraint. By 1850 prosperous New Yorkers, particularly younger ones, were wallowing in luxury with a nonchalance unknown among prior generations. Much of this took place in private, behind Italianate walls, but some uppertens didn't hesitate to flaunt their wealth. They adopted theatrical forms of conspicuous display, which provided yet another reason to live in town, not the suburbs.

"The first thing, as a general rule, that a young Gothamite does is to get a horse; the second, to get a wife," wrote Charles Astor Bristed, only half jokingly, about elite New York males' passion for fine horses. Young men loved harnessing their blood chestnut colts and beautiful bays, then heading over to Third Avenue, Manhattan's de facto exercise and racing track. From where the town's cobblestones ended, Third's newly macadamized surface, flanked by soft earthen trails for trotters, ran north for nearly five uninterrupted miles to Harlem Bridge. Every day from three o'clock until dark, fast horses and fast men climbed steadily up the gradual hills, then quick-timed to the bottom, where convivial taverns awaited, as well as blacksmiths and coachmakers who could repair a broken wheel or replace a lost shoe. Trotting—taken up by the likes of Cornelius Vanderbilt and magazinist Robert Bonner—remained a passion for Bowery B'hoys as well, and impromptu, interclass drag races were not unheard of.

Private equipages, modest in the early 1830s, grew increasingly ostentatious. (Carriage showrooms and harness shops took over the tiny hamlet of Great Kill, on a creek at what is now 42nd Street, and the area above it renamed the Longacre, after London's equestrian hub.) Four-in-hand carriages were everywhere, their horses driven "chequered"—steeds of matching color arrayed diagonally. In winter, fancy cutters and family sleighs were de rigueur, and wealthy families, wrapped in bearskin robes, rode up to Wintergreen's in Yorkville for sherry flips. "One would hardly believe he was in a republican country," said one guidebook author, "to see the escutcheoned panels of the carriages, the liveried coachmen, and the supercilious air of the occupants of the vehicles, as they go pompously and flaringly by."

Bourgeois brownstones were showy too, but their exteriors were sobriety itself compared to their extravagant interiors. Affluent New Yorkers might easily spend ten thousand dollars on furniture for a single room, reported Lydia Maria Child. "Foreign artistic upholsterers assert that there will soon be more houses in New York furnished according to the fortune and taste of noblemen, than there are either in Paris or London." Henry Parish's mansion off Union Square had half a dozen period reception rooms decorated with Italian statuary, Gobelin tapestries, and Sèvres porcelain. The mistress of a hundred-thousand-dollar mansion on Fifth Avenue slept in a bed inlaid with pearls and draped with satin and lace.

Portraits of family members, living or dead, often lined these walls, signifying (or confecting) tradition, but more and more elites began collecting old masters to adorn their parlors or private galleries. To serve them, especially after the American Art-Union was scuttled, European dealers began setting up branch offices—the House of Goupil dispatched Michael Knoedler from Paris to New York in 1846—which stimulated the growth of American dealerships as well.

Wealthy households were rich in mechanical marvels, too. An ad for a dwelling off Union Square in 1846 ticked off the new essentials: "Croton water, range, boiler, bath, water closets, . . . furnace, dumb waiter from basement to attic, gas, and every other improvement introduced into modern built houses of the first class." Water taps, now on every floor, splashed into marble washbasins. Bathing and toilet facilities (virtually unknown outside the major hotels before 1842) supplanted chamber pots and privies. Central heating arrived: cellar furnaces fired with Pennsylvania coal forced hot air through pipes and tin ducts up to cast iron or brass registers (though the upstairs bedrooms still relied on fireplace coal grates).

Maintaining these mechanical marvels required lots of labor power. In the case of central heating, a servant had to rake out the furnace, throw away the ashes, stoke it with coal twice a day, and bank the cinders at night. Fuel and ash had to be carried to and from the new stoves, and the icebox water pan needed emptying. Furniture also demanded upkeep. The very wealthiest families might have six or eight servants, including a cook, butler, waiter, parlor maid, upstairs maid, laundress, houseman, and coachman, though most elites had less than half this number.

The upper class adorned their persons with as much care as they did their houses, though men and women now took different stances on the question of fashion. Most businessmen did not devote undue time or attention to clothing, and indeed considered those who paid attention to fashion as ne'er-do-wells or fools. They simply wrapped themselves in loosely cut waistcoats and frock coats of increasingly somber hue: nineteen out of twenty were of black broadcloth, with claret or mulberry acceptable for weddings. Dark stovepipe hats dignified most heads, while at the neck bourgeois gentlemen sported a "modern high & pointed shirt collar, that fearful sight to an approaching enemy" (or so said Walt Whitman, he of the open-necked shirt). The business suit had arrived—a class costume tailor-made for sedentary activities, in contrast to eighteenth-century gentrywear, which had befitted more active pursuits like hunting, riding, dueling, and dancing. Only when businessmen donned militia uniforms were they allowed to dazzle and display their physical attractions.

One subset of male New Yorkers did keep the older love of plumage alive. "Dandies"—usually sons of the wealthy—promenaded on Broadway and attended fashionable events dressed in up-to-the-minute Euromodes, with an attention to detail (monocles, canes, gold chains) that contemporaries considered effeminate. Dandies were also pioneers, however, as they began sporting mustaches in the 1840s, a full decade before luxuriant beards became generally acceptable.

Most of the pleasures and burdens of dressing up fell to the ladies. In public, genteel women still went about virtually veiled, muffled head to limb in bonnets, shawls, skirts, and gloves, all of muted colors. In two venues only did women discard such self-effacement and display their silks and satins: when promenading on Broadway; and at Easter-time, when some fine ladies began showing off their new dresses in an unofficial after-church stroll along uppertendom's Fifth Avenue.

At home or church, however, as at dinner parties, balls, the opera, and summer spas, wealthy New York women demonstrated clear mastery of the latest French fashions. Fabrics grew steadily more voluptuous (gauze, tulle, organdy, brocade, velvet) and their colors more intense (crimson, maroon, purple). Hemlines on stylish gowns and dresses fell steadily as skirts ballooned outward on layer after layer of petticoats—as many as fourteen. Changing tastes (and the arrival of the sewing machine) required and supplied more and more ruffles, fringes, flounces, lace, and artificial flowers, and sent dressmakers into a frenzy of braiding, pleating, puffing, and tucking. By the late fifties skirts ran to six feet in diameter (department stores widened their aisles accordingly), and a cotton dress required thirty to forty yards of material on the average; counting petticoats and other undergarments, the total could reach a hundred yards or more, eight times what it would have been half a century earlier.

Society women escaped utter immobilization only through the introduction of the cage crinoline, an undergarment into which were sewn narrow steel hoops capable of supporting the massed weight of the garments above. A godsend in helping one walk, the crinoline could all too easily get tangled up in carriage wheels, and wind gusts could blow a woman off her feet. Even more problematic were the tightly laced corsets that produced the stylish eighteen-inch waist, along with headaches, fainting spells, and assorted internal disorders.

The vast consumption of assorted fabrics was a great boon to the city's dry-goods trade but a breathtaking expense to the consumer. James Fenimore Cooper, writing to his wife in the winter of 1850, described a party where one woman wore "a dress that cost, including jewels, thirty thousand dollars"—a fantastic sum at a time when skilled mechanics and craftsmen took home between $1.25 and $2.00 a day in wages.

Jewelery embellished many a costume—Mrs. Belmont attended the opera wearing a gold crown decorated with "clusters and flowers of emeralds and rubies, spangled with dew-drops of diamonds"—and among those hastening to supply these new needs were two young New Englanders, Charles L. Tiffany and John P. Young. Back in 1837 they had opened a stationery and dry-goods shop on Broadway, then slowly switched to more spectacular offerings as the boom took off. At first Tiffany and Young offered only imported goods: English silver and Continental crystal, gold jewelry, and Swiss watches. In 1848, a year of European revolutions, the firm purchased the jewels of Maria Amelia, wife of the recently deposed French king, and put them on display, winning for Tiffany the title "King of Diamonds." That same year the firm's new goldsmithing shop began producing its own jewelry, and three years farther on the company acquired New York City's leading silver manufacturer (and adopted its "Tiffany blue" packaging). By 1854 it had moved to an Italianate white marble palazzo at 550 Broadway, just north of Prince, in the heart of the elite shopping district.

Once properly bejewelled, only a touch of perfume was needed—and by 1858 there were six perfume manufacturers in the city, advertising their wares via scent-soaked cards—and mademoiselle was ready for a ball at Delmonico's. There she could flaunt her shoulders, display alluring décolletage and voluptuous (if possibly padded) curves, and set her crinoline swinging, revealing a flash of ankle. This was all the more likely as the tempo of dances quickened in the 1840s, with tearing polkas now complementing the waltzes and quadrilles. As George Templeton Strong informed his diary in December 1845 after a gathering at Mrs. Mary Jones's: "Polka for the first time brought under my inspection. It's a kind of insane Tartar jig performed to a disagreeable music of an uncivilized character."

The marriages that flowed from these mating rituals were not prearranged; indeed romantic love had never been more highly touted. However, by excluding all but young men of appropriate status and wealth, upper-class families practically guaranteed their daughters' choices would be appropriate. In 1856 37 percent of New York's wealthiest were directly interrelated.

At-home festivities had increased in number and opulence since Mr. and Mrs. Henry Brevoort had set the pace with their famous 1840 costume ball. The grandest *affaire de luxe* of the new era was the costume ball that took place in 1854 in the Lafayette Place mansion of Mrs. William Colford Schermerhorn. Sparing no expense, that redoubtable lady redecorated her house to resemble the Versailles Palace in the age of Louis XV, then invited six hundred of the city's richest citizens to dress up like French courtiers for an evening of dining and dancing.

France set the trends in cuisine as well, with Delmonico's as transmission belt. The Beaver Street establishment remained the preferred setting for balls, assemblies, and family dinners until well into the 1850s. In 1856 the restaurant added an uptown venue on Broadway and Chambers Street. At lunch the new eatery soon drew local influentials like A. T. Stewart (whose store was across the street) and Henry Raymond (whose *Times* would settle across the park). In the evening, families strolled down from upper Broadway for social dining. At either location, those eager to explore the creations of Robert

Beauvilliers and Carême could be sure Delmonico's was offering the latest in Parisian dining.

Upper-class entertainments were rehoused in new settings. Wealthy audiences packed into the grand new Lyceum Theater, on Broome and Broadway, where James William Wallack had established a resident company in 1852 and begun staging English productions with his son, Lester Wallack, as leading man. Laura Keene, a local actress who had worked for Wallack, launched her own company in 1856 in a new playhouse on Broadway just below Bleecker. Her polished productions in the 1858–59 season included the drama *Our American Cousin*, which would be upstaged by tragedy half a decade later when taken on the road to Washington, D.C.

As a bulwark of refinement, however, nothing held out more promise than the establishment of a new opera house in Astor Place. Although they had long shied away from it as an expression of aristocratic decadence, upper-class New Yorkers finally acquired a taste for opera. This was thanks partly to the lyricism of Verdi, Bellini, Donizetti, and other contemporary composers, and partly to the impact of visiting European singers who began flocking to New York via the speedy new steamships and dazzling audiences at the Park Theater and Niblo's Gardens. Equally weighty was upperten's expectation that an opera house would provide, in Nathaniel Parker Willis's words, "a substitute for a general drawing room—a refined attraction which the ill-mannered would not be likely to frequent, and around which the higher classes might gather, for the easier interchange of courtesies, and for that closer view which aides the candidacy of acquaintance."

Designed by Isaiah Rogers (architect of the Astor House, among other buildings), the new Astor Opera House pioneered a frankly elitist organization of theatrical space. The pit was "aristocratized" (Willis's term) by replacing the usual benches with fixed, upholstered, and numbered chairs sold only by subscription. Above the pit rose two tiers of open boxes, also reserved exclusively for subscribers, where patrons could see and be seen by the entire assembly. A gallery at the very top of the house provided general-admission benches for five hundred people; accessible by a single narrow staircase, this plebeian "cockloft" was almost completely quarantined from the genteel zones below. On opening night in November 1847, amid blazing jewels and rustling silk, New York's haut monde signaled their approval by turning out en masse for a performance of *Ernani*. (Brooklynites quickly set to creating equivalent venues, among them the Athenaeum [1853], the Philharmonic Society [1857], and the Academy of Music [1859–61].)

New York's upper classes now lacked but one thing: a house organ to provide respectful coverage of their doings. Society reportage remained monopolized by James Gordon Bennett's sardonic reflections in the *Herald* until 1846, when Nathaniel Parker Willis and his old *Mirror* partner, George Pope Morris, launched the *Home Journal* (later *Town and Country*). The *Home Journal* announced its intention of keeping New York City's "more refined individuals" apprised of all that was "new, charming, or instructive in the brilliant circle of city life." *Home Journal* featured talk of the town columns like "Prittle Prattle," "The Season and Society," and "Uptown Correspondence," the latter done with the aid of wealthy society ladies (whose lives a grateful Willis then chronicled in serial features). The magazine also provided dramatic and musical reviews, literary notices, and, for gentlemen, digests of the week's news condensed "in small compass." To report the doings of England's haut monde, it excerpted London society journals, and French affairs were covered in "Parisian Chit-Chat," much of it translated (possibly by Edgar Allan Poe) from New York City's own French-language paper, the *Courrier des Etats-Unis*.

On the whole, uppertendom was quite comfortable with success and indulged in fine wines, fast horses, and voguish clothing with no discernible traces of guilt. Yet in certain quarters, republican suspicions of aristocratic luxury retained considerable sway. Cold-water Yankees had long differed with pleasure-loving Knickerbockers about the proper use of wealth, and still did. Nor had old-stock spokesmen quite resigned themselves to the new monied's ascendancy, and lampooning the pretensions of Fifth Avenue vulgarians became itself a mark of respectability. James K. Paulding, Irving's collaborator on *Salmagundi*, dryly observed that when invited to dinner "I ate out of a set of China, my lady assured me cost seven hundred dollars, and drank out of glasses that cost a guinea a piece. In short, there was nothing on the table of which I did not learn the value."

Industrialists too tended to decry the growth of luxury, in part because they saw themselves as useful producers, in contrast to superfluous financiers. Peter Cooper, one of New York's richest men, continued to live at Fourth Avenue and 28th Street even after the New York and Harlem Rail Road began parking cattle cars in front of his house. Even after he moved to Gramercy Park in 1850, Cooper disdained ostentation, dressed simply, and limited the family to two servants; when his wife bought an elaborate carriage, he exchanged it for a more frugal model.

Principled objections to high living required principled rejoinders, and some prestigious churchmen endeavored to supply them. The Rev. Henry W. Bellows, minister of All Souls, editor of the *Christian Enquirer*, and a founder of the Century Association, addressed such issues in *The Moral Significance of the Crystal Palace* (1853) and other widely touted tracts. Bellows had no brief for the mere pursuit of money, and he blasted aristocratic foppery. He insisted, on the other hand, that the enterprise of self-interested Christian businessmen had brought wealth and progress to the republic, that the desire for material goods would promote hard work among the poor, and that possessing goods was as morally beneficial as pursuing them. Poverty, to his way of thinking, had nothing to recommend it.

Even Nathaniel Parker Willis agreed that a proper aristocracy had to rest on more than wealth and fashion. He reminded readers that refinement was the true hallmark of respectability, and he called for creation of "a class whose opinion is entitled to undeniable weight—a class whose judgement is made up from elevated standards." Without the authority conferred by refinement, no local elite would be ever be able to provide a "breakwater" to the dangers posed by the "ignorant and vicious classes."

Nevertheless, many of the city's haute bourgeoisie found it uncomfortably hard to reconcile upperten lifestyles with their still-cherished beliefs in political equality (for white men), equality of opportunity, the fairness of market relationships, the possibility of social mobility, and the purported insignificance of class divisions in republican America.

Uppertendom seemed even more problematic to the petite bourgeoisie, newly enlarged and newly self-conscious, which the boom had summoned into being. New York's middling strata would split on the luxury issue, some opting for fierce republican disapproval, others for fawning emulation. Most, however, sought to carve out a position that, while drawing the line at aristocratic frippery, nevertheless sought to find some common ground with the city's most powerful people, ground they discerned in the theory and practice of "respectability."

THE RESPECTABLE CLASSES

A state census completed in 1855 fixed the population of New York City at just under 630,000 people, about 215,000 of whom were gainfully employed. Perhaps 30 percent of these were members of a many-layered middle class, though the 30 percent figure varies markedly depending on which social clusters get classified as middle class, something on which observers did not (and still don't) agree.

Nearly everyone placed professionals in the middle class—after setting aside those few whose wealth and connections placed them in uppertendom. This group included traditional practitioners like doctors, lawyers, clergy, and teachers, and newcomers like the members of the American Society of Civil Engineers (1852) and the American Institute of Architects (1857). Lesser merchants, along with small independent businessmen, were usually considered another middle-class contingent: clothiers, grocers, barbers, druggists, shopkeepers, restaurateurs, undertakers, and dealers in commodities as varied as books, cattle, oysters, coal, or stone.

Clerical workers, though employees, were generally but not always accorded (lower) middle status. Some of these—bank tellers, accountants, bookkeepers, cashiers, and copyists like Bartleby—handled the surging paperwork in the city's (by 1856) seventy-five banks, ninety insurance companies, and brokerage houses (130 on Wall and William streets alone). Another set acted as management assistants, staffing the headquarters of railroad, shipping, publishing, mining, or manufacturing companies. Thus the Novelty Iron Works had eighteen departments, and each was headed by a foreman who reported to a "front office" presided over by a superintendent and eleven clerks. A third complement served in the great retail establishments and thus included the two hundred clerks and salespeople who worked the floors at Brooks' Brothers Broadway emporium. Taken together, the nearly fourteen thousand clerical workers constituted New York City's third largest workforce category after servants and laborers.

It proved hardest of all to situate those in the upper ranks of the artisanal economy: "mechanics of the better class" or small contractors and manufacturers. In 1855, when one Yorkville resident said his community was "mostly made up from the middle class," he referred not only to neighboring merchants, brokers, bookkeepers, and clerks but also to master masons, carpenters, printers, and bookbinders. Other contemporaries, however, set skilled workers apart from professionals, managers, and clerical workers, pointing to marked contrasts in their work and lives.

Middle-class workspaces differed sharply from artisanal workshops. In the financial district, men spent their days in quiet, clean, even elegant "offices" (a word that began to replace "countinghouse" in the 1850s, the same decade in which dealers in office supplies first appeared in city directories). One of New York's earliest offices erected as such was the Trinity Building (1853). A five-story, double-width structure, enormous for the time, it replaced an eighteenth-century sugar house just north of Trinity Church. The commercial Trinity, like the ecclesiastical one, was an Upjohn-designed edifice whose very architecture proclaimed its occupants genteel.

Inside such buildings—and retail equivalents like Stewart's Marble Palace—clerks and professionals seldom encountered manual workers. The same was true outside, on the streets and in the lunch-hour restaurants of the financial or shopping districts. As they made their way home on omnibuses and commuter trains, middling people again traveled in different circles from the bulk of walk-to-work laborers. Even in the industrial world, firms began to carve out separate workspaces for nonmanual employees, accessible by separate entrances.

Middle-class employees dressed differently from manual laborers. Salesmen in fancy retail stores were expected to be indistinguishable from patrons, both in clothing and bearing. Cashiers and bookkeepers not only had to look the part but could afford to, as salaried workers were usually better compensated than artisans and laborers. True, some old-fashioned firms still paid clerks less, considering them merchants-in-training. But most office workers were Bartlebys now—permanent wage-workers—solaced with annual salaries that could run as high as two thousand dollars. Professionals, lesser merchants, and small proprietors could earn considerably more.

These higher incomes allowed many to attain a modest version of haut bourgeois status. In the colonial era, the middling sorts had stood far closer to poor plebeians than to aristocratic elites. The new middle class repositioned itself much closer to the upper echelons, starting with how and where its members lived.

Middle-class families couldn't afford mansions or grand row houses, but thousands managed to purchase or rent a red brick dwelling, or even a brownstone with showy facade, albeit a narrower model. Where the *bon ton* enjoyed twenty-five-foot fronts, upper-middle-class residents settled for twenty- or eighteen-foot widths, while lower-middle-class buyers squeezed into structures but fourteen to twelve and a half feet wide. Still, most could afford amenities—indoor plumbing, Croton water, cast-iron stoves, gas lights, and plaster walls—that would have been considered the height of opulence only a decade or two earlier (and were still out of reach of the majority of their fellow citizens).

Middling families could live "above Bleecker" too—not in the upperten enclaves running up Manhattan's spine but along the flanking avenues and streets that lay between the wealthy center and the working-class riverfronts. The most affordable opportunities lay far uptown, in areas still under construction. These once distant venues had become newly accessible with the rapid spread of street railways, hastened by the invention in 1852 of a grooved rail that lay flush with the pavement. By decade's end horsecars were rolling smoothly up and down Third, Sixth, Eighth, and Ninth avenues and crosstown at 8th, 14th, and 23rd streets. They carried a hundred thousand passengers a day, and allowed middle-class commuters to get downtown in less than forty-five minutes, though traveling conditions were admittedly less than optimal. "The seats being more than filled," one paper observed, "the passengers are placed in rows down the middle, where they hang on by the straps, like smoked hams in a corner grocery." Nevertheless rapid transit promoted rapid infill of Manhattan's open spaces. By 1860 the island was solidly blanketed with residences as far north as 42nd Street. In another four years, over half the city's population would live above 14th Street—the northern frontier as recently as the mid-1840s.

Middling sorts were a major presence in the new territories. On the west side they settled from west Greenwich Village and Clement Moore's Chelsea up to the moderately priced brownstone row houses William B. Astor erected in the mid-40s between Broadway and Ninth Avenue. On the east side, old-fashioned but respectable three- or four-story brickfronts were to be had in the 20s, east of Third Avenue, and "handsome dwellings" between 30th and 45th streets could be rented for three to four hundred dollars per annum—beyond the means of most clerks but within the budget of a frugal professional family of four.

Even uptown, however, many middle-class New Yorkers could not afford a home of their own and had to settle for sharing space with others. "Part of a house to let"—read one 1854 ad, describing an opportunity in the west 30s near Ninth Avenue—"the upper part of a first-class house with modern improvements to a small genteel family." Such quarters might be rented for $160 to $300 in the 1850s, too high for a mechanic making a thousand a year, but accessible to a middle-class person making twice that.

Others turned to boardinghouses. Doctors, lawyers, professors, and lower merchants—especially when single or married without children—might place an ad stating their preferences in the *Herald, Tribune,* or *Times,* or peruse there the communiqués from proprietors seeking appropriate renters ("family must be small and of the highest respectability"). Boardinghouses ran the gamut from former mansions of Knickerbocker patricians, replete with furnished parlors, pianofortes, and "all modern improvements," to dingy and warren-like barracks offering lodging, meals, threadbare carpets, and cockroaches to dry-goods clerks.

All of them had their drawbacks, however, said Thomas Butler Gunn in his humorous but instructive *Physiology of New York Boarding Houses* (1857). These ranged from landladies trying to palm off unmarried daughters, to thunderous snorers in adjoining apartments, to pious gatekeepers who locked up at eleven and refused to give out latchkeys. Even in the best of circumstances, multifamily dwellings were ultimately inconsistent with the middle-class desire for a "genuine home." As one little girl replied when asked where her parents lived: "They don't *live*; they BOARD."

For those priced out of domesticity in Manhattan, a proper independence could be purchased at the cost of trekking greater distances. Some made their way north to the growing railway communities of Mott Haven, Morrisania, and Fordham. But far greater numbers of clerks, shopowners, teachers, and youthful professionals migrated east to Brooklyn. After 1853 a steamboat ferry connected Wall and Montague streets, supplementing the older Fulton Ferry to downtown Brooklyn and the South Ferry to Atlantic Avenue (where it linked with the LIRR). By the mid-1850s the giant Union Ferry Company had consolidated most such nautical operations, and its vessels, carrying as many as six hundred passengers at a penny a ride, shuttled an estimated seventy thousand commuters to and from Manhattan each day.

A building frenzy struck Brooklyn in the 1850s (to which Whitman and his brothers made their small contribution). Twenty-six hundred new structures—balloon-frame houses and inexpensive row houses—went up during 1851 alone. Middle-class people filtered into the interstices of affluent Brooklyn Heights. Others migrated to South Brooklyn (embracing parts of today's Cobble Hill, Boerum Hill, and Carroll Gardens), where it was possible for a dry-goods clerk to rent a narrow row house with a large back yard for two hundred dollars a year. Bolder souls could travel farther east to the brownstones of Fort Greene or to East New York, where in 1853 ads proclaimed: "Now every family can own a home." Far to the south lay the respectable community of Fort Hamilton, with its own episcopal St. John's Church; here, in the 1840s, Robert E. Lee was a vestryman and Thomas (later Stonewall) Jackson was baptized.

Middle-class communities, like wealthy enclaves, sought ecclesiastical anchors. In mixed-class districts they often made use of churches established by their more affluent neighbors. On Brooklyn Heights professionals and clerks might join an Episcopalian stronghold of the older-monied elite, whose fortunes flowed from land. Or they might associate themselves with the richest of the mercantile elite who worshiped along with the Low family at the Unitarian Church of the Saviour, Minard Lafever's brownstone Gothic masterpiece. But the middle class had an anchor of its very own in Brooklyn Heights—the largest and most influential church in all Brooklyn, all New York, and some said all the nation.

Plymouth Church was a breakaway from Brooklyn's first Congregational venue, the Church of the Pilgrims, a conservative bastion of New Englanders led by the Rev. Richard Salter Storrs. In search of a more potent pastor, Plymouth's founders reached across the country to Indianapolis, where they found Henry Ward Beecher, himself of New England stock, and brought him east to serve.

When Beecher arrived in 1847, Plymouth consisted of fewer than two dozen members, but soon his bravura preaching was pulling in crowds (including an enraptured Walt Whitman). A large-framed man, Beecher had a powerful voice and was a master of the anecdotal and colloquial: some called him a combination of St. Paul and Phineas T. Barnum. When Plymouth burned down in January 1849, it was rebuilt according to Beecher's specifications—along lines pioneered by Charles Grandison Finney—with a central platform instead of a pulpit and with seats arranged in a giant semicircle. This format would allow his "social and personal magnetism" to work better, Beecher said. "I want the audience to surround me," he told the architect, "so that I shall be in the centre of the crowd, and have the people surge all about me."

The barnlike sanctuary on Orange Street was completed in January 1850—barely adequate, it turned out, for within another few years Plymouth's membership stood at twelve hundred, there was a waiting list of over two thousand, and the deacons had figured out how to distribute the communion bread and wine to fifteen hundred worshipers in under ten minutes. So many people came over from Manhattan to hear Beecher that on Sundays the Fulton Street Ferry came to be known as "Beecher's Ferry." His ministerial range was magnified, moreover, by New York's national-circulation newspapers, which covered Beecher consistently, and by the *Independent*, a Congregational journal for which he himself wrote regularly.

Beecher was successful because his message suited the membership. Although Plymouth's trustees included a few of Brooklyn's wealthiest merchants, its congregants and visitors were predominantly middle class. Many (perhaps three-fourths) were newly arrived in Brooklyn and New York. Like Rufus Griswold, clerk in a business house, they were doing well in the marketplace but feeling socially isolated, fearful of wandering into wicked ways. Griswold immediately felt "at home" in Beecher's church, in part because the minister's liberal, barely denominational Protestantism presented virtually no doctrinal barriers to admission.

Beecher's lack of concern for old dogmas and rigid creeds appealed to young men and women who themselves had broken with their past. His amiable and urbane theology also offered a comforting contrast to the faith of their parents, with its emphasis on human depravity and damnation. Beecher did not try to frighten them with strident Calvinist warnings about the wrath of Jehovah. He spoke instead of human perfectibility, a benevolent Deity, and the beauty of the natural order.

Beecher insisted, moreover, on Christians' responsibility for their fellows, a position with great appeal for those who wanted to be socially respectable *and* socially responsible. Plymouth thus provided a welcome contrast to elite churches like Grace

Episcopal, which middle-class spokesmen like journalist James Parton lambasted as little more than ecclesiastical clubs, designed "for the accommodation of persons of ten thousand a year, and upward."

Beecher, like Finney before him, believed that people could and should contribute both to their own salvation and to society's. Indeed he went Finney one better. The older evangelist (whom Beecher invited to preach at Plymouth in 1849) sought social reform through conversion, not legislation; he declined to "get up a Christian party in politics." Beecher, however, engaged in direct political action. Each year, just before Plymouth's sale of pews, he restated his outspoken support for abolition and women's rights, so that congregants would have no cause for later complaint about their investment.

Beecher also helped parishioners negotiate the oft-conflicting claims of morality and business. He vigorously denounced speculative and corrupt practices and demanded that trade be conducted according to the highest standards. Yet he insisted that "religion and commerce stand together," with "one working from a divine nature, and the other from a selfish; but both together conferring benefaction." He also helped his flock deal with the prosperity attending their worldly success. Counseling against either extravagance or penuriousness, he defended frugality and discipline, while reassuring his audiences that affluence as such presented no obstacle to God's grace and might well be a sign of divine approbation. A love of true beauty—as opposed to superficial fashion—was evidence of inner refinement. And true refinement—not mere aristocratic display—was evidence of Christian grace.

GENTEEL PERFORMANCES

Middle-class New Yorkers who set out to demonstrate refinement by acquiring beautiful commodities found handcrafted luxury items unaffordable. Mass-produced versions, however, were well within their reach—and satisfyingly beyond the grasp of cruder classes below. Their parlors now bloomed with framed chromolithographs, machine-woven floral carpets, machine-pressed glassware, mahogany bureaus, wallpaper, ottomans, sofas, chairs, tables, and books. Perhaps even a modest upright piano.

Commodities were problematic, however. Those in the middling ranks who really *did* hanker to keep pace with the rich were doomed to be outspent and outclassed, their imitation luxuries branding them an imitation bourgeoisie. Those who made a point of denouncing "profligacy and waste in the upper classes" (as middle-class tribune Horace Greeley put it) worried that they themselves might be succumbing to what Greeley called "the shameless ostentation which reigns in our dwellings and furniture, the boundless luxury which presides at our entertainments, [and] the premature exposure of our young men to the contact of a vicious and rotten civilization."

In either case it was imperative to demonstrate that goods signified grace, not vulgarity. And the best way to do so was by *acting* in a refined manner—displaying graceful manners, polished conversation, a self-assured bearing, a genteel sensibility. Assuming such virtues, however, especially for those new to citified or bourgeois ways, required study and practice. Fortunately, a small army of experts was ready and eager to advise them. The publishing industry churned out etiquette books—over one hundred between 1830 and 1860—aimed at upwardly striving urbanites or those who were wealthy but socially challenged urbanites. The courtesy-book authors, along with popular fiction writers, codified and inculcated standards of polite behavior, counseling novices how to dress, how to dine, how to walk, how (and how often) to bathe. Magazine editor Nathaniel Parker Willis also set out to "instruct" and "refine" readers in what he called the "vital middle class" that lay between "wealth and poverty." Willis offered articles on posture and dress, answers to questions about social do's and don't's, and endless exhortations to embrace "TASTE and ELEGANCE."

Parlors were crucial performance spaces. Here neophytes, by paying and receiving visits properly, could display their newfound delicacy of feeling, capacity for embarrassment, and rigorous self-control—acting "naturally" all the while, as if to the manners born. Hundreds of rules governed these events. You arrived at the stroke of the clock— "if you are a moment later, your character is gone"—and presented your calling card. On entering the house, you never thumped into the parlor, breathing hard, but prepared yourself first in an offstage dressing room, until "every part of your person and dress" was "in perfect order." Next, your entrance: "A graceful bearing, a light step, an elegant bend to common acquaintance . . . are all requisite to a lady." Gentlemen, for their part, were warned against offering their seat to the newly arrived lady—body warmth was offensive—and instructed to avoid "ill-bred" or "indecent" subjects of conversation. At table, as in conversation, all participated in making other players look good; should one spill wine on one's dress, one was not to "exhibit peculiar or violent emotion," and others were to tactfully ignore the faux pas.

Death was the final performance, and mourning manuals—advice books on bereavement—counseled that the capacity to experience deep grief was a sign of true gentility. As never before, the bourgeoisie (haute and petite alike) wept over their dead and developed a sentimental reverence for keepsakes, relics, "locks of shining hair." 1846 witnessed the invention of the Frederick and Trump corpse cooler, indispensable for the expanding profession of undertaker who prepared the deceased—affixing cosmetics, wiring limbs in a "natural" position, inserting false teeth—until a polite visitor could give the formerly vulgar corpse the ultimate accolade: "He looks asleep." Widows (though not widowers) were expected to wear mourning for two years, just as, in general, the burdens of refinement fell most heavily on women. It was a virtual prerequisite for middle-class (as for upperten) status that the male breadwinner spare his wife from work outside the household. She was installed instead as priestess of the home, where her task was to provide a serenely pastoral sanctuary from the urban jungle. In theory this was achieved by effortless emanations of her character; in fact it took a tremendous amount of hard work.

Usually the middle-class housewife had help, though seldom as much as was available to wealthy women. In 1855 New York had thirty-one thousand domestics, the largest category of women workers. This vast pool allowed one family out of every four to employ at least one servant. The ability to command at least some labor power— perhaps a cook or maid—became another virtually defining characteristic of middle classness.

To help the housewife manage these servants, a host of advisers was standing by. Often the how-to books and ladies' magazines counseled mistresses to take a tough line vis-à-vis their employees. Complaints about refractory or inexperienced help became common coin, a way respectable women could instantly establish a class camaraderie. Elizabeth Cady Stanton was heard to say that one day she'd surely be hanged for "breaking the pate of some stupid Hibernian for burning my meat or pudding on some company occasion."

Advice books also aided women in managing other aspects of their increasingly

BRIDGET.—"Indade, Misthress Smith isn't in the House. She tould me to tell you so, this very minit, when she set her eyes on you."

PEGGY.—"Please, Ma'am, Cook is dressin' for the ball to-night, and says would you lend her a brooch, and a pair of bracelets, and a scarf, and a wreath."

"The Miseries of Mistresses," cartoon views of the "servant problem" from *Harper's New Monthly Magazine* of 1857. Among middle- and upper-class New Yorkers, the alleged foibles of Irish maids like "Bridget" and "Peggy" were a running joke. (© Collection of The New-York Historical Society)

complex households. Housewifery was becoming a "profession," wrote Catharine Beecher, Henry Ward Beecher's sister, and she along with other writers would help women master it. They discussed how to do (or oversee) the cleaning, cooking, health care, and childrearing and how to sort out the new technology of stoves, illuminants, furnaces, and sewing machines.

As women's work expanded, it became less valued, in part because it was unpaid, in part because, as home was meant to be the antithesis of the workplace, labor there was not something to be acknowledged. Indeed the success of women's work was often measured by its invisibility. The veiling of domestic labor's contribution was accompanied by an insistence on women's importance as civilizing agents. Home, one minister wrote, was the place where "fighters, with their passions galled, and their minds scarred with wrong—their hates, disappointments, grudges, and hard-worn ambitions—may come in, to be quieted and civilized." Housewives, that is, were expected to instruct their husbands in matters of sensibility, in part by crafting an environment that exerted a refining and spiritualizing influence.

As women guided their husbands, so they molded their children, lavishing increasing nurturance on fewer offspring. It was the father's duty to pay for formal schooling. It was the mother's to impart the character traits, table manners, conversation styles, dress codes, and spiritual wherewithal required to retain and transmit the family's position in the middle class. In shaping their children, it was argued, women shaped the country. Mothers, said one minister, would decide "whether we shall be a nation of refined and high minded Christians" or "a fierce race of semi-barbarians."

Middle-class men were not entirely irrelevant to the civilizing process. They enrolled in literary discussion societies, went to concerts, and attended lyceum lectures, which in the mid-fifties almost surpassed theaters in popularity. Clerks flocked to talks sponsored by the Mercantile Library Association, which, still going strong, had over four thousand members by 1853. Formal associations were equally decorous. The International Order of Odd Fellows, which had once featured convivial gatherings in taverns, now forbade drinking and promoted individual self-improvement.

In physical pursuits, too, middle-class men hewed to respectable activities. Some exercised at gyms (by 1860 there were seven in operation). Others attended regattas, trotting meets, and pedestrian races. But it was on the new frontier of participatory sports that a handful of New Yorkers, in search of an appropriate after-work pastime, invented a game that would sweep the country, and eventually the world.

Cricket, played informally in the city since the Revolution, got organized, in a small way, with the formation of the St. George Cricket Club in 1839–40. The members were all Englishmen, mostly merchants and agents of English import houses, along with some skilled craftsmen. But the sport grew very slowly in the 1840s and 1850s. Despite the *Times*'s praise of it as a "manly, healthy and invigorating exercise," its complexity, professionalism, and English associations limited its appeal.

In 1842, however, white-collar workers who lived near Madison Square and Murray Hill came up with an alternative. In a vacant lot at 27th and Madison Avenue they began playing a version of the children's game known variously as one-old-cat, stool ball, bat and ball, base ball, or rounders—the latter being the others' English forerunner. Popular since its arrival early in the century, rounders and its cognates involved four bases in diamond formation and a "feeder" who tossed balls to a "striker." After several years of informal play, Alexander Joy Cartwright, a shipping clerk who later opened a bookstore and stationery shop, proposed to his fellows that they constitute themselves the Knickerbocker Base Ball Club. The group—almost all of them businessmen, professionals, or clerks like Cartwright—drew up a constitution and wrote down a set of formal rules for the game. After being forced out of their playing field by resurgent uptown development, the Knickerbockers rented a site at the Elysian Fields across the Hudson in Hoboken. In June 1846, using the new rules, they took on their first challenger, a group called the New York Club.

Slowly the game caught on. The Gothams (originally the Washingtonians) began play in the early 1850s at the St. George Cricket Club's ground in Harlem. By 1854 the Eagles and Empires had taken the field, as had, across the river in South Brooklyn, the Excelsiors. Like the Knickerbockers, most of these clubs were comprised of middle-class men and were more fraternal organizations than competitive teams. Club members met off as well as on the field, with postgame collations at their favorite hotel or restaurant, and in the winter at suppers, promenades, skating parties, soirees, and an annual ball. Most games were intramural, with only an occasional match game, initiated by written challenge, the winner of which got to keep the game ball in its trophy case. The clubs insisted on decorum and gentlemanly behavior, emphasizing their self-control in contrast to working-class raucousness.

In the late fifties the game took off. By 1858 there were seventy-one clubs in Brooklyn and twenty-five in Manhattan; others on Long Island and New Jersey brought the metropolitan area total to 125. 1858 saw the establishment of a National Association of Base Ball Players to refine rules, resolve disputes, and control the game's development. The title may have seemed a bit grandiose, as the constituents were all local teams, but the wording was fair enough, for Brooklyn and New York City had between them become the acknowledged capital of the sport. For a time, the "New York" game was rivaled by "Philadelphia" and "Massachusetts" varieties. But all the leading sports journals—like Porter's *Spirit of the Times* and the *New York Clipper*—were located here, and they gave tremendous nationwide coverage to epic contests played by "New York" rules; among these was the first intercity all-star match, in 1858, in which New York beat Brooklyn in a best-two-out-of-three series at the Fashion Course (to which tens of thousands paid admission, another first). With over a million readers devouring such stories, and sports papers issuing series on the history of the game, and baseball editor Henry Chadwick of the *Brooklyn Daily Eagle* devising a scoring system, the metropolitan version of the game soon became standard throughout the nation. In yet another indication of the city's imperial outreach and cultural clout, its native sport had become the national pastime.

Even as it careened toward a more competitive, commercial format, baseball remained predominantly a middle-class affair. In the late fifties roughly a quarter of the players were businessmen and professionals. Half were clerks and small proprietors (occupationally based teams of schoolteachers, physicians, even clergymen had become popular). But the percentage of artisanal ballplayers had also risen rapidly. Skilled workers now constituted a quarter of the players in Manhattan and an even larger component in Brooklyn, though virtually no laborers had time for baseball. But if by 1860 baseball had become a sport that straddled cultural boundaries, it is a sign of the degree to which the game had been indelibly molded by its middle-class progenitors that newcomers like butchers and volunteer firemen, who leaned toward more rowdy pursuits, accepted the rules, conventions, and even the adherence to decorum laid down by their predecessors. The spread of baseball, some thought, was a triumph of the civilizing process.

The respectable classes had carved out a social and psychological location for themselves vis-à-vis the uppertens, by stressing their shared gentility while disavowing undesirable aristocratic elements. But in moving closer to the city's elite they distanced themselves culturally as well as physically from the less respectable orders. They could play ball with artisans who accepted their standards of propriety but had only scorn for mechanics who did not. With refinement open to all, they reasoned, the lower sorts had only themselves to blame for their vulgarity.

By mid-century organs of middle-class opinion like *Harper's Monthly* were making ever more condescending references to manual laborers: their sun-darkened skin, tattered clothes, rough hands, mental sluggishness, even their "bestial" character. The widening cultural divide was enormously exacerbated by the fact that, in an astonishingly short period of time, the class landscape had been drastically rearranged. Most merchants, professionals, shopkeepers, and clericals could consider themselves socially superior, not simply because the city's laboring force still worked with its hands but because, augmented by a torrent of immigrants, it had become overwhelmingly alien in tongue and habit.

42

City of Immigrants

Ireland, the summer of 1845: the air reeked with a sickly odor of decay as the potatoes blackened and died. Nearly a third of the crop rotted that year, nearly all of it the next. Starving men and women ate grass, then died along the roads. Skeletal children grubbed the fields in search of food, their faces "bloated yet wrinkled and of a pale greenish hue." Before the famine ended five years later, as many as a million and a half people would perish, most of them poor laborers and cotters.

England, whose imperial exactions had led to the crisis, now worsened it. The British government required relief committees to sell rather than give food to the starving, lest charity foster dependency. It permitted cattle and grain to flow out of Ireland rather than tamper with the free market. It supported Protestant landlords in evicting over half a million tenants. (Soon, crowed the *London Times*, "a Celtic Irishman will be as rare in Connemara as is the Red Indian on the shores of Manhattan.") Of the two million sons and daughters of Eire who eventually escaped the devastation, perhaps three of every four headed for the United States. Crammed below decks in "coffin ships" by shipmasters bent on maximizing returns, more than one in every ten didn't survive the journey.

Thousands of peasants in the southern and western German states also fell victim to the potato blight and made their way to Bremen, where they booked passage for the United States. Joining them were thousands of other Germans: small proprietors forced off the land by agricultural depression, spinners and handloom weavers unable to compete with English textiles flooding down the Rhine, skilled shoemakers and furniture makers facing proletarianization, and handfuls of merchants and manufacturers frustrated by economic stagnation and political repression.

Emigration from German states accelerated following the suppression of the short-lived revolutions of 1848. The recapture of Berlin by forces loyal to the Prussian monarchy precipitated a flight of craft workers, small shopkeepers, and intellectuals, all of whom had backed a program of radical social and economic change: universal suffrage, socialized workshops, a minimum wage, a ten-hour day. They too set their sights on America. *Kein König da*, said the republicans among them—no king there. "Since Capital so commands Labor in the Fatherland," explained a group of radicals departing Baden, they would go to a new country "where the reverse relationship prevails."

In the gray industrial towns and villages of England rose still another stream of emigrants, including unemployed handicraft workers, disgruntled factory hands, and defeated Chartists. A largely working-class movement, Chartism had hoped to secure economic justice through political reforms: universal manhood suffrage, secret balloting, and annual Parliaments. In 1848, after a decade of having their petitions rejected by Parliament, Chartists talked about linking up with European revolutionaries, but a combination of internal division and government suppression squelched their attempt to march on Parliament. Many fled to America, scant steps ahead of the police, beaten yet unrepentant. (Similarly defiant were the defeated Italian veterans of the 1849 war for independence from Austria, among them Giuseppe Garibaldi, who settled on Staten Island in 1850.)

Irish peasants, German craftsmen, English Chartists—America was their common destination, and it was New York, now the principal western terminus of transatlantic traffic, where they converged. Between 1820 and 1839, better than 667,000 immigrants had arrived in the United States. Some 501,000 (75 percent) of them entered at the Port of New York, a yearly average of around 25,000. Between 1840 and 1859, however, the total number of immigrants soared to 4,242,000. Forty percent were Irish, 32 percent were German, and 16 percent were English. Three out of every four entered at New York, approximately 157,000 per year on the average. In 1854 alone, setting a record that stood for decades, the United States accepted 428,000 immigrants. Of that number, roughly 319,000 (75 percent) descended on Manhattan—more than the entire population of the city in 1840!

Only a minority of these immigrants became permanent residents. Every year, as a general rule, perhaps three of every five departed immediately for the interior. Others moved on after a short stay. Of the more than three million immigrants who passed through the city between 1840 and 1860, maybe one in five or six remained—but this was enough to help drive the population of New York City from 313,000 to 814,000 and that of Brooklyn from 11,000 to 267,000, an aggregate increase of some 757,000 people. In 1845 Manhattan had been half the size of Paris; by 1860 it had over a million inhabitants and had pulled even with the French metropolis.

New York's surging population wasn't wholly the result of foreign immigration. The villages of New England, New Jersey, and Long Island continued to export men and women to the city, as they had since the 1790s. The pace of this migration quickened during the 1830s and 1840s as a ramifying network of canals and railroads brought New York's older agricultural hinterlands into direct competition with more productive farmsteads around the Great Lakes and west toward the Mississippi. Thousands of marginal growers and stockmen left the land altogether and went to Manhattan in hopes of making new lives for themselves; others joined a burgeoning corps of farm laborers, wandering between town and country in search of seasonal employment, here successful, there obliged to subsist "on the good-nature of relatives, landlords, or grocers, so long as they can, and then make their choice between roguery and beggary." Also on the move were numerous small-town craftsmen and retailers whose livelihoods had been destroyed by the expansion of urban manufacturing.

Although native migrants (sometimes called "buckwheats") had a good deal in common with their immigrant counterparts—above all, the confusion and resentment of lives thrown into disarray by the advent of new capitalist economies—it was the immigrants, more alien and far more visible, who had the most profound impact on New York. By 1855 over half the city's residents hailed from outside the United States: 176,000 from Ireland, another ninety-eight thousand from Germany, and thirty-seven thousand from England, Wales, or Scotland. Two of every three adult Manhattanites had been born abroad.

New York City was no novice at handling large-scale immigration, but never before had it confronted anything like this inundation. Where the English had overborne the Dutch in a century-long evolutionary process, this demographic revolution took but twenty years. It was as if a second city had sprung up, virtually overnight—not encamped across the river but superimposed atop the older metropolis. Newcomers in such numbers would not be stirred and dissolved in some metropolitan melting pot.

RECEPTION CENTER

By the early 1840s up to forty passenger ships might drop anchor off Manhattan every day, the biggest carrying as many as a thousand men, women, and children in steerage. As lighters and steamboats shuttled their cargoes to shore, bedlam engulfed the water-front. Clattering wagons careened around heaps of boxes and crates. Newsboys, ped-dlers, apple sellers, and hot-corn girls elbowed noisily through the crowds. Throngs of bewildered newcomers milled about, searching for friendly faces and familiar voices. "Runners" wearing bright green neckties and speaking in thick accents competed to channel their "fellow countrymen" to boardinghouses along Greenwich Street—charg-ing them exorbitantly or robbing them outright—or booked them passage to points further west at rates that were the envy of swindlers everywhere. Hundreds, penniless and half starved, wandered into town, where they begged for food and hunkered in doorways.

Besides the din and disorder and sheer misery of it all, large numbers of those com-ing ashore had been exposed to typhus, cholera, smallpox, and other infectious diseases that ran rampant on immigrant ships. Under state legislation dating back to the 1790s, the visibly sick should have been dropped off at the marine hospital in Tompkinsville, Staten Island, until doctors certified their fitness to enter the city. Many captains regarded the law as a time-consuming nuisance and either ignored it altogether or sur-reptitiously landed passengers in places like Perth Amboy, New Jersey, from where they easily made their way to Manhattan.

When city authorities proved unwilling or unable to provide even minimal protec-tion to the new immigrants, associations of older ones stepped forward. The German Society set up an office on Fulton Street, and the Friendly Sons of St. Patrick busied itself with its compatriots' problems. Most notably, the Irish Emigrant Society (1841) offered information about jobs and lodgings, filed complaints against charlatans, protested shipboard conditions, remitted money and prepaid tickets back to Ireland, and in 1850 established an Emigrant Industrial Savings Bank.

For all their energy, the private German and Irish organizations were quickly overwhelmed, and they demanded and got greater state support. In 1847, overcoming bitter opposition from politicians and would-be predators, they prevailed on Albany to create a Board of Commissioners of Emigration. The panel included the mayors of Brooklyn and New York, the presidents of the German and Irish Emigrant Societies, and six gubernatorial appointees (six of the original ten were members of the Friendly Sons). The legislature empowered the new board to organize and reform the entire process: inspecting inbound vessels, helping immigrants find work, and arranging food, lodging, and medical care for those who had been in America for less than the five-year naturalization period. Funds to pay for it all were gathered by taxing the captain of each arriving vessel a dollar per passenger.

The commission would receive considerable criticism in the coming years. More than a few members had vested interests of one kind or another in the immigrant traffic, and periodic investigations turned up evidence of persons in their care being victimized by poor medical care, bad food, and dirty lodgings. But overall the commissioners accomplished a great deal, starting with a mammoth emergency medical relief program for the thousands of arriving sick and destitute. In 1847 they set up the Emigrant Refuge and Hospital on Ward's Island, rapidly expanding it from a handful of temporary buildings until by the mid-1850s it was the largest hospital complex in the world.

In 1855 the commissioners converted Castle Garden into the Emigrant Landing Depot. The nation's first immigrant reception center significantly reduced the abuses to which newly arrived aliens had been subjected for years. After ships had passed through the Quarantine Station, six miles below the city, they anchored off the Castle Garden pier, where they were inspected by medical officers and customs officials, and their passengers were barged to the great stone rotunda. Here, clerks of the Emigration

Immigrants arriving at the new Emigrant Landing Depot, formerly Castle Garden. From *Frank Leslie's Illutrated Newspaper*, December 29, 1855. Here some seven million immigrants, mostly Irish and German, would enter the United States over the next thirty-five years. (© Collection of The New-York Historical Society)

Commission supervised the collection and weighing of baggage, enforced uniform porters' fees, steered travelers to approved agents of railroad and steamship companies, and maintained an official cashier to prevent price-gouging, extortion, and other frauds. In conjunction with labor contractors and manufacturers, the commissioners opened an Intelligence Bureau and Labor Exchange in Castle Garden and began sending tens of thousands of unskilled immigrants every year to the interior to take work on farms and construction crews, in mines and factories, as laborers and domestic servants.

Nowhere, however, would the torrent of immigrants have greater impact than in New York City itself. The new arrivals would transform every aspect of life in the metropolis—its patterns of work, housing, religion, politics, and gender—and nowhere would the impact be more dramatic than in the arena of class relationships. Some of the better-off immigrants filtered or fought their way into the city's upper and middling ranks, but the overwhelming mass of them piled into the laboring classes, ousting or overbearing their predecessors in almost every trade. By the late 1850s New York's predominantly Anglo-Protestant middle and upper classes would confront a reconstituted working class of which better than three-fourths were foreigners.

IMMIGRANTS AT WORK

New York's had long been a niche economy, its sectors colonized by competing social groups. Newcomers broke into (or were repulsed from) particular occupations depending on the skills and resources they brought with them and the degree of resistance or encouragement they faced from those already entrenched.

Bourgeois occupations remained relatively open to new arrivals, particular those with access to foreign capital or commodities. These included Gustav Schwab, who represented North German Lloyd, a steamship line that began direct service from Bremen to New York; Bavarian emigré Joseph Seligman, who in 1846 opened a successful dry-goods importing house; and B. Westermann and Company, who distributed German books, pamphlets, and periodicals to the rapidly growing German-American market. By 1855 fully 25 percent of New York's top ten thousand taxpayers hailed from foreign countries.

Fewer lawyers, pharmacists, ministers, and teachers migrated—the professional and clerical middle class remained 85 percent native born—but there were openings for people to service their respective ethnic communities. German journalists and editors found work at the many papers that sprang up to serve the German-language community. Twenty-eight appeared between 1850 and 1852 alone, including the *New Yorker Staats-Zeitung*, published by Oswald Ottendorfer of Moravia, who had fought on the barricades of Vienna in 1848: by 1860 it claimed the largest circulation of any German paper in the world. German doctors were in great demand to staff the Ward's Island establishment, and by the mid-1850s they constituted an estimated one-third of New York's physicians. Abraham Jacobi, who arrived shortly after being released from prison for his role in the Revolution of 1848, was readily accepted by his American counterparts and began a lengthy career promoting the new field of pediatrics at the College of Physicians and Surgeons.

The shopkeeping portion of the city's middle class, by contrast, was completely transformed, in considerable measure because the immigrants' arrival coincided with, and further exacerbated, a breakdown of New York's public market system. Guided by the new laissez-faire mentality, the municipality allowed existing markets to deteriorate—apart from Washington Market, which was so lucrative the city replaced it with a larger one—and refused to build new ones in the emerging uptown areas (the farthest north the system reached was 10th Street).

This nonexpansion policy created a vacuum, which thousands of small retailers—chiefly immigrants—rushed to fill. Many started as peddlers: Irish women hawked vegetables from streetcorner stands, Germans purveyed small manufactured goods, and Italians sold fruit and flowers. Increasingly, however, Irish, Polish Jews, and arrivals from the mercantile regions of the lower Rhine valley opened independent corner grocery stores. By the mid-1850s the grocery business was dominated by Germans, some of whom had come with capital from the old country, others of whom worked their way up from peddling. Many in turn purchased their supplies from immigrant German farmers who commenced market gardening along the Brooklyn shore from Williamsburgh to Astoria, on well-tilled farms in Flatbush, and even in the pastures, meadows, and woodlands of upper Manhattan. Germans also made substantial inroads as butchers, tobacconists, and newsstand dealers, and by 1855 there were fifteen hundred German bakers, including nine Jewish bakers who could prepare matzohs for Passover.

Immigrants moved into the dry-goods trade as well. Long-bearded Jews, recently arrived from Bavaria, Bohemia, Moravia, and Posen, opened used clothing stores along Chatham and Baxter Streets, creating a bazaar-like atmosphere where haggling was the rule. The Irish ran secondhand shops too but dealt more in iron, brass, and copper: by 1855 224 of the city's 245 junk dealers were immigrants. Successful secondhand clothiers often moved on to establish their own dry-goods stores. By the end of the 1850s German-Jewish shops lined Houston, Division, Bowery, Grand, and lower Broadway. Irish clothiers were fewer in number (eighty-one out of the city's 403 in 1855) but did very well indeed. By the 1850s Patrick Rogers of County Tyrone, who arrived in 1836 as

This cluster of second-hand clothing shops along Chatham street reflected the movement of new immigrants—in this instance German Jews—into small-scale retailing during the 1850s. (© Museum of the City of New York)

a half-trained tailor, was running a prosperous men's clothing store at Nassau and Fulton, with a retail salesroom and a wholesale warehouse that dealt with merchants across the United States. And Charles Knox, a genius at self-promotion, rose from a basement contracting business to being New York's best-known hatter, personally fitting out rich Manhattanites with new silk toppers and purveying his goods to the nation.

Dealing alcohol was another route to middle-class status. Irish constituents of Tammany Hall found it particularly easy to get a liquor license from the Board of Aldermen. Many opened porter houses for day laborers, cartmen, and sailors, while others started taverns frequented by skilled artisans, clerks, and tradesmen. Germans specialized in beer halls and wine gardens. Most of these were "lokals," lively family venues whose regulars came from particular neighborhoods, trades, vereins (organizations), or old country regions, but some were mammoth enterprises. The Deutsches Volksgarten, Atlantic Gardens, and Lindenmuller's Odeon could seat twelve to seventeen hundred in frescoed halls, and the Concordia and Germania included meeting halls, bars, ballrooms, billiard rooms, and bowling alleys. Liquor flowed as well in half a dozen German-owned hotels, most famously Eugen Lievre's Shakespeare on Duane Street, rendezvous for literati, freethinkers, and socialists. According to Police Chief Matsell, fifty-five hundred establishments were licensed to sell liquor in 1855.

For all these entrepreneurial successes, the great majority of immigrants wound up in the manual labor force. Indeed they *became* the manual labor force: by 1855, only twenty-four thousand native-born whites (17 percent) were doing artisanal or unskilled labor, and a significant proportion of these were clustered in a handful of occupations, notably building and printing.

Immigrants dominated some trades by virtue of special skills. German brewers brought a new product with them. New Yorkers were accustomed to English top-fermented ales, porters, and stouts, which tended to spoil in the hot American summers. Frederick and Maximilian Schaefer, immigrants from Prussia, brought over some bottom-floating yeasts and began producing German lager at a brewery on Fourth Avenue between 50th and 51st streets. Lagers were more highly carbonated, less heavy and less intoxicating, and they kept better. By the 1850s New York had gone mad for lager, and competitors had launched operations in Williamsburgh, Bushwick, and the Bronx, where land was cheaper. By 1860 forty-six breweries were in operation, most consisting of a brewmaster and five to ten workers.

Pianomaking was another specialized trade in which Germans excelled. In 1849 Heinrich Steinweg dispatched his son, then facing reprisals for revolutionary activities, to New York City. His glowing reports about Manhattan's status as center of the growing U.S. piano industry fetched the elder Steinweg and family in 1850, and in 1853 they formed Steinway and Sons. (Steinweg anglicized the company name, because English pianos were reckoned the best, but kept his German name for some time and didn't bother learning English.) His timing proved perfect, as refined New Yorkers were demanding parlor accoutrements, and when sales blossomed, Steinway and Sons purchased (in 1858) a site virtually next door to Schaefer's brewery. The firm installed enormous steam boilers and a Corliss engine to run the plant's saws, lathes, planes, and elevators, becoming the first industry in New York to mechanize on such a grand scale; by 1860 the company employed three hundred workers.

Cigarmaking had been a substantial industry in Hamburg and Bremen, but in the 1850s the German men (many of them Jewish) who handcrafted expensive cigars faced competition from poorly paid rural women churning out a cheaper product. Thousands migrated to New York City, and soon the old tobacco town became the capital of the North American cigar industry.

English machinists were in great demand to design and develop machine tools— a virtually brand-new trade requiring a knowledge of mathematics, metallurgy, and engineering. English, Scottish, or Welsh printers did well too, constituting nearly half the city's total in 1855. German printers brought their own fonts and printed prayer books and wedding certificates for German-Jewish synagogues; they also worked for German book, newspaper, and magazine publishers and for English periodicals, like *Frank Leslie's*, that started up German editions. (In 1851 Charles Dana, Greeley's associate at the *Tribune*, made a bid for German readers by hiring Karl Marx as a European correspondent.)

For many of these skilled craftsmen, life in boomtime New York was a distinct improvement on their former condition. In 1851, attempting to demonstrate immiseration, the *Tribune* printed a workingman's budget that allowed "only" 2.8 pounds of "butchers meat" (roasts and chops, not innards) per person weekly. But an annual consumption of 146 pounds of meat was three times that available to London's workers, and well-nigh unimaginable to new arrivals from devastated Ireland, used to grains and tubers. Enough Irish ate themselves sick on arrival for the Shamrock Society to warn against an "abundance of animal food to which [they were] unaccustomed." Refugees' letters back to Ireland reveled in relating the sheer quantity, variety, and cheapness of food in the mouthwatering metropolis.

Many skilled workers could also afford inexpensive furniture (a bed, some chairs, a chest), a stove, perhaps even a swatch of carpet from Hiram Anderson, the Bowery dealer who billed himself as "Carpet Merchant of the People." Better-paid Irish craftsmen could afford good quality ready-to-wears: "I wear as good a suit of cloths as any Gentleman in the City of Cork, and twenty dollars' worth of a watch in my pocket," said an Irish boxmaker in 1852.

These luxuries, to be sure, were tentatively held: the slightest dip in the economy and the watches were off to the pawnshop. And most immigrant craftsmen fared far less well. German and Irish tailors, woodworkers, and shoemakers had fled proletarianization, hoping to reestablish themselves as traditional artisans. But the same capitalizing process was at work in New York and was accelerated by their arrival. Some highly skilled German furniture makers, many with experience in the finest Paris workshops, did obtain custom craft work in firms like Duncan Phyfe's. Most, however, cranked out cheap chairs and cabinets in small "slaughter shops," with one to five employees. These outfits, competing desperately to sell their products at wholesale auctions or to large mercantile houses, underbid rivals by driving down wages so steeply that where in 1836 cabinetmakers had made from twelve to fifteen dollars a week, a decade later the majority made less than five. Shoemakers were reduced to putting-out work in cellar workshops, aided by their families.

The garment industry—the city's largest—was utterly reconstituted. By 1855 95 percent of New York's tailors had been born abroad; of that number 55 percent were Germans, 34 percent Irish. Some became petty contractors, bidding (and underbidding) for the right to transform the precut cloth supplied by big companies into finished suits and shirts. Some became cutters in the large firms. Most, however, sewed at home for a contractor, at piece rates so low that by the 1850s journeyman tailors, aided by their wives and children—"A tailor is nothing without a wife, and very often a child" went a maxim of German craftsmen—worked sixteen hours a day but seldom cleared more than ten dollars for a seven-day week.

Some Irish garment manufacturers did far better. Daniel Devlin came to New York in 1844 from Donegal, married the daughter of a wealthy Irish American, and did custom tailoring for the city's leading Catholics. Devlin also pioneered in manufacturing quality discount clothing—he was one of the first in the city to use the new sewing machine—and his line proved popular with upwardly mobile immigrants. By the late 1850s Devlin and Company's store, at the corner of Broadway and Warren, was the biggest men's clothier in New York after Brooks Brothers. But Devlin's accomplishments rested on a huge force of chiefly Irish workers—150 in-house cutters and clerks, and two thousand out-work tailors who labored in their boardinghouses. Devlin paid his men better than average wages by the standard of the day, but that standard was in free fall and soon plunged to seventy-five cents a day.

Female seamstresses might make as little as seventy-five cents a *week*—when they could find work at all in the highly seasonal and competitive industry. By 1855 two-thirds of New York's dressmakers, seamstresses, milliners, shirtmakers and collarmakers, embroiderers, and those who turned out artificial flowers for the high-fashion hats of wealthy ladies, were foreign born (64 percent of them Irish, 14 percent German). Living right at the edge, some occasionally fell over. Two German sisters, Cecelia and Wanda Stein, migrated to New York in 1852, both unmarried, Wanda the mother of an illegitimate child. They labored at doing embroidery, but in 1855 their employer went out of business; times being particularly hard, they couldn't find other work. With the rent due and the larder empty, having borrowed all they could and being unwilling to take up whoring, the sisters spent their last pennies on some flowers, spruced up their dreary room, and got into their bed with the six-year-old, and all took a terminal drink of prussic acid.

Below the ranks of these skilled and semiskilled immigrants lay the battalions of Irishmen and German laborers whose sheer muscle power, as even the most xenophobic New Yorkers were prepared to agree, rapidly transformed the cityscape. In 1855 Irish immigrants made up 87 percent of New York's unskilled laborers; it was the largest single occupation for Irish males. Some slotted into existing industrial hierarchies at the bottommost ranks: at the Novelty Iron Works, they were hired for such part-time jobs as moving a newly cast thirty-five-ton bed plate through the yard and hoisting it into a ship's hull. Irishmen also carved out particular niches, especially in construction and transport, often at the expense of African Americans.

With construction booming, Irishmen opened lumberyards, stoneyards, and coalyards and established themselves as building contractors—ethnic middlemen who assembled and managed work crews. By 1860 there were 166 incorporated construction companies. These outfits afforded better-paid jobs for carpenters, masons, and stonecutters skilled in using the new planing machines and steam-powered stone-dressers. However, they relied chiefly on thousands of Irish laborers for the raw manpower needed to complete the Croton Aqueduct High Bridge, build the Hudson River Railroad from Manhattan's West Side up through the northernmost Bronx, and double-track the New York and Harlem up the Bronx River Valley to White Plains. In Brooklyn, Irishmen filled in the boggy Red Hook marshlands, erected the new docks there, deepened the Buttermilk Channel, and enlarged Fort Hamilton. In Queens they drained meadowlands, filled swamps, and drove turnpike roads east from Hallet's Cove to Flushing Creek (one them being today's Astoria Boulevard) and south along the riverbank over Newtown Creek's first bridge through Greenpoint on to Williamsburgh (including today's Vernon and Manhattan avenues).

Irishmen reigned supreme in horse-reliant transport. They sat atop hacks, omnibuses, stages, and horsecars—in foul as well as fair weather—and piloted private coaches around town, often suited up in livery. Many found jobs taking care of animals—one agrarian skill transferable to the city—and by 1855 Irishmen accounted for 84 percent of immigrant hostlers. After 1849, when the Common Council, urged by businessmen seeking improved transport, ended ancient restrictions on the trade, Anglo- and Dutch-American one-horse entrepreneurs found themselves in competition with capitalist carting companies who hired immigrant wage-workers. By 1855 there were over eight thousand cartmen (up from thirty-four hundred in 1840), and the bulk of them were Irish.

Irishmen took over New York's docks as well. "Along the wharves, where the colored man once done [*sic*] the whole business of shipping and unshipping," noted one African-American newspaper, "there are substituted foreigners or white Americans." On any given day five or six thousand of these "alongshoremen" moved mountains of cargo off ships and around the port, roaming from pier to pier for the "shape-ups" at which native-born stevedores amassed work crews. The work was hard, poorly paid, and erratic. While waiting for ships to arrive or weather to clear, men hung around local saloons, took alternate jobs as teamsters, boatmen, or brickmakers, and relied on the earnings of their wives and children.

Others went to sea. Here too their arrival noticeably whitened the labor force. Captains relied increasingly on waterfront crimps to assemble crews, and these men, often Irish proprietors of taverns or boardinghouses, tended to favor their own. Black sailors were pushed to the bottom of an already wretchedly exploitative industry. (The glorious clippers were known to seamen as "blood boats.")

It was much the same with service jobs. Gardeners on upperten estates overlooking the Hudson and Harlem rivers were 90 percent German, Scots, or French by 1855, and immigrants made deep inroads on traditionally black niches in barbering and hotel and restaurant work. Immigrant women competed with blacks for positions as hotel maids, waitresses, cooks, nurses, and washerwomen. By 1855 more than twenty-five "intelligence offices" were placing streams of applicants as household domestics, usually young, single, and recently arrived Irish girls in need of a place to stay as well as work. It was hard work, and the fifteen- or sixteen-hour days, six and a half or seven of them a week, brought in only four to seven dollars a month plus room and board. Still, it seemed better than sweatshop labor, and by 1855 Irish women made up 92 percent of a domestic workforce once overwhelmingly black. "Every hour," wrote black spokesman Frederick Douglass in 1853, "sees us elbowed out of some employment to make room for some newly-arrived emigrant from the emerald isle, whose hunger and color entitle him to special favor." There was precious little satisfaction in noting that "in assuming our avocation," as Douglass put it, the Irish have "also assumed our degradation."

SETTLING IN

People had marveled at the almost overnight construction of uppertendom's fashionable *quartier*, but they were boggled by the emergence of a huge German metropolis within their precincts. If Manhattan's Germans had set up their own city in 1855, it would have been the fourth largest urban agglomeration in the United States—third largest if joined by Brooklyn's Germans. New York City had become one of the three capitals of the German-speaking world, outranked only by Berlin and Vienna.

Roughly half these newcomers were crowded into a mammoth ethnic enclave known as Kleindeutschland (Little Germany). The phenomenon was new to New York, new to the United States. Never before had tens of thousands of foreigners, to whom the English language and American ways were virtually unknown, congregated in such close quarters.

At first, the nucleus of Kleindeutschland lay within a five-block span between Canal Street and Rivington Street. The cobbled or unpaved north-south arteries of Elizabeth, Bowery, Chrystie, Forsyth, and Eldridge were lined with two- to four-story buildings (many of wood) behind which, reached by a maze of alleyways, lay internal courtyards crowded with industrial workshops. From this initial base camp, immigrants pushed north above Houston toward 14th Street in the 1840s and 1850s and east from Third Avenue, through the alphabet avenues, down toward the East River shore, which grew dense with breweries, coalyards, factories, shipyards, and slaughterhouses.

To outsiders Kleindeutschland, with its wealth of German shops, seemed a uniformly Teutonic mass, but the area was far from homogeneous. Quite apart from the admixture of Irish, English, and older American residents, the "German" residents in fact hailed from very different cultural and linguistic regions. "Germany," after all, was a patchwork of thirty states, and on close inspection Kleindeutschlanders dissolved into a welter of Plattdeutsche and Hessians, Bavarians and Prussians. They were fragmented and spatially sorted along religious lines too. German Jews, for example, concentrated at first in the area bounded by Grand, Stanton, Ludlow, and Pitt. It was here, on Norfolk Street between Rivington and Delancey, that Anshe Chesed built its synagogue in 1849. In the 1850s Jews pressed north with their fellow Germans.

The remainder of the new Germans headed for the urban frontier and formed villages composed substantially of countrymen, much as did their peers who settled in Argentina and Chile. In Manhattan, Yorkville was the leading outer enclave. Between 76th and 100th streets—north of the fire district—cheap wooden housing was available. It was also possible to find work close by or to commute downtown by horsecar. In Brooklyn, Germans constituted two-thirds of the population of Williamsburgh as early as 1847, and Bushwick became known as Dutchtown, from a phonetic rendering of "Deutsch." Those without local jobs in the tailoring shops or shipyards could float to work, reading their *Long Island Zeitung*, on steam ferries that arrived every five minutes at Kleindeutschland's Grand Street. Up in Westchester, Gouverneur Morris II—his ancient manor lands now profitably accessible from Manhattan via the New York and Harlem Rail Road—began to sell off parcels to Germans, among others, and they flocked to villages like Morrisania, Mott Haven, Port Morris, and Melrose.

In Queens, College Point emerged as an industrial town that might well have been transplanted from Germany's Ruhr region. After Conrad Poppenhusen's Hamburg vat dyeing business was destroyed by fire, he moved his family to Williamsburgh in 1843 and began manufacturing whalebone brushes, combs, and corset stays. Just as whaling declined in the early 1850s, Poppenhusen learned that Charles Goodyear had figured out how to transform natural rubber into a whalebone substitute. As Goodyear was also strapped for funds, Poppenhusen loaned him considerable sums in return for rights to his discovery. He then established the Enterprise Rubber Works at pastoral College Point and developed a company town around it. He drained marshes, built a cobble-stone road to Flushing, brought in water, streets, and gas, and built homes for the employees whom Poppenhusen's agents recruited from among the disembarking German immigrants. The little town grew from a few hundred in 1853 to over a thousand in 1855 and two thousand by 1860.

Germans also flocked to satellite cities in New Jersey. Between 1840 and 1860 Newark's population soared from seventeen thousand to seventy-two thousand, Jersey City grew from three thousand to thirty thousand, and Hoboken boomed as well. Substantial percentages of these new urbanites were German (and Irish) immigrants— 40 percent in the case of Jersey City—attracted to the manufacturing establishments of Essex and Hudson counties.

Irish immigrants were less densely concentrated. Their only counterpart to imposing Kleindeutschland was the dilapidated stronghold of the Five Points. Here Hibernians clustered by kin and county—a clutch of Corkonians on Mulberry Street, a cluster of Kerryonians on Baxter. But while the Sixth Ward was more Irish than ever, most African Americans having departed, it remained home to Germans, Italians, Chinese, some remaining blacks, and a multinational assortment of sailors.

Rather than joining their compatriots, most incoming Irishmen settled wherever they could find work. As this was usually on far-flung construction projects, their communities were dispersed throughout the metropolitan region. In the Bronx, Irish laborers who built the Croton High Bridge settled in Highbridge; those who worked on the New York and Harlem opted for villages along its path—Melrose, Morrisania, Tremont; and those driving the Hudson River Railroad into the northwestern Bronx gravitated to Kingsbridge. In Queens, those building turnpikes and draining meadows were drawn to Astoria's "Irishtown," whose local byways bore names like Emerald or Shamrock Street. In Brooklyn, "Irish Town" referred chiefly to the substantial enclave around the Navy Yard, but there were others. Brooklyn Irish laid out Bedford's streets and horsecar lines, then stayed on as residents (immigrants constituted 70 percent of Bedford's population in 1855, and three-fourths of these were Irish). Red Hook housed the Irishmen who built and worked its docks, brickyards, distilleries, warehouses, and factories. By 1855, out of Brooklyn's total population of 205,250, roughly a hundred thousand were foreign born (47 percent compared to Manhattan's 51 percent), and of these fifty-seven thousand were Irish, twenty-six thousand German, and eighteen thousand English.

The diversity of immigrant settlements was matched by the variety of housing conditions. While some immigrants' dwellings were quite substantial, certainly superior to those they had just fled, overall the standard of working-class accommodations in New York City went into steep decline. The 1837–43 depression had virtually halted new construction, so the vast numbers of newcomers were rolling into a seriously understocked city. Propertied New Yorkers responded to the sudden and intensive demand for shelter either by cramming newcomers into existing housing or by building a new kind of structure, the "tenant house" or tenement, designed specifically as a multifamily worker dwelling.

In lower Manhattan, especially around the Five Points, cramming was the strategy of choice. Landlords converted frame houses built for single artisan families into rabbit-warrened boardinghouses, jammed renters in, then jammed some more into sheds and stables. By 1850 an estimated twenty-nine thousand people, most of them Irish, had become unwilling troglodytes, living in cellars, often with two or three families sharing a single soggy space. The Five Points' Old Brewery alone housed hundreds of poor Irish and blacks.

Kleindeutschland too was carved up and stuffed full: the elegant five- or six-story buildings on the north end of Tompkins Square (now Der Weisse Garten) that developers had hoped would house the native upper classes were sliced and diced into crowded rooming houses. But in Little Germany, the cumulative market power of even poorly paid laborers and artisans was so great that tenement construction became profitable. Some of the new three- to five-story buildings, especially along Avenues A through D, were solid brick structures. Many, however, were, as former mayor Hone put it, "so slightly built that they could not stand alone, and, like drunken men, require the support of each other to keep them from falling." Many were in insalubrious locations, stuffed into back lots, nearly flush with the walls of existing houses and privies. Most were stripped-down, amenity-free versions of the row houses developers were raising for the middle and upper classes elsewhere around town. Most lacked "modern improvements," apart from stoves, and were seldom linked up with water or sewer mains: working people used bedpans and privies long after the respectable classes had switched to water closets.

Tenement areas were intensely crowded. A tenement twenty-five feet wide and seventy feet deep might have twenty-four two-room apartments, each with a ten-by-ten-foot "parlor," facing street or yard, and a windowless interior eight-by-ten-foot room, big enough for a bed. Such buildings would house a minimum of twenty-four families (plus boarders), but often more—one all-black tenement contained forty families—and when they were organized as boardinghouses for sailors and laborers, densities shot up higher still. Such crowding magnified the dangers of fire and disease, and indeed mortality rates began climbing sharply in the working-class wards.

Given these alternatives, large numbers of immigrants preferred to squat in shantytowns on the periphery of the city. At Dutch Hill, a promontory at 40th Street and First Avenue overlooking Turtle Bay (now the United Nations), Germans and Irish lived in log cabins and recycled railroad cars, the men laboring in nearby quarries, the women and children gathering rags and bones. Farther north lay Harlem—a "third or fourth-rate country village," the Board of Aldermen called it in 1838, whose lands were worn out after centuries of use, and whose marshes reeked so badly they could "knock the breath out of a mule!" Yet Harlem was also full of lovely hills, woods, brooks, and meadows with river views, and the land was cheap or free. Irish families built one-and two-story frame houses around 125th Street in the 1850s or squatted on mud flats at the river's edge in cottages pieced together from bits of wood, twigs, barrel staves, old pipes, and tin cans hammered flat. Many raised animals for local markets—geese, cows, horses, goats and such a profusion of hogs that the area around 125th Street was known as Pig's Alley.

Along the west side, after the Hudson River Railroad opened along Eleventh Avenue in 1851, many threw up shanties in vacant lots between 37th and 50th (the future Hell's Kitchen). Here they raised pigs and goats, scavenged for food and firewood, hired out as day laborers, and found jobs in the industrializing area. Further north, so many Irish families planted themselves in the African-American community of Seneca Village (bounded by 82nd and 86th streets and Seventh and Eighth avenues)

By mid-century, unable to find adequate housing in the city, thousands of immigrants were crowding into shantytowns scattered around upper Manhattan, safely outside the municipal fire limits. (© Museum of the City of New York)

that by 1855 they constituted a third of it. One of the first to arrive was Pat Plunkitt, an Irish immigrant laborer whose wife, Sara, gave birth to George Washington Plunkitt, later a political luminary. Another was an itinerant veterinarian named Croker, who plied his trade among the area's animals and sired little Richard, the future boss of Tammany Hall.

Many immigrants simply bedded down in the streets. One 1850 account reported that "six poor women with their children, were discovered Tuesday night by some police officers, sleeping in an alleyway, in Avenue B, between 10th and 11th streets. When interrogated they said they had been compelled to spend their nights where ever they could obtain any shelter. They were in a starving condition, and without the slightest means of support." After the establishment of the Police Department in 1845, precinct houses began accommodating homeless people. In one six-month period during 1853 they sheltered roughly twenty-five thousand, a number that would rise dramatically in hard times.

JEWS AND HUGHES

Through the 1830s New York had remained a Protestant town. The 1840s and 1850s immigration ended that dominance forever. Jews went from being an ecclesiastical sliver (five hundred in 1825) to a respectable religious minority of forty thousand by 1859. Catholics, a respectable minority in the 1830s, became the largest denomination in the city—with two hundred thousand congregants in 1855—and a temporal power in metropolitan affairs.

The mass migration of Jews to New York City was triggered when various German states, especially Bavaria, imposed severe economic and social restrictions, making business, travel, and even marriage increasingly difficult. With the arrival of thousands of

German- or Yiddish-speaking Jews, the number of synagogues rose rapidly, reaching a total of twenty-seven by 1860. The immigration also created considerable internal strains in what had been a relatively harmonious population. German Jews, especially the more educated and wealthy among them, objected to holding services in Hebrew, which few understood. They also wanted preaching by a rabbi, the introduction of instrumental music, and the integration of sexes. Those inclined toward such practices organized their own "reform" congregation—Emanu-El (God Is with Us)—which soon acquired its own "temple" (first on Chrystie, then on 12th Street) and its own cemetery (at Cypress Hills on Long Island). By the 1850s Emanu-El was challenging "orthodox" Shearith Israel and B'nai Jeshurun for leadership of the Jewish community.

Many German Jews, as verein-minded as other Kleindeutschlanders, flocked to secular groups as well. By 1849 the combined membership of the fifty-odd Jewish organizations—charitable, social, and fraternal—exceeded by far the combined membership of the synagogues. Among the most important was the Independent Order of B'nai B'rith (Sons of the Covenant). It resembled the Odd Fellows and Masons in providing members with mutual aid and burial benefits, and by 1860 it had ten lodges and a thousand members. A Jewish press emerged as well. The *Asmonean*, the first successful Jewish weekly in the United States, was joined, in 1857, by the *Jewish Messenger*. In 1855 the "Jews' Hospital in the City of New York" opened its doors (it would be known after 1866 as Mount Sinai). Initially a project of the older Portuguese and English, it soon added immigrant Germans to its board and became the most prominent Jewish organization in New York City. All factions attended its charity banquets and balls; the spectacular affair at Niblo's in 1858, graced by the mayor's presence, was the most extravagant event of its kind ever organized by New York Jews.

The emergence of a full-blown Jewish community raised relatively few hackles among other religious communities in a city where congregants of Shearith Israel had long been a respected presence. Anti-Semitic caricatures of Chatham Street's clothing dealers and pawnbrokers were prevalent, to be sure. A character in Melville's *Redburn* recalls "walking up Chatham-street" and seeing "a curly-headed little man with a dark oily face, and a hooked nose, like the pictures of Judas Iscariot." But most found it hard to distinguish German Jews from other Germans, and when they did, it was apparent that the newcomers were intent on fashioning a brand of Judaism that would be "acceptable" to the gentile majority. By 1856 Temple Emanu-El had switched from German to English.

Where the arrival of the German Jews—modest in numbers and demeanor—provoked no backlash, the arrival of hundreds of thousands of Irish immigrants provoked strenuous anti-Catholic outbursts. Yet the newcomers were by and large only nominally Catholic. Most cleaved to pre-Christian Celtic peasant traditions. In Ireland, the official dogmas about sex and sin that would characterize the postfamine Church had, as yet, made inroads only among better-off tenant farmers. Peasants continued to hold boisterous celebrations, wakes, and saint's-day festivals that appalled the clergy, who were spread far too thinly (one priest per three thousand parishioners in 1840) to have more than marginal influence.

This state of affairs was reproduced in New York City. Many immigrants were ignorant of the simplest Catholic rituals and skipped even Sunday Masses; those inclined to go couldn't afford pew rents, an American invention. Most hewed instead to rituals like wakes—festive and largely social events that left no room for a priest. The metropolitan hierarchy and the more affluent and anglicized among the laity were eager to church the immigrants, to be sure, but Catholicism was even weaker in New York than in the old country: here there were only eight churches, and one priest for every eight thousand Catholics.

John Hughes, self-proclaimed "bishop and chief" of the Irish community, set out to transform this situation. With considerable assistance from the international Catholic community, he succeeded brilliantly in welding his scattered and dispirited countrymen and women into a coherent body. One of the first great "brick and mortar" priests, Hughes embarked on a mammoth building program, particularly in the uptown industrial wards into which his would-be parishioners were moving. He provided churches for the railroad builders who settled in Harlem and Yorkville villages, built the Church of Annunciation at Manhattanville (1853) for the Hudson River Railroad crews, and erected St. Paul's on 59th Street for the shantytown squatters on the city's western edge in 1858. By the 1860s nine new Catholic churches had been organized between 14th and 42nd streets, the overall total had gone from eight to thirty-one, and plans had been set in motion to erect a spectacular new St. Patrick's Cathedral on Fifth Avenue.

Nor were outlying areas neglected. St. Raymond's, established in 1843, was the first Catholic church in the Bronx. In southern Brooklyn, St. John the Evangelist was founded in 1846, with services held in nearby stables until its tall wooden structure at 21st Street off Fifth Avenue was dedicated in 1851. Two years later Brooklyn became a separate diocese under Bishop John Loughlin.

German Catholics presented a special problem. Hughes opposed "national parishes." He want to preside over a unified community, not a congeries of ethnic ghettoes. Nor was Hughes comfortable with the Germans, whose piety was of a fervent counter-reformation variety. Nevertheless, when the Germans pushed to construct their own churches and use their own language, Hughes did not stand in their way. In 1844 Manhattan Redemptorists raised the Church of the Most Holy Redeemer, whose original wooden structure was replaced in 1851 with what German New Yorkers called their "cathedral," and indeed Most Holy Redeemer's 250-foot tower dominated the Kleindeutschland skyline. In all, seven German churches were established by 1860, along with mutual aid groups independent of those provided by the Irish-dominated Catholic hierarchy.

Hughes's second priority was to train a cadre of priests and nuns. To this end he built St. John's College (later Fordham) on 106 acres near the Village of Fordham, twelve miles north of the city, newly accessible by railroad. Opened in 1841, presided over by the Rev. John McCloskey (later, New York's first cardinal), St. John's began preparing young men from wealthier Irish families for the priesthood and other professions. Hughes knew, however, that he had neither the priests nor the money to sustain such an institution, so he turned to the Jesuits, his worries about allowing such a powerful religious order into his bailiwick overridden by his desire to have the prestigious organization run his college. The Jesuits, finding the idea of a base in New York City appealing, purchased Fordham from the diocese in 1846. The following year they opened St. Francis Xavier, on West 16th Street in Manhattan, also to prepare men for the priesthood, the bar, and the medical professions. The same goals motivated the Christian Brothers to launch Manhattan College in 1849. All three institutions would be supported by—and in turn help create—a Catholic middle class. For females, Hughes arranged for the Madames of the Sacred Heart to begin the Academy of the Sacred Heart (1841), which moved in 1847 to the grounds of Jacob Lorillard's estate in Manhattanville. By 1850 local graduates and arrivals from Europe had brought the ratio of priests to parishioners down from one to eight thousand to (a still overwhelmed) one per forty-five hundred.

Hughes's third enterprise was to bring the children of the immigrants into the Faith. With the city and state having refused financial support to Catholic schools, the bishop made organizing parochial schools his top priority. A crash program, which ran up an immense diocesan debt, brought the number of Catholic schools to twenty-eight by 1854, embracing ten thousand pupils. A decade later, fifteen thousand students were attending twelve select and thirty-one Catholic free schools in New York, and there were another twenty-eight institutions in the Diocese of Brooklyn.

To staff these schools, Hughes traveled to Ireland, England, and France seeking help from religious teaching orders. Several accepted his call. In 1848 the Christian Brothers from France opened their first two schools for boys, St. Vincent de Paul's Academy on Canal Street and De La Salle Academy on 2nd Street near Second Avenue; the order would run many others. For instructing girls, Hughes relied on nuns from, among others, the Sisters of Mercy, Sisters of Notre Dame, Sisters of the Good Shepherd, and, above all, Sisters of Charity.

Mother Seton's Sisters of Charity had become legendary in New York City for their work during the cholera epidemic of 1832. Like the other orders, it was not under Hughes's direct control. In 1846, however, thirty-two of the fifty sisters chose to form a separate community, the Sisters of Charity of St. Vincent of Paul. Now they reported directly to the bishop (and their superior, Mother Angela Hughes, the bishop's youngest sister). At his direction, the women organized the Academy of Mount St. Vincent. In 1847 they purchased the Jacob Dyckman estate at McGowan's Pass, five miles north of the city in the vicinity of 105th Street and Fifth Avenue. By the mid-1850s their convent had seventy sisters (half of them Irish born), eleven Irish servant girls, nine male employees (also Irish), several buildings with classrooms for nuns, and a free school for local children. In 1856 they moved again, to a fifty-acre tract fifteen miles from City Hall in Westchester County. Once part of Frederick Phillipse's confiscated lands, the Hudson River estate had been home most recently to the celebrated actor Edwin Forrest. In 1847 he had built Font Hill there, a Norman castle. Now it became part of Mount St. Vincent de Paul. By 1859 a great new red brick building housed a convent for novices and an academy for training the teachers who would staff many of the city's parochial schools (and other welfare institutions) from that day to this.

Last, Hughes secured ample final resting space for his parishioners. In 1848 the church purchased the old Alsop estate on the Maspeth side of Penny Bridge, which traversed Newtown Creek. Here Calvary Cemetery was laid out, and for the convenience of funeral corteges, steamboat service was inaugurated from East 23d Street. Other cemeteries quickly followed, such as Holy Cross in Flatbush (1849) and Mount Olivet on the old Hallett Estate in Maspeth (1851).

By 1850, reflecting Hughes's accomplishments, and the importance the Vatican increasingly attached to New York, the city was chosen to be an archdiocese, and Hughes was appointed its first archbishop. For all this, the Irish did not unreservedly accept Hughes as their chieftain. Hughes was certainly a hero to many working-class Irishmen—he had arrived a penniless laborer like themselves and yet achieved great things—and many in the Irish middle class, who saw him as savior and sponsor, snapped up busts of the Bishop turned out by a Greenpoint porcelain factory. Yet the majority of his parishioners were still only nominally in the fold. In the 1850s at least half the Sixth Ward Irish rarely attended Mass. Many parents were reluctant to send their children to parochial schools, fearing this would hamper their futures in the wider city. Substantial numbers preferred the public schools, which had also expanded vigorously and were now ward controlled, hence, in Irish neighborhoods, no longer a threat to their faith. Hughes also met resistance when he moved to seize power from the lay trustees who by custom and state law controlled church property. Their insistence on maintaining a democratic pattern of church governance left him at odds with many professionals, small businessmen, and skilled artisans, key elements of the fledgling Irish middle class.

The bishop also faced considerable opposition to his political stance on international issues. New York's hierarchy had already assumed the conservative cast that would characterize it for the next century, in part because the clergy had to compete with arriving radicals for the loyalty of the immigrant masses. In 1848 a group known as Young Ireland, impatient with Daniel O'Connell's failure to end English rule, seized on news of the revolution in France to organize for a rising. In New York City radical nationalists held rallies, raised money, purchased arms, and formed militia companies for anticipated action overseas.

New York's Irish-American republicans emerged as an alternative and at times oppositional voice. In 1849 Patrick Lynch launched the *Irish-American*, a moderate nationalist weekly. Its circulation soared from twenty thousand in 1854 to forty thousand by decade's end, and it was widely read aloud in Irish taverns. Lynch maintained an uneasy truce with Hughes, but he insisted that Irish-Americans believed firmly in the separation of church and state, and he grew incensed when nativists characterized Irish republicans as tools of an autocratic church. Hughes managed for a time to isolate those who advocated armed struggle against the British, but in 1858 militants formed the Fenian Brotherhood, a transatlantic underground organization devoted to raising money, arms, and soldiers for a future rebellion. The Fenians' numbers were small, and their attention was focused primarily on exile politics, but they would yet play a major part in the affairs of New York City.

RUDE B'HOYS

These divisions within the Catholic community were largely lost on nativists, from whose perspective it seemed that Hughes had constructed a monstrous phalanx and become its spiritual and temporal dictator. Their anxieties were further fueled by New York's newfound favor with the Vatican and by some intemperate remarks Hughes made in November 1850 before leaving for Rome to receive the pallium of office from the pope. In a sermon at St. Patrick's Cathedral, "The Decline of Protestantism and Its Causes," Hughes announced the coming triumph of Rome over Protestant nations everywhere, including America. Such missionary fervor confirmed many nativists' worst fears.

Beleaguered white artisans, in particular, facing an avalanche of immigrants and speeded-up proletarianization, reacted with hostility. Some organized the American Laboring Confederacy, whose paper, the *Champion of American Labor*, spoke out bitterly against the "swarms of needy adventurers, cut-throats and paupers of European jails and poor-houses, that, like the locusts of Egypt," were ravaging the New York labor market. In trade after trade, an 1847 petition argued, employers had beaten down wages "by reason of their having the cheap pauper labor of Europe ready at hand, to work for that price if Americans refuse."

Stopping or slowing the onrush seemed the only answer. If the government, through its tariff and other policies, could extend protection to "rich capitalists, to mammoth manufacturers, extensive railroad speculators and contractors in the public works," why not protect workers by putting a tariff on people as well as commodities? In the boom era, however, most erstwhile allies were nowhere in sight or actively opposed to immigration restriction. Many old-timers recognized that the faucets of imported labor power were fixed in a wide-open position, that the New York working class would soon be dominated by immigrants, and that nativism was a strategy without a future. Some native-born artisans, accordingly, set out to make common cause with English Chartists, German socialists, and Irish nationalists. Others would nevertheless continue to press restrictionist demands, and street violence would flare up in the 1850s.

Whenever the crackle of street fighting subsided—or perhaps precisely when it was most furious—combative young American, German, and Irish workingmen discovered they had much in common. Many shared a visceral distaste for bourgeois culture, with its exaltation of piety and sobriety, self-control and industriousness, female domesticity and refined respectability. Many working-class men did embrace such virtues, of course, but others rejected definitions of male success that poorly paid proletarians found increasingly impossible to meet.

Some immigrants were drawn to the party of the refined; others joined the ranks of the rude boys—and transformed them into "b'hoys." The b'hoy was a multiethnic construction, part native American rowdy, part Irish "jackeen," part German "younker" (Kleindeutschland grocery clerks who expressed their Americanness by greasing their hair and wearing loud checked clothes to dance halls, rather than wearing the old costumes and singing the old songs with their elders in the beer halls).

This new youth culture fashioned its self-image not at work but at play—and the bastion of b'hoydom was the Bowery, long a site of rough sports for adolescents and apprentices, more recently a center of commercial entertainment. After work, rambunctious young men, free of family responsibilities and with enough money in their pockets to indulge the less expensive pleasures, rolled out of their bachelor boardinghouses in the surrounding heavily male wards and headed for the Bowery's theaters, brothels, and dance halls.

They were usually clad in colorful attire, not bourgeois black—either the red flannel of their volunteer fire company, the costume of their gang, or the regalia of a working-class dandy. B'hoys loved dressing "high," in mocking parody of Broadway's exquisites—sidelocks heavily greased with soap, stovepipe hat perched on head, cigar or chaw in mouth, red shirt, black silk tie, flaring trousers, high-heeled calfskin boots. And they preened and promenaded with swaggering bravado, not proper decorum: "He rolls down the Bowery a perfect Meteor," said one observer.

Florid body language found its counterpart in "flash talk." The word "slang," meaning "illegitimate language," first came into use around 1850, and Boweryites introduced slang terms by the bushelful: "chum," "kick the bucket," "going on a bender," "pal," "blow-out," and "So long!" "Many of slang words among fighting men, gamblers, thieves, prostitutes, are powerful words," Walt Whitman observed, and his poetry so reflected their defiant vitality that more than one reviewer observed: "He is the 'Bowery Bhoy' in literature."

Many spent the bulk of their time in taverns, which the immigrants completely refashioned. In the 1840s the traditional English-style artisanal gathering place, where craftsmen passed a leisurely evening drinking ale and brandy and playing checkers, dominoes, or billiards, gave way to rural-Irish-style establishments, usually named for the owner. Most often found in a corner store or perhaps a cellar, these taverns—more often called "saloons" by the 1850s—consisted of a single long room dominated by a long straight bar along one wall. The saloons had few seats, which made it easier to accommodate the midday crushes of customers fostered by saloonkeepers who handed out free food to those purchasing beer—usually German lager. At night saloons served as jumping-off points from which to barhop, a peripatetic custom that allowed newcomers to learn their way around the neighborhood.

Though weddings and wakes were often celebrated at saloons, they were mainly centers of rough male conviviality. Amid a fog of tobacco smoke, men drank and spat, cursed and quarreled, played cards and told tales and offered toasts to the likes of Daniel O'Connell. The men treated one another in turn, spending lavishly what little they had to demonstrate their honor and bonhomie.

Lost honor, conversely, rapidly led to barroom brawls. Taverns became sites of ritual battles, in which men aired out personal quarrels, displayed courage, vindicated honor by shedding blood, and sustained reputation by demonstrating ferocity and support for chums. Macho touchiness, often heightened by differences of religion and ethnicity, made defending cultural turf a matter of personal—or collective—pride. Volunteer fire companies also offered a chance for real heroics and colorful display, and in the 1850s immigrants joined them in large numbers (the Irish were 14.7 percent of the firemen in 1850 and 37.8 percent in 1860). Battles between these volunteers escalated as well, in part because Irish immigrants brought over from Connaught and Munster the Gaelic peasant tradition of faction fights.

Neighborhood ethnic-based gangs, headquartered at a saloon or corner liquor grocery, also afforded opportunities to bolster identities in the metropolitan flux. Fights between gangs, especially at times of nativist anxiety, could be ferocious affairs, featuring stomping, brass-nailing, eye-gouging, and nose-biting their enemies. Guns began to appear too, for by mid-century cheap, concealable revolving pistols were becoming available. Yet the code of the streets still decreed that a true reputation for grit and toughness had to be won barehanded. And it was precisely the value placed on fisticuffs—by immigrant and native alike—that accounted for one of the Bowery's most spectacular contributions to the larger life of the city.

THE MANLY ART

Organized boxing (as opposed to mere brawling) originated in eighteenth-century Britain, where it appealed to both plebeian respect for raw physical courage and aristocratic fascination with ritual combat. Immigrants and merchant seaman brought the sport across the Atlantic in the early years of the nineteenth century, and during the 1820s a handful of prizefights took place in the United States. Around the same time, New York gentlemen began to experiment with "sparring" when William Fuller built a gym in the city and offered to teach law-abiding citizens to defend themselves on the streets against "insolent ruffians and blackguards." Respectable opinion in the city ran strongly against the brutality of the ring, however, and local authorities exerted themselves to suppress scheduled bouts (in 1824 the King's County sheriff had dispersed a Coney Island crowd with bayonets).

Fed by ethnic and communal rivalries, "the detestable practice of prize fighting" continued nonetheless to grow in popularity. After 1840 boxing contests and exhibitions became weekly events in New York, thanks in large part to the arrival that year of James "Yankee" Sullivan, an Irishman who had a minor career scrapping in the London prize ring. Sullivan set up the Sawdust House, a Bowery saloon where pugilistically inclined immigrants could slake their thirst, watch a fight or two and swap stories about the great bouts of bygone days.

Two years later, on August 29, 1842, ten steamboats ferried more than six thousand people to Hart's Island in Long Island Sound for a bare-knuckle fight between Sullivan and William Bell. This was a rendezvous guaranteed to grab public attention, for not only was Bell an Englishman, he was also a sparring master who made his living teaching the "good people of Brooklyn" how to defend themselves against foreigners. In the end, after twenty-four rounds and thirty-eight minutes, Professor Bell proved no match for the hard-hitting Sullivan.

The event sent boxing enthusiasm soaring in the city. Fans packed into the Arena, a new saloon on Park Row, for nightly sparring matches, but the sport soon received a serious setback. Sullivan's victory had helped him promote a second Anglo-Irish fight, two weeks later in White Plains, between Thomas McCoy and Christopher Lilly. This time the Englishman, Lilly, emerged victorious—except that it took him a grueling two hours and forty-one minutes, and he beat his opponent to death, with McCoy literally drowning in his own blood in the 118th round. Outraged by this first fatality in an American ring, the authorities moved quickly to indict all concerned for riot and manslaughter. Lilly's friends hustled him out of the country, but Sullivan was packed off to Sing Sing after a sensational trial, crowded with urban street fighters and flashily dressed gamblers, in the White Plains courthouse.

An all-out press attack ensued on prizefighting as an attempt by immigrant barbarians to infect American youths—Greeley's *Tribune* led the pack against these "festival[s] of fiends"—but it proved impossible to keep down. By the late 1840s the thousands of arriving Irish immigrants underwrote a resurgence of such magnitude that boxing swiftly became the most important spectator sport in the country, and New York City became its national headquarters.

The revival was marked by the great fight in 1849 between Sullivan, now out of jail, and Tom Hyer, a native American butcher. As the sport was still illegal, the combatants had to travel south, to Maryland, and even there were forced to dodge local authorities and throw their hats into a hastily constructed ring. Hyer won the brief (sixteen-round) slugfest, and the new telegraph lines flashed the results to the metropolis. Newsboys hawked bundles of papers, lithographers sold pictures of the fighters, and saloonkeepers (especially at Hyer's haunt, the Fountain House on Park Row) did a booming business in postbellum merriment.

In the 1850s dozens of bouts took place each year, along with hundreds of sparring exhibitions. A sporting community blossomed, composed of fight connoisseurs, retired pugilists, and active boxers who opened taverns and sporting houses like Jim Gidding's Old Crib and James Regan's Clipper Shades. Boxing became big business. The saloonkeepers at the heart of the pugilistic community became entrepreneurs: they arranged bouts, gave odds, took bets, chartered steamboats, sold railroad tickets. Fight managers whipped up public excitement by publishing challenges in the paper (an echo of the old aristocratic dueling practice). Publishers played to the new audience by putting out cheap popular pamphlets like *The Life and Battles of Yankee Sullivan* (1854).

Boxing did not, for the most part, attract the upper classes. There was, to be sure, a coterie of sporting lawyers, brokers, editors, doctors, and clerks who attended the fights, as well as a wider circle of genteel men who followed them in print. Gentry enthusiasts were known as the "fancy," from which "fan." But for working-class pugilists and participants, boxing was far more than a thrilling diversion. For the winners, it could be the ticket out of poverty into the middle-class realm wherein saloonkeepers dwelled. And in a world where ordinary men felt increasingly powerless, a tough guy who battled to the top could become an instant hero to those still trapped below.

UNDERWORLD

Betting at ringside allowed b'hoys to display their skill as gamblers, demonstrating their courageous willingness to lose all. Gambling was also a major avocation in most saloons and public houses and, as an affair among friends, had an ancient lineage in the city. Now, however, gambling went pro. Full-time sharpers had begun filtering into New York back in the 1820s, plying its taverns, hotels, and racetracks. The first successful gambling house—a modest place with a few tables for dice, cards, and checkers—had been established in 1825, aptly enough on Wall Street, near the old Tontine Coffee House. Dozens more opened in the 1830s, featuring faro, roulette, and dice and card games. But it was during the 1840s, Bennett's *Herald* charged in 1850, that the city became "the great head quarters of the gamblers in this country." Greeley believed at least five hundred "gambling hells" were in nightly operation, with vast numbers of "ropers-in"—sometimes moonlighting policemen—haunting New York's hotels, barrooms, brothels, and businesses, steering potential patsies toward their employer's "hell."

From the world of gamblers and boxers it was but a short step down to New York's underworld, a term warranted by the numbers of criminals at work in the city, the emergence of a rough-hewn infrastructure of criminal operations, and the development among the fraternity of villains of a language peculiarly their own.

Chief of Police George Matsell compiled a 128-page *Vocabulum; or, The Rogue's Lexicon* (1859) whose words and phrases, arranged from *A* to *Z*, hint at the rich variety of opportunities (and perils) the port afforded the criminally inclined. Examples from the *A*-to-*B* range include "Air and Exercise" (working in the stone quarry at Blackwell's Island or Sing Sing), "Amusers" (who use snuff or peppers to blind and rob victims), "Anglers" (who steal from store windows), "Badger" (one who robs a man's pocket after he's been enticed into bed with a woman), "Bat" (a prostitute who only walks the streets at night), "Boodle" (a quantity of counterfeit money), and "Booked" (arrested). Matsell also observed that this was a multiethnic jargon, spoken no matter what the thief's nationality. The chief noted somewhat pridefully that in New York thieves "from all parts of the world congregate."

Hangouts emerged that were patronized more or less exclusively by the criminal classes. One-Armed Charley, a noted thief, opened the Hole in the Wall, which became a place where robbers could meet with fences to plan jobs. Usually these fences were junkmen who moved stolen goods under cover of their normal operations, but there were innovators in this field too, like Fredrika 'Marm' Mandelbaum, who now launched her long career by peddling looted goods door to door. There were also noted female robbers. One-Armed Charley selected as his lieutenant "Gallus Mag," a ferocious six-plus-footer who held her skirt up with galluses (suspenders). In addition to her considerable abilities as a mugger, Mag ran a tight ship at the Hole in the Wall. Seizing the ear of an excessively rowdy gangster in her teeth, she would drag him to the street or bite it off altogether and add it to the collection of pickled ears she kept in a jar behind the bar.

Much of the city's crime was undertaken by individual entrepreneurs who hung around the waterfront, mugging boozy sailors as they exited dockside dives. Others sent female coconspirators to lure hapless landsmen to deserted piers or alleys, where they were struck on the head with a slung-shot (a rudimentary blackjack), their pockets rifled, and their unconscious bodies tossed in the river, sometimes with fatal results. One homeless German immigrant was coshed, robbed of twelve cents, and thrown over the Battery wall, where he was found, frozen, in river ice the next morning. Murders remained a rarity, however—at least solved murders. There were only thirteen homicide convictions in the entire city between 1838 and 1851 (roughly one a year), so that when another thirteen were registered between 1852 and 1854, with guns increasingly in evidence, the city trembled. "Horrible murders, stabbings, and shootings," the *New-York Atlas* reported in August 1854, "are now looked for, in the morning papers, with as much regularity as we look for our breakfast."

Some of the upsurge in fatalities could be traced to the burgeoning activities of so-called river pirates, gangs of professional predators who seized on the opportunities presented by the bustling port. Police Chief Matsell claimed in 1850 that there were over four hundred such robbers, organized into roughly fifty gangs, though his figures may well have been inflated in order to win creation of a harbor police force. Some river pirates simply prowled the wharves, snatching up unguarded property. Others were more venturesome—like the Daybreak Boys, named for their youthfulness (most were under eighteen) and their penchant for predawn operations. The Daybreakers would depart their headquarters (a gin mill at Slaughter House Point), head to the waterfront, and row to their objectives—ships at anchor—with muffled oars and greased locks. Once aboard, they rifled the cargo, rowed their booty ashore (at times to Brooklyn), and sold it off to fences. Between 1850 and 1852, it was claimed, the Daybreak Boys stole a hundred thousand dollars in property. Their career ended abruptly when, in the fall of 1852, a trio of Daybreakers shot a watchman who had surprised them on board his ship. Caught and convicted, Nicholas Howlett, nineteen, and William Saul, twenty, were condemned to death by the court but hailed as heroes by the Boweryites. When they were hanged in January 1853, hundreds showed up in the Tombs courtyard to shake hands with the condemned men on the scaffold.

"IF I DON'T HAVE A MUSS SOON, I'LL SPILE"

The b'hoys also adored theater, and immigrants were quickly incorporated into popular audiences. (Linguistic differences did generate a degree of ethnic segregation: the Bowery Amphitheater was rebuilt in 1854 as the twenty-five-hundred-seat Stadttheater, which presented classical German dramas, popular comedies, musicals, melodramas, and farces.) At a plebeian playhouse, the *Spirit of the Times* observed in 1847, "the pit is a vast sea of upturned faces and red flannel shirts, extending its roaring and turbid waves close up to the foot-lights on either side." The most eager pushed onto the boards themselves, "chanking peanuts and squirting tobacco juice upon the stage."

Shakespeare remained a major staple of popular theater, but burlesques based on life in New York grew rapidly in working-class esteem. William Mitchell's Olympic Theater became the most popular venue in town, in part for its low prices, in part for its regular diet of lampoons, parodies, and travesties involving well-known city figures and activities. In the 1843 *Macbeth Travestie*, for example, the king and attendants appeared as "nabobs of the 15th ward," while the witches resembled the New York's market women.

Minstrelsy in particular, said the *Literary World* in 1849, "convulse[d] the b'hoys and their seamstress sweethearts." By the 1850s there were ten major minstrel halls or "Ethiopian Opera Houses" in town, and some became semipermanent features of the cultural landscape. E. P. Christy's Minstrels (at Mechanics Hall) and Hooley's Minstrels (in Brooklyn) each played for ten years straight. Minstrelsy too was a variety of social travesty. Its routines ridiculed the self-importance, pretentiousness, and hypocritical morality of New York's middle and upper classes. One performer usually stood in for a nabob or reformer, whose high-flown diction the other actors delighting in puncturing, often via lewd buffoonery. Immigrants too took their knocks. To the dismay of Irish actors and the Irish-American press, comedians got easy laughs portraying stage Hibernians as ignorant, pugnacious, and drunken buffoons.

The foibles of stage Africans—whites in blackface, of course—received no such leniency. Vicious derision of blacks remained integral to the art form (albeit alloyed with fascination and envy). It afforded artisans and immigrant audiences, who feared their declining economic status might be seen as racial slippage, a chance to collectively display their whiteness by dissing their only inferiors. Whitman, a great fan of minstrelsy, was one of the few to see the racial intermingling underlying the insistence on racial separation—blendings at work behind the backs of the performers. One visitor to a black tavern observed that "in the negro melodies you catch a strain of what has been metamorphosed from such Scotch or Irish tune, into somewhat of a chiming jiggish air." While Whitman suggested such musical confluence presaged a "native grand opera in America," it was tap dancing that would later emerge from the admixture, in the Five Points, of African and Irish dance traditions.

Audiences that laughed at Zip Coon or chuckled at Paddy positively roared for Mose. In 1848 Francis Chanfrau took to the stage at the Olympic wearing a version of the standard fire-laddie outfit, complete with red shirt, stovepipe hat, and soaplocked hair. At first, there was puzzled silence. Then Chanfrau took his cigar out, spit into the wings, and growled, "I ain't a-goin' to run wid dat machine no more!" There was an instant "yell of recognition" from the pit and galleries. And well there might have been, for Benjamin A. Baker, the playwright, had put the Bowery itself on the boards. The play—*A Glance at New York in 1848*—revolved around a young Connecticut greenhorn who fell into a series of scrapes with assorted loafers and sharpers, from which he was extricated by Mose.

Baker realized he had a good thing going and redrafted the play, called it *New York as It Is,* and put Mose at its center. "I'm bilein' over for a sousin' good fight with someone somewhere," Mose bellowed. "If I don't have a muss soon, I'll spile." But Mose the tough guy was also Mose the protector of the weak. If pugilism was his avocation, firefighting was his mission in life. The plebeian hero rescued babies from burning

Mary Taylor and F. S. Chanfrau in the roles of
Mose and his ladyfriend, Lize, in the premier
of "A Glance at New York," 1848. (The New York
Public Library for Performing Arts)

buildings (played out onstage with elaborate sets and props), defended Bowery folk
against urban corruption, saved Linda the cigar girl from molesters, helped a rural
migrant cheated by city slickers, and—antiaristocratic hero that he was—thwarted
effete and wicked gentlemen. The rough realism was a smash, crowds turned the theater
into a frolicsome madhouse, and *New York as It Is* became one of the greatest successes
in the history of the Manhattan stage.

The fictional b'hoy's nationality was ambiguous. In Baker's play Mose was obviously a native-born worker, though the character also invoked Moses Humphrey, a well-
known fire laddie, brawler, and Irish Catholic printer at the *Sun*. But Mose was generally perceived as not an ethnic but an urban type—appropriately enough given that b'hoy
youth culture, for all its internal stresses and strains, was a conglomerate affair. A mix of
social fact and literary convention, Mose was the New York rude boy writ large, but as
he liked to think of himself: opinionated, rowdy, but virtuous withal.

Over the next two years, as seven different Mose plays went on the national circuit,
the image of Big Mose cohered into a cultural identity recognizable across the country.
Lithographed reproductions of scenes from the plays then turned Mose into an international figure. The Bowery B'hoy—riotous and vociferous habitué of fire companies
and theaters and prizefights and street corners—became as well known as the Wall
Street Banker.

In the 1850s Mose cohered into a fabulous semimythic figure of the sort made popular by Davy Crockett ("half-horse, half-alligator, a little touched with snapping turtle"), and he took his place alongside the likes of Mike Fink, swaggering riverboatsman. This urban Paul Bunyan was said to be eight feet tall, with ginger hair, a two-foot-wide beaver hat, and hands like hog hams, and he toted a fifty-gallon keg of ale as a canteen. He had the strength of ten: he could uproot iron lampposts and use them to smite rival gang members, lift a horsecar and carry it for blocks, leap the East River to Brooklyn with ease, and swim the Hudson in two mighty strokes (with six he could circumnavigate Manhattan).

As Mose grew larger than life, his roots in an adversarial milieu became fuzzed, his Boweryite critique of New York's elite blurred. But there would be no such ambiguity in 1849, when Mose's acolytes declared theatrical war against uppertendom and its associated thespians. That year real, not stage, blood ran through the streets of the city.

43

Co-op City

On May 7, 1849, William Charles Macready, the famous British actor, opened in *Macbeth* at the Astor Opera House. Macready did not go over well with many in the audience, who greeted him with wild hissing and a hail of rotten eggs. He did, to be sure, have his supporters, who cried, "Shame, shame!" cheered, and waved handkerchiefs. But Macready's opponents responded relentlessly with loud groans, cries of "Down with the codfish aristocracy!" and a barrage of potatoes, apples, lemons, and copper coins. The remainder of the first act and all of the second proceeded in "dumb show," the actors pantomiming their lines rather than trying to make themselves heard over the din. But then the crowd escalated. They howled and stomped on the newly installed red plush chairs, then hurled one from the second tier into the orchestra, whose occupants promptly fled. That did it for Macready. Escaping out the back door, he promptly and indignantly announced his intention to take the next steamship back to England and civilization.

Theater riots were commonplace in New York, and Bennett's *Herald* was not alone in dismissing the affair as innocent and customary; an attorney would later note that "the right of hissing an actor has been exercised from time immemorial." In the theater, consumers were sovereigns, their riotous displeasure attended to instantly. The May 7 affair was unusual, and about to get a good deal more so.

The objections to Macready went far beyond his acting style, though that was part of it. Macready had adopted a subdued, scholarly, genteel approach to his art, particularly in Shakespearean performances. He disdained vulgarity and wanted to elevate acting to the status of refined profession. Edwin Forrest, the great American tragedian worshiped by New York's working-class theatergoers, had a very different method. His was a muscular, histrionic style that matched the demands of Bowery melodrama. Forrest specialized, moreover, in playing superpatriotic yeoman heroes who fought tyrants (domestic and foreign) and rescued helpless women. Like Mose, he incarnated b'hoy-dom's self-image.

These contesting styles soon blossomed into personal animosity. Macready had let it be known that he thought Forrest lacked "taste." Forrest, during a tour of Britain in 1846, had loudly hissed Macready in midperformance. The ensuing feud had been eagerly followed by the penny press, which showcased the combatants as it did pugilists and politicians. When Macready came to the states again, Forrest inflamed the rivalry by playing in competing productions during his tour, which culminated in New York City.

The contest had more serious overtones. The actors, in the popular imagination, were stand-ins for larger and more explosive issues. Macready was strongly identified with England and its aristocracy, at just the moment when New York's Irish were at the height of their rage over the famine and Britain's suppression of Young Ireland's rebellion. When Forrest, at his own May 7 performance of Macbeth at the Broadway Theater, spoke Macbeth's line "What rhubarb, senna or what purgative drug will scour these English hence?" the entire audience rose and cheered for many minutes.

Boweryites were even more furious about the theater chosen for Macready's performance, the recently erected Astor Opera House. Its founders' intention of creating an exclusive atmosphere—the dress code stipulated "freshly shaven faces, evening dress, fresh waistcoats, and kid gloves"—were well known and vehemently objected to by Boweryites. As a minstrel songwriter put it in 1849: "De Astor Opera is anoder nice place; / If *you* go thar, jest wash your face! / put on your 'kids,' and fix up neat, / For dis am de spot of de *eliteet*!"

"De spot" itself was provocative. During the recent metropolitan expansion, two parallel avenues had been driving north, constituting the cultural spines of two different class worlds. On the west: Broadway, with its retail shops, department stores, monster hotels, and porpoise-parade of the fashionable. On the east: the Bowery, the thorough-fare of sportsmen, dandies, gangsters, and fire laddies. The thoroughfares, however, were not exactly parallel. At one point—Astor Place, just south of Union Square—the two avenues, and worlds, collided. And at just that point of convergence, capping it and in a sense claiming it, entrepreneurs had erected a splendid opera house for the exclusive enjoyment of the Broadway world's most self-proclaimedly aristocratic segment.

It was the combination of the "English" Macready and the "aristocratic" opera house that had so aroused the ire of native American and Irish immigrant alike, but it was not these animosities that made the May 7 affair (and its explosive aftermath) remarkable. What made this fracas different was the response of the city's upper classes.

They were not amused. Against the frightening backdrop of the 1848 European revolutions and the alarmingly autonomous politics and culture of New York's working-class quarters, the theater riot no longer seemed innocent. It appeared to signal a new aggressiveness, a willingness to break out of the Bowery world and invade Broadway's. The elite had built an institution behind whose august portals they could take refuge from the vulgarity of the streets. Now a senseless mob had violated their inner sanctum. The barbarians were at—indeed well past—the gates. It was too much. It was time to act. It was time to draw a line and say thus far and no farther.

Forty-seven of the city's most prominent citizens sent Macready a joint letter urging him to return to the opera house stage. They assured him "that the good sense and respect for order prevailing in this community will sustain you on the subsequent nights of your performance." Macready agreed. Then they published the letter in the papers. Their gauntlet thus thrown down, they set about assembling the firepower necessary to sustain their challenge. They turned to the newly elected Whig mayor, Caleb S. Woodhull, and insisted he protect the lawful rights and personal liberty of actor Macready.

At a City Hall meeting on the morning of Thursday, May 10, with Macready scheduled to reappear that evening, Police Chief Matsell informed Mayor Woodhull that he lacked the force to quell a serious riot. Terrified of chaos on his second day in office, the mayor ordered General Charles Sandford, commander of the military forces in New York City, to have his men ready in Washington Square Park. Sandford called out two hundred of the elite's crack militia, the Twenty-seventh Regiment—since 1847 renumbered and renamed as the Seventh Regiment—along with two troops of horse, one troop of light artillery, and two companies of hussars, 350 men altogether. In addition, 150 police were placed inside the theater and another hundred on its perimeter; still more were dispatched to guard nearby homes of the wealthy.

The Bowery responded to the challenge. Captain Isaiah Rynders swung into action. Forrest's most ardent backer, the man who had distributed tickets to barroom habitués and mobilized hundreds more for the initial May 7 affair, and the Tammany stalwart who had made a career out of exploiting resentment against the social and cultural elite, Rynders now salivated at the chance to embarrass the new Whig administration. Devising a handbill, he had copies printed, delivered to a Park Row tavern, and then distributed to runners, who on Wednesday, May 9, posted them at saloons and eateries throughout the city. "SHALL AMERICANS or ENGLISH RULE IN THIS CITY?" it demanded to know, and it called on all workingmen to "express their opinions this night at the ENGLISH ARISTOCRATIC OPERA HOUSE!" It was signed by the "American Committee," a group headed by Rynders's chief assistant, Ned Buntline, author the previous year of *Mysteries and Miseries of New York*, saga of a city riven along class lines.

Tickets to the performance, along with marching orders, were handed out to assorted b'hoys at Jim McNulty's saloon, on the corner of Chatham Square and Dover Street. By show(down) time, Rynders's activists were in place, under Judson's field management, and thousands more had turned out to watch or participate; the majority were native born, but there was a considerable minority of Irish immigrants—butchers and laborers united in mutual Anglo-aristophobia.

Tight security screened out many of Rynders's ticket holders, and their yells about discrimination against those who didn't have "kid gloves and a white vest, damn 'em!" merged with the general roar. The play commenced promptly at 7:30. Anti-Macready forces as promptly disrupted it. The actors went into dumb-show mode while police made their way through the audience, seizing and arresting protestors.

Outside, the crowd, now grown to ten thousand, began hurling paving stones, which smashed through the windows and sailed into the audience. Massing their ranks, the crowd rammed at the doors, intent on breaking in. The police, way out of their depth, called on the militia for support, which arrived at 9:15 P.M. and took up positions. The crowd pressed forward, wrestling with the militia. Matsell warned the crowd that force would be used, a notification drowned out by enraged voices crying, "Burn the damned den of the aristocracy!" One fellow in a red flannel shirt bared his breast, screaming, "Fire, fire you damned sons of bitches; you durs'n't fire, you durs'n't fire."

Soldiers fire on rioters outside the Astor Place Theater, May 10, 1849. Lithograph by Nathaniel Currier.
(© Collection of The New-York Historical Society)

But they did, first in the air, then directly into the bodies massed in front of them. Moving up Astor Place, they discharged several more volleys, working relentlessly now to clear the area.

When it was over, eighteen of the crowd lay dead, none of them Rynders's men, most bystanders. Four more would die within the week. Over 150 were wounded or injured, and 117 were arrested, mostly workingmen: coopers, printers, butchers, carpenters, servants, sailmakers, machinists, clerks, masons, bakers, plumbers, and laborers. Of the twenty-two killed, seven were Irish laborers.

Friday, May 11, the day after the riot, the streets bristled with a display of civilian and military power: a thousand special deputies, two thousand infantry, a squadron of cavalry, four troops of horse artillery. Handbills went up around town calling for a mass rally at City Hall Park that evening, and at six P.M. an enraged crowd cheered speakers who condemned the mayor, police, and military. Rynders declared that mass murder had been perpetrated "to please the aristocracy of the city at the expense of the lives of inoffensive citizens—to please an aristocratic Englishman backed by a few sycophantic Americans. (Loud cries of indignation.)" Mike Walsh called for a murder prosecution, told the crowd to arm itself in future frays and said that only his high respect for the law restrained him from urging the crowd to emulate their European counterparts and mount the barricades. Several thousand auditors boiled out of the park, roaring for vengeance, and marched up to Astor Place to confront the troops again. They hurled stones from behind hastily erected barricades, but the militia leveled their muskets, fixed bayonets, and charged, and the crowd dispersed. The June Days were not to be replayed in Manhattan. Not yet.

The danger passed, the gentry rejoiced. The old Whig warhorse James Watson Webb applauded the troops in his *Courier and Enquirer* and underscored a larger message the bloody affair had delivered: "The promptness of authorities in calling out the armed forces and the unwavering steadiness with which the citizens obeyed the order to fire upon the assembled mob, was," Webb declared, "an excellent advertisement to the Capitalists of the old world, that they might send their property to New York and rely upon the certainty that it would be safe from the clutches of red republicanism, or chartists, or communionists [*sic*] of any description."

Some tender-hearted souls looked askance at the use of force—surely republics didn't do this sort of thing! The *Democratic Review* noted that more lives had been lost than in many of the Mexican War battles in which b'hoys had served as volunteers. Nathaniel Parker Willis, of all people, noted in his upperten *Home Journal* that the riot was a protest "from *Mose* and the soap-lock-ery" against "aristocratizing the pit" and suggested the rich "be mindful where its luxuries offend."

Future entertainment entrepreneurs would follow Willis's advice, especially once the opera house itself proved a casualty of the affair. Burlesque shows were soon calling it the "Massacre Opera House" at "DisAster Place"; when it reopened in September, attendance was dismal, and it was eventually sold off. The upper classes relocated their sanctum a bit farther north, to the more defensible precincts of Union Square. In 1853 Moses H. Grinnell (a staunch Macready supporter) and others formed a corporation to build the Academy of Music at 14th Street and Irving Place. Embodying the grandest metropolitan ambitions, it was the largest opera hall in the world when it opened in 1854. Like the ill-fated Astor, it boasted a plush interior and a small number of private boxes. But in a manifest bit of caution, enhanced by the need to fill the space, many of the four thousand seats were priced inexpensively, and management forswore all claims to aristocratic exclusiveness, insisting rather that its mission now was to cultivate taste and knowledge among the citizenry at large.

In the immediate aftermath of the riot, however, Judge Charles Patrick Daly, who presided over the trial of those arrested, pushed hard for their conviction, to serve notice that the old republican acceptance of crowd actions as inevitable, even legitimate, even functional, had come to a definitive end. Judson, convicted, got a year in jail and was treated as a hero on his release. Rynders got off with the help of attorney John Van Buren, the former president's son, a sign from Tammany that the party would look after its own.

What was clear to all concerned was that the Astor Place affair signaled (in the *Herald*'s words) a "collision between those who have been styled the 'exclusives,' or 'upper ten,' and the great popular masses." It was left to a reporter from Philadelphia to sum up the newly hardened positions. The riot, he wrote, "leaves behind it a feeling to which this community has hitherto been a stranger—an opposition of classes—the rich and the poor—white kids and no kids at all; in fact, to speak right out, a feeling that there is now, in our country, in New York City, what every good patriot has hitherto felt it his duty to deny—a *high* class and a *low* class."

The riot at Astor Place, a frenzied challenge to the cultural authority of New York's nascent bourgeoisie, was swiftly followed by a far more disciplined attack on its right to set the city's economic agenda. Since at least the 1820s—the heyday of Thomas Skidmore, Fanny Wright, and the Workingmen's Party—plebeian New Yorkers had been fashioning analyses and programs to contest the degradation of their working and living conditions. Now another upheaval got underway, rooted in prior protests but boosted by thousands of feisty immigrant agitators who contributed their own radical traditions and energies. Laissez-faire polemics, it turned out, were not the only ideas capable of crossing the Atlantic.

TENANTS VERSUS LANDLORDS

One way to improve the quality of life in New York City, said the "land reformers," was to get a lot of New Yorkers to leave town. Given the vast numbers surging into what was still an overwhelmingly rural continent, this approach had many advocates, but the leading tribune was George Henry Evans. The old workingmen's spokesman of the 1830s had retreated to a New Jersey farm during the depression era, where he pondered the work of Tom Paine and Thomas Skidmore. Evans became convinced that labor's problems, at home and work, were chiefly due to its swollen ranks. A surplus of workers allowed bosses to dictate low wages; a surplus of people seeking shelter allowed landlords to extract high rents. It followed that moving substantial numbers from city to country would improve the lot of those who stayed behind as well as those who departed. The chief obstacle, as Evans saw it, was that landlords—often large speculative companies based in New York City—were hogging the public domain out west.

The solution was to use labor's political power to break the grip of land monopolists as President Jackson had broken the reign of bank monopolists. In 1844 Evans organized the National Reform Association, whose slogan was "Vote Yourself a Farm." The idea was to give publicly owned land to actual settlers, free of charge, while barring speculators and absentee landlords. The government—crucially—would also subsidize construction of republican villages and build government-owned railroads to get settlers to them.

Immigrant radicals also liked land reform. In 1840 Thomas Ainge Devyr, who had been a leader of the Chartist movement in Newcastle-upon-Tyne, escaped to Brooklyn, where he began agitating for free public land grants, government-owned railroads, and laws restricting wealth and landownership, and in 1844 linked up with Evans's National Reformers.

Evans and Devyr were soon joined by Hermann Kriege, a Westphalian journalist and member of the outlawed Communist Bund der Gerechten (which later would publish the *Communist Manifesto*). Kriege arrived in New York in 1845 and formed the Sozialreformassoziatin (Social Reform Association), which drew nearly a thousand members, making it the city's leading verein. The SRA soon had its own newspaper, the *Volks-Tribun*, and a Social Reform Halle on Grand Street that would remain one of Kleindeutschland's most important public meeting places for decades to come. Kriege backed Evans's free-land-for-settlers campaign, and soon land reform societies had germinated in New York and cities across the country. This popular demand for access to western lands partly accounts for the enthusiasm with which many New York workers greeted imperial expansion into Mexico and Oregon.[1]

---

1. New York workingmen's egalitarian imperialism was surpassed by editors, politicians, and businessmen who smelled profits from speculation, trade, and investments. Moses Beach, editor of the *Sun*, howled for annexation of Mexico in order to provide access to silver mines, banking rights in Mexico City, new commercial markets, and a fresh field for canal and railroad construction. Indeed New York City boasted the greatest concentration of those who insisted it was America's Manifest Destiny to seize the rest of the continent. "The extension of the republic to the uttermost extremities of this vast division of the earth," Bennett argued in the *Herald*, "must now be seen as natural, justifiable and safe as the extension of New York to the Harlem River."

For most city workers, however, garnering western lands at gunpoint, while perhaps symbolically satisfying, remained basically irrelevant. Without government support—as yet nowhere in sight—escape to the West was utterly impractical. Indeed some critics, who believed emigration schemes sidestepped rather than confronted New York's housing problems, proposed tackling the land issue in the city itself. Mike Walsh, the Irish Protestant editor of the *Subterranean* (and Evans's sometimes ally), believed that urban crowding was "the cause of more vice and misery, more suffering in every way, sickness, debauchery, seduction, assaults, and even murder, than all other causes put together." But rather than blasting western monopolists, Walsh took aim at the most powerful landlords in New York City: Trinity Church and John Jacob Astor. Walsh declared Astor a "worthless wealthy drone" whose rent extortions amounted to a "legalized system of plunder," and Trinity's property, Walsh wrote in 1845, should be confiscated for public use, beginning with St. John's Park. To encourage the Common Council to action, he blazed a direct action trail by climbing over the park's fence and tromping on forbidden ground.

Astor's death in 1848 at the age of eighty-five provoked others to pointed commentary. Bennett reprinted Astor's will on the *Herald*'s front page and charged that at least half the estate's enormous value was unearned. It was, rather, a by-product of the general rise in the value of New York City real estate, which in turn was due primarily to improvements effected by the city's working people. Yet the millionaire's legacy—apart from a bequest of four hundred thousand dollars for an Astor Library—passed not to New Yorkers in general but to Astor's family, creating in the process a most unrepublican dynasty. Greeley took the occasion to propose limiting individual ownership of city land to a thousand acres. He also urged passage of an income tax law, on the grounds that it had been unjust for city government "to protect Mr. Astor's houses, lands, ships, stocks, etc.," without having exacted recompense from him commensurate to his income.

Such demands, which already transgressed the bounds of the politically possible, paled next to those promulgated by the Tenant League. In February 1848, with landlords cashing in on economic recovery and immigrant desperation, Irish radicals and native land reformers established what they hoped would become a citywide organization of wage-earning tenants. Its goal, they declared, was to attack the "system of landlordism" as "one of the most blighting curses that ever was inflicted on the human race." Specifically, the Tenant League called on the legislature to limit landlord profit from rents to 7 percent of the property's assessed valuation, guarantee security of possession to tenants who paid their "legal rents," impose a city tax of 3 percent on all unimproved lots (to discourage owners from keeping them off the market for speculative purposes), and halt the incorporation of building companies, which allowed combinations of capitalists to oppress the poor.

Picking up on Evans's ideas but applying them locally, the Tenant League urged New York City to sell its public "common lands" only to those who did not already own other lots; this would allow urban "homesteaders" to build their own houses on city soil. The league also asked the legislature to forbid the renting of cellar apartments and the building of rear houses that left no part of the lot uncovered. It called for repeal of the northward extension of the fire limits, calling it a "scheme of speculators" to push Irish shanty dwellers off leased land. It denounced Moving Day—still going strong—as a landlord trick to raise rents each May. It formed lodgers' leagues and kept track of landlords who evicted tenants and charged high rents, creating a counterpart to the land-lords' blacklist of delinquent tenants. Finally, it demanded the city establish a housing code and oversee landlord compliance.

The Tenant League proposals, which flew in the face of laissez-faire ideology and the interests of the wealthy, proved beyond the ability of the radicals to organize. There would be no direct collective confrontation by tenants of landlord power in this era. Poor people unable to keep up with burgeoning rents settled for individual but achiev-able tactics—fleeing without paying, or searching out ever more squalid quarters. But ideas like rent control and taxation of speculative profits had been placed on the metro-politan agenda. They'd be back.

TOWARD A COOPERATIVE METROPOLIS

In the meantime, the working-class quarters were afire with even more startling chal-lenges to the metropolitan status quo. For decades Europe had been buzzing with a vari-ety of "socialist" notions, nowhere more so than in Paris, where Charles Fourier's sweeping indictment of capitalist civilization as one based on fraud, waste, and exploita-tion resonated widely. So did his proposal that dissenters should withdraw into cooper-ative communities—"phalanxes," he called them—that would be the seeds of an alter-native society.

Fourierism had reached New York during the panic years, courtesy of Albert Bris-bane. The idealistic son of a wealthy upstate merchant and landowner, Brisbane was no intellectual; he always looked, said Whitman, "as if he were attempting to think out some problem a little too hard for him." But if his versions of Fourier's teachings were glib, he promulgated them with tremendous energy and swiftly won a crucial convert in Horace Greeley. During 1842 and 1843, the editor gave Brisbane regular access to the *Tribune*'s front page and added his own explanations and plaudits for Fourierism.

Horace Greeley was no socialist. A staunch Whig, he was convinced that capitalist growth would eventually benefit the working-class, that the interests of employers and employees were ultimately in harmony, and that strikes raised the specter of class con-flict and should be vigorously opposed. But Greeley was not prepared to dismiss depression-spawned misery as an inevitable by-product of the free market, and he refused to root the plight of wage-earners in their own moral deficiencies. Greeley reported so regularly on foul conditions in the capitalizing trades that his archrival, Bennett, took him to task in the *Herald* for "eternally harping on the misery, destitution and terrible sufferings of the poor of this city."

It was, however, primarily from the middling classes that Greeley and Brisbane won most support—from people who concurred with their analysis of the negative impact of the "system of Free Competition" on life in the city. Charles Dana, Greeley's assis-tant, deplored its economic fallout ("periodical crises and bankruptcies"), its psycho-logical repercussions ("killing cares, harassing anxieties, hopes blasted, and unforeseen reverses and ruin"), and its ethical iniquity (fostering selfishness and duplicity). Most alarming was its tendency to concentrate economic and political power in fewer and fewer hands. Fourier had predicted that capitalism would lead to "Commercial and Industrial Feudalism," with producers in bondage to large corporations and banking houses. His American disciples pointed to New York City, with its "ascendancy of a monied oligarchy and a commercial feudality" and attendant "degradation of the labor-ing classes," as clear vindication of the master's theories.

Greeley didn't buy Fourier's solutions, but he did believe that a moderate version, dubbed Associationalism, would sort out the problems of capitalist society without impinging on property rights or fueling class resentments. If artisans simply pooled their talents and money and established cooperative workshops, they could control their working conditions, retain the profits of their labor, preserve republican traditions of mutuality, and still survive in the larger free market economy.

As promulgated by middle-class activists, Associationalism drew some modest support from urban mechanics—a band of Brooklyn artisans organized the first American phalanx—and the city's most effective cooperative was established by professional musicians. In 1842 the men who played in local theaters created the New York Philharmonic, a self-governing and profit-sharing orchestra. The Philharmonic, significantly, was 42 percent German at its inception, a percentage that leapt to nearly three-quarters with the arrival of revolutionary exiles, who brought with them not only a proclivity for cooperatives but considerable experience in their formation.

When Louis Philippe abdicated in February of 1848, the Parisian working class, so instrumental in his overthrow, won establishment of a Second Republic with adult male suffrage. But socialist (or "red") republicans like Louis Blanc had pressed for more profound changes, including a guaranteed "right to work" in government-backed "cooperative" workshops. Blanc's message had wide appeal in 1848. The provisional government emptied Clichy prison of debtors and converted it to a cooperative association in which some two thousand tailors made uniforms for the new national guard. Soon saddlers, spinners, cabinetmakers, masons—eventually more than 120 Parisian trades—had formed nearly three hundred production cooperatives, which collectively enrolled some fifty thousand members. Some were brilliantly successful, others failed miserably, but all alarmed the moderate republican leadership and horrified the bourgeoisie. Few co-ops long survived the terrible "June Days" when barricades went up and workers battled the army until being crushed in fighting that killed or injured over ten thousand.

When the refugees from this and other upheavals poured into New York City, among their ranks was Wilhelm Weitling, a German tailor. Like thousands of his mobile countrymen, Weitling had spent time in Paris learning the skills of his trade and the language of socialism and had fought on the barricades in forty-eight. Now, in Manhattan, he proposed that New York workers create producer cooperatives, which would in turn sell their goods to a worker-run Trade-Exchange Bank. Co-op workers would be paid in paper money, valid in worker-run stores and warehouses, which would sell both finished products and raw materials. The profits gained from cutting out capitalists and middlemen would be plowed back into expanding the cooperative sector until, eventually, competitive capitalism would be superseded by a cooperative commonwealth. As vehicles for this transformation, Weitling launched the Arbeiterbund (Workers League) in 1849 and a newspaper called *Die Republik der Arbeiter (Worker's Republic)* the following year.

Weitling's initiatives resonated in New York's German community, where most people, whatever their politics, were culturally predisposed toward organizations. British radicals, too, were familiar with producers' cooperatives, which had been established in the north of England, and natives had already been inspired by the associationist and Fourierist movement of the mid-1840s.

Among the most powerful and militant groups to get behind the idea was the Turnverein—the gymnastics society—which combined a passion for physical culture with socialist activism. Thousands of Turners had fought in the 1848 uprisings. Now, as refugees, they formed the New Yorker Socialistischen Turnverein, whose newspaper, the *Turn-Zeitung*, promoted a wide range of radical programs, including Weitling's. Together with English Chartists, Irish nationalists, and American Associationalists, the Germans set to work establishing cooperatives, and soon Manhattan blossomed with associations of tailors, cabinetmakers, upholsterers, cigarmakers, confectioners, shipwrights, bakers, shoemakers, and grocers.

In addition, the activists combined cooperative formation with labor organizing. In 1850, inspired by the ongoing degradation of the trades and by an inflationary spiral touched off by an influx of California gold that sent prices and rents climbing, newcomers and old-timers alike resurrected New York City's union movement, all but demolished by the 1837–43 depression. (The *Turn-Zeitung* ran a series of historical articles informing readers about the 1830s labor movement in their adopted city.) This combination of resurgent unionism and militant cooperationism touched off an "uprising"— replete with mass rallies, marches on City Hall, and some bloody confrontation with the forces of order—that in a very modest way echoed the stormy June Days of Paris.

"WE DID NOT EXPECT TO FIND IN THIS FREE COUNTRY A RUSSIAN POLICE"

In March 1850 German cabinetmakers fanned out through the working-class wards, posting handbills in immigrant boardinghouses calling for a union and a strike. In short order two thousand had walked off work, marched around the laboring districts in grand parades, and forced many masters to increase wages and change work rules. By April unions had blossomed in almost every trade. Greeley reported on their meetings—the just-minted New-York Printers Union elected him its president—and promoted the new cooperatives as well. Weitling too was everywhere, giving speeches, penning exhortations in the *Republik der Arbeiter*. By month's end he had brokered formation of a Central Commission of the United German Trades, comprised of seventeen unions representing forty-five hundred members.

The Irish community's dander was up too. Irish tailors and hatters flocked to labor organizations or organized them where they didn't exist. Irishmen were prominent in initiatives by blacksmiths, boilermakers, porters, shoemakers, and construction workers. The *Irish-American* came out for co-ops, declaring that "the principles of Association, can, alone" better the conditions of labor. Unskilled workers took the biggest steps forward. Back in 1843 Irish builders had helped establish the Laborers Union Benevolent Association, New York's first mutual aid society by and for the unskilled. By 1850 it had enlisted over six thousand workers—many of them famine refugees, many with organizational skills honed in battling landlords. By far the largest organization of wage earners in the city, it supported the striking craft workers and called its own men out on behalf of higher wages and an end to the sweating system in the building trades.

Bosses and businessmen were convinced this upheaval was the work of outside agitators—Bennett's *Herald* blamed the "vast importations of foreign socialists"—and indeed the overseas influence was decisive. But these "alien" ideas had local analogues. It was, after all, the "American" Brotherhood of the Union that in 1850 denounced the competition fostered by "capitalists, monopolists and tyrants" as tending to "divide, distract, and degrade Labor, and render the laborer and the mechanic a mere tool of those whose only God is Gold."

During the upheaval, workers strove with considerable success to overcome national divisions. Many remembered 1846, when five hundred Irish laborers at the new Atlantic Docks had struck for an eighty-seven-cent hour and a ten-hour day, only to be replaced by greenhorn Germans provided to boss stevedores by the elite German Society, to the fury of German workers. Cabinetmakers issued their constitution in German, French, and English versions ("for the accommodation of all nations") and conducted proceedings in several languages. German shoemakers forbade members to scab on their English brethren and adopted parallel wage demands. In virtually none of these cases, however, did labor ecumenicism stretch far enough to embrace African Americans or women.

New York's white male workers of the world united more formally on June 5, 1850, when eighty-three delegates, representing seventy unions and twenty-eight reform groups, formed the Industrial Congress. The new organization sought an eight-hour day, a minimum wage on public works projects, and direct city hiring of workers rather than the use of private contractors. It also backed the land reformers' initiatives, favoring a homestead law to open the West and a housing law at home to oversee construction and inspection of tenements to ensure they met appropriate standards of public health. Industrial Congress delegates also urged the municipal government to foster cooperatives, establish a labor exchange, and build reading rooms and public baths throughout the city. Such demands would remain at the core of New York's labor movement for the remainder of the century.

The Industrial Congress also supported embattled strikers. On July 10, 1850, a mass meeting of German, Irish, and American tailors proposed a scale of prices, and on the fifteenth some nine hundred tailors turned out to enforce it. On July 22 three hundred strikers, most Germans, marched to the Nassau Street offices of Longstreet and Company, one of New York's largest clothing manufacturers, a firm notorious for low wages and antiunionism. A brawl ensued. Police waded in with nightsticks and arrested the strikers. Organized labor swung into action. On the twenty-seventh thousands swarmed to City Hall Park for a rally. Radicals and unionists denounced the police ("We did not expect to find in this free country a Russian police," declared the Central Committee), and the Industrial Congress started a campaign to boycott any clothing firm that rejected the tailors' bill of prices. At another City Hall rally, on August 3, some went farther and called for a general strike. If butchers and bakers were to cut off supplies, "then the aristocrats will all starve," one militant argued, for "they are the drones and the idlers."

On August 4 three hundred German tailors marched to 38th Street and Ninth Avenue, where strikebreaking subcontractors were at work. There, according to the *Staats-Zeitung*, police attacked the tailors; according to English papers, tailors ransacked the nonunion outfit. All agreed that a melee ensued, in which two tailors were killed and dozens severely wounded. Thirty-nine unionists were convicted of rioting and dispatched to prison. For the first time in U.S. history, urban American workers had died at the hands of the forces of order in a trade dispute. The event only outraged and strengthened the strikers. By month's end almost every employer had come to terms with the union, and three thousand German and Irish tailors had formed a Cooperative Union Tailoring Establishment.

But this would be cooperation's high-water mark. Marx and Engels—Weitling's opponents in the European radical wars—had derided such efforts as utopian wishful thinking, and in New York, certainly, their tough-minded analysis proved correct. Businessmen attacked cooperative shops as the opening wedge of socialism. Wholesalers refused to buy their goods. Banks denied them capital or credit. The legislature wouldn't grant co-ops the legal protections it afforded corporations, leaving individual members liable for collective losses. And with artisan-run shops unwilling to slash their own pay to subsistence levels, they were unable to compete with capitalists willing and able to exploit cheap immigrant outworkers.

By 1852 such obstacles had become evident to all, and mass defections produced a general collapse. Those co-ops that survived did so by accepting individualistic approaches. The one thousand members of Industrial Home Owners Society Number One (1849), determined to escape the orbit of Manhattan land monopolists, bought a 367-acre tract in Westchester County along the New Haven Railroad line, divided up the land into a gridwork of quarter-acre parcels, then distributed plots by lot. As of 1854 these suburban pioneers had built over three hundred homes, planted shade trees, built a commercial section around the railroad station, and incorporated their community as Mount Vernon. This was the kind of land reform that bankers and builders could live with, and legislators had no hesitation in authorizing such associations to incorporate; by 1852 there were nearly seventy. In 1859, similarly, Germans set up the Deutsche Sparbank, and within a year ten thousand depositors—the majority of them tailors, shoemakers, cabinetmakers, and grocers—had put in $2.5 million. For now, the most "cooperative" enterprises would be the corporations themselves, but the vision of a cooperative municipality survived and would be resuscitated repeatedly.

The unions proved far more durable. Some, on winning their immediate goals, did lapse into dormancy or continue on as mutual benefit societies only. But with employers constantly reneging on recent agreements, and inflation biting deeply into wages (the cost of necessities rose 30 percent between 1853 and 1854), unions old and new continued to launch strikes. The mid-1850s witnessed initiatives by omnibus drivers, horsecar drivers on the Third Avenue Railroad, pilots of the Union Ferry Company, Erie Railroad workers, hatmakers, cigarmakers, coopers, printers (now part of a nationwide organization, their local known as Typographical Union No. 6), hotel waiters, drygoods clerks, housepainters, machinists, carpenters, gilders, typesetters, and the German Pianomakers Union of New York City, proud possessors of the flag carried by journeyman pianomakers of Paris "upon the barricades during the stormy days of the French Revolution."

Good interethnic relations remained an important goal. The Longshoremen's United Benevolent Society, formed in 1852, had fourteen hundred members by 1854. Though overwhelmingly Irish, the Longshoremen's Union boasted a banner decorated with the flags of France, Germany, the Netherlands, Sweden, Ireland, Denmark, Hungary, and Italy, all bound together under an American flag and the word "Unity." African Americans, again, were conspicuously excepted.

Many, though by no means all, of these strikes were successful. Influential bourgeois opinion tolerated nonviolent protests; there was so much money floating around that union demands seemed both legitimate and affordable. As *Harper's* put it in the summer of 1853: "It is reasonable and natural, that in view of the splendid trappings of our growing houses, and our metropolitan hotels, that the gas-fitters, and cordwainers and ladies' shoemakers, and saloon-servants should hold out their hands for their share of the excess."

Many unionists accordingly stuck to fighting for wages and work rules and avoided larger political initiatives: this was the guiding philosophy of a new central labor congress established in 1853, the Amalgamated Trades Convention. However, others continued to believe that only broad-based pressure on city and state authorities would effect fundamental change.

Joseph Weydemeyer was among the leaders of those calling for creation of a full-fledged labor party. Newly arrived in 1851, Weydemeyer was a former Prussian army officer who had been converted to socialism and was now a close colleague of Marx and Engels. In New York, Weydemeyer first wrote for the *Turn-Zeitung*, then (by January 1852) established *Die Revolution*, which that spring published Marx's masterly postmortem of the 1848 Revolution, *The Eighteenth Brumaire of Louis Bonaparte*.

In March 1853 Weydemeyer put out a call "To the Workers of All Trades!" for a March meeting at Mechanics Hall, to which eight hundred German-American housepainters, tailors, shoemakers, cabinetmakers, cigarmakers, Turners, and members of Weitling's Workers League responded. Those assembled endorsed formation of the Amerikanische Arbeiterbund (American Workers League). It issued a call for what by now had become the standard set of working-class cultural, political, and economic demands. These included the ten-hour day, abolition of child labor, free higher education and day care, opposition to temperance, enactment of a mechanic's lien law, unification of workers across national lines, and establishment of political clubs in working-class wards in order to "strive for the organization of the working class into a cohesive and independent political party." The organization established a base of support in Kleindeutschland and German communities in Brooklyn, Williamsburgh, and Staten Island but failed to reach much beyond them, although an Irish Societies Convention also emerged in 1853 to push for some of the same reforms.

Though nothing like the scenarios envisioned by enthusiastic immigrant revolutionaries would come to pass, their campaigns, coupled with the Astor riot and patently appalling slum conditions, would have a tremendous impact on reform-minded members of the city's upper classes, the men and women who though reaping the benefits of the boom were increasingly alarmed by some of its consequences.

44

Into the Crazy-Loved
Dens of Death

As New York's propertied classes surveyed the new metropolitan landscape, their pride in the city and its power was laced with a sour frustration, even revulsion. All around them stretched noisome urban marchlands where the writ of gentility hadn't run in years—Five Points, Corlear's Hook, Dutch Hill, the black enclave around Bancker Street, Kleindeutschland, the Hudson River waterfront, and the sprawling eastside industrial precincts between 14th and 23rd streets—nurseries every one of unionism, radicalism, Catholicism, pugilism, vice, squalor, and disease. Take care, respectable citizens, when you descend into these haunts of "rum-degraded human beings," warned Solon Robinson in *Hot Corn* (1854), a popular collection of sunlight-and-shadow vignettes. "You may meet someone, perhaps a man, perhaps a woman, who in their drunken frenzy may thrust you, for the very hatred of your better clothes, or the fear that you have come to rescue them from their crazy-loved dens of death."

In fact no part of town seemed safe anymore. Prostitutes, homeless urchins, vagabonds, beggars, and other "social rats" had free run of the streets, and legislators investigating conditions in Corlear's Hook worried that the cancerous horrors of the slums were spreading relentlessly through New York's "veins and arteries." If nothing were done, they continued, "the heart and limbs of the city will sooner or later suffer, as surely as the vitals of the human system must suffer by the poisoning or disease of the smallest vehicle." Once bucolic suburbs weren't immune from infection either, thanks to the ease of travel by railroad and steamboat. On summer Sundays and holidays, growled George Templeton Strong, "the civic scum" washed over Long Island, Staten Island, and New Jersey. "All conveniently accessible hotels and boarding houses are overrun by the vermin that hot weather roasts out of its homes in towns." Most of his friends, Strong added, never went out at night without a revolver.

Every year, indeed, brought shocking new testimony—from physicians, health inspectors, hospitals and medical dispensaries, orphanages, courts, police officials, and legislative commissions—that confirmed a horrifying expansion of poverty and disease and crime in the metropolis. Yet concerned elites were no longer certain what they could or should do about it. Many held fast to traditional moralizing while others found the pressure of circumstances (and working-class radicalism) forcing them to reconsider some cherished assumptions about the causes of poverty and the role of government in responding to it.

"PENITENTIAL TEARS"

The merchants and industrialists who ran the Tract Society and Bible Society continued trying to convert tenement dwellers, particularly Catholic ones, to Protestant piety and bourgeois social virtues, though increasingly they shifted from relying on volunteers (who found the immigrant localities "very repulsive") to using full-time salaried workers. To churn out bulk shipments of Holy Writ for Sunday schools, poorhouses, prisons, orphanages, and immigrant depots—and to manage what was increasingly a worldwide crusade—the American Bible Society erected a grand new Bible House that took up the entire block between Third and Fourth avenues and 8th and 9th streets.

The Home Missionary Society similarly kept on spreading gospel civilization to heathen savages from the African veldt to the American West and working for the Christian redemption of New York City. They were joined in this by Episcopalians (who revived their Missionary Society) and Congregationalists (Beecher's Plymouth Church opened several waterfront missions), but the boldest initiative came from the Ladies' Home Missionary Society (LHMS) of the Methodist Episcopal Church.

In 1850, backed by wealthy contributors like Daniel Drew and Anson G. Phelps, the LHMS opened a Five Points Mission in a rented room diagonally across from the infamous "Old Brewery." There, under the leadership of the Rev. Louis M. Pease, the ladies ran prayer meetings and Bible study classes, opened a charity day school, sponsored temperance speakers, and went out to comfort the sick. Closely attuned to the virtues of publicity, they issued regular accounts of their work—filled with stories of miraculous conversions and deathbed repentances—and on Thanksgiving Day paraded hundreds of scrubbed Sunday school students before benefactors. Then the ladies fed their charges turkey dinners, inaugurating a ritual that would lead, a decade later, to Thanksgiving's establishment as an official (and feminized) holiday.

In 1852, drawing again on the ample resources of Phelps and Drew and on a thousand-dollar contribution from the Common Council, the LHMS purchased the Old Brewery itself and announced that the notorious "pest-house of sin" would be replaced with a proper "school of virtue." To dramatize its demolition, the LHMS ran candle-lit tours of the rookery's fetid interior, "where miserable men, women, and children . . . moodily submitted to the gaze of the strangers in that community of degraded outcasts." The residents were then evicted and the building razed; in its place rose the new Five Points Mission, complete with chapel, schoolrooms, baths, and twenty apartments for the homeless—a bow to the poor's material needs.

Some missionaries learned unexpected things in the working-class quarters. One day, the Rev. Pease was preaching to a group of "profligate" women—"respectably, some even genteelly dressed," he remembered, "yet their character was readily perceived." Suddenly they turned on him. "Don't talk to us of death and retribution and perdition before us; we want no preacher to tell us all that," they cried. "Give us work and wages!" These "sotted wretches," Pease discovered, could not afford to pay the security deposit clothing manufacturers required before handing out garments to sew. Pease decided to help. Converting the mission's evening prayer room into a daytime sewing workshop, he collected the piecework himself and offered employment to all who would pledge themselves to temperance and a moral life. The LHMS, believing Pease had gone too far, denounced him as a Fourierist and severed their relationship. But Pease won the backing of the Episcopal Church of the Ascension, and in 1854 his new Five Points House of Industry set up shop on Anthony Street.

By the late 1850s there were seventy-six missions in the metropolis, almost saturating the working-class quarters, yet for all this earnest activity, there was a growing sense that it was little more than an expensive dead end. A vigorous and self-assured working-class culture seemed to shrug off evangelical efforts as easily as did Middle Eastern Muslims. In 1855, when New York's population was 629,924, there were only 138,678 communicants in metropolitan churches.

And of these over half, 78,488, were Catholics, a statistic not calculated to warm Protestant hearts. The Irish, long inured to proselytizing by British Protestants, kept evangelicals firmly at bay—a task made easier by the missionaries' obvious disdain for what they regarded as a cult of medieval superstition and idolatry. (In their determination to guard Christian souls from the clutches of Rome, evangelicals forbade inmates of their homes and shelters to see a priest, even if they were on their deathbeds.) Catholics boycotted "Old Pease's School," cursed the redoubtable ladies of the LHMS, and threatened bodily harm to representatives of the Tract Society.

Besides such grass-roots opposition, the evangelicals had the Catholic hierarchy to contend with. Redeeming the poor from "bondage" to Protestant charity was "the noblest work for Catholic charity," said their spokespaper *Freeman's Journal*, and the Church set out to establish a rival aid network. In 1846 Father Varela, pastor of Transfiguration, introduced the St. Vincent de Paul Society to New York City; other parishes quickly established chapters or started their own missions. In 1849 the Sisters of Mercy opened a House of Mercy, which accommodated two hundred destitute women each evening and gave food and clothing to great numbers of the needy. That same year Archbishop Hughes, infuriated that Protestant hospitals blocked priests from visiting Catholic patients, got the Sisters of Charity to launch St. Vincent's Hospital. (The German Sisters of the Poor would follow suit with St. Francis Hospital.) St. Vincent's charged a modest admission, in part to remove the stigma of receiving charity, and by 1858 a physician at New York Hospital admitted that "most of our domestic servants prefer" St. Vincent's.

Catholic and Protestant elites saw eye to eye, however, on the evils of demon rum, being dispensed (as of 1849) at 5,780 licensed liquor groceries, porter houses, taverns, and fancy saloons. The New-York Temperance Society and Bishop Hughes alike welcomed Cork's famous Father Theobald Mathew to Manhattan, where he spent much of a year preaching against alcohol and inspiring formation of the Roman Catholic Total Abstinence and Benevolent Society. Even pleasure-loving Knickerbocker patricians listened more attentively now to temperance claims that "the cheap wines of France" had been responsible for "insubordination and revolution" in 1848.

Yet here too reformers found themselves up against formidable opponents, starting with the immigrants themselves. When advocates opened a mission next door to a German beer garden in 1860, its outraged customers "evinced their displeasure by throwing water into the open windows, shouting, making noises in the hall, casting stones against the door, and other disorderly conduct; so that the aid of the police became necessary." In addition, alcohol purveyors ranging from merchant importers to waterfront barkeepers mobilized into a formidable pressure group—the Liquor Dealers Protective Union had eight hundred members by 1855—and sponsored mass meetings to mobilize antiprohibition sentiment.

Balked, temperance advocates turned to the state. "Ought law to conform to public sentiment," Horace Greeley rhetorically asked delegates assembled in 1853 for the World's Temperance Convention, "or ought law to be based upon essential righteousness, and then challenge a public sentiment to act in conformity therewith?" The reformers answered by successfully pressuring the state legislature into passing the 1855 Act for the Prevention of Intemperance, Paupers, and Crime, a law that, among other things, authorized keeping persons arrested for public drunkenness locked up until they agreed to testify as to the source of their intoxicant. The statute aroused immense hostility in New York City, touching off mass rallies at Tammany Hall and bringing declarations from Bennett's *Herald* that it would ruin New York business to the benefit of wet New Jersey. The mayor refused to enforce the law, and in 1856 the state appellate court declared it unconstitutional.

Setbacks in missionary and temperance work were accompanied by abject failure to check the spread of gambling. Jonathan Harrington Green, a reformed gambler turned professional lecturer on tricks of the sharpster's trade, helped set up a New York Association for the Suppression of Gambling (ASG) in 1850. The board of ministers and businessmen directed executive agent Green to undertake a thorough survey of the problem. He reported back that there were 6,126 gambling houses in town—defined broadly enough to include the first-class "hells" where rich merchants played faro in luxurious surroundings, the dimly lit "penny-poker dens" where small-time thieves congregated, the lottery offices, the policy offices, and indeed anywhere bets were placed, including ten-pin alleys, billiard rooms, saloons, cockfighting pits, and shooting galleries. Green also noted the rarity of arrests: in the previous six years a grand total of fifty-nine people had been indicted for gambling.

The ASG professed great concern about the impact of these establishments on vulnerable young men, and it was true enough that gambling, like much else in New York, had rapidly shifted its nature in recent years. In the past, most recreational betting had been done with peers; monies won generally remained in circulation within the neighborhood. Now much of the wagering went on in commercial settings, organized by oftunscrupulous professionals who lived off customers' losses. But Green and the ASG proved to be less troubled by gambling's impact on youths than by its consequences for employers. In general, they bemoaned the gambling-propagated lust for quick wealth that was undermining the industry and sobriety businessmen wanted in their labor force. In particular, they bewailed the rising number of gambling-addicted clerks who dipped into their employers' tills to make up losses.

Green's contemporary, a young merchant named George H. Petrie, had visited London for business and to see the Crystal Palace, discovered the Young Men's Christian Association there, and brought it back to New York in 1852 to "ralley around the young stranger and save him from the snares of this wicked city." With the help of Mercer Street Presbyterian's Rev. Isaac Ferris, Petrie set up a temporary sanctuary in two rooms on the third floor of the old New York City Lyceum at 659 Broadway. Clerical workers, many of them new to the city, flocked to the YMCA, attracted by its library and meeting place, network of friends and surrogate family, and help in finding housing, churches, and jobs with YMCA businessman backers. Such men, in turn, responded warmly to the argument (cogently expressed by the Rev. George W. Bethune at the second annual meeting in 1854) that the organization was "a principle of insurance to their interests," a way "to make their servants—I mean those who are in their employ—faithful to their duty."

For all its promise, the "Y"—which would itself evolve in unexpected directions—was not intended to transform the immigrant masses in the present but to contend with them in the future. It was wonderful, Bethune said, that "after all this infusion of foreign admixture, the Anglo-Saxon element pervade[s] and rules" New York, but maintaining that predominance required advance planning. The YMCA would train up what Bethune called a cadre of men "calm, resolute, armed, drilled and prepared for the fight, taking their position as the guardians of the city," but even if successful, such troops could have no immediate impact on a rapidly deteriorating situation.

"TO EXPEL IDLENESS AND BEGGARY FROM THE CITY"

The "scientific reformers" at the Association for Improving the Condition of the Poor were not doing much better than the moralizers they tended to belittle. By the early fifties the AICP, with roughly four thousand contributing members—including some of the greatest bankers, merchant princes, and industrialists of the day—was the most influential organization of its kind in New York. Its program of centralized philanthropy to manage city indigents was in full swing; nearly four hundred employed visitors had logged hundreds of thousands of visits; and executive secretary Robert Milham Hartley professed himself mightily pleased with the elaborate structure. "Its machinery," Hartley boasted, "though extensive, is easily managed, and works with admirable precision, economy and effect." Surely it couldn't fail "to expel idleness and beggary from the city." Here, he crowed, was America's answer to the recently published *Communist Manifesto*.

Hartley *had* succeeded in expelling many of the most wretched from the city, in a sense. They'd been swept from Manhattan's streets and dispatched to Blackwell's Island, by 1850 a 1.75-mile-long laboratory for scientific management of the classified poor. Yet no matter how many grand (and costly) new establishments got constructed on Blackwell's, they were immediately (and expensively) swamped with inmates, 60 percent of them Irish. Many were elderly discharged domestics who, having spent their lives in service, had no children to look after them nor community support networks to rely upon in their old age. Between 1853 and 1856, caring for the seven thousand people crammed into the new almshouse drove the costs of operation up by 240 percent, from $385,000 to $925,000.

The sick and immigrant poor, meanwhile, were shoehorned into Bellevue Hospital. Of the 3,728 admissions in 1850, 2,596 had been born in Ireland and only 647 were native born. A substantial minority were relegated to the floors until a new wing, added in 1855, brought the number of beds to twelve hundred; by the mid-1850s Bellevue was treating four to five thousand patients annually. The place had a fearsome reputation, however, partly because the private hospitals and other poor-relief institutions continued to dump their terminal cases there and then slander the facility for its mortality rate. Ardent efforts brought in-house deaths down somewhat, but in the late 1850s Bellevue remained rat-infested, lice-ridden, and, like many of the other overcrowded institutions, wracked by epidemics of puerperal fever (which carried off parturient women) and ophthalmia (which led to blindness in large numbers of children).

Public and private reformers made heroic efforts to respond to the crisis. A tiny smallpox hospital was opened on Blackwell's southern tip in 1848, then replaced by a much larger version in 1856. The Blackwell's Island Lunatic Asylum, a mammoth and intricately designed hospital at the northern apex, was the largest such institution in the country when it opened in 1839 but was quickly overburdened with inmates; it was replaced by two new buildings in the late 1840s. Three-fourths of these inmates were immigrants, two-thirds of whom were Irish. Insanity proved especially prevalent among young immigrant women, one sympathetic physician wrote, who were simply overwhelmed by "the combined moral and physical influences of their leaving the homes of their childhood, their coming almost destitute to a strange land, and often after great suffering."

The idle and dissolute—"paupers" and "vagrants"—were sent to the new (1855) workhouse, which reformers had been clamoring for for years. There they were set to productive labor, isolated from the respectable almshouse poor with whom they had once been promiscuously mixed. The utterly "debased" and "depraved" were incarcerated in the fortresslike penitentiary near the island's southern end, with one wing for males, another for females; at times, however, the crush of vagrants in the workhouse was so great that its overflow—twenty-five hundred people in 1851—had to be confined along with the convicts.

Most of these establishments imposed a rigorous and moralistic order on their "inmates." They required the able-bodied to work: men labored in the quarry, rowed ferryboats to the mainland, and were on occasion loaned out to clean sewers; women cooked, washed, ironed, sewed; expectant mothers scrubbed floors. But these tasks, originally intended to inculcate values while offsetting costs, soon degenerated into devices for maintaining discipline or imposing a punitive routine. Rehabilitation had given way to warehousing.

"IDLE AND VICIOUS CHILDREN OF BOTH SEXES"

The reform community's greatest efforts were devoted to rescuing children of the poor—now, more than ever, considered a threat to civic stability. In 1849 George Matsell, New York's chief of police, alerted residents to a "deplorable and growing evil" that threatened the very survival of the city. "I allude," he wrote, "to the constantly increasing number of vagrants, idle and vicious children of both sexes, who infest our public thoroughfares." The three-hundred-pound Matsell was detested in working-class neighborhoods—Mike Walsh called him "a degraded and pitiful lump of blubber and meanness"—but his warning inflamed the imaginations of middle- and upper-class reformers. The Rev. Edwin Chapin quite agreed that "the children of the Poor create an appeal to *prudential* considerations," as they "form a large proportion of those groups known in every city as 'The Dangerous classes.'"

By the late 1840s children under fifteen constituted almost one-third of the city's population (comparable to London's 31.9 percent though far more than Paris's 19.6 percent). The virtual disappearance of apprenticeship with its provision of room, board, and steady work had freed many from traditional constraints, and working-class families, who expected children to earn their keep from early on, routinely sent their young into unsupervised street trades.

Even more alarming than the swarms of children working the streets were those who lived on them as well. Many were orphans—poor parents often died young—but others simply didn't like working-class family life, with its enforced sharing and cooperation, its parental discipline, often its parental violence. The streets beckoned the discontented with their alluring range of things to buy and places to go; even boys with homes slept out for weeks at a time, swelling the ranks of vagrant children.

The AICP's solution was similar to the one they fashioned for adult immigrants: round the children up, then slot them, depending on character, into reformatories, schools, or bourgeois-type homes. To accomplish the first goal, the AICP drafted a model Truancy Law and, with help from the Female Guardian Society, got the state legislature to pass it in 1853. The law empowered police to arrest vagrant children between the ages of five and fourteen. If they proved to be orphans, they were to be made wards of the state and institutionalized. If not, they were to be turned over to their parents, who were enjoined to send them to school—an injunction given teeth by making school attendance a condition of family relief. If parents still failed to live up to their responsibilities, authorities were authorized to seize the children "and place them under better influences, till the claim of the parent shall be re-established by continued sobriety, industry and general good conduct."

The legislation was less effective than it might have been in banning children from the streets, as it was so harsh that in practice many policemen refused to make arrests. But those who were picked up in the dragnet got consigned to a range of specialized institutions.

The hard cases were packed off to the House of Refuge, founded in 1824 and still going strong, though newly relocated in 1854 to Randall's Island. There, isolated from the wicked city and adult prisoners alike, youthful vagrants were set to laboring alongside convicted juvenile delinquents and rebellious sons and defiant daughters who had been committed by their working-class parents. In the House of Refuge, the AICP noted approvingly, twelve-year-olds were "trained in habits of industry" by being compelled to make sixty pairs of ladies' shoes a day, which sold briskly in retail shops, undercutting adult shoemakers.

The AICP did worry, however, that inmates who were hardened reprobates would drag down into delinquency those who were as yet merely vagrant and neglected. So the organization proposed and helped institute the New York Juvenile Asylum (1851), dedicated to teaching disobedient and idle children "self-discipline of body, mind, and heart" and then apprenticing them to employers. The asylum, unfortunately, proved no more effective an agency of reform than did the House of Refuge, and it too came to serve primarily a custodial function.

The reformers vested their major hopes for saving the salvageable in the school system, which underwent a major reorganization in these years. The Public School Society, the private board that had been running the free schools with public money, was subordinated to, and then in 1853 subsumed by, the popularly elected Board of Education. The public system launched an ambitious building program, constructing some schools capable of holding a thousand or more, and hired women as teachers, to keep costs down. Most innovatively, the board, seeking to provide an alternative to theaters and saloons, provided an evening school program that by 1856 had enrolled nearly fifteen thousand, some four thousand of whom were females, taught in separate classes.

The board's pedagogical agenda remained that of the old Public School Society—the president announced in 1852 that he sought the "cultivation of habits of ready obedience"—and many of the new ward-school teachers, old PSS veterans, brought along their emphasis on mechanical memorization and Protestant indoctrination. The schools, accordingly, had a mixed record in accessing the immigrant poor. Over half of those registered never showed up, and perhaps fifty thousand went utterly unprovided for. What the institutions did best was protect and encourage children of middle-class character; youths who failed to measure up were weeded out rather than reformed.

The Sunday School Union had its own problems with the immigrant poor, though it did reaffirm (in 1856) its commitment to the "wretched progeny" of the "refuse population of Europe" as well as the "offcast children of American debauchery, drunkenness, and vice." However, as the union admitted, "our object has always been to reach the masses, but we cannot get to them." More and more, the Sunday schools became adjuncts of middle-class congregations, and most outposts in the working-class districts were eventually written off as failures.

The era's most creative educational initiatives were aimed at older youths and adults. In 1846 the Board of Education's Townsend Harris, a prosperous crockery merchant, proposed establishing a college for those who "have been pupils in the common schools." It would offer studies relevant for the "active duties of operative life" rather than the classics courses Columbia and NYU considered preparatory for "the Pulpit, Bar, or the Medical profession." The Free Academy was authorized in 1847 by an act of the legislature, but under pressure from "friends of the present expensive colleges [who] dislike it and are trying to crush it," its fate was made conditional on winning a referendum.

In a whirlwind thirty-day campaign, Tammany posted placards all over town urging a "Free Academy for the poor man's children" while Whigs opposed the idea on several grounds. Some complained of the cost. Others suggested that workers lacked the intellectual capacity to absorb higher education or, conversely, that they *would* absorb it and then become "too proud of their superior education to work either as clerks or mechanics, or to follow any active business except what is termed professional." After all, as "Plain Truth" argued, "in every organism there must be diversity of members. There will be head, and hands, and—we must venture to say it—feet, too." Finally there was the blanket ideological objection that the proposed expansion of free public services was really the opening wedge of a "mongrel Fourierism."

Overriding these plaints, the citizenry passed the Free Academy referendum by 19,305 to 3,409. Architect James Renwick was set to designing a Gothic structure on Lexington and 23rd, and at the formal opening, in January 1849, a speaker hailed the "system of popular education for the common man" as solid evidence of the "growing democratization of American life." Mike Walsh denied this, predicting that few laboring-class children would ever grace its Gramercy Park precincts, for most could not afford not to work, and the academy, while free, offered no stipends. Walsh's prediction proved only slightly overstated. Talented sons of laborers, cartmen, craftsmen, and clerks did enter (though few from the ranks of Irish or German immigrants), but most were indeed forced by indigence to drop out and take jobs. The vast majority of graduates were scions of merchants, ministers, lawyers, doctors, brokers, or clergymen, and most were of English, Dutch, or Huguenot descent. Nor were any graduates women, no matter what their ethnic and class credentials, for despite an 1854 legislative grant of authority to extend free higher education to females, raucous opposition within and outside the board blocked formation of the female Normal School (later Hunter College) for another decade and a half.

Peter Cooper set out to do better. Long inspired by the adult education programs offered by lyceums and mechanics' institutes in the United States and abroad, Cooper, while PSS leader, had helped inaugurate the public schools' evening classes back in 1848. Now he decided to erect an institute that would offer free education in the mechanical arts and sciences, with an emphasis on practical education, for men and women of the working classes. In 1853, on a plot of land between Astor Place, Third Avenue, Seventh Street, and Fourth Avenue, he laid the cornerstone for Cooper Union; he spent $600,000 completing it over the next five years. Its open-admission night classes were available to all comers, regardless of previous education; those lacking rudimentary knowledge were sent to the public evening schools. Two thousand people responded avidly—clerks, salesmen, bookkeepers, machinists, carpenters, and cabinetmakers predominated—filling every class immediately, though over six hundred soon dropped out. The courses were coed—though 95 percent of the students were male—and Cooper also opened a daytime Women's School of Design to teach engraving, lithography, drawing, and painting on china. Cooper Union's program was strictly nonsectarian, despite Cooper's strong history of opposition to Catholics' receiving state funds for education, and the school drew high praise from Bishop Hughes. The Great Hall, to the alarm of some, became a place where civic issues were debated from many (including radical) points of view. And its well-stocked reading room—unlike those of the neighboring Astor Library (which opened at 6th and Lafayette in 1854) or the Mercantile Library (now housed in the old Astor Opera House) or the New York Society Library (newly installed on University Place in 1856)—was kept open until ten P.M., making it accessible to working people.

WESTWARD HO! (CHILDREN'S VERSION)

Despite the defects of existing child-saving programs, the Rev. Charles Loring Brace insisted that this was a time for decisive action, not despair. Brace believed, as did the moralizers and schoolmen, that the "existence of such a class of vagabond, ignorant, ungoverned children" represented a massive danger "to the value of property" and even "the permanency of our institutions." But his mission work with the Rev. Pease in the Five Points had convinced him that "the old technical methods—such as distributing tracts, and holding prayer-meetings, and scattering Bibles"—were now useless. "The neglected and ruffian class which we are considering are in no way affected directly by such influences as these. New methods must be invented for them."

Brace also dissented sharply from the AICP approach. The street urchin, Brace agreed, having "grown up ignorant of moral principle as any savage or Indian," would eventually "poison society," yet while fearing those he called "barbarians" and "street rats" Brace also admired the "independence and manly vigor" of the newsboys, bootblacks, match sellers, even the petty thieves. Their creative entrepreneurial energy suggested they might be little businessmen in the making—if only they could be instilled with a " 'sense of property,' and the desire of accumulation, which, economists tell us, is the base of all civilization."

Clearly the first step was to isolate urchins from their working-class milieu—the "engine runners, cock fighters, pugilists, and pickpockets," the "low theatres, to which he is passionately attached," the "vicious career of [his] parents." But the next step, Brace insisted, was not to place them in asylums or schools, whose obsession with "drilled and machine-like" conformity would only break their spirit and render them "unused to struggle."

The better solution was to extract them from the city altogether and ship them off to the interior, where they would be boarded in "kind Christian *homes in the country*." This would submit them to the moral tutelage of some pure woman: "No influence, we believe, is like the influence of a *Home*." It would also set them to work, having the additional advantage of sending "laborers where they are in demand" while relieving "the over-crowded market in the cities." Clumped in New York, the children were a festering menace; dispersed over the continent, their individualism and opportunism could be put to good account.

To this end, in 1853 Brace set up the Children's Aid Society, on Astor Place on Fourth Avenue (near the headquarters of the AICP and the YMCA). At first, after screening both children and potential families, it shipped youths to farms in the nearby countryside. Later, when the railroad system penetrated deeper into the interior, they were sent all the way to Illinois, Michigan, and Iowa. By 1860 the society had placed out 5,074.

Brace's approach attracted a good deal of support from socially prominent merchants, bankers, and lawyers (though not, despite some help from the Unitarians, from the ministerial community, a sign of the growing secularization of the reform movement). Working people were of a more mixed mind. The program had its appeals: enterprising youths were attracted to its promise of a western adventure; emigration schemes were in the air; and the Irish, in particular, were well accustomed to seasonal migrations of adolescents as farm laborers and domestic servants. On the other hand, there was a widespread (and often justified) sense that the children were being exploited as cheap labor by shrewd western farmers. And unlike the land reformers' voluntary homesteading plan, the Children's Aid Society approach had the unappealing aspect of something *done* to one. Moreover, just as African Americans had long resisted Colonization Society efforts to "solve" the racial problem by deporting them en masse, Catholics vigorously resented a policy that seemed, in the words of the *Freeman's Journal*, to be "seizing them in the name of charity and of religion, and carrying them away to be brought up aliens to the Catholic faith."[1]

The New York Archdiocese, accordingly, redoubled its own children-saving efforts. By 1858 the assets of its massive parochial school system were valued at over two million dollars, and soon there were nearly fifteen thousand attending twelve select schools and thirty-one free schools. Some of these were artfully counterplaced: when crowds of

---

1. The anti-Catholic animus hampered even Brace's more radical efforts. Having explored the Italian section of the Five Points and discovered that poor Italian parents were indenturing their children to "Padrones" who exploited them as organ grinders, bootblacks, and flower-sellers, the CAS tried to break the traffic and started a night school for Italian children in 1855. But parents kept their children away in fear they would be converted to Protestantism.

Catholic parents prevented children from entering Pease's House of Industry in the fall of 1853, they redirected their youngsters to a parochial school that had been deliberately set up nearby. New orphanages rose, to prevent Catholic children being consigned to Protestant asylums and "brought up in hatred of that religion which was the only and last consolation of their dying parents!" The most spectacular countermeasure was launched in 1863 when the enormous Catholic Protectory was inaugurated on 114 acres of farmland in the Bronx—a rural training center where city boys could be rescued from the wicked city and the Children's Aid Society alike.

ENTER THE ENVIRONMENTALISTS

In 1842 John H. Griscom, a learned and pious Quaker physician who served on the AICP's first executive committee, issued a scorching report on sanitary conditions in the city. Griscom had seen the effects of living in cellars and tenements close up during his years of service at the New York Dispensary and New York Hospital, and after he was appointed to John Pintard's old post of city inspector in 1842, he embarked on a comprehensive survey of city health.

Griscom concluded that a good deal of metropolitan mortality was avoidable. To his mind, "first among the most serious causes of disordered general health" was the city's crowded and poorly ventilated housing, especially its rear courts and cellars (he found some that housed as many as forty-eight persons), and he bitterly condemned the cupidity of those who had taken advantage of abject destitution to convert their basements "into living graves for human beings." Griscom's second-ranked killer was the omnipresent filth, which resulted from obscenely overused facilities (often fifty people shared a single privy) and from abysmal drainage and sewerage.

After carefully demonstrating the connection between unsanitary living conditions and poor health, Griscom argued for preventive action. Like his predecessors, he wanted common nuisances eliminated. But he went farther, citing studies of Edwin Chadwick and other English health reformers, and urged construction of a comprehensive sewage and drainage system and free provision of Croton water to the entire population. Griscom also sought public regulation of housing. Going far beyond the existing fire-related statutes, he asked for legislation to protect residents "from the pernicious influence of badly arranged houses and apartments." Griscom wanted to require landlords to provide tenants with adequate space and fresh air (at least ten cubic feet per minute per adult). He urged banning the use of cellars, limiting the number of residents per building, and holding landlords accountable for keeping buildings clean. To ensure compliance, he proposed replacing politically appointed health wardens with nonpolitical medical experts—a Health Police, authorized to make routine inspections and, if necessary, close down places found unfit for human habitation.

The aldermen did not take kindly to Griscom's proposals, which among other things would lop off lots of patronage positions, and the doctor was not reappointed as city inspector. But a group of reformers including Peter Cooper put together a fund to publish an expanded version of his 1842 study, and *The Sanitary Condition of the Laboring Population of New York*—a landmark in the history of public health—came out in 1845.

Among Griscom's many striking departures from conventional bourgeois wisdom was his refusal to blame the poor for their wretched housing. He knew that lack of fresh water and adequate sanitation made it impossible for residents to keep clean and pious homes, even if they wanted to, and he even declined to blame laboring men for escaping from such hovels to the grogshops. For Griscom, dirt was a symptom of poverty, not its cause.

On the other hand, he didn't blame the rich, as the land reformers did. Rather he appealed to them to provide decent housing, not just as "a measure of humanity, of justice to the poor," but as a matter of self-interest. Bad housing meant sick workers, and sick workers meant lower profits, higher relief outlays, and higher taxes. Ultimately, too, slums fostered the growth of "a class in the community more difficult to govern, more disposed to robbery, mobs, and other lawless acts, and less accessible to the influence of religious and moral instruction." Griscom was convinced that such rational appeals would have weight because the problem seemed to stem from lack of understanding: "One half of the world does not know how the other half lives."

The comfortable half didn't pay much attention to Griscom, however, until rudely reminded of the costs of inaction. In June 1849, scant weeks after the riot in Astor Place, James Gilligan, an Irish laborer, was found dead, sprawled on the dirt floor of a rear basement room he shared with four women on Orange Street; by next day three of his fellow tenants were dead too.

The previous December the packet ship *New York* had arrived in quarantine from Le Havre with cholera as a passenger. Three hundred steerage customers had been hastily sequestered in commandeered customs warehouses, but many escaped to the city in small boats. Within a week cases had begun appearing in crowded immigrant boardinghouses. The cold winter had slowed its spread; now the disease roused itself and leapt out of the Points, sending the city into plague mode. The Board of Health struggled to find space for a makeshift hospital; turned down everywhere, they seized a colored public school. Railroads and steamships pulled in with no passengers aboard. Hotels emptied out. Business stopped.

The wealthy escaped to the country, leaving the disease to claim over five thousand of their poorer compatriots (another 642 died in Brooklyn). Bodies lay in the streets for days. Eventually they were rowed over to Randall's Island and dumped in an open trench, at which point a gruesome public health device came into play as thousands of rats swam over and gnawed the flesh from the carcasses before they rotted.

As in 1832, many declared the cholera God's retribution for sin—notably that of being Catholic. (Had not over 40 percent of the casualties been born in Ireland?) Indeed the *Herald* was amazed to find victims "among the respectable, *including even ladies*." Overall, however, the cholera—together with the Astor riot and rising radicalism—strengthened the hand of those who argued that moralizing was no longer a sufficient response to social crisis. The relationship between ethics and environment had to be reconceptualized as an interactive rather than a one-way affair. "The physical and moral are closely allied," announced the liberal Protestant *New York Independent* in 1850, trying out the new thinking: "The habit of living in squalor and filth engenders vice, and vice, on the other hand, finds a congenial home in the midst of physical impurities." Poor people tended to be sick people, a group of state officials noted, and vice versa. Even Hartley began to temper his moralizing and to admit that substandard housing, inadequate sanitation, and other environmental or circumstantial factors might be causes as well as consequences of poverty.

The implication for action, Charles Loring Brace concluded robustly, was that "Material Reform and Spiritual Reform must mutually help one another." But the for-

Another pig round-up, from *Frank Leslie's Illustrated Newspaper*, August 13, 1859.
(© Collection of The New-York Historical Society)

mer would prove as difficult to obtain as the latter, especially as the municipality and
state, smitten with laissez-faire, had dismantled much of their eighteenth-century regulatory apparatus. Still, the patent social breakdown registered by the crudest of social
indicators—corpses stacked like cordwood—gave newly enthused reformers the chance
to make a considerable impact on the urban landscape.

Starting with hogs. The 1849 catastrophe jolted the city into taking up arms once
again against the immemorial foe. Overcoming sometimes violent resistance by impoverished owners, the police flushed five to six thousand pigs out of cellars and garrets and
drove an estimated twenty thousand swine north to the upper wards that summer. (At
the same time, in an exterminating frenzy spurred on by municipal bounties, 3,520 stray
dogs were killed in the streets, mostly by small boys with clubs.) The authorities, moreover, kept up their campaign year after year, banishing from lower Manhattan (in
1851–2) all bone-boiling works (along with the putrefying carcasses piled high in
their yards). In the late 1850s Hog Town was invaded and the westside piggery complex
between 50th and 59th streets dismantled. By 1860 New York's porkers had been
definitively exiled north of 86th Street and transformed into a distinctively "uptown"
menace.

Cows were another story. Absent refrigeration, the city's on-the-hoof meat supply
had to be kept close at hand. Besides, the Common Council was reluctant to limit the
entrepreneurship of powerful butchers. An 1853 ordinance did ban cattle drives south
of 42nd Street (at least in the daytime), but that still left 206 slaughterhouses open for
business, which butchered over 375,000 animals annually (usually draining excess blood
to the gutters). Then there were the eleven public markets, the 531 private markets or
butcher shops, the tanneries with their piles of putrid hides, and the beasts—usually
five thousand a year—who simply dropped dead in the streets from natural causes. In
August 1853 alone, the city's contract scavenger reported clearing away 690 cows, 577

horses, 883 dogs, 111 cats, fourteen hogs, and six sheep—plus 1,303 tons of "butchers offal" and sixty-two tons of refuse bones from the slaughterhouses.

Then there was shit. The mercantile boom had vastly expanded the horse-based transport system—in 1854, there were 22,500 horses pulling public vehicles alone and countless others hauling private ones—collectively plopping tons of manure in the streets each day. Humans contributed their share via thousands of overflowing privies and cesspools, especially in the densely overpopulated tenement districts, where absentee landlords were disinclined to waste profits on tenant amenities, and tenants lacked money to pay privy cleaners. Where night scavengers did make pickups, they often spilled much of their cargo along the lanes as they jounced their way to the waterfront. There they dumped their loads onto (or off of) the wharves, where poorly designed slips held the effluent fast to the shore and were themselves rendered almost impassable to vessels, to say nothing of the stench.

That New York was drowning in garbage was in large measure a by-product of the explosive and unregulated growth that few were willing to impede. But the problem was compounded by the city's having turned street cleaning over to private contractors in 1842, convinced this would bring improved service and lower costs. In the real world, collection contracts were often handed out as political plums to recipients who felt little compunction to make more than token swabs on the main streets; or they were awarded to the lowest bidders, often unprincipled sorts who hadn't the slightest intention of doing any work whatever.

Ironically, Croton water, so recently hailed as savior, only made matters worse. The rich built water closets in profusion, which when flushed with Croton water overflowed their cesspools even more rapidly. They consequently clamored for the right to plug directly into the sewers, which had been built for draining storm water from the streets. In 1845 the Common Council permitted such hookups. However, the pipes had been laid at right angles or awkward grades that could handle swift-moving rain runoff but couldn't cope with thick and sluggish wastewater. The result: impenetrable blockages, clogged pipes, and rampant flooding.

This problem was in turn resolved—in part—by building new sewers. The drawback here was that sewers, financed by assessments on adjacent property owners, were built only when resident proprietors or speculative realtors petitioned for them. Unlike the water supply, which had been designed as a system and paid for out of the common treasury, sanitation was reserved to those who could afford it. Sewer pipes slithered up Lexington, Second, and Third, where horsecar lines had facilitated better home construction, but most Irish and German areas remained bereft. Even where trunk lines did penetrate working-class quarters—along Stanton, Rivington, Delancey, Broome, and Grand—landlords refused to connect up with them, just as they resisted paying the Croton Aqueduct Department's installation fee and its annual water rent of ten dollars. In 1854, however, in yet another concession to environmentalists, the Common Council ruled that residences had to be connected to sewer lines. And in 1856 it passed an ordinance limiting construction of new buildings to lots serviced by drains.

Nevertheless, in 1857 (the AICP noted), only 138 miles of the city's five hundred miles of paved streets had been sewered. This left two-thirds of all New Yorkers still reliant on backyard and basement privies, whose overflow continued to seep to the water table, infect public wells used by the poor, flood cellars, and leave missionaries and physicians routinely horrified to find children playing and mothers hanging the wash in yards coated with human excrement and swarming with flies. Against all this, the pioneering Bath and Wash House opened by the AICP in 1852 was a worthy but woefully insufficient response.

Foul milk, like foul water, proved durable and deadly. Dairy herds, like beef cattle, had to be kept near consumers and were most densely concentrated on the west side near 16th Street. Often, to keep costs low, they were placed next to distilleries, allowing "swill," the boiling-hot waste product of fermentation, to be fed directly into stable troughs in the cramped quarters. Swill had nutritive value but required supplementation with hay and grain. Few profit-conscious owners bothered to provide it. Nor were they overly concerned that disease ran rampant among their confined herds. They continued extracting thin blue milk from rotting and ulcerous cows until the animals died (at which point they were sold for meat). Then they doctored the product with magnesia, chalk, and stale eggs and passed it on to consumers, felling infants by the thousands.

Griscom and Hartley campaigned vigorously against swill milk, proposing city inspection, but neither city nor state was inclined to interfere with the workings of the free market, especially when the wealthy could afford good milk from farms in Westchester and Queens. By 1856 an estimated two-thirds of all milk sold in New York City was coming from distillery dairies. In 1858 Frank Leslie began a visual exposé in his *Illustrated Weekly Newspaper*, depicting the milking of sick cows, detailing dairymen's profits, and decrying lobbyist payoffs to aldermen. The Common Council reluctantly authorized an investigation, then dropped the matter. Not until 1862 would environmentalists win a swill-milk law from the state legislature, and it proved to be full of loopholes.

TENEMENT TROUBLES

Housing reformers too ran into brick walls, though some of their difficulty in finding a solution stemmed from their own misdiagnosis of the problem. John Griscom had focused his ire on the "merciless inflation and extortion of the *sublandlord*." The AICP agreed that slumlords tended to be unscrupulous immigrants or, at best, first-generation Americans—petty exploiters, often operators of saloons, brothels, and gambling dens—difficult to distinguish, in other words, from their wretched tenants.

It was true that large landlords commonly sublet their buildings to middlemen, leaving to them the chore of extracting high rents, rather as big garment shops left small contractors to do the direct sweating of labor. It was also true that many of these intermediaries were lower-middle-class proprietors (grocers, tavern keepers, building tradesmen) who had jumped into the real estate game or were professional real estate agents (often unemployed building tradesmen) who for a 5 percent commission let apartments and collected rent. In either case, landed grandees were effectively distanced from their tenants, few of whom knew that their ultimate landlord might be an Astor.

But the bottom line was determined from above: sublandlords had to pay chief landlords what Griscom blandly termed "a sum that will yield a fair interest on the costs." But "fairness" was defined in relation to the returns their capital could fetch elsewhere. New York's bourgeoisie had many outlets for accumulated cash—finance, industry, transportation, and western lands—and would invest in local real estate only if they could garner comparable profits. The same logic dominated the building industry, where the newly incorporated construction companies bid for capital from individuals and institutions; forced to pay high interest rates, building companies cut costs elsewhere, usually by slashing wages of construction workers, lowering housing standards, or both.

Griscom nevertheless believed he could convince "the benevolent capitalist" to build decent housing at a fair rate of profit. The AICP vigorously promoted a bricks-and-mortar discussion among builders and capitalists by circulating plans of "model" tenements gleaned from English sources. Well maintained and properly managed, it was argued, they could bring the owner a legitimate 6 percent return. Alas, even respectable Christian businessmen preferred to invest in upper-class housing that brought in 10 percent, new tenement housing that could garner 15 to 25 percent, or old crammed-up artisan housing that could reap 50 to 75 percent, though much of that had to be split with others.

When distressingly few businessmen stepped forward to begin construction, the AICP decided, again taking its cues from English and Continental philanthropists, to do the job itself. In 1855, after frustrating delays and false starts, it opened the largest multiple dwelling yet built in New York City, a six-story structure for eighty-seven families at Mott and Elizabeth streets, just north of the Five Points. Known as the Working-men's Home and often described as the city's first model tenement, it had water closets on each floor, gas lighting, and Croton water. All the apartments were rented to African-American New Yorkers, since "they are usually forced into the worst kind of dwellings, and are deprived of most special privileges, and consequently were specially deserving commiseration." The experiment wasn't successful, however. Though many rooms lacked windows, and all were absurdly cramped (bedrooms measured eight feet by seven and a half), rents, ranging from $5.50 to $8.50 per month, proved too high for most tenants yet too low to ensure the promised 6 percent. After a dozen years of losing money (and continuing trouble with the "inmates"), the Workingman's Home was sold to the Five Points House of Industry as a residence for working women.

As it became clear that tenement reform wouldn't attract private investors, the AICP began to consider the need for government regulation of the housing market. Joined by fire insurers, who thought a stricter building code would reduce their risk exposure, by concerned physicians, who were also seeking to enhance their standing as public experts, and merchants worried about the city's sinking reputation as a healthy place to do business, the environmentalists persuaded the legislature's Tenement House Committee to launch a full-scale investigation in 1856.

The legislators proceeded to immerse themselves (à la Dickens) in places like Corlear's Hook and were duly shocked. "Though expecting to look upon poverty in squalid guise, vice in repulsive aspects, and ignorance of a degraded stamp," the investigators recounted in conventional sunshine-and-shadow prose, "we had not yet formed an adequate conception of the extremes to which each and all of these evils could reach." The committee's Tenant House Report of 1857 declared that housing in New York's Tenth Ward was "without room sufficient for civilized existence" and that some dwellings in the Eleventh Ward were so bad "it is astounding that everyone doesn't die of pestilence."

The legislators, however, were no more prepared than Griscom or the AICP to ask tough questions about the larger economic order that gave rise to the slums. The mismatch between rising rents and falling wages was not on the table. Nor was the premise that housing had to be provided as a commodity: the land reformers' notion of government-underwritten urban homesteads was literally unthinkable. They did, however, recommend passage of regulatory housing laws, and their work led to the drafting of the state's first housing code.

Drafting, but not adoption: the prospect of regulation raised an enormous hue and cry from builders and owners, forcing the legislature to retreat, and another decade would pass before it summoned the nerve to try again. Housing was left to market forces—with the predictable result that the thirty-four blocks along Fifth Avenue between Washington Square and 42nd Street housed a mere four hundred families in virtually agoraphobic comfort (twelve families per block) while on the East Side seven hundred families jammed themselves into one tenement block.

When added to inaction on the garbage and sewage fronts, the result (said a legislative committee) was that "death is making an alarming inroad upon [our] population." Cholera raced through the tenements again in 1852. Typhus, an immigrant disease of dirt and overcrowding, grew endemic, then turned epidemic in 1852. Deaths from consumption (tuberculosis) soared in the black and immigrant communities. Between 1845 and 1854 the citywide mortality rate hovered at an all-time high of forty deaths per thousand city residents, and the gap between bourgeois and working-class districts widened dramatically: in 1855 the Sixth Ward had the highest death rate in New York. The flood of corpses manifested itself in a grisly version of the law of supply and demand. With the number of unclaimed bodies growing faster than medical schools' need for cadavers, their prices dropped accordingly. Corpses had cost twenty-five dollars in the early 1800s, but in 1848 a certain Dr. Reese was selling bodies of dead patients as a sideline at five dollars apiece.

The infant mortality figures were particularly horrifying. Pulmonary diseases drove the rate to a record high of 166 per thousand between 1850 and 1854, with the casualties (the AICP noted) "chiefly amongst the children of the poor, in the most filthy parts of the city." Between 1850 and 1860 more than half of those under the age of five died each year—seven of every ten under the age of two—figures equal to the worst of the English factory districts.

By 1856 more New Yorkers were dying each year than were being born. Without the continuing torrent of immigration, said the city inspector, "the city would in a few years be depopulated."

"LUNGS OF THE CITY"

In the end, only one environmentalist enterprise succeeded fully, though its public health component would constitute a small part of a project that for a wide variety of other reasons enlisted the backing of some very powerful New Yorkers.

In October 1848, only months after the revolution in the streets of Paris, landscape architect Andrew Jackson Downing proposed the creation in New York of a mammoth (five-hundred-acre) People's Park. Until then Downing had concentrated on providing country gentlemen with picturesque retreats and editing the *Horticulturist*. But the European upheavals alarmed him. They seemed to herald similar convulsions in a New York that, to his dismay as an old-school republican, had been dividing up into social classes that no longer comingled one with the other as they once had. New York desperately needed a place where classes could regain comity. Parks, he thought, would facilitate interactions no longer available on the street. Such social intercourse, Downing believed, would, as reformers wished, uplift the lower orders. "Every laborer is a possible gentleman," Downing argued. It wanted only "the refining influence of intellectual and moral culture," which a park might make available, to raise up "the man of the working men to the same level of enjoyment with the man of leisure and accomplishment." In addition, Downing said, coupling his concerns to the demands of the growing public health movement, the park's material as well as moral environment would be beneficial: the open space would serve as the "lungs of the city."

Merchant and AICP sponsor Robert Bowne Minturn reached a similar conclusion by a somewhat different route. After returning in the winter of 1849–50 from an eighteen-month grand tour, he and his wife, Anna Mary Minturn, were struck, as so many other well-off travelers had been, with the mortifying contrast between what Downing called New York's "mere grass-plots of verdure" and Europe's grand green spaces. Minturn became the nucleus of a group of largely Whig gentlemen, many of whom had made their fortunes in international trade, that came to agree that Manhattan needed a public space worthy (as William Cullen Bryant put it) "of the greatness of our metropolis."

A proper park, these gentlemen said, would advance New York's commercial interests, counter the attractions (like Brooklyn's Green-Wood) offered by rival cities, and offer a pastoral and healthy retreat from the disorderly city. It would also provide the respectable classes a place to promenade that was far from crowded Broadway, where cultivated ladies like Anna Minturn were finding themselves "stared out of countenance by troupes of whiskered and mustachioed chatterers" (a *Post* correspondent noted). Even better, a spacious park would allow the gentility to roll about in their fabulous new carriages, rectifying what Nathaniel Parker Willis had long ago singled out as New York's great deficiency "as a metropolis of wealth and fashion": the "lack of a *driving park*."

Placing a park at the spot favored initially—the 150-acre plot bounded by 66th, 75th, Third Avenue, and the East River known as Jones' Wood—would, moreover, reap additional advantages. Uptown property owners had been expressing considerable dismay at finding Irish, German, and African Americans forced northward along with hogs, bone-boiling establishments, and dung heaps. The Harlem Rail Road, too, was fostering a rapid growth of up-island brickworks, ropewalks, and paint manufactories. By removing a substantial chunk of uptown territory from the marketplace, landowners believed, a park would protect their terrain from further encroachment. Establishing the "character" of the surrounding neighborhood would also "materially improve Real estate" and make possible the profitable construction of terraced villas like those facing Regent's Park in London.

Unfortunately, the Joneses and Schermerhorns who owned the Wood were unwilling to sell, scenting bigger profits in more commercial and river-oriented uses. So in 1851 James Beekman, a wealthy Whig state senator, who himself owned property near Jones' Wood and was generally regarded as uptown's representative in the legislature, introduced a bill to seize the land by eminent domain. Backed by Minturn and other prominent merchants and bankers, Beekman's proposal passed quickly into law.

Despite this fast start, the Jones' Wood plan now triggered vigorous opposition from other downtown merchants who castigated it (said one irate *Tribune* contributor) as "a scheme to enhance the value of up-town land." Fiscally conservative gentlemen like U.S. Senator Hamilton Fish also objected to the way Beekman's plan shifted the method of paying for the park: away from the traditional practice of assessing the neighboring landowners who would be the chief beneficiaries, and toward putting the burden on all taxpayers. There were additional reservations about the unnervingly massive and worrisomely precedent-setting expansion of state intervention in the land market.

Unionists, land reformers, and environmental reformers had their own objections. The Industrial Congress was on record as saying that if the city was to build parks, they should be placed in "vacant squares in the more thickly populated districts"; Mike Walsh and others were particularly keen to enlarge the Battery as a people's promenade. The *Staats-Zeitung* also preferred "many smaller parks in different parts of the city" to one big one for "the heirs of the Upper Tendoms," and it rejected as "complete humbug" the claim that a landscape park three miles north of the congested center would somehow lower the mortality rate. Dr. Griscom agreed that eight parks of a hundred acres each, or sixteen of fifty, "would certainly be less aristocratic; more democratic, and far more conducive to the public health." Better, said physician and land reformer Hal Guernsey, to use the public's money for building cheap homesteads on uptown land.

Finally, upper *westside* landowners made clear that they too were unhappy about the growth of immigrant and poor communities in their domain—places like Seneca Village—and demanded a park in their neck of the woods lest it soon "be covered with a class of population similar to that of Five Points" (as uptown assistant alderman Daniel Tiemann put it). They proposed an alternative, more "central" mid-island location, whose rocky topography made it unsuitable for building houses, grading streets, or digging sewers. The land would be much cheaper, and the municipal corporation already owned 135 acres in the area. It would therefore be possible to build a much bigger park, indeed one of the largest in the world, that would have "ample room for riding and driving therein with Horses and Carriages."

After two years of debate and maneuver, the coalition backing the central park location won out. In 1853 the state agreed to use eminent domain to take 778 acres (expanded to 843 a decade later) from the 561 proprietors who controlled the site, 20 percent of which was owned by three families. Over the next two years a commission of estimate surveyed and assessed the thirty-four thousand lots, finally authorizing payment of five million dollars for the parcels (three times what advocates had claimed the entire park would cost). Compromising on the funding mechanism, it decreed that one-third of the expense would have to be covered by assessing adjacent landowners, generating screams and (ultimately unsuccessful) lawsuits from men like Archibald Watt, who nevertheless cleared a 1500 percent profit on land he'd bought only twenty years earlier. The sixteen hundred or so Irish, Germans, and blacks who lived on the land—dismissed and disparaged as "vagabonds and scoundrels"—were evicted by 1857, though the Sisters of Charity were allowed to remain in their Mount St. Vincent retreat until 1859.

Also in 1857 the state legislature established a Board of Commissioners of the Central Park, which sponsored a competition for choosing the park's layout, touching off a new controversy over design. The commissioners were drawn to Downing's old vision of a park that could foster interclass harmony, but many in the city either doubted that such coexistence was possible or feared that comingling would end with the lower orders imposing their vicious habits on their betters. The *Times* detested the notion of providing Boweryites with free access: "As long as we are governed by the Five Points, our best attempts at elegance and grace will bear some resemblance to jewels in the snouts of swine. Rather the Park should never be made at all if it is to become the resort of rapscalians." Far better, some said frankly, to design a space that catered to distinctly upper-class needs—a new trotting course for sporting types, a carriage drive for the fashionable, a pastoral space cleansed of commercial excess and social disorder for the genteel—which would also anchor northern Fifth Avenue as a residential preserve for the wealthy.

Tribunes of popular culture like *Frank Leslie's Illustrated Newspaper* countered by calling on the commissioners not to "allocate to aristocratic pride and exclusiveness, a place which they may strut and parade in a solitary state, but [to create] a spot for all classes of our fellow citizens" that would allow "the labouring classes to have cafe concerts, cirques, ambulatory exhibitions, and shooting galleries." The *Irish News* wanted a "commons" area—in the vein of such pleasure gardens as Niblo's or the Elysian Fields—that would allow for plebeian pleasures like picnics, festivals, sports, games, militia drills, theaters, fireworks, and circuses.

In the end the commissioners chose the Greensward Plan offered by Frederick Law Olmsted, whom they had just appointed superintendent of the park, and Calvert Vaux, a London-born architect who had suggested the competition idea to them in the first place.

Olmsted, son of a prosperous dry goods merchant from Hartford, had been set up by his father on a 125-acre Staten Island farm (on Raritan Bay) as a scientific agriculturalist. He had also written on rural design for Downing's *Horticulturalist* (including a piece on Liverpool's Birkenhead Park), published travel books on the social landscape of England and the American South, and in 1855 become a managing editor of *Putnam's Magazine*, which by 1857 was foundering. When family friend and park commissioner Charles Elliott encouraged him to apply for the position directing the park's labor force, he swiftly gathered endorsements from editors, writers, reformers, and friends, including Brace, Greeley, Cooper, and Irving.

One thing that helped him secure the position was his anti-laissez-faire conviction—very much in tune with the newest reform currents—that properly designed environments like English-style landscaped parks could elevate the character and condition of the poorer classes. Olmsted was also convinced of the value of class intermixing and in 1854 had urged his Yale chum and traveling companion Charles Loring Brace to "get up parks, gardens, music, dancing schools, reunions which will be so attractive as to force into contact the good and the bad, the gentlemanly and the rowdy."

Vaux thought in similar terms. Trained as an architect in London, Vaux had attracted the attention of Andrew Jackson Downing, who in 1850 recruited him to run the architectural wing of his flourishing landscape-gardening practice. After Downing died in 1852, Vaux carried on his practice, then moved to New York in 1856, joined the National Academy of Design and the Century Association, and helped found the American Institute of Architects. He too adopted an environmentalist position and in 1857 urged municipal authorities to underwrite wholesome rational play—"public baths, gymnasiums, theatres, music halls, libraries, lecture rooms, parks, gardens, picture galleries, museums, schools"—as activities that would ensure "a refinement in popular education" and "good taste."

When Vaux decided to enter the Central Park competition, he invited Superintendent Olmsted—whom he had met at Downing's home in Newburgh—to join him, chiefly for his on-site familiarity with the topography. During the winter of 1857–58 they worked on a plan that would apply their social philosophy to the barren and rocky mid-Manhattan terrain. Evenhandedly rebuffing both working class desires for ball fields and aristocratic longings for a raceway, their Greensward Plan proposed a reformer's vision—a space designed to school both patrician and plebeian cultures by transmitting, almost subliminally, civilized values and a "harmonizing and refining influence."

To achieve this, they called for exiling the normal business of urban life to beyond the park's perimeter. Coal carts, butchers' carts, dung carts, and fire engines that had to cross the park were to be diverted to sunken transverse roads (rather as servants and tradesmen were kept out of sight in genteel mansions). Also banished was Manhattan's grid, and with it the kind of streets that were "staked off," as Olmsted put it, "with a rule and pencil in a broker's office." Here therapeutically romantic curves were to be the rule. Pedestrians and carriages would meander along paths affording ever-changing vistas, rather like a succession of Cole or Durand canvasses, intended to invoke decorous contemplation of nature, in the manner of Bryant's poems. In addition to spectatorship of civilizing scenery, the plan encouraged genteel pastimes such as skating and boating and was particularly attentive to the needs of ladies. The park was to be a sanctuary, a retreat from the city's competitiveness and congestion akin to the bourgeois-home-as-domestic-refuge, a place to set aside at least temporarily the "habit of mind, cultivated in commercial life, of judging values by the market estimate." For all this sniping at the marketplace, Olmsted, in particular, stressed that Central Park would "greatly accelerate the occupation of the adjoining land," pleasing wealthy Fifth Avenue landowners, and increase tax revenues, a claim calculated to warm the hearts of city officials.

The Greensward Plan was far less welcoming to the working classes. It banned not only their conventional recreations but their republican political culture. Olmsted and Vaux forbade martial displays, civic processions, and public oratory. The Mall was reserved for promenades: silent and apolitical encounters. Nor, for all the emphasis on the virtue of interclass mixing, was there much of it. Transport was neatly segregated: the middle class moved through the park space by carriage and horse, the working class on foot.

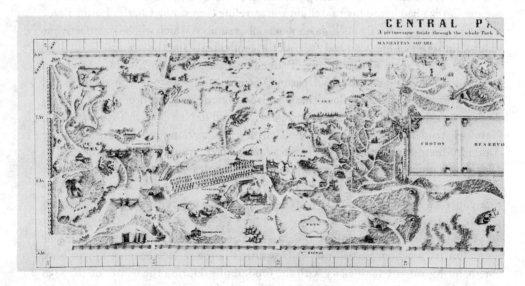

Central Park, New York, "a picturesque guide through the whole Park showing all the improvements up to June 1865." (Map Division. The New York Public Library. Astor, Lenox and Tilden Foundations)

Olmsted also took patrician anxieties about potential plebeian rambunctiousness to heart. "A large part of the people of New York are ignorant of a park, properly so-called," he wrote. "They need to be trained to the proper use of it." Doubting that the park's deep structure would sufficiently discipline the unruly, Olmsted established regulations that, in marked contrast to the laissez-faire streets of the city, soon blanketed the park terrain with 125 varieties of directive and injunctive signs and posters. He also instituted park police—"keepers"—who would "respectfully aid an offender toward a better understanding of what is due to others, as one gentleman might manage to guide another."

For the time being, an apparatus to enforce proper canons of behavior was hardly necessary. The nascent park was too far north of the Bowery, and public transport too expensive, for it to attract many laborers apart from those busy constructing it. But the design and regulatory structure reassured the elite that it would in time become a gathering ground for the civilized. The value of surrounding property skyrocketed accordingly: by 1860 assessed values had risen by two-thirds of their 1856 levels.

This complacency was in fact misplaced. Working-class citizens would soon be contesting Greensward notions of proper usage. However, to the degree that Central Park did for the moment remain an upper-class playground, it represented yet another defeat for the larger reform project. Once again a cultural enterprise designed to mitigate the divisiveness of metropolitan life had served only to exacerbate it.

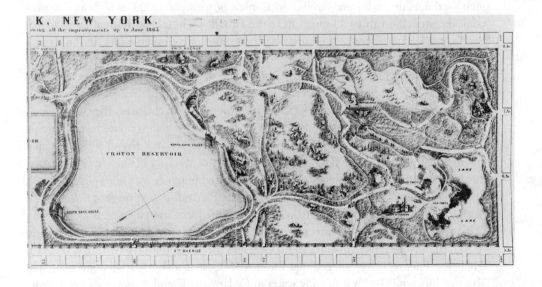

Feme Decovert

N ew York in the 1840s and 1850s was an intensely
     homosocial city. Men clubbed, ate, drank, rioted,
     whored, paraded, and politicked together, clus-
tered together in boardinghouses and boards of directors, even slept together. Whitman
spent much of his time in the company of handsome young workingmen, occasionally
bringing them home for the evening, and whether or not he and they engaged in sexual
intimacies, other men certainly did.

New York provided many opportunities for same-sex encounters. Vast numbers of
men lived outside traditional families in all-male boardinghouses. Casual acquaintances
could be struck up in bathhouses near the Broadway hotels, at bohemian bars like
Pfaff's, in theaters, aboard ships, along wharves, while strolling in parks, and in church
(in 1846 two men who had met in a house of worship lived together for three months in
a boardinghouse, engaging in nightly "carnal intercourse"). Passing references to "male
prostitutes" suggest more strictly commercial options were available.

When reports of "buggery" or "sodomy" cropped up in the press they were usually accompanied by traditional abuse. Thus in 1846 the *Herald* excoriated a respectable
storekeeper who had been caught "in one of those revolting and disgraceful acts which
are nightly practiced on the Battery or in the vicinity of the City Hall." City authorities,
however, were remarkably unconcerned. Consensual buggery was seldom prosecuted
by public officials. There were only five arrests for sodomy throughout the 1850s.
Authorities usually intervened only in cases involving force and violence, underage participants (in 1857, a man was arrested for committing sodomy with boys aged eleven to
fourteen), or indecent exposure, punishing less the "act" than its visibility. In 1846,
when one Thomas Carey alleged that Edward McCosker, a young Irish policeman, had
accosted him while he "was making water in Cedar Street" and "commenced indecent-

ly feeling his privates," the mayor, after a hearing, dismissed McCosker from the force but took no criminal action.

Homosexuality wasn't a crime. It didn't even exist. The very notion of "homosexuality"—understood as a category describing a person's sexual *being*—was not invented until the eighties. And while same-sex *acts* still fell under ancient proscriptions, "consenting to sodomy" would not be criminalized in New York law until the end of the century. In an era when passionate male bonding was universal, and all-male gatherings the norm, a little buggery between friends might well have been taken as an extension of existing norms rather than a flagrant transgression of them.

What really alarmed critics of same-sex behavior was males who adopted "feminine appearance and manners"—men like Peter Sewally, a.k.a. Mary Jones, a black New Yorker who lived in a Greene Street brothel where he cooked, greeted patrons, and dressed in female clothes because, he explained, he "looked so much better in them." The unnerving thing about cross-dressing was that it transgressed the frontier between gender domains, which same-sex displays of affection reinforced.

Males were the most vociferous about keeping spheres separate—no surprise, given that the distribution of gender perquisites so heavily favored their sex. But upper-

"The Man Monster"—Peter Sewally, a.k.a. Mary Jones (1836).
(© Collection of The New-York Historical Society)

and middle-class women spent much of their time weaving and sustaining densely homosocial associational networks, forming intense friendships, hugging, kissing, sleeping with, and ardently proclaiming their love for one another. They trooped to one another's homes for visits and teas. They offered extensive support at crucial moments in a woman's life: marriage, pregnancy, birth, nursing. They spent entire days on joint shopping trips, moved in with one another while husbands were away, shared summer vacations. They apprenticed their daughters in housewifery and motherhood at a time when apprenticeship in the male trades was collapsing. They built together a world that provided the emotional warmth and connection absent from the increasingly stiff relations across the gender divide.

City space manifested these delineations. The downtown worlds of politics and business remained physically off limits to ladies, and many of the civic parades that trooped through lower Manhattan streets were totally masculine events. When genteel women ventured out into heterosexual terrain, they found a network of safe spaces and corridors awaiting them. By the 1850s New York had a Ladies' Oyster Shop, a Ladies' Reading Room, a Ladies' Bowling Alley; banks and post offices had special ladies' windows. There was even a ladies' eatery: Taylor's, at Broadway and Franklin Street, grew from being a humble ice creamery to serving three thousand women on the average weekday at over a hundred black walnut tables ("the restaurant of the age," the *Herald* called it). Olmsted made sure that when his Central Park skating rink opened in 1858 it included a "ladies' pond" where the timid could tumble without blushing, and his park regulations strictly prohibited "boisterous or indecent conduct or language."

Much as many bourgeois women may have appreciated the provision of such accommodations, and others may have found honor, dignity, even a modicum of power in presiding over their sphere, others felt increasingly restless and constricted. As they watched male fields of action expand so dramatically in the boom years, the balance between the gender spheres was coming to seem increasingly unequal, even unjust.

"THE UTTER IDLENESS OF THE LADY CLASS"

Nowhere was this new sensibility more in evidence than in the separate sphere of women's literature that had emerged, in the 1840s and 1850s, with such astonishing rapidity. The books that hundreds of thousands of female buyers boosted to bestseller status (dwarfing Dickens's sales) included domestic novels that explored the pleasures and trials of running a modern household (including struggles with servants and husbands), dreamy romances that celebrated decked-out and adored young heroines, weepy tales of dying children, and illustrated guides to the latest fashions. Much of what made it into print accepted, even glorified, the sentimental stereotypes of female passivity. Susan Warner's 1850 blockbuster *The Wide Wide World* urged readers to seek spiritual strength in submission and obedience, and that same year author Grace Greenwood defined the feminine genius as "timid, doubtful and clingingly dependent; a perpetual childhood."

Yet what was most striking about the new women's literature was how angry much of it was, how full of complaints about what one 1856 novel called "that living death to which it is the fashion to consign females of the wealthy middle-class." "I feel like rushing out," said a character in Charlotte Chesebro's *Children of Light* (1853). "But here I am, only a woman—a housekeeper . . . to be kept in my 'proper sphere' and 'place,' and never to stir an inch out of it in any direction, for fear that all creation would turn against me, and hunt me down, as they would a wild beast!" Many novelists fumed at men they saw as jailers. A host of masculine villains paraded through their plots—neglectful fathers, cruel husbands, and assorted gamblers, alcoholics, philanderers, failures, or murderers—with whom courageous and creative women did combat or from whom they fled.

Authors ritually agreed that the "Home" was "woman's empire" and that the work women did there raising republican children was indispensable, but in go-ahead New York City, the action was patently elsewhere. Urban society celebrated producers—the men who made ships, built railroads, traded stocks and commodities, got on with business. Some New York women, too, were censorious of what one British visitor called "the utter idleness of the lady class." Novelist Catharine Sedgwick found her peers as little trained for the actual business of life "as if we had been born in the royal family of Persia." Women didn't choose idleness, insisted Lydia Maria Child, they were pressed into it.

What particularly galled writer and editor Child was the dictum that women "must not study, because gentlemen do not admire literary ladies." Worse, the conventional male assessment (particularly that of medical "experts") held that mental acuity wasn't really possible for women, driven as they were by their wombs, not their heads. But growing numbers of women were in fact receiving rigorous intellectual training at institutions around the metropolitan area. The Brooklyn Collegiate Institute for Young Ladies insisted its charges be educated "as carefully, as substantially, and as liberally" as men, and the Rutgers Female Institute, incorporated in 1838, taught belles lettres, history, mathematics, and philosophy. Such academies were not intended to prepare graduates for careers or roles in the public realm, to be sure, but rather to help them attract and later assist the right kind of husband. Yet without denying their special responsibilities to home and family, some ladies began to argue they should be allowed to enter the occupations and professions into which their brothers were flocking.

The notion that respectable and educated females might undertake gainful employment ran up against the reality that, as an 1846 article in the feminist *Advocate for Moral Reform* put it bluntly: "Men have monopolized almost every field of labor. They have taken the learned professions, they have entered every department which commerce opens, and indeed, almost every place where skill and talent is required, they have excluded women." While the city's flourishing publishing industry had proved hospitable to women, other suitable professions were growing *more* restrictive, notably medicine.

Childbirth had long been a jealously guarded female domain. New York midwives had to swear they would not reveal "any matter Appertaining to your Office in the presence of any Man." Since the development and use of obstetrical forceps, however, male doctors had begun to assist midwives at difficult births and then, slowly, to displace them in the birthing room. To consolidate control over this lucrative practice, they refused to train midwives in the new methods, claiming women were too emotional to make cool judgments in medical emergencies. Midwives dwindled, male obstetricians multiplied.

They did not, however, sweep the field, in part because examinations by male doctors continued to outrage female modesty. Many physicians were forced to communicate with their patients on delicate issues through elderly female intermediaries. In this context, female doctors constituted a serious threat, one reason women were barred from medical college. Those who did receive medical training attended unorthodox institutions, like the New York Hydropathic and Physiological School, which in 1856 graduated thirty males and twenty females. Such women could be dismissed as quacks. Dr. Elizabeth Blackwell could not.

Blackwell, an English immigrant, had gotten into an upstate medical school and received the first American M.D. degree ever conferred on a woman. But when she returned to New York City in 1851, physicians prevented her from practicing in city hospitals and dispensaries, and she became the target of hate mail. In 1853 Blackwell opened what would become the New York Infirmary for Women and Children, in a one-room dispensary on 7th Street near Tompkins Square. She would be assisted by Dr. Marie Zackrzewska, former chief midwife of Prussia's largest hospital, who had emigrated to New York City convinced that "only in a republic can it be proved that science has no sex." Poor women flocked from all over Manhattan and Brooklyn to this first medical charity in the United States staffed by female physicians. The New York Infirmary took root, despite vitriolic opposition from the city's male medicos, though its efforts to add a women's medical college would be thwarted until 1868. It would be the Women's Hospital of New York (1855), organized by male physicians to treat female disorders, that would receive significant appropriations of money and land from state and city.

A FAMILY WAGE

Working-class women faced quite a different problem. The same booming economy that was tempting some of the lady class into the workplace was driving poorer women into it willy-nilly.

Many female Irish refugees, large numbers of whom came over on their own, tried to reconstruct familiar domestic arrangements, but a good man, any man, was hard to find. Though Irish females only slightly outnumbered males on the immigrant ships, in New York there were 125 women of marrying age for every hundred men. The demand for Irish brawn was continental in scope, and many males swirled in and out of the city to great construction projects in surrounding states and points west. "The immense majority," noted a New York Irish paper in 1859, were "as yet but a mere floating population, migrating from place to place, wherever they may find a market for their labor." Irishwomen, on the other hand, found it relatively easy to get jobs as domestic servants with affluent New Yorkers and tended to stay in the metropolis. The gender imbalance created by male mobility was exacerbated by male mortality, as dangerous jobs chewed up Irish laborers.

Germans, whose flight was less chaotic, found it easier to reconstruct existing families and create new ones. Though early in the exodus 60 percent of the mostly youthful arrivals were male, by the late 1850s the gender ratio had evened out at fifty-two to forty-eight, and over two-thirds of the community were settled down in families. As a general rule, the higher uptown in Kleindeutschland one went, the more likely one was to find married couples predominating over boardinghouse singles. Yet those who did marry hardly lived middle-class lives. Some skilled craftsmen's wives could afford to tend to their parlors, but with male incomes low and sporadic, women had to work if their families were to get beyond the basics or, in some cases, even to survive. Taking in boarders was one solution: over half the working women in the Sixth Ward over thirty did so in 1855. Taking in garment piecework was another, and young unmarried German daughters worked alongside their parents in tenement workshops. Even then, poor immigrant wives were, of necessity, out and about the town far more than their middle-class counterparts. And many immigrant women were forced to live and work in other people's families: servants boarded with employers in sufficient numbers to give the genteel wards a decidedly feminine majority.

Among Irish women, moreover, the ranks of those who *could* not marry were increasingly bolstered by those who *would* not, or who delayed doing so as long as possible. Violence, drink, poverty, desertion: all these devalued matrimony for Irish women, continuing a Famine-generated retreat from traditional marriage patterns. Males and females in Ireland increasingly led sex-segregated lives—in the family circle, at church, and in places of recreation—and convents flourished in post-Famine Ireland. They thrived in New York too, because they offered sisters an appealing combination of spiritual fulfillment, power, respect, significant work (most orders being activist, not contemplative), and freedom from subordination to husbands and the dangers of childbirth.

A growing numbers of jobs—products of the city's development as a publishing, communications, manufacturing, and fashion center—provided young and childless women with the wherewithal to survive outside traditional family units. For exploited seamstresses, this autonomy could be a miserable experience. For the old, the frail, and those with children, life without male support could be catastrophic. But others carved out a decent independence by doing "women's work," such as hairdressing, photo-graphic tinting, etching, engraving, jewelry making, cameo cutting, enameling, toymak-ing, and bookselling. In addition, the city's commitment to public education (and its desire to cut costs) created new opportunities. The ensuing demand for teachers was increasingly met by women, who worked for far less than male counterparts, and soon three-quarters of the thousand public school teachers were women.

Such jobs allowed single young females to live apart from parents. One survey of single working women in 1855 found over half living on their own in boardinghouses or sharing tenement rooms with siblings, cousins, or workmates. Conditions could be spar-tan, even harsh, with half a dozen factory girls crammed into a single garret. On the other hand, they were no longer obliged to cook, wash, haul water, and carry wood for their parents after they had finished their paid jobs for the day.

Efforts to improve wages and working conditions in female trades continued to go nowhere. Not only did the great labor upheavals of the 1850s almost completely exclude women, but the Industrial Congress adopted rigid positions on "woman's place" and said female wage work was "incompatible with the true dignity and nature of woman." The real solution was for men to be paid a "family wage" that would allow them to keep their wives at home, as did the men of the bourgeoisie.

Some German socialists adopted a feminist stance. Weitling's *Republik der Arbeiter* formally acknowledged women's rights, and the labor societies he led included a few women—among them Mathilde Giesler Anneke, daughter of a wealthy Westphalian landlord and mine owner. Estranged from her class, she married forty-niner Fritz Anneke, arrived in 1852, joined Weitling's organization, and regularly lectured at work-ers' vereins in New York City and Williamsburgh on her view "that the social question could only be solved by the emancipation of women." Few rank-and-file socialists agreed. The hausfrau should be a companion but stick to guarding the proletarian family. German radicals defended the family wage and scorned feminists as dupes of

Manchesterian liberal economics, thus elevating domesticity to the status of scientific principle.

That this stubborn rearguard battle to keep women out of wage-work would prove costly was already evident in the printing trade. Male typesetters were understandably dismayed that mechanization had allowed poorly paid young women to replace highly skilled men, but rather than include them in the union, men argued women should be banned from the business. The result was that in 1853, when the union struck the *Day-Book*, it had little recourse after the publisher established crash typesetting courses for women and hired graduates as strikebreakers.

"... GROWS RICH ON THE HARD LABORS OF OUR SEX."

By decade's end, women's trade unionism had been obliterated; it would not revive until the twentieth century. With working women unable to speak for themselves, some middle-class feminists proposed to speak for them. "Every woman in misfortune," wrote Caroline Kirkland, "is the proper object of care to the happier and safer part of her sex." Indeed, Kirkland suggested, "women should consider themselves as a community, having special common needs and common obligations." But the effort to throw womanly bridges across the class divide would prove far more difficult than nascent feminists imagined.

In 1845 the all-female editorial staff of the *Advocate of Moral Reform*, newspaper of the American Female Moral Reform Society, declared that "the ordinary rate of wages for female labor is unjust and oppressive." They excoriated male employers who "drive the young and unfriended to dens of shame, while they fill their coffers with the avails of unrequited toil." Catharine Beecher (Henry Ward's sister) was less flowery and more specific. "Capitalists at the East avail themselves of this excess of female hands," Beecher wrote. They got work from poor women "at prices that will not keep soul and body together; and then the articles thus made are sold for prices that give monstrous profits to the capitalist, who thus grows rich on the hard labors of our sex."

In 1848, the Reform Society established a four-story Home for the Friendless and House of Industry, uptown on Fifth Avenue between 29th and 30th streets. Here the "unprotected female whose only crime is poverty and the need of employment" could learn a trade as well as the precepts of religion and morality. The American Female Guardian Society, as it now renamed itself, also established an Industrial School for those too poor to attend public school, which taught sewing and provided free lunches. The idea was quickly replicated at a German Industrial School, a Brooklyn Industrial School, and across the United States.

Even these limited efforts by affluent women to reach out across class lines to their poorer sisters were—as in the case of analogous projects by their male counterparts—hampered by elite fears and prejudices. The notion of laboring women as active and equal partners was unimaginable. The lady class would succor shivering seamstresses, but only if they bore their ills in silence and maintained a grateful and deferential demeanor to their benefactors. Proper recipients, moreover, had to uphold (or at least aspire to) bourgeois domestic standards, keeping their houses and raising their children in a manner of which ladies approved. But as this was virtually impossible in the clamorous and grimy tenement quarters, genteel visitors tended to see Five Points females as less than truly women. Above all, there was the religious gulf, drawn deep and wide. For

Class lines are enforced in a fashionable store, from *Harper's Weekly*, January 8, 1859. (© Collection of The New-York Historical Society)

Protestant missionary women, Catholics were priest-ridden heathen with whom no accommodation short of conversion was possible.

In the end, while genteel feminists did provide tangible services to immigrant women, they themselves were the primary beneficiaries. Reform projects justified respectable women's claim on city space. Social housekeeping was deemed a legitimate extension of women's sphere into the public arena, accepted (at times hailed) by wealthy males of their own class. It allowed them to create and run large, complex organizations that commanded considerable assets. Like the women writers who (with the help of readers) had secured a position in the marketplace, so female reformers (with the help of reformees) secured a place in the civic and charitable arena. A feminist alliance would remain elusive, however, not least because women of different classes were as far apart on issues of sexuality as they were on those of economics and theology.

CITY OF ORGIES

In 1857 the Reverend William Berrian had been for three decades the rector of Trinity Church, the most prestigious pulpit in the United States. In a sermon that year he admitted to his congregation that "during a ministry of more than fifty years I have not been in a house of ill-fame more than ten times!" Perhaps even more remarkable than this pronouncement by such a model Christian was the fact that what startled his listeners was not that he had gone whoring at all but that he had gone so infrequently. For the years of his ministry had seen a luxuriant growth of prostitution in New York City—marked by the widespread patronage of eminently respectable bourgeois men— to the point that the metropolis had become the wide-open national capital of commercialized sex.

In the 1840s and 1850s, when Broadway between Canal and Houston streets

"Hooking a Victim," streetwalkers on Broadway, c. 1850. The adoption of the term *hooker* as a synonym for prostitute may have been inspired by the proliferation of brothels and streetwalkers on the Corlear's Hook waterfront. (© Museum of the City of New York)

emerged as the city's grand shopping and entertainment boulevard, New York's bawdy houses trekked northward too. They clustered directly behind the commercial strip, in the small cobbled streets of Mercer, Greene, Howard, and Wooster—present-day SoHo. In the evening, scant hours after the afternoon promenade of fashionable ladies, Broadway filled with fashionable streetwalkers, who sauntered past the hotels, paused at the gas-lit shop windows, loitered outside the theater entrances. As the fifties wore on, these *femmes de pavé* invaded the daylight, cruising Broadway after shopping hours, casting inviting glances at passersby.

The SoHo brothels, most of them run by entrepreneurial madams, were stylish affairs, noted for attractive women, luxurious furniture, fine liquor, and black servants, some of whom doubled as piano players. Different houses had distinctive clienteles (southerners, Germans, Astor House visitors) and particular specialties: Mrs. Hathaway's "fair Quakeresses," Mrs. Everett's "beautiful señoritas [who] are quite accomplished," Miss Lizzie Wright's "French belles." Carnally inclined males kept abreast of the possibilities by perusing handbooks such as Charles DeKock's *Guide to the Harems*, Free Lovyer's [*sic*] *Directory of the Seraglios*, and Butt Ender's *Prostitution Exposed*. They could also consult the newspapers, the calling cards brothels dropped off at hotels, or the city directories (in 1855 sixty-nine women listed themselves as "prostitute").

The ethnic composition of women "on the town" reflected the larger transformation in working-class demographics. In 1855 Dr. William Sanger, chief resident physician at Blackwell's Island Hospital, carried out a statistical survey with the aid of the police. He estimated the total number of prostitutes as 7,860. Of these 38 percent were country girls (most of whom worked in brothels), while 35 percent were Irish and 12 percent German (most of whom plied the streets). These numbers included children. Not only was pedophilia a popular gentleman's vice, but the likelihood of contracting disease and producing pregnancy was thought to be lessened by intercourse with pre-pubescent girls. Conveniently, the age of menarche was approximately fifteen, the age of consent but ten.

Dr. Sanger administered a questionnaire to two thousand prostitutes, asking survey participants why they had entered the trade. Many cited "destitution," which had usually resulted from being seduced, abandoned, widowed, orphaned, or otherwise deprived of male support. But a sizable percentage cited "inclination"; they preferred prostitution to a father's or husband's drunken abuse, a mother's nagging, the monotony of a rural existence, or the miserably paid life of a seamstress or servant. Where the latter might make two or three dollars a week, an elite courtesan could pull in ten to fifty dollars for a single trick. As the city's highest-paid women workers, they were able to avail themselves of fancy clothes and urban entertainments. Prostitution had innumerable drawbacks—syphilis and gonorrhea not the least of them—but it afforded poor women their best chance for autonomy.

The demand for commercial sex, like its supply, had broadened dramatically since the 1820s. New York was inundated with transient males: country storekeepers, gentleman travelers, and suburban ferry commuters. Roughly sixty thousand ship crewmen (oystermen, steamboat deckhands, sailors from whalers and naval vessels, canal boatmen) passed through town each year by the late 1850s. Thousands of single male immigrants settled here, and hundreds of thousands more paused in the city on their way west.

Workingmen seeking sex could find it in Kleindeutschland basement bars, Five Points interracial brothels, and the waterfront area of Corlear's Hook, where half-exposed women sat on stoops of tenements and former mansions along Walnut, Water, Pearl, and Cherry streets, beckoning nautical males and men from the nearby shipyards, coal dumps, sawmills, and ironworks.

A prominent new venue was the "concert saloon," a hybrid entertainment place that combined music, drink, and sex. The concert saloon had emerged in the depressed 1840s when taverns drummed up business by converting back rooms or cellars into small concert halls, which put on specialty acts to encourage drinking. By the 1850s many old theaters or three- or four-story brownstones were being rigged up with a long bar and a curtainless stage at the rear. The entertainment was a pastiche of French vaudeville, Italian opera, German beer garden, and English theater. When vocalists sang, the audience, waiters, and "waiter girls" (frequently full- or part-time prostitutes) joined in the chorus. Between acts, performers sat in the audience and solicited customers for prostitution in private rooms upstairs.

In SoHo, at the top of the commercial sex chain, second-class brothels for clerks and "the higher class of mechanics" could be found near the district's lower end. Farther north lay the rows of patrician and middle-class establishments, which were, the *Tribune* noted, "frequently visited by gentlemen of the best standing," a category including "aldermen, judges, lawyers, assemblymen, state officers, country merchants, and others." From Saturday night through the Lord's Day and on into Monday morning, SoHo's streets were filled with expensive carriages. The sidewalks were lined as well, with young men who had strolled over from Broadway, all camped out in front of their favorite brothels waiting their turn. Editor Walt Whitman contended that nineteen of every twenty males—including "the best classes of Men" in Brooklyn and New York—visited brothels regularly.

Some men justified brothels as "safeguards to the virtue of maidens, wives, and widows, who would otherwise be exposed to violence and outrage." "Sporting men" went farther and celebrated brothel culture, calling it an essential part of sophisticated urbanity. Their ranks included stylish Bowery soaplocks, young clerks on the make, and "fast" gentlemen who set up their shopgirl, milliner, or servant "sweethearts" in brownstone apartments. Sporting males detested matrimony, which turned men into "captives" of women, and read sporting papers like the *Flash*, the *Libertine*, the *Rake*, the *Whip*, and the *National Police Gazette*, which featured up-to-date information about New York underworld offerings (along with ads for the cure of venereal disease).

Many respectable women were enraged that their husbands and brothers so casually flaunted a sexual code that women were forbidden to transgress. Theoretically both sexes of the bourgeoisie agreed on finding in sexual repression a badge of their moral superiority to class inferiors. True, it was supposedly easier for women to adhere to these standards—medical texts insisted that most "are not very much troubled with sexual feelings of any kind"—so marriage manuals urged wives to assist husbands in subduing their passions. Some husbands went along with the dictates of propriety or agonized over their lapses when they didn't, but many cheerfully bifurcated their sexual lives, turning for fun to working-class women who embraced sexual pleasure, or were forced by circumstances to pretend they did.

With males' self-assumed prerogatives negating whatever control respectable women had gained over the sexual system, they set out to rein in prostitution. The traditional approach—redeeming or rescuing prostitutes, thus helping dry up supply— was carried on by the Female Benevolent Society, founded in the early thirties. In 1838 the society built a refuge in Yorkville, several miles outside the city, where residents could learn useful trades. It also began to take in the "friendless female orphan, when no way is left for her to obtain a livelihood but that of prostitution."

Other women reached out to prostitutes in prison or immediately upon their release. The male Prison Association of New York set up a Female Department, which later, having come to believe "women could work best independently for the redemption of their own sex," split off to form the Women's Prison Association (1854). These ladies opened a refuge on Tenth Avenue for former inmates; it housed over a hundred women, on condition they forsook smoking, drinking, and cursing and took up sewing, laundering, and "religious study." The ladies promised to "whisper hope to [each ex-convict] amid her despair, teach her lessons of self-control, instill into her ideas of purity and industry"—then get her a job as a maid. In its first twenty years the refuge sheltered 2,961 women and placed 1,083 with private families, finding only 480 to be "unworthy" or hopelessly recidivist.

Reformers also crusaded tirelessly against male "licentiousness." "Every man who will sport with female virtue," declared the *Advocate*, should be fixed with "an eternal stigma." Virtuous females were asked to boycott seducers: "Let them be regarded as enemies to the sex." The Female Moral Reform Society turned to state power to rein in forward males. After a lengthy struggle, including a petition campaign that drew thousands of "virtuous mothers and daughters" from around the state, the legislature passed an Act to Punish Seduction as a Crime (1848). "Any man who shall under promise of marriage seduce and have illicit connection with any unmarried female of previous chaste character shall be guilty of a misdemeanor," the law proclaimed. But with redress available only to women willing to prove their virtue in court, and with the "testimony of the seduced female, unsupported by other evidence," being insufficient for conviction, the seeming triumph fizzled. It was a rare year in which more than one or two rakes were arrested under its provisions.

Prostitution per se was not outlawed by statute, but the police could and did arrest "all common prostitutes who have no lawful employment" as vagrants or "disorderly persons" and send them to either the almshouse or penitentiary for six months. However, though the police periodically raided Sixth Ward brothels and often hauled in streetwalkers from predominantly immigrant areas, elite brothels were almost never disturbed: the New York district attorney charged a grand total of seven during the entire decade of the 1850s.

Prostitution proved irrepressible because New York males supported it, patrons and profiteers alike. The latter included landlords who collected hefty rents from madams, municipal tax collectors who skimmed their share of landlord revenues, and two new beneficiaries: pimps and politicians. Madams had begun hiring men to protect their employees from assault by drunken packs like the one, forty strong, that in 1851 trashed Catherine Cauldwell's place on Lispenard Street. But streetwalkers were far more vulnerable and were soon dominated by their protectors. By the 1850s pimps had become a common sight, lounging in front of the monster hotels or in nearby bars, waiting for women to hand over their earnings.

Politicians too leeched off sex workers. The local ward bosses who relied on muscle to dominate the polls also used it to extort revenue, often in conjunction with local police. Tammany gang leaders like Isaiah Rynders and Thomas Hyer levied tribute from brothels, saloons, and gambling dens and in return extended them "protection." In 1850, when police rounded up brothel keepers in the Points, Alderman Patrick Kelly scurried to their aid.

By mid-century prostitution had become deeply imbricated in the business life of the city. Dr. Sanger calculated its aggregate annual revenues as exceeding three million dollars and if liquor sales and rental income were added, the figure doubled, to an annual cash value just below the garment industry's $7.5 million. For all the feminists' efforts, New York would remain a "city of orgies."

"MISTRESS OF ABOMINATIONS"

While respectable women fruitlessly battled the sex trades, they barely held their own in another arena, control of their own fertility. The average number of children born to white New Yorkers surviving to menopause continued to decline, dropping from seven or eight in 1800 to five in 1860. But abortion, one of the leading weapons in women's birth control arsenal, came under heavy censure, touching off a public struggle over sexuality in the city.

Abortions were legal if done before "quickening"—a woman's first awareness of fetal movement, usually late in the fourth month. Given most people's assumption that a fetus was not human before this, the procedure's morality was not generally an issue. Most considered abortion akin to contraception, and white, married, native, middle- and upper-class Protestants dramatically expanded their reliance on it in this era. Catholics aborted far less frequently—their lower rate and later age of marriage provided an effective substitute—but there is no evidence of any public activity against abortion by the city's Catholic leadership. By the end of the 1850s, according to one estimate, perhaps 20 percent of all New York pregnancies were being aborted, a substantial increase from earlier in the century.

Since 1828, however, abortion *after* quickening had been a crime. A person convicted of performing one—though not the woman herself—could be found guilty of second-degree manslaughter and given a year in jail or a hundred-dollar fine. This law, passed at the insistence of regular doctors, stipulated that postquickening abortions could be done legally if necessary to save the mother's life, though only if two regular doctors attested to such necessity. The law, part of a larger package physicians had pushed through the state legislature in an effort to clamp down on their "irregular" competitors, had little practical effect throughout the 1830s.

Indeed, at decade's end abortion had become a public commercial enterprise. Practitioners began advertising in newspapers. In March 1839 a notice in the *Sun* suggested it was neither moral nor desirable for families of any class to grow beyond their means, nor was it necessary "when a simple, easy, healthy, and certain remedy is within our control." Those interested in limiting the size of their families need only come by the Liberty Street office of Mrs. (soon to be Mme.) Restell and pick up some pills, which could "be used by married or single, by following directions."

Mme. Restell was the public persona of Ann Lohman, an English immigrant seamstress who had married Charles Lohman, a printer at Bennett's *Herald* and an avowed admirer of Robert Dale Owen's writings on birth control. Charles and Ann set to producing preventive pills and powders—not placebos but potent drugs. If they didn't work, as they often didn't, Mme. Restell offered more extensive services along with "private and respectable board." For an income-adjusted fee (twenty dollars for the poor, a hundred for the wealthy), she would use instruments to pierce the amniotic sac and induce a miscarriage, at which point the woman would go for further treatment to her regular doctor.

Restell was a spectacular success, especially with the carriage trade. Soon she had six pill outlets in the city, an enlarged Greenwich Street lying-in facility for aborting a fetus or bearing a child, branch agencies in Newark, Philadelphia, and Boston, and salesmen on the road marketing her abortifacients and making referrals to the New York clinic. Rivals set up shop, including a Madame Costello, who also pretended to a Parisian background, and a Mrs. W. H. Maxwell, whose clinic on Greene Street offered abortions, treatment for venereal disease, and a "sanctuary to which to flee" for the unfortunate.

Commercialization afforded new ease of access for women seeking abortions, but it also brought their changing sexual habits forcibly to public attention. Before 1840 there had been virtually no mention of abortion in the popular press. Now one George W. Dixon, owner and editor of a weekly named the *New York Polynathos*, started a campaign to expose Restell as a malefactor. Dixon, a self-appointed scourge of lax public morals, was less concerned with the life of the fetus or health of the mother than with the presumed threat to female virtue. Spouses could now commit adultery without detection, Dixon warned. Worse, a man about to wed a professed maiden could well discover that "Madame Restell's Preventive Powders have counterfeited the hand writing of Nature; you have not a medal, fresh from the mint, of sure metal; but a base, lacquered counter, that has undergone the sweaty contamination of a hundred palms."

In 1841 a carman with the Harlem Rail Road claimed his dying wife had accused

Restell of a botched abortion. Restell was arrested, accused of murder, and confined to the Tombs. In the end, however, she was convicted of only two minor infractions, and the publicity garnered her additional business. She was indicted again in 1844; though none of her wealthy clients dared defend her in public, Restell boldly argued her own case in letters to the public press and again got off without serious penalty.

As she grew wealthier Restell took a certain delight in her notoriety. She rode daily along Broadway in a showy carriage with four superb horses and a liveried coachman, brushing aside press depictions of her as a "she devil." But now Restelle came up against more powerful enemies. Medical doctors had been arguing that a fetus was alive from the point of conception, not the moment of quickening. Abortions were therefore immoral at any stage and should be recategorized as murder and outlawed. Doctors also claimed abortions were dangerous (and there *were* incompetent and avaricious practitioners, though the operation remained far less hazardous than childbirth). Physicians backed Dixon's charge that abortion fostered sexual license among females; "Madame Restell," one doctor claimed, "offered to those who would not control their appetites, impunity." Doctors neglected to mention their concern that female abortionists were undermining male efforts to dominate the lucrative new field of obstetrics and gynecology.

Physicians set out to persuade the state legislature to criminalize the procedure and eradicate New York City's burgeoning reputation as the nation's abortion capital. Dr.

THE FEMALE ABORTIONIST.

Madame Restell demonized in the *Police Gazette*, March 13, 1847. She is shown holding a bat with a dead baby in its jaws. (American Antiquarian Society)

Gunning S. Bedford, professor of midwifery and diseases of women and children at the University of New York, led the attack. He and his colleagues had substantial influence, and the combination of medical pressure and sensational publicity won passage of a new abortion law in May 1845. It declared the death of a fetus or its mother to be second-degree manslaughter if quickening had taken place, a crime punishable by four to seven years in the state prison. It also made the mother herself liable for seeking and submitting to an abortion or for performing one on herself—an unprecedented revocation of women's common-law immunity from punishment.

With law in hand, press and physicians stepped up their assaults. The new *National Police Gazette* denounced abortionists as murderers and alleged they ran a lucrative side business selling their victims' bodies to surgical clinics. Dixon, Restell's old nemesis, incited the public to force her from the city, and in February 1846 a crowd of several hundred descended on her Greenwich Street quarters, yelling, "Where's the thousand children murdered in this house?" and "Hanging's too good for the monster!" Forty policemen, commanded by Chief Matsell, prevented mayhem, but city authorities proceeded to station men outside her office who followed callers home and noted down names and addresses.

In 1847 Restell was arrested again, indicted for manslaughter in the second degree, and tried before a crowded courtroom that included numerous lawyers from other states, among them Senator Stephen A. Douglas of Illinois. Dr. Bedford was a leading prosecution witness at this first highly publicized abortion trial in U.S. history. Restell was found guilty, though only of a misdemeanor, and to the applause of spectators, she was sentenced to a year on Blackwell's Island. It seemed a decisive victory for antiabortion forces.

It wasn't. Restell did easy time—a featherbed instead of the usual straw mattress, food from the keeper's table—and after she was freed, in June 1849, promptly resumed her advertisements and practice. More remarkably, throughout the 1850s the authorities and general populace alike virtually ceased hostilities against her and her competitors. Some attributed this to behind-the-scenes support from a combination of influential gentleman-patrons and to politicians and policemen won over by campaign contributions and bribes. Restell was certainly wealthy enough to afford payoffs. In spring 1857 she and her husband bought the northeast corner of Fifth Avenue and 52nd Street—outbidding Archbishop Hughes, who had wanted to build an official residence there—and began erecting a mansion. Now, to the prelate's dismay, the future St. Patrick's Cathedral would have the city's foremost abortionist as its neighbor.

Abortion thus remained in place as a leading option for women seeking birth control. But if the women who used such services were relieved, the feminists crusading against prostitution were not. Like Dixon, they feared its regularization would facilitate adultery (though they feared husbands would be the errant parties). Indeed in 1847 the American Female Moral Reform Society had rejoiced at the arrest of Mme. Restell, the "mistress of abominations," and visited the "heroine of licentiousness" in her cell to encourage her to Christian contrition—with singular lack of success.

So female reformers turned to promoting alternatives to abortion, though once again their initiatives were hampered by religious and class convictions. New York City lacked a lying-in hospital where unwed mothers could bear illegitimate children and receive medical attention in private. Many European cities had such institutions, so as not to box pregnant women into choosing between abortion and disgrace. In Catholic

Ireland, Dublin's lying-in hospitals freely admitted all of the thousands who applied each year, never asking if they were married. The New York Asylum for Lying-In Women on Orange Street also offered poor pregnant women a midwife's services and postpartum care, but the "lady managers" accepted only "reputable married" females—lest they encourage "criminal improvidence"—and demanded references in advance, ideally from a "respectable New York citizen." Once admitted, moreover, patients were treated like servants: forbidden to have visitors, to leave without permission, or to use liquor or profane language. A female matron enforced deference and decorum, with violators subject to dismissal. After delivery, the asylum placed many of the mothers as wet nurses with respectable women, assuring prospective employers that their candidates' breasts were in good condition and that "their characters [had] already [been] investigated by the Visiting Committee."

The sole alternative to the asylum was the almshouse, and poor women preferred the former to the latter. It was nearer their homes, was reputedly safer, and protected them from having to associate (and be associated) with prostitutes, and its wet-nurse employment service provided them with a year-long "situation," even if it did require they nurse only their employer's baby and farm out their own. Most avoided both if possible.

New York had no place that would take in foundlings, either. No hospital (again excepting Bellevue) would accept deserted or abandoned children, or even admit a sick child under two. Bellevue paid poor women to care for these unwanted children—usually less than it cost them to do so—with the result that nearly 90 percent of those farmed out died. According to the Almshouse commissioner, nearly one thousand babies perished each year between 1854 and 1859.

Awakened to this situation by a personal experience, Mary Delafield DuBois, wife of a well-to-do Gramercy Park lawyer, joined with Anna R. Emmet, wife of a famous New York specialist in the diseases of women and children, and in May 1854 they opened a Nursery for the Children of Poor Women in a small house on St. Mark's Place. It became the first institution in the country devoted primarily to day care, taking in the children of working women (including wet nurses) so their mothers could "go out to service." Yet here too the pioneers drew back from establishing a Dublin-style open-door institution. They would only accept the progeny of an unwed woman if it was her first lapse and she could demonstrate victimhood: "The mother must produce evidence of having borne a good character until the dark shadow of him who ruined her fell across her path."

Beyond these efforts, women unhappy with existing sexual codes and practices would not or could not go. Public discussions about erotic matters remained difficult or impossible, and only those wrapped head to toe in the mantle of purity dared address such issues at all. It was left to a tiny handful—the men and women of the Free Love movement—to issue a more frontal challenge to the conventional order, and the rough handling they received served as a warning to others to keep silent.

Free Lovers rejected coercion in sexual relations, whether from male lust or legally prescribed duties of marriage. Stephen Pearl Andrews, a philosopher influenced by anarchism and Fourierism, argued that only "passional attraction"—spiritual holy love—should bind two individuals. The state had no business in the bedroom. Legal marriage, like many other governmental or religious institutions, was inherently enslaving, little more than a form of legalized prostitution, and ought to be abolished. Decisions about engaging in sexual relations should be left to the "well developed conscience," with women having an absolute right to refuse such connections.

Free Lovers by no means advocated promiscuity. Most considered themselves particularly chaste and pure and rejected sex apart from procreation. Respectable sorts assumed the opposite and denounced them as sexual libertines. When Andrews and Fourierist Albert Brisbane founded the New York Free Love League in 1853, Henry Raymond's *New York Times* accused its five to six hundred members of holding regular "orgies" at its 555 Broadway clubhouse, though his own news columns admitted that, whatever their theories, their social events were refined gatherings, little different from "an ordinary family party." But it was precisely the theory that alarmed Raymond, who saw in it an assault on the family; he kept up his sensational coverage and prodded police into raiding the club and arresting some members. The cases were thrown out of court, and the circle continued in existence, but from then on, respectable and conventional feminists would find themselves charged with being Free Lovers, stifling further discussion.

New York women thus faced substantial obstacles when they tried to loosen some of the constraints that bound them. They were barred from most professions, banned from labor unions, balked in their efforts to limit prostitution, excluded from many public activities and spaces. City life did afford women new avenues of expression, however, wherever an expansion of female possibilities suited the needs of the marketplace.

"FASHION'S DESPOTIC RULE"

As rapidly as republican simplicity was scrapped in urban architecture, it waned even faster in the field of feminine attire. Nowhere was this more striking than in New York City, capital of America's clothing industry and portal for *la mode parisienne*. Fashion was the affluent woman's metier, a way to display her expertise (as well as her husband's wealth). Devotees of fashion redeployed old words to describe new looks: "elegant" gained currency from 1845, "stunning" from 1849, and "chic" from 1856.

The pursuit of fashion also validated expanded female claims on city space. Shopping was irreproachably legitimate, and respectable women could wander the Broadway commercial district without reproach in search of commodities. This "midtown" terrain, easily accessible from uptown's female zone yet satisfactorily distant from downtown's all-male turf, emerged as an acceptable heterosexual domain (as would Central Park).

Fashion provided women farther down the social scale with expanded employment opportunities. Quite apart from the thousands employed in the garment industry itself, milliners and dressmakers blossomed, most of whom affected fancy French names, though most were Irish working class. They subscribed to French fashion magazines, kept up with current French designers, and maintained correspondents in Paris who dispatched dress dolls in the latest styles. Cosmeticians did a thriving trade too, now that New York women had abandoned the old republican association of painted faces with aristocrats or whores. Some professional hairdressers in the 1850s opened their own shops, and others were attached to hotels for out-of-towners, but most still attended wealthy patrons in their homes. On New Year's Eve hairdressers went from house to house, crimping with heating irons, working through the night until noon next day when visiting began; those clients done early might sit up all night so as not to spoil their hairdos.

Working women were consumers too. Immigrants might arrive at Castle Garden in traditional costume, but those who could afford it shed such garb with great alacrity and slipped into something fashionable. Stylish dress could signal one's aspirations, attract an upward-striving husband, and erase (or at least smudge) sartorial discrepancies of class. When Irish maids donned hoopskirts and flowered bonnets, one observer noted, they were "scarcely to be distinguished from their employers." Irritated mistresses agreed, and some insisted their employees wear costumes adapted to their station in life.

Democratization of fashion led to contestation as well as imitation. The bourgeois model of beauty favored a pale-complexioned, heart-shaped face with a "rosebud" mouth (the right degree of pucker was obtained by repeating the mantra "peas, prunes, and prisms"). It required a tiny eighteen-inch waist (whose stylish circumference was achieved with the aid of straitlaced corsets). Bowery g'hals paid little attention to these conventions. They opted for the "plump and hearty" look, reported George Foster, and whenever they thought about the "poor, pale-faced creatures of Broadway, they actually and heartily pity them."

Shopgirls, milliners, and dressmakers' assistants—professionally well versed in prevailing styles—mischievously parodied elite fashions. They adopted startling color combinations, ornate hats, and elaborate decorations even gaudier than those favored by the wealthy. By recycling fashions of the 1820s, they essayed a retro look. G'hals, like ladies, promenaded in public space, sashaying along the Bowery after working hours with girlfriends or young men, indulging the pleasures of city life, reveling in new freedom from customary constraints.

Yet fashion could restrain women as well as liberate them, and a largely female band of feminists, writers, editors, reformers, and advice givers pointed to its more problematic aspects. They found prevailing styles cumbersome and imprisoning. Layers of petticoats weighed down the wearer, long skirts dragged through the mud, and corsets were positively hazardous to health. Emily Thornwell, in her *Lady's Guide to Perfect Gentility in Manners, Dress and Conversation* (1856), was one of many who deplored tight lacing as causing coughing, consumption, headaches, heart palpitation, deformed ribs, uterine and spinal disorders, and "an extreme heaving of the bosom, resembling the panting of a dying bird."

Fashion was unrepublican, the handmaiden of aristocratic luxury and self-indulgence. It valued consumption over production, appearance above character, idleness over industry. "Do we not see females in every fashionable circle," queried Mrs. A. J. Graves in her *Woman in America* (1843), "who fill no loftier station in social life, and who live as idly and as uselessly as the gorgeously attired inmates of the harem?"

Fashion was expensive. It undid hardworking husbands. Magazine writers often depicted bankrupt businessmen as victims of their wives' pursuit of lavish wardrobes. The pursuit itself opened women to ridicule. Anna Cora Mowatt's popular play *Fashion* (1845) presented a parvenu Mrs. Tiffany who, in her attempts to become a woman of fashion, made a complete fool of herself until set straight by Adam Trueman, her virtuous friend from the country.

Stylish women, finally, were slaves to fashion, which is why feminist reformers attuned to the politics of dress declared that "our sex should rise above subserviency to fashion's despotic rule." Determined to take grass-roots control of the mode, the women boldly proposed an alternative costume. Picking up on a gymnastic uniform promoted by the New York City *Water-Cure Journal* during the 1840s, two upstate women, Elizabeth Cady Stanton and Amelia Bloomer (editor of the *Lily*, a temperance paper) began to wear and publicize a seemlier version in 1851. It consisted of a simple woolen dress, shortened to midcalf or knee, worn over billowing Oriental pantaloons— a blend of Turkish and Quaker. Soon many feminists were wearing the reform attire, which journalists promptly labeled "bloomers."

The initiative came under instant and ferocious attack. Men were outraged to see women wearing trousers, a patent transgression of gender boundaries. Little boys wore dresses until five years of age, when they ritually signaled their departure from the female community by donning trousers. Strong women who disagreed with their husbands had long been accused of trying to "wear the breeches." Men jeered at bloomer wearers in the street. Boys pelted them with snowballs in winter, apple cores in summer. They were the butt of vicious caricatures and sexist jokes.

Women didn't much care for the new style either. Conservative women saw it as a threat to their sphere. Fashionable ladies sniffed because it hadn't come from Paris and no society leader (or even actress) would take it up. Style-conscious working-class women agreed: when a manufacturer of painted window shades urged his female employees to wear bloomer dress, as their voluminous skirts were brushing against the still-wet product, they refused, accepting dismissal rather than don the outfit. Truth to tell, even Bloomerites found the costume unattractive, and when the hoop skirt arrived, bearing the endorsement of Empress Eugénie of France, Bloomer herself adopted it, declaring that its doing away with heavy petticoats was an acceptable enough reform. Stanton hung on alone until 1853, then gave up.

Soon the hoop skirt was all the rage. With firms like Douglass and Sherwood of Broadway churning out four thousand of them daily, it was clear that the bloomer movement had run up against more than gender stereotyping and bad design. The fashion system was as deeply imbricated in New York City's economy as was prostitution, and the profitable matrix of designers, department stores, fashion entrepreneurs, garment manufacturers, and the clothing trade would prove highly resistant to tampering.

"LINDOMANIA" AND "HIGH-FLYER STAMPEDES"

In the world of commercial entertainment it was much the same. The imperatives of profit opened new pathways for city women, though only if they stayed within prescribed patterns and places of consumption.

Barriers tumbled quickest in the midtown entertainment district. Where it had been quite improper for a woman of refinement to enter a public eating house, feeding ladies became a lucrative business. Some restaurants allowed mixed dining, others arranged special accommodations (ladies' dining rooms, separate ladies' entrances), and some (notably ice cream parlors like Taylor's) became completely identified as women's spaces. The explosion in the number of women travelers speeded this transformation, as such visitors were obliged to eat in public. Many of the new hotels established reserved drawing rooms. Astor House went farther, refusing to admit any lady unless accompanied by a gentleman: while this offended reputable single women, it effectively excluded prostitutes.

The presence or absence of prostitutes was key to theatrical developments too. Playhouses wanted to draw more respectable women. They courted such ladies by installing special lobbies in which they could promenade between acts and by keeping lights on halfway during performances so they could take one another's measure. But the third tier remained a galling obstacle, and many women boycotted theaters that retained one. Instead they flocked to musical venues like the Astor Opera House, the Academy of Music, and the New York Philharmonic Society, where, as Lydia Maria Child noted, "no degraded corner is reserved for unveiled vice." Seeking respectable patronage, the Park Theater substituted a "family circle" for its third tier in 1848. Most theaters refused to follow suit. Convinced that the presence of prostitutes was crucial to profitability, many handed out free tickets in the brothels.

It was left to the shrewdest impresario of them all to demonstrate the lucrative possibilities in marketing respectability. P. T. Barnum had observed that women patrons considered content as crucial as audience. When Lola Montez came to town, her reputation as mistress of the king of Bavaria preceded her, and when she appeared onstage as dancer or actress, New York's ladies were as one in boycotting her scandalous person. So, in the late 1840s, Barnum sanitized his American Museum. He banned prostitutes, prohibited liquor, cracked down on raucous audiences, and cleaned up his acts. He introduced matinees and continuous performances and pointedly featured "moral" presentations: scriptural dramas, the occasional Shakespeare play "shorn of its objectionable features," and temperance melodramas like *The Drunkard* (1850), which ran without interruption for over a hundred performances, breaking all New York records. Women and entire families streamed in, proving to Barnum's satisfaction that he was tapping new portions of the populace.

The readiness of ladies to attend recitals of European concert artists suggested that still fatter profits lay in finer art. In 1849 Barnum began preparations to bring over Jenny Lind, a Swedish singer. Since her 1844 debut in the Berlin Opera House, Lind had gone from triumph to musical triumph while establishing a reputation for piety, modesty, charitable good works, and a spotless private life. Barnum enticed her across the Atlantic with a guarantee of $150,000 (plus very considerable expenses) for 150 concerts, which Lind, herself no mean bargainer, required him to bank in advance. Barnum mortgaged all he owned and borrowed more. Then he set out to guarantee success.

Barnum launched an unprecedented press campaign to acquaint Americans with Lind's voice—and, more important, her virtues—concentrating on winning over homemakers and charity ladies and writers of sentimental fiction. Biographies from N. P. Willis and George Foster emphasized Lind's morals rather than her musicianship, stressing "her intrinsic worth of heart and delicacy of mind."

Next Barnum orchestrated her arrival. In September 1850 he arranged one of the most tremendous welcomes in the history of New York City. Thousands swarmed to the Canal Street dock from which Lind, pelted with flowers and accompanied by twenty companies of firemen, was conveyed under triumphal arches to the Irving House Hotel opposite A. T. Stewart's store; there 150 musicians serenaded her into the wee hours. In the next days, Barnum had Lind visit Brady's gallery, meet Archbishop Hughes, and stop in at the *Herald* to see its Hoe presses at work. "Reputation was manufactured for her, by wholesale," a rival impresario grumped, and Barnum gleefully agreed: Lind "would have been adored if she had had the voice of a crow."

The first concert was held September 11 at Castle Garden. The huge event—five thousand turned up—was handled with perfect decorum. A hundred hired policemen kept order; color-coded tickets matched color-coded seats. Willis rhapsodized at "the clockwork precision" with which people were seated and the "quiet dignity of their egress." When Lind gave local New York charities her share of the evening's profits—ten times what she'd made in any single European appearance—Hone declared that "New York is conquered; a hostile army or fleet could not effect a conquest so complete."

As Lind moved out into the country, to continued adulation, some commentators expressed concern at the rampant "Lindomania." Barnum's ability to whip up publicity was a wholly new order of event. He had made use of an assortment of New York institutions—press, photography, hotels—to transform reputation into commodity, to package the first superproduct in the emerging marketplace of popular commercial culture. "Jenny Lind is a celebrity," said one magazine, using a noun of relatively recent coinage, and there were those who worried that the business of celebrity creation might prove to have its downsides.

Barnum had demonstrated something else. Lind's earnings were unprecedented in the history of American entertainment. Her New York concerts alone grossed nearly $290,000. Barnum personally cleared half a million on her tour and became a rich man. Clearly, conventional androcentrism had been proved wrong. Big bonanzas awaited those who tailored their entertainments to the precepts of bourgeois morality, and particularly to the hitherto underestimated audience of respectable females.

The entertainment marketplace also welcomed working-class women. German immigrant men and women piled together into immense beer halls like the Deutscher Volksgarten, the Atlantic Gardens, and Lindenmuller's Odeon where, at rough tables and wooden benches, surrounded by gaudily painted frescos, they drank, sang, and watched amateur theatricals. Women were also present at melodrama, burlesque, and blackface performances, dime museums, ice cream parlors, oyster shops, and lecture halls. But they were most in evidence (as was true for the bourgeoisie) in venues devoted to music, especially dance halls.

Dancing in the past had usually been held under organizational auspices—the annual balls of fire companies, militia units, and political clubs. Now it became a commercial proposition. Girls were admitted free; men paid twenty-five cents. Seamstresses and servants threw themselves into dances that were as acrobatic as they were graceful. George Foster noted that the "high-flyer stampedes" drew the East Side's "unmarried womanhood" in all their finest clothes and declared that "New York is undoubtedly the greatest place for dancing in all Anglo Saxdom."

On the Bowery, g'hals could enjoy a pleasurable evening away from the prying eyes of neighbors or keep an eye out for a permanent partner, amid a far wider constituency of eligible men than was accessible through family and community networks. Such independence could be risky. The crowds that shielded her from neighborhood scrutiny also left her exposed to seduction-bent males. Some of the b'hoys extended a rough courtesy to women and adopted a protective stance, particularly against "aristos"— gentleman rakes looking to pick up working girls. But there were plenty of working-class sporting men, for whom conquest remained a source of self-esteem. Many still considered women in public a scant step from prostitution. They were quick to assume that women in dance halls were "rowdy girls," willing to trade sexual favors for the provision of beer and oysters. Ruffians often hung around fire stations and rumshops, insulting and abusing women passing by. "Bloods" camped out on street corners, shouting out: "An Angel, by H——s!" "Dam'd fine girl, by g—d!" "Where do you lodge, my dear?" Predatory tavern rowdies and waterfront gangs dragged off lone women, especially those who appeared both vulnerable and independent, and subjected them to brutal group rapes, a male prerogative known as "getting our hide." Such belligerence served as a stark reminder that women's newfound access to public space remained subject to masculine veto.

FEME DECOVERT

When Lydia Maria Child asserted that women's legal status was akin to that of slaves, the analogy seemed more compelling than when white working-class men used it. Female subordination, after all, was deeply inscribed in the law, and had been since the British Empire overrode Holland's more tolerant approach to gender issues. Quite apart from not being allowed to vote, the doctrine of *feme covert* meant that a married woman could not sign contracts, control her own earnings or inherited property, or be the legal guardian of her children. Her legal identity was subsumed in her husband's. Under the law, as a later judicial summary recalled, "the husband and wife were one and the husband was the one."

In the 1840s feminist New Yorkers began to protest this state of affairs, starting with the laws blocking women from owning property. The premise underlying such statutes, the *Advocate* said in 1846, was that "women do not know enough to take care of [property], and therefore the laws and customs of society virtually say they shall have none to protect." Radical feminists argued that "free Christian enlightened women" needed their property and earnings if they were not to be forced into economic subservience. More conservative women emphasized that such a right would protect wives against drunks and gamblers who would squander their property.

Initially, legislators resisted, leery of undermining the sexual order, but it was increasingly clear that the vicissitudes of contemporary capitalism dictated some gender adjustments. The first convincing arguments for a married women's property bill were made during the Panic of 1837, in the context of debtor relief. Too many respectable families had been wiped out after husbands sank their wives' money into ill-chosen investments. Given the growing centrality of stocks and credit to New York's economy, was it really wise for a wife's property to be subject to her husband's debts?

This was part of a larger problem: *feme covert* was hampering development of new kinds of capitalist industry. Life insurance companies had been stymied because wives were not allowed to own life insurance in their own names or to hold any benefits they received free from claims by their husbands' creditors. In 1840 New York State had solved both problems with a stroke of the legislative pen, simultaneously giving the life insurance business a boost and feminists their first triumph.

Another powerful group of males—scions of old and propertied families—had a different problem, keeping the family fortune from falling into the hands of predators. Since the seventeenth century, when the English gentry had first grappled with this problem, wealthy New York clans had been insulating a wife's property by conveying it to a trustee, reserving to the wife powers that ranged from full authority over her property to complete dependence on the designated trustee. In 1844 Philip Hone's daughter Emily married Frederic G. Foster, but Hone made Frederic De Peyster the trustee over the dowry she brought, and her husband was forbidden to touch the principal.

New York's equity judges had been going along with this modification of *feme covert*, but obtaining their approval on a case-by-case basis was a costly and cumbersome business, and even wealthy gentlemen preferred to have such rights guaranteed across the board. It was an era, moreover, when republican-minded citizens and lawyers sought to scrap equity courts as feudal and colonial remnants and to replace arbitrary judge-made law with a uniform statutory code. They succeeded in 1846, when the state constitutional convention abolished the office of chancellor and put equity under jurisdiction of the common-law courts.

It was in this context that a small but aggressive group of feminist campaigners, led by Elizabeth Cady Stanton and Ernestine Rose, a recently arrived Polish-Jewish immigrant, struck up an alliance with patrician and propertied men and pushed for a married women's property statute. Women had long been aware that prenuptial contracts held great potential for them, in that a woman with assets (and the permission of her intended husband) could create a trust that she herself controlled. When Sarah Willis ("Fanny Fern") took James Parton as her third husband, he signed an agreement stipulating that her property and the proceeds of her writing would belong solely to her and her children. However, few women had the assets or legal sophistication to negotiate such a bargain, and feminists wanted the same rights granted to all.

Resistance to such legislation came from those who feared the gender consequences might outweigh economic benefits. Might not husband and wife come to see their interests as antithetical? Might not a wife compete with her husband in trade? Become the partner of his business rival? Might not such a law incite women to invade bench, bar, pulpit, and dissecting room? Supporters of the law countered that it was not an attack on the economic foundations of patriarchy but rather a way to extend men's ability to protect dependent women. Their arguments carried the day, and in 1848 the state legislature made a wife's possessions her own and not subject to her husband's debts.

The women's rights advocates who gathered that summer in the upstate New York town of Seneca Falls hailed the law but recognized its limitations. Wives might control their property, but husbands continued to command their earnings. Besides, taken as a whole, marriage still entailed the surrender of a woman's legal personality. They pressed on.

Further successes came in areas where women's desires dovetailed with the needs of powerful businessmen. In 1850 a new law allowed married women to control their bank deposits. The act was primarily designed to protect the banks and keep a wife's deposits out of reach of her husband's creditors, but it further enhanced women's financial standing. Next year the legislature decreed that a married woman who owned stock could vote it herself, making all stockholders equal regardless of sex or marital status. Again, this pleased wealthy fathers, who were bequeathing stocks to their daughters.

What did not please them, or nearly any males, was the next proposition women advanced: that all people capable of owning property should be allowed to vote. In 1848 a bare majority of the delegates at Seneca Falls had agreed to include Elizabeth Cady Stanton's call for the suffrage in their Declaration of Sentiments. Over the next decade, as it became ever clearer that moral suasion had failed to transform men or society and that electoral politics were becoming the crucial instruments for resolving national and local issues, more and more feminists began demanding access to the ballot. Such claims were greeted with tremendous hostility, and nowhere more so than in New York City.

Since 1850, inspired by the Seneca Falls meeting, feminists had begun holding annual Women's Rights Conventions. The first three met upstate or outside New York altogether, but in 1853, attracted by the opening of the Crystal Palace and the simultaneous gatherings of the Anti-Slavery Society and the World's Temperance Convention (whose clergyman organizers excluded women), organized feminism ventured into the metropolis for the first time.

On September 6 three thousand delegates from eleven states as well as England and Germany packed into the Broadway Tabernacle on Worth Street. Female speakers shared the platform with male abolitionist luminaries in town for their own meeting. Together they advocated women's right to enter public life, to engage in any profession, to wear what they chose (Lucy Stone donned "bloomers"), and to vote. Men, they declared, must be forced to abandon their privileges by an aroused public sentiment.

But "public" sentiment—if one was to judge by the crowds that jammed their way into the galleries—was cholerically against them. The audience interrupted each speaker with shouts, hisses, stomping, cheering, rude remarks, and free-for-all fights. Sojourner Truth, back in town for the event, handled the rowdies pretty well: "We'll have our rights," she warned. "You may hiss as much as you like, but it is comin'." Soon, however, cacophony reigned again, and amidst a yelling, laughing uproar, the meeting was forced to adjourn.

Greeley and Bryant condemned the crowds, but the *Times*, the *Herald*, and the *Courier* applauded them. James Watson Webb of the *Courier* jeered at the "antiquated and very homely females" who "made themselves ridiculous by parading the streets in company with hen-pecked husbands, attenuated vegetarians, intemperate Abolitionists and sucking clergymen, who are afraid to say 'no' to a strong-minded woman for fear of infringing upon her rights." Even men as sympathetic as Whitman found feminism unnerving. "What a queer medley of women's rights meetings at present!" he wrote in 1858 in the *Daily Times*. "Women in breeches and men in petticoats—white, black, and cream-colored—atheists and free-lovers, vegetarians and Heaven knows what—all mixed together, 'thick and slav,' until the mixture gets a little too strong, we should think, even for metropolitan stomachs."

Many women also remained unconvinced or in active opposition. Some traditionalists simply denounced women's rights as contrary to divine law, but others argued that deep-rooted social inequalities made it extremely difficult to survive without a man. Where male antifeminists balked at sharing their prerogatives, females feared losing the few they had. "Women never aim so suicidal a blow against their own interest," wrote one women's magazine, "as when they try to do away with or revolt against . . . [the] doctrine of their inferiority," for in so doing, they "absolve the lords of creation from that protection which they are so willing to afford."

Working-class women were not so much opposed as indifferent to the feminist project. Upper- and middle-class calls for feminine solidarity meant little to tenement mothers and factory girls, especially given the condescension and religious bullying many feminists displayed in the autonomous women's institutions they established, and for the moment these sets of sisters would remain unaligned. Indeed some feminists resorted to anti-immigrant rationales, hoping to win over wealthy men and women. Stanton and Susan B. Anthony toured the summertime spas at Saratoga and Ballston, arguing that female suffrage would bolster Anglo-Saxon civilization and win passage of temperance laws. Stanton complained to the state legislature that the current suffrage arrangements exalted "the ignorant and vulgar above the educated and refined—the alien and the ditch-digger above the authors and poets of the day." But legislators held the line. The inferiority of women (and the necessity of maintaining their public subordination) was one thing on which men of different classes could agree.

Progress came only when feminists trimmed their demands to seek, as the *New York Times* delicately put it, the "legal protection and fair play to which women are justly entitled" while abandoning "the claims to a share of political power which the extreme advocates of Women's Rights are fond of advancing." Finally, in May 1860, the legislature accepted a bill drafted by Susan B. Anthony that permitted a wife to own property acquired by "trade, business, labor, or services," to be the joint guardian of her children, and to bring legal actions in her own name (and to *be* sued as well). Every provision of this act had been a specific goal of the women's movement.

At the Tenth National Women's Rights Convention, held on May 10 and 11, 1860, at New York's new Cooper Institute (with historian Mary Louise Booth serving as secretary), feminists were jubilant about this triumph. They would soon find that its effects were limited, as judges undid in the courts gains won in the public arena. *Feme covert* was buried deep within the Anglo-American legal tradition and would prove hard to root out.

46

Louis Napoleon and
Fernando Wood

After the defeat of the workers' uprising in June 1848, a frightened French bourgeoisie and peasantry elected Louis Napoleon to the presidency, then acquiesced when he overthrew the newly established republic and declared himself head of a Second Empire. As Napoleon III he swiftly established an authoritarian state and then, power secured, commenced the reconstruction of Paris.

In June 1853 the emperor handed a map of the capital to Baron Georges Eugène Haussmann, his newly appointed prefect of the Department of the Seine. On it he had sketched a network of wide, straight boulevards he wanted Haussmann to ram through the old city center. His goals were threefold: to unblock clotted medieval capillaries that were obstructing the circulation of commodities; to shift the city's primary link to the outside world, from the Seine River to railheads converging on Paris from the countryside; and to forestall future construction of barricades and allow the emperor to mow down his enemies with artillery.

Haussmann duly plowed Napoleonic avenues straight from the new train stations to the commercial center, treating Paris as an engineering obstacle. The process deindustrialized much of the inner city and forced many working people to the periphery. As one class went out, another came in. The bourgeoisie roosted along the new boulevards in grand new apartment houses—modeled on the *palais* of urban aristocrats—whose heights and facades were reassuringly regulated by the state.

The state also undertook massive infrastructure projects: it built Les Halles and other giant markets, dug an enormous maze of underground galleries with space for sewers, water lines, and gas pipes; and made the Bois de Boulogne—with its curving roads, lakes, and bridle and pedestrian paths (some staked out by the emperor himself)—the new standard for metropolitan parks. Indeed command of the authoritarian state was crucial to every aspect of this urban renewal enterprise, from overbearing small property owners who resisted improvements, to mobilizing a scheme of debt financing, to promoting better housing for working people in an attempt to win their support.

The Parisian model would be copied repeatedly in the ensuing decades, not only by French provincial cities but by Brussels, Stockholm, Barcelona, and Madrid; soon Mexico City would be graced by Parisian boulevards (courtesy of the French-installed Emperor Maximillian). But it would not be copied in New York. There would be no grand design, for there was no grand designer, no political authority able or willing to unilaterally reorganize the flow of people and goods or impose a unified order of architecture. New York's bourgeoisie, inconvenienced but not as yet significantly threatened from below, retained their republican distaste for centralized authority. When Lajos Kossuth came to town in 1851, the leader of Hungary's rebellion against Austrian and Russian despotism was given a hero's welcome at Castle Garden, on a par with those afforded Washington and Lafayette.

New York's merchants, bankers, and industrialists were content to pursue their interests within the framework of a democratic polity, in part, because they had done so quite successfully, certainly at the national and state levels. Though differing sectors of the city's propertied classes had different and sometimes opposing interests, and though New Yorkers in Washington had to negotiate with southern slaveholders and western farmers, and in Albany to tussle with upstaters—overall, the results had been satisfactory. Governments provided banking and currency legislation, tariff laws, protection for investments (especially in western land), judicial procedures for enforcing contracts, land for railroads, and subsidies for steamship operators. Much of their port's expansion in this era was underwritten by the federal government. The U.S. Coastal Survey charted a new channel into the harbor; federal engineers cleared away obstructions in the Hudson and East rivers; federal largesse underwrote lighthouses and provided half a million dollars for work on the harbor's forts and Navy Yard. Clearly, there seemed to be no inherent contradiction between capitalism and popular suffrage.

To sustain their access to and influence upon national and state governments, bourgeois New Yorkers participated personally in government, often serving as congressmen or state legislators. Chiefly, however, the wealthy worked in and through political parties, though continuing to differ on which was more suited to their interests. In the early 1850s, perhaps 75 to 90 percent of the merchants, industrialists, and bankers active in party politics were Whigs—attracted particularly by that party's support for infrastructure development. Still, the oft repeated line "The Democratic merchants could have easily been stowed in a large Eighth Avenue railroad car" was seriously overstated, for New Yorkers were powers in the Democratic Party too (beguiled by its anti-tariff policies, among other things). Democrats, like Whigs, established their national headquarters in New York, for ease of access to campaign contributors and organizational talent: banker August Belmont, head of the Democratic National Committee, was instrumental in running and bankrolling James Buchanan's presidential campaign.

TAMMANY'S TOWN

In New York City itself, however, the upper classes were far more ambivalent about democratic politics. From their perspective, municipal government had fallen into the wrong hands. Once upon a time wise and enlightened gentlemen like themselves had ruled in the public interest. Now, as they saw it, sleazy self-interested politicians had secured a lock on local affairs.

The mayoralty, to be sure, remained a bulwark of respectability throughout the period, as both parties felt impelled to select leading businessmen as nominees. The problem lay with the Common Council. Between 1838 and 1850, the percentage of merchants serving in this body dropped by half, to 15 percent. The ranks of aldermen and assistant aldermen were dominated by ambitious petty entrepreneurs (slaughter-house operators, grocers, dealers in coal or hardware) or skilled craft workers (boat-builders, carpenters, printers, sailmakers, hatters, tailors, saddlers, bakers, and chair-makers). Many councilmen, officeholders, and party activists had their political base in the liquor trade; it was said that one way to break up a meeting of Tammany's Executive Committee was to open the door and yell, "Your saloon's on fire!"

Such men rose to power not from boardrooms or drawing rooms but from the intensely maculinist working-class streets. Rising politicians like William Magear Tweed often developed personal followings—as the gentry once had—by displaying their courage and generosity in leading volunteer fire companies. Tweed, born in 1823 to a Protestant, third-generation Scottish-American family, grew up on Cherry Street, studied bookkeeping, worked in the brushmaking business in which his father owned stock, then joined the family chairmaking firm. A brawny young man with clear blue eyes, an amiable smile, and a fabulous memory for names and faces, Tweed was a gregarious chap (and a good dancer to boot). In 1847 he enlisted in the International Order of Odd Fellows; he was later initiated as a Mason and in 1849 joined some friends in organizing a fire company. He seems to have chosen its name—the Americus Engine Company, Number 6 (more popularly known as "Big Six")—and its symbol as well, a snarling red tiger. In 1850, Big Six's seventy-five red-shirted, intensely clannish members elected him foreman, and Tweed, dashingly attired in white firecoat, led his loyal men in "running with the machine" to battle blazes. Unfortunately they also battled other companies, and in 1850 chief engineer Alfred Carson, who personally accused Tweed of leading an ax-wielding assault on rivals, managed to get him expelled. Still, his exploits had provided a stepping-stone into politics, by bringing the vigorous and ambitious twenty-six-year-old businessman to the attention of Seventh Ward Democratic politicians. In 1850 they ran him for assistant alderman. It was a Whig year, and Tweed lost, but the following year he ran for alderman and won, embarking on a fateful career.

Like fire companies and saloons, gangs were important recruiting grounds for party activists. Candidates for ward offices were chosen at wide-open, walk-in primaries, held in local saloons and hotels. These meetings also selected the ward's delegates to nominating conventions, which in turn proposed candidates for state offices, county offices, city departments, city judgeships, the U.S. Congress, and the mayoralty—at a time when nomination was often tantamount to election. Those intent on dominating these gatherings—held during August and September, when respectable folk were out of town—simply packed them. For the requisite muscle, political entrepreneurs turned to "shoulder-hitters," the same men who for a price would keep opponents from the polls and guard (or stuff) ballot boxes.

Political gangs were, in their own way, open to talent. In the late 1840s John Morrissey, a Troy ironworker, came down to New York, walked into Captain Rynders's Empire Club, and offered to fight any man in the house. He was immediately beaten to a pulp, but Rynders—Tammany boss of the Sixth Ward—admired his bravado and offered him a spot as a shoulder-hitter and emigrant runner (a task that involved meeting immi-

Boss Tweed as foreman of "Bix Six." Engraved
portrait. (© Museum of the City of New York)

grants at the docks, getting them naturalized, and finding them homes and jobs, in
return for their votes).

The Whig *Tribune* was correct in claiming that Democrats regularly rigged elections with the aid of "a dozen of beastly ruffians in each ward, hired to do the voting and
knock down any one who should presume to interfere with the play." But Whigs too
turned to gang leaders, like "Butcher Bill" Poole, a celebrated brawler and eye gouger
who ran his own Ninth Ward gambling and drinking place. A nasty piece of work,
whom even his friends considered deceitful and bloodthirsty, Poole periodically set his
thugs to contesting Morrissey's men at the polls, until his assassination in Stanwix Hall
in 1855, which some suspected Morrissey of masterminding.

Once successful, an alderman had much more to offer his followers than bonhomie
and booze. Tammany councilmen, in particular, were ardent in protecting immigrants
and their customs and regularly denounced nativists as "bigots and fanatics in religion."
They also attended diligently to immigrant sensitivities: green flags and much bombast
flew from the steps of Tammany Hall on St. Patrick's Day. The newcomers were not
naive about the depth of this commitment, but, as the *Irish American* noted, though the
Democrats had their anti-Irish prejudices, at least "they act as if they loved us."

In the end, however, patronage was the lubricant that kept the still-rickety political machines in running order. The mayor appointed all policemen but had to choose them from a nominating list submitted by ward aldermen; the need for annual reappointment kept cops attentive to councilmen's wishes. Supporters could also be rewarded with carting licenses, saloon licenses, and appointments as health wardens, street sweepers, and a myriad of other minor city positions. Councilmen handed out municipal contracts for school, dock, sewer, and street construction to builders, utilities contractors, stone-masons, and carpenters (a good many of them Irish), who returned the favor by mobilizing their grateful employees at election time.

Aldermen, imbued with the era's entrepreneurial spirit, also asked what government could do for them, and found many answers. They could require contractors to present padded bills and then split the excess among themselves. They could award contracts to firms run by relatives, or in which they were partners, or owned entirely by themselves. The really big money, however, came from the ability of a newly autonomous *political* elite to force the city's *economic* elite to pay for things it had once commandeered more directly. Market-oriented politicians set about selling off public assets to the highest bidder.

There was plenty to sell. The Common Council merrily leased out city piers, sold off profitable riverfront properties, and granted ferry franchises to a favored and responsive few. Corruption was hardly new, of course—"There never was a time when you couldn't buy the Board of Aldermen," Tweed once remarked—but it was the arrival of the street railroads, with their attendant scramble for franchises, that brought civic chicanery to new heights (or depths).

Since the Harlem Line had been initiated back in the 1830s, aldermen had generally rejected requests to run horsecars through the city's streets, usually at the behest of politically influential omnibus operators determined to avoid competition. As the potential profits in accommodating the railroad interests became clear, they changed their minds. First, however, they had to beat back proposals that the city itself lay out a unified rail system, to keep fares low and earn profits for the city. Laissez-faire aldermen indignantly denounced public ownership—it would never be able to impose "a system of responsibility that private enterprise alone can arrange and insist upon"—and then got down to the lucrative business of handing out franchises to clamorous (and rivalrous) entrepreneurs.

The turnaround on railroads largely coincided with the accession to power—in the November 1851 elections—of brushman-chairmaker William Tweed and a host of other petty entrepreneurs including a tobacconist, saloonkeeper, stonecutter, butcher, saddler, timber dealer, fishmonger, fruit vendor, and proprietor of a livery stable: men who had watched their "betters" get rich and were determined to get their cut. Working amid the cloud of lobbyists that swarmed each day about City Hall, the Common Council set about earning its nickname of the "Forty Thieves."

Among other initiatives during their two-year run for the money (1852–53), the magistrates spurned an offer to pay the city fifty thousand dollars for the exclusive right to collect dead animals from the streets and gave the contract instead to one W. B. Reynolds, paying *him* sixty-three thousand a year (out of which, a grand jury later found, he made disbursements to aldermen and the city inspector). The Common Councilmen leased city-owned piers at giveaway rents to favorites. They sold off Gansevoort Market, among the most valuable pieces of real estate in the city, for much less than it was worth, allegedly pocketing between forty-five and seventy-five thousand dollars for themselves. Witnesses testified before a grand jury that ferry leases were awarded in return for payoffs. In the case of the Wall Street ferry, the aldermen overrode the mayor's veto and gave the plum to Jacob Sharp, one of their favorites, for much less than other applicants were willing to pay, then lowered his rental costs still farther the following year. Council members also perfected the art of "ringing the bell"—proposing nuisance ordinances that brought the threatened parties running with payoffs.

Most significant, 1852 brought a deluge of railroad projects, and an obliging council liberally handed out charters—which were to be held in perpetuity—on terms unfavorable to the city. One line up Second Avenue went to a group that included Tweed's father-in-law; another, up Third, was awarded to a combination that included prominent Democratic politicians. Thus did the council establish—without even minimal planning, much less coordination on a Haussmannesque scale—the transportation system that would dominate the city for decades. In addition, its charters created quasi-monopolistic agglomerations of corporate power, like the Third Avenue line (capitalized at over a million dollars), whose impact on the city, including the flagrant corruption of civic politics, would long outlast Tweed and his cohort.

MUNICIPAL POLITICS INDICTED

Many businessmen pragmatically accommodated themselves to this de facto partnership with politicos. For those in a position to outbribe their rivals, the situation had the positive advantage of allowing their money to talk loudest. Councilmen were also useful at ensuring that unwanted things did *not* happen. Whether from principled attachment to laissez-faire dictums or inspired by more tangible inducements, aldermen routinely blocked government actions (housing codes, labor laws, horsecar construction) that might hamper favored entrepreneurs. In 1850, against the backdrop of widespread radical and union agitation, a newly established Gas Consumers Association demanded the Common Council build and operate a municipal gas plant. Hostility to the two old monopolies that divided the business had long been building. The rates of the New York Gas-Light Company (1823), which supplied districts south of Grand Street, and the Manhattan Gas-Light Company (1830), which handled territory north of Grand, were much higher than those charged by counterparts in Philadelphia. Friendly authorities quashed the program for public power, however, and indeed forestalled the chartering of any new competitors—until 1855, when powerful entrepreneurs won establishment of Harlem Gas and Metropolitan Gas. Even then, City Bank's Moses Taylor, a Manhattan Gas director, proved able to negotiate an amicable agreement with the new outfits, forestalling potentially ruinous competition (and lower gas prices as well).

If particular enterprisers were prepared to treat corruption as a routine cost of doing business, a far broader constituency was enraged by what it considered a more pernicious consequence: higher taxes. The Forty Thieves managed to increase city spending by 70 percent in their two years—including a marked upswing in expenditures for gas and lamps, street cleaning, and the purchase of real estate (up 400 percent)—and taxes had jumped accordingly, up by 54 percent between 1850 and 1853. The Common Council had also raised money by drawing on new techniques of railroad finance to sell revenue anticipation bonds. This practice had been going on since 1843, but where it once covered just 27 percent of the city's expenditures it now (by 1856) paid for 47 percent of a sharply higher outlay, calling into question the security of investments in city bonds.[1]

Lost in the outcry of property-owning taxpayers was any awareness that while corruption certainly siphoned off funds, most city money went for street extension and paving, police stations and prisons, and many other items for which the bourgeoisie itself had pushed. Alderman Tweed, responding to critics at the end of his term, noted indignantly that half the appropriations made by the Common Council in 1853 were for mandated items, especially the almshouse and schools. "I ask the people," Tweed went on, "if a city such as ours, daily receiving an immense population of the idle, degenerate, vicious, and good from all parts of the world, could be governed at less expense?"

Reformers worried about more than taxes, however. They were dismayed by what they saw as the Forty Thieves' encouragement of lawlessness and disorder. In the summer of 1852, for instance, the aldermen used their judicial powers to discharge over fifteen hundred of the two thousand men arrested for street fighting and disorderly conduct—many of them loyal party activists—at just the moment when an epidemic of "garotting" (mugging) seemed to be sweeping Manhattan. Reformers were also appalled that council-dominated police officers were taking money to leave underground entrepreneurs alone. This was evident from the throngs of thimble-riggers and three-card monte men who worked the streets openly (and particularly thickly near City Hall) and from the gambling joints on Barclay, the Bowery, and Ann Street (between Broadway and Nassau) that were jammed with volunteer firemen, shoulder-hitters from Tammany Hall around the corner, and gangsters from the Bowery and the Points.

Cordial relations with politicians were key to the gamblers' survival, and indeed the line between the two was often hard to spot. After working for Rynders, John Morrissey went on to a career as a bare-knuckle prizefighter; he took on Yankee Sullivan in an indecisive brawl in 1853, which the umpire gave to Morrissey, and no sooner had he become top dog of the boxing world than he opened his own faro parlor and taproom. Michael Norton, another pugilistic politician, established an entire community of outlaws on the far westerly end of Coney Island (soon known as Norton's Point), which quickly attracted gamblers, sporting men, and others with a distaste for law and order.

If bourgeois New Yorkers were alarmed at losing control of the police—an increasingly critical government agency, given employers' strained dealings with labor unions in the mid-1850s—they were equally dismayed by deficiencies in the fire department. Between 1837 and 1848, notwithstanding the introduction of Croton water, New York suffered twenty-five hundred fires, and some of the worst took place in downtown business wards: the great blaze of 1845, which rivaled that of 1835, destroyed one hundred buildings. Disgusted observers blamed brawling (à la Tweed), the companies' steadfast refusal to introduce steam engines (the first was not adopted until 1857 and was the gift

---

1. Working-class spokespeople also protested corruption. Mike Walsh excoriated the "wirepullers" who rigged nominating meetings to choose corrupt hacks who would hand out city or state contracts to their buddies. He denounced Captain Rynders as an unprincipled hireling. He decried the rising costs of campaign spending, which meant, in effect, that no one could get elected who wasn't either already rich or who "basely sells himself to corrupt and wealthy men." This fury stemmed from the larger conviction that the supposed Democrats were betraying the larger interests of working people under the guise of pseudo-populist rhetoric. The fact was, he insisted, that "no man can be a good political democrat without he's a good social democrat." But Walsh himself was incorporated into the machine and sent off to Congress, and he was snared by the party's coalition with southern interests (and his scorn for northern hypocrisy about wage-labor) into a defense of slavery. Finally he became a political pawn; his movement collapsed by 1850, and Walsh himself came to a wretched end in 1859.

of a fire insurance company), and, most of all, the councilmen who protected the politically potent firemen.

Environmentalist reformers joined the indictment of municipal politics. They insisted that inefficiencies in sanitation, and thus the soaring mortality rates, stemmed from aldermanic disbursal of cleaning and scavenging contracts to incompetents or crooks. In 1852 John Griscom denounced as well the failure of council-appointed health wardens to enforce such sanitary laws as existed. Merchants in general increasingly feared (as one said in 1854) that "men will go with reluctance to make money in a city where pestilence or violence renders life unsafe."

The growing power of politicians, moreover, seemed to coincide worrisomely with the growing public presence of immigrants. The St. Patrick's Day parade had been a small and insignificant affair up until 1849, when it suddenly swelled to a reported fifteen hundred marchers, in part because of a feisty newcomer, the Laborers United Benevolent Association. By 1851 seventeen societies, including other new labor organizations, had formed a Convention of Irish Societies, which reorganized the parade under a grand marshal. By 1853 it had grown big enough to bring city business to a virtual standstill and politically puissant enough so that when St. Patrick's Day paraders tromped into City Hall Park, they were reviewed by the mayor and city officials.

Such acknowledgment grated on nativist nerves, but it was when the Irish decided that same year to march on July 4 as well—staking a claim to American nationalism—that violence erupted. Anti-Catholics had been wrought up already by the arrival in June 1853 of papal nuncio Monsignor Gaetano Bedini, a notorious reactionary who had helped brutally suppress the 1849 republican revolution in Rome. Nativists were convinced his mission was (as Bishop Hughes had boasted) to subjugate the American republic. Tempers were taut, therefore, when the Ancient Order of Hibernians announced it would hold its own Independence Day parade, which would then link up with the official one.

Early on the Fourth, five hundred marchers clad in green scarves and green badges set out from the Hibernians' headquarters, arrayed in eight divisions. Proceeding west on 14th Street toward Eighth Avenue they held aloft a twelve-foot-high banner depicting George Washington shaking hands with Daniel O'Connell. At 10:30 A.M., the Hibernians reached Abingdon Square in Greenwich Village, a community still dominated by native-born artisans and professionals. An altercation with a stagecoach driver annoyed at having his way blocked by Catholics exploded into violence. Led by a notorious nativist gang called the Short Boys, a huge crowd of local nativists, including local volunteer firemen summoned by ringing bells, descended on the marchers, screaming, "Kill the Catholic sons of bitches!" and brandishing knives. A mass of enraged men— Hibernians in green scarves, nativists in red shirts—were swirled in battle when the unabashedly nativist Ninth Ward police arrived and waded in against the Hibernians. Scores of Irish were bloodied, their Washington-O'Connell banner was shredded, and thirty of their number were subsequently indicted for riot.

Street skirmishes became commonplace that fall when evangelical Protestant preachers, most of them obscure artisans and laborers, ventured into Irish neighborhoods spewing incendiary views about the "Scarlet Whore of Babylon" and the morals of Irish women. Other preachers held forth at the East River shipyard owned by Mayor Jacob Westervelt, where they were hailed by throngs of cheering Protestants and heckled by crowds of Catholics, in assemblages reaching twenty thousand people.

Kleindeutschland too was on the move, as were its enemies. For their 1851 celebration of Pentecost, commemorated in Germany by festivals in the woods, some ten to twelve thousand assembled at City Hall Park, then crossed to Hoboken. The Short Boys showed up and overthrew tables and insulted females until a disciplined contingent of Turners in sharply pressed white uniforms drove them off. When the revelers headed back to the ferry, however, the Short Boys struck again, reinforced by Jersey nativists armed with pistols, swords, clubs, and spike-covered poles. The Turners launched a counterattack, and a sanguinary two-hour battle ensued; at least one was killed and dozens wounded before the military arrived from Jersey City.

The Turners promptly demonstrated their fearlessness by returning to Hoboken for their own Turnfest, a gymnastics jamboree. It became an annual event, one of the most popular in German New York, and from then on Turners marched at the head and tail of almost all Kleindeutschland parades (except religious processions). In addition, the Germans formed *Schützenvereine* (shooting clubs) and militia companies. By 1853 there were seventeen hundred German militiamen, 28 percent of the city's total force; added to the twenty-six hundred Irish militiamen and contingents of French, Scotch, Italians, Portuguese, and Jews, this meant that more than two-thirds of New York's six thousand uniformed militia were foreign born. The immigrants were establishing their rights to city space; their enclaves would not be ghettos.

REFORM

In this atmosphere not only did Napoleon and Haussmann look good, but some New York elites looked with interest at a direct action model pioneered by their counterparts in San Francisco. In 1849 and 1851 the prominent men of that city had organized a Committee of Vigilance, which issued warnings to criminals, then banished some and hung others. Dissolved in 1853, it was reborn in 1856 as the San Francisco Vigilance Committee, still dominated by leading merchants. It not only hung crooks and shut up gambling houses but fought corruption in city government—by which it meant wresting control from the dominant Irish Catholic Democratic machine. This had been set in place back in 1849, when David C. Broderick, an old Tammany hand and Gold Rush migrant, had transplanted Manhattan's political methodology, especially its ward-based apparatus, to the West Coast. Not only were the bulk of the vigilantes middle- and upper-class Protestants—either Whigs or nativists—but most of their victims were Catholics.

In New York, though some were tempted by vigilante or authoritarian models, most opted for exclusionary devices. In 1849 a group of nativists founded the Order of the Star Spangled Banner, a secret society with clandestine meetings, rituals, signs, distress calls, and handshakes. In 1853 the group was informally christened "Know-Nothings" by E. Z. C. Judson (Astor riot leader) after their habitual response to questions about their underground operations. The Know-Nothings' aboveground operation, the American Party, aimed to eliminate all foreigners and Catholics from public office, to impose a twenty-one-year residency requirement for naturalization (time enough to reeducate victims of papist and monarchist delusions), to deport foreign paupers and criminals, to require Bible reading in the public schools, to ban the use of foreign languages from schools and public documents, and to break up all military companies "founded on and developing foreign sympathy."

The nativists won support among respectable New Yorkers too, some of whom had been wondering if the city's newest residents weren't perhaps beyond redemption—so inferior to their predecessors, both morally and physically, as to constitute a separate species. Watching an Irish crew dig the cellar for his new home, George Templeton Strong remarked on the "prehensile paws supplied them by nature with evident reference to the handling of the spade and the wielding of the pickaxe." The occupants of Union Square town houses and Fifth Avenue mansions were in fact nearly obsessed by the "brutish" or "simian" physiognomy of the Irish, vesting it with a range of political and social meanings: that Paddy was born, not made; that his physical and moral defects were hereditary; that like blacks, Indians, and women, he was inherently unsuited for republican citizenship. Yet despite some mutterings about disfranchising the immigrants, the city bourgeoisie still lacked the inclination to abandon republicanism—or the power to do so had it wished. Instead it chose to do combat in the political arena.

In 1852 William Dodge, John Harper, Stephen Whitney, and others determined to recapture the municipal ship from the pirates who had boarded and seized it launched not a vigilante group but a City Reform League. By March 1853 Peter Cooper had signed on as President (he would lead the reform movement for the next twenty years) and a host of dignitaries had agreed to serve as vice-presidents—including shipbuilder William Webb, rentier Peter Stuyvesant, Simeon Baldwin (then president of the Merchants' Exchange), banker Moses Taylor, *Times* editor Henry Raymond, and several merchants, like William Aspinwall and Henry Grinnell, whose own methods in winning federal mail subsidies wouldn't have borne close examination. Blasting the use of muscle and corruption, denouncing municipal extravagance, and warning that high taxes would drive businessmen out of the city, they set about the work of reform.

First they changed the charter. The City Reform League prevailed on the legislature to propose, and the electorate to ratify (in June 1853), a drastic reduction in aldermanic power. The Board of Assistant Aldermen was scrapped altogether and replaced by a sixty-man, annually elected Board of Councilmen—on the theory that so many councilmen could not be "bribed but in battalions." (The penalties for bribery were strengthened, just in case.) This body was given charge of all legislation regarding expenditures—the aldermen being limited to suggesting amendments—and required to award all contracts in excess of $250 to the lowest bidder at public auctions.

On the law-and-order front, the councilmen were stripped of their right to sit as judges in municipal courts and lost the power to appoint policemen. Control of the force shifted to a Board of Commissioners (mayor, recorder, and city judges). Also in 1853, the police were given permanent tenure during good behavior and ordered into blue uniforms; in 1854, arrests jumped 40 percent.

The new charter also strengthened the mayor somewhat, by giving him a stronger veto that only two-thirds majorities of both legislative chambers could override. But the city's chief magistrate was no Bonaparte. Since 1849 the nine executive departments had been controlled by independently elected heads, not answerable to the mayor, and they, not he, controlled most patronage, in conjunction with the legislature.

The charter secured, the City Reform League turned to the fall 1853 elections and backed those members of the regular parties (mainly Whigs) who agreed to run as reformers. In the nativist atmosphere, the reformers did well, with victory at the polls stemming in large part from a de facto alliance with the resurgent anti-immigrant movement. The Forty Thieves were swept out of office and into obscurity—except for

William Tweed, who in 1852, while still an alderman, had run for Congress and won. The reformers were ecstatic; reclaiming the polity from the politicians seemed eminently feasible.

Holding it proved tougher. The new councilmen didn't grant questionable franchises, nor did they interfere with the newly reorganized police department, yet neither did they succeed in holding down spending. Paying for those new policemen and the burgeoning school system helped boost taxes 25 percent higher in 1854 and 1855 than in Tweed's two-year term. The disgusted Reform League repudiated its political progeny.

Worse, their alliance with the nativists, and the temperance forces active at the same time, tarnished their image, giving them a narrow and persecuting taint. Given that by 1855 nearly half of the eighty-nine thousand legal voters in New York City were naturalized immigrants, this boded ill. Their reputation was further sullied by continuing nativist street violence. In June 1854 a sailor named John S. Orr, calling himself the Angel Gabriel, clad himself in a long white gown, flourished a brass trumpet, and led a crowd of a thousand nativists to Brooklyn on Catholic-bashing expeditions. The Irish fought back with clubs and stones, then guns came into play, forcing Brooklyn's mayor to call in the National Guard. Such disorders helped speed Know-Nothingism to total collapse the following year.

In addition, the reform movement split apart in 1854 when a critical mass of the membership, especially old Democrats like Peter Cooper and William Havemeyer, decided that Tammany had come up with a candidate they could live with: a businessman of considerable wealth and a reformer who promised to clean up New York City with Napoleonic efficiency.

"OUR CIVIC HERO"

Fernando Wood had commenced his business career in the 1830s, as the owner of a grocery and grogshop near the waterfront, and his political career in 1840, when his immigrant longshoreman patrons sent him to Congress for a term. Returning to New York, Wood had invested his liquor store profits in three small sailing vessels and, by the late 1840s, established himself as a shipping merchant, leasing ships and engaging in the coastal trade with southern markets. A sharp practitioner, he was accused of fraud in 1839; although not convicted, he would be dogged from then on by a (probably deserved) reputation for duplicity. Nevertheless, Wood did well in the Gold Rush trade and parlayed his profits—and the comfortable inheritance of his second wife, Anna Richardson—into a still greater fortune by adroit land speculation. Beginning in 1848 with a substantial upper west side tract, he bought land and built and sold homes, offices, and stores in nearly every ward. ("I never yet went to get a corner lot," Tweed said later, "that I didn't find Wood had got in ahead of me.") These profits in turn were pyramided into investments in banks, railroads and insurance companies, and by the end of the 1850s he was a millionaire.

In 1850 Wood ran for mayor as a "true friend of the Irish" but was beaten back, partly by allegations of business dishonesty: Wood, Philip Hone wrote, "instead of occupying the mayor's seat, ought to be on the rolls of the State Prison." But in 1854 he recaptured the Democratic nomination and won, despite hysterical opposition from nativists to the candidate of Rum and Rowdyism. His strongest support came from the working-class wards (particularly the Irish Sixth, where he harvested four thousand more votes than there were voters). His enemies, however—a combination of prohibitionists, Know-Nothings, and Whigs—secured control of the Common Council and many of the critical patronage-dispensing departments.

Until the very day of his inauguration, January 1, 1855, many considered Wood the incarnation of evil, a Cataline with a long and sorry record. Yet immediately on taking office, Wood became the very model of a reforming mayor. He announced his intention to establish frugal government and maintain public order. He commenced a modest crusade against prostitution in lower Broadway and violators of Sunday closing laws. He went on to call for clean streets, new stone municipal docks, effective building codes, sanitary police, market inspectors, metering of an expanded Croton water system, uptown steam railroads (and uptown development in general), a new City Hall, a full-size Central Park (resisting would-be trimmers), and creation of a great university and a free academy for young women. All in all he championed a thorough reconstitution of the city that would, he said, make New Yorkers proud of their "citizenship in this metropolis" and enable them to "say with Paul of Tarsus, 'I am a citizen of no mean city.'"

Even beyond this astonishing advocacy of proposals advanced over the years by Griscom, Cooper, and others, Wood announced a determination to *govern*. Just as Louis Napoleon was beginning his top-down reconstruction of Paris, the new mayor declared he would vigorously make use of the powers provided his office by the new charter to bring efficiency and order to New York, and indeed appealed for still greater authority. "I am satisfied," he proclaimed, "that no good Government can exist in a city like this, containing so many thousands of the turbulent, the vicious, and the indolent, without a Chief Officer with necessary power to see to the faithful execution of the laws." In the short term, Wood set out to turn the newly reformed police department into a highly centralized and disciplined civic army, connecting all station houses to the chief's office by telegraph. The *Tribune* was thrilled at the department's new capability "of being quickly concentrated by the magical telegraph wires on any given part of the city" and pronounced it "a terrible warning to . . . the ruffianism which has so long beset our city."

The reformers rubbed their eyes, convinced they were dreaming. But no, Wood had been transformed. He even *looked* the part: tall, erect, urbane, with a commanding presence. Strong was amazed that this "man whose former career shews him a scoundrel of special magnitude" had become "our Civic Hero."

Not everyone was entranced. The more astute reformers noticed that Wood's antivice crusades were highly selective. His men rounded up streetwalkers but left brothels alone, raided the grubbier gambling dens but not the fashionable establishments, and bypassed Sunday saloonkeepers who voted the right way. Nor did hard core prohibitionists appreciate the deft way he finessed a draconian 1855 temperance law, casting his refusal to enforce it on constitutional rather than proliquor grounds. In addition, his monopolization of patronage, reputed use of strong-arm tactics at the polls, and repeated demands for an increase in his constitutional power (especially greater control over the police) seemed to some to herald a turn to French-style despotism.

Equally disturbing was his continuing popularity with the immigrant laboring classes. Wood established a "Complaint Book" in which citizens could register charges against crooked or exploiting employers, or obnoxious policemen and public officials. He appointed Irishmen to the police in growing numbers (by 1855, they constituted 27 percent of the force and outnumbered native-born members in heavily Irish wards).

Temperance, but no Maine Law, A. Fay's 1854 depiction of the interior of the Gem Saloon, a fashionably rococo
establishment that stood on the corner of Broadway and Worth Street. The top-hatted man shaking hands in
the center is Mayor Fernando Wood, who opposed adoption of a state prohibition law and subsequently
refused to enforce it on constitutional grounds. (The Metropolitan Museum of Art. The Edward W. C. Arnold
Collection of New York Prints, Maps and Pictures)

Most alarming of all, when the economy buckled, Wood called for aiding the unemployed with public assistance and public jobs.

In the winter of 1854–55, the great boom faltered badly. A string of commercial
failures and a flurry of frauds and defalcations failed to touch off a full-scale depression
but did precipitate a recessionary crisis. Factories, shipyards, and the building trades
laid off massive numbers of employees. As a cold wave drove the temperature to minus
ten Fahrenheit, charities tried to succor the suffering. Soup kitchens set up by rich merchants fed twelve thousand a day—A. T. Stewart opened one in the basement of his
Marble Palace—but most relief givers were quickly overwhelmed. The AICP warned
in January it had nearly exhausted its treasury helping some fifty thousand needy, and
issued what for the laissez-faire organization was a humiliating plea to the Municipal
Almshouse Department to increase public spending on outdoor relief.

Meanwhile, thousands were listening to more radical solutions to their plight. Rallies in City Hall Park and elsewhere around the city hailed speakers who denounced
unemployment, high prices and rents, and speculators in land and bread. Mass meetings passed resolutions calling on the city to "secure to us our right to labor" by providing jobs on public works, including an immediate start to construction on the Central
Park reservoir "to furnish employment to those who do not covet the degradation of
beggary." Demonstrators called for an urban homestead act, asking the Common
Council to distribute common lands to workers and appropriate half a million dollars
with which to build "inalienable homes." They also wanted evictions of the destitute
stopped, with landlords to be indemnified out of public funds, and a three-million-dollar loan fund established to transport idled workers west. These were hardly extrava-

Labor demonstration in City Hall Park, demanding
relief for the unemployed. From an 1855 nativist tract,
The Crisis; or, the Enemies of America Unmasked.
(Courtesy of American Social History Project.
Graduate School and University Center. City University
of New York)

gant demands, one shoemaker noted, at a time when "Louis Napoleon had given four
millions and a half to build houses for the workingmen."

The unemployed rebuffed the wealthy's offer of charity and insisted on public aid
as a citizen's right. "Need pounds with heavy fists on the door of public attention,"
thundered Wilhelm Weitling, "which has offered only beggars-soup in response. Beggars-soup! Beggars-soup!! In America it has already come to that."

The *Herald* recoiled from demonstrations by "unwashed and greasy workmen" and
attacked their presuppositions. It was a fallacy, the paper argued, that it was the business
of the state to care for the unemployed. "This principle, which is of French origin, has
been widely disseminated among the operative classes by a set of political imposters." It
was absurd; it flew in the face of modern science: "To render any class or set of men
responsible for the existing state of things is obviously to ignore the first principles of
political economy."

Labor spokesman William West countered such laissez-faire objections from
the standpoint of a well-thought-out, alternative moral economy. It was obvious that
"private capital is insufficient to satisfy the demands of labor," West said in laying a
mass meeting's proposals before the Common Council. "Unless you, therefore, substitute the public for private capital, in the employment of these thousands of compulsori-
ly idle workmen, it must be apparent that the men cannot live except upon charity
(which they will not ask and are very reluctant to receive) or by theft (which is their last
alternative)."

Reformer Peter Cooper agreed, and in an open letter urged that the city either provide land or put men to work quarrying marble for the construction of new docks and piers. Even the *Times* came out cautiously for public works, while denouncing demonstrators as a "miscellaneous crowd of alien chartists, communists and agrarians." But it was Mayor Wood who spoke most boldly of all, in his January 1855 inaugural during the height of the panic winter. "Do not let us be ungrateful as well as inhuman," said the mayor, who supported Cooper's dock-work plan. "Do not let it be said that labor, which produces every thing, gets nothing and dies of hunger in our midst, while capital, which produces nothing, gets every thing, and pampers in luxury and plenty."

These opposing worldviews, poised for an all-out clash, never arrived at a confrontation. The economy lurched upward again. Unions returned to narrowly focused issues. Some radicals, discouraged, moved elsewhere: Joseph Weydemeyer headed west to agitate in 1856.

Wood pressed ahead with his reform program. When opponents in the state legislature threatened to curtail his power, particularly over the police, Wood was supported by two mass meetings of the wealthy and powerful including William Havemeyer, James Watson Webb, Commodore Vanderbilt, Horace Greeley, and City Reform League president Peter Cooper. Even the *Times*, more critical than most, remained beguiled by Wood's energetic course: "Most of the objects of a city administration are far better carried out," it declared in best Napoleonic style, "by a vigorous and arbitrary police system than by a representative assembly." As his term ran out, a hundred wealthy bankers and merchants asked Wood to run again in 1856. Which he did, defeating his Know-Nothing opponent with heavy support from the East Side's German and Irish precincts, helping send that party into steep and rapid decline. Taking no chances, Wood had also released some patrolmen from normal duties to help with his campaign and furloughed others on election day so that friendly hoodlums had a free hand menacing opposition voters. Despite some outcries, these lapses were not enough to alienate the bulk of the respectable classes, most of whom were overjoyed that Wood seemed capable of maintaining an electoral mandate from the poor at so little cost to the rich.

STATE OVER CITY

Balked in New York City, die-hard nativists, temperancites, and good-government men turned to Albany, where they staged not a Napoleonic coup but something almost as effective.

Upstate New York was a much more congenial stamping ground for such reformers. Not only were nativist and temperance forces far stronger in the countryside, but widespread rural animosity toward the burgeoning metropolis had created a host of potential allies. Upstaters denounced what seemed to them an urban trampling of the rights of man. On the one hand there was the expanding power of New York's monied classes and the "subtle invading power of [its] gigantic corporations," which actively threatened Christian and republican America. On the other there was the deplorable barbarism of the poor and the power of the political demagogues. Saving the republic required that the metropolis be brought under control of the good people of the state. As one upstate legislator declared in 1853, "the time has come when it is to be settled whether New York City is an empire—a community by itself."

The vehicle for achieving an upstate-downstate alliance was a new political formation, the Republican Party. A northern phenomenon, it came together in New York

State in September 1855 when a mix of Seward Whigs, Free Soil Democrats, and disaffected Know-Nothings joined hands on a variety of national issues, chiefly resistance to the western expansion of southern slavery. In the fall of 1856 state voters elected a Republican governor, John Alsop King (son of Rufus King and brother of banker James Gore King), and a Republican majority in the Assembly. In short order, Republicans in Albany set out to wrest New York City from the Democrats. Some were driven by dreams of harvesting its rich fields of patronage and building up their new organization. Others were reformers determined to implement their program from the State level. All were convinced that as masters of the state they had the legal authority to become masters of the city.

A series of recent decisions by the New York Court of Appeals had put paid to Manhattan's lingering claims to special status as a municipal corporation, with independent powers derived from colonial-era charters. City property, the judges ruled, was held entirely in trust for the public. The corporation as such had no inherent authority over even the city's streets, and the state legislature could interfere at will in its affairs. The government of New York City—like that of even the smallest upstate village—existed only to the extent the state granted it governmental authority.

In ruling thus, the judges completed a legal revolution, begun back in the 1780s, that distinguished between public and private corporations. The two had long been considered kin in both having rights—rooted in charters—which in varying degree insulated them from central authorities. Now only private corporations (as fictive persons) were deemed to have rights against the state and immunities from legislative intervention. Municipal "corporations," their name to the contrary notwithstanding, were declared mere agencies of the state, with no legal autonomy whatever. In 1857 the legislature underscored its awareness of the new legal situation by declaring itself free to intervene at will in the affairs of the municipality—and promptly proceeding to do so.

The legislature changed the city charter yet again—although this time, unlike earlier revisions, it was not submitted to the people of New York for their approval. Again, the Common Council was stripped of power, this time over finances, with authority to administer the city's real estate, audit its accounts, oversee its disbursements, and collect its taxes being transferred to the comptroller. Again, ostensibly, the mayoralty was strengthened, this time by being given the power to appoint and remove most heads of departments, with consent of the aldermen. But in fact the legislature took dead aim at the office and its current occupant. Mayor Wood was required to stand for reelection in December 1857—his term slashed in half while the comptroller, a Republican, was allowed to finish out his second year. Then the legislature erected a series of state agencies to administer city affairs that were utterly free from control by municipal representatives (and the immigrant masses to whom they owed allegiance). When added to the already existing state boards that oversaw the almshouse, the asylums, and the Croton Aqueduct, these new institutions gave Albany control over three-fourths of New York City's budget.

The new agencies spanned a wide spectrum of public affairs. The New York Harbor Commission was given control of the port, including authority to block further encroachments into the rivers by defining a permanent bulkhead line. Command of the building of the city's new park, together with its enormous patronage opportunities, was handed over to a Board of Commissioners of the Central Park, a self-perpetuating entity appointed by the state legislature. Another body was given the right to administer construction of a proposed new City Hall.

At the urging of environmentalists, the legislators expanded the purview of the Croton Aqueduct Department beyond its existing responsibility for water supply and sewerage to include street pavements, pumps, and privy vaults, but in leaving intact the Common Council's cojurisdiction over public works, they thwarted the department's ability to impose systemic reforms. In Brooklyn, however, they created a Board of Sewer Commissioners and empowered it "to devise and carry into effect a plan of drainage and sewerage for the whole city, upon a regular system," which it did. In addition, a local Board of Water Commissioners oversaw establishment during 1856–58 of a system that tapped streams and ponds on the southern shore of Long Island (leased or purchased by the City of Brooklyn), ran the water through a brick conduit (along today's Conduit Avenue), and pumped it up the glacial moraine (at today's Force Tube Avenue) into Ridgewood Reservoir (in today's Highland Park) from which it flowed down to the city in iron mains. A secondary distributing reservoir atop the higher Prospect Hill (within today's Mount Prospect Park near Flatbush Avenue and Eastern Parkway) supplied those parts of Brooklyn above the level of Ridgewood.

State Republicans were able to make as much headway as they did because state Democrats were divided into contending factions, and those who feared Wood's growing power—he was being talked of as the next Democratic candidate for governor—were prepared to back Republican wing-clippers. In the city itself, many Tammanyites, fearing that Wood's ascension would help immigrants expand their base in the machine, considered him a greater threat than the Republicans, who were weak in the metropolis itself.

Among Wood's Democratic opponents was William Tweed, who had returned from two unhappy and undistinguished years in the House of Representatives, a largely forgotten man. Determined to bid for power by striking at the existing leader, Tweed was given his chance by the Republicans, who in their eagerness to curb metropolitan power unwittingly provided him with a base of operations. In yet another reform, legislators enhanced the power of the New York County Board of Supervisors, created as a check on city government, by giving it authority to audit county expenditures, supervise public works, oversee taxation and the various city departments, and appoint the inspectors of elections. In an effort to underline the purity of their intentions, they incautiously made the twelve-person board (six elected, six appointed by the mayor) bipartisan. Among those who climbed on board in 1857 was William Tweed. Within a year he had formed a "ring," a combination with other equally unscrupulous supervisors, which began levying a systematic 15 percent tribute on all vendors who furnished the county with supplies. Tweed also used his new status to dramatically enhance his standing among ward leaders and to promote friends to office, including, by 1858, George Barnard (recorder), Peter Sweeny (district attorney), and Richard Connolly (county clerk).

In the meantime, Republican reformers, unaware of what they had spawned, decided to press on with their campaign against the miscreant metropolis. Utterly heedless of the possible impact on even sympathetic Democrats, they proceeded to pass two acts, on April 15 and 16, 1857, that drew a moral line and provided the muscle to make the city toe it.

Their new Liquor Excise Law was an attempt to circumvent judicial decisions that had stymied their 1855 effort at straight-out prohibition of alcohol. The act required saloonkeepers to obtain a license. Applicants had to submit, to a Board of Excise Commissioners, vouchers attesting to their good moral character signed by thirty resident freeholders (those with absolute ownership of an estate), post a bond, and provide boarding facilities and stables. The *Herald* surmised such requirements would force out of business thirteen of every fourteen saloons in the city, and probably ninety-nine of every hundred in the lower wards where few freeholders lived. The law also banned the sale of liquor on Sunday or election days, further foreclosing working-class access to spirits, and—in a quasi-feminist intervention into hitherto sacrosanct family life—provided that on a wife's complaint, a husband could be put on a list of known drunkards to be distributed to all liquor dealers.

Republicans, perfectly aware that if enforcement was left to New York's current municipal leadership (i.e., Mayor Wood) it would swiftly become a dead letter, passed a complementary piece of legislation, the Metropolitan Police Act, which shifted effective control of the force from the (Democratic) mayor to a Metropolitan Police Commission controlled by (chiefly Republican) state appointees. The new law also dropped the requirement that officers serve in the ward where they resided, seeking (as had London) to sever the connections between cops and communities. The new commissioners—whose domain included Kings, Richmond, and Westchester counties as well as Manhattan—were given tremendous powers. Not only had they authority to enforce the Sunday closing laws, but they had complete control over the election machinery of New York and Brooklyn.

This legislative one-two punch produced instant furor. In May 1857 a Democratic mass meeting in City Hall Park attacked the Republican "principle of governing by boards" as despotic. Just the right word, thought the *Irish News*, which denounced the Republican laws as "specimens of despotic legislation which Louis Napoleon, with his legion of spies, a garroted press and an army of mercenary bayonets at his back, would hardly attempt in Paris."

Democrats were not alone in their outrage. *Harper's* said the laws resembled those imposed "on revolted districts or conquered places." The *Herald* evoked city-versus-country sentiments when it branded the upstate legislators as "archaeological curiosities" who "daren't trust themselves alone with a loaded pistol, or a gin bottle, or a pretty girl . . . without a good stout law to protect them and keep them in bounds."

But it was Mayor Wood who emerged as municipal champion. Blasting the excise law as "another of the encroachments upon individual rights for which the dominant party are so much distinguished," he called for resistance to an insolent state centralism that would make of New York a "subjugated city" and plunge its citizens into a "feeble state of vassalage." Claiming the laws violated home rule rights guaranteed by the Dongan and Montgomerie charters, Wood ordered all policemen to reject the authority of the new metropolitan commissioners, at least while he instituted legal proceedings to get the law declared unconstitutional. Those who defied him he fired.

To bolster his position, Wood got the Common Council to establish a separate Municipal Police force, composed of all pre-1857 officers, under direct mayoral control. There were now *two* official departments, and between late May and mid June 1857 policemen of the various wards were forced to choose up sides. In the end about eight hundred cops and fifteen captains stayed with Wood's Municipals and three hundred cops and seven captains opted for the Metropolitans (splitting more or less on ethnic lines). Each of the rival forces then proceeded to fill up its vacancies (again ethnically, the Mets tending to appoint Anglo-Americans, the Munis leaning toward the foreign born).

Chaos ensued. Criminals had a high old time. Arrested by one force, they were rescued by the other. Rival cops tussled over possession of station houses. The opéra bouffe climax came in mid-June when Metropolitan police captain George W. Walling attempted to deliver a warrant for the mayor's arrest, only to be tossed out by a group of Municipals. Armed with a second warrant, a much larger force of Metropolitans marched against City Hall. Awaiting them were a massed body of Municipals, supplemented by a large crowd (characterized by George Templeton Strong as a "miscellaneous assortment of suckers, soaplocks, Irishmen, and plug uglies officiating in a guerrilla capacity"). Together, the mayor's supporters began clubbing and punching the outnumbered Metropolitans away from the seat of government. "The scene was a terrible one," a *Times* reporter wrote; "blows upon naked heads fell thick and fast, and men rolled helpless down the steps, to be leaped upon and beaten till life seemed extinct." The Metropolitans gained the day after the Seventh Regiment came to its rescue, and the warrant was served on Wood. This setback for the mayor was followed by another: on July 2 the Court of Appeals ruled in favor of the state law. Wood knuckled under and disbanded the Municipals late in the afternoon of July 3, leaving the Metropolitans in possession of the field.

The ultrareformers had triumphed over Wood, but it proved to be a shaky victory. Exactly how shaky became clear the very next day.

July 4, 1857, promised, like most Independence Days, to be given over to massive parades, democratic rhetoric, hard drinking, and street brawls. The unenviable task of maintaining a minimal degree of order and decorum was now to be shouldered entirely by the Metropolitans. Their ranks were notably untested. The victorious department refused to hire those who had backed the losing side, choosing instead to swear in a host of special officers, with little or no experience, to flesh out their ranks. All in all, no more than a hundred had had even a month's experience.

When a small party of Mets patrolling the Chatham Square area in the predawn hours suddenly found themselves under attack by a crowd of young men and boys, they broke and ran. One sought shelter in the saloon headquarters, at 40 Bowery, of the Bowery Boys, a nativist gang, who succeeded in repelling the assailants. At this point, the Dead Rabbits—the Irish Sixth Ward gang whose members were known as ardent Wood supporters—opened up another front on Bayard Street, between Mulberry and Elizabeth; together with the neighborhood's Irish inhabitants, they attacked a group of thirty Metropolitans. Once again, the on-the-job trainees had to be rescued by a phalanx of two hundred Bowery Boys. While the policemen straggled away from the scene, the gangs and their supporters escalated their encounter. Barricades went up, assembled out of carts, barrels, lumber; brickbats flew (women, it was said, gathered and broke up stones and carried them to their menfolk on the front lines or atop the tenement roofs); then the guns came out. The battle raged for hours, drawing thousands to the scene, and was ended only by the exhaustion of the participants. Twelve died outright or soon thereafter, and thirty-seven were injured. It was the worst riot since Astor Place back in 1849.

The next day, Sunday, violence flared again, but this time it was put down by the

The Dead Rabbits barricade on Bayard Street, from *Frank Leslie's Illustrated Newspaper*, July 18, 1857.
(© Collection of The New-York Historical Society)

National Guard (with Metropolitans placed at the head of the regiments). The streets were swept clean. The Sunday closing laws were enforced.

On Thursday, July 9, fifteen hundred turned out for a meeting at Hamilton Square that had been called to consider "effecting a division of the state, by organizing a new one from the five southern counties." The mayor showed up but told the crowd it must obey the legislature's laws. (As a potential gubernatorial candidate, secession of city from state was not, at this point, in his interest.) Passions lowered to a simmer.

They boiled over again the following Sunday, July 12, this time in the heart of Kleindeutschland, at Avenue A and 4th Street. Several thousand Germans taunted the Metropolitans and met their efforts to close saloons and clear streets with clubs and brickbats. Reinforcements—three regiments and most of the police force, massed five abreast—drove them back; a blacksmith was killed in the process. The next day a funeral procession, ten thousand strong, marched up Broadway under a banner reading OPFER DER METROPOLITAN-POLIZEI (victim of the Metropolitan Police), accompanied by a dirge-playing band. A mass meeting denounced the tyrannical laws.

Order was restored. But no one, least of all the police, imagined that popular hatred of the new laws, and their defenders, had been other than driven underground for the moment. The superintendent of the Metropolitans recommended that ten officers in each ward be armed with revolvers—"for the suppression of riots." Ominously, the state decided to build a new armory at 35th Street and Seventh Avenue, more than a mile closer to City Hall (and the Sixth Ward) than the existing one.

It seemed as if long-accumulating tensions were coming to a head, as if a cultural crossroads had been reached. On one side was the growing immigrant working class, with its own culture, its own politics. On the other side was a wealthy and anxious bourgeoisie, trying not very successfully to impose its vision of domestic and civic relations on those below.

For a time, it had looked as if Mayor Wood might be able to mediate this clash, but the upstate victory of the ultrareformers had put him in an impossible position. Either he enforced the liquor and police laws and lost his immigrant constituency, or he rejected reform and lost the fragile support of the rich and powerful. Faced with that choice he opted to secure his political base. In this he succeeded; in October, Wood, an idol to Democratic voters, gained Tammany's renomination for the mayoral race. But the summer's events had cost him dearly. Many reformers now turned away from him. Still, Wood might have been able to salvage the situation; he retained important upper-class support. But at just this point, the city was rocked by an economic earthquake that made glaringly apparent just how deep the fissures in civic life had become, just how wide a gap now yawned between the contending cultures, and just how unbridgeable they were by even the most heroic of political efforts.

47

The Panic of 1857

At the end of August 1857, little more than a month after the Dead Rabbits riot, the New York branch of the Ohio Life Insurance and Trust Company suddenly closed its doors. It soon transpired that the putatively rock-solid institution had been deftly looted by its manager, Edwin C. Ludlow. Worse, it had made loans with abandon to speculators playing the stock market—and done some gambling itself in railroad stocks, which had been gliding steadily downward. Since the Crimean War had ended the previous year—restoring Western Europe's access to Russian grain—demand for American wheat had dropped steadily, shipments east had tapered off considerably, and railroad earnings (and stock prices) had dipped disappointingly. Farmers and merchants too had been squeezed; by the spring of 1857 metropolitan merchants found it difficult to collect on midwestern debts.

In August, unfortunately for Ohio Life, European farmers harvested a bumper crop, and the sudden glut threatened to further depress world farm prices. Worried midwestern businessmen had begun telegraphing New York banks, including Ohio Life, asking for the return of their surplus funds (which they had, as was customary, parked in the metropolis to garner high interest rates). Ohio Life, courtesy of Mr. Ludlow, was caught short, and the firm failed, leaving behind seven million dollars in debts. But Ohio Life had not been the only New York financial institution shoveling out shakily secured loans—indebtedness had reached an all-time high earlier in August—and many Manhattan banks had loaned funds to Ohio Life. Now, finding themselves suddenly and dangerously overextended, the banks panicked. Terrified that soon other institutions (or even their own) might be proved rotten, they demanded payment of all matured loans from all their debtors. In the ensuing fiscal *sauve qui peut*, "stony-hearted directors and inflexible cashiers" refused (as George Templeton Strong noted) to make loans on promissory notes or bills of exchange, despite pitiful pleading from straitened merchants, and went so far as to demand certified checks from even the bluest of their blue chip customers. The banks thus jammed on the credit brakes at precisely the moment businessmen were in direst need of accommodation. The financial institutions, especially banks newly hatched during the boom, saved themselves but forced merchants into bankruptcy.

Panic spread quickly. "The Foundations of financial confidence appear to have been knocked from under the Stock and Money markets," worried the *Times*. In the days that followed, hundreds of other firms failed as well, and panicky brokers were observed pummeling one another with their fists on the floor of the Stock Exchange. Each day brought new lists of failures or suspensions, with each misfortune posted in large type on the bulletin boards in front of newspaper offices, attracting crowds. Handbills with the latest lists of broken banks and suspect banknotes were cried about in the streets by boys at "a penny a piece."

Depositors lined up to withdraw gold. By mid-September the specie reserves of New York banks had shrunk from $94.5 million (in August) to $75.8 million. Desperate to augment their holdings, they demanded payment from stockbrokers of call loans, exacerbating the crisis at the Exchange, and pressed small banks in the interior for payment, generating a widening pool of failures. New York bankers hoped a forthcoming gold shipment from California would relieve the pressure, but just at the moment when everyone was scrambling for specie, and a heavy payment was due English creditors, word came that the steamer *Central America* had gone down on September 12 in a terrible hurricane, with the loss of four hundred passengers and crew, and $1.6 million worth of precious metal. The catastrophe precipitated a new wave of failures.

Now the banking system itself began to buckle. Philadelphia's institutions suspended—refused to honor their legal commitment to redeem paper for gold—and banks across the nation were forced to follow suit, with legislators duly authorizing their actions. As credit dried up, manufacturing and transport wound down, construction ceased, produce was neither demanded nor shipped, and prices of western staples and southern cotton plummeted. By the first week of October, the nation's trade was at a standstill. Only New York banks held out, and they were under siege, with tens of thousands of noteholders thronging Wall Street demanding redemption. "We seem foundering," Strong wrote on October 10. "People's faces in Wall Street look fearfully gaunt and desperate."

The "excitement today is fearfull," Brown Brothers officials advised their London partners on October 13. "Some banks have stopped and we don't know whether the balance can hold out." Broadway omnibuses were packed with people trying to get downtown. By three P.M. eighteen banks had suspended specie payments, and crowds milled from Water to Broadway, numb with fear and disbelief. Prices plunged on the stock market as investors dumped thousands of shares in a vain race to stay ahead of the avalanche. As sell orders were telegraphed to exchanges elsewhere, the crisis spread like a "malignant epidemic" across the country. Soon almost half the brokers on Wall Street, including Jacob Little, were wiped out.

The "bursting of bubbles in New York," the *Chicago Tribune* had soothed at first, "need not alarm anybody in the West," for regional prosperity rested on solid foundations. But as the panic radiated outward from the metropolitan center, howls were heard

Wall Street, Half Past 2 O'clock, October 13, 1857, by James H.
Cafferty and Charles G. Rosenberg. Among the nervous bankers
and brokers gathered outside the Merchants Exchange are
Cornelius Vanderbilt, on the far right with a walking stick, and
Jacob Little, in the light coat, center. (© Museum of the City of
New York)

around the country. The *New Orleans Crescent* railed against New York—"the centre of
reckless speculation, unflinching fraud and downright robbery"—the city whose "rotten bankruptcies" were "permeating and injuring almost every solvent community in
the Union." The impact proved far greater than that, however.

The panic soon reached London and Paris, affecting more than a third of the stocks
traded on Lombard Street and the Bourse. In Britain, only Bank of England intervention held the line. Modern communications sped the panic along to northern Germany,
then Scandinavia, leaving a trail of bankruptcies and unemployment. From Europe, the
crisis hopscotched back across the Atlantic to South America. Though the ensuing
depression had many causes, New Yorkers could (had they wished) have taken a perverse pride in having managed to trigger a crisis of the entire world capitalist system.
Karl Marx, then ensconced in the British Museum writing the *Grundrisse*, forerunner
to *Das Kapital*, was ecstatic. To Friedrich Engels he wrote: "Despite my financial distress, I have not felt so cozy since 1848." Engels's response was similarly gleeful: "The
general aspect of the Exchange here was most delicious in the past week. The fellows
grow black in the face with rage at my suddenly rising good spirits."

"APPALLING PICTURE OF SOCIAL WRETCHEDNESS"

Spirits recovered rapidly on Wall Street, however, as suspension of specie payments, in freeing banks from the pressure of their own creditors, gave them time to bolster their reserves. This they did with dispatch, and by December 14 New York had gone back on a hard money standard. Several financiers had meanwhile seized the opportunity to profit from the failure of others: Moses Taylor, president of City Bank, gobbled up railroad stocks and the city's largest gas company; Commodore Vanderbilt began to move in on financially troubled railroads, starting with the New York and Harlem, a course that within a decade would make him master of the mighty New York Central; and his partner-to-be Leonard Jerome became a millionaire by the simple expedient of selling short during the crisis.

For everyone else in New York, however, the recession was just getting under way. By December 985 merchants had failed, with losses totaling $120,000,000, and the shock waves from their collapse had toppled many other kinds of enterprises.

J. A. Westervelt and Company defaulted; one of the city's largest shipbuilding firms, it was headed by a former mayor. Maritime construction collapsed in general, laying off between two-thirds and three-quarters of the city's shipbuilders. The clipper ship industry, already weakened by tremendous competition from railroads and steamers, would never recover from the panic, and the city's merchant marine, which lost federal subsidies in 1858, went into steady decline, losing much of its mail, passenger, and freight traffic to British rivals within a few years.

The New York and Erie Rail Road was forced into receivership, halting work on its Jersey City terminal. Foundries laid off hundreds of mechanics. Four-fifths of the city's coopers lost their jobs. Textiles were badly hurt: the giant Hanford and Lewis collapsed, Brooks Brothers let go a thousand workers; the mantilla and cloak industry collectively laid off two thousand more. Garment workers who retained their jobs found their wages cut from $1.25 to eighty-five cents a day. Retailers suffered accordingly. "Almost every shop has its placards," said Strong "announcing a great sacrifice, vast reduction of prices, sales at less than cost," and, as in 1837, the stock of bankrupt tradesmen was snapped up by more fortunate merchants. Even "Chinamen who peddle cigars" and Italian "organ grinders" were hard hit, noted Bryant's *Post*.

The communications world was pummeled. *Putnam's Magazine* went under, and Putnam's publishing house nearly followed, but Washington Irving helped rescue it by giving Putnam the plates for his Collected Edition. The printers' union lost two-thirds of its members by 1858; female lithographers were virtually wiped out. Cyrus Field's paper business suspended, and only his neighbor Peter Cooper kept him afloat.

The building boom halted abruptly, leaving even Fifth Avenue mansions half completed and masses of construction laborers out of work. Merchant princes cut costs by firing servants in droves. Seagoing black cooks and stewards found themselves drydocked in the Coloured Sailors Home—its proprietor wrote—given "the great revulsion in the commercial affairs."

By September 1857 estimates of New York unemployment ran as high as forty thousand. By late October *Hunt's Merchant Magazine* calculated the figure in Manhattan and Brooklyn had risen to a hundred thousand. As word on local conditions reached Europe, immigration damped down from 460,474 in 1854 to 123,126 in 1858.

Unions proved powerless to halt or slow the devastation. Indeed most laboring organizations broke up altogether, and trade union activity virtually ceased. Out-of-work mechanics pawned their tools; women their household goods, with one paper noting that "many a worthy home this winter will be half-stripped of the cherished things on which the good wife had prided herself." Army recruiters were besieged by unemployed men. Women had no such option, though their need was greater—the contraction having cut female employment by almost half, versus 20 percent for males. At one point in midpanic, an advertisement ran for girls willing to work in the West, and within a week, over a thousand applied. Other "opportunities" lay closer to home: Dr. William Sanger estimated that the recession drove perhaps a thousand women to street whoring, and the numbers of women in prison rose accordingly.

Joblessness meant homelessness: adamant landlords turned out those who didn't pay their rents. The AICP estimated that during three severe winter months of 1857–58 forty-one thousand were forced to seek shelter in police stations. Thousands more were forced out of respectable lodgings into crowded tenement apartments, and slum conditions surged. Industrial Home Owners Society Number One foundered in the hard times, as did many of the cooperatives, caught between soaring interest rates and assorted swindlers, and many participants lost their life savings.

One thing that did *not* collapse was the price of food, as the breakdown of the credit system prevented eastward shipments of western grain. Standing amid the economic ruins, even the AICP's Hartley was forced to admit that New York "presented a more appalling picture of social wretchedness than was probably ever witnessed on this side of the Atlantic" and that "we were now brought to realize something of the distress which, at times, has often been experienced in European cities."

"PAPER BUBBLES OF ALL DESCRIPTIONS"

Analyses of the crisis varied. James Waddell Alexander, pastor of New York's largest Presbyterian church, announced that the panic was God's work. Many Wall Streeters agreed and hied to their churches to pray for relief. By mid-winter, merchants and clerks were jamming lunch-hour prayer meetings at the local John Street Methodist Church. The *Journal of Commerce* encouraged more readers to participate: "Steal awhile away from Wall Street / and every worldly care, / And spend an hour about midday / in humble, hopeful prayer." By February 1858 the noonday prayer meetings were attracting huge crowds. Soon a full-scale revival was in progress, an urban camp meeting in which bookkeepers and bankers, their wives, and their children huddled together and sang the old hymns, trying to create an island of stability amid the economic storm.

Horace Greeley adopted a structural explanation, though lacing his economic analysis with a dose of moralism, and the *Tribune* editor's listing of presumed causes is all the more impressive for having been issued in the summer of 1857, several weeks before the collapse. One of the country's biggest problems, Greeley argued, was its excess of imports over exports, an imbalance he believed had been fueled by the buying binge of luxury-mad New Yorkers (and other Americans), who expended millions "in fine homes and gaudy furniture" and "hundreds of thousands in the silly rivalries of fashionable parvenus in silks, laces, diamonds." These purchases had been made possible, Greeley further suggested, by the booming sale of railroad securities and the tremendous levels of speculation in stocks and real estate ("government spoilations, public defaulters, paper bubbles of all descriptions").

The ill effects of this adverse balance of payments, the fiscally astute James Gordon

Bennett noted, had been staved off by exporting California gold and importing European capital. But this precarious equilibrium had begun to wobble in the mid-1850s, when Europeans had begun to cut back sharply on investment in the midwestern railroad boom. Capital transfers to the United States dropped from fifty-six million dollars in 1853 to twelve million dollars in 1856. Partly this was in intelligent response to signs of an overheated American economy; the Barings started to liquidate their holdings after the 1854 mini-crisis, and British funds shuttled into less speculative, often more remunerative English securities. The money was also needed at home for imperial expenses: the Crimean War, campaigns in China and Persia, and the suppression of the Indian Mutiny of 1857. The selloff helped drive down the price of shares on the New York Exchange, which in turn weakened the American banking system by reducing the value of assets supporting it. Bennett feared that the drying up of European capital might force the railroads into bankruptcy, then drag down the poorly capitalized banks. "What can be the end of all this," he wrote before the crisis, "but another general collapse like that of 1837, only upon a much grander scale? The same premonitory symptoms that prevailed in 1835–6 prevail in 1857 in a tenfold degree."

Bennett, Greeley, and many others put particular emphasis on the overbuilding of the railroad system. The expansion had been at the core of prosperity, but the free-for-all way the job was done undermined that prosperity. Railroad company promoters issued vast amounts of watered stock, way beyond what actual assets or dividends could support. Legislatures were pressured (or bribed) into granting charters, buying bonds, and donating land to underwrite the construction of unnecessary and overlapping lines. Promoters formed construction companies and awarded themselves contracts, siphoning off profits.

The superheated expansion—pointed out J. S. Gibbons in his 1859 postmortem, *The Banks of New-York, Their Dealers, the Clearing House, and the Panic of 1857*—had been underwritten by a too liberal granting of credit, engineered by the new banks and the booming Stock Exchange. Between 1851 and 1853 alone, twenty-seven new banks had been established, most of whose aggregate capital of over sixteen million dollars was fictitious book debt. Nevertheless, the banks attracted new deposits, upon which they issued additional credit, until by August 1857 over forty million dollars were out in loans, a good two-thirds of which Gibbons deemed ill advised.

Easy money encouraged speculation: as the boom wore on, greater profits were to be won by financing, promoting, and speculating in railroads than by building them. "All confidence is lost, for the present, in the solvency of our merchant-princes—and with good reason," wrote Strong, as "it is probable that every one of them has been operating and gambling in stocks and railroad bonds." Speculation spilled easily into manipulation; men like Jacob Little made fortunes in short selling, arranging rumors to drive stock prices down, and then clean up. (Bennett's warnings were in part ignored because he was associated with Leonard Jerome, who, as a bear, stood to benefit if stock prices were driven down by gloomy prognosticators.) From manipulation to straight-out corruption was but a short and easy step. Editor Freeman Hunt grew convinced that it was now necessary "to deal with every man and woman, so far as business is concerned, as if they were rogues."

WOOD REDUX

New Yorkers disagreed on how to respond to the crisis. On October 21 a thoroughly

alarmed *New York Times* wondered if perhaps the metropolis needed a civic hero to rescue it—a Louis Napoleon who would put the unemployed to work rebuilding the city
into a second Paris. The very next day, Mayor Fernando Wood, with at least one eye on
the upcoming elections, volunteered for the role, proposing to the Common Council
that the city both accelerate existing projects and launch new ones. Specifically, he
urged the municipal government to build and grade streets, construct engine houses
and police stations, repair docks, construct a new reservoir, forge ahead swiftly on the
new Central Park, and buy fifty thousand barrels of flour, and a similar amount of corn-
meal and potatoes, to be given to laborers on the public works in lieu of money. The cost
of this crash program would be covered by issuing long-term 7 percent bonds,
redeemable in fifty years.

To mobilize the upper classes behind this agenda, Wood argued that it was in their
self-interest. Only swift action could prevent another 1837 riot or 1848 Paris-style
upheaval. "Give no man excuse for violence or depredation upon property, that he must
have bread for his children," Wood counseled. "If the present want of employment
continues many must rely upon either public or private charity, and I fear that not a few
will resort to violence and force rather than submit to either of these precarious and
humiliating dependences."

At the same time, Wood appealed to the affluent's sense of responsibility, in language (echoing his 1854 remarks) that was also calculated to demonstrate his sympathy
for the poor. "In the days of general depression," Wood argued, workers "are the first
to feel the change, without the means to avoid or endure reverses. Truly it may be said
that in New York those who produce everything get nothing, and those who produce
nothing get everything." "Is it not our duty," Wood asked, "to provide some way to
afford relief?"

Some merchants supported his program, if not his rhetoric. John Dix, a prominent
railroad financier who knew whereof he spoke, acknowledged that men of his class had
engaged in frenetic speculation, were partly to blame for the panic, and had a responsibility to help their innocent victims: though he condemned the mayor for inflammatory
language that might "excite the laborer against the capitalist, the rich against the poor."

Others totally rejected the proposal. The *Evening Post* castigated its political
premise: "Despotic governments do incur such obligations," Bryant's paper said, "but
our republican system of government . . . incurs no obligation to take care of the vicious
and the thriftless and improvident." The notion that the state should provide work, the
Post fulminated, was "one of the most monstrous doctrines ever broached in revolutionary France." There was, perhaps, a duty "to relieve the poor and to succor the distressed," but that was "a Christian duty, not a political duty."

For all the talk of succoring the distressed, the rich—held firmly in check by the
Association for the Improvement of the Condition of the Poor—did less of it than ever.
The AICP loathed Wood's proposals, fearing his "words would excite the harassed
unemployed rather than allay their fears and lead to humble forbearance." Hartley was
determined that in 1857, unlike 1854, almsgiving would be kept in private and tight-
fisted hands. He successfully blocked formation of independent ward relief committees, which freed him from having to set up rival AICP branch offices in working-class
neighborhoods. He was thus able to force the unemployed to travel to a central office,
where trained personnel imposed rigorous means tests, which three-fourths of those

applying for aid failed. Though eight thousand families were given assistance in October this was 25 percent *fewer* than had been helped in the previous prosperous year, a statistic of which Hartley later boasted. The AICP also made some ineffectual efforts to find jobs for the unemployed with farmers outside the city; and Charles Loring Brace of the Children's Aid Society, too, urged the jobless be directed "into one great channel—that of EMIGRATION." But Hartley's main suggestion was that the laboring classes "bear with manliness what they must bear."

"WE WANT WORK!"

Albert Komp, James McGuire, and Ira B. Davis thought differently. In October 1857 Komp, an associate of Joseph Weydemeyer's, gathered together some fellow radical forty-eighters into a Kommunisten Klub, which in turn helped revive the dormant Amerikanische Arbeiterbund. The Germans then joined forces with McGuire, an Irish labor leader, and Davis, an old Loco Foco man and cooperative movement activist, in an effort to organize the unemployed of all nations. As McGuire said, "If one man suffer, it don't matter whether he is an all American or a foreigner—they all suffer."

This working-class movement claimed state assistance as a right, not as charity or patronage, a call that resonated powerfully even amongst nonsocialists, especially in an Irish immigrant community profoundly scarred by the recent Great Hunger. As the *Irish News* wrote: "When famine stares fifty thousand workmen in the face—when their wives and little ones cry to them for bread, it is not time to be laying down stale maxims of economy, quoting Adam Smith, or any other politico-economical old fogy."

Tired of upper-class bickering while the crisis deepened, the revived American Workers League announced a "work and bread" demonstration to protest the Common Council's failure to act on Mayor Wood's suggestions. On November 5 four thousand radicals, unionists, and land reformers gathered in Tompkins Square and marched to City Hall Park behind a banner emblazoned ARBEIT! (work). While a speaker perched on the fountain basin pointed out that "ladies throng Broadway every day buying silk robes, while the wives and children of honest laborers are starving," a "Mass Petition for the Unemployed" was presented to Mayor Wood.

"Every human being has a RIGHT to live," it declared, "not as a mere charity, but as RIGHT, and governments, monarchical or republican, MUST FIND work for the people if individual exertion prove not sufficient." Specifically the unemployed demanded a program of public works at a guaranteed minimum wage, aimed at launching the new Central Park, sewering the city's streets, "or any other public works so indispensable for the sanitary condition of the people and the comfort and safety of the wealthy themselves." They also called for municipal construction of low-income housing on city-owned land and for an injunction against evictions of the unemployed. When Wood responded he would give the petition to the aldermen the following week, a spokesman named Bieler said of the massed jobless outside, "We cannot warrant that, their patience being exhausted, they will not help themselves by employing physical power with its accompanying brutalities." Thus prompted, Wood passed on the plea that evening, and the councilmen announced they would advertise for bids to undertake the project of leveling Hamilton Square.

The next day, November 6, the fight was carried to Wall Street. A procession of five thousand chanting, "We want work," trooped to the steps of the Merchants' Exchange and demanded bankers lend funds to businessmen who would employ the poor. Workingmen, a blacksmith named Bowles warned, did not intend to starve while tens of millions in specie was lying unused.

Crowds were bigger than ever on Monday, November 9, and demonstrators flooded into City Hall itself. Councilmen agreed to authorize a $250,000 bond issue for Central Park but rejected further direct relief. Wood, himself troubled by the growing throngs, now decided to post police guards around government buildings and—remembering 1837—the flour warehouses. The next day, when another mass meeting at Tompkins Square dispatched a delegation to confer with the mayor, it found City Hall Park ringed by three hundred police and stocked with a brigade of militia. A few blocks further south, moreover, the federal government had deployed soldiers and sailors under Mexican War hero General Winfield Scott to guard the Custom House and Sub-Treasury Building.

Despite the array of armed might and editorial calls to "shoot down any quantity of Irish or Germans" necessary—"Rioters, like other people, have heads to be broken," cried the *Herald*, "and bodies to be perforated with ball and steel"—thousands again swarmed into Tompkins Square, and this time some of the desperately hungry broke discipline and launched a bread riot, seizing bakers' wagons and invading food shops. Increasingly, however, protesters redirected their attention uptown, gathering in front of Superintendent Frederick Law Olmsted's office carrying white muslin standards reading WORK/ARBEIT and WE WANT WORK and demanding men be hired from their ranks. The park commissioners, however, were also inundated with four thousand letters from job seekers, and in conjunction with local politicians they proceeded to divide up the patronage positions among this vaster body. By January 1858 a thousand men had been set to work clearing debris from the site; ten months later twenty-five hundred were so employed; by the following year, on a peak day in September 1859, thirty-six hundred were laboring away.

WOOD REMOVED

The winning of job openings—together with the patent inability to wrest further assistance from city government—dissipated the protest movement. By the end of November 1857, the crowds in Tompkins Square had virtually disappeared, and so had the massed police and military presence. Nevertheless, Wood's combination of class rhetoric and public welfare cost him his remaining elite support. He was now, in their eyes, thoroughly identified with the subterranean city ("the *canaille*" in Strong's word).

Days after the first demonstrations, and a scant three weeks before the December 1 election, powerful merchants in the Democratic Party's inner circle bolted. Men like August Belmont, John A. Dix, William Havemeyer, and John Van Buren made common cause with Republicans, former Know-Nothings, and leaders of the old civic reform movement like Peter Cooper. A Wall Street mass meeting of merchants, industrialists, and bankers—claiming "our metropolis is the worst governed city in Christendom"— nominated Almshouse Governor Daniel F. Tiemann, a Democrat and wealthy German-American paint manufacturer, to run against Wood. Disgruntled Tammanyites (including William Tweed) were happy Tiemann was of their party, Republicans liked his opposition to slavery, and Know-Nothing men applauded his well-known nativism (tempered by a German background).

Spurned by the upper class, Wood garnered support from the organized workers.

Ira B. Davis denounced the Wall Street Democratic renegades, noting that none had objected when the state government bailed out the banks: apparently what was "virtuous in them" was "a crime in Mayor Wood or the workingmen." At a meeting in Steuben Hall on November 26, James McGuire announced: "We mean to make labor the plaintiff and capital the defendant."

In the December election, Wood carried the heavily German and Irish eastside wards, but enough Democrats deserted him (especially in Tweed's ward) to narrowly cost him the election. The fusion coalition's 51.4 percent to 48.6 percent victory was probably aided as well by Republican state-appointed election inspectors, who closed the polls before workmen could leave their jobs to vote.

Over the next two years, business conditions slowly improved. Specie stocks rose as gold shipments began arriving again. Credit eased, and trade expanded steadily if unevenly, with far stronger European demand for cotton than for wheat. Foreign capitalists cautiously began buying securities again, though foreign laborers remained bearish and immigration stayed low. With a reviving economy—by spring 1859 the worst was clearly over—the labor movement girded itself to restore wages to their prepanic level. A new German labor federation was established in 1859, paced by cabinetmakers and pianomakers, and it embarked on a series of strikes.

Still, the fierce animosities the panic had fanned subsided for the moment, muted by exhaustion, political catharsis, and rising public and private employment. But the divisions the crisis had illuminated did not knit themselves up; fear and rancor smoldered, awaiting only a new crisis to rekindle them. It was not long in coming, for even as New York was congratulating itself for having survived the economic maelstrom, a political hurricane was about to slam into the city.

48

The House Divides

The Panic of 1857, coming on top of the frenzied expansion of the boom years, increased the pressure on the nation's poorly soldered-together political system. The weakest seam did not lie along the Mason-Dixon line; in their direct dealings, North and South had managed to maintain the balancing act begun two generations earlier at the Constitutional Convention. Rather the crisis came out west, where the vast territories won from Mexico in 1848 were proving difficult to digest. In 1850 another deal was cobbled together, whose provisions included admission of California as a free state and the passage of a Fugitive Slave Act facilitating the extradition of escapees. But powerful forces in both slave and free states were no longer willing to settle their differences by a Solomonic divvying up of the spoils of empire. Neither side was willing to be excluded from the trans-Mississippi territory; increasingly, each side wanted it all.

During the long period of prosperity the South had gotten expansionist. As British industrial demand sent cotton prices soaring, planters sought to spread slave production west, along with the legal and political support system slavery required. They were seconded in this by white small farmers, squeezed into marginality by the pressures of competition with big planters and hoping migration would improve their condition. Even though some of the new western lands were not fertile grounds for cotton production, the planters nevertheless wanted new slave states carved out of them in order to maintain the balance of political power in the Congress and Electoral College.

The North had promoted expansion as well. Dynamic capitalists had grand visions of an integrated and nationwide industrial economy, stitched together by rail lines; they also dreamed, less loftily, of speculative bonanzas in cheap government lands. Small farmers wanted to reserve the new states for "free labor": they didn't want to compete with huge factories-in-the-fields staffed by slave labor and suffer the fate of southern poor whites.

The North was also growing more culturally aggressive. To the liberal bourgeoisie the global capitalist boom seemed conclusive proof that slave societies were contrary to history's march—morally undesirable, economically inefficient, and doomed. While "respectable opinion" still backed away from the abolitionist call to assault the institution in its southern lair, it listened with increasing enthusiasm to the new Free Soil movement's counsel: leave slavery alone in its heartland but block its westward expansion; penned up, it would eventually die.

Far-sighted Southerners experienced anticipatory suffocation and demanded immediate breathing room. Some went beyond insisting on the right to open new plantations in the West to calling for equal access to the North itself—regaining the right, for instance, to travel freely with their slaves. They grew ever more vehement, too, in their insistence on an explicit veto power over Democratic Party policy and federal government activity and successfully blocked programs many northerners desired: a protective tariff, a homestead bill, a northern transcontinental rail route. On the cultural front southern ideologues matched the North's denigration of their society with a vigorous defense of paternalistic slavery as morally *superior* to heartless capitalism.

As each side grew more convinced that the nation could no longer exist half slave and half free, that it must become all one thing or all the other, the divided American house began to crumble. In the end it was the center—the Kansas-Nebraska Territory—that failed to hold. On January 4, 1854, Senator Stephen Douglas (Democrat from Illinois) introduced a bill looking toward the entry of the territory into the Union, which left the question of its slave or free status entirely up to a vote by local residents. This sounded democratic ("popular sovereignty" he called it), but in fact it shredded the old Compromise of 1820 in which Congress had banned slavery in that part of the continent no matter what the desires of its residents. This (to Free Soil eyes) treacherous blow, together with ensuing proslavery initiatives such as the 1857 Supreme Court Dred Scott decision, which barred Congress from forbidding the transport of slaves to northern states, seemed conclusive evidence of a Slave Power design to make slavery lawful in *all* the states, North as well as South.

Free Soilers decided that if slavery in Kansas was to be decided by its residents they would rush northern settlers to the territory in time for the vote. Southerners countered with their own westward race. In short order, rival groups of settlers, in a kind of election riot writ large, were shooting their way toward majoritarian status. It was in outraged response to the bloodbath in Kansas that the Republican Party had crystallized—a definitively sectional organization that fused antislavery Whigs and Democrats. It also had a strong (though not dominant) nativist streak. Republicans tended to see the Roman Church and the Slave Power as corporate monoliths that restricted individual freedom and to condemn Irish immigrants and white planters alike for lack of economic enterprise or self-discipline.

The new party ran General John C. Frémont for president in 1856 on a platform dedicated to northern capitalist and small farmer interests (tariffs, homesteads) and the extirpation of the "twin relics of barbarism" (slavery and Mormon polygamy). Frémont lost, but the party picked up powerful adherents. New York's William Seward signed on; the Whig senator had been an early opponent of the Slave Power and by 1858 was convinced that "an irrepressible conflict between opposing and enduring forces" was at hand.

The idea of an irrepressible conflict between North and South did not warm many hearts in New York, that most southern-connected of northern cities, and the metropolis would prove to be a fierce opponent of Republicanism-with-a-capital-R. But the new party's antisouthern militancy did attract two strategically placed constituencies, whose affiliation would have resounding local impact: the tiny African-American community and a small but extremely influential coterie of professionals and businessmen.

BLACK REPUBLICANS

In 1860 the city's 12,574 African Americans had no territorial base, no cultural stronghold. The Irish had pushed them out of the Five Points, and they were strewn about the city in isolated, vulnerable clumps. Some had migrated east to streets abutting the East River docks. Others (perhaps about five thousand) had drifted north to the area bounded by Houston on the north and Canal on the south, concentrating in Greenwich Village streets—Minetta Lane, Bleecker, Thompson, Sullivan, and MacDougal—near to jobs as servants for the Washington Square gentry. Others still, perhaps fifteen hundred, had pressed on farther, into blocks west of Sixth Avenue between 23rd and 40th streets, or to Seneca Village before it was dismantled to make way for Central Park.

In Brooklyn more than a hundred black families had trekked out to Weeksville and Carrville, the settlements begun on former farmland back in the 1830s and 1840s, to Crow Hill (the future Crown Heights), and to Fort Greene, where work was to be found in the nearby shipyards. Here too the black population was dwarfed by the inrush of white immigrants: where in 1800 one of every three people in Kings County had been black, by 1860 the proportion had dropped to less than one in fifty. In Staten Island a black community grew up at Sandy Ground (near today's Woodrow) in the late 1830s, after free blacks migrated north from the Eastern Shore of Maryland to work the oyster beds in nearby Prince's Bay. In Queens there were African-American communities in Flushing, Newtown (in today's Corona), and Jamaica (near the Green at today's Douglas Avenue between 171st and 175th streets).

Work opportunities had continued to contract. In 1852 the newly formed Longshoreman's United Benevolent Society announced its intention to reserve waterfront jobs to its own (overwhelmingly Irish) membership and to "such white laborers as they see fit to permit upon the premises." By 1855 few blacks worked the docks, apart from occasional strikebreaking stints under the protection of city police. It was much the same with other unskilled positions. As the *African Repository* reported in 1851, "the influx of white laborers has expelled the Negro almost en masse from the exercise of the ordinary branches of labor. You no longer see him work upon buildings, and rarely is he allowed to drive a cart of public conveyance. White men will not work with him."

For black women domestic service remained an option, though in 1855 only 3 percent of the city's servants were African Americans, and many of these worked either for the very rich or in brothels, as laundresses, charwomen, and maids. Black men did hold on to jobs as waiters in the dining rooms and kitchens of the great hotels and restaurants and, indeed, organized a union that won higher wages. Other remaining possibilities included laboring for Brooklyn and Queens farmers, going to sea, and working in skiffs for white oystermen (as did the Sandy Grounders) culling mollusks with iron rakes.

Despite—and in response to—these handicaps, a semiautonomous African-American community flourished, organized around black churches. Methodists remained numerically dominant. Mother Zion's new 1840 edifice was perhaps the largest black-owned Protestant house of worship in the world, and AMEZ churches formed the nuclei of communities at Weeksville, Sandy Ground (near Crabtree Avenue), and Flushing (still extant in a downtown parking lot).

Presbyterians, fewer in number, were extremely influential, thanks in part to the dynamic series of leaders who succeeded Sam Cornish as pastor of the First Colored Presbyterian Church. The Rev. Theodore Wright stayed nineteen years and transformed a struggling institution into a formidable establishment, and when he died in 1847, the community held a mammoth funeral march. Under the Rev. James W. C. Pennington—an escaped slave who had worked as a blacksmith, taught himself to read and write, and became a teacher and minister—the church changed its name to Shiloh Presbyterian and moved to a building at Prince and Marion that could hold sixteen hundred.

Pennington was followed by Henry Highland Garnet, whose family had also escaped to New York from a Maryland plantation. Garnet's father, a shoemaker, became an important member of the African Methodist Episcopal Church and sent his son to the African Free School #1, until financial straits forced the youth to sea in 1829 as a cabin boy. While Henry was away, a relative of Garnet's master came to their home determined to seize them all. His father and mother jumped from an upper-story window and escaped. His sister was caught and taken before the city recorder but with the help of white abolitionists was able to prove herself a resident of the city. Henry returned to find the family home abandoned, the furniture destroyed or stolen, and his father still in hiding. Enraged, he bought a huge knife and dashed up and down Broadway hunting for slavecatchers, until his friends spirited him out of town to save his life. Garnet became a militant abolitionist and pursued a ministerial career under the wing of Theodore Wright. After holding pastorates upstate and winning acclaim for an incendiary address at the 1843 National Negro Convention in which he urged armed uprising on southern bondsmen, Garnet assumed Wright's old pulpit in 1855.

In the meantime, Charles B. Ray, another blacksmith turned clergyman, had established the tiny Bethesda Congregational Church (1845), having previously served as editor and proprietor of New York's *Colored American*, the short-lived (1837–41) successor to *Freedom's Journal*. Yet another important newcomer emerged in 1847, when six Brooklyn residents who were members of Manhattan's Abyssinian Baptist Church bought lots in downtown Brooklyn and erected the Concord Street Baptist Church of Christ.

New York's African-American churches were too poor to support substantial social welfare programs, but their members did take a hand in supporting an establishment, dedicated to the black community, that had been founded by white Quaker women. In 1836 Anna M. Shotwell and her niece May Murray had discovered two little Negro orphans on the steps of an old house. On learning that no existing nurseries accepted blacks and that the almshouse relegated black children to a squalid cellar, the women established a Colored Orphan Asylum, got the Common Council to donate twenty lots on Fifth Avenue between 43rd and 44th streets, and by 1843 had opened an impressive structure there, the first of its kind in the United States.

The Colored Orphan Asylum received support from the city, the state, and private organizations (when the old Manumission Society finally dissolved in 1849, it transferred all its assets to the asylum). The black community too gave aid, via regular collections at Mother Zion, St. Philip's, and Abyssinian Baptist and an occasional fair by "Colored Friends" of the institution. In addition, James McCune Smith, the city's leading black doctor, served as its attending physician throughout the era. Smith, born in New York City of free black parents in 1813, had been educated at the African Free School, tutored privately in the classics, and in 1832 had gone to Scotland for a five-year course of study at the University of Glasgow, earning three degrees. On his return, though barred by white doctors from the New York Academy of Medicine, Smith practiced medicine and ran an apothecary shop.

This cadre of black ministers and doctors organized a remarkable number of ad hoc and ongoing organizations. When southern spokesman and Secretary of State John C. Calhoun alluded snidely to the "vice and pauperism of the African race in the north," a protest meeting designated Dr. Smith to draft a pamphlet that took vigorous and well-documented exception to Calhoun's remarks.

When education for black children was neglected by the city, the New York Society for the Promotion of Education Among Colored Children (whose president was Charles B. Ray) won some modest improvements from the Board of Education, though not the dismantling of segregated schools they sought.

Antisegregationist activists made greater headway combating discriminatory practices in public transportation. Black ministers had long protested omnibus and horsecar company policies that forced black passengers to ride outside on the front platform or wait for a vehicle bearing the sign COLORED PEOPLE ALLOWED IN THE CAR—known as a "Jim Crow" car after Daddy Rice's minstrel character, which had become an all-purpose derogatory label for blacks. Many walked rather than be humiliated, but this option had grown more onerous as the city expanded: the Rev. Wright's fatal illness was brought on from the exhaustion of walking miles uptown to see prospective donors and then miles back downtown, "under the full muzzle of the July or August sun."

The first major breakthrough came thanks to the gritty determination of a twenty-four-year-old schoolteacher. On a Sunday afternoon in July of 1854, Miss Elizabeth Jennings, on her way to play the organ at services of the First Colored Congregation Church on Sixth Street near the Bowery, attempted to board a Third Avenue car at Pearl and Chatham. The conductor told her to wait for the colored car, but after an altercation he grudgingly allowed her entrance, though saying: "Remember, if any passenger objects, you shall go out, whether or no, or I'll put you out." Jennings's response—"I am a respectable person, born and brought up in New York, and I was never insulted so before"—roused in turn the conductor's ire: "I was born in Ireland and you've got to get out of this car," he said. She refused, he tried dragging her out, she clung to the window. He called on the driver to help, and together they pried her loose and threw her to the street. Though badly hurt, Jennings climbed back on. Finally the driver galloped his horses down the street until he found a policeman, who ejected her.

The young woman reported this to her church and to her father, Thomas Jennings, a successful tailor with a long record of activism in the black community. Born in New York in 1798, Jennings had dug trenches to help protect the city during the 1812 war, worked in the African Society for Mutual Relief, and helped found the Abyssinian Baptist Church. Now the Jenningses sued the Third Avenue line and were represented by attorneys from the firm of Culver, Parker, and Arthur, including Chester A. Arthur, a twenty-four-year-old recent law school graduate and future president of the United States. When the case came to trial in February 1855, the judge instructed the jury that the company was a common carrier and bound to carry all respectable persons, including "colored persons, if sober, well-behaved, and free from disease." The jury awarded Jennings $225. After this, most Manhattan railroads ceased discrimination.

Most, but not all. When Shiloh's Rev. Pennington, encouraged by Jennings's victory, set about testing other lines, he was forcibly expelled from a Sixth Avenue car. Three weeks later blacks organized the Legal Rights Association—with Thomas Jennings as president—to raise funds for Pennington's (and similar) cases. When this suit reached Superior Court in December 1856, however, the judge decided for the company, saying it had every right to decide who rode its cars. The decision encouraged the Eighth Avenue Railroad to hold fast to segregation until 1856, when Peter S. Porter, treasurer of the Legal Rights Association, after being beaten, kicked, and banged about "most ferociously," brought suit and won an out-of-court settlement allowing blacks to ride on the same terms as whites.

The African-American community's most ardent struggle, however, was (as it long had been) against slavery itself. Blacks were active in the American and Foreign Anti-Slavery Society. In addition, numbers attended mass abolitionist meetings like those held in Morris Grove, Brooklyn; supported the nationalist *Weekly Anglo-African*, founded in 1859 by two black printers in the city; worked in the Liberty Party; and helped raise funds for the defense and repatriation of the Mendi Africans who had seized their slave ship, *La Amistad*, and secured their freedom.

Their riskiest enterprise was harboring runaway slaves and helping them on their way to Canada. The New York Vigilance Committee was still going strong—presided over by Wright, then Ray—with funds gathered by Garnet and Pennington on speaking tours in the British Isles and at annual fairs black women held at the Broadway Tabernacle. New York became a major way station on the Underground Railroad; Ray dealt with over four hundred runaways in one fifteen-month period during 1848–49. City blacks provided sanctuary, food, and clothing—in private homes, in the Mutual Relief Hall (said to have a secret room the length of the building), in the boardinghouse on Dover Street run by passionate abolitionist William P. Powell for "the better class of colored seamen," and in the churches of Manhattan and Brooklyn: notably Mother Zion, Siloam Presbyterian, Bridge Street Methodist, and Concord Baptist.

After 1850, when President Fillmore signed the Fugitive Slave Law, their work became considerably more dangerous. As the act applied ex post facto to former runaways, many escapees who had remained in New York now fled town—the number of blacks in the city dropped from 13,815 in 1850 to 11,840 in 1855—or went to ground. In 1850 James Hamlet, a thirty-year-old fugitive, had been working for the past three years as a porter for the merchant firm of Tilton and Maloney. Seized on the street, Hamlet was arrested and returned to his Baltimore owner, leaving behind his wife and two children. Days later, on October 2, 1850, enraged blacks and sympathetic whites crowded into Mother Zion for a protest meeting. Presiding officer William P. Powell asked: "You are told to submit peacefully to the laws; will you do so? (No, no.) You are told to kiss the manacles that bind you; will you do so? (No, no, no.)" Eight hundred dollars was raised to purchase Hamlet's freedom, and on October 5 five thousand blacks cheered, sobbed, and sang hymns as they welcomed him home to New York.

Despite these occasional successes, the 1850s were dark days for African-Americans. Even some of the most militant began to abandon hope for a future in the United States and to reconsider their opposition to colonization. Henry Highland Garnet, despite his impeccable antislavery credentials, had become convinced, as had many western land reformers before him, that emigration might provide opportunities unavailable in New York City. In the summer of 1858 Garnet became the first president of the African Civilization Society, a group that included wealthy whites, and he promoted efforts to develop black colonies in Africa.

Garnet was vigorously opposed by those like Frederick Douglass, Dr. James McCune Smith, and the Rev. James Gloucester (of Brooklyn's Siloam Presbyterian Church) who preferred to stay and struggle within the political arena. This was no easy matter, however, as most blacks were still barred by stiff property requirements from voting at all. Such eligible voters as existed had organized themselves, in 1838, as the Colored Freeholders of the City and County of New York. During the 1840s and 1850s they met periodically with other such groups from around the state to demand universal suffrage. By the late 1850s there were forty-eight local suffrage clubs in Manhattan, eighteen in Brooklyn, and an umbrella organization, the New York State Suffrage Association. In 1860 they succeeded in getting the legislature to submit the question to the voters. James Gordon Bennett—who the year before had called for the reenslavement of northern blacks—rallied the opposition, urging "white men" not "to consummate the act of self-degradation which will bring them down to the level of . . . the niggers of the Five Points." The referendum lost by only 337,900 to 197,000 at the state level. But in New York City, it was rejected by 95 percent of the voters.

Given this generally dismal situation, it is not surprising that the rise of the Republican Party kindled hopes in the black community. In September 1858, at a New York Negro Suffrage Convention, the majority urged the state's eleven thousand eligible black electors to vote Republican to ensure the "defeat and ruin of the so-called Democratic party, our most inveterate enemy." But Garnet noted that Republicans loudly protested they had no intention of abolishing slavery in the South and that even those who did support equal suffrage rights, such as Horace Greeley, routinely disparaged blacks as "indolent, improvident, servile and licentious." Garnet counseled support for the Radical Abolitionist Party, the favorite of white abolitionists like the Tappans. Nevertheless, African Americans would overwhelmingly identify with—and be identified with—the Republican Party, to such a degree that it would be called by its enemies the "Black Republican" Party.

WHITE REPUBLICANS

Among the city's earliest white converts to Republicanism were journalists and ministers. Before taking up his Central Park duties, Frederick Law Olmsted had won prominence as a commentator on the southern way of life. In a series of books about his travels below the Mason-Dixon line, Olmsted had cast a critical eye on the world the slaveholders had made, less for its effect on suffering slaves than for its inefficiency. Horace Greeley of the *Tribune* stressed slavery's barbarity more than its supposed unprofitability. Citing British and Dutch precedents, he pronounced slavery a retrograde movement, contrary to the laws of motion of Christian civilization, and condemned planters—who loved posturing as cavaliers—as violent, degraded, and ignorant. Greeley also condemned New York's support for slavery—"In order to line our pockets, must we utterly stifle our souls?"—and was seconded in this by William Cullen Bryant of the *Post*, who departed the Democrats for ceasing "to serve the cause of freedom and justice."

The Rev. Henry Ward Beecher had swung into the Free Soil camp in the mid-1840s, though he remained opposed to abolitionism and feared liberating the South's "vast horde of undisciplined Africans." In 1848, however, Beecher began appearing at the Broadway Tabernacle, crucible of the antislavery crusade, and speaking out with Lewis Tappan and Frederick Douglass. After 1850 he urged defiance of the Fugitive Slave Act—"We are determined to break any law that commands us to enslave or re-enslave a man, and we are willing to take the penalty"—and he began holding sensational (and titillating) mock "slave auctions" at Plymouth Church, in which weeping men and women of his prosperous Brooklyn congregation heaped cash and jewels on collection plates to buy the freedom of light-skinned young women and children. Beecher also called on New Yorkers to extend the rights of citizenship to their own black citizens and refused to ride any streetcar line in Brooklyn that segregated its passengers. When Kansas became a battleground, he told northern emigrants heading there that "Sharpe's rifles are a greater moral agency than the Bible," and soon the Free Soilers smuggling guns to the territory took to calling them "Beecher's Bibles." By 1856 Plymouth was hosting the most radical abolitionists—like Wendell Phillips, who had been refused a venue by virtually every church and hall in both cities—and in that same year he became a Republican (his congregation gave him two months off to campaign for Frémont).

Republicanism made inroads in the business community too. Some Wall Streeters —particularly financiers promoting a transcontinental railroad and merchants whose trade dealings were not southern oriented—joined Beecher in attacking attempts to introduce slavery into Kansas. Such men gave financial aid to send free-state settlers to the territory or turned out for protest meetings in City Hall Park, and some entered the

Beecher Selling a Slave Girl from Plymouth Pulpit. (General Research. The New York Public Library. Astor, Lenox and Tilden Foundations)

new Republican Party. These were chiefly former Whigs, like clothing manufacturer and merchant George Opdyke, sugar and coffee importer Edwin Morgan, banker Simeon Draper, and flour and tea merchant George Griswold, though Democrats too joined up, like Isaac Sherman, a millionaire involved in western trade and railroads. Others were led to the Republican fold via their religious convictions, including William Dodge and Pelatiah Perit.

In the 1856 presidential campaign, a small nucleus under the leadership of Moses H. Grinnell set out to win Wall Street converts. In addition to offering a moral and cultural critique of the South, they stressed the practical business advantages a Republican victory might bring. They invited N. P. Banks, speaker of the House of Representatives and a recent convert to Republicanism, to address a crowd of twenty thousand from the steps of the Merchants' Exchange. Banks argued that the election of Democrat James Buchanan would hurt trade with Cuba (because a prosouthern administration would try to annex it for slavery), block a northern transcontinental rail route in favor of a southern one (diminishing New York's chances of capturing the China trade), and slow up river and harbor improvements.

Banks's appeal failed. The critique of the South might tug at moral and cultural heartstrings and speak to particular practical interests, but the facts of New York's situation dictated a continuing southern alliance.

METROPOLITAN DIXIECRATS

Whatever their private views about the southern social order, the city's key economic actors—the shipowners who hauled cotton, the bankers who accepted slave property as collateral for loans, the brokers of southern railroad and state bonds, the wholesalers who sent goods south, the editors with large southern subscription bases, the dealers in tobacco, rice, and cotton—all had come to profitable terms with its slave economy. Their attitude had been reinforced by the aftermath of the Panic of 1857, when the South rebounded far more quickly than did the West—clear evidence that European demand for cotton was higher than that for foodstuffs. "Cotton is King," said the editor of *Scientific American* in 1858.

One merchant spelled out the implications to Samuel J. May, a prominent abolitionist: "Mr. May, we are not such fools as not to know that slavery is a great evil, a great wrong. But a great portion of the property of the Southerners is invested under its sanction; and the business of the North, as well as of the South, has become adjusted to it. There are millions upon millions of dollars due from Southerners to the merchants and mechanics alone, the payment of which would be jeopardized by any rupture between the North and the South. We cannot afford, sir, to let you and your associates endeavor to overthrow slavery. It is not a matter of principles with us. It is a matter of business necessity," he concluded: "We mean, sir, to put you abolitionists down, by fair means if we can, by foul means if we must."

May's correspondent perhaps overstressed the cynicism of the prosouthern commitment. Many businessmen had close personal as well as commercial ties to southern planters and refused to stereotype them as barbarian slaveocrats. New York merchants vacationed with planters at Saratoga and other watering spots, intermarried with them, and, for all their official republican disapproval of aristocratic manners, were themselves often closet cavaliers. In October 1860, when the nineteen-year-old Prince of Wales (later Edward VII) and a retinue of British peers paid the city a visit, the elite fell all over itself to do him honor. Shops closed down. Business was paralyzed. A huge crowd turned out to acclaim the procession of the resplendent prince and his party up Broadway (with the notable exception of Colonel Michael Corcoran's Sixty-ninth Irish Regiment, which refused to join the line of march). At a grand ball next evening at the Academy of Music, a glittering crush of nabobs gathered to jostle and squeeze the royal person—so many that a section of the floor collapsed.

But interests remained fundamental to the alliance, including some quite nasty ones. From January of 1859 to August 1860, nearly one hundred vessels left New York harbor on slave trade business. Many had been built here, as shipbuilders hurt by the panic turned to the production of slavers. The profits could be enormous—$175,000 on a single voyage—as steamers could carry many more slaves than had the old sailing vessels.

While it was commonly held that some of biggest merchants in the city were in the trade, it was hard to pin this down. Merchants were unwilling to admit to their own participation in the illegal trade. Transactions were carried out through Cuban go-betweens, and captains used Spanish or Portuguese crews. But merchants were not reticent when it came to opposing all efforts—such as Seward's in the Senate—to get more effective control over the trade. At the annual meeting (in May 1860) of so pious an organization as the American Tract Society, Daniel Lord and Hiram Ketchum led a large group of merchants in shouting down a resolution condemning the slave trade. And the *Day-Book* was indignantly amazed that anyone could find fault "simply because somebody takes a few niggers from the jungles of Africa to Cuba."

Given this matrix of interest and ideology, most New York City merchants worked through the decade to banish the slavery issue from politics. The Kansas controversy did provoke a temporary outcry, in large measure because it seemed southerners were not keeping faith with the sectional truce, but for most the militancy didn't last. The rise of the Republican Party seemed a far deadlier threat to the Union, and few New York City Whig merchants followed Seward, Weed, and Grinnell into the new party. In the 1856 campaign, therefore, most old-line Whigs either sat out the election or voted for Democrats and Know-Nothings; Frémont came in a poor third. Upstate, however, went overwhelmingly Republican, and Frémont carried New York by the huge majority of eighty thousand votes. That year was also the one in which Republican John King won the governorship and Republicans in the Albany legislature began hacking away at New York City home rule.

Democratic merchants continued to press hard for conciliation with a South given to ever-escalating threats of secession. In October 1859—at a mass meeting in Cooper Union attended by two thousand merchants—August Belmont, William B. Astor, Moses Taylor, William F. Havemeyer, and attorney Samuel J. Tilden organized the Democratic Vigilant Association, dedicated to battling Seward's Republicans and convincing the South that New York merchants could still be depended on.

Republicanism found few adherents among workers, either. The artisan radicals who had been drawn to abolitionism in the 1830s had been alienated in the 1840s with its domination by upper-class evangelists, their inveterate enemies. By the 1850s few laboring groups strongly opposed slavery, apart from the Communist Club and several of the *Turnvereine* (whose defense squads protected antislavery meetings); fewer still joined the Republicans.

Like businessmen, workingmen believed that New York's economy, and thus their jobs, depended on a southern connection that Republicanism endangered. There were other bases for antipathy. Many Republicans were anti-immigrant bigots. Working people were also deeply suspicious of the Republican project of creating a nationwide "free labor" regime. To the Republicans, it seemed, "freedom" meant simply self-ownership, the fact of not being a slave. A laborer was fully "free," Republicans argued, when he was able to sell his labor, able to move from job to job in accordance with the changing demands of the marketplace.

Some Republicans—like Abraham Lincoln, a rising Republican luminary in Illinois—admitted that wage-work was incompatible with true freedom but argued that the free labor system allowed workers to climb out of their dependent and propertyless situation. This notion made sense to Lincoln's (and Seward's) rural and small-town constituency of farmers, craftsmen, and small businessmen; it didn't resonate in the big city, where most workers were trapped in permanent proletarian status, and knew it.

Workers also resisted Republican doctrine that unions were despotic institutions, on a par with the Slave Power and the Catholic Church in their coercion of individuals. Workers, the new party said, like reformers of old, would do better to advance themselves individually, by adopting proper habits and values. To people who depended on collective modes of organization and action for survival, this smacked of pious hypocrisy, especially when it came from wealthy employers.

Finally, white workers rejected Republicanism because it was Black Republicanism. Working-class racism, already deeply held, was strengthened each time employers used African Americans as strikebreakers; that their own racial animus helped sustain the divisions that facilitated this practice was not an easily achieved insight.

When opponents of Republicanism looked about for a vigorous champion, the likeliest candidate—back from the political dead—appeared to be Fernando Wood. In 1858 Wood had bolted Tammany Hall and organized his own independent Democratic organization, known as Mozart Hall, after its meeting place at the corner of Bond Street and Broadway. In 1859 he ran again for mayor, with the powerful support of Bennett's *Herald*.

This time it was his opponents who were divided. The monied members of the Democratic Vigilant Association, including Belmont, Tilden, and Havemeyer, demanded that Tammany nominate one of their own, on pain of withholding vital funding. The Hall selected Havemeyer, allowing Wood to present himself as the protector of the true Democrat, the workingman, and the immigrant, against the "kid glove, scented, silk stocking, poodle-headed, degenerate aristocracy." Republicans tried to fuse with Tammany, but the deal fell through and they ran their own candidate, George Opdyke, a wealthy importer. Wood blistered the Republicans for interfering with home rule in New York City and for threatening to estrange the South. "The South is our best customer," Wood declared. "She pays the best prices, and pays promptly." When the *Times* raised the old charge of excessive ambition—Wood wanted to become "Our Municipal Emperor," Raymond said—the ex-mayor retorted: "Better have an iron rule than no rule at all, as is now." When Wood won (with 38.3 percent to Havemeyer's 34.6 percent and Opdyke's 27.4 percent), his victory was hailed in the South by such organs as the *Richmond Examiner*.

All things considered, it was not altogether inappropriate that what would become the South's national anthem had its premiere in New York City that year. Dan Emmett's "I Wish I Was in Dixie's Land" was first aired at the April 4, 1859, performance of

Bryant's Minstrels in Mechanics Hall. It was then published by the New York firm of Firth, Pond and Co. and later made its way down south. (In a further irony, Emmett may have drawn upon the work of the Snowden Family Band—an African-American touring group—in composing the song.)

JOHN BROWN'S BODY

The metropolis was committed to the status quo. As ever, however, the status quo refused to stand still. On October 16, 1859, convinced that "the crimes of this guilty land, will never be purged away, but with Blood," John Brown struck at Harper's Ferry.

Some New Yorkers had known of Brown's plan. He had appealed to Henry Highland Garnet and Frederick Douglass for help, but African-American abolitionists had decided against participating in what seemed a suicidal exercise. When Douglass met with Brown just before the raid, however, he did pass along a contribution of twenty-five dollars from Elizabeth and James Gloucester (pastor of Brooklyn's Siloam Presbyterian Church) and their letter of support urging Brown "to do battle to that *ugly foe* of slavery."

New York's white abolitionists, adhering to their nonviolent principles, had also backed away from John Brown. "Would not one Uncle Tom do more good by his pious submission to God," Lewis Tappan had said to Brown's request for arms, "than a score or a hundred men who should act exactly opposite?"

But from the moment news of Brown's raid and capture arrived in New York on October 18, and through the ensuing weeks of his trial, the black and white abolitionist community was alive with prayer and sympathy meetings. Thomas Hamilton, editor of the *Weekly Anglo-African*, staunchly defended Brown's right of insurrection, and "the colored women of Brooklyn" wrote Brown in his Virginia jail cell that we "recognize in you a Saviour commissioned to redeem us, the American people, from the great National-al sin of Slavery." When Brown was hanged, on December 2, Henry Highland Garnet's Shiloh Church held a large memorial meeting, and the colored women of Brooklyn and New York sent donations to the martyr's widow and to the wife of his black compatriot, Lewis Leary. At the Broadway Tabernacle Church, Henry Ward Beecher produced the chains that had bound Brown to the scaffold, threw them to floor, stomped them with his heel, and cried, "The fate of the slaver states!"

Mainstream reaction was something else again. Businessmen denounced Brown as a madman. Bennett's *Herald* said the "lawless violence" tolerated by Republicans on the Kansas frontier had come back east to haunt them. Fernando Wood excoriated Brown as a "fiend" and his "fanaticism" as a threat to the Union. The Democratic Vigilant Association called the raid a logical outgrowth of Sewardism and urged the business community to show the South they repudiated Republicanism's pernicious principles.

The South didn't bother waiting. New York drummers were expelled from several states. Many firms canceled outstanding northern orders. Others called for boycotting abolition-tainted firms and shifting business to "friendly" concerns.

Thoroughly alarmed, several thousand metropolitan businessmen gathered at the Academy of Music on December 19 to denounce Brown's crimes and Seward's ideas. Leading merchants thronged the speaker's platform. The night rang with vigorous defenses of slavery as a positive good, ordained by nature.

49

Civil Wars

The atmosphere in New York was still poisonous when Abraham Lincoln came to town two months later. Lincoln, having emerged as a serious contender for the 1860 Republican nomination, had attracted the attention of Horace Greeley and William Cullen Bryant, on the lookout for a candidate to block Seward. The Young Men's Central Republican Union of New York City (a group run by such youngsters as Bryant and Greeley) originally intended to have him speak at Beecher's Plymouth Church in Brooklyn but shifted the venue to the more overtly political Cooper Union in New York. Lincoln's run through the celebrity production mill also included a stop at Mathew Brady's studio for an official campaign portrait.

In his talk at Cooper Union Lincoln disavowed Brown, struck a conciliatory pose toward the South, and denied the Republican Party was a sectional organization. But he also remained adamant on the need to stop the expansion of slavery, emphasized there were overarching moral issues at the crux of the sectional confrontation, and displayed oratorical gifts—"Let us have faith that right makes might"—that thrilled his audience. By the time he boarded a train for New England, Lincoln had demonstrated that a western man had appeal in the East, a crucial step toward his triumph at the Chicago convention.

In the ensuing campaign, most Republicans wrote off New York City as a lost cause and indeed boasted of their antiurban animosity in a bid for rural support. Campaigning in the West, Seward reminded audiences that "there is no virtue in Pearl Street, in Wall Street." Greeley's *Tribune* said the "moneybags of Wall Street" feared Lincoln because the "rich Jews and other money lenders," along with the "great dry goods and other commercial houses," were in league with slaveholders.

Some Republican politicians did try to make headway in the metropolis itself. They argued that the West—finally recovered from the 1857–59 recession—might be a better market, and political partner, than the South. They emphasized Republican support for internal improvements and tariffs, positions that won over some industrialists.

Still, most leading businessmen worked for Lincoln's defeat. The richest bankers and largest merchants forced contending Democratic candidates to fuse into a joint Union ticket, then promoted it vigorously. One group of dirty tricksters rigged a stock market panic, hoping to scare the country into thinking a Republican victory would create financial chaos. Anti-Lincoln editors escalated their racist rhetoric. The *New York Daily News*, edited by Fernando Wood's brother, Benjamin, said that if Republicans won, "we shall find negroes among us thicker than blackberries swarming everywhere," and Bennett warned workingmen that "if Lincoln is elected you will have to compete with the labor of four million emancipated negroes."

On election day thousands of stores closed and hung out signs urging patrons to vote the Union (Democratic) ticket. Many businesses circularized their employees, saying that if Lincoln were elected "the South will withdraw its custom from us and you will get little work and bad prices." New Yorkers gave the Union ticket a majority of thirty thousand and cast 62 percent of their votes for candidates other than Lincoln. The Republican *Tribune* blamed the showing on the "very general enlistment of the Mercantile and Capitalist classes in the Fusion cause."

But once again, success in the city was negated by Republican landslides upstate, which in turn helped put Lincoln over the top nationwide. Southerners read the Republican triumph as undermining their ability to veto federal threats to their institutions. South Carolina moved toward secession.

In New York, on December 15, over two thousand panicky city merchants crowded into a Pine Street establishment to draft a resolution of conciliation and reassurance to southern leaders, stressing their racial solidarity: one merchant declared that "if ever a conflict arises between races, the people of the city of New York will stand by their brethren, the white race." They vowed to defend slaveowner rights in the Union but declared that if southerners chose secession they should be allowed to depart in peace.

GRASS IN THE STREETS?

On the day before Christmas South Carolina swept out of the Union. Other Deep South states followed over the ensuing weeks. By early February the rebels had formed a government, the Confederate States of America.

One of the first rebel projects was to repudiate debts owed the North, with Manhattan's businessmen the principal target. Southern nationalists remembered that New Yorkers, with their charges for credit, commodities, insurance, shipping, and storage, had creamed off forty cents of every dollar Europeans paid for southern cotton. As the *Vicksburg Daily Whig* put it, New York "sends out her long arms to the extreme South; and with avidity rarely equalled, grasps our gains and transfers them to herself—taxing us at every step and depleting us as extensively as possible without actually destroying us." Now revenge was at hand. "What would New York be without slavery?" James Dunmore De Bow asked, and answered gleefully: "The ships would rot at her docks; grass would grow in Wall Street and Broadway, and the glory of New York, like that of Babylon and Rome, would be numbered with the things of the past."

Southern secessionists, in calculating whether they could win a military test of strength with the North, factored in what they believed to be the inherent contradictions and structural weaknesses of capitalism. These included Wall Street's financial instability—vividly witnessed in the 1857 panic—and the class and ethnic conflicts evident in New York City.

During the 1860 campaign, militant secessionist Edmund Ruffin concocted an eerily prescient fantasy he called *Anticipations of the Future to Serve as Lessons for the Present Time*. "When the Civil War began," Ruffin's narrator-in-the-future recalled, "loss of the lucrative southern trade caused massive unemployment in the industrial cities of the North." The jobless organized vast demonstrations, which turned into riots. At first these were put down by police and militia, with heavy loss of life. But "with the northern forces suffering military defeat and the northern government floundering in financial difficulties, the number of unemployed rose and the price of food spiraled." The city of New York "broke into open rebellion. Banks were broken open and their vaults robbed. Churches were looted. The avenues were filled with terrified refugees, struggling to escape the mob. . . . Drunk and gorged with plunder, the mob set the city on fire. A high wind whipped the flames into a hurricane of fire, and when morning came New York was a blackened, charred ruin." In the end, riots in other towns forced the northern government to abandon its efforts to conquer the South.

Ruffin's first predicted catastrophe arrived as if on cue. Triggered by the interruption of southern commerce, a panic struck New York City in 1861 that in some respects was more severe than that of 1857. Southern debts went unpaid, ruining northern creditors. Merchandise went unordered, and newspapers filled with ads from merchants frantically trying to sell goods originally destined for southern ports. Prices of commodities dropped steadily. Money dried up despite cooperative efforts by bankers to halt the panic. The *Herald* computed northern losses at $478 million. President Buchanan tried to reassure the city's capitalists and bankers by appointing one of their own, John A. Dix, as secretary of the treasury. But the crisis worsened. Some, like the Rev. Henry Bellows, feared secession was triggering social breakdown, "driving our populace into panic for bread and violence toward capital and order."

In early January two delegations—one Republican, one Democratic—left for Washington to plead for compromise with the South. Both efforts failed. At month's end thirty metropolitan leaders tried again, clambering aboard a special train with a monster memorial signed by forty thousand New York businessmen. Despite a respectful hearing from Republican congressmen over supper at Willard's Hotel, they made little impact. Indeed the Republicans soon introduced the Morrill tariff, which raised duties sharply, in some cases by 100 percent.

Some New Yorkers tried to use their financial muscle to force Republicans to compromise, saying they would otherwise refuse to buy the government's loans. Enraged Republicans countered that if a few wealthy businessmen tried to negate the democratic will, the government would issue bonds directly to the people: Horace Greeley said money could "be raised without difficulty, and in spite of Wall Street." The would-be capital strike collapsed.

LINCOLN REDUX

At this juncture, on February 19, Abraham Lincoln, on his way to Washington to be inaugurated, made his second visit to New York City. He arrived at three P.M. on the Albany train at the Hudson River Railroad Company depot on 30th Street at Tenth Avenue. From here he was taken, in a procession of hackneys escorted by the Metropolitans, past crowds almost equal to the turnout for the prince of Wales, to Astor House, across from City Hall Park. Nearby buildings were thick with spectators. Barnum's Museum across the way was bedecked with bright flags and banners. From the top of a Broadway omnibus gridlocked in traffic, Walt Whitman watched Lincoln step out on the sidewalk, stretch his arms and legs, and scan the crowd of thirty to forty thousand. There was, he remembered, "a sulky, unbroken silence. . . . I had, I say, a capital view of it all, and especially of Mr. Lincoln, his look and gait—his perfect composure and coolness—his unusual and uncouth height, his dress of complete black, stovepipe hat push'd back on the head, dark-brown complexion, seam'd and wrinkled yet canny-looking face, black, bushy head of hair, disproportionately long neck, and his hands held behind him as he stood observing the people. He look'd with curiosity upon that immense sea of faces, and the sea of faces return'd the look with similar curiosity."

The next morning at eight o'clock, accompanied by Thurlow Weed and James Watson Webb, Lincoln was driven to the Fifth Avenue home of Moses Grinnell's daughter, where he breakfasted with a hundred of the city's most prosperous merchants. Present were the leading Republican proponents of compromise. Someone remarked to Lincoln on the number of assembled millionaires, pointedly underscoring the city's financial clout. "Oh, indeed, is that so?" countered Lincoln deftly, underscoring his political muscle. "Well, that's quite right. I'm a millionaire myself. I got a minority of a million in the votes last November."

During the remainder of the day Lincoln made short remarks to Mayor Wood and the City Council before huge throngs at City Hall while his wife visited Barnum's and received ladies at the Astor House. At night he took in an evening reception, an elaborate dinner, a performance of Verdi's new *Un ballo in maschera* at the Academy of Music (to which he wore black kid gloves, a gaffe at which the press snickered next day), and a midnight serenade. The following day he left for Washington.

A week later anxious businessmen followed him there. William E. Dodge, industrialist and financier, explained that New Yorkers were nervous about the position he would take toward the South in his forthcoming inaugural and wanted to know "whether the grass shall grow in the streets of our commercial cities." Lincoln responded pleasantly that "if it depends upon me, the grass will not grow anywhere except in the fields and meadows." But when Dodge pressed him, asking if this meant he would yield to the just demands of the South, Lincoln replied grimly that the Constitution must be "respected, obeyed, enforced, and defended, let the grass grow where it may."

THE REPUBLIC OF NEW YORK?

Stymied by Lincoln's intransigence, some New Yorkers argued that if the Union could not be preserved, the southern states should be allowed to depart in peace, and the city should follow them out the door.

Back in January Mayor Wood had proposed to the Common Council that if the Union dissolved, New York should consider declaring—in the words of the Dongan Charter—that "New York be, and from henceforth forever hereafter shall be and remain, a free city of itself." Wood considered the national Republican assault on southern institutions, and the state Republican dismantling of metropolitan home rule back in 1857, to be co-evil assaults on local self-government. A declaration of independence by Manhattanites would liberate them from the meddling and plundering of upstate Puritans and free them as well from federal-dictated tariffs. By making theirs a duty-free port—apart from a nominal levy on imports that would cover the cost of local government and allow the abolition of local taxes—New Yorkers would retain an "uninterrupted intercourse with every section," including "our aggrieved brethren of the slave states," and rise to new heights of prosperity.

While Wood's idea was denounced publicly, it was debated privately in business circles. It had its appealing points. Some cited Hamburg, Lubec, Bremen, and Frankfurt as models. Rumors spread that some merchants were moving beyond contemplation to action. John Forsyth, a Confederate commissioner, wrote Confederate President Jefferson Davis that influential and wealthy men planned to seize the federal government's Navy Yard, warships, and forts.

Nothing of the sort materialized. Most businessmen calculated that New York's departure would simply trigger a further round of secessions, and the city would soon find itself cut off from West and South alike by tariff walls. Besides, the city hadn't the material base to sustain independence. As Lincoln dryly remarked, it would be "some time before the front door sets up house-keeping on its own account."

Wood's fantasy died abruptly in March 1861 when the provisional government of the Confederacy announced its tariff policy. After April 1 duties on imports arriving via New Orleans, Charleston, or Savannah would be lowered to half the rates federal law required New York City to impose. It would soon be cheaper for St. Louis or Cincinnati to import European goods through southern ports. The certain result, wrote a horrified *New York Times*, would be that "we shall not only cease to see marble palaces rising along Broadway, but reduced from a national to a merely financial metropolis, our shipping will rot at the wharves, and grass will grow in the streets." Worse still, the Confederacy abrogated federal coastal trading laws, thus expanding foreign access to southern ports, allowing the new nation (as the *Charleston Mercury* put it) to bypass the "New York money changers" and "trade directly with our customers."

Faced with the specter of the South's appending itself to the British Empire, the repudiation of millions in outstanding debts, and the disruption of trading and financial networks built up over a century, New York's bourgeoisie, virtually overnight, opted for war.

BEAT! BEAT! DRUMS!

At 4:30 A.M., before dawn on the morning of April 12, 1861, Edmund Ruffin pulled the lanyard on one of the shore batteries aimed at federal troops occupying Fort Sumter in Charleston harbor. Twenty hours later and eight hundred miles to the north, Walt Whitman heard the report. At midnight, walking down Broadway after leaving a performance of Verdi's *A Masked Ball*, he bought a paper from newsboys crying an extra and stopped to read the story under the gaslights outside the Metropolitan Hotel. Civil war had begun.

On Monday, April 15, Lincoln declared that an "insurrection" existed in the South and called on seventy-five thousand men to volunteer for three months to put it down. That very evening a group of "the largest capitalists and most influential citizens" (according to the *Tribune*) met on Pine Street and set up a committee to organize a gigantic mass meeting on Saturday, April 20. Throughout the week the business community's various institutions—the Stock Exchange, the Board of Currency, the Clearing House and, on Friday, the Chamber of Commerce, in the largest assembly in its history—gathered to say farewell to conciliation. "We are either for the country or for its enemies," proclaimed the Chamber's president. The Seventh Regiment, composed of young merchants, bankers, professional men, and clerks, left its Tompkins Market armory and marched down Broadway to the Jersey City ferry and off to defend the city of Washington, at that point virtually cut off and wide open to Confederate attack.

On Saturday the twentieth, what was reputedly the largest assemblage ever seen on the continent—somewhere between 100,000 and 250,000 people—flooded into Union Square. (In the war years, Union Square would replace City Hall Park as the center of civic life.) It was, all agreed, "a red, white and blue wonder." Five stands swathed in the official colors groaned with speakers (including Major Robert Anderson, the hero of Sumter). The new bronze statue of Washington was wrapped in the flag that had been fired upon at Sumter. And Broadway emporiums from Stewart's (at Reade) to Lord and Taylor's (at Grand) were similarly bedecked as the city's trade and benefit societies marched behind bands and flags of their own. Virtually every workshop in the city sent a delegation to the rally.

The meeting (as banker John Austin Stevens recalled) had been planned and orchestrated toward having the populace entrust "the guidance of their action" to "the merchants of the city, the chief representatives of its wealth and influence." As expected, those assembled ratified establishment of a Union Defense Committee (UDC), composed of thirteen Democratic and twelve Republican businessmen. These gentlemen set about launching the war effort.

On Sunday, April 21, Lincoln, impressed by the New Yorkers' dispatch, surreptitiously ordered the transfer of two million federal dollars into UDC hands, with which to unofficially purchase arms, steamships, and supplies and to use in enlisting and dispatching troops to open the road to Washington. At the urging of none other than

The Great Union Meeting in Union Square, April 20, 1861. (© Collection of The New-York Historical Society)

Mayor Wood, recent advocate of municipal secession, the Board of Aldermen authorized borrowing another million and a half from the Bank of New York and other financial institutions to pay for volunteers and for the relief of their families while they were away. Within a week the UDC started funneling this $3.5 million into chartering ships, procuring supplies, and forwarding troops to Annapolis in armed convoys via the Potomac River and Chesapeake Bay. New York was established as headquarters of the army's Department of the East, and four military depots were set up to process recruits. By Tuesday, April 23, six regiments had been dispatched. The following weeks witnessed virtually continuous ceremonies honoring departing troops. Bowery photographers did a booming business printing thousands of pictures of new soldiers decked out in their "regimentals." By the end of 1861 the UDC had placed sixty-six New York regiments in the field and aided almost twelve thousand volunteers' dependents.

THE B'HOYS AT WAR

The German community was aflame with war fever. A huge meeting at Steuben House on the Bowery had already established enlistment stations all through Kleindeutschland. Three-fourths of the New York Socialistischen Turnverein signed up, forming an all-Turner outfit, and many other units—such as the Seventh Volunteer Regiment (Steuben Guard) and Colonel Louis Blenker's German Rifles—were also manned by veterans of the 1848 Continental wars. Blenker's Regiment received a regimental flag at City Hall from Mrs. August Belmont, feasted at the Bowery's Atlantic Garden on sausage, dark bread, and beer, then set off to war.

Hungarians and Swiss flocked to join George D'Utassy's First Foreign Rifles, which swiftly merged with the Italian Legion formed by Alexander Repetti (who had served under Giuseppe Garibaldi in the Italian reunification struggle of 1848–49). The merged unit—the Garibaldi Guard—followed European practice and equipped wives of members as *vivandières*. Dressed in red flannel basques and blue skirts, it was their job to lead troops in dress parade and sometimes into battle, as well as to serve as nurses, cooks, laundresses, soldiers' confidantes, and matrons of the company in camp. Several young working women from Jersey City ran away from home to serve, marrying men on the spot in order to sail with the Garibaldians. Escorted to the dock and off to war by the Teutonic and Germania societies, they would later be followed by the DeKalb Regiment, composed entirely of German clerks, and by the Polish Legion.

No group surpassed the Irish in enthusiasm. The Sixty-ninth, which had refused to honor the prince of Wales, voted unanimously to enlist under Michael Corcoran. Within days, an additional sixty-five hundred were pleading to serve under the Donegal-born Fenian leader. On April 23 the regiment was blessed by Archbishop Hughes at St. Patrick's Cathedral and marched off to the ferry. After their ninety-day service was up, which included honorable duty at First Bull Run, they returned to the Battery on July 27 for an uproarious welcome from Irish fire companies, the Ancient Order of Hibernians, the Sons of Erin, and bands blaring "The Cruiskeen Lawn" and "St. Patrick's Day in the Morning." Most reenlisted immediately and inspired yet another wave of Irish to join up.

Corcoran himself, wounded and captured at First Bull Run, didn't make it back to New York until August 1862, when Lincoln got him exchanged. In his absence Thomas Francis Meagher organized an Irish Brigade. Meagher had been a leader of the Young Ireland agitation of the 1840s. Exiled to Tasmania, he escaped to New York, where he

The Irish Sixty-ninth Regiment departing for the war, April 23, 1861. Old St. Patrick's Cathedral, facing Mott Street, is at the right. Hibernian Hall, "the Irish Headquarters," is the two-story building with dormer windows on Prince Street in the left center. The large building with two wings on the left is the St. Patrick's School, run by the Sisters of Charity. (© Collection of The New-York Historical Society)

set up a law practice and led anti-British agitation among the immigrants. Now Meagher recruited thousands into the brigade's three regiments; Irish women sewed it flags and banners; Daniel Devlin furnished its uniforms free of charge; and the troops departed in late 1861.

When Corcoran returned from Confederate prison to a triumphal welcome in 1862—the kitchen help for miles around flooded to the streets to welcome their hero, noted young Joseph Choate, partner in a Wall Street law firm—he promptly organized yet another four new regiments into an Irish Legion. Corcoran would command its four thousand members—who received an en masse outdoor blessing from Archbishop Hughes—as a brigadier general until his death in 1863.

For many Irish, joining up had political overtones. Patriotic participation, some hoped, would forever silence nativist charges that Hibernian Catholics were unworthy of citizenship. Recruiting posters also emphasized that the war was a blow against England, natural ally of the Confederate "cotton lords." Many noted, too, that Union army training would serve them well in Ireland's coming war of liberation. For others, volunteering was part lark and part escape from hard times. It was impossible to get work in the panic spring and summer of 1861, and many followed suggestions in the *Herald* to sign up for the soldier's pay of thirteen dollars a month. These companies, extremely rambunctious, constantly tested the limits of military authority.

Billy Wilson's Boys, the Sixth Regiment, were a case in point. Wilson, an ex-pugilist and ex-alderman, recruited his volunteers at a dogfighting and ratbaiting house in White Street. His pugnacious men, armed with slung-shots and seven-inch knives, envisioned the war as an adventurous brawl-writ-large. In their camp on Staten Island, they trained by scrapping with other regiments, plundering the neighborhood, and drinking prodigiously.

Equally notorious were the men of the Eleventh Regiment (the Fire Zouaves). Composed largely of volunteer fire laddies, the unit was commanded by Ephraim Elmer Ellsworth, the man who popularized the uniform of the Franco-Algerian Zouaves: red billowing trousers, loose tunics, sashes, and turbans. These b'hoys went boisterously off to war and, on arriving in Washington, promptly broke into taverns, ordered meals, and charged them to Jeff Davis. They redeemed themselves in Washingtonian eyes, however, when a building next to Willard's Hotel caught fire. Ellsworth's men, quartered nearby in a wing of the Capitol, leapt out the windows, broke into the engine houses, and reached the spot before the city's firemen were even awakened, saving the whole structure. More to the point, they fought well at Bull Run, though after the rout hundreds melted away and returned to New York, denouncing their officers who had fled the scene of battle. The regiment was reorganized, and though it remained refractory and brawled repeatedly, in the end it returned to the fray.

African-American troops were conspicuously absent from that fray, though not for lack of trying. Back in May, black New Yorkers had started drilling on their own in a privately hired hall. Chief of Police Kennedy warned them that "they must desist from these military exercises, or he could not protect them from popular indignation and assault." In July the community tried again. Three regiments of black soldiers were offered to Governor Morgan for the duration of the war. The black population of the state guaranteed their arms, clothing, equipment, pay, and provisions. The governor declined.

Overall, however, the outpouring of metropolitan manpower and firepower was tremendous. Walt Whitman was ecstatic. In a new poem (*Beat! Beat! Drums!*) that he read aloud at Pfaff's in September, Whitman claimed that the "torrents of men" he'd seen marching off that summer represented "DEMOCRACY" in all its primal energy: "I have witness'd my cities electric; I have lived to behold man burst forth, and warlike America rise."

ENTREPÔT AND WORKSHOP

The South was furious at its former ally. A Richmond Dispatch editorial entitled "Execrable New York" proclaimed it the inferior of "Sodom, to which, on account of its horrible profligacy of morals, it has often been likened," because Sodom, unlike New York, had had at least one principled man "amid an unclean and accursed generation." The *Charleston Courier*—railing at "the treacherous cowardice and hypocrisy of [its] merchants and Mammon-worshippers"—declared that "the interests of Christianity, civilization, humanity, and intelligent self-government, require that New York, the metropolis of shoulder-hitters, prize-fighters, blackguards and mercantile gamblers should be blotted from the list of cities."

For a time it looked as if the *Courier* would get its wish. Southern crowds menaced the offices of northern firms until their occupants packed up and returned home. The Confederacy prohibited the payment of debts to northerners. Even merchants who refused to repudiate announced a suspension of remittances until the war's end. By July trade had virtually ceased.[1]

1. Some New Yorkers let go of their profitable southern links with great reluctance. Trading in southern state

Severed from its southern connection, New York's manufacturing economy crashed, too. The East River shipyards and ironworks came to a standstill. Boot and shoe production was drastically curtailed. Half the two thousand workers in the carriagemaking trade, heavily dependent on southern slaveocrat orders, were laid off. The dry-goods business was prostrated—the hoop skirt trade had sent 75 percent of its product to southern belles—and by summer one-fourth of the jobbers in Manhattan had gone under. Even the ice industry was crippled by lack of orders from the South.

With thirty thousand idled, droves of workingmen requested commitment to the workhouse. The superintendent of the outdoor poor got ten thousand applications for coal. Hundreds of homeless sought shelter in police stations. In July two thousand German workers demanded municipal public works programs. It looked like 1857 had come round again.

By fall, however, war had resurrected and reoriented the economy. Wheat began surging into the city. In 1860 and 1861 European (and particularly British) crops failed, while at the same time, the American West produced bumper harvests and great quantities of livestock. With the Mississippi closed by war—paddle wheels on sixteen hundred steamboats had stopped turning—westerners shifted from rivers to railways. Freight tonnage and passenger usage expanded rapidly on established East-West lines like the Pennsylvania, the Erie, and the New York Central. Demand spurred the strengthening of old lines—the Hudson River Railroad spanned the Hudson at Albany with a revolutionary two-thousand-foot long iron bridge—and induced construction of new ones. British capital and fifteen thousand British laborers and engineers were dispatched from Europe to lay tracks for the Atlantic and Great Western. It ran from Cincinnati through the newly discovered and already booming oil fields of Pennsylvania, and on to Salamanca in western New York, where it connected with and revivified the half-defunct Erie, cutting Cincinnati–New York travel time to less than a week. Looking ahead to still grander vistas, New Yorkers, including Dix, Dodge, and A. A. Low (now president of the Chamber of Commerce), assumed key roles in the federal government's 1862 incorporation of the Union Pacific, which they planned to run to the eastern border of California. Together with the flood of waterborne traffic—Great Lakes and Erie Canal tonnage was still twice that of the New York Central and Erie combined—the new routing finished off New Orleans as a contender for leading export center. Atlantic seaboard competitors fell even farther behind: while exports of wheat, wheat flour, and corn from New York City mounted from nine million bushels annually to fifty-seven million, Philadelphia limped along with a mere five million, Boston with but two.

The amber waves of grain that rolled into the harbor flowed right out again to European ports. To speed the wheat on its way, merchants at Brooklyn's Atlantic Dock deployed the first floating elevators. These could remove, weigh, bag, and reload grain from canal boats onto steamers at the rate of five thousand bushels per hour. Hundreds

bonds at the Merchants' Exchange terminated only at the end of 1861. Gazaway Lamar, acting on a secret commission from the Confederacy, was able to buy a thousand muskets in Manhattan, and though the ship sending them south was seized by the Metropolitan Police—Mayor Wood apologized but noted his lack of authority over the state-run body—it was released when the governor of Georgia threatened to seize New York vessels in Savannah harbor. Some clothiers surreptitiously sewed southern uniforms, even after Sumter, and agent Lamar got the National Bank Note Company to print up Confederate bonds and ship them to Alabama. Still, these were exceptions.

of Irish grain shovelers were fired; the company boasted that thousands more would go. In July 1862 two thousand shovelers, organized by the Grain Workers Protective Association, joined three thousand longshoremen and stevedores in a strike to demand the machines be abandoned. The grain merchants used scabs from ships' crews around the harbor to break the strike, something the grain workers would remember.

The West shipped cattle along with wheat. By the summer of 1862, Illinois alone was forwarding two thousand head a week. The city was overrun with cows being driven through the streets to more than two hundred uptown slaughterhouses. By 1864 over two million beasts were being butchered annually in New York (more than in Chicago) and the air reeked from boiling bones and rendering fat. Lumber came rolling in too, more than enough to sustain Brooklyn's building boom. Sugar poured in, enough to warrant the opening of six new refineries during the war. The Havemeyer family rose to prominence as the sugar business became one of the city's largest industries. Oil gushed in. Within a scant few years of the 1859 discovery of black gold in Titusville, millions of barrels were flowing out of northwestern Pennsylvania to the nation's two hundred new oil refineries. Twenty-five of these still-small (ten-man) operations were in the metropolitan area, notably in Williamsburg and Greenpoint along the East River and Newtown Creek, where they produced "kerosene," the cheapest illuminant ever known. By 1863 almost half a million barrels of petroleum product were being exported from New York.

Shipbuilding, like almost every other city industry, was stoked by war contracts. As early as August 1861 the *Tribune* noted that local yards were busy producing a new gunboat fleet for the navy, refitting old steamers and merchantmen for war, and meeting businessmen's demand for vessels to handle the exploding coastal, lake, and river trade. "Recently so idle and empty, [they] once more resound with the cheery hum of labor and the new music of the adze and anvil." Soon four thousand men were at work in Brooklyn's Navy Yard alone.

Skilled machinists were in great demand to develop and repair naval machinery. By 1863 the great ironworks—Neptune, Fulton, Morgan, Novelty, Continental, Allaire, Delamater, and McLeod—were turning out vertical and horizontal engines, boilers, furnaces, plates, and anchors. At the Novelty works twelve hundred men were kept busy refitting the *Roanoke* with a thousand tons of armor and three revolving turrets for fifteen-inch guns, while simultaneously making a beam engine for a Pacific mail steamship and machinery for three side wheel steamers.

The maritime engineering triumph of the war years came at Thomas F. Rowland's huge Continental Iron Works along the Greenpoint waterfront at Calyer and West streets. In 1861, while most of its fifteen hundred hands were producing gun carriages and mortar beds for the Navy, the company began work on a design by Swedish engineer John Ericsson for an ironclad warship. Ironclads were an old idea. The United States had flirted with them during the Mexican War, and French success with them in the Crimean War (1854–56) had led the English and French navies to pour millions into their construction. The *Monitor*, launched at Greenpoint on January 30, 1862, was also a success: it fought the Confederate's *Merrimac* to a standoff on March 9 and generated a host of additional government contracts for Continental.

Underwritten by federal dollars and protected by federal tariffs, New York manufacturers of every description expanded rapidly. Cooper, Hewitt turned out gun carriages and gun-barrel iron; Phelps, Dodge, and Company churned out iron forgings and castings; the Hendricks Brothers Copper Rolling Mills worked at full capacity throughout the war. Conrad Poppenhusen's Enterprise Rubber Works in College Point flourished on orders for hard rubber flasks, cups, and buttons. City carriagemakers produced hundreds of ambulances and baggage wagons for the Quartermaster General's Department. War galvanized Brooklyn's fledgling pharmaceutical industry too. Edward Robinson Squibb, a former navy doctor, manufactured drugs (including ether) for the military, first in rented quarters on Furman Street, then in additional buildings on Columbia and Vine streets in order to handle the bulk orders of bandages, splints, and panniers (baskets of medicines and surgical instruments). Charles Pfizer, who had immigrated in 1848 and established a chemical manufacturing plant in Williamsburg on Bartlett Street, similarly expanded to meet wartime demand.

War orders and the tariff on foreign ready-mades boomed the clothing trades too. A. T. Stewart's army and navy contracts netted him nearly two million dollars annually during the conflict, and Brooks Brothers received its first contract from the New York State Military Board—for twelve thousand uniforms—as early as April 1861. Brooks Brothers also pioneered the use of "shoddy" when, discovering it lacked enough suitable cloth, it resorted to using shredded rags that were rolled, glued, and smoothed into ersatz cloth. When artisan tailors alerted government officials to the fact that the contractor was "fitting out soldiers with suits of clothing that disgraced the State" while paying a "grinding standard of wages," the firm replaced the inferior goods. However, many of those who snared subsequent contracts were speculators who had influence and connections, but no experience in the business. After taking a hefty cut of the appropriated funds, they subcontracted the work to jobbers who, to extract their own profit, jammed wages down, demanded blistering rates of production from artisans and female outworkers, and scrimped on materials. This became apparent when shoddy uniforms fell to pieces in the rain, leaving soldiers almost naked. The army also marched on shoddy shoes. Even the New York Chamber of Commerce later admitted that local contractors had sold the government great numbers of boots whose soles, made of pine chips pasted over with thin leather, dropped off after a half-hour's hike. Contractors also supplied rotten blankets, tainted pork, glued knapsacks that came apart in rain, and even shoddy horses: stables on 24th Street—in collusion with inspectors—fobbed off partially blind nags on the cavalry at premium prices.

War boosted the communications industry. New technology allowed newspapers to bring the fighting vividly before the literate public, and as Sabbatarian reservations crumpled, special Sunday editions offered detailed recounting of battles. The press reached the illiterate as well: the dailies, and especially *Harper's Weekly, Frank Leslie's Illustrated Newspaper*, and the *New York Illustrated News*, carried Currier and Ives etchings or sketches by artists that graphically portrayed battlefields, soldiers, and hospitals. The soldiers themselves were mass consumers, and it was rumored that during the battle of Antietam newsboys hawked the latest extras to the troops.

The war did deal a severe blow to one sector of the city's economy. New York's merchant marine—badly buffeted in 1857 and 1858—was finished off by Confederate cruisers. After 284 captures by southern privateers (sixty-four by the dreaded *Alabama* alone) and the inevitable hike in insurance rates, most American and overseas traders had transferred to foreign flags. The total value of goods carried in U.S. vessels sank from $507 million in 1860 to $185 million in 1864. By war's end three-fourths of the commerce in New York's harbor was carried by foreign lines, and most of the steamship lines that serviced the city were heavily subsidized British and German firms.

Overall, however, the war forged powerful new bonds between metropolitan manufacturing and the national state—neatly symbolized by the Bronx-built Capitol dome set in place in 1863—which wrought a revolution in productivity. The industrial output of New York City almost outpaced that of the entire Confederacy.

GREENBACKS AND GOLDBUGS

By July 1861 the Union was nearly broke. Secretary of the Treasury Salmon P. Chase had two million dollars on hand to meet federal needs he estimated at $320 million. He turned to the banks. In August, after a week-long conference in Manhattan, a consortium of financiers from New York, Boston, and Philadelphia—headed by Moses Taylor of City Bank and James Gallatin of National Bank—agreed to lend the government $150 million. Charging a 7.3 percent rate of interest, compared to the 5 to 6 percent they got from railroad companies, the consortium began with a first installment of $50 million, of which New York's share was $29.5 million, apportioned among thirty-nine of the city's fifty banks. Secretary Chase took the loan in gold (the government was, by law, not allowed to accept bank deposits). This quickly depleted the banks' reserves, especially given the hoarding of gold that had commenced with the war. By December 30, 1861, the New York banks had ceased making specie payments, and bankruptcy was at hand.

So Congress authorized the treasury to print money. In February 1862 the government began issuing legal tender "greenbacks," and by March 1863 it had authorized $450 million worth. The arrival of the nation's first uniform currency did not stop state banks from continuing to print a bewildering array of notes, which also served as money, so to regularize the currency, Congress reorganized the entire banking system in February 1863. The law created the new status of "national bank"—chartered directly by the federal government and required to obey certain rules and regulations. Many state-chartered banks, particularly in New York and other eastern cities, were hostile to the new system, as the inducements didn't seem to warrant accepting federal regulation. Finally, in 1865, they were bludgeoned into acquiescence by the imposition of a stiff tax on state bank notes. For all their grumbling, Manhattan bankers soon found the new national system, which quickly came to center in the metropolis, to be highly lucrative.

To raise money to pay the interest on its bonds and back its greenbacks, the Republican administration instituted taxes on manufactured products and on professional and business activities and initiated a 3 percent levy on incomes over eight hundred dollars. When these revenues failed to bring in enough funds, the government decided to borrow from the general public. Secretary Chase appointed Philadelphia financier Jay Cooke as the nation's investment banker. He organized a syndicate of the ablest investment houses in several cities (Livermore, Clews, and Company was the New York choice), and this group in turn hired twenty-five hundred subagents who hawked the treasury's "five-twenties" in almost every town and village. For a time Cooke's bond drive, which brought in a million dollars a day, proved sufficient. During the war's last grueling years, however, expenditures soared to over $3.73 million a day, and the government was again forced to rely heavily on New York financial houses to sell bonds and negotiate loans.

The Civil War gave the city's bondholders and bankers—as it had local manufac-turers—a tremendous stake in the fortunes of the federal government. By 1863 the Chamber of Commerce added to its list of reasons for putting down the rebellion the "vast pecuniary obligation" the war itself had created, noting Union defeat would put "in jeopardy one thousand millions or more of public debt." Command of the fiscal sinews of war in turn would give the northern commercial classes, especially the Man-hattan bourgeoisie, ever greater influence over affairs of state.

The flood of government greenbacks and the large issue of short-term interest-bearing notes made money abundant, facilitated the war boom, and ignited the financial exchanges. The stock market fluctuated wildly with the military situation. When McClellan landed his army on the peninsula, stocks rose; the first reverses brought them down; they rose with the fall of New Orleans; they dropped with defeats on the Chickahominy. Yet through all the gyrations—which afforded fertile field for specula-tors—the direction of the market was unmistakably up. In the space of two years, the overall value of stocks on the New York market increased by two hundred million dollars.

Merchants, dowagers, and clergymen accordingly flocked to Wall Street. In Janu-ary 1862 the *Tribune*'s financial editor wrote that "the excitement in stock circles today we have never seen equalled in our very long experience of the street. . . . The intense desire to buy almost any kind of securities amounted almost to insanity. . . . The oldest members of the Board cannot remember such a day of rampant speculation." The bull market was further fueled by margin buying. Stock buyers could put up as little as 10 percent (at times even 3 percent) of the purchase price in cash. Banks were only too willing to lend the rest at up to 10 percent interest. Stockbrokers were delirious: by 1863 they were averaging three thousand dollars a week in commissions.

One beneficiary of the war boom was the New York Stock Exchange, which received a permanent home after flitting for years from stables to attics along Wall, Hanover, William and Beaver streets. In 1863 a group of brokerage firms incorporated a building company, hired architect John Kellum to design a Tuscan palazzo-style struc-ture, bought a site for it two blocks west from where the Exchange had started back in 1792, purchased iron and stone from the Cornell Works and the East Chester Marble Company, and had the building finished a few months after Appomattox.

THE SHODDY ARISTOCRACY

In March of 1863 William Dodge wrote a friend in England: "Things here at the North are in a great state of prosperity. You can have no idea of it. The large amount expended by the government has given activity to everything and but for the daily news from the War in the papers and the crowds of soldiers you see about the streets you would have no idea of any war. Our streets are crowded, hotels full, the railroads, and manufactur-ers of all kinds except cotton were never doing so well and business generally is active."

New York's upper classes made money in quantities never before seen or even imagined. In 1863 the upper 1 percent of income earners (sixteen hundred families) garnered about 61 percent of the city's wealth. And where in 1860 there had been a few dozen millionaires in the city, by war's end there would be several hundred, some of them worth over twenty millions.

In celebration of their expanded or newly minted fortunes, the rich went on a shop-ping binge. After striking successful deals at the Astor House, speculators decked out in velvet coats, gold chains, breast pins, and rings dined at Delmonico's on partridge stuffed with truffles. The "shoddy aristocracy" paraded down Fifth Avenue on Sundays or trotted around the new Central Park in their shiny equipages wearing thousand-dollar camel's hair shawls. Contractor parvenus gloried in liveried servants and imported luxuries. In 1862 the genteel Maria Daly was horrified to hear that "a saddler's wife went to Tiffany and Young's . . . and ordered the greatest quantity of pearls and diamonds and plate."

Among the most prodigious shoppers was Mary Lincoln. When Congress appropriated twenty thousand dollars for her to redecorate the White House, she hastened to New York City's department stores, overspent her budget, then pleaded with bureaucrats to make up the difference without telling her husband. Throughout the war she went on repeated and increasingly pathological spending sprees in the metropolis. Mrs. Lincoln was driven by personal demons, but in milder form, her ardent consumerism became commonplace.

The grand symbol of the wartime boom was A. T. Stewart's "New Store." Abandoning his Marble Palace on Broadway and Chambers, Stewart had architect John Kellum design a structure farther uptown on a plot bounded by Broadway and Fourth Avenue, 9th and 10th streets, just across Astor Place from Cooper Union. The New Store was of cast iron (produced at the Hudson shoreline by the Cornell Iron Works). Painted white, the building rose five stories around a great rotunda. Its graceful molded arches in the Venetian manner—Stewart compared them to "puffs of white clouds"—also permitted rows upon rows of windows, and the building featured two thousand panes of French plate glass.

Stewart put no displays in the ground-floor windows, relying instead on views of the shoppers within to draw additional customers. On opening day, November 10, 1862, crowds entering the largest retail store in the world found countless orderly displays, laid out with "military precision," *Harper's Monthly* noted approvingly, and an army of five hundred clerks and cash boys (who ran back and forth between cashier and clerk) waiting to serve them. On the first floor customers could purchase silks, dress goods, men's furnishings, linens, and domestics' clothing. Here the wealthy could buy outfits for balls (like the glittering 1863 reception for officers of the Russian fleet at the Academy of Music) or for the summer season. Though the prices tended to the staggering, the less well heeled could find bargains at the calico and remnant counters.

The upper floors were devoted to production, not consumption. On the fourth, 500 seamstresses and dressmakers labored in well-lit, well-ventilated workrooms considered the finest in the city, though annual wages ranged only from $100 to $250. The fifth floor was given over to a linen service that employed another three hundred women. The store thus had nearly a thousand employees, neatly segregated by gender—eight hundred women or girls on the production side, a hundred supers, cashiers, bookkeepers, ushers, porters, clerks, and cash boys on the consumption end—though as the war generated a male labor shortage, women entered the sales force for the first time. In some ways the cast-iron palace, the largest worksite under one roof in the city, resembled a gigantic factory. Reviewers noted the clerks were placed on a strict regimen during their twelve-hour days and that Stewart treated his "employees as cogs in the complicated machinery of his establishment. . . . The men are numbered and timed." All the latest technology was deployed: steam engines heated all the floors, pumped water to the laundry, and powered the sewing machines in the carpet-manufacturing department. At night the building was brilliantly illuminated by gaslight chandeliers.

In summer many New Yorkers traveled north to Saratoga on Daniel Drew's sumptuous new steamboats. There the women arranged fancy dress balls while the men indulged in liquor, races, and gambling at establishments created by John Morrissey, the Democratic politico, boxer, casino operator, and now turfman.

In fall, back in the city, the great hotels were glittering and crammed. Hundreds of contented Republican males packed the Astor House's smoke-filled, gas-lit Rotunda Bar each evening, to banter and drink tap-beer and eat roasted meat before heading out for evening expeditions. Pleasure seekers might take in the theater, the city's flourishing bawdy houses, or an opera at the Academy of Music. After 1862, they could dine at Lorenzo Delmonico's latest and most luxurious restaurant, in the converted Moses Grinnell mansion at Fifth and 14th, one block west of Union Square.

For the ladies, there were days at the milliner's or department stores. Wartime fashion ran to carriage cloaks of moire or amber velvet, to sable or mink furs, and to gowns of organdy, grenadine, and brocade silks in deep and brilliant magenta, gold, or fuchsia. Hoop skirts blocked traffic, which is why Mme. Demorest's Imperial "dress-elevator" was immensely popular: its weighted strings allowed women to raise or lower their skirts at will, thus clearing New York's mud and slush.

Even charitable occasions could be turned into festivals of consumption. In April 1864 the U.S. Sanitary Commission held a Metropolitan Sanitary Fair to raise money for its activities. Organized by the wives of leading businessmen, it was held in two buildings erected at Union Square (with interior decoration by the young architect Richard Morris Hunt). For three weeks, an estimated ten to thirty thousand daily shoppers thronged the stalls, raising $1,365,000.

The extravagance did provoke some opposition. A *Harper's* 1864 article called "The Fortunes of War" denounced the "suddenly enriched contractors, speculators, and stock-jobbers" who were "spending money with a profusion never before witnessed in our country, at no time remarkable for its frugality." The magazine rebuked those who used gold and silver dust to powder their hair and noted caustically that the price of a dinner at Delmonico's or Maison Dorée could "support a soldier and his family for a good portion of the year." At a May 1864 Cooper Union meeting called by the Women's Patriotic Association for Diminishing the Use of Luxuries, various speakers denounced the purchase of foreign superfluities while young men were dying on the Potomac, and all assembled pledged to reject imported luxuries. But the campaign was a flop: many promoted republican simplicity, but few were prepared to practice it.

REFORMERS AT WAR: THE SANITARY COMMISSION

Reformers—environmentalists and moralists alike—saw the great contest as an opportunity to educate the United States into a grander understanding of nationhood. In New York City they had fought to promote the public welfare. Now the war would allow them to apply, on a continental scale, ideas and programs they had developed while fighting metropolitan poverty and squalor.

The object of their reform efforts was the Union Army. Armies, they believed, were like cities: in both, vast numbers of men, mostly undisciplined workers, were packed into small deprived environments, which threatened their health, morals and lives. The organizational instrument they established to reform military life was a commission in many ways analogous to the commissions Republicans had established in the late 1850s to reform New York City.

The genesis of the U.S. Sanitary Commission lay in the response of northern women to the outbreak of war. By 1861 thousands of ladies, exhorted by women's magazines, had gathered at one another's homes or in churches to make bandages for the troops. Upper-class ladies worked for the Seventh Regiment at George Templeton Strong's, and Henry Ward Beecher's church kept a dozen sewing machines going. In addition, Dr. Elizabeth Blackwell, seeing the need for nurses, began giving two-month training courses in her infirmary, and at Bellevue or New York Hospital, then sending volunteers on to Washington.

Soon, several elite women decided these efforts needed coordination. Dr. Blackwell joined with Mrs. William Cullen Bryant, Mrs. Peter Cooper, and "Ninety-Two of the Most Respected Ladies" in calling for an oversight organization. On April 26 four thousand women gathered at the Cooper Union to form the Women's Central Association of Relief for the Sick and Wounded of the Army. The twenty-four-year-old Louisa Lee Schuyler, a member of the Rev. Henry Bellows's fashionable All Souls Unitarian Church on Gramercy Park, became the key organizer.

They soon found that federal administrators paid women little heed, so they turned to Bellows, Strong, and some prominent male physicians for assistance in gaining official approval and establishing a working relationship with military authorities. These men prepared a report for Lincoln that adopted an expert, "scientific" approach. Analyzing data generated by the British and French Commissions of the Crimean War, they observed that during that conflict (1854–56) an estimated 22 percent of British war deaths (30 percent for the French) had stemmed from possibly preventable disease.

In June, Stanton and Lincoln authorized establishment of the Sanitary Commission as a semiofficial agency to take charge of the health and welfare needs of the army. The organizers established a committee of associates, composed mainly of Republican bankers and merchants, to help solicit funds. The initial stake came from life insurance companies; many communities had taken out policies for local volunteers, so the firms stood to benefit from decreases in soldier mortality.

Their next move was to establish the predominance of their male, professional, and highly centralized staff over the volunteer women already organized in benevolent associations in most of the cities and small towns of the north. By 1863 the Sanitary Commission had become the mediator between these women's groups and the military, circulating information on hospital and army supply requirements to thousands of local Soldiers Aid societies. The commission also investigated troop, camp, and hospital conditions and established an elaborate battlefield relief system, introducing reform methods into the government bureaucracy.

The sanitary commissioners proved extremely effective. They also made a lot of enemies by their insistence that discipline and subordination should be imposed on unruly armies, as on unruly cities. They thought Lincoln's pardoning of condemned deserters smacked of just the kind of fuzzy-minded and indiscriminate charity they had battled in New York. Female volunteers, in turn, resented the male commissioners' domination of the one public arena, charity, in which women had established some authority and objected to the commission's use of agents who were paid fifteen hundred to four thousand dollars annually when soldiers were getting $156. Nor did the commission members' wealth, professionalism, Republicanism, or residence in New York City endear them to the mass of the volunteers.

Many switched their support to another Manhattan operation, the U.S. Christian Commission, founded November 16, 1861, by the YMCA. Its leadership was an interlocking directorate of the American Bible Society, the American Tract Society, and the Sunday school and temperance movements, with its New York Committee chaired by the indefatigable William Dodge. The Christian Commission's concern was the "Spiritual Good of the Soldiers." Its methods too grew out of approaches to the urban poor long since worked out by tract societies and missionaries. Pious and devoted volunteers—1,375 of them—distributed religious literature and medical supplies directly to the wounded men in the hospitals, rather than, like the Sanitary Commission, to doctors for distribution as they saw fit.

CARNAGE AND CLASS

Meanwhile, New York's working classes were experiencing the world's first modern war in all its horror. What had seemed at first a lark or a living became a ghastly death trap. Between April and November 1862—at Shiloh, Seven Days, Second Bull Run, Antietam—tens of thousands were killed or maimed. In December came the disaster at Fredericksburg when the blundering General Ambrose Burnside led the Army of the Potomac in a suicidal charge against Confederate entrenchments. The Fifty-first New York Volunteers were ordered to advance over a narrow plain so well covered, said a southern gunner, that "a chicken could not live in that field when we open on it."

Among the ninety-six hundred Union wounded at Fredericksburg (though luckily not among the 1,284 who died there) was Walt Whitman's brother George. Walt hurried from Brooklyn to Virginia. On arriving, the author of *Beat! Beat! Drums!* had his first direct encounter with war: an immense heap of amputated arms and legs ("cut, bloody, black and blue, swelled and sickening"). Whitman would stay on for the next three years as a volunteer worker, make six hundred visits to hospitals, comfort soldiers, and record images of a war that resembled nothing so much as the cattle pens of New York City: "a great slaughter-house & the men mutually butchering each other"; a "butchers' shambles" replete with "groans and screams" and the "odor of blood."

As city soldiers were shot to pieces—the Irish Brigade and the Garibaldi Guard virtually ceased to exist by 1863—the bright marching songs gave way to mournful ballads. Around the campfires survivors sang sentimental songs of home: "Shall I Never See My Mother," "It Was My Mother's Voice," "Mother, I'll Come Home Tonight." The sheet music sales of "Weeping, Sad and Lonely; or, When This Cruel War Is Over" (published in 1863 by Sawyer and Thompson of Brooklyn) reached nearly a million.

Word of the dreadful course of events quickly got back to the northern metropolis a thousand miles or more behind the lines. Newspaper reports and pictures finished off the "picnic" image of the early days of the war as the press routinely printed catalogs of death and disfiguration ("Thomas Mcguire, Co. A, leg amp"; "M. Riley, Co. C, groin"; "H. Mcilainy, Co. I, forehead, severe"). Still more direct testimony was furnished by the thousands of hobbling wounded on the city's streets, the incessant funeral processions, and the many deserters who had fled the wanton waste of life for the anonymity of the big city, rather than return to their small hometowns, where certain arrest awaited them. The city's hospitals, moreover, were jammed with wounded soldiers, notably Bellevue—whose Dr. Stephen Smith produced the pocket text *A Handbook of Operative Surgery*, which became a standby in Union field hospitals—and the special military hospital set up in Central Park at the former Mount St. Vincent, where nursing duties were given over to the Sisters of Charity.

All these sources made abundantly clear that at the front, pay was not only low but late (and arrears of up to a year were disastrous to those with families dependent on them); that soldiers were gouged by the sutlers who sold them tobacco, ink, stamps; and that nativist bigots ruled some of the camps. Army General Orders required attendance at religious services of the commander's choice (despite Archbishop Hughes's plea that soldiers be free to attend or not). The tendency of Republican officers to use their rank to impose their views was particularly objectionable at a time when the southern press dwelt on the foreign character of the northern armies (calling the Germans Huns and the Irish barbarians) and debated whether to grant such savages prisoner-of-war status or simply to hang them outright when captured.

Word also got back to New York that if officers weren't bigoted, they were incompetent. Whitman was not alone in believing that many of the deaths were unnecessary: he called Burnside's Fredericksburg operations "the most complete piece of mismanagement perhaps ever yet known in the earth's wars." The root of the problem, it seemed clear, was that most of those who raised, and therefore led, the volunteer regiments early in the war were not military professionals (who remained segregated in the regular army) but wealthy businessmen, socially prominent gentlemen, or successful politicians. Their only qualifications were their connections to the state governors who commissioned colonels and brigadiers. Many proved corrupt as well as incompetent, extorting money by making up fraudulent payrolls, forcing their men to answer to fake names, and pocketing their pay.

As word got back, enthusiasm for enlistment fell. The recruiting tent in City Hall Park was shut down for lack of business. And the federal government, faced with similar manpower problems throughout the North, began to explore the possibility of instituting a draft.

50

The Battle for New York

Working people in the city had their own miseries to contend with as the war ground on. In the boom's first flush, jobs had been plentiful, especially for skilled workers, and wages decent even for manual laborers (a dollar a day versus forty-three cents in the army). People had been able to put a little something away in savings banks. But paper money, scarcity of goods, and incessant profiteering led to rampant inflation. Between 1860 and 1863 currency depreciated by 43 percent while wages rose a mere 12 percent. Beef nearly doubled in price; rents jumped 15 to 20 percent, coal went up more than 30 percent.

Wives and children of the absent volunteers found much of the money the Common Council had appropriated for their care rerouted to supplies and troops. As the relief program sagged, women demonstrated at City Hall and the homes of councilmen; in December 1861, when public relief was halted for a time, some two hundred desperate women gathered in Tompkins Square to insist that "you have got me men into the souldiers, and now you have to kepe us from starving." Community self-help efforts—like a Jones' Wood "festival" that drew sixty thousand who paid twenty-five cents apiece to aid those widowed and orphaned by the Battle of Bull Run—proved at best temporary expedients.

Shelter was a growing problem. During the war construction of housing declined sharply, just as expanding commercial and industrial operations ate into working-class territory in lower Manhattan. Those displaced jammed into uptown districts like the Fourth Ward (at 290,000 people per square mile, now the most densely populated place on earth), or the teeming East Side and West Side factory districts, or shantytowns above 50th Street, where thousands of squatters lived among the rocks and ravines. Working-class quarters grew steadily more wretched. An 1863 AICP report found the housing "dark, contracted, ill constructed, badly ventilated and disgustingly filthy." Eighteen thousand lived in cellar apartments with floors of putrid mud.

In response, working people revived the labor movement and pushed for a greater share of wartime profits. In the fall of 1862 the city's ship joiners and caulkers, coppersmiths, and hat finishers went on strike, launching the "advanced wages movement." Leather workers in the Swamp walked out, as did men at the Manhattan Gas Works near the East River. By the spring of 1863 there were 133 union locals, up from thirty the previous year. Though small, they did well. When custom tailors went out in March, most first-class shops conceded at once (with the fateful exception of Brooks Brothers). Carpenters, pianomakers, and machinists also struck successfully for higher wages. Three thousand mostly Irish longshoremen walked off work, citing the "enormous prices of every article," and won an increase, despite the government's bringing in prisoners from Governors Island to load army transports, protected by troops with fixed bayonets.

Employers and their spokesmen fought back. Horace Greeley, despite his long history of support for working people, insisted that workmen had a right to combine and refuse the wages employers offered but were not entitled to strike. The *U.S. Economist and Dry Goods Reporter* branded work stoppages as "despotic on the business of their employers." Labor was a commodity like any other. Its price should be set by the natural laws of supply and demand.

To boost supply and weaken labor's bargaining ability, employers brought additional workers to the city. Most focused on Europe—during the war Secretary of State Seward's consuls abroad often acted as emigrant agents—but some, like Peter Cooper, urged Lincoln to send up southern blacks. A Tammany mass meeting censured employer efforts "to bring hoards of Blacks from the South, as well as Whites from Europe, to fill the shops, yards and other places of labor and by that means compel us to compete with them for support of our families."

Employers also repeatedly hired strikebreakers to defeat the new unions. African-American New Yorkers were used in disputes at the Staten Island ferry, the Custom House, and, most particularly, on the waterfront. In March 1863 laborers at the Erie Railroad's Hudson River docks struck, seeking a share of the company's vaulting prosperity. The railroad hired blacks to move the cotton bales accumulating at Pier 36 at the foot of Duane Street, until a thousand white strikers drove them off.

Increasingly, white workers argued that blacks had no legitimate claim whatever on laboring jobs. In August 1862 two to three thousand people from predominantly Irish South Brooklyn threatened to burn the Watson and Lorillard tobacco factories at the foot of Sedgwick Street unless several hundred black women and children left the plants. When the companies refused, they besieged the buildings and were only prevented from setting fires to "roast the niggers alive" by the arrival of police.

THE POLITICS OF EMANCIPATION

To these growing strains along class and race lines was added the shock of emancipation. In September 1862, when Lee's invasion of Maryland was turned back at Antietam, Lincoln used the good news to issue a Preliminary Emancipation Proclamation. On January 1, 1863, the Proclamation itself was promulgated, though it freed no slaves, applying as it did only to areas beyond the reach of federal power.

New York City's blacks and abolitionists were nevertheless ecstatic. At an "Emanci-

pation Jubilee" at Cooper Union, Henry Highland Garnet read the Proclamation aloud
to a cheering crowd. Lewis Tappan, the now seventy-five-year-old patriarch of the
city's antislavery movement, gave a moving review of the long history of the struggle in
what would prove to be his last public appearance.

Black and white abolitionists were considerably less enthusiastic about Lincoln's
zealous campaign to get African Americans to leave the country voluntarily. An emigra-
tionist minority applauded a late 1862 Lincoln-promoted plan to transport five thousand blacks to Île à Vache, a small island off Haiti, until the effort, run under contract by
Leonard Jerome and other prominent New York businessmen, proved a disastrous failure. But most New York blacks flatly rejected the colonization project. The Colored
Citizens of Queens County notified Lincoln that America was their native country and
they had no intention of leaving it. Emancipation, rather, spurred black demands to join
the army and fight for the total liberation of the slaves.

Emancipation also roiled the city's political waters. Republicans had been of two
minds on slavery. Many of those who joined up before the war held fast to their moral
and cultural repugnance for the institution and followed the "radical" lead of Greeley's
New York Tribune in opposing it and welcoming Lincoln's commitment to ending it.
For the bulk of the old Whigs who had belatedly clambered aboard the Republican
Party and nested in its "conservative" wing, where they took their political cues from
Henry Raymond's editorial page, the war had little to do with slavery. As the *Times*
argued: "The issue is between anarchy and order,—between Government and lawlessness,—between the authority of the Constitution and the reckless will of those who
seek its destruction." Still, most conservative Republicans went along with the president on emancipation, with varying degrees of enthusiasm or distaste, accepting it as a
necessary wartime measure that would expedite restoration of the Union.

Democrats were more thoroughly divided, much as they had been before the fighting broke out. "War Democrats"—who included prominent businessmen and the bulk
of Tammany Hall politicians, among them Tweed—favored fighting on to victory but
opposed partisan Republican legislation and the Lincoln administration's erosion of
civil rights. "Peace Democrats," rooted in Fernando Wood's Mozart Hall, wanted to
restore the Union as it had existed before the war, with slavery intact, though a more
extreme wing was prepared to accept peace without reunion. These divisions had
already cost their party the mayoralty in 1861, when Tammany's C. Godfrey Gunther
and Mozart's Wood divided the Democratic vote, allowing Republican George
Opdyke—a wealthy dry-goods importer, banker, and broker and a leader in the Union
Defense Committee—to capture City Hall with barely more than one-third of the vote.
This had led to various overtures looking toward restoration of party unity.

But emancipation appalled the Peace Democrats, who saw it as a fundamental alteration of war aims. They now hoisted a militantly antiwar banner, under which gathered
old Democrats unhappy with wartime Republican domination, merchants and
financiers disturbed at the increasing power of the national state, and considerable
numbers of white working-class people angry at wartime inequities.

Emancipation also alienated the Catholic Church hierarchy. Up till then Archbishop Hughes had been friendly with the administration, especially Seward, his old ally on
the education issue. Hughes had even served as Lincoln's semiofficial envoy to the Vatican and to France (he met with Napoleon III and Empress Eugénie), where he pleaded
the Union cause and urged nonrecognition of the Confederacy. But emancipation

alarmed conservative men who had long argued slavery was an evil to be borne, that abolitionism smacked of a revolutionary violation of property rights, and that the anti-slavery movement was inextricably linked to militant nativist Protestants.

In the fall 1862 elections, after the Preliminary Proclamation, Peace Democrats bid for power. In the city, ex-mayor Wood and his supporters denounced the administration as "fanatical, imbecile, and corrupt" and openly urged resistance to emancipation. At the state level, Peace Democrat Horatio Seymour (allied to New York Central Railroad interests) adopted a similar stance, favoring restoration of the Union by granting all possible concessions to the South. Both resorted to a shrill racism, protesting that emancipation substituted "niggerism for nationality." In the context of growing unhappiness with the costs of the war, Democrats carried every ward in the city, Wood won a congressional seat, and Seymour captured the governorship.

The peace movement continued to build after the full Proclamation was issued. On February 6, 1863, at Delmonico's, a group of Democratic and ex-nativist businessmen led by financier August Belmont launched the Society for the Diffusion of Political Knowledge. Other luminaries included the venerable Samuel F. B. Morse (president), Governor Seymour, and corporate attorney Samuel J. Tilden. The organization published antiwar and antiemancipation tracts in which they suggested that freeing the slaves would ruin the South (and indirectly the North) by undermining its ability to compete with slave economies like Brazil or Cuba. Pamphleteers attacked the rising war debt, the government's military strategy, and the Republican Party's centralizing project and agitated for a negotiated peace and a revocation of emancipation. Belmont also promoted these ideas in the *New York World*, a newspaper edited by twenty-seven-year-old Manton Marble, which he, Tilden, and other rich Democrats underwrote.

In addition, in his capacity as Democratic Party national chairman, Belmont began grooming the cashiered General George McClellan to challenge Lincoln in 1864. After being fired, McClellan moved to New York City and began working with Chairman Belmont on building a presidential candidacy. He took with him as his aide Lieutenant George Armstrong Custer, who now received his first introduction to the financial, political, and journalistic elite of the metropolis.

While the Society for the Diffusion of Political Knowledge took the (relatively) high road, the popular press launched a gloves-off campaign that mixed racism, solidarity with labor, attacks on war profiteers, and, increasingly, calls for peace. At various points the Lincoln administration banned "Copperhead" papers from the mails. Republican infringements of civil liberties generated more support for Peace Democrats. The Lincoln administration suspended habeas corpus and arrested or detained hundreds. In New York City political prisoners were housed in Fort Lafayette, just off the Brooklyn shore from Fort Hamilton. When Ohio Democrat Clement L. Vallandigham was indicted for seditious oratory, Fernando Wood chaired a meeting at Cooper Institute in his support.

June 1863 was the high point of antiwar activism in the city. Wood held a massive Peace Convention at Cooper Union on June 3—of which James Gordon Bennett's *Herald* approved, auguring a new respectability—and orators pounded home the ideas that the war was a rich man's fight, that it was undermining the Constitution, and that it would flood the North with southern blacks.

Few of New York's wealthy backed Wood's movement. Nor, despite the Peace Democrats' intensive efforts at wooing urban workmen, did any laboring organizations or leaders "go Coppery." Rather the surging peace movement alarmed and galvanized prowar activists. "Two years ago," one wrote, "you could walk the entire length of Broadway without stepping on a snake," whereas now "New York swarms with Copperheads" engaged in the "slimy errand" of helping rebellion. Three Sanitary Commission leaders—Strong the lawyer, Olmsted the intellectual, and Bellows the minister—called for a hard-line organization to combat Copperheadism. They were worried that Wood and Belmont's operations might mislead Europeans into assuming the wealth and culture of the American metropolis were arrayed with the rebellion. Strong wanted to show France and England that the war was "not waged by the rabble of the North, or by politicians, but that the intelligent, cultured, gentlemanly caste sustains it."

Dismissing Belmont and his crowd as "vulgar parvenus," Olmsted and friends set out to form a club of "descendants and almsbearers of the old dukes of our land." Launched on February 24, 1863, the new Union League Club included pedigreed New Yorkers, leading literati, and sixty-six of the business elite, among them Robert Minturn, the city's top shipping merchant, who became the club's first president. By May it had 350 members, including (in Strong's words) the leading "representatives of capital and commerce." By war's end the Union League Club embraced eight hundred of the city's most wealthy and well established merchants, lawyers, bankers, and professionals. The club leased, redecorated, and strung telegraph lines into an elegant house on Broadway and 17th Street, facing Union Square. It quickly became the place to banquet visiting dignitaries and meet to run the war effort.

The Union League Club quickly took on the Peace Democrats, setting up a Loyal Publication Society. Over the next two years, it distributed, to the army and civilians alike, nine hundred thousand copies of ninety pamphlets (in German and French as well as English). Fierce nationalists, the club members argued that only a strong central state could win the war and establish continental prosperity. In 1863 Olmsted proposed establishing a magazine to spread this gospel, to be called, appropriately enough, the *Nation*. For the moment, however, it relied on *Harper's Weekly*, which George William Curtis took over in 1863 and brought into the Republican camp. Locally, the Union League Club established the Loyal National League, which organized committees in each ward to mobilize mass support and held rallies at Cooper Institute or in Union and Madison squares.

THE DRAFT

In mid-1863, with the city rancorously divided, Confederates invaded the North. On June 27 Lee's Army of Northern Virginia moved up the Shenandoah Valley, crushed the Union garrison at Winchester, and crossed over the Potomac, and by June 29 it was within ten miles of Harrisburg, the capital of Pennsylvania. Thousands of troops poured out of New York City to join General George Meade's army, which, on July 1, engaged Lee at the town of Gettysburg.

The emergency left the city virtually stripped of defenses. General John Wool, commander of the army's Department of the East, reported to Governor Seymour that he had only 550 men in eight forts and almost no military vessels in the harbor. The city was wide open to invasion by southern ironclads. If Lee eluded Meade he could be in Jersey City, and at New York's throat, in a matter of days.

To make matters worse—far worse—it was at just this moment that the federal government's new draft law was to go into effect. Back in March, reacting to heavy losses, dwindling recruitment, and soaring desertion rates, Congress had passed the National Conscription Act. The legislation authorized government agents to go house-to-house, enrolling all men aged twenty to thirty-five (and all unmarried men thirty-five to forty-five), and then hold a lottery to choose draftees from this pool. The law also created federal provost marshals in each congressional district and gave them unprecedented power to summarily arrest draft evaders, draft resisters, and deserters. Finally, in a crude assertion of class privilege, the law provided that draftees could provide a substitute to fight in their place or pay three hundred dollars—a prohibitive sum for working people—for the government to use as a recruiting bounty. In short order an advertisement, appearing daily in New York City newspapers, announced that "gentlemen will be furnished promptly with substitutes by forwarding their orders to the office of the Merchants, Bankers and General Volunteer Association."

This was not a popular law in New York. It represented, together with emancipation and the new tariff and banking laws, yet another massive increase in the intrusion of the federal government into the city's communities, workplaces, even households. It did not go unnoted that the three-thousand-dollar shawl A. T. Stewart had imported for Secretary Chase's daughter now represented the price of ten men's lives. The argument advanced by Republican organs like the *Times* and *Harper's*—that businessmen had to stay home and run production—failed to convince many Boweryites.

The enrollment process proceeded peacefully enough in May and June, in part because leading Democrats like Governor Seymour vowed to initiate legal challenges to the act's constitutionality. Seymour also argued, correctly as it turned out, that Republicans had set unfairly high quotas for the heavily Democratic metropolis. Other voices counseled harsher tactics. The editor of the *Catholic Metropolitan Record*, John Mullaly, encouraged armed resistance. Even Seymour, at a mass protest meeting on July 4 at the Academy of Music, used words he would later regret, telling the crowd: "Remember this—that the bloody and treasonable and revolutionary doctrine of public necessity can be proclaimed by a mob as well as by a government." On July 4 news of the Union victory at Gettysburg began to trickle in over the telegraph wire, but the general jubilation was tempered by reports of the heavy casualties among local soldiers.

One week later, on Saturday, July 11, the lottery commenced. Seymour had failed even to get it postponed. Anticipating trouble, and still without military resources to back up the police, the authorities chose to begin the process on the city's periphery, at the Ninth District Headquarters on Third Avenue and 47th Street, an area of vacant lots and isolated buildings. It went reasonably well. While a large but good-tempered crowd watched, the provost marshal read off names drawn from a large barrel. By late afternoon, 1,236 draftees had been selected, at which point the office closed, leaving the remainder of the two-thousand-man quota to be filled two days later.

The next morning, working-class families pored over the names published in the Sunday papers. In bars and taverns around the city, men discussed their response over glasses of whisky, and large numbers of working-class wives and mothers (the *Herald* reported) "mingled their wildest denunciations against the conscription law." A variety of protest activities were decided upon for the next day, Monday, July 13.

DAY ONE

Between six and seven in the morning, four hours before the lottery was scheduled to begin again, hundreds of workers from the city's railroads, machine shops, shipyards, and iron foundries, together with building and street laborers working for uptown contractors, began to stream up the West Side along Eighth and Ninth avenues. Beating copper pans as if they were gongs—a tactic familiar from labor protests—they closed shops, factories, and construction sites, moved on to a brief meeting in Central Park, and then marched, with NO DRAFT placards aloft, toward the provost marshal's office on Third Avenue. There they linked up with downtown committees, which, in similar fashion, had closed Allaire's, the great novelty works on 14th Street, and a dozen or more foundries and machine shops along the East Side waterfront. At 10:30, with a huge crowd gathered outside, the selection process started up, guarded by sixty hurriedly gathered police.

At this point another group arrived: the Black Joke Engine Company No. 33, in full regalia. The volunteer firemen, enraged at having lost their traditional exemption from military service, had decided over the weekend not only to halt the proceedings but to destroy all evidence that members of their unit had been drafted. They stoned the building, drove off the police, smashed the draft wheel, poured turpentine everywhere, fired the structure, and then drove away the arriving fire companies.

Word of all this reached the provost marshal's general bureau headquarters. A thirty-two man squad of the Invalid Corps (composed of wounded or disabled veterans reassigned to light guard duties) was dispatched uptown on a Third Avenue horsecar through jeering and ever thicker crowds. Finally they were ordered to detrain, form a line across the avenue, and march north toward the burning draft office. When they reached 43rd Street they were met with a fusillade of paving stones. They broke and ran. A similar experience awaited Police Superintendent John Kennedy. On hearing of the attack he hurried most of the way uptown by buggy, then tried to walk the remainder of the way up Lexington through the now huge throngs around the Ninth District Office. After he was identified by a former policeman, the crowd beat Kennedy about the head until he was unrecognizable.

By now the day had grown hot and humid; it made one feel "as if you had washed yourself in molasses and water," one participant recalled. The streets fumed with the usual rotting debris and excrement, the stench worsened by the stifling heat and humidity. Tremendous numbers of people poured out of the tenements. Crowd members began to isolate the area, cutting down telegraph poles that connected local police precincts to the Central Office. They stopped Second and Third Avenue Railroad cars. New Haven commuter trains were stoned, then Irish women crowbarred up the tracks of the Fourth Avenue line above 42nd Street. Rioters pulled down fences surrounding vacant lots to make clubs. The skirmishes spread into the east 40s around Third and Lexington. As small isolated detachments of police reserves were sent into the area they were routed and stomped, their bodies stripped, their faces smashed. Homes suspected of giving refuge to fleeing policemen were burned. Fury at the Metropolitans, banked for years, blazed up viciously.

Targets identifiable as Republican came under attack. A crowd entered the Columbia College grounds on Fifth Avenue at 49th Street, knocked on the door of President Charles King's house demanding to know if a Republican lived there, and were stopped from burning the building down only by the intervention of two Catholic priests. Farther down Fifth, a crowd menaced Republican Mayor Opdyke's house until dissuaded by Democrats. Sumptuous Fifth Avenue mansions were sacked, looted, and burned. George Templeton Strong, watching the stoning of a house on Lexington off 45th rumored (wrongly) to be Horace Greeley's, concluded that "the beastly ruffians were masters of the situation and of the city."

Some of the crowd now hived off downtown toward an armory at 21st Street and Second Avenue, really a rifle factory operated by a son-in-law of Mayor Opdyke, which contained a thousand weapons. The rioters so far had had few guns. The Broadway Squad arrived to defend the armory but soon found themselves surrounded and stoned by thousands of men and women. Strong, who had followed along, depicted a crowd of Irish day laborers, including "low Irish women, stalwart young vixens and withered old hags . . . all cursing the 'bloody draft' and egging on their men to mischief." Finally they stormed and occupied it around four P.M. and began carrying off carbines. When police reinforcements arrived, the crowd torched the building, trapping some rioters inside on the upper floors; of the thirteen who died at the armory, ten perished in the fire.

At about the same time, an ugly second front opened up across town, as crowds hitherto focused on rich whites turned their fury on poor blacks. Patrick Merry, an Irish cellar digger, led two to three hundred men and boys down Broadway to West 29th Street where, at five o'clock, they burned the deserted Eighth District provost marshal's office. Then they began attacking homes of African Americans in the west 30s. The race riot had gotten under way.

Bands of Irish longshoremen, with quarrymen, street pavers, teamsters, and cart-men following along, began chasing blacks, screaming, "Kill all niggers!" Blacks were dragged off streetcars and stages around City Hall. The owner of a colored sailors' boardinghouse on Roosevelt Street in the Fourth Ward was robbed and stripped, his building fired. Maria Prince's boardinghouse in Sullivan Street was trashed, as rioters dug up paving stones, smashed the windows, and ransacked it. A crowd tried to attack black waiters at Crook's Restaurant in Chatham Street but was repulsed. Uptown, at Fifth Avenue and 43rd, rioters attacked the Colored Orphan Asylum, screaming, "Burn the niggers' nest." The 237 children (most under twelve years old) escaped—young Paddy McCafferty heroically shepherding them to the 20th Precinct house—while the crowd smashed pianos, carried off carpets and iron bedsteads, uprooted the trees, shrubs, and fences, then set the building ablaze. Crowds would attack other moral reform projects, even those not associated with blacks. They stoned the Magdalene Asylum on Fifth at 88th Street and burned down the Five Points Mission.

When night fell, the racial assaults worsened. Some blacks were attacked on the corner of Varick and Charlton streets by a crowd led by an Irish bricklayer. One of the pursued turned, shot the bricklayer with a pistol, and escaped; the maddened crowd grabbed one of the others, lynched him, and then burned the corpse. Gangs attacked and torched waterfront tenements, dance houses, brothels, bars, and boardinghouses that catered to black workingmen. Furniture was burned in sidewalk bonfires. Bands of small boys would mark the victims' houses by stoning windows, then return with older men to finish the job. Racially mixed couples, white women who consorted with blacks—anyone who defied taboos on "amalgamation" was specially targeted. By mid-week rioters had virtually emptied the downtown waterfront of blacks.

That same evening crowds moved toward the intellectual heartland of Republicanism, Newspaper Row, across from City Hall Park, where Greeley's *Tribune* and Raymond's *Times* had their headquarters. Raymond had used his influence to get Gatling guns from the army, which he set up in the north windows. Raymond manned one himself; millionaire speculator Leonard Jerome, a leading *Times* shareholder, took another.

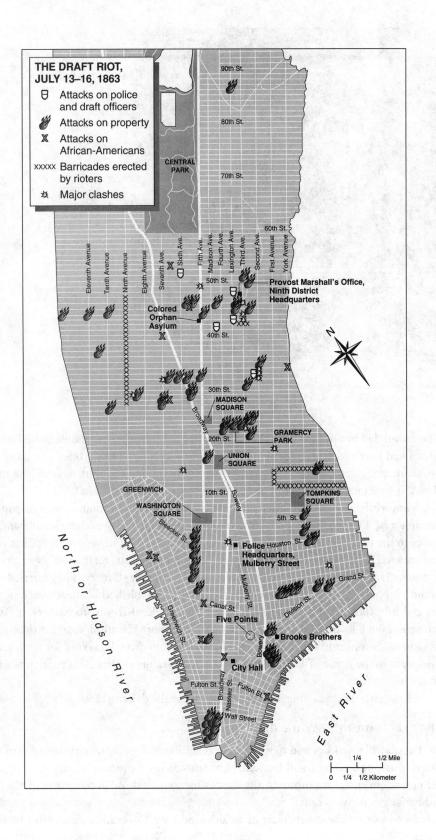

**THE DRAFT RIOT,
JULY 13–16, 1863**

⊌ Attacks on police
and draft officers

🔥 Attacks on property

✗ Attacks on
African-Americans

xxxxx Barricades erected
by rioters

✻ Major clashes

CENTRAL
PARK

90th St.

80th St.

70th St.

60th St.

Eleventh Avenue
Tenth Avenue
Ninth Avenue
Eighth Avenue
Seventh Avenue
Sixth Ave.
Fifth Ave.
Madison Ave.
Fourth Ave.
Lexington Ave.
Third Ave.
Second Ave.
First Avenue
York Avenue

50th St.

**Provost Marshall's Office,
Ninth District
Headquarters**

**Colored
Orphan
Asylum**

40th St.

30th St.

Broadway

**MADISON
SQUARE**

20th St.

**GRAMERCY
PARK**

**UNION
SQUARE**

Bowery

xxxxxxxxxxx
xxxxxxxxxxxxxxx

GREENWICH

10th St.

**TOMPKINS
SQUARE**

**WASHINGTON
SQUARE**

Bleecker St.

5th St.

✻ **Police**
Headquarters,
Mulberry Street

Houston St.

Grand St.

Greenwich St.

Mulberry St.

Division St.

✗ Canal St.

Five Points

Bowery

Brooks Brothers

✗

✗ **City Hall**

Fulton St.

Broadway
Nassau St.
Fulton St.

Wall Street

North or Hudson River

East River

N

0   1/4   1/2 Mile

0   1/4   1/2 Kilometer

Lynching on Clarkson Street, from *Harper's Weekly*, July 21, 1863.
(© Museum of the City of New York)

The crowd, led by a waiter from Astor House, attacked the less well defended *Tribune*, which had barricaded itself with bales of printing paper. They stoned the building, broke in, and started a fire but were driven off by police brought in from the quiet Brooklyn precincts.

Meanwhile, a debate had broken out among the authorities about how to respond to the upheaval. During the day, Mayor Opdyke's approach of dispatching small bands of police to the uptown working-class wards had proven drastically counterproductive; it had enraged the crowds and provoked massive and murderous retaliation. Now Strong and some Union League Club colleagues proposed another strategy. They hurried over to the St. Nicholas Hotel, where General Wool had established his headquarters, and begged him to declare martial law and summon federal troops to enforce it. Wool refused, though he did order troops moved in from Fort Hamilton to assist the police. Disgusted, Strong and the others telegraphed Lincoln directly, asking for troops, and then went to the home of David Dudley Field in Gramercy Park, where friends gathered with muskets.

At eleven P.M., drenching, cooling rain brought the day to a close.

THE BATTLE FOR NEW YORK CITY

As Tuesday dawned hot and dry, crowds crystallized all over the city, broke into gun shops to arm themselves, and launched firefights against a variety of targets. Far from being random anarchic outbursts, the attacks focused on those in command of the new industrial and political order.

Rioters swept the streets clear of wealthy individuals—readily identifiable by their clothes and bearing. ("There goes a $300 man!" "Down with the rich men!") They attacked genteel homes and trashed (more often than stole) the fancy furniture.

They lit into Republican enterprises. Crowds attacked and sacked Brooks Brothers, hated for being hard employers and shoddy contractors, went after German clothing stores along Grand Street, and would have marched on Wall Street had it not been the best-defended area in the entire city. Customs House workers prepared bombs with forty-second fuses. Employees of the Bank Note Company readied tanks of sulfuric acid to spill on attackers. At the Sub-Treasury Building on the corner of Nassau Street, guns and bottles of vitriol were passed out to employees stationed at windows, troops with howitzers were stationed nearby, and a gunboat was anchored at the foot of Wall Street.

The crowds, particularly the women, beat policemen and soldiers, the agents of upper-class and federal power. After Colonel Henry O'Brien of the Eleventh New York Volunteers used a howitzer to clear Second Avenue and killed a woman bystander and a child, the crowds (when they found him the next day) beat his face to a pulp, then stripped, tortured, and shot him in the head and hung his broken body from a lamppost.

Rioters began erecting barricades, cordoning off their waterfront neighborhoods from center-island bourgeois districts. On the East Side, industrial metal trades workers used cut-down telegraph poles, carts, wagons, lumber, boxes, bricks, and rubbish to run a line along First Avenue (particularly solid from 11th to 14th streets) and along Third Avenue on up to 26th Street—areas with high concentrations of large metal-working establishments. On the West Side, waterfront laborers drew their lines along Ninth Avenue, most solidly from 36th to 42nd streets, from where they could dominate most of the Upper West Side. To hinder the summoning of outside reinforcements, they cut telegraph lines—as Indians did out west—and assaulted ferry slips and railroads.

Rioters also pursued the race war. Brandishing poles and clubs, they hunted blacks on the streets, mauled them along the docks, went after black workers in restaurants and hotels. They attacked black homes and stores around Bleecker and Carmine streets,

Sacking Brooks Brothers Clothing Store at Catherine and Cherry Streets, from *Harper's Weekly*, August 1, 1863. (© Collection of The New-York Historical Society)

except where blacks tore down chimneys for bricks to hurl at attackers or, as in Minetta Lane, guarded their homes with guns.

Divisions now appeared in the rioters' ranks. Many original protesters had envisioned at most a one-day antidraft demonstration, and certainly not a general onslaught on private property. Large numbers of them—particularly the Germans, though many Irish Catholics and native Protestants as well—abandoned violence and even joined with the authorities. Squads of *Turnverein* and *Schutzenverein* patrolled the streets of Kleindeutschland. Volunteer fire companies (including the Black Joke men who had started the riot) turned out to defend their neighborhoods against riot and arson. Crowds, at times led by Irish priests like Father Treanor of Transfiguration, intervened to halt lynch mobs.

While the battle raged on the streets, two sharply opposed factions within the city's upper classes argued over how to respond to the uprising. On one side were those businessmen and Democratic officials who, in effect, treated the riots as an appeal to elites to respect and protect customary working-class rights and privileges. Governor Seymour dispatched gentlemen and clergymen to negotiate face-to-face with the crowds, displaying the confidant paternalism of the old upper class. On Tuesday morning he himself, flanked by Tammany leaders A. Oakey Hall and William Tweed, pledged a large crowd at City Hall (whom he addressed as "My Friends") that he would work for postponement of or relief from the draft, while repudiating violence.

Republican journals, merchants, financiers, and industrialists saw the riot as a full-scale challenge to the political and social order at precisely the moment when—given the Union's doubtful military prospects—such an uprising might actually precipitate European intervention. Their prescription was simple: "Crush the mob!" howled Tuesday's *Times*. Merchants and bankers gathered at Wall Street to demand federal imposition of martial law, "an immediate and terrible" display of federal power.

Rioters and militia fighting at the barricades on First Avenue, from *The Illustrated London News*, August 15, 1863. (© Collection of The New-York Historical Society)

At noon Mayor Opdyke asked Secretary of War Stanton for troops. Stanton complied that evening, but had the request come even a day earlier it would have put him in a difficult spot. After Gettysburg, Lee's army, wounded and dangerous, had remained in the area, and Union forces had been tied down in blocking a possible move northward. As it happened, Lee escaped south across the Potomac the night of Monday the thirteenth, leaving Stanton free to divert five regiments.

Troops began arriving Wednesday evening, a day of atrocities during which crowds had hanged, drowned, and mutilated black men, looted and burned black homes up and down Sixth Avenue, and attacked Republican mansions and Protestant missions. In Brooklyn hundreds of men, including some disgruntled ex-employees, invaded the Atlantic Docks and burned two of the hated grain elevators, and along the East River north and east of Fulton Street, blacks were beaten and killed, their houses ransacked and destroyed.

Promptly on arrival, the soldiers from Pennsylvania took up arms against the rioters, aided by volunteer companies set up by merchants and bankers who mobilized their employees. Fighting continued all Wednesday night and throughout the next day. Troops assaulted "infected" districts, using howitzers loaded with grapeshot and canister (primitive fragmentation bombs) to mow down rioters and engaged in fierce building-by-building firefights. Rioters defended their barricaded domains with mad desperation. Faced with tenement snipers and brick hurlers, soldiers broke down doors, bayoneted all who interfered, and drove occupants to the roofs, from which many jumped to certain death below.

By Thursday evening it was all over. The city filled with six thousand troops. Seventh Regiment pickets manned Third Avenue. The Eighth Regiment Artillery Troop trained mountain howitzers on streets around Gramercy Park. The 152nd New York Volunteers set up camp in Stuyvesant Square. By Friday telegraph lines were being repaired, West Side rails relaid. Omnibuses and horsecars ran. Laborers returned to work. It was over.

AFTERMATHS

Contemporaries believed that a thousand people had died, though in the end only a body count of 119 could be verified. To participants, no doubt, it had seemed like another Gettysburg; perhaps the tremendous death tolls on the battlefields made overstatements credible. But even adopting the smaller number, the New York City draft riots had been the largest single incident of civil disorder in the history of the United States.

The response to the riots was relatively mild, certainly not on a par with the bloody reaction to the earlier 1848 uprisings in Paris. There were no mass sentencings, no mass executions of rioters, though some of the Union League crowd thirsted for all-out reprisals. George Templeton Strong declared: "I would like to see war made on Irish scum as in 1688." Herman Melville, who would move back to New York City from his tranquil Berkshire retreat that fall, conjured up similar images in his poem "The House Top, a Night Piece, July 1863," which concluded that "the town is taken by its rats."

The images haunting Republican minds—of barbaric, subhuman savages tearing down a civilized city—certainly invited retribution, but Republicans were not in charge, War Democrats were. Republicans had asked Lincoln to declare martial law and install General Benjamin F. Butler as military governor (they applauded his rigorous suppres-

sion of treason during an 1862 stint running New Orleans). But Lincoln feared alienating conservative Democrats and perhaps provoking the New York City regiments who
had loyally done riot duty but might well balk at imposing Republican military rule.
Rejecting the advice of Republican hard-liners, the president turned military control of
New York over to General John Adams Dix, a Democrat (and financier) of impeccable
credentials, appointing him commander of the Department of the East.

This strategy also required, and received, the cooperation of Tammany Hall and its
chairman and grand sachem, William Tweed. Tammany, whose patriotic prowar credentials were well established, denounced transgressions against property and lawlessness, while at the same time signaling its willingness, and demonstrating its ability, to
protect local rioters from excessive federal vengeance. Tammanyite District Attorney
A. Oakey Hall and Recorder John T. Hoffman indicted and prosecuted the rioters
vigorously, becoming in the process among the most popular politicians of the era,
though the postriot trials they directed through August and September eventually let
most offenders off, and of the sixty-seven who were convicted, only a handful got
lengthy jail terms.

Meanwhile, Dix ordered a formidable show of force and started up the draft
machinery again. Ten thousand federal troops from Meade's army were brought in,
including three batteries of artillery from the Virginia front. Battalions bivouacked in
Madison and Washington squares. Squads marched up and down city streets. Republicans were pleased at the display. When the selection process began again on August 19,
this time in the Republican stronghold of Greenwich Village, perfect peace reigned in
the metropolis.

As well it might have, for the Democrats had completely defanged the draft. Governor Seymour and Samuel J. Tilden had gotten the Lincoln administration to reduce the
quota from twenty-six to twelve thousand men. The Democrat-controlled Common
Council appropriated three million dollars to pay bounties and relief to anyone drafted,
but Mayor Opdyke vetoed it (even as his own son, conscripted, bought his way out).
The Board of Supervisors then created its own Exemption Committee and appropriated two million dollars with which it could buy substitutes for poor men with dependent
families and for municipal service workers (police, fire, militia), virtually guaranteeing
that few conscripts who did not want to serve would be compelled to do so. On this crucial committee, dispensing life and money, sat William Tweed.

In the riot's aftermath, the mass of the Irish and German working class began to
disassociate themselves from Peace Democrats. That fall Seymour was replaced in the
governor's mansion by Republican Reuben Fenton, and the following year Wood lost
his seat in Congress, though antiwar sympathy remained powerful enough to vote fur
merchant, pacifist, and dissident Democrat C. Godfrey Gunther into City Hall. Not
until 1865 would enough of the electorate rally decisively enough behind Tammany's
red, white, and blue banner to elect Tweed's candidate, John Hoffman, to the mayor's
office.

Blocked from vengeance, Republicans got back at the rioters more indirectly, at first
through their principled support for the rioters' African-American victims. During the
riot itself, many Protestant clergymen had courageously given blacks refuge, and merchant families had protected their servants. But blacks needed more organized assistance. Many had fled the city permanently—throughout the summer, one could still see
blacks walking north up the Hudson along the railroad tracks—resulting in a 20 percent

drop in their numbers in the metropolis, to 9,945 in 1865. But many, an estimated five thousand, were still camped in temporary havens (Blackwell's Island, police stations) or on the outskirts of the city (the hills, woods, and swamps of New Jersey; the barns and outhouses of farmers in eastern Brooklyn or Morrisania; the African-American communities of Weeksville and Carrsville, whose armed residents had taken in hundreds of refugees).

The week after the riots, William Dodge and others established the Merchants' Committee for the Relief of the Colored People Suffering from the Late Riots. At a central receiving depot on East 4th Street, they handed out clothing and money to almost six thousand black laborers, longshoremen, and female servants. Setting aside their usual insistence on discriminating between worthy and undeserving recipients, the Merchants' Committee turned the evaluation procedure over to the Rev. Garnet. The merchants thus demonstrated acceptance of their paternal responsibility to their "loyal" dependents, the churchgoing, respectable black poor, who, unlike the Catholic Irish, shared their language and culture. Indeed some efforts were made to have the upper classes reverse their recent hiring practices and employ black rather than Irish servants.

In a far more satisfying response to rioters, Republicans gave blacks not alms but guns. At one point during the upheaval, when Union League members huddled impotently in their barricaded headquarters, they vowed that if they escaped alive they would send a regiment of black troops to the front, first marching them through the very streets then ruled by the rioters. Now they made good their pledge. By December 19, 1863, they had formed the thousand-man-strong Twentieth Regiment United States Colored Troops, billeted it on Rikers Island, and begun building the Twenty-sixth.

The Union League Club and the black community's moment of triumph came on March 5, 1864. The Twentieth, clad in Union blue, disembarked at East 36th Street and marched with muskets and fixed bayonets to a gigantic rally in Union Square. There Charles King, the Columbia College president whose house had come close to being incinerated during the riots, addressed the officers and men. He presented them with a flag and a parchment scroll inscribed by the club members' "Mothers, Wives and Sisters" (names including Astor, Beekman, Fish, Jay, and Van Rensselaer). From there the regiment, led by the now recovered Superintendent Kennedy and a force of a hundred Metropolitans, marched down Broadway, past applauding throngs, to the Canal Street dock, where it boarded a steamer bound for New Orleans. The *Times* rejoiced, noting that where "eight months ago the African race in this City were literally hunted down like wild beasts," now they marched in solid platoons "with waving handkerchiefs, with descending flowers, and with the acclamations and plaudits of countless beholders."

Countless other beholders watched too, infuriated but helpless. The *Herald* was livid at the "miscegenation" represented by the "daughters of Fifth Avenue" presenting the black troops their regimental colors. Nor was the point of the black and upper-class alliance lost on the Workingmen's United Political Association, which asserted: "The very object of arming the negroes is based on the instinctive idea of using them to put down the white laboring classes." Many upper-class conservatives, like Maria L. Daly, wife of a Democratic judge, were distressed at the move to punish the Irish and support the blacks. She was "very sorry and much outraged at the cruelties inflicted," Daly wrote, but added: "I hope it will give the Negroes a lesson, for since the war com-

The Twentieth U.S. Colored Infantry presented with its colors, March 5, 1864, from *Frank Leslie's Illustrated Newspaper*, March 26, 1864. (© Collection of The New-York Historical Society)

menced, they have been so insolent as to be unbearable. I cannot endure free blacks. They are immoral with all their piety."

More pragmatic whites came to accept the idea of black enlistment. When General Thomas F. Meagher gave a banquet for veterans of the Irish Brigade at Irving Hall in January 1864, they hailed a new song written by Charles Graham Halpine. An Irish-born journalist, Halpine, while serving as an officer in the Sixty-ninth, had begun publishing morale-raising minstrel-type pieces for the *Irish American* featuring the fictional hero "Private Miles O'Reilly of the Forty-seventh New York Volunteers." In his latest ditty, titled "Sambo's Right to Be Kilt," the final stanza went:

> Though Sambo's black as the ace of spades,
> His finger a thrigger can pull,
> And his eye runs sthraight on the barrel-sights
> From undher its thatch of wool.
> So hear me all, boys darlin',
> Don't think I'm tippin' you chaff,
> The right to be kilt we'll divide wid him,
> And give him the largest half!

These proved to be prescient verses, in that black soldiers would experience ferocious discrimination in the ranks. Until the war's end they got paid less, collected no federal bounties, obtained little help for their families from the government, seldom became officers, were organized in segregated regiments, and were assigned largely to menial labor—though an incredible 37 percent of their total number would die. Nor did the administration hasten to protect black soldiers who surrendered to Confederate forces from being butchered on the spot or sold into slavery. Despite all this, New York's African Americans signed up at a rate twice that the army had forecast, inspired by their antislavery convictions, and for some military service would provide unprecedented opportunities for exercising leadership.

The episode of the black troops was satisfyingly cathartic, but it was clear to upper-class reformers that a longer-term response to the upheavals was necessary. The Association for Improving the Condition of the Poor, now presided over by James Brown of the Brown Brothers banking and trading firm, asserted that the riots proved beyond all doubt the existence of a "dangerous class" in New York City. The "terrible demonstration written in blood" required renewed elite attention to the task of "moral and physical elevation of these ignorant, semi-brutalized masses."

A Citizens Association was founded. Presided over by popular War Democrat Peter Cooper, it included industrialists and merchants of different party backgrounds, from Democrat August Belmont to conservative Republicans Hamilton Fish and William Dodge. The association, picking up on prewar approaches, called for environmentalist reforms like housing legislation, noting that the rioters had come from overcrowded quarters, but these initiatives would not really begin to take effect until after the war was over.

BACK TO BUSINESS

The draft riots would leave long-term scars, but in the short run their impact was overridden by the war boom, which roared on unabated, offering countless ways of making fabulous amounts of money.

Trading with the enemy—an old New York City staple—again became big business. Congress had legalized trading in cotton with the rebel states, and by late in the war, despite outcries from Union generals, cotton purchased in the Confederacy for twelve to twenty cents a pound in gold was selling in the North for $1.90 per pound. The Treasury Department licensed factors to do the deals. Thurlow Weed, the powerful Republican politician, could ensure that licenses flowed to traders willing to cut him in. Weed also helped those who shipped bales illegally, and eventually hundreds of thousands of them flowed into New York from captured Confederate towns like Memphis, Vicksburg, and New Orleans.

Land speculation reaped great bounties. The Homestead Act permitted the sale of unsurveyed land at $1.25 an acre, and syndicates of New York businessmen took up millions of acres. The government also handed out vast tracts of public land to railroad corporations to encourage development; General Dix's Union Pacific did particularly well in this regard.

Stockbrokers engaged in frenzied profit-taking. "Money is pouring into Wall Street from all parts of the country," wrote the *Herald*, a scant two weeks after the draft riots. By 1864 the old system of auction trading could no longer accommodate the flood of business. A breakaway group of brokers established the Long Room on Broad Street, where stocks could be traded continuously and hundreds of transactions could take place simultaneously. In addition, "curb brokers" (also known as "guttersnipes") traded in the streets from after the New York Stock Exchange's five P.M. closing until the sun went down. One businessman opened an Evening Exchange, providing the only place in the world where securities could be traded twenty-four hours a day.

Stock manipulation reached new heights, best exemplified by the great Harlem Corner, which culminated just after the riots. Commodore Vanderbilt had discovered that the charter of the old Harlem Railroad gave it the right (with the approval of the Common Council) to lay tracks anywhere in the city. Vanderbilt took control of the company and set out to build a line down the full length of Broadway. Secret negotiations brought the aldermen on board: they bought chunks of Harlem stock, approved the franchise, and watched happily as their shares surged from 60 to 116. But then, foolishly, the aldermen decided to doublecross the Commodore. They sold Harlem short— betting that the stock would go down—then rescinded the franchise, and the price plummeted. Before they could take their profits, however, Vanderbilt and his partner, Leonard Jerome, reentered the market and bought up every share of Harlem in sight until they had it all—had "cornered the market." In August, when Harlem peaked at 179, the bleeding bears were forced to take disastrous losses.

Great profits were made gambling on stocks. "We fellows in Wall Street had the fortunes of war to speculate about and that always makes great doings on a stock exchange," recalled Daniel Drew fondly: "It's good fishing in troubled waters." But far greater fortunes were to be won by gambling on gold.

With government greenbacks unsecured by precious metal, their value plunged and soared depending on the bulletins from the battlefield. In terms of greenbacks, therefore, gold behaved just like a stock. It could be traded. Fortunes could be made (and lost) gambling on its value. Many held such trading in moral disrepute. Currency, after all, was not just a stock, it was the lifeblood of the economy and the sinews of war. But to traders, gold stocks were a source of profit—whether they went up *or* down. When the Union Army won, making the future of greenbacks rosier, their value relative to gold rose (i.e., the price of gold measured in greenbacks fell). This suited bearish investors. Those bullish on gold, on the other hand, prayed for Confederate successes and sang "Dixie" lustily in the Exchange whenever they got one.

Such unpatriotic amorality led the New York Stock Exchange to forbid its members from dealing in gold. This barely halted the trade for an instant. The dealers began migrating from one basement to another along Wall, William, and Broad—now in an ill-lit den called the Coal Hole, next in Gilpin's News Room, and finally, in the winter of 1864, in their own home, the New York Gold Exchange at the corner of William Street and Exchange Place (the Gold Room, it was popularly called). At the height of the speculative frenzy, the Gold Room was crammed with frantic dealers—a "rat-pit in full blast," said one observer—while outside speculators lined up in the street, "ankle-deep in slush."

The key to success in the Gold Room was information. Knowledge of a battle's outcome obtained an hour before one's competitors could be parlayed into a phenomenal fortune. At first, brokers haunted the wire services. Then they built their own: by 1863 private wires brought military results to New York's financial district before they reached Lincoln in the White House. J. P. Morgan installed the first such wire in his office, and as his operator was a friend of Grant's telegrapher, he easily kept abreast of the latest military movements. By 1864 Wall Streeters had spies in the Confederate high command and could learn southern battle plans before colonels in the Army of Virginia did.

As Union fortunes slumped in the summer of 1864, with Grant stalled in Virginia and Sherman stymied in Georgia, gold reached an all-time high of $280 an ounce. Some began to argue that "Jeff Davis" speculators were even more interested in undermining

U.S. currency than in reaping their spectacular profits. Philadelphia's Jay Cooke was convinced that New York City was a "hotbed of Southern sentiment and scheming" and that its moneymen were out to ruin the credit of the government.

"What do you think of those fellows in Wall Street, who are gambling in gold at such a time as this?" Lincoln asked Governor Andrew G. Curtin of Pennsylvania. "They are a set of sharks," Curtin replied. "For my part," said Lincoln, banging his clenched fist on the table, "I wish every one of them had his devilish head shot off!" In a crackdown, Secretary Chase dashed up to New York and drove the gold price down— for a time—by selling millions of dollars' worth of specie. Congress tried to outlaw speculative gold contracts altogether, but the act proved utterly unavailing and was swiftly repealed.

Even labor began to benefit from the boom, despite employers having undertaken an anti-Union offensive. The Boss Barbers, Master Coopers, Master Shipwrights, and Iron Founders aggressively sought to reduce wages, increase hours, and, if possible, destroy the fledgling labor organizations. In 1864 the Pianoforte Manufacturers Association, led by Charles Steinway and D. Decker, spearheaded the fight against piano workers, locking out three thousand workmen.

This initiative had run into stiff labor resistance. Goaded by soaring prices, rising rents, and new taxes, workers organized more unions and launched strikes, drawing in the city's various ethnic communities. Germans were particularly energetic, organizing the cigarmakers, pianomakers, tailors, and varnishers. Irish public works and transport laborers went on strike four months after the draft riots. In October 1864 five thousand machinists walked out of the Novelty, Allaire, and Delameter works (all had important military contracts) and demanded a 25 percent increase. When employers rejected this, two thousand workers turned out and by December had largely succeeded.

In April 1864 employers introduced a bill in the state legislature to outlaw strikes altogether. The newly constituted Workingmen's Union, an umbrella organization led by William Harding, an immigrant English coach painter and president of the Coachmakers Union, rallied in Tompkins Square to protest the antistrike bill. On April 7 mechanics and laborers paraded down Third Avenue with banners, flags, and transparencies, cheered by thousands on the sidewalks. Workers from Williamsburg, Brooklyn, Hoboken, and Jersey City joined them in Tompkins Square, until their numbers had swelled to fifty-thousand. Under this pressure, the initiative was defeated.

The latter years of the war were heady ones for labor. For the first seven months of 1864 not a single trade-wide strike failed. And despite continuing inflation and the dreadful conditions of much of the workforce, steady employment, rising wages, soldiers' bounties, and relief payments to families meant that thousands of New York City's poor had more money than ever before.

THE ELECTION OF 1864

In the summer of 1864, Abraham Lincoln's reelection was very much open to question. The war news was gloomy, the progress of Grant's and Sherman's armies slow and terribly costly. With Lincoln's private approval, Horace Greeley had engaged in peace discussions with Confederate representatives at Niagara Falls. In New York City several prominent businessmen deserted the prowar coalition to support the Democratic candidate, George McClellan. Then, in September, Sherman occupied Atlanta, and Sheridan began drubbing Jubal Early's forces in the Shenandoah Valley. At a stroke the situation changed. McClellan's early lead was erased, and Lincoln now had an excellent chance of winning. City businessmen rallied to his campaign, which was masterminded by Thurlow Weed from the Astor House.

The impending Lincoln victory meant the war would go on until the South capitulated, and it would be Republicans who would guide the reconstruction of the postwar political order. Some desperate Confederates decided to disrupt the election process by terrorizing northern cities. The idea was to have Confederate sappers team up with disaffected Copperheads to wreak havoc. For New York City the plans were particularly grandiose. Confederate Secret Service men would infiltrate the country from Canada, make their way to the metropolis, and set off fires around town, hopefully triggering another uprising like the draft riots. Copperheads then would seize federal buildings, throw General Dix in a dungeon, raise the Confederate flag over City Hall, and take New York out of the Union and into an alliance with the Richmond government.

When rumors of the plot reached New York City, Governor Seymour pooh-poohed them, insisting that New York State could handle any untoward developments. But Stanton and Seward decided to send federal troops to the metropolis to secure the electoral process. As commander they chose General Benjamin F. Butler, a fantasy come true for reformers and Republicans. The no-nonsense Butler was just the man to deal with spies, rioters, Tammany bully-boys, and Peace Democrats.

On November 5 regulars from the Army of the Potomac docked in the harbor, the first of a mixed force of five thousand that included reliable New England and New York units. On the seventh the last of the volunteers disembarked in a drizzling rain and stowed their baggage in Brooklyn's Fort Hamilton or at Fort Richmond on Staten Island. Butler set up his headquarters in a twelve-room suite in the brand-new Hoffman House off Madison Square, built on the ruins of stores burned down in the draft riots. Here he established a sixty-wire telegraph center, connecting him to the War Department in Washington, to every major city in New York State, and to every police station and polling place in New York City.

Unbeknownst to Butler, a band of Confederate agents mingled in the crowd outside the Hoffman House watching the bustling military activities. The rumors, for once, had been true. Led by a pair of ex-cavalrymen from Morgan's Raiders, the sappers had entered the country at Niagara Falls, ridden the rails to New York, checked into various hotels and boardinghouses, obtained Greek Fire (a mixture of phosphorus and bisulfide of carbon that ignited on contact with air) from a sympathetic chemist on Washington Place, and met every few days in public places like the recently opened Central Park.

Butler issued General Order No. 1, calling for a peaceful election, and then lay low as the campaign entered its culminating weekend. On Friday night the Republicans paraded, in a chaos of hacks, kettledrums, and wagons festooned with bunting and slogans, from Madison Square to Union Square, converted for the occasion into a temporary coliseum with bandstands (decked with Chinese lanterns) on all four sides. On Saturday night General McClellan (whose home was on East 34th Street) presided over a Democratic parade and rally at Madison Square, three times as large as the Republican effort, culminating in a torchlight parade and fireworks and an address by McClellan from the balcony of the Fifth Avenue Hotel. Monday, the day before the election, the "monied men of the city" rallied for Lincoln, at a gathering in front of the Customs

House near Wall Street. According to the *Times*, three-fourths of the capital of the city was represented.

On Tuesday, election day, Butler deployed his troops in low profile, aboard transports, ferryboats, revenue cutters, and tugs anchored along the waterfront. Butler concentrated on key points: Wall Street, the telegraph cable over the North River, the High Bridge, Mackerelville, and the Battery. Backup troops were stationed on Governor's Island, ready "to be landed at once in spite of barricades and opposition." But there was no opposition. The only crowds were those who gathered in Newspaper Row to hear men call down election bulletins from upper-story telegraph rooms. New York, as Butler cabled Washington, was "the quietest city ever seen."

Lincoln carried New York State (by a whisker) and the nation (by a plurality) but lost the metropolis (by a landslide: 73,716 to 36,687, though his percentage was not much lower than in 1860). City Republicans did better in federal elections, sending industrialist William Dodge and Henry Raymond of the *Times* to Congress. Peace Democrats fared poorly: Seymour was ousted from the governorship, and Fernando Wood fell before a Tammany onslaught.

Butler's troops left the Hudson for the James, but Butler himself tarried a bit, to be wined and dined by the rich, the powerful, and the grateful. At a Fifth Avenue Hotel banquet he was given ovations and a pair of silver spurs. Beecher proposed he be a presidential candidate in 1868. He departed in a glow on November 15.

As it turned out, the congratulations were premature. The plot to burn New York had been deferred, not canceled. It had also changed its character. Copperhead supporters of the original project dropped out, disheartened by, among other things, Sherman's sacking of Georgia. As the Confederate cause now seemed irretrievably lost, nothing could be gained by a rising. But the Confederate officers, reading about Sheridan's scorching of the Shenandoah Valley, switched rationales. They would revenge the desolated South by ravaging the North, beginning with gay, rich, and carefree New York City. They would start by incinerating the opulent symbols of the city's wealth, its glittering hotels. With luck, and a good wind, they might burn New York to the ground.

On the night of November 25, the conspirators set their fires in thirteen major hotels, chiefly along Broadway, including the Astor House, the Metropolitan, and the St. Nicholas (the thousand-room palace where Dix's Department of the East was headquartered). For good measure, the Confederates kindled would-be conflagrations in Barnum's Museum, Niblo's Theater, the Winter Garden, and assorted Hudson River docks, lumberyards, stores, and factories, before making good their escape to Canada.

As blazes broke out all along Broadway, terrified crowds poured into the street. Wooden houses were evacuated in a frenzy. Police wagons and fire engines fought their way through dense crowds of people screaming, "Find the rebels! Hang them from a lamppost! Burn them at the stake!"

Despite the panic, the fires were promptly extinguished, though not before causing four hundred thousand dollars' worth of damage. The incident captured world headlines but did not affect the course of the war. New York City detectives tracked the conspirators down in Canada and arrested one, Robert Kennedy, when he reentered the United States trying to return south. Tried as a spy, he was found guilty and hanged in Fort Lafayette in March 1865. His fate was symbolic. That same March the death knell of the Confederacy itself could be heard tolling in New York.

PEACE

On March 6 a procession seven miles long snaked its way through the streets of lower Manhattan—a "National Jubilee" hailing Lincoln's second inaugural, recent Union victories, and impending Confederate defeats. Marchers included huge numbers of troops, the city's volunteer fire companies, scores of German, Italian, and Irish community organizations, businesses and banks, insurance and express companies, typographers, pianomakers, steam fitters, tailors—even elephants and camels. Patriotism and commerce mingled: *Harper's* sniffed that for all too many businesses the "chief object in participating in the festival was the opportunity to advertise their wares." Some commercials were done with knowing wit, like the sign for McAuliffe's Irish whiskey: DON T AVOID THE DRAUGHT. In echoes of earlier days, sailors carried model boats, one of a full-rigged ship, another of the *Monitor*. Others proclaimed the future: OIL IS KING NOW, NOT COTTON read one display.

On April 3, businessmen standing on the corner of Pine and William read on the *Commercial Advertiser*'s bulletin board that Richmond and Petersburg had been captured the day before. Broadway became an instant river of cheering, singing men. Flags waved, guns saluted. On April 11 word came that Grant had run Lee to ground at Appomattox, and again the city exploded.

But the night of April 14 wrenched New York into an abrupt change of mood. Lincoln had been shot and died the next morning, Good Friday. Whitman, reading the news in black-bordered papers, crossed to Manhattan and walked up Broadway past shuttered stores hung in black. Toward noon, he recalled, it began to rain: "Black clouds driving overhead. Lincoln's death—black, black black—as you look toward the sky—long broad black like great serpents."

The city prepared for Lincoln's final visit. The Committee of Arrangements included A. T. Stewart, Moses Grinnell, William Dodge, and William Tweed. The funeral train left Washington on April 21. It stopped at Baltimore, Harrisburg, Philadelphia. From New Jersey the party was ferried to Manhattan. The ships in the harbor were draped in black muslin. At the Desbrosses Street dock the body was placed in a glass hearse drawn by six gray horses. Accompanied by a German society singing a funeral ode, the procession, headed by General Dix and the Seventh Regiment, moved across Canal and down Broadway to a black-draped City Hall, where it was put on a catafalque. Lines formed to pay last respects.

The city shut down for the day. Businesses closed, courts adjourned. At the Nineteenth Street Synagogue, the Rev J. J. Lyons led the Nahan Neshomen, the prayer for the dead, the first time such a ceremony was ever held in the United States for a non-Jew. Mourning was not unanimous, however. Strong reported hearing of a dozen cases where "celtic handmaidens" had been summarily discharged for rejoicing at the news. Gramercy Park House similarly dismissed a number of waiters for approving of the assassination.

The next day, April 25, a sixteen-horse funeral car led by eighteen bands paced its way from City Hall up Broadway to 14th Street, across Union Square to Fifth Avenue, and north to the Hudson River Railroad Depot. At the rear walked a small group of "freedmen." This human postscript represented a last-minute compromise. The Common Council had excluded blacks from participating in the march at all, and they had organized their own ceremonies, featuring Frederick Douglass, at Cooper Institute. But the Union League Club protested. Interceding with Stanton and the local police, they got permission for a token representation to bring up the rear.

At four P.M., the train pulled out of the station for Albany. The Civil War in New York City was over.

Lincoln's funeral cortege turning up Broadway, April 25, 1865. To the right, a huge banner draped across the front of City Hall reads: "The Nation Mourns." It was said that a million people watched the procession. (© Collection of The New-York Historical Society)

51

Westward, Ho!

With the guns silenced, New York's exporters, importers, shippers, and bankers set out to repair their severed southern connections. Cotton might no longer be king, but as the country's leading export it remained, the *Times* noted, "a magnate of the very first rank." To restore the antebellum status quo as quickly as possible, New York businessmen overwhelmingly supported President Andrew Johnson's policies. They applauded the president's grant of amnesty to most ex-Confederates, accepted a quick return of southern representatives to Congress, and raised no objections when state legislatures passed "Black Codes" imposing virtual peonage on freed slaves.

Less than a year after the fighting ended, though, leniency had reaped few rewards. When New York City's Chamber of Commerce commissioned an envoy, Thomas N. Conway, to canvass the old Confederacy for prospects and to let former rebels know that "money in vast quantities was awaiting a chance of safe and profitable investment," Conway turned in a gloomy assessment. There were, he reported, planters desperate for funds to restart operations, merchants eager to hook up with old trading partners, and would-be southern industrialists who needed northern capital to build railroads, erect textile mills, and exploit mineral resources. But enthusiasm from the few was offset by hatred from the many. There was no way, Conway reported, that New Yorkers "could live and safely conduct business in any section of the South." Nor were serious profits likely. Whites were obsessed with subordinating the newly freed blacks, and looming racial turmoil would make southern labor unproductive and unreliable.

Conway's predictions were quickly confirmed. In May 1866 Memphis whites fired and pillaged hundreds of black homes, churches, and schools, gang-raped black women on the streets, and murdered dozens of black men. In July a massacre in New Orleans left thirty-eight dead and 146 wounded. These events shocked and angered many New

York businessmen. So did the decision by "reconstructed" states to send Confederate congressmen, Confederate generals—even the Confederacy's vice-president!—to represent them in Washington. Presidential reconstruction, it seemed, was letting southerners win back politically what they had lost on the battlefield.

These developments strengthened the radical wing of the Republican Party, which had been arguing for much tougher treatment of the South. Freedmen, radicals argued, should be granted political and civil rights, and former Confederate leaders should be disfranchised. The most militant radicals called for expropriating ex-slaveholders' lands and dividing them up among poor whites and blacks. Radicalism had attracted few New Yorkers outside the Union League Club or the city's African-American community, but the appalling news out of the South enhanced the appeal of harsher measures.

Riding the surge of resentment, Radical Republicans swept to national triumph in the fall 1866 elections, capturing two-thirds majorities in both houses of Congress. In 1867 they imposed military rule on the South. Federal troops oversaw enrollment of voters, this time with blacks included and most Confederate officials excluded. The newly reconstituted state governments ratified the Fourteenth Amendment—a guarantee of equal rights (short of suffrage) for all citizens, to be overseen by the national government—and embarked on social reforms.

Propertied northerners balked at any confiscation of planter lands, however, and by the time the 1868 presidential campaign got under way, New York Republican conservatives believed reconstruction had gone far enough. Democrats believed it had gone too far. Selecting Horatio Seymour, New York's wartime governor, as their presidential standard-bearer, they denounced Republicans for subjecting the South to rule by "a semi-barbarous race of blacks" who longed to "subject the white women to their unbridled lust." Conservative Republicans, seeking a candidate who would accept the new status quo but foreswear dramatic new departures, turned to Ulysses S. Grant. Indeed the Grant candidacy was born and bred in New York City, launched by such businessmen as A. T. Stewart, Cornelius Vanderbilt, William B. Astor, and Hamilton Fish. The general lost the metropolis, still stubbornly Democratic, but carried the nation.

Under federal protection, southern governments tried hard to attract northern investment. They extended munificent aid to railroad corporations, exempted new industries from taxes, leased convict labor to entrepreneurs, repealed usury laws, and proved as susceptible as their northern and federal counterparts to being bribed by businessmen. One Georgia legislator got a "loan" of thirty thousand dollars from Harper and Brothers in exchange for a promise to have the new state school system adopt its textbooks.

Yet most New York capitalists shied away from the South. They financed some cotton production (some merchants even acquired their own plantations) and put some money into railroads, the Texas cattle industry, and Florida's nascent tourist business. Merchants restored the flow of cotton bales through the Hudson River seaport and on to Europe, driving exports from a puny six million pounds in 1865 to over three hundred million pounds by 1873. But with disfranchised, infuriated whites organizing the paramilitary Ku Klux Klan and launching insurrectionary forays against the reconstructed governments, the South seemed "the last region on earth"—as George Templeton Strong formulated dominant opinion—in which "a Northern or European capitalist [would] invest a dollar."

WALL STREET AND THE WEST

As their hopes for the former Confederacy withered, New York businessmen grew ever more enthusiastic about the West, eyeing the enormous opportunities opened up by the thrust of railroads across the Mississippi toward California. Before the Civil War only a scant six thousand miles of track had been laid. By 1869 the engineers and work gangs of the Union Pacific and Central Pacific had driven their converging lines toward a golden-spiked conjuncture, and competitors were proliferating rapidly. By 1873 twenty-four thousand miles of track had been laid; by 1877, seventy-nine thousand miles. Railway expansion not only created a truly national marketplace but spurred a cascading industrial development. The demand for rails and railroad bridges galvanized iron manufacturing, summoned the steel industry into being, and touched off mining booms from Pittsburgh to Colorado. These industrial and extractive operations, in turn, attracted vast numbers of immigrant workers, accelerated urban development, and fostered commercial agriculture.

New Yorkers would be deeply involved in the industrialization of the West. The metropolis would finance, promote, and publicize the region's feverish development, funnel its products to Europe, distribute imported commodities to its populace, serve as portal for the millions rushing westward, and consume vast quantities of its agricultural and industrial products. Soon four of the country's seven great arteries to the interior (the Erie Canal and the Central, Pennsylvania, and Erie railroads) would be pouring western goods into New York's harbor—grain, meat, lumber, coal, and iron, both for local consumption and for transshipment to Europe and a growing Latin American market. In return New York merchants would ship westward burgeoning quantities of

The torrent of western wheat that descended on the city after the Civil War would prompt the New York Central Railroad to erect this enormous grain elevator on the Hudson River at Sixty-First Street in 1879. (© Collection of The New-York Historical Society)

northeastern industrial products—shoes from Lynn, rifles from Springfield, clothing from Manhattan itself—and the most essential item of all: money.

Dime novels depicted western settlement as the result of ambitious efforts by innumerable individuals—family farmers and cantankerous cowboys—but pioneering the continent also demanded a far more organized mobilization of resources. Mining, lumbering, steelmaking, railroad building, cattle ranching, and "bonanza" farming were enormously expensive, requiring investment capital on a colossal scale.

Government provided much of the funding (and, of course, the requisite military muscle). No fears of socialism or debilitating dependency hindered entrepreneurs from seeking handouts. Washington and local states gave subsidies, credits, and over a hundred million acres of land to mining companies and railroads, free of charge. The legislative largesse was intended to foster economic development, consolidate the national territory, and, less high-mindedly, to line the pockets of officeholders, as evidenced by the spectacular scandals of the Grant administration.

It also provided a huge windfall for the New York bourgeoisie, who had invested so heavily in such enterprises. Industrialists turned to Manhattan to tap into eastern and European capital pools. Paced by the rapid growth of trading in railroad stocks, Wall Street's money markets expanded rapidly. By 1868 over three billion dollars' worth of securities were sold at the New York Stock Exchange, an even larger volume at the Open Board, and still more at the curb. Additional trading at the Gold Exchange, Produce Exchange, and Petroleum Exchange swelled New York's capital markets until they outranked all their American competitors combined.

Industrialists turned less often now than they had before the war to the city's merchants, more often to its financiers. Brokerage houses proliferated in downtown Manhattan, especially after the invention of the stock "ticker," patented in 1867, allowed them to access price information from exchange floors. The crucial financing institutions, however, were the great banking firms, especially those with solid European connections, and the most critical technology was the Atlantic cable, which, restored to life in 1866, made instantaneous communication with overseas investors possible.

Once again foreigners began pouring vast sums into the American economy—the setbacks of 1857, like those of 1837, now merely a hazy memory. In 1853 fifty-two million dollars' worth of U.S. railroad stocks and bonds had been held outside the country. By 1869 the figure had jumped to $243 million and was accelerating rapidly. Altogether, in that year, Europeans held over $1.46 billion of American securities.

Tremendous power accrued to firms that could raise and funnel funds from Europe into the U.S. economy. Some were old, established operations, like the House of Belmont, with its ties to the House of Rothschild, but new ones emerged as well, the most outstanding being the father-son team of Junius Spencer Morgan and John Pierpont Morgan.

The elder Morgan ran the largest and wealthiest American bank in London. A highly respected firm, it had long specialized in underwriting the sale of British iron to American railroads. But Junius aspired to the loftier plateau of investment banking, where Barings and Rothschilds dwelled. Morgan had developed close ties with leading railroad entrepreneurs (and iron consumers) like Commodore Vanderbilt. When galloping American iron production and steep American tariffs drastically curtailed this trade, Junius shifted easily into underwriting railroad issues.

Like any other European-based concern, J. S. Morgan and Company needed reliable information about the great American West. Junius turned to his son, Pierpont, whom he had long been grooming for the business. After being schooled in Switzerland and Gottingen, Pierpont had started work in a conservative Wall Street firm during the panic year of 1857. Brilliant but rash, the burly young man with the handlebar mustache and intense gaze alarmed his employers, and when they refused to make him a partner Morgan formed his own firm in 1861.

Pierpont composed lengthy letters to his father on America's political and financial condition (and reported in person to London each spring), but he also found time to participate in the speculative scramble of the war years. (When drafted, he'd purchased a substitute, whom he jocularly referred to as "the other Pierpont Morgan.") He became a regular denizen of the Gold Room, cleared $160,000 on a market-rigging scam, and financed some speculators who purchased five thousand obsolete rifles from a government armory in New York and resold them to government troops in Missouri at six times the price. Junius, dismayed, orchestrated an alliance with a sober banker thirty years Pierpont's senior, and Dabney, Morgan, and Company became his New York agent.

As his father moved into railroad financing, Pierpont set out to investigate the frontier first hand. Boarding a train in July 1869—a scant few weeks after the first transcontinental line had gone into operation—he and his new wife, Fanny (daughter of the successful lawyer Charles Tracy), headed for the Far West. After a twelve-day stopover in Chicago, during which he met with officials of the major railroads, he pressed on through Nebraska in one of George Pullman's recently invented luxury sleeping cars. From his window he spotted Pawnee warriors, wagon trains, and U.S. Cavalry scouts. Then the train notched through the Rockies at South Pass and descended into California, where Morgan spent an additional month, as the guest of prominent Western businessmen, deepening his firsthand knowledge of the emerging American rail system.

In 1871, when Dabney retired, Junius arranged for a new Pierpont partner: Anthony Drexel, a leading Philadelphia banker, who was well aware that the center of financial activities lay in New York City. Two years later, the firm of Drexel, Morgan, and Company moved to a brand-new six-story marbled building on the corner of Wall and Broad streets (the land alone had cost a record-breaking $349 per square foot). The new company, in alliance with Morgan Senior, was perfectly positioned to market railroad and government bonds to English clients and swiftly became one of the leading houses on Wall Street.

England was not the only source of investment capital flowing into New York City. Germany too shipped vast quantities to Wall Street, and this afforded an opening for several German Jewish concerns that had made the transition from commerce to banking. The most influential was the firm of J. and W. Seligman. Joseph Seligman and his brothers, having done well in California commerce, had moved into banking by trading their West Coast bullion on the New York gold market in the 1850s. They quit just in time to keep their fortune from being wiped out by the 1857 panic and bought a clothing factory just in time to take advantage of wartime government contracts. When, to their dismay, they were paid with Union bonds instead of specie, they learned how to convert the paper into hard cash by selling the securities to wealthy contacts in Frankfurt and Amsterdam.

The Seligmans' expertise caught the eye of the secretary of the treasury, who enlisted their aid in marketing tens of millions of new government notes abroad. It proved much easier to raise money among Germany's numerous Union sympathizers than in the City of London, whose cotton connections left it cool to the North. When the war was over, the brothers established an international banking house, frankly modeled on the Rothschilds'. Various Seligman brothers were dispatched to Paris, Frankfurt, London, San Francisco, and New Orleans, and in 1869 the House of Seligman became the first German Jewish bank to enter the railway security business.

Close on their heels came another firm that had emerged out of wartime profit-making. Abraham Kuhn, a German Jewish immigrant, had founded a prosperous dry-goods business in Cincinnati. He was joined, after 1848, by a distant relative, Solomon Loeb, son of a Worms wine dealer. During the war they made a fortune providing uniforms and blankets to the Union Army. After Appomattox, they took their capital of half a million dollars to New York City and opened Kuhn, Loeb, a private banking establishment in Nassau Street. Kuhn soon retired to Germany, but the mother country supplied a more than ample replacement when Jacob Schiff, scion of an ancient Frankfurt family of scholars and bankers, joined the firm in 1875.

In the 1870s investment banking firms like Drexel, Morgan, the Houses of Belmont and Seligman, and Kuhn, Loeb constituted New York's financial elite, partly because they channeled such huge amounts of capital into western industrialization, but also because they were known as ethical operators. Not that they weren't ruthless businessmen, but they did tend to adhere to a gentlemanly code that emphasized discretion, honest agency, and restraint in competition with one another. These standards worked to their advantage and the city's: by garnering the trust of distant investors they sustained New York's reputation as a reliable haven for foreign capital.

THE SCARLET WOMAN OF WALL STREET

Not all New York financiers were honorable men. Ever since the days of Hamilton and Duer, the market had inevitably been a magnet for those who hoped to profit by manipulating the market itself. Prudential investment and speculative rascality were the Castor and Pollux of Wall Street.

The Panic of 1857 wiped out most of the older generation of traders, and the Civil War brought to prominence a breed of brash gamblers, men who played big-stakes games with cutthroat earnestness. In the postwar years, these travelers down Wall Street's dark side were fortified by an atmosphere of feverish growth, a virtual absence of regulation, and a political system in New York City that facilitated skullduggery.

John Duer's most notorious incarnations in this era were the improbable trio of Daniel Drew, Jim Fisk, and Jay Gould. Drew, now in his seventies, was one of the few survivors from prewar days, having been a leading Wall Street figure since 1838, when he'd given up driving cattle and turned to manipulating stock. Jim Fisk—tall, florid, and fat—was a vulgarian even by the lights of a gaudy age. With his pomaded and waved light brown hair, his loud suits, his frilled shirtfront garnished with huge diamonds, and his theatrical style, he looked like the huckster he had in fact once been. During the war Fisk wangled contracts to sell dry goods to the government and smuggled cotton through the Union lines. At war's end he came to New York, bet and blew a fortune speculating on Wall Street, and started anew as a broker handling work for Daniel Drew. He soon demonstrated that behind the genial Falstaffian buffoonery lay a speculative freebooter of the first order.

Jay Gould was not a man who, by his appearance, would shock polite New York (indeed he married into it and set up a model family life on Fifth Avenue). Small, thin, intense, and abstemious, Gould was an enigma, not a peacock, but in his own way quite as amoral as his friend and colleague Fisk. Gould grew up poor and sickly in upstate New York, first visiting New York City in 1853 when he came down to exhibit his grandfather's better mousetrap at the Crystal Palace. He entered the leather business, moved to New York to deal in the Swamp, then shifted into the stock market as a "guttersnipe," teaching himself the tricks of an increasingly nasty trade. Learning how to control big enterprises with small holdings, Gould became a consummate litigant and a master of the arts of deception and bribery. He would soon become the most hated man in America.

Cornelius Vanderbilt was no Alexander Hamilton—he had zero qualms about speculative wheeling and dealing—but since he'd shifted from river to rails, by gaining control of the Harlem during the Civil War, he had been a model entrepreneur. Devoting himself to improving the old line's management and equipment, by 1866 he had turned the Harlem into a going concern, but one whose future profitability, he realized, was imperiled by competition from the Hudson line. Vanderbilt, accordingly, bought control of the Hudson by purchasing its shares on the open market, in partnership with Leonard Jerome and John M. Tobin. Then he coordinated the former rivals' schedules and rates.

Now it became apparent that the success of his combined operation, which ran to Albany, was at the mercy of yet another road, the New York Central, which controlled the traffic with Buffalo, the junction point with midwestern commerce. Vanderbilt decided to take over the Central too. Buying a minority holding on the open market, he proceeded to convince key Central stockholders—notably John Jacob Astor Jr.—that only by linking up with his roads and letting him manage the conjoint operation would the Central be able to stand up to *its* competitors for the western trade. By 1867 he had become president and was operating the Hudson and Central as an effective New York-to-Buffalo unit.

The roads flourished and paid high dividends. Vanderbilt accordingly issued a vast amount of new stock, nearly doubling the capitalization, arguing that the additional certificates were justified by anticipated earnings. Others had "watered" stock this way, but only to make quick speculative profits; Vanderbilt plowed much of the proceeds back into improvements.

In his new position as commander of the consolidated Central lines, Vanderbilt confronted yet another competitor, the old Erie Rail Road. It too ran from New York City to the Great Lakes. The Erie, moreover, was controlled by his old steamboat rival Daniel Drew, beneath whose pious and austere Methodist exterior beat the heart of a shark. Drew had repeatedly jerked the road's stock price up or down, as suited his market gambit of the moment, and had launched periodic rate wars to win freight traffic away from the Central.

In 1867 Vanderbilt set out to capture Erie and oust Drew. Drew, seconded by new board members Fisk and Gould, prepared to repel the hostile takeover. The Commodore began by secretly buying up Erie stock, through dummy agents. To block Drew and company from issuing more stock, which would make his buyout harder, Vanderbilt prevailed upon Justice George G. Barnard of the Supreme Court, a Tammany man renowned for his favors to wealthy petitioners, to enjoin Erie from increasing its capitalization. But Drew, Fisk, and Gould evaded the ban and secretly threw millions of dollars of new Erie stock on the market, in effect churning out certificates as fast as Vanderbilt's unsuspecting brokers could buy them. "If this printing-press don't break down," chortled Fisk, "I'll be damned if I don't give the old hog all he wants of Erie."

Vanderbilt soon discovered the ruse but grimly kept buying, driving the price ever higher. Meanwhile, he got Judge Barnard to authorize the arrest of the Erie's directors for contempt of court. Drew, Fisk, and Gould, one jump ahead of the law, gathered together the company records, baled up over seven million dollars' worth of greenbacks, and literally decamped with the corporation, fleeing by ferry through the fog to Jersey City. There they set up headquarters at Taylor's Hotel (promptly dubbed "Fort Taylor"), hired policemen and roughs to protect them from Vanderbilt vengeance, and settled in for a lengthy stay.

The Erie directors now opened up a second front. Their agents in Albany introduced a bill into the state legislature that would, in effect, retroactively legalize all their questionable stock issuances. The proposed bill also shrewdly forbade Vanderbilt from merging the Central and the Erie, on the grounds that it would create a monopoly that would leave the poor and working class vulnerable to price-gouging. While the Erie's newfound concern for the poor probably changed few votes, legislators did pay close attention to New York City's merchants, who also feared, and vigorously protested, a Vanderbilt-dominated future.

Winning Chamber of Commerce support gave the triumvirate high hopes for success, but, taking no chances, Gould traveled to Albany, reportedly with a trunk full of thousand-dollar bills, set up shop in the Delavan House, and began buying votes. The Commodore swiftly dispatched counterbribery agents, among them William Tweed, who installed themselves on another floor of the same hostelry. Legislators shuttled back and forth in search of the highest bidder. With the Erie's treasury close at hand, Gould's was the more bottomless wallet, and Vanderbilt's troops deserted him, even Tweed—who was rewarded for his treachery with lavish supplies of Erie stock, netting him $650,000 in all. The desired legislation passed.

Vanderbilt didn't give up. He met secretly with Drew, who—miserable in New Jersey and ready as ever to sell out his partners—whined his way back into the Commodore's good graces and initiated a deal. In return for Vanderbilt's withdrawing his lawsuits and allowing the exiles to come home, Erie would buy back a hefty chunk of his recently purchased stock, even though it would add millions to the company's debt and leave it virtually bankrupt.

Drew left the road to Gould and Fisk—and two new board appointees, Tweed and his henchman Sweeney—and the duo settled into control of Erie. At Fisk's urging, they purchased for their headquarters the floundering Pike's Opera House (at Eighth Avenue and 23rd Street). The top floors became offices; the bottom part—now festooned with frescoes and gilded balustrades—became the Grand Opera House, a theater in which Fisk, wearing his impresario hat, staged extravaganzas. The flamboyance disturbed Gould, who preferred anonymity, but Fisk was in his element. He installed his mistress Josie in a nearby house, and she presided over regular champagne and poker soirees for Boss Tweed, Judge Barnard, and others in what people now called the "Erie Ring."

Gould proceeded to wring a fortune from the supposedly squeezed-dry railroad by spreading false rumors that sent Erie's stock quote dancing in the direction he desired. In the course of one audacious scam Gould fleeced his quondam partner Drew so thoroughly that he was forever washed up as a major Wall Street figure. Gould's gambits, however, deeply disturbed the Erie's English bondholders, and they asked August Belmont to organize his ouster from the presidency. Gould, in a brilliant maneuver, had the ever complaisant Judge Barnard throw the road into receivership and appoint him its caretaker.

At this point the Erie buccaneers came up against a worthier opponent. Determined to take over a small but strategically located upstate New York railroad, Gould and Fisk began buying its stock on the market. The desperate directors turned for help to Pierpont Morgan. The ensuing contest was a bruiser, the highlight of which was a shootout for control of a railway station in Binghamton. Fisk recruited a small army of eight hundred gang members from the Five Points; Morgan countered with recruits from the Bowery; and in the ensuing free-for-all, at least eight men were shot before the state militia intervened. Morgan's forces triumphed, and Fisk returned to New York, famously remarking that "nothing is lost save honor."

Morgan solidified his clients' position by arranging for a friendly merger with a larger company, then sought and obtained a seat on the board of directors of the consolidated company. It was Morgan's first such position, and it marked the beginning of a portentous new relationship between financiers and industrialists.

Gould's railroad predations had seriously annoyed conservative bankers like Morgan, but his next venture, an audacious foray into high finance, horrified and enraged them. In 1869 Jay Gould set out to corner the nation's gold supply. Given the centralization of finances in lower Manhattan, this was not an impossible dream. The supply of gold in the city was less than twenty million dollars' worth, and it could all be purchased on credit. Once he had it in his hands, Gould could drive the price sky high. City merchants who needed the metal for their international dealings, and bearish speculators who had foolishly promised to sell gold at a lower figure, would be at his mercy.

The treasury could easily break such a corner by selling some of its vast holdings in the market, instantly driving the price down. Gould, to prevent the newly installed Grant administration from intervening against him, convinced the president that a corner was in the national (and Republican Party's) interest. If the price of gold went up, American farmers could more easily sell their wheat abroad; railroads would profit from the increased grain shipments; and farmers and railroads were key Republican constituencies. Q.E.D.

Grant agreed, and with the president on board, Gould and Fisk began buying gold. As their army of brokers drove the price steadily higher, howls of outrage reached the White House. Sensing impending doom, Gould began secretly *selling* gold, even while encouraging Fisk to keep buying and bulling its price. Bears, facing utter disaster, pleaded with the government to sell gold. On September 24, 1869, soon to remembered as Black Friday, crowds of businessmen and merchants facing ruin jammed New Street. As Fisk bought and Gould secretly sold, gold inched up, accompanied by shrieks from the bears, to 145, 150, 155. Then, at noon, with brokers crumpling, transactions flying, and the crowd outside so enraged the militia was ordered into readiness, the government dumped gold on the market, sending the price plummeting. Slipping away from the chaos, Gould and Fisk holed up in their heavily defended Opera House headquarters while the reverberations rocked the city.

Scores of smaller dealers failed, one broker shot himself to death, and the market collapsed, threatening a full-scale panic. "Over the pallid faces of some men stole a deadly hue," wrote the *Herald*, "and almost transfixed to the earth, they gazed on vacancy. Others rushed like wildfire through the streets, hatless and caring little about stumbling against their fellows." One man who kept his head was Jim Fisk, who escaped ruin by the simple expedient of repudiating all his contracts and hiding behind Tammany-supplied judges.

Gould kept his head too but lost what was left of his reputation. The collapse of the Gold Corner didn't precipitate a full-scale depression, but hundreds of businesses failed, and thousands of workers were laid off. They would remember Jay Gould, and the emerging national labor movement would be indelibly affected by this encounter with finance capitalism run amuck. Nor was the press pleased with the turmoil. The *Times* led a journalistic assault that fastened to Gould forever the character of a sinister and poisonous predator. New York City's reputation suffered as well. Wartime gambling in the Gold Room had cast the metropolis in a baleful light; Gould's escapade further blackened its image.

But the men most alienated by the mess Gould had made of the financial markets were the elite directors of conservative banking houses, particularly J. P. Morgan. Gould's machinations distressed Pierpont both as a matter of business aesthetics and personal interest—his own firm of Dabney, Morgan, and Company was bruised by Black Friday—and in years to come he would dedicate himself to imposing his particular brand of order on the national economy.

THE WEST AND WALL STREET

From the West's perspective, the differences between Wall Streeters were less compelling than their similarities, given that most bankers and merchants were determined to restore "hard money." During the Civil War, the government had churned out greenbacks—paper money not exchangeable for gold—in such massive quantities that the postbellum era inherited an inflated currency. This distressed the banking community, which had never liked greenbacks, finding them all too vulnerable to politicians with printing presses. Merchants hated them, for though legal tender in America they were non grata in Europe and ensnared international traders in endless difficulties.

Seeking a quick return to the gold standard, New York City's bankers and merchants hailed a Johnson administration plan to make greenbacks "as good as gold" by withdrawing them from circulation and literally burning them up. Eventually, with scarcity, their value would swell to market equivalence with precious metal, and gold and paper could once again be made interconvertible.

Western farmers and businessmen loathed the idea. With their capital-starved region in the midst of a gigantic expansion, there was not enough currency in circulation as it was. They protested a policy that would drive them into deeper dependency on Wall Street. Entrepreneurs in the iron and steel industry—who had done quite well under wartime inflation—denounced this plot by "money lenders" to throttle "productive capital." Eastern manufacturers agreed. They organized the American Industrial League (1867), installed Peter Cooper as its first president, and complained that contraction would choke the economy into depression.

Western fury at Wall Street was intensified by the perceived inequities of the banking system. Congress had authorized nationally chartered institutions to issue banknotes that could circulate as money but allocated this credit-creating right on a regional basis, giving by far the bulk of it to New York and New England. By 1866 the per capita circulation of banknotes in New York was $33.30; in the Midwest, $6.36; in

Arkansas, fourteen cents. This too forced West and South to turn east to finance their own expansion.

The new national financial system had further exacerbated regional inequalities by creating a three-tiered pyramid of banks. At the bottom were "Country Banks," required for safety's sake to keep a portion of their capital in a bank located in one of seventeen "Reserve Cities." These institutions, in turn, were mandated to keep half of *their* required reserves at a bank in the "Central Reserve City"—i.e., Manhattan. This generated additional outcries against "the money power" that was being "centralized in New York."

Westerners were even more unhappy with the government's solution to the bond problem. During the war, Washington had been forced to offer high rates of interest, payable in gold, to those who purchased bonds. By 1869 there were over $1.6 billion of these in circulation. The government now announced that it would pay off the principal in gold too, even though most bonds had been purchased with greenbacks worth fifty to sixty cents at best. This would give bondholders a tremendous windfall profit (akin to that received by New York speculators in the aftermath of the Revolutionary War). Westerners denounced the plan, noting that the great bulk of notes were held by wealthy individuals and financial institutions. One protest pamphlet depicted a sybaritic "Mr. Bond" sitting in his parlor, smoking imported Havanas, downing French champagne, and gloating over tax-free bonds that brought in 11 percent a year, while out west, a disabled union veteran groaned under the high taxes imposed to pay off the corpulent Mr. Bond.

In 1867 Western animosity crystallized around a "soft money" proposal to pay off the bonds in greenbacks, the same depreciated currency with which they had been purchased. "Hard money" forces—centered in New York City—went wild. Academic economists weighed in with treatises about the immutable laws of classical economics. Ministers like Henry Ward Beecher preached sermons on the sanctity of specie and the wickedness of paper money. (Beecher's text: "Thou shalt not steal.")

The money issue became central to the 1868 presidential campaign. The Democratic Party held its national convention in New York, the first in the city's history. A bruising battle pitted a strong western contingent backing paper, against eastern Democrats led by national chairman August Belmont, Samuel J. Tilden, and Horatio Seymour (all intimately tied to Wall Street financial circles), who insisted on government's moral obligation to redeem in gold. In the end, Seymour got the nomination, only to lose to Grant and the Republicans, who had more decisively declared themselves for hard and moral money. Their word proved to be their bond. On taking office, Republicans immediately passed the Public Credit Act (in March 1869), which pledged to redeem bonds in coin and to make greenbacks as good as gold, as soon as possible.

To raise the massive supply of specie required for a return to the gold standard, the government planned to sell $1.4 billion worth of federal bonds, the largest securities transaction of the decade. For help, the government turned to a syndicate dominated by New York's international bankers, including the Seligman Brothers (who had close ties to Grant and strong connections abroad), August Belmont and Company (acting on behalf of the English Rothschilds), and Drexel, Morgan (representing Junius Spencer Morgan of London). Syndicate members succeeded brilliantly, accruing hefty profits in the process, and on January 2, 1879, the country went back on the gold standard, a Wall Street triumph bitterly resented in the West.

Reconstructing New York

Southern planters and western greenbackers were far from being the sole concerns of the city's propertied classes in the immediate aftermath of the Civil War. Memories of the terrible draft riots remained raw. The lower three-fifths of New York's population seemed still in thrall to poverty, ignorance, alcohol, Romanism, and the Democratic Party, which some Republicans now believed tainted with treason as well as venality.

The Union League Club's Committee on Municipal Reform, established in October 1865, caught the prevailing mood among groups like the Citizens Association and Chamber of Commerce when it wondered: "Is there not a member of this Club who had not had fleeting moments of longing for a temporary dictator who would sweep these bad men from our municipal halls and cleanse this Augean stable of its accumulated corruption?" Some Republicans were indeed convinced that setting the city to rights would require methods as vigorous as those employed in reconstructing Georgia or Mississippi, and they yearned for the dispatch of federal troops to New York.

But most preferred to resume the strategy, launched just before the war, of using the state legislature to override and supplant local government, thus bypassing politicians and encrusted special interests. Handing power to state commissions staffed with professionals, moreover, would allow reformers to assess and redress civic wrongs by using "scientific" studies of municipal problems.

Drs. Griscom and Sanger had pioneered the idea of scientific surveys and statistical analyses of municipal problems back in the forties and fifties. The wartime success of agencies like the Sanitary Commission had greatly strengthened reformers' confidence that the fruits of social intelligence could be brought to bear upon previously intractable urban ills. Now, in the postwar era, "social science" (argued E. L. Godkin in the *Nation*) could be fully brought to bear on "the arrangement and management" of city life. The new optimism was caught by William Cullen Bryant in an *Evening Post* editorial. "Thoughtful men," Bryant said, no longer believed that urban growth was beyond "the control of scientific thought." Instead they were focusing their attention on "the important problem of how to plan and how to build a city so as best to accommodate business and promote health."

Many businessmen were prepared to support such initiatives. Even laissez-faire stalwarts who, before the war, had balked at any legislative infringement on property or profits experienced a change of heart after the draft riots. The Citizens Association, formed in that upheaval's aftermath and heavily stocked with civic leaders, would now push hard for substantial government intervention in an all-too-free marketplace.

FIRE

One of the city's most serious problems was its ongoing flammability. Reformers blamed the volunteer firefighters, whom they now set out to replace with a professional fire department. The volunteers were newly vulnerable to assault, as their prewar reputation for rowdyism had been reinforced by the behavior of some in their ranks during the draft riots. After Appomattox, moreover, their brawling had reached intolerable new heights. In one August 1865 shootout at a fire scene, two men were killed and eighty wounded, while the building they had come to rescue burned to char and cinders. For the insurance companies, which had to cover such losses, and for the local merchants, who were forced to pay premiums higher than anywhere else in the United States or Europe, the volunteer system was inexcusably inefficient. Republican reformers were also well aware that the companies were prime recruiting resources for the Democratic Party.

Republican legislators accordingly introduced a bill to replace the forty thousand volunteers with a thousand-man professional fire department, to be equipped with the horse-drawn, steam-powered pumpers that brawny volunteers had long resisted. In hearings on the bill, the insurance industry presented the damning evidence they had systematically collected that demonstrated exactly how costly the old amateur order was to the city and its property owners. Other urban centers, the insurance companies noted, had established professional departments, and the statistics made clear how much more effective Baltimore and Cincinnati's systems were. Twenty-three banks, 109 insurance companies, and thirteen thousand citizens filed petitions on the measure's behalf. Businessmen complained that having worker-volunteers down tools and race off whenever the fire bells rang was "incompatible with any steady pursuits of industry." The police commissioner testified about rowdyism. Moral reformers charged that volunteers, who were allowed to bed down in the firehouses at public expense, had been bedding down with prostitutes, converting stations to de facto whorehouses.

The existing Board of Fire Commissioners offered feeble rebuttals but was ill equipped to controvert such charges. Sputtering was no match for statistics. The bill passed, weathered an immediate lawsuit challenging its constitutionality, and went briskly into effect. The new fire commissioners, moving swiftly to establish discipline, replaced competition between companies with a centralized command. The old system of summoning assistance by ringing the City Hall bell was replaced by an extensive network of fireboxes (by 1873 there were 548 boxes on Manhattan, connected by 612 miles of telegraph wire). Within a few years, annual losses from fire, and the amount of settlements paid out by insurance companies, had both dropped sharply, to widespread relief and applause.

HEALTH

Reformers also succeeded in establishing a Metropolitan Board of Health. Dr. John H. Griscom, who first called for creating a sanitary police back in the 1840s, had kept hammering at the issue throughout the 1850s and had been joined by other activist physicians like Joseph M. Smith, president (from 1854) of the New York Academy of Medicine. The doctors helped organize a New York Sanitary Association in 1859, which brought physicians together with civic-minded businessmen like Peter Cooper to agitate for change. The Association for Improving the Condition of the Poor signed on to the crusade, spurred like other reformers by the draft riots. "The mobs that held sway in our city," the Citizens Association agreed, had been generated in "overcrowded neglected quarters."

In 1864 the Citizens Association submitted a proposal for action to the state legislature. It went nowhere. The most vigorous resistance came, ironically, from the city inspector's office (Griscom's old department), which had oversight of sanitation. Inspectors opposed further transfer of municipal authority to Albany, partly on home-rule principle, primarily to hold on to their hefty level of funding (some of which they apparently diverted into the pockets of legislators who voted against reform). Antireformers also claimed that charges of unsanitary conditions were vastly overblown.

Griscom blasted his old department, noting that since he'd left twenty years earlier, its expenses had shot up, and so had the city's mortality rate. In terms of public health, Griscom charged, New York had regressed to London's position two centuries earlier. To counter opponents with solid statistics, militant physicians organized a Council of Hygiene and Public Health and initiated a block-by-block, tenement-to-tenement survey of Manhattan. Dividing the city into twenty-nine districts, the council assigned each a doctor, who visited every building and put to every family a written schedule of questions. Artists went along, sketched conditions, and prepared illustrations. The mammoth study (it ran to seventeen volumes) was then condensed to a five-hundred-page *Sanitary Report*, published in June 1865.

The report startled even those hardened by two decades of such surveys. The examiners had discovered that smallpox—a preventable disease—was rampant in the city; they turned up fifteen hundred cases in their first few days investigating. The Council of Hygiene called on the city to replace its voluntary (and disorganized) vaccination efforts with a compulsory program. But smallpox was only a small part of the story. Where Philadelphia's death rate per thousand was twenty and London's was twenty-two, New York City's stood at thirty-three. This meant that thirteen thousand people were dying each year from diseases and conditions that were probably avoidable. And for each death there were twenty-eight cases of disease: in some tenements, 50 to 70 percent of the residents were sick at any given moment. This added up to a vast amount of preventable illness and—a fact the council underscored for the business community—a corresponding loss of work hours.

By 1865 the Citizens Association had distributed two million sanitarian tracts in every part of town, sponsored many public meetings, and once again introduced a health bill in the legislature. Incorporating provisions of England's public health laws, it urged that a nonpolitical board of experts be given extraordinary powers to clean up

Scavengers on the Beach Street dumping barge, *Harper's Weekly*, September 29, 1866. Here, the paper said, men, women, and children dug through "the refuse of respectable folk" to find anything that could be used or sold to junk dealers. (Library of Congress)

unsanitary conditions. Union League Club members testified on the bill's behalf. Once again it was blocked by municipal bureaucrats and politicians and by those who resisted giving government agencies substantial power over property rights. The legislature did, however, authorize New York City's Croton Aqueduct Department to devise a plan for the systematic sewering of all Manhattan, free from interference by the Common Council.

At just this point, cholera tugged at the legislators' sleeves. In August of 1865 newspapers announced that the disease had reached Europe and was heading west. In November a steamship arrived with sixty cases aboard. A cold winter retarded its movement, but alarmed state lawmakers realized that in spring the plague might well scythe through New York's tenement population and then, as in the past, press on to devastate Syracuse, Rochester, and Buffalo. In February 1866, therefore, Albany created a Metropolitan Board of Health and gave it extraordinary powers to fight the scourge. The new board could order any person deemed a health threat removed from home to hospital. It could order property owners to rectify unhealthy conditions. Such orders could be enforced by the police or the board's own officers.

When spring came the board sent an army of agents marching through town, making house-to-house inspections and cleaning and disinfecting privies, cellars, and yards. It commissioned new street-cleaning contracts and oversaw the removal of vast amounts of filth from the city's streets (160,000 tons of manure from vacant lots alone). It got the city's butchers to clean up slaughterhouses and agree to their eventual removal north of 40th Street. The water supply was improved. New standards were imposed on the milk industry.

The mobilization helped keep New York's death toll under five hundred—one-tenth the fatalities of 1849, despite a one-third increase in population since then—while Cincinnati lost twelve hundred, St. Louis thirty-five hundred. New York had erected a milestone in the history of public health, but it was clear to reformers that securing their victory would require systematic attention to the city's built environment as well.

HOUSING

The war had exacerbated the city's housing crisis. New construction had limped badly while immigrants continued to pour in (over 150,000 in 1863 alone). With peace, demobilized veterans swarmed back home, and steamers disgorged ever greater numbers of newcomers. The 1865 report of the Council of Hygiene and Public Health demonstrated just how crowded the tenement districts were. Out of New York's seven-hundred-thousand-plus residents, 495,592 individuals were tenanted in 15,309 multifamily dwellings, an average of roughly seven families per building. Many of these five-or six-story tenements had each floor carved into eighteen rooms, organized like compartments on a train, hence the expression "railroad flats." Only two of these tiny rooms got direct sunlight (if the facade faced south), and interior cubbyholes were without ventilation, unless an extravagant builder included air shafts. Thousands more tenants were crammed into the back buildings landlords continued to insert behind tenements, often jammed up against their rear wall. In the Fourth Ward, the population density reached 290,000 per square mile.

Things got rapidly worse. In 1867 the legislature authorized another investigation. Again, statistics were amassed. Fifty-two percent of Manhattan's tenements were "in a condition detrimental to the health and dangerous to the lives of the occupants." Their deficiencies included insufficient ventilation, absence of light, lack of fire escapes, and terrible drainage. (When the tide came in, a basement in a filled-in swampland area could fill to a depth of twelve inches, high enough "to keep the children of the occupants in bed until ebb-tide.")

With rotten conditions came rising rents, which jumped 50 to 100 percent within a year after Appomattox, feeding a profit stream that flowed upward to the great propertied families from whom many slumlords leased their lands. Priced out of even tenement housing, the very poorest drifted to uptown shantytowns or, like Jacob Riis, a young and unemployed Danish immigrant, slept in doorways.

In March 1865 Germans near Tompkins Square held a mass meeting and called on the legislature to regulate rents; a year later they renewed their demands. The Council of Hygiene and Public Health called for strict public regulation of tenements. Radical Republicans supported imposition of minimum standards. The conservative Republican *Times* and Democratic *World* agreed, with the latter's editor, stunned by the investigations, declaring that "of all the diabolical, horrid, atrocious, fiendish, and even hellish systems of money-making ever invented by the mind of man, the tenement-house system of this city, is the most horrible."

In 1866 Albany enlarged New York's Department of Buildings, giving it a full-time staff, and established standards for municipal construction, creating the nation's first comprehensive building code. In 1867 the legislature passed the Tenement House Law, New York's first regulation of working-class housing. Modeled in key respects on London's 1848 Lodging-House Act, the act limited the number of persons permitted to reside in a given amount of space. It required that every room in new buildings have ventilation and that transoms be installed in older ones. It decreed the installation of fire escapes and the provision of one water closet for every twenty residents (one per hun-

Clearing Out a "Dive," *Harpers Weekly*, July 12, 1873. Basement
dwellers often clashed with the Board of Health's Sanitary Inspectors,
who were empowered to throw them out and dispose of their
possessions. (Library of Congress)

dred then being the norm). It outlawed domestic animals (except dogs and cats). It forbade renting out cellar apartments less than seven feet high. And it made landlords
liable to a daily fine for every uncorrected violation cited by the new Metropolitan Board
of Health, which was given enforcement responsibility.

Most landlords, builders, and real estate companies soon discovered, however, that
the Tenement House Law was loosely worded and loophole-ridden. A fire escape "or
some other means of egress" was required—a wooden ladder might do. Cesspools were
forbidden—except where unavoidable. Ventilation for a dark inner room could be provided by a window to an outer one. "Tenements" were legally defined as buildings with
more than three families, though many of the worst ones contained only that number.

Despite these obvious concessions to real estate interests, the law was a remarkable
stride forward. Reformers had made private housing a matter of public concern and
authorized government intervention to protect tenant health and welfare. The Metropolitan Board of Health pursued its duties vigorously, suing scores of city landlords for
code violations in over three thousand units in 1868 alone, and in succeeding years managed to cut the cellar-dweller population in half. Slowly, dilapidated wooden housing
gave way to new brick tenements constructed under the reformed building codes.

CITY BUILDING

"Generally the public works that have heretofore been carried out on this island have
been conceived on too narrow and limited a scale," said Andrew Haswell Green in 1865,
"We need not go off the Island," he amplified a year later, "to see lamentable results of
the want of largeness of ideas in the attempts that have been made to provide for the
growing wants of a great people," If "the planning of a city" were to be "done with any
degree of foresight," Green insisted in 1867, it was imperative to transfer authority to
"some body with comprehensive powers." The body he had in mind was his own Central Park Commission, and the powers he had in mind were Haussmannesque—nothing

less than authority to plan and oversee the expansion of all city services into northern Manhattan, and even Westchester.

Suggestions from Andrew Haswell Green commanded respect among New York's landed wealthy, for he had long since proven his devotion to their larger interests. Since 1844 the former wholesale clerk had been a partner in Samuel Tilden's law firm, where he worked closely with the eminent corporate attorney then urging consolidation on the railroad industry. Green himself offered investment advice and management services to owners of New York's great estates. He won their trust with his expertise, his pious Protestantism (a legacy of his Massachusetts upbringing), his extreme frugality (bordering on miserliness), and his pugnacious conviction that government should rest with the propertied, not the politicians. He himself had entered politics as an anti-Wood Democrat, been appointed by state Republicans to the Central Park Commission in 1857, and served ever since with distinction.

Though he shared many of the values of the reformers, professionals, and journalists then debating the proper "arrangement and management" of cities in periodicals like the *Journal of Social Science*, Green approached city building as a businessman rather than an intellectual. Well aware that property owners balked at infringements of their prerogatives, Green argued that comprehensive and orderly development would enhance the value of their property.

This approach resonated among members of the organized real estate "industry" that was now emerging in New York City. Businessmen concerned with property and its purveyance formed trade journals, like the *Real Estate Record and Builders' Guide* (1868), and established landowners' associations in various parts of town. Their goal was to systematize New York's haphazard approach to urban development and to discipline the city's chaotic real estate market, in the interest of enhancing profitability.

Such men cast envious eyes at contemporary Paris. "Despotic governments are generally bad governments," the *Guide* averred, "but when one hears of the marvels Napoleon has accomplished in Paris . . . , it makes us wish that he, or some one like him, could be made Emperor of New York for about ten years." Would-be developers at the *Guide* were particularly enamored of the French capital's stunning public improvements and stated baldly that "we want a Haus[s]mann who will do for New York what that great reconstructor did for Paris."

Uptown boosters attracted to this vision founded the West Side Association (WSA) in 1866 to promote extensive improvements in the area north and west of Central Park—the Badlands of Manhattan. Craggy slopes, running streams, and malarial pools marked the bleak and rocky land. It was barely accessible to downtown civilization: a single horsecar trudged along Eighth Avenue up to 84th Street, where it gave up, turned around, and trudged back. Intrepid travelers heading farther north could take a stagecoach up the Bloomingdale Road (now Broadway), but there wasn't much to see in these parts. The hamlets of Harsenville, Manhattanville, and Carmansville. Some miniature farms. Some squatter shacks occupied by poor immigrants, refugees from Central Park, and assorted outlaws. Some asylums, hospitals, institutional homes, country churches.

In the collective mind's eye of the WSA, however, the inhospitable terrain looked very different. The elevated plateau afforded magnificent views of the Hudson to the west and the splendid new Central Park to the east, and river breezes provided a salubrious climate. If the rugged topography were tamed—drained, roads and sewers put through, gas and water lines installed, scenic parks and tree-lined promenades created,

West Ninety-fourth Street, looking west across West End Avenue toward Riverside Drive, c. 1889. Although real estate promoters began to target the Upper West Side soon after the Civil War, development was slow. (© Museum of the City of New York)

centers of culture and learning sprinkled here and there—it might one day replace lower Fifth Avenue as New York's luxury *quartier*.

To hasten such a glorious future into existence, WSA boosters, ably led by lawyer-developer William Martin, petitioned the state legislature to give Andrew Haswell Green and the Central Park Commission (CPC) authority to transform the upper western wilds into a residential gentry preserve. Albany Republicans had already shown their willingness to expand the CPC's powers: In 1864 it had been asked to extend the park's pleasure drives above its northern boundary by turning Seventh Avenue into a shaded carriage way; in 1865 legislators charged it with fixing up upper Sixth Avenue and making over the old Bloomingdale Road into a tree-lined, Parisian-style "Boulevard."

In 1866, with Martin and the WSA applying the pressure, Albany gave the go-ahead for the CPC to develop a street and property plan for all territory above 155th Street (ungridded in the 1811 blueprint). In succeeding months and years, the legislature steadily expanded the CPC's mandate to include platting streets, designing ne works of parkways and promenades (including a grand Riverside Boulevard along the top of the bluff, and a racing lane for elite horseowners), arranging for parks (Morningside and Riverside), laying out suburban districts, improving up-island riverfronts, dredging a shipping canal at Spuyten Duyvil, and arranging for bridge and road connections across the Harlem River. Not only did the CPC now dominate the city-building process for all of Manhattan Island north of 59th Street and west of Central Park, but Green also took charge of forming a general street plan for the adjacent regions of the Bronx—still part of Westchester County.

Green now called for the annexation of western Westchester; "unity of plan for improvements on both sides of the river is essential," he said. This was soon arranged. In 1873 voters were asked to authorize the incorporation of the area, including Kingsbridge, West Farms, and Morrisania, into New York City. Then-Mayor Havemeyer opposed the plan, which he attributed to "speculators on both sides of the Harlem

River." Where would it all end, he asked: "Once entered on the mainland, where can we stop?" He was voted down, however, as Westchesterites opted overwhelmingly for access to the city's police, fire, water, sewage, and street-building services, while Manhattanites agreed with one newspaper editor who declared it "the manifest destiny of this great commercial emporium to spread in ever-widening circles over adjacent counties." And many voiced hopes of moving the "laboring classes" to "neat and comfortable cottages," accessible via "cheap workmen's trains." With the formal acquisition in 1874 of what would long be known as the "Annexed District," New York entered on the first phase of its imperial expansion.

With the Central Park Commission established as the nation's first de facto planning agency, the Prospect Park Commission emerged as a close runner-up. In Brooklyn, Andrew Haswell Green's counterpart was James Samuel Thomas Stranahan. An upstate New Yorker who settled in Brooklyn in 1844, Stranahan had made a fortune as a railroad contractor, become a principal investor in the Atlantic Docks and the Union Ferry, and served as a trustee of the Brooklyn Academy of Music and the Long Island Historical Society.

In 1859 the *Eagle* had argued that if Brooklyn were "no longer to be a suburb of New York" it needed to develop "extensive and well cultivated Public Parks." Mayor Powell agreed the following year, noting that "to attract a large population, it is indispensable that something else should be provided than interminable rows of brick houses along long lines of dusty streets, for these alone can never constitute a great city." Stranahan, public-minded capitalist, took up the challenge. He gathered other prominent citizens into a South Brooklyn Association and argued strongly for a mammoth three-hundred-acre park, one grand enough to entice Manhattan taxpayers to Brooklyn. The group proposed to locate it on Prospect Hill, an elevated area already a favorite with "pic-nic parties" and easily accessible via Flatbush Avenue, Kings County's major thoroughfare.

In 1860 the state legislature, following its Central Park procedure, created a Board of Commissioners (headed by Stranahan), which in January 1865, again following in Manhattan's footsteps, invited Calvert Vaux to prepare a plan of development. Vaux, soon accompanied by Olmsted, produced a design the commissioners believed would "hold out strong inducements to the affluent to remain in our city" rather than be drawn away by the "seductive influences of the New York park." In May 1866 the two, now the landscape architects and superintendents of the park, began directing the labor of hundreds of stonecarvers, masons, earth movers, and tree planters. Work proceeded rapidly during the late 1860s. Portions were opened in 1867 and 1868, and the work was essentially completed by the early 1870s, when even George Templeton Strong was forced to admit that Prospect Park was "a most lovely pleasure" and that in trees and views it "beats Central Park ten to one." The Brooklyn populace was equally pleased: in 1873 the park received 6,700,000 visits.

Stranahan, now known as the Haussmann of Brooklyn, followed Green's lead by extruding his commission's power beyond the park's boundaries, moving steadily from park design to urban planning. In 1868 Olmsted and Vaux proposed creating a "parkway neighborhood" surrounding Prospect Park that would offer "more wealthy and influential citizens" the rural satisfactions of air, space, and abundant vegetation. The commission was given extraordinary powers to open and improve streets, take property, and restrict land use. Though most of the costly project never came to fruition, it did eventually leave one major legacy: two grand "park-ways" radiating out from Prospect Park, for which Olmsted and Vaux cited Louis Napoleon's Avenue de l'Impératrice as precursor. To the east, stretching to the city's frontier, ran Eastern Parkway—a tree-lined dual carriageway quite like Manhattan's Boulevard—and the equally magnificent Ocean Parkway, which ran south to the sea.

In 1870 the legislature embarked on its last and most ambitious venture into urban reconstruction by appointing a Staten Island Improvement Commission to transform the malaria-plagued and hard-to-reach territory into New York's premier suburb. A "committee of experts," including Olmsted (an old Staten Island hand) and architect Henry Hobson Richardson, offered a fourteen-point, multimillion-dollar scheme to drain lowlands, improve ferry service, and build a comprehensive network of roads and parks, as well as suburban domestic neighborhoods, for the "class of people . . . able and willing to pay an advanced price for land and for improvements." The island's far-flung villages, however, proved unwilling to underwrite the experts' approach, and though piecemeal improvements were undertaken, the grand plan was never implemented.

WHITE MEN SHALL RULE AMERICA!

New York radicals' boldest intervention in civic affairs involved political rather than physical reconstruction. In tandem with Republican initiatives in the South and other states, New York's radicals pressed for giving the black population the right to vote. African Americans, in their churches, newspapers, and state conventions, had been demanding the suffrage as a fair return for their war service, and many radicals agreed a debt was due. The elimination of the existing $250 property qualification, moreover, might add eleven thousand blacks to the rolls, virtually all of whom would vote Republican. This was a bloc of considerable consequence, given that Republican Governor Reuben Fenton had won by only eight thousand votes in 1864 and that Democratic presidential candidate Horatio Seymour would carry the state by just nine thousand votes in 1868. The bulk of these potential Republicans, moreover, lived in the Democratic strongholds of New York City and Brooklyn.

Radicals first raised the issue at the state constitutional convention in 1867. Democrats, spearheaded by Henry C. Murphy of Brooklyn, resisted furiously. Playing a "scientific" race card, Murphy trotted out a "craniological" analysis that purported to prove the existence of superior and inferior breeds of man. Giving blacks the vote, Murphy argued, would lead to social equality, race mixing, and the collapse of civilization. Republicans countered that granting political rights would lessen the likelihood of amalgamation—which they too rejected—by granting blacks dignity. "There is no danger," one radical argued, "of the intermingling of the race by a man who respects his own blood."

Democrats pressed their racist campaign during the November 1867 elections. Banners at Tammany campaign rallies read NO SUFFRAGE NOR NEGRO EQUALITY! WHITE MAN'S GOVERNMENT FOR WHITE MEN! WHITE MEN SHALL RULE AMERICA! Riding the backlash, Democrats handily captured the state assembly and missed retaking the state senate by a mere two votes. When a proposed state constitutional amendment authorizing black suffrage was finally submitted to the electorate, in November 1869, the *Daily Eagle* asked the white man in the street: "Are you willing to declare by your vote that you are exactly and precisely the equivalent of a negro, neither more nor less?" The answer was a resounding no. New York repulsed black voting by 70.4 percent.

THE END OF RADICAL RECONSTRUCTION IN NEW YORK

The same 1869 election that defeated black suffrage gave Tweed Democrats control of both the Assembly and the Senate, completing their conquest of the state (Tweed's protégé, New York Mayor John Hoffman, had captured the governorship in 1868). Tammany's forces, marshaled by Grand Sachem Tweed, a state senator since 1867, now proposed a new city charter that would restore home rule to the metropolis by abolishing all the new state commissions and transferring their functions to ten departments controlled by the city (and Tweed). After thirteen years, power over the police force would be returned to the municipality, along with dominion over its own health, fire prevention, education, public works, charities, buildings, and docks. The proposed charter further strengthened City Hall, making all department heads mayoral appointees, and further hedged the Common Council, requiring it to muster a three-fourths vote on all bills involving expenditures. The charter also allowed the city virtually unlimited borrowing power for specified improvements.

Reformers were surprised but delighted. Tweed had proposed a simplified, centralized, fiscally responsible, and potentially effective city government. Peter Cooper of the Citizens Association strongly urged passage. So did the Union League Club, Horace Greeley, and a long list of prominent businessmen headed by banker James Brown and rentier John Jacob Astor. Even the Republican minority supported it, either reassured by promises that a strong voter registration law would be enacted or won over by hard cash—some six hundred thousand dollars' worth, Tweed later admitted. Governor Hoffman signed the charter into law in April 1870. In May Democrats easily won charter-mandated special elections for the Common Council, sweeping all fifteen aldermanic slots (one going to a budding politico named George W. Plunkitt).

Despite their acquiescence on the charter, Republicans, like their Klan-beleaguered southern counterparts, were not prepared to accept Tammany's electoral triumph without protest. Since 1868 Republicans had been compiling statistical evidence of Tammany wrongdoing. They leveled charges of straight-out fraud (some wards had more voters than residents), and they accused Tammany of mass-producing new citizens. Tammany Judge McCunn naturalized 2,109 petitioners in one day, a rate of three per minute—with "as much celerity," the *Tribune* observed caustically, "as is displayed in converting swine into pork at a Cincinnati packing house."

Republicans appealed to Washington, where their party still reigned. A sympathetic Republican Congress investigated in 1869 and agreed that "crimes against the elective franchise" had been committed. The "crimes" were only metaphorical, however, because Tammany practices contravened no existing law. Congress closed this loophole in 1870 with two pieces of legislation. An Enforcement Act—aimed at crushing both Ku Klux Klan resistance to southern Reconstruction governments and Tammany-style practices in northern cities—imposed penalties for obstructing or intimidating voters and authorized federal marshals or troops to supervise elections. A second law, the Naturalization Act, extended the waiting period between naturalization and voting by six months and established machinery to supervise voter registration.

New York Republicans used the new legislation to full effect in 1870. Federally appointed officials scrutinized registration proceedings and clapped some Democrats in jail even before election day. On October 25 President Grant ordered several regiments to the city's harbor forts and dispatched two warships to the East and Hudson rivers.

Democrats portrayed themselves as martyred defenders of civil rights and home rule. At a torchlight parade, Tweed told fifty thousand partisans to scrupulously obey the law on November 8. Tammany more or less followed orders—the courts created only two thousand new citizens, compared to the sixty thousand they'd turned out two years earlier—and Republicans had to admit it was a fair election. Which made the results—a total Democratic sweep—all the more galling.

The new charter had established a powerful municipal government, but that power belonged to Tweed. The trio of Tweed and his comrades Mayor A. Oakey Hall and Comptroller Richard Connolly constituted the new Board of Supervisors that controlled city finances, and Mayor Hall swiftly appointed his colleagues to high offices as well. Tweed himself presided over the Department of Public Works, a consolidation of the former Street Department and Croton Aqueduct Board. And one of Tweed's closest advisers, Peter Sweeny, took charge of the powerful Central Park Commission, now folded into a Department of Public Parks.

With control over parks, public health, and tenement regulation now removed from their hands, the elite stewards, who in their own minds stood for professional expertise, moral refinement, and the public welfare, worried that their regulatory state would be dismantled. In some cases, they were right. The new Metropolitan Board of Health became a haven for hacks and rapidly waned in effectiveness, and the Tenement House Law, easily evaded by bribing compliant inspectors, went largely unenforced.

Yet Tammanyites didn't scuttle all their predecessor's initiatives. In particular, they made the city-building project their own, though turning it to their own purposes. The reformers had seen their primary constituency (in the words of one association) as the bourgeoisie in general—"the class who have the largest pecuniary stake in the good order of the city and who also command its moral forces." The politicians were certainly prepared to extend municipal benefits to businessmen who were willing (or forced) to pay for them, but they also sought power and profit by dispensing patronage to working-class clients and siphoning off benefits for themselves.

Democrats backed public works projects far more grandiose than anything the Republican planners had promoted, to maximize the jobs they could hand out and the money they could pull in. Embracing a far more comprehensive and centralized approach to wielding municipal power than the laissez-faire Democratic Party had been accustomed to, Tammany politicians together with their bourgeois allies set out to reshape the urban landscape once again.

City Building

William Martin of the West Side Association was delighted with Tweed's rise to power, convinced that under a Democratic regime "the great public works on this Island would be vigorously pushed forward." Yet in his part of town, the pace of progress remained languorous at best. Olmsted was not asked to submit a plan for Riverside Park until 1875, and work began only in 1877. Masses of laborers did begin transforming the old Bloomingdale Road into the grand new Boulevard, laying out two fifty-foot-wide carriageways, broad sidewalks, and a thirty-foot-wide planted median, but that project alone wasn't enough to transform the drowsing countryside. In 1876 a *Herald* reporter found its lower extremities lined with saloons and shanties and its upper reaches, around 100th Street, used mainly by the occasional cowherd leading his charges to pasture.

There were many reasons for the sluggish pace of West Side development, but the most critical was the Tweed men's fixation on the opposite side of Central Park, a function in part of their heavy real estate investments in the area. The property owners who formed the East Side Association in 1868 had several things going for them. What their territory lacked in grandeur, it made up for in lower construction costs. The terrain from 59th to 110th, between Fifth and Third avenues, was relatively easy to grade, dig up, and build upon, and the Harlem Plains (north of 110th) were more accessible still.

Tendrils of civilization, moreover, had already climbed higher up Manhattan's East Side than its West. The New York and Harlem Rail Road up Fourth Avenue had opened up the area in the 1830s. In the 1850s horsecars came to Third Avenue, and by the 1860s it was lined with detached frame buildings, shops, and occasional groups of row houses. Horsecars ran along Second Avenue too, all the way up to 122nd, providing access to Harlem's modest cottages. By Tweed's time, with newcomers spilling westward along 125th Street, Harlem seemed ripe for full-scale development.

The East Siders' battle plan was straightforward: settle working-class families in brownstones and tenements along the arterial avenues, salt the transverse streets with row houses for the middle class, and entice the wealthy to Fifth Avenue mansions fronting the new Central Park. Hopefully the obstacles and nuisances littering the territory—shantytowns and slaughterhouses, breweries and quarries, stockyards and garbage dumps—would be forced over to the industrializing East River waterfront.

Tweed proved a perfect partner. As commissioner of the Department of Public Works, he authorized miles of sewer, water, and gas pipelines, appointed first-rate professionals to oversee the enterprise, and told them to build the best. Tammany sent civil engineer Alfred Craven to study European waste disposal systems, then sanctioned the use of technologically innovative vitrified tubing. Tweed appointed Edward H. Tracy chief engineer (he'd worked on the Croton Aqueduct under Jervis), and Tracy laid out the new underground network as a coordinated, unified system, in sharp contrast to the downtown jumble.

Next came roads. By 1873 over a thousand men in the pay of the Department of Public Works were laying out miles of hundred-foot-wide macadamized avenues (made using successive layers of stone broken into pieces of nearly uniform size) and substantial streets, at least fifty feet wide, with the key crosstown connectors (at 57th, 79th, and 86th) twice that size. The city also fostered development by leasing or giving away land to hospitals, schools, and museums—Mount Sinai, a Sisters of Mercy foundling hospital, the Normal (later Hunter) College—and encouraged Harlem's improvement by laying out Mount Morris Park at 120th and Lenox.

Contracting firms, employing great numbers of skilled construction workers, followed behind the public works crews and began erecting speculative housing. Much of it—aimed at middle class and better-off Irish and German workers—consisted of three-story brick row houses with brownstone fronts, equipped with gas, Croton water, and indoor toilets. Even the four-story tenements lining Third, Second, and First avenues were several notches up from those blanketing the Lower East Side, though shady, marginal operators perpetrated some inferior work. Municipal expansion allowed the Democratic Party to establish solid relationships with uptown contractors, brickmasons, stonemasons and plasterers, many of them Irish-American.

New housing blotted out the old. At Dutch Hill—the shantytown on 42nd Street at the East River—the city broke up the hundreds of one-room shacks, cobbled together out of old timbers and tin roofing, that had housed over a thousand full-time residents. Old mansions tumbled. The Astors' former estate at the foot of East 88th was torn down, as was the 1763 Beekman country home on East 51st Street. Workingmen digging the cellar for a building at Lexington and 104th Street uncovered a graveyard for British soldiers.

The construction boom sent land prices spiraling, and rumors of transit development sparked further hikes. Investors, convinced current values would be doubled or tripled in months, paid outrageous asking prices. Turnover was brisk, profits were taken quickly, and among the biggest profit-takers was William Tweed. He and his cronies bought heavily in uptown lands, especially in Yorkville and Harlem, and their properties became prime beneficiaries of—and spurs to—their many projects. In 1869, for example, Tweed and some friends bought the entire block bounded by Fourth, Madison, 68th, and 69th, had the city lay water pipes, and watched happily as their investment soared. Some bonanza hunters didn't wait for actual construction. In 1869 Terence Farley, a contractor and well-connected Tweed alderman, acquired a corner lot at Madison and 68th; the city announced the impending arrival of sewers and water mains; and within two weeks of his purchase, Farley sold out for a substantial profit. Tweed had West Side investments too, but his East Side ventures were three times as big, which likely accounts for some of the delay in launching West Side public works. There were others who argued that progress on mapping, coordinating, integrating, and upgrading the maze of disintegrating sewer pipes in lower Manhattan was unduly delayed by the pressure of real estate promoters pushing uptown expansion.

But Tweed's speculative exploits were matched by solid accomplishment. In the mid-1870s the *Real Estate Record and Builders' Guide* rhapsodized that "from One Hundred and Tenth street to Harlem river, from St. Nicholas avenue to the East river, the Boulevards and cross-streets are laid out and improved in the highest style of Tammany Art—opened, regulated, curbed, guttered and sewered, gas and water mains laid, with miles and miles of Telford-McAdam pavement, streets and avenues brilliantly lighted by fancy lamp-posts." Tammany had made the region "one of the most desirable and picturesque localities for residence."

Tweed had done his job well but expensively, with padded contracts inflating real construction costs. Some of the money came from city-levied property taxes, authorized by Tweed's charter, whose collection was overseen by the Tweed-dominated Board of Apportionment. Most, however, was borrowed by selling interest-bearing bonds on the open market. In 1867 New York had already owed thirty million dollars—for Croton, for Central Park, and for Civil War draft-related expenditures—but the debt tripled by 1871, to nearly ninety million dollars, with two-thirds of the increase coming between 1869 and 1871.

Much of this capital flowed from wealthy private investors—old-monied merchants and Civil War profiteers—who with stock market waters roiled by the likes of Jay Gould sought the more sheltered investment harbor of municipal bonds. City bankers were pleased to underwrite the public works program, which generated fat commissions and a hefty 7 percent rate of interest (payable, as was the principal, in gold). Trust companies and savings banks blossomed after the war, many boasting Tammany-affiliated officers, and these repositories for the spectacular fortunes accumulated during the boom bought up fifty million dollars' worth of city and county bonds by 1871. The international capital markets were another novel source. The Houses of Belmont and Seligman were skilled at financing railroads. Now they marketed New York City, selling its bonds in London, Frankfurt, and Paris.

RAPID TRANSIT

The one piece of infrastructure upper Manhattan still sorely lacked was a transportation system that could speed uptown residents to downtown jobs. On the East Side, the old New York and Harlem line, now part of the Vanderbilt empire, was a limited and unpopular resource. Property owners along Fourth Avenue had long been dismayed by the steam locomotives chugging up and down their thoroughfare, spewing smoke and cinders, and though Vanderbilt did open stations at 86th and 110th streets, rail access wasn't nearly sufficient. Nor was the old horsecar system. By 1872 Third Avenue cars built to carry twenty-two riders bulged with sixty or more during rush hour, and it could take an hour and a half to get to Wall Street. West Siders wailed that without fast transportation their area (as one promoter put it) would remain a "howling wilderness of vacant lots and rocks and morasses" from "which only death and the tax-gatherer will extract any harvest." Here Tweed's ambitions were the most vaulting. He planned to build a colossal, elevated Viaduct Railroad that would run along tracks mounted on massive masonry arches, forty feet high. Starting at a grand terminal he envisioned across from City Hall, two trainways would drive northward, plowing through the middle of blocks rather than along the avenues. One would proceed up the East Side paralleling Third Avenue to Harlem, the other up the West Side alongside Sixth Avenue to Spuyten Duyvil, thus encircling Manhattan Island. The cost was projected to be millions of dollars per mile.

In 1871 the Democratic legislature and Democratic Governor Hoffman authorized Tweed to charter the New York Railway Company and provided that after an initial subscription by private capitalists, the city treasury would contribute five million dollars to start construction. The company, moreover, was to be exempted from all taxes and assessments, could build anywhere it chose, and could condemn and raze anything in its path. With such extensive powers in hand, Tweed attracted the wealthiest capitalists in the city to the line's board of directors—including A. T. Stewart, August Belmont, Abram Hewitt, Joseph Seligman, and J. J. Astor—as well as prominent press barons James Gordon Bennett Jr., Horace Greeley, and Oswald Ottendorfer.

Not surprisingly, Tweed reacted crankily to competition from Alfred Ely Beach, editor-publisher of the *Scientific American*, who in 1868 had slipped a bill through the legislature permitting him to install an underground system of pneumatic tubes using compressed air. Beach claimed they would blow letters and parcels between Wall Street and a planned new post office at City Hall, but in fact he intended blowing *people* to and fro. From the basement of Devlin's clothing store at Murray Street, Beach had workers dig a nine-foot-wide tunnel twenty feet below Broadway, smuggling out the dirt after dark, that ran one block north, to Warren Street. Next, to ensure the popular acclaim that would overwhelm resistance from corrupt politicians, Beach installed a gas-lit entryway, a platform with frescoed walls, settees, and a grand piano, and a luxuriously upholstered twenty-two-person car. In February 1870 a huge rotary blower began propelling passengers smoothly back and forth—a public relations triumph that drew four hundred thousand riders that year, at twenty-five cents each. Nevertheless, the combination of Tweed's opposition, protests from powerful Broadway landlords who feared for their buildings' foundations, technical difficulties, and reluctance of private investors to undertake the enterprise led to its demise.

Charles T. Harvey had better luck. Back in 1867 he had received legislative permission to erect an experimental single-track elevated line on a half-mile stretch of Greenwich Street (just north from Battery Place). By June 1868 Harvey's scheme was precariously operational, with cables attached to stationary engines shuttling a car back and forth. Harvey was ruined in Jay Gould's Black Friday, but three years later, after several corporate reorganizations and abandonment of the pulley system, steam locomotives of the New York Elevated Railway Company began regular service along the single elevated track that ran up Greenwich and along Ninth Avenue to the 30th Street station of the Hudson River Railroad. For all its flaws—the engines belched sparks and inundated pedestrians below with ashes—the elevated railroad had proven its practicability. The future seemed rosy to uptown Manhattan's promoters, with the disturbing exception of the competitive behemoth rising across the East River.

BOSSES, BOOSTERS, AND BRIDGEMAKERS

Brooklyn was booming. Most new development still closely hugged the waterfront, especially industries with large land requirements; Havemeyer and Elder's mammoth sugar refineries; Appleton's printing and bookbinding establishment near the Navy Yard, manned by six hundred workers; Williamsburg breweries, far larger now than before the war; Mayor Martin Kalbfleisch's Bushwick Chemical Works; the score of refineries in Greenpoint along Newtown Creek, like Charles Pratt's, which processed oil shipped east by rail and floated to their front doors. Around these giants hundreds of smaller concerns clustered: in 1865 Brooklyn had five hundred factories; by 1870, a thousand; by 1880, over five thousand.

Residential districts near the waterfront also did well. The Brooklyn Heights and Cobble Hill complex expanded farther into South Brooklyn (today's Carroll Gardens) in these prosperous years. But interior territories near the new Prospect Park languished. Back in the 1850s Edwin C. Litchfield had assembled a seven-acre stretch of land that sloped downward from the crest of Prospect Hill. Construction of Prospect Park in the 1860s gave him hope that he could lure wealthy families into buying large plots and constructing grand urban town houses along its borders, villas like his own Alexander Jackson Davis-designed Grace Hall. Unfortunately, buyers showed insufficient interest in paying the kind of prices Litchfield had in mind, so, with the patience of the long-term developer, he settled down to wait. (He would in fact die, in 1884, before prices reached a satisfactory level.)

Other developers, encountering similar resistance from the well-to-do, tried to attract people of more moderate means. They tried to pull buyers from downtown Brooklyn or Williamsburg, both of which were rapidly changing into immigrant industrial or commercial districts, and to attract middle-class Manhattanites, who were being priced out of New York by escalating rents and land prices. Developers of Windsor Terrace had some success enticing buyers to streets stretching from Prospect Park's southwestern border down to Green-Wood Cemetery. But Kensington's developers did less well, while those who purchased large tracts south of the park around Ocean Avenue did downright poorly. Similar difficulties plagued Charles S. Brown, who

Oil Refineries on Newtown Creek, from *Harper's Weekly*, August 6, 1881. (© Collection of The New-York Historical Society)

bought land way to the east of the park, a place he immodestly christened Brownsville. Brown hadn't really imagined his domain becoming a middle-class suburb, what with the unpleasant smells wafting up from the marshes and bone-boiling plants of Jamaica Bay, but even working-class customers proved scarce.

Brooklyn's bosses and boosters, like those promoting uptown Manhattan, believed that poor transportation was the source of their city's problems, and they set about rectifying the situation.

Boss Tweed's Brooklyn counterpart was Boss Hugh McLaughlin, master of the Kings County Democratic Party. McLaughlin, whose parents had come from Ireland early in the century, had worked, variously, as whip boy in a ropewalk, waterfront gang leader, fishmonger, and master foreman in the Navy Yard before becoming a full-time professional politician. McLaughlin looked a bit like Tweed—he was almost as tall and fat—and he too concentrated on facilitating public improvements, then profiting from insider information about the direction of the path of progress. Real estate deals would make him a millionaire, but, unlike Tweed, he would avoid ostentation and continue to dress "like a Canarsie clam baker."

McLaughlin's chief colleague was William C. Kingsley, Brooklyn's most prosperous contractor. Kingsley made a fortune paving streets and installing sewers, then branched out into dealing in lumber and granite. He bought real estate, forged close ties to the Fulton Street banks and insurance companies, became publisher of the *Brooklyn Eagle*, and emerged as a major power in the city.

McLaughlin, Kingsley, and other boosters like J. S. T. Stranahan had been delighted with the Prospect Park Commission's work. Kingsley's companies did a great deal of the park's construction business, and Boss McLaughlin managed to buy up land where Vaux and Olmsted intended to place their grand plaza at the park's Flatbush Avenue entrance. But when the park failed to galvanize Brooklyn's interior development they refocused their attention on the transport problem.

Viewed by night from one of Brooklyn's lofty lookouts, the harbor sparkled romantically with the gaily colored lights of ferries plying their way back and forth from Atlantic Street to South Street, from Wall to Montague, from Fulton to Fulton. And Whitman's masterpiece "Crossing Brooklyn Ferry" was an exuberant hymn to its daytime glories. But practical men saw the system as a bottleneck, not a marvel, and the icy winter of 1866–67, which crippled river traffic, only underscored the problem.

A bridge over the East River at its narrowest point seemed the obvious solution. It would help farmers and brewers get their wares to market, perhaps even attract customers to Fulton Street shops, and, above all, allow Manhattanites to live in Brooklyn and work in New York. But would-be bridgebuilders confronted formidable obstacles. The East River, a tidal estuary prone to surging currents, was dauntingly wide, and conventional bridges would block the flow of maritime commerce. Only a suspension bridge of hitherto unachieved dimension—high enough to afford clearance to even the tallest sailing ships, and long enough to overleap the treacherous currents—had a chance of succeeding, and only John Augustus Roebling had a chance of building it.

In his native Germany, Roebling had studied architecture, hydraulics, and bridge construction—and philosophy, with Hegel, who thought Roebling one of his brightest pupils. In 1831 he had migrated to the United States, joined a farming colony, worked as a canal engineer, and developed a wire cable, which he used in building iron bridges that allowed America's proliferating rail lines to surmount its abundant rivers. At Niagara Falls locomotives shuttled serenely across the great gorge on Roebling's breathtaking International Suspension Bridge. Contacted by promoters of the East River crossing, Roebling laid out a magisterial plan. He would build the longest suspension bridge in the world, eighty feet in width (as spacious as Broadway, he liked to point out) with plenty of room for cable cars. The span would be supported by steel cables strung over two massive masonry towers—which if built would be the largest structures ever built on the North American continent—and the cables would be rooted to onshore seven-story stone anchorages.

If technical obstacles seemed bridgeable, political currents remained treacherous. In 1867, when William Kingsley broached the idea of chartering the New York Bridge Company, he turned to State Senator Henry Cruse Murphy, point man in Albany for Brooklyn's Democrats. Son of a Brooklyn judge, Murphy had had a distinguished legal and diplomatic career, helped found the *Brooklyn Eagle* back in 1841, served as Brooklyn's mayor and congressman, and taken part in the city's economic evolution, most recently as a developer of Coney Island (another potential bridge beneficiary).

Murphy designed a charter for the Bridge Company that would fix its capital stock at five million dollars and authorize the City of Brooklyn to subscribe three millions' worth and the City of New York one-and-a-half million, with the rest to be taken up by private shareholders. Brooklyn authorities, he knew, would do their part. The key problem lay in Manhattan, where the phalanx of promoters and politicians booming the upper island worried a bridge would siphon off potential home buyers. In addition, New York warehouse owners feared loss of business, and its taxpayers fretted at the enormous costs involved. But only one voice counted in the end, and it belonged to William M. Tweed. To find out if New York aldermen would accept a half-price deal, Murphy paid Tweed a visit. Tweed allowed as how the aldermen would probably come around if encouraged by sixty thousand dollars or so. Murphy authorized the expenditure—according to Tweed, though Murphy denied the story—and Kingsley provided the cash, carried over from Brooklyn in a carpetbag.

To recompense Tweed, hardly interested in such paltry rewards, Kingsley bought up and gave over roughly half the outstanding private stock to the Boss and two Tammany colleagues. The stock was incredibly valuable because under Murphy's charter, only private stockholders had voting rights. The cities, which would put up 90 percent of the capital, were to be, in the truest sense, dummy partners. For Tweed, this opened up magnificent vistas—jobs for constituents, kickbacks from contractors—a treasure chest that would more than offset any potential damage to his uptown investments.

This tawdry but obligatory business behind them, the Bridge Company (Henry Murphy, president; William Kingsley, chief contractor) set to work. Roebling, named chief engineer in 1867, gathered a crack crew and had just about completed preliminary planning when, on June 28, 1869, an accident crushed the tip of his foot, which led to lockjaw, seizures, a coma, and death on July 22. The company passed the engineer's mantle to his son, Washington, who had worked on bridges for the Union Army and, at his father's request, visited Europe in 1867 to study the use of pneumatic caissons.

Young Roebling's first task was to design and oversee the construction of just such caissons—essentially huge, watertight, submersible boxes that could shelter work crews while they dug down in search of bedrock on which to erect the giant towers. In May

1870 the first caisson was floated four miles down the East River from the Webb and Bell yards to just beside the Fulton ferry slip. Now, invisible to onshore watchers, the mostly Irish, German, and Italian laborers set to work under limelights—calcium lamps normally used for stage lighting or nighttime political rallies—boring their way down through traprock and basalt, at fewer than six inches a week. To speed the process, workers using long steel drills hammered holes in the obdurate rock, tamped them full of blasting powder, and set them off. Working around the clock (three eight-hour shifts every day except Sunday), the rate of descent accelerated to twelve to eighteen inches a week, and the bottom was soon reached.

In May 1871, while the Brooklyn tower rose ponderously out of the water, the process began again on the deeper, more difficult New York side. Now to the grueling work and foul odors were added incidents of a strange and painful disease. Laborers found blood spurting from their noses and mouths and fell prey to terrible cramps, which so contorted their bodies that the ailment was named "the bends." As the shaft sank deeper, workers began to die (young Al Smith, who lived near the construction site, listened to neighborhood talk of their horrible deaths). The company hired a doctor to investigate and while he never quite identified the cause—nitrogen bubbles trapped in the blood—he more or less stumbled on the solution, a slower transition from compressed to normal atmosphere. He urged a five-to-six-minute exit procedure (twenty minutes would have worked), but with the company in a hurry to finish and

Building the Brooklyn Bridge, 1877 engraving. (© Collection of The New-York Historical Society)

workers in a hurry to get out, they settled on a two-to-three-minute transit—so men kept dying.

On May 8, galvanized by the terrifying conditions, the caisson men struck for an increase in pay: three dollars for their four-hour stints. The Bridge Company agreed to $2.75, which the men angrily turned down, but when Kingsley announced he would fire them all, the strike collapsed. Roebling, aware laborers were at their limits, gave orders on May 18 to halt further digging, chancing that the level already reached, though not bedrock, would provide a sturdy enough base. Now the final stages commenced—though without Roebling. His health crushed by the ordeal, he spent the next several years in European spas and in Trenton, New Jersey, trying in vain to recover, but all the while directing the ongoing work via letters to his on-site assistants.

In June 1875 the Brooklyn tower was finished. Little over a year later the last stone was set in place on its New York counterpart. As crowds watched on both shores—it was the "best attended circus in the world," said the *Tribune*—the first cables were strung over the tops of the immense towers, taller even than the spire of Trinity Church. Finally, on Friday, August 25, Master Mechanic E. F. Farrington, an agile sixty-year-old, donned a linen suit and a new straw hat and climbed into a little seat attached by pulley to the wire rope. Then, as tens of thousands cheered, cannons roared, church bells clanged, and tugs shrilled their whistles, Farrington was hauled aloft to the flag-bedecked top of the Brooklyn tower, sailed serenely across the river (lifting his hat from time to time), and then brought safely down, twenty-two minutes after his departure, on the tumultuous Manhattan shore. The bridge's span would take years more to complete, and the 1876 mini-Festival of Connection would be dwarfed by the official one in 1883, but it was as plain as the sparkling August day that a momentous conjuncture had been wrought.

CONSTRUCTING QUEENS

The great postwar boom roused even slumbering Queens. Here, however, no formidable state commission would undertake large-scale planning, nor would an alliance of powerful politicians and private investors direct large-scale development. It was, rather, an ill-judged action of Brooklyn's that proved to be the crucial agent of change.

Since 1832 the Long Island Rail Road (LIRR) to Jamaica and points beyond had run east along Atlantic Street (later Avenue) from Brooklyn's South Ferry. Objections to the smoky and dangerous steam engines and to the cargoes of manure they hauled had forced the line (in 1844) to submerge its first two thousand feet of tracks in a tunnel under Atlantic. In 1859, however, responding to years of continuing complaint from area merchants and homeowners, the state legislature banned steam locomotives from Brooklyn altogether.

In 1861, accordingly, the tunnel was sealed up (and eventually forgotten, only to be rediscovered in 1980). The LIRR moved its operations to Queens. For its new depot, the company chose Hunter's Point, an easy ferry crossing from Manhattan's 34th Street and already, since the 1850s, western terminus of a railroad from Flushing. From Hunter's Point, the company ran a line directly to Jamaica, where it linked up with the main road on to Greenport. By the early 1870s rival rail lines connected the Hunter's Point hub with Rockaway and Whitestone, and a turnpike (now Jackson Avenue and Northern Boulevard) had been pushed through to Flushing.

Long Island's commuter and commercial traffic quickly reoriented itself along the new rail and road arteries. Many of Brooklyn's warehouses, stores, hotels, and banks closed or relocated. Kings' loss proved Queens' gain. Soon Hunter's Point resembled a western boomtown. Entrepreneurs built hotels, saloons, boardinghouses, kerosene refineries, and coal and lumber yards. A massive depot with engine houses and machine shops went up. Housing, churches, and schools arrived.

Like many western towns, Hunter's Point developed a grandiose vision of its future. In 1869 it launched a drive to incorporate itself as Long Island City, an entity with imperial ambitions. Leading businessmen lobbied Albany. So did the pastor of St. Mary's Church, whose Catholic congregation included the town's Irish factory and railroad workers. In 1870 the state legislature decreed a shotgun wedding between industrial Hunter's Point, aristocratic Ravenswood, and affluent Astoria. In 1872 the county seat was transferred from Mineola to the new Long Island City, and by 1876 a grand new courthouse had been completed at Thomson and Jackson avenues.

It soon became apparent, however, that ambition had outrun reality. Vast marshes separated the new city's component regions. These marshes, once drained by tidal flows, were now fouled with factory and slaughterhouse effluvia and had become breeders of endemic malaria. Some heroic (and lucrative) draining and filling was undertaken, but the task was beyond the fledgling city's means. Though the Long Island Rail Road tried to knit together a transportation infrastructure by acquiring its competitors, it failed. Long Island City, moreover, was as politically fragmented as it was spatially divided, riven by endless contention between wealthy families to the north and immigrant workers to the south.

Lacking a nucleus around which to crystallize, Queens, as in the past, would be developed by discrete local initiatives—chiefly, in this era, company towns launched by big-city industrialists, and residential suburbs founded by speculators. The preeminent postwar company town was developed by William Steinway. After the Civil War, Steinway and Sons' success at marketing its upright pianos outgrew the production capacities of its 52nd Street factory in Manhattan. Steinway was also concerned to shelter his workforce from "the machinations of the anarchists and socialists, who," he said, "were continually breeding discontent among our workmen and inciting them to strike."

In 1870 Steinway began buying up farms and estates in northeastern Astoria overlooking Bowery Bay. He acquired four hundred acres of the most lightly taxed land in the city, including woodland, salt meadows, and open fields in virtually primeval condition, plus half a mile of waterfront property. At water's edge he constructed a pianoforte production complex, which included an iron and brass foundry, a steam sawmill, boiler and engine houses, and a large building for making iron frames. On the waterfront, an enclosed dock and basin could hold millions of square feet of lumber—the logs floated in and kept moist while awaiting processing—and receive barge deliveries of foundry sand and pig iron.

Steinway set up summer quarters in the old Pike mansion overlooking the bay (the family wintered at Gramercy Park). His German laborers camped out in Long Island City hotels or commuted from Yorkville via the 92nd Street ferry (soon known as the Piano Ferry), where they were picked up by stage and brought to the factory. In 1873 Steinway began building a town—grading, leveling, and macadamizing the roads at his expense. Private money also built the waterworks, installed the sewer system, constructed a railroad spur, and installed a telegraph line connecting the new facilities with the Fourth Avenue factory and the 14th Street showrooms. Finally, Steinway's Astoria

Homestead Company erected frame houses for sale to workingmen and more substantial homes for "well-to-do refined people."

Steinway's efforts were matched by Florian Grosjean. After outgrowing his Manhattan factory, which churned out tin cooking utensils, Grosjean settled on Woodhaven Village (bounded by today's 95th and 97th avenues, Woodhaven Boulevard, and 85th Street, in what is now Ozone Park). Here Grosjean built a new factory, over a hundred workers' cottages (half he sold, half he rented), a hotel, shops, churches, a market, and a school. By 1873 Woodhaven—which was accessible by rail (along Atlantic Avenue) and wagon (along the Jamaica highroad)—had become a going concern.

Corona, on the other hand, was a residential development, not a factory town. In 1867 music publisher Benjamin W. Hitchcock had successfully launched the village of Woodside. Now the peripatetic developer moved east (along today's Roosevelt Avenue) to West Flushing, home since the 1850s of the Fashion racetrack. Hitchcock bought twelve hundred lots, christened the area Corona, prevailed on the Flushing Rail Road to open a station at National Avenue, and, after a brisk sales campaign in 1870, sold off hundreds of lots (P. T. Barnum bought two).

Next, in 1871, Hitchcock organized the New York Suburban Building Society, offering loans to the land buyers (repayable in easy ten-dollar monthly installments) to help them build on their plots. (Adding a western touch, he called this the "homestead system.") So many "homesteaders" erected homes that professional builders and masons from nearby Flushing flocked in, and Hitchcock had to install a sawmill to keep up with demand. The paraphernalia of social life followed: a firehouse, stores, saloons, meeting halls. A Catholic church went up on the former racetrack's property in 1872, and a Sunday school was opened by the president of the Bank of New York, who owned a mansion nearby. In 1873 the well-established village, having met the requirement of six hundred people within one mile, was crowned with a post office. In 1875 the restless Hitchcock floated farther east to begin yet another project.

HIGH FINANCE

In the wide-open spaces of Queens, Brooklyn, and uptown Manhattan, planned developmental initiatives were the norm. Lower Manhattan, by contrast, evolved out of countless calculations and decisions by an astounding number of participants, none of whom was capable of exercising a decisive influence. Businesses jockeyed for position, with the real estate market serving as the principal sorting mechanism; the soaring costs of land, assessments, and rents reserved the most valuable space for the most prosperous users. Through a ceaseless process of tearing down and building up, the once compact business district was rapidly reconstructed and broken down into discrete clusters devoted to particular functions: finance, communication, shipping, retailing, and commercial entertainment.

The financial district grew both laterally (it now stretched to City Hall) and perpendicularly (beginning its ascent toward the sky). Hundreds of private banks and trust companies were founded in the late 1860s and early 1870s, and they spawned scores of new headquarters buildings, like Drexel, Morgan's at Wall and Broad. Brokerage firms multiplied like bees and settled into rented office space; their agents hived together at the New York Stock Exchange, John Kellum's Tuscan palazzo.

Galvanized by the wartime risks of military service, the life insurance business had surged as well. The assets of New York companies (who controlled some 85 percent of the national market) multiplied eleven times during the postwar decade, rising to nearly a quarter of a billion dollars. Growth led to a spate of headquarters construction by the likes of Equitable, Mutual, and New York Life.

The burgeoning office district was not, however, primarily built and tenanted by the corporations directing western development—railroads, mines, oil—but by the host of businesses and professionals that sprang up to serve their needs. Corporate law firms multiplied (by 1870 there were two and a half times the number of lawyers as in the mid-1850s boom). Express firms expanded their outreach. American Express, which had concentrated on transport of goods, currency, and securities in New York State, now offered services nationwide and moved into the former Taylor's building—the 1850s "restaurant of the age" had closed in 1866—on Broadway and Franklin. Lewis Tappan's old Mercantile Agency, wholly owned since 1859 by R. G. Dun, soon had twenty-eight branch offices in the nation's major commercial centers and over ten thousand reporters or investigators handling the five thousand requests for information that poured in each day. The tremendous demand for credit information on ever more distant clients kept the rival Bradstreet Agency booming as well.

Railroad and telegraph revolutions transformed the marketing of commodities too. Old-style cotton factors, who had extended credit to planters, were replaced by jobbers, who bought cotton directly at southern railheads and resold it to British or New England textile mills. In 1870 the New York Cotton Exchange was established, allowing these brokers to collectively standardize grades of cotton, inspect samples, and begin a market in futures, to reduce risk. In 1873 the Butter and Cheese Exchange opened on Greenwich Street, near the railroad terminals where dairy shipments arrived; here too buyers and sellers met to examine products, negotiate prices, and get information on future crop prospects. The New York Produce Exchange similarly let merchants examine samples from individual lots of grain, and in 1874 it established trading pits for such transactions.

All these businesses, and swarms of others, needed two things: proximity to one another—as profitability depended on access to information, markets, and capital resources—and space, for their burgeoning staffs of administrative and clerical workers (Equitable Life, in addition to top management, administrators, and agents, had two hundred clerks processing policies). The only way to achieve both proximity and space, given downtown's circumscribed terrain and sky-high land prices, was by thinking big and building tall. Before the war, five-stories was the rule, and commercial life was carried on primarily at ground level—in streets and showrooms, at sales counters, on exchange floors. After the war, office buildings went vertical, climbing to unprecedented heights—six stories, seven, eight. "Our business men are building up to the clouds," one newsman exclaimed.

The elevator made this possible. Lift technology had improved since the vertical screw used at the Fifth Avenue Hotel. Now the "steam and drum" method was available. Steel wire cables were run over a drum at the top of the shaft, which was then revolved to raise or lower the cab. An alternative model hauled the cage up and down the shaft by looping its wire cable over a pulley, then attaching a wrought-iron bucket almost as weighty as the cage. When filled with water from a tank, the bucket descended by gravity, pulling the cage up. At the bottom, an operator emptied the bucket, shifting the weight balance in favor of the cage, which then descended and pulled the bucket back up.

The "Metropolitan Steam Safety Elevator" in Lord and
Taylor's store at Broadway and 20th Street. (Courtesy of Otis
Elevator)

Elevators made upper floors profitable, bringing in the rents required to offset the
rising cost of land. Directors of Equitable Life were skeptical of consulting-engineer
George Post's plans to make their proposed seven-and-a-half-story headquarters at
Broadway and Cedar into New York's first office structure with steam passenger elevators. They were reassured somewhat when the young man rented an upper-floor suite of
offices at twice the market value to demonstrate his confidence. Two months after it
opened in 1870, Equitable easily leased out the fifty upper story rooms to financial and
legal firms, and four months later Post sold his lease for a profit of six thousand dollars.
Multitudes came to ride the iron-framed building's elevators to see the panoramic view
afforded by this first example of what in time would be called a skyscraper.

Tall buildings raised stylistic problems, and possibilities too. Many owners played it
safe, commissioning structures modeled on the commercial palazzos of the 1850s. A
more adventurous solution was to make the building "modern" by topping it with a
mansard (or "French") roof. This transformed "Italianate" into "Second Empire,"
drawing on the cachet of Napoleon III's France and the elegance of Haussmann's Paris.
Continental Life introduced the mansard roof to the business district at 100-102 Broadway; New York Life Insurance Company followed suit; and Mutual, to stay in vogue,
was forced to call John Kellum back to add two mansarded stories.

COMMUNICATION GIANTS

The Second Empire solution was also adopted by the federal government for its new
post office, which went up in City Hall Park in 1875. The tremendous increase in business correspondence, the emergence of the railroad mail car, and Congress's approval of

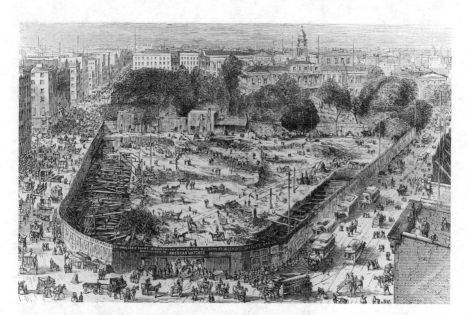

Construction of the new Post Office, *Harper's Weekly*, October 23, 1869. (© Collection of The New-York Historical Society)

free urban delivery in 1863 had channeled staggering amounts of mail into the metropolitan area. Some six million letters were delivered locally in fiscal year 1867–68 alone, despite complaints that it was easier to get mail to Boston than to Gramercy Park. The post office was still headquartered in the dark, overcrowded, seventeenth-century Middle Dutch Church on Nassau Street, where it had moved in 1845. So when Alfred B. Mullet was asked to build a new central post office he thought big and raised a colossal Second Empire structure in City Hall Park; widely hated for overshadowing City Hall itself, it was contemptuously nicknamed "the Whale."

A more revolutionary architectural development lay two blocks south, at Broadway and Dey, where, in 1872, the cornerstone was laid for what was about to become the nation's tallest office building and home to the nation's first continental-scale enterprise: Western Union. The company had done well in the war, receiving massive government subsidies and fourteen thousand miles of government-built lines, and in 1866 had merged with its leading rivals, using massive quantities of Cornelius Vanderbilt's money, and relocated to New York City. Its virtual monopoly on national telegraphic communications gave Manhattan the technological wherewithal to monitor capital and commodity movements on a national scale and also helped triple the volume of messages between Manhattan and Europe by 1875. New York's lock on the new information order was further secured with a December 1865 compact between Western Union and the Associated Press, in which each agreed not to patronize one another's competitors or accept clients who did.

When Western Union commissioned construction of a nerve center to coordinate its over 12,600 offices—and to reflect its wealth and glory—it turned to Equitable's George Post. The architect-engineer had several novel problems to solve, stemming from the building's projected height, a hitherto unimaginable ten stories—notably the question of how to design surfaces lifted far beyond any street watcher's ability to grasp them. Post opted for a tripartite organization that would become standard for tall towers. A massive base—required by masonry construction, which needed thicker walls to support additional higher stories—supported a shaft section, boldly striped with red pressed brick and granite. Atop this was perched a showpiece capital—a Renaissance palace—and a clock tower, which featured a ball, synchronized with the Naval Observatory in Washington, that fell precisely at noon, allowing mariners in the harbor to set their chronometers and ground-level businessmen to adjust their watches.

When completed in 1875, the Western Union building stood at 230 feet, featured one of the first hydraulic-gravity elevators, and had its own wells beneath the cellar, from which water could be pumped to the roof by steam pumps in case of fire. The office, which housed one hundred telegraph operators in the vast open reaches of the eighth floor, was open 24 hours a day and brilliantly illuminated through the night. New York had become a city at least part of which never slept.

The great newspapers too began to climb skyward. Most still congregated just east of City Hall Park amid a thicket of magazines, news agencies, job printers, type foundries, lithographers, engravers, bookbinders, stationers, and publishing houses. The day's copy (much of it taken from the telegraph wires) was assembled at night, and the giant basement steam presses rumbled until the predawn hours. Newsboys, some of whom slept on nearby streets, picked up the still-warm sheets and began their sunrise deliveries. The newspapers, already voracious consumers of space, with their extensive staff and bulky presses, were also expanding rapidly. This dictated larger headquarters, for purposes of practicality and for competitive display.

James Gordon Bennett's *Herald* launched the process. When Barnum's American Museum burned down in July of 1865—a spectacular blaze, which left a dead whale in the street for two days—Bennett decided to erect a showpiece building on its Broadway and Ann Street site. He selected architect John Kellum, who by 1867 had turned out another of the mansarded Second Empire structures that were now the rage.

Perhaps Bennett's project, together with Oswald Ottendorfer's construction of new quarters for his *Staats Zeitung* at the corner of Chatham and Tryon, inspired Greeley to outdo them all and trump even Western Union. He commissioned Richard Morris Hunt—the first American architect trained at the Ecole des Beaux-Arts in Paris—to raise an *eleven*-story mansarded building, the Tribune Tower, on the corner of Nassau and Spruce. Like Post, Hunt divided his granite and brick structure into an imposing base, a repetitious shaft, and a dramatic summit: a clock-campanile that, when completed in 1875, soared to 260 feet, now within nine yards of Trinity's crown.

RAIL COMPLEX

Some of Louis Napoleon and Baron Haussmann's most dramatic interventions in the Parisian cityscape had been designed to integrate the French capital into the national rail network. Cornelius Vanderbilt, whose consolidated lines now connected the western heartland to the heart of Manhattan, similarly realized that to maximize his system's efficiency, he (and his son William) would have to complement their rail building with city building.

Vanderbilt's primary effort lay far uptown, where he decided to build a passenger terminal that would service both the Central and Hudson road (which ran down Tenth Avenue) and the Harlem and New Haven lines (which ran down Fourth Avenue to the shed at 26th Street). Ridership on the three roads had doubled in the 1860s, a function of increased suburban commuting and an increase in long-haul travelers, enticed by new luxuries such as through-ticketing, sleepers, diners, and parlor cars.

Neither existing terminal seemed suitable. Tenth was too far west, and 26th too far south, given that the city still required that any train running below 42nd Street be hauled by horsepower, not steam power. So Vanderbilt settled on Fourth Avenue and 42nd Street as a suitably central location. To make the East Side venue accessible to his West Side line, he had tracks laid along the north bank of the Harlem River from Spuyten Duyvil to Mott Haven. This allowed Hudson trains coming south from Albany to enter the city via the Harlem's Fourth Avenue route.

Construction of Grand Central Depot began in 1869. It took two years and three million dollars to finish, a sum raised partly by selling off the old station at 26th Street, which was soon converted into the first Madison Square Garden. When the depot opened in 1871, the five-acre complex included a brick and granite neo-Renaissance station, twelve parallel tracks, and an immense iron vaulted shed, the largest enclosed space on the North American continent and a close runner-up to London's St. Pancras as the biggest train station in the world.

After Grand Central Depot opened, a hundred trains rattled to and fro each day, creating such a din that Columbia College, near the tracks at 49th Street, couldn't conduct classes. Under mounting pressure, Vanderbilt agreed to sink the tracks—if the city came up with half the six-million-dollar price tag. The municipality grumbled but paid, and by 1876 the tracks dropped below ground at 56th, not to emerge again until 96th. With his usual keen eye for developmental possibilities, Vanderbilt began buying up land cheaply along the still-unappealing Fourth Avenue—the future Park Avenue.

Way downtown, meanwhile, Vanderbilt was building a new freight terminal for the Central and Hudson. He purchased the once exclusive suburb of St. John's Park from Trinity Church and its co-owners for a million dollars. In its place he erected a massive three-story granite structure, topped with a 150-foot bronze pediment memorializing his achievements on land and sea, featuring a giant statue of himself. ("As a work of art," grumbled George Templeton Strong after the 1868 opening, "it is bestial.")

The new terminal revolutionized the Lower West Side. An enormous complex of grain depots, stockyards, and stables arose along the waterfront. Here, also, midwestern cattle, sheep, and hogs—fifteen thousand head each week—were dispatched in efficient new assembly-line abattoirs and dressed for transshipment to European markets.

The transport complex acted as like an enormous magnet, pulling wholesalers and related businesses west from old haunts near the East River seaport. Access to the national rail grid had already transformed commercial relations between New York and the interior. Before the war, rural shopkeepers had made semiannual pilgrimages to Manhattan to purchase imported consumer goods for the coming season at Pearl Street auction houses. With the spread of rail and telegraph links, the city went to the countryside instead. Wholesale merchants—jobbers—bought goods en masse from manufacturers; unlike the old commission merchants, jobbers actually took title to the commodities, pleasing manufacturers, who no longer had to await a final sale for payment. Then merchants like A. T. Stewart and H. B. Claflin established nationwide sales networks of "drummers." In the late forties such men had drummed up business from country merchants lodged at Broadway hotels. Now they swarmed west and south, displaying samples, reporting back on changing demand. Rural stores and urban shops then wired in orders to jobbers, who dispatched shipments immediately to the buyer's doorstep, no longer constrained by the seasons. The same rail-and-wire system would make it feasible for rival jobbers to emerge in the midwestern cities themselves, and soon Chicago, Cincinnati, and St. Louis would be major dissemination centers in their own right.

Many mercantile establishments fled the venerable East Side slips. South Street would remain the port's ground zero, but wholesalers, express companies, packing-box firms, and dry-goods commission merchants set up shop on the West Side near the freight depot. Economical and efficient cast-iron warehouses, equipped with the newest in freight elevators and "modelled after the sumptuous palaces of Italy," went up due west of City Hall and then north to Canal, and on into today's SoHo. These new warehouses—over two hundred went up in the Fifth Ward alone in the postwar decade—quickly filled with midwestern farm staples, New England manufactured products, and luxury goods from Europe and East Asia.

Other wholesalers followed the dry-goods giants. The city's hardware district had migrated from upper Pearl to Chambers by 1877, and the iron shops from lower Broadway to Washington and West. Only the leather-goods traders remained in their ancient territory: the Swamp (bounded by Beekman, Gold, Frankfort, and the East River). Workshops too tagged along. Processing and consumer-finishing manufactories flourished, finishing goods that moved in and out of the warehouses. Extra loft space was turned over to pieceworkers making boxes, notions, artificial flowers, or cigars.

LADIES' MILE

The spread of warehouses and factories bumped fashionable retailers from Broadway below Houston northward toward Union Square. A. T. Stewart had pioneered this transition during the war, when he shifted operations from his Chambers Street Marble Palace to his New Store at Broadway and 9th Street. Now competitors overleaped him, spilling into Union Square itself and pressing on toward Madison Square.

Some department stores opted for Broadway. Arnold Constable remoored itself just north of Union Square, on Broadway at 19th Street in 1868, and Lord and Taylor soon resettled a block farther uptown, in an ornate cast-iron five-story structure, replete with steam elevators fitted out with divans and plush carpets.

Others preferred Sixth Avenue, well serviced by horsecars. At 14th and Sixth, Rowland Macy expanded his original shop by taking over adjacent stores and adding departments rapidly. Macy, a close friend of P. T. Barnum, used his talent for publicity to draw clientele, producing thematic exhibits and fashioning elaborate Christmas extravaganzas that featured a store Santa and illuminated window displays, introduced in 1874. His competitors used architecture as publicity, erecting gigantic palaces of consumption. Majestic cast-iron frigates lined Sixth by the 1870s, including Hugh O'Neill's Byzantine-style building, domed and painted yellow and burnt umber, along with Altman's, Best, and Stern Brothers, the latter a two-hundred-foot-wide, seven-story monster on 23rd Street.

In the wake of these frigates sailed the sloops and schooners of retailing. Many moved into the basements and parlor floors of Union Square mansions and brownstones, none more than twenty years old, but vacated now by wealthy families fleeing north to Gramercy Park and Murray Hill. Silversmiths, dry-goods stores, confectionery shops, F. A. O. Schwarz, and W. and J. Sloane were among the newcomers. Tiffany's purchased the Church of the Puritans, demolished it, and in 1870 had Kellum

R. H. Macy's store, corner of Sixth Avenue and Fourteenth
Street, from Devorkin, *Great Merchants of Early New York*.
(The Collection of Macy's)

put up a cast-iron palace that boasted a storage vault where the affluent could leave their
plate and jewels during the summer Saratoga season.

The cast-iron arcades and glass show windows attracted armies of shoppers, mainly women. Broadway and Sixth were choked with female-filled victorias, landaus,
broughams, and coupes during afternoon hours, and the sidewalks thronged with elegantly attired women, promenading and perusing the windows. So emphatically female
an area was eventually dubbed the Ladies' Mile. The women were served by armies of
salesclerks, mainly male (though increasing numbers were female), whose lot was a
difficult one, as authoritarian management banned talking and imposed six-day weeks
and lengthy hours. During Christmas, when Macy's stayed open till eleven, male clerks
would often not bother going home but curl up in their bluish-gray uniforms and sleep
on the counters.

RIALTO

As department stores relocated to the Union-Madison Square area, another flock of
northwardly migrating institutions, the city's theaters, were touching down in the same
terrain. Theaters and emporiums coexisted amicably, in part because each increasingly
resembled the other. Stores had a new dramatic flair, and theaters, induced by new
opportunities out west, adopted the latest marketing techniques.

Railroads wrought a revolution in the New York stage. For over a century, the basic
unit of theatrical business had been the stock company. A Broadway or Bowery manag-

er—often a prominent actor—would buy a theater, equip it with sets and costumes, and engage a resident company to perform plays in repertory. Such companies did survive in the postwar world. Lester Wallack's theater, on Broadway and 13th Street, was considered by many the finest stock company in town, and it offered a steady diet of British Restoration comedies and the occasional romantic melodrama. Edwin Booth, who had retired temporarily after his brother John Wilkes assassinated Lincoln, returned to the New York stage in 1866 to thunderous ovations. He used his profits to open Booth's Theater on Sixth Avenue and 23rd Street, a technologically sophisticated and magnificently florid Second Empire temple to Shakespeare. Another prewar giant fared less well: the younger generation wrote off Edwin Forrest as a "ranter," and he gave his final New York performance in 1871.

Stock companies themselves were on the way out, along with the minstrel outfits. The future lay with the "combination" system. A star or manager would pull together an ensemble for a single play. It would showcase in New York, then take to the road on the new rail networks and tour the country. When the run was over, the company disbanded, and the promoter reinvested his profits (if any) in another New York production. The city had become a manufacturer of dramatic commodities.

This transformation of the entertainment industry affected the theater district's location and structure. Before the war, playhouses had been beaded along Broadway and the Bowery, with the Academy of Music on 14th Street at the apex. Now entrepreneurs—drawn by the crowds of shoppers in Ladies' Mile—opened playhouses between Union and Madison squares, along Broadway and Sixth Avenue, with the idea of renting them out for the length of a booked run.

The new combination system also required a complex array of support services. Since the tools of the theatrical trade—costumes, props, scenery—were no longer owned by each house, they had to be rented for each particular performance. Specialized businesses met the need, beginning with the Eaves Costume Company, formed by a former actor, which furnished wigs and beards, boots and shoes, tights and swords.

Actors too had to be assembled on a show-by-show basis. At first this was done in an impromptu way, with deals cut on benches in Union Square (known to some as the "slave market") or in nearby restaurants. Then professional talent brokers emerged, theatrical agents who mediated between actors and impresarios. They too set up offices around the square (the first being the Simmonds and Wall Dramatic Agency in 1875). To stay near the action, hundreds of young actors settled into theatrical boardinghouses nearby.

Actors aiming for the big time, and stars who kept their image brightly burnished, both turned to stage photographers like Napoleon Sarony, who opened his famous Union Square studio in 1871. Here actors posed in costume, with arresting props, before painted backgrounds, while the "father of artistic photography" worked his flamboyant magic, deepening New York's capacity to manufacture "celebrities."

Publicity was crucial to theaters, and the increased competition spawned a flourishing poster and playbill business. This in turn boosted the theatrical printing industry, which also turned out tickets, which were hawked by scalpers who wandered the Rialto crying, "I have seats in the front!" Printers ran off new trade newspapers, which covered the drama industry, playscripts, in great demand out in the country, and sheet music, for sale to middle-class families with parlor pianos, likely purchased at Steinway's Union Square showroom.

Trade papers, scripts, and music alike were also sold at the bookstores that clustered in the Rialto. Agosto Brentano, a Sicilian immigrant, had for years run a newspaper stand in front of the New York Hotel. In 1860, gambling his earnings, he bought in bulk an issue of the *London Times* recounting the Heenan–Sayer fight. With the windfall profits he garnered selling these to sporting men, Brentano opened a larger stand in Union Square. After amassing capital selling foreign and domestic papers, he branched into books and playscripts, opening Brentano's Literary Emporium in 1876. It became a popular rendezvous for the theatrical elite, as did specialty shops like Gustave Schirmer's and Samuel French and Son; another favorite haunt was the Lambs Club (1874), which met in restaurants around Union Square.

Rialto restaurants also drew evening crowds of theatergoers and men-about-town. Many local oyster and chop houses—like Shakespeare Inn and Browne's Greenroom—were opened by actors. Italian restaurants catered to Italian singers from the Academy of Music. As ever, the preeminent establishment was the ever prescient Delmonico's at Fifth Avenue and 14th Street, where it hosted champagne and canvasback dinner parties—*pre* and *après* the theater—for wealthy patrons of Wallack's and the Academy of Music. In 1876, sensing another impending shift in the center of theatrical gravity, Delmonico's closed its 14th Street operation and moved to sumptuous quarters at 26th Street.

DOWNTOWN DOWNSIDES

Lower Manhattan had emerged as a well-oiled business machine, whose discrete parts related synergistically. Capital, legal expertise, trade information, wholesale goods had easy access to one another. Commodities flowed smoothly from train station to warehouse to workshop to emporium or harbor. But while the marketplace had in many respects reordered the cityscape to meet the needs of the new economic order in a rational way, vexing irrationalities remained.

Nowhere were these more manifest than in the streets. As property values rose, and buildings rose with them, more people and goods were accommodated in the commercial quarters. As a result, traffic levels—chaotic enough before the war—now approached the point of paralysis. Costly paralysis, the *Real Estate Record and Builders' Guide* noted, as it forced merchants "to pay as much for the removal of a load from Courtlandt to Canal street as is required to bring it from Chicago to New York." When to gridlock were added spectacular accumulations of garbage—filth that sometimes reached knee level—the judgment of the *Evening Post* that "New York is the most inconveniently arranged commercial city in the world" was uncomfortably close to the mark.

Some of the disarray was a consequence of success: the terrific increase in flow of bulky agricultural goods, fuel, and manufactured products. Much of the muck followed from the still-unavoidable reliance on horses—forty thousand of them, who each working day generated some four hundred tons of manure, twenty thousand gallons of urine, and almost two hundred carcasses—exacerbated by municipal incompetence and corruption in garbage removal. Some difficulties stemmed from cramming a nineteenth-century economy into a seventeenth-century matrix of narrow and crooked former cowpaths. Others were the fault of the grid's blithe disregard of Manhattan's topography, or actual exacerbation of its shortcomings, as in emphasizing north-south arteries over east-west river-to-river connections. (Only Fulton Street spanned the lower island, and it perforce slammed head on into the torrent of eighteen thousand vehicles that daily made their way up and down Broadway, to say nothing of the flood of pedestrian shoppers.)

Some of the problems reflected limits of the era's technology. The city did replace cobblestones in Broadway, Wall, and West streets, among other key arteries, but replacements were not necessarily improvements. With asphalt still decades away, Department of Public Works officials relied on the "Belgian" method of setting granite blocks in sand. The slabs were durable (if horrifically noisy), but as they shifted in their foundations they produced a jarring, undulating ride; "carriages," reported one French visitor, "appear to rise and fall as if on a troubled sea."

Much of the difficulty lay in the inability to bring concerted public power to bear on the issue. Many of the city's business leaders, public officials, and journalists—thoroughly disgusted with the effects of the preceding generation's laissez-faire policies—clamored for a sustained and systematic approach to coordinating essential improvements in the built environment. "NO PIECEMEAL IMPROVEMENT WANTED," blared the *Guide* in 1870: "What is wanted is one, general, comprehensive plan for . . . the thoroughfares of the whole city." But the resistance of property holders to any constraints on short-term profitability, and the tremendous number of interested and competing parties, few if any of whom were willing to subordinate their interests to some larger vision, raised insurmountable obstacles to reform.

The docks provided a particularly egregious case in point. Thrown up in slipshod manner during the prewar boom, then neglected and abused, by the mid-1860s fewer than 10 percent were in good or fair repair. Docks periodically collapsed from the weight of merchandise piled high on rotting timbers or were swept away by the current. Wharves were too short and narrow for the era's larger vessels and increased volume. They lacked such modern improvements as the steam-powered hoists commonplace at seaports in Europe, along the eastern seaboard, and across the East River. Unsheltered and unsecured, they were subject to weather, fire, and theft.

Ship captains could wait a week to land cargoes; without paying bribes, they could wait forever. Municipal piers adhered to the strategy of underpricing rivals by keeping rents and wharfage costs low, but this failed to generate enough income to maintain, much less upgrade, them. Regulation was inconsistent or absent and occasionally perverse: the Albany legislature, to boost the toll-earning capacity of the state's waterway system, reserved the lower East River for its canal boat fleet, which clogged the piers around Coenties Slip, hindering deliveries of western grain.

Shipping continued to slip away to Brooklyn's modernized facilities. Following the huge financial success of the Atlantic Docks, extensive waterfront improvements flowered after the war. The vast Erie Basin complex at Red Hook sped barged-in grain to Liverpool steamers using steam-driven elevators. Public works complemented private metamorphoses, transforming Wallabout Bay marshlands into the Kent Basin municipal docks. From Main Street to Red Hook Point, three thousand vessels (not counting canal boats) tied up each year, disgorging molasses, sugar, coffee, hides, and wool into the burgeoning warehouse districts and grain into elevators capable of storing fifteen million bushels.

Frustrated Manhattan merchants cried out for port improvements. For a city that had "a whole country tributary to its power, a whole nation concerned in its welfare," said the Citizens Association, it was astonishing how little New York had done "to improve the commercial advantages which nature affords." The group sponsored a meeting of indignant merchants in 1867, which proposed formation of a state Harbor Commission to unite the Manhattan and Brooklyn waterfronts. Other merchants, shipowners, and marine insurers formed a New York Pier and Warehouse Company to build and lease a complex of stone quays, iron piers, and dockside stores with steam hoists and railheads.

The rise of Tweed's Democracy scuttled these plans—the machine was not willing to forego the patronage possibilities inherent in waterfront development—but Tammany proposed an even more ambitious agenda of publicly sponsored and planned development.[1] Tweed's 1870 charter created a strong, centralized, municipal Department of Docks, which sent engineers to London and Liverpool to study current approaches and commissioned General George C. McClellan to design a master plan. McClellan proposed a waterfront revamping similar to Tweed's projected Viaduct Railway in grandeur and potential cost. It called for ringing the riverside, from the Upper West Side round to Corlear's Hook, with a massive masonry bulkhead, a grand waterfront highway, and a uniform system of piers, with all private wharves to be absorbed by the city.

Some land acquisitions began in 1872, but the project soon slowed to a crawl. Owners of waterfront property, including some of wealthiest men in New York City, fought the project. Transport magnates like Vanderbilt lobbied hard to be given control of dock improvements, but rivals and concerned merchants blocked that initiative too. Other merchants agitated for complete deregulation rather than municipalization. In the end, the multitudinous shipowners, wharf owners, insurance firms, canal interests, rail lines, ferry companies, real estate promoters, wholesalers, and assorted corporations and individuals were utterly unable to agree on a collective solution. The very diversity of competing forces led to stalemate.

And worse. Land values stagnated along the East River waterfront, reflecting the rapid decline of the East Side shipyards and the rise of superior portside facilities in Brooklyn and New Jersey. Low-cost land attracted space-hungry industrial users— breweries, stables, refineries, grain and construction mills, coalyards—which further devalued the area, leading to disinvestment and accelerating squalor. The result was a downtown landscape that, for all its efficiencies and its lucrative centers of finance, communication, wholesaling, and retailing, coexisted with an inefficient public sphere and decaying, overcrowded communities.

---

1. The legislature did intervene in harbor affairs after an 1871 study by the U.S. Coastal Survey revealed that refuse dumping was fast filling up key harbor channels. Albany prohibited casting of wastes into the Hudson and East rivers, Upper New York Bay, and parts of Raritan Bay, though authorizing dumping in Lower New York Bay south of the Narrows, if okayed by the new state office of shore inspector. They also shut down the official garbage dump site established at Oyster Island in 1857 and shifted it to the southeastern side of Staten Island, though by 1877 much refuse was also being used as fill in Bayonne, New Jersey, and Newtown Creek.

54

Haut Monde
and Demimonde

In May 1871 the *New York Times* observed that elaborate preparations for the ball honoring Grand Duke Alexis of Russia had "kept all the aristocracy and respectability of this good city in a fever of expectation for weeks." Now, as instructed by the Reception Committee (which included John Jacob Astor, William Henry Vanderbilt, August Belmont, and John Pierpont Morgan), workmen at the Academy of Music were hoisting into position the evening's decorative centerpiece: two huge banners, one portraying Czar Alexander abolishing serfdom, the other Abraham Lincoln holding up the Emancipation Proclamation. Elite New Yorkers would thus proclaim their commitment to human liberty, while at the same time asserting their parity with the aristocratic classes of Europe.

Since the Revolution, Manhattan's elite had been torn between a lifestyle that befit their sober republican principles and one that displayed their increasing wealth and confidence. In the affluent fifties they had tilted toward public preening; now, in the gilded sixties and seventies, they lurched toward outright ostentation. The adoption of ducal levels of display was driven by tremendous self-assurance—engendered by their victory in war, mastery of the peacetime economy, and unprecedented accumulation of wealth. (After 1873, moreover, their riches would no longer be subject to federal exactions, thanks to successful lobbying and legal challenges by the Anti-Income Tax Association of New York, led by Astor, Belmont, Morgan, and others among the grand duke's welcoming party.)

The New York haute bourgeoisie's postwar passion for gilded display also reflected recent shifts in power, wealth, and cultural authority within its ranks. The frenzied industrialization and financial speculation unleashed by combat and reconstruction had weakened those in the elite whose prewar preeminence had come from trade. Sea-based merchants remained numerically superior among their peers—in 1870 38 percent of those whose combined personal and real property was assessed at more than fifteen thousand dollars dealt in commerce or retail trade—but land-and-rail-based industrialists (16 percent) and financiers (6 percent) were often richer, stronger, and more central to the city's changing economy.

These factions mixed and mingled in their social and business dealings, to be sure, and in some respects an ever more homogenized bourgeois culture was emerging. But important stylistic distinctions remained—with old-monied merchants tending toward the understated, and new monied industrialists and financiers favoring the flamboyant. Given the latter groups' new resources and the intensely competitive nature of Manhattan's elite socializing, customary constraints fell rapidly away. Upper-class rituals came to resemble those of European—and especially French—aristocrats, far more than they did those of antebellum American republicans. Nowhere was the penchant for princely display more evident than among those metropolitan millionaires who pursued their city's long-standing love affair with fine horses with heightened fervor, even as they presided over an industrialization of transportation that would terminate the equestrian age.

HOT TO TROT

After a hard morning fighting Gould, Fisk, and Drew in the Erie War, Cornelius Vanderbilt would harness up his team, drive north of Central Park to Harlem Lane (later St. Nicholas Avenue), and spend the afternoon happily racing heats against other whooping and screaming brokers and lawyers—to the cheers of sightseers on porches of inns along the route. Vanderbilt might well find Robert Bonner of the *Ledger* awaiting him with his new champion trotter, Dexter (for whom he had paid an incredible thirty-three thousand dollars). Certainly his partner Leonard Jerome would be there, a horse fancier of such intensity that he housed his team in a black walnut-paneled stable complete with wall-to-wall carpeting—lodgings that rivaled Napoleon III's Mews in

Fast Trotters on Harlem Lane N.Y., by Currier & Ives, 1870. (© Museum of the City of New York)

Paris, where Jerome had attended races with French dandies. August Belmont, when not selling railroad or municipal bonds, would be behind his sulky, urging on his prize horses. The actor Lester Wallack and even the Rev. Henry Ward Beecher were known for their fast teams. Indeed so famous an institution was Harlem Lane that when General Grant first visited New York after the war he immediately asked to be taken uptown to see the spectacle.

A more sedate type of horse-mania was the carriage promenade through Central Park. In the late afternoon the aristocracy climbed aboard their coaches and entered the park at Fifth Avenue and 59th Street; by four P.M. the miles of drives were alive with carriages, so many that "a stranger would think that the whole of New York was out on a grand trotting spree to see which had the fastest pair of horses or the gayest and most costly equipage."

This mode of elite socializing—an elaboration of the Broadway promenade of the 1850s—embraced both sexes. While plenty of men were delighted to demonstrate that they could afford to curtail their working day, women were more available for these fashionable parades, especially as Central Park was a thoroughly controlled environment, insulated from the indignities of urban street life. By the 1870s even young unmarried women could drive through the park—with a friend, with a suitor, even alone, albeit not without raising an eyebrow or two. As May King Van Rensselaer later recalled, "When I drove the first pony phaeton ever seen on Fifth Avenue, members of the Union Club, as I passed, shook their heads and feared the young Miss King was rather 'fast.'"

Vehicles varied by class clique. The old patriciate of Jays, Livingstons, and Stuyvesants favored stately black broughams, or perhaps a landau, hauled by huge fat horses. The smart set, who relied more on wealth than pedigree to establish their position, adopted the barouches favored by the Empress Eugénie. The avant-garde, taking their cues from Leonard Jerome and August Belmont, piloted coaches with *two* pairs of fine horses, a feat requiring some skill at four-in-hand driving. Not to be outdone by anyone, Jim Fisk, the King of Flash, would roll out from his stables just behind the Erie's Opera House headquarters, driving *six*-in-hand—three pairs of white and black horses—with a coach adorned in front by two black postilions in white livery, and in the rear by two white footmen in black livery.

Jerome and others also organized the more formal Coaching Club, which sponsored semiannual parades organized according to strict protocols. Drivers dressed in bottle-green cutaways with brass buttons and tall white hats and were accompanied by ladies under frilly parasols. When all was ready members would roll four-in-hand up Fifth Avenue, past crowds of gawking onlookers, many clutching *The Tally-ho*, a pamphlet that identified the heraldic colors of each participant. Gossip columnists reported on the doings for those who couldn't afford the trip uptown.

The pleasures of coaching, with its opportunities for social primping, and of trotting, with its hard-driving manly competitions, merged neatly in thoroughbred racing. Before the war, as sectional relations curdled, southern horse breeders had refused to send their steeds to northern competitions, and the sport had declined. Now southerners were back at Saratoga, and New York turfmen returned to building up racing stables.

What they lacked, however, was a proper setting, Long Island's Union Course and Fashion Park having been taken over by the hoi polloi. Leonard Jerome, a familiar of Parisian courses, set out to fill the need. In 1865 he and wealthy horse fanciers August

Belmont and William Travers formed the American Jockey Club (AJC). Jerome then purchased a 230-acre Bathgate estate in Fordham and laid out a track, an eight-thousand-seat grandstand, and a clubhouse patterned after elaborate European models. With his brother, Lawrence, Jerome had a wide avenue cut from Macomb's Dam to the track (today at the bottom of Jerome Park Reservoir). Local authorities named it Murphy Avenue, after a local alderman, but Lawrence's infuriated wife ordered bronze plates bearing the words JEROME AVENUE and had them riveted in place—a fait accompli in which the authorities acquiesced.

Jerome Park opened on September 25, 1866. Everyone was there: old money and new, swells and politicos, Vanderbilt and Fisk, Tweed and Morrissey, sportsmen from around the country, all in white hats and gloves. Grant was guest of honor. Ladies attended too—"ladies of fashion, ladies domestic, ladies professionally literary, ladies of birth and culture" (in the words of a *Harper's* reporter). They felt protected in Jerome's elegant clubhouse, despite the presence of people who arrived via the Harlem Rail Road, and their participation rendered racing both fashionable and respectable.

Too fashionable, some thought. Complaints emerged about the AJC's "aristocratic" policies. Opponents sniped at its governing clique of fifty life members, calling it the "House of Lords," and objected to having the main section of the grandstand restricted to members only. The AJC dealt with such adverse press by inducting publishers (Henry Raymond, Manton Marble, and James Gordon Bennett Jr.) into the ruling group and permitting nonmembers to enter the club section if introduced by a member. But mainly they hung tough: "Racing is for the rich," Belmont said bluntly.

Racing was also faster than ever. The AJC abandoned four-mile heats in favor of the British system of "dashing" over short distances, an "urban" approach that emphasized speed. In 1867 the Belmont Stakes was inaugurated, named for the AJC's first president, and the size of prize monies mounted steadily. Soon New York's purses, largest in the nation, were drawing entrants from around the country, and the metropolis had reemerged as the capital of American thoroughbred racing.

Nonequestrian clubs blossomed too, as bourgeois men refurbished old sanctuaries and created new ones—venues one observer classified as "anti-matrimonial and anti-domestic" havens. Merchants and lawyers of impeccable pedigree indulged in the sedentary pleasures of conversation and dining at the Union Club, now resituated at Fifth Avenue and 21st Street. Its ten-year waiting list so grated on blueblood potential applicants that Alexander Hamilton, John J. Astor, and Philip Schuyler formed the Knickerbocker Club in 1871, and gentlemen of the Democratic persuasion turned to August Belmont's Manhattan Club (1865) in the old Benkard residence on Fifth Avenue.

Many of the newly monied flocked to the New York Yacht Club—though the group drew the line at accepting Jay Gould—and their ever bigger boats, including schooners of over two hundred tons, encouraged millionaire members Jerome, Bennett, and Pierre Lorillard to launch racing on a transatlantic scale. Other vigorous Knickerbockers (including some young Roosevelts and DePeysters) were inspired by the London Athletic Club to open a New York version in 1868, and soon the New York Athletic Club was sponsoring track and field meets. Sporting men also turned to the New York Racquet Club or got caught up in the velocipede (early bicycle) craze of 1868 and formed associations dedicated to its development.

When such wholesome diversions palled, gentlemen could gamble at any of a dozen new luxury casinos, equal to Europe's finest. Here one could dine in splendor—the sumptuous meals and choice wines were free—and then repair to the glass-domed, velvet-carpeted, rosewood-furnished gaming rooms for high-stakes faro and roulette (Belmont reputedly lost sixty thousand dollars in one night). Old-fashioned Knicker-bockers considered even the grandest of these establishments, John Morrissey's on 24th Street near the Fifth Avenue Hotel, to be somewhat indecent. They had not forgotten Morrissey's brawler origins or Tammany ties. But the frisson of such connections appealed to sporting men like Vanderbilt, Jerome, and Belmont, who had no hesitations about racing Morrissey's team up at Harlem Lane or playing at his tables.

New York clubmen seeking new ways to shatter old constraints on conspicuous consumption adopted recreational hunting, that favorite pastime of European aristo-crats. The ever energetic Bennett Junior, assisted by his good friend General Phil Sheri-dan, organized one such expedition in 1871. The party whose sleeping car chugged out of the newly completed Grand Central Depot in mid-September included such mem-bers of the "fastest society set" as Leonard Jerome, John G. Hecksher, Carrol Liv-ingston, and J. Schuyler Crosby. Awaiting them at Fort McPherson, Nebraska, was a supply train of sixteen wagons to carry tents and provisions (including ice for the wine), three hundred Fifth Cavalry troopers to ward off Indians, and a guide, gorgeously resplendent in a white buckskin suit and crimson shirt, by the name of William Freder-ick Cody—better known, since the 1869 New York publication of Ned Buntline's dime novel about him, as Buffalo Bill. The "dudes" proceeded to "rough it" in style, shooting up behemoths, dining under prairie sunsets on filet of buffalo aux champignons, and leaving behind campsites littered with Mumm's champagne bottles. Buffalo Bill made such a hit with the New Yorkers that they invited him to the metropolis, where for six weeks he was trotted around town from party to party. Hostesses lionized him, papers reported his every word, and Cody became the smash hit of the social season, the quin-tessence of western equestrian chic.

LES GIRLS

The unbuttoned, not to say raucous, sexual hedonism of upper-class males—in marked contrast to the growing prudishness of the merely well-to-do—was yet another way that the haute bourgeoisie pleasurably demarcated itself in the Gilded Age. New peaks of public promiscuity were attained at masked balls (also known as French balls), which began just after the war when the Cercle Français de l'Harmonie started hosting wild parties at the Academy of Music, New York's sanctum sanctorum of high culture. Nou-veau riche Wall Street brokers in fancy dress rubbed elbows and much else with the city's assembled demimondaines, attired in costumes that exposed much, if not all, of their persons. As the champagne flowed, modesty was abandoned and the parties esca-lated to Mardi Gras levels. In the words of an amazed *World* reporter attending one such event, women were caught up and tossed in the air, then fallen on by a "crew of half-drunken ruffians, and mauled, and pulled, and exhibited in the worst possible aspects, amid the jeers and laughter of the other drunken wretches upon the floor." There was, he recounted, "not a whisper of shame in the crowd," nor did such press strictures halt the carryings-on. Indeed they expanded, as clubmen and courtesans flocked to the frolics—in 1876 over four thousand attended one event—and they would grow even larger in succeeding decades.

Public theaters too became sites of sexual display, the likes of which had not been seen since "living tableaux" had been suppressed before the war. In 1866 Niblo's Garden booked *The Black Crook*, a balletic musical spectacle. The unprecedented display of female flesh by lightly clad "coryphees" packed the house, night after night, until nearly five hundred performances had shattered all box office records in New York City—and the sale of men's opera glasses had reached an all-time high.

Two years later the Lydia Thompson Burlesque Company arrived at Wood's Museum (Broadway and 30th Street), four British blondes who sang, danced, winked, leered, and satirized conventional manners with raucous impertinence. These prototypical "showgirls"—voluptuous departures from the ethereal feminine ideal—were soon followed by dancers of the opéra bouffe companies, fresh from the boulevards of Paris. Offenbachian events climbed steadily in popularity, capped, during the 1874 winter season, by the triumphant arrival of the cancan. Crowds came to see dancers expose their colorful garters and ruffled drawers.

With the showgirl came the man-about-town, as wealthy, famous, and often married men vied with one another for the attentions of dancers or singers. The richest—the Belmonts and Jeromes—openly "sponsored" singers, showering them with flowers and jewelry, investing their money for them, and driving them around town, while their wives looked the other way or, as in Jerome's case, were packed off to Paris. Jim Fisk, whose wife languished in Boston, did things in his usual spectacular way. Apart from his many liaisons, culminating in a soon-to-be-fatal affair with Josie Mansfield, Fisk set up

"Paris in New York," from Van Every, *Sins of New York*. "The shameless antics and contortions indulged in by the lively damsels of la Belle France, at the Cercle de l'Orpheon masquerade ball at the Academy of Music—free champagne and Offenbachian music puts life and mettle in feminine heels." (General Research. The New York Public Library. Astor, Lenox and Tilden Foundations)

entire companies in his Grand Opera House, becoming the city's first "angel." Soon the playboy-showgirl nexus was as prevalent in Manhattan as it was in Paris.

Churchmen fulminated against "French indecencies" and attempted to suppress the "leg shows," but they flourished, ironically, in response to the successful prewar crackdown on immorality in conventional theaters, with "disreputable" women expelled from audiences now popping up onstage.[1] An equally unintended consequence of suppressing "third tier" prostitution was the birth of the concert saloon, forerunner of the New York nightclub. These boozy and licentious variety halls thrived on the patronage of Civil War soldiers on furlough, prompting moralists to persuade the city to require in 1862 that all theatrical and musical performing spaces be licensed and that the sale of liquor and employment of "waitresses" be banned wherever a curtain separated performers from customers. Entrepreneurs of leisure promptly dove through this loophole by inaugurating nightspots that featured a raised platform in the rear, a piano, and an open dance floor surrounded by tables and chairs. In larger establishments, balconies overlooked the floor and "stage" and were ringed with private rooms.

By 1872 there were roughly eighty of these concert saloons in New York City, many of them with names—Cremorne, Strand, and Buckingham Palace—that evoked the London scene. They featured traditional entertainment turns drawn from French vaudeville, Italian opera, and German beer gardens—and a novel form of audience participation, encouraged by the legally mandated absence of curtains. Patrons sang along with the chorus, singers sat at tables between acts or danced with customers, and "waiter-girls" with low bodices, short skirts, and high tasseled red boots took orders for drinks at the tables. They often sold sex as well, and waiter-girls, many of whom had been camp followers during the war, might accompany a guest to one of the upstairs rooms or arrange an assignation in a nearby brothel.

Concert saloons appealed to males of all classes but tended to be segregated by social rank. Some fast young gentlemen liked to go slumming, dropping in at working-class haunts like Billy McGlory's Armory Hall on Hester Street, a thrilling but potentially dangerous experience. At McGlory's, parties of uptown visitors could sit in a special balcony above the dance floor and gaze in fascination at brawls between gangsters and thugs, but they might also be robbed on leaving.

Most gentlemen, therefore, stuck to concert saloons like the Gaiety, on Broadway near Houston, which advertised its audience as "respectable, though by no means stilted in manners," or the Louvre, on Broadway and 23rd, a marble-columned establishment with an ornate mirrored bar, where rich men could more safely meet beautiful demimondaines or waiter-girls. But the most popular spot—famous throughout the country—was Harry Hill's, on Houston just east of Broadway.

Hill, born in Epsom, England, had been working there as a jockey and horse trainer when in 1850 a visiting American turfman invited him to manage a model horse farm in Astoria. Hill did so for two years, then moved to Manhattan and opened his own sporting house. After the war Hill's place drew "judges, lawyers, merchants, members of

---

1. The continuing ecclesiastical hostility to the theater was famously manifested at the end of the 1860s when an old actor by the name of George Holland died, and the rector of a fashionable Fifth Avenue church declined to hold a funeral for him. He did, however, recommend asking at "the little church around the corner," which obliged the bereaved thespian community. That establishment, the Church of the Transfiguration at 29th Street just east of Fifth, retains to this day its identification with the city's theatrical profession.

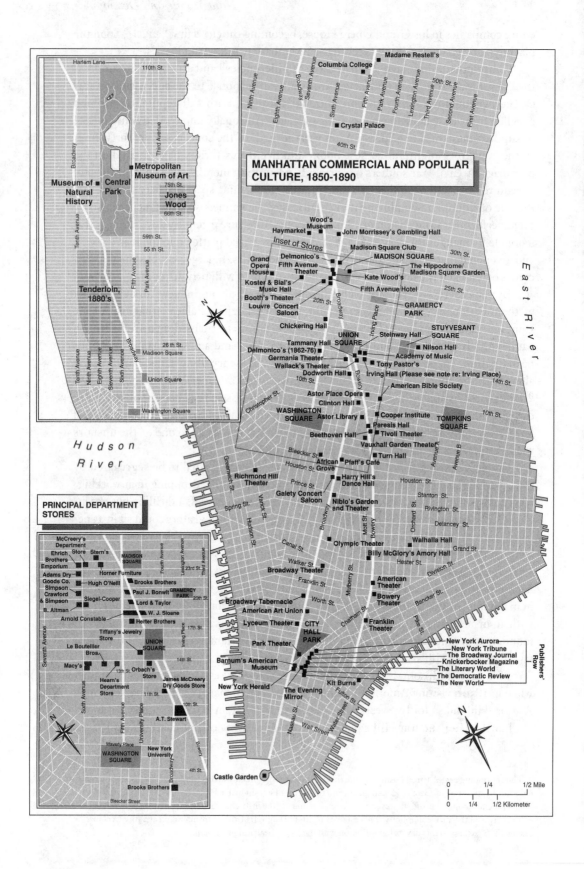

MANHATTAN COMMERCIAL AND POPULAR CULTURE, 1850-1890

Main map labels:

Madame Restell's
Columbia College
Harlem Lane
110th St.
Third Avenue
Broadway
Seventh Avenue
Sixth Avenue
Fifth Avenue
Park Avenue
Fourth Avenue
Lexington Avenue
Third Avenue
Second Avenue
First Avenue
50th St.
Ninth Avenue
Eighth Avenue
Crystal Palace
40th St.

Inset (upper left):

Museum of Natural History
Central Park
Metropolitan Museum of Art
75th St.
Jones Wood
66th St.
59th St.
55th St.
Tenderloin, 1880's
Broadway
Tenth Avenue
Ninth Avenue
Eighth Avenue
Seventh Avenue
Sixth Avenue
Fifth Avenue
Park Avenue
26th St.
Madison Square
Union Square
Washington Square

Central map:

Wood's Museum
Haymarket
John Morrissey's Gambling Hall
Madison Square Club
Inset of Stores
Delmonico's
MADISON SQUARE
30th St.
Grand Opera House
Fifth Avenue Theater
The Hippodrome/Madison Square Garden
Koster & Bial's Music Hall
Kate Wood's
Booth's Theater
Fifth Avenue Hotel
25th St.
Louvre Concert Saloon
GRAMERCY PARK
Chickering Hall
STUYVESANT SQUARE
Steinway Hall
UNION SQUARE
Nilson Hall
Tammany Hall
Delmonico's (1862-76)
Academy of Music
Germania Theater
Tony Pastor's
Wallack's Theater
Dodworth Hall
Irving Hall (Please see note re: Irving Place)
10th St.
Christopher St.
Astor Place Opera
American Bible Society
Clinton Hall
14th St.
WASHINGTON SQUARE
Astor Library
Cooper Institute
TOMPKINS SQUARE
Beethoven Hall
Paresis Hall
Tivoli Theater
10th St.
Vauxhall Garden Theater
Turn Hall
Bleecker St.
Houston St.
African Grove
Pfaff's Café
Avenue B
Avenue A
Richmond Hill Theater
Prince St.
Harry Hill's Dance Hall
Houston St.
Galety Concert Saloon
Niblo's Garden and Theater
Stanton St.
Rivington St.
Spring St.
Delancey St.
Greenwich St.
Varick St.
Hudson St.
Olympic Theater
Walhalla Hall
Grand St.
Canal St.
Billy McGlory's Amory Hall
Hester St.
Walker St.
Broadway Theater
American Theater
Division St.
Franklin St.
Bowery Theater
Worth St.
Broadway Tabernacle
American Art Union
Franklin Theater
Lyceum Theater
CITY HALL PARK
Park Theater
New York Aurora
New York Tribune
The Broadway Journal
Barnum's American Museum
Knickerbocker Magazine
The Literary World
The Democratic Review
The New World
New York Herald
Kit Burns
The Evening Mirror
Castle Garden
Wall Street
Water Street
Fulton St.
Nassau St.
Publishers' Row
East River
Hudson River

Inset (lower left): PRINCIPAL DEPARTMENT STORES

McCreery's Department Store
Ehrich Brothers Emporium
Stern's
MADISON SQUARE
Fourth Avenue
Lexington Avenue
Third Avenue
23rd St.
Adams Dry Goods Co.
Horner Furniture
Simpson Crawford & Simpson
Hugh O'Neill
Brooks Brothers
Paul J. Bonwit
GRAMERCY PARK
Siegel-Cooper
Lord & Taylor
20th St.
B. Altman
W. J. Sloane
Arnold Constable
Herter Brothers
17th St.
Tiffany's Jewelry Store
UNION SQUARE
Irving Place
Le Boutellier Bros.
14th St.
Seventh Avenue
Macy's
Hearn's Department Store
13th St.
Orbach's Store
James McCreery Dry Goods Store
11th St.
Sixth Avenue
Fifth Avenue
University Place
10th St.
A.T. Stewart
Waverly Place
WASHINGTON SQUARE
New York University
Bowery
Broadway
4th St.
Brooks Brothers
Bleecker Street

0   1/4   1/2 Mile
0   1/4   1/2 Kilometer

Congress and the State Legislature, doctors and other professional men" who liked to mingle with pugilists, politicians, and the racetrack crowd and to dance and drink with fast women (not all of them professionals). Harry's prominent patrons were reassured by the proprietor's tight surveillance—a prominent sign warned that "no one violating decency, will be permitted to remain in the room"—and his provision of a private room in which to sober up, lest they be waylaid by thugs outdoors.

It was getting ever harder to "violate decency," however, as the continuing relaxation of standards helped expand the commercial sex industry rapidly. After the Civil War, brothels traipsed north along with the department stores and theaters, pursuing their upwardly mobile clientele and fleeing a SoHo now overrun with factories and warehouses. Scores of whorehouses remained behind on Crosby, Howard, and Grand to service the arriving working class, but others overleaped the Rialto to the area above Madison Square, where a raft of new hotel construction was in progress. By the early 1870s the Fifth Avenue Hotel, which had once been a venturesome frontier outpost, found competitors springing up north of it along Broadway and Fifth Avenue. Visiting congressmen, military officers, coal mine operators, and railroad magnates could take their pick among the Hoffman House on 24th Street, the Brunswick (favorite of the horsey set) on 26th, the Victoria at 27th, the Gilsey House at 29th, the Grand at 31st, and—just opposite Vanderbilt's Grand Central Depot on 42nd Street—the Grand Union Hotel.

Anywhere that hotels went, the whores were sure to follow. On West 25th Street, the so-called Seven Sisters opened seven adjacent brothels in a residential brownstone neighborhood. The Sisters sent engraved invitations to sojourners whose arrival was announced in the press. Guests, often attired in formal evening clothes, were received by girls as well versed in society etiquette as in the tricks of their trade; some were accomplished pianists or singers. Josie Woods, proprietor of an exquisite brothel, donned elegant dresses, wore magnificent diamonds, went to Saratoga in the summers, rode in the Central Park carriage promenades, and kept open house on New Year's Day to receive her aristocratic neighbors (and clients).

The police accommodated the spread of prostitution, for a price. By 1876 the system of payoffs was so notorious that when police captain Alexander S. "Clubber" Williams was transferred to the 29th Precinct, he almost drooled with delight: "I've been having chuck steak ever since I've been on the force," said Clubber, "and now I'm going to have a bit of tenderloin." His bon mot, then most applicable to the mid-20s between Sixth and Seventh, would come to characterize the entire area between Fifth and Eighth avenues from 23rd to 57th streets—known for the next two generations as the Tenderloin or, alternatively, as Satan's Circus.

ON THE AVENUE

The new fascination with aristocratic French taste, architecture, and costume also pervaded the sumptuous residences and lavish private entertainments of Manhattan's haute bourgeoisie, whose precincts were once again in motion. The commercial invasion of Union Square, and the transformation of elegant row houses on Fifth Avenue's side streets into boardinghouses for the merely middle class, squeezed the rich northward. Soon even Madison Square began to give way on its western edge to shops, clubhouses, and boardinghouses willing to pay tremendous rents, though the square's eastern side remained lined with fancy residences. Murray Hill remained a secure haven for the moment, and the fashionable quarter between 23rd and 34th quickly filled with well-appointed town houses. Increasingly, however, the rich migrated to the area between Sixth and Third, from the 30s through the 50s, particularly along the vertical axes of Madison, Park, and above all Fifth Avenue.

The latest luxury area's upper boundary was staked out in 1869 by an unlikely pioneer, Mrs. Mary Mason Jones. This seventy-year-old dowager of impeccable pedigree—Edith Wharton, her niece, would use her as the model for Mrs. Manson Mingot in *The House of Mirth*—abandoned her venerable Waverly Place establishment and moved to the northeast corner of Fifth Avenue and 57th Street. The locale, despite its proximity to the new Central Park, was still undeveloped and filled with shantytowns, slaughterhouses, charitable institutions, the unfinished Catholic cathedral, and, at Fifth and 52nd, the home of abortionist Mme. Restell, now known as the "wickedest woman in New York." Nevertheless, Mrs. Jones's mansion, and the new Grand Army Plaza the Tweed regime thoughtfully provided in 1870, were soon surrounded by fine homes of fashionable Fifth Avenoodles (as the irreverent called them).

Fine homes, as before the war, meant three-or four-story Italianate structures (at $75,000 to $150,000 each), only now they had to be topped with a mansard (or "French") roof. As one commentator noted in 1868, "no man who wants a fashionable house, will be without it," and some now hopelessly passé Federal, Greek, and Gothic houses were accordingly recapped.

A few pathbreakers built urban chateaux. Leonard Jerome's flamboyant six-story mansion at 32 East 26th Street included a six-hundred-seat theater (for performances by his protégées), a breakfast room seating seventy, and a white and gold ballroom with fountains that spouted champagne and eau de cologne. A. T. Stewart's white marble Parisian *hôtel*, when finished in 1869, was the largest dwelling in New York City and featured a seventy-five-foot-long art gallery for his superb collection. Most wealthy Manhattanites still preferred comfortingly monolithic streetscapes to individualistic architectural statements, though their plain brownstone fronts masked increasingly extravagant interiors. Gilt-covered walls, marble, mirrors, frescoes, bric-a-brac, cabinets of porcelain curiosities, and ponderous furniture upholstered with opulent fabrics became standard issue along the avenue.

The social events held in these mansions grew ever more elaborate and competitive. The season just after the war featured six hundred balls, for which seven million dollars was laid out for dresses and jewelry. The ultimate arbiters of fashion were still European monarchs, though less Victoria now (since her beloved Albert died in 1861, she had taken to mourning clothes) than the Empress Eugénie. Her every move was monitored and interpreted by Mme. Demorest, the reigning monarch of New York fashion, in her *Demorest's Illustrated Monthly Magazine* and *Mme. Demorest's Mirror of Fashions* (as well as in, after 1867, the new *Harper's Bazaar*). Madame's correspondents reported instantly on every new Worth gown the empress wore to a Tuileries ball, and in New York the imperial styles were reproduced, exhibited in semiannual shows, and sold as finished garments or as patterns for seamstresses to follow. (Mme. Demorest's 14th Street workshops generated tons of these multicolored tissue-paper patterns and distributed them throughout the country via three hundred agents and by catalog mailings). The more daring fashions of the Parisian demimondaines received similar treatment, though modulated appropriately for American women (in Mme. Demorest's words, stripped of "coarseness or exaggerations" so as not "to vitiate and deprave the public taste"). In fashion, as in finance, New York remained Europe's gateway to the American continent.

Fashion dictated the demise of the crinoline and the birth of the bustle. Dresses (both day and evening) gradually flattened in front while gathering at the back, assisted by the bustle, a half-cage or puff filled with horsehair or stiffened gauze and net. (This was not a new invention, having been favored in the eighteenth century, when it was known more forthrightly as a "false bum.") Dresses cascaded down over this precipice to flow out (by the mid-1870s) into a trailing train. This appendage proved something of a safety hazard as, in an age of open fireplaces, it tended to catch fire while the wearer was dancing. Ladies' advice books urged fireproofing trains with a mixture of whitening and starch.

While it was acceptable to flaunt wealth by having diamonds sown into one's dress, moralists did raise alarms at the way 1870s fashions—and their underlying corsets, bustles, and breast-heavers—created a voluptuous display of propped-up bosoms. In 1868 Harriet Beecher Stowe launched a violent attack on "*outré* unnatural fashion," claiming that despite all Demorest's modifications, trends were being set by "the most dissipated foreign circles"—those immoral Parisian demimondaines who "live[d] only for the senses," lacked "family ties," and adorned themselves "to attract men and hide the ravages of dissipation." Such admonitions got nowhere. Indeed, very rich women began buying some of the forty gowns they would need each Season directly from Worth in Paris, at twenty-five hundred dollars a dress.

Dresses like these were too good to waste on small private parties, and social events increasingly switched to more public spaces. In the early 1870s Archibald Gracie King gave a debutante ball for his daughter at Delmonico's; Belmont threw one there in 1875 for his daughter that was reportedly "more splendid than the famous one given the previous year in London by the Prince of Wales." The only thing better than outdoing European aristocrats was marrying them. The first "dollar princesses" appeared as cash-poor Eurocrats lined up to wed Manhattan's daughters: among the first was Leonard Jerome's Jennie, who, after lengthy negotiations over her dowry, was married off to Lord Randolph Churchill in 1874.

Substantial wardrobes were de rigueur as well for appearances at theater and concert hall. Wealthy New Yorkers mingled with other classes in the Union Square Rialto. They would take in an opera there at the Academy of Music, which in addition to offering luscious music—the hall hosted the American premieres of *Aida* (1873), *Lohengrin* (1874), *Die Walküre* (1877), and *Carmen* (1878)—provided a place for debutante daughters to meet eligible gentlemen during the intervals. Boxes at the Academy were as eagerly sought after as seats on the Stock Exchange.

Stalls at Wallack's, the nation's leading playhouse, were in equal demand, and first nights in particular brought out the aristocracy of wealth in full plumage. Concerts similarly drew the wealthy to Union Square. At Irving Hall, designed (in 1860) for "miscellaneous entertainments of a high character," one could hear both the Philharmonic Society—the old German co-op—and Theodore Thomas's new orchestra. Thomas had been brought to America in 1845, at the age of ten, by his German parents. During the Civil War the young man, with the aid of wealthy backers, founded and trained his own orchestra, paying the musicians a regular salary rather than sharing box office takings as the Philharmonic's members did. This stable income allowed Thomas's artists to rehearse and play together on a full-time basis, and the well-drilled performers soon surpassed their part-time competitors. The new group also felt freer to go beyond the Philharmonic's more old-fashioned (but crowd-pleasing) repertoire: it was the Thomas Orchestra that introduced Schubert's *Unfinished Symphony* to America in 1867.

Both orchestras soon deserted Irving Hall in favor of the new Steinway Hall (1866), an exceptionally comfortable three-thousand-seat theater the piano manufacturer opened at the rear of his showroom on 14th Street. It also became the favorite stage for touring opera singers (Christine Nilsson made her American concert debut there in 1870), instrumentalists (such as Anton Rubinstein, the legendary Russian pianist), and lecturers (Dickens, on his 1867 visit, read selections from *Christmas Sketches, Pickwick Papers*, and *Nicholas Nickleby*).

MCCALLISTER AMONG THE PATRIARCHS

The trouble with the torrent of competitive postwar socializing was that it dissolved society into a welter of competing epicenters, none of which seemed to hold. Its innermost precincts—swollen but manageable in the 1850s—were now (as May King Van Rensselaer recalled) "assailed from every side by persons who sought to climb boldly over the walls of social exclusiveness." Arriviste hostesses, backed by their husbands' cash, threw ever more lavish and unorthodox affairs. Mrs. Paran Stevens (her husband a real estate tycoon) held parties on Sunday nights! Scandalized matrons ostracized her, but gentlemen flocked to her parlor. Mrs. William Colford Schermerhorn, a still more disturbing renegade, drew guests to her Madison Square drawing room with musicales.

Men were equally combative. Jerome, Belmont, and wealthy clubman William R. Travers each engaged Lorenzo Delmonico to offer the most perfect dinner, at any cost. His Silver, Gold, and Diamond affairs were so equally magnificent that Jerome, to win the race, gave each lady in attendance a gold bracelet. Still worse was the way a social unknown like millionaire importer Edward Luckemeyer could barge his way into society with a *coup de table*. Luckemeyer simply gave Charles Delmonico free rein (and ten thousand dollars), and *voilá*. Seventy-two distinguished guests turned out to boggle at the gigantic oval dining table, of virtually ballroom size, landscaped with flowers, with a thirty-foot lake at its center, upon which paddled four swans from the new Prospect Park.

In the 1870s only one family had the financial and social resources to bring some order to this chaos: the Astors. John Jacob had passed on his land and liquid assets to William Backhouse Astor, who during his lifetime had doubled his inheritance by assiduous extraction of rents from his acres and tenements. When he died in the mid-1870s, he in turn bequeathed roughly forty million dollars to his two heirs, John Jacob III and William. John Jacob (elder of the two) received two-thirds of the estate, but neither he nor his wife was willing to take on the role of social dictator. Nor was William—a playboy who spent his days at the track, or pursuing women, or yachting in distant waters. It was his frustrated and furious wife, Caroline, possessed of wealth and status too (she was a Schermerhorn), who set out to impose her authority on New York society.

As her chamberlain she chose Ward McCallister, a man who became known as the "Autocrat of Drawing Rooms" but was really more a steward of the elite, on the order of Isaac Brown. McCallister's own pedigree was most unaristocratic; the son of a Savannah attorney, he had moved to New York in the 1840s and worked as a bookkeeper. Society-struck, and desperate to break into the inner circles, McCallister found he lacked the economic wherewithal or social cachet to sustain a position among the smart set.

Resolved to correct both deficiencies, he went to California, made a modest fortune, and married an heiress. Then he traveled extensively in Europe, memorizing the manners of the great courts and studying heraldry, genealogy, and cookery.

After the war, McCallister came to Caroline's attention through his elaborate Newport parties and his revival, in the winter of 1866–67, of cotillion suppers—an old New York tradition dating back to the colonial-era Dancing Assembly. The metropolitan patriciate was delighted at the idea of a secure space in which its daughters could meet eligible men. In the winter of 1872–73, McCallister, with Caroline Astor as special adviser, executed his masterstroke, the creation of the Patriarchs. He selected a group of twenty-five men, headed by the Astor brothers, that included both Old Knickerbockers and newly monied—a group that collectively commanded unrivaled respect. Each Patriarch was invested with the right and responsibility of inviting four ladies and five gentlemen to periodic Patriarch's Balls. Fastidious exclusion soon made these affairs the city's cultural pinnacle, the goal of every social climber. They were also—along with balls given by the Assembly, the old guard, and the Cercle de l'Harmonie—attended by representatives of the press. Reporters wrote up the parties for the society pages, and artists sketched the scenes for *Harper's Weekly*, *Frank Leslie's*, or *Ballous's Pictorial*, making it a matter of public record as to who was in, and who was out. The city's facilities for creating celebrities were now applied to the social elite.

Grand public spectacles were complemented by more private weekly dinner parties at Mrs. Astor's Fifth Avenue and 34th Street mansion. These elaborate rituals further helped to discipline the chaos of social life, especially as practiced by playboys like her husband. They began and ended at precise times. Exact gastronomic rules were enforced. Topics tolerated in other mansions were banished; food, wine, horses, yachts, cotillions, and marriages were the only acceptable subjects.

"STILL DESTITUTE OF SUCH AN INSTITUTION"

Though art was not on Mrs. Astor's list of approved topics, for many in the elite world the amassing of great collections had long been an important tactic in the struggle for social preeminence. But the galleries established before the war by mercantile men had been chiefly for private consumption. Now industrial and financial elites decided to marry their pursuit of personal collections with a new emphasis on creating museums in which to display their treasures publicly. By providing the city with cultural institutions more lavish than any the old elites had created—merging connoisseurship with civic stewardship—they would exalt their own status while enhancing the city's reputation.

The Hudson River painters remained popular in the city—Asher Durand still sold well—but chroniclers of the Catskills were now surpassed by those who captured the glories of the great West. In 1859 Albert Bierstadt had explored the Rockies. After his return he moved to New York City and took a room in the Richard Morris Hunt-designed Tenth Street Studio Building—the first structure in the United States or Europe designed as a place for artists to live, work, and exhibit. Bierstadt's heroic canvasses, like *A Storm in the Rocky Mountains* (1866), generated a host of private commissions (at from five to thirty-five thousand dollars each) from fashionable men of means.

Bierstadt's work could be seen at the National Academy of Design, now in a new and highly praised Venetian Gothic building at Fourth Avenue and 23rd Street, but that building, indeed all current artistic showplaces, seemed insufficient to wealthy New

Yorkers determined to match the best that Europe could offer. John Jay, descendant of the governor and chief justice, convinced the Union League Club that the city needed a permanent public art gallery. The club's Art Committee, headed by George Palmer Putnam, included Samuel P. Avery, the respected art dealer then helping William Vanderbilt and other millionaires form their private collections. The committee convoked a public meeting in late 1869, out of which in January 1870 came the Metropolitan Museum of Art—a title no other city would have assumed. Its trustees and officers commingled prominent businessmen and lawyers with leading artists like poet-editor Bryant, architect Hunt, and landscaper Olmsted.

The Metropolitan's new president, John Taylor Johnston, set out to obtain for the institution a "more or less complete collection of objects illustrative of the History of Art from the earliest beginnings to the present time." He made some early headway by buying up the private collections of Europeans made desperate for funds by the outbreak of the Franco-Prussian War (rather as Tiffany had done with jewels). He exhibited these prizes in rented quarters on the Rialto—the former Douglas Cruger mansion at 128 West 14th Street—preserving its elite status by remaining closed on evenings and Sundays, the only times most working people could attend.

The influential trustees next set their sights on a permanent home. As so often, they found in Tweed a helpful associate. Tweed prevailed on the state legislature to assign the museum a portion of Central Park, in the low 80s off Fifth Avenue—far from the downtown rabble and close to other new cultural institutions. Among these was the Lenox Library (1875), at Fifth Avenue and 71st Street, which Richard Morris Hunt had designed for the scholarly book collector and millionaire rentier James Lenox. Up till then Lenox had piled his volumes in a carelessly kept-up town house that appalled his wealthy neighbors. Now he made his eighty-five thousand books accessible (providing a half-million-dollar endowment to care for them), though only to scholars. Ground was broken in 1874 for the Metropolitan Museum—an institution built on municipal land, supported with public funds, but controlled by private trustees—and it would move into its new quarters in 1880.

Across Central Park, a group of prominent men set out to build an American Museum of Natural History, modeled on European institutions and inspired by the Museum of Comparative Zoology that Louis Agassiz had created at Harvard in 1860. Albert Bickmore, an Agassiz student, proposed to wealthy amateur members of the Lyceum of Natural Sciences that they purchase two large private natural history collections then up for sale and use them as the core of a new establishment. Theodore Roosevelt Sr., a leading glass importer and amateur naturalist, agreed to help; he got J. P. Morgan and corporate attorney Joseph Choate involved, and the enterprise was launched.

The founders were prominent men—A. T. Stewart, James Brown, and William Dodge, in addition to Roosevelt, Morgan, and Choate—though not yet of the highest rank in New York society, not quite on a par with Rhinelanders, Livingstons, or Stuyvesants. Creating a natural history museum would strengthen their social position while underscoring their commitment to newly prized scientific values. It would also, as they stressed in their fund-raising appeals, rectify the disgraceful situation that "nearly all the capitals of Europe and more important cities in our own land" had natural history museums, "while New York, notwithstanding its metropolitan position, is still destitute of such an institution." Again, public assistance proved crucial. Samuel Tilden was dispatched to broach the idea to Tweed, who quickly secured a charter in 1869. The operation established temporary quarters in the Central Park Arsenal and opened to the public in 1871.

The trustees encouraged other-than-wealthy visitors, but with little success, so they too pressed the city for land on which to build an attractive permanent home. After they presented Tweed with a petition signed by men who collectively owned over half the taxable real estate in New York City, the museum was given the use of Manhattan Square, a rocky patch on the wild West Side covered with rocks and stagnant pools. Convinced (correctly) that the municipality would pick up the bill, the trustees forged ahead, got Calvert Vaux and Jacob Wrey Mould to design a huge structure, and pressed on with its construction. By 1874 the enterprise was far enough along for President Grant to come up from Washington and preside over laying the cornerstone. In haute culture, as well as in more frivolous enterprises, the haute bourgeoisie was making its mark on Manhattan.

55

The Professional-
Managerial Class

In 1868 James Dabney McCabe's *The Secrets of the Great City: A Work Descriptive of the Virtues and Vices, the Mysteries, Miseries, and Crimes of New York City* proposed that "the middle class, which is so numerous in other cities, hardly exists at all here." New York, said McCabe, had only two classes—"the poor and the rich."

Such a perception was understandable, given the glaring visibility of the city's social extremities, but wrong. Somewhere between a quarter and a third of the population were middle class, an amorphous strata encompassing a wide range of conditions and occupations. Its upper ranks were composed of professionals and managers: doctors, lawyers, editors, professors, architects, landscape architects, civil servants, librarians, reporters, engineers, advertising executives, corporate administrators, lesser merchants, nurses, dentists, retailers, ministers, entrepreneurs, department store buyers, realtors, and artists. At its less affluent end lay growing numbers of shopkeepers, schoolteachers, clerks, and salespeople.

Its boundaries were fuzzy. At the top, the Gilded Age middle class bled imperceptibly into the haute bourgeoisie, with the border peopled by independently wealthy professionals descended from mercantile and landholding families. At bottom, the line between clerks and the more prosperous members of the skilled working class could be hard to discern, especially as clerical workers might well earn less than shipwrights or masons. Generally, however, a lower-middle-class New Yorker would probably take home two thousand dollars a year while a mechanic would be happy to make half that. It is only when looking at the *mentalité* of this new middle class—its values and ideologies, rooted in changing patterns of work and culture—that its contours come more sharply into focus.

NOBLE PROFESSIONS

The professionals and managers who set the tone and tenor of middle-class life believed that mind was mightier than muscle. As organizers and officers in the Civil War, they had mobilized manpower and deployed resources, initiatives crucial to the military effort. Such experiences gave them the psychic wherewithal to challenge the traditional republican conviction that all value flowed from artisanal or agricultural labor—that he who worked with head, not hand, was probably a social leech.

The increasing complexity of postwar technical and organizational projects further demonstrated the growing centrality—and enhanced the valuation—of skilled intellectual labor. The Brooklyn Bridge had continued to rise even as its engineer-designer lay sick abed, and Washington Roebling himself had drawn the appropriate conclusion: "When it comes to planning, one mind can in a few hours think out enough work to keep a thousand men employed for years." Grasping the underlying concepts behind everyday empirical experience elevated professionals above the once vaunted "amateur" (the dismissive word "amateurish" dates from this period) and made them indispensable to the "running" (another contemporary neologism) of modern civilization.

New York City, in particular, spawned many such specialists, and their growing numbers generated a reassuring sense of collective authority. Upper-echelon professionals, moreover, were independent agents, with far greater control over the nature and conditions of their labor than was usual in the now heavily proletarianized city; this too strengthened class confidence.

In the seventies confidence was reinforced by organization. Before the war many professions had been on the defensive, their efforts to set standards and control access to their ranks traduced as aristocratic. Now, newly nerved, they strengthened existing professional bodies and created new ones. Lawyers, doctors, engineers, and architects came together to restrict membership to candidates they designated as qualified and who pledged allegiance to a common code of conduct.

Lawyers multiplied rapidly in the postwar era, though firms remained relatively small. Bidwell and Strong, which represented Steinway and Sons, Wells Fargo, and Western Union Telegraph, consisted of six attorneys and four assistants in 1878. Lawyers served many functions in the new order: defending railroads in court, serving as board directors, working as lobbyists (bridging the worlds of business and government), representing speculators and empire builders, managing real estate interests, advising social and cultural organizations, and handling trusts, estates, and, especially in New York City, the complicated affairs of the new nationally oriented corporations.

Involvement in corporate warfare, however, brought the Bar into serious disrepute. Drew, Fisk, and Gould hired a team of forty-plus attorneys to run legal interference for them in the Erie War, while an opposing regiment of lawyers handled Vanderbilt's machinations. The Bench too had been tarnished by its abetting of financial and political skullduggery: in 1867 the distinguished attorney James T. Brady accused Tweed crony Judge Barnard of corruption, to his face in open court.

Many lawyers, notably George Templeton Strong of Bidwell and Strong, blamed not corporate capitalism but the 1846 state constitution, which had abolished the old distinctions between attorneys, solicitors, and counselors, placed all lawyers on the same nominal footing, and adopted simplified and unexacting licensing procedures. It had also made judgeships elective rather than appointive positions. The result, Strong believed, had been a "progressive debasement of the Bar & Bench." The swollen legal fraternity was no longer "learned & dignified" but rather ranked "next below that of patent-medicine mongering." Strong believed reform required replacing apprenticeship with a law school education. He devoted himself accordingly to expanding Columbia College's School of Law, and by the 1880s it was one of the two largest in the United States.

Other reform-minded lawyers—Samuel Tilden and William Evarts chief among them—decided that only a new and exclusive group restricted to "the more worthy of the profession" could remedy the situation, given their inability to control access to the field itself. If New York City were to remain the commercial and monetary capital of the United States, Tilden warned, "it must establish an elevated character for its Bar, and a reputation throughout the country for its purity in the administration of justice." To police their own ranks, define the boundaries of acceptable conduct, aid attorneys in standing up to judges (and the political machines that elected them), and make the law a "noble profession" and not merely a "trade with the rest," they and others created the Association of the Bar of the City of New York (1870). Rigorous admission procedures and hefty fees allowed the "worthy" to exclude the "uncouth in manners and habits, ignorant even of the English language, jostling and crowding and vulgarizing the profession." A year after its formation, the self-selected and overwhelmingly Anglo-Saxon Protestant founders had admitted only 450 out of New York's approximately four thousand lawyers to their ranks. Grievance and screening committees were established to exercise some control over the behavior of attorneys and judges. The association's pioneering effort at self-regulation was swiftly and widely copied throughout the country, and Manhattanites proved instrumental in forming the American Bar Association in 1878.

The New York chapter of the American Institute of Architects, under the presidency (after 1869) of Richard Morris Hunt, similarly sought to winnow out those it considered unprofessional and to impose order and standards on practitioners. It recruited only trained architects—often from well-to-do families able to pay for their education—while rejecting older craftsmen who had worked their way up from the ranks of carpenters and masons. The group thus denied membership to John Kellum, perhaps the most employed architect of the day, on the ground that he was merely an unskilled draftsman. Indeed Kellum's very popularity counted against him: the new men found him too "commercial," too willing to defer to the wishes of his prosperous clients, too reluctant to improve his employers' tastes by bringing to bear the authority of his professional credentials.

In the 1870s "regular" doctors made another effort to impose their methods and approaches on the practice of medicine. The New York Medico-Legal Society prepared a bill in 1872 authorizing the County Medical Society to license all physicians, thus allowing the American Medical Association's allopathic physicians to define their homeopathic rivals as quacks, effectively putting them out of business. The bill passed, but, heeding widespread opposition, Governor Hoffman vetoed it, arguing that only the marketplace should regulate medical practice. A compromise measure passed in 1874, but physicians remained dissatisfied. In the meantime their public-oriented colleagues organized separately: Dr. Edward H. Janes, the city's sanitary inspector from 1866 until his death in 1893, helped found the American Public Health Association in 1872.

New Yorkers and Brooklynites were particularly prominent in the movement to professionalize civil engineering, as so many leading practitioners were graduates of the area's many public works projects. Faced with a flood of self-proclaimed engineers in the late 1860s, promoters pushed to create a "proper association, admission to which should only be possible to accomplished and competent men." In 1867 they established the American Society of Civil Engineers (ASCE). J. P. Kirkwood and Julius Adams, the engineers of Brooklyn's sewer system, served as the ASCE's first president and vice-president, respectively, and Alfred W. Craven, John B. Jervis, and other Croton veterans became prominent members. Indeed seven of the first eight presidents were either permanent employees of New York City or did consulting work for it. The organization established its permanent home in Manhattan, holding meetings and social functions in offices at the Chamber of Commerce Building, and started regular publication of a professional journal in 1872.

The ASCE thrived, boasting 212 members by 1871. Participation was restricted to men who had been actively employed for five or more years in a supervisory capacity, though less experience was acceptable for those who had completed a college course of study. Before the war New York's engineers had trained on the job or in apprenticeships; mastery of the fundamentals of math, physics, and mechanics had been deemed unnecessary to solving most technical problems. In 1864, however, Thomas Egleston founded Columbia's School of Mines, which, despite its name, pioneered broad-based scientific education for engineers as well as geologists, and in 1869 the school began offering four-year courses in civil engineering. Mechanical engineers too, most of whom had emerged from machine shops, set about distinguishing themselves from mere "mechanics," by forming in New York City the American Society of Mechanical Engineers (1880).

One of the greatest obstacles to even organized engineers' winning professional autonomy was their continuing subordination to the political authorities who controlled public works, but here too there were breakthroughs. In 1860, when Mayor Wood fired Alfred W. Craven, chief engineer of the Croton Aqueduct, Craven fought back vigorously, arguing that he had the technical know-how required to run the city's water and sewer systems, and the mayor did not. Craven won his point both legally (he was reinstated) and in the court of public opinion, where the mayor was denounced for putting politics above efficiency.

Professionalization spread among corporate managers too, particularly in the expanding railroad industry. Managers of competing companies, striving to rationalize a hodgepodge system, came together to standardize operating procedures and equipment, then continued to meet regularly. A growing sense of professional kinship transcending corporate loyalties gave rise to groups like the American Society of Rail Road Superintendents and the National Association of General Passenger and Ticket Agents.

At the other end of the middle-class spectrum, which consisted of employees rather than professionals and managers, postwar developments in the municipal economy swelled the ranks of clerical and sales forces. Insurance companies, banks, mercantile and stock exchanges, post offices and express agencies, credit rating firms, shipping and railroad companies, newspapers, large-scale manufacturers, and wholesaler jobbers—all these required sizable numbers of bookkeepers, cashiers, accountants, and clerks to staff them. The burgeoning of department stores, fashion and piano showrooms, and elegant retail outlets similarly required growing numbers of stockroom employees and salesmen—and, gradually, saleswomen: in 1869 A. T. Stewart's began to employ "American ladies of refinement and culture" to stand behind the counters.

Such workers seldom organized on the model of the professional organizations; most didn't organize at all. What bound them together, rather, were common experiences and shared values. Most worked in "clean" environments—the giant new downtown office buildings—rather than grubby factories, grimy warehouses, or messy construction sites, and most of them dressed accordingly. Junius Browne, watching the morning ferry passengers disembark in 1869, noted that the first contingent— "mechanics with their flannel and check shirts"—was followed by platoons of salesmen, accountants, and clerks after seven A.M., at which time "the shirts of the passengers begin to whiten and raiment to improve." Many of these white-collared workers believed, as an 1868 commentator in *Galaxy* put it, that "manual labor is disreputable" even though it often paid better than head work (masons earned twice what clerks did). To further distinguish themselves from mechanics and laborers, the lower middle classes adopted appropriate modes of personal conduct—taking their cultural cues from professionals and managers when deciding how and where to live their lives.

HOME SWEET APARTMENT

Manhattan's middle classes had their own territorial enclaves, spatially distinct from both Hell's Kitchen and Fifth Avenue. They settled in the West Village, in Chelsea, along cross streets in the rectangle bordered by 14th, 59th, Eighth, and Second, and on the Upper East Side and Harlem. Their travels to and from work downtown helped swell the annual ridership on New York's thirteen streetcar lines to 150 million by 1873, up fourfold since 1860, despite crammed conditions on the commuting cars (it "would not be decent to carry live hogs thus," huffed Horace Greeley). Shopping soon followed them northward, and dry-goods stores spread up Third, Sixth, and Eighth avenues, making them the commercial thoroughfares of middle-class neighborhoods.

When they could afford to, middling New Yorkers purchased their own homes. In the postwar years, however, clericals and even professionals found this increasingly difficult to do. Soaring land prices put single-family twenty-five-foot-wide row houses out of reach. Middle-class salaried employees making two thousand dollars a year could seldom afford a ten- to eighty-thousand-dollar town house, and for a skilled mechanic making an annual thousand dollars it was quite impossible.

Many abandoned private ownership altogether and became boarders. As commerce marched into Union Square, the rich decamped northward, and their elegant town houses along lower Fifth and Madison avenues were subdivided and converted into respectable boardinghouses for doctors, lawyers, professors, and smaller merchants. Rooms here might cost from twelve to fifteen dollars a week in 1869. Hotels were another option, and those willing to settle for modest accommodations had a wide choice. By 1869 the construction boom had boosted the total number of metropolitan hotels to between seven and eight hundred, many of which offered rooms for residents as well as for transients. Boardinghouses on side streets offered even cheaper accommodations, which salaried clerks could afford. As Dickens observed on his 1867–68 visit, there were "300 boarding houses in West 14th Street, exactly alike, with 300 young men, exactly alike, sleeping in 300 hall bedrooms, exactly alike, with 300 dress suits, exactly alike, lying on so many chairs, exactly alike, beside the bed."

But the growing middle class did not *like* such housing. *Respectable* people lived in a "home" of their own, not jumbled up with strangers. Multifamily dwellings smacked of tenement life. Boardinghouses, with their centrally cooked and commonly eaten meals, threatened family integrity; wives might mingle promiscuously with others while husbands were off at work. Enforced intimacy mocked middle-class values of family privacy and the sanctity of the home.

The first "apartment houses" were built to solve this spatial and cultural conundrum. New Yorkers had been hearing about so-called French Flats, the grand buildings lining Haussmann's new boulevards, and most of what they heard was negative. French Flats were too public; they came with a nosy concierge; they lacked most features of a proper Anglo-Saxon home. Some magazine writers did note their advantages: everything was on one floor, eliminating the need to squeeze up and down a brownstone's narrow stairway; they were more spacious and easier to clean; the nosy concierge looked after things when owners summered out of town. Still, prevailing opinion was opposed. "Gentlemen," as one of the breed irately put it, "will never consent to live on mere shelves under a common roof!"

It took the combined prestige and power of the city's most francophiliac architect and a gentleman of unimpeachable social standing to pierce the armor of conventional opinion. Rutherfurd Stuyvesant was as patrician as you could get in New York. His father, Lewis Rutherfurd, was merely a distinguished astronomer. But his mother was a direct descendant of Petrus Stuyvesant and had transmitted the family fortune to Rutherfurd (on the condition that he spurn patrilineality and adopt his mother's last name). Stuyvesant had admired apartment houses in Paris, and in 1869 he hired Richard Morris Hunt, whom he had met in France, to create one for him on a four-row-house-wide stretch of 18th Street between Irving Place and Third Avenue. Each of the first four floors had four separate apartments, and the fifth was reserved for artists' studios. To the astonishment of many, the apartments, overseen by a French-style concierge, were rented immediately, by young couples of impeccable "old Knickerbocker" credentials.

Hunt next constructed a far grander apartment house for Paran Stevens (whose wife's parties were then scandalizing more staid society matrons). The striking marble-trimmed, mansard-capped, eight-story building, when completed in 1872, occupied the entire south side of 27th Street between Fifth Avenue and Broadway and was one of the largest buildings in the city. Stevens House had eighteen suites, each with parlor, dining room, kitchen, butler's pantry, bedrooms, dressing rooms, and bathroom—along with steam elevators that rose to an attic where servants' quarters were available. Stevens had overreached, and his luxury operation was soon converted into a more modest apartment hotel, but the Second Empire edifice remained a New York cultural and technological landmark.

Now socially certified, the French Flat began to catch on. By the mid-1870s, with a dozen or so up or in the planning stages, especially around the lower border of Central Park, the New York City Buildings Department adopted "French Flat" as an official category. The term, like "apartment house," implied a larger and better-quality edifice than "tenement," and to underscore the class status of their residents, the new buildings took toney names like Osborne, Knickerbocker, Berkeley, and Saratoga.

The as yet limited number of apartment houses could shelter only a relative handful, however, and many middle-class home and status seekers, in pursuit of an immediate solution, decided to cross the East River. The wealthiest professionals took up quarters in Brooklyn Heights or Cobble Hill, mingling with old New England merchants and new-monied businessmen. Others settled in Fort Greene (particularly around Washington Park, where contractor William Kingsley built his home in 1867) or in Clinton Hill (where oil magnate Charles Pratt erected a mansion in 1875). Less costly accommodations could be found in Boerum Hill or in row houses with deep front gardens along the streets around Carroll Park, an area developed after 1869. The least-well-paid members of the middle class could turn to the lower Park Slope area, between Third and Sixth avenues, though it was unattractively interlaced with the light industrial establishments spreading outward from the Gowanus Canal.

Those willing to travel farther could settle in growing Bedford. Speculators and builders advertised the area as the "Garden of Brooklyn," perfect for the "refined and select" middle class. Single-family Gothic-style frame houses with gas, hot and cold water, indoor plumbing, and, in some cases, gardens, grape arbors, and apple trees, could be had in South Bedford for between five and ten thousand dollars. These new homes were deliberately situated away from the LIRR stops on Atlantic Avenue and the horsecar line on Fulton Street, even though 50 percent of Bedfordites commuted all the way into Manhattan, a two-and-a-half-mile journey that took about an hour and cost thirteen cents. Catching a ride to the city entailed a long walk, but it seemed worth it to preserve, for the moment, the area's bucolic character. To the north, by contrast, row houses and tenements clustered around the Flushing and Myrtle Avenue lines of the Brooklyn City Rail Road. Their cars transported native-born lower-middle-class clerical workers to Manhattan or to Brooklyn's City Hall and Fulton Street commercial districts.

Some professionals were drawn to the Queens suburban frontier, to places like the new railroad community of Richmond Hill, named for a London suburb. New York attorney Albon Platt Man built it in 1869 along the wooded hills of the terminal moraine and ensured its class character by barring such "nuisances" as factories, warehouses, and tenements. But in the 1860s and 1870s, Kings seemed preferable to Queens, as residents could visit local analogues of New York City's cultural institutions (Brooklyn Academy of Music, Brooklyn Club, Mercantile Library, Long Island Historical Society) and were close to Prospect Park, Green-Wood Cemetery, and more distant rural diversions. A Brooklyn Heights resident could leave his Manhattan office at three o'clock, return on the Wall Street ferry, dine at four, then take a leisurely drive to the outskirts of town. Residents and realtors began to boast that Brooklyn was a middle-class paradise, free from urban ills and evils, a complacency that required ignoring the tenements of detested "micks" on the flats south of the Navy Yard.

Brooklyn was indeed something of a paradise for the African-American middle-class. Though the vast majority of black Brooklynites consisted of manual laborers, the city was also home to a small elite of professionals (doctors, lawyers, journalists, ministers, and teachers) and businesspeople (dressmakers, undertakers, carpenters, barbers, tailors). Some were affluent enough to invest in real estate during the 1870s, via the Excelsior Land Association of Brooklyn, and some owned substantial middle-class dwellings, complete with pianos, libraries, and pictures of Lincoln, John Brown, and AME Bishop Richard Allen.

The presence of this African-American elite was felt most strongly in Brooklyn's black churches, which moved away from religious enthusiasm toward a more urbane and intellectual Christianity. Their trained and educated ministers focused heavily on promoting learning, literacy, and culture. Concord Baptist, Bridge Street African Wesleyan Methodist Episcopal (AWME), and Siloam Presbyterian took the lead in providing libraries, classes, lectures, and concerts of classical music. The black Brooklyn community also developed autonomous institutions, like the Howard Colored Orphan Asylum (1866), the African Civilization Society, which began publishing the newspaper *Freedman's Torchlight* the same year, and the Zion Home for Colored Aged (1869).

THE CULTIVATED LIFE

In the 1870s Harriet Beecher Stowe wrote novels about New York life—like *We and Our Neighbors; or, the Record of an Unfashionable Street* (1875), which featured heroines like Eva, "a child of wealth and fashion" whose father had gone bankrupt. Eva married a journalist, moved to an unfashionable street, made do with only one servant, and moderated her expectations to middle-class levels. Referring to the posh Elmores she said: "We must keep in sight of them. All I ask is to be *decent*. I never expect to run into the extremes those Elmores do."

Middling New Yorkers adhered to values that, like their jobs and residencies, set them off from vulgar lower classes and dissipated upper ones. "Decent" was an imprecise term, more or less interchangeable with "genteel," "cultured," "refined," "civilized," "respectable," and "cultivated," but all the near-synonyms suggested an earned status. "Cultivation" implied self-development, a purposeful pursuit of "higher things." It prized intellect and sensibilities tutored in arts, letters, and manners. It was an identity rooted in education rather than in labor or wealth.

Not that the middle class had anything against wealth as such: prosperity was an indispensable precondition for gentility. Indeed it was the growing purchasing power of the postwar middle class that allowed ever greater numbers of New Yorkers to acquire the trappings of gentility: to live in tasteful homes in good neighborhoods, wear respectable clothes, attend refined schools, cultivate the arts and graces. Only "mere" or "vulgar" wealth was objectionable, wasted as it was on display rather than development, squandered in private hedonism rather than promotion of the public good.

Wherever they settled, therefore, middle-class New Yorkers decorated their quarters with objects that betokened their cultivation. Art galleries à la A. T. Stewart were out of the question, but mass-produced artwork was readily available. In his studio at 212 Fifth Avenue, John Rogers fashioned sculptural tableaux in clay, then churned out reproductions in plaster and bronze, which sold throughout the city and, via advertising and railroad delivery, across the continent. Rogers used industrial methods to evoke preindustrial life—*The Village Post-Office, Coming to the Parson*—along with more topical, even political themes, which balanced realism and sentimentality. Contemporary critics noted that his was not a "high art" but lauded the "Rogers groups" for their "elevated meaning" and "true feeling," which were "alike satisfying to head and heart." Metropolitan middle-class parlors were embellished as well with Currier and Ives chromolithographs that limned the triumphal expansion of Christian American civilization out west and hailed the triumph of a middle-class order in New York City.

As cultural possessions piled up in the parlor, along with machine-made upholstery, drapery, and carpeting and heavily carved furniture, they demanded an increasing level of maintenance. The haute bourgeoisie solved this problem with platoons of servants, but most of the middle class could at best afford but one. This required the housewife to take a professional approach to increasing the efficiency of such domestic labor as she had available. Advice books had been telling wives to manage households scientifically since the 1840s, but now the audience for such counsel had grown large enough to support an ongoing journalistic advocacy. Thus Eunice Beecher wrote a regular domestic advice column for the *Christian Union* in the 1870s, in which she aimed to help a woman "conduct her household as a business, prepare herself for it as a man prepared for his life work."

When they turned from work to play, more and more middle-class New Yorkers could afford to take in the same operatic and theatrical performances at the Rialto as did the haute bourgeoisie. But they also enjoyed more modest pastimes, like group singing in their parlors or reading aloud from genteel magazines like *Harper's Weekly* and *Scribner's*. Lectures were popular too: the uplifting or scientific ones at Chickering Hall (Fifth Avenue and 18th Street) and the effusions of humorists like Artemus Ward at Dodworth Hall (just north of Grace Church).

The new Central Park attracted many middling Manhattanites. When flags flew on omnibuses and horsecars, or one heard that "the ball is up in the Park," it meant that the pond at 59th Street was frozen over and one could go skating (at night the area was illuminated by calcium lights). Park officials enforced respectable behavior, and regulations said that "any person observing any act of indecorum may signalize a park-keeper by holding aloft or waving a handkerchief." Middle-class New Yorkers couldn't afford private carriages, but they could rent one from a livery stable for a dollar or two an hour, at least for special occasions. Families of clerks, prosperous shopkeepers, young professionals, and independent artisans (especially Germans) also went for walks, strolled through the Ramble, and took their children to the nascent zoo at the Arsenal. On summer Saturday afternoons, when most of "the mechanic and laboring classes" were still at work, Dodworth's band concerts attracted crowds of forty-five thousand or more to the Mall. These assemblages, the papers noted, were composed of the "orderly, well-conducted and respectable," the kinds of people (said the *Tribune*) "whose tastes are above grog shops and lager bier gardens but whose pockets are not equal to Newport or Saratoga."

Those who could afford the bicycles produced by several city manufacturers—which retailed for a stiff fifty dollars to three times that—could take classes in biking at the new Velocinasium. Here, the *Scientific American* observed in 1869, "on any weekday evening may be seen upward of a hundred and fifty gentlemen—doctors, bankers, merchants, and representatives from almost every profession—engaged in this training school preparatory to making their appearance upon the public streets and fashionable promenades."

Shopkeepers, clerks, and skilled craftsmen (especially butchers) dominated the city's baseball fields, hailing the sport as a healthful outdoor exercise. Amateur outfits continued to flourish, and by 1867, with the return of veterans who had played in the army, there were over one hundred clubs in Brooklyn and Manhattan, many formed by companies and colleges. But baseball had begun its own professionalization process during the war, when William H. Cammeyer opened the Union Grounds in Brooklyn's Eastern District, providing a rent-free playing field to three clubs but charging a ten-cent admission fee to watch the games. His success inspired a competitor in the Capitoline Grounds (once part of the old Lefferts farm). Now the clubs that drew the biggest crowds demanded a share of the gate; to attract greater attendance they sought more proficient players; athletes, in turn, demanded pay to play and proved willing to engage in "revolving"—jumping from one team to another that paid better.

By the late 1860s baseball had become a business, an urban entertainment commodity with Brooklyn and New York City at its center. The metropolitan area was a major market for recruitment: when a Cincinnati Red Stocking triumph in 1869 ended the local area's domination of baseball, most of the Reds proved to be New Yorkers.

The huge crowds that came to contests were predominantly drawn from the city's middling ranks. In part this was simply because the fees (twenty-five to fifty cents) and costs of travel to out-of-city fields effectively barred unskilled laborers. It was also due to baseball's peculiarly white-collar charms, its appeal to middle-class sensibilities. An extremely orderly game, full of reassuring rules and penalties for infractions, baseball grew ever more "scientific" in nature as it professionalized. This was reflected on the field, in growing levels of specialization, training, and discipline and in the invention of new techniques: Dicky Pearce, the Atlantics' star shortstop, became the first to employ the bunt as an offensive weapon. Even fandom required new levels of cerebration. Henry Chadwick, editor of the *Chronicle*, invented box scores and began calculating batting averages. Spectators could now peruse the reports, tables, and statistics in the sporting press and follow players and teams in a methodical fashion. The commentary of sports journalists in turn expanded the available information pool—the *New York National Police Gazette*, a major source, was widely available in hotels, barbershops, and saloons—and helped educate habitués in the finer points of observation.

The respectable middle class knew the kinds of entertainment it didn't like, as well: the sordid goings-on in Kit Burns's rat pit. The American Society for the Prevention of

"City Enormities—Every Brute Can Beat His Beast," from *Frank Leslie's Illustrated Newspaper*, October 28, 1865. This depiction of cartmen abusing a horse is said to have prompted the formation of the ASPCA, which used it for many years to rally support among the urban middle classes. (General Research. The New York Public Library. Astor, Lenox and Tilden Foundations)

Cruelty to Animals (ASPCA)—a strictly New York City concern despite its expansive name—had been founded in 1866 by Henry Bergh, son of wealthy shipbuilder Christian Bergh. Addressing a crowded Clinton Hall meeting of the American Geographical and Statistical Society, Bergh had denounced the cruelties practiced upon urban animals, particularly by the brutish (and Irish) lower classes, and urged New Yorkers to follow England's example in tackling the problem organizationally and legislatively. The backing of wealthy bourgeois gentlemen (Astor, Fish, Belmont) and leading ministers (the Unitarian "Pope" Henry Bellows) won the ASPCA a charter and gained passage of restrictive laws, but the rank-and-file supporters of the organization were mainly middle class.

The ASPCA took out after lower-class blood sports, deploring both their cruelty and their waste of working-class time. It repeatedly raided Kit Burns's establishment, forcing sportsmen to shift to pits in Brooklyn, Williamsburg, and Hoboken, and in subsequent decades largely succeeded in driving animal sports from the city. Except, that is, for the upper-class pastime of fox-hunting.

In addition to denouncing particular forms of working-class play, many professionals scorned the communal culture of the immigrant streets. Frederick Law Olmsted objected to "young men in knots of perhaps half a dozen in lounging attitudes," who rudely obstructed sidewalks or descended into a "brilliantly lighted basement, where they find others of their sort, see, hear, smell, drink, and eat all manner of vile things." Proper neighborliness did not consist in sitting about on doorsteps or curbstones while children "dodge[d] about at play," but rather in sitting at the "tea-table with neighbors and wives and mothers and children, and all things clean and wholesome, softening and refining."

RAGS TO 'SPECTABILITY RELIGION

More than ever, middle-class families hewed to distinctively middle-class creeds and denominations, clustering in neighborhood Methodist, Baptist, Congregational, Presbyterian, and Episcopalian churches and having little to do with Catholicism unless they were Irish or German. Middling New Yorkers harkened particularly to the teachings of three theologians whose messages resonated with special force within their social stratum: the Rev. Henry Ward Beecher, the Rev. Dwight L. Moody, and the Rev. Horatio Alger Jr.

In the postwar years Henry Ward Beecher was at the top of his form. His exuberant oratorical performances pulled crowds of Manhattanites across the river on Sunday mornings (on "Beecher boats") to drink in his Plymouth Church sermons alongside Brooklyn brokers, small businessmen, professionals, clerks, bookkeepers, and skilled laborers. The "Hercules of American Protestantism" made twenty thousand dollars a year—equal to the president's salary—supplemented with income from writing articles for the secular and religious press, penning a bestselling novel, and giving lectures.

Part of Beecher's attraction lay in his long-standing ability to successfully negotiate tensions in middle-class ideologies, as in his continuing reassurances to privileged audiences that social inequalities generated by the free market system were divinely sanctioned and morally justifiable. Now, in the postwar age of Darwin, Beecher demonstrated a capacity to reconcile religion with reason—coequal polestars for his middle-class followers. Confronted with hard evidence from geologists, paleontologists, and biologists that challenged traditional biblical teachings, Beecher responded by accepting the new findings, formally embracing Darwin in 1882, though implicitly he had done so much earlier. Beecher argued that Science and Religion were not really in conflict, as evolution was God's work. God was imminent in Nature, and His Laws might be grasped by the rational mind, but His Divine Essence was Love, and that could only be captured by contemplation of Nature's beauty. God could therefore be best discerned, Beecher suggested, by the refined and the sensitive, attributes that (like knowledge and education) could be cultivated. It was possible, accordingly, for people to "ripen" by their own efforts to a "nobler plane," attaining a level at which they were naturally attracted to love and goodness and cleaved to proper behavior as a matter of course, not coercion.

Organizing the process of elevating masses of middling men and women to such an exalted status was central to the work of Dwight L. Moody, the era's most influential evangelical preacher, and in 1875 Moody decided to undertake a jumbo-scale revival in Beecher's Brooklyn, one that would dwarf the efforts of prewar predecessors like Charles Grandison Finney. As a young man, Moody had moved from Massachusetts to Chicago, become a successful shoe salesman and usurious moneylender, and worked for the Chicago YMCA. After a conversion experience, he became an itinerant revival preacher in the midwest, then rocketed to fame after a successful 1873–75 tour of England, Scotland, and Ireland, along with Ira D. Sankey, his musical director, who led congregants in old hymns and taught them new ones.

On his return, Moody launched the revival in Brooklyn. Demonstrating a mastery at organizing urban camp meetings, the evangelist converted a huge skating rink to a six-thousand-seat auditorium, advertised extensively with posters and newspapers, and accommodated reporters on the platform who in turn related the services at great length. The following year, 1876, he worked out of New York City's mammoth Hippodrome, the remodeled Harlem Railroad Depot at 26th and Madison whose adaptation cost a substantial ten thousand dollars, plus a fifteen-hundred-dollar weekly rental.

Moody's ministry was financed by the very wealthy (William E. Dodge, Cornelius Vanderbilt II, J. P. Morgan). As one journalist observed, a Moody revival was "a vast business enterprise, organized and conducted by businessmen, who have put money into it on business principals for the purpose of saving men." They applauded his views, which, though short on doctrine, suggested that urban suffering was due to city folk having drifted away from God and could best be addressed by seeking personal salvation through Jesus and avoiding sins such as drunkenness, Sabbath-breaking, and theatergoing or other "worldly amusements."

Moody's meetings were themselves fabulous middle-class entertainments. Immense crowds, often ten thousand or more, jammed and overflowed his arenas, aided by the streetcar companies, which built special tracks to their doors. The hymnbook and photograph vendors, the common singing, the mixing with pious strangers: these afforded a social outlet sorely needed by those required to abjure wicked commercial pleasures.

Such guilt-free get-togethers were particularly attractive to recently arrived, country-bred, evangelically oriented young men who had perhaps secured an office job but whose status and social networks still seemed fragile and insecure. One such newcomer was Horatio Alger, a recently secularized man of the cloth. Born in 1832 in Revere, Massachusetts, Alger went to Harvard, tried unsuccessfully to make a living as a professional writer for the Boston weeklies, then finally, and somewhat reluctantly, entered

Cambridge Theological School to prepare himself for the ministry. Alger spent the war years preaching. On the side, he wrote patriotic verse and a juvenile novel, *Frank's Campaign*, "to show how boys can be of most effectual service in assisting to put down the Rebellion." In 1864 he settled down as a Unitarian pastor in Brewster, Massachusetts, but his ministry ended abruptly two years later, after an investigation by church authorities determined that the pastor had been engaging in "unnatural crimes" with young boys in the parish. Alger, admitting he had been "imprudent," left town on the next train.

Moving to New York, Alger rented a room in a cheap hotel on St. Mark's Place and set about making a career as a writer, though at first his articles and novels garnered good reviews but disappointing sales. In the meantime he had begun to study the habits of New York's "street Arabs" and to aid the work of the Newsboys' Lodging House. A project inaugurated by Charles Loring Brace's Children's Aid Society, it provided dormitory space at Fulton and Nassau where newsboys and bootblacks could lodge for a nickel a night. Alger's experiences provided him with material that, once fictionalized, proved the making of him as a writer.

In 1867 the Boston editor of a children's magazine, *Student and Schoolmate*, began bringing out monthly installments of Alger's *Ragged Dick; or, Street Life in New York*. Dick, the bootblack hero, is ragged indeed, but a youth of enterprise and ambition. By chance (and luck plays as much a part as pluck in Alger's novels) Dick is hired by a wealthy merchant to guide his rural nephew, Frank, around the city. Dick initiates the country lad into the ways and wiles of the city. He takes Frank (and the reader) on an extensive tour of Manhattan, alerting Frank to urban perils: "A feller has to look sharp in this city, or he'll lose his eye-teeth before he knows it." At the same time, Frank introduces Dick to refined speech and dress and awakens his latent desire to rise in the world. Dick announces his intention to "try to grow up 'spectable." To ready himself for a job "in an office or counting room," he takes up lodgings, opens a savings account, and gets some new clothes. At this point, his past looms up in the person of Micky Maguire, an Irish Five Points tough, who accuses Dick of "putting on airs" and picks a fight. When Maguire (a boy of "impetuous" Irish nature) strikes out "wildly," Dick (a model of "quiet strength and coolness") fells the bully with "adroit" and "measured" blows. From here on Dick never looks back, and in the end he gets a Pearl Street counting-room job (at ten dollars a week), becomes Richard Hunter, Esq., and moves to "a nicer quarter of the city."

Dick's trajectory is not from rags to riches but from rags to 'spectability. Alger's sermons, like those of Beecher and Moody, honored not robber-baron rapacity but middle-class diligence. He counseled ambitious young boys to make themselves useful and acceptable to potential employers—to prepare themselves, as it were, for the dispensation of economic grace. Alger's secularized vision of salvation demanded ongoing subordination, not manly independence, as illustrated by the once scrappy Dick's now humble response to his job offer: "I'll try to serve you so faithfully, sir, that you won't repent having taken me into your service." His was a creed for clerks.

THE POLITICS OF DECENCY

The question of how to apply science to society—particularly the affairs of New York City—posed a conundrum for the middle class in general, and its intellectuals in particular. On the one hand, there was continuing enthusiasm in the postwar years for "scientific governance": action by experts, armed with up-to-date statistical information, to improve urban conditions. On the other hand, "social Darwinism" won many advocates; this credo, as expounded by Herbert Spencer, the English philosopher, and William Graham Sumner, the Yale sociologist, suggested that evolution's natural workings should not be interfered with by misguided state-based activists, even in the name of science, compassion, or justice. In the 1860s and 1870s New York's college-educated professionals veered back and forth between purposive social action and a revitalized laissez-faire, but people of both persuasions agreed the government of New York City was in the wrong hands.

Disgruntled observers believed the public sector responded all too readily to particularistic political and economic interests. Politicians pandered to the urban proletariat, dispensing largesse to alien immigrant voters, and self-serving businessmen barged their way into the legislative process, buying what favors they needed. Both streams of corruption commingled in the ample person of Boss Tweed—crony of Jay Gould, patron of the Irish, enemy of good government. There were, to be sure, sanitary engineers, landscape architects, educators, and physicians sprinkled throughout city government who had carved out positions of some independence—witness Croton engineer Craven—but trained intellectuals were generally shunted aside or forced to make dishonorable compromises with ignorant politicians.

What New York needed, argued the American Social Science Association (1865), was a neutral corps of experts, along the lines of the English civil service, in which Oxford and Cambridge graduates found respected positions administering the realm. To achieve it, the association called for civil service reform—taking public jobs away from party spoilsmen and giving them to qualified professionals—and a campaign got underway in which George William Curtis, political editor of *Harper's Weekly*, assumed the leading role.

Social Darwinists like E. L. Godkin also supported civil service reform. Godkin, a middle-class Protestant born in Northern Ireland, had emigrated to New York in 1856, having received a rigorous training in classical political economy at Queens College, Belfast. He began a career as free-lance journalist and, in 1865, accepted editorship of the *Nation*, which Olmsted had urged the Union League Club to establish. Godkin used his magazine pulpit to warn cultivated middle-class readers about looming threats to laissez-faire. Manufacturers wanted tariffs, which would disrupt the free flow of trade between nations. Greenbackers sought to block restoration of the gold standard, the only rational form of specie. The labor movement wanted to tamper with the "eternal laws of political economy" by imposing an eight-hour day, as preposterous an idea as legislating against the attraction of gravity. For Godkin, the most "scientific" government was the one that governed least, and bureaucrats of the proper persuasion would be far superior to Tammany hacks. In this Godkin had the fervent backing of bourgeois taxpayers who believed that politicians were spending extravagant sums of city money—their money—on public projects.

With both hands-off and hands-on advocates concurring that government should be turned over to (in Godkin's words) "thoughtful, educated, high-minded men," representatives of both perspectives inched their way toward the conclusion that universal suffrage was the major stumbling block to professionalizing government.

One strategy for curtailing the influence of the urban masses was advanced by Simon Sterne, a New York lawyer and University of Heidelberg graduate who promoted the English idea of "cumulative voting," a nostrum calculated to restore the influence of the educated minority. Others proposed giving extra weight to the ballots of college graduates or establishing literacy tests to screen out the uncultivated. Godkin suggested giving propertied taxpayers power to veto city expenditures adopted by "the representatives of mere numbers" or treating the city as a corporation and letting only those who held stock in it vote.

Though suffrage restriction remained a minority prescription, it won some sympathy in the most surprising quarters. In *Democratic Vistas* (1871) Walt Whitman denounced the terrible deficiencies of America's democratic society in the age of Grant and Tweed. Looking his times "searchingly in the face," Whitman found himself unable to "gloss over the appalling dangers of universal suffrage"—the "half-brained nominees," the "savage, wolfish parties," the governments "saturated in corruption, bribery, falsehood, maladministration." Most distressing of all was the fate of his beloved cities, New York and Brooklyn. Certainly there was still much to admire: the "oceanic amplitude and rush," the "hurrying, feverish, electric crowds," the "costly and lofty new buildings." But these aesthetic delights could not outweigh the "demonism of greed," the "robbery and scoundrelism," and the ascension of "a mob of fashionably dressed speculators and vulgarians" whose antics were matched only by the "plentiful meanness and vulgarity" of the masses below. The city had betrayed the promise of its artisanal republican youth, and Whitman could summon up only a nebulous hope for its moral renaissance.

"WOMEN: THEIR RIGHTS AND NOTHING LESS"

The booming metropolitan economy opened up opportunities for middle-class women to make their mark in professional and managerial positions—particularly those geared toward serving other women. Jane Cunningham Croly was a regular news columnist who published collections of her pieces under the pen name "Jennie June." Dr. Clemence Lozier was a highly regarded obstetrician who had established the New York Medical College and Hospital for Women in 1863, from which Dr. Susan Smith, daughter of a Weeksville pork merchant, graduated in 1870 to become New York's first female African-American doctor, and later founder of a Women's Hospital and Dispensary in Brooklyn. Dr. Mary Putnam Jacobi, daughter of George Palmer Putnam, studied medicine in Paris, taught at the Women's Medical College, and in 1872 would found the Women's Medical Association of New York City. Ellen Louise Demorest's *Mirror of Fashions* by now had sixty thousand readers, some as far away as mining settlements in Colorado and isolated farms in the Midwest. Sarah Payson Willis (Fanny Fern), now nearly sixty, was still the greatest circulation draw at Robert Bonner's *Ledger*, and Margaret Getchell, general manager of Macy's, was responsible for many of the firm's innovations.

Despite these individual successes, which built on the prewar legislative victories that allowed wives to keep their own earnings, middle-class females in general found themselves repeatedly thwarted in efforts to crack male monopolization of professional positions. When three women applied to Columbia Law School, one trustee responded, "No woman shall degrade herself by practicing law, in New York especially, if I can save her."

One such snub precipitated a collective reaction. On the occasion of Charles Dickens's second visit to the metropolis, the New York Press Club decided to pay him homage with a fancy Delmonico's dinner. Women, including journalist Croly, were barred. Croly, along with Willis, proposed forming a woman's club, in counterpoint to the male havens lining Fifth Avenue, in which women could support one another's initiatives and careers. Several of the best-known professional women had already begun meeting periodically at Sunday evening receptions held in the oak-paneled library of Alice and Phoebe Cary, two poet sisters. The core group quickly incorporated Sorosis—the first such organization in the country—and by April 1868 its members were meeting regularly in a second-floor room at Delmonico's. The idea of a woman's club triggered widespread derision, but the lampooning soon died down, in part because many members' husbands were powerful men. By 1870 Sorosis included thirty-eight writers, six editors, twelve poets, six musicians, two artists, ten lecturers, four professors, nine teachers, two physicians, and one historian.

Many in the group were feminists and freethinkers, including Jacobi, Matilda Joslyn Gage, and Paulina Wright Davis, and in 1869 Sorosis leaders helped organize a Woman's Parliament in New York City. The body established committees to deal with education, household reform, health reform, and newspaper work for women, among others. It lasted only a year but was resurrected, in 1873, as the Association for the Advancement of Women, again at the initiative of Sorosis. The association sponsored the first Woman's Congress, to which it invited all who "have conquered an honorable place in any of the professions or leading reforms of the day." Over four hundred women from eighteen states came to New York, all from upper- or middle-class backgrounds, and they concentrated on problems specific to professional women, like having "two careers." They applauded the ongoing expansion opportunities in women's education—that same year the Normal College of the City of New York (1869), the teachers' training institution presided over by Thomas Hunter, moved into a neo-

Anatomy Lesson at the New York College for Women, 1870, from *Frank Leslie's Illustrated Newspaper*, April 16, 1870. (© Collection of The New-York Historical Society)

Gothic building at 68th and Lexington—but delegates also demanded the opportunity to be educated for all professions and businesses.

Professional women in New York City also provided a powerful constituency for the broader feminist movement now revitalized by Susan B. Anthony and Elizabeth Cady Stanton. Both had been based in New York since Henry Stanton won appointment as deputy collector of the Custom House in 1862. The Stantons had settled into a brownstone on West 45th Street, a block from the Colored Orphan Asylum, and Anthony boarded with them. Like many other women, the duo had subordinated feminist concerns for the duration of the war—even when the state legislature took advantage of the temporary abeyance of feminist pressure to gut several provisions of the Married Women's Property Act. After Appomattox and the Thirteenth Amendment's abolition of slavery, they decided to press on for the emancipation of women, and in particular the right to vote.

In 1866 Stanton became the first woman to run for Congress—having noted that though females were disfranchised, nothing in the Constitution forbade them from holding office. A symbolic breakthrough, her campaign in New York City's Eighth District was an electoral flop, garnering but two score votes.

In 1867 Stanton and Anthony organized a lobbying and petition campaign to pressure the state constitutional convention—then considering black male suffrage—into extending the privilege to women too. Granted a hearing by Horace Greeley's Committee on Suffrage, they parried a barrage of jibes and objections, including Greeley's jocular query whether the women—given that "bullet and ballot go together"—were "ready to fight." "We are ready to fight, sir, just as you fought in the late war," Stanton snapped back, "by sending our substitutes." In the end the convention refused to grant female suffrage, an innovation "so openly at war with a distribution of duties and functions between the sexes."

The campaign for women's suffrage drew this satirical response from Currier & Ives, known variously as *The Age of Brass* or *The Triumph of Women's Rights*. (© Museum of the City of New York)

The women fared no better at the federal level. When former abolitionists set out to guarantee the vote for black males by passing the Fifteenth Amendment to the Constitution, Stanton and Anthony supported them but insisted that suffrage for women be included in the demand. Rebuffed by hitherto staunch supporters like Wendell Phillips, who announced that "this hour belongs to the negro," Stanton and Anthony countered that Phillips's definition of "negro" left out half the African-American race and that by smuggling the word "male" into the Constitution, the proposed new amendment was actually taking a step backward. Their protests proved unavailing, and many abolitionist women (mostly in Boston) supported Phillips's argument that burdening black suffrage with women's rights would sink it.

Balked by Republicans, Stanton and Anthony turned to Democrats, in the process embracing racist justifications for their cause. Arguing that white men should accept women as allies against the supposed perils of black supremacy, they joined forces with the flamboyant millionaire George Francis Train and campaigned for enfranchising Beauty, Virtue, and Intelligence to counter freedmen's Muscle, Color, and Ignorance. Many of their colleagues felt shamed by this appeal, but Stanton and Anthony argued that the Republican Party was a sinking ship, and "rats—that is female rats ought to know enough to leave." Yet when they appealed for support at the national Democratic Party convention in 1868, Stanton was literally laughed out of Tammany Hall.

Renewing their search for allies, Stanton and Anthony discovered their true constituency: middle-class women like themselves, particularly those living in New York City. Using funds provided by their rich ally George Francis Train, they launched a feminist journal, the *Revolution*, from offices in the Woman's Bureau, a large town house near Gramercy Park established by Elizabeth B. Phelps as a meeting center for New York women. With Anthony managing and Stanton editing, they brought out the first issue in January 1868, its masthead proclaiming, "Men Their Rights and Nothing More—Women Their Rights and Nothing Less." Train, a militant Fenian, departed soon after for Ireland, leaving Stanton and Anthony the sole directors of the paper.

The *Revolution*, promising that "not only the ballot, but bread and babies will be discussed," embraced a whole panoply of gender-related issues. The editors resurrected the radical feminist heritage by publishing the work of Frances Wright and Mary Wollstonecraft. They boldly tackled the divorce issue, which Stanton had first raised, to great consternation, at the Tenth Woman's Rights Convention in 1860, and again urged that marriage be treated not as a sacred pact but as a civil contract, easily dissolvable in the event of desertion, drunkenness, insanity, cruelty, adultery, and even simple incompatibility.

Setting the divorce issue in a still larger framework, the editors argued that women needed to become independent so they could marry and remain married out of choice, not economic necessity. This in turn required equal rights under law, the vote, coeducation in schools and colleges, and fundamental changes in society's attitudes about men, women, and the nature of their relationships. To this end, the editors took up subjects usually considered anathema in respectable publications, including sex education, infanticide, rape, wife beating, and prostitution. In 1867 the duo had protested when the Metropolitan Board of Health, picking up on Dr. Sanger's antebellum proposal, recommended fighting venereal disease (which had spread dramatically during the war years) by legalizing and registering prostitutes and requiring they be regularly inspected. Questioning why men who visited the prostitutes were to be immune from such public surveillance, they denounced the proposal as an insult to women, got the bill killed, and in 1871 beat back another attempt to pass what Anthony called a "Social Evil Bill."

The *Revolution*'s editors also mobilized for action around the suffrage issue. At an 1869 meeting in the Woman's Bureau, they and their supporters formed the National Woman's Suffrage Association—an avowedly feminist-first body whose officers were all women—to press for passage of a Sixteenth Amendment to guarantee female access to the ballot. It was supplemented the following year by the New York City Woman Suffrage Association (1870), formed by Dr. Clemence Lozier and Charlotte Wilbour, president of Sorosis, beginning what would be a decades-long struggle to win the franchise locally.

The *Revolution*'s militant policies won significant support from New York City's professional women. Many in Sorosis were quite prepared to take up daring subjects: club members discussed abortion and prostitution, and Dr. Mary Putnam Jacobi lectured about the need to abolish female ignorance concerning sexual physiology. Dr. Anna Densmore, vice-president of the New York City Woman's Club, gave scientific lectures for women on physiology and in 1868 got Board of Education approval to train female public school teachers to pass on such information to their students.

Other women were alarmed or repelled by material they considered far too controversial. In addition, former antislavery activists denounced Stanton and Anthony's continuing resort to race (and class) bigotry. When the Fifteenth Amendment passed Congress in February 1869, making no provision for women, Stanton denounced it as an "open, deliberate insult to American womanhood to be cast down under the iron-heeled peasantry of the Old World and these slaves of the New."

At the same moment they were being challenged by relatively conservative women, Stanton and Anthony found themselves confronting Victoria Woodhull, a feminist who was in some respects more radical—and certainly more flamboyant—than they were. Born poor in the frontier hamlet of Homer, Ohio, Woodhull had spent her youth roaming the Midwest with a traveling family medicine show—telling fortunes, communing with spirits, practicing faith healing and animal magnetism. With her sister Tennie C. (or Tennessee) Claflin she came to New York after the war and struck up an alliance with Cornelius Vanderbilt (Tennessee's physical ministrations warmed the old man's bones while Victoria's seances consoled him over the loss of his wife). Vanderbilt's remarriage suspended more intimate relations, but the grateful millionaire set them up on Wall Street. Woodhull, Claflin, and Co., the first woman's brokerage firm in the all-male New York financial world, was a great success, its rise in no way impeded by the sisters' well-known association with the Commodore, and the women made a small fortune.

They did not, however, rest on these professional laurels, but instead entered the world of radical politics. In 1870 they started their own newspaper, *Woodhull and Claflin's Weekly*, which took up the deeply scandalous (and deeply misunderstood) issue of Free Love. Widely seen as a commitment to unbridled lechery, it was, in fact, a feminist challenge to men's sexual prerogatives under prevailing gender rules. Free Lovers attacked the double standard and insisted men be held to the same high levels of moral purity that were required of women. In some respects, Woodhull's position was not far removed from that of those who had challenged the convention of marriage ("We are all free lovers at heart," Stanton said). The *Revolution*, quite as often as *Wood-*

hull and Claflin's Weekly, carried demands for a woman's "control over her own person, independent of the desires of her husband."

If some of Woodhull's ideas weren't shocking, her manners certainly were. Woodhull was a feminist for the age of flash, as shrewd about publicity as Barnum, as brash in personal style as Jim Fisk. Her personal appearance violated gender proprieties: short hair, skirts that reached only her shoe tops, jackets of mannish cut, bright-colored neckties. Worse still, Woodhull argued that people might have more than one "natural mate," which raised the theoretical possibility of extramarital pursuits (in Victoria's case, apparently, not merely theoretical), and she took a positive view of sexual pleasure, even when not aimed at procreation, and indeed agitated openly for legalized prostitution and birth control. Mainstream feminists did not approve of contraceptive devices (though many used them) for fear their widespread adoption would increase male promiscuity. They were wary of abortion (though many had them) because they were associated with frivolous society women, demimondaines, and the poor and because they too could be used by men to escape the consequences of their cavortings.

Given her notoriety, when Woodhull plunged into the suffrage movement, many in the American Woman Suffrage Association and even some in the National Woman's Suffrage Association (including Stanton) were dismayed. But Woodhull quickly earned some kudos. She presented a memorial to the House of Representatives arguing that the Fourteenth Amendment's extension of suffrage to blacks provided ample constitutional grounds for granting it to women, and she proposed that women take direct action at polling places and assert their right to vote. Woodhull's speech and battle plan met with tremendous acclaim and catapulted her to a leadership position in the suffrage movement. Objections by those scandalized by association with such a forward woman were brusquely dismissed by Stanton: "We have had women enough sacrificed to this sentimental, hypocritical prating about purity," she said scathingly. "If Victoria Woodhull must be crucified, let men drive the spikes and plait the crown of thorns."

In 1872 Stanton went so far as to back Woodhull's proposal to use the May meeting of the National Woman's Suffrage Association in Steinway Hall to launch a third political party, of which Woodhull would be the presidential candidate. The new People's Party platform, as leading feminists envisioned it, would merge their crusade for the enfranchisement of women with the movement that, for the past several years, had been pressing for the emancipation of labor.

Eight Hours for
What We Will

Postwar prosperity revitalized the labor movement. German tradesmen (nearly a quarter of the city's working population) were particularly energetic. Their individual unions—woodworkers, machinists, tailors, cigarmakers, waiters, silverplaters, and bookbinders—confederated in an umbrella organization, the Arbeiter Union. English-speaking workers, led by printers and building tradesmen, formed their own citywide central, the Workingmen's Union. Irish organizations flourished too, both the Longshoremen's Union and the Laborers United Benevolent Society, which, with its myriad divisions (brown-stone cutters and blue-stone cutters, marble cutters and marble-polishers, hod carriers and derrickmen, sawyers and quarrymen), was the largest labor organization in the city. Seventy thousand were involved in this union resurgence. A larger proportion of the metropolitan working population enrolled in trade unions between 1865 and 1873 than during any other period of the nineteenth century.

City unions launched 249 trade-wide strikes between 1863 and 1873, some of them, like the 1868 bricklayers' walkout, involving several thousand workers. Some trades were particularly militant and persistent: Steinway's pianomakers struck in 1863, 1864, twice in 1865, and again in 1869. From 1866 on the Association for Improving the Condition of the Poor published yearly reports on "Labor Movements and Strikes."

Many contests were for higher wages, as workers fought to keep ahead of rising costs. They also sought a fair share of the period's tremendous profits, most of which accrued to the owners of capital, who flagrantly displayed their riches for all to see. Capitalists groused at these demands. A. A. Low told the Chamber of Commerce that the only real danger to "the prosperity of our port and our city" was "the combinations of men who seek continually to advance the prices of labor beyond what employers can afford to pay." But pay they did. Rolling in money, employers could easily afford to purchase labor peace. Wages in the strategically critical construction trades nearly doubled in the 1860s.

THE EIGHT-HOUR DAY

Another labor objective—one that inspired much stiffer resistance from employers—was to cut the working day from ten to fourteen hours down to eight. In May 1865 the Workingmen's Union launched the eight-hour campaign with a monster picnic in Jones' Wood attended by fifty thousand. In December a packed mass meeting of over fifty unions at Cooper Institute turned thousands away. The following April an immense rally jammed Union Square.

Speakers at these events—men like Brooklynite William Harding, president of the coachmakers—argued that an eight-hour day would ease the crushing workload that made laborers slaves to their jobs. "Labor-saving" machines should start saving labor, rather than just increasing profits. Eight hours for work and eight for sleep would leave eight more in which to develop their human capacities, to be with their families, to get some fun out of life. The working class should get to enjoy the pleasures of the city. There was, Harding reminded his audiences, a fine picture gallery in the Cooper Institute, but not one in twenty workingmen had time to see it. A band gave concerts in Central Park, but artisans hadn't time to hear it. "Should it not," he asked, "play for the mechanics in this republic as well as for the millionaire?" Shorter hours would make it feasible for workers to live farther away from their jobs and escape the tenement districts. Shorter hours would cut unemployment, by requiring more workers to maintain existing production levels. Shorter hours would ward off depressions, by boosting wages and increasing purchasing power.

Moving beyond speechmaking, the Workingmen's Union petitioned New York State to pass an eight-hour law. In April 1866 shipyard workers at the Greenpoint yards launched a strike for the eight-hour day. It was broken, but the sounds of labor's growing militancy were heard up in Albany. State legislators disagreed on how to respond. The ruling Radical Republicans had demonstrated, in the cases of the fire department and the Board of Health, that they were prepared to use government to redress social ills. They liked the eight-hour issue's potential to attract Democratic workmen to their party. They appreciated the argument that laborers would use the extra time to improve their character as citizens and workers.

But Radicals worried about intervening in capital-labor relations. The idea went beyond guaranteeing the equality of individuals and smacked of "class legislation," which might open the door to more extreme proposals. Some lawmakers were convinced that workers would use their leisure time to drink themselves into a stupor. Others argued that hours legislation violated both the "natural law" of supply and demand and the "liberty" of the worker. "This is a free country," said one Republican, "and everybody ought to be allowed to work just as long as he pleases."

They settled on a spurious compromise, embodied in the Eight Hour Law of April 1867. The legislation set eight hours as the legal length of a working day but allowed longer workdays if arranged by "mutual consent." If a laborer worked "overtime," moreover, he or she was not entitled to extra compensation. Nor did the state create an administrative agency to monitor compliance. Employers ignored the law.

Unions decided to enforce it on their own. At the beginning of the 1868 construction season, over two thousand bricklayers struck for a 20 percent reduction of hours (from ten to eight), to be partly offset by a 10 percent cut in wages (from $5.00 to $4.50). Boss masons fought back furiously, supported by investors and clients like Vanderbilt who would brook no impediment to the breakneck and profitable pace of construction. They organized an employers' association, advertised in other cities for replacement workers, and sued the journeymen under state conspiracy laws.

Other workers, realizing a crucial test of strength was at hand, rallied to the builders' support. When bricklayers at the new Arnold Constable site insisted on a shorter workday, plasterers and painters walked off as well. Traveling committees went to Brooklyn, Jersey City, and Philadelphia, dissuaded scabs from coming, and got union locals there to provide money and roughly a thousand jobs for their beleaguered New York comrades. The Workingmen's Union organized a mammoth street procession, headed by two thousand bricklayers, and held a militant rally at Cooper Institute. By 1869 a majority of builders were working eight hours. So were federal employees at the Navy Yard, thanks to the Radical Republican Congress and the Grant administration.

The gains proved difficult to sustain, however, thanks in part to Jay Gould. In the slump that followed the unraveling of his gold corner in September 1869, many employers successfully forced hours back up to ten, so the unions turned again to politics. In the fall of 1869, claiming that "both of the existing parties are corrupt, serving capital instead of labor," the Workingmen's Union, the Arbeiter Union, and the Irish unions combined to run independent labor candidates. Their electoral initiative was defeated, as were others in 1870 and 1871, so they had to rely on workplace battles to wring concessions on wages and hours from employers.

MARXISTS, FEMINISTS, AND THE MONEY POWER

Many unionists believed labor's ills were exacerbated by the financial system. New York workers watched the shenanigans on the Stock Exchange, probed the impact of the new banking system, and called for a change in monetary policy. Before the war labor had fought for hard money against the depreciated paper notes issued by banks. Now, with bondholders clamoring for a return to the gold standard, unions backed paper currency. What linked labor's old "hard" and new "soft" money programs was the insistence that control over currency should be taken from banks and given to government.

The soft money policy was adopted by the new National Labor Union, established in 1866, when officers of nine national unions—all residents of the metropolitan area— met in New York City. The union aimed to coordinate labor activity on a continental scale, support the eight-hour day, and fight the "Money Power." When Republicans (and Wall Street Democrats) triumphantly passed the Public Credit Act guaranteeing a return to specie payments, many workingmen decried a bondholder victory engineered (they were darkly convinced) by "the Rothschilds and their agents here."

Another set of participants in the postwar labor movement, the German socialists, supported both the eight-hour day and currency reform but argued that such piecemeal single-issue strategies were doomed from the start, that only a broad-based attack on the entire capitalist order could succeed. The sole survivor of the prewar movement, Friedrich Sorge's Communist Club, affiliated itself with Karl Marx's International Workingmen's Association (IWA) and in the late 1860s received reinforcements when radical brewers, metalworkers, and printers arrived from Germany. Radical intellectuals arrived as well—followers of Ferdinand Lassalle—who proposed organizing cooperatives, a shopworn approach to which they gave a new twist. Co-ops, Lassalleans argued, could compete with capitalist firms if they got financing from the state, so workers should use the ballot to attain political power.

In 1868 New York's Marxists and Lassalleans joined forces and plunged into politics. Their platform called for the eight-hour day, currency reform, a progressive income tax, and equal rights for men and women. They got nowhere electorally. But digging in for the long haul, they reconstituted themselves as Section 1 of the IWA, with Sorge as secretary. The IWA, headquartered at Broome and Forsythe (near Fanny Wright's 1829 Hall of Science), had strong links to the German trade unions, and it became the backbone of a renewed socialist movement in New York City. Like other German-American vereins, the socialists created an array of neighborhood clubs, chiefly organized by socialist women, who arranged bake fests, musical performances, "hen parties," excursions, and events at the socialist-owned Germania Hall in the Bowery.

Their very success at rooting themselves in Kleindeutschland concerned the ever practical Marx, who sent word from London that the nascent American socialist movement had better expand beyond "foreigners residing in the U.S." Sorge protested this characterization, calling his members "adopted citizens," but others admitted that "we Germans do not mingle with Americans in public." In July 1871, accordingly, two "American sections" were admitted to the International.

The leaders of Sections 9 and 12 were indigenous (and mostly elderly) New York land reformers and labor activists. Some had been engaged in radical politics since the era of the Loco Focos. They included John Commerford, the chairmaker who had presided over the National Trades Union in 1835, Lewis Masquerier, who had helped George Henry Evans found the National Reform Association in 1844, and Stephen Pearl Andrews, the now sixty-year-old abolitionist, anarchist, mystic, Free Lover, and leader of a circle that included Victoria Woodhull and Tennessee Claflin.

These survivors of the successful crusade against slavery were determined to create a fully egalitarian society. Andrews and his comrades were radical democrats, convinced that extending citizenship rights to blacks and women was the best way to right society's wrongs. They also supported a vast range of other reforms—universal religion, universal language, universal world government—some with distinctly crankish aspects. They ardently opposed monopolies, landlords, politicians, and clerics but were also, as Marxists noted with alarm, hostile to class-based movements and sought the "Scientific Reconciliation of Labor and Capital." Yet it was clear to the Germans that, all in all, the American sections' democratic egalitarianism and experience with direct action made them a potentially potent addition. For the moment, the IWA flourished—by the end of 1871 there were thirty-three sections, with five thousand members—and it received the endorsement of the English-speaking New York Workingmen's Assembly led by the sympathetic William J. Jessup.

Working women, on the other hand, though they would have liked to join the resurgent labor movement, continued to be unwelcome. So some responded positively when, as before the war, they received offers of help from middle-class women—this time not religious reformers but suffrage leaders. Stanton and Anthony turned to workers in their search for allies. The *Revolution* embraced the eight-hour day and greenbackism, agreed that the working class was the source of all wealth, accepted that the rich had stolen their wealth from those who created it, and declared that strikes were legitimate tools of working people.

As part of their new concern for the condition of working women in New York City, feminists investigated the situation of seamstresses at A. T. Stewart's department store, and in 1868, Anthony and Stanton established the Workingwoman's Association, initially composed chiefly of female typographers who worked in The *Revolution*'s shop. Publishers confronting strikes by the all-male National Typographical Union had made a practice of training women as compositors, employing them as scabs, then firing (or demoting) them once the men were brought to terms. This had created a pool of semiskilled, semitrained women floating around the industry, whom Anthony through the typographers offered to help organize. The female printers decided to take her up on it, though nervous about being tagged "strong-minded" women of a Bloomer persuasion.

Though Stanton and Anthony hoped the Workingwoman's Association would in the long run establish unions in every industry employing women and forge a cross-class alliance behind women's suffrage, in the short term the group provided Anthony with the credentials she needed to join the National Labor Union, whose members she wished to lobby on behalf of women's rights. The NLU accepted her as a delegate to the New York City convention in 1868, in part because it too was looking for allies. But as soon as Anthony raised feminist issues, it became clear this would be a difficult coalition to cement. The NLU's base of skilled white craft workers saw working women as competitors. They also believed women were "created" to be "the presiding deity of the home circle," as one NLU leader argued, there to "console us in our declining years."

What shattered the alliance was a labor conflict that pointed up the gap between middle-class feminists and working-class unionists. The National Typographical Union, impressed with the new militancy of female printers, moved to placate and incorporate them. They were accepted as an NTU local, and when male printers struck the *World*, the women refused to replace them. But now Anthony stepped forward as a

The Upstairs Sewing Room at A.T. Stewart's store on Broadway at Tenth Street, *Frank Leslie's Illustrated Newspaper*, April 24, 1875. While middle- and upper-class women thronged the emporiums of Ladies' Mile below, regiments of working-class seamstresses toiled under the watchful eyes of male supervisors. (© Collection of The New-York Historical Society)

strikebreaker. She offered the Workingwoman's Association as a place where publishers could train women to be scabs, arguing (as did employers) that it was only seeking new opportunities for females. Printers at the national convention in 1869 demanded Anthony's ouster, and got it.

The Workingwoman's Association did not last much longer, but its existence marked an important development. In the past, the conventional linkages between upper- and lower-class women—charitable enterprises launched by ladies—had been one-sided and condescending. The Workingwoman's Association, though riddled with mutual misunderstandings, suggested the possibility of a more coequal coalition.

WALKING TO WORK

Even with improved wages, the bulk of the working class—still unable to afford public transportation—had to live near their jobs. For most this meant Manhattan's rim, the tenement-lined streets leading back from the docks into a mixed terrain of heavy industry and light manufacture. The twenty-five thousand ironworkers walked to great foundries rooted on the East and Hudson river shorelines, near their rail and sea lifelines. Clothing sweatshops sprouted in the Lower East Side wards to be near their cheap labor supplies (some women outworkers rarely left their tenements at all). Bohemian cigarmakers too worked at home now that cigar molds made it possible to do so.

The proximity of community to industry cast a pall over daily life. Admixed with foundries and factories were reeking gasworks, putrid slaughterhouses, malodorous railyards, rotting wharves, and stinking manure piles, which gave the working-class quarters their distinctively fetid quality. In the Lower (predominantly Irish and German) East and West Side wards, the stench was compounded by Tweed's inaction. The race to develop the uptown wards left scant energy or public capital available to rescue the downtown districts, many built on filled-in swampland. Poorly designed sewage pipes were left to spew their putrefying contents into cobblestoned streets, where they mingled with animal wastes, and where at night homeless children slept in abandoned carts and wagons. Cholera and other diseases devastated such streets. In 1866 the death rate reached 195 per thousand in the worst blocks. Even the cantankerous George Templeton Strong muttered, "It is shameful that men, women and children should be permitted to live in such holes."

Those who could, moved. Conditions were far better in the newer tenements of Yorkville or Harlem, if one had the cash for a horsecar commute downtown or found a job in the factories, stoneyards, or gas tanks moving north along the East River. But sleazy conditions crept uptown too, as speculators threw up rookeries on the damp and low-lying streets leading from First Avenue down to the waterfront. The area's many vacant lots were used as garbage dumps, through which poor women and children scavenged, and stables from near and far dropped their loads at colossal manure heaps. Conditions on the far West Side were no better. The immigrant residential areas abutting the railyards, factories, and the stinking Manhattan Gas Works at 18th and Tenth were so bad that their upper reaches, around the west 30s and 40s, became known as Hell's Kitchen (the name borrowed from an old Corlear's Hook dive or perhaps a local gang).

Other workers fled Manhattan for Brooklyn. Conditions were marginally better in the factory-warehouse districts along the Red Hook waterfront and around the Gowanus Canal, and considerably so in the growing downtowns of Brooklyn proper, Williamsburg, and Greenpoint and in the upper stretches (around Myrtle Avenue) of

Bushwick and Bedford. Other laborers settled on the new urban frontiers: the blue-collar, oil-worker town of Hunter's Point (soon Long Island City), the company town of Steinway, or industrial villages like College Point, Woodhaven, and Mott Haven in the Bronx. In 1869 the German Cabinetmakers Association of New York cooperatively purchased five East Astoria farms, covering ninety-one acres; in 1870 they opened a hotel and a shooting gallery that within two years had blossomed into Scheutzen Park, a seven-acre grove complete with woodland, shooting galleries, and dancing pavilions.

Working women had special problems finding housing. Those who entered service were provided for, of course, though the "new conveniences" seldom reached the top-floor servants' quarters, whose inhabitants still washed weekly in a tub in the kitchen. Clothing workers continued to pool their low wages and rent a garret or tenement room. But the ranks of single laboring women had grown greatly in the backwash of civil war, a function of mass widowhood, economic dislocation, and a dearth of marriageable men. And many boardinghouses—the chief mainstay of single men—refused to accept single women.

Middle-class reformers made some efforts on their behalf. The Female Christian Home and Ladies Christian Association (later the YWCA) founded a Young Woman's Home to promote the "temporal moral and religious welfare of women, particularly of young women dependent on their own exertions for support." The Five Points House of Industry, aided by the state, remodeled the old six-story tenement on Elizabeth Street, built in 1855 by the AICP as a "Workmen's Home," and renamed it the Home for Working Women. It provided its five hundred boarders and employees with six dormitories, a large dining room, parlors with donated pianos and organs, a sewing room, and a library with daily papers, but it required character references to enter and attendance at prayers to stay.

These initiatives served as models for A. T. Stewart, who wanted to repay his debt to the women who had made his fortune (and perhaps encourage his current employees to remain unmarried longer, and help expand his fortune farther). Stewart built a magnificent hotel for working women of good character on Fourth and 32nd. Its sumptuous apartments, for a thousand women, put it on a par with the city's top hotels, and Stewart planned to rent them at an affordable $2.50 a week for room and board. But Stewart died in 1876, and his executors upped the charges to seven dollars—knocking out seamstresses and dry-goods clerks but accommodating teachers, bookkeepers, and governesses. When it still continued to lose money, it was shut down altogether after a scant two months of philanthropic life and reopened as a luxury hotel.

COLORED QUARTERS

Relations between working-class blacks and whites did not improve in the decade after the draft riots, and labor's new solidarity did not extend across racial lines. When Susan B. Anthony asked why unions didn't lower their barriers to women, a baffled printer replied: "You might as well ask why we don't send for the colored men or the Chinese to learn the trade." White contractors and work gangs collaborated in keeping black workers from the docks, pits, and quarries and in terrorizing those who did get hired, even though the costs of such racial exclusion kept mounting. An 1866 strike by Greenpoint shipyard workers had been successful—until black caulkers were brought in from Portsmouth, Virginia, to replace them, which further poisoned relations.

In 1869 blacks demanded an "equal right to labor with all other classes of our fellow citizens," calling the exclusion policy "strong evidence of the power which the spirit of slavery and caste still holds over the mind of our white fellow citizens." The sole positive response came from Section 1 of the IWA, the only white citywide labor group that actively promoted the organization of black workers—one reason the National Colored Labor Convention sent a delegate to the 1870 Paris Congress of the First International.

Excluded from the mechanical trades—a machinist with Admiral Farragut found he couldn't get a job in the city—blacks remained sequestered in the laboring and service sectors as longshoremen, laundresses, sailors, waiters, barbers, cooks, servants, coachmen, or porters or in a handful of skilled crafts jobs. Excluded from the unions, laborers, longshoremen, and artisans gathered in the New York African Society for Mutual Relief, founded in 1808 and still going strong, while black caterers, coachmen, barbers, and seamen formed their own organizations.

Despite the generally dismal circumstances, the city's shrunken black community began to regenerate itself. At war's end there were but 14,804 African-Americans in New York and Brooklyn combined, five thousand fewer than in 1840, and they constituted a scant 1.4 percent of the total population. The populace grew 26.7 percent between 1865 and 1870 and jumped by another 53.6 percent over the next decade, partly through natural increase and partly via the flow of immigrant freedmen who began to trickle north, primarily from Virginia.

Internal migration was more dramatic. In the 1860s and 1870s, though some blacks still lived in Greenwich Village, like "sardines in a box in rickety-old houses," many more had migrated to enclaves in Hell's Kitchen. These were among the meanest areas in the city but were within walking distance of such longshore and service jobs as remained open to them. Churches relocated accordingly. St. Mark's Methodist Episcopal and Bethel African Methodist Episcopal moved uptown. New congregations opened as well, like Mount Olivet Baptist, which appealed particularly to southern newcomers. Philanthropists followed too. The Quakers' New York Colored Mission settled on West 30th Street to seek the "religious, moral and social elevation of the Colored People"; it offered Sunday school, Bible classes, aid for the sick and underfed, and a nursery school to get children out of apartments "while laundry work was carried on."

Brooklyn had been attracting blacks since the draft riots, though here too numbers remained small. In 1870, out of a total Brooklyn population of approximately 420,000, roughly fifty-six hundred were African Americans, and they were scattered across widely separated communities. The Fort Greene Park area, south and east of the Navy Yard, and the stretch along Atlantic Avenue to the western border of Bedford both witnessed black development in these years. The black enclave at Weeksville-Carrville still hosted 650 in 1875, though much of the area was destroyed when Eastern Parkway and other streets were cut through the area, and it soon lost its African-American character.

HAVING FUN

New York's working people divided along racial and ethnic lines at play as well as at work and in their residential quarters, in part because so many leisure-time activities were themselves structured around existing communal institutions: fraternal orders, benevolent societies, political and social clubs, militias and rifle clubs, unions, churches, and family groups.

After the war Kleindeutschland's Germans enhanced the already considerable number of spaces devoted to community pastimes, adding Walhalla Hall, Beethoven

Hall, and a new Turn Halle, among many others. Here German confectioners, uphol-sterers, barbers, horseshoers, morocco dressers, and goldworkers could hold their fall and winter balls.

German (and Irish) associations also traipsed en masse to pleasure spots around the metropolitan area. At first, the favorite Manhattan venue was Jones' Wood, where the Schermerhorn and Jones families had leased their grounds to entrepreneurs who estab-lished a commercial picnic ground and hotel there. The proprietors then rented out the space to ethnic, social, athletic, and religious groups, who arranged their own excur-sions or festivals. Germans arrived in great numbers—by steamboat or the Second and Third Avenue street railways—to dance to German music, watch gymnastic exhibi-tions, and drink lager beer. The Scottish Caledonian Society held track and field games at Jones' Wood, and Irish church groups and temperance societies held annual excur-sions and fund-raising picnics.

Improved transport made trips farther afield practical too. The Journeymen Plumbers traveled (along with Wallach's Brass Band) by steamboat and barge up the Hudson to hold their annual picnics at Dudley's Grove. Nearby rural Queens County was even more popular. Every Sunday four to five thousand would cross to Hunter's Point on the 34th Street ferry and fan out to various country retreats for picnics. On one fine afternoon in 1872 so many Germans flocked to Schuetzen Park to hear the Prussian Guard Band play that over a thousand were turned away. Steamers ferried massive crowds directly to weekend resorts like Witzel's twenty-seven-acre establishment at College Point for eels, clams, and beer and to Coney Island, whose west end was an increasingly popular destination.

Working people avoided the new Central Park at first—aside from special occasions like July 4—as Olmsted's rules forbidding German singing society picnics or Irish church suppers made it clear that visitors were welcome only on bourgeois terms. Things changed when Tweed's charter transferred power from state to city. The Tweed regime did not, as the *New York Times* was convinced it would, turn the park over to rowdies, peddlers, and prostitutes. Tammany politicians actually improved the park—while lining their pockets and those of well-connected contractors. It also loosened park rules, expanded permissible activities, and added new attractions like boat rentals, Sun-day pony rides (though religious groups blocked Sunday concerts), and a children's carousel, turned by a blind mule in the basement. Above all the Democrats renovated the Arsenal Zoo in 1870. By 1873 park attendance had jumped 43 percent, and the zoo, a free attraction, was the destination of roughly one of every four visitors (especially after circus owners like P. T. Barnum began quartering animals there). Working-class visitation continued to soar in the late 1870s, as the Sixth Avenue El cut twenty minutes off travel time from downtown and more working people had moved within walking dis-tance. Sundays in the park were now dominated by working-class visitors, especially Germans.

Alongside these communal activities the city's expanding commercial culture attracted people on a more individual basis. On Saturday evening, their week's wages in hand, working people still headed for the Bowery. From its lower reaches in the Five Points up to its northern end where it spilled into the Union Square Rialto area, the Bowery was aflame with gas-lit clusters of white, red, blue, and green glass globes. The street itself was filled with entertainers: four- or five-piece German bands playing waltzes and schottisches, organ grinders with gaudily attired monkeys, black quartets singing spirituals, street vendors hawking hot corn and fresh oysters (the latter served raw, with pepper sauce, for a penny apiece). Illuminated signs—a good half now in German—pinpointed the tremendous variety of indoor attractions, including the *Lagerbier* saloons, the *Weinstuben* ("Grosses Conzert, Eintritt Frei"), and huge establishments like the Atlantic Garden where German families sang songs of the fatherland or listened to orchestras perform Strauss, Wagner, and Beethoven.

Popular theaters—including the old Bowery, still going strong—offered melodramas like *The Three Fast Men, or New York by Daylight and Gaslight* and dramatized stories from the *New York Weekly* like *Bertha, the Sewing Machine Girl*. Many featured elaborate special effects and mechanisms, such as trains, fires, and live animals. Some houses specialized in Irish dramas in which virtuous peasant girls and high-minded patriots joined forces to confound designing English dukes. As in prior generations, actors engaged in colloquies with the peanut-and-sausage-munching audiences (families held mini-picnics in the second tier). Marching down front after a particularly patriotic speech, they would demand, "Isn't that so, boys?" and receive an earsplitting affirmation. Other houses presented musical extravaganzas, burlesque, and French opéra bouffe.

Bowery dime museums presented mechanical contrivances, flea circuses, and wax figures: one such establishment had a fake Dante's Inferno peopled by the likes of Tweed, Gould, and Henry Ward Beecher. A panorama building housed a Gettysburg cyclorama where audiences stood while unfolding canvases depicted the clash of armies (accompanied by narration from a uniformed veteran). Lent's New York Circus at 14th Street (just across from the elite's Academy of Music) boasted equestrian rings—larger than Astley's in London or the Cirque Napoleon in Paris—where one could see horseback riders, high-wire artists, clowns, and animal acts.

"Variety" shows refused to specialize in any one popular entertainment form but mixed them all. Starting in 1865 Tony Pastor, a former clown and veteran concert saloon entertainer, ran one out of an old Bowery theater. Tony Pastor's was known as a bar-free family house, a place to take one's maiden aunt. It mixed blackface minstrelsy, clog dances, magicians, acrobats, tableaux vivants, sing-alongs with Tony, and plays presenting idealized pictures of life on the Lower East Side (like *The Little Fraud*, in which Ned Harrigan and Tony Hart made their first appearance in September of 1872).

Tammany Hall merged politics and entertainment, already stylistically similar, in its new headquarters (1868) just off Union Square at 141 East 14th Street. The Tammany Society kept only one room for itself, renting the rest to entertainment impresarios: Dan Bryant's Minstrels, a German theater company, classical concerts and opera. The basement—in the French mode—offered the Café Ausant, where one could see tableaux vivant, gymnastic exhibitions, pantomimes, and Punch and Judy shows. There was also a bar, a bazaar, a Ladies' Cafe, and an oyster saloon. All this—with the exception of Bryant's—was open from seven till midnight for a combination price of fifty cents.

All-male audiences could enjoy raunchier entertainments. After 1874 Robinson Hall presented the cancan—"funny, frenchy, spicy and sparkling"—which was such a hit the theater changed its name to Parisian Varieties. This inspired the Columbia Café to open in 1875 with "the Latest Parisian Novelties," including risqué pieces like *Cleopatra's Amours* and *Fifty Nice Girls in Naughty Sketches*. The competition soon generated full-fledged girly shows—"spicy French Sensations" such as *Beautiful Min-*

uet Dances from the Jardin Mabille, Paris and *The Sultan's Harem, or Secrets of the Seraglio.*

Raunchier still—and far more participatory—were the concert halls at the Bowery's lower end, in the Five Points, or along the waterfront. Many were gas-lit basement dives—like Sailor's Welcome Home or the Jolly Tar—which cajoled sailors through their red-curtained doors down to rooms where pianos rolled and drinks were brought to bare tables by waiter-girls. Other desires could usually be accommodated on the premises—in gambling rooms, cockpits, boxing rings, or ersatz seraglios complete with women in Turkish costumes.

Finally, there were the real workshops of commercial sex, brothels geared to male laborers. The female laborers here worked in unappealing conditions. The madams, entrepreneurs of sex, charged their girls—the appropriate term, as many of the whores were between ten and fifteen—weekly board and took half their income. Given their vested interest in productivity, the madams insisted on a high-volume, high-turnover strategy. On Saturday and Sunday nights lines formed outside the most successful houses. One Stakhanovite of sex serviced fifty-eight men in three hours. The more routine (but still strenuous) rate averaged between from seventy to a hundred encounters a week, at one to two dollars for ten to fifteen minutes in the sack.

OLD SLEUTH AND BUFFALO BILL

Sensational fiction was another working-class pleasure—quite different from the genteel fiction served up in *Harper's* or *Scribner's*—which New York publishers specialized in generating. The front counters of corner groceries sold story papers like Beadle and Adams's *Saturday Journal* and George Munro's *Fireside Companion*. Aimed at the

Inside John Allen's Dance House on Water Street, *Frank Leslie's Illustrated Newspaper*, August 8, 1868. Allen provided small rooms in the rear of the house for prostitution, each of which he equipped with a Bible. In 1868, he began allowing prominent evangelists to hold prayer meetings in his establishment, which soon lost its clientele and was converted into a revival hall. (General Research. The New York Public Library. Astor, Lenox and Tilden Foundations)

entire family, they offered eight pages of illustrated adventure stories and domestic romances, usually three or four serialized episodes per issue. The installments were then collated and reprinted as pamphlet novels selling for a nickel or ten cents and packaged in "libraries."

The form was pioneered by Erastus Beadle, a small New York City publisher of ten-cent song and etiquette books, who in 1860 began bringing out a weekly series of pamphlet novelettes known as Beadle's Dime Novels. During the Civil War these handy, pocket-sized (four by six inches, a hundred pages) "yellow-backs" became enormously popular with young soldiers. Beadle published four million by 1865. Competitors sprang up immediately. George Munro, a clerk in the Beadle enterprise, started his own operation in 1863, and by the 1870s his firm had become one of the largest mass-fiction publishers in the country.

Dime novel entrepreneurs employed journalists, teachers, and clerks to hack out formulaic literary commodities. The intended audience was composed of skilled craftsmen, factory workers, and laborers, at times sorted out ethnically, as with the Ten Cent Irish Novels and George Munro's Die Deutsche Library, though none addressed blacks. Many serials spoke to young female domestic servants, but the overwhelming targets were young men and boys.

The papers and booklets, heavily advertised, were distributed nationally by the monopolistic American News Company (formed in 1864) along the new trunk railway lines. But their premier audience, and often premier subject, lay in the city itself, especially in the case of crime thrillers. In this Poe-initiated genre, a professional villain, often of "foreign" blood, was tracked down and jailed, murdered, or banished back to his "foreign" clime by a stern and paternal detective. The most famous, Old Sleuth, first appeared in the 1872 "Old Sleuth, the Detective; or, the Bay Ridge Mystery," in George Munro's *New York Fireside Companion*. The New York private eye (his card read "Sleuth, Detective") was a spectacular success. Crime dimes—like Alger's books—helped demystify the city. They showed, as the plot rolled along, how to secure a cheap room, open a bank account, go shopping, and avoid con men. They also provided a vicarious peek at upper-class exotica such as masked balls and Fifth Avenue mansions.

Western adventures, another wildly popular genre, were also churned out en masse in the metropolis. The West had long been promoted by city-based land reformers as a rural Utopia of small republican farm communities. The dime novel West—peopled by savages, scouts, desperadoes, and dance hall madams—was a more individualistic place, where white men could make a new start, a world of gambling, gold, and guns where—unlike the city—masters of property and capital were not in control. Out west unfettered heroes like "Ralph Rockwood, the Reckless Ranger" or "Deadwood Dick" and even "Calamity Jane" triumphed over greedy villains—often bankers. The most triumphant of all was Buffalo Bill.

In 1869 the publishers of the *New York Weekly* signed Astor Place riot veteran Edward Z. C. Judson—better known as Ned Buntline—to write a series of sensational westerns. On a trip to interview Frank North, a well-known frontier scout, Buntline ran across William S. Cody, whom he considered a more promising candidate, gave him a more crowd-pleasing cognomen, and began writing. In December *Buffalo Bill, the King of Border Men* appeared in New York, the first of 550 dime novels about Cody to follow.

By the time Cody came to New York City (in 1872) as Bennett Junior's guest, Buntline had turned out three sequels and produced a play. When Cody took in the perfor-

mance at Niblo's Gardens—and received an ovation—he realized the commercial possibilities of becoming the author of his own melodramas, rather than a star in someone
else's. Jettisoning Buntline, whose bombastic style had become a liability, he took on as a
press agent Major John M. Burke, one of the earliest geniuses of publicity.

For the 1873–74 season, Cody joined forces with Wild Bill Hickok—another metropolitan media star, who had shot to fame after publication of an article in *Harper's
Monthly*—persuading him to come to New York and play himself. Cody sent precise
instructions: "You will land in New York at the 42nd St. depot. To avoid getting lost in
the big city, take a cab at the depot and you will be driven to the hotel in a few minutes.
Pay the cabman two dollars. These New York cabmen are regular holdup men, and your
driver may want to charge you more, but do not pay more than two dollars under any
circumstances." The cabbie charged him five, and Hickok refused stoutly. When the
cabbie announced he would "take the rest out of your hide," the long-haired Hickok
flattened him with a roundhouse swing. Despite this impressive entrance, Hickok
couldn't make the jump to performer for the metropolitan masses. He found "making a
show of yourself" ridiculous and embarrassing and finally headed back west. Cody,
however, was making a fortune with his growing repertory of western dramas, ground
out by Bowery hacks on a piecework basis, and the Buffalo Bill Combination launched
an eleven-season run.

UNDERWORLD

Like their detective hero Old Sleuth, dime novel aficionados found plenty of criminality close to home. The laboring quarters were the primary stomping grounds for the
city's gangs—though "gangsters" was increasingly the more appropriate term—and
host to a newly professionalized criminal fraternity that grew up on the underside of
working-class life.

The old Bowery Boys and Dead Rabbits, for all the mayhem they inflicted (mainly
on each other), had not been really *criminal* organizations. They were, rather, part of the
rowdy republican universe; the same skilled craftsmen and laboring men often turned
up as volunteer firemen or militia units serving semicivic functions.

Now, however, following the lead of antebellum river pirates, many gangs preyed
professionally on citizens and businesses. They broke into houses in daylight, beat and
robbed strangers by night, levied tribute on merchants and factory owners, stole from
warehouses and railroad yards. The piers remained a favorite thieving ground, with
their piles of unprotected goods heaped up for easy plunder. An estimated million dollars' worth of merchandise was stolen annually in the late 1860s by river thieves like the
Hell's Kitchen Gang headquartered around Eighth Avenue and 34th.

Some of the post-Appomattox crime wave was the doing of battle-hardened veterans, familiars of pain and death, but the period also saw a rapid growth of juvenile and
teenage gangs (now called "hoodlums," a word newly arrived from San Francisco). New
legions erupted from the slum streets: the Baxter Street Dudes; the Nineteenth Street
Gang (on Tenth Avenue); the Fourth Avenue Tunnel Gang (denizens of the 34th to
42nd Street horsecar conduit, led by young Richard Croker). Some were willing to contract out their violent services if the price was right: the Whyos, early pioneers of mayhem for money, would blacken eyes, break jaws, shoot legs off, or "do the big job" all
according to an established scale of prices.

Crude criminality was countered by crude policing. Before patrolman Alexander S.

Williams graduated so gleefully to the Tenderloin, the huge former ship's carpenter had worked the Houston Street and Broadway area. On his first day out he selected two of the toughest local hoods, knocked them cold with his club, and hurled them through the window of their favorite saloon. Reportedly averaging a fight a day for the next four years, Clubber Williams (as he soon became known) was promoted in 1871 to captain in the Gas House district, home to the Gas House Gang. Williams formed a strong-arm squad that proceeded to club local gangsters senseless, with or without provocation. "There is more law in the end of a policeman's nightstick," Clubber reflected, "than in a decision of the Supreme Court."

Street gangs were arguably less significant in New York's outlaw annals than a much smaller confraternity of criminals who dwelt in the working-class world but modeled themselves on the professional classes above them. Eschewing brute force, these more resourceful outlaws prized planning and analysis, and they scanned the contemporary landscape for entrepreneurial opportunities. Happily for them, almost every new enterprise developed by legitimate businessmen could also be considered a novel source of profit by their netherworld counterparts. As the postwar economy grew more specialized and sophisticated, so did those who preyed upon it.

With the tremendous expansion in the circulation of easily negotiable paper—greenbacks and federal bonds—and concomitant increase in everyday impersonal commercial transactions, a crew of sophisticated counterfeiters, forgers, and white-collar con artists sprang into being. The City Bank forked over seventy-five thousand dollars in exchange for a check purportedly signed by Cornelius Vanderbilt. Liquid assets had to be shuttled about the financial districts, so gangs waylaid messengers carrying money or securities between banks or, on a grander scale usually associated with the Wild West, hijacked rail shipments: the Tenth Avenue Gang boarded an express train of the Hudson River Rail Road at Spuyten Duyvil and got away with an iron box stuffed with greenbacks and government bonds.

As an ever-growing number of banks filled up with deposits, safecrackers and bank robbers made New York City their national headquarters. Some people called the robbery of Rufus Lord's Exchange Place office in 1867, in which a three-man team made off with cash and securities worth over a million dollars, the first "truly professional" crime. But that isolated coup was as nothing compared to the body of work sustained over years by George Leonidas Leslie (or Western George, as he was known) and his colleagues. This Ohio immigrant lived a remarkable double life. At one moment he was an independently wealthy man-about-town, known for his impeccable manners, his tailoring, his love of books, and his membership in several excellent clubs. At other moments he headed a highly sophisticated gang of bank robbers whose careful preparations—obtaining architect's plans of the building under scrutiny, or constructing special burglars' tools—helped pull off perhaps a hundred jobs like the robbery, in 1869, of the Ocean National Bank at Greenwich and Fulton, which netted them over three-quarters of a million dollars. Beginning in 1875, Western George spent three years preparing for his master heist, a knockover of the Manhattan Savings Institution on Bleecker and Broadway, arrangements that included purchasing a duplicate of the Manhattan's vault in order to ferret out its weak spots. In the end his team of specialists made off with nearly three million dollars, though it turned out that not all the bonds were negotiable.

Not all the opportunities afforded by the city were on this munificent scale, but there was as much work available for the minnows of crime as for the whales. Crowded streetcars became traveling meccas for the hordes of pickpockets (and, on occasion, the hijacking of an entire vehicle). Packed department stores turned into stamping grounds for light-fingered ladies. Commercial sex offered great opportunities for panel game entrepreneurs, some of whom, like Shang Draper, were highly organized: he had thirty salaried women working out of his saloon on Sixth Avenue between 29th and 30th streets enticing drunks to a house with sliding panels behind which confederates waited to relieve preoccupied marks of their possessions. Even old-fashioned muggers got up-to-date by purchasing knockout drops—chloral hydrate or morphine—from one of Diamond Charley's traveling salesmen; a teaspoon's worth in the victim's beer saved time and muscle.

Professionals avoided violence as much as possible; of the forty-eight murders in 1868, almost all were committed by "youthful ruffians." The best ones avoided drink and drugs, kept themselves in shape, and exchanged tips and tricks only with one another. Slowly a professional community emerged among the perhaps twenty-five hundred full-time criminals. Certain concert saloons became well-known hangouts, like Paddy Quinn's Island No. 10, on Catherine Street just off the Bowery, or Bill Varley's joint, in the basement of a Bowery hardware store.

This community had a distinctive hierarchy of criminal careers, ranked by skill and daring. Robbery, the premier form, had its own subspecialties: bank robbers ranked from bank-sneaks of the first class at the top down through damper-sneaks, safe-blowers, safe-bursters, and, the lowest grade, safe-breakers. Somewhere near the bottom in the community's estimation dwelt the ghouls—grave robbers like the ones who snatched A. T. Stewart's remains shortly after they were buried in St. Mark's, and demanded a ransom of twenty thousand dollars from his widow, which the hard-nosed lady took a good two years to pay. The Vanderbilts took Stewart's postmortem dilemma very much to heart and had Richard Morris Hunt design them an impregnable mausoleum on Staten Island.

Fencing too got professionalized in this period. Pawnbrokers and junk dealers still operated, but the smart thieves and prominent pickpockets like William Burke (better known for his later western exploits as Billy the Kid) patronized sophisticated operators like Rosenburg, who fronted as a respectable jeweler on the lower Bowery, or Traveling Mike, who frequented the Thieves Exchange (near Broadway and Houston).

The state-of-the-art practitioner, however, the queen of fences, was unquestionably Fredericka "Marm" Mandelbaum. This 250-pound, black-bonneted matron got her start after the war running teams of young pickpockets, supplying them bail if arrested and fencing their harvest from a clapboarded wing behind her haberdashery store at Clinton Street on the corner of Rivington. In time Marm concentrated on financing and directing operations of gangs of bank and store burglars, though, being a proto-feminist in her own way, she always found time to help female pickpockets, blackmailers, and con women get their careers off the ground. She particularly enjoyed throwing fancy dinner parties, à la Mrs. Astor, for members of the criminal fraternity.

One reason Marm Mandelbaum could dine in relative repose, despite the perils of her profession, was that she had the law firm of Howe and Hummel on an annual retainer of five thousand dollars. Big Bill Howe and Little Abe Hummel were as odd a pair, in their way, as Fisk and Gould were in theirs, and equally at the top of their field—the newly specialized profession of criminal law. Howe, like Fisk, was given to gaudy attire and clusters of diamonds and was also a master showman. In the courtroom his inspired rhetoric or ready tears worked wonders for his clients, famous and shady alike. The Gould-like Hummel—small, tidy, and precise—sported not gems but a death's head watch charm and was master of the more subtle legal maneuvers.

Behind the lawyers were policemen and politicians. The Gilded Age witnessed an elaboration of the linkages between crime and politics established before the war. Politicos turned to gangsters for an election-day supply of muscle power and repeaters. Bill Varley's joint was not only the resort of well-known burglars, it was also election headquarters for the energetic campaigns of electoral fraud waged during 1868 and 1870. Bribery and corruption of law enforcement officers became as commonplace as it was in the mainstream business world. The newly professionalized underworld nexus of criminals, fences, lawyers, police, and politicians would grow and deepen in coming generations, but the fundamental structure had been put in place.

57

The New York
Commune?

Since the war, New York's elite had been spell-
bound by Paris, glittering capital of Napoleon
III's Second Empire. Shedding centuries of
anglophilia, they had passionately pursued all things French, from apartment houses
to mansard roofs, from boulevards to ball gowns, from the cancan to the Crédit Mobil-
iér. Now, in the summer of 1870, they were riveted by the rise and fall of the Paris
Commune.

Bismarck's rising empire had declared war on France, crushed Napoleon's troops,
and captured the emperor himself. (In Kleindeutschland enthusiasm for Prussian victories reached delirious levels.) Napoleon and Eugénie's empire reeled, then toppled. The
mass of Parisians demanded a republic that would fight on. They got a provisional government, led by haut bourgeois republicans, that only reluctantly prosecuted the war.
The Prussians laid siege to Paris and, over the ensuing bitter winter, starved and froze it
into submission. In January 1871 the provisional government agreed to an armistice and
gave way to a new government, chosen by rural Frenchmen, dominated by landed gentry and royalists and headed by Adolphe Thiers, who accepted a humiliating surrender.
But when Thiers's troops tried to disarm the Parisian national guard, they failed, and he
and his government fled the city.

Power passed to the Commune of Paris. Its officials were primarily professionals; its
chief supporters craftsmen, laborers, and poor women, who were particularly active in
street demonstrations. Within days Thiers's army launched a second siege of Paris. In
May, after bombarding the city's fortifications, his troops entered the city and attacked
the barricades the people of Paris had erected around their quartiers and arrondisse-
ments. In the next gruesome week of street fighting, Thiers's forces made free use of
incendiary shells, and the Communards burned great swatches of the city to slow the
advancing troops. At the climax, vengeful troops slaughtered thousands of Parisians out

of hand, and maddened and despairing Communards shot those they had held as hostages—including the archbishop of Paris—and torched hated public buildings. The victors, urged on by a frightened and frenzied bourgeois press, launched a "Communard hunt," assembling new-made corpses in great piles at which wealthy women gleefully poked with parasols. "Trials" found thirteen thousand guilty and meted out sentences of death, imprisonment, forced labor, and deportation. Final body count: seventy hostages, 877 soldiers, and over twenty-five thousand Parisians.

New York radicals supported the Parisians. The American sections of the International expressed sympathy for the fight against the Thiers government, and Victoria Woodhull led a dramatic march in memory of the Commune. Exiles who escaped the carnage were welcomed and organized into a French section of the IWA. German socialists too supported the Commune, at the cost of much of their popularity in pro-Bismarck Kleindeustchland. The labor movement's *Workingman's Advocate* printed Marx's blistering defense of the Commune, *The Civil War in France*.

Wealthy New Yorkers, however, were horrified by the red flags, the socialist speeches, the carnage of Bloody Week. Many hailed the violent suppression; George Templeton Strong professed delight that the "foot of the bourgeoisie is on the neck of the dreaded and hated Rouges at last," rendering them powerless, "if anything short of extermination" could do so.

Equally horrifying was the thought that such scenes might be reenacted in New York. Godkin's *Nation* saw the socialist specter "gaining among the working-classes all over the world" and declared one had to be "wilfully blind" to "imagine that America is going to escape the convulsion." Charles Loring Brace insisted that "there are just the same explosive social elements beneath the surface of New York as of Paris," and the *Times* concurred. The "terrible *proletaire* class" had already shown its revolutionary head during the draft riots, the *Times* recalled, when for a few days in 1863, "New York seemed like Paris, under the Reds in 1870." Now matters were arguably worse, as there were "communist leaders and 'philosophers' and reformers" in New York, ready to stir up the "seething, ignorant, passionate, half-criminal class" who "hate and envy the rich." Should "some such opportunity occur as was present in Paris," we should soon see "a sudden storm of communistic revolutions even in New York such as would astonish all who do not know these classes."

ORANGE AND GREEN

In early July 1871 a group of Protestant Irish-Americans—the Loyal Order of Orange—requested police permission to march through the city streets to celebrate the Battle of the Boyne. Irish Catholic organizations protested that the parade would be an insult to their community and pointed to the Orangemen's behavior the previous July 12, when they had marched up Eighth Avenue to Elm Park on 92nd Street. As they went they had taunted residents of Hell's Kitchen, Irish Catholic laborers laying pipelines in 59th Street, and others who were broadening the boulevard farther uptown. They'd spewed epithets and sung insulting tunes, such as "Croppies, Lie Down," whose refrain ended: "Our foot on the neck of the Croppy we'll keep." A crowd of enraged workmen followed along and attacked the Elm Park picnickers with stones and clubs. Shots were exchanged, and eight people were killed.

Such disgraceful scenes, the Catholics argued, must not be repeated. The Orangemen sought "race ascendancy," argued Patrick Ford, Galway-born editor of the recently established *Irish World*. They hoped, in league with the nativist "Anglo-American element," to make the United States a thoroughly "Saxon" nation. But the United States, Ford argued, articulating what would emerge as a major strand of metropolitan thought and feeling, was in fact a multicultured construction—"a *political*, not a *natural*, nation." "This people are not one," Ford insisted. "In blood, in religion, in traditions, in social and domestic habits, they are many." It was wrong, therefore, to ask non-English residents to "ignore their own identity and origin" and "become *Yankees* first, before they can be regarded as Americans."

City authorities agreed, noting that the use of abusive language or gesture in public streets was a misdemeanor and that courts had declared no organization had the right to provoke violence by inflaming the passions of other groups. On July 10, with Tweed's backing, Police Superintendent James J. Kelso forbade the parade. Irish organizations and Archbishop John McCloskey (who had succeeded John Hughes on his death in 1864) applauded the decision.

Now Protestants protested. The next day, indignant Wall Street businessmen lined up outside the Produce Exchange to sign a petition denouncing the edict. Leading newspapers raged at the cowardly surrender to a Catholic mob and demanded an instant reversal. Protestant New Yorkers viewed the parade issue through the prism of events in France. Thus the *Herald* argued that Irish Catholic outcries against Orangemen manifested "the same spirit which prompted the Paris Commune."

Protestants also feared that Catholic political power menaced republican liberties, an old worry recently revived by Pope Pius IX's Syllabus of Errors (1864), eighty in all, that condemned such tendencies of the bourgeois era as naturalism, rationalism, separation of church and state, liberty of conscience, and (error number eighty) the notion that "the Roman Pontiff can and ought to reconcile himself and come to terms with progress, liberalism and modern civilization." The *Times* suggested that Catholics intended to set up a state church and drive Protestants "to take shelter in holes and cor-

"The American River Ganges: The Priests and the Children," by Thomas Nast, *Harper's Weekly*, September 30, 1871. (General Research. The New York Public Library. Astor, Lenox and Tilden Foundations)

ners," and Thomas Nast, cartoonist for *Harper's*, fashioned images of mitred crocodiles slithering up on the beaches of America.

These anxieties had been boosted by Tammanyite Mayor Abraham Oakey Hall, who had taken to reviewing the St. Patrick's Day parade in full Irish regalia, showing up at balls in bottle-green flytail coats and emerald silk shirts, and jocularly claiming his initials really stood for "Ancient Order of Hibernians." Tweed and company had, moreover, authorized state and city aid to parochial schools and Catholic private charities: the Church got nearly $1,500,000 from public sources between 1869 and 1871. To the *Tribune* it seemed quite apparent that the Irish, "under the leadership of Mr. William M. Tweed, had taken possession of this City and State." Superintendent Kelso's order banning the Orange Parade seemed brutal confirmation of this.

Protestants also fought the banning order because it gave comfort to Irish nationalists, Fenians chief among them. After the war, the Fenians had come up from underground, declared themselves a sovereign government-in-exile, and hoisted their harp-and-sunburst flag over the old Moffat mansion (opposite Union Square), now their capitol. A faction led by William R. Roberts, a wealthy New York dry-goods merchant, pushed to capture British Canada and hold it hostage for Irish independence. This would hopefully embroil the United States in an Anglo-American war, during which Ireland could break for freedom.

This program roused tremendous enthusiasm among New York's working-class Irish. In March 1866 over a hundred thousand turned out for a Fenian rally in Jones' Woods—despite the opposition of Archbishop McCloskey. The savings of domestics and longshoremen (not, for the most part, the more conservative Irish middle classes) helped purchase a cache of arms from the U.S. government. But money, enthusiasm, and some tacit support from American officials still fuming at England's Confederate leanings were no substitute for military competence, and the Fenian invasion forces were easily routed by Canadian militiamen.

This invasion fiasco stimulated the growth of the Clan na Gael (founded 1867), a far more disciplined and secretive organization. Because Irish nationalists retained broad popular support, they were vigorously wooed by Tammany politicians, and Grant Republicans gave them federal jobs in New York City. But leading Irish exiles aligned themselves with the International, which strongly supported Irish independence. Ford of the *Irish World* linked the nationalist cause to radical enthusiasms by denouncing the "money interest" as "a huge boa constrictor" that "has wound itself about the nation, crushing its bones and sucking the life blood from its heart."

This combination of concerns about Commune-style radicalism, Irish Catholicism's growing power in the city, and the emergence of left-leaning Irish nationalism generated intense elite pressure on Tammany to reverse its stand and let the Orangemen parade. Tweed, already feeling the heat from some initial exposés of Tammany corruption, decided he had no choice but to acquiesce. Governor Hoffman came down from Albany on the eleventh and, after conferring with Tweed and Hall, rescinded Kelso's decision. He also ordered regiments of National Guardsmen and cavalry to guard the marchers the following day.

SLAUGHTER ON EIGHTH AVENUE

July 12 dawned bright and hot. Five thousand troops reported to their armories at seven A.M. Some were old hands at this kind of thing—notably the elite Seventh Regiment. At the other extreme was the new-minted Ninth Regiment, a Jim Fisk creation. The master of Erie had bankrolled the troop but put far more energy into its scarlet-coated hundred-piece band than into imparting military discipline. Most Guardsmen were Protestant employees of the city's financial and business firms (the Irish Sixty-ninth would be kept in its armory all day). Most shared their employers' fear or hatred of the tenement house denizens whose paths they would cross that day. In addition to the military, fifteen hundred policemen gathered at headquarters in Mulberry Street.

Catholic forces readied themselves as well. For a week there had been vigorous debates in nationalist circles about how to respond should a parade go forward. Ancient Order of Hibernians lodges around New York and Brooklyn had called for violent resistance. Some had undergone street drills in preparation. Fenian leaders were in unusual agreement with the Catholic hierarchy that violence would only make the Irish appear incapable of self-government, but neither priests nor moderate nationalists had much influence that morning.

From all over the city groups of people made their way toward Lamartine Hall, on the northwest corner of Eighth Avenue and 29th Street, where the Orangemen were forming up their tiny contingent. The Green forces came from scattered worksites: longshoremen from East River docks, laborers from the Jackson and Badgers Foundry on 14th Street, plasterers, Boulevard workers, quarrymen at Mount Morris, Central Park laborers, men doing repairs on the Third Avenue Railroad or digging sewers in Fourth Avenue or manning the Harlem Gas Works. They came from a morning mass meeting at Hibernian Hall—Ancient Order of Hibernians headquarters, at Prince and Mulberry—where there had already been a violent clash with the Eighty-fourth Regiment and the police (except for two "copps" who had refused to fight fellow Irishmen and been promptly fired and jailed). And, of course, they came from the working-class quarters, from Mackerelville (around 13th Street between First Avenue and Avenue A), from Yorkville, from Brooklyn, and—in greatest numbers—from Hell's Kitchen.

By 1:30 crowds lined both sides of Eighth Avenue, from 21st to 33rd, and jammed the cross streets. Most were laborers, wearing the long black coats and dirty white shirts of their calling. Many neighborhood women mingled in the crowd, and others took up positions at windows and on roofs (reminding one reporter of "the Paris *petroleuse*").

Now the troops and police arrived and took up their positions, to jeers and hisses. At two o'clock, the Orange women and children were sent off, and the men donned their regalia (often with pistols under their coats) and formed up in 29th Street. The men of the Eighty-fourth Regiment, to make clear their unabashed sympathy with the marchers, placed their caps on their bayonets and cheered. The Orangemen were now surrounded by regimental units—the Seventh in front, Sixth and Ninth in rear, Twenty-second and Eighty-fourth to the sides. After some preliminary street clearing by mounted and club-wielding police, a cannon was fired, the band played "The Star-Spangled Banner," the Orangemen unfurled their purple silk banner of the Prince Glorious on horseback, and the parade set off.

Almost immediately, to howls of "Give them hell, the infernal Englishmen!" a shower of stones, bricks, bottles, and old shoes was unleashed. Some militiamen fired musket shots, pistols were fired from the crowd, police charged and clubbed the bystanders, and the parade moved ahead. A block further on came more stones and sniper fire; Seventh Regiment soldiers responded, on command, with sporadic shots. Eighth Avenue ahead of the line of march grew choked with crowds. The procession

"The Orange Riot of July 12th," from *Frank Leslie's Illustrated Newspaper*, July 29, 1871. This view shows the soldiers firing into protesters massed on the east side of Eighth Avenue near 24th Street. (Courtesy of American Social History Project. Graduate School and University Center. City University of New York)

halted. One woman broke through the troops and tore the regalia off an Orangeman before being pushed back at bayonet point, shrieking and raging. The police smashed into the crowd ahead, bashing heads open. Stones and crockery rained down from rooftops and windows. More gunshots rang out. Two Eighty-fourth Guardsmen were hit. The troops, without orders and without warning, began blasting volleys at point-blank range into the throngs along the sidewalk at 24th Street. Other regiments began firing indiscriminately into the screaming and terrified crowds. Mounted police followed up with charges.

The parade re-formed ranks. The band struck up a festive Orange tune, banners were lifted aloft, and the assemblage ground on. The police had to batter their way into 23rd Street, where immense numbers had regrouped at Booth's Theater, but the parade successfully negotiated the left turn and headed east, its rear protected from angry crowds, until it reached Fifth Avenue, where, for a moment, it entered a different world: at the Fifth Avenue Hotel, two to three thousand well-dressed people cheered lustily. Further ovations greeted them as they made their way south along Fifth Avenue. Then marchers and troops and police entered Rialto territory at 14th Street. Once again they had to wade through hissing and jeering crowds (except for Protestant oases like the American Bible Society building, from which girls merrily waved orange ribbons). Wearily they made their way across town toward Cooper Union, where finally, at four o'clock, they shed their regalia and quietly dispersed.

Back at Eighth Avenue it was quiet too, apart from the groans of the injured and dying and the lamentations of priests and women. A shaken *Herald* correspondent found the steps of a basement barbershop "were smeared and slippery with human blood and brains while the landing beneath was covered two inches deep with clotted gore, pieces of brain, and the half digested contents of a human stomach and intestines." The walls of a butter store, he observed, were "speckled with bullet marks and splashed with blood," and the sidewalk in front was "thickly coated with a red mud."

Over sixty civilians were killed outright or later died from wounds. Over one hundred were wounded (and another hundred arrested). Most were Irish laborers, but there were many German and American casualties. Twenty-odd policemen were injured by stones, clubs, and rocks, and four were shot, none fatally. Three Guardsmen were killed (possibly by wild firing from other troops) and twenty-two injured. One Orangeman was wounded.

The next day twenty thousand Irish mourners converged on Bellevue's morgue, adjacent to the outpatient dispensary for the poor, to pay respects. Massive funeral processions, composed of somber delegations from the Society of the Immaculate Conception, St. Patrick's Mutual Alliance, and the Ancient Order of Hibernians in white mourning scarves, traveled by the Greenpoint ferry to Brooklyn's Calvary Cemetery. There were other, angrier responses to what Ford's *Irish World* called the "Slaughter on Eighth Avenue." The Brooklyn Irish hanged Governor Hoffman in effigy in a parade down Hamilton Avenue, and barroom poets composed ballads like "The Great Orange Massacre." There were, however, prominent nationalists—Fenians and Irish Brigade Association leaders from the ranks of business and the professional classes—who distanced themselves from the whole affair, a sign of divisions to come.

The day after the riot, fashionable men and women rode along Eighth Avenue in comfortable carriages, matching up street corners or buildings with descriptions in the morning papers. But the forces of order, while triumphant, were also in a fury. One banker declared that the riot eclipsed "the worst religious outrage of the Commune." A *Times* editor found it final proof that the "Dangerous Classes" cared nothing for "our liberty or civilization" other than to "come forth in the darkness and in times of disturbance, to plunder and prey on the good things which surround them." Police Commissioner (and banker) Henry Smith only regretted "that there were not a larger number killed." As he explained to the *Tribune*, "in any large city such a lesson was needed every few years. Had one thousand of the rioters been killed, it would have had the effect of completely cowing the remainder."

Democratic authorities got no points for having ordered out the troops. Their "criminal weakness and vacillation," the *Tribune* charged, had encouraged the mob in the first place. One of the reasons many in the upper and middle classes had grudgingly acquiesced in Tammany's hold on power was its presumed ability to maintain political stability. That saving grace was gone: Tweed could not keep the Irish in line. The time had come, said Congregational minister Merrill Richardson from the pulpit of his fashionable Madison Avenue church, to take back New York City, for if "the higher classes will *not* govern, the lower classes *will*."

TWEED TOPPLED

Six months earlier, Tweed had seemed impregnable, despite assaults by the *New York Times* and the vitriolic *Harper's Weekly* cartoons of Thomas Nast, which portrayed Tweed as a leering hulk of corruption and Tammany's inner circle as a conspiratorial Ring. The campaign, long on invective, was short on facts, and the *Times* insisted the city's books be examined. Just before the election, Mayor Hall established a blue ribbon panel of six businessmen with unimpeachable reputations—including rentier John

Jacob Astor, banker Moses Taylor, and Marshall O. Roberts of the West Side Association—and gave them access to municipal accounts. On election eve, the panel issued its findings. The books had been "faithfully kept," avowed these leading beneficiaries of Tweed's policies, and the debt levels were manageable. Tweed and his men swept to victory.

Accordingly, 1871 had looked to be a very good year. On New Year's Day, A. Oakey Hall was again sworn in as mayor, and John T. Hoffman took office as governor. With luck, by 1872, Hoffman would be president, Hall would move up to governor, and Tweed would become a United States senator. The annual Americus Club Ball, held in early January at Indian Harbor, Connecticut (near Tweed's summer place at Greenwich), was a jubilant affair. As late as May, Tweed was still riding high. On May 31 he arranged a spectacular wedding, at Trinity Chapel, for his daughter Mary Amelia. At the Delmonico's-catered reception that followed at Tweed's Fifth Avenue (and 43rd Street) mansion, guests brought a vast outpouring of dazzling gifts (including forty sets of sterling silver). Tammany's growth-oriented coalition, like the Gilded Age boom itself, was in fine fettle.

Within weeks, however, the visceral response to the Commune and the Orange Riot had rallied support for the war the *Times* and *Harper's* were waging against Tweedite corruption. On July 22, ten days after the Boyne Day battle, the *Times* began publishing solid evidence of Ring rascality, turned over to the paper by an aggrieved insider. Day after day, publisher George Jones reproduced whole pages from the cooked account books of James Watson, who until his recent death in a sleighing accident up in Harlem Lane had been the Ring's trusted bookkeeper. The series culminated in a special four-page supplement, on July 29, that quickly sold out its run of two hundred thousand copies. Under screaming headlines—"Gigantic Frauds of the Ring Exposed"—the paper detailed Watson's system of kickbacks. Contractors on public projects padded their bills and slipped the overcharge back under the table. The surcharge to the city usually ranged from 10 to 85 percent, though on occasions it soared to truly empyrean heights of corruption. One member of a Tweed-affiliated club was paid $23,553.51 for furnishing thirty-six awnings, boosting the per-awning price from the market rate of $12.50 to a Ring rate of $654.26. Construction of the county courthouse allowed for an orgy of such creative accounting, and the building wound up costing four times as much as the Houses of Parliament and twice the price of Alaska.

The *Times* stories brought to a head a growing international crisis of confidence in New York City's ability to pay its debts. Earlier in the year, rumors of mismanagement had so undermined trust that only the unimpeachable credentials of the city's underwriters were keeping New York's securities afloat. Now overseas bankers refused to extend further credit. The Berlin stock exchange struck the city's bonds from its official list.

This jolted New York's financial and mercantile community into action. Mammoth interest payments on outstanding debt were due in weeks, and in a few months twenty-five million dollars' worth of short-term notes would come due for payment. If the city's credit collapsed, noted Henry Clews, a leading private banker, every bank in New York might go down with it. It was time, Clews said, to oust "this brazen band of plunderers, root and branch."

On a Monday evening in early September, after the elite had returned from their summer vacations, a great reform meeting was held at Cooper Union. In attendance, besides Republicans, nativists, civil service reformers, and frightened financiers, were powerful upper-class Democrats, like corporate lawyer Samuel J. Tilden, who had been forced to take a back seat to Tweed; Germans, led by *Staats-Zeitung* editor Oswald Ottendorfer, who had felt pushed aside by the Irish; and those small property owners, merchants, and manufacturers who feared Tammany corruption would hike taxes and pauperize them.

The meeting quickly agreed that the "wisest and best citizens" should take control of the city government—as intellectuals and reform groups had been arguing since the draft riots. Extremists, Godkin of the *Nation* among them, talked cholerically of forming a Vigilance Committee to lynch Tweed. Cooler heads established instead an Executive Committee of Citizens and Taxpayers for Financial Reform of the City, popularly known as the Committee of Seventy. Chaired by sugar refiner William Havemeyer, and packed with Bar Association lawyers, it decided to bring Tweed down by choking off the city's funds. Setting up offices in the Brown Brothers building—making the banking house de facto center of city government—the committee spearheaded a concerted refusal by a thousand property owners to pay municipal taxes until the books of the city were audited. On September 7 they went before Judge Barnard, who now deserted his former comrades and gave them an injunction that barred Comptroller Connolly from issuing new bonds or spending any money. As Tweed later noted, this "destroyed all our power to raise money from the banks or elsewhere and left us trapped." Crowds of workmen now gathered at City Hall demanding their pay—a crisis relieved only temporarily by Tweed's handing out fifty thousand dollars from his own pocket. Organized labor turned against him too, even those in the construction trades who had benefited mightily from his programs. On Wednesday, September 13, eight thousand workmen marched in the rain to City Hall to denounce Tammany rule.

Five days later, Comptroller Connolly jumped ship. At Committee of Seventy insistence, he appointed Tilden associate Andrew Haswell Green as acting comptroller. Escorted by a hollow square of mounted policemen, Green took possession of the office, giving investigators access to Ring financial records and further isolating Tweed. (Barnard allowed the city to borrow from the banks again, but only departments not under Tweed's control.) At the end of October Green and Tilden traced money from city contractors directly to Tweed's bank account, and the following day Tweed was arrested, though immediately released on a million dollars bail.

Tweed appealed to the ballot box and held rallies on the Lower East Side, to no avail. In the November 1871 elections—with the polls closely guarded—Tweed retained his state senate seat (and he would remain a Robin Hood hero, "poverty's best screen," to his local constituents), but most of his associates were defeated by wide margins. Ring members large and small slipped out of the city for foreign climes. Tweed stood his ground. Indicted in December, he was arrested, forced to resign his powerful public works position, and voted out as grand sachem of Tammany.

His personal world unraveled too. In January 1872 his old comrade Jim Fisk was fatally shot, while walking up the marble staircase of the Grand Central Hotel, by Edward S. Stokes, the spendthrift son of a prominent New York family, who had taken up with Fisk's mistress Josie Mansfield. As he lay dying, Tweed (out on bail) was at his side. Another bedside mourner was Jay Gould, who had his own problems, stemming directly from Tweed's fall. The Erie president's powerful enemies had been circling, but he had successfully fended them off with the aid of Tweed's judges. Now Tweed was forced to resign from the Erie board of directors, Judge Barnard was impeached and convicted (at the insistence of the Bar Association), and Gould's position became untenable. He too was forced to resign.

Though his power was shattered, Tweed continually wriggled out of reach of his prosecutors. His trial in January 1873 ended with a hung—some said bribed—jury. In November 1873 he fared less well and was sentenced to a twelve-year term. But after a year in jail, the decision was reversed, and in January 1875 he was released. His enemies immediately slapped him with a civil suit to recover six million of his ill-gotten gains. Unable to come up with the three-million-dollar bail, he was reincarcerated and languished in Ludlow Street Jail. The monotony was broken, however, by repeated home furloughs. In the course of one of these, he escaped and made his way to Florida, then to Cuba, then (disguised as a seaman) attempted to flee to Spain. Arrested by Spanish authorities, Tweed was delivered to an American warship for return to New York. Back again in the Ludlow Street Jail, and now desperate, he agreed to testify (in return for his freedom) about the workings of the Ring. After he did so at great length, however, vengeful authorities (including now-governor Tilden) refused to release him. His spirit broken, he died in prison, of a combination of diseases, on April 12, 1878.

To consolidate their takeover of municipal power, the Committee of Seventy ran their own chairman, William Havemeyer, for the mayoralty in 1872. Havemeyer, now sixty-eight, had been mayor in 1848–49 and didn't like much of what had happened since then. Elected to City Hall in a divided campaign, Havemeyer and Comptroller Andrew Haswell Green imposed a vigorous retrenchment policy on New York. They laid off city workers and cut salaries of government officials, hoping to drive out professional politicians and draw in public-spirited elites. They jammed the brakes on development to cut costs and lower the taxes of the propertied classes who were Havemeyer's biggest supporters. Work on the uptown boulevards ceased. Grading of West Side thoroughfares was halted. The viaduct railway was scuttled. Central Park expansion (and maintenance) was curtailed, and work on the proposed Riverside and Morningside parks was pushed off into the future. The elaborate plans to develop the waterfront were canceled and a cheaper, more circumscribed plan adopted. Declaring the city "finished," the mayor even argued that New York should refuse any further assistance to the Brooklyn Bridge, then rising in the East River.

Also in 1872, some of the outraged businessmen and professionals who had toppled Tweed tried to displace the corruption-ridden Grant administration. The collection of dissidents formed a third party, called themselves Liberal Republicans, and nominated the sixty-one-year-old Horace Greeley to run against President Grant. The Democratic Party seconded Greeley's nomination, hoping to ride his coattails to the White House—against the better judgment of Democratic national chairman August Belmont, who thought the Greeley nomination "one of those stupendous mistakes which it is difficult even to comprehend." Belmont was right. Grant, the old war hero, aided by boom-time prosperity and a last spurt of northern outrage at Klan outrages, won every northern state. Few municipal reformers backed Greeley, whom they saw as too close to the Democratic Party. They endorsed independent candidates instead, including Frederick Law Olmsted for vice-president. The city's bourgeoisie stuck with Grant. "I was the worst beaten man that ever ran for that high office," Greeley lamented. Weakened by the arduous campaign and depressed over the death of his wife just before election, Horace Greeley came home to his beloved New York City to find that Whitelaw Reid had seized control of the *Tribune* in his absence. Broken in spirit, he died three weeks later on November 29, 1872.

BACK TO THE TEN-HOUR DAY

Having crushed Tweed, the forces of order lit into the labor movement, which, in the spring of 1872, had launched its strongest bid yet to institute the eight-hour day. Building trades struck first and, to their delight, got a boost from President Grant. Bricklayers working on the new post office had complained to him about ten-hour workloads. Grant, with one eye on the upcoming elections, denounced this violation of the federal eight-hour law and issued an Executive Proclamation entitling them to overtime pay. This galvanized other construction workers to join the strike, and by early June most small building contractors had knuckled under.

Inspired by these successes, other workers downed tools and walked off. Soon twenty thousand—including plumbers, upholsterers, pianomakers, masons, marble cutters, quarrymen, tin and slate roofers, sugar refiners, and gas men—were fighting for the eight-hour day. The city's employers dug in their heels, and the test of wills spiraled upward into a near-general strike—the biggest labor conflict in New York's history thus far—pitting a hundred thousand workers from fifty-two crafts (two-thirds of the manufacturing workforce) against a newly unified manufacturing elite supported by most of the city's bourgeoisie.

The fiercest clashes came in the woodworking trades. In May militant German journeymen of the Furniture Workers League shut down various woodworking factories. On the other side were the piano manufacturers, who ran the most highly mechanized and subdivided woodworking trades. The most vigorous opposition came from

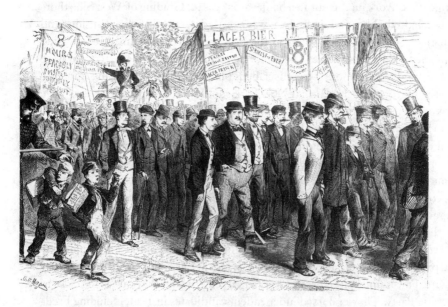

The Eight-hour Movement—Procession of Workingmen on a "Strike," in the Bowery, June 10, 1872, from Frank Leslie's Illustrated Newspaper, *June 29, 1872. Note that many marchers are smoking cigars. Cigar-making remained a major source of employment in New York, although production was shifting from small craft shops to factories and tenement houses. (Courtesy of American Social History Project. Graduate School and University Center. City University of New York)*

Steinway and Sons, a firm far larger and wealthier than most of the vulnerable cabinet-maker shops who had given in to union demands. Seeking to head off trouble, the company offered workers at its Fourth Avenue plant an increase in pay if they would stick with ten hours. When some accepted, a mass meeting of piano workers (held June 5) denounced the rank-breakers and marched, thousands strong, to ring the factory and muscle the ten-hour men away. Steinway called on the new probusiness city government for police protection, and got it. "Captain Gunner arrived with about 80 men," William Steinway noted in his diary, "who charged on the strikers and clubbed them on the arms and legs, they running as fast as their legs can carry them."

With momentum faltering, the Iron and Metal Workers League called out its fifteen thousand members, and the strike revved up again. Crowds of blacksmiths surrounded J. B. Brewster's Carriage Factory and the Singer Sewing Machine's plant—both bastions of the ten-hour day in metallurgy—and brass founders, pattern makers, wireworkers, pen and pencil makers, church organ builders, brewery workers, packinghouse butchers, and bakers entered the fray.

Now employers organized. On June 18 the industrialists and building contractors joined forces with the woodworking bosses and, at a meeting of over four hundred employers, formed an Executive Committee of the Employers of the City, dedicated to smashing the eight-hour movement—now depicted as the stalking horse for something far worse. As one steam pump manufacturer harangued the meeting: "I see behind all this the specter of Communism. Our duty is to take it by the throat and say it has no business here."

Soon, indeed, employers brought in the police, who sent platoons, then battalions of men, many of them recent veterans of the Orange Riot suppression, to club picketers away from plants and open avenues for scabs. One after another the strikes crumbled. Steinway and Singer triumphed. The iron men surrendered in July. Many earlier gains were lost, and apart from some in the building trades, most New York workers were forced back to a ten-hour regimen by jubilant employers.

SPECIAL AGENT ANTHONY COMSTOCK

With the municipality's political and economic order under control, reformers set out to restore decency to its moral affairs, with the earnest young Anthony Comstock serving as point man. Comstock, another New England migrant come to the big city, had been born in 1844 to a once-affluent New Canaan farm family come on hard times, from whom he received a rock-ribbed upbringing as stony as their Connecticut soil. With the outbreak of civil war he joined the army, only to discover it full of "wicked men" who swore and drank. His vigorous opposition to such pursuits did not endear him to his comrades—indeed he discerned a "feeling of hatred" on the part of his fellow soldiers—but, convinced that his critics were "under Satan's power," he prayed earnestly, if ineffectually, for their conversion.

After the war, like Horatio Alger, Comstock left Connecticut for New York, where he moved into a rooming house and found work as a porter in a dry-goods store. In a career that Ragged Dick would have envied, he was promoted to shipping clerk and in 1869 made salesman. By 1871 his salary had climbed from five to twenty-seven dollars a week. He used the five hundred dollars he had saved as down payment on a house in Brooklyn, married the daughter of a New York businessman, and joined the Clinton Avenue Congregational Church.

For all Comstock's success, what most occupied his attention was the shocking behavior of his fellow clerks. Comstock didn't think himself a stuffed shirt—he was fond of practical jokes (of the exploding cigar variety)—but he drew the line at drinking, gambling, whoring, and particularly pornography (a "moral vulture," which "steals upon our youth in the home, school, and college, silently striking its terrible talons into their vitals, and forcibly bearing them away on hideous wings to shame and death"). Early in 1872 he tried to shut down a circulating library of "vile books," only to have a policeman warn the owner. Comstock got him dismissed from the force, then teamed up with a reporter from the *Tribune*, toured the Ann Street and Nassau Street porn purveyors, and organized a (well-publicized) police raid.

The muttonchopped one-man vice squad now came to the attention of Morris Ketchum Jesup, merchant, banker, railroad financier, and president of the Young Men's Christian Association. Under Jesup's leadership, the YMCA had been taking a carrot-and-stick approach to combating the deleterious impact of the brothels, gambling dens, saloons, and "licentious books" that distracted young men from serving their employers, saving their money, and rising in the world. In 1868 the Y had built a grand new residence for unmarried men, at Fourth Avenue and 23rd Street, which offered lectures, classes, reading rooms, parlors, and a picture gallery. Additionally, its members had gone to Albany and got the legislature to ban obscene material.

Jesup, himself a Connecticut immigrant of devout but impoverished background intent on imposing an unambiguous moral code on the metropolis, took an instant liking to Comstock. On May 9, 1872, Jesup invited him to meet a group of YMCA backers—leading businessmen (including J. P. Morgan), clergy, and lawyers, men as determined to restore decency to cultural affairs as political ones. They agreed to support his work as a vice fighter by giving him a stipend to supplement his income and a clerk.

Much buoyed by this powerful backing, Comstock now took on Victoria Woodhull, who had been more or less constantly pilloried since her emergence as a feminist spokesperson, with associates and relatives of Henry Ward Beecher prominent among the assailants. On November 2, 1872, she struck back with an article in *Woodhull and Claflin's Weekly* intended to "burst like a bombshell into the ranks of the moralistic social camp." That it did. Within hours New Yorkers were scrambling to read "The Beecher-Tilton Case," in which Woodhull laid bare the story of Henry Ward Beecher's adultery with Mrs. Elizabeth Tilton, the wife of Theodore Tilton, one of his closest friends and associates.

Woodhull condemned not Beecher's philandering but his hypocrisy. This was, after all, the minister who had maligned Jim Fisk as a "glaring meteor, abominable in his lusts and flagrant in his violation of public decency." Indeed Woodhull praised Beecher's "physical amativeness," claiming him (with tongue in cheek) as a covert member of the Free Love ranks, and urging him to accept a leadership role in its future endeavors.

Beecher frostily ignored the piece, but Anthony Comstock did not. He approached the district attorney (a leading member of Beecher's Plymouth Church) with a request for an arrest warrant on grounds that Woodhull and Claflin had violated state law by sending obscene literature—the exposés in the *Weekly*—through the mails. The DA found the argument compelling, and Comstock, in what would prove to be the opening salvo of a decades-long campaign to suppress public discussion of sexual matters, summoned two police officers to his aid, arrested both Woodhull and her sister, and had them incarcerated in the Tombs, where they spent the month of November. When

In 1872, while doing battle against Comstock and Beecher, Woodhull campaigned for President on the People's Party ticket, with Frederick Douglass as her running mate. This scene, reprinted from M. F. Darwin's pamphlet, "One Moral Standard for All," depicts her nomination at Apollo Hall on May 10 of that year. (© Collection of The New-York Historical Society)

released on bail in December, Woodhull promptly circulated the hot issue on the black market and gave a dramatically unrepentant speech. Comstock arrested her again. She got herself bailed out again. He grabbed her a third time in February, but after a June 1873 trial, a judge threw out the charges, saying the 1872 law didn't apply to newspapers.

Woodhull now expanded her attacks on the sexual hypocrisy of New York's male bourgeoisie. She publicly exposed the Rabelaisian masked balls—those gatherings of "the *best* men" and "the worst women in our city" in which the boxes of the Academy of Music were used "for the purpose of debauching debauched women; and the trustees of the Academy know this."

While Woodhull pressed onward, Comstock pressed for stronger legislative weaponry. In January 1873, again with powerful YMCA backing, he traveled to Washington to lobby for federal legislation that would ban obscenity from the mails. His timing was excellent. The Grant administration, swamped by corruption scandals, was in no position to be seen supporting immorality. It didn't hurt that federal authorities were more dependent than ever on access to New York capital, access controlled by the likes of YMCA stalwart J. P. Morgan. After Comstock exhibited some obscene books and postcards to (putatively) shocked congressmen, they swiftly passed (and the president signed, on March 3, 1873) what soon became known as the Comstock Law. The U.S. government, virtually without debate, had gone into the censorship business.

To enforce the act, Congress instituted the office of special agent of the United States Post Office and gave the job to Comstock. He accepted it, without pay, and would keep it for the next forty-one years of a career devoted (as he said) to hunting down violators "as you hunt rats, without mercy." Roaming New York City—and, by rail, other cities—armed with warrants, revolver, and handcuffs, he broke down doors, arrested the inhabitants, and confiscated smut. By January 1874 he had seized a small mountain of it—130,000 pounds of books, 194,000 "bad pictures and photographs," and fifty-five hundred indecent playing cards. No publishers were safe—even those previously considered respectable. Comstock kept Frank Leslie, editor of the well-known weekly, under arrest for advertising obscene books until Leslie promised not to print whatever he disapproved of. He arrested the editor of *Fireside Companion* for issuing dime novels that Comstock found excessively racy (in later years, Horatio Alger would find his works proscribed).

Comstock steadily broadened his definitions of obscenity. He banned any depiction, no matter how indirect, of the act of intercourse; one arrestee "had box containing figures of hen and rooster which by pulling out lid placed it in indecent posture and was offensive to decency." He banned any discussion of sexual acts, words for sexual parts, or overly frank discussion of changes in the institution of marriage. He arrested Dr. E. B. Foote, author of *Medical Common Sense*, a book filled with criticism of sexual taboos that had, by 1870, sold 250,000 copies. "Obscene," said Comstock, and his was the opinion that counted.

Comstock's backers were a bit dismayed by this whirlwind of action, especially as some of it generated bad publicity for the YMCA. But they had no intention of abandoning their urban vigilante: though nervous at the notoriety, they applauded the action. After generations of fruitless exhortation, here was someone who would, if need be, *coerce* people into proper behavior. The *Times* too applauded the assumption of public power into private hands; true, it resembled the work of "vigilance committees, regulators, or lynch policemen," but that was a point in its favor.

Still, this was not the sort of image appropriate to the YMCA. The solution was to cut Comstock loose and set up a new organization just to support his crusade. In May 1873 the New York Society for the Suppression of Vice was incorporated, with Anthony Comstock as agent and secretary. Behind him was a blue ribbon board. It included Jesup, J. P. Morgan, William Dodge Jr. (heir to the Phelps-Dodge copper fortune), Samuel Colgate (head of the New Jersey soap business), Alfred S. Barnes (the textbook publisher), and lawyer William C. Beecher (Henry Ward's son).

Comstock now expanded his purview to encompass the behavior of New York's bourgeois women.

"THE SLAUGHTER OF THE INNOCENTS"

After the war the American Medical Association had renewed its prewar efforts to suppress abortion. Doctors asserted abortion was morally wrong, in itself and because it helped women evade their maternal duties. An 1868 study found perhaps two hundred full-time abortionists at work in the metropolis and estimated that one out of five New York City pregnancies ended in abortion. This latter number—which included many reputable married females of the better classes—suggested a widespread selfishness, claimed Dr. Horatio Storer, a leader of the crusade to punish both those who performed the operation and the women who sought it. Ladies, Storer said, were aborting simply to seek "the pleasures of a summer's trips and amusements." By diminishing the native Protestant birth rate, moreover, they were allowing immigrant Catholics to advance demographically. It was time, therefore, to reaffirm that woman's place was in the nursery, and certainly not, some doctors muttered privately, in medical school.

In 1868 the State Medical Society pressured the New York legislature into passing the first antiabortion legislation in twenty-two years. The act banned all advertisements alluding either to abortion or birth control. The following year a still tougher law made the destruction of a fetus—at any stage—manslaughter in the second degree, a great victory for physicians. It made little dent, however, in the widespread belief than an early abortion was a woman's right. City practitioners—notably Madame Restell—continued to thrive. Indeed the brazen Restell regularly turned up at afternoon carriage promenades in Central Park, in a coach pulled by a matchless team of Cuban horses.

The concatenation of Commune, Orange Riot, Tweed prosecution, and labor crackdown drastically changed the moral and political climate. In 1871 the *New York Times* launched a full-scale attack on abortions, at the same time, and in much the same spirit, as the paper's assault on Tweed (whose regime, the *Times* was convinced, connived to keep the trade going). After undercover reporters visited and exposed some of the sleazier of the city's practitioners, arrests were made, and prosecutors damned defendants in flaming language. One lawyer, referring to Restell's mansion-office on Fifth Avenue, spoke of "that den of shame in our most crowded street, where every brick in that splendid mansion might represent a little skull."

At the height of this whipped-up public indignation—concurrent with the October 1871 arrest of Tweed—a young girl, victim of a botched abortion, was found stuffed in a trunk that had been mailed to Chicago. It was traced back to one Rosenzweig, promptly labeled the Fiend of Second Avenue, who was tried, convicted, and almost lynched. Many abortionists fled the city, and many papers stopped carrying the ads of those (like Madame Restell) who remained.

It was in this context that Anthony Comstock not only joined the antiabortion crusade but declared war on contraception generally. He attacked those who advertised abortions on the grounds that references to female complaints and cures, however delicately phrased, were obscene and arrested those who manufactured or retailed "rubber goods for immoral purposes."

Comstock's job was made easier in April 1872, when, after the Rosenzweig affair, the state legislature made the abortion-related death of a fetus or woman a crime punishable by up to twenty years. It also banned advertisement, manufacture, or sale of abortion-inducing materials. The following year he made sure that the Comstock Law banned contraceptive devices from the mail, and in June 1873 he got Albany to make the mere possession of obscene matter, including "any drug or medicine, or any article whatever, for the prevention of conception, or for causing unlawful abortion," punishable by three months to two years at hard labor. By the end of the year he had confiscated 3,150 boxes of pills and powders used by abortionists and 60,300 "articles made of rubber for immoral purposes" and had thrown several abortionists—though still not Madame Restell—into jail.

The response of New York's bourgeois women to Comstock's campaign was mixed. Elizabeth Cady Stanton and Susan B. Anthony's National Woman's Suffrage Organization protested an initiative, spearheaded by male businessmen and male professionals, that sought to foreclose women's access to abortions and information about sex, and muzzle feminist publications and periodicals. Others were intimidated into silence or actively supported Comstock's crusade as the lesser of two evils. Middle- and upper-class women had been unhappy about the rampant commercialization of sex in New York City. The flagrant spread of concert saloons and brothels provided, in effect, an alternative sexual structure to the family. It facilitated husbandly philandering and freed many men from matrimony altogether. The feminist magazine *Hearth and Home* complained in 1871 that 125,000 young single men in New York City refused to marry, preferring to live indecent lives and patronize "lower and more infamous" forms of amusement. As contraception and abortion helped sustain this freewheeling system, Comstock's imposition of respectability helped suppress it.

Feminists who had been ardent proponents of spreading knowledge about sexual physiology rejected Comstockery. The many women who found such openness alarming, on the other hand, were prepared to take shelter in Comstock-inspired prudery. And despite the new access of a handful of females to the professions, women remained economically dependent on men and quite aware that, while individual freedom could bring relief from oppressive customs and laws, it could also pitch women into a competitive world in which the deck was stacked against female players.

The fate of those who transgressed conventional boundaries provided a scary object lesson. Victoria Woodhull's challenge to Henry Ward Beecher was a case in point. The reverend denied his adultery, and many in his congregation rallied around him and denounced his accusers. When Tilton finally sued his former friend for alienation of his wife's affections, it led to a sensational 1875 trial, which ended, after six months of testimony, in a hung jury. While respectable opinion didn't completely exonerate the minister, he soon recovered most of his standing in the community. Beecher boats continued to ferry crowds to Plymouth Church on Sundays; he still got a thousand dollars per lecture, while Elizabeth Tilton was hounded into oblivion. The double standard had survived a most vigorous challenge.

It would be left to a small but highly vocal band of sex radicals to contest, on libertarian principles, the new coercive circumspection. Ezra Heywood (author of "Cupid's Yoke") and Robert Ingersoll (who founded the National Liberal League in 1876) struggled against the right of church and state to limit expression of sexual ideas. They boldly printed and distributed "obscenities" and challenged the vice crusaders' attempt to force discussion of sex and contraception behind closed doors. Comstock went after them too and, after a few temporary setbacks, emerged triumphant. In New York City, De Robigne Mortimer Bennett, an iconoclastic, anticlerical freethinker, helped mount an effort to repeal the Comstock Law that gathered over fifty thousand signatures. But Comstock, who considered Bennett "everything vile in Blasphemy and Infidelism," nailed him for mailing an "obscene" scientific pamphlet (*How do Marsupials Propagate?*) and in 1879 got a landmark decision against him.

Another prominent casualty was Victoria Woodhull, attacked not only by Comstock but by her comrades in the IWA. In the aftermath of the disastrous 1872 strike, the International Workingmen's Association fell into internal warfare between immigrant socialists and American radicals. The Germans thought their native-born allies' attachment to temperance chauvinistic, their professions of spiritualism preposterous, and their devotion to greenbacks ludicrous, but most of all the Germans had no sympathy with the Americans' feminism. The Americans found German atheism excessively materialistic, considered socialist devotion to the gold standard incomprehensible, and insisted "the extension of equal rights of citizenship to women must precede any general change in the relationship between capital and labor." The IWA purged itself of feminists and "fanatics" but, fatally weakened by internal discord and external defeat, eked out an existence for only a few more years, then limped into history. Woodhull's last attempt to rally feminists and assorted reformers was her People's Party presidential campaign in 1872, which was crushingly defeated. After this the women's movement would distance itself from radicalism. So would Woodhull, who in 1876 packed herself off to England, married a nobleman, repudiated her scandalous Free Love views, and settled into respectability and good works.

Among the last holdouts was the sixty-seven-year-old Ann Lohman—Madame Restell. As late as 1878 she was still running her business on Fifth Avenue (though dispensing only pills, not abortions, that industry having been driven underground and turned over to the unscrupulous and the untrained). Comstock, calculating that the once immune Restell was now safely isolated by the new repressive moral climate, called on her incognito, got her to sell him a contraceptive device, and arrested her. He also made sure that every paper in town was invited to witness her arraignment at Jefferson Market Police Court. Restell managed to post bond, though with considerable difficulty as most people were afraid to be publicly associated with her. As the weeks before her trial dragged on, with the press lambasting her daily, she became convinced Comstock would succeed in hounding her back into prison. Rather than accept such a fate, she lay down in her tub, filled it half full, and slit her throat from ear to ear. The *New York Times* declared it "a fit ending to an odious career."

58

Work or Bread!

At ten o'clock on Thursday morning, September 18, 1873, leading Wall Street bankers and brokers gathered at the New York office of Jay Cooke and Co. The Philadelphia-based investment banking house had long been considered one of the strongest in the country, but it was now teetering at the edge of bankruptcy, and Cooke's men pleaded for an immediate transfusion of funds. Their pleas were refused. At eleven o'clock, they closed their doors and telegraphed the bad news to Cooke in Philadelphia. He promptly shut down the entire concern. A titan of American finance had crumpled.

When news of Cooke's suspension was announced on the floor of the New York Stock Exchange, "a monstrous yell went up and seemed to literally shake the building." Now "dread seemed to take possession of the multitude," the *Tribune* reported. Brokers began trampling one another to sell off stocks that were suddenly, terrifyingly vulnerable.

All that day and all the next, as a *Nation* reporter observed from the gallery, a "mad terror" swept through the "great crowds of men [who] rushed to and fro trying to get rid of their property, almost begging people to take it from them at any price." Jay Gould reigned jubilant amid the carnage. Having gauged the market correctly and bet on a massive decline, he had already made an instant fortune and now sought to claw down prices even farther. Vanderbilt, champion of the bulls, bought desperately to buoy prices. He protected his New York Central but was unable to do much more. Many Vanderbilt concerns were battered down, and Gould (with his ally Russell Sage) scooped them up. Brokerage firms failed on all sides. Banks buckled. On Friday, despite a pelting rain, a "seething mob" filled Broad Street. Frenzied depositors surged through the mud to remove their funds from banks whose vaults were stuffed with railroad bonds deteriorating in value by the minute. One broker moaned that the unfolding catastrophe was the "worst disaster since the Black Death."

By Saturday the governors of the Exchange had had enough. At eleven o'clock they shut down trading "for an indefinite period." Wall Street, in its extremity, turned to Washington for help. President Grant and Secretary of the Treasury Richardson hustled north to take charge. At a crisis conference in the Fifth Avenue Hotel, bankers, brokers, merchants, manufacturers, and railroad men—laissez-faire scruples jettisoned for the moment—pleaded with Grant to deposit twenty to forty million greenbacks in the city's banks. The administration judged that such an action would exceed its authority, but it did agree to buy government bonds in the open market, injecting some currency into the system.

It wasn't enough. Next week the Exchange stayed closed, but crowds bought and sold sinking securities on the streets. Bank runs multiplied (as did defalcations by bank officials). Brokerage houses collapsed. By the following Friday, most of the major banks and insurance companies, and almost all the second-rank institutions, had shut down. The panic spread rapidly from New York to the rest of the country. Chicago, its banks paralyzed, was reduced to barter.

TAKING STOCK

Reporters besieged Vanderbilt asking what had gone wrong. The ill-tempered Commodore blamed the crisis on excessive railroad promotion. "There are," he argued, "many worthless railroads started in this country without any means to carry them through." To raise money, entrepreneurs had turned to "respectable banking houses in New York, so called," who affixed them with "a kind of moral guarantee of their secureness" and sold the bonds in Europe. But the roads, many of which went "from nowhere to nowhere," soon got into difficulties. "If people will carry on business in this madcap manner," he concluded, "they must run amuck."

Vanderbilt had a point. To convince investors to buy his Northern Pacific Railroad stocks, Jay Cooke had had public relations experts crank out stories that the bleak right-of-way through the Dakota and Minnesota territories was in fact a "vast wilderness waiting like a rich heiress to be appropriated and enjoyed." Cooke's campaign formed the basis for Mark Twain and Charles Dudley Warner's *Gilded Age*, a satire on boom-time ethics. Cooke enticed some immigrants with his planted fairy tales, but nowhere near enough. Investments fell off. To save his existing stake, Cooke cooked books, corrupted politicians, and milked capital to meet debt payments. Rivals spread rumors of his deteriorating position. Bond sales dwindled to nothing, European creditors called in their notes, and the Northern Pacific went bankrupt, dragging the House of Cooke down with it.

The Northern Pacific's story, though larger than life, was not atypical. Far more roads had been built than the transport market demanded. Many ran at a loss most of the year, hoping to make up deficits during harvest time's mass movement of crops to markets. But they could never squeeze enough profits out of the farmers, who, themselves confronting lower commodity prices, vigorously resisted railroad exactions. This left the heavily indebted lines highly vulnerable to contraction elsewhere in the economy.

Another source of strain was the now familiar end-of-boom diversion of capital into speculative channels. *Bankers Magazine* had fretted at all the money pouring into the call market, pursuing interest rates that ranged from 12 to 24 percent. These funds, in turn, had fueled the sporting of bulls (including Vanderbilt) and bears (such as Gould and Sage). Wall Streeters had become convinced that crises like those of 1837 and 1857 were no longer possible as governmental safeguards had been erected. The secretary of the treasury had been given so much power, said the *Herald*, that "it is difficult to conceive of any condition of circumstances which he cannot control."

Among the many things the secretary could not control were the capital markets of Europe. The American rail boom had been sustained by overseas funds, but overexcited European investors had spiraled off into a wild speculative binge, often snapping up absurd or fraudulent prospectuses. One Viennese journalist expected any day to see a company formed "to transport the aurora borealis in pipelines to St. Stephen's square." And it was in Austria that the great Panic of 1873 started. It spread to Berlin, jumped to Paris and Amsterdam, then slammed into London. European markets lost interest in American railroad stocks, and it was this, together with seasonally tight money and news of widespread corruption, that brought down the New York market.

Beyond this lay still vaster problems with the global capitalist economy. Since the 1840s it had been powered by the international development of the railway system, which in turn had stimulated coal-, iron-, and steam-based industrialization. In the 1870s the limits of that expansion were reached, and the world economy tumbled into a slump of unprecedented proportions. The U.S. economy, more globally integrated than ever, tumbled with it. The depression would last from its inception in 1873 until a partial recovery in 1879, with effects far more disastrous than those of any slump before it. The fifty-one hundred bankruptcies of 1873 rose to 10,478 in 1878. By 1876 half the nation's railroads—twenty-one thousand miles' worth—had defaulted on their bonds and were in receivership. Blast furnaces shut down. Farmers were foreclosed. Within a year an estimated three million people were unemployed.

WORK OR BREAD!

New York City's economy fell apart with frightening speed. Wall Street brokerage houses took the first hits, but the damage swiftly spread to other financial institutions that had invested heavily in railroad stocks and bonds. Life insurance companies crumbled: of the thirty-two companies chartered since 1861, only eight remained in 1877. A score or more savings banks collapsed as well. Investment bankers too were gloomy: "Everything looks dark," August Belmont wrote his son in October 1873. It was impossible for him to "imagine the utter prostration of all business."

The real estate bubble burst. Inflated values collapsed; the equities of thousands of property owners were wiped away, one industry spokesman wrote, "as with a sponge." An avalanche of foreclosure proceedings drove down land values, and lots near Fifth Avenue that fetched a hundred thousand dollars in 1873 went for forty thousand in 1876, if they found a buyer at all. Row after row of middle-class houses, thrown up so confidently, now went begging. Fully half the speculators who had built them were, said the *Real Estate Record and Buyers' Guide* in 1875, "swept out of sight [by the] momentous and unprecedented crisis." Construction projects declined 70 percent between 1871 and 1877. The grand plans for uptown improvement went into hibernation. The boom on the metropolitan frontier deflated. Small investors who had bought Queens lots in the auction sales of 1870–73 couldn't pay their taxes and were foreclosed. Promoters went bankrupt. The development of Queens came to a complete stop.

In Manhattan the blight spread from the financial district up lower Broadway, which by 1876 was plastered with FOR LET placards. Many former wholesale stores were now occupied by auction marts selling off bankrupts' goods. Two years later, "vacant shops, stores and manufactories," the mayor reported, "stare at us in every street." Steinway agreed that "business seems to be perfectly dead," with "not a single order coming in."

As usual, most people's loss was some people's gain. Sharks cruised the roiled stock market waters, snapping up sinking securities. Jay Gould emerged the master of Western Union. The young George F. Baker bought out the majority shareholder of First National Bank. Drexel, Morgan made a substantial profit in 1873, and with Jay Cooke removed, the big treasury offerings would now go to them, to New York's other Yankee house, Morton, Bliss, and to the two major German-Jewish firms run by Seligman and Belmont. In the land market too, as prices scraped bottom, well-heeled buyers moved in to scarf up bargains: Belmont was active; so was newcomer William Rockefeller.

As usual, working people bore the brunt of things. By the winter of 1873–74, 25 percent of the city's labor force had lost their jobs, and the wages of the rest declined steadily. Hunger and homelessness spread. The shanty-dwelling population of the West Side burgeoned. Thousands sought shelter on the floors of police stations or almshouses. The New York Commissioners of Charity relief rolls soared. "Formerly," one official said, "[we confined] relief to women. Now the men come to us hungry with hollow cheeks. . . . It is terrible, terrible." Too terrible for some: in August 1875, Andreas Fuchs, a forty-year-old shoemaker, shot himself to death in Central Park, leaving a note for his wife and children that explained, "I have no work and do not know what to do."

As in prior depressions, hard times stirred popular discontent. Workingmen disliked charity. The YMCA sold "dinner tickets" to New York businessmen to give to the unemployed, but the New York Workingmen's Central Council rejected "crumbs that

Station House Lodgers, engraving by Winslow Homer, *Harper's Weekly*, February 7, 1874. (© Collection of The New-York Historical Society)

fall from the tables of the rich." Nor did they like the police lodgings—"living charnel houses" that reeked "with filth and vermin."

The Spring Street International (the American reformers recently expelled from the IWA) argued that the unemployed were entitled to better, as a matter of right. The government had showered aid and assistance on the wealthy; now it should "legislate for the good of all, not the few." In October 1873 it proposed a comprehensive anti-depression program. New York should provide public employment on street and park improvements and in building a rapid transit system. The city should also establish municipally owned markets where people could buy necessities at cost.

Such ideas rapidly gained popularity. The Workingmen's Central Council announced plans for a mass meeting to demand "Work or Bread." J. P. McDonnell, an Irish Fenian and socialist, argued in the *New York Sun* that to make "wealthy citizens and law-makers" listen, labor should mount the "greatest demonstration ever held in New York." Leading trade unionists endorsed the idea. So did German socialists, currency reformers, and neighborhood mass meetings around the city (including one of fifteen hundred French workers and refugees from the Commune). Wagons paraded through the streets with placards announcing the December 11 gathering at Cooper Institute. On the appointed day four thousand crammed their way in, leaving thousands more outside, as speakers analyzed the nature of the depression (in German and English) and how to respond to it.

Many blamed the financial system. Bankers and brokers—the "moneyocracy"—had obtained special privileges by corrupt deals with politicians, then used their ill-gotten wealth to "speculate in stocks, money, gold, or other commodities." These operations had brought on the crisis that now endangered the producing classes and the republic itself. One long-term answer was to set limits on the accumulation of personal wealth, at a maximum of three hundred thousand dollars, by imposing a graduated income tax. In the short run, the city should undertake massive street, pier, and park improvements and construct housing for the homeless.

Socialists at the Cooper meeting offered similar prescriptions and added some novel ones, including suspension of evictions for nonpayment of rent during the coming winter and dispensation of a week's supply of food or money to distressed families. Peter J. McGuire, a young socialist carpenter, later endorsed the meeting's no-violence pledge but argued that if relief were not forthcoming, then "a provisional committee" in each ward should "take food" to keep people from starving and "send the bills to the city for collection."

The Cooper meeting appointed a fifty-man Committee of Safety—nomenclature borrowed from the Paris Commune—and selected German, French, Irish, and American representatives. The committee organized ward clubs of the unemployed throughout the city and called for a meeting with city authorities. When Mayor Havemeyer did get together with a delegation of workers, it became clear that they inhabited different universes. Havemeyer expressed concern for the men's plight but suggested, none too subtly, it was their own fault for not having prepared themselves for such contingencies. "I know that it is hard for you to be out of employment," he said, "but don't you think that workingmen should lay up something for a rainy day?" "Yes, sir," a delegate replied, "that's all very well, but workingmen can't save much out of their wages. Rents are so high; and then many of us can only work four or five days out of a week." The mayor responded with homilies: "Men who get rich, gentlemen, are men who save.

When a man has $100 in a bank he becomes a capitalist." His father (a wealthy sugar manufacturer), Havemeyer remarked pointedly, "didn't go to the beer shops and theaters every night." Besides, public works meant higher taxes and the "confiscation" of property and so were out of the question.

The press was even less diplomatic. The *New York Graphic* said that "there is no point in railing at the rich nor in scowling at the capitalists nor in condemning corporations simply because one's stomach is empty and he happens to be dinnerless." The paper went on to snarl, "Whining and whimpering are as useless as they are disgusting." The *Times* loftily lectured the unemployed on the hard facts of political economy. The "natural laws of trade" were "working themselves out." Governments could "only watch the process." Finally, "things must regulate themselves."

TOMPKINS SQUARE

"Things" got rapidly worse. Unemployment rose as the thermometer dropped, and the Committee of Safety issued a call to all "in sympathy with the suffering poor" to rally in Tompkins Square on January 13, 1874, and then march on City Hall to demand a municipal contribution of a hundred thousand dollars to a Labor Relief Bureau for the unemployed.

The press, badly alarmed, insisted the meeting be suppressed as a "communist agitation." The Committee of Safety was adopting the "favorite tactics of the worst class of European socialists," and on behalf of the unemployed—a "thriftless and improvident" lot. More hysterically (or cynically), it was asserted that leaders of the defeated Commune had smuggled diamonds—stolen from the churches of Paris—into the city to buy ammunition and bombs to launch a revolution. The Department of Parks had already given permission to use the square, but the Police Board, composed of wealthy entrepreneurs and powerful politicians, forced it to renege at the last minute. Word of the revocation did not reach the working-class quarters.

The next morning, by eleven o'clock, over seven thousand people had turned out despite below-freezing temperatures. The ten-acre park was filled, and the crowd, which included many women and children, overflowed into the surrounding streets. One corner of the square was occupied by twelve hundred resolute members of the German Tenth Ward Workingmen's Association.

At that moment the police commissioner and a squad of patrolmen marched into the square. Announcing, "Now, you all go home, right away!" they immediately waded into the assemblage with clubs flailing. The crowd scattered "like wild birds" except for the German workers, who battled back until mounted police drove them from the square. As the demonstrators fled into adjacent streets, a *Sun* reporter noted, the police kept "close at their heels, their horses galloping full speed on the sidewalks," their batons flailing. One zealous young German socialist, Justus Schwab, marched boldly back to the square waving the red flag of the Commune, only to be attacked and arrested. The police continued clubbing groups of workers for hours, Samuel Gompers remembered, in "an orgy of brutality," until, finally, the area was cleared and still.

The Tompkins Square clash was a minor affair materially—a few score bloodied heads and arrested bodies—but a major one symbolically. It hardened attitudes on both sides of the class divide and shaped larger patterns of response to the depression.

Organized labor bitterly attacked the police, asserting their rights of free assembly and free speech had been violated. Iron molders rejected the way "every protest, peti-

Police charge the Tompkins Square demonstrators, from *Frank Leslie's Illustrated Newspaper*, January 31, 1874. (Library of Congress)

tion, or demand of labor is met with the cry of 'Commune.'" Unions and ethnic organizations raised funds for the arrested, tried and failed to oust the police board, and held protest meetings. The *New York Graphic* and the *New York Sun*—both editorial antagonists of the unemployed movement—similarly condemned the "clubbing of innocent and peaceful men."

Such reactions were exceptional. The authorities, the press, and the upper and middle classes were virtually united in their satisfaction with the outcome. Mayor Havemeyer was delighted: "Nothing better could have happened," he declared. The police commissioner was elated: "It was the most glorious sight I ever saw the way the police broke and drove that crowd. Their order was perfect as they charged with their clubs uplifted."

The press was convinced that vigorous action had forestalled a host of horrors. Behind the Tompkins Square "rabble," the *World* was sure, stood "the red spectre of the commune." The *Times* reported (incorrectly) that all those arrested were "foreigners," which at least proved that communism was not a weed of "native growth." Religious spokesmen were even more ferocious, with one prominent clergyman vowing that if workers "lift their hands against law, order, and good government, they will be mowed down like grass before a scythe."

The depression overrode middle-class republican inclinations to respect the "rights of labor," or even labor's right to public protest. Also set aside was the notion that capital and labor shared a fundamental harmony of interest. In smaller cities and towns the urban middle classes would continue to harbor older republican convictions and even blame the newly rich for many of the nation's ills. But in New York City a social and cultural chasm had opened up, and for the moment, most of the middle class jumped to the side of the rich and powerful.

In this atmosphere employers rapidly mopped up remaining union resistance. In October 1874 stevedoring companies united to humble the longshoremen's union. After a five-week strike, the union's power on the docks was shattered. Wages plummeted to twenty-five cents an hour; they would not return to their 1874 levels for another forty years. Whitelaw Reid, Greeley's successor at the *Tribune*, proved as ruthless an employer as editorialist, slashing his printers' wages and replacing construction workers on the new *Tribune* building, when they struck in 1874, with Italian laborers.

The city did its part. Police smuggled spies into labor and socialist meetings, pressured landlords to evict radical groups, broke up picket lines. The city also (in 1876) laid off many public employees, hiring day laborers through private contractors instead, resulting in reductions of wages by as much as 65 percent. This in turn helped dampen wages in the private sector.

In these circumstances, union militancy melted away. When the Cigar Makers Union rank and file complained of their leaders' inaction, they begged members to "remember the adage that prudence is the better part of valor." Members chose instead to melt away themselves. New York City's labor movement was not utterly destroyed, as it had been in 1837 and 1857, but by the late 1870s its rolls had shrunk from forty-five thousand to five thousand.

RETRENCHMENT

In the chaotic aftermath of Tweed's fall, wealthy Democratic Party leaders like Tilden, Belmont, and Hewitt—coming to be known as "Swallowtails" for the cut of their fashionable coats—demanded a housecleaning. To refurbish Tammany's image they selected former city sheriff John Kelly as the new leader. Kelly was a shrewd choice. "Honest John" had not been implicated in the scandals. As a deeply religious Catholic, a respectable Murray Hill resident, and a relative-by-marriage of Archbishop John McCloskey (who in 1875 was appointed the first American cardinal), Kelly had strong support in the immigrant community, especially among the Irish middle class.

Once installed, Kelly consolidated the Tammany hierarchy, formalized and centralized its lines of command, muted the power of working-class ward heelers, weeded out remaining Tweed supporters, and by 1874 had become the acknowledged boss of a revitalized machine. Setting out to topple the nonpartisan and deeply unpopular Mayor Havemeyer—who had given total support to Comptroller Andrew Haswell Green's slashing cutbacks, which had only accelerated after the onset of the depression—Kelly ran William H. Wickham, a prominent and Tammany-connected diamond merchant. Wickham campaigned on a platform of kick-starting the economy (and aiding the poor) with a vast program of public works, while simultaneously reassuring the taxpaying community he would continue reducing expenditures.

Wickham won, as did the Democrats generally, and after January 1875 New York City was again in Tammany hands. The mayor made an initial effort to fulfill his pledge by appointing developer William Martin—eager as ever to launch public building programs—to run the Parks Department. But the landowners, insurance companies, trust companies, and savings banks—whose property investments had dropped drastically in value during the depression—fervently resisted new municipal programs, and their agent, Comptroller Green, stonily pressed on with retrenchment.

Kelly sought Green's removal, to restart the flow of patronage. But Green's patron, Swallowtail-in-Chief Samuel Tilden, had just been elected governor and was now the presumptive presidential nominee of the Democratic Party. Tammany, accordingly, backed off and committed itself to retrenchment. Even when Green's term expired in December 1876, and Kelly himself took over as comptroller, the Tammany leader adamantly opposed demands from developers, labor unions, and radicals for a depression-combating program of public works. Indeed, determined to win the business community's confidence, Kelly cut Green's austerity budget even further, reducing the city's debt.

Taxes declined too, despite complaints by city and state tax commissioners and several legislative investigations that the city's wealthy, far from being fiscally overburdened, were flagrantly evading their fair share of such taxes as existed. Real estate in the mid-1870s was seldom assessed at more than 60 percent of its value—less in the case of the Astor family and Trinity Church—and evasion of even shrunken impositions was commonplace. "Personalty" income got off even more lightly, despite the fact that in the postwar era the value of such holdings—money, goods, debts due, bonds, mortgages, and public or corporate stocks—had grown far faster than landed wealth. City tax commissioners conservatively estimated local personalty to be worth between two and three billion dollars, even though in 1879 only eighty-nine hundred people on the tax rolls admitted having any such holdings at all. Liquid portfolios, moreover, were even more grossly undervalued than real estate, via subterfuges like shifting taxable capital into nontaxable forms, or more straightforwardly through fraud and perjury.

Not only did William H. Vanderbilt pay taxes on half a million dollars of personalty income, though his total such holdings were estimated at forty million, but his New York Central railroad, while reporting a capital of $143 million, paid taxes on only twenty-two million. Corporations in general proved particularly skillful tax dodgers, deliberately violating the rules by cooking books, establishing phony indebtedness, or simply by bribing tax collectors. Investigators calculated that corporate evasion alone cost the state and city millions each year, but the notion of increasing revenues rather than cutting expenses was not to be placed on the political table.

"CHARITY RAGES LIKE AN EPIDEMIC"

In their continuing search for new ways to slice the budget, reduce taxes, and restore investor confidence, municipal officials turned their attention instead to the burgeoning relief budget. In 1873 five thousand families had been receiving public assistance; by 1874 twenty-four thousand were being aided. In March of that year, Mayor Havemeyer, aware that Tweed's Department of Charities and Correction had been implicated in corruption, and convinced that the level of "destitution and suffering" did not seem "to warrant the interference of the Municipal authorities," announced the suspension of all public outdoor relief from July through December. Aid resumed for a time on Mayor Wickham's watch, in the hard winter of 1875. But in 1876, pressed by welfare reformers, the new Board of Estimate and Apportionment—which included the mayor, comptroller, and president of the Department of Taxes and Assessments—announced that such assistance would henceforth be permanently discontinued, apart from cash stipends to the blind and fuel handouts to the proven poor (an exemption that pleased Democratic coal merchants). The Board of Aldermen protested, saying there were "more needy and deserving poor in this city than ever before in any one winter, rendered so in consequence of the general prostration of business," but the post-Tweed-charter reform of 1873 had rendered them powerless in the matter. Outdoor relief would not return to New York City for nearly sixty years.

The termination of assistance to the poor in their own homes did not increase the almshouse population, as the commissioner of Charities and Correction took steps to ensure that indoor relief remained an unenticing alternative. "Care has been taken," he noted, "not to diminish the terrors of this last resort of poverty, because it has been deemed better that a few should test the minimum rate at which existence can be preserved, than that the many should find the poor-house so comfortable a home that they would brave the shame of pauperism to gain admission to it." Spending on almshouse inmates actually dropped, to a per capita twelve cents a day.

Brooklyn too tightened its municipal belt, insofar as the poor were concerned. When relief rolls began to climb after 1874, the city slashed its per capita expenditures so that actual outlays stayed relatively steady, despite the growing number of recipients. Handouts took the form of either food (flour, potatoes, rice, tea, sugar) or coal, never both in the same week, and never in amounts exceeding a dollar per week per family of four. Critics attacked the inclusion of tea and sugar as profligate and debated deleting coal, which though cheaper to give out was often sold by recipients for cash to buy other commodities. Soon, not to be outdone by their neighbors across the river, Brooklyn reformers began demanding the total abolition of outdoor relief. Not only was it a symbol of wasteful public spending, but corruption had been uncovered in the (Democratic) Department of Charity, which the (Republican) County Board of Supervisors was determined to end.

Leading the crusade was Seth Low, the youthful and independently wealthy Republican whose grandfather had founded Brooklyn's Association for Improving the Condition of the Poor (AICP). Low and his allies urged that, as an experiment, outdoor relief be phased out over a two-year period, disbursing only coal in 1876–77, then nothing the following year. In the winter of 1876–77, however, the charity commissioners protested, noting that starving people were congregating at warehouses where food was stored, begging they be opened. When the commissioners took it upon themselves in mid-January to vote an emergency appropriation and give out flour and potatoes, enraged reformers denounced them in editorials. The Board of Supervisors subtracted the appropriation from the commissioners' salaries; in 1878, it succeeded in shutting down the program altogether.

Low acclaimed welfare reform as a great success—and it did launch his political career—on the grounds that money had been saved, and corruption curtailed, without any increase in suffering of the poor. It was true that some with other sources of income, who had been fraudulently obtaining relief, carried on much as before. It was also true that there was no great increase in the poorhouse population (jammed as it already was) and that some of the poor who borrowed, pawned, and lived on credit from landlords, grocers, or kin managed to get by for a year or two. But it was true as well that hunger and cold sent many to the city's hospitals or police station basements; that many impoverished parents sent their children to asylums, where they cost the county forty dollars a month rather than one or two dollars in home relief payments; and that while women sought jobs as live-in servants, many men took to the streets seeking charity or work—and triggering a new round of complaints by reformers.

OF BEGGARS AND TRAMPS

In May 1874 the American Social Science Association organized a conference of charitable organizations, at which participants denounced the increase in street begging and petty crime, clucked about "imposter paupers" on the charity rolls, and deplored the way "charity assisted labor in the combat to keep up wages." Not only were beggars (aided by soft-hearted benefactors) nullifying the law of supply and demand by refusing to sell their labor at whatever price employers were willing to pay, but the police were abetting them in their malingering. Under existing statutes, officers of the law could, at their own discretion, summarily arrest vagrants and lock up them up pending trial in police court, usually without benefit of jury, with suspects presumed guilty unless they could give "a good account of themselves." Those found guilty, in deliberations that seldom lasted more than a minute, were taken to the workhouse and set to hauling coal, breaking stone, laying pipes, and making bricks—a procedure workingmen protested as a throwback to fugitive slave laws. Reformers found the process satisfactory in theory but claimed that the police were insufficiently zealous and that judges too often acquitted the poor; and indeed, although vagrancy arrests in New York City soared in the depressed 1870s, not all those arraigned were convicted.

Reformers were ever more exercised by "tramps," a new and pejorative word for the homeless unemployed (one of its earliest uses occurred in the *New York Times* in February 1875). The term referred to those who boarded in the cheapest lodging houses in the winter or bedded down in doorways, docks, empty warehouses, or Central Park, or along the Battery, on tolerable nights. When the weather turned bitter, many resorted to the verminous police basements. Touring one of them, a *Herald* reporter noted that his flickering gas lamp sent "feeble rays through the laden air and every ray touches a pile of rags which in the morning will hatch out a tramp." The stations gave lodging on a one- or two-night basis, forcing users to move repeatedly to a new precinct (hence their label of "revolvers"). In 1874 and 1875 thirty thousand were said to be so circulating.

In the summer many of the unemployed roamed the surrounding countryside, looking for handouts or doing chores for farmers' wives in return for food and shelter. Those few who bullied or stole what they wanted had their crimes splashed across the front pages, and out of these stories was conjured up the "tramp evil." The press routinely treated the homeless not as victims but menaces. Some papers defined "tramp" in racial terms—as an urban Indian—or, in the words of one professional, "a lazy, incorrigible, cowardly, utterly depraved savage." The *Times* suggested that readers worried about tramps "procure a large dog who understands how to insert his teeth where it will do the most good."

Finally, the scientific reformers were dismayed, as they had been for decades, by New Yorkers' stubborn penchant for undisciplined benevolence. Mayor Havemeyer had felt free to suspend outdoor relief in part because he was convinced that the needs of the poor were being "adequately met by private donations and the various Christian and charitable institutions." Many churches indeed struggled to help during the depression. Thirty-four free soup kitchens fed five to seven thousand daily, and missions provided refugees from the freezing streets with shelter (and sermons). The St. Vincent de Paul Society declared: "Let all strangers be received and welcomed as Christ himself."

Such efforts infuriated the AICP. Appalled at the "outgush of morbid sympathy," the organization applauded the end of public outdoor relief and urged an end to scatter-shot beneficence as well. "Charity," agreed the *World*, "rages like an epidemic," and to what end? It only encouraged "idleness and dependence in the lower classes" and gave "impetus to worthlessness and vagrancy" by making "begging more profitable than labor." Cutting off charity, on the other hand, would ensure that "the large class drawn hither by the possibility of living without work should be compelled to return to the country, where their hands are needed, by the stern necessity to work or starve." E. L. Godkin declared in the *Nation*, "Free soup must be prohibited," and "all classes must learn that soup of any kind, beef or turtle, can be had only by being paid for."

The AICP was partly mollified when, after 1876, the city's Board of Estimate and Apportionment began giving large sums of municipal money directly to a few private charities—the AICP chief among them—on the grounds that they would provide home relief (as they already did institutional relief) more efficiently. The AICP had resisted the idea at first, but when its expenses almost doubled in the depression's first year as its income from contributions dropped, it decided (in December 1876) to accept the new policy of public subsidies with private controls, then through careful scrutiny managed to disqualify the majority of the approximately sixty thousand who were stripped of public aid.

But reformers believed that more concerted and coordinated action was needed to bring down vagrancy and beggary, and the State Charities Aid Association (SCAA), established in 1872 by Louisa Lee Schuyler, pillar of the wartime Sanitary Commission, took the lead in generating fresh thinking. The SCAA, another private organization with public responsibilities, had accepted the task of visiting and inspecting all charitable institutions receiving state aid. Now, in 1877, it summoned a grand assemblage of charity reformers at the fashionable Saratoga Springs resort.

Almost all those present agreed that tramps were socially defective beings. One person did suggest there might be a connection between the depression and homelessness, but the idea that tramps couldn't find work was generally decried as absurd. Some, notably eugenicist Richard T. Dugdale of the New York Prison Association, argued that vagrancy and pauperism were hereditary traits, and one conference participant drew the obvious conclusion: "I don't think a pauper has any right to marry nor do I think the State has a right to allow him." There was also interest in Charles Loring Brace's proposal of a pass system (like one used in England) that would require tramps to carry papers certifying they were genuinely unemployed and looking for work.

In the end, the preferred (if not so fresh) solution was the one advanced by the SCAA's Committee on Able-Bodied Paupers, set up the previous year to investigate the tramp problem, under the chairmanship of Josephine Shaw Lowell, whose prominence at the gathering was itself remarkable. In 1855 Josephine Shaw had moved with her family from Boston to Bard Avenue, near West New Brighton, on Staten Island. The wealthy and patrician Shaws, despite their Fourierist and abolitionist convictions, moved easily into New York's genteel society, and Josephine's older sister soon married George William Curtis, editor of *Harper's Weekly*. The Civil War tore her comfortable existence to pieces. An ardent Unionist, she joined a branch of the Sanitary Commission and threw herself into war work. Her brother, Robert Gould Shaw, was soon cut down while leading the first African-American regiment in action in South Carolina; and the following year, her husband, Charles Russell Lowell, died in battle. Widowed at twenty, Josephine Shaw Lowell would wear black (and keep her hair tightly coiled) for the rest of her days.

After working in Virginia with the Freedmen's Relief Association, Lowell was invited by Louisa Lee Schuyler to join a committee visiting Bellevue and other hospitals. She then helped found the SCAA and made the investigation of able-bodied paupers her specialty. She came to public attention in 1876 after an infant died at the breast of Julia Deems, a young woman who had been nursing her baby on the freezing city streets while asking alms from Christmas crowds. When the *Tribune* suggested this was a shocking demonstration of social indifference, Lowell wrote a spirited letter insisting that the real fault lay with the errant Mr. Deems, with lax enforcement of the beggary laws by the police department, and with New Yorkers who opted for "indiscriminate almsgiving" over providing appropriate shelter.

In the same year, and in a similar vein, Lowell completed her SCAA report, which suggested that the key to solving the tramp problem was recognizing that they were not only "vicious and idle" but carriers of moral contagion, capable of infecting others. To limit the "corrupting influence of these worthless men and women," they should be "committed, until reformed, to district work-houses, there to be kept at hard-labor, and educated morally and mentally." This analysis so impressed Governor Tilden that he appointed her the first woman commissioner of the New York State Board of Charities.

In a step toward accomplishing Lowell's program, the SCAA prevailed upon New York City to end the police department's program of giving free lodging. Those deemed "worthy" were sent to special lodging houses like that established in 1876 by the Night Refuge Association of New York in the Old Strangers Hospital, on Avenue D and 10th Street. The vast majority were arrested as vagrants and jailed. Soaring prison occupancy rates prompted Lowell, in March 1878, to again appeal to the state legislature to construct workhouses.

In 1879 she proposed a law to incarcerate all women under thirty who had been arrested for misdemeanors or who had produced two illegitimate children. To prevent them from transmitting their "moral insanity" to others, they would be sentenced to a reformatory, under the exclusive management of women, where, under "tender care," the "weak and fallen creatures" would undergo rehabilitation. "The very character of the women must be changed"—they must "learn to enjoy work"—and as this could not be done overnight, the reformatories should be places "where, if necessary they may spend years." Though the legislature refused to embark on an extensive building program of either workhouses or female reformatories, it did pass an Act Concerning Tramps in 1880 that imposed imprisonment at hard labor in the nearest penitentiary for up to six months.

DISPENSING WITH DEMOCRACY

In 1874 Governor Samuel Tilden, elected in large measure on the strength of his role in prosecuting Tweed, set up a commission to study the "decay of municipal government." Its members included intellectuals and influentials, like *Nation* editor E. L. Godkin and railroad lawyer Simon Sterne, who had been arguing for some years that the root of New York City's problems was an insufficiently fettered franchise. In March 1877, after nearly two years of deliberation, the commission revealed what it thought should be done.

It called for a constitutional amendment that would establish a Board of Finance, to be elected solely by men who paid taxes on property worth over five thousand dollars or an annual rent higher than $250. This board would appoint all financial and legal officers of the city and take control over all municipal revenues and expenditures. The rest of the citizenry could still participate in electing the mayor and Board of Aldermen, but these worthies would be effectively stripped of their power to distribute public goods and services. The city would become more like a business corporation, where ultimate authority was reserved to those who provided the capital, in this case the leading taxpayers. The proposed Board of Finance would in effect institutionalize the power the bourgeois Committee of Seventy had temporarily seized during the fight against Tweed. It would guarantee, Sterne explained, that New York's propertied elite "would no longer find themselves in contest with the loafer element, which would eventually outnumber and beat them."

The commission's proposals were an instant hit in upper-class circles. The Chamber of Commerce, the New York Stock Exchange, the Produce Exchange, the Cotton Exchange—indeed every leading business organization—endorsed them enthusiastically. So did Astor, Vanderbilt, Dodge, Havemeyer, and leading newspapers like the *Times*, the *Herald*, and the *Tribune*, whose publisher Whitelaw Reid opined that "ignorant voters" were "as dangerous to the interests of society as the communists of France."

At a mass meeting held April 7, 1877, to rally support for the amendment, speakers hammered away at the necessity of taking power away from the "the idle, the vicious and the scheming politicians." They dismissed as "preposterous" the idea that "a mere majority should direct how the public expenses, paid by the minority, should be regulated." Democracy, acceptable for a small town, was lunacy in a large city like New York. Most towns, after all, had an "intelligent, orderly American population," whereas Manhattan was filled with dependent proletarians and "desperadoes from all ends of the earth." (Nor was it much better across the East River: the *World* believed that the "uncivilized classes in Brooklyn are quite as murderous as the savage in Montana.")

Urged on by Governor Tilden, the state legislature passed the proposed amendment in the fall of 1877. Under existing rules, if it passed again the following year it would go into effect. In the fall of 1878, unfortunately, New York City voters gave Tammany Hall a controlling influence in the state legislature and the Common Council. Despite John Kelly's heretofore extraordinary willingness to court businessmen's approval, he recognized the Tilden Commission's suffrage restriction plan for what it was—a device to dethrone politicians by disfranchising their electoral base—and when the proposed constitutional amendment came up for reconfirmation, it was scuttled. For the moment, neither the propertied nor the new-model politicians could rule without the other, and an uneasy power-sharing arrangement was cobbled together in which Kelly maintained control of the party, and the wealthy contented themselves with strategic positions in the government and on independent boards and commissions.

A MONUMENTAL ASIDE

During the period when the city's political and economic elite were striving mightily to rein in democracy and the immigrant masses, New York City played host to an object that would become the quintessential emblem of them both. Auguste Bartholdi, one of the many Frenchmen who had arrived in New York in 1871, was not a Communard seeking refuge but a sculptor seeking a site. Bartholdi was the emissary of a group of activist French intellectuals, of moderate republican stamp, who were intent on erecting a monumental statue in the United States, dedicated to liberty, to commemorate the upcoming centennial of 1776. The leader of this group was Édouard-René Lefebvre de Laboulaye, a prolific writer who had produced a three-volume *Histoire des États-Unis* and a book, *Paris in America*, about a Parisian transported to Manhattan.

Laboulaye was fascinated with the United States because he saw it—especially after the northern victory—as the kind of ideal republic he wanted to establish in France. He had worked to liberalize Napoleon's reign from within, and after the fall of the empire he became a republican member of the royalist-dominated National Assembly. To advance his cause he fastened on the idea of having a collaborative Franco-American group erect a statue in America, far enough away to avoid provoking a monarchist back-lash, yet close enough to foster (by association) a republican image for France. Hence Bartholdi's scouting mission. In addition to meeting with American notables, he inspected various locations and found his ideal spot on Bedloe's Island, situated in what was now unquestionably the gateway to the United States, the harbor of New York City.

The project advanced slowly during the 1870s. In 1873, in a kind of test case, the French government commissioned Bartholdi to execute a larger-than-life bronze statue of Lafayette, to give to New York City for having sent aid to Paris after it had been besieged by the Germans in the winter of 1870–71. It would be delivered and erected in Union Square for the 1876 centennial of the American Revolution.

By 1875 Laboulaye and his colleagues had gained the ascendancy and established the Third Republic. Now a French-American Union was created (with Laboulaye head-ing the French side), and Bartholdi forged ahead with producing a prudent Statue of Liberty, one that embodied republican ideals but steered clear of any taint of the Com-mune. The initial fragmentary result—Liberty's hand and torch—destined for display at the Philadelphia Centennial, was first parked in Madison Square, where New Yorkers could enter and climb to a viewing platform. Lest anyone mistake the symbolism, Laboulaye underlined that Bartholdi's figure "does not hold an incendiary torch, but a beacon which enlightens."

FAREWELL TO RECONSTRUCTION

As the metropolitan bourgeoisie worked to wrest power from the urban masses, they grew ever more understanding of, and sympathetic to, the efforts by southern elites to recapture power from Reconstruction governments. New York Democrats hoping to restore their prewar southern allies to power had long sought to topple Radical Republi-can regimes, routinely denouncing them (in the *World*'s words) as "Semi-Barbarians Led into Horrible Excesses by the Very Scum of Northern Carpetbaggism." Now many Republicans, alarmed by their own urban barbarians, had come to agree. George Tem-pleton Strong, who had long backed Grant's policies, now excoriated southern govern-ments as "nests of corrupt carpetbaggers upheld by a brute nigger constituency"—the equivalent of New York City's "celtocracy." The *Tribune*, the *Nation*, *Scribner's*, *Harp-er's*—all began to depict Reconstruction as a monstrous inversion of the natural order, in which the men of "intelligence and culture" had been sidelined by the lower orders.

Many white Republicans also thought it was time to stop courting electoral disaster by supporting blacks. In 1869 their party had backed black suffrage and been trounced at the polls. In 1873 African-American Republicans led by Henry Highland Garnet got Albany legislators to pass a statewide Civil Rights Act, which outlawed the exclusion of blacks from "full and equal enjoyment of any accommodation, advantage, facility, or privilege furnished" by public conveyances, innkeepers, theaters, public schools, or places of public amusement and expunged the word "white" from previous statutes. In 1874 their party was again crushed at the polls. The remnants of support for Reconstruction collapsed. It was time, said the Best Men of the North, to come to an understanding with the Best Men of the South, end misguided reform efforts, and unite in defense of property.

The presidential election of 1876 became the vehicle for arranging this detente. Samuel Tilden, the Democratic nominee, was not a personally popular figure. "Silk-Stocking Sammy," even his associates agreed, was vain, ambitious, cold, and aloof. But Tilden had won credit for his part in breaking Tweed. He was also a rich man—having made his fortune reorganizing bankrupt railroad lines and representing the likes of Gould and Fisk—and he was backed by rich Swallowtails like August Belmont and Abram Hewitt.

Tilden's opponent, Rutherford B. Hayes, had his own wealthy backers in New York City, but Tilden was a Democrat and a favorite son, and by the closing minutes of November 7, after having spent the evening at Everett House on Union Square tallying votes, it seemed clear he had carried city, state, and country. Tilden returned to his Gramercy Park home, where a crowd gathered at his doorstep acclaimed him as the next president. In the early morning hours of November 8, however, someone at Republican headquarters discerned a possibility of reversing the popular victory in the Electoral College, if Republicans in three southern states took appropriate action. Telegraphs were dispatched from New York to this effect, starting a chain of events that led, in March 1877, to Hayes's selection as the next chief executive and the swift abandonment of Reconstruction.

THE GREAT STRIKE

For the New York bourgeoisie, the president's pulling of federal troops out of southern politics and back to their barracks came not a moment too soon, as it meant that ample firepower would now be available to deal with the nationwide rail strike that broke out four months after Hayes was inaugurated.

The depression had exacerbated cutthroat competition between those railroads that had survived the crash. Fierce rate wars led to savage losses and repeated attempts to arrange a lasting truce. But invariably some opportunistic free enterpriser pursuing short-term profits—Jay Gould notable among them—would break ranks shortly after a price-fixing accord was reached. On those rare occasions when it seemed that rail executives might actually succeed in collectively hiking their rates, shippers and merchants protested, especially in New York City. In 1874, after forty rail lines agreed to a rate-boosting Saratoga Compact, the New York Chamber of Commerce and the Cheap Transportation Association attacked the Erie and the New York Central for their participation, claiming it would harm New York City's trade. This in turn led to the spectacle of the presidents of the two roads denouncing the "destructive communistic characteristics" of the New York Chamber of Commerce.

The primary alternative to raising prices was cutting wages, and it was a wage reduction that sparked a skirmish at Martinsburg, West Virginia, on July 16, 1877, which spread to Baltimore, then Pittsburgh, then to most major cities in the country. The struggle of railroad workers to reverse depression-era losses attracted support from other unionists and from the disaffected urban poor. Heavy-handed military responses provoked counterviolence, which in some cities—especially Pittsburgh—crescendoed to full-scale urban warfare.

The strike spread to the Erie and Central lines. Buffalo railmen went out and were joined by sympathetic factory workers, and the struggle spread east to Rochester, Syracuse, and Albany. The governor declared martial law, Albany was ringed with troops, and the great conflict seemed about to roll south into New York City—but it didn't. Part of the reason was that the metropolis was not really a railroad town; neither rail companies nor rail unions occupied the same commanding position as they did in smaller cities. But there were other reasons for the city's escape from the national cataclysm: a phenomenal mobilization of military might directed at would-be strikers and supporters, and, in sharp contrast to other urban battlegrounds, a closure of ranks and hearts by the upper and middle classes against the urban working class and its depression-era hardships.

As the strike spread, New York opinion makers had waxed ever shriller in denouncing it. The *Tribune* saw the strikers as "Communistic and law defying, against all law, order, and civilization," and if the upheaval spread to New York City, it should be "met by the shooting of every rioter within range of a musketball." The Congregational journal the *Independent* was more bloodthirsty still: "If the club of the policeman, knocking out the brains of the rioter, will answer, then well and good; but if it does not promptly meet the exigency, then bullets and bayonets, canister and grape" were the proper remedy: "Napoleon was right when he said the one way to deal with a mob is to exterminate it."

Congregationalist Henry Ward Beecher, still a moral tribune despite his recent contretemps, gave two sermons on the strike in mid-July. Though agreeing that the "oppressed" working class was entitled to organize "for mutual protection against the mutual selfishness of employers and of capital," he denounced the railroad strikers. Their effort was immoral because it contested the workings of "natural law," which was "on the side of the largest, always, whether men would have it so or not; and no meddling on their part can interrupt it." To this Spencerian outburst he added divine benediction, asserting that God "has meant that great shall be great and that little shall be little," and the poor must "reap the misfortunes of inferiority." Besides, he told his comfortable Plymouth parishioners, the poor's misfortunes weren't all *that* great. "It is true that a dollar a day is not enough to support a man and five children, if the man insists on smoking and drinking beer. Is not a dollar a day enough to buy bread? Water costs nothing. [Laughter] Man cannot live by bread [alone], it is true; but the man who cannot live on bread and water is not fit to live." More laughter, capped by applause.

Three days after Beecher's second sermon, the Workingmen's Party was scheduled to hold a strike support meeting in Tompkins Square. Railroad executive William H. Vanderbilt wrote mayor Smith Ely urging him not to allow it, but the mayor refused. The authorities did, however, cancel all police leaves, call out the First and Second divisions of the New York National Guard, summon the men of the Seventh Regiment back from vacation, connect Tompkins Square to armories by telegraph wires, garrison the New York Central roundhouse and depot, place two gatling guns at the heads of Wall and Pine, and dispatch seventy-five volunteers to defend the subtreasury. Frederick Law Olmsted surrounded Central Park headquarters with loaded howitzers. The Treasury Department, anxious about the millions stored in the Custom House, arranged for troops to be transferred to New York garrisons. The navy secretary sent a vessel that could, if necessary, clear the streets surrounding the Custom House. When told streets in the financial district were too crooked, Evarts responded: "The big guns will straighten them." Finally, with over a thousand sailors and marines at the ready, and an estimated eight thousand rifles and twelve hundred clubs in place, New York was ready to put down a "Communist riot."

On the evening of July 25, in the glare of hundreds of torches and calcium light at each corner of Tompkins Square Park, a crowd of twenty thousand turned out to hear socialist orators hold forth from a platform draped with an American flag. (All speeches were repeated in German at a second stand.) David Conroy, labor union leader, opened the giant rally saying: "I hope and trust that you, fellow citizens and workingmen will show to the press of New York tonight that you are an orderly people and that you are no rioters." Temperate speeches followed, expressing sympathy with the railroad strikers. An address to President Hayes was proposed, decrying the fact that all the government had offered workers hard hit by depression was "the hangman's rope and the soldier's bullet." There were calls for "political revolution through the ballot box" and the nationalization of transport, communication, and banks. John Swinton, editorial writer for the *New York Sun*, attacked Beecher's recent effusions as particularly unseemly coming from a man who made thirty thousand dollars a year.

After two hours, just as the meeting adjourned, policemen charged in, clubbing people without apparent provocation, yet without sparking resistance. As Emmons Clark of the Seventh Regiment summed up, the "large and dangerous assemblage in Tompkins Square was inspired with a wholesome terror" and "sullenly dispersed."

In the strike's aftermath, the War Department began constructing a system of armories in major cities. The labor press bitterly opposed the notion of establishing a standing army. The *New York Sun* said it presaged a "radical revolution of our whole republican system of government." Even the *Commercial and Financial Chronicle* opposed the armory program, fearing the military could be used "against business itself."

But an armory program had already been launched in New York City. The Seventh Regiment had been pushing for new quarters since 1873 and in 1874 had asked the city to provide them the plot of land bounded by 66th, 67th, Fourth, and Lexington. In 1875, after the state legislature authorized New York City to spend money erecting new armories, the aldermen appropriated $350,000 and assigned the desired parcel. Then budget cutter Andrew Haswell Green vetoed the expense, and the regiment decided to build the armory itself. At first subscriptions were slow, despite the *Tribune*'s exhortation that "banks, insurance and trust companies, in fact all the large corporations of every kind, owe to themselves as well as to the regiment, ample aid in this matter." Then came the 1877 strike, and money poured in. John Jacob Astor, A. T. Stewart, William H. Vanderbilt, Brown Brothers, Harper Brothers, Singer Manufacturing Company, Equitable Life, and Drexel, Morgan were among the many benefactors. In the end it cost $589,000, twice the sum raised for the Statue of Liberty, but when it opened in November 1879 it was the finest armory in the world. Its huge hall, ample enough to accommodate regimental maneuvers, was stoutly defended by a bronze gate, a bronze portcullis, and a solid oak door half a foot thick. Loopholes for riflemen enfiladed all approaches, and two or three gatling guns could be quickly mounted in the tower to sweep Fourth Avenue.

The Seventh Regiment Armory was only the first of many to follow, but for all the bourgeoisie's readiness to militarize Manhattan, many of its leading figures—John Pierpont Morgan chief among them—were becoming convinced that this was not a viable long-term solution to the problems and divisions wracking city and country. Morgan was appalled by the chaos of the national economy. Unrestrained competition, rate wars, depressions, strikes, and warfare in the streets—this was not the way to attract European investors for American securities. As the depression hit bottom, Morgan busied himself with developing an alternative: the consolidation of the continental economy under the aegis of a manageable number of large-scale corporations, manageable, that is, by him and his fellow investment bankers in New York City. As Morgan reorganized many of the era's failed railroads, he took care to obtain seats on the boards of the new, more powerful companies he fashioned. In 1879 the New York Central itself passed into Morgan's control, after he brokered the sale of 250,000 shares owned by Commodore Vanderbilt's heirs. Slowly he and his fellow financiers were accumulating unheard-of levels of power. The consolidation of a nationwide corporate economy under the control of Manhattan bankers in the next two decades would have enormous consequences for the global economy, for the United States, and, perhaps above all, for New York City.

PART FIVE

INDUSTRIAL CENTER AND CORPORATE COMMAND POST (1880–1898)

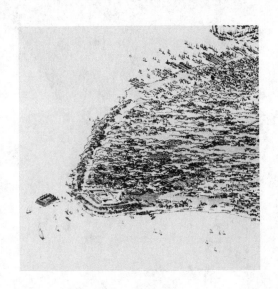

Greater New York birdseye view, especially drawn and painted for the *New York Tribune*. (General Research. The New York Public Library. Astor, Lenox and Tilden Foundations)

59

Manhattan, Inc.

In 1879 the national and metropolitan economies swung upward again. Reconstruction was over, the South was wide open for investment, and cotton billowed north again. Out west, the U.S. Army was winning its way to the rich trans-Mississippi territories, and within a decade obstinate Apache, Nez Perce, and Oglala Sioux resistance would be only a memory, the stuff of Wild West shows and dime novels. Farmers were reaping bountiful harvests, just as European crops were coming up short. The balance of trade turned favorable. For the first time in thirty years New York's bankers, merchants, and industrialists faced no significant obstacles to profit-making. Years of depression had crippled unions. Wages were down, the working day up. Activist judges intervened in economic disputes with admirable partiality on the side of capital. Municipal government was no longer wasting taxpayer money on outdoor relief or public works. The federal government too was in splendid hands. The gold standard was back, the income tax was no more, interest rates were down. Not surprisingly, railroad construction exploded. The need for iron horses to shuttle settlers west, and wheat and ore east, seemed limitless. Annual track construction spun up from 2,665 miles in 1878 to a staggering 11,569 in 1882, inducing tremendous output from steel mills, iron mines, the entire industrial sector.

The capital demands of this railroad "boom"—a word first used in this era to describe economic acceleration—revived Wall Street. From 1879 on, frock-coated, silk-hatted brokers jostled and pushed at the New York Stock Exchange, buying and selling millions' worth of stocks amid a great din. Outside, along Nassau, Pine, and William streets, outdoor curb traders created a bedlam of their own, while all around them bank messengers and telegraph boys with yellow envelopes darted to and fro amid the throng. Trading continued at fever pitch through 1882, boosted by the willingness of brokers to extend margin credit—an investor could buy a stock by putting down a mere 10 percent of its purchase price—and by the return of European investors who had sworn they would never again buy American stocks even if endorsed by angels.

But the railroad wars revived as well. Rival barons had agreed to a new "pool" in 1877—a cartel to curtail competition, fix prices, and divvy up markets. Unenforceable at law, the arrangement was soon in tatters. Supply rapidly outstripped demand. When one line proved a route's profitability, others jumped in and built another, forcing the established firm to slash rates. Profits spiraled downward. Faced with catastrophe, the roads formed new pacts, only to find them quickly violated by predators.

The biggest shark of all was Jay Gould. With fellow manipulators like Russell Sage, Gould bought up western lines, puffed their stock, sold out at profitable highs, and turned a final profit by selling short on the way down. Gould joined pools, then sabotaged them without compunction, precipitating yet another round of conflict.

By the early 1880s each major line was struggling to transform itself into a giant, self-contained, nationwide system capable of withstanding all possible rivals. Gould expanded his core lines in all directions and by 1882 owned over fifteen thousand miles of road, 15 percent of the national trackage. William Vanderbilt retaliated with his own massive expansion program. So did Henry Villard and the group of New Yorkers— including August Belmont, Robert Goelet, and the young Edward H. Harriman—who controlled the Illinois Central. But all this did was reproduce the warfare at a higher level.

By 1883 the combat was buffeting Wall Street. At first there were just isolated failures: high-flying financiers like Henry Villard plummeted suddenly into bankruptcy. Then, as competition blighted earnings, rail stocks declined, and iron stocks dipped downward. Alarmed European capitalists retreated again across the Atlantic. Rumors spread of an impending collapse. The president of the Exchange asserted that "the situation now is in no respect like that which preceded the panic of 1873"—a sure sign of trouble.

By 1884 the contraction had become so pronounced, the speculative marketplace so vulnerable, that anything might have triggered disaster. In the event, the unwitting precipitant turned out to be Ulysses S. Grant Sr.

After the war, an unscrupulous young man named Ferdinand Ward had plunged into the stock market and scored with a series of modestly successful speculations. On the strength of this, Ward persuaded Ulysses "Buck" Grant Jr., airhead son of the ex-president, that he could make him a millionaire overnight. Grant and Ward, stockbrokers, was born. Next, the smooth-talking Ward convinced Grant Senior—the general had moved to New York City in 1881 and settled into a brownstone on 66th Street— that he could advance his son's career by joining the firm too. Then Ward went to James D. Fish, president of the Marine National Bank, and hinted lucrative government contracts were on the way to the ex-president's firm. Fish took the bait and advanced large sums of depositors' money, which Ward used for stock market speculations.

Ward, unfortunately, bet on a bullish market just as stocks turned bearish. He lost heavily but continued to pay dividends to Grant and Ward's investors—including the Grants—by arranging further loans from Marine Bank. The Grants, *père et fils*, thought themselves rich.

In April 1884, with both Ward and Marine Bank desperate for funds, Ward went to the credulous general and said the bank, and thus his brokerage house, were in a spot of temporary trouble. Could the general borrow $150,000 from William Vanderbilt to tide things over? Grant did as requested, though Vanderbilt, who like most rich business-men had a great affection for Grant, said: "To you—to General Grant—I'm making this loan, and not to the firm."

Grant turned the check over to Ward, who promptly cashed it, pocketed the funds, and prepared to flee the city. He didn't move quickly enough. Fish announced the Marine Bank's failure. Crowds of enraged depositors milled outside its closed doors, baying for Fish's head. They organized a posse, captured Ward, and clapped both in Ludlow Street Jail. When word reached Grant at his G&W office, the stunned old man, a dead cigar clutched between his lips, hobbled out into the street and headed home, as cynical Wall Streeters doffed their hats out of respect for the tragedy unfold-ing before them.

More banks collapsed. Eminent directors were revealed to have stolen millions and plunged, ineptly, into railroad securities. Stocks nosedived. Panic swept the district. Bro-kerage houses failed. High rollers were laid low: Gould himself came close to collapse.

General Grant went bankrupt. The public, correctly convinced he had known nothing of his partner's swindles, offered sympathy and cash. Grant, down to his last eighty dollars, accepted reluctantly. Greatly distressed about his debt to Vanderbilt, he signed over his properties, medals, and presidential memorabilia to the financier. Van-derbilt refused to accept them, until Grant pointed out that creditors would take them anyway; the magnate turned the medals over to the government.

Detail from *The Panic of 1884*, from *Harper's Weekly*, May 24, 1884. (Library of Congress)

At this darkest hour Grant recalled a request by *Century Magazine* that he write articles on the Civil War. He produced a series of successful pieces, then landed a book contract for his memoirs. In 1885 Grant learned he had contracted terminal throat cancer. Despite great suffering, he pushed on and finished the book—later a spectacular success and the salvation of his heirs—before dying on July 23, 1885.

His adopted city did better by him in death than it had in life. Grant's body lay in state at City Hall for three days, then embarked on a six-mile-long funeral procession through the city's streets, past an estimated million and a half spectators, to a temporary tomb on Riverside Drive. The following year, the Department of Parks authorized creation of a permanent memorial and gravesite, and after April 27, 1897, when Grant's Tomb was finally dedicated, the old soldier finally lay in peace beside the Hudson.

THE CORPORATE SOLUTION

The stock market chaos of 1884 proved less catastrophic than the breakdowns of 1819, 1837, 1857, and 1873—in part, the *Nation* observed, because previous crises had broken upon good times "like thunderclaps out of a clear sky." In the mid-1880s, however, business had already slumped, and unemployment had risen to 7.5 percent from its normal 2.5 percent. The panic's limited impact was also due to prompt and decisive action by the financial community itself, now far better prepared to meet such crises. The Clearing House pumped credit into the system, and dozens of banks and brokerage firms were hauled back from the precipice. One of the coolest and boldest players was J. P. Morgan, who stepped in and purchased stocks almost as fast as panicked speculators sold them, thus helping restore confidence. When the crisis passed, Morgan had emerged as Wall Street's preeminent leader.

Morgan, chewing on his big cigar, surveyed the bloody economic battlefield from the mahogany partners' room at 23 Wall and decided it was time to end the railroad wars. Morgan had himself participated in them vigorously, bankrolling combatants and mending casualties, both highly lucrative endeavors. But the London investors he represented were fed up, as he barked at one recalcitrant railroad president: "Your roads! Your roads belong to my clients!" With competitive conflagrations now threatening Wall Street itself, Morgan and other New York investment bankers decided to intervene aggressively.

On a hot and muggy July day in 1885 a clutch of railroad executives boarded Morgan's 165-foot, black-hulled steam yacht, the *Corsair*. While the vessel cruised up and down the Hudson River, the banker spelled out his displeasure at the "fever for building and extending competitive lines." The assembled magnates agreed to reject unbridled competition and establish spheres of influence. But the "Corsair Compact," like previous pools, lasted little more than a year. The wars commenced again, this time with the Vanderbilts as rate cutters and Gould promoting stability. There seemed no way to quit the free enterprise merry-go-round, so the ride spun on, propelled by fear of failure, accumulated rancor and mistrust, monumental egoism, and the sheer exhilaration and momentum of combat. In 1887 matters worsened further when farmers, passengers, small businessmen, and the New York City merchants assembled in the National Anti-Monopoly League convinced Congress to outlaw pools altogether. Wars of unparalleled ferocity chewed up earnings, and the economy tipped downward once more. In 1888 Morgan summoned the presidents of sixteen major roads to the library of his Madison Avenue mansion and hammered out another pact—which quickly crumbled.

Industrialists, facing much the same dilemma, had meanwhile invented the "trust," a legal device they believed might solve the problem. Oil refiner John D. Rockefeller and his leading rivals had joined forces in a Standard Oil cartel that used its collective domination of processing capacity and railroad transportation to force thousands of combative oil producers to stabilize prices, with William Rockefeller dispatched to New York City to handle the Standard's export operations. When competitors threatened to bypass this arrangement by launching pipelines that would pump crude oil directly to New York Bay for refining and export, the Standard fought back. It gained control of most independent metropolitan-area outlets—folding Charles Pratt's Astral Oil company (which Rockefeller had bought up secretly in 1874) with other Hunter's Point and Newtown Creek operations into Standard Oil Company of New York (SOCONY)—and ran its own pipeline from the Pennsylvania oil fields to newly centralized operations in Bayonne, New Jersey.

The problem was that this enormous enterprise lacked a legal and administrative superstructure—until 1882, when New York attorney Samuel C. T. Dodd conceived the Standard Oil Trust. Shareholders of the cartel's now forty companies exchanged their stock for certificates in the trust, which in turn was authorized to "exercise general supervision over the affairs of the several Standard Oil Companies" out of a unified headquarters in New York City. Here, clearly, was an outfit that knew how to overcome competition, and indeed boasted of it: "The day of combination is here to stay," John D. declared. Industrial consolidation, he announced, was a step up the evolutionary ladder. It represented the "survival of the fittest," Rockefeller said, "the working out of a law of nature and a law of god."

Inspired by the Standard's example, ten other processing industries established trusts and all but two located their central offices in New York City. In 1887 Elihu Root, corporate attorney and pillar of the Manhattan Bar, helped Henry O. Havemeyer wring competition out of one of New York's oldest industries. Seventeen metropolitan sugar refining companies, representing 78 percent of the nation's capacity, came together in a Sugar Trust, which consolidated its members' production and purchasing and proceeded to drive remaining competitors out of business, a process it acclaimed as advancing "the common good."

Small businessmen, farmers, and consumers disagreed. They denounced trusts for raising prices and concentrating power. In 1890 these opponents won passage of the Sherman Act, which declared the trustee device an illegal restraint of trade. Gloomy businessmen faced another murderous round of free enterprise.

At this juncture, Wall Street attorneys James Brooks Dill and William J. Curtis (a partner in Sullivan and Cromwell) took a new tack. Dill drafted a law that permitted one manufacturing company to purchase and hold stock in any other company "manufacturing and producing materials necessary to its business." In effect it allowed competitors to combine in a single corporate body. This simple and elegant solution was enacted by the New Jersey state legislature after Dill and Curtis, both Jersey residents, convinced the governor it would attract new corporations and strengthen the state's budget. It soon passed judicial muster, as courts found that elements of a single firm, no matter how large, could act in concert without their association constituting an illegal restraint of trade.

Between 1890 and 1893 half a hundred companies converted to the corporate holding company form. Some were old trusts, forced into reformatting by the Sherman Act:

when the Sugar Trust was declared illegal in 1889 and ordered dissolved, Root recommended the Havemeyers try incorporation, and within a few years the new American Sugar Refining Company controlled nearly 98 percent of the national output. Some of the new corporations were "Morganized" railroads, formed when J. P. Morgan and other New York City investment bankers reassembled bankrupt competitors into viable corporate entities, set up their headquarters in Manhattan, and pocketed million-dollar fees and directorships for their trouble. Some were metropolitan wholesale merchants—like H. B. Claflin's—who had discovered the virtues of the corporate form.

Some of the new corporations were industrial concerns, like the American Tobacco Company (1890), a newcomer to New York. In the mid-1880s James Buchanan Duke, a North Carolina chewing tobacco manufacturer, switched to cigarette production. Duke relocated his operations to Manhattan—the largest urban tobacco market in the nation and an industry center since Pierre Lorillard had opened his snuff factory on Chatham Street back in 1760. Backed by lines of credit from New York financial houses, Duke opened a massive factory at First Avenue and 38th Street, using cheap female labor and fifteen of the new Bonsack machines capable of producing 120,000 cigarettes a day. By 1889 he was rolling over eight hundred million cigarettes annually. The following year Duke subsumed his five leading competitors into his giant new ATC corporation (and a few years later P. Lorillard Company as well).

The financial community rapidly thawed its frosty attitude toward "industrials." Bankers and brokers had long considered manufacturing operations too small or too unstable to warrant investment. Through the 1880s the New York Stock Exchange had refused to list industrials, with the single exception of the Pullman Palace Car Company. Now funds flowed to newly merged companies. By 1897 eighty-six industrial corporations, each capitalized for over a million dollars, had been formed and financed, most of them on Wall Street. Mining and petroleum stocks traded in unprecedented numbers. Foreigners plunged in too and by the early 1890s had sunk roughly three billion dollars into U.S. firms, up 50 percent since 1883. Poor's, Moody's, and Dun's began publishing analyses of the new corporations, and many began filing annual reports with the Exchange.

It seemed, finally, that a stable future was coming into being, one in which incorporation would replace competition, antagonistic companies would be consolidated, and their oversight operations would be centralized—in New York City, emerging capital of an emerging corporate economy.

ASSOCIATES AND AGENTS

In the 1880s and 1890s many industrial and railroad magnates relocated themselves—as well as their corporations—to Manhattan. Cleveland's John D. Rockefeller joined his brother William in 1884. Collis P. Huntington came in from California; the Armours arrived from Chicago; Andrew Carnegie shifted from Pittsburgh. They and their companies were drawn, chiefly, by the gravitational pull of money. They wanted direct access to the great investment banks and their connections to vast pools of domestic and foreign capital. New York was host to virtually all the leading firms: Drexel, Morgan (which in 1895 became J. P. Morgan and Company); August Belmont and Company (run after his death in 1890 by his son August Junior); Kuhn, Loeb (led, after the original partners retired in 1885, by Jacob Schiff); and the Seligmans, Lehmans, and Speyers. Even Boston banks like Lee, Higginson and Kidder, Peabody felt obliged to open outlets in New York.

Some newcomers entered the banking world themselves. The Rockefellers cycled their oil profits into the National City Bank, Moses Taylor's old operation until his death in 1882. From 1891 it was in the steady hands of the steely James Stillman (two of whose daughters married sons of William Rockefeller), and Standard Oil connections and cash would make National City Bank a power in the city.

Manhattan was attractive to businessmen for other reasons too, especially its great assemblage of experts. Among the vast array of talented metropolitan professionals, none were more crucial to the emerging corporate order than lawyers. Since George Templeton Strong died in 1875, firms like his had been joined by a host of crack legal firms. They specialized in providing legal, managerial, and financial advice to large corporate clients on a regular basis, not just at the point of litigation. Indeed many corporate attorneys withdrew from trial work altogether, dealing instead with the growing number of regulatory state agencies that corporations were answerable to, or serving as businessmen's emissaries and lobbyists (shuttling back and forth between Washington or Albany and New York City), or serving in public office themselves.

Lower Manhattan grew thick with corporate law firms. Bangs and Stetson, ancestor of Davis, Polk, and Wardwell, boasted Francis Lynde Stetson, known as J. P. Morgan's attorney general for his work counseling the financier on industrial and railroad reorganizations. When Grover Cleveland lost the White House in 1888, he moved to New York City and worked at Bangs, Stetson, forming close alliances with Morgan and other financiers before returning to Pennsylvania Avenue in 1892.

Morgan also turned to William Nelson Cromwell of Sullivan and Cromwell (1879), as did Henry Villard and E. H. Harriman. Anderson, Adams, and Young (1866)—later Milbank, Tweed, Hadley, and McCloy—became the "Rockefeller firm" in 1888 when George Welwood Murray brought in John D. as a client; Murray remained his legal adviser and confidant for decades. Joseph Choate counseled Standard Oil and American Tobacco, Elihu Root advised big sugar, and future legal giant Henry Lewis Stimson got his start advising railroad and streetcar companies.

Most firms remained modest in size—five partners constituted a large operation—but some of them, Strong would have been glad to know, began to replace the old apprenticeship system, which had relied on unpaid law clerks, with a more professional approach. Walter S. Carter's firm, Chamberlain, Carter, and Hornblower, began hiring graduates of elite law schools as paid "associates," who specialized in particular departments (corporate, real estate, trusts and estates) and served as the pool from which future partners were drawn. Among the first recruits and graduates was Paul D. Cravath, a brilliant Columbia Law graduate who would later develop the new approach so extensively at his own firm that it became known as the "Cravath system." At the same time, law schools and the "white shoe" firms they fed became ever more socially exclusive. There were a few Jewish or Catholic organizations, and after 1890 women were admitted to NYU Law School, but the new procedure helped make Wall Street law firms into overwhelmingly white, Protestant, upper- or middle-class, Republican, and male bastions.

New York's attractiveness to corporations was enhanced by its advertising industry, which underwent a transformation akin to the legal profession's. Advertising had a

The throng of top hats in this downtown lunchroom conveys the ever-increasing density—and thoroughly masculine tone—of the city's business district during the 1880s. *Harper's Weekly*, September 8, 1888. (© Collection of The New-York Historical Society)

dubious reputation in the postwar era, due in part to its most prominent clients: the patent medicine manufacturers who laced their products with alcohol and opium. Business self-promotion seemed Barnumesque; it smacked of desperation and unsoundness. Even the best agencies, like Samuel Pettengill, New York's and the country's largest, shilled for newspaper and magazine publishers and lied shamelessly about circulation figures to wrest higher rates from advertisers.

George P. Rowell enhanced the industry's image when he began bringing out annual editions of *Rowell's American Newspaper Directory*, which provided reasonably accurate figures on circulation and rates for over five thousand U.S. and Canadian papers. By evaluating media, he shifted the business toward representing advertisers rather than publishers. In 1888 Rowell started a trade journal, *Printer's Ink*, that advertised the very notion of advertising. In the same year, Pear's Soap obtained clerical benediction for its product, and for the practice of promotion itself, from Henry Ward Beecher's cautious testimonial: "If cleanliness is next to Godliness, soap must be considered as a means of Grace, and a clergyman who recommends moral things should be willing to recommend soap."

Carlton and Smith, another New York agency, also gained respectability by convincing Methodist magazines that running ads was both wise and virtuous. By 1870 the firm worked with four hundred religious weeklies, many of them headquartered in New York. William Carlton's young assistant James Walter Thompson followed this up by persuading genteel journals like *Scribner's* and *Harper's* that they too could carry ads without losing integrity or offending subscribers. In 1878 Thompson bought Carlton out and renamed the agency after himself.

"Advertising is the steam propeller of business success," Rowell claimed, and giant corporations and insurance companies agreed. They turned to professionals like Thompson, and the growing number of firms clustered around Newspaper Row, to create copy rather than simply broker it. Consumer goods manufacturers used ads to familiarize a national market with their product's "brand name." In the mid-1870s a New York firm, Enoch Morgan's Sons, peddled its scouring soap by adopting a Latin-sounding brand name (Sapolio) and giving retailers pamphlets that sang its praise in verse penned by Bret Harte, then scratching out a marginal living in the metropolis. In 1884 the firm hired a professional advertiser to place its proverbs ("Be Clean!" "Sapolio Scours the World") in publications across the country, posted them in streetcars, and blazoned them on a huge sign in New York harbor.

Companies relied on metropolitan agencies to promote *types* of products too. Admen taught consumers to prefer breakfast cereals in boxes, rather than scooped from grocers' barrels; to shave themselves, rather than patronize barbers. By 1889 Duke's American Tobacco Company was spending eight hundred thousand dollars a year to expand the cigarette-smoking public, win tobacco chewers and cigar smokers over to the newer product, and force retailers to distribute his merchandise. Ad agencies placed Duke propaganda in papers and periodicals, on billboards around the city, in programs for theatergoers and handbills at ballfields and boxing matches. In the 1890s other corporate manufacturers used professional pitchmen to launch new commodities, and campaigns designed for Procter & Gamble and Colgate-Palmolive, Pabst and Postum, Coca-Cola and Cream of Wheat, similarly dwelt on the compatibility of their wares with modern urban lifestyles.

The number of ad agencies swelled from forty-two in 1870 to over four hundred by the end of the 1890s. Like law firms, they grew larger and more internally specialized. At J. Walter Thompson's, "account executives" supervised copywriting for particular companies, then liaised with their counterparts in the corporation's sales and marketing divisions, and with the advertising departments of New York's newspapers as well. In the 1870s the daily press had gotten less than one-third its income from advertisements. As journalism's costs increased, papers relied more heavily on such revenues, which jumped to 44 percent of income by 1880 and 55 percent by 1900. The ratio of editorial to ad matter swung from seventy-thirty to fifty-fifty in the same period, and self-promotional gambits flourished as papers sought to assemble an audience to sell to advertisers.

TALL TOWERS

Burgeoning professional and corporate concerns needed lots of office space. Continental-scale companies like American Tobacco had to control the flow of product from factory to retailer, oversee sales agents throughout the country, maintain a large central depot in New York, audit costs, manage labor, track inventory, compile reports, pay taxes, and initiate legal transactions. Companies with international outreach, like I. M. Singer and Company—led by Edward Clark since 1876, the year after Singer's death—established agencies in Latin America, Canada, and the Far East, which dispatched reports back to the central office in New York City. Sales, purchasing, legal, auditing, and manufacturing departments, in turn, required ever-expanding support staffs: typists and stenographers to handle intra- and extra-company correspondence, clerks to file it all, office boys to handle miscellaneous chores.

Particular entities had special space needs. Insurance companies needed to keep huge record bases for premium and claims payments, manage investments, and develop actuarial statistics. In the case of a company like Metropolitan Life, which sold "industrial insurance" to workers, headquarters had to direct the army of agents who sold policies and collected premiums each week. Law firms needed bigger libraries as national reporting of case law expanded the number of publications to be researched. Specialized segments of the import-export fraternity (iron and metal, petroleum, produce, cotton, coffee, and coal) needed their own gathering places; no longer would a single Merchants' Exchange do.

To meet this demand, Manhattan's real estate industry—itself newly organized and housed in a Real Estate Exchange (1883)—generated a tremendous volume of commercial construction, much of it now in red brick neo-Renaissance rather than Second Empire, though mansard roofs remained popular. Some construction was commissioned, but much was erected "on spec" for rental to bankers, brokers, and railroad and insurance companies; the building boom created havens for capital in more ways than one.

The result was a dramatic enlargement—horizontally and vertically—of the city's business district. The high cost of land encouraged tall towers. "Real estate capitalists," according to "Sky Building in New York," an 1883 article in *Building News*, had "suddenly discovered that there was plenty of room in the air, and that by doubling the height of its buildings the same result would be reached as if the island had been stretched to twice its present width."

In 1882 the cornerstone was laid for George Post's mammoth, arcaded Produce Exchange. Over the next two years, it rose at the corner of Broadway and Beaver—site of Peter Stuyvesant's weekly "Monday Market"—until it loomed ten stories tall over Bowling Green. In 1884 William Rockefeller commissioned a headquarters to house the new Standard Oil Trust at 24-26 Broadway, and two years later its ten stories were filled with managers and employees directing the production, refining, and marketing of oil. By the end of the 1890s over three hundred buildings nine or more stories tall would have gone up in Manhattan.

Though such structures did not overtop the previous era's Tribune and Western Union buildings, they did surpass them in technology. Most lofty predepression structures had been masonry buildings, whose thick weight-supporting walls ate up floor space and dictated small windows. Post's Produce Exchange used cage construction: iron columns and girders carried the weight of the floors, allowing exterior walls to get slimmer. Post also experimented with "skeleton" construction for some of the walls, using a metal frame to support them as well.

New York ambled farther into the technological future in 1888, when Bradford Lee Gilbert, an experienced railroad station architect, announced he would raise an eleven story building, 158 feet tall, that relied completely on skeletal construction. His decision was immediately attacked by architects, engineers, newspapers, and public officials who believed such a structure would be precarious. Gilbert defended himself by pointing to recent engineering developments. Gustave Eiffel, for example, had just designed an internal steel-and-wrought-iron armature for the 151-foot Statue of Liberty (completed in 1886) that could withstand a wind load factor of fifty-eight pounds per square foot. At 50 Broadway, Gilbert would use the most up-to-date wind bracing, using iron diagonals in each bay to transmit wall weight through girders and columns down to the footings and foundation of timber piles driven forty feet down to hardpan.

Despite the skeptics, Gilbert's Tower Building won a city construction permit and overcame the worries of the owner, who feared his narrow building (only twenty-one feet wide) might well blow over. One blustery Sunday morning, the usual gawkers were watching laborers work on the building's tenth story, when the weather turned really fierce. Throngs poured down to Broadway expecting to see the thin tower topple. As the wind howled, Gilbert clambered to the top, lowered a plumb line, and discovered to his great satisfaction that the building vibrated not at all.

Gilbert's design ambitions were less daring than his technological ones. Eschewing the approach favored by Chicagoans of having exteriors "honestly" match construction principles, Gilbert swathed the slender base in rusticated stone and enslabbed the remainder with a conventional facade. Just looking at the completed Tower Building in 1889, one would never have known that New York had entered a new era. But after Joseph Pulitzer's building was finished the following year, there would be no mistaking the fact.

In 1888 the *New York World*'s publisher had the great satisfaction of buying up French's Hotel at Park Row and Frankfort Street and having it torn to pieces. During the Civil War, the elegant establishment had ejected Pulitzer, then a newly arrived Hungarian immigrant and volunteer Union Army cavalryman, because his frayed uniform annoyed the fashionable guests. Pulitzer had grand plans for the site. In the previous few years, his newspaper had dwarfed the circulation of James Gordon Bennett's *Herald* and Charles Henry Dana's *Sun*. Now he would have George Post erect an edifice that would dwarf his competitors' nearby buildings, though it would not be as technologically sophisticated as Gilbert's Tower Building, as Post opted here for cage construction.

On December 10, 1890, the governor and mayor teamed up to celebrate the opening of Pulitzer's dazzling 309-foot structure—the tallest building in the world. The *World* tower was topped by a glittering gilded dome, which now would be the first thing to strike the eye of passengers on vessels arriving in the harbor. It was also the first building to overshadow Trinity Church (284 feet), physical ratification of the passage of metropolitan power from sacred to secular. At the top was Pulitzer's huge semicircular office with three great windows, frescoed ceilings, and walls of embossed leather. One wag reportedly got off the elevator at the top floor and in a loud voice asked, "Is God in?" The editors on the eleventh floor were delighted to find they could lean out the windows and "spit on the *Sun*."

Appropriately enough, in the years following Pulitzer's coup, the term "skyscraper" first gained common currency. It was not a novel word, having had a long history of other associations. Since the eighteenth century it had been used to describe the triangular sails, set above the royals in calm latitudes, called skyscrapers or moonrakers due to their great height. Now, in the early 1890s, it fastened itself irrevocably to the tall buildings sprouting up in lower Manhattan. The new principle of skeletal construction won official sanction, building laws were revised appropriately, and the city made clear its willingness to tear down old masonry structures and erect steel ones, to the delight of ironmasters like Andrew Carnegie and Abram Hewitt.

More was involved here than a prosaic expansion of commercial office stock. In succeeding so admirably in overarching its competitors—making runts of the *Times*,

Herald, Sun, and even the *Tribune,* whose campanile peaked at a paltry 260 feet—the World Building broke new cultural as well as material ground. Pulitzer's publishing success owed as much to his paper's exuberant self-advertising and ferociously competitive spirit as to its innovative content. His architectural initiative extended this warfare onto a new terrain. The World Building was more than a mere office building; it was a corporate self-proclamation, a brand name shouting itself in iron and stone, a shrewd Barnumesque statement by a man well aware that appearances could constitute reality.

Other corporate moguls would follow Pulitzer's lead and seek their own boardroom-eyries. It would be a few years yet before the process accelerated sharply, but soon a corporate competition for sensational self-presentation—and rentable floor space— would be unleashed. The ensuing frenzied space race would drive New York spectacularly skyward.

The city's silhouette was also transformed in these years by two devices that became (and have remained) two of New York's most distinguishing features: water tanks and steam pipes.

As commercial buildings rose to six stories, beyond the reach of fire ladders, and then even higher, beyond the reach of fire hoses dependent on Croton-generated water pressure, the fire department, city government, insurance industry, and tall-tower occupants grew steadily more alarmed, especially when it became clear how quickly flames shot up elevator and air shafts. Western Union, whose building was among the first to confront this problem, had adopted an extremely costly solution. The company dug wells seventy feet deep in its cellar and installed powerful steam pumps to drive the water up through iron mains to the roof, from which heavy streams of water could be played on surrounding buildings. This was not a practical solution to mounting fire losses—which in the dry-goods district alone surpassed six million dollars between 1877 and 1882, less than a third of which had been covered by reluctant insurers. In the latter year the burning of the former World Building on Park Row produced four hundred thousand dollars in damages and twelve deaths, starkly underscoring the peril.

Water sprinklers were part of the answer. The Parmelee Automatic Sprinkler, a heat-triggered device connected to piping installed on each floor, was introduced in 1874 and replaced in 1881 by the improved Grinnell Sprinkler. But sprinklers, as much as hydrants and hoses, required a sure source of pressurized water. The solution, adopted at first on a piecemeal basis, was to have barrelmakers construct a bulky wooden water tank, which looked like a huge washtub on stilts, up on the roof, where it gravity-fed water into the sprinkler pipes that wove back and forth through the building beneath. Fire insurance companies lowered rates on buildings that installed these tanks. In the 1890s, companies emerged to build them (of which two remain, the Rosenwach Tank Company and Isseks Brothers). And the city's Building Code was amended to require them (or a cellar pump equivalent) on all buildings over 150 feet tall.

Another solution to problems raised by tall buildings was the creation of a network of underground steam pipes to heat them. If each of the new behemoths had a separate heating plant, their gargantuan coal requirements, which would have to be delivered through narrow downtown streets, would soon have rendered the area impassable. To obviate the problem, the New York Steam Company, formed by a merger of competitors in 1881, got a Common Council franchise to lay such pipelines (for which it paid a paltry hundred dollars a year) and in 1882 supplied its first customer, the United Bank

Installing district steam heating mains, *Scientific American*, November 19, 1881. (© Collection of The New-York Historical Society)

Building at Wall and Broadway. By year's end sixty-two clients in the Wall Street area had signed on to be connected to the Steam Company's boiler plant at Dey and Greenwich. By 1886 it had 350 customers and five miles of mains, and to this day visitors are periodically startled to see clouds of steam erupt from beneath the streets, as if the city rested on a foundation of geysers.

HIGH ROLLERS

Conduits below were matched by conduits above, as the system of elevated railroads was spurred to fruition by the need to accommodate the city to the growth of corporate enterprise. Rapid transit made the skyscrapers possible by ferrying vast numbers of uptown workers to the downtown high-rise business district, and indeed the "els" accelerated tall-tower construction by driving property values sky high and making efficient use of space ever more desirable.

During the depression, the availability of cheap labor had galvanized promoters to win passage of a Rapid Transit Act (1875), which authorized handing out franchises to private entrepreneurs, and by the early 1880s locomotives were steaming up and down Manhattan. On Ninth Avenue, Charles Harvey's old road, rebuilt and extended, reached 81st Street in mid-1879, spurring long-delayed development on the Upper West Side. By 1881 the track continued on to 110th Street, where, at the spine-tingling height of sixty-three feet, it swerved giddily eastward to Eighth Avenue, then loped on up to the Harlem River at 155th. At 53rd Street a crosstown feeder linked the Ninth Avenue line to the Metropolitan (formerly the Gilbert) Elevated Railway, whose trains chugged at twelve miles an hour up from Rector Place to Sixth Avenue and on to Central Park.

After December 1878 the New York Elevated Railroad Company's Third Avenue El stretched from South Ferry up to 129th Street. The company obligingly ran cars all through the night—"Owl Trains" every 15 minutes—which conveyed homeward late workers in the newspaper offices or carousers out on the town, rolling northward across the gloomy and still largely untenanted Harlem flats while the lights of Astoria twinkled across the water in the distance. From 1880 it was paralleled by the Manhattan Railway Company's Second Avenue road that ran north from Chatham Square.

The new transport lines were not restricted to Manhattan. At first, Third Avenue El passengers bound for the Bronx could only transfer—for a separate fare—to the so-called Huckleberry Line, a horsecar that meandered along the Annexed District's Third Avenue so slowly that passengers could hop off, pick huckleberries in the fields, and reboard the same car. After 1886, however, the Suburban Rapid Transit Company (1880) ran an elevated service that crossed the Harlem River on an iron drawbridge and (by 1891) traveled up Bronx's Third Avenue through Mott Haven, Melrose, and Morrisania to 177th, spurring a building boom along the corridor. Passengers bound for the

Steam engines at the Franklin Square Station of the Second Avenue El. At the left are the offices of Harper & Brothers, the largest publishing house in the United States at the time. *Harper's Weekly*, September 7, 1878. (© Collection of The New-York Historical Society)

Annexed District could also connect with the New York and Northern (which became the New York Central's Putnam Division) running up through Highbridge, Morris Heights, and Kingsbridge. Or they could catch the New York and Harlem Railroad, whose ash-spewing locomotives carried them up the Bronx's central corridor, past Mott Haven's solid brick clock-towered station, through Melrose, Morrisania, Tremont, Fordham, Williamsbridge, and on past Woodlawn's country mansion station with its landscaped flower beds, to White Plains and points north. Wealthy folk could simply hop the Hudson line to Riverdale.

Southbound travelers, once they reached the Brooklyn Bridge—which opened with great fanfare in 1883—could take a cable-drawn car, which commenced operation in 1885, from Park Row to Sands Street. From there—also after 1885, when Mayor Seth Low helped inaugurate it—Brooklyn Elevated Company trains (the city's first) ran through downtown to Lexington Avenue, then headed east to Broadway and Gates. A rival, the Kings County Elevated Rail Road, established service along Fulton Street to Nostrand Avenue by 1888, to Brownsville by 1891, and to East New York and the city line in 1893. By that year Brooklyn's elevated system was complete, differing companies having built the Bay Ridge, Myrtle Avenue, and Broadway lines. These trains handled over thirty million passengers annually, most of them commuting from homes in Brooklyn to jobs in Manhattan.

Different lines served different clientele and had correspondingly different styles. Manhattan's Sixth Avenue El, which transported a predominantly middle-class ridership, was built for delight as well as convenience. Its dainty green stations, topped by graceful iron pavilion roofs, were designed by landscape artist J. F. Cropsey to simulate tasteful cottages and contained heated, gas-lit waiting rooms for gentlemen and for ladies. The trains that pulled up were equally ornamental, their Pullman palace-style cars manned by conductors in braided blue flannel uniforms.

The Third Avenue line, a working-class conveyance, was not quite as spiffy, though it had its devotees. The Marches—a fictional middle-class couple in William Dean Howells's *Hazard of New Fortunes* (1890)—were thrilled by the theatricality of nighttime rides on it, by the "fleeting intimacy you formed with people in second-and third-floor interiors." You might see, as you passed their windows: "a family party of workfolk at a late tea, some of the men in their shirt-sleeves; a woman sewing by a lamp; a mother laying her child in its cradle; a man with his head fallen on his hands upon a table; a girl and her lover leaning over the windowsill together." At 42nd Street, the Marches noted, you could look south along the long stretch of "track that found and lost itself a thousand times in the flare and tremor of the innumerable lights." The couple gazed in fascination at "the coming and going of the trains marking the stations with vivider or fainter plumes of flame-shot steam."

Not everyone was quite so taken with the trains. Many of those in the windows the Marches swept by complained furiously about ear-splitting noise, soot and cinders, and those "plumes of flame-shot steam"—which seemed far less picturesque at close quarters. Stephen Crane, stirred to more mordant imagery than Howells's, wrote of the darkened Bowery where "elevated trains with a shrill grinding of the wheels stopped at the station, which upon its leglike pillars seemed to resemble some monstrous kind of crab squatting over the street." The truly powerful denizens of Fifth, Park, and Madison had already banned elevateds from their avenues. Finally, in 1883, some of the more affluent owners of properties abutting existing lines sued the elevateds and won, the

Court of Appeals ruling they had been illegally deprived of "light, air and access." The prospect of a series of heavy damage payments effectively halted all further elevated construction in built-up sections of Manhattan.

Apart from this victory, disgruntled citizens made little headway in attaining redress of grievances because of the elevateds' structure of ownership. At first, the spurt of el building in New York had paralleled the outburst of railroad construction on the national level and involved many of the same players. Rival financiers, aware of the elevateds' enormous potential, had taken control of them and engaged in the same free-for-alls that characterized rail warfare at the continental level. In New York City, however, the combatants were able to come together and obtain the monopoly control—and bonanza profits—that eluded them in the national arena.

The early contenders had leased their shares to a holding company, the Manhattan Elevated Railway Company. Jay Gould and Russell Sage swallowed it up in 1881 by driving its stock price down, then buying it up. They continued to use it as a financial plaything, much as Gould, Fisk, and Drew had done the Erie: heavily watering its stock; clearing millions on market manipulations. Some people kicked up a fuss, but Gould bought legislators, corrupted judges, and expanded his control, taking over the Third Avenue line too.

Private control and public interest clashed again in 1883, when the state legislature passed a bill to lower the monopoly's fares from ten cents (and five cents at rush hour) to five cents all day. The bill was popular, but the Manhattan's owners denounced it as an attack on property rights. They were backed by Drexel, Morgan, William H. Vanderbilt, and fifty other leading capitalists, who successfully petitioned Governor Cleveland to veto the offending legislation.

Gould and Morgan failed, however, in their effort to turn Battery Park into a switchyard and elevated loop. The intense anger generated by the Manhattan's attempt at appropriating the only park accessible to the Lower East Side's working-class families was compounded by the company's maladroit dismissals of its opponents as tramps, rascals, and immigrants. Tammany Hall, usually in the Manhattan's pocket, had to back away from it on this one, and the company abandoned its plan.

Popular protest might stop a Manhattan Company initiative but it couldn't start one. By the late 1880s success had bred crowding, especially on the East Side lines—crowding that swelled to dangerous dimensions at rush hour. Station platforms got so jammed that passengers, unable to fight their way out of cars during the all-too-brief stops, were often carried one or two stations beyond their destination, while pickpockets fingered through their possessions. Given the absence of competition, and the presence of handsome dividends paid regularly on heavily watered stock, Gould, Sage, and Morgan had no incentive to relieve the miserable conditions, and so they didn't.

If monopoly had drawbacks, so did competition, as became clear during the horsecar wars. The thirty-two rival street lines, whose routes often underlay the new elevated tracks, had been damaged by their overhead rivals but still made money. They did so by scrimping on upkeep (the cars were dirty and badly ventilated, their straw-strewn floors full of vermin). They also slashed labor costs (drivers and conductors worked sixteen-hour days, constantly exposed to the weather, for beggarly wages, conditions that would lead to violent labor upheavals in 1886). In addition, the lines still operated on perpetual franchises they had cozened out of compliant aldermen over the previous half century, for which they paid little or nothing to the city. Highly parochial and viciously competitive, each refused transfer privileges to its rivals. Journeys, accordingly, were badly splintered: traversing Manhattan at 14th Street required three car changes and four separate fares.

The horsecar wars spilled into municipal and state politics in the mid-1880s. Jacob Sharp, the wealthiest and shrewdest of the streetcar magnates, had been trying for thirty years to get a franchise allowing his Broadway and Seventh Avenue Railroad, which ran from 59th Street to Union Square, to use lower Broadway to reach the Battery. Though long blocked by powerful Broadway retailers and real estate princes like the Stewarts, Astors, and Goelets, by 1883 Sharp was close to having his way with a tractable state legislature. Suddenly a new rival emerged, the New York Cable Railway Company, composed of a group of businessmen that included Thomas Fortune Ryan, a Virginia-born, Irish-American stockbroker and protégé of a Standard Oil partner. The cable interests, who planned to substitute horsepower for horses, also wanted a Broadway franchise.

In Albany, in 1884, Sharp's lawyer, Francis Lynde Stetson (whom he shared with J. P. Morgan), introduced supportive legislation, while Sharp's lobbyist, "Whisky" Halloran, disbursed two hundred thousand dollars to the legislators, handily outbribing the cable forces. Matters now shifted to the ever pliable Board of Aldermen, to whom Sharp gave half a million. To do battle effectively, Ryan added William Collins Whitney to his board of directors. Whitney, a dapper young attorney, was wise in the ways of local politics, having served as the city's corporation counsel from 1875 to 1882, and been prominent among the Swallowtail Democrats. He was also well connected, having married Flora Payne, sister of his Yale roommate (and Standard Oil partner) Oliver Payne.

Whitney drew a group of Philadelphia millionaires into the Cable syndicate and easily topped Sharp's bribe to the aldermen, coming up with $750,000, but stumbled in offering only half in cash and the rest in bonds in the new company; the politicos accepted Sharp's all-cash incentive. Whitney recovered quickly, however. Announcing that had the franchise been sold at public auction he would have offered the city a million-dollar annual rental for it, he demanded an investigation of exactly why the aldermen were planning to give it away for a feeble forty thousand. In the ensuing uproar, an inquiry led to the indictment and conviction (or flight to Canada) of many of the now infamous "boodle" aldermen (their leader got nine years' hard labor in Sing Sing). Sharp himself was sentenced to four years in the slammer, but the Court of Appeals reversed the verdict on technicalities and ordered a second trial, which Sharp avoided by his timely demise in 1888.

Whitney, Ryan, and the Philadelphians, left in possession of the field, consolidated their control over New York's surface transit system. They organized a holding company, the Metropolitan Traction Company, at the suggestion of Francis Lynde Stetson and their chief legal counsel, Elihu Root. (Of him Whitney reputedly said: "I have had many lawyers who have told me what I cannot do; Mr. Root is the only lawyer who tells me how to do what I want to do.") Using the techniques of national merger makers, the Metropolitan began buying, leasing, or conquering the independent horsecar companies, issuing vast amounts of heavily watered stock as it went. By 1897 it would control nearly every line in Manhattan.

As fast as they were acquired, Whitney and Ryan welded their roads into an integrated system. They instituted highly popular free transfers that finally made it possible to travel long distances for a nickel. They also understood that true rationalization required mechanization: the horse would have to go. By 1892 they had, at great expense, installed a cable line along Broadway. Powered by a steam engine in the basement of the handsome new nine-story Cable Building at Broadway and Houston, two endless steel strand loops ran, taut and humming, just below street level, one down to Bowling Green, the other up to 36th Street. Once a motorman gripped the cable, his streetcar was jerked along at thirty miles per hour, far faster than horses.

There were problems, however. Speed couldn't be varied at corners, so cars whipped passengers around spots like Dead Man's Curve at Union Square, gongs clanging wildly. Accidents—which were frequent—required stopping the belt, halting traffic all along the line. And when the forty-ton cables broke, which was often, they were not easy to replace. In short order the experiment would be declared a failure. Further problems emerged when George Gould, who succeeded to control of Manhattan Elevated when his father died in 1892, proceeded to declare war on the Metropolitan, a struggle whose consequences would reverberate into the next century. Most disturbing of all, while the street railway franchises proved enormously profitable to their owners, the city received virtually nothing by way of financial return, and speculators like Gould had no interest in promoting orderly and planned development in advance of existing settlement.

Still, for all their drawbacks, the city's combined transport facilities helped weld Manhattan and its surrounding suburbs into an integrated regional economic unit. The Manhattan Elevated carried 75.6 million passengers in 1881; by 1891 it was conveying 196.7 million; and by the latter year, counting all means of travel, well over a million people poured into New York each day and flowed back home each night. Titans and typists, merchants and clerks, insurance men and accountants, storekeepers and shop-girls, lawyers and advertisers and journalists—they streamed, in their hundreds of thousands, across the Brooklyn Bridge to Brooklyn Heights, Bedford, and Bay Ridge; boarded the Staten Island ferry to New Brighton, where they caught trains out to Arrochar and Bowmans; clambered on cars at Grand Central that whisked them north to Yonkers, White Plains, and New Rochelle; ferried east to the Long Island Rail Road terminus at Hunter's Point and west to Jersey for connections to Newark and Morristown. The great human tide ebbed to a hundred domestic destinations, regathered its energies, and was transported next morning back to the tall-tower workplaces, in time for the opening of yet another business day.

60

Bright Lights, Big City

In the 1880s New York got wired for sound and light, and the whirlwind rise of the electrical industry, and its equally rapid consolidation by New York financiers, was a telling sign of the times. It was probably inevitable, in the absence of government funding, that electrification, the largest industrial investment in the nation's history, would be pioneered in the metropolis. Wall Street's capital pools were here. So were the new corporations, who swiftly realized that electric power worked synergistically with tall towers and rapid transit to increase the velocity and efficiency of business operations. Manhattan also had a well-established tradition of innovation. Its interlocking commercial and civic cultures had nurtured Fulton's steamboat and Morse's telegraph into fruitful life, and now, in the corporate-professional postwar decades, a diverse mix of financiers, engineers, workers, lawyers, and publicists stood equally ready to promote scientific experimentation and harvest its most profitable applications. The city's cosmopolitan openness to new ways of doing things, moreover, guaranteed a swift embrace of electric opportunities by leading economic, social, and cultural actors. *Son et lumière* would thus transform everyday urban life at the same time it strengthened the emerging corporate order and New York's claim to be its capital.

HELLO, CENTRAL

In the early 1870s Western Union, the New York-based communications giant, was having technical difficulties. It had solidified its grip on the country's telegraphic system, crushed efforts to create a government-run service, and, in alliance with the Associated Press, come to dominate the flow of information to the nation's newspapers. But success had generated a staggering increase in the volume of messages, clogging the system. As a result, many telegraphers—the cantankerous, tobacco-chewing, hard-drinking, iconoclastic, peripatetic, and poorly paid men who worked the wires in stations across the country—had taken to spending their off-hours trying to strike it rich by inventing a "duplex," a device to send two messages over the same wire at the same time.

Thomas Alva Edison was one of the tinkering telegraphers. He had displayed a bent for experimentation as a child in rural Ohio and developed a rudimentary mastery of mechanics and electricity in his years of wandering from one midwestern post to another. In the late 1860s, having been fired repeatedly for tying up lines for his research or alienating workmates with crude practical jokes, Edison was living in Boston, working on a duplex. He made ends meet by traveling to New York City, buying up stock tickers (just recently invented), and reselling and installing them for Boston financial firms. Beginning in 1869 he spent more and more time in New York, working on improving the ticker. He soon devised Edison's Universal Printer, which was snapped up by Wall Street companies, becoming another of the technological struts supporting Manhattan's financial preeminence.

In the summer of 1870 Edison ran across Daniel H. Craig, a bitter enemy of Western Union, who hired Edison to invent a way to automate telegraphic transmission. Funded by Philadelphia financiers eager to undercut the giant Manhattan firm, Craig set up the long-impoverished Edison in a large workshop in Newark, stocked with the finest machines and tools. Together with a draftsman, a machinist, and some theory picked up in a course at Cooper Union, Edison created a working duplex, then began designing a quadruplex that would allow one line to do the work of four.

News of this invention factory reached Western Union, then under Vanderbilt control. The firm summoned the twenty-four-year-old to company headquarters and proposed to help him perfect his device and let him test his models on Western Union lines. When Edison succeeded, however, the Vanderbilts refused his asking price for the rights. Aware that his Philadelphia backers had been weakened by the Panic of 1873, they figured the inventor would come to terms. They were right: with his debts mounting, Edison gravitated, as he always would, to where the money was that would fund his experiments and sustain his household, and in the crunch, the money proved to be in New York, not Philadelphia.

Edison moved from Newark twelve miles south to the farming village of Menlo Park, remote yet easily accessible to Manhattan (it stood three hundred yards from the railroad station). Here he established the first significant industrial research laboratory in the United States. Edison now spewed out inventions—cooking up plans, and sometimes models, for electric pens, dental drills, and fax machines. Occasionally he would break for a weekend jaunt to New York, dining with his wife at Delmonico's and spending the night at the Astor House, or carousing with cronies at music halls and theaters, losing himself in the Bowery's nighttime throng.

In early 1877, in Boston, Alexander Graham Bell transmitted vocal sounds—conversation itself—over the long lines. Bell exhibited the instrument in New York, giving lecture-demonstrations at Chickering Hall. Western Union assigned Edison to producing an improved apparatus, which they hoped would be distinctive enough to ward off patent infringement suits. Edison came up with a receiver that could amplify sounds more loudly. He arranged a long distance concert and had piano selections wired in from Philadelphia to a huge audience, including Professor Bell, jammed into Steinway Hall. By December the device was in production by the new American Speaking Telegraph Company, hustled into existence by Western Union investors, and Edison, at thirty-three, was one of the richest men in the country. But Western Union lost the ensuing legal and technological war and, threatened on its flank by Jay Gould, agreed to stay out of telephony if the Bell forces would stay out of telegraphy. Local telephone service therefore came to the metropolis under the corporate aegis of the Boston-based American Bell Corporation.

In May 1878 American Bell licensed a Metropolitan Telephone and Telegraph Company to commence service in an area thirty-three miles in all directions from City Hall. In March 1879 subscribers—who paid sixty dollars a year, soon upped to $150—were linked together by New York's first telephone "exchange," at 82 Nassau Street, and listed in the first directory, a small card listing 252 names. To reach a subscriber users turned a crank, lifted the earpiece, and asked the "operator" to connect them. At first, following the telegraph industry model, young men were used as operators, but their rowdy switching-room behavior—they drank beer, fought, and swore at customers—proved ill adapted to an industry that still had to seduce clients away from telegraphy. Native-born white women came presocialized with the proper decorum, and the new "Hello Girls" proved successful at soothing irate customers (equipment and connections being frustratingly unreliable). Many clients came to consider "Information" operators like Miss Katherine M. Schmitt, who joined the company in 1882, as being what she described as a "combination of personal-service bureau and general

The Cortlandt Street Board of the New York Telephone Company, 1894, by which time women "operators" were the norm. Observed a writer in the *Metropolitan Magazine*: "It may seem, to one visiting the operating room of a telephone exchange, that the girls appear uncomfortably like prisoners. The galley-slave of old, bound to his oar by chains, was not held closer to his work than these, with their curious headgear of steel bands and black auricles, and the short stretch of wire which holds them, literally by the head, at their places in front of the switchboard." (General Research. The New York Public Library. Astor, Lenox and Tilden Foundations)

guide to the city of New York." Schmitt routinely fielded queries such as "Where is the fire?" "Did anyone call me while I was out?" and "How do I get to Central Park?"

By the mid-1890s there were twelve exchanges, each of which averaged 150,000 calls a day. Residential subscribers accounted for only 10 percent of this traffic, however, as household phones were far too expensive for most people (service was available at banks and drugstores). Only after the Bell patents expired in 1894, and independent companies rushed in, would phone service become more accessible.

Businesses, however, leapt to install the new instruments, with banks, brokers, professionals, the Stock Exchange, dry-goods firms, publishers, jewelers, and druggists leading the way. Phones promoted internal organizational coherence as well as communication with the outside world. Bankers and brokers scattered them through their offices. Department stores put instruments at sales counters. Factories installed them to keep the main office in touch with shop foremen. Engineers ran vertical wires along rising skyscrapers to allow contractors below to confer with foremen aloft. Once a tall tower was built, moreover, telephones eliminated the need for messengers to be endlessly riding up and down elevators to deliver telegrams. This helped make upper-story offices as profitable as ones nearer the ground. After long distance service arrived—New York was connected to Boston in 1884, Philadelphia in 1885, and Chicago in 1892—it also became easier for corporations headquartered in Manhattan to direct their far-flung operations.

Telephones were also deployed to help guard the central business district itself. In 1880 Chief Inspector Thomas Byrnes, head of the police department's detective bureau, established a protective cordon around the Wall Street community, declaring Fulton Street a "Dead Line" south of which criminals (of the blue-collar variety) would not be tolerated. Using the new telephone, he connected Mulberry Street Headquarters to every station house. More conventionally, Byrnes saturated the financial district with police and maintained an elaborate system of underworld informants. Grateful businessmen like Jay Gould dispensed market tips, helping Byrnes accumulate a fortune of $350,000 on an annual salary of two thousand.

While New Yorkers were adopting the telephone, Edison was making other breakthroughs in sound, including a machine that could register and print voice patterns. By December 1877 his apparatus repeated words spoken into it in a faint metallic tone. With Barnumesque attention to publicity, he took the machine—the sound writer or "phonograph"—to the Manhattan offices of *Scientific American*. As one astonished participant recalled, Edison "turned a crank, and the machine inquired as to our health, asked how we liked the phonograph, informed us that *it* was very well, and bid us a cordial good night." On January 2, 1878, the machine went on display at the Western Union building. People came, heard, and were convinced.

Edison brimmed over with moneymaking ideas for the phonograph. He licensed two Brooklyn men to incorporate it into clocks and watches that would call out the time, wake people up, and emit advertising messages. He groped toward stereo by working up a two-sided disk, both sides of which could be played simultaneously. He aimed to market an educational toy phonograph that would help children learn the alphabet. And to promote the new machine in the most colossal manner possible, Edison proposed that when the Statue of Liberty finally rose on Bedloe's Island, a phonograph be put in its mouth so that it could talk and whistle to ships passing by in the harbor.

LET THERE BE LIGHT

In 1879 New York's Common Council decided to experiment with arc lighting. Back in 1808 Humphrey Davy had discovered that when an electric current arced across the space between two carbon electrodes, it heated the carbon points to white heat, giving off a powerful incandescent light. For many decades this "arc light" found only intermittent uses, as carbons burned up rapidly and batteries were prohibitively expensive. By the 1870s, however, the development of electric generators had reduced the cost of power and a device had been invented to automatically replace burned out rods. Arc lights were now deployed here and there in Europe—St. Petersburg's Winter Palace and Nevski Drive; Paris's Place de la Concorde and Arc de Triomphe—and even more so in the United States, where Charles F. Brush's company erected huge "sun towers" in several western cities. The towers were cheaper to install than hundreds of lampposts, and it was believed that the carpet of illumination they spread equally through all parts of town was somehow a more democratic, more American light.

New York City's Gas Commission authorized the Brush Electric Light Company to set up a generating station at 25th Street, consisting of two Corliss steam engines and two dynamo-electric generators. These would power a series of arc lights along Broadway. Each was mounted on a twenty-foot-tall ornamental cast-iron post, one per block, between the lower end of Union Square, opposite Delmonico's, and Madison Square. On December 20, 1880, the boulevard was bathed in brilliant light—a Broadway show that garnered rave reviews.

The Brush Electric lights on Broadway, near Madison Square. This view looks south across 23rd Street, with Fifth Avenue on the right. The clock tower, which stood outside the Fifth Avenue Hotel, remains to this day. (© Collection of The New-York Historical Society)

During 1881 the city commissioned lights for Fifth Avenue and the crosstown streets of 14th and 34th. In addition it tried out "sun towers" in Union and Madison squares—160-foot masts topped with clusters of arc lights. The system was far from perfect, and storms often triggered power failures, but progress in driving back the darkness seemed evident.

Over the next few years, electric arc illumination spread along selected streets. By 1886 fifteen hundred lamps were in operation on Fourth, Fifth, and Seventh avenues, between the Battery and 59th Street, and up the thoroughfares flanking Central Park. Brush Electric Light (and soon its rivals) also began stringing wires on street poles and delivering power to illuminate industrial and commercial spaces: factories, railroad stations, building construction sites, Gansevoort Market Square, wharves, and the lobbies of hotels, theaters, office buildings, and department stores. The brilliant lights offered security for a burgeoning nightlife and drew vast numbers of visitors to commercial establishments.

At first there was no equivalent change in domestic lighting, even though by the 1870s gas light was rapidly falling from public favor. Once celebrated as a clean energy source, it now seemed impure, dirty, unhygienic. Gas jets produced headaches by eating oxygen and giving off ammonia, sulphur, and carbon dioxide, and they blackened ceilings and wrecked parlors with their soot. But arc lights were too dazzling for domestic use. Gas light was measured in the dozens of candlepower, arc light in the thousands. Unlike gas, moreover, an arc's intensity could not be varied, and though they didn't use up oxygen, their carbons gave off noxious fumes as they burned.

In 1878 Thomas Edison announced to the press that New York's interiors would not be left in flickering half-light much longer. He intended to develop an incandescent lamp—not "a large light or blinding light, but a small light having the mildness of gas." On the strength of this pronouncement, the Vanderbilts, heavy investors in the gas business, decided it was time to switch horses. They offered to form a company that would help Edison develop his ideas. The inventor, now canny in the ways of Wall Street, retained a high-powered corporate attorney, and a deal was hammered out.

A consortium of capitalists set up the Edison Electric Light Company to issue three hundred thousand dollars in stock, of which Edison would hold $250,000. The businessmen put up fifty thousand in cash to get him started experimenting. The twelve-member board of directors included Vanderbilt representatives, Western Union delegates, and J. P. Morgan himself (Drexel, Morgan would be the company's banker). Henry Villard, flamboyant railroad financier, invested in the firm and urged his German banker connections to do likewise. In Vienna, Baron Rothschild got wind of events and sent August Belmont out to Menlo Park to investigate. Morgan himself crossed the Hudson to negotiate a deal for lighting Great Britain and Europe. And all this before Edison had generated much more than brash and unsupported promises.

Edison, supremely confident, spent a hefty portion of his advance money erecting a greatly expanded workshop, as well as an elegant library, with plush leather furniture, in which to greet visiting plutocrats from New York. Then he set to work, and in December 1879, syndicate members were invited out to a demonstration of what Edison had wrought. As the financiers watched in awe, globes decorated with flowers and papier-mâché glowed evenly and steadily, with the intensity of a gas jet, roughly twenty-five watts of luminosity.

During the following year, Edison prepared for the electrification of New York

City. He laid out in the Menlo Park fields a grand mockup grid of Manhattan's streets, replete with four hundred of the new lights. After a test performance in December 1880, to which he invited an enthralled Sarah Bernhardt, Edison was ready for New York's officialdom. He gave a gala demonstration to assorted aldermen and commissioners, followed by a Delmonico-catered feast, at which he explained his intention to install subterranean electric wires in the square mile stretching from Wall Street to Canal. The assembled worthies gave Edison three hip-hip-hurrahs and, two weeks later, permission to lay his power mains.

Edison now transferred operations to Manhattan, taking over a four-story brownstone on lower Fifth Avenue near 14th Street. He illuminated it with a hundred globes, making it the first building in New York lighted exclusively by electricity and an irresistible nighttime beacon for residents. He also dismantled the Menlo Park machine shop and relocated it at Roach's ironworks. To house the power station, he purchased two old buildings at 255-57 Pearl Street, near the Fulton Fish Market, though he professed to be flabbergasted at the $155,000 asking price for what he considered "the worst dilapidated street there was."

With expenses soaring, financiers complaining, and rivals emerging, Edison reduced his target area to the fifty square blocks encompassed by Spruce, Nassau, Wall, and the East River—a territory that contained New York's key financial, commercial, and manufacturing establishments and backed up on City Hall and Printing House Square. Throughout the summer, from eight at night until four in the morning, his men dug fifteen miles of trenches, laid the massive, solid copper power mains, and insulated them with a mix of Trinidad asphalt, linseed oil, paraffin, and beeswax. By fall new, improved, twenty-seven-ton generators, named "Jumbos" after Barnum's giant elephant, were in place at the Pearl Street Station.

Finally, on September 4, 1882, the dynamos fed power—"direct current"—into the system. Eight hundred lamps winked on in two score locations, including the *New York Times* and the Drexel, Morgan building, where Edison himself, sporting a new Prince Albert coat, presided over the epochal event.

BRIGHT LIGHTS

The first private house in the city to convert entirely to incandescent lighting was J. P. Morgan's Madison Avenue mansion. Despite an explosive mishap that scorched the walls and carpets, the banker professed great pleasure; less so his neighbors, annoyed by the clanking of the generator installed in his garden. The Vanderbilts wired all three of their uptown palaces, though William H. backslid to gas after some mechanical disruptions. Within a year over five hundred wealthy homes were electrified: New York's bourgeoisie now glowed in the dark with new intensity.

Houses of commerce switched to electricity with dispatch. The New York Stock Exchange installed three "electroliers" of sixty-six lamps each above the main trading floor. Scant steps away, at Broad and Exchange Place, the new nine-and-a-half-story Mills Building (1883) became the first office building in the city, and likely in the world, to have its own electric generation plant: it powered the 5,588 lights in quarters rented by bankers, brokers, and railroad and insurance companies and in the top-floor restaurant. In 1889 the first electric elevators began gliding up and down, and by the following year they were being purchased in lieu of hydraulic models. The first escalator would follow a decade later.

Industry lit up too. Machine shops, piano factories, sugar refineries, and newspaper plants went incandescent. Edison talked eagerly about converting 240,000 sewing machines to electricity: "In the tenement-house districts our business will be simply enormous," he enthused. Manufacturers and financiers—the sorts who joined Edison in becoming members at the new and exclusive Electric Club (1886)—boasted that direct current would make it possible to significantly lengthen the working day, a prospect not greeted with universal acclaim.

What did delight almost everyone was the electrification of nightlife. Department stores shifted from gas to bulbs in the late 1880s. Freed from fear of fire, their window displays now shimmered in the night air, lending new glamour to commodities, providing virtual theaters for audiences passing by. Actual theaters seized on Edison's lights too. In 1883 Niblo's Garden featured "novel lighting effects by the Edison Electric Light Company," including an illuminated model of the new Brooklyn Bridge and chorus girls who flourished electric wands.

The lady in the harbor went electric too. In 1886, when the Statue of Liberty was officially dedicated, its hand was brilliantly illuminated—too much so for mariners, and it had to be toned down—and its base was garlanded with eight-thousand-candlepower lamps. On a more domestic note, a New York Edison vice-president lit up his Christmas tree with incandescent colored globes, creating an instant popular sensation.

Hotels, restaurants, cafes, and shops—all beckoned customers with their radiance. Even shady places opted for the spotlight: Edison personally installed electric lights at Harry Hill's, and the enterprising "French Madame" screwed bulbs into sockets on her doorstep. Illumination spilled down from the elevateds, which lit up their station platforms. It shone in from luminous Hudson River steamers and the yachts of the Bennetts and Goulds. Electric nights drew throngs of festive boulevardiers to the streets, linking its big-city image indelibly to the bright lights of its avenues. This identification was fixed forevermore with the emergence, in the mid-1890s, of what people began calling the "Great White Way"—a stretch of Broadway between 23rd and 34th streets that began to blaze with electric advertisements. The first large illuminated sign—a fifty-foot-high and eighty-foot-wide display at Madison Square—used fifteen thousand lights, which winked on and off in a sequence controlled by an operator in a shanty on a nearby roof, to trumpet Coney Island hostelries. It was soon superseded by a forty-five-foot-long Heinz ("57 Varieties") pickle, outlined in bright green bulbs against an orange background, easily visible a mile away.

In 1887 Mayor Hewitt declared that nocturnal effulgence had become essential for the "prevention of crime" and the preservation of "the good order of the city." So quickly had New York grown accustomed to electric street lights that whenever they went off in substantial numbers, extra police were ordered out as a matter of course.

The alacrity with which New York adopted the new technology did have its drawbacks. Most notably it generated a vast and proliferating network of wires that threatened to bury Manhattan. Western Union, Bell Telephone, the Gold and Stock Ticker Company, the Brush, United States, and East River Electrical Lighting companies, the fire department, police department, and private burglarproofing companies who installed alarm systems—all these strung their power lines on poles or across rooftops. As firms rarely deigned to share space, the streets were soon festooned with posts, each between fifty and ninety feet tall, each carrying a dozen to two score crosstrees, each crosstree bearing perhaps twenty wires. Some poles groaned with the weight of two hundred strands.

Increasing numbers of these snapped, dropping writhing live wires to the street below. In 1884 the legislature, impressed by the success of Edison's underground operations, insisted that all other electrical supply systems be buried as well. The telephone, telegraph, and lighting companies ignored the order. Four years later, the blizzard of 1888 deposited twenty-two inches of snow on the streets and coated the wires with ice, sending them crashing down, terrifying the city. Mayor Grant led an ax-and-nipper patrol around town, slashing at the wire tentacles, but the Brush Company threatened to leave the city, and Jay Gould, now Western Union's chieftain, got an injunction.

The public's growing anxiety was heightened by Edison's war against George Westinghouse, who was promoting "alternating current." This rival system could be used to transmit power at high voltage from generating stations sited near waterfalls or dams hundreds of miles away, bypassing Edison's entire patented system of direct current stations, which had to be located near their customers. Edison issued shrill warnings about the danger of high voltage lines, and, in the fall of 1887, when the state legislature asked for his help in inventing a more humane method of execution, he set aside his opposition to capital punishment and arranged some public demonstrations with test animals—using alternating current. When a competition was held to name the

In response to the huge demand for telephones and electricity during the 1880s, a forest of utility poles sprang up along the streets of downtown Manhattan. (Consolidated Edison)

method, candidates included "electromort" and "electricide" (Edison held out for "Westinghoused") but in August 1890 a convicted murderer was "electrocuted" for the first time, a bungled job that produced an "awful spectacle." "They could have done it better with an axe," Westinghouse said.

In October 1889 a Western Union lineman had been electrocuted on a wire grid-iron in the heart of the business district. Thousands watched as the body dangled from overhead lines for nearly an hour, its mouth spitting blue flame. The next day the mayor ordered unsafe wires chopped down. It took another two months for incensed public uproar to overcome corporate legal stonewalling, but finally the poles began to fall. By 1894 there would still be lots to bury, but New York's Board of Electrical Control announced that millions of feet of wire had been banished belowground and that Manhattan now possessed a sixteen-hundred-mile-long electrical arterial system from which 6,790 arc lamps, 268,000 incandescent lamps, and nearly ten thousand telephones drew sustenance.

USEFUL AND UNUSEFUL UTILITIES

While working on the electric light, Edison, aware that his generator run in reverse could serve as a motor, took a break from his primary experiments, purchased some secondhand horsecar tracks, and built a model roadbed one-third of a mile long. Then he mounted a twelve-horsepower dynamo on a truck, installed brushes on the wheels to pick up current from the rails, and on May 13, 1879, gleefully rolled along at twenty miles per hour in a horsecar filled with twenty passengers. Railroad companies clamored for Edison to develop his invention, and the president of the Long Island Rail Road offered tracks for testing, but though Edison did work now and then on an electric locomotive, there just weren't enough hours in the day.

It was Frank Sprague, an academically trained electrical engineer who'd worked for Edison then struck out on his own, who invented a superior motor and installed it successfully in Richmond, Virginia. In the late 1880s Sprague electrified New York's Fourth Avenue street railway line between the post office and 86th Street. In the 1890s, driven by competition, first the Third Avenue line and then the Metropolitan Street Railway Company began the enormously expensive process of switching their motive power. The Manhattan Company, however, under Gould, Sage, and Morgan, refused to follow suit. Sprague had successfully tested a system for electrifying New York's elevateds back in 1886, but the complacent monopoly proved no more willing to invest in installing the requisite six-hundred-volt third rail than they were in relieving crowding. The Manhattan would stick with steam into the next century, nearly a decade after Chicago had junked its heavy and dirty steam engines.

Brooklynites' problem was not corporate recalcitrance but excessive zeal. Brooklyn streetcar companies, not hampered by Manhattanites' abhorrence of high wires, strung power lines above their tracks. The first conversions were completed in 1890, and within five years trolleys had almost completely replaced horsecars throughout the city, an extremely mixed blessing. Horsecars clopped along at six miles per hour. Electric cars could hurtle through streets at a terrifying thirty miles per hour, carrying three times the number of passengers, but though they had the weight and power of locomotives, their brakes were still those of a horsecar. Worse, companies set out to maximize profits by increasing the number of trips required for drivers to earn their daily wage, forcing them to careen through streets at near maximum speed. The result was carnage. By

1895 trolleys had killed 105 and maimed 407, most of them children, and become a symbol of random death. Calls for the municipalization of transit companies would grow steadily.

There were calls as well for the municipalization of the power supply. Once bourgeois neighborhoods and homes were wired, street and domestic lighting in Manhattan diffused at glacial pace because electric lighting was treated as a commodity, not (as in some European cities) a subsidized public service. Poor streets and outlying areas like Harlem would remain gas-lit until well into the twentieth century, and a blend (in William Dean Howells's words) of "the moony sheen of the electrics mixing with the reddish points and blots of gas" would long characterize the Manhattan nightscape. Working people couldn't afford electricity in their houses—a bulb alone cost a dollar, half a day laborer's wages—or gas either: kerosene lamps remained their mainstay for illumination, and kerosene or coal stoves served for cooking and heating.

Gas itself grew more expensive as the industry grew less competitive. During the 1880s Manhattan's many gas companies, panic stricken at the arrival of electricity, moved to conglomerate their operations. Primacy of place was seized by the Consolidated Gas Company (1884), a holding company organized by H. H. Rogers of Standard Oil, with backing from William Rockefeller and National City Bank. Consolidated Gas gained sufficient complete control of the marketplace to jack up prices—25 percent in 1885 alone—and deliver poorer quality gas, while paying high dividends on wildly overcapitalized stock. William Rockefeller also gained a power base in Brooklyn's gas industry, and once again the price went up and the product declined.

Substantial gas users such as hotel owners grew increasingly restive at the steady monopolization of the industry. Establishing a Gas Consumers Association, they called for the state legislature to investigate the situation; the resulting report denounced rampant stock watering and excessive profit-taking. In 1886 the state passed a bill lowering the maximum price from $1.75 to $1.25 per thousand cubic feet, though a reputed seventy thousand dollars in gas company bribes spread around Albany warded off threats to Consolidated itself. Gasmen proved unable to freeze out powerful new competitors, however. In 1894 the New York and East River Gas Company (1893) built a tunnel under the East River from Long Island City, permitting delivery of Ravenswood gas to Manhattan, and both Russell Sage and J. P. Morgan weighed in with new companies. Outfits like these exerted sufficient pressure to lower prices enough to satisfy big users, and the issue of gas reform was taken off the table.

Morgan achieved a clearer preeminence in electricity than the Rockefellers did in gas. In May 1889 Henry Villard set about consolidating Edison's various American properties into a new Edison General Electric Company, capitalized at twelve million dollars. The initial stock offering, handled by Drexel, Morgan, was parceled out among various German and American banking concerns, and Morgan became the major investor in his own right. The merger provided Thomas Edison with enormous sums to run his laboratory—and to improve his living standard: he leased a Gramercy Park mansion, bought a yacht, and expanded both his investment portfolio and waistline.

In 1890 Edison General president Henry Villard set out to end what he considered the "ruinous competition" between his company and the other major players in the new electric universe. Villard first worked out a price-fixing agreement, but it was nullified by the Sherman Anti-Trust Act. He then tried to persuade Edison to merge with his enemies, but Edison objected that "no competition means no invention." Events were no longer in the Wizard's control, however. Morgan arranged a grand consolidation that in November 1892 pulled rivals together into General Electric, more popularly if less affectionately known as the Electric Trust. A scant fourteen years after Edison had invented a practical electric light, General Electric and Westinghouse between them had swallowed all competitors and controlled the market in generating equipment, transformers, meters, motors, and lighting apparatus. Edison, distraught at his loss of control and the obliteration of his name, announced he would "not be held responsible for the acts of an organization in which my voice is but one amongst a great many."

Capital-intensive electrification helped make the old republican competitive free enterprise order seem hopelessly inefficient and quixotic, as the AC-supplied electric grid made feasible ever bigger generating stations for the centralized supply of power. The financial grid would make entrepreneurial autonomy seem equally outmoded and facilitate the concentration of economic power in a handful of centralized financial institutions.

Electrification-cum-corporatization would also force the issue of how vital city services were to be delivered onto the metropolitan agenda. Should energy provision remain in private and largely unregulated hands, to be distributed to citizens on the basis of their ability to pay? Or should the city and state again become more active agents in the production and distribution of social goods, the model New York had followed in the development of its water and canal systems? And if so, would countering private corporate power perhaps require the metropolitan area to construct a civic grid, connecting the various independent political constituencies scattered around the harbor? These were murky issues, and it would take more than an Edison to illuminate them.

61

Châteaux Society

In the winter of 1883 Mrs. William Kissam Vanderbilt, born Alva Smith of Mobile, launched an assault on New York Society's inner circle—still presided over by Caroline Astor and Ward McCallister—by announcing a fancy dress affair intended to eclipse the Patriarch's Balls over which the reigning duo presided. The Vanderbilt fete would inaugurate the new château, at Fifth Avenue and 52nd Street, that she and her husband had commissioned from beaux-arts master Richard Morris Hunt, expressly to outclass the brownstones lower down the avenue.

Hunt had long been wishing New Yorkers would take an architectural leap forward. Now, with three million dollars at his command, he showed them how to do it, producing a palatial residence that, in the opinion of the *Times*, went way beyond anything "heretofore attempted in New York." Well aware how mock-castles like Chambery and Chenonceaux had delighted the parvenu bankers and merchants of the Renaissance, Hunt erected an adaptation of Francis I's sixteenth-century Château de Blois, filled it full of Renaissance and medieval furniture, tapestries, and armor, and had it ready for Alva's ball in 1883.

The city's elite gave itself over to a flurry of preparations. A hundred-plus dressmakers labored night and day for weeks. Groups of young women practiced "quadrilles"—complex dance presentations—among them Miss Caroline (Carrie) Astor and her friends, who planned to appear as pairs of stars. As daughter of the Queen of Society, she simply assumed, rashly, that her invitation was on the way.

It was not. As the magic night of March 26 approached, Mrs. Vanderbilt casually let it be known that no invitation would be forthcoming for the charming Miss Astor as, alas, she had never properly made her acquaintance, or that of her mother. The queen surrendered forthwith. A footman in Astor-blue livery was dispatched from the 34th Street mansion to deliver, a mile up Fifth Avenue, an engraved calling card to a servant in Vanderbilt-maroon livery. With her arrival in society thus duly certified, Alva Vanderbilt authorized a return delivery of the last of the twelve hundred invitations.

The affair, as every New York paper blared in front-page next-day stories, was the grandest social event to date in the city's history. The barely completed halls and rooms, lined with roses, orchids, palm fronds, and bougainvillea, had been transformed into a tropical wonderland. The Louis XV salon was resplendent with Gobelin tapestries, and wainscoting ripped from old French châteaux. The triumphant hostess, costumed as a Renaissance princess, welcomed her equally gorgeously attired guests—including an array of Mary Stuarts, Marie Antoinettes, and Queen Elizabeths; her brother-in-law Cornelius was dressed as Louis XVI, but his wife, more au courant, came as The Electric Light. Alva presided happily over a spectacular dinner and a round of dancing. Many gave highest accolades to Mrs. S. S. Howland's group for their Hobby-Horse Quadrille, in which the dancers appeared mounted on life-size model horses made of genuine hides, but Mrs. Vanderbilt perhaps warmed most to the graceful moves of Carrie Astor's Star Quadrille.

FROM THE FOUR HUNDRED TO THE TWO THOUSAND

By her grudging accommodation of Vanderbilts and other new Medici, Mrs. Astor preserved her hegemony for another decade. She became, in fact, something of a national institution. Over the next years, as the country followed with awe (or outrage) the shimmering doings of New York Society, Mrs. Astor's verdicts and edicts as conveyed by the press—her remarks invariably couched in the third person—enthralled readers from coast to coast.

With the assistance of her chamberlain, Ward McCallister, she sustained, for a time, an unfortunately enlarged but still acceptably exclusive inner circle. In 1888 McCallister opined to a *Tribune* reporter that the core group was in fact small enough to fit comfortably into Mrs. Astor's ballroom: "Why, there are only about 400 people in fashionable New York Society. If you go outside that number you strike people who are either not at ease in a ballroom or else make other people not at ease. See the point?" This pronunciamento created something of a stir and led to rampant speculation about who was (or was not) included on the gilded list of "the Four Hundred." Finally, on the occasion of Mrs. Astor's ball of February 1, 1892, McCallister issued a more precise inventory to the *New York Times*. It contained a mere 273 names, drawn mostly from the community of Patriarch's Ball invitees.

Wealthy would-be socialites denounced this magisterial accounting with all the fervor of populists attacking railroad pools, and in a sense naming the Four Hundred was an attempt to create a Social Trust. But the ranks of the wealthy, augmented by millionaire arrivistes from around the nation, had swelled far beyond the bounds of Mrs. Astor's ballroom. As in the larger economy, competitive forces proved too fierce to be contained by informal mechanisms that had worked for generations.

Mrs. Astor's regime began to come unglued. Powerful rivals carped, mocked, and rejected her rule. Mrs. Burton Harrison, in 1895, said flat out: "I am an unbeliever in the body corporate which, for want of a better term has come to be popularly known as the Four Hundred of New York." Fortunately another mechanism had evolved as a way to delineate a Society now clearly numbered in the thousands, not the hundreds.

Maurice M. Minton, an enterprising blueblood, had pointed the way by printing up his mother's visiting list and merging it with another to form the *Society-List and*

Club Register. In 1887 this example, and that of the recently introduced telephone directory, inspired Louis Keller to launch *The Social Register*. Keller, independently wealthy (though just barely), had his eye on more remunerative possibilities. With the support of friends at the Union and Calumet clubs, he assembled a list of nearly two thousand socially prominent names and printed it up as a handsome book with orange and black binding. To make it indispensable, he included addresses, telephone numbers, maiden names, wives' names by previous marriages, clubs, colleges, places of summer residence, and names of yachts—everything one needed to keep up with old friends and screen potential new ones. (To get the lowdown on highbrow enemies, one could also turn, after 1885, to the pages of *Town Topics*, a Society scandal sheet that tattled about upcoming divorces and impending bankruptcies, using information secured from Fifth Avenue butlers and chambermaids. Fortunately one could forestall the display of dirty laundry by bribing the editor into discretion.)

With the advent of *The Social Register*, dictatorship gave way to an accommodating bureaucracy; now thousands could make the social grade. But with outspending one's rivals the only definitive route to preeminence, a steady inflation in extravagance ensued as members of opposing cliques scrambled to convert Wall Street revenue into Fifth Avenue social standing. Dinner parties corkscrewed upward in lavishness—black pearls in oysters, cigars rolled in hundred-dollar bills, lackeys in knee breeches and powdered wigs. These glittering affairs attracted platoons of elegantly attired jewel thieves, whose takings were kept to a minimum by equally nattily dressed police detectives supplied by Inspector Byrnes, the same man whose Dead Line cordoned off Wall Street by day.

The Drive—Central Park—Four O'Clock, from *Harper's Weekly*, May 19, 1883. Upper-class New Yorkers still regarded an afternoon drive in the park as an opportunity to see and be seen, but ascertaining who belonged to "society" was becoming increasingly difficult. (© Collection of The New-York Historical Society)

TO THE OPERA HOUSE

The social wars raged as fiercely on the male side, though here the front line ran through the opera house. Old-guard families had undergirded their position by cornering the market on Academy of Music boxes. From these seemingly secure perches, Bayards and Beekmans, Cuttings and Schuylers, and a few properly patinaed former upstarts like August Belmont had peered down contentedly on tycoons in the seats below. When William H. Vanderbilt offered a whopping thirty thousand dollars for a box in 1880, the old set snubbed him as they had his father, the Commodore, before him.

Vanderbilt embarked on a grand flanking movement. First he gathered together a formidably monied strike force, including many of the most powerful figures in the emerging corporate economy—his sons William Kissam and Cornelius II, J. P. Morgan, William Rockefeller, Jay Gould, William C. Whitney, George F. Baker—as well as some older patricians like Ogden Goelet, Adrian Iselin, and William Rhinelander. Then Vanderbilt announced they would construct a new opera house, as grand as those of Milan and Vienna, and eclipse the 14th Street bastion forevermore.

Belmont and company panicked and offered to add twenty-six boxes to the Academy's existing eighteen, but it was too late. Way uptown, at Broadway and 39th Street, a mammoth edifice slowly took shape, the grandly named Metropolitan Opera House, capable of seating over thirty-six hundred people, and accommodating wealthy patrons in *seventy* opulent boxes. On opening night, October 22, 1883, with *Faust* as the inaugural performance, these were packed with opera lovers whose collective worth was estimated at $540 million. "The Goulds and the Vanderbilts and people of that ilk," wrote the *New York Dramatic Mirror*, "perfumed the air with the odor of crisp greenbacks."

The Metropolitan was an instant triumph. The doomed Academy of Music hung on gamely a few more years, then folded with an announcement from its manager that "I cannot fight Wall Street." Musically its early years were somewhat shakier. To fill the huge hall, the Metropolitan called on Leopold Damrosch, a devout Wagnerian. Damrosch devoted the 1884 season almost entirely to German opera. Singers were imported from Bayreuth. This appealed to the city's massive German population, but boxholders loathed the new music, couldn't see one another's finery in the Wagnerian gloom, and bustled and gabbled throughout the performances. When rebuked by the Germans below, the directors maintained that the stockholders had a perfect right to disturb whomever they wished. Conductor Anton Seidl, who had assisted Wagner at Bayreuth, replaced Damrosch on his death in 1885 and maintained the German program for several more years, until a full-scale revolt brought back Italian and French opera.

In the symphonic world, musically inclined industrialists and financiers were having problems of a different sort with the New York Philharmonic. The old German cooperative presented only half a dozen concerts each year. As the orchestra couldn't guarantee members full time work, they spent most of their time playing at balls and dances; hence their performances were less than highly polished, though much improved after Theodore Thomas was taken on as conductor. Neither their less than professional standards nor traditional repertoire bothered old-fashioned elites, but both failed to satisfy new tycoons. A capitalist combine including Vanderbilt, Rockefeller, Morgan, and Carnegie underwrote a rival, the New York Symphony Orchestra (1878), another Leopold Damrosch project. Orchestra war ensued. In one notable sally

Damrosch stole the American premiere of Brahms's First Symphony from under Thomas's nose.

On Leopold's death in 1885, his son Walter succeeded to Symphony leadership, and the younger Damrosch convinced Andrew Carnegie that what the group needed was a permanent home—the Metropolitan Opera House being inadequate for orchestral performances. Carnegie agreed to support construction of a first-class concert hall. On May 5, 1891, a vaguely Italian Renaissance structure—including the velvet-lined, acoustically superb Music Hall, as it was then known—opened at another untraditionally uptown venue, Seventh Avenue and 57th Street. Nestled in their boxes, subscribers Whitney, Rockefeller, Frick, and, of course, Carnegie himself heard Episcopal Bishop Henry Codman Potter say that while in European countries culture often depended on state patronage, "it is a happy omen for New York that a single individual can do so princely a thing." Then they and their guest of honor, Pyotr Ilich Tchaikovsky—the symphonic giant had been lured by Carnegie with a fee of twenty-five hundred dollars—listened to Walter Damrosch and the New York Symphony Orchestra inaugurate a five-day festival.

New money thrust its way into the world of men's clubs with equal dispatch. In this case it was the Union Club—the city's most prestigious—that gave offense. Patrician members had opened its exclusive doors just enough to allow a few newly monied to squeeze inside, but the rate of access was far too slow for those clamoring to be admitted. This time it was J. P. Morgan who assembled the group of *refusés*. Again, a new edifice was built, a regally scaled Italianate structure. Again, the newcomer was grandly titled the Metropolitan. And again, its backers situated the building, which opened in 1894, far uptown from the center of established clubdom—at Fifth Avenue and 60th Street.

CHÂTEAUX COUNTRY

Hunt's château for the Vanderbilts proved an epochal success. Previous elites had rejected efforts, by A. T. Stewart and Leonard Jerome, to break the brownstone mold. But the eighties' elite loved the Vanderbilt mansion's scale, materials, and ornate sensuousness. They hailed it as a liberation from what their own Edith Wharton would call New York's "mean monotonous streets," lined with buildings "of a desperate uniformity of style" and a "universal chocolate-coloured coating of the most hideous stone ever quarried."

Not all the elite was swept off its feet, to be sure. In 1882 J. P. Morgan was making a decent half million a year and could well have afforded something ostentatious. But Morgan despised fashion and vulgar display (except in yachts) and opted for a brownstone at Madison and 36th, in the no longer cutting-edge Murray Hill. And when the staunchly Baptist John D. Rockefeller arrived in town, he too settled in a brownstone, albeit one within blocks of the Vanderbilt château.

Nevertheless, Hunt would be kept busy until the day he died fashioning urban mansions for the rich, and their homes away from home as well. During the late 1880s and 1890s—as the elite fled Saratoga for Newport—Hunt constructed colossal summer places for them, like the Marble House for William Kissam Vanderbilt, and the Breakers for his brother Cornelius II. Indeed so great was the flow of commissions from avid haute bourgeois househunters that it begat a whole new generation of New York architects, of whom perhaps the most influential were Stanford White and Charles McKim.

McKim studied at the Ecole des Beaux Arts in 1867–70, came back to work in H. H. Richardson's New York office, then drifted out of Richardson's Romanesque orbit into that of Hunt's Renaissance. When the Vanderbilt 52nd Street chateau went up, it seized his imagination; he got into the habit, he later recalled, of walking up Fifth Avenue late at night to admire it and "always slept better for enjoying the sight." But even during the 1870s McKim had begun designing town houses in what was coming to be called the Queen Anne style, based loosely on English Renaissance sources. He also came to love the architecture of England's American colonies—McKim was among the first to appreciate eighteenth-century vernacular buildings—and he held in high regard the civic decorum and classical orderliness of New York's Federal structures.

Stanford White traveled a similar trajectory. Born in New York in 1853, he grew up in the city's artistic and reform community. His father, Richard Gant White, was a cosmopolitan essayist who penned articles on music, art, literature, the stage, and English life and manners for the *Galaxy, Nation*, and *Century* magazines. The elder White was also a friend of Calvert Vaux and Frederick Olmsted. It was through Olmsted that young White got an apprenticeship in Richardson's firm in 1872, replacing McKim, who had opened his own firm in collaboration with William Mead. Seven years later, White joined the other two, and the trio of McKim, Mead, and White would dominate New York's architectural scene for the next generation.

The firm, a brilliant combination of talents, was described as a vessel of which McKim was the hull, White the sails, and Mead the rudder and anchor. McKim, who styled himself "Bramante," produced restrained, fine designs. Mead organized the staff along the same lines as the other corporate and professional headquarters then going up in Manhattan, and by 1892, with 120 draftsmen, it was the largest architectural office in the world. White provided drama and flair—both in his work and his personal life—and brought in most clients.

White, the self-styled Benvenuto Cellini of the profession, was indeed a renaissance man. Apart from his architectural work, he painted, designed furniture and jewelry, collected antiques. He was also a man-about-town—he loved making a grand entrance at the opera in cape and red mustache—and was a vigorous, not to say ubiquitous clubman. His various memberships allowed him to mingle with moguls and pull in commissions from Knickerbockers and nouveaux riches alike. The firm's list of clients included Astors, Fishes, Goelets, Morgans, Pulitzers, Stuyvesants, Vanderbilts, and Villards.

McKim, Mead, and White didn't monopolize the field; they shared it with a formidable array of practitioners—including William Ware, Richard Upjohn, James Renwick, LeBrun, and others who formed, in 1881, the Architectural League of New York, seeking to elevate their skills to Ecole des Beaux Arts standards. Devoted to European models, many used books of photographs they had snapped on their grand tours to convince clients of the accuracy of their imitations. No stylistic consensus emerged; rather the new generation ransacked all European history.

The Vanderbilt-Hunt collaboration inspired, and the eighties' upturn made feasible, a building boom in town houses. Even the mid-1880s recession spurred construction, as investors frightened by chaos in the stock market shifted their capital into real estate. Soon upper Fifth was chock-a-block with millionaires—Harry Payne Whitney, Charles Harkness, Jay Gould, Collis P. Huntington, Benjamin Altman, Robert Goelet, Solomon Guggenheim, Russell Sage—and even the Astors, followers now rather than leaders, abandoned lower Fifth. The queen had Hunt build her a white French Renais-

Fifth Avenue north from 65th Street, 1898. The château that Hunt designed for Caroline Astor stands on the near corner, anchoring a line of mansions that stretches uptown as far as the eye can see. (© Museum of the City of New York)

sance palace at 65th Street, where she lived out the closing years of her reign. William Waldorf Astor sidled northward to a cream-colored Touraine château at the corner of 56th, three blocks south of the great complex of luxury skyscraper hotels clustered around 59th that included the Plaza, the Savoy, and his own seventeen-story New Netherland Hotel.

Some plutocrats pressed slightly eastward, to Madison Avenue, though not so far as the newly (1888) and misleadingly renamed "Park" Avenue, still fatally blemished by ventilation holes belching smoke and steam from the trains below. In 1882 McKim, Mead, and White started on a complex—between 50th and 51st, just behind the recently opened St. Patrick's Cathedral—of six town houses grouped around a court. Their client, railroader Henry Villard, got a monumental Italian Renaissance structure, based on the Cancelleria in Rome, outwardly austere, richly embellished on the inside. Unfortunately for Villard, as the buildings were going up he was suffering career reverses. During the 1884 panic he moved into the unfinished house, hoping to save on hotel bills, but angry crowds besieged him there, as they hunted down Ward and Fish elsewhere in the city. After a few weeks Villard moved out, never to return, and in 1886 he sold the complex to *Tribune* publisher Whitelaw Reid.

The Seventh Regiment's new armory at 66th Street facilitated elite expansion into heretofore drowsy Lenox Hill. The French medieval-style fortress (with elegant interior for the unit's social functions designed by White and Louis Comfort Tiffany) guarded against the concentration of working-class Germans and Irish stretching from Third Avenue down to the East River, providing a sense of security for the northward-streaming rich. Elegant mansions went up, interspersed with rows of individualized Queen

Anne town houses sporting facades with square and polygonal bows and bays, and oriels of every shape.

Lenox Hill remained Society's outer periphery until the 1890s, when mansions advanced up Fifth to Prospect Hill, encouraged by the new Eighth Regiment Armory (1894) on Park Avenue between 94th and 95th, which bulwarked the area against laboring masses to the east. Even so, only a handful of the wealthy—chiefly Germans like the Rupperts, Untermeyers, and Ehrets—braved such proximity to the tenement world.

Not everyone in Châteaux Country could afford a grand-scale mansion, and some who could afford luxurious-but-not-magnificent accommodations found the cooperative apartment house an appealing alternative. In 1880 Philip G. Hubert, a French emigré architect, organized his first Hubert Home Club, a device for allowing "gentlemen of congenial tastes, and occupying the same social positions in life," to buy shares in a joint stock company, which then bought land and erected an apartment building. Each cooperator got a perpetual lease to an apartment, its size dependent on how much he put in (costs ranged from ten to fifty thousand dollars). Each was assessed a share of the combined operating expenses: taxes and insurance, light and heat, janitors and elevator boys. Each got the right to approve, together with other leaseholders, the mere tenants to whom some suites were rented in order to pay off the mortgage.

The cooperative apartments of the 1880s, as well as those raised wholly by speculators for rental purposes, were a cut above the French Flats of the previous generation. They were huge—eight to twelve stories in height, as tall as or taller than most downtown skyscrapers. They were elaborate, châteauesque, awash in turrets and gables. The suites, which could include as many as twenty rooms, came with the parlors and reception rooms that guaranteed cachet. They offered all sorts of conveniences, grand public spaces and courtyards, dining facilities, and building staffs that, as *Harper's* noted in 1882, allowed families to make do with half the usual number of servants.

Luxury apartments tended to cluster in or near already affluent areas and to bear distinguished-sounding names. There was the Gramercy (1883) at Gramercy Park, the Berkshire (1883) on Madison at 52nd behind St. Patrick's, and the Chelsea (Hubert's most popular project), an immense, red-bricked, multigabled cooperative on West 23rd near Seventh Avenue.

The densest concentration, however, lay just south of Central Park. Hubert's first Home Club, the Rembrandt, went up on West 57th Street in 1882, next to the future site of Carnegie Hall. Nearby were the Plaza at 59th Street, the Osborne Apartments at Seventh and 57th, and the grandest of them all, completed in 1885, the Central Park Apartments (a.k.a. the Navarro Flats, after their builder) at Seventh and 59th. From a distance the Navarro appeared a single Moorish mass of turrets and dormers. In fact it consisted of eight ten-story personalized towers, each with its own entrance and name (Granada, Valencia, etc., hence yet another nickname, the Spanish Flats), all of them wrapped around a tremendous courtyard filled with trees, flowers, and fountains. Each apartment had its own floor; most had views of Central Park. It was by all accounts the largest and most elegant apartment house in the world.

The *Real Estate Record and Builders' Guide* called these behemoths "tenements of the rich," and with the cost of ground and building easily topping a million dollars, most cooperative shareholders were among the city's most affluent. But very well off professionals and managers could handle the rental prices: a ten-room in the Spanish Flats could be had for eighteen hundred dollars a year, and the Chelsea, which rented out thirty of its ninety apartments, embraced an even wider spectrum of tenants.

There was, however, another alternative for venturesome members of the "comfortable bourgeoisie": the "American Belgravia" of the Upper West Side. In 1879 Edward S. Clark, the Singer Sewing Machine magnate now branching out into real estate development, read his paper entitled "The City of the Future" to members of the West Side Association. Clark argued that pulling the right sorts of people northward required a mix of single-family homes and some truly striking apartment houses, where "the principle of economic combination should be employed to the greatest possible extent."

Clark delivered the latter in grand fashion in his Dakota Apartments (1884). "Dakota" was synonymous with distance and wealth—gold having been discovered in the far-off territories in the 1870s—and Clark's monumental Renaissance palace, looming over Central Park at 72nd Street in splendid isolation, embodied both. The nine-story structure by Henry Hardenbergh boasted a *cour d'honneur* manned by a concierge and an interior courtyard large enough to accommodate a carriage turnaround. Occupants of the fifty-eight suites (which ranged from four to twenty rooms) had access to

The Dakota Apartments, from *Frank Leslie's Illustrated Newspaper*, September 7, 1889. As affluent residents flocked to the West Side, the shanties quickly disappeared. (General Research. The New York Public Library. Astor, Lenox and Tilden Foundations)

hotel-style amenities, a wine cellar, a large dining room for private parties, and addition-al rooms under the mansard roof for Irish cooks and coachmen. It was fully rented by the day of its completion, peopled not with millionaires or fashionables (not a single tenant made the *Social Register* in 1887) but prosperous professionals and businessmen, many of them associated with the arts.

The Dakota fixed the West Side's character not only in spawning a rash of western-named buildings—the Wyoming, Yosemite, Nevada, and Montana—but in helping draw the affluent to town houses that went up along the avenues (some with suitably upgraded names: Eleventh became West End Avenue in 1880; Eighth became Central Park West in 1883). No chocolate brownstone uniformity here, but rather individual-ized, eclectic, historical styles, jumbling together Jacobean, French Gothic, and Dutch Renaissance. Indeed McKim, Mead, and White touched off a Dutch Colonial revival in 1885, with their row houses on West End and 83rd, and soon the area resembled a new New Amsterdam. Better still, by 1893 (*King's Handbook of New York City* reported)—while the Four Hundred were not in evidence—the West End locale had become "to a certain extent fashionable," so much so that "even society countenances it."

MANHATTAN RENAISSANCE

To decorate their interiors—the term "interior decoration" dates from the late 1870s—the wealthy patronized local artists as well as local architects, commissioning craftsmen to design walls, windows, and woodwork. The flood of orders fostered formation of a small, interlocking network of artists whose work gave luster to the city's, and the elite's, cultural reputation. Indeed the rich generated such a swirl of activity that they half convinced themselves, in the words of one artist, "that the days of the Italian Renaissance were revived on Manhattan Island."

The Vanderbilts, again, were among the foremost patrons, with Cornelius II assembling a platoon of artists to decorate his mansion. For glasswork he turned to John La Farge. The New York-born son of a cultivated French family, La Farge had studied in France, where he'd been inspired by impressionists, Japanese prints, and stained glass. On his return he invented (and patented) an opalescent glass and produced fabu-lous windows and ceiling panels. For sculptural details Cornelius turned to La Farge's friend and collaborator, Augustus Saint-Gaudens. Son of a French father and Irish mother, Saint-Gaudens too was brought up in New York, where he studied at Cooper Institute before attending the Ecole des Beaux Arts, and now provided Vanderbilt with Renaissance ornamental motifs.

Vanderbilt also employed the firm of Associated Artists, formed in 1879 by Louis Comfort Tiffany. Tiffany's atelier was a mix of Renaissance workshop and corporate headquarters. Each partner had his own department—fabrics and wallpapers, carving and wood decoration, textiles and embroideries—the whole presided over by the mas-ter. Tiffany also ran the glass department and, like La Farge, patented novel production processes. These craftsmen, following the path of contemporary professionals, formed their own organizations (like the Society of Decorative Art, 1877), their own social groups (like the Tile Club, 1877), and their own schools and periodicals.

In fact, however, Manhattan Medici imported the bulk of their artwork from Europe, turning to professional art consultants to certify their purchases. Among the most prestigious were Joseph and Henry Duveen, English-based importers of antique porcelain. Sensing a lucrative market opening up in New York, the Duveens started a branch operation in Manhattan. Henry brought over high-quality porcelain, silver, tiles, and tables, and business began to click the day Stanford White wandered into the store. White introduced Duveen to his wealthy friends, notably J. P. Morgan, then in the market for tapestries to cover the vast walls of his new mansion and furniture to cover its floors. Happily for all concerned, rich aristocrats were junking tapestries left and right, in favor of William Morris wallpaper, and clearing out their old armor and furniture. Joel stripped and shipped noble interiors to Henry's Fifth Avenue offices, and Henry cultivated new clients, like department store magnate Benjamin Altman, whom he began assisting in 1888.

In the world of painting and sculpture, would-be collectors had, until the mid-1880s, turned to local dealers like Michael Knoedler, Jean-Baptiste Goupil, and Samuel P. Avery, whose styles tended toward the private and personal. The boom years changed all this, generating a vigorous and highly visible art market pioneered by Thomas Kirby, an art auctioneer of long standing. Kirby's profession, like advertising, had a somewhat shady reputation, which may account for his invariably impeccable appearance: wing collar, cutaway morning suit, and clipped, pointed imperial beard. In 1883 Kirby joined forces with two men who ran an art gallery on the south side of Madison Square, transforming it into the American Art Association (AAA), a salon "for the Encouragement and Promotion of American art." When his 1887 sale of the late A. T. Stewart's collection fetched over half a million dollars, the AAA was firmly established as the city's foremost marketplace for sales of fine art, antiques, rare books, and jewels.

For all Kirby's talk about the "Promotion of American art," however, he and his buyers were fixated on Europe. But within those parameters he was willing to take some chances. In 1886 the AAA arranged to have the famous dealer Paul Durand-Ruel send over 289 works of modern French art. The first massive French impressionist show in the United States included oils by Renoir, Manet, Degas, and Pissaro, among many others. The New York press was underwhelmed—"Is this Art?" asked the *Times*—but the perceptive Durand-Ruel found New Yorkers were far more open to his painters than Parisians had been at first, and the following year he opened his own gallery at 297 Fifth. Impressionist collectors like Louisine and Henry Osborne Havemeyer—awash in Sugar Trust money—soon proved him right, and New York became established as modern art's portal to America.

PORK INTO PORCELAIN

In March 1880 President Hayes joined frock-coated trustees, and their wives in silk dresses, in dedicating the Metropolitan Museum of Art's new building. To reach the entrance of Calvert Vaux and Jacob Wrey Mould's barnlike, red brick structure, guests had to troop along a boardwalk that ran from Fifth Avenue to the main entrance on the building's west side. Once they were settled, Joseph C. Choate, one of New York's leading corporate attorneys, addressed the distinguished conclave.

He stressed the civic purposes of the new museum. It would not, as in Europe, be a plaything for wealthy connoisseurs—a "mere cabinet of curiosities which should serve to kill time for the idle"—but rather a democratic institution that by its "diffusion of a knowledge of art in its higher forms of beauty would tend directly to humanize, to educate and refine a practical and laborious people."

Choate also pointed to the benefits awaiting the museum's patrons. New York's rich could gain personal immortality by converting some of their fortunes—transient and perishable in any event—into a more permanent legacy. Wall Street, he enthused, should "convert pork into porcelain, grain and produce into priceless pottery, the rude ores of commerce into sculptured marble, and railroad shares and mining stocks—things which perish without the using, and which in the next financial panic shall surely shrivel like parched scrolls—into the glorified canvas of the world's masters, that shall adorn these walls for centuries."

Choate's stress on public benefits was politic. The museum, though privately owned, had been built with municipal largesse, including the parcel of Central Park on which it sat and the half-million dollars that had paid for its construction. But while director Luigi Cesnola believed the museum a source of "civilizing, refining, and ennobling influences," the *Tribune* suggested that "from the very beginning it has been an exclusive social toy, not a great instrument of education."

The Met had developed a snobbish reputation, in large part because most of the public couldn't get in. On Sunday, the one day the purported audience of working-class citizens could attend, the doors were shut fast by a board of trustees dominated by stoutly Sabbatarian Presbyterians. As early as 1881 ten thousand petitioned the Department of Parks to force the Met to open on Sundays, an appeal supported by almost every paper in the city and by reformers who argued that the museum could aid the "struggle against gigantic vices" by allowing access to its uplifting precincts. The Met trustees held firm for a decade, caving in only when the state legislature threatened to block a proposed North Wing expansion. On the first open Sunday, May 31, 1891, twelve thousand came, and Sunday remained the institution's most popular day ever after.

The museum nevertheless continued to cultivate wealthy art collectors, whose donations were a crucial source of accessions, and their artistic preferences shaped the museum's collections. William H. Vanderbilt liked sugary canvases of landscapes, allegories, and scenes of the wealthy at leisure, like the aptly titled work by Erskine Nicol called *Looking for a Safe Investment*. Henry Gudron Marquand, who had made a fortune in real estate, banking, and railroading, assembled an important collection of Van Dycks, Rembrandts, Hals, and Vermeers, which, when lent to the Met in 1888, instantly put the institution in the forefront of American museums. Most art that reached the museum was safely conventional in style and subject. At one point a group of young turk trustees pushed for including some of the impressionists, but the revolt on behalf of "advanced canvases" was put down by an old guard led by Marquand, Dodge, Rhinelander, and (trustee since 1888) J. P. Morgan.

So far as local painters were concerned, the Manhattan Medici were at best lukewarm patrons. Director Cesnola dismissed complaints by New York artists unrepresented in the Metropolitan as crassly self-interested men who wanted the museum to be "a kind of marketplace where their works were to be sold at exorbitant prices and permanently exhibited as their professional advertisement." This dismissal—a sharp contrast to their underwriting of decorative artists—was the odder because many youthful painters were producing just the kind of academic work that moguls seemed to favor. Yet the elite passed them by, preferring to patronize the London-based John Singer Sargeant, who in 1887 began painting full-blown portraits in New York City.

The truly unconventional did worst of all. One of the founding members of the Society of American Artists—a breakaway group from the National Academy of Design—was Albert Pinkham Ryder, a red-bearded, dreamy-eyed visionary. Ryder had begun his art career in the customary way, studying at the National Academy and setting up a studio near Washington Square. But after 1880 he was drawn to New York's "nightbird" tradition, best exemplified by Poe, and his canvases veered toward the romantic, the mysterious, even the sinister. He loved to walk around the city at night, soaking up the effects of moonlight on clouds, though his work never dealt with metropolitan "reality" in any but the most mediated way. Ryder was ignored by critics and public alike.

MAKING HISTORY

In the mid-1870s, as de facto editor of the *New York Sketch Book of Architecture*, Charles McKim reprinted images of old Manhattan treasures, especially Mangin and McComb's City Hall, which he called the "most admirable public building in the city." In revaluing the city's built remains, McKim helped fashion a turn toward the past, one that particularly appealed to old Knickerbocker and mercantile families who couldn't muster the financial resources for the social arms race. "Life here," rued Frederic J. DePeyster in the early 1890s, "has become so exhausting and so expensive that but few of those whose birth or education fit them to adorn any gathering have either strength or wealth enough to go at the headlong pace of that gilded band of immigrants and natives, 'The Four Hundred.'"

There were, of course, many old-timers who could well afford to "go the pace." Descendants of Knickerbockers and merchant princes who owned large amounts of Manhattan real estate had profited from the city's transformation into a corporate headquarters. Others had invested wisely in the new industrials. When the *Tribune Monthly* published a list of millionaires in 1892, a respectable one-fifth of the names belonged to antebellum families: Livingstons, Schermerhorns, Rhinelanders, Stuyvesants, Astors, Beekmans, DePeysters, Morrises, and Van Rensselaers. Even more tellingly, 60 percent of the leaders of New York's national corporations, investment banks, and railroads were descendants of old-monied families.

Still, out of penury or principle, many of those caught up in the status struggle emphasized what they had and upstarts didn't—a pedigree. Ever since the confrontation in the 1820s between Knickerbockers and New Englanders, bluebloods at bay had organized social bastions based not on wealth, or even accomplishment, but on heredity. Now the St. Nicholas Society (1835) and the Knickerbocker Club (1871) were joined by a host of others, like the Society of the Sons of the Revolution in the State of New York (1884) and the Holland Society (1885), which required a colonial ancestor in each member's closet. As Knickerbocker Robert B. Roosevelt told the Holland Society men in 1886, theirs was a haven for the "old residents of New York"—a race, added William D. DeWitt, that was "being outnumbered and overrun in its own land."

Soon such sanctuaries abounded, and members snuggled into their pedigrees, hunted up coats of arms at the Genealogical Society, and burnished their forebears' image the better to shine by reflected glory. Patrician women—like those in the New York chapter of the Daughters of the American Revolution (organized at Sherry's in 1891)—reenacted colonial teas using their ancestors' cups and wearing their great-grandmothers' gowns.

Some ancestral societies, however, adopted a more activist stance toward New York's history. Noting (with Frederic DePeyster) that "the mighty city of today knows little or nothing of our traditions," the old guard turned to publicly promoting them. They placed tablets at historic sites, raised commemorative statues in public parks, and in 1889 began publishing *Old New York*, a journal of city history and antiquities. Documentary reclamation projects got underway as well: in 1891 the state legislature authorized verbatim republication of the colonial laws, and in 1894 the Society of Iconophiles set out to publish both contemporary and facsimiles of early views of New York.

A string of city histories appeared, some in the elegiac vein pioneered by Abram Dayton's *Last Days of Knickerbocker New York* (1882), others works of substantial scholarship, much though not all of it written by women. Martha Lamb's *History of the City of New York* was published beginning in 1877; in 1884, Benson J. Lossing published his two-volume *History of New York City*; and Mariana Griswold Van Rensselaer penned historical essays for *Century Magazine*, which prefigured her later two-volume study of the seventeenth-century city.

Many female historians stuck to the history of women's sphere, writing, as had antebellum scribbling novelists, about home and hearth. Gertrude Lefferts Vanderbilt declared, in her *Social History of Flatbush* (1880), that "as a woman, I have inclined to the social side of life, and have endeavored to record the changes which time has made among the people in their homes and at the fireside." Alice Morse Earle, a member of the Society of the Colonial Dames, did the same in *Colonial Days in Old New York* (1896). And the redoubtable May King Van Rensselaer made clear, in *The Goede Vrouw of Mana-ha-ta at Home and in Society*, 1609–1760 (1898), that while "history is generally written by men, who dwell on politics, wars, and the exploits of their sex," she would chronicle "household affairs, women's influence, social customs and manners."

Old-monied men and women also embraced historic preservation, a decidedly un–New York sort of enterprise. Provoked by the latest spasm of vanishing churches, inns, and houses, preservationists rallied in 1889 to save Alexander Hamilton's Grange by shifting it to a new location. And in 1892, when the 1763 Rhinelander Sugar House at Duane and Rose was demolished, a portion of the building was reerected, together with an inscription, alongside the old Van Cortlandt house up in the Bronx.

Their most heroic campaign helped save City Hall. By 1893 efforts to tear it down and build anew had gotten as far as an architectural competition for its replacement. In 1894 the Sons of the American Revolution published a piece by Andrew Haswell Green calling for "The Preservation of the Historic City Hall of New York," and that year Green and Frederic J. DePeyster organized what would become the American Scenic and Historic Preservation Society. *Harper's* ratified the effectiveness of their intensive protests when it declared: "The majority of cultivated persons in New York would regard the demolition of City Hall not only as a municipal calamity, but as an act of vandalism."

Old-guard New Yorkers did not stand alone on the ramparts of history. Fashionable members of Châteaux Society also exhibited a penchant for the bygone days of pre-Reformation and Renaissance opulence, and some tycoons responded to the Knickerbockers' lineage challenge by purchasing instant pedigrees through marriage into titled European families. Clara, adopted daughter of railroad magnate Collis P. Huntington, wed Prince von Hatzfeld Wildenburg in 1889. Florence, offspring of corporate lawyer John H. Davis, became the second marquise of Dufferin and Ava in 1892. And in 1895 Pauline, daughter of horsecar magnate William C. Whitney, became the baroness Queensborough.

Dukedoms didn't come cheap. Impecunious earls insisted on a quid pro quo for their bloodline transfusions. It cost $5.5 million to ransom the daughter of the despised

Jay Gould into respectability. Even this outlay paled before the transatlantic exchange of assets arranged between Alva and William Kissam Vanderbilt and the ninth duke of Marlborough. In 1895 they virtually bludgeoned their daughter, Consuelo, to the St. Thomas altar and gave her away in the most spectacular nuptials in New York social annals. "Gave" is perhaps not the right word, given that compensation for His Grace included fifty thousand shares of Beech Creek Railway, the rehabilitation and maintenance of Blenheim Palace, and the construction of Sutherland House in London—an eventual Vanderbilt outlay of over ten million dollars.

In the right circumstances, the newly monied could be drawn into celebrating local history as well. In 1874 the country had kicked off a series of centennial commemorations by honoring the Continental Congress's first meeting in Philadelphia. By 1883 it was New York's turn. To celebrate the hundredth anniversary of Britain's exodus from the city, the metropolis revived Evacuation Day—the local holiday that; apart from a brief Tammany-inspired revival in the mid-1860s, had been pretty much supplanted by Independence Day before the Civil War. New Yorkers with Revolutionary ancestry claimed a special role in these ceremonies, but William Astor and William Vanderbilt helped finance the festivities too. The culmination of the event was the unveiling of John Quincy Adams Ward's twice-life-size statue of Washington on the front steps of the Sub-Treasury, site of Federal Hall. Ward, unusually, depicted Washington as civilian gentleman rather than martial equestrian, a decision that pleased the bankers and brokers over whose Wall Street community the genteel bronze Washington would now preside.

Evacuation Day redivivus proved mere prelude to a full-blown reenactment, six years later, of Washington's inauguration in 1789. The old-guard New York Historical Society and New York Society of the Sons of the Revolution again tried to preempt the event, but by now the wider New York bourgeoisie had developed a passion for local history almost as strong as their romance with the Renaissance and the world of Marie Antoinette. The Chamber of Commerce demanded a role in the planning, as did many others—so many that in 1887 two hundred interested parties merged in an ecumenical Committee of Citizens, which proceeded to fashion a glittering three-day event honoring the Court of Washington and the Court of Contemporary New York.

The pageantry began on April 29, 1889, with the arrival of President Benjamin Harrison from Washington City. He reprised his predecessor's cross-harbor voyage from New Jersey on a replica of the original barge, crewed by shipmasters from the New York Marine Society, the organization that had conducted Washington to Manhattan a century earlier. Landfall was followed by a march up Wall Street, a formal reception for four thousand of New York's business and professional elite at the Lawyers' Club, and a more intimate French feast for sixty at Café Savarin, whose souvenir menu listed the names of the City Council of yore (noting pointedly the absence of "Divvers, Flynns or Sheas").

Evening brought seven thousand guests to the Metropolitan Opera House for a grand Centennial Ball. Ladies and gentlemen, selected by Ward McCallister after a careful genealogical search, opened the gala by doing a Centennial Quadrille in colonial costume. To no one's surprise, Mrs. William Astor led the dance, brilliant in diamonds and a Worth creation. Some women did wear gowns "after the colonial period," but far more New York aristocrats favored apparel from the courts of Louis XV and XVI.

Not all the events were so exclusive. A reenactment of the swearing-in, which featured an address by New York Central's Chauncey Depew, attracted huge numbers of spectators, as did the Grand Military Parade. An estimated million people, vast numbers of whom had poured in by excursion trains, watched as fifty thousand members of various state militias marched from Wall Street up to the heart of Châteaux Country at 59th and Fifth. Finally, at the tail end of the events, a second float-filled parade allowed participation by those so far restricted to spectating. Immigrant societies, butchers in knee breeches brandishing sausages, plasterers tossing new-made busts of Washington to the crowd, firemen, policemen, and the sachems of Tammany Hall predominated here, though the accent remained aristocratic.

In the end, the colonial revival provided a way for new money to bow to old money's values, while old money acknowledged newcomers' superior resources. Perhaps appropriately, its most lasting legacy proved to be the practice of collecting "antiques"—a craze for amassing historical commodities having been ignited by the six-week-long Centennial Loan Exhibition of old gold and silver plate arranged by a Metropolitan Museum curator at the Metropolitan Opera House. New money also made its way into the Historical Society. While it was Rufus King's grandson who presided over the sanctum for much of this era, the drive for a costly new building, planned for Central Park West between 76th and 77th, made the participation of Cornelius Vanderbilt and J. P. Morgan particularly welcome.

INCLUSIONS

Upper-class New Yorkers had other settings—boarding schools, country clubs, exclusive resorts, elite universities, and Protestant churches—in which blood and money could forge a common culture. In the 1880s and 1890s, these elite institutions displayed both a new cosmopolitanism and a new parochialism, the first evidenced by a willingness to mix and mingle with provincial and professional elites, the second by the rise of anti-Semitism.

Magnates and Knickerbockers alike sent their sons to exclusive, usually Episcopalian private schools. They didn't mind that nearly all the influential prep schools of the 1880s and 1890s were more in Boston's than New York's cultural orbit. Nor did they object to their sons mixing with wealthy young men, from around the country, who would one day would join with them in owning and managing the corporate economy. Together they learned classics, sports, and social graces, while developing the habits of command and taste for public service that would become the hallmarks of their class.

From boarding school the elite-in-training headed on to college. Columbia remained a patrician citadel, with old-line mercantile supporters like the Lows and Schermerhorns joined by industrialists and financiers, but increasingly both elite branches found the college too parochial. Roosevelts and Fishes, who had for generations sent their sons to Columbia and served as its trustees, now opted for Harvard or Princeton or Yale, and Morgans and Vanderbilts followed in their footsteps.

Like prep schools, colleges brought New Yorkers into fruitful contact with youthful members of the propertied and professional classes from around the nation. Elite scions bonded in Greek-letter fraternities like Delta Kappa Epsilon (both Theodore Roosevelt and J. P. Morgan were members). This facilitated formation of "old boy" alumni networks that would help bind together a class capable of withstanding the centrifugal forces of competitive capitalism. Ivy League schools also served as socializing and recruiting grounds for senior subalterns, the managers who would run the banks, mercantile houses, and industrial corporations, along with leading lawyers, architects, and physicians.

An "old girl" network emerged too, as elites, especially affluent professionals, expanded educational opportunities for their daughters. These institutions tended to be closer to home, especially the new primary and secondary schools like Dwight School (1880), Brearley (1884), and Miss Spence's School for Girls (1892). When Columbia refused to admit females, Barnard College (1889) became the first secular institution in New York City to grant a BA to women.

Ecclesiastically speaking, Episcopalianism remained the favored denomination of both new and old Protestant elites. Henry Codman Potter, who became Episcopal bishop of New York in 1887, was pastor to the smart set and had several relatives on Ward McCallister's Four Hundred list. He loved officiating at weddings between English aristocrats and the New York rich, and when he traveled to church conventions he rode in J. P. Morgan's private railroad car. The General Theological Seminary expanded rapidly under Eugene Augustus Hoffman, its dean from 1879. Hoffman, descendent of an old Dutch family and owner of real estate worth millions, was said to be the richest clergyman in the world and was widely known as a sporting parson for his love of shooting and fishing and his active membership in the New York Riding Club.

Many believed that St. Thomas, on Fifth Avenue at 53rd Street, now surpassed Grace Church as the city's most fashionable. It was certainly more sumptuous than ever after its reworking by Stanford White. (Other Episcopal Churches would strive for most sumptuous status, with the Church of the Ascension at Fifth Avenue and 10th Street employing the combined talents of Stanford White, La Farge, Louis Saint-Gaudens and D. Maitland Armstrong, and White designing an elaborate portal for St. Bartholomew's at Madison and 44th.) Membership in St. Thomas was kept exclusive by charging pew rents of $500–700. On Easter Sunday, ladies of the church began parading up Fifth Avenue in all their finery, carrying the spectacular flower arrangements used for the service to patients at nearby St. Luke's Hospital.

Way uptown, moreover, plans were under way for the erection of the biggest religious edifice in the city, indeed in the country—indeed in the western hemisphere. Bishop Potter took the first steps toward building the Cathedral of St. John the Divine at the end of the 1880s. The cathedral project gained important support from both prestigious Knickerbocker families and the more recently monied; the biggest contributors included John Jacob Astor, August Belmont, Cornelius Vanderbilt, and the man described as "the financial and spiritual force behind the project," J. P. Morgan.

EXCLUSIONS

The obverse of inclusion being exclusion, the upper class identified itself by the kinds of people to whom it denied access: Catholics and African Americans, of course, but increasingly, departing from prior patrician practice, Jewish New Yorkers as well. During the first postwar decades, most wealthy German Jews had lived amicably among their class counterparts in integrated neighborhoods. They sustained their own institutions, of course. They attended the Byzantine-towered Temple Emanu-El (1868) on Fifth Avenue and 43rd, sent their children to the Sachs Collegiate Institute (1871) on West 59th Street, and joined their own men's club, the Harmonie Gesellschaft (1852). Many emphasized their Germanness: the Loebs and Lehmans spoke German at home, followed German affairs closely, vacationed at German spas, employed German governesses. But this cultural clustering was not the result of anti-Semitic rebuffs by their

Fifth Avenue neighbors, as was evident from the ongoing memberships of assorted Seligmans, Hendrickses, Lazaruses, and Nathans in such exclusive precincts as the Union, the Union League, and the Knickerbocker clubs.

In 1877, moreover, when banker Joseph Seligman arrived at Saratoga Springs by private railroad car only to be turned away from the Grand Union Hotel by Judge Hilton, executor of A. T. Stewart's estate (and soon-to-be hotel magnate), the incident produced widespread condemnation. *Harper's* and the *Tribune, Daily Graphic, Commercial Advertiser, Sun*, and *Herald* all denounced anti-Jewish snobbery. When one hundred leading Jewish merchants successfully boycotted Stewart's Department Store—also administered by Hilton—a *Puck* Christmas editorial offered "all honor to the Jews for their manly stand in this instance."

The hotel did not, however, withdraw its exclusion policy, and indeed the practice spread. Starting in 1878 the Greek-letter societies at the City College of New York (as the old Free Academy had been renamed in 1866) barred Jewish members, something Bernard Baruch (class of '89) would long remember. And in 1879 Austin Corbin banned Jews from Manhattan Beach Hotel, explaining that such "detestable and vulgar people" were driving away respectable guests. Again, most New York papers denounced Corbin's policy as mean-spirited, even shockingly un-American, and in 1881 the New York civil rights code that prohibited discrimination in public places for reasons of race was amended to include reasons of creed.

Nevertheless, anti-Semitic social ostracism grew steadily more acceptable during the 1880s, and by the early 1890s it had become a social given. In 1892 Theodore Seligman was blackballed when he sought to join the Union League Club—of which his father had been a founder—without eliciting a word of protest from members like Elihu Root and J. P. Morgan. This precipitated the resignation en bloc of all other Jewish members, many of long standing. Yet this time, while the *Evening Post* regretted Christians' refusal to associate with even well-bred Jews, it also allowed as how people really shouldn't try to push in where they weren't wanted. Sephardic aristocrats and German financiers alike found doors around town slamming shut: Jews were excluded from the *Social Register*, banned from Four Hundred functions (not one was invited to the 1892 ball), and rejected from private schools. Some affluent Jews responded by assimilating all the more thoroughly; others circled their own wagons more tightly and established a "Hebrew Select" society.

Social exclusion fostered economic segregation. With prep schools explicitly geared to turning out Anglo-Saxon "Christian Gentlemen," and colleges giving preference to sons of alumni, and few if any Jews (or Catholics, or African Americans) being accepted at top clubs, it became difficult, if not impossible, to accumulate the requisite old-boy connections, and banks, corporations, and law firms became Anglo-Saxon Protestant enclaves. Shoved to the side, Jews would advance only in industries they already controlled (merchandising and one wing of the investment banking community) or in fields still open to entrepreneurial innovation (entertainment and mass communications).

Yet the sequestration of elite Jewry would prove no more fatally corrosive of upper-class solidarity than the internecine combat between Astors and Vanderbilts or the acid rivalries of merchants and financiers. For all their internal conflicts, the issues uniting wealthy New Yorkers were far more compelling than those that divided them, and in the mid-1880s none was more urgent than the challenge issued to their political and economic authority from a very different part of town.

62

"The Leeches Must Go!"

In the industrial precincts of the East and West sides, the metropolitan labor movement had revived along with the quickened economy. The world of German socialism, in particular, had been newly reinvigorated by the arrival of thousands of immigrants fleeing Bismarck's repression. Newcomers slipped comfortably into various of the German-speaking craft unions leagued together in the United German Trades. Many also joined the Socialist Labor Party (SLP), as the old Workingmen's Party was now called, and indeed political and labor organizations overlapped substantially—with the Brewery Workers, a pioneering industrial union, making significant gains under socialist leadership. German socialism, with its labor lyceums and schools for children, was deeply rooted in, though largely limited to, Kleindeutschland.

A second constellation of unionists, known as the "pure and simple" variety, concentrated on mustering skilled workers into disciplined craft-based organizations. Cigarmakers, led by Samuel Gompers, were the strongest advocates of this approach. Gompers, born in 1850 in London's East End to Dutch-Jewish parents, was brought to New York in 1863. He spent his teens and twenties helping his father make cigars in their East Side tenement apartment. He attended lectures and classes at Cooper Union, joined debating clubs and the Odd Fellows, and developed a fierce attachment to the fledgling Cigarmakers Union. In the early days, he and his intimate associates—men like Adolph Strasser and Peter J. McGuire—shared the socialists' conviction that unions should struggle for the ultimate transformation of society at the same time as they fought to improve working conditions in the present.

The depression years changed his thinking. Watching (and dodging) rampaging policemen at Tompkins Square in 1874 convinced Gompers that those in power would not shrink from violently repressing radical challenges to the existing order. His conviction was deepened by the hysterical response of police, press, and pulpit to the Great Strike of 1877 and by the failure of the Cigarmakers' own walkout that year.

If capitalism were here to stay, then working people, Gompers believed, and particularly skilled craftsmen, should prepare themselves for a long-haul struggle. Following the example of British trade unions, he and Strasser (in 1879) revamped the Cigar Makers' International Union's structure on "businesslike" lines. Charging high dues, they built up a tough and self-sufficient organization, with ample reserves for strike funds and sick benefits.

The new model union bade farewell to what it now saw as the socialists' utopian fantasies. It would fight only for carefully delimited targets: better wages, hours, working conditions. Gompers made clear to capitalists that they had nothing fundamental to fear from unions such as his. At a Senate investigation in 1883, Strasser was asked what the Cigar Makers' ultimate ends were. "We have no ultimate ends," he replied. "We fight only for immediate objects—objects that can be realized in a few years."

The Cigar Makers' new policy set them on a collision course with the Knights of Labor, the largest working-class organization in the city. The Knights, formerly a clandestine operation, had flowered with the economy: national enrollment had shot from under ten thousand in 1878 to over seven hundred thousand by 1886. American workers were attracted by the Knights' hybrid attention to the immediate and the utopian. Despite Grand Master Terrence V. Powderly's disapproval of strikes—he thought them too easily crushed—the Knights walked out repeatedly in the mid-1880s in pursuit of very specific goals, often with considerable success. But the Knights were also convinced that capitalism—and its associated evils of degraded crafts, fevered competition, rapacious individualism, and urban squalor—threatened the artisan-yeoman republic. They believed that an alliance of the "producing classes" could regenerate America and transform it into a cooperative commonwealth.

The Knights regarded exclusionary craft unions like the Cigar Makers as shortsighted. Labor had to organize not just skilled craftsmen but semiskilled industrial workers and unskilled day laborers as well. The Knights were ecumenical on other fronts too, embracing Protestants and Catholics, whites and blacks, natives and immigrants, men and women. When Knights of Labor telegraphers struck Western Union in 1883, they demanded equal pay for equal work, well aware that females made up a quarter of the Morse operators at 195 Broadway. The Knights' definition of the "producing classes" was so all-encompassing that it included manufacturing employers as well. Indeed the only people *not* entitled to sup at labor's table were bankers, brokers, speculators, gamblers, and liquor dealers.

Most New York workers adopted one or another of these positions, and sometimes more than one. Many individual Socialist Labor Party members joined the New York Knights, even though they felt culturally and politically ill at ease there. In socialist eyes, the Knights failed miserably to grasp the inevitability of class struggle, and its temperance schemes dismayed lager-loving Germans. Gompers' Cigar Makers opposed the Knights altogether, resenting their embrace of semiskilled working men and women who, in the cigar trade, were replacing skilled craftsmen like themselves. They also thought it foolish to treat bankers rather than industrialists as labor's chief enemy.

THE FIRST LABOR DAY

In January 1882 Robert Blissert, an activist in the Knights of Labor and the Tailors

Union, led a rally at Cooper Union that led to formation of a citywide trades' assembly. Within weeks, a core group of a dozen unions had constituted the Central Labor Union (CLU) of New York, Brooklyn, and Jersey City. The CLU grew as rapidly and spectacularly as had the Knights (who composed roughly half the CLU's members). By 1884 thirty-six unions were affiliated. By 1886, spurred by the mid 1880s panic and recession, over two hundred organizations, representing perhaps fifty thousand workers, had joined New York's "parliament of Labor."

The Central Labor Union, like the Knights, was ecumenical. Its ranks included craft-based printers and builders, industrialized brewers and machinists, and unskilled (and unorganized) salesclerks and day laborers. Its aims were equally variegated. The CLU demanded the eight-hour day, an end to child labor, equal pay for equal work, government- (not bank-) issued currency, the abolition of tramp laws, and, quite grandly, an end to "all class privileges."

To make its new voice heard in the wider city, the CLU revived the tradition of artisanal festivals and parades, which had once been integral to New York's working-class world. The CLU proposed that one day each year be set aside as a holiday dedicated to and celebrated by working people, and under its aegis the United States' first Labor Day parade was held on September 5, 1882. Wearing their regalia and hoisting transparencies, the contingents formed up in Park Place near City Hall. The Jewelers Union of Newark led off smartly behind their own band. Then came the bricklayers in their white aprons, the jewelers in derby hats and dark suits, and a group seven hundred strong from Big Six (the typographical union). The marchers were festive but sober; no drinking was allowed. They carried mottos proclaiming: LABOR BUILT THIS REPUBLIC AND LABOR SHALL RULE IT, NO MONEY MONOPOLY, and (most shocking to next day's dailies), PAY NO RENT. Twenty thousand strong they strode north past Broome and Canal streets to Union Square, as hundreds of seamstresses at windows along the route waved hand-

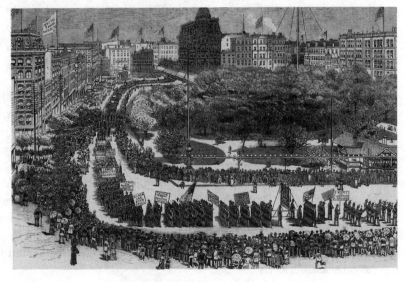

Union Square Demonstration, September 5, 1882—the first Labor Day parade in the United States. As the head of the column passes the reviewing stand on the north side of the park (17th Street), thousands more can be seen marching up Broadway in the distance. *Frank Leslie's Illustrated Newspaper*, September 16, 1882. (Library of Congress)

kerchiefs and blew kisses. Finally, after passing by a reviewing stand filled with labor dignitaries, the participants adjourned, via the elevated, to an uptown picnic at Elm Park. There they danced to jigs played by Irish fiddlers and pipers and were serenaded by the Bavarian Mountain Singers while the flags of Ireland, Germany, France, and the USA flapped in the autumn air.

The following year, in an effort to broaden its constituency, the CLU reached out in two directions. On March 20, 1883, it sponsored an enormous gathering at Cooper Union to commemorate the recent death of Karl Marx. Most speakers were socialists, but the packed crowd was composed of workers of many ideologies, nationalities, and trades, who joined in raising funds to publish an English-language edition of the *Communist Manifesto*. Their second initiative was to induct Henry George into the Knights of Labor.

PROGRESS AND POVERTY

A few weeks after the bloody finale of the Great Railroad Strike of 1877, with New York and the country still mired in depression, Henry George, a young San Francisco newspaperman, sat down to write a book. He was determined to make sense of the awful economic storms that periodically wracked the republic and to grapple as well with the terrible paradox of misery amidst plenty.

The short and scrappy redhead—friends called him the bantam cock—had been battered by economic depressions for most of his life. His father had published Episcopalian books until hard times drove him out of business and thrust the family into poverty. He himself had taken up the printer's trade, only to be pitched into unemployment by the depression of 1857. After the war he founded a penny paper with reformist principles; his sheet decried the way America's bountiful riches flowed into the pockets of a few. In 1869 George made a trip to New York City, in a failed attempt to get a franchise from the Associated Press. The metropolitan experience underscored for him just how profound the contrast could be between "monstrous wealth" and "debasing want." Then came the crash of '73, which sank his theretofore successful paper. Thus galvanized, and with shoestring support from a job inspecting gas meters, he wrote *Progress and Poverty: An Inquiry into the Cause of Industrial Depressions and of Increase of Want with Increase of Wealth*.

George blamed crises on the "principle of competition upon which society is now based." Under conditions of competition, American individualism, which he valued highly, too easily degenerated into "cruel selfishness and monstrous greed." The republic had to reject cutthroat competition and become "a family, in which the weaker brethren shall not be remorselessly pushed to the wall."

George also blamed hard times on the growth of monopolies, and the worst monopolists were landlords—parasites who cornered an irreplaceable resource and exacted outrageous charges for its use. When an increase in population and productive resources made land more valuable, landlords creamed off most of the benefit. Worst of all were speculators who deliberately held property off the market until its price reached unconscionable levels.

It was landlords' gouging, George asserted, that forced factory owners to cut workers' wages, in order to offset the high cost of land. The solution was straightforward: tax the landlords and confiscate all their unearned profits. This one single tax would generate such phenomenal revenues that the country could eliminate all other taxes. Unfettered entrepreneurs would then be able to pay fair wages. Capital and labor would be reconciled; strikes and poverty would become things of the past. The single tax would also "lessen crime, elevate morals, and carry civilization to yet nobler heights."

George mailed off his manuscript to publishers in New York City. Harpers and Scribner's turned it down, but D. Appleton and Company agreed to print some copies if George supplied the plates. The book received little attention in the press, however, so in August 1880 the forty-one-year-old author moved to New York City to promote it, as well as to look for work. He soon made modest headway on both fronts. The book received a series of notices that, while hardly all favorable—the *Times* and *Nation* damned it—attracted enough attention to land him several journalistic assignments. George brought his family east and relocated to a porter's lodge on the outlying Kingsbridge Road.

The one really enthusiastic review for *Progress and Poverty* came from Patrick Ford's *Irish World*. Ford liked George's analysis of American conditions, and even more its relevance to Ireland's current dilemmas. In the late 1870s crop failures, rack-renting, and mass evictions had revived fears of famine. Two hundred thousand angry tenants organized the Irish Land League, which demanded a halt to evictions and the transfer of property from aristocratic landlords to working farmers. The league was led by Michael Davitt, a militant Fenian and son of an evicted tenant farmer, and Charles Stuart Parnell, a wealthy Protestant landlord who had been fighting for home rule.

In 1880 Parnell came to New York City to raise funds and organize American branches. He was spectacularly successful. Catholic Irish Americans and mainstream Protestants alike gave him a jubilant reception and bountiful patronage, and by September 1881 the new American Land League had over fifteen hundred branches. In New York City the Catholic hierarchy, Tammany Hall, and the Irish-American middle class—many of whom had condemned Fenianism—rallied to the Land League, reassured by Parnell's brand of constitutional and parliamentary nationalism. At the same time, the day laborers and servant maids for whom Ford was the leading spokesman were fired with enthusiasm for Davitt's radical antilandlordism. It was this wing of Irish-American nationalism that found Henry George's work compelling. Ford printed up a cheap edition of *Progress and Poverty*, and soon working-class chapters of the Land League were studying it avidly.

In October 1881 Ford dispatched George to Ireland as a special correspondent. Soon he was wiring back articles castigating English despotism and landlord oppression. He also lectured around the Irish countryside, blossomed into a commanding orator, was arrested by the authorities, and returned to New York an Irish-American working-class hero.

Many in the Knights of Labor now took George's teachings to heart. Grand Master Powderly, himself of Irish descent and prominent in the Land League, promoted *Progress and Poverty* vigorously, sponsoring lectures by George around New York and out west. Though not convinced the single tax was the answer to all labor's problems, Powderly applauded George's raising of the land issue.

For his part, George was cautious about linking up with the union movement, given his convictions about the harmony of interest between capital and labor. But the Knights' old republican belief in the essential unity of the producing classes mirrored his own, and the tangible injustices he had witnessed on his travels moved him emotionally, so George joined the ranks of the workingmen.

"CHRIST HIMSELF WAS BUT AN EVICTED PEASANT"

Among George's new admirers was Father Edward McGlynn, the Soggarth Aroon (Gaelic for "Priest of the People"). McGlynn, a New Yorker born and bred of Irish immigrant parents, had begun his ministry in a Civil War military hospital. He worked his way up from a floating ministry to Irish squatters, assigned him by Archbishop Hughes, to pastorship of the beautifully frescoed St. Stephen's on East 28th Street, between Lexington and Third avenues, spiritual center of the largest and one of the poorest parishes in the city. McGlynn had long sought to promote the material as well as spiritual needs of his parishioners, and when he read *Progress and Poverty*, it explained to him why all his efforts on behalf of poor parishioners had come to nought. A magnetic speaker, the enormously popular McGlynn teamed up with George in speaking out against Irish and American landlordism, from secular as well as sacred pulpits. "Christ himself was but an evicted peasant," McGlynn asserted, fashioning an Irish Catholic counterpart to Protestant workingmen's veneration of "Jesus the brother carpenter who banned money changers from the temple."

McGlynn was also a venturesome theologian, and he headed a remarkable group of New York City clerics who were urging democratization on a local hierarchy that was traveling rapidly in the opposite direction.

New York's Catholic Church was thriving. Over 40 percent of Manhattan's population (and a somewhat smaller percentage of Brooklyn's) was now Catholic, and Catholics accounted for perhaps three-quarters of the city's active churchgoers. With nearly four hundred priests and perhaps two hundred churches and chapels, the archdiocese was unquestionably the largest in the United States. In 1875 the Vatican had recognized New York's importance, when Pius IX sent a red hat across the Atlantic to John McCloskey, Archbishop Hughes's successor. And on May 25, 1879, the cardinal, with forty-five archbishops and bishops in attendance, had sung a dedication Mass, before an immense crowd of dignitaries, at the high altar of the finally completed St. Patrick's Cathedral—now the most imposing ecclesiastical edifice in New York City.

Cardinal McCloskey died in 1885. Power passed to New York's third archbishop, Michael Corrigan. Corrigan was the son of a Dublin cabinetmaker who had emigrated to Newark in 1829 and become, by the 1850s, a prosperous wholesale grocer, liquor dealer, and real estate investor, one of the wealthiest Catholics in the city. Michael, born in 1839, had grown up in the comfortable world of the emerging Irish middle class. In 1859 Corrigan studied for the priesthood at the new American College in Rome, where his prefect was the strappingly masculine Edward McGlynn, who apparently looked down on the bookish Corrigan, a slight that would be remembered. Ordained in Rome, Corrigan returned to America and rose to become bishop of Newark in 1873, where he stayed until summoned in 1880 by McCloskey to help administer the huge and rapidly growing archdiocese of New York.

In 1885, now himself archbishop, Corrigan found himself pitted against his old nemesis McGlynn, on matters both sacred and secular. Corrigan had moved swiftly to centralize ecclesiastical authority, but McGlynn, like many priests in New York, thought the American Church should adopt a more democratic style, one better suited to the American people. Corrigan also believed that New York's Catholics should band together socially, and he launched a massive parochial-school building program, with Democratic Party backing. McGlynn, however, decried Corrigan's goal of withdrawing into a Catholic ghetto, publicly opposed state aid to parochial schools, and decried the Church's alliance with Tammany. The pastor of St. Stephen's urged Catholics to break down differences with their fellow citizens rather than erect new barriers between them.

The two men did not see eye to eye on labor issues either. McGlynn wanted the Church to actively support working-class organizations like the Knights and CLU. The archbishop, like others of the affluent Irish upper middle class, was a strong supporter of the status quo and gratified that upper-class Protestants had come to see the Church as a source of stability. It was appropriate, Corrigan thought, for workers to want improved conditions, but they should wait patiently for such improvements to come their way, rather than engage in militant and clerically unsupervised self-help. Corrigan even urged a ban on the Knights of Labor but was thwarted by more liberal bishops in other cities.

Finally, Corrigan opposed political radicalism of any stripe. He was at one with the Council of Trent in condemning the "false doctrines or negations which flourish in our time and eat like a cancer into society." These included agnosticism, materialism, naturalism, rationalism, any doctrine proposing that civil power issued from the people and not from God, and—most emphatically—"socialism and communism, the twin monsters threatening the social order of mankind." When McGlynn took up with Henry George—a close-enough socialist to Corrigan's way of thinking—it was the last straw. McGlynn, for the moment, was muzzled.

DYNAMITE!

The confluence of Catholic radicalism, Irish nationalism, and labor militancy greatly strengthened the ability of working-class organizations—and working-class neighborhoods—to bring pressure to bear on obdurate employers. When relatively powerless workers like bakers, store clerks, freight handlers, cloakmakers, or unskilled cigarmakers struck for shorter hours or union recognition, they were now backed both by the Central Labor Union and by newly energized communities.

Sometimes this support reached riotous dimensions. In March 1886 the miserably exploited horsecar drivers and conductors of the Dry Dock line along Grand Street went on strike to lower their sixteen-to-seventeen-hour workday (with no time off for dinner) to twelve. Organized labor raised funds to back the drivers' efforts, and when on March 4 the city sent policemen to escort scab operators, sympathetic neighborhood crowds blockaded the tracks with barricades of wagons and rubbish. The superintendent of police now dispatched 750 men (25 percent of the force) to aid the company, posting five hundred along Grand Street and a phalanx of 250 around a car as it edged out of the stables. Now (as *Harper's Weekly* noted) thousands of neighborhood residents and factory girls "groaned, hissed, and jeered from the sidewalks, while from every window there were angry jabbering and shaking of fists." Crowds heaped coal, lumber, cobblestones, and bricks on the tracks while throwing rocks, eggs, and rotten vegetables at the police. When three hundred officers charged and clubbed protestors at Forsyth Street, rioters overturned and fired cars, but police bulled the car through from river to river.

In response the CLU that evening voted a citywide "tie-up" of every streetcar line, and the next day over sixteen thousand drivers, conductors, and stablemen refused to show up for work. Surface transit was utterly paralyzed, and though the elevateds kept running they couldn't handle the overload. When the Dry Dock Company gave in, it

March 4, 1886: club-wielding policemen attempt to clear Grand Street of striking
streetcar workers and their supporters. *Harper's Weekly*, March 13, 1886.
(© Collection of The New-York Historical Society)

touched off wild celebratory parades, cheered by thousands of men, women, and children waving blankets, sheets, flags, and brooms. The horsecar corporations had the last
word, however, when the Third Avenue line beat back a strike, aided by indictments
against union leaders and a mammoth police presence provided by the city, despite the
recent revelations that Jacob Sharp, the company's owner, had won special privileges via
massive bribery of the Board of Aldermen and that his company had cheated the city
out of a million dollars in back taxes.

Since the depression of the 1870s, violence had been an ever-increasing fact of life
for New York's laboring classes. Year after year platoons of police cracked skulls, broke
up meetings, and smashed picket lines while press and politicians acquiesced or
applauded wildly. Nationally, too, employers employed squads of Pinkertons to combat
strikers: Jay Gould was thought to have boasted he could "hire one half of the working
class to kill the other half." Some New York German socialists responded by forming
Lehr-und-Wehr Verein (education and defense societies). Resolved to never again be
beaten or shot without resisting, they trained, drilled, and, on special occasions,
marched in the streets. Such activities proved particularly appealing to newly arrived
German immigrants, who had experienced at first hand Bismarck's antisocialist laws,
which disbanded unions, suppressed newspapers, and arrested radicals. They too were
determined to draw the line.

In Lower East Side cafes and saloons where intellectuals, writers, workers, and students hung out, there was talk of going farther, of taking the offensive, of launching an
armed struggle to rip up the old order "root and branch." When the Socialist Labor
Party denounced such notions, dissidents formed the Social Revolutionary Club.
Derided as "anarchists," they adopted the name as a badge of pride. Their headquarters
was First on First—Justus Schwab's saloon at First Avenue and 1st Street, a tiny beer
hall with a bas-relief of Marat behind the bar. Schwab, the Social Revolutionary Club's

president, was a tall, powerfully built man who had raced through Tompkins Square in 1874 waving the Commune's red flag, and when he sang the "Marseillaise" at First on First, his deep voice rattled the glasses on their shelves.

The anarchists remained a tiny, unknown sect devoted to drill and discussion until December 18, 1882. Then, after a terrible crossing, a steamship out of Liverpool limped into Pier 38 at the foot of King Street and unleashed Johann Most on the American scene. Schwab and his associates had invited the famous European comrade. They hastened him to a mass meeting at Cooper Union, where Most delivered a flaming speech that electrified his listeners, then set off on a national speaking tour that within six months transformed the anarchist movement into a national presence. Back in New York City, Most set up his newspaper *Die Freiheit* on William Street and issued pamphlets filled with apocalyptic appeals to violence.

The quickest route to the Cooperative Commonwealth, Most explained, lay through a field of capitalist corpses. "The best thing one can do with such fellows as Jay Gould and Vanderbilt is to hang them on the nearest lamp-post." Dynamite was his favorite panacea. Dynamite would enable ordinary workmen to stand up to police, Pinkertons, and militias, even armies. As gunpowder had brought down feudalism, so dynamite would blow up capitalism.

In 1884 Most took a job in a Jersey City dynamite factory to explore its mysteries, and in July 1885 he issued a seventy-four-page booklet, *Revolutionary War Science: A Little Handbook of Instruction in the Use and Preparation of Nitroglycerine, Dynamite, Gun-Cotton, Fulminating Mercury, Bombs, Fuses, Poisons, etc., etc.* In this manual of urban guerrilla warfare, Most explained how to destroy bridges, capture arsenals, and sabotage telegraph and railroad lines. He also offered helpful tips on exterminating the bourgeoisie (the whole "reptile brood"), recommending that charges be placed at "an opulent banquet" or "a ball where monopolists are assembled."

Some anarchists were excited by this verbal ferocity, despite, or perhaps because of, its being all talk: Most had never thrown a bomb, placed a charge, or hanged a single capitalist. During the miserable mid-eighties, years of recession and repression, *Revolutionary War Science* sold like lager at picnics and meetings around town, at ten cents a copy. Serialized in the anarchist press, it roused readers across the country. Young Emma Goldman, a seamstress up in Rochester, decided to move to New York City and ask Most to help her become an anarchist.

Overwhelmingly, however, New York workers were repelled by Most's posturing. Schwab and the local anarchists broke with him, branding his fulminations dangerous and immoral. The socialists and the Knights would have nothing to do with him. But by matching the levels of rhetorical violence that middle- and upper-class spokesmen had employed routinely since the depression of the 1870s, Most provided an all too convenient symbol for those intent on portraying all challenges to the status quo as lethal menaces.

The press made Most into an archetypal terrorist. Cartoonists like Nast (of anti-Tweed fame) pilloried him constantly. Joseph Keppler of *Puck* used him as model for a bewhiskered foreign-looking anarchist, bomb in one hand, pistol in the other, though Most usually dressed in a business suit and had neatly trimmed hair. These images, along with characterizations of anarchists as "reptiles" and "leeches" worthy of extermination, raised the rhetorical stakes. General Sherman, now a resident of West 71st Street, foresaw an imminent and "armed contest between Capital and Labor" as the "better classes are tired of the insane howlings of the lower strata, and they mean to stop them."

MAY DAY!

It was in this venomous atmosphere, on May 1, 1886, that organized labor launched a nationwide offensive. The tremendous growth of the Knights of Labor, and a run of successful strikes in 1884 and 1885, had given unionists the idea that perhaps a general strike would win the eight-hour day.

Across the country over three hundred thousand turned out. In New York City forty-five thousand walked off work, including streetcar conductors, cigarmakers, building tradesmen, pianomakers, and machinists. Many of the strikes were swiftly successful. Others were ferociously resisted, particularly after May 3, when in Chicago's Haymarket Square someone exploded a bomb amid policemen who were attacking an anarchist demonstration. The *New York Times* blamed the police deaths on the "doctrine of Herr Johann Most"—who was promptly arrested—and called for the application of "hemp, in judicious doses." The Knights of Labor scrambled to distance itself from the affair, denouncing the anarchists accused of inciting the crime as "wild beasts." It did them no good; public sympathy was abruptly alienated by the Haymarket bombing, and the eight-hour movement went down to defeat.

More alarming, Central Labor Union organizers were convicted and jailed for using a boycott. The tactic had its roots in the Irish practice—developed during the land wars of 1879–83—of cutting off social intercourse with rack-renting and evicting landlords. New York City's workers used it against employers, targeting their products rather than their persons. With so many consumer goods locally produced for local sale, working-class boycotts that disciplined businessmen through the marketplace were often more effective than strikes. By the mid-1880s, the CLU had mounted scores of them successfully against recalcitrant employers who made or sold beer, bread, cigars, shoes, hats, clothing, and house furnishings. An alarmed press and pulpit denounced the tactic as (in *Harper's* words) a "new form of terrorism." Businessmen brought criminal prosecutions, and by 1886 over a hundred tailors, bakers, musicians, and waiters had been arrested and indicted.

In the latest instance, Knights of Labor musicians had called for, and the CLU had sanctioned, a boycott against George Theiss, proprietor of a beer garden on East 14th Street. Workers also boycotted beer produced by George Ehret's brewery, because Theiss's hall served it, and canceled picnics at Jones' Wood, because it sold Ehret's beer. Ehret, feeling the pressure, arranged a sit-down that ended in mutual concessions and a deal. Despite this a grand jury charged the five CLU negotiators with conspiracy and extortion, and they were sentenced, on July 2, 1886, to terms ranging up to four years in Sing Sing prison.

"HONEST LABOR AGAINST THIEVING LANDLORDS AND POLITICIANS"

Within two weeks the CLU decided to enter politics, something labor had not done effectively since the 1830s, when the Workingmen's Party, similarly infuriated by court decisions, had taken to the hustings. Badly burned then, and in minor forays since, organized workingmen had shunned the electoral arena. The CLU itself banned politicians, lawyers, and public officials from membership. It refused to elect a permanent president lest he sell out the organization to a political party. But employers' ease of access to police and courts convinced union men that control of city government was an indispensable prerequisite to workplace organizing.

In August the CLU called all city labor organizations to a meeting, and on the appointed day 402 delegates, representing 165 groups and over fifty thousand wage-earners, formed a United Labor Party (ULP). Over the next two months it hammered out a platform and considered candidates. Finally, on September 23, after a mighty speech by Father McGlynn, it nominated Henry George as its candidate for mayor of New York City.

George had been chary of making the race. When a CLU committee first visited him at his new home up in Harlem, he declined the honor, dubious about a third party's chances in a city where even Republicans were perennial runners-up. A nervous Tammany inadvertently decided George by sending secret emissaries to offer him a safe congressional seat if he declined the nomination. He couldn't be elected, the delegation explained, but "his running will raise hell." That settled it for the truculent George: "You have relieved me of an embarrassment," he responded. "I do not want the responsibility and the work of the office of Mayor of New York, but I do want to raise hell!" He would run, but only if the new party demonstrated its potential strength by getting thirty thousand backers to pledge their support in writing.

On October 5, 1886, George worked his way through the mammoth crowds outside Cooper Union and in the jam-packed interior, finally reaching the Great Hall. There he mounted a stage decorated with sheaves of petitions, arranged like floral offerings, that contained over thirty-four thousand signatures. Formally accepting the ULP nomination for mayor, George addressed the party's three major concerns: labor, politics, and land.

He ratified the platform's call for higher pay, shorter hours, better working conditions, government ownership of railroads and telegraph, and an end to "officious intermeddling of the police with peaceful assemblages," adding his own denunciation of "industrial slavery."

He declared that "this government of New York City—our whole political system—is rotten to the core." Politicians had made a trade out of assembling votes and selling them to powerful interests; revelations about horsecar magnate Jacob Sharp's scandalous bribery of boodle aldermen back in 1884 were front-page news just then, with twenty-two aldermen (Democrats, Republicans, and Independents alike) having been arrested. What business got in return was police protection, lax enforcement of housing and health codes, friendly judges, and fat franchises. To purify the political order, working-class voters had to sever ties to all the established parties and choose candidates from their own ranks, not what John Swinton called the "fleecing classes."

Finally, George applied *Progress and Poverty*'s analysis to metropolitan landlordism. "Why," he asked, "should there be such abject poverty in this city?" What is it that "forces girls upon the streets and our boys into the grog shops and then into the penitentiaries"? The answer was insanely high levels of rent. New Yorkers sweated for landlords because Manhattan real estate had long since been monopolized: "We are toiling, perhaps, for Mrs. Astor" or "the heirs of some dead Dutchman." The majority of those piled in tenement barracks, as Peter McGuire had noted, had "paid by way of rent enough to purchase for themselves, not only one house but several," yet they remained at the mercy of landlords who could and did get an eviction order from a district court judge if rent was three days late.

Worse, while New Yorkers were penned up in the tenement districts—"nowhere else in the civilized world are men and women and children packed together so closely"—there was plenty of empty land available, "miles and miles and miles of land all around this nucleus. Why cannot we take that and build houses upon it for our accommodation?" Because land monopolists were warehousing it, waiting for its price to rise. Taxing their properties would force landlords to disgorge vacant but valuable land and make it available to working people. "There is no good reason whatever why every citizen of New York should not have his own separate house and home; and the aim of this movement is to secure it."

Taxing away the unearned profits of the idle rich would also generate enormous revenues, which could be used to improve city services, particularly in education and transit. George was grateful to Peter Cooper for providing the hall in which they now met, but education for working people should be a matter of right, not charity. The people of New York should establish *twenty* Cooper Institutes, and pay for them out of "our own estate." Streetcars and elevateds should be taken out of the hands of men like Jay Gould and Jacob Sharp and be operated as a public service. "We could take those railroads and run them free, let everybody ride who would, and we could pay for it out of the increased value of the people's property."

THE "TAILBOARD" CAMPAIGN

George had proposed an alternative way to run the city and urged formation of a new governing coalition to run it. Now United Labor Party troops poured into the streets to do electoral battle. The German socialists came on board. So did Sam Gompers and the Cigarmakers, albeit reluctantly. Quite apart from the prominence of so many Knights and socialists in the movement, Gompers and his colleagues believed all politicians were crooks and would sell out labor's interests to the highest bidder. Even if the ULP did elect candidates pledged to prolabor measures, executives would refuse to enforce such laws, or the courts would quickly reverse them. Nevertheless, the "pure and simple" men were as enraged as other workers by the blatant police and judicial support for capital. Given the phenomenal support building up in the working-class districts for George, it seemed that perhaps this crusade would be able to make some fundamental changes in New York City.

The George campaign set up headquarters in the Colonnade Hotel on Broadway (near 8th Street) and translated the enormous amateur enthusiasm into a formidable electoral army. To finance the challenge, union members across the city were assessed twenty-five cents a head. Heaps of pennies poured in, and the candidate could often be seen at headquarters helping roll coins for distribution to campaign managers around town.

Since Tammany ward heelers held sway in saloons, the new organization took to the streets, shop floors, and union halls. Drawing on the CLU's logistical experience with organizing boycotts, parades, and mass demonstrations, the ULP created an apparatus of neighborhood meetings, streetcorner rallies, campaign clubs, Assembly District organizations, and trade legions—an entire political counterculture.

With the exception of *John Swinton's Paper*, Ford's *Irish World*, and the socialists' *New Yorker Volkszeitung*, every paper in the city opposed George. One of the campaign's major complaints was that "the same centers of power that have seized the reins

of government . . . have also grasped the press by the throat." The campaign accordingly launched its own daily, the *Leader*, staffed by eager volunteers from the other papers;
by mid-October it circulated to forty thousand readers.

Using the elevateds, the candidate whirled around the city addressing labor unions,
Irish nationalists, Catholic parish fairs, German *Turnverein*, and middle-class social
reformers. On one typical day, George talked at the opening of a church fair at St.
Cecilia's (106th Street between Third and Lexington), spoke at Waiters Union No. 3 at
40th Street and Third Avenue, addressed a mass meeting of eight thousand at Third
and 42nd, marched with the Henry George Bohemian Club, and hopped the el downtown to a tumultuous meeting in Chickering Hall.

Even more striking was the "tailboard" campaign in which speakers rumbled by
horsecart from one street throng to another, talking from a makeshift backseat podium.
From breakfast to midnight, campaign orators hit the docks, factory yards, elevated stations, churches, and tenement districts. They addressed shoppers by day and, with the
aid of torches, carousers at night. Speakers drew on a host of notables, including Father
McGlynn, Knights leader Terrence Powderly, editor Patrick Ford, liberal Protestant
minister Walter Rauschenbusch, and Columbia professor Daniel DeLeon, but the tail-
boarders also included men of purely local renown. Some were shop-floor and neighborhood activists addressing mass audiences for the first time. Others were merchants,
lawyers, doctors, or teachers, drawn into unprecedented coalition with organized labor
by George's synthesis of piety and political economy.

As the campaign rolled on, and volunteer poll workers began training to counter
the ward bosses' election day "hirelings," it was clear to the entire city—and to the
nation, and to Europe, where the campaign was covered via cable—that something
extraordinary was happening in the streets of New York. There had not been such a
challenge to the established order since the Sons of Liberty contested merchant control
of the city in colonial days. The Workingmen's Party of the 1830s had flamed out quickly; the draft riots of 1863 had been terrifying but undisciplined and ultimately repress-
ible. Now the possibility that had always lurked in a democratic polity seemed finally to
have materialized: working people would use the polls to advance their class interest.

THE COLLEGE-BRED TRIBUNE

The prospect caused consternation among the propertied classes. The "present revolt
of the working men of this city," the Union League Club declared, had "become a matter of the first importance." To battle George, Fifth Avenue sent into the ring another
scrappy young bantamweight, named Theodore Roosevelt. The very name Roosevelt
was reassuringly redolent of old New York, indeed old New Amsterdam. After the family's plate glass business had boomed with Manhattan's postwar expansion, it shifted
much of its capital into banking, investment, and city real estate. When Cornelius died
in 1871, he left Theodore Senior over a million dollars and a mansion on 57th Street off
Fifth Avenue.

In 1876 Theodore Junior, aged seventeen, had gone off to Harvard, not Columbia as
had innumerable Roosevelts before him. Despite his unprepossessing appearance—five
feet eight inches, 125 pounds, a thin and piping voice, thick spectacles, and a laugh
described by his mother as an "ungreased squeak"—his impeccable upper-class credentials and deep pockets got him into the best clubs. He worked hard too, immersing him-

self in laissez-faire political economy. After graduating in 1880 Teddy married, entered Columbia Law School, and joined the social whirl of New York's ultrafashionables, dining at Mrs. Astor's and dancing at Ward McCallister's Patriarch's Balls.

On October 10, 1882, Roosevelt invited a score of "respectable, well educated men" to his home at 55 West 45th Street to launch a City Reform Club. He told the press that the club intended that "the respectable, educated, refined young men of this city should have more weight in public matters." Membership would "be restricted to that class in the community from which its members have hitherto been chosen," that is, wealthy, native-stock, Protestant businessmen or professionals. In this the club certainly succeeded: a newsman at one meeting noted that the chairman officiated in full evening dress with white butterfly tie, and of the thirty-eight men present, thirty-six carried canes, thirteen wore kid gloves, and twenty-two parted their hair in the middle.

The City Reform Club planned to elect "honest and capable men" who, once installed, would "administer their offices on business principles as opposed to party methods." In October 1882 Roosevelt himself ran for the state assembly, in a campaign during which, he prided himself, he never pandered to the populace or "paid for a drink or entered a saloon"—admittedly easier to do in a district where one did not have to deal with "the vast majority of the vicious and illiterate population." Roosevelt later depicted his run as a daring departure from the ideals and practices of his class, but his own social set hailed him as a "college-bred tribune," and he received strong backing from such clubmen and business leaders as Joseph H. Choate, J. P. Morgan, Elihu Root, and Morris K. Jessup.

Once elected—at twenty-three he was the youngest member of the legislature—TR set about making his mark. "He came in," one Albany politico recalled, "as if he had been ejected by a catapult." The assemblymen chortled at the foppish, bespectacled dandy who sought attention by calling, "Mr. Spee-kar!" in falsetto. Teddy, for his part, considered his new colleagues to be "vicious, stupid-looking scoundrels," though he soon got on well with (and was indeed fascinated by) the machine politicians.

Placed on the powerful City Affairs Committee, Roosevelt worked hard for his wealthy constituents. He opposed salary increases for New York police and firemen, opposed establishing a minimum wage of two dollars a day for municipal workers, and opposed Knights of Labor attempts to improve working conditions for railroad men. Hailed in city clubs as a watchdog, denounced in labor circles as a silk-stocking tool, he announced grandly that "I represent neither capital nor labor," and at times he did prove hard to type, as when he bitterly denounced Jay Gould as a member "of that most dangerous of all dangerous classes, the wealthy criminal class."

On another occasion, Samuel Gompers of the Cigarmakers Union proposed a bill to outlaw tenement house cigar work, and it was referred to a subcommittee where Roosevelt was expected to make short work it. Gompers, however, presented evidence of horrifying conditions that he had gleaned from a house-to-house survey of the bohemian tenements, disguised as a book agent selling a set of Dickens. The union leader offered to take Roosevelt around to see for himself, and the dapper young legislator agreed. The tour shocked Roosevelt profoundly. To the amazement of his colleagues and constituents, and to Gompers's delight, he supported the bill despite its being "in a certain sense a socialistic one" and got it signed into law. It was soon overturned by the courts, however, partly on the grounds it endangered the cigarmaker's "morals by forcing him from his home and its hallowed associations."

Mainly, however, Roosevelt concentrated on Good Government. His first success was a law reorganizing Brooklyn's government that stripped the appointment power from the aldermen, Boss McGlaughlin's creatures, and gave it to the mayor, along with authority to sack his appointees. He chaired a committee that investigated Manhattan's governance, found it "absolutely appalling," and in 1884 won passage of civil service reform.

With this triumph, his legislative career came to a sudden and tragic end. After his wife Alice died of Bright's disease, almost simultaneously with the death of his mother from typhoid fever, Roosevelt resigned, sold his house, and spent much of the next two years in the Dakota Territory. But in 1886, when his old constituents needed a candidate to take on Henry George, Teddy rode out of retirement. Nominated by Chauncey Depew at a convention presided over by corporation lawyer Elihu Root, Roosevelt promised an end to municipal corruption and the beginning of businesslike administration. The *New York Times* endorsed him and predicted the "uptown vote" would rally "to effectually squelch communism and socialism."

Soon, indeed, Wall Street businessmen organized a Roosevelt Club, and the Stock Exchange, Produce Exchange, Real Estate Exchange, and Iron and Metal Exchange promised their support. The Union League Club endorsed him. Dry-goods men held rallies. With the setting up of Roosevelt campaign headquarters at the Fifth Avenue Hotel, Fifth Avenue's white knight, now known familiarly as the "Cowboy Candidate," was well launched.

BOSSES, BISHOPS, AND THE MAN OF IRON

The roster of mayoral candidates was not yet complete, however. The organized working class and the organized bourgeoisie had sent in contenders. But the Irish-American middle class, whose nascent power was manifested through the Democratic Party and the Catholic Church, two warily interlaced institutions, had at least as much riding on the outcome.

In the late 1870s and early 1880s, John Kelly had centralized and disciplined Tammany beyond Tweed's fondest imaginings. He also continued the business community's program of cutbacks, thus enhancing the Democracy's standing and making it a more respectable outlet for middle-class Irish ambitions. Kelly did not, however, command sufficient financial resources to do without the well-heeled Swallowtail Democrats. From their Manhattan Club headquarters, now housed in A. T. Stewart's old marble mansion on Fifth Avenue and 34th Street, men such as iron and steel manufacturers Abram Hewitt and Edward Cooper, corporate attorney Samuel Tilden, and banker-railroad investor August Belmont still wielded great power. These Protestant businessmen and professionals had access to campaign funds, a social standing that reassured the city's creditors, an avenue to newspapers, a capacity to dispense patronage in their own enterprises, and powerful connections to the national Democratic Party.

Indeed it was national politics that motivated the Swallowtails to contest Tammany for power in the city. As importers and exporters, manufacturers who relied on imported raw materials, bankers, and railroad investors, they were vitally interested in lower tariffs, hard money, and federal aid to commerce through improved harbors, harbor defenses, coastal surveys, and foreign consulates. Given the equilibrium between Democrats and Republicans at the federal level, New York State was often the most important swing state in a presidential election, and with New York City casting a larger proportion of its state's vote than any other American city, it had provided the margin of national victory in 1880 and 1884, had come close to doing so in 1876, and would again in 1888 and 1892. It was no surprise that the major parties repeatedly nominated candidates for president and vice-president who might attract metropolitan voters.

Tammany had strengthened itself vis-à-vis the Swallowtails by expanding its political base in the burgeoning Irish middle class—appealing to its fraternal organizations and actively cultivating an ethno-religious identity. Under Kelly, who married Cardinal McCloskey's niece, the Democratic Party arranged for public funding of parish activities, particularly parochial schools. In 1880 Kelly's forces elected Swallowtail William R. Grace, perhaps America's most successful Irish immigrant. Grace had left his family's prosperous County Cork estate, went to sea, roved the world, and ended up in Peru, working for a ship chandler's firm, of which he and his brother eventually took control. He moved to New York City in 1865 and founded his own firm, W. R. Grace and Company, to cooperate with his brother's operation and made a vast fortune supplying the Peruvian military and in the South American trade. His election as the city's first Irish Catholic mayor, over the vocally expressed concerns of Protestants that he would help Archbishop Corrigan build a parochial school empire, helped cement Tammany-Church relations.

Kelly died in June 1886, just before the mayoral race got underway, and was replaced at the party's helm by Richard Croker, his right-hand man and former Tammany bruiser. Croker, born in 1843 in Clonakilty, Ireland, was brought to New York at the age of three. The family had lived in Seneca Village until his father got a veterinarian job with an East Side horsecar line. After a year's schooling, young Croker worked in the Harlem Railroad's machine shop and later as engineer on a steamboat. A formidable fighter, Croker also led the Fourth Avenue Tunnel Gang, whose members served as Tammany musclemen and repeaters. He cast his first ballot in 1864, in fact seventeen of them, and in 1868 he became an alderman at age twenty-five. In 1873, thanks to his new patron Kelly, he was elected coroner of New York; ten years later he was made fire commissioner, and in 1886 Croker stepped into the leadership—and into a full-blown crisis.

The United Labor Party presented a potentially mortal threat to the nexus of Catholics, Democrats, and the Irish-American middle class, if it succeeded in reorganizing New York City politics along class rather than ethnic lines. George was backed by Land League nationalists like Patrick Ford and Michael Davitt and by radical priests like Father McGlynn. If the Irish working class followed their lead and abandoned Tammany, it would leave the bosses high and dry. In addition, many an Irish alderman, grocer, and saloonkeeper was deeply invested in uptown real estate, and such men, perhaps even more than upper-class landlords, were banking on precisely the kind of speculative profits that George threatened to tax away.

Croker understood that solid Swallowtail backing was essential to defeating George, so he insisted on nominating ironmaster Abram Hewitt, the impeccably respectable leader of that opposing faction. The Democratic candidate proceeded to attack the very notion of a labor party as an attempt "to organize one class of our citizens against all other classes." Between capitalists and laborers "there never is and never can be any antagonism," but if the working classes "as they are called" ever did need special representation, they had their trade unions to speak for them.

Unions were perfectly legitimate bodies, Hewitt admitted, though he himself thought "self-help is the remedy for all the evils of which men complain." Certainly Hewitt had a deeper sympathy for workingmen than many of his peers, certainly more than did Theodore Roosevelt. A paternalistic employer, he had kept mills open and men employed during recessions. As congressman during the Great Strike of 1877, he hadn't howled for blood but held congressional hearings, which demonstrated that industrial interests had cheated and abused labor.

Being the son-in-law of the revered Peter Cooper won him additional support among the city's laboring classes, and Hewitt held up his family's support for Cooper Union as an example of responsible charity. He went so far as to criticize the Astors for failing to devote their "unearned increment" to public purposes. He even agreed with George that the city ought to provide education and recreational facilities out of its own coffers. The way to obtain the needed funds, however, was not by taxing land, which Hewitt noted shrewdly would put the burden on modest property holders as well as millionaires. Instead the city should tax the *mansions* of the wealthy, a levy he was sure the rich wouldn't mind paying once Tammany was vanquished.

To working-class constituents Hewitt insisted that despite his considerable wealth, he wasn't the millionaire's candidate: "These rich Republicans and these rich millionaires—nay, have they not at the Union League Club indorsed Mr. Roosevelt?" At the same time he crudely appealed to the fears of the propertied classes, indicting the United Labor Party as "anarchists, nihilists, communists, socialists" who were "enemies of civilization and social order." George's theories, if put into practice, would recall "the horrors of the French Revolution and the atrocities of the Commune." These accusations, though false, proved effective.

Stung by such charges, and with three days left in the campaign, the United Labor Party arranged a grand parade to demonstrate its responsibility. On Saturday, October 30, tens of thousands converged on the Bowery and formed into disciplined ranks. As the Printers Legion led off toward Cooper Union, a light mist gave way to heavy rain. Undeterred, hoisting their bedraggled banners and transparencies, unionists fed into the line of march, forming a human river, two miles long, of tailors, plumbers, painters, brass workers, framers, street railway workers, Cuban cigarmakers, Italian fruit handlers, Bohemian single taxers, and German cooperationists (pushing a huge broom, with which to sweep the election).

As they strode into Union Square, in a cold and drenching downpour, their signs—illuminated by sputtering torches, calcium lights, and colored fires—were clearly visible: THE WORKERS OF THE CITY ARE NOT ANARCHISTS! THE SPIRIT OF '76 STILL LIVES! and George's own campaign slogan: HONEST LABOR AGAINST THIEVING LANDLORDS AND POLITICIANS—THE LAND BELONGS TO THE PEOPLE! As they swung into the last leg heading toward Tompkins Square, their chants rang out over the driving storm: "Hi! Ho! The leeches must go!" and "George! George! Hen-ry George!"

The next day, Sunday, an alarmed Tammany Hall turned to the Church for assistance. Archbishop Corrigan was loathe to appear in cahoots with Boss Croker, but the situation was critical. Only the hierarchy could possibly counter McGlynn's enormous influence. On September 29 Corrigan had forbidden McGlynn from speaking at a scheduled George rally at Chickering Hall. McGlynn insisted on fulfilling his commitment, telling the archbishop that "I, in view of my rights and duties as a citizen, which were not surrendered when I became a priest, am determined to do what I can to support Mr. George." Two days later, Corrigan suspended McGlynn. The pastor of St. Stephen's made no more speeches for the rest of the campaign but continued to make highly visible appearances at United Labor Party rallies.

The vicar-general, the Right Rev. Monsignor Thomas S. Preston, was authorized to make a forceful preelection statement of Church policy. "The great majority of the Catholic clergy of this city," Preston asserted, "are opposed to the candidacy of Mr. George." Gleeful Tammanyites reproduced Preston's statement and handed it out on Sunday morning in front of Catholic churches.

DENOUEMENT

On Tuesday, November 2, voters trooped to the polls while a mute McGlynn rode through the streets with George, and United Labor Party volunteers oversaw the election process as well as they were able. Hewitt won with 90,552 votes. George came second with 68,110. Roosevelt finished last with 60,435.

George ran best among the second-generation German-and Irish-American working classes of the Lower East Side and Hell's Kitchen. He did especially well with Catholics, who provided perhaps five-sixths of his support. But the poorest, most recent immigrants in the gashouse and slum districts along the East River—motivated by the carrot of Tammany patronage and the stick of Church denunciation—went with Hewitt. George talked well, but these were practical people, and it was the Democratic Party, and its associated network of tenement-world notables like saloonkeepers, grocers, builders, and contractors, that responded most effectively to their day-to-day needs with jobs, credit, legal help, and holiday handouts.

Roosevelt's vote was down by as much as twenty thousand from the usual Republican level. Apparently many wealthy Republican voters, terrified at the prospect of a George victory, switched to Hewitt, who did well in the silk-stocking districts and middle-income wards.

Despite the loss, George and his supporters were ecstatic. Labor editor John Swinton pointed out that they had "struck a blow truly astounding under the circumstances." The *World* agreed that it was "an extraordinary thing for a man without political backing, without a machine, without money or newspaper support" to have polled so many votes. The defeated candidate was convinced that the future was his. "This is the Bunker hill," George crowed. "We have lit a fire that will never go out."

In fact the flame flickered for a year or two, sputtered, and died. The United Labor Party ran George in 1887 for statewide office, but during the campaign the 1886 coalition fragmented into its constituent parts.

First to go were the socialists. George and his single-tax followers, never comfortable with their militant class politics, soon read the Germans out of the party. The socialists retreated to their base in Kleindeutschland, where, amid the post-Haymarket wave of nativist hysteria, they languished, isolated, demoralized, riven by factional brawls. Within a few years, German hegemony in the Socialist Party and socialist press was finished, but not before they passed the torch to a new generation of New Yorkers—chiefly Jewish immigrants—who would carry the red banner into a new century.

The Knights of Labor never recovered from being tagged with the anarchist label. In the red scare that followed Haymarket, the organization disintegrated almost as rapidly as it had grown. Gompers and the business unionists went their own way, now *totally* persuaded that workers should shun politics. Gompers threw all his energies into building up the new American Federation of Labor. In the 1890s he would accept the free market economy, viciously attack former socialist comrades, and, despite his earlier inclination for a multiethnic, multiracial organization, preside over the growth of an exclusionary bastion for craft workers. The cigarmakers would fail to overcome the structural problems in their industry—tenement shops remained and flourished—but they would win the eight-hour day and a steady increase in pay.

The year 1887 also witnessed the collapse of Catholic support for class-based politics. Archbishop Corrigan saw to that. After the election he issued a pastoral letter counseling parishioners to adopt "the loving docility that becomes dutiful children" and "give no ear to those, whoever they may be, who preach a different Gospel." Father McGlynn responded by giving weekly orations to crowds of two to three thousand people in which he insisted that bishops, even the pope, shouldn't interfere with American Catholics' exercise of their political rights. After some priests gave McGlynn guarded support, Corrigan and the Vatican decided to heed an adviser who said, "Dr. McGlynn must be put down or the Archbishop of New York might as well not be Archbishop of New York."

McGlynn was summoned to Rome, refused to go, and in January 1887 was removed from his post at St. Stephen's. Thousands paraded in his support. He told the throng he would not obey the pope. On July 3 he was excommunicated. The archbishop circulated a pledge of loyalty for the priesthood to sign. Some refused and found themselves exiled to upstate parishes. So effectively did Corrigan assert the hierarchy's power that no Catholic clergyman in New York would ever again repeat McGlynn's defiance.

Corrigan went after the rebel priest's lay supporters too. He told Catholics that George's writings were "false and pernicious"—he tried to get them placed on the Index—and forbade attendance at meetings of the Anti-Poverty Society, McGlynn's secular reform vehicle. Corrigan ousted supporters of George from the thousand-member Catholic Club, making it a bulwark of lay support for archdiocesan officials. The pressure was so fierce that even Patrick Ford took the *Irish World* back into the fold. As Corrigan warred on liberalism in theology and social practice, he also emerged as a major backer of the Vatican. The archbishop strongly pushed Peter's Pence collections among his wealthier parishioners, an important source of income now that the Papal States had been lost. He also agreed to manage Vatican investments, yet another manifestation of New York's importance as a financial center. By the time Corrigan was finished, the metropolis had been solidly established as the bastion of conservatism in the American Church.

As to the candidates themselves: George, after his disappointing 1887 loss, and an abortive attempt to build a national labor party, formed local clubs to promote the single-tax movement and worked for free trade within the Democratic Party. One of his most ardent followers, Philip G. Hubert, founded the cooperative apartment movement, thus making the Chelsea Hotel an indirect Georgian legacy.

Roosevelt went back to reform work and served as a federal civil service commissioner between 1889 and 1895. He would be heard from again.

Hewitt, the victor, began his mayoralty by pushing a program of harbor, street, and rapid transit improvements designed to aid commerce and provide public works jobs. But his administration soon ran aground. When balked in his reforms, Hewitt, a notoriously obstinate and ill-tempered man given to fits of pique and bursts of anger, vituperatively turned on his 1886 constituents. Having at first channeled Croker some patronage, he cut off the supply. Having made bows to working people, he denounced the Knights of Labor.

Most dramatic, Hewitt reverted to his nativist roots. He pushed for a literacy test and a twenty-one-year naturalization period for immigrants and decreed the closing of small saloons on Sundays. He flatly refused to review the St. Patrick's Day Parade, something every mayor had done for thirty-seven years. He even refused to fly the shamrock flag at City Hall that day and starchily told his largely Irish Board of Alder- men that "America should be governed by Americans" and that those who preferred another flag should go back where they came from. In the end, it was Hewitt who was sent back where he came from. Croker refused to renominate him, and when the Swal- lowtails ran him as an independent, he was trounced at the polls.

THE NEW TAMMANY HALL

The biggest winner of the Henry George election was Tammany Hall, which learned a great deal from its near-loss. What impressed Democrats most about the United Labor Party was not its principles but its organization—the network of union locals, Knights of Labor assemblies, and labor clubs the upstart party fielded. They noticed that one Tammany ward that held its own in 1886 had done so by adopting elements of the ULP approach. Henry Purroy, boss of the Twenty-fourth Ward up in the Annexed District, had established a clubhouse in place of the usual saloon. Purroy had also involved the voters' wives and children on excursions, clambakes, and the like, making the party as much a cultural organization as a political one.

After 1886 Tammany extended this approach throughout the city. By 1893 there was a clubhouse in every Assembly District, all of them linked in the Associated Tam- many Societies, with a *Tammany Times* to report on their activities. The clubs replaced the personal and perishable followings of saloonkeepers and gang leaders and gave a bureaucratic underpinning to the machine. They also gave the party an air of respectability, making it more like the American Legion or the Elks than a bunch of brawlers. Clubs also strengthened the leadership, by making it difficult for insurgents without club endorsements to break into politics. Those who wanted construction and carting work or clerical and professional jobs with the city were well advised to join their local party association, as patronage rewards were now reserved for those who labored long and hard in clubhouse vineyards.

There was patronage aplenty under the dispensation of Croker's protégé Hugh J. Grant, the man who rebuffed Hewitt's try for a second term in 1888. Grant, the first New York-born, Irish-American mayor, came from solid middle-class stock. His immi- grant father had accumulated a string of successful saloons and left him a substantial inheritance. Grant graduated from St. Francis Xavier and Columbia Law, invested in Upper West Side real estate, built a base of support among Irish-American fraternal organizations, and became a Tammany District Leader and loyal Crokerite—a whole new route to municipal power.

Croker renominated Grant, got him reelected in 1890, then passed the baton to Thomas Francis Gilroy in 1892. Gilroy's rise was even more heavily dependent on the machine, as his background was more plebeian than his predecessor's. The Irish-born Gilroy, brought to New York as a child, attended public school, worked as a printer's apprentice, then worked his way up through the political ranks, serving as a Tweed mes- senger boy, holding a series of county and court clerkships, becoming district leader on the Upper East Side, then, in 1886, rising to undersheriff of New York County, before being elevated to the mayoralty.

Grant gave virtual control of all city offices and contracts to Croker, who started by making himself city chamberlain at twenty-five thousand dollars a year. With patronage resources beyond anything Kelly or Tweed ever dreamed of, Croker strengthened his control over political officials. No longer would Tammany leaders have to bribe Democratic aldermen into doing their bidding; from 1888 on the complaisant board took its orders from Croker.

Command over twelve thousand city workers also gave the machine a source of campaign funds (via mandatory assessments) and a vast reservoir of election day labor power. This electoral army was supplemented with the aid of a quarter-million dollars of public money allotted to "poll watching." Technically controlled by police captains in each precinct, it was doled out to voters at the direction of District Leaders, with perhaps 20 percent of the Democratic electorate on the receiving end. City government had, to a significant degree, become an affair of patrons and clients.

This process of consolidation—like the one taking place in the corporate world— was never complete. Croker could not rule absolutely because District Leaders retained power in their own domain. He would have to deal with proconsuls like Big Tim Sullivan, baron of the Bowery, and George Washington Plunkitt, boss of Hell's Kitchen. Archbishop Corrigan, who carried out a parallel consolidation in the ecclesiastical realm, did far better than either Croker or Morgan.

Tammany's new strength did allow its Irish-American leaders to crush their longtime partner-opponents, the Swallowtail Democrats, and their stronghold, the County Democracy, expired in 1892. Independence required Irish-American politicians to develop alternate sources of income. One solution was the establishment of an informal "vice tax," with the machine offering police protection to gamblers and prostitutes in exchange for cash. Payoffs helped fill Tammany coffers from the late 1880s on, but as the politicians would soon discover, such revenue came with risks of its own.

The other source of working capital was the business community. The rise of powerful corporate entities was aided by, and in turn encouraged, the parallel centralization of political power. In the past, businessmen in search of favors had bribed individual aldermen or state legislators, not Tammany bosses. When Jacob Sharp went after his Broadway franchise, almost all the boodle board lined up for a cut, which was annoying, expensive, and problematic, as one could never be sure the bribed would stay bought. Now men like William Whitney could go straight to the top and achieve in a day what had taken Sharp years.

The utilities became Tammany's greatest source of income. Whitney and Ryan of the Manhattan Elevated Railroad provided top politicos with hefty lawyer's fees, stock market tips, contracts for their construction companies, and pieces of the action in Metropolitan's financial deals. They were amply repaid with valuable franchises, maintenance of high fares, and blockage of utilities reform. Upstate too, after Tammany solidified control of both houses in 1892, corporations seeking favors paid "campaign contributions" to him, not legislators, and Croker then distributed the largesse. Republican boss Thomas Platt adopted the same system and indeed worked closely with Croker.

The old shanty dweller did quite well in the new order. He joined the elite and adopted its favorite hobby of raising thoroughbred horses. By the end of 1893 Croker had a $250,000 stock farm, $103,000 worth of race horses, and an eighty-thousand-dollar mansion on Fifth Avenue. Like other monopolists, he justified his personal gains by pointing to larger social benefits. As he explained the merits of his new system to Lincoln Steffens, a young reporter: "A business man wants to do business with one man, and one who is always there to remember and carry on the business." *The Bankers Magazine* agreed: bosses were mercenaries, no doubt, but they offered "financial corporations" the protection of "a Rob Roy who could control the legislative marauders."

Croker made peace with the city's working class as well. Tammany arranged some legislative overtures that redressed some of labor's grievances, and between 1887 and 1894 laws improved working conditions for streetcar workers and provided for arbitration of some labor disputes. But Democratic interventions tended more toward the rhetorical than the substantive. Tammany became the Friend of the Working Man, but not of workingmen. Democratic Party energies—over and under the table—concentrated on maintaining a pro-business climate, particularly low taxes and freedom from regulation. Thomas Byrnes's police continued to deal ferociously with labor unrest and break up radical meetings while tolerating grafters and boodlers. Armories proliferated, like the Twenty-second Regiment's fortified new home at 67th and Broadway (1890), which had slits for cannons and a main entrance that afforded easy passage for cavalry troops. By the mid-1890s New York had 12,800 National Guardsmen, specially trained in riot suppression, and available too as a strikebreaking force, as its mostly middle-class members had been carefully screened. "Are you connected in any way with any labor organization?" each applicant to Brooklyn's Forty-seventh Regiment was asked, and anyone who responded positively was rejected.

The new Democratic Party would be of but not for labor. The failure of Henry George's campaign meant there would be no Labor Party in New York City of the sort taking shape in Britain and Germany. Nevertheless, as Teddy Roosevelt observed dolefully after the 1886 election, while the large vote for George did "not mean a new party," it did constitute, "unfortunately, a new element to be bid for by the old parties."

The alliance of Irish-, German-, and Anglo-American workers forged in the labor and political wars of the mid-1880s had laid out an agenda for transforming the city. It had sought changes in work, transportation, communication, housing, taxation, health care, sanitation, charity, education, policing, and the organization of politics—stressing the need for government provision of social services by using tax revenues or undertaking full-scale "municipalization" of private businesses.

In 1886 the labor radicals failed to force Tammany, much less Albany, to significantly address their concerns. But reinforcements were arriving. Ships in the harbor had begun disembarking tens of thousands of Germans, Irish, and Britons, along with hundreds of thousands of Eastern European Jews and Southern Italians. Once again, as in the 1840s and 1850s, a vast second city was rising alongside the existing one.

At first this would hamper radical initiatives, as the newcomers had no shared history with New York's established workforce, had not forged links in the course of common struggle, and often had but limited command of English. But many brought militant traditions of their own and quickly discovered interests in common. When working-class New Yorkers succeeded in overcoming the latest set of barriers to cooperation, the pressures on Tammany would mount once again, until, in the new century, the machine would find itself forced into adopting policies advanced by the radicals of '86.

63

The New Immigrants

Between 1865 and 1873 over two hundred thousand migrants had arrived in New York City each year. The depression pummeled these numbers downward—in 1877 only sixty-three thousand immigrants passed through Castle Garden— but with the return of prosperity the influx soon set new records.

The old state-run system for processing newcomers buckled, and in 1890 the new federal Bureau of Immigration took over the task. The bureau, surveying the harbor for a site to replace the overburdened Castle Garden, settled on Ellis Island, newly swollen with landfill, and on January 1, 1892, the new immigration station began screening steerage passengers. First- and second-class arrivees were handled onboard ship and allowed to disembark directly on Manhattan. That first year, 445,987 passed through Ellis. By 1897 some 1,500,000 had threaded their way through examinations designed to weed out criminals, lunatics, and potential paupers.

The great bulk of new immigration came from old sources, with German migration actually reaching its peak in the 1880s. Farmers and farm laborers came from Germany's north and east, uprooted by the ongoing commercialization of agriculture and declining wheat prices. Artisans undercut by factory production left towns and villages, found industrial centers in Silesia and the Ruhr valley as yet unable to accommodate them, and crossed the Atlantic in force (some fleeing the antisocialist laws).

In the 1880s 1,445,181 Germans arrived, constituting 27.5 percent of the total incoming migrant stream, and of these, fifty-five thousand stayed in New York City, a figure that doubled in the 1890s. The German-born population rose steadily from 119,964 (in 1860) to 151,203 (in 1870), 163,482 (in 1880), and 210,723 (in 1890), before leaping to its peak (in 1900) at 324,224.

Collectively—and German unification made provincial groups more conscious of their commonalities—German New York stood third behind Berlin and Vienna as a German-speaking metropolis. Kleindeutschland continued to bulk large as a cultural community—so many lived within its German universe that assimilation proceeded quite slowly—but its spatial boundaries shifted. Kleindeutschland proper shrank to a truncated parallelogram bounded by 14th, Grand, Broadway, and the East River. Second-generation Germans continued their uptown exodus to the East Side (between Central Park and the river) and to Brooklyn (especially Williamsburg), where over one-third the German population lived.

Irish emigration was rekindled too, as agricultural depression in the late 1870s raised the specter of another famine. Emerald Isle reinforcements kept the combined Irish-born population of New York and Brooklyn hovering above the quarter-million mark, rising slightly from 260,450 in 1860 to 275,156 in 1890 (an estimated seventy thousand of them Gaelic speakers). While this represented a decline in natal Irish people as a percentage of the total population—from 24 percent to 12 percent—New Yorkers of Irish extraction constituted some 40 percent of the city in the mid-1880s, 5 percent more than the second-ranked German Americans. The metropolitan area thus retained a pronounced Irish flavor, with the heaviest concentrations in Manhattan's Hell's Kitchen (between 34th and 57th streets, Ninth and Twelfth avenues) and in Brooklyn's Navy Yard and Red Hook areas.

Not all newcomers came through Castle Garden or Ellis Island. African Americans continued to leave the South—over eighty thousand departed between 1870 and 1890, over a hundred thousand in the 1890s alone—and the small but steady influx began to replenish both New York's and Brooklyn's black communities. Still, the two cities had just 60,666 African Americans resident in 1900—less than 2 percent of the total population. In addition, there were 3,552 foreign-born blacks on hand in 1900, most of them recently arrived from the West Indies, the largest such settlement in the United States. The Tenderloin and San Juan Hill in the west 60s hosted the majority of black Manhattanites.

Despite obvious differences, all these groups shared two broad characteristics: their members came, by and large, from small-town or rural hinterlands thrown into turmoil by an advancing capitalist global economy, and they were tossed abruptly into an urban American environment for which they had little preparation. In both these regards, they had much in common with three more novel streams of arriving immigrants: Eastern European Jews, southern Italians, and Chinese.

SHTETLS UNDER SIEGE

For centuries the Jews of the Russian empire had been channeled, by law and prejudice, into particular spaces and particular functions. Territorially, they had been restricted to the Pale of Settlement, which stretched from the Ukraine on the Black Sea up to Lithuania on the Baltic. Within the Pale Jews had been tied to shtetls—market towns—where they provided services to the surrounding peasantry. Shtetl Jews ran shops and weekly markets; peddled goods to the countryside; administered inns, mills, taverns, and estates; and worked as tailors, cobblers, cabinetmakers, metalworkers, weavers, tanners, watchmakers, and bakers.

Jewish islands in a gentile sea, the shtetls survived through community self-help, disciplined religious devotions, and maintenance of rigid class and gender hierarchies. An elite alliance of learned scholars and the wealthy organized rituals and regulations in the holy language of Hebrew. These leaders looked down on the mass of laborers, denigrating both their trades and their language—a vernacular dialect, just coming to be known as Yiddish, borrowed from German and other European tongues. Lowest in prestige were the women, whose labor made men's study possible but who were themselves barred from becoming scholars. Wives managed fiscal affairs, worked in markets and shops, peddled, made their own and their children's clothes, ran the home, performed household religious rituals, and took charge of charity.

The shtetls survived internal strains and external pressures, but imperial liberalization, intended to drag Russia into the Western capitalist world, proved their undoing. Emancipation of the serfs in 1863 undercut Jews who had served as agents of the nobility. Railroads brought the products of urban (particularly German) factories to the Pale, supplanting rough-hewn artisanal output. Trains also brought cheaper grain from faraway markets, debilitating the peasant economy that sustained the shtetls. City-based commercial and financial enterprises grew, undermining shtetl merchants and moneylenders.

Artisans were hardest hit. Tailors, cobblers, hatmakers—their skills obsolete—found themselves proletarianized. Even with wives and daughters working alongside them, they sank to the status of *luftmenschen*—men who lived on air—or lower still, to the ranks of the *schnorrers* (beggars). In some shtetls half the population was dependent on charity. To all this was added an intolerable population squeeze. Where there had been one million Jews in the Pale in 1800, there were a suffocating four million in 1880.

So Jews left the impoverished towns and villages and made their way to industrializing cities like Warsaw, Lodz, Bialystok, and Grodno. Some escapees went farther still, to America, that magical land that apparently respected labor and rejected religious oppression. But very few went to such lengths. The Orthodox rejected it as a *trayf* (ritually unclean) country, whose Jews had no respect for Orthodox traditions. Russified Jewish radicals preferred to stay and help populists and socialists transform all Russia.

Then came March 1, 1881. Czar Alexander's imperial carriage was rumbling along a St. Petersburg street, flanked by Cossack guards, when a young man threw a bomb among the horses' legs. Unharmed, Alexander stepped to the street to survey the situation. Now a second man charged him and detonated another bomb, mortally wounding the czar.

The Jewish community of St. Petersburg laid a silver wreath on Alexander's bier in thanks for his modest lightening of Russia's oppression of their people. But the assassination touched off a wave of reaction against their coreligionists. The peasantry identified Jews with rapacious capitalism, despite the fact that most Jews were among its casualties, while the rich blamed them for radical attacks on the established order.

Pogroms broke out, organized massacres unhindered and at times instigated by the government. Jews were beaten, killed. Jewish shops, dwellings, warehouses, and synagogues were attacked and destroyed. The worst violence took place in bulging urban centers like Yelizabetgrad, Kiev, and Warsaw. Over the next decade, new czarist policies imposed forced relocations, banned access to certain professions, restricted admission to the educational system, and, in 1891, forcibly expelled Jews from Kiev, Moscow, and other Russian cities.

These pogroms and policies precipitated flight, with many Jews opting for America. In 1881–82, thousands bolted from southern Russia across the Austrian border to Brody. From there European Jewry's charitable organizations passed many along to Bremen or Liverpool, where they boarded steamers heading to New York City. Over the next two decades, tens of thousands more made the trek on their own, escaping both sporadic repression and steady economic impoverishment.

In the 1870s roughly forty thousand Eastern European Jews had come to the United States. In the 1880s over two hundred thousand came; in the 1890s over three hundred thousand followed suit. Roughly 70 percent would settle in New York City, the major port of entry. In 1870 there had been about sixty thousand Jews in the metropolis, and by 1880 about eighty thousand. By the early 1890s that number had more than doubled, to nearly 170,000, and by the end of the decade it had reached 290,000—a phenomenal inrush that troubled New York's long-established German-Jewish community.

OCCIDENTALS, ORIENTALS

In the context of the rising anti-Semitism that characterized the late 1870s and early 1880s city, New York's German Jews, especially the more affluent among them, worried that the arriving masses would further undermine their decades-long drive for social acceptance. Such anxieties were not unreasonable. At first the wider metropolis rallied against Russian barbarism and anti-Semitism: a large protest meeting at Chickering Hall in 1882 denounced the pogroms, and the *Commercial Advertiser* suggested reprisals against the czarist regime. At the same time, however, faced with refugees who were far poorer and more exotic than had been imagined, less sympathetic opinions surfaced. A two-page cartoon in *Judge* that year depicted a "Ceremony of taking down the last sign of the Christians in New Jerusalem (Formerly New York)".

The temptation was therefore strong to underscore the differences between German "Hebrews," still widely respected, and "low-class Jews," who were increasingly suspect. Thus the Rev. Dr. J. Silverman complained in an 1889 lecture at Temple Emanu-El that the newcomers were "a standing menace" because their "loud ways and awkward gesticulations are naturally repulsive and repugnant to the refined American sensibilities." The "thoroughly acclimated American Jew," the *Hebrew Standard* agreed, "is closer to the Christian sentiment around him than to the Judaism of these miserable darkened Hebrews."

Real differences did exist. In Europe, those inspired by the Haskalah—an earlier German-Jewish enlightenment that had reconciled Jewish tradition to Western culture—had long rejected the power that shtetl rabbis, *melamdim* (teachers), and scholars retained in community affairs, considering it rigid and reactionary. In New York, many haut bourgeois Reform Jews, whose modes of observance had been moving steadily closer to those of their Protestant confreres, considered the Orthodox immigrants little better than fanatics. And even the Conservative Jews—those who balked at the Reform project and founded the Jewish Theological Seminary in 1886—were far more liberal in their theology than the arriving immigrants.

German Jews, moreover, had long contrasted their own progressive "Occidental civilization" with Russian "Orientalism." Now, made prouder than ever of their German inheritance by the triumphs of Bismarck's empire, many sought to distinguish themselves from Eastern Europeans on all fronts. They derided Yiddish as a "piggish jargon" and ridiculed newcomers as "kikes," as their names often ended in *ki*. Many detested the immigrants' dress and habits, which they thought unhygienic, and found them clannish, backward, and alien. To cultural disdain they added the class contempt that investment bankers and genteel merchants had for peddlers and tailors.

For all this, the Jewish old guard was torn between its class aspirations and its religious loyalties and increasingly began to respond to the combined pull of compassion, kinship, and *zedakah*, the charity required of every observant Jew. Emma Lazarus was the daughter of Moses Lazarus, a wealthy Sephardic New York sugar manufacturer and a founding member of the Knickerbocker Club. She was stung to read a piece in the *Century* magazine that bordered on blaming the victims of the 1881 riots for their own misfortunes, and she wrote a tart rebuttal. When those raising funds for the Statue of Liberty read it, they invited Lazarus to contribute a poem. In December 1883 she read her "New Colossus" at the National Academy of Design, a verse that reformulated the monument's meaning from spreading enlightenment to embracing immigrants. Unlike the forbiddingly masculine Colossus of Rhodes, Lazarus wrote, America's monument was a welcoming woman with "mild eyes"—a "Mother of Exiles"—who stood at "our sea-washed, sunset gates," our "golden door," lifting a lamp to beckon the "homeless" and the "tempest-tost"—whom she also characterized as the "wretched refuse" of Europe's "teeming shore."

Convinced that without some direct intervention on their part, that the city's ambivalent acceptance of "wretched refuse" might not long continue, and that they themselves would be irretrievably associated with the newcomers, New York's wealthy German Jews, for all their misgivings, shouldered responsibility for their impoverished and outlandish coreligionists. Jacob Schiff, B'nai B'rith, the Baron de Hirsch Fund, and the Union of American Hebrew Congregations (among others) underwrote the Hebrew Emigrant Aid Society's establishment of temporary shelters at Greenpoint and set up another barracks encampment on Ward's Island, in the grounds of the old lunatic asylum. A fledgling United Hebrew Charities extended direct aid to settlers, reaching one in ten. In 1892 the newly established Hebrew Immigrant Aid Society stationed a representative on Ellis Island to mediate with immigration officials and hand out advice bulletins to newcomers.

Traditionally, *zedakah* was blind. Donors did not know the identity of recipients and vice versa. This precluded using charity to influence or control beneficiaries. But influence was precisely what German-Jewish givers wanted—as did their counterparts in Protestant charities like the Association for Improving the Condition of the Poor or the Children's Aid Society. The immigrants "must be Americanized in spite of themselves," one uptowner wrote in the *Jewish Messenger*, "in the mode to be prescribed by their friends and benefactors."

In June 1889 a group including Jacob Schiff, Isaac Seligman, and Isidor Straus began to raise funds for a Hebrew Educational Alliance. It was conceived, in the consolidating spirit of the day, as a merger of the Hebrew Free School Association, the Young Men's Hebrew Association (which Oscar Straus had helped found in 1874 as a counterpoint to the Christian organization), and the Aguilar Free Library (founded for new arrivals in 1886, with the goal of "uplifting the mental and moral tone of a class that woefully lacks refining influences").

The organizers quickly deleted "Hebrew" from the Educational Alliance, which opened its five-story yellow brick building at Jefferson Street and East Broadway in 1891. They did, however, sponsor Hebrew classes for boys and girls, lest parents send them to a *cheder* (religious school), "where the general surroundings, considered from hygienic, moral and Americanizing standpoints," as the organization put it in 1894, "are of the very type which it is the chief aim of the Alliance to extirpate." They drew the line at Yiddish, though, banning its use until the end of the century. Within these parameters, the institute developed pioneering and popular programs—summer camps and arts classes and English and civics programs—which became a model for citizenship courses in public schools.

To another set of German Jews—merchants and manufacturers—the new immigrants seemed less a burden to uplift than a czar-sent opportunity. German Jews had come a long way from the secondhand shops of Baxter and Chatham Street: they now owned 80 percent of all retail and 90 percent of all wholesale clothing firms in the city. To these men, and the garment manufacturers who supplied their wares, the Eastern Europeans constituted a phenomenal supply of cheap labor. Some uptown philanthropies, like the United Hebrew Charities (UHC), stayed in close contact with leading manufacturers and actually funneled greenhorns into the garment business. The UHC gave quick and limited training to new arrivals, steered them to the shops, and on occasion deployed them to break strikes.

There was little need for coercion, however. Unskilled immigrants were well aware that the road to survival led literally to the garment district. Once past customs, most newcomers walked from the Battery up Broadway, turned right up Park Row at the General Post Office, and continued straight ahead along East Broadway, until they arrived at its conjuncture with Canal and Essex streets, a spot later known as Seward Square. Settling near there left them perfectly positioned to find work, for Canal Street was the center of the wholesale trade and Grand Street, two blocks north, was the axis of retailing.

In the 1880s New York's textile trades were undergoing yet another transition, which the Eastern Europeans spurred. In the mid-nineteenth century, men's clothing production had shifted from custom tailoring to ready-to-wear. In the 1880s it was women's wear's turn. The breakthrough came in cloakmaking; in the 1890s shirtwaist, skirt, and dress manufacturing followed suit. The number of women's clothing establishments ballooned from 230 in 1880 to 3,429 twenty years later, while men's shops continued their expansion, rising from 736 to 2,716 in the same period.

Production of both men's and women's clothing involved increasing mechanization and microdivision of labor. Before the Civil War, merchant-manufacturers had parceled out handcut fabric to skilled German and Irish craftsmen who, with the aid of their families, manually assembled the finished goods at home. Now German-Jewish manufacturers used the new rotary cutting machine (1874) to slice up materials in great quantities. Some finished up the garments in their own factories, employing young unmarried women (only 2 percent of Jewish wives worked outside their homes). But rents were high and the business seasonal, so ninety-seven out of a hundred cloak and suit houses turned cloth bundles over to German-Jewish or, increasingly, Russian-Jewish contractors, for transformation into ready-to-wear garments at a negotiated price.

A contractor then set up a workspace in a rented loft or his own tenement apartment. He rented or bought sewing machines—fifty to a hundred dollars would buy a few used Singers—or required employees to bring their own. Finally he supervised, and usually worked alongside, teams of eight to twenty semiskilled workers, ideally just off the boat. Labor in these "sweatshops" was broken down into thirty or more tasks, with machine work done by operators and needlework, basting, finishing, felling, and pressing reserved for the less skilled.

By 1895 there were roughly six thousand sweatshops in New York City and nine hundred in Brooklyn, employing perhaps eighty thousand workers. Given such fierce competition, few contractors did well. Each had to underbid the other, forcing all to operate so close to the margin that a slack season or a general economic downturn could wipe them out. In some years as many as one-third failed. Those who survived did so by relentlessly exploiting their workers. Contractors demanded six fourteen- to sixteen-hour days a week and drove wages down from fifteen dollars a week in 1883 to seven dollars in 1885.

Immigrant Jews accepted such conditions partly because the sweatshop environment was culturally compatible. They were not (always) forced to labor on the Sabbath; they could work with *landsmen* (fellow countrymen); they could keep their households intact—the family that sweated together stayed together. But mainly they had no choice in the matter. Many were unskilled, in poor health, and locked in competition with one another. Each day at eight A.M. the unemployed shaped up at the corner of Hester and Ludlow streets; the din of negotiating gave it the name of the Khazzer-Mark (pig market).

THE LOWER EAST SIDE

As newcomers poured in, Kleindeutschland morphed into the Lower East Side. The original Jewish quarter rapidly expanded outward from its core near the Canal, Hester, and Grand Street job markets. It spread west to the Bowery, east and south toward the river and warehouse districts, still Irish strongholds, and north to Delancey and beyond, pushing the remaining Germans ahead of it into the now shrunken "Dutchtown" that ran from Houston to 14th Street.

Within this terrain, ethnic subdivision was the rule. So many Russians clustered around the Canal to Grand Street core that by 1890, the old Tenth Ward, once predominantly German, was 70 percent Russian Jewish. Galicians roosted from Grand up to Houston; Hungarians occupied blocks north of Houston and east of Avenue B.

Inside this new if unofficial Pale, density soared as landlords subdivided old row houses into five or six apartments and stuffed in tenants. One house at Essex and York, split into sixteen apartments, warehoused two hundred. Bathrooms were scarce, coal and wood remained the main sources of fuel, kerosene provided lighting, and blocks of ice furnished refrigeration. More spacious five- or six-story tenements went up to house the slightly more affluent, offering reasonably adequate plumbing, heating, and ventilation. But their higher rents forced tenants to take in boarders, and soon these structures too were packed. By 1890 the Tenth Ward had 524 people per acre, the highest density in the city. Within ten years the figure would rise to seven hundred per acre, a rate that topped Bombay's as highest in the world.

Jews stayed packed like herrings in a barrel in part because they couldn't afford to commute. When job opportunities did open up in more hospitable surroundings, some moved out with alacrity. In the 1880s one such destination was Brownsville, in a faroff and still undeveloped section of Brooklyn. The little village of one- and two-family houses lay at the outlying end of Vaux and Olmsted's Eastern Parkway, where it ran into Pitkin Avenue. Here, just west of the orchards and farm fields beyond Rockaway Avenue, a Jewish real estate agent invested in local lots in the mid-1880s, persuaded some cloakmakers to set up shop, and began constructing rows of frame houses for workers (a hundred dollars down, ten dollars a month). By 1892 a Jewish community of four thousand Russians and Poles, complete with synagogues and fraternal organizations, had taken root.

Other newcomers followed trails blazed by Germans and headed to Williamsburg, to Yorkville (where cigar factories provided work), and to Harlem, where by 1890 thirteen hundred Russian and Polish Jews had settled into the Irish-German neighborhood west of Third Avenue. But in such outposts they would remain minorities, whereas the Lower East Side was emerging as a world the Jews had remade for themselves.

Concentration had its benefits. It guaranteed ethnic predominance and cultural familiarity. The streets were packed with *landsmen*, the stores emblazoned with Yiddish signs, the backyards stocked with chickens—it might have been Odessa. Street and cafe grapevines provided information about jobs. Housewives purchased fish, milk, tin, and bits of cloth from the omnipresent pushcarts. It required almost no capital to rent a cart, stock it at the Canal Street wholesalers, and make the rounds. Soon these peripatetic retailers settled down themselves. Hester Street, nestled between Grand and Canal, became the unofficial peddlers' concourse, jam-packed from end to end, patronized by immigrants familiar with European street markets. Soon Grand, Orchard, and Rivington had become open-air bazaars as well. Sex too was for sale here, and by the 1890s Jewish prostitutes worked Allen, Houston, and Delancey streets.

Some peddlers rose to become shopkeepers and served as grocers, bakers, and kosher butchers to the burgeoning community and the wider metropolis. By 1888 perhaps half the city's four thousand meat retailers and three hundred meat wholesalers

E. Idell Zeisloft, who published this photograph of Hester Street in *The New Metropolis* (1899), described it as "the wonderful market of the Ghetto. See it on Thursday afternoon and evening and Friday morning, when all the housewives are making their purchases for the Shabbas . . . a most picturesque spectacle." (General Research. The New York Public Library. Astor, Lenox and Tilden Foundations)

were Jewish. At a time when other eastern cities had come to depend on midwestern abattoirs, New York's demand for kosher meat sustained the metropolis as an important slaughtering center, and one firm, Schwartzchild and Sulzberger, emerged as a meatpacking giant. By 1890, a mere decade after mass settlement got underway, there were forty-three bakeries, fifty-eight bookshops, and 112 candy stores belonging to East European Jews. The latter dispensed seltzer, a less expensive version of soda water. It was tremendously popular among the generally nonalcoholically inclined Jews, prized as a complement to rich kosher diets (*belchwasser*, it was often called), and when mixed with chocolate syrup and milk, it got magically transformed into an "egg cream," neither of which it contained.

Orthodox Jews tried to resurrect the shtetl's religious life. They founded synagogues in profusion. Many were little more than storefronts or tenement rooms. Others were housed in recycled Protestant churches or German-Jewish synagogues. An exalted few were custom built: in 1886, the Herter brothers produced a glorious Moorish-Gothic-Romanesque temple at 14 Eldridge Street for the Polish Congregation Khal Adas Jeshurun. It was the first to be raised by Eastern European Jews on the Lower East Side.

With the synagogues came *talmudai torah* (religious schools), *chedarim* (Bible and Hebrew classes for young boys), and *mikvehs* (ritual baths). Key shtetl figures resurfaced as well: *shohets* (ritual slaughterers), *mohels* (circumcisors), and *hazzan* (cantors). Newspapers devoted to traditional ways flowered: the *Yidishe Gazetn* (1874), *Yidishe Tseitung* (1870), *Yidisher Tageblatt* (1890s). So did *chavarot* (mutual benefit societies) and *landsmanshaftn* (self-help groups organized on hometown lines, of which Bialystoker Center was the first). These organizations—housed in attics, basements, and storefronts—provided financial aid, funeral and cemetery benefits, loans, and communal centers.

Re-creating the Old World in the New proved difficult. Leaders were scarce: few Orthodox rabbis emigrated, and indigent scholars were forced to work. Followers were even harder to come by. Many *luftmenschen* immigrants had already been drawn to secularism in Europe. Now, in New York, many abandoned the old customs in a drive to become "regeleh Yankees": men stopped daily prayers, shed skullcaps, trimmed or shaved beards and sidelocks, and donned Prince Alberts, starched collars, and neckties. Young men were attracted to secular educational institutions, and a small trickle of East European Jews managed to join the several dozen German-Jewish boys who entered City College each year, at a time when the average class numbered fifty. Bernard Baruch graduated in 1889, and in the following years New York Jews developed a close attachment to the institution at Lexington and 23rd, despite its mediocre faculty, its Protestant moralism, and occasional anti-Semitic episodes.

Women doffed wigs and kerchiefs and adopted American fashions. Some even began to question shtetl dogmas about female inferiority, now that they were in a country that considered women elevated creatures. They were less taken, however, with the bourgeois American notion that women should be homebound and passive, accustomed as they were to breadwinning roles. By the early 1890s an estimated twenty thousand young Jewish women, largely American born, were employed as saleswomen, milliners, typists, bookkeepers, stenographers, and public or private school teachers.

By and large, Jewish secular radical intellectuals would have more impact on their countrymen than did Orthodox traditionalists. At first, however, intoxicated by New

York's cosmopolitanism and their newfound freedom from shtetl and czarist controls, the intellectuals devoted most of their attention to debating one another. Some were attracted by socialism, with its optimism, universalism, impressive learning, and ethical appeal, and Tammany was startled in 1886 by the heavy turnout of Jewish voters for Henry George. Others, like Emma Goldman, opted for anarchism. Goldman, a Lithuanian immigrant who had been sewing overcoats in Rochester for several years, arrived in New York during the summer of 1889 with a sewing machine and five dollars, rented a room on Suffolk Street, and plunged immediately into the political scene, determined, like Russian heroines, to "go to the people."

Inspired by the impromptu refusal (in 1882) of a group of newly arrived Jewish immigrants to scab on striking Irish longshoreman, the city's German socialists began holding mass meetings on Rivington Street. Abraham Cahan, a brash young Lithuanian immigrant and former cell member of Vilna's Narodnaya Volya, argued successfully that such lectures, to be effective, must be given in Yiddish. This led, with German socialist assistance, to the formation in 1886 of the *New Yorker Yiddishe Volks-Zeitung* and in 1888 of the United Hebrew Trades (UHT), both dedicated to helping the "Jewish proletariat . . . free itself more quickly from the filth of the pig market."

The UHT grew swiftly, due in large part to the efforts of Cahan, Morris Hillkowitz (later Hillquit), a twenty-year-old recently arrived shirtmaker who helped unionize tailors, cloakmakers, and pressers, and the flamboyant Joseph Barondess, self-styled king of the cloakmakers. Barondess affected the haughty, not to say arrogant, manners of a bohemian aristocrat, satisfying his followers' yearning for dramatic militancy, rather as Mike Walsh had done for the Irish half a century earlier. In the 1890 May Day celebrations, Barondess, mounted on a white horse, led his three thousand cloakmakers in a grand parade of nine thousand Jewish workers that marched to the "Marseillaise" up to Union Square, greeted by cheering bystanders waving red banners from windows.

Histrionics aside, with the aid of assistants like Emma Goldman, Barondess in 1890 led a strike by cutters and contractors against the Cloak Manufacturers Association and stood firm as well against the determined opposition of the United Hebrew Charities, which, when asked to extend relief to locked-out cloakmakers, reportedly said: "If they strike on account of their union, let them suffer for it . . . let them starve." ("Better the whip of *Fonye* [the Tsar]," snarled the *Arbeiter Zeitung*, "than the charity of Eighth Street.") In the end, Meyer Jonassen, New York's leading clothing manufacturer and a wealthy uptown German Jew, was forced to boost wages and recognize the union, though the terms excluded women, who were the bulk of his factory employees.

In the volatile garment industry, successes proved hard to sustain. Concessions were withdrawn, agreements broken. The year following Barondess's triumph, one of the largest manufacturers sent work to nonunion shops out in Jamaica, and Barondess himself was thrown in jail on a trumped-up charge. By the end of the 1890s, after a decade of intense activity and ferocious strikes, which were often widely supported in the community, little more than 15 percent of the garment workers belonged to unions.

Irish and German workingmen were slow to take Jewish unionists into their councils. To be sure, Yiddish speakers like Cahan were now invited to take a place alongside German and Irish orators at May Day parades, and the United German Trades helped promote the fledgling United Hebrew Trades. But it was hard to gainsay the fact that Jews were steadily if indirectly pushing German tailors and Irish dressmakers out of work. The older unionsts were even less happy with the Italians.

MEZZOGIORNO MISERIA

Steaming into New York harbor alongside vessels bearing Jewish immigrants were boats from Naples carrying refugees from southern Italy. In crucial respects their immigrant cargoes could not have been less alike. The Eastern Europeans were predominantly families, Jewish, and urban; the Italians mainly bachelors, Catholic, and rural. But both populations had been shaken out of entrenched situations by the economic and political storms sweeping across the European landscape.

Where the Jews had been trapped in the shtetls, southern Italians were mired in the isolated valleys and lowlands formed by the mountain chains into which the *mezzogiorno* was divided. Within these provincial pockets, society was frozen in a quasi-feudal mode. A handful of aristocrats owned the bulk of the land and exacted profit and prestige from peasant tenants as their forebears had done for centuries. With the higher clergy and professionals, they formed a tiny ruling elite, utterly uninterested in agricultural improvements. As a result, the *contadini* (peasants who leased land or owned small plots) and the *giornalieri* (day laborers) worked the soil essentially as their Roman ancestors had, with wooden plows.

The area also suffered from primitive housing conditions, illiteracy (perhaps the highest rate in Europe), microdivision of farm plots, an absence of public welfare programs, limited diet, earthquakes, deforestation, soil erosion, malaria, and harsh sirocco winds blowing up from North Africa. The result was *La Miseria*—a miserable, impoverished way of life.

To survive, local communities hunkered down into tight defensive units whose loyalties and interests traveled no farther than the sound of the village church bell. The bedrock institution was the intensely patriarchal family, whose members, with good reason, distrusted all outside and higher powers, ecclesiastical as well as secular. The southern Italians were dug into the baked soil as deeply as their olive and chestnut trees. As with the shtetl Jews, it took a powerful confluence of outside events to dislodge them.

Italian unification provided much of the impetus. The northerners dominating the new nation considered southerners little better than African barbarians, and just as available for colonial plundering. The authorities failed to provide roads or schools, which could help eliminate backward conditions, but siphoned off in taxes what capital and resources existed. Unification also abolished customs barriers and thus opened up the *mezzogiorno* to northern and European economic penetration.

Exposure to developed capitalism proved disastrous. Free trade destroyed fledgling industries. Commercial agriculture foundered too, as the inefficient orange and lemon growers of Calabria, Sicily, and Basilicata faced ruinous competition from growers in Florida and California.

Meanwhile—as in Eastern Europe—the population mounted steadily, rising 25 percent from the 1870s to the 1890s. Overpopulation, like unemployment, disease, oppression, and neglect, contributed to the growing realization that the region had been sentenced to lingering death. Beginning slowly in the 1870s, therefore, and picking up steam in the 1880s and 1890s, southern Italian cultivators and laborers and a smaller number of artisans began making their way to the United States. Overwhelmingly—between 75 and 90 percent depending on the year—they were single men between the ages of fourteen and forty-four, though single women also came, intent perhaps on earning a dowry and improving their prospects of finding a good husband when they returned. Overwhelmingly they were poor: in 1892 the average Italian arrived in America with eleven dollars in his pocket. And virtually all arrived in New York City.

MANHATTAN COLONIA

From the beginning of the Civil War until 1880, Italian immigration to the United States had never exceeded thirty-five hundred a year, predominantly from the northern provinces. Then, from 1881 to 1890, the average annual figure jumped to over thirty thousand. In the succeeding decade, Italians poured in at an annual average rate of sixty-five thousand, becoming the most numerous ethnic group entering the United States.

Not all Italians who landed at Castle Garden or, later, Ellis Island stayed in New York. But enough did to transform it into the Italo-American capital of the United States. In 1850 there had been a grand total of 833 Italians in the metropolis. By 1880 the figure had climbed to twenty thousand (of whom twelve thousand were foreign born). By 1900, after two decades of immigration and local reproduction, there would be a quarter-million Italian Americans living in New York City.

Residence meant something different for Italians than it did for Jews. Many young Italian men thought of themselves as migrant workers, perched here only temporarily. Many planned to and did return to Italy once they had saved enough to set themselves up with a farm; others retreated across the Atlantic for a breather—or permanently—when faced with economic adversity. Altogether during these decades perhaps forty-three of every hundred immigrants went back, becoming known, to those who had never left, as *Americani*.

Even while in-country, their primary mission of making money quickly led them to consider New York more home base than home. They moved about the country to wherever the jobs were, with their precise destinations arranged by *padroni*, the Italian equivalent of the Jewish garment contractors. The *padroni* packaged up gangs of Italian laborers in New York (and sometimes in Italy itself) and supplied them to corporate employers around the country, in mines, agriculture, railroads, and construction sites. During the winter, or in hard times, thousands of these seasonal laborers would either return to Italy or camp out in New York City.

Others never left the metropolis, where a substantial and growing number of jobs were available. Transplanted peasants avoided factory jobs, considering them physically confining, socially unrespectable, and personally demeaning, but they flocked to hard physical labor on the city's docks, roads, rapid transit lines, aqueducts, and building sites.

This invasion of New York's labor market met with mixed reactions from established workers. In the building trades the Italian takeover of casual day labor work (their share zoomed from 15 percent in 1883 to 75 percent in 1893) was accepted by Irish and German immigrants and their sons, who were busy consolidating their hold on the more highly skilled crafts of carpentering, plastering, and masonry. In public works, too, older immigrants gave ground with relative grace, abandoning such unskilled and unpleasant jobs as garbage scow trimming, ditch digging, snow shoveling, excavation, sewer laying, and hod carrying—until by 1890 perhaps 90 percent of the laborers employed by the Department of Public Works were Italian. Certain "service" jobs were also rapidly Italianized. By 1894 the great majority of barbers and streetcorner fruit vendors were Italians, as were 97 percent of the bootblacks—the latter job, like organ grinder assistant, reserved for children.

Other job niches were hotly contested. In the late 1880s and early 1890s, resolved to crack the Irish monopoly on longshore jobs, dock bosses began hiring Italians—especially during strikes—to take over the more menial work. The Italians were prepared to scab because they were transients, with little stake in transforming local labor conditions, and because they resented the union's discriminatory policies: its high fees, arduous apprenticeships, and obvious lack of interest in trying to win them over. This led to violent conflicts at job sites and to enduring bad blood between the two groups. Relations were better in the skilled trades, where Italian shoemakers, masons, bricklayers, stonecutters, and marble workers joined unions or mutual aid societies.

Italian women took jobs outside their homes in small tobacco or candy factories or in noxious shops where they glued paper boxes together. The great majority stayed (or were kept) at home in cramped tenements where they looked after kin and boarders or did needle-trades outwork. For wages one-third less than the already abysmal compensation paid Jewish seamstresses, they felled and finished garments or made artificial flowers.

To save money to bring over their wives, sisters, and parents, Italian men accepted wretched living conditions, especially as the meanest Manhattan life was often an improvement on what they'd left behind. They headed for slum streets just west of the Bowery (between Canal and Houston), where earlier poor Italian immigrants had settled in among the Irish, and worked as scavengers, selling their rags, bones, and cans to nearby junk dealers. By the late 1890s Italians had supplanted the Irish along Mulberry, Mott, Hester, Prince, and Elizabeth streets, making the "Mulberry Bend" area the most concentrated Italian "colony" in the city.

Slum landlords welcomed the new arrivals: no matter how cramped and squalid the housing, they paid their rent and seldom complained. A three-room apartment (at twelve dollars a month) might house sixteen: a husband, wife, four daughters, two sons, and eight male lodgers. A two-room apartment (eight dollars a month) could hold eleven: a widow, her son, and nine male lodgers.

As Mulberry Bend filled to bursting, the colony threw off satellite settlements. Some were virtually contiguous: newcomers spread north and west of Houston into Greenwich Village south of Washington Square, pushing remaining blacks out of the former Little Africa toward the Tenderloin. Others left Manhattan altogether. In Brooklyn they clustered near the Hamilton Ferry, along Union and President streets, near the docks, warehouses, and factories of Red Hook. Newcomers also went to Williamsburg, Greenpoint, Fort Greene, the Navy Yard area, and Sunset Park; by the end of the 1890s there were also small colonies in Astoria, Long Island City, and Flushing.

The preeminent offshoot was up in East Harlem. Italians came to northern Manhattan in the 1870s when an Irish American contractor building the First Avenue trolley tracks imported them as strikebreakers, and a workers' shantytown sprang up along the East River on 106th Street. As construction opportunities expanded in the booming Harlem community, Italians made their way to the wide-open uptown spaces. Wide open didn't mean pastoral: the area stank from gasworks, stockyards, and tar and garbage dumps. By the mid-1880s four thousand had arrived. They boarded with families or pooled expenses in all-male rooming houses where they shared cooking and washing, even made their own wine. By the end of the 1890s Italians had pushed north

A Black and Tan Dive on Thompson Street, photograph by Jacob Riis. As Italians moved into Greenwich Village, Riis wrote, the neighborhood once known as "Africa" was "fast becoming a modern Italy." (© Museum of the City of New York)

to 115th Street and west to Third Avenue, pressing hard against Irish, German, and Jewish neighborhoods.

Italian Harlem, unlike Mulberry Bend, was new enough for residents to leave their mark on it. *Paesani* settled near one another—Neapolitans between 106th and 108th, Basilicatans from 108th to 115th, Aviglianese at First Avenue and 112th—but a broader Italian community also emerged, with distinctive sights, sounds, and smells. The populace resisted Americanization (few became citizens), eschewed the English language (perhaps a third couldn't make themselves understood to natives), and foreswore Yankee clothing (women wore peasant costumes with red bandannas or yellow kerchiefs; men clung to traditional garb). People stuck close to the cultural shelter of the colony and when they traveled to lower Manhattan were apt to say: "I have been down to America today."

Community leadership fell to those who organized relations with "America": the *padroni* and the *banchiere*. The latter group was composed of immigrants who, having acquired some capital as grocers, barbers, or saloonkeepers, now set up as bankers. In addition to lending and changing money and transmitting funds to the old country, the *banchiere* provided a wide array of services, acting as travel agents, scribes, marriage brokers, and legal advisers. Together with the small number of better-off professionals—doctors, dentists, pharmacists, merchants, and lawyers—the *banchiere* and *padroni* dominated colony life. These *prominenti*, who owned or financed the mutual aid societies, community organizations, and ethnic newspapers, were highly conservative, concerned about their status, and antagonistic to working-class efforts at self-help. The leading newspaper, *Il Progresso Italo-Americano*, was founded in 1879 by Carlo Barsotti, a wealthy contractor-*padróne* who styled himself "his excellency Chevalier Carlo Barsotti." Under his leadership, the paper pugnaciously opposed unions, independent political parties, and any laws that would regulate *banchiere* or *padroni*. The leading mutual aid association, the Società Italiana di Beneficenza (1882), was also under the thumb of wealthy *prominenti* like its banker-*padróne* president, Commendatore Louis V. Fugazy ("Papa Fugazy"). In the ecclesiastical arena, however, immigrant workers took matters into their own hands.

THE MADONNA OF 115TH STREET

To the Irish hierarchy and Irish parishioners, their new coreligionists seemed barely Catholic at all. They seldom came to church, apart from baptisms, weddings, and funerals. In 1884 Archbishop Corrigan noted that of fifty thousand Italians in the New York area, not more than twelve hundred attended mass. In addition, the newcomers refused to contribute to the building programs Corrigan promoted, and they rejected his parochial schools in favor of the free public school system. The Italians had no great respect for priests, even their own, and were given to ribald speculations about clerical sins and to denunciations of priests as lazy hangers-on. Socialists objected to the Church's identification with wealthy landowners, nationalists to its opposition to Italian unification.

To the Irish, such "Catholics" seemed more than half pagan. Yet the Italians were capable of amazing devotion. The immigrant men filled their rooms with sacred images—pictures and statues of the Virgin and their hometown patron saints—which they either brought with them or sent home for. In their thousands of cramped rooms, laboring men set up little shrines at which they offered prayers for families left behind. Such intensely personal devotions were considered acceptable, if unorthodox. Far more shocking to Irish-American clerics was the way such practices spilled into the streets.

In the summer of 1881 immigrants from Polla formed a mutual aid society named after the Madonna del Carmine, the town's protectress. The following year they began annual *feste* in her honor. From 1883 these were held behind a 111th Street boardinghouse, at a little chapel in the back yard where ragpickers sorted, washed, and packed their daily hauls. In 1884 the confraternity—a lay organization—obtained from Polla a statue of the Madonna and turned their *festa* into a popular celebration.

The growing cult alarmed Bishop Corrigan and the Irish hierarchy. Now fully alive to the "Italian problem," the archdiocese invited to New York the Pallottine fathers who had been ministering to Italian immigrants in London. Their first priest, Father Emiliano Kirner, arrived in 1884 and was given care of the little 111th Street chapel. Father Kirner soon discovered the East Harlemites wanted to build a more beautiful and dignified residence for their patroness. He encouraged them, and soon the locals established the all-male Congregazione del Monte Carmelo della 115ma Strada. Its laborers and junkmen, after their own exhausting workdays were over, threw themselves into erecting a church with their own hands. When the masons' union objected to the use of free labor, neighborhood women took over the job.

The Church of Our Lady of Mount Carmel was the first Italian-built church in Manhattan. But because it was situated on the border with the Irish and German community, and the bulk of the funds for its construction had come from older immigrants, Italians were sent to the basement to worship. La Madonna too, her gown now covered with precious stones, was placed in *la chiesa inferiore*.

This exile to the lower depths rubbed against Italian sensibilities—already raw from their dealings with Irish foremen and contractors, or with Irish nuns who placed Italian parochial school children in the rear of the room. In part as spiritual defiance, the festival, and others that now sprouted around the city, grew to enormous proportions by the 1890s. Thousands flocked to the food and games, bands and dancing, costumes and parades. The gathering also provided a stabilizing center for dislocated migrants, and by parading La Madonna through the neighborhood's streets and parks they put their cultural stamp on a piece of the alien New York world.

The archdiocese remained dismayed by the cult's "pagan" quality, its barefoot faith, its flashy street religiosity. They resented the dominance of the Mount Carmel society over the *festa*, correctly seeing it as a lay challenge to ecclesiastical control over immigrant religious life. They were also unsettled by feast-day inversion of patriarchal proprieties. Normally, Italian street life was dominated by men, who milled in front of their regional and social clubs, playing boccie and card games, but during the *festa* of La Madonna women commanded the streets. Finally they feared the *festa* would hinder Italians' Americanization, a concern shared by German Jews vis-à-vis their Russian coreligionists.

In 1887 Archbishop Corrigan called for clerical reinforcements. He asked Rome and religious orders for additional Italian priests and encouraged the Missionary Sisters of the Sacred Heart to work here. With the pope's particular blessing, Mother Frances Xavier Cabrini arrived with a few sisters in 1889, founded an orphanage, and opened Columbus Hospital in 1892. New Italian parishes were established, joining Mount Carmel and the Franciscans' 1866 Church of St. Anthony of Padua in Greenwich Village. Corrigan authorized eight Italian churches, including the Scalabrinians' Saint Joachim on the Lower East Side's Roosevelt Street in 1888 and the Jesuits' Missione Italiana della Madonna di Loreto, established in 1891 on Elizabeth Street.

Still, the disconcerting 115th Street *festa* continued. The matter was referred to higher levels. Unfortunately for Irish prelates, the decisive precincts were in Italy. In the next decade East Harlemites petitioned Pope Leo XIII to elevate their Mount Carmel shrine to the dignity of a sanctuary under the special protection of the Virgin. Only two such existed in the New World: Our Lady of Guadalupe in Mexico and Our Lady of Perpetual Help in New Orleans. The pontiff would decide that the devotion met two of the formal requirements for coronation: evidences of favors granted the devout by the Virgin and popularity of the cult. Leo waived the third criterion, antiquity, perhaps on the grounds that in New York, where everything moved so fast, twenty years was the equivalent of two hundred in Europe. More likely, Leo was well aware that the crowning asserted the authority of the Roman-centered papacy over Irish-American prelates, and in America's most modern city to boot. And so, before an enormous crowd in Jefferson Park, the Madonna of 115th Street would receive her crown, made in New York out of the melted-down golden rings, brooches, and family heirlooms contributed by grateful immigrants. After decades of uncertain commitment to the American metropolis, the Italians, symbolically as well as demographically, had arrived.

CHINATOWN

Although the Chinese came in minuscule numbers, compared to the great waves of Southern and Eastern Europeans, the establishment of the first Asian-American community in New York City triggered powerful responses of fascination and fear. For all the tensions evoked among old-stock New Yorkers by the emergence of Polish and Italian enclaves, as Europeans they shared far more with one another than any of them did with men and women from the opposite side of the planet.

There had long been a floating population of Chinese merchants and mariners in Manhattan, for the same sea lanes that carried tea, silk, and porcelain brought traders and transient sailors. By the 1850s a tiny handful, fewer than 150, had established a quasi-permanent presence.

Some, like Ah Sue, served Asian travelers. Cook and steward on a Hong Kong–New York packet line, Ah Sue had wearied of maritime travel and in 1847 opened a modest tobacco and candy store on Cherry Street. He operated as well a small boarding-house for the Chinese, Japanese, Filipino, Hindu, Maori, Hawaiian, Malay, and Annamese seamen whose vessels docked a few blocks away. More boardinghouses emerged, hosting other seamen who switched to land labor, usually in hopes of making a fortune and returning to China. Work was hard to come by, however, and many resorted to peddling cigars and Chinese candies around City Hall Park and the Bowery. Becoming familiar figures, they were collectively referred to as John Chinaman.

At the other end of the tiny group's class spectrum were men like Quimbo Appo. Having survived the British bombing of Shanghai during the Opium Wars, Appo took to the trade routes, tried his luck in the newly opened goldfields of California, then moved to New York and in a Spring Street store began retailing tea, the city's major Chinese import. Like other merchants, Appo mastered English speech and American mores as a requirement of doing business. With no Chinese women in town, Appo, like between a fourth and a third of the resident Chinese men, married a local woman, the Irish-American Catherine Fitzpatrick; wedlock between Irish "apple women" and Asian cigar peddlers was particularly common. Such unions ruffled racists, but the tiny numbers of Chinese involved did not raise the kinds of anxiety black-white "amalgamation" did.

After the Civil War, the community grew somewhat—reaching at most two thousand by 1880—with newcomers arriving from China by way of Cuba. When slavery was banished from British and Spanish colonies, sugar planters in Peru, Guiana, Brazil, Cuba, and Jamaica imported "coolie" laborers from impoverished sections of south China, a practice widely denounced in the United States as cruel and inhuman. In the 1860s Cuban cigarmakers recruited some of these Chinese from the sugar fields to work as hand rollers, a task at which they became expert. Given abysmal wage levels, many then traveled north on the thriving Cuban-New York trade routes. In the city, pioneer Cuban-American cigar manufacturers snapped up the highly skilled Chinese, paying some of them more than they did Germans.

This growth in the number of permanent and land-based residents fostered the emergence of an inland "Chinese Quarter," moving away from the Fourth Ward docks into the Sixth Ward blocks above Chatham Square. Along Baxter Street and lower Mott, where it spilled into Chatham Square, a small number of stores, boardinghouses, mutual aid associations, and shrines emerged to serve the community.

In 1872 Wo Kee, a former Hong Kong merchant, moved his general goods store from Oliver to Mott, dropping the first commercial anchor in the area that would soon be known as Chinatown. A *Sun* reporter, visiting the store in 1880, marveled at the array of goods crammed into front and back rooms of the former residence: Chinese medicines, incense sticks, jade bracelets, dried shark fins, ducks split and baked in peanut oil, opium and pipes for smoking it, silks, and "exquisite" teas, some of which was served to customers by the proprietor while he calculated sums on his abacus. Wo Kee's establishment was a social club and entertainment center as well. Men could shop, get mail, pick up tips on work opportunities, gamble in one basement room, lounge and eat in another. Upstairs there were sleeping quarters, with eleven bunk beds for twenty-two people and small rooms for use by cigarmakers. Other such multipurpose centers opened, often catering to people from the same clan and territory.

Soon the little complex received another and far larger demographic infusion, this time from California. Tens of thousands of Chinese, overwhelmingly unskilled peasants from rural Guangdong (Canton) and Fukien, had come to America to build the transcontinental railroad. Its completion in 1869 threw twenty thousand of them out of work. Most of them returned to California, where many entered the hand laundry business. When the depression of the 1870s struck California, many white workers scapegoated the Chinese, whom they considered unwitting capitalist tools. Animosities exploded into violence—pogroms of a sort—and led California to enact punitive anti-immigrant provisions. Many Chinese fled east along the transcontinental link they themselves had constructed.

Their arrival in the New York region in the late 1870s and early 1880s galvanized a new metropolitan industry. Each week, in Belleville, New Jersey, Captain James Hervey's Passaic Steam Laundry Factory machine-washed and hand-ironed six thousand shirts newly manufactured in the garment factories of New York City. Considering his workforce of Irish women to be obstreperous in their wage demands, and finding it hard to snare sufficient numbers of greenhorns on trips to Castle Garden, Captain Hervey imported sixty-eight Chinese from San Francisco, sneaking them into his factory compound by dead of night. This touched off protest rallies in Tompkins Square Park against coolie labor. And in the end, the Chinese too proved unsatisfactory, peeling off, as their contracts expired, to open their own hand laundries.

At first "washee washees," as metropolitan journalists referred to them, were few in number, perhaps thirty by 1877. In 1879, with the West Coast exodus underway, a *Sun* reporter found two hundred hand laundries in Manhattan. By 1888 Wong Ching Foo, a scrappy bilingual journalist-lecturer who wrote about and defended New York's Chinese, estimated there were over two thousand such laundries in New York, with another eight or nine hundred in Brooklyn. There was, he explained, no other way to make money as surely and quickly, given "the prejudice against the race." Start-up costs were low, perhaps a hundred dollars, and the average laundryman could save a nest egg of fifteen hundred or two thousand dollars, sell the laundry to relatives flocking in from the West Coast or Hong Kong, and return to China. Soon nearly every street and avenue in New York was festooned with signboards bearing good-luck names painted in flaming red.

The 1890 census counted 2,048 Chinese in the city, though the true figure was probably four to five times that. Of these, less than 20 percent lived in Chinatown, mostly cigarmakers who worked in the vicinity or merchants, clerks, barbers, doctors, and professional gamblers. Many in the Chatham Square area lived in dormitories, set up in the cheapest parts of dilapidated private houses, further divided into cubicles for those who could afford minimal privacy, with the rest stuffed into tri-tiered bunks, often two to a bed (three-per-bedders got rock-bottom rates of $1.50 to three dollars a week).

Most Chinese, however, were scattered about the city, domiciled in quarters attached to the hand laundries where many spent 80 percent of their lives. Others lived in mansions of the uptown rich, who had taken to hiring male Chinese house servants— there were still virtually no Chinese women in the city—to replace refractory Irish girls.

Chinatown Restaurant, 1896. (General Research. The New York
Public Library. Astor, Lenox and Tilden Foundations)

Isolated and lonely—the only Asian faces they were likely to see were peddlers from
Mott Street who carried in provisions—these men were also vulnerable to harassment
by gangs, and there were several race-based murders. For them, Chinatown was the
source of companionship as well as commodities. Laundry workers would flock to Mott
Street in the evenings, or on Sunday, to socialize, gamble, smoke opium, get mail, hear
news of their home villages.

The neighborhood grew only slightly in size—inching into Pell, Bayard, Doyer,
and Canal—but its internal organization got considerably more complicated. By 1888
there were at least thirty all-purpose store-centers in Chinatown, now often run not by
an individual entrepreneur but by mutual aid and protection societies known as *fang*
(house), organized by kin or area of origin. These houses provided temporary lodging
and financial assistance and sponsored social events and cultural festivals. They also
provided deceased members with proper burials in a plot at Green-Wood Cemetery—
or, rather, temporary interment, as men came periodically from San Francisco and, for a
price, exhumed bodies, collected and packed the bones, and shipped them to Canton
and on to home villages for a truly proper burial.

The neighborhood also developed a quasi-criminal wing, as mah-jongg and card
games gave way to organized fan-tan gambling, especially after the arrival of Tom Lee.
Wong Ah Ling, as he was known before he changed his name, had been a labor contractor in California, moved on to St. Louis, where he became a citizen, and arrived in New
York in 1879. Lee did well in the tea and silk trade business, in manufacturing cigars,
and in less legal pursuits as well. In 1880 he and some colleagues incorporated the Lung
Gee Tong—translated for legal purposes as "the Order and Brotherhood of Masons"—
and established a headquarters at 4 Mott. The Lung Gee Tong (later famous as the On
Leong Tong) was a lodge of the Triads, or Sam Hop Hui, an underground oppositional
society reputedly founded in the seventeenth century by Buddhist monks seeking to
return China to Han rule. ("Oppose the Qing, Restore the Ming" was their slogan.)

Staunchly nationalist, the secret brotherhood was involved in various revolutionary movements in China; in New York City their muscle was devoted, among other things, to establishing a criminal underworld.

Tom Lee, identifying himself as "the President of the Chinese Society of this city," wined and dined prominent members of the Democratic Party and won de facto recognition from Tammany Hall as the leader of Chinatown. The only organized opposition to Lee came from the Christian Chinese. In 1875 Sara Goodrich of the Fourth Avenue Presbyterian Church established a mission at Pearl Street that provided English-language classes every evening and religious instruction in Chinese on Sundays, by a missionary back from Canton. By 1883 there were ten Sunday schools operating in Manhattan and another eight in Brooklyn, with a combined enrollment of about six hundred. There was also a Chinese Young Men's Christian Association and the first independent Chinese church in New York, founded by Huie Kin, a Lane Theological Seminary graduate who arrived in 1885 to work with the Presbyterian schools. He and others dressed as workmen, infiltrated gambling houses, got to know the proprietors, had warrants made out, and took part in ensuing police raids. But the charges were almost invariably dismissed, and the shuttered houses did not remain so long.

The emergence of organized "vice" contributed to a sharp change in the wider city's attitude toward the Chinese community. The former high esteem for Chinese goods and culture turned to fear and loathing in the late 1870s, and early nineteenth-century images of clever craftsmen transmuted into harsh portraits of cunning deceivers. Wong Ching Foo, who in 1883 launched the first (and short-lived) Chinese-language newspaper in New York, the *Chinese American*, lectured at Steinway Hall and published articles in leading magazines championing the community's reputation, but to no avail.

Part of the reason for this sharp shift of perspective, ironically, was opium consumption. The drug that the West had forced into China at gunpoint, that had been the making of many New York fortunes, and that was widely hawked to middle-class Americans in the form of laudanum-laced patent medicines, cough syrups, and child quieters, came to be considered an evil substance to which Chinese were peculiarly addicted and which they used to subvert the morals of decent white women. Newspapers that had once treated pipe smoking light-heartedly now presented stories about the ruination of adolescent girls, headlined "Horrors of the Opium Dens" and accompanied by drawings of white women reclining alongside yellow men in collective stupor.

The fact that the Chinese had laid claim to an occupational niche that left them isolated from the wider society, against their earlier integrationist inclinations, was used as proof that they were racially inassimilable. Racist images of ravenous Chinese who would devour rats, cats, and dogs mingled with fears that yellow hordes would gobble up American jobs. Labor leaders like Samuel Gompers, whose cigar workers had actually encountered Chinese competition, called for race-based exclusion rather than making an effort to organize the Asians. The combination of middle-class revulsion and working-class animosity won passage in 1882 of the Chinese Exclusion Act.

The law had serious repercussions in New York City. Though it allowed for class exemptions—officials, diplomats, scholars, teachers, students, merchants, and tourists could enter the country—they were denied citizenship, the right to vote, and thus inclusion in the political life of the city and country. The law also indirectly barred Chinese from the licensed professions, most of which required citizenship. It forced Chinese already here to obtain residence certificates, in effect internal passports, which branded them permanent aliens and left them peculiarly subject to political, social, and economic exploitation, especially if they had entered illegally. Finally, the law erected gender barriers, barring Chinese laborers from bringing their wives to the United States and making it extremely difficult even for members of the "exempt classes" to do so. This guaranteed the perpetuation and exacerbation of a gender imbalance that went way beyond the merely lopsided; it would lead to formation of what would become known as a "bachelor society."

In response, New York's Chinatown turned farther inward. In 1883 all the city's *fang* and clan associations combined into an umbrella organization called the Zhonghua Gong Suo, a group that for much of the next century would serve as Chinese New York's unofficial but extremely potent local government. In 1887 its officials purchased a building on Mott Street, and Tom Lee, now styled as "Chairman of the Chinese Municipal Council," raised twenty-five thousand dollars for a new structure. When the building finished in 1890, the organization incorporated itself under state law and came to be called the Chinese Consolidated Benevolent Association of the City of New York (CCBA).

The CCBA was not a conventional Chinese institution transplanted to the metropolis but a local response to local conditions. The organization became the place where groups and powerful individuals settled disputes. It allocated business sites to hand laundries and required them to maintain a fixed schedule of prices. It kept records of leases and business contracts and posted on the board in front of its headquarters notices about partnerships formed and businesses or goods up for sale. Its agents watched docks and rail stations to make sure no one left town without settling debts. It acted as liaison to the rest of the city and defended community interests in municipal forums.

New Yorkers, spared by the 1882 act and its 1892 extension from invasion by "Mongolian hordes," now embarked on their own invasion of Chinatown. To adventurous uptowners the area's "evils" seemed attractively exotic, and the early 1890s witnessed a "slumming" craze. Moses King's 1893 guidebook urged a visit to Mott, Pell, and Doyers—a veritable Chinatown "with all the filth, immorality, and picturesque foreignness which that name implies." Genteel visitors trooped to the area's restaurants and the new "chop suey" houses that sprang up. The wilder ones sampled the forbidden pleasures of opium den and fan-tan parlor. All the activity finally created the sin-and-violence-drenched climate originally imagined to exist, as rowdy white Boweryites flocked to local bordellos, petty criminals took up residence, drunks and bravos engaged in combat, and tong extortionists preyed on Chinese (though never on white) businessmen.

The Chinese community was unique among the new immigrant groups in having its entire community turned into a cultural commodity. Jews and Italians did attract lovers of the "picturesque" to their neighborhoods, and they experienced the larger community's scorn as well as its curiosity, but they were never subjected to anything quite like the indignities suffered by the Chinese. But the various communities did share something else: a capacity for artistic creativity that, in mutual interaction, would work a cultural revolution in New York City.

64

That's Entertainment!

If an energetic couple had decided to hike from one end of Coney Island to the other on a summer Sunday in the late 1880s, their five-mile journey would have taken them through four wildly diverse communities.

Landing at the old steamboat dock on Coney's extreme western edge would have plunged them into seedy old Norton's Point. Though now grandly renamed the West End, it remained a year-round colony of crooks and unfortunates where, in season, rowdies congregated for prizefights, gambling, and prostitution. Respectable sorts gave the area a wide berth.

About a mile and half along the beach, past thickening numbers of bathhouses and makeshift eateries, our trekkers would have arrived in West Brighton and found themselves engulfed in noise—brass bands, hand organs, the shrieking whistles of arriving and departing steamers and locomotives, and the happy chatter of tens of thousands of merrymakers. The throngs poured out from Culver Plaza, where the Prospect Park and Coney Island Rail Road, popularly known as the Culver Line (a name that lives on to mystify today's F line riders), debouched Brooklynites. Manhattanites headed for West Brighton could take a steamer to Bay Ridge and transfer to the New York and Sea Beach Railroad (1879), for a round-trip fare of only a quarter.

In West Brighton our visitors, if keen on gaining a panoramic overview, could have headed for the three-hundred-foot Iron Tower, which Andrew Culver had carted back from the Philadelphia Centennial Exposition, and ascended by elevator to a vantage point higher than Trinity's steeple.

If hungry, they might have hustled directly to Charles Feltman's Ocean Pavilion, a gigantic restaurant-cum-entertainment center. In the early 1870s Feltman, a German immigrant, had opened a shanty stand at the beach and begun selling clam roasts, ice

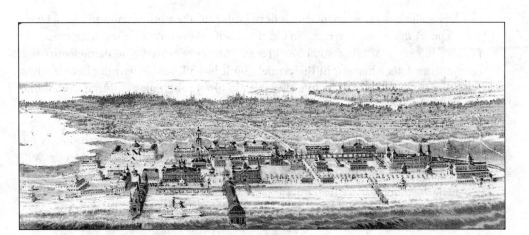

Coney Island Panorama, c. 1880. From its low end at Norton's Point (on the far left), through West Brighton, Brighton Beach, and Manhattan Beach (on the far right), Coney's atmosphere became progressively more refined. (© Collection of The New-York Historical Society)

cream, lager beer, and what *Harper's* would call a "weird-looking sausage, muffled up in the two halves of a roll and smoking hot from the vender's grid-iron."

From Feltman's, they might have walked to see the Elephant, a wood-framed, tin-skinned hotel, 150 feet long and 122 feet high. It had thirty-four rooms in its head, stomach, and feet, a cigar store in one foreleg, a diorama in the other, and a dairy stand in its trunk. "Seeing the Elephant" became New Yorkese for going down to Coney. Equally dazzling landmarks were the two-thousand-foot Iron Piers, erected by steamboat companies in 1879 and 1881, amusement centers on a par with those at Blackpool and Brighton, England.

If our visitors sought excitement, they could have headed for the chaotic and exhilarating carnival quarter. West Brighton's beachfront properties had been leased and subleased into tiny plots, on which small immigrant businessmen, showmen, and venders had erected hundreds of pavilions, platforms, tents, kiosks, sheds, and shanties. Here visitors could play with lung testers, throw rings at cane stubble, shoot clay ducks, and try to hit a Negro on the nose (his head, stuck through a hole in a cloth, bobbing and weaving to elude the balls). They could get their pictures taken, their fortunes read, their strength tested, their weight guessed. As exiled Cuban revolutionary Jose Martí, entranced by Coney Island, reported to a Bogotá newspaper in 1881, "to North Americans to weigh a pound more or less is a matter of positive joy or real grief."

If our hikers were venturesome souls, they might have beelined for the mechanized rides, advertised in the *World*'s Sunday edition by amusement entrepreneurs like Peter Tilyou and his son, George. Merry-go-rounds were an old divertissement but had been steam powered only since 1865. And only since the mid-1870s had Charles I. D. Looff, a German immigrant carver who worked out of a small Gravesend factory, been crafting the fabulous animals and birds that adorned West Brighton's carousels. In 1883 the first Loop-the-Loop opened for scary (and occasionally mortal) business. In 1884 its offspring the roller coaster was born, the progeny of LaMarcus A. Thompson. His trains, which tore up and down a giant steel structure, were an amalgam of the switchback railroads used in coal mines and the new elevateds crisscrossing the cities.

The roller coaster momentarily relieved riders of their inhibitions, providing welcome opportunities for romance. So did the beach. Many on the strand were tenement families in search of wholesome sea breezes. Mothers rented blue flannel suits and coarse straw hats, changed in the crudely built but affordable bathing houses, then cozied with their husbands while their all too often tubercular children buried one another in the sand. Singles displayed a more boisterous intimacy. At antebellum resorts each sex had taken its turn in the ocean on a fixed time schedule; in the 1880s they tumbled in together. Thousands, of both genders, shed cumbersome beach outfits for tighter-fitting, more revealing costumes and jettisoned much of their reserve as well, with women hugging fellows met minutes before.

Fellows wanting more than hugs repaired, as did flashily dressed sporting men, to the "Gut," a ten-square-block area up toward West 8th Street, in whose wooden shanties and sheds more carnal appetites were attended to. The Gut's brothels, dance halls, peep shows, and gambling dens provided plentiful helpings of sin, though not without peril. Knockout drops flowed freely, while crooks and swindlers found it easy to avoid the none too vigilant oversight of the Gravesend police.

Teeming West Brighton might well have reminded our sightseeing couple of the Bowery—indeed one of the principal saloon-lined thoroughfares was called "the Bowery"—and it was, overwhelmingly, a working-class pleasure ground. Skilled craftsmen and small shopkeepers tended to come on organized outings; garment workers, clerks, saleswomen, and servants came on their own or in small groups. Many were on Saturday half-holidays, the new summertime practice of closing at one P.M. adopted in the

The Coney Island Roller Coaster. *Frank Leslie's Illustrated Newspaper*, July 24, 1886. (General Research. The New York Public Library. Astor, Lenox and Tilden Foundations)

late 1880s by numbers of manufacturing and retail establishments. Others were at Coney on unpaid holidays: when broiling summer days turned Brooklyn's iron foundries, sugar refineries, and glassworks into infernos, owners shut them down.

If our revelers had stayed on into the evening, they could have tried "Electric Bathing" in the flare of the arc lights newly installed along the shore, or gone to one of the well-lit music halls and open-air theaters, often managed by Irish barkeeps from New York. There they could have seen and heard pianists, dancers, female impersonators, ballad singers, and comedy acts as broad as the beach. These establishments provided jobs for thousands of recent immigrants, many of whom became full-time Coney residents. They worked as bartenders, cooks, bathhouse keepers, musicians, domestic servants, vendors, and hotel waiters (many of the latter listing their occupation as artist or actor). The percentage of blacks in the year-round population—8.3 percent—was far higher than in Brooklyn or New York, though their numbers at the beach were far fewer.

If our hypothetical hikers had torn themselves away from West Brighton and pressed on east, they would soon have reached a relatively empty stretch of beach, paralleled by a tree-lined concourse and bisected by Ocean Parkway—Coney Island's Great Divide. Roughly three-quarters of a mile from the Elephant, they would have come upon the grounds of the enormous, low-slung, mansarded, stick-style Brighton Beach Hotel.

Our travelers had entered Brighton Beach—a different world from West Brighton, and differently peopled too. Sitting on the great hotel's broad verandas, strolling on its vast lawns down to the boardwalk at surf's edge, or listening (after 1888) to Anton Seidl direct serenades at the bandstand were large numbers of what one 1890 paper called "good middle-class Brooklynites." Brighton drew businessmen and their families, doctors and lawyers, white-collar office workers, clerks in insurance firms, and salesmen with manufacturing companies.

Brighton Beach reflected the unified vision and ownership of William A. Engeman, a New York-born carpenter who had made a wartime fortune selling mules to the Union Army. Captivated by Coney and its pecuniary possibilities, Engeman tracked down the various owners of two hundred acres of marshland and sand dunes and bought them out cheap. Then he constructed the four-hundred-foot-wide, two-story Brighton Beach Bathing Pavilion (ready for the 1878 season), and the following year he opened the Brighton Beach Racetrack, a mile-long course that by 1882 was netting him two hundred thousand dollars a year.

Meanwhile, a powerful consortium of Brooklyn businessmen and politicians—including Henry Murphy and William Kingsley of the New York and Brooklyn Bridge Company—had bought half of Engeman's property and on it erected the Brighton Beach Hotel. The group also built the Brooklyn, Flatbush, and Coney Island Railroad to deliver passengers to its doorstep, placing BF&CI stations conveniently near middle-class Bedford, Clinton Hill, Ocean Hill, and Prospect Park. Brooklynites could train down for a music programme and be home by a reasonable hour, or entire families could settle in for the summer while husbands commuted to work in the cities. The hotel also attracted racing devotees, including Wall Street high rollers, politicians, actresses, and socialites.

Finally, if our trekkers had headed eastward one more time, they would have crossed another half-mile gap, then come upon two magnificent edifices: the Manhattan Beach Hotel with its turreted roofs and pinnacles, and the moorish Oriental Hotel, replete with fanciful minarets. It would not, however, have been easy for our beach-combers to have got near these palaces, as a high fence surrounded the area, and Pinkertons at the private railway station monitored arriving coaches of the New York and Manhattan Beach Railway to screen out undesirables.

Manhattan Beach was the brainchild (and property) of New York railroad magnate and banker Austin Corbin. In the depressed 1870s he had picked up over five hundred acres of shorefront marshland for $16,500 and given it a glamorous name. Then he inaugurated the railway that whisked Manhattanites directly to his two hotels within an hour. To ensure exclusiveness, he charged the highest prices in the country. To ensure even greater exclusiveness, he banned Jews in 1879.

Corbin's hostelries succeeded in attracting an elite clientele, almost up to Newport standards. The Oriental drew leading businessmen, visiting aristocrats, famous entertainers, and powerful politicians. The Manhattan Beach Hotel attracted a racier crowd—notably members of the Coney Island Jockey Club, whose leaders August Belmont Jr., Leonard Jerome, Pierre Lorillard Jr., and William K. Vanderbilt organized the nearby Sheepshead Bay Racetrack in 1880, helping make Kings County one of the nation's top turf centers.

PLEASURE AND COMMERCE

Coney Island, in the space of a decade, had leapt from marshy obscurity to preeminence among the world's beach resorts. It was remarkable for its size and for its segmentation—the way its component parts were sorted and sequenced by class, from "low" to "high," with each zone governed by its own conventions. Even more remarkable—and alarming, to guardians of the traditional order—was the way West Brighton encouraged unconventional behavior. Reformers called it "Sodom by the Sea." They were upset by the doings in the Gut, of course, but also by the spooning on the beach, the frolicking in the waves, the way people acted (said one shocked observer) "precisely as if the thing to do in the water was to behave exactly contrary to the manner of behaving anywhere else."

West Brighton was also disconcerting in the connections it was fostering among New York's immigrants. On Sunday ethnic groups that during the week were segregated by work or neighborhood mixed and mingled at the shore. At Coney's rides and beaches, diverse peoples swam, ate, played, and rode together, encouraging development of an interethnic—albeit white—"New York" sensibility, an eclectic camaraderie that paralleled and perhaps undergirded such multiethnic entities as the Central Labor Union and Henry George campaign. Ever since Petrus Stuyvesant's day, the city's upper classes had tried to suppress plebeian ways of having fun that appeared to undermine established authority. But this quest took on added importance in the 1880s, a time when unions, Catholics, ethnic nationalists, and new immigrants—the very people gamboling and gambling at West Brighton—were boldly challenging the city's political, economic, and religious status quo.

In this context, what seemed most unnerving about West Brighton was its unembarrassed air, the way it exuded a sense of entitlement to a band on the city's recreational spectrum. The entire structure of Coney Island seemed to reinforce this claim. All the communities, after all, had undergone their explosive development simultaneously, and they shared the same strand. This temporal and territorial equivalency suggested a moral and cultural equality—as if styles, tastes, and practices at either end of the beach were equally "legitimate."

Worse, West Brighton's wayward ways seemed impervious to criticism or correction, in part because its cultural independence was sustained by powerful businessmen. Entrepreneurs of leisure, since the tavern keepers of New Amsterdam, had always resisted regulation. But never before had entertainment been such big business.

Among those developing amusement parks around the metropolitan area were transportation, real estate, and brewery magnates. Pleasure gardens had become all but extinct in Manhattan, victims of rising land values, but were being reborn, in far grander format, on the urban periphery. Their developers sought to increase traffic on streetcar lines, lure consumers to selling grounds, and enhance property values. In the early 1880s Bowery Bay (site of today's La Guardia Airport), then far from the nearest village, had been a popular Queens destination for picnickers. In 1886 piano potentate and nearby land baron William Steinway, along with brewery industrialist George Ehret, transformed the isolated strand into Bowery Bay Beach (renamed North Beach in 1891). Soon it was festooned with beer halls, supplied exclusively by Ehret, and swarming with tens of thousands of patrons, who arrived on Steinway-owned mass transit. North Beach grew ever more boisterous, yet ever more profitable, and its owners ever more averse to bluenose interference. And big businessmen had more clout than their smaller predecessors.

This was particularly evident at Brighton and Manhattan Beach, which even more than West Brighton represented substantial investment by large-scale capitalists. Most East End amusements were dignified and genteel, to be sure, but the racetracks, on which much hotel patronage depended, were (in the opinion of reformers) nearly as subversive of public morals as the Gut. In 1877 state legislation had banned the old auction betting system, in hopes of curbing racing. Instead it nourished a new variety of betting, done by at-the-track bookmakers. The growing ranks of professional gamblers, together with the rich horsemen of the Coney Island Jockey Club, formed another influential constellation in favor of cultural laissez-faire.

Both ends of Coney, moreover, had powerful political protectors. The island was beyond the jurisdiction of either New York or Brooklyn—legally an appendage of the independent town of Gravesend, which was the bailiwick of John Y. McKane. A stout-framed, red-bearded man, McKane had been born in County Antrim in 1841, had been brought up in Gravesend from 1843, and worked as a farmhand and as a clam digger in Sheepshead Bay, then opened his own carpentry shop. He went into politics and with the help of fellow Irish immigrants supplanted the old Dutch town leaders. Between 1878 and 1893 McKane *was* Coney's government. He was effective at delivering water and electricity and disposing of sewage. He was also corrupt, assisting those businesses that hired his construction firm, which is to say virtually every hotelier on the beach. McKane permitted gambling throughout West Brighton—making the occasional raid, to quiet moral critics, after warning the targets he was coming. He also protected the tracks from overzealous enforcement of the penal codes, in alliance with sportsmen and gamblers who had their own lines to the Democratic Party.

All these phenomena—the growing vigor of a multiethnic popular culture, the rapid commercialization of entertainment on a hitherto unmatched scale, the emergence of novel kinds of mass amusement forms, the loosening during leisure time of constraints that governed elsewhere in the city—were present elsewhere in the New York's far-flung and fast-flowering world of entertainment. In Manhattan, as in Coney, the clashing and blending enclaves of commercial culture were laid out quite tidily along a spatial axis. Here the journey from "low" to "high" ran south to north, rather than west to east. A tourist determined to grasp the city's complete range of entertainment possibilities would have to begin in the raunchy and interethnic precincts of the Bowery; travel to the Union Square Rialto, now home to the novel and interlinked phenomena of vaudeville and pop music; head on to the peculiarly multipurpose, multiclass venue of Madison Square Garden; and finally reach "Broadway," the newly transplanted center of the "legitimate" stage (unless a wrong and westward turning had plunged the unwary into Satan's Circus).

ALL THE WORLD'S ONSTAGE

The Bowery, long the heartland of working-class amusements, had been flagging a bit, weakened by competition from new forms of entertainment, amusement parks among them. Melodramas, downtown's favorite performance style, were still in evidence, to be sure. Each night on the Bowery boards, working-class heroes triumphed over rich men whose pockets were stuffed with bonds, and poor but pure shopgirls or seamstresses escaped the villain's machinations (as in Charles Foster's *Bertha, the Sewing Machine Girl*). Many plays, as before the war, used the city as backdrop, with offerings such as *The Waifs of New York*, *Outcasts of a Great City*, and the inspirational *Tom Edison the Electrician*. But what revivified Bowery theater in the 1880s and 1890s, infusing it with terrific new energy, was the establishment of zestful new immigrant communities, which had imported new cultural traditions and the audiences to sustain them.

Yiddish theater, born in Odessa and Bucharest in the late 1870s, blossomed in New York City in the 1880s and 1890s. Amateur companies took the lead, their actors shuttling between stage and sweatshop. The first production came in 1882, and soon there were regular weekend shows at the Bowery Garden, National, and Thalia theaters, starring unknowns like sixteen-year-old Boris Tomashefsky. In 1884, a year after czarist Russia banned Yiddish theater, professional companies were performing in playhouses along the Bowery, and they flourished over the next decade.

Yiddish melodrama provided glamorous diversion and emotional communion for tenement dwellers and a sense of empowerment for the politically impotent. Ghetto audiences cheered historical spectacles of Jewish heroism, oohed and aahed at tableaux of ancient kings and prophets, shouted denunciations of villains, howled with laughter at tomfoolery and clownishness, demanded popular songs be repeated, and often kept performances running till midnight.

The plays were packed with topical references to life along East Broadway, helping greenhorns learn their way around an alien land. They also evoked heartbroken recollections of loved ones left behind; Tomashefsky always worked a mama song (like "A Letter to Mother") into his plays no matter what the subject. Masters of bricolage, these Lower East Side playwrights ransacked all European drama for bits of theatrical business and mingled opera tunes and synagogue chants with abandon. They desacralized Shakespeare with a vengeance, domesticating the Bard, turning Capulets and Montagues into feuding Jewish sects; after the first Yiddish *Hamlet* the crowd was so pleased it called for the author. In the 1890s, a new generation of performers and intel-

Poster advertising a performance of *King Solomon* at the Thalia Theater. (Library of Congress)

lectuals—notably playwright Jacob Gordin and actor Jacob Adler—warred against cheap "three-hankie" melodramas and called for "serious" theater. But even then Yiddish drama would remain grand and flamboyant, an affair of shouts and whispers, deeply in touch with the lives of ordinary immigrants.

Popular Italian dramaturgy followed an almost identical course. Amateur actors took to the stage in 1882, with a farce at Concordia Hall. Soon there were several theatrical clubs in action, like the Circolo Filo-Drammatico Italo-Americano (1885), which played in halls like the Bowery's Germania Assembly Rooms, and offered special performances on saints' days in church basements. Like their Yiddish counterparts, Italian actors offered long and varied evenings: thrilling melodramas, commedia dell'arte skits, Pulcinella farces, songs and dances in Neapolitan or Sicilian, and comedies like *Pasquale, You're a Pig*. Again, theatrical pastiche was the norm, with Schiller, Sardou, and an Italianized Shakespeare sharing time with local dramas set in Little Italy. In the 1890s Italian theater too entered a more polished phase with the arrival of professional actors lured by the popularity of the *circolo* groups. Antonio Maiori, who came in 1892 and established a company, had a harder time of it than Jacob Adler, however, as opera remained the art form of choice in the community.

New York Chinese theater began with professionals. In June 1889 the traveling Swin Tien Lo (Most Sublime Company) arrived from San Francisco and performed at the Windsor Theater on the Bowery. In 1893 the community got its own company when a wealthy merchant rented a Doyers Street basement, hired thirty actors, and opened a Cantonese theater.

VARIETY: THE SPICE OF BOWERY LIFE

While these cultural stewpots bubbled on their separate burners, the Bowery's variety stage—another pastiche performance form—was absorbing many of their assorted traditions into a more commercialized culture.

Variety emerged as a distinct branch of the entertainment industry only in the 1870s and 1880s, but the presentation of brief entertainment bits by singers, dancers, and monologuists had long been part of New York's theatrical tradition. Until the fifties, variety acts had been interpolated in, or ancillary to, the main dramatic event. Then managers determined to upgrade their houses banished comics and song-and-dance men. Variety acts quickly resurfaced inside minstrelsy and became standard elements of the concert saloon repertoire. When minstrelsy began to fade away—in 1883, for the first time in forty years, New York City was without a resident minstrel troupe—and concert saloons came under attack for harboring prostitution, variety came into its own.

Variety was strictly a downtown affair, housed in Bowery showcases like the London Theatre, Miner's Bowery, and the Globe Museum. These houses jumbled acts together in a way calculated to please a diverse constituency. Minstrels too had presented a succession of turns, but all were performed by members of the same troupe. Variety assembled a mélange of performers, a division of labor that allowed for greater range and specialization. The result was a potpourri of entertainment bits, unconnected by persona or plot, that drew upon a host of plebeian entertainments. From the *Turnverein* and *Harmonie-Bund* came gymnastic and musical routines; the circus provided animal acts and acrobats; dance competitions supplied Lancashire and hornpipe clogs and jigs.

Variety's staples were its songs and comic sketches. Skits were often ribald and physical, geared to the male and working-class audience. Performers set their topical gags and routines in the city's saloons, sidewalks, and shipyards. The most popular bits were ethnically oriented, with performers mimicking New York's diverse populations, doing Irish turns and Dutch (German) shtick.

Black comics were not numerous in variety. African Americans did pour into minstrelsy in these years, on the strength of the argument that they could "act the nigger"—depict grotesque caricatures of plantation slaves—"with greater fidelity," as the *Clipper* argued of Haverly's Colored Minstrels, "than any 'poor white trash' with corked faces can ever do." White comics fled to variety, where they did their old dialect putdowns of shiftless and irresponsible darkies or used blackface as a cover for raunchier humor than they could get away with if clad only in their own white skins.

As new immigrant groups arrived they were quickly added to the cast of comic characters, with sharp-witted Jews, song-loving Italians, and opium-smoking Chinamen tossed in among the pugnacious Irishmen, lazy Africans, beer-drinking Germans, tight-fisted Scots, and ignorant farm rubes who peopled the virtual Lower East Side. These personas varied from good-humored to derogatory, benign to malignant, and the songs and spiels conveyed both the antagonisms and alliances between groups. Most variety skits never rose above one-dimensional stereotyping, but some did, and in the process gave rise to a new entertainment form, the ethnic sitcom.

"PROMINENT TYPES WHICH GO TO MAKE UP LIFE IN THE METROPOLIS"

Edward "Ned" Harrigan, born in New York in 1845, left home at eighteen to become a traveling song-and-dance man. Tony Hart (originally Anthony J. Cannon), born ten years later, left an Irish slum in Worcester, Massachusetts, and also took to the stage. They teamed up in 1871 and, for the next nine years, settled into Josh Hart's Theatre Comique, a variety house at 514 Broadway. Soon they were among the most popular performers in New York City.

Where other variety houses rejuvenated their weekly bills by bringing in all new acts, the Theatre Comique relied on Harrigan and Hart to constantly turn out fresh bits themselves. The talented Harrigan wrote comedy sketches in profusion, as well as lyrics for the songs to accompany them. For fresh scenes and characters, Harrigan turned to the Lower East Side. His "The Mulligan Guards," one of over forty sketches he churned out in the team's first three seasons, was a takeoff on the city's hundred-plus immigrant "target companies," pseudomilitary outfits that on Sundays donned home-made uniforms and went to Jones' Wood or Hoboken, where they marched, caroused, and shot at targets.

Harrigan's loving spoof was a smash success, and in 1879 he began turning out a series of full-length plays that developed the character of Dan Mulligan, along with his family, friends, and ethnic neighbors—the "prominent types," said Harrigan, "which go to make up life in the metropolis." In fashioning his characters, who were of far greater range and depth than the traditional stereotypes, Harrigan took to the streets to catch "the living manners as they rise." His daughter, Nedda, remembered him following people around, learning their walk and talk, observing how and where they lived, at times buying the clothes off their backs to use as costumes. Harrigan used realistically painted backdrops to set his scenes on Lower East Side streets, in the Mulligans' dining room, in black-run barbershops where men gathered to talk sports.

Harrigan and Hart's comedies were no more into a grim realism than was melodrama or minstrelsy, nor did they completely transcend stereotyping. Harrigan's Irish were rowdy, garrulous, quick tempered, intemperate; his Germans were slow witted, stubborn, coarse eaters, heavy drinkers; his blacks loved to dress up in overly elaborate costumes, use long words, and mangle syntax. Yet all these characters had redeeming qualities. The Irish came off best, no doubt: Paddy, though given to drink and disorder, was also witty and generous, hardworking and brave. Remarkably, Harrigan's black barbers and servants were equally complex and, though played for laughs like everyone else, weren't subjects of ridicule. The Chinese came off much the worst: rat-eating, opium-smoking, pidgin-English laundrymen with a penchant for stealing clothing.

Perhaps most significant, Harrigan and Hart's assorted characters got on with one another—rather as did many of their real-life contemporaries at West Brighton, or in the CLU, or in the George campaign, or on the Tammany picnics organized by Big Tim Sullivan. H&H's Lower East Siders also exuded a collective sense of downtown's self-worth and power, particularly in relation to the snooty uptown sorts, that appealed to heavily ethnic working-class audiences.

SEX REDIVIVUS

As ethnicity reigned in the melodrama and variety houses, burlesque was ruled by

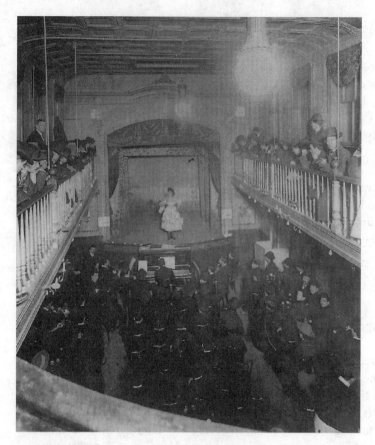

A Bowery concert saloon, with a "re-fined singing and dancing act" in progress, c. 1890. (© Collection of The New-York Historical Society)

raunch. Lydia Thompson and her impertinent "British Blondes" had created an uproar back in 1868 as much for their streetwise language, male impersonations, and mockery of bourgeois culture as for their revealing costumes. Since then burlesque had been stripped of its more radical components and gone downtown, downscale, and downhill. The dozens of troupes that sprang up in Thompson's wake eliminated cutting-edge criticism and stuck to displaying female bodies to male audiences—the "leg business"—though women on Bowery stages "peeled" only down to their tights.

Sex was the mainstay of concert saloons too, like old Harry Hill's, on Houston and Mulberry, which still offered alcohol and licentious entertainment to male audiences, attracting rugged Bowery types, celebrities like Bennett Junior and Edison, and slummers out for a walk on the sinful side, hoping to pick up immigrant girls. But the Bowery's range of sensual possibilities—like the diversity of its ethnic-based offerings—was expanded in this era by new arrivals on the scene, the men called "Nancys" and "fairies." Ralph Werther, who occasionally went by the name of Jennie June (the celebrated fashion magazinist), moved to the metropolis in 1882 in part because "in New York one can live as Nature demands without setting every one's tongue wagging." Werther, a middle-class student, attended college uptown but spent much of his free time, usually in drag, at the Columbia Club on the Bowery at 5th Street. Better known as Paresis Hall—paresis being a medical term for the insanity one could supposedly contract by consorting with fairies—the establishment resembled most working-class variety haunts. It had a modest barroom and a small beer garden out back and offered nightly music and comedy routines. Here, however, the performers were men, often of upper- or middle-class background, painted, powdered, and attired in evening dresses, who sang (according to one disapproving observer) "songs with immoral lyrics" that encouraged lewd dances and other acts of depravity. Male prostitutes solicited men at tables, and the upper two floors had small rooms that could be rented by the hour or the night.

There were several such nightspots downtown. Charles Nesbitt, a medical student from North Carolina who visited the city around 1890, went on a slummer's tour and stopped in at beer gardens along the Bowery where, he later recalled, "male perverts, dressed in elaborate feminine evening costumes, 'sat for company'" and were compensated, as were waiter-girls, with commissions on the drinks clients bought them. The Slide, where waiters with rouged necks sang filthy ditties in falsetto voices, was often recommended by city-smart types to tourists in search of Sodom and Gomorrah.

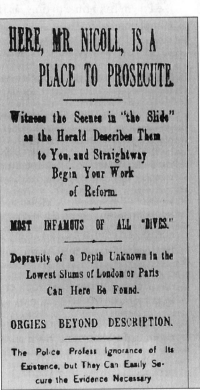

HERE, MR. NICOLL, IS A PLACE TO PROSECUTE.

Witness the Scenes in "the Slide" as the Herald Describes Them to You, and Straightway Begin Your Work of Reform.

MOST INFAMOUS OF ALL "DIVES."

Depravity of a Depth Unknown in the Lowest Slums of London or Paris Can Here Be Found.

ORGIES BEYOND DESCRIPTION.

The Police Profess Ignorance of Its Existence, but They Can Easily Secure the Evidence Necessary

AT MIDNIGHT IN "THE SLIDE."

Headline and drawing from the *New York Herald*, January 5, 1892. Wrote a reporter for the paper: "Let a detective be opportuned by people from a distance to show them something outre in the way of fast life, the first place he thinks of is the Slide, if he believes the out-of-towner can stand it." (General Research. The New York Public Library. Astor, Lenox and Tilden Foundation)

The Slide was also, however, a place where fairies felt free to socialize with one another as well as tourists. By the 1890s they had established a community in the interstices of the working-class neighborhood. Nesbitt attended a ball at Walhalla Hall, a Lower East Side establishment popular with local ethnic social clubs. There he found some five hundred male couples waltzing sedately and quite a few "masculine looking women in male evening dress" dancing with other women. So many seemed of "good" background, Nesbitt marveled, that he could almost imagine himself "among respectable people."

Ralph Werther reported at least one instance in which solidarity went beyond mere socializing. In 1895 he was invited to join a little club called Cercle Hermaphrododitos, open only to those who "like to doll themselves up in feminine finery." Its goal was to unite for defense "against the world's bitter persecution"—making it conceivably the first homosexual rights organization in the United States. Persecution was less prevalent in the working-class neighborhoods than in uptown quarters, the fairies found; Werther enjoyed good relations with Irish and Italian youths. But while Bowery males tolerated these sexual newcomers, they did not respect them, and gang members brutalized them from time to time, as they did the Chinese, well aware their victims would not complain to police.

PASTORIZED VARIETY

Traveling up the Bowery or Broadway brought amusement seekers to the Union Square Rialto, center of a very different kind of cultural production. Union Square remained the hub of the nation's theatrical industry, and managers and actors lived by the hundreds in area apartments and theatrical boardinghouses. The stock company system completed its collapse in this era. Lester Wallack's group disbanded in 1887, leaving just Augustin Daly's old troupe and one newcomer, Charles Frohman's Empire Theater Stock Company. The stage was now completely given over to combination companies, the assembled-to-order groups that went out on prearranged tours. In the 1881–82 season 138 companies took to the road. In 1894–95 234 groups were hoofing their way across the country, and variety artists and minstrel performers were also assembling troupes and traveling. As the combination system grew ever more reliant on big-name attractions, duly certified success on the New York stage grew ever more critical.

Actors did not leave such crucial notices to chance. Thespians led vivid lives, fashioned personal legends and glamorous personas, and employed dramatic agents to publicize their reputations across the country. Richard d'Oyly Carte, the entrepreneur who produced Gilbert and Sullivan's *Patience* at the Standard, arranged for Oscar Wilde, whose "aesthetic" movement the play spoofed, to tour the country giving talks. His prospectus promoting Wilde to out-of-town booking agents promised that "he will be first announced, advertised, and worked up in N.Y. City." Ballyhooing techniques had developed since P. T. Barnum packaged Jenny Lind. New York talent brokers now drew on methods advertising executives used to market brand-name corporate products. Theatrical portraits of famous personalities were displayed everywhere—in shop windows, hotels, restaurants—and cheaper reproductions graced cards inserted in cigarette packages.

Union Square's specialization in theatrical marketing, coupled with its proximity to genteel precincts, made it the crucible for the emergence of vaudeville, a new entertainment form that would soon sweep the city and the country. The impresario most responsible for this development was the fat, genial, and handlebar-mustachioed Antonio "Tony" Pastor, a master of the variety stage who set out in the 1880s to change its image. At the age of twelve, Pastor, born in Greenwich Village in 1834, gave his first paid performance, as a blackface minstrel singer, at Barnum's Museum. Later he joined the circus as an acrobat, singer, and clown, then returned to New York, where he sang topical songs at a Broadway saloon. In 1865 he took over the old Volk's Garden at 201 Bowery and rechristened it Pastor's Opera House; there he ran a successful variety show for many years.

In 1881 he moved up to Union Square, opening Tony Pastor's New Fourteenth Street Theater in Tammany Hall. Following in Barnum's footsteps, Pastor decided to repackage variety—a brash, plebeian, and male-oriented entertainment form—and make it suitable for a broader and more profitable audience, one that crossed class and gender lines. Union Square was ideally situated for such an initiative, as vast numbers of respectable women came every day to the area's shops and to Ladies' Mile, thriving a scant few blocks away. The Sixth Avenue Elevated had poured customers onto the strip that ran from Macy's at 14th Street up to McCreery's at 23rd. More giant department stores went up in the 1880s and 1890s, each determined to outdo the others as a spectacular stage for marketing goods.

Pastor launched an ad campaign, aimed at wives, sisters, and sweethearts, announcing the birth of "clean variety." He barred liquor, banned prostitutes, and sheared the entertainment itself of excessive vulgarity. Once again a cultural entrepreneur had set out to buff the rough edges off downtown culture in order to sell it to uptown audiences. A new form required a new name, and Pastor's 1881 advertisements proclaimed "the first specialty and vaudeville theater of America, catering to polite tastes." Variety was associated with drink, sex, and the working class; "vaudeville" had French associations and suggested respectability and "class."

There was in fact no structural difference between variety and vaudeville, each being a series of acts strung together, but Pastor's vaudeville was more "tasteful." His offerings included demure dancers, blackface comics, spoofs of uptown light operas, Irish acts, magic lantern shows, puppetry, city sketches ("The Mysteries of Gotham," "The Bowery by Day and Night"), and Tony himself, singing favorites like "Lula, the Beautiful Hebrew Girl" or "Sarah's Young Man" ("On her I grew love sick / She was a domestic / And lived in a mansion / On Washington Square.")

Pastor, though a great success, at first had little wider impact—most variety stages continued much as before—largely because the performer-manager had no ambitions beyond his own theater. It would take an empire builder to press the transformation farther. At the time Pastor was launching vaudeville, Benjamin Franklin Keith came to town to work at Bunnell's Museum, one of the fifty dime museums flourishing in New York City in the late 1870s and early 1880s. Keith was not a performer but an entrepreneur, and after a year at Bunnell's, displaying collections of human curiosities, wax figures, and two-headed chickens, followed by a year on the road with P. T. Barnum's circus, he opened his own Pastor-style vaudeville operation, the New York Dime Museum, in Boston in 1883. Over the next decade, Keith worked out and standardized the vaudeville formula, while his partner, Edward F. Albee, designed special-purpose theaters.

By the time Keith and Albee moved into New York's Union Square Theater in 1893, they had industrialized the master's approach. The Union Square offered "continuous performance," repeating acts throughout the day. Each was no less than seven and no more than twenty minutes long and fit for family viewing. The theater itself was refined too, staffed with a corps of boy ushers in Turkish costumes and with ladies' room maids in lace caps and frilly aprons. Perhaps most important, the managers hired bouncers to cope with any men or boys who, accustomed to stag-house laxity, might shout obscenities at female performers from the galleries. They also banned smoking, hat wearing, whistling, stamping, spitting on the floor, and crunching peanuts. Not surprisingly, Brighton Beach and Manhattan Beach established tasteful music halls in which they offered patrons the new and respectable vaudeville.

THE ROOTS OF TIN PAN ALLEY

Union Square's sheet music houses had long served primarily as distribution agencies for established songwriters, but in the 1880s, in tandem with the rise of vaudeville, they began producing what one advertised as "Songs Written to Order." In 1886 Witmark and Sons, a Jewish firm like many of the new companies, segued from commercial printing into sheet music publishing and song production. The youthful brothers quickly discovered that test marketing before live audiences was the key to success. At first they kept the operation in the family: Julius, "the boy soprano," became a popular performer at Tony Pastor's, and gave stage-play to songs Isidore wrote. Those that caught on were quickly printed up and marketed.

As new entrepreneurs poured into the business, song salesmanship became a ferociously competitive affair. Rival song "pluggers" stalked popular vaudeville vocalists, snared them on streetcorners, and sang them their songs amid the passing throng. To get real stars to work their ditties into an act, pluggers would buy them drinks or dinners in Union Square restaurants, pay their board bill, purchase their railroad tickets to distant cities. They also wooed bandleaders, managers, and waiters, hired boys in the galleries to take up the chorus, and got organ grinders to spread their melodies throughout the city. In addition, they cultivated the growing number of vaudeville agents who worked in the Union Square area booking agencies supplying acts and songs to theaters and amusement parks across the country.

In the 1890s the stakes and purses grew larger, as evidenced by the Cinderella success of Charles K. Harris. Like most free-lance songwriters, Harris was at the bottom of the emerging industry, way below publishers and performers. When the Witmarks offered him an eighty-five-cent royalty check for one effort, the enraged Harris opened his own company and began churning out melodramatic songs about women wronged and vice reproved. In 1892 Harris wrote "After the Ball," a pathetic tale of a young man doomed to eternal bachelorhood ("Long years have passed, child, I've never wed / True to my lost love, though she is dead.") Harris got songstress May Irwin to introduce it at Tony Pastor's, and within a few years it sold over two million copies.

Other million-plus sellers followed in the early 1890s, with some of the biggest hits packaging and marketing images of life in New York. "The Bowery" (1892), first sung in the musical comedy *A Trip to Chinatown*, was about the misadventures of a genteel young man who, on his first visit to the metropolis, disregarded advice to stay away from the working-class boulevard:

Oh, the night that I struck New York, I went out for a little walk.
Folks who are onto the city say, better far that I took Broadway.

But I was out to enjoy the sights: there was the Bowery ablaze with lights;
I had one of the Devil's own nights, I'll never go there any more.

In succeeding verses the hapless tourist is bilked at an auction, bounced from a variety hall, and battered in a bar ("I struck a place that they called a dive. I was lucky to get out alive"), with each crisis punctuated by the pointed refrain: "I'll never go there any more."

More appealing metropolitan portraits were furnished by "The Sidewalks of New York" (1894) and "The Band Played On" (1895), the latter a song about Matt Casey's stylish social club in a rented hall where on Saturday night he and his cronies would grease the floor with wax, don their Sunday clothes, and waltz with strawberry blondes. Most of the big hits were waltzes, with lyrics that got to the point as quickly as an advertisement and memorably melodic choruses that made it easy for audiences and parlor performers to sing along.

These blockbuster successes, which kept New York life in the nation's ear, inspired dozens of other songwriting firms to try their hand. Most continued to locate around 14th Street, until the flourishing Witmark brothers moved uptown to West 28th Street, nearer the new theatrical district. By the late 1890s almost every major music publisher had followed them, creating a new center for the popular music industry soon to be dubbed Tin Pan Alley.

BIG TENT ON MADISON SQUARE

While Union Square mediated between Bowery and Broadway, Madison Square, a few blocks north, accommodated both simultaneously.

Ever since the old New York and Harlem Rail Road shed at Madison and 26th had been rendered obsolete by Grand Central Depot, the Vanderbilt family had leased the old terminus to various theatrical entrepreneurs. In 1873 P. T. Barnum used the premises, remodeled as the Great Roman Hippodrome, for performances of the world's first three-ring circus. Later, bandmaster Patrick S. Gilmore rented it for boxing matches, marathon running races, and the first Westminster Kennel Club Show (1877).

In 1879 William Kissam Vanderbilt reasserted family control over the site and rechristened it Madison Square Garden, appropriating for indoor halls a word long associated with outdoor "pleasure gardens." In the early 1880s Vanderbilt focused on sports events, relying heavily on six-day-long marathon runs and boxing "exhibitions" featuring John L. Sullivan. But in 1885 a clampdown on the still illegal sport cut off that income stream, and events like the National Horse Show, which started that year, failed to replace it. Vanderbilt decided to raze his "patched-up, grimy, drafty, combustible old shell" and sell out to a syndicate of titans that included J. P. Morgan (president), Andrew Carnegie, James Stillman, and W. W. Astor.

Their Madison Square Garden Company raised over $1.5 million, solicited Stanford White to design the new structure, and launched construction with a workforce of over a thousand men. Eleven months later, one of the largest public entertainment halls in the world opened its doors. Its vast buff-and-yellow base, girdled by pedestrian arcades and embellished with terra-cotta, was crowned by a three-hundred-foot-plus-tall tower modeled on Seville's Moorish Giralda. Exceeded in size only by Pulitzer's World Building, the tower became an instant attraction and emblem of New York City. After 1891 elevators carried the public to a loggia, from which stairs provided access to an observation platform 289 feet above the street that afforded bird's-eye views of the metropolis, and on higher still to a two-person perch at the 304-foot level. At the pinnacle, a Saint-Gaudens statue of Diana was unveiled on November 1, 1891, with a grand illumination of red fire, colored lights, and rockets. When the bombs bursting in air revealed that Diana was nude, moralists condemned it as an outrage, but J. P. Morgan liked it, and it stayed.

The Garden offered bourgeois audiences orchestral performances, light operas, and romantic comedies in the Garden Theater, as well as an array of deluxe facilities including a ballroom-concert hall, an adjoining supper room-foyer, a restaurant, men's and women's withdrawing rooms, and a roof garden enclosed in glass that could be removed during the summer. The Garden's colossal amphitheater—with 110 boxes and brilliant illumination from incandescent lamps—became home to elite affairs like the annual National Horse Show, the first big event of each season, and the Westminster Kennel Club Show. After 1891 it hosted the annual French Ball, still an unbuttoned affair. At the 1894 ball, New York clubmen tossed laughing courtesans, bare bosomed, from the dance floor into lower boxes. On one occasion, the bediamonded Miss Western, a leading madam, held court in the Astor family's private box—in the Queen's very seat—as hundreds of males passed by to pay her homage.

As a financial proposition, however, the Garden was a disaster. Elites alone couldn't support the lavishly equipped complex, which seated five thousand (twelve thousand at special events) and cost $240,000 a year to maintain. Stanford White tried fashioning some large-scale popular entertainments—re-creations of Shakespeare's House and the Globe Theatre—and the management brought in P. T. Barnum's and John Ringling's circuses. Madison Square Garden thus became an institution that oscillated, from night to night, between patrician and plebeian entertainments.

SATAN'S CIRCUS

North and west of Madison Square lay the sin-drenched Tenderloin—or Satan's Circus, as the clergy were fond of calling it. It started at Sixth and 23rd, where since 1879 Bryant's Opera House, one of the last minstrel venues in the city, had been leased by Adam Bial and John Koster for their Koster and Bial's Music Hall. A glorified concert saloon, where patrons in balcony boxes or at ground-floor tables could drink and watch Lillian McTwobucks do a Bowery version of the cancan or listen to barrelhouse baritones, Koster and Bial's was rather tame, though the *Times* called it "lurid." A few blocks north things were considerably lustier.

The notorious Haymarket, on Sixth just south of 30th, had a veneer of outward decency. It forbade its wealthy clientele from close-up dancing with prostitutes and expelled working-class girls who turned out for an evening's fun if they displayed their ankles. At the same time, it thoughtfully provided curtained galleries behind which discreet sex could be practiced. Visiting firemen or men-about-town could also repair to the Haymarket's balcony level, where cubicles featured sex exhibitions or "circuses."

Elite bordellos too had ensconced themselves in the Tenderloin, having pursued their respectable clients northward, like camp followers in the train of an army. As fashionable theaters had now banned third-tier operations, prostitutes met their patrons at the doors of the Metropolitan Opera House or Wallack's or Daly's and escorted them to nearby establishments, like the almost solid row of whorehouses on West 29th Street.

An evening of high culture was hardly a prerequisite for commercial sex, however. Elevated railroads put the area within easy reach of distant patrons. The same el that brought respectable women to shop at genteel department stores by day brought respectable men by night to shop for women. "Ladies' Mile" took on a different meaning at night, as Sixth Avenue between 14th and 34th streets became a brightly lit whore's promenade. A block farther west, patrols of black prostitutes gave the strip of Seventh Avenue between 23rd and 40th streets the name of "African Broadway."

Gambling resorts too settled here in the 1880s and 1890s. Of New York's hundreds of faro banks and policy shops, most of the first-class houses were Tenderloin operations. John Daly, the city's kingpin gambler, had been drawn to New York from Troy by the success of John Morrissey, and his famous house at 39 West 29th, open since 1878, paid a rumored one hundred thousand dollars in annual protection. The era's rising star was Richard A. Canfield, who had started as a poker-room operator in Providence, traveled to Monte Carlo and European spas to learn how aristocrats gambled, then moved to New York. In 1888 Canfield opened the Madison Square Club at 22 West 26th; a more dignified, luxurious, and honest operation than was customary at the time, it would soon win him international renown.

BEST OF BROADWAY

Those who left Madison Square Garden but stuck to the straight and narrow northward path found themselves in the heartland of the "legitimate" stage, which had fled the old Rialto to upper Broadway between 23rd and 42nd. The chain of theaters began with the Lyceum (1885), the first New York playhouse lighted by electricity, which had been personally installed by Edison. Augustin Daly, the first to gamble on a northward drift, had relocated his stock company to Broadway and 30th in 1879, and Lester Wallack had followed close behind in 1882. Then came the Bijou, the Abbey, the Casino (famed for its Moorish design and novel roof garden), and the Empire, at the very edge of Longacre (not yet Times) Square. By the early 1890s this once sparsely settled stretch of Broadway was ablaze with electric lights and thronged by crowds of middle- and upper-class theater, restaurant, and cafe patrons.

What kept these houses packed—even during the blizzard of 1888—was partly New Yorkers' traditional devotion to the stage, partly a great surge in out-of-town tourists and businessmen who stayed at the nearby hotels, and partly the greatly improved transportation network of ferries, elevateds, and streetcars, which expanded the accessible theatrical hinterland. Communication technology helped: prosperous Manhattanites with call boxes connected by wire to the nearest telegraph office for summoning a messenger boy to pick up a telegram could also use their device to order tickets from Daly's Theater, which then were delivered by hand.

For the most part, the content in these new playhouses was as respectable as their audiences. The Lyceum was the favorite haunt of the Four Hundred who, dressed in formal evening attire, took in its drawing-room dramas. Fashionable audiences packed Daly's for its lavish productions of Shakespeare and mingled during the intervals in its richly furnished lobby. Arthur Sullivan and W. S. Gilbert's *H.M.S. Pinafore* opened at the Standard in January 1879—they arrived for a visit and were given a gala reception at the Lotos Club—but the Casino became the city's new temple of light opera, drawing many patrons clad in the new tailless evening coat, the "tuxedo." Frohman's did well with English and European comedies and dramas. While some of these offerings could approach the mildly risqué, uptown promoters assured bourgeois audiences their plays met minimum standards of decency.

Edwin Booth, New York's (and America's) greatest tragedian, strove to make thespians as well as theater more respectable. Society packed the playhouses but kept players at arm's length, even the most highly reputed. Sarah Bernhardt's 1880 American debut at Booth's Theater was the talk of the town a year before she arrived, and the haute monde paid up to forty dollars a ticket to see her, but ladies refused to invite her to their homes, and her Century Association reception was for men only.

Booth, impressed by London's Garrick Club, where actors mixed with fashionable society, decided that a New York counterpart would help in "the elevation of the stage." In 1888 he and his friends bought a stately 1845 house on Gramercy Park, had Stanford White remodel it, and reopened it as the Players Club. Actors flocked to its subdued and dignified precincts. Those of too bohemian a bent were blackballed; they could, however, betake themselves to the Lambs Club, a more uninhibited and convivial watering hole, or to Keens Chophouse, which Albert Keen, the Lambs' manager, had opened on 36th Street in 1885.

This trend toward respectability was hailed by important voices in the larger theatrical community. The city's leading trade paper, the *New York Mirror* (1879; later the *Dramatic Mirror*), urged players to attend church every Sunday. And the genteel drama critic at the *Tribune* exhorted the profession "to instill, to protect, and to maintain purity, sweetness, and refinement in our feelings, our manners, our language, and our national character."

For all this, there was nothing like a whiff of forbidden sensuality to sell tickets, and the boundary between Broadway and the Tenderloin proved a porous one. A series of ravishing overseas visitors such as Lily Langtry and Sarah Bernhardt took to the boards, and the arrival of glamorous Lillian Russell turned out to be a classic case of downtown infiltrating uptown.

Russell was born Helen Louise Leonard in Clinton, Iowa, in 1861. At age two she was taken to Chicago by her father, a newspaperman, and her mother, Cynthia Leonard, a strong-willed feminist and crusader for women's rights, and placed in the Convent of Sacred Heart for eight years; she first studied music in church choirs. In 1877 Helen's mother, eager to work with the suffrage and socialist movements, took her seventeen-year-old daughter with her to New York. Intending Helen for an opera career, Leonard placed her with famed teacher Leopold Damrosch and then plunged into feminist work: in 1888 she would become the first woman to run for mayor of New York City. Helen, equally strong willed, abandoned her lessons and joined a chorus, where she caught the eye and ear of Tony Pastor. The variety entrepreneur assigned her a new name and launched her career with a major role in *The Pie-rats of Penyan*, a vaudeville burlesque of uptown operettas.

Russell soon shifted from satire to the real thing, landing a role in Gilbert and Sullivan's *Patience*. In short order the silvery-voiced singer had become the Casino's resident light opera prima donna and was pulling down a salary on a par with those of steel executives and Wall Street brokers. Sexually magnetic—her 165 pounds corseted into the requisite hourglass figure—Russell became one of the most lusted after women in America, with tycoons pleading to drink champagne from her slippers, yet all the while she maintained a reasonably respectable cachet.

The genteel theater, for all its reservations about actors, public sensuality, and the commercialization of sex, itself dabbled in the "leg-itimate" business (as one downtown burlesque show chortled). Its marketing of personalities, moreover, was directly tied in with the marketing of commodities. The daily doings of famous actresses were chronicled in the women's magazines, and their choice of clothes, jewelry, and millinery began to set national trends. Women adopted their coiffures and tried to imitate their figures (for a time Bernhardt's "spiral silhouette" banished the bustle). Makeup moved out of theatrical dressing rooms into respectable parlors, beauty shops became almost as common as barbershops, and photographs of Lily Langtry's flawless complexion soon graced ads for Pear's soap.

PULITZER'S WORLD

Manhattan and Coney islands were incubating a new mass commercial culture, but their assorted entertainment zones were strung out over such distances that it was hard for even the most diligent pedestrian to grasp the new phenomenon as a whole. There was one source, however, that even armchair investigators could easily consult and master: Joseph Pulitzer's *New York World*, which was itself a prize example of the new order.

After the Civil War Pulitzer had moved to St. Louis, worked as a reporter for a German-language paper, got into politics, practiced law, formed the *Post and Dispatch*, and become a successful publisher. By 1883 he was ready to tackle New York again, but the city's field of metropolitan dailies was a crowded one, filled with such potent competitors as Dana's *Sun*, Bennett Junior's *Herald*, George Jones's *New York Times*, and Whitelaw Reid's *Tribune*—just among the morning papers.

There was also the *World*, once the organ of Swallowtail Democrats, now Jay Gould's plaything. Deep in the red, it nevertheless had an Associated Press franchise and a Democratic lineage in a Democratic town, so Pulitzer bought it from the hard-bargaining financier for an outrageous $346,000, payable in installments. Pulitzer had his foothold in Manhattan, and a staggering debt as well. Simply to survive he needed a fantastically rapid rise in circulation.

He got it. When he took over in 1883 the World was selling perhaps fifteen thousand copies a day. It passed the sixty thousand mark in a matter of months. The *Herald*, *Times*, and *Tribune*, acting like rival railroad magnates, slashed their prices to keep up, but to no avail. Within a scant two years the *World*'s circulation topped 150,000, and in 1890 Pulitzer capped his triumph by erecting the world's tallest building.

Pulitzer succeeded by navigating the course charted back in the 1830s by those master pilots of the penny press, Bennett Senior and Benjamin Day. He also seized on the possibilities of the 1880s: the industrialization of communications technology, the techniques developed by the advertising business, and the strategies deployed by the mass entertainment entrepreneurs on Coney Island, the Bowery, Broadway, and Union Square.

The *World* adopted a breezy and colloquial style. "Condense, condense!" Pulitzer commanded his reporters, following admen in opting for the simple nouns, vivid verbs, and short sentences that made the paper accessible to immigrants learning the language. When chastised by E. L. Godkin of the *Evening Post* for breaking with genteel conventions, Pulitzer replied: "I want to talk to a nation, not to a select committee."

World news stories scrapped leisurely chronology for snappy analysis, putting the who-what-when-where-and-why into an easily graspable lead paragraph. This, together with smaller pages, was a boon to hurrying commuters, explained a trade paper in 1887, as New Yorkers "read largely in the horse cars, the elevated railroads and the omnibuses"—crowded and noisy venues. "We do not want a paper which requires a whole conveyance in which to turn its pages."

Pulitzer reformatted the front page. Even penny press papers like the *Herald* and the *Sun* had stayed with single-column headlines, simply adding subheads to denote particularly important stories. The *World* went with multicolumn banners that contemporaries likened to department store displays designed to grab shoppers' attention.

He plunged into pictures. Graphics had long been central to weekly magazines and illustrated papers like *Frank Leslie's*, and in 1880 the *New York Daily Graphic* had supplemented its zinc etchings and photoengraved line illustrations with the first halftone photograph ever reproduced in a New York newspaper, a picture labeled "Shantytown." But in the regular daily press, it was Pulitzer who first routinely deployed images to accompany text—an enhancement that, like bold heads and terse prose, appealed to the barely or recently literate. He also furthered the development of cartoons (the *Daily News* had run a strip since 1884) and broke new ground in 1894 with the first colored comic strip—also, curiously, called "Shantytown." This was followed by the introduction of "Hogan's Alley," featuring a hairless, single-toothed street urchin dressed in flowing yellow robes. The "Yellow Kid" would be spun off as a strip in its own right.

Pulitzer's content, like his style, appealed to a mass audience. Immediately on assuming control, he had called his inherited, dignified staff together and announced: "Gentlemen, you realize that a change has taken place in the *World*. Heretofore you have all been living in the parlour and taking baths every day. Now I wish you to understand that, in future, you are all walking down the Bowery." This unnerving prospect prompted several on-the-spot resignations, allowing Pulitzer to bring in replacements from his St. Louis paper.

Pulitzer, like Harrigan and Hart, drew on working-class life for material. The *World* chronicled ordinary people, using human interest stories to spotlight and dignify members of the metropolitan crowd. Pulitzer's reporters routinely quoted the kind of New Yorker who had rarely appeared in print before, like the gashouse laborer who had just learned of the existence of Central Park and attended a Sunday concert there: the *World* passed on to the world his remark that "to-day I have been as happy as a king." Graphically too the paper was broad gauged. It filled its pages with visages of hotel clerks, artists, cooks, and cops, as well as portraits of judges, politicians, and financiers. The paper also practiced skillful tribal journalism, scorning the English on behalf of Irish readers, providing Kleindeutschland with news of Bismarck's doings, and paying close attention to Jewish holidays for patrons on the Lower East Side. Pulitzer covered, as well, aspects of commercial culture usually relegated to specialized journals like the *Spirit of the Times, Clipper*, and *Police Gazette*; he inaugurated a sports page in the 1880s.

The *World* treated as front-page news such dramatic moments in the life of the city as the Festival of Connection marking the opening of the Brooklyn Bridge. It promoted investigative reporting: *World* reporter Nellie Bly (née Elizabeth Cochrane) feigned insanity, got herself committed to the Blackwell's Island Asylum, and wrote up a story on the abominable conditions there that led to a grand jury investigation.[1] Pulitzer certainly exploited sentiment for the sake of sales, but his paper also promoted public generosity and helped foster an ethos of civic solidarity.

Pulitzer made his paper news as well as newsmaker. In 1885 the Statue of Liberty languished unassembled in France, efforts to raise money for a pedestal having stalled. Crying, "Let us not wait for the millionaires to give this money," Pulitzer appealed to "the people" to rescue the monument and avoid an "irrevocable disgrace to New York City." Tens of thousands of small contributions rolled in, the pedestal was constructed, and, in the process, the *World* became associated indelibly with the enterprise (Pulitzer even incorporated the statue into the paper's nameplate).

The *World* took great pains to attract women readers, a constituency most dailies gave scant attention. Pulitzer understood, as did manufacturers and purveyors of consumer goods, that in the 1880s women did most household purchasing, and their patronage was therefore the key to attracting advertisers. The *World* accordingly argued that "what the New York woman of the higher order is likely to have as her special denotement is style," unlike her Boston sister who was "severely intellectual or burdened with scholarship." Maintaining this stylish lead was a difficult and never-ending process, and the *World* was there to help.

The *World* also walked a fine line between the prudery demanded by genteel opinion and a sale-boosting prurience. The paper's pages, for all their surface propriety, were suffused with erotic innuendo, sternly condemning sinfulness in general while recounting in detail the doings of particular sinners. The *World* served up scandals, particularly when they involved the respectable and prosperous, and waged campaigns against prostitution, abortionists, variety shows, and opium dens—campaigns simultaneously sanctimonious and titillating.

Pulitzer adopted a similar strategy in depicting violence, wrapping concupiscent accounts of bloody deeds in pious disapproval. Sensational headlines—"Who Murdered Mrs. Bush?"—dragged attention to graphic coverage of gruesome incidents, often accompanied by precisely labeled crime-scene sketches ("Bed Covered with Blood"; "Sink in Which the Knife was Found"). Executions were featured because judicial murders were simultaneously gory ("Dragged Resisting to a Prayerless Doom") and legitimate. Reviving an ancient urban practice, the very first issues of the revamped *World* carried lurid accounts of executions, dwelling on the last hours of condemned killers.

If Pulitzer paid extravagant attention to most sensational aspects of the urban underworld, affording bourgeois readers the opportunity for armchair slumming, he provided equal opportunity voyeurism in the *World*'s society pages, peeps inside the grand chateaux that afforded the twin pleasures of virtuous condemnation and vicari-

---

1. On November 14, 1890, Bly left New York City aiming to travel around the world in fewer than the eighty days it had taken Jules Verne's fictional Phileas Fogg. After a brief stop at Amiens to interview Monsieur Verne (who said she'd never make it), she dashed eastward while the *World* watched breathlessly, chronicling her race against time, whipping up excitement, and running "Your Nellie Bly Guessing Match," in which readers were urged to estimate the number of days and hours she would take. The winning number proved to be seventy-two. When Bly arrived back in the city, thousands cheered and cannons were fired, as if her circumnavigation, like the opening of the Erie Canal or the Atlantic Cable, warranted a full-fledged Festival of Connection, which in a way it did. Pulitzer transformed Bly's hoisting of the *World*'s circulation figures *itself* into news. He began publishing daily circulation statements, transforming business exigency into popular drama, while simultaneously underscoring the *World*'s reputation as an advertising vehicle.

ous sybaritism. The paper attacked the culture of the "watered-stock aristocracy" and lit into the ostentatious glitter of the new and "vulgar wealthy," denouncing their urban chateaux, Newport palaces, and valet-guarded boxes at the Metropolitan Opera House. It was equally scathing about the old guard, ruthlessly lampooning the "snobocracy" and its pretensions to noble lineage.

Pulitzer also kept a critical edge on reporting about the everyday life of the working classes. Proclaiming that the *World* would henceforth be "dedicated to the cause of the people rather than that of purse potentates," he ran stories on squalid tenement housing, impure milk, infant mortality, female and child labor, and strikes. In one of the earliest instances of what would later be called muckraking, Pulitzer denounced Rockefeller's Standard Oil as "the most cruel, impudent, pitiless, and grasping monopoly that ever fastened upon a country," and his crusades for antitrust legislation helped pass the Sherman Act in 1890.

The *World* pointed out and excoriated the connection between big money and politicians—if they were Republican politicians. In the 1884 presidential race, when 180 financiers attended a sumptuous Delmonico's dinner for candidate James G. Blaine, the *World* denounced "the Royal Feast of Belshazzar." A huge front-page political cartoon depicted Blaine and the "Money Kings"—with precise caricatures of Gould, Vanderbilt, Astor, Depew, Carnegie, Seligman, Sage, and others shown drinking "Monopoly Soup" and downing "Lobby Pudding," heedless of the pleas of an unemployed worker, his emaciated wife, and his ragged child for crumbs from the groaning board. The *World* also made much of Blaine's meeting, earlier the same day, with a group of Protestant New York clergymen at the Fifth Avenue Hotel. The spokesman, the Rev. Samuel D. Burchard of the Murray Hill Presbyterian Church, had suggested the Democrats were the party of "rum, Romanism and rebellion." A tired Blaine failed to contradict the remark, a silence the *World* converted to vigorous assent to a proposition that affronted Catholic citizens.

Despite its sharp, even shrill attacks on great wealth, the World was not a radical paper. It railed at the Rockefellers but rejected socialism and anarchism, arguing that an enlightened capitalism could avoid class warfare if—with the help of the press—it rid itself of excesses. For all its quarrels with corruption, it was a staunch Democratic Party organ. In the 1886 mayoralty campaign it supported Abram Hewitt, not Henry George.

The *World* was a triumph, but Pulitzer proved unable to enjoy it. Long burdened with psychological problems (he was probably a manic depressive), his eyes and nerves deteriorated, forcing him to spend much of his time in a darkened room, and he became extremely sensitive to unexpected sounds. In his later years, the man who had mastered and marketed the city's cacophonous commercial culture would retreat to a McKim, Meade and White mansion on 73rd Street; its utterly noise-proofed annex—double walls packed with mineral wool, and triple-glass windows—served as Pulitzer's refuge from the slightest city sound, a burden the neurotic publisher now found intolerable.

65

Purity Crusade

The Great Fire broke out first in Murray Hill, where enraged and drunken mobs sacked and torched the mansions of millionaires. Then hungry men from the Bowery began pouring into fashionable restaurants, gorging themselves, setting the eateries ablaze, and moving on to loot and burn. Perched atop an elevated railroad platform, a reporter watched the conflagration spread out from Fifth Avenue in "billows and waves and worlds of smoke and flame." The fires roared south, incinerating the great newspaper offices, sending rivers of now-molten lead type flowing out from Franklin Square. Finally the inferno swept into the poor and industrial districts, and soon "the oil, the gas, the rum, the thousands of filthy things which man in his drunken greed had allowed to accumulate on the face of the island appealed to heaven for purification," and purification was at last attained when the colossal firestorm, having consumed hundreds of thousands of lives, seared on and on till it "burned and burned and burned to the very bed-rock!"

Or such was the premise of popular writer Joaquin Miller's *The Destruction of Gotham*, issued by Funk and Wagnalls in the year of the Henry George campaign. While Miller's book added luster to his reputation, as apocalyptic literature it was soon eclipsed by Ignatius Donnelly's *Caesar's Column* (1889), which would sell a quarter-million copies and become one of the century's bestsellers. Donnelly depicted New York City, a century in the future, as being locked in a death struggle between the Oligarchy, a cabal of acquisitive and vicious Hebrew capitalists who had seized wealth and power through "subtle combinations," and the Brotherhood of Destruction, composed of "vast, streaming swarms" of beaten-down proletarians of all nations, commanded by the Italian-born giant Caesar Lomellini. After Lomellini's forces routed the evil Oligarchs with "dynamite bullets," the "brutal and ravenous multitude"—with no one left to keep order—broke loose "like a huge flood, long damned up" and flowed "full of foam and terror" in every direction. Maddened men chased well-dressed individuals "like hounds after a rabbit," tore them apart, and whirled the dead bodies to delighted spectators, who hauled them off in gory chariots to Union Square. There, by the light of blazing bonfires, the drunken victors set sixty thousand prisoners ("merchants professional men, etc.") to stacking and cementing a quarter-million cadavers into a colossal column of corpses—"in commemoration of the death and burial of modern civilization."

Like Miller, Donnelly saw cities—New York in particular—as breeding million-aires, tramps, and urban Armageddon. "The classes from which we have most to fear," agreed Josiah Strong in *Our Country* (1891), "are the two extremes of society—the dangerously rich and the dangerously poor." Like other popular Cassandras, Strong, who was secretary of the Congregationalist American Home Missionary Society, emphasized that "a mighty emergency is upon us"—us being the country's imperiled Protestant middle classes, who were fast losing any ability to rein in either irresponsible monopolists or "ignorant and vicious" aliens.

In New York itself, the comfortable middle classes were finding the final decades of the nineteenth century a strange and perplexing time. They knew they lived amid unprecedented progress and prosperity. Yet everywhere they beheld portents of danger: poverty, corruption, licentiousness, militant unionism, political radicalism, open strife between capital and labor, and a surge of immigrants so vast and alien that it was hard to imagine what would become of the old Anglo-Saxon republic.

Badly buffeted by the upheavals of the mid-1880s—the recession, the rise of the Knights of Labor, the great strikes for the eight-hour day, the burgeoning immigration, the near-triumph of the Henry George campaign, and the Haymarket bombings—many middle-class New Yorkers would enlist in movements dedicated to warding off the now so frequently prophesied apocalypse. Some would direct their energies toward checking the unbridled growth of corporate power, others would concentrate on constraining or transforming the disorderly poor, and others still would find their self-assigned mission of preserving order and civility in urban affairs leading them in both directions at once.

ARMIES OF SALVATION

Among those most rattled by contemporary disorders were metropolitan ministers, to whom it had become grimly apparent that Protestantism had lost any influence with the urban working class. This conviction was aired and ratified in December 1888 at a Chickering Hall Christian Conference organized by prominent clergymen. Minister after minister stood up to testify that New York's Protestant churches, by moving north with their uptown congregations, had abandoned the lower city to Catholicism, Judaism, secularism, anarchism, and socialism.

In *Modern Cities and Their Religious Problems* (1887), Samuel Lane Loomis suggested another reason that the masses of immigrant workingmen avoided Protestant services apart from lack of proximity: their (misguided) conviction that these were "the churches of the capitalists," simply because they were "usually attended and sustained by persons of means and intelligence." The deplorable consequence was that most laborers (overwhelmingly Catholic) "never breathed a Christian atmosphere" and—separated from good influence—fell prey to drink, crime, and anarchism.

Some evangelicals still hoped that old-time proselytizing would solve the problem.

The Sunday school movement and urban revivalists pressed ahead with renewed vigor, while the New York Mission and Tract Society updated its publications and, with substantial Chamber of Commerce support, tried aggressively to convert the Jews. But the immigrant wards seemed impervious to such efforts.

There *were* Protestants who had more of an impact, though their successes were of limited comfort to the established ministry; their advance guard had arrived on Wednesday, March 10, 1880. A Pioneer Party of the Salvation Army had marched down the gangplank of the steamer *Australia* at Castle Garden, singing hymns and carrying a flag emblazoned BLOOD & FIRE NEW YORK NO. 1—to the amazement of a curious throng of bystanders and reporters who mistook them at first for a traveling concert troupe.

Founded two years earlier in England by Methodist William Booth, the Salvation Army had taken evangelical aim at the most destitute members of the London poor, then decided to expand to America. A company of seven female volunteers was dispatched under the command of trusted Booth lieutenant George Scott Railton, a former clerk turned full-time missionary. Immediately on arrival the little vanguard set out to "wed ourselves to the fate and fortunes of the so-called dangerous classes." Spurning offers of church pulpits, they scandalized respectable opinion by accepting a proposition from the notorious Harry Hill to "do a turn" at his music hall that Sunday. The ensuing revival service—covered in the *World* under the headline "A Peculiar People amid Queer Surroundings"—was treated by most of Harry's clientele as a great joke. But one participant, a well-known Manhattan drunkard known as Ash-Barrel Jimmy, was wrested from the Devil's grip that day, becoming the Army's first American convert. Word of this miracle brought large crowds to hear Jimmy's "testimony" and, soon, that of other reformed drunkards. When the Army's rented halls overflowed, they took their meetings to the streets.

Uniformed soldiers of the Salvation Army conducting a worship service, *Harper's Weekly*, April 3, 1880. (© Collection of The New-York Historical Society)

The Army promoted its orthodox Wesleyan message of grace, forgiveness, and love—and total war on drink—with novel methods. Stirring brass bands, drums, and tambourines, clearly audible over the din of city traffic, attracted passers-by. So did the rousing versions of religious texts set to popular melodies, including barroom ballads, love songs, vaudeville ditties, and minstrel tunes. Ranks and titles gave a new sense of importance and purpose to converts. So did the handsome blue uniforms (and black straw bonnets for women), which made all soldiers, even those too poor to purchase decent clothing, equal participants in the Great Salvation War. Women, who quickly advanced to leadership positions, were attracted in great numbers. The Army displayed a Barnumesque flair for publicity, as when they burned the Devil (the Enemy Commander) in effigy. And they showed a canny, Pulitzerian grasp of effective public prose by hewing to the injunction "Everything short, sharp, striking, vigorous."

The Army supplemented its psychic and spiritual appeal with tangible social benefits. The October 1886 issue of its weekly publication, the *War Cry*, announced the opening in Brooklyn of a Rescue Home for Fallen and Homeless Girls, a haven for husbandless pregnant women, the most desperate of outcasts from respectability. In 1889 they opened a "creche" on Cherry Street where infant care was provided for mothers at work or in jail, a shoestring program sustained by donated pennies, baby clothes, and rice. The same year the Army began sending pairs of "Slum Sisters" to the streets. The women helped stroke victims, washed babies, cooked meals for invalids, and dressed the dead for the undertaker. Salvation Army girls, often alerted by bartenders, entered Bowery saloons or dance halls and rescued girls stupefied from drink or drugs, fighting off men who wanted to keep them there. The program was hailed even by the cynical as an angelic ministry.

At Christmas time in 1891, the Army opened a Cheap Food and Shelter Depot in the basement of a deserted old Baptist church on Bedford and Downing streets. At this New York Lighthouse men could get a box bed and a shower for seven cents (half that charged by commercial lodging houses, for much cleaner, safer, and drunk-free surroundings). A restaurant served staples for pennies. The totally penniless could work for the shelter for two hours in the morning, splitting wood, which was then sold to poor families. Soon larger quarters were opened on Front Street, with attendance at evangelical meetings a prerequisite for coffee and buns. Before long their urban enterprises included day nurseries and Salvage Brigades that collected old clothes, hired the poor to repair them, and sold them to the needy.

This combination of material and spiritual aid was spectacularly successful. The crusade expanded rapidly—by 1890 the Salvation Army was established in forty-three states—with national headquarters at the Brooklyn Lyceum. But such success did not please genteel church leaders. They were offended by the Army's hoopla and made uncomfortable by its bumptious vitality, which they felt degraded the Christian heritage. While there was some admiration for its expanding social program, overall they found plebeian Protestantism—and its biblical literalism—hard to swallow.

"FRIENDLY VISITORS"

The welfare reforms of the 1870s, by halting municipal outdoor relief and handing public monies over to private agencies for disbursal, guaranteed that metropolitan charity would be governed by well-worn axioms: poverty most often stemmed from individual moral and character defects (probably hereditary), and the task of scientific charity was to dispense assistance, cautiously and grudgingly, to the deserving while incarcerating or rehabilitating the remainder.

In 1881 State Board of Charities commissioner Josephine Shaw Lowell surveyed the city's existing private charities in the light of this flinty perspective and found too many of them "wasteful" and "encouraging pauperism and imposture." New York's alms enterprise remained insufficiently coordinated, despite the decades-long efforts of the Association for Improving the Condition of the Poor (AICP). "So important a business as the administration of charity has become in New York City," Lowell concluded, "requires to be carried on on business principles."

In 1882, accordingly, Lowell launched the New York Charity Organization Society (COS), modeled on the London Society for Organizing Charitable Relief and Repressing Mendicity (1869), established by professionals intent on curtailing indiscriminate almsgiving by aristocratic West Enders. As the group's "guiding spirit" she presided over a thoroughgoing amalgamation of Protestant almsgiving organizations and families. Emerging as something of a Charity Trust—the philanthropic equivalent of Standard Oil—New York COS pooled the resources of over five hundred churches and societies and nearly a thousand private families, embracing old monied (Robert W. De Forest was president) and new (J. P. Morgan was a generous patron). In 1893 this consolidating impulse received architectural expression when COS erected a United Charities Building (on Fourth Avenue and 22nd Street) and persuaded other charitable organizations such as the Mission and Tract Society, the Children's Aid Society, and the AICP to move in with them (merging with the latter in all but name).

To block multiple handouts, COS established a centralized Registry Bureau to which outdoor relief agencies, asylums, churches, and the city's Department of Public Charities and Correction sent in data on their clients. By 1887 COS had accumulated data on nearly ninety thousand families and 27,400 houses "occupied by the dependant and disreputable classes." By the mid-1890s, when COS had files on 170,000 families or individuals, it was making the information freely available, by return mail, not only to agencies considering giving relief but to prospective employers, landlords, banks, and even the police. (Under Seth Low, the Brooklyn Bureau of Charities set up a similar master index to weed out welfare cheats.)

COS tightened standards. "Gratuitous charity," Lowell said, "works evil rather than good." Authorizing assistance for a widow with infants might make her life easier, but then the mother might, "by being relieved of anxiety for them, lose her love for the children." Giving a handout to an unemployed man might get him through tough times but also teach "the dreadful lesson that it is easy to get a day's living without working for it." COS, accordingly, was quite selective in its help (far more stringent than the Department of Charities and Correction had been), and it turned down the majority of applicants after probing investigations revealed that character flaws underlay their poverty. Paupers, Lowell argued, should be discouraged from reproducing themselves: while "every person born into a civilized community has the right to live," the community had the right to see that "incompetent and dangerous persons shall not, so far as can be helped, be born to acquire this right to live upon others."

Lowell relied on volunteers, believing the AICP had lost touch with the poor after it switched to using salaried visitors in 1879. COS promoters believed the urban poor had degenerated morally in large part because they had been cut off from the elevating influence of their moral betters. The job of reknitting the urban fabric could best be undertaken (one charity expert argued) not by hired professionals but by "noble-hearted women of the wealthier class," who would bring the poor under "the firm though loving government of heroic women."

The volunteers—"friendly visitors"—who were urged to help their assigned charges depart the "ranks of idlers" by setting a personal example, by diffusing strength of character across class lines, by making the recipient more like the visitor: honest, thrifty, sober. "If we do not furnish the poor with elevating influences," the COS argued, "they will rule us by degrading ones." The proto-caseworkers were urged to avoid soft-heartedness. "All charity must tend to raise and elevate the moral nature," Lowell reminded her troops, "even if the process be as painful as plucking out an eye or cutting off a limb."

The return of hard times in the mid 1880s brought renewed demands for aid to the unemployed, presenting the COS with its first major challenge. It succeeded in keeping charitable relief to a bare minimum, though Lowell's efforts in 1883 to convince the Board of Apportionment "that they can safely cut off the City coal and trust to private charity to make up any necessary claims" were blocked in part due to objections by Tammany-connected coal merchants. It did establish a wood yard on East 24th Street in 1884, but the organization made clear this was not done "with any idea of providing work at fair prices for the unemployed, but purely as a means by which to test the good faith of those seeking relief under the plea of inability to procure work." Tickets were printed up and sold to charitable persons, who in turn could give them to street beggars in lieu of cash. Each entitled a man to a "day's work" cutting wood. When finished he would be given fifty cents or, if homeless, two meals and a night's lodging.

To ensure the poor did not escape its stern concern by panhandling, COS established a Committee on Mendicancy, which hired "Special Agents" who were empowered by the city to arrest beggars. In 1885 they hauled seven hundred before the police justices, then stayed to make sure they were punished under the vagrancy statutes. The police notified COS when such miscreants were released from the Blackwell's Island Workhouse, and it published a bulletin listing the names and aliases of all known street beggars at large. COS offered as well to investigate and deal with all "Begging-Letter Writers"—the unemployed having gotten into the habit of sending their former employers pleading missives.

COS inveighed too against the city's policy of providing emergency housing in verminous police station basements, lest encouraging the shiftless in their idleness set the working poor a bad example. Lowell's group was never able to choke off the practice altogether—Tammany police were unwilling to give up their supply of voters—but it did get the legislature, in 1886, to authorize establishment of a Municipal Lodging House (on First Avenue) which would give food and a night's lodging (no more than three times in any one month) in return for labor in the COS wood yard. As a corollary, police stations within one mile of the house were forbidden to provide shelter.

"The task of dealing with the poor and degraded has become a science," said Lowell with some satisfaction—but problems remained. There was the ongoing sniping from those who called COS the "Society for the Suppression of Benevolence." There was the contradiction between their goal, of restoring the poor to independence, and their method, of granting relief only to those who did as they were told. There was also a dismaying lack of heroic women volunteers—the requirement of being both loving friend and prying investigator put some people off—forcing the COS to resort to paid agents. The biggest problem, however, lay in dealing with the children of the "poor and degraded."

SAVE THE CHILDREN

More than ever—given the new "scientific" literature on the heritability of crime, poverty, insanity, and drunkenness—the Protestant welfare establishment was determined to prevent poor and working-class parents from passing on their lax morals and distaste for work to their offspring. "To keep such families together," wrote charity reformer Charles Hoyt, "is contrary to sound policy; the sooner they can be separated and broken up, the better it will be for the children and for society at large"—a view endorsed officially by the Protestant female reformers of the State Charities Aid Association (SCAA) in 1879.

Charles Loring Brace and his Children's Aid Society (CAS) had continued doing their best in this regard. By the mid-1890s Brace had dispatched over ninety thousand poor children to Protestant homes in the Midwest so American women could raise them in proper surroundings. CAS surveys reported these children were happily growing into independent adulthood—though in fact a disturbing number seemed to be wending their way back to New York and reestablishing relations with their families.

The Society for the Prevention of Cruelty to Children (SPCC) was empowered to take more definitive action than Brace's group could. A spinoff of Henry Bergh's old American Society for the Prevention of Cruelty to Animals, the SPCC had been established in 1874 by ASPCA lawyer Elbridge Gerry. An all-male, all-elite, and overwhelmingly Protestant organization, it searched out children deemed neglected or abused, prosecuted the parents, and turned the youths over to an appropriate agency (after 1881 it was given actual law enforcement power).

The problem lay in finding an appropriate agency. In the old days, such youths would have been consigned to an institution like the almshouse or the House of Refuge, but asylums had fallen out of favor. Rather than educating and redeeming their youthful charges, they were now believed to expose them to further degradation. Indeed, in 1875 the SCAA had won passage of a Children's Act removing all two-to-sixteen-year-olds from poorhouses. In large measure the law was aimed at parents who, after public outdoor relief was terminated, began entering poorhouses with their children, thus maintaining their negative influence. The new legislation required parents entering poorhouses to surrender their children, who would then be transferred to orphanages, from which they could be passed on to decent foster homes.

Unfortunately for this schema, the male Irish Catholics who had just assumed control of Tammany Hall under Honest John Kelly proved newly powerful enough to insist that the law require children be placed only in institutions controlled by persons of the same religious faith. Catholic nuns moved swiftly to turn their convents into refuges from Protestant childsavers, and did so with public money. Within a year, the number of children in orphanages and asylums nearly doubled. Soon thousands of poor Catholic parents, who had been loathe, even in extremis, to send their children to hated Protestant institutions, were turning to the new Catholic ones, treating them as free and temporary boarding schools. Such families knew that the sisters believed poverty a misfortune to be alleviated, not a condition to be reformed, and while they might resent the nuns for requiring compulsory attendance at Mass, they knew that once they were back on their feet, the sisters would funnel their children home to them again.

By 1885 nuns were rearing over 80 percent of the city's dependent youths and had won effective control of the metropolitan child care system. Josephine Shaw Lowell and her COS and CAS colleagues were appalled. For all their professions of nonsectarianism, anti-Catholicism ran deep in the childsaving movement; the Children's Aid Society refused to place Catholic or Jewish children with Catholic or Jewish families, as they weren't proper homes.

The nuns, moreover, had successfully challenged the hard-won right of Protestant women to mother the children of the immigrant poor, which in turn had justified their own entry into public life. The SCAA fought hard in the mid-1880s to dismantle the convent-based system, arguing it led to child abuse or sowed the seed of "pauper poison." But Tammany and the archdiocese backed the nuns. So did such powerful Protestant male groups as Gerry's SPCC, because the women religious were unquestionably efficient, and cheap—having taken a vow of poverty—which meant a saving of tax dollars.

THE WAR ON SIN

Protestant reformers were deeply disturbed by the wide-open wickedness of New York's teeming entertainment quarters. Saloons were everywhere—the city seemed awash in liquor—and one Methodist speaker at the 1888 Chickering Hall conference noted that where there was but one Protestant church for every 4,464 inhabitants, the saloon-to-inhabitant ratio was one to 150. What was particularly galling to genteel opponents was the de facto legalized status of commercialized vice. The *National Police Gazette* reported regularly on the fancy life of theaters, gambling dens, and bordellos, and a new generation of sunshine-and-shadow writers provided salacious details on dives and opium dens.

The refusal to pay even decent tribute to the opinions of the respectable drove conservative feminists and cultivated gentlemen ("upright men and virtuous women" in the terminology of the day) into banding together to purify New York City. Rejecting laissez-faire in the moral realm as others were discarding it in the sphere of economics, purity reformers called for greater public regulation of private behavior.

The New York Committee for the Suppression of Legalized Vice, a key organization of the purity movement, was generaled by Aaron Macy Powell and Abigail Hopper Gibbons, two old veterans of the abolitionist crusade (Powell had been an editor of the *Anti-Slavery Standard*). They set out to free their "fallen sisters" from a "white slavery" as evil as the black slavery that preceded it.

In this they took their cues from England, where since the 1870s a coalition of middle-class nonconformists, feminists, and radical workingmen had been calling for repeal of Britain's Contagious Diseases Act (1864), which effectively legalized and regulated commercial sex. The British movement received an enormous boost in 1885 with the publication, in the *Pall Mall Gazette*, of a series by W. T. Stead entitled "The Maiden Tribute of Modern Babylon." Stead had investigated the traffic in young girls in London's vice emporiums and claimed to have actually bought a virgin on the black market. His accounts were inflammatory, prurient, and factually dubious but, coming on top of a decade of moral mobilization, touched off a popular uproar.

The New York Committee, for its part, forced the American Medical Association to drop its plan for municipal regulation of prostitution. Instead the physicians agreed to advocate chastity as the best, indeed the only, defense against venereal disease. The

New York Committee also launched petition campaigns demanding the age of consent be increased from ten, a figure that had come to seem shockingly low to the middle classes, whose members increasingly deferred the age of matrimony. Upward revision would also block brothels from legally recruiting scarcely adolescent girls, leading many working-class fathers along with the Knights of Labor to back the campaign. New York State raised the age of consent from ten to sixteen in 1889 and upped it again to eighteen in 1895—the only eastern state to do so. Now sexual behavior once merely improper was illegal.

For a short time, during the administrations of Mayors Grace and Hewitt—at the height of the transatlantic excitement over the Stead exposé—purity crusaders also succeeded in getting the municipality to wage limited war on prostitution and gambling. In October 1886 Mayor Grace authorized police raids on leading concert saloons and on the West 27th Street brothels, even those under the protection of police Captain Alexander "Clubber" Williams. Mayor Hewitt continued the campaigns and drove many prostitutes out of the concert saloons, leading them to set up operations in tenements around the city.

But these efforts were of limited reach and effectiveness. They had no impact at all on brothels outside the Tenderloin, and within it the primary consequence of raids— which reformers called "shake-ups" and madams called "shake-downs"—was to increase the price of doing business, thus funneling additional funds to the Tammany machine.

To surmount such obstacles, purity reformers, like their charity counterparts, began gathering law enforcement into their own hands, establishing private preventive societies to ride herd on lax public officials. "In some degree," the New York *Times* observed, "our voluntary associations for the prevention of various evils resemble vigilance committees, regulators, or lynch policemen."

Anthony Comstock's Society for the Suppression of Vice (SSV) served as censorship squad. Armed with federal authority and the backing of Morris Jessup, J. P. Morgan, and other members of the Chamber of Commerce, Comstock patrolled library bookshelves, scrutinized the city's printed pages for anything that might corrupt youthful morals, and kept would-be purveyors of birth control information in line.

Steadily expanding his definition of obscenity, Comstock began attacking art he deemed unfit for the public eye. "Nude paintings and statues," he cautioned, "are the decoration of infamous resorts, and the law-abiding American will never admit them to the sacred confines of his home." Lest passers-by be tempted by lascivious statuary in art gallery windows, Comstock warned dealers not to display naked pictures where the public could see them. In 1887, however, when he raided the Herman Knoedler Art Gallery on Fifth Avenue for violating this dictate, he was sharply rebuked by the *Times* and warned not to become "a social nuisance almost as pestilent as that which he exists to abate." Comstock shrugged off such protests and pressed ahead. In 1890 he invaded the shop of Eugene Caret, a new art dealer on Broadway, and insisted he remove a photograph of an offending Rodin statue; the frightened dealer sold off his stock and left on the next boat.

Comstock's SSV, along with Elbridge Gerry's SPCC and Presbyterian minister Howard Crosby's SPC (the Society for the Prevention of Crime he founded in 1878), also arranged raids on concert saloons, dance halls, brothels, rat pits, and Coney Island's Gut in a determined—but largely unsuccessful—effort to suppress "immoral behavior." Comstock became an early pioneer in the repression of "fairies," "mollie coddles," and "androgynes," in the parlance of the day. But while the growing attention of vice reformers did lead to an increase in sodomy prosecutions in the 1880s and 1890s and to a shutdown of the Slide in 1892, for the most part same-sex hangouts like Paresis Hall continued to receive (and pay for) the protection of the police.

The reformers' war on gambling garnered only modest victories. In 1877 the state legislature had banned the old auction pool betting system, but succeeded mainly in promoting bookmaking, a system in which bettors selected a horse at publicly posted odds. Now neighborhood bookies sprang up, offering their services to gamblers who couldn't afford a trip to the track, at such male bastions as newsstands, barbershops, saloons, and "poolrooms" (off-track betting parlors). Results were received immediately throughout the city via Western Union, which in 1890 paid sixteen hundred dollars a day to each New York track for the exclusive right to transmit results. Despite this overhead Western Union's racing department became the most profitable part of the company.

In 1887 the Rev. Thomas de Witt Talmage, minister of the Central Presbyterian Church of Brooklyn, teamed up with Comstock (along with New York racetrack interests) in winning passage of the Ives Anti-Poolroom Law, which forbade off-track betting but authorized thirty days of wagering at tracks each year. Despite the Ives law, and the Saxton Act of 1893, which made keeping poolrooms a felony, they continued to operate with virtual impunity. Comstock managed to instigate the occasional police raid, but poolroom clerks were usually forewarned of such events and, if caught, usually acquitted by Tammany judges. Indeed, by the mid-1890s Big Tim Sullivan and other Tammany honchos ran organized bookmaker and poolroom syndicates.

Those out to purify civic life made more headway against boxing. Influence and payoffs enabled "exhibition" bouts in the early 1880s—John L. Sullivan began fighting in such events at Madison Square Garden in 1882—but in 1884 and 1885 reformers got police to break up Sullivan's fights there, local promoters gave up the business, and the sport's locus shifted to New Orleans. In the early 1890s, however, local prizefighting revived, mainly at Coney Island, under the auspices of boss John Y. McKane. The Gravesend politico also owned the Coney Island Athletic Club (organized in May 1892 by Kings County machine politicians), which became the leading boxing club in the United States (though in 1893 public pressure did force it to cancel a world championship heavyweight bout between Jim Corbett and Charley Mitchell).

Efforts to ban alcohol made limited progress, despite the emergence of the Women's Christian Temperance Union (WCTU). In the 1880s the WCTU employed a missionary evangelist to meet immigrants as they landed in New York City and distribute temperance literature in sixteen languages. But despite some local strength in Brooklyn, the WCTU's attitude toward immigrants—Willard in the 1890s advocated immigration restriction to block the "influx into our land of more of the scum of the Old World, until we have educated those who are here"—foreclosed support in New York's ethnic wards. Teddy Roosevelt's old City Reform Club—down by 1887 to a dozen active members, including Henry Stimson—struggled to enforce a law requiring saloons within two hundred feet of polling places be closed on election day, with minimal success. Liquor interests were deeply imbricated in local politics, and vice versa: of the 1,002 political meetings held in New York City on the local level in 1886, nearly eight hundred were held in saloons. The best reformers could manage was passage of a Temperance Education Law that provided for compulsory drug education in the schools.

Balked in extending their moral mantle over the public at large, some Protestant reformers concentrated on protecting their coreligionists' ranks. Benjamin DeCosta, a New York Episcopal minister, met with purity reformers, including Stead, on a visit to England. Their work seized his imagination, particularly the efforts of the White Cross Society, newly established by the Church of England. This organization had already converted thousands of respectable workingmen to the cause of a single standard—chastity for both sexes—and DeCosta hurried home to establish the White Cross Army in New York. The organization recruited young people, who pledged themselves to sexual abstinence before marriage. Once enrolled—and a single White Cross meeting in 1888 attracted a thousand members—participants were sent out (often in tandem with YMCA cadre) to disseminate purity literature to other youth groups in the city. White Cross counselors also provided sex education, which consisted chiefly in assisting young men to refrain from illicit activities.

Refuges that provided alternatives to commercial culture were central to this strategy. In January 1887 the YWCA began to offer home-havens in the dangerous city. The first Y, at 7 East 15th Street, provided educational classes, a free lending library, and wholesome entertainments. The Children's Aid Society expanded its program of lodging houses for newsboys and industrial schools for working-class boys and girls.

In 1884 Grace Hoadley Dodge, wealthy young philanthropist and Sunday School teacher, organized the 38th Street Working Girls Society to isolate members from exposure to the street, cheap dance halls, theaters, and, in general, male cupidity. Adopting the model of the burgeoning women's club movement, Dodge provided clubhouses—nineteen of them within ten years—salted with moral education (emphasizing "purity of life, dutifulness to parents, faithfulness to employers and thrift") and peppered by exposure to the "refined influences" of ladies of her class. These retreats also provided more tangible benefits: libraries, entertainment, doctors, insurance, and classes in cooking, sewing, hygiene, childrearing, and household management. The clubs attracted mainly American-born women—carpet and silk factory workers, salesgirls and dressmakers, telegraph operators and stenographers—who were more open than the immigrants to the Anglo-American ideals of the reformers.

DECENTEST NATION

For many in the Protestant middle class, Culture itself came to constitute a refuge—albeit a somewhat secularized one—especially after Matthew Arnold came to visit in 1883. The celebrated English poet and essayist was well known in the city for his 1869 indictment, in *Culture and Anarchy*, of Britain's fragmentation into selfish class fractions. English workers, Arnold had said, threatened social chaos by demanding greater power, as did aristocrats by their complacent defense of a privileged status quo. The British middle class, which should have been a stabilizing force, had abandoned the public good for an individualistic and spiritually impoverished pursuit of riches. Chaos might yet be forestalled, Arnold argued, if Anarchy were combated by Culture—the pursuit of beauty and intelligence, "sweetness and light."

Arnold brought a similar warning and appeal to New York, beginning with a lecture in Chickering Hall. As the New World was even more complacent, philistine, and anarchic than the Old, it was the duty of America's saving remnant—its cultivated gentlefolk—to promote the "elevated and beautiful" and to ennoble the public by transforming "the administration, the tribunals, the theatre, the arts." When Arnold took this message on the national lecture circuit, he would be condemned as just another snooty Englishman disparaging American manners. But many of New York's genteel intellectuals received him warmly, for they saw his prescriptions as legitimating a mission they had already embraced: ennobling, elevating, and purifying the metropolitan literary scene.

One of Arnold's many admirers was Richard Watson Gilder, editor of the *Century* magazine. Gilder, a minister's son from New Jersey, had come to New York in 1870 to work on the old *Scribner's*. Under his editorship it became independent of the publishing firm and changed its name to the *Century*. By the mid-eighties, the finely printed, beautifully illustrated journal circulated to 250,000, chiefly among the nation's middle classes, and it had established a reputation as perhaps the best-edited magazine in the world.

And among the prissiest. Gilder's method of raising public standards of taste and morality required the production of bloodless pages. As custodian of genteel culture he sought out the delicate and the refined and stood guard against the vulgar and the vernacular. Walt Whitman, though a personal friend, was banned from the *Century*'s pages; a bit of Mark Twain's *Huckleberry Finn* snuck in, but only after Gilder deleted references to nakedness, blasphemy, and smells and emended all improper phraseology (changing "in a sweat" to "worrying"). To those who accused him, and Americans, of prudishness, Gilder replied: "It may be that this accusation is well-founded. If so, we can only say that this is the price we pay for being, on the whole, the decentest nation on the face of the globe."

Gilder's values and ambitions were widely shared by the editors of New York's (and Boston's) genteel monthly magazines. Champions of convention and restraint, grace and serenity, they fed their readers a stately diet of English fiction, biography, travel, and cozy columns addressed to the "gentle reader" from the "Editor's easy chair"—a mix popular since Washington Irving's day. A similar tone marked the output of the leading publishing houses, notably that of Charles Scribner's Sons, under the literary control of William Crary Brownell.

Brownell, born in 1851 to a comfortable Episcopalian family, was a devout Arnoldian disciple who feared New York City was disintegrating into anarchy. Brownell advanced this thesis most forcefully in 1884 after returning from France, which he applauded as a model of an integrated public culture. There the institutions and architecture of public life imposed discipline and constraint on individuals. By comparison, America's metropolis was chaotic. Paris made people Parisians. New York generated only a "characterless individualism," a "noisy diversity" with no "effect or ensemble."

From 1888 on Brownell made the House of Scribners into a fortress of Culture, seeking out writers who combined "strength" and "refinement," whose fiction and poetry reflected and espoused morality, truth, and beauty. Other great publishing houses joined him, with editors and publishers circulating in a Manhattan milieu that encompassed not only professional writers and critics but also a larger and highly sociable circle embracing amateur authors, artists, architects, cultivated businessmen, polished professionals, and learned university professors and administrators. These gentlemen, and a few ladies, gathered together to dine, talk, and listen in an interlocking network of clubs and institutions.

Genteel women remained the bulwark of Culture and the market for decent literature they had been for decades. Convinced they had a biological affinity for the beautiful and the uplifting, they took up their Arnoldian assignment of promoting art, culture, and Protestantism as redemptive antidotes to the centrifugal tendencies of a male-dominated economy. In the 1880s and 1890s the women's club movement started by Sorosis burgeoned, developing self-improvement salons, islands of refined sociability for discussion of literature and art. In 1890 Jane Cunningham Croly and the New York Sorosis women linked literary clubs with alumnae associations, civic reform societies, mothers' groups, and needlework guilds into a national network of female organizations, the General Federation of Women's Clubs.

Editors of "family journals" and leading publishers were extremely sensitive to the wishes of this enormous and ever more organized reading public. They kept their content "innocent as milk" partly out of the conviction that ladies would brook no deviation from genteel standards, and indeed when editors did transgress, they were swiftly brought to task. Even Gilder's carefully expurgated version of *Huckleberry Finn* brought protests, and when *Harper's* published du Maurier's *Trilby* in January 1893 it produced a storm of criticism and canceled subscriptions.

Restrictions on subject matter hastened an ossification of genteel culture. In a collective averting of eyes from indelicate matters, those who dealt with everyday city life or wrote in the vernacular were dismissed as vulgarians. When the Anglo-Saxon literati did deign to focus on immigrant working people, it saw them through picturesque or sentimental lenses.

This policing of the cultural landscape, by producers and consumers alike, was not exactly what Arnold had had in mind. For all his tendencies toward elitist snobbery, he had challenged an array of comfortable middle class convictions. But in the hands of the metropolitan gentility, Culture was transformed from critique to possession, ownership of which served as a credential of class standing.

"HEY, WHISKERS!"

On February 14, 1892, at the Madison Square Presbyterian Church, the Rev. Charles Parkhurst gave a most unusual Sunday sermon. The tall, slender, bewhiskered minister launched a vitriolic attack on Mayor Grant and his Tammany cohorts. They were, Parkhurst thundered, nothing more than a pack of "polluted harpies that, under the pretense of governing this city, are feeding day and night on its quivering vitals. They are a lying, perjured, rum-soaked and libidinous lot." The mayor, Parkhurst continued, together with District Attorney De Lancy Nicoll and the entire police department, were pillars of organized crime, linked in an "official and administrative criminality that is filthifying our entire municipal life, making New York a very hotbed of knavery, debauchery and bestiality." Frustrated by the purity crusade's setbacks—Parkhurst was a vigorous supporter of Comstock's SSV—he declared that apparently "every effort to make men respectable, honest, temperate, and sexually clean is a direct blow between the eyes of the Mayor and his whole gang of drunken and lecherous subordinates."

Mayor Grant challenged Parkhurst to prove his charges. DA Nicoll hauled him before a grand jury and demanded to see his evidence. Parkhurst was forced to admit he had none, apart from newspaper clippings of journalistic exposés. The jury then formally denied his charges of police complicity and rebuked him for character assassination. Most of the press denounced Parkhurst as a vulgarian, and Pulitzer's *World* cautioned him about "the bearing of false witness."

The humiliated minister now set out to assemble evidence that would stand up in court. He would descend into the city's lower depths so he could himself serve as a first-hand witness to New York's degradation. In Parkhurst's person, gentility would go toe-to-toe with vice; culture would meet anarchy head on.

Parkhurst, of course, was treading a well-beaten path. Dickens, Brace, and a host of sunshine-and-shadow journalists had long been prowling New York's nether regions. There was even precedent for nocturnal meanderings by men of the cloth. Parkhurst's fellow Presbyterian, Brooklyn's Rev. Talmage, had been touring the nighttime metropolis ever since he had read Charles Loring Brace's *Dangerous Classes* and decided that "I, as a minister of religion, felt I had *a divine commission to explore the iniquities of our cities.*" Talmage had policemen pilot him around brothels and saloons. He then recounted his findings in vivid (and racy) talks that drew as many as five thousand to the vast Brooklyn Tabernacle. These sensational sermons were then reprinted in newspapers and collected in books like *The Night Sides of City Life* (1878) and *The Masque Torn Off* (1880).

Parkhurst was no mere sensationalist, and he set about his task methodically. Now president of the Society for the Prevention of Crime, he turned to his righteous and wealthy membership for funds and legal advice. Then, with a zealous young parishioner, John Langdon Erving, he engaged Charles Gardner, a private detective, as guide to New York's underworld (for six dollars a night plus expenses). The bemused Gardner disguised the pair. He eliminated Parkhurst's "aroma of the pulpit" by soaping his hair and dressing him as a tough. He gave similar treatment to Erving, a dandy whose initial notion of deep cover was to put on last year's suit. Then the trio boarded the Third Avenue El at 18th Street and rode it down—literally and figuratively—to Franklin Square.

The slumming party soon made its way to a Cherry Street dance hall filled with sailors and laborers where a nineteen-year-old girl's greeting to Parkhurst was "Hey, whiskers, going to ball me off?" Nothing daunted, Parkhurst and company pressed on. During the rest of the evening, and over several succeeding nights, the trio took in a five-cent Park Row lodging house, a whiskey saloon, an opium den in Chinatown, a stale beer dive in the Italian section, and other horrors. Always Parkhurst pressed bravely ahead, demanding to be shown "something worse." They stopped in at a dance hall. "Coarseness was everywhere. The girls sat upon the laps of men, and in no way rejected any advance, no matter how vile it was."

On to Nigger Johnson's colored dance house, where white girls waltzed with blacks and black girls cavorted lasciviously with whites (accompanied by piano, harp, violin, and piccolo). In a Tenderloin house, five girls stripped and did a "dance of nature." (At one point, Gardner later testified, the girls played leapfrog. "Did you join in this leapfrog business?" he was asked. "Yes," he answered, "I was the frog." This gave rise to a popular concert hall ditty, borrowing from a current song hit, that went: "Dr. Parkhurst on the floor / Playing leapfrog with a whore / Ta-ra-ra-Boom-de-ay / Ta-ra-ra-Boom-de-ay.")

"Show me something worse," Parkhurst commanded. Finally the minister had his circuits completely blown at Scotch Ann's Golden Rule Pleasure Club on West 3rd.

Descending to the basement, they found it subdivided by partitions into cubicles, each furnished with a table and two chairs, in one of which sat a boy with a painted face, a high falsetto, and the airs of a young girl. At this the good doctor turned on his heel and fled at top speed, gasping: "Why, I wouldn't stay in that house for all the money in the world."

On March 13, 1892, Parkhurst ascended his pulpit and described to a jammed church the nature of life in the "disgusting depths of this Tammany-debauched town"—"rotten with a rottenness that is unspeakable and indescribable." In addition to his own evidence he now waved affidavits gathered by Gardner's private detectives attesting to the fact that at least 254 Manhattan saloons and thirty brothels had been doing business on the previous Lord's Day.

At first, many ministers, papers, and politicians professed greater dismay at the impropriety of Parkhurst's expedition than at his findings. But soon a grand jury indicted two brothel keepers and summoned Police Board members on the carpet. Though it concluded the officials were merely incompetent rather than legally culpable, the police were sufficiently alarmed to promote the highly regarded Chief Inspector Thomas F. Byrnes to superintendent. Promising a crackdown on vice, Byrnes soon shifted police captains around and began closing saloons on Sundays. Paresis Hall was forced to close.

Pressing ahead, Parkhurst called a mass meeting in May 1892 and organized the City Vigilance League, modeled on the Manchester City Vigilance League. Its goal—the "perfection of municipal government"—was to be achieved by establishing a massive grass-roots surveillance operation. In each Assembly district a vigilance group would monitor its neighborhood for violations of sanitary, excise, or morals regulations.

Parkhurst was neither bigot nor fundamentalist—a believer in evolution, he favored a liberal interpretation of the Bible—and he strove to make the Vigilance League a collective effort of Protestants, Catholics, and Jews who "mingle harmoniously in its councils, and co-operate in its work." (When Theodore Seligman was blackballed from the Union League Club that year, Parkhurst said the group would doubtless have excluded Moses.) But if Parkhurst was not bigoted, other crusaders certainly were. In any event, the demand for blue laws dismayed the immigrants, the Germans in particular, and made allies hard to come by.

Even Parkhurst's short-term hopes were blasted when yet another Tammanyite, Thomas F. Gilroy, was elected mayor in 1892. It was clear that barring extraordinary circumstances—or the formation of a wider political coalition—New York's government, and thus its moral landscape, would remain unpurified.

66

Social Gospel

To a growing number of middle-class Protestant reformers, neither Parkhurst, Comstock, the Charity Organization Society nor the Salvation Army was attuned to the scale or complexity of New York's problems. All these activists, in one way or another, focused on promoting personal salvation or constraining individual behavior, when what was really needed was a theological perspective that confronted issues at a societal level—a "social gospel" that rejected the inevitability of snarling conflict between capital and labor, spurned an inhumane laissez-faire acceptance of urban immiserization, and rejected competitive selfishness as the path to progress. Nothing less would reverse working people's disaffection from the civic status quo or forestall their adoption of radical solutions for metropolitan ills.

Social gospel sentiments emerged in most Protestant denominations, though most Presbyterians and Methodists stuck to fostering individual redemption through prayer, frugality, temperance, and hard work. Baptists, still largely a rural sect, were slow to take up urban problems, though in New York City men like Walter Rauschenbusch began coming to grips with metropolitan realities. Before he came to New York in 1886 as pastor of the Second German Baptist Church, Rauschenbusch later recalled, he had "had no idea of social questions." But in New York, "among the working people, my social education began." In Hell's Kitchen, "when I began to apply my previous religious ideas to the conditions I found, I discovered they didn't fit." Laissez-faire came to seem heartless and selfish, Rauschenbusch became a strong Henry George supporter, and he would go on to formulate a theology of social reform.

Congregationalist Lyman Abbott, who also took part in the George campaign, succeeded to the prestigious pulpit of Brooklyn's Plymouth Church after Henry Ward Beecher died in 1887. Abbott also assumed editorship of the *Christian Union*, a leading religious weekly, which became *the Outlook* in 1893. Abbott signaled a major change in his denomination's approach when he argued that "individualism is the characteristic of simple barbarism, not of republican civilization," and that "with all the good that competition has wrought, the principle is now a destructive one."

It was the Episcopal Church, however, a sect that to all appearances was more interested in Society than in a social gospel, that took the lead in jettisoning laissez-faire ethics and tackling the city's social problems. Henry Codman Potter, rector of fashionable Grace Church since 1868 and bishop of the Diocese of New York since 1887, had long been known as the favorite clergyman of the smart set, and he had devoted much of his attention to a sumptuous church building and beautification program. Despite some complacent clubbiness, however, churches in the Anglican communion had a long track record of taking seriously the obligations of the rich to the poor, a tendency nourished by New York Episcopalians' ongoing connections to British Anglicans, who had never completely abandoned the old medieval dream of a society guided and led by their Church. When the mid-1880s depression had led to massive demonstrations in Britain and the growth there of a socialist movement (thanks in part to Henry George's speaking tours), English church leaders responded by turning to a more social Christianity.

In New York, moreover, many Episcopalian laymen were drawn from the ranks of the emerging corporate elite—the very bankers and businessmen who were rejecting laissez-faire ethics in the economic marketplace. Nowhere were the consequences of this connection exemplified more dramatically than at St. George's Church. Erected in 1848 on then-exclusive Stuyvesant Square (and rebuilt there after it burned down in 1865), by the 1880s the brownstone Romanesque Revival church was in trouble. Its Protestant parishioners had dwindled away, leaving it adrift in a sea of Catholics and Jews, facing empty pews and mounting debts. Trinity could survive without a constituency by living off its tenement rent rolls, but St. George's had either to reach out or move on. Digging in their heels, the remaining vestrymen—led by Senior Warden John Pierpont Morgan—named the Rev. William Stephen Rainsford as the new rector in 1883.

The thirty-three-year-old Rainsford, a Dublin native with a Cambridge education, had worked in urban ministries since the 1870s and developed strong views on the crisis of urban Protestantism. It was, he said, essential to confront the fact that "the whole aspect of the modern Protestant churches, in our large cities at least, is repellent to the poor man." When interviewed for the position at St. George's, Rainsford had proposed to Morgan that the church deemphasize doctrine and open itself up to the poor by abolishing pew rentals and offering a variety of secular programs. "Done," said Morgan, who agreed to make up any resulting deficits. The vestry poured resources into recreational and educational facilities, including choirs, an industrial school, a boys' club, and a Girls' Friendly Society. These activities, together with Rainsford's vigorous social preaching, attracted over seven thousand people to one or another program by the end of the decade.

CHRISTIAN RADICALS

St. George's was an outstanding example of an "Institutional Church" designed to "reach the masses," but there were more radical departures afoot within New York Episcopalianism. Some proposed the church go beyond providing social services to working-class parishioners, to forging an alliance with working-class activists dedicated to restructuring capital-labor relations.

In 1881 the Rev. James Otis Huntington had founded the Order of the Holy Cross, a semimonastic organization, and settled on the Lower East Side. Though a Harvard graduate from an elite background, Father Huntington startled his colleagues by joining the Knights of Labor and becoming an ardent supporter of Henry George. He began reporting on union meetings for the Episcopal press and promoting George's single tax in church circles. In 1884 the semiofficial but prestigious Church Congress invited George to talk on the topic "Is our Civilization Just to Workingmen." In the 1886 campaign, Father Huntington addressed street crowds from the back of trucks while wearing his priestly robes; he was second only to Father McGlynn in providing clerical assistance.

Other church leaders now began to address the issues Huntington raised. Bishop Potter himself had been dissatisfied for some time with the rabid antilabor ferocity of many theologians. He had said, apropos of the repression of the Great Strike of 1877, that "we shall not finally silence the heresies of the communist with the bullets of the militia." In 1886 he issued a pastoral letter that, while denouncing boycotts, admitted the justice of workingmen's demands. He particularly rejected the laissez-faire argument that labor was a commodity "to be bought and sold, employed or dismissed, paid or underpaid, as the market shall decree."

Reminding his clerics that "in New York centers the capital that controls the traffic, and largely the manufactures, of this new world," Potter pointed out that "in your congregations are many of those who control that capital." It was their duty to make clear to those who employed labor and reaped its benefits that "wealth brings with it a definite responsibility . . . that luxury has its decent limits . . . that class-churches and class-distinctions of kindred kinds have nearly destroyed in the hearts of many of the poor all faith in the genuineness of a Religion."

The bishop's letter provoked widespread discussion among New York's Episcopal clergy and laity and led, the following year, to formation of the Church Association for the Advancement of the Interests of Labor (CAIL). With Potter, Huntington, and thirty-eight other bishops serving as vice-presidents, CAIL became the first powerful Protestant group to actively defend labor's right to organize. More, it declared solidarity with labor's struggle against slums, sweatshops, and child labor. Starting in 1891 Trinity held an annual celebration called Labor Sunday, tied to the new Labor Day, to which the Knights of Labor were invited to send delegates, and in which a red flag was borne in procession. Perhaps more impressive, given the vestry's traditional tight-fistedness, was the decision of the diocese that same year to allocate church printing only to firms that paid union rates. In 1893 CAIL established a Board of Arbitration, with coequal representatives from capital, labor, and the public, to help settle strikes.

Others adopted still more radical stances. William Dwight Porter Bliss, a Boston Episcopalian clergyman, member of the Knights, and enthusiastic follower of Henry George, formed, in 1889, the Society of Christian Socialists, which soon started a chapter in New York City. The Bliss group advocated the eight-hour day, free technical education for workers, higher education for women, public employment of the unemployed, a municipal program of public housing and slum clearance, municipal ownership of public utilities, and national ownership of railroads, telegraphs, and mines.

There was in many of these initiatives a somewhat facile optimism, a reluctance to confront hard realities of power, a comforting conviction that there were no opponents to be overcome but only misguided adversaries to be enlightened. Nevertheless the Episcopalians' pleas for social solidarity constituted a dramatic break with the bleak tooth-and-claw approach to which other Protestants had and still adhered.

CREED INTO DEED

If not all Protestants were social gospelites, neither were all social gospelites Protestant. The reform wing of Judaism—which assembled in Pittsburgh in 1885—expressed its concern about the "evils of the present organization of society." But the forefront of the Jewish movement was occupied by a small number of highly assimilated activists, among whom the most preeminent was Felix Adler.

Adler, born in Germany in 1851, was brought to New York in 1857 when his father, Samuel Adler, was called to the rabbinate of Temple Emanu-El. The family settled near Stuyvesant Square, where his father raised him in the emerging Reform tradition, and his mother involved him in her work with such Jewish charities as the Hebrew Orphan Asylum. Felix was disappointed with Columbia College, finding it mired in Christian parochialism, and much preferred his graduate work at the Universities of Berlin and Heidelberg, where he was exposed to the problems of industrial society and a variety of proposed solutions.

Back in New York, Adler scotched expectations he would succeed his father in the Emanu-El pulpit when, in 1873, he preached a sermon called "The Judaism of the Future." In it he embraced a secular, activist, and universalistic philosophy, rejecting prayer, ritual, and theology. Beginning in 1876 the austere Dr. Adler delivered Sunday morning lectures in Standard Hall on the need to translate "creed into deed" by struggling for social justice. The following year, the Society for Ethical Culture was incorporated, with Adler as its "lecturer"; its board, chaired by Joseph Seligman, included trustees ranging from Henry Morgenthau Sr. to Samuel Gompers.

Over the next decade, the Ethical Culture Society initiated a series of social innovations, including a free kindergarten, a district nursing program, and a Workingman's School. Adler also fought political corruption, advanced the cause of progressive education, and, most notably, took up the issue of tenement house reform.

In 1884 Adler called for revision of the badly flawed 1879 Tenement House Law. This piece of legislation had emerged from an 1878 architectural competition to design a tenement, twenty-five by one hundred feet, that would maximize both investor profits and tenant satisfaction. The judges (who included Dr. Potter) awarded first prize to James Ware's "dumbbell" design. Ware's wasp-waisted building had front and rear wings, connected by a narrow hall containing the stairways, an arrangement that allowed light to filter dimly into the stairwell through airshafts on either side.

As the 1879 housing legislation required that every tenement bedroom have a window opening directly onto a street, a yard, or an acceptable substitute—like the airshaft of the Ware design—the law quickly made the dumbbell tenement a terrible reality for hundreds of thousands of tenants. Landlords packed four families into each of the five or six floors, with each family (plus boarders) squashed into a three-or four-room apartment, the "bedrooms" of which measured seven by eight and a half feet. The airshafts—noisy with the quarrels of twenty-plus families and noisome from the cooking odors of twenty-plus kitchens—became garbage dumps and firetraps, which shot flames up from one story to the next.

In his 1884 lecture "The Helping Hand of Government," Adler called for state intervention against such substandard housing. As workers could not build tenements for themselves, "the law of morality and common decency binds the Government to see to it that these houses shall not prove fatal to the lives and morality of the inmates." If houses were overcrowded, the state "must compel a reduction of the number of inmates, enforce renovation at the expense of the landlord, and where that is no longer possible, must dismantle the houses and remove them from existence."

Adler nevertheless believed that the private market could provide affordable and decent housing for working people, if philanthropic investors would agree to settle for profit margins lower than the market rate. Here he followed Brooklyn housing reformer Alfred Tredway White, who in 1877–79 had erected the low-rent Home Buildings and Tower Buildings along Hicks and Baltic streets using plans similar to Sir Sidney Waterlow's 1863 Industrial Dwellings Company of London: blocks of sunlit, well-ventilated apartments with a courtyard in the center.

White hoped his limited dividend project had demonstrated that private capital could solve the housing crisis, and Adler's 1885 effort—he helped found the Tenement House Building Company of New York—was intended to spur the model housing movement along. The company restricted profits to 4 percent and constructed six tenements on Cherry Street. When the 108 two- or three-room apartments opened in December 1887, many Russian Jews were attracted by the moderate rents, as well as the separate toilets for each two apartments, nine free baths, kindergarten room, roof playground, common laundry room, and superintendent.

Neither these nor other model tenements that followed, however, would usher in a new housing order, as these investment schemes failed to challenge the basic economic arrangements shaping land use in New York City. Inflated land costs remained high, and the small capitalists who dominated the building industry were not able or willing to settle for 4 or 5 percent when they could get a 15 percent rate of return. The dumbbells would continue to constitute the overwhelming majority of new working-class housing; by 1900 there would be 13,600 of them below 14th Street, twenty-eight thousand above.

SUPPING SORROW WITH THE POOR

In 1886 Stanton Coit, an Episcopalian turned Ethical Culturalist, spent three months in England living at the recently founded Toynbee Hall, which he soon decided was an exemplary application of Adler's creed-into-deed philosophy. Since the 1870s a stream of wealthy young Oxford men had been residing in London's East End during vacation periods to "sup sorrow with the poor." After publication in 1882 of *The Bitter Cry of Outcast London*, an exposé of slum life, sporadic visits no longer seemed sufficient, and a new Universities Settlement Association (1884) opened Toynbee Hall. To it flocked students inspired by Matthew Arnold's faith in the redeeming influence of culture. Through clubs, classes, lectures, and concerts they would uplift the laboring man. Through investigations of neighborhood conditions, they would improve his material lot.

Returning to Manhattan just as the 1886 mayoral campaign was gearing up, Coit prevailed on Adler's Ethical Culture Society to help establish the New York Neighborhood Guild. In a four-room tenement apartment at 146 Forsyth Street, in a mixed German, Irish, and Jewish neighborhood, Coit worked to provide private services to the poor and to organize the poor themselves to demand better public ones. Coit was soon joined by Charles B. Stover, a social gospel man par excellence. A graduate of the Union Theological Seminary, Stover had been a mission worker on the Bowery, directed the Ethical Culture Society's model tenement house, and helped organize the Society of Christian Socialists. When Coit departed in 1888 to accept a ministerial position in London, Stover became head of what would be renamed the University Settlement.

Soon idealistic and well-bred young men were flocking to the slums. In 1891 a group of Episcopalian laymen—backed financially by Robert Fulton Cutting, J. P. Morgan, and Cornelius Vanderbilt—established East Side House at 76th Street and the East River in an Irish and German neighborhood. In 1892 the Educational Alliance opened its doors, with support from Jacob Schiff, Isaac Seligman, and Isidor Straus. In 1895 alumni of the Union Theological Seminary began the Union Settlement in a tenement at 202 East 96th. Brooklyn joined the movement in 1889, when Maxwell House was established on Concord Street by members of the Second Unitarian Church. These and other groups established kindergartens, libraries, clubs, classes, concerts, gyms, and playgrounds and helped organize neighborhoods to press for public baths, parks, and cooperative stores.

At first the settlements were all-male enterprises, but in 1889 Vida Scudder, an impassioned young Wellesley instructor who had visited Oxford and been inspired by English developments, joined with alumnae from Wellesley, Smith, Vassar, and Bryn Mawr to establish the College Settlement at 95 Rivington Street, in a predominantly Jewish neighborhood. For well-bred females to live among the poor was unprecedented. The first visitor was a policeman who, convinced the women were opening a whorehouse, promised to leave them alone if they paid him the customary contribution. The press sneered at the project. "Seven Lilies have been dropped in the mud," one paper observed, "and the mud does not seem particularly pleased."

Widespread disapproval didn't stop over eighty college women from applying for residency. The settlement house movement was made to order for this first generation of female graduates, who, having stepped outside restrictive domesticity, found it hard to step back into it. Settlement houses offered a means to live outside the bourgeois home and to extend the freedom and comradeship of student years. The Rivington Street women, who furnished their building with pictures, books, and a piano, noted that "upstairs, in our rooms, it seemed as if we were back in college again."

For all their challenges to bourgeois gender roles, settlement house women insisted on their place in the genteel world. They were, after all, embarked on an unimpeachably proper project—the purveying of elite culture to their plebeian neighbors—and early programs had a distinctly Arnoldian aspect. Art exhibitions diffused a sense of beauty; a Good Seed Club for girls taught about flowers; a Hero Club for boys showed how the Knights of the Round Table had learned to be "chivalrous and true." Some classes taught the art of serving tea from a silver service or accepting calling cards on a tray, prompting Thorstein Veblen to remark caustically that settlement workers seemed intent on the "incubation, by precept and example, of certain punctilios of upper-class propriety in manners and customs."

Soon enough, however, they were providing more vital services, no one more so than Lillian Wald, who in 1893 convinced Sophia Loeb and Jacob Schiff to underwrite a visiting nurse service. Wald, raised in a comfortable bourgeois Rochester family, came to study at New York Hospital's School of Nursing in 1889. After graduating in 1891 she worked for a year at an orphan asylum, enrolled for a time in Elizabeth Blackwell's Women's Medical College, then taught a course in home nursing at an East Side program run by Mrs. Loeb.

Stunned by the suffering and poverty, Wald decided to move there permanently. Charles Stover of the University Settlement guided Wald around the neighborhood; she joined a Social Reform Club discussion group that included Felix Adler; she stayed for a time at the College Settlement on Rivington Street; then she won Schiff's backing for establishing the visiting nurse service with Mary Brewster, a friend from nursing school, out of a fifth-floor apartment on Jefferson Street. Called the Nurses' Settlement, it would be renamed the Henry Street Settlement when it relocated in 1895.

Wald and Brewster were by no means the first women to offer medical services to poor communities. Catholic nuns had long been in the field, and in the years after Father McGlynn founded the Anti-Poverty Society in 1887—an organization that merged Christian morality with secular reform in much the way Protestant social gospelers did—the number of hospitals under Catholic auspices steadily increased. (Mother Frances Xavier Cabrini's Columbus Hospital for Italian immigrants opened in 1892.) What the Nurses' Settlement offered was nonsectarian care—Wald originated the term "public health nurse"—and the women provided it in patients' homes, a service for which they charged next to nothing, or nothing at all. Wald and Brewster were pioneers, as well, in searching out tuberculosis victims, supplying them with sputum cups and disinfectant, and teaching them how to protect others from infection.

Daily life in the slums nudged Wald—and most other settlement workers—toward an ever more sympathetic and sophisticated understanding of the roots of poverty. Like social gospelers generally, they began to jettison moralistic explanations of poverty in favor of sociological ones. They shed as well the nativism and maternalism/paternalism that had characterized previous generations of genteel reformers. Increasingly, they got caught up in workplace and trade union struggles. In time, settlement workers would take the lead in campaigns for sanitation, industrial regulation, public education, better housing, parks and playgrounds, gyms and camps, and women's rights. From being missionaries *to* the poor they became advocates *for* the poor.

THE WHITE LIST

The changing character of genteel reform in New York—its new willingness to see poverty as a social rather than individual problem and its preference for engaged activism over pious exhortation—was registered with unusual clarity in the metamorphosis of Josephine Shaw Lowell. From being a chilling anticharity crusader in the 1860s and 1870s, she blossomed in the 1880s and 1890s into a warm advocate of social reform.

What appears to have started her down the road from Auntie Scrooge to militant activist was eloquent denunciations of her Charity Organization Society issuing from the social gospel ranks, notably from the Rev. Dr. B. F. DeCosta, Episcopal minister of the Church of St. John the Evangelist, a founder of CAIL, and a close friend of Father Huntington. COS, said DeCosta in 1884, was "the meanest humbug in the city of New York" and was engaged in a "heartless oppression of the unfortunate." "While the rich are allowed systematically to rob the poor," he charged, "we have a Society carried on at a large cost to prevent the poor from robbing the rich." COS closed ranks against DeCosta and other critics, but the charges rankled, fostering grave internal dissension among board members who felt uncomfortable about the prominence of "repressive and disciplinary work."

Lowell would also be deeply influenced by Henry George, though in her case the connection was an intensely personal one. Before her father, Francis George Shaw, died in 1882, the old Fourierist and radical abolitionist found his moral energies rekindled by George's writings, so much so that he funded the printing of a thousand copies of *Progress and Poverty* for distribution to libraries. Shaw became George's financial angel and made him virtually a member of the family. Josephine found George's views to be far closer to the compassionate and religious values that had drawn her into the antislavery movement than were the secular Darwinian beliefs held by the men with whom she worked in the charity movement. By 1885 George's explication of the connections between unemployment and poverty had so colored her thinking that in a speech at the Congregational Club, pointedly entitled "The Bitter Cry of the Poor in New York," Lowell declared that "if the working people had all they ought to have we should not have the paupers and criminals."

Lowell's rethinking was furthered by a belated recognition of just how difficult it was for young working women to survive in New York City. This insight was pressed upon her by a nineteen-year-old labor organizer named Leonora O'Reilly, whose background was light-years removed from the genteel Mrs. Lowell's. O'Reilly grew up on the Lower East Side in the 1870s and 1880s in a household of Irish rebels. As a child she was enchanted by the reminiscences of family friend Victor Drury, who was an acquaintance of Marx, had fought with Mazzini for Italian independence, and had survived the Paris Commune. In 1881, aged eleven, she went to work in a collar factory; in 1886, aged sixteen, she was recruited into the Knights of Labor by another Commune fighter and O'Reilly family friend, Jean Baptiste Hubert.

Soon O'Reilly helped organize a Working Women's Society to investigate and expose conditions in the clothing trades. They leveled a litany of charges at manufacturers, ranging from locked doors in tenement house sweatshops to unsanitary working conditions. But what touched off a public uproar was their description of life in the great department stores.

The picture was indeed a pathetic one. Within a decade of the founding of Macy's, the retail sales trade was relying on women—chiefly young girls—for 80 percent of its labor force. Managers liked them because lady customers could discuss intimate apparel with them, because they seemed more demure and less dishonest, but mainly because they could be paid less than men. The shopgirls (as they were known despite their desire to be called salesladies) typically made five to six dollars a week (cash girls might take home $1.50). Layoffs were common. One New York store regularly fired women after five years' satisfactory service to forestall demands for increased salary. Discipline was harsh and arbitrary. At Macy's sitting was forbidden while at work (and work, in busy seasons, could fill a sixteen-hour day). Lateness was fined. "Unnecessary conversations" could lead to instant dismissal. Facilities were squalid.

O'Reilly and the Working Women's Society took these facts to several middle-class women, including Helen Campbell, whose 1882 book *The Problem of the Poor* had described her work in a waterfront mission where she discovered that working-class women's wages were simply too low to qualify as a livelihood. Campbell, daughter of a New York attorney, had followed up with an influential 1886 series in the *Tribune* giving a first-person account of a bitter woman garment worker. Next year she produced a book, *Prisoners of Poverty: Women Wage-Earners, Their Trades and Their Lives*, that used vivid, indeed sensationalist, prose and the new methods of social science to expose, in telling and documented detail, conditions in the needle trades and department stores; it also attacked hard-hearted clergymen for ascribing the resulting poverty to vice.

O'Reilly also turned to Josephine Shaw Lowell for help. Lowell and Campbell arranged a mass meeting at which the young activist and others presented their case, and Father Huntington exhorted the middle-class audience to help "correct the social evil that permits their unfortunate sisters to be so frightfully overworked and badly paid." By 1889 Lowell was so won over—what the "poor want is fair wages and not little doles of food," she wrote her sister-in-law—that she resigned from the State Board of Charities and threw all her formidable energies into supporting the Working Women's Society. She had decided that helping the "five hundred thousand wage earners in this city, 200,000 of them women and 75,000 of those working under dreadful conditions or for starvation wages," was more important than harrying the twenty-five thousand dependents of the city's charities.

In 1891 she, Campbell, and Dr. Mary Putnam Jacobi organized the New York City Consumers' League. Lowell became its first president, the board met in her home, and its offices were established in the United Charities Building. Taking a leaf out of the Central Labor Union's book, the women proposed boycotting department stores and retail shops that did not treat employees properly. Lowell argued that just as "most decent people object to buying stolen goods, even though they get them very cheap," so in the case of products of sweated labor, the "time and strength of the people who made them have been virtually stolen, even though under the forms of law." During the abolitionist crusade women shoppers had given up slave-made cotton and sugar; now they should forgo goods identified by the league as made by exploited women.

Rather than promulgate a blacklist of stores to avoid, the league drew up a White List of stores to patronize. Only eight of the large department stores were included as dealing fairly with their employees. The White List was published in the papers, printed on postal cards and mailed to four thousand names taken from the *Social Register*, and placed in the ladies' parlors of the twenty largest hotels.

As with the settlement house organizers, the Consumers' League women's analysis and programs grew steadily more sophisticated. Soon they would be involved in campaigns seeking state intervention to ensure adequate health and safety and to regulate maximum hours and minimum wages. Lowell began denouncing capitalists' "arbitrary and tyrannical way toward the workers," encouraging workers to form unions, and defending strikes as legitimate. In 1893 she joined Bishop Potter and Felix Adler on CAIL's Board of Arbitration.

Despite her new insights, Lowell remained committed to the premise that direct aid to the poor was "evil." Awareness of the structural roots of poverty only deepened her animosity, now reinforced by a conviction that charity handouts allowed employers to underpay workers, thus hindering efforts to attain a living wage. Lowell had, nevertheless, traveled far enough from her earlier stance to declare at an 1895 charities conference that "if the charity organization societies of the country are going to take the position of defenders of the rich against the poor which I do think is the danger which stands before us, then I shall be very sorry that I ever had anything to do with the work."

REALISTS

In the literary world, too, dissatisfaction with reigning genteel conventions produced some startling defections, none more so than that of William Dean Howells, who until the mid-1880s had been a pillar of authorial propriety, an outsider turned ultimate insider. As a self-educated country boy in rural Ohio, Howells had adulated from afar the literary elite of genteel Boston—Emerson, Longfellow, Lowell—and just after the Civil War he came east to join their ranks. Hired as assistant editor of the prestigious *Atlantic* magazine, Howells became its editor by 1871; after a successful decade, he resigned to devote full time to writing novels and critical essays.

Most of Howells's early work mirrored his Boston Brahmin colleagues' in its sunny and genial optimism. As late as 1886, in a review of Dostoevsky, Howells invited his fellow novelists "to concern themselves with the more smiling aspects of life, which are the more American." As prudish as any of the genteel elite, he was uncomfortable with Zola and "bad French morality" and argued that novels should "make the race better and kinder." He had, however, become discomfited with the moralizing prettiness of much contemporary fiction and was attracted, like his good friend Henry James, to Turgenev. Making tentative gestures toward "realism," he began dwelling to an unusual degree on matters of everyday life.

He also began spending more and more time in New York City, where, he wrote his father, there was "more for me to see and learn." He published much of his new work (like *The Rise of Silas Lapham*) in the *Century* and, in 1885, agreed to author a regular "Editor's Study" column in *Harper's*. But it was the events of 1886–87 that converted Howells into a self-conscious renegade from the ranks of the proper. In the latter year he broke ranks with his genteel colleagues to speak out on behalf of the condemned Haymarket anarchists, the only leading American man of letters to do so, and he was subjected to scathing attack and shunned by friends. His interest in social issues ripened, he read Tolstoy, William Morris, and the Fabian socialists and grew increasingly estranged from laissez-faire orthodoxy and "our competitive civilization." In 1888, at the age of fifty, he left Boston and moved to Manhattan.

After settling in at 330 East 17th Street (just across Stuyvesant Square from St. George's Episcopal Church and a short walk from the Lower East Side), he began exploring the city by foot and train. Howells was exhilarated by its noisy ebullience. "At the bottom of our wicked hearts," he wrote James in London, "we all like New York," and he confided his intention "to use some of its vast, gay, shapeless life in my fiction." He got his chance almost immediately when his new publisher, J. W. Harper, asked him for "a powerful presentation of the life of our great metropolis, social, educational, economical, political," one that would treat "the rich & the poor, the idler & the worker," and "command the interest of all classes." Howells's response was *A Hazard of New Fortunes*, serialized in *Harper's* beginning March 2, 1889. *Hazard*, the first novel to present a fully rendered portrait of the metropolis, was, Howells wrote, the "first fruit of my New York life."

Hazard broadened the boundaries of the permissible in fiction as Pulitzer's *World* had in news. Its panorama of city life included German Marxists, striking workingmen, natural gas millionaires, Christian socialists, advertising experts, and restaurateurs. But the central figures were a genteel middle-class couple—the Howells-like Basil March and his wife Isabel—who throughout the novel, in confrontation with the giant metropolis, come to realize the limits of their genteel worldview.

The Marches, like Howells, move from Boston to New York, where Basil is to work on a new literary magazine. Once ensconced in a Manhattan apartment, the Marches venture out, on foot and elevated, into nongenteel parts of the city—voyages they find "unfailingly entertaining." In Washington Square and the Lower East Side, they encounter a vast and "picturesque" hive of "nationalities, conditions, and characters."

Their fascination with metropolitan bustle, however, is a superficial and condescending one, Howells suggests, as if the ragged poverty of Italian immigrants "existed for their appreciation." Glints of other ways of seeing flit through March's mind—"he had read that they are worked and fed and housed like beasts"—but like most of respectable society, March didn't much trouble himself about "what these poor people were thinking, hoping, fearing, enjoying, suffering; just where and how they lived; who and what they individually were."

The remainder of the novel recounts March's awakening to social and civic consciousness, an evolution paralleling Howells's own. He is exposed to Conrad Dryfoos, an Episcopalian social worker (modeled on Father Huntington) who in helping the poor in their tenement houses has provided for the Church a "way back to the early ideals of Christian brotherhood." March comes to see New York as a "lawless, Godless" society, whose planless "play of energies" yields only a "fierce struggle for survival" in which the stronger preside over "the mutilation, the destruction, the decay, of the weaker." The novel swirls to a violent denouement—set against a streetcar strike modeled on the real ones of 1886—in which March is forced to acknowledge his connectedness to, and complicity in, a world of which he had hitherto been only a spectator.

HOW THE OTHER HALF LIVED

The following year saw the arrival of another realistic book dedicated to probing life in New York City, this one the product of Jacob Riis, who had arrived in New York in 1870 as a hopeful twenty-one-year-old Danish immigrant, only to plunge, with the metropolis, into the great depression. Despite his cultivated background and his acquired skills as a carpenter, Riis had lived from job to job, often from hand to mouth. Some nights found him sleeping in the doorways and ashbins of Mulberry Bend and the Five Points. Once he was rolled in a Church Street police station men's shelter. For a time, with dismal appropriateness, he survived by selling copies of Charles Dickens's *Hard Times* door to door.

Finally, in 1877, Riis had landed a position at the *New York Tribune*, soon becoming its police reporter. For the next eleven years he worked out of an office across from the Mulberry Street Police Headquarters. He wrote Pulitzerian-type pieces on the people of the slums, articles that tugged at readers' heartstrings, made them smile, taught them moral lessons. But for all his portrayal of the miseries of slum life, and his growing contacts with genteel reform-minded people, Riis—now a self-made man—had little patience with or sympathy for most slum dwellers. In the early 1880s, he publicly hailed Josephine Shaw Lowell's COS; in an 1883 article about tramps, wrote severely: "As to the man who will not work, let him starve."

Privately, however, he was coming to think the COS approach harsh, cold, and patronizing and to wonder if collective prevention was not as necessary as individual cures. This rethinking was spurred when, in 1884, he covered Felix Adler's lectures on the housing crisis, and as the 1880s wore on, Riis's critiques of urban injustice grew sharper. He wrote a column called "Gotham Doings" for a Wisconsin newspaper in which he wrote mockingly about Mrs. Astor's Patriarch's Balls. He expressed admiration for Henry George and published pieces in the United Labor Party campaign newspaper, though in the end he voted for Teddy Roosevelt. He applauded the emergence of the settlement movement. And in 1888, after accompanying a sanitary inspector on a dreadful slum tour, he decided he must present the facts of slum life to a wider audience than Adler had been able to reach. He had seen sights, he wrote, that "gripped my heart until I felt that I must tell of them, or burst, or turn anarchist."

To reach out more effectively, the new convert to the social gospel seized upon two recent technological developments. In 1885 George Eastman had invented the handheld "detective" camera, which could be carried about in a valise, and some Germans had invented a flashgun that burned magnesium powder, creating a brilliant (if dangerous) flare. Together, the two instruments allowed Riis to take pictures indoors, making it possible to hurl javelins of artificial sunshine into the darkest shadows. He began making nocturnal patrols around the city. Accompanied by the police, he would burst into the haunts of the poor and explode his flash in their faces, then vanish—as he explained to the *Sun* in 1888—before the photographees "could collect their scattered thoughts."

The photographs garnered in this fashion broke sharply with genteel pictorial conventions. The predominant images of street children were typified by the sentimental paintings of New York artist J. G. Brown, picturesque portraits of cuddly scrubbed urchins—the subjects often posed in the studio. Riis's pictures of street children or down-and-out lodgers, in bold contrast, were less image than evidence, very different from the Byron Company's photographic celebrations of property and from the guidebook photographs that touted city treasures. He got behind the fashionable dwelling fronts to disclose the internal partitions and rear houses installed by rack-renting landlords.

In January 1888 Riis gave a two-hour lecture at the Society of Amateur Photographers, illustrated with a hundred lantern slides of homeless people, street children, and crowded tenements, ending with images of Bellevue Hospital, the New York Morgue, and the pauper graveyard on Hart's Island. He spoke again in February at the Broadway Tabernacle, and among the deeply impressed audience was the Rev. Parkhurst, who helped Riis to other engagements at churches in Manhattan, Brooklyn, and Jamaica. In May, Lyman Abbott asked him to contribute two articles to the *Christian Union*.

In 1889 Riis began writing more pieces that played on the theme of two New Yorks, one prosperous and respectable, the other "uneasy, suffering, threatening anarchy and revolt." He named one such essay in *Scribner's* "How the Other Half Lives," a phrase often used before, notably by Dr. Griscom back in 1845. The following year, he bundled the pieces together into an illustrated book of the same title. *How the Other Half Lives* (1890) was an instant success, so much so that Riis abandoned regular newspaper work and became a free-lance journalist, reformer, and lecturer.

Part of the book's popularity was fortuitous: it appeared the same year as Ward McCallister's *Society as I Have Found It*, which touted the Four Hundred's opulence and was compared, devastatingly, with Riis's work by many reviewers. The *Other Half* also fit neatly into the established sunshine-and-shadow tradition; indeed Riis's literary strategy came straight from Dickens's *American Notes*, one of his favorite books. The narrator offers the reader an armchair guided tour of the underworld.

"Leaving the Elevated Railroad where it dives under the Brooklyn Bridge at Franklin Square," Riis wrote, "scarce a dozen steps will take you where we wish to go. . . . We have turned the corner from prosperity to poverty." Suppose we look into a Cherry Street tenement, he continued. "Be a little careful, please! The hall is dark and you might stumble over the children pitching pennies back there. Not that it would hurt them; kicks and cuffs are their daily diet. They have little else. Here where the hall turns and dives into utter darkness is a step, and another, another. . . . Here is a door. Listen! That short hacking cough, that tiny, helpless wail—what do they mean?" (A dying infant, of course). "With half a chance it might have lived but it had none. That dark bedroom killed it." The slum was death to virtue as well, though Riis was always amazed at finding "sweet and innocent girls" there; he theorized they survived only because "inherent purity revolts instinctively from the naked brutality of vice as seen in the slums."

To a critical Christianity, Riis married the progressive scientism of photographic proof and statistical data. An *Other Half* tenement room was never just stiflingly hot; it was 115 degrees. The Elizabeth Street lodging station had enough cubic air space for ten men but crammed in forty-eight. Where sixteen or seventeen people out of every thousand died from cholera in the uptown wards, 195 per thousand so perished in the slums. Over nine thousand homeless young men lodged nightly along Chatham Street and the Bowery, between City Hall and Cooper Union. One of every ten New Yorkers ended up in the potter's field.

Riis's book obviously sympathized with the poor, but he never tumbled over into too alarming (or too radical) an identification with his subjects. He remained a detached gentleman, someone with whom genteel readers could identify, and he presented the poor as victims—worthy of pity but not respect. The photographs underlined the distance between guide and local denizen by their flash-and-run quality. Spotlit in the sudden glare, Riis's subjects tended to register fright and surprise, creating a victimesque aura of helplessness about them. He was far less pleased with daytime shoots of forewarned subjects: smiling at the camera, they appeared at ease in surroundings Riis declared intolerable.

If his photographs were sometimes presumptuous, his prose was often contemptuous. Slum dwellers were "shiftless, destructive, and stupid, in a word they are what the tenements made them." He accepted the genteel premise that working people were incapable of "aspiration above the mere wants of the body." The tenement houses, he believed, "have no aesthetic resources. If any are to be brought to bear on them, they must come from the outside." Fundamental change would require that the immigrants be Americanized, as *he* had been: the title of his autobiography would be *The Making of an American*. One of the worst aspects of the slums was that they slowed this process by encouraging a clannish defensiveness.

When Riis surveyed the Lower East Side neighborhoods—that "queer conglomerate mass of heterogeneous elements"—he often deployed stereotypes or slurs. The Italians were "gay, light-hearted"; African Americans were sensual and superstitious; and as to Russian Jews—who were still "where the new day that dawned on Calvary left them standing, stubbornly refusing to see the light"—"money is their God," and their attachment to "thrift" was at once the community's "cardinal virtue and its foul disgrace." The Chinese "in their very exclusiveness and reserve . . . are a constant and terrible menace to society": he ridiculed their customs unmercifully, expressing particular horror at white girls' submission to Chinamen's lusts. Only one group seemed more threatening, Lincoln Steffens reported, recalling his deeply pious friend's response when an assistant brought news of a police raid on a resort of fairies. " 'Fairies!' Riis shouted, suspicious. 'What are fairies?' And when Max began to define the word Riis rose up in a rage. 'Not so,' he cried. 'There are no such creatures in this world.' He threw down his pencil and rushed out of the office."

For all his country man's recoil from metropolitan cosmopolitanism, Riis had absorbed more than a touch of Henry George's values and analysis. In the *Other Half*, he rejected explanations of immigrant viciousness that looked to intemperance or individual moral failings; instead he insisted that environment in general, and bad housing in particular, was the determining factor in their moral fall.

Riis lit into landlords with Georgian fervor. He argued that the horrors they perpetuated "come near to making the name of landlord as odious in New York as it has become in Ireland." The tenement mess was the "evil offspring of public neglect and private greed." He called on his genteel readers to help rectify the situation, if not from love of their fellow man, than from fear of him. One of the most striking images in *How the Other Half Lives* is the account of a poor ragged man standing on Fifth Avenue and 14th Street. He builds up a head of rage at the fashionable driving by in their carriages, oblivious to "those little ones crying for bread around the cold and cheerless hearth." All at once, the man "sprang into the throng and slashed around him with a knife, blindly seeking to kill, to revenge."

Very much in the vein of the era's apocalyptic novels, Riis warned the propertied classes that their neglect had bred "a proletariat ready and able to avenge the wrongs of their crowds." The restless, pent-up multitudes "hold within their clutch the wealth and business of New York, hold them at their mercy in the day of mob-rule and wrath." "The sea of a mighty population, held in galling fetters, heaves uneasily in the tenements," he cried, and "if it rise once more, no human power may avail to check it." How to forestall such an explosion? At points Riis argued in social gospel fashion for rejecting laissez-faire and asserting the public good.

In the end, however, Riis backed away from state-centric proposals and called on the real estate industry itself to remedy the situation. "The greed of capital that wrought the evil must itself undo it." Landlords must be shown that building better housing for the poor was both the Christian thing to do and in their own economic interest. The safest way forward, Riis argued, was Alfred Tredway White's proposal that "the intelligent and wealthy portion of the community" provide homes for the working classes.

"STRIKE AT A GIVEN SIGNAL"

In large measure, Riis's reluctance to resort to state power was based on the fact that government was in the grip of Tammany Hall. Many in the social gospel movement shared his conviction—as did the purity crusaders under Parkhurst—that existing city and state administrations were problems, not solutions. By the early 1890s, therefore, both wings of genteel reform seemed equally stymied. There was a widespread readiness to support state initiatives on both moral and economic fronts—even the new

American Economic Association (1886) denounced "laissez-faire as an excuse for doing nothing while people starve" and called government "an educational and ethical agency whose positive aid is an indispensable condition of human progress"—but the state seemed out of reach.

In 1891 Walter Vrooman, a reporter for the *New York World*, urged formation of a Union for Concerted Moral Effort. "Only by *union*," wrote Vrooman, "can the moral forces of society defend themselves against aggressive evil." Disparate reformers had to link up—allowing "myriads of hammers" to "strike all at a given signal"—and act together "according to intelligent plan." It was in this spirit that the City Club was incorporated, in April 1892, to take up the work of Theodore Roosevelt's all but dormant City Reform Club in pressing for honest, efficient government. City Club trustees included August Belmont, Robert Fulton Cutting, Richard Watson Gilder, John Jacob Astor, J. P. Morgan, Cornelius Vanderbilt, and assorted Roosevelts, Stuyvesants, Jays, Grinnells, and Lows. Over half were in the *Social Register*; many were Union League, Century, or University club members; and all could afford annual dues stiff enough to maintain a magnificent clubhouse on Fifth Avenue, large enough to accommodate all of the several hundred members.

The City Club also set out to establish more broadly based nuclei throughout the city, around which to mobilize reform strength and disseminate reform ideas. Within two years, there was at least one Good Government Club in nearly every Assembly district. With headquarters and outposts thus established, the forces of Good Government—embracing the moral reform wing under Parkhurst and the social reform wing of social gospelers and settlement workers—were ready to mount a unified campaign to wrest political power from Tammany Hall. In their diversity, Good Government men and women (dubbed "goo-goos" by irreverent opponents) bore remarkable resemblance to the working-class confederation that had rallied around Henry George almost a decade earlier. Unlike George, however, this set of reformers would triumph, thanks in part to their formidable assets but even more to the fact that, at just this juncture, the great economic wheel of fortune took another downturn.

67

Good Government

The Panic of 1893—unlike those of 1873, 1857, and 1837—did not come as a sudden shock. Americans had seen it brewing since 1890 when Baring Brothers, England's (and the world's) mightiest banking house, had crumpled, the victim of overoptimistic loans to Argentina. The Baring crisis had punctured the late 1880s boom and brought hard times to Western Europe. Americans watched anxiously for signs the financial storm was striking out across the Atlantic—rather as they had once scanned the horizon for cholera epidemics.

For three years, European crop failures buoyed up the U.S. economy, as America's wheat farmers reaped bumper profits from overseas sales. But prosperity didn't last. Hard-pressed Europeans cut back investments in American industry, and when their agriculture revived, the balance of payments reversed course. U.S. gold reserves began draining away, and the resulting capital stringency put intolerable pressure on an already vulnerable economy, which now began to crack at its weakest points.

In February 1893 the Philadelphia and Reading Railroad failed, a victim of reckless empire building. Its demise heightened fears that the entire overbuilt and shoddily financed rail network might topple too. In May the National Cordage Company went under. Known colloquially as the Twine Trust, its collapse exposed the precariousness of even the biggest American enterprises.

In June the credit system seized up. Over the summer stock prices scudded downward, drawing crowds to brokerage houses to watch their fortunes melt away. Banks, mainly in the South and West, began to founder. Calling home their reserves on deposit in New York City, they created near-insolvency in the nation's money center. Before the summer was out 141 national banks had failed, and hundreds more state banks, private banks, savings banks, and loan, trust, or mortgage companies soon followed them into oblivion.

The sharp credit contraction sent debt-ridden or cash-strapped transportation and industrial corporations over the edge. During 1893 companies crashed with terrifying frequency. By year's end nearly sixteen thousand businesses had gone belly-up, the worst-ever toll in U.S. history. Among the felled firms were institutions that controlled over a third of the nation's rail system. J. P. Morgan and his fellow financiers worked mightily, and profitably, reorganizing failed lines and bringing them under banker control. Virtually every bankrupt road east of the Mississippi was eventually "Morganized," and by decade's end most of the country's trackage would be combined into six huge systems controlled by Wall Streeters.

The panic raised the curtain on a five-year depression. Foreign and domestic investors sat on their funds, and the economy languished accordingly. With roughly 20 percent of the nonagricultural work force unemployed, class warfare broke out as some corporations sought worker givebacks and others seized the opportunity to crush unions altogether. Federal troops and state militias battled miners and railroad workers in uprisings spanning a score of states and involving hundreds of thousands.

In New York City, layoffs commenced during the summer of 1893 and reached fearsome levels during the freezing winter months. In January 1894 Mayor Thomas F. Gilroy ordered police to make a house-to-house canvass. They found about seventy thousand unemployed, of whom about 25 percent were female. An additional twenty-five thousand were reported down and out in Brooklyn. Destitution among African Americans was particularly terrible, and the Colored Mission reported people "were found actually dying of want." The disaster was only partly mitigated by a collapse in prices—sensational ads proclaimed "slaughtered" prices and "sacrificed" goods—though deflation brought no joy to tradesmen or manufacturers.

The mayor's report found that twenty thousand were homeless as well as jobless. People piled up in parks and squares, in the Salvation Army Hall, on Blackwell's Island, and in Bowery lodging houses. In February 1894 Stephen Crane, impersonating a tramp, spent a night in a Bowery flophouse and reported, in "An Experiment in Misery," on the men who lay there "in death-like silence, or heaving and snoring with tremendous effort, like stabbed fish."

Some charitable and business groups estimated a lower total unemployment figure, some settlement houses a higher one, but few disputed the mayor's conclusions that there were an "unprecedentedly large number of people unable to secure employment" and that "distressing destitution and hardship are imminent in thousands of homes among those worthy and willing to work."

DEALING WITH HARD TIMES

As early as August 1893, angry socialists and unionists (especially cigarmakers, carpenters, typographical workers, and the United Hebrew Trades) began collecting food, establishing soup kitchens, and organizing "hunger demonstrations" on the East Side and in Union Square. In addition, the Socialist Labor Party, the Central Labor Union, Gompers's American Federation of Labor (AFL), and Barondess's cloakmakers all petitioned the state and city to provide direct emergency relief and set up public works projects. "When the private employer cannot or will not give work, the municipality, state, or nation must," the AFL declared.

Anarchists favored more direct action. During one August demonstration, Emma Goldman told a crowd of thousands that rather than tamely petitioning the authorities,

Mealtime at the Female Almshouse on Blackwell's Island, c. 1897. (© Museum of the City of New York)

they should march by the homes of the wealthy and demand relief. On another occasion she addressed a jobless audience (in German) at the Golden Rule Hall. According to one witness she told them: "If you are hungry and need bread, go and get it. The shops are plentiful and the doors are open."

Such militancy provoked hysteria among the respectable. The *New York Times*, which preferred to leave depression relief to traditional charities, was terrified by the effect "the appalling nonsense of creatures like Goldman" had on the "hatchet-faced, pimply, sallow-cheeked, rat-eyed young men of the Russian-Jew colony." The paper called for an immediate suspension of immigration (which they failed to get) and the immediate incarceration of Emma Goldman (which followed hard upon their demand). As usual, muzzling created a martyr. While in the Tombs awaiting trial, Goldman gave an interview to Nellie Bly of Pulitzer's *World*. The anarchist leader's sincerity and conviction enchanted Bly, who presented her to readers as a "little Joan of Arc." This didn't help Goldman at her October trial—she was found guilty of inciting a riot, which all agreed hadn't happened—but after ten months in Blackwell's Island Penitentiary, she was welcomed back to the Lower East Side by a crowd of thousands, besieged by reporters, and swamped with nationwide invitations to lecture.

The city, as per reigning policy, did next to nothing. The Department of Charities and Correction gave aid to the blind and free coal to the poor but ceased doling out food and clothing as the result of pressure from groups like the Charity Organization Society. The COS and the Association for Improving the Condition of the Poor were, however, shocked by the magnitude of the crisis, and admitted what they had denied in previous downturns: that the unemployed were not shiftless louts but simply unable to support themselves. Josephine Shaw Lowell now agreed that the plight of the poor was "not due usually to moral or intellectual defects on their own part, but to economic causes over which they could have had no control, and which were as much beyond their power to avert as if they had been natural calamities of fire, flood or storm."

Lowell, aided by Lillian Wald and Jacob Riis, set up the East Side Relief Committee in cooperation with COS, settlement workers, unions, churches, and the St. Vincent de Paul Society. The committee, headquartered in the College Settlement on Rivington Street, established a "relief-by-work" program. Work tickets were given to trade unions, churches, and charities for distribution to known heads of families.

Under the supervision of trained social workers, recipients were given "continuous, hard and underpaid" work. Men received a dollar for a seven-hour day spent cleaning streets, removing garbage and carcasses from stables, lofts, and yards, and cleaning and whitewashing tenements. Women got seventy cents for eight hours of sewing clothes for the Red Cross. Nevertheless, demand for relief-work from desperate East Siders far exceeded the supply. Seldom were more than a thousand aided at any given time; and by the following spring no more than five thousand men and women had been helped, less than 10 percent of the unemployed.

The COS also chartered a Provident Loan Society, which made loans to the needy (when secured by personal property) at 1 percent a month, better terms than were available from pawn shops or moneylenders. And its Wayfarer's Lodge on West 28th Street allowed the homeless to stay in facilities superior to Bowery flophouses for up to a week, in exchange for a stint of woodchopping.

Yet for all these new departures, Lowell and her COS colleagues were not prepared to abandon their opposition to public works or soup kitchen handouts. Such policies would only foster dependency in the recipients—"their souls must not be sacrificed in the efforts to save their bodies"—and the charity establishment feared attracting "an army of vagrants" to the city. There was, in fact, no sign of New York's becoming a mendicant Mecca. Quite the opposite: as in most depressions, word spread swiftly in Europe that America and its leading metropolis were poor job prospects. Immigration plummeted from sixty-five thousand in 1892 to twenty-five thousand in 1893 to thirteen thousand in 1897—and among some groups more people left than arrived.

The Charity Organization Society's stringent policy of giving direct aid only after rigorous investigation had weeded out "indolent vagrants" from worthy unemployed generated tremendous public animosity. One woman, enraged at the treatment given her mother, wrote asking, "When you get to the gates of Heaven how will you feel when God will say go down to hell for a week until the committee meets to see if you . . . are worthy enough to enter Heaven." St. Vincent de Paul and the United Hebrew Charities rejected strict scrutiny of disaster-overwhelmed applicants as mean-spirited and gave relief on what the COS considered an indiscriminate basis. Indeed New Yorkers of various stripes, from a variety of motives, raised and distributed over three million dollars' worth of "irresponsible relief," making the metropolis the most generous of all U.S. cities in responding to the harsh depression.

Many businessmen gave unstintingly during the crisis—out of decency, Christian or Jewish conviction, a sense of richesse oblige, or a prudent desire to prevent a potentially explosive situation from deteriorating further. J. P. Morgan was particularly active. He served as treasurer of the forthrightly named Committee of Prominent and Wealthy Citizens and joined with others in forming a Business Men's Relief Committee.

Nathan Straus, co-owner of Macy's with his brother Isidor, was also partner with Abraham Abraham in Abraham and Straus, the largest dry-goods store in the city. The German-Jewish philanthropist established several depots where fuel and foodstuffs

The "breadline" at Fleischmann's Model Vienna Bakery, Broadway at 9th Street, from E. Idell Zeisloft, *The New Metropolis* (1899). (© Collection of The New-York Historical Society)

were bagged in bundles and sold, below cost, at five cents each. He also opened three apartment buildings that provided accommodations at five cents a night and established restaurants that offered five-cent meals.

Yeast manufacturer Louis Fleischmann sold sweet rolls and coffee (by day) at his Model Vienna Bakery next to Grace Church on Broadway. At midnight, Fleischmann's distributed a third of a loaf of bread to all comers—giving popular currency to the term "breadline." Stephen Crane spent a night on the breadline during a blizzard in preparation for writing his classic story "Men in the Storm," which *Arena* published in October 1894.

Businessmen's generosity was spurred in part by the emergence of a new and competitive source of charity: the popular press, self-proclaimed tribunes of the people. In August 1893 Joseph Pulitzer's *World* declared a well-publicized war on hunger. It established a Free Bread Fund, which sent wagons—emblazoned with the paper's logo—rumbling through the tenement streets. These gave away free loaves (one and a quarter million by winter's end) to long lines of the hungry, which formed each day—handing them out with no investigation whatever: "That you are hungry is credential enough." To pay for the program, the *World* turned to the public, as it had during the Statue of Liberty fund drive. Pulitzer yoked sensational stories of individual distress with sentimental appeals for funds, and contributions rolled in from individuals, clubs, theater and ballgame benefits, and Bread Fund Boxes left on store counters. Colorful follow-up accounts (from a roving Nellie Bly, among others) recounted for readers the impact of their donations on recipients.

Not to be outdone, the *Herald*, in December, announced a Free Clothing Fund, and on New Year's Day the *Tribune*, the city's highest-priced and most conservative paper, established a Coal and Food Fund. *Tribune* editor Whitelaw Reid did assure his wealthy readers that his fund, unlike its profligate competitors, would work closely with existing charities and carefully investigate all recipients to be sure they were sober, devout, and thoroughly destitute (had pawned all their available household effects).

Mrs. Lowell, dismayed by the efforts of businessmen, was incensed at the philanthropy of the press (the *Tribune*'s effort excepted). Handing out "something for nothing" was bad enough, but far worse was the papers' calculated commercialism, the way "a desire to help those in distress was blended with the advertising indulged in at their expense." Lowell denounced the publicizing of recipients' names as "a further degradation, a moral stripping naked of the suffering of the poor, which was cruel in the extreme." The *World*, in rebuttal, chided the COS for its niggardly inhumaneness and bureaucratic pettifoggery and claimed the Bread Fund was the "most direct, simple, and useful of charities."

While philanthropists squabbled, politicians heeded the demands of the distressed and established a program of public works—though with considerable reluctance and considerable debate. Democrats, longtime supporters of laissez-faire, backed away from the issue. Despite Mayor Gilroy's call for a government jobs program, his administration did no more than solicit funds from municipal employees and saloonkeepers for distribution to traditional charities. During the first depression winter, Big Tim Sullivan—appointed District Leader of the Bowery area by Boss Croker in 1892—began a tradition of feeding thousands of poor people a free Christmas dinner (turkey, ham, stuffing, potatoes, bread, beer, pie, and coffee). As many as five thousand, mostly single men from neighborhood lodging houses, were feted at his Comanche Clubhouse headquarters, while local vaudeville singers offered entertainment.

At the state level, however, Democratic Governor Roswell P. Flower, a Wall Street banker in civilian life, flat-out rejected demands for public works. "It is not the province of the government to support the people," he declared. That way lay "corruption, socialism, and anarchy." In Washington, the Democratic Congress similarly ignored calls by Gompers's AFL to hire the unemployed to construct a canal across Nicaragua, improve the Mississippi, and irrigate arid western lands. Democratic President Grover Cleveland concurred with Governor Flower that "while the people should support their Government its functions do not include the support of the people."

But Flower came under tremendous pressure from the Central Labor Union and from social gospel reformers; twenty thousand attended a Madison Square Garden conference at which Felix Adler, William Rainsford, and Sam Gompers, among others, called for public works projects. Finally, facing looming electoral disaster—Republicans had capitalized on depression distress to capture the legislature in 1893—Governor Flower grudgingly signed a bill in February 1894 that authorized New York City's Parks Department to spend up to one million dollars on public improvements. Soon hundreds of men were at work along Cathedral Parkway, in Morningside and Riverside parks, and at Manhattan Square, though the CLU complained that work tickets had been cornered by Tammany politicians and were being sold at a profit. Squabbles over patronage kept over half the funds from being expended.

With the return of good weather in spring 1894, nearly all the funds, relief programs, and work projects were dismantled, and for the remainder of the depression of the 1890s, New York City's unemployed were left to the attentions of churches, conventional charities, and official public agencies.

REVOLT OF THE PRIVILEGED

The depression gave the heretofore stymied coalition of moral and political reformers its chance to win power. Democrats paid the traditional penalty of incumbency during hard times, and Republicans, in fusion with dissident Democrats, swept into office. Their sequence of triumphs began in 1893 in Brooklyn, where rebellious lawyers, professionals, and businessmen challenged Boss Hugh McLaughlin, still running the city and county from the back of Kerrigan's Auction Rooms on Willoughby Street.

Peppery attorney and gadfly William Jay Gaynor took the lead. Of Irish and English descent, Gaynor had studied for the priesthood at De la Salle Institute and taught with the Christian Brothers but left the Church before taking his vows. Turning to the law, he was admitted to the bar in 1871 and got his start in Flatbush, where he represented with equal fervor the saloonkeepers of East New York and the bluenose opponents of roadhouses that catered to weekenders en route to Coney Island. By the mid-1880s, Gaynor's firm, now housed in Montague Street near City Hall, was representing far more influential Brooklynites, like Abraham Abraham, whom he helped to set up Abraham and Straus, and William Ziegler, who ran the multimillion-dollar Baking Powder Trust. By 1886, worth nearly a million himself, the blue- and cold-eyed lawyer who parted his reddish-brown hair in the middle was comfortably ensconced in a Park Slope brownstone.

Though a Democrat, the cantankerous Gaynor had been repeatedly riled by Boss McLaughlin's shadier activities. Backed by Ziegler's zeal and money, Gaynor battled the padding of public payrolls and brought a variety of taxpayers' suits to block giveaways of franchises for elevateds and streetcars. As the personification of honest government, Gaynor became an extremely popular man with Brooklyn's respectable classes.

In the 1893 mayoral campaign, McLaughlin renominated the scandal-tainted David A. Boody for a second term. Gaynor, together with other dissident Democrats like Edward Shepard, endorsed the Republican candidate, businessman Charles A. Schieren, who was popular with the city's Germans and the brewing interests, and Gaynor himself became a fusion candidate for justice of the state supreme court.

In the course of campaigning, Gaynor called attention to the fraudulent electoral practices of McLaughlin henchman John Y. McKane, boss of the independent town of Gravesend and its appendage, Coney Island. McKane routinely registered Coney's large summertime population—cooks, waiters, barkeeps, stableboys—as permanent residents, then cast their votes for them. Out of a total Gravesend population of 8,418, 6,218 were registered to vote when, as Gaynor argued, the figure, after subtracting women and minors, should have been closer to 1,628. With the election less than two weeks away, Gaynor sent a crew of clerks to copy the registration books so the names could be checked. McKane denied them access. With five days to go, Gaynor got a writ ordering the list be made available, but when his representatives stepped off the train at Gravesend they were pounced on by a posse (led by the barrel-chested McKane himself), roughed up, and booked as vagrants. Finally, on election day, Gaynor sent six carriages' worth of inspectors to monitor the vote counting, only to be knocked down by armed police and locked up in the jail's privy, while McKane maintained a tight cordon around the town's sole polling place all day.

A firestorm of outrage, fanned by the press of both cities, helped sweep fusion candidates Schieren and Gaynor into office. The overwhelming victory—though due as much to hard times as to boss rule—spelled the beginning of the end for McLaughlin's reign. Within weeks of Schieren's accession it was noted that Remsen Street, where McLaughlin lived, had gone from being the cleanest street in Brooklyn to the one least visited by sanitation men. McKane suffered a far harsher fate. His enemies compelled Governor Flower to bypass the Kings County DA and appoint two special prosecutors (Edward Shepard and Benjamin F. Tracy, leaders of the Brooklyn bar), and in January 1894 McKane was convicted of election fraud and sentenced to six years' hard labor in Sing Sing. To complete the overthrow of ring rule, the dissidents pushed for and won, in May 1894, the annexation of Gravesend by Brooklyn, transferring to central authorities control over its patronage and police—and jurisdiction over Coney Island, which reformers like St. Clair McKelway, editor of the *Brooklyn Daily Eagle*, believed would bring an end to the "wholesale licensing of every form of bestial immorality."

In Manhattan, too, machine Democrats would be driven from office by a Republican-dominated reform coalition, with an investigation of the New York City police department serving as the springboard to victory. Tammany had assumed that the Rev. Parkhurst's spectacular challenge had been effectively squelched back in 1892. However, the dogged vice reformer, with the aid of powerful Chamber of Commerce supporters, got Republican party boss Thomas Platt (a regular attendant at Parkhurst's Madison Square church) to launch a probe into Democratic municipal corruption. The work of the investigating committee, chaired by Republican State Senator Clarence Lexow of Nyack, was momentarily foiled when Tammanyite Governor Flower vetoed its funding appropriation, but the Chamber of Commerce rescued the inquiry by agreeing to cover its costs.

By March 1894 the Lexow Committee, operating out of the Tweed Courthouse on Chambers Street, was poring over evidence accumulated by Parkhurst's City Vigilance League. It went on to dig up a good deal more dirt over the course of nearly a year's rooting about in the city's underworld. Eventually 10,576 pages of testimony compiled from 678 witnesses made clear the price Tammany had exacted for protecting outlawed interests. Politicians and police officers had been systematically shaking down saloons, brothels, abortionists, and gambling dens. Some policemen justified the practice as a way of making back the money they had been forced to ante up to buy their jobs in the first place. Others, like Clubber Williams, pointed to prevailing upper-class mores, cheerfully admitting he had made no attempt to close disorderly houses in the Tenderloin because, "well, they were fashionable." Williams also admitted to having a half-dozen large bank accounts, a yacht, and a Cos Cob, Connecticut, estate; he told Lexow he'd made his money speculating in building lots in Japan. Not all police witnesses were so chattily cooperative. One police captain, the soon-to-be-notorious William S. Devery, turned aside most questions with the insouciant assertion that "touchin' on and appertainin' to that matter, I disremember."

Police corruption was matched by police lawlessness: investigators turned up evidence of involvement in counterfeiting and confidence scams, pervasive election frauds, voter intimidation, and the systematic brutalizing of newer immigrants: clubbings of Eastern and Southern Europeans in Irish-American-dominated police stations were so routine they were known colloquially as "slaughterhouses." The poor suffered additionally from police collaboration with landlords, strikebreaking employers, and assorted racketeers. The Lexow exposures received nationwide press coverage, sharing head-lines with depression-era strikes and marches of the unemployed.

Parkhurst, who attended every session, was thrilled by his vindication. Now he longed to go farther and overthrow Tammany itself. He was seconded in this ambition by the mercantile and financial titans of the Chamber of Commerce. These gentlemen saw in the police scandals and the depression an opportunity to rid themselves of Tammany rule and take back control of the city.

In September, at a Madison Square Garden meeting called by the Council of Good Government Clubs, a constellation of Chamber of Commerce luminaries—including J. P. Morgan, Cornelius Vanderbilt, William E. Dodge, Abram Hewitt, Jacob Schiff, James Speyer, Morris K. Jesup, Gustav Schwab, and Elihu Root—engineered the for-mation of a Committee of Seventy (so named to evoke the group that had toppled Tweed).

Under its banner the Committee of Seventy established a formidable campaign operation, run out of the Chamber of Commerce building, on behalf of their mayoral candidate, William L. Strong. A millionaire dry-goods merchant turned banker, Strong was a longtime member of the Union League Club and former president of the Busi-ness Men's Republican Club. His inner core of supporters were similarly wealthy Yan-kee Protestant Republicans, most of whom were active in the City Club, Good Govern-ment Clubs, Civil Service Reform Association, and various moral reform agencies. In addition, Josephine Shaw Lowell, at Parkhurst's suggestion, organized a Women's Municipal League, which drew in the wives of many prominent reformers. University Settlement workers carried Strong's campaign into immigrant and Tammany strong-holds. The one hundred constituent organizations of the German American Reform Union signed on too, angered by the numerically inferior Irish Americans' grip on Tammany.

Tammany countered by nominating German-Jewish dry-goods merchant Nathan Straus, philanthropic hero of the previous depression winter. But the reformers drove Straus from the field, threatening him with social ostracism for his disreputable affilia-tion with Boss Croker: nine days after his nomination he withdrew and embarked on an extended vacation to Europe. A desperate Tammany drafted former mayor Hugh Grant, a reluctant candidate, having been himself badly tarred by the Lexow exposés. Grant would run an apathetic campaign.

The reformers, on the other hand, launched an energetic effort built around their twin themes of moral and political reform. The Rev. Parkhurst bore the standard for purification. Hurling denunciations at Tammany's Lexow-exposed connivance in vice and corruption, he summoned supporters to "fight the devil" with the "incisive edge of bare-bladed righteousness." Parkhurst's calls to reject cultural laissez-faire and embrace moral unity—or impose it, if necessary—rallied some but repelled others. Alarmed Catholics scented a revived nativism, and several priests would condemn the fusion ticket at preelection masses, echoing, albeit from a different perspective, the Church's anti-George efforts of 1886.

Businessmen concentrated more on secular concerns. They promised a reform administration that would run the city government "solely in the interests of efficiency and economy." Proponents of a "businessmen's administration" stressed that ending extravagance and corruption would diminish the tax burden on property owners. They also offered inducements to working-class voters. A reformed city would be a cleaner city (with improved street sweeping, garbage disposal, and public baths), a pleasanter city (more small parks), a smarter city (more public schools), a healthier city (more TB prevention programs and a vigilant health board), and an efficient city (more use of experts, better rapid transit, an expanded civil service).

In November 1894 New Yorkers voted at sites monitored by the over two thousand poll watchers put in the field by the now twenty-four Good Government Clubs. Strong won decisively, reaping nearly three votes for every two cast for Grant. The bulk of his support came from uptown silk-stocking wards and from the Yorkville, Harlem, and Upper West Side preserves of middle-class Germans. Strong also made some inroads in downtown, depression-disaffected, working-class districts, racking up substantial backing from Jewish voters (though many Jewish protest votes went to socialist candidates). The bulk of the Irish stayed loyal to Tammany. On the state level, Republican Levi Morton (a millionaire Manhattan banker) won the governorship, and Republicans completed their sweep, begun the previous year, of the legislature and virtually all state elective offices. The same electoral upheaval cost Democrats control of both houses of Congress.

Announcing he would run the city on purely "business principles," Strong embarked on a three-year term that would span the remainder of the depression. The twin goals of the new mayor's reform administration—efficiency and moral order—were soon apparent in the work of his appointees.

COLONEL WARING CLEANS THE STREETS

Strong handed command of the Department of Street Cleaning to Colonel George Edwin Waring Jr., a Civil War veteran. It was a brilliant choice. Waring was a sanitation engineer of high repute; he had directed the drainage of Central Park and had helped design and construct sewer systems in cities all over the United States. Waring was also of impeccable social standing, well known in the clubs and social circles of New York and Newport. Finally, he had long evidenced a steely determination that appealed to the new administration.

Waring inherited a department notorious for its inefficiency. Created in 1881, it had coped poorly with dirt, ashes, garbage, snow, and the 2.5 million pounds of manure and sixty thousand gallons of urine the city's horses deposited each and every day along New York's 250-plus miles of paved streets. Its problems stemmed from insufficient funding, inadequate authority, and intermittent public cooperation. It didn't help that sweepers were primarily Tammany patronage appointees—hired and fired on the whims of politicians—and reportedly spent much of their workday in saloons.

Waring decided that before cleaning the streets he would clean up his men. A longtime devotee of martial virtues, Waring insisted employees purchase and don white duck uniforms and caps. He then paraded them down Fifth Avenue, twenty-seven hundred strong, in strict military order, their new commissioner prancing ahead on horseback. Waring posted rigorous new regulations—no entering saloons, no foul language, no neglecting of horses—and carried out personal inspection tours to see they were obeyed. He rallied his troops, honoring them as "soldiers of the public" who were "defending the health of the whole people," then led them into battle.

Not all troopers were thrilled. Some sanitation workers denounced their uniforms as badges of servitude; it was embarrassing to be caricatured as a "Waring White Angel." More to the point, they resented Waring's arbitrary and dictatorial ways, notably his wage cuts. One of his earliest acts was to chop sweepers' annual salaries from $720 to $600 a year, feasible enough given that Italian laborers were readily available in the open market for $350 a year. (Waring marveled at how well suited Italians were for garbage work, calling them "a race with a genius for rag-and-bone-picking and for sub- sisting on rejected trifles of food.") Nor were workers pleased by his ruthless suppres- sion of Knights of Labor resistance to such cuts. ("Strikes will not be tolerated for one moment.") But Waring's war on Tammany also brought workers benefits: they no longer had to contribute time, labor, and money to the machine. And Waring estab- lished an arbitration scheme—a joint management-labor board—which, though clearly an antiunion device, worked to the reasonable satisfaction of most employees.

The results were spectacular. Obstructions, particularly unharnessed vehicles, were briskly removed. Waring forced city trucking firms to stop leaving wagons on the streets for days or weeks; he objected to them because "thieves and highwaymen made them their dens, toughs caroused in them, both sexes resorted to them, and they were used for the vilest purposes." Streets were scoured—those on the East Side as well as Fifth Avenue. Violators of the sanitary code were promptly arrested. Snow, once left to pile into mountains of grunge, was shoveled away. *Harper's* proudly published before- and-after photos.

Waring also imposed a recycling program, something hitherto sabotaged by munic- ipal lethargy and political corruption. Since 1882 the garbage collected by cartmen had been taken to riverside dumps, where it was loaded or "trimmed" on scows by private

"Specimens of Colonel Waring's splendid work in street cleaning, before and after he began, 1893–95," *Harper's Weekly*, June 22, 1895. (© Collection of The New-York Historical Society)

operators who paid for the privilege of picking out old shoes, carpets, paper, rugs, rags, and bones, which they sorted, baled, and sold—rags and paper to paper mills, bones to soda makers, iron to junk dealers and on to foundries. The remainder was hauled out into the harbor and dumped. Since 1871, it had been against state law to offload into the Harlem or East rivers or the Upper Bay, but south of the Narrows was still acceptable. By the late 1880s, however, ocean-dumped garbage was killing oyster and clam beds and drifting back to beaches. Redirecting the refuse to Riker's Island's landfills brought furious complaints from Queens, Manhattan, and Bronx residents sickened by the terrible odors.

To solve all these problems at once, Waring in 1896 required that householders put out their ashes, their garbage (organic animal and vegetable wastes), and their rubbish (drystuffs such as paper, cardboard, tin cans, bottles, shoes, carpets) in separate containers. Mayor Strong assigned him forty policemen to ensure compliance. Department employees then sent ashes—along with street sweepings (mainly dirt)—to be dumped at Riker's Island rather than at sea, along with rubbish, once it had been scavenged by scow trimmers for salable items. Finally, Waring contracted with the New York Sanitary Utilization Company to pick up garbage and take it to a plant on Barren Island in Jamaica Bay. There "digestors" cooked and stewed it until oil and grease were separated out for sale to manufacturers, and the residue was dried and ground into fertilizer.

Though ocean dumping was thus cut to a minimum, Waring did nothing to tackle the growing problem of industrial pollution. Hunter's Point chemical plants continued to pour toxic by-products into Dutch Kills and Newtown Creek. Oil leaks and spills created a constant danger of petroleum vapor conflagration there, and in Newark Bay as well, but as one Queens newspaper noted, "the petroleum industry is of such overwhelming magnitude and importance and is operated by such heavy combinations of capital that it is doubtful whether even by an appeal to the State Legislature" the practice could be halted.

Nevertheless, reformers adored Waring: he was their first star. He demonstrated that despite Tammany taunts about goo-goo ineffectiveness, reformers could *deliver*. The man provided businesslike nonpolitical efficiency, fostered civic pride, advanced a godly cleanliness, and, via a ruthless paternalism, kept labor in line and productive. For having so thoroughly proved there were viable alternatives to machine rule, they would in 1898 elect him president of the City Club.

GERM WARFARE

A less dazzling star in the reform firmament, but one of arguably even greater importance, was Dr. Hermann Biggs, a holdover from the Tammany regime whom Strong and company had the good sense to retain and encourage. Biggs, who had studied at Bellevue Hospital Medical College and in German laboratories, was by 1885 running Bellevue's new Carnegie Lab, working as the hospital's (and city's) pathologist, and serving as visiting physician at the workhouse and almshouse while maintaining a sizable private practice.

In 1889, after reviewing the work of German bacteriologist Robert Koch, Biggs wrote a landmark report for the Health Department concluding that tuberculosis was communicable and thus preventable. As the disease was acquired by direct transmission of bacilli, usually by dried and pulverized sputum floating dustlike in air, regular disinfection of wards and houses with tubercular patients, as well as rigorous inspections of the city's meat and milk supply, might make serious inroads against a disease that killed more than six thousand New Yorkers each year but was largely ignored because it was endemic rather than epidemic. Many doctors resisted this view, however, and by the early 1890s virtually the only health workers acting on the theory were the women at the Nurses' Settlement.

Biggs hammered away at the idea that given Koch's and French chemist Louis Pasteur's breakthroughs in microbiology, and the new ability to isolate infectious organisms, "public health is purchasable." The city could, within natural limits, determine its own death rate. New York authorities were slow to react until the summer of 1892, when cholera again stalked its way westward from Persia and Russia to the ports of Europe. By August it reached Hamburg, killing thousands. On August 30 the steamship *Moravia* arrived in New York. Twenty-two passengers had died en route. Ten days later another steamer reported thirty-two deaths at sea.

Now—in addition to imposing a rigorous quarantine, readying a floating hospital, and placing a corps of physicians and nurses on alert—the Health Department established a Division of Pathology, Bacteriology, and Disinfection under the direction of Dr. Biggs. When the disease struck, his laboratory examined the feces of suspected infectees for traces of the cholera spirillum, confirming or denying questionable diagnoses. Once a case was confirmed in the lab, Health Department crews were dispatched to the lodgings of the stricken, which were scrubbed and fumigated, and the patient's clothes and bedding treated or burned. The department also marched a small army into the tenement districts to clean streets and vacant lots, scour thirty-nine thousand tenements, flush water pipes with disinfectant, and pass out circulars on prevention and treatment in English, German, French, Spanish, Italian, and Yiddish.

Only nine people died. The epidemic—which had killed twenty-five hundred *a day* in Russia for weeks at a time—had been completely defeated. Never again would this particular scourge gain a foothold in New York City. But the mobilization was even more significant for what it kicked off: a series of pioneering municipal efforts at preventive medicine.

Biggs declared war on diphtheria, a massive child killer whose victims often died a lingering death from suffocation. Using new methods of diagnosis he proved that nearly half the cases thought to be diphtheria weren't—a crucial discovery, because quarantining such patients with the really diseased could kill them. Biggs now established a system of mass diagnosis. The division supplied culture tubes free and picked them up by messenger each evening; doctors could phone the lab next day for results.

In 1894 Biggs, while in Europe, learned of a new diphtheria antitoxin. Using first his own money, then proceeds from a *Herald* fund drive, and finally a substantial appropriation from the Board of Estimate, Biggs began producing the antitoxin from horses; he was the first to do so outside Europe. In 1895 the antitoxin halted an epidemic at the New York Infant Asylum. Biggs began giving it away free to doctors for use with poor patients and sold the surplus to drugstores to fund continued research. The serum brought an immediate and sharp decline in mortality rates, gaining an international reputation for New York City's Health Department.

Biggs also won acceptance for a more aggressive campaign against tuberculosis. The Health Department put out multilingual educational leaflets. It launched an anti-spitting campaign, instituted inspections for tubercular meat, and required dispensaries and public institutions to report the names of patients with TB (and requested doctors do so voluntarily). It was the beginning of a drive that in ensuing years would eliminate the "great white plague" as a major cause of death in New York City.

The city made great gains against typhoid, too, after investigations confirmed that a major culprit was the city's milk supply. Since the anti-swill milk campaigns of the 1850s and 1860s, producers and wholesalers had invented more subtle ways to adulterate their product. Filthy conditions, warm temperatures, and the lengthy trip from cow to consumer rendered the product lethal. In the 1890s, philanthropist Nathan Straus halved the death rate in the city's infant asylum on Randall's Island by using pasteurized milk. He and the Henry Street Settlement went on to establish pure milk stations for needy infants, further helping bring down the whopping infant mortality rate. After 1893, the city also experimented with chlorinating the water supply, a procedure that would slowly win favor in coming decades.

The Strong administration took steps as well to implement the establishment of public baths, for which reformers had long been calling. In 1888 the Department of Public Works's fifteen outdoor baths were tremendously popular with the poor, drawing an average 2.5 million males and 1.5 million females during the limited season (June 10–October 1) they were open. The baths afforded youthful patrons recreational relief from broiling summers, though as the city's goal was promotion of cleanliness it imposed a twenty-minute time limit on their use, leading boys to travel from one to the other, dirtying themselves on the way to gain access. But as river water grew ever more polluted by sewage—despite Waring's garbage reforms, liquid effluvia was still channeled into surrounding waterways—and as the baths were in any event closed most of the year, calls were raised for indoor, all-weather washing facilities stocked with filtered and purified water.

The most vigorous proponent of public baths was Simon Baruch (father of Bernard)—a German immigrant, surgeon, and professor of hydrotherapy at the College of Physicians and Surgeons. After visiting the impressive German municipal bath systems in the late 1880s, Baruch began a campaign stressing that baths, in addition to benefiting the poor and helping create "civic civilization" out of "urban barbarism," were in the interest of "the better situated classes": no longer unwashed, the employees, servants, laborers, and tradespeople next to whom they sat on crowded cars would not carry so many deadly germs. At Baruch's urging, the AICP, long interested in such programs, erected a People's Baths in 1891, charging a five-cent fee for use of the twenty-three showers and three bathtubs (the Colgate Company donated free soap samples). Though the program was well patronized, Tammany governments proved uninterested in expanding it. It was not until 1895 that the state legislature mandated a campaign, and Mayor Strong constituted a committee to press ahead.

HOUSING FRONT

In housing, the reform administration moved to enact recommendations of a state-established Tenement House Committee chaired by *Century* editor Richard Watson Gilder. During 1894, with Gilder's close friend Jacob Riis serving as unofficial adviser and settlement house workers acting as investigators, the committee examined dwelling places and took public testimony from housing experts, health inspectors, landlords, and residents. They discovered that over 70 percent of the city's population of roughly 1,800,000 now lived in multifamily domiciles, four-fifths of which were tenement houses, vast numbers of which were experiencing the familiar litany of housing ills, including high rates of disease, terrific overcrowding, and a lack of accessible parks and play-grounds.

The Gilder Committee debated a variety of potential solutions. Felix Adler, picking up where Henry George had left off, recommended the municipality purchase low-cost land in still undeveloped outlying areas, then lease it cheaply to individuals or companies, who would in turn provide low-income housing. European cities were moving in this direction, as the researches of Elgin Ralston Lovell Gould made clear. Gould, a professor of political science at Columbia, made a thorough survey of domestic and overseas approaches (which he would publish in 1895 as *The Housing of the Working People*). Gould reported that many English, Scottish, German, and Belgian cities were either building low-cost worker housing themselves or providing loans to cooperatives pledged to do so. Some cities, like Frankfurt, had planned their own deconcentration by buying up undeveloped peripheral land to forestall its acquisition by speculators.

Gould himself rejected such efforts as "bad principle and worse policy." The state should set standards below which no housing could fall but leave its provision to market forces. Chairman Gilder agreed that municipal housing initiatives would be an "unjustifiable interference with private enterprise," as did Jacob Riis, who was also squarely in the entrepreneurial tradition. Gilder did embrace a policy of reform through demolition, urging that bad buildings, especially rear tenements, be destroyed, thus creating open spaces for neighborhood parks. Felix Adler counterargued that the committee was focusing too much on destruction and not enough on building new housing, without which slum clearance would amount to depriving poor people of desperately needed shelter. In addition, the value of new parks would be swiftly neutralized by crowding spawned by new tenements.

Gilder's approach dominated the committee's report of January 1895, as well as the Tenement House Act of 1895, passed to implement its proposals. The new law increased the Board of Health's power to vacate and demolish and streamlined the process for implementing condemnation orders. When the board actually attempted a campaign against rear tenements, however, landlords and developers challenged its new powers and won court decisions affirming that renters had no right to light and air.

Demolition too made little headway. The 1895 law authorized the razing of tenements and the issuance of three million dollars in bonds toward building parks and playgrounds in their stead. But only in the case of Mulberry Bend—thanks to Jacob Riis's impassioned and persistent denunciation of it as "the foul core of New York's slums"—did Mayor Strong order buildings vacated and destroyed (their owners were paid a total of $1.5 million). Even then it took two more years of Riis's nudging before Columbus Park opened on the site.

Mayor Strong did put the Building Department in charge of a professional architect, Stevenson Constable, who began subjecting plans of builders and contractors to thorough examination before issuing permits. Under Tammany, the department had been a plum for party faithful, as building tradesmen routinely paid inspectors bribes to get around vexing requirements. Constable, like Waring, demanded inspectors don uniforms, stay out of saloons during working hours, and crack down on slipshod construction methods. Wrathful builders, architects, and contractors managed to bog down the campaign, and the results proved negligible.

Public approaches floundered in part because housing reformers, pursuant to their analysis and inclinations, put most of their energy into private programs. Made aware, from the limited follow-up to model housing initiatives like those of White and Adler, that small builders were unlikely ever to house the poor and laboring classes, many in the Strong administration believed that corporate philanthropy was the answer. Concentrated capital could work on the grand scale required and could afford to settle for moderate profits.

In 1896, accordingly, an independent Committee on Improved Housing was set up—with Richard Watson Gilder as chair—to sponsor an architectural competition for structures covering large lots (two hundred by four hundred feet, rather than the tiny twenty-five by a hundred specified in the dumbbell competition). Then a City and Suburban Homes Company was established to provide wage-earners with "improved, wholesome homes at current rates." It counted among its directors and officers both leading housing activists (such as Gould, Gilder, Riis, Adler, White, and Rainsford) and wealthy philanthropists (among them Cornelius Vanderbilt II, Isaac N. Seligman, Darius Ogden Mills, and the brothers W. Bayard Cutting and Robert Fulton Cutting), and received additional financial support from the Astor, Low, Morgan, Rockefeller, and Schiff families.

City and Suburban Homes was capitalized at a million dollars (J. P. Morgan helped issue its stock), and its dividends were limited to 5 percent. For its first venture the company had architect Ernest Flagg design the Clark Estate, a complex of six-story buildings on a site given by Mrs. Alfred Corning Clark, heir to the Singer fortune, in exchange for shares in the company. When completed in 1898, its 373 apartments, at West End Avenue and Amsterdam between 68th and 69th streets, each had its own toilet, laundry, and tubs.

Yet where City and Suburban led, few followed, as big capital had many investment outlets far less troublesome and more lucrative than low-rent housing. By the end of the 1890s the model tenement movement had built only two thousand units, which housed no more than ten thousand people. In the same period, the housing industry built twenty thousand units into which 750,000 people were crammed.

ROOSEVELT CRACKS DOWN

Mayor Strong's police commissioner, Theodore Roosevelt, would achieve a notoriety that equalled Waring's, but his accomplishments would be more problematic. Since his defeat in the 1886 mayoral election, Roosevelt had kept busy. He toured Europe with his new wife, Edith, then came home to set up his Sagamore Hill estate at Oyster Bay. He took up duties as a federal civil service commissioner. He wrote history prolifically, turning out a celebratory volume entitled *The Winning of the West*, a biography of Gouverneur Morris, and, in 1891, a *History of New York City*.

Roosevelt's municipal biography, a scholarly potboiler, was enlivened by enthusiastic "bullys" for historic virtue and stern condemnations of historic vice (the "unscrupulous rich" and the "vicious and ignorant poor" garnering almost equal opprobrium). He applauded with particular vigor the efforts of the police and troops who had attacked the Civil War draft rioters "with the most wholesome desire to do them harm," professing his delight that "over 1200 rioters were slain—an admirable object lesson to the remainder."

In 1895 Roosevelt added a late-breaking postscript to the second edition of his city history hailing the resurgence of the reform movement he had helped foster. If this was his way of indicating a desire to return to the metropolitan fray, his wish was swiftly granted. Mayor Strong, determined to put a strong hand at the police department tiller, summoned Roosevelt back from his long exile. He would never leave the spotlight again.

Roosevelt soon discovered his authority was nowhere near as clear-cut as Waring's. The major legislative upshot of the Lexow exposés had been a Platt-dictated law requiring the four-man Police Board to be composed equally of Democrats and Republicans (giving Platt assured access to police patronage and the election machinery). Roosevelt was thus only one of four commissioners, though his colleagues promptly elected him president. To the public eye, however, Roosevelt seemed totally in charge, an impression the publicity-conscious politician eagerly cultivated.

Roosevelt lunged into action. First he arranged for the resignation of Lexow-disgraced Superintendent Byrnes and Inspector "Clubber" Williams. (Byrnes would launch a detective agency on Wall Street; Clubber entered the insurance business and would die a multimillionaire). Roosevelt and his colleagues established a merit system for appointments and promotions and added two thousand new recruits to the force—many from out of town, few of them Irish Catholics. In 1897 he would announce—prematurely, as it turned out—that "the old system of blackmail and corruption has been almost entirely broken up." Roosevelt also raised morale and encouraged excellence by handing out medals for heroism and partially modernizing the department: telephone call boxes on streets allowed cops to communicate with station houses; a Bicycle Squad added mobility.

Like Waring, TR set out to exercise personal authority over a refractory workforce. He delighted in making surreptitious nocturnal tours of the city, accompanied only by his friend (and publicist) Jacob Riis (whom Roosevelt had sought out after reading his *Other Half*). Dressed in black cloaks and wide-brimmed hats, the duo crept up on errant bluecoats sneaking beers in saloons, nabbing them while their mustaches were still drenched with incriminating foam.

In 1896 Roosevelt ordered an investigation of the decades-old practice of police stations offering shelter to the homeless—urged on by Riis, who had unpleasant memories of his experiences in them when still a penniless immigrant. The filthy condition of the lodgings was apparent. And his chief of police swore that 98 percent of the more than sixty thousand homeless people who had resorted to them during the past year were the "lazy, dissipated, filthy, vermin-covered, disease-breeding and disease-scattering scum of the city's population." So Roosevelt adopted the Charity Organization Society's long-standing position that the lodgings were "a fruitful encouragement to vagrancy" and shut them down. After the pitching of thousands into homelessness in mid-depression generated cartoons in the popular press of heartless men shivering outside closed police stations, the city set up a Municipal Lodging House in a rented factory, but it sheltered only two hundred men. In the meantime, Roosevelt had established "tramp and beggar squads" to harry habitual mendicants.

Roosevelt also kept a close rein on labor activists as part of his determination to "keep in order the turbulent portion of the population." Lincoln Steffens reported on "brutal clubbings of East Side strikers," and Roosevelt himself applauded his police for "clubbing right and left" in the course of breaking up a horsecar strike. Compared to

Byrnes-era attacks on strikers, however, the Strong regime was relatively mild. TR was willing to hold discussions with labor leaders, an openness that won him points.

Roosevelt and Strong's comparative evenhandedness was glaringly underscored by the actions of the reform regime across the East River, where Mayor Schieren presided over the most violent labor conflict in Brooklyn's history, the closest the metropolitan area came to such gunslinging affairs as Homestead, Pullman, and Coeur d'Alene.

Brooklyn's notorious trolley companies had long imposed execrable pay and working conditions, in part to wring out enough profits to pay dividends on mountains of watered stock, in part to recoup the massive investments they'd made converting from horsepower to electricity. Finally, in January 1895, Knights of Labor motormen and conductors walked out, bringing passenger service to a complete halt. The companies advertised for replacement workers in cities across the country. Soon men made desperate for work by hard times flocked to Brooklyn, and a few cars began running. Now thousands of strike supporters in working-class communities came forward—the trolley firms were widely hated—and crowds began sabotaging the newly vulnerable electric lines. The mayor deployed the police, who protected scabs and raided union headquarters, but they didn't act quickly enough to suit the companies, in part because many policemen sympathized with the Knights, in part because protecting the far-flung operations stretched them thin.

Strike supporters went to court to demand the companies be required to resume full service, on pain of having their charters revoked. Judge Gaynor, who had often denounced the trolley firms for greed and corruption, issued the requested writ. Public service corporations, he ruled, had a duty to the people that transcended their obligation to stockholders. "If they can not get labor to perform those duties at what they offer to pay, then they must pay more, and as much as is necessary to get it." The strikers were overjoyed; the *New York Times* denounced Gaynor's decision as "anarchistic"; and the Brooklyn City Council moved to revoke the charters. But Mayor Schieren—whose company, it was noted, supplied the trolleys with electric belts—vetoed the measure.

He also called in the militia, for the first time in Brooklyn's history, and then drew in the First Brigade from New York City, amassing seventy-five hundred soldiers in all. Confronted by angry stone-throwing crowds, the militiamen responded with bayonet charges in which at least two civilians were killed and many wounded. In February the strike was called off. Many clergymen bitterly denounced calling out the militia—including William Rainsford, despite J. P. Morgan's heavy investments in trolley companies.

Commissioner Roosevelt won plaudits for avoiding such ferocity, but he drew furious condemnation for his efforts at enforcing Parkhurstian levels of social purity. Convinced, appropriately enough, that the core of police corruption lay in the system of extorting payments from illicit entrepreneurs for the privilege of noninterference, Roosevelt, though not himself a prohibitionist, declared war on Sunday sin. Beginning in June 1895, saloons, brothels, and gambling dens doing business on the Lord's Day were raided, shut down, boarded up. Sabbatarians, whose campaigns since the 1850s had come to nought, were thrilled, and the Parkhurst-led wing of the Strong coalition cheered Roosevelt on.

But the campaign incensed the German community. They had not voted for Good Government to have their "Continental Sunday" afternoons—spent in beer gardens listening to Strauss waltzes—branded as immoral and banned. Labor unions noted pointedly that while there were over eight thousand arrests annually for excise violations, only 104 violators of the factory laws were hauled off to jail in 1895, shrinking to twenty-one in 1896. The popular press, meanwhile, complained of Roosevelt's shutting off the poor man's recreation while allowing champagne suppers at the Union League Club. Teddy delighted in facing down "the wrath of the asinine herd." On one occasion, having accepted an invitation to personally review a mammoth protest parade of outraged Germans, he bantered good-naturedly with the marching legions, who shook empty beer steins at him as they passed by.

Strong's Jewish supporters were also outraged. Strict enforcement of blue laws penalized the thousands of sabbath observers who chose to work on Sundays, and Roosevelt's insistence on cracking down on those who violated anti-pushcart laws generated much talk of abandoning reform and going back to corruptible Tammanyites.

The person most dismayed by TR's vigorous efforts was Mayor Strong. Never an ardent moralist, he had led the city's liquor dealers to believe he would accept a half-dry Sunday as a compromise. Now, fearing the destruction of his electoral coalition, Strong tried to rein in his appointee, only to find Roosevelt had the bit firmly between his formidable teeth. The best Strong could do, given the then-limited authority of a mayor, was to distance himself publicly from his rogue commissioner. "I found," he told one gathering, "that the Dutchman whom I had appointed meant to turn all New Yorkers into Puritans." Roosevelt's response was to raid Sherry's, a watering hole of the wealthy, thus alienating the rich as well as the poor.

In the end, the courts (deliberately) and the legislature (inadvertently) rode to the rescue of Sunday drinkers. Magistrates began interpreting very broadly indeed a statute that allowed liquor to be served if it accompanied a meal; one judge ruled that seventeen beers and a pretzel satisfied the law. The legislature, intent on shutting down this loophole, opened up a far bigger one. Senator John W. Raines achieved passage in 1896 of a bill that permitted Sunday sale of liquor with meals, but only in "hotels," defined as establishments with at least ten bedrooms. Saloons swiftly added the requisite number of rooms and then, to cover remodeling costs, rented the cubicles out to prostitutes or unmarried couples. Roosevelt, indirectly, had managed to engineer a quantum leap forward in the city's quotient of sin.

Denounced now from all sides—apart from the loyal Parkhurst—with a forced removal from office in the offing, the ever practical Roosevelt decided it was time to move on. In April 1897 he gratefully accepted the offer of an assistant secretaryship of the navy from newly elected President William McKinley, and bounded off to glory.

POPULISTS AND GOLDBUGS

TR's job switch was made possible by the Republican Party's having emerged victorious from a titanic struggle with populism, a triumph that owed much to Teddy and his New York City colleagues.

The depression had provided an opportunity for Republicans to take on the regnant Democratic administration of Grover Cleveland. But the presidential election of 1896 proved to be far more than a conventional political contest. To contemporaries it seemed a cosmic clash, worthy of the Book of Revelation, pitting West against East, silver against gold, and populists against plutocrats in a battle for the soul of the republic.

Over the previous decade, as the world marketplace flooded with agricultural products, farmers in the South and West found that wheat, which had sold for a dollar a bushel in 1870, now fetched anywhere from sixty cents to a dime. Loath to blame the market itself, they attacked those they believed took unfair advantage of them: the great railroad companies, mercantile middlemen, land speculators, commodity brokers, local bankers, and behind and above all these the "Money Kings of Wall Street" who controlled the nation's credit and currency systems.

In the 1880s and early 1890s, agriculturalists in the cotton South and wheatfield Midwest established a cooperative movement—the Farmers Alliance—dedicated to bypassing the corporate world headquartered in New York City. Pushing to develop alternative systems of distribution, credit, and exchange, the farmers called for government ownership of the railroads, granaries, banks, and telegraph companies and demanded that government regulate privately owned companies to outlaw monopoly, collusion, and price-fixing. Seeking nothing less than to transform the United States into a "cooperative commonwealth," the mass movement entered politics in 1892 and organized the People's Party (becoming known as "populists").

In response, the western wing of the Democratic Party, while sidestepping most People's Party demands as too radical, fastened on one small piece of the populists' currency program: the call for "free silver." A global shortage of gold, coupled with a rising demand for its use, had driven up its value and that of currencies pegged to it. This forced borrowers to repay loans in ever more valuable currency. Debtors reasoned that if silver were made an official U.S. currency alongside gold and coined in unlimited quantities, the resulting inflation would raise depressed prices and profits. Rocky Mountain silver-mine owners liked this idea and backed Democratic politicians who promoted it—men like the silver-tongued Nebraskan William Jennings Bryan.

New York City became the stronghold of the opposing "goldbug" forces. When the Panic of 1893 led holders of greenbacks and bonds to cash in their paper for gold, draining the federal government's specie reserves, Wall Streeters got newly reelected President Cleveland, whose campaign J. P. Morgan and others had funded, to replenish the federal strongbox by repeatedly selling bonds for fresh supplies of gold. Syndicates organized by Morgan and August Belmont Jr. sold the bonds to European investors (notably the English Rothschilds) and to local capitalists (notably New York banks, trust companies, and life insurance companies). In each case, however, the treasury's gold swiftly flowed right back out again, sometimes to be used again in the next round of bond purchases, a highly profitable loop.

Populists and western Democrats denounced the bond sales as short-term ripoffs—"A Wicked Deal. Rothschilds, Morgan, and Belmont Skin the Country," squawked the *Atlanta Constitution*—and as part of a long-term conspiracy to prop up the gold standard. At the 1896 Democratic convention in Chicago, silverites challenged New York goldbug control of the party. Bryan denounced the attempt to crucify Americans on a cross of gold and issued his famous antiurban philippic: "You come to us and tell us that the great cities are in favor of the gold standard; we reply that the great cities rest upon our broad and fertile prairies. Burn down your cities and leave our farms, and your cities will spring up again as if by magic; but destroy our farms and the grass will grow in the streets of every city in the country." Delegates cheered, Cleveland and his New York backers were overthrown, and the Democratic Party rallied behind Bryan and free silver. The People's Party, despite concerns that Bryan was insufficiently radical, backed the Democrats, and a grand climactic showdown between "the People" and "Wall Street" got underway.

Wealthy New Yorkers too saw 1896 as an electoral Armageddon. From their perspective, the inflationary proposals of agrarian primitives, antimodern provincials, crackpot economists, and hayseed cranks were dangerous, immoral, little short of theft. Currency panaceas took no account of the realities of life in a gold-standard world—only Latin Americans and other backward peoples used silver—and thus imperiled international trade. Worse, by striking at the heart of the credit superstructure, they threatened to abort modern capitalism—and with it, modern civilization.

Hatred of Bryan and silver reached acrid levels. The Rev. Parkhurst called on the "solid intelligent integrity of the country" to "grind its heel relentlessly and unpityingly into the viperous head that is lifting itself up in venomous antagonism not only to this Government, but in venomous antagonism to all government."

Horrified by the silver hordes sweeping in out of the West, Wall Street erected golden barricades. Abandoning the Democrats, they piled into the Republican Party and met candidate William McKinley's campaign manager with open wallets. Morgan dined with him on board the *Corsair* and pledged a quarter-million dollars. Standard Oil matched this, and contributions from New York-based corporations and insurance companies helped swell the GOP's war chest to an unprecedented and astronomical three-million-plus dollars (Bryan managed a mere three hundred thousand).

The Republican millions bankrolled a political advertising campaign that sent hundreds of speakers into the field, coordinated the work of metropolitan papers and churches, and printed and distributed millions of pamphlets, broadsides, and booklets. Employers formed sound-money clubs and pressured workers into attending "educational" meetings. Republicans wrapped themselves in the flag too. On the Saturday before the November election, New York was swathed in patriotic bunting and festooned with Old Glories. While 750,000 looked on, a huge column of a hundred thousand professionals, businessmen, and their employees (volunteered or dragooned), each holding aloft a flag, marched in a monster parade organized by the Sound Money Association. Children, their chests covered with badges attesting allegiance to the gold standard, sang derisive songs about greenbacks.

Bryan carried the fight to the temple of the moneychangers. Though he was reviled from press and pulpit with unprecedented ferocity, working people packed Madison Square Garden hoping to hear the great orator give a stem-winding speech. Bryan disappointed them, reading a prepared, "statesmanlike," two-hour address to the packed and sweltering house; many in the audience melted away.

Bryan's problems went beyond the heat. The populist vision of a republic of small freeholders had little to offer the mass of metropolitan wage-laborers in the mid-1890s. German and Jewish socialists and anarchists were put off by the populists' evangelical convictions and prohibitionist culture. Unionists like Gompers reasoned that the farmers were themselves employers of wage-labor and so unworthy of support. Tammany did endorse the national ticket and turned out such (largely Irish working-class) support as Bryan got. Gold Democrats of course bolted the party; even Pulitzer's *World* refused to back the Nebraskan.

Bryan lost both New York and Brooklyn, the first Democratic presidential candidate to do so since 1848. So thorough was McKinley's triumph that the greenback critique of finance capitalism dropped out of the national discourse (aided by the discovery of gold in the Yukon and South Africa, which increased the money supply and relieved the currency stringency). Once in power, the Republicans passed a tariff, wrote the gold standard into law, and gathered Theodore Roosevelt to their collective bosom.

FUSION DEFUSED

What McKinley's victory did not do was restore prosperity. The depression dragged on. So did class tensions, as was evidenced in the winter of 1897 when Mrs. Bradley Martin, having read of the sufferings of the poor, decided to throw a ball "to give an impetus to trade." With colossal symbolic ineptitude—and at a cost of $370,000—the Bradley Martins rented the ballroom of the Waldorf Hotel and transformed it into a replica of Versailles. Mr. Bradley Martin dressed up as Louis XV, and Mrs. Bradley Martin—attired as Mary Queen of Scots (replete with a massive ruby necklace once worn by Marie Antoinette)—perched herself on a throne while liveried lackeys announced the seven hundred moneyed guests who incautiously flocked to the affair. With anarchists rumored to be planting bombs, the windows were boarded up, and the police kept massed spectators at bay. Editors, clergymen, college debating societies, and Democratic politicians denounced the heartless extravagance. New York authorities doubled the Bradley Martins' tax assessment. Hounded out of town by the storm of notoriety, the couple moved permanently to England after receiving a sendoff by a dinner of unrepentant multimillionaires.

The Bradley Martin fiasco helped usher New York City Republicans out of power, though the problems confronting the Good Government coalition in 1897 were manifold. Just as the Henry George coalition, having failed to win office in 1886, had flown apart in 1887, the reformers discovered that victory could be equally problematic, and their alliance fissured into its component parts.

Roosevelt's liquor policy drove the Germans back to the Democrats, and his rigorous Sabbatarianism alienated Jewish supporters. Strong's disbursal of patronage to Republicans enraged purist nonpartisans, and his handouts to independent Democrats enraged Boss Platt. The former sat out the 1897 campaign in high-minded disgust. The latter decided to run as the Republican candidate, fatally splitting the anti-Tammany forces (possibly in collusion with Boss Croker, as they had a mutual interest in getting rid of pesky reformers). Mayor Strong himself declined a bid for reelection; his own business having failed, he was eager to refurbish his private affairs.

The reform enterprise did not disintegrate completely, however. With the upcoming mayoral election as spur, the hard core of the coalition decided to build a permanent third party devoted to the pursuit of municipal power. They named their vehicle the Citizens Union. The new organization included the leaders of organized charity, with Robert Fulton Cutting as the party's chair. Businessmen and professionals occupied leadership and financial backer positions, with Morgan, Speyer, Dodge, Schiff, and Hewitt, and such luminaries of the Bar as Joseph Choate and Elihu Root, in prominent positions. The Good Government Clubs were converted into Citizens Union district headquarters. And around this nucleus clustered crucial auxiliaries: Protestant clergymen, reform-minded women, and settlement house workers, with James Reynolds of University Settlement serving as executive director.

For a standard bearer the Citizens Union chose Seth Low. The stout and stolid burgher—a former two-term mayor of Brooklyn and currently president of Columbia University—seemed an ideal choice. Low took a leaf from George's 1886 campaign and demanded the Citizens Union gather a convincing number of preelection pledges of support. This done, he accepted the nomination, as had George, at a Cooper Union rally, only in this case the frock-coated candidate was escorted to the podium by the president of the Bar Association, and his audience consisted of wealthy, respectable, and well-educated bankers and lawyers, merchants and professionals, ladies and clergymen.

To their central plank of opposition to bossism, Citizens Union leaders, aware of the need for outreach, held out an olive branch to respectable laborers (a group its City Club predecessors had ignored in 1894) by gingerly supporting an eight-hour law for city workers and for employees in private businesses with city contracts. Low was chosen in part for his work with the Church Association for the Advancement of the Interests of Labor—he had won plaudits as a labor mediator—and his chairmanship of the board of trustees of the University Settlement Society, which had developed close connections with East Side labor organizations.

The Citizens Union's chances were given an unexpected lift by the startling return to politics of Henry George. Nominated by a coalition of dissident Democrats, union leaders, single taxers, and social reformers, the old warrior, despite a recent heart attack, launched a wrathful campaign, promising to throw Croker in jail if he won. Low's backers were thrilled, thinking the maverick effort might siphon off Tammany support; George himself admitted he would be satisfied if he threw the election to Low.

This possibility was torpedoed by George's death. With less than a week to go in the campaign, the fragile reformer had maintained a strenuous pace. One night he spoke four times; the next day he succumbed to a stroke. One hundred thousand filed past his bier in Grand Central Palace, while an equal number thronged outside. The *World* described the massive crowds as comparable only to those for Lincoln. Father McGlynn gave the eulogy, to tumultuous applause, and then a catafalque drawn by sixteen black-draped horses drew the coffin down Madison Avenue to City Hall, over the Brooklyn Bridge, and on to burial in Green-Wood Cemetery. Over him would be erected, by popular subscription, a granite monument engraved with a quote from *Progress and Poverty*. George's son picked up his father's fallen banner, but he lacked dynamism and would garner few votes.

Labor had nowhere to turn but to Tammany, and Boss Croker made it easy for them. He nudged the Democratic Party slightly to the left, pledging not to use the police or courts against strikers, agreeing to grant the eight-hour day to city workers, promising fair treatment for municipal employees (in lieu of Waring's paternalism), and guaranteeing opportunities for local boys to work their way up in city jobs (unlike TR's reliance on out-of-towners). Croker also affirmed the Democrats' long-standing commitment to moral laissez-faire and proclaimed the common people's ability to run New York City without the aid of the "better element."

As its candidate, Tammany chose Robert A. Van Wyck, an obscure municipal court judge. With no independent base, no money, no personal pizazz, indeed nothing much more going for him than a venerable city name, Van Wyck was a perfect Croker creature. District leaders rallied their troops behind him at a rousing ratification meeting to fireworks and the strains of a band booming out "There'll Be a Hot Time in the Old Town To-Night."

Tammany swept Van Wyck into office, outpolling the other three candidates combined. Still, Low and the Citizens Union did creditably well on the Upper East and West sides and in Central Harlem. Low remained hopeful about the future. "If 10 righteous men could save Sodom," he argued, the thousands in his corner "will yet bring about good government in the City of New York." For now, however, the day belonged, as it had back in 1886, to Tammany Hall, and its partisans marched through the streets joyously chanting, "Well, well, well, Reform has gone to Hell!"

68

Splendid Little War

"This country needs a war," proclaimed Theodore Roosevelt in 1895 as, against a background of unremitting depression, he and others among the New York elite began clamoring for imperial expansion. Though war was touted as a way to end unemployment, it was emphasized even more as a way to scour away the barnacles of corruption and money-grubbing that had corroded the American spirit. War would toughen the nineties' generation as the Civil War had toughened its parents'—that bloodbath having taken on a nostalgic glow, especially to those who hadn't fought it, after the passage of thirty years.

The notion that Empire would revive the sterner virtues of the Founding Fathers appealed to upper-class males who felt cooped up in enervating offices by day and confined in stifling parlors by night, who feared that, deprived of opportunities for manly heroism, they were growing effete, even effeminate—a dangerous development, surrounded as they were by anarchists, ruffians, immigrants, strikers, and criminals. Literary fashions reflected these fears, first the 1880s cult of the cowboy (of which TR had been an early disciple), then the 1890s fancy for medieval knights, the new rough riders on the plains of bourgeois fantasy. Bookstores and genteel magazines like *Harper's*, *Scribner's*, and *Century* were flooded with historical romances about Saxon warriors and chivalric aristocrats.

Armchair activism was complemented by a vogue of physical vigor, as TR counseled his enfeebled upper-class-mates to adopt a more strenuous life. Sports—the "modern chivalry"—would toughen up a "delicate, indoor genteel race" by providing a "saving touch of honest, old-fashioned barbarism." Others urged youth to enlist in the proliferating Protestant boys' groups, which drilled martial virtues into the next generation.

But the best antidote to civilization was imperialism. Jingoistic New Yorkers craved the psychic satisfactions of Empire, reveling in the potential glory of conquering exotic territories and ruling over dusky races with pomp and panoply. Imperialism would allow simultaneously for the exercise of a restorative barbarism and the refurbishment of republican virtue. America had moral responsibilities abroad, said Josiah Strong, secretary of the Congregational Home Missionary Society. The American Anglo-Saxon had an inherited genius for imperial exploits; he was "divinely commissioned to be, in a peculiar sense, his brother's keeper"; it was the *duty* of the fittest "race" to bring civilization, Christianity, and the rule of law to backward peoples.

In prior generations, such values had been given expression in the course of exercising the country's Manifest Destiny to govern the continent—a saga Roosevelt limned in his *Winning of the West* (1889)—but with the trans-Mississippi frontier closing down, the rejuvenating benefits of conquest could only be achieved overseas. Expansionists, accordingly, applauded each step in this direction, particularly the thrilling actions of President Cleveland in 1895, when he confronted Britain over Venezuela and put some muscle back in the Monroe Doctrine.

The Venezuelan crisis did, however, foreshadow serious divisions within New York's upper classes over imperialism. Where Roosevelt was ecstatic and hoped the confrontation with Britain might lead farther—perhaps to the conquest of Canada— Joseph Pulitzer organized a "peace crusade" against "jingoes" (Roosevelt itched to put him in jail). Some Wall Streeters, too, deprecated war with Britain, leading the *New York Times* to snarl at such "patriots of the ticker." "If they were heeded," the *Times* said, "American civilization would degenerate to the level of the Digger Indians, who eat dirt all their lives and appear to like it."

There were those on Wall Street who argued that a selfless pursuit of Anglo-Saxon duty could be combined with the restoration of sagging profit margins. Many believed "overproduction" responsible for the great slump. U.S. capitalism's ability to supply goods seemed to have outraced the American market's ability to consume them, leading some to look overseas for adequate outlets for their products. Several New York City companies had demonstrated a correlation between economic health and foreign sales: Standard Oil of New York supplied over 70 percent of the world's kerosene, Duke's Tobacco Trust rolled cigarettes for the global millions, and Singer sent sewing machines to factories and sweatshops the world over.

New Yorkers were also exporting money. In the 1880s bankers and industries had begun to make loans to foreign governments, invest in overseas ventures, and set up branches abroad. The 1890s depression, in diminishing domestic opportunities, spurred calls to accelerate the process, and Americans increased their investments abroad by almost $250 million during hard times. In the course of expanding their export of capital and commodities, however, New Yorkers kept running up against entrenched Europeans. In the Far East, a conglomerate of American oil, rail, sugar, steel, and banking interests (with participation by Harriman, Schiff, Carnegie, and Rockefeller) put together a million-dollar American China Development Corporation in 1895, but it lagged far behind the British and was threatened by expanding German interests.

In Latin America, New Yorkers were in a stronger position. The city had long imported substantial quantities of Caribbean and Central and South American goods, carried northward by generations of shippers from the Griswolds to Grace. By the end of the century, metropolitan families were consuming one pound of coffee per week, bananas had become a customary delicacy, and the city's parlors and Palm Rooms were festooned with tropical products.

Dictator Porfirio Díaz had thrown Mexico open to New York capital; his agents hosted a dinner at Delmonico's and successfully enlisted railroad investments from the likes of Collis P. Huntington, Grenville M. Dodge, Russell Sage, and Jay Gould. J. P. Morgan's firm made loans to Peru and participated in Argentine development; William R. Grace engaged in banking and shipping operations in South America; William Rockefeller of Standard Oil had interests in Brazil.

A New York syndicate had bought up the Dominican Republic's debt in 1892, taken control of its finances, and launched the San Domingo Improvement Company. In Cuba the great Yankee metropolis, long intimately involved in the island's commercial affairs, had increased its presence after the last great upheaval against Spanish rule. The Ten Years War of 1868–78 had bankrupted many Cuban planters and opened the way to substantial investment by wealthy New Yorkers, including Henry Havemeyer's Sugar Trust. By the mid-1890s, American investment in Cuba alone surpassed 50 million dollars, ten million more than Carnegie's annual profit from steel. And by 1898 U.S. capitalists had sunk $350 million into the Caribbean and Central America.

Nevertheless, Europeans still dominated the hemisphere's markets and supplied the bulk of its credit requirements, and in the depression years some New Yorkers cast hungry eyes southward. If "we could wrest the South American markets from Germany and England and permanently hold them," wrote the *Bankers' Magazine* in 1894, "this would be indeed a conquest worth perhaps a heavy sacrifice."

Increasingly, Roosevelt and others demanded that the U.S. government play rough on behalf of its entrepreneurs. Europe had inaugurated a new age of imperialism—the word itself first became current in the 1890s—and in the last quarter of the nineteenth century had swallowed up a fifth of the earth's surface, including most of Africa and much of the Far East. The United States must get into the great game and compete vigorously or risk being cut off from markets and raw materials in a world increasingly carved up into colonies or protectionist blocs. The global economy was a dog-eat-dog world, and America should concentrate on biting.

Fortunately the country had developed some teeth since the 1880s, when an antiquated navy left the country at the mercy of foreign fleets, and a Spanish or Chilean armada, *Leslie's Weekly* noted, could have anchored off Coney Island and bombed Madison Square. In the late 1880s and early 1890s, two New Yorkers had helped oversee creation of a powerful American fleet. The initiatives of financier William Whitney, secretary of the navy in Cleveland's first administration, had been carried on by his successor in Harrison's Republican administration, Benjamin Franklin Tracy. A leading lawyer (and friend and ally of Tom Platt), Tracy believed the Gulf of Mexico and the Pacific were the coming theaters of naval action, and he promoted construction of armored steel battleships as American interests there were "too important to be left longer unprotected." When the first naval squadron departed for Europe from New York harbor in 1889, Tracy invited Whitney to attend in a show of bipartisan support.

By 1897, this apparatus was to some degree under the control of Assistant Secretary of the Navy Theodore Roosevelt, and jingoists had high hopes that President McKinley would surpass his predecessors in boldness, perhaps by securing a base in the Philippines and making Manila an American Hong Kong. Hawaii was another leading candidate for imperial enterprise. The *Tribune*, under the editorial helmsmanship of

Whitelaw Reid (who had been Republican vice-presidential nominee on the losing 1892 ticket), declared that "the necessity for new markets is now upon us" and urged attaining sovereignty over Hawaii for its sugar, rice, and usefulness as a naval base and coaling station.

All that was missing was a war.

PRO PATRIA

The most likely venue for a military joust was Cuba—once again in rebellion against Spain. Not only was it a mere ninety miles from America's shores, but the revolution itself, conveniently enough, was being run out of New York City.

After the upheavals of the 1870s, many Cuban rebels had fled to exile in Manhattan, where they joined Irish, German, and Russian immigrants in plotting the overthrow of their respective home-country governments. Since his arrival in 1880, the leader of the Cuban exile community had been poet and writer José Martí. Taking up quarters in a boardinghouse at 51 West 29th Street, Martí supported himself as a journalist—filing insightful copy on *norteamericano* culture and politics, especially New York City's, to various Latin American newspapers.

Martí also built a revolutionary movement based on the growing Cuban cigarworker communities in U.S. cities, particularly New York, where the cigar trade was booming. By 1894 its three thousand factories (five hundred of them owned by Hispanics) provided jobs for the Cuban immigrants who settled into Yorkville and Chelsea boardinghouses. Many of these workers joined Martí's Partido Revolucionario Cubano, bought its newspaper *Patria*, and flocked to Clarendon Hall to listen to the eloquent apostle and his colleagues.

Martí also drew support from New York's small but growing Puerto Rican community. A tiny *colonía* had grown up in the city in the eighteenth century; by 1830 a Sociedad Benéfica Cubana y Puertorriqueña, composed of merchants from the islands, promoted trade exchanges. They did well. By 1897 roughly two-thirds of Puerto Rico's sugar exports came to the United States and only about one-third went to Spain. With the sugar came the sons and daughters of the island's mercantile and creole *hacendado* class—as students, exiles, and fomenters of separation from Spain.

Puerto Rico had also planned a rebellion in 1868. Directed from New York by Ramón Emeterio Betances and others, the rising was discovered and swiftly snuffed out. In the ensuing decades exile leaders like the fiery Eugenio María de Hostos established organizations and newspapers (including the evanescent *La Voz de Puerto Rico*) to carry on the struggle among immigrant cigarmakers, artisans, and laborers. Many joined the Puerto Rican branch of Martí's party and organized their own political-cultural clubs. One such activist was Arthur Schomburg, newly arrived in the city in 1891 at age seventeen. Schomburg earned a living as an elevator operator, bellhop, porter, and printer, took night classes at Manhattan Central High, and helped organize Las Dos Antillas (the Two Islands), a club on Third Avenue that collected money, weapons, and medical supplies for an armed struggle.

In January 1895 Martí issued the order for an uprising, smuggling it down to Havana rolled inside a cigar. Although he was frail and ill, Martí himself headed south, ending his long New York exile, and was killed in action that May. Despite this and other setbacks, the rebellion soon established itself in Santiago Province. It launched an effective guerrilla campaign that torched mills, ranches, and plantations, some of them

American owned. The Spanish empire struck back by herding farm families off the land into concentration camps and cities, where thousands died of disease and malnutrition.

Back in New York City, the insurgent government established a junta to generate U.S. support for the war effort. It was led by Tómas Estrada Palma, who worked out of the Wall Street-area office of a sympathetic and prominent New York lawyer. The junta organized mass meetings (including a week-long Cuban-American Fair at Madison Square Garden in May 1896). It cultivated contacts with investors, merchants, and politicians. And it issued news releases, many of which prettified the struggle for American readers or fabricated guerrilla triumphs out of thin air. To raise money for the war, the New York leadership also set up a Cuban League for local supporters. Militants like Teddy Roosevelt and Charles A. Dana of the *Sun* were members; so were conservative businessmen like J. Edward Simmons, former president of the New York Stock Exchange, railroad chief Chauncey M. Depew, and John Jacob Astor.

Americans were receptive to the junta's message. Schoolbook accounts of inquisitors and conquistadors had convinced many of the inherent depravity of Spaniards. Others equated the Cuban struggle for freedom with the USA's own War of Independence.

Particular interests had particular reasons for urging American involvement. The AFL, led by Gompers's Cigarmakers Union, called for support short of war. Metropolitan sugar and shipping interests, appalled at the damage to their property and disruption of their business, sought to end the fighting, either by pressuring Spain into conceding autonomy or by annexing the island outright. Leading Wall Streeter Frederick R. Coudert admitted that "it makes the water come to my mouth when I think of the state of Cuba as one in our family." Yet many metropolitan businessmen remained wary of being pulled into war.

"BLOOD, BLOOD, BLOOD!"

Those still on the fence about Cuba found it increasingly hard to stay there, given the blasts of prorebel publicity emanating from the New York City press. Joseph Pulitzer had counseled moderation during Cleveland's saber-rattling over Venezuela in 1895, but he favored Cuban self-government and steered the *World* toward support of the rebellion. His relatively temperate campaign was soon outdone by one of typhoon proportions issuing from a competing New York newspaper under the control of William Randolph Hearst.

Hearst, born in San Francisco in the midst of the Civil War, had been fortunate in his parents. George Hearst had accumulated a fortune in silver and copper mining, as well as the proceeds from a million-acre ranch in Porfirio Díaz's Mexico, and Phoebe Hearst provided a disciplined Episcopalian upbringing. After an aborted Harvard education he headed to New York City, beelined his way to the World Building, and spent a year there apprenticing in journalism. Then he returned home, turned the *San Francisco Examiner* into a profitable reform sheet, and, in 1895, decided to run a newspaper in New York City. His mother, who had inherited her husband's estate in 1891, sold off $7.5 million of her shares of Anaconda Copper and turned the proceeds over to William.

Hearst moved to Manhattan, took up quarters in Madison Square, and bought the *Morning Journal*, a paper operating out of the Tribune Building on Park Row. The *Journal*, once a scandal sheet known informally as the "chambermaids' delight," had now, under more proper but less profitable management, sunk to a circulation of seventy-seven thousand (the *World*'s was 450,000). Hearst dropped the *Journal*'s price to a penny, expanded its size, imitated the *World*'s format, and stole away its reporters by offering fabulous salaries and byline credits. Hearst adopted Pulitzer's social and political stances and went them one better. When Pulitzer gave away free bread to the unemployed, the *Journal* set up a soup kitchen and passed out free sweaters. Pulitzer was a power in the Democratic Party; Hearst replaced him in 1896 by backing Bryan.

Pulitzer riled New York society, but Hearst appalled it, and backs turned when the blond, racily dressed six-footer strode into the Metropolitan Club. He didn't care. Nor did his phenomenal expenses trouble him overly, his pockets being far deeper than his debts. Besides, the *Journal*'s circulation shot up to 430,000 within a year, leaping past the *Herald, Sun, Tribune*, and *Times*. The vigorous young Hearst, who worked in his office late into the evening, was clearly gaining on Pulitzer, now a half-blind nervous wreck, running his operations from his yacht while cruising the world in a search for quiet harbors.

Much of the *Journal*'s success stemmed from Hearst's support for the Cuban rebellion—like Pulitzer's, a mix of conviction and calculation—and his campaign slipped steadily away from conventional standards of truth in journalism. Hearst stirred fact with fiction and poured the resulting prose into a mold of pure melodrama, one that played explosively with the gender conventions of his culture. For the *Journal*, the heart of the matter was that villainous Spaniards were brutalizing noble Cubans, and the *heart* of the heart of the matter was that lustful Spanish brutes were ravishing pure Cuban women.

In February 1897 Richard Harding Davis, a romantic-fiction writer turned war correspondent, filed a dispatch reporting that Spanish police had boarded a U.S. vessel bound from Havana to Tampa and strip-searched three female Cuban passengers thought to be carrying messages to insurgent leaders in New York City. Next to this inflammatory text Hearst placed an incendiary image: a half-page drawing, done in distant Manhattan by Frederic Remington, showing one of the women, naked, surrounded by Spanish officers. A five-column screamer headline demanded: "Does Our Flag Protect Women?" The issue sold nearly a million copies. That the women had in fact been searched by matrons, as the *World* soon discovered and trumpeted, did nothing to still the uproar.

Next Hearst claimed that an imprisoned eighteen-year-old Cuban girl, Evangelina Cosio y Cisneros (known as Miss Cisneros in the States), had been jailed for trying to defend her honor against the advances of "a beast in uniform." Hearst launched a campaign to free Evangelina from jail, where the molested maiden with her "white face, young, pure and beautiful," languished "among the most depraved Negresses of Havana." (Few Americans realized that in some areas four-fifths of the guerrilla forces were of African descent, and the yellow press did little to enlighten them.)

Hearst arranged a jailbreak, brought Cisneros to New York, met her in the harbor on his steam launch, introduced her to hundreds of dignitaries at a Delmonico's reception, and presented her to the masses at Madison Square Garden, accompanied by searchlights, fireworks, and bands. The affair was so compellingly staged that the president, who had canceled his *Journal* subscription in disgust at its reportage, felt obliged to invite the Cuban Joan of Arc to the White House.

Faced with Hearst's triumphs, Pulitzer abandoned restraint. *World* reporters began recounting ghastly horror stories—some true, many fraudulent. ("Blood on the road-sides, blood in the fields, blood on the doorsteps, blood, blood, blood!") The two papers whipped themselves into a competitive frenzy—matching the fervor of the old railroad wars, with text, not trackage, the product—and the Associated Press carried the copy to the country. Increasingly both editors began to push for war.

War eluded them, in part because the president, unlike armchair warriors Hearst and Roosevelt, was old enough to remember the carnage of the Civil War. When Spain made conciliatory gestures, McKinley responded positively (to the fury of Roosevelt, who declared the president had the backbone of a chocolate eclair). In addition, the official goal of the New York-based Cubans was not war but American recognition of the Cuban belligerency, a crucial step toward acknowledging independence. Some, like Estrada Palma, leaned toward American military intervention, believing it would keep more radical elements in the liberation army from taking power and "give confidence to American capitalists, who may lend us the money necessary for the reconstruction of the country." But others feared war would lead to annexation, not independence.

Wall Street also still favored peace. Most businessmen feared war would interrupt trade, endanger currency stability, and torpedo a fledgling recovery. Their reluctance generated nationwide opprobrium. Roosevelt denounced the "craven fear and brutal selfishness of the mere money-makers." Some Democrats joined in the baying, claiming that New York moneymen, by putting profits over people, were blocking a humanitarian crusade. The clamor reached such dimensions that Elihu Root advised McKinley not to "retard the enormous momentum of the people bent upon war" lest he bring the silverites to power.

McKinley and the metropolitan community held firm until the pressure of events overwhelmed them. An indiscreet letter from a Spanish diplomat was passed to Hearst, who ran it under banner headlines. A week later the battleship *Maine* (a product of the Brooklyn Navy Yard) was blown up in Havana's harbor, and the papers screamed for war. When a Spanish cruiser paid New York a courtesy call, the *World* warned of treachery, claiming "her shells will explode on the Harlem River and in the suburbs of Brooklyn." Circulations soared, the *Journal*'s passing the million mark.

The clamor and instability convinced many businessmen that peace was proving as debilitating as war. Leading figures like John Jacob Astor, William Rockefeller, Stuyvesant Fish, and Thomas Fortune Ryan adopted a more belligerent stance. In late March J. P. Morgan declared nothing further could be obtained from arbitration. Many others were converted, reported the *Wall Street Journal*, after the moderate Senator Proctor assured them that the terrible conditions in Cuba were not just the imaginings of the yellow press and that it was not inevitable that Cubans—the Spanish once removed—would be revolutionary. On March 25 a leading New York journalist and McKinley adviser sent him a telegram arguing that "big corporations here now believe we will have war. Believe all would welcome it as relief to suspense." Two days later, the president presented an ultimatum to Spain; on April 11 he sent a message to Congress asking for "forcible intervention"; on April 25 the United States formally declared war.

As in the Civil War, the city immediately shed ambivalence and donned patriotic bunting. Regiments formed up and marched down Fifth Avenue, crowds cheering, flags flapping, bands playing Sousa marches. Harbor defenses were bolstered to ward off a feared invasion by the Spanish fleet. New York bankers organized popular loan drives to fund the war effort. New York newspapers, whose communication systems were superi-

Watching the Bulletin-Boards on Park Row at the Time of Dewey's Great Battle of Manila Bay, from E. Idell Zeisloft, *The New Metropolis* (1899). (General Research. The New York Public Library. Astor, Lenox and Tilden Foundations)

or to Washington's, relayed information to the military: the secretary of the navy first learned of Commodore George Dewey's victory at Manila Bay from the *World*.

Volunteer troops so clogged the transport system that rival regiments had to elbow their way toward the front lines. Teddy embarked for Havana with his Rough Riders—a collection of cowboys and clubmen—with six spare sets of glasses sewn to his uniform and one inside his hat.

Each of the two yellow press contenders was now printing 1,250,000 issues a day. Hearst chartered a steamship, sailed a reportorial regiment into Cuban waters, and filed his own copy. The *World* sent a crack squadron of investigators, including Stephen Crane, but the novelist's forthright realism got Pulitzer into trouble. When the author of *The Red Badge of Courage* filed a critique that mentioned the shaky conduct of some New York volunteers, the *Journal* charged slander ("Slurs on the Bravery of the Boys of the 71st") and forced the *World* to back down.

Still, Cuba provided some with a chance for heroics. Roosevelt led his men up Kettle Hill, a small outcropping below the principal enemy fortifications on San Juan Ridge, and shot a Spanish officer with his pistol. Even Hearst—barred by McKinley from military status—managed to capture prisoners.

Within weeks the war was over, both Cuba and Puerto Rico taken. New Yorkers went wild over America's emergence as an imperial power. The metropolis offered now-Admiral Dewey, the war's greatest hero, a homecoming on a scale not seen since its greeting to Lafayette. The artistic community collaborated in creating a mammoth triumphal arch (out of lath and plaster) at Madison Square, the city's reigning civic center. When the North Atlantic Squadron steamed into New York harbor on September 29, 1899—its progress upriver marked by a *Journal* balloon that released showers of color-

Sampson and Schley Leading the Fleet into New York Harbor, August 20, 1898, painting by Fred Pansing. On July 3, two days after Roosevelt and the Rough Riders captured San Juan Hill, the U.S. naval forces under Rear Admiral William T. Sampson and Commodore Winfield S. Schley destroyed the Spanish fleet off Santiago. Their triumphant return to New York—here they fire a salute while steaming up the Hudson past Grant's Tomb—was only a dress rehearsal, however, for the adulation showered on Admiral Dewey himself a year later. (© Museum of the City of New York)

coded confetti over Grant's Tomb—it touched off two days of frenzied adulation. The spectacle hailed the emergence of America as a new Roman Empire, and underscored New York's position as its de facto capital.

WINNERS AND LOSERS

Like all wars, the struggle with Spain had its winners and losers. The losers, apart from the 379 killed and sixteen hundred wounded in action, included the more than five thousand soldiers who had died from yellow fever, malaria, or typhoid and the enormous number still suffering from such diseases. Twenty thousand such casualties were ensconced in a great hospital camp at Montauk Point, where they were ministered to by New York matrons, young girls, and such nurses as could be spared from Bellevue, Roosevelt, Presbyterian, and other hospitals, themselves packed with casualties.

Some were victims of badly preserved beef. One such was Achille La Guardia who would later die of it, leaving his son Fiorello enraged at corporate malfeasance. Other casualties included Stephen Crane—his Cuban stint had broken his health, and he would die in 1900 from TB—and George Waring, who went to Cuba to deal with yellow fever, contracted it himself, and died shortly after returning to New York City.

Topping the winners' list was Teddy Roosevelt. The Rough Rider wrote up his war memoirs (which Mr. Dooley—the fictional commentator created by Finley Peter Dunne—remarked should have been titled *Alone in Cuba*). In 1898 Roosevelt stumped for the governorship as a war hero, won, served two years, irritated state Republican boss Platt no end, and was accordingly bounced upstairs to serve as McKinley's running mate in the successful 1900 campaign. When McKinley was assassinated the following year, TR assumed the office, completing a run-up from police commissioner of New York City to president of the United States in four and a half years flat.

Among the other big winners was a potpourri of New York City businessmen. With Cuba an unofficial American protectorate, the Sugar Trust expanded operations, aided by Elihu Root, longtime legal counsel to the Havemeyers; now, as newly appointed secretary of war, he oversaw the island's military occupation and worked to lower U.S. tariffs on Cuban sugar. Low tariffs, coupled with America's asserted right of military intervention, its possession of a naval base on the island, and its eagerness to improve Cuba's roads and public health, unleashed a torrent of U.S. investment. The Sugar Trust and its competitors bought up vast tracts of the best land and erected million-dollar mills. In a decade the Havemeyer-dominated Cuban-American Sugar Company had created the largest sugar plantation in the world.

Other New York City companies also steamed down to the Caribbean. The Tobacco Trust built the world's largest factory in Havana, and its affiliate, the American Cigar Company, soon dominated 90 percent of the export trade in Havana cigars. A group of New York capitalists took over manganese mining. The Cuba Company, a syndicate formed in 1900, had the Cuba Central Railroad up and running by 1902. Another Wall Street syndicate won control of the Havana Street Railway. And Manhattan's North American Trust Company was appointed the occupying government's fiscal agent; in time, it evolved into the Banco Nacionál de Cuba, which would dominate the island's financial system. The Yankee invasion had a tremendous impact on Cuba's society as well as its economy: the elite was cut in, the rural middle classes were wiped out, and the peasantry was reduced to seasonal wage-work. Protests were suppressed by the marines.

Puerto Rico was made an official American colony, and its residents were granted limited local participation in government. U.S.-dominated sugar and tobacco production supplanted the old coffee-based agronomy and pumped profits off-island, perpetuating or worsening poverty. Within a decade of the occupation, four U.S. corporations produced 50 percent of all sugar cultivated in Puerto Rico, and the island's inclusion in the Coastwise Shipping Act had given the United States a monopoly over Puerto Rican commerce. When Samuel Gompers returned from a 1904 visit, he told a New York press conference: "In all my life I have never witnessed such misery, sickness, and suffering." In 1917 Puerto Ricans would be made citizens—a step of great significance for the future of New York City, as, dislodged from the land, earning some of the lowest wages in the world in exchange for ten- to twelve-hour days, some of these new citizens would begin to migrate from the edge of America's new empire to its center.

America's war with Spain provided one final benefit: it helped boost the country out of depression. The initial upward shove had come in 1897 when simultaneous crop disasters in Europe, Asia, and South America drove the price of American wheat to a dollar a bushel. Ecstatic farmers paid off burdensome mortgages and started a round of heavy purchases. Agricultural traffic boosted railroad earnings and spurred the iron and steel industry. The next year brought not only wartime government spending but discoveries of gold in South Africa and the Yukon. The combination of stimuli jolted the economy into action. Factories started up, the stock market reached its highest level in years, the unemployed began trooping back to work, and the country clambered its way toward prosperity.

69

Imperial City

O n New Year's Eve, with 1897 turning into 1898, thousands of New Yorkers cascaded into lower Manhattan's streets despite a cold and driving rain. Soaked but celebratory, they were gearing up for one of the greatest Festivals of Connection in the city's history. This time they would not be hailing New York's insertion into some larger grid—as they had on completion of the Erie Canal or the Atlantic Cable—but rather the city's new internal linkages, its own municipal consolidation. At midnight, the nation's first- and fourth-largest cities would merge into a supercity— Greater New York—that would encompass not only Manhattan and Brooklyn, but Queens, Staten Island, and the Bronx as well. Other metropolises had been engaging in similar combinations, but New York's would be the grandest—a municipal counterpart of the giant corporations busily being born.

The master of ceremonies, oddly, was not Mayor Strong. The lame-duck reformer had grumpily suggested holding a funeral service for the old city rather than a jamboree for the new one. When this met with widespread derision, William Randolph Hearst had stepped forward to volunteer as producer and ringmaster. The publisher raised funds (mostly from his own pocket), purchased fireworks by the cartload, enlisted military and civic groups and marching and singing societies, and arranged for a spectacular parade. An immense crowd formed up in Union Square, umbrellas aloft, well fortified by visits to local saloons, and prepared to accompany the long line of brilliantly illuminated floats down to City Hall, itself bedecked with hundreds of electric lights.

For all the rejoicing, mutters and imprecations could be heard in many quarters. The road to Consolidation Eve had not been an easy one. Some Brooklynites felt like victims of an imperial expansion they had tried and failed to halt. Tammany Hall was exceedingly ambivalent, despite the fact that Croker and company would control the new colossus, thanks to Van Wyck's triumph in the recent mayoral election; the pols couldn't help being suspicious of an enterprise so largely engineered by their Republican and reformer enemies. And even consolidation's sponsors, the businessmen and professionals over at the Chamber of Commerce and the Citizens Union, were lukewarm about their creation and apprehensive about the future. This mélange of mixed feelings was the legacy not only of the previous decade of struggle but of two centuries of interurban rivalry.

ANNEXATION AND ITS ENEMIES

Manhattan had first gained dominance over Brooklyn when the Dongan Charter (1686) and Montgomerie Charter (1730) granted it domain over the East River and its ferry traffic, effectively depriving Brooklyn of control over its own waterfront. When Brooklyn pursued city status in the early 1830s, New York resisted, to maintain its lucrative privileges and because (as Manhattan officials argued) constituting a "distinct and rival commercial community" would lead to "contentions, inconvenience and other calamities." Besides, Brooklyn was obviously destined to be folded into the larger and wealthier city, and making it a separate polity would only impede the inevitable. Brooklyn community leaders successfully demanded independence, insisting that "between New York and Brooklyn, there is nothing in common, either in object, interest, or feeling— nothing that even apparently tends to their connexion."

In 1857 the two cities were subjected to something of a shotgun wedding when the state combined their police, fire, and health departments into joint metropolitan boards. There were those who hoped the merger of functions might evolve into a more thoroughgoing consolidation, and indeed it was from one of these supra-boards that conglomeration's strongest champion emerged. It was in the course of pursuing Haussmannesque authority for the Central Park Commission—allowing it to plan and develop bridges, roads, and sewers on both sides of the Harlem River—that Andrew Haswell Green first developed the arguments he would promote for the next forty years. And it was in the course of convincing uptown and Westchester property owners that comprehensive development was in their mutual interest that Green began to assemble a constituency powerful enough to translate his ideas into action.

In 1868, when Green was proposing that Manhattan should annex the portion of the mainland just across the Harlem River, he alluded to what for him was the obvious end point of such an initiative: formation of a metropolitan totality out of the discrete political entities grouped around the harbor. It was, he asserted, desirable to bring "the City of New York and the County of Kings, a part of Westchester County and a part of Queens and Richmond, including the various suburbs of the City, under one common municipal government, to be arranged in departments under a single executive head."

In 1870 Green's plans seemed to have been short-circuited by Tweed's city charter, which abolished the state boards and deprived Green of his power base. But Tweed, in his own way, was a master planner too. Following Green's logic, he gave his new Department of Public Parks the power to expand street mapping into Morrisania and West Farms and eastward to the Bronx River. Meanwhile powerful Westchester residents like Colonel Richard M. Hoe and Lewis G. Morris, whose interests were entwined with those of Manhattan, had taken up Green's cry for full-scale annexation. They wanted New York to build connecting bridges and perhaps even deepen the Harlem River into a viable link between the Jersey railheads and Long Island Sound, thus making Port Morris a major transportation hub.

BROOKLYN AND QUEENS,
1850-1898

BRONX

LONG
ISLAND
SOUND

Wards
Island

Rikers
Island

FLUSHING
BAY

Whitestone

LITTLE
NECK
BAY

College
Point

Astoria

East
River

Steinway

BOWERY
BAY

Bayside

MANHATTAN

Jackson
Heights

Flushing

Northern
Boulevard

NEW
JERSEY

Long Island City

Corona

Bellerose

Hudson River

Hunter's
Point

QUEENS COUNTY

Newtown
Creek

Queens
Village

Greenpoint

Maspeth

Middle
Village

Jamaica

Hollis

Brooklyn
Navy Yard
(WALLABOUT BAY)

St. Albans

Jericho
Turnpike

Brooklyn
Bridge

Williamsburg

Ridgewood

Fulton St.

Weeksville

Bushwick

Long Island
Rail Road

Atlantic
Avenue

Fort
Greene

Carrville

Woodhaven

Richmond
Hill

Governors
Island

Brooklyn

Bedford

Atlantic
Basin
Erie
Basin

Red
Hook

Park
Slope

Brownsville

Eastern
Parkway

East
New
York

New
Lots

UPPER
NEW YORK
BAY

Prospect
Park

KINGS COUNTY

Green-wood
Cemetery

Flatbush

Canarsie

Bay
Ridge

Borough
Park

Flatbush
Avenue

New
Utrecht

Flatlands

Kings
Highway

Bensonhurst

Fort Hamilton

JAMAICA
BAY

Gravesend

Sheepshead
Bay
Racetrack

Far
Rockaway

LOWER
NEW YORK
BAY

Ocean
Parkway

Brighton
Race Track

Manhattan
Beach

Norton's
Point

West
Brighton

Coney
Island

Rockaway
Inlet

Brighton
Beach

ATLANTIC
OCEAN

0   1   2 Miles

0   1   2 Kilometers

Manhattanites were divided about annexation. Using arguments that would be recycled repeatedly during the next decades of debate, downtowners balked at underwriting Bronx-based competitors, though their objections were partly alleviated when local property owners agreed to shoulder half the improvement costs. They also protested the notion of paying to enhance the quality of life for suburban commuters who deserted the city each night. Proponents countered that annexation would corral the fleeing middle class back into the taxpaying fold, provide room for downtown to expand, and boost upper Manhattan's real estate values. Put to the electoral test in November 1873, annexation passed overwhelmingly, and on January 1, 1874, the city's territory jumped from fourteen thousand to twenty-one thousand acres, its thirty to forty thousand new citizens assembled in two new wards.

Not coincidentally, consolidation sentiment surfaced in Brooklyn that year. In 1874 a cohort of property owners, developers, and businessmen (including such potentates as J. S. T. Stranahan, D. D. Litchfield, and A. A. Low) formed the Municipal Union Society of the City of Brooklyn and the County of Kings. These gentlemen sought a merger between the two great cities and the five county towns. Union, they argued, would enhance property values, sustain the area's commercial supremacy, and end boundary disputes. But even after they pointed out the benefits achieved by annexationist movements in Paris, London, Boston, and Philadelphia, public response in Brooklyn remained unenthusiastic, and consolidation, though it passed the Assembly, was defeated in the Senate.

Further such efforts were derailed by the depression of the 1870s. Andrew Haswell Green busied himself with estate management and with projects that secured de facto if not de jure linkages. Green was one of the original commissioners of the Brooklyn Bridge—as was Stranahan, who on opening day in 1883 prophesied that its bonds of steel would usher in political union. Green also helped get a bridge thrown across the Harlem River at 183rd Street in 1886 and was appointed in 1890 to a commission charged with planning a railroad bridge across the Hudson.

In the meantime, the harbor's constituent communities had undergone such a degree of interlacing that the editor of the 1880 census's volumes on social statistics suggested that a greater city had in effect already come into being. The population was separated "by physical and political lines," he said, but as these "have had little influence on the character of the people, their industries, or their modes of life," it "seemed proper" to consolidate the data on them under "the one head of 'The Metropolis' which they constitute."

"IMPERIAL DESTINY"

A statistical consolidation had been wrought, but it was only after the Henry George campaign that Manhattan elites, jolted by the challenge of the radical and labor movements to their vision and command of New York City, wholeheartedly joined Green's campaign, and his project began to rumble toward realization.

In 1887 the New York Chamber of Commerce officially urged that Brooklyn be added to New York. The assembled merchants expressed concern that the port was losing ground to the more efficient facilities of New Orleans, Baltimore, Boston, and Philadelphia—and between 1880 and 1890 New York did indeed suffer an absolute and relative decline in its percentage of the country's exports and imports. The slovenly state of metropolitan infrastructure—decaying docks, clogged streets, and turtle-paced transit systems—was costing the city its competitive edge. But efforts to coordinate port administration, build new bridges, and improve city services were thwarted by divided political jurisdictions. The chamber considered competition between the area's municipalities to be annoyingly irrational, much as big businessmen were rethinking the virtues of economic competition. As an aid to planning piers, wharves, warehouses, and transportation, the chamber urged putting "New York and its environs under one general scheme of municipal rule."

In 1888 the *Real Estate Record and Builders' Guide*, organ of New York's propertied interests, also came out for consolidation. Only a centralized authority, it argued, could push through the improvements that would boost land values and provide insurance companies, savings banks, and estate trustees with profitable investment opportunities.

That same year Mayor Hewitt, himself a Chamber of Commerce stalwart, issued a proposal for a vast and coordinated program of public improvements and sketched a grand vision of New York's future. "With its noble harbor protected from injury, and the channels of its approach straightened and deepened"; with its wharves and docks improved and its streets paved and cleansed; with "cheap and rapid transit throughout its length and breadth" and "salubrious and attractive parks" sprinkled throughout the area; and with a system of taxation "so modified that the capital of the world may be as free to come and go as the air of heaven"—then, Hewitt said, "the imagination can place no bounds to the future growth of this city in business, wealth, and the blessings of civilization." Indeed New York's "imperial destiny as the greatest city in the world is assured by natural causes, which cannot be thwarted except by the folly and neglect of its inhabitants."

For all its upbeat energy, this "imperial" urban vision—like those of nationalist jingoes, railroad magnates, and corporate financiers—was also fueled by fear. Inaction might leave the field to rival empire builders, which in New York's case meant Chicago. In 1889 Chicago swallowed up 133 square miles of suburban terrain, and when the 1890 census was tallied, the results showed the midwestern metropolis (population 1,100,000) gaining fast on Manhattan (1,515,000).

The *Real Estate Record* assessed the threat bluntly: "New York would undoubtedly lose a great deal in prestige the world over—and in actual dollars and cents, too—should Chicago or any other city on the continent count a larger population." European banking and export firms might shift their American branches to the heartland; corporate headquarters would soon follow, taking professional firms along; the market prices of stocks and commodities would get set in the interior; manufacturing would steal away; New York's property values would scud downward. Doomsayers recalled how the power and prestige of Philadelphia, once America's chief city, had slowly bled away once it was surpassed numerically by its Hudson River rival.

If Chicago became the first city in population, moreover, it might relegate New York to secondary status in other spheres—those of arts, culture, and politics. This fear took tangible form in 1890, when Congress gave the midwesterners the go-ahead to host a giant celebration of the four hundredth anniversary of Columbus's voyage. The idea of a World's Fair had been broached back in 1882, and ever since the two colossi had been competing for it furiously. Defeat seemed another doleful indicator of metropolitan decline.

How to hold the front rank? Immigration was important but inconstant and slow. Green underscored the fact that Chicago, like Paris and London (which had obtained a regional government with establishment of the London County Council in 1888), had "become great and prosperous, not alone by accumulation of number, within their first restricted bounds, but by expansion, annexation, and consolidation"—and the city's leading businessmen agreed.

GREEN'S DREAM OF NEW YORK

With the Chamber of Commerce opting for decisive measures, Andrew Haswell Green turned to the state legislature in 1890 and got it to establish a Greater New York Commission to examine the issue of consolidation. The new body quickly elected Green president and Stranahan vice-president, and in a series of addresses and memorials that year, Green proceeded to lay out, with great sweep and power, the arguments on its behalf.

Green began at the beginning, the prelapsarian age when the area's European settlers had lived in harmony with one another. The three islands they settled—Manhattan, Long, and Staten—remained "in close indissoluble relation" at the mouth of the great river, serving as common "buttresses and breakwaters of a capacious harbor." Then came the Fall. Natural unity gave way to artificial divisions: states, cities, counties. Waterways became walls, as residents perversely turned them from "bonds of union" into "symbols of division."

But it was absurd to treat rivers as barriers. Green pointed out that the chief cities of the world—London, Amsterdam, Prague, Vienna—were municipally and commercially unified by rivers. Paris alone boasted twenty-seven spanning bridges. Far more troubling was that under existing political arrangements, protection of the navigable water system—the concern of all—had become the duty of none. Fragmentation of authority led to pollution and subversion of the area's single greatest asset, even though all were affected equally by the decay. The tides marched through all the municipalities, collecting and distributing everywhere "offal and sewerage loaded with contagion," and "exotic microbes, bacteria, and all variety of poisonous germic life" were not hemmed in by city boundaries.

Such harbor-level problems—garbage, smoke, stench, bad drainage, noxious manufactories—could not be attended to by municipalities in hostile array. In the absence of a supra-government that could make a corrective plan for the entire port, the area would continue to suffer from the depredations of a vast number of private "marauders, who by encroachment, appropriation and misuse, deplete the general system to transfuse its vitalities into some niggard scheme of individual profit."

This situation was as unnecessary as it was ridiculous. Perhaps long ago, when it seemed there would not be enough commerce to go around, there might have been some sense in a hoarding of territorial advantages. But with benefits now clearly illimitable, interests had become interlocking; the prosperity of one territory promoted that of the others. Brooklyn's lawyers did more business in New York courts than in their own, and its merchants' mansions were paid for with profits from their New York-based trade. The reverse was also true: the waterfront from Astoria to Bay Ridge was largely owned, developed, and used by New York merchants.

If all could swim together, they could sink together too. One common problem was the port's vulnerability to modern foreign fleets. Wherever the next war came from, Green warned, "New York must first answer at the muzzle of the gun." It was essential that it "be allowed to answer at the muzzle of another gun as heavy as that by which we shall be challenged." Local divisions only impeded the combined effort that alone could induce the national government to provide adequate defenses.

Access to the interior was another common predicament. Green reminded the citizenry that New York had become the nation's chief emporium not simply because it commanded foreign commerce but because it controlled routes to continental markets. Norfolk's was a better harbor, but it remained a summer watering place because it lacked inland connections. The Hudson seaport had long relied on its Erie edge, but that was no longer enough, as modern engineering skill whittled away mountainous impediments. New connections were essential—crucially, a bridge across the Hudson—and only a Greater New York could muster the resources to act without waiting for state or national governments.

Planning the city's physical development was as critical as arranging its commercial future. New York had to prepare for the immigrants who would clearly be flooding in for the foreseeable future, not just from overseas, but from the countryside. The percentage of the U.S. population living in cities had been rising steadily since 1790. Urbanization was rapidly speeding up as machine farming dispensed with field labor and city factories attracted former agricultural workers. If the process of incorporating this populace were left to pell-mell development, the results would be as inadequate to the needs of future generations as the colonial-era streets and alleys of lower Manhattan were to the present one.

Planning the whole area as a single unit—as Green had on a smaller scale while head of the Central Park Commission—would ensure better relations between centers and suburbs. Only if a Greater City controlled its outlying territories could it reserve them for, say, healthful parks, rather than having them eaten up piecemeal. Only a Greater City could solve the "difficult question of taxation of non-residents that now exists," with people on the periphery drawing sustenance from New York's commerce but contributing little to its governance.

If taxpayers could easily cross city lines, so could rogues and criminals. Lawbreakers were truly "cosmopolitan," Green noted, heedless of political boundaries, and disorderly persons often overwhelmed small towns. Only a unified metropolitan police command could check them.

There were other, more dangerous criminals on Green's mind: he believed New York was in mortal peril from "lawless enterprise," by which he meant modern combinations of capital—"leagues, guilds, combinations, federations, monopolies, pools and trusts." For a man who'd spent much of his career helping Samuel Tilden arrange giant mergers—or perhaps precisely because of that experience—Andrew Haswell Green was extremely wary about the growth of corporations.

Their rise and impact was nowhere more evident than in cities, where "people live, move, and have their being by sufferance of the corporate power." A citizen buys food from one, water from another, light from a third, and heat from a fourth, works on the road of a fifth, is paid in bills from a sixth, has his life insured by a seventh, and is buried in the grounds of an eighth. Green was not hostile to "modern forms of corporate contrivances" but insisted they "must be regulated and controlled by governmental intervention."

The consequences of insufficient public purview were most apparent in the case of Green's bête noire, railroad corporations—one he shared with merchants, populists, labor unions and social gospelers. While it was true that their lines made cities possible by allowing them to draw upon the resources and markets of a vast hinterland, they also "usurp[ed] control over approaches from the interior by land" and forced their way into the city, plowing through areas of their own choosing, laying tracks with no regard for street patterns, topography, or the public welfare. Their decisions, moreover, were laying down "lines of abnormal development or desolation," deciding the character "of future growth or decay"; yet "if there are any who dispute their right, there are none to resist their might."

The populace massed in cities represented a potentially countervailing power, but at a time when all private interests, "actuated by selfish motives," were tending to consolidation, the only interests *not* combining were "our unselfish, thoughtless peoples, and their fatuous municipalities, which in broken form, carry on desultory and futile war against the organized forces of relentless and absentee capitalism." For all his angry declamations about "popular rights" being subordinated to "corporate power," however, Green had nothing much to say about actual people, and the issues like slums and sweatshops that agitated working people didn't make it onto his agenda.

Green was hopeful about the future outcome of this war "between the corporate power and the power of the people" because he discerned evolutionary laws at work in the history of great cities, and of New York especially—laws that were the counterpart of those that had led to creation of the great corporations. Both developments were equally part of mankind's great progression from barbarism to civilization.

But if Green was hopeful, he wasn't smug. There were no guarantees that "the scheme of civilization, even in the hands of the Caucasian race, is beyond the hazards of deterioration." Faulty government—and tribal (read: Tammany) divisions—jeopardized progress. New York unfortunately still had "our Sachems" who, clinging to traditions of barbaric times, "seek to preserve their clans and clanships." Only through struggle could evolutionary destiny be attained, Green exhorted: "The encounter is one between the retreating forces of the tribal system and the coming forces of the cooperative system, between barbaric tradition and educated aspiration, to which there can be but one result, when the frontier lines of the Manhattan, the Montauks and the Raritans shall be obliterated, and New York, Brooklyn, Long Island City and Staten Island shall be one politically as they are already in every other relation."

Finally, in the Rooseveltian spirit of the times, Green urged New York to recognize and grasp its imperial destiny. He realized there were carpers who believed his unification project was irrational, a lusting after magnitude for its own sake. But magnitude was already there, its real dimensions hidden but not erased by the sham separation into contending municipalities. New York had become, in fact, the second city in the world but was refusing to claim its title. It should do so, joyously. "Cities are the crowns, the signs, the factors of empire," Green proclaimed, and "the imperial city has won an honorable renown throughout the world which all her colonies may proudly inherit and which they cannot avoid accepting." For all his upbeat assertions—and in the case of such impolitic references to Brooklyn's secondary status, precisely because of them—Green's cosmic vision was about to collide with local realities.

IMPERIUM OR COLONY?

Green and his Greater New York commissioners now proceeded to map out the precise dimensions of their proposed super-city. They included all New York State territories fronting on the harbor, added enough of Queens to embrace potential rival ports such as

Jamaica and Little Neck bays, and threw in enough of Kings and Westchester counties to provide housing for uncounted future generations.

Next Green and his colleagues pushed for legislative authorization of a merger. This smoked out the opposition: upstate Republicans, who feared creating a monster metropolis; Tammany politicians, who shuddered at the thought of trying to organize such a vast territory; northern Manhattan and North Side (Bronx) developers, who dreaded a diversion of resources to Canarsie and Flatlands. But the most obdurate opponents came from Brooklyn itself. More precisely, they came from the old Anglo-Protestant community centered in Brooklyn Heights.

These worthies had a peculiar relationship with Manhattan. They were well aware that Brooklyn was fundamentally dependent on New York: part bedroom suburb, part industrial hinterland, part agrarian supplier, part commercial backup. Yet they also maintained and treasured a separate identity, organized in large part around their difference from and presumed superiority to the metropolis. Protestant middle-class Brooklynites liked to think they embodied New England virtues, seasoned, mildly, with a dash of Dutch character. Theirs was a "city of homes and churches." It was free from millionaires and the fashionably wicked ways of Fifth Avenue; free from the huddled immigrant masses and the squalor of Five Points or Hell's Kitchen; free from the sordid pleasures of the Tenderloin and the Bowery; free from the corruptions of Tammany ward heelers; and free from the fast pace of scurrying big-city life. Yet, withal, it was not provincial. The town prided itself on its modern cultural appurtenances: parks, opera houses, clubs, educational institutions, newspapers, a historical society, and, on the drawing boards, a museum that would surpass the Metropolitan. Keeping Manhattan at river's length would preserve this lovely way of life.

This was, however, a badly overstated case. It is true that the big rich stayed mainly in Manhattan, though the Pratts, Lows, and Pierreponts were no pikers. But the percentage of non-Protestants in each city, while different (52.7 percent in New York to 40 percent in Brooklyn), hardly justified such sweeping characterizations. The working-class Irish around the Navy Yard, the Germans of Williamsburg, the Italians of Red Hook, the Jews of Brownsville, the African Americans of Fort Greene may have been out of sight (from the perspective of the Montauk Club or the Church of the Pilgrims) but they were hardly out of power, as repeated failures to impose a Dry Sunday attested.

There was, moreover, still another Brooklyn to contend with, the developmental powerhouse centered in the commercial section around City Hall. Montague Street's residential buildings had given way to banks, real estate offices, insurance companies, and law firms (like Gaynor's). New public buildings were everywhere—most strikingly a Hall of Records and a huge Romanesque Revival post office. Fulton Street by 1893 was crowded with hotels, warehouses, newspaper offices, theaters, and stores. Real estate values had zoomed to such levels that the downtown mercantile district was flowing farther from the piers, a development fostered by the traffic funneling in over the Brooklyn Bridge. A new satellite commercial district had emerged between City Hall and Flatbush Avenue, thick with Romanesque department stores, power stations, fire headquarters, libraries, and churches.

Yet the piers remained crucial to this booming Brooklyn—the thriving termini of great transatlantic fleets, vessels from South and Central America, domestic coastal freighters. In one week in 1886, the ships along Brooklyn's wharves and piers had carried a combined cargo of roughly 45,000 tons, compared to the mere 12,000 or so tons' worth tied up at New York during the same seven days. By 1897 an average of four thousand ships unloaded cargoes annually.

Manufacturing and the processing of agricultural commodities reached record levels. Half the sugar consumed in the United States was refined in Brooklyn; almost all the oil for the Atlantic seaboard was refined in Williamsburg and Long Island City (along with plants in New Jersey). Bakeries and breweries drew from grain elevators with four times the capacity of Manhattan's, and its myriad ironworks and factories made Brooklyn the fourth largest industrial city in the country.

The economic expansion that had commenced with the opening of the Brooklyn Bridge had pulled in a huge workforce—the city's population had gone from 570,000 in 1880 to 800,000 by 1890, and in 1894 it was approaching 900,000. This demographic explosion had in turn generated a frenzied building boom. Construction of genteel housing was rampant from Brooklyn Heights to Fort Greene, to the newly (at last) fashionable Park Slope. Williamsburg was thriving, and Greenpoint's population had tripled (from twenty-three to seventy-five thousand) between 1880 and 1890. New Utrecht, only recently a farming town, had been transformed by the arrival of the Second Avenue Trolley, and thousands of houses were going up in real estate developments named Bensonhurst, Blythebourne, Bay Ridge Park, and Van Pelt Manor.

Most of the people presiding over this Brooklyn, and the spectacular run of prosperity it had been enjoying, craved consolidation because without it—they knew—it was all going to come to a halt. Roused to action by a William Gaynor speech at the Montauk Club, promerger merchants, bankers, real estate developers, large retailers, warehousers, lawyers, speculators, manufacturers, hotel proprietors, and streetcar company presidents came together, at a public meeting in the Real Estate Exchange, and organized the Brooklyn Consolidation League (BCL, 1893) to fight for ties with Manhattan. Launching a massive propaganda campaign, the BCL would issue two million pieces of literature, nearly all of them insisting Brooklynites face up to some unpleasant facts of life.

The Brooklyn Bridge, linchpin of the new prosperity, was a casualty of its own wild success. In 1890 over forty million people used it, roughly a quarter million each day. The thousands of Brooklynites descending on it at rush hour made it a human maelstrom. Men fought women and children for places in the cars, and the weaker were forced to walk over or take the ferry. Brooklyn and Williamsburg merchants clamored for additional East River bridges, but New York's commercial and political establishments were hostile; Mayor Grant, not atypically, worried in 1889 that the benefits of new construction would accrue wholly to Brooklynites.

The bridge was symbolic of other irrationalities. There was no through transport across it. Manhattan transit cars traversed the bridge, dumped their passengers, turned around and returned to Manhattan; and vice versa for Brooklyn trolleys. Neither the Metropolitan nor the BRT was prepared to establish the coherent, integrated, and vastly expanded rapid transit system that was patently key to keeping real estate values surging.

The transport dilemma, however, was as nothing compared to the water crisis. Brooklyn was about to run dry. In 1896 its water system was delivering ninety-four million gallons a day. Sober estimates suggested demand would reach that level within three years; some people were already experiencing shortages. Wells had been sunk down to suck water from layers of gravel 150 feet deep, and the city was pumping in fifty million gallons a day from the wells, ponds, and streams of Long Island, but the only remaining expedient—imperial expansion eastward—was about to be foreclosed.

In January 1896 Alfred Tredway White, then serving as commissioner of city works, urged Brooklyn to buy land in central Suffolk, suggesting that eastern Long Island's streams, and the watershed beneath its pine barrens, might well bring in an additional eighty million gallons a day. But Suffolk farmers, baymen, and homeowners had no intention of letting that happen, having witnessed the ecological impact of extractions to date. They had been forced to dig their own wells deeper and deeper to reach the sinking water table; oystermen's creeks were filling up with mud; ponds were turning into stagnant bogs teeming with the germs whose significance had recently become menacingly apparent. In June 1896, accordingly, Suffolk went to Albany and got a law preventing Brooklyn from drawing off its water without the approval of a majority of the county supervisors. This meant that for the foreseeable future, Brooklyn had reached its limit. Without a new source of supply, it could look forward to outbreaks of pestilence or an unquenchable conflagration that might lay half the city in ashes.

New York, meanwhile, was swimming in water. The original Croton Aqueduct's capacity of ninety million gallons a day had been exceeded by the early 1880s. Thanks to lobbying efforts by Andrew Haswell Green, among others, a New Croton Aqueduct had been authorized in 1883, begun in 1885, come partially on line in 1891, and fully completed in 1893. It had already expanded carrying capacity to three hundred million gallons daily, and plans were afoot to expand the Croton watershed itself by building new dams and reservoirs. Even without these, the new system, when added to the former Croton's ninety million and the Bronx River's twenty million, could supply roughly four hundred million gallons per day, enough to support four million people, or a million more than the combined population of both Brooklyn and New York. Immediate relief via connecting pipes under the East River was therefore only a consolidation away—an argument deployed with equal cogency and force in Queens and Staten Island. Even the *Brooklyn Daily Eagle*, one of the staunchest Brooklyn *independista* organs, came out for a merger of the two cities' water supplies, though nothing else.

Water, the BCL noted, wasn't the only thing about to be in short supply. Development to date had required immense expenditures on roads, lighting, sewer mains, and the like, but Brooklyn would soon be unable to afford any of these. In 1884 New York State—in line with the post-Tweed fiscal clampdown engineered by, among others, the tight-fisted Andrew Haswell Green—had forbidden cities or counties from incurring a debt greater than 10 percent of the assessed value of its property. The postbridge expansion had been very costly for Brooklyn; apart from its layouts for basic infrastructure, it had assumed obligations for the $1.2 million purchase of Wallabout Market from the U.S. government, and it was about to be burdened with the debts of several Kings County towns. As a result, Brooklyn was bumping up against its debt ceiling. Some banks had already rejected its bonds, the depression was not helping its revenues, and it seemed that rather than expanding city services Brooklyn would have to contract them, laying off clerks, teachers, policemen, firemen, and other employees. The gloomiest observers talked of impending bankruptcy.

The problem, most agreed, was Brooklyn's narrow revenue base, composed essentially of residential housing. In 1891 Brooklyn's population was fully half that of New York's, but it had only a fourth as much taxable property. New York was home to the big corporations—even railroads and steamship companies that did business in Brooklyn paid taxes in Manhattan—and it housed their offices too: in one year a single New York skyscraper paid more taxes than five hundred homes in Brooklyn.

In 1894, accordingly, New York was still fifty-five million dollars below its debt limit and it could sell its bonds for a negligible 3.9 percent. Brooklyn, meanwhile, had been forced to curtail its per capita spending, which was down to $9.75 a head, compared to New York's $22.46, while raising taxes steadily: Brooklynites paid an average of $2.85 per hundred dollars of property to Manhattanites' $1.82. To irate citizens who said the wealthy could well afford still higher taxes, the BCL counterargued that owners would invariably pass such increases on to renters, cutting demand, slowing building, and in the end mainly hurting construction workers, tradesmen, clerks, and shopgirls.

Consolidation, on the other hand, would allow construction of yet another cross-river pipeline, this one to Wall Street's capital pool. The resultant money flow would fertilize bridges, tunnels, waterworks, parks, roadways, rapid transit, and jobs. It would also lower taxes for property owners, with the slack picked up by underassessed Manhattanites—as lawyer Edward C. Graves pointed out in a winning BCL pamphlet called "How Taxes in Brooklyn Can Be Reduced One-Half."

Finally, to those concerned with moral order and good government, the league argued that unification would not bring what one paper called the "horde of plug-ugly politicians that control New York" streaming across the bridge; rather, the combination of the virtuous of Brooklyn with the best men of Manhattan would overwhelm the politicos. Greater New York would be so immense that no Ring could possibly control it. And to those who feared the evils of Manhattan's slums and costs of welfare, Edward Bradford of the BCL wrote that there was no escaping such ills in any event. A man might "withhold charity, but he cannot dodge taxes swelled by crime and pauperism," and every breeze was freighted with tenement-spawned germs.

THE GREAT DEBATE

In March 1893, William Gaynor led a two-hundred-man BCL delegation on board a charter train to Albany, where they presented all these weighty arguments to the legislature, only to see the measure killed by Brooklyn's representatives, who took their orders from Boss McLaughlin. At this the BCL plunged into politics, merging with that fall's Good Government, anti-McLaughlin, anti-McKane crusade. Both causes triumphed together, and the new delegation of Brooklyn's representatives was solidly behind consolidation. When Andrew Haswell Green submitted a bill in February 1894 that called for submitting the issue to a nonbinding yea-or-nay referendum, it sailed through both houses and was signed into law by Governor Flower.

Now the Pros and Cons took their case to the electoral marketplace, and the battle-ground widened. In Manhattan, among the forces calling for a yes vote were the City Club, the Good Government Clubs, the leading commercial associations, and most major papers, including the *World, Herald, Sun, Tribune*, and the *Times*. Adding to consolidation's appeal among these wealthy and powerful men was the argument advanced by municipal efficiency advocates like Albert Shaw, who suggested—rather as Hamilton had a century earlier—that creating a metropolitan-scale government, with at-large elections, would allow "representatives of the best elements of business life" to edge out the politicians who excelled at ward-level combat. Shaw pointed to the new London County Council as a model for Greater New York, noting that there "were no saloon keepers or ward bosses in this London council."

Consolidation was thus presented as a device for achieving the circumscription of democracy that the "best men" had been seeking ever since the Tilden Commission— led by Green's mentor back in 1877—had urged municipal power be vested in taxpayers only. Simon Sterne, a lawyer who had served on that body, was now in the forefront of consolidationist advocates, arguing that "we must stop organizing on the basis of arbitrary population and organize on the basis of interests, and let the elected few or the chosen few who are at the top of these interests ipso facto go into government."

For the Manhattan masses, proponents stressed the benefits of lebensraum. Better-off clerks, bookkeepers, salesmen, mechanics, and operatives, suggested the *Real Estate Record*, would be able to flee congested apartments to modest free-standing cottages available in Brooklyn at twenty-five dollars per month, or two-family houses at ten dollars per month. While this would not eradicate the slums, it would separate "the industrious and self-respecting poor" from "the less regenerate people by whom they are surrounded."

This prospect also appealed to the development-minded in Brooklyn, but it terrified those who feared the unworthy might follow hard on the heels of the respectable. In part to soothe such fears, and win additional backing for a yes vote in the referendum, the city's new Republican-Fusion leadership embarked on its own campaign of urban imperialism. In 1894, to extend the sway of Good Government over the rest of Kings County, Brooklyn called for annexation of the seventeenth-century Dutch and English towns that still retained their independence. Gaining control over Gravesend's Coney was of particular concern, said the *Eagle*, for "the rescue of the island from barbarism, brigandage and bestiality requires that it be made part of the limits and jurisdiction of Brooklyn." Gravesend, Flatbush, and New Utrecht became wards of the city that year, and in 1896 the last remaining town, Flatlands, would be gathered in, making Greater Brooklyn coterminus with Kings County.

Given the Brooklyn Consolidation League's multidimensional and extremely well funded campaign, it appeared that even in Brooklyn the referendum was heading for easy passage. A BCL canvass of selected districts that spring showed 64 percent of voters in favor of consolidation.

Then came the Lexow investigation of corruption among Manhattan's police and politicians, and many Brooklynites backed away from the idea. Between May and November of 1894, as the exposés dragged on, hundreds of columns and cartoons appeared in the anticonsolidation press warning of the horrors that would flow from incorporation into a Tammany-run super-city. Republicans, in particular, took fright at the prospect of having their new-minted victory overridden and being forced to relinquish power to Democratic crooks and connivers.

In November 1894 the referendum went to the voters.

In Manhattan, 96,938 voted for consolidation, 59,959 against. The Pro forces did best in upper- and middle-class districts and among native born and more assimilated German and Irish Americans; they did worst in poor districts and Tammany strongholds.

In Queens, over 60 percent of the electors voted for consolidation, with the greatest tallies being registered in the urbanized areas closest to Manhattan. Long Island City, in particular, was counting on reaping such benefits as a Blackwell's Island bridge, a bevy of new streets, and the assumption by Manhattan of its substantial debt, product of both honest construction and blatant thievery. Such resistance as there was in Queens came from its sparsely settled periphery, though only Flushing failed to cast a majority in favor.

On Staten Island, the results were crisply clear: 5,531 for consolidation, 1,505 against.

In the eastern districts of the Bronx: Mount Vernon declined, by a large majority; Westchester said no, but only by one vote; Eastchester, Pelham, and the remainder of the territory said yes, convinced of amalgamation's benefits by the flurry of improvements that had begun in 1890, when the state transferred development oversight from the Department of Parks to a local group, the Department of Street Improvements of the Twenty-third and Twenty-fourth Wards. This body had gotten lots of streets paved and sewers built and had extended the grid throughout the area's irregular terrain. The new North Side Board of Trade (1894) pushed successfully for consolidation to keep the process in motion.

The referendum passed in Brooklyn too, but by less than the proverbial whisker. The final tally was 64,744 for merger and 64,467 against—a winning margin of 277 out of 129,211. Ironically, it was the newly conquered colonies of Gravesend and New Utrecht that, in voting heavily for consolidation, overcame the negative majority in Brooklyn's imperial center.

A benevolent "Father Knickerbocker" welcomes "Brooklyn" to the family of Greater New York after the 1894 referendum. Another two years would pass, however, before opposition to consolidation on both sides of the East River had been finally defeated. (Brooklyn Historical Society)

The result emboldened opponents, who immediately after the election organized a League of Loyal Citizens, assembled their own roster of bankers, merchants, landlords, reformers, and clergymen, and launched a campaign to block consolidation at the state level. In pamphlets, circulars, leaflets, and a weekly bulletin called *Greater Brooklyn*, the Loyal Leaguers attacked Manhattan as a social and political failure (citing Jacob Riis to good effect); expressed doubts that a Manhattan-dominated Greater New York would ever dispense Brooklyn its fair share of anything; reiterated its objection to being swamped (as the Rev. Dr. Storrs of the Church of the Pilgrims put it) by a flow from Manhattan to Brooklyn of the "political sewage of Europe"; and expressed a desire not to "vote away our religion" and to remain "a New England and American city."

The Loyalists appealed as well to traditions of local self-government and against a centralizing state, rather as had the Antifederalists a century earlier. They also sought to rouse middle-class ire against big developers on both sides of the East River. Thus *Eagle* editor St. Clair McKelway declared that in Brooklyn, every plain citizen was "the political peer of every capitalist or of every lot boomer," that they preferred homes to tenements and houses to mansions, and that as residents of a "manly city" they would not "sell their rights or dodge their responsibilities for dirty money, no matter how high it be heaped."

Finally, Loyalists appealed to municipal patriotism, wrapping themselves in the flag of Brooklyn, recalling with St. Clair McKelway the glorious days when "Washington's army saved the Union's life and afterward were able to beat the consolidation attempted against American liberty." Seeking to tap popular levels of affection for Brooklyn, they denounced those consolidationist-minded gentlemen as being people who (in Storrs's opinion) considered the city as a mere convenience on the order of a trolley car.

A disgusted Andrew Haswell Green dismissed the Loyalist campaign as a mix of "senile sentimentalism" and cynical manipulation by officeholders who hoped to "stay the wheels of beneficent progress by a display of flags and banners, the din of brass bands, and other claptrap, to capture the thoughtless and unwary." Whatever it was, it worked, and in 1895 the Loyalists, claiming a membership of fifty thousand, stormed Albany and succeeded in setting aside the referendum's verdict. The merger movement—apart from a decision that year to bring the eastern Bronx on board—was dead.

ENDGAME

Then Boss Thomas Collier Platt revived it. As Republicans in 1894 had made a strong showing in all local municipalities, Platt had high hopes of capturing the first mayoralty of Greater New York. He believed he could enhance his party's chances by combining Tammany-prone Manhattan with more Republican-friendly Brooklyn. Consolidation might also strengthen Platt's hand against excessively independent Republican reformers like Mayors Strong and Schieren, who had sorely disappointed the boss in matters of patronage. Indeed he had received fewer political plums from the likes of Strong, Waring, and Roosevelt than he had from Tammany Hall. Perhaps, Platt reasoned, he might re-establish state-run commissions to seize control of police, fire, and public works departments from the reformers, at the very least until a supra-city charter took effect. Finally, by stepping forward as the Father of Greater New York, Platt could demonstrate to his big business backers how capable he was of energetic leadership on their behalf.

In 1896, accordingly, Platt rammed a bill through the legislature calling for consolidation of precisely the territories Green's commission had proposed, to take effect as of January 1, 1898. The new law also empowered Republican Governor Levi Morton to appoint a nine-member panel to draft a new charter. As required by the state constitution, the bill was submitted to mayors of the affected cities.

Brooklyn's Frederick Wurster vetoed it. So did Mayor Strong. Poised on the brink of victory, the Chamber of Commerce crowd allied to the Strong administration had gotten cold feet. Maybe the deal was *too* favorable to Brooklyn. Maybe Manhattan taxpayers would get stuck with the tab for improvements in the Bronx or be forced to shoulder debts racked up by profligate villages in Queens. The Union League Club, the City Club, the Reform Club, the Association of the Bar, the Real Estate Exchange, the Board of Trade and Transportation—all counseled delay.

Platt shut his ears and pressed ahead relentlessly with repassage. The recalcitrant mayors were overridden on April 22. Now last-standers from both sides of the river descended on Governor Levi Morton, pleading for a veto. But Levi Morton very much wanted to be president, and Thomas Collier Platt was the only man who could obtain the nomination for him at the Republican convention upcoming in five weeks' time. Morton signed on May 11, 1896. Greater New York had arrived, though apart from its spatial boundaries, no one had the slightest idea of what it would look like.

Only now did the governor appoint a Charter Commission—ten Republicans and five Democrats. It included both notable consolidationists like Andrew Haswell Green (though he would fall sick and be unable to participate in the drafting process) and a strong contingent from Brooklyn (which Platt was anxious to placate). The members were virtually all lawyers, politicians, and men of property; there were no representatives of labor.

These gentlemen prepared an immense and rambling document that represented a series of compromises. It strengthened the mayor and the Board of Estimate and maintained the position of independently elected comptroller—features applauded by taxpayers and bondholders. It retired the Common Council, after more than two hundred years of service, and replaced it with a two-chambered municipal assembly. This body, together with the five newly instituted borough governments (complete with elected borough presidents) was intended to satisfy the desire of Brooklyn's Loyal Leaguers for decentralized, local self-government. It also gave Boss Platt four potential footholds outside Manhattan should Tammany manage to hold on to New York County.

The charter commissioners pleased home rulers by shifting the right to grant street railway franchises from the state legislature to the municipal assembly and permitting the city to impose conditions on owners of shoreline property. Developers and planners appreciated creation of a Board of Public Improvements, with modest powers to coordinate public works throughout the city. Housing reformers applauded the charter's call for a commission to establish a uniform building code for all five boroughs. And charity reformers were delighted when Commissioner Seth Low wrote in a provision that explicitly banned all outdoor relief (apart for subsidies to the blind)—including the spirit-sapping free handouts of fuel supplies they had been trying to outlaw for over a decade. The charter would thus force Richmond and Queens to terminate their relief programs, and Manhattan to cut off coal.

Though New York Good Government forces assailed the final product, Brooklynites professed general satisfaction (or exhaustion), and with Croker's support Platt got the nine-hundred-page document safely through the legislature by March 23, without, he boasted, "the crossing of a 't' or the dotting of an 'i.'" After one last stubborn mayoral veto from William Strong had been overcome, the Charter of Greater New York was presented to Governor Frank Black for his signature, which he affixed on May 5, 1897.

By the rainy evening of December 31, 1897, therefore, the city was poised for transformation.

TOWARD THE TWENTIETH CENTURY

Marching through soggy streets, the parade of revelers poured into City Hall Park, brilliantly illuminated by five hundred magnesium lights. Bands and choral societies regaled them (while competing for silver cups, with Tony Pastor and his fellow judges straining to hear over the wind and din). As midnight approached, the rain turned to damp snow. When Trinity's bells chimed the hour, Hearst's coordinated cacophony rolled over the assembled merrymakers. A battery of field guns near the post office boomed out a hundred-gun salute. Red and green flares and aerial bombs soared aloft. The city's tugs and ferries shrieked their whistles. And as the throng (led by German singing societies) joined in singing "Auld Lang Syne," Mayor James Phelan of San Francisco pressed a button that sent a charge of electricity hurtling across the continent to unfurl Greater New York's new blue and white flag atop City Hall. At the same moment, the glum crowd assembled outside what was now merely Brooklyn's Borough Hall fell silent, marking their city's passing.

A colossus had been born. Over three million strong, over three hundred square miles huge, larger than Paris, gaining on London, New York was ready to face the twentieth century. But when the fireworks faded away and the crowds dispersed, what—apart from an end to free coal for the poor—would consolidation mean for the city and its people?

Consolidation, which would take many forms other than the merely municipal, would be key to the new century's first decades. As we will see, J. P. Morgan and his colleagues would press relentlessly ahead with the process, begun in the 1880s, of consolidating rival companies into giant corporations. A great merger movement from 1897 to 1904 would forge the modern American capitalist economy, of which New York City would be the headquarters, its ever taller skyscrapers affording the new order both shelter and symbolic expression.

Greater New York would undertake mammoth building projects, creating the infrastructure of bridges, subways, railways, water tunnels, and power lines that would make consolidation a reality, not just a constitutional artifact. Its populace, swollen by massive immigration, would move out along the new rapid transit lines, filling out Brooklyn, creating an instant city in the Bronx.

Culture wars would continue, with the upper and middle classes consolidating their museums and libraries and housing them in grand Roman Imperial temples, for their own enjoyment and to elevate the retrograde. The city's commercial culture would also expand, however, giving rise to such novelties as cabarets, nickelodeons, and Times Square, all of which genteel reformers would vainly attempt to rein in.

Businessmen and professionals would continue their efforts, intermittently successful, to wrest control of municipal politics from Tammany Hall, while middle-class reformers would struggle to refurbish the civic order by consolidating the agencies of public health, law enforcement, housing, welfare, and schooling.

A new generation of socialists, unionists, feminists, artists, African-American activists, and settlement workers would come together: to criticize corporate power; to protest and improve working conditions in shops and factories; to suffer from and fight against unemployment, poverty, and high rents; to organize a series of mammoth general strikes that would force Tammany into taking up a progressive agenda; to promote a radical assault against the ramparts of genteel culture; to win suffrage for women; and, after a race riot in 1900, to generate a civil rights coalition that would contest Jim Crow at home and throughout the country.

New York's financiers and industrialists, finally, would steadily expand New York's imperial outreach, their efforts reaching an apotheosis during the First World War, when the United States was transformed from a debtor to a creditor nation and its leading metropolis began to replace London as the fulcrum of the global economy, emerging as heir presumptive to the title of Capital of the World.

References

INTRODUCTION TO SOURCES AND SUGGESTIONS FOR FURTHER READING

A synthesizer, looking back, sees a thief's shadow. Our book draws upon thousands of studies made by myriad specialists who in the last generation have rewritten the city's history. It is they who produced the strands of scholarship that we have woven into a narrative.

In the resource notes that follow, we have space to offer only the most truncated acknowledgment of the immense debt we owe those upon whose research and insights we have relied. The alphabetized author and date listings are intended only to suggest those works we found most valuable in sorting our way through the subject of each particular section. This approach does not allow us to differentiate between those interpretations we support and follow and those which we disagree with but nevertheless consider provocative or informative. Under these circumstances, it is more important than usual to insist that those we cite are to be held blameless for our infelicities of analysis and errors of fact. As to the latter, we acknowledge that this work, by its very scope, will inevitably contain mistakes and misstatements, and we invite correction and comment (bouquets as well as brickbats). Readers can email us at gotham@oup-usa.org.

Finally, a note, for those who might be interested, about the nature of our scholarly collaboration. It began a quarter century ago, when we jointly wrote, in 1972, a lengthy essay on the American Revolution. In the early 1980s, we embarked on this study of New York City. The end product is the result not only of years of discussion and debate but of decades of mutual support and sustenance without which this daunting enterprise would never have come to fruition. Our method of work involved one of us doing the reading, researching, structuring, and writing of a chapter, then passing it to the other, whose commentary, critique, and at times additional research, new writing, or rewriting, would inform the second, third, or however many drafts it took until both partners were basically satisfied with the result. The authors' contributions of intellect and energy are therefore so interlaced that each page bears the mark of their affiliation.

Practical considerations, however, demanded a rough division of labor and attained expertise. Accordingly, Burrows took primary responsibility for producing drafts of chapters 1–26—essentially the seventeenth, eighteenth, and early nineteenth centuries. Wallace did the same for the Introduction and for the remainder of the nineteenth-century material (embracing chapters 27–69). The story of the twentieth century, which swelled to such dimension that it required a volume of its own, has been and will be tackled by MW alone.

We consulted several indispensable reference works so often that it would be tiresome to mention them in each of the section notes that follow. They are Jackson, *Encyclopedia of New York* (1995), Kouwenhoven, *Columbia Historical Portrait of New York* (1953), and Stokes, *Iconography of Manhattan* (1915–28). For the city's history in the seventeenth and eighteenth centuries, we likewise made heavy and repeated use of the primary materials collected by Fernow (1887, 1897, 1902–7, 1907), Lincoln (1894), Hastings and Corwin (1901–16), O'Callaghan, 1849, 1853–87, 1868), Osgood (1905), and Van Laer (1974).

INTRODUCTION

Allen, 1990; Atkins, 1973; Botkin, 1976; Bubrinski, 1995; Clarkson, 1915; Clouston, 1903; Conrad, 1984; Cunningham, 1889; Fox, 1899; Francis, Jr., 1986; Hazlitt, ed., 1866; Irving, 1984; Jagendorf, 1950; Kahrl, ed., 1965; Kandell, 1988; Kane, 1989; Knickerbocker, 1968; Miller, 1886; Opie and Opie, 1997; Paulding, 1839; Pearson, 1991; Stapleton, 1910; Throsby, 1677; Tyrell, 1991; Walter, 1988

PART ONE:
LENAPE COUNTRY AND NEW AMSTERDAM TO 1664

CHAPTER 1:
FIRST IMPRESSIONS

Andrews, 1908; Andrews, 1984; Bayer, 1925; Boyle,

1969; Burnaby, 1904; Danckaerts and Sluyter, 1867; Denton, 1966; Earle, 1938; Habert, 1949; Honour, 1975; Innis, 1902; Jameson, 1909; Kessler and Rachlis, 1959; Lipinsky, 1958; McManis, 1972; Meinig, 1966; Morison, 1971–74; Murphy, 1969; Raesly, 1945; Rink, 1986; Van der Donck, 1841; Van Gelder, 1982; Van Rensselaer, 1898; Wolley, 1902

Immigrant Ice: Barlow, 1969; Boyle, 1969; Cressy, 1966; Homberger, 1994; Joyce, 1988; Kieran, 1959; McPhee, 1983; Miller, 1970; Nicholas, 1988; Raymo and Raymo, 1989; Rensberger, 1976; Schuberth, 1968; Suggs, 1966; Van Diver, 1985; White, 1987

Where the Lenapes Dwell: Axtell, 1981; Axtell, 1982; Axtell, 1987; Axtell, 1992; Berkhofer, 1978; Brasser, 1971; Ceci, 1990; Cronon, 1983; Farb, 1968; Gehring, Starna, and Fenton, 1987; Gibson, 1980; Grumet, 1981; Grumet, 1995; Hauptman and Knapp, 1977; Jacobs, 1972; Jacobs, 1974; Jaffe, 1975; Jameson, 1909; Jennings, 1975; Jennings, 1979; Kammen, 1975; Kraft, 1986; Kupperman, 1980; Lurie and Leacock, 1971; Martin, 1978; Miller and Hamell, 1986; Pearce, 1965; Salisbury, 1982; Salisbury, 1996; Sauer, 1971; Sauer, 1980; Strong, 1997; Trelease, 1960; Trelease, 1962; Trelease, 1969; Washburn, 1971; Washburn, 1975; Wessel, 1981; Wolf, 1982

Lazy and Barbarous People: Brasser, 1971; Bridenbaugh, 1981; Ceci, 1990; Cronon,

1983; Denton, 1966; Etienne and Leacock, 1980; Farb, 1968; Gehring and Grumet, 1987; Gehring, Starna, and Fenton, 1987; Gibson, 1980; Grumet, 1980; Grumet, 1981; Grumet, 1995; Grumet, 1996; Hauptman and Knapp, 1977; Jacobs, 1974; Jaffe, 1979; Jameson, 1909; Jennings, 1975; Jennings, 1979; Kammen, 1975; Kraft, 1986; Kupperman, 1980; Lodwick, 1849; Lurie, 1959; Lurie, 1971; Lurie and Leacock, 1971; Miller and Hamell, 1986; Pearce, 1965; Pyne, 1997; Richter, 1992; Richter, 1983; Rink, 1986; Salisbury, 1982; Salisbury, 1996; Sauer, 1971; Sauer, 1980; Starna, 1986; Strong, 1997; Suggs, 1966; Trelease, 1960; Trelease, 1962; Trelease, 1969; Washburn, 1971; Washburn, 1975; Wessel, 1981; Wolf, 1982; Wolley, 1902

The Fur Trade: Burke, 1986; Dennis, 1994; Fenton, 1971; Hunt, 1940; Josephy, 1958; Krech, 1981; Lipinsky, 1958; Martin, 1978; McBride, 1994; Murray, 1938; Norton, 1974; Richter, 1983; Richter, 1992; Starna, 1986; Strong, 1997; Trelease, 1960; Trelease, 1962; Trelease, 1969; Vecsey, 1986

CHAPTER 2:
THE MEN WHO BOUGHT MANHATTAN

Asher, 1860; Burke, 1986; Grumet, 1981; Hart, 1959; Heckwelder, 1841; Jameson, 1909; Murphy, 1972; Norton, 1974; Strong, 1997

Mighty Amsterdam: Anderson, 1974a; Anderson, 1974b; Bachman, 1969;

Barbour, 1950; Bayer, 1925; Boxer, 1965; Braudel, 1981; Condon, 1968; Davies, 1961; Dillon, 1981; Francis, 1986; Goslinga, 1971; Huey, 1988; Israel, 1989; Israel, 1995; Kistemaker, 1983; Masselman, 1963; Murphy, 1972; Murray, 1938; Newton, 1933; Norton, 1974; Raesly, 1945; Rink, 1986; Scammell, 1981; Schama, 1987; Smit, 1970; Smith, 1973; Van Deusen, 1991; Van Loon, 1928; Wallerstein, 1974; Weslager, 1961; Wilson, 1968

The West India Company: Bachman, 1969; Barbour, 1950; Condon, 1968; Davies, 1961; Francis, 1986; Jameson, 1909; Rink, 1986; Smith, 1973

New Netherland: Bachman, 1969; Baird, 1985; Bayles, 1915; Burke, 1986; Butler, 1983; Ceci, 1990; Condon, 1968; Davies, 1961; Duffy, 1968; Fayden, 1993; Hart, 1959; Israel, 1977; Israel, 1989; Jameson, 1909; Kavenagh, 1973; Kenney, 1975; Maika, 1995; Norton, 1974; Rink, 1978; Rink, 1986; Smith, 1973; Wright, 1973; Zwierlein, 1910

Farms or Factories?: Bachman, 1969; Bayer, 1925; Burke, 1986; Condon, 1968; Jacobs, 1972; Jameson, 1909; Jennings, 1975; Kammen, 1975; Norton, 1974; Rink, 1986

War and Wampum: Boyle, 1969; Brasser, 1971; Burke, 1986; Ceci, 1980; Ceci, 1990; Cronon, 1983; Francis, 1986; Gehring, 1980; Grumet, 1995; Hauptman and Knapp, 1977; Jacobs, 1972; Jacobs, 1974; Jameson, 1909; Lodwick, 1849; Lowensteyn,

1984; McBride, 1994; Norton, 1974; Otto, 1995; Richter, 1992; Rink, 1986; Salisbury, 1982; Strong, 1997; Taxay, 1970; Vecsey, 1986

New Amsterdam: Bayles, 1915; Francis, 1986; Gehring, 1980; Grumet, 1981; Hunt, 1940; Jameson, 1909; Jennings, 1975; Quinn, 1993; Rink, 1986; Starna, 1986

CHAPTER 3:
COMPANY TOWN

Bayles, 1915; Cohen, 1992; Condon, 1968; Davies, 1961; De Jong, 1968; Dubois, 1884; Goodfriend, 1978; Jameson, 1909; Kammen, 1975; Kavenagh, 1973; Kenney, 1975; Kessler and Rachlis, 1959; Kruger, 1985; McManus, 1966; Nissenson, 1937; Postma, 1990; Raesly, 1945; Schama, 1987

Patroons and Puritans: Bachman, 1969; Condon, 1968; Goslinga, 1971; Rink, 1978; Rink, 1986

The Case for Colonization: Bachman, 1969; Condon, 1968; Jameson, 1909; Rink, 1986

Personnel and Chattel: Bakker, 1995; Berlin, 1996; Bridenbaugh, 1966; Cohen, 1992; Foote, 1993; Goodfriend, 1978; Goodfriend, 1992; Janvier, 1894; Kessler and Rachlis, 1959; Kruger, 1985; McManus, 1966; Rink, 1981; Rink, 1986; Swan, 1990; Swan, 1993; Wilder, 1994

Wild West on the Hudson: Biemer, 1983; Cohen, 1981; Cohen, 1992; Davies, 1961; Foglesong, 1986; Foote, 1993; Gehring and Grumet, 1987; Goodfriend, 1978; Goodfriend, 1992; Harlow, 1931; Hershkowitz, 1965; Innis, 1902; Jameson, 1909; Kenney, 1975; Kruger, 1985; McLaughlin, 1981; Narrett, 1988; Narrett, 1992; Raesly, 1945; Riker, 1983; Rink, 1981; Rink, 1986; Rink, 1994; Schama, 1987; Singleton, 1909; Strong, 1842; Van der Zee, 1978; Van Deusen, 1991; Van Rensselaer, 1898; Van Rensselaer, 1909; Wagman,

1983a; White, 1953; Wilcoxen, 1984; Zwierlein, 1910

Development: Bridenbaugh, 1966; Duffy, 1968; Innis, 1902; Jameson, 1909; Kross, 1983; Kruger, 1985; Maika, 1995; Otto, 1995; Riker, 1852; Riker, 1904; Rink, 1986; Seymann, 1939; Singleton, 1909; Wilder, 1994; Wright, 1973

Disaster: Biemer, 1981; Boyle, 1969; Brasser, 1971; Ceci, 1990; Cronon, 1983; Denton, 1966; Gibson, 1980; Grumet, 1981; Hauptman and Knapp, 1977; Innis, 1902; Jameson, 1909; Lodwick, 1849; Lowensteyn, 1984; Macleod, 1928; Norton, 1974; Otto, 1995; Raesly, 1945; Richter, 1983; Richter, 1992; Rink, 1986; Starna, 1986; Strong, 1997; Trelease, 1960; Wagman, 1979; Wessel, 1981; Williams, 1995

Losing Ground: Bachman, 1969; Biemer, 1981; Biemer, 1983; Waller, 1975; Winthrop, 1996

CHAPTER 4:
STUYVESANT

Goslinga, 1971; Kenney, 1975; Kessler and Rachlis, 1959; Raesly, 1945; Rink, 1986; Smith, 1973; Van der Zee, 1978

Town Building: Bridenbaugh, 1966; De Jong, 1970; Duffy, 1968; Gehring, 1991; Innis, 1902; Jameson, 1909; Kammen, 1975; Kessler and Rachlis, 1959; Kilpatrick, 1912; Raesly, 1945; Rink, 1986; Schneider, 1938; Singleton, 1909; Van Rensselaer, 1909; Van Zwieten, 1996; Weidner, 1974

A Well-Regulated Economy: Barbour, 1950; Berlin, 1996; Blackmar, 1989; Ceci, 1980; Davies, 1961; Davis, 1991; De Jong, 1968; Dunn, 1972; Fayden, 1993; Goodfriend, 1978; Goodfriend, 1992; Hobhouse, 1986; Hodges, 1988; Innis, 1902; Jameson, 1909; Kessler and Rachlis, 1959; Kruger, 1985; Maika, 1995; Mintz, 1985; Moss, 1985; Postma, 1990; Quinn, 1993; Richter, 1992; Rink,

1986; Rink, 1987; Rink, 1994; Sheridan, 1974; Swan, 1990; Syrett, 1954; Van den Boogaart, 1986; Van der Zee, 1978; Wagman, 1983a; White, 1953; White, 1956; Wright, 1973

"Persons of Quality": Biemer, 1983; Burke, 1986; Cohen, 1981; Cooper, 1968; Innis, 1902; Kilpatrick, 1912; Maika, 1995; McCormick, 1989; Narrett, 1992; Raesly, 1945; Riker, 1904; Riker, 1981; Rink, 1986; Schama, 1987; Singleton, 1909; Wagman, 1983a, Wagman, 1983b; White, 1956

Common Folk: Bayles, 1915; Bridenbaugh, 1966; Burke, 1978; Hodges, 1988; Kessler and Rachlis, 1959; Newman, 1993; Raesly, 1945; Riker, 1904; Riker, 1981; Rose, 1988; Schama, 1979; Schama, 1987; Singleton, 1909; Van den Boogaart, 1986; Van der Zee, 1978; Van Deusen, 1991; Wagman, 1983

The Negroes' Lot: Davis, 1991; Foote, 1993; Innis, 1902; Jameson, 1909; Kessler and Rachlis, 1959; Kruger, 1985; Moss, 1985; Newman, 1993; Swan, 1990; Wilder, 1994

CHAPTER 5:
A CITY LOST, A CITY GAINED

Cohen, 1992; Earle, 1938; Gehring, 1991; Innis, 1902; Kammen, 1975; Hertzberg, 1989; Katz, 1983; Kessler and Rachlis, 1959; Raesly, 1945; Riker, 1904; Rink, 1986; Schama, 1987; Singleton, 1909; Van der Zee, 1978; Van Deusen, 1991; Van Rensselaer, 1909; Wilder, 1994; Zwierlein, 1910

Servants of Baal: De Jong, 1968; Faber, 1994; Goodfriend, 1992; Hertzberg, 1989; Innis, 1902; Israel, 1989; Jameson, 1909, Kessler and Rachlis, 1959; Marcus, 1970; Pool, 1955; Pratt, 1967; Raesly, 1945; Rink, 1986; Smith, 1973; Van der Zee, 1978; Waller, 1975

"Our Great Muscovy Duke": Biemer, 1981; Biemer, 1983; Ellis, 1997; Fernow, 1902–7;

Innis, 1902; Jameson, 1909; Kammen, 1975; Kavenagh, 1973; Kessler and Rachlis, 1959; Kilpatrick, 1912; Maika, 1995; Narrett, 1988; New-York Historical Society, 1886; Raesly, 1945; Reynolds, 1984; Riker, 1983; Rink, 1986; Seybolt, 1918; Seymann, 1939; Syrett, 1954; Teaford, 1975; Van der Zee, 1978; Van Rensselaer, 1898; Wagman, 1983b; Waller, 1975; White, 1953; Wright, 1973

The Struggle for Power: Jameson, 1909; Kavenagh, 1973; Raesly, 1945; Rink, 1986; Seybolt, 1918; Seymann, 1939; Teaford, 1975; Wagman, 1983b; White, 1953, Wright, 1973

Imperiled Periphery: Biemer, 1981; Cohen, 1981; Cohen, 1992; Danckaerts and Sluyter, 1966; De Jong, 1968; Dilliard, 1974; Dubois, 1884; Earle, 1938; Goodfriend, 1992; Grumet, 1996; Harlow, 1931; Hauptman and Knapp, 1977; Hunt, 1940; Innis, 1902; Kammen, 1975; Kenney, 1975; Kessler and Rachlis, 1959; Kross, 1983; McLaughlin, 1981; Merwick, 1980; Nooter, 1995; Raesly, 1945; Riker, 1982; Rink, 1986; Rink, 1991; Rink, 1994; Salisbury, 1982; Singleton, 1909; Strong, 1842; Strong, 1997; Trelease, 1960; Van den Boogaart, 1986; Van der Donck, 1968; Van Gelder, 1982; Van der Zee, 1978; Wagman, 1979; Wessel, 1981; Williams, 1995; Wright, 1973; Wright, 1980

James Stuart, Duke of York: Andrews, 1934–38; Biemer, 1983; Calder, 1981; Dunn, 1972; Israel, 1989; Kessler and Rachlis, 1959; Mowrer, 1960; Raesly, 1945; Riker, 1982; Ritchie, 1977; Shomette and Haslach, 1988; Van der Zee, 1978; Van Rensselaer, 1909; Waller, 1975

New York, New York: Andrews, 1934–38; Balmer, 1989a; De Jong, 1968; Israel, 1989; Kessler and Rachlis, 1959; Kruger, 1985; Maika, 1995; Moss, 1985; Mowrer, 1960; Murphy, 1969; Quinn, 1993; Raesly, 1945; Ritchie, 1977; Shomette and Haslach,

1988; Van der Zee, 1978; Van Rensselaer, 1909

PART TWO:
BRITISH NEW YORK
(1664–1783)

CHAPTER 6:
EMPIRE AND OLIGARCHY

Andrews, 1934–38; Goebel and Naughton, 1943; Goebel, 1969; Goodfriend, 1992; Greene, 1996; Kavenagh, 1973; Maika, 1995; Pennypacker, 1944; Pratt, 1967; Ritchie, 1977; Van der Zee, 1978; Van Rensselaer, 1898; Van Rensselaer, 1909

Collaborators: Balmer, 1983; Balmer, 1989a; Bayles, 1915; Biemer, 1983; Danckaerts and Sluyter, 1966; Earle, 1938; Ellis, 1997; Fabend, 1994; Greene, 1996; Harlow, 1931; Kavenagh, 1973; Kessler and Rachlis, 1959; Kupp, 1974; Maika, 1995; Matson, 1987; Murrin, 1988; Narrett, 1992; Reynolds, 1984; Ritchie, 1977; Severini, 1981; Singleton, 1909; Steele, 1986; Stern, 1974; Still, 1956; Van Rensselaer, 1898; Van Rensselaer, 1909; White, 1987

Dissidents: Andrews, 1934–38; Archdeacon, 1976b; Balmer, 1983; Balmer, 1989a; Biemer, 1983; Johnson, 1965; Kavenagh, 1973; Kim, 1970; Lovejoy, 1972; McCormick, 1989; McKinley, 1900; Mowrer, 1960; Nooter, 1995; Pratt, 1967; Reich, 1953; Riker, 1982; Ritchie, 1977; Stern, 1974; Van Rensselaer, 1909; Waller, 1975

New Orange: Balmer, 1989a; De Jong, 1975; Israel, 1989; Reich, 1953; Ritchie, 1977; Shomette and Haslach, 1988; Van der Zee, 1978; Van Rensselaer, 1909

Andros: Bridenbaugh, 1966; Greene, 1996; Hodges, 1982; Kammen, 1975; Kavenagh, 1973; McCormick, 1989; Peterson, 1917; Reich, 1953; Ritchie, 1977; Severini, 1981; Van Rensselaer, 1909; Webb, 1976; Webb, 1984

The Covenant Chain: Cohen, 1992; Gehring and Grumet,

1987; Jennings, 1975; Jennings, 1984; Martin, 1985; McCormick, 1989; Richter, 1992; Webb, 1984

New York in 1680: Archdeacon, 1976b; Bayles, 1915; Cohen, 1974; Danckaerts and Sluyter, 1966; Davis, 1991; Denton, 1966; Goodfriend, 1992; Hodges, 1982; Kruger, 1985; Looney, 1982; Lovejoy, 1972; Matson, 1987; McCormick, 1989; McLaughlin, 1981; Murrin, 1988; Reich, 1953; Ritchie, 1977; Van Rensselaer, 1909; White, 1956; Wolley, 1902

Standing More on Nature than Names: Andrews, 1934–38; Archdeacon, 1976b; Biemer, 1983; Danckaerts and Sluyter, 1966; Ellis, 1997; Fabend, 1997; Goodfriend, 1992; Lovejoy, 1972; McCormick, 1989; McLaughlin, 1981; Merwick, 1981; Morris, 1935; Narrett, 1988; Narrett, 1992; Reich, 1953; Ritchie, 1977; Roeber, 1991; Shammas, 1987; Shammas, et al., 1987; Sheridan, 1974; Smith, 1983; Stern, 1974; Strong, 1842; Van Rensselaer, 1909

CHAPTER 7:
JACOB LEISLER'S REBELLION

Andrews, 1934–38; Kammen, 1975; Kennedy, 1930; Phelan, 1933; Van Rensselaer, 1909

The Reorganization of Government: Andrews, 1934–38; Biemer, 1983; Duffy, 1968–74; Hartog, 1983; Hodges, 1982; Kammen, 1975; Kavenagh, 1973; Lovejoy, 1972, McCormick, 1989; Merwick, 1981; Murrin, 1988; Narrett, 1988; Narrett, 1992; Phelan, 1933; Reich, 1953; Ritchie, 1977; Seymann, 1939; Singleton, 1909; Still, 1956; Van Rensselaer, 1909

The Gathering Storm: Archdeacon, 1976b; Biemer, 1983; Bosher, 1995; Butler, 1983; Christoph, 1994; Cray, 1988a; Cray, 1988b; Goodfriend, 1992; Kierner, 1992; Kim, 1970; Kim, 1978; Leder, 1961; Levinson, 1961; Mark, 1965; Monaghan,

1935; Murrin, 1988; Narrett, 1988; Nissenson, 1937; Pound, 1975; Ritchie, 1977; Steele, 1986; Still, 1956; Van Rensselaer, 1909

A Glorious Revolution: Lovejoy, 1972; McCormick, 1989; Ritchie, 1977; Van Rensselaer, 1909

"this confused businesse": Andrews, 1915; Andrews, 1934–38; Archdeacon, 1976b; Leder, 1961; Lovejoy, 1972; McCormick, 1978; McCormick, 1989; McCully, 1982; Merwick, 1989; Murrin, 1988; Nash, 1976; Reich, 1953; Ritchie, 1977; Sosin, 1982; Steele, 1986; Stern, 1974; Van Rensselaer, 1909; Webb, 1966

Leisler and the Leislerians: Andrews, 1915; Archdeacon, 1976a; Archdeacon, 1976b; Balmer, 1989a; Balmer, 1989b; Fabend, 1994; Howe, 1990; Leder, 1954; Lovejoy, 1972; Maika, 1994; Mason, 1949; McCormick, 1989; Mowrer, 1960; Narrett, 1992; Nooter, 1995; Raesly, 1945; Reich, 1953; Ritchie, 1977; Sosin, 1982; Stern, 1974; Van Rensselaer, 1909; Voorhees, 1989; Voorhees, 1994a; Voorhees, 1994b; White, 1956

"Kill him! Kill him!": Archdeacon, 1976b; Hodges, 1982; Kierner, 1992; Leder, 1961; Leder, 1955; McCormick, 1989; Nash, 1976; Peckham, 1964; Peterson, 1917; Reich, 1953; Richter, 1992; Ritchie, 1977

"For they have devoured Jacob": Balmer, 1989a; Biemer, 1983; Bonomi, 1971; Budd, 1978; Goebel and Naughton, 1943; Greenberg, 1974; Johnson, 1965; Leder, 1952; McCormick, 1989; Narrett, 1992; Reich, 1953; Ritchie, 1977; Van Rensselaer, 1909; Voorhees, 1994a

CHAPTER 8:
HEATS AND ANIMOSITYES

Church and State: Andrews, 1956; Archdeacon, 1976b; Balmer, 1981; Balmer, 1988; Balmer, 1989a; Balmer, 1989b; Biemer, 1983; Bonomi, 1971; Bonomi, 1986; Bridenbaugh, 1966; De Jong, 1975; Earle, 1938; Fowler, 1981; Fox, 1926;

Goodfriend, 1992; Greenberg, 1974; Greenberg, 1975; Hodges, 1982; Kammen, 1975; Kavenagh, 1973; Kemp, 1969; Kilpatrick, 1912; Leamon, 1963; Leder, 1960; Lodwick, 1849; McCormick, 1989; Miller, 1843; Morehouse, 1973; Nooter, 1995; Olson, 1973; Phelan, 1933; Pointer, 1988; Pool, 1955; Pratt, 1967; Reich, 1953; Roeber, 1991; Sosin, 1985; Still, 1956; Waller, 1960; White, 1956

The Pirates of New York: Andrews, 1956; Bayles, 1915; Bonomi, 1971; Fox, 1926; Goodfriend, 1992; Harlow, 1931; Johnson, 1963; Judd, 1975; Kammen, 1975; Leamon, 1963; Leder, 1961; Lydon, 1970; McCormick, 1989; Miller, 1843; Monaghan, 1935; Morris, 1952; Nash, 1976; Rediker, 1987; Reich, 1953; Risjord, 1981; Ritchie, 1986; Ritchie, 1988; Singleton, 1902; Valentine, 1853; Waller, 1960; White, 1956

The Anglicization of City Life: Andrews, 1956; Bayles, 1915; Bridenbaugh, 1966; De Jong, 1975; Eames, 1928; Earle, 1938; Gilje, 1987; Goebel, 1969; Goodfriend, 1992; Harlow, 1931; Howe, 1990; Kammen, 1970; Kammen, 1975; Katz, 1968; Levinson, 1961; Mintz, 1985; Phelan, 1933; Plumb, 1967; Rediker, 1981; Reynolds, 1984; Ritchie, 1986; Rosen, 1987; Shaw, 1981; Singleton, 1902; Steele, 1986; Straka, 1973

"Trumpet and Drumms": Balmer, 1989a; Balmer, 1989b; Bayles, 1915; Budd, 1978; De Peyster, 1879; Fox, 1926; Howe, 1990; Kammen, 1975; Klein, 1964; Knittle, 1970; Leamon, 1963; Leder, 1961; Leder, 1971; McCormick, 1989; Reich, 1953; Runcie, 1969; Sosin, 1985; Varga, 1960; Waller, 1960; White, 1956

The Strange Career of Captain Kidd: Earle, 1938; Leder, 1954; Leder, 1961; Miller, 1843; Morris, 1935; Ritchie, 1986

"A very well humourd Affable Gent.": Archdeacon, 1976b;

Balmer, 1981; Balmer, 1988; Balmer, 1989a; Bayles, 1915; Bonomi, 1994; Bonomi, 1998; Earle, 1938; Ellis, 1997; Hodges, 1986; Howe, 1990; Katz, 1983; Kemp, 1969; Kierner, 1992; Kim, 1970; Leder, 1961; McAnear, 1967; Nooter, 1995; Olson, 1973; Pratt, 1967; Reich, 1953; Sheridan, 1981; Sosin, 1985; Valentine, 1853; Van Rensselaer, 1898

Political Interests: Bonomi, 1971; Craven, 1968; Egnal, 1988; Ellis, 1997; Goebel, 1969; Jennings, 1984; Johnson, 1963; Kammen, 1975; Katz, 1968; Katz, 1970; Klein, 1964; Klein, 1966; Kramnick, 1968; Leder, 1960; Leder, 1961, Lustig, 1995; Lydon, 1961; Maika, 1995; Nash, 1976; Olson, 1973a; Olson, 1973b; Pares, 1956; Peckham, 1964; Reich, 1953; Sosin, 1985; Steele, 1986; Valentine, 1853; Van Rensselaer, 1985; Waller, 1960; White, 1956

CHAPTER 9:
IN THE KINGDOM OF
SUGAR

Davisson and Bradley, 1971; Kammen, 1975; Kouwenhoven, 1953; Wilkenfeld, 1977

White Gold, Black Slaves: Brock, 1975; Calder, 1981; Davis, 1991; Dunn, 1972; Henretta and Nobles, 1986; Hobhouse, 1986; Kruger, 1985; Liss, 1983; McCusker, 1978; Mintz, 1985; Pares, 1956; Price, 1974; Sheridan, 1970; Sheridan, 1974; Steele, 1986

The West Indian Connection: Archdeacon, 1976b; Bridenbaugh and Bridenbaugh, 1972; Bruchey, 1966; Davisson and Bradley, 1971; Duffy, 1974; Dunn, 1972; Goodfriend, 1992; Jaher, 1982; Kammen, 1975; Kierner, 1992; Marcus, 1970; McCusker and Menard, 1985; Mintz, 1985; Monaghan, 1935; Narrett, 1988; Pares, 1956; Rediker, 1987; Reich, 1953; Risjord, 1981; Rosen, 1992; Scoville, 1866; Sheridan, 1974; Singleton, 1902; Steele, 1986; Still, 1956; White, 1956; Wilkenfeld, 1978

The Town that Trade Built: Archdeacon, 1975; Bayles, 1915; Bridenbaugh, 1966; Bruchey, 1966; Davisson and Bradley, 1971; DeVoe, 1970; Goodfriend, 1992; Kammen, 1975; McCusker and Menard, 1985; McKee, 1935; Still, 1956; White, 1956; Wilkenfeld, 1977; Wilkenfeld, 1978

City of Slaves: Archdeacon, 1975; Bonomi, 1971; Cray, 1988; Cray, 1988; Davis, 1991; Dillard, 1972; Fox, 1926; Goodfriend, 1992; Kammen, 1975; Kruger, 1985; Lydon, 1978; McCormick, 1989; McKee, 1935; McManus, 1966; Moss, 1985; Narrett, 1989; Newman, 1993; Smith, 1983

"Bonny Country": Balmer, 1989a; Bender, 1987; Bonomi, 1971; Butler, 1983; Calder, 1981; Cray, 1988a; Cray, 1988b; Crimmins, 1905; Dickson, 1966; Doyle, 1981; Faber, 1992; Goodfriend, 1989; Goodfriend, 1992; Goodfriend, 1996; Graham, 1956; Grinstein, 1945; Hamlin, 1939; Hamlin and Baker, 1959; Hershkowitz, 1976; Hershkowitz and Meyer, 1968; Kammen, 1975; Keys, 1967; Kierner, 1992; Klein, 1964; Klein, 1978; Knittle, 1970; Leder, 1971; Lustig, 1983; Lustig, 1995; Marcus, 1970; Maury, 1853; McGregor, 1888; McKee, 1935; Miller, 1985; Mintz, 1985; Morris, 1935; Morris, 1978; Narrett, 1989; Nash, 1979; Otterness, 1994; Pool, 1952; Pool, 1955; Pryde, 1935; Roeber, 1993; Rosenwaike, 1972; Scott and Stryker-Rodda, 1975; Sheridan, 1974; Smith, 1978; Van Rensselaer, 1985; Wells, 1973; White, 1956

An Epitaph for Dutch New York: Archdeacon, 1976b; Balmer, 1989a; Benson, 1964; Bonomi, 1971; Bridenbaugh, 1948; Butler, 1983; Cohen, 1971; Cohen, 1992; De Jong, 1975; Dunshee, 1952; Earle, 1938; Fabend, 1991; Fabend, 1997; Gehring, 1984; Goebel, 1969; Goodfriend, 1992; Greenberg, 1974; Harlow, 1931; Harrington, 1933; Hershkowitz and Meyer, 1968; Janvier, 1894; Jordan,

1977; Kemp, 1969; Kierner, 1992; Klingberg, 1940; Krassner, 1985; Maury, 1853; Maxson, 1920; Miller and Johnson, 1963; Narrett, 1988; Narrett, 1992; Nooter, 1995; Norton, 1980; Pointer, 1988; Roeber, 1991; Rosenwaike, 1972; Singleton, 1902; Sweeney, 1992; Tanis, 1967; Wacker, 1986; Wertenbaker, 1949

CHAPTER 10:
ONE BODY CORPORATE
AND POLITIC?

Kavenagh, 1973; McAnear, 1967

"A Free City of Itself": Andrews, 1900; Archdeacon, 1976b; Black, 1967; Edwards, 1967; Gilje, 1987; Goebel, 1969; Hartog, 1983; Hodges, 1986; Hodges, 1988; Kavenagh, 1973; Kent, 1956; Klein, 1964; McAnear, 1967; McKee, 1935; Peterson, 1917; Seybolt, 1918; Teaford, 1975; Varga, 1960; Wagman, 1983b; Wilkenfeld, 1971; Williamson, 1960

Deference or Indifference?: Archdeacon, 1976b; Blackmar, 1989; Bonomi, 1971; Duffy, 1968–74; Flexner, 1980; Fox, 1926; Goodfriend, 1992; Greene, 1996; Hartog, 1983; Howe, 1990; Kammen, 1975; Katz, 1968; Klein, 1964; McKee, 1935; Morgan, 1988; Narrett, 1988; Nash, 1976; Peterson, 1917; Rothschild, 1990; Varga, 1960; Wagman, 1983b; Wilkenfeld, 1976; Wilkenfeld, 1978

The Master's Voice: Cray, 1988a; Duffy, 1968–74; Edwards, 1967; Ekirch, 1987; Goodfriend, 1992; Greenberg, 1974; Kavenagh, 1973; Kross, 1983; McKee, 1935; Mohl, 1969; Morris, 1935; Narrett, 1988; Peterson, 1917; Richardson, 1970; Ross, 1988; Rothman, 1990; Schneider, 1980; Seybolt, 1918; Smith, 1947; Van Rensselaer, 1909; Wilkenfeld, 1976; Wilkenfeld, 1978

The City and the Poor: Cray, 1988a; McKee, 1935; Mohl, 1969; Narrett, 1988; Ross, 1988; Schneider, 1980

"a terror to others": Cohen,

1971; Cohen, 1974; Cohen, 1992; Davis, 1991; Goodfriend, 1992; Graydon, 1979; Greenberg, 1974; Higginbotham, 1978; Hodges, 1986; Kavenagh, 1973; Kemp, 1969; Klingberg, 1940; Kobrin, 1971; Kross, 1983; Kruger, 1985; Lustig, 1995; Lydon, 1978; McKee, 1935; McManus, 1966; Olson, 1973b; Riker, 1982; Scott, 1961; Sheridan, 1974; Skemer, 1975; Trelease, 1960; Vanderbilt, 1881

CHAPTER 11:
RECESSION, REVIVAL,
AND REBELLION

Bridenbaugh, 1966; Calder, 1981; Countryman, 1981a; Cray, 1988a; Cray, 1988b; Davis, 1973; Davis, 1985; Duffy, 1968–74; Greenberg, 1974; McKee, 1935; Nash, 1976; Rosenwaike, 1972; Ross, 1989

The Party of the People: Bailyn, 1967; Bayles, 1915; Bonomi, 1971; Henderson, 1982; Hershkowitz and Meyer, 1968; Jacobson, 1965; Katz, 1968; Klein, 1963; Klein, 1964; Lustig, 1995; Nash, 1976; Rankin, 1965; Varga, 1960; Wertenbaker, 1949; White, 1956

The Case of the Poor Printer: Bayles, 1915; Botein, 1985; Hershkowitz and Meyer, 1968; Kammen, 1975; Katz, 1963; Katz, 1968; Katz, 1970; Katz, 1971; Levy, 1960; Lustig, 1995; Morris, 1952; Nash, 1976; Singleton, 1902; Steers, 1968; Wertenbaker, 1949

"Such a Struggle I Never Saw": Bayles, 1915; Bonomi, 1971; Jordan, 1977; Cray, 1988a; Cray, 1988b; Katz, 1968; Lustig, 1995; Olson, 1973a

"Gethsemane! Gethsemane!": Bushman, 1970; Duer, 1867; Fowler, 1981; Hodges, 1988; Kammen, 1975; Klingberg, 1940; Pratt, 1967; Vedder, 1898

"G—d d—n all the white people": Chase, 1983; Davis, 1985; Davis, 1991; Goodfriend, 1992; Harris, 1993; Hershkowitz and Meyer, 1968; Horsmanden,

1971; Sheridan, 1974; Szasz, 1967

CHAPTER 12:
WAR AND WEALTH

Anderson, 1972; Bridenbaugh, 1971; Buffington, 1933; Harris, 1993; Nash, 1976; Peckham, 1964

Spoils of War: Abbott, 1974; Bridenbaugh, 1971; Buffington, 1933; Byard, 1989; DeVoe, 1970; Egnal, 1988; Gilje, 1987; Harlow, 1931; Harrington, 1933; Harrington, 1935; Hershkowitz, 1976; Hershkowitz and Meyer, 1968; Hodges, 1986; Janvier, 1984; Kim, 1970; Lydon, 1961; Lydon, 1968; Marcus, 1970; McKee, 1933; McKee, 1935; Narrett, 1989; Nash, 1976; O'Conor, 1938; Rediker, 1981; Swanson, 1991; White, 1956; Whiteman, 1971

Industry and Empire: Bruchey, 1965; Bruchey, 1966; Calder, 1981; Coleman, 1977; Egnal, 1985; Egnal, 1988; Fox, 1967; Harrington, 1933; Henretta and Nobles, 1986; Kammen, 1970; Kierner, 1992; Kouwenhoven, 1953; Lorillard, 1960; Price, 1980; White, 1956

Refinement: Alexander, 1938; Bender, 1987; Breen, 1986; Breen, 1992; Bridenbaugh, 1948; Bushman, 1993; Calvert, 1992; Earle, 1938; Garrett, 1978; Gerardi, 1978; Gottesman, 1938; Henderson, 1982; Kierner, 1988; Kierner, 1992; Klein, 1963; Klein, 1967; Klingenberg, 1940; Kraus, 1949; Narrett, 1988; Norton, 1980; Odell, 1927–49; Rankin, 1965; Silverman, 1976; Singleton, 1902; Sweeney, 1992; Wertenbaker, 1949; White, 1956; Wilkenfeld, 1978; Wright, 1957

Genteel Resorts: Abbott, 1974; Bayles, 1915; Black, 1984; Breen, 1986; Bushman, 1983; Chappell, 1992; Dunshee, 1952; Earle, 1938; Garrett, 1978; Gottesman, 1938; Harlow, 1931; Harrington, 1935; Harris, 1993; Henderson,

1982; Hershkowitz and Meyer, 1968; Kierner, 1988; Kierner, 1992; McAnear, 1967; McKendrick, et al., 1982; Mintz, 1970; Mintz, 1985; Monaghan, 1935; Narrett, 1988; O'Conor, 1938; Price, 1974; Reynolds, 1984; Scoville, 1863–66; Severini, 1981; Singleton, 1902; Sweeny, 1992; Wertenbaker, 1949; White, 1956; Wilkenfeld, 1978

Politics Among Gentlemen: Bender, 1987; Benson, 1964; Countryman, 1981a; Dillon, 1949; Doyle, 1981; Egnal, 1988; Ford, 1902; Gerardi, 1977–8; Gilje, 1987; Humphrey, 1976; Keep, 1909; Kierner, 1992; Kim, 1970; Klein, 1963; Klein, 1971a; Klein, 1971b; Klein, 1993; Launitz-Schurer, 1981; Lustig, 1995; Mark, 1965; McCaughey, 1980; Miller, 1985; Nelson, 1979; Pratt, 1967; Schneider, 1980; Singleton, 1902; Upton, 1969; Van Rensselaer, 1898

Wages of War: Bayles, 1915; Benson, 1964; Bridenbaugh, 1971; Gilje, 1987; Gottesman, 1938; Hodges, 1986; Jennings, 1988; Jordan, 1977; Lemisch, 1977; Lydon, 1961; Lydon, 1968; McKee, 1933; McKee, 1935; Narrett, 1989; Nash, 1976; Rediker, 1981; Singleton, 1902; Swanson, 1991; White, 1956; Whiteman, 1971; Wilkenfeld, 1978

Municipal Improvements: Bridenbaugh, 1971; Cray, 1988a; DeVoe, 1970; Dunshee, 1952; Edwards, 1967; Greenberg, 1974; Hodges, 1986; Klein, 1963; Richardson, 1970; Rosen, 1950; Schneider, 1938–41; Schneider, 1980

Artisanal Wards: Abbott, 1974; Bayles, 1915; Benson, 1964; Blackmar, 1989; Boydston, 1990; DeVoe, 1970; Hodges, 1986; Jordan, 1977; McEllhenny, 1982; McKee, 1935; Morehouse, 1973; Rothschild, 1990

CHAPTER 13:
CRISES

Bridenbaugh, 1971; Dructor, 1975; Edwards, 1967; Egnal, 1985; Egnal, 1988; Goodfriend, 1996;

Harrington, 1935; Henretta and Nobles, 1986; Nash, 1976; Rogers, 1974; Walton and Shepherd, 1979; Wertenbaker, 1948; Wilkenfeld, 1977; Wilkenfeld, 1978

Newcomers: Bailyn, 1986a; Bailyn, 1986b; Bayles, 1915; Bridenbaugh, 1971; Calder, 1981; Countryman, 1981a; Doyle, 1981; Earle, 1938; Edwards, 1967; Gilje, 1987; Greenberg, 1974; Harrington, 1935; Knollenberg, 1960; Mason, 1966; Mohl, 1969; Nash, 1976; Odell, 1927–49; Rankin, 1965; Singleton, 1902; Wertenbaker, 1949; Wilkenfeld, 1976

Policy: Calder, 1981; Calhoon, 1973; Egnal, 1988; Johnson and Syrett, 1968; Kammen, 1975; Kierner, 1992; Kim, 1970; Klein, 1960; Knollenberg, 1960; Lustig, 1995

Resistance: Egnal, 1988; Gilje, 1988; Kammen, 1975; Lustig, 1995; Mohl, 1971; Morgan, 1953; Scull, 1882; Shy, 1965; Wertenbaker, 1948

Riotous Proceedings: Becker, 1909; Christen, 1968; Engleman, 1953; Gerlach, 1972; Gilje, 1987; Lemisch, 1997; Morgan, 1953; Nash, 1976; Ranlet, 1986; Scull, 1882; Singleton, 1902; Wertenbaker, 1948

Sons of Liberty: Champagne, 1967; Champagne, 1975a; Champagne, 1975b; Christen, 1968; Countryman, 1981a; Launitz-Schurer, 1981; MacDougall, 1977; Maier, 1980; Morais, 1939; Nash, 1976; Wertenbaker, 1948

"Our port is shut up": Alexander, 1938; Becker, 1909; Bonomi, 1971; Christen, 1968; Countryman, 1976b; Countryman, 1981a; Egnal, 1988; Ernst, 1993; Gerlach, 1972; Gilje, 1987; Jensen, 1968; Kim, 1970; Kim, 1982; Lynd, 1967; Mark, 1965; Ranlet, 1986; Scull, 1882; Singleton, 1902

Repeal: Egnal, 1988; Gilje,

1987; Scull, 1882; Upton, 1969

CHAPTER 14:
THE DEMON OF DISCORD

Christen, 1968; Gilje, 1987; Launitz-Schurer, 1981; Olm, 1974

The Transformation of Politics: Bonomi, 1971; Champagne, 1963; Champagne, 1975a; Christen, 1968; Egnal, 1988; Friedman, 1965; Gerlach, 1972; Kammen, 1975; Launitz-Schurer, 1981; Leder, 1962–63; Lustig, 1995; Nash, 1976; Varga, 1956; Wertenbaker, 1948

A City "Alive to God": Dillon, 1949; Fowler, 1981; Goodfriend, 1996; Klein, 1993; Maxon, 1920; McEllhenney, 1992; Pointer, 1988; Pratt, 1967; Upton, 1969; Vedder, 1898; Wilkenfeld, 1978

The Wilkes of America: Bayles, 1915; Boyer, 1973; Champagne, 1975a; Christen, 1968; Egnal, 1988; Gilje, 1987; Lustig, 1995; Ranlet, 1986; Scull, 1882

Nonimportation Defeated: Champagne, 1975a; Christen, 1968; Countryman, 1981a; Egnal, 1988; Maier, 1980; McKee, 1935; Ranlet, 1986; Upton, 1969; Wertenbaker, 1948

"A New Flame Kindling in America": Bridenbaugh, 1971; Calder, 1981; Christen, 1968; Countryman, 1981a; De Pauw, 1974; Dickson, 1966; Egnal, 1988; Gerlach, 1972; Graham, 1956; Greenberg, 1974; Labaree, 1975; Lustig, 1995; Mason, 1966; Mintz, 1970; Nash, 1976; Nelson, 1990; Still, 1956; Wertenbaker, 1948.

The "New Arcadia" of Liberty: Christen, 1968; Countryman, 1981a; Kerber, 1980; Lustig, 1995; Lynd, 1967; Mason, 1966; Norton, 1980; Wertenbaker, 1948

The Continental Association: Alexander, 1938; Ammerman, 1974; Christen, 1968; Countryman, 1981a; Lustig, 1995; Odell,

1927–49; Rankin, 1965; Wertenbaker, 1948

Whigs of the Old Stamp: Ashton, 1976; Balmer, 1989a; Benton, 1975; Black, 1984; Calhoon, 1973; Champagne, 1975a; Countryman, 1976a; Countryman, 1981a; Crary, 1973; De Jong, 1975; Dructor, 1975; Egnal, 1988; Ernst, 1993; Flick, 1969; Gerardi, 1978; Hull, et al. 1978; Judd, 1975; Judd, 1983; Kammen, 1976; Klingle, 1979; Launitz-Schurer, 1981; Lustig, 1995; Mason, 1966; McNamara, 1995; Pointer, 1988; Potter, 1983; Pratt, 1967; Ranlet, 1986; Smith, 1969–71; Tiedemann, 1983; Tiedemann, 1984; Tiedemann, 1988; Warnock, 1988; Wertenbaker, 1948; Wright, 1975

"The Mob Begin to Think and Reason": Adams, 1976; Alexander, 1938; Becker, 1966; Griswold, 1856; Klein, 1983; Mintz, 1970; Monaghan, 1935; Morris, 1973; Wertenbaker, 1948; Young, 1967

CHAPTER 15:
REVOLUTION

Champagne, 1975a; Christen, 1968; Countryman, 1981a; Egnal, 1988; Judd, 1983; Launitz-Schurer, 1981; Lustig, 1995; Mason, 1966; Mitchell, 1962; Nelson, 1990; Nelson, 1991; Ranlet, 1986; Schachner, 1947; Smith, 1969–71; Tyler, 1975; Wertenbaker, 1948

"Good and Well-Ordered Governments": Bliven, 1972; Countryman, 1981a; Egnal, 1988; Flick, 1969; Gilje, 1987; Lustig, 1995; Mason, 1966; Mintz, 1970; Wertenbaker, 1948

Yankee Doodle Comes to Town: Abbott, 1929; Alden, 1951; Bangs, 1968; Billias, 1964; Bliven, 1972; Christen, 1968; Fleming, 1776; Flexner, 1968; Flick, 1969; Higginbotham, 1971; Luke and Venables, 1976; Lustig, 1995; MacDougall, 1977; Maier, 1972; Mason, 1966; Mather, 1913; Moore, 1969; Nelson, 1979; Potter, 1983; Ranlet, 1986; Shy, 1976;

Still, 1956; Wertenbaker, 1948

"People Treading on Their Leaders' Heels": Egly, 1981; Flick, 1969; Flexner, 1968; Flexner, 1980; Gallagher, 1995; Gilje, 1987; Johnston, 1971; Lustig, 1995; Lynd, 1967; Mason, 1966; Ranlet, 1986; Schaukirk, 1979

"I Thought All London Was Afloat": Bangs, 1968; Bliven, 1972; Blumenthal, 1952; De Pauw, 1975; Flexner, 1968; Flick, 1969; Gerlach, 1972; Gruber, 1972; Lynd, 1967; Marston, 1987; Mason, 1966; Pratt, 1967; Scheer and Rankin, 1957; Wall, 1975; Wertenbaker, 1948

Such Unsoldierly Conduct: Abbott, 1929; Doyle, 1981; Fleming, 1776; Flexner, 1968; Flick, 1969; Gallagher, 1995; Gruber, 1972; Higginbotham, 1971; Koke, 1975; Mackenzie, 1979; Scheer and Rankin, 1957; Wertenbaker, 1948

The Battle of Brooklyn: Balderston and Syrett, 1975; Black, 1991; Dann, 1980; Flexner, 1968; Flick, 1969; Gallagher, 1995; Graydon, 1979; Gruber, 1972; Gruber, 1986; Hayes, 1995; Johnston, 1971; Kruger, 1985; Leggett, 1979; Manders, 1978; Nelson, 1979; Peckham, 1974; Sabine, 1954; Sabine, 1973; Scheer, 1962; Scheer and Rankin, 1957; Tucker, 1975; Vanderbilt, 1881

The Fall of New York: Black, 1991; Fleming, 1975; Flexner, 1968; Gruber, 1972; Gruber, 1986; Johnson, 1976; Johnston, 1897; Johnston, 1971; Paltsits, 1975; Scheer and Rankin, 1957; Serle, 1940; Still, 1956; Wagner, 1963; Wertenbaker, 1948

Heaven in Flames: Crary, 1973; Ellis, 1997; Fleming, 1975; Flexner, 1968; Graydon, 1979; Johnston, 1897; Kerber, 1980; Mackenzie, 1979; Moore, 1969; Scheer and Rankin, 1957; Wertenbaker, 1948

Finale: Billias, 1975; Bonwick, 1977; Booth, 1973; De Pauw, 1975; Engle, 1976;

Plumb, 1986; Scheer and Rankin, 1957

CHAPTER 16:
THE GIBRALTAR OF
NORTH AMERICA

Barck, 1966; Cohen, 1974; De Pauw, 1975; Flexner, 1980; Flick, 1969; Gerlach, 1972; Johnson, 1976; Keep, 1909; Klein, 1983; Klingle, 1979; Kruger, 1985; Lorenz, 1972; Luke and Venables, 1976; Mason, 1966; Mather, 1913; Ranlet, 1986; Ritchie, 1975; Silverman, 1976; Tiedemann, 1987; Vail, 1975; Wertenbaker, 1948

"Toujours de la gaieté": Barck, 1966; Dructor, 1975; East, 1938; Graydon, 1979; Harlow, 1931; Johnson, 1976; Lorenz, 1972; Moore, 1969; Ridge, 1988; Ritchie, 1975; Schaukirk, 1979; Silverman, 1976; Spalding, 1932; Wertenbaker, 1948

"Every Negro Who Shall Desert the Rebell Standdard": Davis, 1991; Hodges, 1987; Johnson, 1976; Klingle, 1979; Kruger, 1985; McKee, 1935; Narrett, 1988; Nash, 1992; Watson, 1846

Herrings in a Barrel: Barck, 1966; Conway, 1986; Conway, 1990; Eddis, 1972; Flexner, 1980; Flick, 1969; Gilje, 1987; Graydon, 1979; Hodges, 1987; Klein, 1983; Klein and Howard, 1983; Klingle, 1979; Leary, 1975; Marcus, 1970; Onderdonk, 1894; Pennypacker, 1930; Pennypacker, 1939; Pool, 1952; Pool, 1955; Ranlet, 1986; Ritchie, 1975; Schaukirk, 1979; Still, 1956; Upton, 1969; Wertenbaker, 1948

"Blood-Sucking Harpies": Conway, 1990; De Pauw, 1974; Flexner, 1980; Klein, 1980; Klein, 1983; McNamara, 1995; Nelson, 1990; Schaukirk, 1979; Silverman, 1976; Young, 1977

"Kennel, Ye Sons of Bitches!": Blatchford, 1865; Booth, 1973; Bray and Bushnell, 1978; Dunshee, 1952; Gilje and Rock, 1992; Graydon, 1979; Hawkins, 1979; Hayes, 1995; Lemisch, 1969; Onderdonk, 1894;

Ranlet, 1986; Watson, 1846; Wertenbaker, 1948

"One General Scene of Ravage and Desolation": Balderston and Syrett, 1975; Barck, 1966; Booth, 1973; Buck, 1995; Conway, 1986; Conway, 1990; Crary, 1975; De Pauw, 1974; Dunkak, 1988; Fingerhut, 1983; Graydon, 1979; Hodges, 1887; Hufeland, 1926; Johnson, 1976; Judd, 1983; Kammen, 1982; Kelsay, 1984; Kemble, 1885; Kim, 1993; Klein and Howard, 1983; Klingle, 1979; Luke and Venables, 1976; McNamara, 1995; Mintz, 1970; Norton, 1980; Parmet, 1967; Ranlet, 1986; Reynolds, 1960; Riker, 1982; Shy, 1975; Tiedemann, 1976; Waller, 1975; Wertenbaker, 1948

"Curses Upon Their King": Barck, 1966; Booth, 1973; Conway, 1990; Crary, 1959; De Pauw, 1974; Ernst, 1983; Fingerhut, 1983; Flexner, 1980; Judd, 1983; Kemble, 1885; Klein and Howard, 1983; Mason, 1966; Pennypacker, 1930; Pennypacker, 1939; Ranlet, 1986; Schaukirk, 1979; Still, 1956; Upton, 1969; Wertenbaker, 1948

The State of New York: Adams, 1980; Barck, 1966; Bielinski, 1975; Cochran, 1932; Countryman, 1981a; Countryman, 1981b; Dangerfield, 1960; Ernst, 1983; Flick, 1969; Graymont, 1972; Hartog, 1983; Kaminski, 1993; Kammen, 1976; Kelsay, 1984; Kierner, 1992; Kruger, 1985; Lynd, 1967; Main, 1973; Mason, 1966; Mintz, 1970; Mitchell, 1962; Monaghan, 1935; Overall, 1887; Polf, 1977; Pratt, 1967; Quarles, 1961; Ranlet, 1986; Scoville, 1863–66; Upton, 1969; Wertenbaker, 1948; Wright, 1984; Young, 1967; Zeichner, 1940

Evacuation Day: Balderston and Syrett, 1975; Bayles, 1915; Ernst, 1983; Flexner, 1968; Gilje, 1987; Kaminski, 1993; Mather, 1913; Pomerantz, 1938; Ranlet, 1986; Silverman, 1976; Tiedemann, 1987; Wright, 1984

PART THREE:
MERCANTILE TOWN
(1783–1843)

CHAPTER 17:
PHOENIX

Alexander, 1938; Crowley, 1993; Dangerfield, 1960; Griswold, 1856; Hershkowitz, 1990; Lynd, 1967; Mason, 1966; Monaghan, 1935; Nettels, 1962; Pomerantz, 1938; Pound, 1931

Radical Resurgence:
Alexander, 1938; Champagne, 1975a; Cooke, 1960; Countryman, 1981a; Dangerfield, 1960; East, 1938; Garrett, 1978; Gilje, 1987; Hartog, 1983; Humphery, 1976; Kaminski, 1993; Kierner, 1989, Lynd, 1967; Main, 1973; Mason, 1966; Mohl, 1969; Nevins, 1969; Odell, 1927–49; Pomerantz, 1938; Pool, 1955; Pratt, 1967; Prescott and Zimmerman, 1972; Ranlet, 1986; Silverman, 1976; Smith, 1984; Smith, 1989; Spaulding, 1932; Tiedemann, 1987; Wilkenfeld, 1978; Willis, 1967; Young, 1967

New New Yorkers:
Armbruster, 1929; Black, 1984; Cress, 1975; Davis, 1965; Duffy, 1968–74; East, 1938; Ernst, 1989; Haeger, 1991; Harlow, 1931; Hartfield, 1993; Hartog, 1983; Henderson, 1974; Jaher, 1982; Jones, 1975; Jones, 1987; Jones, 1992; Lomask, 1979–82; Main, 1965; Mason, 1966; Matson, 1987; Matson, 1989; Meehan, 1906; Monaghan, 1935; Parmet, 1967; Peters, 1984; Pomerantz, 1938; Porter, 1931; Pratt, 1967; Rosenwaike, 1972; Ryan, 1935; Scoville, 1863–66; Smith, 1989; Spaulding, 1932; Stiles, 1867–70; Still, 1956; Young, 1967

Phocion Speaks: Cooke, 1960; Dangerfield, 1960; Horton, 1939; Kent, 1898; Lynd, 1967; Kline, 1973; Mitchell, 1962; Spaulding, 1932

The Empress of China: Barck, 1966; Cochran, 1932; Countryman, 1981a; East, 1938; Fischer, 1965; Matson, 1989; McDonald, 1958; Smith, 1984; Smith, 1989;

Spaulding, 1932; Wright, 1984; Young, 1967

CHAPTER 18:
THE REVOLUTION
SETTLEMENT

Alexander, 1938; Champagne, 1975; Cooke, 1960; Countryman, 1981a; Kline, 1973; Lynd, 1967; Matson, 1987; Mitchell, 1962; Morris, 1935; Nevins, 1969; Pomerantz, 1938; Spaulding, 1932; Willis, 1967; Young, 1967

Rapprochement: Barck, 1966; Cochran, 1932; Cooke, 1960; Countryman, 1981; Crowley, 1993; De Pauw, 1966; Hartog, 1983; Lynd, 1967; Main, 1973; Matson, 1987; McDonald, 1958; Mohl, 1969; Pomerantz, 1938; Ranlet, 1986; Smith, 1989; Spaulding, 1932; Willis, 1967; Young, 1967

The Radical Retreat:
Alexander, 1938; Benton, 1975; Champagne, 1975; Countryman, 1981; Ernst, 1983; Fingerhut, 1983; Flick, 1969; Lynd, 1967; McDonald, 1958; Overall, 1987; Pomerantz, 1938; Pratt, 1967; Spaulding, 1932; Young, 1967; Zeichner, 1940

Estate Sales: Blackmar, 1989; Countryman, 1981a; Dangerfield, 1960; Davis, 1965; East, 1938; Harlow, 1931; Lynd, 1967; Main, 1973; McDonald, 1958; Pomerantz, 1938; Ranlet, 1986; Spaulding, 1932; Yoshpe, 1939; Young, 1967

Order out of Confusion:
Cooke, 1960; Countryman, 1981a; Hartog, 1983; Murrin, 1980; Spaulding, 1932

Daughters of Liberty: Basch, 1982; Berg, 1978; Blackmar, 1989; Booth, 1973; Boydston, 1990; Burrows and Wallace, 1972; Countryman, 1981a; De Pauw, 1974; De Pauw, 1975; Fliegelman, 1982; Gilje and Rock, 1992; Kann, 1991; Kerber, 1980; Kerber, 1992; Lewis, 1987; Norton, 1980; Rock, 1979; Scoville, 1863–66; Spalletta, 1955; Stansell, 1986; Vanderbilt, 1881; Wilson, 1976

Emancipation: Cooke, 1960; Gilje, 1987; Johnson, 1930; Kaplan, 1989; Kruger, 1985; Main, 1973; McManus, 1966; Monaghan and Lowenthal, 1943; Narrett, 1988; Nash, 1992; Pomerantz, 1938; Roediger, 1991; Wegelin, 1969; White, 1991; Zilversmit, 1967

CHAPTER 19:
THE GRAND FEDERAL
PROCESSION

Cochran, 1932; De Pauw, 1966; Kaminski, 1993; Kline, 1973; Matson, 1987; McDonald, 1958; McDonald, 1965; Miner, 1921; Mitchell, 1962; Monaghan, 1935; Pomerantz, 1938; Spaulding, 1932

"What are you, boy, FEDERAL or ANTI-FEDERAL?": Boyd, 1976; Brooks, 1967; Burrows, 1966; Cochran, 1932; Cooke, 1960; De Pauw, 1966; Jeffrey, 1971; Kaminski, 1988; Kaminski, 1993; Kenyon, 1966; Kline, 1973; Lynd, 1963; Main, 1973; McDonald, 1958; Miner, 1921; Monaghan, 1935; Pomerantz, 1938; Spaulding, 1932; Webking, 1987; Wood, 1974

Vox Populi: Barck, 1966; Boyd, 1976; Brooks, 1967; Burrows, 1966; Countryman, 1981a; De Pauw, 1966; Ernst, 1968; Ernst, 1989; Kaminski, 1988; Kaminski, 1993; Kent, 1898; Kenyon, 1966; Lynd, 1963; Lynd, 1967; McDonald, 1958; Monaghan, 1935; Pomerantz, 1938; Rutland, 1955; Spaulding, 1932; Still, 1956

The Federal Ship Hamilton:
Alexander, 1938; Bell, 1962; Brooks, 1967; Countryman, 1981a; Dangerfield, 1960; De Pauw, 1966; Ernst, 1989; Lynd, 1967; McDonald, 1958; Pomerantz, 1938; Smith, 1989; Spaulding, 1932; Wilentz, 1983

Inauguration Day:
Alexander, 1938; Bernstein, 1989; Bickford and Bowling, 1989; Bowling, 1990; Boyd, 1976; Countryman, 1981a; Den Boer, 1989; Flexner, 1968; Griswold, 1856;

Kaminski, 1993; Kenyon, 1966; Maclay, 1965; Miller, 1960; Monaghan and Lowenthal, 1943; Pomerantz, 1938; Riley, 1990; Silverman, 1976; Smith, 1989; Spaulding, 1932; Young, 1967

CHAPTER 20:
CAPITAL CITY

Alexander, 1938; Bender, 1987; Bowling, 1990; Dangerfield, 1960; Davis, 1965; Elkins and McKitrick, 1993; Ernst, 1968; Garrett, 1978; Gilder, 1938; Griswold, 1856; Harlow, 1931; Harris, 1968; Manzo, 1986; Mitchell, 1962; Monaghan, 1935; Monaghan and Lowenthal, 1943; Pomerantz, 1938; Reynolds, 1984; Silverman, 1976; Smith, 1989

A "Vortex of Folly and Dissipation": Blau, 1973; Bowling, 1990; Brissot, 1964; Dangerfield, 1960; Davis, 1965; Elkins and McKitrick, 1993; Ernst, 1968; Ernst, 1993; Flexner, 1968; Griswold, 1856; Kammen, 1982; Maclay, 1965; Monaghan, 1935; Monaghan and Lowenthal, 1943; Pomerantz, 1938; Silverman, 1976; Smith, 1989; Still, 1956; Wecter, 1937; Young, 1967

Moneyed Men: Alexander, 1938; Bates, 1962; Bruchey, 1965; Cooke, 1964; Davis, 1965; Ernst, 1993; Graydon, 1979; Jones, 1992; Matson, 1987; Matson, 1989; Mitchell, 1962; Young, 1967

The Compromise of 1790:
Allen, 1990; Bender, 1987; Bickford and Bowling, 1989; Bowling, 1971; Bowling, 1991; Charles, 1961; Cooke, 1970; Davis, 1965; Ernst, 1968; Griswold, 1856; Jefferson, 1970; Kammen, 1982; Maclay, 1965; Miller, 1960; Mitchell, 1962; Pomerantz, 1938; Risjord, 1976; Young, 1967

The Problem of Manufactures: Appleby, 1984; Barck, 1966; Carman, 1933; Clark, 1916–28; Gilje and Rock, 1992; Monaghan and Lowenthal, 1943; Nelson, 1979; Pomerantz, 1938; Smith, 1989;

Strickland, 1971, Wilentz, 1984; Young, 1967

Scriptomania: Davis, 1965; East, 1938; Hurst, 1978; Jones, 1992; Kennedy, 1989; Matson, 1987; Matson, 1989; Miller, 1960; Nelson, 1979; Sobel, 1968; Young, 1967

Panic: Dangerfield, 1960; Davis, 1965; Ernst, 1993; Gilje, 1987; Harris, 1968; Jones, 1992; Matson, 1987; Matson, 1989; Mitchell, 1962; Pomerantz, 1938; Sobel, 1968; Sterling, 1979; Werner and Smith, 1991; Young, 1967

Under the Buttonwood Tree
Blau, 1973; Cochran, 1981; Davis, 1965; De Peyster, 1855; Friedman, 1990; Gardner, 1982; Geisst, 1997; Harris, 1968; Hemming, 1905; Kouwenhoven, 1953; Miller, 1960; Pomerantz, 1938; Scoville, 1863–66; Severini, 1981; Sobel, 1970; Sterling, 1979; Warshaw, 1929; Werner and Smith, 1991

CHAPTER 21:
REVOLUTIONS FOREIGN
AND DOMESTIC

Babb, 1954; Blau, 1973; Brillat-Savarin, 1926; Childs, 1940; Hickey, 1982; Hunt, 1988; James, 1962; Jones, 1927; Kennedy, 1989; Kouwenhoven, 1953; Pomerantz, 1938; Raddin, 1940; Raddin, 1953; Sheehan, 1955, Tarry, 1981; Watson, 1846; White, 1988; Young, 1967

Wars and Rumors of Wars: Albion, 1961; Blau, 1973; Davison, 1964; De Conde, 1966; Lampard, 1986; Miller, 1960; Perkins, 1967; Pomerantz, 1938; Young, 1967

Republican Spirits: Ammon, 1973; Bender, 1987; Blackmar, 1989; Blau, 1973; Booth, 1859; Bushman, 1992; Dangerfield, 1960; Durey, 1987; Durey, 1997; Ernst, 1968; Francis, 1866; Furman, 1937; Gilje, 1987; Gronowicz, 1987; Harlow, 1931; Hatcher, 1940; Hodges, 1986; Irwin, 1968; Kaestle, 1973; Kaminski, 1993; Link, 1942; Maclay, 1965; McClung, 1958;

Miller, 1960, Mohl, 1969; Monaghan, 1935; Mushkat, 1971; Paulson, 1953; Raddin, 1953; Rock, 1979; Rock, 1989; Scoville, 1863–66; Smith, 1989; Still, 1956; Wansey, 1796; Wecter, 1937; Wilentz, 1983; Wilentz, 1984; Young, 1967

The Democratic-Republicans: Blau, 1973; Hatcher, 1940; Kaminski, 1993; Miller, 1960; Kaestle, 1973; Kline, 1983; Link, 1942; Lomask, 1979–82; McClung, 1958; Mushkat, 1971; Pomerantz, 1938; Rock, 1979; Rock, 1989; Scoville, 1863–66; Young, 1967

Broken Heads: Blau, 1973; Combs, 1970; Dangerfield, 1960; Gilje, 1987; Hurst, 1978; Kennedy, 1989; Kline, 1983; Lomask, 1979–82; Miller, 1960; Mitchell, 1962; Monaghan, 1935; Pomerantz, 1938; Rorabaugh, 1986; Thorburn, 1845; Young, 1967

"As Good As Any Buggers": Blau, 1973; Gilje, 1987; Hodges, 1986; Pomerantz, 1938; Young, 1967

Black Cockades: Dangerfield, 1960; DeConde, 1966; Gilder, 1938; Gilje, 1987; Miller, 1960; Monaghan, 1935; Pomerantz, 1938; Shuffelton, 1985; Shulim, 1964; Smith, 1965

Federalists in Retreat: Blau, 1973; Bickford and Bowling, 1989; Bobbe, 1933; Dangerfield, 1960; Davis, 1955; DeConde, 1966; Ernst, 1968; Evans, 1952; Gilje, 1987; Hall, 1934; Hatcher, 1940; Hodges, 1986; Horton, 1939; Kaminski, 1993; Katz, 1963; Kline, 1983; Lomask, 1979–82; Miller, 1960; Mitchell, 1962; Monaghan, 1935; Mushkat, 1971; Pomerantz, 1938; Rock, 1979; Rock, 1989; Smith, 1965; Syrett, 1960; Wecter, 1937; Willis, 1967; Young, 1967

"Political Equality and the Corporation": Blackmar, 1989; Bobbe, 1933; Bowden, 1980; Chambers, 1963; D'Innocenzo, 1974; Fischer, 1965; Fox, 1965; Hartog, 1983; Hatcher, 1940; Hodges, 1986; Kline, 1983;

Lomask, 1979–82; Mitchell, 1962; Morgan, 1969; Pomerantz, 1938; Reynolds, 1984; Rock, 1979; Rock, 1989; Seybolt, 1918; Siry, 1990; Syrett and Cooke, 1960; Teaford, 1975; Willis, 1967; Young, 1967

Interview in Weehawken: Fox, 1965; Kline, 1983; Lomask, 1979–82; Mitchell, 1962; Slaughter, 1985; Syrett and Cooke, 1960

CHAPTER 22:
QUEEN OF COMMERCE,
JACK OF ALL TRADES

Albion, 1961; Bjork, 1967; Blau, 1973; De Conde, 1966; Haeger, 1991; Jaher, 1982; Lampard, 1986; Luke, 1953; Miller, 1960; Nelson, 1987; Nettels, 1962; Peters, 1984; Pomerantz, 1938; Sellers, 1991; Smelser, 1968; Still, 1956; White, 1991

Connections: Albion, 1961; Bjork, 1967; Booth, 1859; Bowling, 1990; Bushman, 1983; Cornog, 1988; Davis, 1965; Davison, 1964; Duffy, 1968–74; East, 1938; Ernst, 1968; Ernst, 1993; Frug, 1984; Hammond, 1957; Harlow, 1931; Hartog, 1983; Jaher, 1982; Kline, 1983; Lampard, 1986; Lockwood, 1976; Luke, 1953; Mohl, 1969; Peters, 1984; Pomerantz, 1938; Rosenberg, 1971; Scoville, 1863–66; Shaw, 1966; Smith, 1989; Syrett and Cooke, 1960; Teaford, 1975; White, 1987; Willis, 1967

Riding the Wave: Albion, 1961; Ellis, 1991; Haeger, 1991; Jaher, 1982; Scoville, 1863–66; Simon, 1978; Willis, 1967

Concomitants of Commerce: Albion, 1961; Allen, 1990; Blackmar, 1989; Blau, 1973; Bone, 1973; Evans, 1952; Hartog, 1983; Luke, 1953; Moehring, 1981; Nettels, 1962; Pomerantz, 1938; Rosenwaike, 1972; Still, 1956; Strickland, 1971; Wall, 1994; Wansey, 1796; Young, 1967

Down to the Sea in Ships: Haeger, 1991; Hanyan, 1972; Morrison, 1903; Philip, 1985; Porter, 1931; Whiteman, 1971

Capitalizing Crafts: Appleby, 1984; Barck, 1966; Blackmar, 1989; Carman, 1933; Davidson, 1977; Dyer, 1915; Fox, 1967; Gilje, 1989; Gilje and Rock, 1992; Gowans, 1976; Hartog, 1983; Lorillard, 1960; McClelland, 1990; Monaghan and Lowenthal, 1943; Nelson, 1979; Pomerantz, 1938; Rock, 1979; Rock, 1989; Rorabaugh, 1986; Smith, 1989; Strickland, 1971; Teaford, 1975; Wilentz, 1984; Young, 1967

The End of Slavery: Blackburn, 1988; Blackmar, 1989; Blau, 1973; Blockson, 1987; Bolster, 1997; Cohen, 1992; Countryman, 1981a; Cray, 1986; De Voe, 1970; Freeman, 1966; George, 1973; Gilje, 1987; Gilje and Rock, 1992; Gilje and Rock, 1994; Hanyan, 1972; Johnson, 1930; Kaplan, 1989; Kruger, 1985; Litwack, 1961; Main, 1973; McManus, 1961; McManus, 1966; Nash, 1988; Perlman, 1971; Pomerantz, 1938; Rock, 1979; Rock, 1994; Roediger, 1991; Rosenwaike, 1972; Strickland, 1971; Thorburn, 1845; Watson, 1846; White, 1986; White, 1988; White, 1989b; White, 1991; White, 1994; Wilder, 1994; Young, 1967; Zilversmit, 1967

Progress and Poverty: Blackmar, 1979; Blackmar, 1989; Cray, 1988a; Cray, 1988b; Gilje and Rock, 1992; Harlow, 1931; Kaestle, 1973; Lynd, 1964; Mohl, 1969; Pomerantz, 1938; Rock, 1979; Stansell, 1986; White, 1991; Wilkenfeld, 1978; Wilentz, 1984; Willis, 1967

CHAPTER 23:
THE ROAD TO CITY HALL

Blackmar, 1989; Blackmar, 1995; Duffy, 1968–74; Gilje and Rock, 1992; Goldman, 1997; Harlow, 1931; Kammen, 1982; Mitchill, 1807; Moehring, 1981; Mohl, 1969; Pomerantz, 1938; Rosenwaike, 1972; Schechter and Tripp, 1990; Teaford, 1975; Vail, 1954; Young, 1967

Shaking Hands with Death: Blau, 1973; Duffy, 1968–74;

Duffy, 1966; Harlow, 1931; Mohl, 1969; Pernick, 1972; Pomerantz, 1938; Raddin, 1940; Raddin, 1953; Robbins, 1964; Thorburn, 1845; Young, 1967,

Excrement and Frog-Spawn: Duffy, 1968–74; Goldman, 1997; Harlow, 1931; Janvier, 1894; Mack, 1947; Pomerantz, 1938; Smith, 1989

Water: Blake, 1956; Duffy, 1968–74; Ginsberg, 1968; Goldman, 1997; Hammond, 1957; Hanyan, 1972; Harlow, 1931; Hartog, 1983; Hunter, 1989; Kline, 1983; Lockwood, 1976; Moehring, 1981; Pomerantz, 1938; Reubens, 1957, 1958; Weidner, 1974; White, 1987

Fire: Duffy, 1968–74; Gilje and Rock, 1992; Ginsberg, 1968; Lockwood, 1976; Pomerantz, 1938

Poverty: Cray, 1988a; Mohl, 1969; Pomerantz, 1938

Up the River: Buckley, 1984; Cunliffe, 1968; Gilje, 1987; Hirsch, 1992; Janvier, 1984; Kraus, 1949; Lewis, 1963; Lewis, 1965; Miller, 1962; Miller, 1980; Miller, 1990; Mohl, 1970b; Monaghan and Lowenthal, 1943; Pickett, 1969; Pomerantz, 1938; Rienders, 1976; Rothman, 1990; Watson, 1846; White, 1991

Departments and Debts: Duffy, 1968–74; Pomerantz, 1938

City Hall: Blackmar, 1989; Cornog, 1988; Dunshee, 1952; Goldstone and Dalrymple, 1974; Gowans, 1976; Harris, 1966; Holloway, 1928; Janvier, 1894; Kennedy, 1989; Kouwenhoven, 1953; Lockwood, 1972; Lockwood, 1976; Pomerantz, 1938; Reynolds, 1984; Sloan and Anthony, 1968; Tauranac, 1979; Walsh, 1996; Whiffen and Koeper, 1981

CHAPTER 24:
PHILOSOPHES AND PHIL-
ANTHROPISTS

Baily, 1856; Batterberry, 1973; Blackmar, 1989; Bushman, 1983; Collins,

1946; Cook, 1887; Dangerfield, 1960; Evans, 1952; Gilder, 1938; Hartog, 1983; Henderson, 1982; Kennedy, 1989; Kouwenhoven, 1953; Luke, 1953; Lynd, 1964; Monaghan, 1935; Monaghan and Lowenthal, 1943; Pomerantz, 1938; Smith, 1989; Still, 1956; Thorburn, 1845

Parlor Society: Baily, 1856; Bayles, 1915; Blackmar, 1989; Blumin, 1989; Boydston, 1990; Bushman, 1983; Collins, 1946; Cook, 1887; Dudden, 1983; Ellis, 1997; Gilje and Rock, 1992; Hall, 1934; Horton, 1939; Kerber, 1989; Kouwenhoven, 1953, Lockwood, 1972; Luke, 1953; Lynd, 1964; Monaghan, 1935; Monaghan and Lowenthal, 1943; Morgan, 1969; Pomerantz, 1938; Raddin, 1954; Roche, 1971; Roediger, 1991; Scott, 1933; Smith, 1989; Still, 1956; Vail, 1954; Willis, 1967; Young, 1967

Learned Men and Cultivated Women: Axelrod, 1985; Basch, 1982; Bender, 1987; Blackmar, 1989; Blau, 1973; Blumin, 1989; Bobbe, 1933; Bottoroff, 1985; Canary, 1970; Clawson, 1989; Cronin, 1973; Cutler, 1972; Dangerfield, 1960; Duffy, 1966; Gilje and Rock, 1992; Griffin, 1960; Hall, 1934; Hanyan, 1972; Heale, 1968; Heale, 1971; Heale, 1973; Heale, 1976; Hopkins, 1975; Horton, 1939; Jaher, 1982; Jensen, 1968; Kann, 1991; Kerber, 1980; Krause, 1977; Leary, 1975; May, 1976; Nevins, 1969; Raddin, 1940; Nord, 1988; Norton, 1980; Philip, 1985; Pomerantz, 1938; Raddin, 1953; Robbins, 1964; Roche, 1971; Rosenberg, 1971; Rosenthal, 1985; Sterling, 1959; Still, 1956; Vail, 1954; Young, 1967

Cultivating Citizens: Gottesman, 1959; Harris, 1966; Hedges, 1965; Kerber, 1980; Miller, 1966; Mondello, 1968; Norton, 1980; Pomerantz, 1938; Rosenthal, 1985; Taft, 1947; Vail, 1954

"Active Exertions & Useful Improvements": Boylan,

1986; Brooks, 1944; Foster, 1960; Griffin, 1960; Hall, 1934; Heale, 1968; Heale, 1976; Kaestle, 1973; Kerber, 1980; Lomask, 1979–82; Miller, 1962; Mohl, 1969; Morais, 1934; Norton, 1980; Pomerantz, 1938; Rosenberg, 1971

"The Slow Process of Education & Religious Instruction": Allen, 1990; Coleman, 1974; Cutler, 1972; Dunlap, 1930; Elliot, 1985; Foster, 1960; Hatch, 1989; Heale, 1968; Hofstadter, 1965; Horton, 1939; Kaestle, 1973; Kierner, 1992; Koch, 1933; Mann, 1994; Matthews, 1991; Mohl, 1969; Mohl, 1970a; Mohl, 1970b; Monaghan and Lowenthal, 1943; Morais, 1934; Pickett, 1969; Pomerantz, 1938; Rock, 1989; Rosenberg, 1971; Siry, 1990; Thistlethwaite, 1959; Walters, 1990; Willis, 1967; Young, 1967

The Picture of New York: Mitchill, 1807

CHAPTER 25:
FROM CROWD TO CLASS

Duffy, 1968–74; Gilje, 1987; Hofstadter and Wallace, 1970; Monaghan, 1935; Pomerantz, 1938

Working Neighborhoods: Blackmar, 1989; Boyer, 1993; Foote, 1993; Freeman, 1966; Harlow, 1931; Gilje, 1994; Gilje, 1996a; Gilje, 1996b; Gilje and Rock, 1992; Kroessler, 1991; Kruger, 1985; Miller, 1990; Mohl, 1969; Pomerantz, 1938; Rock, 1979; Stiles, 1867–70; Wall, 1994; White, 1991; Wilder, 1994

Five Points: Blackmar, 1989; Dunshee, 1952; Gilje and Rock, 1992; Pomerantz, 1938; Rock, 1979

Turmoil in the Trades: Blackmar, 1989; Bolster, 1997; Durey, 1987; Durey, 1997; Gilje, 1989; Gilje and Rock, 1992; Hodges, 1986; Mohl, 1969; Monaghan and Lowenthal, 1943; Nord, 1988; Odell, 1927–49; Pomerantz, 1938; Raddin, 1940; Raddin, 1953; Rock, 1979; Rock, 1989; Stevens, 1913; Thorburn, 1845;

Wansey, 1796; Wilentz, 1984; Young, 1967

Infidels and Evangelicals: Andrews, 1985; Blau, 1973; Carwardine, 1972; Carwardine, 1978; Foner, 1976; Fruchtman, 1994; Gilje, 1987; Gilje and Rock, 1992; Gribbin, 1972; Griffin, 1960; Harlow, 1931; Hatch, 1989; Hawke, 1974; Keane, 1995; Koch, 1933; Kring, 1974; Morais, 1934; Newman, 1993; Pomerantz, 1938; Rock, 1989; Schultz, 1995; Sellers, 1928; Siry, 1990; Walters, 1990; Wilentz, 1984; Young, 1967

Out from the Back of the Church: Blockson, 1987; Bolster, 1997; Cohen, 1992; Countryman, 1981a; Cray, 1986; Earle, 1938; Freeman, 1966; George, 1973; Gilje and Rock, 1992; Gravely, 1983; Hardie, 1827; Harlow, 1931; Hatch, 1989; Johnson, 1930; Jordan, 1968 ; Kaplan, 1989; Kruger, 1985; McManus, 1966; Nash, 1988; Perlman, 1971; Pomerantz, 1938; Roff, 1986; Rosenwaike, 1972; Sellers, 1928; Sernett, 1975; Stansell, 1986; Strickland, 1971; Thorburn, 1845; Walker, 1993; White, 1986; White, 1988; White, 1989a; White, 1989b; White, 1991; White, 1994; Wilder, 1994; Wilentz, 1984

"Irishtown": Doyle, 1981; Ellis, 1997; Gilje, 1987; Gilje, 1996a; Gilje and Rock, 1992; Greene, 1987; Hagan, 1923; Haines, 1829; Hartfield, 1993; Meehan, 1906; Mohl, 1969; Otter, 1995; Pomerantz, 1938; Postgate, 1932; Pratt, 1967; Rock, 1989; Smith, 1989; Walsh, 1996; Wilentz, 1984

"Honest Folks in the Pit": Blau, 1973; Blackmar, 1989; Bolster, 1997; Brooks, 1944; Brown and Ment, 1980; Buckley, 1984; Canary, 1970; Culhane, 1990; De Voe, 1970; Dudden, 1994; Dunlap, 1930; Ellis, 1979; Gilje and Rock, 1992; Grimsted, 1968; Harlow, 1931; Henderson, 1982; Johnson, 1975; Johnson, 1985; Kaestle, 1973; Kasson, 1990; Leary, 1948; Leary, 1975; Levine, 1988; Monaghan and Lowenthal,

1943; Morgan, 1969; Odell, 1927–49; Otter, 1995; Pomerantz, 1938; Pye, 1991; Rock, 1979; Rock, 1989; Silverman, 1976; Smith, 1989; Stiles, 1867–70; Taft, 1947; Thorburn, 1845; Vail, 1956; White, 1991; Wilentz, 1984

"The Life of a Citizen in the Hands of a Woman": Arnold, 1989; Blackmar, 1979; Blackmar, 1989; Bolster, 1997; Boydston, 1990; Davidson, 1977; De Voe, 1970; Dudden, 1994; Franchot, 1985; Gilje, 1987; Gilje and Rock, 1992; Harlow, 1931; Hone, 1927; Kerber, 1980; Monaghan and Lowenthal, 1943; Nash, 1988; Norton, 1980; Pomerantz, 1938; Stansell, 1986; Wall, 1994

CHAPTER 26:
WAR AND PEACE

Adams, 1947; Cook, 1887; Ellis, 1997; Gilje, 1987; Haeger, 1991; Perkins, 1961; Smelser, 1968; Tchen, 1990; W.P.A., 1941

O Grab Me: Cray, 1988a; Daitsman, 1963; Folsom, 1991; Gilje, 1987; Gilje and Rock, 1992; Goldstone and Dalrymple, 1974; Guernsey, 1889; Haeger, 1991; Hodges, 1986; Irwin, 1968; Janvier, 1894; Kaplan, 1987; Mohl, 1969; Nettels, 1962; Perkins, 1961; Pomerantz, 1938; Schneider, 1938–41; Smelser, 1968; Spivak, 1979; Still, 1956; Tauranac, 1979

"Bread or Work": Folsom, 1991; Gilje and Rock, 1992; Schneider, 1938–41

Unlawful Combinations and Riotous Assemblies: Boydston, 1990; Carwardine, 1972; Carwardine, 1978; Ernst, 1968; Fox, 1965; Gilje, 1987; Gilje and Rock, 1992; Greene, 1987; Hagan, 1923; Haines, 1829; Postgate, 1932; Rock, 1989; Stevens, 1913; Still, 1956; Walsh, 1996; Wilentz, 1984; W.P.A., 1941

"Much Exultation Among the Federalists": Alexander, 1969; Bayles, 1915; Bender, 1987; Bobbe, 1933; Cray, 1988a; Dangerfield, 1960; D'Innocenzo, 1974; Ernst, 1968; Fischer, 1965; Fox,

1965; Hammond, 1957; Hodges, 1986; Irwin, 1968; July, 1951; Mohl, 1969; Mushkat, 1971; Rock, 1989; Strum, 1981

Diedrich Knickerbocker: Adkins, 1930; Batterberry, 1973; Bayles, 1915; Bender, 1987; Black, 1974; Bowden, 1980; Bowden, 1981; Brooks, 1944; Buckley, 1984; Callow, 1967; Conrad, 1984; Cooper, 1968; Evans, 1952; Hedges, 1965; Herold, 1926; Irving, 1965; Leary, 1975; Marx, 1983; Myers, 1976; O'Connell, 1994; Paulding, 1867; Pomerantz, 1938; Reynolds, 1984; Seelye, 1991; Taft, 1947; Wilson, 1976

Internal Improvements: Allen, 1993; Blackmar, 1989; Blackmar, 1995; Bobbe, 1933; Brown, 1964; Cohen and Augustyn, 1997; Dunshee, 1952; Fischer, 1965; Fox, 1965; Gilje, 1987; Hanyan, 1972; Hartog, 1983; Irving, 1984; Irwin, 1968; Janvier, 1894; July, 1951; Koolhaas, 1978; Lockwood, 1976; Miller, 1962; Miller, 1990; Mintz, 1970; Mushkat, 1971; Perkins, 1961; Plunz, 1990; Pound, 1975; Reps, 1965; Rock, 1989; Shanor, 1988; Shaw, 1966; Smelser, 1968; Sutcliffe, 1981; Taylor, 1992; Van Leeuwen, 1988; White, 1987

The Mayor Who Would Be President: Alexander, 1969; Brown, 1964; Ernst, 1968; Fischer, 1965; Fox, 1965; Gilje, 1987; Guernsey, 1889; Hammond, 1957; Hanyan, 1972; Irwin, 1968; July, 1951; Mintz, 1970; Mushkat, 1971; Nevins, 1922; Perkins, 1961; Prescott and Zimmerman, 1972; Rock, 1989; Sellers, 1991; Siry, 1990; Smelser, 1968; W.P.A., 1941

The War of 1812: Bobbe, 1933; Bolster, 1997; Booth, 1859; Brown, 1964; Cleveland, 1985; Ernst, 1968; Freeman, 1966; Guernsey, 1889; Haeger, 1991; Hammond, 1957; Horsman, 1969; Irwin, 1968; Jonas, 1982; Mohl, 1969; Morrison, 1909; Rock, 1989; Sellers, 1991; Smelser, 1968; Still, 1956; Wall, 1994; Walsh, 1996; Werner, 1991; White, 1991; Wilder, 1994; W.P.A., 1941

Peace! Peace! Peace!: Bayles, 1915; Sellers, 1991; Still, 1956

CHAPTER 27:
THE CANAL ERA

Albion, 1939; Gilchrist, 1967; Lindstrom, 1988; Sellers, 1991

The Wedding of the Waters: Carp, 1986; Gunn, 1988; Hanyan, 1972; Miller, 1962; Seelye, 1991; Shaw, 1966; Shaw, 1990; Siry, 1990; Stone, 1825; Wilentz, 1984

Under Steam and Sail: Albion, 1939; Browder, 1985; Condit, 1980–81; Coombe, 1991; Cudahy, 1990; Flexner, 1964; Haeger, 1991; Hartog, 1983; Horwitz, 1977; Howard, 1984; Hoyt, 1962; Hutchins, 1941; Lane, 1942; Morrison, 1909; Patterson, 1989; Philip, 1985; Pred, 1973; Seelye, 1991; Sellers, 1991; Smith, 1989; Tchen, 1992; Weld, 1950

Emporium: Albion, 1939; Bayles, 1915; Bixby, 1972; Blumin, 1989; Blunt, 1817; Brooks Brothers, 1918; Brooks Brothers, 1943; Collins, 1934; Cooper, 1963; De Voe, 1970; Devorkin, 1987; Dodge, 1987; Dunshee, 1952; Evans, 1952; Gilder, 1938; Gilje and Rock, 1992; Greene, 1834; Greene, 1837; Gunn, 1988; Kidwell, 1974; Larkin, 1988; Lockwood, 1976; Lowitt, 1954; Lurkis, 1982; McKay, 1934; Moehring, 1981; Pomerantz, 1938; Rosebrock, 1975; Severini, 1981; Shumway, 1975; Somerville, 1983; Stott, 1990; Stotz, 1948; Thomas, 1967; W.P.A., 1941; Wyatt-Brown, 1969

The Word from Manhattan: Albion, 1939; Barth, 1982; Bixby, 1972; Blunt, 1817; Brown, 1971; Charvat, 1959; Crouthamel, 1989; Exman, 1965; Greene, 1837; Lehmann-Haupt, 1951; Mushkat, 1971; Overton, 1925; Pred, 1973; Sarna, 1981; Schiller, 1980; Schudson, 1978; Sobel, 1965; Tebbel, 1972–81

Industrial Revolutions: Albion, 1939; American Sugar, 1918; Blunt, 1817;

Clark, 1916–28; Coombe, 1991; Exman, 1965; Gilje and Rock, 1992; Haswell, 1896; Morrison, 1909; Porter and Livesay, 1971; Pred, 1966; Pred, 1972; Sachs, 1988; Stansell, 1986; Stott, 1990; Whiteman, 1971; Wilentz, 1984

Wall Street: Albion, 1939; Carosso, 1970; Cleveland, 1985; Fox, 1992; Gilchrist, 1967; Gunn, 1988; Haeger, 1981; Haeger, 1991; Hammond, 1957; Hidy, 1949; Jaher, 1982; Jenks, 1927; Keller, 1963; Levinson, 1961; Miller, 1962; Morrison, 1973; Myers, 1931; Nevins, 1934; Olmstead, 1976; Porter, 1931; Rezneck, 1968; Rothbard, 1962; Scoville, 1863–66; Sellers, 1991; Severini, 1981; Sobel, 1975; Sylla, 1967; Tucker, 1991; Werner and Smith, 1991; Wilkins, 1989; Ziegler, 1988

Land Lords: Blackmar, 1989; Boyer, 1993; Brown, 1971; Byard, 1989; Chapin, 1917; Cooke, 1995; Cowles, 1979; Fox, 1965; Gardner, 1994; Garrett, 1978; Gates, 1981; Haeger, 1991; Haswell, 1896; Limpus, 1940; Lockwood, 1976; Miller, 1990; Moehring, 1981; Parton, 1858; Patterson, 1935; Pessen, 1973; Porter, 1931; Rosenzweig and Blackmar, 1992; Shachtman, 1991; Simon, 1978; Sinclair, 1984; Tauranac, 1985; Trager, 1987; Wecter, 1937

On the Heights of Brooklyn: Armbruster, 1929; Cooke, 1995; Everdell and MacKay, 1973; Jackson, 1985; Lancaster, 1961; Snyder-Grenier, 1996; Stiles, 1867–70; Weld, 1938
"The London of the New World": Blunt, 1817; Conkin, 1980; Fox, 1992; Gilchrist, 1967; Hartog, 1983; Hodges, 1986; Moehring, 1981; Nord, 1984; Stiles, 1867–70; Trollope, 1832

CHAPTER 28:
THE MEDICI OF THE REPUBLIC

Adelman, 1990; Albion, 1939; Amory, 1960; Blumin, 1989; Brooks, 1944; Buckley, 1984; Cunliffe, 1976;

Dayton, 1882; Garrett, 1978; Hardie, 1827; Haswell, 1896; Henderson, 1973; Henderson, 1986; Jaher, 1982; Jentz, 1977; John, 1990; Kasson, 1990; Lang, 1922; Miller, 1967; Stankowski, 1978; Trollope, 1832; Weinbaum, 1979; Wilentz, 1984; Wyatt-Brown, 1969

E Pluribus Unum: Banner, 1983; Bender, 1993; Blackmar, 1989; Boydston, 1990; Churchill, 1970; Danforth, 1974; Dayton, 1882; Gilder, 1938; Greene, 1837; Grinstein, 1945; Hall, 1992; Harvey, 1995; Kasson, 1990; Kidwell, 1974; Landau, 1982; Lindsley, 1984; Lockwood, 1972; Lockwood, 1976; Milbank, 1989; Miller, 1962; Moehring, 1981; Pessen, 1972; Pessen, 1973; Ryan, 1990; Shank, 1956; Taylor, 1966; Trollope, 1832; Wall, 1994; Whiteman, 1971; Wilentz, 1984

Spheres of Influence: Blackmar, 1989; Blumin, 1989; Boydston, 1990; Kasson, 1990; Larkin, 1988; Lockwood, 1976; Wall, 1994

The Domestication of Christmas: Blackmar, 1989; Haswell, 1896; Moore, 1818; Nissenbaum, 1996; Patterson, 1935; Patterson, 1956

Parlor Business: Blackmar, 1989; Bushman, 1993; Dudden, 1983; Gowans, 1976; Halttunen, 1982; Kasson, 1990; Katzman, 1978; Ryan, 1990; Stott, 1990

True Republicans: Albion, 1939; Colden, 1825; Cooper, 1963; Gilder, 1938; Haswell, 1896; Huxtable, 1964; Jenkins, 1992; Kennedy, 1985; Kennedy, 1989; Landau, 1982; Mack, 1949; Nathan, 1965; Newton, 1942; Nolan, 1934; Pierson, 1938; Somkin, 1967

Civic Patrons: Auchincloss, 1989; Ayres, 1993; Bender, 1987; Brown, 1971; Callow, 1967; Cole, 1994; Foshay, 1990; Howat, 1972; Leary, 1975; Lees, 1985; Miller, 1966; Miller, 1973; Myers, 1974; Rebora, 1990; Staiti

and Reynolds, 1982; Taylor, 1992; Tebbel, 1972–81

Nature and Nostalgia: Auchincloss, 1989; Ayres, 1993; Beard, 1953; Bender, 1987; Brooks, 1944; Bryant, Sands and Verplanck, 1828–30; Buckley, 1984; Callow, 1967; Colden, 1825; Gates, 1987; Hills, 1974; July, 1951; Landy, 1970; Leary, 1975; Lees, 1985; Lowenthal, 1976; Myers, 1987; Pierson, 1938; Pilat, 1941; Shank, 1956

CHAPTER 29:
WORKING QUARTERS

Gilje, 1987; Gilje and Rock, 1992; Nissenbaum, 1996

Working Quarters: Blackmar, 1989; Blumin, 1989; Boydston, 1990; Boyer, 1993; Browder, 1985; Buckley, 1984; Bushman, 1993; Gardner, 1979; Gilje and Rock, 1992; Haswell, 1896; Hodges, 1982; Hodges, 1986; Jentz, 1977; Larkin, 1988; Mack, 1949; Pernicone, 1973; Stiles, 1867–70; Stott, 1990; Tchen, 1990; Wall, 1994; Weld, 1950; Weld, 1938; Wilentz, 1984

Women at Work: Blackmar, 1989; Boydston, 1990; Dudden, 1983; Gilje, 1987; Gilje and Rock, 1992; Hartog, 1983; Ryan, 1990; Stansell, 1986; Stott, 1990; Wall, 1994

"the vilest rabble, black & white, mixt together": Blackmar, 1989; Bolster, 1997; Connolly, 1977; Foote, 1993; Freeman, 1966; Gilje, 1987; Haswell, 1896; Hoffman, 1976; Kroessler, 1991; Miller, 1985; Richards, 1970; Rosenberg, 1962; Rosenzweig and Blackmar, 1992; Walker, 1993; Weld, 1938; White, 1991

They Gathered at the River: Carwardine, 1972; Dolan, 1975; Farley, 1908; Gilje, 1987; Grinstein, 1945; Haswell, 1896; Hatch, 1989; Johnson, 1994; Mack, 1949; McCadden, 1969; Smith-Rosenberg, 1971; Stiles, 1867–70; Swift, 1989; Weld, 1950; Weld, 1938; Whiteman, 1971; Wilentz, 1984

On the Town: Blackmar,

1989; Buckley, 1984; Gilfoyle, 1992; Hill, 1992; Whiteaker, 1977

"Let's Liquor": Blumin, 1989; Browder, 1985; Gilje and Rock, 1992; Jentz, 1977; Miller, 1985; Otter, 1995; Pernicone, 1973; Rock, 1979; Rorabaugh, 1979; Sellers, 1991; Stiles, 1867–70; Stott, 1990; Weld, 1938; Wilentz, 1984

On the Bowery: Adelman, 1990; Buckley, 1984; De Voe, 1970; Dizikes, 1993; Gilfoyle, 1992; Gilje, 1987; Gilje and Rock, 1992; Harlow, 1931; Haswell, 1896; Otter, 1995; Shank, 1956; Stiles, 1867–70; Wilentz, 1984

Jump Jim Crow: Blunt, 1817; Buckley, 1984; Foote, 1993; Garrett, 1978; Gilje, 1987; Harlow, 1931; Harris, 1968; Jentz, 1977; Levine, 1988; Lott, 1993; Marshall, 1958; McArthur, 1984; Odell, 1927–49; Roediger, 1991; Saxton, 1990; Thompson, 1997; Toll, 1976

Running with the Machine: Asbury, 1928; Buckley, 1984; Calhoun, 1973; Dayton, 1882; Gilje, 1987; Ginsberg, 1968; Haswell, 1896; Hodges, 1982; Jentz, 1977; Limpus, 1940; Morrison, 1909; Weinbaum, 1979; Wilentz, 1984

CHAPTER 30:
REFORMS AND REVIVALS

Abramovitz, 1988; Blunt, 1817; Boyer, 1978; Bridges, 1984; Cray, 1988; Griffin, 1960; Heale, 1971; Jaher, 1982; Katz, 1986; Klips, 1980; Lubove, 1968; Miller, 1985; Mohl, 1971; Pascu, 1980; Pickett, 1969; Rothman, 1971; Rothman, 1989; Sellers, 1991; Smith-Rosenberg, 1971; Stiles, 1867–70; Weinbaum, 1979

Urban Missionaries: Berg, 1978; Blackmar, 1989; Blumin, 1989; Davis, 1979; Foster, 1960; Fowler, 1981; Ginzberg, 1990; Jackman, 1964; Jentz, 1977; Johnson and Wilentz, 1994; Mohl, 1971; Sellers, 1991; Smith-Rosenberg, 1971; Whiteaker, 1977; Wilentz, 1984; Wyatt-Brown, 1969

Spreading the Good News: Blunt, 1817; Foster, 1960; Grinstein, 1945; Hatch, 1989; Kaestle, 1973; Katz, 1986; Lehmann-Haupt, 1951; Miller, 1962; Nord, 1984; Smith-Rosenberg, 1971; Stiles, 1867–70; Tebbel, 1972–81; Weld, 1938; Wyatt-Brown, 1969

Off to School: Bender, 1987; Blumin, 1989; Blunt, 1817; Boyer, 1978; Boylan, 1988; Bridges, 1984; Buetow, 1970; Cooke, 1995; Fowler, 1981; Freeman, 1966; Harris, 1968; Heale, 1971; Jaher, 1982; Kaestle, 1983; Kaestle, 1973; Katz, 1986; Lowitt, 1954; Mohl, 1971; Pascu, 1980; Pettit, 1991; Ravitch, 1974; Smith-Rosenberg, 1971; Stiles, 1867–70; Tyack, 1974; Walker, 1993; Weld, 1938; Wilentz, 1984

Juvenile Delinquents: Heale, 1971; Lewis, 1965; Pickett, 1969; Pierson, 1938; Rothman, 1989; Rothman, 1971

The Bellevue Institution: Blackmar, 1989; Dowling, 1982; Gilje, 1996; Grinstein, 1945; Hardie, 1824; Hardie, 1827; Haswell, 1896; Heale, 1971; Katz, 1986; Klips, 1980; Lewis, 1965; Marx, 1983; Masur, 1989; Moehring, 1981; Mohl, 1971; O'Grady, 1930; Rosenberg, 1987; Rothman, 1971; Rothman, 1989; Russell, 1945; Schneider, 1938–41; Starr, 1957; Sutton, 1874; Weinbaum, 1979; Whiteman, 1971

On to Blackwell's Island: Bender, 1987; Hardie, 1827; Klips, 1980; Pierson, 1938

CHAPTER 31:
THE PRESS OF
DEMOCRACY

Bender, 1987; Brooks, 1944; Dickinson, 1992; Eckhardt, 1984; Fruchtman, 1994; Ginzberg, 1994; Jentz, 1977; John, 1990; Keane, 1995; Osborne, 1966; Pascu, 1980; Pessen, 1967; Rosenberg, 1962; Ryan, 1990; Saxton, 1990; Smith-Rosenberg, 1971; Stansell, 1986; Tucher, 1994; Wilentz, 1984

Aristocrats and Democrats: Gilje, 1996; Jaher, 1982;

Peterson, 1966; Pomerantz, 1938; Sellers, 1991; Strum, 1981; Wilentz, 1984; Williamson, 1960

Tammany Democracy: Allen, 1993; Blackmar, 1989; Bridges, 1984; Brunson, 1989; Danforth, 1974; Fox, 1965; Freeman, 1966; Gelfand, 1975; Gunn, 1988; Haswell, 1896; Hershkowitz, 1960; Jaher, 1982; July, 1951; Kaestle, 1983; Moehring, 1981; Mushkat, 1971; Pessen, 1973; Peterson, 1966; Pickett, 1969; Roediger, 1991; Sellers, 1991; Stott, 1990; Wallace, 1968; Werner, 1928; Wilentz, 1984

Workers and "Bosses": Albion, 1939; Blackmar, 1989; Blumin, 1989; Boydston, 1990; Conkin, 1980; Gilje, 1987; Gilje and Rock, 1992; Lehmann-Haupt, 1951; Pessen, 1967; Roediger, 1991; Stansell, 1986; Stevens, 1913; Stott, 1990; Wilentz, 1984

Workingmen's Advocates: Blackmar, 1989; Boydston, 1990; Bridges, 1984; Brown, 1971; Coleman, 1974; Ernst, 1949; Gilchrist, 1967; Ginzberg, 1994; Gorelick, 1981; Hartog, 1983; Hodges, 1982; Hodges, 1986; Hofstadter, 1943; Hugins, 1960; Jentz, 1977; Kaestle, 1973; Mohl, 1971; Pascu, 1980; Pessen, 1967; Roediger, 1991; Saxton, 1990; Sellers, 1991; Teaford, 1975; Tucher, 1994; Tyack, 1974; Wilentz, 1984

The Sun Shines for All: Barth, 1982; Bender, 1987; Bergmann, 1995; Blunt, 1817; Brown, 1971; Buckley, 1984; Butler, 1992; Crouthamel, 1989; Henkin, 1995; Hershkowitz, 1960; Lott, 1993; Reynolds, 1988; Richards, 1970; Saxton, 1990; Schiller, 1980; Schudson, 1978; Stansell, 1986; Stott, 1990; Tucher, 1994; Weinbaum, 1979; Whitby, 1984; Wilentz, 1984

Exhilarating the Breakfast Table: Banner, 1983; Bergmann, 1995; Crouthamel, 1989; Haswell, 1896; Juergens, 1966; Kluger, 1986; Mushkat, 1971; Tucher, 1994

A Glance At New York: Greene, 1837; Marx, 1983

CHAPTER 32:
THE DESTROYING DEMON
OF DEBAUCHERY

Carwardine, 1972; Ginzberg, 1990; Hardman, 1987; Hatch, 1989; Howe, 1971; Johnson and Wilentz, 1994; Mohl, 1971; Sellers, 1991; Smith-Rosenberg, 1971; Stansell and Wilentz, 1994; Swerdlow, 1976; Thomas, 1989; Wall, 1994; Whiteaker, 1977; Wyatt-Brown, 1969

Onward, Christian Soldiers: Bender, 1987; Blumin, 1989; Bridges, 1984; Foster, 1960; Fowler, 1981; Gilje and Rock, 1992; Handy, 1987; Miller, 1962; Nichols, 1963; Nord, 1984; Patterson, 1956; Smith-Rosenberg, 1971; Swift, 1989

Spirit versus Spirits: Bernstein, 1990; Blackmar, 1989; Blumin, 1989; Boyer, 1978; Foshay, 1990; Mohl, 1971; Pickett, 1969; Rorabaugh, 1979; Sellers, 1991; Stiles, 1867–70; Tyrrell, 1979; Weld, 1938; Weld, 1950; Wilentz, 1984; Wyatt-Brown, 1969

"The Destroying Demon of Debauchery": Berg, 1978; Brooks, 1944; Bushman, 1993; Cohen, 1992; Gilfoyle, 1992; Jentz, 1977; Larkin, 1988; Le Duc, 1939; Nissenbaum, 1980; Otter, 1995; Pivar, 1973; Roediger, 1991; Rothman, 1989; Ryan, 1990; Sellers, 1991; Smith-Rosenberg, 1983; Stansell, 1986; Whiteaker, 1977; Wyatt-Brown, 1969

"Is it not more likely the work of a woman?": Berg, 1978; Buckley, 1984; Cohen, 1992; Crouthamel, 1989; Gilfoyle, 1992; Greene, 1834; Hill, 1992; Kluger, 1986; Schiller, 1980; Srebnick, 1995; Stansell, 1986; Tucher, 1994

CHAPTER 33:
WHITE, GREEN, AND
BLACK

The Coming of the Green: Buetow, 1970; Cohalan, 1983; Cooke, 1995; Dolan, 1975; Ernst, 1949; Gilje,

1996; Haswell, 1896; Hodges, 1986; McCadden, 1969; Miller, 1985; O'Connor, 1989; Ravitch, 1974; Ridge, 1988; Roediger, 1991; Stiles, 1867–70; Tebbel, 1972–81; Walsh, 1996

"Popery ought always to be loathed and execrated": Billington, 1938; Dickinson, 1992; Gilje, 1987; Gilje, 1996; Hershkowitz, 1960; Jentz, 1977; Knobel, 1986; Ravitch, 1974; Scisco, 1901; Weld, 1950; Wyatt-Brown, 1969

"Damned Irish!": Feldberg, 1980; Fox, 1965; Gilje, 1987; Gilje, 1996; Grimsted, 1972; Hershkowitz, 1960; Litwack, 1961; Prince, 1985; Weinbaum, 1979; Werner, 1986

Life Along the Color Line: Blackmar, 1989; Bolster, 1997; Boylan, 1988; Brown, 1971; Buckley, 1984; Coleman, 1982; Curry, 1981; Dann, 1971; Foote, 1993; Freeman, 1966; Garrett, 1978; George, 1973; Gilfoyle, 1992; Gilje, 1987; Gilje and Rock, 1992; Harris, 1968; Haswell, 1896; Hershkowitz, 1960; Hodges, 1982; Hodges, 1986; Ignatiev, 1995; Kaestle, 1973; Kaestle, 1983; Kerber, 1967; Litwack, 1961; Lowitt, 1954; Ottley and Weatherby, 1967; Painter, 1996; Pascu, 1980; Richards, 1991; Sellers, 1991; Seyfried, 1995; Stiles, 1867–70; Swift, 1989; Walker, 1993; Weinbaum, 1979; Werner, 1986; Wilentz, 1984; Wilson, 1991

"Crush this hydra in the bud": Carter, 1964; Feldberg, 1980; Gilje, 1987; Grimsted, 1972; Hardman, 1987; Kerber, 1967; Prince, 1985; Quarles, 1969; Ratner, 1968; Richards, 1970; Sellers, 1991; Sorin, 1978; Swift, 1989; Weinbaum, 1979; Werner, 1986; Wyatt-Brown, 1969

White Slaves and "Smoked Irish": Blackmar, 1989; Bolster, 1997; Cooper, 1969; Gilje, 1987; Hodges, 1986; Ignatiev, 1995; Jentz, 1981; Litwack, 1961; Lott, 1993; Otter, 1995; Roediger, 1991; Saxton, 1990; Sellers, 1991;

Swift, 1989; Wall, 1994

"He called my Saviour a nigger!": Feldberg, 1980; Gilfoyle, 1992; Gilje, 1987; Grimsted, 1972; Kerber, 1967; Prince, 1985; Ratner, 1968; Richards, 1970; Swift, 1989; Weinbaum, 1979; Wyatt-Brown, 1969

The Railroad that Ran Underground: Blockson, 1994; Freeman, 1966; Gilje, 1987; Gilje and Rock, 1992

CHAPTER 34:
RAIL BOOM

Blunt, 1817; Condit, 1980–81; Dayton, 1882; Dodge, 1987; Dolan, 1975; Dunshee, 1952; Fox, 1992; Garmey, 1984; Gates, 1981; Greene, 1837; Gunn, 1988; Haeger, 1991; Harlow, 1931; Haswell, 1896; Hershkowitz, 1960; Hugins, 1960; Jackson, 1985; Jaher, 1982; Kroessler, 1991; Lockwood, 1976; Mack, 1949; Marx, 1983; Miller, 1990; Moehring, 1981; Pred, 1980; Saint, 1992; Schaeffer, 1975; Sellers, 1991; Stiles, 1867–70; Stoff, 1989; Stott, 1990; Taylor, 1966; Trollope, 1832; Wall, 1994

Smokestacks and Speculators: Browder, 1985; Chandler, 1977; Clark, 1916–28; Condit, 1980–81; Coombe, 1991; Greene, 1834; Gunn, 1988; Hammond, 1957; Haswell, 1896; Hidy, 1949; Jaher, 1982; Perret, 1982; Sobel, 1965; Stott, 1990; Werner and Smith, 1991; Whiteman, 1971; Ziegler, 1988

Pioneers of Capital: Albion, 1939; Crouthamel, 1989; Fox, 1965; Haeger, 1981; Hammond, 1957; Hershkowitz, 1960; Jaher, 1982; July, 1951; Miller, 1967; Mushkat, 1971; Remini, 1988; Sellers, 1991; Wilentz, 1984; Wilkins, 1989; Zelizer, 1979; Ziegler, 1988

Bank War: Brown, 1971; Callow, 1967; Cleveland, 1985; Crouthamel, 1989; Fox, 1965; Gatell, 1966; Gilchrist, 1967; Gunn, 1988; Haeger, 1981; Hammond, 1957; Haswell, 1896; Hershkowitz, 1960;

Huxtable, 1964; July, 1951; McFaul, 1972; Miller, 1962; Moehring, 1981; Newton, 1942; Remini, 1988; Sellers, 1991; Severini, 1981; Sushka, 1976; Temin, 1969

Bank Riot: Albion, 1939; Brooks, 1944; Brown, 1971; Clark, 1916–28; Danforth, 1974; Fox, 1965; Gilje, 1996; Hammond, 1957; Jaher, 1982; July, 1951; Kaplan, 1996; Mushkat, 1971; Weinbaum, 1979; Wilentz, 1984

City Builders: Albion, 1939; Bender, 1993; Blackmar, 1989; Blunt, 1817; Boyer, 1993; Brooks, 1944; Buckley, 1984; Bushman, 1993; Cooke, 1995; Dayton, 1882; Fox, 1965; Garmey, 1984; Gilder, 1938; Greene, 1837; Gunn, 1988; Haeger, 1991; Harlow, 1931; Haswell, 1896; Landau, 1982; Lockwood, 1976; Mack, 1949; McGrane, 1924; Miller, 1962; Moehring, 1981; Patterson, 1935; Rosenwaike, 1972; Rosenzweig and Blackmar, 1992; Saint, 1992; Severini, 1981; Simon, 1978; Still, 1982; Stott, 1990; Taylor, 1966; Thompson, 1946; Trager, 1987; Wall, 1994; Werner and Smith, 1991

Second City: Conklin, 1983; Cudahy, 1990; Gardner, 1979; Hall, 1898; Hartog, 1983; Hershkowitz, 1960; Hoffman, 1976; Kroessler, 1991; Landesman, 1977; Patterson, 1989; Rainone, 1985; Schoenebaum, 1977; Snyder-Grenier, 1996; Stankowski, 1978; Stiles, 1867–70; Weld, 1938; Weld, 1950

Good Times: Amory, 1960; Banner, 1983; Blumin, 1989; Buckley, 1984; Bushman, 1993; Dizikes, 1993; Fairfield, 1873; Garrett, 1978; Haswell, 1896; Hershkowitz, 1960; Pessen, 1972; Pessen, 1973; Rorabaugh, 1979; Scoville, 1863–66; Thompson, 1946; Townsend, 1936; Wecter, 1937

CHAPTER 35:
FILTH, FEVER, WATER, FIRE

Armstrong, 1976; Blackmar, 1989; Corey, 1994; Gilje and Rock, 1992; Ginsberg, 1968;

Goldman, 1997; Hartog, 1983; Haswell, 1896; Hodges, 1982; Hodges, 1986; Limpus, 1940; Lockwood, 1976; Moehring, 1981; Smith-Rosenberg, 1971; Wall, 1994; W.P.A., 1938b

Cholera: Blackmar, 1989; Brown, 1971; Dolan, 1975; Duffy, 1968–74; Foote, 1993; Freeman, 1966; Hershkowitz, 1960; Hoyt, 1962; Klips, 1980; Larkin, 1988; McCadden, 1969; Moehring, 1981; Nissenbaum, 1980; Plunz, 1990; Pred, 1973; Rosenberg, 1962; Smith-Rosenberg, 1971; Sokolow, 1983; Starr, 1957; Tebbel, 1972–81; Wilentz, 1984; Wyatt-Brown, 1969

Water: Blake, 1956; Calhoun, 1973; Costello, 1887; Gilje and Rock, 1992; Ginsberg, 1968; Hartog, 1983; Lockwood, 1976; Miller, 1990; Moehring, 1981; Plunz, 1990; Rosenberg, 1962; Weidner, 1974

Fire: Calhoun, 1973; Costello, 1887; Foshay, 1990; Ginsberg, 1968; Ginsberg, 1971; Haswell, 1896; Hodges, 1982; Miller, 1962; Mohr, 1973; Stiles, 1867–70; Werner and Smith, 1991; Wilentz, 1984

Phoenix: Blackmar, 1989; Buckley, 1984; Gunn, 1988; Haswell, 1896; Lockwood, 1976; Miller, 1962; Moehring, 1981; Plunz, 1990; Rosebrock, 1975; Severini, 1981; Spann, 1986b; W.P.A., 1938b

Fevered Finance: Briggs, 1839; Cleveland, 1985; Gatell, 1966; Gunn, 1988; Hammond, 1957; McGrane, 1924; Mushkat, 1971; Sellers, 1991; Werner and Smith, 1991

CHAPTER 36:
THE PANIC OF 1837

Boydston, 1990; Cleveland, 1985; Commons, 1910–11; Gilje, 1987; Hammond, 1957; Hershkowitz, 1960; Hofstadter, 1943; Lewis, 1965; Morrison, 1909; Mushkat, 1971; Pessen, 1967; Richards, 1970; Roediger, 1991; Sellers, 1991; Stansell, 1986; Stott,

1990; Tucher, 1994; Walkowitz, 1993; Werner, 1986; Wilentz, 1984; Wilkins, 1989

"Down with Monopolies!": Bender, 1987; Bridges, 1984; Brown, 1971; Buckley, 1984; Byrdsall, 1842; Eckhardt, 1984; Fox, 1965; Gilchrist, 1967; Ginsberg, 1968; Greene, 1837; Gunn, 1988; Harlow, 1931; Haswell, 1896; Hershkowitz, 1960; Hodges, 1982; Hodges, 1986; Hofstadter, 1943; Jentz, 1977; Mushkat, 1971; Pessen, 1967; Roediger, 1991; Schiller, 1980; Schlesinger, 1945; Sellers, 1991; Stotz, 1948; Vidal, 1973; Weinbaum, 1979

"To Hart's flour store!": Bridges, 1984; Byrdsall, 1842; Greene, 1837; Hershkowitz, 1960; Hodges, 1986; Hugins, 1960; Lockwood, 1976; Weinbaum, 1979; Werner, 1986; Wilentz, 1984

"The volcano has burst and overwhelmed New York": Blackmar, 1989; Brunson, 1989; Byrdsall, 1842; Clark, 1864; Conklin, 1983; Eckhardt, 1984; Folsom, 1991; Gardner, 1979; Garmey, 1984; Ginsberg, 1968; Greene, 1834; Haeger, 1981; Hammond, 1957; Haswell, 1896; Hershkowitz, 1960; Hoffman, 1976; Kroessler, 1991; Landesman, 1977; Lockwood, 1976; McGrane, 1924; Nevins, 1927; Pessen, 1978; Pred, 1973; Rainone, 1985; Rezneck, 1968; Richards, 1970; Rosenzweig and Blackmar, 1992; Sellers, 1991; Sobel, 1988; Stiles, 1867–70; Stott, 1990; Weinbaum, 1979; Wyatt-Brown, 1969

Causes and Remedies: Blackmar, 1989; Bridges, 1984; Cleveland, 1985; Crouthamel, 1989; Fox, 1965; Gatell, 1966; Gunn, 1988; Haeger, 1981; Hammond, 1957; Hershkowitz, 1960; Hidy, 1949; McFaul, 1972; McGrane, 1924; Miller, 1962; Pessen, 1978; Rezneck, 1968; Sellers, 1991; Sobel, 1988; Temin, 1969; Werner and Smith, 1991; Whiteman, 1971; Wilkins, 1989; Ziegler, 1988

From Boom to Bust: Auchincloss, 1989; Bender, 1987; Blackmar, 1989; Folsom, 1991; Grund, 1959; Hammond, 1957; Hershkowitz, 1960; Lockwood, 1976; McGrane, 1924; Miller, 1962; Miller, 1973; Patterson, 1935; Rezneck, 1968; Schneider, 1938–41; Sellers, 1991; Siles, 1986; Stevens, 1913; Stott, 1990; Whiteman, 1971; Wilentz, 1984

CHAPTER 37:
HARD TIMES

Barth, 1982; Beckert, 1995; Billington, 1938; Folsom, 1991; Jentz, 1977; Kaestle, 1973; Katz, 1986; Rezneck, 1968; Schneider, 1938–41; Shaftel, 1978; Smith-Rosenberg, 1971; Spann, 1986b; Tucher, 1994; Weinbaum, 1979

The Politics of Laissez-Faire: Bridges, 1984; Brown, 1971; Brunson, 1989; Byrdsall, 1842; Coleman, 1974; Crouthamel, 1989; Folsom, 1991; Fox, 1965; Freeman, 1966; Gatell, 1966; Gunn, 1988; Haeger, 1981; Hammond, 1946; Hammond, 1957; Hartog, 1983; Hershkowitz, 1960; Hodges, 1982; Hodges, 1986; Hofstadter, 1943; Howe, 1971; Jaher, 1982; July, 1951; Klips, 1980; Kluger, 1986; McFaul, 1972; McGrane, 1924; Miller, 1967; Moehring, 1981; Mushkat, 1971; Mushkat, 1971; Meyers, 1965; Myers, 1901; Rezneck, 1968; Schneider, 1938–41; Scisco, 1901; Sellers, 1991; Shaw, 1990; Sobel, 1988; Spann, 1986b; Teaford, 1975; Temin, 1969; Thompson, 1946; Walker, 1993; Werner, 1928; Werner and Smith, 1991; Wilkins, 1989

"Water! Water!": Armstrong, 1976; Blake, 1956; Clark, 1864; Cooke, 1995; Ellis, 1997; Ginsberg, 1968; Goldman, 1997; Larkin, 1990; Limpus, 1940; Lockwood, 1976; Mack, 1949; Moehring, 1981; Olmstead, 1976; Rosenzweig and Blackmar, 1992; Ryan, 1990; Weidner, 1974; Wilentz, 1984

Rum, Revivals, . . .: Blumin,

1989; Buckley, 1984; Dolan, 1975; Harlow, 1931; Hatch, 1989; Jentz, 1977; Johnson and Wilentz, 1994; Mack, 1949; Numbers and Butler, 1987; Painter, 1996; Reynolds, 1988; Rezneck, 1968; Rorabaugh, 1979; Sellers, 1991; Stott, 1990; Wilentz, 1984

. . . and Romanism: Billington, 1938; Brown, 1976; Buetow, 1970; Cooney, 1984; Crouthamel, 1989; Dolan, 1975; Farley, 1908; Fox, 1965; Gorelick, 1981; Kaestle, 1973; Lott, 1993; Pascu, 1980; Ravitch, 1974; Scisco, 1901; Shaw, 1977

The Return of the Natives: Billington, 1938; Buckley, 1984; Clark, 1864; Fox, 1965; Hershkowitz, 1960; Miller, 1985; Mushkat, 1971; Roediger, 1991; Scisco, 1901; Stott, 1990; Wilentz, 1984

Roach Guards and Dead Rabbits: Asbury, 1928; Bridges, 1984; Brown, 1976; Gorn, 1984; Grund, 1959; Harlow, 1931; Hershkowitz, 1960; Kaplan, 1996; Limpus, 1940; Myers, 1901; Sante, 1991; Srebnick, 1995; Stott, 1990; Weinbaum, 1979; Wilentz, 1984

"A civic ARMY": Bacon, 1939; Buckley, 1984; Costello, 1885; Gilje, 1987; Ginsberg, 1971; Hoffman, 1976; Klips, 1980; McCullough, 1983; Miller, 1977; Moehring, 1981; Newton, 1942; Richardson, 1970; Spann, 1986b; Srebnick, 1995

Bottomfeeders: Albion, 1939; Barth, 1982; Black, 1981; Blackmar, 1989; Collier, 1994; Gardner, 1979; Haeger, 1981; Hammond, 1957; Harris, 1968; Haswell, 1896; Jackson, 1985; Maynard, 1983; Nissenbaum, 1996; Norris, 1978; Porter, 1931; Resseguie, 1964; Stiles, 1867–70; Wyatt-Brown, 1969

"Laugh and Grow Fat": Auchincloss, 1989; Barnes, 1974; Bergmann, 1995; Brown, 1971; Buckley, 1984; Crouthamel, 1989; Dizikes, 1993; Freeman, 1966;

Garrett, 1978; Harlow, 1931; Harris, 1973; Kluger, 1986; Lehmann-Haupt, 1951; Lott, 1993; Reynolds, 1988; Saxton, 1990; Shank, 1956; Simon, 1978; Tebbel, 1972–81; Toll, 1976; Tucher, 1994; Walker, 1993

PART FOUR:
EMPORIUM AND
MANUFACTURING CITY
(1844–1879)

CHAPTER 38:
FULL STEAM AHEAD

Albion, 1939; Birmingham, 1984; Bunker, 1979; Carr, 1963; Carse, 1961; Caughey, 1962; Clark, 1910; Cray, 1978; Croffut, 1975; Cudahy, 1990; Cutler, 1961; Cutler, 1930; Hall, 1992; Hartog, 1983; Hobsbawm, 1975; Hodges, 1982; Howard, 1984; Howe and Matthews, 1926/27; Hoyt, 1962; Jackson, 1985; Laing, 1966; Manchester, 1924; Moehring, 1981; Morrison, 1903; Morrison, 1909; Nevins, 1927; Scroggs, 1916; Slotkin, 1985; Spann, 1986b; Stampp, 1990; Stiles, 1867–70; Taylor, 1966; Tchen, 1992; Whipple, 1987; Wright, 1968

Rail: Browder, 1985; Carosso, 1987; Chandler, 1977; Condit, 1980–81; Gunn, 1988; Lowit, 1954; Spann, 1986a

Dollars and Dry Goods: Beckert, 1995; Bonner, 1924; Browder, 1985; Carosso, 1987; Chandler, 1954; Chandler, 1977; Chernow, 1990; Cleveland, 1985; Clough, 1946; Hammack, 1982; Hodas, 1974; Jaher, 1982; Keller, 1963; Lockwood, 1976; Norris, 1978; Severini, 1981; Sobel, 1965; Sobel, 1988; Spann, 1986a; Spann, 1986b; Strasser, 1989; Tchen, 1993; Werner and Smith, 1991; Zelizer, 1979

Iron Age: Abbot, 1851; Albion, 1939; American Sugar Refining Company, 1918; Armbruster, 1942; Beckert, 1995; Bixby, 1972; Brown and Ment, 1980; Bunker, 1979; Cook, 1913; Degler, 1952; Furer, 1965; Gayle, 1974; Goldman, 1997; Hecht, 1978;

Hobsbawm, 1968; Hobsbawm, 1975; Jenkins, 1912; Jonnes, 1986; Kroessler, 1991; Ment, 1979; Ment, 1980; Morrison, 1909; New York (N.Y.), 1973; Sachs, 1988; Schoenebaum, 1977; Schwartz, 1972; Seyfried, 1985; Shaw, 1990; Spann, 1986b; Stankowski, 1977; Stankowski, 1978; Steinmeyer, 1975; Stiles, 1867–70; Stott, 1990; Weitzenhoffer, 1986; Whiteman, 1971

Metropolitan Manufacturing: Brandon, 1977; Clark, 1930; Degler, 1952; Ernst, 1949; Mack, 1949; Malon, 1981; Mitchell, 1992; Nadel, 1990; New York (N.Y.), 1973; Sachs, 1988; Spann, 1986b; Stansell, 1986; Stott, 1990; Wilentz, 1984

Palaces of Consumption: Agnew, 1983; Boyer, 1985; Chandler, 1977; Devorkin, 1987; Elias, 1992; Gardner, 1979; Gayle, 1974; Morris, 1975; Resseguie, 1964; Resseguie, 1965

A Palace of Crystal: Brand, 1991; Hornung, 1970; Jayne, 1990; Koolhaas, 1978; Petersen, 1945; Post, 1983; Reynolds, 1995

Palaces for Travelers: Boyer, 1985; Buckley, 1984; Gayle, 1974; Kouwenhoven, 1953; Morris, 1975; Steen, 1970

The Pigeon Perspective: Bergmann, 1995; Brand, 1991; Kasson, 1990; Kelley, 1996; Kouvenhowen, 1953; Marx, 1983

CHAPTER 39:
MANHATTAN, INK

Bender, 1987; Carter, 1968; Czitrom, 1982; Garmey, 1984; Gilder, 1938; Harlow, 1936; Hindle, 1981; Nevins, 1927; Prime, 1874; Sobel, 1965; Staiti and Reynolds, 1982, 1989; Tarr, 1987

"Extra, Extra, Read all About It!": Bernstein, 1984; Blondheim, 1994; Brown, 1951; Crouthamel, 1989; Henkin, 1995; Hoe, 1902; Kluger, 1986; Lears, 1995; Lehmann-Haupt, 1951; Malon, 1981; Pred, 1973; Reynolds, 1988; Saxton,

1990; Schudson, 1978; Sellers, 1991; Spann, 1986b; Tebbel, 1972–81; Whitby, 1984

A Pageant of Text: Henkin, 1995

Book Mart: Barnes, 1974; Beckert, 1995; Bridges, 1984; Buckley, 1984; Callow, 1967; D'Emilio, 1988; Denning, 1987; Douglas, 1977; Exman, 1965; Hoffman, 1949; Kray, 1982; Lehmann-Haupt, 1951; New York (N.Y.), 1973; Papke, 1987; Reynolds, 1988; Sellers, 1991; Spann, 1986b; Tebbel, 1972–81; Tompkins, 1985; Warner, 1987; Widmer, 1993; Zboray, 1993

"The Centre of Literary Power": Bender, 1987; Buckley, 1984; Denning, 1987; Gilmore, 1985; Malon, 1981; Marx, 1983; Miller, 1966; Morris, 1975; Papke, 1987; Reynolds, 1988; Saxton, 1984; Saxton, 1990; Schiller, 1980; Sellers, 1991; Spann, 1986b; Srebnick, 1995; Warren, 1992; Zboray, 1993

Young America: Bergmann, 1995; Bernstein, 1984; Douglas, 1977; Miller, 1966; Sellers, 1991; Widmer, 1993

Art in the Age of Mechanical Reproduction: Bergmann, 1995; Brown, 1993; Buckley, 1984; Callow, 1967; Crouthamel, 1989; Degler, 1952; Dudden, 1983; Hales, 1984; Henkin, 1995; Kasson, 1990; Klein, 1995; Kowenhoven, 1953; Meredith, 1946; Miller, 1966; Miller, 1990; New York (N.Y.), 1973; Prime, 1874; Reynolds, 1988; Spann, 1986b; Staiti and Reynolds, 1989; Trachtenberg, 1989; Welling, 1978; Widmer, 1993

CHAPTER 40:
SEEING NEW YORK

Bender, 1987; Bergmann, 1995; Brand, 1991; Buckley, 1984; Callow, 1967; Conrad, 1984; Cooke, 1995; Kelley, 1996; Kray, 1982; Miller, 1973; O'Connell, 1994; Reynolds, 1988; Robertson-Lorant, 1996; Saxton, 1990; Stansell, 1986; Williams, 1973; Zweig, 1984

Crowds and Civilization:
Barth, 1982; Bergmann,
1995; Brand, 1991; Kasson,
1990; Kovenhoven, 1953;
Marx, 1983; Spann, 1986b;
Van Leeuwen, 1988

*Lonely Crowds, Confidence
Men*: Baym, 1995;
Bergmann, 1969; Buckley,
1984; Child, 1845; Gilder,
1938; Halttunen, 1979;
Harlow, 1931; Henkin, 1995;
Kasson, 1990; Kelley, 1996;
Kluger, 1986; Lears, 1995;
Leary, 1975; Lees, 1985;
Marx, 1983; Miller, 1977;
O'Connell, 1994; Reynolds,
1995; Robertson-Lorant,
1996; Ryan, 1990; Spann,
1986b; Stiles, 1867–70;
Trachtenberg, 1989; Tucher,
1994

Unquiet Bones: Ayres, 1993;
Beard, 1953; Booth, 1859;
Brodhead, 1853–71; Curry,
1853; Guy, 1935; Kammen,
1979; Lawrence, 1906;
Moulton, 1843; New York
City Common Council,
1841–70; O'Callaghan,
1846–48; Scoville, 1863–66;
Vail, 1954; Valentine,
1853

Mysteries of the City: Berg,
1978; Bergmann, 1995;
Blackmar, 1989; Blumin,
1984; Blumin, 1989; Buckley,
1984; Denning, 1987;
Dickens, 1961; Kasson,
1990; Kelley, 1996; Lott,
1993; Marx, 1983; Papke,
1987; Reynolds, 1988;
Reynolds, 1995; Ryan, 1990;
Saxton, 1990; Srebnick,
1995

Man of the Crowd: Berg,
1978; Bergmann, 1995;
Brand, 1991; Jenkins, 1912;
Jonnes, 1986; Kasson, 1990;
Kray, 1982; Lees, 1985;
Meredith, 1946; Miller,
1973; Morris, 1987; Moss,
1963; Papke, 1987; Parry,
1933; Reynolds, 1988;
Saxton, 1990; Silverman,
1991; Sokolow, 1983; Spann,
1986b; Srebnick, 1995;
Tebbell, 1972–81; Widmer,
1993

"Dollars Damn Me": Bender,
1987; Bergmann, 1995;
Boydston, 1990; Boyer, 1978;
Brand, 1991; Bremner, 1956;
Conrad, 1984; Douglas,
1977; Exman, 1965;
Gilmore, 1985; Hardwick,
1983; Johnson and Wilentz,

1994; Kasson, 1990; Kazin
and Finn, 1989; Kelley, 1996;
Kray, 1982; Lears, 1995;
Lees, 1985; Lott, 1993;
Masur, 1989; Matthiessen,
1941; Melville, 1996; Miller,
1973; O'Connell, 1994;
Parker, 1996; Post-Lauria,
1996; Reynolds, 1988;
Robertson, 1996; Rogin,
1983; Srebnick, 1995;
Trachtenberg, 1982; Trimpi,
1987; Tucher, 1994; Wall,
1994; Zelnick, Winter
1979–80; Zweig, 1984

"My City!": Allen, 1969;
Allen, 1993; Bender, 1987;
Berry, 1983; Brand, 1991;
Brooks, 1944; Brown, 1971;
Brown and Ment, 1980;
Buckley, 1984; Callow, 1992;
Christman, 1963; Conrad,
1984; Cooke, 1995; Dolan,
1975; Douglas, 1977;
Erkkila, 1989; Harrington,
1973; Holloway, 1921; Howe,
1986; Kray, 1982; Lott, 1993;
Lynch, 1985; Machor, 1987;
Marx, 1983; Miller, 1990;
Miller, 1989; Morris, 1975;
Museum of the City of New
York, 1990; Parry, 1933;
Pilat, 1941; Reynolds, 1988;
Reynolds, 1995; Robertson,
1996; Rubin, 1973; Saxton,
1990; Thomas, 1987;
Whitman, 1950; Whitman,
1973; Zweig, 1984

CHAPTER 41:
LIFE ABOVE BLEECKER

Adelman, 1990; Beckert,
1995; Bender, 1987; Boyer,
1985; Brown, 1924; Buckley,
1984; Croffut, 1975; Elias,
1992; Garmey, 1984; Hoyt,
1962; Jaher, 1982; July, 1951;
Klein, 1987; Lockwood,
1976; Miller, 1967; Morris,
1975; Nevins, 1927; Nevins
and Thomas, 1952; Pessen,
1973; Spann, 1986b; Wecter,
1937

*". . . fled by dignified degrees
up Broadway"*: Blackmar,
1989; Blackmar, 1991;
Bristed, 1852; Brown, 1924;
Buckley, 1984; Frick, 1983;
Garmey, 1984; Goldstone
and Dalrymple, 1974; Jaher,
1982; Landy, 1970;
Lockwood, 1972b;
Lockwood, 1976; Miller,
1967; Moehring, 1981;
Morris, 1975; Nevins, 1927;
Simon, 1978; Spann, 1986b;
Tauranac, 1985; Thompson,
1946; Trager, 1990; Warren,
1992; Wecter, 1937

Suburbs and Summer Spots:
Brooks, 1944; Hartog, 1983;
Jackson, 1985; Jenkins, 1912;
Lockwood, 1972b;
Lockwood, 1976;
Schoenebaum, 1977; Scobey,
1992; Simon, 1972

*"I never saw such luxury and
extravagance"*: Adelman,
1990; Albion, 1939; Allen,
1991; Banner, 1983; Berg,
1978; Black, 1981; Bristed,
1852; Brooks, 1944; Brown,
1924; Buckley, 1984;
Bushman, 1993; Coleman,
1972; Elias, 1992;
Gernsheim, 1981; Graves,
1843; Gunn, 1857;
Henderson, 1986; Kasson,
1990; Larkin, 1988; Levine,
1988; Lockwood, 1972b;
Lockwood, 1976; Lowitt,
1954; Mayer, 1983; Miller,
1967; Morris, 1975; Nevins,
1927; Pessen, 1973; Spann,
1986b; Still, 1956; Stone,
1982; Thomas, 1987;
Warren, 1992; Watson, 1992;
Wecter, 1937

The Respectable Classes:
Barth, 1982; Blumin, 1985;
Blumin, 1989; Boydston,
1990; Boyer, 1985; Bridges,
1984; Buckley, 1984;
Bushman, 1993; Clark, 1978;
Cromley, 1990; Curtis, 1853;
Douglas, 1977; Duduit,
1983; Gardner, 1979; Gunn,
1857 ; Halttunen, 1979;
Jackson, 1985; Kasson, 1990;
Kirsch, 1989; Livingston,
1994; Lockwood, 1972b;
Lockwood, 1976;
McCullough, 1983;
McLoughlin, 1970; Ment,
1979; Nevins, 1927;
O'Hanlon, 1982; Rosenberg,
1987; Ryan, 1982; Schwartz,
1972; Simon, 1972; Spann,
1986; Stiles, 1867–70;
Stuart-Wortley, 1851; Waller,
1982; Wecter, 1937; Wolfe,
1994

Genteel Performances:
Adelman, 1990; Auser, 1969;
Banner, 1983; Blumin, 1989;
Boydston, 1990; Buckley,
1984; Bushman, 1993;
Cromley, 1990; Douglas,
1977; Dudden, 1983;
Goldstein, 1992; Green,
1986; Halttunen, 1979;
Henderson, 1986; Kirsch,
1989; Lang, 1922;
Lieberman, 1995;
Lockwood, 1972b; Miller,
1967; Ryan, 1982; Sklar,
1973; Ward, 1994

CHAPTER 42:
CITY OF IMMIGRANTS

Coleman, 1972; Cutler, 1961;
Diggins, 1972; Diner, 1996;
Dolan, 1975; Ernst, 1949;
Gunn, 1857; Hendin, 1993;
Kraut, 1996; Marraro, 1949;
Miller, 1985; Nadel, 1990;
Rosenwaike, 1972;
Schneider, 1994; Shaw, 1977;
Spann, 1986b; Stott, 1990;
Taylor, 1966; Tchen, 1992;
United States, 1961; W.P.A.,
1938a

Reception Center: Beckert,
1995; Coleman, 1972;
Degler, 1952; Diner, 1996;
Duffy, 1968–74; Ernst, 1949;
Kraut, 1996; Levine, 1992;
Spann, 1986b; Still, 1956;
Wust, 1984

Immigrants at Work:
Anderson, 1976; Bernstein,
1984; Blumin, 1989; Bolster,
1997; Curry, 1853; Degler,
1952; Devlin, 1996; Diner,
1996; Ernst, 1949; Furer,
1973; Gilfoyle, 1992;
Grinstein, 1945; Hertzberg,
1989; Hodges, 1982; Hodges,
1996; Ignatiev, 1995;
Jackman, 1964; Jenkins,
1912; Jonnes, 1986; Kaplan,
1996; Lapham, 1977; Levine,
1992; Lieberman, 1995;
Lockwood, 1976; Melville,
1983; Miller, 1967;
Moehring, 1981; Nadel,
1990; Nadel, 1991;
O'Donovan, 1969; Quiroga,
1989; Stansell, 1986;
Steinmeyer, 1975; Stott,
1990; Sunset Park
Restoration Committee,
1980?; Supple, 1957; Tchen,
1993; Tebbel, 1972–81;
Truax, 1952; Wilentz, 1984

Settling In: Blackmar, 1989;
Blumin, 1989; Boydston,
1990; Coleman, 1972; Cooke,
1995; Cromley, 1990; Diner,
1996; Dolan, 1975; Dunshee,
1952; Ernst, 1949; Grinstein,
1945; Hecht, 1978; Hodges,
1996; Jenkins, 1912; Jonnes,
1986; Judd, 1995; Lapham,
1977; Lockwood, 1972b;
Lockwood, 1976;
McCullough, 1983; Ment,
1979; Ment, 1980; Nadel,
1990; North, 1951; Osofsky,
1966; Pernicone, 1973;
Scharf, 1886; Scherzer, 1982;
Schoenebaum, 1977;
Schwartz, 1972; Seyfried,
300; Simon, 1972; Stansell,
1986; Still, 1956; Stott,
1990

Jews and Hughes: Billington, 1938; Brown and Ment, 1980; Buetow, 1970; Buhle, 1987; Burns, 1969; Comfort, 1906; Cooke, 1995; Cudahy, 1990; Diner, 1996; Dolan, 1975; Ernst, 1949; Farley, 1908; Fine and Wolfe, 1978; Grinstein, 1945; Hertzberg, 1989; Hodges, 1996; Hofstadter and Wallace, 1970; Jackson, 1989; Jenkins, 1912; Jonnes, 1986; Kaplan, 1996; Katz, 1986; Kraut, 1996; Kroessler, 1991; Lannie, 1968; Nadel, 1990; O'Grady, 1930; Ridge, 1988; Rosenzweig and Blackmar, 1992; Scharf, 1886; Shaw, 1977; Shea, 1878; Stankowski, 1977; Starr, 1957; Stiles, 1867–70; Sunset Park Restoration Committee, 1980?; Walsh, 1960; Weinbaum, 1979; Wittke, 1952

Rude B'hoys: Allen, 1991; Allen, 1993; Beckert, 1995; Blumin, 1989; Crouthamel, 1989; Devlin, 1996; Diner, 1996; Ernst, 1949; Gorn, 1984; Hertzberg, 1989; Hodges, 1996; Horowitz, 1987; Kaplan, 1996; Lees, 1985; Leuchs, 1928; Lott, 1993; Melville, 1996; Meyer, 1987; Nadel, 1990; Nissenbaum, 1996; North, 1951; Otter, 1995; Reynolds, 1995; Ridge, 1988; Ryan, 1990; Saxton, 1990; Schneider, 1994; Shanet, 1975; Shea, 1878; Spann, 1986; Stott, 1990; Wall, 1994; Wecter, 1937; Wilentz, 1984; Wust, 1984

The Manly Art: Adelman, 1990; Gilfoyle, 1992; Gorn, 1984; Gorn, 1986; Halttunen, 1982; Hodges, 1996; Koolhaas, 1978; Nadel, 1990; Nevins, 1927; Nissenbaum, 1996; Pilat, 1941; Reynolds, 1995; Saxton, 1990; Schiller, 1980; Sellers, 1991; Spann, 1986b; Stott, 1990; Weinstein, 1984

Underworld: Asbury, 1928; Asbury, 1938; Crapsey, 1872; Fabian, 1990; Kaplan, 1996; Matsell, 1859; Nelli, 1976; Sante, 1991; Spann, 1986b; Srebnick, 1995

"If I don't have a muss soon, I'll spile": Allen, 1991; Blumin, 1989; Buckley, 1984; Dorson, 1943; Frick, 1983;

Henderson, 1973; Hodges, 1996; Ignatiev, 1995; Knobel, 1986; Lott, 1993; McConachie, 1992; Nadel, 1990; Nathan, 1962; Odell, 1927–49; Roediger, 1991; Saxton, 1990; Spann, 1986b; Stansell, 1986; Stott, 1990; Tchen, 1993; Toll, 1976; Weinbaum, 1979

CHAPTER 43:
CO-OP CITY

Asbury, 1928; Beckert, 1995; Bergmann, 1995; Blumin, 1989; Brown, 1951; Buckley, 1984; Bushman, 1993; Cooke, 1995; Crouthamel, 1989; Dizikes, 1993; Frick, 1983; Headley, 1970; Henderson, 1973; Hodges, 1996; Kaplan, 1996; Kasson, 1990; Levine, 1988; Lott, 1993; McConachie, 1992; Moody, 1958; Mueller, 1951; Reynolds, 1995; Srebnick, 1995; Weinbaum, 1979

Tenants versus Landlords: Blackmar, 1989; Blumin, 1989; Boston, 1971; Bridges, 1984; Conkin, 1980; Crouthamel, 1989; Ernst, 1949; Freeman, 1966; Grinstein, 1945; Haeger, 1991; Jackson, 1985; Kluger, 1986; Kraut, 1996; Nadel, 1991; Pessen, 1967; Saxton, 1990; Sellers, 1991; Shanet, 1975; Slotkin, 1985; Slotkin, 1973; Spann, 1986b; Tucher, 1994; Zahler, 1941

Towards a Cooperative Metropolis: Degler, 1952; Denholm, 1972; Guarneri, 1988; Harvey, 1985; Hobsbawm, 1975; Horowitz, 1987; Kluger, 1986; Levine, 1992; McKay, 1934; Nadel, 1991; Raynor, 1978; Rude, 1964; Shanet, 1975; Wilentz, 1984

"We did not expect to find in this free country a Russian police": Beckert, 1995; Bernstein, 1984; Bridges, 1984; Degler, 1952; Devlin, 1996; Diner, 1996; Ernst, 1949; Guarneri, 1988; Ignatiev, 1995; Levine, 1992; Ment, 1979; Migliore, 1975; Nadel, 1991; Nadel, 1990; Seyfried, 1984; Spann, 1986b; Stevens, 1913; Stott, 1990; Wilentz, 1984; Wust, 1984; Zboray, 1993

CHAPTER 44:
INTO THE CRAZY-LOVED DENS OF DEATH

Asbury, 1928; Beckert, 1995; Berg, 1978; Child, 1845; Rosenzweig and Blackmar, 1992; Stansell, 1986

"Penitential Tears": Asbury, 1938; Beckert, 1995; Bridges, 1984; Browder, 1988; Crouthamel, 1989; Diner, 1983; Dolan, 1975; Ernst, 1949; Fabian, 1990; Healy, 1992; Hodges, 1996; Horlick, 1975; Kaestle, 1973; Kaplan, 1996; Katz, 1986; Klips, 1980; Kraut, 1996; Macleod, 1983; McCabe, 1868; Rorabaugh, 1976; Rosenberg, 1987; Smith-Rosenberg, 1971; Rothman, 1971; Shaw, 1977; Spann, 1986b; Stott, 1990; Weinbaum, 1975; Weinbaum, 1979

"To Expel Idleness and Beggary from the City": Bremner, 1956; Brieger, 1978; Crouthamel, 1989; Diner, 1983; Duffy, 1968–74; Ernst, 1949; Hodges, 1996; Klips, 1980; McLachlin, 1970; Smith-Rosenberg, 1971; Rosenwaike, 1972; Russell, 1945; Spann, 1986b

"Idle and Vicious Children of Both Sexes": Beckert, 1995; Berg, 1978; Newt Davidson Collective, 1974; Duffy, 1968–74; Gorelick, 1981; Grinstein, 1945; Hodges, 1996; Mack, 1949; Pickett, 1969; Quiroga, 1989; Rudy, 1949; Ryan, 1990; Schneider, 1938–41; Stansell, 1986

Westward Ho! (Children's Version): Bellingham, 1983; Brace, 1872; Buckley, 1984; Buetow, 1970; Degler, 1952; Diner, 1983; Dolan, 1975; Katz, 1986; Marraro, 1949; O'Grady, 1930; Quiroga, 1989; Schneider, 1938–41; Spann, 1986b; Stansell, 1986

Enter the Environmentalists: Blackmar, 1989; Blackmar, 1995; Bluestone, 1991; Blumin, 1989; Boydston, 1990; Duffy, 1968–74; Freeman, 1966; Goldman, 1997; Hodges, 1996; Kaplan, 1996; Kraut, 1996; Lockwood, 1976; Loop, 1964; Moehring, 1981; Peterson, Fall 1979; Pickett, 1969; Quiroga, 1989;

Rosenberg, 1962; Smith-Rosenberg, 1971; Rosenberg and Rosenberg, 1968; Rosenzweig and Blackmar, 1992; Shaftel, 1978; Spann, 1986b; Stansell, 1986; Starr, 1957; Stiles, 1867–70; Stott, 1990; Tarr, 1979; Wilentz, 1984; Williams, 1991

Tenement Troubles: Blackmar, 1989; Blackmar, 1995; Bremner, 1958; Duffy, 1968–74; Gardner, 1979; Jackson, 1976; Nadel, 1990; Plunz, 1990; Stansell, 1986

"Lungs of the City": Adelman, 1990; Bernstein, 1984; Buckley, 1984; Bushman, 1993; Garrett, 1978; Green, 1986; Henkin, 1995; Kelley, 1996; Roper, 1973; Rosenzweig and Blackmar, 1992; Scobey, 1989; Scobey, 1992; Spann, 1986b

CHAPTER 45:
FEME DECOVERT

Banner, 1983; Berg, 1978; Bushman, 1993; D'Emilio, 1988; Gilfoyle, 1992; Hill, 1992; Kasson, 1990; Katz, 1983; Lockwood, 1976; Lynch, 1985; Reynolds, 1995; Ryan, 1990; Stansell, 1986; Wall, 1994; Wecter, 1937

"The utter idleness of the lady class": Banner, 1983; Baym, 1995; Belden, 1849; Berg, 1978; Boydston, 1990; Brewer, 1987; Butcher, 1989; Child, 1845; Clifford, 1992; Cogan, 1989; Douglas, 1977; Ernst, 1949; Graves, 1843; Karcher, 1994; Levine, 1992; Quiroga, 1989; Reynolds, 1995; Robertson, 1996; Rudy, 1949; Sellers, 1991; Srebnick, 1995; Stansell, 1986; Stiles, 1867–70; Tompkins, 1985; Tucher, 1994; Urbanski, 1994; Walker, 1993; Walsh, 1977

A Family Wage: Banner, 1983; Boydston, 1990; Brewer, 1987; Buhle, 1981; Cogan, 1989; Degler, 1952; Devlin, 1996; Diner, 1983; Diner, 1996; DuBois, 1978; Dudden, 1983; Hodges, 1996; Lerner, 1977; Levine, 1992; Lott, 1993; Nadel, 1990; Pernicone, 1973; Schneider, 1994; Stansell, 1986; Stevens, 1913; Tchen, 1993

". . . grows rich on the hard labors of our sex.": Asbury, 1928; Beckert, 1995; Berg, 1978; Boyer, 1978; Cogan, 1989; Dolan, 1975; Dudden, 1983; Freedman, 1981; Hodges, 1996; Kaplan, 1996; Katz, 1986; McCauley, 1992; O'Grady, 1930; Quiroga, 1989; Smith-Rosenberg, 1971; Ryan, 1990; Spann, 1986b; Stansell, 1986; Strasser, 1989; Urbanski, 1994; Whiteaker, 1977

City of Orgies: Allen, 1991; Berg, 1978; Boyer, 1978; Browder, 1988; Buckley, 1984; D'Emilio, 1988; Gilfoyle, 1992; Henderson, 1973; Hill, 1992; Kaplan, 1996; Marx, 1983; McConachie, 1992; Nadel, 1990; New York (N.Y.), 1973; Reynolds, 1995; Ryan, 1990; Sellers, 1991; Stansell, 1986; Urbanski, 1994; Whiteaker, 1977

"Mistress of Abominations": Browder, 1988; Crouthamel, 1989; D'Emilio, 1988; Duffy, 1968–74; Gilfoyle, 1992; Gordon, 1976; Leach, 1980; Miller, 1990; Mohr, 1978; Morris, 1975; Olasky, 1986; Parry, 1933; Quiroga, 1989; Srebnick, 1995; Stoehr, 1979; Waller, 1982

"fashion's despotic rule": Allen, 1991; Banner, 1983; Berg, 1978; Boyer, 1985; Buckley, 1984; Child, 1845; Cogan, 1989; Ellington, 1869; Hill, 1992; Kasson, 1990; Leach, 1980; Lockwood, 1976; McConachie, 1992; Morris, 1975; Ryan, 1990; Scobey, 1992; Shanet, 1975; Stansell, 1986; Stuart-Wortley, 1851; Thomas, 1967

"Lindomania" and "High-flyer Stampedes": Berg, 1978; Buckley, 1984; Dayton, 1882; Dizikes, 1993; Harris, 1973; Hodges, 1996; Horowitz, 1987; Kaplan, 1996; Kasson, 1990; McConachie, 1992; Parry, 1933; Ryan, 1990; Srebnick, 1995; Stansell, 1986

Feme Decovert: Basch, 1982; Berg, 1978; Blackmar, 1989; Boylan, 1990; Cogan, 1989; Crouthamel, 1989; Douglas, 1977; Gilfoyle, 1992; Ginzberg, 1986; Gurko, 1974; Hersh, 1978; Meyer,

1987; Painter, 1996; Reynolds, 1995; Sicherman, et al., 1980; Stansell, 1986; Stanton, Anthony, and Gage, 1881–1922; Swerdlow, 1976; Walker, 1993

CHAPTER 46:
LOUIS NAPOLEON AND
FERNANDO WOOD

Boyer, 1985; Bridges, 1984; Danforth, 1974; Gronowicz, 1998; Guarneri, 1988; Harvey, 1985; Hobsbawm, 1975; Jaher, 1982; McGerr, 1986; Pinkney, 1958; Shefter, 1993; Spann, 1986a; Spann, 1986b

Tammany's Town: Allen, 1993; Anbinder, 1987; Beckert, 1995; Blumin, 1989; Bridges, 1984; Brown, 1976; Callow, 1966; Gorn, 1984; Hershkowitz, 1977; Hodges, 1996; Moehring, 1981; Mollenkopf, 1981; Montgomery, 1967; Mushkat, 1990; Myers, 1901; Reynolds, 1995; Spann, 1986b; Summers, 1987; Werner, 1928

Municipal Politics Indicted: Albion, 1939; Beckert, 1995; Blackmar, 1989; Buckley, 1984; Callow, 1966; Cleveland, 1985; Diner, 1996; Duffy, 1968–74; Ginsberg, 1968; Harlow, 1931; Hodas, 1976; Hofstadter and Wallace, 1970; Kaplan, 1996; Klips, 1980; Rosenzweig and Blackmar, 1992; Sante, 1991; Spann, 1986b; Stiles, 1867–70; Stott, 1990; Stotz, 1948; Urbanski, 1994; Wilentz, 1984

Reform: Anbinder, 1987; Baker, 1983; Baker, 1990; Barth, 1982; Beckert, 1995; Berg, 1978; Brown, 1966; Buckley, 1984; Carman, 1919; Gorn, 1984; Gronowicz, 1998; Hodges, 1986; Hofstadter and Wallace, 1970; Kaplan, 1996; Knobel, 1986; Mack, 1949; Miller, 1977; Moehring, 1981; Mushkat, 1990; Pickett, 1969; Rosenzweig and Blackmar, 1992; Saxton, 1990; Spann, 1986b; Srebnick, 1995; Stott, 1990; Summers, 1987; Wilentz, 1984

"Our Civic Hero": Anbinder, 1987; Beckert, 1995;

Blackmar, 1989; Browder, 1988; Brown, 1976; Folsom, 1991; Hill, 1992; Levine, 1992; Mushkat, 1990; Nadel, 1990; Nadel, 1991; Reynolds, 1995; Richardson, 1970; Rosenzweig and Blackmar, 1992; Rudy, 1949; Scobey, 1989; Spann, 1986b; Stampp, 1990

State over City: Allen, 1991; Anbinder, 1987; Asbury, 1928; Beckert, 1995; Bridges, 1984; Brown, 1976; Buckley, 1984; Callow, 1966; Chalmers, 1969; Crouthamel, 1989; Duffy, 1968–74; Hartog, 1983; Ment, 1979; Miller, 1977; Moehring, 1981; Mushkat, 1990; Nadel, 1990; North, 1951; Otter, 1995; Rorabaugh, 1976; Rosenzweig and Blackmar, 1992; Seyfried, 1985; Snyder-Grenier, 1996; Spann, 1986b; Stansell, 1986; Stiles, 1867–70; Stott, 1990; Summers, 1987; Tarr, 1979; Weinbaum, 1975

CHAPTER 47:
THE PANIC OF 1857

Black, 1981; Browder, 1985; Crouthamel, 1989; Gibbons, 1859; Huston, 1987; Norris, 1978; Stampp, 1990

"appalling picture of social wretchedness": Adelman, 1990; Banner, 1983; Barth, 1982; Bolster, 1997; Folsom, 1991; Garmey, 1984; Hendrickson, 1979; Hodas, 1976; Huston, 1987; Jackson, 1985; Jaher, 1982; Lebhar, 1952; Lockwood, 1972; Moehring, 1981; Nadel, 1990; Nadel, 1991; Rush, 1920; Stampp, 1990; Stansell, 1986; Stott, 1990; Tebbell, 1972–81; Winkler, 1934

"paper bubbles of all descriptions": Clark, 1978; Crouthamel, 1989; Fishlow, 1966; Gibbons, 1859; Hobsbawm, 1975; Huston, 1987; Jaher, 1982; Nadel, 1991; Spann, 1986b; Temin, 1975; Van Vleck, 1943; Waller, 1982

Wood Redux: Beckert, 1995; Bernstein, 1984; Blackmar, 1989; Bridges, 1984; Degler, 1952; Folsom, 1991; Huston, 1987; Levine, 1992; May, 1949; Moehring, 1981; Mushkat, 1990; Nadel, 1991;

Nadel, 1990; Rosenzweig and Blackmar, 1992; Ryan, 1990; Stampp, 1990

"We Want Work!": Bernstein, 1984; Bridges, 1984; Degler, 1952; Huston, 1987; Klebaner, 1960; Rosenzweig and Blackmar, 1992

Wood Removed: Anbinder, 1987; Beckert, 1995; Huston, 1987; Lapham, 1977; Levine, 1992; Mushkat, 1990; Rosenzweig and Blackmar, 1992; Walker, 1993

CHAPTER 48:
THE HOUSE DIVIDES

Bernstein, 1984; Foner, 1970; Foner, 1980; Hobsbawm, 1975; Brewer, 1976; McKay, 1990; Slotkin, 1985; Taylor, 1961

Black Republicans: Aptheker, 1951; Beard, 1993; Berg, 1978; Blockson, 1994; Bolster, 1997; Cook, 1974; Crouthamel, 1989; Dann, 1971; Dudden, 1983; Foner, 1983; Foote, 1993; Freeman, 1966; Gronowicz, 1998; Harris, 1968; Hershkowitz, 1960; Hirsch, 1931; Hodges, 1996; Hutchinson, 1972; Hutton, 1993; Ignatiev, 1995; Klips, 1980; Lee, 1943; Litwack, 1961; Lockwood, 1976; Man, 1951; Maynard, 1983; Ment, 1980; Mitchell, 1959; Mitchell, 1992; Ottley and Weatherby, 1967; Ovington, 1911; Quarles, 1969; Rainone, 1985; Scheiner, 1965; Stansell, 1986; Stiles, 1867–70; Swift, 1989; Taylor, 1994; Walker, 1993; Werner, 1986; Wesley, 1939; Wilder, 1994

White Republicans: Beckert, 1995; Bernstein, 1984; Booraem, 1983; Brown, 1971; Foner, 1975; Fredrickson, 1965; Gienapp, 1987; Lott, 1993; Marx and Engels, 1937; McLoughlin, 1970; Migliore, 1975; Mushkat, 1971; Nadel, 1991; Richards, 1970; Roediger, 1991; Saxton, 1990; Sellers, 1991; Whitby, 1984; Wilder, 1994; Wyatt-Brown, 1969

Metropolitan Dixiecrats: Anbinder, 1992; Bernstein, 1984; Browder, 1985; Crouthamel, 1989; Foner, 1975; Foner, 1982; Foner,

1980; Hamm, 1979; Lee, 1943; Man, 1951; McKay, 1990; McLoughlin, 1970; Migliore, 1975; Mushkat, 1971; Sacks and Sacks, 1993; Schluter, 1913; Slotkin, 1985

John Brown's Body: Dann, 1971; Hutchinson, 1972; Quarles, 1969; Slotkin, 1985; Swift, 1989; Walker, 1993; Wilder, 1994; Wyatt-Brown, 1969

CHAPTER 49:
CIVIL WARS

Bernstein, 1984; Degler, 1952; Foner, 1968; Foner, 1975; Genovese, 1965; Genovese, 1971; Hofstadter, 1948; McKay, 1990; Migliore, 1975; Moore, Jr., 1966; Randall, 1945; Ryan, 1975; Trachtenberg, 1989

Grass in the Streets?: Bernstein, 1984; Foner, 1968; Hammond, 1957; Hammond, 1970; Hershkowitz, 1977; Migliore, 1975; Ruffin, 1860; Ryan, 1990; Slotkin, 1985

Lincoln Redux: Kaplan, 1980; Lee, 1943; McKay, 1990; Oates, 1977; Randall, 1945; Zweig, 1984

The Republic of New York?: Anbinder, 1987; Beckert, 1995; Bernstein, 1984; Lee, 1943; McKay, 1990; Migliore, 1975; Mushkat, 1990

Beat! Beat! Drums!: Adams, 1958; Beckert, 1995; Browder, 1985; Catalfamo, 1989; Clark, 1864; Devlin, 1996; Ellis, 1997; Foner, 1968; Furer, 1973; Harlow, 1931; Hershkowitz, 1977; Hobsbawm, 1975; Kaplan, 1980; McKay, 1990; Migliore, 1975; Miller, 1985; Montgomery, 1967; Nadel, 1990; Ridge, 1988; Spann, 1996

The B'hoys at War: Bernstein, 1984; Foner, 1975; Frederickson, 1965; Kaplan, 1980; Lee, 1943; Migliore, 1975

Entrepôt and Workshop: Attie, 1987; Beckert, 1995; Bernstein, 1984; Browder, 1985; Brown and Ment, 1980; Cook, 1974; Costello, 1967; Cruden, 1972; Fite,

1976; Foner, 1968; Hecht, 1978; Hobsbawm, 1975; Hutchins, 1941; Jackson, 1984; Jonnes, 1986; Lapham, 1977; Lee, 1943; Livingston, 1994; McKay, 1990; Migliore, 1975; Nevins, 1959–70; New York (N.Y.), 1973; Poole, 1915; Rischin, 1962; Rosenzweig and Blackmar, 1992; Singer, 1986; Snyder-Grenier, 1996

Greenbacks and Goldbugs: Beckert, 1995; Browder, 1985; Cleveland, 1985; Gische, 1979; Hammond, 1957; McKay, 1990; Montgomery, 1967; Sharkey, 1959; Shefter, 1993; Sobel, 1965; Supple, 1957; Winkler, 1934

The Shoddy Aristocracy: Adelman, 1990; Asbury, 1938; Attie, 1987; Barth, 1982; Boyer, 1985; Browder, 1985; Cruden, 1972; Fite, 1976; Gardner, 1979; McKay, 1990; Migliore, 1975; Nevins, 1959–70; Ross, 1963; Sobel, 1965; Thomas, 1967

Reformers at War: The Sanitary Commission: Attie, 1987; Fredrickson, 1965; Kaplan, 1980; McKay, 1990; Migliore, 1975; Smith, 1957

Carnage and Class: Cruden, 1972; Fredrickson, 1965; Griffin, 1990; Hershkowitz, 1977; Kaplan, 1980; Kouwenhoven, 1953; Lee, 1943; Lonn, 1951; McKay, 1990; Nevins, 1959–70; Ryan, 1975; Slotkin, 1985; Spann, 1996; Starr, 1957

CHAPTER 50:
THE BATTLE FOR NEW YORK

Beckert, 1995; Bernstein, 1984; Costello, 1967; Cruden, 1972; Fite, 1976; Lee, 1943; Man, 1951; McKay, 1990; Migliore, 1975; Montgomery, 1967; Spann, 1996; Wilder, 1994

Politics of Emancipation: Anbinder, 1987; Aptheker, 1951; Attie, 1987; Beckert, 1995; Bernstein, 1984; Callow, 1966; Cook, 1974; Fehrenbacher, 1987; Frederickson, 1965; Hershkowitz, 1977; Hutchinson, 1972; Marx, 1937; McKay, 1990; Migliore, 1975;

Montgomery, 1967; Mushkat, 1971; Mushkat, 1990; Slotkin, 1985; Wyatt-Brown, 1969

The Draft: Bernstein, 1984; Cook, 1974; Costello, 1967; Lee, 1943; Migliore, 1975; Montgomery, 1967; Ryan, 1990

Day One: Bernstein, 1984; Brown, 1976; Cook, 1974; McKay, 1990; Ryan, 1990; Spann, 1996

The Battle for New York City: Bernstein, 1984; Brooks Brothers, 1943; Cook, 1974; Costello, 1967; Hodges, 1996; Livingston, 1994; McKay, 1990; Montgomery, 1967; Snyder-Grenier, 1996

Aftermaths: Beckert, 1995; Bernstein, 1984; Callow, 1966; Duffy, 1968–74; Frederickson, 1965; Hershkowitz, 1977; Maynard, 1983; McKay, 1990; Migliore, 1975; Montgomery, 1967; Mushkat, 1990; Roediger, 1991; Scobey, 1989; Seraile, 1977; Slotkin, 1985; Spann, 1996

Back to Business: Browder, 1985; Chernow, 1990; Costello, 1967; Cruden, 1972; Fite, 1976; Klein, 1986; Lee, 1943; McKay, 1990; Nevins, 1959–70; Sobel, 1965

The Election of 1864: Brandt, 1986; Longacre, 1984; McKay, 1990; Migliore, 1975; Mohr, 1973; Van Deusen, 1947; Zornow, 1954

Peace: Boyer, 1985; Hershkowitz, 1977; Kaplan, 1980; Kouwenhoven, 1953; McKay, 1990; Migliore, 1975

CHAPTER 51:
WESTWARD, HO!

Beckert, 1995; Bernstein, 1984; Coben, 1962; Field, 1982; Foner, 1988; Katz, 1968; Migliore, 1975; Montgomery, 1967; Scobey, 1989

Wall Street and the West: Beckert, 1995; Black, 1981; Carosso, 1970; Carosso, 1976; Chernow, 1990; Cook,

1974; Katz, 1968; Klein, 1986; Lane, 1942; Montgomery, 1967; Simon, 1978; Supple, 1957

The Scarlet Woman of Wall Street: Browder, 1985; Callow, 1966; Carosso, 1970; Chandler, 1977; Chernow, 1990; Gordon, 1988; Klein, 1986; Lane, 1942; Morris, 1975; Scobey, 1989; Sharkey, 1959; Trager, 1990; Unger, 1964

The West and Wall Street: Foner, 1988; Gische, 1979; Montgomery, 1967; Sharkey, 1959; Slotkin, 1985; Trachtenberg, 1982; Unger, 1964

CHAPTER 52:
RECONSTRUCTING NEW YORK

Bernstein, 1984; Migliore, 1975; Scobey, 1989; Waugh, 1992

Fire: Calhoun, 1973; Costello, 1887; Ginsberg, 1968; Mandlebaum, 1965; Moehring, 1981; Mohr, 1973

Health: Corey, 1994; Duffy, 1968–74; Goldman, 1997; Hershkowitz, 1977; Kaplan, 1975; Kaplan, 1979; Mandlebaum, 1965; Mohr, 1973; Peterson, 1979; Rosenberg, 1962; Rosner, 1995; Scobey, 1989; Williams, 1991

Housing: Bender, 1987; Costello, 1967; Cromley, 1990; Lane, 1974; Lubove, 1962; Moehring, 1981; Plunz, 1990; Schiesl, 1977; Simon, 1978

City Building: Boyer, 1985; Cooke, 1995; Foord, 1913; Hall, 1898; Kaplan, 1975; Kaplan, 1979; Lane, 1942; Leng and Davis, 1930–33; MacCracken, 1905; Mazaraki, 1966; Real Estate Record, 1898; Roper, 1973; Rosenzweig and Blackmar, 1992; Salwen, 1989; Schwarz, 1972; Schyuler, 1986; Scobey, 1989; Simon, 1972; Steinmeyer, 1975; Stone, 1969; Syrett, 1944

White Men Shall Rule America!: Field, 1982; Foner, 1988; Mohr, 1973; Scheiner, 1965

The End of Radical Reconstruction in New York: Beckert, 1995; Bernstein, 1984; Coben, 1962; Cohen, 1976; Field, 1982; Foner, 1988; Gordon, 1993; Henderson, 1976; Katz, 1968; Kolchin, 1967; Migliore, 1975; Mohr, 1973; Mushkat, 1988; Scheiner, 1965

CHAPTER 53:
CITY BUILDING

Bernstein, 1984; Boyer, 1985; Gardner, 1979; Goldman, 1997; Gordon, 1977; Harvey, 1981; Hood, 1993; Lane, 1942; Lockwood, 1976; Mandlebaum, 1965; McCullough, 1972; Moehring, 1981; Mohr, 1973; Morris, 1975; Real Estate Record, 1898; Rosenzweig and Blackmar, 1992; Scobey, 1989; Shanor, 1988; Simon, 1978; Teaford, 1984; Trachtenberg, 1982; Trager, 1987; Trager, 1990

Rapid Transit: Boyer, 1985; Derrick, 1979; Fischler, 1976; Hood, 1993; McCullough, 1972; Sullivan, 1995; Walker, 1970

Bosses, Boosters, and Bridgemakers: Chandler, 1977; Cooke, 1995; Hershkowitz, 1977; Lightfoot, 1981; Mandlebaum, 1965; McCullough, 1972; Schoenebaum, 1977; Schuyler, 1986; Simon, 1972; Syrett, 1944

Constructing Queens: Condit, 1980–81; Diamond and Ricciardi, 1983; Hecht, 1978; Kroessler, 1991; Lieberman, 1995; Seyfried, 1986; Seyfried, 1985; Seyfried, 1984; Singer, 1986

High Finance: Barth, 1982; Bender, 1987; Chandler, 1977; Costello, 1967; Czitrom, 1982; Gabler, 1988; Gardner, 1979; Garside, 1939; Gayle, 1974; Harlow, 1936; Henderson, 1986; Herskowitz, 1977; Klein, 1986; Kluger, 1986; Landau and Condit, 1996; Lane, 1942; Lockwood, 1976; Mandlebaum, 1965; Markham, 1987; McCullough, 1972; Moehring, 1981; Papke, 1987; Real Estate Record,

1898; Scobey, 1989; Silver, 1967; Syrett, 1944; Trager, 1990

Communication Giants: Gardner, 1979; Harlow, 1936; Klein, 1986; Landau and Condit, 1996; Mandlebaum, 1965; Papke, 1987; Real Estate Record, 1898; Scobey, 1989; Weisman, 1970; Weisman, 1953

Rail Complex: Condit, 1980–81; Lane, 1942; Scobey, 1989; Trager, 1990

Ladies' Mile: Abelson, 1989; Barth, 1982; Boyer, 1985; Chandler, 1977; Cooke, 1995; Devorkin, 1987; Frick, 1983; Gardner, 1979; Hobsbawm, 1975; Hower, 1943; Lockwood, 1976; Montgomery, 1967; Scobey, 1989

Rialto: Boyer, 1985; Corey, 1994; Frick, 1983; Henderson, 1986; Lockwood, 1976; Morris, 1975; Scobey, 1989

Downtown Downsides: Bernstein, 1984; Mandlebaum, 1965; Moehring, 1981; Scobey, 1989

CHAPTER 54:
HAUTE MONDE AND DEMIMONDE

Beckert, 1995; Langenderfer, 1980; Rosenzweig and Blackmar, 1992

Hot to Trot: Adelman, 1990; Asbury, 1938; Barth, 1982; Beckert, 1995; Birmingham, 1967; Boyer, 1985; Fabian, 1990; Leslie, 1954; Lockwood, 1976; McCullough, 1972; Morris, 1975; Riess, 1989; Rosenzweig and Blackmar, 1992; Sante, 1991; Scobey, 1992; Sell and Weybright, 1955; Simon, 1978; Slotkin, 1985; Wecter, 1937; Wright, 1983

Les Girls: Allen, 1991; Gilfoyle, 1992; Lockwood, 1976; McCabe, 1868; Morris, 1975; Odell, 1927–49; Ross, 1963; Seyfried, 1986; Simon, 1978; Snyder, 1989

On the Avenue: Beckert,

1995; Birmingham, 1967; Boyer, 1985; Canton, 1975; Cromley, 1990; Frick, 1983; Gardner, 1979; Lockwood, 1972; Lockwood, 1976; Moehring, 1981; Real Estate Record, 1898; Ross, 1963; Scharnhorst, 1985; Simon, 1978; Steele, 1985

McCallister Among the Patriarchs: Beckert, 1995; Dudden, 1983; Frick, 1983; Gardner, 1979; Gates, 1981; Morris, 1975; Rosenzweig and Blackmar, 1992; Thomas, 1967; Wecter, 1937

"still destitute of such an institution": Bender, 1987; Blaugrund, 1982; Clark, 1954; Dizikes, 1993; Frick, 1983; Gardner, 1979; Hellman, 1969; Kennedy, 1968; Morris, 1975; Rosenzweig and Blackmar, 1992; Simon, 1978; Trachtenberg, 1982

CHAPTER 55:
THE PROFESSIONAL-MANAGERIAL CLASS

Beckert, 1995; Blumin, 1985; Blumin, 1989; Montgomery, 1967; Walker, 1979

Noble Professions: Beckert, 1995; Bledstein, 1976; Calhoun, 1960; Chandler, 1977; Coon, 1947; Duffy, 1990; Gardner, 1979; Goldman, 1997; Horlick, 1975; Lockwood, 1976; Martin, 1970; McAdam, 1897–99; McCullough, 1972; Montgomery, 1967; Noble, 1977; Powell, 1988; Scobey, 1989; Teaford, 1984

Home Sweet Apartment: Cromley, 1990; Hawes, 1993; Kroessler, 1991; Lockwood, 1976; McCullough, 1983; Morris, 1975; Plunz, 1990; Scheiner, 1965; Schoenebaum, 1977; Scobey, 1989; Snyder-Grenier, 1996; Syrett, 1944; Taylor, 1994; Wilder, 1994

The Cultivated Life: Adelman, 1990; Barth, 1982; Bledstein, 1976; Costello, 1967; Dudden, 1983; Foner, 1988; Frick, 1983; Goldstein, 1992; Kaufman, 1972; Morris, 1975; Riess, 1989; Rosenzweig and Blackmar, 1992; Smith, 1967; Strasser, 1989; Trachtenberg, 1982; Turner, 1980; Ward, 1994

Rags to 'Spectability Religion: Beckert, 1995; Cawelti, 1967; Clark, 1978; Douglas, 1977; Duduit, 1983; Findlay, 1969; Johnson, 1973; Klein, 1986; McCullough, 1983; McLoughlin, 1970; Scharnhorst, 1985; Simon, 1978; Slotkin, 1985; Syrett, 1944; Trachtenberg, 1982; Wagenknecht, 1972; Waller, 1982

The Politics of Decency: Bannister, 1979; Beckert, 1995; Bender, 1987; Bernstein, 1984; Fine, 1964; Foner, 1988; Fredrickson, 1965; Haskell, 1977; Hobsbawm, 1975; Leach, 1980; Mandlebaum, 1965; Milne, 1956; Montgomery, 1987; Ross, 1991; Slotkin, 1985; Sproat, 1968; Teaford, 1984; Trachtenberg, 1982; Waugh, 1992; Whitman, 1949

"Women: Their Rights and Nothing Less": Banner, 1980; Barry, 1988; Blair, 1980; Boyer, 1985; Buhle, 1981; Buhle, 1987; Cooke, 1995; Costello, 1967; D'Emilio and Freedman, 1988; Devorkin, 1987; DuBois, 1978; Foner, 1988; Gabriel, 1998; Gardner, 1979; Gardner, 1994; Goldsmith, 1998; Gordon, 1976; Griffith, 1984; Lane, 1942; Leach, 1980; Morris, 1975; Paterson, 1955; Ross, 1963; Sears, 1977; Solomon, 1985; Stanton, 1898; Stanton, Anthony and Gage, 1881–1922; Truax, 1952; Underhill, 1995

CHAPTER 56:
EIGHT HOURS FOR WHAT WE WILL

Beckert, 1995; Costello, 1967; McKivigan and Robertson, 1996

The Eight-Hour Day: American Social History Project, 1989; Aptheker, 1951; Bernstein, 1984; Costello, 1967; Foner, 1988; Malon, 1981; Mohr, 1973; Montgomery, 1967; Montgomery, 1987; Schneider, 1994; Scobey, 1989; Singer, 1986

Marxists, Feminists, and the Money Power: Banner, 1980; Barry, 1988; Beckert, 1995; Bernstein, 1984; Boyer, 1985;

Buhle, 1987; Costello, 1967; Foner, 1988; Gardner, 1979; Gilfoyle, 1992; Gordon, 1976; Lieberman, 1995; Malon, 1981; Morris, 1975; Schneider, 1994; Scobey, 1989; Sears, 1977; Sharkey, 1959; Unger, 1964

Walking to Work: Bruce, 1877; Costello, 1967; Gardner, 1979; Harlow, 1931; Hecht, 1978; Moehring, 1981; Montgomery, 1967; O'Connor, 1958; Schoenebaum, 1977; Seyfried, 1984

Colored Quarters: Aptheker, 1951; Bernstein, 1984; Connolly, 1977; Costello, 1967; DuBois, 1978; Foner, 1988; Scheiner, 1965; Seraile, 1991a; Seraile, 1991b; Snyder-Grenier, 1996; Taylor, 1994; Wilder, 1994

Having Fun: Frick, 1983; Gilfoyle, 1992; Hecht, 1978; Kroessler, 1991; McCabe, 1868; McConachie, 1992; Morris, 1975; Rosenzweig and Blackmar, 1992; Scobey, 1989; Seyfried, 1984; Snyder, 1989

Old Sleuth and Buffalo Bill: Denning, 1987; Papke, 1987; Trachtenberg, 1982
Underworld: Asbury, 1928; Bruce, 1877; Campbell, 1900; Crapsey, 1872; Harlow, 1931; Hartsfield, 1985; Johnson, 1979; Papke, 1987; Peterson, 1983; Richardson, 1970; Rovere, 1947; Sante, 1991; Scobey, 1989; Sutton, 1874; Van Every, 1930; Walling, 1887; Wunsch, 1976

CHAPTER 57:
THE NEW YORK
COMMUNE?

Beckert, 1995; Bernstein, 1984; Bruce, 1877; Castells, 1978; Cherry, 1950; Costello, 1967; Edwards, 1971; Harvey, 1985; Herreshoff, 1967; Montgomery, 1967; Scobey, 1989; Slotkin, 1985; Williams, 1968

Orange and Green: Brown, 1966; Buhle, 1987; Gordon, 1977; Gordon, 1993; Mandlebaum, 1965; McKivigan and Robertson, 1996; Montgomery, 1967;

Slotkin, 1985

Slaughter on Eighth Avenue: Bernstein, 1984; Clark, 1864; Costello, 1967; Gordon, 1993; Headley, 1970; Mandlebaum, 1965

Tweed Toppled: Beckert, 1995; Bender, 1987; Bernstein, 1984; Callow, 1966; Carosso, 1987; Foner, 1988; Gardner, 1979; Hershkowitz, 1977; Katz, 1968; Klein, 1986; Mack, 1949; Mandlebaum, 1965; Mazaraki, 1966; McCullough, 1972; Moehring, 1981; Montgomery, 1967; Morris, 1975; Mushkat, 1988; Powell, 1988; Teaford, 1984; Trachtenberg, 1982

Back to the Ten-Hour Day: Bernstein, 1984; Bruce, 1877; Costello, 1967; Lieberman, 1995; Mohr, 1973; Montgomery, 1967; Yellowitz, 1978

Special Agent Anthony Comstock: Beckert, 1995; Beisel, 1997; Boyer, 1968; Browder, 1988; Brown, 1993; D'Emilio and Freedman, 1988; Duduit, 1983; Johnson, 1973; Leach, 1980; Morris, 1975; Sears, 1977; Waller, 1982

"The Slaughter of the Innocents": Browder, 1995; Buhle, 1981; Buhle, 1987; Costello, 1967; DuBois, 1978; Foner, 1977; Fox, 1993; Herreshoff, 1967; Leach, 1980; Mohr, 1973; Montgomery, 1967; Waller, 1982

CHAPTER 58:
WORK OR BREAD!

Browder, 1985; Foner, 1988; Lane, 1942; Sobel, 1988; Sobel, 1965; Unger, 1964

Taking Stock: Beckert, 1995; Chernow, 1990; Fels, 1959; Gordon, 1982; Hobsbawm, 1975; Lane, 1942; Livingston, 1987; Livingston, 1994; Rezneck, 1968; Scobey, 1989; Slotkin, 1985; Sobel, 1988

Work or Bread!: Beckert, 1995; Bender, 1987; Boyer, 1985; Carosso, 1987; Chernow, 1990; Feder, 1936; Folsom, 1991; Foner, 1988;

Gutman, 1965; Mandlebaum, 1965; Moehring, 1981; O'Donnell, 1995; Real Estate Record, 1898; Reznock, 1968; Rosenzweig and Blackmar, 1992; Salwen, 1989; Seyfried, 1985; Sobel, 1988; Unger, 1964

Tompkins Square: Bender, 1987; Bernstein, 1956; Bruce, 1877; Gutman, 1965; Gutman, 1965; Montgomery, 1987; Rezneck, 1968; Ringenbach, 1973; Trachtenberg, 1982

Retrenchment: Bender, 1987; Cohen, 1976; Lui, 1993; Mandlebaum, 1965; Mazaraki, 1966; Moehring, 1981; Mushkat, 1988; Ringenbach, 1973; Scobey, 1989; Shefter, 1993; Teaford, 1984; Yearley, 1970

"Charity Rages Like an Epidemic": Kaplan, 1978; Lui, 1993; Mandlebaum, 1965; Rezneck, 1968; Ringenbach, 1973; Slotkin, 1985; Waugh, 1992

Of Beggars and Tramps: Beckert, 1995; Bruce, 1877; Denning, 1987; Fitzgerald, 1992; Foner, 1988; Kaplan, 1978; Katz, 1983; Katz, 1986; Kurland, 1971; Lui, 1993; Mandlebaum, 1965; Moehring, 1981; Reznick, 1968; Ringenbach, 1973; Schneider, 1938–41; Slotkin, 1985; Stanley, 1992; Trachtenberg, 1982; Trattner, 1983; Waugh, 1992

Dispensing with Democracy: Beckert, 1995; Bender, 1987; Bernstein, 1984; Erie, 1988; Foner, 1988; Kaplan, 1978; Mandlebaum, 1965; McGerr, 1986; Mushkat, 1988; Rosenzweig and Blackmar, 1992; Slotkin, 1985; Teaford, 1984

A Monumental Aside: McCabe, 1868; Unrau, 1984

Farewell to Reconstruction: Cohen, 1976; Foner, 1988; Mushkat, 1988; Slotkin, 1985; Trachtenberg, 1982

The Great Strike: Beckert, 1995; Bernstein, 1956; Brown, 1966; Bruce, 1877; Carosso, 1987; Chandler, 1977; Clark, 1864; Cohen, 1976; Duduit, 1983; Flick,

1939; Fogelson, 1989; Foner, 1977; Foner, 1988; Garmey, 1984; Hershkowitz, 1977; Kluger, 1986; Lane, 1942; Mack, 1949; Mandlebaum, 1965; Mushkat, 1988; Papke, 1987; Ringenbach, 1973; Roper, 1973; Scheiner, 1965; Scobey, 1989; Slotkin, 1985; Trachtenberg, 1982; Trager, 1990; Waugh, 1992; Woodward, 1951

PART FIVE:
INDUSTRIAL CENTER AND
CORPORATE COMMAND
POST (1880–1898)

CHAPTER 59:
MANHATTAN, INC.

Aronowitz, 1983; Carosso, 1987; Chandler, 1977; Cohen, 1976; Fels, 1959; Hobsbawm, 1987; Livingston, 1986; Sklar, 1988; Slotkin, 1985; Sobel, 1988; Stokes, 1928; Trachtenberg, 1982

The Corporate Solution: Bannister, 1979; Beckert, 1995; Brown and Ment, 1980; Carosso, 1987; Chandler, 1977; Chernow, 1990; Dean, 1957; Donnelly, 1982; Fels, 1959; Fine, 1964; Gordon, 1982; Hammack, 1982; Hower, 1943; Klein, 1986; Kluger, 1996; Kobler, 1988; Kroessler, 1991; Leopold, 1954; Lisagor, 1989; Livingston, 1986; McAdam, 1897–99; McCabe, 1868; Myers, 1931; Nevins, 1940; Sklar, 1988; Swaine, 1946; Tomsich, 1971; Trachtenberg, 1982; Wecter, 1937; Winkler, 1934

Associates and Agents: Barth, 1982; Beckert, 1995; Dean, 1957; Fox, 1984; Hammack, 1982; Hobsbawm, 1987; Hobson, 1984; Hodgson, 1990; Jaher, 1982; Kluger, 1996; Lears, 1995; Lisagor, 1989; Norris, 1990; Parrini, 1969; Pope, 1983; Powell, 1988; Schudson, 1984; Seyfried, 1984; Starret, 1938; Strasser, 1989; Swaine, 1946; Trachtenberg, 1982; Winkler, 1934

Tall Towers: Beckert, 1995; Boyer, 1985; Burchard and Bush-Brown, 1961; Costello, 1887; Derrick, 1979; Domosh, 1985; Donner, 1990; Finney, 1970; Gibbs, 1976; Goldberger, 1981;

Hammack, 1982; Hendin, 1993; Kessner, 1977; Klein, 1986; Landau and Condit, 1996; Lisagor, 1989; Lockwood, 1976; McCabe, 1868; McShane, 1979; Morris, 1975; Myers, 1974; New York Steam Corporation, 1932; Snyder-Grenier, 1996; Starrett, 1928; Stern, 1900; Still, 1956; Van Leeuwen, 1988

High Rollers: Bobrick, 1981; Boyer, 1983; Bronx Museum, 1986; Carosso, 1987; Chandler, 1977; Cheape, 1980; Derrick, 1979; Donnelly, 1982; Fischler, 1976; Fox, 1977; Hammack, 1982; Hirsch, 1948; Klein, 1986; Mandlebaum, 1965; McCabe, 1868; McCullough, 1981; Moerhing, 1981; Morris, 1975; Nye, 1990; Skolnik, 1971; Snyder-Grenier, 1996; Stern, 1900; Sullivan, 1995; Tabb, 1984; Ultan, 1985; Walker, 1970; Wecter, 1937

CHAPTER 60:
BRIGHT LIGHTS, BIG CITY

Hello, Central: Barnouw, 1966; Chandler, 1977; Cleveland, 1985; Dean, 1957; Garnet, 1985; Green, 1990; Josephson, 1969; Klein, 1986; Landau and Condit, 1996; Lisagor, 1989; Lockwood, 1976; Morris, 1975; Pool, 1977; Rudolph, 1986; Schlesinger, 1933; Van Leeuwen, 1988

Let There Be Light: Abelson, 1989; Bruce, 1987; Carosso, 1987; Conot, 1979; Cromley, 1990; Harlow, 1936; Millard, 1990; Nye, 1990; Rudolph, 1986; Schivelbusch, 1988; Trachtenberg, 1982

Bright Lights: Abelson, 1989; Burchard and Bush-Brown, 1961; Cheape, 1980; Gilfoyle, 1992; Landau and Condit, 1996; McCabe, 1868; Morris, 1975; Nye, 1990; Trager, 1990

Useful and Unuseful Utilities: Barth, 1982; Carosso, 1987; Chandler, 1977; Chernow, 1990; Cleveland, 1985; Collins, 1934; Daley, 1959; Hodas, 1976; Hurwitz, 1943; Lurkis, 1982; Myers, 1974; Novick, 1976; Nye, 1990; Rudolph, 1986; Stotz, 1948;

Sullivan, 1995; Teaford, 1984

CHAPTER 61:
CHÂTEAUX SOCIETY

Beckert, 1995; Lasch, 1973; Livingston, 1986; Livingston, 1994; Morris, 1975; Nye, 1990; Wecter, 1937

From the Four Hundred to the Two Thousand: Amory, 1960; Beer, 1941; Chernow, 1990; Douglas, 1991; Hammack, 1982; Jaher, 1982; McCabe, 1868; Morris, 1975; Schiesl, 1977; Stern, 1900; Trachtenberg, 1982; Wecter, 1937

To the Opera House: Bannister, 1979; Dizikes, 1993; Henderson, 1973; Horowitz, 1987; Jaher, 1982; Kasson, 1990; Kolodin, 1966; Levine, 1988; Mayer, 1983; Mueller, 1951; Raynor, 1978; Schickel, 1960; Shanet, 1975; Trager, 1987; Wecter, 1937

Châteaux Country: Bacon, 1986; Baker, 1980; Baker, 1989; Boyer, 1985; Burchard and Bush-Brown, 1961; Chernow, 1990; Cooke, 1995; Cromley, 1990; Fairfield, 1985; Fogelson, 1989; Gowans, 1976; Hawes, 1993; Landau and Condit, 1996; Lockwood, 1976; Lowe, 1992; McCabe, 1868; Morris, 1975; Mumford, 1971; Norton, 1984; Presa, 1981; Roth, 1983; Stern, 1900; Trager, 1987; Wecter, 1937; Wilson, 1983

Manhattan Renaissance: Beard, 1993; Beer, 1941; Brooklyn Museum, 1979; Carosso, 1987; Conrad, 1984; Fogelson, 1989; Gowans, 1976; Hammack, 1982; Hoopes, 1979; Mayer, 1958; Mumford, 1971; Naifeh and Smith, 1976; Norton, 1984; Simpson, 1986; Trachtenberg, 1982; Trager, 1987; Watson, 1983; Weitzenhoffer, 1986

Pork into Porcelain: Ayres, 1993; Barth, 1982; Brown, 1955; Jaher, 1982; Kraus, 1980; McCabe, 1868; Morris, 1975; Simpson, 1986; Tompkins, 1970

Making History: Beard, 1993; Bender, 1987; Bernstein,

1989; Bluestone, 1991; Dayton, 1882; Gilmartin, 1994; Hammack, 1982; Harris, 1970; Harris, 1990; Hobsbawm, 1987; Hosmer, 1965; Jaher, 1982; Marling, 1988; McNamara, 1997; Page, 1995; Stern, 1900; Vail, 1954; Wecter, 1937

Inclusions: Baltzell, 1987; Beckert, 1995; Cookson and Persell, 1985; Fox and Lears, 1983; Hobsbawm, 1987; Jaher, 1982; Levine, 1988; Livingston, 1986; McCabe, 1868; McLachlin, 1970; Stern, 1983; Wecter, 1937

Exclusions: Beer, 1941; Diner, 1992; Gorelick, 1981; Hammack, 1982; Higham, 1988; Howe, 1976; Kobler, 1988; Mayo, 1988; McSeveney, 1972; McWilliams, 1948; Rischin, 1962; Wecter, 1937

CHAPTER 62:
"THE LEECHES MUST GO!"

Aronowitz, 1983; Barnes, 1915; Beckert, 1995; Buhle, 1987; Devlin, 1996; Fink, 1983; Foner, 1988; Foner, 1975; Gabler, 1988; Gompers, 1984; Gutman, 1977; Hurwitz, 1943; Klein, 1986; LaFeber, 1963; Lieberman, 1995; McSeveney, 1972; Mendel, 1989; Mollenkopf, 1992; O'Donnell, 1995; Ringenbach, 1973; Schneider, 1994; Scobey, 1989; Seretan, 1979; Trachtenberg, 1982; Trautmann, 1980; Walkowitz, 1993; Ware, 1929

The First Labor Day: Foner, 1973; McKivigan and Robertson, 1996; Montgomery, 1987; Watts, 1983

Progress and Poverty: Beckert, 1995; Blackmar, 1989; Blythe, 1983; Boyer, 1978; Bremner, 1956; Donnelly, 1982; Fine, 1964; Foner, 1980; George, 1900; Hammack, 1982; Hellman, 1987; O'Donnell, 1995; Rezneck, 1968; Scobey, 1989; Jones, 1971; Thomas, 1983; Trachtenberg, 1982

"Christ Himself Was But an Evicted Peasant": Bell, 1937;

Cohalan, 1983; Curran, 1978; Donnelly, 1982; Fairfield, 1985; Hammack, 1982; Hellman, 1987; Howells, 1976; Mendel, 1989; Montgomery, 1987; O'Donnell, 1995; Shanaberger, 1993

Dynamite!: Avrich, 1988; Beckert, 1995; Donner, 1990; Fogelson, 1989; Glickman and Glickman, 1984; Harlow, 1931; Kosak, 1987; O'Donnell, 1995; Trautmann, 1980; Ware, 1929; Wexler, 1984

May Day!: Anderson, 1976; Avrich, 1984; Avrich, 1988; O'Donnell, 1995

"Honest Labor Against Thieving Landlords and Politicians": Atkins, 1947; Beckert, 1995; Hammack, 1982; Hellman, 1987; Mollenkopf, 1992; O'Donnell, 1995; Scobey, 1989; Sullivan, 1995; Trachtenberg, 1982

The "Tailboard" Campaign: Hammack, 1982; Hellman, 1987; Mollenkopf, 1992; O'Donnell, 1995; Post and Leubuscher, 1887; Rezneck, 1968; Scobey, 1984; Scobey, 1989; Speek, 1917

The College-Bred Tribune: Beckert, 1995; Bender, 1987; Collier, 1994; Donnelly, 1982; Fox and Lears, 1983; Gompers, 1984; Hammack, 1982; Hurwitz, 1943; Kurland, 1971; McCabe, 1868; McCullough, 1981; Morris, 1979; Roosevelt, 1891; Schiesl, 1977; Skolnik, 1971; Slotkin, 1985; Sullivan, 1995; Teaford, 1984; Tomsich, 1971; Wecter, 1937

Bosses, Bishops, and the Man of Iron: Allen, 1993; Beckert, 1995; Bernstein, 1984; Binder, 1995; Cohalan, 1983; Curran, 1978; Czitrom, 1991; Donnelly, 1982; Gibson, 1951; Gilfoyle, 1992; Hammack, 1982; Hurwitz, 1943; Martí, 1975; McCabe, 1868; McCullough, 1972; McGerr, 1986; McSeveney, 1972; Montgomery, 1987; Nadel, 1990; Nevins, 1935; O'Donnell, 1995; Post and Leubuscher, 1887; Rezneck, 1968; Rosenwaike, 1972; Rosenzweig and Blackmar,

1992; Shefter, 1993; Speek, 1917; Stoddard, 1931; Trachtenberg, 1982; Werner, 1928

Denouement: Avrich, 1988; Beckert, 1995; Curran, 1978; Donnelly, 1982; Hammack, 1982; Hellman, 1987; Higham, 1988; Martí, 1975; Mendel, 1989; Nevins, 1935; Norton, 1984; Rumbarger, 1989; Scobey, 1989; Speek, 1917; Sullivan, 1995; Trachtenberg, 1982; Ware, 1929; Werner, 1928

The New Tammany Hall: Beckert, 1995; Binder, 1995; Cheape, 1980; Donnelly, 1982; Donner, 1990; Erie, 1988; Fairfield, 1985; Fogelson, 1989; Gronowicz, 1991; Gronowicz, 1998; Hammack, 1982; Hellman, 1987; Hirsch, 1948; Hirsch, 1978; Hurwitz, 1943; James, 1993; McNickle, 1993; McSeveney, 1972; O'Donnell, 1995; Riordon, 1948; Shefter, 1976; Shefter, 1978; Skolnik, 1971; Sullivan, 1995; Teaford, 1984; Thomas, 1932; Thomas, 1983; Trachtenberg, 1982; Waugh, 1992; Werner, 1928; Zeisloft, 1899

CHAPTER 63:
THE NEW IMMIGRANTS

Aronowitz, 1973; Bayor and Meagher, 1996; Binder, 1995; Gordon, 1982; *Harvard Encyclopedia*, 1980; Higham, 1988; Hobsbawm, 1987; Lapham, 1977; McCaffrey, 1996; McSeveney, 1972; Mendel, 1989; Miller, 1985; Nadel, 1990; Nilsen, 1996; Rosenwaike, 1972; Scheiner, 1965; Schneider, 1994; Schudson, 1978; Stokes, 1928; Trachtenberg, 1982; Unrau, 1984; Wilder, 1994

Shtetls under Siege: Binder, 1995; Ewen, 1985; *Harvard Encyclopedia*, 1980; Hertzberg, 1989; Howe, 1976; Kessner, 1977; Kosak, 1987; Mendel, 1989; New York Historical Society, 1970; Rischin, 1962; Rosenwaike, 1972; Sanders, 1969; Sanders, 1988

Occidentals, Orientals: Binder, 1995; Cooke, 1995; Cremin, 1988; Dain, 1972; Fierstien, 1990; Goodman,

1979; Gorelick, 1981; Goren, 1970; Gurock, 1979; *Harvard Encyclopedia*, 1980; Howe, 1976; Kosak, 1987; Mayo, 1988; McCabe, 1868; Mendel, 1989; Rischin, 1962; Rosner, 1982; Sanders, 1969

The Lower East Side: Binder, 1995; Bluestone, 1991; Cooke, 1995; Diner, 1992; Ewen, 1985; Fried, 1980; Gorelick, 1981; Gurock, 1979; Hammack, 1982; Harlow, 1931; Howe, 1976; Joselit, 1983; Kessner, 1977; Kosak, 1987; McNickle, 1993; Mendel, 1989; O'Donnell, 1995; Rischin, 1962; Rosenwaike, 1972; Sanders, 1969; Schudson, 1978; Snyder-Grenier, 1996; Trautmann, 1980; Wexler, 1984

Mezzogiorno Miseria: Brown, 1986; Ewen, 1985; Fenton, 1957; Gabaccia, 1984; *Harvard Encyclopedia*, 1980; Hendin, 1993; Hobsbawm, 1987; Mendel, 1989; Pozzetta, 1971; Tomasi, 1975; Unrau, 1984

Manhattan Colonia: *Harvard Encyclopedia*, 1980; Hendin, 1993; Kessner, 1977; McCullough, 1983; Mendel, 1989; Ment and Donovan, 1980; Montgomery, 1987; Orsi, 1985; Osofsky, 1966; Pozzetta, 1971; Rosenwaike, 1972; Snyder-Grenier, 1996

The Madonna of 115th Street: Brown, 1986; Cohalan, 1983; Curran, 1978; Di Giovanni, 1983; Donnelly, 1982; Hendin, 1993; Higham, 1988; McCabe, 1868; McCullough, 1983; Mendel, 1989; Orsi, 1985; Pozzetta, 1971; Sullivan, 1992; Tomasi, 1975; W.P.A., 1938b

Chinatown: Beck, 1898; Binder, 1995; Bonner, 1997; Chen, 1941; Gardner, 1894; Gong and Grant, 1930; *Harvard Encyclopedia*, 1980; Hobsbawm, 1987; Hsiong, 1939; Leinenweber, 1969; Light, 1974; Mendel, 1989; Tchen, 1990; Tchen, 1992; Tchen, 1996; Torres, 1995

CHAPTER 64:
THAT'S ENTERTAINMENT!

Hammack, 1982; Kasson,

1978; Koolhaas, 1978; Martí, 1975; McCabe, 1868; Mendel, 1989; Pilat, 1941; Snyder-Grenier, 1996; Stern, 1983; Weinstein, 1984

Pleasure and Commerce: Bronx Museum, 1986; Czitrom, 1991; Garrett, 1978; Kasson, 1978; Kroessler, 1991; Lieberman, 1995; Martí, 1975; Mendel, 1989; Pilat, 1941; Riess, 1989; Rosenzweig and Blackmar, 1992; Seyfried, 1984; Snyder, 1989; Snyder-Grenier, 1996; Thomas, 1969; Weinstein, 1984; Younger, 1978

All the World's Onstage: Bonner, 1997; Harlow, 1931; *Harvard Encyclopedia*, 1980; Heintze, 1990; Howe, 1976; Kaufman, 1990; McArthur, 1984; McConachie, 1992; Mendel, 1989; Rischin, 1962; Sanders, 1988; Slobin, 1982; Snyder-Grenier, 1996; Sogliuzzo, 1985

Variety: the Spice of Bowery Life: Allen, 1991; Barth, 1982; Gilbert, 1940; Gilfoyle, 1992; Gorn, 1986; Harlow, 1931; Howe, 1976; Huggins, 1973; Marks, 1934; Mendel, 1989; Nasaw, 1993; Ottley and Weatherby, 1967; Pilat, 1941; Rischin, 1962; Snyder, 1989; Tchen, 1992; Toll, 1976; Woll, 1989; W.P.A., 1938b; Zellers, 1971

"Prominent Types Which Go to Make up Life in the Metropolis": Allen, 1991; Alpert, 1991; Brown, 1966; Gilbert, 1940; Hamm, 1979; Henderson, 1986; Josephson, 1969; Kahn, 1955; Lott, 1993; Marks, 1934; Moody, 1980; Rischin, 1962; Snyder, 1989; Taylor, 1992; Tchen, 1992; Woll, 1989

Sex Redivivus: Chauncey, 1989; Erenberg, 1981; Gilfoyle, 1992; Gorn, 1986; Katz, 1983; Lewis, 1988; McCabe, 1868; Miller, 1990; Morris, 1975; Pivar, 1973; Sante, 1991

Pastorized Variety: Allen, 1991; Barth, 1982; Beer, 1941; Gilbert, 1940; Hamm, 1979; Huggins, 1973; Marks, 1934; Morris, 1975; Snyder, 1989; Toll, 1976; W.P.A., 1938b; Zellers, 1971

The Roots of Tin Pan Alley: Bergreen, 1990; Erenberg, 1981; Furia, 1990; Goldberg, 1930; Hamm, 1979; Harlow, 1931; Huggins, 1973; Jasen, 1993; Johnson, 1933; McArthur, 1984; Meyer, 1977; Slobin, 1982; Snyder, 1989; Whitcomb, 1987

Big Tent on Madison Square: Asbury, 1938; Boyer, 1985; Chauncey, 1989; Durso, 1979; Garrett, 1978; Gilfoyle, 1992; Koolhaus, 1978; Lowe, 1992; Moody, 1980; Riess, 1989; Stern, 1983

Satan's Circus: Asbury, 1928; Asbury, 1938; Erenberg, 1981; Gilfoyle, 1992; Gorn, 1986; Lewis, 1988; McCabe, 1868; Morris, 1975; Pivar, 1973; Sante, 1991; Stern, 1983

Best of Broadway: Allen, 1991; Barth, 1982; Boyer, 1985; Burke, 1972; Frick, 1983; Hammack, 1982; Henderson, 1973; Henderson, 1989; McArthur, 1984; McCabe, 1868; Morris, 1975; Stern, 1983; Taylor, 1991; Trager, 1987; Wecter, 1937

Pulitzer's World: Barth, 1982; Buhle, 1987; Chauncey, 1989; Cole, 1979; Filler, 1976; Fox, 1984; Fox and Lears, 1983; Gorn, 1986; Hofstadter, 1955; Juergens, 1966; Lewis, 1978; Pope, 1983; Ryan, 1990; Schudson, 1978; Schudson, 1984; Swanberg, 1967; Taylor, 1992; Trachtenberg, 1982; Trachtenberg, 1989

CHAPTER 65:
PURITY CRUSADE

Bannister, 1979; Boyer, 1978; Donnelly, 1960; Jaher, 1964; Mayo, 1988; Miller, 1886; Strong, 1891; Trachtenberg, 1982

Armies of Salvation: Boyer, 1978; Campbell, 1900; Cross, 1967; Davis, 1967; Harlow, 1931; Magnuson, 1977; May, 1949; McKinley, 1980; McKinley, 1986

"Friendly Visitors": Bender, 1987; Boyer, 1978; Bremner, 1956; Ehrenreich, 1985; Gordon, 1988; Hammack, 1982; Higham, 1988; Jaher,

1982; Kaplan, 1978; Katz, 1986; Kurland, 1971; Lubove, 1965; Lui, 1993; Ringenbach, 1973; Rischin, 1962; Stanley, 1992; Stewart, 1911; Taylor, 1963; Ward, 1989; Waugh, 1992; Zeisloft, 1899

Save the Children: Boyer, 1978; Comfort, 1906; DiDonato, 1960; Fitzgerald, 1992; Gilfoyle, 1992; Katz, 1986; O'Grady, 1930; Schneider, 1938–41; Waugh, 1992; Zeisloft, 1899

The War on Sin: Beer, 1941; Beisel, 1997; Bernstein, 1984; Bordin, 1981; Boyer, 1978; Chauncey, 1989; Chernow, 1990; Crane, 1979; Czitrom, 1991; Erie, 1988; Fabian, 1990; Fishman, 1980; Fox, 1989; Gilfoyle, 1986; Gilfoyle, 1992; Gordon, 1988; Hammack, 1982; Howe, 1976; Johnson, 1973; Kasson, 1978; Kasson, 1990; Katz, 1983; Lewis, 1988; Papke, 1987; Peiss, 1985; Pivar, 1973; Richardson, 1970; Riess, 1989; Ryan, 1990; Skolnik, 1971; Trachtenberg, 1982; Walkowitz, 1992; Weinstein, 1984; Wunsch, 1976

Decentest Nation: Barth, 1982; Beer, 1941; Bender, 1987; Bendroth, 1985; Blair, 1980; Bordin, 1981; Boyer, 1978; Brown, 1966; Conrad, 1984; Douglas, 1977; Ellmann, 1987; Fox and Lears, 1983; Fox, 1989; Gordon, 1976; Hammack, 1982; Hobsbawm, 1987; Kasson, 1990; Lasch, 1973a; Leonard, 1932; Levine, 1988; Livingston, 1986; May, 1959; McCullough, 1981; Morris, 1975; Perry, 1984; Pivar, 1973; Raleigh, 1957; Rubin, 1991; Smith-Rosenberg, 1985; Stern, 1983; Taylor, 1994; Tomsich, 1971; Trachtenberg, 1982

"Hey, Whiskers!": Chauncey, 1989; Crane, 1979; Fox, 1977; Gardner, 1894; Gilfoyle, 1992; Greenberg, 1988; Katz, 1983; Knerr, 1957; Lewis, 1988; Reynolds, 1995; Trachtenberg, 1982; Werner, 1957

CHAPTER 66:
SOCIAL GOSPEL

Boyer, 1978; Campbell,

1900; Carosso, 1987; Chernow, 1990; Fine, 1964; Fishburn, 1981; Fox and Lears, 1983; Hartsfield, 1985; Higham, 1988; Hurwitz, 1943; Jaher, 1982; Jaher, 1964; McCabe, 1868; Miller, 1985; Moulton, 1964; Rischin, 1962; Wagenknecht, 1972; Wecter, 1937

Christian Radicals: Fine, 1964; Hurwitz, 1943; Keyser, 1910; Rischin, 1962; Scudder, 1940; Waugh, 1992

Creed into Deed: Boyer, 1978; Cromley, 1990; Friess, 1981; Gurock, 1979; Guttchen, 1974; Kraus, 1980; Plunz, 1990; Rischin, 1962; Scobey, 1989; Trachtenberg, 1982

Supping Sorrow with the Poor: Bordin, 1981; Boyer, 1978; Brown, 1986; Cohalan, 1983; Cook, 1913; Davis, 1967; DiDonato, 1960; Ewen, 1986; Fox and Lears, 1983; Gorelick, 1981; Groshen, 1989; Hammack, 1982; Howe, 1976; Johnson and Wilentz, 1994; Katz, 1986; Kraus, 1980; Lubove, 1962; O'Donnell, 1995; Paulding, 1937; Quiroga, 1989; Rosenberg, 1987; Rousmaniere, 1980; Smith-Rosenberg, 1985; Waugh, 1992

The White List: Barth, 1982; Bender, 1987; Benson, 1986; Bremner, 1956; Dye, 1980; Fitzgerald, 1992; Katz, 1986; Sklar, 1995; Stewart, 1911; Tax, 1980; Ward, 1989; Waugh, 1992

Realists: Avrich, 1984; Bender, 1987; Bremner, 1956; Conrad, 1984; Giamo, 1989; Howells, 1976; Kazin, 1942; May, 1959; Morris, 1975; Scobey, 1989; Slotkin, 1985

How the Other Half Lived: Boyer, 1978; Bremner, 1956; Conrad, 1984; Davis, 1967; Fried, 1990; Giamo, 1989; Harlow, 1931; Higham, 1988; Hurwitz, 1943; Katz, 1983; Kroessler, 1991; Lane, 1974; Page, 1995; Perry, 1984; Riis, 1890; Schudson, 1978; Trachtenberg, 1982; Trachtenberg, 1989; Ward, 1989

"Strike at a Given Signal": Boyer, 1978; Hammack,

1982; Jaher, 1982; Kaplan, 1978; Knerr, 1957; Muccigrosso, 1968; Schiesl, 1977; Skolnik, 1971; Sullivan, 1995; Waugh, 1992

CHAPTER 67:
GOOD GOVERNMENT

American Social History Project, 1989; Beer, 1941; Boyer, 1978; Chernow, 1990; Conrad, 1984; Feder, 1936; Fels, 1959; Hoffman, 1970; Howe, 1976; LaFeber, 1963; Navin and Sears, 1955; Osofsky, 1966; Painter, 1987; Rezneck, 1968; Rischin, 1962; Roth, 1983; Sklar, 1988; Sobel, 1965; Sobel, 1988; Waugh, 1992; White, 1982

Dealing with Hard Times: Barth, 1982; Boyer, 1978; Burgess, 1962; Carosso, 1987; Czitrom, 1991; Erie, 1988; Feder, 1936; Fine, 1964; Gordon, 1982; Higham, 1988; Hoffman, 1970; Jaher, 1982; Kaplan, 1978; Katz, 1986; Kosak, 1987; Lane, 1974; Leinenweber, 1969; Linderman, 1974; May, 1949; McCormick, 1981; Mendel, 1989; Museum of the City of New York, 1990; Osofsky, 1966; Painter, 1987; Presa, 1981; Rezneck, 1968; Ringenbach, 1973; Rosenzweig and Blackmar, 1992; Skolnik, 1971; Stewart, 1911; Swanberg, 1967; Taylor, 1963; Waugh, 1992; Wexler, 1984; White, 1982; Zeisloft, 1899

Revolt of the Privileged: Beer, 1941; Boyer, 1983; Boyer, 1978; Corey, 1994; Czitrom, 1991; Donner, 1990; Finegold, 1985; Fox, 1977; Hammack, 1982; Howe, 1976; Jaher, 1982; Jeffers, 1994; Knerr, 1957; Lane, 1974; Lui, 1993; McCormick, 1981; McSeveney, 1972; Morris, 1975; Muccigrosso, 1968; Nevins and Krout, 1948; O'Connor, 1963; Rischin, 1962; Schiesl, 1977; Skolnik, 1971; Sullivan, 1995; Swanberg, 1967; Syrett, 1944; Taylor, 1963; Teaford, 1984; Thomas, 1969; Waugh, 1992; Weinstein, 1984; White, 1982; Williams, 1991

Colonel Waring Cleans the Streets: Armstrong, 1976;

Corey, 1994; Knerr, 1957; Kroessler, 1991; Krogius, 1978; Loop, 1964; McSeveney, 1972; Melosi, 1981; O'Donnell, 1995; Pozzetta, 1971; Scobey, 1989; Skolnick, 1968; Skolnik, 1971; Teaford, 1984; Trachtenberg, 1982; Zeisloft, 1899

Germ Warfare: Duffy, 1990; Duffy, 1968–74; Fee, 1995; Kraus, 1980; Lubove, 1962; Rischin, 1962; Skolnik, 1971; Starr, 1957; Starr, 1982; Teaford, 1984; Williams, 1991

Housing Front: Bacon, 1986; Bender, 1987; Boyer, 1978; Carosso, 1987; Davis, 1967; Dolkart, 1988; Knerr, 1957; Lane, 1974; Lubove, 1962; Page, 1995; Plunz, 1990; Rischin, 1962; Rosenzweig and Blackmar, 1992; Schiesl, 1977; Stern, 1983; Teaford, 1984; Tomsich, 1971; Zeisloft, 1899

Roosevelt Cracks Down: Asbury, 1938; Beer, 1941; Boyer, 1978; Filler, 1976; Fogelson, 1989; Gilfolyle, 1992; Hammack, 1982; Harbaugh, 1963; Henry, 1991; Howe, 1976; Hurwitz, 1943; Jeffers, 1994; Katz, 1986; Knerr, 1957; Kosak, 1987; Kraus, 1980; Lane, 1974; McCormick, 1981; McSeveney, 1972; Mendel, 1989; Moulton, 1964; Museum of the City of New York, 1990; Rischin, 1962; Schiesl, 1977; Sullivan, 1995; Swanberg, 1961; Swanberg, 1967; Syrett, 1944; Thomas, 1969

Populists and Goldbugs: Beer, 1941; Buhle, 1987; Carosso, 1987; Carosso, 1970; Fels, 1959; Goodwyn, 1976; Hammack, 1982; Hammond, 1970; Harvey, 1963; Hobsbawm, 1987; Hofstadter, 1955; Jones, 1964; LaFeber, 1963; Linderman, 1974; Livingston, 1986; May, 1959; McSeveney, 1972; Painter, 1987; Sklar, 1988; Sobel, 1988; Swanberg, 1961; Trachtenberg, 1982; White, 1982; Zeisloft, 1899

Fusion Defused: Boyer, 1978; Cerillo, 1969; Erie, 1988; Gordon, 1982; Hammack, 1982; Hellman, 1987;

Hoffman, 1970; Knerr, 1957; Kurland, 1971; McSeveney, 1972; O'Connor, 1963; Schiesl, 1977; Skolnik, 1971; Swanberg, 1961; Thomas, 1969; Waugh, 1992; Wecter, 1937; Weiss, 1968; Zeisloft, 1899

CHAPTER 68:
SPLENDID LITTLE WAR

Bannister, 1979; Beer, 1941; Boyer, 1978; Carosso, 1987; Chandler, 1977; Fels, 1959; Foner, 1972; Hall, 1898; Healy, 1988; Hirsch, 1948; Hobsbawm, 1987; Hofstadter, 1967; Kiernan, 1978; Klein, 1986; La Feber, 1963; Lears, 1981; Leopold, 1954; Linderman, 1974; Livingston, 1986; Magdoff, 1969; McCullough, 1981; Myers, 1931; Painter, 1987; Pratt, 1936; Rischin, 1962; Sanchez-Korrol, 1983; Sklar, 1988; Strong, 1891; Trachtenberg, 1982; Williams, 1969

Pro Patria: Foner, 1972; *Harvard Encyclopedia*, 1980; Healy, 1988; Kiernan, 1978; Linderman, 1974; Maldonado-Denis, 1972; Sanchez Korrol, 1983; Sinnette, 1989; Turton, 1986;

Vega, 1984; Wakefield, 1960

"Blood, Blood, Blood!": Barth, 1982; Crane, 1979; Foner, 1972; Healy, 1988; Juergens, 1966; Leinenweber, 1969; Linderman, 1974; Pivar, 1973; Schudson, 1978; Swanberg, 1961

Winners and Losers: Beisner, 1968; Bogart, 1989; Brooklyn Museum, 1979; Carosso, 1987; Ciucci, 1979; Fels, 1959; Foner, 1972; Gordon, 1982; Healy, 1988; Hobsbawm, 1987; Hodgson, 1990; Hoffman, 1970; Kiernan, 1978; Leopold, 1954; Linderman, 1974; Magdoff, 1969; May, 1959; McNamara, 1997; Morris, 1975; Painter, 1987; Sanchez-Korral, 1983; Shefter, 1993; Sklar, 1988; Skolnik, 1971; Starr, 1957; Vega, 1984; Waugh, 1992; Welch, 1979; White, 1982; Winkler, 1934; Zeisloft, 1899

CHAPTER 69:
IMPERIAL CITY

Annexation and Its Enemies: Graves, 1894; Hall, 1898; Hammack, 1982; Kaplan, 1975; Kaplan, 1979;

MacCracken, 1905; Mazaraki, 1966; Schroth, 1974; Scobey, 1989; Stiles, 1867–70; Stone, 1969

"Imperial Destiny": Graves, 1894; Green, 1896; Hammack, 1982; Kaplan, 1975; Kroessler, 1991; Skolnik, 1971; Trachtenberg, 1982

Green's Dream of New York: Foord, 1913; Green, 1896; Hammack, 1982; Kaplan, 1975; Kaplan, 1979; MacCracken, 1905; Mazaraki, 1966;

Imperium or Colony?: Bradford, 1894; Brooklyn League of Loyal Citizens, 1895; Costello, 1887; Fitzpatrick, 1927; Graves, 1894; Hall, 1898; Hammack, 1982; Jenkins, 1912; Kaplan, 1975; Knerr, 1957; Kroessler, 1991; Mazaraki, 1966; McCormick, 1981; Moehring, 1981; Rosenwaike, 1972; Skolnik, 1971; Sullivan, 1995; Syrett, 1944; Thomas, 1969; Weidner, 1974; Weinstein, 1984

The Great Debate: Bradford, 1894; Erie, 1988; Fitzpatrick, 1927; Graves, 1894; Hall,

1898; Hammack, 1982; Hirsch, 1948; Jenkins, 1912; Kaplan, 1975; Knerr, 1957; Kroessler, 1991; Mazaraki, 1966; McCormick, 1981; McSeveney, 1972; Moehring, 1981; Nevins and Krout, 1948; Rosenwaike, 1972; Skolnik, 1971; Sullivan, 1995; Syrett, 1944; Teaford, 1984; Thomas, 1969; Weinstein, 1984

Endgame: Backus, 1895; Bronx Museum, 1986; Cook, 1913; Fitzpatrick, 1927; Foord, 1903; Foord, 1913; Hall, 1898; Hammack, 1982; Jeffers, 1994; Kaplan, 1975; Kaplan, 1978; Kroessler, 1991; Krout, 1948; Lubove, 1962; Lui, 1993; MacCracken, 1905; Mazaraki, 1966; McCormick, 1981; Syrett, 1944; Waugh, 1992

Toward the Twentieth Century: Banker's Magazine, 1902

MAPS:

Rendered maps throughout the text: Grumet, 1981; Homberger, 1996; Cohen and Augustyn, 1997.

Bibliography

Abbreviations

AHR	The American Historical Review	NYHS	New-York Historical Society
AQ	American Quarterly	NYHSQ	The New-York Historical Society Quarterly
JAH	The Journal of American History	PSQ	Political Science Quarterly
NYH	New York History	WMQ	The William and Mary Quarterly

Abbott, Carl. (1974) "The Neighborhoods of New York, 1760–1775." *NYH* 55: 35–74.

Abbott, Jacob. (May 1851) "The Novelty Works." *Harper's New Monthly Magazine* 2.

Abbott, Wilbur C. (1929) *New York in the American Revolution.* New York.

Abelson, Elaine S. (1989) *When Ladies Go A-Thieving: Middle-Class Shoplifters in the Victorian Department Store.* New York.

Abramovitz, Mimi. (1988) *Regulating the Lives of Women: Social Welfare Policy from Colonial Times to the Present.* Boston.

Adams, Henry. (1947) *The Formative Years: A History of the United States During the Administrations of Jefferson and Madison,* edited by Herbert Agar. Boston.

———. (1958) *The Great Secession Winter of 1860–61, and Other Essays,* edited by George Hochfield. New York.

Adams, Willi Paul. (1976) "'The Spirit of Commerce Requires that Property be Sacred': Gouverneur Morris and the American Revolution." *Amerikastudien* 21: 310–34.

———. (1980) *The First American Constitutions: Republican Ideology and the Making of the State Constitutions in the Revolutionary Era.* Chapel Hill, NC.

Adelman, Melvin L. (1990) *A Sporting Time: New York City and the Rise of Modern Athletics, 1820–1970.* Urbana, IL.

Adkins, Nelson Frederick. (1930) *Fitz-Greene Hallack: An Early Knickerbocker Wit and Poet.* New Haven, CT.

Agnew, Jean-Christophe. (1983) "The Consuming Vision of Henry James." In *The Culture of Consumption: Critical Essays in American History, 1880–1980,* edited by Richard Wightman Fox and T. J. Jackson Lears. New York.

Aiken, John R. (1991) *Utopianism and the Emergence of the Colonial Legal Profession: New York, 1664–1710, A Test Case.* New York and London.

Albion, Robert. ([1939]1984) *The Rise of New York Port, 1815–1860.* Boston and New York.

Alden, John Richard. (1951) *General Charles Lee: Traitor or Patriot?* Baton Rouge, LA.

Alexander, DeAlva S. ([1909]1969) *A Political History of the State of New York.* Vol. 1, 1774–1832. New York.

Alexander, Edward P. (1938) *A Revolutionary Conservative: James Duane of New York.* New York.

Allen, David Y. (1991) "Dutch and English Mapping of Seventeenth-Century Long Island." *The Long Island Historical Journal* 4: 45–62.

Allen, Gay Wilson. (1969) *Walt Whitman.* Rev. ed. Detroit.

Allen, Irving Lewis. (1993) *The City in Slang: New York Life and Popular Speech.* New York.

Allen, Oliver. (1990) *New York, New York: A History of the World's Most Exhilarating and Challenging City.* New York.

———. (1993) *The Tiger: The Rise and Fall of Tammany Hall.* New York.

Allen, Robert C. (1991) *Horrible Prettiness: Burlesque and American Culture.* Chapel Hill, NC.

Alpert, Hollis. (1991) *Broadway! 125 Years of Musical Theatre.* New York.

American Social History Project. (1989) *Who Built America? Working People and the Nation's Economy, Politics, Culture, and Society.* 2 vols. New York.

American Sugar Refining Company. (1918) *A Century of Sugar Refining in the United States, 1816–1916.* New York.

Ammerman, David. (1974) *In the Common Cause: American Response to the Coercive Acts of 1774.* Charlottesville, VA.

Ammon, Harry. (1973) *The Genêt Mission.* New York.

Amory, Cleveland. (1960) *Who Killed Society?* New York.

Anbinder, Tyler. (1987) "Fernando Wood and New York City's Secession from the Union: A Political Appraisal." *NYH* 68: 67–92.

———. (1992) *Nativism and Slavery: The Northern Know-Nothings and the Politics of the 1850s.* New York.

Anderson, Perry. (1974a) *Lineages of the Absolutist State.* London.

———. (1974b) *Passages from Antiquity to Feudalism.* London.

Anderson, Samuel K. (1972) "Public Lotteries in Colonial New York." *NYHSQ* 56: 133–46.

Anderson, Will. (1976) *The Breweries of Brooklyn: An Informal History of a Great Industry in a Great City.* Carmel, NY.

Andrews, Charles McLean, comp. (1915) *Narratives of the Insurrections, 1675–1690.* New York.

———. (1934–38) *The Colonial Period of American History.* 4 vols. New Haven, CT.

Andrews, Doris E. (1985) "Popular Religion and the Revolution in the Middle Atlantic Ports: The Rise of the Methodists, 1770–1800." Ph.D. diss., University of Pennsylvania.

Andrews, Kenneth R. (1984) *Trade, Plunder and Settlement: Maritime Enterprise and the Genesis of the British Empire, 1480–1630.* New York.

Andrews, Wayne. (1956) "A Glance at New York in 1697: The Travel Diary of Dr. Benjamin Bullivant." *NYHSQ* 40: 55–73.

Andrews, William Loring. (1893) *The Bradford Map: The City of New York at the Time of the Granting of the Montgomerie Charter.* New York.

———. (1900) *James Lyne's Survey, or, as it is more commonly known, the Bradford Map.* New York.

———. (1908) *Jacob Steendam, Noch Vaster: A Memoir of the First Poet in New Netherland.* New York.

Appleby, Joyce. (1984) *Capitalism and a New Social Order: The Republican Vision of the 1790s.* New York.

Aptheker, Herbert, ed. (1951) *A Documentary History of the Negro People in the United States.* New York.

Archdeacon, Thomas. (1976a) "Anglo-Dutch New York, 1676." In *New York: The Centennial Years,* edited by Milton M. Klein. Port Washington, NY.

———. (1976b) *New York City, 1664–1710: Conquest and Change.* Ithaca, NY.

Armstrong, Ellis L., ed. (1976) *History of Public Works in the United States, 1776–1976.* Chicago.

Armbruster, Eugene. (1918) *Bruijkleen Colonie.* New York.

———. (1929) *The Olympia Settlement in Early Brooklyn, New York.* New York.

———. (1942) *Brooklyn's Eastern District.* New York.

Arnold, Marybeth Hamilton. (1989) "'The Life of a Citizen in the Hands of a Woman': Sexual Assault in New York City, 1790–1820." In *Passion and Power: Sexuality in History,* edited by Kathy Peiss, Christina Simmons, and Robert A. Padgug. Philadelphia.

Aronowitz, Stanley. (1973) *False Promises: The Shaping of American Working-Class Consciousness.* New York.

———. (1983) *Working-Class Hero: A New Strategy for Labor.* New York.

Asbury, Herbert. (1928) *The Gangs of New York: An Informal History of the Underworld.* New York.

———. (1938) *Sucker's Progress: An Informal History of Gambling in America from the Colonies to Canfield.* New York.

Asher, G. M. ([1860]1963) *Henry Hudson the Navigator.* New York.

Ashton, Rick J. (1976) "The Loyalist Congressmen of New York." *NYHSQ* 60: 95–106.

Atkins, Gordon. (1947) "Health, Housing and Poverty in New York City, 1865–1898." Ph.D. diss., Columbia University.

———. (1973) *The Merry Tales of the Wise Men of Gotham.* Oadby, UK.

Attie, Rejean. (1987) "A Swindling Concern: The United States Sanitary Commission and the Northern Female Public, 1861–1865." Ph.D. diss., Columbia University.

Auchincloss, Louis, ed. (1989) *The Hone and Strong Diaries of Old Manhattan.* New York.

Auser, Cortland P. (1969) *Nathaniel P. Willis.* New York.

Avery, Kevin J., and Peter L. Fodera. (1988) *John Vanderlyn's Panoramic View of the Palace and Gardens of Versailles.* New York.

Avrich, Paul. (1984) *The Haymarket Tragedy.* Princeton, NJ.

———. (1988) *Anarchist Portraits.* Princeton, NJ.

Axelrod, Alan. (1985) "John Blair Linn." In *American Writers of the Early Republic,* edited by Emory Elliott. Detroit.

Axtell, James. (1981) *The European and the Indian: Essays in the Ethnohistory of Colonial North America.* New York.

———. (1982) "Bronze Men and Golden Ages: The Intellectual History of Indian-White Relations in Colonial America." *Journal of Interdisciplinary History* 12: 663–75.

———. (1987) "Colonial America Without the Indians: Counterfactual Reflections." *JAH* 73: 981–96.

———. (1988) *After Columbus: Essays in the Ethnohistory of Colonial North America.* New York.

Ayres, William, ed. (1993) *Picturing History: American Painting, 1770–1930.* New York.

Babb, Winston C. (1954) "French Refugees from Saint Domingue to the Southern United States: 1791–1810." Ph.D. diss., University of Virginia.

Bachman, Van Cleaf. (1969) *Peltries or Plantations: Economic Policies of the Dutch West India Company in New Netherland, 1623–1639.* Baltimore.

Backus, Truman J. (1895) *Against Consolidation: An Address.* Brooklyn.

Bacon, Mardges. (1986) *Ernest Flagg: Beaux Arts Architect and Urban Reformer.* Cambridge, MA.

Bacon, Selden Daskam. (1939) "The Early Development of American Municipal Police: A Study of the Evolution of Formal Controls in a Changing Society." Ph.D. diss., Yale University.

Bailey, Paul. (1962) *Early Long Island.* Westhampton Beach, NY.

———. (1982) *The Thirteen Tribes of Long Island.* Syosset, NY.

Baily, Francis. (1856) *Journal of a Tour in Unsettled Parts of North America in 1796 & 1797.* London.

Bailyn, Bernard. (1967) *Ideological Origins of the American Revolution.* Cambridge, MA.

———. (1986a) *The Peopling of British North America: An Introduction.* New York.

———. (1986b) *Voyagers to the West: A Passage in the Peopling of America on the Eve of the Revolution.* New York.

Baird, Charles W. (1985) *History of the Huguenot Emigration to America.* Baltimore.

Baker, Jean H. (1983) *Affairs of Party: The Political Culture of Northern Democrats in the Mid-Nineteenth Century.* Ithaca, NY.

Baker, Paul R. (1980) *Richard Morris Hunt.* Cambridge, MA.

———. (1989) *Stanny: The Gilded Life of Stanford White.* New York.

Baker, Paula. (1990) "The Domestication of Politics: Women and American Political Society, 1780–1920." In *Women, the State, and Welfare,* edited by Linda Gordon. Madison, WI.

Bakker, Peter. (1995) "First African into New Netherland, 1613–1614." *de Halve Maen* 67: 50–53.

Balderston, Marion, and

David Syrett, eds. (1975) *The Lost War: Letters from British Officers During the American Revolution.* New York.

Balmer, Randall H. (1981) "From Rebellion to Revivalism: The Fortunes of the Dutch Reformed Church in Colonial New York, 1689–1715." *de Halve Maen* 56: 6ff.

———. (1982) "From Rebellion to Revivalism: The Fortunes of the Dutch Reformed Church in Colonial New York, 1689–1715." Part 2. *de Halve Maen* 56: 10ff.

———. (1983) "Anglo-Dutch Wars and the Demise of Dutch Reformed Power, 1664–1682." *de Halve Maen* 58: 5ff.

———. (1988) "Schism on Long Island: The Dutch Reformed Church, Lord Cornbury, and the Politics of Anglicization." In *Authority and Resistance in Early New York*, edited by William Pencak and Conrad Wright. New York.

———. (1989a) *A Perfect Babel of Confusion: Dutch Religion and English Culture in the Middle Colonies.* New York.

———. (1989b) "Traitors and Papists: The Religious Dimension of Leisler's Rebellion." *NYH* 70: 341–72.

Baltzell, Digby E. (1987) *The Protestant Establishment: Aristocracy and Caste in America.* New Haven, CT.

Bangs, Edward, ed. ([1890]1968) *Journal of Lieutenant Isaac Bangs, April 1 to July 29, 1776.* New York.

Bankers' Magazine. (1902) "The Financial Center of the World." *Bankers' Magazine* 64: 172–75.

Banner, Lois. (1980) *Elizabeth Cady Stanton: A Radical for Woman's Rights.* Boston.

———. (1983) *American Beauty.* New York.

Bannister, Robert C. (1979) *Social Darwinism: Science and Myth in Anglo-American Social Thought.* Philadelphia.

Barbour, Violet. (1950) *Capitalism in Amsterdam in the Seventeenth Century.* Baltimore.

Barck, Oscar T., Jr. ([1931]1966) *New York City During the War for Independence: With Special Reference to the Period of British Occupation.* New York.

Barlow, Elizabeth. (1969) *The Forests and Wetlands of New York City.* Boston

Barnes, Charles B. (1915) *The Longshoremen.* New York.

Barnes, James J. (1974) *Authors, Publishers and Politicians: The Quest for an Anglo-American Copyright Agreement, 1815–54.* Columbus, OH.

Barnouw, Erik. (1966) *A History of Broadcasting in the United States, Vol. 1: A Tower of Babel: To 1933.* New York.

Barry, Kathleen. (1988) *Susan B. Anthony: A Biography of a Singular Feminist.* New York.

Barth, Gunther. (1982) *City People: The Rise of Modern City Culture in Nineteenth-Century America.* New York.

Basch, Norma. (1982) *In The Eyes of the Law: Women, Marriage and Property in Nineteenth-Century New York.* Ithaca, NY.

Bates, Whitney K. (1962) "Northern Speculators and Southern State Debts: 1790." *WMQ* 19: 30–48.

Batterberry, Michael, and Ariane Batterberry. (1973) *On the Town in New York: A History of Eating, Drinking, and Entertainments from 1776 to the Present.* New York.

Bayer, Henry G. (1925) *The Belgians: First Settlers in New York and in the Middle States.* New York.

Bayles, W. Harrison. (1915) *Old Taverns of New York.* New York.

Baym, Nina. (1995) *American Women Writers and the Work of History, 1790–1860.* New Brunswick, NJ.

Bayor, Ronald H., and Timothy J. Meagher, eds. (1996) *The New York Irish: Essays Toward a History.* Baltimore.

Beard, James F., Jr. (1953) "The First History of

Greater New York: Unknown Portions of Fenimore Cooper's Last Work." *NYHSQ* 37: 109–45.

Beard, Rick, ed. (1987) *On Being Homeless.* New York.

Beard, Rick, and Leslie Cohen Berlowitz, eds. (1993) *Greenwich Village: Culture and Counterculture.* New Brunswick, NJ.

Beck, Louis J. (1898) *New York's Chinatown: An Historical Presentation of Its People and Places.* New York.

Becker, Carl L. (1909) *The History of Political Parties in the Province of New York, 1760–1776.* Madison, WI.

———. ([1935]1966) "John Jay and Peter Van Schaack." In *Everyman His Own Historian.* New York.

Beckert, Sven. (1995) "The Making of New York City's Bourgeoisie, 1850–1886." Ph.D. diss., Columbia University.

Beer, Thomas. (1941) *Hannah, Crane, and the Mauve Decade.* New York.

Beisel, Nicola Kay. (1997) *Imperiled Innocents: Anthony Comstock and Family Reproduction in Victorian America.* Princeton, NJ.

Beisner, Robert L. (1968) *Twelve Against Empire: The Anti-Imperialists, 1898–1900.* New York.

Belden, E. Porter. (1849) *New-York, Past, Present, and Future: Comprising a History of the City of New York, a Description of Its Present Condition, and an Estimate of Its Future Increase.* New York.

Bell, Stephen. (1937) *Rebel, Priest, and Prophet: A Biography of Dr. Edward McGlynn.* New York.

Bell, Whitfield J. (1962) "The Federal Processions of 1788." *NYHSQ* 46: 5–39.

Bellingham, Bruce. (1983) "The 'Unspeakable Blessing': Street Children, Reform Rhetoric and Misery in Early Industrial Capitalism." *Politics and Society* 12: 303–31.

Bender, Thomas. (1987) *New York Intellect: A History of Intellectual Life in New York City, from 1750 to the*

Beginnings of Our Own Time. Baltimore.

———. (1988) "The Emergence of the New York Intellectuals: Modernism, Cosmopolitanism, and Nationalism." Paper presented at Conference on the History of Budapest and New York: 1870–1930. Budapest.

———. (1993) "Washington Square in the Growing City." In *Greenwich Village: Culture and Counterculture*, edited by Rick Beard and Leslie Cohen Berlowitz. New Brunswick, NJ.

Bendroth, Margaret Lamberts. (1985) "The Social Dimensions of 'Woman's Sphere': The Rise of Women's Organizations in Late-nineteenth-century Protestantism." Ph.D. diss., The Johns Hopkins University.

Benson, Adolph, ed. (1964) *Peter Kalm's Travels in North America.* 2 vols. New York.

Benson, Susan Porter. (1986) *Counter Cultures: Saleswomen, Managers, and Customers in American Department Stores, 1890–1940.* Urbana, IL.

Benton, William A. (1975) "Peter Van Schaack: The Conscience of a Loyalist." In *The Loyalist Americans: A Focus on Greater New York*, edited by Robert East and Jacob Judd. Tarrytown, NY.

Berg, Barbara J. (1978) *The Remembered Gate: Origins of American Feminism: The Woman and the City, 1800–1860.* New York.

Bergmann, Hans. (1969) "The Original Confidence Man," *AQ* 21: 560–77.

———. (1995) *God in the Street: New York Writing from the Penny Press to Melville.* Philadelphia.

Berkhofer, Robert F., Jr. (1978) *The White Man's Indian: Images of the American Indian from Columbus to the Present.* New York.

Berlin, Ira. (1996) "From Creole to African: Atlantic Creoles and the Origins of African-American Society in Mainland North America." *WMQ* 53: 251–88.

Bergreen, Laurence. (1990)

As Thousands Cheer: The Life of Irving Berlin. New York.

Bernstein, Iver. (1990) *The New York City Draft Riots*. New York.

Bernstein, Rachel Amelia. (1984) "Boarding-House Keepers and Brothel Keepers in New York City, 1880–1910." Ph.D. diss., Rutgers University.

Bernstein, Richard B. (1989) "The Inauguration of George Washington." In *Well Begun: Chronicles of the Early National Period*, edited by Stephen L. Schechter and Richard B. Bernstein. Albany, NY.

———. (1989) *Where the Experiment Began: New York City and the Two Hundredth Anniversary of George Washington's Inauguration*. New York.

Bernstein, Samuel. (1956) "American Labor in the Long Depression, 1873–1878." *Science and Society* 20: 60–82.

Berry, Faith. (1983) *Langston Hughes, Before and Beyond Harlem*. Westport, CT.

Bickford, Charlene, and Kenneth R. Bowling. (1989) *Birth of the Nation: The First Federal Congress, 1789–91*. New York.

Bielinski, Stefan. (1975) *Abraham Yates, Jr., and the New Political Order in Revolutionary New York*. Albany, NY.

Biemer, Linda. (1981) "Lady Deborah Moody and the Founding of Gravesend." *The Journal of Long Island History* 17: 18–41.

———. (1983) *Women and Property in Colonial New York: The Transition from Dutch to English Law, 1643–1727*. Ann Arbor, MI.

Billias, George A., ed. (1964) *George Washington's Generals*. New York.

———. (1975) "Pelham Bay: A Forgotten Battle." *Narratives of the Revolution in New York*. New York.

Billington, Ray Allen. (1938) *The Protestant Crusade, 1800–1860: A Study of the Origins of American Nativism*. New York.

Binder, Frederick M. and David M. Reimers. (1995) *All the Nations Under Heaven: An Ethnic and Racial History of New York City*. New York.

Birmingham, Stephen. (1967) *"Our Crowd": The Great Jewish Families of New York*. New York.

———. (1984) *"The Rest of Us": The Rise of America's Eastern European Jews*. Boston.

Bixby, William. (1972) *South Street*. New York.

Bjork, Gordon C. (1967) "Foreign Trade." In *The Growth of the Seaport Cities, 1790–1825*, edited by David Gilchrist. Charlottesville, VA.

Black, David. (1981) *The King of Fifth Avenue: The Fortunes of August Belmont*. New York.

Black, George Ashton. (1967) *The History of Municipal Ownership of Land on Manhattan Island*. 2nd ed. New York.

Black, Jeremy. (1991) *War for America: The Fight for Independence, 1775–1783*. New York.

Black, Mary. (1984) *New York City's Gracie Mansion: A History of the Mayor's House, 1646–1942*. New York.

Black, Michael L. (1974) "Political Satire in Knickerbocker's *History*." In *The Knickerbocker Tradition: Washington Irving's New York*, edited by Andrew Myers. Tarrytown, NY.

Blackburn, Robin. (1988) *The Overthrow of Colonial Slavery, 1776–1848*. London.

Blackmar, Elizabeth. (1979) "Re-walking the 'Walking City': Housing and Property Relations in New York City, 1780–1840." *Radical History Review* 21: 131–48.

———. (1989) *Manhattan for Rent, 1785–1850*. Ithaca, NY.

———. (1991) "Uptown Real Estate and the Creation of Times Square." In *Inventing Times Square: Commerce and Culture at the Crossroads of the World*, edited by William R. Taylor. New York.

———. (1995) "Accountability for Public Health: Regulating the Housing Market in Nineteenth-Century New York City."

In *Hives of Sickness: Public Health and Epidemics in New York City*, edited by David Rosner. New Brunswick, NJ.

Blair, Karen J. (1980) *The Clubwoman as Feminist: True Womanhood Redefined,, 1868–1914*. New York.

Blake, Nelson Manfred. (1956) *Water for the Cities: A History of the Urban Water Supply Problem in the United States*. Syracuse, NY.

Blatchford, John. (1865) *The Narrative of John Blatchford, Detailing His Sufferings in the Revolutionary War, While a Prisoner . . .* New York.

Blau, Alan Lee. (1973) "New York City and the French Revolution, 1789–1797: A Study of French Revolutionary Influence." Ph.D. diss., City University of New York.

Blau, Joseph L. (1974) "Religion and Politics in Knickerbocker Times." In *The Knickerbocker Tradition: Washington Irving's New York*, edited by Andrew B. Myers. Tarrytown, NY.

Blaugrund, Annette. (1982) "The Tenth Street Studio Building: A Roster, 1857–1895." *American Art Journal* 14: 64–71.

Bledstein, Burton. (1976) *The Culture of Professionalism: The Middle Class and the Development of Higher Education in America*. New York.

Bliven, Bruce. (1955) *Battle for Manhattan*. New York.

———. (1972) *Under the Guns: New York, 1775–1776*. New York.

Blockson, Charles L. (1987) *The Underground Railroad*. New York.

———. (1994) *Hippocrene Guide to the Underground Railroad*. New York.

Blondheim, Menahem. (1994) *News over the Wires: The Telegraph and the Flow of Public Information in America, 1844–1897*. Cambridge, MA.

Bluestone, Daniel. (1991) "Destruction and Preservation: Historical Memory in Flatbush New York, 1830–1930." Unpublished manuscript.

———. (1992) "The Pushcart Evil." In *The Landscape of Modernity: Essays on New York City, 1900–1940*, edited by David Ward and Olivier Zunz. New York.

Blumenthal, Walter Hart. (1952) *Women Camp Followers of the American Revolution*. Philadelphia.

Blumin, Stuart M. (1984) "Explaining the New Metropolis: Perception, Depiction, and Analysis in Mid-nineteenth-century New York City." *Journal of Urban History* 11: 7–38

———. (1989) *The Emergence of the Middle Class: Social Experience in the American City, 1760–1900*. New York.

———. (1985) "The Hypothesis of Middle-Class Formation in Nineteenth-century America: A Critique and Some Proposals." *AHR* 90: 299–338.

Blunt, Edmund M. (1817) *The Stranger's Guide to the City of New York*. New York.

Blythe, Ronald. (1983) *Characters and their Landscapes*. San Diego.

Bobbé, Dorothie. (1933) *De Witt Clinton*. New York.

Bobrick, Benson. (1981) *Labyrinths of Iron: A History of the World's Subways*. New York.

Bogart, Michele H. (1989) *Public Sculpture and the Civic Ideal in New York City, 1890–1930*. Chicago.

Bolster, W. Jeffrey. (1997) *Black Jacks: African American Seamen in the Age of Sail*. Cambridge, MA.

Bone, Kevin, Mary Beth Betts, and Stanley Greenberg. (1997) *The New York Waterfront: Evolution and Building Culture of the Port and Harbor*. New York.

Bonner, Arthur. (1997) *Alas! What Brought Thee Hither? The Chinese in New York, 1800–1950*. Madison, NJ.

Bonner, William Thompson. (1924) *New York, the World's Metropolis, 1623/4–1923/4*. New York.

Bonomi, Patricia U. (1966) "Political Patterns in Colonial New York City: The General Assembly Election of 1768." *PSQ* 81: 432–47.

———. (1971) *A Factious*

People: Politics and Society in Colonial New York. New York.

———. (1974) "Local Government in Colonial New York: A Base for Republicanism." In *Aspects of Early New York Society and Politics*, edited by Jacob Judd and Irwin Polishhook. Tarrytown, NY.

———. (1986) *Under the Cope of Heaven: Religion, Society, and Politics in Colonial America.* New York.

———. (1994) "Lord Cornbury Redressed: The Governor and the Problem Portrait." *WMQ* 51: 106–18.

———. (1998) *The Lord Cornbury Scandal: The Politics of Reputation in British America.* Chapel Hill, NC.

Bonwick, Colin. (1977) *English Radicals and the American Revolution.* Chapel Hill, NC.

———. (1986) "English Radicals and American Resistance to British Authority." In *Resistance, Politics, and the American Struggle for Independence*, edited by Walter Conser. Boulder, CO.

Booraem, Hendrik. (1983) *The Formation of the Republican Party in New York: Politics and Conscience in the Antebellum North.* New York.

Booth, Mary L. (1859) *History of the City of New York, From Its Earliest Settlement to the Present Time.* New York.

Booth, Sally Smith (1973) *The Women of '76.* New York.

Bordin, Ruth. (1981) *Woman and Temperance: The Quest for Power and Liberty, 1873–1900.* Philadelphia.

Bosher, J.F. (1995) "Huguenot Merchants and the Protestant International in the Seventeenth Century." *WMQ* 52: 77–102.

Boston, Ray C. (1971) *British Chartists in America, 1839–1900.* Manchester, UK.

Botein, Stephen, ed. (1985) *"Mr. Zenger's Malice and Falsehood": Six Issues of the New York Weekly Journal, 1733–34.* Worcester, MA.

Botkin, Benjamin. (1976) *New York City Folklore.* New York.

Bottoroff, William K. (1985) "Elihu Hubbard Smith." In *American Writers of the Early Republic*, edited by Emory Elliot. Detroit.

Bowden, Mary Weatherspoon. (1980) "Cocklofts and Slang-whangers: The Historical Sources of Washington Irving's *Salmagundi*." *NYH* 61: 133–60.

———. (1981) *Washington Irving.* Boston.

Bowling, Kenneth R. (1971) "Dinner at Jefferson's: A Note on Jacob E. Cooke's 'The Compromise of 1790.'" [With Cooke rebuttal.] *WMQ* 28: 629–48.

———. (1989) "New York City: The First Federal Capital." In *Well Begun: Chronicles of the Early National Period*, edited by Stephen L. Schechter and Richard B. Bernstein. Albany, NY.

———. (1990) "New York City, Capital of the United States, 1785–1790." In *The World of the Founders: New York Communities in the Federal Period*, edited by Stephen L. Schechter, Wendell Tripp, and Thomas E. Burke. Albany, NY.

———. (1991) *The Creation of Washington, D.C.: The Idea and Location of the American Capital.* Fairfax, VA.

Boxer, Charles R. (1965) *The Dutch Seaborne Empire, 1600–1800.* New York.

Boyd, Steven R. (1976) "The Impact of the Constitution on State Politics: New York as a Test Case." In *The Human Dimensions of Nation Making: Essays on Colonial and Revolutionary America*, edited by James Kirby Martin. Madison, WI.

Boydston, Jeanne. (1990) *Home and Work: Housework, Wages, and the Ideology of Labor in the Early Republic.* New York.

Boyer, Christine. (1983) *Dreaming the Rational City: The Myth of American City Planning.* Cambridge, MA.

———. (1985) *Manhattan Manners: Architecture and Style, 1850–1900.* New York.

———. (1993) "Straight Down Christopher Street: A Tale of the Oldest Street in Greenwhich Village." In *Greenwich Village: Culture and Counterculture*, edited by Rick Beard and Leslie Berlowitz. New Brunswick, NJ.

Boyer, Lee R. (October 1973) "Lobster Backs, Liberty Boys, and Laborers in the Streets: New York's Golden Hill and Nassau Street Riots." *NYHSQ* 57: 281–308.

Boyer, Paul. (1968) *Purity in Print: The Vice-Society Movement and Book Censorship in America.* New York.

———. (1978) *Urban Masses and Moral Order in America, 1820–1920.* Cambridge, MA.

Boylan, Anne M. (1984) "Women in Groups: An Analysis of Women's Benevolent Organizations in New York and Boston, 1797–1840." *JAH* 71: 497–523.

———. (1986) "Timid Girls, Venerable Widows and Dignified Matrons: Life Cycle Patterns among Organized Women in New York and Boston, 1797–1840." *AQ* 38: 779–97.

———. (1988) *Sunday School: The Formation of an American Institution, 1790–1880.* New Haven, CT.

———. (1990) "Women and Politics in the Era Before Seneca Falls." *The Journal of the Early Republic* 10: 363–82.

Boyle, Robert H. (1969) *The Hudson River: A Natural and Unnatural History.* New York.

Brace, Charles Loring. (1872) *The Dangerous Classes of New York.* New York.

Bradford, Edward A. (1894) *Great York.* Brooklyn.

Brand, Dana. (1991) *The Spectator and the City in Nineteenth-century American Literature.* New York.

Brandon, Ruth. (1977) *A Capitalist Romance: Singer and the Sewing Machine.* Philadelphia.

Brandt, Nat. (1986) *The Man Who Tried to Burn New York.* Syracuse, NY.

Brasser, T.J.C. (1971) "The Coastal Algonkians: People of the First Frontier." In *North American Indians in Historical Perspective*, edited by Eleanor Leacock and Nancy Lurie. New York.

Braudel, Fernand. (1981) *Civilization and Capitalism, 15th–18th Century.* 3 vols. New York.

Bray, Robert, and Paul Bushnell, eds. (1978) *The Diary of a Common Soldier in the American Revolution, 1775–1783. An annotated edition of the military journal of Jeremiah Greenman.* Dekalb, IL.

Breen, T. H. (1992) "'Baubles of Britain': The American and Consumer Revolutions of the Eighteenth Century." In *Of Consuming Interests: The Style of Life in the Eighteenth Century*, edited by Cary Carson, Ronald Hoffman, and Peter J. Albert. Charlottsville, VA.

———. (1986) "An Empire of Goods: The Anglicization of Colonial America, 1690–1776." *Journal of British Studies* 25: 467–99.

Bremner, Robert Hamlett. (1956) *From the Depths: The Discovery of Poverty in the United States.* New York.

———. (1958) "The Big Flat: History of a New York Tenement House." *AHR*, 64: 54–62.

Brewer, Eileen Mary. (1987) *Nuns and the Education of American Catholic Women, 1860–1920.* Chicago.

Bridenbaugh, Carl, ed. (1948) *Gentleman's Progress: the Itinerarium of Dr. Alexander Hamilton, 1744.* Chapel Hill, NC.

———. (1966) *Cities in the Wilderness: The First Century of Urban Life in America, 1625–1742.* New York.

———. (1971) *Cities in Revolt: Urban Life in America, 1743–1776.* New York.

———, and Roberta Bridenbaugh. (1972) *No Peace Beyond the Line: The English in the Caribbean, 1624–1690.* New York.

———. (1981) "The Old and New Societies of the

Delaware Valley in the Seventeenth Century." In *Early Americans*, edited by Carl Bridenbaugh. New York.

Bridges, Amy. (1984) *A City in the Republic: Antebellum New York and the Origins of Machine Politics*. New York.

Brieger, Gert H. (1978) "Sanitary Reform in New York City: Stephen Smith and the Passage of the Metropolitan Health Bill." In *Sickness and Health in America*, edited by Judith Leavitt and Ronald Numbers. Madison, WI.

Briggs, Charles F. (1839) *Adventures of Harry Franco*. New York.

Brillat-Savarin, Jean Anthelme. (1926) *The Physiology of Taste, or Meditations on Transcendental Gastronomy*. New York.

Brissot de Warville, Jacques Pierre. ([1792]1964) *New Travels in the United States of America, 1788*. Translated by M. S. Vamos and D. Echeverria. Cambridge, MA.

Bristed, Charles Astor. (1852) *The Upper Ten Thousand: Sketches of American Society*. New York.

Brock, Leslie. (1975) *The Currency System of the American Colonies, 1700–1764*. New York.

Brodhead, John Romeyn. (1853–71) *History of the State of New York*. New York.

Bronx Museum of the Arts. (1986) *Building a Borough: Architecture and Planning in the Bronx, 1890–1940*. New York.

Brooklyn League of Loyal Citizens. (1895) Pamphlet No. 7. New York.

Brooklyn Museum. (1979) *The American Renaissance, 1876–1917*. New York.

Brooks Brothers. (1918) *Brooks Brothers Centenary, 1818–1918*. New York.

———. (1943) *A Chronicle Recording One Hundred Twenty-Five Years, 1818–1943*. New York.

Brooks, Robin. (1967) "Alexander Hamilton, Melancton Smith, and the Ratification of the Constitution in New York."

WMQ 24: 339–58.

Brooks, Van Wyck. (1944) *The World of Washington Irving*. New York.

Browder, Clifford. (1985) *The Money Game in Old New York: Daniel Drew and His Times*. Lexington, KY.

———. (1988) *The Wickedest Woman in New York: Madame Restell, the Abortionist*. Hamden, CT.

Brown, Charles Henry. (1971) *William Cullen Bryant*. New York.

Brown, Francis. (1951) *Raymond of the Times*. New York.

Brown, Henry Collins. (1922) *Old New York: Yesterday and Today*. Baltimore.

———. (1924) *Fifth Avenue Old and New, 1824–1924*. New York.

———. (1935) *Brownstone Fronts and Saratoga Trunks*. New York.

Brown, Joshua. (1976) "The 'Dead Rabbit'-Bowery Boy Riot: An Analysis of the Antebellum New York Gang." Master's thesis, Columbia University.

———, and David Ment. (1980) *Factories, Foundries, and Refineries: A History of Five Brooklyn Industries*. Brooklyn.

———. (1993) "'Frank Leslie's Illustrated Newspaper': The Pictorial Press And the Representations of America, 1855–1889. Ph.D. diss., Columbia University.

Brown, Mary Elizabeth. (1991) "The Adoption of the Tactics of the Enemy: The Care of Italian Immigrant Youth in the Archdiocese of New York, 1890s–1920s." In *Immigration to New York*, edited by William Pencak, Selma Berrol, and Randall M. Miller. Philadelphia.

Brown, Roger H. (1964) *The Republic in Peril: 1812*. New York.

Brown, T. Allston. (1903) *A History of the New York Stage*. 3 vols. New York.

Brown, Thomas. (1966) *Irish-American Nationalism, 1870–1890*. Philadelphia.

Bruce, Robert V. (1959) *1877: Year of Violence*. Indianapolis.

———. (1987) *The Launching of Modern American Science, 1846–1876*. New York.

Bruchey, Stuart. (1965) *The Roots of American Economic Growth, 1607–1861: An Essay in Social Causation*. New York.

———, ed. (1966) *The Colonial Merchant: Sources and Readings*. New York.

Brunson, B. R. (1989) *The Adventures of Samuel Swartwout in the Age of Jefferson and Jackson*. Lewiston, NY.

Bryant, William Cullen, R. C. Sands, and G. C. Verplanck. (1828–30) *Talisman*. New York.

Bubrinski, Kevin. (1995) *The Power Places of Kathmandu*. Rochester, VT.

Buck, Sarah. (1995) "An Inspired Hoax: The Antebellum Reconstruction of an Eighteenth-Century Long Island Diary." *The Long Island Historical Journal* 7:191–204.

Buckley, Peter G. (1984) "To the Opera House: Culture and Society in New York City, 1820–1860." Ph.D. diss., State University of New York at Stony Brook.

Budd, Martin. (1978) "The Legal System of 1691." In *Courts and Law in Early New York*, edited by Leo Hershkowitz and Milton Klein. Port Washington, NY.

Buetow, Harold. (1970) *Of Singular Benefit: The Story of Catholic Education in the United States*. London.

Buffington, Arthur H. (1933) "The Colonial Wars and Their Results." In *History of the State of New York*, vol. 2, *Under Duke and King*, edited by Alexander C. Flick. New York.

Buhle, Mari Jo. (1981) *Women and American Socialism, 1870–1920*. Urbana, IL.

Buhle, Paul. (1987) *Marxism in the United States: Remapping the History of the American Left*. London.

Bunker, John. (1979) *Harbor and Haven: An Illustrated History of the Port of New York*. Woodland Hills, CA.

Burchard, John, and Albert Bush-Brown. (1961) *The Architecture of America: A*

Social and Cultural History. Boston.

Burgess, Charles O. (1962) "The Newspaper as Charity Worker: Poor Relief in New York City, 1893–1894." *NYH* 43: 249–53.

Burke, Gerald L. (1956) *The Making of Dutch Towns: A Study in Urban Development from the Tenth to the Seventeenth Centuries*. London.

Burke, John. (1972) *Duet in Diamonds: The Flamboyant Saga of Lillian Russell and Diamond Jim Brady in America's Gilded Age*. New York.

Burke, Peter. (1978) *Popular Culture in Early Modern Europe*. New York.

Burke, Thomas E. (1986) "The New Netherland Fur Trade, 1657–1661: Response to Crisis." *de Halve Maen* 59:1ff.

Burnaby, Rev. Andrew. (1904) *Travels Through the Middle Settlements in North America in the Years 1759 and 1760*, edited by Rufus R. Wilson. New York.

Burns, James A. (1969) *The Principles, Origin and Establishment of the Catholic School System in the United States*. New York.

Burrows, Edwin G. (1966) "The Meaning of Federalism and Anti-Federalism: New York and the Constitution." M.A. thesis, Columbia University.

———, and Michael Wallace. (1972) "The American Revolution: The Ideology and Psychology of National Liberation." *Perspectives in American History* 6: 167–306.

Bushman, Claudia. (1992) *America Discovers Columbus: How an Italian Explorer Became an American Hero*. Hanover, NH.

Bushman, Richard L., ed. (1970) *The Great Awakening: Documents on the Revival of Religion, 1740–1745*. New York.

———. (1993) *The Refinement of America: Persons, Houses, Cities*. New York.

Butcher, Patricia Smith. (1989) *Education for Equality: Women's Rights Periodicals and Women's Higher*

Education, 1849–1920. New York.

Butler, Jon. (1983) *The Huguenots in America.* Cambridge, MA.

Butler, Marilyn. (1992) "Hidden Metropolis: London in Sentimental and Romantic Writing." In *London—World City, 1800–1840,* edited by Celina Fox. New Haven, CT.

Byard, Spencer. (1989) *The Legend of the Hall-Edwards Inheritance: A Recurrent Delusion.* New York.

Byrdsall, Fitzwilliam. (1842) *The History of the Locofoco, or Equal Rights Party.* New York.

Calder, Angus. (1981) *Revolutionary Empire: The Rise of the English-Speaking Empires from the Fifteenth Century to the 1780s.* New York.

Calhoon, Robert McCluer. (1973) *The Loyalists in Revolutionary America, 1760–1781.* New York.

Calhoun, Daniel Hovey. (1960) *The American Civil Engineer: Origins and Conflict.* Cambridge, MA.

Calhoun, Richard. (1973) "From Community to Metropolis: Fire Protection in New York City, 1790–1875." Ph.D., Columbia University.

Callow, Alexander B., Jr. (1966) *The Tweed Ring.* New York.

Callow, James T. (1967) *Kindred Spirit: Knickerbocker Writers and American Artists, 1807–1855.* Chapel Hill, NC.

Callow, Philip. (1992) *From Noon to Starry Night: A Life of Walt Whitman.* Chicago.

Calvert, Karin. (1992) "The Function of Fashion in Eighteenth-Century America." In *Of Consuming Interests: The Style of Life in the Eighteenth Century,* edited by Cary Carson, Ronald Hoffman, and Peter J. Albert. Charlottesville, VA.

Campbell, Helen. (1900) *Darkness and Daylight: or, Lights and Shadows of New York Life. A Woman's Pictorial Record of Gospel, Temperance, Mission, and Rescue Work.* Hartford, CT.

Canary, Robert H. (1970) *William Dunlap.* New York.

Canton, Jay. (1975) "A Monument of Trade: A. T. Stewart and the Rise of the Millionaire's Mansion in New York." *Winterthur Portfolio* 10: 165–98.

Cantor, Mindy, ed. (1982) *Around the Square, 1830–1890: Essays of Life, Letters, and Architecture in Greenwich Village.* New York.

Carman, Harry J. (1919) *The Street Surface Railway Franchises of New York City.* New York.

———. (1933) "The Beginnings of the Industrial Revolution." In *History of the State of New York,* vol. 5, *Conquering the Wilderness,* edited by Alexander C. Flick. New York.

Carosso, Vincent P. (1970) *Investment Banking in America: A History.* Cambridge, MA.

———. (1976) "A Financial Elite: New York's German-Jewish Investment Bankers." *American Jewish Historical Quarterly* 66: 67–78.

———. (1987) *The Morgans: Private International Bankers, 1854–1913.* Cambridge, MA.

Carp, Roger Evan. (1986) "The Erie Canal and the Liberal Challenge to Classical Republicanism, 1785–1850." Ph.D. diss., University of North Carolina at Chapel Hill, NC.

Carr, Albert H. Z. (1963) *The World and William Walker.* New York.

Carse, Robert. (1961) *The Moonrakers: the Story of the Clipper Ship Men.* New York.

Carson, Cary, Ronald Hoffman, and Peter J. Albert, eds. (1992) *Of Consuming Interests: The Style of Life in the Eighteenth Century.* Charlottesville, VA.

Carter, Ralph. (1964) "Black American or African: The Response of New York City Blacks to African Colonization, 1817–1841." Ph.D. diss., Clark University.

Carter, Samuel, III. (1968) *Cyrus Field: Man of Two Worlds.* New York.

Carwardine, Richard. (1972)

"The Second Great Awakening in the Urban Centers: An Examination of Methodism and the 'New Measures.'" *JAH* 59: 327–40.

———. (1978) *Transatlantic Revivalism: Popular Evangelicalism in Britain and America, 1790–1865.* Westport, CT.

Castells, Manuel. (1978) *City, Class, and Power.* New York.

———. (1983) *The City and the Grassroots: A Cross-cultural Theory of Urban Social Movements.* Berkeley, CA.

Catalfamo, Catherine Christine. (1989) "The Thorny Rose: The Americanization of an Urban, Immigrant, Working Calss Regiment in the Civil War: A Social History of the Garibaldi Guard. Ph.D. diss., University of Texas, Austin.

Caughey, John Walton, and LaRee Caughey, eds. (1962) *California Heritage: An Anthology of History and Literature.* Los Angeles.

Cawelti, John G. (1967) *Apostles of the Self-Made Man: Changing Concepts of Success in America.* Chicago.

Ceci, Lynn. (1980) "The First Fiscal Crisis in New York." *Economic Development and Cultural Change.* 28: 839–47.

———. (1990) *The Effect of European Contact and Trade on the Settlement Pattern of Indians in Coastal New York, 1524–1665.* New York.

Cerillo, Augutus, Jr. (1969) "Reforms in New York City: A Study of Urban Progressivism." Ph.D. diss., Northwestern University.

Chalmers, Leonard. (1969) "Tammany Hall, Fernando Wood, and the Struggle to Control New York City, 1857–59." *NYHSQ* 53: 7–13.

Chamber, William N. (1963) *Political Parties in a New Nation: The American Experience, 1776–1809.* New York.

Champagne, Roger. (1963) "Family Politics versus Constitutional Principles:

The New York Assembly Elections of 1768 and 1769." *WMQ* 20: 57–79.

———. (1967) "Liberty Boys and Mechanics of New York City, 1764–1774." *Labor History* 8: 115–35.

———. (1975a) *Alexander McDougall and the American Revolution in New York.* Schenectady, NY.

———. (1975b). "The Military Association of the Sons of Liberty." In *Narratives of the Revolution in New York.* New York.

Chandler, Alfred D., Jr. (1954) "Patterns of Railroad Finance, 1830–50." *Business History Review* 28: 248–63.

———. (1977) *The Visible Hand: The Managerial Revolution in American Business.* Cambridge, MA.

Chapin, Anna Alice. (1917) *Greenwich Village.* New York.

Chappell, Edward A. (1992) "Housing a Nation: The Transformation of Living Standards in Early America." In *Of Consuming Interests: The Style of Life in the Eighteenth Century,* edited by Cary Carson, Ronald Hoffman, and Peter J. Albert. Charlottesville, VA.

Charles, Joseph. (1961) *The Origins of the American Party System.* New York.

Charvat, William. (1959) *Literary Publishing in America, 1790–1830.* Philadelphia.

Chase, Jeanne. (1983) "The 1741 Conspiracy to Burn New York: Black Plot or Black Magic?" *Social Science Information.* 22: 969–81.

Chauncey, George. (July 1, 1986) "Gay Male Society in the Jazz Age." *Village Voice:* 29–30, 32.

———. (1994) *Gay New York: Gender, Urban Culture, and the Making of the Gay Male World, 1890–1940.* New York.

Cheape, Charles W. (1980) *Moving the Masses: Urban Public Transportation in New York, Boston, and Philadelphia, 1880–1912.* Cambridge, MA.

Chen, Julia I. Hsuan. (1974) *The Chinese Community in New York: A Study in*

Their Cultural Adjustment, 1920–1940. San Francisco.

Chernow, Ron. (1990) *The House of Morgan: An American Banking Dynasty and the Rise of Modern Finance.* New York.

Cherry, George L. (1950) "American Metropolitan Press Reaction to the Paris Commune of 1871." *Mid-America: An Historical Review* 32: 3–12.

Child, Lydia Maria. (1845) *Letters from New York: Second Series.* New York.

Childs, Frances S. (1940) *French Refugee Life in the United States, 1790–1800: An American Chapter of the French Revolution.* Baltimore.

Christen, Robert J. (1968) "King Sears, Politician and Patriot in a Decade of Revolution." Ph.D. diss., Columbia University.

Christoph, Peter R. (1994) "Social and Religious Tensions in Leisler's New York." *de Halve Maen* 57: 87–92.

Churchill, Allen. (1970) *The Upper Crust: An Informal History of New York's Highest Society.* Englewood Cliffs, NJ.

Ciucci, Giorgio, et al. (1979) *The American City: From the Civil War to the New Deal.* Translated by Barbara Luigia La Penta. Cambridge, MA.

Clark, Arthur Hamilton. (1910) *The Clipper Ship Era: An Epitome of Famous American and British Clipper Ships, Their Owners, Builders, Commanders, and Crews, 1843–1869.* New York.

Clark, Clifford E., Jr. (1978) *Henry Ward Beecher: Spokesman for a Middle-Class America.* Urbana, IL.

Clark, Eliot Candee. (1954) *History of the National Academy of Design, 1825–1953.* New York.

Clark, Emmons. (1864) *History of the Second Company of the Seventh Regiment (National Guard).* New York.

Clark, Evans. (1930) *Financing the Consumer.* New York.

Clark, Victor S. (1916–28) *History of Manufactures in the United States.* 2 vols. Washington, DC.

Clarkson, Grosvenor. (1915) *Why Gotham? The Story of a Name.* New York.

Clawson, Mary Ann. (1989) *Constructing Brotherhood: Class, Gender, and Fraternalism.* Princeton, NJ.

Cleveland, Harold B. et. al. (1985) *Citibank, 1812–1970.* Cambridge, MA.

Clifford, Deborah Pickman. (1992) *Crusader for Freedom: A Life of Lydia Maria Child.* Boston.

Clough, Shepard B. (1946) *A Century of Life Insurance: A History of the Mutual Life Insurance Company of New York, 1843–1943.* New York.

Clouston, W. A. (1903) *The Book of Noodles: Stories of Simpletons; or, Fools and Their Follies.* London.

Coben, Stanley. (1962) "Northeastern Business and Radical Reconstruction: A Re-Examination." In *The Economic Impact of the Civil War,* edited by Ralph Andreano. Cambridge, MA.

Cochran, Thomas C. (1932) *New York in the Confederation: An Economic Study.* Philadelphia.

———. (1981) *Frontiers of Change: Early Industrialization in America.* New York.

Cogan, Frances B. (1989) *All-American Girl: The Ideal of Real Womanhood in Mid-nineteenth-century America.* Athens, GA.

Cohalan, Florence D. (1983) *A Popular History of the Archdiocese of New York.* Yonkers, NY.

Cohen, David Steven (1974) *The Ramapo Mountain People.* New Brunswick, NJ.

———. (1981) "How Dutch Were the Dutch of New Netherland?" *NYH* 62: 43–60.

———. (1992) *The Dutch-American Farm.* New York.

Cohen, Patricia Cline. (1992) "Unregulated Youth: Masculinity and Murder in the 1830s City." *Radical History Review* 52: 933–52.

Cohen, Paul E. and Robert T. Augustyn. (1997) *Manhattan in Maps, 1527–1995.* New York.

Cohen, Roger Alan. (1976) "The Lost Jubilee: New York Republicans and the

Politics of Reconstruction and Reform, 1867–1878." Ph.D. diss., Columbia University.

Cohen, Ronald D. (1969) "The Hartford Treaty of 1650: Anglo-Dutch Cooperation in the Seventeenth Century." *NYHSQ* 53: 311–32.

———. (1972) "The New England Colonies and the Dutch Recapture of New York, 1673–74." *NYHSQ* 56: 54–78.

Cohen, Sheldon S. (1971) "Elias Neau, Instructor to New York's Slaves," *NYHSQ* 55: 7–27.

Colden, Cadwallader D. (1825) *Memoir, Prepared at the Request of a Committee of the Common Council of the City of New York and Presented to the Mayor of the City, at the Celebration of the Completion of the New York Canals.* New York.

Cole, John Y. (1979) "Storehouses and Workshops: American Libraries and the Uses of Knowledge." In *The Organization of Knowledge in Modern America, 1860–1920,* edited by Alexandra Oleson and John Voss. Baltimore.

Cole, Thomas. (1994) *Thomas Cole: Landscape into History.* Edited by William H. Truettner and Alan Wallach. New Haven, CT.

Coleman, D. C. (1977) *The Economy of England, 1450–1750.* London.

Coleman, Peter J. (1974) *Debtors and Creditors in America: Insolvency, Imprisonment for Debt, and Bankruptcy, 1607–1900.* Madison, WI.

Coleman, Terry. (1972) *Going to America.* New York.

Coleman, Willie Mae. (1982) "Keeping the Faith and Disturbing the Peace: Black Women from Anti-Slavery to Women's Suffrage." Ph.D. diss., University of California, Irvine.

Collier, Peter, and David Horowitz. (1994) *The Roosevelts: An American Saga.* New York.

Collins, Frederick Lewis. (1934) *Consolidated Gas*

Company of New York. New York.

———. (1946) *Money Town: A History of Manhattan's Golden Mile.* New York.

Combs, Jerald R. (1970) *The Jay Treaty: Political Battleground of the Founding Fathers.* Berkeley, CA.

Comfort, Randall. (1906) *History of Bronx Borough, City of New York.* New York.

Commons, John R., et al., eds. (1910–11) *A Documentary History of American Industrial Society.* Cleveland.

Condit, Carl W. (1980–81) *The Port of New York.* 2 vols. Chicago.

Condon, Thomas J. (1968) *New York Beginnings: The Commercial Origins of New Netherland.* New York.

Conkin, Paul. (1980) *Prophets of Prosperity: America's First Political Economists.* Bloomington, IN.

Conklin, William J., and Jeffrey Simpson. (1983) *Brooklyn's City Hall.* New York.

Conley, Patrick and John P. Kaminski, eds. (1988) *The Constitution and the States: The Role of the Original Thirteen in the Framing and Adoption of the Federal Constitution.* Madison, WI.

Connolly, Harold X. (1977) *A Ghetto Grows in Brooklyn.* New York.

Conot, Robert. (1979) *A Streak of Luck.* New York.

Conrad, Peter. (1984) *The Art of the City: Views and Versions of New York.* New York.

Couser, Water, ed. (1986) *Resistance, Politics, and the American Struggle for Independence.* Boulder, CO.

Conway, Stephen. (1986) "To Subdue America: British Army Officers and the Conduct of the Revolutionary War." *WMQ* 43: 381–407.

———. (1990) "'The Great Mischief Complain'd of': Reflections on the Misconduct of British Soldiers in the Revolutionary War." *WMQ* 47: 370–90.

Cook, Adrian. (1974) *The Armies of the Streets: The New York City Draft Riots of 1863.* Lexington, KY.

Cook, Clarence, ed. (1887) *A Girl's Life Eighty Years Ago: Selections from the Letters of Eliza Southgate Bowne*. New York.

Cook, Harry. (1913) *The Borough of the Bronx, 1639–1913: Its Marvelous Development and Historical Surroundings*. New York.

Cooke, Hope. (1995) *Seeing New York: History Walks for Armchair and Footloose Travelers*. Philadelphia.

Cooke, Jacob E. (1960) "Alexander Hamilton's Authorship of the 'Caesar' Letters." *WMQ* 17: 78–85.

———, ed. (1964) *The Reports of Alexander Hamilton*. New York.

———. (1970) "The Compromise of 1790." *WMQ* 27: 523–45.

Cookson, Peter W., Jr., and Caroline Hodges Persell. (1985) *Preparing for Power: America's Elite Boarding Schools*. New York.

Coombe, Philip Walter. (1991) "The Life and Times of James P. Allaire, Early Founder and Steam Engine Builder." Ph.D. diss., New York University.

Coon, Horace. (1947) *Columbia: Colossus on the Hudson*. New York.

Cooney, John. (1984) *The American Pope: The Life and Times of Francis Cardinal Spellman*. New York.

Cooper, Henry S., Jr. (1968) "The Man Who Invented Dutch New York" In *New York, N.Y.: An American Heritage Extra*, edited by David G. Lowe. New York.

Cooper, James Fenimore. (1963) *Notions of the Americans Picked Up by a Travelling Bachelor*. New York.

———. (1969) *The American Democrat: A Treatise on Jacksonian Democracy*. New York.

Corey, Steven Hunt. (1994) "King Garbage: A History of Solid Waste Management in New York City, 1881–1970." Ph.D. diss., New York University.

Cornog, Evan W. (1988) "To Give Character to Our City: New York's City Hall." *NYH* 69: 389–423.

Costello, Augustine E. ([1885] 1972) *Our Police Protectors: History of the New York Police from the Earliest Period to the Present Time.* Montclair, NJ.

———. (1887) *Our Firemen: A History of the New York Fire Departments, Volunteer and Paid*. New York.

Costello, Lawrence. (1967) "The New York City Labor Movement, 1861–1872." Ph.D. diss., Columbia University.

Countryman, Edward. (1976a) "Consolidating Power in Revolutionary America: The Case of New York, 1775–1783." *Journal of Interdisciplinary History* 66: 45–78.

———. (1976b) "'Out of the Bounds of the Law': Northern Land Rioters in the Eighteenth Century." In *American Revolution: Explorations in the History of American Radicalism*, edited by Alfred Young. DeKalb, IL.

———. (1981a) *A People in Revolution: The American Revolution and Political Society in New York, 1760–1790*. Baltimore.

———. (1981b) "Some Problems of Power in New York, 1777–1782." In *Sovereign States in an Age of Uncertainty*, edited by Ronald Hoffman and Peter J. Albert, Washington, D.C.

Cowles, Virginia S. (1979) *The Astors*. New York.

Crane, Stephen. (1979) *Maggie: A Girl of the Streets*, edited by Thomas A. Gullason. New York.

Crapsey, Edward. (1872) *The Nether Side of New York, or, the Vice, Crime, and Poverty of the Great Metropolis*. New York.

Crary, Catherine S. (1959) "The Tory and the Spy: The Double Life of James Rivington." *WMQ* 16: 61–72

———. (1973) *The Price of Loyalty: Tory Writings from the Revolutionary Era*. New York.

———. (1975) "Guerrilla Activities of James DeLancey's Cowboys in Westchester County: Conventional Warfare or Self-Interested Freebooting?" In *The Loyalist Americans: A Focus on Greater New York,* edited by Robert East and Jacob Judd. Tarrytown, NY.

Craven, Wesley Frank. (1968) *The Colonies in Transition, 1660–1713*. New York.

Cray, Ed. (1978) *Levi's*. Boston.

Cray, Robert E., Jr. (1986) "Forging a Majority: The Methodist Experience On Eastern Long Island, 1789–1845." *NYH* 67: 285–303

———. (1988a) *Paupers and Poor Relief in New York City and Its Rural Environs, 1700–1830*. Philadelphia.

———. (1988b) "Poverty and Poor Relief: New York City and Its Rural Environs, 1700–1790." In *Authority and Resistance in Early New York*, edited by William Pencak and Conrad Wright. New York.

Cremin, Lawrence. (1988) *American Education: The Metropolitan Experience, 1876–1980*. New York.

Cress, Lawrence D. (1975) "Whither Columbia? Congressional Residence and the Politics of the New Nation, 1776 to 1787." *WMQ* 32: 581–600.

Cressy, George B. (1966) "Land Forms." In *Geography of New York State*, edited by John Thompson. New York.

Crimmins, John D. (1905) *Irish-American Historical Miscellany Relating Largely to New York City*. New York.

Croffut, William Augustus. (1975) *The Vanderbilts and the Story of their Fortune*. New York.

Cromley, Elizabeth Collins. (1990) *Alone Together: A History of New York's Early Apartments*. Ithaca, NY.

Cronin, James E. (1949) "Elihu Hubbard Smith and the New York Friendly Club, 1795–1798." *Publications of the Modern Language Association* 64: 471–79.

———. (1949) "Elihu Hubbard Smith and the New York Theater (1793–98)." *NYH* 31: 136–48.

———, ed. (1973) *The Diary of Elihu Hubbard Smith (1771–1798)*. Philadelphia.

Cronon, William. (1983) *Changes in the Land: Indi-ans, Colonists, and the Ecology of New England*. New York.

Cross, Robert D., ed. (1967) *The Church and the City, 1865–1910*. Indianapolis.

Crouthamel, James L. (1989) *Bennett's New York Herald and the Rise of the Popular Press*. Syracuse, NY.

Crowley, John E. (1993) *The Privileges of Independence: Neomercantilism and the American Revolution*. Baltimore.

Cruden, Robert. (1972) *The War that Never Ended: The American Civil War*. Englewood Cliffs, NJ.

Cudahy, Brian J. (1990) *Over and Back: The History of Ferryboats in New York Harbor*. New York.

Culhane, John. (1990) *The American Circus: An Illustrated History*. New York.

Cunliffe, Marcus. (1968) *Soldiers and Civilians: The Martial Spirit in America 1775–1865*. Boston.

———. (1976) "Frances Trollope, 1780–1863." In *Abroad in America*, edited by Marc Pachter.

Cunningham, Robert Hays, ed. (1889) *Amusing Prose Chap-Books*. London.

Curran, Robert Emmett. (1978) *Michael Augustine Corrigan and the Shaping of Conservative Catholicism in America, 1878–1902*. New York.

Curry, Daniel. (1853) *New York: Historical Sketch of the Rise and Progress of the Metropolitan City of America*. New York.

Curry, Leonard. (1981) *The Free Black in Urban America, 1800–1850: The Shadow of the Dream*. Chicago.

Curtis, George William. (1853) *The Potiphar Papers*. New York.

Cutler, Carl C. (1930) *Greyhounds of the Sea: The Story of the American Clipper Ship*. Annapolis, MD.

———. (1961) *Queens of the Western Ocean: The Story of America's Mail and Passenger Sailing Lines*. Annapolis, MD.

Cutler, William W. (1972) "Status, Values, and the Education of the Poor: The Trustees of the New York Public School Society, 1805–53." *AQ* 24: 69–85.

Czitrom, Daniel J. (1982) *Media and the American Mind: From Morse to McLuhan.* Chapel Hill, NC.

———. (1991) "Underworlds and Underdogs: Big Tim Sullivan and Metropolitan Politics in New York, 1889–1913." *JAH* 78: 536–58.

Dain, Phyllis. (1972) *The New York Public Library: A History of Its Founding and Early Years.* New York.

Daitsman, George. (1963) "Labor and the 'Welfare State' in Early New York." *Labor History.* 4: 248–56.

Daley, Robert. (1959) *The World Beneath the City.* Philadelphia.

Danckaerts, Jaspar, and Peter Sluyter. ([1867] 1966) *Journal of a Voyage to New York* [1679–80]. New York.

Danforth, Brian. (1974) "The Influence of Socioeconomic Factors upon Political Behavior: A Quantitative Look at New York City Merchants, 1828–1844." Ph.D. diss., New York University.

Dangerfield, George. (1960) *Chancellor Robert R. Livingston of New York, 1746–1813.* New York.

Daniels, Doris Groshen. (1989) *Always a Sister: The Feminism of Lillian D. Wald.* New York.

Dann, John C., ed. (1980) *The Revolution Remembered: Eyewitness Accounts of the War for Independence.* Chicago.

Dann, Martin E. (1971) *The Black Press, 1827–1890.* New York.

Davidson, Marshall. (1977) *New York: A Pictorial History.* New York.

Davies, D.W. (1961) *A Primer of Dutch Seventeenth Century Overseas Trade.* The Hague.

Davis, Allen Freeman. (1967) *Spearheads for Reform: The Social Settlements and the Progressive Movement, 1890–1914.* New York.

Davis, Hugh H. (1979) "The American Seamen's Friend Society and the American Sailor, 1828–1838." *American Neptune* 39: 45–57.

Davis, Joseph S. ([1917] 1965) "William Duer, Entrepreneur, 1747–99." In *Essays in the Earlier History of American Corporations.* 2 vols. New York.

———. ([1917] 1965) *Essays in the Earlier History of American Corporations.* 2 vols. New York.

Davis, Ralph. (1973) *The Rise of the Atlantic Economies.* Ithaca, NY.

Davis, Thomas J. (1985) *A Rumor of Revolt: The "Great Negro Plot" in Colonial New York.* New York.

———. (1991) "New York's Long Black Line: A Note on the Growing Slave Population, 1676–1790." Reprinted in *Coming and Becoming: Pluralism in New York State History,* edited by Wendell Tripp. Cooperstown, NY.

Davison, Robert A. (1964) *Isaac Hicks: New York Merchant and Quaker, 1767–1820.* Cambridge, MA.

Davisson, William, and Lawrence Bradley. (1971) "New York Maritime Trade: Ship Voyage Patterns, 1715–1765." *NYHSQ* 55: 309–17.

Dayton, Abram C. (1882) *Last Days of Knickerbocker Life in New York.* New York.

De Conde, Alexander. (1966) *The Quasi-War: The Politics and Diplomacy of the Undeclared War with France, 1797–1801.* New York.

De Jong, Gerald F. (1968) "Dominie Johannes Megapolensis, Minister to New Netherland." *NYHSQ* 52: 7–47.

———. (1970) "The 'Ziekentroosters' or Comforters of the Sick in New Netherland." *NYHSQ* 54: 339–59.

———. (1975) *The Dutch in America.* Boston.

De Pauw, Linda Grant. (1966) *The Eleventh Pillar: New York State and the Federal Constitution.* Ithaca, NY.

———. (1974) *Four Traditions: Women of New York During the American Revolution.* Albany.

———. (1975) *Founding Mothers: Women of America in the Revolutionary Era.* Boston.

De Peyster, Frederick. (1855) *History of the Tontine Building.* New York.

———. (1879) *The Life and Administration of Richard, Earle of Bellomont . . . from 1697 to 1701.* New York.

De Voe, Thomas F. (1970) *The Market Book: A History of the Public Markets of the City of New York.* New York.

Dean, Arthur Hobson. (1957) *William Nelson Cromwell, 1854–1948: An American Pioneer in Corporation, Comparative and International Law.* New York.

Degler, Carl Neumann. (1952) "Labor in the Economy and Politics of New York City, 1800–1850." Ph.D. diss., Columbia University.

D'Emilio, John, and Estelle B. Freedman. (1988) *Intimate Matters: A History of Sexuality in America.* New York.

Den Boer, Gordon. (1989) "The First Federal Elections." In *Well Begun: Chronicles of the Early National Period,* edited by Stephen L. Schecter and Richard B. Bernstein. Albany, NY.

Denholm, Anthony. (1972) *France in Revolution, 1848.* New York.

Denning, Michael. (1987) *Mechanic Accents: Dime Novels and Working-Class Culture in America.* London.

Dennis, Matthew. (1994) *Cultivating a Landscape of Peace: Iroquois-European Encounters in Seventeenth-Century America.* Ithaca, NY.

Denton, Daniel. (1966) *A Brief Description of New York* [1670]. New York.

Derrick, Peter. (1979) "The Dual System of Rapid Transit." Ph.D. diss., New York University.

Devlin, William E. (1996) "Shrewd Irishmen: Irish Entrepreneurs and Artisans in New York's Clothing Industry, 1830–1880." In *The New York Irish,* edited by Ronald H. Bayor and Timothy J. Meagher. Baltimore.

Devorkin, Joseph. (1987)

Great Merchants of Early New York: "The Ladies' Mile." New York.

Di Donato, Pietro. (1960) *Immigrant Saint: The Life of Mother Cabrini.* New York.

Di Giovanni, Stephen Michael. (1983) "Michael Augustine Corrigan and the Italian Immigrants." Ph.D. diss., Gregorian Pontifical University.

Diamond, Robert, and Vincent R. Ricciardi. (1983) *The Atlantic Avenue Tunnel.* Brooklyn.

Dickens, Charles. (1961) *American Notes for General Circulation.* Introduction by Christopher Lasch. Greenwich, CT.

Dickinson, H. T. (1992) "Radical Culture." In *London—World City, 1800–1840,* edited by Celina Fox. New Haven, CT.

Dickson, R.J. (1966) *Ulster Emigration to Colonial America, 1718–1775.* London.

Diggins, John P. (1972) *Mussolini and Fascism: The View from America.* Princeton, NJ.

Dillard, J.L. (1972) *Black English: Its History and Usage in the United States.* New York.

Dilliard, Maud Esther. (1974) "A Village Called Midwout." *The Journal of Long Island History.* 11: 6–24.

Dillon, Clarissa F. (1981) "A Survey of the Dutch in the Delaware Valley in the Seventeenth Century." *de Halve Maen,* 1ff.

Dillon, Dorothy. (1949) *The New York Triumvirate.* New York.

Diner, Hasia R. (1983) *Erin's Daughters in America: Irish Immigrant Woman in the Nineteenth Century.* Baltimore.

———. (1992) *A Time for Gathering: The Second Migration, 1820–1880.* Baltimore.

———. (1996) "'The Most Irish City in the Union': The Era of the Great Migration." In *The New York Irish,* edited by Ronald H. Bayor and Timothy J. Meagher. Baltimore.

D'Innocenzo, Michael. (1974) "The Popularization of Politics in Irving's New York." In *The Knickerbocker Tradition*, edited by Andrew B. Myers. Tarrytown, NY.

Dix, Morgan, ed. (1898) *A History of the Parish of Trinity Church in the City of New York*. New York.

Dizikes, John. (1993) *Opera In America: A Cultural History*. New Haven, CT.

Dodge, Phyllis. (1987) *Tales of the Phelps-Dodge Family: A Chronicle of Five Generations*. New York.

Dolan, Jay P. (1975) *The Immigrant Church: New York's Irish and German Catholics, 1815–1865*. Baltimore.

Dolkart, Andrew S., and Sharon Z. Macoska. (1988) *A Dream Fulfilled: City and Suburban's York Avenue Estate*. New York.

Domosh, Mona. (1985) "Scrapers of the Sky: The Symbolic and Functional Structures of Lower Manhattan." Ph.D. diss., Clark University.

Donnelly, Ignatius. (1960) *Caesar's Column: A Story of the Twentieth Century*. Cambridge, MA.

Donnelly, James Francis. (1982) "Catholic New Yorkers and New York Socialists, 1870–1920." Ph.D. diss., New York University.

Donner, Frank. (1990) *Protectors of Privilege: Red Squads and Police Repression*. Berkeley, CA.

Dorson, Richard. (1943) "Mose the Far-Famed and World-Renowned." *American Literature* 15: 288–300.

Douglas, Ann. (1977) *The Feminization of American Culture*. New York.

Douglas, George H. (1991) *The Smart Magazines: 50 Years of Literary Revelry and High Jinks at Vanity Fair, the New Yorker, Life, Esquire, and the Smart Set*. Hamden, CT.

Dowling, Harry. (1982) *City Hospitals: The Undercare of the Underprivileged*. Cambridge, MA,.

Doyle, David Noel. (1981) *Ireland, Irishmen and Revolutionary America, 1760–1820*. Dublin.

Dructor, Robert Michael (1975) "The New York Commercial Community:

The Revolutionary Experience." Ph.D. diss., University of Pittsburgh.

Dubois, Anson. (1884) "A History of the Town of Flatlands." Reprinted from Stiles, *Illustrated History of Kings County*. Pamphlet. Brooklyn.

DuBois, Ellen Carol. (1978) *Feminism and Suffrage: The Emergence of an Independent Women's Movement in America, 1848–1869*. Ithaca, NY.

Dudden, Faye E. (1983) *Serving Women: Household Service in Nineteenth-century America*. Middletown, CT.

———. (1994) *Women in the American Theater: Actresses and Audiences, 1790–1870*. New Haven, CT.

Duduit, James Michael. (1983) "Henry Ward Beecher and the Political Pulpit." Ph.D. diss. Florida State University.

Duer, William A. (1867) *Reminiscences of An Old New Yorker*. New York.

Duffy, John. (1966) "An Account of the Epidemic Fevers that Prevailed in the City of New York from 1791 to 1822." *NYHSQ* 50: 333–64.

———. (1968) *A History of Public Health in New York City, 1625–1866*. Vol. 1. New York.

———. (1974) *A History of Public Health in New York City, 1866–1966*. Vol. 2. New York.

———. (1990) *The Sanitarians: A History of American Public Health*. Urbana, IL.

Dunkak, Harry M. (1988) "A Colonial and Revolutionary Parish in New York: St. Paul's Church, Eastchester." *Anglican and Episcopal History* 57: 397–426.

Dunlap, William. (1930) *Diary of William Dunlap, 1766–1839*. 3 vols. New York.

Dunn, Richard S. (1972) *Sugar and Slaves: The Rise of the Planter Class in the English West Indies, 1624–1713*. Chapel Hill, NC.

Dunshee, Kenneth Holcomb. (1952) *As You Pass By: Old Manhattan through the Fire Laddies' Eyes*. New York.

Durey, Michael. (1987)

"Thomas Paine's Apostles: Radical Emigres and the Triumph of Jeffersonian Republicanism." *WMQ* 44: 661–88.

———. (1997) *Transatlantic Radicals and the Early American Republic*. Lawrence, KS.

Durso, Joseph. (1979) *Madison Square Garden: 100 Years of History*. New York.

Dye, Nancy Schrom. (1980) *As Equals and as Sisters: Feminism, the Labor Movement, and the Women's Trade Union League of New York*. Columbia, MO.

Dyer, Walter A. (1915) *Early American Craftsmen*. New York.

Eames, Wilberforce. (1928) *The First Year of Printing in New-York: May, 1693 to April, 1694*. New York.

Earle, Alice Morse. (1938) *Colonial Days in Old New York*. New York.

East, Robert. (1938) *Business Enterprise in the American Revolutionary Era*. New York.

———, and Jacob Judd, eds. (1978) *The Loyalist Americans: A Focus on Greater New York*. Tarrytown, NY.

Eckhardt, Celia Morris. (1984) *Fanny Wright: Rebel in America*. Cambridge, MA.

Eddis, William. (1792) *Letters from America, Historical and Descriptive, Comprising Occurrences from 1769 to 1777, Inclusive*. London.

Edwards, George W. ([1917] 1967) *New York as an Eighteenth-Century Municipality, 1731–1776*. Port Washington, NY.

Edwards, Stewart. (1971) *The Paris Commune, 1871*. Chicago.

Egly, T. W. (1981) *History of the First New York Regiment*. Hampton, NH.

Egnal, Marc. (1985) "The Economic Development of the Thirteen Continental Colonies, 1720–1775." *WMQ* 32: 191–222.

———. (1988) *A Mighty Empire: The Origins of the American Revolution*. Ithaca, NY.

Ehrenreich, John H. (1985) *The Altruistic Imagination:*

A History of Social Work and Social Policy in the United States. Ithaca, NY.

Ekirch, A. Roger. (1987) *Bound for America: The Transportation of British Convicts to the Colonies, 1718–1775*. New York.

Elias, Stephen N. (1992) *Alexander T. Stewart: The Forgotten Merchant Prince*. Westport, CT.

Elkins, Stanley, and Eric McKitrick. (1993) *The Age of Federalism: The Early American Republic, 1788–1800*. New York.

Ellington, George (pseud.). (1869) *The Women of New York, or, The Under-world of the Great City*. New York.

Elliot, Emory, ed. (1985) *American Writers of the Early Republic*. Detroit.

Ellis, David M. (1979) *New York: State and City*. Ithaca, NY.

———. (1991) "The Yankee Invasion of New York, 1783–1850." Reprinted in *Coming and Becoming: Pluralism in New York State History*, edited by Wendell Tripp. Cooperstown, NY.

Ellis, Edward Robb. ([1966] 1997) *The Epic of New York City*. New York.

Ellis, Joseph J. (1979) *After the Revolution: Profiles of Early American Culture*. New York.

Ellmann, Richard. (1987) *Oscar Wilde*. New York.

Engelman, F.L. (1953) "Cadwallader Colden and the New York Stamp Act Riots." *WMQ* 10: 560–65.

Engle, Paul. (1976) *Women in the American Revolution*. Chicago.

Erenberg, Lewis A. (1981) *Steppin' Out: New York Nightlife and the Transformation of American Culture, 1890–1930*. Westport, CT.

Erie, Steven P. (1988) *Rainbow's End: Irish-Americans and the Dilemmas of Urban Machine Politics, 1840–1985*. Berkeley, CA.

Erkkila, Betsy. (1989) *Whitman: The Political Poet*. New York.

Ernst, Robert. (1944) "The Economic Status of New York City Negroes, 1850–1863." *Negro History Bulletin*. 12: 131–43.

———. (1949) *Immigrant Life in New York City, 1825–1863.* New York.

———. (1968) *Rufus King: American Federalist.* Chapel Hill, NC.

———. (1983) "A Tory-eye View of the Evacuation of New York." *NYH* 64: 377–94.

———. (1989) "The Long Island Delegates and the New York Ratifying Convention." *NYH* 70: 55–78.

———. (1993) "Isaac Low and the American Revolution." *NYH* 74: 133–57.

———. (1994) "Nicholas Low: Merchant and Speculator in post-Revolutionary New York." *NYH* 75: 357–72.

Etienne, Mona, and Eleanor Leacock, eds. (1980) *Women and Colonization: Anthropological Perspectives.* New York.

Evans, Meryle R. (1952) "Knickerbocker Hotels and Restaurants, 1800–1850." *NYHSQ* 36: 377–410.

Everdell, William R., and Malcolm MacKay. (1973) *Rowboats to Rapid Transit: A History of Brooklyn Heights.* Brooklyn.

Ewen, Elizabeth. (1985) *Immigrant Women in the Land of Dollars: Life and Culture on the Lower East Side, 1890–1925.* New York.

Ewers, Hans-Jurgen, John B. Goddard, and Horst Matzerath, eds. (1986) *The Future of the Metropolis: Berlin, London, Paris, New York.* Berlin.

Exman, Eugene. (1965) *The Brothers Harper: A Unique Publishing Partnership and Its Impact upon the Cultural Life of America from 1817 to 1853.* New York.

Fabend, Firth. (1991) *A Dutch Family in the Middle Colonies, 1660–1800.* Rutgers, NJ.

———. (1994) "'According to Holland Custome': Jacob Leisler and the Lookermans Estate Feud." *de Halve Maen* 67: 1–8.

———. (1997) "The Synod of Dort and the Persistence of Dutchness in Nineteenth-Century New York and New Jersey." *NYH* 77: 273–300.

Faber, Eli. (1992) *A Time For Planting: The First Migration, 1654–1820.* Vol. 1 of *The Jewish People in America.* Baltimore.

Fabian, Ann. (1990) *Card Sharps, Dream Books, and Bucket Shops: Gambling in Nineteenth-century America.* Ithaca, NY.

Fabre, Genevieve, and Robert O'Meally, eds. (1994) *History and Memory in African-American Culture.* New York.

Fairfield, Francis Gerry. (1873) *The Clubs of New York.* New York.

Fairfield, John D. (1985) "Neighborhood and Metropolis: The Origins of Modern Urban Planning, 1877–1935." Ph.D., diss., University of Rochester.

Farb, Peter. (1968) *Man's Rise to Civilization: As Shown By the Indians of North America from Primeval Times to the Coming of the Industrial State.* New York.

Farley, John M. (1908) *History of St. Patrick's Cathedral.* New York.

Fayden, Meta Patricia (1993) "Indian Corn and Dutch Pots: Seventeenth-Century Foodways in New Amsterdam/New York City." Ph.D. diss., City University of New York.

Feder, Leah H. (1936) *Unemployment Relief in Periods of Depression: A Study of Relief Measures in American Cities, 1857 Through 1922.* New York.

Fee, Elizabeth, and Evelyn M. Hammonds. (1995) "Science, Politics, and the Art of Persuasion: Promoting the New Scientific Medicine in New York City." In *Hives of Sickness: Public Health and Epidemics in New York City*, edited by David Rosner. New Brunswick, NJ.

Fehrenbacher, Don Edward. (1987) *Lincoln in Text and Context: Collected Essays.* Stanford, CA.

Feldberg, Michael. (1980) *The Turbulent Era: Riot and Disorder in Jacksonian America.* New York.

Fels, Rendigs. (1959) *American Business Cycles, 1865–1897.* Chapel Hill, NC.

Fenton, Edwin. (1957) "Immigrants and Unions: A Case Study of Italians and American Labor, 1870–1920." Ph.D. diss., Harvard University.

Fenton, William N. (1971) "The Iroquois in History." In *North American Indians in Historical Perspective*, edited by Eleanor Leacock and Nancy Lurie. New York.

Fernow, Berthold, ed. (1887) *New York in the Revolution.* Albany, NY.

———. (1897) *The Records of New Amsterdam from 1653 to 1674.* 7 vols. New York.

———. (1902–7) *The Minutes of the Orphanmasters Court of New Amsterdam.* New York.

———. ([1907] 1970) *Minutes of the Executive Board of the Burgomasters of New Amsterdam.* New York.

Field, Phyllis F. (1982) *The Politics of Race in New York: The Struggle for Black Suffrage in the Civil War Era.* Ithaca, NY.

Fierstien, Robert E. (1990) *A Different Spirit: The Jewish Theological Seminary of America, 1886–1902.* New York.

Filler, Louis. (1976) *The Muckrakers.* University Park, PA.

Findlay, James F. (1969) *Dwight L. Moody, American Evangelist, 1837–1899.* Chicago.

Fine, Jo Renee, and Gerard Wolfe. (1978) *The Synagogues of New York's Lower East Side.* New York.

Fine, Sidney. (1964) *Laissez Faire and the General-Welfare State: A Study of Conflict in American Thought, 1865–1901.* Ann Arbor, MI.

Finegold, Kenneth. (1985) "Progressivism, Electoral Change and Public Policy: Reform Outcomes in New York, Cleveland and Chicago." Ph.D. diss., Harvard University.

Fingerhut, Eugene R. (1983) *Survivor: Cadwallader Colden II in Revolutionary America.* Washington, DC.

Fink, Leon. (1983) *Workingmen's Democracy: The Knights of Labor and American Politics.* Urbana, IL.

Finney, Jack. (1970) *Time and Again.* New York.

Fischer, David Hackett. (1965) *The Revolution of American Conservatism: The Federalist Party in the Era of Jeffersonian Democracy.* New York.

Fischler, Stan. (1976) *Uptown, Downtown: A Trip Through Time on New York's Subways.* New York.

Fishburn, Janet Forsythe. (1981) *The Fatherhood of God and the Victorian Family: The Social Gospel in America.* Philadelphia.

Fishlow, Albert. (1966) *American Railroads and the Transformation of the Antebellum Economy.* Cambridge, MA.

Fishman, Eric. (1980) "New York City's Criminal Justice System, 1895–1932." Ph.D. diss., Columbia University.

Fite, Emerson David. (1976) *Social and Industrial Conditions in the North During the Civil War.* Williamstown, MA.

Fitzgerald, Maureen. (1992) "Irish-Catholic Nuns and the Development of New York City's Welfare System, 1840–1900." Ph.D. diss., University of Wisconsin, Madison.

Fitzpatrick, Benedict. (1927) *The Bronx and Its People.* New York.

Flaherty, David H., ed. (1969) *Essays in the History of Early American Law.* Chapel Hill, NC.

Fleming, Thomas. (1975) *1776: Year of Illusions.* New York.

Flexner, James Thomas. (1964) *Steamboats Come True: American Inventors in Action.* New York.

———. (1968) *George Washington in the American Revolution, 1775–1783.* Boston.

———. (1970) *George Washington and the New Nation, 1783–1793.* Boston.

———. (1980) *States Dyckman: American Loyalist.* Boston.

Flick, Alexander C. ([1901] 1969) *Loyalism in New York During the American Revolution.* New York.

———, ed. (1933) *History of the State of New York.* 10 vols. New York.

———. (1939) *Samuel Jones Tilden: A Study in Political Sagacity.* New York.

Fliegelman, Jay. (1982) *Prodigals and Pilgrims: The American Revolution against Patriarchal Authority, 1750–1800.* Cambridge, MA.

Fogelson, Robert. (1989) *America's Armories: Architecture, Society, and Public Order.* Cambridge, MA.

Foglesong, Richard E. (1986) *Planning the Capitalist City: The Colonial Era to the 1920s.* Princeton, NJ.

Folsom, Franklin. (1991) *Impatient Armies of the Poor: The Story of Collective Action of the Unemployed, 1808–1942.* Niwot, CO.

Foner, Eric (1970) *Free Soil, Free Labor, Free Men: The Ideology of the Republican Party Before the Civil War.* New York.

———. (1976) *Tom Paine and Revolutionary America.* New York.

———. (1980) *Politics and Ideology in the Age of the Civil War.* New York.

———. (1988) *Reconstruction: America's Unfinished Revolution, 1863–1877.* New York.

Foner, Philip S. (1968) *Business and Slavery: The New York Merchants and the Irrepressible Conflict.* New York.

———. (1972) *The Spanish-Cuban-American War and the Birth of American Imperialism, 1895–1902.* New York.

———, ed. (1973) *When Karl Marx Died: Comments in 1883.* New York.

———. (1975) *History of the Labor Movement in the United States.* 2nd ed. New York.

———. (1977) *The Great Labor Uprising of 1877.* New York.

———. (1982) *Organized Labor and the Black Worker, 1619–1973.* 2nd ed. New York.

———. (1983) *History of Black Americans: From the Compromise of 1850 to the End of the Civil War.* Westport, CT.

Foord, John. (1903) *The Life and Public Services of Simon Sterne.* New York.

———. (1913) *The Life and Public Services of Andrew Haswell Green.* Garden City, NY.

Foote, Thelma Wills. (1991) "Black Life in Colonial Manhattan, 1664–1786." Ph.D. diss., Harvard.

———. (1993) "Crossroads or Settlement? The Black Freedmen's Community in Historic Greenwich Village, 1644–1855." In *Greenwich Village: Culture and Counterculture,* edited by Rick Beard and Leslie Cohen Berlowitz. New Brunswick, NJ.

Ford, Paul Leicester. (1902) *Journal of Hugh Gaine.* 2 vols. New York.

Forster, Robert and Jack P. Greene, eds. (1970) *The Preconditions of Revolution in Early Modern Europe.* Baltimore.

Foshay, Ella M. (1990) *Luman Reed's Picture Gallery: A Pioneer Collection of American Art.* New York.

Foster, Charles J. (1960) *An Errand of Mercy: The Evangelical United Front, 1790–1837.* Chapel Hill, NC.

Fowler, Dorothy Ganfield. (1981) *A City Church: The First Presbyterian Church in the City of New York, 1716–1976.* New York.

Fox, Arthur William. (1899) *A Book of Bachelors.* Westminster, UK.

Fox, Celina, ed. (1992) *London—World City: 1800–1840.* New Haven

Fox, Dixon Ryan. ([1919] 1965) *The Decline of Aristocracy in the Politics of New York, 1801–1840,* edited by Robert V. Remini. New York.

———. (1926) *Caleb Heathcote, Gentleman Colonist: The Story of a Career in the Province of New York, 1692–1721.* New York.

———. (1940) *Yankees and Yorkers.* New York.

Fox, Kenneth. (1977) *Better City Government: Innovation in American Urban Politics, 1850–1937.* Philadelphia.

Fox, Maxwell. (1960) *Lorillard and Tobacco: 200th Anniversary, P. Lorillard Company, 1760–1960.* New York.

Fox, Richard Wightman, and T. J. Jackson Lears, eds. (1983) *The Culture of Consumption in America: Critical Essays in American History, 1880–1980.* New York.

Fox, Richard Wightman. (1991) "The Discipline of Amusement." In *Inventing Times Square: Commerce and Culture at the Crossroads of the World,* edited by William R. Taylor. New York.

———. (1993) "Intimacy on Trial: Cultural Meanings of the Beecher-Tilton Affair." In *The Power of Culture: Critical Essays in American History.* Chicago.

Fox, Stephen. (1984) *The Mirror Makers: A History of American Advertising and Its Creators.* New York.

Franchot, Jenny. (1985) "Susanna Haswell Rowson." In *American Writers of the Early Republic,* edited by Emory Elliott. Detroit.

Francis, John W. (1857) *Old New York During the Last Half Century.* New York.

———. (1866) *Old New York: Or, Reminiscences of the Past Sixty Years.* New York.

Francis, Jr., Peter. (1986) "The Beads That Did Not Buy Manhattan Island." *NYH* 67: 5–22.

Fredrickson, George M. (1965) *The Inner Civil War: Northern Intellectuals and the Crisis of the Union.* New York.

Freedman, Estelle B. (1981) *Their Sisters' Keepers: Women's Prison Reform in America, 1830–1930.* Ann Arbor, MI.

Freeman, Rhoda. (1966) "The Free Negro in New York City During the Pre-Civil War Era." Ph.D. diss., Columbia University.

Frese, Joseph, and Jacob Judd, eds. (1979) *Business Enterprise in Early New York.* Tarrytown, NY.

Frick, John W., Jr. (1983) "The Rialto: A Study of Union Square, the Center of New York's First Theater District, 1870–1900." Ph.D. diss., New York University, 1983.

Fried, Albert. (1980) *The Rise and Fall of the Jewish Gangster in America.* New York.

Fried, Lewis. (1990) *Makers of the City.* Amherst, MA.

Friedman, Bernard. (1965) "The New York Assembly Elections of 1768 and 1769: The Disruption of Family Politics." *NYH* 46: 3–24.

———. (1970) "The Shaping of Radical Consciousness in Provincial New York." *JAH* 56: 781–801.

Friedman, Maxine. (1990) *Wall Street: Changing Fortunes.* New York.

Friess, Horace. (1981) *Felix Adler and Ethical Culture: Memories and Studies.* New York.

Fruchtman, Jack. (1994) *Thomas Paine: Apostle of Freedom.* New York.

Frug, Gerald E. (1980) "The City as a Legal Concept." *Harvard Law Review* 93: 1059–154.

———. (Summer 1984) "Property and Power: Hartog on the Legal History of New York City." *American Bar Foundation Research Journal,* 673–91.

Furer, Howard B. (1965) *William Frederick Havemeyer: A Political Biography.* New York.

———, comp. and ed. (1973) *The Germans in America, 1607–1970: A Chronology and Fact Book.* Dobbs Ferry, NY.

Furia, Philip. (1990) *The Poets of Tin Pan Alley: A History of America's Great Lyricists.* New York.

Furman, Gabriel. (1937) "How New York City Used to Celebrate Independence Day." *NYHSQ* 21: 93–96.

Gabaccia, Donna R. (1984) *From Sicily to Elizabeth Street: Housing and Social Change Among Italian Immigrants, 1880–1930.* Albany, NY.

Gabler, Edwin. (1988) *The American Telegrapher: A Social History, 1860–1900.* New Brunswick, NJ.

Gabriel, Mary. (1998) *Notorious Victoria: The Life of Victoria Woodhull, Uncensored.* Chapel Hill, NC.

Gabriel, Ralph H. ([1921] 1968) *The Evolution of Long Island: A Story of Land and Sea.* Port Washington, NY.

Gallagher, John J. (1995) *The Battle of Brooklyn, 1776.* New York.

Garber, Marjorie B. (1993) *Vested Interest: Cross Dressing and Cultural Anxiety.* New York.

Gardner, Chas G. ([1894] 1931) *The Doctor and the Devil, or Midnight Adventure of Dr. Parkhurst.* New York.

Gardner, Deborah S. (1979) "The Architecture of Commercial Capitalism: John Kellum and the Development of New York, 1840–75." Ph.D. diss., Columbia University.

———. (1982) *Marketplace: A Brief History of the New York Stock Exchange.* New York.

———. (1994) *Cadwalader, Wickersham and Taft: A Bicentennial History, 1792–1992.* New York.

Garmey, Stephen. (1984) *Gramercy Park: An Illustrated History of a New York Neighborhood.* New York.

Garnet, Robert. (1985) *The Telephone Enterprise: The Evolution of the Bell System's Horizontal Structure, 1876–1909.* Baltimore.

Garrett, Thomas Myers. (1978) "A History of Pleasure Gardens in New York City, 1700–1865." Ph.D. diss., New York University.

Garside, Alston Hill. (1939) *Cotton Goes to Market: A Graphic Description of a Great Industry.* New York.

Gatell, Frank Otto. (1966) "Sober Second Thoughts on Martin Van Buren, the Albany Regency, and the Wall Street Conspiracy." *JAH* 53: 19–40.

Gates, John D. (1981) *The Astor Family.* Garden City.

Gates, Robert Allan. (1987) *The New York Vision: Interpretations of New York City in the American Novel.* Lanham, MD.

Gayle, Margot, and Edmund V. Gillon, Jr. (1974) *Cast-Iron Architecture in New York City: A Photographic Survey.* New York.

———, and Robin Lynn. (1974) *A Walking Tour of Cast-iron Architecture in SoHo.* New York.

Gehring, Charles. (1980) "Peter Minuit's Purchase of Manhattan Island—New Evidence." *de Halve Maen* 54: 6ff.

———. (1984) "The Survival of the Dutch Language in New York and New Jersey." *de Halve Maen* 58: 7ff.

———, and Robert S. Grumet. (January 1987) "Observations of the Indians from Jaspar Danckaerts's Journal, 1679–1680." *WMQ* 44: 104–20.

———, William A. Starna, and William N. Fenton. (1987) "The Tawagonshi Treaty of 1613: The Final Chapter." *NYH* 68: 373–94.

———, ed. (1991). *Laws and Writs of Appeal, 1647–1663.* Syracuse, NY.

Geisst, Charles R. (1997) *Wall Street: A History.* New York.

Gelfand, Mark I. (1975) *A Nation of Cities: The Federal Government and Urban America, 1933–1965.* New York.

Genovese, Eugene D. (1965) *The Political Economy of Slavery: Studies in the Economy and Society of the Slave South.* New York.

———. (1971) *In Red and Black: Marxian Explorations in Southern and Afro-American History.* New York.

George, Carol V. R. (1973) *Segregated Sabbaths: Richard Allen and the Emergence of Independent Black Churches, 1760–1840.* New York.

George, Henry, Jr. (1900) *The Life of Henry George, by His Son.* New York.

Gerardi, Donald F.M. (1977–78) "The King's College Controversy, 1753–56, and the Ideological Roots of Toryism in New York." *Perspectives in American History* 11: 147–96.

Gerlach, Larry, ed. (1972) *The American Revolution: New York as a Case Study.* Belmont, CA.

Gernsheim, Alison. (1981) *Victorian and Edwardian Fashion: A Photographic Survey.* New York.

Giamo, Benedict. (1989) *On the Bowery: Confronting Homelessness in American Society.* Iowa City.

Gibbons, James S. (1859) *The Banks of New York: Their Dealers, the Clearing House, and the Panic of 1857.* New York.

Gibbs, Kenneth Turney. (1976) "Business Architectural Imagery: The Impact of Economic and Social Changes on Tall Office Buildings, 1870–1930." Ph.D. diss., Cornell University.

Gibbs, Kenneth T. (1984) *Business Architectural Imagery in America, 1870–1930.* Ann Arbor, MI.

Gibson, Arrell Morgan. (1980) *The American Indian: Prehistory to the Present.* Lexington, MA.

Gibson, Florence E. (1951) *The Attitudes of the New York Irish Toward State and National Affairs, 1848–1892.* New York.

Gienapp, William E. (1987) *The Origins of the Republican Party, 1852–1856.* New York.

Gilbert, Douglas. (1940) *American Vaudeville, Its Life and Times.* New York.

Gilchrist, David T., ed. (1967) *The Growth of Seaport Cities, 1790–1825.* Charlottesville, VA.

Gilder, Rodman. (1938) *The Battery.* Boston,

Gilfoyle, Timothy. (1986) "The Moral Origins of Political Surveillance: The Preventive Society in New York City, 1867–1918." *AQ* 38: 637–52.

Gilfoyle, Timothy J. (1992) *City of Eros: New York City, Prostitution, and the Commercialization of Sex, 1790–1920.* New York.

Gilje, Paul A. (1987) *The Road to Mobocracy: Popular Disorder in New York City, 1763–1834.* Chapel Hill, NC.

———. (1988) "Republican Rioting." In *Authority and Resistance in Early New York*, edited by William Pencak and Conrad Wright. New York.

———. (1989) "Culture of Conflict: The Impact of Commercialization on New York Workingmen, 1787–1829." In *New York and the Rise of Capitalism,*

edited by William Pencak and Conrad Wright. New York.

———, and William Pencak, eds. (1992) *New York in the Age of the Constitution, 1775–1800.* Rutherford, NJ.

———, and Howard B. Rock, eds. (1992) *Keepers of the Revolution: New Yorkers at Work in the Early Republic.* Ithaca, NY.

———, and Howard B. Rock. (1994) "'Sweep O! Sweep O!': African-American Chimney Sweeps and Citizenship in the New Nation." *WMQ* 61: 507–38.

———. (1996a) "The Development of an Irish Community in New York City before the Great Migration." In *New York Irish*, edited by Ronald Bayor and Timothy Meagher. Baltimore.

———. (1996b) "On the Waterfront: Maritime Workers in New York City in the Early Republic, 1800–1850." *NYH* 77: 395–426.

Gilmartin, Gregory F. (1994) *Shaping the City: New York and the Municipal Art Society.* New York.

Gilmore, Michael T. (1985) *American Romanticism and the Marketplace.* Chicago.

Ginsberg, Stephen F. (1968) "The History of Fire Protection in New York City, 1800–1842." Ph.D. diss., New York University.

———. (1971) "The Police and Fire Protection in New York City: 1800–1850." *NYH* 52: 133–51.

Ginzberg, Lori D. (1986) "Moral Suasion Is Moral Balderdash': Women, Politics, and Social Activism in the 1850s." *JAH* 73: 601–22.

———. (1990) *Women and the Work of Benevolence: Morality, Politics, and Class in the Nineteenth-century United States.* New Haven, CT.

———. (1994) "Fanny Wright." In *The American Radical*, edited by Mari Jo Buhle, Paul Buhle, and Harvey J. Kaye. New York.

Gische, David M. (1979) "The New York City Banks and the Development of the National Banking System." *American Journal of Legal History* 23: 21–67.

Glickman, Toby, and Gene Glickman. (1984) *The New York Red Pages: A Radical Tourist Guide*. New York.

Goebel, Julius Jr., and T. R. Naughton. (1944) *Law Enforcement in Colonial New York: A Study in Criminal Procedure, 1664–1776*. New York.

Goebel, Julius, Jr. (1969) "The Courts and the Law in Colonial New York." In *Essays in the History of Early American Law*, edited by David H. Flaherty. Chapel Hill, NC.

Goldberg, Isaac. (1930) *Tin Pan Alley: A Chronicle of the American Popular Music Racket*. New York.

Goldberger, Paul. (1981) *The Skyscraper*. New York.

Goldman, Joanne Abel. (1997) *Building New York's Sewers: Developing Mechanisms of Urban Management*. West Lafayette, IN.

Goldsmith, Barbara. (1998) *Other Powers: The Age of Suffrage, Spiritualism, and the Scandalous Victoria Woodhull*. New York.

Goldstein, Warren. (1992) *Playing for Keeps: A History of Early Baseball*. Ithaca, NY.

Goldstone, Harmon H., and Martha Dalrymple. (1974) *History Preserved: A Guide to New York City Landmarks and Historic Districts*. New York.

Gompers, Samuel. (1984) *Seventy Years of Life and Labor: An Autobiography*, edited by Nick Salvatore. Ithaca, NY.

Gong, Eng Ying, and Bruce Grant. (1930) *Tong War!* New York.

Goodfriend, Joyce D. (1978) "Burghers and Blacks: The Evolution of a Slave Society at New Amsterdam." *NYH* 59: 125–44.

———. (1989) "A New Look at Presbyterian Origins in New York City." *American Presbyterian* 67: 199–207.

———. (1989) "The Social Dimensions of Congregational Life in Colonial New York City." *WMQ* 46:

252–78.

———. (1992) *Before the Melting Pot: Society and Culture in Colonial New York City, 1664–1730*. Princeton, NJ.

———. (1996) "'Upon a Bunch of Straw': The Irish in Colonial New York City." In *The New York Irish: Essays Toward a History*, edited by Ronald H. Bayor and Timothy J. Meagher. Baltimore.

Goodman, Cary. (1979) *Choosing Sides: Playground and Street Life on the Lower East Side*. New York.

Goodwyn, Lawrence. (1976) *Democratic Promise: The Populist Moment in America*. New York.

Gordon, David M., Richard Edwards, and Michael Reich. (1982) *Segmented Work, Divided Workers: The Historical Transformation of Labor in the United States*. Cambridge, UK.

Gordon, John. (1988) *Scarlet Woman of Wall Street: Jay Gould, Jim Fisk, Cornelius Vanderbilt, the Erie Railway Wars, and the Birth of Wall Street*. New York.

Gordon, Linda. (1976) *Woman's Body, Woman's Right: A Social History of Birth Control in America*. New York.

———. (1988) *Heroes of Their Own Lives: The Politics and History of Family Violence*. New York.

Gordon, Michael A. (1977) "Studies in Irish and Irish-American Thought and Behavior in Gilded Age New York City." Ph.D. diss., University of Rochester.

———. (1993) *The Orange Riots: Irish Political Violence in New York City, 1870 and 1871*. Ithaca, NY.

Gorelick, Sherry. (1981) *City College and the Jewish Poor: Education in New York, 1880–1924*. New Brunswick, NJ.

Goren, Arthur. (1970) *New York Jews and the Quest for Community: The Kehillah Experiment, 1908–1922*. New York.

Gorn, Elliott J. (1986) *The Manly Art: Bare-Knuckle Prize Fighting in America*. Ithaca, NY.

Gorn, Elliott J. (1987) "'Good-bye Boys, I Die a

True American': Homicide, Nativism, and Working-class Culture in Antebellum New York City." *JAH* 74: 388–410.

Goslinga, Cornelius C. (1971) *The Dutch in the Caribbean and on the Wild Coast, 1580–1680*. Gainesville, FL.

Gottesman, Rita S. (1938) *The Arts and Crafts in New York, 1726–1776: Advertisements and News Items from New York City Newspapers*. New York.

———. (1959) "New York's First Major Art Show: As Reviewed By Its First Newspaper Critic in 1802 and 1803." *NYHSQ* 43: 289–305.

Gowans, Alan. (1976) *Images of American Living: Four Centuries of Architecture and Furniture as Cultural Expression*. New York.

Graham, Ian C.C. (1956) *Colonists from Scotland: Emigration to North America, 1707–1783*. Ithaca, NY.

Gravely, Will B. (1983) "African Methodisms and the Rise of Black Denominationalism." In *Rethinking Methodist History*, edited by Russell E. Richey and Kenneth E. Rowe. Nashville.

Graves, Mrs. A. J. (1843) *Woman in America: Being an Examination into the Moral and Intellectual Condition of American Female Society*. New York.

Graves, Edward C. (1894) *The Greater New York: Reasons Why*. Brooklyn.

Graymont, Barbara. (1972) *The Iroquois in the American Revolution*. Syracuse, NY.

Graydon, Alexander. ([1846] 1979) *Memoirs of His Own Time: With Reminiscences of the Men and Events of the Revolution*. Philadelphia.

Green, Andrew H. (1896) *New York of the Future: Addresses and Writings by Andrew H. Green*. New York.

Green, Harvey. (1986) *Fit for America: Health, Fitness, Sport and American Society*. New York.

Green, Martin. (1988) *New York 1913: The Armory Show and the Paterson Strike Pageant*. New York.

Green, Venus. (1990) "The Impact of Technology upon Women's Work in the Telephone Industry, 1880–1980." Ph.D. diss., Columbia University.

Greenberg, David F. (1988) *The Construction of Homosexuality*. Chicago.

Greenberg, Douglas. (1974) *Crime and Law Enforcement in the Colony of New York, 1691–1776*. Ithaca, NY.

———. (1975) "The Effectiveness of Law Enforcement in Eighteenth-Century New York." *American Journal of Legal History* 19:173–207.

Greene, Asa. (1834) *The Perils of Pearl Street, Including a Taste of the Dangers of Wall Street, by a Late Merchant*. New York.

———. (1837) *A Glance at New York*. New York.

Greene, Jack P. (1992) *Imperatives, Behaviors, and Identities: Essays in Early American Cultural History*. Charlottesville, VA.

———. (1996) "Coming to Terms with Diversity: Pluralism and Conflict in the Formation of Colonial New York." In *Interpreting Early America: Historiographical Essays*. Charlottesville, VA.

Greene, Victor R. (1987) *American Immigrant Leaders, 1800–1910: Marginality and Identity*. Baltimore.

Gribbin, William. (1972) "Republican Religion and the American Churches in the Early National Period." *The Historian* 35: 61–74.

Griffin, Clifford Stephen. (1960) *Their Brothers' Keepers: Moral Stewardship in the United States, 1800–1865*. New Brunswick, NJ.

Griffin, William D. (1990) *The Book of Irish Americans*. New York.

Griffith, Elisabeth. (1984) *In Her Own Right: The Life of Elizabeth Cady Stanton*. New York.

Grimsted, David. (1968) *Melodrama Unveiled: American Theater and Culture, 1800–1850*. Chicago.

Grimsted, David. (1972) "Rioting in Its Jacksonian Setting." *AHR* 77: 361–97.

Grinstein, Hyman B. (1945) *The Rise of the Jewish*

Community of New York, 1654–1860. Philadelphia.

Griswold, Rufus Wilmot. (1856) *The Republican Court, or American Society in the Days of Washington.* Boston.

Gronowicz, Anthony. (1987) "Whatever Happened to New York City Political Radicalism in the Revolutionary and Constitutional Eras?" Paper presented at New-York Historical Society conference.

———. (1991) "Labor's Decline with New York City's Democratic Party from 1844–1884." In *Immigration to New York,* edited by William Pencak, Selma Berrol, and Randall M. Miller. Philadelphia.

———. (1998) *Race and Class Politics in New York City Before the Civil War.* Boston.

Gruber, Ira. (1986) "America's First Battle: Long Island, August 27, 1776." In *America's First Battles, 1776–1965,* edited by Charles Heller and William Stofft. Lawrence, KS.

———. (1972) *The Howe Brothers and the American Revolution.* New York.

Grumet, Robert S. (1980) "Sunksquaws, Shamans, and Tradeswomen: Middle Atlantic Coastal Algonkian Women During the 17th and 18th Centuries." In *Women and Colonization: Anthropological Perspectives,* edited by Mona Etienne and Eleanor Leacock. New York.

———. (1981) *Native American Places Names in New York City.* New York.

———. (1995) *Historic Contact: Indian People and Colonists in Today's Northeastern United States in the 16th through 18th Centuries.* Norman, OK.

———. (1996) "Suscaneman and the Matinecock Lands, 1653–1703." In *Northeastern Indian Lives, 1632–1816.* Amherst, MA.

Grund, Francis Joseph. (1959) *Aristocracy in America: From the Sketch-book of a German Nobleman.* New York.

Guarneri, Carl J. (1991) *The Utopian Alternative: Fourierism in Nineteenth-*

century America. Ithaca, NY.

Guernsey, Rocellus S. (1889) *New York City and Vicinity During the War of 1812–15.* 2 vols. New York.

Gunn, L. Ray. (1988) *The Decline of Authority: Public Economic Policy and Political Development in New York State, 1800–1860.* Ithaca, NY.

Gunn, Thomas Butler. (1857) *The Physiology of New York Boarding Houses.* New York.

Gurko, Miriam. (1974) *The Ladies of Seneca Falls: The Birth of the Woman's Rights Movement.* New York.

Gurock, Jeffrey S. (1979) *When Harlem Was Jewish.* New York.

Gutman, Herbert G. (1965) "The Failure of the Movement by the Unemployed for Public Works in 1873." *PSQ* 80: 254–76.

———. (1965) "The Tompkins Square 'Riot' in New York City on January 13, 1874: A Re-Examination of Its Causes and Its Aftermath." *Labor History* 6: 44–70.

———. (1977) *Work, Culture and Society in Industrializing America.* New York.

Guttchen, Robert S. (1974) *Felix Adler.* New York.

Guy, Francis Shaw. (1935) "Edmund Bailey O'Callaghan: A Study in American Historiography." Ph.D. diss., Catholic University of America.

Habert, Jacques. (1949) *When New York Was Called Angoulême.* New York.

Haeger, John D. (1981) *The Investment Frontier: New York Businessmen and the Economic Development of the Old Northwest.* Albany, NY.

———. (1991) *John Jacob Astor: Business and Finance in the Early Republic.* Detroit.

Hagan, Horace H. (1923) *Eight Great American Lawyers.* Oklahoma City, OK.

Haines, Charles G. (1829) *Memoir of Thomas Addis Emmet.* New York.

Hales, Peter B. (1984) *Silver Cities: The Photography of American Urbanization,*

1839–1915. Philadelphia.

Hall, Courtney Robert. (1934) *A Scientist in the Early Republic: Samuel Latham Mitchill, 1764–1831.* New York.

Hall, Edward Hagaman. (1898) *A Volume Commemorating the Creation of the Second City in the World.* New York.

Hall, Lee. (1992) *Common Threads: A Parade of American Clothing.* Boston.

Halttunen, Karen Lee. (1982) *Confidence Men and Painted Women: A Study of Middle-Class Culture in America, 1830–1870.* New Haven, CT.

Hamlin, Paul M. (1939) *Legal Education in Colonial New York.* New York.

———, and Charles Baker, eds. (1959) *Supreme Court of Judicature of the Province of New York, 1691–1704.* Charlottesville, VA.

Hamm, Charles. (1979) *Yesterdays: Popular Song in America.* New York.

Hammack, David. (1982) *Power and Society: Greater New York at the Turn of the Century.* New York.

Hammond, Bray. (1946) "The Chestnut Street Raid on Wall Street, 1839." *Quarterly Journal of Economics* 61: 605–18.

———. (1957) *Banks and Politics in America from the Revolution to the Civil War.* Princeton, NJ.

———. (1970) *Sovereignty and an Empty Purse: Banks and Politics in the Civil War.* Princeton, NJ.

Handy, Robert T. (1987) *A History of Union Theological Seminary in New York.* New York.

Hanyan, Craig R. (1972) "De Witt Clinton and Partisanship: The Development of Clintonianism from 1811 to 1820." *NYHSQ* 56: 109–131.

———, with Mary L. Hanyan. (1996) *De Witt Clinton and the Rise of the People's Men.* Montreal.

Harbaugh, William Henry. (1963) *The Life and Times of Theodore Roosevelt.* New York.

Hardie, James. (1824) *The History of the Tread-Mill.* New York.

———. (1827) *Description of*

the City of New York (Population, Institutions, History, Commerce). New York.

Hardman, Keith. (1987) *Charles Grandison Finney, 1792–1875: Revivalist and Reformer.* Syracuse, NY.

Hardwick, Elizabeth. (1983) *Bartleby in Manhattan, and Other Essays.* New York.

Harlow, Alvin Fay. (1931) *Old Bowery Days: The Chronicles of a Famous Street.* New York.

———. (1936) *Old Wires and New Waves: The History of the Telegraph, Telephone, and Wireless.* New York.

Harrington, Michael. (1973) *Fragments of the Century.* New York.

Harrington, Virginia. (1933) "The Colonial Merchant's Ledger." In *History of the State of New York.* Vol. 2, *Under Duke and King,* edited by Alexander C. Flick. New York.

———. (1935) *The New York Merchant on the Eve of Revolution.* New York.

Harris, Bill. (1989) *The History of New York City.* New York.

Harris, Gale, et al. (1993) *African Burial Ground and the Commons Historic District Designation Report.* New York.

Harris, M. A. (1968) *A Negro History Tour of Manhattan.* New York.

Harris, Neil. (1966) *The Artist in American Society: The Formative Years, 1790–1860.* New York.

———, ed. (1970) *The Land of Contrasts: 1880–1901.* New York.

———. (1973) *Humbug: The Art of P. T. Barnum.* Boston.

———. (1981) "Cultural Institutions and American Modernization." *Journal of Library History* 16: 28–47.

———. (1990) *Cultural Excursions: Marketing Appetite and Cultural Tastes in Modern America.* Chicago.

Hart, Simon. (1959) *The Prehistory of the New Netherland Company: Amsterdam Notarial Records of the First Dutch Voyages....* Amsterdam.

Hartfield, Anne. (1993)

"Profile of a Pluralistic Parish: Saint Peter's Roman Catholic Church, New York City, 1785–1815." *Journal of American Ethnic History.* 12: 30–59.

Hartog, Hendrik. (1983) *Public Property and Private Power: The Corporation of the City of New York in American Law, 1730–1870.* Chapel Hill, NC.

Hartsfield, Larry K. (1985) *The American Response to Professional Crime, 1870–1914.* Westport, CT.

Harvard Encyclopedia of American Ethnic Groups. (1980) Cambridge, MA.

Harvey, David. (1978) "The Urban Process Under Capitalism: A Framework for Analysis." *International Journal of Urban and Regional Research* 21: 101–32.

———. (1985) *Consciousness and the Urban Experience: Studies in the History and Theory of Capitalist Urbanization.* Baltimore.

———. (1985) *The Urbanization of Capital: Studies in the History and Theory of Capitalist Urbanization.* Baltimore.

Harvey, John. (1995) *Men in Black.* Chicago.

Harvey, William Hope. (1963) *Coin's Financial School.* Edited by Richard Hofstadter. Cambridge, MA.

Haskell, Thomas L. (1977) *The Emergence of Professional Social Science.* Urbana, IL.

Hastings, Hugh, and Edward T. Corwin, comps. (1901–16) *Ecclesiastical Records: State of New York.* 7 vols. Albany.

Haswell, Charles H. (1896) *Reminiscences of an Octogenarian of the City of New York (1816–1860).* New York.

Hatch, Nathan O. (1989) *The Democratization of American Christianity.* New Haven, CT.

Hatcher, William B. (1940) *Edward Livingston: Jeffersonian Republican and Jacksonian Democrat.* University, LA.

Hauptman, Laurence M., and Ronald G. Knapp. (1977) "Dutch-Aboriginal Interaction in New

Netherland and Formosa: An Historical Geography of Empire." *Proceedings of the American Philosophical Society* 121: 166–82.

Hawes, Elizabeth. (1993) *New York, New York: How the Apartment House Transformed the Life of the City (1869–1930).* New York.

Hawke, David Freeman. (1974) *Paine.* New York.

Hawkins, Christopher. ([1864] 1979) *The Adventures of Christopher Hawkins, Containing Details of His Captivity . . . Escape from the Jersey Prison Ship.* New York.

Hayes, Michael. (1995) "General Nathaniel Woodhull and the Battle of Long Island." *The Long Island Historical Journal* 7: 166–77.

Hazlitt, W. Carew, ed. (1866) *The Merry Tales of the Mad Men of Gotham.* London.

Headley, Joel Tyler. (1970) *The Great Riots of New York, 1712–1883.* Indianapolis.

Heale, M.J. (1968) "Humanitarianism in the Early Republic: The Moral Reformers of New York, 1776–1825." *Journal of American Studies* 2: 161–75.

———. (1971) "The New York Society for the Prevention of Pauperism, 1817–1823." *NYHSQ* 55: 154–76.

———. (1973) "Patterns of Benevolence: Charity and Morality in Rural and Urban New York, 1783–1830." *Societas* 3: 337–59.

———. (1976) "From City Fathers to Social Critics: Humanitarianism and Government in New York, 1790–1860." *JAH* 63: 21–41.

Healy, David. (1988) *Drive to Hegemony: The United States in the Caribbean, 1898–1917.* Madison, WI.

Healy, Kathleen, ed. (1992) *Sisters of Mercy: Spirituality in America, 1843–1900.* New York.

Hecht, Robert A. (1978) *A History of College Point, N.Y.* New York.

Heckwelder, John. (1841) "Indian Tradition of the

First Arrival of the Dutch at Manhattan." *NYHS Collections.* 2nd ser., vol. 1: 71–74. New York.

Hedges, William L. (1965) *Washington Irving: An American Study, 1802–1812.* Baltimore.

Heinze, Andrew R. (1990) *Adapting to Abundance: Jewish Immigrants, Mass Consumption, and the Search for American Identity.* New York.

Heller, Charles, and William Stofft, eds. (1986) *America's First Battles, 1776–1965.* Lawrence, KS.

Hellman, Geoffrey. (1969) *Bankers, Bones and Beetles: The First Century of the American Museum of Natural History.* Garden City, NY.

Hellman, Rhoda. (1987) *Henry George Reconsidered.* New York.

Hemming, H. G. (1905) *Hemming's History of the Stock Exchange.* New York.

Henderson, H. James. (1974) *Party Politics in the Continental Congress.* New York.

Henderson, Mary C. (1982) *The City and the Theater: New York Playhouses from Bowling Green to Times Square.* Rev. ed. New York.

———. (1986) *Theater in America.* New York.

———. (1989) *Broadway Ballyhoo: The American Theater Seen in Posters, Photographs, Magazines, Caricatures, and Programs.* New York.

Henderson, Thomas M. (1976) *Tammany Hall and the New Immigrants: The Progressive Years.* New York.

Hendin, Josephine Gattuso. (1993) "Italian Neighbors." In *Greenwich Village: Culture and Counterculture,* edited by Ride Beard and Leslie Cohen Berlowitz. New Brunswick, NJ.

Hendrickson, Robert. (1979) *The Grand Emporiums: The Illustrated History of America's Great Department Stores.* New York.

Henkin, David. (1995) "City Reading: The Written Word and the Urban Public in New York City, 1825–1866." Ph.D. diss., University of California, Berkeley, CA.

Henretta, James A., and Gregory H. Nobles. (1986) *Evolution and Revolution: New American Society, 1600–1820.* Lexington, MA.

Henry, Sarah M. (1991) "The Strikers and Their Sympathizers: Brooklyn in the Trolley Strike of 1895." *Labor History* 32: 329–53.

Herold, Amos L. (1926) *James Kirke Paulding: Versatile American.* New York.

Herreshoff, David. (1967) *American Disciples of Marx: From the Age of Jackson to the Progressive Era.* Detroit.

Hersh, Blanche Glassman. (1978) *Slavery of Sex: Feminist-Abolitionists in America.* Urbana, IL.

Hershkowitz, Leo. (1960) "New York City, 1834–1840: A Study in Local Politics." Ph.D. diss., New York University.

———. (1962) "The Native American Democratic Association in New York City, 1835–36." *NYHSQ* 46: 41–60.

———. (1965) "The Troublesome Turk: An Illustration of Judicial Process in New Amsterdam." *NYH* 46: 299–310.

———, and Isidore S. Meyer, eds. (1968) *Letters of the Franks Family (1733–1748).* Waltham, MA.

———. (1976) "Some Aspects of the New York Jewish Merchant Community, 1654–1820." *American Jewish Quarterly* 66: 10–34.

———. (1977) *Tweed's New York: Another Look.* Garden City, NY.

———, and Milton Klein, eds. (1978) *Courts and Law in Early New York.* Port Washington, NY.

———. (1990) "Federal New York: Mayors of the Nation's First Capital." In *World of the Founders: New York Communities in the Federal Period,* edited by Stephen L. Schechter and Wendell Tripp. Albany, NY.

———. (1991) "Some Aspects of the New York Jewish Merchant in Colonial Trade." In *Migration* and Settlement: Proceedings of the Anglo-American Jewish Historical Conference, edited by Aubrey Newman. London.

Hertzberg, Arthur. (1989) *The Jews in America: Four Centuries of an Uneasy Encounter: A History.* New York.

Hickey, Donald R. (1982) "America's Response to the Slave Revolt in Haiti, 1791–1806." *Journal of the Early Republic* 2: 361–80.

Hidy, Ralph W. (1949) *The House of Baring in American Trade and Finance: English Merchant Bankers at Work, 1763–1861.* Cambridge, MA.

Higginbotham, Don. (1971) *The War of American Independence: Military Attitudes, Policies, and Practice, 1763–1789.* New York.

Higginbotham, A. Leon, Jr. (1978) *In the Matter of Color: Race and the American Legal Process, the Colonial Period.* New York.

Higham, John. (1988) *Strangers in the Land: Patterns of American Nativism, 1860–1925.* 2nd ed. New Brunswick, NJ.

Hill, Marilynn Wood. (1992) *Their Sisters' Keepers: Prostitution in New York City, 1830–1870.* Berkeley, CA.

Hills, Patricia. (1974) *The Painters' America: Rural and Urban Life, 1810–1910.* New York.

Hindle, Brooke. (1981) *Emulation and Invention.* New York.

Hirsch, Adam J. (1992) *The Rise of the Penitentiary: Prisons and Punishment in Early America.* New Haven, CT.

Hirsch, Leo H., Jr. (1931) "The Negro and New York, 1783–1865." *Journal of Negro History* 16: 382–473.

Hirsch, Mark David. (1948) *William C. Whitney: Modern Warwick.* Hamden, CT.

———. (1978) "Richard Croker." In *Essays in the History of New York City*, edited by Irwin Yellowitz. Port Washington, NY.

Historical Brooklyn: A Series of Illustrated Booklets Covering Brooklyn's Six Original Villages. (1946) Brooklyn.

Hobhouse, Henry. (1986) *Seeds of Change: Five Plants That Transformed Mankind.* New York.

Hobsbawm, Eric. (1962) *The Age of Revolution, 1789–1848.* New York.

———. (1968) *Industry and Empire: The Making of Modern English Society, 1750 to the Present Day.* New York.

———. (1975) *The Age of Capital, 1848–1875.* New York.

———. (1987) *The Age of Empire, 1875–1914.* New York.

———. (1994) *The Age of Extremes: The History of the World, 1914–1991.* New York.

Hobson, Wayne K. (1984) "Symbol of the New Profession: Emergence of the Large Law Firm, 1870–1915." In *The New High Priests: Lawyers in Post-Civil War America*, edited by Gerard W. Gawalt. New York.

Hodas, Daniel. (1976) *The Business Career of Moses Taylor: Merchant, Finance Capitalist and Industrialist.* New York.

Hodges, Graham Russell. (1986) *New York City Cartmen, 1667–1850.* New York.

———. (1986) "The Rights and Privileges of Citizens: Racial and Ethnic Struggle for Deregulation of Occupations in Early . . ." Paper presented at Organization of American Historians Conference.

———. (1987) "Black Revolt in New York City and the Neutral Zone, 1775–1783." Paper presented at New-York Historical Society Conference.

———. (1988) "Afro-Americans at Work in New York and New Jersey, 1640–1783." Paper presented at New-York Historical Society Conference.

———. (1988) "Legal Bonds of Attachment: The Freemanship Law of New York City, 1648–1801." In *Authority and Resistance in Early New York*, edited by William Pencak and Conrad Wright. New York.

———. (1996) "'Desirable Companions and Lovers':

Irish and African Americans in the Sixth Ward, 1830–1870." In *The New York Irish: Essays Toward a History*, edited by Ronald H. Bayor, and Timothy J. Meagher. Baltimore.

Hodgson, Godfrey. (1990) *The Colonel: The Life and Wars of Henry Stimson, 1867–1950.* New York.

Hoe, Robert. (1902) *A Short History of the Printing Press.* New York.

Hoffmann, Charles. (1970) *The Depression of the Nineties: An Economic History.* Westport, CT.

Hoffman, Edwin D. (1949) "The Bookshops of New York City, 1743–1948." *NYH* 30: 53–65

Hoffman, Jerome. (1976) *The Bay Ridge Chronicles.* Brooklyn.

Hofstadter, Richard. (1943) "William Leggett, Spokesman of Jacksonian Democracy." *PSQ* 58: 581–94.

———. (1948) *The American Political Tradition and the Men Who Made It.* New York.

———. (1955) *The Age of Reform: From Bryan to F.D.R.* New York.

———. (1965) *The Paranoid Style in American Politics and Other Essays.* New York.

———. (1967) "Cuba, the Philippines, and Manifest Destiny." In *Essays in American Diplomacy*, edited by Armin Rappoport. New York.

———, and Michael Wallace, eds. (1970) *American Violence: A Documentary History.* New York.

Hoffman, Ronald, and Peter J. Albert, eds. (1981) *Sovereign States in An Age of Uncertainty.* Washington, DC.

———. (1989) *Women in the Age of the American Revolution.* Charlottesville, VA.

Holloway, Edward Stratton. (1928) *American Furniture and Decoration: Colonial and Federal.* Philadelphia.

Holloway, Emory, ed. (1921) *The Uncollected Poetry and Prose of Walt Whitman.* Garden City, NY.

Homberger, Eric. (1994) *The Historical Atlas of New York City.*

———. (1994) *Scenes from the Life of a City: Corruption and Conscience in Old New York.* New Haven, CT.

Hone, Philip. (1927) *The Diary of Philip Hone, 1828–1851.* Edited by Allan Nevins. 2 vols. New York.

Honour, Hugh. (1975) *The New Golden Land: European Images of America from the Discoveries to the Present Time.* New York.

Hood, Clifton. (1993) *722 Miles: The Building of the Subways and How They Transformed New York.* New York.

Hoopes, Donelson F. (1979) *Childe Hassam.* New York.

Hopkins, Vivian. (1975) "The Empire State—De Witt Clinton's Laboratory." *NYHSQ* 59: 7–44.

Horlick, Allan S. (1975) *Country Boys and Merchant Princes: The Social Control of Young Men in New York.* Lewisburg, PA.

Hornung, Clarence P., comp. (1970) *The Way It Was: New York, 1850–1890.* New York.

Horowitz, Joseph. (1987) *Understanding Toscanini: How He Became an American Culture-God and Helped Create a New Audience for Old Music.* New York.

Horsman, Reginald. (1969) *The War of 1812.* New York.

———. (1985) *The Diplomacy of the New Republic, 1776–1815.* Arlington Heights, IL.

Horsmanden, Daniel. ([1810] 1971) *The New York Conspiracy*, edited by Thomas J. Davis. Boston.

Horton, John T. (1939) *James Kent: A Study in Conservatism, 1763–1847.* New York.

Horwitz, Morton J. (1977) *The Transformation of American Law, 1780–1860.* Cambridge, MA.

———. (1993) *The Transformation of American Law, 1870–1960: The Crisis of Legal Orthodoxy.* New York.

Hosmer, Charles B., Jr. (1965) *Presence of the Past: A History of the Preservation Movement in the United States Before Williamsburg. New York.

Howard, David Sanctuary. (1984) *New York and the China Trade.* New York.

Howat, John K. (1972) *The Hudson River and Its Painters.* New York.

Howe, Adrian. (1990) "The Bayard Treason Trial: Dramatizing Anglo-Dutch Politics in Early Eighteenth-Century New York City." *WMQ* 47: 57–89.

Howe, Daniel Walker. (1971) "The Evangelical Movement and Political Culture in the North During the Second Party System." *JAH* 77: 1216–39.

———. (1979) *The Political Culture of the American Whigs.* Chicago.

Howe, Irving. (1976) *World of Our Fathers.* New York.

———. (1986) *The American Newness: Culture and Politics in the Age of Emerson.* Cambridge, MA.

Howe, Octavius T., and Frederick C. Matthew. ([1926/27] 1986) *American Clipper Ships.* New York.

Howells, W. D. (1976) *A Hazard of New Fortunes.* Bloomington, IN.

Hower, Ralph. M. (1943) *History of Macy's of New York, 1858–1919: Chapters in the Evolution of the Department Store.* Cambridge, MA.

Hoyt, Edwin P. (1962) *The Vanderbilts and Their Fortunes.* Garden City, NY.

Hsiong, George L. (1939) *Chinatown and Her Mother Country.* New York.

Huey, Paul R. (1988) "The Archaeology of Colonial New Netherland." In *Colonial Dutch Studies,* edited by Eric Nooter and Patricia Bonomi. New York.

Hufeland, Otto. (1926) *Westchester County During the American Revolution, 1775–1783.* N.P.

Huggins, Nathan. (1973) *Harlem Renaissance.* New York.

Hugins, Walter. (1960) *Jacksonian Democracy and the Working Class: A Study of the New York Workingmen's Movement, 1829–1837.* Stanford, CA.

Hull, N.E.H., Peter C. Hoffer, and Steven L. Allen. (1978) "Choosing Sides: A Quantitative Study of the Personality Determinants of Loyalist and Revolutionary Political Affiliation in New York." *JAH* 65: 344–66.

Humphrey, David C. (1976) *From King's College to Columbia, 1746–1800.* New York.

Hunt, Alfred N. (1988) *Haiti's Influence on Antebellum America: Slumbering Volcano in the Caribbean.* Baton Rouge, LA.

Hunt, George T. (1940) *The Wars of the Iroquois: A Study in Intertribal Trade Relations.* Madison, WI.

Hunter, Gregory S. (1989) "The Manhattan Company: Managing a Multi-Unit Corporation in New York, 1799–1842." In *New York and the Rise of American Capitalism,* edited by William Pencak and Conrad Wright. New York.

Hurst, James Willard. (1978) "Alexander Hamilton, Law Maker." *Columbia Law Review* 78: 483–547.

Hurwitz, Howard Lawrence. (1943) *Theodore Roosevelt and Labor in New York State, 1880–1900.* New York.

Huston, James Lynn. (1987) *The Panic of 1857 and the Coming of the Civil War.* Baton Rouge, LA.

Hutchins, John G. B. (1941) *The American Maritime Industries and Public Policy, 1789–1914.* Cambridge, MA.

Hutchinson, Earl Ofari. (1972) *Let Your Motto Be Resistance: The Life and Thought of Henry Highland Garnet.* Boston.

Hutton, Frankie. (1993) *The Early Black Press in America, 1827 to 1860.* Westport, CT.

Huxtable, Ada Louise. (1964) *Classic New York: Georgian Gentility to Greek Elegance.* New York.

Ignatiev, Noel. (1995) *How the Irish Became White.* New York.

Innis, J. H. (1902) *New Amsterdam and Its People.* New York.

Irving, Washington. ([1809] 1965) *Knickerbocker's History of New York.* New York.

———. (1984) *History,* Tales and Sketches.* Library of America.* ed. New York.

Irwin, Ray W. (1968) *Daniel D. Tomkins: Governor of New York and Vice President of the United States.* Charlottesville, VA.

Israel, Jonathan I. (1977) "A Conflict of Empires: Spain and the Netherlands, 1618–1648." *Past and Present* 76: 34–74.

———. (1989) *Dutch Primacy in World Trade, 1585–1740.* New York.

———. (1995) *The Dutch Republic: Its Rise, Greatness, and Fall, 1477–1806.* New York.

Jackman, Eugene T. (1964) "Efforts Made Before 1825 to Ameliorate the Lot of the American Seaman: With Emphasis on His Moral Regeneration." *American Neptune* 24: 109–18.

Jackson, Anthony. (1976) *A Place Called Home: A History of Low Cost Housing in Manhattan.* Cambridge, MA.

Jackson, Kenneth T. (1984) "The City Loses the Sword: The Decline of the Major Military Activity in the New York Metropolitan Area." In *The Martial Metropolis: U.S. Cities in War and Peace, 1900–1970,* edited by Roger W. Lotchin. New York.

———. (1985) *Crabgrass Frontier: The Suburbanization of the United States.* New York.

———, and Camilo J. Vergara. (1989) *Silent Cities: Evolution of the American Cemetery.* Princeton, NJ.

———, ed. (1995) *The Encyclopedia of New York City.* New Haven, CT.

Jacobs, Wilbur R. (1972) *Dispossessing the American Indian: Indians and Whites on the Colonial Frontier.* New York.

———. (1974) "The Tip of an Iceberg: Pre-Columbian Indian Demography and Some Implications for Revisionism." *WMQ* 31: 123–32.

Jacobson, David L. (1965) *The English Libertarian Heritage.* Indianapolis.

Jaffe, Herman J. (1979) "The Canarsee Indians: The Original Inhabitants." In Brooklyn U.S.A,* edited by Rita S. Miller. New York.

Jagendorf, M. A. (1950) *The Merry Men of Gotham.* New York.

Jaher, Frederic Cople. (1964) *Doubters and Dissenters: Cataclysmic Thought in America, 1885–1918.* London.

———. (1982) *The Urban Establishment: Upper Strata in Boston, New York, Charleston, Chicago, and Los Angeles.* Urbana, IL.

James, C. L. R. (1962) *The Black Jacobins: Toussaint L'Ouverture and the San Domingo Revolution.* New York.

James, Edward T., et al., eds. (1971) *Notable American Women, 1607–1950.* Cambridge, MA.

James, Marquis. (1993) *Merchant Adventurer: The Story of W. R. Grace.* Wilmington, DE.

Jameson, J. Franklin, ed. (1909) *Narratives of New Netherland, 1609–1664.* New York.

Janvier, Thomas A. (1894) *In Old New York.* New York.

Jasen, David A. (1993) *Tin Pan Alley: The Composers, the Songs, the Performers and Their Times.* New York.

Jayne, Thomas Gordon. (1990) "The New York Crystal Palace: An International Exhibition of Goods and Ideas." Master's thesis, University of Delaware.

Jeffers, H. Paul. (1994) *Commissioner Roosevelt: The Story of Theodore Roosevelt and the New York City Police, 1895–1897.* New York.

Jefferson, Thomas. (1970) *The Anas of Thomas Jefferson.* New York.

Jeffrey, William, Jr. (1971) "The Letters of Brutus—A Neglected Element in the Ratification Campaign of 1787–88." *University of Cincinnati Law Review* 40: 644–46.

Jenkins, Ian. (1992) "'Athens Rising Near the Pole': London, Athens and the Idea of Freedom." In *London—World City, 1800–1840,* edited by Celina Fox. New Haven, CT.

Jenkins, Stephen. (1912) *The

Story of the Bronx. New York.

Jenks, Leland. (1927) *The Migration of British Capital to 1875*. New York.

Jennings, Francis. (1975) *The Invasion of America: Indians, Colonialism, and the Cant of Conquest*. New York.

———. (1979) "Anthropological Foundations for American Indian History." *Reviews in American History*, 486–93.

———. (1984) *The Ambiguous Iroquois Empire*. New York.

———. (1988) *Empire of Fortune: Crowns, Colonies, and Tribes in the Seven Years War in America*. New York.

Jensen, Merrill. (1968) *The Founding of A Nation: A History of the American Revolution, 1763–1776*. New York.

Jentz, John B. (1977) "Artisans, Evangelicals, and the City: A Social History of Abolition and Labor Reform in Jacksonian New York." Ph.D. diss., City University of New York.

———. (1981) "The Anti-Slavery Constituency in Jacksonian New York City." *Civil War History* 27: 101–22.

John, Richard R. (1990) "Taking Sabbatarianism Seriously: The Postal System, the Sabbath, and the Transformation of American Political Culture." *Journal of the Early Republic* 10: 517–67.

Johnson, Claudia. (1975) "That Guilty Third Tier: Prostitution in Nineteenth Century Theaters." *AQ* 27: 575–84.

———. (1985) "William Dunlap." In *American Writers of the Early Republic*, edited by Emory Elliott. Detroit.

Johnson, David R. (1979) *Policing the Urban Underworld: The Impact of Crime on the Development of the American Police, 1800–87*. Philadelphia.

Johnson, Herbert A. (1963) *The Law Merchant and Negotiable Instruments in Colonial New York. 1664–1730*. Chicago.

———. (1965) "The Advent of Common Law in Colonial New York." In *Law and Authority in Colonial America*, edited by George Billias. New York.

———, and David Syrett. (1968) "Some Nice Sharp Quillets of the Customs Law: The *New York* Affair, 1763–1767." *WMQ* 25: 432–51.

Johnson, James Weldon. (1930) *Black Manhattan*. New York.

———. (1933) *Along This Way: The Autobiography of James Weldon Johnson*. New York.

Johnson, Jeremiah. (1976) "Recollections of Incidents of the Revolution of the Colonies Occurring in Brooklyn." Edited by Thomas W. Field Part 1. *Journal of Long Island History* 12: 5–21.

———. (1976) "Recollections of General Johnson." Edited by Thomas W. Field Part 2. *Journal of Long Island History* 13: 21–41.

Johnson, Paul E., and Sean Wilentz. (1994) *The Kingdom of Matthias: A Story of Sex and Salvation in Nineteenth-Century America*. New York.

Johnson, Richard Christian. (1973) "Anthony Comstock: Reform, Vice and the American Way." Ph.D. diss., University of Wisconsin, Madison.

Johnston, Henry P. ([1878] 1971) *The Campaign of 1776 Around New York and Brooklyn*. New York.

———. (1897) *The Battle of Harlem Heights, September 16, 1776*. New York.

Jonas, Manfred, and Robert V. Wells, eds. (1982) *New Opportunities in a New Nation: The Development of New York After the Revolution*. Schenectady, NY.

Jones, Charles W. (1978) *Saint Nicholas of Myra, Bari, and Manhattan: Biography of a Legend*. Chicago.

Jones, Gareth Stedman. (1971) *Outcast London: A Study in the Relationship Between Classes in Victorian Society*. Oxford.

Jones, Howard Mumford. (1927) *America and French Culture: 1750–1848*. Chapel Hill, NC.

Jones, Robert F. (1975)

"William Duer and the Business of Government in the Era of the American Revolution." *WMQ* 33: 393–415.

———. (1987) "Economic Opportunism and the Constitution in New York State: The Example of William Duer." *NYH* 68: 357–72.

———. (1992) *"The King of the Alley": William Duer, Politician, Entrepreneur, and Speculator, 1768–1799*. Philadelphia.

Jones, Stanley L. (1964) *The Presidential Election of 1896*. Madison, WI.

Jonnes, Jill. (1986) *We're Still Here: The Rise, Fall, and Resurrection of the South Bronx*. Boston.

Jordan, Jean P. (1977) "Women Merchants in Colonial New York." *NYH* 58: 412–39.

Jordan, Winthrop D. (1968) *White Over Black: American Attitudes Toward the Negro, 1550–1812*. Chapel Hill, NC.

Joselit, Jenna W. (1983) *Our Gang: Jewish Crime and the New York Jewish Community, 1900–1940*. Bloomington, IN.

Josephson, Matthew, and Hanna Josephson. (1969) *Al Smith, Hero of the Cities: A Political Portrait Drawing on the Papers of Frances Perkins*. Boston.

Josephy, Alvin M. (1958) *The Patriot Chiefs: A Chronicle of American Indian Resistance*. New York.

Joyce, Arthur A. (1988) "Early/Middle Holocene Environments in the Middle Atlantic Region: A Revised Reconstruction." In *Holocene Human Ecology in Northeastern North America*, edited by George Nicholas. New York.

Judd, Jacob. (1959) "The History of Brooklyn, 1834–1855: Political and Administrative Aspects." Ph.D. diss., New York University.

———. (1971) "Frederick Philipse and the Madagascar Trade." *NYHSQ* 55: 354–74.

———, and Irwin Polishook, eds. (1974). *Aspects of Early New York Society and Politics* Tarrytown, NY.

———. (1975) "Frederick Philipse III of Westchester County: A Reluctant Loyalist." In *Loyalist Americans: A Focus on Greater New York*, edited by Robert East and Jacob Judd. Tarrytown, NY.

———. (1983) "The Unknown Philip Van Cortlandt: Loyalist." *NYH* 64: 395–408.

Juergens, George. (1966) *Joseph Pulitzer and the New York World*. Princeton, NJ.

July, Robert William. (1951) *The Essential New Yorker, Gulian Crommelin Verplanck*. Durham, NC.

Kaestle, Carl F. (1973) *The Evolution of an Urban School System: New York City, 1750–1850*. Cambridge, MA.

———. (1983) *Pillars of the Republic: Common Schools and American Society, 1780–1860*. New York.

Kahn, E. J., Jr. (1955) *The Merry Partners: The Age and Stage of Harrigan and Hart*. New York.

Kahrl, Stanley J., ed. (1965) *Merie Tales of the Mad Men of Gotham*. Evanston, IL.

Kaminski, John P. (1988) "Adjusting to Circumstances: New York's Relationship with the Federal Government, 1776–1788." In *The Constitution and the States: The Role of the Original Thirteen in the Framing and Adoption of the Federal Constitution*, edited by Patrick Conley and John P. Kaminski. Madison, WI.

———. (1993) *George Clinton: Yeoman Politician of the New Republic*. Madison, WI.

Kammen, Michael. (1970) *Empire and Interest: The American Colonies and the Politics of Mercantilism*. Philadelphia.

———. (1975) *Colonial New York: A History*. New York.

———. (1976) "The American Revolution as a *Crise de Conscience*: The Case of New York." In *Society, Freedom, and Conscience: The Coming of the Revolution in Virginia, Massachusetts, and New York,* edited by Richard M. Jellison. New York.

———. (1979) "The Rediscovery of New York's History, Phase One." *NYH* 60: 375–406.

———. (1982) "'The Promised Sunshine of the Future': Reflections on Economic Growth and Social Change in Post-Revolutionary New York." In *New Opportunities in a New Nation: the Development of New York after the Revolution,* edited by Manfred Jonas and Robert V. Wells. Schenectady, NY.

Kandell, Johnathan. (1988) *La Capital: The Biography of Mexico City.* New York.

Kane, Bob. (1989) *Batman & Me.* New York.

Kann, Mark E. (1991) *On the Man Question: Gender and Civic Virtue in America.* Philadelphia.

Kaplan, Barry Jerome. (1975) "A Study in the Politics of Metropolitanization: The Greater New York City Charter of 1897." Ph.D. diss., State University of New York at Buffalo.

———. (1978) "Reformers and Charity: The Abolition of Public Outdoor Relief in New York City, 1870–1898." *Social Service Review* 52: 202–14.

——— (1979) "Andrew H. Green and the Creation of a Planning Rationale: The Formation of Greater New York City, 1865–1890." *Urbanism Past and Present* 8: 32–39.

Kaplan, Justin. (1980) *Walt Whitman: A Life.* New York.

Kaplan, Lawrence S. (1987) *Entangling Alliances with None: American Foreign Policy in the Age of Jefferson.* Kent, OH.

Kaplan, Michael. (1996) "The World of the B'Hoys: Urban Violence and the Political Culture of Antebellum New York City, 1825–1860." Ph.D. diss., New York University.

Kaplan, Sidney. (1989) *The Black Presence in the Era of the American Revolution.* Amherst, MA.

Karcher, Carolyn L. (1994) *The First Woman in the Republic: A Cultural Biography of Lydia Maria Child.* Durham, NC.

Kasson, John F. (1978) *Amusing the Million: Coney Island at the Turn of the Century.* New York.

———. (1990) *Rudeness and Civility: Manners in Nineteenth-century Urban America.* New York.

Katz, Irving. (1968) *August Belmont; A Political Biography.* New York.

Katz, Jonathan. (1976) *Gay American History.* New York.

———. (1983) *Gay/Lesbian Almanac: A New Documentary.* New York.

Katz, Michael. (1983) *Poverty and Policy in American History.* New York.

———. (1986) *In the Shadow of the Poorhouse: A Social History of Welfare in America.* New York.

Katz, Stanley Nider, ed. (1963) *A Brief Narrative of the Case and Trial of John Peter Zenger . . . by James Alexander.* Cambridge, MA.

———. (1968) *Newcastle's New York: Anglo-American Politics, 1732–1753.* Cambridge, MA.

———. (1970) "Between Scylla and Charybdis: James DeLancey and Anglo-American Politics in Early Eighteenth-Century New York." In *Anglo-American Political Relations, 1675–1775,* edited by Alison Olson and Richard Brown. New Brunswick, NJ.

———, ed. (1971) "A New York Mission to England: The London Letters of Lewis Morris to James Alexander, 1735–1736." *WMQ* 28: 439–84.

Katzman, David. (1978) *Seven Days a Week: Women and Domestic Service in Industrializing America.* New York.

Kaufman, Martin. (1972) "Henry Bergh, Kit Burns, and the Sportsmen of New York." *New York Folklore Quarterly* 28: 15–20.

Kaufman, Rhoda Helfman. (1990) *The Yiddish Theater in New York and the Immigrant Jewish Community: Theater as a Secular Ritual.* Ann Arbor, MI.

Kavenagh, W. Keith, ed. (1973) *Foundations of Colonial America: A Documentary History.* Vol. 2: *The Middle Atlantic Colonies.* New York.

Kazin, Alfred. (1942) *On Native Grounds: An Interpretation of Modern American Prose Literature.* New York.

———, and David Finn. (1989) *Our New York.* New York.

Keane, John. (1995) *Tom Paine: A Political Life.* Boston.

Keep, Austin B. (1909) *The Library in Colonial New York.* New York.

Keller, Morton. (1963) *The Life Insurance Enterprise, 1865–1910: A Study in the Limits of Corporate Power.* Cambridge, MA.

Kelley, Wyn. (1996) *Melville's City: Literary and Urban Form in Nineteenth-century New York.* New York.

Kelsay, Isabel T. (1984) *Joseph Brant, 1743–1807: Man of Two Worlds.* Syracuse, NY.

Kemble, Stephen. (1885) *The Stephen Kemble Papers. NYHS Collections.* Vols. 16–17. New York.

Kemp, William Webb. ([1913] 1969) *The Support of Schools in Colonial New York by the Society for the Propagation of the Gospel in Foreign Parts.* New York.

Kennedy, John H. (1930) *Thomas Dongan, Governor of New York.* New York.

Kennedy, John Michael. (1968) "Philanthropy and Science in New York City: The American Museum of Natural History, 1868–1968." Ph.D. diss., Yale University.

Kennedy, Roger G. (1985) *Architecture, Men, Women, and Money in America: 1600–1860.* New York.

———. (1989a) *Greek Revival America.* New York.

———. (1989b) *Orders From France: The Americans and the French in a Revolutionary World, 1780–1820.* New York.

Kenney, Alice P. (1975) *Stubborn for Liberty: The Dutch in New York.* Syracuse, NY.

Kent, James. (1836) *The Charter of the City of New York, with Notes Thereon.* New York.

Kent, William. (1898) *Memoirs and Letters of James Kent.* Boston.

Kenyon, Cecelia, ed. (1966) *The Antifederalists.* Indianapolis.

Kerber, Linda K. (1967) "Abolitionists and Amalgamators: The New York City Race Riots of 1834." *NYH* 48: 28–39.

———. (1980) *Women of the Republic: Intellect and Ideology in Revolutionary America.* Chapel Hill, NC.

———. (1989) "'History Can Do It No Justice': Women and the Reinterpretation of the American Revolution," In *Women in the Age of the American Revolution,* edited by Ronald Hoffman and Peter J. Albert. Charlottesville, VA.

———. (1992) "The Paradox of Women's Citizenship in the Early Republic: The Case of Martin v. Massachusetts, 1805." *AHR* 97: 349–78.

Kessler, Henry H., and Eugene Rachlis. (1959) *Peter Stuyvesant and His New York.* New York.

Kessner, Thomas. (1977) *The Golden Door: Italian and Jewish Mobility in New York City, 1880–1915.* New York.

Keys, Alice Mapelsden. (1967) *Cadwallader Colden: A Representative Eighteenth Century Official.* New York.

Keyser, Harriette A. (1910) *Bishop Potter, the People's Friend.* New York.

Kidwell, Claudia B., and Margaret C. Christman. (1974) *Suiting Everyone: The Democratization of Clothing in America.* Washington, DC.

Kieran, John. (1959) *A Natural History of New York City.* Boston.

Kiernan, Victor Gordon. (1978) *America, the New Imperialism: From White Settlement to World Hegemony.* London.

Kierner, Cynthia A. (1988) "Becoming Gentlefolk: Anglicization, Consumption, and Elite Culture in Pre-Revolutionary New York." Paper presented at Siena College conference.

———. (1989) "Landlord and Tenant in Revolutionary New York: The Case of Livingston Manor." *NYH* 70: 133–52.

———. (1992) *Traders and Gentlefolk: The Livingstons of New York, 1675–1790.* Ithaca, NY.

Kilpatrick, William H. (1912) *The Dutch Schools of New Netherland and Colonial New York.* Washington, DC.

Kim, Sung Bok. (1970) "A New Look at the Great Landlords of Eighteenth Century New York." *WMQ* 27: 581–614.

———. (1978) *Landlord and Tenant in Colonial New York: Manorial Society, 1664–1775.* Chapel Hill, NC.

———. (1982) "The Impact of Class Relations and Warfare in the American Revolution: The New York Experience." *JAH* 69: 326–46.

———. (1993) "The Limits of Politicization in the American Revolution: The Experience of Westchester County, New York." *JAH* 80: 868–89.

Kirsch, George B. (1989) *The Creation of American Team Sports: Baseball and Cricket, 1838–72.* Urbana, IL.

Kistemaker, Renee. (1983) *Amsterdam: The Golden Years, 1275–1795.* New York.

Klebaner, Benjamin J. (May 1960) "Poor Relief and Public Works During the Depression of 1857." *The Historian* 22: 264–79.

Klein, Carole. (1987) *Gramercy Park: An American Bloomsbury.* Boston.

Klein, Maury. (1986) *The Life and Legend of Jay Gould.* Baltimore.

Klein, Milton. (1960) "Prelude to Revolution in New York: Jury Trials and Judicial Tenure." *WMQ* 17: 439–62.

———, ed. (1963) *The Independent Reflector, or Weekly Essays on Sundry Important Subjects . . . by William Livingston and Others.* Cambridge, MA.

———, ed. (1964) *The Politics of Diversity: Essays in the History of Colonial New York.* Port Washington, NY.

———. (1966) "Politics and Personalities in Colonial New York." *NYH* 47: 3–16.

———. (1967) "The Cultural Tyros of Colonial New York." *South Atlantic Quarterly* 66: 218–32.

———. (1971a) "Archibald Kennedy: Imperial Pamphleteer." In *The Colonial Legacy,* Vol. 2: *Some Eighteenth-Century Commentators,* edited by Lawrence Leder. New York.

———. (1971b) "William Livingston's *A Review of the Military Operations in North America.*" In *The Colonial Legacy,* Vol. 2: *Some Eighteenth-Century Commentators,* edited by Lawrence Leder. New York.

———, ed. (1976). *New York: The Centennial Years.* Port Washington, NY.

———. (1978) "Shaping the American Tradition: The Microcosm of Colonial New York," *NYH* 59: 173–97.

———. (1980) "An Experiment that Failed: General James Robertson and Civil Government in British New York, 1779–1783." *NYH* 61: 229–54.

———. (1983) "Why Did the British Fail to Win the Hearts and Minds of New Yorkers?" *NYH* 64: 357–76.

———, and Ronald W. Howard, eds. (1983) *The Twilight of British Rule in Revolutionary America: The New York Letter Book of General James Robertson, 1780–83.* Cooperstown, NY.

———. (1990) *The American Whig: William Livingston of New York.* New York.

Klein, Rachel N. (1995) "Art and Authority in Antebellum New York City: The Rise and Fall of the American Art-Union." *JAH* 81: 1534–1561.

Kline, Mary-Jo, ed. (1973) *Alexander Hamilton: A Biography in His Own Words.* New York.

———, ed. (1983) *Political Correspondence and Public Papers of Aaron Burr.* 2 vols. Princeton, NJ.

Klingberg, Frank J. (1940) *Anglican Humanitarianism in Colonial New York.* Philadelphia.

Klingle, Philip (1979) "King's County During the American Revolution." In *Brooklyn U.S.A,* edited by Rita S. Miller. New York.

Klips, Stephen. (1980) "Institutionalizing the Poor: The New York City Almshouse, 1825–1860." Ph.D. diss., City University of New York.

Kluger, Richard. (1986) *The Paper: The Life and Times of the New York Herald Tribune.* New York.

———. (1996) *Ashes to Ashes: America's Hundred-Year Cigarette War, the Public Health, and the Unabashed Triumph of Philip Morris.* New York.

Knerr, George F. (1957) "The Mayoral Administration of William L. Strong." Ph.D. diss., New York University.

Knickerbocker, Diedrich [Washington Irving]. (1868) *A History of New York.* New York.

Knittle, Walter A. ([1937] 1970) *Early Eighteenth Century Palatine Emigration.* Baltimore.

Knobel, Dale T. (1986) *Paddy and the Republic: Ethnicity and Nationality in Antebellum America.* Middletown, CT.

Knollenberg, Bernhard. (1960) *Origin of the American Revolution: 1759–1766.* New York.

Knudson, Jerry W. (1969) "The Rage Around Tom Paine: Newspaper Reaction to His Homecoming in 1802." *NYHSQ* 53: 34–63.

Kobler, John. (1988) *Otto the Magnificent: The Life of Otto Kahn.* New York.

Kobrin, David. (1971) *The Black Minority in Early New York.* Albany, NY.

Koch, G. Adolf. (1933) *Religion of the American Enlightenment.* New York.

Koke, Richard J. (1975) "The Struggle for the Hudson: The British Naval Expedition under Captain Hyde Parker and Captain James Wallace, July 12–August 18, 1776." In *Narratives of the Revolution in New York.* New York.

Kolchin, Peter. (1967) "The Business Press and Reconstruction." *Journal of Southern History* 33: 183–96.

Kolodin, Irving. (1966) *The Metropolitan Opera, 1883–1966.* New York.

Koolhaas, Rem. (1978) *Delirious New York: A Retroactive Manifesto for Manhattan.* New York.

Kosak, Hadassah. (1987) "The Rise of the Jewish Working Class, New York, 1881–1905." Ph.D. diss., City University of New York.

Kouwenhoven, John Atlee. (1953) *The Columbia Historical Portrait of New York.* Garden City, NY.

Kraft, Herbert C. (1986) *The Lenape: Archaeology, History, and Ethnography.* Newark, NJ.

Kramnick, Isaac. (1968) *Bolingbroke and His Circle: The Politics of Nostalgia in the Age of Walpole.* Cambridge, MA.

Krassner, Nancy. (1985) "The Dutch-English Language Controversy." *de Halve Maen* 59: 1ff.

Kraus, Harry P. (1980) *The Settlement House Movement in New York City, 1886–1914.* New York.

Kraus, Michael. (1949) *The Atlantic Civilization: Eighteenth-Century Origins.* Ithaca, NY.

Krause, Sideny J., ed. (1977) *The Novels and Related Works of Charles Brockden Brown.* Kent, OH.

Kraut, Alan M. (1996) "Illness and Medical Care Among Irish Immigrants in Antebellum New York." In *The New York Irish,* edited by Ronald H. Bayar and Timothy J. Meagher. Baltimore.

Kray, Elizabeth. (1982) *Four Literary-Historical Walks.* New York.

Krech, Shepard, ed. (1981) *Indians, Animals, and the Fur Trade: A Critique of Keepers of the Game.* Athens, GA.

Kreider, Harry J. (1942) *Lutheranism in Colonial New York.* New York.

———. (1949) *The Beginnings of Lutheranism in New York.* New York.

Kring, Walter Donald. (1974) *Liberals Among the*

Orthodox: Unitarian Beginnings in New York City, 1819–1939. Boston.

Kroessler, Jeffrey A. (1991) "Building Queens: The Urbanization of New York's Largest Borough." Ph.D. diss., City University of New York.

Krogius, Henrik. (1978) "The Collection on [*sic*] Garbage." *Seaport* 12: 4–11.

Kross, Jessica. (1983) *The Evolution of An American Town: Newtown, New York, 1642–1775*. Philadelphia.

Krout, John A. (1948) "Framing the Charter." In *The Greater City: New York, 1898–1948*, edited by Allen Nevins and John A. Krout. New York.

Kruger, Vivienne L. (1985) "Born to Run: The Slave Family in Early New York, 1626–1827. " Ph.D. diss., Columbia University.

Kupp, Jan. (1974) "Aspects of New York-Dutch Trade Under the English, 1670–1674." *NYHSQ* 58: 139–47.

Kupperman, Karen O. (1980) *Settling with the Indians: The Meeting of English and Indian Cultures in America, 1580–1640*. Totowa, NJ.

Kurland, Gerald. (1971) *Seth Low: The Reformer in an Urban and Industrial Age*. New York.

Kuroda, Tadahisha. (1988) "New York and the First Presidential Election: Politics and the Constitution." *NYH* 69: 318–51.

Labaree, Benjamin Woods. (1975) *The Boston Tea Party*. New York.

LaFeber, Walter. (1963) *The New Empire: An Interpretation of American Expansion, 1860–1898*. Ithaca, NY.

Laing, Alexander. (1966) *Clipper Ships and their Makers*. New York.

Lampard, Eric E. (1986) "The New York Metropolis in Transformation: History and Prospect. A Study in Historical Particularity." In *The Future of the Metropolis: Berlin, London, Paris, New York*, edited by Hans-Jurgen Ewers, John B. Goddard, and

Horst Matzerath. Berlin.

Lancaster, Clay. (1961) *New York's First Suburb: Old Brooklyn Heights*. Rutland, VT.

Landau, Sarah Bradford. (1982) "Greek and Gothic Side by Side: Architecture around the Square." In *Around the Square, 1830–1890: Essays on Life, Letters, and Architecture in Greenwich Village*, edited by Mindy Cantor. New York.

———, and Carl W. Condit. (1996) *Rise of the New York Skyscraper, 1865–1913*. New Haven, CT.

Landesman, Alter F. (1977) *A History of New Lots, Brooklyn to 1887*. Port Washington, NY.

Landy, Jacob. (1970) *The Architecture of Minard Lafever*. New York.

Lane, James B. (1974) *Jacob A. Riis and the American City*. Port Washington, NY.

Lane, Wheaton Joshua. (1942) *Commodore Vanderbilt: An Epic of the Steam Age*. New York.

Lang, Ossian. (1922) *History of Freemasonry in the State of New York*. New York.

Langenderfer, Harold Q. (1980) *The Federal Income Tax, 1861–1872*. 2 vols. New York.

Lannie, Vincent P. (1968) *Public Money and Parochial Education: Bishop Hughes, Govenor Seward, and the New York School Controversy*. Cleveland.

Lapham, James Sigurd. (1977) "The German-Americans of New York City 1860–1890." Ph.D. diss., St. John's University.

Larkin, F. Daniel. (1990) *John B. Jervis: An American Engineering Pioneer*. Ames, IA.

Larkin, Jack. (1988) *Reshaping of Everyday Life, 1790–1840*. New York.

Lasch, Christopher. (1973a) "The Moral and Intellectual Rehabilitation of the Ruling Class." In *The World of Nations*. New York.

———. (1973b) *The World of Nations: Reflections on American History, Politics, and Culture*. New York.

Launitz-Schurer, Leopold.

(1981) *Loyal Whigs and Revolutionaries: The Making of the Revolution in New York, 1765–1776*. New York.

———. (1984) "Feudal Revival or Republican Government: An Interpretation of the Loyalist Ideology of William Smith of New York." *Australian Journal of Politics and History* 30.

Lawrence, Richard Hoe. ([1906] 1911) *Valentine's Manuals: A General Index*. New York.

———, comp. (1930) *History of the Society of Iconophiles of the City of New York*. New York.

Le Duc, Thomas H. (1939) "Grahamites and Garrisonites." *NYH* 20: 189–91.

Leach, William. (1980) *True Love and Perfect Union: The Feminist Reform of Sex and Society*. New York.

Leacock, Eleanor, and Nancy Lurie, eds. (1971). *North American Indians in Historical Perspective*. New York.

Leamon, James. (1963) "Governor Fletcher's Recall." *WMQ* 15: 527–42.

Lears, T. J. Jackson. (1981) *No Place of Grace: Antimodernism and the Transformation of American Culture, 1880–1920*. New York.

———. (1995) *Fables of Abundance: A Cultural History of Advertising in America*. New York.

Leary, Lewis. (1948) "St. George Tucker Attends the Theater." *WMQ* 5: 369–97.

———. (1975) "John Blair Linn." "Samuel Low: New York's First Poet." "The Education of William Dunlap." "Washington Irving: An End and A New Beginning." In *Soundings: Some Early American Writers*. Athens, GA.

Leavitt, Judith W., and Ronald L. Numbers, eds. (1978) *Sickness and Health in America*. Madison, WI.

Lebhar, Godfrey M. (1952) *Chain Stores in America: 1859–1950*. New York.

Leder, Lawrence H. (1952) "Records of the Trials of Jacob Leisler and His Associates." *NYHSQ* 26: 431–57.

———. (1954) "Captain Kidd and the Leisler Rebellion." *NYHSQ* 38: 48–53

———. (1954) "The Unorthodox Dominie: Nicholas Van Rensselaer." *NYH* 35: 166–76.

———. (1955) "'Like Madmen through the Streets': The New York City Riot of June, 1690." *NYHSQ* 39: 405–15.

———. (1960) "The Politics of Upheaval in New York, 1689–1709." *NYHSQ* 44: 413–27.

———. (1961) *Robert Livingston (1654–1728) and the Politics of Colonial New York*. Chapel Hill, NC.

———. (1962–63) "The New York Assembly Elections of 1769: An Assault on Privilege." *Mississippi Valley Historical Review*. 49: 675–82.

———. (1971) "Dongan's New York and Fletcher's London: Personality and Politics." *NYHSQ* 55: 28–37.

Lee, Basil Leo. (1943) *Discontent in New York City, 1861–1865*. Washington, DC.

Lees, Andrew. (1985) *Cities Perceived: Urban Society in Europe and American Thought, 1820–1940*. New York.

Leeuwen, Thomas A. P. van. (1988) *The Skyward Trend of Thought: The Metaphysics of the American Skyscraper*. Cambridge, MA.

Leggett, Abraham. ([1865] 1979) *The Narrative of Major Abraham Leggett*. New York.

Lehmann-Haupt, Hellmut, ed. (1951) *The Book in America*. New York.

Leinenweber, Charles. (1969) "Immigration and the Decline of Internationalism in the American Working Class Movement, 1864–1919." Ph.D. diss., University of California, Berkeley, CA.

Lemisch, Jesse. (1968) "Jack Tar in the Streets: Merchant Seamen and the Politics of Revolutionary America." *WMQ* 25: 371–407.

———. (1969) "Listening to the 'Inarticulate': William Widger's Dream and the

Loyalties of American Revolutionary Seamen in British Prisons." *Journal of Social History* 3: 1–28.

———. (1997) *Jack Tar vs. John Bull: The Role of New York's Seamen in Precipitating the Revolution.* Hamden, CT.

Leng, Charles W., and William T. Davis, (1930–1933) *Staten Island and Its People.* 5 vols. New York.

Leonard, Chilson. (1932) "Arnold in America: A Study of Matthew Arnold's Literary Relations with American and of His Visits to This Country in 1883 and 1886." Ph.D. diss., Yale University.

Leopold, Richard William. (1954) *Elihu Root and the Conservative Tradition.* Boston.

Lerner, Gerda, ed. (1977) *The Female Experience: An American Documentary.* Indianapolis.

Leslie, Anita. (1954) *The Remarkable Mr. Jerome.* New York.

Leuchs, Frederick A. H. (1928) *The Early German Theatre in New York, 1840–1872.* New York.

Levine, Bruce. (1992) *The Spirit of 48: German Immigrants, Labor Conflict, and the Coming of the Civil War.* Urbana, IL.

Levine, Lawrence W. (1988) *Highbrow/Lowbrow: The Emergence of Cultural Hierarchy in America.* Cambridge, MA.

Levinson, Leonard Louis. (1961) *Wall Street: A Pictorial History.* New York.

Levy, Leonard. (1960) "Did the Zenger Case Really Matter? Freedom of the Press in Colonial New York." *WMQ* 17: 35–50.

Lewis, Alfred Allan. (1978) *Man of the World: Herbert Bayard Swope: A Charmed Life of Pulitzer Prizes, Poker, and Politics.* Indianapolis.

Lewis, Jan. (1987) "The Republican Wife: Virtue and Seduction in the Early Republic." *WMQ* 44: 689–721.

Lewis, Steven L. (1988) "Gay Masquerade: Male Homosexuals in American Cities, 1910 to 1940."

Ph.D. diss., Western Michigan University.

Lewis, W. David. (1963) "Newgate of New-York: A Case History (1796–1828) of Early American Prison Reform." *NYHSQ* 47: 137–71.

———. (1965) *From Newgate to Dannemora: The Rise of the Penitentiary in New York, 1796–1848.* Ithaca, NY.

Leyburn, James G. (1962) *The Scotch-Irish: A Social History.* Chapel Hill, NC.

Lieberman, Richard K. (1995) *Steinway and Sons.* New Haven, CT.

Light, Ivan. (1974) "From Vice District to Tourist Attraction: The Moral Career of American Chinatowns, 1880–1940." *Pacific Historical Review* 43: 367–94.

Lightfoot, Frederick S. ed. (1981) *Nineteenth-century New York in Rare Photographic Views.* New York.

Limpus, Lowell M. (1940) *History of the New York Fire Department.* New York.

Lincoln, Charles Z., ed. (1894) *The Colonial Laws of New York from the Year 1664 to the Revolution.* 5 vols. Albany, NY.

Linderman, Gerald F. (1974) *The Mirror of War: American Society and the Spanish-American War.* Ann Arbor, MI.

Lindsley, James Elliott. (1984) *This Planted Vine: A Narrative History of the Episcopal Diocese of New York.* New York.

Lindstrom, Diane. (1988) "Economic Structure, Demographic Change, and Income Inequality in Antebellum New York." In *Power, Culture, and Place: Essays on New York City,* edited by John Hull Mollenkopf. Princeton, NJ.

Link, Eugene P. (1942) *Democratic-Republican Societies, 1790–1800.* New York.

Lipinsky, Lino S. (1958) *Giovanni da Verrazzano: The Discoverer of New York Bay.* New York.

Lisagor, Nancy, and Frank Lipsius. (1989) *A Law unto Itself: The Untold Story of the Law Firm Sullivan and Cromwell.* New York.

Liss, Peggy K. (1983) *Atlantic Empires: The Network of Trade and Revolution, 1713–1826.* Baltimore.

Litwack, Leon F. (1961) *North of Slavery: The Negro in the Free States, 1790–1860.* Chicago.

Livingston, E. A. (1994) *President Lincoln's Third Largest City: Brooklyn and the Civil War.* Glendale, NY.

Livingston, James. (1986) *Origins of the Federal Reserve System: Money, Class, and Corporate Capitalism, 1890–1913.* Ithaca, NY.

———. (1987) "The Social Analysis of Economic History and Theory: Conjectures of Late Nineteenth-Century American Development." *AHR* 92: 69–95.

———. (1994) *Pragmatism and the Political Economy of Cultural Revolution, 1850–1940.* Chapel Hill, NC.

Lockwood, Charles. (1972a) "The Bond Street Area." *NYHSQ* 56: 309–320.

———. (1972b) *Bricks and Brownstone: The New York Rowhouse, 1783–1929: An Architectural and Social History.* New York.

———. (1976) *Manhattan Moves Uptown: An Illustrated History.* Boston.

Lodwick, Charles. (1849) "Letter from New York, 1692." *NYHS Collections,* 2nd ser., vol. 2: 243–50.

Lomask, Milton. (1979–1982) *Aaron Burr.* 2 vols. New York.

Longacre, Edward G. (1984) "The Union Army Occupation of New York City, November 1864." *NYH* 65: 133–58.

Lonn, Ella. (1951) *Foreigners in the Union Army and Navy.* Baton Rouge, LA.

Looney, Jefferson. (1982) "Social Mobility and Capital Accumulation on Proprietary Long Island." *de Halve Maen* 56: 4ff.

———. (1983) "Social Mobility and Capital Accumulation on Proprietary Long Island, Part II." *de Halve Maen* 57: 12ff.

Loop, Anne S. (1964) *History and Development of Sewage*

Treatment in New York City. New York.

Lorenz, Alfred Lawrence. (1972) *Hugh Gaine: A Colonial Printer-Editor's Odyssey to Loyalism.* Carbondale, IL.

Lorillard and Company. (1960) *Lorillard and Tobacco: 200th Anniversary.* New York.

Lorini, Alessandra. (1991) "Public Rituals, Race Ideology, and the Transformation of Culture: The Making of the New York African-American Community. Ph.D. diss., Columbia University.

Lott, Eric. (1993) *Love and Theft: Blackface Minstrelsy and the American Working Class.* New York.

Lovejoy, David S. (1972) *The Glorious Revolution in America.* New York.

Lowe, David G., ed. (1968) *New York, N.Y.: An American Heritage Extra.* New York.

———. (1992) *Stanford White's New York.* New York.

Lowensteyn, P. (1984) "The Role of the Dutch in the Iroquois Wars." *de Halve Maen* 58: 1ff.

Lowenthal, David. (1976) "The Place of the Past in the American Landscape." In *Geographies of the Mind: Essays in Historical Geography,* edited by David Lowenthal and Martyn J. Bowden. New York.

Lowitt, Richard. (1954) *A Merchant Prince of the Nineteenth Century: William E. Dodge.* New York.

Lubove, Roy. (1962) "The Progressives and the Prostitute." *Historian* 24: 308–30.

———. (1962) *The Progressives and the Slums: Tenement House Reform in New York City, 1890–1917.* Pittsburgh.

———. (1965) *The Professional Altruist: The Emergence of Social Work as a Career, 1880–1930.* Cambridge, MA.

———. (1968) *The Struggle for Social Security, 1900–1935.* Cambridge, MA.

Lui, Adonica Yen-Mui. (1993) "Party Machines,

State Structure, and Social Politics: The Abolition of Public Outdoor Relief in New York City, 1874–1898." Ph.D. diss., Harvard University.

Luke, Myron. (1953) *The Port of New York, 1800–1810: Foreign Trade and the Business Community*. Hempstead, NY.

———, and Robert W. Venables. (1976) *Long Island in the American Revolution*. Albany, NY.

Lurkis, Alexander. (1982) *The Power Brink: Con Edison, a Centennial of Electricity*. New York.

Lurie, Nancy O. (1959) "Indian Cultural Adjustment to European Civilization." In *Seventeenth-Century America: Essays in Colonial History*, edited by James Smith. Chapel Hill, NC.

———. (1971) "The World's Oldest On-Going Protest Demonstration: North American Indian Drinking Patterns." *Pacific Historical Review*. 40: 311–32.

———, and Eleanor Leacock. (1971) *North American Indians in Historical Perspective*. New York.

Lustig, Mary Lou. (1983) *Robert Hunter, 1666–1734: New York's Augustan Statesman*. Syracuse, NY.

———. (1995) *Privilege and Prerogative: New York's Provincial Elite, 1710–1776*. Madison, NJ.

Lydon, James G. (1961) "Barbary Pirates and Colonial New Yorkers." *NYHSQ* 45: 281–89.

———. (1968) "The Great Capture of 1744." *NYHSQ* 52: 255–69.

———. (1970) *Pirates, Privateers, and Profits*. Upper Saddle River, NJ.

———. (1978) "New York and the Slave Trade, 1700–1774." *WMQ* 35: 375–94.

Lynch, Michael. (1985) "'Here Is Adhesiveness': From Friendship to Homosexuality." *Victorian Studies* 29: 67–96.

Lynd, Staughton. (1963) "Abraham Yates's History of the Movement for the United States Constitution." *WMQ* 20: 223–45.

———. (Fall 1964) "The

Mechanics in New York Politics, 1774–1788." *Labor History* 5: 225–46.

———. (1967) *Class Conflict, Slavery, and the United States Constitution: Ten Essays*. Indianapolis.

MacCracken, Henry Mitchell. (1905) *Andrew Haswell Green: A Memorial Address*. New York.

MacDougall, William L. (1977) *American Revolutionary: A Biography of General Alexander McDougall*. Westport, CT.

Machor, James L. (1987) *Pastoral Cities: Urban Ideals and the Symbolic Landscape of America*. Madison, WI.

Mack, Edward Clarence. (1949) *Peter Cooper, Citizen of New York*. New York.

MacKenzie, Frederick. ([1930] 1979) *Diary of Frederick MacKenzie*. Cambridge, MA.

Maclay, William. ([1927] 1965) *The Journal of William Maclay: United States Senator from Pennsylvania, 1789–1791*. New York.

Macleod, David I. (1983) *Building Character in the American Boy: The Boy Scouts, YMCA, and Their Forerunners, 1870–1920*. Madison, WI.

Macleod, William C. (1928) *The American Indian Frontier*. New York.

Magdoff, Harry. (1969) *The Age of Imperialism: The Economics of U.S. Foreign Policy*. New York.

Magnuson, Norris. (1977) *Salvation in the Slums: Evangelical Social Work, 1865–1929*. Metuchen, NJ.

Maier, Pauline. (1972) *From Resistance to Revolution: Colonial Radicals and the Development of American Opposition to Britain, 1765–1776*. New York.

———. (1980) *The Old Revolutionaries: Political Lives in the Age of Samuel Adams*. New York.

Maika, Dennis J. (1994) "Jacob Leisler's Chesapeake Trade. *de Halve Maen* 67: 9–14.

———. (1995) "Commerce and Community: Manhattan Merchants in the Seventeenth Century." Ph.D.

diss., New York University.

Main, Jackson Turner. (1965) *The Social Structure of Revolutionary America*. Princeton, NJ.

———. (1973) *Political Parties Before the Constitution*. Chapel Hill, NC.

Maldonado-Denis, Manuel. (1972) *Puerto Rico: A Socio-Historic Interpretation*. Translated by Elena Vialo. New York.

Malon, Patrica Evelyn. (1981) "The Growth of Manufacturing in Manhattan, 1860–1900: An Analysis of Factoral Changes and Urban Structure." Ph.D. diss., Columbia University.

Man, Albon P., Jr. (1951) "Labor Competition and the New York Draft Riots of 1863." *Journal of Negro History* 36: 375–405.

Manchester, H. H. (1924) "A History of the Warehouse: VII, Early America, Part I: New York and Brooklyn, 1800–1850." *Distribution and Warehousing* 22: 38–40.

Manders, Eric I. (1978) *The Battle of Long Island*. Monmouth Beach, NJ.

Mandlebaum, Seymour. (1965) *Boss Tweed's New York*. New York.

Mann, Bruce H. (1994) "Tales from the Crypt: Prison, Legal Authority, and the Debtor's Constitution in the Early Republic." *WMQ* 51: 183–202.

Manzo, Bettina, ed. (1986) "A Virginian in New York: The Diary of St. George Tucker, July–August, 1786." *NYH* 67: 177–98.

Marcus, Jacob R. (1970) *The Colonial American Jew*. 3 vols. Detroit.

Mark, Irving. (1965) *Agrarian Conflicts in the Colony of New York, 1711–1775*. 2nd ed. New York.

Markel, Howard. (1997) *Quarantine!: East European Jewish Immigrants and the New York City Epidemics of 1892*. Baltimore.

Markham, Jerry W. (1987) *The History of Commodity Futures Trading and Its Regulation*. New York.

Marks, Edward B. (1934) *They All Sang: From Tony Pastor to Rudy Vallee*. New York.

Marling, Karel Ann. (1988) *George Washington Slept*

Here: Colonial Revivals and American Culture, 1876–1986. Cambridge, MA.

Marraro, Howard R. (1949) "Italians in New York in the 1850s, Part I." *NYH* 30: 181–203.

———. (1949) "Italians in New York in the 1850s, Part II." *NYH* 30: 276–303.

Marshall, Herbert, and Mildred Stack. (1958) *Ira Aldridge, the Negro Tragedian*. New York.

Marston, Jerrilyn Greene. (1987) *King and Congress: The Transfer of Political Legitimacy, 1774–1776*. Princeton, NJ.

Martí, José. (1975) *Inside the Monster: Writings on the United States and American Imperialism*. New York.

Martin, Calvin. (1978) *Keepers of the Game: Indian-Animal Relationships and the Fur Trade*. Berkeley, CA.

———. (1985) "The Covenant Chain of Friendship, Inc.: America's First Great Real Estate Agency." *Reviews in American History*. 14–20.

Martin, George. (1970) *Causes and Conflicts: The Centennial History of the Association of the Bar of the City of New York, 1870–1970*. Boston.

Martin, James Kirby, ed. (1976) *The Human Dimensions of Nation Making: Essays on Colonial and Revolutionary America*. Madison, WI.

Marx, Karl. (1972) *On America and the Civil War*.

———, and Frederick Engels. (1937) *The Civil War in the United States*. Edited by Richard Enmale. New York.

Marx, Paul A. (1983) "This Is the City: An Examination of Changing Attitudes Toward New York as Reflected in its Guidebook Literature." Ph.D. diss., Harvard University.

Mason, Bernard. (1949) "Aspects of the New York Revolt of 1689." *NYH* 30: 165–80.

———. (1966) "Adjustment to a War Economy: Entrepreneurial Activity in New York During the Revolution." *Business History Review* 40: 190–212.

———. (1966) *The Road to Independence: The Revolutionary Movement in New York, 1773–1777.* Lexington, MA.

Masselman, George. (1963) *The Cradle of Colonialism.* New Haven, CT.

Masur, Louis P. (1989) *Rites of Execution: Capital Punishment and the Transformation of American Culture, 1776–1865.* New York.

Mather, Frederick G. (1913). *The Refugees of 1776 from Long Island to Connecticut.* Albany, NY.

Matsell, George W. (1859) *Vocabulum: or, The Rogue's Lexicon.* New York.

Matson, Cathy. (1987) "Commerce After the Conquest: Dutch Traders and Goods in New York City, 1664–1764." Part 1. *de Halve Maen* 59: 8ff.

———. (1987) "Commerce After the Conquest: Dutch Traders and Goods in New York City, 1664–1764." Part 2. *de Halve Maen* 60: 17ff.

———. (1987) "Liberty and Union: Two Views of the New York City Economy in the 1780s." Paper presented at New York Historical Society Conference.

———. (1989) "Public Vices, Private Benefit: William Duer and His Circle." In *New York and the Rise of American Capitalism*, edited by William Pencak and Conrad Wright. New York.

Matthews, Jean V. (1991) *Toward a New Society: American Thought and Culture, 1800–1830.* Boston, MA.

Matthiessen, F. O. (1941) *American Renaissance: Art and Expression in the Age of Emerson and Whitman.* London.

Maury, Ann. (1853) *Memoirs of a Huguenot Family: Translated and Compiled from the Original Autobiography of the Rev. James Fontaine.* New York.

Maxson, Charles Hartshorn. (1920) *The Great Awakening in the Middle Colonies.* Chicago.

May, Henry F. (1949) *Protestant Churches and Industri-*

al America. New York.

———. (1959) *The End of American Innocence: A Study of the First Years of Our Own Time, 1912–1917.* New York.

———. (1976) *The Enlightenment in America.* New York.

Mayer, Grace. (1958) *Once upon a City: New York from 1890 to 1910.* New York.

Mayer, Martin. (1983) *The Met: One Hundred Years of Grand Opera.* New York.

Maynard, Joan, and Gwen Cottman. (1983) *Weeksville Then and Now: The Search to Discover, the Effort to Preserve, Memories of Self in Brooklyn, New York.* New York.

Mayo, Louise. (1988) *The Ambivalent Image: Nineteenth-Century America's Perception of the Jew.* Rutherford, NJ.

Mazaraki, George Alexander. (1966) "The Public Career of Andrew Haswell Green." Ph.D. diss., New York University.

McAdam, David, et al., eds. (1897–1899) *History of the Bench and Bar of New York.* 2 vols. New York.

McAnear, Beverly. (1967) *The Income of the Colonial Governors of British North America.* New York.

McArthur, Benjamin. (1984) *Actors and American Culture, 1880–1920.* Philadelphia.

McBride, Kevin A. (1994) "The Source and Mother of the Fur Trade: Native-Dutch Relations in Eastern New Netherland." In *Enduring Traditions: The Native Peoples of New England*, edited by Laurie Weinstein. Westport, CT.

McCabe, James. (1868) *Lights and Shadows of New York Life.* Philadelphia.

McCadden, Joseph, and Helen McCadden. (1969) *Father Varela: Torch Bearer from Cuba.* New York.

McCaffrey, Lawrence J. (1996) "Forging Forward and Looking Back." In *The New York Irish*, edited by Ronald H. Bayor and Timothy J. Meagher. Baltimore.

McCaughey, Elizabeth P. (1980) *From Loyalist to*

Founding Father: The Political Odyssey of William Samuel Johnson. New York.

McCauley, Bernadette. (1992) "'Who Shall Take Care of Our Sick?' Roman Catholic Sisterhoods and Their Hospitals, New York City, 1850–1930." Ph.D. diss., Columbia University.

McClelland, Nancy. (1919) *Duncan Phyfe and the English Regency, 1795–1830.* New York.

McClung, Robert M., and Gale S. McClung. (1958) "Tammany's Remarkable Gardiner Baker: New York's First Museum Proprietor, Menagerie Keeper, and Promotor . . ." *NYHSQ* 42: 143–69.

McConachie, Bruce A., and Daniel Friedman, eds. (1985) *Theatre for Working-class Audiences in the United States, 1830–1980.* Westport, CT.

McConachie, Bruce A. (1992) *Melodramatic Formations: American Theater and Society, 1820–1870.* Iowa City.

McCormick, Charles H. (1978) "Governor Sloughter's Delay and Leisler's Rebellion, 1689–1691." *NYHSQ* 62: 238–52.

———. (1989) *Leisler's Rebellion.* New York.

McCormick, Richard L. (1981) *From Realignment to Reform: Political Change in New York State, 1893–1910.* Ithaca, NY.

McCullough, David. (1972) *The Great Bridge.* New York.

———. (1981) *Mornings on Horseback.* New York.

McCullough, David W. (1983) *Brooklyn—and How It Got That Way.* New York.

McCully, Bruce T. (1982) "Governor Francis Nicholson, Patron *Par Excellence* of Religion and Learning in Colonial America." *WMQ* 39: 310–33.

McCusker, John J. (1978) *Money and Exchange in Europe and America, 1600–1775: A Handbook.* Chapel Hill, NC.

———, and Russell Menard, eds. (1985) *The Economy of British Ameri-*

ca, 1607–1789. Chapel Hill, NC.

McDonald, Forrest. (1958) *We the People: The Economic Origins of the Constitution.* Chicago.

———. (1965) *The Formation of the American Republic, 1776–1790.* Baltimore.

McEllhenny, John G. (1992) *United Methodism in America: A Compact History.* Nashville.

McFaul, John M. (1972) *The Politics of Jacksonian Finance.* Ithaca, NY.

McGerr, Michael G. (1986) *The Decline of Popular Politics: The American North, 1865–1928.* New York.

McGrane, Reginald Charles. (1924) *The Panic of 1837: Some Financial Problems of the Jacksonian Era.* Chicago.

McGregor, Robert Kuhn. (1988) "Cultural Adaptation in Colonial New York: The Palatine Germans of the Mohawk Valley." *NYH* 69: 5–34.

McKay, Ernest. (1990) *The Civil War and New York City.* Syracuse, NY.

McKay, John P., Bennett D. Hill, and John Buckler. (1979) *A History of Western Society.* Boston.

McKay, Richard C. (1934) *South Street: A Maritime History of New York.* New York.

McKee, Samuel. (1933) "The Economic Pattern of Colonial New York." In *History of the State of New York*, ed. by Alexander C. Flick. 2: 247–82.

———. (1935) *Labor in Colonial New York, 1664–1776.* New York.

McKendrick, Neil, John Brewer, and J.H. Plumb. (1982) *The Birth of a Consumer Society: The Commercialization of Eighteenth-Century England.* Bloomington, IN.

McKinley, Albert E. (1900) "The Transition from Dutch to English Rule in New York." *AHR* 6: 693–724.

McKinley, Edward. (1980) *Marching to Glory: The History of the Salvation Army in the United States of America.* San Francisco.

———. (1986) *Somebody's Brother: A History of the Salvation Army Men's*

Social Service Department, 1891–1985. Lewiston, NY.

McKivigan, John R., and Thomas J. Robertson. (1996) "The Irish American Worker in Transition, 1877–1914: New York City as a Test Case." In *The New York Irish,* edited by Ronald H. Bayor and Timothy J. Meagher. Baltimore.

McLachlan, James. (1970) *American Boarding Schools: A Historical Study.* New York.

McLaughlin, William John. (1981) "Dutch Rural New York: Community, Economy, and Family in Colonial Flatbush." Ph.D. diss., Columbia University.

McLoughlin, William G. (1970) *The Meaning of Henry Ward Beecher: An Essay on the Shifting Values of Mid-Victorian America, 1840–1870.* New York.

McManis, Douglas R. (1972) *European Impressions of the New England Coast, 1497–1620.* Chicago.

McManus, Edgar J. (1961) "Antislavery Legislation in New York." *Journal of Negro History.* 46: 207–16.

———. (1966) *A History of Negro Slavery in New York.* Syracuse, NY.

McNamara, Brooks. (1997) *Day of Jubilee: The Great Age of Public Celebrations in New York, 1788–1909.* New Brunswick, NJ.

McNamara, Patrick. (1995) "'By the Rude Storms of Faction Blown': Thomas Jones, a Long Island Loyalist." *Long Island Historical Journal* 7: 178–90.

McNickle, Chris. (1993) *To Be Mayor of New York: Ethnic Politics in the City.* New York.

McPhee, John. (1983) *In Suspect Terrain.* New York.

McSeveney, Samuel T. (1972) *The Politics of Depression: Voting Behavior in the Northeast 1893–1896.* New York.

McShane, Clay. (1979) "Transforming the Use of Urban Space: A Look at the Revolution in Street Pavements, 1880–1924." *Journal of Urban History* 5: 308–39.

McWilliams, Carey. (1948) *A Mask for Privilege: Anti-Semitism in America.* Boston.

Meehan, Thomas F. (1906) "Some Pioneer Catholic Laymen in New York—Dominick Lynch and Cornelius Heeney." U.S. Catholic Historical Society. *Historical Records and Studies* 4: 285–301.

Meinig, Donald W. (1966) "The Colonial Period, 1609–1775." In *Geography of New York State,* edited by John Thompson. Syracuse, NY.

Melosi, Martin V. (1981) *Garbage in the Cities: Refuse, Reform, and the Environment, 1880–1980.* College Station, TX.

Melville, Herman. (1983) *Redburn, His First Voyage: White-jacket, or, the World in a Man-of-War; Moby-Dick, or, The Whale.* New York.

———. (1996) *Pierre, or, The Ambiguities.* New York.

Mendel, Ronald. (1989) "Workers in Gilded Age New York and Brooklyn, 1886–1898." Ph.D. diss., City University of New York.

Ment, David. (1979) *Building Blocks of Brooklyn: A Study of Urban Growth.* New York.

———. (1979) *The Shaping of a City: A Brief History of Brooklyn.* Brooklyn.

———, and Mary S. Donovan. (1980) *The People of Brooklyn: A History of Two Neighborhoods.* Brooklyn.

Meredith, Roy. (1946) *Mr. Lincoln's Camera Man: Mathew B. Brady.* New York.

Merwick, Donna. (1980) "Dutch Townsmen and Land Use: A Spatial Perspective on Seventeenth-Century Albany, New York." *WMQ* 37: 53–78.

———. (1981) "Becoming English: Anglo-Dutch Conflict in the 1670s in Albany, New York," *NYH* 62: 389–414.

———. (1989) "Being Dutch: An Interpretation of Why Jacob Leisler Died." *NYH* 79: 373–404.

Meyer, Donald. (1987) *Sex and Power: The Rise of Women in America, Russia,* Sweden, and Italy. Middletown, CT.

Meyer, Hazel. (1977) *The Gold in Tin Pan Alley.* Westport, CT.

Meyer, Michael A. (1987) "German-Jewish Identity in Nineteenth-Century America." In *The American Jewish Experience,* edited by Johnathan D. Sarna. New York.

Meyers, Marvin. (1965) *The Jacksonian Persuasion: Politics and Belief.* Stanford, CA.

Migliore, Paul Renard. (1975) "The Business of Union: The New York Business Community and the Civil War." Ph.D. diss., Columbia University.

Milbank, Caroline Rennolds. (1989) *New York Fashion: The Evolution of American Style.* New York.

Millard, A. J. (1990) *Edison and the Business of Invention.* Baltimore.

Miller, Christopher L., and G.R. Hamell. (1986) "A New Perspective on Indian-White Contact: Cultural Symbols and Colonial Trade." *JAH* 73: 311–28.

Miller, Donald L. (1989) *Lewis Mumford: A Life.* New York.

Miller, Douglas T. (1967) *Jacksonian Aristocracy: Class and Democracy in New York, 1830–1860.* New York.

Miller, Joaquin. (1886) *The Destruction of Gotham.* New York.

Miller, John. (1843) *A Description of the Province and City of New York . . . in the Year 1695.* London.

Miller, John C. (1960) *The Federalist Era, 1789–1901.* New York.

Miller, Kenneth D., and Ethel Prince. (1962) *The People Are the City: 150 Years of Social and Religious Concern in New York City.* New York.

Miller, Kerby A. (1985) *Emigrants and Exiles: Ireland and the Irish Exodus to North America.* New York.

Miller, Lillian B. (1966) *Patrons and Patriotism: The Encouragement of the Fine Arts in the United States, 1790–1860.* Chicago.

Miller, Martin B. (1980) "Dread and Terror: The Creation of State Penitentiaries in New York and Pennsylvania, 1788–1838." Ph.D. diss., University of California, Berkeley.

Miller, Nathan. (1962) *The Enterprise of a Free People: Aspects of Economic Development in New York State During the Canal Period, 1792–1838.* Ithaca, NY.

Miller, Perry, and Thomas H. Johnson, eds. (1963) *The Puritans.* 2 vols. New York.

Miller, Perry. (1973) *The Raven and the Whale: The War of Words and Wits in the Era of Poe and Melville.* Westport, CT.

Miller, Rita S. (1979) *Brooklyn, U.S.A.* Brooklyn.

Miller, Robert Moats. (1985) *Harry Emerson Fosdick: Preacher, Pastor, Prophet.* New York.

Miller, Terry. (1990) *Greenwich Village and How It Got that Way.* New York.

Miller, Wilbur R. (1977) *Cops and Bobbies: Police Authority in New York and London, 1830–1870.* Chicago.

Miller, William J. (1970) *The Geological History of New York State.* Port Washington, NY.

Milne, Gordon. (1956) *George William Curtis and the Genteel Tradition.* Bloomington, IN.

Miner, Clarence E. (1921) *Ratification of the Federal Constitution by the State of New York.* New York.

Mintz, Max M. (1970) *Gouverneur Morris and the American Revolution.* Norman, OK.

Mintz, Sidney W. (1985) *Sweetness and Power: The Place of Sugar in Modern World History.* New York.

Mitchell, Broadus. (1957, 1962) *Alexander Hamilton.* 2 vols. New York.

Mitchell, Joseph. (1959) *The Bottom of the Harbor.* Boston.

———. (1992) *Up in the Old Hotel and Other Stories.* New York.

Mitchill, Samuel Latham. (1807) *The Picture of New York, or The Traveller's Guide Through the Commercial Metropolis of the United States.* New York.

Moehring, Eugene P. (1981) *Public Works and the Pat-*

tern of Urban Real Estate Growth in Manhattan, 1835–1894. New York.

Mohl, Raymond. (1969) "Poverty in Early America, a Reappraisal: The Case of Eighteenth-Century New York City." *NYH* 50: 5–27.

———. (1970a) "The Humane Society and Urban Reform in Early New York, 1787–1831." *NYHSQ* 54: 30–52.

———. (1970b) "Humanitarianism in the Preindustrial City: The New York Society for the Prevention of Pauperism." *JAH* 57: 576–99.

———. (1971) *Poverty in New York, 1783–1825.* New York.

Mohr, James C. (1973) *The Radical Republicans and Reform in New York During Reconstruction.* Ithaca, NY.

———. (1978) *Abortion in America: The Origins and Evolution of National Policy, 1800–1900.* New York.

Mollenkopf, John. (1981) "Community and Accumulations." In *Urbanization and Urban Planning in Capitalist Society,* edited by Michael Dear and Allen J. Scott. London.

———. (1992) *A Phoenix in the Ashes: The Rise and Fall of the Koch Coalition in New York City Politics.* Princeton, NJ.

Monaghan, Frank. (1935) *John Jay.* New York.

———, and Marvin Lowenthal. (1943) *This Was New York: The Nation's Capital in 1789.* Garden City, NY.

Mondello, Salvatore. (1968) "John Vanderlyn." *NYHSQ* 52: 161–83.

Montgomery, David. (1967) *Beyond Equality: Labor and the Radical Republicans, 1862–1872.* New York.

———. (1987) *The Fall of the House of Labor: The Workplace, the State, and American Labor Activism, 1865–1925.* Cambridge, UK.

———. (1993) *Citizen Worker: The Experience of Workers in the United States with Democracy and the Free Market During the Nineteenth Century.* New York.

Moody, Richard. (1958) *The Astor Place Riot.* Bloomington, IN.

———. (1980) *Ned Harrigan: From Corlear's Hook to Herald Square.* Chicago.

Moore, Barrington, Jr. (1966) *Social Origins of Dictatorship and Democracy: Lord and Peasant in the Making of the Modern World.* Boston.

Moore, Clement Clarke. (1818) *A Plain Statement, Addressed to the Proprietors of Real Estate, in the City and County of New-York, by a Landholder.* New York.

Moore, Frank, comp. (1969) *Diary of the American Revolution.* 2 vols. New York.

Morais, Herbert M. (1934) *Deism in Eighteenth Century America.* New York.

———. (1939) "The Sons of Liberty in New York." In *The Era of the American Revolution,* edited by Richard B. Morris. New York.

Morehouse, Clifford P. (1973) *Trinity: Mother of Churches.* New York.

Morgan, Edmund S. (1953) *The Stamp Act Crisis: Prologue to Revolution.* Chapel Hill, NC.

———. (1988) *Inventing the People: The Rise of Popular Sovereignty in England and America.* New York.

Morgan, Helen M., ed. (1969) *A Season in New York 1801: Letters of Harriet and Maria Trumbull.* Pittsburgh.

Morison, Samuel Eliot. (1971–74) *The European Discovery of America.* 2 vols. New York.

Morris, Edmund. (1979) *The Rise of Theodore Roosevelt.* New York.

Morris, Jan. (1987) *Manhattan '45.* New York.

Morris, Richard B., ed. (1935) *Select Cases of the Mayor's Court of New York City, 1674–1784.* Washington, DC.

———, ed. (1939) *The Era of the American Revolution.* New York.

———. (1952) *Fair Trial: Fourteen Who Stood Accused, from Anne Hutchinson to Alger Hiss.* New York.

———. (1973) "John Jay and the Radical Chic

Elite." In *Seven Who Shaped Our Destiny: The Founding Fathers as Revolutionaries.* New York.

———. (1978) "The New York City Mayor's Court." In *Courts and Law in Early Colonial New York,* edited by Leo Hershkowitz and Milton Klein. Port Washington, NY.

Morrison, Grant. (1973) *Isaac Bronson and the Search for System in American Capitalism, 1789–1838.* New York.

Morrison, John Harrison. (1903) *History of American Steam Navigation.* New York.

———. (1909) *History of New York Ship Yards.* New York.

Morris, Lloyd R. (1975) *Incredible New York.* New York.

Moss, Richard S. (1985) "Slavery on Long Island: Its Rise and Decline During the Seventeenth through Nineteenth Centuries." Ph.D. diss., St. John's University.

Moss, Sidney P. (1963) *Poe's Literary Battles.* Durham, NC.

Moulton, Elizabeth. (1964) *St. George's Church, New York.* New York.

Moulton, Joseph W. (1843) *New York 170 Years Ago.* New York.

Mowrer, Lilian T. (1960) *The Indomitable John Scott: Citizen of Long Island, 1632–1704.* New York.

Muccigrosso, Robert. (1968) "The City Reform Club: A Study in Late-Nineteenth-Century Reform." *NYHSQ* 52: 235–54.

Mueller, John H. (1951) *The American Symphony Orchestra: A Social History of Musical Taste.* Bloomington, IN.

Mumford, Lewis. (1971) *The Brown Decades: A Study of the Arts in America, 1865–1895.* New York.

Murphy, Henry Cruse. (1969) *Anthology of New Netherland; or, Translations from the Early Dutch Poets of New York, with Memoirs of their Lives.* Port Washington. NY.

———. (1972) *Henry Hudson in Holland.* New York.

Murray, Jean E. (1938) "The Early Fur Trade in New

France and New Netherland." *Canadian Historical Review* 29: 365–77.

Murrin, John M. (1980) "The Great Inversion, or Court versus Country: A Comparison of the Revolution Settlements in England (1688–1721) and America (1776–1816)." In *Three British Revolutions, 1641–1776,* edited by J. G. A. Pocock. Princeton, NJ.

———. (1988) "English Rights as Ethnic Aggression: The English Conquest, the Charter of Liberties of 1683, and Leisler's Rebellion in New York." In *Authority and Resistance in Early New York,* edited by William Pencak and Conrad Wright. New York.

Museum of the City of New York. (1990) *Within Bohemia's Borders: Greenwich Village, 1830–1930.* New York.

Mushkat, Jerome. (1971) "Epitaphs by Mordecai Noah." *NYHSQ* 55: 253–71.

———. (1971) *Tammany: The Evolution of a Political Machine, 1789–1865.* Syracuse, NY.

———. (1981) *The Reconstruction of New York Democracy, 1861–1874.* Rutherford, NJ.

———. (1990) *Fernando Wood: A Political Biography.* Kent, OH.

Myers, Andrew B. (1974) *The Knickerbocker Tradition: Washington Irving's New York.* Tarrytown, NY.

———, ed. (1976) *A Century of Commentary on the Works of Washington Irving.* Tarrytown, NY.

Myers, Gustavus. (1901) *The History of Tammany Hall.* New York.

———. (1907–10) *History of the Great American Fortunes.* 3 vols. Chicago

———. (1943) *History of Bigotry in the United States.* New York.

———. ([1900] 1974) *History of Public Franchises in New York City.* New York.

Myers, Kenneth. (1987) *The Catskills: Painters, Writers, and Tourists in the Mountains, 1820–1895.* Yonkers, NY.

Myers, Margaret G. (1931) *The New York Money*

Market: Vol. I: Origins and Development. New York.

Nadel, Stanley. (1990) *Little Germany: Ethnicity, Religion and Class in New York City, 1845–80.* Urbana, IL.

———. (1991) "From the Barricades of Paris to the Sidewalks of New York." In *Immigration to New York,* edited by William Pencak, Selma Berrol, and Randall M. Miller. Philadelphia.

Naifeh, Steven W. (1976) *Culture Making: Money, Success and the New York Art World.* Princeton, NJ.

Narratives of the Revolution in New York: A Collection of Articles from the New-York Historical Society Quarterly. (1975) New York.

Narrett, David E. (1988) "Dutch Customs of Inheritance, Women, and the Law in Colonial New York City." In *Authority and Resistance in Early New York,* edited by William Pencak and Conrad Wright. New York.

———. (1988) "A Zeal for Liberty: The Antifederalist Case Against the Constitution in New York." *NYH* 69: 285–317.

———. (1992) *Inheritance and Family Life in Colonial New York City.* Ithaca, NY.

Nasaw, David. (1993) *Going Out: The Rise and Fall of Public Amusements.* New York.

Nash, Gary B. (1976) "Urban Wealth and Poverty in Pre-Revolutionary America." *Journal of Interdisciplinary History* 6: 545–84.

———. (1979a) "The New York Census of 1737: A Critical Note on the Integration of Statistical and Literary Sources." *WMQ* 36: 428–35.

———. (1979b) *The Urban Crucible: Social Change, Political Consciousness, and the Origins of the American Revolution.* Cambridge, MA.

———. (1988) *Forging Freedom: The Formation of Philadelphia's Black Community, 1720–1840.* Cambridge, MA.

———. (1992) *Race and Revolution: Essays on American Colonial and Revolutionary Society.* Urbana, IL.

Nathan, Hans. (1962) *Dan Emmett and the Rise of Early Negro Minstrelsy.* Norman, OK.

Nathan, Rosemary. (1965) "A Study of the Reactions in New York State to the Greek War for Independence, 1821–1830." Master's thesis, Hunter College.

Navin, Thomas R., and Marian V. Sears. (1955) "The Rise of a Market for Industrial Securities, 1887–1900." *Business History Review* 29: 105–38.

Nelli, Humbert S. (1976) *The Business of Crime: Italians and Syndicate Crime in the United States.* New York.

Nelson, John R. (1979) "Alexander Hamilton and American Manufacturing: A Reexamination." *JAH* 65: 971–75.

———. (1987) *Liberty and Property: Political Economy and Policymaking in the New Nation, 1789–1812.* Baltimore.

Nelson, Paul David. (1987) *William Alexander, Lord Stirling.* University, AL.

———. (1990) *William Tryon and the Course of Empire: A Life in the British Imperial Service.* Chapel Hill, NC.

———. (1991) "William Tryon Confronts the American Revolution, 1771–1780." *Historian* 53: 267–84.

Nelson, William H. (1964) *The American Tory.* Boston.

Nettels, Curtis. (1962) *The Emergence of a National Economy, 1775–1815.* New York.

Nevins, Allan. (1922) *The Evening Post: A Century of Journalism.* New York.

———. ([1924] 1969) *The American States During and After the Revolution, 1775–1789.* New York.

———. (1934) *History of the Bank of New York and Trust Company, 1784–1934.* New York.

———. (1935) *Abram S. Hewitt: With Some Account*

of Peter Cooper. New York.

———. (1940) *John D. Rockefeller: The Heroic Age of American Enterprise.* New York.

———, and John A. Krout, eds. (1948) *The Greater City: New York, 1898–1948.* New York.

———. (1959–1971) *The War for the Union.* 4 vols. New York.

New York City Common Council. (1841–1870) *Manual of the Corporation of the City of New York.* New York.

New-York Historical Society. (1886) *The Burghers of New Amsterdam and the Freemen of New York, 1675–1866. NYHS Collections for the Year 1885.* New York.

New-York Historical Society. (1970) *City of Promise: Aspects of Jewish Life in New York, 1654–1970.* New York.

New York (N.Y.) Landmarks Preservation Committee. (1973) *SoHo–Cast Iron Historic District Designation Report.* New York.

New York Steam Corporation. (1932) *Fifty Years of New York Steam Service: The Story of the Founding and Development of a Public Utility.* New York.

Newman, Aubrey, ed. (1991) "Migration and Settlement." *Proceedings of the Anglo-American Jewish Historical Conference.* London.

Newman, Renee. (1993) "Pinkster and Slavery in Dutch New York." *de Halve Maen* 56: 1–8.

Newt Davidson Collective. (1974) *Crisis at CUNY.*

Newton, Arthur P. ([1933] 1967) *The European Nations in the West Indies, 1493–1688.* New York.

Newton, Roger Hale. (1942) *Town and Davis, Architects: Pioneers in American Revivalist Architecture, 1812–1870.* New York.

Nicholas, George P. (1988) "Ecological Leveling: The Archaeology and Environmental Dynamics of Early Postglacial Land Use." In *Holocene Human Ecology in Northeastern North America.* New York.

Nichols, Robert Hastings. (1963) *Presbyterianism in*

New York State: A History of the Synod and its Predecessors.* Philadelphia.

Nilsen, Kenneth E. (1996) "The Irish Language in New York, 1850–1900." In *The New York Irish,* edited by Ronald H. Bayor and Timothy J. Meagher. Baltimore.

Nissenbaum, Stephen. (1980) *Sex, Diet and Debility in Jacksonian America: Sylvester Graham and Health Reform.* Westport, CT.

———. (1996) *The Battle for Christmas.* New York.

Nissenson, Samuel G. (1937) *The Patroon's Domain.* New York.

Noble, David F. (1977) *America by Design: Science, Technology, and the Rise of Corporate Capitalism.* New York.

Nolan, J. Bennett. (1934) *Lafayette in America Day by Day.* Baltimore.

Nooter, Eric, and Patricia U. Bonomi, eds. (1988) *Colonial Dutch Studies: An Interdisciplinary Approach.* New York.

Nooter, Eric. (1995) "Between Heaven and Earth: Church and Society in Pre-Revolutionary Flatbush, Long Island." Ph.D. diss., Vrije Universiteit, Amsterdam.

Nord, David Paul. (May 1984) "The Evangelical Origins of Mass Media in America, 1815–1835." *Journalism Monographs* 88: 1–31.

———. (March 1988) "A Republican Literature: A Study of Magazine Reading and Readers in Late Eighteenth-Century New York." *AQ* 40: 42–64.

Norris, James D. (1978) *R. G. Dun and Co., 1841–1900: The Development of Credit-reporting in the Nineteenth Century.* Westport, CT.

———. (1990) *Advertising and the Transformation of American Society, 1865–1920.* New York.

North, Edgerton G. (1951) *The First Hundred Years, 1851–1951: An Account of the Founding and Growth of the Williamsburgh Savings Bank.* Brooklyn.

Norton, Mary Beth. (1980) *Liberty's Daughters: The*

Revolutionary Experience of American Women, 1750–1800. Boston.

Norton, Thomas, and Jerry E. Patterson. (1984) *Living It Up: A Guide to the Named Apartment Houses of New York.* New York.

Norton, Thomas Elliot. (1974) *The Fur Trade in Colonial New York, 1686–1776.* Madison, WI.

———. (1984) *100 Years of Collecting in America: The Story of Sotheby Parke Bernet.* New York.

Novick, Sheldon. (1976) *The Electric War: The Fight over Nuclear Power.* San Francisco.

Numbers, Ronald L., and Jonathan M. Butler. (1987) *The Disappointed: Millerism and Millenarianism in the Nineteenth Century.* Bloomington, IN.

Nye, David E. (1990) *Electrifying America: Social Meanings of a New Technology, 1880–1940.* Cambridge, MA.

O'Callaghan, Edmund Bailey. (1846–1848) *History of New Netherland, or New York Under the Dutch.* 2 vols. New York.

———, ed. (1849) *Documentary History of the State of New York.* 4 vols. Albany, NY.

———, ed. (1853–87) *Documents Relative to the Colonial History of the State of New-York.* 15 vols. Albany, NY.

———, ed. (1868) *Laws and Ordinances of New Netherland, 1638–1674.* Albany, NY.

O'Connell, Shaun. (1994) *Remarkable Unspeakable New York: A Literary History.* Boston.

O'Connor, John P. (1989) "The Shamrock, The First Irish-American Newspaper." *New York Irish History* 4: 4–5.

O'Connor, Richard. (1958) *Hell's Kitchen: The Roaring Days of New York's Wild West Side.* Philadelphia.

———. (1963) *Court Room Warrior: The Combative Career of William Travers Jerome.* Boston.

O'Conor, Norreys J. (1938) *A Servant of the Crown in England and North America, 1756–1761.* New York.

O'Donnell, Edward Thomas. (1995) "Henry George and the 'New Political Forces': Ethnic Nationalism, Labor Radicalism, and Politics in Gilded Age New York City." Ph.D. diss., Columbia University.

O'Donovan, Jeremiah. (1969) *A Brief Account of the Author's Interview with His Countrymen.* New York.

O'Grady, John. ([1930] 1971) *Catholic Charities in the United States: History and Problems.* New York.

O'Hanlon, Timothy. (1982) "Neighborhood Change in New York City: A Case Study of Park Slope, 1850–1980." Ph.D. diss., City University of New York.

Oates, Stephen B. (1977) *With Malice Toward None: The Life of Abraham Lincoln.* New York.

Odell, George C. D. (1927–1949) *Annals of the New York Stage.* 15 vols. New York.

Olasky, Marvin. (1986) "Advertising Abortion During the 1830s and 1840s: Madame Restell Builds a Business." *Journalism History* 13: 49–55.

Olm, Lee E. (1974) "The Mutiny Act for America: New York's Noncompliance." *NYHSQ* 58: 188–214.

Olmstead, Alan L. (1976) *New York City Mutual Savings Banks, 1819–1861.* Chapel Hill, NC.

Olson, Alison Gilbert. (1973a) *Anglo-American Politics 1660–1775: The Relationship Between Parties in England and Colonial America.* New York.

———. (1973b) "Governor Robert Hunter and the Anglican Church in New York." In *Statesmen, Scholars, and Merchants: Essays in Eighteenth-Century History,* edited by Anne Whiteman, J.S. Bromley, and Peter Dickson. Oxford.

Onderdonk, Henry, Jr. (1849) *Revolutionary Incidents of Suffolk and Kings Counties.* New York.

Opie, Iona, and Peter Opie, eds. (1997) *The Oxford Dictionary of Nursery Rhymes.* Oxford.

Orsi, Robert. (1985) *The Madonna of 115th Street: Faith and Community in Italian Harlem, 1880–1950.* New Haven, CT.

Osborne, John Walter. (1966) *William Cobbett: His Thought and His Times.* New Brunswick, NJ.

Osgood, Herbert L., ed. (1905) *Minutes of the Common Council of the City of New York, 1675–1776.* 8 vols. New York.

Osofsky, Gilbert. (1966) *Harlem: The Making of a Ghetto: Negro New York, 1890–1930.* New York.

Otter, William. (1995) *History of My Own Times,* edited by Richard B. Stott. Ithaca, NY.

Otterness, Philip. (1994) "The New York Naval Stores Project and the Transformation of the Poor Palatines." *NYH* 75: 133–56.

Ottley, Roi, and William J. Weatherby, eds. (1967) *The Negro in New York: An Informal Social History.* New York.

Otto, Paul A. (1995) "New Netherland Frontier: Europeans and Native Americans along the Lower Hudson River, 1524–1664." Ph.D. diss., Indiana University.

Overall, C. S. (1987) "New York State versus Loyalists of New York State: An Analysis of Loyalist Petitions of 1783 and 1783." Paper presented at New-York Historical Society conference.

Overton, Grant. (1925) *Portrait of a Publisher, and the First Hundred Years of the House of Appleton, 1825–1925.* New York.

Ovington, M. (1911) *Half a Man: The Status of the Negro in New York.* New York.

Pachter, Marc, and Frances Wein, eds. (1976) *Abroad in America: Visitors to the New Nation, 1776–1914.* Reading, MA.

Page, Max. (1995) "The Creative Destruction of New York City: Landscape, Memory, and the Politics of Place, 1900–1930." Ph.D. diss., University of Pennsylvania.

Painter, Nell. (1987) *Standing at Armageddon: The United States, 1877–1929.* New York.

———. (1996) *Sojourner Truth: A Life, a Symbol.* New York.

Paltsits, Victor Hugo. (1975) "The Jeopardy of Washington, September 15, 1776." *Narratives of the Revolution in New York.* New York.

Papke, David Ray. (1987) *Framing the Criminal: Crime, Cultural Work, and the Loss of Critical Perspective, 1830–1900.* Hamden, CT.

Pares, Richard. (1956) *Yankees and Creoles: The Trade between North America and the West Indies before the American Revolution.* Cambridge, MA.

Parker, Hershel. (1996) *Herman Melville: A Biography.* Baltimore.

Parmet, Herbert. (1967) *Aaron Burr: Portrait of an Ambitious Man.* New York.

Parrini, Carl P. (1969) *Heir to Empire: U.S. Economic Diplomacy, 1916–1923.* Pittsburgh.

Parry, Albert. (1933) *Garrets and Pretenders: A History of Bohemianism in America.* New York.

Parton, James. (1858) *The Life and Times of Aaron Burr.* 5th ed. New York.

Pascu, Elaine Weber. (1980) "From the Philanthropic Tradition to the Common School Ideal: Schooling in New York City, 1815–1832." Ph.D. diss., Northern Illinois University.

Patterson, Jerry E. (1989) *The Vanderbilts.* New York.

Patterson, Samuel White. (1935) *Old Chelsea and Saint Peter's Church: The Centennial History of a New York Parish.* New York.

———. (1955) *Hunter College: Eighty-five Years of Service.* New York.

———. (1956) *The Poet of Christmas Eve: A Life of Clement Clarke Moore, 1779–1863.* New York.

Paulding, James Kirke. (1839) *The Merry Tales of the Three Wise Men of Gotham.* New York.

———. (1938) *Charles B. Stover.* New York.

Paulding, William I. (1867) *Literary Life of James K. Paulding.* New York.

Paulson, Peter. (1953) "The Tammany Society and the Jeffersonian Movement in New York City, 1795–1800." *NYH* 34: 50–68.

Pearce, Roy Harvey. (1965) *The Savages of America: A Study of the Indian and the Idea of Civilization.* Rev. Ed. Baltimore.

Pearson, Roberta E., and William Uricchio, eds. (1991) *The Many Lives of the Batman: Critical Approaches to a Superhero and His Media.* New York.

Peckham, Howard H. (1964) *The Colonial Wars, 1689–1762.* Chicago.

———, and Charles Gibson, eds. (1969) *Attitudes of Colonial Powers Toward the American Indian.* Salt Lake City.

———, ed. (1974) *The Toll of Independence: Engagements and Battle Casualties of the American Revolution.* Chicago.

Peiss, Kathy. (1985) *Cheap Amusements: Working Women and Leisure in Turn-of-the-Century New York.* Philadelphia.

———, Christina Simmons, and Robert A. Padguy, eds. (1989) *Passion and Power: Sexuality in History.* Philadelphia.

Pencak, William, and Conrad Wright, eds. (1988) *Authority and Resistance in Early New York.* New York.

Pennypacker, Morton. (1930) *The Two Spies: Nathan Hale and Robert Townsend.* Boston.

———. (1939) *General Washington's Spies on Long Island and in New York During the American Revolution.* New York.

———. (1944) *The Duke's Laws: Their Antecedents, Implications, and Importance.* New York.

Perkins, Bradford. (1961) *Prologue to War: England and the United States, 1805–1812.* Berkeley, CA.

———. (1967) *The First Rapprochement: England and the United States, 1795–1805.* New York.

Perlman, Daniel. (1971) "Organizations of the Free Negro in New York City, 1800–1860." *Journal of Negro History* 56: 18–97.

Pernick, Martin S. (1972) "Politics, Parties, and Pestilence: Epidemic Yellow Fever in Philadelphia and the Rise of the First Party System." *WMQ* 29: 559–86.

Pernicone, Carol [Groneman]. (1973) "The 'Bloody Ould Sixth': A Social Analysis of a New York City Working-class Community in the Mid-nineteenth Century." Ph.D. diss., University of Rochester.

Perret, Geoffrey. (1982) *America in the Twenties: A History.* New York.

Perry, Lewis (1984) *Intellectual Life in America: A History.* Chicago.

Pessen, Edward. (1967) *Most Uncommon Jacksonians: The Radical Leaders of the Early Labor Movement.* Albany, NY.

———. (1972) "Philip Hone's Set: The Social World of the New York City Elite in the 'Age of Egalitarianism.' " *NYHSQ* 56: 285–300.

———. (1973) *Riches, Class, and Power Before the Civil War.* Lexington, MA.

———. (1978) *Jacksonian America: Society, Personality, and Politics.* Rev. ed. Homewood, IL.

Peters, Nathan. (1984) "The Growth of the Port of New York, 1790–1800: A Look at Vessel Turn Around Time." Ph.D. diss., University of Wisconsin.

Peterson, Arthur E. (1917) *New York as an Eighteenth Century Municipality, Prior to 1731.* New York.

Peterson, Jon. (1979) "The Impact of Sanitary Reform upon American Urban Planning, 1840–1890." *Journal of Social History* 13: 88–103.

Petersen, L. A. (1945) *Elisha Graves Otis, 1811–1861, and His Influence upon Vertical Transportation.* New York.

Peterson, Merrill D. (1966) *Democracy, Liberty and Property: The State Constitutional Conventions of the 1820's.* New York.

Peterson, Virgil W. (1983) *The Mob: 200 Years of Organized Crime in New York.* Ottawa, IL.

Pettit, Marilyn Hilley. (1991) "Women, Sunday Schools, and Politics: Early National New York City, 1797–1827." Ph.D. diss., New York University.

Phelan, Thomas P. (1933) *Thomas Dongan: Colonial Governor of New York, 1683–1688.* New York.

Philip, Cynthia Owen. (1985) *Robert Fulton: A Biography.* New York.

Pickett, Robert S. (1969) *House of Refuge: Origins of Juvenile Reform in New York State, 1815–1857.* Syracuse, NY.

Pierson, George Wilson. (1938) *Tocqueville and Beaumont in America.* New York.

Pilat, Oliver, and Jo Ranson. (1941) *Sodom by the Sea: An Affectionate History of Coney Island.* New York.

Pinkney, David H. (1958) *Napoleon III and the Rebuilding of Paris.* Princeton, NJ.

Pivar, David J. (1973) *Purity Crusade: Sexual Morality and Social Control, 1868–1900.* Westport, CT.

Plumb, J. H. (1967) *The Origins of Political Stability: England, 1675–1725.* Boston.

———. (1986) "British Attitudes toward the American Revolution." In *Resistance, Politics, and the American Struggle for Independence, 1765–1775,* edited by Walter Conser. Boulder, CO.

Plunz, Richard A. (1990) *A History of Housing in New York City: Dwelling Type and Social Change in the American Metropolis.* New York.

Pocock, J. G. A., ed. (1980) *Three British Revolutions, 1641–1776.* Princeton, NJ.

Pointer, Richard W. (1988) *Protestant Pluralism and the New York Experience: A Study of Eighteenth-Century Religious Diversity.* Bloomington, IN.

Polf, William A. (1977) *1777: The Political Revolution and New York's First Constitution.* Albany, NY.

Pomerantz, Sidney Irving. (1938) *New York, an American City, 1783–1803: A Study of Urban Life.* New York.

Pool, David de Sola. (1952) *Portraits Etched in Stone: Early Jewish Settlers, 1682–1831.* New York.

———, and Tamar de Sola Pool. (1955) *An Old Faith in the New World: Portrait of Shearith Israel, 1654–1954.* New York.

Pool, Ithiel de Sola, ed. (1977) *The Social Impact of the Telephone.* Cambridge, MA.

Poole, Ernest. (1915) *The Harbor.* New York.

Pope, Daniel. (1983) *The Making of Modern Advertising.* New York.

Porter, Glenn, and Harold Livesay. (1971) *Merchants and Manufacturers: Studies in the Changing Structure of Nineteenth-century Marketing.* Baltimore.

Porter, H. C. (1979) *The Inconstant Savage: England and the North American Indian, 1500–1660.* London.

Porter, Kenneth Wiggins. (1931) *John Jacob Astor, Business Man.* Cambridge, MA.

Post, Louis F., and Fred C. Leubuscher. (1887) *Henry George's 1886 Campaign: An Account of the George-Hewitt Campaign in the New York Municipal Election of 1886.* New York.

Post, Robert C. (1983) "Reflections of American Science and Technology at the New York Crystal Palace Exhibition of 1853." *Journal of American Studies* 17: 337–56.

Postgate, R. W. (1932) *Dear Robert Emmet: A Biography.* New York.

Post-Lauria, Sheila. (1996) *Correspondent Colorings: Melville in the Marketplace.* Amherst, MA.

Postma, Johannes M. (1990) *The Dutch in the Atlantic Slave Trade, 1600–1815.* New York.

Potter, Janice. (1983) *The Liberty We Seek: Loyalist Ideology in Colonial New York and Massachusetts.* Cambridge, MA.

Pound, Arthur. (1931) *Native Stock: The Rise of the American Spirit Seen in Six Lives.* New York.

———. ([1935] 1975) *The Golden Earth: Manhattan's*

Landed Wealth. New York.

Powell, Michael J. (1988) *From Patrician to Professional Elite: The Transformation of the New York City Bar Association.* New York.

Pozzetta, George Enrico. (1971) "The Italians of New York City, 1890–1914." Ph.D. diss., University of North Carolina at Chapel Hill, NC.

Pratt, John W. (1967) *Religion, Politics, and Diversity: The Church-State Theme in NYH* Ithaca, NY.

Pratt, Junius. (1936) *Expansionists of 1898.* Baltimore.

Pred, Allan R. (1966) *The Spatial Dynamics of United States Urban Industrial Growth, 1800–1914.* Cambridge, MA.

———. (1972) "Manufacturing in the American Mercantile City, 1800–1840." In *Cities in American History,* edited by Kenneth T. Jackson and Stanley K. Schultz. New York.

———. (1973) *Urban Growth and the Circulation of Information: The United States System of Cities, 1790–1840.* Cambridge, MA.

———. (1980) *Urban Growth and City Systems in the United States, 1840–1860.* Cambridge, MA.

Presa, Donald G. (1981) "The Development and Demise of the Upper West Side Row House: 1880–1980." Paper produced for Columbia University School of Architectural Planning. New York.

Prescott, Frank W., and Joseph F. Zimmerman. (1972) *The Council of Revision and the Veto of Legislation in New York State, 1777–1782.* Albany, NY.

Price, Jacob M. (1974) "Economic Function and the Growth of American Port Towns in the Eighteenth Century." *Perspectives in American History.* 8: 121–86.

———. (1980) *Capital and Credit in British Overseas Trade: The View from the Chesapeake, 1770–1776.* Cambridge, MA.

Prime, Samuel Irenaeus. (1874) *The Life of Samuel F. B. Morse.* 2 vols. New York.

Prince, Carl E. (1985) "'The Great 'Riot Year': Jacksonian Democracy and Patterns of Violence in 1834." *Journal of the Early Republic* 5: 1–20.

Pryde, George S. (1935) "Scottish Colonization in the Province of New York," *NYH* 16: 138–57.

Pye, Michael. (1991) *Maximum City: The Biography of New York.* London.

Pyne, Stephen J. (1997) *Fire in America: A Cultural History of Wildland and Rural Fire.* Rev. ed. Seattle, WA.

Quarles, Benjamin. (1961) *The Negro in the American Revolution.* Chapel Hill, NC.

———. (1969) *Black Abolitionists.* New York.

Quinn, Doris C. (1993) "Theft of the Manhattans" [1664]. *de Halve Maen* 56: 25–30.

Quiroga, Virginia Anne Metaxas. (1989) *Poor Mothers and Babies: A Social History of Childbirth and Child Care Hospitals in Nineteenth-century New York City.* New York.

Raddin, George G., Jr. (1940) *An Early New York Library of Fiction.* New York.

———. (1953a) *Hocquet Caritat and the Early New York Literary Scene.* Dover, NJ.

———. (1953b) *Hocquet Caritat and the Gênet Episode.* Dover, NJ.

———. (1953c) *The New York of Hocquet Caritat and His Associates, 1797–1817.* Dover, NJ.

———. (1954) "The Music of New York City, 1797–1804." *NYHSQ* 38: 478–99.

Raesly, Ellis Lawrence. (1945) *Portrait of New Netherland.* New York.

Rainone, Nanette, ed. (1985) *Brooklyn Neighborhood Book.* Brooklyn.

Raleigh, John Henry. (1957) *Matthew Arnold and American Culture.* Berkeley, CA.

Randall, J. G. (1945) *Lincoln, the President: From Springfield to Gettysburg.* Gloucester, MA.

Rankin, Hugh F. (1965) *The Theater in Colonial America.* Chapel Hill, NC.

Ranlet, Philip. (1986) *The New York Loyalists.* Knoxville, TN.

Ratner, Lorman. (1968) *Powder Keg: Northern Opposition to the Antislavery Movement, 1831–1840.* New York.

Ravitch, Diane. (1974) *The Great School Wars: New York City, 1805–1973.* New York.

Raymo, Chet, and Maureen E. Raymo. (1989) *Written in Stone: A Geological and Natural History of the Northeastern United States.* Chester, CT.

Raynor, Henry. (1978) *Music and Society Since 1815.* New York.

Real Estate Record Association. (1898) *History of Real Estate, Building and Architecture in New York City During the Last Quarter of a Century.* New York.

Rebora, Carrie J. (1990) "The American Academy of the Fine Arts, New York, 1802–1842." Ph.D. diss., City University of New York.

Rediker, Marcus. (1981) "'Under the Banner of King Death': The Social World of Anglo-American Pirates, 1716–1726." *WMQ* 38: 203–27.

———. (1987) *Between the Devil and the Deep Blue Sea: Merchant Seamen, Pirates and the Anglo-American Maritime World, 1700–1750.* New York.

Reich, Jerome. (1953) *Leisler's Rebellion: A Study of Democracy in New York, 1664–1620.* Chicago.

Remini, Robert Vincent. (1988) *The Life of Andrew Jackson.* New York.

Rensberger, Boyce. (1976) "The Region As Reliquary." *New York Times,* October 24.

Reps, John W. (1965) *The Making of Urban America: A History of City Planning in the United States.* Princeton, NJ.

Resseguie, Harry E. (1964) "A. T. Stewart's Marble Palace—The Cradle of the Department Store." *NYHSQ* 48:131–62.

———. (1965) "Alexander Turney Stewart and the Development of the Department Store, 1823–1876." *Business History Review* 39:301–22.

Reubens, Beatrice G. (1957, 1958) "Burr, Hamilton and the Manhattan Company." *PSQ* 72: 578–607, 73: 100–25.

Reynolds, David S. (1988) *Beneath the American Renaissance: The Subversive Imagination in the Age of Emerson and Melville.* New York.

———. (1995) *Walt Whitman's America: A Cultural Biography.* New York.

Reynolds, Donald M. (1984) *The Architecture of New York City: Histories and Views of Important Structures, Sites, and Symbols.* New York.

Reynolds, John. (1960) *Long Island: Behind the British Lines During the Revolution.* Setauket, NY.

Reynolds, Larry J. (1984) *James Kirke Paulding.* Boston.

Rezneck, Samuel. (1968) *Business Depressions and Financial Panics: Essays in American Business and Economic History.* New York.

Richards, Leonard L. (1970) *Gentlemen of Property and Standing: Anti-abolition Mobs in Jacksonian America.* New York.

Richardson, James F. (1970) *The New York Police, Colonial Times to 1901.* New York.

Richter, Daniel K. (1983) "War and Culture: The Iroquois Experience." *WMQ* 40: 528–59.

———. (1992) *The Ordeal of the Longhouse: The Peoples of the Iroquois League in the Era of European Colonization.* Chapel Hill, NC.

Ridge, John T. (1988) *The St. Patrick's Day Parade in New York.* New York.

Rienders, Robert. (1976) "Militia and Public Order in Nineteenth-Century America." *Journal of American Studies* 11: 81–101.

Riess, Steven A. (1989) *City Games: The Evolution of American Urban Society and the Rise of Sports.* Urbana, IL.

Riis, Jacob. (1890) *How the*

Other Half Lives. New York.

Riker, David M. (1983) "Surgeon Hans Kierstede of New Amsterdam." *de Halve Maen* 57: 11–13; 24–25.

———. (1989) "Govert Loockermans: Free Merchant of New Amsterdam." *de Halve Maen* 62: 4–10.

Riker, James. (1904) *Revised History of Harlem: Its Origins and Early Annals.* New York.

Riker, James, Jr. ([1852] 1982) *The Annals of Newtown, in Queens County, New-York.* New York.

Riley, John P. (1990) "George Washington's Inaugural Trip to New York." In *Well Begun: Chronicles of the Early National Period,* edited by Stephen L. Schechter and Richard B. Bernstein.

Ringenbach, Paul T. (1973) *Tramps and Reformers, 1873–1916: The Discovery of Poverty in New York.* Westport, CT.

Rink, Oliver A. (1978) "Company Management or Private Trade: The Two Patroonship Plans for New Netherland." *NYH* 59: 5–26.

———. (1981) "The People of New Netherland: Notes on Non-English Immigration to New York in the Seventeenth Century." *NYH* 62: 5–42.

———. (1986) *Holland on the Hudson: An Economic and Social History of Dutch New York.* Ithaca, NY.

———. (1987) "Unraveling a Secret Colonialism." Part 1. *de Halve Maen* 60: 13ff.

———. (1987) "Unraveling a Secret Colonialism." Part 2. *de Halve Maen* 60: 8ff.

———. (1994) "Private Interest and Godly Gain: The West India Company and the Dutch Reformed Church in New Netherland, 1624–1664." *NYH* 75: 245–64.

Riordon, William L. ([1905]1948) *Plunkitt of Tammany Hall: A Series of Very Plain Talks on Very Practical Politics, Delivered by Ex-Senator George Washington Plunkitt, the Tammany Philosopher, from*

His Rostrum, the New York County Court-house Bootblack Stand. New York.

Rischin, Moses. (1962) *The Promised City: New York's Jews, 1870–1914.* Cambridge, MA.

Risjord, Norman K. (1976) "The Compromise of 1790: New Evidence on the Dinner Table Bargain." *WMQ* 33: 309–14.

———. (1981) "Blackbeard the Pirate: The Story of Edward Teach." In *Representative Americans: The Colonists.* Lexington, MA.

Ritchie, Carson I. A., ed. (1975) "A New York Diary of the Revolutionary War." *Narratives of the Revolution in New York.* New York.

Ritchie, Robert C. (1977) *The Duke's Province: A Study of New York Politics and Society, 1664–1691.* Chapel Hill, NC.

———. (1986) *Captain Kidd and the War Against the Pirate.* Cambridge, MA.

———. (1988) "Samuel Burgess, Pirate." In *Authority and Resistance in Early New York,* edited by William Pencak and Conrad Wright. New York.

Robbins, Christine Chapman. (1964) *David Hosack: Citizen of New York.* Philadelphia.

Robertson-Lorant, Laurie. (1996) *Melville: A Biography.* New York.

Roche, John F. (1971) "The Uranian Society: Gentlemen and Scholars in Federal New York." *NYH* 52: 121–32.

Rock, Howard B. (1979) *Artisans of the New Republic: The Tradesmen of New York City in the Age of Jefferson.* New York.

———, ed. (1989) *The New York City Artisan, 1789–1825: A Documentary History.* Ithaca, NY.

———. (1994) "Confrontation in Gotham: The Sweep and the Fop." *NYH* 75: 157–72.

———, Paul A. Gilje, and Robert Asher. (1995) *American Artisans: Crafting Social Identity, 1750–1850.* Baltimore.

Roeber, A. G. (1991) "'The Origin of Whatever Is Not English Among Us': The Dutch-speaking and Ger-

man-speaking Peoples of Colonial British America." In *Strangers Within the Realm: Cultural Margins of the First British Empire,* edited by Bernard Bailyn and Philip D. Morgan. Chapel Hill, NC.

———. (1993) *Palatines, Liberty, and Property: German Lutherans in Colonial British America.* Baltimore.

Roediger, David R. (1991) *The Wages of Whiteness: Race and the Making of the American Working Class.* London.

Roff, Sandra S. (1986) "The Brooklyn African Woolman Benevolent Society Rediscovered." *African Americans in New York History and Life,* 55–58.

Rogers, Alan. (1974) *Empire and Liberty: American Resistance to British Authority, 1755–1763.* Berkeley, CA.

Rogin, Michael Paul. (1983) *Subversive Genealogy.* New York.

Roosevelt, Theodore. (1891) *New York: A Sketch of the City's Social, Political, and Commercial Progress from the First Dutch Settlement to Recent Times.* London.

Roper, Laura Wood. (1973) *FLO: A Biography of Frederick Law Olmsted.* Baltimore.

Rorabaugh, W. J. (1976) "Rising Democratic Spirits: Immigrants, Temperance, and Tammany Hall, 1854–1860." *Civil War History* 22:138–57.

———. (1979) *The Alcoholic Republic: An American Tradition.* New York.

———. (1986) *The Craft Apprentice: From Franklin to the Machine Age.* New York.

Rose, Peter G. (1987) "Dutch Colonial Foodways." *Journal of Gastronomy* 4: 3–19.

Rosebrock, Ellen Fletcher. (1975) *Counting-House Days in South Street: New York's Early Brick Seaport Buildings.* New York.

Rosen, Deborah A. (1987) "The Supreme Court of Judicature of Colonial New York: Civil Practice in Transition, 1691–1760." *Law and History Review* 5: 13–47.

———. (1992) "Courts and

Commerce in Colonial New York." *American Journal of Legal History* 36: 139–63.

Rosen, George. (1950) "Politics and Public Health in New York City, 1838–1842." *Bulletin of the History of Medicine.* 24: 441–61.

Rosenberg, Charles. (1962) *The Cholera Years: The United States in 1832, 1849, and 1866.* Chicago.

———, and Carroll S. Rosenberg. (1968) "Pietism and the Origins of the American Public Health Movement: A Note on John H. Griscom and Robert M. Hartley." *Journal of the History of Medicine* 23: 16–35.

———. (1987) *The Care of Strangers: The Rise of America's Hospital System.* New York.

Rosenthal, Bernard. (1985) "Charles Brockden Brown." In *American Writers of the Early Republic,* edited by Emory Elliott. Detroit.

Rosenwaike, Ira. (1972) *The Population History of New York City.* Syracuse, NY.

Rosenzweig, Roy, and Elizabeth Blackmar. (1992) *The Park and the People: A History of Central Park.* Ithaca, NY.

Rosner, David. (1982) *A Once Charitable Enterprise: Health Care in Brooklyn and New York, 1885–1915.* New York.

———, ed. (1995) *Hives of Sickness: Public Health and Epidemics in New York City.* New Brunswick, NJ.

Ross, Dorothy. (1991) *The Origins of American Social Science.* New York.

Ross, Ishbel. (1963) *Crusades and Crinolines: The Life and Times of Ellen Curtis Demorest and William Jennings Demorest.* New York.

Ross, Steven J. (1988) "'Objects of Charity': Poor Relief, Poverty, and the Rise of the Almshouse in Early Eighteenth-Century New York City." In *Authority and Resistance in Early New York,* edited by William Pencak and Conrad Wright. New York.

Roth, Leland. (1983) *McKim, Mead and White, Architects.* New York.

Rothbard, Murray. (1962) *The Panic of 1819: Reactions and Policies*. New York.

Rothman, David. (1990) *The Discovery of the Asylum: Social Order and Disorder in the New Republic*. Rev. ed. Boston.

Rothman, Flora. (1989) *Bad Girls/Poor Girls: A New York History of Social Control from the Alms House to Family Court*. Ph.D. diss., City University of New York.

Rothschild, Nan A. (1990) *New York City Neighborhoods: The 18th Century*. New York.

Rousmaniere, John P. (1980) "Cultural Hybrid in the Slums: The College Woman and the Settlement House, 1889–1894." In *Women's Experience in America*, edited by Esther Katz and Anita Rapone. New Brunswick, NJ.

Rovere, Richard H. (1947) *Howe and Hummel: Their True and Scandalous History*. New York.

Rubin, Joan Shelley. (1991) *The Making of Middlebrow Culture*. Chapel Hill, NC.

Rubin, Joseph Jay. (1973) *The Historic Whitman*. University Park, PA.

Rude, George F. E. (1964) *The Crowd in History: A Study of Popular Disturbances in France and England, 1730–1848*. New York.

Rudolph, Richard, and Scott Ridley. (1986) *Power Struggle: The Hundred-Year War over Electricity*. New York.

Rudy, S. Willis. (1949) *The College of the City of New York: A History, 1847–1947*. New York.

Ruffin, Edmund. (1860) *Anticipations of the Future, to Serve as Lessons for the Present Time*. Richmond, VA.

Rumbarger, John J. (1989) *Profits, Power and Prohibition: Alcohol Reform and the Industrializing of America, 1800–1930*. Albany, NY.

Runcie, John D. (1969) "The Problem of Anglo-American Politics in Bellomont's New York," *WMQ* 26: 191–217.

Rush, Thomas E. (1920) *The Port of New York*. Garden City, NY.

Russell, William Logie. (1945) *The New York Hospital: A History of the Psychiatric Service, 1771–1936*. New York.

Rutland, Robert A. (1955) *The Birth of the Bill of Rights, 1776–1791*. Chapel Hill, NC.

Ryan, Leo. (1935) *Old St. Peter's: The Mother Church of Catholic New York, 1785–1935*. New York.

Ryan, Mary P. (1975) *Womanhood in America: From Colonial Times to the Present*. New York.

———. (1982) *The Empire of the Mother: American Writing About Domesticity, 1830 to 1860*. New York.

———. (1990) *Women in Public: Between Banners and Ballots, 1825–1880*. Baltimore.

Sabine, W. H. W. (1954) *Suppressed History of General Nathaniel Woodhull*. New York.

———. (1973) *Murder, 1776, and Washington's Policy of Silence*. New York.

Sachs, Charles. (1988) *Made on Staten Island: Agriculture, Industry and Suburban Living in the City*. Staten Island, NY.

Sacks, Howard L., and Judith Rose Sacks. (1993) *Way Up North in Dixie: A Black Family's Claim to the Confederate Anthem*. Washington, DC.

Saint, Andrew. (1992) "The Building Art of the First Industrial Metropolis." In *London—World City, 1800–1840*, edited by Celina Fox. New Haven, CT.

Salisbury, Neal. (1982) *Manitou and Providence: Indians, Europeans and the Making of New England, 1500–1643*. New York.

———. (1996) "The Indians' Old World: Native Americans and the Coming of Europeans." *WMQ* 53: 435–58.

Salwen, Peter. (1989) *Upper West Side Story: A History and Guide*. New York.

Sanchez-Korrol, Virginia E. (1983) *From Colonia to Community: The History of Puerto Ricans in New York City, 1917–1948*. Westport, CT.

Sanders, Ronald. (1969) *The Downtown Jews: Portraits of an Immigrant Generation*. New York.

———. (1988) *Shores of Refuge: A Hundred Years of Jewish Emigration*. New York.

Sante, Luc. (1991) *Low Life: Lures and Snares of Old New York*. New York.

Sarna, Jonathan D. (1981) *Jacksonian Jew: The Two Worlds of Mordecai Noah*. New York.

Sauer, Carl Ortwin. (1971) *Sixteenth-Century North America: The Land and the People as Seen by the Europeans*. Berkeley, CA.

———. (1980) *Seventeenth-Century North America*. Berkeley, CA.

Saxton, Alexander. (1984) "Problems of Class and Race in the Origins of the Mass Circulation Press." *AQ* 36: 211–34.

———. (1990) *The Rise and Fall of the White Republic: Class Politics and Mass Culture in Nineteenth-century America*. London.

Scammell, G. V. (1981) *The World Encompassed: The First European Maritime Empires, c. 800 to 1650*. Berkeley, CA.

Schachner, Nathan. (1947) "Alexander Hamilton Viewed by His Friends: The Narratives of Robert Troup and Hercules Mulligan." *WMQ* 4: 203–25.

Schaeffer, K. H., and Elliott Sclar. (1975) *Access for All: Transportation and Urban Growth*. Harmondsworth, UK.

Schama, Simon. (1979) "The Unruly Realm: Appetite and Restraint in Seventeenth Century Holland." *Daedalus* 108: 103–24.

———. (1987) *The Embarrassment of Riches: An Interpretation of Dutch Culture in the Golden Age*. New York.

Scharf, John Thomas. (1886) *History of Westchester County*. Philadelphia.

Scharnhorst, Gary. (1985) *The Lost Life of Horatio Alger, Jr.* Bloomington, IN.

Schaukirk, Rev. Ewald G. ([1887] 1979) *Occupation of New York City by the British*. New York.

Schechter, Stephen L., Wendell Tripp, and Thomas E. Burke, eds. (1990) *The World of the Founders: New York Communities in the Federal Period*. Albany, NY.

Scheer, George F., and Hugh F. Rankin (1957) *Rebels and Redcoats*. New York.

———, ed. (1962) *Private Yankee Doodle*. New York.

Scheiner, Seth M. (1965) *Negro Mecca: A History of the Negro in New York City, 1865–1920*. New York.

Scherzer, Kenneth. (1992) *The Unbounded Community: Neighborhood Life and Social Structure in New York City, 1830–1875*. Durham, NC.

Schickel, Richard. (1960) *The World of Carnegie Hall*. New York.

Schiesl, Martin J. (1977) *The Politics of Efficiency: Municipal Administration and Reform in America, 1800–1920*. Berkeley, CA.

Schiller, Dan. (1980) *Objectivity and the News*. Philadelphia.

Schivelbusch, Wolfgang. (1988) *Disenchanted Night: The Industrialization of Light in the Nineteenth Century*. Berkeley, CA.

Schlesinger, Arthur Meier (1945) *The Age of Jackson*. Boston.

Schlesinger, Arthur M., Jr. (1933) *The Rise of the City, 1878–1898*. New York.

Schluter, Hermann. (1913) *Lincoln, Labor and Slavery: A Chapter from the Social History of America*. New York.

Schneider, David M. (1938–1941) *The History of Public Welfare in New York State*. 2 vols. Chicago.

———. (1980) "The Patchwork of Relief in Provincial New York." In *Compassion and Responsibility: Readings in the History of Social Welfare Policy in the United States*, edited by Frank R. Bruel and Steven J. Diner. Chicago.

Schneider, Dorothee. (1994) *Trade Unions and Community: The German Working Class in New York City, 1870–1900*. Urbana, IL.

Schoenebaum, Eleanora. (1977) "Emerging Neighborhoods: The Development of Brooklyn's Fringe

Areas, 1850–1930." Ph.D. diss., Columbia University.

Schroth, Raymond A. (1974) *The Eagle and Brooklyn: A Community Newspaper, 1841–1955*. Westport, CT.

Schuberth, Christopher J. (1968) *The Geology of New York City and Environs*. Garden City, NY.

Schudson, Michael. (1978) *Discovering the News: A Social History of American Newspapers*. New York.

———. (1984) *Advertising, the Uneasy Persuasion: Its Dubious Impact on American Society*. New York.

Schultz, Ronald. (1995) "Alternative Communities: American Artisans and the Evangelical Appeal, 1780–1830." In *American Artisans: Crafting Social Identity, 1750–1850*, edited by Howard B. Rock, Paul A. Gilje, and Robert Asher. Baltimore.

Schuyler, David. (1986) *The New Urban Landscape: The Redefinition of City Form in Nineteenth-century America*. Baltimore.

Schwartz, Joel. (1972). "Community Building on the Bronx Frontier, Morrisania, 1848–1875." Ph.D. diss., University of Chicago.

Scisco, Louis D. (1901) *Political Nativism in New York State*. New York.

Scobey, David. (1984) "Boycotting the Politics Factory: Labor Radicalism and the New York City Mayoral Election of 1884 [*sic*]." *Radical History Review* 28–30: 280–325.

———. (1989) "Empire City: Politics, Culture, and Urbanism in Gilded-Age New York." Ph.D. diss., Yale University.

———. (1992) "Anatomy of the Promenade: The Politics of Bourgeois Sociability in Nineteenth-century New York." *Social History* 17: 203–227.

Scott, Eleanor. (1933) "Early Literary Clubs in New York City." *American Literature* 5: 7ff.

Scott, Kenneth. (1961) "The Slave Insurrection in New York in 1712." *NYHSQ* 45: 43–74.

———, and Kenn Stryker-Rodda. (1975) *Denizations, Naturalizations, and Oaths of Allegiance in Colonial New York*. Baltimore.

Scoville, Joseph A. (1863–1866) *The Old Merchants of New York City*. 5 vols. New York.

Scroggs, W. O. (1916) *Filibusters and Financiers: The Story of William Walker and his Associates*. New York.

Scudder, Vida Dutton. (1940) *Father Huntington, Founder of the Order of the Holy Cross*. New York.

Scull, G. D., ed. (1882) *The Montresor Journals*. New York.

Sears, Hal D. (1977) *The Sex Radicals: Free Love in High Victorian America*. Lawrence, KS.

Seelye, John. (1984) "'Rational Exultation': The Erie Canal Celebration." *Proceedings of the American Antiquities Society* 94: 241–67.

———. (1991) *Beautiful Machine: Rivers and the Republican Plan, 1755–1825*. New York.

Sell, Henry Blackman, and Victor Weybright. (1955) *Buffalo Bill and the Wild West*. New York.

Sellers, Charles C. (1928) *Lorenzo Dow: The Bearer of the Word*. New York.

Sellers, Charles Grier. (1991) *The Market Revolution: Jacksonian America, 1815–1846*. New York.

Seraile, William. (1977) "New York's Black Regiments during the Civil War." Ph.D. diss., City University of New York.

———. (1991a) "Brooklyn's Colored Society: A Minister's Observation, 1876–1877." *Afro-Americans in New York Life and History* 15: 43–52.

———. (1991b) *Voice of Dissent: Theophilus Gould Steward (1843–1924) and Black America*. Brooklyn.

Seretan, L. Glen. (1979) *Daniel DeLeon: The Odyssey of an American Marxist*. Cambridge, MA.

Serle, Ambrose. (1940) *The American Journal of Ambrose Serle*, edited by E. H. Tatum, Jr. San Marino, CA.

Sernett, Milton C. (1975) *Black Religion and American Evangelicalism: White Protestants, Plantation Missions, and the Flowering of Black Christianity, 1787–1865*. Metuchen, NJ.

Severini, Lois. (1983) *The Architecture of Finance: Early Wall Street*. Ann Arbor, MI.

Seybolt, Robert F. (1918) *The Colonial Citizen of New York: A Comparative Study of Certain Aspects of Citizenship Practices . . .* Madison, NJ.

Seyfried, Vincent. (1982) *Queens: A Pictorial History*. Norfolk, VA.

———. (1984) *300 Years of Long Island City, 1630–1930*. Garden City, NY.

———. (1985) *The Story of Queens Village*. Queens, NY.

———. (1986) *Corona: From Farmland to City Suburb, 1650–1935*. Staten Island, NY.

———. (1995) *Elmhurst: From Town Seat to Megasuburb*. New York.

Seymann, Jerrold, ed. (1939) *Colonial Charters, Patents and Grants to the Communities Comprising the City of New York*. New York.

Shachtman, Tom. (1991) *Skyscraper Dreams: The Great Real Estate Dynasties of New York*. Boston.

Shackel, Paul A. (1985) "Conspicuous Consumption and Class Maintenance: A Case Example from the Nicoll Site, Islip, Suffolk County." In *Historical Archaeology of Long Island. Part I: The Sites*, ed. by Gaynell Stone and Donna Ottusch-Kianka.

Shaftel, Norman. (1978) "A History of the Purification of Milk in New York, or, 'How Now, Brown Cow.'" In *Sickness and Health in America*, edited by Judith W. Leavitt and Ronald L. Numbers. Madison, WI.

Shammas, Carole. (1987) "English Inheritance Law and Its Transfer to the Colonies." *American Journal of Legal History* 31: 145–63.

———, et al., eds. (1987) *Inheritance in America: From Colonial Times to the Present*. New Brunswick, NJ.

Shanaberger, Manuel Scott. (1993) "The Reverend Dr. Edward McGlynn: An Early Advocate of the Social Gospel in the American Catholic Church." Ph.D. diss., University of Virginia.

Shanet, Howard. (1975) *Philharmonic: A History of New York's Orchestra*. New York.

Shank, Theodore, Jr. (1956) "The Bowery Theatre, 1826–1836." Ph.D. diss., Stanford University.

Shanor, Rebecca Read. (1988) *The City that Never Was: Two Hundred Years of Fantastic and Fascinating Plans that Might Have Changed the Face of New York City*. New York.

Sharkey, Robert. (1959) *Money, Class, and Party: An Economic Study of Civil War and Reconstruction*. Baltimore.

Shaw, Peter. (1981) *American Patriots and the Rituals of Revolution*. Cambridge, MA.

Shaw, Richard. (1977) *Dagger John: The Unquiet Life and Times of Archbishop John Hughes of New York*. New York.

Shaw, Ronald E. (1966) *Erie Water West: A History of the Erie Canal, 1792–1854*. Lexington, KY.

———. (1990) *Canals for a Nation: The Canal Era in the United States, 1790–1860*. Lexington, KY.

Shea, John Gilmary, ed. (1878) *The Catholic Churches of New York City*. New York.

Sheehan, Arthur, and Elizabeth O. Sheehan. (1955) *Pierre Toussaint: A Citizen of Old New York*. New York.

Shefter, Martin. (1976) "Emergence of the Political Machine: An Alternative View." In *Theoretical Perspectives on Urban Politics*, edited by Willis D. Hawley, et al. Englewood Cliffs, NJ.

———. (1977) "New York City's Fiscal Crisis: The Politics of Inflation and Retrenchment." *Public Interest* 48: 98–127.

———. (1978) "The Electoral Foundations of the Political Machine: New York City, 1884–1897." In *The History of American Electoral Behavior*, edited by Joel Silbey, Allan G. Bogue, and William H. Flanigan. Princeton, NJ.

——. (1993) "New York City and American National Politics." In *Capital of the American City: National and International Influence of New York City*. New York.

——. (1994) "Political Incorporation and the Extrusion of the Left: The Insertion of Social Forces into American Politics." In Martin Shefter, *Political Parties and the State: The American Historical Experience*. Princeton, N.J.

Sheridan, Eugene R. (1981) *Lewis Morris, 1671–1746: A Study in Early American Politics*. Syracuse, NY.

Sheridan, Richard. (1970) *The Development of the Plantations to 1750: An Era of West Indian Prosperity, 1750–1775*. Barbados.

——. (1974) *Sugar and Slavery: An Economic History of the British West Indies, 1623–1775*. Baltimore.

Shomette, Donald G., and Robert D. Haslach (1988) *Raid on America: The Dutch Naval Campaign of 1672–1674*. Columbia, SC.

Shuffelton, Frank. (1985) "John Daly Burk." In *American Writers of the Early Republic*, edited by Emory Elliott. Detroit.

Shulim, Joseph I. (1964) *John Daly Burk: Irish Revolutionist and American Patriot*. Philadelphia.

Shumway, Floyd M. (1975) *Seaport City: New York in 1775*. New York.

Shy, John. (1965) *Toward Lexington: The Role of the British Army in the Coming of the American Revolution*. Princeton, NJ.

——. (1975) "The Loyalist Problem in the Lower Hudson Valley: The British Perspective." In *The Loyalist Americans: A Focus on Greater New York*, edited by Robert A. East and Jacob Judd. Tarrytown, NY.

——. (1976) *A People Numerous and Armed: Reflections on the Military Struggle for American Independence*. New York.

Sicherman, Barbara, et al., eds. (1980) *Notable Ameri-*

can Women: The Modern Period. Cambridge, MA.

Siles, William H., ed. (1986) "Quiet Desperation: A Personal View of the Panic of 1837." *NYH* 67: 89–92.

Silver, Nathan. (1967) *Lost New York*. Boston.

Silverman, Kenneth. (1976) *A Cultural History of the American Revolution*. New York.

——. (1991) *Edgar A. Poe: Mournful and Never-ending Remembrance*. New York.

Simon, Donald E. (1972) "The Public Park Movement in Brooklyn, 1824–1873." Ph.D. diss., New York University.

Simon, Kate. (1978) *Fifth Avenue: A Very Social History*. New York.

Simpson, Colin. (1986) *Artful Partners: Bernard Berenson and Joseph Duveen*. New York.

Sinclair, David. (1984) *Dynasty: The Astors and Their Times*. New York.

Singer, Aaron. (1986) *Labor Management Relations at Steinway and Sons, 1853–1896*. New York.

Singleton, Esther. (1902) *Social New York Under the Georges, 1714–1776*. New York.

——. (1909) *Dutch New York*. New York.

Sinnette, Elinor Des Verney. (1989) *Arthur Alfonso Schomburg, Black Bibliophile and Collector: A Biography*. New York.

Siry, Steven E. (1990) *De Witt Clinton and the American Political Economy: Sectionalism, Politics, and Republican Ideology, 1787–1828*. New York.

Skemer, Don C. (1975) "New Evidence of Black Unrest in Colonial New York." *Journal of Long Island History* 12: 46–49.

Sklar, Kathryn Kish. (1973) *Catharine Beecher: A Study in American Domesticity*. New Haven, CT.

——. (1995) *Florence Kelley and the Nation's Work*. New Haven, CT.

Sklar, Martin J. (1981) "The Corporate Ascendancy and the Socialist Acquiescence: An Inquiry into Strange Times." *The Maryland Historian* 12: 49–59.

——. (1988) *The Corpo-*

rate Reconstruction of American Capitalism, 1890–1916: The Market, the Law, and Politics. Cambridge, MA.

Skolnick, Richard. (1968) "George Edwin Waring, Jr.: A Model For Reformers." *NYHSQ* 52:4: 354–78.

——. (1971) "The Crystallization of Reform in New York City, 1890–1917." Ph.D. diss., Yale University.

Slaughter, Thomas P. (1985) "Conspiratorial Politics: The Public Life of Aaron Burr." *New Jersey History* 103: 68–85.

Sloane, Eric, and Edward Anthony. (1968) *Mr. Daniels and the Grange*. New York.

Slobin, Mark. (1982) *Tenement Songs: The Popular Music of Jewish Immigrants*. Urbana, IL.

Slotkin, Richard. (1973) *Regeneration Through Violence: The Mythology of the American Frontier, 1600–1860*. Middletown, CT.

——. (1985) *The Fatal Environment: The Myth of the Frontier in the Age of Industrialization, 1800–1890*. New York.

Smelser, Marshall. (1968) *The Democratic Republic, 1801–1815*. New York.

Smit, J. W. (1970) "The Netherlands Revolution," In *The Preconditions of Revolution in Early Modern Europe*, edited by Robert Forster and Jack P. Greene. Baltimore.

Smith, Abbot Emerson. (1947) *Colonists in Bondage: White Servitude and Convict Labor in America, 1607–1776*. Chapel Hill, NC.

Smith, George L. (1973) *Religion and Trade in New Netherland: Dutch Origins and American Development*. Ithaca, NY.

Smith, Henry Nash, comp. (1967) *Popular Culture and Industrialism, 1865–1890*. New York.

Smith, Hiram Leroy. (1989) "Emigration and the Development of the Passenger Trade from the British Isles to New York 1818–1845." Ph.D. diss., Syracuse University

Smith, James Morton, ed. (1959) *Seventeenth-Century America: Essays in Colonial History*. Chapel Hill, NC.

——. (1965) *Freedom's Fetters: The Alien and Sedition Laws and American Civil Liberties*. Ithaca, NY.

Smith, Joseph H. (1978) "Adolpe Philipse and the Chancery Resolves of 1727." In *Courts and Law in Early New York*, edited by Leo Hershkowitz and Milton Klein. Port Washington, NY.

Smith, Philip Chadwick Foster. (1984) *The Empress of China*. Philadelphia.

Smith, Samuel Stelle. (1983) *Lewis Morris: Anglo-American Statesman, ca. 1613–1691*. Atlantic Highlands, NJ.

Smith, Thomas E. V. (1889) *The City of New York in the Year of Washington's Inauguration*. New York.

Smith, Timothy Lawrence. (1957) *Revivalism and Social Reform in Mid-nineteenth-century America*. New York.

Smith, William. (1969–71) *Historical Memoirs . . . of William Smith*. 2 vols. New York.

Smith-Rosenberg, Carroll. (1971) *Religion and the Rise of the American City: The New York City Mission Movement, 1812–70*. Ithaca, NY.

——. (1985) *Disorderly Conduct: Visions of Gender in Victorian America*. New York.

Snyder, Rob. (1989) *Voice of the City: Vaudeville and Popular Culture in New York*. New York.

Snyder-Grenier, Ellen M. (1996) *Brooklyn! An Illustrated History*. Philadelphia.

Sobel, Robert. (1965) *The Big Board: A History of the New York Stock Market*. New York.

——. (1968) *Panic on Wall Street: A History of America's Financial Disasters*. New York.

——. (1970) *The Curbstone Brokers: The Origins of the American Stock Exchange*. New York.

——. (1975) *N.Y.S.E.: A History of the New York*

Stock Exchange, 1935–1975. New York.

Sogliuzzo, A. Richard. (1985) "Shakespeare, Sardou, and Pulcinella: Italian-American Working-Class Theatre in New York, 1880–1940." In *Theatre for Working-class Audiences in the United States, 1830–1980*, edited by Bruce A. McConachie and Daniel Friedman. Westport, CT.

Sokolow, Jayme A. (1983) *Eros and Modernization: Sylvester Graham, Health Reform, and the Origins of Victorian Sexuality in America*. Cranbury, NJ.

Solomon, Barbara Miller. (1985) *In the Company of Educated Women: A History of Women and Higher Education in America*. New Haven, CT.

Somerville, Duncan S. (1983) *The Aspinwall Empire*. Mystic, CT.

Somkin, Fred. (1967) *Unquiet Eagle: Memory and Desire in the Idea of American Freedom, 1815–1860*. Ithaca, NY.

Sorin, Gerald. (1978) *The New York Abolitionists: A Case Study of Political Radicalism*. Westport, CT.

Sosin, Jack. (1982) *English America and the Revolution of 1688: Royal Administration and the Structure of Provincial Government*. Lincoln, NE.

———. (1985) *English America and Imperial Inconstancy: The Rise of Provincial Autonomy, 1696–1715*. Lincoln, NE.

Spalletta, Mateo. (1955) "Divorce in Colonial New York." *NYHSQ* 39: 422–40.

———. (1978) "Divorce in Colonial New York." In *Courts and Law in Early New York*, edited by Leo Hershkowitz and Milton Klein. Port Washington, NY.

Spann, Edward K. (1986a) "Gotham in Congress: New York's Representatives and the National Government, 1840–1854." *NYH* 67: 305–30.

———. (1986b) *The New Metropolis: New York City, 1840–1857*. New York.

———. (1996) "Union Green: The Irish Commu-

nity and the Civil War." In *The New York Irish*, edited by Ronald H. Bayar and Timothy J. Meagher. Baltimore.

Spaulding, E. Wilder. (1932) *New York in the Critical Period, 1783–1789*. New York.

———. (1938) *His Excellency George Clinton, Critic of the Constitution*. New York.

Speek, Peter A. (1917) *The Single Tax and the Labor Movement*. Madison, WI.

Spivak, Burton. (1979) *Jefferson's English Crisis: Commerce, Embargo, and the Republican Revolution*. Charlottesville, VA.

Sproat, John G. (1968) *The Best Men: Liberal Reformers in the Gilded Age*. New York.

Srebnick, Amy Gilman. (1995) *The Mysterious Death of Mary Rogers: Sex, and Culture in Nineteenth-century New York*. New York.

Staiti, Paul J., and Gary A. Reynolds. (1982) *Samuel F. B. Morse*. New York.

———. (1989) *Samuel F. B. Morse*. Cambridge, MA.

Stampp, Kenneth. (1990) *America in 1857: A Nation on the Brink*. New York.

Stankowski, Barbara W. (1977) *Maspeth: Our Town*. Maspeth, NY.

———. (1978) *Old Woodhaven: A Victorian Village*. Flushing, NY.

Stanley, Amy Dru. (1992) "Beggars Can't Be Choosers: Compulsion and Contract in Postbellum America." *JAH* 78: 1265–93.

Stansell, Christine. (1986) *City of Women: Sex and Class in New York, 1789–1860*. New York.

———, and Sean Wilentz. (1994) "Cole's America: An Introduction." In *Thomas Cole: Landscape into History*, edited by William Truettner and Alan Wallach. New Haven, CT.

Stanton, Elizabeth Cady, Susan B. Anthony, and Matilda Joslyn Gage, eds. (1881–1922) *History of Woman Suffrage*. 6 vols. New York.

———. (1898) *Eighty Years and More: Reminiscences, 1815–1897*. New York.

Stapleton, Alfred. (1910) *All About the Merry Tales of Gotham*. 2nd ed. Nottingham, UK.

Starna, William A. (1986) "Seventeenth-Century Dutch-Indian Trade: A Perspective from Iroquoia." *de Halve Maen* 59: 5ff.

Starr, John. (1957) *Hospital City*. New York.

Starr, Paul. (1982) *The Social Transformation of American Medicine*. New York.

Starrett, Col. W. A. (1928) *Skyscrapers and the Men Who Built Them*. New York.

Starrett, Paul. (1938) *Changing the Skyline: An Autobiography*. New York.

Steele, Ian K. (1986) *The English Atlantic, 1675–1740: An Exploration of Communication and Community*. New York.

Steele, Valerie. (1985) *Fashion and Eroticism: Ideals of Feminine Beauty from the Victorian Era to the Jazz Age*. New York.

Steers, Don. (1968) *The Counsellors: Courts and Crimes of Colonial New York*. New York.

Steinmeyer, Henry G. (1975) *Staten Island, 1524–1898*. Rev. ed. Staten Island.

Sterling, David L. (1959) "John Pintard (1759–1844): The First City Inspector of New York." *NYHSQ* 43: 453–63.

———. (1979) "William Duer, John Pintard, and the Panic of 1792." In *Business Enterprise in Early New York*, edited by Joseph Frese and Jacob Judd. Tarrytown, NY.

Steen, Ivan D. (1970) "Palaces for Travelers, New York City's Hotel in the 1850s." *NYH* 51: 269–86.

Stern, Robert A. M., Gregory Gilmartin, and John Montague Massengale. (1983) *New York 1900: Metropolitan Architecture and Urbanism, 1890–1915*. New York.

Stern, Steve. (1974) "Knickerbockers Who Asserted and Assisted: The Dutch Interest in New York Politics, 1664–1691." *NYHSQ* 58: 113–38.

Stevens, George A. (1913) *New York Typographical Union No. 6: A Study of a Modern Trade Union and Its Predecessors*. Albany, NY.

Stewart, James Brewer. (1976) *Holy Warriors: The Abolitionists and American Slavery*. New York.

Stewart, William R. (1911) *The Philanthropic Work of Josephine Shaw Lowell*. New York.

Stiles, Henry R. (1867–1870) *A History of the City of Brooklyn*. 3 vols. New York.

———, ed. (1884) *The Civil, Political, Professional and Ecclesiastical History of County of Kings and City of Brooklyn, N.Y., 1683–1884*. 3 vols. New York.

Still, Bayrd. (1956) *Mirror for Gotham: New York as Seen by Contemporaries from Dutch Days to the Present*. New York.

———. (1982) "The Washington Square Neighborhood, 1830–1855." In *Around the Square, 1830–1890: Essays on Life, Letters, and Architecture in Greenwich Village*, edited by Mindy Cantor. New York.

Stoddard, Lothrop. (1931) *Master of Manhattan: The Life of Richard Croker*. New York.

Stoehr, Taylor, ed. (1979) *Free Love in America: A Documentary History*. New York.

Stoff, Joshua. (1989) *The Aerospace Heritage of Long Island*. Interlaken, NY.

Stokes, I. N. Phelps, comp. (1915–1928) *The Iconography of Manhattan Island, 1498–1909*. 6 vols. New York.

Stone, Gaynell, and Donna Ottusch-Kianka, eds. (1985). *The Historical Archaeology of Long Island. Part I: The Sites*. Stony Brook, NY.

Stone, Jill (1982) *Times Square: A Pictorial History*. New York.

Stone, Richard. (1969) "The Annexation of the Bronx, 1874." *Bronx County Historical Society Journal* 6: 1–24.

Stone, William L. (1825) *Narrative of the Festivities*

Observed in Honor of the Completion of the Grand Erie Canal. New York.

Stott, Richard Briggs. (1990) *Workers in the Metropolis: Class, Ethnicity, and Youth in Antebellum New York City, 1820–1860.* Ithaca, NY.

Stotz, Louis. (1948) *History of the Gas Industry.* New York.

Straka, Gerald M. (1973) *A Certainty in the Succession, 1640–1815.* New York.

Strasser, Susan. (1989) *Satisfaction Guaranteed: The Making of the American Mass Market.* New York.

Strickland, William. (1971) *Journal of a Tour in the United States of America, 1794–1795*, edited by the Rev. J. E. Strickland. New York.

Strong, George Templeton. (1952) *The Diary of George Templeton Strong, 1820–1875.* Edited by Allan Nevis and Milton Helsey Thomas. New York.

Strong, John A. (1997) *The Algonquian Peoples of Long Island from Earliest Times to 1700.* Interlaken, NY.

Strong, Josiah. (1891) *Our Country: Its Possible Future and Its Present Crisis.* New York.

Strong, Thomas Morris. (1842) *The History of the Town of Flatbush.* New York.

Strum, Harvey. (1981) "Property Qualifications and Voting Behavior in New York, 1807–1816." *Journal of the Early Republic* 1: 347–72.

Stuart-Wortley, Emmeline. (1851) *Travels in the United States, Etc., During 1849 and 1850.*

Suggs, Robert C. (1966) *The Archaeology of New York.* New York.

Sullivan, Joseph Patrick. (1995) "From Municipal Ownership to Regulation: Municipal Utility Reform in New York City, 1880–1907." Ph.D. diss., Rutgers University.

Sullivan, Mary Louise. (1992) *Mother Cabrini, "Italian Immigrant of the Century."* New York.

Summers, Mark W. (1987) *The Plundering Generation: Corruption and the Crisis of*

the Union, 1849–1861. New York.

Sunset Park Restoration Committee. (1980?) *Sunset Park: A Time Remembered.* Brooklyn.

Supple, Barry E. (1957) "A Business Elite: German-Jewish Financiers in Nineteenth-century New York." *Business History Review* 31: 43–78.

Sushka, Marie E. (1976) "The Antebellum Money Market and the Economic Impact of the Bank War." *Journal of Economic History* 36: 8009–35.

Sutcliffe, Anthony. (1981) *Towards the Planned City: Germany, Britain, the United States, and France, 1780–1914.* New York.

Sutton, Charles. (1874) *The New York Tombs.* New York.

Swaine, R. T. (1946) *The Cravath Firm.* New York.

Swan, Robert J. (1990) "The Black Presence in Seventeenth-Century Brooklyn." *de Halve Maen* 63: 1–6.

———. (1993) "First Africans into New Netherland, 1625 or 1626?" *de Halve Maen* 56: 75–81.

Swanberg, W. A. (1961) *Citizen Hearst: A Biography of William Randolph Hearst.* New York.

———. (1967) *Pulitzer.* New York.

Swanson, Carl E. (1991) *Preditors and Prizes: American Privateering and Imperial Warfare, 1739–1748.* Columbia, SC.

Sweeney, Kevin M. (1992) "High-Style Vernacular: Lifestyles of the Colonial Elite." In *Of Consuming Interests: The Style of Life in the Eighteenth Century,* edited by Cary Carson, Ronald Hoffman, and Peter J. Albert. Charlottsville, VA.

Swerdlow, Amy. (1976) "Abolition's Conservative Sisters: The Ladies' New York Anti-Slavery Societies, 1834–1840." Paper presented at Third Berkshire Conference.

Swierenga, Robert P. (1994) *The Forerunners: Dutch Jewry in the North American Diaspora.* Detroit.

Swift, David. (1989) *Black Prophets of Justice: Activist*

Clergy Before the Civil War. Baton Rouge, LA.

Sylla, Richard. (1967) "Forgotten Men of Money: Private Bankers in Early U.S. History." *Journal of Economic History* 27: 173–88.

Syrett, Harold. (1944) *The City of Brooklyn, 1865–1898: A Political History.* New York.

———. (1954) "Private Enterprise in New Amsterdam." *WMQ* 9: 536–50.

———, and Jean G. Cooke, eds. (1960) *Interview in Weehawken: The Burr-Hamilton Duel as Told in the Original Documents.* Middletown, CT.

———, ed. (1961–79) *The Papers of Alexander Hamilton.* 26 vols. New York.

Szasz, Ferenc. (1967) "The New York Slave Revolt of 1741: A Reexamination." *NYH* 48: 215–30.

Tabb, William K., and Larry Sawers. (1984) *Marxism and the Metropolis: New Perspectives in Urban Political Economy.* New York.

Taft, Kendall B., ed. (1947) *Minor Knickerbockers.* New York.

Tanis, James. (1967) *Dutch Calvinist Pietism in the Middle Colonies: A Study in the Life and Theology of Theodorus Jacobus Frelinghuysen.* The Hague.

Tarr, Joel. (1979) "The Separate and Combined Sewer Problem: A Case Study in Urban Technology Design Choice." *Journal of Urban History* 5:309.

———, Thomas Finholt, and David Goodman. (1987) "The City and the Telegraph: Urban Telecommunications in the Pre-Telephone Era." *Journal of Urban History* 14: 38–80.

Tarry, Ellen. (1981) *The Other Toussaint: A Modern Biography of Pierre Toussaint: A Post-Revolutionary Black.* Boston.

Tauranac, John. (1979) *Essential New York: A Guide to the History and Architecture of Manhattan's Important Buildings, Parks, and Bridges.* New York.

———. (1985) *Elegant New*

York: The Builders and the Buildings, 1885–1915. New York.

Tax, Meredith. (1980) *The Rising of the Women: Feminist Solidarity and Class Conflict, 1880–1917.* New York.

Taxay, Don. (1970) *Money of the American Indians and Other Primitive Currencies of the Americas.* New York.

Taylor, Clarence. (1994) *The Black Churches of Brooklyn.* New York.

Taylor, George Rogers. (1966) "The Beginnings of Mass Transportation in Urban America: Parts I and II." *Smithsonian Journal of History* 1: 31–54.

Taylor, Lloyd C. (1963) "Josephine Shaw Lowell and American Philanthropy." *NYH,* 44: 336–64.

Taylor, William Robert. (1961) *Cavalier and Yankee: The Old South and American National Character.* New York.

———, ed. (1991) *Inventing Times Square: Commerce and Culture at the Crossroads of the World.* New York.

———. (1992) *In Pursuit of Gotham: Culture and Commerce in New York.* New York.

Tchen, John Kuo Wei. (1990) "New York Chinese: The Nineteenth-century Pre-Chinatown Settlement." In *Chinese America: History and Perspectives.* San Francisco.

———. (1992) *New York Before Chinatown: The Formation of an American Political Culture, 1784–1882.* New York.

———. (1996) "Quimbo Appo's Fear of Fenians: Chinese-Irish-Anglo Relations in New York City." In *The New York Irish,* edited by Ronald H. Bayar and Timothy J. Meagher. Baltimore.

Teaford, Jon C. (1975) *The Municipal Revolution in America: Origins of Modern Urban Government, 1650–1825.* Chicago.

———. (1984) *The Unheralded Triumph: City Government in America, 1870–1900.* Baltimore.

Tebbel, John William. (1972–1981) *A History of*

Book Publishing in the United States. 4 vols. New York.

Temin, Peter. (1969) *The Jacksonian Economy.* New York.

———. (1975) "The Panic of 1857." *Intermountain Economic Review* 6: 1–12.

Thistlethwaite, Frank. (1959) *The Anglo-American Connection in the Early Nineteenth Century.* New York.

Thomas, George. (1989) *Revivalism and Cultural Change: Christianity, Nation Building, and the Market in the Nineteenth-century United States.* Chicago.

Thomas, John L. (1983) *Alternative America: Henry George, Edward Bellamy, Henry Demarest Lloyd, and the Adversary Tradition.* Cambridge, MA.

Thomas, Lately. (1967) *Delmonico's: A Century of Splendor.* Boston.

———. (1969) *The Mayor Who Mastered New York: The Life and Opinions of William J. Gaynor.* New York.

Thomas, M. Wynn. (1987) *The Lunar Light of Whitman's Poetry.* Cambridge, MA.

Thomas, Norman, and Paul Blanshard. (1932) *What's the Matter with New York: A National Problem.* New York.

Thompson, D. G. (1946) *Ruggles of New York: A Life of Samuel B. Ruggles.* New York.

Thompson, George, Jr. (1997) *The African Theater and James Hewlett: A Documentary Study.* Northwestern UP.

Thompson, John, ed. (1966) *Geography of New York State.* New York.

Thorburn, Grant. (1845) *Fifty Years Reminiscences of New York.* New York.

Throsby, John. ([1677] 1797) *Thoroton's History of Nottinghamshire.* London.

Tiedemann, Joseph S. (1976) "Patriots by Default: Queens County, New York, and the British Army, 1776–1783." *WMQ* 43: 35–63.

———. (1983) "Queens County, New York, Quak-

ers in the American Revolution: Loyalists or Neutrals?" *Historical Magazine of the Protestant Episcopal Church* 52: 215–28.

———. (1984) "Communities in the Midst of the American Revolution: Queens County, New York." *Journal of Social History* 18: 644–46.

———. (1987) "Loyalists and Conflict Resolution in Post-Revolutionary New York: Queens County as a Test Case." *NYH* 68: 27–44.

———. (1988) "A Revolution Failed: Queens County, New York, 1775–1776." *AHR* 75: 417–444.

Toll, Robert. (1976) *Blacking-Up.* New York.

Tomasi, Silvano. (1975) *Piety and Power: The Role of the Italian Parishes in the New York Metropolitan Area, 1880–1930.* Staten Island, NY.

Tomkins, Calvin. (1970) *Merchants and Masterpieces: The Story of the Metropolitan Museum of Art.* New York.

Tompkins, Jane. (1985) *Sensational Designs: The Cultural Work of American Fiction, 1790–1860.* New York.

Tomsich, John. (1971) *A Genteel Endeavor: American Culture and Politics in the Gilded Age.* Stanford, CA.

Torres, Andres. (1995) *Between Melting Pot and Mosaic: African Americans and Puerto Ricans in the New York Political Economy.* Philadelphia.

Townsend, Reginald T. (1936) *Mother of Clubs: Being the History of the First Hundred Years of the Union Club of the City of New York, 1836–1936.* New York.

Trachtenberg, Alan. (1982) *The Incorporation of America: Culture and Society in the Gilded Age.* New York.

———. (1989) *Reading American Photographs: Images as History, Mathew Brady to Walker Evans.* New York.

Trager, James. (1987) *West of Fifth: The Rise and Fall of Manhattan's West Side.* New York.

———. (1990) *Park Avenue:*

Street of Dreams. New York.

Trattner, Walter I. (1983) *Social Welfare or Social Control? Some Historical Reflections on Regulating the Poor.* Knoxville, TN.

Trautmann, Frederic. (1980) *The Voice of Terror: A Biography of Johann Most.* Westport, CT.

Trelease, Allen W. (1969) "Dutch Treatment of the American Indian, With Particular Reference to New Netherland." In *Attitudes of Colonial Powers Toward the American Indian,* edited by Howard Peckham and Charles Gibson. Salt Lake City.

———. (1960) *Indian Affairs in Colonial New York: The Seventeenth Century.* Ithaca, NY.

———. (1962) "Indian-White Contacts in Eastern North America: The Dutch in New Netherland." *Ethnohistory* 9: 137–46.

Trimpi, Helen P. (1987) *Melville's Confidence Men and American Politics in the 1850s.* Hamden, CT.

Tripp, Wendell, ed. (1991) *Coming and Becoming: Pluralism in New York State History.* Cooperstown, NY.

Trollope, Frances. (1832) *Domestic Manners of the Americans.* London.

Truax, Rhoda. (1952) *The Doctors Jacobi.* Boston.

Tucher, Andie. (1994) *Froth and Scum: Truth, Beauty, Goodness, and the Ax Murder in America's First Mass Medium.* Chapel Hill, NC.

Tucker, David M. (1991) *The Decline of Thrift in America: Our Cultural Shift from Saving to Spending.* New York.

Tucker, Louis L., ed. (1975) "'To My Inexpressible Astonishment': Admiral Sir George Collier's Observations on the Battle of Long Island." In *Narratives of the Revolution in New York.* New York.

Tully, Alan. (1994) *Forming American Politics: Ideals, Interests, and Institutions in Colonial New York and Pennsylvania.* Baltimore.

Turner, James. (1980) *Reckoning with the Beast: Animals, Pain, and Humanity*

in the Victorian Mind. Baltimore.

Turton, Peter. (1986) *José Martí: Architect of Cuba's Freedom.* London.

Twomey, Richard J. (1989) *Jacobins and Jeffersonians: Anglo-American Radicalism in the United States, 1790–1820.* New York.

Tyack, David B. (1974) *The One Best System: A History of American Urban Education.* Cambridge, MA.

Tyler, J. E. (1975) "A British Whig's Report from New York on the American Situation, 1775." In *Narratives of the Revolution in New York.* New York.

Tyrrell, Ian R. (1979) *Sobering Up: From Temperance to Prohibition in Antebellum America, 1800–1860.* Westport, CT.

Tyrrell, William Blake. (1991) *Athenian Myths and Institutions: Words in Action.* New York.

Ultan, Lloyd, and Gary Hermalyn. (1985) *The Bronx in the Innocent Years, 1890–1925.* New York.

Underhill, Lois Beachy. (1995) *The Woman Who Ran for President: The Many Lives of Victoria Woodhull.* Bridgehampton, NY.

Unger, Irwin. (1964) *The Greenback Era: A Social and Political History of American Finance, 1865–1879.* Princeton, NJ.

United States. Bureau of the Census. (1961) *Historical Statistics of the United States.* Washington, DC.

Unrau, Harlan. (1984) *Ellis Island, Statue of Liberty National Monument, New York–New Jersey.* 3 vols. Washington, DC.

Upton, L. F. S. (1969) *The Loyal Whig: William Smith of New York and Quebec.* Toronto.

Urbanski, Marie, ed. (1994) *Margaret Fuller: Visionary of the New Age.* Orono, ME.

Vail, R. W. G. (1954) *Knickerbocker Birthday: A Sesqui-centennial History of the New-York Historical Society, 1804–1954.* New York.

———. (1956) *Random Notes on the History of the*

Early American Circus. Barre, MA.

———. (1975) "The Loyalist Declaration of Dependence of November 28, 1776." In *Narratives of the Revolution in New York.* New York.

Valentine, David T. (1853) *History of the City of New York.* New York.

Van den Boogaart, Ernst. (1986) "The Servant Migration to New Netherland, 1624–1664." In *Colonialism and Migration: Indentured Labor Before and After Slavery,* edited by P. C. Emmer. Dordrecht.

Van der Donck, Adriaen. ([1841] 1968) *A Description of the New Netherlands.* Edited and translated by Thomas F. O'Donnell. Syracuse, NY.

Van der Zee, Henri, and Barbara Van der Zee. (1978) *A Sweet and Alien Land: The Story of Dutch New York.* New York.

Van Deusen, Arie T. (1991) *Plain Lives in a Golden Age: Popular Culture, Religion, and Society in Seventeenth-Century Holland.* New York.

Van Deusen, Glyndon G. (1947) *Thurlow Weed, Wizard of the Lobby.* Boston.

Van Diver, Bradford B. (1985) *Roadside Geology of New York.* Missoula, MT.

Van Every, Edward. (1930) *Sins of New York, As Exposed by the Police Gazette.* New York.

Van Gelder, Roelof. (1982) "'A Richly Blessed Land Where Milk and Honey Flows': New Netherland Seen by Dutch Eyes." In *The Birth of New York: Nieuw Amsterdam, 1624–1664,* edited by Boudewijn Bakker et al. New York.

Van Laer, Arnold J. F., ed. (1974) *New York Historical Manuscripts: Dutch.* Baltimore.

Van Leeuwen, Thomas A. P. (1988) *The Skyward Trend of Thought: The Metaphysics of the American Skyscraper.* Cambridge, MA.

Van Loon, Hendrik W. (1928) *Adriaen Block: Skipper, Trader, Explorer.* New York.

Van Rensselaer, Mrs. John King. (1898) *The Goede Vrouw of Mana-ha-ta: At Home and in Society, 1609–1760.* New York.

Van Rensselaer, Maria Schuyler. (1909) *History of the City of New York in the Seventeenth Century.* 2 vols. New York.

Van Vleck, George W. (1943) *The Panic of 1857: An Analytical Study.* New York.

Van Zwieten, Adriana. (1996) "The Orphan Chamber of New Amsterdam." *WMQ* 53: 319–40.

Vanderbilt, Gertrude Lefferts. (1881) *Social History of Flatbush.* New York.

Varga, Nicholas. (1956) "The New York Restraining Act: Its Passage and Some Effects, 1766–1768." *NYH* 37: 233–58.

———. (1960) "Election Procedures and Practices in Colonial New York." *NYH* 41: 249–77.

Vecsey, Christopher. (1986) "The Story and Structure of the Iroquois Confederacy." *Journal of the American Academy of Religion* 54: 79–106.

Vedder, Henry C. (1898) *A History of the Baptists in the Middle States.* Philadelphia.

Vega, Bernardo. (1984) *Memoirs of Bernardo Vega: A Contibution to the History of the Puerto Rican Community in New York,* edited by Cesar Andreu Iglesias. Translated by Juan Flores. New York.

Vidal, Gore. (1973) *Burr: A Novel.* New York.

Voorhees, David W. (1989) "Leisler's Pre-1689 Biography and Family Background." *de Halve Maen* 62: 1–7.

———. (1994a) "The 'Fervent Zeale' of Jacob Leisler." *WMQ* 51: 447–72.

———. (1994b) "Hearing . . . What Great Success the Dragonnades in France Had': Jacob Leisler's Huguenot Connections." *de Halve Maen* 67: 15–20.

Wacker, Peter O. (1986) "The Dutch Culture Area in the Northeast, 1609–1800." *New Jersey History* 104: 1–21.

Wagenknecht, Edward. (1972) *Ambassadors for Christ: Seven American Preachers.* New York.

Wagman, Morton. (1979) "Wolfert Gerritsen van Couwenhoven and the Founding of New York." *Journal of Long Island History* 15: 5–22.

———. (1983a) "Liberty in New Amsterdam: A Sailor's Life in Early New York." *NYH* 64: 101–20.

———. (1983b) "The Origin of New York's City Government: From Proprietary Control to Representative Democracy." *de Halve Maen* 57: 6ff.

Wagner, Frederick. (1963) *Submarine Fighter of the American Revolution: The Story of David Bushnell.* New York.

Wakefield, Dan. (1960) *Island in the City: Puerto Ricans in New York.* New York.

Waldstreicher, David L. (1994) "The Making of American Nationalism: Celebrations and Political Culture, 1776–1820." Ph.D. diss., Yale University.

Walker, George E. (1993) *The Afro-American in New York City, 1827–1860.* New York.

Walker, James Blaine. (1970) *Fifty Years of Rapid Transit, 1864–1917.* New York.

Walker, Nancy A. (1993) *Fanny Fern.* New York.

Walker, Pat, ed. (1979) *Between Labor and Capital.* Boston.

Walkowitz, Daniel J. (1993) "The Artisans and Builders of Nineteenth-century New York: The Case of the 1834 Stonecutters' Riot." In *Greenwich Village: Culture and Counterculture,* edited by Rick Beard and Leslie Berlowitz. New Brunswick, NJ.

Walkowitz, Judith R. (1992) *City of Dreadful Delight: Narratives of Sexual Danger in Late-Victorian London.* Chicago.

Wall, Alexander J. (1975) "New York and the Declaration of Independence." In *Narratives of the Revo-lution in New York.* New York.

Wall, Diana diZerega. (1994) *The Archaeology of Gender: Separating the Spheres in Urban America.* New York.

Wallace, Michael. (1968) "Changing Concepts of Party in the United States: New York, 1815–1828." *AHR* 74: 453–91.

Waller, Altina Laura. (1982) *Reverend Beecher and Mrs. Tilton: Sex and Class in Victorian America.* Amherst, MA.

Waller, George M. (1960) *Samuel Vetch: Colonial Enterpriser.* Chapel Hill, NC.

Waller, Henry D. ([1899] 1975) *History of the Town of Flushing.* Harrison, NY.

Wallerstein, Immanuel. (1974) *The Modern World-System I: Capitalist Agriculture and the Origins of the European World-Economy in the 16th Century.* New York.

———. (1974) *The Modern World System II: Mercantilism and the Consolidation of the European World-Economy, 1600–1750.* New York.

———. (1988) *The Modern World-System III: The Second Era of Great Expansion of the Capitalist World-Economy, 1730–1840s.* New York.

Walling, George W. (1887) *Recollections of a New York Chief of Police.* New York.

Walsh, Marie De Lourdes. (1960) *The Sisters of Charity of New York, 1809–1959.* 3 vols. New York.

Walsh, Mary Roth. (1977) *"Doctors Wanted, No Women Need Apply": Sexual Barriers in the Medical Profession, 1835–1975.* New Haven, CT.

Walsh, Walter J. (1996) "Religion, Ethnicty, and History: Clues to the Cultural Construction of Law." In *The New York Irish,* edited by Ronald H. Bayor and Timothy J. Meagher. Baltimore.

Walter, E. V. *Placeways: A Theory of the Human Environment.* Chapel Hill, NC.

Walters, Kerry S., ed. (1990) *Elihu Palmer's "Principles*

of Nature": Text and Commentary. Wolfboro, NH.

Walton, Gary M., and James F. Shepherd. (1979) *The Economic Rise of Early America*. New York.

Wansey, Henry. (1796) *The Journal of an Excursion of the United States of North America in the Summer of 1794* . Salisbury, UK.

Ward, David. (1989) *Poverty, Ethnicity, and the American City, 1840–1925: Changing Conceptions of the Slum and the Ghetto*. New York.

———, and Olivier Zunz, eds. (1992) *The Landscape of Modernity*. New York.

Ward, Geoffrey C. (1994) *Baseball: An Illustrated History*. New York.

Ware, Norman. (1924) *The Industrial Worker, 1840–1860*. Boston.

———. (1929) *The Labor Movement in the United States, 1860–1895*. New York.

Warner, Susan. (1987) *The Wide, Wide World*. New York.

Warnock, James. (1988) "Thomas Bradbury Chandler and William Smith: Diversity Within Colonial Anglicanism." *Anglican and Episcopal History* 57: 272–97.

Warren, Joyce W. (1992) *Fanny Fern: An Independent Woman*. New Brunswick, NJ.

Warshaw, Robert Irving. (1929) *The Story of Wall Street*. New York.

Washburn, Wilcomb. (1971) "History, Anthropology, and the American Indian." *Pacific Historical Review* 42: 261–81.

———. (1975) *The Indian in America*. New York.

Watson, John F. (1846) *Annals and Occurrences of New York City and State in the Olden Time*. Philadelphia.

Watson, Peter. (1992) *From Manet to Manhattan: The Rise of the Modern Art Market*. New York.

Watts, Theodore F. (1983) *The First Labor Day Parade, Tuesday, September 5, 1882: Media Mirrors to Labor's Icons*. Silver Spring, MD

Waugh, Joan. (1992) "Unsentimental Reformer: The Life of Josephine Shaw Lowell." Ph. D. diss., University of California, Los Angeles.

Webb, Stephen Saunders. (1966) "The Strange Career of Francis Nicholson." *WMQ* 23:513–48.

———. (1976) "The Trials of Sir Edmund Andros." In *Human Dimensions of Nation Making*, edited by James Martin. Madison, WI.

———. (1984) *1676: The End of American Independence*. New York.

Webking, Robert H. (1987) "Melancton Smith and the *Letters from the Federal Farmer*." *WMQ* 44: 510–28.

Wecter, Dixon. (1937) *The Saga of American Society: A Record of Social Aspiration, 1607–1937*. New York.

Wegelin, Oscar. ([1915] 1969) *Jupiter Hammon, American Negro Poet: Selections from His Writings and a Bibliography*. New York.

Weidner, Charles H. (1974) *Water for a City: A History of New York City's Problem from the Beginning to the Delaware River System*. New Brunswick, NJ.

Weinbaum, Paul O. (1975) "Temperance, Politics, and the New York City Riots of 1857." *NYHSQ* 59: 246–70.

———. (1979) *Mobs and Demagogues: The New York Response to Collective Violence in the Early Nineteenth Century*. Ann Arbor, MI.

Weinstein, Laurie, ed. (1994) *Enduring Traditions: The Native Peoples of New England*. Westport, CT.

Weinstein, Stephen Frederick. (1984) "The Nickel Empire: Coney Island and the Creation of Urban Seaside Resorts in the United States." Ph.D. diss., Columbia University.

Weisman, Winston. (1953) "New York and the Problem of the First Skyscraper." *Journal of the Society of Architectural Historians* 12: 13–20.

———. (1970) "A New View of Skyscraper History." In *The Rise of an American Architecture*, edited by

Edgar Kaufmann Jr. New York.

Weiss, Nancy Joan. (1968) *Charles Francis Murphy, 1858–1924; Respectability and Responsibility in Tammany Politics*. Northampton, MA.

Weitzenhoffer, Frances. (1986) *The Havemeyers: Impressionism Comes to America*. New York.

Welch, Richard E. Jr. (1979) *Response to Imperialism: The United States and the Philippine-American War, 1899–1902*. Chapel Hill, NC.

Weld, Ralph Foster. (1938) *Brooklyn Village, 1816–1934*. New York.

———. (1950) *Brooklyn Is America*. New York.

Welling, William. (1978) *Photography in America: The Formative Years, 1839–1900*. New York.

Wells, Robert V. (1973) "The New York Census of 1731." *NYHSQ* 57: 255–59.

Werner, John M. (1986) *Reaping the Bloody Harvest: Race Riots in the United States During the Age of Jackson, 1824–1849*. New York.

Werner, M. R. (1928) *Tammany Hall*. Garden City, NY.

———. (1957) *It Happened in New York*. New York.

Werner, Walter, and Steven T. Smith. (1991) *Wall Street*. New York.

Wertenbaker, Thomas Jefferson. (1948) *Father Knickerbocker Rebels: New York City During the Revolution*. New York.

———. (1949) *The Golden Age of Colonial Culture*. Ithaca, NY.

Weslager, C. A. (1961) *Dutch Explorers, Traders, and Settlers in the Delaware Valley, 1609–1664*. Philadelphia.

Wesley, Charles H. (1939) "The Negroes of New York in the Emancipation Movement." *Journal of Negro History* 24: 65–103.

Wessel, Thomas R. (1981) "Agriculture, Indians, and American History." In *The American Indian, Past and Present*, edited by Roger Nichols. New York.

Wexler, Alice. (1984) *Emma Goldman: An Intimate Life*.

New York.

Whiffen, Marcus, and Frederick Koeper. (1981) *American Architecture, 1607–1976*. Cambridge, MA.

Whipple, A.B.C. (1987) *The Challenge*. New York.

Whitby, Gary Lamar. (1984) "The New York Penny Press and the American Romantic Movement." Ph.D. diss., University of Iowa.

Whitcomb, Ian. (1987) *Irving Berlin and Ragtime America*. New York.

White, Gerald T. (1982) *The United States and the Problem of Recovery After 1893*. University, AL.

White, Norval. (1987) *New York: A Physical History*. New York.

White, Philip L. (1953) "Municipal Government Comes to Manhattan." *NYHSQ* 37: 146–57.

———. (1956) *The Beekmans of New York in Politics and Commerce, 1646–1877*. New York.

White, Shane. (1986) "Impious Prayers: Elite and Popular Attitudes towards Blacks and Slavery in the Middle Atlantic States, 1783–1810." *NYH* 67: 261–83.

———. (1988) "'We Dwell in Safety and Pursue Our Honest Callings': Free Blacks in New York City, 1783–1810." *JAH* 75: 445–70.

———. (1989a) "Pinkster in Albany, 1803: A Contemporary Description." *NYH* 70: 191–99.

———. (1989b) "A Question of Style: Blacks in and Around New York City in the Late Eighteenth Century." *Journal of American Folklore* 102: 23–44.

———. (1991) *Somewhat More Independent: The End of Slavery in New York City, 1770–1810*. Athens, GA.

———. (1994) "'It Was a Proud Day': African-Americans, Festivals, and Parades in the North, 1741–1834." *JAH* 81: 13–50.

Whiteaker, Larry H. (1977) "Moral Reform and Prostitution in New York City, 1830–1860." Ph.D. diss., Princeton University.

Whiteman, Anne, J. S. Bromley, and Peter Dickinson, eds. (1973) *Statesmen, Scholars, and Merchants: Essays in Eighteenth-Century History*. Oxford.

Whiteman, Maxwell. (1971) *Copper for America: The Hendricks Family and a National Industry, 1755–1939*. New Brunswick, NJ.

Whitman, Walt. (1949) *Democratic Vistas*. New York.

———. (1950) *Walt Whitman of the New York Aurora: Editor at Twenty-two: A Collection of Recently Discovered Writings*, edited by Joseph Jay Rubin and Charles H. Brown. Westport, CT.

———. (1963) *Walt Whitman's New York: From Manhattan to Montauk*, edited by Henry M. Christman. New York.

———. (1973) *Leaves of Grass: Authoritative Texts, Prefaces, Whitman on his Art, Criticism*. Edited by Sculley Bradley and Harold W. Blodgett. New York.

Widmer, Edward Ladd. (1993) "Young America: Democratic Cultural Nationalism in Antebellum New York." Ph.D. diss., Harvard University.

Wilcoxen, Charlotte. (1984) *Seventeenth-Century Albany: A Dutch Profile*. Rev. ed. Albany, NY.

Wilder, Craig Steven. (1994) "A Covenant With Color: Race and the History of Brooklyn, New York." Ph.D. diss., Columbia University.

Wilentz, Sean. (1983) "Artisan Republican Festivals and the Rise of Class Conflict in New York City, 1788–1837." In *Working-Class America: Essays on Labor, Community, and American Society*, edited by Michael Frisch and Daniel Walkowitz. Urbana, IL.

———. (1984) *Chants Democratic: New York City and the Rise of the American Working Class, 1788–1950*. New York.

Wilf, Steven Robert. (n.d.) "Anatomy of an Execution: New York City,

1797." Unpublished manuscript.

Wilkenfeld, Bruce M. (1971) "The New York City Common Council, 1689–1800." *NYH* 52: 249–73.

———. (1976a) "New York City Neighborhoods, 1730." *NYH* 57: 165–82.

———. (1976b) "Revolutionary New York, 1776." In *New York: The Centennial Years, 1676–1976*, ed. by Milton M. Klein. Port Washington, NY.

———. (1977) "The New York Shipowning Community, 1715–1764." *American Neptune* 37:50–65.

———. (1978) *The Social and Economic Structure of the City of New York, 1695–1796*. New York.

Wilkins, Mira. (1989) *The History of Foreign Investment in the United States to 1914*. Cambridge, MA.

Williams, James Homer. (1995) "Great Doggs and Mischievous Cattle: Domesticated Animals and Indian Relations in New Netherland and New York." *NYH* 76: 245–64.

Williams, Marilyn Thornton. (1991) *Washing "The Great Unwashed": Public Baths in Urban America, 1840–1920*. Columbus, OH.

Williams, Raymond. (1973) *The Country and the City*. New York.

Williams, Roger L., ed. (1968) *The Commune of Paris, 1871*. New York.

Williams, William Appleman. (1969) *The Roots of the Modern American Empire: A Study of the Growth and Shaping of Social Consciousness in a Marketplace Society*. New York.

Williamson, Chilton. (1960) *American Suffrage: From Property to Democracy, 1760–1860*. Princeton, NJ.

Willis, Edmund P. (1967) "Social Origins of Political Leadership in New York City from the Revolution to 1815." Ph.D. diss., University of California, Berkeley.

Wilson, Charles. (1968) *The Dutch Republic and the Civilisation of the Seventeenth Century*. New York.

Wilson, Clint C. (1991) *Black Journalists in Paradox: Historical Perspectives and Current Dilemmas*. New York.

Wilson, Joan Hoff. (1976) "The Illusion of Change: Women and the American Revolution." In *The American Revolution: Explorations in the History of American Radicalism*, edited by Alfred Young. DeKalb, IL.

Wilson, Richard Guy. (1983) *McKim, Mead, and White, Architects*. New York.

Wilson, Rufus R. (1947) *New York in Literature: The Story Told in Landmarks of Town and Country*. Elmira, NY.

Winkler, John Kennedy. (1934) *The First Billion: The Stillmans and the National City Bank*. New York.

Winthrop, John. (1996) *The Journal of John Winthrop*, edited by Richard S. Dunn, James Savage, and Laetitia Yeandle. Cambridge, MA.

Wittke, Carl. (1952) *Refugees of Revolution: The German Forty-Eighters in America*. Philadelphia.

Wolf, Eric R. (1982) *Europe and the People Without History*. Berkeley, CA.

Wolfe, Gerard R. (1994) *New York: A Guide to the Metropolis: Walking Tours of Architecture and History*. 2nd ed. New York.

Woll, Allen. (1989) *Black Musical Theatre: From Coontown to Dreamgirls*. Baton Rouge, LA.

Wolley, Charles. ([1679] 1902) *A Two Years' Journal in New York*, edited by Edward G. Bourne. Cleveland.

Wood, Gordon S. (1974) "The Authorship of the *Letters from the Federal Farmer*." *WMQ* 31: 299–308.

Woodward, C. Vann. (1951) *Reunion and Reaction: The Compromise of 1877 and the End of Reconstruction*. Boston.

W.P.A. (1938a) Federal Writers' Project of the Works Progress Administration (later, Work Projects Administration). *The Italians of New York*. New York.

———. (1938b) *New York Panorama: A Companion to the WPA Guide to New York City*. New York.

———. ([1939], 1982) *The WPA Guide to New York City*. New York.

———. (1941) *A Maritime History of New York*. Garden City, NJ.

Wright, Carol. (1983) *New York: Blue Guide*. New York.

Wright, Conrad E. (1984) "Merchants and Mandarins: New York and the Early China Trade." In *New York and the China Trade*, edited by David Howard. New York.

Wright, Esmond. (1975) "The New York Loyalists: A Cross-Section of Colonial Society." In *The Loyalist Americans: A Focus on Greater New York*, edited by Robert A. East and Jacob Judd. Tarrytown, NY.

Wright, Esther Clark. (1984) "The Evacuation of the Loyalists from New York in 1783." *Nova Scotia Historical Review* 4: 5–27.

Wright, Langdon G. (1973) "Local Government and Central Authority in New Netherland." *NYHSQ* 57: 7–29.

———. (1980) "In Search of Peace and Harmony: New York Communities in the Seventeenth Century." *NYH* 61: 5–22.

Wright, Louis B. (1957) *The Cultural Life of the American Colonies, 1607–1763*. New York.

———. (1968) *Life on the American Frontier*. New York.

Wunsch, James Lemuel. (1976) "Prostitution and Public Policy: From Regulation to Suppression, 1858–1920." Ph.D. diss., University of Chicago.

Wust, Klaus. (1984) *Guardian on the Hudson: The German Society of the City of New York, 1784–1984*. New York.

Wyatt-Brown, Bertram. (1969) *Lewis Tappan and the Evangelical War Against Slavery*. Cleveland.

Yearley, Clifton K. (1970) *The Money Machines: The Breakdown and Reform of Governmental and Party

Finance in the North, 1860–1920. Albany, NY.

Yellowitz, Irwin, ed. (1978) *Essays in the History of New York City: A Memorial to Sidney Pomerantz.* Port Washington, NY.

Yoshpe, Harry B. (1939) *The Disposition of Loyalist Estates in the Southern District of the State of New York.* New York.

Young, Alfred. (1967) *The Democratic Republicans of New York: The Origins, 1763–1797.* Chapel Hill, NC.

———, ed. (1976) *The American Revolution: Explorations in the History of American Radicalism.*

DeKalb, IL.

Young, Philip. (1977) *Revolutionary Ladies.* New York.

Younger, William Lee. (1978) *Old Brooklyn in Early Photographs, 1865–1929.* New York.

Zahler, Helene Sara. (1941) *Eastern Workingmen and National Land Policy, 1829–1862.* New York.

Zboray, Ronald J. (1993) *A Fictive People: Antebellum Economic Development and the American Reading Public.* New York.

Zeichner, Oscar. (1940) "The Loyalist Problem in New York after the Revolution." *NYH* 21: 284–302.

Zeisloft, E. Idell, ed. (1899) *The New Metropolis: 1600—Memorable Events of Three Centuries—1900; from the Island of Manahat-ta to Greater New York at the Close of the Nineteenth Century.* New York.

Zellers, Parker. (1971) *Tony Pastor: Dean of the Vaudeville Stage.* Ypsilanti, MI.

Zelizer, Viviana A. Rotman. (1979) *Morals and Markets: The Development of Life Insurance in the United States.* New York.

Zelnick, Stephen. (1979–80) "Melville's 'Bartleby': History, Ideology, and Literature." *Marxist Perspectives* 2: 74–92.

Ziegler, Philip. (1988) *The Sixth Great Power: A History of One of the Greatest of All Banking Families, the House of Barings, 1762–1929.* New York.

Zilversmit, Arthur. (1967) *The First Emancipation: The Abolition of Slavery in the North.* Chicago.

Zornow, William Frank. (1954) *Lincoln and the Party Divided.* Norman, OK.

Zweig, Paul. (1984) *Walt Whitman: The Making of the Poet.* New York.

Zwierlein, Frederick J. (1910) *Religion in New Netherland, 1623–1664.* Rochester, NY.

Acknowledgments

One measure of how long this project has gone on is that so many of the people we most wanted to read the finished product are no longer around to do so.

For EGB that list includes my grandmother, Eleanor Cary Lemon, as well as my grandfathers, Prof. Millar Burrows of Yale University and the Rev. William Philip Lemon, scholars as well as men of faith, each of whom had set aside a place on his shelves for such a book as *Gotham*. I am sorry that Gerard Mutsaers, a Dutchman who took such pride in escorting friends around the Netherlands, did not live long enough to read about the role of his native country in the city's early history.

Among the family members whose absence I (MW) most regret are my mother, Margaret Wallace (I miss her joyful curiosity and unflagging support), my father, Aaron Wallace (I miss his wit and political empathy), and my uncle, Sol Isaacs (who, until his death at ninety-five, was still sharing laser-sharp memories of life as a New York garment presser and union man). Among mentors and friends I wish were here to share the satisfaction are Richard Hofstadter, a man who asked big questions and answered them with artistry and authority; Joe Murphy, former CUNY chancellor, crusader for working class educational opportunity and a strong supporter of this book; Herb Gutman, Raphael Samuel, Warren Susman, and Edward Thompson—model activist intellectuals all; and Tony Lukas, David Varas, and Elliot Willensky, who were looking forward to *Gotham* but departed way before their time.

Happily, there are vast numbers still around to share our delight and receive our thanks, beginning with those closest to us, those who've endured The Book, helped us to survive it, and—mainly—shared and enriched our lives.

There is no one to whom I (EGB) am more beholden for firm anchorage and steady encouragement than my wife, Pat Adamski. Our life together began more than two decades ago with a rollicking late-night jaunt up Fifth Avenue, and it was during one of our many subsequent urban reconnaissances that I decided to launch a course at Brooklyn College on the history of the city. I am humbled by the thought that even while building her own distinguished career as a legal scholar and educator, she also found the time and energy to bear with me during the years that followed, as *Gotham* struggled toward completion. There are no words to encompass my wonder at the loving patience of our children, Matt and Kate, who have waited their entire lives for "daddy's book" to be done, unaware of how many times their presence revived my spirits and kept me going until it was, in fact, done. My parents, E. G. Burrows and Gwenyth L. Burrows, not only brought me up to value good books and good writing but seemed to understand why *Gotham* required so long to finish. I am much obliged as well to Eric McKitrick and Richard Hofstadter, my teachers at Columbia University, whose guidance, praise, and friendship made all the difference to a young graduate student.

My (MW) wife, Hope Cooke—wise counsellor, historical compeer, voluptuous playmate (for the full encomium see my *Mickey Mouse and Other Essays on American Memory*)—shared my love of the city and pleasure in exploring its past and present. Hope also provided me with a new family—Hope Leezum, Palden, and Kesang, and now our grandchildren, Khendum and Diki. My sister, Penny, offered sibling love and helped keep me laughing. Anne Leiner was my wise, caring, and transformative counsellor. Marion Skelly and Lauree Wise were skillful healers when mind-and-body flagged. My old friend Bob Padgug has been waiting for this book as long as he can remember. Finally, some long overdue thanks to a trio of teachers—Eric McKitrick, who among other lessons taught me I didn't yet know how to write; Jim Shenton, who through example and exhortation got me into the history business; and Walter Metzger, who one day, without realizing it, broached the concept of a life project.

It's quite insufficient to thank Frances Goldin for being our "agent." She is as much a "principal" in this project as we are—third paddle in our canoe. Frances is, to be sure, a superb literary representative, but her personal steadfastness and politically principled support were as important as her skillfulness. Without her deep caring, astonishing patience, and resolute determination this book would not likely have seen the light of day.

Many mavens helped us negotiate the churning currents of the big city's publishing industry. Vincent Virga, novelist, historian, and photo editor par excellence, was our crucial pillar and counsellor during many critical moments. The late Jerry Kaplan understood immediately what we wanted to do and opened the first of what would be many doors. Andre Schiffrin and Peter Dimock provided wise tactical and strategic advice. David Klein, Robert Youdelman, Leon Friedman, Bardyl Tirana, and Kellis Parker helped steer us through some legal rapids. Eddie Ellis offered the fruits of his encyclopedic labor and much of his library. Marty Duberman pointed us to Frances, and Sydelle Kramer, Frances's associate, pointed out a productive path at a fork in the road. We thank too those in the publishing world who had faith in us at an earlier stage—Jim Silberman, Dominick Anfuso, Michael Denneny, Aaron Asher, Philip Pochoda, Arthur Samuelson—and we thank those who didn't, for spurring us to greater effort.

All praise to Laura Brown, publisher at Oxford University Press, for having the courage and enthusiasm to tackle such a massive project and for doing so with such gusto and expertise. Sheldon Meyer, a richly experienced editor of the old school (long may it prosper), helped us slim down our manuscript from preposterous to merely gargantuan proportions. The artistry and commitment of India Cooper added luster to the copyediting profession. Susan Day, Brandon Trissler, Adam Bohannon, Pat Burns, Joellyn Ausanka, Mary Ellen Curley, and Russell Perreault formed the team that took *Gotham* from hard drive to hard copy.

Both of us work in a great if currently beleaguered institution, the City University of New York, and we would like to thank our respective colleges and colleagues for their many years of support.

At Brooklyn College, EGB has had the good fortune to share an office with an old friend, Don Gerardi, whose encyclopedic knowledge of the city's religious history proved indispensable on more than one occasion. Teo Ruiz and Tim Gura, eminent teachers as well as deep-dyed New Yorkers, have been generous and loyal comrades, off campus and on. During his year as a visiting professor at Brooklyn, Peter Charles Hoffer read the first half of the manuscript with uncommon diligence and kept reminding me to let go of it. As a graduate student, Sara Gronim untangled some puzzling aspects of Kieft's war; as a new colleague, she has willingly shared her work on Jane Colden and the study of science in eighteenth-century New York. Thanks, too, to Christoph Kimmich, former chairman of the History Department, Provost of the College, and now interim Chancellor of the University, who has been a sturdy advocate of this and other scholarly projects. A tip of the hat, finally, to the many hundreds of students who have joined me over the years in History 44 ("Burrows on the Boroughs," as one of them called it): your boundless curiosity about the city's past and your steadfast belief in its future should be an example to us all.

I must also pay my respects to a small coterie of Gothamites who, though not at Brooklyn College, vetted great blocs of manuscript and responded with such good grace to my appeals for additional assistance that they might as well have occupied offices just down the hall: Charles Gehring of the New Netherland Project in Albany; Milton Klein, prolific doyen of early New York historians; Howard Rock, who also freely shared his collection of New York pictures; and David Voorhees, editor of *de Halve Maen* and the Jacob Leisler Papers.

At MW's John Jay College of Criminal Justice, President Gerald Lynch has been a staunch backer of this enterprise and over the years has put the resources of the College behind it. Former Vice President John Collins was long a beamish supporter. In recent years Provost Basil Wilson, an ardent sponsor of intellectual enterprise at the College, arranged crucial time off for writing. My heartfelt thanks to them and to former Dean John Cammett and once-and-future Chairman Isidore Silver (for bringing me to Jay a quarter century ago) and to colleagues past and present who buoyed me up over the long years of Gothamizing: Bob Banowicz, Paul Brenner, Blanche Wiesen Cook, Eli Faber, Dan Gasman, Mary Gibson, Carol Groneman, Ann Lane, Jacob Marini, Gerry Markowitz, Joe O'Brien, Bill Preston, Jay Sexter, and Howard Umansky, among many others. I want in particular to salute my students, who in their extraordinary diversity and their determined pursuit of education (often under the most difficult of circumstances) truly represent what's best about New York. In teaching them, I learned a great deal about our city and discovered new and better ways to tell its story.

We have been jointly and severally fortunate in receiving financial assistance, which afforded us that most precious of resources, time. In this project's long foreground, MW was assisted by a 1976 Victor Rabinowitz Foundation grant, and in 1980 the authors together received a Research Fellowship from the National Institute for Humanities— another beleaguered and worthy public institution. In *Gotham*'s latter days, the Wolfe Institute for the Humanities at Brooklyn College gave EGB a year off in 1992–93; the N.E.H. gave MW a College Teaching Fellowship in 1993, and the American Council of Learned Societies awarded him a fellowship in 1994. The authors and Oxford University Press would like to thank Furthermore . . . , the publication program of The J.M. Kaplan Fund, which helped leaven our texty loaf with a grant to enhance its graphics component. A special thank-you to Joan Davidson of Furthermore . . . .

Libraries! Treasuries of source material and constellations of knowledgeable and helpful souls. Wayne Furman, who runs the Allen Room—the New York Public Library and Frederick Lewis Allen's superlative gift to authors—provided us with our indispensable home away from homes and a direct pipeline into the NYPL's magnificent collections. Mark Piel, spirited director of an even more venerable local institution, the New York Society Library (1754), repeatedly extended himself, and his material, on our behalf. The New-York Historical Society—yet another threatened scholarly institution and indeed one that nearly foundered during the course of this project—offered invaluable resources. So did the Brooklyn Historical Society and the Museum of the City of New York. EGB is grateful to the staff of the Brooklyn College Library, past and present, who have so often extended themselves to retrieve obscure materials. MW offers special thanks to the Lloyd Sealy Library at John Jay College, whose superb staff over the years—including Marilyn Lutzker, Eileen Rowland, Bob Grappone, Tony Simpson, Bonnie Nelson, Kathy Halloran, Janice Dunham, Marvie Brooks—assembled a deep and rich collection of metropolitania.

The authors have also drawn upon scores of specialized libraries and of history museums as well. Among them are the Abigail Adams Smith Museum, Bronx County Historical Society, Bronx Museum of the Arts, Ellis Island Immigration Museum, Engineering Societies Library, Fort Wadsworth, General Society of Mechanics and Tradesmen Library, Harbor Defense Museum, Historic Richmond Town, Jewish Museum, King Manor Museum, Lower East Side Tenement Museum, Masonic Hall Library and Museum, Merchants' House Museum, Morris-Jumel Mansion, Museum of Chinese in America, New York Transit Museum, New York City Fire Museum, Police Academy Museum, Queens Historical Society, Schomburg Center for Research in Black Culture, Skyscraper Museum, South Street Seaport, Valentine-Varian House, and the Weeksville Society.

We have been helped in accumulating primary and secondary source materials by David Paskin, Kesang Namgyal, Marcia Caro, Jacqueline Talamas, and Nuria Agullo. Thanks also to Marilyn Atkins-Nelson and Ana Argueta.

Our greatest debt—apart from that we owe the legions of scholars upon whose work we have drawn—is to those friends, colleagues, and family members who took out often inordinate amounts of time to read portions of this opus as it issued from our computers. In the beginning there was Roy Rosenzweig, himself a scholar of the city and a preeminent practitioner of public history. Roy read reams of our earliest prose, offered first-rate criticism, and gave encouragement and enthusiasm when it counted most. Roy was followed by many others who contributed advice, information, and many other kinds of support. We've been helped by outstanding academics from a wide variety of fields and by tour guides, history buffs, political activists, architects, lawyers, engineers, journalists, union leaders, and historic preservationists, among many others.

With regrets for lacking space to give them adequate personal recognition, we salute and thank Jean-Christophe Agnew, David Amram, Jeanie Attie, David Birnbaum, Dan Bluestone, Pat Bonomi, Steve Brier, Josh Brown, Ric Burns, Paul Byard, Barbara Cohen, Page Cowley, Jacques D'Amboise, Bruce Davidson, Susan Davis, Gloria Deák, Vicki DeGrazia, Kanak Mani Dixit, Joe Doyle, Edward Robb Ellis, Jason Epstein, Liz Fee, Joe Fried, Deborah Gardner, Marvin Gelfand, Eugene Genovese, Brendan Gill, David Gordon, Christopher Gray, Carolyn Grimstead, Herb Gutman, John Halpern, Erich Hartmann, Susan Henderson, Ken Jackson, Brooks Jones, Alfred Kazin, Derek Keene, Thomas Kessner, Barbara Kirshenblatt-Gimblett, Jeff Kroessler, Richard Lieberman, Tony Lukas, Harry Magdoff, Pedro Mateos, David Melville, Mike Merrill, Simon Middleton, Jane Miliken, Sandy Miller, John Mulligan, Charles Musser, Palden Namgyal, David Nasaw, De Nederlandsche Bank, Peter Neill, Paul Otto, Chimie Pemba, T. T. Pemba, Mike Pertschuk, the members of the Radical History Review Collective, Paul Resnik, Dick Roberts, Dan Schiller, Dinitia Smith, Deborah Solbert, Peter Solbert, Paul Sweezey, Bill Tabb, Walter Thabit, Danny Walkowitz, Margaret Wallace, Suzanne Wasserman, Jon Wiener, Sean Wilentz, Bill Wise, Alan Wolfe, and Sally Yarmolinsky.

In the home stretch, supplementing Sheldon Meyer's sharp-eyed rereadings, three people plowed through the entire manuscript. Eric Foner brought his wide-ranging historical expertise to bear and provided a sweeping and reassuring assessment. Betsy Blackmar, a penetrating scholar of the city, gave the manuscript a brilliant, cranky, loving, and tough-minded going over—exactly what it needed. For Hope Cooke, herself a virtuoso metropolitan historian (see her *Seeing New York*), this was but the latest journey through these pages, having read every preceding draft, and her final insights were as invaluable as all her earlier ones.

Index of Names

Index of Subjects

Rent (continued)
George's views about, 1099; and immigrants, 1123; in late nineteenth century, 933, 959, 1024, 1078, 1099, 1174; of luxury apartments, 1078; in mid-nineteenth century, 770, 807, 846; and Panic of 1857, 846; for piers, 949; in post-revolutionary New York, 301
Representation: and ratification of Constitution, 289, 290
Republican Motherhood, 284–85, 799
Republicanism: and art world, 379; artisanal, 394–95, 553; betrayal of, 980; and blacks, 400; and class issues, 324, 372, 518; in colonial and revolutionary New York, 221, 231, 244, 257, 275; and consumerism, 879; and Crash of 1873, 1026; and Democratic-Republicans, 323; in early nineteenth century, 315–19, 320, 323, 324, 330, 465–67, 507, 509–11, 518; and education, 509–10; in 1830s, 543, 553; and elites, 465–67; in France, 320, 395, 397, 1034; and gender, 283, 284; and immigrants, 543; and Irish, 401, 752, 1004–5; in late nineteenth century, 1004–5, 1026, 1034; and manifest destiny, 652; in mid-nineteenth century, 829, 830, 835; and money and banking, 304–5; and morality, 301; and neutrality, 318; and organized labor, 414; and patriotism, 405; and politics, 394–95; and poor/poverty, 394–95; in post-revolutionary New York, 278, 280, 283, 284, 295, 301, 304–5, 306; and prisons, 366; radical, 396–97, 510–11; and ratification of constitution, 295; and religion, 396–97; and selection of federal capital, 301; in 1790s and early 1800s, 366, 372, 379, 394–95, 396–97, 401, 405; and slavery, 553; and Statue of Liberty, 1034; and Tammany societies, 316; and Tories, 278, 317–18; and unemployment, 1026; and voting, 330; and women's role in society, 407; and working class, 317

Republicans: blacks as, 857, 858–60, 862, 1034; and Catholics, 853, 862; and city-state relations, 835–36, 837, 838; and Civil War, 864, 865, 866, 867, 869, 876, 879, 880, 885, 886, 888, 889–90, 893, 894, 895–97, 902, 903; and Consolidation, 1220, 1227, 1231, 1233, 1234; and consumerism, 879; and Crash of 1873, 1029; and draft riot, 889–90, 893, 894, 895–97; and elections of 1860, 864–65; and elections of 1864, 901–3; and elections of 1886, 1099; and entertainment, 1154; and events leading to Civil War, 853, 854, 857, 858–60, 861–62, 863; and financial system, 988; and Good Government, 1191–94, 1201, 1203, 1205, 1206; and immigrants, 853, 862; and Irish, 853; in late nineteenth century, 983, 987, 988, 1005, 1010, 1029, 1034–35, 1047, 1099, 1105, 1106, 1109, 1154; 1191–94, 1201, 1203, 1205, 1206; in mid-nineteenth century, 835–36, 850, 851, 853, 854, 857, 858–60, 861–62, 863; and municipal government, 1109; and organized labor, 988; and Panic of 1857, 850; and Panic of 1861, 866; and poor relief, 1029; and Reconstruction, 1034–35; and reform, 880; rise of, 857, 861; and slavery, 853, 858–60, 862, 885; and toppling of Tweed, 1010; war chest of, 1205; and Whigs, 860; and Wood administration, 850, 851
Rescue Home for Fallen and Homeless Girls, 1158
Reservoirs, 848, 954
Restaurants, 323, 437, 723–24, 814, 947, 948. *See also* Delmonico's restaurant
Retailers: and British occupation of New York, 247; as Clinton supporters, 257; in colonial New York, 124, 125, 181, 183, 187, 188, 192; and commercial expansion, 437; in early nineteenth century, 330, 339–40, 437, 487, 530; and economy, 192; in 1830s, 600, 607; entertainment for, 487, 1134; and evangelical religion, 530; in Hanover Square, 183;

houses for, 188; immigrants as, 739–40; and land prices, 187; in late nineteenth century, 970, 974, 1057, 1134; as loyalists, 219; in mid-nineteenth century, 739–40, 845; and middle-class, 970, 974; and money, 308; and Panic of 1857, 845; and politics, 152, 181, 267; in post-revolutionary New York, 257, 267, 308; and resistance to British policies, 205; in revolutionary New York, 219, 229; in 1790s and early 1800s, 372; and transportation, 1057; voting by, 330; women as, 183; workplace of, 142. *See also* Department stores
Revenue Act (1764). *See* Sugar Act
Reviewing literature/plays, 684
Revolution of 1830, 567–68
Revolution (journal), 983–85, 989, 990
Revolution Settlement, 283
Revolutionary New York: blockade of, 251; British evacuate, 259–61; British occupation of, 245–59; British troops return to, 228–29, 231–44; burnings of, 241–42, 250; as center of British power in America, 246; collapse of government in, 223–24; corruption in, 251–52; fall of, 240–44; as headquarters for British troops, 228; population of, 245; port closed in, 224; Provincial Congress assumes control of, 223–24; social life in, 247–48, 249; and suspension of hostilities, 256, 257; Tory flight from, 224, 226, 227, 230; vulnerability of, 226, 234; Washington abandons, 241–42
Revolutions of 1848, 657, 762, 769, 895
Rhinelander Sugar House, 1084
Rhode Island, 28, 63, 121, 285, 292
Rhynder Street, 439
Rialto. *See* Theater
Richmond: in colonial New York, 91, 103–4, 128, 219–20; and Consolidation, 1220, 1234; delegates to Provincial Congress from, 225; in early and mid-nineteenth century, 581, 838; and

ratification of Constitution, 291, 293; slavery in, 285
Richmond Hill, 178, 229, 324, 338, 447, 448, 972
Richmond Road, 8
Rickett's Equestrian Circus, 369, 379, 406
Ridgewood Reservoir, 837
Riker's Island, 656, 897, 1196
Ringling circus, 1148
River pirates, 757
River Road. *See* Pearl Street
Riverdale, 718, 1055
Riverside Drive, 1044
Riverside Park, 929, 1011, 1190
Rivington Street, 364, 532, 745, 787, 1000, 1118, 1120, 1176, 1188
Roach Guards, 633
Roach's ironworks, 1065
Robberies, 999, 1000
Robinson Hall, 995
Rockaway, 5, 230, 937
Rockaway Avenue, 1117
Rockaway Indians, 5, 8, 68
Roller coasters, 1133–34
Roosevelt Avenue, 939
Roosevelt Club, 1103
Roosevelt Hospital, 1217
Roosevelt Island, 29, 32
Roosevelt Street, 340, 347, 359, 391, 890, 1126
Rose Hill, 178
Rose Street, 363, 413, 559, 1084
Rosenburg Jewelers, 1000
Rosenwach Tank Company, 1052
Rosenzweig affair, 1017
Rossville, 662
Rotunda, 468
Rotunda Bar, 879
Rough Riders, 1216
Row houses, 747, 972
Royal African Company, 71, 120, 126
Royal African Regiment, 249
Royal Exchange: building of, 176
Royal Irish Regiment, 225
Royal Navy: and Anglo-Dutch relations, 71; and British occupation of New York, 250; and British return to New York, 235; in "Burgis View," 112; deserters from, 182; in early nineteenth century, 315, 326; and French and Indian War, 191; impressment by, 182, 193, 315, 409–10; and Napoleonic Wars, 326, 409–10; and resistance to British policies, 204; and rum, 119; Station Ship, 112, 118; suppliers for, 270
Royal Society, 10
Rule of 1756, 315